NINETEENTH EDITION

SCHROEDER'S ANTIQUES PRICE GUIDE

Edited by Sharon & Bob Huxford

COLLECTOR BOOKS
A Division of Schroeder Publishing Co., Inc.

The current values in this book should be used only as a guide. They are not intended to set prices, which vary from one section of the country to another. Auction prices as well as dealer prices vary greatly and are affected by condition as well as demand. Neither the editors nor the publisher assumes responsibility for any losses that might be incurred as a result of consulting this guide.

Searching For A Publisher?

We are always looking for knowledgeable people considered experts within their fields. If you feel that there is a real need for a book on your collectible subject and have a large comprehensive collection, please contact Collector Books.

COLLECTOR BOOKS
P.O. Box 3009
Paducah, Kentucky 42002-3009

Introduction

As the editors and staff of *Schroeder's*, our goal is to compile the most useful, comprehensive, and accurate background and pricing information possible. We strive to suggest values based on traditional market sales rather than Internet auctions which are notoriously erratic. Our guide encompasses nearly five hundred categories, many of which you will not find in other price guide. Our sources are varied; we use auction results and dealer lists, and we consult with national collectors' clubs, recognized authorities, researchers, and appraisers. We have by far the largest Advisory Board of any similar publication on the market. Each year we add several new advisors and now have over 450 who cover almost all our categories. They go over our computer print-outs line by line, deleting listings that are misleading or too vague to be of merit; they often send background information and photos. We appreciate their assistance very much. Only through their expertise and experience in their special fields are we able to offer with confidence what we feel are useful, accurate evaluations that provide a sound understanding of the dealings in the marketplace today. Correspondence with so large an advisory panel adds months of extra work to an already monumental task, but we feel that to a very large extent this is the foundation that makes *Schroeder's* the success that it has become.

Our Directory, which you will find in the back of the book, lists each contributor by state. These are people who have allowed us to photograph various examples of merchandise from their show booths, sent us pricing information, or in any way have contributed to this year's book. If you happen to be traveling, consult the Directory for shops along your way. We also list clubs who have worked with us and auction houses who have allowed us to use photographs from their catalogs.

Our Advisory Board lists only names and home states, so check the Directory for addresses and telephone numbers should you want to correspond with one of our experts. Remember, when you do, *always* enclose a self-addressed, stamped envelope (SASE). Thousands of people buy our guide, and hundreds contact our advisors. The only agreement we have with our advisors is that they edit their categories. They are in no way obligated to answer mail. Some are dealers who do many shows a month. The time they spend at home may be very limited, and they may not be open to contacts. There's no doubt that the reason behind the success of our book is their assistance. We regret seeing them become more and more burdened by phone and mail inquiries. We have lost some of our good advisors for this reason, and when we do, the book suffers and consequently, so do our readers. Many of our listed reference sources report that they constantly receive long distance calls (at all hours) that are really valuation requests. If they are registered appraisers, they make their living at providing such information and expect a fee for their service and expertise.

If you find you need more information than *Schroeder's* provides, there are other sources available to you. Go to your local library; check their section on reference books. Museums are public facilities that are willing and able help you establish the origin and possibly even the value of your particular treasure. In today's world of e-commerce, there are many websites you may visit that are full of pertinent, up-to-date information. Check the yellow pages of your phone book. Other cities' phone books are available from either your library or from the telephone company office. Look under the heading *Antique Dealers*. Those who are qualified appraisers will mention this credit in their advertisement. But remember that if you sell to a dealer, he will expect to buy your merchandise at a price low enough that he will be able to make an appreciable profit when he sells it. Once you decide to contact one of these appraisers, unless you intend to see them directly, you'll need to take photographs. Don't send photos that are under- or overexposed, out of focus, or shot against a background that detracts from important details you want to emphasize. It is almost impossible for them to give you a value judgement on items they've not seen when your photos are of poor quality. Shoot the front, top, and the bottom; describe any marks and numbers (or send a pencil rubbing), explain how and when you acquired the article, and give accurate measurements and any further background information that may be helpful.

The auction houses listed in the Directory nearly all have a staff of appraisal experts. If the item you're attempting to research is of the caliber of material they deal with, they can offer extremely accurate evaluations. Of course, most have a fee. Be sure to send them only professional-quality photographs. Tell them if you expect to consign your item to their auction. If you disagree with the value they suggest, you are under no obligation to do so.

Nearly five hundred categories are included in our book. We have organized our topics alphabetically, following the most simple logic, usually either by manufacturer or by type of product. If you have difficulty in locating your subject, consult the index. Our guide is unique in that much more space has been allotted to background information than in any other publication of this type. Our readers tell us that these are features they enjoy. To be able to do this, we have adopted a format of one-line listings wherein we describe the items to the fullest extent possible by using several common-sense abbreviations; they will be easy to read and understand if you will first take the time to quickly scan through them.

The Editors

Editorial Staff

Editors
Sharon and Bob Huxford

Research and Editorial Assistants
Michael Drollinger, Nancy Drollinger, Donna Newnum, Loretta Suitors

Layout
Beth Ray, Terri Hunter, and Donna Ballard

Cover Design
Beth Summers

On the front cover:
Calendar, 1916, 13x32" framed, $2,000.00; string holder, cherries, chalk, $95.00–115.00; chestnut ice box, gallery top and brass spigot, $1,500.00–2,000.00; Alexander Scarlett, 17", $1,450.00; basket with handle, Sandwich, Duncan and Miller, no established value (has been reproduced); Woodland Cornucopia, Hull, W10–11" yellow to green, $175.00–210.00.

On the back cover:
Nippon vase, 10", $880.00.

Listing of Standard Abbreviations

The following is a list of abbreviations that have been used throughout this book in order to provide you with the most detailed descriptions possible in the limited space available. No periods are used after initials or abbreviations. When two dimensions are given, height is noted first. If only one dimension is listed, it will be height, except in the case of bowls, dishes, plates, or platters, when it will be diameter. The standard two-letter state abbreviations apply.

For glassware, if no color is noted, the glass is clear. Hyphenated colors, for example blue-green, olive-amber, etc., describe a single color tone; colors divided by a slash mark indicate two or more colors, i.e. blue/white. Teapots, sugar bowls, and butter dishes are assumed to be 'with cover.' Condition is extremely important in determining market value. Common sense suggests that art pottery, china, and glassware values would be given for examples in pristine, mint condition, while suggested prices for utility wares such as Redware, Mocha, and Blue and White Stoneware, for example, reflect the probability that since such items were subjected to everyday use in the home they may show minor wear (which is acceptable) but no notable damage. Values for other categories reflect the best average condition in which the particular collectible is apt to be offered for sale without the dealer feeling it necessary to mention wear or damage. For instance, advertising items are assumed to be in excellent condition since mint items are scarce enough that when one is offered for sale the dealer will most likely make mention of that fact. The same holds true for toys, banks, coin-operated machines, and the like. A basic rule of thumb is that an item listed as VG (very good) will bring 40% to 60% of its mint price — a first-hand, personal evaluation will enable you to make the final judgement; EX (excellent) is a condition midway between mint and very good, and values would correspond.

Am ....American
appl ....applied
att ....attributed to
bbl ....barrel
bk ....back
bl ....blue
blk ....black
brn ....brown
bulb ....bulbous
bsk ....bisque
b3m ....blown 3-mold
C ....century
c ....copyright
ca ....circa
cb ....cardboard
Chpndl ....Chippendale
CI ....cast iron
compo ....composition
cr/sug ....creamer and sugar
c/s ....cup and saucer
cvd ....carved
cvg ....carving
dbl ....double
decor ....decoration
dk ....dark
Dmn Quilt ....Diamond Quilted
drw ....drawer
dtd ....dated
dvtl ....dovetail
emb ....embossed, embossing
embr ....embroidered
Emp ....Empire
eng ....engraved, engraving
EPNS ...electroplated nickel silver
EX ....excellent
Fed ....Federal
fr ....frame, framed
Fr ....French
ft, ftd ....foot, feet, footed
G ....good
gr ....green
grad ....graduated
grpt ....grain painted
H ....high, height
Hplwht ....Hepplewhite
hdl, hdld ....handle, handled
HP ....hand painted
illus ....illustration, illustrated by
imp ....impressed
ind ....individual
int ....interior
Invt T'print ..Inverted Thumbprint
irid ....iridescent
L ....length, long
lav ....lavender
ldgl ....leaded glass
litho ....lithograph
lt ....light
M ....mint
mahog ....mahogany
mc ....multicolor
MIB ....mint in box
MIG ....Made in Germany
MIP ....mint in package
mk ....mark
MOC ....mint on card
MOP ....mother-of-pearl
mt, mtd ....mount, mounted
NE ....New England
NM ....near mint
NRFB ....never removed from box
NP ....nickel plated
opal ....opalescent
orig ....original
o/l ....overlay
o/w ....otherwise
Pat ....patented
pc ....piece
ped ....pedestal
pk ....pink
pnt ....paint
porc ....porcelain
prof ....professional
QA ....Queen Anne
re ....regarding
rfn ....refinished
rnd ....round
rpl ....replaced
rpr ....repaired
rpt ....repainted
rstr ....restored
rtcl ....reticulated
rvpt ....reverse painted
s&p ....salt and pepper
sgn ....signed
SP ....silverplated
sq ....square
std ....standard
str ....straight
sz ....size
trn ....turned, turning
turq ....turquoise
uphl ....upholstered
VG ....very good
Vict ....Victorian
W ....width
wht ....white
w/ ....with
w/o ....without
X, Xd ....cross, crossed
yel ....yellow
(+) ....has been reproduced

A B C Plates

Children's plates featuring the alphabet as part of the design were popular from as early as 1820 until after the turn of the century. The earliest English creamware plates were decorated with embossed letters and prim moralistic verses, but the later Staffordshire products were conducive to a more relaxed mealtime atmosphere, often depicting playful animals and riddles or scenes of pleasant leisure-time activities. They were made around the turn of the century by American potters as well. All featured transfer prints, but color was sometimes brushed on by hand to add interest to the design.

Be sure to inspect these plates carefully for damage, since condition is a key price-assessing factor, and aside from obvious chips and hairlines, even wear can substantially reduce their values.

For further information we recommend *A B C Plates & Mugs, Identification and Value Guide*, by Irene and Ralph Lindsay (Collector Books). Our advisor for this category is Dr. Joan George; she is listed in the Directory under New Jersey.

Ceramic

Aesop's Fables, Hare & Tortoise, mc transfer, unmk, 6½" 185.00
Archery, mc transfer, J&G Meakin, 5¼" 140.00
August, shepherd w/lamb, mc transfer, unmk, 7¼" 135.00
Baseball, gr transfer, Staffordshire, 6¼", EX 350.00
Bear w/cubs, mc transfer, BPCo, 7½" 250.00
Bears playing ball, mc transfer on porc, Smith Phillips, 6½" 125.00
Cats playing cards at table, mc transfer, unmk German, 7" 100.00
Crane & toad, mc transfer, ABCs in center of plate, unmk, 7¼" .140.00
Crusoe Rescues Friday, brn transfer, Staffordshire, 7¼", VG 140.00
Crusoe Viewing the Island, mc transfer, #69963, 7¼" 140.00
Destruction of Pharoah, mc transfer, #106738, 7¼" 150.00
Dog, mc transfer, unmk (English), 7¼" 175.00
Dogs (3) walking tightrope, mc transfer, Elsmore & Son, 8" 155.00
Feeding the Donkey, blk transfer, emb rim, Powell & Bishop, 7" .100.00
Floral transfer, mc transfer, emb rim, unmk, 7" 135.00
Flowers That Never Fade, Cheerfulness, blk transfer, Meakin, 5¾" .150.00
Four Is for the Fowls, bl transfer, unmk, 6½" 155.00
Frolics of Youth, Young Artist, mc transfer, unmk, 8" 150.00
Gleaners, mc transfer, unmk, 6" 145.00
Horse portrait, monochrome, W Adams & Co, 7¼" 120.00
January, red transfer, Staffordshire, 5¾", EX 125.00
Little Bo Peep, blk transfer, HC Edmiston, England, 6" 125.00
Lovers, mc transfer of couple in interior scene, unmk, 5¾" 115.00
Man plowing w/horses, mc transfer, J&G Meakin, 4½" 130.00
Man w/Alpine horn & dog, blk transfer, unmk, 6" 115.00
Plow Deep While..., Franklin's Proverbs, blk transfer, unmk, 8" ...135.00
Punch & Judy w/dog, brn transfer, CA & Sons, 7¼" 135.00
Rider Rents Horse, mc transfer w/dmn center, CA & Sons, 7½" .145.00
Sunbonnet girls making pie crust, Smith Phillips, 7" 125.00
Titmouse (pr), mc transfer, ABCs at right side of plate, 7" 135.00
Weasel, blk transfer, Wm Adams & Co, Tunstall, 7" 135.00
Young Charioteer, mc transfer, emb rim, unmk, 5½" 140.00

Glassware

ABCs (pnt/emb), milk glass, unmk, 7", from $50 to 60.00
Child's face (Emma), vaseline, unmk, 8" 30.00
Christmas Eve, unmk, 6", from $175 to 200.00
Clock face, w/months, days & ABCs, unmk, 7", from $50 to 60.00
Clock face w/numerals & ABCs, unmk, 7", from $50 to 60.00
Ducks, deep yel, unmk, 6", from $60 to 70.00
Fan center, scalloped rim, unmk, 6", from $65 to 75.00
Numerals in center, carnival glass, unmk, 7½", from $90 to 120.00
Rooster, unmk, 6", from $65 to 75.00
Sancho Panza & Dapple, unmk, 6", from $50 to 60.00
8-pointed dmn center, unmk, 6¼", from $50 to 60.00

Tin

ABCs around rim, deep dish, unmk, 6", from $15 to 25.00
ABCs around rim, unmk, 6¼", from $60 to 95.00
After Supper Run a Mile, litho, Kemp Mfg Co, Toronto, 6" 175.00
Cats (2) w/yarn basket, litho, Ohio Art Co, 4¼", from $65 to ..110.00
Her Majesty Queen Victoria, unmk, 8" 300.00
Liberty, unmk, 5½", from $110 to 150.00
Lion, unmk, 2⅞" 300.00
Mary Had a Little Lamb, unmk, 7¾", from $130 to 160.00
Peter Rabbit, litho, unmk, 7¾" 350.00
Simple Simon Met a Pieman..., Tudor Plate Oneida Community, 6", up to 95.00
Who Killed Cock Robin, unmk, 7¾", from $130 to 150.00

Abingdon

From 1934 until 1950, the Abingdon Pottery Co. of Abingdon, Illinois, made a line of art pottery with a white vitrified body decorated with various types of glazes in many lovely colors. Novelties, cookie jars, utility ware, and lamps were made in addition to several lines of simple yet striking art ware. Fern Leaf, introduced in 1937, featured molded vertical feathering. La Fleur, in 1939, consisted of flowerpots and flower-arranger bowls with rows of vertical ribbing. Classic, 1939–40, was a line of vases, many with evidence of Chinese influence. Several marks were used, most of which employed the company name. In 1950 the company reverted to the manufacture of sanitary ware that had been their mainstay before the Art Ware Division was formed.

Highly decorated examples and those with black, bronze, or red glaze usually command at least 25% higher prices.

For further information we recommend *Abingdon Pottery Artware 1934–1950, Stepchild of the Great Depression*, by Joe Paradis (Schiffer).

Rose plate, aqua matt, 12", $150.00.

#030, vase, Chang, bronze 225.00
#098, figurine, upright goose, 1934-50, 3½" 40.00
#116, vase, Classic, 10", from $20 to 25.00
#117, vase, Classic, gr, 10" 35.00
#118, vase, powder bl, hdls, 10" 25.00
#120, planter w/bow, bl 20.00
#151, flowerpot, 6" 22.00
#152, vase, yel, 8¾" 22.00
#305, bookends, sea gull, 9¼", pr 80.00
#321, bookends, Cossack/Russian, blk, 6½" or 8½", pr 95.00
#324, vase, bottle form, yel w/wht int, 3¾" 110.00
#370, bookends, Cactus, 6", pr 65.00

#374, planter/bookends, Cactus, lt gr, 7", pr 100.00
#377, wall pocket, Morning Glory, ivory, 9x6¼" 45.00
#388, figurine, pouter pigeon, 4½" 40.00
#392, vase, Morning Glory, 5½" 35.00
#393, bowl, Morning Glory, 7" 35.00
#400, tea tile, geisha, sq, 5" 50.00
#408, bowl, leaf, beige, 1937, 6½" 50.00
#412, vase, Volute, wht, 1937-40, 15½" 125.00
#416, figurine, peacock, 7" 95.00
#422, vase, Fern Leaf, wht, 10" 30.00
#428, bookend, Fern Leaf, 5½" 45.00
#429, vase/candle holder, Fern Leaf, 8" 25.00
#435, wall pocket, Tri-Fern, 9", from $135 to 150.00
#444, planter bookends, dolphin, decor, 5¾", pr 50.00
#450, bowl, Asters, flared rim, oval, 11½" L 55.00
#452, bowl, Asters, 9x14½" 45.00
#453, vase, Asters, 8" 25.00
#460, bowl, Panel, 8" 25.00
#463, vase, Star, 7" 18.00
#469/#470, figurines, Dutch boy & girl, 1939-40, 8", pr 50.00
#474, cornucopia, yel, 5½" 18.00
#476, window box, 10½" H 20.00
#482, dbl cornucopia, peach, 11" 50.00
#484, fan vase w/bow, bl, 8¼" 35.00
#486, vase, Acanthus, silver o/l birds on peach, 11" 150.00
#487, floor vase, Egret, 14" 145.00
#497, figurine, Blackamoor, w/decor, 7½" 95.00
#501, bowl, Shell, pk, sm 22.50
#505, candle holder, Shell, dbl, 4" 20.00
#507, vase, Shell, wht, oval, 7½" 25.00
#509, ashtray, elephant, 5½" 50.00
#510, ashtray, donkey, 5½" 50.00
#512, vase, Swirl, gr, 9" 20.00
#513, vase, Swirl, 9", from $15 to 25.00
#514, vase, Swirl, chartreuse, 11", from $25 to 35.00
#515, vase, gold rim & hdls, 6¾" 45.00
#520, vase, gr, 9" 25.00
#522, vase, Barre, 9" 35.00
#528, bowl, Hibiscus, bl, 15" 40.00
#532, bowl, console; gold trim, 14½" L, from $25 to 35.00
#532 & #575, console set, bl, 3-pc 25.00
#533, bowl, Shell, yel, 12", from $22 to 25.00
#536, bowl, Regency, gr, 7x9x5" 40.00
#547, figurine, heron, tan 68.00
#552, vase, squatty, 13" 40.00
#557, vase, pk, draped design, 11" 40.00
#563, urn, coral w/wht decor, 9" 35.00
#564, bowl, Scallop, pk, 11" 18.00
#568, mint compote, pk, ftd, 1942-47, 6" dia 28.00
#569D, cornucopia, bl w/decor, 10" L 27.50
#571, figurine, goose, blk, 5" 40.00
#572, figurine, pelican, gr, 5" 55.00
#573, figurine, penguin, decor, 5½" 40.00
#576, window box, gr, 12¼" L 25.00
#581, vase, dbl cornucopia; bl, 8½" 45.00
#593, vase, bowknot, bl, 9" 35.00
#596, vase, sea horse 65.00
#610, bowl, Shell, 9" 25.00
#616D, vase, Cactus, w/sleeping Mexican man, 6½" 38.00
#620, vase, anemones, daisies & tulip, bl w/gold, from $30 to 35.00
#629, vase, Poppy, 6½" 30.00
#640, wall pocket, Triad, 5½", from $40 to 45.00
#652, planter, puppy, decor, 6¾" 25.00
#654, vase, Tulip, 6½" 20.00
#659, vase, Hackney, 8½" 30.00
#667, planter, gourd, 5½" 20.00
#675D, wall pocket, matchbox form, 5½" 50.00
#681/#682, sugar bowl & creamer, Daisy 48.00
#699, wall pocket, apron, 6" 50.00
#711, wall vase, carriage lamp, 10" 25.00
#714, candle holders, Star, 4¼", pr 30.00
#3906, figurine, shepherdess & faun, blk, 11½" 250.00

Cookie jar, #471, Little Ol' Lady (Black face), 1942, 7½", from $375.00 to $400.00. (Photo courtesy Ermagene Westfall)

Cookie jar, #471, Old Lady, plain, 1942 ....210.00
Cookie jar, #495, Fat Boy 250.00
Cookie jar, #549, Hippo, decor, 1942 ....250.00
Cookie jar, #561, Baby, Blk 300.00
Cookie jar, #588, Money Bag 75.00
Cookie jar, #602, Hobby Horse 185.00
Cookie jar, #611, Jack-in-Box, from $275 to 325.00
Cookie jar, #622, Miss Muffet 205.00
Cookie jar, #651, Choo Choo (Locomotive) 150.00
Cookie jar, #653, Clock, 1949 ....100.00
Cookie jar, #663, Humpty Dumpty, decor 250.00
Cookie jar, #664, Pineapple 95.00
Cookie jar, #665, Wigwam, from $250 to 300.00
Cookie jar, #674, Pumpkin, 1949 ....250.00
Cookie jar, #677, Daisy, 1949 ....50.00
Cookie jar, #678, Windmill, from $200 to 225.00
Cookie jar, #693, Little Girl, from $60 to 75.00
Cookie jar, #694, Bo Peep, from $250 to 275.00
Cookie jar, #695, Mother Goose, from $295 to 350.00
Cookie jar, #696, Three Bears, from $90 to 100.00

Adams

Wm. Adams, whose potting skills were developed under the tutelage of Josiah Wedgwood, founded the Greengates Pottery at Tunstall, England, in 1769. Many types of wares including basalt, ironstone, parian, and jasper were produced; and various impressed or printed marks were employed. Until 1800 'Adams Co.' or 'Adams' impressed in block letters identified the company's earthenwares and a fine type of jasper similar in color and decoration to Wedgwood's. The latter mark was used again from 1845 to 1864 on parian figures. Most examples of their product found on today's market are transfer-printed dinnerwares with ornate backstamps which often include the pattern name and the initials 'W.A. & S.' This type of product was made from 1820 until about 1920. After 1890 the word 'England' was included in the mark; 'Tunstall' was added after 1896. From 1914 through 1940, a printed crown with 'Adams, Estbd 1657, England,' identified their products. From 1900 to 1965, they produced souvenir plates with transfers of American scenes, many of which were marketed in this country by Roth Importers of Peoria, Illinois. In 1965 the company affiliated with Wedgwood. Although there were other Adams potteries in Staffordshire, their marks incorporate either the first name initial or a partner's name and so are easily distinguished from those of this company. See also Adams Rose; Flow Blue; Spatter; Staffordshire; Tea Leaf.

Candlestick, Cries of London, 3½", pr 90.00
Cup & saucer, Casino, lt bl transfer, mini 50.00
Cup & saucer, Sower, red transfer, 6" dia 90.00
Plate, Caledonia, purple transfer, 10⅝", NM 110.00
Plate, Dr Syntax Bound to a Tree, pearlized rim, 9½" 60.00
Plate, unidentified scenic view, dk bl, scalloped, 6¾", EX 120.00
Platter, Lake George, red transfer, 13¼", EX 350.00
Relish, Woodland Lovers, dk bl, fruit hdls, unmk, rstr, 6⅝" 135.00
Teapot, Oriental scenic view, dk bl transfer, 7¼" 415.00

Adams, Matthew

In the 1950s a trading post located in Alaska contacted Sascha Brastoff to design a line of porcelain with scenes of Eskimos, Alaskan motifs, and animals indigenous to that country. These items were to be sold in Alaska to the tourist trade.

Brastoff selected Matthew Adams to design the Alaska series. Pieces from the line he produced have the Sascha B mark on the front; some have a pattern number on the reverse. They did not have the rooster backstamp. (See the Sascha Brastoff category for information on this mark.)

After the Alaska series was introduced and proved to be successful, Matthew Adams left the employment of Sascha Brastoff and opened his own studio. Pieces made in his studio are signed Matthew Adams in script and may have the word Alaska on the front. Where his studio (or studios) was is unknown at the present time, but a 'Made in Alaska' paper label has been found, suggesting that he may have worked from that location. Our advisor for this category is Marty Webster; he is listed in the Directory under Michigan. Feel free to contact Mr. Webster if you have any further information.

Vase, Eskimo, 13½", minimum value $250.00. (Photo courtesy Jack Chipman)

Ashtray, husky, #061, 13x10" 40.00
Ashtray, polar bear, blk & wht, free-form, 7x12" 35.00
Bowl, console; glacier on bl, 12x20" 165.00
Bowl, Eskimo child, lt gr, 3-ftd, #138a, 4x6" 40.00
Bowl, iceberg on lid, #158, 4x6½" 75.00
Bowl, mountain sheep (ram), dk bl w/wht image, 3-ftd, #138, 3½" .50.00
Bowl, polar bear on gr, free-form, 7½" L 50.00
Charger, caribou on dk bl, 18" 150.00
Cookie jar, mother & child on brn 75.00
Creamer & sugar bowl, walrus, 5" 125.00
Jar, walrus on lt bl, w/lid, #1492, 7½" 50.00
Mug, Eskimo child, yel bkground, 4" 30.00
Platter, house, 12" 45.00
Shakers, Eskimo child & walrus, ice bl, teardrop shape, 5½", pr ..35.00
Tile, seal, wht & bl bkground w/gold accents, 8½x10" 60.00
Vase, Alaskan mountains/sea/sky, bl/gray/blk/gold, 17x6" 160.00
Vase, bear on yel, oval rim, #126, 7x4½" 65.00
Vase, caribou/elk, sky bl w/gold streaks, 4½x2¾" 30.00
Vase, mother & child on teal, cylindrical, 17" 165.00
Vase, reindeer, 4½" 45.00
Vase, walrus on gr & wht, tumbler shape, #143a, 4x3½" 25.00

Adams Rose, Early and Late

In the second quarter of the nineteenth century, the Adams and Son Pottery produced a line of hand-painted dinnerware decorated in large, red brush-stroke roses with green leaves on whiteware, which collectors call Adams Rose. Later, G. Jones and Son (and possibly others) made a similar ware with less brilliant colors on a gray-white surface.

Unless otherwise noted, our values are for items in mint condition or nearly so; be sure to discount prices for damage.

Bowl, late, 2¾x5⅜" 50.00
Bowl, late, 3x6¼" 70.00
Bowl, sauce; early, 1⅛x4⅞" 150.00
Bowl, vegetable, late, oval, 2x9¾x7", EX 90.00
Coffeepot, late, 8" 875.00
Creamer, early, yel panels, 5¾" 825.00
Creamer, late, scalloped rim, 4⅝" 210.00
Pitcher, early, scrolled hdl & rim, rpr, 9", VG 235.00
Pitcher, late, scalloped rim, 6½" 235.00
Pitcher, water; late, scalloped rim, 7½" 400.00
Plate, early, lt stains, 9" 220.00
Plate, late, mk Adams, 9½" 90.00
Plate, mk Adams, 10½" 145.00
Plate, toddy; mk Adams, 5" 350.00
Platter, mk Adams, 13½" 385.00
Soup plate, late, 9" 150.00
Sugar bowl, late, w/lid, 6" 350.00
Tea bowl & saucer, early 350.00

Advertising

The advertising world has always been a fiercely competitive field. In an effort to present their product to the customer, every imaginable gimmick was put into play. Colorful and artfully decorated signs and posters, thermometers, tape measures, fans, hand mirrors, and attractive tin containers (all with catchy slogans, familiar logos, and often-bogus claims) are only a few of the many examples of early advertising memorabilia that are of interest to today's collectors.

Porcelain signs were made as early as 1890 and are highly prized for their artistic portrayal of life as it was then . . . often allowing amusing insights into the tastes, humor, and way of life of a bygone era. As a general rule, older signs are made from a heavier gauge metal. Those with three or more fired-on colors are especially desirable.

Tin containers were used to package consumer goods ranging from crackers and coffee to tobacco and talcum. After 1880 can companies began to decorate their containers by the method of lithography. Though colors were still subdued, intricate designs were used to attract the eye of the consumer. False labeling and unfounded claims were curtailed by the

Pure Food and Drug Administration in 1906, and the name of the manufacturer as well as the brand name of the product had to be printed on the label. By 1910 color was rampant with more than a dozen hues printed on the tin or on paper labels. The tins themselves were often designed with a second use in mind, such as canisters, lunch boxes, even toy trains. As a general rule, tobacco-related tins are the most desirable, though personal preference may direct the interest of the collector to peanut butter pails with illustrations of children, or talcum tins with irresistible babies or beautiful ladies. Coffee tins are popular, as are those made to contain a particularly successful or well-known product.

Perhaps the most visual of the early advertising gimmicks were the character logos, the Fairbank Company's Gold Dust Twins, the goose trademark of the Red Goose Shoe Company, Nabisco's ZuZu Clown and Uneeda Kid, the Campbell Kids, the RCA dog Nipper, and Mr. Peanut, to name only a few. Many early examples of these bring high prices on the market today.

Our listings are alphabetized by product name or, in lieu of that information, by word content or other pertinent description. When no condition is indicated, the items listed below are assumed to be in excellent condition, except glass and ceramic items, which are assumed mint. Remember that condition greatly affects value (especially true for tin items). For instance, a sign in excellent or mint condition may bring twice as much as the same one in only very good condition, sometimes even more. On today's market, items in good to very good condition are slow to sell, unless they are extremely rare. Mint (or near-mint) examples are high.

We have several advertising advisors; see specific subheadings. For further information we recommend *Zany Characters of the Ad World* by Mary Jane Lamphier; *Advertising Character Collectibles* by Warren Dotz; *Value Guide to Advertising Memorabilia, Second Edition*, by B.J. Summers; *The World of Beer Memorabilia* by Herb and Helen Haydock; and *Encyclopedia of Advertising Tins, Vol. II*, by David Zimmerman. *Huxford's Collectible Advertising* and *Garage Sale and Flea Market Annual* by Sharon and Bob Huxford are other good references. All of these books are available at your local bookstore or from Collector Books. See also Advertising Dolls; Advertising Cards; Automobilia; Coca-Cola; Banks; Calendars; Cookbooks; Paperweights; Posters; Sewing Items.

Key:
- cb — cardboard
- cl — celluloid
- fs — flange sign
- lcs — litho on canvas sign
- pp — pre-prohibition
- ps — porcelain sign
- sf — self-framed
- tc — tin container
- ts — tin sign

Aunt Jemima Pancake Flour, cardboard stand-up diecut, minor fading and soiling, 20x12½", $375.00.

A-Treat, sign, diecut cb, Santa in sleigh, 22x28", EX 75.00
AC Spark Plugs, fs, w/3 chained product panels, dtd 9/47, NM+ .300.00
Acme Boots, cb trifold, hunting party/elk, 23x37", EX 150.00
Adams Pure Chewing Gum, jar, etched glass, ca 1915, NM+ 110.00
Alka-Seltzer, neon on rvpt glass case, bl, 7x27x6", EX+ 400.00
Altes Beer, display, hand-held bottle, plaster, EX 150.00
American Line/Red Star Line, letter opener, metal, 3x12", EX .230.00
Anheuser-Busch, display figure, waiter, chalkware, 20", EX 190.00
Arden Milk, sign, aluminum, diecut Ardie figure, 36", VG 400.00
Athleta Hose Supporters 15¢, display, tin, wood-tone, 18x10", VG ..330.00
Aunt Hannah's Bread, jigsaw puzzle, 1932, 7½x8½", EX 45.00
B-1 Lemon-Lime Soda, thermometer, tin, More Zip..., 17", NM .65.00
Backwith Co, sign, paper/cb, Doe-Wah-Jack profile, 14x10", EX+ ..150.00
Baker's Chocolate, poster, girl w/tray, fr, 36x26", NM 300.00
Bata Super Bullets Sneakers, display sneaker, plaster, 24", VG ..250.00
Beech-Nut Baby Food, sign, cb stand-up, kids, 1905, 10", EX ...300.00
Beech-Nut Gum, display case, tin, 4-tier, 15x6x7", VG+ 850.00
Beehive Overalls, pocket mirror, trademk girl, oval, NM 300.00
Bickmore's Gall Cure, diecut cb trifold, 3 scenes, 34x50", NM .450.00
Big Ben Tobacco, pocket tin, clock, EX 950.00
Big Ben Tobacco, pocket tin, horse, EX 40.00
Black Cat Cigarettes, diecut ts, head on yel circle, 51x48", VG+ ..550.00
Blatz Beer, display figure, bottle man, VG+ 75.00
Blatz Beer, display figure, keg man, EX 100.00
Borden's, needle book, 1940s, 5¼", EX 55.00
Borden's Ice Cream, thermometer, tin, 1960s, 25", NM 500.00
Borden's Milk, ts, Elsie on bl/wht, 28x20", NM 300.00
BT Babbitt's Cleanser, sign, cb trolley, lady's image, 11x22", VG ...70.00
Bubble-Up, ts, ...Has Pa-Zazz!, bottle cap on bl, 12x28", NM 125.00
Buckeye Harvesting Machines, fan, cb, 4 heart shapes, 6x9", EX ...50.00
Budweiser, display figure, Bud Man, hard foam, 19", NM 165.00
Budweiser, radio, can shape, EX (NM box) 30.00
Budweiser, sign, cb, emb, Clydesdales/wagon, 1909, 10x26", VG+ ..80.00
Budweiser, sign, neon, bl, 9x28", NM 315.00
Bull Durham, sign, tin, Prize Winners, orig fr, 36x36", NM 7,500.00
Bunnies Salted Peanuts, store tc, red, rnd, 10-lb, VG+ 250.00
Bunte Marshmallows, tc, rnd w/pry lid, bl/wht, ca 1914, 4-oz, VG ..100.00
Bunte Marshmallows, tc, rnd w/pry lid, wht, 5-lb, 10x13" dia, EX+ .450.00
Burma-Shave, ts, red w/stenciled phrase, 6-pc, 1930s, NM 700.00

Buster Brown

Buster Brown was the creation of cartoonist Richard Felton; his comic strip first appeared in the *New York Herald* on May 4, 1902. Since then Buster and his dog Tige (short for Tiger) have adorned sundry commercial products but are probably best known as the trademark for the Brown Shoe Company established early in this century. Today hundreds of Buster Brown premiums, store articles, and advertising items bring substantial prices from many serious collectors.

Balloon inflatable head, w/cape & pants, EX 750.00
Clicker, Shoes, emb tin, silver-tone, BB & Tige, EX 11.00

Clock, glass face and front with metal frame, light-up, Pam Clock Co., 15" dia, working, EX, $925.00.

Container, Mustard, cb w/tin top & bottom, red, 2-oz, EX 75.00

Display, Shoes, diecut tin, BB in wheeled shoe, 2-pc, 24", VG .4,000.00
Display, Shoes, diecut tin, Tige jumping for cracker, 2-pc, 40", G ...2,000.00
Display, Shoes, mechanical, for store window, 36x36", EX 575.00
Display figure, plastic doll on base, clothed, 34", VG 55.00
Display rack, Shoes, diecut tin, BB straddling Tige, 12", EX+ ..1,200.00
Mask, Bread, paperbrd, BB winking, 8½x11", EX 100.00
Painting box, paper on cb, Milton Bradley, 1910, 10½x7x¾", EX 50.00
Pin-bk button, Bread, phrase on fence, 1½", EX 35.00
Plaque, Shoes, bas-relief plaster, BB & Tige w/name, 19x18", EX ..340.00
Rug, w/Tige, yel w/bl border, 47" dia, VG 375.00
Sign, cb, Shoes, diecut school bus, stand-up, 20x69", EX 60.00
Sign, cb hanger, Bread, BB writes phrase on chalkbrd, 11x8", EX .200.00
Sign, flange, Shoes, Get Them Here, BB w/shoe, 24x16", G ..1,800.00
Sign, wood, Quality Children's Clothes, 2-sided, 19x43", VG ...125.00

BVD Union Suits, ts, beveled, man/phrase, 1920s, 13x9", EX ...200.00
Canada Dry, clock, Pam, 1962, 15" dia, EX 500.00
Canada Dry, door plate, porc, phrase/bottle, 1950s, 14", EX 150.00
Canada Dry, sign, light-up box, ...5¢ a Glass, 1930s, 7x14", NMIB 400.00
Canadian Club 5¢ Cigar, sign, cb, phrase/oval image, 14x21", NM ..50.00
Carnation Milk, bookmk, cb, Panama-Pacific Expo, 1915, 7", NM ..65.00
Carta Blanca, tip tray, girl in pigtails, 4½" dia, EX 60.00
Carter's Overalls, porc sign, train, red/wht/bl, 6x15", EX+ 1,350.00
Caterpiller, clock, Time To Buy..., glass/metal, 15" dia, EX 325.00
Cenol Mothproofing, plaster moth figure, 24", VG 150.00
Ceresota Flour, jigsaw puzzle, 6 factory views, 1900, 7x9", EX ...125.00
Champagne Velvet Beer, charger, cherubs/colonial party, 24", EX ..600.00
Chase & Sanborn, jigsaw puzzle, store scene, 1910, 6x8", EX 50.00
Chero-Cola, pocket mirror/pin holder, cl, rnd, EX+ 35.00
Chesterfield, pocket tin, paper label, oval portrait, EX+ 100.00
Christo Cola, paperweight, metal turtle w/cl top, EX 150.00
Circus Club Marshmallows, tc, set of 6 animals, G+ to EX+ 935.00
Cities Service, pocket mirror, cartoon serviceman, 2" dia, EX 90.00
Cities Service, winterfront, cb, fr, 13x21", EX 50.00
City Club Crushed Cubes, pocket tin, VG+, from $175 to 200.00
Clabber Girl Baking Powder, banner, cloth, yel/bl/yel, 18x36", EX+ ..50.00
Clark's Peanut Butter, pail, 1-lb, EX+, from $320 to 500.00
Clark's Teaberry Gum, dish w/ped base, vaseline glass, 7", NM+ .55.00
Clark's Teaberry Gum, ts, A Happy Thought..., 9x12", EX 180.00
Cloverbloom Butter, display cottage w/cows, cb, 16x31", EX 200.00
Conoco Gasoline, sign, porc, minuteman, 2-sided, 25" dia, EX ..2,950.00
Consolidated Biscuit Co, toy house biscuit box, cb, 1932, 9x5", EX .85.00
Cott, sign, cb, ZaZa Gabor at table, 22x32", NM+ 125.00
Crawford Cooking Ranges, yardstick, VG 65.00
Curtis' Pepsin Gum, sign, diecut cb, girl on box, 1890s, 9x7", EX .850.00
Cuticura Soap, sign, cb, Medicinal..., tortoise-shell fr, 16", EX+ ..60.00
Cuticura Talcum Powder, tc, sample, EX 50.00

Dan Patch Rye, reverse-painted sign, pre-WWI era, 34x24", NM, $5,000.00.

Dad's Root Beer, clock, cap logo, light-up, gold/wht fr, 16" sq, EX ..200.00
Dad's Root Beer, sign, bottle on tray, 1940s-50s, 29x13", EX 280.00
Decoret, string holder, tin, 19x13", EX 2,035.00
DeLaval, broom holder, tin, 1911, 3" dia, EX 325.00
DeLaval, fs, diecut metal separator, 1913, VG 1,300.00
DeLaval, thimble, 1910, EX 475.00
Delco, fs, battery shape w/bl ribbon, diecut, 17x23", NM 350.00
Dentyne Chewing Gum, toothbrush holder, figural boy, 1930s, NM+ ...275.00
Deodo Powder, sign, diecut cb, nude/product tin, 1920s, 25", VG+ ..130.00
Devilish Good Cigar, ts, None Better/5¢, open box, 10x14", EX+ 500.00
DeVoe's Sweet Smoke, pocket tin, NM 500.00
Diamond Tire Service, fs, diecut tire atop emblem, 27x17", EX .1,100.00
Donald Duck Beverages, ts, head image, bl/wht, 20x28", EX+ ..365.00
Donald Duck Bread, ts, head/loaf/phrase, 1940s-50s, 20x39", EX .350.00
Donald Duck Coffee, can, pry lid, sample, 2½x3", EX 475.00
Donald Duck Lime Cola, bottle carrier w/6 7-oz bottles, cb, EX+ ..90.00
Donald Duck Peanut Butter, jar bank, clear glass figural head, NM ..65.00
Dr Caldwell's Syrup Pepsin, push plate, porc, yel/blk, 7x4", EX .210.00

Dr. Pepper

A young pharmacist, Charles C. Alderton, was hired by W.B. Morrison, owner of Morrison's Old Corner Drug Store in Waco, Texas, around 1884. Alderton, an observant sort, noticed that the drugstore's patrons could never quite make up their minds as to which flavor of extract to order. He concocted a formula that combined many flavors, and Dr. Pepper was born. The name was chosen by Morrison in honor of a beautiful young girl with whom he had once been in love. The girl's father, a Virginia doctor by the name of Pepper, had discouraged the relationship due to their youth, but Morrison had never forgotten her. On December 1, 1885, a U.S. patent was issued to the creators of Dr. Pepper. Our advisor for Dr. Pepper is Craig Stifter; he is listed in the Directory under Illinois.

Art plate, girl looking right, rare, EX 900.00
Bottle opener, metal, diecut lion's head, 3", EX 85.00
Bottle opener/spoon, The Friendly Pepper Upper, EX+ 385.00
Bottle topper, Edith Luce, NM 250.00
Bottle topper, Virginia Kavanagh, NM 220.00
Clock, Art Deco style, rvpt glass, 1930s, 17x22", NM 3,700.00
Clock, bottle cap, plastic w/metal bk, light-up, 12" dia, EX 70.00
Clock, octagonal, neon, rvpt glass, EX+ 1,200.00
Decal, Please Pay When Served, 1930s-40s, 8x9", EX+ 200.00
Drinking glass, flared w/etched logo, 1910s, NM 1,200.00
Fan, cb w/wood hdl, girl w/bottle on knee, Earl Morgan art, EX ..75.00
Fan pull, cb, beach girl w/umbrella, G 80.00
Match holder, tin, party scene w/Buster serving bread, 7x2", VG ..400.00
Menu board, tin, yel panel atop chalkbrd, 1940s, 27x19", VG ..250.00
Postcard, Free! 6 Bottles of Dr Pepper, red/gr/wht, NM 15.00
Sign, cb, Madelon Mason w/sign & bottle, 1940s, 19x32", G+ .100.00
Sign, cb hanger/stand-up, carhop/soldier, 1940s, 6x12", NM+ ...275.00
Sign, flange, Fountain/Drink DP, panel atop oval, 1961, 15x22", NM ...750.00
Sign, porc, Drink DP, wht on red w/wht edge, rnd corners, 9x24", NM ..160.00
Sign, porc, Drink DP/Good for Life!, 1930s-40s, 11x27", EX+ ..275.00
Sign, porc, 10-2-4/Drink DP, red/wht, 10" dia, NM 750.00
Sign, tin, Drink DP/Good for Life, red/wht, emb, 1936, 7x20", VG+ .350.00
Stick pin, diecast brass head, 2¼", NM 165.00
Syrup jug, clear glass w/paper label, screw cap, VG+ 120.00
Thermometer, tin, Hot or Cold/Enjoy..., red/wht, 1950s, 16", EX .175.00
Tray, You'll Like It To!, w/graphics, 1930s-40s, VG+ 280.00

Drewry's Old Stock Ale, statue, plaster, Mounty/horse/bottle, EX 100.00
Duluth Imperial Flour, ts, phrase/Black baker, wood fr, 28x21", VG ...1,000.00
Dutch Boy, sign, canvas bk, The Dutch Boy Painter, fr, 24x12", EX ..275.00
Dutch Java Coffee, pocket mirror, Secret of Happiness, 2" dia, EX+ ...50.00

Effinger Fine Beer, tray, waiter/lettering, deep rim, 12" dia, VG+ 100.00
Egyptian Deities Cigarettes, sign, paper, queen, fr, 29x21", EX ..525.00
El-Bart Dry Gin, sign, paper, girl on beach, gold fr, 46x33", G ..3,000.00
Elgin Watches, sign, rvpt glass, gold on blk, 30x24", EX 250.00
Empire Pilsner Style Beer, coaster, 2-sided, 4½" dia, VG+ 85.00
Esso, bank, tiger figure, hard rubber, 8", NM 45.00
Esso, pocketknife, gas pump shape, globe top, metal, 3", EX 230.00
Essolube, jigsaw puzzle, Foiled by Essolube, Dr Seuss, 11x17", EX ..65.00
Eureka Spool Silk, cabinet, wood, w/clock, 24x23x16", EX 1,300.00
Evinrude Motor Co, tip tray, lady in boat, deep rim, 4" dia, NM .400.00
Eye Fix, tip tray, lady/cherub, HD Beach litho, 4" dia, VG 325.00
Fairbank's Fairy Soap, display box, Fairy Christmas, 16x17x9", EX ..160.00
Fairway Cocoa, tc, sq, slip lid, paper label, boy/girl, EX+ 65.00
Fairway Peanut Butter, pail, str-sided, 14-oz, EX+ 1,290.00
Fairway Quick...Oats, container, cb, chef/elves, 2-lb 10-oz, EX 65.00
Farmers Fire Insurance Co, sign, rvpt, metallic/blk, fr, 33", VG .750.00
Favorite Cigarettes, trolley sign, cb, baseball, fr, 10x19", VG .1,250.00
Federal Cartridge Co, sign, sf cb, dogs in field, 1937, 17x19", VG+ ..55.00
Federal Club Coffee, can, slip lid, paper label, 1-lb, EX 300.00
Fehr's Malt Tonic, ts, nymph/cherubs, gold trim, sf oval, 29", G ..800.00
Fern Glen Rye, sf ts, I'se in a Perdickermunt, 33x23", EX 2,250.00
Ferris Waists, sf ts, mother/daughter, 23x17" oval, EX+ 2,300.00
Fisk Tires, bank, Fisk Boy, ceramic, M 55.00
Fisk Tires, display figure, Fisk Boy, compo, 32", EX 800.00
Fisk Tires, radiator front, cb, Fisk Boy, 1926, 11x21", VG 130.00
Five Roses Flour, door plate, porc, wht, 12x4", NM 375.00
Forty Four (44) 5¢ Cigars, sign, diecut cb Indian scout, 32x21", VG .260.00
Frank's Choice Cigars, sign, paper, 4 kids in woods, fr, 18x25", EX 330.00
Frostie Root Beer, menu brd, tin, slots, 1950, 12x36", NM 500.00
Frostie Root Beer, thermometer, dial type, 12" dia, M 125.00
Frostie Root Beer, thermometer, tin, 1950s, 35", NM 225.00
Full Dress Tobacco, pocket tin, flat top, brn, VG 215.00
Full Dress Tobacco, pocket tin, flip top, gold, EX 200.00
FW Cook Brewing Co, ts, elderly gent w/brew, fr, 30x23", EX ...650.00
Gail & Ax Navy Tobacco, sign, paper, sailor, fr, 40x31", VG 800.00
Garland Stoves & Ranges, match holder, diecut tin, 7x4", EX+ .225.00
GE, ashtray, Power Groove, ceramic fluorescent tube, 1950, EX .40.00
Gem Damaskeene Razor, clock, wooden case w/pendulum, 27", EX .1,150.00
Gillett's Flavoring Extracts, display cabinet, 34x21", VG 1,000.00
Gold Soap, ps, Extra Large/Extra Good, 1915-20, 26x20", EX ...550.00
Goody Orange Drink, bottle topper, diecut cb, bottle cap, EX 30.00
Goody Root Beer, bottle topper, diecut cb, boy's head, NM 48.00
Goodyear, fs, diecut metal tire shape, 2-sided, 34x22", VG 950.00
Goodyear Motorcycle Tires, fs, porc diecut cyclist, 11x24", EX 13,200.00
Gorden Dye Hosiery, sign, paper, ladies showing ankles, 27x13", EX ..900.00
Grads Cigarettes, thermometer, tin, wht on red, 39", NM 100.00
Grand Prize Beer, display, Pale Dry Pete w/bottle, plaster, G 140.00
Grant's Cherry Whiskey, ts, 2 gents outside pub, 13x10", EX+ ..150.00
Grape Nuts, string holder, tin, 1910s, 12", VG 160.00
Grape Ola, ts, Drink.../It's Real..., w/graphics, 1920s, 20x28", VG ..300.00
Grapette, clock, rnd light-up, bottle in center, 1940s, NM+ 400.00
Grapette, ps, Grapette Soda on red/wht/bl oval, 10x17", EX 300.00
Great Majestic Ranges, plaque, bas-relief gesso, 1915, 49x37", EX ..3,000.00
Great West Cut Plug, lunch box, red, VG+ 85.00
Green River Whiskey, ts, She Was Bred..., fr, 33x45", EX 1,100.00
Greyhound Atlantic Lines Ticket Office, pc, 2-sided, 1930s, 30", VG ..1,600.00
Gulf, thread container/thimble, metal, 2", EX 300.00
Gulf Gasoline, blotter, There Is More Power..., w/graphics, 4x6", EX ..65.00
Hambone Mild & Mellow 5¢ Cigar, menu brd, cb, 20x13", NM 120.00
Hamilton Brown Shoe Co, watch fob/compass, brass, EX 75.00
Hamm's Beer, light-up display building w/slant roof, VG 150.00
Hand Bag Cut Plug, lunch box, tin, VG+ 200.00
Hanley Export Beer, chalkware display hand w/bottle, 1940s, 14", EX+ .140.00
Happy Hour Coffee, can, screw lid, sample, 2" dia, EX+ 350.00
Harvard Brewing Co, ts, Victorian lady in exotic room, 45x36", EX+ .1,750.00
Hassan Cork Tip Cigarettes, sign, cb, man in fez, fr, 30x23", EX ..235.00
Heptol Splits, tip tray, cowboy/horse, Russell, 1904, 4" dia, EX .285.00
Hickory Children's Garters, sign, wood, boy/girl/umbrella, 18", VG ..350.00
High-Toned 3¢ Cigar, ts, emb diecut Yellow Kid, 20", VG 800.00
Hills Bros Coffee, thermometer, porc, HB man, red/wht, 21x9", EX .500.00

Hires

Charles E. Hires, a drugstore owner in Philadelphia, became interested in natural teas. He began experimenting with roots and herbs and soon developed his own special formula. Hires introduced his product to his own patrons and began selling concentrated syrup to other soda fountains and grocery stores. Samples of his 'root beer' were offered for the public's approval at the 1876 Philadelphia Centennial. Today's collectors are often able to date their advertising items by observing the Hires boy on the logo. From 1891 to 1906, he wore a dress. From 1906 until 1914, he was shown in a bathrobe; and from 1915 until 1926, he was depicted in a dinner jacket. The apostrophe may or may not appear in the Hires name; this seems to have no bearing on dating an item. Our advisor for Hires is Craig Stifter; he is listed in the Directory under Illinois.

Banner, Enjoy a Hires Float/Only 50¢..., canvas, 32x42", EX 125.00
Bottle, salesman's sample, amber, ca 1910, 3", NM 200.00
Bottle carrier, wood w/dvtl corners, Quarter Case, VG+ 30.00
Bottle topper/bottle, diecut cb, 10¢ Off/Try a Real Black Cow, EX .15.00
Clock, rnd, Drink Hires..., light-up, glass face, 15", EX 385.00
Clock, sq w/curved top/bottom, logo/mug, blk fr, EX 75.00
Coupon, Free Drink, image of Hires Boy, VG+ 38.00
Dispenser, ceramic hourglass shape w/finial, orig spigot, 13", EX .1,750.00
Dispenser, metal box w/flat lid, 1940s, 22x12x16", VG+ 300.00
Drinking glass, curved top, etched, Enjoy Hires..., NM+ 160.00
Mug, ceramic, tapered, Hires Boy in tux, phrase, Mettlach, 5", NM .325.00
Mug, ceramic bbl shape w/Hires Boy, Mettlach, 4", EX+ 275.00
Mug, ceramic hourglass shape w/Hires Boy on wht, 4", EX 200.00
Recipe folder, boy looking at Hires sign, VG 20.00

Sign, cardboard, easel back, party scene, 16x12", NM, $225.00.
(Photo courtesy Autopia, Inc.)

Sign, cb, For Finer Flavor, lady/food tray, 12" dia, NM 160.00
Sign, cb, Hires to You/Tuned to Good Taste, 16x28", EX+ 200.00
Sign, cb, The Right Note..., girl at piano, fr, 39x34", VG 475.00
Sign, rvpt glass, Drink...For Thirst & Cheer, 33x25", VG 6,500.00
Sign, sf tin oval, Drink Hires, 2 ladies, Meyers art, 1915, 20x24", G ...250.00
Sign, tin, Ask for Hires in Bottles, wht on bl, 10x28", VG+ 135.00
Sign, tin, bottle shape, 1950s, 22", M 200.00
Sign, tin, bull's-eye logo, emb, 24" dia, EX 125.00
Sign, tin, We Serve...RJ.../Fountain Service, 2-sided, 15x16", VG .475.00
Sign, tin flange, ...Made w/Roots..., check-mk logo, 12x14", EX ..325.00
Syrup bottle, rvpt octagonal label, emb knob lid, 13", EX 825.00
Thermometer, tin, Drink Hires, lt bl w/wht stripes, 27", EX+ 325.00

Thermometer, tin bottle shape, Since 1876 label, 29", NM 250.00
Trade card, bust image of girl w/paper hat, M 18.00
Trade card, bust image of lady, Haskell Coffin, 1917, NM+ 60.00
Tray, Just What the Doctor Ordered..., ca 1914, 13" dia, G 350.00

Holsum Bread, push bar, pnt tin, red diecut loaf on bl bar, NM ..200.00
Honey Krust Bread, string holder, tin panels, 16x13", VG 300.00
Honeymoon 5¢ Cigar, rvpt sign, silver on blk, fr, 12x19", NM ..425.00
Hood's Sarsaparilla, jigsaw puzzle, Rainy Day/Balloon, 2-sided, NM+ 70.00
Hood Tire Dealer, ps, diecut man w/flag down & hand up, 71", VG+ .1,100.00
Humble, pc, diecut Oil Drop Man saluting, 48x24", EX 1,600.00
Hunt Pen Co Round Pointed Pens, case, wood/glass, 11", NM .300.00
Illinois Watch Co, sign, rvpt train, blk on gold, 13x22", EX 400.00
Indian Rock Ginger Ale, ts, emb, bottles flank phrase, 12x36", G+ ..200.00
Indianapolis Brewing Co, tip tray, bottle on red, 1905-10, NM .100.00
Indianapolis Glove Co, thermometer, wood, keyhole shape, 11x4", VG ..100.00
Ingersoll Watches, fs, porc, diecut pocket watch, 17x9", VG 220.00
IW Harper Whiskey, sign, canvas, Parting Gift, 1912, fr, 34x46", EX 1,500.00
IW Harper Whiskey, sign, Vitrolite, dog/cabin, 1909, 28x22", NM .1,850.00
Java Coffee Mills, pocket mirror, wht on bl, oval, EX 40.00
Jests, thermometer, porc, mascot's head/name/product, 36", EX ...550.00
Jewel Shop, pocket mirror, lettering w/decorative border, oval, VG .60.00
JG Davis Co's Granite Flour, bill hook, Don't Forget..., 6", EX .200.00
John Deere, clock, rnd light-up, glass front/metal fr, 15", NM ...600.00
Joseph Glennon's New Brewery, art plate, Lenore, Meek litho, 10", VG ..100.00
Jumbo Brand Peanut Butter, measuring cup, tin, gr, 12-oz, VG+ ..1,100.00
Kayo, ts, Tops in Taste..., graphics, yel/bl, 1930s, 24x14", EX 425.00
Kellogg's, blotter, Toasted Corn Flakes..., boy saluting, 3x6", EX .25.00
Kellogg's, jigsaw puzzle, Keep Going w/Kellogg's, boy ball player, M 60.00
Kellogg's, salesman's ad booklet, Superman/War Planes, 8-pg, EX ..1,450.00
Kelly Springfield Tires, magazine ad, Lotta Miles, fr, 9x7", NM+ ..20.00
Kelly Tires, fs, 2-sided circle, girl waving, 24" dia, VG+ 4,000.00

Kendall Motor Oil, oil can, enamel on steel, 20x12", EX, $400.00. (Photo courtesy Dunbar Gallery)

Kennebec Canoes, display model, canvas w/gold name, 63", VG .7,750.00
Kessler Whisley, display baseball figure, compo, scarce, 47", VG .1,000.00
King Midas Flour, string holder, tin, 1908, 20x14", EX+ 1,400.00
Kist, ts, bottle cap, red/wht/blk, dtd 6-59, 15" dia, EX+ 170.00
Klingzon Cleaner, bill hook, cl, 6x3", EX 275.00
Knapsack Matches, vendor, wood/glass panels, 8-sided, 1892, 11", G .600.00
Knox Sparkling Gelatin, sign, diecut cb, 4-sided, 16x15x10", EX .2,000.00
Kool Cigarettes, display, Willy in top hat, compo, 1930s, 14", EX 600.00
Laquerwax, sign, diecut cb stand-up, car/product, 30x22", EX ...250.00

Levi's, display cowboy figure, 1960s, 30", EX 2,500.00
Life Savers, display box, tin, 2-tier, 10x11x8", VG 250.00
Lime Cola, banner, canvas, Drink...in Bottles, 10x49", EX 80.00
Little Boy Blue Bluing, dispenser, tin, 1920s, 19x4", NM+ 250.00

Log Cabin Syrup

Log Cabin Syrup tins have been made since the 1890s in variations of design that can be attributed to specific years of production. Until about 1914, they were made with paper labels. These are quite rare and highly prized by today's collectors. Tins with colored lithographed designs were made after 1914. When General Foods purchased the Towle Company in 1927, the letters 'GF' were added.

A Cartoon series, illustrated with a mother flipping pancakes in the cabin window and various children and animals declaring their appreciation of the syrup in voice balloons, was introduced in the 1930s. A Frontier Village series followed in the late 1940s. A schoolhouse, jail, trading post, doctor's office, blacksmith shop, inn, and private homes were also available. Examples of either series today often command prices of $125.00 to $200.00 and up.

Bank, glass cabin shape, EX 40.00
Container, plastic wigwam, yel letters, 1950, 2x2" dia 9.00
Spoon, SP, log cabin on tree trunk stem, ca 1910, NM 65.00
Syrup tin, animal skin on door, 1909-14, label, ½-gal, EX 180.00
Syrup tin, bear in doorway, 1930s, 5", VG+ 160.00
Syrup tin, boy in doorway, 1918, paper label, sample, EX 350.00
Syrup tin, boy in doorway, 1918, paper label, 1-gal, EX 275.00
Syrup tin, boy in doorway, 1918, 4", EX+ 200.00
Syrup tin, boy in doorway, 1930s, 5", EX+ 140.00
Syrup tin, Dr RU Well, 4", EX+ 360.00
Syrup tin, Express Office, 5", EX+ 170.00
Syrup tin, frontier boy w/lasso, red shutters, bl door, 4", EX+ 300.00
Syrup tin, frontier family, gold shutters, 5", EX+ 220.00
Syrup tin, Frontier Inn, 6", NM 200.00
Syrup tin, Frontier Jail, 4", EX+ 225.00
Syrup tin, frontier woman/girl in doorway, red shutters, 4", EX .250.00
Syrup tin, girl in doorway, 1930s, 5", EX+ 150.00
Syrup tin, red sign nailed to cabin wall, 1950s, 58-oz, EX+ 135.00
Syrup tin, Trading Post, 6", EX+ 200.00
Syrup tin, wigwam, rare, 4", EX 1,625.00

Lucky Star Ginger Ale, ts, bottle shape, 20x6", NM 100.00
Madison Cigar Mfg Co, sign, paper, Indian maiden, 1906, fr, 30", NM .730.00
Mammoth Salted Peanuts, tc, blk on wht, 10-lb, 11", G 200.00
Maryland Club Mixture, pocket tin, flat top, EX+ 250.00
Maryland Club Mixture, pocket tin, vertical, curved flip top, EX .315.00
Mason-Heflin Co, jigsaw puzzle, coal truck, 1930, 4¾x6½", EX ..60.00
Maxwell House Coffee, sign, cb, phrase/graphics, 1921, 9x11", EX+ ..225.00
Maxwell House Iced Tea, dispenser, ceramic bbl w/spigot, 13", VG 300.00
Mayo's Tobacco, lunch box, collapsible, EX+ 250.00
Mission Beverages/Orange, fs, bottle cap shape, 1940s-50s, 19", NM ..375.00
Mother's Bread, display case, oak w/glass front, rail top, 39x51", VG ..500.00
Mother's Oats, sign, paper, The Naughty Boy, fr, image: 23x16", VG .250.00
Moxie, clock, figure-8, Baird, rstr, 31" 1,500.00
Moxie, fan, cb, Rocking Horse/Moxie Man, 1922, NM 75.00
Moxie, thermometer, tin, red, w/Moxie Man, 1953, 25x10", EX+ ..700.00
Moxie, ts, Drink Moxie, depicts horsemobile, rare, 27x39", G ..2,100.00
Moxie, umbrella/parasol, red/blk on wht, rare, EX 350.00
Munsing Union Suits, fs, man, diecut scrolled border, 15x18", VG ...3,500.00
Nehi, clock, glass/metal, Drink...& Other Flavors, 15" dia, NM ...325.00
Nehi, fs, Drink...Ice Cold, diecut bottle/yel panel, 1940s, 13x18", NM 525.00
Nehi, ts, emb, ...Quality Beverages, bottle on wht, 1940s, 20x6", EX ...100.00

Nesbitt's, sign, cb, ...California Orange, barbecue, 1940s, 24x36", EX ...250.00
Nesbitt's, thermometer, tin, yel/orange on blk, 1938, 23", EX ...200.00
NuGrape, fs, oval, hand-held bottle, 14x20", EX 200.00
NuGrape, tray, draped woman w/bottle, 1925, 13x11", VG 85.00
Oak Motor Oil, ps, gr/wht/blk/red, tree graphics, 20" dia, NM ..1,500.00
Ohio Match Co, paperweight/mirror, aerial factory view, rnd, EX+ ..90.00
Oilzum Motor Oil, banner, Escape to No Wear/Oilzum Man, 1950s, 26", M ..500.00
Oilzum Motor Oil, clock, Choice of..., light-up, Pam, 15" dia, NM .525.00
Old Mission Lager, tray, deep rim, C Shonk litho, 12" dia, VG+ .220.00
Old Virginia Cheroots, sign, paper, cowboy, fr, 25x17", NM 625.00

Old Crow

Old Crow Whiskey items have become popular with collectors primarily because of the dapper crow dressed in a tuxedo, top hat, etc., that was used by the company for promotional purposes during the 1940s through the 1960s. However, there is a vast variety of Old Crow collectibles, some of which carry only the whiskey's name. In the 1970s ceramic decanters shaped like chess pieces were available; these carried nothing more than a paper label and a presentation box to identify them. In 1985, the 150th anniversary of Old Crow, the realistic crow that had been extensively used prior to 1950 re-emerged.

Very little Old Crow memorabilia has been issued since National Distillers Products Corporations, the parent company since 1933, was purchased by Jim Beam Brands in 1987. No reproductions have surfaced, although a few fantasies have been found where the character crow was borrowed for private use. Our advisors for Old Crow collectibles are Judith and Robert Walthall; they are listed in the Directory under Alabama.

Plaque, ceramic plate with applied 4¾" character crow, 8", NM, $125.00. (Photo courtesy Judith and Robert Walthall)

Ashtray, Bakelite, 3½", NM 25.00
Bank, wooden bbl, 1985, 6", EX 15.00
Booklet, Mixing Guide & Almanac, drink recipes, etc, EX 15.00
Booklet, Mixing Magic, drink recipes, etc, EX 10.00
Bottle opener, metal, bottle shape, 2⅝", NM 30.00
Dice, I Buy, You Buy, EX 30.00
Dice cup, Bakelite, blk w/yel lettering, felt-lined, NM 100.00
Display, bkbar; ceramic Broken Leg Mug holds bottle, 5¼", NM ..100.00
Doorstop, wood, 2-D crow, 21", EX 125.00
Figure, compo, 1940s, 11½", EX 125.00
Figure, plastic, blk-banded wht base, 1960s, 10", EX 45.00
Figure, plastic, on rocking base, 1950s, 9", EX 95.00
Glass, Bourbon; crow & lettering in blk on clear, 4⅞", NM 5.00
Jigger, lettering in blk on clear glass, no crown, NM 5.00
Label, bbls, etc, gold/red/blk/wht, 1905, about 4¾" sq, NM 15.00
Lipstick tissue booklet, Cub Products, 1⅞x3", unused 25.00
Pitcher, ceramic, Broken Leg decor, NM 35.00
Playing cards, Two Crows...Good Luck..., 1967, 2 decks, M 50.00
Punch bowl, Hall, ceramic, w/10 cups & ladle, gold trim, MIB .250.00
Stirrer, plastic, full-figure crow on end, from $1 to 3.00
Thermometer, metal, rnd dial, gold/red/blk/wht, 9x13", EX 100.00
Thermometer, Taste the Greatness of..., red/wht/blk, 13½", EX ...200.00

Orange Crush, clock, rvpt glass, 1930s, 16" dia, NM 1,600.00
Orange Crush, menu board, blkbrd bottom, 1954, 28x19", VG+ .250.00
Orange Crush, sign, diecut cb bottle stand-up w/Crushy, 30", NM .140.00
Orange Kist, bottle topper, cb, bl lettering on orange half, EX 26.00
OshKosh, display, cb cutout, Uncle Sam in real overalls, 77", NM ..2,150.00
Pabst, sign, neon, name in bl ribbon logo, NM 100.00
Pabst Blue Ribbon Beer, display figure, boxer in ring, pot metal, VG ...100.00
Pabst Brewing Co, match safe, brass, button release, VG 40.00
Pastime Plug Tobacco, store bin, tin, blk on red, Ginna, EX+ ...340.00
Paul Bunyan Coffee, can, key-wind lid, red, 1-lb, EX+ 330.00
Paul Jones Clean Cut Tobacco, pocket tin, bl, NM 2,450.00
Paul Jones Pure Rye Whiskey, ts, Comrades for 81 Yrs, 1903, 29x22", EX ...900.00
Pear's Soap, sign, paper, 3 girls playing, WS Coleman art, 32x23", VG ...350.00
Pennzoil, lollipop sidewalk sign, porc, red CI base, 60", EX 850.00

Pepsi-Cola

Pepsi-Cola was first served in the early 1890s to customers of Caleb D. Bradham, a young pharmacist who touted his concoction to be medicinal as well as delicious. It was first called 'Brad's Drink' but was renamed Pepsi-Cola in 1898. Various logos have been registered over the years. The familiar oval was first used in the early 1940s. At about the same time, the two 'dots' (indicated in our listings by '=') between the words Pepsi and Cola became one, though more recent items may carry the double-dot logo as well, especially when they're designed to be reminiscent of the old ones. The bottle cap logo came along in 1943 and with variations was used through the early '60s. Our advisor for Pepsi is Craig Stifter; he is listed in the Directory under Illinois.

Ashtray, chrome bowl w/enameled bottle cap, 1956, 3½" dia, EX+ ..75.00
Ballpark vendor, wood, red/wht on bl, 1950s, 6x19", NM 325.00
Bottle carrier, cb, Bigger-Better, w/6 full 12-oz bottles, 1945, EX .190.00
Bottle carrier, wood 6-pack w/dowel hdl, 1940, EX 100.00
Bottle topper, Pepsi & Pete, 1930s, 14x12", EX+ 700.00
Change purse, leather, Drink...The World's Best Drink, rare, EX ...275.00
Clock, bottle cap on yel, light-up, Swihart, 1950s, 15" dia, NM .450.00
Clock, Drink...Light Refreshment, light-up, 1950s, 17" dia, NM .600.00
Clock, Say Pepsi Please, light-up, 1960s, 18x12", EX 80.00
Dispenser, red/wht/bl, streamline, 1950s, NM 600.00
Display rack, wire, 3-tier w/diecut cap, 1940s, 42x22", VG 175.00
Door push bar, Enjoy...Iced, yel/wht stripes, porc, 30", EX 225.00
Door push plate, Enjoy..., P-C bottle caps, yel/wht, 1954, 14", EX+ ..230.00
Drinking glasses, Pepsi & Pete Safedge Tumblers, box of 6, EX+ .775.00
Fan, cb w/wooden hdl, Pepsi & Pete, 1940, 12", NM+ 120.00
Lighter, can shape, diagonal stripes, 1960s, EX+ 50.00
Menu board, tin w/red rope on wood-look fr, 1940s, 27x20", EX .150.00
Menu board, wood, sign w/ribbon above dbl slots, 1940s, EX 750.00
Miniature 6-pack, cb carrier w/6 glass swirl bottles, 2½", EX 70.00
Paperweight, glass, rectangular w/rnd corners, VG 50.00
Radio, fountain dispenser, red/wht/bl, 1950s, EX+ 375.00
Sign, cb, The Am Beverage, girl in profile, fr, 1907-08, 27x21", G+ .4,000.00
Sign, cb, The Light Refreshment, girl w/parakeet, 1957, 11x25", EX+ .150.00
Sign, cb, Think Young...Say Pepsi Please, Black pr, 14x30", VG .40.00
Sign, cb cutout, Pepsi cops inspecting bottle, 1941, EX+ 650.00

Sign, cl button, Ice Cold...Sold Here, 1930s-40s, 9", EX 425.00
Sign, masonite, bottle cap, 48", EX+ 325.00
Sign, porc, bottle cap, 19", EX 325.00
Sign, porc, Drink...Iced, cap on yel, 1950s, 12x29", NM 500.00
Sign, sf cb, Certified Quality, lady lounging, 1940s, 22x28", EX .750.00
Sign, tin, bottle cap, 1960s, unused, 19", NM 325.00
Sign, tin, bottle shape, 5¢, 45", EX 1,400.00
Sign, tin, Drink, bottle bursting through yel bkground, 20x27", VG+ .335.00

Sign, tin, More Bounce to the Ounce, 1950s, NM, $475.00. **(Photo courtesy Craig Stifter)**

Standee, cb, grocer offering bottle from 6-pack, 1930s, 68", VG+ ..875.00
Thermometer/mirror, rvpt glass, fr, 1930s, 22x10", EX 1,850.00
Tip tray, 1910, EX+ 1,400.00
Toy truck, plastic Ford, 5 cases, red/wht/bl, 1960s, 7½", EX 250.00
Tray, ...Bigger & Better, w/stylized flowers, 11x14", EX 50.00

Peter Pan Fresh Bread, screen door sign, triangular, EX 150.00
Peter Rabbit Peanut Butter, pail, gr, VG 225.00
Peters Weatherbird Shoes, display, plaster rooster, 24", EX 500.00
Pfeiffer's, display figure, chalkware, Johnny Pheiffer w/flute, EX ..50.00
Piccadilly Little Cigars/10 Minute Havanas, sf ts, couple, 21x13", EX ..250.00
Piedmont Cigarettes, folding chair, wood w/porc sign, EX 190.00

Planters Peanuts

The Planters Peanut Co. was founded in 1906. Mr. Peanut, the dashing peanut man with top hat, spats, monocle, and cane, has represented Planters since 1916. He took on his modern-day appearance after the company was purchased by Standard Brands in November 1960. He remains perhaps the most highly recognized logo of any company in the world. Mr. Peanut has promoted the company's products by appearing in ads; on product packaging; on or as store displays, novelties, and premiums; and even in character at promotional events (thanks to a special Mr. Peanut costume).

Among the favorite items of collectors today are the glass display jars which were sent to retailers nationwide to stimulate 'point-of-sale' trade. They come in a variety of shapes and styles. The first, distributed in the early 1920s, was a large universal candy jar (round covered bowl on a pedestal) with only a narrow paper label affixed at the neck to identify it as 'Planters.' In 1924 an octagonal jar was produced, all eight sides embossed, with Mr. Peanut on the narrow corner panels. On a second octagon jar, only seven sides were embossed, leaving one of the large panels blank to accommodate a paper label.

In late 1929 a fishbowl jar was introduced, and in 1932 a beautiful jar with a blown-out peanut on each of the four corners was issued. The football shape was also made in the 1930s, as were the square jar, the large barrel jar, and the hexagon jar with yellow fired-on designs alternating on each of the six sides. All of these early jars had glass lids which after 1930 had peanut finials.

In 1937 jars with lithographed tin lids were introduced. The first of these was the slant-front streamline jar, which is also found with screened yellow lettering. Next was a squat version, the clipper jar, then the upright rectangular 1940 leap year jar, and last, another upright rectangular jar with a screened, fired-on design similar to the red, white, and blue design on the cellophane 5¢ bags of peanuts of the period. This last jar was issued again after WWII with a plain red tin lid.

In 1959 Planters first used a stock Anchor Hocking one-gallon round jar with a 'customer-special' decoration in red. As the design was not plainly evident when the jar was full, the decoration was modified with a white under-panel. The two jars we've just described are perhaps the rarest of them all due to their limited production. After Standard Brands purchased Planters, they changed the red-on-white panel to show their more modern Mr. Peanut and in 1963 introduced this most plentiful, thus very common, Planters jar. In 1966 the last counter display jar was distributed: the Anchor Hocking jar with a fired-on large four-color design such as those that appeared on peanut bags of the period. Prior to this, a plain jar with a transfer decal in an almost identical but smaller design was used.

Some Planters jars have been reproduced: the octagon jar (with only six of the sides embossed), a small version of the barrel jar, and the four peanut corner jar. Some of the first were made in clear glass with 'Made in Italy' embossed on the bottom, but most have been made in Asia, many in various colors of glass (a dead giveaway) as well as clear, and carrying only small paper stickers, easily removed, identifying the country of origin. At least two reproductions of the Anchor Hocking jar with four-color designs have been made, one circa 1978, the other in 1989. Both, using the stock jar, are difficult to detect, but there are small differences between them and the original that will enable you to make an accurate identification. With the exception of several of the earliest and the Anchor Hocking, all authentic Planters jars have 'Made in USA' embossed on the bottom, and all, without exception, are clear glass. Unfortunately, several paper labels have also been reproduced, no doubt due to the fact that an original label or decal will greatly increase the value of an original jar. Jar prices continue to remain stable in today's market.

In the late 1920s, the first premiums were introduced in the form of story and paint books. Late in the 1930s, the tin nut set (which was still available into the 1960s) was distributed. A wood-jointed doll was available from Planters Peanuts stores at that time. Many post-WWII items were made of plastic: banks, salt and pepper shakers, cups, cookie cutters, small cars and trucks, charms, whistles, various pens and mechanical pencils, and almost any other item imaginable. In recent years the company, now a division of Nabisco, has continued to distribute a wide variety of novelties.

Note that there are many unauthorized Planters/Mr. Peanut items. Although several are reproductions or 'copycats,' most are fantasies and fakes. Our advisors for Planters Planters are Judith and Robert Walthall; they are in the Directory under Alabama.

Key:
al — aluminum
cc — common colors
(green, light blue, red, tan)
MrP — Mr. Peanut
okl — octagon knob lid
pfl — peanut finial lid
pl — plastic
pm — papier-mache
pnut — peanut

Ashtray, gold-plated metal w/MrP figure, 50th Anniversary, 6x5", MIB 130.00
Badge, employee's, metal, space for name, 1½x2", EX 300.00
Bank, MrP figure, pl, cc, 9", EX, from $10 to 20.00
Bank, MrP figure, pl, yel/blk/wht, 1991, 9", NM 10.00
Bank, MrP head labeled ...Vender Bank, pl, 1950s, EX, from $350 to ..450.00
Belt, Nabisco Dinah Shore Invitational Golf Tournament, 1984, MIB ...40.00
Booklet, Planters War Atlas (WWII), 10x13" 45.00
Bucket, wood, 25-lb, paper label, early, EX 750.00

Cardboard box, blue and white on orange, held 24 bags of 5¢ salted peanuts; 2½x7½x8½", with fold-out diecut and box top, 1930, NM, $600.00. (Photo courtesy Judith and Robert Walthall)

Cookie cutter, MrP figure bowing or tipping hat, red pl, EX 20.00
Dish, pressed glass, MrP in center, 5½", M (+) 20.00
Display box, cb, 24 5¢ Bags, 1950s, 2½x6x5", M 60.00
Display statue, pot metal, MrP on base w/2 peanuts, 7½", EX ...600.00
Doll, MrP, jtd wood, yel body, bl hat, blk/wht limbs, 8½", NM .250.00
Fork & spoon set, salad; wood w/ceramic figural hdls, MIB 115.00
Jar, Barrel, pfl, paper label, 1935, 12¼", EX 250.00
Jar, Fishbowl, okl, no label, 1929, 12½", EX 75.00
Jar, Fishbowl, okl, Planters on base, orig label, 12½", VG, $150 to ..175.00
Jar, Football, pfl, 1931, 8½", EX 225.00
Jar, Four Peanut Corner, pfl, 1932, 14" (+) 225.00
Jar, Octagon, 6 sides emb, pfl, clear & colors, repro 35.00
Jar, Octagon, 7 sides emb, okl, no label, 12", EX (+) 85.00
Jar, Octagon, 8 sides emb, okl, 1924, 12", EX (+) 250.00
Mug, ceramic, 75th Anniversary, heat sensitive, unused, 1981, M .15.00
Mug, MrP head, cc pl, M, from $5 to 15.00
Mug, Wilton Armatele, w/emb MrP, 1983, M 20.00
Nodder, MrP figure, compo, 6½", MIB 150.00
Oven mitt, MrP figure, MIP 10.00
Pin, MrP figure, wooden, 1¾", MOC 80.00
Plate, Wilton Armatele, ...Since 1906 logo, 2,000 made, 1981, 6", M ..75.00
Poster, paper, Planters MrP Sale/Stock Up..., 1950s, 15x36", EX .85.00
Puppet, hand; MrP figure, rubber, tan w/blk hat/monocle, early, 6", EX ...750.00
Shakers, MrP figures, china w/rhinestone monocles, 4½", M, pr ...150.00
Toy, windup MrP, pl, cc, 1950, working, 8½", EX 350.00
Tray, ...Since 1906, premium, oval, 1982, 12x15", M 25.00
Umbrella, yel/bl, single image of MrP, 1982, M 40.00

Popsicle, sign, cb cutout, Buck/Wilma facing 5¢ Popsicle, EX ...1,450.00
Post Toasties, sign, cb, Sweet Memories, Bryson art, 1909, 24x17", EX ..535.00
Pratt's Veterinary Remedies, cabinet, wood/tin front, 33x17", VG 2,300.00
Prestone Anti-Freeze, thermometer, dial type, 1930s-40s, NM+ ..300.00
Prince Albert Tobacco, charger, tin, man/pocket tin, 24" dia, G ..450.00
Proctor & Gamble, clock, wht face/bl numbers/name, sq, NM ..200.00
Pur-Ox Syrups, fan, cb, 2 couples at dinner, NM 110.00
Putnam Dyes, fan, cb w/wooden hdl, peacock, 1930s, NM 25.00
Quaker State Motor Oil, clock, light-up, Ask for..., 16" sq, MIB .90.00
Quaker State Motor Oil, sign, paper, lady counting change, 34x58", EX+ ..100.00
Quisp Cereal, figurine, Quisp Rabbit, cermaic, 5", NM 150.00

RCA Victor

Nipper, the RCA Victor trademark, was the creation of Francis Barraud, an English artist. His pet's intense fascination with the music of the phonograph seemed to him a worthy subject for his canvas. Although he failed to find a publishing house who would buy his work, the Gramophone Co. in England saw its potential and adopted Nipper to advertise their product. The painting was later acquired and trademarked in the United States by the Victor Talking Machine Co., which was purchased by RCA in 1929. The trademark is owned today by EMI in England and by General Electric in the U.S. Nipper's image appeared on packages, accessories, ads, brochures, and in three-dimensional form. You may find a life-size statue of him, but all are not old. They have been manufactured for the owner throughout RCA history and are marketed currently by licensees, BMG Inc. and Thomson Consumer Electronics (dba RCA). Except for the years between 1968 and 1976, Nipper has seen active duty, and with his image spruced up only a bit for the present day, the ageless symbol for RCA still listens intently to 'His Master's Voice.' Many of the items have been reproduced in recent years. Exercise care before you buy.

The recent phenomenon of Internet auctions has played havoc with prices paid for Victor and RCA Victor collectibles. Often prices paid for online sales bear little resemblance to the true value of the item. Reproductions are often sold as old on the Internet and bring prices accordingly. It is common knowledge that auction prices, more often than not, are inflated over sales made through traditional sales outlets. The Internet has exacerbated the situation by focusing a very large number of buyers and sellers through the narrow portal of a modem. The prices here are intended to reflect what one might expect to pay through traditional sales. Our advisor for RCA Victor is Roger R. Scott; he is listed in the Directory under Oklahoma.

Sign, porcelain, double-sided, RCA Radiola Dealer, black, white, red, and yellow, 19x14½", NM, $575.00. (Photo courtesy Autopia, Inc.)

Bank, Nipper, felt over pot metal, mk Radio Corp of Am, 6", NM ...125.00
Buckle, His Master's Voice, brass, Nash Tiffany 25.00
Chair, NP pipe fr w/armrest, plastic bk/seat, logo on bk, M 100.00
Curtains, RCA 40.00
Figure, Nipper, chalk, Victor, 4" 40.00
Figure, Nipper, crystal, Fenton, 4" 60.00
Figure, nipper, molded plastic, 36", EX 235.00
Figure, Nipper, papier-mache, 14" or 18", from $200 to 400.00
Figure, Nipper, papier-mache, 36" 600.00
Figure, Nipper, plaster, 14½x7½x5", VG (not repro) 200.00
Necktie, Nipper, M 20.00
Needle tin, Nipper, 3-color, NM, from $25 to 50.00

Pin-bk button, I Support Nipper, 1930s, ½", EX ...45.00
Pin-bk button, Nipper Fan Club ...50.00
Plate, Nipper, collector's edition ...50.00
Puzzle record, Victor, MIP ...100.00
Radiotrons man, Cameo Doll Co, jtd wood, 1920s, 15", M ...900.00
Record brush, Lucite hdl, in faux leather snap case ...30.00
Record display, dog & phonograph, chalk ...150.00
Shakers, dog & RCA phonograph, plastic, pr ...45.00
Shakers, Nipper, Lenox, 3", pr ...55.00
Shakers, Radio Corp of Am, 1940s, pr ...40.00
Sign, plastic/metal, light-up, 1940s, 15x37", EX ...200.00
Sign, porc, Authorized Dealer..., 1940s, 18x24", EX ...165.00
Sign, porc, record shape w/trademark image on red label, 24", VG ...300.00
Sign, tin, Nipper Listening, fr, 13½x19", G ...500.00
Watch fob, EX ...30.00
Water glass, etched Nipper, set of 6 ...100.00

Rabbit's Foot Baking Powder, tc, pry lid, paper label, unused, EX ...775.00
Rainbo Bread, push bar, diecut tin loaf on bl bar, 9x32", EX+ ...200.00
Red Devil, clock, ...Time To Polish, wood fr, 1930s, 16x16", EX ..150.00
Red Devil's Lighter Fluid, thermometer, tin, wht, 12", MIB ...160.00

Red Goose Shoes

Realizing that his last name was difficult to pronounce, Herman Giesceke, a shoe company owner resolved to give the public a modified, shortened version that would be better suited to the business world. The results suggested the use of the goose trademark with the last two letters, 'ke,' represented by the key that this early goose held in his mouth. Upon observing an employee casually coloring in the goose trademark with a red pencil, Giesceke saw new advertising potential and renamed the company Red Goose Shoes. Although the company has changed hands down through the years, the Red Goose emblem has remained. Collectors of this desirable fowl increase in number yearly, as do prices. Beware of reproductions; new chalkware figures are prevalent.

Card game, Cities, incomplete, w/box, VG ...18.00
Clock, light-up, glass/metal, Pam, dtd Nov 1954, 14½" dia, NM+ ...550.00
Clock, light-up, glass/metal, Telechron, 1930s-40s, NM ...400.00
Dispenser, Golden Egg, cb & papier-mache goose, kid prizes, EX .325.00
Figure, chalkware goose, red, wht emb name, gr base, 12", NM+.400.00
Figure, plaster goose, red, giveaway, 4", NM+ ...40.00
Glider, paper goose, red, 9", NM ...10.00
Globe, world; metal, w/stand, 9x6" dia, EX ...165.00
Pull toy, elephant, wood, 4x3½", VG ...100.00
Pull toy, fish, 7", EX ...55.00
Punch-out book, Chimpanzee Show, St Louis Zoo, 10x10", NM .25.00
Rug, Half the Fun of Having Feet, gold/gray, rare, 27x59", EX ..325.00
Ruler, wooden fold-up, 24", VG ...25.00
Sign, cb stand-up, goose, 10x6", NM ...20.00
Sign, neon goose shape on wht oval, 1930s-40s, 24x12", NM+ ..1,900.00
Sign, porc, yel name on red goose/yel ground/red border, 17x12", EX .250.00
Sign, tin, ...For Boys & Girls, yel/red, 13x19", VG ...110.00
Sign, wood, Red Goose Boots, stenciled, zigzag ends, 5½x24", EX .35.00
String holder, CI goose, 11x17", VG ...1,900.00
Welcome mat, rubber, VG ...50.00

Red J Tobacco, store tc, red, 6½x6½x4", VG+ ...60.00
Red Raven, charger, tin, lady hugging RR, 24" dia, VG ...450.00
Red Raven, tip tray, lady hugging RR, rnd, EX ...150.00
Red Raven, tip tray, RR w/glass & bottle, rectangular, EX ...100.00
Red Rock Ginger Ale, pocket mirror, lady w/bottle, oval, EX ...140.00
Red Rose Tea, push bar, porc, wht on red, 1950s-60s, 3x30", NM ...150.00
Red Seal Batteries, thermometer, porc, bl, curved top, 1920s, 27", G+ ..100.00
Reddy Kilowatt, apron, She Loves Me/Reddy pulling daisy petals, M ..40.00
Reddy Kilowatt, measuring glass, red on clear glass, 1930s, 4¾", M ...42.00
Reddy Kilowatt, sign, diecut hardbrd figure, red/wht, 10x9", VG ...115.00
Rising Sun Stove Polish, sign, paper, garden lady, Ottman, 29x13", VG ..350.00
Robin Hood Flour, display figure, chalkware, 15", EX ...150.00
Rockford Watches, tip tray, bust of pretty lady, oval, EX+ ...220.00

Roly Poly

The Roly Poly tobacco tins were patented on November 5, 1912, by Washington Tuttle and produced by Tindeco of Baltimore, Maryland. There were six characters in all: Satisfied Customer, Storekeeper, Mammy, Dutchman, Singing Waiter, and Inspector. Four brands of tobacco were packaged in selected characters; some tins carry a printed tobacco box on the back to identify their contents. Mayo and Dixie Queen Tobacco were packed in all six; Red Indian and U.S. Marine Tobacco in only Mammy, Singing Waiter, and Storekeeper. Of the set, the Inspector is considered the rarest and in near-mint condition may fetch more than $1,000.00 on today's market.

Dutchman, Dixie Queen, EX ...400.00
Inspector, Dixie Queen, VG ...500.00

Inspector, Dixie Queen, NM, from $1,000.00 to $1,100.00.

Inspector, Mayo, EX ...700.00
Inspector, Mayo, G ...375.00
Mammy, Mayo, NM+ ...850.00
Satisfied Customer, Mayo, VG+ ...425.00
Singing Waiter, Mayo, EX ...600.00
Storekeeper, Mayo, EX ...500.00

Rose Bud Coffee, tc, slip lid, sample, 2x2x3", EX ...450.00
Round Oak Stoves, grocery list brd, cb, Doe-Wah-Jack, 15x5", EX+ ..115.00
Royal Cord Tire/Red Special Tube, fan, cb tire shape, 12x7", EX ...130.00
Royal Crown Cola, clock, rnd w/rainbow marquee, light-up, 32", EX .1,300.00
Royal Crown Cola, picnic cooler, yel/red metal box, 20x18x12", EX ...150.00
Royal Crown Cola, thermometer, tin, red w/yel arrow, 1960s, 26", NM .275.00
Royal Crown Cola, ts, The Fresher Refresher, rnd corners, 28x8", NM ..125.00
Ruhstaller's Gilt Edge Beer, tray, man/2 ladies, 13x13", EX ...700.00
Sauer's Flavoring Extracts, clock, New Haven regulator, VG+ ..1,050.00
Schlitz Beer, paperweight, glass, brewery scene in glass, rnd, VG .100.00
Schlitz Beer, sign, paper, Purity, gesso/wood fr, 38x28", NM ...1,650.00

Schrafft's Chocolates, display shelf, diecut lady w/sign, rstr, 30" ..700.00
Schroeder's HT Whiskey, ts, I'se in a Perdickermunt, sf, 33", EX ..1,300.00
Sea Foam Baking Powder, sign, paper, ladies swimming, 20x12", G .275.00
Segars Bulldog, sign, cb, bulldog, J Merriam art, 1900, fr, 15", EX 470.00
Senate Beer, ashtray, metal dish/3 diecut metal bottles, 5" dia, EX ...140.00
Sensible Tobacco, lunch box, slip lid, dbl swing hdls, EX+ 50.00
Sharples, match holder, tin, The Pet of the Dairy, 7x2", NM 745.00
Sharples, pot scraper, The 1909 Tubulars Are Better..., EX 235.00
Shell, jigsaw puzzle, Jimmy Dolittle flying Shell plane, 10x14", NM ...340.00
Shell, winterfront, diecut cb logo, Starts Quickly, 13x21", G+ 65.00
Shell Gasoline/Motor Oil, thermometer, porc, yel/red, 27", NM+ ...3,500.00
Sherwin-Williams Paints, fs, diecut porc logo, 48x33", NM 700.00
Silver Dust Flour, thermometer, porc, wht/bl, 16x4", EX 300.00
Silver Moon Brand Coffee, can, slip lid, paper label, 1-lb, EX+ ..500.00
Sinclair, ashtray, chrome Dino in irregular shallow dish, 2x7", EX 70.00
Singer Sewing Machines, Singer Buffalo Puzzle, ca 1890, 7x11", EX+ .330.00
Singer Sewing Machines, ts, logo, emb, 2-sided, fr, 36", VG ..1,500.00
Skelly, fan, 3 cb bell-shaped foldouts w/graphics, VG 220.00
Smith Bros Cough Drops, blotter, blk/wht, 7x12", M 20.00
Smith Bros Cough Drops, paperweight, CI cough drop, 2x1", EX 135.00
Smith Bros Cough Drops, trolley sign, cb, 2 boys/5¢ ad, 18x28", EX .180.00
Snow King Baking Powder, bag holder, metal, 17", VG 1,300.00
Socony Motor Oils, paperweight/mirror, cl, 3½" dia, EX 160.00
Sparrow Chocolates, tip tray, girl standing on chair, EX 400.00
Squeeze, sign, diecut cb stand-up, man/boy fishing in boat, 20", NM ..450.00
Squires, ts, We Recommend..., pig in sf oval, 24x20", EX 1,500.00
Squirrel Brand Peanut Butter, tc, pry lid, 27-oz, NM 175.00
Squirt, display figure, Squirt Kid/bottle, 1947, 13", EX 650.00
Squirt, thermometer, boy sips from swirl bottle, wht, 14", EX 350.00
Star Soap, cb hanger, 2 diecut babies on swing, 10x5", EX+ ..1,300.00
Stegmaier Malt Extract, match holder, tin, 4 bottles, VG+ 85.00
Sterling Dark Tobacco, store tin, rnd w/sq slip lid, gr, NM 350.00
Sterling Motor Oil, tc, corner spout, diagonal grip hdl, 1-gal, VG ..100.00
Sterling Pilsner Beer, display bottle, glass, 2 labels, 20", VG 70.00
Stewart Clipping Machine, ts, 2 men/horse, beveled, 1900, 15x18", NM 825.00
Sun Crest, clock, light-up, glass/metal fr, Telechron, 1940s, EX+ ..350.00
Sun Crest, thermometer, tin bottle shape, 17", EX+ 220.00
Sun Crest, ts, bottle-cap shape, Get Tanle-ated..., 1950s, 36", NM ..165.00
Sun Cured Crushed Tobacco, pocket tin, scarce, VG+ 1,760.00
Sun Cured Tobacco, pocket tin, paper label, EX+ 200.00
Sunbeam Bread, push bar, loaf shape, Batter Whippers, 9x20", NM 250.00
Sunbeam Bread, sign, cb stand-up, Miss Sunbeam/umbrella, 26", NM .700.00
Sunny Boy Peanut Butter, pail, red on cream, 16-oz, VG 120.00
Sunoco, key holders, metal gas-pump design, Ladies'/Mens', EX, pr ..210.00
Superior Peanut Butter, pail, circus scenes, 12-oz, EX+ 600.00
Sure Shot Chewing Tobacco, store tin, 5x10x15", EX 850.00
Sweet Orr Work Clothes, standee, cb, man holding sign, 60", NM .800.00
Sweet Violet Cube Cut, pocket tin, wht, EX+ 3,000.00
Sweetheart Soap, display, baby in pk wicker basket, electric, NM+ .1,300.00
Swing's Coffee, display, automated Black man, 29", EX 2,300.00
Texaco, banner, Texaco Presents Eddie Cantor..., 35x56", G+ 60.00
Texaco, print, Summer Skies, John MacGilchrist, 1930, 10x9", EX ..200.00
Texaco, standee, cb, Eddie Cantor/2 Scottie dogs, 1930s, 64", EX 575.00
Texaco Fire Chief, winterfront, cb, helmet on bl, fr, 13x21", VG 100.00
Texaco Gasoline/Filling Station, ps, 1915, 42" dia, EX 2,500.00
Tiny-Tot Toilet Powder, tc, baby on scalloped oval, NM 75.00
Tiny-Tot Toilet Powder, tc, plain-edge oval, 6½", EX+ 70.00
Town Crier Flour, match holder, cl w/tin fr, red/wht/bl, 3x2", NM 65.00
Treasure Steel Ranges, sign, canvas, Her Three Treasures, 49", EX 1,320.00
Triple AAA Root Beer, ts, bottle shape, 45", NM+ 100.00
Turkish Dyes, cabinet, wood/cb front, stenciled marquee, 28", EX .360.00
Turkish Trophies Cigarettes, sign, paper, girl, fr, 36x27", EX 700.00
Twin Oaks Mixture, pocket tin, flip top, sample, EX 115.00
Twix Cookie Bars, glass jar, Keep On Movin'..., NM 70.00
Tydol/Veedol, pocket mirror, colored birthstone border, 2" dia, EX ..80.00
Uncle John's Syrup, sign, cb cutout, hanger, 5-pc, 24x40", NM+ 600.00
Uncle Tom's Chewing Gum, display box, paper/cb, Mint, 2x9", EX ..300.00
Uneeda Bakers, standee, cb, boy in slicker w/box, 51", EX 775.00
Uneeda Biscuit, letter opener, diecut metal boy, 8", VG 60.00
Union Leader Cut Plug, milk can, red, 9", EX 235.00
Union Leader Smoking Tobacco, ts, pocket tin image, 13x11", NM+ 200.00
Union Mills Flour, sign, paper, baby in basket, fr, 17x21", EX ...280.00
Union Petroleum Co/Mineral Lard Oil, pocket mirror, 4" dia, NM 110.00
US Marine Cut Plug, sign, cb, sailor in porthole, fr, 33x24", VG 2,100.00
US Tires, clock, serviceman's head in center, 1914, 18" dia, NM+ .2,500.00
USACuba, cigar box, 5 Cents, image of Tampa/Havana, VG 100.00
Vacuum Oil, match safe, bbl on cl center, plated ends, 1x2", NM ..180.00
Valina Brand Coffee, pail, factory scene/rabbit, ca 1890, VG 690.00
Van Houten's Cocoa House, sign, decal on Vitrolite, fr, 24x19", EX+ ...2,780.00
Veedol, ts, diecut female ice skater, dtd 11-57, 18", NM+ 1,400.00
Velvet Tobacco, sign, paper, lady standing on 2 horses, fr, 44", G ...800.00
Vernor's Ginger Ale, thermometer, dial type, gr/yel, 12" dia, NM ..300.00
Viking Snuff, dispenser, wht/red on bl, 1950s, 15", NM 100.00
Voight Brewery, match safe, metal, striker on reverse, VG 100.00
Wainwright Brewing Co, sign, paper, tavern scene, 14x22", EX ...400.00
Wak-Em Up Coffee, pail, gr, 10-lb, VG 260.00
Walk-Over Shoes, display, diecut tin, factory/man/woman, 9x15", EX ..950.00
Walker's Soaps, string holder, CI beehive shape, 5", G 225.00
Walla-Walla Pepsin Gum, glass jar, emb Indian Chief, 13", EX .465.00
Walter A Wood Rake, sign, paper, farm boy/girl, 1880s, 11x14", EX ..220.00
Walter's Gold Label Beer, tray, pie-pan rim, waitress, 13" dia 340.00
Ward's, pot scraper, wht/blk/gold on red, EX+ 500.00
Ward's Vitamin Bread, thermometer, porc, curved top, EX 750.00
Waterford Carriage Co, sign, paper, 3 rows of carriages, 36x21", VG ...75.00
Waverly Oils & Gasoline, fs, red/wht/bl porc bbl, 10x16", NM+ ...3,250.00
Welch Juniors, ts, bottle/grapes on red/bl, 1931, 14x20", NM+ .675.00
Welch's, trolley sign, cb, men lined up/lady, 1910-15, 21", EX+ ...375.00
Welch's Grape Juice, pin, cl/metal, bottle/grapes, 1", EX 100.00
Western Ammunition, sign, paper, Bob White, LB Hunt art, 24x16", VG 700.00
Westinghouse Mazda Lamps, Toonerville masks, cb, set of 4, 1920s, EX ...100.00
Weyman's Cutty Pipe, store tin, Foil Package, gr, 14x10x10", EX ...375.00
Wheaties, bowl, wht ceramic, red letters/athletes silhouettes, NM+ .30.00
Wheaties, sign, cb, Am Flyer Electric Train promo, bl/wht, 14x22", VG .15.00
Whistle, clock/display, masonite/wood, elf/bottle/slogan, 24", EX .825.00
Whistle, fan, diecut cb, photo image of boy, 1936, EX 115.00
Whistle, pocket mirror, 1940s, 2x3", NM 150.00
Whistle, thermometer, tin, 2 elves w/bottle, 20", NM 850.00
White Goose Coffee, can, red, tall, 1-lb, NM 1,300.00
White Horse Scotch Whisky, bust of colonial man, plaster, VG+ 100.00
White Rock Table Water, art plate, fairy, box fr, 1881, 18x18", EX ...3,000.00
Whiz Service Center, display stand, metal, 4-shelf, 54x32x21", VG 300.00
Whiz White Rubber Tire Coating, ts, lady in roadster, 17x12", VG+ ...400.00
Wishing Weel Orange, thermometer, tin, yel, 1961, 41", NM ...200.00
Witch Soap, ps, witch on broom/phrase on bl, fr, 26x38", EX ...1,900.00
Wonder Bread, ts, loaf shape, 1950s, 20x42", EX 185.00
Wrigley's, display box, cb, 2-tiered, 1930s-40s, 7", NM 350.00
Wrigley's, trolley sign, cb, In Bond!..., man/pack, 10x20", EX ...100.00
Wrigley's Juicy Fruit Gum, match holder/striker, pnt metal, 5", VG ...90.00
Xtra Brau, tap knob, ball shape, blk/wht, VG+ 150.00
Yale Mixture, humidor, ceramic, dk bl glaze, emb name, NM 150.00
Yeast Foam, sign, cb, girl w/jack'o lantern, fr, 26x21", VG 1,550.00
Yellow Kid Scrip/Pulver Co Inc, gum wrapper, 3x4", EX+ 250.00
Younger's Tartan Beer, display figure, beared man, rubber, 9", NM ...100.00
Yucatan Gum, display box, tin, yel/red, 6x5x7", EX+ 400.00
Zang's Tonic, tape measure, cl, lady in profile, EX 100.00
Zeno's Quality Ice Cream, sidewalk sign, porc, metal fr, 28x20", EX ...550.00
Zig Zag Confections, match safe, Can't Be Matched, VG+ 150.00
Zodenta for the Teeth, toothbrush holder, aluminum, wall-mount, EX ...220.00

7-Up

The Howdy Company of St. Louis, Missouri, was founded in 1920 by Charles L. Grigg. His first creation was an orange drink called Howdy. In the late 1920s Howdy's popularity began to wane, so in 1929 Grigg invented a lemon-lime soda called Seven-Up as an alternative to colas. Grigg's Seven-Up became a widely accepted favorite. Our advisor for this category is Craig Stifter; he is listed in the Directory under Illinois.

School Zone curb sign, double-sided metal, 61½x24", EX, $1,900.00.

Bill hook, cl button, I'd Hang for a Chilled 7-Up, EX+ 35.00
Bottle topper w/bottle, cb, Easter Fresh Up, EX 25.00
Broom stand, 2-legged rack w/sign, 1940s, 28x20", EX+ 700.00
Clock, gr neon, sq w/glass front & metal fr, 15x15", EX 375.00
Matchbook, 7-Up/The Uncola, M 8.00
Mechanical pencil, bottle in liquid on end, EX+ 40.00
Menu brd, wood-tone tin, oval logo, slotted, 1940s, 23x9", EX .225.00
Money clip, enameled dollar symbol w/logo, M 30.00
Music box, can shape, plays Love Story theme, NM 50.00
Sign, cb hanger, Season's Greetings, 3-D, w/bottle, 2-sided, EX+ ...48.00
Sign, Glo-Glass, Drink 7-Up/Take Some Home, 1930s, 4x10", NM+ ...775.00
Sign, porc, Fresh Up w/7-Up, rnd corners, 20x28", NM 475.00
Sign, sf cb, The All-Family Drink!, w/baby, 1956, 13x23", NM+ ...100.00
Sign, tin, Real 7-Up Sold Here, w/bubbles, raised rim, 14" dia, G+ .230.00
Sign, tin bottle shape w/wet look, 2-sided, 44x13", EX 300.00
Thermometer, rnd dial type, 7-Up Likes You on red dot, 10", NM .150.00
Tie clip, enameled logo on bar, EX 15.00
Toy truck, tin, friction, driver in dome cab, 1950s, 9", EX+ 335.00
Tumbler, aluminum, w/7-Up logo, 5", EX+ 45.00

Advertising Cards

Advertising trade cards enjoyed great popularity during the last quarter of the nineteenth century when the chromolithography printing process was refined and put into common use. The purpose of the trade card was to acquaint the public with a business, product, service, or event. Most trade cards range in size from 2" x 3" to 4" x 6"; however, many are found in both smaller and larger sizes.

There are two classifications of trade cards: 'private design' and 'stock.' Private design cards were used by a single company or individual; the images on the cards were designed for only that company. Stock cards were generics that any individual or company could purchase from a printer's inventory. These cards usually had a blank space on the front for the company to overprint with their own name and product information.

Four categories of particular interest to collectors are:

Mechanical — a card which achieves movement through the use of a pull tab, fold-out side, or movable part.

Hold-to-light — a card that reveals its design only when viewed before a strong light.

Diecut — a card in the form of something like a box, a piece of clothing, etc.

Metamorphic — a card that by folding down a flap shows a transformed image, such as a white beard turning black after use of a product.

For a more thorough study of the subject, we recommend *Reflections 1* and *Reflections 2* by Kit Barry; his address can be found in the Directory under Vermont. *Victorian Trade Cards* by Dave Cheadle (Collector Books) is another fine reference. Values are given for cards in near-mint condition.

Allen & Ellis, 'Our Trotter' chewing tobacco, running horse 45.00
Archimedean Lawn Mower, man mowing, woman seated w/book .25.00
Babbitt Soap, boy as Continental soldier 7.00
Babbitt Soap, boy handing box to girl over garden wall 7.00
Buchan's Carbolic Toilet Soap, naked water nymph w/swans 12.00
Buchan's Disinfecting Soap No 11, boy & girl washing dog 12.00
Capewell Horse Nail Co, 6 shoe nails as border around text 20.00
Champion Abdominal Supporter, Uncle Sam/Liberty on bicycles .10.00
Charter Oak Lawn Mower, girl mowing, seated woman sewing ...30.00
Corrugated Stove Pipe Elbow, kitchen before & after using elbow ..20.00
Currier & Ives, Monroe Chief trotter 60.00
Curtis Davis Welcome Soap, boy, man w/basket on arm, horse 5.00
Curtis Davis Welcome Soap, Cupid giving soap box to 2 women ..6.00
Curtis Davis Welcome Soap, fountain, man, woman, peacock 6.00
Curtis Davis Welcome Soap, man & woman admiring baby 6.00
Dingman's Electric Soap, bl-sashed girl in soap box boat w/sail 8.00
Fisk White Prussian Soap, child, red hat, blond curls, bl shirt 6.00
Frash & Co Continental Champagne, grapes, glass & 2 bottles ...20.00
Gem City Tobacco Wks, 'Spotted Fawn,' fawn in woods 45.00
Golding Bros Hatters, 9 hat-people foot racing 35.00
Haas Hog & Poultry Remedy, 'The Original Hen-pecked' 40.00

Heinz, diecut of chef w/Heinz tomato soup in large pickle, $30.00. (Photo courtesy Dave Cheadle)

Hunt's Remedy, Dr holding beaker w/seated patient & woman ...25.00
Hurd's Magical Mixture for Easy Washing, butterfly diecut 6.00
Kirk & Co Soaps, Belgian woman in native dress w/postage stamp ..6.00
Kirk Soap Makers, man handing flower to woman, 'Magnolia' 6.00
Kirk Soap Makers, queen on washtub throne 6.00
Kirk Soap Makers, reindeer sleigh, 'Wht Russian' 6.00
Knockabout Club Books, tri-scenes of outdoors 12.00
Lautz Bros Master Soap, baby w/rattle on cushion 12.00

Lavine Soap, boy w/soap wagon, woman, 2 women doing laundry .6.00
Lavine Soap, 4 children w/sailboat in washtub, sign painter 6.00
Morgan's Sons' Sapolio Soap, tambourine diecut w/woman's head ..6.00
Morgan's Sons' Sapolio Soap, woman w/baby cleaning bathtub ...12.00
Morgan's Sons' Sapolio Soap, 2 women cleaning 3 statues 12.00
Morgan's Sons' Sapolio Soap, 3 women in kitchen washing dishes .12.00
Morgan's Sons' Sapolio Soap, 4 women cleaning vases & wall 12.00
National Lead Co Paints, house showing effect of paints 20.00
Nicholson's Liquid Bread, nurse w/sick man 25.00
One Hundred Years Hence, 'Submarine Excursions' 75.00
Pan American Exposition, woman in waterfall, rainbow 25.00
Parker Bros Shotguns, trapshooting range scene 85.00
Pettit's Eye Salve, boy in box w/finger on closed eye 20.00
Price's Flavoring Extract Vanilla, jungle scene, oversz 35.00
Renne's Pain Killing Magic Oil, man tossing bottles to the sick ..15.00
Royal Brand Fish Delicacies, family picnic, products pictured 12.00
Royal Glue, 'The US Capitol, Washington DC' 12.00
Ryan's Menagerie, man in cage w/3 lions 45.00
Ryan's Menagerie, 2 trapeze artists 45.00
Sing Fat Co Oriental Bazaar, dragon w/Chinese words 12.00
Soapine, Chinaman doing laundry, 'Me Wash-ee all Clean-ee' ...12.00
Soapine, girl by rocks on beach w/toy shovel & bucket 6.00
Sparking Spray Gloss Starch, 2 children, woman, Black woman .15.00
Steikel Smith Spice Co, spice plants, fancy lettering 15.00
Tanglefoot Fly Paper, man w/box, woman in kitchen w/flies 15.00
Tulip Soap, apple blossoms & grass 4.00
Universal Fashion Co Patterns, 2 women, child, dog at seashore ...8.00
Vegetable person, beet (or cabbage) as man on bicycle 20.00
Vegetable person, beets as man in bowler w/cane & 2 women 18.00
Vegetable person, cabbage as woman w/basket on arm 18.00
Vegetable person, carrot as man w/top hat & cane 18.00
Vegetable person, celery as woman w/parasol 18.00
Vegetable person, corn as Indian, 'A Corned Indian' 20.00
Vegetable person, corn as woman w/hat 18.00
Vegetable person, cotton as Black woman, 'A Cotton Ball' 20.00
Vegetable person, cotton bush w/Black woman's head on top 20.00
Vegetable person, cucumber as man in straw hat 18.00
Vegetable person, onion as man w/hands to head 18.00
Vegetable person, pear as man, 'My First Ap-pear-ance' 15.00
Vegetable person, pear as schoolgirl 20.00
Vegetable person, plum as Black man playing banjo 20.00
Vegetable person, potato as Irish man w/stick & knapsack 18.00
Vegetable person, tobacco leaf as man seated & smoking cigar 18.00
Vegetable person, tomato as man in top hat, The Mikado 20.00
Vegetable person, turnip as man w/bald head 18.00
Vegetable person, watermelon as Black man sitting w/dog 20.00
Vegetable person, watermelon as man 18.00
Vegetable person, wheat sheaf as woman, 'A Nice S'wheat Girl' .18.00
Vegetable person, wheat sheaf as woman, 'A S'wheat Girl' 15.00
Young & Larabec Crackers, woman & child w/winged sprite 50.00

Advertising Dolls and Figures

Whether your interest in ad dolls is fueled by nostalgia or strictly because of their amusing, often clever advertising impact, there are several points that should be considered before making your purchases. Condition is of utmost importance; never pay book price for dolls in poor condition, whether they are cloth or of another material. Restoring fabric dolls is usually unsatisfactory and involves a good deal of work. Seams must be opened, stuffing removed, the doll washed and dried, and then reassembled. Washing old fabrics may prove to be disastrous. Colors may fade or run, and most stains are totally resistant to washing. It's usually best to leave the fabric doll as it is.

Watch for new dolls as they become available. Save related advertising literature, extra coupons, etc., and keep these along with the doll to further enhance your collection. Old dolls with no marks are sometimes challenging to identify. While some products may use the same familiar trademark figures for a number of years (the Jolly Green Giant, Pillsbury's Poppin' Fresh, and the Keebler Elf, for example) others appear on the market for a short time only and may be difficult to trace. Most libraries have reference books with trademarks and logos that might provide a clue in tracking down your doll's identity. Children see advertising figures on Saturday morning cartoons that are often unfamiliar to adults, or other ad doll collectors may have the information you seek.

Some advertising dolls are still easy to find and relatively inexpensive, ranging in cost from $1.00 to $100.00. The hard plastic and early composition dolls are bringing the higher prices. Advertising dolls are popular with children as well as adults. For a more thorough study of the subject, we recommend *Advertising Dolls with Values* by Myra Yellin Outwater (Schiffer). Our advisor for this category is Jim Rash; he is listed in the Directory under New Jersey. Values are for dolls in near mint condition; be sure to discount prices for soil, missing parts, wear, or damage of any type.

A&W Root Beer, bear, 1975, plush, 13", EX, from $25 to 35.00
Admiral Appliances, Admiral, vinyl, 7", M 15.00
Alka-Seltzer, Speedy, pnt rubber, Canadian, 5", EX 215.00
Alka-Seltzer, Speedy, squeeze vinyl, 1960, 8", EX 600.00
Allied Van Lines, 1970s, stuffed cloth, 18", NM 30.00
Bazooka, Bazooka Joe, 1973, stuffed cloth, EX 20.00
Betty Crocker, Kenner, 1974, stuffed cloth, 13", VG 20.00
Big Boy, bank, 1973, vinyl, 9", EX 30.00
Bradford Restaurant, Bucky Bradford, vinyl, NM, from $35 to 45.00
Campbell's Soups, Campbell girl as cheerleader, 1967, vinyl, 8", EX .75.00
Cap'n Crunch, plush, 14", NM 75.00
Chips Ahoy, girl in bl dress/cookie hat, vinyl, 4½", NM+ 20.00
Chocks Vitamins, Charlie Chocks, 1960s, stuffed cloth, 18", EX ...25.00
Coca-Cola, Buddy Lee, 1950s, compo, EX 875.00
Cracker Jack, boy, Ideal, 1917, compo & cloth, orig, 14", EX 325.00
Cream of Wheat, Rastus, printed stuffed cloth, premium, NM+ ..150.00

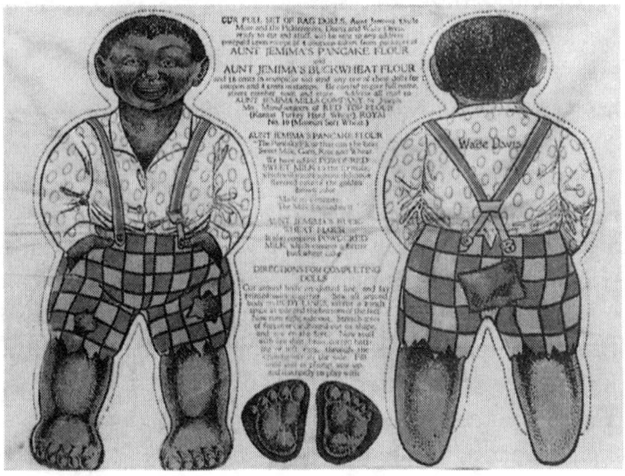

Davis Milling Co. (Now Quaker Oats), Wade (Aunt Jemima's son), uncut cloth, ca 1910, 12x18", $250.00. (Photo courtesy Myla Perkins)

Eskimo Pie, boy, Chase Bag Co, 1975, stuffed cloth, 15", NM 25.00
Frostie Root Beer, 1972, stuffed cloth, 16", EX 25.00
Grandma's Cookies, bank, 1970, plastic, 7½", NM 30.00
Green Giant, Jolly Green Giant, 1960s, stuffed cloth, 16", EX 30.00
Green Giant, Little Sprout display, inflatable vinyl, 1970s, 24", NM ...65.00
Jordache Jeans, cheerleader, Mego, 1981, 12", NRFB 30.00
Keebler, Elf, 1981, stuffed cloth, 24", VG 30.00

Kellogg's, Tony the Tiger, squeeze vinyl, 9", NM+ 25.00
Kellogg's, Toucan Sam, vinyl, jtd, 1984, 6¼", NM 45.00
Meow Mix, cat, 1970s, vinyl, NM 45.00
Michelin, Michelin Man holding baby, squeeze vinyl, 6½", EX ..200.00
Miss Clairol, Glamour Misty, Ideal, 1965, rpl robe, 12", VG 35.00
Mr Bubble, vinyl, 10", M 35.00
Mr Clean, vinyl, all wht, 1960s, NM+ 135.00
North American Van Lines, Mary Ann, MIB 70.00
Pappy Parker's Fried Chicken, hillbilly, 1970s, vinyl, NM 45.00
Pillsbury, Poppin' Fresh, plush, USA, 1982, NM+ 40.00
Pizza Hut, Pete, 1969, vinyl, NM 55.00
Raid, Raid Bug, purple plush, 1989, NM 40.00
Sprite, Lucky Lymon, vinyl, 1980s, MIB 35.00
Star-Kist, Charlie Tuna, plush, premium, 1983, NM 40.00
Tango Orange Drink, Tango VooDoo, vinyl, MIB 55.00
Tastee Freeze, Miss Tastee Freeze, 1950s, hard plastic, 7", NM 20.00
Travelodge, Sleepy Bear, squeeze vinyl, 1970s, 5½", M 45.00
TW Grant Co, Bucky Bradford, vinyl, 1970s, 9", NM 15.00
United Airlines, Menehune of Hawaii, bank, vinyl, 9", M 150.00

African Art

African art does not consist of a single class of objects. Rather, these often powerful images and objects are carved by many varying African tribes and groups across the central continent; each item represents specific cultural and spiritual functions and meanings. Many kinds of materials are used including wood, metal, fiber, ivory, and bone. Large numbers of these items are now being produced and sold to the tourist trade, but authentic African art is generally considered to consist of objects which were used in cultural and/or religious activities. The items listed here are authentic, in good condition, without provenance, and considered to be of average aesthetic quality. Scott Nelson, a collector of African art, is our advisor; his address is listed in the Directory under New Mexico.

Basket, Nigeria, open fiber w/cowrie shells, 8x10" 175.00
Beads, trade; ceramic, string of 20 ....100.00
Bracelet, Ashanti, bronze, knobs..35.00
Cloth, Kuba, geometric design, 18" sq..175.00
Comb, Ashanti, bird's head surmount, 4".....................................200.00
Container, Luba, gourd, wooden figural stopper............................90.00
Divination board, Yoruba, animals, 20" dia.................................475.00
Doll, Ashanti, figural, 7" 275.00
Doll, Mossi, abstract human figure 275.00
Door, Dogon, granary, human figures, 26".................................1,500.00
Drum, Hemba, geometric designs, 22" 275.00
Earrings, Masai, beaded, 6"...175.00
Figure, Baule, standing female, 14" 350.00
Figure, Dogon, crouched male, 10"...850.00
Figure, Yoruba, pnt colonial, 12" 175.00
Goldweight, Ashanti, bronze turtle 125.00
Hat, Kuba, fiber, blk pnt 175.00
Headdress, Bamana, Tchi-wara (antelope), horizontal.................675.00
Headrest, Luba, supporting human figure 5" 475.00
Heddle pulley, Senufo, bird surmount, 5".....................................375.00
Ibejis, Yoruba, 9", pr. 375.00
Knife, throwing; Kuba, curved blade, 14".....................................175.00
Lock, Bamana, door, 2 figural surmounts, 14" 675.00
Mask, Bamana, N'Tomo, 14" 375.00
Mask, Dan, human face, 15" 375.00
Mask, Dogon, Kanaga, 26" 500.00
Mask, Karumba, polychrome, antelope, 21" 475.00
Mask, Mende, helmet, female initiation, 12" 875.00
Mask, Pende, human face, 8" 375.00
Pendant, Yoruba, ivory human figure, 4".......................................900.00
Pipe, Cameroons, elephant, brass, 14"..275.00
Ring, Dogon, bronze, horse & rider..275.00
Slingshot, Baule, animal head, 5" 85.00
Stool, Lega, human figural supports, 13" 675.00
Whisk, Yoruba, human figure, wood & horsehair, 12" 275.00

Agata

Agata is New England peachblow (the factory called it 'Wild Rose') with an applied metallic stain which produces gold tracery and dark blue mottling. The stain is subject to wear, and the amount of remaining stain greatly affects the value. It is especially valuable (and rare) on satin-finish items when found on peachblow of intense color. Caution! Be sure to use only gentle cleaning methods.

Currently rare types of art glass have been realizing erratic prices at auction; until they stabilize, we can only suggest an average range of values. In the listings that follow, examples are glossy unless noted otherwise. A condition rating of 'EX' indicates that the stain shows a slight amount of wear. Our advisors for this category are Betty and Clarence Maier; they are listed in the Directory under Pennsylvania. See also Green Opaque.

Bowl vase, flared petal rim, EX color/VG stain, 3x5" 735.00
Celery vase, sqd/scalloped rim, M mottling, 6½" 950.00
Condiment set, 2-pc, EX mottling; unmk SP 5¼" fr 2,500.00
Cruet, NM mottling 2,000.00
Cruet, trifold rim, bulbous stopper, worn 750.00

Finger bowl, EX mottling and gold tracery, 2½x5¼", $685.00. (Photo courtesy Betty and Clarence Maier)

Finger bowl, EX mottling 500.00
Finger bowl & underplate, M mottling, set of 6 ....7,200.00
Pitcher, milk; sq mouth, EX mottling, 6¼" 850.00
Pitcher, milk; sq rim, sparce mottling, 6¼" 725.00
Pitcher, water; sqd spout, allover mottling, 7", from $3,100 to ..3,700.00
Pitcher, water; 8¾", +6 tumblers 8,300.00
Toothpick holder, ovoid 1,600.00
Toothpick holder, sq top, EX mottling 1,000.00
Toothpick holder, 3-corner rim, 2" 625.00
Tumbler, EX color & mottling, 3¾", from $600 to 750.00
Tumbler, juice; EX color, EX spots/stain, 4" 1,000.00
Tumbler, scattered bl spots, 3¾" 400.00
Tumbler, whiskey; EX mottling, 2½" 900.00
Vase, lily; EX color & mottling, 6" 885.00
Vase, lily; EX color & mottling, 7" 950.00
Vase, lily; subtle decor, 7" 345.00
Vase, scalloped top, M mottling, 6½x3½" 1,200.00
Vase, stick neck, VG mottle to lower half, minor wear, 8¾" 725.00
Vase, waisted tricon rim, M mottling, 3½" 1,600.00

Akro Agate

The Akro Agate Co., founded in 1914 primarily as a marble maker, operated in Clarksburg, West Virginia, until 1951. Their popular wares included children's dishes, powder jars, flowerpots, and novelty items along with the famous 'Akro Aggies.' Much of their glass was produced in the distinctive marbleized colors they called Red Onyx, Blue Onyx, etc.; solid opaque and transparent colors were also produced. Most of the wares are marked with their trademark, a crow flying through the letter 'A' holding an Aggie in its beak and one in each claw. Other marks include 'J.P.' on children's pieces, 'J.V. Co., Inc.,' 'Braun & Corwin,' 'N.Y.C. Vogue Merc Co. U.S.A.,' 'Hamilton Match Co.,' and 'Mexicali Pickwick Cosmetic Corp.' on novelty items. In 1936 Akro obtained the molds from the Balmer-Westite Co. of Weston, West Virginia. Westite produced a similar line of products for several years. Their ware is drab in color when compared to Akro and is generally unmarked. The embossed Westite logo does appear occasionally on the bottoms of some pieces. Westite is commonly accepted as a companion collectible of Akro.

For more information we recommend *The Collector's Encyclopedia of Children's Dishes* by Margaret and Kenn Whitmyer. Our advisor for miscellaneous Akro Agate is Albert Morin; he is listed in the Directory under Massachusetts.

Chiquita

Creamer, gr opaque, 1½" 5.00
Cup, any opaque color other than gr, 1½" 14.00
Plate, transparent cobalt, 3¾" 7.00
Saucer, any opaque color other than gr, 3⅛" 5.00
Set, gr opaque, 22-pc, MIB 125.00
Sugar bowl, baked-on colors, 1½" 8.00
Teapot, baked-on colors, w/lid, 3" 22.00

Concentric Rib

Creamer, sm, opaque colors other than gr or wht, 1¼" 16.00
Cup, sm, gr or wht opaque, 1¼" 5.00
Plate, sm, gr or wht opaque, 3¼" 4.50
Saucer, sm, opaque colors other than gr or wht, 2¾" 2.50
Set, sm, opaque colors other than gr or wht, 8-pc, MIB 54.00

Concentric Ring

Creamer, lg, any opaque color, 1⅜" 16.00
Cup, sm, bl marbleized, 1¼" 35.00
Cup, sm, cobalt transparent, 1¼" 35.00
Plate, lg, cobalt transparent, 4¼" 20.00
Saucer, sm, any opaque color, 2¾" 3.50
Set, lg, bl marbleized, 21-pc, MIB 745.00
Set, sm, cobalt transparent, 16-pc, MIB 480.00
Teapot, sm, bl marbleized, w/lid, 3⅜" 125.00

Interior Panel, Stippled Interior Panel

Cereal, lg, lemonade & oxblood, 3⅜" 45.00
Cereal, lg, yel opaque, 3⅜" 45.00
Creamer, sm, bl & wht marbleized, 1¼" 35.00
Creamer, sm, pk lustre, 1¼" 35.00
Cup, lg, gr transparent, 1⅜" 18.00
Cup, lg, lemonade & oxblood, 1⅜" 50.00
Pitcher, sm, gr lustre, 2⅞" 20.00
Plate, lg, bl & wht marbleized, 4¼" 20.00
Plate, sm, gr & wht marbleized, 3¾" 18.00
Saucer, lg, pk lustre, 3⅛" 4.00
Saucer, sm, azure bl or yel, 2⅜" 7.00
Set, lg, azure bl or yel opaque, 21-pc, MIB 550.00
Set, lg, gr & wht marbleized, 21-pc, MIB 550.00
Set, sm, red & wht marbleized, 8-pc, MIB 200.00
Teapot, lg, gr lustre, w/lid, 3¾" 45.00
Teapot, lg, red & wht marbleized, w/lid, 1⅞" 125.00
Teapot, sm, pk lustre, w/lid, 3⅜" 30.00

J.P. (Made for J. Pressman Company)

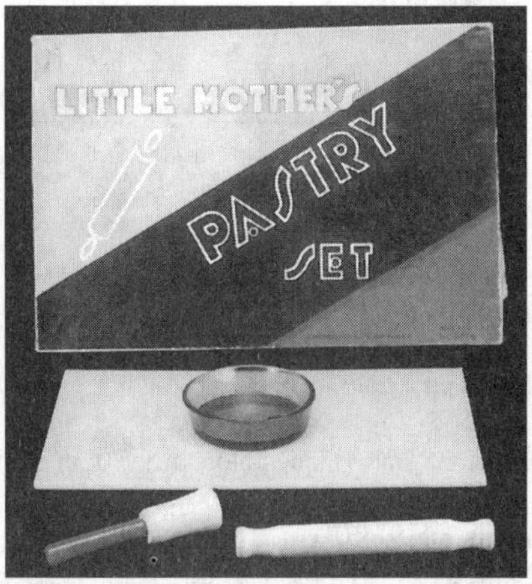

J.P. (made for J. Pressman Company), Little Mother Pastry Set, MIB, $250.00. **(Photo courtesy Margaret and Kenn Whitmyer)**

Cereal, lg, baked-on colors 11.00
Creamer, lg, gr transparent, 1½" 60.00
Cup, lg, cobalt w/ribs, 1½" 14.00
Plate, lg, lt bl or crystal, 4¼" 20.00
Saucer, lg, baked-on colors, 3¼" 1.50
Set, lg, baked-on colors, 21-pc, MIB 200.00
Sugar bowl, lg, red or brn transparent, w/lid, 1½" 80.00
Teapot, lg, gr transparent, w/lid, 2¾" 90.00

Miss America

Creamer, wht, 1¼" 50.00
Cup, orange & wht, 1⅝" 60.00
Cup, wht, 1⅝" 40.00
Plate, orange & wht, 4½" 50.00
Saucer, orange & wht, 3⅝" 15.00
Set, forest gr, 17-pc, MIB 700.00
Set, wht, 17-pc, MIB 550.00
Sugar bowl, wht, w/lid, 2" 80.00
Teapot, forest gr, w/lid, 3¼" 175.00

Octagonal

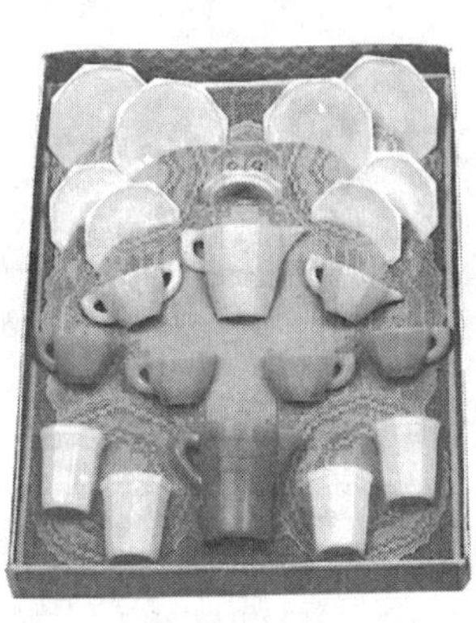

Octagonal, small, twenty-one piece set, $195.00.

Creamer, sm, dk gr, 1¼" 16.00
Cup, sm, lime gr, 1¼" 27.00
Pitcher, sm, bl or wht, 2¾" 22.00
Plate, lg, gr or wht, 4¼" 4.00
Plate, sm, bl or wht, 3⅜" 6.00
Saucer, lg, lemonade & oxblood, 3⅜" 6.00
Set, lg, mixed opaque colors, 17-pc, MIB 200.00
Set, sm, mixed opaque colors, 16-pc, MIB 180.00
Teapot, lg, pumpkin, closed hdl 80.00
Tumbler, sm, pumpkin or yel, 2" 20.00

Raised Daisy

Creamer, sm, yel, 1¼" 75.00
Cup, sm, bl, 1¼" 100.00
Plate, sm, bl, 3" 25.00
Saucer, sm, beige, 2½" 9.00
Sugar bowl, sm, yel, 1¼" 75.00
Teapot, sm, bl, w/lid, 2⅜" 200.00
Tumbler, sm, beige, 2" 25.00

Stacked Disc

Creamer, sm, opaque colors other than gr or wht, 1¼" 16.00
Cup, sm, gr or wht, 1¼" 6.00
Pitcher, lg, gr or wht, 2⅞" 18.00
Plate, sm, gr or wht, 3¼" 4.00
Saucer, lg, opaque colors other than gr or wht, 2¾" 4.00
Set, sm, gr or wht, 21-pc, MIB 130.00
Sugar bowl, lg, gr or wht, 1¼" 10.00
Teapot, sm, opaque colors other than gr or wht, w/lid, 3⅜" 18.00
Tumbler, sm, gr or wht, 2" 8.50

Stacked Disc and Interior Panel

Cereal, lg, gr transparent, 3⅜" 30.00
Creamer, lg, any opaque color, 1⅜" 25.00
Creamer, sm, cobalt transparent, 1¼" 45.00
Cup, sm, pumpkin, 1¼" 16.00
Plate, sm, cobalt transparent, 3¼" 14.00
Saucer, lg, gr transparent, 3¼" 7.00
Saucer, sm, bl marbleized, 2¾" 14.00
Set, lg, any opaque color, 21-pc, MIB 425.00
Set, sm, 7-pc water, cobalt transparent, MIB 150.00
Sugar bowl, sm, opaque cobalt, 1⅞" 35.00
Tumbler, sm, gr transparent, 2" 20.00

Stippled Band

Stippled Band, large, all green transparent: Cup, 1½", $8.00; Saucer, 3¼", $2.50; Plate, 4¼", $6.00.

Creamer, lg, amber transparent, 1½" 25.00
Creamer, sm, gr transparent, 1¼" 35.00
Cup, lg, azure transparent, 1½" 35.00
Pitcher, sm, amber transparent, 2⅞" 18.00
Plate, lg, amber transparent, 4¼" 8.50
Set, lg, azure transparent, 17-pc, MIB 450.00
Set, sm, amber transparent, 7-pc, MIB 78.00
Set, sm, gr transparent, 28-pc, MIB 250.00
Sugar bowl, lg, amber transparent, w/lid, 1⅞" 35.00
Sugar bowl, sm, gr transparent, 1¼" 35.00
Teapot, sm, gr transparent, w/lid, 3⅜" 25.00
Tumbler, sm, amber transparent, 1¾" 11.00

Miscellaneous

Ashtray, Atlantic Foundry, hexagonal, rare 750.00
Ashtray, Camel Cigarette, amber, very rare 2,500.00
Ashtray, car w/suction cup, 10 panels 85.00
Ashtray, clubs (card symbol), bl w/crow trademk, 4" dia 275.00
Ashtray, Hamilton match holder, amber 85.00
Ashtray, Hotel Lincoln, bl 95.00
Ashtray, oxblood/wht, 3" sq 20.00
Ashtray, Shell, bl/wht 12.50
Ashtray, TX Centennial 1936, rare 1,500.00
Basket, gr/wht, 2-hdl 38.00
Bell, Fine Rib, crystal 65.00
Bell, ivory/custard 95.00
Bell, orange, rare 400.00
Bowl, #320 Graduated Dart 250.00
Bowl, #322 Stacked Disc, bl, ftd 40.00
Bowl, finger; 18 int panels, rare, 4" 250.00
Bowl, fruit; marbleized, ftd, rare 650.00
Candlestick, Lander finger ring, wht w/perfume candle 35.00
Candlesticks, gr, 3¼", pr 250.00
Candlesticks, marbleized, 3¼", pr 600.00
Cornucopia, #765, gr/wht marbleized 16.00
Cornucopia, #765 Niagara Falls 65.00
Cornucopia, NYC Vogue Merc, crystal, rare 125.00
Flowerpot, #292 Ribbed Top, marbleized 10.00
Flowerpot, #295 Combo, any color, rare 295.00
Flowerpot, #297 Ribs & Flutes, marbleized 15.00
Flowerpot, #298 Plain Band, orange 30.00
Flowerpot, #300 Banded Dart, blk 150.00
Flowerpot, #308 Grandaddy, yel 300.00
Flowerpot, #1309, ivory w/Mexican decor, rare 350.00
Flowerpot, #1311, orange 195.00
J Vivaudou, #329 apothecry jar, blk 85.00
J Vivaudou, #333 puff box, marbleized, rare 350.00
J Vivaudou, mortar & pestle jar, wht, MIB 95.00
Jardiniere, #306 Graduated Dart, royal bl w/scalloped top 85.00
Jardiniere, #314 Narrow Ledge, blk 200.00
Jardiniere, bell shape, yel, 4¾" 85.00
Knife, AERFLO grid style, crystal, from $60 to 75.00
Knife, AERFLO grid style, forest gr transparent 400.00
Lamp, crystal, 5-pc 35.00
Lamp, gr, 3-pc 185.00
Lamp shade, marbleized 265.00
Marbles, #116 Popeye, set in yel box 1,000.00
Marbles, Akro Chinese Checkers, set in box 45.00
Marbles, 100 #00 Glassies, in box 200.00
Planter, #651 Graduated Dart, orange 95.00
Planter, #657 Lily, any color 28.00
Powder jar, Apple, orange 375.00
Powder jar, Colonial Lady, bl transparent, very rare 2,000.00
Powder jar, Scottie dog, wht 95.00
Shot glass, Mr Boston, yel, very rare 2,500.00
Tire ashtray, US Rubber, crystal 65.00
Tire pen holder, Goodrich, bl/wht marbleized 185.00

Tumbler & tray set, gr, transparent, rare 650.00
Urn, Beaded Top, any color 12.00
Vase, #311 Ribs & Flutes, marbleized 250.00
Vase, #317, tab hdls, orange 135.00
Westite, ashtray, gr, hexagonal 35.00
Westite, flowerpot, #303, marbleized, 6" 200.00
Westite, pot stand, blk, sq 100.00
X-14, milk pitcher, bl, very rare 1,200.00

Alamo Pottery

Alamo art pottery (1945 – 1951) was a division of the Alamo Pottery of San Antonio, Texas, which otherwise produced only sanitary ware (bathroom fixtures). The art pottery division was founded by Jake Rowe, Richard Potter, and Bruce Blunt. They produced vitreous china items which have survived the decades without crazing and with the high gloss glazes still gleaming as if new. (Mrs. Potter was a valuable resource in compiling information about Alamo history.)

Rowe, Potter, and Blunt developed glazes, processes, and mold shapes from which came styles and colors that ran the gamut from elegant, classically styled vases to whimsical figurals, and from pale translucent aquas and yellows to bold crayon greens, blues, and yellows. The vast majority of the pieces are monochromatic, and the rare sponge- or spatter-ware pieces are at a premium.

Alamo is usually marked with a mold number (from 701 to 908, and P-2, P-3, and presumably P-1). Many also have an oval Alamo Pottery ink stamp in either black or blue. Bottoms are generally unglazed, although a few pitchers with glazed bottoms have been observed. Flea bites in the glaze are fairly common and unless excessive are tolerated by most collectors. Crazing and staining in the vitreous china pieces (there are a few items which are not vitreous) are nonexistent, and virtually all interiors are fully glazed. These items were originally intended for the floral trade, and most sold for less than $3.00.

The art pottery division of Alamo closed in 1951 due to high costs of storing and shipping. Rowe, Potter, and Blunt moved to Gilmer, Texas, and founded Gilmer Pottery (see Gilmer listing), which produced many items often mistaken for Alamo. Our advisor for this category is Suzanne Knight; she is listed in the Directory under Texas.

Ashtray, #800 ....18.00
Bowl, #730, duck, rabbit & bear 33.00
Bowl, #766, rings, 2¾x6" 30.00
Bowl, #767, rings, 3x7" 15.00
Bowl, #772, tulip form, 2¾x3½" 16.00
Bowl, #773, tulip form, 2¾x3½" 16.00
Bowl, #774, tulip form, 3" 16.00
Bowl, #775, tulip form, 3½x9" 18.00
Bowl, #776, tulip form, 4x12" 20.00
Bowl, console; Delphinium Blue, #775, 3¼x9" dia 22.50
Figurine, baby diaper w/hole for pin 113.00
Figurine, high-top baby shoe 55.00
Figurine, swan, #725, 5½x5" 40.00
Figurine, toilet, 4½" 30.00
Flowerpot, #728-6, not vitreous, 5x6¼" 21.00
Flowerpot, #729-10, not vitreous, 8½x10½" 39.00
Flowerpot, #829-5, diagonal waves, 5" 10.00
Flowerpot, #829-6, diagonal waves, 6" 12.00
Flowerpot, #829-7, diagonal waves, 7" 20.00
Flowerpot, #829-8, diagonal waves, 8" 25.00
Flowerpot, #829-10, diagonal waves, 10" 70.00
Pitcher, #759, modified octagon, 7¼x7½" 40.00
Pitcher, #760, 4 diagonal sweep indentations, 7½x8½" 40.00
Planter, #734, oval, 2x8½x4" 14.00
Planter, #735, oval, 2¼x11½x6½" 14.00
Planter, #736, oval, 2¾x15x10" 20.00
Planter, #737, 3¾x6x6" 20.00
Planter, #769, rings, 4½x8" 26.00
Planter, #770, rings, 3x9½x6" 18.00
Planter, #771, 3¼x12x7" 34.00
Planter, #777, tulip form, 2¾x6½" 18.00
Vase, #701, grapes & Pan, hdls, 5¾x6½" 54.00
Vase, #704, wht w/bl sponging (rare), 8x4" 236.00
Vase, #705, 8" 18.00
Vase, #706, 12x6" 58.00
Vase, #709, 11½x6½" 92.00
Vase, #716, 11" 41.00
Vase, #718, rnd base, sq top, 8½x5½" 45.00
Vase, #719, rnd base, sq top, 9¾x5½" 43.00
Vase, #721, 6x4" 15.00
Vase, #722, flares to 5½" at top, 7½" 17.00
Vase, #723, 9" 33.00
Vase, #732, hdls, 7½x8" 48.00
Vase, #733 (1 of 2 fan vases), 7x7" 40.00
Vase, #741, 10" 50.00
Vase, #743, 15x6", from $77 to 180.00
Vase, #746, cornucopia, 7¾" 45.00
Vase, #900-10, flares to 5¼" at top, 10" 44.00
Vase, #900-5, flares to 6¼" at top, 5" 20.00
Vase, #900-7, flares to 7" at top, 7" 20.00
Vase, #901-7 ....52.00
Vase, #902-10 ....27.00
Vase, #902-5 ....8.00
Vase, #906-10 ....27.00
Vase, #906-10, 10x7¼" 91.00
Vase, #939 (1 of 2 fan vases), 6x12" 30.00
Vase, bottom smaller than top, #704, 8x4" 258.00
Vase, P-2, ink stamped #, 6½" 48.00
Vase, P-2, yel w/blk spatters (rare), 6½" 83.00
Vase, P-3, str sides, vertical ribs, 12½" 66.00
Wall pocket, fish figural 110.00

Alexandrite

Alexandrite is a type of art glass introduced around the turn of the century by Thomas Webb and Sons of England. It is recognized by its characteristic shading, pale yellow to rose and blue at the edge of the item. Although other companies (Moser, for example) produced glass they called alexandrite, only examples made by Webb possess all the described characteristics and command premium prices. Amount and intensity of blue determines value. Our advisors for this category are Betty and Clarence Maier; they are listed in the Directory under Pennsylvania.

Jack-in-the pulpit vase, intense colors, 4¾", $2,000.00. **(Photo courtesy Gene Harris)**

Bowl & underplate, sq rim, 5", 2½x6" 2,000.00

Finger bowl, Honeycomb, crimped/ruffled, 3¾", +underplate ...2,200.00
Toothpick holder, molded peacock feathers, 3¼" 1,000.00
Tumbler, juice; 6-panel bowl, wafer base, EX color, 3" 985.00
Vase, mushroom shape w/wide flange, EX color, 2½x4½" 1,600.00
Vase, Optic Honeycomb, ovoid w/flared ruffled top, 4¼" 1,250.00
Wine, purple rim (average color), amber body, stem, base, 4½" .1,100.00

Almanacs

The earliest evidence indicates that almanacs were used as long ago as Ancient Egypt. Throughout the Dark Ages they were circulated in great volume and were referred to by more people than any other book except the Bible. *The Old Farmer's Almanac* first appeared in 1793 and has been issued annually since that time. Usually more of a pamphlet than a book (only a few have hard covers), the almanac provided planting and harvesting information to farmers, weather forecasts for seamen, medical advice, household hints, mathematical tutoring, postal rates, railroad schedules, weights and measures, 'receipts,' and jokes. Before 1800 the information was unscientific and based entirely on astrology and folklore. The first almanac in America was printed in 1639 by William Pierce Mariner; it contained data of this nature. One of the best-known editions, Ben Franklin's *Poor Richard's Almanac*, was introduced in 1732 and continued to be printed for twenty-five years.

By the nineteenth century, merchants saw the advertising potential in a publication so widely distributed, and the advertising almanac evolved. These were distributed free of charge by drug stores and mercantiles and were usually somewhat lacking in information, containing simply a calendar, a few jokes, and a variety of ads for quick remedies and quack cures.

Today their concept and informative, often amusing, text make almanacs popular collectibles that may usually be had at reasonable prices. Because they were printed in such large numbers and often saved from year to year, their prices are still low. Most fall within a range of $4.00 to $15.00. Very common examples may be virtually worthless; those printed before 1860 are especially collectible. Quite rare and highly prized are the Kate Greenaway 'Almanacks,' printed in London from 1883 to 1897. These are illustrated with her drawings of children, one for each calendar month. See also Greenaway, Kate.

1890, Warner's Safe Cure Almanac, colorful cover, EX, $10.00.

1857, Greeley's Tribune Almanac & Political Register, VG 5.00
1866, Brown's, Father Time cover, 73-pg, 3½x5", EX 9.00
1866, Old Farmer's, Robert B Thomas, EX 7.00
1873, Wright's Pictorial Family, EX 5.00
1877, Clarks' ABC (Anti Bilious Compound), VG 4.00
1884, Morse's Indian Root Pill Book of Fun, EX 9.00
1885, Merchant's Gargling Oil Dream & Fate Book, VG 8.00
1918, Dr Herrick's Family Medicine Co, EX 4.00

Aluminum

Aluminum, though being the most abundant metal in the earth's crust, always occurs in combination with other elements. Before a practical method for its refinement was developed in the late nineteenth century, articles made of aluminum were very expensive. After the process for commercial smelting was perfected in 1916, it became profitable to adapt the ductile, nontarnishing material to many uses.

By the late '30s, novelties, trays, pitchers, and many other tableware items were being produced. They were often handcrafted with elaborate decoration. Russel Wright designed a line of lovely pieces such as lamps, vases, and desk accessories that are becoming very collectible. Many who crafted the ware marked it with their company logo, and these signed pieces are attracting the most interest. Wendell August Forge (Grove City, Pennsylvania) is a mark to watch for; this firm produced some particularly nice examples and upwardly mobile market values reflect their popularity with today's collectors. In general, 'spun' aluminum is from the '30s or early '40s, and 'hammered' aluminum is from the '50s.

For further information, refer to *Collectible Aluminum, An Identification and Value Guide* (1997 updated values), by our advisor for this category, Everett Grist; he is listed in the Directory under Tennessee. Another excellent reference is *Hammered Aluminum, Hand Wrought Collectibles*, by Dannie Woodard, see the Directory for Texas.

Ashtray, tulips, 3 rests curve into ft, Rodney Kent, 5½" dia 10.00
Basket, cake; flowers, hammered, twist hdl, Canterbury Arts, 12" 30.00
Basket, hexagonal w/upturned edges, dbl loop hdl, Continental, 9" dia .12.00
Basket, polished w/twisted hdl, serrated rim, Buenilum, 9" 15.00
Boot jack, heavy construction, hand-rubbed, W August Forge 90.00
Bowl, floral spray, hammered, shallow, Canterbury Arts, 8" 20.00
Bowl, fruit/flowers, hammered, rolled hdls, Cromwell, 12" 18.00
Bowl, leaf design, fluted rim, heart hdls, Designed Aluminum, 13" .16.00
Bowl, pine cone, shallow, W August Forge, 7½" 25.00
Bowl, shallow, curvilinear design, hammered, Canterbury Arts, 11" .18.00
Bread tray, bamboo, bamboo hdls, Everlast, oval, 11" 18.00
Bread tray, fruit, fluted rim, hdls, unmk (Cromwell style), 8x13" .12.00
Buffet server, hammered, 6 glass inserts, Keystone Ware, 10x15" .35.00
Candelabrum, triple w/twisted & looped stem, Buenilum, 13½" .45.00
Candle holders, mums, Continental, 4½", pr 20.00
Candy dish, apple blossoms, w/lid, W August Forge, 7" dia 40.00
Candy dish, pine cones, upturned/crimped, coiled hdl, unmk, 6" sq .5.00
Casserole, plume design, hammered, hdls, w/lid, Everlast, 9¼" 12.00
Casserole, tulip, hammered, floral/ribbon hdls, ftd, Rodney Kent ...22.00
Chafing dish, tulip bud finial, hammered, Rodney Kent 25.00
Cigarette box, applied duck figure, Laird Argental, 3x5½x1½" ...75.00
Coaster set, tulip form, w/holder, unmk (Rodney Kent) 20.00
Cocktail shaker, mums, hammered, Continental, 12" 50.00
Coffee set, server/sugar/creamer/tray, mums, hammered, Continental 135.00
Compote, floral/fruit, 3 sections, Cromwell, 6" 12.00
Creamer & sugar bowl, hammered, angle hdls, Everlast 15.00
Goblet, hammered, stemmed, unmk 6.00
Hurricane lamp, fluted base w/loop hdl, crystal globe, Everlast, 6" .32.00
Ice bucket, hammered, angled hdls, w/lid, Canterbury Arts, 8" ...45.00
Lazy Susan, stemmed roses, hammered, Continental 20.00
Leaf dish, floral & leaf, upturned edges, coiled hdl, Continental ...9.00
Leaf dish, sailing ship, tall scrolled hdl, World Hand Forge 15.00
Magazine rack, water fowl scene, hammered/rubbed, W August Forge 200.00
Pie plate holder, buttercups & leaves, beaded hdls, Everlast, 10" .16.00
Pitcher, hammered w/polished band, looped ice guard, Continental 27.00
Punch bowl w/ladle, grapes, hammered, W August Forge, 15½" ..125.00
Silent butler, bittersweet, rnd, W August Forge, 7½" 35.00

Table lamp, brushed, tall/tapered, rnd base, red shade, 24x14" ... 300.00
Tray, apple blossoms, decorative corners, W August Forge, 12x18" ... 40.00
Tray, celery; apple blossoms, notched edge, W August Forge ... 20.00
Tray, English fruit pattern, Cromwell, 14" dia ... 27.00
Tray, fruit bowl, polished hammered effect, hdl, Cromwell, 15" dia ... 27.00
Tray, hammered, dowels in coiled hdls, glass dish, Buenilum, 11" dia ... 15.00
Tray, pine cones, sq w/center loop hdl, hand rubbed, W August Forge ... 30.00
Tray, sandwich; dogwood, canted corners, W August Forge, 11" ... 75.00
Tray, sandwich; ribbon-tied bouquet, Designed Aluminum, 12" ... 16.00
Tray, schooner, hammered, rolled hdls, Arthur Amour, 9x14" ... 50.00
Tray, tidbit; bamboo, bamboo hdl, 2-tier, Everlast ... 18.00
Tray, tidbit; dogwood, fluted rim, Designed Aluminum, 6" dia ... 6.00
Tray, wagon train scene w/horseman, rectangular, Arthur Armour ... 175.00
Tray, 3 horses rearing, scalloped rim, hdls, Arthur Armour ... 45.00
Tumbler, hammered, Everlast ... 5.00
Vase, dogwood/butterflies, weighted base, Arthur Armour, 12" ... 85.00
Wastebasket, bittersweet, W August Forge ... 150.00

AMACO, American Art Clay Co.

AMACO is the logo of the American Art Clay Co. Inc., founded in Indianapolis, Indiana, in 1919, by Ted O. Philpot. They produced a line of art pottery from 1931 through 1938. The company is still in business but now produces only supplies, implements, and tools for the ceramic trade.

Values for AMACO have risen sharply, especially those for figurals, items with Art Deco styling, and pieces with uncommon shapes. Our advisor for this category is Virginia Heiss; she is listed in the Directory under Indiana.

Bowl, blue, scroll handles, #170, 2½x7" across handles, $150.00.

Bust of woman, turq, #144, 7" ... 160.00
Figurine, bear, seated, blk gloss, #197, 5" ... 250.00
Figurine, goose, standing, bl gloss, 5½" ... 125.00
Figurine, puma, seated, bl gloss, 4¾" ... 150.00
Figurine, woman's head, bl gloss, #144, 7" ... 160.00
Ginger jar, bl gloss, #131, 9" ... 225.00
Vase, cobalt matt, hdls, #2, 4½" ... 45.00
Vase, dk bl matt w/gold trim, trumpet form, #72, 6" ... 160.00
Vase, gr gloss w/tall sq hdls, #50 ... 150.00
Vase, gr matt w/silver, #86, 9x8½" ... 235.00
Vase, gray & bl crystalline, #31, 7½" ... 115.00
Vase, lt bl matt, corseted, #73, 6¼" ... 110.00

Amberina

Amberina, one of the earliest types of art glass, was developed in 1883 by Joseph Locke of the New England Glass Company. The trademark was registered by W.L. Libbey, who often signed his name in script within the pontil.

Amberina was made by adding gold powder to the batch, which produced glass in the basic amber hue. Part of the item, usually the top, was simply reheated to develop the characteristic deep red or fuchsia shading. Early amberina was mold-blown, but cut and pressed amberina was also produced. The rarest type is plated amberina, made by New England for a short time after 1886. It has been estimated that less than 2,000 pieces were ever produced. Other companies, among them Hobbs and Brockunier, Mt. Washington Glass Company, and Sowerby's Ellison Glassworks of England, made their own versions, being careful to change the name of their product to avoid infringing on Libbey's patent. Prices realized at auction seem to be erratic, to say the least, and dealers appear to be 'testing the waters' with prices that start out very high only to be reduced later if the item does not sell at the original asking price. A lot of amberina glassware is of a more recent vintage — look for evidence of an early production, since the later wares are worth much less than glassware that can be attributed to the older makers. Generic amberina with hand-painted flowers will bring lower prices as well. Our values are taken from auction results and dealer lists, omitting the extremely high and low ends of the range. Our advisor is Debby Maggard; she is listed in the Directory under Ohio. See also Libbey.

Basket, gold sprigs, amber hdl w/worn gold, 3½x7¾" ... 250.00
Basket, Swirl, HP decor, amber ft, roped hdl, 11" H ... 400.00
Bowl, Daisy & Button, Hobbs Brockunier, 1⅝x4" sq ... 125.00
Bowl, Dmn Quilt, irregular folded top, 3x5½" ... 100.00
Bowl, lobed rim, NE Glass, 2x4½" ... 165.00
Bowl, melon ribs, flaring rim, flint, 5" ... 175.00
Bowl, Swirl, ruffled, 2½x7½" ... 115.00
Bowl vase, Dmn Quilt, 3-lobe rim, 2¼x4½" ... 300.00
Butter dish, Daisy & Button, 4x5¼" ... 450.00
Celery, Dmn Quilt, sq scalloped rim, 6¼" ... 225.00
Celery, Invt T'print, crimped rim, 6" ... 225.00
Celery boat, Daisy & Button, Hobbs Brockunier, 14" ... 500.00
Celery vase, Dmn Quilt, NE Glass, 6½" ... 400.00
Celery vase, Dmn Quilt, sq top, NE Glass, 6¼" ... 200.00
Condiment set, sm Raindrop, cruet/pr shakers in Pairpoint fr ... 1,500.00
Cracker jar, Invt T'print, amber knob finial, Hobbs, 8x5¾" ... 750.00
Cruet, invt ribbing, 2 Dmn Quilt bands, chestnut form w/clear hdl ... 200.00
Cruet, Invt T'print, faceted stopper, NE Glass, 6¾" ... 500.00
Cruet, Invt T'print, trefoil spout, EX color, att Mt WA, 5½" ... 500.00
Cruet, Invt T'print, 6" ... 200.00
Cruet, Swirl, amber faceted stopper, NE Glass, 6" ... 495.00
Cruet, Swirl, tricorner top, amberina ball stopper, 6¾" ... 300.00
Custard cup, paneled sides, reeded hdl, NE Glass, 2⅛x2½" ... 225.00
Finger bowl, fluted rim, NE Glass ... 225.00
Finger bowl, ribbed/ruffled, NE Glass ... 150.00
Mug, amber spun rope hdl, 2⅝x2⅞" ... 65.00
Mug, Swirl, amber hdl, 3¾x3" ... 55.00
Pitcher, Daisy & Button, str sides, Hobbs Brockunier, 5" ... 300.00
Pitcher, Dmn Quilt, melon ribs, 10", +6 tumblers ... 400.00
Pitcher, Invt T'print, amber hdl, NE Glass, 3" ... 175.00
Pitcher, Invt T'print, dimpled sides, amber hdl, 5¾x4½" ... 175.00
Pitcher, Invt T'print, sq rim, clear reeded hdl, 5½" ... 175.00
Pitcher, Invt T'print, tricon top, amber hdl, 8½x6½" ... 250.00
Pitcher, melon ribbed w/herringbone pattern, ruffled, 8½" ... 300.00
Pitcher, Optic Rib, amber hdl, 10x4¾" ... 235.00
Pitcher, Swirl, amber appl hdl, 7⅞x4½" ... 165.00
Pitcher, Swirl, bulbous, reeded hdl, 9" ... 300.00
Pitcher, tankard; Invt T'print, att NE Glass, 8¾" ... 600.00
Pitcher, tankard; paneled, 5" ... 250.00
Pitcher, trifold top, high amberina hdl, Midwest, 4½" ... 100.00
Punch cup, Dmn Quilt, amber reeded hdl, 2½" ... 100.00
Punch cup, Invt T'print, amber hdl, 3" ... 50.00
Spooner, Dmn Quilt, petticoat shape, Mt WA, 4" ... 500.00
Toothpick holder, Baby Invt T'print, fuchsia, sqd top, 2½" ... 300.00
Toothpick holder, Baby Invt T'print, 3-lobe rim, 2¼x2½" ... 325.00
Toothpick holder, Daisy & Button, tricorner, 2¾" ... 275.00
Toothpick holder, Dmn Quilt, EX fuchsia, tricon top, NE Glass ... 300.00

Toothpick holder, Dmn Quilt, fuschia, NE Glass 150.00
Toothpick holder, Dmn Quilt, ovoid w/short neck, Mt WA 285.00
Toothpick holder, Dmn Quilt, sqd rim, NE Glass, 2⅜" 295.00
Toothpick holder, Invt T'print, sqd rim, Mt WA, 2½" 285.00
Tray, ice cream, Daisy & Button, 5½" dia 85.00
Tumbler, Dmn Quilt, EX color 150.00
Tumbler, Dmn Quilt, fuchsia, NE Glass, set of 6 ....240.00
Tumbler, Dmn Quilt, HP floral, 3½" 130.00
Tumbler, Invt T'print 45.00
Tumbler, Invt T'print, mc floral, 4" 125.00
Vase, Dmn Quilt, amber rigaree collar, ruffled rim, 3¼" 150.00
Vase, Dmn Quilt, EX color, sqd rim, NE Glass, 6¾" 345.00
Vase, Dmn Quilt, netted design, corset form, sq rim, 7¼" 135.00
Vase, HP florals, cylindrical, ground pontil, 6⅞x3⅞" 195.00
Vase, jack-in-pulpit; rigaree collar, ball near base, 8½" 100.00
Vase, lily; EX color, 10" 800.00
Vase, lily; NE Glass, 8" 650.00
Vase, lily; ribbed, 8" 215.00
Vase, lily; Swirl, w/gold flowers, appl amber coil/ft, 12" 245.00
Vase, Optic Dmn, roll-down fuchsia rim, 6¾" 300.00
Vase, Swirl, appl coil, amber appl ft, 8½x3" 185.00
Vase, swirled & dimpled body, pinched neck, rigaree collar, 3½" ...450.00
Vase, trumpet form, fold-over appl amber rim, 20" 950.00

Plated Amberina

Cruet, amber cut stopper, 7x3½", $2,500.00; Lily vase, tricon rim, slim trumpet form, 9", $5,000.00; Tumbler, embossed ribs, 3¾", $1,650.00.

Creamer, 3x4½" 3,250.00
Cruet, uniform color, well ribbed, amber hdl/stopper, 7" 2,500.00
Mug, amber hdl 2,300.00
Plate, ruffled, 6⅝" 1,300.00
Punch cup, 2¾" 3,750.00
Shade for hanging lamp, extremely rare, 14" 12,000.00
Tumbler, vertical ribs, EX color, 4" 1,650.00

American Bisque

The American Bisque Pottery operated in Williamstown, West Virginia, from 1919 to 1982. The company was begun by Mr. B.E. Allen and remained an Allen-family business until its sale in 1982. Figural pottery was produced from approximately 1937 until about the time the pottery closed.

American Bisque pottery is often identified by the 'wedges' or dry-footed cleats on the bottom of the ware. Many cookie jar designs are unique to the American Bisque Company, such as cookie jars with blackboards and magnets, cookie jars with lids that doubled as serving trays, and cookie jars with 'action pieces' which show movement. American Bisque pieces are very collectible and are available in a broad variety of color schemes; some items are decorated with 22–24k gold. Many items are modeled after highly popular copyrighted characters.

For further information, we recommend *American Bisque, Collector's Guide with Prices*, by Mary Jane Giacomini (Collector Books).

Cookie jars, Popeye the Sailor Man, unmarked, from $1,000.00 to $1,200.00. (Photo courtesy Ermagene Westfall)

Ashtray, Flintstones, ea 110.00
Ashtray, free-form, Marietta Modern line, mk 715-A (APCO) ...20.00
Ashtray, tepee form, airbrushed glazes, 6¼" 36.00
Bank, Boy/Girl Turnabout, unmk (APCO), 9" 175.00
Bank, Casper, USA, from $350 to 375.00
Bank, Chick, unmk, 6½" 40.00
Bank, Diaper Pin Pig, gold trim, mk USA, 9" 175.00
Bank, Elephant on Tub, unmk, 6" 45.00
Bank, Fluffy Cat, gold neck bow, unmk (APCO), 5¾" 45.00
Bank, Little Audrey, unmk, 8¼" 775.00
Bank, Popeye (head) 350.00
Bank, Snowman (head), unmk, 6½" 32.00
Bank, Yarn Doll, USA, from $30 to 35.00
Christmas tree plate, cold pnt & gold trim, unmk, 14½" 75.00
Condiment jar, any figural head, ea 65.00
Cookie jar, Animal Crackers (Cookies), wht/mc cylinder, mk USA, 8" ..35.00
Cookie jar, Bear, eyes closed, w/indented dots, unmk, 11¾" 85.00
Cookie jar, Beehive, plain, mk USA, 9½" 50.00
Cookie jar, Bell (Ring for Cookies), mk USA, 10" 50.00
Cookie jar, Casper the Friendly Ghost, mk, 13½", minimum value 1,000.00
Cookie jar, Castle, mk Cardinal 310 USA, 11½" 175.00
Cookie jar, Cat on Side of Box, w/tail finial, mk USA, 10¼" ...145.00
Cookie jar, Cheerleaders (Have a Cookie), #802, 11" 325.00
Cookie jar, Chef Head, #603, 7½" 425.00
Cookie jar, Churn, red cold pnt flowers, mk USA, 10", from $25 to ...35.00
Cookie jar, Clown on Stage, #805, 9¾" 775.00
Cookie jar, Coffee Pot, pine cones, side hdl, mk USA, 9½" 50.00
Cookie jar, Coffee Pot, red flowers, bail hdl, mk USA, 10" 45.00
Cookie jar, Coffee Pot (Cookies), gold trim, bail hdl, 9½" 95.00
Cookie jar, Collegiate Owl, plain, mk USA, 11½" 85.00
Cookie jar, Cookie Bus (Cookieville Bus Co), mk Cardinal USA, 7½" ...350.00
Cookie jar, Cookie Safe, mk Cardinal 309 USA, 10½" 110.00
Cookie jar, Cookie Time Clock, mk USA 203, 9" 150.00
Cookie jar, Cookies of This World (Space Man/Spaceship), mk USA, 10" 775.00
Cookie jar, Cup of Chocolate w/Marshmallows, mk USA, 9¼" ..85.00
Cookie jar, French Poodle, maroon, mk USA, 10½", from $100 to ..125.00
Cookie jar, Graduate, #303, mk Cardinal USA, 9" 125.00
Cookie jar, Hands in Pockets Cat, chartreuse, mk USA, 1½" ...120.00
Cookie jar, Hands in Pockets Elephant, mk USA, 10½" 160.00
Cookie jar, Hands in Pockets Elephant, unmk, 8¾" 145.00
Cookie jar, Hands in Pockets Pig, chartreuse, mk USA, 11" 120.00

Cookie jar, Jack-in-the-Box, mk USA, 12" 150.00
Cookie jar, Kittens on Beehive, mk USA 65.00
Cookie jar, Liberty Bell, mk USA, 9¾", from $110 to 125.00
Cookie jar, Oaken Bucket, brn w/yel ladle finial, mk USA, 10" 125.00
Cookie jar, Pennsylvania Dutch Boy, unmk, 11½" 425.00
Cookie jar, Pennsylvania Dutch Girl, unmk, 11¼" 375.00
Cookie jar, Picnic Basket, #601, 6¾" 325.00
Cookie jar, Pig (Dancing), cold-pnt indented dots, 11½" 125.00
Cookie jar, Poodle on Side of Box, w/bone finial, mk CJ 5 USA, 10" ...145.00
Cookie jar, Rooster, openings in tail, cold pnt, unmk, 12½" 85.00
Cookie jar, Rooster, solid tail, cold pnt, mk USA, 11", from $50 to .60.00
Cookie jar, Sack of Cookies, #307, mk Cardinal USA, 10" 60.00
Cookie jar, Saddle, no blackboard, unmk, 12" 275.00
Cookie jar, Sandman Cookies (TV Bedtime), #801, 9¾" 285.00
Cookie jar, Santa Claus, winking, cold-pnt red hat, mk USA, 9¾" ...400.00
Cookie jar, Sea Bag, birds & anchor, w/cord hdl, mk USA, 10¼" 175.00
Cookie jar, SS Kookie Elephant, unmk, 11¾" 175.00
Cookie jar, Strawberry, mk Sears Exclusive Patent Pending, 8¾" ...35.00
Cookie jar, Tall Bus (After School Cookies), mk USA, 11" 175.00
Cookie jar, Tall Train, mk USA, 12" 200.00
Cookie jar, Tall Truck (Cookie Truck), mk USA 744, 11½" 75.00
Cookie jar, Tall Truck (Cookie Truck), mk USA 744, 13" 100.00
Cookie jar, Train Engine, gold trim, mk USA 200, 7½x11¾" 95.00
Cookie jar, Treasure Chest, closed lid, mk USA, lg 200.00
Cookie jar, Treasure Chest, open lid w/coins & jewels, mk USA, sm ...175.00
Flower frog, swans, APCO, 5¾" 28.00
Lamp, Baseball Boy, unmk, 7½" 35.00
Lamp, Chick, cold pnt, 6¾" 35.00
Lamp, Zebra, APCO, 7¼" 40.00
Pitcher, ball shape w/strawberry decor, cold pnt, mk USA, 6¾" ..35.00
Pitcher, Pig, cold pnt, 8" 150.00
Planter, Dutch Girl w/Wooden Shoe, unmk, 6" 8.00
Planter, Elephant in Basket, unmk, 3¾" 10.00
Planter, Elf on Mushroom, unmk, 6" 30.00
Planter, Elf Reclining by Log, unmk, 2¾" 10.00
Planter, Farmer Pig w/Corn, unmk (APCO), 6½" 8.00
Planter, Fish, bl/wht, unmk (APCO), 3¼" 18.00
Planter, Happy Fish, unmk, 4¾" 25.00
Planter, Lovebirds & Nest, unmk, 6½" 14.00
Planter, Pig Sleeping, mk USA (APCO), 2½" 18.00
Planter, Snow White, mk, 6½" 115.00
Planter, Three Little Pigs, unmk, 5½" 24.00
Planter, Yarn Doll w/Block, unmk, 5¾" 20.00
Refrigerator jug, emb floral decor, gold trim, unmk (APCO), 8¾" ...150.00
Refrigerator jug, swirled, emb floral decor, gold trim, APCO, 8¾" ...150.00
Shakers, Elephants, unmk (APCO), 3½", pr 18.00
Shakers, Strawberries, w/blossom-&-leaf tops, leaf bottoms, 3", pr .16.00
Shakers, Strawberries, w/blossom-&-leaf tops, leaf bottoms, 5", pr .25.00
Teapot, swirl pattern, APCO, 6" 30.00
Toothpick holder, wht vertical ribs w/hdls, gold trim, APCO, 2½" 20.00
Vase, Calla Lilly, gold trim, unmk (APCO), 6" 22.00
Vase, Cornucopia, rose motif, gold trim, unmk (APCO), 5" 24.00
Vase, Philodendron Leaves, gold trim, unmk, 7¼" 28.00
Wall pocket, Hurricane Lamp, mk USA (APCO), 6" 24.00
Wall pocket, Pluto w/Cart, mk, 6¾" 120.00

American Encaustic Tiling Co.

A.E. Tile was organized in 1879 in Zanesville, Ohio. Until its closing in 1935, they produced beautiful ornamental and architectural tile equal to the best European imports. They also made vases, figurines, and novelty items with exceptionally fine modeling and glazes. See also Tiles.

Bookends, cherub seated on swag, rabbit below, shield-shape bk, pr ..300.00
Bowl, eagle on rock w/wings out at side, gr, high-glaze, mk 285.00
Inkwell, matt blk & silver, dbl, w/logo 255.00
Tray, monks/wine bbl, emb/mc, 5x6½", EX 75.00
Vase, gr & brn gloss, 7", NM 100.00
Vase, yel-gr crystalline w/lt irid, hdls, 9" 160.00

American Indian Art

That time when the American Indian was free to practice the crafts and culture that was his heritage has always held a fascination for many. They were a people who appreciated beauty of design and colorful decoration in their furnishings and clothing; and because instruction in their crafts was a routine part of their rearing, they were well accomplished. Several tribes developed areas in which they excelled. The Navajo were weavers and silversmiths, the Zuni, lapidaries. Examples of their craftsmanship are very valuable. Today even the work of contemporary Indian artists — weavers, silversmiths, carvers, and others — is highly collectible. Unless otherwise noted, values are for items with no obvious damage or excessive wear (EX/NM). For a more thorough study we recommend *Arrowheads and Projectile Points*, *Indian Axes*, *Indian Artifacts of the Midwest*, and *Collector's Guide to Indian Pipes, Identification and Values*. All four have been written by our advisor, Lar Hothem; you will find his address in the Directory under Ohio.

Key:
bw — beadwork
dmn — diamond
p-h — prehistoric
s-s — sinew sewn

Apparel and Accessories

Before the white traders brought the Indian women cloth from which to sew their garments and beads to use for decorating them, clothing was made from skins sewn together with sinew, usually made of animal tendon. Porcupine quills were dyed bright colors and woven into bags and armbands and used to decorate clothing and moccasins. Examples of early quillwork are scarce today and highly collectible.

Early in the nineteenth century, beads were being transported via pony pack trains. These 'pony' beads were irregular shapes of opaque glass imported from Venice. Nearly always blue or white, they were twice as large as the later 'seed' beads. By 1870 translucent beads in many sizes and colors had been made available, and Indian beadwork had become commercialized. Each tribe developed its own distinctive methods and preferred decorations, making it possible for collectors today to determine the origin of many items. Soon after the turn of the century, the craft of beadworking began to diminish.

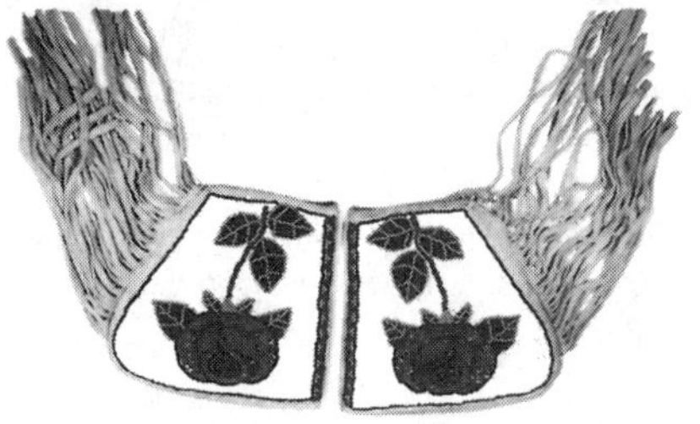

Cuffs, Kootenai full-beaded floral design with long fringe, ca 1920, 8x8", $175.00.

Belt, Sioux, tacked leather w/s-s war shirt strip, 1900s, 36x2" ...500.00
Blouse, Navajo, bl velvet w/silver concho buttons, 1940s 200.00
Bonnet, Blackfoot, horned 'wormy' ermine, bw/tacked brow band, 1880s 4,000.00
Breech clout, leather w/mc ribbonwork, 1940s, 16x3" 25.00
Cap, Plains Sioux, full bw lazy stitched on corduroy, 1910s, 5" H .900.00

Coat, Shawnee, Fr-style dbl cape, pony beads/fringe, 19th C .15,000.00
Dress, Cheyenne, buckskin, outstanding bw, fringe, 1920s, 54x32" ...3,100.00
Dress, Great Lakes, rows of tin cone dangles, 1920s, sm 500.00
Dress, Nez Perce, trade cloth w/geometric bw yoke, ribbons, 1900s .1,100.00
Dress, Sioux, buckskin, bw yoke, tin cones, fringe, leggings, 1940s ..2,100.00
Gauntlets, Flathead, tanned buckskin w/floral bw & fringe, 1920s 275.00
Gauntlets, Lakota, tan hide w/mc bw & fringe, 12", pr, EX 850.00
Gauntlets, Plateau, unusual cutouts w/bw designs on wool, 1920s, 16" .850.00
Gauntlets, Santee, full bw front & bk on soft buckskin, 1930s, 18" 850.00
Hat, Eastern Woodlands Iroquois, velvet panels w/bw, 7½" 650.00
Hat, Iroquois, blk velvet w/floral bw on top & sides, 1880s, 5x6" .1,100.00
Hat, Yakima, fez w/full bw of cut beads w/eagles/salmon/flags, 20th C ...550.00
Jacket, Cree, tanned moose hide, floral bw/fringe, 1950, sm 150.00
Jacket, scout; Crow, pony & seed bw strips on red Mountie wool .3,250.00
Leggings, Blackfoot, red stroud w/bw, ermine/bell dangles, 1900s, 33" ..900.00
Leggings, Blackfoot, wht buffalo hide w/bw strips, 1900s, 36x16" 700.00
Leggings, Ponca, bl trade cloth w/bw strips & trim, 31" 350.00
Leggings, Sioux, trade cloth, s-s bw strips, 1910s, 26x14" 600.00
Moccasins, Arapaho, bw tops/trim, concho buttons, high-top, 1920s, 11" ...425.00
Moccasins, Arapaho, s-s full bw geometrics, 1890s, 10x4" 450.00
Moccasins, Assiniboine, full bw geometrics on top, 1880s, 8x3" ..900.00
Moccasins, Blackfoot, geometric bw toes, soft soles, 1900s, 10" .500.00
Moccasins, Cheyenne, mc bw on wht leather, 10" 600.00
Moccasins, Cheyenne, s-s ochred antelope hide, buffalo soles, 1870s .1,200.00
Moccasins, Comanche, s-s, hard soles, heel fringe, 1880s, doll sz, 3" 500.00
Moccasins, Iroquois, heavy floral embr, bw flaps, 1880s, 10" 300.00
Moccasins, Nez Perce, floral bw, brass buttons, high-top, 1915, 11" ...275.00
Moccasins, Oto, bw on hide, parfleche soles, ca 1900, 6¼" 1,000.00
Moccasins, Plains, bw bands of wht enclose bl fields, 7" 330.00
Moccasins, Plains, mc bw, 11" 1,125.00
Moccasins, Plains Cree, s-s hide w/floral bw, hard soles, 1880s, 9" 550.00
Moccasins, Santee Sioux, s-s hide w/mc floral quillwork, 1870s, 10" .650.00
Moccasins, Seneca, bw toe & flaps on hide, 1870s, 9" 475.00
Moccasins, Sioux, buffalo sole, s-s w/bifurcated tongues, cones, 1890s ...1,000.00
Moccasins, Sioux, full bw s-s on buffalo hide, 1880s, 10½" 1,200.00
Robe, tanned buffalo hide, mc pnt sunburst, 20th C, 56x61" 500.00
Sash, Great Lakes, assumption type, finger woven, 1860s, 44x8" .225.00
Trousers, Sioux, s-s parade type, full bw, ca 1900, boy's sz, 16" ..5,000.00
Vest, Kiowa, bw stars & geometric strips on blk cloth, 1900, 27" .150.00
Vest, Ojibway, velvet panels w/mc bw, 1890s, 22x20" 700.00
Vest, Santee Sioux, dyed floral & quilled figures, ca 1900, 18" .1,100.00
Vest, Sioux, crossed Am flags, 1910, baby sz, 8x5" 700.00
Vest, Sioux, full bw, inscribed & dtd 1903, 21x19" 5,500.00
Vest, Sioux, s-s full bw front & bk on buffalo hide, 1890s, adult 4,000.00
Vest, Sioux, s-s/full bw on buffalo hide, warrior figures, 1880s, lg ...19,000.00

Bags and Cases

The Indians used bags for many purposes, and most display excellent form and workmanship. Of the types listed below, many collectors consider the pipe bag to be the most desirable form. Pipe bags were long, narrow, leather and bead or quillwork creations made to hold tobacco in a compartment at the bottom and the pipe, with the bowl removed from the stem, in the top. Long buckskin fringe was used as trim and complemented the quilled and beaded design to make the bag a masterpiece of Indian art.

Apache, awl, bw on ochred hide, brass buttons, 1870s, +bone awl .900.00
Apache, bw on hide, ca 1900, 14x16" 550.00
Apache, medicine, bw sides: turtle effigy/geometrics, 1880s, 9½x4" ..1,600.00
Arapaho, pipe, s-s sheep hide, quilled slate, fringe, 19th C, 39" 7,000.00
Arapaho, strike-a-lite, bw front, trade beads/tin cones, 1880s, 5½" .475.00
Blackfoot, holster, bw cross/hourglass on leather, 1900s, 10x4" .325.00
Cheyenne, shot pouch, bw cross on wht, buffalo hide, 1880s, 4½" .550.00
Cheyenne, tepee, s-s buffalo hide, cones/horsehair drops, 1870s, pr ..12,000.00
Cheyenne, tobacco, s-s, bw ea side, fringed, 1880s, 16x6" 700.00
Comanche, strike-a-lite, bw front w/cross, tin cones, 1880s, 6" ...400.00
Crow, knife sheath, Sundance bw, bw edge, 1880s, 5¼x2" 150.00
Crow, parfleche, mineral pnt on elk hide, 1800s, 26x12", pr ..2,500.00
Crow, parfleche, pnt geometrics, fold-over type, 1890s, 6x5" 250.00
Crow, pipe, hourglass bw on hide w/fringe, 1880s, 30x7" 1,300.00
Gros Ventre, shot pouch, s-s w/full bw font & bk, 19th C, 4½" ..425.00
Gros Ventre, strike-a-lite, bw (seed), tin cones/fringe, 1880s, 5" .400.00
Kiowa, strike-a-lite, full bw, brass cones, twisted fringe, 1870s, 5" .600.00
Lakota, belt pouch, geometric bw, fringe/tinklers, 1900s, 20" 500.00
Mandan, pipe, quilled lines & slats on side, fringe, 1920s, 32" ..475.00
Nez Perce, floral bw, fringe, rectangular, 1930s, 18x10" 250.00
Plains, Peace Medal pouch, full quillwork on buckskin, 1890s, 4x5" .150.00
Plains, tepee, bw ends, tin cones, horsehair dangles, 1890s 2,000.00
Plateau, coin, floral bw on steel bw ground, 19th C, 3¼" 110.00
Plateau, full bw w/5 star designs, rectangular, 1910s, 20x11" 275.00
Sioux, knife, s-s buffalo hide w/quilled tin cones, 1880s, 7½" 550.00
Sioux, mc floral quillwork, 1890s, 4½x4½" 225.00
Sioux, pipe, geometric & floral quillwork on hide, 1890s, 27" ..1,900.00
Sioux, pipe, s-s, bw ea side, quill-wrapped w/fringe, 1910s, 36" .1,200.00
Sioux, pipe, s-s, full quillwork (pictorial), 1920s, 44x6" 2,500.00
Sioux, pipe, s-s buffalo hide w/quillwork buffalo head, 1860s, 17" .1,800.00
Sioux, pouch, 3-sided, fine fringe, seed bw floral, 1880s, 7" 600.00
Teton Sioux, pipe, s-s buckskin w/bw, fringe/ochre, 1880s, 35" ..3,250.00
Ute, strike-a-lite, bw front/bk, tin tinklers, yel ochre, 1880s, 5" ..375.00

Baskets

In the following listings, examples are basket form and coiled unless noted otherwise.

Apache, beehive decor, 1940s, 2x10" 700.00
Apache, blk geometrics (striking), 1930s, 5x18" 3,500.00
Apache, burden, fringe, tin cones, 1930s, 8x7" 425.00
Apache, medicine, mc waterbirds, 1930s, 6x15" 325.00
Apache, olla, mc geometrics/half dmns, ca 1925, 12x15" 1,500.00
Apache, star fret & arrow point decor, 1935, 3x13" 1,900.00
Apache, tray, central flower, stepped design, 1920s, 18x6" 2,500.00
Apache, tray, human & animal figures, 1920s, 10" 1,000.00
Apache, tray, 16 different stick figures/4 crosses, 1920s, 19x4" ..5,000.00
Apache, triangles & crosses, 1940s, 2x6" 300.00
Cowlitz, storage, embricated w/mc geometrics, 1880s, 14x15" .2,000.00
Hopi, central blossom, ca 1970, 11" 225.00
Hopi, wicker, mc, 1930s, 11½x13¾" 475.00
Hupa, woman's 'hat,' muted mc decor, 1920s, 3x7" 350.00
Mono, bowl, dbl row of geometrics, 1925, 5½x11½" 800.00
Mono, bowl, 3 blk off-set lines, 1930s, 14x6" 650.00
Paiute, seed gathering, conical w/banded decor, 1910s, 7x7" 275.00
Pima, birds & human figures, 1935, 4x7" 550.00

Pima, bowl, geometric designs, ca 1920s, 7x17", $775.00.

Pima, geometric pattern, shallow, 3¼x14", EX 225.00
Pima, horsehair, classic fret decor, ca 1975, ½x4½" 325.00

Pima, horsehair, 3 snakes/9 friendship figures, 1975, ½x3¼" 650.00
Pima, horsehair w/mc geometrics, 1975, 2x2" 275.00
Pima, olla, fret decor, 1920s, mini, 4½x4½" 650.00
Pima, stepped geometrics, 1920s, 5x13" 350.00
Pima, storage, whirling log decor, 1935, 9x14" 600.00
Pima, tray, geometric pinwheel decor, 3½x12¾", EX 650.00
Pima, tray, geometric stepped pattern, 4x15½", EX 1,250.00
Pomo, boat shape, stair-step decor, single rod, 1910s, 2x3½" 375.00
Pomo, gift, fully feathered, 1930s, ¾x2" 400.00
Pomo, horizontal striped rows, 1920s, 3x6½" 950.00
Salish, embricated Frazier River w/mc chevrons, 1910s, 9x14x8" .275.00
Second Mesa, deer & geometric decor, 1950s, 4x8¼" 275.00
Shasta, brn bands on beige, ca 1930, 4x9" 475.00
Tlingit, mc false embr decor, ca 1910, 4x5" 325.00
Tulare, shoulder, 4 rattlesnake bands, 1930s, 4½x8" 3,000.00
Washo, flame & cross decor, att Tootsie Dick, 1920s, 4x7½" ..2,250.00
Yokut, doll cradle, red bud & willow, 1920s, 5x11" 190.00
Yurok, bowl, parallelogram decor, openwork top, 1920s, 5x7" ...800.00

Blades and Points

Relics of this type usually display characteristics of a general area, time period, or a particular location. With study, those made by the Plains Indians are easily discerned from those of the West Coast. Because modern man has imitated the art of the Indian by reproducing these artifacts through modern means, use caution before investing your money in 'too good to be authentic' specimens.

Adena, blk flint, sturdy design, Woodland, OH, 3½" 90.00
Adena, Robbins variety, dk bl Upper Mercer, Woodland, OH, 4⅝" ...160.00
Agate Basin, tan flint, typical form, Late Paleo, 4⅛" 500.00
Bifurcate, faded bl flint, Archaic, 3" 125.00
Clovis, chert, reworked tip, Paleo, 1x2" 45.00
Dalton, wht Burlington chert, resharpened, Paleo, 1x2⅝" 175.00
Dickson, lt flint w/bl swirls, Hopewell/Middle Woodland, MO, 3½" ...225.00
Fulton turkey-tail, Red Ochre, hornstone, thin, Woodland, IN, 3⅝" ...350.00
Godar, wht-tan chert, EX length, Archaic, IL, 4" 60.00
Hardin, gray flint, barbed, resharpened, Archaic, IN, 3x⅞" 20.00
Hopewell, wht chert, Middle Woodland, IL, 3½x2⅛" 40.00
Mason, creamy flint w/pk wash, Early Woodland, IN, 4½" 165.00
Notched base, lt brn flint, Archaic, IL, 3x2" 30.00
Palmer, tan chert, Early Archaic, MO, 1½x1¼", from $50 to 60.00
Rice side-notch, red & pk flint, Archaic, MO, 3¼x1⅛", up to ...40.00
Sedalia, gray chert, EX patina, Archaic, IL, 5¼", minimum value ...200.00
Snyders, red/pk chert, Middle Woodland, IN, 4x2¼", from $200 to ..275.00
Stanfield, tan flint w/brn streaks, thin, Archaic, IN, 1¼x4¼" ...145.00
Thebes, tan chert, Archaic, MO, 6" 1,000.00
Turkey-tail, red ochre, bull's-eye hornstone, Woodland, 4¾" 800.00

Ceremonial Items

Bag, shoulder; Chippewa, floral bw/tube beads/fringe, 1890s, 39" .1,600.00
Bells, dance; Yacqui, nut shell type, rare, ca 1870, pr 155.00
Breast plate, Sioux, hair pipe bone/bead/rawhide spacers, 1890s, 38" .1,100.00
Drum, Crow, hide-covered, pnt traces, 1910s, 16" 100.00
Drum, Peyote, CI kettle w/hide cover & rope tie downs, 1910s, 10" .350.00
Drum, Taos, hide-covered hollow log, 1950s, 13x7" 70.00
Fan, Iroquois, wild turkey feathers, bw cloth hdl, 1880, 14x12" ..325.00
Fan, Kiowa, feathers w/bw hdl & twisted hide fringe, 1900s, 22" .650.00
Feast bowl, Sioux, cvd bird effigy, burled hardwood, 1860s, 6x11" ..275.00
Feast dish, Seminole, wooden, ca 1900, old native rpr, 19x36" ..110.00
Feast spoon, Great Lakes, cvd wood, 1860s, 25x5" 225.00
Fetish, Cheyenne, umbilical, bw turtle, fringe on ft, 20th C, 5x4" ...225.00
Fetish, Cheyenne, umbilical, full bw, s-s, 1870s, 7" 600.00
Fetish, Sioux, mc bw turtle, 1920s, 2x5" 200.00
Leggings, Stomp Dance; turtle shells & leather, 1890s, 11" 450.00
Mask, Cayuse Horse, muslin lined, pony beads, 19th C, 28x34" .3,750.00
Mask, Navajo, buckskin/felt/abalone/horsehair, 12x11½", EX ...1,000.00
Rattle, Kiowa, peyote gourd/bw shaft/horsehair top/fringe, 1900, 22" ...250.00
Shirt, Ghost Dance, muslin w/buffalo fetish/ermines/bundles, 20th C ..100.00
Skirt, Hupa, basketry w/shells o/l & fringe, 1900s, 26x18" 2,500.00

Dolls

Blackfoot, hide face, shell-decor dress, bw moccasins, 1930s, 12" ...550.00
Cochiti, Storyteller, 10 babies, Martha Arquero, 7x6½" 325.00
Crow, fully costumed, 1930s, 9" 700.00
Hopi, Kachina, Ahote, ca 1940, 8x4" 200.00
Hopi, Kachina, Black Ogre, 1-pc, ca 1940, 14x7" 325.00
Hopi, Kachina, Chavero Black Ogre w/knife & shield, 1975, 20" ..325.00
Hopi, Kachina, Eagle Dancer, action cvd, much detail, 1970s, 19" ..275.00
Hopi, Kachina, Kayemsai, 1940s, 14x7" 325.00
Hopi, Kachina, Ogre, long hair, snake-dancer skirt, 1975, 18" ..325.00
Hopi, Kachina, One Ear, blk, old style, 1-pc, ca 1960, 15x4" 325.00
Hopi, Kachina, One Horn, ca 1940, 6x4" 280.00
Hopi, Kachina, Warrior, ca 1940, 10x5" 325.00
Hopi, Kachina, White Buffalo w/rattle & bowl, 1970s, 17" 300.00
Hopi, Kachina, White Ogre, w/knife & staff, Natumya, 1975, 16" ..425.00
Sioux, bw hide face, bw dress/leggings/moccasins, 1900s, 9x5" ..500.00
Sioux, female w/hide face, human hair, buckskin dress, 1880s, 13" ..1,400.00
Sioux, full mc bw, w/moccasins/belt/ear drops, 1920s, 9½" 450.00
Sioux, leather face, human hair, beaded dress, leggings, 1900s, 14" ...550.00
Zuni, Kachina, EX cvg, ca 1940, 13" 175.00

Domestics

Blanket, central star, brns & tans, minor damage, 48x84" 135.00
Blanket, chief's, 3rd Phase, hand loomed, fine weave, 1890s, 53x66" 3,750.00
Blanket, Haida, button type w/eagles, I Collison, 1940, 50x60" ...450.00
Blanket, Navajo, Third Phase Chief's, homespun wool, ca 1910, 76x55" ..3,000.00
Blanket, Nez Perce, trade cloth w/mc floral bw, 1910s, 34x60" ..500.00
Blanket, Rio Grande Chimayo, central design/end stripes, 52x73" 150.00
Blanket, saddle; Sioux, s-s buffalo hide w/bw/bells/fringe, 1880s, 72" .2,500.00
Blanket, Sioux, dk bl w/s-s geometric-decor strip, 1900, 76x62" 1,400.00
Blanket, Sunday saddle; Germantown yarn, ca 1940, 28x48" 225.00
Bridle, Sioux, s-s w/full bw, quilled drops & conchos, 1880s 700.00

Cradle cover, Sioux, sinew-sewn hide, geometric multicolor glass tube beads, cowrie shell suspensions, 1880s, 19", $1,500.00.

Container, Penobscot, birchbark w/classic designs, 1880s, 7x8" .325.00
Cradle, Cheyenne, bw wrap style on buckskin carrier on brds, 1920s 6,000.00
Cradle, Cheyenne, s-s, bw dogs/thunderbird, cloth bottom, 1880s, 38" ..2,750.00

Cradle, Cheyenne, s-s bw top, bl stroud cloth bottom, 1880s, 37" ...3,500.00
Cradle, Winnebago, wooden, ca 1900, 27x13" ...375.00
Ladle, NW Coast, cvd wood w/raven hdl, abalone eyes, 1950s, 15" ..200.00
Spoon, Plains, bent horn, 1890s, 8x2½" ...60.00
Tepee, Arapaho, muslin, pnt horses & ghost dancers, 1890s, 59x34" .8,500.00

Jewelry and Adornments

As early as 500 A.D., Indians in the Southwest drilled turquoise nuggets and strung them on cords made of sinew or braided hair. The Spanish introduced them to coral, and it became a popular item of jewelry; abalone and clam shells were favored by the Coastal Indians. Not until the last half of the nineteenth century did the Indians learn to work with silver. Each tribe developed its own distinctive style and preferred design, which until about 1920 made it possible to determine tribal origin with some degree of accuracy. Since that time, because of modern means of communication and travel, motifs have become less distinct.

Quality Indian silver jewelry may be antique or contemporary. Age, though certainly to be considered, is not as important a factor as fine workmanship and good stones. Pre-1910 silver will show evidence of hammer marks, and designs are usually simple. Beads have sometimes been shaped from coins. Stones tend to be small; when silver wire was used, it is usually square. To insure your investment, choose a reputable dealer.

Bracelet, Navajo, turq & silver cluster, VM Begay, 1980, 6½x3" .170.00
Bracelet, Navajo, 3-strand, turq & silver, 1950s, 6" ...75.00
Breast plate, Plains, bone hair pipes w/brass/glass bw/mirrors, 1885 ...700.00
Breast plate, Sioux, bone hair pipe w/trade bead dangles, 19th C, 49" ..950.00
Buckle & bolo tie, Navajo, silver & lapiz, 1995 ...500.00
Choker, Plains, bones & trade beads w/hide spacers, 1910s, 13" ...100.00
Earrings, silver, spoon-hdl type, 1920x, 2x½" ...15.00
Hair drop, Kiowa, German silver w/eng silver Peyote bird, 1870s, 51" ..900.00
Hair drops, quilled medicine-wheel type, cone dangles, 1920s, pr ..50.00
Necklace, Crow, bw loops w/tacks/1 concho/tin cones, 1900s, 16x14" ..850.00
Necklace, multi-strand lapis heishi, lapis tabs, 1890s, 16" ...200.00
Necklace, Navajo, silver w/naja motif, lg naja w/lg turq, 1940, 30" ...200.00
Necklace, Navajo, silver w/pendant cross & lg turq stone, 1940, 34" ...375.00
Necklace, Navajo, turq & silver cluster squash blossom, 1980, 32" ...400.00
Necklace, Pueblo, wrought silver beads, 1 lg/18 sm crosses, 1940s, 28" .450.00
Necklace, shells w/dance woman inlay, silver chain, 1950s, 24" ..75.00
Necklace, Shoshone, full bw pendant on bone & bead strand, 1950, 44" ...60.00
Necklace, Sioux, 3-strand brass bead+whiteheart/cowrie shells, 1880s ...200.00
Necklace, 7-strand red tubular coral, wrap style, 1980, 28" ...150.00

Pipes

Pipe bowls were usually carved from soft stone, such as catlinite or red pipestone, an argilaceous sedimentary rock composed mainly of hardened clay. Steatite was also used. Some ceremonial pipes were simply styled, while others were intricately designed naturalistic figurals, sometimes in bird or frog forms called effigies. Their stems, made of wood and often covered with leather, were sometimes nearly a yard in length.

Catlinite bowl carved with snake capturing frog, wooden polychromed corkscrew stem, Lake/Woodlands, 28½" long, EX, $3,100.00.

Catlinite, cvd buffalo effigy w/cvd twist stem, 1890s, 28" ...950.00
Catlinite, eagle effigy bowl, cvd catlinite stem, 1890s, 25" ...800.00
Catlinite cvd horse bowl, wooden stem w/pigment, Sioux, 20th C, 30" ..275.00
Catlinite openwork, quillwork/feather/horsehair stem, Sioux, 1890s ...1,200.00
Catlinite T bowl, new wooden stem, Sioux, 20th C, 35x5" ...200.00
Gr stone bird shape, Mound Builder ceremonial, p-h, 6x3" ...200.00
Pipe tomahawk, brass presentation, inscribed 1775 US, 17x7" ...1,100.00
Stone owl effigy bowl, p-h, newer wooden stem, 23x3" ...110.00

Pottery

Indian pottery is nearly always decorated in such a manner as to indicate the tribe that produced it or the pueblo in which it was made. For instance, the designs of Cochiti potters were usually scattered forms from nature or sacred symbols. The Zuni preferred an ornate repetitive decoration of a closer configuration. They often used stylized deer and bird forms, sometimes in dimensional applications.

Acoma, canteen, foliate star in umber, 1930s, 5¼x4½" ...190.00
Acoma, jar, stylized Pueblo birds, ca 1950, 11x11" ...475.00
Acoma, olla, classic design, Loretta Joe, 1980, 13x14" ...1,000.00
Acoma, olla, fine linear & geometric decor, 1930s, 10x9" ...450.00
Acoma, seed jar, linear star decor top, Lucy Lewis, 1970s, 5x8" .850.00
Anasazi, bowl, mc stylized birds, p-h, 5x11" ...425.00
Anasazi, ladle, blk-on-wht geometrics, p-h, 8x4" ...225.00
Anasazi, pitcher, blk on wht, animal head on lip, p-h, 7x6" ...550.00
Anasazi, pitcher, blk on wht, dog-head protrusion, p-h, 7x7" ...650.00
Anasazi (Bidahochi), bowl, mc parrot decor, p-h, 4x10" ...300.00
Cochiti, water jar, birds/floral/foliage decor, ca 1900, 10x9" ...325.00
Hopi, jar, mc geometrics, sgn by Frogwoman, 6x6½" ...330.00
Hopi, jar, old Nampeyo designs, 1910s, 9x6" ...300.00
Jeddito, bowl, p-h, 8½" ...700.00
Nampeyo, jar, stylized feathers, ca 1965, 4x4" ...180.00
Quapaw, figurine, human effigy w/mc pnt geometrics, p-h, 7x4" ..300.00
Quapaw, vessel, 4 female effigy figures in relief, p-h, 11x8" ...700.00
Santa Clara, bowl, blkware, Avenu, Linda Tafoya, 1975, 4x5" ..325.00
Santa Clara, bowl, blkware, Avenu, Rosalie & Joe, 1950, 4x8" .450.00
Santa Clara, jar, blkware, fingerprints at rim, 1890s, 7½x10" ...400.00
Santa Clara, olla, old style, red w/indented thumbprints, 1930s, 10x9" .550.00
Santo Domingo, bowl, birds, Arthur & Hilda Coriz, 1980, 5x6" ...125.00
Santo Domingo, canteen, birds, Arthur & Hilda Coriz, 1980, 5x6" ..125.00
Santo Domingo, dough bowl, foliage, ca 1900, 4x8" ...125.00
Santo Domingo, olla, geometrics, Arthur & Hilda Coriz, 1985, 10x11" ...500.00
Zia, olla, birds & rainbows all around, ca 1975, 9x11" ...425.00
Zuni, jar, mc stylized birds, ca 1900, 6x7½" ...375.00

Pottery, San Ildefonso

The pottery of the San Ildefonso pueblo is especially sought after by collectors today. Under the leadership of Maria Martinez and her husband Julian, experiments began about 1918 which led to the development of the 'black-on-black' design achieved through exacting methods of firing the ware. They discovered that by smothering the fire at a specified temperature, the carbon in the smoke that ensued caused the pottery to blacken. Maria signed her work (often 'Marie') from the late teens to the 1960s; she died in 1980. Today a piece with her signature may bring prices in the $500.00 to $4,500.00 range.

Bowl, blkware, geometric, Juanita Vigil, 3½x5¼" ...175.00
Bowl, blkware, serpent, Rose, 1935, 3x5" ...300.00
Corn meal container, blkware, simple design, Romona, 1930, 2½" ...335.00
Jar, blkware, butterflies, sgn Marie & Julian, 7x9" ...2,200.00
Jar, blkware, feather, Marie & Julian, ca 1925, 5x6" ...1,600.00
Jar, blkware, serpents, Rose, 12x9" ...1,300.00

Jar, mc feathers, Blue Corn, ca 1975, 5x5" 700.00
Olla, 3-color, shouldered form, Maria Martinez, 1930s, 8½x9" .1,300.00
Pot, blkware, bear claw, Blue Corn, 1954, 4" 195.00
Vessel, blkware, zig-zag band, Blue Corn, 2½x3" 245.00

Rugs, Navajo

Chinle, alternating bands of waterbirds & solid colors, 1935, 102x75" ..750.00
Cornstalk/birds/symbols on natural homespun wool, 1920s, 48x65" ...8,000.00
Crystal, crisp geometrics, natural wool, 1920s, 62x36" 325.00
Crystal, dbl central lozenge, ca 1930, 78x51" 1,500.00
Crystal, dmn & central lozenge, 1930s, 56x37" 200.00
Crystal, mc dmn in dmn pattern, 1920s, 86x58" 1,300.00
Crystal, ornate arrangement of elements, 4-color, 1930s, 68x44" .700.00
Crystal, vegetal dye, hand spun, 1978, 116x72" 1,200.00
Crystal Area, waterbirds on natural wool, ca 1945, 44x76" 300.00
Crystal Trading, dmns & triangles, mc on tan, 1915-25, 54x79" ..715.00
Ganado, dmns & stepped blocks, mc on natural, ca 1945, 67x37" ...500.00
Ganado, terraced dmns & stepped blocks, mc on gray, 78x42" ..660.00
Ganado, 3 serrated dmns, 4-color, 1920-30, 43x66" 440.00
Ganado Red, complicated geometrics, 1930s, 74x49" 1,000.00
Ganado Red serape design, Louise Mike, 1985, 60x47" 950.00
Geometric figures/3 dmns, natural wool, JB Moore, 1915, 91x66" ...2,250.00
Klagetoh, red central lozenge, 1920s, 62x30" 1,100.00
Klagetoh, Sunrise pattern, 5-color, ca 1950, 31x54" 275.00
Teec Nos Pos outline w/angular geometrics, bright mc, 1930s, 84x56" 1,700.00
Two Grey Hills, Alberta Henderson, 1990, 24x34" 300.00
Two Grey Hills, 2-dmn central lozenge, mc geometrics, 1965, 49x79" .750.00
Two Grey Hills w/geometric design, natural wool, 1920s, 108x58" ..900.00
Western Reservation, Teec Nos Pos outline influence, 1945, 44x73" ..350.00
Wide Ruins, borderless, earthy vegetal colors, 1960s, 52x34" 425.00
Yei design w/blk feather border, 1940s, 47x92" 1,900.00
4-figure picture, 1920s, 33x49" 1,600.00

Shaped Stone Artifacts

Bannerstone, banded slate, butterfly type, Archaic, OH, 6" W .2,000.00
Bannerstone, banded slate, extended-wing type, IN, 7" W 500.00
Bannerstone, banded slate, unnotched wings, Archaic, 2½x3½" ..800.00
Bannerstone, ferruginous quartzite, bottle type, Archaic, MO, 2x2¼" .1,100.00
Bannerstone, glacial slate, geniculate type, Archaic, OH, 2½x6½" .4,000.00
Bannerstone, glacial slate, pick type, center hole, 1x5½" 500.00
Bannerstone, glacial slate, tubular type, Archaic, IN, 4" 500.00
Bannerstone, gr & wht hardstone, triangular, Archaic, IN, 2½" L .800.00
Bannerstone, gr banded slate, reel type, Archaic, KY, 1¾x4⅞" ...1,400.00
Bannerstone, hardstone, hourglass type, Archaic, OH, 2x3⅛" ..1,000.00
Birdstone, popeye hardstone type, Archaic, IN, 3", from $400 to ..500.00
Birdstone, tan banded slate, animal type, Archaic, IN, 2⅝" 300.00
Discoidal, Salt River, mottled hardstone, Woodland, MO, 1x4" dia ..650.00
Gorget, Adena, banded slate, expanded center, Woodland, OH, 4½" L ...350.00
Gorget, hematite, Archaic, MO, 1¼x2½" 200.00
Pendant, banded slape, thin, Woodland, IN, 3¼" 125.00
Pendant, banded slate, bell type Woodland, IL, 3⅝x1½" 225.00
Pendant, banded slate w/4 tallies, teardrop, Woodland, OH, 4⅞" ..165.00
Pendant, blk hardstone, 21 tally mks, Archaic, 1¼x2⅛" 150.00
Pendant, red slate, shovel type, Late Hopewell, IN, 4" 400.00

Tools

Adz, dk diorite, grooved, Archaic, OH, 4½" L 200.00
Adz, lt chert, Archaic, IN, 2x5½" 40.00
Axe, dk hardstone, ¾-groove, chisel type, Archaic, IN, 9" L 800.00
Axe, gr hardstone, full grove, Archaic, MO, 5-lb, 4⅝x8¼" 200.00
Axe, gr hardstone, ¾-groove, Archaic, 6-lb+, 4¼x8¼" 900.00
Axe, gr speckled hardstone, ¾-groove, Archaic, OH, 4⅛" 150.00
Axe, streaked hardstone, ¾-groove, Archaic, 4¼" H 300.00
Celt, brn speckled hardstone, Woodland, IN, 5¾x2½" 95.00
Celt, gr slate, Archaic, IL, 4⅜x2x1⅛" 25.00
Celt, gray chert, Mississippian, IN, 7⅛x2" 150.00
Celt, greenstone, Woodland, IL, 4½x1⅞" 50.00
Celt, wht limestone, grooved, Woodland, MO, 5½x2" 200.00
Drill, Burlington chert, Woodland, 1" drill section, MO 85.00
Drill, chalky wht flint, Archaic, IL, 4x1½" 175.00
Drill, dvtl/St Charles, cream flint, Archaic, MO, 2¼" 95.00
Drill, narrow blade, wht chert, Archaic, MO, 2⅛x11/16" 45.00
Drill/perforator, dk gray flint, Archaic, IL, 3x⅞" 100.00
Fishhook, polished bone, Archaic, IN, 1⅞x2" 150.00
Hammer/maul, hardstone, full groove, Archaic, 2⅛x2½x3¾" ...125.00
Hoe, chert, Mississippian, IL, 5¾x4¼" 275.00
Hoe, Mill Creek chert, notched, Mississippian, IL, 5½" 400.00
Hook, Haida, wood, all orig, ca 1870, 5x3" 175.00
Lanceolate, red-brn flint, Archaic, MO, 3x1" 30.00
Maul, hardstone, full groove, Archaic, 3⅛x5" 100.00
Maul, pk/gray/blk hardstone, full groove, Archaic, IN, 5x7x4" ..295.00
Maul, tan/brn quartzite, ¾-groove, Archaic, 3x4" 125.00
Pestle, quartzite, knobbed type, Archaic, OH, 7" 1,000.00
Pestle/seed grinder, polished, slight damage, Archaic, OH, 5½" ...150.00
Pick/chisel, gray hardstone, 1 blade-like end, Archaic, 5⅞" 165.00
Plummet, gray hematite, grooved top, Archaic, IL 300.00
Scraper, antler wrapped w/rawhide, 20th C, 11x1½" 35.00
Spade, off-wht flint, polished, narrow blade, Mississippian, 8⅞" L ...125.00
Ulu (cutting blade), NW Coast, slate blade, wood hdl, early, 5x3" ..175.00

Weapons

Bow, Osage, ochred/sinew-bkd, 19th C, 43", +3 steel-tip arrows ...1,300.00
Club, Apache, grooved stone, pnt rawhide-covered hdl, 1890s, 31" 550.00
Club, Great Lakes, cvd wood ball head w/iron blade, 1900s, 21x5" ..250.00
Club, Plains, catlinite head w/pewter inlay, bw hdl, 1890s, 30x7" 450.00
Club, Plains, dmn-shaped stone, bw on wooden hdl, 1910s, 16x3" ..100.00
Club, Plains, egg-shaped stone, pnt rawhide hdl, 1880s, 18x7" ..350.00
Club, Plains, egg-shaped stone w/bw rawhide hdl, 1880s, 21x5" 375.00
Club, Plains, grooved stone axe head, bw hdl, 1900s, 27x4" 300.00
Club, Sioux, stone, egg shape w/bw hdl, 1890s, 15x4" 200.00
Lance, forged steel point, gr trade-cloth cover, 1880s, 80" 1,100.00
Tomahawk, iron w/brass tacks, wire-wrapped hdl, 1880s, 14x7" ..700.00
Tomahawk, Plains, iron pipe head w/rpl tacked wooden stem, 1890s, 18" .600.00

Miscellaneous

Atlatl thrower, Pacific Northwest, cvd wood, p-h, 19x2" 300.00
Box, Iroquois, cloth w/bw birds/animals/etc, bw fringe, 1880s, 7x5x5" .275.00
Box, Navajo, silver w/stamping & turq cabochons, 1955, 2x4½" .900.00
Game, pins & bones, Sioux, SD, ca 1900, 18" 350.00
Painted hide, Sioux, ledger drawing style, 1890s, 40x41" 1,500.00
Painting, Navajo, horse & rider w/dog, H Begay, 1960, 13½x10½" ...250.00
Peace medal, James Buchanan, dtd 1857, full bw neckpc, 30" ...650.00
Peace medal, John Tyler, dtd 1841, floral bw neck pc, 33" 375.00
Photo, Jack Red Cloud, sgn Billy Walker, ca 1908, 7x9" 550.00
Photo, White Swan, Crow, Rhinehart #38, ca 1900, 11x14" 150.00
Sculpture, sterling, Indian hunter, on wooden base, 1930, 8x5" ..200.00

American Painted Porcelain

The American china-painting movement can be traced back to an extracurricular class attended by art students at the McMicken School of Design in Cincinnati. These students, who were the wives and daughters of the city's financial elite, managed to successfully paint numerous porcelains for display in the Woman's Pavilion of the 1876 United States Centennial Exposition held in Philadelphia — an amazing feat considering the high technical skill required for proficiency, as well as the length of time and multiple firings necessary to finish the ware. From then until 1917 when the United States entered World War I, china painting was a profession as well as a popular amateur pursuit for many people, particularly women. In fact, over 25,000 people were involved in this art form at the turn of the last century.

Collectors and antique dealers have discovered American hand-painted porcelain, and they have become aware of its history, beauty, and potential value. Until now, there was no all-inclusive source to turn to for information on this subject. *American Painted Porcelain: Collector's Identification & Value Guide* and *Antique Trader's Comprehensive Guide to American Painted Porcelain* by Dorothy Kamm are the culmination of a decade of research; we recommend them highly for further study.

Though American pieces are of high quality and commensurate with their European counterparts, they are much less costly today. Generally, you will pay as little as $10.00 for a 6" plate and less than $50.00 for many other items. Values are based on aesthetic appeal, quality of the workmanship, size, rarity of the piece and of the subject matter, and condition. Age is the least important factor, because most American painted porcelains are not dated. (Factory backstamps are helpful in establishing the approximate time period an item was decorated, but they aren't totally reliable.) See Clubs and Newsletters for information regarding *Dorothy's Kamm's Porcelain Collector's Companion*, each issue of which contains comprehensive material expounding on artists, patterns, dating, and functions of china.

Our advisor for this category is Dorothy Kamm; she is listed in the Directory under Florida.

Condiment set (four-piece), 7⅜x4½" tray, salt and pepper shakers, and toothpick holder, poppy border, ca 1891 – 1914, from $45.00 to $55.00. (Photo courtesy Dorothy Kamm)

Bar pin, brass-plated bezel, 1½" W, from $25 to 35.00
Belt buckle brooch, oval, 1¾x2⅛", from $90 to 115.00
Bonbon bowl (depending on size), from $18 to 85.00
Bowl, fruit; from $60 to 80.00
Box, 4¾" dia, from $50 to 75.00
Brooch, brass-plated bezel, oval, 2x1½", from $55 to 75.00
Brooch, gold-plated bezel, 1½" dia, from $35 to 45.00
Brooch/pendant, heart shape, gold-plated bezel, 2x1¾", from $50 to .75.00
Cake plate, from $35 to 75.00
Candlestick, from $45 to 125.00
Celery tray, from $35 to 75.00
Creamer & sugar bowl, from $30 to 65.00
Cruet, from $60 to 80.00
Cuff pin, rectangular, brass-plated bezel, ¼x1⅛", from $12 to 18.00
Cup & saucer 45.00
Cup & saucer, bouillon; from $35 to 45.00
Ewer (depending on size), from $100 to 150.00
Gravy boat, from $55 to 75.00
Handy pin, brass-plated bezel, 1½", from $30 to 40.00
Hatpin holder, from $88 to 98.00
Jam jar, from $30 to 50.00
Jardiniere (depending on size), from $65 to 375.00
Mug, from $30 to 75.00
Napkin ring, from $10 to 25.00
Pendant, gold-plated bezel, 1" dia, from $50 to 75.00
Pin tray, from $30 to 50.00
Pitcher, lemonade; from $175 to 225.00
Plate, 6", from $10 to 35.00
Plate, 8", from $35 to 65.00
Salt cellar, from $20 to 40.00
Scarf pin, medallion, brass-plated bezel & shank, 1¼" dia, $35 to ..65.00
Shakers, pr, from $20 to 30.00
Shirtwaist button, 1" dia, from $20 to 40.00
Shirtwaist set, brooch, brass-plated mts, 1¾"+cuff links, $150 to ..250.00
Stein, from $75 to 95.00
Tea or coffee set, ea set, from $175 to 300.00
Vase, 6-7", ea, from $45 to 65.00
Whiskey set, ears of corn, sgn, Surquist, 1903-17, 8-pc, $300 to .400.00

Amphora

The Amphora Porcelain Works in the Teplitz-Turn area of Bohemia produced Art Nouveau-styled vases and figurines during the latter part of the 1800s through the first few decades of the twentieth century. They marked their wares with various stamps, some incorporating the name and location of the pottery with a crown or a shield. Because Bohemia was part of the Austro-Hungarian empire prior to WWI, some examples are marked Austria; items marked with the Czechoslovakia designation were made after the war. All decoration described in the listings that follow is hand painted unless otherwise indicated. Our advisor for this category is Jack Gunsaulus; he is listed in the Directory under Michigan.

Chalice, 3 Wisemen, stars/geometrics, 3-hdl, oval mk 395.00
Ewer, fern leaves, sgn, mk, #3430, 7½" 150.00
Pitcher, flower medallion on bl, glossy cobalt hdl, 7½" 85.00
Planter, flowers & vines in relief, brn matt, hdls, 5x7" 225.00
Vase, bird in tree, mc matt & gloss, hdls, mk, 7⅛" 100.00
Vase, blkberry branches on mottled ochre w/gold, 8¼x11", NM .1,500.00
Vase, cvd yel rose on brn mottle, sqd neck-to-body hdls, 7x9" ..325.00
Vase, dragon figure, yel/tan/gold on mauve mottle, #4548 50, 20" .5,750.00
Vase, enfolded by lg winged dragon, bronze irid, 17", EX 5,000.00
Vase, floral, mc on lt gr, ovoid, waisted neck, 12", EX 300.00
Vase, floral, mc w/jeweled centers, bulbous, incurvate rim, 5½" .700.00
Vase, floral band emb top/base, hdls w/cutouts, drip glaze, 17" ..250.00
Vase, flowers, cobalt w/gold on wht, curved lines, 8¼" 300.00
Vase, flowers (thick/appl) at rim, scene, 4 low hdls, 7½", EX 290.00
Vase, gold-lined butterfly reserve, dbl gold hdls, ftd, 8" 650.00
Vase, hawk on tree/floral spray, hdls, #d, 13⅛" 275.00
Vase, heron (lg)/geometrics, mc enamel on bsk, hdls, 13" 350.00
Vase, jewels/spider web/bees/butterflies, gold on irid, 7½" 850.00
Vase, lady's profile, gold outlines, 7" 850.00
Vase, lady's profile/flowers, 4-lobe neck w/irregular top, 13" ...1,700.00
Vase, leafy branch, gold on pk to gr, ornate gold hdls, 13" 325.00
Vase, leaves, mc on gr w/wht at shoulder, Holland, 9" 160.00
Vase, leaves (lg/swirling) form sm high hdls, violet irid w/gold, 16" .750.00
Vase, leaves form 4 hdls, bl irid mottle on mauve, #3858 42, 10" 350.00
Vase, modern patterns emb at base & rim, 4-hdl, unmk, 10⅜" ..100.00
Vase, Nouveau lady's portrait, bottle shape, #492, 5½x3¾" 400.00
Vase, roses & fired-on gold, buttressed hdls, 7", NM 225.00

Vase, rtcl top w/4 dragonflies at rim, 8 below, 4-loop hdls, 6" .1,200.00
Vase, trees, lg/deeply cut bk, brn tones, 17½", EX 1,200.00
Vase, twig w/wht 5-dot flowers on gr mottle, gold snake hdl, 9" ...550.00
Vase, 2 sides: 3-D eagle w/gold head, vertical scroll bands, 13" ..800.00

Animal Dishes With Covers

Covered animal dishes have been produced for nearly two centuries and are as varied as their manufacturers. They were made in many types of glass (slag, colored, clear, and milk glass) as well as china and pottery. On bases of nests and baskets, you will find animals and birds of every sort. The most common was the hen.

Some of the smaller versions made by McKee, Indiana Tumbler and Goblet Company, and Westmoreland Specialty Glass of Pittsburgh, Pennsylvania, were sold to food-processing companies who filled them with prepared mustard, baking powder, etc. Occasionally one will be found with the paper label identifying the product and processing company still intact.

Many of the glass versions produced during the latter part of the nineteenth century have been recently reproduced. In the 1960s, the Kemple Glass Company made the rooster, fox, lion, cat, lamb, hen, horse, turkey, duck, dove, and rabbit on split-ribbed or basketweave bases. They were made in amethyst, blue, amber, and milk glass, as well as a variegated slag. Kanawha, L.G. Wright, and Imperial made several as well. It is sometimes necessary to compare items in question to verified examples of older glass in order to recognize reproductions. Reproduction is continued today.

For more information, we recommend *Covered Animal Dishes* by our advisor, Everett Grist, whose address is in the Directory under Tennessee. In the listings below, when only one dimension is given, it is the greater one, usually length. See also Greentown and other specific companies.

Cat on wide-rib base, milk glass, 5½" 50.00
Chick on basketweave base, milk glass, Westmoreland, child sz, 2" ..15.00
Chicks in oblong basket, milk glass w/pnt details, 2¼x4¼" 325.00
Dog, bl w/wht head, bl wide-rib base, 5¼" 65.00
Dolphin, transparent (clear or colored), sawtooth edge, repro 45.00
Dove & hand on rectangular lacy base, milk glass, Westmoreland .150.00
Duck, Atterbury; milk glass, Patent Apld For, 11" 245.00
Duck, milk glass, US Glass, 8" 125.00
Duck, Pin-Tail; on split-rib base, bl opaque, Kemple, 5½" 125.00
Duck, Swimming; colors other than wht or bl, Vallerysthal, 5" .120.00
Duck on cattail base, milk glass, 5½" 120.00
Duck on flange base, milk glass, LG Wright 50.00
Elephant, clear, standing, Co-operative Flint Glass Co, 9" 25.00
Elephant on rib base, milk glass, unmk, 5½" 1,300.00
Fish, collared base, frosted, Central Glass 150.00
Fish, Entwined; lacy Atterbury base, milk glass, lid dtd 1889, 6" ..170.00
Fish, Flat; gr transparent 75.00
Fox, Ribbed; milk glass, on lacy Atterbury base, dtd, 6¼" 175.00
Hen, milk glass, Vallerysthal, 2" 20.00
Hen (str head), clear, unmk Imperial Glass, sm 15.00
Hen (str head), marigold carnival, Indiana Glass (+) 25.00
Hen on basketweave base, Golden Sunset, Westmoreland, 3½" ..30.00
Hen on lacy base, milk glass w/bl marbled bk, Atterbury 300.00
Hen on sleigh, milk glass, Westmoreland Specialty, 5½" 85.00
Hen w/chicks on split-rib base, milk glass w/pnt comb, unmk, 5½" .165.00
Lamb on picket fence base, milk glass, Westmoreland Specialty ..95.00
Lion, British; milk glass, emb title on base, unmk, 6¼" 195.00
Lion on dmn base, milk glass, Westmoreland, 8" 135.00
Lion on picket fence base, milk glass w/bl head, Westmoreland, 5½" ...125.00
Mother Eagle, milk glass, Westmoreland 100.00
Owl on basketweave base, amber, LG Wright, 5½" 35.00
Rabbit, Jack; clear, att Flaccus 95.00
Rabbit, milk glass w/red glass eyes, Atterbury, dtd Aug 6, 1889, 6" .110.00
Rabbit, mule eared; picket fence base, milk glass (+) 40.00
Rat on egg, milk glass, Vallerysthal 225.00
Robin on nest base w/ped ft, bl opaque, mk Vallerysthal 90.00
Rooster (standing), Antique Blue, Westmoreland, 8½" 85.00
Rooster on basketweave base, bl opaque, Westmoreland, lg 125.00
Rooster on nest, red slag, LG Wright, 5½" 95.00
Rooster on ribbed base, milk glass, Westmoreland, 5½" 35.00
Rooster on wide-rib base, wht w/bl head, Westmoreland, 5¼" 70.00
Squirrel on ribbed base, milk glass, unmk McKee, 5½" 185.00
Swan, Block; clear frosted, 7" 120.00
Swan, raised wing; milk glass, molded eyes, Westmoreland 85.00
Turtle, dk amber, knobby bk, LG Wright, lg 95.00
Turtle, on scroll base w/2 hdls, milk glass, unmk, 7½" 185.00
Turtle on basketweave base, purple slag, LG Wright, 5½" 50.00

Appliances, Electric

Antique electric appliances represent a diverse field and are always being sought after by collectors. There were over one hundred different companies manufacturing electric appliances in the first half of the twentieth century; some were making over ten different models under several different names at any given time in all fields: coffeepots, toasters, waffle irons, etc., while others were making only one or two models for extended periods of time. Today collectors and decorators alike are seeking those items to add to a collection or to use as accent pieces in a period kitchen. Refer to *Toasters and Small Kitchen Appliances* published by L-W Book Sales for more information. If you're especially interested in vintage fans, we recommend *The Collector's Guide to Electric Fans* by John Witt. Toaster collectors will enjoy *Collector's Guide to Toasters & Accessories* by Helen Greguire. (The latter two books are published by Collector Books.)

Always check the cord before using and make sure the appliance is in good condition, free of rust and pitting. The prices below are for appliances in good to excellent condition. Prices may vary around the country.

If you have any questions regarding antique appliances, feel free to contact our advisor, Jim Barker; he is listed in the Directory under Pennsylvania.

Table stove, Armstrong, white enamel, with broil pan and insert, toast rack, waffle iron and egg poacher, Patented Oct. 9, 17 Apr. 23, 18 Dec. 12, 22, No 813, complete, $185.00.
(Photo courtesy Helen Greguire)

Broiler, Royal Master #1-A, hammered aluminum, 1930s, 20" 35.00
Chafing dish, electric, GE #78732 ....195.00
Chafing dish, Simplex #1220 ....145.00

Chafing dish, SP, Universal E840 ....120.00
Coffee maker, Heat Master, ceramic, ivory w/silver lines 125.00
Coffee urn, Jos Heinrichs Solid Copper 135.00
Coffee urn, Universal E9189 ....65.00
Coffee urn, Universal E9269 ....85.00
Coffee urn, Westinghouse #284244 ....65.00
Dripolator, Sunbeam Coffee Master, chrome, spherical, 12" 35.00
Egg cooker, Rochester, chrome, ovoid w/stick hdl, 1915 ....45.00
Fan, Adams Bagnal, Jandus #48091, C-fr oscillator, 12" blades ..1,600.00
Fan, Bersted Eskimo, cobweb guard, 16" blades, 1946 ....25.00
Fan, Dayton, CI housing, tab-ft base, 8" blades, 1910 ....250.00
Fan, Emerson #66548-AL, overlapping blades, X guard, '40s 35.00
Fan, Emerson #94646-B, concentric wires in guard, 12" blades 12.50
Fan, GE #19X263, 10" blades, 2-speed, 1928 ....20.00
Fan, GE #427220 Sidewinder Oscillator, 16" blades, 1909 ....1,500.00
Fan, GE #49X719, 10" blades, octagonal guard, oscillating, '39 ...20.00
Fan, GE AK-Ford D #181327, 12" blades, ribbed base, 1903 ....180.00
Fan, Gilbert #A-325, 10" blades, lt bl, aluminum base, 1946 ....25.00
Fan, Peerless #G-1, 12" blades, CI ribbed base, 1905 ....1,600.00
Fan, Singer Ribbonaire, portable, Bakelite, ribbon blades, 10" ..175.00
Fan, StarRite, octagonal guard, 10" brass blades, gr base, 1933 ....75.00
Fan, Westinghouse #8-SFN-30, 9" blades, 3-speed, non-oscillating ..35.00
Heater, GE, 2-bulb type 124.00
Heater, Hotpoint 116A16 ....75.00
Heater, REX 125.00
Heater, Simplex Sunbowl 45.00
Heater, Westinghouse Cozy Glo 45.00
Hot plate, Bersted Mfg, bl & wht mottled graniteware, 2-burner, EX ..65.00
Hot plate, GE, Disk Stove, 1920s, 6" dia 45.00
Hot plate, gr & wht speckled graniteware, NM 75.00
Hot plate, Westinghouse, lt gr graniteware, 1906, NM 85.00
Iron, AM Electric Htr Co 75.00
Iron, Dominion #35 ....75.00
Iron, Electrex United Drug Co 40.00
Iron, GE Type CF-5 ....125.00
Iron, GE Type 5-13 ....55.00
Iron, L&H #101 ....35.00
Iron, Security Iron #165 ....65.00
Iron, Simplex GE #819F77 ....35.00
Iron, Universal E7193 ....35.00
Kettle, GE #20801 ....65.00
Kettle, Manning Bowman #14767 ....55.00
Kettle, Universal E971 ....65.00
Mixer, Builtwell, bl/wht housing, ribbed Chalaine Blue bowl 150.00
Mixer, Chicago Electric, Jade-ite cylindrical base 60.00
Mixer, GE #10-A, Bakelite hdl, 2 bowls, 1938 ....50.00
Mixer, Hamilton Beach, juicer top, Seville Yellow bowls 200.00
Mixer, Vidrio, cobalt bl cylindrical base 150.00
Mixer, Vidrio, gr glass cylinder base 60.00
Oven, Eureka, sq front door w/canted top corners, table-top 145.00
Pencil sharpener, Swingline Electro-Pointer, gray plastic 75.00
Percolator, GE Simplex #814p41 ....45.00
Percolator, GE Spiderweb design 65.00
Percolator, Manning-Bowman, #636, fluted bands, 1930s, 12" 40.00
Percolator, Manning-Bowman, chrome w/red Bakelite hdls 65.00
Percolator, Polar Ware, red enamel ware 150.00
Percolator, Samson-United, ceramic, orange/gr flowers, 1930s 75.00
Percolator, Universal, chrome w/eng festoons, Bakelite hdls 40.00
Percolator, Universal E9435 ....50.00
Popcorn popper, Excel 85.00
Popcorn popper, Fire-King, chrome w/blk plastic hdl/legs 40.00
Popcorn popper, Knapp, aluminum w/glass dome lid, 1930s 20.00
Popcorn popper, Master Co Loeb Co, NYC 95.00
Stove, Armstrong, table-top, NP/graniteware, 1917, NM 65.00
Stove, Wilwear #4-5A - 110V, NP, table-top, no control 20.00
Teapot, Farber Bros, elongated w/tan Bakelite hdl & knob 55.00
Teapot, Manning-Bowman, lg Bakelite wing hdl, ball-bearing base ...100.00
Toaster, Coleman #2 ....125.00
Toaster, Corona E1312 ....45.00
Toaster, Danby Electric Co, Canada 75.00
Toaster, Electrahot #38 ....65.00
Toaster, Kalorik 85.00
Toaster, Kookenette 155.00
Toaster, Landers E5946 ....85.00
Toaster, Landers E7542 ....135.00
Toaster, Manning-Bowman #1229 ....85.00
Toaster, Perfection Electric, horizontal type 95.00
Toaster, Royal Rochester #13260 ....65.00
Toaster, Security Electric #192 ....75.00
Toaster, Simplex GE 816T26 ....65.00
Toaster, Super Electric #444, Art Deco 85.00
Toaster, Thermax E35412 ....65.00
Toaster, Universal E3612 ....65.00
Toaster, Universal E7722 ....75.00
Toaster, Universal E79312 ....55.00
Toaster, Westinghouse TL-14 ....38.00
Toaster, Westinghouse TO-71 ....55.00
Toaster, Westinghouse TTC-74 ....75.00
Toaster, White Cross Reversible 95.00
Toaster/hot plate, no mk, chrome, burner ea end, 1938 ....150.00
Toastwich, Sunbeam #B5, makes sandwiches, 1930s, 4½x11x7" 165.00
Vacuum cleaner, Electrolux, ca 1940s 25.00
Vacuum cleaner, Hamilton Beach, upright, 1937, H Dreyfuss design ..100.00
Vacuum cleaner, Hoover Dustette, hand model, 1936 ....65.00
Waffle iron, Knapp-Monarch, NP body, blk wood hdls, 1930s 18.00
Waffle iron, Manning-Bowman, Homelectrics, on stand, 1920s ..30.00
Waffle iron, Universal, band of rings, Bakelite knob, +tray 25.00
Washing machine, Norleigh Diamond #55, wooden, ca 1914 ...150.00
Washing machine, Portland, wooden w/wringer, ca 1912 ....125.00
Whipper, Knapp Monarch, Modern, 3-cup glass bottom, 1930s, 8" .25.00
Wringer, National Premium, galvanized fr, cog wheels, 1895 ....50.00

Arequipa

The Arequipa Pottery operated from 1911 until 1918 at a sanitorium near Fairfax, California. Its purpose was two-fold: therapy for the patients and financial support for the institution. Frederick H. Rhead was the originator and director. The ware, made from local clays, was often hand thrown, simply styled and decorated. Marks were varied but always incorporated the name of the pottery and the state. A circular arrangement encompassing the negative image of a vase beside a tree is most common.

Examples are evaluated according to quality of artwork; size and shape are less important. Those done by Rhead himself are most desirable.

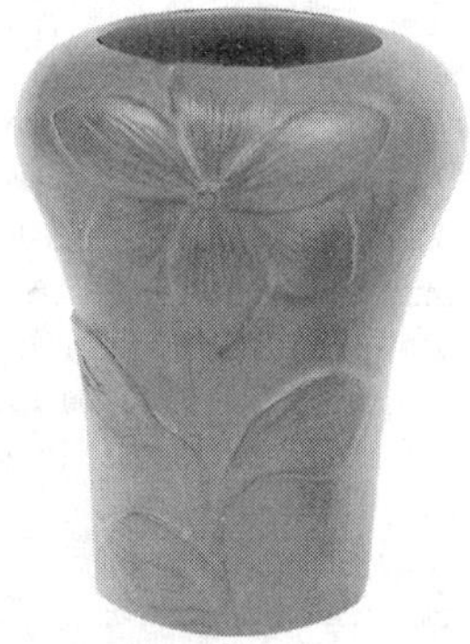

Vase, deeply carved flowers and leaves on brown matt, signed MIW, marked, repair to rim, 5½", $425.00. (Photo courtesy Treadway Gallery)

Bowl, bl matt, sgn/dtd 1912, 9½" 190.00
Bowl, dk gr/blk matt, incurvate, 5" 160.00
Bowl, gr & dk bl w/emb eucalyptus branches, KH?11, 2¼x6½" ..800.00
Bowl, purple matt w/lt gr & bl highlights, sgn/dtd 1912, 6½" 230.00
Vase, avocado matt w/yel buds & squeeze-bag vines, 1912, 7½" ..4,000.00
Vase, berries on plant pnt on bl-gray, AP/1911, 4¼x7" 600.00
Vase, dusty mauve matt, shouldered, #105, 5½" 300.00
Vase, rose matt, shouldered, incurvate, 5½", NM 350.00
Vase, suspended bl matt, waisted, pnt sgn, EX quality, 8" 1,600.00

Argy-Rousseau, G.

Gabriel Argy-Rousseau produced both fine art glass and quality commercial ware in Paris, France, in 1918. He favored Art Nouveau as well as Art Deco and in the '20s produced a line of vases in the Egyptian manner, made popular by the discovery of King Tut's tomb. One of the most important types of glass he made was pate-de-verre. Most of his work is signed. Items listed below are pate-de-verre unless noted otherwise.

Bowl, raspberry vines, clear/purple frost, 4" 2,100.00
Pendant, pate-de-verre flowers on 2" frosted disc 1,150.00
Plaque, 2 tigers amid rayed panels, 7x6" 5,750.00
Vase, Les Rainures, gr/bl streaks, pate-de-crystal, mk, 8¼" 3,165.00
Vase, thistle blossoms/leaves, rose on gray frost, 6" 3,400.00

Art Deco

To the uninformed observer, 'Art Deco' evokes images of chrome and glass, streamlined curves and aerodynamic shapes, mirrored prints of pink flamingos, and statues of slender nudes and greyhound dogs. Though the Deco movement began in 1925 at the Paris International Exposition and lasted to some extent into the 1950s, within that period of time the evolution of fashion and taste continued as it always has, resulting in subtle variations.

The French Deco look was one of opulence — exotic inlaid woods, rich material, lush fur and leather. Lines tended toward symmetrical curves. American designers adapted the concept to cover every aspect of fashion and home furnishings from small inexpensive picture frames, cigarette lighters, and costume jewelry to high-fashion designer clothing and exquisite massive furniture with squared or circular lines. Vinyl was a popular covering, and chrome-plated brass was used for chairs, cocktail shakers, lamps, and tables. Dinnerware, glassware, theaters, and train stations were designed to reflect the new 'Modernism.'

The Deco movement made itself apparent into the '50s in wrought iron lamps with stepped pink plastic shades and Venetian blinds. The sheer volume of production during those twenty-five years provides collectors today with fine examples of the period that can be bought for as little as $10.00 or $20.00 up to the thousands. Chrome items signed 'Chase' are prized by collectors, and blue glass radios and tables with blue glass tops are high on the list of desirability in many areas.

Those interested in learning more about this subject will want to read *Collector's Guide to Art Deco* by Mary Frank Gaston; and *Affordable Art Deco, Identification and Value Guide*, by Ken Hutchinson and Greg Johnson. (Both are published by Collector Books.) See also Bronzes; Chase; Frankart; Jewelry; Lalique; Radios; etc.

Ashtray, bl glass decorated w/chrome sailboat, mk FD Co, Am, 5" dia ..60.00
Ashtray, HP ceramic head in bathing cap, Japan, 6" 30.00
Ashtray w/cigarette & match holders, copper w/Indian motif, 3-pc .250.00
Bed, brass w/sunbursts on head/ftbrd, ca 1930, 43x49" 290.00
Belt buckle, scalloped edge w/rainbow shades of gr & gold, German .25.00
Bowl w/flower frog, copper bowl w/pot-metal nude, 12" dia 350.00
Chandelier, alabaster & wrought iron, drum-shaped shade, 32x18" dia ...3,350.00
Clock, bronze box on lg flat base, digital, Silvercrest, 1930s, 19" L ..250.00
Clock, gr ceramic dmn-&-stepped fan shape, St Clements, 1925, 12" .225.00
Clock table; silver/gray face w/rays, Frankl/Telechron, 8x5" 650.00
Coffee service, pot/warmer/creamer/sugar/tray, brass, Doryln, 1930s ..400.00
Console bowl, blk glass w/silver ped base 50.00
Console bowl & candlesticks, chrome w/olive Bakelite ped bases, 3-pc ..150.00
Desk set, bronze calendar & envelope holders, mk Silvercrest, Am 125.00
Figurine, Russian dancer, bronze & ivory, rpt boots, ca 1930, 12" 5,175.00
Figurine, woman w/ball & greyhound on base, mk Pecchioli, 25" L 325.00
Figurine, 2 birds on base, high gloss gr glaze, sgn Ch Lemanceau .350.00
Frame, beveled glass w/etched floral & leaf design, 1940s, 17x15" ..100.00
Hairbrush, brn plastic stepped design 25.00
Incense burner, cast metal Egyptian man kneeling on cushion, France ..375.00
Incense burner, CI sun-dial form w/floral & geometric designs, 6½" .175.00
Lamp, bronze cold-pnt clown w/ivory face at base, Austria, 12" .835.00
Lamp, cobalt glass & chrome airplane form w/chrome supports, table sz ..575.00

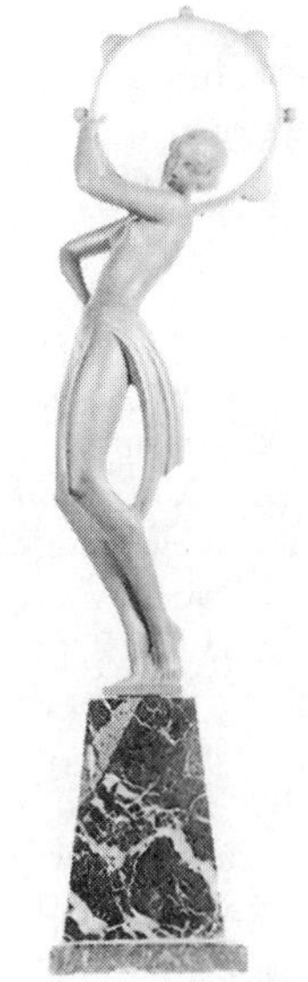

Lamp, draped maiden supports tambourine on shoulders, marble base, signed Fayral, 24", $2,400.00.

Lamp, geometric, stepped ftd base, metal, mk Armour Bronze, 1928 ...160.00
Lamp, metal nude leans on draped glass panel, Fayral, 16" 2,300.00
Lamp, nude sunbather draped on dome base w/half-ball shade, chrome .150.00
Magazine rack, chrome scrolled heart on scrolled base, Revere .160.00
Pen holder, rnd chrome & red streamline sundial form 75.00
Picnic jug, polished aluminum w/blk enamel bands, bail hdl 40.00
Pipe stand, bronze nude in diving position w/holder on bk, unmk ...250.00
Pitcher & bowl, ceramic, blk & rose dmn design, Keller & Guerin .350.00
Plaque, cut-out oval image of Diana & hound in steel & gesso .450.00
Sconce, brass graduated triple circles on rnd wall base, 10" 175.00
Sculpture, alabaster nude & fawn, Italian, 14" L 230.00
Table, side; rnd Bakelite top on chrome curved strap legs, Howell ...400.00
Tea cart, chrome curvilinear frwork w/smoky glass top & shelf ..800.00
Teapot, chrome bowl shape w/6 ball ft on rnd base, Catalin hdl & knob .150.00
Teapot, chrome over ceramic, Bakelite finial, Ellgrave, +sug/cr .230.00
Torchere, etched bowl shade, aluminum & Bakelite std, 56", EX ...100.00
Tray perfume; silver cameo center on bl glass w/chrome trim, 9x12" ..35.00
Tray, rvpt glass pane over foil on chrome, 16x10" 500.00
Vase, foil under mc enamel straps/arcs, Faure Limoges, 8¾" ...3,450.00
Vase, stylized floral on textured gray, ceramic, L Dage/France, 11x9" ...200.00
Wastebasket, tin octagonal shape w/pnt design 60.00

Art Glass Baskets

Popular novelty and gift items during the Victorian era, these one-of-a-kind works of art were produced in just about any type of art glass in use at that time. They were never marked. Many were not true production pieces but 'whimsies' made by glassworkers to relieve the tedium of the long work day. Some were made as special gifts. The more decorative and imaginative the design, the more valuable the basket. Our advisor for this category is Deborah Maggard; she is listed in the Directory under Ohio.

Note: Prices on art glass baskets have softened due to the influence of the Internet which has made them much more accessible.

Amber w/peach-orange stripes & mica, melon ribs, 10½x7½" ..200.00
Amethyst overshot, twisted rope hdl, crimped/ruffled, 8x7½" ...120.00
Bl o/l w/mica flakes, clear thorn hdl, 9¼x5¾" ...225.00
Bl opal cased, melon ribbed, Xd hdl, 2 rows Hobnails, 11x11" ..300.00
Bl to clear cased, V-shaped hdl, Hobnails on melon shape, 11x11" ..110.00
Chartreuse cased Hobnail, sm, 5x3½" ...75.00
Clambroth opaline w/pk snake loop around hdl, gold rim, 6½x6" .150.00
Cranberry w/emb rib int, rigaree at rim, ftd, 9x5" ...110.00
Cream opaque, appl amber/pk floral branch, amber loop hdl, 9" .150.00
Dmn Quilt MOP, bl, frosted ruffle & hdl, 6x4½" ...400.00
Honeycomb, rubena, clear ruffled rim, sq thorny hdl, 9x5½" 175.00
Latticinio stripes, rose/wht in clear, 3 ft, 8¾x7" ...850.00
Lt gr custard w/appl florals, gr twist hdl, sm ...115.00
Mahog red to cherry to lt yel, wht int, loop hdl, 7½x8" ...250.00
Peachblow w/appl amber ft & thorn hdl, 6" dia ...175.00
Pk Herringbone MOP, ribbed body, frosted thorn hdl, 7x5½" ...250.00
Pk opal w/appl wht flower, clear ruffle & twist hdl, 6¾x4½" 225.00
Pk to wht cased, amber thorn hdl, pulled-in sides, 5¾x7x4" 85.00
Pk to wht cased, ribbed, thorn hdl, 7x7" ...125.00
Pk to wht cased w/ruffle, clear rope hdl, 6½" ...125.00
Rose to lt pk cased, V-shaped clear hdl, 8" ...85.00
Sapphire bl w/clear ft, petal edge & twist hdl, 9x5" ...150.00
Spangle, bl o/l w/mica, clear ruffle, rope hdl, 9" dia ...125.00
Spangle, bl over wht w/mica, ruffled rim, twisted loop hdl, 6½" .150.00
Spangle, bl/tan w/mica, wht ext, Jack-in-pulpit lip, 12x8" 200.00
Spangle, butterscotch w/gold flecks, wht int, clear edge, 8" 70.00
Spangle, cranberry cased w/mica, clear ruffle & hdl, 7½" 150.00
Spangle, yel over wht w/mica, ribbed & reeded, pointed hdl, 7x7" .180.00
Spatter, brn/gr on wht, 7-point rim, thorn hdl, 7½x6" ...200.00
Spatter, mc, clear loop hdl, 2 rows Hobnails, rectangular, 6½x6" ..200.00
Spatter, mc, thorn hdl, appl crystal rim, 8½x6" ...100.00
Spatter, pk/yel, 8-point rim, clear thorn hdl, 6x6½" ...245.00
Spatter, sapphire bl w/wht, bl thorn hdl, 6-point rim, 6x6" 175.00
Spatter, turq bl w/bl thorn hdl, 6½" ...100.00
Spatter, wine/bl/gold/wht, clear twist thorn hdl, ruffled, 7x6" 125.00
Tomato red to yel w/crystal rim, low, thorn hdl, 7¾x8¾" 200.00
Vasa Murrhina, 3-layer: amber/ivory spots & mica/pk, X hdl, 11x10" .300.00
Wht satin Hobnail w/pk int, crimped rim, wishbone ft, 5½x4" .200.00
Wht w/amber trim, appl red cherries & mc leaves, 7½x5" 130.00
Yel/gr/wht swags w/gold, crystal hdl, 9½" ...250.00

Art Nouveau

From the famous 'L'Art Nouveau' shop in the Rue de Provence in Paris, 'New Art' spread across the continent and belatedly arrived in America in time to add its curvilinear elements and asymmetrical ornamentations to the ostentatious remains of the Rococo revival of the 1800s. Nouveau manifested itself in every facet of decorative art. In glassware Tiffany turned the concept into a commercial success that lasted well into the second decade of this century and created a style that inspired other American glassmakers for decades. Furniture, lamps, bronzes, jewelry, and automobiles were designed within the realm of its dictates. Today's market abounds with lovely examples of Art Nouveau, allowing the collector to choose one or several areas that hold a special interest. Our advisor for this category is Steven Whysel; he is listed in the Directory under Florida. See also Bronzes; Galle; Jewelry; Loetz; Tiffany; Silver; specific manufacturers.

Lamp, gilt bronze, lady wrapped in lilies on marble base, ca 1910, 21", $1,850.00. (Photo courtesy Steven Whysel)

Box, brass w/emb glass-set flower & vine, 2-drw, 5½x15x8" 350.00
Box, mixed woods inlay, country scene, sgn Galle, 14x8x5", VG ...1,950.00
Casket, brass-inlaid burl walnut, cartouch form, 8½" L ...430.00
Clock, desk; gilt-metal & glass w/red enamel, Chelsea, 4½" 460.00
Clock, wht metal, lady's head w/flowing hair, Seth Thomas, 12" .300.00
Compote, metal std: lady figural, bowl: lime opal, 15x10" 335.00
Frame, gilt brass, lady's head & leaves on fr, EX, 6½x5" ...125.00
Plaque, lady w/flowers, gilt-bronze w/ebony/MOP fr, ca 1895, 20x10" ...1,000.00
Tray, copper/brass, flower form w/hdls, WMF, 10¼x5", EX 250.00
Tray, pewter, lady's head, leaf shape, 14x9", EX ...300.00
Tray, SP, wave pattern w/child & lizard, floral hdl, WMF, 11" L ...440.00
Vase, seated nymph, gr/brn cold pnt, marble base, 8¾x4½" 400.00

Arts and Crafts

The Arts and Crafts movement began in England during the last quarter of the nineteenth century, and its influence was soon felt in this country. Among its proponents in America were Elbert Hubbard (see Roycroft) and Gustav Stickley (see Stickley). They rebelled against the mechanized mass production of the Industrial Revolution and against the cumulative influence of hundreds of years of man's changing taste. They subscribed to a theory of purification of the styles: that designs be geared strictly to necessity. At the same time they sought to elevate these basic ideals to the level of accepted 'art.' Simplicity was their virtue; to their critics it was a fault.

The type of furniture they promoted was squarely built, usually of heavy oak, and so simple was its appearance that as a result many began to copy the style which became known as 'Mission.' Soon factories had geared production toward making cheap copies of their designs. In 1915 Stickley's own operation failed, a victim of changing styles and tastes. Hubbard lost his life that same year on the ill-fated *Lusitania.* By the end of the decade the style had lost its popularity.

Metalware was produced by numerous crafts people, from experts such as Dirk van Erp and Albert Berry to unknown novices. Prices for Arts and Crafts accessories rose dramatically in 1988, but by the beginning of 1991 leveled off and (in some cases) dropped. Metal items or hardware should not be scrubbed or scoured; to do so could remove or damage the rich, dark patina typical of this period. Our advisor for this category is Bruce Austin; he is listed in the Directory under New York. See also Roycroft; Silver; Stickley; specific manufacturers.

Note: Values for metal items reflect the worth of examples that retain their original patina, unless otherwise indicated in the description.

Key: h/cp — hammered copper

Folding screen, Limbert #43-L, oak with Moroccan goat leather panels, original finish, 73x68", G, $3,850.00. (Photo courtesy Jackson's Auctions)

Armchair, Limbert, 3-slat bk, drop-in seat, label, 37", VG 300.00
Armchair, Limbert #1935, 5-slat bk, saddle seat, rfn, 39x26", VG ...550.00
Armchair, Limbert #8073, 2 curved bk slats, leather seat, 35", VG ..200.00
Armchair, oak, V crest/5-slat bk, orig leather, rfn, 37" 700.00
Bed, 5 vertical slats in head/ftbrd, 48x57x78" 850.00
Boat, van Erp, pierced & h/cp, dk patina, 7x10½x6" 1,100.00
Bookcase, Paine, 3 glass doors ea w/ldgl top panel, 59x60", VG .2,200.00
Bookends, Carence Crafters, flower stalks, gr on brass, 5x7" 325.00
Bowl, Harry Dixon, h/cp, heavy gauge, 11" 1,100.00
Bowl, Heintz, bronze w/silver floral, hdls, 11½" 550.00
Bowl, Kalo, hammered silver, mk, 5" 375.00
Bowl, van Erp, h/cp, 2½x6" 500.00
Bowl, van Erp, h/cp, 8½" 600.00
Box, cigarette; Carl Sorensen, h/cp, 4 buttressed ft, cleaned, 6" ..350.00
Box, h/cp, w/straps & rivets, 5x10x7", VG 450.00
Box, Heintz, bronze w/silver geometrics, 4" 200.00
Box, stamp; van Erp, h/cp, hinged domed lid, 5" 325.00
Box, van Erp, h/cp, 3½x6" 1,000.00
Cabinet, china; Limbert #1466, copper strap hinges, 56x48", EX .6,500.00
Cabinet, smoking; Limbert, door, copper hdw, shelf, rfn, 36" .1,000.00
Candlestick, Jesse Preston, bronze, #8, 13" 2,500.00
Candlesticks, brass, 2 scrolled holders, conical bases, 11x8", pr ...6,500.00
Candlesticks, hammered brass, 9x8½", pr 225.00
Candlesticks, Jarvie, bronze, ovoid bobeches, 11½", pr 1,100.00
Candlesticks, Jessie Preston, brass w/bobeches, 13x8" dia, pr .3,250.00
Candlesticks, Tudric, hammered pewter, mk, 6½", pr 275.00
Chair, bicycle; #79, leather bk, shaped seat, slab base, 42" 1,100.00
Chair, Limbert #931, 3-slat bk, new leather, brand, EX 750.00
Chair, lounge; Old Hickory, woven seat, bk w/pine poles, 40" .1,000.00
Chair, Morris; JM Young #186, flat-arm, 5-slat sides, 40", EX ..3,500.00
Chair, Morris; Knaus, flat arms w/5 slats, rstr leather seat, 38" .2,000.00
Chair, Morris; shaped flat arms over wide slat, sq posts, G 400.00
Chair, side; Limbert, H bk over 1 slat, orig leather, mk, 35" 250.00
Chair, side; 4-slat bk, arched rail, solid seat, 36", 12 for 1,000.00
Chair set, Limbert #1821 (5)/#1825 (arm), brand, VG 2,900.00
Charger, Benedict Studios, h/cp, emb organic forms, 20" 2,500.00
China cabinet, Limbert, corbels under side shelves, 59x44" ...3,750.00
China cabinet, Limbert, 2-door, ea w/2 sm panes at top, 60x38" .4,000.00
China cabinet, Limbert #428, trapezoidal, glazed doors/sides ..4,250.00
Clock, grandfather's; keyed tenons, porc face, 80x22x15", VG .2,200.00
Clock, Tudric, hammered pewter, 3x4", EX 850.00
Coal scuttle, h/cp, wrought-iron hdls/top, pyramidal lid, 19x18" ..550.00
Coat rack, oak w/5 swivel iron hooks, Make Yourselves..., 11x41" ...250.00
Curtains, linen, stylized trees, red/gold on natural, 2 panels ...1,000.00
Desk, drop-front, 2 drws over 2, foliate hdw, rfn, 46x36" 1,800.00
Desk, Lifetime #8567, drop-front, drw & shelf, h/cp hdw, 45x33" 1,200.00
Desk, Limbert, drop-front, 2-shelf, sq cutouts, rfn, 51x22" 2,700.00
Desk, Limbert #718, letter holder ea side pen tray, 2-drw, VG .1,000.00
Desk, Mission Oak style, slant lid, dvtl drw, open base, sq legs, 42" ..330.00
Desk set, Benedict, brass w/appl scarab, 8-pc 325.00
Desk set, Heintz, bronze w/silver flowers, Pat Aug 27.12, 10-pc ..375.00
Fire screen, mesh w/riveted brass bands, unmk, 23x48" 425.00
Footstool, Barber Bros, new leather seat, retouched, 13x13", VG ...110.00
Footstool, drop-in leather cushion, 4-slat sides, 16" L, VG 260.00
Footstool, Limbert #205½, cut-out/shaped slab sides, 20" W 1,200.00
Frame, Heintz #1103, bronze w/silver o/l, 3½x5" 250.00
Humidor, Benedict (att), h/cp, curled brass legs, lt cleaning, 10" L ..300.00
Humidor, Heintz, bronze w/silver geometrics, 2½x8½x3½" 550.00
Humidor, Heintz, bronze w/silver Viking ship, 3x10x6" 450.00
Humidor, van Erp Studios, sterling, hinged lid, 5x14½x8¾" ..5,750.00
Inkwell, van Erp, h/cp, EX form, 2½x4½" sq 300.00
Lamp, desk; van Erp, h/cp, conical shade w/later paper panels, 19" ...4,000.00
Lamp, desk; van Erp, h/cp, 11" domical mica shade, after 1915, 11" .6,900.00
Lamp, floor; rattan, 20" dia dome w/woven border, 73", VG 130.00
Lamp, floor; wrought iron, brass-fr tulip shade w/HP florals, 57" ...1,300.00
Lamp, Heintz, bronze w/silver floral, 13½" 2,600.00
Lamp, Heintz, bronze w/silver foliage, orig linen shade, 10x8¾" .1,500.00
Lamp, Heintz, bronze w/silver pine cone, 11" 2,300.00
Lamp, Prairie School, rvpt 12" shade; HP scene in base panels, 19" ..2,000.00
Lamp, van Erp, h/cp, 4-socket base, 4-panel mica shade, 19x21" ...55,000.00
Lamp, van Erp, h/cp trumpet base, 4-panel mica shade, 18x16½" .14,000.00
Lamp, van Erp, h/cp w/mica shade, bulbous, 4-socket, 22x21½" 65,000.00
Lamp, van Erp, 4 mica panels in 16½" h/cp fr; 4-arm std, 16½" 20,000.00
Lamp, 16" 5-panel (rpl) mica shade; h/cp bulbous std, 17" 1,500.00
Lamp, 17" 8-panel slag glass shade; bronzed metal std, 22", EX ..1,200.00
Lantern, h/cp & mica, tapered cylinder, domed top, 23" 4,300.00
Letter holder, Twichell, h/cp w/enamel ship, 4x5½" 375.00
Letter opener, Carence Crafters, h/cp w/nickel wash, 8" 200.00
Magazine rack, Lakeside Craftshop, cut-out sqs & arches, 38x14" ...1,100.00
Magazine stand, Limbert #300, 4-shelf, canted sides, mk, 37", VG ..1,100.00
Magazine stand, Limbert #301, 2-shelf, arched toe brd, 39" ...1,100.00
Magazine stand, Tobey Furniture, 4-shelf, rpl leather, rfn, 44", VG ...1,100.00
Mirror, h/cp, 21½" dia 100.00
Mirror, h/cp w/gr & bl enamel disks ea corner, 35x19" 2,000.00
Plant stand, Limbert, ebon oak line w/4 caned panels, rfn, 34" .2,100.00
Plant stand, Limbert, sq top over arched apron, brand, 27x12" .800.00
Plant stand, sq top on tapered stem w/ped base, rfn, 29x12" 250.00
Plate, Art Crafts Shop #212, copper w/HP strawberries, 8¾" 850.00
Print, woodblock; 2 swans on water, Hans Frank, dbl-matted, 12x14" .1,200.00
Rocker, Karpen Furniture, 9 cutouts under ea arm, reuphl, 37" ...1,100.00
Rocker, leather-uphl 5-slat hump-bk, shaped arms, tacks, 33" .1,150.00
Rocker, Limbert, 4-slat bk, rpl uphl seat/bk, brand, 36" 800.00
Rocker, 4-slat bk, corbel supports under arms, reuphl, 36" 200.00
Rug, drugget style, geometric, 4-color, 51x83", VG 130.00
Settle, Lifetime, Puritan, 10-slat bk, leather seat, rfn, 74", VG ..900.00
Sideboard, Limbert, gallery top, door ea side, 4-drw, 53", EX .4,500.00
Sideboard, Limbert, 2 half-drws amid 2 doors over drw, mirror, 48x48" ..2,000.00
Sideboard, Limbert, 3 sm drws/3 doors over linen drw, 45x57" .3,250.00
Sideboard, Limbert #1445, 3 drws/2 doors over long drw, 46x60" ...5,000.00
Sideboard, oak, gallery shelf w/mirror, 54" L, VG 490.00
Spoon, Handicraft Guild, h/cp, pierced work, 8" 700.00
Table, dining; Limbert, 48" dia top, sq ped w/4 ft, brand 1,900.00
Table, dining; Limbert #1487, intricate base, 54" dia+4 orig leaves 7,500.00
Table, dining: Limbert #403, 5 cut-out/shaped slab legs, 50" ..2,500.00
Table, lamp; Limbert #148, rnd top, splayed legs, brand, 29x30" ...3,000.00
Table, library; Lifetime, corbels on legs, slat sides, 54", VG 900.00
Table, library; Limbert, 30x45" oval top, cut-out sides, rfn 2,100.00
Table, library; Limbert #1132, lift-top, blind drw, 29x42x26", VG ...1,600.00
Table, library; oak, 1 drw opens from either side, 30x42x27" 500.00

Table, library; thru posts, 2-drw, 4 slats ea side, 43", G 800.00
Table, Limbert, 8-sided top, splayed legs, dbl-keyed tenons, 45" dia ...2,500.00
Table, Rittenhouse, splayed trn pine legs, 30x30" dia 200.00
Table, sofa; oak on twisted iron legs w/curls, rfn, 31x33x16" 750.00
Table, wrought-iron w/brass-insert top, low shelf, 26x20" dia .1,600.00
Tankard, Tudric, hammered pewter, whiplash hdl, 4½" 80.00
Tea set, Liberty Tudric, hammered pewter, 4-pc+tray 2,800.00
Tea/coffee set, Tudric, pewter w/turq enamel cabochons, blk hdls, 4-pc .950.00
Tray, Art Crafts Shop, copper, HP berries & leaves, #202, 22x8½" 475.00
Tray, dresser; Jarvie, h/cp w/emb linear decor, cleaned, 6x12" ...1,500.00
Tray, h/cp in brass, cut-out brass hdls, 13x10" 425.00
Tray, hammered brass, repousse snails, 9½" 375.00
Tray, van Erp, h/cp, raised hdls, 15" dia 1,200.00
Tray, van Erp, h/cp, 6" dia 275.00
Trunk stand, Limbert, 6-slat top, mk, orig finish, 18x26x16" ..1,000.00
Umbrella stand, Oak Craft, slatted cylinder, rpl pan, 27x10" 350.00
Vase, bud; h/cp, riveted hdl, 10¾x5½" 475.00
Vase, Harry Dixon, h/cp, 7" 900.00
Vase, Heintz, bronze, 8¼x4¼" 345.00
Vase, Heintz, bronze w/silver branch, 5" 225.00
Vase, Heintz, bronze w/silver cherry branches, pitting, 6" 90.00
Vase, Heintz, bronze w/silver floral, #3703, 15" 900.00
Vase, Jarvie, h/cp, 5", VG 350.00
Vase, Jauchen's Olde Copper Shop, h/cp, bottle form, 10½x5" ..1,100.00
Vase, Silvercrest, bronze w/silver cattails, 10½" 350.00
Vase, Tudric, hammered pewter, open hdls, 7½" 350.00
Vase, van Erp, h/cp, bulbous, rare red patina, 5x5¾" 1,400.00
Vase, van Erp, h/cp, spherical w/rolled rim, 7½x9½" 4,000.00
Vase, van Erp, h/cp, waisted cylinder, 1915, 7⅝" 2,185.00
Vase, van Erp, h/cp, 3½x4½" 600.00
Vase, van Erp, h/cp, 4½" 1,100.00
Vase, Zimmermann, patinated copper, ftd/ribbed V-form, 7x12" ...2,500.00
Wastebasket, Lakeside Craft Shops, 12 slats w/in band, 15x11", G .300.00
Woodblock print, Wm S Rice, Buoy, orange/bl/gr, 1936, 5½x4½"+fr ..700.00

Attwell, Mabel Lucie

Born in London in 1879, Mabel Lucie Attwell put her talent in illustration and design toward many outlets. Merchandise ranging from children's books and dinnerware, postcards, advertising, dolls, calendars, and greeting cards were marketed under her direction. She also designed a line of china called Nursery Ware for the Shelley China Company (see also Shelley). Our advisor for this category is David Ehrhard; he is listed in the Directory under California.

Lucie Attwell's Fairy House Money Box, tin litho, 8", $85.00.

Book, Alice in Wonderland, L Carroll, Tuck & Sons, 12 plates .200.00
Book, Children's Stories by Lucie Attwell, Whitman 100.00
Creamer & sugar bowl, BooBoo 380.00
Figurine, BooBoo on a puppy, Shelley, 4" 650.00
Figurine, BooBoo w/mushroom 700.00
Figurine, Bride 1,000.00
Figurine, Little Mermaid 700.00
Figurine, Toddler, girl w/doll in hand, Shelley 1,000.00
Handkerchief set, Lucie Atwell's Picture Hankys, M 165.00
Nursery Ware, bowl, Bobby Bear Went to the Moon..., Shelley, 5" .100.00
Nursery Ware, bowl, Look at This Wee Jolly, Shelley 200.00
Nursery Ware, plate,, We've Just Come From..., oval, Shelley ...250.00
Nursery Ware, teapot, flying plane scene & verse, Shelley 250.00
Print, Evacuation of School Children..., Aug 1939, from book .125.00
Print, Fairies Are Mischiefing Dorothy Dell, 4x6" 75.00
Print, Muvver's Pretty Pet 700.00
Print, Working on the Act, 8x10" 70.00
Tin container, Little Friends, Huntley Palmer, 1 of 6, 5" dia 35.00

Austrian Glass

Many examples of fine art glass were produced in Austria during the times of Loetz and Moser that cannot be attributed to any glasshouse in particular, though much of it bears striking similarities to the products of both artists.

Vase, cameo, Deco lily & leaves, purple on bl irid, 12" 575.00
Vase, gr irid w/glass thread o/l, long neck, 10" 60.00
Vase, gr irid w/6 pulled elements, bulbous, 6" 260.00
Vase, purple/yel swirls w/pulled irid, pinched neck, 5" 145.00
Vase, red irid w/bl & gr pulled decor, pinched/twisted, 12¼" 250.00
Vase, red irid w/cream/burnt orange pulled decor, flared rim, 7¼" ..260.00

Austrian Ware

From the late 1800s until the beginning of WWI, several companies were located in the area known at the turn of the century as Bohemia. They produced hard-paste porcelain dinnerware and decorative items primarily for the American trade. Today examples bearing the marks of these firms are usually referred to by collectors as Austrian ware, indicating simply the country of their origin. Of those various companies, these marks are best known: M.Z. Austria; Victoria, Carlsbad, Austria (Schmidt and Company); and O. & E.G. (Royal) Austria. Of these three companies, Victoria, Carlsbad, Austria, is the most highly valued.

Though most of the decorations were transfer designs which were sometimes signed by the original artist, pieces marked Royal Austria were often hand painted and so indicated alongside the backstamp.

Collectors should note that in our listings transfer decorations showing 'signatures' (sgn), such as 'Wagner,' 'Kauffmann,' 'LeBrun,' etc., were not actually painted by those artists but were merely based on their original paintings. Our advisor for this category is Mary Frank Gaston.

Bowl, hazelnuts, 4-ftd, incurvate, MZ, 4x8" 80.00
Butter pat, wht porc w/etched floral on gold, Royal Austrian, 3½" ...10.00
Butter pat, wht porc w/pk & yel roses & gr leaves, scalloped, 3¼" ..10.00
Butter pat, wht w/HP bl floral, sq w/canted corners, mk, 3" 16.00
Dresser tray, violets & leaves, gold border, Osborne, 14½" 100.00
Figurine, lady dressed for winter walk, 6½" 200.00
Figurine, Nouveau lady, elaborate detail, EX quality, 17" 325.00
Pitcher, Easter Lily, Schoner, 1903-05, 7½" 700.00
Shakers, gold bands, 1905-10, 3¾", pr 45.00
Tray, dresser; allover gold Rose & Daisy, 1938, 10" L 50.00
Tray, lady w/long flowing hair on rim, lg water lilies, 8" 190.00
Tray, pastel floral, scalloped rim, 12x8" 35.00
Vase, floral, rtcl, griffin hdls, 14½x7" 395.00
Vase, gr irid dbl-bulb w/4 hdls, Hellosine Ware, 11½", NM 300.00

Vase, lily petals appl below rim, vertical stems, 20", NM, pr **750.00**
Vase, shamrocks, gold harp, Schonig, MZ, 6" **40.00**

Autographs

Autograph collecting, also known as 'philography' or 'love of writing,' used to be a hobby shared by a few thousand dedicated collectors. But in recent years, autograph collecting has become a serious pursuit for more than 2,000,000 collectors worldwide. And in the past decade, more investors are adding rare and valuable autograph portfolios to their traditional investments. One reason for this sudden interest in autograph investing relates to the simple economic law of supply and demand. Rare autographs have a 'fixed' supply, meaning that unlike diamonds, gold, silver, stock certificates, etc., no more are being produced. There are only so many Abraham Lincoln, Marilyn Monroe, and Charles Lindbergh autographs available. In the meantime, it's estimated that more than 20,000 new collectors enter the market each year, thus creating an ever-increasing demand. Hence, the rare autographs generally rise steadily in value each year. Because of this scarcity, a serious collector will pay over $10,000.00 for a photograph signed by both Wilbur and Orville Wright, or as much as $25,000.00 for a handwritten letter by George Washington.

But by far, the majority of autograph collectors in the country do it for the love of the hobby. A polite letter and self-addressed, stamped envelope sent to a famous person will often bring the desired result. And occasionally one receives not only an autograph but a nice handwritten letter thanking the fan as well!

In terms of value, there are five general types of autographs: 1) mere signatures on an album page or card; 2) signed photographs; 3) signed documents; 4) typed letters signed; and 5) handwritten letters. The signatures are the least valuable, and handwritten letters the most valuable. The reasoning here is simple: with a handwritten letter, not only do you get an autograph but the handwritten message of the person as well. And this content can sometimes increase the value many times over. A handwritten letter of Babe Ruth's thanking a fan for a gift might fetch a few thousand dollars. But if the letter were to mention Ruth's feelings on the day he retired, it could easily sell for $10,000.00 or more.

Today the Internet has become a popular way to buy and sell autographs. A word of warning: Be very careful when buying over the Internet. It is an easy way for unscrupulous forgers to sell their fakes and disappear. Teenagers need to be especially aware that many of the 'signed' photos on the Internet of Sarah Michelle Gellar, Brad Pitt, Katie Holmes, Leonardo DeCaprio, Kate Winslett, and many others are either signed by secretaries or are outright forgeries. Make sure the Internet dealer offers a full money-back guarantee of authenticity and belongs to one of the major autograph organizations. Ask how long the dealer has been in business and for personal references if possible. Remember the old Latin warning, 'caveat emptor,' let the buyer beware.

There are several major autograph collector organizations where members can exchange celebrity addresses or buy, sell, and trade their autographed wares. Philography can be a fun and rewarding hobby. And who knows! In ten or twenty years, those autographs you got for free could be worth a small fortune!

Our advisor for autographs is Tim Anderson; he is listed in the Directory under Utah.

Key:
ADS — handwritten document signed
ALS — handwritten letter signed
ANS — handwritten note signed
AQS — autograph quotation signed
CS — counter signed
DS — document signed
ins — inscription
ISP — inscribed signed photo
LH — letterhead
LS — signed letter, typed or written by someone else
PLH — personal letterhead
sig — signature
SP — signed photo

Agnew, Spiro T; ISP, ¾-length portrait, bold sig **75.00**
Baker, Josephine; ISP, blk & wht, 6x3¾", VG **400.00**
Bogart, Humphrey; SP, scene from movie, blk & wht, 8x10" .**1,250.00**
Boone, Richard; SP, 8x10" glossy **65.00**
Brooks, Mel; SP, half-bust pose, blk & wht **18.50**
Bush, Barbara; ISP, color portrait in bl suit **85.00**
Cagney, James: ISP, half-bust portrait, ca 1930s, 5x7", +mailer .**125.00**
Channing, Carol; ISP, sipping from huge cup, ca 1958, 4x5" **25.00**
Cogan, Kevin; ISP, color, 6½x4½" **15.00**
Coolidge, Calvin; SP, by Harris & Hewig, in fr **150.00**
Coolidge, Grace; sig on White House card, w/orig envelope **65.00**
Dietrich, Marlene; SP, in peignoir, blk & wht, 8x10" **100.00**
Dreyfus, Richard; SP, color, 8x10" **25.00**
Eisenhower, Dwight D; LS, on White House stationery, to Bing Crosby ..**400.00**
Falwell, Jerry; DS on cover **15.00**
Gable, Clark; ISP, as Rhett Butler, 8x10" **1,200.00**
Garner, John Nance; bold sig on card **65.00**
Gish, Lillian; sig on book: Dorothy & Lillian Gish, 1973 ....**75.00**
Glenn, John; SP **45.00**
Grant, Julia Dent; sig clipped from letter, 1x4½" **150.00**
Grant, US; DS, countersigned w/Sec of War, 1869 ....**990.00**
Hepburn, Katharine; ISP, sexy pose, sepia tone, 8x10" **500.00**
Heston, Charlton; SP, as Moses, color **100.00**
Hutton, Betty; SP, blk & wht, ca 1940 ....**35.00**
Irwin, Hale; ISP, color, 8x10" **25.00**
Johnson, Andrew; DS, w/EM Stanton, dtd 1866 ....**1,500.00**
Johnson, Andrew/Stanton, Edwin; DS on parchment, 1866 ..**1,000.00**
Johnson, Lyndon B; sig on luncheon program/menu **150.00**
King George II, DS, 1727 ....**325.00**
Lincoln, Abraham; DS as president, w/EM Stanton, dtd 1863, EX ...**5,225.00**
Lincoln, Abraham/Cameron, Simon; DS on parchment, ca 1861 ....**4,300.00**
Long, Huey P; DS, w/gold state seal, 11x5½" **195.00**
MacArthur, Douglas; SP, full-face pose in uniform, 7x10" **695.00**
Madonna, ISP, in low-cut gown, gold ink, early, 8x10" **175.00**
Mailer, Norman; LS on personalized letterhead, 5/17/88, 8x10" ..**48.50**
Marx, Groucho; cut sig w/blk & wht photo, EX **150.00**
McGovern, George; SP, candid half bust **25.00**
McKinley, William; cut sig, on 1x4½" sheet in fr **145.00**
Michener, James A; ANS on 5x3" bookplate, w/trademk stamp ..**48.50**
Mitchum, Robert; SP, blk & wht **75.00**
Murphy; Audie; SP, in jacket & tie, color, 6x7½" **115.00**
Polk, James K; DS, countersigned by Sec of War, 1848 ....**935.00**
Powell, Colin; LS, as Chairman of Joint Chiefs of Staff, 1993 ...**100.00**
Rickenbacker, Eddie; ISP, sitting at desk, bold sig, 1967 ....**250.00**
Rogers, Roy; sig on card **40.00**
Roland, Gilbert; ISP, macho pose, sepia, ca 1935 ....**45.00**
Roosevelt, Eleanor; ALS on White House stationery, 1940, 14x19" .**250.00**
Simpson, OJ; ISP, official San Francisco 49ers photo, 5x8" **125.00**
Stevenson, Adlai E; bold sig on sm heavy card **20.00**
Stone, Milburn; ANS on card, scarce **95.00**
Tierney, Gene; SP, blk & wht **45.00**
Truman, Bess W; sig (bold) on White House card **195.00**
Truman, Harry S; LS, to University president, 1-pg, 1959 ....**140.00**
Westmoreland, William C; sig on book cover: A Soldier Reports ..**25.00**
Williams, Esther; SP, in shorts, blk & wht **25.00**
Williams, Robin; SP, as Mrs Doubtfire, blk & wht **35.00**

Automobilia

While some automobilia buffs are primarily concerned with restoring vintage cars, others concentrate on only one area of collecting. For instance, hood ornaments were often quite spectacular. Made of chrome or nickel plate on brass or bronze, they were designed to represent the 'winged maiden' Victory, flying bats, sleek greyhounds, soaring eagles, and a host of other creatures. Today they often bring prices in the $75.00 to $200.00 range. R. Lalique glass ornaments go much higher!

Horns, radios, clocks, gear shift knobs, and key chains with company emblems are other areas of interest. Generally, items pertaining to the classics of the '30s are most in demand. Paper advertising material, manuals, and catalogs in excellent condition are also collectible.

License plate collectors search for the early porcelain-on-cast-iron examples. First year plates (e.g., Massachusetts, 1903; Wisconsin, 1905; Indiana, 1913) are especially valuable. The last of the states to issue regulation plates were South Carolina and Texas in 1917, and Florida in 1918. While many northeastern states had registered hundreds of thousands of vehicles by the 1920s making these plates relatively common, those from the southern and western states of that period are considered rare. Naturally, condition is important. While a pair in mint condition might sell for as much as $100.00 to $125.00, a pair with chipped or otherwise damaged porcelain may sometimes be had for as little as $25.00 to $30.00.

Our advisor for this category is Leonard Needham; he is listed in the Directory under California. For more information we recommend *American Automobilia: An Illustrated History and Price Guide* by Jim and Nancy Schaut. See also Gas Globes and Panels.

Badge, Buffalo Auto Show 1913 & open roadster, pnt metal **40.00**
Badge, chauffeur; IL, 1948 ....**35.00**
Banner, Chevrolet Task-Force Trucks/New 1956..., cloth, 33x91", VG ...**70.00**
Blotter, Buick, car in landscape, 1924, 4x9", NM **28.00**
Blotter, Dodge Bros Trucks, dock scene/truck/1929 calendar, EX .**85.00**
Blotter, Oldfield (Barney) Tires, early #14 race car/phrase, 3x6", EX **215.00**
Brochure, Packard, 1925 Luxurious Motoring, mechanical, 11x6", EX ..**150.00**
Brochure, 1936 Oldsmobile sales, EX **45.00**
Brochure, 1980 Ford Fairmont **12.00**
Calendar, Hupmobile, 1926, cars/sailboats/people, complete, 31", EX ..**160.00**
Calendar attachment, Chevrolet Motor Co, car on base, 3x5", EX **275.00**
Cap, Harley-Davidson, cloth w/embr wings logo, 1930s **250.00**
Catalog, Buick Valve-In-Head Motor Cars, 1915, 32-pg, EX **110.00**
Catalog, Indian Motorcycles, 1916, schoolboy on cycle, 24-pg, G ..**800.00**
Catalog, showroom; 1963 Chevrolet, all models, interiors, etc **12.00**
Clock, Buick, cloisonne radiator shape, nonworking, 6x4", EX .**350.00**
Clock, Cadillac, sq light-up desk type, ca 1960, 9x10", NM **200.00**
Clock, Cadillac Sales, octagonal, glass/metal, 18x18", VG **600.00**
Clock, Hudson Super Size auto dealer's, 1920s **325.00**
Clock, Indian Motorcycles, octagonal, neon/metal/glass, 18", EX .**1,500.00**
Clock, Oldsmobile Service, neon, octagonal, 18", VG **700.00**
Clock, Packard Motor, Master Salesman 1926, radiator form, 5x4", VG .**500.00**
Compact mirror, Dodge Bros Coupe, bl shading into yel, 2" dia, EX **360.00**
Directional signal kit, Universal, Dbl S Corp, MIB **75.00**
Display, Pontiac, wire figural Indian head logo, 1930s, 20x47", M ...**275.00**
Display, 1953 Ford Models, light-up, wood, steel trim, 36½", EX **425.00**
Flyer, Harley-Davidson Model 125 Motorcycle, 1932-38, 7x11", EX .**16.00**
Hat, Yellow Cab, blk webbing/orange leatherette trim, 1930, EX ..**300.00**
Hood ornament, Mack Bulldog, VG **40.00**
Hood ornament, Super Chief, illuminated Indian head, 1950, 4", NMIB ...**125.00**
Hood ornament, Winged Flight, chrome/bl Lucite, 1937-48, MIB .**125.00**
Hubcap, Model T Ford, screws on, 1918-25, M **10.00**
Jigsaw puzzle, Dodge Bros New Eight.../Six Sedan, 2-sided, 1932, EX ..**100.00**
Jigsaw puzzle, Studebaker Vehicles, 2-sided, 1890, 7x6", EX **200.00**
Lamp, side; Ford script, Edmonds & Jones, 1914-17, 4½" **50.00**
Lamp shade, Chevrolet, plastic stained-glass look, 15" dia, VG .**250.00**
License plate, California 1914, porc, wht on red, EX **300.00**
License plate attachment, Ford, cartoon cop, metal, 4x7", EX **20.00**
License plate attachment, Hudson 6, tin, sleek bird, 4x14", EX ..**110.00**
License plate attachment, Jaguar Driver's Club, metal, 5", EX+ ..**70.00**
License plate attachment, Pacific Coast Auto Assoc, cloisonne, VG ..**50.00**
License plate attachment, top hat/gloves/cane, tin, 6x9", VG+ .**275.00**
Lighter, Buick, pressed tin car, Occupied Japan, 5", EX **220.00**
Manual, 1935, Hudson 8, owner's **30.00**
Manual, 1948 Pontiac, owner's **40.00**
Matchbook, Oldsmobile, various ads/car photos, 1956, M, ea **8.00**

Moto-meter, Buick-Boyce, glass and metal, Moto-meter Co. Inc., Long Island...USA, missing thermometer, 5½x7x2½", EX, $110.00.

Pamphlet, Harley-Davidson Motorcycles & Sidecars, 1923, 12-pg, EX **75.00**
Paperweight, Packard, brass emblem w/emb car & lettering, 3½", EX+ .**325.00**
Paperweight/mirror, Mack, shows gasoline dray, red/wht, 2½", EX **415.00**
Paperweight/mirror, Yellow Taxi Co, 3½", EX **440.00**
Photo, Prosperity Train, 190 Buicks on train, 1915, 14x24", EX ..**700.00**
Photo, 1920 Hudson, 4 deer tied on car, 2 hunters, 10x8" **16.50**
Pin, Chevrolet Corvette Owner, rnd, metal, 1955-56, NM **260.00**
Pin, Nash Millionaire Holiday, celluloid, red/wht/gr, 1934, 2¼" **8.50**
Pocket mirror, Elmore, early auto/dealer, 2x3" oval, VG+ **990.00**
Pocket mirror, Paterson '30,' early auto, blk/wht, 2x3" oval, EX .**550.00**
Pocket mirror, Willys-Knight Indianapolis Dealers, red/wht/bl/gold .**200.00**
Pocket watch, Harley-Davidson, silver-tone, 1920s, EX **725.00**
Pocketknife, Chevrolet, plastic casing w/logo, 3½", EX **20.00**
Pocketknife, Ford, bl logo on red plastic casing, 3½", EX **40.00**
Postcard, Nash Ambassador 600, shows auto/advertising, NM **30.00**
Postcard, Ormand Daytona Racers, mc cars, 1909, EX **10.00**
Postcard, Overland Model 83 Touring Car side view, 1909, NM .**10.00**
Poster, Ford, 1939 Baseball All-Stars, w/photos/stats, 32x17", EX .**650.00**
Promotional car, 1968 Oldsmobile Toronado **85.00**
Radiator cap, dog bone, Boyce Motometer, beveled glass, 3" **55.00**
Radiator cap, The Wiggler Spinner, metal/rubber base, 4" dia, EX ...**230.00**
Radiator mascot, Pierce Arrow, diecut metal circle & arrow, 4", VG+ ..**170.00**
Radiator mascot, Thomas Flyer, eagle on globe, metal, 4¾", EX .**350.00**
Radiator nameplate, DeSoto, enameling w/crest, 1930, 2x1¼" **20.00**
Radiator nameplate, Earl (ca 1907-08), 8-sided, recessed letters ..**25.00**
Radiator nameplate, Ford, Ford in silver on bl enamel oval, 1932 ...**18.00**
Radiator nameplate, Oldsmobile on wht, 1935, 3x5" **18.00**
Radiator nameplate, 1910 Hupmobile 6, brass letters w/6 below .**30.00**
Radiator nameplate, 1914 Lexington, bl & wht enamel, 1x4" **35.00**
Screwdriver, Harley-Davidson, NP hdl w/eng lettering, 5", EX .**115.00**
Sign, Buick Lubricare, neon/porc, diecut top, 19x68", NM+ ..**1,600.00**
Sign, Cadillac Authorized Service, porc, 42" dia, EX **1,500.00**
Sign, Chevrolet dealership, neon w/clock, 1930s, NM **1,200.00**
Sign, DeSoto Authorized Dealer, metal emblem, 16x36", VG ...**235.00**
Sign, Dodge Bros/Detroit USA, stained glass, 48x48", EX **2,200.00**
Sign, Edsel Service, arrow shape, light-up, 2-sided, 72", M **1,200.00**
Sign, Ford Genuine Parts, oval, NM **500.00**
Sign, Ford oval logo, neon/porc, wht on bl, 2-sided, 24x48", EX ..**2,000.00**
Sign, GMC Trucks, neon, Deco housing, wall-mount, 44x72x8", NM ...**4,250.00**
Sign, Hudson, neon on porc Deco housing w/dmn logo, 48x102", EX **1,400.00**
Sign, Jaguar Sales & Service, porc emblem, maroon, 2-sided, 41", EX **1,200.00**
Sign, Lincoln, diecut porc shield, red/wht/bl, 26x16", EX **650.00**
Sign, Nash, neon over name/border, 27x63x8", NM **1,900.00**

Sign, OK, neon flasher, 24" dia, EX 1,000.00
Sign, Oldsmobile Service, porc, globe symbol, 2-sided, 60" dia, EX .850.00
Sign, Pontiac/Master Salesman, molded emblem, gold/bl/red, 36x39", EX ..375.00
Sign, Studebaker, rvpt, Welcome/logos, gold/wht, fr, 8x48", EX ...475.00
Sign, Studebaker Service, porc, 1930s, 42" 1,200.00
Sign, Western Auto Associate Store, emb tin arrow, red, 33x9", EX 110.00
Sign, Willys Cars/Trucks/Jeeps, neon/porc, 36x72", EX 1,000.00
Stick pin, Indian Motorcycles, metal, Indian head, ½", EX 180.00
Table, Chrysler/Plymouth/Dodge DeSoto, wood fold-down, 26" sq, VG ..330.00
Thermometer, Chevrolet Covair/OK, emb tin, wht, 16", MIB ..150.00
Thermometer, United Motors Service, wood, blk/red on wht, 15", VG ..45.00
Tip tray, Maxwell Automobiles, gold/brn wood-tone, 4" dia, EX ..360.00
Watch fob, Cadillac, blk duck cloisonne emblem, w/strap, NM ..200.00
Watch fob, Ford emblem, metal w/bl cloisonne, 1x2" oval, EX+ .50.00

Autumn Leaf

In 1933 the Hall China Company designed a line of dinnerware for the Jewel Tea Company, who offered it to their customers as premiums. Although you may hear the ware referred to as 'Jewel Tea,' it was officially named 'Autumn Leaf' in the 1940s. In addition to the dinnerware, frosted Libbey glass tumblers, stemware, and a Melmac service with the orange and gold bittersweet pod were available over the years, as were tablecloths, plastic covers for bowls and mixers, and metal items such as cake safes, hot pads, coasters, wastebaskets, and canisters. Even shelf paper and playing cards were made to coordinate. In 1958 the International Silver Company designed silverplated flatware in a pattern called 'Autumn' which was to be used with dishes in the Autumn Leaf pattern. A year later, a line of stainless flatware was introduced. These accessory lines are prized by collectors today.

One of the most fascinating aspects of collecting the Autumn Leaf pattern has been the wonderful discoveries of previously unlisted pieces. Among these items are two different bud-ray lid one-pound butter dishes; most recently a one-pound butter dish in the 'Zephyr' or 'Bingo' style; a miniature set of the 'Casper' salt and pepper shakers; coffee, tea, and sugar canisters; a pair of candlesticks; an experimental condiment jar; and a covered candy dish. All of these china pieces are attributed to the Hall China Company. Other unusual items have turned up in the accessory lines as well and include a Libbey frosted tumbler in a pilsner shape, a wooden serving bowl, and an apron made from the oilcloth (plastic) material that was used in the 1950s tablecloth. These latter items appear to be professionally done, and we can only speculate as to their origin. Collectors believe that the Hall items were sample pieces that were never meant to be distributed.

Hall discontinued the Autumn Leaf line in 1978. At that time the date was added to the backstamp to mark ware still in stock in the Hall warehouse. A special promotion by Jewel saw the reintroduction of basic dinnerware and serving pieces with the 1978 backstamp. These pieces have made their way into many collections. Additionally, in 1979 Jewel released a line of enamel-clad cookware and a Vellux blanket made by Martex which were decorated with the Autumn Leaf pattern. They continued to offer these items for a few years only, then all distribution of Autumn Leaf items was discontinued.

It should be noted that the Hall China Company has produced several limited edition items for the National Autumn Leaf Collectors Club (NALCC): a New York-style teapot (1984); an Edgewater vase (1987, different than the original shape); candlesticks (1988); a Philadelphia-style teapot, creamer and sugar set (1990); a tea-for-two set and a Solo tea set (1991), a donut jug, and a large oval casserole. Later came the small ball jug, one-cup French teapot, and a set of four chocolate mugs. Other special items over the past few years include a sugar packet holder, a chamberstick, and an oyster cocktail. Additional items are scheduled for production. All of these are plainly marked as having been made for the NALCC and are appropriately dated. A few other pieces have been made by Hall as limited editions for an Ohio company, but these are easily identified: the Airflow teapot and the Norris refrigerator pitcher (neither of which was previously decorated with the Autumn Leaf decal), a square-handled beverage mug, and the new-style Irish mug. A production problem with the square-handled mugs halted their production. The company then issued a regular conic-style mug with a round handle. Additional items available now are a covered onion soup, tall bud vase, china kitchen memo board, and egg drop-style salt and pepper shakers with a mustard pot. They have also issued a deck of playing cards and Libbey tumblers. See *Garage Sale & Flea Market Annual* (Collector Books) for suggested values for club pieces. Our advisor for this category is Gwynne Harrison; she is listed in the Directory under California.

Teapot, New York, club piece from 1984, 536 made, from $600.00 to $700.00. (Photo courtesy NALCC)

Apron, oilcloth 700.00
Baker, cake; Heatflow clear glass, Mary Dunbar, 1½-qt 65.00
Baker, French; 3-pt 20.00
Baker, oval, Fort Pitt, 12-oz ind 225.00
Baker/souffle, 4½" 50.00
Bean pot, 1-hdl 1,000.00
Bean pot, 2-hdl, 2¼-qt 250.00
Blanket, Vellux, bl, full sz 200.00
Book, Mary Dunbar cookbook 30.00
Bottle, Jim Beam, w/stand 130.00
Bowl, cereal; 6½" 12.00
Bowl, cream soup; 2-hdl 35.00
Bowl, flat soup; 8½" 20.00
Bowl, fruit; 5½" 6.00
Bowl, grease; w/lid 20.00
Bowl, mixing; New Metal, 3-pc set 275.00
Bowl, refrigerator; metal w/plastic lids, 3 for 275.00
Bowl, Royal Glas-Bake, set of 4 ....200.00
Bowl, soup; Melmac 20.00
Bowl, vegetable; divided, 10½", from $90 to 125.00
Bowl, vegetable; oval, w/lid, 10" 75.00
Bowl, vegetable; rnd, 9" 150.00
Bowl, vegetable; Royal Glasbake, milk wht, divided 125.00
Bowl cover set, plastic, 8-pc: 7 assorted covers in pouch 90.00
Bread box, metal, from $400 to 500.00
Butter dish, 1-lb, regular 500.00
Butter dish, ¼-lb, regular, ruffled top, from $175 to 250.00
Butter dish, ¼-lb, sq top, rare 1,200.00
Butter dish, ¼-lb, wings top 1,800.00
Cake safe, metal, motif on top & sides, 5" 50.00
Cake safe, metal, side decor only, 4½x10½", from $35 to 45.00

Cake stand, metal base, orig box, $150 to 225.00
Candle holder, Christmas, club pc, 1994 ....125.00
Candle holder, club pc, 892 made, 1989, pr 250.00
Candlestick, metal, 4", pr 100.00
Canister, brn & gold, wht plastic lid 10.00
Canister, metal, rnd, w/coppertone lid, set of 4, from $500 to 800.00
Canister, metal, rnd, w/matching lids, set of 3, from $200 to 300.00
Carafe, glass & metal, Douglas, minimum value 300.00
Casserole, Royal Glas-Bake, rnd, milk wht w/clear glass lid 90.00
Casserole, Tootsie, w/lid, rnd, 2-qt 45.00
Catalog, Jewel, hardbound 50.00
Clock, electric 550.00
Coaster, metal, 3⅛" 8.00
Coffee dispenser/canister, metal, wall type, 10½x19" dia 400.00
Coffee maker, 9-cup, w/metal dripper, 8" 45.00
Coffee percolator, electric, all china, 4-pc 350.00
Coffeepot, Jewel's Best, 30-cup 600.00
Coffeepot, Rayed, 8-cup 45.00
Cookware, New Metal, 7-pc set 650.00
Creamer, New Style 25.00
Creamer & sugar bowl, Rayed, 1930s style 80.00
Cup & saucer, regular 6.00
Custard cup, Heatflow clear glass, Mary Dunbar, from $40 to 60.00
Custard cup, Radiance 10.00
Dripper, metal, for coffeepot 25.00
Flatware, silverplated, ea 35.00
Flatware, silverplated, serving pc, ea 100.00
Fondue, complete set 200.00
Fork, pickle; Jewel Tea 75.00
Gravy boat, w/underplate (pickle dish) 55.00
Hot pad, metal, oval, 10¾", from $12 to 15.00
Hot pad, metal, red or gr felt-like bking, rnd 20.00
Hurricane lamp, Douglas, w/metal base, pr 600.00
Loaf pan, Mary Dunbar, from $90 to 125.00
Mug, beverage 60.00
Mug, chocolate; club pc, 1,500 made, 1992, 4-pc set 100.00
Mustard, condiment set, 3-pc 100.00
Napkin, ecru muslin, 16" sq 50.00
Pickle dish or gravy liner, oval, 9" 25.00
Pie plate, Heatflow, clear glass, Mary Dunbar, from $45 to 60.00
Pie plate, 9½" 35.00
Pitcher, syrup; club pc, 1995 ....95.00
Pitcher, utility; 2½-pt, 6" 25.00
Place mat, paper, scalloped, set of 8, from $150 to 325.00
Plate, Melmac, 7" 20.00
Plate, 10" 18.00
Plate, 7¼" 10.00
Plate, 8" 18.00
Plate, 9" 12.00
Platter, 11½" 28.00
Platter, 13½", from $25 to 28.00
Pressure cooker, Mary Dunbar, metal 225.00
Sauce dish, serving; Douglas, Bakelite hdl, w/warmer base 600.00
Saucepan, w/lid, 2-qt 100.00
Saucer, Ruffled-D, regular 3.00
Shakers, Casper, regular, pr 30.00
Shakers, range, hdl, pr 30.00
Shelf liner, paper, 108" roll 50.00
Shoe polish, wht 55.00
Sifter, metal 400.00
Spray, No-Dust 50.00
Sugar bowl, Old Style, 3½" 40.00
Tablecloth, cotton sailcloth w/gold stripe, 54x54", from $100 to 150.00
Tablecloth, cotton sailcloth w/gold stripe, 54x72", from $125 to 150.00
Tablecloth, ecru muslin, 56x81", from $300 to 500.00
Tablecloth, plastic 150.00
Teapot, Aladdin 70.00
Teapot, long spout, 1935-42 ....70.00
Teapot, Newport, dtd 1978, from $175 to 200.00
Teapot, Rayed, long spout, 1978, from $800 to 1,600.00
Teapot, Solo, club pc, 1,400 made, 1991 ....100.00
Tidbit tray, 3-tier 100.00
Tin, cocoa 70.00
Tin, fruitcake; wht or tan 10.00
Tin, spice 70.00
Toaster cover, plastic, fits 2-slice toaster 50.00
Towel, tea; cotton, 16x33" 60.00
Toy, Jewel Truck, gr, from $350 to 425.00
Toy, Jewel Truck Semi Trailer, brn, from $1,000 to 1,600.00
Toy, Jewel Van, brn, Buddy L, from $400 to 650.00
Tray, glass, wood hdl, 19½x11¼", from $100 to 130.00
Tray, metal, oval 100.00
Tumbler, Brockway, 9-oz, 13-oz or 16-oz, ea 45.00
Tumbler, frosted, 14-oz, 5½" 20.00
Tumbler, frosted, 9-oz, 3¾" 32.00
Tumbler, gold frost etched, flat or ftd, 10-oz, ea 75.00
Tumbler, gold frost etched, flat or ftd, 15-oz, ea 75.00
Tumbler, Libbey, gold & frost on clear, 10-oz 75.00
Vase, bud; sm or regular decal, 6" 225.00
Vase, Edgewater, club pc, 626 made, 1987 ....350.00
Waffle iron, Manning-Bowman 95.00
Warmer base, oval 200.00

Aviation

Aviation buffs are interested in any phase of flying, from early developments with gliders, balloons, airships, and flying machines to more modern innovations. Books, catalogs, photos, patents, lithographs, ad cards, and posters are among the paper ephemera they treasure alongside models of unlikely flying contraptions, propellers and rudders, insignia and equipment from WWI and WWII, and memorabilia from the flights of the Wright Brothers, Lindbergh, Earhart, and the Zeppelins. See also Militaria. Our advisor for this category is John R. Joiner; he is listed in the Directory under Georgia.

Pan American Airlines, Japanese tin friction airplane, 1950s, 7½" wingspan, MIB, $75.00. (Photo courtesy Dunbar Gallery)

Bag, Japan Air Lines, wht w/red logo, 1964, 11½x11" 25.00
Bag, Western, golf, red w/wht logo, 1982, 48", M 20.00
Book, Kennedy Airport Picture History, 1981, 200-pg 15.00
Bottle, liquor; KLM Airlines, house shape, EX 30.00
Dish, Flying Tiger Airline, 25th Anniversary, emb brass, 1970, 6½" 32.00
Fan, folding; CAAC Airline, 2 cats decor, bamboo, 9¼" closed 40.00
Glass, wine; Iran Air, crystal w/wht logo, ca 1970, 4" 25.00

Guide, Official Airline; N Am ed, 1959, 980-pg, 8x11", VG 105.00
Labels, luggage; US/Foreign, 1950s, 50 in orig envelope, 1950s, NM .90.00
Magazine, Airline Passengers Association News, 1976, EX 12.00
Model, Capitol Airlines, 8½x9½" span, on Lucite stand 30.00
Model, Douglas DC3, Eastern Airlines, Corgi, 7½" span, w/stand .40.00
Model, Western Air Lines, DC-10, Air Jet Models, 11" 35.00
Model, Western Air Lines, 737-200, Air Jet Models, 5⅞" 25.00
Model, Western Air Lines, 737-300, Manning Models, 6¼" 27.00
Model, 727, Hughs Air, from travel agency, 32" L, on stand 390.00
Mug, Eastern Airline, dk bl w/logo & Eastern in wht, 4x3" 35.00
Pin, Goodyear Blimp, silver-tone metal, 1¼" L 15.00
Plate, Regent Air, gold logo w/blk & gold border, mk Spode, 8" .30.00
Playing cards, Mexicana Airlines, NM (sealed box) 14.00
Postcard, Constellation Speedbird, BOAC, 1950s, 6x4¼", EX 32.00
Postcard, TCA Air Canada, flight map, 1956, 6x4¼", VG+ 25.00
Program, Lindbergh souvenir, Fargo ND, EX 45.00
Ribbon, Lindbergh & crossed flags, red/wht/bl silk, w/orig backing ..150.00
Schedule, 27 different airlines, fares/map, 1929, EX 50.00
Sheet music, Amelia Earhart's Last Flight, portrait cover, 1939 ....20.00
Slide rule, Airline Flight Calculator, plastic, 1940s, 10¼" 35.00

Baccarat

The Baccarat Glass company was founded in 1765 near Luneville, France, and continues to this day to produce quality crystal tableware, vases, perfume bottles, and figurines. The firm became famous for the high-quality millefiori and caned paperweights produced there from 1845 until about 1860. Examples of these range from $300.00 to as much as several thousand. Since 1953 they have resumed the production of paperweights on a limited edition basis. Our advisors for this category are Randall Monsen and Rod Baer; their address is listed in the Directory under Virginia. See also Bottles, Commercial Perfume; Paperweights.

Atomizer, cranberry floral on frost, metal top, maroon bulb, 7" .200.00
Bottle, scent; Rose Tiente, Pinwheel, 6x2½" 95.00
Bottle, scent; Swirl, bl, swirl stopper, 5¾x2¼" 90.00
Bottle, wine; Rose Tiente, Zipper, cut paneled neck, 10x5" 235.00
Brandy snifter, sgn, 5½x4" 45.00
Candelabra, center tulip vase w/2 arms, prisms, 23x12" 500.00
Candelabra, faceted spear, 2-light, beaded rnd base, 24x12" ...1,500.00
Compote, crystal w/crystal bobeches 1,100.00
Cruet, sapphire, HP floral/gold medallion, spherical body, 9x5" ...235.00
Fairy lamp, Rose Tiente, Pinwheel, dome on matching plate, 6" ..250.00
Figurine, cat, amber, 3x3" 110.00

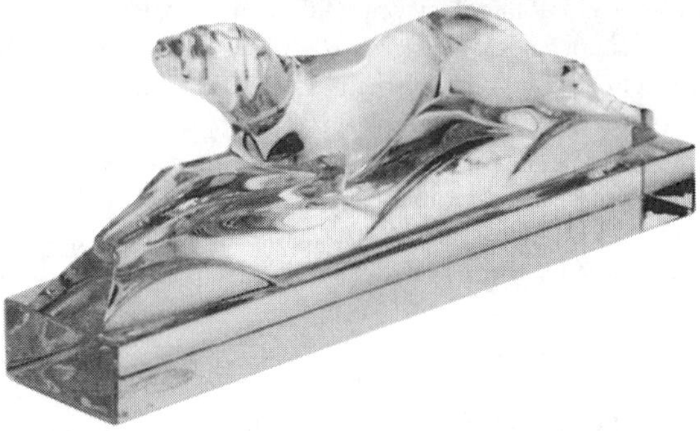

Figurine, greyhound on rectangular base, crystal, marked, 7¼", $195.00.

Figurine, Loving Doves, #2100916, 2⅞x3⅞" 125.00
Figurine, unicorn, recumbent w/head against chest, 3¼x4½" 115.00
Stem, wine; Perfection, 4¾" 65.00
Tumbler, cut, 4" 30.00
Vase, bud; cut crystal 150.00

Badges

The breast badge came into general usage in this country about 1840. Since most are not marked and styles have changed very little to the present day, they are often difficult to date. The most reliable clue is the pin and catch. One of the earliest types, used primarily before the turn of the century, involved a 't-pin' and a 'shell' catch. In a second style, the pin was hinged with a small square of sheet metal, and the clasp was cylindrical. From the late 1800s until about 1940, the pin and clasp were made from one continuous piece of thin metal wire. The same type, with the addition of a flat back plate, was used a little later. There are exceptions to these findings, and other types of clasps were also used. Hallmarks and inscriptions may also help pinpoint an approximate age.

Badges have been made from a variety of materials, usually brass or nickel silver; but even solid silver and gold were used for special orders. They are found in many basic shapes and variations — stars with five to seven points, shields, disks, ovals, and octagonals being most often encountered. Of prime importance to collectors, however, is that the title and/or location appear on the badge. Those with designations of positions no longer existing (City Constable, for example) and names of early western states and towns are most valuable.

Badges are among the most commonly reproduced (and faked) types of antiques on the market. At any flea market, ten fakes can be found for every authentic example. Genuine law badges start at $30.00 to $40.00 for recent examples (1950–1970); earlier pieces (1910–1930) usually bring $50.00 to $90.00. Pre-1900 badges often sell for more than $100.00. Authentic gold badges are usually priced at a minimum of scrap value (karat, weight, spot price for gold); fine gold badges from before 1900 can sell for $400.00 to $800.00, and a few will bring even more. A fire badge is usually valued at about half the price of a law badge from the same era and material. Our advisor for this category is Gene Matzke; he is listed in the Directory under Wisconsin.

Brookline Police, NP brass w/scrollwork/sunburst, ca 1890, EX ...85.00
Constable, NP octagon w/blk enamel, pin-bk, 1880s, 2x2" 60.00
Deputy Sheriff Madera Co #5, SP shield, pin-bk, 1900s, 1¾" 85.00
Officer Supreme Court NY, 10k gold filled, eagle-top sunburst .100.00
Police, NP shield w/blk enamel, ca 1800s, 2" 60.00
Police Chief, Los Angeles, silver star w/copper & enamel, 1900 ..300.00
Private Detective, NP shield w/center star, 1920s, EX 60.00
Seaboard Air Line Railway Police, NP brass, 1920s 45.00
State of SC, State Parks, state seal, gold 40.00
State Security, SC Ports Authority, state seal, silver 50.00
Taxi Driver NY, emb letters/#s, 1938 ....15.00
TX-Mexican Railway Police, state seal, gold, used 65.00
Washington DC Bicentennial Police, NP, emb eagle/Capitol building ...150.00

Banks

As always true, the continuing impact of auctions shows in the listings. Again, condition, condition, condition is what is driving the market. The spread between a bank in good condition and an excellent or original condition example continues to widen. It is imperative that you realize the importance of paint and the completeness of a bank. Also some banks have a wide margin of value based on color variations. It becomes more and more important that you attend as many shows and auctions as possible. Direct contact with collectors and knowledgeable dealers is the only way you can get a feel for prices and the desirability of banks, both mechanical and still. Banks continue to hold their value. However, it is becoming extremely important for collectors to understand the market.

Let's take a look at the price variations possible on an Uncle Sam mechanical bank. If you find one with considerable paint missing but with some good color showing, the price would be around $1,000.00. If it has repairs or restoration, the value would drop to something like $800.00 or less. If you had another example, and it had two thirds of its original paint and no repairs, it would be priced around $1,800.00. One with minor nicks and 90% of the original paint could go as high as $3,500.00. Or if you find one that is in near-original paint and has no repairs, $5,000.00 would not be out of line. This should help you see what causes price variations. After considering all of these factors, remember the final price is always determined by what a willing buyer and seller agree on for a specific bank.

The category of mechanical banks is unique. Along with cast-iron toys, they are among the most outstanding products of the Industrial Revolution and are recognized as some of the most successful of the mass-produced products of the nineteenth century. The earliest mechanicals were made of wood or lead, but when John Hall introduced Hall's Excelsior, a cast-iron mechanical bank, it was an immediate success. J. & E. Stevens produced the bank for Hall and soon began to make their own designs. Several companies followed suit, most of which were already in the hardware business. They used newly developed iron-molding techniques to produce these novelty savings devices for the emerging toy market. Mechanical banks reflect the social and political attitudes of the times, racial prejudices, the excitement of the circus, and humorous everyday events. Their designers made the most of simple mechanics to produce banks with captivating actions that served not only to amuse but to promote the concept of thrift to the children. The quality of detail in the castings are truly remarkable. The most collectible examples were made during the period of 1870 to 1900; however, they continued to be made until the early days of World War II. J. & E. Stevens, Shepard Hardware, and Kyser and Rex are some of the more well-known manufacturers; most made still banks as well.

Still banks are widely collected, and you can literally choose from thousands of banks. No one knows exactly how many different banks were made, but at least three thousand have been identified in the various books published on the subject. Cast-iron examples still dominate the market, but the lead banks from Europe are growing in value. Tin and early pottery banks are drawing more interest as well. American pottery banks which were primarily collected by Americana collectors are becoming more important in the still bank field. This market has not been as volatile as the mechanical banks, but the number of collectors is growing. The auction market on still banks is not as extensive as with the mechanicals, but some nice examples do turn up. Collectors and dealers are still the best source.

Book of Knowledge Banks were produced by John Wright (Pennsylvania) from circa 1950 until 1975. Of the thirty models they made during those years, a few continued to be made in very limited numbers until the late 1980s; these they referred to as the 'Medallion' series. (Today the Medallion banks command the same prices as the earlier Book of Knowledge series.) Each bank was a handcrafted, hand-painted duplicate of an original as was found in the collection of The Book of Knowledge, the first children's encyclopedia in this country. Because the antique banks are often priced out of the range of many of today's collectors, these banks are being sought out as affordable substitutes for their very expensive counterparts. It should also be noted that China has reproduced banks with the Book of Knowledge inscription on them. Buyers should take extra caution when investing in Book of Knowledge banks and purchase through a reputable dealer who offers a satisfaction guarantee as well as a guarantee that the bank is authentic.

As both value and interest continue on the increase, it becomes even more important to educate one's self to the fullest extent possible. We recommend these books for your library: *The Dictionary of Still Banks* by Long and Pitman, *The Penny Bank Book* by Moore, *Penny Banks Around the World* by Don Duer, and *The Bank Book* by Norman. If you are primarily interested in mechanicals, *Penny Lane*, a book by Davidson, is considered the most complete reference available. It contains a cross-reference listing of numbers from all other publications on mechanical banks.

In the listings that follow, banks are identified by L for Long, G for Griffith, M for Moore, N for Norman, D for Davidson, and W for Whiting.

Our advisor for mechanicals is Diane Patalano, listed in the Directory under New Jersey; Dan Iannotti (for Book of Knowledge) is listed under Michigan; and our still bank advisor is Larry Egelhoff, who is listed in the Directory under Indiana.

Key:
CI — cast iron
NPCI — nickel-plated cast iron
EPCI — electroplated cast iron

Advertising

Snappy Service Copper & Brass Sales, red, white, and blue figural, 6¼", NM, $125.00.

Chevrolet, tin globe, The Symbol of Savings, Chein, EX 60.00
Chrysler, Mr Fleet, vinyl figure, 1970s, NM 350.00
Dodge, metal barrel shape, Switch to Dodge..., 3", EX 50.00
Eureka gas stove, M-1350, pnt tin, 5¼", EX 60.00
GE refrigerator, M-1331, pnt CI, 4¼", EX 100.00
Hotpoint electric stove, M-1346, CI/tin, wht pnt, 6", EX 575.00
Kelvinator refrigerator, CI/tin, wht pnt, 4¼", EX 80.00
Kelvinator Silver Anniversary refrigerator, pnt wht metal, 4⅛", M .120.00
Mayflower refrigerator, M-1681, pnt CI, 5⅛", EX 340.00
Mellow furnace, M-1363, pnt CI, 3¾", NM 80.00
Norge stove, M-1339 (similar), pnt wht metal, 3½", EX 130.00
Red Goose School Shoes, goose, M-628, pnt CI, 3¾", EX 300.00
Rexair vacuum cleaner, pnt wht metal, 5¼", NM 45.00
Roper stove, M-1341, CI/tin, worn wht pnt, 3¾" 140.00
Sinclair dinosaur, M-777 variant, wht metal w/bronze pnt, 8½", EX ...90.00
Singer sewing machine, M-1368, tin/steel, faded decals, 5¼" 230.00
Wonder Bread loaf, plastic, M 15.00
Zenith radio, M-823, wht metal, 3¾", EX 45.00

Book of Knowledge Banks

Always Did 'Spise a Mule (Boy on Bench), M 395.00
Always Did 'Spise a Mule (Jockey), NM 285.00
Artillery Bank, NM 295.00
Boy on Trapeze, NM 425.00
Bulldog, M 250.00
Butting Buffalo, NM 325.00
Cabin Bank, NM 285.00

Cat & Mouse, M 375.00
Creedmoor Bank, M 325.00
Dentist, NM 250.00
Eagle & Eaglets, M 425.00
Humpty Dumpty, MIB 295.00
Indian & Bear, M 425.00
Jonah & Whale, M 275.00
Leaping Frog, MIB 325.00
Magician, NM 325.00
Milking Cow, NM 295.00
Organ Bank, Boy & Girl, M 335.00
Owl Turns Head, M 250.00
Paddy & Pig, M 325.00
Punch & Judy, M 325.00
Tammany, NMIB 325.00
Teddy & Bear, NM 335.00
Trick Pony, NMIB 325.00
Uncle Remus, MIB 395.00
Uncle Sam, M 325.00
US & Spain, M 275.00
William Tell, M 325.00
World's Fair, scarce bronze version, NM 350.00

Mechanical

Always Did 'Spise a Mule, Bench; N-2940, pnt CI, Stevens, 1897, EX ..2,600.00
Always Did 'Spise a Mule, Bench; N-2940, pnt CI, Stevens, 1897, G .700.00
Always Did 'Spise a Mule, Jockey; N-2950, pnt CI, Stevens, EX ..2,200.00
Boy Robbing Bird's Nest, N-1360, pnt CI, Pat 1875, VG 1,250.00
Boy Scout Camp, N-1370, pnt CI, Stevens, ca 1915, VG 4,500.00
Boy Stealing Watermelon, N-2380, G 715.00
Bulldog, N-1430, pnt CI, Stevens, 1880, EX 1,400.00
Bulldog, N-1430-A, pnt CI, glass eyes, 1880, 7⅝", VG 165.00
Cabin, N-1610, pnt CI, Stevens, 1885, EX 825.00
Cat & Mouse, N-1700, pnt CI, Stevens, 1891, rpl plate, VG .1,400.00
Chief Big Moon, N-1740, pnt CI, Stevens, 1899, VG 1,650.00
Clown on Globe, N-1930, pnt CI, yel base, Stevens, 1890, rprs, G .1,000.00
Creedmore, N-2000, pnt CI, rpr to gun & arm, G 300.00
Darktown Battery, N-2080-A, pnt CI, VG 3,500.00
Dinah, N-2150-A, short sleeves, pnt CI, Harper, 1911, VG 825.00
Dinah, N-2150-B, long sleeves, pnt CI, Harper, 1911, G+ 400.00
Dog on Turntable, N-2170, pnt CI, VG 525.00
Dog on Turntable, N-2170-A, rpt CI, Judd, 1870s, G 300.00
Eagle & Eaglets, N-2230, CI w/worn pnt, Stevens, 1883, rpr, 8" ..385.00
Eagle & Eaglets, N-2230, pnt CI, Stevens, 1883, VG 1,000.00
Elephant, Man Pops Out; N-2280-A, pnt CI, Enterprise, 1884, EX .650.00
Elephant, 3 Stars; N-2340, pnt CI, ca 1884, EX 650.00
Elephant & 3 Clowns, N-2250, pnt CI, Stevens, 1883, EX 2,300.00
Frog on Base, N-2530, pnt CI, gr & wht, Stevens, 1872, EX ..1,150.00
Frog on Base, N-2530, pnt CI, red & yel, Stevens, 1872, G 350.00
Frog on Rock, N-2520, pnt CI, Kilgore, 1920s, EX 600.00
Frogs, Two; N-2540, pnt CI, Stevens, 1882, rpl leg, G 700.00
Hall's Excelsior, N-2710, pnt CI, red, Stevens, 1869, rstr 350.00
Hall's Liliput, N-2740, pnt CI, yel version, Stevens, 1877, VG .600.00
Humpty Dumpty, N-2900, CI, worn pnt, VG 1,000.00
Indian Shooting Bear, N-2980-A, pnt CI, Stevens, ca 1900, EX .2,800.00
Jolly N, High Hat; N-3130 (similar), pnt CI, VG 500.00
Jolly N, High Hat; N-3290-A, pnt CI, Starkies, EX 700.00
Jolly N, N-3270, pnt aluminum, Starkies, EX 165.00
Jolly N, N-3270, pnt CI (poor pnt), Pat 1920, 6", G 500.00
Jonah & the Whale, N-3490, pnt CI, Shepard, rpl parts, G 400.00
Jonah & the Whale, N-3490, pnt CI, Shepard, 1890, VG 3,000.00
Lion & Monkeys, N-3650, pnt CI, VG 1,200.00
Magic, N-3730, pnt CI, wht & bl version, Stevens, 1886, G 600.00
Magic, N-3730, pnt CI, wht & bl version, Stevens, 1886, VG .1,600.00
Mammy & Child, N-3790-A, CI, red version, Kyser & Rex, 1884, VG ..2,400.00
Monkey, N-3960, pnt CI, Hubley, VG, from $450 to 550.00
Mule Entering Barn, N-4030, pnt CI, Stevens, 1880, VG 1,200.00
Multiplying Bank, M-1184, pnt CI (possible touchup), 6½", EX ..1,700.00
New Creedmore, N-4220, pnt CI, VG 500.00
Novelty, N-4260, pnt CI, Stevens, 1873, EX 1,300.00
Organ Bank, Cat & Dog; N-4320, pnt CI, Kyser & Rex, 1881, rpl hat .650.00
Organ Bank, Medium; N-4330, pnt CI, Kyser & Rex, 1881, VG ..600.00
Organ Bank, Medium: N-4330, pnt CI, Kyser & Rex, 1881, EX .1,200.00
Organ Grinder & Bear, N-4350-A, CI, rpt roof, Kyser & Rex, 1890s, EX .3,800.00
Owl Turns Head, N-4380, brn w/yel eyes, EX 700.00
Owl Turns Head, N-4380-B, wht, Stevens, 1880, VG+ 1,650.00
Paddy & Pig, N-4400, pnt CI, Stevens, VG 1,300.00
Paddy & Pig, N-4400, pnt CI, Stevens, 1885, EX 2,400.00
Paddy & Pig, N-4400 variation (red coat), CI, rstr pnt 350.00
Panorama, N-4410, pnt CI, Stevens, 1876, VG 5,500.00
Pump & Bucket, N-4700, CI, worn pnt, rpl hdl 525.00
Punch & Judy, N-4740, pnt CI, Shepard, 1884, G, from $725 to ...850.00
Punch & Judy, N-4740, pnt CI, Shepard, 1884, VG 1,600.00
Rabbit in Cabbage, N-4790-A, pnt CI, Kilgore, 1925, EX, $700 to .800.00
Rooster, N-4920, pnt CI, Kyser & Rex, 1880s, EX 700.00
Santa Claus, N-5010, pnt CI, Shepard, 5⅞", NM 5,280.00
Santa Claus, N-5010, rpt CI, Shepard, 5⅞", G 470.00
Snap It, N-5160, pnt CI, EX 425.00
Speaking Dog, N-5170, pnt CI, maroon base, Shepard, 1885, G .700.00
Speaking Dog, N-5170, pnt CI, Shepard, EX, from $3,500 to .3,800.00
Squirrel & Tree Stump, N-5270, pnt CI, Mechanical Novelty, 1881, NM ...2,400.00
Stump Speaker, N-5370, pnt CI, Shepard, 1886, VG 1,200.00
Tabby, N-5410, pnt CI, ca 1887, VG+ 825.00
Tammany, N-5420, pnt CI, Stevens, 1873, EX 800.00
Tammany, N-5420-B, pnt CI, Pat 1873, lt rust, VG 300.00
Trick Dog, N-5610, pnt CI, yel & brn base, Hubley, G, from $400 to .500.00
Trick Dog, N-5610, pnt CI, yel & brn base, Hubley, VG 775.00
Trick Pony, N-5640, rpt CI, Shepard, 1885, G 475.00
Uncle Remus, N-4730, pnt CI, EX 2,700.00
Uncle Sam, N-5740, pnt CI, Shepard, 1886, VG 1,430.00
Uncle Sam Bust, N-5750, pnt CI, NM 3,000.00
Uncle Tom, Star; N-5780-D, pnt CI, Kyser & Rex, 1882, G 450.00
Watchdog, N-5890, pnt CI, Stevens, 1880s, G 250.00
William Tell, N-5940, pnt CI, Stevens, rpl trap, VG 550.00
William Tell, N-5940, pnt CI, Stevens, 1896, EX 1,000.00

Registering

Barrel, M-921, pnt CI, 4", EX 240.00
Bean Pot, M-951, pnt CI, 3", EX 210.00
Beehive, M-618, pnt CI, 5⅜", VG 145.00
Bestmaid, tin litho, 4¾" 75.00
Burdick Cash Register, pnt steel, 4¾", EX 30.00
Captain Marvel, dime register, tin litho, 2½", NM 300.00
Children Emptying Bank, tin litho, 4⅜", NM 35.00
Dandy Self Registering Savings Bank, tin litho, 4¾", NM 360.00
El Tio Sam Cinco Centavos, pnt steel, 5⅜", NM 85.00
Imperial 3-Coin, pnt CI, 4½", NM 360.00
Kam Kap Save-O-Matic, pnt steel, 6¾", EX 25.00
Mother & Child Emptying Bank, tin litho, 5", EX 50.00
Nickel Register, M-951, worn NP w/red pnt, 4" 55.00
Prince Valiant, dime register, tin litho, 2½", EX+ 270.00
Thrifty Elf, dime register, tin litho, 2⅝", VG 85.00
Time Registering, N-5550, pnt CI, EX 450.00
Treasury Dime Bank, Union Savings & Loan, tin litho, 2½", NM .525.00
Uncle Sam, dime register, tin litho, 2⅝", NM 560.00
Uncle Sam, M-1290, sheet steel w/blk & gold, 6¼" 40.00

Uncle Sam, quarter register, pnt steel, 5⅜", EX 25.00
Valiant Savings & Register, pnt steel, 6⅛", NM 100.00

Still

Alamo, M-1187, CI, worn pnt, 1⅞", VG 370.00
Alice in Wonderland, M-1323, brass, 4½", EX 50.00
Auto (Chevrolet), M-1509, pnt wht metal, 2⅜", NM 140.00
Basset Hound, M-380, pnt CI, 3⅛", NM 1,050.00
Battleship Maine, M-1441, rpt CI, 5¼" 400.00
Battleship Oregon, M-1452, CI, worn pnt, 4⅞" 340.00
Bear Stealing Pig, M-693, pnt CI, 5½", G 525.00
Bear Stealing Pig, M-693, pnt CI, 5½", NM 1,600.00
Bear w/Honey Pot, M-717, pnt CI, 6½", EX+ 165.00
Black Boy, 2-Faced; M-83, CI, old blk pnt, 4⅛" 130.00
Blackpool Tower, M-984, CI, worn pnt, 7⅜", VG 220.00
Bugs Bunny at Bbl, M-270, pnt wht metal, 5½", NM 75.00
Bulldog, Seated; M-396, CI, worn pnt, 3⅞", G 80.00
Bulldog, Standing; M-429, pnt CI, 5¼", EX 165.00
Buster Brown & Tige, M-241, pnt CI, 5½", NM 500.00
Camel, Kneeling; M-770, pnt CI, 2½", NM 650.00
Capitolist, M-5, pnt CI, 5", EX+ 2,100.00
Captain Kidd, M-38, CI, worn pnt, 5⅝", G 300.00
Castle, M-954, pnt CI, 3", EX 575.00
Cat w/Long Tail, M-369, pnt CI, 4⅜", M 1,250.00
Champion Safe, M-1355, pnt CI, 4⅛", EX 100.00
Chimney Slot Building, M-997, pnt CI, 2⅞", EX 600.00
City Bank w/Paying Teller, M-1907, rpt CI, 5½" 1,550.00
Coin Bank, M-875 variant, pnt CI, 4¼", EX 150.00
Coronation Crown, M-1312, pnt wht metal, 3½", MIB 45.00
Cupola, M-1145, pnt CI, 5½", VG 175.00
Cupola, M-1146, pnt CI, 4⅛", EX 750.00
Cupola, M-1147, pnt CI, 3¼", G 110.00
Devil, 2-Faced; M-31, pnt CI, 4¼", EX, from $525 to 625.00
Donkey, M-500, pnt CI, 6¾", NM 400.00
Donkey w/Blanket, M-488, pnt CI, Kenton, 3⅞", EX 450.00
Double Door Building, M-1125, rpt CI, 5½", VG 70.00
Dutch Boy on Barrel, M-180, CI, worn mc pnt, 5⅝", G 85.00
Dutch Girl w/Flowers, M-181, CI, worn pnt, 5¼" 45.00
Eagle on Globe, Columbia Savings; M-783, wht metal/paper, 5¾", NM .1,900.00
Eiffel Tower, M-1074, pnt CI, 8¾", VG 625.00
Elephant, Deco; M-449, pnt CI, 4⅜", EX 370.00
Elephant, McKinley/Roosevelt; M-453, CI, worn pnt, 2½" 500.00
Elephant, Stiff-Legged; M-469, CI, worn pnt, 3½" 290.00
Elephant on Tub, M-483, CI, worn pnt, 5⅜", G 75.00
Elephant w/Bent Knee, M-447 (similar), CI, worn pnt, 3", G ...330.00
Elephant w/Blanket, M-487, pnt CI, 3⅛", NM 1,200.00
Elephant w/Chariot, M-479, pnt CI, rust on chariot, 4¾", G+ .950.00
Fidelity Trust Vault, M-903, pnt CI, 6½", EX 475.00
Flat Iron Building, M-1159, pnt CI, 8¼", NM 3,200.00
Flat Iron Building, M-1161, pnt CI, 5½", G 400.00
Football Player, M-11, pnt CI, 5⅞", EX 450.00
Gas Stove, M-1349, CI/steel, worn pnt, 5½" 140.00
Gem, N-2570, pnt CI, NM 1,200.00
General Butler, M-54, pnt CI, old rpr, 6½", EX 1,700.00
Globe on Wood Base, M-791, paper/steel/wood, 4¼", EX 35.00
Globe Savings Fund, M-1199, japanned, 7¼", VG 1,700.00
Golliwog, M-16, pnt aluminum, 6", EX 110.00
Golliwog, M-85, pnt CI, 6¼", EX 600.00
Goose, Squatty; M-612 variant, pnt CI, 3⅞", EX 380.00
Graf Zeppelin, M-1428, CI, old worn silver pnt, 6¾", VG 140.00
Graf Zeppelin, M-1428, pnt CI, 6¾", EX 240.00
Hitler Pig, M-305, compo, 4½", NM 175.00
Home Savings, M-1126, CI, 5⅞", VG 250.00
Home Savings w/Dog's Head Finial, M-1237, pnt CI, 5¾", EX, $350 to ..450.00
Honey Bear, M-696, pnt CI, 2½", NM 850.00
Horse Prancing on Platform, M-520, pnt CI, 7¼", VG 90.00
Horse w/Belly Band, M-533 (similar), pnt CI, 4⅛", NM 500.00
Humpty Dumpty, M-338, tin litho, 5¼", M 280.00
Indian in Tepee, M-236, pnt lead, 4⅞", EX 45.00
Kitten w/Bowl, M-349, pnt CI, 4¾", EX 90.00
Knight's Helmet, M-1385, lead, 5", EX 70.00
Lighthouse, M-1115, pnt CI, no trap, 10¼", EX 1,650.00
Lion, Seated; Royal, M-751, pnt CI, 5", EX 850.00
Main Street Trolley w/People, M-1471, pnt CI, recast trap, 3", VG ...350.00
Majestic Radio, M-827, pnt CI, 4½", EX 70.00
Mammy w/Basket, M-175, pnt wht metal, 5¼", M 700.00
Mammy w/Hands on Hips, M-176, pnt CI, 5¼", VG 90.00
Mammy w/Spoon, M-169, pnt CI, slot in legs, 5⅞", EX 370.00
Man on Bale of Cotton, M-37, pnt CI, rstr, 4⅞" 425.00
Mascot, M-3, CI, partial rpt, 5⅞", EX 1,450.00
Nipper, M-376, flocked aluminum, 6", NM 175.00
Owl, Be Wise; M-598, pnt CI, 4⅞", EX 155.00
Pay Phone, M-845, pnt CI, recast trap, 7¾", EX 585.00
Pelican, M-679, pnt CI, 4¾", M 1,550.00
Pet Stove, M-1345 variant, pnt CI, 2¼", VG 40.00
Porky Pig, M-264, pnt CI, 5¾", NM 450.00
Professor Pug Frog, M-311, CI, worn pnt, 3¼" 300.00
Rabbit, Standing; M-574, CI, worn pnt, 6¼" 220.00
Red Ball Safe, M-873, pnt CI, 3", NM 230.00
Rhino, M-721, CI, old gold pnt, 2⅝", VG 200.00
Rooster, M-547, pnt CI, 4⅝", VG+ 180.00
Rumplestiltskin, M-75, pnt CI, 6", EX 350.00
Santa, M-95, wht metal, 5½", EX 25.00
Santa Claus, M-63, pnt CI w/touch-up, Harper, 4⅛", VG 2,100.00
Scottie & 8 Ball, M-429, wht metal, 3¼", NM 200.00
Skyscraper, 6-Post; M-1241, pnt CI, 6½", EX 500.00
Spaniel, Standing; M-418, CI, orig mc pnt, 3¾", EX 270.00
Squirrel w/Nut, M-660, pnt CI, 4⅛", NM 700.00
St Bernard, M-437, CI, brn pnt, AC Williams, 5½x7¾", NM ..100.00
State Bank, M-1078, CI, japanning w/gold & bronze, 8¾", NM ..825.00
State Bank, M-1080, pnt CI, 5⅞", EX 230.00
Statue of Liberty, M-1166, CI, no pnt, 9⅝", G 200.00
Stop Sign, M-1479, pnt CI, 4½", NM 875.00
Stop Sign, M-1481, pnt CI, 5⅝", NM 2,200.00
Teddy Bear, M-698, CI, worn pnt, 2½" 290.00
Three Monkeys, M-743, pnt CI, 3¼", EX 220.00
Town Hall, M-998, pnt CI, rpl turnpin, chipped corner, 4⅝" 245.00
Transvaal Money Box, M-107, CI w/bronze pnt, 6", EX, from $475 to ..550.00
Turkey, M-585, pnt CI, rpl screw, 4¼", EX 290.00
US Mailbox w/Eagle, M-849, pnt CI, 5⅛", VG 110.00
Victorian Cottage, M-992, pnt CI, 4", VG 190.00
Westminster Abbey, M-973, pnt CI, 6¼", G 130.00
Westside Presbyterian Church, M-958, pnt CI, 3¾", VG, $300 to .400.00
Zeppelin on Wheels, M-1431, pnt CI, 2¼", EX 220.00
1890 Tower, M-1198, pnt CI, rpr hinge, 6⅞", VG 575.00
$100,000 Money Bag, M-1262, pnt CI, w/key, 3⅝", EX 330.00

Barber Shop Collectibles

Even for the stranger in town, the local barber shop was easy to find, its location vividly marked with the traditional red and white striped barber pole that for centuries identified such establishments. As far back as the twelfth century, the barber has had a place in recorded history. At one time he not only groomed the beards and cut the hair of his gentlemen clients but was known as the 'blood-letter' as well, hence the red stripe for blood and the white for the bandages. Many early barbers even pulled teeth! Later, laws were enacted that divided the practices of barbering and surgery.

The Victorian barber shop reflected the charm of that era with fancy barber chairs upholstered in rich wine-colored velvet; rows of bottles made from colored art glass held hair tonics and shaving lotion. Backbars of richly carved oak with beveled mirrors lined the wall behind the barber's station. During the late nineteenth century, the barber pole with a blue stripe added to the standard red and white as a patriotic gesture came into vogue.

Today the barber shop has all but disappeared from the American scene, replaced by modern unisex salons. Collectors search for the barber poles, the fancy chairs, and the tonic bottles of an era gone but not forgotten. See also Bottles; Razors; Shaving Mugs.

Book, instructional, Assoc Master Barbers of Am, 1939, 330-pg .28.00
Booster seat, metal, pnt red, vinyl-like seat, EX 45.00
Brush, lather; Old Reliable #9, walnut hdl, early 1900s, EX 12.50
Brush, neck; horsehair bristles, hardwood hdl, ca 1910s, lg, EX ...25.00
Cabinet, oak, 2-drw, pull-down sides & front, cvgs, 17x26, 12" .375.00
Chair, Congress, quarter-sawn wht oak/leather, 1911, EX, minimum .1,500.00
Chair, Paidar #319, 1-lever, ca 1925, EX, minimum value 765.00
Chair, Theo A Kochs, NP CI fr, gr porc arms/lever, ftrest, EX ...650.00
Clippers, Coates' Adjust, Kochs, ca 1898, EX 37.50
Container, comb disinfectant; clear glass w/Barbicide in wht, 11" ..35.00

Globe, two 15" lens in red and white painted metal body, 19½", VG, $600.00.

Jacket, wht cotton duck, collarless, wht buttons, 3-pocket, 1904, EX ..85.00
Latherizier, Lather King Jr, Campbell Products, 5½x8½x3½" 70.00
Massage & shampoo machine, Hugo Melchoir's, in oak dvtl case ..90.00
Massager, Stim-U-Lax Model M3, Oster, EX 30.00
Music box, customer turns in chair, Enesco, 1968, 6½x5" 25.00
Music box, mother w/child in chair, Sweet Adeline, animated, EX .110.00
Pole, metal, rnd front, flat bk, Wm Marvy Co, #4812, 24" 180.00
Pole, stained glass stripes, hexagonal fr, porc top & mt, 31¼" ...550.00
Postcard, int of 4-chair shop, ca 1910, VG (unused) 25.00
Postcard, OK Barber Shop, Birmingham AL, ca 1910, EX 135.00
Shears, Lafayette, hand forged, ca 1910, 8", NM 8.00
Shelf brackets, NP brass, holds 5⅞" W glass, Art Brass Co 80.00
Sign, Out to Lunch, Sappy's Colored Only, 1929 ....55.00
Sign, porc, pole w/Modern Service, ½-rnd, Bob White Sign Co, 48" .315.00
Sterilizer, Renewal #6, Am Sundries Co, 1940s, 4x4x6" 25.00
Strap, honing; leather, chromed buckle 1930s, 24" 150.00
Towel steamer, brass & copper, ftd cylinder w/ball-shaped top, 64" .1,300.00

Barometers

Barometers are instruments designed to measure the weight or pressure of the atmosphere in order to anticipate approaching weather changes. They have a glorious history. Some of the foremost thinkers of the seventeenth century developed the mercury barometer, as the discovery of the natural laws of the universe progressed. Working in 1644 from experiments by Galileo, Evangelista Torrecelli used a glass tube and a jar of mercury to create a vacuum and therefore prove that air has weight. Four years later, Rene Descartes added a paper scale to the top of Torrecelli's mercury tube and created the basic barometer. Blaise Pascal, working with Descartes, used it to determine the heights of mountains; indeed, only later was the correlation between changes in air pressure and changes in the weather observed and the term 'weather-glass' applied. Robert Boyle introduced it to England, and Robert Hook modified the form and designed the wheel barometer.

The most common type of barometer is the wheel or banjo type. Second is the stick type. Modifications of the plain stick would be the marine gimballed type, followed by the laboratory or Kew or Fortin type. Others are the Admiral Fitzroys of which there are twelve or more types. The above all have mercury contained in either glass tubing or wood-box cisterns.

Another type of barometer is the aneroid, working on atmospheric pressure changes. They come in all sizes ranging from 1" in diameter to 12" or larger. They may be in metal or wood cases. There is a Barograph which records on a graph that rotates around a drum powered by a seven-day clock mechanism. Pocket barometers (altimeters) vary in sizes from 1" diameter up to 6" diameter. One final type of barometer is the symphisometer, a modification of the stick barometer used for a limited time and not as accurate as a conventional marine barometer. Our advisor for this category is Bob Elsner; he is listed in the Directory under Florida.

American

Banjo, James Kirby St Neotes, walnut, swan's neck, 19th C, 38" ..400.00
Banjo, Thomas Taber, NY; rosewood, early 19th C, 43½" 1,045.00
Stick, AS & JA, West Rochester NY, walnut w/eng, ca 1840, 35" ...635.00
Stick, Walter Frasier Cleveland OH, walnut, printed dial, 1860s, 40" ..300.00

English

Banjo, A Dodd Glasgow, mahog Wm IV, brass face, 40½", EX ..425.00
Banjo, R Bailey Birmingham, cvd burl walnut, thermometer, 1860, 48" .1,100.00

Other Barometer Types

Aneroid, w/½-rnd thermometer 250.00
Aneroid, 4-6" dia, brass case 150.00
Barograph reading barometer, Negretti & Zambra, mahog 950.00
Pocket barometer (altimeter), w/case, from $200 to 300.00
Sympresometer, Hyman & Co, banjo 1,050.00

Barware

Back in the thirties when social soirees were very elegant affairs thanks to the influence of Hollywood in all its glamour and mystique, cocktails were often served up in shakers styled as miniature airplanes, zeppelins, skyscrapers, lady's legs, penguins, roosters, bowling pins, etc. Some were by top designers such as Norman Bel Geddes and Russel Wright. They were made of silverplate, glass, and chrome, often trimmed with colorful Bakelite handles. Today these are hot collectibles, and even the more common Deco-styled chrome cylinders are often priced at $25.00 and up. Ice buckets, trays, and other bar accessories are also included in this area of collecting.

For further information we recommend *Vintage Bar Ware Identification & Value Guide* by Stephen Visakay, our advisor for this category; he is listed in the Directory under New Jersey.

Sheriden serving set, chromium plated with Catalin trim, Empire shaker (value alone: $550.00) and footed cups on Hercules tray, Revere Copper & Brass Co., Rome, New York, designed by W.A. Welden, ca 1938, complete as shown, $1,500.00. (Photo courtesy Stephen Visakay)

Bar towel, cloth w/Black caricature motif, 1940s, oblong, ea **35.00**
Bar towel, cloth w/mc printed bar motif **18.00**
Bottle opener w/corkscrew, metal parrot form, Melodelite, 1929, 7" .**28.00**
Cigarette dispenser, mini bar w/Black bartender, metal/wood, Fr .**650.00**
Cocktail cup, SP golf bag form, Derby, 1920s, 3" **65.00**
Cocktail glass, Catalin w/chrome & Catalin stem, gr, Nudawn, 5¾" ...**10.00**
Cocktail glass, frosted glass w/sterling rings, ftd, 1930s, 3⅜" **7.00**
Cocktail glass, plastic w/colored spring coil stem, 1950s **7.00**
Cocktail glass, SP ftd rooster figural holder w/cut glass cone insert .**125.00**
Cocktail napkin, rooster print on cloth, colored border, oblong **8.00**
Cocktail picks, barware/bottles in bartender holder, plastic, 7-pc, 6" ...**150.00**
Cocktail picks, domino tops w/domino holder, plastic, 9-pc, 4½" .**75.00**
Cocktail set, bowling ball container+decanter+6 glasses, 1940-50s ..**65.00**
Cocktail set, hammered aluminum, shaker/4 cups/rnd tray, TKF, 1930s .**175.00**
Cocktail set, silver baluster shaker, 12 sm tumblers, Chinese Export ..**1,150.00**
Ice bowl w/tongs, chrome, Russell Wright/Chase, 1930s-40s, 7" dia ...**35.00**
Ice bucket, aluminum ball form w/emb penguins, West Bend, 1941, 8" .**25.00**
Ice bucket, chrome w/porc lining, Bakelite trim, Keystone Ware, 11" ...**75.00**
Mixer, chrome pitcher w/jade Catalin trim, 1928, 52-oz, 10¾" .**250.00**
Pitcher, martini; clear glass w/brn plastic-wrapped hdl, w/stick, 13" ..**45.00**
Pitcher, martini; stainless steel w/walnut hdl, Italy, 9¼" **45.00**
Shaker, aluminum cylinder in anodized bl, 11¼" **75.00**
Shaker, aluminum ftd cylinder w/blk plastic top, 1940s, 12" **55.00**
Shaker, chrome Connoisseur w/cover knob, Manning-Bowman, 1930s, 12" .**95.00**
Shaker, chrome cylinder, Modernist, Royal Hickman, 1930s, 14" .**450.00**
Shaker, chrome cylinder w/horizonal lines, Manning-Bowman, 7½" .**45.00**
Shaker, glass, clear & color, chrome top, 1940s-50s, 14¾" **150.00**
Shaker, glass, cobalt dumbbell w/chrome cap, wire rest, 14" **325.00**
Shaker, glass, gr w/eng rooster, SP top, 1926, 10½" **75.00**
Shaker, glass, Hazel Atlas, mc horizontal stripes, chrome top, 1930s ..**38.00**
Shaker, glass, John Held Jr cartoon art, sgn, 1920s-30s, 11" **200.00**
Shaker, glass, leg form, ruby, chrome top/slipper, Derby Shelton, 16" ...**650.00**
Shaker, glass, orange & yel spatter, glass top, 1930s, 7" **85.00**
Shaker, glass, skyscraper, cobalt cylinder w/sterling trim, 1930s, 16" **200.00**
Shaker, glass, skyscraper, frosted w/sterling bands, 1930s, 16" **100.00**
Shaker, glass, textured, w/silver ship, SP top, cobalt base, '20s, 9" .**110.00**
Shaker, glass w/frosted & sterling Vs, chrome top, 1930s, 12" ...**150.00**
Shaker, NP, eng rooster, pinched bottle, Meriden, 1927, 8¼" **250.00**
Shaker, NP w/hammered finish, Bernard Rice & Sons, 1920s, 13¾" **75.00**
Shaker, SP, eng/stamped ornate design, swing hdl, Silver City, 1890s ...**125.00**
Shaker, SP, golf bag, pour spout/golf ball finial, Geo Berry/Derby **1,100.00**
Shaker, SP, hammered rooster form, tail hdl, Wallace Bros, 1928, 15" ...**1,500.00**
Shaker, SP, rooster head, clear glass bottom, 1920s, 11" **750.00**
Shaker, sterling, hexagonal, Mexico, 42-oz, 13" **300.00**
Shaker, sterling, Modernist pitcher, allover relief sqs, Gorham, 12" .**4,500.00**
Shaker, wooden barrel form w/metal insert, chrome top, 9½" **75.00**
Swizzle sticks, glass w/mc fruit tops, 6-pc, Bohemian, 1930s, 8" ...**18.00**
Traveling bar, brass/chrome, red stripes, 8-pc, Germany, 1928, 14" ..**250.00**
Traveling bar, zeppelin, SP, 19-pc set, Germany, ca 1928, 12" ..**2,500.00**
Tray, metal, enameled cocktail glasses/bubbles, 1930s, 13" dia **35.00**
Tray, metal w/John Held Jr cartoon art, 'Here's How,' 1920s, 12x17" ...**100.00**
Tray, SP w/golf ball hdls, Derby, 1925-30, 9½x15½" **275.00**

Baskets

Basket weaving is a craft as old as ancient history. Baskets have been used to harvest crops, for domestic chores, and to contain the catch of fishermen. Materials at hand were utilized, and baskets from a specific region are often distinguishable simply by analyzing the natural fibers used in their construction. Early Indian baskets were made of corn husks or woven grasses. Willow splint, straw, rope, and paper were also used. Until the invention of the veneering machine in the late 1800s, splint was made by water-soaking a split log until the fibers were softened and flexible. Long strips were pulled out by hand and, while still wet and pliable, woven into baskets in either a cross-hatch or hexagonal weave.

Most handcrafted baskets on the market today were made between 1860 and the early 1900s. Factory baskets with a thick, wide splint cut by machine are of little interest to collectors. The more popular baskets are those designed for a specific purpose, rather than the more commonly found utility baskets that had multiple uses. Among the most costly forms are the Nantucket Lighthouse baskets, which were basically copied from those made there for centuries by aboriginal Indians. They were designed in the style of whale-oil barrels and named for the South Shoal Nantucket Lightship where many were made during the last half of the nineteenth century. Cheese baskets (used to separate curds from whey), herb-gathering baskets, and finely woven Shaker miniatures are other highly-prized examples of the basket-weaver's art.

In the listings that follow, assume that each has a center bentwood handle (unless handles of another type are noted) that is not included in the height. Unless another type of material is indicated, assume that each is made of splint. Prices are subjective and hinge on several factors: construction, age, color, and general appearance.

For further information we recommend *Collector's Guide to Country Baskets* by Don and Carol Raycraft (Collector Books). See also American Indian; Eskimo; Sewing; Shaker.

Apple drying, oak splint, pine fr, 38x14" **700.00**
Buttocks, EX patina w/dk brn color, 6x12½x11" **220.00**
Buttocks, Eye-of-God bent-twig hdl, 6½x14x12" **100.00**
Buttocks, fine weave, set of 5, lg: 52 ribs/sm: 28, 2-5" dia **1,100.00**
Buttocks, grayish patina, minor damage, 12x20" dia **200.00**
Buttocks, med patina, 6½x18x12½" **195.00**
Buttocks, natural patina, 5½x13x12" **140.00**
Buttocks, old scrubbed patina, 5½x11x10" **60.00**
Buttocks, tight weave, EX detail, wide plaited medial band, 8x17x14" **900.00**
Buttocks, woven splint & cane, Eye-of-God bentwood hdl, 8x20x16" **195.00**
Buttocks, 22-rib, EX color, minor damage, 3x6½x5½" **245.00**
Buttocks, 30-rib, old worn patina, minor damage, 8x17x14" **220.00**
Cheese, circular w/5 shaped wooden fixed hdls, 19th C, 7x18" .**800.00**
Cheese, old patina, minor rpr, 21" dia **200.00**
Fruit, open rim hdls, EX patina, 11x16½" **230.00**
Harvest, dbl-wall splint staves, wooden bottom, bushel, 16x22" dia ..**150.00**
Herb drying, open rim hdls, EX patina, 6¼x21" dia **250.00**
Knife & fork, splint, center divider, wood hdl, bl pnt **200.00**
Loom, natural/pk/gr w/varnish, 8¾x9½" **95.00**

Mini, 24-rib, EX patina, 2½x5x4¾" 385.00
Nantucket, minor breaks, 19th C, 11½x13¾" 1,200.00
Nantucket, minor losses to basket & lashing, 3x7¼" 800.00
Nantucket, mk of Jose Formose Reyes w/map of island, 4¼x8½" .2,000.00
Nantucket, mk of R Folger, 6¾x10" 1,380.00
Nantucket, oval, misshapen, 3½x9¾" 500.00
Nantucket, paper label w/poem by buyer, 4½x7½" 2,100.00
Nantucket, purse, cvd ivory whale on lid, 19th C, 10" L 1,000.00
Oblong, w/laced detail on hdl, EX old patina, 15" 200.00
Round, bentwood rim hdls, old patina, 20" H 195.00
Round, 33-rib, EX color, 7½x12" dia 220.00
Round, 33-rib, EX color, 9½x15½" dia 165.00
Rye straw, oval, wear/damage, 5x15x21" 85.00

Batchelder

Ernest A. Batchelder was a leading exponent of the Arts and Crafts movement in the United States. His influential book, *Design in Theory and Practice*, was originally published in 1910. He is best known, however, for his artistic tiles which he first produced in Pasadena, California, from 1909 to 1916. In 1916 the business was relocated to Los Angeles where it continued until 1932, closing because of the Depression.

In 1938 Batchelder resumed production in Pasadena under the name of 'Kinneola Kiln.' Output of the new pottery consisted of delicately cast bowls and vases in an Oriental style. This business closed in 1951. Tiles carry a die-stamped mark; vases and bowls are hand incised. For more information we recommend *Collector's Encyclopedia of California Pottery, Second Edition*, by Jack Chipman (Collector Books).

Bookends, Dutch boy and girl, bronze finish, 5x5½", $550.00 for the pair.

Ashtray, lt bl matt, hexagonal w/emb advertising, 4½", EX 275.00
Bookends, gray matt w/vertical incising 6", EX 200.00
Bookends, 2¾" tiles set on Potter Studio brass mts, pr 350.00
Bowl, bl, flared rim, incised mk, 3¼x7½" 95.00
Bowl, cobalt gloss, 1½x8" 95.00
Bowl, rose, oval, Kineola Kiln mk, 4x12x7" 145.00
Tray, olive gr w/turq int, floriform, #234, 10¾" dia 300.00
Vase, carmel/brn gloss w/bl & gray highlights, 4" 300.00
Vase, cobalt & teal sheer gloss, bulbous, 5x3¾" 550.00
Vase, cobalt semigloss, clay exposed, 5" 475.00
Vase, gr/multi-toned bl matt, spherical, 3½" 375.00
Vase, gray, cylindrical, 9½" 250.00

Battersea

Battersea is a term that refers to enameling on copper or other metal. Though originally produced at Battersea, England, in the mid-eighteenth century, the craft was later practiced throughout the Staffordshire district. Boxes are the most common examples. Some are figurals, and many bear an inscription. Values are given for examples with only minimal damage, which is normal. Our advisor for this category is John Harrigan; he is listed in the Directory under Minnesota.

Bottle, scent; Classical lady musician, glass stopper, 3" 250.00
Box, motto; 'Have Communion w/Few...,' wht, 1⅝" 550.00
Box, motto; 'The Gift Is Small...,' wht, 1⅝" 525.00
Mirror holder, woman at tomb: 'Sacred to Friendship,' 1⅝" dia ...350.00

Bauer

Originally founded in Paducah, Kentucky, in 1885, the J.A. Bauer Company moved to Los Angeles where it was re-established in 1910. Until the 1920s their major products were terra cotta gardenware, flowerpots, and stoneware and yellow ware bowls. During prohibition they produced crocks for home use. A more artful form of product began to develop with the addition of designer Louis Ipsen to the staff circa 1915. Some of his work, a line of molded vases, flowerpots, bowls, etc., was awarded a bronze medal at the Pacific International Exposition in 1916.

In 1930 the first of many dinnerware lines was tested on the market. Their initial pattern, Plain Ware, was well accepted and led the way to the introduction of the most popular dinnerware in their history and with today's collectors, Ring Ware. It was produced from 1932 into the early 1960s in solid colors of jade green, royal blue, dusty burgundy, ivory, Chinese yellow, Delph blue, orange-red, and (in very limited quantities) black or white. Its simple pattern was a design of closely-spaced concentric ribs, either convex or concave. Over the years, more than one hundred shapes were available. Some were made in limited quantities, resulting in rare items to whet the appetites of Bauer buffs today. Other patterns were La Linda, produced during the 1940s and 1950s, and Monterey Moderne, introduced in 1948 and remaining popular into the 1950s (made in pink, black, gray, brown, and green).

After WWII a flood of foreign imports and loss of key employees drastically curtailed their sales, and the pottery began a steady decline that ended in failure in 1962. Prices listed below reflect the California market. For more information we recommend *Collector's Encyclopedia of Bauer Pottery: Identification & Values* (Collector Books) and *The Collector's Encyclopedia of California Pottery, Second Edition*, both by Jack Chipman, our advisor for this category. Mr. Chipman's address may be found in the Directory under California.

In the lines of Ring and Plain ware, pricing depends to some extent on color. Use the low end of our range of values for light brown, Chinese yellow, orange-red, jade green, red-brown, olive green, light blue, turquoise, and gray; the high-end colors are delph blue, ivory, dusty burgundy, cobalt, chartreuse, papaya, and burgundy. Black is 50% higher than the high end; to evaluate white, double the high side. Use the low end of the range to evaluate Monterey items in all colors but Monterey blue, burgundy, and white — those are high-end colors. You'll need to double the high end for black in this line as well as Monterey Moderne. An in-depth study of colors may be found in the books referenced above.

Art Pottery

Flower bowl, dk gr overdrip, low, rare, 10", minimum 800.00
Jardiniere, gr matt, incurvate, 9" 300.00
Jardiniere, gr matt, raised scrollwork/filigree, 10" 500.00
Vase, gr matt, shouldered, short can neck, 5" 200.00
Vase, gr matt, 9" 450.00
Vase, Rebekah, gr satin-matt w/irid splotches, 15", minimum ..1,500.00
Vase (carnation jar), gr satin-matt w/splotches, 24", minimum ..1,500.00

Bauer Atlanta

Ashtray, #8, Russel Wright, minimum 400.00
Ball jug, band of rings encircles bulbous body 145.00
Bowl, centerpiece; #17, minimum 900.00
Bowl, flower; low, Cal-Art, 2x11½" 20.00
Bowl, mantel-pc; #9, minimum 850.00
Butter plateau, rectangular, Co Gardens, minimum 250.00
Candlestick, #14, Russel Wright, minimum 600.00
Sugar bowl, w/spoon as lid, Co Gardens, minimum 175.00
Vase, #2, Russel Wright, 8½", minimum 425.00
Vase, lotus, 11½" 65.00

Brusche Al Fresco and Contempo

Bowl, divided vegetable; Hemlock Gr, 9¼" 30.00
Bowl, vegetable; speckled yel, 7½" 24.00
Creamer, Hemlock Gr 15.00
Creamer, jumbo; Dubonnet 25.00
Plate, dinner; speckled gray, 10" 10.00
Platter, Lime, 10¼" 20.00
Shakers, jumbo, speckled gr, pr 24.00
Sugar bowl, Hemlock Gr 18.00

Cal-Art Pottery

Bowl, gr matt, swirled lines, 8" 40.00
Figurine, duck, feeding, wht matt, 2¼x4¼" 25.00
Figurine, Madonna, wht matt, 10", minimum 150.00
Flower bowl, bl matt, fan shape w/rim pulled down 2X, 10" L 45.00

Matt Carlton

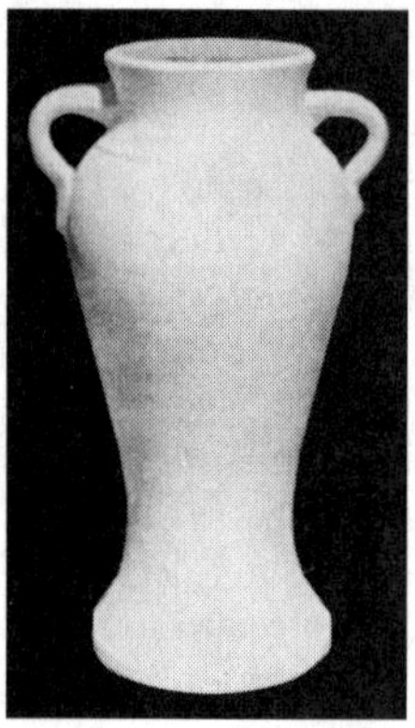

Vase, Rebekah, 10x6", minimum value $800.00.
(Photo courtesy calpots.com)

Basket, orange-red, uncommon shape, 8", minimum 1,500.00
Bowl, jade gr, ruffled/scalloped rim, 3½x7" 85.00
Vase, blk, grooved fan shape w/hdls (rare shape), 10", minimum ..1,500.00
Vase, Delph Bl (uncommon), w/'hands-on-hips' hdls, 14", minimum ...2,500.00
Vase, orange-red, fan shape, 3¾" 75.00
Vase, orange-red, fan shape w/crimped sides, 9½", minimum 750.00
Vase, royal bl, horizontal ridges, twist hdls, 9½", minimum 1,200.00
Vase, wht (uncommon), fan shape w/striations, 6x8", minimum 500.00

Florist and Garden Pottery

Bowl, Chinese Yel, soft rim scallops, oval, 10½" L 85.00
Hanging basket, orange-red, 3 sm rim hdls, 8" 225.00
Jardiniere, Ring, Chinese Yel, 8" 175.00
Oil jar, bl, 16", minimum 500.00
Pot, Pinnacle, olive gr, 10" 85.00
Vase, Chinese Yel, Florist, horizontal bands top & bottom, 18" .150.00

Hi-Fire Pottery

Bowl, Monterey Bl, deep, #211, 10" 85.00
Flower bowl, wht, fluted sides, 3½x11", minimum 200.00
Vase, red-brn, ogee sides, #214, 7" 65.00
Vase, red-brn, slip cast, #219, 5" 45.00
Vase, turq, ovoid, #215, 7" 65.00

Tracy Irwin

Ashtray, str sides w/3 cigarette rests, sm 15.00
Bowl, Indian, blk matt, 1950s, 7x10", minimum 200.00
Bowl, pumpkin; melon ribbed, 5x8" 80.00
Vase, blk matt, fan form, ped ft, 10", minimum 100.00
Vase, low angle to sides, #516, 10" 85.00
Vase, ovoid w/rim pulled into upwards point, #505, 8" 50.00

La Linda

Butter dish, pk matt 65.00
Creamer, old or new style, from $12 to 15.00
Cup, bl matt 18.00
Gravy boat, pk matt 35.00
Plate, dinner; gr 15.00
Platter, yel, oval, 10" 15.00
Shakers, brn, pr 12.00

Monterey

Beverage dispenser, refrigerator; w/lid, from $200 to 300.00
Bowl, fruit; 3-toed, 9", from $45 to 65.00
Candle holder, from $45 to 65.00
Cup, from $18 to 25.00
Plate, dinner; 10½", from $30 to 45.00
Relish plate, 3-compartment, 10", from $60 to 90.00
Sauce boat, lg, from $40 to 60.00
Tray, raffia-wrapped hdl, from $15 to 23.00

Monterey Moderne and Related Kitchenware

Bowl, mixing; olive gr, #18 ....25.00
Bowl, salad/serving; yel, 10½" 35.00
Casserole, ind; chartreuse 25.00
Mug, no hdl (Al Fresco 8-oz tumbler), burgundy 20.00
Pitcher, brn, str sides, 5½" 35.00
Pitcher, chartreuse, angle hdl, 2½-qt 85.00
Plate, salad; gray, 7½" 10.00
Shakers, pk, pr 150.00
Teapot, yel, 6-cup 65.00

Plain Ware

Ashtray, sq, 3", from $45 to 65.00
Ashtray, 4" dia, from $75 to 100.00
Bean pot, 2-qt, from $75 to 100.00
Beer mug, from $125 to 175.00
Bowl, batter; 2-qt, w/hdl, from $85 to 125.00
Bowl, divided vegetable; oval, from $150 to 225.00
Bowl, mixing; #24, from $35 to 50.00
Bowl, nappy, #5, from $30 to 45.00
Bowl, salad; low, 12", from $100 to 150.00
Bowl, salad; 8¼", from $60 to 90.00

Butter dish, rnd, from $150 to 225.00
Butter dish, ¼-lb, from $175 to 200.00
Coffee server, bulbous w/wooden hdl, from $65 to 95.00
Coffee server, open, w/wooden hdl, 6-cup, from $50 to 75.00
Coffeepot, dripolator; from $300 to 400.00
Egg cup, from $160 to 240.00
Gravy bowl, w/attached undertray, from $100 to 125.00
Honey jar, single bee or dbl bee cover, complete, minimum ...2,000.00
Mug, baby; 8-oz, from $30 to 40.00
Pitcher, beer; from $350 to 525.00
Pitcher, restyled, from $100 to 150.00
Pitcher, 2-qt, from $100 to 150.00
Pitcher, 5", from $125 to 175.00
Plate, dinner; 10½", from $65 to 95.00
Plate, relish; 5-compartment, from $85 to 125.00
Plate, salad; 7½", from $30 to 45.00
Pudding dish, #6, 10¼", from $80 to 120.00
Ramekin, any color but blk, from $15 to 20.00
Ramekin, blk 30.00
Sugar bowl, from $45 to 65.00
Sugar bowl, midget, from $75 to 100.00
Sugar shaker, from $200 to 300.00
Teapot, w/wooden hdl, 6-cup, from $150 to 225.00
Tumbler, 6-oz, from $15 to 20.00
Water bottle, 7", from $200 to 300.00

Red, White, and Yellow Ware

Bean pot, brn glazed, w/lid, 4-qt 65.00
Chick font, wht ware, 2-pc, 1-gal 65.00
Churn, wht ware, stamped mk on outside, #2 (2-gal), 13x7" 75.00
Jar, wht ware, open, 4¾" 25.00
Jug, brn glaze, mk, 5-gal 180.00
Mug, yel ware, handmade, 3", minimum 45.00
Pitcher, spongeware, bl on wht, #12, 7¼", minimum 275.00
Pitcher, yel ware, #12, 7¼" 145.00
Pot, laurel wreath emb on redware, 10" 150.00
Spice jar, yel ware, w/lid, #1, 4½" 75.00
Vase, stoneware, bulbous, 4½" 175.00

Ring Ware

Bowl, batter; 2-qt 125.00
Bowl, ice/souffle 300.00
Bowl, mixing; #24 ....50.00
Bowl, salad; low, 14" 240.00
Bowl, vegetable; divided oval 225.00
Bowl, vegetable; oval, 8" 125.00
Candle holder, 2½" 85.00
Cookie jar, minimum 600.00
Creamer, restyled 30.00
Gravy bowl 175.00
Nappy, #8 ....75.00
Plate, dinner; 9" 45.00
Plate, salad; 7½" 45.00
Platter, oval, 9" 45.00
Sugar bowl 65.00
Teapot, blk, 6-cup, minimum 225.00
Tumbler, bbl shape, metal hdl 150.00

Miscellaneous

Ashtray, beige matt, sq w/rests ea side, '50s, 11" 45.00
Ashtray, vase & 'Bauer Pottery' emb in bottom, skillet form 250.00
Oil jar, jade gr, #129, 24", minimum 1,500.00
Oil jar, royal bl, #100, 16", minimum 850.00
Vase, Saxon, yel w/cobalt int, handmade, rare, 12", minimum ..500.00

Bavaria

Bavaria, Germany, was long the center of that country's pottery industry; in the 1800s, many firms operated in and around the area. Chinaware vases, novelties, and table accessories were decorated with transfer prints as well as by hand by artists who sometimes signed their work. The examples listed here are marked with 'Bavaria' and the logos of some of the various companies which were located there.

Demitasse cup and saucer, pink flower transfer, molded and ribbed, Zeh, Scherzer & Co., ca 1900, from $30.00 to $40.00. (Photo courtesy Jim and Susan Harran)

Bottle, scent; Pierro w/urn, flower stopper, glass dauber, 5" 165.00
Bowl, mc flowers w/gold, ZS&Co, lg 85.00
Cake plate, mc roses in yel center, wide rose-colored rim, RC mk ..70.00
Chocolate pot, roses, pk on gr, red lion mk, 9", +4 c/s 225.00
Plate, daisies, gilt, Osborne, 6¾", set of 6 ....40.00
Plate, roses, mc on pastel w/gold, ZS&Co, 12⅜" 70.00
Teapot, alternating panels w/gold, +6 c/s 225.00

Beer Cans

In the early 1930s one of America's largest can-manufacturing companies approached an East Coast brewery with a novel concept — beer in cans. The brewery decided to take a chance on the idea, and in January 1935, the beer can was born.

The 'church key' style can opener was invented at the same time, and early flat top cans actually had instructions on how to use it to open a can.

Canned beer soared in popularity, and breweries scrambled to meet the canning challenge. Since many companies did not have a machine to fill a flat-top can, the cone top was invented. Brewery executives believed its shape would be more acceptable to consumers used to buying bottled beer, and it easily passed through existing bottling machinery. The more compact flat-top can dominated sales, and by the 1950s cone tops were obsolete.

About values: Condition is critical when determining the value of a beer can. Prices quoted are for like-new condition cans, free of rust, dents, scratches, and other damage. Like any collectible, value drops in direct proportion to condition, and off-grade cans are often worth no more than one-half of retail value. Our advisor for this category is Dan Andrews; he is listed in the Directory under California. Information in our descriptions is given in this specific order: 1.) name of brew; 2.) company — may be simply repetitive; and 3.) city/state or state.

A-1, Arizona, Phoenix, flat top 20.00
A-1, National, Phoenix, pull tab 8.00
Alps Brau, Maier, Los Angeles, flat top 60.00
Ballantine, Ballantine, Newark, zip tab, 16-oz 5.00
Ballantine, Bock Ballantine, Newark, pull tab 65.00

Ballantine's Ale, Ballantine, Newark, flat top 25.00
Bavarian's Select, Iroquois, Buffalo, pull tab 22.00
Bel Air, Horlacher, Allentown, flat top 60.00
Berghoff 1887, Berghoff, Fort Wayne IN, cone top, low profile ...45.00
Black Dallas, Walter, Pueblo, pull tab 35.00
Black Label, Carling, Belleville, pull tab 5.00
Blitz Weinhard, Blitz Weinhard, Portland, pull tab 12.00
Boh, Enterprise, Fall River, flat top 40.00
Brut, Lone Star, San Antonio, pull tab 10.00
Burgemeister Draft, Schlitz, Los Angeles, pull tab 5.00
Burger Ale, Burger, Cincinnati, flat top 48.00
Busch Bavarian, Anheuser-Busch, Los Angeles, zip tab, 16-oz 20.00
Cardinal, Cardinal, St Charles, flat top 6.00
Champagne Pilsner, HC Johnson, Lomira, cone top, high profile ...225.00
Chief Oshkosh, Peoples, Oshkosh, pull tab 9.00
Colorado Imperial, Walter, Pueblo, pull tab 24.00
Coors, Coors, Golden, flat top 5.00
Coors Light, Dallas 150th Anniversary, pull tab, tall 12-oz 3.00
Dawnson's Lager Beer, Dawson, New Bedford, flat top 350.00
Drewerys, Drewerys, South Bend, flat top 15.00
Drewerys Bock, Drewerys, South Bend, pull tab 40.00
Drewerys Draft, Associated, Evansville, pull tab 5.00
Eastside Old Tap, Pabst, Los Angeles, flat top, 16-oz 20.00
El Rancho, General, Los Angeles, pull tab 15.00
Encore, Schiltz, Milwaukee, pull tab 5.00
Erin Brew, Standard, Cleveland, flat top 45.00
Falstaff, Falstaff, St Louis, zip tab 5.00
Fitzgerald's Lager, Fitzgerald Bros, Troy, cone top, high profile 80.00
Fort Schuyler, Fort Schuyler, Utica, flat top 45.00
Fox Head Malt Liquor, Fox Head, Sheyboygan, pull tab 28.00
Gablinger's, Forrest, New Bedford, pull tab 6.00
Gibbons, The Lion, Wilkes-Barre, cone top, high profile 65.00
Gipps Amberlin, Gipps, Chicago, flat top 35.00
Golden Lager, Burgermeister, San Francisco, pull tab 30.00
Golden Pilsner, Becker, Ogden, flat top 45.00
Great Lakes, Heileman, La Crosse, pull tab 10.00
Haffenreffer Draught, Haffenreffer, Boston, zip tab 55.00
Hamm's Draft, Hamm, Los Angeles, pull tab, 16-oz 10.00
Heileman's Lager, Heileman, La Crosse, flat top 28.00
Hensler, Hensler, Newark, flat top 195.00
Highlander, Highlander, Seattle, zip tab 15.00
Horton Ale, Horton Pilsner, NY, cone top, low profile 245.00
Huber, Huber, Monroe, cone top, high profile 65.00
Hynne, Walter Pueblo, pull tab 5.00
Iron City Pirates, 1974 TV Schedule, pull tab 3.00
Iroquois, Iroquois, Columbus, pull tab 3.00
Jax Draft, Jackson, New Orleans, pull tab 45.00
Kingsbury Malt Tonic, Kingsbury, Sheyboygan, flat top 9.00
Krueger, Krueger, Cranston, pull tab 3.00
Lite, Meister Brau, Chicago, pull tab, 16-oz 28.00
Milwaukee's Best, Gettelman, Milwaukee, flat top 15.00
Old Bohemian Draft, Eastern, Hammonton, flat top 95.00
Old Craft, Oconto, Oconto, flat top 32.00
Old Tavern, Warsaw, Warsaw, pull tab 12.00
Olympia, Olympia, Olympia, pull tab, 16-oz 12.00
Pearl Draft, Pearl, San Antonio, pull tab 3.00
Peil's, Piel Bros, Brooklyn, flat top, 16-oz 90.00
Rainier Ale, Rainier, San Francisco, flat top 32.00
Rolling Rock, Latrobe, Latrobe, pull tab 3.00
Schiltz, Schiltz, Milwaukee, flat top 15.00
Schlitz Vitamin D, Schlitz, Milwaukee, cone top, low profile 90.00
Steinbeck, Grace Bros, Santa Rosa, flat top 20.00
Stroz Draft, Storz, Omaha, pull tab 32.00
Utica Club, West End, Utica, cone top, high profile 185.00
Wellington Malt Liquor, Walter Pueblo, pull tab, 16-oz 5.00

Bellaire, Marc

Marc Bellaire, originally Donald Edmund Fleischman, was born in Toledo, Ohio, in 1925. He studied at the Toledo Museum of Art under Ernest Spring while employed as a designer for the Libbey Glass Company. During World War II while serving in the Navy, he travelled extensively throughout the Pacific, resulting in his enriched sense of design and color.

Marc settled in California in the 1950s where his work attracted the attention of national buyers and agencies who persuaded him to create ceramic lines of his own, employing hand-decorated techniques throughout. This resulted in the building of a studio in Culver City. He produced high-quality ceramics, often decorated with ultramodern figures or geometric patterns and executed with a distinctive flair. His most famous line was Mardi Gras, decorated with slim dancers in spattered and striped colors of black, blue, pink, and white. Other major patterns were Jamaica, Balinese, Beachcomber, Friendly Island, Cave Painting, Hawaiian, Bird Isle, Oriental, Jungle Dancer, and Kashmir. Kashmir usually has the name Ingle on the front and Ballaire on the reverse.

It is to be noted that Marc was employed by Sascha Brastoff during the 1950s. Many believe that he was hired for his creative imagination and style.

During the period of 1951–1956, Marc was named one of the top ten artware designers by *Giftwares Magazine*. After 1956 he taught and lectured on art, design, and ceramic decorating techniques from coast to coast. Many pieces were one of a kind, commissioned throughout the United States.

During the 1970s he set up a studio in Marin County, California, and eventually moved to Palm Springs where he opened his final studio/gallery. There he produced large pieces with a Southwestern style. Mr. Bellaire died in 1994. Our advisor for this category is Marty Webster; he is listed in the Directory under Michigan.

Platter, reclining woman with blue bird in hand on gray background, 14" long, $175.00.

Ashtray, Bird Isle, asymmetrical, 7x14" 100.00
Ashtray, Pastorale, oblong, 14¼" 200.00
Box, Jamaica, 2 male dancers, w/lid, 6x7½" dia 125.00
Candlestick, Jamaica, man w/bongos, 10½" 175.00
Compote, Bali, ftd, oblong, 8x17" 225.00
Compote, prehistoric cave painting, ftd, oblong, 6x12" 125.00
Creamer & sugar bowl, Pastorale 150.00
Dish, abstract, brn & wht on blk, free-form, 13¼x7¼" 140.00
Dish, Balinese Dancers, lav/bl/burgundy bkground, 7x12" 125.00
Dish, Beachcomber, teardrop shape, 12" L 150.00
Dish, blk dancer on rose, free-form, 16" 160.00
Dish, Jamaica, 1 man w/guitar, 1 w/bongos, divided, 10" 175.00
Dish, Mardi Gras, 3-ftd, #B77-15, 15" 225.00
Dish, Pastorale, divided, 10" 175.00
Figurine, Bali Dancers, fancy wht headdress, 24" 1,200.00
Figurine, Island Bongo Drummer, 8½" 425.00
Figurine, Mardi Gras, man seated, very slim, minimum value ..1,200.00

Figurine, Mardi Gras, man standing, very slim, 30", minimum value .1,200.00
Gravy boat, wht flower w/bl leaves on wht-to-bl, w/underplate ...55.00
Pitcher, Sea Gull, 4½" ...110.00
Plate, exotic pear-shaped floral spray, 10" ...65.00
Plate, Hawaiian King & Queen of the Islands, 15" ...225.00
Plate, Jungle Dancer, 12" ...200.00
Plate, Mardi Gras, hanger on bk, 15" ...250.00
Plate, stylized bird on branch, post-Culver City, 15" ...165.00
Plate, 2 angels, 1 w/harp, post-Culver City, 15", minimum ...400.00
Platter, Jungle Dancer, oval, 18x13" ...250.00
Platter, Oriental-style scene of sampans, egg-shape, 14" ...150.00
Tray, Friendly Island, free-form, w/gold, sgn, lg ...175.00
Vase, bl bird in nest on branch, mk 1959, 11" ...125.00
Vase, stick people, brn & blk, beak-like opening, 12" ...300.00

Belleek, American

From 1883 until 1930, several American potteries located in New Jersey and Ohio manufactured a type of china similar to the famous Irish Belleek soft-paste porcelain. The American manufacturers identified their porcelain by using 'Belleek' or 'Beleek' in their marks. American Belleek is considered the highest achievement of the American porcelain industry. Production centered around artistic cabinet pieces and luxury tablewares. Many examples emulated Irish shapes and decor with marine themes and other naturalistic styles. While all are highly collectible, some companies' products are rarer than others. The best-known manufacturers are Ott and Brewer, Willets, The Ceramic Art Company (CAC), and Lenox. You will find more detailed information in those specific categories. Our advisor for this category is Mary Frank Gaston.

Key:
AAC — American Art China

Vase, large pastel flowers on white, embossed gilt decoration on handles, American Art China Works, 12", $1,000.00. (Photo courtesy Mary Frank Gaston)

Bowl, tiny flowers w/in & w/o, gold trim, AAC, 2½x5" ...365.00
Cream soup, Bouquet, Coxon, w/underplate ...235.00
Cup & saucer, morning glories, Morgan ...155.00
Plate, Bouquet, mixed floral on wht, Coxon, 8" ...200.00
Salt cellar, gold sponging, pk int, scalloped border, AAC, 2½" .125.00
Sugar bowl, soft pk int, gold trim, AAC, 2¼" ...275.00
Vase, floral on wht, gold emb hdls, AAC, 12", pr ...2,000.00

Belleek, Irish

Belleek is a very thin translucent porcelain that takes its name from the village in Ireland where it originated in 1859. The glaze is a creamy ivory color with a pearl-like lustre. The tablewares, baskets, figurines, and vases that have always been made there are being crafted yet today. Shamrock, Tridacna, Echinus, and Thorn are but a few of the many patterns of tableware which have been made during some periods of the pottery's history. Throughout the years, their most popular pattern has been Shamrock.

It is possible to date an example to within twenty to thirty years of crafting by the mark. Pieces with an early stamp often bring prices nearly triple that of a similar but current item. With some variation, the marks have always incorporated the Irish wolfhound, Celtic round tower, harp, and shamrocks. The first three marks (usually in black) were used from 1863 to 1946. A series of green marks identified the pottery's offerings from 1946 until the seventh mark (in gold/brown) was introduced in 1980 (it was discontinued in 1992). The most current mark, the eighth, is blue. Belleek Collector's International Society limited edition pieces are designated with a special mark in red. In the listings below, numbers designated with the prefix 'D' relate to the book *Belleek, The Complete Collector's Guide and Illustrated Reference, Second Edition*, by Richard K. Degenhardt (published by Wallace-Homestead Book Company, One Chilton Way, Radnor, PA 19098-0230). Our advisor for this category is Liz Stillwell; she is listed in the Directory under California.

Key:

A — plain (glazed only)	I — 1863–1890
B — cob lustre	II — 1891–1926
C — hand tinted	III — 1926–1946
D — hand painted	IV — 1946–1955
E — hand-painted shamrocks	V — 1955–1965
F — hand gilted	VI — 1965–3/31/1980
G — hand tinted and gilted	VII — 4/1/1980–12/22/1992
H — hand-painted shamrocks and gilted	VIII — 1/4/1993–current

J — mother-of-pearl
K — hand painted and gilted
L — bisque and plain
M — decalcomania
N — special hand-painted decoration
T — transfer design

Further information concerning Periods of Crafting (Baskets):
1 — 1865–1890, BELLEEK (three strand)
2 — 1865–1890, BELLEEK CO. FERMANAGH (three strand)
3 — 1891–1920, BELLEEK CO. FERMANAGH IRELAND (three strand)
4 — 1921–1954, BELLEEK CO. FERMANAGH IRELAND (four strand)
5 — 1955–1979, BELLEEK® CO. FERMANAGH IRELAND (four strand)
6 — 1980–1985, BELLEEK® IRELAND (four strand)
7 — 1985–1989, BELLEEK® IRELAND 'ID NUMBER' (four strand)
8-12 — 1990 to present (Refer to *Belleek, The Complete Collector's Guide and Illustrated Reference, 2nd Edition*, Chapter 5)

Aberdeen Vase, Flowered, D55-II, A, Lg Sz, 8½" ...950.00
Artichoke Tea Ware Tea & Saucer, D709-III, F ...350.00
Belleek Flower Pot, Flowered, D48-IV, J, Mid Sz, 2½" ...150.00
Bust of Clytie, D14-V, L&B, 11¼" ...600.00
Bust of Joy, D1129-V, L&B, 10½" ...600.00
Bust of Shakespeare, D1131-VII, A, 8½" ...200.00
Bust of Sorrow, D1132-VII, L&B, 10½" ...550.00
Celtic Low Shape Tea Ware Tea & Saucer, D1446&57-II, C ...325.00
Celtic Low Shape Tea Ware Teapot, D1458-V, B ...210.00
Cherub Font, D1110-III, L, Lg Sz ...450.00
Clam Shell & Griffin, D140-I, A, 7" ...1,500.00
Cleary Sugar & Cream, D249-VI, B ...75.00
Cone Flower Pot, D223-V, B, Mid Sz, 4" ...75.00

Dairy Sugar, D251-II, A 90.00
Dolphin & Shell, D137-II, C, 7" 695.00
Earthenware Covered Muffin Dish, D859-II, A 250.00
Earthenware Jelly Mould, D882-I, A, 8" 150.00
Earthenware Telegraph Insulator, D1055-No Mk, A 95.00
Feather Vase, D154-VI, B, Lg Sz, 8½" 175.00
Flowered Spill, D45-V, D, Lg Sz, 5" 110.00
Frog Lily Pad Paperweight, D1526-VI, D, 5¼" L 110.00
Harp Shamrock Tea Ware Butter Plate, D1356-IV, E 95.00
Heart Shape Basket, Flowered, D1259-5, D, Sm Sz 450.00
Henshall's Twig Basket, D120-6, A, Lg Sz, 10x8" 2,400.00
Henshall's Twig Basket, Flowered, D1259-5, D, Sm Sz 450.00
Hexagon Salt, D291-II, B 95.00
Hexagon Twig Cake Plate, hdls, D1264-5, A 600.00
Holly Ware, Santa Claus Mug, D1961-VII, D 95.00
Holly Ware, Sugar, D1965-VII, D 40.00
Holly Ware Cream, D1957-VII, D 50.00
Ivy Sugar & Cream, D241-III, B, Sm Sz 150.00
Leaf Plate, D630-IV, B, Sz 3, 5" 60.00
Limpet Shell Salt, D272-III, B 110.00
Limpet Tea Ware Sugar & Cream, D551&52-V, B, Sm Sz 110.00
Limpet Tea Ware Tea & Saucer, D549-III, B 135.00
Lotus Cream, D244-III, A 90.00
Low Lily Tea Ware Tea & Saucer, D518-II, C 425.00
Mask Tea Ware Coffeepot, D1477-VI, B 225.00
Mask Tea Ware Sandwich Tray, D1492-III, B, 11½" 375.00
Neptune Tea Ware Coffee & Saucer, D420-VI, B 75.00
Neptune Tea Ware Teapot, D415-IV, B, Mid Sz 250.00
New Shell Tea Ware Cream, D1382-V, B, Lg Sz 65.00
Nile Vase, D86-III, B, Sm Sz, 7" 350.00
Oak Leaf Bowl, VIII, F, 8" 70.00
Owl Spill, D1774-V, B, 8¼" 95.00
Pocket Watch Stand, D2097-I, C 3,000.00
Prince of Wales Ice Pail, rstr, D3-I, L, 18½" 3,000.00
Princess Vase, Flowered, D60-V, D, 9" 750.00
Ribbon Sugar & Cream, D243-IV, B 95.00
Rock Spill, D162-IV, B, Mid Sz, 5" 175.00
Scroll Vase, D1779-VI, C, 7" 60.00
Shamrock Biscuit Jar, D541-V, E 225.00
Shamrock Tea Ware Coffeepot, D1319-IV, E 225.00
Shamrock Tea Ware Milk Jug, D390-II, E 300.00
Shamrock Tea Ware Moustache & Saucer, D374-II, H 450.00
Shamrock Trinket Box, D112-III, A, 2" 450.00
Shamrock Trunk Stump Spill, D1224-IV, E, 6¼" 75.00
Shamrock Ware Berry Dish, D1316-III, E, 6½" 125.00
Shamrock Ware Dinner Plate, D1330-III, E, 10½" 150.00
Shamrock Ware Letter Opener, D2011-VII, F 80.00
Shamrock Ware Milk Jug, Flat, D1326-IV, E, Sm Sz 100.00
Shell Cream, D601-I, A, Lg Sz 650.00
Shepherd & Dog Candle Holder, D1603-I, G, 7" dia 3,000.00
Single Root Spill, D151-II, D, 3" 475.00
Sunflower Vase, D188-V, B, 7" 100.00
Thistle Top Vase, Flowered, D1782-III, A, 5¼" 325.00
Thorn Tea Ware Teapot, D759-II, K, 7" L 1,050.00
Thorn Vase, D1784-VII, D, Sm Sz, 4½" 45.00
Toy Shamrock Sugar & Cream, D234-V, E 90.00
Tridacna Tea Ware Butter Plate, D1345-III, B, 5" 100.00
Tridacna Tea Ware Coffeepot, D1346-III, B 425.00
Tridacna Tea Ware Cream, D474-II, Bl, Lg Sz 225.00
Tridacna Tea Ware Teapot, D475-V, B, Lg Sz 200.00
Tub Salt, D290-IV, B, Sm Sz 60.00
Tyrone Vase, D1791-VII, K, 8½" 125.00
Undine Cream, D305-V, B 90.00
Victoria Shell, D128-V, B, 8" 400.00
Wicklow Vase, D1796-VII, C, 6½" 70.00

Bells

Some areas of interest represented in the study of bells are history, religion, and geography. Since Biblical times, bells have announced morning church services, vespers, deaths, christenings, school hours, fires, and community events. Countries have used them en masse to peal out the good news of Christmas, New Year's, and the endings of World Wars I and II. They've been rung in times of great sorrow, such as the death of Abraham Lincoln.

Dorothy Malone Anthony is the author of a series of ten books entitled *World of Bells*. Her address is in the Directory under Kansas. All have over two hundred colored pictures covering many bell categories. See also Nodders; Schoolhouse Collectibles.

Korean gong repro, 12", $120.00. (Original made in Korea about 770 A.D. weighing 7.2 tons.) (Photo courtesy Dorothy Malone Anthony)

Anri 'Bouquet' girl, 4" 70.00
Brass, Australian Condamine 'bull frog,' 5½" 35.00
Brass, Conestoga, 4 bells on metal strap, 12½" H 150.00
Brass, Hindu naga hdl, 5½" 30.00
Brass, Kiwanis speaker's bell, 11" 100.00
Brass, sailor boy holding mechanical bell, 8" 150.00
Brass, Tsar Kolokol replica, 5¾" 175.00
China, American Gothic by Rivershore, 6½" 50.00
China, Methodist 200th Anniversary, wht bsk, 4½" 35.00
China, Paragon, Tree of Kashmir, 4¾" 30.00
China, Staffordshire lady holding teacup, blk & wht, 6" 125.00
Chinese enamel, Foo Dog hdl, 4" 75.00
Colorado alabaster, 4¾" 75.00
Glass, cobalt (tall) w/clear hdl, English, 10½" 250.00
Glass, Lalique, bird hdl w/closed wings, 5" 300.00
Pottery, Todd Warner Arabian camel, 9" 60.00
Pottery, Wedgwood '4 Seasons,' gr 75.00
Pottery, 12 Japanese Zodiac figures, 2-3" 75.00

Bennington

Although the term has become a generic one for the mottled brown ware produced there, Bennington is not a type of pottery, but rather a town in Vermont where two important potteries were located. The Norton Company, founded in 1793, produced mainly redware and salt-glazed stoneware; only during a brief partnership with Fenton (1845–47) was any Rockingham attempted. The Norton Company endured until 1894, operated by succeeding generations of the Norton family. Fenton organized his own pottery in 1847. There he manufactured not only redware and stoneware, but more artistic types as well — graniteware, scroddled ware, flint enamel, a fine parian, and vast amounts of their famous Rockingham. Though from an esthetic standpoint his work rated highly among the country's finest ceramic achievements, he was economically unsuccessful. His pottery closed in 1858.

It is estimated that only one in five Fenton pieces were marked; and although it has become a common practice to link any fine piece of Rockingham to this area, careful study is vital in order to be able to distinguish Bennington's from the similar wares of many other American and Staffordshire potteries. Although the practice was without the permission of the proprietor, it was nevertheless a common occurrence for a potter to take his molds with him when moving from one pottery to the next, so particularly well-received designs were often reproduced at several locations. Of eight known Fenton marks, four are variations of the '1849' impressed stamp: 'Lyman Fenton Co., Fenton's Enamel Patented 1849, Bennington, Vermont.' These are generally found on examples of Rockingham and flint enamel. A raised, rectangular scroll with 'Fenton's Works, Bennington, Vermont,' was used on early examples of porcelain. From 1852 to 1858, the company operated under the title of the United States Pottery Company. Three marks — the ribbon mark with the initials USP, the oval with a scrollwork border and the name in full, and the plain oval with the name in full — were used during that period.

Among the more sought-after examples are the bird and animal figurines, novelty pitchers, figural bottles, and all of the more finely modeled items. Recumbent deer, cows, standing lions with one forepaw on a ball, and opposing pairs of poodles with baskets in their mouths and 'coleslaw' fur were made in Rockingham, flint enamel, and occasionally in parian. Numbers in the listings below refer to the book *Bennington Pottery and Porcelain* by Barret. Our advisors for Bennington (except for parian and stoneware) are Barbara and Charles Adams; they are listed in the Directory under Massachusetts.

Key: c/s — cobalt on salt glaze

Book flask, Life of Kossuth, flint enamel, sm line, 5¾" 575.00
Bottle, Coachman/Toby, Rockingham, brn & orange on tan, 1849 mk, 11" 750.00
Candlestick, flint enamel, flanged base, flaw, 7¾" 385.00
Candlestick, Rockingham, chip, 7¾" 465.00
Cuspidor, flint enamel, brn & tan, 1849 mk, 4x9" 250.00
Cuspidor, flint enamel, brn w/dk gr & bl, emb seashells, 10½" dia .140.00
Cuspidor, Rockingham, imp 1849 mk, 9" dia 250.00
Humidor, flint enamel, emb ribs, Lyman Fenton, ca 1850, 7" 475.00
Inkwell, Rockingham, emb shells, quill holes/central well, 4½" dia .1,400.00
Jar, Toby, lt gr sponging, brn-amber int, 1848 mk, 4½", EX 650.00
Jug, Centennial Augt 16th 1877, brn slip covered, 3¼x2" 50.00
Pitcher, bl & wht, Paul & Virginia pattern, lozenge mk, 9¼" 700.00
Pitcher, flint enamel, brn w/bl & gr on lower ribs, 1849 mk, 12¾" 1,500.00
Pitcher, flint enamel, sm heart at tip of ea rib, Lyman Fenton, 10" 900.00
Pitcher, Graniteware, Wild Rose, Fenton's Works mk, 1845-47, 10¼" 300.00
Pitcher, milk; Rockingham, floral panels, hexagonal, rpr, 6¾" ..150.00
Pitcher, Rockingham, Cupid & Psyche, scalloped rim, rpr, 9¾" ...250.00
Pitcher, Rockingham, hound hdl, emb hunt scenes, 9", EX 475.00
Pitcher, Rockingham, swirled alternate ribs, sm chip on base, 10" ..800.00
Pitcher, Toby, Rockingham, grapevine hdl, Pat 1849 mk, rpr, 6" 350.00
Pitcher, Toby, Rockingham, 6" 250.00
Snuff jar, Toby, Rockingham, lt wear to rim, 19th C, 19th C, 4⅛" ..525.00
Soap dish, Rockingham, acanthus leaves at rim, pierced, 6½" dia 150.00
Wash bowl & pitcher, flint enamel, Scalloped Rib, prof rprs ..1,500.00

Stoneware

Churn, #3/flower, c/s, J&E Norton, rstr line, ca 1859, 15½" 715.00
Crock, #2/birds (Xd), c/s, E&LP Norton, rstr, ca 1880, 9" 1,300.00
Crock, #2/flower, c/s, E&LP Norton, chip, ca 1870, 9" 165.00
Crock, #2/flower, c/s, J&E Norton, stain on bk, ca 1859, 10½" .850.00
Crock, #3/bird on plume, E&LP Norton, rstr, ca 1870, 10½" 450.00
Crock, #3/flower (dbl), c/s, J&E Norton, hairline, ca 1859, 10" 355.00
Crock, #4/flower (dbl), J&E Norton, rstr, ca 1855, 13¾" 415.00
Crock, #5/chicken pecking corn, c/s, J Norton & Co, line/rstr, 13" ...1,300.00
Crock, #6/flower basket, c/s, J Norton, ca 1880, 13" 3,200.00
Crock, cake; #1½/flower, c/s, J Norton & Co, ca 1859, 7", EX ..770.00
Jar, #1½/flower, c/s, E&LP Norton, rpl lid, ca 1870, 10" 300.00
Jug, #1/bird on log, c/s, J&E Norton, ca 1855, 11" 550.00
Jug, #2/flower (triple), c/s, Norton & Fenton, ca 1845, 12½" 580.00
Jug, #2/flower (triple), c/s, Norton & Fenton, rpr, ca 1845, 12½" .385.00
Jug, #3/bird (dbl), c/s, J Norton, spider/chips, ca 1859, 15½" 800.00
Jug, #3/flower, c/s, J&E Norton, stain, ca 1859, 15" 385.00
Jug, #3/flower (stylized), c/s, E&LP Norton, ca 1880, 15½" 220.00
Jug, #3/peacock on stump, c/s, J&E Norton, ca 1859, 15" 2,975.00

Beswick

In the early 1890s, James Wright Beswick operated a pottery in Longston, England, where he produced fine dinnerware as well as ornamental ceramics. Today's collectors are most interested in the figurines made since 1936 by a later generation Beswick firm, John Beswick, Ltd. They specialize in reproducing accurately detailed bone-china models of authentic breeds of animals. Their Fireside Series includes dogs, cats, elephants, horses, the Huntsman, and an Indian figure, which measure up to 14" in height. The Connoisseur line is modeled after the likenesses of famous racing horses. Beatrix Potter's characters and some of Walt Disney's are charmingly re-created and appeal to children and adults alike. Other items, such as character Tobys, have also been produced. The Beswick name is stamped on each piece. The firm was absorbed by the Doulton group in 1973. Our advisor for this category is Nicki Budin; she is listed in the Directory under Ohio.

Condiment set, 1950s, $120.00.

Cheese dish, floral, emb/pnt on gr, flower finial 55.00
Figurine, Amiable Guinea Pig 180.00
Figurine, Anna Maria, Beatrix Potter, gold mk 375.00
Figurine, Benjamin Bunny, Beatrix Potter, V2, brn mk 125.00
Figurine, Benjamin Bunny, ears & shoes out, 2st version 250.00
Figurine, Chesshire Cat 500.00
Figurine, Duchess, Beatrix Potter, 3rd mk, #2601 ....175.00
Figurine, Eeyore, Owl or Piglet, ea 99.00
Figurine, Felia Cat, David Hand, rare 550.00
Figurine, Fish Footman, Alice series 285.00
Figurine, Hunca Munca, Beatrix Potter, C3 ....65.00
Figurine, Jemima Puddleduck, Beatrix Potter, B3 ....65.00
Figurine, Kitty MacBride Racegoer 55.00
Figurine, Miss Moppet, Beatrix Potter, 3B 55.00
Figurine, Mr Alderman Ptolemy, Beatrix Potter, B6 ....65.00
Figurine, Mr Jackson Green Frog, rare 475.00
Figurine, Mr Jeremy Fisher, Beatrix Potter, C3 ....70.00

Figurine, Mrs Tittlemouse, PB1, gold mk 325.00
Figurine, Old English Sheepdog, #453 ....150.00
Figurine, Old Mr Brown, Beatrix Potter, brn mk 75.00
Figurine, Old Woman in Shoe, brn mk 50.00
Figurine, Persian cat, gray, #1867, lg 72.00
Figurine, Pigling Bland, Beatrix Potter, 1st paper label 390.00
Figurine, Siamese kittens, #1296 ....45.00
Figurine, Squirrel Nutkin, Beatrix Potter, brn mk 75.00
Figurine, Susan, Beatrix Potter, ca 1983, 4" 225.00
Figurine, Tabitha Twitchett, Beatrix Potter, B3 ....75.00
Figurine, Tigger, Rabbit or Pooh, ea 125.00
Figurine, Tom Kitten, Beatrix Potter, 1st version, 3B 85.00
Figurine, Tony Weller, #281 ....50.00
Plate, Christmas in Mexico 45.00
Toby jug, Barnaby Rudge 70.00
Toby mug, Sairey Gamp, #372, MIE, 6⅝" 50.00
Toby mug, Scrooge, #372, MIE, 6¾" 25.00

Big Little Books

The first Big Little Book was published in 1933 and copyrighted in 1932 by the Whitman Publishing Company of Racine, Wisconsin. Its hero was Dick Tracy. The concept was so well accepted that others soon followed Whitman's example; and though the 'Big Little Book' phrase became a trademark of the Whitman Company, the formats of his competitors (Saalfield, Goldsmith, Van Wiseman, Lynn, and World Syndicate) were exact copies. Today's Big Little Book buffs collect them all.

These hand-sized sagas of adventure were illustrated with full-page cartoons on the right-hand page and the story narration on the left. Colorful cardboard covers contained hundreds of pages, usually totaling over an inch in thickness. Big Little Books originally sold for 10¢ at the dime store; as late as the mid-1950s when the popularity of comic books caused sales to decline, signaling an end to production, their price had risen to a mere 20¢. Their appeal was directed toward the pre-teens who bought, traded, and hoarded Big Little Books. Because so many were stored in attics and closets, many have survived. Among the super heroes are G-Men, Flash Gordon, Tarzan, the Lone Ranger, and Red Ryder; in a lighter vein, you'll find such lovable characters as Blondie and Dagwood, Mickey Mouse, Little Orphan Annie, and Felix the Cat.

In the early to mid-'30s, Whitman published several Big Little Books as advertising premiums for the Coco Malt Company, who packed them in boxes of their cereal. These are highly prized by today's collectors, as are Disney stories and super-hero adventures.

For more information we recommend *Big Little Books, A Collectors Reference and Value Guide*, by Larry Jacobs (Collector Books). Our advisor for this category is Ron Donnelly; he is listed in the Directory under Alabama.

Note: At the present time, the market for these books is fairly stable — values for common examples are actually dropping. Only the rare, character-related titles are increasing.

Ace Drummond, Whitman #1177, EX 35.00
Adventures of Popeye, Saalfield #1051, 1934, scarce, EX 150.00
Andy Panda & Tiny Tom, Whitman #1425, 1944, EX 25.00
Bambi's Children, Whitman #1497, 1943, VG 45.00
Betty Boop in Miss Gulliver's Travels, Whitman #1158, NM 140.00
Billy the Kid, Whitman #773, 1935, EX 35.00
Buccaneers, Whitman #1646, 1958, VG 15.00
Buck Jones & the Two Gun Kid, Whitman #1404, 1937, EX 35.00
Bugs Bunny & the Pirate Loot, Whitman #1403, 1947, EX 40.00
Buz Sawyer & Bomber 13, Whitman #1415, 1946, VG 35.00
Captain Midnight & the Moon Woman, Whitman #1452, 1943, EX ..75.00
Convoy Patrol, Whitman #1469, 1942, NM 35.00
Dan Dunn & the Border Smugglers, Whitman #1481, 1938, EX .35.00
Dan Dunn on the Trail of Wu Fang, Whitman #1454, 1938, EX .35.00
Dectective Dick Tracy & the Spider Gang, Whitman #1446, EX ..75.00
Dick Tracy & the Boris Arson Gang, Whitman #1163, NM 65.00
Dick Tracy & the Tiger Lily Gang, Whitman #1460, 1949, VG ..35.00
Dick Tracy Returns, Whitman #1495, 1939, NM 75.00
Dick Tracy Solves the Penfield Mystery, Whitman #1137, VG ...55.00
Donald Duck Gets Fed Up, Whitman #1462, NM 70.00
Donald Duck Off the Beam, Whitman #1438, EX 60.00
Donald Duck Up in the Air, Whitman #1486, NM 55.00
Ella Cinders & the Mysterious House, Whitman #1106, NM 55.00
Ellery Queen Adventure of the Last Man Club, Whitman #1406, NM .50.00

Flash Gordon and the Monsters of Mongo, #1166, 1935, VG, $75.00; Buck Rogers 25th Century A.D. in the War With the Planet Venus, Better Little Book, Whitman #1437, 1938, VG, $75.00.

Flash Gordon & the Red Sword Invaders, Whitman #1479, 1945, EX ..70.00
Flash Gordon in the Jungles of Mongo, Whitman #1424, EX 60.00
Flying the Sky Clipper w/Winsie Atkins, Whitman #1108, EX ...30.00
G-Man & the Radio Bank Robberies, Whitman #1434, 1937, EX ...45.00
G-Man Breaking the Gambling Ring, Whitman #1493, 1938, NM .50.00
G-Men on the Job, Whitman #1168, 1935, EX 45.00
Gene Autry in Red Bandits Ghost, Whitman #1461, 1949, EX ..35.00
Gene Autry Special Ranger, Whitman #1428, 1941, EX+ 50.00
Green Hornet Cracks Down, Whitman #1480, NM 135.00
Green Hornet Returns, Whitman #1496, 1941, NM 145.00
Houdini's Big Little Book of Magic, Whitman #715, NM 65.00
In the Name of the Law, Whitman #1124, EX 30.00
Inspector Wade Solves the Mystery of the Red Aces, Whitman #1148, EX ..35.00
Jack Swift & His Rocket Ship, Whitman #1102, EX 50.00
Jane Withers in Keep Smiling, Whitman #1463, EX 45.00
Jim Starr of the Border Patrol, Whitman #1428, EX 25.00
Jimmy Allen in the Air Mail Robbery, Whitman #1143, 1936, EX ..35.00
Joe Palooka's Great Adventure, Whitman #1168, VG 35.00
Jungle Jim & the Vampire Woman, Whitman #1139, 1937, EX+ ..75.00
Junior G-Men, Whitman #1442, 1937, EX 35.00
Katzenjammer Kids in the Mountains, Saalfield #1055, 1934, rare, EX+ 85.00
Kay Darcy & the Mystery Hideout, Whitman #1411, EX 35.00
Li'l Abner in New York, Whitman #1198, 1936, EX 60.00
Little Orphan Anne & Chizzler, Whitman #748, 1933, VG 55.00
Little Orphan Annie & the Mysterious Shoemaker, Whitman #1449, NM ...60.00
Lone Ranger & the Barbary Coast, Whitman #1421, 1944, VG ..30.00
Lone Ranger & the Menace of Murder Valley, Whitman #1465, EX ..40.00
Lone Ranger & the Vanishing Herd, Whitman #1196, NM 60.00
Mandrake the Magician & the Flame Pearls, Whitman #1418, NM ..55.00
Marge's Little Lulu, Alvin & Tubby, Whitman #1429, NM 60.00
Mickey Mouse & Pluto the Racer, Whitman #1128, 1936, EX 75.00
Mickey Mouse & the Lazy Daisy Mystery, Whitman #1433, 1947, EX .60.00
Mickey Mouse & the Stolen Jewels, Whitman #1464, NM 60.00
Mickey Mouse in the Foreign Legion, Whitman #1428, 1940, EX .65.00

Moon Mullins & the Plushbottom Twins, Whitman #1134, VG .35.00
Oswald the Lucky Rabbit, Whitman #1109, EX 60.00
Our Gang on the March, Whitman #1451, 1942, NM 45.00
Perry Winkle & the Rinkydinks, Whitman #1199, EX 40.00
Phantom & the Girl of Mystery, Whitman #1416, NM 60.00
Pinocchio & Jiminy Cricket, Whitman #1435, 1940, NM 65.00
Popeye & Queen Olive Oyl, Whitman #1458, EX 45.00
Popeye Ghost Ship to Treasure Island, Whitman #2008, 1967, VG .10.00
Radio Patrol Outwitting Gang Chief, Whitman #1496, EX 35.00
Red Ryder & Little Beaver on Hoofs of Thunder, Whitman #1400, EX ..50.00
Red Ryder in Circus Luck, Whitman #1466, 1947, EX 35.00
Return of Tarzan, Whitman #1102, 1936, EX 75.00
Return of the Phantom, Whitman #1489, 1942, VG- 60.00
Roy Rogers King of the Cowboys, Whitman #1476, NM 55.00
Scrappy, Whitman #1122, NM 70.00
Skeezix Goes to War, Whitman #1414, EX 35.00
Smilin' Jack & the Jungle Pipe Line, Whitman #1419, EX 45.00
Smitty & Herby Lost Among the Indians, Whitman #1404, 1941, EX .35.00
Snow White & the Seven Dwarfs, Whitman #1460, 1938, VG ..60.00
Tailspin Tommy & the Sky Bandits, Whitman #1494, NM 45.00
Tarzan & the Ant Men, Whitman #1444, 1945, NM 65.00
Terry & the Pirates Shipwrecked on Desert Island, Whitman #1412, EX 45.00
Thumper & the Seven Dwarfs, Whitman #1409, 1944. M, ...70.00
Tim McCoy, the Prescott Kid, Whitman #1152, 1935, VG 40.00
Tim McCoy on Tomahawk Trail, Whitman #1436, EX 35.00
Tim Tyler's Luck, Adventure in the Ivory Patrol, Whitman #1140, VG 40.00
Tom Mix & His Circus on the Barbary Coast, Whitman #1482, 1940, EX .45.00
Tom Mix Plays Lone Hand, Whitman #1173, 1935, VG 45.00
Uncle Sam's Sky Defenders, Whitman #1461, EX 30.00
Uncle Wiggily's Adventures, Whitman #1405, EX 40.00
Wash Tubbs & Captain Easy Hunting for Whales, Whitman #1455, NM .40.00
Wash Tubbs in Pandemonia, Whitman #751, EX 35.00
Zane Grey's King of the Royal Mounted Gets His Man, Whitman #1452, EX ..45.00
Zip Saunders King of the Speedway, Whitman #1465, NM 25.00

Bing and Grondahl

In 1853 brothers M.H. and J.H. Bing formed a partnership with Frederick Vilhelm Grondahl in Copenhagen, Denmark. Their early wares were porcelain plaques and figurines designed by the noted sculptor Thorvaldsen of Denmark. Dinnerware production began in 1863, and by 1889 their underglaze color 'Copenhagen Blue' had earned them worldwide acclaim. They are perhaps most famous today for their Christmas plates, the first of which was made in 1895. See also Limited Edition Plates.

Ashtray, Lily of the Valley, scalloped, free-form, 5" 28.00
Bowl, Sea Gull, w/lid, rnd, 11" 365.00
Bowl, serving; Sea Gull, mk, 9½" 70.00
Bowl, warmer; Sea Gull, 3" 60.00
Cake dish, Sea Gull, ftd, 6" dia 100.00
Candlesticks, Sea Gull, hdls emerge from base, curve to cup, 5", pr .85.00
Cigarette holder, Sea Gull, 2½" dia 22.00
Condiment set, Sea Gull shakers, mustard & 5½" triangular tray ..275.00
Figurine, bird singing, #1852, 3x3" 45.00
Figurine, boy & girl reading, #1567, 4x3½", from $125 to 175.00
Figurine, boy playing accordion, #1991, 9" 250.00
Figurine, boy w/crab near bare toes, #1870, 7¾" 190.00
Figurine, boy w/dog, #1951, 3¾x5x3" 120.00
Figurine, boy w/flute, #1897, 11" 280.00
Figurine, boy w/puppy, #1747, 6¾" 170.00
Figurine, bull, brn & wht, #2121, 8x14" 780.00
Figurine, calf laying down w/head turn bk, #2168, 2x3" 50.00
Figurine, cat, sitting, gray & wht, #1876, 5", from $70 to 100.00
Figurine, catfish, gray, #2144, 4x1¾" 35.00
Figurine, English Pointer puppy, #444, 4½x7" 200.00
Figurine, Eskimo w/arms clasped overhead, #2417, 4½" 100.00
Figurine, Fisherman's Wife, #2233, 8½", from $350 to 425.00
Figurine, girl knitting, #1656, 6⅝" 125.00
Figurine, girl putting milk into milk can, #2181, 8½" 310.00
Figurine, girl w/cat in basket, #4429, 4x4" 140.00
Figurine, girl w/doll, #1526, 3½x4¼", from $90 to 110.00
Figurine, Hans Christian Andersen, #2037, 9½" 380.00
Figurine, Love Refused, #1614, 7", from $165 to 210.00
Figurine, Palace Guard, #2342, 10¾" 240.00
Figurine, penguin, #1821, 3¼x2¼" 50.00
Figurine, polar bear, pacing, 2½x5" 95.00
Figurine, Russian Wolfhound, #1811, 5x12" 340.00
Figurine, sea gull w/fish in mouth, #1808, 2x6" 75.00
Figurine, Two Friends, boy w/bulldog, #1790, 4¾", from $175 to ...250.00
Figurine, Youthful Boldness, couple kissing, #2162, 7½" 260.00
Figurine, 2 boys, #1648, 7¾" 145.00
Gravy boat, Sea Gull, w/hdls, 9" 140.00
Pitcher, Sea Gull, #189, 4" 100.00
Pitcher, Sea Gull, 9" 280.00
Plate, salad; Sea Gull, 7½" 30.00
Plate, Sea Gull, 8½" 40.00
Platter, Sea Gull, w/open hdls, 10½" 70.00
Tray, serving; Sea Gull, rnd, 13" 110.00
Vase, lt brn & beige w/lg leaf decor & Oriental writing 125.00

Binoculars

There are several types of binoculars, and the terminology used to refer to them is not consistent or precise. Generally, 'field glasses' refers to simple Galilean optics, where the lens next to the eye (the ocular) is concave and dished away from the eye. By looking through the large lens (the objective), it is easy to see that the light goes straight through the two lenses. These are lower power, have a very small field of view, and do not work nearly as well as prism binoculars. In a smaller size, they are opera glasses, and their price increases if they are covered with mother-of-pearl (fairly common but very attractive), abalone shell (more colorful), ivory (quite scarce), or other exotic materials. Field glasses are not valuable unless very unusual or by the best makers, such as Zeiss or Leitz. Prism binoculars have the objective lens offset from the eyepiece and give a much better view. This is the standard binocular form, called Porro prisms, and dates from around 1900. Another type of prism binocular is the roof prism, which at first resembles the straight-through field glasses, with two simple cylinders or cones, here containing very small prisms. These can be distinguished by the high quality views they give and by a thin diagonal line that can be seen when looking backwards through the objective. In general, German binoculars are the most desirable, followed by American, English, and finally French, which can be of good quality but are very common unless of unusual configuration. Japanese optics of WWII or before are often of very high quality. 'Made in Occupied Japan' binoculars are very common, but collectors prize those by Nippon Kogaku (Nikon). Some binoculars are center focus (CF), with one central wheel that focuses both sides at once. These are much easier to use but more difficult to seal against dirt and moisture. Individual focus (IF) binoculars are adjusted by rotating each eyepiece and tend to be cleaner inside in older optics. Each type is preferred by different collectors. Very large binoculars are always of great interest. All binoculars are numbered according to their magnifying power and the diameter of the objective in millimeters. 6 x 30 optics magnify six times and have 30 millimeter objectives.

Prisms are easily knocked out of alignment, requiring an expensive and difficult repair. If severe, this misalignment is immediately noticeable on use by the double-image scene. Minor damage can be seen by focusing on a small object and slowly moving the binoculars away from the eye, which will cause the images to appear to separate. Overall cleanliness should be checked by looking backwards (through the objective) at a light or the sky, when any film or dirt on the lenses or prisms can easily be seen. Pristine binoculars are worth far more than when dirty or misaligned, and broken or cracked optics lower the value far more. Cases help keep binoculars clean but do not add materially to the value.

As of 1999, any significant changes in value are due to Internet sales. Some of the prices listed here are lower than would be reached at an online auction. Revisions of these values would be inappropriate at this point for these reasons: First, values are fluctuating wildly on the Internet; 'auction fever' is extreme. Second, some common instruments can fetch a high price at an Internet sale, and it is clear that the price will not be supported as more of them are placed at auction. In fact, an overlooked collectible like the binocular will be subject to a great increase in supply as they are retrieved from closets in response to the values people see at an online auction. Third, sellers who have access to these Internet auctions can use them for price guides if they wish, but the values in this listing have to reflect what can be obtained at an average large antique show. The following listings assume a very good overall condition, with generally clean and aligned optics.

Our advisor for this category is Peter Abrahams, who studies and collects binoculars and other optics. Please contact, especially to exchange reference material (SASE required with written questions). Mr. Abrahams is listed in the Directory under Oregon.

Field Glasses

Fernglas 08, German WWI, 6x39, military gr, many makers 50.00
Folding, modern, hinged flat case, oculars outside 10.00
Folding or telescoping, no bbls, old 100.00
Ivory covered, various sm szs & makers 180.00
LeMaire, bl leather/brass, various szs & makers 25.00
Metal, emb hunting scene, various sm szs & makers 65.00
Pearl covered, various sm szs & makers 90.00
Porc covered, delicate painting, various szs & makers 185.00
US Naval Gun Factory Optical Shop 6x30 ....85.00
Zeiss 'Galan' 2.5x34, modern design look, early 1920s 120.00

Prism Binoculars (Porro)

Barr & Stroud, 7x50, Porro II prisms, IF, WWII 110.00
Bausch & Lomb, 6x30, IF, WWI, Signal Corps 50.00
Bausch & Lomb, 7x50, IF, WWII, other makers same 85.00
Bausch & Lomb Zephyr, 7x35 & other, CF 120.00
Bausch & Lomb/Zeiss, Pat 1897, 8x17, CF 140.00
Crown Optical, 6x30, IF, WWI, filters 65.00
France, various makers & szs, if not unusual 30.00
German WWII 10x80, eyepcs at 45 degrees, 3-letter code (makers) .450.00
German WWII 6x30, 3-letter code for various makers 60.00
Goertz Trieder Binocle, various szs, unusual adjustment 75.00
Huet, Paris 7x22, other sm szs, unusual shapes 80.00
Leitz 6x30 Dienstglas, IF, good optics 65.00
Leitz 8x30 Binuxit, CF, 1950s 150.00
M19, US military 7x50, ca 1980 ....170.00
Nikon 9x35, 7x35, CF, 1950s 85.00
Nippon Kogaku, 7x50, IF, Made in Occupied Japan 150.00
Ross Stepnada, 7x30, CF, wide angle, 1930s 250.00
Ross 6x30, standard British WWI issue 50.00
Sard, 6x42, IF, very wide angle, WWII 800.00
Toko (Tokyo Opt Co) 7x50, IF, Made in Occupied Japan 55.00
Universal Camera 6x30, IF, WWII, other makers same 50.00
US Naval Gun Factory Optical Shop 6x30, IF, filters, WWI 90.00
US Naval Gun Factory Optical 10x45, IF, WWI 210.00
US Navy, 20x120, various makers, WWII & later 2,500.00
Warner & Swasey (important maker) 8x20, CF, 1902 ....250.00
Wollensak 6x30, ca 1940 ....50.00
Zeiss Deltrintem 8x30, CF, 1930s 95.00
Zeiss DF 95, 6x18, sq shoulder, very early 150.00
Zeiss Starmorbi 12/23/42x60, turret eyepcs, 1920s 2,200.00
Zeiss Teleater 3x13, CF, bl, leather 100.00
Zeiss 15x60, CF or IF, various models 800.00
Zeiss 8x40 Delactis, CF or IF, 1930s 240.00

Roof Prism Binoculars

Hensoldt Dialyt, various szs, long tapered bbl, 1930s-80s 130.00
Hensoldt Universal Dialyt, 6x26, 3.5x26, cylindrical, 1920s 100.00
Leitz Trinovid, 7x42 & other, CF, 1960s-80s, EX 475.00
Zeiss Dialyt, 8x30, CF, 1960s 400.00

Birdcages

Birdcages can be found in various architectural styles and in a range of materials such as wood, wicker, brass, and gilt metal with ormolu mounts. Those that once belonged to the wealthy are sometimes inlaid with silver or jewels. In the 1800s, it became fashionable to keep birds, and some of the most beautiful examples found today date back to that era. Musical cages that contained automated bird figures became popular; today these command prices of several thousand dollars. In the latter 1800s, wicker styles came into vogue. Collectors still appreciate their graceful lines and find they adapt easily to modern homes.

Victorian Gothic Revival, carved and painted wood and wire, removable carved acanthus leaf base, nineteenth century, 19¼x20¼x15¾", $1,000.00.

Chinese export, cvd wooden boat form, ornate, ca 1900, 27x17" 500.00
Chinese export, porc/ivory/boxwood/jade/cloisonne mts, 1900s, 27" .425.00
Cvd wood & wirework, Nouveau style, 36" 1,500.00
Folk art w/domed wire top orig red pnt 115.00
Toleware w/old wht pnt, blk & gold highlights, wrought stand, 71" ..250.00
Walnut & wire w/pnt traces, old worn patina, crown crest, 17x11x11" ...600.00
Wicker, crescent moon floor stand 800.00
Wood w/wire bars, trn ft/posts, detailed cornice, pnt, 18" 335.00
Wooden dowels form top & sides, solid wood base, 2 perches, 6" .45.00

Bisque

Bisque is a term referring to unglazed earthenware or porcelain that has been fired only once. During the Victorian era, bisque figurines became very popular. Most were highly decorated in pastels and gilt and demonstrated a fine degree of workmanship in the quality of their modeling. Few were marked. See also Heubach; Nodders; Dolls; Piano Babies.

Black African princess, mc & gold, Fr, 11x3½" 500.00

Boy & girl in chairs, fancy clothes, gold trim, 5¼", pr 145.00
Candlesticks, girl (boy) on base, 2-arm, 8", pr 275.00
Cherubs support rtcl vase, gold trim, 9" 200.00
Cupid & Psyche on demilune base, rstr wing, 9½x12" 250.00
Dog, Spitz, Steinbach, 5½" 140.00
Lady dancing, man w/mandolin, mc, 1880s, 16", pr 365.00
Lamp, boy & girl, dancing bear on balcony, Germany, 11" 150.00
Planter, fox in clothes beside open stump, Germany 135.00

Black Americana

Black memorabilia is without a doubt a field that encompasses the most widely exploited ethnic group in our history. But within this field there are many levels of interest: arts and achievements such as folk music and literature, caricatures in advertising, souvenirs, toys, fine art, and legitimate research into the days of their enslavement and enduring struggle for equality. The list is endless.

In the listings below are some with a derogatory connotation. Thankfully, these are from a bygone era and represent the mores of a culture that existed nearly a century ago. They are included only to convey the fact that they are a part of this growing area of collecting interest. Black Americana catalogs featuring a wide variety of items for sale are available; see the Directory under Clubs, Newsletters, and Catalogs for more information. We also recommend *Black Collectibles* by P.J. Gibbs; and *Black Dolls, Books I* and *II,* by Myla Perkins, all published by Collector Books. See also Cookie Jars; Postcards; Posters; Sheet Music.

Alarm clock, I'm on the Go, child on pot, nonworking, 5x6", VG ..200.00
Alarm clock, travel; Amos 'N Andy, leather-type case, 4", EX ..900.00
Alarm clock, woman washing, cb face, ftd, Waterbury, 6" dia, EX ..650.00
Ashtray stand, butler w/removable tray, pnt CI, 33", VG 500.00
Banner, Here Today! Aunt Jemima..., cloth, 34x58", EX 500.00
Book, Little Black Sambo & Tiger Kitten, Ver Beck, 1935, hardbk, EX .125.00
Book, Pickaninny Twins, Lucy F Perkins, 1st ed, 1931, hardbk, EX ...165.00
Book, Watermelon Pete & Other Stories, E Gordon, 1937, hardbk, EX ...85.00
Bootscraper/shiner, pnt CI Mammy atop, 15x16x9", VG 425.00
Card, get well, Mammy standing on scale, scalloped edge, 1930s, EX ..30.00
Clock, Drink Topsy/City Dairy, tin, 14x14", EX 275.00
Clock, Joe Lewis World Champion, molded copper, electric, 12", EX ..500.00
Clock, Nanny, pnt wood half-figure, eyes move w/pendulum, EXIB 325.00
Coaster, Sambo's Restaurants, paper, Bicentennial, 1776-1976, M .16.00
Cookie jar, Aunt Jemima, plastic, F&F 400.00
Cookie jar, Mammy w/2 kids in tub, ceramic, Wihor #58-91, EX ...200.00
Crate, Blum's Li'l Darkies, stenciled wood, 13x24x11", NM 300.00
Creamer & sugar bowl, Aunt Jemima & Uncle Mose, plastic, F&F .175.00
Crock, Golliwog, Robertson's Preserves, sm 40.00
Desk accessory, sleek brass figure/chained panther, marble base, EX ..125.00
Dice toy (Kobe), wood head w/bug eyes & top hat, 1930s, 3½", EX .150.00
Dispenser, C Sandherger's Old Tub, glass, rvpt ad, 21", EX 5,000.00
Display figure, chalkware, pnt clothing w/real wool cap, 60", EX ..1,800.00
Display figure, papier-mache, dapper man seated, 52", EX 5,000.00
Doll, Gilliwog, Merrythought, from $125 to 250.00
Doll, Golliwog, celluloid face, from $125 to 135.00
Doll, Golliwog, primitive, ca 1920-30, up to 475.00
Doll, Topsy Turvy, stuffed cloth, 1930s, 14", EX 100.00
Figure, boy carrying watermelon on shoulder, chalkware, 25", VG .650.00
Figure, Farmer James, pnt cvd wood, on base, 42½", EX 850.00
Figure, gambler standing on stepped base, bronze, 33", EX 2,000.00
Figure, Mammy Jesse, cvd wood, on base, 42½", EX 850.00
Game, carnival; ball toss, pnt wood bbl w/2 heads, 43x23x6", VG .600.00
Game, carnival; Penny Catch 1¢, cvd wood, 22½" dia, EX 750.00
Game, 1¢ counter-top sport machine, CI/metal/wood base, 16", EX ...700.00
Grocery list pegboard, Recken Ah Needs?, dbl column, 8¼x6", EX ...90.00
Humidor, boy w/arms around watermelon, terra cotta, 12", EX .750.00
Incense burner, baby w/mouth wide open & bottle, pnt brass, 5", VG .350.00
Jug, Honey dat's all Sample 301 (paper label on glass), 1920s, 9", EX ...90.00
Lawn jocky, top hat/wht shirt/red vest/blk pants, pnt CI, 27", VG 475.00
Match holder, boy on 2 baskets w/2 corn-pattern holders, CI, 5", VG .200.00
Match holder, 1895 Atlanta Cotton Expo, 2 boys/bale, metal, 3", EX ..425.00
Mug, Sambo's, name repeated diagonally, 1950s, M 30.00
Noisemaker, litho tin w/dapper dancing figure, 1940s, EX 55.00
Nutcracker, cvd wood, head w/red-pnt lips & earrings, 8½", EX ..500.00
Painting, oil on brd, man by cotton bales, Walker, 8x4", EX ..2,500.00
Peanut dispenser, Smilin' Sam From Alabam, CI, red, 13", EX ..2,000.00
Pillow cover, souvenir of New Orleans w/Black scenes, 1930s, 18", EX .80.00
Pin, figural boy by cooking pot on open fire, emb metal, 2x1", EX .100.00
Pin, gold-tone metal, tintype image, pre- or early 1900s, 1½", EX ..75.00
Pipe rack, brass bust figure in hat & leaf decor, 6x12½", EX 150.00
Place mat, Aunt Jemima, The Story Of...At Disneyland, 1955, EX .35.00
Plaque, Booker T Washington, From Slave Cabin..., brass, 17x13", EX ..100.00
Platter, Golliwog, Joan Allen, from $675 to 695.00
Pocket mirror, celluloid w/metal hdl, photo of 2 women, 3½", EX ..55.00
Postcard, Golliwog, 1924 ....20.00
Print, Blind Man's Bluff, paper litho, Cruikshank, fr, 15x19", VG ..400.00
Print, exterior of cabin/donkey cart, paper litho, fr, 34x25", G ..225.00
Print, Golliwog, Longman's Green & Co, 1904 ....55.00
Recipe book, Fine Old Dixie Recipes, wood cover, 1939, EX 65.00
Recipe booklet, Aunt Jemima, Pancakes Unlimited, 1958, EX 65.00
Scales, Aunt Jemima Breakfast Club, metal, cb face, 8", EX 350.00
Shakers, Aunt Jemima & Uncle Mose, plastic, F&F, 3½", pr 65.00
Shakers, Aunt Jemima & Uncle Mose, plastic, F&F, 5", pr 75.00

Shakers, chef couple, ceramic, St. Anne de Beaupre label on aprons, 4", 3¾", $60.00 for the pair.

Sheet music, Ise Done My Best, man on deck cover, 1933, EX 25.00
Sheet music, Mammy's Little Coal Black Rose, 1916 ....25.00
Soap dish, Mammy w/basket on head, pnt CI, 5", VG 135.00
Spatula, Aunt Jemima Day, plastic hdl, 1940s, EX 45.00
Spice jar, Aunt Jemima, plastic, F&F, from set of 6, ea 50.00
Syrup, Aunt Jemima, plastic, F&F, 5½" 70.00
Tankard, mini souvenir mk Coburg w/native image, ceramic, 1930s, EX ..45.00
Thermos, plastic, repeated Sambo's design, 1970s, EX 65.00
Tin, Had Our Mazawatte, 3 smiling boys w/empty cups, 3-lb, EX ..500.00
Transfers, Aunt Martha's Hot Iron..., #9947, 1930s, unused, MIP ..70.00
Tray, metal, 2 kids ready for bed on turq ground, 6x9", EX 275.00
Weather vane, alligator/boy, pnt tin/wood, wrought iron base, 57", VG .650.00

Black Cats

Made in Japan during the '50s, these novelty cats may be found bearing the labels of several different importers, all with their own particular characteristics. The best known and most collectible of these cats are from the Shafford line. Even when unmarked, they are easily identified by their red bows, green eyes, and white whiskers, eyeliners, and eyebrows. Relco/Royal Sealy cats are tall and slender, and their bow ties are gold with red dots. Wales is a wonderful line with yellow eyes and gold detailing; Enesco cats have blue eyes, and there are other lines as well. When evaluating your black cats, be sure to inspect their paint and judge them accordingly. Paint that is 50% should relate to 50% of our suggested values, which are given for cats in mint (or nearly mint) paint. Enthusiastic bidding on Internet auctions have resulted in much higher prices on the more hard-to-find items as reflected in our listings.

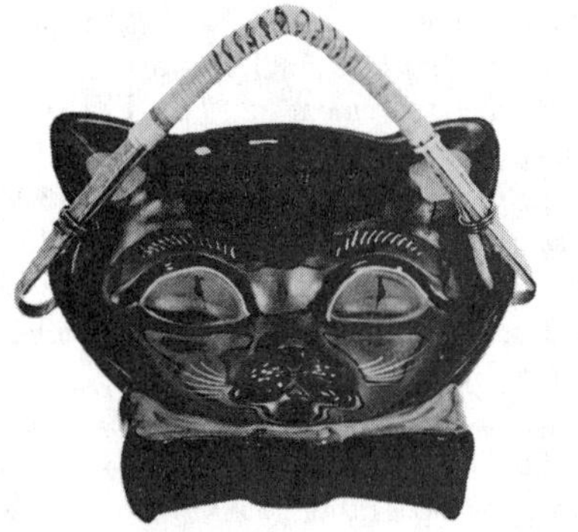

Tray, head shaped, wicker handle, Shafford, rare, $185.00.

Ashtray, flat face, Shafford, hard to find sz, 3¾" 45.00
Ashtray, flat face shape, Shafford, 4½x4½" 18.00
Ashtray, 3-D head, open mouth w/cigarette rest, Shafford 22.00
Cigarette lighter, Shafford, 5½" 175.00
Condiment set, 2 joined heads, J&M bows w/spoons, Shafford, 4" ..95.00
Cookie jar, lg cat head, Shafford, from $80 to 100.00
Creamer & sugar bowl, Shafford 45.00
Cruets, he w/O eyes, she w/V eyes & hair bow, Shafford, pr, $60 to .75.00
Decanter, long cat w/red fish in his mouth as stopper 60.00
Decanter, upright cat holds bottle w/cork stopper, Shafford 50.00
Demitasse pot, tail hdl, bow finial, Shafford, 7½" 165.00
Egg cup, cat face on bowl, ped ft, Shafford, from $95 to 125.00
Fork, emb cat face, gr eyes, from wall-hanging utensil set, Shafford ...125.00
Grease jar, sm cat head, Shafford, from $95 to 110.00
Ice bucket, cylindrical w/emb yel-eyed cat face, 2 szs, ea 75.00
Mug, Shafford, rare lg sz, 4¼", from $70 to 80.00
Mug, Shafford, 3½" 55.00
Pitcher, milk; upright, Shafford 150.00
Planter, cat & kitten in hat, Shafford-like pnt 30.00
Pot holder caddy, 'teapot' cat, 3 hooks, Shafford, from $170 to .195.00
Shaker, long cat, salt in 1 end, pepper in other end, Shafford ...165.00
Shakers, rnd-bodied 'teapot' cat, Shafford, pr, from $125 to 140.00
Shakers, seated, 1 w/head tilted, gr eyes, Shafford, 3¾", pr 25.00
Spice rack, wireware face w/marble eyes, 4 shakers, Shafford 450.00
Spice set, 6 sq shakers in wooden fr, yel eyes 175.00
Strainer, w/cat face, long wood hdl, Shafford 125.00
Teapot, ball-shape body, gr eyes, Shafford, 4-4½" 30.00
Teapot, ball-shaped body, head lid, gr eyes, Shafford, med sz 45.00
Teapot, ball-shaped body, head lid, gr eyes, Shafford, 7" 75.00
Teapot, head w/2 spouts & chambers, wrapped hdl, Shafford, 5", $200 to 250.00
Teapot, panther-like appearance, gold eyes, sm 20.00
Toothpick holder, cat on vase atop hook, Occupied Japan 12.00
Tray, flat face, wicker hdl, Shafford, rare 185.00
Utensil rack, flat-bk cat w/3 slots for utensils, cat only 125.00
Wall pocket, flattened 'teapot' cat, Shafford, scarce, from $125 to .150.00
Wine, emb cat face, gr eyes, Shafford, sm 75.00

Black Glass

Black glass is a type of colored glass that when held to strong light usually appears deep purple, though since each glasshouse had its own formula, tones may vary. It was sometimes etched or given a satin finish; and occasionally it was decorated with silver, gold, enamel, coralene, or any of these in combination. The decoration was done either by the glasshouse or by firms that specialized in decorating glassware. Crystal, jade, colored glass, or milk glass was sometimes used with the black as an accent. Black glass has been made by many companies since the 1600s. Contemporary glasshouses produced black glass during the Depression, seldom signing their product. It is still being made today.

To learn more about the subject, we recommend *A Collector's Guide to Black Glass, Books I and II,* written by our advisor, Marlena Toohey; she is listed in the Directory under Colorado. Look for her newly updated value guide. See also Tiffin, L.E. Smith, and other specific manufacturers.

Bottle, Zodiac, rnd cap, Avon, 1975, 4¾" 5.00
Bottoms Up, nude lying over dome of cup, Guernsey, 1979, 3¼" .25.00
Bowl, console; oval, unknown maker, 12½" 20.00
Bowl, Cornucopia Line #416, New Martinsville, 1941, 12" L 45.00
Candle holder, cat figural, Indiana Glass, ca 1980s, 5" L 20.00
Candlestick, crackled glass, unknown maker, ca 1920s-30s, 7" 25.00
Candlestick, spiral, Viking (Westmoreland mold), 1980s, 7" 28.00
Candlesticks, twisted, #725, Northwood, ca 1920s, 10", pr 150.00
Cigarette box w/match-holder finial, 1900s, 7" 75.00
Curtain tiebacks, unknown maker, ca 1920s-30s, 3½" 45.00
Decanter, poodle, unknown maker, 15" 35.00
Figurine, Venus Rising, Mirror Images by Imperial, 6½" 100.00
Flower frog, raised florals, Greensburg, 1930s, 4¾" 20.00
Flowerpot & saucer, LE Smith, 1930s, 4" H 25.00
Necklace, beads of multiple sizes, 1-strand, 16" 25.00
Oil lamp, w/shade, Taiwan, 1970s, 9" 25.00
Pendant, faceted heart shape, 2" L 38.00
Pilsner, 'Ten Pin,' crystal on blk base, Imperial, 1931, 16-oz 35.00
Plate, Geo WA Bicentennial, LE Smith, 1932, 8¼" 85.00
Plate, Line #99, Diamond Glassware Co of IN PA, 1930s, 8" 10.00
Shakers, Viking, 1980s, 3¼", pr 45.00
Tray, sandwich; w/center hdl, LE Smith, ca 1930s, 10" dia 35.00
Vase, HP floral, 1900s, 6" 60.00
Wine glass, Fostoria, 1978, 8-oz 20.00

Blown Glass

Blown glass is rather difficult to date; eighteenth and nineteenth century examples vary little as to technique or style. It ranges from the primitive to the sophisticated, but the metallic content of very early glass caused tiny imperfections that are obvious upon examination, and these are often indicative of age.

In America, Stiegel introduced the English technique of using a patterned, part-size mold, a practice which was generally followed by many glasshouses after the Revolution. From 1820 to about 1850, glass was blown into full-size three-part molds. In the listings below, glass is assumed clear unless color is mentioned. Numbers refer to a standard reference book, *American Glass,* by Helen and George McKearin. See also Bottles and specific manufacturers. Our advisor for this category is Mark Vuono; he is listed in the Directory under Connecticut. See also Bottles.

Bird feeder, clear w/cobalt knob, smooth base, 5⅞" 50.00
Bird feeder, conical, appl rigaree & bird, pontil, 8" 50.00
Celery vase, bl-gr, appl stem & ft, pontil scar, heavy, 7⅝" 120.00
Compote, dk gr, appl ft, baluster stem, rigaree on rim, 3x5½" ...715.00
Compote, w/lid, ground top lip, 9x8" 140.00
Creamer, cobalt w/gold traces, tooled rim, pontil, appl hdl, 3¼" ..130.00
Creamer, emerald/teal gr, flared rim, appl base, 5" 185.00

Cuspidor, chocolate amber, flared mouth, pontil scar, 4⅜" 180.00
Decanter, amber, cut panels & notches, w/stopper, 11", NM 500.00
Decanter, clear w/gilt Holland scenes, hdls, rigaree, 9¼" 160.00
Decanter, cut neck, wheel-eng sides, w/stopper, 9½" 100.00
Flask, chestnut; med olive gr, pontiled, 4¾" 300.00
Flask, chestnut; yel-olive w/amber tone, flattened, 8⅝" 160.00
Fly trap, clear, dome shape, 3 appl ft, 6" dia 150.00
Fly trap, cranberry red flashing on clear (inside), 3 ft, 6" 350.00
Fly trap, dk grass gr, tooled base, appled neck, 3 ft, 5⅛" 350.00
Fly trap, lt apple gr, 19 vertical ribs, 3 ft, 6¾" 110.00
Fountain, birdcage; aquamarine, appl 'feather' pinched finial, 6" .130.00
Gaffing tool holder, peacock bl, appl base, segmented stem, 4¾" ..575.00
Jar, Pillar mold, frosted neck, w/lid, 6" 300.00
Pan, clear w/cobalt lip, 6¼" 140.00
Pan, folded rim, clear w/bl appl ring, 6" 140.00
Pitcher, dk gr-aqua, pontiled, appl hdl/rigaree, 6¼" 650.00
Pitcher, Lily Pad, aqua, appl hdl, threading on neck, 5½" 350.00
Rolling pin, blk glass w/wht splotches, 14¾" 220.00
Rolling pin, cobalt w/mc pnt decor, open end, 13¼" 90.00
Rolling pin, deep root beer-amber, sheared/ground pontil, 15" ..130.00
Rolling pin, dk chocolate-amber, bubbles, 16¼" 110.00
Rolling pin, dk red amethyst (blk), pnt traces, 15¼" 90.00
Rolling pin, dk turq, tooled end, 15¼" 125.00
Rolling pin, purple amethyst, sheared end is open, 12¼" 140.00
Rolling pin, wht opal w/pnt decor & Forget Me Not, 13½" 100.00
Salt cellar, dk sapphire bl, pontil scar on ft, 2" 160.00
Shot glass, fiery wht opal, 6-sided, pontil, 2¼" 100.00
Sugar bowl, smoky amethyst w/lav ft, w/lid, 7¾" 250.00
Tumbler, dk grass gr, 8-sided, polished pontil, 3½" 775.00
Tumbler, dk sapphire bl w/olive striations, 6-sided, 3⅜" 90.00
Tumbler, molded ribs in base, eng band, 5⅝" 170.00
Vase, bl trumpet form, flared/folded rim, wafer stem, rnd ft, 10" ..6,500.00
Vase, bud; bright gr, tooled rim, rough pontil, 8¼" 110.00
Vase, canary, hex waterfall base, panel & arch bowl, 11⅜", EX .715.00
Vase, Lily Pad, aqua, ear hdls, threaded neck, 6", NM 330.00
Vase, trumpet; amethyst, baluster, folded lip, 9½" 1,980.00
Vase, trumpet; amethyst, 3-knop stem, w/wafers, w/lid, pontil, 13" ..2,750.00
Whimsey baton, clear w/mc spiral bands, 45½" 50.00
Whimsey flip hat, med amber, pontil scar, folded rim, 2½" 95.00
Whimsey flip hat, med amber, pontil scar, tooled rim, 1½" 90.00
Wine, clear, eng name & 1829 marriage date, pontil, 4⅛" 50.00

Blown Three-Mold Glass

A popular collectible in the 1920s, '30s, and '40s, blown three-mold glass has again gained the attention of many. Produced from approximately 1815 to 1840 in various New York, New England, and Midwestern glasshouses, it was a cheaper alternative to the expensive imported Irish cut glass.

Distinguishing features of blown three-mold glass are the three distinct mold marks and the concave-convex appearance of the glass. For every indentation on the inner surface of the ware, there will be a corresponding protuberance on the outside. Blown three-mold glass is most often clear with the exception of inkwells and a few known decanters. Any colored three-mold glass commands a premium price.

The numbers in the listings that follow refer to the book *American Glass* by George and Helen McKearin. Our advisor for this category is Mark Vuono; he is listed in the Directory under Connecticut.

Bowl, GII-19, olive gr, pontiled, att Mutzer, 2x4½" 60.00
Creamer, GII-18, rigaree on hdl finial, 3" 190.00
Creamer, VG-8, flared rim, tooled spout, ribbon hdl, 5" 190.00
Decanter, GI-15, minor stains, 6¾"+stopper 220.00
Decanter, GII-18, pontil scar, flared mouth, orig stopper, 8¼" ..140.00
Inkwell, GII-2, disk mouth, pontiled, 1¾" 225.00
Pan, GI-18, folded rim, pontiled base, 1½x6" 120.00
Pitcher, GII-18, lt bl, appl rib hdl, tooled thumb rest, 2⅞", EX ...80.00
Pitcher, GII-18, pontiled 15-dmn base, ribbed hdl, 3⅛", NM 120.00
Salt cellar, GII-21, sm flakes, 2⅜" 165.00
Syrup, GV-II, star-pattern base, pewter lid, 7¼" 100.00
Tumbler, GI-6, folded rim, ringed base w/pontil, 3" 350.00
Tumbler, GII-18, 5¾" 250.00

Blue and White Stoneware

Salt glaze or molded stoneware was most commonly produced in a blue and white coloration, much of which was also decorated with numerous 'in-mold' designs (some 150 plus patterns). It was made by practically every American pottery from the turn of the century until the mid-1930s. Crocks, pitchers, wash sets, rolling pins, and other household wares are only a few of the items that may be found in this type of 'country' pottery, now one of today's popular collectibles.

Logan, Brush-McCoy, Uhl Co., and Burley Winter were among those who produced it; but very few pieces were ever signed. Naturally, condition must be a prime consideration, especially if one is buying for resale; pieces with good, strong color and fully molded patterns bring premium prices. Normal wear and signs of age are to be expected, since this was utility ware and received heavy use in busy households.

In the listings that follow, crocks, salts, and butter holders are assumed to be without lids unless noted otherwise. Items are in near-mint condition unless noted otherwise. For further information we recommend *Blue and White Stoneware* (1981) by Kathryn McNerney and *Collector's Encyclopedia of Salt Glaze Stoneware* (1997) by Terry Taylor and Terry and Kay Lowrance. See also specific manufacturers.

Bowl, Wedding Ring, ranging in sizes from 2x5" to 4x8", M values from $100.00 to $150.00 each. (Photo courtesy Terry Taylor)

Bank w/Money Bank stencil, coin slot, break to open, 4x3" ...1,200.00
Bean pot, Boston Baked Beans, Swirl, heavy diffused pattern 500.00
Bowl, Apricot, 9½" 95.00
Bowl, mixing; Flying Bird, 4x7½" 350.00
Bowl, Reverse Pyramids w/Reverse Picket Fence, 2½x4½" 95.00
Bowl (milk crock), Apricot, w/hdl 225.00
Box, powder; Wildflower & Fishscale, w/lid 350.00
Butter crock, Apricot, appl wood & wire hdl, w/lid, 4x7" 275.00
Butter crock, Basketweave & Morning Glory, w/lid, 4x7½" 425.00
Butter crock, Cows, appl wood & wire hdl, w/lid, 4½x7¼" 500.00
Butter crock, Daisy & Trellis, orig lid & bail, 4½" 200.00
Butter crock, Dragon Fly & Flower, no lid, 4½x7" 125.00
Butter crock, Draped Windows, 4½x8" 225.00
Butter crock, Grapes & Leaves, dbl ring around rim, 3x6½" 175.00
Butter crock, Lovebirds, w/lid, 5½x6", M 600.00
Butter crock, Peacock, w/lid, 6x6" 575.00

Butter crock, Wild Flower (stenciled), w/lid, 6½x7¼" 175.00
Canister, Basketweave, Cloves, orig lid, 4½" 200.00
Canister, Basketweave, Pepper, orig lid, 4½" 200.00
Canister, Basketweave, Salt, orig lid, 7½" 350.00
Canister, Basketweave, Sugar, orig lid, 7½" 350.00
Canister, Snowflake (stenciled), rpl lid, 6½x5¾" 150.00
Canister set, Basketweave, 9-pc 4,000.00
Chamberpot, Fishscale & Wild Rose, no lid, 5½x9¼" 200.00
Chamberpot, Peacock, 9¾" 1,250.00
Chamberpot, Wildflower & Fishscale, w/lid 525.00
Coffeepot, Bull's Eye, rim chips, 9¾x3¾" (base) 2,550.00
Coffeepot, Oval, Diffused Blue, bl-tipped knob, str sides, 11x4" ..1,500.00
Coffeepot, Swirl, w/lid 900.00
Cookie jar, Brickers, flat button finial, 8x8" 500.00
Cooler, iced tea; Blue Band, flat lid, complete, 13x11" 295.00
Cooler, water; Blue Band, orig lid 250.00
Cooler, water; Cupid, brass spigot, patterned lid, 15x12" 700.00
Cooler, water; Polar Bear, brass NP spigot, rare, 1-gal, 17x15" ..3,100.00
Crock, Lovebird, rstr bail & handgrip, 5½x9" 400.00
Crock, Peacock, rstr bail & handgrip, 5½x9" 500.00
Cup, Wildflower w/emb Ribbon & Bow, 4½x2½" 85.00
Cuspidor, Basketweave & Morning Glory, 5x7½" 125.00
Cuspidor, Butterfly & Shield, 6x7½" 175.00
Cuspidor, Flower Panels & Arches, 7x7½" 250.00
Egg storage crock, Barrel Staves, bail hdl, 5½x6" 235.00
Ice crock, Barrel Staves, rope/tongs/ice block emb, 4½x6" 225.00
Jardiniere, Flowers, hairline, 7⅞" (complete w/stand & crock) 800.00
Meat tenderizer, Wildflower 500.00
Mug, Basketweave & Flower, 5x3" 150.00
Mug, beer; advertising, Diffused Blue, sqd hdl 150.00
Mug, Flying Bird, 5x3" 275.00
Mug, plain 65.00
Pie plate, Blue Walled Brick-Edge star emb base, 10½" 225.00
Pitcher, Acorns, stenciled, 8x6½" 175.00
Pitcher, American Beauty Rose, 10" 500.00
Pitcher, Apricot, 8" 250.00
Pitcher, Barrel, +6 mugs 395.00
Pitcher, Blue Band, plain 200.00
Pitcher, Blue Band Scroll, emb design 300.00
Pitcher, Bluebird, 9x7" 450.00
Pitcher, Castle & Fishscale, 8" 195.00
Pitcher, Cattails, bulbous, 6" 300.00
Pitcher, Cattails, 10" 300.00
Pitcher, Cattails, 9½" 275.00
Pitcher, Cherry Cluster & Basketweave, 10" 375.00
Pitcher, Columns & Arches, 8¾x5" 425.00
Pitcher, Daisy Cluster, 7x7", rare 800.00
Pitcher, Doe & Fawn, bl, 8½" 185.00
Pitcher, Dutch Landscape, stenciled, Diffused Blue, tall 275.00
Pitcher, Eagle w/Shield & Arrows, rare, 8" 800.00
Pitcher, Fishscale & Wild Rose (part of wash set), 10" 160.00
Pitcher, Garden Rose, 9" 500.00
Pitcher, Garden Rose Sponge, 9" 700.00
Pitcher, Girl & Dog, regular bl, 9" 675.00
Pitcher, Girl & Dog, sponge, 7" 900.00
Pitcher, Grape & Shield, 8½x5" 150.00
Pitcher, Grape w/Rickrack, any sz 250.00
Pitcher, Grazing Cows, bl, 7½" 400.00
Pitcher, Grazing Cows, bl, 8" 250.00
Pitcher, Grazing Cows, 6½" 500.00
Pitcher, hot water; Wildflower & Fishscale, sm 150.00
Pitcher, Indian Boy & Girl (Capt John Smith & Pocahontas), 6" ..300.00
Pitcher, Iris, 9" 375.00
Pitcher, Leaping Deer, sponge, 8" 1,200.00
Pitcher, Leaping Deer, 8½" 400.00
Pitcher, Leeping Deer in 1 oval, Swan in other (mfg error), 8" .1,200.00
Pitcher, Lincoln, allover deep bl, 4¾x4¾" 250.00
Pitcher, Lincoln, allover deep bl, 6x4" 300.00
Pitcher, Lincoln, allover deep bl, 7x5" 400.00
Pitcher, Lincoln, allover deep bl, 8x6" 730.00
Pitcher, Lovebird, arc bands, deep color, 8½", EX 500.00
Pitcher, Lovebird, pale color, 8½" 300.00
Pitcher, Monk, dk cobalt 350.00
Pitcher, Peacock 1,500.00
Pitcher, Pine Cone, sponge, rare, 9½" 850.00
Pitcher, Pine Cone, 9½" 750.00
Pitcher, Poinsettia, 6½" 385.00
Pitcher, Rose on Trellis, 8x5½" 225.00
Pitcher, Scroll & Leaf, advertising, 8" 450.00
Pitcher, Shield, prof rpr, 8" 200.00
Pitcher, Swan, in oval, deep color, 8½", EX 400.00
Pitcher, Tulip, 8x4" 350.00
Pitcher, Wild Rose, solid bl, 9x6" 450.00
Pitcher, Wild Rose, sponged bands, 9" 500.00
Pitcher, Windmill & Bush, 9" 225.00
Pitcher, Windmills, 7¼", EX 195.00
Pitcher, Windy City (Fannie Flagg), Robinson Clay, 8½" 450.00
Roaster, Wildflower, domed lid, 8½x12" 225.00
Rolling pin, Blue Band, advertising, Andka, Nebr, 14x4" 900.00
Rolling pin, Blue Band, no advertising, 14x4" 400.00
Rolling pin, Swirl, baker's sz, 16" 1,200.00
Rolling pin, Swirl, orig wooden hdls, 13" 1,200.00
Rolling pin, Wild Flower, advertising, Analomink PA, dtd 1905 ..1,100.00
Rolling pin, Wildflower, plain 375.00
Salt crock, Apricot, no lid 130.00
Salt crock, Butterfly, orig lid 275.00
Salt crock, Eagle, w/lid 575.00
Salt crock, Grapevine on Fence, pale bl, orig lid, 6½x6¾" 300.00
Salt crock, Peacock, w/lid 550.00
Soap dish, Beaded Rose 150.00
Soap dish, cat's head 200.00
Soap dish, Indian in War Bonnet 250.00
Soap dish, Wildflower & Fishscale 150.00
Spice set, Basketweave, 6-pc, w/lids 1,750.00
Teapot, Swirl, dbl wire bail hdl, ball shape, 9x6½" 1,200.00
Toothbrush holder, Bow Tie, stenciled flower 50.00
Toothbrush holder, Wildflower & Fishscale 150.00
Vinegar cruet, 4½x3" 300.00
Wash bowl & pitcher, Rose on Trellis 300.00
Wash bowl & pitcher, Wildflower & Fishscale 500.00
Wash set, Wildflower & Fishscale, complete, 7-pc 2,000.00
Washboard, sponge 400.00
Water bottle, Diffused Blue Swirl, stopper w/cork, 10x5½" 550.00
Whipped cream jar, 4¾x6¾" 475.00

Blue Ridge

Blue Ridge dinnerware was produced by Southern Potteries of Erwin, Tennessee, from the late 1930s until 1956 in twelve basic styles and two thousand different patterns, all of which were hand decorated under the glaze. Vivid colors lit up floral arrangements of seemingly endless variation, fruit of every sort from simple clusters to lush assortments, barnyard fowl, peasant figures, and unpretentious textured patterns. Although it is these dinnerware lines for which they are best known, collectors prize the artist-signed plates from the '40s and the limited line of character jugs made during the '50s most highly. Examples of the French Peasant pattern are valued at double the prices listed below; very simple patterns will bring 25% to 50% less.

Our advisors, Betty and Bill Newbound, have compiled three lovely books, *Blue Ridge Dinnerware, Revised Third Edition,* and *The Collector's Encyclopedia of Blue Ridge, Volumes I* and *II,* all with beautiful color illustrations and current market values. They are listed in the Directory under North Carolina. For information concerning the National Blue Ridge Newsletter, see the Clubs, Newsletters, and Catalogs section of the Directory.

Ashtray, advertising, rnd 70.00
Ashtray, Mallard, box shape, 3½x2½" 50.00
Basket, aluminum edge, 7" 25.00
Bonbon, divided center hdl, china 130.00
Bonbon, flat shell, Pixie 125.00
Bowl, cereal/soup; 6" 25.00
Bowl, flat soup 30.00
Bowl, Square Dancers, 11½" 165.00
Bowl, vegetable; rnd, 8" 25.00
Box, candy; rnd w/lid, rare 170.00
Box, cigarette 90.00
Box, Rose Step, pearlized 90.00
Box, Seaside 180.00
Celery, leaf shape, china 60.00
Celery, Skyline 45.00
Child's feeding dish 150.00
Child's mug 100.00
Chocolate pot 275.00

Coffeepot, Ovoid shape, Rose Marie pattern, from $110.00 to $125.00. (Photo courtesy Betty and Bill Newbound)

Counter sign 375.00
Creamer, demitasse; china 75.00
Creamer, Waffle 20.00
Cup & saucer, demitasse; china 55.00
Cup & saucer, Jumbo 65.00
Cup & saucer, regular 20.00
Deviled egg dish 65.00
Egg cup, Premium 60.00
Jug, batter; w/lid 100.00
Jug, character 700.00
Jug, syrup; w/lid, scarce 115.00
Lazy susan, complete 800.00
Pie baker 40.00
Pitcher, Betsy, china 190.00
Pitcher, Rebecca 185.00
Pitcher, Spiral, 7" 80.00
Plate, artist sgn 600.00
Plate, dinner; 9¼" 22.00
Plate, salad; Bird, 8½" 80.00
Plate, sq, novelty pattern, 6" 90.00
Plate, Square Dance, 14" 250.00
Platter, artist sgn, 15" 1,300.00
Platter, Turkey w/Acorns, 15" 100.00
Ramekin, w/lid, 7½" 40.00
Relish, Charm House 160.00
Relish, loop handle, china 85.00
Relish, Palisades 60.00
Relish, T-hdl 75.00
Salad spoon 50.00
Sconce 90.00
Shakers, Apple, 2¼", pr 40.00
Shakers, Blossom Top, pr 65.00
Shakers, ftd, china, tall, pr 90.00
Shakers, Good Housekeeping, pr 90.00
Shakers, Palisades, pr 30.00
Shakers, Skyline, pr 25.00
Sherbet 25.00
Sugar bowl, Colonial, eared, open 30.00
Sugar bowl, Waffle, w/lid 25.00
Sugar bowl, Woodcrest, w/lid 30.00
Teapot, Mini Ball 200.00
Teapot, Piecrust 130.00
Tidbit, 2-tier 35.00
Tray, snack; Martha 175.00
Vase, bud 175.00
Vase, ruffled top, 9½" 135.00

Blue Willow

Blue Willow, inspired no doubt by the numerous patterns of the blue and white Nanking imports, has been popular since the late eighteenth century and has been made in as many variations as there were manufacturers. English transfer wares by such notable firms as Allerton and Ridgway are the most sought after and the most expensive. Japanese potters have been producing Willow-patterned dinnerware since the late 1800s, and American manufacturers have followed suit. Although blue is the color most commonly used, mauve and black lines have also been made. For further study we recommend the book *Blue Willow,* with full-color photos and current prices, by Mary Frank Gaston, our advisor for this category. In the following listings, if no manufacturer is noted, the ware is unmarked. See also Buffalo.

Bowl, flat soup; Homer Laughlin, 8" 15.00
Bowl, fruit; Royal Doulton, 1902-22, 3½x7" 135.00
Bowl, Japan, 5¾" 8.00
Bowl, oval, Booth's, 10x8" 150.00
Bowl, oval, Hopewell China, 1920-30 ....45.00
Bowl, oval, w/lid, Ridgway, ca 1927, 10x8½" 175.00
Bowl, scalloped edge, Allerton, 5" 15.00
Bowl, vegetable; Worcester (att), ca 1800s, 12" L, EX 170.00
Box, trinket; gold rim, Japan (unmk) 140.00
Butter dish, Royal China, ¼-lb 35.00
Butter dish, w/strainer, England 235.00
Butter pat, English (unmk), 3¼" 40.00
Cake plate, hdls, gold trim, unmk, ca 1880, 9" 65.00
Casserole, w/lid, Homer Laughlin 45.00
Cheese dish, unmk 185.00
Coffee server/warmer, Japan 225.00
Creamer, John Stevenson & Sons 45.00
Creamer & sugar bowl, Fenton 70.00
Creamer & sugar bowl, Johnson Bros 45.00
Cup & saucer, demitasse; lt bl, bone china, Fenton 65.00

Cup & saucer, gold trim, Cauldon, ca 1905-20, 3" 45.00
Cup & saucer, handleless; English (unmk) 75.00
Cup & saucer, Royal 6.00
Cup & saucer, Shenango 40.00
Cup & saucer, Spode 60.00
Egg cup, dbl; Bow-Knot border w/gold, Booth, 4" 65.00
Egg cup, Homer Laughlin 25.00
Gravy boat, attached tray, scalloped, Allerton, 7½" 165.00
Gravy boat, scalloped rim, English (unmk) 125.00
Ladle, soup; English (unmk), 4" dia bowl, 12" 175.00
Lamp, oil; Japan, 7½" 75.00
Meat drain, unmk, ca 1880, 13½x9½" 325.00
Pie dish, unmk, ca 1880, 6½x5" 125.00
Pie plate, Royal China, 10" 30.00
Plate, Allerton, 7" 18.00
Plate, Allerton, 8" 25.00
Plate, Allerton, 9" 35.00
Plate, Doulton, ca 1891-1902, 10½" 55.00
Plate, gold trim, unmk, 1880, 7" 25.00
Plate, Homer Laughlin, 9" 15.00
Plate, rectangular, scalloped, Allerton, 7½x9½" 90.00
Plate, Ridgway, 9¾" 35.00
Plate, Staffordshire Warranted, 10" 45.00
Plate, Wedgwood, 1906, 10", 6 for 250.00
Platter, Allerton, scalloped, 14x11" 225.00
Platter, Allerton, 11¼x9¼" 175.00
Platter, bl C mk (unknown), 14x11" 175.00
Platter, Booth's, 12x9½" 150.00
Platter, England, 12½x10½" 185.00
Platter, Fenton, 10" 95.00
Platter, Fenton, 14" 175.00
Platter, Fenton, 16" 260.00
Platter, JC mk (Joseph Clementson), ca 1841-64, 18x14" 295.00
Platter, Staffordshire, ca 1880, 21½x16½" 525.00
Platter, unmk, ca 1850, 15½x12½", from $185 to 245.00
Platter, well & tree; printed Royal Arms mk, pre-1837, 20½x16½" ..625.00
Platter, Woods & Sons, 1907, 14x11" 250.00
Relish bowl, Stevenson Burleigh 35.00
Relish plate, Japan, from $25 to 35.00
Sauce tureen, appl hdls, w/lid, mk D (Dillwyn & Co?), 7x4½" .185.00
Saucer, gold trim, Charles Ford, Hanley, Staffordshire, 5" 20.00
Shakers, Japan, pr 35.00
Shakers, Royal China, pr 18.00
Snack hound, Japan 75.00
Soup plate, Allerton, 9" 35.00
Spice rack, Japan, lg, 8-pc 275.00
Spice rack, Japan, 6-pc w/holder 195.00
Tea caddy, 8-sided, unmk, ca 1820s, EX 395.00
Tea set, child sz, Made in Japan, ca 1920, 12-pc 165.00
Teapot, Homer Laughlin 60.00
Teapot, Royal China 125.00
Tray, sandwich; Booth's 250.00
Wash bowl & pitcher, Wedgwood 1,450.00
Water server, w/lid, Japan 150.00

Bluebird China

Made from 1910 to 1934, Bluebird China is lovely ware most often decorated with bluebirds flying among pink flowering branches. Another style depicts larger, more slender bluebirds in flight. The latter variety was made by Knowles Taylor Knowles, W.S. George (Derwood), French Co., Sterling Colonial, and Pope Gosser. All of it was inexpensive dinnerware and reached the height of its popularity in the second decade of this century. Many potteries produced it, and shapes differ from one manufacturer to another. Besides the companies we've already mentioned, you'll find the trademarks of Cleveland; Carrolton; Homer Laughlin (today the most expensive, most collected, and most available of all the lines); Limoges China of Sebring, Ohio; Salem; Taylor Smith Taylor; and there are others.

Our advisor for this category is Kenna Rosen; she is listed in the Directory under Texas.

Bowl, berry; Cleveland, ind 12.50
Bowl, deep, Derwood, WS George, 4¾" 25.00
Bowl, deep, Homer Laughlin, 5½" 35.00
Bowl, gravy; w/saucer, Hopewell China 50.00
Bowl, sauce; SP Co, 4½" 12.50
Bowl, soup; PMC Co, 8" 30.00
Bowl, vegetable; Cleveland, 9¾" 45.00
Butter dish, 4½" holder w/in 7" dish, Steubenville 175.00
Butter pat, unmk 15.00
Calendar plate, 1921 advertising pc, ELPCO, 8" 95.00
Canister set, rnd, unmk, 6½x5", 6 for 300.00
Casserole, Homer Laughlin Empress, rnd, w/lid, 8½" 150.00
Casserole, Ostro China, 10½" dia 95.00
Casserole, Pope Gosser, w/lid, 10½x10½" 100.00
Casserole, Royal China Internat'l, 7x11½" 125.00
Casserole, Taylor Smith & Taylor, w/lid, 11x7½" 130.00

Chocolate cup, footed, no mark, 3½", $35.00; Creamer, no mark, 4¼", $25.00.

Coffeepot, Sterling Colonial 150.00
Creamer, Derwood, WS George 30.00
Creamer & sugar bowl, Knowles Taylor Knowles 75.00
Creamer & sugar bowl, SP Co, w/lid 85.00
Creamer & sugar bowl, w/lid, Homer Laughlin 100.00
Cup, coffee; unmk, 3½" 25.00
Cup, tea; unmk 15.00
Cup & saucer, SP Co 25.00
Dish, oval, Hudson, Homer Laughlin, 1x5¼x4" 20.00
Gravy w/underplate, Homer Laughlin, 4x9¾" 75.00
Ladle, sauce; gold scrolling 40.00
Pitcher, water; Salem China, 10" 125.00
Plate, baby's, ELP Co China, 7½x7½" 150.00
Plate, bread; hdls, gold trim, unmk, 10" 150.00
Plate, dessert; Limoges, 6" 8.00
Plate, dinner; Cleveland, 9" 25.00
Plate, dinner; Knowles Taylor Knowles, 9¾" 22.50
Plate, dinner; Wilmer Ware 20.00
Plate, Homer Laughlin, 8½" 35.00
Plate, National China, 8" 22.50

Plate, rtcl, sq, unmk, 9" 35.00
Plate, scalloped, Homer Laughlin, 7¼" 35.00
Plate, Steubenville, 9" 22.50
Platter, Edwin M Knowles, 14½x11" 75.00
Platter, Hopewell China, 13x10" 75.00
Platter, Hopewell China, 17½x13" 100.00
Platter, sqd oval, Carrollton, 17¾x12¾" 95.00
Platter, Thompson Glenwood, 13x10" 75.00
Platter, unmk, 9x7" 45.00
Platter, West End Pottery Co, 15½x11" 100.00
Saucer, Homer Laughlin 5.00
Sugar bowl, Illinois China Co, w/lid, 7x6" 50.00
Syrup, unmk, 4" 35.00
Tea set, CPCo, child sz, 21-pc 400.00
Teapot, Carrollton 250.00
Teapot, ELP Co, 8½x8½" 250.00
Teapot, Homer Laughlin 400.00

Boch Freres

Founded in the early 1840s in La Louviere, Boch Freres Keramis became the foremost producer of art pottery in Belgium. Though primarily they served a localized market, in 1844 they earned worldwide recognition for some of their sculptural works on display at the International Exposition in Paris.

In 1907 Charles Catteau of France was appointed head of the art department. Before that time, the firm had concentrated on developing glazes and perfecting elegant forms. The style they pursued was traditional, favoring the re-creation of established eighteenth-century ceramics. Catteau brought with him to Boch Freres the New Wave (or Art Nouveau) influence in form and decoration. His designs won him international acclaim at the Exhibition d'Art Decoratif in Paris in 1925, and it is for his work that Boch Freres is so highly regarded today. He occasionally signed his work as well as that of others who under his direct supervision carried out his preconceived designs. He was associated with the company until 1950 and lived the remainder of his life in Nice, France, where he died in 1966. The Boch Freres Keramis factory continues to operate today, producing bathroom fixtures and other utilitarian wares. A variety of marks have been used, most incorporating some combination of 'Boch Freres,' 'Keramis,' 'BFK,' or 'Ch Catteau.' A shield topped by a crown and flanked by a 'B' and an 'F' was used as well.

Bowl, geometrics, bl/cobalt on wht crackle, #10L9/#1187, 10" ..435.00
Box, solid/floral rays, blk/gr/mc, 3x5" dia 300.00
Vase, concentric circles, yel/brn/brn, bulbous, rpr, 9" 80.00
Vase, Deco floral, mc on matt ground, #D957, 6¾x11¼" 310.00
Vase, Deco floral on blk vertical panels, blk rim, pillow form, 9" .375.00
Vase, pinwheel/waves/dots, mc on wht crackle, long neck, 9" ...230.00
Vase, ribbons w/fruit & leaves, mc on gray & wht, #683, 17¾" .825.00
Vase, stylized bird/geometric bands, vivid mc, 8x8" 900.00
Vase, wide/scalloped floral top on vertical stripes, 11" 450.00

Boehm

Boehm sculptures were the creation of Edward Marshall Boehm, a ceramic artist who coupled his love of the art with his love of nature to produce figurines of birds, animals, and flowers in lovely background settings accurate to the smallest detail. Sculptures of historical figures and those representing the fine arts were also made and along with many of the bird figurines, have established secondary-market values many times their original prices. His first pieces were made in the very early 1950s in Trenton, New Jersey, under the name of Osso Ceramics. Mr. Boehm died in 1969, and the firm has since been managed by his wife. Today known as Edward Marshall Boehm, Inc., the private family-held corporation produces not only porcelain sculptures but collector plates as well. Both limited and non-limited editions of their works have been issued. Examples are marked with various backstamps, all of which have incorporated the Boehm name since 1951. 'Osso Ceramics' in upper case lettering was used in 1950 and 1951. Our advisor for this category is Leon Reimert; he is listed in the Directory under Pennsylvania.

Ptarmigans, #463, 1962, male: 13¾", female: 9½", on 14" base, $1,800.00 for the pair (at auction).

Alec's Red Rose, ltd ed, 1980, 7" 425.00
American Bald Eagle on branch, Nat'l Audubon Society, 1989 ...660.00
Arizona Queen of Night Cactus, ltd ed, 1976, 10" 600.00
Blue Jay fledgling 200.00
Blue Jays, mother w/2 babies & chameleon, 1966 ....2,200.00
Bluebird fledgling 195.00
Cedar Waxwing, #432 ....160.00
Chickadee fledgling 175.00
Dwarf Rose, #250-50 ....135.00
Gold Finch fledgling 195.00
Hummingbird, #440, 10" 350.00
Kingfisher fledgling 250.00
Magpie fledgling 250.00
Mockingbirds, ltd ed, 10¼" 1,100.00
Mr Lincoln Rose 165.00
Nuthatch on tree w/mushrooms, ltd ed, 1973 ....300.00
Panda Cub, #200-97 ....125.00
Pascali Rose w/Freesias, ltd ed, 1978, 10" 500.00
Queen Elizabeth Rose, on bronze stem 275.00
Red Poll fledgling 250.00
Robin fledgling 195.00
Scissor-tailed Flycatcher, ltd edition, 1977, 13½" 1,375.00
Seal Pup, #40127 ....95.00
Supreme Orchid Cactus w/Horned Toad, ltd ed, 1976, 6½" 400.00
Thoroughbred race horse w/jockey on top, 10½x10¼" 585.00
Tropicana Rose, ltd ed, 1978, 4" 220.00
Woodthrush fledgling 200.00
Yellow-throated Warbler, #431, 9½" 300.00
Yellowhammers, 10¾" 1,400.00

Bohemian Glass

The term 'Bohemian glass' has come to refer to a type of glass developed in Bohemia in the late sixteenth century at the Imperial Court of Rudolf II, the Hapsburg Emperor. The popular artistic pursuit of the day was stone carving, and it naturally followed to transfer familiar procedures to the glassmaking industry. During the next century, a formula was discovered that produced a glass with a fine crystal appearance which lent itself well to deep, intricate engraving, and the art was further advanced.

Although many other kinds of art glass were made there, collectors today use the term 'Bohemian glass' to often indicate clear glass overlaid or stained with color through which a design is cut or etched. (Unless otherwise described, the items in the listing that follows are of this type.) Red or yellow on clear glass is common, but other colors may also be found. Another type of Bohemian glass involves cutting through and exposing two layers of color in patterns that are often very intricate. Items such as these are sometimes further decorated with enamel and/or gilt work.

Beaker, amber, friendship symbols, 1850s, 5¼", NM 250.00
Beaker, amber, Rheinstein Castle scene, 1860s, 5" 275.00
Beaker, amber, stag & castle scene, 1900s, 4½" 80.00
Beaker, amber/cranberry/bl o/l, friendship scenes/flowers, 1860s, 6" ...350.00
Beaker, amethyst w/amber stain, pasty enamel, gold wear, 1860s, 5½" ..325.00
Beaker, cobalt, facets, 1860s, 4¾", NM 265.00
Beaker, cranberry, spa scenes on rnd facets, 1860s, 4" 200.00
Beaker, red, facets w/gold tracery, 1860s, 5" 265.00
Beaker, red, HP duck hunt scene, facets, 1860s, 4" 300.00
Beaker, red, stag & castle scene on fluted body, late, 5" 80.00
Beaker, wht, facets, flake, ca 1875, 4½" 125.00
Beaker, wht, facets, 19th C, 5¾" 175.00
Beaker, wht, HP floral, amber stained/cut panels, 5" 250.00
Beaker, wht to gr o/l, HP floral, oval facets, 1930s, 5½" 95.00
Beaker, wht/clear/bl o/l, facets w/gold tracery, 1860s, 5" 350.00
Beaker, wht/clear/cranberry o/l, facets, 1860s, 5" 285.00
Bottle, wht to cranberry o/l, HP lady, 3 ball ft, 1860s, 6" 6.00
Bottle, wine; ruby, eng grapes vines, pointed stopper, 14", pr 150.00
Goblet, amber, stag scenes, 1900s, 6¼" 125.00
Goblet, bl, enameled lady w/gold, ca 1900, 6" 150.00
Goblet, cranberry, wht glass snake around stem, gold trim, 1860s, 6" ..150.00
Goblet, red, HP butterflies & flowers, faceted stem, 1890s, 6¾" ..200.00
Lustre, red w/floral panels & gold, prisms, 13", pr 800.00
Pokal, red to bl o/l, Bible scenes, reducer lenses, 10" 3,000.00
Powder box, cranberry opaline w/HP foliage & gold, 2¼x4" 300.00
Stein, red, Steinbad scene, reducer lenses, inlaid lid, ½-litre 400.00
Vase, gr, HP floral, 1890s, 14" 100.00

Bookends

Though a few were produced before 1880, bookends became a necessary library accessory and a popular commodity after the printing industry was revolutionized by Mergenthaler's invention, the linotype. Books became abundantly available at such affordable prices that almost every home suddenly had need for bookends. They were carved from wood; cast in iron, bronze, or brass; or cut from stone. Chalkware and glass were used as well. Today's collectors may find such designs as ships, animals, flowers, and children. Patriotic themes, art reproductions, and those with Art Nouveau and Art Deco styling provide a basis for a diverse and interesting collection.

Currently, figural cast-iron pieces are in demand, especially examples with good original polychrome paint. This has driven the value of painted cast-iron bookends up considerably.

For further information we recommend *Collector's Guide to Bookends, Identification and Values,* by Louis Kuritzky, our advisor for this category; he is listed in the Directory under Florida. See also Arts and Crafts; Bradley and Hubbard.

African King, roaring lion, CI, att Littco, ca 1925, 4¼" 85.00
Angelfish, pnt gray metal on stone base, att Hirsch, 1930, 6" 120.00
Angelus Call To Pray, couple in field, pnt gray metal, K&O, ca 1925 ...125.00
Bedouin, CI, gr finish, ca 1925, 5¾" 95.00
Chariot Rounding Bend, CI relief scene, #695, 6¼" 75.00
Classical Cellist, gray metal w/celluloid face, stone base, Hirsch ..225.00
Dante & Beatrice, pnt gray metal, Ronson, 1923, 6" 175.00
Deco Seal, chrome, ca 1930, 6¼" 175.00
Egyptian Face, bronze, ca 1930, 6" 175.00

Elephants with trunks raised, painted cast iron, Connecticut Foundry, ca 1930, 5¾", $75.00. (Photo courtesy Louis Kuritzky)

Elephant Head, gray metal, Jennings Bros, ca 1928, 7" 185.00
End of Trail, rider in relief, CI, Connecticut Foundry, 1928, 5" ...50.00
Eve, female figure w/fruit in hand in relief, CI, ca 1925, 6¾" 110.00
FDR bust, gray metal, Ronson, 1933, 3" 110.00
Flower Basket, CI w/mc pnt, Hubley, ca 1923, 5¾" 175.00
French's Lincoln, seated, gold-pnt CI, Gift House, ca 1924, 6" .195.00
Gazelle, beside tree, CI, Hubley, ca 1925 ....125.00
Hammered Arch Design, copper, C Soreson, ca 1914, 5½" 175.00
Horse on Arc, leaping pose, gray metal, Dodge, ca 1947, 5½" 60.00
Indian Scout, figure on horse, gray metal, Jennings Bros, 1927, 5" .170.00
Lincoln & Tad, CI, ca 1925, 7" 110.00
Lindy, CI, Verona, ca 1928, 6" 110.00
Lorenzl Lady (sits w/book), bronze, Lorenzl Austria, 9" 3,500.00
Lorenzl Lady (sits w/book), gray metal, Ronson, ca 1924, 9" 425.00
Man Reading, chalk on stone base, JB Hirsch, ca 1932, 4½" 125.00
Mermaid, gold on gray metal, ca 1930, 6" 250.00
Mermaids, gray metal on marble base, att JB Hirsch, ca 1925, 5" .275.00
Nude (kneeling), gray metal, 1933 ....140.00
Nude on Sphinx, bronze clad, att Armor Bronze, ca 1925, 6" ...175.00
Nude w/Sash, single-tier ped, iron, X-2, ca 1929, 5" 175.00
Parrot on Book, pnt gray metal, K&O, ca 1928, 6" 125.00
Patriotic Eagle, coated chalk, ca 1970, 5" 20.00
Peacock Splendor, pnt bronze, tail wide, ca 1930, 5¾" 175.00
Penguin Family, birds on base, gray metal, ca 1925, 4¾" 225.00
Pine Cone, bronze w/silver o/l, Heintz Art Metal, ca 1914, 5", up to 400.00
Pioneer Woman, boy at side, pnt gray metal, Jennings Bros, 8½" 300.00
Prancing Greyhound, gold-pnt gray metal, Ronson, 1930, 6" 325.00
Queen of Nile, Egyptian figure, mc pnt, Ronson, 1924 ....475.00
Ride the Waves, sailing ship, brass, Greenblatt Studios, 1925, 5½" .120.00
Ruling Couple, seated Egyptian figures, Bellini Italy, 1980s, 7" .110.00
Russian Wolfhound (seated), CI, gr finish, England, 1925, 6½" .150.00
Scottie on Fence, bronze, ca 1928, 6" 175.00
Shepherdess, relief scenic, gray metal, Pompeian Bronze Co, 1925, 4" 135.00
Slashing Samurai, action figure, gray metal, Ronson, 7⅛" 375.00
Thinker, nude man sits in thoughtful pose, gray metal, Ronson, 5½" ..125.00
Village Blacksmith, figure at work in relief, bronze, 1930s, 5½" ...125.00
Washington Bust, pnt gray metal, Ronson, ca 1932, 5½" 85.00
Ye Olde Inn, Syroco Wood, ca 1940, 6¼" 45.00
10 Commandments, gray metal, LV Aronson, 1922, 3¾", 5" 175.00

Bootjacks and Bootscrapers

Bootjacks were made from metal or wood. Some were fancy figural shapes, others strictly business! Their purpose was to facilitate the otherwise awkward process of removing one's boots. Bootscrapers were handy gadgets that provided an effective way to clean the soles of mud and such. Our advisor for this category is Louis Picek; he is listed in the Directory under Iowa.

Bootjacks

Am Bull Dog, CI pistol shape, folding, blk pnt 90.00
Beetle-shaped jaws, CI, no pnt, ca 1880 ....50.00
Cat silhouette, blk-pnt CI, 10½x10" 295.00
Cricket, CI, no pnt, Webster Bros, Reading PA, 11" 55.00
Heart form w/scalloped sides, CI, 13" L 145.00
Lee Riders advertising, wood w/leather trim, EX 75.00
Naughty Nellie, CI, worn copper pnt, 10½x4½x4½" 135.00
Pine w/sq nails, lg, early 80.00
Sunflower, brass, Musselman's Plug advertising 150.00

Bootscrapers

Aunt Jemima figure atop, CI, rpt, 14½" 285.00
Beetle form, CI, orig pnt, 10½" 85.00
CI, scrolled harp shape, 7⅞x7¼" 40.00
Dachshund, CI, old worn wht pnt, 1900s, 7x22x5" 25.00
Dog, cast steel, blk pnt, simple tooling, 13" 140.00
Dog silhouette, blk-pnt CI, 10½x10" 295.00
Duck, CI, full bodied w/scraper on bk, 14½" L 350.00
Eagle relief & classical lady in oval, CI, Portland Foundry 300.00
Griffins jtd at wings & tails, CI w/marble base, 18" 880.00
Scottie dog, CI, orig pnt, EX 65.00

Borsato, Antonio

Borsato was a remarkable artist/sculptor who produced some of the most intricately modeled and executed figurines ever made. He was born in Italy and at an early age enjoyed modeling wildlife from clay he dug from the river banks near his home. At age eleven, he became an apprentice of Guido Cacciapuotti of Milan, who helped him develop his skills. During the late '20s and '30s, he continued to concentrate on wildlife studies. Because of his resistance to the fascist government, he was interred at Sardinia from 1940 until the end of the war, after which he returned to Milan where he focused his attention on religious subjects. He entered the export market in 1948 and began to design pieces featuring children and more romantic themes. By the 1960s his work had become very popular in this country. His talent for creating lifelike figures has seldom been rivaled. He contributed much of his success to the fact that each of his figures, though built from the same molded pieces, had its own personality, due the unique way he would tilt a head or position an arm. All had eyelashes, fingernails, and defined musculature; and each piece was painted by hand with antiquated colors and signed 'A. Borsato.' He made over six hundred different models, with some of his groups requiring more than one hundred and sixty components and several months of work to reach completion.

Borsato died in 1982. Today, some of his work is displayed in the Vatican Museum as well private collections.

Prices vary according to size and the amount of work involved. Single figures often fetch $1,000.00. Larger pieces, for instance, 'Gypsy Camp' or 'Revelry,' may go from $12,000.00 to as high as $15,000.00. 'Play Gypsy Play' was originally made in the early '30s; a second version followed in the late '40s, and a limited edition was created to mark the 30th anniversary of the date he began his work. Though he planned to make thirty of these limited edition groupings, he died after only thirteen had been completed. This version was larger than the first two and has sold on the secondary market for more than $50,000.00. Various pieces were made in two mediums, gres and porcelain, with porcelain being double the cost of gres. In the listings that follow, our suggested values should be regarded as conservative.

Our advisor for this category is Betty O. Martin, she is listed in the Directory under California.

Large (limited edition) version of 'Play Gypsy Play,' #9 of edition of 13, #1274, 17¼ x 18", minimum value, $50,000.00. (Photo courtesy Betty O. Martin)

Caner, The; man caning chairs w/supplies 1,900.00
Christ's Resurrection, 13th Station of the Cross, 7 figures, 19" .5,000.00
Farmer toting wood on bk w/goat, 8½x11½" 1,200.00
Fisherman, catching a fish w/fish in creel, 6¼x8¼" 900.00
Grandparents, Grandma doing needlework, Grampa smoking pipe, 8" ...1,100.00
Man & woman on bench w/dog, 5⅜x7⅝" 1,200.00
Mother w/child (naked) on bk, tree trunk w/flower on base, 9" ..1,100.00
Siesta's Price, fruit cart, peddler asleep while cash drw is robbed .2,700.00
Sylvan Beauty, lady w/flowers 1,100.00

Boru, Sorcha

Sorcha Boru was the professional name used by California ceramist Claire Stewart. She was a founding member of the Allied Arts Guild of Menlo Park (California) where she maintained a studio from 1932 to 1938. From 1938 until 1955, she operated Sorcha Boru Ceramics, a production studio in San Carlos. Her highly acclaimed output consisted of colorful, slip-decorated figurines, salt and pepper shakers, vases, wall pockets, and flower bowls. Most production work was incised 'S.B.C.' by hand.

Bowl, appl lilies at ruffled rim, 6½" 85.00
Bowl, maroon, appl peony on lid, 6" 85.00
Cup, 3 dinosaur hdls 75.00
Figurine, bluebird male & female, 5", 6½", pr 350.00
Figurine, Penelope, fawn, 6" 85.00
Figurine, shepherdess 155.00
Pitcher, pk lustre florals w/gold centers, beading, 6½" 80.00
Shakers, bride & groom, pr 175.00
Shakers, elephants, pr 95.00
Shakers, man & woman fox hunters, pr 165.00
Shakers, sailor boy & girl, pr 125.00
Sugar shaker, lady figure, 6" 110.00
Vase, appl flowers & leaves, 8" 75.00

Bossons Artware

Bossons closed operations December 1996. The company (located in England) was founded by the late William Henry Bossons in 1944; his son W. Ray Bossons (now deceased) was manager from 1951 until he retired in 1994. It was always owned and managed by the Bossons family, who have stored the only remaining molds (many have been destroyed) and at the present time have no intention of selling them or the Bossons name.

With the company's closing, all Bossons are now categorized as discontinued; as stock holdings are depleted, some are appreciating at a very fast rate. Many that sold in the US for under $5.00 are now in the range of $100.00 to $300.00. Bossons were exported to nearly forty countries around the globe with Canada and the U.S. being the most important importers, and as a result, collector interest is widespread.

Major points to remember:

1) Not all will have the name incised under the collar (e.g., Syrian, Smuggler, Tibetan, and Tyrolean, see *Schroeder's* 17th Ed. for pictures).

2) Many character studies in gypsum plaster are produced in England that are not Bossons; to be specific, Legends, Naturecraft, and those incised 'Made in England.' Fraser-Art products are Bossons, so are products marked Briar Rose and Bossons Ivorex. Osborne Ivorex is not Bossons.

3) Except in very rare cases, all carry the incised copyright: 'Bossons, Congleton, England, World copyright reserved' on the back **and** in most cases under the collars, along with that particular 'Bossons' specific name. **Important:** The copyright date is a mold release date; each Beefeater, for example, will carry the date 1966. This is not the date of manufacture, so it has no bearing on value.

Though they can be used for authentication, a signature is not a critical consideration when determining value; most are the initials of painters, e.g., PB is Phyllis Brightwell. FW (Fred Wright), AB (Alice Brindley), and WRB (W. Ray Bossons) are sculptor/modelers. Mold makers' marks include K (Ken Potts), P (George Proudlove), and D (Damen Smith). In extremely rare instances where the Bossons copyright does not appear, it is sometimes possible to make positive identification using these initials.

Suggestions for evaluating Bossons based on rarity and condition:

A. Determine the copyright (release) date from under the collar or on the back.

B. Length of production helps determine rarity; with few exceptions, the earlier (1958–63) and latest (1986–98) are found in fewer numbers. This information can be found in *Imagical World of Bossons, Vol. 1, 1946–82*, and *Vol. II, 1982–94*, by Dr. Robert E. Davis. (See advisor's Directory listing for information on this publication.) Examples in rare color combinations may be valued at 200% to 300% of retail as indicated in the line listings that follow.

C. Condition is a major factor. If mint and in original colors, a Bossons is worth 100% of its retail value. Premium prices are obtained for only pristine, mint condition Bossons, either factory mint in original boxes or perfectly returned to their original structural and coloring beauty by a professional restoration artist recommended by Bossons.

Beware of fakes and look-alikes; above all, know your dealer. Be aware that Internet auctions are flooded with plaster 'faces' and figures claiming to be Bossons in mint condition which are neither mint nor Bossons.

See Clubs, Newsletters, and Catalogs in the Directory for information about *Bossons Briefs*, the quarterly magazine of the International Bossons Collector' Society (IBCS). Our advisor for this category is Dr. Don Hardisty; since 1984 he has been recommended by Bossons to restore their products. He is listed in the Directory under New Mexico. Visit his website for more information.

Abduhl, 1961-86, widely available today, M, minimum value 55.00
Aruja Barbarossa, 1994-96, (2-yr production), MIB, from $145 to .250.00
Espana (male & female), very desirable, poor condition 600.00
Espana (male & female), very desirable, prof rstr, minimum value .6,000.00
Examples originally valued at $5, many models, from $100 to ...300.00
Examples released ca 1959, rare, from $500 to 1,000.00
Examples released ca 1959, very rare (few examples), minimum value ..10,000.00

Mr. Wang, Left: first edition, sculptor Fred Wright, 1959, Bossons England, no established value; Right: second edition, IBCS special issue, 1995, from $450.00 to $600.00. (Photo courtesy Dr. Don Hardisty)

Punjabi, gr hat (standard color), from $65 to 100.00
Punjabi, yel hat (rare), from $200 to 300.00
Snake Charmer, 1959-64, (once $700-900), EX, now from $300 to ...500.00

Bottle Openers

Around the turn of the century, manufacturers began to seal bottles with a metal cap that required a new type of bottle opener. Now the screw cap and the flip top have made bottle openers nearly obsolete. There are many variations, some in combination with other tools. Many openers were used as means of advertising a product. Various materials were used, including silver and brass.

A figural bottle opener is defined as a figure designed for the sole purpose of lifting a bottle cap. The actual opener must be an integral part of the figure itself. A base-plate opener is one where the lifter is a separate metal piece attached to the underside of the figure. The major producers of iron figurals were Wilton Products, John Wright Inc., Gadzik Sales, and L & L Favors. Openers may be free-standing and three-dimensional, wall hung, or flat. They can be made of cast iron (often painted), brass, bronze, or aluminum.

Numbers within the listings refer to a reference book printed by the FBOC (Figural Bottle Opener Collectors) organization. Those seeking additional information are encouraged to contact FBOC, whose address can be found in the Directory under Clubs, Newsletters, and Catalogs. The items below are all in excellent original condition unless noted otherwise.

Alligator, bronze, F-138, 5" 20.00
Alligator, pot metal, F-137, 2⅜x6" 16.00
Amish Boy, CI, F-31, 4x2" 275.00
Auto Jack, chrome, F-211 ....32.00
Beaver, bronze, F-90, 3½x4¼" 75.00
Billy Goat, aluminum, F-74a, 2¾x1⅞" 15.00
Billy Goat, CI, F-74, 2¾x2¾" 180.00
Canada Goose, bronze, F-105b, 1½x3½" 30.00
Cat, brass, F-95, 2¼x3" 40.00
Cathy Coed, CI, F-35, 4½" 725.00
Cowboy Sign Post, CI, F-14, 4⅛" 60.00
Cowboy w/Guitar, CI, F-27, 4¾" 90.00
Donkey, aluminum, F-60a, 3½x3¼" 15.00
Donkey, brass, F-60, 3¼" 15.00
Elephant, brass, F-48a, 3⅜" 15.00
Elephant, CI, F-48, 3½x2½" 30.00

False Teeth, CI, F-420, 3⅜" 75.00
Fish, abalone, F-164 ....35.00
Flamingo, pot metal, F-119, 4¼x3¼" 120.00
Goat, brass, F-71a, 4¼" 40.00
Hanging Drunk, wall mt, CI, F-415, 5" 80.00
Lamppost Drunk, CI, F-1, 4⅛" 15.00
Lamppost Drunk, mtd on ashtray, F-2 ....20.00
Lamppost Drunk, mtd on marble paperweight, F-1e 32.00
Mademoiselle, lamppost & sign, CI, F-10, 4½" 32.00
Mallard Duck, CI, F-106, 2⅝x3¼" 25.00
Monkey, aluminum, F-89b, 2⅝" 30.00
Parrot, Sm; brass, F-112a, 3" 40.00
Pelican, brass, F-129a, 3¼" 45.00
Signpost Drunk, CI, mtd on ashtray, F-11 ....20.00
4-Eyed Lady, wall mt, CI, F-407 ....130.00
4-Eyed Man, wall mt, CI, F-413 ....60.00

Bottles and Flasks

As far back as the first century B.C., the Romans preferred blown glass containers for their pills and potions. Though you're not apt to find many of those, you will find bottles of every size, shape, and color made to hold perfume, ink, medicine, soda, spirits, vinegar, and many other liquids. American business firms preferred glass bottles in which to package their commercial products and used them extensively from the late eighteenth century on. Bitters bottles contained 'medicine' (actually herb-flavored alcohol), and judging from the number of these found today, their contents found favor with many! Because of a heavy tax imposed on the sale of liquor in seventeenth-century England by King George, who hoped to curtail alcohol abuse among his subjects, bottlers simply added 'curative' herbs to their brew and thus avoided taxation. Since gin was taxed in America as well, the practice continued in this country. Scores of brands were sold; among the most popular were Dr. H.S. Flint & Co. Quaker Bitters, Dr. Kaufman's Anti-Cholera Bitters, and Dr. J. Hostetter's Stomach Bitters. Most bitters bottles were made in shades of amber, brown, and aquamarine. Clear glass was used to a lesser extent, as were green tones. Blue, amethyst, red-brown, and milk glass examples are rare. (Please note that color is a strong factor when pricing bottles. For example, an amber Hostetter's bitters sells for $25.00 or less, but a green variant can bring hundreds of dollars. An aqua scroll flask may bring $50.00, but a cobalt blue variation will command over $1,000.00.)

Perfume or scent bottles were produced abroad by companies all over Europe from the late sixteenth century on. Perfume making became such a prolific trade that as a result beautifully decorated bottles were fashionable. In America they were produced in great quantities by Stiegel in 1770 and by Boston and Sandwich in the early nineteenth century. Cologne bottles were first made in about 1830 and toilet-water bottles in the 1880s. Rene Lalique produced fine scent bottles from as early as the turn of the century. The first were one-of-a-kind creations done in the cire perdue method. He later designed bottles for the Coty Perfume Company with a different style for each Coty fragrance.

Spirit flasks from the nineteenth century were blown in specially designed molds with varied motifs including political subjects, railroad trains, and symbolic devices. The most commonly used colors were amber, dark brown, and green.

From the twentieth century, early pop and beer bottles are very collectible as is nearly every extinct commercial container. Dairy bottles are a relatively new area of interest; look for round bottles in good condition with both city and state as well as a nice graphic relating to the farm or the dairy.

Bottles may be dated by the methods used in their production. For instance, a rough pontil indicates a date before 1845. After the bottle was blown, a pontil rod was attached to the bottom, a glob of molten glass acting as the 'glue.' This allowed the glassblower to continue to manipulate the extremely hot bottle until it was finished. From about 1845 until approximately 1860, the molten glass 'glue' was omitted. The rod was simply heated to a temperature high enough to cause it to afix itself to the bottle. When the rod was snapped off, a metallic residue was left on the base of the bottle; this is called an 'iron pontil.' (The presence of a pontil scar thus indicates early manufacture and increases the value of a bottle.) A seam that reaches from base to lip marks a machine-made bottle from after 1903, while an applied or hand-finished lip points to an early mold-blown bottle. The Industrial Revolution saw keen competition between manufacturers, and as a result, scores of patents were issued. Many concentrated on various types of closures; the crown bottle cap, for instance, was patented in 1892. If a manufacturer's name is present, consulting a book on marks may help you date your bottle.

Among our advisors for this category are Madeleine France (see the Directory under Florida), Mark Vuono (Connecticut), Steve Ketcham (Minnesota), and Monsen and Baer (Virginia). In the listings that follow (most of which have been taken from auction catalogs), glass is assumed to be clear unless color is indicated. Numbers refer to a standard reference book, *American Glass*, by George and Helen McKearin. See also Advertising, various companies; Barber Shop Collectibles; Blown Glass; Blown Three-Mold Glass; California Perfume Company; Czechoslovakia; De Vilbiss; Fire Fighting; Lalique; Medical Collectibles; Sandwich Glass; Steuben; Zanesville Glass.

Key:

am — applied mouth	grd — ground pontil
bbl — barrel	GW — Glass Works
bt — blob top	ip — iron pontil
b3m — blown 3-mold	ps — pontil scar
cm — collared mouth	rm — rolled mouth
fl — filigree	sb — smooth base
fm — flared mouth	sl — sloping
gm — ground mouth	sm — sheared mouth
gp — graphite pontil	tm — tooled mouth

Barber Bottles

Amethyst with white enameling, Bay Rum and mill scene, open pontil, 1880s, 8", $275.00.

Blk amethyst w/wht & gold florals, sb, sm, 7⅞" 600.00
Cobalt rib pattern w/gold Art Nouveau decor, ps, rm, 7⅝" 400.00
Cobalt rib pattern w/wht enameling, ps, sm, 7⅞" 70.00
Coin Spot, cobalt, mc floral, ps, rm, 8⅛" 120.00
Coin Spot, cranberry opal w/wht o/l, melon sided, sb, rm, 8⅜" .150.00
Coin Spot, dk teal bl, melon sided, sb, rm, 8½" 120.00
Coin Spot, wht opal w/melon sides, sb, rm, 7" 65.00
Cranberry opal w/wht stripes, melon sided, sb, fm, 7⅜" 90.00

Daisy & Fern, bl opal sb, rm, 7⅜" 110.00
Daisy & Fern, cranberry opal, melon sides, sb, rm, 7⅛" 170.00
Emerald gr (dk) w/mc enameling, ps, rm, 8⅛" 85.00
Gr rib pattern w/red/yel/wht/gold enameling, ps, sm, 7⅛" 65.00
Grape amethyst w/mc enameling, ps, rm, 8⅛" 85.00
Grass gr frost rib pattern w/wht & gold decor, ps, sm, 7¾" 350.00
Hobnail, cranberry, 8" 175.00
Hobnail, cranberry opal, sm chips, 7" 130.00
Hobnail, turq bl, polished p, rm, sm chips, 7⅛" 50.00
Invt T'print, clear w/cranberry flashing inside, rm, 6¾" 130.00
Label under glass: Fred W Suttle Bay Rum w/roses on milk glass, 10" .220.00
Mary Gregory decor on purple amethyst, Vegederma, ps, rm, 7⅝" 400.00
Milk glass cased w/turq, overall emb dmns, sb, rm, 8¼" 160.00
Milk glass w/mc cherubs, ps, sm, 7⅝" 230.00
Pk-lav rib pattern w/orange/wht/bl enameling, ps, rm, 6⅞" 150.00
Purple amethyst rib pattern, bell form w/mc floral, 7⅝" 70.00
Purple amethyst w/gold Art Nouveau florals, ps, rm, 7⅝" 210.00
Purple amethyst w/wht enameling, sb, sm, 8⅛" 65.00
Purple amethyst w/wht/yel/orange enameling, ps, fm, 7½" 90.00
Red cut to clear w/Bohemian-style decor, sb, 8½" 75.00
Spanish Lace, cranberry opal, polished p, rm, 8⅜" 200.00
Stars & Stripes, cranberry 400.00
T'print, saphire bl w/wht/yel/orange decor, ps, rm, 8⅛" 120.00
Turq bl (dk) w/vertical ribs & mc florals, sb, fm, 8¾" 500.00
Turq frost w/cut oval panels, mc enameling, sb, 7¾" 450.00
Turq w/mc enameling, ps, rm, 8⅛" 80.00
Vertical stripes, wht on clear w/vaseline tint, emb dmns, 7¾" ...210.00
Wht opal, Toilet Water & mc florals, corset waist 350.00
Wht opal w/Toilet Water & mc clover, ps, rm, 8⅝" 120.00
Yel-gr rib pattern, mc floral decor, ps, rm, 7¾" 220.00

Bitters Bottles

Baker's Orange Grove, apricot-puce, sb, sl cm, sm chip, 9½" 300.00
Baker's Orange Grove, cherry-puce, sb, sl cm, 9⅜" 800.00
Brown's Celebrated Indian Herb..., amber, queen, 12", NM 600.00
Bryant's Stomach, dk olive gr, 8-sided lady's leg, ps, dbl cm, 12" ..5,000.00
C Gates & Cos Life of Man, lt gr, 95% orig label, sb, 8" 50.00
Corwitz Stomach..., dk bl-aqua, sb, tm, whittle/bubbles, 7⅝" 200.00
Curtis Cordial Calisaya..., root beer-amber, sb, am, 11½", NM .425.00
CW Roback's Stomach Cincinnati O, amber, bbl, ip, sl cm, 9⅞" ..300.00
Davis Kidney & Liver...Cathartic, golden amber, sb, tm, 10" 200.00
Doyle's Hop...1872 (berries & leaves), yel-gr, semicabin, sb, 9⅞" .300.00
Dr AW Coleman's Antidyspeptic..., emerald gr, ip, sl cm, 9⅛", NM 3,600.00
Dr Bell's Golden Tonic, amber, bell figural, ip, am, 10", NM .9,000.00
Dr Blake's Aromatic..NY, dk bl-aqua, ps, sl cm, 7½", NM 140.00
Dr Geo W Bicknell's..., golden amber, sb, sl cm, chip, 9½" 60.00
Dr Langley's Root & Herb...Boston, yel-amber, sb, am, bubbles, 7" ...300.00
Dr Wood's Sarsaparilla & Wild Cherry, aqua, open p, sl cm, 8¾" 280.00
Edw Wilder's Stomach...KY, semicabin, sb, tm, 9¾" 135.00
F Brown Boston Sarsparilla & Tomato, aqua, ps, sl cm, 9¼" 275.00
Great Tonic Caldwell's Herb..., golden amber, ip, sl cm, 12¾" ..190.00
Hartwig Kantorowicz Posen..., bright grass gr, sb, am, bubbles, 13" ..1,000.00
Holtzermann's Pat Stomach, amber, 4-roof cabin, sb, 9¾" 190.00
Holtzermann's Pat Stomach, red-amber, 4-roof cabin, sb, tm, 9¾" ...230.00
Kelly's Old Cabin Pat 1863, yel-amber, sb, sl cm, chips, 9¼" .1,000.00
Lediard's Celebrated Stomach, bl-gr, sb, sl dbl cm, cleaned, 10" .400.00
Morning (star) Inceptum 5869..., med amber, ip, sl cm, 12½" ...180.00
National, med yel-amber, ear of corn, Pat 1867 on sb, am, 12½" .300.00
Old Dr Townsend's Celebrated..., golden yel-amber, hdld chestnut, 9" 10,000.00
Old Homestead Wild Cherry..., golden yel-amber, cabin, sb, 9⅜" .350.00
Old Sachem...Wigwam Tonic, dk strawberry puce, sb, am, 9⅜", NM ...575.00
Oxygenated For Dyspepsia..., aqua, ps, sl cm, 7½" 120.00
PDH & CO Sazerac Aromatic, milk glass, lady's leg, sb, 12⅛" ..275.00
Professor Geo J Byrne...1870, amber, sb, sl dbl cm, 10¾" 1,200.00
Royal Pepsin Stomach...Sole Agents, red-amber, sb, tm, 3⅞", NM ...230.00
Smyrna Stomach Prolongs Life, golden amber, sb, tm, paneled neck, 9" ..1,000.00
Southern Aromatic Cock Tail..., yel, lady's leg, sb, stain, 12⅝" .600.00
St Drake's 1860 Plant'n X Pat 1862, burgundy, 6-log, 10" 150.00
St Drake's 1860 Plant'n X Pat 1862, dk cherry puce, 6-log, 9⅞" ...250.00
St Drake's 1860 Plant'n X Pat 1862, golden amber, 4-log, 10¼" 210.00
St Drake's 1860 Plant'n X Pat 1862, strawberry puce, 6-log, 10" ...220.00
St Drake's 1860 Plant'n X Pat 1862, yel-amber, 4-log, 10⅛" 240.00
The Fish...Pat 1866, amber, fish figural, sb, am, 11½" 200.00
Wahoo & Calisaya...Jacob Pinkerton..., amber, semicabin, 10⅜" .600.00

Black Glass Bottles

Many early European and American bottles are deep, dark green or amber in color. Collectors refer to such coloring as black glass. Before held to light, the glass is so dark it appears to be black.

Demijohn, dk olive gr, ps, sl cm, crude/bubbles, 12⅝" 220.00
Demijohn, dk tobacco-amber, ps, sl cm, bubbles, 17½" 350.00
Demijohn, med olive gr, ps, sl cm, long neck, 18¾" 90.00
Demijohn, olive gr, kidney shape, ps, sl cm, 2-pc mold, 17⅝" ...210.00
Demijohn, olive gr, ps, sl cm, 21" 120.00
Demijohn, olive-amber, ps, sl cm, bubbles, 11⅜" 140.00
Mallet, dk olive-amber, ps on deep kick-up, am, dullness, 8⅝" ..170.00
Mallet, olive gr w/amber tone, ps, am, ca 1730-40, ½-sz, 6" 775.00
Onion, med olive gr w/mc pnt scenes, ps, am, 7" 400.00
Ribbon seal: LI Knudsen, dk cherry red, sb, dbl cm, 8⅝" 170.00
Seal: Elizir Ue Cullie G, dk olive-amber, sb, am, 7" 100.00
Seal: GR 1801, dk olive-amber, ps, am, high shoulders, 8¾" 500.00
Seal: TC (in shield w/hand), dk olive gr, ps, am, flake, 11" 180.00
Seal: TS Cann Indham 1813, olive gr, ps on deep kick-up, am, 10½" ...425.00
Seal: WS, olive-amber, ps, am, 11¼" 210.00
Square, olive-amber, ps, sm, bubbles, 4¾" 110.00
Wine, dk olive-amber, ps, sl dbl cm, 11⅝" 150.00
Wine, dk olive-amber, ps, wide mushroom mouth, 1770-90, 13⅜" 350.00

Blown Glass Bottles and Flasks

Chestnut flask, bright olive yel, sm, ps, 9¾" 180.00
Chestnut flask, med yel-olive, sm w/appl rim, ps, 7" 160.00
Chestnut flask, yel-olive, sl c/m, ps, 8½" 160.00
Chestnut flask, yel-olive, sm w/appl rim, ps, 5¼" 170.00
Demijohn, golden amber, kidney form, sm w/appl ring, sb, 18½" ...200.00
Demijohn, med emerald gr, kidney form, sl/m, ps, 18½", NM ...260.00
Demijohn, olive-yel, kidney form, sm w/collar, sb, 1830-60, 17" ..150.00
Demijohn, yel, kidney form, sl/m, sb, Am, 1860-80, 17" 260.00
Globular, yel-amber w/olive tone, rm, ps, mini, 1783-1830, 3¼" .700.00

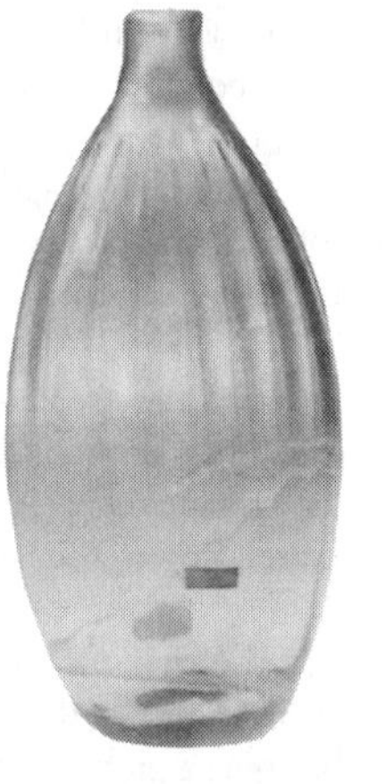

Nurser, greenish aqua, 19 vertical ribs, pontil scar, sheared mouth, American, 1830 – 50, 7¾", NM, $85.00.

Pitkin flask, lt gr, 16 broken swirl ribs, 5¼" 400.00
Pitkin flask, lt yel-olive, 36-broken right-swirl ribs, ps, 5" 325.00
Utility, bright yel-olive, am, ps, 1840-60, 13½" 100.00

Cologne, Perfume, and Toilet Water Bottles

Atomizer, HP landscape & trees on amber & frosty sky, Malo, 5¾" ...225.00
Atomizer, monocrome sepia cottages along water, Mignon, 6" ..200.00
Bl opaque, free-blown, rm, ps, 9" 110.00
Cobalt, free-blown, rm, sb, 11" 130.00
Dk apple gr, 18 vertical ribs w/twists in neck, ps, sm, 3" 95.00
Dk teal bl, 12-sided, sb, rm, 4¾" 85.00
Powder bl opaque, ps, rm, 13¾" 130.00

Commercial Perfume Bottles

One of the most popular and growing areas of perfume bottle collecting is what are called 'commercial' perfume bottles. They are called commercial because they were sold with perfume in them — in a sense one pays for the perfume and the bottle is free. Collectors especially value bottles that retain their original label and box, called a perfume presentation. If the bottle is unopened, so much the better. Rare fragrances and those from the 1920s are highly prized. 'Tis a sweet, sweet hobby. Our advisors are Randy Monsen and Rod Baer; they are listed in the Directory under Virginia.

Bourjois, Glamour, w/gold crown cap, full, 1953, 2½", MIB 55.00
Bourjois, Soir de Paris, bl w/silver cap, 2", Bakelite door case 220.00
Corday, Orchidèe Bleue, replica, 1½", +bl/gold box 88.00
D'Orsay, Fleur de France, disk w/gold label, 2⅜", box 88.00
D'Orsay, Intoxication, pleated replica w/silver cap, 2¼", +box 65.00
Dana, Tabu, sq w/label, blk, cap, near full, 7¼" 90.00
DuBarry, Bunch of Violets, w/plastic base/mermaid cap, 3½" 155.00
Elizabeth Arden, Mèmoire Chèrie, w/gold, 1½", +ornate case 467.50
Elizabeth Taylor, Passion, violet w/molded facets, gold dmn, 12½" 285.00
Estèe Lauder, Cinnabar, foo dog on ped, solid perfume, 2" 575.00
G Hayman, Delicious, rock shape w/snow leopard metal top, factice, 7" ..465.00
Gorgio Beverly Hills, Red, faceted column w/ribbon, 15½" 165.00
Guerlain, Mitsouko, stopper w/plastic tip, front label, 12", MIB ...550.00
Guerlain, Rose du Moulin, gr jar w/flourishes, label, 1907, 1¾" ..90.00
H Carnegie, Carnegie Blue, head/shoulders, mini, 1¾", +box 1,200.00
Halston, Catalyst, clear/frost curvaceous flame-like shape, 14" ..200.00
Jacques Fath, Fath's Love, pleated w/gold cap, 2¾", +box 80.00
Jean Patou, Joy, gold label, logo stopper, 6⅝" 250.00

Lancome, Nativitè, frosted with gold winged angels and rays, Delhomme design, limited edition, 1945, $1,100.00. (Photo courtesy Monsen and Baer)

Lubin Ocèan Bleu, replica, gold cap/label, 2¼", +box 65.00
Lucien Lelong, Siròcco, vial/bottle/stick, travel set, MIB 25.00
Matchabelli, Crown Jewel, gold on clear crown, 1¾", M 275.00
Matchabelli, Windsong, gr/gold/blk enamel crown, factice, 8⅜", NM .1,100.00
Myrugia, Promesa, clear w/gold label/cap, 1½", +box w/dancers front 100.00
N Ricci, Capricci, w/filigree, w/funnel/label, 2⅜", +box 155.00
N Ricci, L'Air du Temps/Capricci/Coeur Joir, replica minis, MIB ...880.00
Paloma Picasso, 2¼" ball in wht plastic abstract form, +box 55.00
R Hudnut, Deauville, scalloped, w/label, 2⅜", silk bag 55.00
Renoir ChiChi, heart w/Bakelite cap, mini, 2", +showgirl box 440.00
Saville, Mischief, blk, 1¾", wht Cupid w/blk cap case 155.00
Saville, Mischief, blk w/silver label, metal cap, 1¾", +egg case .110.00
Schiaparelli, Succès Fou, fig-leaf over pk heart, 2", +box 320.00
Stuart, Perfumatone, 3 minis w/bl caps in pk plastic radio, +box .88.00
V Vivaudou, Lucky Sambo, African caricature cloth sachet, 3¼", +box ..100.00
Worth, Vers le Jour, amber w/molded chevron stopper, mini, 2⅛" ..185.00

Dairy Bottles

Absolutely Pure.../man milking emb, metal closure, pt 300.00
Hampden (cow's head) Creamery Co, tin top, ½-pt 75.00
Lyon Brook Dairy...Bklyn..., sb, tm, metal closure, pt 90.00
NY Dairy Co (shield) emb, tm, metal closure/stopper, qt 65.00
Sanitary Dairy Chisholm ME, ½-pt 5.00
Scotia Pure...& Returned, sb, tm, 20th C, ½-gal 30.00
Speedwell Farm (cow's head), Wash & Return, tin lid, ½-pt 70.00
SV Saquoit Valley (Indian chief) Dairy Co, w/ribs, sb, qt 25.00
TA Spencer Pure...Spring Lake NJ, sun-colored amethystine, qt .35.00
Turner Center System, This Bottle Not Sold..., ½-pt 15.00

Figural Bottles

Artichoke, dk olive gr, Gesetzlich/Geschutzt on sb, 9⅝" 250.00
Bear, clear, Distrie Mercator SA..., sb, tm, 9⅞" 170.00
Benjamin Harrison bust on column, clear frost on blk column, 11¼" ...975.00
Car, clear frost, Depose emb on license plate, sb, 5⅝" 100.00
Clam, med amber, sb, gm, metal screw cap, 5¼" 110.00
Coachman w/pipe & glass, milk glass, sb, 10¼", NM 1,500.00
Fountain, turq shading to clear, Depose on ps base, tm, 10¾" ...575.00
Kummel Bear, olive-amber (blk), sb, am, 11⅛" 35.00
Lady in flowing dress, med gr, Depose, ps, rm, 13⅛" 1,150.00
Man on stump, cobalt, ps, fm, 7⅛" 525.00
Orange, P Bardinet Bordeau, straw yel w/orange tone, sb, 4⅛" 40.00
Ship, clear frost, sb, gm, gold pnt traces, 6¼" 500.00

Flasks

Baltimore/Anchor GW, GXIII-48, golden yel-amber, sb, dbl cm, qt ...500.00
Clasped Hands/Eagle, GIV-42, aqua, sb, sl cm, calabash, 9¼" 65.00
Corn for World/Ear of Corn, GV-16, bright yel-gr, ps, sm, pt .6,250.00
Corn for World/Ear of Corn/Baltimore, GVI-5, yel-amber, qt ..1,900.00
Cornucopia/Urn, GIII-4, yel-amber, ps, sm, pt 100.00
Eagle/Clasped Hands, GXIII-18, med amber, sb, am, pt 625.00
Eagle/Cornucopia, GII-72, olive-amber, ps, sm, pt 150.00
Eagle/For Our Country, GII-54, chocolate tobacco-amber, ps, sm, pt ...4,800.00
Eagle/JKB Masonic Arch, GIV-3, yel topaz to yel-gr, ps, pt 4,100.00
Eagle/Tree, GII-60, aqua, ps, sm, ½-pt 375.00
Flora Temple/Standing Horse, GXIII-23, bl-gr, sb, am, lacks hdl, pt ...425.00
For Pike's Peak Prospector/Eagle, GXI-9, dk bl-aqua, sb, am, pt ..70.00
Franklin/Dyott, GI-94, aqua, ps, sm, pt 190.00
Franklin/Franklin, GI-97, lt gr-aqua, ps, sm, qt 55.00
Horseman/Hound, aqua, sb, dbl cm, pt 95.00
Hunter Fisherman, GXIII-4, med puce, ip, sl cm, calabash, sm stain 300.00
Isabella GW/Sheaf of Wheat, GXIII-56, aqua, ps, sm, pt 180.00
Jenny Lind/Glasshouse, aqua, ps, sl cm, calabash 75.00
Lafayette/TS DeWitt Clinton, med yel-olive, ps, sm, stain, pt ...425.00

Louis Kossuth/US Steam Frigate, GI-112, bl-aqua, ip, calabash .250.00
Lowell RR Horse Drawn Cart/Eagle, GV-10, olive gr, ps, ½-pt .250.00
Masonic Arch/Eagle KCCNC, GIV-18, med yel-amber, ps, sm, pt 875.00
Pikes Peak/Prospector Hunter, GIX-50, root beer-amber, sb, am, pt ..1,050.00
Sheaf of Wheat/Star, dk bl-aqua, ps, sl cm, bubbles, calabash 150.00
Success to RR/Horse Pulling Cart, GV-3, yel-amber, open p, sm, pt ...275.00
Success to RR/Horse Pulling Cart-Eagle, GV-8, olive gr, ps, pt 80.00
Summer Tree/Winter Tree, GX-19, dk bl-aqua, open p, am, qt ...1,650.00
Travelers Companion/Star, med amber, ip, sm, ½-pt 300.00
Union/Clasped Hands Cannon, lime gr, sb, am, stain, pt 500.00
Union/Clasped Hands Eagle, amber, sb, am, ½-pt 160.00
US Battleship Maine, sb, gm, metal screw cap, haze, 5¾" 275.00
Washington/Eagle, GI-26, bl-aqua, ps, sm, stain, qt 180.00
Washington/Taylor, GI-42, lt teal bl, ps, sm, qt 375.00
Washington/Taylor, GI-54, dk yel-olive, ps, sl dbl cm, qt 550.00
Washington/Taylor, GI-55, lt bl gr, ps, am, pt 120.00
Westford Glass Co/Sheaf of Wheat, GXIII-27, dk tobacco-amber, ½-pt 120.00
Westford Glass Co/Sheaf of Wheat, GXIII-35, olive gr, sb, pt ...110.00

Food Bottles and Jars

Berry, bright yel-gr, ps, rm, 11⅛" 325.00
Berry, petal-style sides, w/offset & am, ps, 12", EX 110.00
Extract, Bastine & Co Pure Flavoring Extracts, dk teal gr, sb, 9¾" ..130.00
Food, med gr, wide mouth bbl, ps, folded-down lip, 8¾" 210.00
Mustard, F&B emb opposite sides, am, crude, early, EX 80.00
Peppersauce, cathedral, lt to med gr, 6-sided, sb, dbl cm, 10½" .625.00
Peppersauce, unmk, open pontil, crude, cleaned 80.00
Peppersauce, Wells Miller Provost, rm, crude, 9½" 90.00
Pickle, Arrow Brand Pickles label, yel-amber, sb, tm, 8⅝" 130.00
Pickle, cathedral, dk bl-gr, sb, am, 13¾" 850.00
Pickle, cathedral, dk gr-aqua, am, sb, crude, 11½", NM 200.00
Pickle, cathedral, lt bl-gr, sb, am, 11⅜" 210.00
Pickle, cathedral, med gr, 6-sided, ip, am, whittled, 13¼" 475.00
Pickle, cathedral, RF Atmore, bl-aqua, ip, rm, 11½" 400.00
Pickle, Stoddard 'Cloverleaf,' red-amber, sb, rm, 8¼" 500.00
Wide mouth, bright olive gr, fm, ps, 9⅜" 160.00
Wide mouth, lt apple gr, sheared tm, ps, 13⅛" 150.00
Wide mouth, med olive gr, ps, sm w/tooled lip, 12" 160.00
Wide mouth, yel-olive, sm, sb, 12½" 130.00

Ink Bottles

Harrison's Columbian Ink, cobalt, pontil scar, applied mouth, 1845 – 55, 7", EX, $525.00.

Blown, cobalt, 16 emb ribs, sb, gm, brass ring, hinged lid, 2⅜" .180.00
Boss Patent, lt apple gr, 6-sided, corset waist, open p, rm, 2¾" ..325.00
B3m geometric, dk olive-amber (blk), ps, tm, 1½" 160.00
B3m geometric, med yel-amber, ps, tm, 2¼" 230.00
B3m geometric, yel-olive gr, ps, tooled disc, 1⅞" 250.00
CA RT ER, cobalt, Carter's on sb, 9¾" 110.00
Cabin, sb, tm, lt stain/flakes, 2½" 200.00
Carter's, med gr, sb, am, tooled spout, 5⅛" 120.00
Cottage, Bank of England, aqua, sb, tm, 3⅝" 650.00
Domed, yel-amber w/emb floral, sb, gr, hinged lid, stain 170.00
Estes NY, med bl-gr, 8-sided, open p, am, 6¼" 650.00
Farley's, yel-amber, 8-sided, open p, thin fm, haze, 3¾" 1,000.00
Harrison Columbian, bl-gr, 8-sided, ps, rm, lt stain, 1⅝" 600.00
Harrison Columbian, lt to med bl-gr, 8-sided, ps, rm, 1⅞" 575.00
Harrison Columbian, med apple gr, 8-sided, ps, rm, 2" 700.00
Hover Phila, emerald gr, open p, sl dbl cm, whittled, 7½" 325.00
Hover Phila, lt to med gr w/olive tone, thin fm, 2⅝", NM 150.00
Paperweight, mc pebble base & stopper core, 20th C, 2⅞" 70.00
Pitkin, dk olive gr, disc mouth, ps, 1¾x1⅝" sq 950.00
Pitkin, dk olive gr, 36 broken left-swirl ribs, ps, tm, 1⅞x2⅜" 625.00
Pitkin, olive gr, 36 right-swirl ribs, ps, disc mouth, 1⅝" 500.00
Pitkin, olive-amber, 36 broken left-swirl ribs, ps, 1⅝x2⅛" 560.00
S Fine Blk, med gr, open p, rm, 3", NM 160.00
Teakettle, blk amethyst, sb, sm, sm chip, 2⅛" 400.00
Teakettle, cobalt, 4-sided w/beveled corners, sb, sm, 1⅝" 325.00
Teakettle, cobalt, 8-sided, sb, sm, lt stain, 2" 150.00
Teakettle, cobalt cut to clear in dmns & circles, 2¼" 625.00
Teakettle, cobalt w/brass medal: G Riddle London on top, 2" ...475.00
Teakettle, gr jade cut to clear, flutes & starbursts, 2⅛" 675.00
Teakettle, milk glass w/emb floral, sb, sterling neck ring, 2½" ...275.00
Teakettle, smoky clear w/amethystine tint, sb, sm, 2⅛" 425.00
Teakettle, wht opal w/orig gold & yel pnt on emb floral, sb, 3" ..525.00
Turtle, free-blown, pk-grape amethyst, ps, dbl rm, sm crack, 1¾" ..575.00
Turtle, J&IEM, cobalt, sb, tm, lt stain, 1¾" 800.00
Turtle, J&IEM, med golden amber, sb, tm, dull stain/bruise, 1¾" ...95.00
Turtle, JJ Butler Cin O, aqua, sb, sm, sm stain, 1⅝" 140.00
Umbrella, bl-aqua, 8-sided, ps, rm, 3⅛" 110.00
Umbrella, cobalt, 8-sided, sb, tm, cleaned, 2⅝" 450.00
Umbrella, dk amethyst, 8-sided, open p, rm, shallow chip, 2⅝" ..325.00
Umbrella, olive-amber, 8-sided, ps, rm, crude/bubbles, 2⅜" 170.00
Umbrella, SO Dunbar Taunton, aqua, 8-sided, rm, stain, 2½" 95.00
Umbrella, Water's Troy NY, aqua, 6-sided, open p, rm, stain, 2⅞" .475.00
Umbrella, yel-amber, 8-sided, sb, tm, 2½" 95.00
12-sided, lt moss gr w/puce/amber striations, sb, rm, 2" 450.00
12-sided, med gr, ps, rm, 2⅛" 120.00

Medicine Bottles

Note: Warner's bottles listed below are not American versions, and so are valued higher than those from Rochester, New York.

AJ White Shaker Family Pills..., amber, sb, sm, 2¾" 85.00
Baker's Vegetable Blood & Liver..., red-amber, sb, tm, stain, 10" 350.00
C Heimstreet & Co Troy NY, sapphire bl, 8-sided, ps, 7⅛" 275.00
CGW GPOE, bl-aqua, open p, rm, 99% label, 4⅞" 70.00
Dr Claris' Veterinary Hospital...NY, sb, tm, NM label, 7⅝" 190.00
Dr Davis's Depurative Phila, bl-gr, ip, sl cm, 9¾" 2,700.00
Dr Foster's Anti-Catarrh, dk teal gr, 8-sided bullet, 3¾" 135.00
Dr JS Wood Elixir Albany NY, dk bl-gr tombstone, ip, 8¾" ..4,000.00
Dr S Arnold's Balsam, lt aqua, 8-sided, ps, fm, 2⅜" 160.00
Dr SA Weaver's Canker & Salt Rheum Syrup, aqua, ip, cm, chip, 9⅝" ..60.00
Dr Wistar's Balsam of Wild Cherry..., ice bl, 8-sided, ip, 6⅜" 145.00
Dr Wyncoop's Katjarismic NY, cobalt, ps, sl cm, cleaned, 10⅛" ..4,500.00
Genuine Swaim's Panacea Philadelphia, aqua, open p, sl cm, 7¾" .775.00
Gleet Seven Days Gonorrhea, cobalt, sb base, tm, sm stain, 5" .400.00
Graefenberg & Co Dysentery Syrup NY, aqua, ps, sl cm, 6" 70.00
GW Merchant Chemist Lockport NY, bl-gr cylinder, ip, cm, 7" .250.00
Houcks Vegetable Panacea...TN, dk bl-aqua, sb, dbl cm, 7⅛" ...675.00
Leaven's English Vermin Destroyer, aqua, ps, sl cm, 8⅛" 190.00
LQC Wishart's Pine Tree...1859, emerald gr, sb, sl cm, 9½" 200.00
Malanine Hair Tonic Dodge Brothers, dk purple amethyst, sb, 7⅜" ...675.00

Mathewson Horse Remedy..., bl-aqua, ps, dbl cm, 6½" 135.00
Mrs SA Allen's Worlds Hair...NY, aqua, ps, dbl cm, 6⅝" 95.00
Orcutt's Sure Rheumatic Cure, cobalt, sb, tm, rare, 6⅛" 575.00
RP Spence Drug Co...Knoxville TN, yel-gr, sb, tm, sm stain, 4⅝" .85.00
Southern Cough Syrup...New Orleans, aqua, sb, sl cm, 7⅜" 625.00
Swaim's Panacea Philada, yel-olive, ps, sl dbl cm, 7¾", NM 775.00
Swift's Syphilitic Specific, cobalt strap-side flask, sb, 9⅛" 575.00
Warner's Safe Cure Melbourne Aus..., red-amber, sb, dbl cm, 9⅝" ...90.00
Warner's Safe Cure..., dk olive-gr, sb, am, 9", NM 325.00
WM H Keith & Co Apothecaries San Francisco, dk bl-aqua, 8½" ..135.00
Wynkoop's Katarasmic NY, cobalt, ip, sl cm, 10" 7,250.00
Zollickoffer's Anti Rheumatic Cordial..., amber, sb, tm, chip, 6½" ...50.00

Mineral Water Bottles

Adirondack Spring Westport NY, dk emerald gr, sb, sl dbl cm, qt ..220.00
Congress & Empire...(in fr)-Congress Water, emerald gr, sb, 8" .400.00
Cooper's Well Water..., amber, sb, str dbl cm, stain, qt 110.00
DA Knowlton Saratoga NY, dk olive-gr, sb, sl dbl cm, bubbles, pt .140.00
Deep Rock Spring Trade...NY, aqua, sb, sl dbl cm, pt 210.00
Eureka Spring Co-Saratoga NY, dk emerald gr torpedo, sb, 8⅜" .825.00
Excelsior Spring Saratoga NY, olive-amber, sb, dbl cm, stain, pt .110.00
Gettysburg Katalysine Water, emerald gr, sb, dbl cm, bubbles, qt ..80.00
Gettysburg Katalysine Water, olive gr (rare), sb, dbl cm, qt 120.00
Guilford Mineral GMWS..., dk bl-gr, sb, dbl cm, bubbles, qt 145.00
Guilford Mineral GMWS..., grass gr, sb, sl dbl cm, crude, qt 130.00
Highrock Congress Spring 1767..., dk chocolate-amber, sb, dbl cm, qt ...220.00
Highrock Congress Spring...NY, dk teal, sb, dbl cm, pt 100.00
Highrock Congress Spring...NY, emerald gr, sb, cm, pt 170.00
John Clark New York, olive-amber, b3m, ps, sl dbl cm, qt 160.00
John H Gardner & Son...NY, med teal bl, sb, sl dbl cm, pt 275.00
John H Gardner...NY...Sulphur Water, teal bl, sb, Saratoga type 325.00
Kissinger Water Patterson & Brazeau, yel-lime gr, sb, sl cm, pt .130.00
Massena Spring (bird) Water, med teal bl, sb, dbl cm, qt 150.00
Missisquoi A Springs, dk emerald gr, sb, dbl cm, open bubble, qt .80.00
Missisquoi A Springs, med root beer-amber, sb, dbl cm, bubbles, qt ..140.00
Oak Orchard Acid Springs..., dk bl-gr, sb, dbl cm, qt 200.00
Pacific Congress (arched)/Spring, bl-aqua, Saratoga style 1,600.00
Poland Water...H Ricker & Sons..., Moses figural, 11½" 275.00
Poland Water..Moses Bottle..., yel-olive Moses figural, 12", NM ..130.00
Saint Leon Spring Water...MA, emerald gr, sb, cm, pt, NM 135.00
Saratoga Spring (bkwards S), dk yel-olive, sb, sl dbl cm, qt 110.00
Saratoga Spring (star), orange-amber, sb, sl dbl cm, qt 140.00
St Regis Water Massena Springs, teal bl, sb, dbl cm, qt 160.00
Vermont Spring Saxe & Co Sheldon VT, peach-puce, sb, dbl cm, qt, EX 300.00
Washington Spring Saratoga NY, emerald gr, sb, sl dbl cm, pt ...180.00

Poison Bottles

Lattice & Dmn pattern, cobalt, sb, tm, Poison stopper, 3¾" 130.00
Lattice & Dmn pattern, cobalt, sb, tm, 11¼" 375.00
Poison (owl on mortar & pestle) Owl Drug Co, cobalt, 4⅞" 80.00
Poison Poison, clear w/turq o/l, sb, tm, 5¼" 120.00
Poison Wyeth, amber (rare), sb, am, NM labels, 2¼" 200.00
Skull & X bones De-Dro Gift Flasche..., moss gr, sb, am, 4⅝" ...550.00
Skull & X bones Poison Gift, olive gr, 6-sided, sb, 9¾" 325.00

Sarsaparilla Bottles

Dr Townsend's Albany NY, dk grass gr, ip, sl cm, crude, 9⅜" 240.00
Dr Townsend's Albany NY, emerald gr, ip, sl cm, 9⅝" 325.00
Dr Townsend's Albany NY, olive-amber, ps, sl cm, crack, 9½" 70.00
Log Cabin Rochester NY, amber, sb, 9" 95.00
Log Cabin Rochester NY, root beer-amber, sb, am, 80% label, 9" .170.00

Dr Townsend...New York, blue-green, iron pontil, crude and whittled, 8", $300.00.

Old Dr J Townsend's NY, bl-gr, ip, sl cm, flakes, 9½" 325.00
Old Dr J Townsend's NY, lt to med bl or teal, ip, sl cm, 9¾" 375.00

Soda Bottles

A Ledic Utica..., cobalt, 24-sided teepee form, 7⅝" 1,050.00
AP Smith Charleston (slug plate), cobalt, ip, sl cm, cleaned, 7⅜" .220.00
AP Smith Charleston SC (arch variant), cobalt, ip, am, 7⅝" ...375.00
Babb & Co San Francisco, gr, ip, am, lt stain/chip, 7½" 70.00
Charles Clark Charleston SC..., emerald gr, ip, sl cm, 7¾", NM ..140.00
DL Ormsby NY Union GW Phila, dk cobalt, ip, bt, 7⅜" 550.00
Eagle w/shield motif, lt sapphire bl, ip, sl cm, cleaned, 7⅛" 450.00
Eagle w/shield motif, sapphire bl, ip, sl cm, dug, 7⅜" 475.00
Empire Soda Works Vallejo (eagle), bl-gr, sb, am, 7⅜" 100.00
Fields Superior...Charleston SC, cobalt, 8-sided, ip, sl cm, 7⅝" .325.00
Haas Bros...Napa Soda, dk sapphire bl, sb, am, cleaned, 7⅜" 110.00
J Seedorff Charleston SC, med bl-gr, sb, bt, scratches, 7" 300.00
JA Blaffer & Co New Orleans, dk golden amber, sb, dbl cm, 6⅜" .220.00
John Fehr Reading, bl-gr, ip, appl sl dbl cm, 7" 180.00
John Seedorff Charleston SC, cobalt, ip, am, flake/scratch, 7" ..220.00
John Seedorff Charleston SC, dk sapphire bl, ip, bt, 7⅛" 230.00
John Seedorff Charlston SC, sapphire bl, ip, am, open bubble, 7" ..140.00
New Liberty...(Liberty)...Mark SF, aqua, sb, tm, Hutchinson, 6¾" 60.00
Smith & Fotheringham...Sold, dk sapphire bl, 10-sided, ip, 7½" ..150.00
W Eagle NY Union GW..., sapphire bl, mug base, ip, sl cm, 7½" ..350.00
WHH Chicago, dk chocolate-amber (blk), sb, am, chips, 11⅝" ..65.00

Spirits Bottles

AM Bininger...NY, med amber, cannon, sb, 60% label, 12½" ...550.00
Bininger's Night Cap...NY, med amber, sb, am, 8¼", NM 190.00
Buffalo Old Bourbon (buffalo)...CA, sb, tm, 11⅞" 550.00
Casper's Whiskey...People, cobalt, sb, tm, 13⅜" 400.00
Duffy Formula, med amber, sb, M label/contents, 9⅞" 220.00
Forest Lawn JVH, dk olive gr, ip, am, crude, 7½", NM 400.00
Good Old Bourbon in a Hogs, pig figural, sb, tm, 6⅞" 90.00
Griffith Hyatt & Co Baltimore, tobacco-amber, ps, am, hdl, 7⅛" .475.00
R&S Roehling & Schutz Inc Chicago, 4-roof cabin, 9¾", NM .220.00
Schiedam Schnapps Aromatico, dk olive-amber, sb, sl cm, crude, 9¼" 50.00
Star Whiskey...WB Growel Jr, yel-amber, lg open p, am, hdl, 8", NM 220.00
Udolpho Wolfe's Schiedam...Schnapps, apricot-puce, sb, sl cm, 8¼" 200.00
Warranted Flask From Culpeper Liquor..., clear, strap-sided, qt .375.00

Boxes

Boxes have been used by civilized man since ancient Egypt and

Rome. Down through the centuries, specifically designed containers have been made from every conceivable material. Precious metals, papier-mache, Battersea, Oriental lacquer, and wood have held riches from the treasuries of kings, snuff for the fashionable set of the last century, China tea, and countless other commodities. In the following descriptions, when only one dimension is given, it is length. See also Toleware; specific manufacturers.

Hanging pipe box, poplar with gray-blue over red, scalloped backboard and crest, nailed drawer, 19½", $16,500.00 at auction.

Alabaster, gilt filigree fr w/3 kneeling ladies, Germany, rpr, 5⅜" .165.00
Band, pine w/pnt geometric floral on natural, laced seams, 15" .385.00
Bentwood, ash & poplar w/orig pnt floral decor, tin lacing, 14" ..2,000.00
Bentwood, poplar w/orig wallpaper (squirrels), 18½" 1,100.00
Book shape, gr onyx, brass & wood, sm chips on onyx, 5" 165.00
Bride's, pine, bl pnt w/mc flowers/fruit, old rpr, 19" 880.00
Bride's, pine w/mc floral on brn, figure pnt on lid, 17" 500.00
Bride's, pine w/HP boy pushing girl on swing & flowers, 19x12" .2,000.00
Candle, mahog, screws & wire nails, hinged lid, crest, 12" 330.00
Candle, pine, hinged lid, curved crest, dvtl, rfn, 12¾" 330.00
Candle, pine w/old red, 12" 220.00
Document, burlwood, English, 19th C, 5x12½x9" 100.00
Dome top, beech w/HP birds & flowers on wht, staple hinges, 9" ..1,200.00
Dome top, pine w/brn pnt & striping, mc birds/flowers, 10" 1,900.00
Dome top, pine w/mc pnt floral, loose hinges, 7⅜" 600.00
Dome top, poplar w/brn grpt, yel striping, heart escutcheon, 13" ..1,800.00
Dough, pine & poplar, compartments, 1-brd ends & top, 44" 275.00
Glass, blk amethyst, floral/gilt, ormolu ft/rings, 3x3" dia 185.00
Glass, lime gr w/sanded gold & wht decor, hinged, 2" dia 140.00
Glass, sapphire bl, allover gilt decor, hinged, 2½x4½" 160.00
Glass, sapphire bl, cut vertical panels, glass lid, 3x3¼" 90.00
Glass, sapphire bl w/gold & wht floral etc, 3x4½" dia 170.00
Ivory, HP portrait of King Edward VII, over-fitting lid, 2¾" 400.00
Knife, mahog Geo III, serpentine front, herringbone inlay, 13½" ..635.00
Pantry, red pnt wood, nailed, swing hdl, 19th C, 7x11" dia 545.00
Pine w/mc houses pnt on wht, sliding lid, minor rpr, 8¾" 1,100.00
Pipe, red-washed pine, drw, Am, 19th C, 21¼x5¾x4" 3,000.00
Poplar w/old red, brass escutcheon, appl base, 8½" 600.00
Salt, walnut, dvtl drw, curly maple front, slant top, 12x13x7" ...250.00
Spice, poplar w/old red traces, dvtl, 6-compartment, 12x10" 550.00
Stationery, burl walnut casket form, brass mts, 1890s, 7¼" 200.00
Wallpaper covered, cb sides/top/bottom, lift-off lid, 2x3" dia 700.00
Wallpaper covered, wood lid/bottom, 1840s newspaper, 11" ...2,000.00
Wallpaper covered, wood top/bottom oval, lift-off lid, 9¼", VG ..450.00
Walnut w/old red pnt, primitive, rehinged, 15x15x22" 135.00
Work, mahog veneer w/marquetry, slant lid w/pincushion, 7x12" .275.00

Boyd Crystal Art Glass

This small but productive glasshouse has more than 300 molds and has produced more than 350 colors. They are very collector oriented and alter their mark every five years. In 1978 they used a simple B in a diamond. Today, with four changes behind them, the original mark is now encompassed by four additional lines. Vaseline collectors have increased in number, and many of Boyd's Vaseline pieces (variations include Firefly and Citron) are increasing in value rapidly. Many of Boyd's colors — Golden Delight, Peridot, Pippin Green, and others — fluoresce under black light, and are now highly sought after.

In the near future, watch for price increases for Joey the Horse, as the mold has recently been converted to a carousel horse, preventing further production. Li'l Joe the Horse has met the same fate and is now very limited. As always, satins and hand-painted pieces are commanding 10–50% more than the same items in the regular finish.

Internet exposure and the heightened awareness of Boyd collectibles that resulted have caused an increase in prices of from 5% to 85% in some cases. We will wait to see where they level off before endorsing what may be erratic values. Our advisor for this category is Joyce Pringle; she is listed in the Directory under Texas.

Key: (R) — retired

Airplane, Cobalt Blue Carnival, 3½x4", $25.00. (Photo courtesy Joyce Pringle)

Airplane, Cashmire Pink 14.00
Airplane, Columbus White, HP 25.00
Airplane, Milk Chocolate 16.00
Angel, Cobalt 19.00
Angel, Crystal Carnival 20.00
Angel, Vaseline 32.00
Artie the Penguin, Nile Green 10.00
Artie the Penguin, Ruby Red Carnival (R) 20.00
Artie the Penguin, Vaseline 35.00
Bow Slipper, Buckeye 10.00
Bow Slipper, Peach Whisper 30.00
Bow Slipper, Peackock Blue 8.00
Brian Bunny, Banana Cream (R) 35.00
Brian Bunny, Rubina (R) 18.50
Bunny Salt, Lemonade 25.00
Bunny Salt, Spinnaker Blue 10.00
Candy the Carousel Horse, Aqua Diamond 12.50
Candy the Carousel Horse, Maverick Blue 18.00
Candy the Carousel Horse, Rosie Pink 6.50
Cat on Pillow, Persimmon (R) 20.00
Cat on Pillow, Pippin Green (R) 22.50
Cat on Pillow, Rubina (R) 30.00
Cat Slipper, Alice Blue 25.00
Cat Slipper, Apricot 22.50
Cat Slipper, Lilac 18.00
Chick Salt, Avocado 7.00
Chick Salt, Confetti 42.50
Chick Salt, Frosty Blue 50.00
Chick Salt, Furr Green 20.00

Duck Salt, Copper Glo 25.00
Duck Salt, Harvest Gold 7.50
Elizabeth Doll, Chocolate Carnival (R) 12.00
Elizabeth Doll, Lime Carnival (R) 55.00
Elizabeth Doll, Nile Green (R) 10.00
Hand Dish, Avocado 7.00
Hand Dish, Cashmire Pink 15.00
Hand Dish, Pineapple 20.00
JB Scottie, Cornsilk (R) 18.00
JB Scottie, Ebony (R) 40.00
JB Scottie, Heatherbloom (R) 70.00
JB Scottie, Nutmeg (R) 10.50
JB Scottie, Pocono (R) 22.50
Jeremy Frog, Crystal Carnival (R) 8.50
Jeremy Frog, Nile Green (R) 10.00
Jeremy Frog, Pacifica (R) 18.00
Jewel Heart Box, Apricot 22.50
Jewel Heart Box, Rubina 35.00
Joey the Horse, Bermuda Carnival (R) 60.00
Joey the Horse, Cobalt Carnival (R) 100.00
Joey the Horse, Crown Tuscan (R) 25.00
Joey the Horse, Pippin Green (R) 18.00
Li'l Joe the Horse, Baby Blue (R) 27.00
Li'l Joe the Horse, Crown Tuscan (R) 12.00
Li'l Lucky the Unicorn, Dijon (R) 10.00
Li'l Lucky the Unicorn, Jadite (R) 20.00
Louise Doll, Delphium 25.00
Louise Doll, Firefly 40.00
Louise Doll, Ice Blue 70.00
Lucky the Unicorn, Bermuda 14.00
Lucky the Unicorn, Crystal 25.00
Miss Cotton the Kitten, Chocolate 9.00
Miss Cotton the Kitten, Columbus White 15.00
Miss Cotton the Kitten, Crystal Carnival 10.00
Nancy, Capri Blue 8.00
Nancy, Cobalt Carnival 12.00
Nancy, Peacock Blue Carnival 9.00
Patrick Bear, Country Red (R) 15.00
Patrick Bear, Sunglow (R) 12.50
Pooch, Frosty Blue & Orange 35.00
Pooch, Rosie Pink 8.00
Pooch, Wintergreen 24.00
Sammy Squirrel, Alpine Blue (R) 8.00
Sammy Squirrel, Mulberry Carnival (R) 20.00
Sammy Squirrel, Patriot White Carnival (R) 15.00
Sportscar, Millinium White 10.50
Sportscar, Nutmeg Carnival 12.50
Suee Pig, Baby Blue 20.00
Suee Pig, Candyland 8.00
Suee Pig, Cardinal Red Carnival 18.00
Suee Pig, Thistlebloom 8.00
Taffy the Carousel Horse, Harvest Gold 16.00
Taffy the Carousel Horse, Moss Green 20.00
Taffy the Carousel Horse, Mystique 16.00
Teddy the Tugboat, Bermuda 24.00
Teddy the Tugboat, Daffodil 15.00
Teddy the Tugboat, Mulberry 26.00
Teddy the Tugboat, White, HP 12.00
Tucker, Cashmire Pink (R) 12.00
Tucker, Classic Black Carnival (R) 18.00
Tucker, Cobalt (R) 15.00
Tucker, Ruby Red Carnival (R) 25.00
Turkey Salt, Harvest Gold 7.50
Turkey Salt, Sunkist Carnival 12.00
Zack the Elephant, Flame (R) 60.00
Zack the Elephant, Lemonade (R) 45.00
Zack the Elephant, Moss Green (R) 18.00
Zack the Elephant, Snow (R) 75.00

Bradley and Hubbard

The Bradley and Hubbard Mfg. Company was a firm which produced metal accessories for the home. They operated from about 1860 until the early part of this century, and their products reflected both the Arts and Crafts and Art Nouveau influence. Their logo was a device with a triangular arrangement of the company name containing a smaller triangle and an Aladdin lamp.

Lamps

Banquet, dome shade, 6 brass scrolls as std, 24" 625.00
Gone-w/the-Wind, rose clusters, red on yel, gilt font, 30" 645.00
Prairie School, 16" sq shade w/triangular panels, simple std ...1,300.00
Rvpt 15" shade w/Glasgow roses; same on bronze std, att, 25" .3,500.00
Rvpt/obverse-pnt 18" iris shade; HP floral std 3,500.00
Slag-glass paneled shade w/filigree; metal #10 stick base, 23" 900.00
Slag-glass 14" 8-sided shade; faceted bronze std, 20" 1,400.00
Student, brn slag glass panels w/open leaf border; lyre std, 14" ..800.00

Miscellaneous

Andirons, cast brass & iron w/sunburst finials, #9510, 16½", pr .850.00
Andirons, hammered bronze, steel fire dogs, scrolled base, 29", pr .825.00
Andirons, owl on branch, CI w/glass eyes, 15¼", pr 450.00
Bookends, Beethoven & Chopin, bronze, mk, 6x4½", pr 150.00
Bookends, country gate, CI, 5", pr 125.00
Bookends, Hiawatha & verse, bronze, 6¼", pr 275.00
Bookends, Longfellow & Dickens, w/quotes, bronze, pr 165.00
Bookends, Shakespeare bust, rectangular bkground, CI, 4", pr ..175.00
Bookends, Temple of Isis, bronze finish, mk, 4x5⅞", pr 100.00
Frame, ornate florals, CI w/gold pnt, mk, 17¼x13⅛" 195.00
Inkwell, bronzed CI, Gothic style, mk, 1880-90 ....400.00
Pin tray, rabbit/4-leaf clover, pnt CI, 4x5½" 160.00
Pipe tray, old man smoking pipe, #2167, 5x7½" 125.00
Plant stand, gilt CI w/onyx insert in top, mk, 30x14" sq 360.00
Smoking stand & lamp w/attached match holder/ashtray, mk, 43", VG ...125.00

Brass

Brass is an alloy consisting essentially of copper and zinc in variable proportions. It is a medium that has been used for both utilitarian items and objects of artistic merit. Today, with the inflated price of copper and the popular use of plastics, almost anything made of brass is collectible, though right now, at least, there is little interest in items made after 1950. Our advisor, Mary Frank Gaston, has compiled a lovely book, *Antique Brass and Copper,* with full-color photos. See also Candlesticks.

Coal hod, hammered, relief scenes, 17x16½x15" 220.00
Knife box, paw ft, rtcl sides/divider/bottom, soldered, 11x15" ...770.00
Pail, cast, steel bail hdl, 6x11" 60.00
Posnet, long hdl, pierced end, 3½x4½" dia, 7" hdl 200.00
Sconce, gilt/porc inserts, 4 electric candles w/gold shades, pr 275.00
Settee, wrought & cast, lion finials on bk posts, uphl seats 825.00
Shelf, kettle; EX detail, late 1800s, 11x16x11" 275.00
Shelf, kettle; wrought-iron frwork, pierced apron, 13x16x12" 95.00
Shelf brackets, cast scroll forms, 19th C, 4½x10x7¾", pr 450.00

Standish, Napoleon III casket form w/appl stag, fitted int, 6" 130.00
Tea cart, 2 dbl-plate glass shelves, 1 sm/2 lg wheels, 32x41x23" ..650.00
Teapot, eng floral, handmade, ornate hdl, 1900s, 8½" 275.00
Umbrella stand, repousse w/lion hdls & paw ft, 26¼x17x7½" ...195.00
Wax jack, scissors hdl, ca 1800, 5" 335.00
Wick tender, 19th C, w/tray 45.00

Brastoff, Sascha

The son of immigrant parents, Sascha Brastoff was encouraged to develop his artistic talents to the fullest, encouragement that was well taken, as his achievements aptly attest. Though at various times he was a dancer, sculptor, Hollywood costume designer, jeweler, and painter, it is his ceramics that are today becoming highly regarded collectibles.

Sascha began his career in the United States in the late 1940s. In a beautiful studio built for him by his friend and mentor, Winthrop Rockefeller, he designed innovative wares that even then were among the most expensive on the market. All designing was done personally by Brastoff; he also supervised the staff which at the height of production numbered approximately 150. Wares signed with his full signature (not merely backstamped 'Sascha Brastoff') were personally crafted by him and are valued much more highly than those signed 'Sascha B.,' indicating work done under his supervision. Until his death in 1993, he continued his work in Los Angeles, in his latter years producing 'Sascha Holograms,' which were distributed by the Hummelwerk Company.

Though the resin animals signed 'Sascha B.' were neither made nor designed by Brastoff, collectors of these pieces value them highly. After Sascha Brastoff left the factory in the 1960s, the company retained the use of the name to be used on reissues of earlier pieces or merchandise purchased at trade shows.

In the listings that follow, items are ceramic and signed 'Sascha B.' unless 'full signature' or another medium is indicated.

For further information we recommend *The Collector's Encyclopedia of Sascha Brastoff* by Steve Conti, A. DeWayne Bethany, and Bill Seay; available from Collector Books or your local book store.

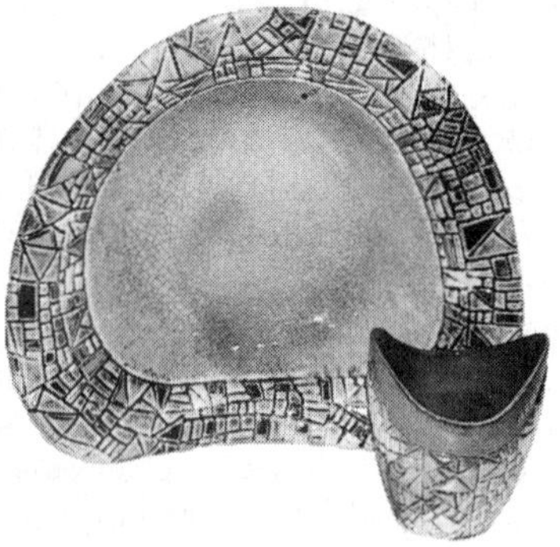

Bowl, Mosaic rim with gold trim, 'crackle' center, 14", $150.00. Matching 5" vase, $100.00. (From the collection of Dennis Hopp)

Ashtray, bl w/geometric bkground, sq w/winged corners, 6" 35.00
Ashtray, floral, enamel on copper, 5" 35.00
Ashtray, Jewel Bird, 7" 35.00
Ashtray, Jewel Bird on blk bkground, rests to 1 side, 5x8¾" 48.00
Ashtray, Poodle, enamel on copper, 8" sq 70.00
Ashtray, Roof Tops, #F2, 8x10¼" 90.00
Ashtray, Roof Tops, free-form, 6¾x5⅜" 40.00
Ashtray, Roof Tops, 7½" sq 60.00
Bowl, Americana, 5½" dia 50.00
Bowl, florals w/gold, lt/dk bl/tan/gr, #F44, 13x4½", from $80 to ..90.00
Box, apples & leaves on gr w/gold highlights, w/lid, 5x3¾" 40.00
Box, Ballet, w/lid, 3x5x8" 150.00
Candlestick, amber-colored resin, 7¾" 35.00
Candlestick, modernistic lines, alternating bands of flowers, 9½" .110.00
Charger, mc fruit, 14" 110.00
Charger, Star Steed on gray w/blk outside rim, 11½" 125.00
Cigarette lighter, leaf pattern, table-top 60.00
Cigarette lighter, Star Steed on bl-gr, cylindrical, #L2, 5½" 75.00
Creamer, Roman Coin 150.00
Cup & saucer, Roman Coin 125.00
Dish, Minos pattern, kidney shape, 1950s, 9" 90.00
Figurine, owl, gr resin, 13½" 350.00
Figurine, pelican, gr resin 310.00
Figurine, rooster, textured/shaded thick gold leaf, sgn, 17" 800.00
Figurine, seal, resin, 9½" L, from $270 to 290.00
Figurine, whale, resin, 12" L, from $190 to 210.00
Jar, Misty Blue, 6" 110.00
Mug, Mosaics, lg 35.00
Pendant, starfish, #1059, w/24" 24k gold chain 85.00
Plaque, fish form & decor, #D-50F, 11½" 75.00
Plate, bread & butter; Roman Coin 50.00
Plate, dinner; Roman Coin 100.00
Plate, Rooster, mc on wht w/yel rim, 10⅛" 80.00
Plate, salad; Roman Coin 75.00
Sculpture, Star Steed, metal, mtd on marble base, 4½x4½" 360.00
Sign, dealer's; gold w/brn & tan decor, gold rooster mk, 10½" ...450.00
Sugar bowl, Roman Coin, w/lid 185.00
Toothpick holder, Alaskan, walrus, 2¾" 25.00
Tray, dancer w/plumes headdress, wht on blk & gray, 7x5" 65.00
Vase, Alaskan, Eskimo, bl bkground, #V4, 6" 50.00
Vase, Alaskan, totem pole, #082, 8⅛" 80.00
Vase, Alaskan, totem pole w/mountain bkground, #047, 8½" 85.00
Vase, Aztec or Mayan totem, gold, bronze & wht, 6¼" 35.00
Vase, Jewel Bird, #F20, 1953-62 mk, 5" 45.00
Vase, Jewel Bird, dk to lt bl, 4-sided, 10x6½" 155.00
Vase, Star Steed, mc w/gold on lt gray w/blk accents, 5x4½" 60.00
Vase, Temple Towers, 10" 150.00
Vase, wagonwheel decor, #V3, 12¼" 120.00

Brayton Laguna

Durlin E. Brayton made handcrafted vases, lamps, and dinnerware in a small kiln at his Laguna Beach, California, home in 1927. He soon married, and with his wife, Ellen Webster Grieve, as his partner, the small business became a successful commercial venture. They are most famous for their amusing, well-detailed figurines, some of which were commissioned by Walt Disney Studios. Though very successful even through the Depression years, with the influx of imported novelties that deluged the country after WWII, business began to decline. By 1968 the pottery was closed. For more information on this as well as many other potteries in the state, we recommend *The Collector's Encyclopedia of California Pottery* by Jack Chipman; he is listed in the Directory under California.

Ashtray, HP ducks, mk, 7" sq 30.00
Bowl, burgundy, wavy lip, handmade, 4" 65.00
Box, cigarette; Dahlias 45.00
Box, Fr peasants, rnd 50.00
Candle holders, Blackamoor, mc w/gold trim, 5", pr 150.00
Candy jar, chicken shape, sm 225.00
Chess pc, Bishop, maroon & gold, 13" 165.00
Chess pc, King & Queen, 12", pr 300.00
Cookie jar, chicken shape, 10" 400.00
Cookie jar, Christina (Swedish Maiden), 11" 550.00
Cookie jar, Mammy, burgundy base, turq bandana (+) 1,300.00
Cookie jar, Matilda 475.00
Cookie jar, Ringmaster, from Pinocchio series 3,100.00

Creamer, Calico Cat 65.00
Dish, partridges on blk branches, #V11, w/lid, 7x8" 250.00
Figurine, abstract man (or woman) w/cat, blk, 21", pr 1,200.00
Figurine, Ann, seated, 4" 85.00
Figurine, Bambi & mother deer, Disney 125.00
Figurine, bartender at bar w/2 customers, Gay '90s 145.00
Figurine, bear seated, front legs apart, 1950s, 3½" 75.00
Figurine, Becky, Childhood series 85.00
Figurine, bedtime couple, Gay '90s 95.00
Figurine, Blackamoor kneeling holding cornucopia, 10" 175.00
Figurine, Calico Dog, 8" 85.00
Figurine, Chinese girl w/baby on bk, mc, Childhood series, 7" 90.00

Figurines, Purple Cow Family: Bull, 6½x11¾"; Cow, 6x8½"; and Calf, 4x6", from $350.00 to $450.00 for the three-piece set. (Photo courtesy Lee Garmon)

Figurine, duck, brn bsk, wht crackle, 5x5½" 55.00
Figurine, elephant, woodtone & wht crackle, ca 1957, 13½" 200.00
Figurine, Ellen, pigtails & hat, Childhood series, 7" 125.00
Figurine, fox, red, #H-57, lg 175.00
Figurine, grouse, red 75.00
Figurine, island girl in sarong 150.00
Figurine, Little Boy Blue 275.00
Figurine, man in top hat & cigar store Indian, ca 1940, 9½" 850.00
Figurine, mule, w/yoke, 7¼x10" 250.00
Figurine, owl, woodtone & crackle, 6" 55.00
Figurine, panther, snarling, jewelled collar, 20", from $175 to 225.00
Figurine, Patti, Childhood series 95.00
Figurine, Pluto, sniffing, Disney, 1930s 150.00
Figurine, quails, B-40/B-41, pr 225.00
Figurine, ringmaster, 8" 85.00
Figurine, rooster, olive gr/drab gold, 17x12" 145.00
Figurine, toucan, mc, 9" 200.00
Figurine, woman in yel dress w/dog, 11" 100.00
Figurine, zebra, sm 100.00
Flower holder, Blackamoor, gold & blk, 8" 75.00
Flower holder, Frances, bl & wht 60.00
Pitcher, owl form, mk, dtd 1941 ....80.00
Planter, baby w/pillow 75.00
Planter, rabbit, sm 75.00
Shakers, Black Chef & Mammy, 5½", pr 130.00
Shakers, Black Chef & Mammy, 6¾", pr 175.00
Shakers, Calico Cat & Gingham Dog, pr 85.00
Shakers, circus tent & animal, pr 375.00
Shakers, Mammy & Chef, sm, pr 125.00
Sugar bowl, Gingham Dog 80.00
Tile, Mexican man sleeping, cacti & tree nearby, 6½" sq 450.00
Toothbrush holder, Gingham Dog 150.00
Vase, lady's head, 9x11" 450.00
Vase, sea horse w/'pocket' on bk, wht w/bl, yel & rose dots, 8½" .115.00
Vase, seafoam bl w/lupines, 15½" 150.00
Vase, Swiss peasant woman w/basket 75.00
Vase, waisted neck, bulbous body, yel, 5½" 250.00
Wall pocket, Blackamoor holding planter over head, 2-pc, NM ..280.00

Bread Plates and Trays

Bread plates and trays have been produced not only in many types of glass but in metal and pottery as well. Those considered most collectible were made during the last quarter of the nineteenth century from pressed glass with well-detailed embossed designs, many of them portraying a particularly significant historical event. A great number of these plates were sold at the 1876 Philadelphia Centennial Exposition by various glass manufacturers who exhibited their wares on the grounds. Among the themes depicted are the Declaration of Independence, the Constitution, McKinley's memorial 'It Is God's Way,' Remembrance of Three Presidents, the Purchase of Alaska, and various presidential campaigns, to mention only a few.

'L' numbers correspond with a reference book by Lindsey. Our advisor for this category is Darlene Yohe; she is listed in the Directory under Arkansas.

American Flag, 38 stars, L-51, 11x8" 235.00
Barley (Cable Edge & Stippled) 65.00
Bible 50.00
Bunker Hill, L-44 ....75.00
Chain w/Star, hdls, 11" 30.00
Cleveland/Thurman, clear/frosted, L-325, 9½x8½" 215.00
Constitution 60.00
Continental (Memorial Hall), hand & bar hdls, 12¾" 60.00
Cupid & Venus, 10½" dia 55.00
Currier & Ives, balking mule 60.00
Egyptian, Cleopatra center, 13" L 55.00
Frosted Lion, Give Us This Day, 12½x9" 175.00
Garden of Eden 45.00
Garfield Drape, We Mourn, L-303, 11½" 55.00
Garfield Memorial, frosted center, L-302, 10" L 47.50
Give Us This Day, Sheaf of Wheat, 11" dia 40.00
Grant, Let Us Have Peace, L-289 ....65.00
Grant, sq, L-291 ....45.00
Grape (It's A Pleasure) 50.00
In Remembrance, frosted, 3 Presidents 59.00
Independence Hall 125.00
Jewel & Dewdrop (Kansas) 55.00
Jeweled Band (Scalloped Tape) 25.00
Let Us Have Peace, amber 65.00
Maltese Cross in Circles 55.00
Merry Christmas, bells in center, shallow bowl shape 75.00
Minerva 50.00
Moses Montifiore, L-239 ....75.00
Niagara Falls, L-489 ....95.00
Old State House, L-32 ....60.00
Preparedness, L-481 ....300.00
Prescott Stark 60.00

Transcontinental Railroad, 9x12", $95.00.

Volunteer, emerald gr, L-101 ....575.00
Warrior 80.00
Washington Centennial, clear Washington center 125.00
Washington Centennial, frosted Washington center 145.00
Wildflower, sq 28.00

Bretby

Bretby art pottery was made by Tooth & Co., at Woodville, near Burton-on-Trent, Derbyshire, from as early in 1884 until well into the twentieth century. Marks containing the 'Made in England' designation indicate twentieth-century examples.

Clock, female face surmount, scroll panels, HP birds, 10" 1,495.00
Tray, woman's head ea end, rose matt, 15" L, EX 160.00
Vase, bee & dragonfly emb on faux-wood brn, rstr ring hdls, 10½" ...165.00
Vase, bird & egg, majolica, ca 1910, 5" 180.00
Vase, Carved Bamboo, appl metal mts, 2 faux gems, #1958, 10⅛" .175.00
Vase, Carved Bamboo, bamboo hdls & appl lizards, #1343, 14⅝", pr ..700.00
Vase, Carved Bamboo, 2-hdl, appl metal mts, #1681, 9⅝" 180.00
Vase, sapphire bl w/swirling irid lines, #2567, 9" 175.00
Vase, shaded/mottled gr, rim-to-hip hdls, incised decor, '20s, 4½" ..90.00

Bride's Baskets and Bowls

Victorian brides were showered with gifts, as brides have always been; one of the most popular gift items was the bride's basket. Art glass inserts from both European and American glasshouses, some in lovely transparent hues with dainty enameled florals, others of Peachblow, Vasa Murrhina, satin, or cased glass, were cradled in complementary silverplated holders. While many of these holders were simply engraved or delicately embossed, others (such as those from Pairpoint and Wilcox) were wonderfully ornate, often with figurals of cherubs or animals or birds. The bride's basket was no longer in fashion after the turn of the century.

Watch for 'marriages' of bowls and frames. To warrant the best price, the two pieces should be the original pairing. If you can't be certain of this, at least check to see that the bowl fits snugly into the frame. Beware of later-made bowls (such as Fenton's) in Victorian holders and new frames being produced in Taiwan.

Our advisor for this category is Deborah Maggard; she is listed in the Directory under Ohio. In the listings that follow, if no frame is described, the price is for a bowl only.

Apricot cased w/floral, swirl ribs, pinched sides/rim, 9½" 225.00
Apricot satin, HP int; Meriden fr, 15" 550.00
Bl cased satin w/HP floral int, ruffled rim 125.00
Bl cased w/butterflies etc; Poole std w/cherub support, 16" 800.00
Bl Herringbone MOP, pk int, mini, 4¼" 145.00
Bl o/l, ruffled, HP wht flowers/gr leaves, 3½x10¾" 210.00
Bl satin, HP floral branches, frilly ruffled rim 350.00
Bl satin w/gold foliage/lav flowers; rstr figural fr, 13½x14" 1,100.00
Bl satin w/wht satin ruffled rim, 4x10½" 100.00
Chartreuse/pk cased satin, HP floral, 4½x10½" 300.00
Clear to bl, Invt Honeycomb, ruffled, HP floral; fr 375.00
Coralene, coral on wht to bl shaded; ftd Meriden fr 550.00
Cream opaque w/rose hibiscus; Meriden base w/2 3-D lions ...1,000.00
Frosted w/florals & Hobnails, crimped; fr w/cockatoo, 11x10½" ..850.00
Gold satin w/birds & floral, clear ruffle, 13"; mk fr 495.00
Ivory w/dk flutes & gilt scrolls; arched Meriden fr w/Cupid 395.00
Lav satin, yel/wht/lav florals, ruffled, 4x10½" 200.00
Lemon w/HP florals & dots, Mt WA; rstr SP fr, 12x10½" 425.00
Maroon to cream cased w/sm flowers, deeply sclloped, 12" 200.00
Peachblow, crimped/folded rim, gold florals, 4½x11" 275.00
Peachblow, glossy, ribbed body, ruffled rim, 4¼x10½" 225.00
Peachblow cased, molded bead swags, rayed ruffled rim 400.00
Pigeon blood to cranberry to custard cased; ftd fr, 14x12" 350.00
Pk cased, mc bird & flowers, ruffled rim, 3x8½x6½" 165.00
Pk cased w/clear & opaque wht ribbon edge, HP floral, 2¾x9¾" ..210.00
Pk cased w/daisies, fluted/ruffled; fr w/3-arch hdl, 11x11" 400.00
Pk cased w/Hobnails, ruffled, 9½"; emb brass base, 7¾" 180.00
Pk Dmn Quilt MOP, rectangular, Mt WA; mk fr, 11x10½" 550.00
Pk frosted Hobnail w/bl rim, oblong; in Derby holder 450.00
Pk satin to clear frost w/HP, folded rim; ftd base, 4x10" 300.00
Pk w/mc pansies & scrolls, clear ruffle, 4x12" 225.00
Rubena frosted satin; grapes on fr, 8½x9½" 450.00
Sapphire bl, ruffled; ornate fr, 10x14" 450.00
Vaseline cased w/HP florals; ornate Meriden fr, 10½x11" 300.00
Wht satin w/gold, scalloped; ornate fr 400.00
Yel cased w/griffin/birds/flowers, Mt WA, 3¾x9½" 900.00
Yel satin w/HP, pk int, 12"; 3 cherubs hold Wilcox fr 2,500.00

Bristol Glass

Bristol is a type of semi-opaque opaline glass whose name was derived from the area in England where it was first produced. Similar glass was made in France, Germany, and Italy. In this country, it was made by the New England Glass Company and to a lesser extent by its contemporaries. During the eighteenth and nineteenth centuries, Bristol glass was imported in large amounts and sold cheaply, thereby contributing to the demise of the earlier glasshouses here in America. It is very difficult to distinguish the English Bristol from other opaline types. Style, design, and decoration serve as clues to its origin; but often only those well versed in the field can spot these subtle variations.

Bottle, barber; fox hunt scene, w/gold, ca 1890s, 7¾" 290.00
Bowl, wht w/pk flashed int, bird on branch, ruffled sq rim, 3" H ..200.00
Box, patch; pk, floral & fans, w/gold, 1x2" dia 150.00
Box, wht, children building snowman, 2⅜x4½" 145.00
Cracker jar, bl, daisies & foliage, SP mts, 6½x4¾" 175.00
Cup, bl, Remember Me in wht, 4¼" 110.00
Lamp, blk, scenic, 31" 175.00
Lustres, florals, ruffled top, 2 rows of prisms, 17", pr 1,200.00
Rose bowl, wht, duck on snowy bank, 4" 150.00
Teapot, cream, water birds in grasses, 5¼x4½" 295.00
Tumble-up, lt yel, violets, sgn V Gherke, 5x2½" 75.00

Vases, Left and right: double profile portraits in reserve with gold on blue, Greek key band at rim and base, 16½", $450.00 for the pair; Center: wild animals and scrolling vines in multicolor on opaque ground with blue and gilt borders, 20", $375.00.

Vase, bl, wht bird, gold trim at notched rim, ped ft, 6¾x2¼" 135.00
Vase, custard, floral, w/gold, 9¾" 65.00
Vase, turq, florals, w/gold, 10½x4", pr 225.00
Vase, wht w/bl int, floral w/bird on branch, ruffled, ftd, 10¾" 70.00

British Royalty Commemoratives

Commemoratives have been issued for royal events since Edward VI's 1547 coronation through modern-day occasions, so it's possible to start collecting at any period of history. Many collectors begin with Queen Victoria's reign, collecting examples for each succeeding monarch and continuing through modern events.

Some collectors identify with a particular royal personage and limit their collecting to that era, ie., Queen Elizabeth's life and reign. Other collectors look to the future, expanding their collection to include the heir apparents Prince Charles and his first-born son, Prince William.

Royalty commemorative collecting is often further refined around a particular type of collectible. Nearly any item with room for a portrait and a description has been manufactured as a souvenir. Thus royalty commemoratives are available in glass, ceramic, metal, fabric, plastic, and paper. This wide variety of material lends itself to any pocketbook. The range covers expensive limited edition ceramics to inexpensive souvenir key chains, puzzles, matchbooks, etc.

Many recent royalty headline events have been commemorated in a variety of souvenirs. Buying some of these modern commemoratives at the moderate issue prices could be a good investment. After all, today's events are tomorrow's history.

For further study we recommend *British Royal Commemoratives* by our advisor for this category, Audrey Zeder; she is listed in the Directory under Washington.

Key:
A/S — Andrew/Sarah
anniv — anniversary
bd — birthday
C/D — Charles/Diana
chr — christening
com — commemorative
cor — coronation
EPNS — electro-plated nickel silver
ILN — Illustrated London News
inscr — inscribed
jub — jubilee
LE — limited edition
mem — memorial
Pr — Prince
Prs — Princess
QM — Queen Mother
wed — wedding
vis — visit

Bank, Elizabeth II jub, crown shape, silver-tone, 4x3½" 45.00
Bank, Geo VI w/Queen & 2 Prs, tin, 1937, 5x3x2" 75.00
Beaker, C/D wed, brn portrait/decor, Doulton, 3½" 75.00
Beaker, Edward VII cor, brn portrait/decor, Doulton 150.00
Beaker, Geo V cor, mc portrait/decor, Mailing, 4" 45.00
Beaker, George VI cor, gray portrait w/mc, Doulton, 4" 85.00
Beaker, Victoria '87 jub, enamel mc portrait/decor, gold bands, 4" .190.00
Bible, Elizabeth II cor, dk bl cover w/gold royal cypher 55.00
Book, Queen Victoria & Her People, Dawe, hard-bk, 1897 ....65.00
Booklet, C/D wed, Royal Wedding Official Souvenir, 11x8" 30.00
Booklet, Prs Elizabeth 1947 wed gifts, 164-pg, 8x5" 35.00
Bookmark, C/D wed, blk portrait/decor, woven silk, orig folder ...30.00
Bookmark, Elizabeth II cor, mc portrait/decor on woven silk 25.00
Bookmark, Prs Diana mem, bl woven silk w/gold 10.00
Bookmark, QM 95 bd, bl leather w/gold, 9x11" 25.00
Bottle, ale; Victoria portrait emb on dk gr glass, 1890s 65.00
Bottle, Elizabeth II jub portrait/decor emb on amethyst glass 45.00
Bottle, gin; George V/Queen Mary figural, clear glass, 13" 225.00
Bottle, Victoria cor, brn crown, beige decor, Imperial Pottery ...750.00
Bowl, C/D wed, mc portrait/decor, bl/gold border, 1x9" 95.00
Bowl, Edward VIII '37, mc portrait/decor, sq w/rnded corners, 5" .45.00
Bowl, Elizabeth II cor, sepia portrait/decor, oval, 1x5x3" 35.00
Bowl, George V jub, blk/wht portrait, mc ship/plane, 6½" 55.00
Bowl, George VI cor, mc portrait/decor, for feeding baby, 6½" 75.00
Bowl, George VI cor, mc portrait/decor, scalloped rim, 5½" 45.00
Bowl, Victoria/Albert 1851, blk/wht portrait w/mc, pk lustre, 3x6" ...250.00
Calendar, Geo VI '39 Canada vis, King/Queen collage, Gibson Coal ad .25.00
Cigarette card album, George V jub, 50 mc cards, WD Wills 60.00
Coin, Edward I 1300s silver penny, ¾" 85.00
Coin, Victoria 1861 farthing, ¾" 15.00
Coin, William IV 1836 silver groat, ⅝" 45.00
Covered dish, QM 30 bd, mc portrait, Rington by Wade, 3½x2" .95.00
Cup & saucer, Edward VII cor, portrait/decor on turq 165.00
Cup & saucer, Edward VIII cor, mc portrait in cor robe, Shelley .65.00
Cup & saucer, Geo V cor, mc portrait/decor, pierced hdl 155.00
Doll, Pr Philip, vinyl, bl uniform, Nisbit, ca 1950, 8½" 150.00
Doll, Prs Anne wed, vinyl, satin dress/veil, Nisbit, 8½" 195.00
Egg cup, Edward VIII 1937, mc portrait/decor, bl ft 55.00
Egg cup, George VI cor, shaded portrait, gold rim, ftd 35.00
Egg cup, QM 90 bd, mc portrait wearing yel, ftd 30.00
Ephemera, C/D wed bus pass, pastel portrait/decor, 4x6" 20.00
Ephemera, Elizabeth II cor coloring book, unused, 14x10½" 50.00
Ephemera, Elizabeth II cor invitation, US Embassy seats/procession rte ..25.00
Ephemera, George V cor, ad label for Royal beverage bottle 20.00
Ephemera, George VI '49 carriage pass to garden party 26.00
Ephemera, Pr William 1982 birth, unused notebook, 4½" 15.00
Ephemera, Prs Anne 1950 portrait, stand-up easel, 5x3" 20.00
Horse brass, C/D wed, emb Pr of Wales feather 25.00
Horse brass, Elizabeth II cor, emb portrait/decor 35.00
Horse brass, Prs Diana mem, Nat'l Horse Brass Society 45.00
ILN Record No, Elizabeth II jub, bl cover/silver decor, 14x10" 55.00
ILN Record No, George V cor, rnd cover/gold decor, 16½x11½" ..175.00
ILN Record No, George V jub, rnd cover/silver decor, 14x10" ..125.00
Jewelry, Elizabeth II pin, mc portrait on MOP, 2⅝" 45.00
Jewelry, George IV 1820 maudy coin, gold bezel w/extended ring ..35.00
Jewelry, George VI cor stickpin, blk/wht portrait, brass bezel 40.00
Jewelry, George VI cor stickpin, brass profile, 1¾" 35.00
Jewelry, Prs Diana key ring, mc portrait, gold-tone chain 25.00
Jewelry, Prs Diana stickpin, mc portrait, 2" 20.00
Jewelry, Queen Victoria coin, gold bezel w/extended ring 35.00
Jug, Victoria '87, blend whiskey, blk portrait on beige stoneware .325.00
Loving cup, Victoria '87 jub, blk portrait/decor, 5¼x8½" 425.00

Loving cup, coronation of Queen Elizabeth II, earthenware, Royal Doulton, 1953, limited edition, 10¾", $950.00.

Magazine, Graphic, Prs Mary 1922 wed, 3/4/22 ....50.00
Magazine, Hello, Charles/Harry in S Africa, 11/15/97 ....12.00
Magazine, Sphere, Prs Marina wed, 12/8/34 ....35.00
Magazine, Sunday Express, Royal Year 1988 ....25.00
Magazine, Telegraph, Remembering Diana, 8/11/98 ....15.00
Medallion, Edward VII 1902 Germany vis, bronze, ⅞" 40.00
Medallion, George III 1761 cor, bronze w/emb portrait, 2¾" 250.00
Medallion, George VI cor, Victoria Hotel giveaway, bronze, 1¾" ...50.00
Medallion, Pr of Wales Open 1887 Jub Exhibit, bronze, 1¾" 125.00
Medallion, Pr of Wales 1841 wed, pot emtal, 2" 95.00
Medallion, Prs Diana mem, 14k gold-plate on silver, ¾", MIB 50.00
Medallion, Victoria 1860 Scottish Volunteers review, 1¾" 195.00

Medallion, Victoria 1887 jub, bronze w/emb portrait, 1½" 60.00
Medallion, Victoria/Albert 1851 Manchester vis, pot metal, 2" ...95.00
Medallion, Victoria/Albert 1858 vis w/Napoleon, brass, ⅞" 75.00
Miniature, C/D wed loving cup, gold portrait/decor, Wade, 2" 50.00
Miniature, Elizabeth II cor, pitcher, copper/brass, 2½" 25.00
Miniature, George V cor pitcher, mc portrait in bl uniform, 2" ...55.00
Miniature, Pr Wm 1st bd plate, mc Diana w/baby, 2¼" 35.00
Miniature, QM 80's plate, mc portrait, purple hat/dress, 2¼" 30.00
Mug, C/D engagement, blk portrait, bl decor, stoneware 55.00
Mug, C/D wed, wht silhouettes, pastel decor, Denby 45.00
Mug, Edward VII cor, brn-tone portrait/decor, Royal Doulton, 4" ..125.00
Mug, Edward VII cor, mc portrait w/mc enamel, gold rim, 2⅛" .110.00
Mug, Edward VIII '37, sepia portrait, mc decor, molded crown hdl .60.00
Mug, Elizabeth II cor, brn portrait, Art-Deco style, Doulton 75.00
Mug, Elizabeth II cor, mc portrait, stylized decor, bbl shape 35.00
Mug, George V cor, mc portrait/decor, fancy hdl, 2⅝" 60.00
Mug, George V jub, sepia portrait, mc decor, silver rim/hdl 55.00
Mug, George VI cor, mc Coat of Arms, lion hdl, Paragon, 3" 75.00
Mug, Pr Charles 50th bd, mc portrait/decor, Chown, LE 50 ....65.00
Mug, Pr William '95 at Eaton College, mc decor, 'W' hdl 155.00
Mug, Prs Diana '95 Argentina vis, mc decor, Chown, LE 50 .....125.00
Mug, Prs Diana 30th bd, mc portrait in 'D' fr, Chown, LE 70 ....155.00
Mug, QM '95 Royal Ascot Ladies Day, portrait, Chown, LE 50 ..110.00
Mug, Victoria 1897, bl & gray portrait/decor, JC&N, 3¼" 195.00
Music box, Prs Diana mem, mc portrait, wood, Ercolano, 7x7" .195.00
Newspaper, Prs Elizabeth 1947 wed, Daily Mirror, 11/21/47 ....25.00
Newspaper, Victoria '87 jub, Daily Graphic, special dbl # 75.00
Novelty, C/D address book, bl cover w/inscription, unused 5.00
Novelty, Elizabeth II cor thermometer, free-standing, brass, 3x3" ...35.00
Novelty, Elizabeth II cor thermos bottle, royal cypher decor 55.00
Novelty, George VI cor napkin ring, emb profile on silver 55.00
Novelty, George VI crumb pan, emb portrait/decor on brass 75.00
Novelty, Prs Diana mem ballpoint pen, mc portrait/decor 10.00
Novelty, Prs Diana tree ornament, std figure, Carlton 25.00
Photo album, C/D wed, mc portrait, red/wht/bl flag bkground, unused 65.00
Photograph, Elizabeth II w/Marilyn Monroe, blk/wht, matted ...135.00
Photograph, George VI 1940 at bomb damage, blk/wht, 8½x5¾" ..25.00
Pin-bk, Edward VII cor, mc portrait/decor, 1¼" 245.00
Pin-bk, Edward VIII cor, blk/wht portrait, red/bl decor, 1¾" 35.00
Pin-bk, Elizabeth II coronation, mc portrait/flag decor, 1¾" 35.00
Pin-bk, George V '35 jub, blk/wht portrait, 1¾" 40.00
Pitcher, Edward VII cor, mc portrait in red uniform, Doulton, 2¾" ...115.00
Pitcher, George V cor, mc portrait/decor, emb rim decor, 8½" ..195.00
Pitcher, George VI cor, emb mc portrait/decor, music box inside 495.00
Pitcher, George VI cor, mc portrait by Van Dyke, gold rim, 3¼" ..50.00
Pitcher, Victoria 1840 wed, mc figure on bl w/copper lustre, 6" .360.00
Pitcher, Victoria 1887 jub, brn tone w/emb decor, Doulton 275.00
Pitcher, Victoria 1897 jub, blk portrait on cobalt w/gold, 5" 195.00
Plate, C/D wed, brn-tone portrait, blk/brn rim, Hornsea, 7¾" 55.00
Plate, C/D wed, cobalt w/gold, Bing & Grondahl, 10" 235.00
Plate, C/D wed, mc portrait/decor, Coalport, LE 500, 10¾" 190.00
Plate, C/D wed, ornate bl/gold decor, Minton, LE 1000 ....330.00
Plate, C/D wed, 24k gold portrait/decor, Prinknash, 6½" 65.00
Plate, Edward VII cor, mc portrait in red uniform, Doulton, 6¾" ..155.00
Plate, Edward VIII '37, brn portrait cor robes, mc decor, T&K, 6" .40.00
Plate, EDward VIII '37, mc portrait in cor robe, Royal Winton, 9" .90.00
Plate, Edward VIII '37, mc portrait in cor robe/crown, 4¾" 55.00
Plate, Elizabeth II '92, Annus Horribilis year, mc decor, 4" 35.00
Plate, Elizabeth II cor, sepia portrait by Wilder, 8¼" 45.00
Plate, George V cor, bl portrait/decor, Worcester, 10½" 150.00
Plate, George V jub, bl portrait, mc decor, silver rim, Melba, 6" ..45.00
Plate, George VI '39, Canada vis, brn portrait/decor, Maddock, 9" .45.00
Plate, Prs Diana '84, name Royal Prs ship, Royal Doulton 195.00
Plate, Prs Diana mem, 5 mc portraits, Wyton, LE 50, 8" 150.00
Plate, Victoria '87 jub, blk/wht portrait on gold star w/mc enamel .290.00
Plate, Victoria '97 jub, blk/wht portrait, mc royal residences, 10" ...295.00
Plate, Victoria cor, standing portrait, mc accents, 8-sided, 6¾" ...1,500.00
Playing cards, C/D wed, mc portrait/decor, single pack, unused ...25.00
Playing cards, Edward VII cor, mc portrait/decor, full deck 95.00
Postcard, Elizabeth II 40th anniv cor, 5 silk o/l cards, Benham 50.00
Postcard, George V on horsebk, blk/wht, cancelled stamp, ca 1912 ..15.00
Postcard, George VI 1939 vis Niagara Falls, mc, unused 15.00
Postcard, Prs Diana '98 Althorp Exhibition w/mem stamp 12.00
Postcards, Queen Alexandra on yacht, blk/wht, ca 1905, used 15.00
Poster, C/D wed, set of 4 in orig com box 75.00
Pressed glass, C/D separation plate, portrait/decor, bl 35.00
Pressed glass, Edward VII cor compote, feather design, clear, 5" .165.00
Pressed glass, Elizabeth II cor plate, portrait, dot design, 6½" 25.00
Pressed glass, George VI cor plate, gold portrait, amber, 9½" 95.00
Pressed glass, Prs Diana mem plate, portrait, irid, 3½" 30.00
Pressed glass, Prs Diana 30 bd plate, portrait, gr, 3½" 30.00
Pressed glass, Victoria '87 jub bowl, crown, clear, 9½" 125.00
Print, Prs Diana mem, mc portrait in formal, fr, 16x20" 30.00
Print, Sarah, Duchess of York, mc portrait, 11¾x8½" 10.00
Puzzle, Prs Diana, mc collage, MIB 55.00
Puzzle, QM 80 bd, mc portrait w/Corgi dog, 19x13" 60.00
Puzzle, Royal Family, comic version, dbl-sided, Buffalo 75.00
Sheet music, Pr of Wales 1863 wed, mc wed scene, for piano 50.00
Sheet music, Princess Mary Adelaide Waltz, 1880 ....20.00
Spoon, C/D wed, Pr Wales feather, mc decor, SP, MIB 20.00
Spoon, Edward VII 1900s w/Fr President, hallmk 80.00
Spoon, George VI '39 Canada vis, emb portrait/decor on SP, 6⅛" ..45.00
Spoon, George VI cor, emb portrait, anointing spoon design 35.00
Spoon, Pr William birth, emb decor/inscription, SP 30.00
Spoon, Victoria '97 jub, emb portrait/decor on sterling, 5½" 150.00
Stamps, C/D wed first day cover, Solomon Islands 20.00
Stamps, Elizabeth II cor, album 107 stamps, White Ace 75.00
Stamps, Prs Diana stamp sheet, formal dress, Togo, 9 on sheet 30.00
Teapot, Edward VII cor, mc portrait in red uniform, Doulton, 2-cup ...210.00
Teapot, George VI cor, sepia King/Queen & 2 Prs, Shelley, 2-cup ..110.00
Teapot, Victoria '87 jub, bl w/gold portrait & mc enamel, 4-cup ..290.00
Teapot stand, George V cor, mc portrait, sepia ship decor, 6" 150.00
Teapot stand, George V jub, mc portrait/decor, silver rim, 6" 95.00
Textile, C/D wed tea towel, blk/wht portrait, mc family tree 35.00
Textile, Edward VII cor, blk/wht portrait on red/wht/bl, 19x26" ..57.00
Textile, Elizabeth II cor woven ribbon, mc decor, 1½ yards 15.00
Textile, Elizabeth II jub place mat, hand embr, 19x13" 25.00
Textile, George V 1916 pillow, blk/wht portrait w/mc, 16x16" 95.00
Textile, George V 1918, blk/wht king & allies, 19x19" 125.00
Textile, George VI cor, blk/wht portrait, mc commonwealth countries 45.00
Thimble, C/D/William '83 New Zealand vis, mc decor, Caverswall ..45.00
Thimble, Pr Willam '83 1st bd, mc portrait/decor, bone china, Fenton ..35.00
Thimble, Prs Diana 30 bd, blk portrait w/mc, Caverswall 45.00
Tin, C/D wed, mc portrait on bl, 8-sided, London Tea Co 45.00
Tin, C/D wed, mc portrait/decor on cream, 4¼x3x3" 35.00
Tin, Edward VII cor, mc portrait on purple, angular shape 195.00
Tin, Elizabeth II cor, mc portrait, rnd, flat, Daintee, 2x4" 30.00
Tin, Elizabeth II cor, mc portrait/decor, Waller/Hartlet, 5x4x1" ...45.00
Tin, Elizabeth II cor, standing portrait in formal gown, 6x4x2" 45.00
Tin, Elizabeth II jub, Coat of Arms, Coleman Mustard, 2x5x4" ...45.00
Tin, George V cor, mc portrait/decor, JS Frye, 6x4x¾" 55.00
Tin, George VI cor, red w/gold portrait/decor, Crawford, 3¼" 35.00
Tin, Pr Wales '33 Morley vis, mc portrait/decor, hinged 85.00
Toby mug, Victoria, HP, L&S, 3" 55.00
Toy dishes, Edward VII 1937, portrait w/mc decor, 3-pc set 95.00
Tray, C/D wed, emb portrait/decor on SP, oval, 9½x6½" 55.00
Tray, Pr William chris, mc Diana holding Pr, wicker sides 120.00
Trinket box, C/D wed, mc portrait/decor, scallop lid, Mason 85.00

Broadmoor

In October of 1933, the Broadmoor Art Pottery was formed and space was rented at 217 East Pikes Peak Avenue, Colorado Springs, Colorado. Most of the pottery they produced would not be considered elaborate, and only a handful was decorated. Many pieces were signed by P.H. Genter, J.B. Hunt, Eric Hellman, and Cecil Jones. It is reported that this plant closed in 1936, and Genter moved his operations to Denver.

Broadmoor pottery is marked in several ways: a Greek or Egyptian-type label depicting two potters (one at the wheel and one at a tile-pressing machine) and the word Broadmoor; an ink-stamped 'Broadmoor Pottery, Colorado Springs (or Denver), Colorado'; and an incised version of the latter.

The bottoms of all pieces are always white and can be either glazed or unglazed. Glaze colors are turquoise, green, yellow, cobalt blue, light blue, white, pink, pink with blue, maroon red, black, and copper lustre. Both matt and high gloss finishes were used.

The company produced many advertising tiles, novelty items, coasters, ashtrays, and vases for local establishments around Denver and as far away as Wyoming. An Indian head was incised into many of the advertising items, which also often bear a company or a product name. A series of small animals (horses, dogs, elephants, lamb, squirrels, a toucan bird, and a hippo), each about 2" high, are easily recognized by the style of their modeling and glaze treatments, though all are unmarked. For more information we recommend *Collector's Encyclopedia of Colorado Pottery*, by Carol and Jim Carlton (Collector Books).

Ashtray, ballerina in center, pk 35.00
Ashtray, toucan or bluejay finial, cobalt bl 55.00
Bean pot, red, w/hdl 75.00
Bookends, sitting Indians, bl, 7", pr 200.00
Cigarette holder, squirrel finial, yel 45.00
Custard, gr 15.00
Figurine, dachshund, Souvenir of Estes Park 40.00
Figurine, horse, 2" 45.00
Paperweight, Indian head, bl matt, rare 55.00
Pitcher, water; matt gr 150.00
Planter, open-mouth bird, bl matt 25.00
Relish tray, 3-section, 10" 45.00
Vase, bud; Mongol Red 35.00
Vase, Longhorn steer, bl matt, 15" 150.00
Vase, matt bl spongeware, 5" 45.00
Vase, pillow; bl to mauve, 6" 55.00
Vase, red swirl, 17" 175.00
Vase, yel w/pine-cone decor, 8" 35.00

Broadsides

Webster defines a broadside as simply a large sheet of paper printed on one side. During the 1880s, they were the most practical means of mass communication. By the middle of the century, they had become elaborate and lengthy with information, illustrations, portraits, and fancy border designs. Those printed on coated stock are usually worth more.

African Redemption Fund, Marcus Garvey, 6x9" 435.00
Army Horses Needed, 1865, 11½x9½" 80.00
Bridge order, All Persons Crossing on Sabbath..., 19th C, 11x9" .315.00
Lecture on Microscope, by Prof WJ Koerstetter, late 19th C, 6x11" .60.00
Magician Frederick E Powell, 1922, 9x6" 50.00
National City & Otay RR Daily Excursions, 1890s, 9x19" 55.00
Presidential candidates 1856, 26x36", matted 750.00
Republic Meeting, 4th Ward Schnectady NY, 1858, 12½x9" 40.00
Traveling Stereopticon show, 1890s, 8x18" 380.00
Woman Suffrage, Justice First Give Mother a Vote, 1915, 6½x12" ...80.00

Bronzes

Thomas Ball, George Bessell, and Leonard Volk were some of the earliest American sculptors who produced figures in bronze for home decor during the 1840s. Pieces of historical significance were the most popular, but by the 1880s a more fanciful type of artwork took hold. Some of the fine sculptors of the day were Daniel Chester French, Augustus St. Gaudens, and John Quincy Adams Ward. Bronzes reached the height of their popularity at the turn of the century. The American West was portrayed to its fullest by Remington, Russell, James Frazier, Hermon MacNeil, and Solon Borglum. Animals of every species were modeled by A.P. Proctor, Paul Bartlett, and Albert Laellele, to name but a few.

Art Nouveau and Art Deco influenced the medium during the '20s, evidenced by the works of Allen Clark, Harriet Frismuth, E.F. Sanford, and Bessie P. Vonnoh.

Be aware that recasts abound. While often esthetically satisfactory, they are not original and should be priced accordingly. In much the same manner as prints are evaluated, the original castings made under the direction of the artist are the most valuable. Later castings from the original mold are worth less. A recast is not made from the original mold. Instead, a rubber-like substance is applied to the bronze, peeled away, and filled with wax. Then, using the same 'lost wax' procedure as the artist uses on completion of his original wax model, a clay-like substance is formed around the wax figure and the whole fired to vitrify the clay. The wax, of course, melts away, hence the term 'lost wax.' Recast bronzes lose detail and are somewhat smaller than the original due to the shrinkage of the clay mold.

Hans Zeissig, L.F.V.A. Die Beamstenschaft 1819 – 1919, maiden reaching to kneeling nude youth, 44", $4,600.00.

A Brandel, classical maiden w/hoop & dove, 29"+marble base ..935.00
Adrioani Cecioni, Cock Captured, child w/rooster, ca 1880s, 20" ..1,840.00
August Moreau, classical maiden, gilt-bronze & ivory, marble base, 9" ..2,875.00
Austria, Knight of Verona, on horsebk in full armor, gilt, 1900s, 17" ..3,750.00
Austria, North African man, mk Tiffany & Co, ca 1910, 18¼" .3,165.00
Austria, Roman head on ped, marble plinth, ca 1900, 9¾" 265.00
Barillot, Pied Piper, ivory face & hands, onyx plinth, 9¾" 1,230.00
Beatris Fenton, Wood-Music, deep olive-gr patina, ca 1930, 39" ..3,470.00
Bergman, Middle Eastern Girl, dancing, marble base, 10" 2,875.00
Busch, Berlin; Greek athlete on blk onyx base, 13" 825.00
Chiparus, girl clown on tiptoes, gold pnt, 9" 1,750.00
Christopher Cairns, Woman in Flames, lt gr patina, 1984, 25" ...500.00
Claire Jeanne Colinet, Juggler, nude female, blk patina, 1930s, 10" .1,100.00
Continentel, Stringing His Bow, draped Hercules w/bow, 21¾" ..1,380.00
Edouard Villanis, Bust of a Woman Seule, 22½" 2,300.00
French, lady w/rose & putti on marble base, gilt, 19th C, 15x10" ...630.00
Georges Gardet, Great Dane, dk brn patina, 5x9½" 1,380.00
Hans Guradze, Jockey Astride Horse, dk brn patina, 12½" 1,100.00
Isadore-Jule Bonheur, Jockey/Steed, brn patina, marble base, 17" .825.00

Miccinglo after Donatello, Ste Cecelia relief plaque, 14x12" 440.00
Otto Marth, lioness attacking wild boar, 12¾" 335.00
Paul Silvestre, faun & goose, gr patina, Susse Freres, 1925, 16x34" ...3,450.00
Pierre Jules Mene, Ibpahim, regal horse, 19th C, 11⅞"+base .5,000.00
Roland, Bacchante riding goat, 1796, 16½" 2,875.00
Russel, Smoking w/Spirit of Buffalo, recast from orig, 5½x9" 185.00
Unknown, bust of lady w/bird on shoulder, gilded, late 1800s, 16" ...575.00
Unknown, Narcissus, male nude w/wine skin over shoulder, 15½" ..635.00
Unknown, nude man w/head in hands, 13½" 450.00
Unknown, woman & girl w/birds & flowers, 20th C, 35x10" .1,375.00

Brouwer

Theophilis A. Brouwer, an accomplished artist even before his interests turned to the medium of pottery, started a small one-man operation in 1894 in East Hampton, New York. Two years later he relocated in Westhampton, where he perfected the technique of fire-painting, learning to control the effects of the kiln to produce the best possible results. In 1925 he founded the Ceramic Flame Company in New York, but it is for his earlier work that he is best known. Brouwer died in 1932.

Vase, multicolor metallic high gloss with violet, blue, and gold iridescent highlights, squat form with short rising rim, incised marks, 4x5½", $950.00.

Vase, frothy amber & gold flames, modeled leaves, 3x3" 1,800.00
Vase, gr/purple flames, str rim, 8½x5¼" 1,600.00
Vase, ivory/brn/mauve flames, spherical, 3¾x3" 2,000.00
Vase, ivory/yel/umber flames, whalebone mk, 3¾x3", NM 700.00
Vase, purple & blk lustre, bulbous, flame mk, 5½x5¼" 800.00
Vase, Seagrass-bl flames, ovoid, mk Flame, 8½x5¼" 1,700.00
Vase, yel/amber/gr irid, rstr, 3x4¼" 600.00

Brownies by Palmer Cox

Created by Palmer Cox in 1883, the Brownies charmed children through the pages of books and magazines, as dolls, on their dinnerware, in advertising material, and on souvenirs. Each had his own personality, among them The Bellhop, The London Bobby, The Chairman, and Uncle Sam. But the oversized, triangular face with the startled expression, the protruding tummy, and the spindle legs were characteristics of them all. They were inspired by the Scottish legends related to Cox as a child by his parents, who were of English descent. His introduction of the Brownies to the world was accomplished by a poem called *The Brownies Ride*. Books followed in rapid succession, thirteen in the series, all written as well as illustrated by Palmer Cox.

By the late 1890s, the Brownies were active in advertising. They promoted such products as games, coffee, toys, patent medicines, and rubber boots. 'Greenies' were the Brownies' first cousins, created by Cox to charm and to woo through the pages of the advertising almanacs of the G.G. Green Company of New Jersey. Perhaps the best-known endorsement in the Brownies' career was for the Kodak Brownie, which became so popular and sold in such volume that their name became synonymous with this type of camera. Our advisor for this category is Anne Kier; she is listed in the Directory under Ohio.

Almanac, G Green Woodbury, Cox illus, 1890 ....25.00
Ashtray, Brownie scene, RS Germany, 1913 ....75.00
Book, Another Brownie Book, NY, 1890, 1st ed, VG 150.00
Book, Brownie Year Book, Cox illus, Century, 1895, EX 100.00
Book, Brownies & Goblins, Grosset Dunlap, no date, hardback, VG ...45.00
Book, Brownies & Prince Florimel, Century, 1918, VG 95.00
Book, Brownies at Home, laminated cover, Dover, 1968, EX 35.00
Book, Brownies at Home, 1942, w/dust cover, VG 35.00
Book, Brownies Round the World, Cox illus, Unwin, 1894, EX ..100.00
Book, Little Goody Two Shoes, 1903, EX 40.00
Book, paint; Santa Claus, w/Brownies, rocking horse, fireplace, 1914, G ..42.00
Book, Queer People, Cox illus, 1894, EX 60.00
Book, Querrie Queers, color plates, EX 125.00
Brownie Blocks, McLoughlin, litho decor, wood box, 13½x11" ..260.00
Candlestick, Bobby, majolica, 7½" 300.00
Candy dish, 15 Brownies, Tufts SP, ball ft, 7x5½" 210.00
Chocolate mold, 2-pc 135.00
Comic sheet, 1907, lg, EX 45.00
Creamer, Scottsman head, majolica, 3¼" 80.00
Cup, emb Brownies, Homan Silver Co, child's, EX 85.00
Cup & saucer, demi; comical action Brownies, Ceramic Art Co ..110.00
Dish, 2 Brownies w/golf clubs, 4" 100.00
Figure, Chinaman, papier-mache head, 9", EX 450.00
Figures, papier-mache w/stick legs, jtd arms, 1900s, 5", EX, 4 for ..1,250.00
Fruit crate label, Brownies collect/distribute orange juice, 10" 45.00
Game, Mysterious Vanishing Drawing, dtd 1929, NM (G box) ...35.00
Game, 9-Pins, 1883, NMIB 1,495.00
Hand mirror, pewter fr w/emb Brownies 195.00
Ice cream bag, Cox illus, 5¢ orig value, 1930s, M 40.00
Knife, silver, deeply molded hdl 85.00
Needle book, Brownies, 1892 World's Fair, rare 65.00
Paper doll, Lion Coffee, Indian Brownie, EX 40.00
Pencil box, rolling-pin shape, 15 Brownies in boat 95.00
Pitcher, Brownies playing golf on tan, china, 6" 155.00
Plate, porc, mk La Francaise, 7" 85.00
Plate, SP, Brownies on rim, 8½" 75.00
Puzzle, Brownies skating, 20-pc, early, fr, 10½x12½" 65.00
Sheet music, Dance of the Brownies 30.00
Sign, emb Brownies on tin, Howell's Root Beer, EX 185.00
Spoon, sterling w/enameled Brownie man finial, demitasse 60.00
Table set, emb Brownies, brass, 3-pc (knife/fork/spoon), no box ..75.00
Table set, emb Brownies, brass, 6", in orig box 90.00
Trade card, Sheriff's Sale Segars, Brownies & product, 5x3" 25.00
Whiskey taster, German head, majolica, 3¼" 85.00

Brush-McCoy, Brush

George Brush began his career in the pottery industry in 1901 working for the J.B. Owens Pottery Co. in Zanesville, Ohio. He left the company in 1907 to go into business for himself, only to have fire completely destroy his pottery less than one year after it was founded. In 1909 he became associated with J.W. McCoy, who had operated a pottery of his own in Roseville, Ohio, since 1899. The two men formed the Brush-McCoy Pottery in 1911, locating their headquarters in Zanesville. After the merger, the company expanded and produced not only staple commercial wares but also fine artware. Lines of the highest quality such as Navarre, Venetian, Oriental, and Sylvan were equal to that of their larger competitors. Because very little of the ware was marked, it is often mistaken for Weller, Roseville, or Peters and Reed.

In 1918 after a fire in Zanesville had destroyed the manufacturing portion of that plant, all production was contained in their Roseville (Ohio) plant #2. A stoneware type of clay was used there, and as a result the artware lines of Jewel, Zuniart, King Tut, Florastone, Jetwood, Krakle-Kraft, and Panelart are so distinctive that they are more easily recognizable. Examples of these lines are unique and very beautiful, also quite rare and highly prized!

After McCoy died, the family withdrew their interests, and in 1925 the name of the firm was changed to The Brush Pottery. The era of hand-decorated art pottery production had passed for the most part, having been almost completely replaced by commercial lines. The Brush-Barnett family retained their interest in the pottery until 1981 when it was purchased by the Dearborn Company.

For more information we recommend *The Collector's Encyclopedia of Brush-McCoy Pottery* by Sharon and Bob Huxford, and *Sanford's Guide to Brush-McCoy Pottery, Books I and II,* written by Martha and Steve Sanford, our advisors for this category, and edited by David P. Sanford. They are listed in the Directory under California.

Of all the wares bearing the later Brush script mark, their figural cookie jars are the most collectible, and several have been reproduced. Information on Brush cookie jars (as well as confusing reproductions) can be found in *The Encyclopedia of Cookie Jars* by Joyce and Fred Roerig; they are listed in the Directory under South Carolina. Beware! Cookie jars marked Brush-McCoy are not authentic.

Cookie Jars

Antique Touring Car 700.00
Boy w/Balloons 800.00
Chick in Nest (+) 400.00
Cinderella Pumpkin, #W32, from $200 to 275.00
Circus Horse, gr (+) 950.00
Clown, yel pants 250.00
Clown Bust, #W49, minimum value 325.00
Cookie House, #W31 ....125.00
Covered Wagon, dog finial, #W30, minimum value (+) 550.00
Cow w/Cat on Bk, brn, #W10 (+) 125.00
Cow w/Cat on Bk, purple, minimum value (+) 1,000.00
Davy Crockett, no gold, mk USA (+) 300.00
Dog & Basket 250.00
Donkey Cart, ears up, #W33, minimum value 800.00
Donkey Cart, gray, ears down, #W33 ....400.00
Elephant w/Ice Cream Cone (+) 500.00
Elephant w/Monkey on Bk, minimum value 5,000.00
Fish, #W52 (+) 500.00

Formal Pig, with rare gold trim, Brush W 7 USA (being reproduced), $475.00. **(Photo courtesy Joyce and Fred Roerig)**

Formal Pig, gr hat & coat (+) 300.00
Gas Lamp, #K1 ....75.00
Granny, pk apron, bl dots on skirt 325.00
Granny, plain skirt, minimum value (+) 400.00
Happy Bunny, wht, #W25 ....225.00
Hen on Basket, unmk 125.00
Hillbilly Frog, minimum value (+) 4,500.00
Humpty Dumpty, w/beany & bow tie (+) 275.00
Humpty Dumpty, w/peaked blk hat & shoes, from $250 to 350.00
Laughing Hippo, #W27 (+), from $750 to 850.00
Little Angel (+) 800.00
Little Boy Blue, #K24 Brush USA, lg (+) 800.00
Little Boy Blue, gold trim, #K25, sm 700.00
Little Girl, #017 (+) 550.00
Little Red Riding Hood, gold trim, mk, lg, minimum value (+) .850.00
Little Red Riding Hood, no gold, #K24 USA, sm 550.00
Night Owl 125.00
Old Clock, #W10 ....165.00
Old Shoe, #W23 (+) 125.00
Panda, #W21 (+) 250.00
Peter, Peter Pumpkin Eater, #W24 ....300.00
Peter Pan, gold trim, lg (+) 800.00
Peter Pan, sm, no gold 550.00
Puppy Police (+) 585.00
Raggedy Ann, #W16, from $475 to 525.00
Sitting Pig (+), from $400 to 450.00
Smiling Bear, #W46 (+) 350.00
Squirrel on Log, #W26 ....100.00
Squirrel w/Top Hat, blk coat & hat 275.00
Squirrel w/Top Hat, gr coat 250.00
Stylized Owl 350.00
Stylized Siamese, #W41, from $400 to 500.00
Teddy Bear, ft apart 250.00
Teddy Bear, ft together 200.00
Treasure Chest, #W28 ....150.00

Miscellaneous

Ashtray, frogs ea side wht bowl, late, 6½", from $75 to 125.00
Ashtray, Onyx (brn), #041, 2x5½", from $40 to 75.00
Ashtray, Onyx (brn), ftd bowl, 6x2", from $40 to 60.00
Bank, frog, 1916, 3½", from $50 to 75.00
Bank, pig w/head trn up, 1956, from $35 to 45.00
Basket, circular, concentric ridges, Deco, wht, 1939 ....100.00
Bottle, Onyx (gr), w/hdl & stopper, 10", from $125 to 175.00
Bowl, Onyx (brn), #055, 2½x5", from $35 to 75.00
Bowl, Zuniart, 2x7", from $450 to 550.00
Bud vase, Bittersweet, 6½", from $30 to 40.00
Bud vase, Bronze Line, 7½", from $20 to 30.00
Candlesticks, Jetwood, #030, 7", pr 800.00
Candlesticks, King Tut, #032, 10", pr, from $1,900 to 2,800.00
Candlesticks, Onyx (brn), 10½", pr, from $125 to 200.00
Carafe, Bronze Line, palette mk #928, from $40 to 50.00
Casserole, Nurock, grape design, #110, wht, from $100 to 175.00
Clock, Onyx (brn), Jugtime, 7", from $150 to 200.00
Cornucopia, Bittersweet, dbl, 4½", from $45 to 75.00
Cuspidor, Willow Ware, 1916, 5½", from $115 to 175.00
Decanter, Wise Bird (owl), #136, 1927, 8", from $225 to 300.00
Flowerpot, Bittersweet, 6½", from $20 to 30.00
Hanging basket, Stardust, scalloped rim, 1957, 4", from $125 to ..150.00
Jardiniere, Florastone, 7½", from $1,000 to 1,200.00
Jardiniere, Jetwood, 9", from $1,000 to 1,200.00
Jardiniere, Moderne Kolorkraft, #260, bl, 10", from $110 to 165.00
Jardiniere, Roman, #250, 1927, 9", from $275 to 350.00
Jardiniere, Vista, 1918, 8", from $400 to 600.00

Jardiniere, Zuniart, #240, 9", from $800 to 1,000.00
Jardiniere & pedestal, Roman, Colonial Mat, 36½" overall ...2,500.00
Jug, Florastone, 10", from $700 to 1,100.00
Mug, Santa head, late 20.00
Nursery light, rabbit sitting upright, bl w/pk ears, late, 10" 30.00
Ornament, turtle, 1930s, 6½", from $50 to 80.00
Patio lantern, siamese cat, wht w/blk tail, 12½", from $45 to 75.00
Pitcher, Amsterdam (Dutch couple kissing), 1916, 7", from $135 to ..200.00
Pitcher, Wise Bird (owl), 1927, 10", from $200 to 275.00
Planter, cactus w/2 removable blossom pots, 1950s 30.00
Planter, Dutch shoe, wht w/red-pnt flower, 1940, from $15 to 25.00
Planter, elephant, cartoon shape, pk w/red face trim, 1939 ....40.00
Planter, horse, stylized form, late 1930s 35.00
Planter, ostrich, mk Brush #109, 1950s, from $25 to 40.00
Planter, rooster, 1956, from $25 to 40.00
Plaque, Zuniart, 11½" dia, from $2,500 ....3,500.00
Rolling pin, bl on wht, wood hdls, 1910, from $150 to 250.00
Salt box, Kolorcraft, wood lid, 1932, 4½", from $50 to 85.00
Tankard, Kolorkraft, #347, cobalt bl, 1928, from $100 to 175.00
Tray, Mt Pelee, dbl bowls w/center hdl, 2x7", from $750 to 1,000.00
Urn, Onyx (brn), w/hdls, 6", from $65 to 85.00
Vase, Art Vellum, #069, 8", from $50 to 75.00
Vase, Bittersweet, ped ft, 8", from $30 to 50.00
Vase, Florastone, #077, 6", from $800 to 1,000.00
Vase, Krakle-Kraft, dragon, rare, 8", from $3,500 to 5,000.00
Vase, Navarre, 9", from $500 to 750.00
Vase, Onyx, #064, 8", from $65 to 110.00
Vase, Princess, w/hdls mid-1960s, 12", from $50 to 75.00
Vase, Vogue, 10", from $175 to 250.00
Wall pocket, dog in doghouse, 1952, from $75 to 100.00
Wall pocket, Wise Bird (owl), 1927, 8", from $165 to 215.00
Window box, Stardust, 4x12", 1957, from $55 to 95.00

Buffalo Pottery

The founding of the Buffalo Pottery in Buffalo, New York, in 1901, was a direct result of the success achieved by John Larkin through his innovative methods of marketing 'Sweet Home Soap.' Choosing to omit the 'middle-man,' Larkin preferred to deal directly with the consumer and offered premiums as an enticement for sales. The pottery soon proved a success in its own right and began producing advertising and commemorative items for other companies, as well as commercial tableware. In 1905 they introduced their Blue Willow line after extensive experimentation resulted in the development of the first successful underglaze cobalt achieved by an American company. Between 1905 and 1909, a line of pitchers and jugs were hand decorated in historical, literary, floral, and outdoor themes. Twenty-nine styles are known to have been made.

Their most famous line was Deldare Ware, the bulk of which was made from 1908 to 1909. It was hand decorated after illustrations by Cecil Aldin. Views of English life were portrayed in detail through unusual use of color against the natural olive green cast of the body. Today the 'Fallowfield Hunt' scenes are more difficult to locate than 'Scenes of Village Life in Ye Olden Days.' A Deldare calendar plate was made in 1910. These are very rare and are highly valued by collectors. The line was revived in 1923 and dropped again in 1925. Every piece was marked 'Made at Ye Buffalo Pottery, Deldare Ware Underglaze.' Most are dated, though the date has no bearing on the value. Emerald Deldare was made on the same olive body and on standard Deldare Ware shapes and featured historical scenes and Art Nouveau decorations. Most pieces are found with a 1911 date stamp. Production was very limited due to the intricate, time-consuming detail. Needless to say, it is very rare and extremely desirable.

Abino Ware, most of which was made in 1912, also used standard Deldare shapes, but its colors were earthy and the decorations more delicately applied. Sailboats, windmills, and country scenes were favored motifs. These designs were achieved by overpainting transfer prints and were often signed by the artist. The ware is marked 'Abino' in hand-printed block letters. Production was limited; and as a result, examples of this line are scarce today.

Commercial or institutional ware was another of Buffalo Pottery's crowning achievements. In 1917 vitrified china production began, and the firm produced for accounts worldwide. After 1956 all of their wares bore the name Buffalo China. Buffalo China (commercial and institutional ware) is being produced today by Oneida Silver Company.

Our advisors for this category are Fred and Lila Shrader; they are listed in the Directory under California.

Key:
BW — Blue Willow C — commercial ware marked

Abino

Bowl, nut; windmill, farm & harbor scenes, 8" 685.00
Creamer, marine scene w/dk clouds, 3¼" 500.00
Mug, shoreline scene w/lighthouse, 2½" 1,500.00
Plaque, sailing ships at sunrise/sunset, 12¼" 650.00
Plate, sm sailboats, distant lighthouse, 8½" 420.00
Tankard, sailing vessels on rough seas, 10¼" 1,340.00
Toothpick holder, shoreline scene, 2¼" 395.00
Vase, ships in choppy water, cylindrical, 7½" 740.00

Deldare

Tray, Emerald, Dr. Syntax Rural Sports, 1911, 12", $1,600.00.

Ashtray/matchbox holder, scenic Art Nouveau 885.00
Bowl, Fallowfield Hunt, Breakfast, 12" 1,250.00
Bowl, Fallowfield Hunt, The Death, 9" 2,800.00
Bowl, fruit; Ye Village Tavern, 9" 475.00
Bowl, sauce; Village Scene, 5¼" 95.00
Candle holder, Emerald, shield-bk, 7" 1,750.00
Candle holder, Village Scene, shield-bk, 5" 800.00
Candle holder, Village Scene, shield-bk, 7" 1,350.00
Candlesticks, Village Scene, 9½" dia, pr 950.00
Chocolate pot, Ye Village Scene, 10" 725.00
Creamer, Emerald, Art Nouveau flowers & leaves, 3" 510.00
Cup & saucer, chocolate; The Fallowfield Hunt 585.00
Cup & saucer, Emerald, Dr Syntax at Liverpool 665.00
Cup & saucer, tea; The Fallowfield Hunt or Ye Olden Days, ea ..295.00
Hair receiver, Ye Village Street, 4½" dia 485.00
Humidor, 'There was an old sailor...,' 8" 1,400.00
Mug, 'Dr Syntax again filled up his glass...,' 4¼" 695.00
Mug, Fallowfield Hunt, At Three Pigeons, 4½" 425.00
Mug, Fallowfield Hunt, mini, 2½" 499.00
Mug, Village Scene, finger rest on top of hdl, child sz, 2½" 1,000.00
Mug, Ye Lion Inn, 3½" 275.00

Pitcher, Emerald, 'Dr Syntax stopt by highway men,' 6" 980.00
Pitcher, Emerald, 'He canter'd by my lady's side...,' 10" 1,200.00
Pitcher, Fallowfield Hunt, The Return, 8½" 545.00
Pitcher, tankard, Fallowfield Hunt, Supper, 12½" 1,000.00
Pitcher, tankard, untitled countryside scene, 10½" 1,990.00
Pitcher, Their Manner of Telling Stories, 6" 425.00
Pitcher, Ye Old English Village, 10" 785.00
Plaque, Ye Lion Inn, pierced for hanging, 12¼" dia 515.00
Plate, At Ye Lion Inn, 6¼", from $55 to 89.00
Plate, calendar; Emerald, 1910, 9½" 1,700.00
Plate, chop; Fallowfield Hunt, The Start, 14" 595.00
Plate, Deldare advertising, 6½" 1,430.00
Plate, Emerald, Dr Syntax...a Discovery, 10", from $650 to 950.00
Plate, Fallowfield Hunt, Breaking Cover, 10" 279.00
Plate, Fallowfield Hunt, The Death, 8½", from $160 to 195.00
Plate, Fallowfield Hunt, The Start, 9¼" 195.00
Plate, rim soup; Fallowfield Hunt, Breaking Cover, 9" 345.00
Plate, Ye Village Gossips, 10" 185.00
Powder jar, Ye Village Street, 4¾" dia, from $550 to 600.00
Relish dish, Ye Olden Times, 6x12" 750.00
Sugar bowl, Emerald, Death of Punch, w/lid 525.00
Sugar bowl, Scenes of Village Life, w/lid & hdl, 4" 275.00
Sugar bowl, Village Scenes, 6-sided & open, no hdl, 4" dia 495.00
Tea tile, Emerald, Dr Syntax Taking Possession, 6" dia 740.00
Tea tile, Fallowfield Hunt, 6" dia 470.00
Teapot, Emerald, Dr Syntax, 4¼" 495.00
Teapot, various Village Scenes, 5¾" 490.00
Tray, calling card; Fallowfield Hunt, tab hdls, 7¾" dia 385.00
Tray, calling card; Mr Pickwick Addresses..., tab hdls, 8" dia 800.00
Tray, dresser; Dancing Ye Minuet, 9x12" 595.00
Vase, Buffalo Oxen by Ralph Stuart, 8½" 8,000.00
Vase, Village Schoolmaster/Village Parson, 8½" 795.00

Miscellaneous

Ashtray/matchbox holder, IMH intertwined w/Masonic emblem ...35.00
Bone dish, BW, crescent shape 75.00
Bowl, fruit; Bonrea, sm, 6" 12.00
Bowl, fruit; BW, sm, 6" 19.00
Bowl, Geranium (bl & wht), w/metal collar & split lid, 7" dia ..145.00
Bowl, gravy; Modjeska, G gold, 3½x6" 58.00
Bowl, soup; Vienna, flat w/rim, 8½" 42.00
Bowl, vegetable; BW, w/lid, 5½x10" 210.00
Bowl, vegetable; Lamare, bl & wht w/rich gold, w/lid, 5½x10" .135.00
Butter pat, Aster Hotel (w/logo), C 29.00
Butter pat, Bluebird 38.00
Butter pat, Bonrea w/rich gold trim 23.00
Butter pat, Boos Bros, yel flowers w/brn stripe 45.00
Butter pat, BW 35.00
Butter pat, Cafe Metropool w/palm trees, C 35.00
Butter pat, Gaudy Willow w/rich gold trim 185.00
Butter pat, Indian Tree, C 11.00
Butter pat, Modjeska, G gold trim 32.00
Butter pat, US Army Medical Department, C 29.00
Butter pat, US Military Academy, West Point, NY, C 49.00
Butter pat, Wilshire/Ebell Club w/rich gold border, C 55.00
Candlestick holder w/finger ring, Hotel Commodore, C, 5½" dia ..85.00
Canister, Rice, bl & wht floral, rpl lid, 7½" 70.00
Canister set, Tea, Coffee, Sugar, wht w/gold, 7" 188.00
Chamber pot, Chrysanthemum, no lid 70.00
Chamber pot, shaded bl w/gold trim 95.00
Child's feeding dish, ABCs on rim, child w/puppies, 7½" 110.00
Child's feeding dish, Campbell Kids scene, faded decal, 7½" 45.00
Child's feeding dish, Campbell Kids scene w/ABC, EX gold, 7½" ..95.00
Chocolate pot, spray of poppies on gr, EX gold 285.00
Compote, Colorido ware, ped ft, C, 6x9" 85.00
Creamer, Multifleure Lamelle, hdl, C, 3½" 55.00
Creamer, Roycroft, ind w/o hdl, C, 3" 295.00
Creamer, Smoke Tree Ranch (on bottom), hdl, C, 3½" 45.00
Creamer, Tom's Dixie Kitchen, hdl, C, 3" 65.00
Cup, punch; Fallowfield scene on Colorido Ware, ped ft, C 65.00
Cup & liner, bouillon; Hotel Astor (w/logo), C 18.00
Cup & saucer, 'Take ye a cup o' kindness...,' oversz, 12-oz 110.00
Cup & saucer, demi; Roycroft Inn, mk Buffalo Pottery 515.00
Cup & saucer, demi; spray of poppies on gr, EX gold 75.00
Cup & saucer, Modjeska, G gold trim 35.00
Cup & saucer, Vienna, rich gold trim 31.00
Fish set, Beck designs, 14" oval platter & 6 9" plates 325.00
Gravy boat, Lamare, rich gold, w/liner 65.00
Jug, Cinderella, mc on brn transfer, 6" 495.00
Jug, Mason, floral, fishermen, Roman ruins, teal-gr transfer, 8" .450.00
Jug, Rip Van Winkle, 6½" 812.00
Jug, The Gunner, teal gr w/gold highlights, 6" 425.00
Jug, Whirl of the Town, mc, 7" 650.00
Pitcher, BW, w/lid, 5½" 175.00
Pitcher, Cairo (yel & pk roses), 7" 65.00
Pitcher, Chicago style, wht w/gold trim, 6" 65.00
Pitcher, Geranium, 5½" 175.00
Pitcher, Gloriana, mc enhancement on bl transfer, 9" 975.00
Pitcher, Robin Hood, mc on brn transfer, 8" 460.00
Pitcher, Roosevelt Bears, 4 different scenes, 8½" 1,750.00
Pitcher, sailor w/lighthouse on other side, bl transfer, 8½" 550.00
Plate, Bonrea w/rich gold trim, 9" 36.00
Plate, chop; Breakfast at Three Pigeons on Blue Lune Ware, 11½" .700.00
Plate, chop; Breakfast at Three Pigeons on Rouge Ware, 11½" .450.00
Plate, Christmas, bl on bl, 1950, 9½" 38.00
Plate, City of Buffalo's Sesquicentennial, bl & wht, 9½" 24.50
Plate, commemorative, Faneuil Hall, Boston MA, 7½" 55.00
Plate, commemorative, Trinity Church, NY, 7½" 60.00
Plate, commemorative, Washington's Home, Mt Vernon, HP 76.00
Plate, Gaudy Willow w/rich cobalt, gr, brn & gold, 9½" 195.00
Plate, grill; BW, C, 11" 29.00
Plate, historical, Capitol Building, teal gr, 10½" 50.00
Plate, historical, Mt Vernon, bl on wht, 10½" 85.00
Plate, Indian Tree, C, 5¼" 9.00
Plate, Pink Willow, C, 5¼" 11.00
Plate, Seneca, w/emb, 9½" 23.00
Plate, USBF, Bureau of Fisheries, C, 6" 38.00
Plate, Vienna, w/rich gold trim, 8" 27.00
Plate, WYCA in gr triangle w/gr border, 1921, C, 8" 26.00
Platter, BW, fancy tab hdls, 18x14" 235.00
Platter, Dr Syntax Advertises for a Wife, bl & wht, 14x11" 299.00
Platter, Salvation Army, C, 7x9½" 155.00
Relish dish, Hotel Astor, gr logo, C, 5x7½" 24.00
Sugar bowl, Vienna, rich gold trim, w/lid 65.00
Teapot, Argyle, no chain or infuser 65.00
Teapot, Argyle, w/orig & complete tea infuser 195.00
Teapot, Geranium, bl & wht, w/orig & complete tea infuser 265.00
Toilet set, Cairo, pitcher+bowl+chamber pot+lid+4 pcs 365.00
Vase, Geranium, bl & wht, rnded shoulders, 4½" 225.00
Vase, Multifleure, flared baluster form, 8" 250.00

Buggy Steps

The recent increased interest in western collectibles has stimulated a renewed awareness in all horse-drawn memorabilia. A good example of this is the buggy step. This device allowed the passenger to enter or exit the vehicle without the driver's assistance. Steps may be hinged, pivoted, adjustable, folding, and spring loaded. The elaborate handwork of the blacksmiths who created them was equal to that of the finest wheelwrights, carpenters, and leather workers involved in the manufacture of early wheeled vehicles (1865–1910). For listings of no-name steps with multiple designs, see previous editions of this book. Prices suggested here are for steps in mint to good condition. Rust, breaks, and pitting reduce their value. Our advisor for this category is John Waddell; he is listed in the Directory under Texas.

Bolt-on (2-hole, sm pad), from $10 to 15.00
Mounted (tee-mt), from $15 to 25.00
Mounted (tri-fork), from $15 to 25.00
Mounted (3-point w/branch), from $25 to 35.00
Name, ornate, scarce, from $50 to 75.00
Special mfg folding stage/carriage, rare, from $120 to 210.00
Surrey (bar & branch arm), lg, from $90 to 135.00

Burmese

Burmese glass was patented in 1885 by the Mount Washington Glass Co. It is typically shaded from canary yellow to a rosy salmon color. The yellow is produced by the addition of uranium oxide to the mix. The salmon color comes from the addition of gold salts and is achieved by reheating the object (partially) in the furnace. It is thus called 'heat sensitive' glass. Thomas Webb of England was licensed to produce Burmese and often added more gold, giving an almost fuchsia tinge to the salmon in some cases. They called their glass 'Queen's Burmese,' and this is sometimes etched on the base of the object. This is not to be confused with Mount Washington's 'Queen's Design,' which refers to the design painted on the object. Both companies added decoration to many pieces. Mount Washington-Pairpoint produced some Burmese in the late 1920s and Gundersen and Bryden in the '50s and '70s, but the color and shapes are different.

Our advisors for this category are Dolli and Wilfred Cohen; they are listed in the Directory under California. In the listings that follow, examples are assumed to have the satin finish unless noted 'shiny.' See also Lamps, Fairy.

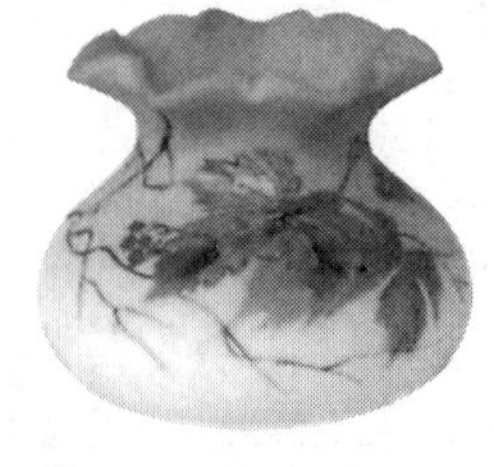

Vase, Webb, foliage and berry decor, crimped flower-form rim, 2¾x3½", $575.00.

Bonbon dish, Mt WA, shiny, heart-shaped rim, 3 yel prunts, 6½" 950.00
Bottle, Mt WA, ribbed cylinder, w/faceted stopper, 5½" 535.00
Bowl, bonbon; Mt WA, sqd rim, optic rib sides, 2x5¼x4½" 285.00
Bowl, bride's; Mt WA, red leaves/wht berries/bl flowers, SP fr, 9" 1,295.00
Bowl, finger; Mt WA, rectangular rim, 2x3½x4¾" 245.00
Bowl, fish in net decor, triangular, 5" dia 995.00
Bowl, ice cream; Mt WA, ruffled top, 4¾" 200.00
Bowl, Mt WA, appl yel drips & edge, flared/folded rim, 2½x6" L 1,600.00
Bowl, Mt WA, ruffled, ftd, rim pulled 3X, berry pontil, 6x6" 1,500.00
Bowl, Mt WA, ruffled, 2¾x9" 935.00
Bowl, Webb, floral branch, triangular, very thin, 2¼x5" 675.00
Bowl, Webb, ruffled corners, 2x6x6" 250.00
Condiment set, Mt WA, ribbed shakers/cruet in mk silver fr 1,750.00
Creamer & sugar bowl, Webb, hexagonal rims, appl vintage 900.00
Cruet, Mt WA, melon ribbed, faceted stopper, 6½" 1,085.00
Cruet, Mt WA, shiny, melon ribbed, mushroom stopper, 7" 1,250.00
Cruet, Mt WA, unfired w/floral branch & gilt, ribbed, 6½" 1,350.00
Cup, punch; Mt WA, waisted (rare shape), 2¾" 335.00
Cup & saucer, demitasse; Mt WA, paper label, 2⅜", 3⅛" 585.00
Fairy lamp/epergne, 4 dome shades/Clarke bases, Webb, 13" mirror, 16" 2,750.00
Fairy lamp/epergne, 6 lilies/dome shade in ruffled base, 11x8" 2,250.00
Lamp, Mt WA, 5 ibis in flight/oasis/sunset, fluid burner, 20x10" 10,350.00
Pitcher, milk; Mt WA, str sides, ear hdl, 7" 935.00
Pitcher, Mt WA, pulled spout, 6" 600.00
Pitcher, Mt WA, ruffled top, 5¼" 550.00
Pitcher, tankard; floral, pnt lines on rim/hdl, mini 750.00
Plate, Mt WA, EX color, 10" 365.00
Plate, Pairpoint, shiny, ca 1920s, 10" 265.00
Plate, shiny, 8" 125.00
Rose bowl, Mt WA, petal top, 2½x2½" 285.00
Sugar bowl, Mt WA, open, pie-crust crimped rim, 3¼" 385.00
Sweetmeat, Mt WA, unfired, pansies on relief stars, SP lid 1,250.00
Toothpick holder, Dmn Quilt, flowers, tricon rim 695.00
Toothpick holder, Mt WA, berries, tricon rim, low 850.00
Toothpick holder, Mt WA, daisies, ribbed, tricon rim 695.00
Toothpick holder, Mt WA, pine cones/needles, sq rim, 3x3" 650.00
Toothpick holder, Mt WA, shiny, bulbous, sq rim 550.00
Toothpick holder, Mt WA, shiny, Dmn Optic, tricon rim, 2½" 585.00
Toothpick holder, Webb, ball shape w/short neck, 2½" 385.00
Toothpick holder, Webb, hexagonal rim, 2½" 385.00
Tumbler, juice; Mt WA, w/curlicue hdl, 3⅞" 225.00
Tumbler, juice; Webb, bbl w/appl berries & foliage, 2¾" 500.00
Tumbler, Mt WA, thin walls, EX color 185.00
Vase, bud; Mt WA, tall ped ft, 9x1½" 1,100.00
Vase, daisies, squat w/collar neck, 3x3" 650.00
Vase, Jack-in-pulpit; Mt WA, ruffled, 6" 400.00
Vase, Jack-in-pulpit; Mt WA, 9" 750.00
Vase, Jack-in-pulpit; Pairpoint, shiny, 5x6¾" 535.00
Vase, lily; Gundersen, 9½" 365.00
Vase, lily; Mt WA, EX color, 12" 850.00
Vase, lily; Mt WA, EX color, 13", from $875 to 935.00
Vase, lily; Mt WA, 8¼" 595.00
Vase, Mt WA, dbl-gourd form, 8" 650.00
Vase, Mt WA, distended neck, ftd, thin hdls, 10" 795.00
Vase, Mt WA, Egyptian style w/hdls, #153, 7" 700.00
Vase, Mt WA, floral, air-trap ribbons, dbl gourd, 7½" 695.00
Vase, Mt WA, gourd shape, 12" 895.00
Vase, Mt WA, gr maiden hair ferns w/gold, stick neck, 9½" 775.00
Vase, Mt WA, ibis/distant pyramids, ovoid, 12" 2,500.00
Vase, Mt WA, lav florals w/beads at rim, 12" 1,500.00
Vase, Mt WA, meadow grass/blossoms w/gold, stick neck, 10" 1,985.00
Vase, Mt WA, shiny, yel rigaree collar & bow, petal top, 4½" 1,750.00
Vase, Mt WA, shouldered w/long neck, 10x5½" 745.00
Vase, Mt WA, stick neck, 5¾" 550.00
Vase, Pairpoint, ruffled goblet form, ca 1920s, 10x7" 735.00
Vase, shiny, fold-out fluted top, 8¾" 350.00
Vase, Webb, birds & flowers on branches, Queen's, 10½" 3,250.00
Vase, Webb, crimped petal-top rim, 2¼" 275.00
Vase, Webb, floral, bulbous w/sq neck, 2¾" 350.00
Vase, Webb, floral, 6-sided top, 3¼" 325.00
Vase, Webb, prunus blossoms, crimped flaring rim, 4½x3" 350.00
Vase, Webb, prunus blossoms, lip pulled 5X, Queen's, 3¾" 400.00
Vase, Webb, red roses/leaves, 6-petal rim, Queen's, 2¾x3½" 480.00
Vase, Webb, trailing ivy, trifold rim, 3½" 350.00
Vase, Webb, 5-pointed crimped top, 3¼" 275.00

Butter Molds and Stamps

The art of decorating butter began in Europe during the reign of

Charles II. This practice was continued in America by the farmer's wife who sold her homemade butter at the weekly market to earn extra money during hard times. A mold or stamp with a special design, hand carved either by her husband or a local craftsman, not only made her product more attractive but also helped identify it as hers. The pattern became the trademark of Mrs. Smith, and all who saw it knew that this was her butter. It was usually the rule that no two farms used the same mold within a certain area, thus the many variations and patterns available to the collector today. The most valuable are those which have animals, birds, or odd shapes. The most sought-after motifs are the eagle, cow, fish, and rooster. These works of early folk art are quickly disappearing from the market.

Molds

Beaver, 3½" dia 195.00
Eagle/stars/foliage, primitive, 3½" dia 195.00
Hen, detailed cvg, rare, 3½" dia 450.00
Rose, deep cvg 110.00
8 sqs w/cvd leaves, acorns/wheat/etc, ftd, 5½x11" 175.00

Stamps

Tulip, deeply carved, chip-carved border with radiating triangles, ca 1830, 4" dia., $270.00. (Photo courtesy Aston Macek Auctioneers and Appraisers)

Acorn w/cap & 2 lg leaves, 4½" dia 150.00
Bird on branch, cvd softwood, 1-pc w/ball-shaped hdl, 3¼" dia ...275.00
Cow, long trn inserted hdl, 2¾" dia 150.00
Cow, poplar, old scrubbed patina, 1-pc trn hdl, 4¼" dia 200.00
Cow & tree, cvd softwood, half-rnd, appl hdl, 7x3½" 1,100.00
Cow & tree, hardwood, weathered, 1-pc trn hdl, 4¼" dia 135.00
Cow & tree, notch-cvd border, 1-pc w/hdl, 4" dia 275.00
Crown-like design, scrubbed, 1-pc trn hdl, 4½" dia 110.00
Dbl-sided, concentric dmns/stylized flower, dmn shape, 5¾" 325.00
Dbl-sided, flower & leaf/leafy branches, 3¼" dia 200.00
Dbl-sided, flower/pinwheel, paddle shape, 3⅝" 625.00
Dbl-sided, star & geometric design/rosette-like design, 5" dia 225.00
Dbl-sided, star flower, lollipop style, worn patina, 8½" 195.00
Dbl-sided, tulip/radial design, EX cvg, 1-pc w/hdl, 4¼" dia 900.00
Eagle, scrubbed poplar, 4" dia 275.00
Eagle (stylized) w/foliage & star, 1-pc, 4⅝" dia 465.00
Eagle w/star, hardwood, old patina, crack, 4" dia 300.00
Eagle w/stars, primitive cvg, lollipop style, 8½" 275.00
Eagle w/wings wide, star at left, notched rim, stick hdl, 7" dia ...875.00
Fish (simple), lollipop style, 7" dia 115.00
Flower (8 petal) & 2 branches w/leaves, cvd softwood, 5½" L ...350.00
Flower & dbl heart, deeply cvd, worn patina, 3⅜x6⅛" 500.00
Flower w/4 petals & sm berries, 1-pc, walnut oval, 5¼x3⅜" 275.00
Flowers (stylized) w/tulip, 1-pc w/knob hdl, 4½" dia 225.00
Flowers in pot w/X-hatching, 1823 on bk, pine, old patina, 4x2⅝" ...300.00
Foliage, rayed rim, 1-pc, trn hdl, 3½" dia 115.00
Grape cluster, scalloped band, oval, 4x6" 200.00
Heart w/deep geometric cvd designs, scrubbed, 5½" dia 220.00
Heart w/foliage & X-hatching, EX cvg, trn hdl, 4⅜" dia 335.00
Hearts (4) & X-hatching, hardwood, old patina, 4¾x4⅝" 400.00
Pineapple, crudely cvd, 3⅞" dia 175.00
Pineapple & foliage, old finish, 1-pc trn hdl, 4¼" dia 185.00
Pineapple & leaves, notch-cvd rim, 7⅛x3⅞" 300.00
Pinwheel, 2-pc hdl, 4⅞" dia 250.00
Plant (stylized) w/cvd dmns & lg leaves, 3¾" dia 175.00
Pomegranate, 1-pc trn hdl, 4¾" dia 125.00
Radial design, 6-lobe, parallel lines, hdl missing, 4⅝" dia 150.00
Radial design, 6-lobe w/tulips, stick hdl, chips, 3¼" dia 200.00
Radial design, 6-lobe w/X-hatching, paddle shape, 3½" dia 250.00
Star flower, old patina, inserted hdl, 4⅞" dia 355.00
Star flower w/zigzag & swags, lollipop style, 7" L 225.00
Sunflower w/2 leaves, trn hdl, 4¼" dia 450.00
Thistle, knob hdl on bk, 2¾x4" dia 110.00
Tulip (stylized), scrubbed, sm knob hdl, age crack, 4" dia 110.00
Tulip & leaves, self-hdl, dtd 1796, PA, 4½x5" 550.00
Tulip & star w/flowers, scrubbed, 1-pc trn hdl, 4⅜" dia 275.00
Tulip & stars, deep cvg, poplar w/old patina, 1-pc trn hdl, 4⅞"dia ...400.00
Tulip cvd in dk walnut wood, lollipop style, 6¾" L 330.00
Tulips (2) w/leaves & notch-cvd border, 6½x4" 950.00
Tulips & stars, cvd maple, oval, 5½x3⅝" 250.00
Wheat sheaf, notch-cvd border, 1-pc w/hdl, 2¾" dia 175.00

Buttonhooks

The earliest known written reference to buttonhooks (shoe hooks, glove hooks, or collar buttoners) is dated 1611. They became a necessary implement in the 1850s when tight-fitting high-button shoes became fashionable. Later in the nineteenth century, ladies' button gloves and men's button-on collars and cuffs dictated specific types of buttoners, some with a closed wire loop instead of a hook end. Both shoes and gloves used as many as twenty-four buttons each. Usage began to wane in the late 1920s following a fashion change to low-cut laced shoes and the invention of the zipper. There was a brief resurgence of use following the 1948 movie 'High Button Shoes.' For a simple, needed utilitarian device, buttonhook handles were made from a surprising variety of materials: natural wood, bone, ivory, agate, and mother-of-pearl to plain steel, celluloid, aluminum, iron, lead and pewter, artistic copper, brass, silver, gold, and many other materials, in lengths that varied from under 2" to over 20". Many designs folded or retracted, and buttonhooks were often combined with shoehorns and other useful implements. Stamped steel buttonhooks often came free with the purchase of shoes, gloves, or collars. Material, design, workmanship, condition, and relative scarcity are the primary market value factors. Prices range from $1.00 to over $200.00, with most being in the $10.00 to $75.00 range. Buttonhooks are fairly easy to find, and they are interesting to display.

Our advisor for this category is Richard Mathes; he is listed in the Directory under Ohio. See also The Buttonhook Society listing in the Directory under Clubs, Newsletters, and Catalogs.

Buttonhook/penknife, ivory side plates, man's 50.00
Collar buttoner, stamped steel, advertising, closed end, 3" 20.00
Glove hook, gold-plated, retractable, 3" 90.00
Glove hook, loop end, agate hdl, 2½" 60.00
Shoe hook, colored celluloid hdl, 8" 15.00
Shoe hook, lathe-trn hardwood hdl, dk finish, 8" 15.00
Shoe hook, SP w/blade, repousse hdl, Pat Jan 5 1892, 5" 40.00
Shoe hook, stamped steel, advertising, 5" 8.00
Shoe hook, sterling, floral & geometrics, 8" 55.00
Shoe hook, sterling, Nouveau lady's face, 6½" 75.00
Shoe hook, sterling, W w/arrow, hammered Florentine decor, mk ..55.00

Shoe hook/shoehorn combination, steel & celluloid, 9" 35.00

Bybee

The Bybee Pottery was founded in 1845 in the small town of Bybee, Kentucky, by the Cornelison family. Their earliest wares were primarily stoneware churns and jars. Today the work is carried on by sixth generation Cornelison potters who still use the same facilities and production methods to make a more diversified line of pottery. From a fine white clay mined only a few miles from the potting shed itself, the shop produces vases, jugs, dinnerware, and banks in a variety of colors, some of which are shipped to the larger cities to be sold in department stores and specialty shops. The bulk of their wares, however, is sold to the thousands of tourists who are attracted to the pottery each year.

Baker, pk splatter, 12¾" 24.00
Candle holder, gr, saucer type w/finger hold 25.00
Canister, speckled bl & wht, w/lid, 4½x5½" dia 25.00
Creamer & sugar bowl, gr w/brn specks, EX 45.00
Figurine, cat, gr & bl sponging, 7" 35.00
Pitcher, aqua-gr, ice lip, 5½" 25.00
Pitcher, bl pastel, tapered hdl w/thumb-press end, 1950s, 5¼" 30.00
Pitcher, ray w/bl specks on top & bl bird on sides, 6" 30.00
Vase, gr matt, 3-hdl, 6" 70.00
Vase, mahog gloss, bulbous w/3 sm hdls, flakes, 7¾" 70.00

Cabat

From beginning experimentation with pottery in New York City around 1940, through several different types of clay, designs, and glazes, and relocation to Arizona, the Rose Cabat 'Feelie,' so named because 'it feels so good,' evolved into present forms and glazes in the late 1950s. Rose was aided and encouraged through the years by her late husband Erni. Their small 'weed pots' are readily recognizable by their light weight, tiny thin necks, and soft glazes. Pieces are marked with a hand-incised 'Cabat' on the bottom.

Vase, Feelie, bl/blk crystalline, 3" 210.00
Vase, Feelie, caramel matt w/mustard flecks, ovoid, 3x1¾" 275.00
Vase, Feelie, gr/yel/purple matt, 3" 200.00
Vase, Feelie, gray/purple/blk matt, 3" 230.00
Vase, Feelie, lav marbled mircocrystalline, 3½" 200.00
Vase, Feelie, lav w/violet/ivory drip, gray matt patches, 3" 300.00
Vase, Feelie, lime gr matt w/tan crystals, 3½" 275.00
Vase, Feelie, lt gr matt/frost, 5 runs w/crystalline, 3½x3" 425.00
Vase, Feelie, lt lime w/tan matt sections, brn at base, 3x3" 225.00
Vase, Feelie, yel microcrystalline, 3½" 225.00

Calendar Plates

Calendar plates were advertising giveaways most popular from about 1906 until the late twenties. They were decorated with colorful underglaze decals of lovely ladies, flowers, animals, birds and, of course, the twelve months of the year of their issue. During the 1950s they came into vogue again but never to the extent they were originally. Those with exceptional detailing, or those with scenes of a particular activity are most desirable, so are any from before 1906.

1904, Happy New Year, Cupid & bell, 8" 50.00
1907, Christmas scenes, 9" 60.00
1908, man & lady on fox hunt w/dog, 9¼" 28.00
1908, pk rose border 30.00
1909, bird carrying ribbon, 8¼" 28.00
1909, Christmas, holly & berries 50.00
1909, monks drinking wine, 9" 55.00
1909, rose center, 8½" 35.00
1910, Betsy Ross, Jersey City 38.00
1910, Fly Fishing 50.00
1910, lighthouse & sailboats 35.00
1911, cherries, pear & apple 28.00
1911, hunter w/dog & quail 40.00
1912, airplane/scenic view, fruit/flower border, 8½", EX 65.00
1912, apples/leaves transfer, DE McNicol, 8¼" 40.00
1912, biplane, Cincinnati grocery 68.00
1912, hot-air balloon, molded/scalloped rim, Sterling, 8" 40.00
1912, Natural Bridge, Westfield, MA 22.00
1912, owl, Augusta IL 35.00
1914, brn transfer sheep: Thoroughbreds, 7¼" 25.00
1914, deer at stream, 7" 35.00
1915, Dutch boy & girl, 'You vill never..., 9½" 30.00
1915, George Washington 32.00
1915, Panama Canal, 8½" 35.00
1919, Am flag, 8" 30.00
1919, WWI airplane/battleships/flags, Peace w/Honor, 8½", EX 70.00
1920, Victory of the Great World War, 1914-1919, 8" 50.00
1929, valentine & flowers 27.50

Calendars

Calendars are collected for their colorful prints, often attributed to a well-recognized artist of the period. Advertising calendars from the turn of the century often have a double appeal when representing a company whose tins, signs, store displays, etc., are also collectible. See also Parrish, Maxfield.

1911, Collins Baking Co., child in chair with puppy and dog, embossed, Kaufman & Strauss Co., Germany, Buffalo, N.Y. U.S.A, complete, $130.00.

1886, Grit Newspaper, cb, boy hawking papers, 11", EX 125.00
1888, Gould Tobacco Co, cb, 2 snowbirds, 11", NM 115.00
1889, Quincy Mutual Fire Insurance Co, cb, cat/3 rats, 10", NM ...575.00
1892, Hood's Sarsaparilla, NM+ 120.00
1892, Singer Sewing Machines, blond girl in straw hat, 9", EX+ .140.00
1893, Hood's Sarsaparilla, M 200.00
1894, Metropolitan Life, diecut cb, girl, filigree border, 12", VG ..40.00
1895, Hood's Sarsaparilla, NM 100.00
1896, Grit Newspaper, cb, girl surrounded by months, 11", EX+ ..150.00
1897, George D Flynn, diecut cb, girl hugging dog, 13½", EX ...185.00
1898, Boston Store, emb diecut cb, 12", EX+ 160.00
1898, Singer Sewing Machines, emb heavy paper, 12", EX 55.00
1899, Grit Newspaper, cb, girl w/flag at mirror, 12", EX 125.00

1900, Fairbank's Fairy Calendar, 13x10", NM 210.00
1900, Woods & Miller, diecut cb, girl w/horseshoe, 17", EX+ ...100.00
1900, Woods & Miller, diecut cb, man on pig's bk, 17", EX+ 140.00
1901, Swift & Co, American Girl, 15", VG 70.00
1901, Youth's Companion, diecut cb, Puritan girl, elongated, EX ...100.00
1902, Good Store, emb cb, boy/girl/rabbit/wheelbarrow, 11", EX+ .145.00
1904, Great Atlantic & Pacific Tea Co, WA McEntee art, 16", G+ .75.00
1904, Hood's Sarsaparilla, EX+ 75.00
1905, A Bauder, diecut cb, boy/girl on wagon fr by roses, 14", EX+ ...175.00
1905, DeLaval Cream Separators, EX 1,100.00
1907, Ed Wilkins (Farm Implements), diecut cb, 12", NM 25.00
1907, Kellogg Iron Works, emb stand-up, 4 caricature men, 8x12", NM .130.00
1908, Theo Wackman Furniture, diecut cb, puppies on ladder, 17", EX ..120.00
1908, Union Ice & Coal Co, Rock Island Ill, girl on phone, 10", EX ..85.00
1909, Independent Tea Co, diecut cb, emb, woman/lilacs, 20", NM .300.00
1909, Peters Cartridge Co, hunt scene, G Muss Arnolt art, 27", G ...165.00
1910, Hanson & Gilbertson The General Merchants, diecut cb, 14", EX ..80.00
1910, Harrington & Richardson Arms Co, GM Arnold art, 27", VG+ .990.00
1912, Hood's Sarsaparilla, VG+ 50.00
1912, Pratt's, cb, lady w/horse, 14", NM+ 400.00
1912, Rising Sun Beer, ladies reading sign posted on tree, 22", EX ...175.00
1914, Gust Werner, paper, girl w/St Bernard, 16", VG+ 70.00
1914, Winchester, 2 dogs pointing/hunter aiming, fr, 30", VG+ ...1,150.00
1916, Mrs LA Wellman Drygoods, diecut cb, girl/flowers, 16", EX ..80.00
1917, A Kostka Grocers, diecut cb, gypsy girl w/puppy, 20", NM .165.00
1917, Peters Cartridge Co, dogs in harvested field, fr, 29", VG .300.00
1919, DeLaval Cream Separators, EX 700.00
1919, Peters Cartridge Co, linen, hunter w/dogs & pups, no pad, EX ...550.00
1919, Uncle Sam Stock Medicine Co, paper, navy fleet, 20", NM 225.00
1922, Dutch Boy Paints, cb, 16", EX 50.00
1922, Johnson Bros General Merchandise, Sunshine Girl, Traver, EX ..50.00
1922, Sunshine Biscuits, Sunshine Girl, Earl Christy art, 18", EX+ ..50.00
1924, Wrigley's PK Chewing Sweet, boy/girl by water, VG 35.00
1925, Remington, Let 'er Rain, 29", EX+ 560.00
1925, Star Brand Shoes/Smith Baker Co, A Bare Chance, 16", G+ ...50.00
1926, Hupmobile, 2 cars/sailboats/people, 31", EX+ 160.00
1926, Peters Cartridge Co, partridges, G Muss-Arnolt art, 20", EX ...550.00
1926, VJ Plew Up-To-Date Shoe Store, diecut cb, girls hugging, NM .70.00
1927, DeLaval Cream Separators, EX 550.00
1927, Nehi, girl on beached boat, wooden fr, 21", EX 200.00
1927, Round Oak Stoves, Indian in canoe, 22", M 150.00
1929, Myers Pumps.../FF Myers & Bro Co, paper, graphics, 50", EX ..265.00
1932, Squire's/Arlington Pork Products, 29", EX 175.00
1935, Goodyear, bear surprising fisherman, NM 25.00
1936, Duplex Bread, cb, toddler, 9", EX 32.00
1937, Jewel Tea, Going to Town, 13", EX+ 28.00
1940, Fox's Bread, paper, boy/girl flirting, 20", EX 170.00
1940, Pure Oil Co, gas station/clouds, 28", VG+ 250.00
1941, Trailways, 24", NM 20.00
1942, Hutchinson's Ice Cream, paper w/metal strips, 29", VG 50.00
1944, John Deere, paper, 2 kids at storefront, 16", EX 60.00
1944, Maas & Steffen Furs, otter in snow, Carlyle Prather, 24", VG .160.00
1946, Kist Beverages, Get Kist for a Nickel, garden girl, 26", NM ...165.00
1946, Maas & Steffen Furs, hunter/dogs/polar bear, fr, 47", NM ...700.00
1946, Orange-Crush, 31", VG 125.00
1947, Jewel Tea Co, Coffee & Grocery Specialists, 13", EX 45.00
1948, Squirt, 4 different girls, 22", EX 100.00
1949, Fisk Tires, Fisk Boy, complete, 33x19", NM 225.00
1951, Dr Pepper, complete, EX+ 100.00
1952, OshKosh Tools, pinup girl on ladder, 32", NM+ 100.00
1952, Sealed Power Piston Ring Sets, paper, Ring Champ, 34", NM .40.00
1953, Mission Beverages, 25", NM 100.00
1957, North Shore Foundry, Joe DiMaggio/boy, Mayo art, 33", EX .70.00
1974, Campbell's Soups, linen, Norcross, 27", M 12.00

Caliente

Caliente was a line of colored dinnerware made by the Paden City Pottery Company in Paden City, West Virginia. It was produced during the 1930s and 1940s in tangerine, yellow, blue, green, and cobalt blue.

Cup and saucer, $15.00.

Bowl, salad; 10" 28.00
Bowl, 5¼" 10.00
Bowl, 9" 20.00
Candle holder 18.00
Creamer 15.00
Cup & saucer 15.00
Plate, dinner; 10" 17.50
Plate, 6" 5.00
Plate, 9½" 10.00
Platter, 12" 25.00
Platter, 14" 28.00
Shakers, pr 25.00
Sugar bowl, w/lid 18.00
Teapot 50.00

California Faience

California Faience was the trade name used by William V. Bragdon and Chauncy R. Thomas on vases, bowls, and other artware produced at their pottery known as 'The Tile Shop' in Berkeley, California, from 1920 to 1930. Faience tile was the principal product of the business during these years and is the favorite with today's collectors. Items in a glossy glaze are rare and therefore more valuable. Tiles were marked 'California Faience' with a die stamp.

Bowl, blk matt, yel/turq gloss int, lotus shape, 1½x9" 100.00
Bowl, mustard matt, cobalt rim, turq int, 12", +candlesticks 200.00
Bowl, raspberry gloss, 5½" 50.00
Trivet, flower basket on cobalt, 5" dia 200.00
Trivet, flower basket on turq, in Dirk Van Erp copper fr, 5" dia 1,200.00
Trivet, flower basket on yel, 5" dia 300.00
Vase, bl gloss over dk red clay, short neck, shouldered, 5" 170.00
Vase, deep bl matt, flaring shoulder, ogee sides, 5½" 600.00
Vase, med bl matt, turq int, ovoid, 8" 325.00
Vase, multi-tone bl gloss over red clay, bulbous bottom, 12" 600.00
Vase, sky bl gloss, 6" 150.00
Vase, thick burgundy matt, incurvate, 4x6½" 850.00
Vase, turq gloss, bulbous, 3½" 175.00

California Perfume Company

D.H. McConnell, Sr., founded the California Perfume Company

(C.P. Company; C.P.C.) in 1886 in New York City. He had previously been a salesman for a book company, which he later purchased. His door-to-door sales usually involved the lady of the house, to whom he presented a complimentary bottle of inexpensive perfume. Upon determining his perfume to be more popular than his books, he decided that the manufacture of perfume might be more lucrative. He bottled toiletries under the name 'California Perfume Company' and a line of household products called 'Perfection.' In 1928 the name 'Avon' appeared on the label, and in 1939 the C.P.C. name was entirely removed from the product. The success of the company is attributed to the door-to-door sales approach and 'money back' guarantee offered by his first 'Depot Agent,' Mrs. P.F.E. Albee, known today as the 'Avon Lady.'

The company's containers are quite collectible today, especially the older, hard-to-find items. Advanced collectors seek 'go with' items labeled Goetting & Co., New York; Goetting's; or Savoi Et Cie, Paris. Such examples date from 1871 to 1896. The Goetting Company was purchased by D.H. McConnell; Savoi Et Cie was a line which they imported to sell through department stores. Also of special interest are packaging and advertising with the Ambrosia or Hinze Ambrosia Company label. This was a subsidiary company whose objective seems to have been to produce a line of face creams, etc., for sale through drugstores and other such commercial outlets. They operated in New York from about 1875 until 1954. Because very little is known about these companies and since only a few examples of their product containers and advertising material have been found, market values for such items have not yet been established. Other items sought by the collector include products marked Gertrude Recordon, Marvel Electric Silver Cleaner, Easy Day Automatic Clothes Washer, pre-1915 catalogs, California Perfume Company 1909 and 1910 calendars, and 1916 Calopad Sanitary Napkins.

There are hundreds of local Avon Collector Clubs throughout the world that also have C.P.C. collectors in their membership. If you are interested in joining, locating, or starting a new club, contact the National Association of Avon Collectors, Inc., listed in the Directory under Clubs, Newsletters, and Catalogs. Those wanting a National Newsletter Club or price guides may contact Avon Times, listed in the same section. Inquiries concerning California Perfume Company items and the companies or items mentioned in the previous paragraphs should be directed toward our advisor, Dick Pardini, whose address is given under California. (Please send a large SASE and be sure to request clearly the information you are seeking; not interested in Avon, 'Perfection' marked C.P.C.'s, or Anniversary Keepsakes.)

Note: Our values are for items in mint condition. A very rare item or one in super mint condition might go for 10% more. Damage, wear, missing parts, etc., must be considered; items judged to be in only good to very good condition should be priced at up to 50% of listed values, with fair to good at 25% and excellent at 75%. Parts (labels, stoppers, caps, etc.) might be evaluated at 10% of these prices.

American Ideal Dbl Compact, brass, powder & rouge, 1921, M ..60.00
American Ideal Toilet Soap, gr box, 2 bars, 1925, M 65.00
Baby Set, toilet water, soap & powder, 1923, M 240.00
Bandoline, cork stopper, 1915, M 55.00
Bay Rum, metal cap, 1929, 16-oz 65.00
Benzoin, metal stopper, 1915, 2-oz or 4-oz, M, ea 75.00
California Baby Soap in box, 1902, M 60.00
Calopad, 12 sanitary napkins, MIB 75.00
Daphne Eyebrow Pencil, metal tube, 1925, M 20.00
Daphne Glycerin Soap, gr box, 2 bars, 1925, M 65.00
Eau De Quinine, shaker cap, 1900, 6-oz, M 65.00
French Perfumes, glass stopper, 1910s, ¼-oz to 4-oz, M, ea 85.00
Gertrude Recordon's Peach Lotion, 1925, MIB 80.00
Little Folks Set, 4 perfume bottles w/corks, 1904, M 300.00
Perfume, glass stopper, ca 1896, 1-oz, M 85.00
Shaving Soap, 1 bar in wrapper, 1905, M 55.00
Toilet Water, glass stopper, 1910, 8-oz, M 75.00
Tooth Powder, metal cone cap, 1908, M 75.00
Trailing Arbutus Brillantine, frosted glass stopper, 1923, M 90.00
Trailing Arbutus...Perfume, metal cap/glass stopper, 1-oz, '23, M ..110.00
Vernafleur Quintette Set, holds 5 items, 1929, M 225.00
Vernafleur Toilet Soap Set, 3 bars, 1928, M 80.00
Violet Almond Meal, glass, metal shaker lid, 1912, M 95.00
Witch Hazel, cork stopper, 8-oz, 1915, M 80.00
Witch Hazel, 1908, 4-oz, 8-oz or 16-oz, M, ea 90.00

Calling Cards, Cases, and Receivers

The practice of announcing one's arrival with a calling card borne by the maid to the mistress of the house was a social grace of the Victorian era. Different messages (condolences, a personal visit, or a good-by) were related by turning down one corner or another. The custom was forgotten by WWI. Fashionable ladies and gents carried their personally engraved cards in elaborate cases made of such materials as embossed silver, mother-of-pearl with intricate inlay, tortoise shell, and ivory. Card receivers held cards left by visitors who called while the mistress was out or 'not receiving.' Calling cards with fringe, die-cut flaps that cover the name, or an unusual decoration are worth about $3.00 to $4.00, while plain cards usually sell for around $1.00.

Case, aluminum, eng floral, ca 1900, 3⅝x2" 30.00
Case, Continental silver, scroll eng, monogram, oblong 80.00
Case, ivory, Oriental cvg, 19th C, 2x4⅛" 350.00
Case, MOP & tortoise shell, silver mts, ivory capped int, 4" L ..155.00
Case, silver, repousee rendition of White House on bk, 19th C ..150.00
Case, sterling w/gold inlay Aztec calendar medallion, 3x5" 85.00
Case, tortoise shell w/appl MOP oak leaf, ca 1890s, 4½x2¾" 165.00
Receiver, brass, Black male figure on base holds basket 450.00
Receiver, Cupid w/lyre among leaves, rstr Reed & Barton SP ...450.00
Receiver, pottery, Nouveau scene of Hotel Astor, German mk, 6¼" ..75.00
Receiver, Racine SP Co, Aesthetic Movement, 6¾x7⅝" 110.00
Receiver, SP, Cupid riding goat emb on bk of tray 350.00
Tray, sterling, floral repousse border, Kirk & Sons, 6½" 110.00

Camark

The Camden Art and Tile Company (commonly known as Camark) of Camden, Arkansas, was organized in the fall of 1926 by Samuel J. 'Jack' Carnes. Using clays from Arkansas, John Lessell, who had been hired as art director by Carnes, produced the initial lustre and iridescent Lessell wares for Camark ('CAM'den, 'ARK'ansas) before his death in December 1926. Before the plant opened in the spring of 1927, Carnes brought John's wife, Jeanne, and stepdaughter Billie to oversee the art department's manufacture of Le-Camark. Production by the Lessell family included variations of J.B. Owens' Soudanese and Opalesce and Weller's Marengo and Lamar. Camark's version of Marengo was called Old English. They also made wares identical to Weller's LaSa. Pieces made by John Lessell back in Ohio were signed 'Lessell,' while those made by Jeanne and Billie in Arkansas during 1927 were signed 'Le-Camark.' By 1928 Camark's production centered on traditional glazes. Drip glazes similar to Muncie Pottery were produced, in particular the green drip over pink. In the 1930s commercial castware with simple glossy and matt finishes became the primary focus and would continue so until Camark closed in the early 1960s. Between the 1960s and 1980s the company operated mainly as a retail store selling existing inventory, but some limited production occurred. In 1986 the company was purchased by the Ashcraft family of Camden, but no pottery has yet been made at the factory.

For further information we recommend *Collector's Encyclopedia of Camark Pottery, Volume I,* by David Edwin Gifford. Our advisor for this category is Tony Freyaldenhoven; he is listed in the Directory under Arkansas.

Ashtray/cigarette holder, bl & wht stipple, 2½" 70.00
Bank, seated pig w/bow tie, wht, w/accents, 6¾" 160.00
Bookends, 2-pc pig, mirror blk, 5¾x10", pr 140.00
Bowl, ivory, fluted w/flared rim, 1st block letter, 2¾x12" 40.00

Bowl, white with embossed foliage, #6, 11", with white two-bird flower frog, $50.00.

Bowl, yel to bl matt, 2x6¼" 250.00
Candlestick, Festoon of Roses, HP on bl/wht, dbl, Lechner, 5¼", ea ...35.00
Candlestick, Iris, yel, rose, or bl, #269 USA, 5¼", ea 25.00
Canoe/flower frog, orange/gr overflow, 11x3¼" & 6¼x¾" 160.00
Cigarette box, HP wht flowers on bright yel, Lechner, 2¾x4¼" ..50.00
Corn bottle, yel & gr, cork stopper, 1st block letter, 7¾" 100.00
Figurine, climbing cat, various colors, 10" or 16", ea, from $60 to ..80.00
Flower bowl, yel to bl matt, 5¼" 500.00
Flower frog, 2 ducks w/wings spread on mound, HP mc, Lechner, 9x6" .300.00
Ginger jar, Old English/Ivory, river scene w/trees, Lessell, 9½ ...900.00
Humidor, bl & wht stipple, w/lid, 1st block letter, 5¾" 100.00
Lamp base, Old English/Gray Blue, river scene w/tree, Lessell, 8" .600.00
Lamp base, Old English/Rose, river scene w/tree, Le-Camark, 8" .500.00
Leaf dish, frosted gr, 1st block letter, 15" 15.00
Pitcher, Autumn matt, sq w/angled hdl & stopper, brn sticker, 7½" ..120.00
Shakers, ship w/removable stacks, #566, 3-pc, 2¾", from $40 to .60.00
Strawberry pot, dripping gr/pumpkin matt, firing chip, 7½" 80.00
Vase, Aztec red mottled, ribbed bulbous form w/sm neck, 10" ...700.00
Vase, bud; gr to bl matt, long trumpet neck, #424, 9½" 250.00
Vase, bud; iris (HP/bas-relief), dbl-gate type, #845R, 6¼" 180.00
Vase, Festoon of Roses on wht/yel, fan shape, Lechner, 7¼" 120.00
Vase, gr crackle, elongated bulbous form, 12¼" 900.00
Vase, ivory, fan shape, 1st block letter, 6" 20.00
Vase, orange crackle, 2-hdld urn, 5¼x7¾" 400.00
Vase, silver lustre, river scene w/pine trees, Le-Camark, 9¾" .1,100.00
Wall plaque, horse head, brn w/blk mane, Lechner, 7" 120.00
Wall pocket, Iris (HP/bas-relief), Lechner, 9", from $300 to 400.00

Cambridge Glass

The Cambridge Glass Company began operations in 1901 in Cambridge, Ohio. Primarily they made crystal dinnerware and well-designed accessory pieces until the 1920s when they introduced the concept of color that was to become so popular on the American dinnerware market. Always maintaining high standards of quality and elegance, they produced many lines that became bestsellers; through the '20s and '30s they were recognized as the largest manufacturer of this type of glassware in the world.

Of the various marks the company used, the 'C in triangle' is the most familiar. Production stopped in 1958. For a more thorough study of the subject, we recommend *Colors in Cambridge Glass* by the National Cambridge Collectors, Inc.; their address may be found in the Directory under Clubs. *Glass Animals and Figural Flower Frogs of the Depression Era* by Lee Garmon and Dick Spencer is a wonderful source for an in-depth view of their particular aspect of glass collecting. They are both listed in the Directory under Illinois. See also Carnival Glass; Glass Animals.

Apple Blossom, crystal, bowl, finger; #3025, ftd, w/plate 30.00
Apple Blossom, crystal, bowl, fruit; tab hdls, 11" 35.00
Apple Blossom, crystal, fruit/oyster cocktail, #3025, 4½-oz 15.00
Apple Blossom, crystal, plate, 8½" 14.00
Apple Blossom, crystal, saucer 4.00
Apple Blossom, crystal, tray, relish; 2-hdl, 7" 15.00
Apple Blossom, pk or gr, bowl, baker; 10" 85.00
Apple Blossom, pk or gr, bowl, nut; 4-ftd, ind, 3" 70.00
Apple Blossom, pk or gr, bowl, 13" 65.00
Apple Blossom, pk or gr, creamer, ftd 22.50
Apple Blossom, pk or gr, pitcher, 76-oz 325.00
Apple Blossom, pk or gr, stem, cordial; #3130, 1-oz 155.00
Apple Blossom, pk or gr, stem, sherbet; #3400, ftd, 6-oz 16.00
Apple Blossom, pk or gr, vase, 2 styles, 8", ea 125.00
Apple Blossom, yel or amber, bowl, fruit; 5½" 18.00
Apple Blossom, yel or amber, bowl, 4-ftd, 12" 70.00
Apple Blossom, yel or amber, pitcher, #3130, 64-oz 250.00
Apple Blossom, yel or amber, plate, bread & butter; 6" 7.00
Apple Blossom, yel or amber, stem, cocktail; #3135, 3-oz 24.00
Apple Blossom, yel or amber, tumbler, #3400, ftd, 12-oz 35.00
Candlelight, crystal, bonbon, #3900/130, ftd, 2-hdl, 7" 35.00
Candlelight, crystal, bowl, #3900/28, ftd, 2-hdl, 11½" 75.00
Candlelight, crystal, candle, #3900/74, 3-light, 6" 62.50
Candlelight, crystal, candy box, #3500/57, 3-part, w/lid 110.00
Candlelight, crystal, comport, #3121, blown, 5⅜" 60.00
Candlelight, crystal, decanter, #1321, ftd, 28-oz 175.00
Candlelight, crystal, plate, #3900/166, rolled edge, 14" 70.00
Candlelight, crystal, relish, #3900/125, 3-part, 9" 47.50
Candlelight, crystal, stem, cherry; #7966, 2-oz 75.00
Candlelight, crystal, stem, sherbet; #3776, low, 7-oz 16.50
Candlelight, crystal, stem, water; #3111, 10-oz 35.00
Candlelight, crystal, tumbler, #3900/115, 13-oz 40.00
Candlelight, crystal, vase, bud; #274, 10" 50.00
Caprice, bl or pk, bonbon, #155, ftd, oval, 6" 42.00
Caprice, bl or pk, bowl, #53, 4-ftd, crimped, 10½" 110.00
Caprice, bl or pk, bowl, salad; #84, shallow, 15" 175.00
Caprice, bl or pk, candlesticks, #1338, 3-light, pr 150.00
Caprice, bl or pk, decanter, #187, w/stopper, 35-oz 425.00
Caprice, bl or pk, pitcher, #179, ball shape, 32-oz 350.00
Caprice, bl or pk, plate, dinner; #24, 9½" 135.00
Caprice, bl or pk, shakers, #96, flat, pr 100.00
Caprice, bl or pk, stem, parfait; #300, blown, 5-oz 225.00
Caprice, bl or pk, tray (for sugar bowl & creamer), #37 ....35.00
Caprice, bl or pk, tumbler, #9, ftd, 12-oz 47.50
Caprice, bl or pk, tumbler, water; #300, ftd, 10-oz 40.00
Caprice, bl or pk, vase, #241, ball shape, 4¼" 115.00
Caprice, bl or pk, vase, #242, ftd, 6" 140.00
Caprice, bl or pk, vase, #343, crimped top, 8½" 325.00
Caprice, crystal, bowl, #61, crimped, 4-ftd, 12½" 35.00
Caprice, crystal, bowl, almond; #95, 4-ftd, 2" 25.00
Caprice, crystal, bowl, salad; #57, 4-ftd, 10" 40.00
Caprice, crystal, candlestick, #67, 2½, ea 15.00
Caprice, crystal, candlestick, #70, w/prism, 7", ea 25.00
Caprice, crystal, comport, #130, low ft, 7" 50.00
Caprice, crystal, creamer, #38, med 11.00
Caprice, crystal, mayonnaise, #106, 3-pc set, 8" 50.00
Caprice, crystal, plate, bread & butter; #21, 6½" 11.00

Caprice, crystal, stem, claret; #301, blown, 4½-oz 50.00
Caprice, crystal, stem, water; #1, 10-oz 27.50
Caprice, crystal, tumbler, #11, ftd, 5-oz 20.00
Caprice, crystal, tumbler, #310, flat, 11-oz, 4¾" 25.00
Caprice, crystal, tumbler, iced tea; #301, blown, 12-oz 20.00
Caprice, crystal, vase, #346, crimped top, 7½" 110.00
Cascade, crsytal, bowl, relish; 2-part, 6½" 13.00
Cascade, crystal, ashtray, 4½" 6.00
Cascade, crystal, bowl, flared, 4-ftd, 10" 25.00
Cascade, crystal, creamer 8.50
Cascade, crystal, plate, salad; 8½" 7.50
Cascade, crystal, stem, cocktail 12.00
Cascade, crystal, tumbler, flat, 5-oz 10.00
Cascade, crystal, vase, 9½" 40.00
Cascade, gr or yel, candlestick, 5" 30.00
Cascade, gr or yel, mayonnaise, w/liner 60.00
Chantilly, crystal, bonbon, 2-hdl, ftd, 7" 17.50
Chantilly, crystal, bowl, 4-ftd, oval, 12" 45.00
Chantilly, crystal, candlestick, 5", ea 18.00
Chantilly, crystal, comport, blown, 5⅜" 37.50
Chantilly, crystal, decanter, ball shape 200.00

Chantilly, crystal, ice bucket, $100.00.

Chantilly, crystal, plate, bonbon; tab hdls, ftd, 8" 15.00
Chantilly, crystal, stem, claret; #3775, 4½-oz 45.00
Chantilly, crystal, stem, cocktail; #3779, 3-oz 25.00
Chantilly, crystal, stem, sherbet; #3625, low, 7-oz 16.00
Chantilly, crystal, stem, water; #3779, 9-oz 22.00
Chantilly, crystal, tumbler, iced tea; #3625, ftd, 12-oz 24.00
Chantilly, crystal, vase, keyhole base, 12" 75.00
Cleo, bl, bowl, comport; 4-ftd, 6" 50.00
Cleo, bl, bowl, pickle; Decagon, 9" 60.00
Cleo, bl, ice tub 125.00
Cleo, bl, plate, 2-hdl, Decagon, 7" 20.00
Cleo, bl, stem, sherbet; #3077, tall, 6-oz 35.00
Cleo, pk, gr, yel or amber, bowl, console; mini, 8" 145.00
Cleo, pk, gr, yel or amber, bowl, console; 12" 40.00
Cleo, pk, gr, yel or amber, bowl, relish; 2-part 22.00
Cleo, pk, gr, yel or amber, pitcher, w/lid, 22-oz 175.00
Cleo, pk, gr, yel or amber, platter, 15" 185.00
Cleo, pk, gr, yel or amber, stem, water; #3115, 9-oz 27.50
Cleo, pk, gr, yel or amber, tumbler, #3115, ftd, 8-oz 25.00
Cleo, pk, gr, yel or amber, vase, 11" 145.00
Decagon, pastel colors, bowl, bouillon; w/liner 7.50
Decagon, pastel colors, bowl, cereal; flat rim, 6" 15.00
Decagon, pastel colors, cup 6.00
Decagon, pastel colors, mayonnaise, w/liner & ladle 20.00
Decagon, pastel colors, salt dip, ftd, 1½" 20.00
Decagon, pastel colors, tray, service; 2-hdl, 13" 25.00
Decagon, red or bl, bowl, belled, 12" 37.50
Decagon, red or bl, bowl, vegetable; rnd, 9" 45.00
Decagon, red or bl, ice tub 55.00
Decagon, red or bl, plate, salad; 8½" 18.00
Decagon, red or bl, stem, cocktail; 3½-oz 22.00
Decagon, red or bl, tumbler, ftd, 10-oz 25.00
Diane, crystal, bitters bottle 145.00
Diane, crystal, bowl, celery/relish; 3-part, 9" 35.00
Diane, crystal, bowl, cereal; 6" 35.00
Diane, crystal, bowl, tab hdls, ftd, 11½" 45.00
Diane, crystal, candlestick, fleur-de-lis; 2-light, 6" 32.50
Diane, crystal, creamer, #3500, pie-crust edge, ind 15.00
Diane, crystal, ice bucket, w/chrome band 75.00
Diane, crystal, plate, 8½" 11.00
Diane, crystal, shakers, flat, pr 35.00
Diane, crystal, stem, cocktail; #3122, 3-oz 20.00
Diane, crystal, stem, oyster/cocktail; #1066, 5-oz 25.00
Diane, crystal, stem, sherbet; #3122, tall, 7-oz 18.00
Diane, crystal, tumbler, #3106, ftd, 3-oz 22.00
Diane, crystal, tumbler, iced tea; #3122, 12-oz 20.00
Diane, crystal, tumbler, juice; ftd, 5-oz 30.00
Diane, crystal, tumbler, sham bottom, 12-oz 35.00
Diane, crystal, vase, globe shape, 5" 45.00
Elaine, crystal, bowl, finger; #3104, w/liner 35.00
Elaine, crystal, bowl, ftd, tab hdls, 11½" 40.00
Elaine, crystal, bowl, pickle/relish; 7" 25.00
Elaine, crystal, candlestick, 5" 20.00
Elaine, crystal, comport, 5½" 30.00
Elaine, crystal, pitcher, ball shape 165.00
Elaine, crystal, plate, dinner; 10½" 65.00
Elaine, crystal, stem, cocktail; #1402, 3½-oz 20.00
Elaine, crystal, stem, creme de menthe; #3104, 2½-oz 125.00
Elaine, crystal, stem, goblet; #3104, 9-oz 25.00
Elaine, crystal, stem, parfait; #3121, low, 5-oz 30.00
Elaine, crystal, tumbler, iced tea; #1402, 12-oz 30.00
Elaine, crystal, vase, ftd, 6" 40.00
Gloria, crystal, bowl, cereal; sq, 6" 18.00
Gloria, crystal, bowl, fruit; 2-hdl, 11" 35.00
Gloria, crystal, bowl, nut; 4-ftd, ind, 3" 55.00
Gloria, crystal, comport, fruit cocktail; 4" 13.00
Gloria, crystal, pitcher, middle indent, 67-oz 150.00
Gloria, crystal, plate, bread & butter; sq 6.00
Gloria, crystal, stem, cocktail; #3035, 3½-oz 17.00
Gloria, crystal, tumbler, #3035, high ft, 5-oz 11.00
Gloria, crystal, vase, keyhole base, 10" 60.00
Gloria, gr, pk or yel, bonbon, 2-hdl, 5½" 32.00
Gloria, gr, pk or yel, bowl, cream soup; w/sq liner 40.00
Gloria, gr, pk or yel, comport, 4-ftd, 6" 40.00
Gloria, gr, pk or yel, ice pail, metal hdl w/tongs 90.00
Gloria, gr, pk or yel, plate, 8½" 15.00
Gloria, gr, pk or yel, saucer, rnd 4.00
Gloria, gr, pk or yel, stem, cocktail; #3035, 3½-oz 27.00
Gloria, gr, pk or yel, stem, sherbet; #3120, tall, 6-oz 16.00
Gloria, gr, pk or yel, sugar bowl, ftd, tall 20.00
Gloria, gr, pk or yel, tumbler, #3115, ftd, 10-oz 25.00
Gloria, gr, pk or yel, tumbler, #3130, ftd, 12-oz 30.00
Imperial Hunt Scene, colors, creamer, ftd 35.00
Imperial Hunt Scene, colors, shakers, pr 150.00
Imperial Hunt Scene, colors, stem, sherbet; #3085, low, 6-oz 22.50
Imperial Hunt Scene, colors, tumbler, #3085, ftd, 12-oz, 5⅜" 40.00
Imperial Hunt Scene, crystal, ice tub 45.00
Imperial Hunt Scene, crystal, stem, water; #1402, 10-oz 40.00
Imperial Hunt Scene, crystal, tumbler, #1402, flat, 15-oz 35.00
Imperial Hunt Scene, crystal, tumbler, #1402, flat, 7-oz 20.00
Mt Vernon, amber or crystal, ashtray, #68, 4" 12.00
Mt Vernon, amber or crystal, bowl, #121, flared, 12½" 35.00

Mt Vernon, amber or crystal, bowl, #126, shallow, 11½" 30.00
Mt Vernon, amber or crystal, bowl, #43, deep, 10½" 30.00
Mt Vernon, amber or crystal, bowl, cereal; #32, 6" 12.50
Mt Vernon, amber or crystal, candelabrum, #38, 13½" 125.00
Mt Vernon, amber or crystal, celery, #98, 11" 15.00
Mt Vernon, amber or crystal, cigarette holder, #66 ....15.00
Mt Vernon, amber or crystal, comport, #11, 7½" 25.00
Mt Vernon, amber or crystal, creamer, #4, ind 10.00
Mt Vernon, amber or crystal, marmalade/honey jar, #74, w/lid 35.00
Mt Vernon, amber or crystal, mustard, #28, w/lid 25.00
Mt Vernon, amber or crystal, plate, bread & butter; #4, 6" 3.00
Mt Vernon, amber or crystal, salt, #102, 2-hdl, oval 12.00
Mt Vernon, amber or crystal, saucer, #7 ....7.50
Mt Vernon, amber or crystal, stem, claret; #25, 4½-oz 13.50
Mt Vernon, amber or crystal, tumbler, #58, tall, 10-oz 12.00
Mt Vernon, amber or crystal, tumbler, #59, tall, 14-oz 22.00
Mt Vernon, amber or crystal, tumbler, cordial; #87, ftd, 1-oz 22.00
Mt Vernon, amber or crystal, vase, #107, squat, 6½" 27.50
Nude stem, amber, wine 300.00
Nude stem, amethyst, claret 140.00
Nude stem, amethyst, mint dish 900.00
Nude stem, amethyst/crystal, cocktail 150.00
Nude stem, carmen, comport, short 495.00
Nude stem, cobalt, ivy ball 550.00
Nude stem, cobalt, wine 550.00
Nude stem, Crown Tuscan, comport, #4 ....145.00
Nude stem, Crown Tuscan, comport, #4, w/gold trim 175.00
Nude stem, crystal, comport, #4 ....125.00
Nude stem, crystal, flying nude bowl, gold trim 325.00
Nude stem, crystal, ivy ball 155.00
Nude stem, crystal, wine 200.00
Nude stem, crystal optic/frost, ivy ball 200.00
Nude stem, crystal/amber, cocktail 145.00
Nude stem, crystal/blk, cocktail (watch for Imperial reproductions) ..125.00
Nude stem, dk gr, ashtray 225.00
Nude stem, pk, brandy 180.00
Nude stem, royal bl/crystal, sauterne 475.00
Nude stem, smoke, cocktail, tall 500.00
Nude stem, Topaz/Crown Tuscan, cocktail 225.00
Nude stem, wine, amethyst 250.00
Nude stem, yel, hoch 450.00
Portia, crystal, bonbon, ftd, 2-hdl, 6" 20.00
Portia, crystal, bonbon, tab hdls, ftd, 7" 25.00
Portia, crystal, bowl, celery/relish; 5-part, 12" 37.50
Portia, crystal, candlestick, 5" 22.00
Portia, crystal, cocktail icer, 2-part 65.00
Portia, crystal, cruet, oil; ball shape, hdld, w/stopper, 6-oz 85.00
Portia, crystal, lamp, hurricane; candlestick base 145.00
Portia, crystal, stem, claret; #3124, 4½-oz 40.00
Portia, crystal, stem, cordial; #3121, 1-oz 60.00
Portia, crystal, stem, cordial; #3130, 1-oz 60.00
Portia, crystal, stem, sherbet; #3121, low, 6-oz 13.50
Portia, crystal, stem, wine; #3130, 2½-oz 35.00
Portia, crystal, tumbler, #3124, 3-oz 15.00
Portia, crystal, tumbler, iced tea; #3126, 12-oz 22.00
Portia, crystal, vase, keyhole ft, 9" 75.00
Rosalie, amber, bowl, 2-hdl, 8½" 25.00
Rosalie, amber, plate, 8⅜" 10.00
Rosalie, bl, pk or gr, bottle, French dressing 140.00
Rosalie, bl, pk or gr, bowl, basket; 2-hdl, 11" 55.00
Rosalie, bl, pk or gr, candlestick, keyhole, 3-light, 6" 55.00
Rosalie, bl, pk or gr, icer, w/liner 60.00
Rosalie, bl, pk or gr, plate, bread & butter; 6¾" 7.00
Rosalie, bl, pk or gr, salt cellar, ftd, 1½" 60.00

Rose Point, crystal, ashtray, #3500/128, 4½" 50.00
Rose Point, crystal, ashtray, #3500/129, sq, 3¼" 55.00
Rose Point, crystal, ashtray, #721, sq, 2½" 32.50
Rose Point, crystal, basket, #3500/55, ftd, 2-hdl, sq, 6" 40.00
Rose Point, crystal, bonbon, #3400/205, cupped, shallow, 6" 60.00
Rose Point, crystal, bowl, #1401/122, 3-part, 10½" 325.00
Rose Point, crystal, bowl, #225, 2-part, blown, 9½" 425.00
Rose Point, crystal, bowl, #3400/1240, 4-ftd, oval, 12" 100.00
Rose Point, crystal, bowl, #3400/47, narrow, crimped, 4-ftd, 13" ..125.00
Rose Point, crystal, butter dish, #3900/52, ¼-lb 175.00
Rose Point, crystal, candle, torchere; #3500/88, flat ftd 185.00
Rose Point, crystal, candlestick, Martha #495, 2-light, 5½" 70.00
Rose Point, crystal, celery, #3400/67, 5-part, 12" 75.00
Rose Point, crystal, comport, #3400/13, 4-ftd, 6" 40.00
Rose Point, crystal, creamer, #3900/40, scalloped edge, ind 20.00
Rose Point, crystal, cruet, oil; #3400/193, hdld, 6-oz 110.00
Rose Point, crystal, hurricane lamp, #1613, w/prisms 400.00
Rose Point, crystal, pitcher, #3400/100, ice lip, 76-oz 200.00
Rose Point, crystal, plate, bread & butter; #3900/20, 6½" 12.00
Rose Point, crystal, plate, dinner; #3900/24, 10½" 135.00
Rose Point, crystal, plate, torte; #3400/65, 14" 150.00

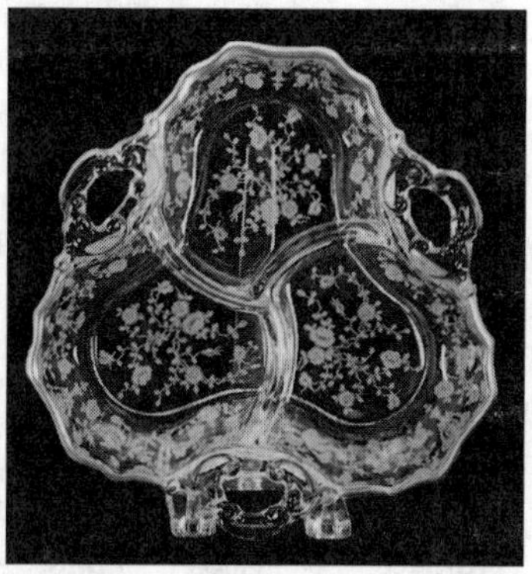

Rose Point, crystal, three-part relish, #3400/91, 8", $40.00.

Rose Point, crystal, relish, #3400/200, 3-part, 11" 57.50
Rose Point, crystal, shakers, #395, w/chrome tops, pr 100.00
Rose Point, crystal, stem, brandy; #3106, rare, ¾-oz 195.00
Rose Point, crystal, stem, water; #3121, 10-oz 35.00
Rose Point, crystal, syrup, #1670, w/drip-stop lid 395.00
Rose Point, crystal, tumbler, #498, str side, 5-oz 50.00
Rose Point, crystal, tumbler, cordial; #3400/1341, 1-oz 95.00
Rose Point, crystal, tumbler, iced tea; #3500, tall ft, 12-oz 35.00
Rose Point, crystal, vase, #3400/102, globe shape, 5" 75.00
Rose Point, crystal, vase, flower; #6004, high ft, 8" 60.00
Square, crystal, bonbon, #3797/164, 7" 13.50
Square, crystal, candle holder, #3797/673, cupped, pr 27.50
Square, crystal, ice tub, #3797/34, 7½" 35.00
Square, crystal, saucer, coffee; #3797/17 ....5.00
Square, crystal, tumbler, wine; #3797, low 15.00
Valencia, crystal, ashtray, #3500/128, rnd, 4½" 18.00
Valencia, crystal, bowl, #1402/88, 11" 40.00
Valencia, crystal, comport, #3500/37, 7" 45.00
Valencia, crystal, pitcher, #3400/141, Doulton, 80-oz 250.00
Valencia, crystal, relish, #3500/13, 4-part, 2-hdl, 15" 90.00
Valencia, crystal, stem, oyster cocktail; #3500, 4½-oz 18.00
Valencia, crystal, tumbler, #3400/115, 14-oz 27.00
Wildflower, crystal, bowl, #3400/4, flared, 4-ftd, 12" 40.00
Wildflower, crystal, bowl, celery/relish; #3900/125, 3-part, 9" 25.00
Wildflower, crystal, bowl, relish; #3400/90, 2-part, 6" 17.50
Wildflower, crystal, candlestick, #3400/638, 3-light 35.00
Wildflower, crystal, hat, #1703, 6" 250.00
Wildflower, crystal, pitcher, #3400/141, Doulton 325.00

Wildflower, crystal, plate, salad; #3900/22, 8" **17.50**
Wildflower, crystal, shakers, #3900/1177, pr **37.50**
Wildflower, crystal, stem, claret; #3121, 4½-oz **45.00**
Wildflower, crystal, vase, #1299, ped ft, 11" **110.00**

Cameo

The technique of glass carving was perfected 2,000 years ago in ancient Rome and Greece. The most famous ancient example of cameo glass is the Portland Vase, made in Rome around 100 A.D. After glass blowing was developed, glassmakers devised a method of casing several layers of colored glass together, often with a light color over a darker base, to enhance the design. Skilled carvers meticulously worked the fragile glass to produce incredibly detailed classic scenes. In the 1700s and 1800s Oriental and Near-Eastern artisans used the technique more extensively. European glassmakers revived the art during the last quarter of the nineteenth century. In France, Galle and Daum produced some of the finest examples of modern times, using as many as five layers of glass to develop their designs, usually scenics or subjects from nature. Hand carving was supplemented by the use of a copper engraving wheel, and acid was used to cut away the layers more quickly.

In England, Thomas Webb and Sons used modern machinery and technology to eliminate many of the problems that plagued early glass carvers. One of Webb's best known carvers, George Woodall, is credited with producing over four hundred pieces. Woodall was trained in the art by John Northwood, famous for reproducing the Portland Vase in 1876. Cameo glass became very popular during the late 1800s, resulting in a market that demanded more than could be produced, due to the tedious procedures involved. In an effort to produce greater volume, less elaborate pieces with simple floral or geometric designs were made, often entirely acid etched with little or no hand carving. While very little cameo glass was made in this country, a few pieces were produced by James Gillinder, Tiffany, and the Libbey Glass Company. Though some continued to be made on a limited scale into the 1900s (and until about 1920 in France), for the most part, inferior products caused a marked reduction in its manufacture by the turn of the century. Beware of new 'French' cameo glass from Romania and Taiwan. Some of it is very good and may be signed with 'old' signatures. Know your dealer! Our advisor for this category is Don Williams; he is listed in the Directory under Missouri. See also specific manufactures.

Key: fp — fire polished

English

Purse bottle, white opaque on blue, metal lid, att Webb, 8½", $2,500.00. (Photo courtesy Jackson's Auctioneers and Appraisers)

Bottle, scent; floral/lilies/leaves, wht on bl, 6½" **1,900.00**
Bottle, scent; oriental branch, wht on bl, 4½" **1,700.00**
Bowl, finger; floral, wht on rose, 5", w/underplate **2,200.00**
Bowl, passion flower/foliage/tendrils, wht/red on frost, 5" H ...**2,100.00**
Bowl, tasseled rope lattice, amber/orange/wht, frost ft, 3½x4½" ...**1,100.00**
Plaque, flowers, wht on citron, 5½x3½" **1,200.00**
Vase, blossoms & stems/butterflies, wht on red, 5" **1,600.00**
Vase, blossoms on convoluted stems, wht on gr, 8" **4,300.00**
Vase, flowers & butterflies, yel/red/wht, spherical, 5¼" **1,800.00**
Vase, flowers & butterfly, wht on bl, 2x2½" **2,500.00**
Vase, flowers & butterfly, yel/red/wht, shouldered, 8½" **4,000.00**
Vase, foliage, wht on turq, 1½", pr **1,265.00**
Vase, morning glories, wht on bl, #784/12, 5¼" **1,200.00**
Vase, morning glories/vines, wht on red, 10" **2,200.00**
Vase, morning glory, wht on citron, mk Cameo #51915, 9" **550.00**
Vase, multifloral/bk: butterfly & bee, wht on red, 5" **1,500.00**
Vase, poppies/butterflies/rose branches, wht on bl, ftd, 8½" ...**2,800.00**
Vase, sweet peas & butterfly, wht on cranberry, waisted, 7x5" ...**1,700.00**

French

Vase, bird in flight, rose on frost, squatty, Delatte, 4x4½" **700.00**
Vase, boats, blk on gr, Michel, 6x2¼" **575.00**
Vase, castle & lake, brn to gr to yel, Michel, 18x5¼" **1,500.00**
Vase, cottage scene, red tones, Michel, 6¼" **700.00**
Vase, Deco triangles, gr mottle on clear, Degue, 18" **925.00**
Vase, floral sprigs, red/bl on pk, ftd ovoid, Degue, 14½" **900.00**
Vase, fuchsias, purple & gr on frost, Arsall, 8" **550.00**
Vase, fuchsias/leaves, brn on citron, Veler, ftd, 8" **150.00**
Vase, leaves, gr on yel, ovoid, Degue, 20" **1,265.00**
Vase, leaves & berries on pk, polished, 6-sided rim, 3x4½" **325.00**
Vase, morning glories, lt on mottled butterscotch, Vierrie..., 5" .**600.00**
Vase, nasturtiums, amethyst/clear, Burgun/Schverer/Cie, 7x7" ..**6,500.00**
Vase, sailboats, red/chocolate on bl-gr to yel, Deveau, 5¾" **600.00**
Vase, scene w/bridge & birds, EX cvg, Arsall, 6½x6" **900.00**
Vase, sunflowers, purple/orange/yel mottle on gray/wht, 8" **1,000.00**
Vase, sunset bayou, oranges/brns on cream frost, Michel, 14" **975.00**
Vase, thistle & crosses, amethyst/frost/martele, bulbous, BS&Co, 7" ..**6,500.00**
Vase, village & lake, pillow shape, Michel, 8" **850.00**

Candle Holders

The earliest type of candlestick, called a pricket, was constructed with a sharp point on which the candle was impaled. The socket type, first used in the sixteenth century, consisted of the socket and a short stem with a wide drip pan and base. These were made from sheets of silver or other metal; not until late in the seventeenth century were candlesticks made by casting. By the 1700s, styles began to vary from the traditional fluted column or baluster form and became more elaborate. A Rococo style with scrolls, shellwork, and naturalistic leaves and flowers came into vogue that afforded the individual silversmith the opportunity to exhibit his skill and artistry. The last half of the eighteenth century brought a return to fluted columns with neoclassic motifs. Because they were made of thin sheet silver, weighted bases were used to add stability. The Rococo styles of the Regency period were heavily encrusted with applied figures and flowers. Candelabra with six to nine branches became popular. By the Victorian era when lamps came into general use, there was less innovation and more adaptation of the earlier styles. See also Silver; Tinware; specific manufacturers.

Bell metal, Neoclassical, sq beaded base, w/pushups, 1790s, 10", pr ...**550.00**
Bell metal, urn-form top, reeded sq base, w/pushup, 1810s, 9", pr ...**485.00**
Brass, belted, dbl-lemon top, NY, early 19th C, 20½", pr **865.00**
Brass, belted shaft, petal base, w/pushup, England, 1790s, 8", pr ...**575.00**
Brass, Coronation 1902, pushups missing, Victorian era, 12⅜", pr **525.00**
Brass, cylindrical cann holds coiled wax taper, 5" **200.00**
Brass, Diamond Prince, w/pushups, Victorian era, 11¾", pr **350.00**

Brass, Diamond Princess, pushups missing, Victorian era, 11", pr ..165.00
Brass, drum base, bulbous stem, rprs, early, 5¾" 440.00
Brass, King of Diamonds, w/pushups, Victorian era, 12", pr, $385 to .415.00
Brass, King of Diamonds, w/pushups, Victorian era, 14", pr 525.00
Brass, machine-tooled classical & floral decor, 19th C, 11", pr ..415.00
Brass, petal base, England, 1750s, rpr, 7½", pr 800.00
Brass, Queen Anne, scalloped base, baluster stem, early, 6¾", pr .900.00
Brass, Queen Anne, scalloped lip & ft, rprs, 8", pr 330.00
Brass, Queen Anne, sq base, not seamed, 8⅜", pr 600.00
Brass, Queen of Diamonds, w/pushups, Victorian era, 11½" 250.00
Brass, rtcl in Moorish taste, Continental, late 19th C, 12⅝" 165.00
Brass, sq base w/4 ft, early, 8¼" 275.00
Brass, sq base w/8-sided segment on stem, 6¾" 300.00
Brass, trn shaft, tall multitiered dome, drip pan, 27", pr 1,450.00
Brass, tulip socket, rnd scalloped base, 5½", pr 385.00
Brass, Victorian, minor rprs, 6½", pr 80.00
Candelabra, gilt-bronze Louis XVI style, 5-light w/cherubs, 21", pr .1,725.00
Candelabra, patinated bronze, Louis XVI style, 6-light, 37", pr 3,750.00
Candelabra, patinated/gilt bronze Emp w/maiden supports, 32", pr ..1,875.00
Candelabra, porc floral plaque insert, gilt bronze, 6-light, 22", pr 1,500.00
Candelabra, SP, 3-light, openwork scroll columns, bobeches, 16", 4 for ..3,000.00
Chandelier, brass, 6 candle arms, ca 1900, 20x23" dia 715.00
Gilt bronze, Gothic Revival, ca 1840, 23½", pr 550.00
Glass, amber w/eng vintage, 10", pr 140.00
Glass, canary, hexagonal, socket appl by wafer to base, 9¾" 230.00
Glass, clambroth, hexagonal, single construction, 7", pr 450.00
Glass, electric bl, hex socket, loop base, 6½" 650.00
Hog scraper, sheet iron, ejector, drip catcher w/hook, 6x4" 140.00
Patinated metal, Egyptian Revival, 19th C, 10½", pr 195.00
Pressed glass, emerald gr, hexagonal, 9¼", NM 800.00
Pressed glass, wht opaque crucifix form, att Cape Cod, 12½" 50.00
Silver, chased swags & florals, Augsburg, 18th C, 7½x4½", pr 750.00
Sticking tommy, wrought iron, tooled & stamped name, 9½" ...150.00
Tin, stamped saucer base w/ring hdl, brass ejector knob, 7" 65.00
Wrought iron, dbl adjustment, tripod w/penny ft, 21½x12", VG ...2,750.00
Wrought iron, spring-loaded splint holder on tripod base, 20" ..470.00

Candlewick

Candlewick crystal was made by the Imperial Glass Corporation, a division of Lenox Inc., Bellaire, Ohio. It was introduced in 1936, and though never marked except for paper labels, it is easily recognized by the beaded crystal rims, stems, and handles inspired by the tufted needlework called candlewicking, practiced by our pioneer women. During its production, more than 741 items were designed and produced. In September 1982 when Imperial closed its doors, thirty-four pieces were still being made.

Identification numbers and mold numbers used by the company help collectors recognize the various styles and shapes. Most of the pieces are from the #400 series, though other series numbers were also used. Stemware was made in eight styles — five from the #400 series made from 1941 to 1962, one from #3400 series made in 1937, another from #3800 series made in 1941, and the eighth style from the #4000 series made in 1947. In the listings that follow, some #400 items lack the mold number because that information was not found in the company files.

A few pieces have been made in color or with a gold wash. At least two lines, Valley Lily and Floral, utilized Candlewick with floral patterns cut into the crystal. These are scarce today. Other rare items include gifts such as the desk calendar made by the company for its employees and customers; the dresser set comprised of a mirror, clock, puff jar, and cologne; and the chip and dip set.

Ashtray, #400/134/1, oblong, 4½" 6.00
Ashtray, #400/174, heart shape, 6½" 15.00
Ashtray set, #400/650, nesting, sq, 3-pc 110.00
Basket, #400/40/0, hdld, 6½" 30.00
Bottle, bitters; #400/117, w/tube, 4-oz 60.00
Bowl, #400/13F, 10" 45.00
Bowl, #400/183, 3-ftd, 6" 60.00
Bowl, #400/5F, rnd, 7" 25.00
Bowl, #400/52B, 2-hdl, 6" 15.00
Bowl, #400/92B, rnd, 12" 40.00
Bowl, cottage cheese; #400/85, 6" 25.00
Bowl, cream soup; #400/50, 5" 42.50
Bowl, lily; #400/75N, beaded rim, ftd, 7½" 295.00
Bowl, relish; #400/215, oblong, 4-part, 12" 115.00
Bowl, relish; #400/217, 2-hdl, oval, 10" 40.00
Bowl, relish; #400/234, divided, sq, 7" 125.00
Bowl, relish; #400/55, 4-part, 8½" 22.00
Bowl, relish; #400/60, 7" 25.00
Bowl, salad; #400/75B, 10½" 40.00
Bowl, vegetable; #400/65/1, w/lid, 8" 295.00
Butter & jam set, #400/204, 5-pc 350.00
Calender, desk; 1947 ....195.00
Candle holder, #400/207, 3-toed, 4½" 75.00
Candle holder, #400/81, w/finger hold, 3½" 50.00
Candle holder, flower; #400/40C, 5" 35.00

Candy box, square decor at rim, round lid, rare, #400/245, 6½", $225.00. (Photo courtesy Gene Florence)

Candy box, #400/59, rnd, 5½" 45.00
Cigarette holder, #400/44, bead ft, 3" 35.00
Clock, rnd, 4" 275.00
Compote, #400/220, 3-bead stem, 5" 70.00
Compote, #400/48F, beaded stem, 8" 80.00
Compote, #400/63B, 4½" 40.00
Creamer, #400/126, beaded hdl, flat 32.50
Creamer, #400/18, domed ft 125.00
Cruet, oil; #400/121, etched Vinegar, w/stopper 60.00
Cruet, oil; #400/274, bulbous bottom, 4-oz 45.00
Cup, punch; #400/211 ....7.50
Decanter, #400/18, w/stopper, 18-oz 395.00
Icer, seafood/fruit cocktail; #400/53/3, 2-pc 95.00
Knife, butter; #4000 ....295.00
Ladle, marmalade; #400/130, 3-bead stem 12.00
Ladle, punch; #400/91 ....30.00
Lamp, hurricane; #400/79, candle base, 2-pc 120.00
Mirror, standing, rnd, 4½" 115.00
Pitcher, juice/cocktail; #400/19, 40-oz 175.00
Plate, #400/145C, crimped, 2-hdl, 12" 32.50
Plate, #400/34, 4½" 6.00
Plate, #400/50, w/indent, 8" 11.00
Plate, #400/52D, 2-hdl, 7½" 10.00
Plate, luncheon; #400/7D, 9" 13.50
Plate, salad; #400/5C, 8" 9.00
Plate, torte; #400/113D, 2-hdl, 14" 30.00
Plate, torte; #400/17D, 14" 42.50

Salt dip, #400/19, 2¼" 11.00
Saucer, AD; #400/77AD 5.00
Shakers, #400/96, bead ft, bulbous, chrome lid, pr 15.00
Snack jar, #400/139/1, bead ft, w/lid 450.00
Stem, claret; #3400, 5-oz 55.00
Stem, claret; #3800 ....32.00
Stem, sherbet; #3800, low 25.00
Stem, sherbet; #400/190, 6-oz 14.00
Stem, wine; #400/109, 5-oz 21.00
Tidbit server, #400/2701, cupped, 2-tier 50.00
Tray, condiment; #400/148, 5¼x9¼" 45.00
Tray, relish; #400/102, 5-part, 13" 75.00
Tumbler, #3400, ftd, 12-oz 17.00
Tumbler, #400/19, 12-oz 22.00
Tumbler, juice; #400/18, 5-oz 37.50
Tumbler, old-fashioned; #400/18, 7-oz 37.50
Tumbler, wine; #400/19, ftd, 3-oz 20.00
Vase, #400/143C, flat, crimped edge, 8" 70.00
Vase, #400/27, bead ft, incurvate rim, 8½" 185.00
Vase, #400/287F, fan shape, 6" 30.00
Vase, bud; #400/107, bead ft, 5¾" 55.00
Vase, rose bowl; #400/142K, 7" 210.00

Candy Containers

Figural glass candy containers were first created in 1876 when ingenious candy manufacturers began to use them to package their products. Two of the first containers, the Liberty Bell and Independence Hall, were distributed for our country's centennial celebration. Children found these toys appealing, and an industry was launched that lasted into the mid-1960s.

Figural candy containers include animals, comic characters, guns, telephones, transportation vehicles, household appliances, and many other intriguing designs. The oldest (those made prior to 1920) were usually hand painted and often contained extra metal parts in addition to the metal strip or screw closures. During the 1950s these metal parts were replaced with plastic, a practice that continued until candy containers met their demise in the 1960s. While predominately clear, they are found in nearly all colors of glass including milk glass, green, amber, pink, emerald, cobalt, ruby flashed, and light blue. Usually the color was intentional, but leftover glass was used as well and resulted in unplanned colors. Various examples are found in light or ice blue, and new finds are always being discovered. Production of the glass portion of candy containers was centered around the western Pennsylvania city of Jeannette. Major producers include Westmoreland Glass, West Bros., Victory Glass, J.H. Millstein, J.C. Crosetti, L.E. Smith, Jack Stough, and T.H. Stough. While 90% of all glass candies were made in the Jeannette area, other companies such as Eagle Glass, Play Toy, and Geo. Borgfeldt Co. have a few to their credit as well.

Buyer beware! Many candy containers have been reproduced. Some, including the Camera and the Rabbit Pushing Wheelbarrow, come already painted from distributors. Others may have a slick or oily feel to the touch. The following list may also alert you to possible reproductions:

Amber Pistol, L #144 (first sold full in the 1970s, not listed in E&A)

Auto, D&P #173/E&A #33/L #377

Auto, D&P #163/E&A #60/L #356

Black and White Taxi, D&P #182/L #353 (A number of metal roofs have appeared. They are different from originals because the white section is more silvery in color than the original cream. These closures are put on original bases and often priced for hundreds of dollars.)

Camera, D&P #419/E&A #121/L #238 (Original says 'Pat Apld For' on bottom, reproduction says 'B. Shakman' or is ground off.)

Carpet Sweeper, D&P 296/E&A #133/L #243 (currently being sold with no metal parts)

Carpet Sweeper, E&A #132/L #242 (currently being sold with no metal parts)

Charlie Chaplin, D&P 195/E&A #137/L #83 (Original has 'Geo. Borgfeldt' on base; reproduction comes in pink and blue.)

Chicken on Nest, D&P #10/E&A #149/L #12

Display Case, D&P #422/E&A #177/L #246 (Original should be painted silver and brown.)

Dog, D&P #21/E&A #180/L #24 (clear and cobalt)

Drum Mug, D&P #431/E&A #543/L #255

Happifats on Drum, D&P #199/E&A #208/L #89 (no notches on repro for closure to hook into)

Fire Engine, D&P 258/E&A #213/L #386 (repros in green and blue glass)

Independence Hall, D&P #130/E&A #342/L #76 (Original is rectangular; repro has offset base with red felt-lined closure.)

Jackie Coogan, D&P #202/E&A #345/L #90 (marked inside 'B')

Kewpie, D&P #204/E&A #349/L #91 (must have Geo. Borgfeldt on base to be original)

Mailbox, D&P #216/E&A #521/L #254 (repro marked Taiwan)

Mantel Clock, D&P #483/E&A #162/L #114 (originally in ruby flashed, milk glass, clear, and frosted only)

Mule and Waterwagon, D&P #51/E&A #539/L #38 (original marked Jeannette, PA)

Naked Child, E&A 546/L #94

Owl, D&P #52/E&A #566/L #37 (original in clear only, often painted; repro found in clear, blue, green, and pink with a higher threaded base and less detail)

Peter Rabbit, D&P #60/E&A #618/L #55

Piano, D&P #460/E&A #577/L #289 (original in only clear and milk glass, both painted)

Rabbit Pushing Wheelbarrow, D&P #72/E&A #601/L #47 (Eggs are speckled on the repro; solid on the original.)

Rocking Horse, D&P #46/E&A #651/L #58 (original in clear only)

Safe, D&P #311/E&A #661/L #268 (original in clear, ruby flashed, and milk glass only)

Santa, D&P 284/E&A #674/L #103 (Original has plastic head; repro is all glass and opens at bottom.)

Santa's Boot, D&P #273/E&A #111/L #233

Scottie Dog, D&P #35/E&A #184/L #17 (Repro has a ice-like color and is often slick and oily.)

Station Wagon, D&P #178/E&A #56/L #378

Stough Rabbit, D&P #53/E&A #617/L #54

Uncle Sam's Hat, D&P #428/E&A #303/L #168

Others are possible. If in doubt, do not buy without a guarantee from the dealer and return privilege in writing.

Our advisor for glass containers is Jeff Bradfield; he is listed in the Directory under Virginia. You may contact him with questions, if you will include an SASE. See Clubs, Newsletters, and Catalogs for the address of the Candy Container Collectors of America. A bimonthly newsletter that offers insight into new finds, reproductions, updates, and articles from over four hundred collectors and members, including all authors of books on candy containers. Dues are $18.00 yearly. The club holds an annual convention in June in Reading, Pennsylvania, for collectors of candy containers.

'L' numbers used in this guide refer to a standard reference series, *An Album of Candy Containers*, Vols 1 and 2, by Jennie Long. 'E&A' numbers correlate with *The Compleat American Glass Candy Containers Handbook* by Eikelberner and Agadjanian, revised by Adele Bowden. D&P numbers refer to *The Collector's Guide to Candy Containers* by Doug Dezso and Leon and Rose Poirier (Collector Books).

Airplane, Musical Toy; red plastic wings, D&P 79/E&A 1/L 331 ...65.00
Airplane, Spirit of Goodwill; Victory Glass, D&P 84/E&A 8/L 320 .....175.00
Apothecary Jar, Old Fashion #1; Hobnail stopper/base, D&P 115/E&A 22 ....75.00
Barney Google by Bbl, trn to left/ft on step, D&P 188/E&A 71 ...1,000.00

Basket, Hanging; clear or milk glass, D&P 291/E&A 81/L 223 ....**40.00**
Betty Lou Toy Town Dairy, cb carrier, D&P 107/E&A 529 ....**200.00**
Binoculars, Victor, brass-plated tin fr, D&P 98/E&A 560/L 624 ...**250.00**
Boat, Colorado; wood/string rigging, D&P 101/E&A 102/L 334 ..**350.00**
Boat, Uruguay; anchor ea side of bow, D&P 105 ....**250.00**

Bus, screw-on closure, seven windows each side, two large headlights, extended bumper, D&P 153, 2⅞x7¼x2", from $300.00 to $400.00. (Photo courtesy Dezso, Poirier, and Poirier)

Bus, NY - San Francisco; D&P 154/E&A 118-2/L 346 ....**600.00**
Cannon, 2-Wheel Mount #2; clear or cobalt, D&P 385/E&A 122/L 534 .**575.00**
Car, Boyd; various colors, D&P 159 ....**30.00**
Car, Coupe — Long Hood w/Tin Wheels; D&P 160/E&A 50/L 357 .**175.00**
Car, Electric Runabout — Open Top; D&P 163/E&A 47/L 356 (+) **80.00**
Car, Hearse #2; open top, D&P 165/E&A 40/L 360 ....**140.00**
Car, Little Sedan; mk 3 DR JS Co & #d, D&P 171/E&A 31/L 374 ...**35.00**
Car, Sedan w/12 Vents; mk VG Co, 90% pnt, D&P 177/E&A 36 ..**125.00**
Car, Tin-Wheeled 2-Door Streamliner; 90% pnt, D&P 180/E&A 63/L 371 ..**160.00**
Cash Register, 4 rows of keys, D&P 420/E&A 135/L 244 ....**450.00**
Cheerful Cholly Clown, cb suit/shoes, compo head, D&P 194/L 530 ..**300.00**
Chicken on Sagging Basket, D&P 14/E&A 148/L 8 ....**75.00**
Circus Wagon, scrollwork between wheels on 1 side, D&P 527/L 439 ..**250.00**
Clarinet, red/wht striped tube at top, D&P 448/E&A 316/L 285 .**35.00**
Clock, Betty Barker Time Teacher; D&P 478 ....**100.00**
Clock, Candy Bank; all plastic, D&P 479 ....**40.00**
Clock, Milk Glass; Roman numerals, 11 o'clock, D&P 483/E&A 162/L 114 ..**250.00**
Coach, Angeline — No Couplers; all orig, D&P 519/E&A 168 .**525.00**
Coal Car — w/Couplers; all orig, D&P 522/E&A 171 ....**400.00**
Colonial Candlestick, hexagonal/paneled, D&P 319/E&A 119-1/L 201 ..**300.00**
Dirigible, Mu-Mu; Bakelite closure, D&P 90 ....**250.00**
Dog, Bulldog w/Rnd Base, Victory Glass, D&P 18/E&A 189/L 15 .**70.00**
Dog, Hound w/Lg Glass Hat; seated, D&P 27/E&A 182/L 22 .....**20.00**
Dog, Scottie, looking str ahead, D&P 35/E&A 184/L 17 (+) **25.00**
Dog by Barrel, LE Smith, D&P 19/E&A 190 ....**200.00**
Dog w/Umbrella, wide opening, D&P 37/E&A 194-2/L 19 ....**50.00**
Don't Park Here USA (sign), D&P 423/E&A 196/L 314 ....**300.00**
Drum Bank, pnt milk glass, emb cannon etc, D&P 389/E&A 195/L 279 ....**300.00**
Duck on Rnd Base (basket), D&P 40/E&A 200 ....**500.00**
Duck on Rope Top Basket (rectangular), D&P 39/E&A 198 ....**80.00**
Elephant, GOP, orig pnt, D&P 43/E&A 206/L 31 ....**250.00**
Felix on Tub, mk c 1922-24/Pat Sullivan, D&P 201/E&A 211-1/L 87 ...**3,500.00**
Fire Engine, Fire Dept in Circle; D&P 253/E&A 215 ....**50.00**
Fire Engine, Lg Boiler; D&P 255/E&A 221 ....**125.00**
Fire Engine, Mini; driver (no steering wheel), D&P 258/E&A 213 (+) ..**25.00**
Fire Engine, 1914 Stough; tin wheels, D&P 262/E&A 223 ....**135.00**
Fire Engine, 3-Dot USA; D&P 260/E&A 220 ....**90.00**
Flapper, hands under china, D&P 203/E&A 227 ....**70.00**
Flossie Fisher's Chair, tin bk/seat, D&P 300/E&A 232/L 128 ....**600.00**
Gas Pump, 23¢ To-Day, D&P 439/E&A 240/L 316 ....**375.00**
Golf Club, DRGM, D&P 425/E&A 244 ....**75.00**
Gun, Kolt; orig pnt, D&P 393/E&A 285/L 151 ....**100.00**
Gun, Medium w/Hook Grip; screw head in grip, D&P 396/E&A 259 ..**35.00**
Gun, Stough's Whistling Jim — Str Grip; D&P 402/E&A 249 ...**25.00**
Gun, Stough's 1939 Pat Pending; D&P 400/E&A 247 ....**25.00**
Gun, Waffle Grip; Stough, D&P 406/E&A 247-1 ....**25.00**
Hansel & Gretel Fairy Pups Salt & Pepper, D&P 22/E&A 193/L 23, pr .**90.00**
Hat w/Tin Brim, various colors, D&P 427/E&A 301/L 166 ....**90.00**
Horn, Stough's 1953; 3 valve buttons, D&P 453/E&A 310/L 283 .**40.00**
House w/Chimney, front dormer, D&P 129/E&A 324/L 75 ....**275.00**
Irish Hat, shamrock on front, D&P 426/E&A 302/L 167 ....**3,000.00**
Jack O'Lantern, Scalloped Edge; orig pnt, D&P 268/L 552 ....**150.00**
Jack O'Lantern, Slant Eyes; orig pnt, D&P 265/E&A 349 ....**225.00**
Kettle on 3 Feet, horizontal ribs/orig closure, D&P 307/E&A 355/L 251 ..**45.00**
Lamp, Inside Ribbed Base; vase-like glass, D&P 331/E&A 367/L 208 ...**150.00**
Lamp, Metal Shade; Stough, D&P 335/L 464 ....**60.00**
Lamp, Mini Kerosene; boot base, D&P 337/L 564 ....**15.00**
Lantern, Aluminum Top & Bottom; beaded ribs, D&P 343/E&A 449/L 560 ..**35.00**
Lantern, Beaded #2, pnt clear or milk glass, D&P 348/E&A 405/L 180 ..**35.00**
Lantern, Beveled Panel; sq panels, D&P 349/E&A 396/L 175 ..**120.00**
Lantern, Dec 20 '04 — Medium; shaker top, D&P 351/E&A 407/L 173 .**30.00**
Lantern, Long Waisted; D&P 356/E&A 402/L 185 ....**25.00**
Lantern, Pat Apld For; Made in USA, D&P 359/E&A 445-1 .....**20.00**
Lantern, Stough's All Glass; D&P 364/E&A 406 ....**25.00**
Lantern, W Glass Co; metal top/base, D&P 375/E&A 451/L 569 ..**45.00**
Lawn Swing, West Bros #2862, all orig, D&P 314/E&A 469/L 135 .**900.00**
Liberty Bell, various colors, orig closure, D&P 94/E&A 87/L 229 ....**125.00**
Locomotive, Curved Line 888; D&P 490/E&A 483 ....**30.00**
Locomotive, Lithographed Closure #3; West Bros, D&P 494/E&A 498 .**90.00**
Locomotive, Little 23; open at cab end, D&P 496/E&A 478 ....**125.00**
Locomotive, Mapother's; D&P 499/E&A 494 ....**325.00**
Locomotive, Sm Plain Screw Cap; D&P 502/E&A 493 ....**175.00**
Locomotive, Stough's E3S Wide Cab; D&P 505/E&A 490 ....**30.00**
Locomotive, 2-Stacker #23; D&P 512/E&A 479 ....**175.00**
Military Cap, D&P 388/E&A 131/L 170 ....**25.00**
Milk Bottle, German, wire closure at neck, D&P 111 ....**100.00**
Mug, Kiddies' Drinking; Millstein, D&P 433/E&A 540/L 258 .....**25.00**
Mug, Victory Glass Co; flat-top hdl w/curl at base, D&P 434/E&A 542 .**15.00**
Nurser, Baby; oval, wood nipple, D&P 118/E&A 554 ....**50.00**
Nurser, Plain Oval; Crosetti, D&P 124 ....**20.00**
Parlor Car, arched windows, D&P 516/E&A 169 ....**325.00**
Pencil, Baby Jumbo; holds real pencil, D&P 218/E&A 567/L 263 .**95.00**
Pipe, Fancy Bowl; cut-glass pattern, various colors D&&P 436/E&A 583 ..**85.00**
Play Packs, Toy Assortment, Christmas; D&P 469 ....**125.00**
Pumpkin Head Policeman Jr, orig pnt, D&P 271/E&A 593/L 164 ..**1,800.00**
Rabbit, Peter; Jeannette, D&P 60/E&A 618/L 55 ....**30.00**
Rabbit w/Aluminum Ears, mk Germany/GesGesch, D&P 63/L 487 .**600.00**
Rabbit w/Feet Together, USA/1-oz Avor, D&P 67/E&A 614/L 52 ....**100.00**
Rabbit w/Legs Apart, mk Contents 1¾ ADV oZ, D&P 71/E&A 612/L 51 ......**125.00**
Racer, Stutz Bear Cat; 10-rib radiator, D&P 474/E&A 639 ....**1,250.00**
Racer #12, D&P 476/E&A 642 ....**220.00**
Refrigerator, coil on top, D&P 309/E&A 650/L 266 ....**6,500.00**
Santa Claus in Banded Coat, Contents 3 oZ ADV, D&P 277/L 97/E&A 669 ..**300.00**
Santa Claus in Dbl Cuff Coat; 1-oz w/bkward z, D&P 278/E&A 671/L 101 ..**150.00**
Santa's Boot — Glass; emb strap, D&P 273/E&A 111/L 233 ....**20.00**
Santa w/Skis, all plastic, D&P 287 ....**20.00**
Settee, Rocking; gilt top edge/arms/risers, D&P 313/E&A 653/L 134 ..**550.00**
Soldier, Doughboy; emb helmet/uniform, D&P 209/L 525 ....**200.00**
Stop & Go, metal post/blades, D&P 441/E&A 706/L 317 ....**400.00**
Table, front drw w/center knob, D&P 316/E&A 714/L 136 ....**900.00**
Tank, 2 Cannons; D&P 413/E&A 723 ....**35.00**
Telephone, Desk; metal ear/mouth pcs, D&P 222/L 581 ....**1,250.00**
Telephone, Glass Receiver — USA; D&P 226/E&A 736/L 290 ..**75.00**
Telephone, Pay Station; plastic w/glass bottle, D&P 235/E&A 120/L 239 ....**250.00**
Telephone, Redlich's Bell/Crank; wood receiver, D&P 238/E&A 752/L 294 ..**350.00**
Telephone, Redlich's Sm Screw Top #2; Pat #, D&P 244/E&A 749/L 296 .....**150.00**

Telephone, Stough's Musical Toy; ringed base, D&P 246/E&A 732/L 310 ....45.00
Telephone, Wood Transmitter; D&P 251/E&A 751/L 308 ....125.00
Tomahawk & Gun, wood hdl, cb head, glass gun, D&P 416 ....60.00
Toonerville Trolley, Fontaine Fox on bottom, D&P 214/E&A 767/L 111 ...800.00
Top, Sm; ½-oz Avor/Made in USA, D&P 443/E&A 776/L 272 .125.00
Uncle Sam by Barrel, slot in closure, 95% pnt, D&P 215/E&A 801/L 112 ..900.00
Village Bank, tin w/insert, D&P 133/E&A 804/L 76B 175.00
Village City Garage, tin w/liner, D&P 136/E&A 811/L 76E 150.00
Village Log Cabin, tin w/insert, D&P 140/E&A 816/L 765 ....500.00
Village School House, tin w/insert, D&P 143/E&A 808/L 7611 .175.00
Watch, Eagle; w/eagle fob, D&P 486/E&A 823/L 122 ....450.00
Watch, Victor; tin face: Pat Aug 12 1913, D&P 487/E&A 824/L 121 ..1,100.00
Windmill, Candy Guaranteed; tin blades, D&P 533/E&A 840 ...1,000.00
Windmill, TG Stough's 1915; D&P 538/E&A 842 ....375.00
Windmill, 5-Window; D&B 535/E&A 844 ....500.00

Miscellaneous

These types of candy containers are generally figural. Many are holiday related. Our advisor for this category is Jenny Tarrant; she is listed in the Directory under Missouri. See also Christmas; Easter; Halloween.

Key: pm — papier-mache

Peter the Pumpkin Bellhop, Germany, 7", EX, $375.00. (Photo courtesy Dunbar Gallery)

Cat, pm w/gesso, mc pnt, glass eyes, red ribbon, rpr, 6" 190.00
Cat, seated, pm w/gesso, worn flocking, glass eyes, old rpr, 4" 100.00
Cat in shoe, compo & gesso w/mc pnt, rpr to ears, 4" 150.00
Cat in shoe, pm & gesso, mc pnt, glass eyes, rprs, 4" 100.00
Ear of corn, molded pottery, gr paper forms husk, unmk Germany, 5⅝" ..125.00
Geo WA, compo, stands on rnd box w/silk flag, Germany, 5" 225.00
Geo WA bust, bottom plug, compo, 2-3" 75.00
Geo WA bust, bottom plug, compo, 4-6" 150.00
Geo WA w/tree stump, compo, Germany, 3-4" 55.00
Geo WA w/tree stump, compo, Germany, 5-7" 85.00
Pig, pm, sleeping, worn/soiled pk flocking, 5⅝" 165.00
St Patrick's Day, Irish man bust, w/plug, compo, Germany, 3-4" ..75.00
St Patrick's Day, Irish man bust, w/plug, compo, Germany, 5-6" ...150.00
St Patrick's Day, Irish man on candy box, compo, Germany, 3½" ..110.00
St Patrick's Day, pig, flocked gr, plug in tummy, wood legs, 3-5" ..225.00
St Patrick's Day, pig, gr, head removes, compo, Germany, 3-5" ..165.00
St Patrick's Day, pig, pk w/shamrock, compo, Germany, 4-6" 155.00
St Patrick's Day, potato, compo, Germany, 3-4" 75.00
Turkey, compo w/metal ft, head removes, Germany, 5" 195.00
Turkey, compo w/metal legs, head removes, Germany, 3½" 125.00

Canes

Fancy canes and walking sticks were once the mark of a gentleman. Hand-carved examples are collected and admired as folk art from the past. The glass canes that never could have been practical are unique whimseys of the glassblower's profession. Gadget and container sticks, which were produced in a wide variety, are highly desirable. Character, political, and novelty types are also sought after as are those with handles made of precious metals.

For more information we recommend *American Folk Art Canes, Personal Sculpture*, by George H. Meyer, Sandringham Press, 100 West Long Lake Rd., Suite 100, Bloomfield Hills, MI 48304. Other possible references are *Canes in the United States* by Catherine Dike and *Canes From the 17th – 20th Century* by Jeffrey Snyder. For information concerning the Cane Collectors Club, see the Directory under Clubs, Newsletters, and Catalogs. Our advisor for this category is Bruce Thalberg.

Bakelite bulldog w/glass light-up eyes, batteries in hdl, Austria .550.00
Bone hdl w/cvd dog's head w/glass eyes, wood shaft, brass ferrule ..250.00
Bone rope-twist cvd hdl, repousse silver ferrule, bamboo shaft, 34" ..165.00
Bone skull w/bow-tie hdl, ivory ring, ebonized shaft, 1890s 575.00
Brass dog leash-whistle hdl mk Blackwell's Pat, ash shaft 1,000.00
Enamel powder compact hdl w/roses & gold, ebony shaft, 1910s ..2,500.00
Gambler's, window top holds 2 dice, ivory inlay, mahog shaft, 1880s .1,350.00
Gold 18k repousse hdl, full-bark malacca shaft, 1860s 1,100.00
Gold-filled hdl w/MOP decor, hardwood shaft w/MOP inlay, 1901 ...375.00
Gold-filled hdl w/repousse floral designs in relief, ebony shaft ...280.00
Gorham sterling L hdl, dk hardwood shaft, ca 1920s 375.00
Ivory, dog & hare relief-cvd ball, gold collar, ebony shaft 650.00
Ivory & MOP hdl w/mc wax lines, rosewood shaft, 1840s 450.00
Ivory bear head hdl w/glass eyes, silver collar, ebony shaft, 1892 .2,500.00
Ivory cvd hdl w/2 horses racing neck & neck, ebony shaft 1,700.00
Ivory cvd skull, 9k gold collar w/London 1865 hallmk, malacca shaft ..900.00
Ivory pistol grip w/cvg, silver ferrule, rosewood shaft 150.00
Meissen porc hdl w/rural scene, brass/iron ferrule, cedar shaft .1,600.00
Staghorn dog w/glass eyes & whistle hdl, silver collar, bamboo shaft ..425.00
Sterling hourglass hdl w/emb decor, horn ferrule, mahog shaft, 1900s ..250.00
Sterling knob w/C scrolls, wht metal/iron ferrule, cherry shaft, 1900s ..225.00
Sterling owl-on-stump hdl w/London 1887 hallmk, rosewood shaft 900.00
Telescoping, SP hdl unscrews for 1-draw scope, hardwood shaft, 1850s .1,400.00
Tortoise-shell knob hdl w/gold, brass ferrule, malacca shaft, 1840s .650.00
Wood, cvd dmn-bk rattlesnake w/glass eyes, mc pnt details, 37" ..250.00
Wood, cvd hawk w/glass eyes hdl, silver collar, malacca shaft, 1890s ..700.00
Wood, cvd hound's head walnut hdl w/glass eyes, hardwood shaft, 1890s ..650.00
Wood, cvd L hdl w/stanhope of Last Supper, silver collar, Fr, 1890s ..500.00
Wood, cvd man's head, mc pnt, 20th C folk art, 42" 165.00
Wood, cvd parrot w/glass eyes hdl, thick malacca shaft, Germany, 1890s ...500.00
Wood, cvd Queen Victoria in lion's mouth hdl, rosewood shaft, 1850s ...900.00
Wood, folk-art fraternal theme w/much cvg, brass ferrule, 1870s .500.00

Canton

Canton is a blue and white porcelain that was first exported in the 1790s by clipper ships from China to the United States, a practice that continued into the 1920s. Canton became very popular along the east coast where the major ports were located. Its popularity was due to several factors: it was readily available, inexpensive, and (due to the fact that it came in many different forms) appealing to the housewife.

The porcelain's blue and white color and simple motif (teahouse, trees, bridge, and a rain-cloud border) have made it a favorite of people who collect early American furniture and accessories. Buyers of Canton should shop at large outdoor shows and up-scale antique shows. Collections are regularly sold at auction. Collectors usually prefer a rich, deep tone rather than a lighter blue. Cracks, large chips, and major repairs will substantially affect values. Prices of Canton have escalated sharply over the last twenty years, and rare forms are highly sought after by advanced collectors. Our advisor for this category is Hobart D. Van Deusen; he is listed in the Directory under Connecticut.

Bowl, cut corners, minor rstr, 19th C, 4¾x9¼" 435.00
Bowl, serving; cut corners, shallow, 2¼x14x11", VG 250.00
Bowl, serving; 2x12", EX 425.00
Bowl, vegetable; almond shape, pine-cone finial, 10½" 225.00
Bowl, vegetable; boars' head hdls, w/lid, 9x14x9", EX 850.00
Bowl, vegetable; pine-cone finial, orange peel glaze, 10" 335.00
Bowl, vegetable; rectangular, w/lid, 4¼x7", EX, pr 500.00
Butter dish, domed lid, pierced insert, rpr 440.00
Creamer, w/leaf-shaped undertray, 4¼", 7¼x5¼", EX 500.00
Dish, almond shape, sm chips, 10½" 110.00
Pitcher, hairline, 19th C, 7¾x6½" 500.00
Pitcher, 4¼" 220.00
Platter, chip, 13¼" 385.00
Platter, cut corners, 17¾x15", from $600 to 700.00
Platter, deep, 19th C, 13¾", EX 375.00
Platter, pierced inset, 19th C, rpr, 17" 700.00
Platter, unglazed base, early, 17", EX 350.00
Platter, well & tree, 19th C, 18", EX 700.00
Platter, 11¼" 300.00
Platter, 11¾", EX 220.00
Platter, 16", EX 440.00
Platter, 17½", from $475 to 550.00
Platter, 19th C, 18½x15¾", EX 750.00
Platter, 8-sided, 15½x12½", EX 450.00
Soup tureen, rectangular, 19th C, 7½x12½x8¼", EX 485.00
Soup tureen, 19th C, 6x10" 865.00
Sugar bowl, ear hdls, mismatched lid, 5⅞" 275.00
Teapot, bbl form, foo dog finial, 19th C, 6½" 865.00
Teapot, bbl form, foo dog finial (mismatched lid), 19th C, 6½" ...700.00
Teapot, twined hdl, mismatched lid, 6½" 415.00
Teapot, 6¼" 500.00
Tray, 10" L 165.00
Warming dish, late 19th C, 9½" 285.00
Warming dish, 19th C, 15⅞" 500.00

Capodimonte

The relief style, highly colored and defined porcelain pieces in this listing are commonly called and identified in our current marketplace as Capodimonte. It was King Ferdinand IV, son of King Charles who opened a factory in Naples in 1771 and began to use the mark of the blue crown N (BCN). When the factory closed in 1834, the Ginori family at Doccia near Florence, Italy, acquired what was left of the factory and continued using its mark. The factory continued until 1896 when it was then combined with Societa Ceramica Richard of Milan which continues today to manufacture fine porcelain pieces marked with a crest and wreaths under a blue crown with R. Capodimonte.

Boxes and steins are highly sought after as they are cross collectibles. Figurines, figure groupings, flowery vases, urns, and the like are also highly collectible, but most items on the market today are of recent manufacture. In the past several years, Europeans have been attending U.S. antique shows and auctions in order to purchase Capodimonte items to take back home, since many pieces were destroyed during the two world wars. This has driven up prices of the older ware. Our advisor for this category is James Highfield; he is listed in the Directory under Indiana.

Bell, child finial, brn crown C 1366/135 mk, 6" 55.00
Bird cage, dancing/singing bird, ca 1970, 9" 85.00
Bottle, perfume; playful cherubs, bronze cork, BCN, 7" 278.00
Box, lady feeding bird, garlands around, BCN, 4½" dia 325.00
Box, peasant scenes w/dogs, Meissen mk, oval, 2¼" 1,500.00
Box, winged cherubs & ladies, egg shape, BCN, 8" 410.00
Casket, couple & floral scenes, R Capodimonte mk, 5x3½x3½" 45.00
Chalice cup, knights on horses fighting, BCN, 9¼" 325.00
Compote, cherubs as 4 Seasons, angel finial, R Capodimonte mk, 9" ..90.00
Cup & saucer, demitasse; chariot, gilt throughout, BCN 92.00
Figurine, monk w/Bible & skull on base, ca 1880, BCN, 6½" ...150.00
Figurines, cherub band, ca 1920, BCN, 4½", 5-pc 105.00
Hand mirror, bronze foliate hdl, ca 1900, 15" 140.00
Nut trays, BCN B Altman & Co, Paris-NY, 3¼x2¾", 4 for 85.00
Pitcher, human face, beard & mustache, BCN, 5½" 200.00
Plaque, shield-making scene, wood & jewled bronze fr, BCN, 18x20" .650.00
Plate, Marie Antoinette portrait, BCN France, 10" 250.00
Stein, knightly battle scene, helmet finial, BCN France, 9" 600.00
Stein, wine party, lion finial, R Capodimonte mk 1535/431 Italy, 10" .100.00
Tankard, drunken men, boar on lid, vintage hdl, BCN, 8½" 300.00
Tankard, lion hunt, lion on lid, elephant hdl, BCN, 7½" 300.00
Tea set, donkey scene, BCN, pot+cr/sug 450.00
Urn, toga ladies dressing, bearded face hdls, BCN, 13", pr 750.00
Vase, cherubs picking apples, 4037 Cemas Capodimonte mk, 11" ..55.00

Carlton Ware

Carlton Ware was the product of Wiltshaw and Robinson, who operated in the Staffordshire district of England from about 1890. During the 1920s, they produced ornamental ware with enameled and gilded decorations such as flowers and birds, often on a black background. In 1958 the firm was renamed Carlton Ware Ltd. Their trademark was a crown over a circular stamp with 'W & R, Stoke on Trent,' surrounding a swallow. 'Carlton Ware' was sometimes added by hand.

Condiment set, three footballs on tray with referee at side, 1920s – 30s, $140.00.

Bell, lady figural, gr & yel dress, 3½x2¼" dia 100.00
Bowl, Rouge Royale, red w/exotic birds & scene in gold, 9" 145.00
Bride's basket, Foxglove, 6x7½x10" 160.00
Cruet set, pea pod, carrot & onion shapes, on oval 9" tray 75.00
Cup, 2 legs as ft, gr shoes, lilac stars on socks, NM 75.00
Dish, Deco silver o/l on bl, dmn form w/wings, 11¾" 40.00
Dish, pk w/yel buttercup, MIE/Australia, 4½" 45.00
Jam dish, Primrose, 5¼" 40.00
Jam dish, Windflower, 4½" 40.00
Marmalade, floral, mc on ivory, pat lid, 5" 90.00
Mug, chocolate; Apple Blossom, w/lid, paper label, 5" 210.00
Night light, blk w/pk floral, W&R #654181, pre-'20, 6½x4½" dia 110.00
Pitcher, orange w/Talouse Lautrec decal ea side, Deco shape, 7x4" 60.00
Pitcher, Rouge Royal, lg bird, gold hdl/trim, 6¾x5" 535.00
Plate, Sunflower, pk, 9½", NM 95.00
Sauce boat, Tomato Ware, gr, MIE/Australia, w/liner 45.00
Sauce jug, Wild Rose, no mk, 2" 20.00
Vase, floral branches on bl w/gold, foo dog finial, 8¾x3½" 375.00
Vase, Oriental scene on dk bl w/gold, #2884, W&R mk, 13" 550.00
Vase, Rouge Royale, red w/bl birds on wht cloud, gilt, 2½x3" dia ..75.00

Carnival Collectibles

Carnival items from the early part of this century represent the lighter side of an America that was alternately prospering and sophisticated or devastated by war and domestic conflict. But whatever the country's condition, the carnival's thrilling rides and shooting galleries were a sure way of letting it all go by — at least for an evening.

For further information on chalkware figures, we recommend *The Carnival Chalk Prize* by our advisor, Thomas G. Morris, who is listed in the Directory under Oregon.

In the shooting gallery target listings below, items are rated for availability from 1 (commonly found) to 10 (rarely found) and all are made of cast iron. Our advisors for shooting gallery targets are Richard and Valerie Tucker; their address is listed in the Directory under Texas.

Chalkware Figures

Abraham Lincoln, bust, ca 1940-50, 12" 55.00
Alice the Goon, ca 1940-45, rare, 10" 120.00
Betty Boop, ca 1930-40, 14½" 295.00
Bulldog, smoking pipe, ca 1935-45, 6½" 20.00
Cat, bank, ca 1935-50, 7" 15.00
Cat, sitting, ca 1935-40, 7¾" 20.00

Charlie McCarthy, copyright Dummy, J.Y. Jenkins, May 3, 1938, 15", $95.00. (Photo courtesy Tom Morris)

Charlie McCarthy, ca 1940-50, 15" 85.00
Circus Horse, ca 1930-40, rare, 16" 195.00
Circus Lion, ca 1930-40, 8x9" 30.00
Clara Bell Cow, ca 1945-50, 11¾" 65.00
Collie w/Ball, ca 1935-45, 7½" 25.00
Comical Cow, mk Edw Botman, ca 1945-50, 6½" 35.00
Cowboy, mk Yippee Jenkins, ca 1943, 15" 95.00
Dog, ashtray, ca 1935-45, 5½" 20.00
Dog, sitting on over-stuffed chair, unmk, 1930-40, 5½" 15.00
Dog in Chair, ca 1930-40, 5½" 35.00
Donald Duck, ca 1934-50, 14" 90.00
Elephant, standing, ca 1930-40, 12½" 12500
Elsie the Cow, ca 1945-50, 6" 45.00
End of the Trail, ca 1930-45, 12" 135.00
Felix the Cat, ca 1925-35, rare, 12½" 245.00
Ferdinand the Bull, flat bk, mk Lisa, ca 1940-40, 8½" 45.00
Hollywood Star, ca 1930-40, 9¾" 50.00
Horse & Clock, ca 1940-50, 13" 145.00
Hunny Bear, bank, mk Disney, ca 1940-50, 10½" 65.00
Indian on Horse, ca 1930-50, 11" 55.00
Kitten, string holder, ca 1930-45, 7¼" 45.00
Lion, ca 1940-50, 4¾" 20.00
Mae West, mk Rainmaker, ca 1936, 14" 145.00
Mickey Mouse, ca 1930-40, rare, 8½" 185.00
Pekingese Dog, ca 1935-40, 7¼x10½" 40.00
Pirate Girl, mk Rainwater, ca 1936, 14¼" 145.00
Pluto, ca 1935-50, 7½" 65.00
Poodle, sittting, ca 1935-45, 8" 20.00
Popeye, ca 1930-50, 18" 195.00
Radio Dog, mk Jenkins, 1924, rare, 9" 195.00
Rin Tin Tin, sitting, ca 1930-40, 7" 20.00
Sgt Bilko (WWII), bank, ca 1945-50, 12" 75.00
Shirley Temple, ca 1935-45, 14½" 190.00
Soldier (WWII), ca 1935-45, 14½" 85.00
Spaniel, sitting, pk, ca 1910-25, rare 135.00
Standing Nude, radio lamp, ca 1940-50, rare, 12" 250.00
Sugar, mk Sugar by Jenkins, ca 1948 ....165.00
Wimpy, ca 1930-50, 16" 175.00
Wishing Well w/Mexican, mk JY Jenkins, ca 1936 ....115.00

Shooting Gallery Targets

Battleship, worn wht pnt, Mangels, 5, 6¼x11⅜", $200 to 300.00
Birds (8) on bar, worn pnt, Mangels, 9, 3½x41½", $700 to 800.00
Bull's-eye w/pop-up duck, old pnt, Quackenbush, 7, 12" dia, $500 to .600.00
Dbl star spinner, worn mc pnt, Mangles, 6, 8x2¾", $200 to 300.00
Dog running, worn wht pnt, Smith or Evans, 6, 6x11", $100 to ..200.00
Duck, detailed feathers, old pnt, Parker, 8, 3¾x5½", $100 to 200.00
Duck, detailed feathers, worn pnt, Evans, 4, 5½x8½", $100 to ...200.00
Eagle w/wings wide, mc pnt, Smith or Evans, 6, 14¾", $650 to ..750.00
Greyhound, bull's-eye, old patina, Parker, 8, 26" W, minimum 1,000.00
Monkey, standing, worn pnt, 10, 9¾x8½", $300 to 400.00
Owl, bull's-eye, wht traces, Evans, 6, 10¾x5⅛", $400 to 500.00
Pipe, old patina, Smith, 1, 5⅜x1¾", value less than 50.00
Rabbit, running, bull's-eye, old patina, Parker, 8, 12x25x1", minimum ..1,000.00
Rabbit, standing, worn pnt, Smith or Mueller, 8, 18x10", $900 to .1,000.00
Reindeer (elk), worn rpt over wht, 7, 10x9", $300 to 400.00
Saber-tooth tiger, old patina, Mangels, 7, 7¾x13", $300 to 400.00
Soldier w/rifle, pnt traces/old patina, Mueller, 5, 9x5", $100 to .200.00
Squirrel, running, old patina, Smith, 4, 5⅛x9¼", $100 to 200.00
Swan, worn wht pnt, Mueller, 7, 5¾x5", $100 to 200.00

Carnival Glass

Carnival glass is pressed glass that has been coated with a sodium solution and fired to give it an exterior lustre. First made in America in 1905, it was produced until the late 1920s and had great popularity in the average American household, for unlike the costly art glass produced by Tiffany, carnival glass could be mass produced at a small cost. Colors most often found are marigold, green, blue, and purple; but others exist in lesser quantities and include white, clear, red, aqua opalescent, peach opalescent, ice blue, ice green, amber, lavender, and smoke.

Companies mainly responsible for its production in America include the Fenton Art Glass Company, Williamstown, West Virginia; the Northwood Glass Company, Wheeling, West Virginia; the Imperial Glass Company, Bellaire, Ohio; the Millersburg Glass Company, Millersburg, Ohio; and the Dugan Glass Company (Diamond Glass), Indiana, Pennsylvania. In addition to these major manufacturers, lesser producers included the U.S. Glass Company, the Cambridge Glass Company, the Westmoreland Glass Company, and the McKee Glass Company.

Carnival glass has been highly collectible since the 1950s and has been reproduced for the last twenty-five years. Several national and state collectors' organizations exist, and many fine books are available on old carnival glass, including *The Standard Encyclopedia of Carnival Glass* by Bill Edwards and Mike Carwile and *Dugan & Diamond Carnival Glass, 1909–1931*, by Carl O. Burns.

Acanthus (Imperial), bowl, smoke pastel, 8-9½" 90.00
Acorn (Millersburg), compote, gr, rare 2,200.00
Acorn Burrs (Northwood), sugar bowl, amethyst, w/lid 200.00
Adam's Rib (Dugan/Diamond), candlestick, marigold, pr 95.00
African Shield (English), toothpick holder, marigold 115.00
American (Fostoria), tumbler, gr, rare 140.00
Apple Tree (Fenton), pitcher, ice bl 400.00
April Showers (Fenton), vase, gr 80.00
Arched Flute (Fenton), toothpick holder, ice gr pastel, scarce ..125.00
Arches & Sand, tumbler, marigold 200.00
Asters, bowl, bl 125.00
Aurora Pearls, bowl, marigold, decor, 2 szs, ea 400.00
Australian Panels (Crystal), creamer, amethyst 70.00
Autumn Acorns (Fenton), bowl, gr, 8½" 110.00
Aztec (McKee), pitcher, marigold, rare 1,300.00
Bamboo Bird, jar, marigold, complete 800.00
Banded Diamonds (Crystal), bowl, amethyst, 9" 125.00
Banded Grape (Fenton), creamer, marigold, mini 75.00
Banded Rose, vase, marigold, sm 175.00
Barbella (Northwood), bowl, vaseline pastel 70.00
Barber Bottle (Cambridge), amethyst or gr, complete 750.00
Barber Bottle (Czech), tray, marigold 50.00
Basket of Roses (Northwood), bonbon, bl, scarce 465.00
Beaded Floral Band, tumbler, marigold 25.00
Beaded Panels (Dugan), compote, bl 350.00
Beaded Panels (Imperial), bowl, marigold, 5" 25.00
Beaded Shell (Dugan), mug whimsey, wht 700.00
Beaded Shell (Dugan), pitcher, marigold 500.00
Beaded Swirl (English), pitcher, milk; bl 90.00
Beads (Northwood), bowl, marigold, 8½" 45.00
Beetle (Argentina), ashtray, bl, rare 475.00
Big Basketweave (Dugan), vase, bl, 8"-14", ea 350.00
Bird & Strawberry, tumbler, marigold, scarce 150.00
Bird w/Grapes (Cockatoo), vase, wall; marigold 75.00
Blackberry Banded (Fenton), hat shape, peach opal 135.00
Blackberry Spray (Fenton), bonbon, bl 45.00
Blackberry Spray VT (Fenton), hat shape, marigold 65.00
Blackberry Wreath (Millersburg), plate, gr, rare, 8" 4,200.00
Blossom & Spears, plate, marigold, 8" 50.00
Blueberry (Fenton), pitcher, bl, scarce 900.00
Booker, mug, marigold 160.00
Border Plants (Dugan), bowl, peach opal, flat, 8½" 180.00
Bouquet (Fenton), pitcher, marigold 285.00
Boutonniere (Millersburg), compote, amethyst 225.00
Braziers Candies, bowl, marigold 650.00
Bride's Vase, vase, marigold, in metal stand 25.00
Britt (Kahula), tumbler, bl, rare 1,000.00
Brocaded Acorns (Fostoria), vase, ice bl pastel 250.00
Brocaded Palms (Fostoria), bonbon, ice gr pastel 55.00
Brocaded Summer Gardens (Fostoria), box, ice bl pastel, w/lid .200.00
Brooklyn Bridge (Dugan), bowl, marigold, unlettered, rare 1,600.00
Bubble Berry, shade, cranberry 75.00
Bull's Eye (US Glass), lamp, oil; marigold 210.00
Bull's Eye & Beads (Fenton), vase, bl, 14-18", ea 150.00
Bull's Eye & Loop (Millersburg), vase, marigold, rare, 7-11", ea ..600.00
Bull's Eye & Spearhead, wine, marigold 90.00
Butterfly (Fenton), ornament, marigold, rare 850.00
Butterfly & Berry (Fenton), bowl, red, ftd, 5" 1,000.00
Butterfly & Berry (Fenton), butter dish, gr, w/lid 300.00
Butterfly & Berry (Fenton), pitcher, wht 1,500.00
Butterfly & Fern (Fenton), tumbler, bl 65.00
Butterfly Bower (Crystal), compote, amethyst 350.00
Buttress (US Glass), pitcher, marigold, rare 450.00
Cane (European), tankard, marigold 170.00
Cane (Imperial), compote, marigold 60.00
Cane & Scroll (Sea Thistle)(English), creamer, marigold 45.00
Cannonball VT, pitcher, bl 285.00
Captive Rose (Fenton), bowl, blk amethyst, 8½-10", ea 250.00
Caroline (Dugan), bowl, banana; bl 125.00
Caroline (Dugan), bowl, marigold, 7"-10" 70.00
Channeled Flute (Northwood), vase, amethyst, 10"-16", ea 75.00
Chatham (US Glass), compote, marigold 75.00
Checkerboard Panels (English), bowl, marigold 70.00
Checkers, butter dish, marigold, 2 szs, ea 200.00
Cherries & Daisies (Fenton), banana boat, bl 1,000.00
Cherry (AKA-Hanging Cherries) (Millersburg), bowl, marigold, 5½" ...75.00
Cherry (Dugan), plate, peach opal, 6" 250.00
Cherry & Cable (Northwood), bowl, marigold, scarce, 5" 75.00
Cherry & Cable Intaglio (Northwood), bowl, marigold, 10" 75.00
Cherubs, toothpick holder, marigold, mini 200.00
Chesterfield (Imperial), candy jar, red, w/lid, tall 300.00
Chesterfield (Imperial), toothpick holder, marigold, hdld 250.00
Chrysanthemum (Fenton), bowl, gr, flat, 9" 200.00
Circle Scroll (Dugan), butter dish, marigold 375.00
Circle Scroll (Dugan), vase whimsey, amethyst, rare 265.00
Colonial Lady (Imperial), vase, amethyst, rare 750.00
Columbia (Imperial), bowl, rose; marigold, rare 200.00
Concave Diamonds (Northwood), tumbler, Celeste Bl 45.00
Concord (Fenton), bowl, bl, scarce, 9" 300.00
Constellation (Dugan), compote, amethyst 350.00
Coral (Fenton), bowl, gr, 9" 275.00
Corinth (Westmoreland), vase, bl opal 550.00
Cornflowers, bowl, marigold, ftd 125.00
Cosmos & Cane (US Glass), bowl, marigold, 5" 40.00
Cosmos & Cane (US Glass), bowl, rose; amethyst, lg 1,200.00
Cosmos VT (Fenton), bowl, red, 9-10", ea 775.00
Country Kitchen (Millersburg), bowl, marigold, rare, 10" 325.00
CR (Argentina), ashtray, marigold 175.00
Crackle (Imperial), bowl, amethyst or gr, 5" 20.00
Crackle (Imperial), bowl, punch; marigold, w/base 55.00
Cuba (McKee), goblet, marigold, rare 50.00
Cut Cosmos (Millersburg), tumbler, marigold, rare 300.00
Cut Dahlia (Jenkins), basket, flower; marigold 185.00
Cut Ovals (Fenton), bowl, smoke pastel, 7-10", ea 75.00
Dahlia, button, gr 20.00
Dahlia (Dugan), tumbler, marigold, rare 90.00
Daisy (Fenton), bonbon, bl, scarce 250.00
Daisy & Plume (Northwood & Dugan), candy dish, marigold, ftd .70.00
Daisy & Plume (Northwood & Dugan), compote, gr, ftd 90.00
Daisy Dear (Dugan), bowl, amethyst 45.00
Dandelion (Northwood), tumbler, gr 85.00
Deep Grape (Millersburg), compote, amethyst, rare 2,200.00
Diamond & Daisy Cut (US Glass), pitcher, marigold, rare 400.00
Diamond & Fan, compote, peach opal 100.00
Diamond Band & Fan (English), cordial set, marigold, complete, rare ..900.00
Diamond Fountain (Higbee), bowl, marigold, scarce 100.00
Diamond Lace (Imperial), bowl, marigold, 10"-11", ea 65.00
Diamond Lace (Imperial), tumbler, amethyst 60.00
Diamond Points (Northwood), basket, bl, rare 2,500.00
Diamond Ring (Imperial), bowl, amethyst, 5" 30.00
Diamonds (Millersburg), tumbler, amethyst 90.00
Diplomat (Fenton), tumbler, marigold, rare 165.00
Dotted Daisies, plate, marigold, 8" 90.00
Double Diamonds, ring tree, marigold 85.00
Double Dolphins (Fenton), bowl, Celeste Bl, 9"-11", ea 65.00
Double Scroll (Imperial), bowl, red 225.00
Double Stem Rose (Dugan), plate, amethyst, ftd, scarce 350.00
Dragon & Lotus (Fenton), bowl, gr, flat, 9" 190.00

Drapery (Northwood), candy dish, aqua 200.00
Drapery VT (Fenton), pitcher, marigold, rare 525.00
Dugan's #1013, vase, peach opal, 8"-13", ea 85.00
Dugan's Flute, vase, amethyst, 7"-13", ea 60.00
Duncan (National Glass), cruet, marigold 600.00
Dutch Mill, plate, marigold, 8" 50.00
EA Hudson Furniture (Northwood), plate, advertising; amethyst ..1,700.00
Elks (Fenton), plate, Atlantic City; bl, rare 1,800.00
Elks (Millersburg), paperweight, gr, rare 3,000.00
Emu (Crystal), bowl, amber pastel, 10", rare 1,400.00
Enameled Panel, goblet, marigold 190.00
Enameled Punty Band, tumbler, marigold, rare 325.00
Enameled Rose of Paradise, tumbler, gr 200.00
English Hob & Button (English), bowl, bl, 7"-10", ea 70.00
Engraved Grape (Fenton), candy jar, marigold, w/lid 85.00
Estate (Westmoreland), creamer, aqua opal 290.00
Etched Deco (Standard), nappy, marigold, hdld 40.00
Exotic Lustre, tumbler, lemonade; marigold, scarce 50.00

Fan-Tail (Fenton), footed bowl, blue, 9", $325.00.
(Photo courtesy Bill Edwards)

Fan-Tail (Fenton), plate, marigold, ftd, rare 5,600.00
Fanciful (Dugan), plate, bl, 9" 650.00
Fancy Cut (English), pitcher, marigold, rare, mini 225.00
Farmyard (Dugan), bowl, gr, scarce, 10" 8,200.00
Fashion (Imperial), pitcher, marigold 150.00
Feather & Heart (Millersburg), pitcher, gr, scarce 850.00
Feather Stitch (Fenton), bowl, marigold, 8½"-10", ea 90.00
Feathered Serpent (Fenton), bowl, bl, 5" 40.00
Fenton's #314, candlesticks, Wisteria, pr 200.00
Fenton's Cherries (Fenton), banana boat, bl, rare 2,750.00
Fenton's Smooth Rays, bowl, marigold, sq, scarce, 9" 100.00
Fentonia Fruit (Fenton), bowl, bl, ftd, 6" 120.00
Field Flower (Imperial), tumbler, red, scarce 1,500.00
File (Imperial & English), bowl, amethyst, 5" 40.00
File (Imperial & English), tumbler, lemonade; marigold, rare .1,000.00
File & Fan, compote, marigold 100.00
Fine Cut & Roses (Northwood), candy dish, bl, ftd 150.00
Fine Cut Rings (English), bowl, marigold, oval 140.00
Fine Rib (Dugan), vase, amethyst, 8"-15", ea 70.00
Fine Rib (Northwood), vase, bl, 7"-14", ea 165.00
Firefly (Moth) (Finland), candlesticks, marigold, pr 90.00
Fish Net (Dugan), epergne, peach opal 350.00
Five Hearts (Dugan), bowl, peach opal, dome base, 8¼" 300.00
Five Lily, epergne, amethyst, metal fittings, complete 250.00
Flared Panel, shade, peach opal 75.00
Fleur-De-Lis (Czech), plate, chop; marigold, rare, 12" 700.00
Flickering Flames, shade, pastel 50.00
Floral & Grape VT (Fenton), tumbler, amethyst 35.00
Floral & Wheat (Dugan), bonbon, bl, stemmed, 2 shapes, ea 250.00
Florentine (Fenton & Northwood), candlesticks, red, lg, pr ...1,100.00
Flowering Dill (Fenton), hat, red 475.00
Fluffy Peacock (Fenton), tumbler, bl 75.00
Flute (Millersburg), vase, bl, rare 2,800.00
Flute (Northwood), creamer or sugar bowl, marigold, ea 75.00
Flute & Cane (Imperial), pitcher, milk; marigold 210.00
Flute #700 (Imperial), tumbler, red 350.00
Footed Prism Panels, vase, gr 120.00
Formal (Dugan), hatpin holder, amethyst, rare 1,100.00
Four Flowers (Dugan), bowl, gr, 8"-11", ea 500.00
Four Pillars (Northwood & Dugan), vase, aqua opal 200.00
Frosted Block (Imperial), bowl, marigold, 6½"-7½", ea 20.00
Frosted Block (Imperial), compote, clambroth 75.00
Frosted Oxford, bobeche, marigold, ea 60.00
Fruit Salad (Westmoreland), cup, punch; peach opal, rare 60.00
Fruits & Flowers (Westmoreland), plate, gr, handgrip, rare, 7" ..250.00
Garden Mums, bowl, amethyst, deep, rnd, rare, 5" 450.00
Garden Path VT (Dugan), plate, chop; marigold, rare, 11" 4,500.00
Gay 90s (Millersburg), pitcher, gr, rare 9,500.00
Georgia Belle (Dugan), tray, card; peach opal, ftd, rare 175.00
Gibson Girl, toothpick holder, marigold 60.00
God & Home (Dugan), pitcher, bl, rare 2,200.00
Goddess of Harvest (Fenton), bowl, bl, rare, 9½" 6,500.00
Golden Cupid, bowl, marigold, rare, 5" 225.00
Golden Pineapple & Blackberries, bowl, marigold, 9" 400.00
Golden Thistle, tray, marigold, rare, 5" 350.00
Good Luck VT (Northwood), bowl, gr, rare, 8½" 450.00
Gothic Arches (Imperial), vase, marigold, rare, 8"-12", ea 125.00
Grape & Cable (Fenton), bowl, red, flat, 8" 750.00
Grape & Cable (Northwood), banana boat, gr, ftd 350.00
Grape & Cable (Northwood), bowl, centerpc; bl, ftd 1,500.00
Grape & Cable (Northwood), sweetmeat, marigold, w/lid 1,900.00
Grape & Cable VT (Northwood), bowl, bl, 6"-8", ea 145.00
Grape & Cherry, bowl, marigold, rare, 8½" 100.00
Grape & Gothic Arches (Northwood), pitcher, marigold 325.00
Grape Leaves (Millersburg), bowl, gr, rare, 9" 900.00
Grape Wreath (Millersburg), bowl, bl, 7½"-9", ea 800.00
Grape Wreath/Multi-Star VT (Millersburg), bowl, gr, 9" 90.00
Grapevine Lattice (Dugan), plate, marigold, 6½"-7½", ea 145.00
Greek Key (Northwood), plate, bl, rare, 9"-11", ea 2,500.00
Greek Key & Scales (Northwood), bowl, marigold, ftd 75.00
Hammered Bell Chandelier, shade, wht 75.00
Harvest Flower (Dugan), pitcher, marigold, rare 2,800.00
Harvest Poppy, compote, amethyst or bl 450.00
Hattie (Imperial), plate, marigold, rare 1,325.00
Headdress, bowl, gr or bl, 9"-10", ea 60.00
Heart & Vine (Fenton), bowl, gr, 8½" 75.00
Hearts & Flowers (Northwood), compote, aqua opal 700.00
Heavy Diamond (Imperial), creamer, marigold 30.00
Heavy Grape (Imperial), bowl, gr, 9"-10", ea 165.00
Heavy Hobnail (Fenton), vase, wht, rare 475.00
Heavy Pineapple (Fenton), bowl, bl, flat or ftd, rare, 10", ea .1,300.00
Heisey Colonial, compote, marigold 80.00
Heron (Dugan), mug, amethyst, rare 425.00
Hex Base, candlesticks, smoke pastel, pr 175.00
Hobnail (Millersburg), pitcher, marigold, rare 3,000.00
Hobnail & Cane (Crystal), compote, amethyst 165.00
Hobnail Soda Gold (Imperial), spittoon, amber pastel, lg 125.00
Hobstar (Imperial), butter dish, amethyst 195.00
Hobstar & Arches (Imperial), bowl, gr, 9" 60.00
Hobstar & Cut Triangles (English), bowl, gr 60.00
Hobstar & Feather (Millersburg), creamer, amethyst or gr, rare .700.00
Hobstar & File, pitcher, marigold, rare 1,700.00
Hobstar & Tassels (Imperial), bowl, teal, scarce, 7"-8", ea 350.00
Hobstar Flower (Imperial), cruet, marigold, rare 400.00
Holiday (Northwood), tray, marigold, scarce, 11" 225.00

Holly (Fenton), plate, red, 9" 3,500.00
Holly Wreath VT (Millersburg), bowl, gr, 8½ " 300.00
Honeycomb & Clover (Fenton), bonbon, bl 40.00
Honeycomb Panels, tumbler, amethyst 175.00
Horse's Head (Horse Medallion) (Fenton), bowl, bl, flat, 7½ " .210.00
Horseshoe, shot glass, marigold 35.00
Hyacinth, lamp, marigold 1,900.00
Illusion (Fenton), bonbon, bl 85.00
Imperial #499 (Imperial), sherbet, red 95.00
Imperial Daisy, shade, marigold 45.00
Imperial Jewels (Imperial), bowl, bl, 4"-6", ea 55.00
Intaglio Ovals (US Glass), bowl, pastel marigold, 7" 75.00
Intaglio Stars, tumbler, marigold, rare 600.00
Interior Swirl, spittoon, bl 140.00
Inverted Prisms (English), creamer, marigold 70.00
Inverted Strawberry (Cambridge), bowl, bl, 9"-10½ ", ea 375.00
Inverted Strawberry (Cambridge), butter dish, amethyst, w/lid ..1,100.00
Inverted Thistle (Cambridge), creamer, marigold, rare 350.00
Iris (Fenton), goblet, buttermilk; amber pastel 80.00
Jack-In-The-Pulpit (Northwood), vase, bl 275.00
Jacobean Ranger (Czech & English), tumbler, juice; marigold ..125.00
Jasmine & Butterfly (Czech), decanter, marigold 100.00
Jeannette's Colonial, bowl, rose; marigold, 5½ " 30.00
Jester's Cap (Westmoreland), vase, peach opal 200.00
Jewels (Dugan), candlesticks, red, pr 275.00
Keg, toothpick holder, gr 25.00
Kitten, paperweight, marigold, rare, mini 250.00
Kittens (Fenton), bowl, bl, 2 sides up, scarce 375.00
Kittens (Fenton), toothpick holder, vaseline pastel, scarce, 3" ..500.00
Kokomo (English), bowl, rose; gr, ftd 60.00
Kookaburra & VTs (Australian), bowl, marigold, 9" 325.00
Large Kangaroo (Australian), bowl, amethyst, 5" 75.00
Late Sunflower (Jeannette), pitcher, milk; marigold 35.00
Lattice (Crystal), bowl, amethyst, 7"-8", ea 145.00
Lattice & Grape (Fenton), pitcher, bl 400.00
Laurel Leaves (Imperial), plate, smoke pastel 65.00
Leaf & Beads (Northwood), bowl, rose; bl, ftd 210.00
Leaf Chain (Fenton), bonbon, amethyst 55.00
Leaf Rays (Dugan), nappy, marigold, spade shape 30.00
Leaf Tiers (Fenton), banana bowl whimsey, marigold 200.00
Leaf Tiers (Fenton), tumbler, bl, ftd, rare 265.00
Lily of the Valley (Fenton), tumbler, bl, rare 275.00
Lined Lattice VT (Dugan), vase, peach opal, 9"-16", ea 250.00
Little Daisies (Fenton), bowl, bl, 8"-9½ ", rare, ea 1,400.00
Little Flowers (Fenton), bowl, amethyst, 9½ " 135.00

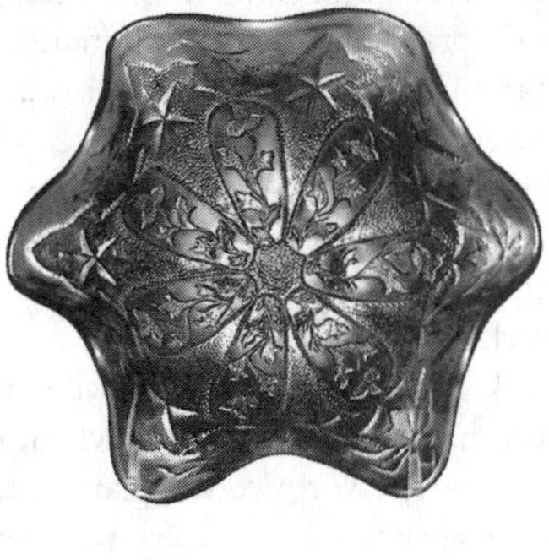

Little Stars (Millersburg), bowl, blue, 7", $3,000.00. (Photo courtesy Bill Edwards)

Long Buttress, pitcher, marigold 400.00
Long Leaf (Dugan), bowl, peach opal, ftd 175.00
Lotus & Grape (Fenton), bonbon, marigold 40.00
Louisa (Westmoreland), bowl, aqua pastel, ftd 65.00
Louisa (Westmoreland), bowl, rose; gr 65.00
Lovely (Northwood), bowl, amethyst, ftd 900.00
Lustre, tumbler, marigold 45.00
Lustre & Clear (Fenton), vase, fan; bl 55.00
Lustre & Clear (Imperial), creamer or sugar bowl, amethyst, ea ..65.00
Lustre Flute (Northwood), cup, punch; marigold or gr 20.00
Lustre Rose (Imperial), bowl, centerpc; marigold, ftd 100.00
Lustre Rose (Imperial), tumbler, marigold 20.00
Mae West (Dugan), candlestick, Celeste Bl 150.00
Malaga (Dugan), bowl, marigold, scarce, 9" 75.00
Many Fruits (Dugan), cup, punch; bl 125.00
Many Stars (Millersburg), bowl, bl, ruffled, scarce, 9" 2,700.00
Maple Leaf (Dugan), pitcher, bl 350.00
Marilyn (Millersburg), pitcher, amethyst, rare 1,000.00
Mary Gregory, bottle, cologne; marigold, rare 175.00
Melon Rib, shakers, marigold, pr 35.00
Memphis (Northwood), bowl, fruit; bl, w/base 2,400.00
Mikado (Fenton), compote, red, lg 7,000.00
Miniature Hobnail, pitcher, marigold, rare, 6" 250.00
Miniature Shell, candle holder, clear, ea 75.00
Mitered Block & Pleats (English), bowl, marigold, 4½ " 25.00
Mitered Ovals (Millersburg), vase, bl, rare 8,000.00
Moongleam (Heisey), tumbler, gr, rare 30.00
Moonprint (Brockwitz), decanter, marigold, w/stopper 250.00
Morning Glory (Imperial), vase, funeral; gr, 16"-22", ea 350.00
Multi-Fruits & Flowers (Millersburg), cup, punch; gr, rare 100.00
Mystic (Cambridge), vase, marigold, ftd, rare 175.00
Nautilus (Dugan-Northwood), creamer, peach opal, rare 175.00
Near-Cut (Northwood), compote, gr 200.00
Nesting Swan (Millersburg), bowl, gr, sq, rare 1,000.00
Night Stars (Millersburg), bonbon, marigold, rare 700.00
Nippon (Northwood), plate, gr, scarce, 9" 800.00
Northern Star (Fenton), plate, marigold, rare, 6½ " 100.00
Nu-Art (Chrysanthemum) (Imperial), plate, amber, rare 1,650.00
Number 270 (Westmoreland), compote, marigold milk glass 100.00
Octagon (Imperial), bowl, amethyst, 8½ " 150.00
Octagon (Imperial), toothpick holder, amethyst, rare 475.00
Ohio Star (Millersburg), vase, wht, rare 5,000.00
Olympic (Millersburg), compote, amethyst, sm, rare 4,800.00
Omera (Imperial), plate, marigold, 8" 50.00
Omnibus, tumbler, bl, rare 550.00
Open Edge Basket (Basketweave) (Fenton), vase whismey, gr, rare .1,200.00
Open Flower (Dugan), bowl, peach opal, flat or ftd, 7" 85.00
Open Rose (Imperial), bowl, rose; gr 125.00
Optic Block, plate, marigold 60.00
Orange Tree (Fenton), bowl, bl, ftd, 5½ " 45.00
Orange Tree (Fenton), bowl, marigold, ftd, 9"-11", ea 100.00
Orange Tree (Fenton), cruet whimsey, bl, rare 2,800.00
Orange Tree (Fenton), cup, punch; gr 50.00
Orange Tree & Scroll (Fenton), pitcher, bl 900.00
Oriental Poppy (Northwood), pitcher, amethyst 750.00
Oval & Round (Imperial), bowl, rose; marigold, rare, lg 175.00
Oxford, mustard pot, marigold, w/lid 75.00
Painted Pansy, vase, fan; marigold 50.00
Palm Beach (US Glass), plate, marigold, rare, 9" 225.00
Panama (US Glass), spittoon, marigold 750.00
Paneled Holly (Northwood), spooner, marigold 55.00
Paneled Tree Trunk (Dugan), vase, gr, rare, 7-12", ea 500.00
Pansy (Imperial), pickle dish, bl, oval 275.00
Panther (Fenton), bowl, bl, ftd, 5" 125.00
Panther (Fenton), bowl, red, ftd, 5" 800.00
Parlor Panels (Imperial), vase, bl, 4"-14", ea 900.00
Peach (Northwood), pitcher, bl 1,300.00
Peach (Northwood), tumbler, marigold 2,000.00
Peacock (Millersburg), bowl, gr, 5" 250.00

Peacock & Grape (Fenton), bowl, red, flat, 8"-9" 1,500.00
Peacock & Urn (Fenton), bowl, bl, 8½ " 225.00
Peacock & Urn (Northwood), bowl, ice cream; bl, 10" 1,200.00
Peacock & Urn & VTS (Millersburg), bowl, amethyst, 9½ " 400.00
Peacock at the Fountain (Northwood), compote, aqua opal, scarce .4,200.00
Peacock Tail (Fenton), compote, bl 50.00
Pearly Dots (Westmoreland), compote, peach opal 150.00
Persian Garden (Dugan), bowl, berry; marigold, 5" 50.00
Persian Garden (Dugan), plate, chop; peach opal, scarce, 13" ..6,000.00
Persian Medallion (Fenton), bowl, gr, 10" 425.00
Persian Medallion (Fenton), plate, bl, 9½ " 1,000.00
Petal & Fan (Dugan), bowl, amethyst, 5" 60.00
Petals & Prisms (English), sugar bowl, marigold, open 65.00
Pillar & Drape, shade, red 625.00
Pinched Swirl (Dugan), bowl, rose; peach opal 135.00
Pine Cone (Fenton), bowl, bl, 6" 65.00
Pineapple (English), bowl, marigold, 7" 60.00
Plaid (Fenton), bowl, marigold, 8¾" 125.00
Plain Jane (Imperial), basket, amethyst 125.00
Plain Rays, compote, amethyst 55.00
Plume Panels (Fenton), vase, red, 7"-12", ea 1,100.00
Poinsettia (Imperial), pitcher, milk; marigold 150.00
Pond Lily (Fenton), bonbon, amethyst or gr 125.00
Poppy (Northwood), pickle dish, aqua opal, oval 1,000.00
Poppy & Fish Net (Imperial), vase, red, rare, 6" 750.00
Poppy Show (Northwood), bowl, bl, 8½ " 1,700.00
Portland (US Glass), toothpick holder, marigold 140.00
Powder Horn (Cambridge), candy holder, marigold 200.00
Premium (Imperial), candlesticks, red, pr 425.00
Primrose (Millersburg), bowl, bl, ruffled, 8¾" 4,500.00
Primrose & Ribbon, shade, marigold 90.00
Prism & Cane (English), bowl, marigold, rare, 5" 45.00
Propeller (Imperial), compote, gr 125.00
Pulled Loop (Dugan), vase, peach opal, 8"-16", ea 65.00
Puzzle (Dugan), compote, wht 125.00
Question Marks (Dugan), cake plate, amethyst, stemmed, rare .275.00
Quill (Dugan), tumbler, marigold, rare 165.00
Ragged Robin (Fenton), bowl, amethyst or gr, scarce, 8¾" 175.00
Rainbow (Northwood), bowl, gr, 8" 75.00
Raindrops (Dugan), bowl, banana; amethyst, 9¾" 150.00
Rambler Rose (Dugan), pitcher, marigold 160.00
Rays (Dugan), bowl, peach opal, 5" 70.00
Rays & Ribbon (Millersburg), bowl, amethyst, sq, scarce 1,000.00
Red Panels (Imperial), shade, red 225.00
Regal Iris (Consolidated), lamp, gone w/the wind; marigold ..3,750.00
Rib & Panel, vase, bl 300.00
Ribbed Holly (Fenton), compote, amethyst 125.00
Ribbon Tie (Fenton), bowl, marigold, 8¼" 100.00
Ribs (Czechoslovakia), bottle, perfume; marigold 110.00
Ripple (Imperial), vase, amethyst, squat, 4"-7", ea 125.00
Rising Sun (US Glass), tumbler, marigold, rare 200.00
Rococo (Imperial), bowl, gr or smoke pastel, 5" 150.00
Roll, tumbler, marigold, scarce 40.00
Rood's Chocolates (Fenton), plate, advertising; amethyst 1,750.00
Rosalind (Millersburg), compote, jelly; gr, rare, 9" 4,000.00
Rose, bottle, wht 125.00
Rose Garden (Sweden & Germany), bowl, rose; marigold, rare, sm ..1,600.00
Rose Show (Northwood), plate, gr, 9½ " 8,000.00
Rose Tree (Fenton), bowl, bl, rare, 10" 3,300.00
Round-Up (Dugan), bowl, amethyst, 8¾" 375.00
Royal Swans (Sowery), vase, marigold, rare 1,500.00
Rustic (Fenton), vase, red, 10"-14", ea 4,300.00
S-Band (aka Broken Chain) (Crystal), bowl, marigold 70.00
Sailboats (Fenton), bowl, gr, 6" 125.00
Scales (Westmoreland), bonbon, bl opal 200.00
Scottie, paperweight, marigold, rare 200.00
Scroll Embossed (Imperial), bowl, amethyst, 4"-7", ea 65.00
Scroll Embossed VT (English), plate, marigold, 7" 165.00
Seacoast (Millersburg), tray, pin; amethyst, rare 900.00
Seaweed, lamp, marigold, 2 szs, ea 250.00
Seaweed (Millersburg), plate, amethyst or gr, rare, 10" 2,500.00
Shanghai (China), tumbler, marigold 50.00

Shell (Imperial), bowl, marigold, 7 – 9", $45.00 each. (Photo courtesy Bill Edwards)

Shell (Imperial), plate, amethyst, 8½ " 1,000.00
Shrine (US Glass), champagne, clear 200.00
Singing Birds (Northwood), bowl, bl, 5" 110.00
Singing Birds (Northwood), mug, marigold, stippled 200.00
Single Flower (Dugan), bowl, banana; peach opal, rare, 9½ " ...375.00
Single Flower (Dugan), hat, gr 65.00
Ski Star (Dugan), bowl, gr, 5" 80.00
Small Blackberry (Northwood), compote, marigold 55.00
Small Rib (Fenton), compote, bl, 4½ " 55.00
Smooth Panels (Imperial), vase, gr, standard shape, 8"-14", ea ..175.00
Smooth Rays (Westmoreland), bowl, bl opal, flat, 6"-9", ea 125.00
Snow Fancy (Imperial), bowl, gr, 5" 60.00
Soda Gold (Imperial), bowl, marigold, 9" 45.00
Soutache (Dugan), lamp, marigold, complete, scarce 350.00
Souvenir Vase (US Glass), vase, peach opal, rare, 6½ " 150.00
Sowerby Wide Panel (Sowerby), bowl, marigold 45.00
Spiderweb (Northwood-Dugan), vase, smoke pastel, 8" 80.00
Springtime (Northwood), bowl, gr, 5" 80.00
Stag & Holly (Fenton), bowl, marigold, ball ft, 9"-13", ea 175.00
Stag & Holly (Fenton), bowl, rose; gr, ftd, scarce 4,600.00
Star (English), bowl, marigold, 8" 50.00
Star & File (Imperial), bowl, marigold, hdld 35.00
Star Fish (Dugan), bonbon, peach opal, hdld, rare 165.00
Star Medallion (Imperial), bowl, smoke pastel, 7"-9", ea 40.00
Star Medallion (Imperial), tumbler, gr, 2 szs, ea 50.00
Star of David (Imperial), bowl, marigold, rnd, rare, 7½ " 300.00
Star of David & Bows (Northwood), bowl, gr, 8½ " 125.00
Star Spray (Imperial), bowl, marigold, 7" 35.00
Starbright, vase, amethyst, 6½ " 45.00
Starburst Lustre (Northwood), bowl, gr 60.00
Stippled Estate (Westmoreland), vase, marigold, 3" 125.00
Stippled Petals (Dugan), bowl, peach opal, 9" 80.00
Stippled Rays (Fenton), bowl, gr, 5"-10", ea 55.00
Stork (Jenkins), vase, wht 90.00
Stork & Rushes (Dugan), bowl, punch; bl, w/base, rare 350.00
Strawberry (Millersburg), bowl, gr, scarce, 8"-10", ea 300.00
Strawberry (Northwood), plate, marigold, stippled, 9" 1,750.00
Strawberry Scroll (Fenton), tumbler, marigold, rare 160.00
Stretched Diamond (Northwood), tumbler, marigold, rare 175.00
Strutting Peacock (Westmoreland), creamer, amethyst or gr 100.00
Summer Days (Dugan), vase, bl, 6" 125.00
Sunflower (Northwood), bowl, gr, 8½ " 165.00
Sungold, epergne, amber pastel 450.00
Sunray, compote, peach opal 60.00

Swirl VT (Imperial), glass juice; marigold 40.00
Swirled Ribs (Northwood), tumbler, amethyst 75.00
Sydney (Fostoria), tumbler, marigold, rare 700.00
Taffeta Lustre (Fostoria), bowl, console; bl, rare, 11" 175.00
Thin & Wide Rib (Northwood), vase, bl, ruffled 115.00
Thin Rib & Drape, vase, gr, 4"-11", ea 200.00
Thistle (Fenton), plate, amethyst, rare, 9" 4,100.00
Thistle Banana Boat (Fenton), banana boat, bl, ftd, scarce 425.00
Threads (Crystal), compote, amethyst 145.00
Three Fruits VT, plate, marigold, 12-sided 150.00
Three Row (Imperial), vase, amethyst, rare 2,900.00
Three-in-One (Imperial), bowl, gr, 8¾" 40.00
Thunderbird (Australian), bowl, marigold, 9½" 350.00
Tiger Lily (Imperial), pitcher, gr 300.00
Tiny Hobnail, lamp, marigold 110.00
Top Hat, vase, wht 50.00
Tornado VT (Northwood), vase, marigold, rare 1,700.00
Tree Bark VT, tumbler, marigold 20.00
Tree of Life, tumbler, juice; marigold, rare 75.00
Tree Trunk (Northwood), vase, funeral; gr, 12-22", ea 4,500.00
Triplets (Dugan), bowl, peach opal, 6"-8", ea 75.00
Tulip (Millersburg), compote, marigold, rare, 9" 750.00
Tulip Scroll (Millersburg), vase, gr, rare, 6"-12", ea 400.00
Twelve Rings, candlestick, marigold 45.00
Twitch (Bartlett-Collins), creamer, marigold 30.00
Two Flowers (Fenton), plate, marigold, ftd, 9" 1,100.00
Two Fruits (Fenton), bowl, marigold, divided, scarce, 5½" 55.00
Two Row (Imperial), vase, amethyst, rare 1,150.00
Venetian, butter dish, marigold, rare 950.00
Vineyard (Dugan), pitcher, peach opal 1,300.00
Vintage (Fenton), bowl, gr or bl, 4½" 40.00
Vintage (Fenton), cup, punch; marigold 25.00
Vintage (Fenton), plate, gr, 8" 450.00
Vintage (Millersburg), bowl, marigold, rare, 9" 625.00
Vintage Banded (Dugan), tumbler, marigold, rare 600.00
Vintage VT (Dugan), bowl, amethyst, ftd, 8½" 175.00
Virginia Blackberry (US Glass), pitcher, bl, rare, sm 950.00
Waffle Block (Imperial), basket, powder bl, hdld, 10" 150.00
Waffle Block (Imperial), spittoon, marigold, scarce 75.00
War Dance (English), compote, marigold, 5" 120.00
Water Lily & Cattails (Fenton), pitcher, bl 5,500.00
Water Lily & Cattails (Northwood), tumbler, bl 700.00
Western Thistle, tumbler, bl, rare 200.00
Wheels (Imperial), bowl, marigold, 8"-9" 50.00
Whirling Leaves (Millersburg), bowl, gr, tri-cornered, 10" 550.00
White Elephant, ornament, wht, rare 350.00
Wide Panel (Fenton), vase, gr, 7"-9", ea 50.00
Wide Panel (Millersburg), bowl, marigold, scarce, 9" 95.00
Wide Rib (Northwood), vase, funeral; marigold, 15"-22", ea 300.00
Wild Blackberry (Fenton), bowl, gr, scarce, 8½" 225.00
Wild Loganberry (Westmoreland), goblet, peach opal 150.00
Wild Rose (Northwood), bowl, horehound, ftd, open edge, 6" 300.00
Wild Strawberry (Northwood), bowl, bl, rare, 6" 225.00
Windmill (Imperial), bowl, amethyst or gr, 5" 25.00
Windmill (Imperial), pickle dish, amethyst 200.00
Wine & Roses (Fenton), pitcher, cider; marigold, scarce 675.00
Wishbone (Northwood), plate, marigold, flat, rare, 10" 2,000.00
Wishbone & Spades (Dugan), bowl, amethyst, 5" 250.00
Woodlands, vase, marigold, rare, 5" 225.00
Wreath of Roses (Dugan), rose bowl whimsey, marigold 100.00
Wreath of Roses (Fenton), bowl, punch; peach opal, w/base 2,200.00
Wreathed Cherry (Dugan), bowl, bl, oval, 5" 125.00
Zig Zag (Millersburg), bowl, gr, rnd or ruffled, 9½" 425.00
Zip Zip (English), flower frog holder, marigold 60.00
Zippered Heart (Imperial), bowl, amethyst, 9" 110.00

Carousel Figures

For generations of Americans, visions of carousel horses revolving majestically around lively band organs rekindle wonderful childhood experiences. These nostalgic memories are the legacy of the creative talent from a dozen carving shops that created America's carousel art. Skilled craftsmen brought their trade from Europe where American carvers took the carousel animal from a folk art creation to a true art form. The 'golden age of carousel art' lasted from 1880 to 1929.

There are two basic types of American carousels. The largest and most impressive is the 'park style' carousel built for permanent installation in major amusement centers. These were created in Philadelphia by Gustav and William Dentzel, Muller Brothers, and E. Joy Morris who became the Philadelphia Toboggan Company in 1902. A more flamboyant group of carousel animals was carved in Coney Island, New York, by Charles Looff, Marcus Illions, Charles Carmel, and Stein & Goldstein's Artistic Carousel Company. These park-style carousels were typically three, four, and even five rows with forty-five to sixty-eight animals on a platform. Collectors often pay a premium for the carvings by these men. The outside row animals are larger and more ornate and command higher prices. The horses on the inside rows are smaller, less decorated and of lesser value.

The most popular style of carousel art is the 'country fair style.' These carousels were portable affairs created for mobility. The horses are smaller and less ornate with leg and head positions that allow for stacking and easy loading. These were built primarily for North Tonawanda, New York, near Niagara Falls, by Armitage Herschell Company, Herschell Spillman Company, Spillman Engineering Company, and Allen Herschell. Charles W. Parker was also well known for his portable merry-go-rounds. He was based in Leavenworth, Kansas. Parker and Herschell Spillman both created a few large park-style carousels as well, but they are better known for their portable models.

Horses are by far the most common figure found, but there are two dozen other animals that were created for the carousel platform. Carousel animals, unlike most other antiques, are oftentimes worth more in a restored condition. Figures found with original factory paint are extraordinarily rare and bring premium amounts. Typically, carousel horses are found in garish, poorly applied 'park paint' and are often missing legs or ears. Carousel horses are hollow. They were glued up from several blocks for greater strength and lighter weight. Bass and poplar woods were used extensively.

If you have an antique carousel animal you would like to have identified, send a clear photograph and description along with a LSASE to our advisor, William Manns, who is listed in the Directory under New Mexico. Mr. Manns is the author of *Painted Ponies*, containing many full-color photographs, guides, charts, and directories for the collector.

Key:
IR — inside row
MR — middle row
OR — outside row
PTC — Philadelphia Toboggan Company

Coney Island-Style Horses

Carmel, IR jumper, unrstr 4,800.00
Carmel, MR jumper, unrstr 8,500.00
Carmel, OR jumper w/cherub, rstr 26,500.00
Illions, IR jumper, rstr 5,200.00
Illions, MR stander, rstr 9,200.00
Looff, IR jumper unrstr 3,200.00
Looff, OR jumper, unrstr 17,000.00

Stein & Goldstein, IR jumper, unrstr 4,700.00
Stein & Goldstein, MR jumper, rstr 9,000.00
Stein & Goldstein, OR stander w/bells, unrstr 29,000.00

European Horses

Anderson, English, unrstr 3,500.00
Bayol, French, unrstr 3,000.00
Heyn, German, unrstr 3,500.00
Hubner, Belgian, unrstr 2,800.00
Savage, English, unrstr 2,900.00

Menagerie Animals (Non-Horses)

Dentzel, bear, unrstr 28,000.00
Dentzel, cat, unrstr 37,000.00
Dentzel, deer, unrstr 13,500.00
Dentzel, lion, unrstr 45,000.00
Dentzel, pig, unrstr 9,000.00
E Joy Morris, deer, unrstr 10,000.00
Herschell Spillman, cat, unrstr 12,500.00
Herschell Spillman, chicken, portable, unrstr 7,000.00
Herschell Spillman, dog, portable, unrstr 6,500.00
Herschell Spillman, frog, unrstr 20,000.00
Looff, camel, unrstr 10,000.00
Looff, goat, rstr 15,000.00
Muller, tiger, rstr 32,000.00

Philadelphia-Style Horses

Dentzel, IR 'topknot' jumper, unrstr 5,500.00
Dentzel, MR jumper, unrstr 12,700.00
Dentzel, OR stander, female cvg on shoulder, rstr 32,500.00
Dentzel, prancer, rstr 9,500.00
Morris, IR prancer, rstr 7,000.00
Morris, MR stander, unrstr 9,500.00
Morris, OR stander, rstr 16,000.00
Muller, IR jumper, rstr 5,700.00
Muller, MR jumper, rstr 12,000.00
Muller, OR stander, rstr 42,000.00
Muller, OR stander w/military trappings 75,000.00
PTC, chariot (bench-like seat), rstr 8,900.00
PTC, IR jumper, rstr 4,000.00
PTC, MR jumper, rstr 12,800.00
PTC, OR stander, armored, rstr 52,000.00
PTC, OR stander, unrstr 29,500.00

Portable Carousel Horses

Allan Herschell, all aluminum, ca 1950 ....500.00
Allan Herschell, half & half, wood & aluminum head 1,500.00
Allan Herschell, IR Indian pony, unrstr 2,500.00
Allan Herschell, OR, rstr 3,200.00
Allan Herschell, OR Trojan-style jumper 3,800.00
Armitage Herschell, track-machine jumper 2,800.00
Dare, jumper, unrstr 3,000.00
Herschell Spillman, chariot (bench-like seat) 3,800.00
Herschell Spillman, IR jumper, unrstr 2,400.00
Herschell Spillman, MR jumper, unrstr 2,900.00
Herschell Spillman, OR, eagle decor 4,500.00
Herschell Spillman, OR, park machine 10,000.00
Parker, MR jumper, unrstr 4,200.00
Parker, OR jumper, park machine, unrstr 7,500.00
Parker, OR jumper, rstr 5,800.00

Carpet Balls

Carpet balls are glazed china spheres decorated with intersecting lines or other simple designs that were used for indoor games in the British Isles during the early 1800s. Mint condition examples are rare.

Bl w/wht sponge, NM+ 160.00
Brn w/wht sponge or stripes, NM 90.00
Red w/wht sponge, EX 80.00
Wht w/blk or brn sponge or stripes, EX/EX+ 85.00
Wht w/gr & blk stripes, EX+ 110.00
Wht w/red or yel stripes, NM+ 115.00
Wht w/red stripes, EX+ 85.00

Cartoon Art

Collectors of cartoon art are interested in many forms of original art — animation cels, sports, political or editorial cartoons, syndicated comic strip panels, and caricature. To produce even a short animated cartoon strip, hundreds of original drawings are required, each showing the characters in slightly advancing positions. Called 'cels' because those made prior to the 1950s were made from a celluloid material, collectors often pay hundreds of dollars for a frame from a favorite movie. Prices of Disney cels with backgrounds vary widely. Background paintings, model sheets, storyboards, and preliminary sketches are also collectible — so are comic book drawings executed in India ink and signed by the artist. Daily 'funnies' originals, especially the earlier ones portraying super heroes, and Sunday comic strips, the early as well as the later ones, are collected. Cartoon art has become recognized and valued as a novel yet valid form of contemporary art. In the listings below all cells are gouache on celluloid unless noted otherwise.

Key:
WB — Warner Brothers
WD — Walt Disney Productions

Animation Cel, Full Color

Partridge Family, original animation cel from cartoon, with framed holder, $80.00. (Photo courtsey American Pie Collectibles)

Bugs Bunny & Friends, in marching band, WB seal, 9x7" 85.00
Dudley Doright, w/Horse & Nell, w/HP bkground, Jay Ward, 8x10" ..340.00
Goofy & nephew of Donald Duck, WDP, 1980, overall in fr: 17x14" .160.00
Lion King, Hakuna Matata w/friends, 12x10" 100.00
Snow White & 7 Dwarfs, Huntsman, WD, ca 1937, 5½x5½ " .1,095.00
Steel & America, Donald Duck w/rope, WD, in fr 1,000.00
Tom (cat) running, MGM, 1963, 11x36", VG 150.00
Ugly Duckling, stepping out of egg, WD, 6½ x6½ " 1,035.00
Woody Woodpecker, W Lantz Studio, golfing scene, 1991, 17x21" ...115.00

Miscellaneous

Comic strip, BC, 12-panel, inscr by Johnny Hart, 1992, 16x11"+fr .115.00
Sericel, Beauty & Beast on staircase, Disney seal, 13x10"+fr 140.00

Cartoon Books

'Books of cartoons' were printed during the first decade of the twentieth century and remained popular until the advent of the modern comic book in the late '30s. Cartoon books, printed in both color and black and white, were merely reprints of current newspaper comic strips. The books, ranging from thirty to seventy pages and in sizes from 3½" x 8" up to 11" x 17", were usually bound with cardboard covers and were often distributed as premiums in exchange for coupons saved from the daily paper. One of the largest of the companies who printed these books was Cupples and Leon, producer of nearly half of the two hundred titles on record. Among the most popular sellers were *Mutt and Jeff*, *Bringing Up Father*, and *Little Orphan Annie*.

Mutt and Jeff, #6, Bud Fisher, 1919, VG, $75.00; Charlie McCarthy, '...So Help Me, Mr. Bergen,' 1938, EX, $60.00.

Bringing Up Father, #4, Cupples & Leon, EX+ 105.00
Bugs Bunny, 50 Years & Only 1 Gray Hair, Freleng & Jones, 11x9" .25.00
Buster Brown, F Stokes, 1902-03, 25-pg, 16x11", EX 145.00
Buster Brown, Happy Days, Cupples & Leon, 1911, 20-pg, 16x11", VG .40.00
Felix the Cat, McLoughlin, 1926, 10¼x9½ ", EX 135.00
Felix the Cat, McLoughlin, 1931, EX 200.00
Little Orphan Annie Never Say Die, Cupples & Leon, VG 45.00
Tillie the Toiler, #4, Cupples & Leon, EX 65.00

Cash Registers

From 1884 until 1916, the National Cash Register Company dominated the field with a massive over-choice of styles and functions. Before the termination of the 'antique styles,' 1,600,000 registers had been built. An inexpensive, painted-on woodgrain patterned steel cabinet replaced the ornate plates, though the mechanisms remained unchanged. Serial numbers were consecutive, making dating simple. Many registers were chopped up for brass shell casings in the two world wars, and as a result, those that remained became more attractive to collectors. Of the NCRs, scholars speculate that about half of them survive. Add to that the many other existing brands, and it is estimated that there are nearly two million registers to discover.

Register values are fixed by a machine's scarcity and charm, including add-on fixtures such as brass or glass topsigns, clocks, and personalized nameplates. National used eight designs on metal registers and four on inlaid wood machines.

The condition code of registers in this column is quite simple: Good (G), Very Good (VG), and Mint (M), restored by a professional. About 20% variation in prices can be attributed to geography and buyer/seller differences.

Internet web pages have jumped into the pricing fray, sometimes creating a carnival-like frenzy when prices aren't fixed. *Schroeder's* will provide a standard but also be mindful of permanent changes generated by the Internet.

An excellent book on cash registers is *Antique Cash Registers, 1880–1920*, by Bartsch and Sanchez (Mr. Bartsch's address may be found in our Directory under Oregon).

Dial, emb brass, emb pattern on drw, 25", EX 6,500.00
Monitor #1A, wood w/CI Amount of Sale sign, ca 1900, 9x13x14" ...415.00
NCR #1, Am detail adder, VG 2,650.00
NCR #2 or #3, inlaid oak or mahog, scarce 2,250.00
NCR #3, mahog inlay, deep wood drw, ca 1886, VG 4,500.00
NCR #5, narrow scroll, glass topsign, M 2,750.00
NCR #7 or #8, detail adder, fleur-de-lis, VG 850.00
NCR #13 or #14, Ionic CI, 1899, G 750.00
NCR #30, bronze, total adder, 13 keys, VG 2,000.00
NCR #33, 1903, VG 900.00
NCR #47, oak w/mahog inlay, up to $6, VG 2,250.00
NCR #50, Renaissance design, orig clock, M 2,500.00
NCR #52, Renaissance design, orig clock, extended base, VG .2,900.00
NCR #52 or #52¼, Renaissance design, extended base, no clock, VG 2,500.00
NCR #64, Bohemian pattern, iron, 25-key, 1901, VG 600.00
NCR #78, custom built to eliminate bk window, NP, 1902, VG ..950.00
NCR #129-130, bronze, VG 950.00
NCR #130, Art Nouveau cabinet, M 1,600.00
NCR #135, Art Nouveau pattern, CI, 31-key, 1905, VG 600.00
NCR #215 or #216, bronze fleur-de-lis, VG 1,200.00
NCR #226, rare bilingual topsign, VG 900.00
NCR #250 or #251, bronze, VG 1,200.00
NCR #312, #313, or #317, dolphin pattern, VG 800.00
NCR #322, #323, or #327, marble 3 sides, extended base, M .2,500.00
NCR #322, #323, or #327, marble 3 sides, extended base, VG .1,500.00
NCR #324, VG 700.00
NCR #332, #333 or #349, orig topsign, M 1,150.00
NCR #332, #333 or #349, orig topsign, VG 550.00
NCR #336, brass, M 950.00
NCR #337, dolphin design, M 950.00
NCR #338, dogwood pattern, English numerals, CA, 1910-16, VG .475.00
NCR #360, 37 keys, rings to $60, 1908-09, M 1,500.00
NCR #441, #442, Empire design w/quartered-oak base, M 1,750.00
NCR #441, Empire pattern, M 1,750.00
NCR #441E, electric, VG 1,250.00
NCR #442E-L, EX orig 1,800.00
NCR #452E, electric, M 2,000.00
NCR #522, 2-drw, electric bar model, 1910-16, M 2,500.00
NCR #522, 2-drw, electric bar model, 1910-16, VG 1,800.00
NCR #711-#717, mahog-grain finish on steel, M 275.00
NCR #1054, glass automatic w/box attachment, 1910-16, M .1,200.00

Cast Iron

In the mid-1800s, the cast-iron industry was raging in the United States. It was recognized as a medium extremely adaptable for uses ranging from ornamental architectural filigree to actual building construction. It could be cast from a mold into any conceivable design that could be reproduced over and over at a relatively small cost. It could be painted to give an entirely versatile appearance. Furniture with openwork designs of grapevines and leaves and intricate lacy scrollwork was cast for gardens as well as inside use. Figural doorstops of every sort, bootjacks, trivets, and a host of other useful and decorative items were made before the 'ferromania' had run its course. See also Kitchen, Cast-Iron Bakers and Kettles; and other specific categories.

Armchair, ferns, old pnt surface, 19th C, VG 300.00
Armchair, ferns, old rpr/silver rpt, Carr label 330.00
Bench, foliage, curved bk, cabriole legs, 1890s, 37" 350.00

Birdhouse, 2-story, old red pnt w/gold trim, Victorian, 13x12x10" .1,750.00
Box, potpourri; worn mc pnt w/transfer portrait, figural finial, 8" .145.00
Fountain, putto on shell, storks/frogs/turtles/etc, 1850s, 84x74" .4,125.00
Fountain, 3-part, shell top, cherub figure support, 82x40" 500.00
Garden seat, vintage, pierced seat, vining legs, 28x38" 300.00
Gate, triple urn finial, classic decor w/medallions, 40x36", pr ...935.00
Griddle, wrought-iron bail hdl, 14¾" dia 110.00
Gypsy kettle, 3 triangle ft, sqd hdl mts on shoulder, 10x10" 85.00
Hitching post, horse's head finial, 1850s 220.00
Hitching post, jockey on plinth, hand out, mc rpt, 37" 550.00
Jardiniere, Am Rococo, foliate swags & shells, late 19th C, 32½ " L ..165.00

Garden planter, rusted patina, $1,565.00. (Photo courtesy Jackson's Auctions)

Planter, acanthus leaves, sq base w/cherubs' heads, 48x36" dia .1,565.00
Planter, urn shape, X-hatch decor, sq base, 26x19"dia, pr 600.00
Settee, ferns, Carr label, worn rpt, 39" 660.00
Settee, vintage, pierced seat, old pnt, 1890s, 33x43x15" 230.00
Stag on rectangular base old worn wht layers, 62" 3,850.00
Stove finial, w/rtcl lid & eagle, 10½ " 100.00
Table, trestle supports ea w/Washington bust, limestone top, 34" ..715.00
Tie rod element, dome shape, 16 swirled-out segments, 6¼x2" ...65.00
Umbrella stand, English sailor on plinth, coiled-rope holder, 28" ..825.00

Castor Sets

Castor sets became popular during the early 1700s and continued to be used through the late Victorian era. Their purpose was to hold various condiments for table use. The most common type was a circular arrangement with a center handle on a revolving pedestal base that held three, four, five, or six bottles. A few were equipped with a bell for calling the servant. Frames were made of silverplate, glass, or pewter. Though most bottles were of pressed glass, some of the designs were cut, and on rare occasion, colored glass with enameled decorations was used as well. To maintain authenticity and value, castor sets should have matching bottles. Prices listed below are for those with matching bottles and in frames with plating that is in excellent condition (unless noted otherwise). Note: Watch for new frames and bottles in clear, cranberry, cobalt, and vaseline Inverted Thumbprint as well as reproductions of Czechoslovakian cut glass bottles. These have recently been appearing on the market. Our advisor for this category is Deborah Maggard; she is listed in the Directory under Ohio.

3-bottle, Am Shield; pewter fr w/eagle, mini, child sz 125.00
3-bottle, Daisy & Button; SP fr w/toothpick holder finial 175.00
3-bottle, Gothic Arch, orig stoppers; pewter fr 115.00
4-bottle, amberina w/eng decor; orig SP fr 1,000.00
4-bottle, Bellflower, single fine; w/pewter fr 400.00
4-bottle, cranberry, orig stoppers; pressed glass holder 400.00
4-bottle, cut; in silver Geo III fr w/scrolling hdls, 1852 ....1,200.00
4-bottle, King's Crown, ruby stain; orig glass stand 350.00
4-bottle, Log & Star, amber; orig ped-base SP fr 275.00
5-bottle, Bellflower, single vine; w/pewter fr 625.00
5-bottle, b3m, GI-24; orig SP fr 70.00
5-bottle, etched amberina, cut amberina stoppers; gilt fr, EX .2,200.00
5-bottle, etched; Japanese-motif SP fr, bird at top 245.00
5-bottle, wreath design w/brite-cut SP fr w/call bell 350.00
6-bottle, Daisy & Button, ornate rstr Wilcox fr revolves 375.00
6-bottle, Honeycomb; ornate Tufts fr, 18", EX 335.00
6-bottle, Sawtooth; ornate Meriden fr, call bell, dtd 1888, EX ..495.00
6-bottle+mustard, etch; T&M Ward SP fr revolves, 18" 1,500.00
6-bottle+2 castors, cut, silver mts; Harris silver fr, 9x11x8" 1,500.00
7-bottle, Chrysanthemum, cut; Gleason ftd fr w/movable doors ..1,750.00
7-bottle, cut crystal; gadrooned/shell border Geo III SP fr 495.00

Catalina Island

Catalina Island pottery was made on the island of the same name, which is about twenty-six miles off the coast of Los Angeles. The pottery was started in 1927 at Pebble Beach, by Wm. Wrigley, Jr., who was instrumental in developing and using the native clays. Its principal products were brick and tile to be used for construction on the island. Garden pieces were first produced, then vases, bookends, lamps, ashtrays, novelty items, and finally dinnerware. The ware became very popular and was soon being shipped to the mainland as well.

Some of the pottery was hand thrown; some was made in molds. Most pieces are marked Catalina Island or Catalina with a printed incised stamp or handwritten with a pointed tool. Cast items were sometimes marked in the mold, a few have an ink stamp, and a paper label was also used. The most favored colors in tableware and accessories are 1) black (rare), 2) Seafoam and Monterey Brown (uncommon), 3) Toyon Red (orange), 4) other brights, and 5) pastels with a matt finish.

The color of the clay can help to identify approximately when a piece was made: 1927 to 1932, brown to red (Island) clay (very popular with collectors, tends to increase values); 1931 to 1932, an experimental period with various colors; 1932 to 1937, mainly white clay, though tan to brown clays were also used on occasion.

Items marked Catalina Pottery are listed in Gladding McBean. For further information we recommend *The Collector's Encyclopedia of California Pottery, Second Edition*, by Jack Chipman (Collector Books).

Dinnerware

Catalina Island, bowl, berry 45.00
Catalina Island, bowl, cereal 75.00
Catalina Island, bowl, fruit; ftd, sq, 13" 180.00
Catalina Island, bowl, vegetable; rnd, 8½ " 145.00
Catalina Island, candle holder, low 95.00
Catalina Island, coffee server, slanted opening, w/lid, rare 300.00
Catalina Island, coffeepot, Deco style, rare 325.00
Catalina Island, compote, ftd, lg 225.00
Catalina Island, cup, coffee/tea 55.00
Catalina Island, cup mug, demi 45.00
Catalina Island, custard cup 50.00
Catalina Island, mug, 6" 55.00
Catalina Island, pitcher, squat base, 9" 250.00
Catalina Island, plate, bread & butter; coupe design, 6" 25.00
Catalina Island, plate, chop; #622, 17½ " 200.00
Catalina Island, plate, dinner; wide rim, 10½ " 75.00
Catalina Island, plate, rolled rim, 12½ " 100.00
Catalina Island, plate, salad; 7" 45.00
Catalina Island, salt cellar 50.00
Catalina Island, saucer, 6½ " 20.00
Catalina Island, sugar bowl, w/lid 80.00

Catalina Island, teapot, traditional English style 275.00
Catalina Island, tumbler, 4" 35.00
Catalina Island, wine cup, hdld 35.00
Rope Edge, casserole, w/lid 95.00
Rope Edge, creamer 40.00
Rope Edge, cup & saucer 50.00
Rope Edge, plate, chop; 13½ " 95.00
Rope Edge, plate, dinner; 10½ " 35.00
Rope Edge, plate, salad; 8½ " 30.00
Rope Edge, sugar bowl 50.00
Rope Edge, teapot 225.00

Miscellaneous

Ashtray, cowboy hat form, Catalina Blue, red clay 195.00
Ashtray, fish form, turq, #551, 5x7" 200.00
Ashtray, goat beside tray, bl, 4", minimum value 375.00
Ashtray, Mexican sleeping, cold pnt on gr matt 325.00
Bookend, monk, Descanso Green, ca 1932, 5x4", minimum value .500.00
Bowl, console; turq, 10¼x12", +pr triple candlesticks 275.00
Bowl, fruit; gr, 3-ftd, 11" 325.00
Bowl, pearly wht, #703 ....125.00
Bowl, Starlight, #710, 13" 100.00
Bowl, yel/gr, oval, fluted, 17" 175.00
Candle/flower holders, #606, pr 150.00
Candlesticks, turq, 5½ ", pr 350.00
Carafe, red, early red clay 200.00
Coaster, plain, bl, red clay 35.00
Match safe, flying fish emblem in relief, rectangular 200.00
Planter, Cat-Lina, turq 250.00
Planter, fish motif, 3½ x3½ " 175.00
Plate, HP Mexican scene, mk, ca 1932, 11½ ", minimum value ..600.00
Vase, bl crystalline, shouldered, trumpet neck, 10½ " 375.00
Vase, bl matt, #601, 7" 200.00
Vase, cafe-au-lait, #618, 8" 225.00
Vase, ivory satin, wht clay, #610, 7½ " 225.00
Vase, oxblood gloss, shouldered, 10½ " 375.00
Vase, red, #322 ....325.00
Vase, stepped body, angle hdls, Monterey Brown, brn clay, mk .375.00
Vase, Toyon Red, hdls, 8x2½ " 350.00
Vase, yel, Deco design w/hdls, red clay, 1927-32, 9x5½ " 375.00
Wall pocket, seashell form, turq, mk 250.00

Catalogs

Catalogs are not only intriguing to collect on their own merit, but for the collector with a specific interest, they are often the only remaining source of background information available, and as such they offer a wealth of otherwise unrecorded data. The mail-order industry can be traced as far back as the mid-1800s. Even before Aaron Montgomery Ward began his career in 1872, Laacke and Joys of Wisconsin and the Orvis Company of Vermont, both dealers in sporting goods, had been well established for many years. The E.C. Allen Company sold household necessities and novelties by mail on a broad scale in the 1870s. By the end of the Civil War, sewing machines, garden seed, musical instruments, even medicine, were available from catalogs. In the 1880s Macy's of New York issued a 127-page catalog; Sears and Spiegel followed suit in about 1890. Craft and art supply catalogs were first available about 1880 and covered such varied fields as china painting, stenciling, wood burning, brass embossing, hair weaving, and shellcraft. Today some collectors confine their interests not only to craft catalogs in general but often to just one subject. There are several factors besides rarity which make a catalog valuable: age, condition, profuse illustrations, how collectible the field is that it deals with, the amount of color used in its printing, its size (format and number of pages), and whether it is a manufacturer's catalog versus a jobber's catalog (the former being the most desirable).

Owl Drug Company Mail Order Catalogue, San Francisco, ca 1910, illustrations, 10x6¾", EX, $400.00 at auction.

AH Luckenbill, headstones & grave markers, 1820s, 18-pg, EX ..25.00
Aldens, summer sale, 1949, 188-pg, VG 25.00
Avery Co, steam traction engines/attachments, 1914, 44-pg, VG .225.00
Bellas Hess & Co, lady's clothing, 1913, 212-pg, VG 38.00
Benj T Crump, harness & saddlery, 1941, 96-pg, 8¼x11", EX 45.00
Black & Decker Mfg Co, portable electric tools, 1939, 34-pg, G+ .18.00
Boston Store, ladies cloaks/capes/suits, 1898, 24-pg, VG 50.00
Bristol Co, electrical supplies, 1916, 26-pg, 8x10", VG 30.00
Butler Bros, home goods & toys, 1932, 272-pg, VG 75.00
Carpenter & Bayles Inc, hickory hdls for tools, 1922, 6-pg, G 22.00
Charles Sadek Import Co, HP Andrea China giftware, 1940s, 42-pg, VG .60.00
Chevrolet Motor Division, accessories, 1966, 20-pg, 4x8" 17.50
CJ Lundstrom Mfg Co, sectional filing cabinets, early, 8-pg, G+ .17.00
Cleveland Foundry Co, cooking stoves, 1900, 19-pg, VG 50.00
David Cook, Sunday school supplies & holiday, 1933, 135-pg, VG ...60.00
Deering Harvester Co, binder twine, Chicago, 1900, 24-pg, 4½ x6" ..23.00
Delta Mfg Co, motor-driven tools, 1934, 48-pg, G 22.00
Domestic Sewing Machine, machines & accessories, 1888, 28-pg, VG ...22.00
Eastman Kodak, cameras, 1925, 64-pg, EX 25.00
FW Woolworth Co, 40th Anniversary souvenir, 1919, 32-pg, G .33.00
Genuine Bangor Slate Co, slate items, PA, 1906, 72-pg, EX 22.50
Glanz, Behm & Herring, rugs & carpet, 1927, 76-pg, VG 34.00
Goldblatt Tool, general tools, 1956, 80-pg, VG 15.00
Graves Electric Supply Co, decorative lighting, 1950, 32-pg, G ..21.00
Great Lakes Products, fishing gear, ca 1950s, 8-pg, G 10.00
HC Evans, gambling equipment & supplies, 1929, 64-pg, EX 85.00
Honeyman Jewelry Co, Zodiac rings, ca 1930, 28-pg, G+ 24.00
Illinois Prison Board, prisoner-made furniture, 1908, 76-pg, VG ...100.00
International Harvester, cream separators, Chicago, 1930, 71-pg, VG ..16.00
Jason Weiler-Baird North, jewelry, 1933, 174-pg, G 34.00
John G Hardy, luggage, 1946, 32-pg, VG 25.00
John Palmer Co, Ltd, Moosehead brand footwear, 1929, 32-pg, G .19.00
John Wannamaker, ladies' clothes, 1920, 98-pg, VG 36.00
King & Hamilton Co, farm elevators, early, 44-pgs, G 32.00
Kuehne Mfg Co, kitchen furniture, 1937, 80-pg, VG 34.00
Lafayette Radio, #65, radios/parts/equipment, 1937, 152-pg, VG ...50.00
Lamson's of Toledo, Christmas, clothing & etc, 1965, 48-pg, VG ..15.00
LC Orrell & Co, painting supplies, 1924, 64-pg, VG 16.00
Lowe Brothers Co, porch & deck pnt, ca 1930, 4-pg, VG 10.00
Metro Mfg Co, Bingo equipment, ca 1940s, 18-pg, VG+ 45.00
Mid-Western Sport Togs, sports clothes, 1942, 24-pg, EX 30.00
Milburn Wagon Co, #104, farm wagons/gears/carts/etc, 1908, 92-pg, VG .225.00
Milton Bradley Co, school supplies, 1922, 124-pg, VG 32.00
Mitchell-Bissell, machinery items, 1927, 108-pg, VG 32.00
Montgomery Ward, general merchandise, 1932, 68-pg, VG 12.50
Musicians Supply Co, violins & supplies, ca 1930, 26-pg, VG 46.00
National Cloak & Suit, Fall & Winter fashions, 1914, 328-pg, VG ..125.00

Nicholas-Beasley Airplane Co, motors/parts/supplies, 1929, 200-pg, VG .150.00
Pilot Electric Mfg Co, radio parts, 1930, VG 20.00
Progress Tailoring Co, coats/capes/etc, 1897, 32-pg, VG 30.00
RCA Victor, Bluebird phonograph records, 1943, 500-pg, VG 50.00
Remington Arms Co, firearms, 1912, EX 65.00
Scout Executive, clothing & equipment, 1928, 42-pg, EX 32.00
Sears Roebuck, #125, fashion/general/toys, 1912, 1458-pg, VG .225.00
Sears Roebuck, Fall & Winter merchandise, 1940, 1182-pg, VG ..38.00
Sears Roebuck, general merchandise, 1922, 1176-pg, VG 95.00
Selby, Starr & Co, agricultural scales, 1889, 16-pg, G 41.00
Seng Co, furniture hardware, 1914, 32-pg, VG 34.00
SH Reese, police equipment, 1948, 42-pg, G+ 71.00
Sidney Shepard & Co, stove-related items, 1881, 24-pg, VG 68.00
Spencer Tracy Co, men's fashions, 1912, 16-pg, G 23.00
Star Rare Coins, 1930, 208-pg, VG 40.00
Storrs & Harrison Co, fruits/flowers/vegetables, 1887, 142-pg, G ..16.00
Strelitz Bros, watches, Chicago, ca 1900, 30-pg, VG 30.00
Syracuse Chilled Plow Co, sulky & gang plows/harrows/etc, 1929, EX .35.00
Unadilla Silo Co, yard & garden items, 1920s, 8-pg, VG 22.00
United Indurated Fibre Co, household items, 1890, 16-pg, VG ...18.00
Walter C Gold, Keystone grinding wheels, 1919, 111-pg, G 15.00
Westinghouse Electric Corp, appliances, ca 1953, 19-pg, G+ 19.00
Work Bros & Co, men's clothes, Chicago, 1892, 120-pg, VG 42.50
York Machinery & Supply, tools & accessories, 1951, 526-pg, EX ..18.00

Ceramic Art Company

Jonathan Coxon, Sr., and Walter Scott Lenox established the Ceramic Art Company in 1889 in Trenton, New Jersey, where they produced fine belleek porcelain. Both were experienced in its production, having previously worked for Ott and Brewer. They hired artists to hand paint their wares with portraits, scenes, and lovely florals. Today artist-signed examples bring the highest prices. Several marks were used, three of which contain the 'CAC' monogram. A green wreath surrounding the company name in full was used on special-order wares, but these are not often encountered. Coxon eventually left the company, and it was later reorganized under the Lenox name. See also Lenox. Our advisor for this category is Mary Frank Gaston.

Salt cellar and pepper shaker, floral with gold, lavender mark, $125.00 for the set. (Photo courtesy Mary Frank Gaston)

Bowl, finger; gold leaves & flowers on gr, scalloped rim 130.00
Chocolate pot, marine life w/gold, mermaid spout & hdl, 12" .1,400.00
Coffeepot, gold wash w/silver o/l, pegasus mk, 7½ ", +cr/sug 175.00
Cream soup cup & saucer, Tridacna w/gold, 2", 5½ " 150.00
Creamer & sugar bowl, cobalt bl w/silver o/l, wreath mk, w/lid .200.00
Cup, demitasse; gold-paste floral, ring hdl, 2" 100.00
Cup, loving; roses on gr, 3 pk hdls w/gold, purple mk, 8" 350.00
Decanter, Scotch, cobalt w/silver o/l, silver hdl & stopper, 4" ...300.00
Inkwell, chrysanthemums w/gold (nonfactory), sq, 4½ " H 175.00
Jug, Rye, brn & gr w/silver o/l, palette mk 200.00
Jug, Scotch, brn w/silver o/l, wreath mk 175.00
Jug, yel & purple pansies, artist sgn, gold spout/hdl, mk, 6" dia .300.00
Loving cup, violets on wht, 3 hdls w/child's head finials, 8½ " ..650.00
Mug, apples on orange ground (nonfactory decor), 6" 125.00
Mug, brn w/silver o/l, wreath mk, 5½ " 250.00
Mug, gr hops, artist sgn, palette mk, 4¾" 75.00
Mug, musketeer on brn, palette mk, 5½ " 80.00
Mug, roses & sorority emblem, gold hdl, palette mk, 5½ " 75.00
Salt cellar, swan form w/gilt trim, w/plain wht spoon 225.00
Shakers & mustard jar, lt gr w/silver o/l, wreath mk, 3" 350.00
Stein, monks eating in cellar, copper/sterling lid, mk, ½-liter ...600.00
Tankard, apple blossoms, gold hdl, palette mk, 14" 350.00
Tankard, gr & purple grapes, gold hdl, palette mk, 14" 275.00
Tankard, lady in wispy gown w/flower wreath, Heidrich, unmk, 13" ..1,200.00
Vase, herons reserves (3) w/gold borders, shouldered, 22" 600.00
Vase, lady's portrait on maroon, turq beading, mk, 15" 1,500.00
Vase, shell form w/snail hdls & emb decor, no pnt decor, 6x7" ..300.00
Vase, wht neck to shaded purple lustre, mk, 3¾" 125.00

Ceramic Arts Studio, Madison

The Ceramic Arts Studio Company began operations sometime prior to the 1940s, but it was about then that Betty Harrington started marketing her goods through this company. Betty Harrington was the designer primarily responsible for creating the line of figurines and knickknacks that has become so popular with collectors. There were two others — Ulli Rebus, who not only designed several of the animals and various other pieces but taught Betty the art of mold-making as well; and Ruth Planter, who's work may have been limited to 'Sonny' and Honey.' About 65% of these items are marked, but even unmarked items become easily recognizable after only a brief study of their distinctive styling and glaze colors. At least eight different marks were used, among them the black ink stamp and the incised mark: 'Ceramic Arts Studio, Madison, Wisc.' A paper sticker was used in the early years.

After the 1955 demise of the company in Madison, the owner (Ruben Sand) went to Japan where he continued production under the same name using many of the same molds. After a short time, the old molds were retired, and new and quite different items were produced. Most of the Japan pieces can be found with a Ceramic Arts Studio backstamp. The Japan identification was often on a paper label and can be missing. Japan pieces are never marked Madison, Wisc., but not all Madison pieces are either. Red or blue backstamps are exclusively Japanese.

Another company that also produced figurines operated at about the same time as the Madison studio. It was called Ceramic Art (no 's') Studio; do not confuse the two.

A second and larger building in the C.A.S. complex in Madison was for the exclusive production of metal accessories. The creator and designer of this related line was Zona Liberace, Liberace's stepmother, who was art director for the line of figurines as well. These pieces are rising fast in value and because they weren't marked can sometimes be found at bargain prices. They were so popular that other ceramic companies bought them to complement their own lines, so they may also be found with ceramic figures other than C.A.S.'s.

Our advisor for this category is BA Wellman; his address can be found under Massachusetts. Mr. Wellman encourages collectors to write him with any new information concerning company history and/or production. He sends John Canfield a 'thank you' for helping us with this year's updates. See also Clubs, Newsletters, and Catalogs.

Bank, Mr & Mrs Blankety Blank, 4½ ", pr 215.00
Bell, Lillibelle, 6½ " 95.00
Bell, Winter Bell, 5¼" 90.00
Birdbath, 4½ " 100.00
Bowl, Bonita; paisley shape, 3¾" L 65.00
Bowl, spice; aqua, rnd/stylized, 5¼" 80.00
Candle holder, Bedtime Girl, 4¾" 95.00

Figurine, Accordion Boy, 5" 80.00
Figurine, Alice, sitting on knees, 4½ " 200.00
Figurine, Aphrodite, 7¾" 195.00
Figurine, Archibald Dragon, 8" 275.00
Figurine, Autumn Andy, 5", from $85 to 95.00
Figurine, baby elephant, 3¼" 75.00
Figurine, Bali-Hai, standing, topless 200.00
Figurine, Bali-Hai, standing, 8" 100.00
Figurine, Balinese Man, 9½ " 135.00
Figurine, Beth, 5" 45.00
Figurine, Blessing Angel, hand down, 5¾" 100.00
Figurine, boy w/cactus & Mexican girl, 7", 6½ ", pr 150.00
Figurine, Bright Eyes, cat, 3" 40.00
Figurine, bunny, 1¾" 50.00
Figurine, Carmen & Carmelita, 7¼", 4¼", pr 95.00
Figurine, chipmunk, 2" 45.00
Figurine, Colonial Man, 6½ " 65.00
Figurine, Daisy Donkey, 4¾" 130.00
Figurine, Dance Moderne Man & Woman, 9½ ", pr 145.00
Figurine, Dutch Love Boy & Girl, 5", pr 95.00
Figurine, Egyptian Woman, 9½ " 325.00
Figurine, Fire Man & Fire Woman, 11¼", pr 295.00
Figurine, giraffe mother & baby, very rare, 6½ ", 5½ ", pr 185.00
Figurine, Guitar Boy, 5" 75.00
Figurine, Gypsy Man & Woman, 6½ ", 7", pr 150.00
Figurine, Harem Girl, kneeling, 4½ " 70.00
Figurine, Hiawatha, on 1 knee, 3½ " 100.00
Figurine, Isaac & Rebekah, 10", pr 250.00
Figurine, kitten w/ball, cat family #2, 2" 45.00
Figurine, lamb w/bow, 4" 65.00
Figurine, leopards, fighting, 3½ ", 6¼" L, pr, from $250 to 295.00
Figurine, Lillibeth, 6" 35.00
Figurine, Little Bo Peep, 5½ " 35.00
Figurine, Little Boy Blue, 4½ " L 35.00
Figurine, Little Miss Muffet #2, 4" 80.00
Figurine, lovebirds, 1-pc, 2¾" 45.00
Figurine, Lover Boy, 4½ " 65.00
Figurine, Lu-Tang & Wing Sang, 6", pr 110.00
Figurine, Lucindy, 7" 60.00
Figurine, Modern Colt, stylized, 7½ " 200.00
Figurine, monkey, scratching bug, 4" 95.00
Figurine, Mrs Skunky, 3" 55.00
Figurine, Peek-A-Boo Pixie, 2½ " 65.00
Figurine, Pekingese, 3" 95.00
Figurine, Pepita, Pan-American, 4½ " 45.00
Figurine, Peter Pan & Wendy, 5¼", pr 250.00
Figurine, Peter Rabbit, 3¼" 100.00
Figurine, Petrov & Petrushka, 5", 5¼", pr 100.00
Figurine, Pioneer Sam & Suzie, 5½ ", 5", pr 95.00
Figurine, Pixie, on toadstool, 4" 50.00
Figurine, Pixie, riding snail, 2¾" 65.00
Figurine, Pixie Girl, kneeling, 2½ " 65.00
Figurine, Pixie Girl, waving, 4¼" 65.00
Figurine, Polish Boy & Girl, 6½ ", pr 120.00
Figurine, Praying Boy Angel, on knees, 3¼" 100.00
Figurine, pup, playing, collie family #1, 2¼" 45.00
Figurine, pup, sleeping w/bone, collie family #2, 2" L 45.00
Figurine, Saucy Squirrel w/jacket, 2¼" 95.00
Figurine, Smi-Li & Mo-Pi, 6", pr 60.00
Figurine, Square Dance Boy & Girl, 6½ ", 6", pr 175.00
Figurine, Squeaky Squirrel, 3¼" 75.00
Figurine, St Francis w/extended arms, 7" 150.00
Figurine, Toby Horse, 2¾" 110.00
Figurine, Water Man & Woman, 11½ ", pr 495.00
Figurine, Wee Dutch Boy & Girl, 3", pr 35.00
Figurine, Wee Eskimo Boy & Girl, 3¼", 3", pr 70.00
Figurine, Wee Swedish Boy & Girl, 3¼", 3", pr 65.00
Head vase, African Woman, 7¾" 195.00
Head vase, Barbie, blond, 7" 175.00

Head vase, Bonnie, 7", $175.00.

Head vase, Mei-Ling, 5" 125.00
Miniature, Aladdin's lamp, 2" L 75.00
Miniature, pitcher, Buddha; bsk, Wedgwood, 3½ " 65.00
Miniature, teapot, grapes, glazed, 2" 75.00
Plaque, Attitude & Arabesque, 9½ ", 9¼", pr 135.00
Plaque, Comedy & Tragedy masks, 5", pr 165.00
Plaque, Greg & Grace, 9½ ", 9", pr 120.00
Plaque, Harlequin & Columbine, 8", pr 225.00
Plaque, Manchu & Lotus, 8", pr 190.00
Plaque, Shadow Dancers A & B, 7", pr 185.00
Plaque, Zor, 9" 65.00
Shakers, bear mother & cub, brn, snuggle, 4¼", 2¼", pr 90.00
Shakers, kangaroo mother & joey, 4¾", 2½ ", pr 160.00
Shakers, Mr & Mrs Penguin, 3¾", pr 95.00
Shakers, Sabu & Elephant, 2¾", 5", pr 265.00
Shakers, Santa Claus & Christmas tree, 2¼", pr 150.00
Shakers, Thai & Thai-Thai, snuggle, 5" L, pr 145.00
Shakers, Wee Chinese Boy & Girl, 3", pr 35.00
Shakers, Wee Elephant Boy & Girl, 3½ ", 3¼", pr 55.00
Shelf sitter, boy w/dog, 4¼" 70.00
Shelf sitter, canary, 5" 65.00
Shelf sitter, cowboy, 4¾" 85.00
Shelf sitter, En Pos & En Repos, 4½ ", pr 195.00
Shelf sitter, Fluffy, cat family #1, 4¾" 65.00
Shelf sitter, Harmonica Boy, 4" 75.00
Shelf sitter, Jack & Jill, 4¾", 5", pr 85.00
Shelf sitter, Maurice & Michelle, 7", pr 165.00
Shelf sitter, Nip & Tuck, 4¼", 4", pr 60.00
Shelf sitter, Pete & Polly Parrot, 7½ ", pr, from $165 to 185.00
Shelf sitter, Sun-Li & Sun-Lin, 5½ ", pr 95.00
Shelf sitter, Tuffy, cat family #2, 5¼" 90.00
Vase, bud; bamboo, 6" 25.00

Metal Accessories

Arched window for Madonna & Child, 14" 80.00
Artist palette w/shelves, left & right, 13" across 95.00
Beanstalk for Jack, rare 165.00
Birdcage w/perch for birds, 14" 85.00
Corner spider web for Miss Muffet, flat blk, 4" 95.00
Diamond-shaped box, flat blk, 15½ x14" 55.00
Frame w/shelf, 22" sq 55.00
Musical score, flat blk, 14x12" 90.00
Pocket step shelf, w/planter, rnd, 8" 75.00
Pyramid shelf 75.00

Rainbow arch w/shelf, blk, 13½ x19x5½ " 120.00
Sofa, for Maurice & Michelle, 10x3¾" 65.00
Star for an angel, flat blk 80.00
Triple ring shelves 125.00

Chalkware

Chalkware figures were a popular commodity from approximately 1860 until 1890. They were made from gypsum or plaster of Paris formed in a mold and then hand painted in oils or watercolors. Items such as animals and birds, figures, banks, toys, and religious ornaments modeled after more expensive Staffordshire wares were often sold door to door. Their origin is attributed to Italian immigrants. Today regarded as a form of folk art, nineteenth century American pieces bring prices in the hundreds of dollars. Carnival chalkware from this century is also collectible, especially figures that are personality related. For those, see Carnival Collectibles.

Bank, pear shape, yel w/red, wood stem, side slot, 3¾" dia 350.00
Cat, seated, old worn mc pnt, 9⅞" 1,400.00
Cat, sleeping, old mc pnt w/minor damage, rpr, 12" 400.00
Cat, worn mc pnt, gr plinth, sm chips on base, 5¾" 165.00
Deer, recumbent, mc pnt, 5½ ", pr 935.00
Stag, reclining, 3-color pnt, on base, minor wear, 10x8½ " 750.00

Champleve

Champleve, enameling on brass or other metal, differs from cloisonne in that the design is depressed or incised into the metal, rather than being built in with wire dividers as in the cloisonnè procedure. The cells, or depressions, are filled in with color, and the piece is then fired.

Vase, Arhats & Buddhist emblems, hexagonal, Meiji, 20" 400.00
Vase, birds & flowers, hdls w/bird heads, Made in Japan, 12x7½ " .150.00
Vase, elaborate pattern, mc on med bl, 7" 110.00
Vase, floral w/animal heads, Made in Japan, 9½ x6" dia 135.00
Vase, Taotie masks/dragons/scrollwork, dragon hdls, 11½ " 160.00

Chase Brass & Copper Company

Chase introduced this logo in 1928. The company incorporated in 1876 as the Waterbury Manufacturing Company. It was located in Waterbury, Connecticut. This location remained Chase's principal fabrication plant, and it was here that the 'Specialties' were made.

CHASE

In 1900 the company chose the name Chase Companies Inc., in honor of their founder, Augustus Sabin Chase. The name encompassed Chase's many factories. Only the New York City sales division was called Chase Brass and Copper Co., but from 1936 on, that name was used exclusively.

In 1930 the sales division invited people to visit their new Specialties Sales Showroom in New York City 'where an interesting assortment of decorative and utilitarian pieces in brass and copper in a variety of designs and treatments are offered for your consideration.' Like several other large companies, Chase hired well-known designers such as Walter Von Nessen, Lurelle Guild, the Gerths, Russel Wright, and Dr. A Reimann. Harry Laylon, an in-house designer, created much of the new line.

From 1930 to 1942 Chase offered lamps, smoking accessories, and housewares similar to those Americans were seeing on the Hollywood screen — generally at prices the average person could afford.

Besides chromium, Chase manufactured many products in a variety of finishes, some even in silver plate. Many objects were polished or satin-finished brass and/or copper.

After World War II Chase no longer made the Specialties line. It had represented only a tiny fraction of this huge company's production. Instead they concentrated on a variety of fabricated mill items. Some dedicated Chase collectors even have shower heads, faucet aerators, gutter pipe, and metal samples. Is anyone using Chase window screening?

Chase products are marked either on the item itself or on a screw or rivet. Because Chase sold screws, rivets, nails, etc. (all with their logo), not all items having these Chase-marked components were actually made at Chase. It should also be noted that during the 1930s, China produced good quality chromium copies; so when you're not absolutely positive an item is Chase, buy it because you like it, understanding that its authenticity may be in question. Remember that if a magnet sticks to it, it's not Chase. Brass and copper are not magnetic, and Chase did not use steel.

Prior to 1933 Chase made smoking accessories for the Park Sherman Co. Some are marked 'Park Sherman, Chicago, Illinois, Made of Chase Brass.' Others carry a Park Sherman logo. It is believed that the 'heraldic emblem' was also used during this period. Many items are identical or very similar to Chase-marked pieces. Produced in the 1950s, National Silver's 'Emerald Glo' wares look very similar to Chase pieces, but Chase did not make them. It is very possible that National purchased Chase tooling after the Chase Specialties line was discontinued.

For further study we recommend *Chase Complete, Chase Catalogs 1934 & 1935, 1930s Lighting – Deco & Traditional by Chase,* all by Donald-Brian Johnson and Leslie Pina (Schiffer); *Art Deco Chrome, the Chase Era; Art Deco Chrome, Book 2, A Collectors' Guide to Industrial Design in the Chase Era,* both by Richard Kilbride (Mrs. Kilbride is listed in the Directory under Connecticut); and *Art Deco Chrome* by James Linz (Schiffer).

In the listings that follow, examples are polished unless noted satin. For further information contact the Chase Collector's Society, listed in the Directory under Clubs, Newsletters, and Catalogs. Our advisor for this category is Barbara Endter; she is listed in the Directory under New York.

Diplomat Coffee Set #17029, chromium with black plastic handles and knobs, without tray, designer: Walter Von Nessen, ca 1933 – 1941, from $280.00 to $300.00. (Photo by Dale Endter, courtesy Barbara Endter)

Ash receiver, Antelope, frosted glass w/chrome trim, #881, 4½ " ..115.00
Ash receiver, Autumn Leaf, copper, #28009, 5½ ", from $40 to ..45.00
Ashtray, Golfer's, H Reichenbach, #890, 4¼" dia, from $45 to ...55.00
Ashtray, Marionette, #304, from $30 to 40.00
Ashtray, Tennis, #892, 4¼" dia, from $65 to 75.00
Bar caddy, chromium, #90141, from $10 to 15.00
Beer mug (keg), copper/chromium, #90042, from $25 to 30.00
Bell, Brittany, brass, #13002 ....75.00
Bookends, stylized cats, brass, #17042, 7⅜", pr, from $475 to 500.00

Bowl, berry; w/spoon, chrome w/wht Bakelite, #90083, 10", from $60 to ..70.00
Bowl, sauce; Lotus, w/tray & ladle, chrome, #17045, from $40 to .45.00
Buffet server, chrome w/Bakelite, electric, #27011, 11x18", $150 to ..175.00
Candlestick, Diana, #17116, 3⅝", from $80 to 100.00
Candy box, Three Layer, w/cherry knob, #90104, 4¾" 85.00
Casserole/Hot Server, chrome w/wht Bakelite, electric, #90115, $140 to ...150.00
Cheese server, chrome w/wood insert, w/lid, #09009, 14" dia, $90 to .100.00
Cigarette box, Floral, gold/mc enamel inlay, #17097, from $125 to ...150.00
Coasters, Danube, copper or chrome, #17072, 3¾", set of 4 ....50.00
Coffee set, Continental, W Von Nessen, #17054, 3-pc, from $210 to ..250.00
Coffeepot, Continental, chrome w/Bakelite, #17051, 9⅜", $175 to .200.00
Compote, Octagonal, satin copper, #15002, 3⅛" H, from $150 to .175.00
Cruet set, ribbed glass w/chrome trim, #26009, 8", from $250 to .275.00
Flower cultivator (indoor), brass & copper, #12333, from $40 to ..45.00
Flower jar, brass, #11151, 3½", from $45 to 55.00
Flowerpot, Rippled, #04007, 6⅛", from $40 to 45.00
Foot scraper, brass, #90033, from $275 to 300.00
Hot plate, Continental, chrome w/Bakelite, electric, #90109, $275 to ..300.00
Humidor, Cannon Ball, #17094, from $125 to 150.00
Ice bowl, Antarctic, #17108, 7", from $100 to 125.00
Jigger & swizzler set, High Hat/Niblick, chrome, L Guild, 5-pc, $60 to .70.00
Lighter, Fireball, chromium on pnt, Schulze, #851, 2½", from $50 to ...60.00
Mint/Nut Dish, #29003, chrome, Gerths, from $30 to 40.00
Mustard, Jubilee Globe, copper (or chrome) & wht, #90070, 4", $45 to .55.00
Napkin clips, Animal, chrome/Bakelite, #90105 (— 08), ea, $65 to 75.00
Pitcher, Tavern, copper w/brass, Von Nessen, #17026, 10¼", $230 to ..250.00
Plant bowl, Pendant, copper, w/chain hanger, #04004, 6¼" dia ..45.00
Relish dish, Savory, chrome tray w/glass insert, #90054, 12" dia ..85.00
Relish dish, Savory, w/tray/glass insert/jam jar/lid/spoon, $150 to ..160.00
Sconce Light (Candle), copper & brass, #16003, 7⅞", from $35 to ..45.00
Shakers, Skyway, chrome w/wht Bakelite bases, #17095, pr 35.00
Smoking stand, Lazy Boy, chrome w/red compo, #17031, 22x14", $400 to ..450.00
Syrup jug, Jubilee, w/tray, glass & chrome, #26004, from $65 to ..75.00
Tray, for beer mug, copper, #09011, 8¾" dia, from $35 to 45.00
Tray, Tiffin, copper or chrome w/blk hdls, #17027, 12x18", $180 to ...200.00
Tray/cup holders, Carefree Set, chrome or brass, #08003, 5-pc, $125 to ..150.00
Vase, Trophy, chrome, #03005, 9" 75.00
Watering can, Niagara, Gerths, #05004, 8⅜", from $65 to 75.00
Wine cooler, Bacchus, copper or brass, hdls, #27015, 8½", $550 to ..600.00

Chelsea Dinnerware

Made from about 1830 to 1880 in the Staffordshire district of England, this white dinnerware is decorated with lustre embossings in the grape, thistle, sprig, or fruit and cornucopia patterns. The relief designs vary from lavender to blue, and the body of the ware may be porcelain, ironstone, or earthenware. Because it was not produced in Chelsea as the name would suggest, dealers often prefer to call it 'Grandmother's Ware.' Our advisor for this category is Mary Frank Gaston.

Grape, bowl, 8" 35.00
Grape, coffeepot, stick hdl, 2-cup, 7" 75.00
Grape, creamer 35.00
Grape, cup & saucer 35.00
Grape, egg cup 25.00
Grape, pitcher, milk, 40-oz 60.00
Grape, plate, 6" 12.00
Grape, plate, 7" 18.00
Grape, plate, 8" 20.00
Grape, sugar bowl, w/lid 50.00
Grape, teapot, octagonal, 10" 125.00
Grape, teapot, 2-cup 75.00
Grape, waste bowl 40.00
Sprig, cake plate, 9" 40.00
Sprig, cup & saucer 40.00
Sprig, pitcher, milk 60.00
Sprig, plate, dinner 25.00
Sprig, plate, 7" 18.00
Thistle, butter pat 15.00
Thistle, cup & saucer 35.00
Thistle, plate, 7" 15.00
Thistle, sugar bowl, 8-sided, w/lid, 7½" 45.00

Chelsea Keramic Art Works

The Chelsea Keramic Art Works Robertson and Sons Pottery was established in 1872 in Chelsea, Massachusetts, by several members of the Robertson family, including Hugh C. Robertson who later formed the Dedham Pottery. Though their very early artware utilized a redware body, by the late 1870s it was replaced with yellow or buff burning clay. A line called Bourg-la-Reine (underglazed slip-decorated ware with primarily blue and green backgrounds) was produced, though not to any great extent. Other pieces were designed in imitation of Asian metalware, even to the extent that surfaces were 'hammered' to further enhance the effect. Occasionally live flora was pressed into the damp vessel walls to leave a decorative impression. They also made glazed plaques and tiles. Hugh C. Robertson ran the pottery alone after 1884 and labored to re-create the ancient Ming-era blood-red glaze. Although world acclaim greeted his rediscovery of what he then called 'Robertson's Blood,' his red-glazed vases cost too much to produce and bankruptcy followed in 1889. Supported by wealthy Boston art patrons, Hugh's pottery reopened in 1891 as the Chelsea Pottery U.S., and began using his other 1880s rediscovery, the crackle glaze, producing cobalt blue-decorated dinnerware. When this firm moved to Dedham in 1895 the ware became known as Dedham Pottery. From 1875 to 1880 the pottery was marked Chelsea Keramic Art Works Robertson and Sons in either two or three impressed lines. Earlier pieces were not marked. The impressed mark CKAW in a diamond formation was also used between 1875 and 1889. From 1891 through 1895 the impressed letters CPUS in a cloverleaf was utilized for the new firm. After the move to Dedham, only new Dedham Pottery marks were used. See also Dedham Pottery.

Bowl, speckled brn over glossy bl, mk, 4¼" dia, NM 100.00
Ewer, bl & brn flambe, squat, mk, 11" 550.00
Plate, Early Pineapple, bl/wht crackle, CPUS, 10" 400.00
Plate, Horse chestnut, CPUS, 8¾" 200.00
Plate, Rabbit, bl/wht crackle, CPUS, 10¼" 300.00
Plate, Rabbit, bl/wht crackle, CPUS/EE, 8½" 250.00
Plate, Sailboat, X repeating border, CPUS, 8½" 3,100.00
Plate, Upside Down Dolphin & Baby, bl/wht crackle, CPUS, 8½" ..1,300.00
Vase, frothy oxblood, experimental, H Robertson, CKAW, 8¾x4" 1,600.00
Vase, gr mottled gloss, fluted, bottle neck, CKAW, 4¼" 350.00
Vase, insects/leaves etc, appl/cvd, sq, 7x2½" 1,100.00
Vase, oxblood orange peel, bottle shape, unmk, 8¼x3½" 1,600.00

Cherokee Pottery

Made and sold in Oklahoma through tribal-owned facilities at an industrial development sponsored in part by the Bureau of Indian Affairs, this pottery may be marked Cherokee in angular-style lettering or with the outline of an Indian head.

Basket, blk, Indian head mk, 8¼" 50.00
Vase, dk pk, 11" 65.00
Vase, tan & blk matt, hdls, 8" 35.00

Chicago Crucible

For only a few years during the 1920s, the Chicago (Illinois) Crucible Company made a limited amount of decorative pottery in addition to their regular line of architectural wares. Examples are very scarce today; they carry a variety of marks, all with the company name and location.

Vase, gr matt, 4 gourd-shaped side elements w/openings at waist, 9" .600.00
Vase, gr mottle over olive matt, sq rim, elongated gourd, 8", NM 350.00
Vase, suspended brn/gr matt, twisted, long neck, 8" 350.00
Vase, swirled leaves on gr, capped acorn form, 9", EX 800.00
Vase, vertical leaves, brn matt, shouldered, 6½ " 375.00
Vase, vertical leaves, textured bl, shouldered, 6½ " 500.00

Children's Books

Children's books, especially those from the Victorian era, are charming collectibles. Colorful lithographic illustrations that once delighted little boys in long curls and tiny girls in long stockings and a lot of ribbons and lace have lost none of their appeal. Some collectors limit themselves to a specific subject, while others may be far more interested in the illustrations. First editions are more valuable than later issues, and condition and rarity are very important factors to consider before making your purchase. For further information we recommend *Collector's Guide to Children's Books, 1850–1950, Volumes Two* and *Three*, by Diane McClure Jones and Rosemary Jones; and *Whitman Juvenile Books Reference & Value Guide* by David and Virginia Brown. Both are available from Collector Books or your local bookstore.

Adventures of Chillee Um-Gum, Colle, Grosset, 1938, VG 25.00
Adventures of Teenie Weenies, Donahey, Rand McNally, '40s Jr ed, VG 50.00
Ali Baba & the Forty Thieves, Mansbridge, Rewick & Otley, 1920s, VG ...15.00
Alice's Adventures in Wonderland, L Carroll, Dodd Mead, 1922 ed, VG .160.00
Apron-String, Gates, Sully & Kleinteich, 1917, 306-pg, VG 10.00
At the Foot of Windy Low, Justus, Volland, 1930, EX 45.00
Betty Grable & the House of Cobwebs, Whitman, 1947, 250-pg, EX .25.00

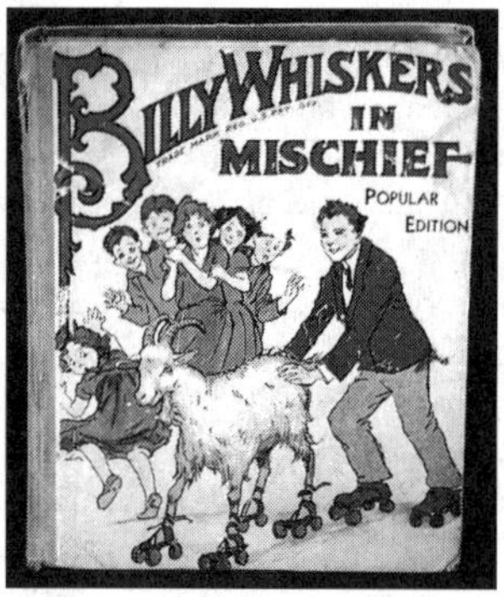

***Billy Whiskers in Mischief,* Popular Edition, copyright 1926, EX, $25.00.**

Brushwood Boy, Kipling, Doubleday, 1907 ed, 73-pg, VG 40.00
Buffalo Bill the Boys' Friend, Sherwood, Whitman, 1917, 246-pg, EX ..15.00
Cecily (Elf Goldihair), Helm, Lippincott, 1924, 298-pg, VG 55.00
Children's Mother Goose, Donahey, Reilly & Lee, 1921, VG ...125.00
Christmas Posy, Mrs Molesworth, MacMillam, 1888, EX 50.00
Circus Boy, War on Wheels, Snow, Whitman, 1958, EX 25.00
Confessions of a Daddy, Butler, Century, 1907, 107-pg, VG 30.00
Delicia & Adolphus, Newman, Rand McNally, 1938, EX 35.00
Dick Tracy Meets the Night Crawler, Gould, Whitman, 1945, 247-pg, EX ...25.00
Enchanted Castle, Hartwell, Altemus, 1906, 1st ed, VG 95.00
F Troop, Great Indian Uprising, Johnston, Whitman, 1967, 214-pg, EX ..18.00
Ginny Gordon & the Missing Heirloom, Whitman, 1950, 249-pg, EX 10.00
Great Jug, Raphael, Reilly Lee, 1936, 136-pg, EX 45.00
Invisible Scarlet O'Neil, Stamm, Whitman, 1943, 248-pg, EX 30.00
Janet Lennon at Camp Calamity, Meyer, Whitman, 1962, 212-pg, EX ..15.00
Johnny Gruelle's Golden Book, Gruelle, Donahue, 1929 ed, 79-pg, VG .45.00
Jolly Jingle Picture Book, Jackson, Rand McNally, 1937, VG 65.00
Ladder of Rickety Rungs, O'Donnell, Volland, 1923, EX 60.00
Life & Adventures of Peter Wilkins, Paltock, Dent, 1928, 324-pg, EX .50.00
Little Men, Alcott, Whitman, 1940, 234-pg, EX 12.00
Little Miss Wardlaw, Gray, Nelson, 1899, 445-pg, VG 20.00
Little Peachling, Faulkner, Wise-Parslow, 1928, 91-pg, VG 40.00
Macaroni Tree, Amsden, Hebberd, 1927, VG 40.00
Magic Ink Pot, Edith, Macmillan, 1928, 208-pg, VG 85.00
Magic Rug, A'Aulaire, Doubleday, 1931, VG 50.00
Nils, D'Aulaire, Doubleday, 1948, VG 45.00
Outcasts, Fraser, Scribner, 1901, 138-pg, VG 15.00
Outdoor Girls at Cedar Ridge, Hope, Whitman, 1931, 214-pg, EX .16.00
Pan & His Pipes..., Cather, Victor, 1916, 80-pg, VG 20.00
Patch Pants the Tailor, Christian, John Martin's House, 1947, VG ..30.00
Peter Teeter Stories, Schwetzky, Thompson, 1904, EX 75.00
Pinocchio in Africa, Cherubini, Ginn Once-Upon-A-Time, 1911, VG .20.00
Purr & Miew, Leet, Saalfield, 1931, 60-pg, EX 55.00
Raggedy Ann in the Snow Castle, Gruelle, 1946, VG 45.00
Real McCoys & Danger at the Ranch, Fannin, Whitman, 1961, 212-pg, EX ..15.00
Red Ryder & the Thunder Trail, McGill, Whitman, 1956, 282-pg, EX .15.00
Rin Tin Tin & the Call to Danger, Whitman, 1957, 282-pg, EX .18.00
Romance of the Moon, Mitchell, Holt, 1886, EX 45.00
Rover Boys on Treasure Isle, Winfield, Whitman, 1909, 287-pg, EX .15.00
Roy Rogers & the Enchanted Canyon, Whitman, 1954, 282-pg, EX .25.00
School Boy, Holmes, Houghton, 1879, 79-pg, VG 45.00
Seven Peas in the Pod, Bailey, Little Brown, 1919, VG 35.00
Silver Buckle, Crumpton, Altemus, 1899, 89-pg, VG 20.00
Six Girls, Irving, Estes, 1884, VG 30.00
Snow Baby, Peary, Stokes, 1901, 84-pg, EX 95.00
Tales From Shakespeare, Lamb, Dutton, 1909, EX 120.00
Tar Baby, Harraden, Appleton, 1904 ed, 190-pg, VG 150.00
Tarzan of the Apes, Whitman, 1964, 285-pg, EX 15.00
When Little Things Go Rhyming, Knobel, Rand McNally, 1916, EX ..30.00
Winifred West, Channing, Wilde, 1901, 271-pg, VG 15.00
Wynken, Blynken & Nod, Field, Whitman, 1941 ed, VG 40.00

Children's Things

Nearly every item devised for adult furnishings has been reduced to child size — furniture, dishes, sporting goods, even some tools. All are very collectible. During the late 1600s and early 1700s, miniature china dinnerware sets were made both in China and in England. They were not intended primarily as children's playthings, however, but instead were made to furnish miniature rooms and cabinets that provided a popular diversion for the adults of that period. By the nineteenth century, the emphasis had shifted, and most of the small-scaled dinnerware and tea sets were made for children's play.

Late in the 1800s and well into the 1900s, toy pressed glass dishes were made, many in the same pattern as full-scale glassware. Today these toy dishes often fetch prices in the same range as those for the 'grown-ups'!

Authorities Margaret and Kenn Whitmyer have compiled a lovely book, *The Collector's Encyclopedia of Children's Dishes*, with full-color photos and current market values; you will find their address in the Directory under Ohio. See also A B C Plates; Blue Willow; Clothing; Stickley; etc.

Key: ds — doll size

China

Tea set, Happifats, marked Rudolstadt, serves seven, EX, $245.00 at auction. (Photo courtesy Diane Jones/Rosemary Jones)

Bowl, vegetable; Fancy Loop, gr on yel, w/lid, unmk English, 2½ " ..60.00
Casserole, Humphrey's Clock, bl on wht, Ridgway's, w/lid 125.00
Casserole, Scenes From House That Jack Built, Florence Cook, 8½ " 150.00
Comport, Bluebird, Choisy & LeRoi, 4¼" 75.00
Creamer, Dutch Children, lustreware, Made in Japan 11.00
Creamer, House That Jack Built, Germany, 3⅜" 35.00
Creamer, Old Moss Rose 18.00
Creamer, Roman Chariots, bl & wht, Cauldon England, 2" 45.00
Creamer, Snow White, Made in Japan, Walt Disney Enterprises, 1937, 2" .28.00
Creamer & sugar bowl, Humphreys' Clock, bl on wht, Ridgway ..75.00
Creamer & sugar bowl, Mary Had a Little Lamb, Brentleigh Ware .24.00
Cup & saucer, Butterfly, Made in Japan, 4⅞" 8.00
Cup & saucer, Friends, mc transfer, gr rim, Germany 28.00
Cup & saucer, Mini Floral, mc on wht, England, 2⅛", 4⅜" 13.00
Cup & saucer, Orient, bl & wht, England, 3", 4¼" 28.00
Cup & saucer, Roman Chariots, bl on wht, Cauldon 45.00
Cup & saucer, Silhouette Children, Czechoslovakia, 1⅞", 3¼" ..12.00
Ladle, Greek Key, brn on wht, Ridgway Sparks & Ridgway, 5" 15.00
Mug, Blind Man's Bluff, mc transfer, 2½ " 120.00
Mug, Catherine, brn transfer, 2¾" 250.00
Mug, Football, blk transfer w/mc, 2½ " 130.00
Plate, Barnyard Animals, Germany, 5½ " 14.00
Plate, Basket, Salem China, 6¼" 7.00
Plate, Dutch Children on tan lustre, Japan 3.50
Plate, Father Christmas & the Children, Germany, 5" 25.00
Plate, Holly, Germany, early 1900s 25.00
Plate, Kite Fliers, bl & wht, English, 3½ " 48.00
Plate, Myrtle Wreath, bl & wht, JM&S, 3¾" 12.00
Plate, Nursery Rhyme, red on cream, W&Co Hanley, 5" 18.00
Plate, Pink Open Rose, Made in England, 4½ " 7.00
Plate, Standing Pony, mc transfer w/gr lustre, Germany 20.00
Plate, Sunset, Japan, 4¼" 5.00
Plate, Tiger Hunt, bl transfer, emb floral rim, 4¾" 130.00
Platter, Athens, bl on wht, Davenport, mid-1800s, 5½ " 40.00
Platter, Butterfly, England, 6¼" 18.00
Platter, Rhodesia, Ridgway's Royal Semi-Porcelain, 6⅛" 55.00
Platter, Rosamond, flow bl, Bistro England, 4¼" 60.00
Soup bowl, Fishers, CE&M, 4" 22.00
Sugar bowl, Godey Prints, Salem China, 2¼" 12.00
Sugar bowl, Merry Christmas w/pk lustre, w/lid, Germany, 3⅝" ..50.00
Sugar bowl, Orient, bl on wht, w/lid, unmk English, 3½ " 32.00
Sugar bowl, Sunset, Made in Japan, w/lid, 3⅛" 13.00
Teapot, Basket, flow bl, England, 4¼" 145.00
Teapot, Blue Banded, Dimmock & Co, 3¾" 100.00
Teapot, Gumdrop Tree, Southern Potteries, 6½ " 200.00
Teapot, mc floral, Nippon, 3¼" 27.00
Teapot, Mickey Mouse, Japan, 3¾" 125.00
Teapot, Pink Rose, Germany, 6¼" 60.00
Teapot, Saint Nicholas, mc transfer, Germany, 5½ " 250.00
Teapot, Teddy Bear, Germany, 6½ " 200.00
Tray, Dimity, gr on cream, England, 4½ " dia 22.00
Tureen, Calico, brn on cream, 3¾" 60.00
Waste bowl, Amherst Japan, Oriental floral decor, England, 4½ " ...95.00
Waste bowl, By the Mill, brn on wht, Methvin & Sons 40.00
Waste bowl, Punch & Judy, bl & wht, unmk, 2⅛" 70.00

Furniture

Examples with no dimensions given are child size unless noted doll size.

Armchair, director-style, cvd swan's-head arm terminals, pnt 600.00
Bed, mahog trn posts, arched tester fr, 1900s, rprs, 39x40x22" ...110.00
Bed, pine tall-post, red pnt, flat tester, disc ft, 48x70x32" 1,100.00
Bench, cut-out silhouette ends, old mc pnt, some wear, 12x12x7" ...1,265.00
Chair, Am Late Fed bamboo-trn, spindle bk, rush seat 110.00
Chair, ice cream; pnt iron w/wooden seat, 21", pr 100.00
Chair, mahog, velvet-uphl seat, English, 22" 360.00
Chest, Emp, curly cherry & walnut, 3-drw, scrolled ft, 13" 900.00
Chest, pnt pine, 6-brd, NE, 1820-30s, 12½ x25x13" 575.00
Cradle, bentwood, 2 wheels, orig red pnt w/silver striping, 54" .600.00
Cradle, bentwood w/ivory fittings, 39x41", EX 440.00
Cradle, cherry/poplar, cut-out details, scrolled crest, 44" 350.00
Cradle, mahog, w/hood, cut-out rockers, scrolled details, 44" .1,100.00
Cradle, pine, arched hood, dvtl rockers, old gr pnt, 18th C 400.00
Cradle, pine, cut-out rockers, splayed sides, rprs, 36" 170.00
Cradle, pine, orig red & blk grpt, dvtl, w/hood, rprs, 40" 150.00
Cradle, pine w/grpt, paneled hood, scrolled sides, 1800s, ds 350.00
Cradle, pine w/worn bl, paneled slats w/cutouts, 31" 500.00
Cradle, pnt CI, wood slat bottom, Vict, 21x37", EX 350.00
Cradle, poplar w/old gr pnt & yel striping, ds, 10¼" 245.00
Cradle, walnut, scroll bk, shaped rockers, rfn, 19th C, 21x39x18" ..230.00
Cradle, walnut, worn finish, dvtl, old rpr to rocker, 42" 165.00
Crib, mahog Am Fed, trn legs, brass casters, 50x30x48" 500.00
Cupboard, 2 doors/shelf/2 drws, pnt wood, 1930s, 45" 900.00
Dresser, oak w/serpentine top drw+2, brass pulls, mirror, 26" 600.00
Highchair, Am Windsor, probably southern, 19th C, EX 385.00
Highchair, mahog Chpndl style, c/b ft, cabriole legs, 39" 440.00
Highchair, mixed woods w/cane bk & seat, Vict, EX 250.00
Highchair, Windsor, old red pnt, shaped seat, trn legs, 36" 1,000.00
Highchair, 2-slat ladder-bk, splint seat, cvd/curved legs, 34" 900.00
Recamier, oak fr, classical style, reuphl, late 19th C, 15x40" 300.00
Rocker, bentwood, orig finish, ca 1924, EX 95.00
Rocker, slat-bk, split wood seat, 19th C 90.00
Rocker, wing-bk, pine w/old red stain, rpl rocker, 25" 200.00
Sofa, Emp, horsehair uphl, New London CT, 1840s, 40" 2,000.00
Table, drop-leaf, old yel pnt w/brn & red striping, 11x16"+leaves .300.00
Table, walnut, 8-sided top w/ornate cvd 4-leg base, 4½ x5x5" ...375.00

Glass

Arched Panel, pitcher, cobalt, 3¾" 150.00
Arrowhead & Oval, creamer 20.00
Arrowhead & Oval, spooner 20.00
Arrowhead & Oval, table set, 4-pc 135.00
Austrian, creamer, vaseline 200.00
Austrian, sugar bowl, clear, w/lid, 3¾" 175.00
Banded Portland, pitcher, water; blush 55.00
Banded Portland, pitcher, water; yel 50.00
Beaded Scroll, creamer 90.00
Beaded Swirl, sugar bowl, amber or cobalt, w/lid, 3¾", ea 125.00
Braided Belt, butter dish, milk glass w/decor 300.00

Button Panel, butter dish, clear w/gold, 4" 110.00
Button Panel, creamer 50.00
Button Panel, spooner 50.00
Buzz Saw, creamer, 2⅜" 25.00
Clear & Diamond Panels, butter dish, gr, 2⅞" 65.00
Clear & Diamond Panels, spooner, gr 35.00
Colonial, creamer, gr 22.00
Colonial, spooner 35.00
Colonial, sugar bowl, olive or emerald gr, w/lid, 3", ea 45.00
Colorado, creamer, gr w/gold 30.00
Dewdrop, butter dish, bl or amber, 2⅝", ea 190.00
Diamond Band, mug 15.00
Doyle #500, mug, amber, 2" 40.00
Dutch Boudoir, bowl, bl opaque, 1⅛" 120.00
Euclid, spooner 30.00
Fernland, sugar bowl, w/lid, 3" 30.00
Galloway, pitcher, clear w/gold, 3⅞" 35.00
Hawaiian Lei, butter dish, 2¼" 40.00
Hawaiian Lei, creamer 20.00
Hawaiian Lei, spooner 25.00
Heisey Sawtooth Band, spooner 75.00
Heisey Sawtooth Band, spooner, ruby flashed 85.00
Hickman, condiment set, complete 45.00
Hobnail & Thumbprint, creamer 40.00
Hobnail & Thumbprint, creamer, bl 55.00
Horizontal Threads, butter dish, clear w/ruby stain, 1⅞" 120.00
Horizontal Threads, creamer 40.00
Horizontal Threads, creamer, ruby 50.00
Kitten, banana dish, marigold 185.00
Lacy Medallion, sugar bowl, gr w/gold 40.00
Liberty Bell, mug 150.00
Mardi Gras, spooner 45.00
Menagerie, spooner, bl 200.00
Michigan, butter dish, clear w/gold, 3½ " 150.00
Michigan, pitcher, water 40.00
Michigan, pitcher, water; clear w/gold 50.00
Mitered Block, creamer 14.00
Nursery Rhyme, bowl, master berry 90.00
Nursery Rhyme, pitcher, 4¼" 120.00
Optic, creamer 20.00
Optic, creamer, gr 30.00
Oval Star, punch bowl 55.00
Pattee Cross, tumbler, 1¾" 14.00
Pennsylvania, creamer, gr 110.00
Pennsylvania, spooner 50.00
Pert, butter dish, 2¾" 125.00
Pillar, mug 12.00
Plytec, punch bowl 30.00
Portland, pitcher, water; clear w/gold 25.00
Puritan, mug 16.00
Rex (Fancy Cut), punch cup, 1¼" 27.00
Rex (Fancy Cut), spooner 35.00
Rose in Snow, mug, appl hdl 35.00
Standing Lamb, butter dish, frosted 950.00
Sultan, butter dish, 3¾" 125.00
Tappan, butter dish, 3" 34.00
Tappan, spooner 22.00
Thumbelina, punch bowl 35.00
Thumbelina, punch bowl, w/4 cups 65.00
Thumbelina, spooner, creamer & sugar bowl, w/lid 70.00
Two Band, spooner, 2⅞" 60.00
Wee Branches, spooner 85.00
Wheat Sheaf, berry set, 5-pc 60.00
Wheat Sheaf, wine jug, 4⅛" 75.00
Wild Rose, punch bowl, milk glass 95.00
Wild Rose, punch cup, 1¼" 25.00
Wild Rose, spooner, milk glass 60.00

Miscellaneous

Carriage, wood & steel fr, wooden wheels, cloth top, ds, 36" 385.00
Carriage, wood w/metal fittings, orig pnt, wooden wheels, 26x29" .300.00
Drum, emb tin, pnt eagle & banner, wooden bands, 7¾x10" 440.00
Kitchen scale, tin litho, mk Germany, early 1900s, 3½ " 125.00
Noisemaker, oak & pine, unpnt rachet style, late 19th C, 18x17x3½ " ..75.00
Perambulator, pnt decor wood/leather/CI, Am, 1860s, 41x55x24" 460.00
Piano stool, seat adjusts, splay legs/ball ft, red traces 140.00
Rattle, SP brass urn shape w/ivory hdl 100.00
Rattle, 4 NP bells on leatherized cloth straps, trn hdl, 6" 150.00
Rattle, 4 tin bells on twisted wires, trn wood hdl, 8¼" 165.00
Rocking horse, old red & brn rpt, rpl mane/tail/harness, 35" L ..330.00
Sled, pnt wood w/Little Red Riding Hood reserve, 19th C, 35" 460.00
Sled, wood fr w/iron runners, gr/red/mustard pnt, 1890s, 34" 800.00
Sled, wood/metal, gilt scrolls, mc village, name, 1880, 26" 200.00
Tea set, pewter, 2½ " pot w/cr/sug & 4 c/s, EX 100.00
Waffle iron, pnt & NP CI, wood hdls, 7¾", EX, from $100 to ..125.00
Wagon seat, ash w/old finish, 2-slat bk, splint seat, 23x23" 660.00
Wheelbarrow, pnt wood w/squirrel stencil, Paris ME USA No 2, 38" .260.00
Wheelbarrow, wood w/mc landscape scenes w/gold, 19th C, 33" L 500.00

Chintz

'Chintz' is the generic name for English china with an allover floral transfer design. This eye-catching china is reminiscent of chintz dress fabric. It is colorful, bright, and cheery with its many floral designs and reminds one of an English garden in full bloom. It was produced in England during the first half of this century and stands out among other styles of china. Pattern names often found with the manufacturer's name on the bottom of pieces include Florence, Blue Chintz, English Roses, Delphinium, June Roses, Hazel, Eversham, Royalty, Sweet Pea, Summertime, and Welbeck, among others.

The older patterns tend to be composed of larger flowers, while the later, more popular lines can be quite intricate in design. And while the first collectors preferred the earthenware lines, many are now searching for the bone china dinnerware made by such firms as Shelley. Prices are already formidable and rising. You can concentrate on reassembling a favorite pattern, or you can mix two or more designs together for a charming, eclectic look. Another choice may be to limit your collection to teapots (the stacking ones are especially nice), breakfast sets, or cups and saucers. For further information we recommend *Charlton Book of Chintz, I, II,* and *II,* by Susan Scott. Our advisor is Mary Jane Hastings; she is listed in the Directory under Illinois. See also Shelley.

Florence, teapot, eight-cup, minimum value $1,800.00. (Photo courtesy Mary Jane Hastings)

Apple Blossom, butter pat, scalloped, James Kent, 3¼" 80.00
Apple Blossom, celery tray, James Kent, 13x6½ " 245.00
Apple Blossom, nut dish, sq, James Kent, sm 85.00

Balmoral, bonbon, scalloped, hdls, Royal Winton 295.00
Balmoral, coffeepot, Albans shape, Royal Winton 950.00
Balmoral, teapot, Albans shape, 6-cup 850.00
Balmoral, teapot, stacking; 3-pc set, Royal Winton 1,500.00
Bedale, relish canoe, int/ext pattern, Royal Winton 295.00
Bedale, teapot, Elite shape, 6-cup 650.00
Beeston, jam pot & liner, Rheims shape, Royal Winton 395.00
Beeston, relish canoe, Royal Winton 495.00
Blue Tulip, teapot, Countess shape, Royal Winton, 4-cup 135.00
Blue Tulip, vase, bud; Gem shape, Royal Winton 240.00
Cheadle, bowl, dk pk, Ascot shape, 8¼" sq 250.00
Cheadle, creamer & sugar bowl, Raleigh shape, Royal Winton .225.00
Cheadle, cruet set, shakers/mustard/tray, Clover Leaf shape 475.00
Cheadle, cup & saucer, Raleigh shape, Royal Winton 175.00
Cheadle, jug, Raleigh shape, Royal Winton 4½ " 375.00
Cheadle, plate, Royal Winton, 7" 165.00
Chelsea, teapot, breakfast; Countess shape, Royal Winton 495.00
Chelsea, teapot, stacking, Delamere shape, 3-pc, 5½ " 1,500.00
Cotswald, bedside set, Countess shape, 6-pc, NM, from $1,200 to .1,500.00
Cotswald, jug, Albans shape, Royal Winton, 5" 575.00
Cranstone, bowl, salad; SP rim, Rheims shape, 4¼x8" sq 800.00
Crocus, cake plate, tab hdls, Royal Winton, 9" 245.00
Crocus, candy dish, wht, Gordon shape, w/lid, 8" 495.00
Crocus, coffeepot, Albans shape, wht, 8" 800.00
DuBarry, cup & saucer, James Kent 95.00
DuBarry, egg cups (4) & underplate 395.00
DuBarry, nut dish, ruffled, James Kent, sm 85.00
DuBarry, plate, James Kent, 8" 90.00
DuBarry, toast rack, scalloped edges, 4-slice, James Kent 395.00
Eleanor, coffeepot, Albans shape, Royal, 8" 800.00
Eleanor, plate, pleated edge, Royal Winton, 8" 145.00
Eleanor, plate, Royal Winton, 7" 125.00
Eleanor, teapot, Albans shape, Royal Winton, 4-cup 650.00
Eleanor, toast rack, 4-slice, Queen shape, Royal Winton, 2½ x7" ..365.00
English Rose, bowl, dessert; Royal Winton 135.00
English Rose, butter pat, Trefu shape, Royal Winton 125.00
English Rose, plate, Royal Winton, 7" 175.00
English Rose, sugar bowl, Royal Winton, 1¾" 115.00
English Rose, toast rack, 4-slice, Royal Winton 525.00
Estelle, basket, Dudley shape, 4½ " 395.00
Estelle, cake plate, open hdls, Royal Winton, 10⅛x9⅜" 200.00
Estelle, hot water pot, Albans shape, 7" 600.00
Estelle, plate, Royal Winton, 7" 115.00
Evesham, cup & saucer, Raleigh shape, Royal Winton 225.00
Evesham, plate, Athena shape, Royal Winton, 7" 250.00
Evesham, toast rack, 2-slice, 2¼x4½ " 350.00
Evesham, wall pocket, Nita shape, Royal Winton 1,400.00
Fireglow, coffeepot, Perth shape, Royal Winton 950.00
Fireglow, flower vase, wht, no wire mesh, Gem shape, 4¾" 250.00
Fireglow, toast rack, wht, 2-slice, Queen shape, 2½ x4½ " 275.00
Floral Feast, bedside set, Royal Winton, 5-pc 850.00
Floral Feast, creamer & sugar bowl, Royal Winton 195.00
Floral Feast, plate, sq, Royal Winton, 4" 85.00
Floral Feast, teapot, Royal Winton, 4-cup 650.00
Florence, butter pat, Trefu shape, Royal Winton, 4x4½ " 155.00
Florence, cheese keeper, Dane shape, 4x6½ " 520.00
Florida, candlestick, 8¼" 545.00
Hazel, bowl, cut-out hdls, Royal Winton, 1¼x5½ x4½ " 145.00
Hazel, breakfast set, Royal Winton, complete w/tray 1,550.00
Hazel, butter dish, Ascot shape, rectangular, 6" L 200.00
Hazel, cake plate, Saville shape 325.00
Hazel, compote, ftd, Royal Winton, 2x6¼" 295.00
Hazel, cruet set, shakers/mustard/tray, Cloverleaf shape 550.00
Hazel, jug, Dutch shape, Royal Winton, 4" 425.00
Hazel, shakers, Acme shape, Royal Winton, pr 195.00
Hazel, vase, bud; Clyde shape, Royal Winton, 3¾" 275.00
Heather, jug, wht hdl, 5" 285.00
Heather, teapot, Lord Nelson, lg 500.00
Julia, coffeepot, Albans shape, Royal Winton 2,500.00
Julia, compote, ftd, Royal Winton, 2¾x6½ " 525.00
Julia, compote, Lily shape, Royal Winton 775.00
Julia, creamer & sugar bowl, Ascot shape, Royal Winton 425.00
Julia, cup & saucer, Ascot shape, Royal Winton 245.00
Julia, jam pot & liner, Ascot shape, Royal Winton 425.00
Julia, plate, Ascot shape, Royal Winton, 6" 175.00
Julia, plate, Royal Winton, 7" 225.00
Julia, relish, unknown shape, 2-part, 5x9" 350.00
Julia, sweetmeat dish, Royal Winton, 6x4½ " 135.00
Julia, toast rack, 4-slice, Royal Winton, 7" 595.00
Julia, tray, sandwich; Royal Winton, 10x6" 395.00
Lilac Time, cup & saucer, gr trim, Empire 110.00
Lilac Time, plate, Empire, 7" 95.00
Majestic, bowl, mayonnaise; Royal Winton 185.00
Majestic, creamer & sugar bowl, Ascot shape, Royal Winton 195.00
Majestic, creamer & sugar bowl, Countess shape, Royal Winton .195.00
Majestic, cup & saucer, demitasse; can shape 225.00
Majestic, jug, Globe shape, 4¼" 425.00
Majestic, mint boat & underplate, Era shape, 2¼" 300.00
Majestic, plate, Ascot shape, 7" 125.00
Majestic, plate, Athena, 6" 125.00
Marguerite, basket, Hampton shape, Royal Winton, 4" 250.00
Marguerite, cheese keeper, bl trim, Royal Winton, 7½ x6¼" 395.00
Marguerite, plate, Royal Winton, 6¼" 60.00
Marguerite, plate, Royal Winton, 8" 70.00
Marguerite, teapot, Countess shape, 4-cup 400.00
Marina, cheese keeper, 3½ x6" 230.00
Marina, creamer & sugar bowl, Lord Nelson 135.00
Marina, jug, milk; Globe shape, Lord Nelson, 4½ " 300.00
Marina, jug, milk; Globe shape, 5" 495.00
Marina, teacup & saucer, gold trim, Lord Nelson 120.00
Marina, teapot, Lord Nelson, 6-cup 385.00
Marina, teapot, stacking; 3-pc, Lord Nelson, from $650 to 800.00
Marion, candy box, Candy Box shape, 5½ x4" 495.00
Marion, plate, Royal Winton, 7" 155.00
May Festival, candy dish, dk bl bkground, Gordon shape, w/lid, 8" .425.00
May Festival, vase, bud; blk bkground, Lune shape, 4¾" 100.00
Mayfair, basket, Rowsley shape, Royal Winton, 5" 395.00
Mayfair, creamer, Countess shape, Royal Winton, 3" 95.00
Mayfair, cup & saucer, Raleigh shape, Royal Winton 145.00
Mayfair, jam pot, Chelsea shape, ceramic lid, w/liner, 4" 295.00
Mayfair, jug, Raleigh shape, Royal Winton, 4½ " 475.00
Mayfair, plate, Ascot shape, Royal Winton, 8" 185.00
Mayfair, plate, Royal Winton, 7" 145.00
Nantwich, coffeepot, Albans shape, Royal Winton 1,000.00
Nantwich, sandwich tray, Ascot shape, 12x6½ " 250.00
Old Cottage, biscuit barrel, unknown shape, 5¾" 700.00
Old Cottage, coffeepot, Perth shape, 8" 775.00
Old Cottage, cup & saucer, demitasse; Royal Winton 100.00
Old Cottage, jug, Royal Winton, 4½ " 300.00
Old Cottage, plate, chop; Royal Winton, 12" 245.00
Old Cottage, plate, Royal Winton, 10" 145.00
Old Cottage, plate, Royal Winton, 8" 110.00
Old Cottage, platter, rectangular, Royal Winton, 12x10½ " 295.00
Old Cottage, platter, Royal Winton, 13" dia 300.00
Old Cottage, platter, Royal Winton, 14x10¼" 375.00
Old Cottage, soup & saucer, 2-hdl, Royal Winton 125.00
Pink Chintz, dish, serving; 3-part w/center hdl, Crown Ducal, 11" ..375.00
Pink Chintz, plate, Crown Ducal, 7½ " 145.00

Rosalynde, nut dish, scalloped sq, James Kent 75.00
Rosalynde, toast rack, 4-slice, James Kent 350.00
Rosetime, cup & saucer, Lord Nelson 110.00
Rosetime, jug, Lord Nelson, 5" 525.00
Rosetime, jug, milk; Globe shape, Lord Nelson, 4" 395.00
Rosetime, plate, 8-sided, Lord Nelson, 6½ " 125.00
Rosetime, plate, 8-sided, Lord Nelson, 7½ " 155.00
Rosetime, plate, 8-sided, Lord Nelson, 8½ " 175.00
Royal Brocade, creamer, Lord Nelson, 3" 95.00
Royal Brocade, teapot, stacking, 6½ " 475.00
Royalty, butter dish, Ascot shape, 3x6" sq 400.00
Royalty, cake plate, cut-out hdls 375.00
Royalty, creamer, Ascot shape, Royal Winton 125.00
Royalty, cup & saucer, Royal Winton 175.00
Royalty, mint boat, no liner, Royal Winton 175.00
Royalty, plate, Ascot shape, Royal Winton, 8¾" 175.00
Royalty, plate, Royal Winton, 7" 135.00
Rutland, bedside set, 5-pc 900.00
Rutland, relish, 3-part, Gem shape, 8" 295.00
Somerset, butter pat, Royal Winton, 4¼" 85.00
Somerset, jug, milk; Globe shape, bl trim, 4½ " 625.00
Somerset, mint boat & stand, Royal Winton 365.00
Somerset, nut dish, bl trim, ftd, no chintz inside, Bow shape, 3½ " .240.00
Somerset, pie plate & server, 10" 460.00
Somerset, plate, Royal Winton, 6" 115.00
Somerset, plate, Royal Winton, 8" 175.00
Somerset, relish canoe, Royal Winton, 11" 330.00
Spring, cheese keeper, Rex shape, Royal Winton 595.00
Spring, plate, wht bkground, Royal Winton, 8" 175.00
Spring, plate, 10-sided, Royal Winton, 8" 195.00
Summertime, coffeepot, Ascot shape, 8½ " 950.00
Summertime, creamer & sugar bowl, Royal Winton, mini, pr ...215.00
Summertime, cup & saucer, King shape, Royal Winton 110.00
Summertime, egg cup, dbl; Royal Winton 155.00
Summertime, hot water pot, Countess shape, 5½ " 650.00
Summertime, jar, Gordon shape, w/lid, Royal Winton, 8½ " 695.00
Summertime, jug, Royal Winton, 4½ " 345.00
Summertime, plate, Ascot shape, Royal Winton, 6" 90.00
Summertime, plate, Ascot shape, Royal Winton, 8" 115.00
Summertime, plate, Athena shape, Royal Winton, 7" 100.00
Summertime, plate, muffin; Royal Winton 145.00
Summertime, platter, Ascot shape, Royal Winton, 14½ x11" 395.00
Summertime, relish, cone shape, 10½ " 300.00
Summertime, teapot, Ascot shape, 4-cup 650.00
Summertime, teapot, Ascot shape, 6-cup 650.00
Summertime, teapot, Elite shape, 4-cup 650.00
Summertime, vase, Gem shape, 6" 395.00
Sunshine, candy box, 2x4x3½ " 350.00
Sunshine, compote, Lily shape, Royal Winton, lg 450.00
Sunshine, cup & saucer, Royal Winton 155.00
Sunshine, teapot, Albans shape, Royal Winton, 2-cup 725.00
Sunshine, teapot, yel wash, Albans shape, 4-cup 850.00
Sweet Pea, bonbon, ftd, 2½ x7¼" 295.00
Sweet Pea, bowl, Crown shape, Royal Winton, lg 595.00
Sweet Pea, bowl, Kipling shape, Royal Winton, 5¾x4" 155.00
Sweet Pea, bowl, Royal Winton, 6½ " 130.00
Sweet Pea, bowl, serving; Royal Winton, 2½ x9" 325.00
Sweet Pea, bowl, tab hdl, Royal Winton, 6x5" 110.00
Sweet Pea, butter dish, Ascot shape, 3x6" sq 425.00
Sweet Pea, compote, Lily shape, Royal Winton, 6⅛x3⅜" 395.00
Sweet Pea, cup & saucer, demitasse; Albans shape, Royal Winton .135.00
Sweet Pea, cup & saucer, grandfather's; Royal Winton 250.00
Sweet Pea, cup & saucer, Royal Winton 155.00
Sweet Pea, jug, milk; Globe shape, 5" 650.00
Sweet Pea, plate, Ascot shape, Royal Winton, 6" 145.00
Sweet Pea, shakers, bulbous, ftd, Royal Winton, pr 195.00
Sweet Pea, trivet, Ascot shape, 5¾" sq 245.00
Victorian Rose, creamer & sugar bowl, Ascot shape, Royal Winton .195.00
Victorian Rose, cup & saucer, Raeigh shape, Royal Winton 165.00
Victorian Rose, shakers, Fife shape, Royal Winton, pr 185.00
Victorian Rose, shakers, Fife shape, 2½ ", pr, +6" tray 250.00
Victorian Rose, tray, Royal Winton, 8x5" 275.00
Welbeck, bowl, salad; SP rim, Rheims shape, 4x8" 650.00
Welbeck, bowl, vegetable; Ascot shape, 9¼" sq 460.00
Welbeck, cup & saucer, Albans shape, Royal Winton 300.00
Welbeck, jam pot, Rheims tall shape, w/lid & liner, 4" 515.00
Welbeck, muffineer, SP lid, Ascot shape, 3½ x7" sq 495.00
Welbeck, plate, Royal Winton, 8" 195.00
Welbeck, vase, bud; Royal Winton, 3¾" 275.00
White Crocus, teapot, Albans shape, Royal Winton, 2-cup 650.00
White Crocus, teapot, stacking; 3-pc set, Royal Winton 1,200.00

Chocolate Glass

Jacob Rosenthal developed chocolate glass, a rich shaded opaque brown sometimes referred to as caramel slag, in 1900 at the Indiana Tumbler and Goblet Company of Greentown, Indiana. Later, other companies produced similar ware. Only the latter is listed here. See also Greentown. Our advisors for this category are Jerry and Sandi Garrett; they are listed in the Directory under Indiana.

Barber bottle (cologne), Venetian, w/stopper 650.00
Bowl, Aldine, oval, w/lid 1,650.00
Bowl, Beaded Triangle, 4½ " 350.00
Bowl, Shield w/Daisy & Button, 8⅜" dia 1,300.00
Bowl, 5-fluted 325.00
Butter dish, Fleur-de-lis 775.00
Butter dish, Wild Rose w/Bowknot 575.00
Butter dish, Wild Rose w/Scrolling, child sz 700.00
Candle holder, griffin 2,500.00
Carafe, Chrysanthemum Leaf 2,500.00
Compote, Chrysanthemum Leaf, 4½ " dia 400.00
Compote, Melrose, 7¼" dia 275.00
Covered dish, lamb (+) 2,250.00
Creamer, Cattail & Water Lily 475.00
Creamer, Rose Garland 1,350.00
Cruet, Geneva, w/stopper 1,250.00
Cuff box, 4½ " H 500.00
Hatpin holder, Orange Tree 800.00
Lamp, Cloverleaf 1,250.00
Mug, Swirl 600.00
Nappy, Navarre, hdld 300.00
Orange bowl, Grape & Cable 3,500.00
Pitcher, File 2,000.00
Pitcher, milk; Feather 1,300.00
Pitcher, Rose Garland 3,000.00
Salt dip, master; Honeycomb, 3½ " dia 650.00
Sauce dish, Melrose, scalloped edge, 3¾" dia 250.00
Sauce dish, Wild Rose w/Bowknot 125.00
Shaker, Beaded Triangle 475.00
Shaker, Geneva 350.00
Spooner, Sultan (aka Wild Rose w/Scrolling), child sz 325.00
Sugar bowl, Fleur-de-lis, w/lid 325.00
Syrup jug, Geneva, metal lid 650.00
Tray, comb & brush; Venetian, 8x10" 450.00
Tray, ring; Venetian, 4x5" 400.00
Vase, Beaded Triangle, 6¼" 250.00

Christmas Collectibles

Christmas past . . . lovely mementos from long ago attest to the ostentatious Victorian celebrations of the season.

St. Nicholas, better known as Santa, has changed much since 300 A.D. when the good Bishop Nicholas showered needy children with gifts and kindnesses. During the early eighteenth century, Santa was portrayed as the kind gift-giver to well-behaved children and the stern switch-bearing disciplinarian to those who were bad. In 1822 Clement Clark Moore, a New York poet, wrote his famous *Night Before Christmas*, and the Santa he described was jolly and jovial — a lovable old elf who was stern with no one. Early Santas wore robes of yellow, brown, blue, green, red, white, or even purple. But Thomas Nast, who worked as an illustrator for *Harper's Weekly*, was the first to depict Santa in a red suit instead of the traditional robe and to locate him the entire year at the North Pole headquarters.

Today's collectors prize early Santa figures, especially those in robes of fur or mohair or those dressed in an unusual color. Some early examples of Christmas memorabilia are the pre-1870 ornaments from Dresden, Germany. These cardboard figures — angels, gondolas, umbrellas, dirigibles, and countless others — sparkled with gold and silver trim. Late in the 1870s, blown glass ornaments were imported from Germany. There were over 6,000 recorded designs, all painted inside with silvery colors. From 1890 through 1910, blown glass spheres were often decorated with beads, tassels, and tinsel rope.

Christmas lights, made by Sandwich and some of their contemporaries, were either pressed or mold-blown glass shaped into a form similar to a water tumbler. They were filled with water and then hung from the tree by a wire handle; oil floating on the surface of the water served as fuel for the lighted wick.

Kugels are glass ornaments that were made as early as 1820 and as late as 1890. Ball-shaped examples are more common than the fruit and vegetable forms and have been found in sizes ranging from 1" to 14" in diameter. They were made of thick glass with heavy brass caps, in cobalt, green, gold, silver, red, and occasionally in amethyst.

Although experiments involving the use of electric light bulbs for the Christmas tree occurred before 1900, it was 1903 before the first manufactured socket set was marketed. These were very expensive and often proved a safety hazard. In 1921 safety regulations were established, and products were guaranteed safety approved. The early bulbs were smaller replicas of Edison's household bulb. By 1910 G.E. bulbs were rounded with a pointed end, and until 1919 all bulbs were hand blown. The first figural bulbs were made around 1910 in Austria. Japan soon followed, but their product was never of the high quality of the Austrian wares. American manufacturers produced their first machine-made figurals after 1919. Today figural bulbs (especially character-related examples) are very popular collectibles. Bubble lights were popular from about 1945 to 1960 when miniature lights were introduced. These tiny lamps dampened the public's enthusiasm for the bubblers, and manufacturers stopped providing replacement bulbs.

Feather trees were made from 1850 to 1950. All are collectible. Watch for newly manufactured feather trees that have been reintroduced.

For further information concerning Christmas collectibles, we recommend *Christmas Ornaments, Lights, and Decorations, A Collector's Identification and Value Guide, Volumes I* through *III*, by George Johnson, available from Collector Books or your local bookstore.

Note: Values are given for bulbs that are in good paint, with no breaks or cracks, and in working order. Examples termed 'mini' measure no more than 1½". When no condition is mentioned in the description, assume values are for examples in EX/NM condition except paper items; those should be assumed NM/M.

Bulbs

Angel, standing in long robe, clear, Japan, ca 1925, 2½ ", up to ..70.00
Apple, celluloid, ca 1915-25, 1¾", from $30 to 40.00
Banana w/face, milk glass, Japan, 1950s, 2¾", from $30 to 40.00
Bear, sitting, milk glass, Japan, 1950s, 2¾", from $75 to 85.00
Bear w/hands on chest, milk glass, Japan, mini, from $40 to 50.00
Bird in birdhouse, milk glass, Japan, 1935-50, 1½ ", from $25 to .30.00
Bulldog in vest, milk glass, Japan, 2¾", from $90 to 110.00
Carriage lantern w/exhaust tip, clear, 4-sided, 2¼", up to 75.00
Cat, beckoning, clear, Japan, 1925, 2½ ", from $20 to 25.00
Cat w/ball, milk glass, Japan, 2¼", from $70 to 80.00
Children in shoe, milk glass, Japan, 1950s, 2¼", from $70 to 80.00
Clown w/mask, milk glass, Japan, 1950s, 3", from $25 to 35.00
Cottage in hillside, milk glass, Japan, ca 1950, 2¼", from $50 to ..60.00
Doc (dwarf), milk glass, Diamond Brite, Disney, Japan, from $50 to ..60.00
Duck, dressed, milk glass, Japan, 1920-55, 2¼", from $25 to 30.00
Elephant sitting on ball, milk glass, Japan, 2¾", from $40 to 50.00
Flower in seashell, milk glass, 10-petal, Japan, 2¼", from $75 to .85.00
Frog, clear, Mazda, 2¼", from $30 to 35.00
Fruit basket, milk glass, Japan, 2¾", from $25 to 35.00
Girl in snowsuit, clear, Japan, 2¼", from $25 to 35.00
Humpty Dumpty, milk glass, Parmount, Japan, 2½ ", from $30 to ..40.00
Indian chief, clear, European, 3¼", from $250 to 275.00
Lion, clear, detailed mane, on haunches, 2¼", from $150 to 175.00
Little Orphan Annie, milk glass, Japan, 1935-55, from $35 to 45.00
Man in moon on star, milk glass, Japan, 1950s, 2", from $25 to ...30.00
Mother dog & pup (Scotties), milk glass, Japan, 1950s, 2", from $65 to ..75.00
Oceanliner, milk glass, Japan, 1950s, 2¾", from $100 to 125.00
Parrot, clear, Japan, mini, from $20 to 25.00
Peacock, feathered disk behind emb bird, milk glass, Japan, 2¼" ..65.00
Pear, celluloid, 1915-25, 2¼", from $30 to 40.00
Pear, clear, ca 1920, 2¼", from $20 to 30.00
Pelican, milk glass, Japan, 1950s, 2¼", from $30 to 35.00
Pig in dress, milk glass, molded sripes, Japan, 2", from $60 to 80.00
Queen of Hearts, milk glass, Parmount, Japan, 2¾", from $25 to ..35.00
Roly poly boy, milk glass, Japan, 2½ ", from $25 to 35.00
Sailor boy w/parrot, celluloid, 1915-25, 4", from $50 to 60.00

Santas, painted milk glass, 3½ – 4": Full figure, $25.00; Head only, $35.00; 'Santa Scenes,' $60.00 each. (Photo courtesy Margaret and Kenn Whitmyer)

Santa (Am style) w/tree, wht fluted base, 5", NM 50.00
Santa (German-style in robe) w/tree & toys, 9", NM 250.00
Santa (German-style) w/bag & tree, wht fluted base, 5", NM 50.00
Santa (3-faced), milk glass, Japan, 2¼", from $20 to 30.00
Santa face on bell, milk glass, 2-sided, Japan, 1¾", from $15 to ..20.00
Santa head, milk glass, Japan, 1930-50, 1½ ", from $18 to 22.00
Santa head in chimney, milk glass, Japan, 2¼", from $20 to 25.00

Snowman w/stick, milk glass, Japan, 1930-55, 2-2½", from $15 to .20.00
Squirrel, milk glass, Japan, 1950s, 2", from $30 to 35.00
Squirrel eating nut, clear, US, mini, from $70 to 80.00

Candy Containers

Antelope head, Dresden, 3-D, natural, 3¼", from $375 to 425.00
Ball, printed paper on cb, HP decor, pre-1950s, 3", from $30 to ..40.00
Basketball, cb w/imitation leather seams, 1½-2", from $65 to 75.00
Bear head, Dresden, natural, 3-D, 3", from $425 to 475.00
Bell, paper w/scrap decor, US, 1930s, 5½", from $25 to 35.00
Boot, lady's high heeled; satin over cb, 1950s, 5½", from $30 to ..50.00
Boot, red plastic, Merry Christmas, Rosbro, 1955, 4", from $5 to ..6.00
Carp (fish), Dresden, gold/silver, 3-D, 7¼" L, from $450 to 500.00
Carrying case, emb paper, appl hdl/straps, 2", from $125 to 150.00
Champagne bottle, papier-mache w/net covering, 3", from $175 to 200.00
Clock, printed paper, Czar on horse, Russia, 1930s, 4", from $110 to ..125.00
Clown's hat, mc paper, pointed top, appl Dresden stars, 3" 225.00
Cockatiel head, Dresden, gold/silver, 3-D, 2½", from $375 to ..400.00
Cornucopia, plain paper w/litho, sm, from $15 to 25.00
Cornucopia, w/scraps & tinsel, 6-8", ea, from $50 to 75.00
Cow's head, Dresden, natural, 3-D, appl ears/horns, 2¾", $450 to ..495.00
Dog's head, Dresden, gold/silver, 3-D, 2½", from $475 to 550.00
Heart, red glazed paper, appl scrap angel or Cupid, 1-2", from $45 to ..50.00
Horse's leg, Dresden, gold/silver, 3-D, 3", from $350 to 375.00
Liberty shield, fabric-covered paper, 1920s, 3¾", from $50 to 75.00
Rabbit, Dresden, natural, 3-D, 2", from $275 to 300.00
Santa, compo face/hands, bl compo legs, fur beard, Germany, 8½" ..675.00
Santa, felt coat, fur beard, opens at waist, compo, Germany, 4" ..325.00
Santa, felt coat, fur beard, opens at waist, compo, Germany, 5" ..375.00
Santa, felt coat, fur beard, opens at waist, compo, Germany, 6" ..425.00
Santa, felt coat, fur beard, opens at waist, compo, Germany, 7" ..475.00
Santa, felt coat, fur beard, opens at waist, compo, Germany, 8" ..525.00
Santa, felt coat, fur beard, opens at waist, compo, Germany, 9" ..575.00
Santa, felt coat, fur beard, opens at waist, compo, Germany, 10" .625.00
Santa (cotton) on train, cb w/mica, front pulls out, Japan, 6" L .185.00
Santa in sled w/running deer, hard plastic, Am, 1950s, 4" L 25.00
Santa on bell, papier-mache/mica, bl robe, Germany, 6" 295.00
Santa on house, cotton batten/paper litho, Japan, 4" 95.00
Santa on log pile, compo w/fur beard, felt coat, Germany, 5" 325.00
Santa on skis, hard plastic, EX details, Am, 1955, 3½" 10.00
Snowman on log, felt/papier-mache & cb, side opens, 4" 195.00
Stork, Dresden, natural, 3-D, candy sack at bk, 4", from $250 to .275.00
Suitcase, printed paper w/appl leather straps, metal latch, 4" 65.00
Turkey, Dresden, natural, 3-D, 4x3½", from $225 to 250.00
Violin, paper litho, appl neck, opens in bk, 3", from $90 to 110.00

Ornaments

Angel, Dresden, gold/silver, flat, crepe-paper skirt, 3½ x6" 130.00
Angel, Dresden, gold/silver, flat, 4", from $90 to 110.00
Angel child, hard plastic, Germany, 4", from $8 to 9.00
Angel head, scrap only (no tinsel), 2-3½", from $3 to 8.00
Angel heads (2) on bell, dbl-sided scrap w/tinsel, 4¾", from $25 to .35.00
Angel w/ribbon (flying), scrap only (no tinsel), 8", from $30 to ..40.00
Angel w/songbook, scrap w/tinsel, 7", from $30 to 40.00
Angel w/spun glass wings, mirror image reverse, 5¼", from $40 to .50.00
Baby crying, paper doll, 2¼" scrap, Germany, 5-6" overall 5.00
Ball, celluloid, made in 2 parts, w/loop, 1930s, 2¾", from $5 to 6.00
Ball w/filigree & holly leaves, hard plastic, Bradford, 1955 ....2.50
Bead chain, plastic, rnd or oval, Japan or China, 1960s-70s, up to ..3.00
Bear, Dresden, natural, dbl-sided, 2¼", from $250 to 295.00
Berry basket, Dresden, gold/silver, flat, 2", from $25 to 35.00
Bird, litho on cb, flat, sm, from $20 to 35.00
Bird w/chalk body, Dresden, gold/silver, 3-D, 4½" wingspan 125.00
Buffalo, Dresden, natural, dbl-sided, 3¾" L, from $275 to 300.00
Clown boy, scrap (no tinsel), in gold oval fr, 3½", from $10 to ..15.00
Crescent moon, Dresden, gold/silver, flat, w/scrap angel, 4½" 75.00
Crescent moon & star, litho on cb, flat, med, from $40 to 60.00
Deer, celluloid, Japan, 3-3½", from $7 to 8.00
Deer (running doe), Dresden, gold/silver, flat, 4¼", from $110 to .125.00
Donkey, Dresden, natural, dbl-sided, 2½", from $175 to 200.00
Dove on olive branch, scrap w/tinsel, 6½ x7", from $40 to 50.00
Eagle, Dresden, gold/silver, flat, 2¼" wingspan, from $20 to 25.00
Elephant, fluorescent plastic, mk USA, 1940s-50s, 4¼", from $6 to ..8.00
Fan, Dresden, gold/silver, flat, 2x3½", from $30 to 40.00
Father Christmas head w/holly, scrap w/tinsel, 4¾", from $20 to .30.00
Flounder (fish), Dresden, gold/silver, dbl-sided, 3½" 300.00
Garland, paper honeycomb, folds flat, 2¾-9½" W, ea, from $6 to 7.00
Horse, Dresden, gold/silver, flat, 4½" W, from $90 to 110.00
Icicle, fluorescent plastic, flanged, 1940s-50s, 4¾-5", w/loop 2.00
Icicle, twisted; clear plastic, Am, ca 1960s, 5" 1.00
Lion stalking, Dresden, gold/silver, 3-D, 4¾" L, from $400 to ...450.00
Medallion, Diamond; Dresden, gold/silver, flat, 5½", from $60 to ..80.00
Nativity scene, scrap foldout, Germany, 7x4½", from $10 to 15.00
Palm in urn, Dresden, gold/silver, flat, 3x1½", from $35 to 50.00
Peacock w/trailing feathers, Dresden, gold/silver, 3-D, 3" 335.00
Peasant boy w/cake, scrap paper doll, Germany, 8½" 25.00
Polar bear on ice, Dresden, natural, dbl-sided, 2", from $175 to ..200.00
Rosette, scrap ea side w/spun glass, dbl-sided, 4-5¾", from $35 to ..50.00
Santa, scrap w/spun glass skirt, tree over shoulder, 4½" 25.00
Santa in heart fr w/toys & tree, scrap w/tinsel, 4½", from $35 to 45.00
Santa in train, scrap only (no tinsel), 6¾", from $100 to 125.00
Santa light cover, hard plastic, Am, 1950s, 4¾", from $15 to 18.00
Santa standing on dome, celluloid, Irwin, 1930-40, 3½", from $40 to .50.00
Snow children (5) w/toys, scrap w/tinsel, 12", from $150 to 175.00
Snow girl w/muff, scrap w/spun glass skirt/Dresden stars, Germany, 12" ..150.00
Star in ring, hard plastic, ca 1950, 3¾" 5.00
Swan, Dresden, swimming, gold/silver, flat, 7", from $80 to 100.00
Tiger, Dresden, natural, 3-D, 2½", from $250 to 275.00
Woman skier, paper w/spun glass skirt, Germany, 12" 75.00

Miscellaneous

Christmas light, Starburst, bright yellow-green, smooth base, 3⅞", $85.00.

Candle clip, bell, emb detail & decor, 2", from $40 to 45.00
Candle clip, emb geometric designs, 1½-2½", from $3 to 8.00
Candle clip, girl w/basket held out before her, 2", from $100 to ..110.00
Candle clip, grape cluster, emb details, insert at leaves, 1½" 40.00
Candle holder, acorns/leaf, tin litho, clip, 2-2½", from $60 to 65.00
Candle holder, angel w/trumpet, tin litho, clip, 3", from $125 to 140.00
Candle holder, boy's-head molded glass shade, clip, 3", from $375 to ..425.00
Candle holder, cherub w/rose, tin litho, clip, 2", from $80 to 90.00
Candle holder, Chinaman's-head molded glass shade, clip, 3", $300 to .350.00
Candle holder, dbl-weighted pendulum w/roses, clip, 1890s, 4-6", up to ..70.00

Candle holder, girl w/doll, tin litho, clip, 2½ ", from $125 to 140.00
Candle holder, glass apple ornament weight, clip, ca 1905, 3", up to .55.00
Candle holder, molded glass ribbed shade, clip, 3½ ", $75 to 85.00
Candle holder, pendulum weight, clip, sm drip pan, US, 1870-90, 5½ " .15.00
Candle holder, tin/lead reflector weight (butterfly), clip, 2½ " 80.00
Christmas light, Daisy pattern, lt gr, emb G in 6-pointed star 65.00
Christmas light, Dmn Quilt, amber, squat, from $20 to 30.00
Christmas light, Dmn Quilt, cobalt, Pain's Pat 1885, from $90 to .100.00
Christmas light, fishnet, lt gr, Stiegel type, 3½ " 85.00
Christmas light, grape cluster, clear, Hearn Wright, 4" 145.00
Fence, feather, per section, from $25 to 35.00
Fence, wood, per section, from $10 to 35.00
Fence, wood pickets w/gr rpt, wire nails, hinged corners, 11x22x22" .60.00
Kugel, ball, amber, ribbed, worn, 4" 160.00
Kugel, ball, bl, brass hanger, 10" dia 1,000.00
Kugel, ball, cobalt, w/brass hanger, 5¾" 300.00
Kugel, ball, cranberry, brass hanger, 3¼" 220.00
Kugel, ball, cranberry, brass hanger, 8" dia 800.00
Kugel, ball, red, brass hanger, 3¾" 600.00
Kugel, berry, unsilvered cobalt, brass hanger, 4¼" dia 600.00
Kugel, grapes, amber, brass hanger, 4¼" 350.00
Kugel, grapes, cobalt, brass hanger, 4¼" 500.00
Kugel, grapes, lt silvery gr, brass hanger, 4" 400.00
Kugel, grapes, med gr, brass hanger, lt wear, 4¼" 300.00
Kugel, grapes, med gr, brass hanger, 4¾" 575.00
Kugel, silver, brass hanger, worn silvering, 8" dia 140.00
Lantern, metal, 6 pierced sides, Germany, 1930s, 1½ ", up to 75.00
Lantern, metal fold-up w/cut-out panels, celluloid insert, 1920, 4" ..35.00
Santa, Belsnickle, papier-mache, old rpt/rprs, 15" 275.00
Santa, celluloid, Germany or Japan, 3-6", ea, from $35 to 150.00
Santa, Roly Poly, HP compo, red top/bl bottom, Germany, 1910, 5", EX ...330.00
Santa w/bag & wreath, HP hollow plaster, 5¼", NM 40.00
Santa w/bag on bk, HP bsk, 4", NM 40.00
Tree, bubble light; paper needles, 1950s-early '60s, 24" 155.00
Tree, feather; Germany, Japan or US, 7-12", from $75 to 90.00
Tree, feather; Germany, Japan or US, 13-23", from $95 to 120.00
Tree, feather; Germany, Japan or US, 32-36", from $155 to 185.00
Tree, feather; Germany, Japan or US, 38-46", from $220 to 295.00
Tree, feather; Germany, Japan or US, 56-62", from $355 to 450.00
Tree, feather; West Germany, gr w/red berries, 15" 250.00
Tree stand, CI w/red & gr poinsettias, 8-light, Noma, 1928 ....75.00
Tree stand, metal, 4-leg, electrified, mk 250V, 1920s-30s 35.00
Tree stand, metal cone w/Santa at chimney scene, Noma, 1928 ..185.00
Tree stand, plaster Santa head, 11½ ", from $300 to 350.00
Tree stand, steel, electrified, musical, Cameo, 1960s, 13" 15.00
Tree stand, steel w/3 detachable legs, 8-Light Automatic, MIB ...35.00
Tree top, angel w/flower, mold/free blown, Germany, early, 4" ...265.00
Tree top, Angel-Glo w/magic wand, plastic, long dress, 1949, 7" .15.00
Tree top, candelabra w/dangles, metal w/jewels & snowflakes, 1910s, 8" ..200.00
Tree top, glass point w/plastic figure, Germany, 1950s, 10" 30.00
Tree top, glass points w/single or dbl ball, 9-14", from $2 to 8.00
Tree top, point on ball, plastic, Bradford/Italy, 1970s-80s, 12" 3.00
Tree top, Santa w/arms in sleeve, blown, 9", from $150 to 175.00
Tree top, star (5-point), metal, Riby, 1880s, 7¾", from $200 to ..225.00
Tree top, 5-point tin star w/red & wht light bulbs, 1930s, 8x7", NM .25.00

Chrysanthemum Sprig, Blue

This is the blue opaque version of Northwood's popular pattern, Chrysanthemum Sprig. It was made at the turn of the century and is today very rare, as its values indicate. Prices are influenced by the amount of gold remaining on the raised designs. Our advisors are Betty and Clarence Maier; they're listed in the Directory under Pennsylvania.

Bowl, berry; sm 325.00
Bowl, master fruit; 10½ " W 600.00
Butter dish 1,250.00
Butter dish, lt in color 500.00
Celery 600.00
Compote, jelly 600.00
Condiment tray, rare, VG gold 750.00
Creamer 385.00
Cruet, EX gold, from $975 to 1,200.00
Pitcher, water 1,100.00

Cruet set, see listings below for individual values. (Photo courtesy Mildred and Ralph Lechner)

Shakers, pr 450.00
Spooner, from $300 to 350.00
Sugar bowl, M gold, w/lid, 7" 475.00
Toothpick holder 450.00
Tumbler 350.00

Cincinnati Art Pottery

Established circa 1880, this pottery initially experimented in the newly developed underglaze Cincinnati faience but soon abandoned these efforts and instead began producing a different kind of ware. Among its products were Hungarian Faience (embossed designs painted in various colors on light-toned grounds), Portland Blue Faience (named for the rich blue glaze used in its production), and the pottery's most famous line, Kenzota (an ivory faience primarily decorated with flowers). The company remained in business in Cincinnati, Ohio, until shortly after 1890.

Vase, floral, mc on multi-tone brn, sgn, att, 8", NM 150.00
Vase, morning glories, mauve/bl on yel to bl, hdls, 12x10" 500.00

Circus Collectibles

The 1890s were the golden age of the circus, when Barnum and Bailey's parades transformed mundane city streets into an exotic never-never land inhabited by trumpeting elephants with jeweled gold head-gear strutting by to the strains of the calliope that issued from a fine red- and gilt-painted wagon extravagantly decorated with carved wooden animals of every description. It was an exciting experience. Is it any wonder that collectors today treasure the mementos of that golden era? See also Posters.

Key:
B&B — Barnum & Bailey RB — Ringling Bros.

Card, Christmas; elephant w/rider cover, RB/B&B, 1925-26, EX ...30.00
Costume, clown's baggy pants, shoes, tie, etc, +makeup kit, '30s ..150.00
Mug, RB/B&B Circus World, park scenes, 1970s, 6½" 18.00
Postcard, Christmas; elephant w/clown & Santa, 7¼x4", EX 35.00
Postcard, 2 ladies & moon w/2 horses & riders, early, mc, EX 30.00
Program, RB/B&B, 1958, VG 18.00
Program, 1944, clown looks up at lady on horse, VG 30.00
Wagon crest, cvd eagle w/lioness & dolphins, losses, VG 650.00

Clarice Cliff

Between 1928 and 1935 in Burslem, England, as the director and part owner of Wilkinson and Newport Pottery Companies, Clarice Cliff and her 'paintresses' created a body of hand-painted pottery whose influence is felt to the present time.

The name for the oevre was Bizarre Ware, and the predominant sensibility, style, and appearance was Deco. Almost all pieces are signed. There were over 160 patterns and more than 400 shapes, all of which are illustrated in *A Bizarre Affair — The Life and Work of Clarice Cliff*, published by Harry N. Abrams, Inc., written by Len Griffen and Susan and Louis Meisel.

Note: Non-hand-painted work (transfer printed) was produced after World War II and into the 1950s. Some of the most common names are 'Tonquin' and 'Charlotte.' These items, while attractive and enjoyable to own, have little value in the collector market. Our advisors for this category are Wilfred and Dolli Cohen; they are listed in the Directory under California.

Pitcher, Fantasque, orange and black flowers, 7¾x7", $1,295.00.

Candlesticks, Fantasque, Melon, mc w/brn outline, 3¼", EX, pr .1,380.00
Creamer & sugar bowl, Aureau, mc flowers, Bizarre, 2¾", 2¼" .200.00
Cup, Chintz, orange/brn/blk, ca 1932, 3⅝" 460.00
Cup & saucer, Melon, gr, globe shape, NM 850.00
Cup & saucer, tea; Farmhouse, mk Bizarre, NM 610.00
Dinner service, Ravel pattern Bizarre Ware, 35-pc (partial) set ...1,150.00
Honey pot, Blue Chintz, beehive shape, mk, 4" 625.00
Jam pot, Melon, overlapping fruit, w/lid, prof rstr, 4" 700.00
Pin dish, Inspiration Persian, 3¾" dia 375.00
Pitcher, Fantasque, Autumn (Balloon Trees), mc, sq base, 5⅛", NM ..925.00
Pitcher, Fantasque, Trees & House (Alpine), 8-sided, 6⅜" 1,725.00
Plate, Autumn, Cafe-Au-Lait, 8½" 550.00
Plate, dinner; Forest Glen, 10⅜x8¼" 475.00
Plate, Fantasque, Autumn (Balloon Trees), mc w/orange bands, 10" ..1,725.00
Plate, Fantasque Fruit, Ledo shape, ca 1930, 8¾" 630.00
Plate, freehand sketch of church, hills & trees, 9" 500.00
Plate, Melon, gr, 9" 1,150.00
Plate, prancing horse, dk bl & brn on wht, brn rim, 8" 500.00
Plate, Woodland, Honeyglaze, 9" 450.00
Shaker, Trees & House (Alpine), teepee shape, Bizarre, 5¾" .1,380.00
Sugar sifter, Marguerite, orange flower on gr, conical, 5½" 875.00
Sugar sifter, Secrets Bonjour 1,150.00
Teapot, Bizarre, trees on invt cone, orange/yel/blk, 4½", NM ..2,185.00
Teapot, Teepee, conical form, totem hdl, brave spout, moose on body, 7" ..900.00
Vase, Crocus, elongated oval form, flared rim, 8", pr 700.00
Vase, vine, leaves & clouds in relief, gr/brn/gold on tan, 7" 350.00

Cleminson

A hobby turned to enterprise, Cleminson is one of several California potteries whose clever hand-decorated wares are attracting the attention of today's collectors. The Cleminsons started their business at their El Monte home in 1941 and were so successful that eventually they expanded to a modern plant that employed more than 150 workers. They produced not only dinnerware and kitchen items such as cookie jars, canisters, and accessories, but novelty wall vases, small trays, plaques, etc., as well. Though nearly always marked, Cleminson wares are easy to spot as you become familiar with their distinctive glaze colors. Their grayed-down blue and green, berry red, and dusty pink say 'Cleminson' as clearly as their trademark. Unable to compete with foreign imports, the pottery closed in 1963. For more information we recommend *The Collector's Encyclopedia of California Pottery, Second Edition*, by Jack Chipman (Collector Books).

Bread tray, Distlefink, 12½" 35.00
Butter dish, Distlefink, w/lid 50.00
Butter dish, lady, w/bottom plate 38.00
Clothes sprinkler, Chinese man, 8" 40.00
Cookie jar, Cookbook 225.00
Cookie jar, Gingerbread House 140.00
Covered jar, Chinese man, stamped mk 60.00
Cup, Spectator Sport, man carrying team flag, 3¾x4½" 25.00
Gravy bowl, Distlefink, w/ladle, 5½" 50.00
Lazy susan, Galagray, 7-pc, on revolving tray 55.00
Marmalade, flowerpot w/strawberry finial, 4" 30.00
Match safe, Cherry, NM 35.00
Pie bird, in-mold initials, 4½", from $25 to 40.00
Pitcher, bird, Distlefink, 9½" 60.00
Plaque, 1903 Packard, pierced 17.50
Plate, Apple, 8¼" 25.00
Plate, chip 'n dip; Dips 'n Chips in pastel colors, EX 50.00
Plate, crowing rooster, 9½" 30.00
Plate, flowers & butterflies, 7" 40.00
Plate, fruit or flowers, ca 1948, 7½", ea 30.00
Plate, God Bless Our Happy Home, yel/red/blk/bl, 6" 30.00
Shakers, artist palette, stamped mk, 6¼", pr 75.00
Spoon rest, floral, 8½" 25.00
String holder, floral decor & verse, 5¾" W 45.00
String holder, house shape, wall hanging, 6½" 75.00
Sugar shaker, lady, wht blouse, yel dress, X-striped apron, 6½" ...40.00
Toothpick holder, butler, stamped mk, 4½" 50.00
Tray, Galagray, 12" 25.00
Wall decoration, kettle shape, w/verse, detachable hdl, 9" 45.00
Wall decoration, teapot, verse, bl w/blk lid & hdl, 8½x8" 40.00
Wall pocket, fireplace bellows, 10½" 40.00
Wall pocket, key form, Welcome Guest, 7¼" 35.00
Wall pocket, kitty in a basket 80.00
Wall pocket, little house on top of the world, 8" W 50.00

Clewell

Charles Walter Clewell was a metal worker who perfected the technique of plating an entire ceramic vessel with a thin layer of copper or bronze treated with an oxidizing agent to produce a natural deterioration of the surface. Through trial and error, he was able to control the degree of patina achieved. In the early stages, the metal darkened and if allowed to develop further formed a natural turquoise-blue or green corrosion. He worked alone in his small Akron, Ohio, studio from about 1906, buying undecorated pottery from several Ohio firms, among them Weller, Owens, and Cambridge. His work is usually marked. Clewell died in 1965, having never revealed his secret process to others.

Prices for Clewell have advanced rapidly during the past few years along with the Arts and Crafts market in general. Right now, good examples are bringing whatever the market will bear.

Bookends, shield-bk candle holders, brn/gr patina, 6½ ", pr ...**2,100.00**
Covered dish, copper-clad, rivets, cleaned patina, 6½ " dia **200.00**
Jardiniere, #403-215, gr/bl/orange/brn patina, 7½ x10½ " **3,750.00**
Jardiniere, #418-2-9, copper clad w/verdigris, 5¼x6½ " **950.00**
Mug, copper clad w/MP/1908 medallion, emb mk, 4½ " **150.00**

Vase, poppies and pods in relief, reticulated area on side, deep golden and brown patina, paper label, rare, 13½", $2,600.00.

Vase, #131, gr/brn/bl patina, hdls, 4½ " **750.00**
Vase, #272-2-6, orange/gr/bl patina, 11" **1,300.00**
Vase, #300-25, copper clad w/verdigris, spherical, 5x4¼" **1,100.00**
Vase, #302-6, orange/gr/bl patina w/drip effect, 11½ " **1,300.00**
Vase, #320-24, gr/bl/orange patina, flared shoulders, 6" **2,000.00**
Vase, #323-6, copper clad w/fine verdigris, 8¾x7" **1,100.00**
Vase, #331-6, copper clad w/verdigris, ovoid, 6x3" **475.00**
Vase, #351-24, copper clad w/verdigris, classic form, 7½ x3½ " .**1,900.00**
Vase, #397-2-6, copper & gr patina, drip effect, 4½ " **1,100.00**
Vase, #426-26, orange/brn/gr/bl patina, 18" **8,500.00**
Vase, #439-2-6, verdigris & bronze patina, faceted, 10x3½ " ..**2,400.00**
Vase, #441-47, gr/bl/orange/brn patina, shouldered/ftd, 6½ " .**2,300.00**
Vase, #463-26, brn to verdigris, classic shape, 8½ x7" **1,800.00**
Vase, #469, gr/bl/orange/brn patina, shouldered, 8½ " **2,300.00**
Vase, #485-215, gr/bronze patina, 11x8" **1,500.00**
Vase, #5-2-6, copper clad w/fine verdigris, 10¼x4¼" **1,700.00**
Vase, copper clad w/fine verdigris, unmk, 10x5" **1,000.00**
Vase, orange/gr/bl patina, 19" **6,000.00**

Clews

Brothers Ralph and James Clews were potters who operated in Cobridge in the Staffordshire district from 1817 to 1835. They are best known for their blue and white transfer-printed earthenwares, which included American Views, Moral Maxims, Picturesque Views, and English Views. A series called *Three Tours of Dr. Syntax* contained thirty-one different scenes with each piece bearing a descriptive title. Another popular series was *Pictures of Sir David Wilkie* with seven prints. (Though we once thought that the Don Quixote series was made by Clews, new information seems to indicate that it was made instead by Davenport.) Both printed and impressed marks were used, often incorporating the pattern name as well as the pottery. See also Staffordshire, Historical.

Creamer, Christmas Eve, dk bl transfer, 5½ " **265.00**
Pitcher, Basket Vase & Floral, dk bl transfer, 5" **250.00**
Pitcher, Water Girl, dk bl transfer, rstr chips, 4¾" **350.00**
Plate, Birdcages, red transfer, 10¾" **190.00**
Plate, Dr Syntax Turned Nurse, dk bl transfer, 7¾", EX **400.00**
Platter, Shepherd Boy Rescued, dk bl transfer, Don Quixote, 13", EX .**300.00**
Platter, The Valentine, dk bl transfer, 17", EX **935.00**
Teapot, floral pattern w/vase/basket/box, mk, mid-19th C, 6" ...**150.00**
Tureen, sauce; Repose in Woods, dk bl transfer, EX **725.00**

Clifton

Clifton Art Pottery of Clifton, New Jersey, was organized ca 1903. Until 1911 when they turned to the production of wall and floor tile, they made artware of several varieties. The founders were Fred Tschirner and William A. Long. Long had developed the method for underglaze slip painting that had been used at the Lonhuda Pottery in Steubenville, Ohio, in the 1890s. Crystal Patina, the first artware made by the small company, utilized a fine white body and flowing, blended colors, the earliest a green crystalline. Indian Ware, copied from the pottery of the American Indians, was usually decorated in black geometric designs on red clay. (On the occasions when white was used in addition to the black, the ware was often not as well executed; so even though two-color decoration is very rare, it is normally not as desirable to the collector.) Robin's Egg Blue, pale blue on the white body, and Tirrube, a slip-decorated matt ware, were also produced.

Teapot, Indian Ware, stamped #s, 6" **150.00**
Vase, Crystal Patina, #128, 1905, 7⅛" **150.00**
Vase, Crystal Patina, bottle shape, #158, 9½ x4½ " **350.00**
Vase, Crystal Patina, bottle shape, 1906, 7" **150.00**
Vase, Crystal Patina, bottle shape, 1907, 8½ x5" **225.00**
Vase, Crystal Patina, bulbous, 6½ " **100.00**
Vase, Crystal Patina, classic shape, 1915, 8" **150.00**
Vase, Indian Ware, geometric eagles in blk, Chevon AZ, 9" **350.00**
Vase, Indian Ware, geometrics, brn/beige, Homolobi, #217, 2x3½ " .**100.00**
Vase, Indian Ware, 4 Mile Ruin AZ, buff/blk/brn, 8½ x11" **500.00**
Vase, silver o/l floral on gr/tan crystalline, teardrop form, 7" **650.00**

Clocks

In the early days of our country's history, clock makers were influenced by styles imported from Europe. They copied the European's cabinets and reconstructed their movements — needed materials were in short supply; modifications had to be made. Of necessity was born mainspring motive power and spring clocks. Wooden movements were made on a mass-production basis as early as 1808. Before the middle of the century, brass movements had been developed.

Today's collectors prefer clocks from the eighteenth and nineteenth centuries with pendulum-regulated movements. Bracket clocks made during this period utilized the shorter pendulum improvised in 1658 by Fromentiel, a prominent English clock maker. These smaller square-face clocks usually were made with a dome top fitted with a handle or a decorative finial. The case was usually walnut or ebony and was sometimes decorated with pierced brass mountings. Brackets were often mounted on the wall to accommodate the clock, hence the name. The banjo clock was patented in 1802 by Simon Willard. It derived its descriptive name from its banjo-like shape. A similar but more elaborate style was called the lyre clock.

The first electric novelty clocks were developed in the 1940s. Lux, who was the major producer, had been in business since 1912, making wind-up novelties during the '20s and '30s. Another company, Mastercrafter Novelty Clocks, first obtained a patent to produce these clocks in the late 1940s. Other manufacturers were Keebler, Westclox, and Columbia Time. The cases were made of china, Syroco, wood, and plastic; most were animated and some had pendulettes. Prices vary according to condition and rarity.

Except for the novelty clocks whose values are on the increase, clock prices have been stable for several years. Unless noted otherwise, values are given for eight-day time only clocks in excellent condition. Clocks that have been altered, damaged, or have had parts replaced are worth considerably less.

Our advisor is Bruce A. Austin; he is listed in the Directory under New York. Our novelty clock advisors is Anita Levi (Allegheny Mountain Antiques Gallery); she is listed in the Directory under Pennsylvania.

Key:

br — brass	reg — regulator
dl — dial	rswd — rosewood
esc — escapement	TS — time & strike
mcr — mercury	wt — weight
mvt — movement	vnr — veneer
OG — ogee	2nds — seconds
pnd — pendulum	

Calendar Clocks

Arthur Pequegnat, school, short drop, rfn oak, 1920, 26½" **225.00**
Ingraham, parlor, walnut, rstr/rfn, ca 1881, 21½" **875.00**
Ingraham Ionic, perpetual, rpl dl, rswd case, 1886, 30" **1,150.00**
Ithaca No 2 Reg, dbl-dl, 2-wt, walnut w/burl, 1875, 48" **1,450.00**
New Haven Bank Reg, pressed oak case, 1910s, 33" **400.00**
New Haven Fashion No 9, rpt dl, rfn walnut, 1889, 32", VG **750.00**
Southern Fashion No 6, walnut, blk dls, long pnd, rfn, 1880s, 31" ..**1,600.00**

Novelty Clocks

Airplane, Bakelite & chrome, Mastercrafters, from $175 to **225.00**
Bobbing Chicks, metal case, various colors, United, from $35 to ..**50.00**
Continental, CI, blinking eye, Bradley & Hubbard, 1860s, 17", VG .**1,000.00**
Cowboy w/Rope, metal, wooden base, United, from $100 to **150.00**
Davy Crockett, metal, United, 10" **650.00**
Fireplace, plastic, Mastercrafters, from $60 to **90.00**
Good Luck, horseshoe, Lux, orig chrome plating (M), 1955, 8", NM .**150.00**
Hula Girl & Drummer, wooden, United, from $200 to **250.00**
Parachute, New Haven, not running, 1889, 8", VG **160.00**
Rocking Horse (Rancho), compo, Haddon, from $150 to **200.00**
Sambo, blinking eyes, pnt dl, Germany, 1950s, 10" **200.00**
Sambo, CI, blinking eyes, rpt case, rstr dl, ca 1860s, 16" **900.00**
Swinging Playmates, plastic, w/fence, Mastercrafters, from $100 to .**125.00**
Topsy, CI, blinking eyes, German lever mvt & dl, 1900s, 17" **957.00**
Waiter w/towel & wine bottle, Lux, ca 1935, 6¼" **300.00**
Water Wheel (L style), plastic, Spartus, from $20 to **50.00**

Shelf Clocks

Adler, Vienna-style reg, porc dl, center pnd, 1900, 34" **400.00**
Angelus, strikes 6 am/noon/6 pm w/call to prayer, 1875, 18", G .**600.00**
Ansonia Gloria, prof rfn, bronze w/verdigris, 1895, 28½" **4,100.00**
Ansonia Pompeii, top garniture, porc dl, rpl pnd, rpt, 1904, 17" ..**275.00**
Ansonia Radical, porc case w/HP & gold, open mvt, ca 1900, 11½" ..**550.00**
Ansonia Royal Bonn, china, floral sprays, porc dl, rprs, 16" **550.00**
Ansonia Tunis, orig porc dl, walnut case, 1885, 14" **300.00**
Atkins & Downs, rvpt scene, eagle crest, pnd window, 38" **450.00**
Birge & Full, 4 candlestick steeple-on-steeple, rstr, 1845, 26" ..**3,500.00**
Birge & Ives, faux tortoise shell column triple decker, 1832, 37" ...**800.00**
Birge Peck & Co, brass strap mvt, Girard Collage tablet, 32" **350.00**
Black Forest, cvd pheasant/chicks/flowers, wood dl, 1875, 30" ..**4,500.00**
Boston Delphus, crystal reg, tandem wind mvt, 1892, rstr, 11" ..**925.00**
Brewster & Ingrahams, Pomeroy mvt, visible balance, 30-hr, 1850, 11" .**850.00**
Charles Houre, carriage alarm, cylinder platform, porc dl, 1810s, 6" .**225.00**
Charles Houre Petit Sonnerie, repeat w/alarm, 1900, 5¼" **1,000.00**
Chauncey Jerome, 30-hr, orig tablet, pnt dl, mahog, 1844, 26" .**150.00**
Chelsea, house strike mantel reg, bronze case, 1921, 9½" **425.00**
Eli Terry, Fed mahog pillar & scroll, rvpt scene, 1822, 23" **7,475.00**
Eli Terry & Sons, wooden works, cvd ft/splat, 1830s, rstr, 36" ...**1,000.00**
English for Bigelow Kennard, 2-tune/8-bell/5-gong/3-fusee, 1890, 26" ...**3,600.00**
F Kroeber, br over CI, floral decor, porc dl (G), 1890, 11" **600.00**
F Kroeber, Polaris, walnut, orig label, ca 1875, 24" **400.00**
F Kroeber, porc china, restrained pnd, orig dl, 1890s, 10" **350.00**
F Kroeber, Rattan, 30-hr time/alarm, br NP 'bamboo' case, 6½" ...**350.00**
Fr, bronzed/gilded spelter lady w/broken pot, porc dl, 1890, 24" ..**700.00**
Fr, cast br, TS on bell, 12-cartouch dl, 1890, 10" **550.00**
Fr, crystal reg w/oversz mercury pnd, HP dl, CJCC mvt, 13" **500.00**
Fr, skeleton type, pnd suspended over mvt, dome, 1890s, 15" ..**1,000.00**
Fr, 4-columm Emp style, ebony w/br inlay, pnd, 1890, 18" **250.00**
Fr/Bigelow Kenard & Co, crystal reg, porc dl, oversz pnd, 1900, 15" .**1,300.00**
Harris & Harrington, mahog tambour, cvd scrolls, porc dl, 12½" **350.00**
Harris & Harrington, mahog tambour, cvd sides/scrolls, porc dl, 8" **330.00**
HJ Davies Surprise, walnut carriage, ca 1875, mini, 6" **300.00**
Ingraham Arch Column, TS/alarm, Pomeroy mvt, ca 1859, 17" .**300.00**
Ingraham Grecian, rswd w/walnut bezels (rfn), 1875, 15" **350.00**
Ingraham Ionic, orig gilt, TS, 1890, 21½" **450.00**
JC Brown, Bristol CT, cvd rswd w/gilt, 1850s, 8¼x6x2½" **3,000.00**
Jerome, cottage w/alarm, gutta percha inserts/rswd vnr, 16" **300.00**
Jerome (att), burled vnr, orig moon hands, rstr dl, 1850s, 16" ...**525.00**
JJ Beals, steeple-on-steeple, rpt dl, repolished case, 1850, 24" ..**1,400.00**
Junghans, quarter strike mvt, gilt dial, mahog case, 16" **450.00**
Kienzle, Berlin style 'free swinger,' winged dl, pnd, 1910s, 24" ..**250.00**
Kitchen, walnut Vict, br works, alarm/key/pnd, rprs, 21" **140.00**
L Leleu Valenciennes, spelter figure on marble base, 1890s, 17" .**450.00**
La Mysterieue, 30-hr, wheel drive, exposed works, 1910s, 10" ...**550.00**
Mark Lane, pillar & scroll, rstr tablet, old dl, ca 1825, 32" **800.00**
Mueller, hunter figural, gold rpt, paper dl, 23" **350.00**

Napoleon III ormolu and patinated bronze-mounted black marble mantel clock, Boul & Mountmart 17 Paris Chimes, ca 1855, 27½x20x8", $2,750.00.

New Haven Gothic Gem, 30-hr TS, orig dl/tablet, 1880, 17" ...**150.00**
Norris North, Classical mahog & stencil, rvpt scene, 1825, 24" .**4,500.00**
Plato, lantern shape, shaft turns to reveal time cards, 1902, 7" ..**200.00**
Pool Executive, self-impulse battery, blk case/dome, 1919, 10½" ..**250.00**
Riley Whiting...CT, stencing, children tablet, 1835, 28" **1,500.00**
Samuel Terry Pillar & Scroll, repro (EX) tablet, rpl dl, 1825, 32" ...**1,400.00**
Seth Thomas, Emp No 0, pnd, runs/strikes, EX gilt, 1910s, 10¾" .**300.00**
Seth Thomas, short stenciled column, rpl tablet, 1835, 31" **550.00**
Seth Thomas, 2 cherubs play below street clock, #8064, 19" **600.00**
Seth Thomas Adamintine, 2-bell 'Ding-Dong' strike, 1910s, 11" ..**250.00**
Seth Thomas Emp No 18, crystal reg, floral dl, ca 1910, 12" **350.00**

Seth Thomas Emp No 300, crystal reg, brushed br, pnd, 1910, 10" ..225.00
Seth Thomas Lincoln, orig dl, pnd, rfn walnut, 1890, 27" 2,250.00
Seth Thomas Parlor No 1, rpt dl, orig tablet, rswd, 1865, 31" ...400.00
Seth Thomas St Paul, imperfect rprs, worn finish, 1886, 21" 450.00
Seth Thomas Turin, #48-J rnd mvt, gong, porc dl/hands/pnd, 1910, 9" ...225.00
Silas B Terry Emp style, wt drive, 1845, 27½ " 5,300.00
Solomon C Spring, Extra 8-day Rolling Pinion, rswd, 1865, 31" ...400.00
Spencer Wooster & Co, orig rvpt tablets, wood dl, mahog, 1830, 34" .1,800.00
Sperry & Shaw, 30-hr bevel front, wooden dl, orig tablet, 1845, 26" 200.00
Terry & Andrews, iron front, orig decor, lyre mvt, 1850s, 14" ...175.00
Waltham, house strike reg, Gothic-style case, 1910s, 13" 500.00
Waterbury, Lansing, kitchen type, walnut, pnd/hands/alarm, 21" ..135.00
Welch Spring & Co Patti, orig tablet, trn rswd, 1875, 19", VG .875.00
Welch Spring & Co Patti, rpl hand, orig finish, 1875, 19", VG 1,000.00
Winterhalder & Hofmeier, 8-bell/3-fusee, golden oak, 1880, 28" ..3,500.00
WS Johnson...NY, steeple, rpl floral tablet, 1850s, 19", VG 250.00
Zappler (Austrian), 30-hr, br facade w/scrolls & eagle, 1810s, 7" .200.00

Tall Case Clocks

A Willard, Chpndl bombe case, mahog/vnr, calendar, 105" .15,400.00
B Willard, cherry Chpndl, br works/face, calendar, 89" 38,500.00
Cherry PA Chpndl, fluted ¼-columns, bonnet w/br mts, 100" 14,300.00
Eli Willard, Hplwht mahog w/inlay, calendar, ¼-columns, 94" 33,000.00
Elliot London, mahog Gothic Revival, br works, 97", EX 7,700.00
English, figured mahog vnr w/inlay, rope cvgs, eagle finials, 83" 3,245.00
Ephm Barber, MA, pine w/old dk red rpt/red trim/yel striping, 80" ..3,400.00
I Grotz, curly maple Chpndl, rosettes/trn finials, 103" 28,600.00
S Willard, Hplwht Roxbury, mahog/inlay, provenance, 97" ..77,000.00
S Willard, mahog Hplwht, inlay fans/fluted columns/calendar, 94" ..55,000.00
Simon Willard, Fed mahog w/inlay, 1790-1810, 89" 42,550.00
Walnut, dvtl bonnet w/molded cornice, paneled base, PA, 1910s, 90" ..5,000.00
Walnut Country Sheraton, appl moldings, dvtl bonnet, rpt face, 94" 3,300.00

Wall Clocks

Andre Speth a la Charite, emb br facade & pnd, 56" 935.00
Ansonia Gallery No 1, Arabic dl, dk oak case, 1915, 23" dia .1,400.00
Ansonia Hiogo, dbl octagon, walnut case, crystal pnd, rpl dl, 24" ...200.00
Ansonia Melody Chime No 1, mahog, 3-train mvt, ca 1920, 32" ...625.00
Ansonia Reg No 6, porc crystal w/gold trim, 1900, 17½ " 2,600.00
Ansonia Royal Bonn Hanging Porc No 3, much gold, 1900, 19" ..15,000.00
Attleboro, hatch-type 'Baltimore' banjo, 1860s, much rstr, 33" .950.00
Austrian Grand Sonnerie, 3-wt, cvd walnut, 1875, 55" 2,500.00
Austrian Grand Sonnerie, 3-wt, late Biedermeier, 1850s, 43" ..3,800.00
Austrian Grand Sonnerie, 3-wt, serpentine case, 1860, 62" ...7,200.00
Austrian Grand Sonnerie, 3-wt, walnut 2-door design, 1890, 50" ..3,750.00
Chauncey Jerome Octagon Extra, 8" dl, EX patina, 1850, 12" ...625.00
E Howard No 5, banjo, orig tablets, rpt dl, 1880, 29" 1,900.00
E Howard No 5, mahog banjo, 1925, 29" 2,100.00
EN Welch, Eclipse, walnut gingerbread, TS/alarm, 28", EX 400.00
Fed mahog, banjo, rvpt harbor scenes, MA, 1820s, 37" 1,000.00
German, Art Nouveau reg in Berliner style, free-swing pnd, 1900, 40" ...675.00
German, cuckoo & quail, pears & grapes motif, 1920s, 26" 325.00
Gilbert Admiral, pressed oak, short drp, rpl dl, rstr/rfn, 27" 250.00
Grand Sonnerie Dwarf, short pnd, full-sz dl, orig cvgs, 1880, 43" .2,800.00
Hamburg Am, spring-drive reg in Vienna style, 1910, 38" 550.00
Ingraham, Nyanza, cherry-color banjo, paper dl, 1915, 39" 275.00
Ingraham Landau, Mission Oak, orig dl, rprs, 1915, 38" 300.00
Joseph Ives Mirror, iron plate mvt, rpl tablets, rpt dl, 1820, 57" .1,600.00
Lenzkirch Style No 81, spring reg, 14-day, porc dl, 1870, 17½ " 525.00
Moncrieff, 2-fusee, mahog drop dl w/cvg, baluster pillars, 1850, 23" ..850.00
New Haven Vienna, orig dl, 1890, much rstr, 50" 625.00
Pequegnat, oak store reg, clear tablet, orig dl, 1915, 35½ " 300.00
Prentice skillet shape w/Waterbury mvt, bronze #s, 1920s, 23" ..135.00
Reg, E Howard Boston, oak w/figure, pnd, 65x19" 1,750.00
Sessions, open spring mvt, Betsy Ross' house on tablets, 1925, 26" ..200.00
Sessions mini store reg, rpl paper dl, orig tablet, rstr, 1920s, 20" .225.00
Seth Thomas Office No 14, 30-day rnd dl, quartered oak, 1930s, 18" ..675.00
Seth Thomas Reg No 17, NP accessories, pnd, 1890, 68" 5,000.00
Seth Thomas Reg No 18, rfn oak case, 1900, 54", +provenance .2,800.00
Seth Thomas Reg No 2, prof rpt dl, 1890, rstr, 36" 1,200.00
Seth Thomas Reg No 6, all orig hdw, rstr case, 1880, 49" 2,100.00
Simon Willard, banjo, Fed mahog w/inlay, ca 1810, 29¼" ...12,650.00
Simon Willard's Pat, banjo, presentation style, drop pendant, 44" ...1,500.00
Vienna 1-wt reg, porc dl, rfn case, 1860, 33" 1,075.00
Vienna 1-wt reg, porc dl, walnut Alt Deutsch-style case, 1890, 34" .750.00
Waltham Reg No 34, rpl oak baffle, clear tablet, ca 1925, 32" ..900.00
Waterbury, 10" Drop, lt rswd (rfn) case, orig dl, 1910s, 22" 250.00
Waterbury Regent, long drop schoolhouse, rosewood, all orig, 1910, 31" ...300.00
Waterbury Willard No 3, wt banjo, tablet flakes, 1910, 43" 900.00
Wm L Gilbert, Columbia, walnut, worn orig tablet, 1890s, 37½ " .700.00

Cloisonne

Cloisonne is a method of decorating metal with enameling. Fine metal wires are soldered onto the metal body following the lines of a predetermined design. The resulting channels are filled in with enamels of various colors, and the item is fired. The final step is a smoothing process that assures even exposure of the wire pattern. The art is predominately Oriental and has been practiced continuously, except during war years, since the sixteenth century. The most excellent examples date from 1865 until the turn of the century. The early twentieth century export variety is usually lightweight and the workmanship inferior. Modern wares are of good quality and are produced in Taiwan as well as China.

Several variations of the basic art include plique-a-jour, achieved by removing the metal body after firing, leaving only the transparent enamel work; foil cloisonne, using transparent or semitranslucent enameling over a layer of embossed silver covering the metal body of the vessel; wireless cloisonne, made by removing the wire dividers prior to firing; and cloisonne executed on ceramic, wood, or lacquer rather than metal.

Vases, peonies and flowering fruit trees on blue, baluster forms, China, 24", $900.00 for the pair.

Charger, birds on fruiting branches, mc on bl, 12" 150.00
Jar, birds on cobalt, 2½ " 55.00
Rice bowl, wht fruit blossoms, 4½ " 20.00
Teapot, mc floral w/butterflies, China, ca 1900, 3" 95.00
Vase, birds/insects/foliage, bronze base, 10", pr 475.00
Vase, brass urn form w/mythological beast hdls, 19th C, 15" 395.00
Vase, flowers & buds on red w/butterflies, Japan, 1930s, 5" 65.00
Vase, pastel florals, silver wire, Meiji, 14¾", EX 250.00
Vase, scrolling mc floral, elephant head hdls, China, 1790s, 15" ..800.00

Clothing and Accessories

More and more collectors are getting involved in the fascinating field of antique, vintage, and collectible clothing, once considered the realm of museum curators and historical societies. Today's collector is highly discriminating; most specialize in certain types of clothing or certain historical periods. This makes it important to know exactly how old an item is before determining a value. Gone are the days when it was sufficient to broadly categorize a dress as simply 'Victorian' or 'old,' as clothing from certain historical periods has increased in value faster than examples from other eras. A mistake in dating an item can cause a loss of several hundreds of dollars on the collectors' market. For example, prices for special-occasion dresses of the Civil War era have skyrocketed in recent years. Another big jump in market value is being seen in dresses of the late 1870s and early 1880s. Meanwhile, prices of dresses from the 1890s and 1900s have remained fairly stable.

Once the age of an item of clothing is ascertained, three other factors come into play in determining a price. The first is condition, as a noticeable rip or stain will devalue an item just as surely as a crack will devalue a glass vase. The second factor is quality: is it well made or made by a famous designer? Were fabrics and trimmings expensive or elaborate? Generally speaking, the more elaborate the item, the higher the value. The third factor is size. Today a large portion of collectors are searching for items which they can wear, therefore extremely small sizes are somewhat less valuable than larger ones.

For further information as well as an easy-to-use guide for dating women's clothing, we recommend *Antique & Vintage Clothing: A Guide to Dating and Valuation of Women's Clothing, 1850–1940*, by our advisor, Diane Snyder-Haug, available from Collector Books or your local bookstore. Our values are for items of ladies' clothing in excellent condition unless otherwise described.

Key:

cap/s — cap sleeves	ms — machine sewn
embr — embroidery	n/s — no sleeves
hs — hand sewn	plt — pleated
l/s — long sleeves	s/s — short sleeves

Apron, bl & wht gingham, ms 25.00
Apron, crochet, wht, 19x17" w/bl ribbon ties 30.00
Apron, wht cotton w/tulip pockets & rickrack trim, 18" 7.50
Bib, wht cotton w/hand quilting & sm pocket, crochet edge, 19th C, 10" ..28.00
Bloomer costume, 1890-1920, from $125 to 225.00
Blouse, bright bl silk w/blk beads, l/s, bk closure, 1960s, NM 35.00
Blouse, lingerie style, 1920s, from $45 to 125.00
Bodice, w/o skirt, plain or elegant, 1890s, from $45 to 95.00
Bonnet, baby's, Irish lace w/pk silk lining, ca 1900 ....35.00
Camisole, 1900s, from $40 to 65.00
Coat, boy's, wool, single-breasted, rolled lapels, 1910s 100.00
Coat, girl's, gray broadcloth, notched collar, puff/s, 1910s 120.00
Coat, girl's, sailor collar, dbl-breasted, ca 1910, from $200 to 225.00
Coat, mohair w/mink tail clasp, ca 1938 ....100.00
Coat, wool, shawl collar, roll-up/s, belt tie, 1960s 65.00
Collar, man's, wht cotton, stiffly starched, 1900s, from $10 to 12.00
Dress, blk silk/brocaded silk chemise w/belt, l/s, ca 1921 ....50.00
Dress, child's, wht polished cotton w/red trim & embr hearts, 1930s .65.00
Dress, christening: wht cambric w/lace, handmade, ca 1900 ....155.00
Dress, Christmas plaid, n/s, wide tie belt, zipper, 1960s, NM 32.00
Dress, cotton eyelet bodice, full skirt, s/s, 1950s, EX 45.00
Dress, cotton floral, strapless, full skirt, 1950s, EX 32.50
Dress, cotton voile w/underslip, ribbons, spaghetti straps, 1960s ..32.50
Dress, crepe chemise w/asymmetrical hem, lace yoke, 1927 ....65.00
Dress, day; brn & wht silk w/lace, sm train, pagoda/s, 1903 ....325.00
Dress, day; checked wool, jet buttons, l/s, ca 1868, EX 250.00
Dress, day; cotton & wool, Peter Pan collar, l/s, w/cape, ca 1909 .295.00
Dress, day; cotton sm print, simple style, l/s, ca 1863, EX 145.00
Dress, day; cotton w/crochet lace, sailor collar/2-tier skirt, 1917 ..145.00
Dress, day; satin/velvet, tie-bk skirt, stand-up collar, l/s, 1870s ..425.00
Dress, day; wht cotton batiste w/crochet lace, pearl buttons, 1908 .325.00
Dress, day; wht cotton batiste w/lace & much trim, 1900s, from $300 to .800.00
Dress, day; wht linen, front pearl buttons, l/s, bustle, 1885 ....100.00

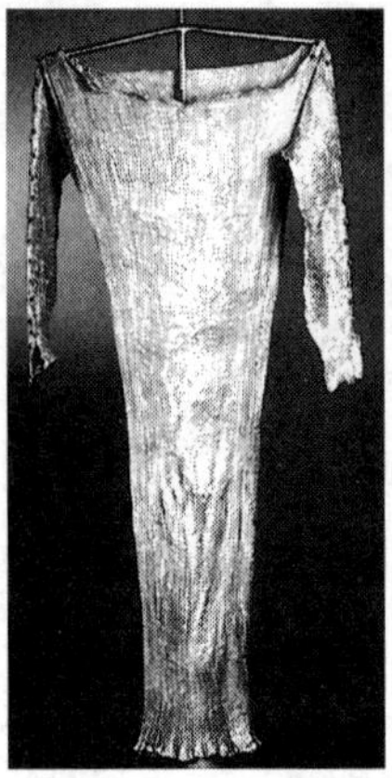

Dress, evening; Fortuny, blue silk, Venetian beads on shoulders and sleeves, $1,250.00.

Dress, evening; coral silk w/sequins/beads/rhinestones, train, 1914 ..330.00
Dress, evening; cut velvet, backless, cape/s, 1930s 295.00
Dress, evening; sheer muslin, Bertha cape w/flower, 1860s, EX ..235.00
Dress, evening; silk, balloon/s w/netting, w/corset, 1890s 195.00
Dress, evening; silk floral, puffed/s, long skirt, 1940s, EX 80.00
Dress, everyday; chemise w/little trim, 1920s, from $40 to 75.00
Dress, everyday; colors other than wht, 1900s, from $85 to 250.00
Dress, everyday; little or no trim, 1890s, from $95 to 125.00
Dress, everyday; little trim, 1910s, from $65 to 200.00
Dress, everyday; little trim, 1930s-40s, from $35 to 75.00
Dress, girl's, cotton batiste w/embr yoke, high neck, l/s, 1910s ..175.00
Dress, girl's, cotton batiste w/embr yoke, sash, l/s, 1910s 215.00
Dress, girl's, lacy shawl collar, drop waist, s/s, 1910s 150.00
Dress, girl's, organdy w/lace & ruffles, 1930s, sm 25.00
Dress, girl's, wide collar, box-pleat front w/drop waist, 1910s 100.00
Dress, mourning; blk w/netting trim/lace/ribbons, 1900s 300.00
Dress, navy bl chemise w/lace yoke & jabot, 1930s 35.00
Dress, polka-dot satin, strapless w/built-in 'bra,' 1950s, M 35.00
Dress, satin A-line, s/s, ribbon trim at waist, 1950s, EX 32.50
Dress, satin floral top w/full plt skirt, rnd neck, l/s, 1960s, EX 32.50
Dress, silk floral w/drop waist, cap/s, flared skirt, 1940s 35.00
Dress, special occasion; elaborate trim, 1910s, from $250 to 400.00
Dress, special occasion; elegant trim, 1890s, from $325 to 800.00
Dress, special occasion; velvet/rayon, V neck, puff/s, 1930s 190.00
Dress, special occasion; 1930s-40s, from $75 to 400.00
Dress, special occasion; 2 or more fabrics, bustle, 1880s, $200 to .800.00
Dress, tea; cotton print w/satin bodice & lace, Watteau train, 1890s ..500.00
Dress, teen girl's, drop waist, plt skirt, collar, s/s, 1930s 100.00
Dress, walking; sm collar, lace & ribbon trim, puff/s, 1890s 150.00
Dust coat, sack style, ca 1915 ....95.00
Fur coat, dk ranch mink, Bergdorf-Goodman, full-length, sm ...3,500.00
Fur muff, ranch mink w/Bakelite bangle attached to wrist, M 45.00
Gloves, blk leather w/top stitching, 1952, 9½ ", pr 12.50
Gloves, wht leather, ca 1940, 10", EX, pr 7.50
Hat, blk felt w/appl flowers, face netting, 1940s, EX 30.00
Hat, boy's, Bowler style, ca 1912 ....25.00
Hat, cloche style, 1920s, from $25 to 95.00
Hat, helmet-shape w/velvet trim/beads/feathers/ribbons, 1880s .130.00
Hat, little trimming 1850-1910, from $20 to 125.00

Hat, ornate trimmings, 1850-1915, from $95 to 200.00
Hat, red wool w/leather band & feather trim, 1960s, MIB 25.00
Hat, spoon bonnet w/netting & ostrich feathers, 1865 ....125.00
Hat, straw (navy), flat w/wide brim, 1950s 32.00
Hat, velvet toque w/cloth flowers/sequins/beads/feather, 1890s .195.00
Hat, wool helmet style w/feather decor, 1940s, EX 20.00
Jacket, beaded wool brocade, shoulder pads, l/s, 1940s, NM 80.00
Jacket, blk velvet, l/s, sm collar, 1950s, EX 55.00
Jacket, man's, checked wool, single-breasted, wide lapel, 1940s ...22.50
Jacket, teen girl's, plaid wool w/low cloth belt, dolman/s, 1910s ...100.00
Knickers, youth's, lined wool, 1920s 40.00
Necktie, polyester silk, med-wide, 1960s, from $5 to 7.50
Necktie, silk floral, wide style, 1950s, from $12 to 15.00
Nightgown, ivory satin w/lace-trimmed bodice, 1940s 32.50
Pants suit, polyester dbl knit, wide legs, l/s, 1970s 12.50
Petticoat, wht linen, dbl-flounce hem, deep lace, 1900s 195.00
Play suit, girl's, drop waist, bloomers, ca 1910, from $200 to 275.00
Robe, pk chiffon w/lace trim & bow at front, 1950s, NM 40.00
Romper, child's, linen, wht collar, 1920s, EX 85.00
Shawl, paisley, Civil War era, EX, from $300 to 400.00
Shawl, plaid wool, 19th C, 124x62" 50.00
Shirtwaist, wht transparent cotton batiste, 1900s, from $85 to ..300.00
Shoes, baby's, wht lace-ups, 1940s-50s 15.00
Shoes, Charm Step, blk patent 17.50
Shoes, child's, Gophers, pigskin 12.50
Shoes, Cushionized Shoes, brn lace-up style, 1940s 25.00
Shoes, girl's, leather strap pumps, 1930s-40s, pr 25.00
Shoes, high heels, open toes & heels, bk strap, 1950s, pr 25.00
Shoes, high-heel pumps w/rhinestone clips, 1960s, M 17.50
Shoes, Hug Tite, blk lace-up style 21.00
Shoes, man's, blk leather w/felt top, buttons, 1900s, up to 90.00
Shoes, man's, leather, lace-up style, 1930s-40s, pr, from $20 to 25.00
Shoes, platform high-heels, tooled leather, 1940s, NM 45.00
Shoes, silver-colored high-heels w/ankle straps, 1940s, pr 22.50
Shoes, Wellco Foam Tread slippers, furry '50s style 15.00
Skirt, circle style w/lacy net over silk, 1950s, M 32.50
Skirt, navy felt, flared, appl circles resembling buttons, 1950s 35.00
Slip, blk taffeta, Flex-O-Skirt, 45", M 27.50
Slip, gathered crinoline 'cancan' style, elastic waist, 1950s 18.00
Slip, wht silk, lace trim, dainty straps, 1960s 12.50
Suit, boy's, bl serge w/paneled front, linen bow at neck, 2-pc, 1900s .150.00
Suit, boy's, pleated shirt, str short pants w/buttons, 1910s 130.00
Suit, boy's, short pants button to shirt, s/s, 1930s, up to 45.00
Suit, boy's, wool knickerbockers, wide lapel, 1930s 85.00
Suit, lady's, linen w/embr cutwork & lace, Vict, 2-pc 100.00
Suit, lady's, tan cotton w/lace inserts, collar, l/s, 1940s, EX 55.00
Suit, man's, dk wool, tailor-made, 1910s, from $185 to 235.00
Suit, man's, striped wool, 2-button jacket, cuffed pants, 1930s ..150.00
Sweater, angora & wool print, l/s, 1950s, NM 15.00
Sweater, fluffy 'cashmere' w/mink collar, 1950s 55.00
Sweater, wht wool w/appl flowers & gold & wht beads, 1950s, NM .48.00
Sweater, wool w/mink collar, ca 1936 ....45.00
Swimsuit, boy's, 2-pc, 1930s-40s, from $50 to 60.00
Waistcoat, beaded/embr florals & leaves, ca 1800, EX 300.00
Waistcoat, embr silk w/monkeys/flowers etc, English, 18th C, 32" .600.00

Cluthra

The name cluthra is derived from the Scottish word 'clutha,' meaning cloudy. Glassware by this name was first produced by J. Couper and Sons, England. Frederick Carder developed cluthra while at the Steuben Glass Works, and similar types of glassware were also made by Durand and Kimball. It is found in both solid and shaded colors and is characterized by a spotty appearance resulting from small air pockets trapped between its two layers.

Plate, pk to opal mottle, att Monart, 7" 35.00
Vase, orange & yel-brn, Kimball, cylindrical, #1998-12, 12x5½" ..625.00
Vase, orange/opal w/clear ft, tapered, #2011-18K Dec 7, 8½" ...275.00
Vase, wht mottle w/blk base, Kimball, K #20140-12 Dec-O, 11½" .275.00

Cobalt Glass

Cobalt glass is characterized by its deep transparent blue color obtained by mixing cobalt oxide and alumina into the batch. It may be found in free-blown, mold-blown, and pressed glassware. See Blown Glass.

Box, HP farm scene, hinged lid, 2¼x3" dia 165.00
Box, wht scrolls/leaves, hinged, ormolu ft, 4x4¾" dia 200.00

Cologne, eight-rib, two applied rings, mushroom stopper, 5⅝", $355.00. (Photo courtesy Garth's Auctions, Inc.)

Creamer, gold flowers/trim, clear hdl, ogee sides, 3½" 175.00
Night light, ball shape, brass shade, 5½ x3½" dia 165.00
Spoon holder, Punty & Ellipse (Monroe), 5" 1,000.00
Vase, allover wht lacy decor, ormolu ft, 6x3", pr 200.00
Vase, in ornate SP fr w/fruit etc mk JB2461, Vict, 9" 170.00
Vase, wht/gilt enamel, jardiniere & pedestal shape, 7½" 125.00

Coca-Cola

J.S. Pemberton, creator of Coca-Cola, originated his world-famous drink in 1886. From its inception the Coca-Cola Company began an incredible advertising campaign which has proven to be one of the most successful promotions in history. The quantity and diversity of advertising material put out by Coca-Cola in the last one hundred years is literally mind boggling. From the beginning, the company has projected an image of wholesomeness and Americana. Beautiful women in Victorian costumes, teenagers and schoolchildren, blue- and white-collar workers, the men and women of the Armed Forces, and even Santa Claus have appeared in advertisements with a Coke in their hands. Some of the earliest collectibles include trays, syrup dispensers, gum jars, pocket mirrors, and calendars. Many of these items fetch prices in the thousands of dollars. Later examples include radios, signs, lighters, thermometers, playing cards, clocks, and toys — particularly toy trucks.

In 1970 the Coca-Cola Company initialed a multimillion-dollar 'image-refurbishing campaign' which introduced the new 'Dynamic Contour' logo, a twisting white ribbon under the Coca-Cola and Coke trademarks. The new logo often serves as a cut-off point to the purist collector. Newer and very ardent collectors, however, relish the myriad of items marketed since that date, as they often cannot afford the high prices that the vintage pieces command. For more information we recommend *Petretti's Coca-Cola Collectibles Price Guide* (available from Nostalgia Publications whose address you will find under Auctions in the Directory); *Huxford's Collectible Advertising, Fifth Edition; BJ Summers' Guide to Coca-Cola, Second Edition,* and *B.J. Summers' Pocket Guide to*

Coca-Cola; also *Coca-Cola Commemorative Bottles* by Bob and Debra Henrich. You may wish to call our advisor for this category, Craig Stifter; he is listed in the Directory under Illinois.

Key:
CC — Coca-Cola   tm — trademark

Reproductions and Fantasies

Beware of reproductions! Prices are given for the genuine original articles, but the symbol (+) at the end of some of the following lines indicate items that have been reproduced. Warning! The 1924, 1925, and 1935 calendars have been reproduced. They are identical in almost every way; only a professional can tell them apart. These are *very* deceiving! Watch for frauds: genuinely old celluloid items ranging from combs, mirrors, knives, and forks to doorknobs that have been recently etched with a new double-lined trademark. Still another area of concern deals with reproduction and fantasy items. A fantasy item is a novelty made to appear authentic with inscriptions such as 'Tiffany Studios,' 'Trans Pan Expo,' 'World's Fair,' etc. In reality, these items never existed as originals. For instance, don't be fooled by a Coca-Cola cash register; no originals are known to exist! Large mirrors for bars are being reproduced and are often selling for $10.00 to $50.00.

Of the hundreds of reproductions (designated 'R' in the following examples) and fantasies (designated 'F') on the market today, these are the most deceiving.

Belt buckle, no originals thought to exist (F), up to 10.00
Bottle, dk amber, w/arrows, heavy, narrow spout (R) 10.00
Bottle carrier, wood, yel w/red logo, holds 6 bottles (R) 10.00
Clock, Gilbert regulator, battery-op, ¾-sz, NM+ (R) 175.00
Cooler, Glascock Jr, made by Coca-Cola USA (R) 350.00
Doorknob, glass etched w/tm (F) 3.00
Knife, bottle shape, 1970s, many variations (F), ea 5.00
Knife, fork, or spoon w/celluloid hdl, newly etched tm (F) 5.00
Letter opener, stamped metal, Coca-Cola for 5¢ (F) 3.00
Pocket watch, often old watch w/new face (R) 10.00
Pocketknife, yel & red, 1933 World's Fair (F) 2.00
Sign, cb, lady w/fur, dtd 1911, 9x11" (F) 3.00
Soda fountain glass holder, word 'Drink' not orig (R) 5.00
Thermometer, bottle form, DONASCO, 17" (R) 10.00
Trade card, copy of 1905 'Bathtub' foldout, emb 1978 (R) 25.00

The following items have been reproduced and are among the most deceptive of all:

Pocket mirrors from 1905, 1906, 1908, 1909, 1910, 1911, 1916, and 1920

Trays from 1899, 1910, 1913, 1914, 1917, 1920, 1923, 1925, 1926, 1934, and 1937

Tip trays from 1907, 1909, 1910, 1913, 1914, 1917, and 1920

Knives: many versions of the German brass model

Cartons: wood versions, yellow with logo

Calendars: 1924, 1925, and 1935

These items have been marketed:

Brass thermometer, bottle shape, Taiwan, 24"

Cast-iron toys (none ever made)

Cast-iron door pull, bottle shape, made to look old

Poster, Yes Girl (R)

Button sign, has one round hole while original has four slots, most have bottle logo, 12", 16", 20" (R)

Bullet trash receptacles (old cans with decals)

Paperweight, rectangular, with Pepsin Gum insert

1930 Bakelite radio, 24" tall, repro is lighter in weight than the original, of poor quality and cheaply made

1949 cooler radio (reproduced with tape deck)

Tin bottle sign, 40"

Fishtail die-cut tin sign, 20" long

Straw holders (no originals exist)

Coca-Cola bicycle with cooler, fantasy item: the piece has been totally made-up, no such original exists

1914 calendar top, reproduction, 11¼x23¾", printed on smooth-finish heavy ivory paper

Countless trays — most unauthorized (must read 'American Artworks; Coshocton, OH.')

Centennial Items

The Coca-Cola Company celebrated its 100th birthday in 1986, and amidst all the fanfare came many new collectible items, all sporting the 100th-anniversary logo. These items are destined to become an important part of the total Coca-Cola collectible spectrum. The following pieces are among the most popular centennial items.

Bottle, gold dipped, 100th Anniversary, 1986, 6½-oz, EX, $45.00.
(Photo courtesy B.J. Summers)

Bottle, gold-dipped, in velvet sleeve, 6½-oz 75.00
Bottle, Hutchinson, amber, Root Co, ½-oz, 3 in case 375.00
Bottle, International, set of 9 in plexiglas case 500.00
Bottle, leaded crystal, 100th logo, 6½-oz, MIB 150.00
Medallion, bronze, 3" dia, w/box 100.00
Pin set, wood fr, 101 pins 300.00
Scarf, silk, 30x30" 40.00
Thermometer, glass cover, 14" dia, M 35.00

Coca-Cola Originals

Ashtray, glass, Have a Coke/Drink C-C on rim, rnd, M 30.00
Bank, dispenser form, red, w/single glass, EX+ 375.00
Banner, canvas, Drink C-C.../bottle graphic, 1910, 16x70", VG+ ..4,000.00
Blotter, 1913, Pure & Healthful..., bottles flank oval, G 15.00
Blotter, 1929, The Pause That Refreshes, couple toasting, VG+ .35.00
Blotter, 1936, 50th Anniversary/1886-1936, EX+ 35.00
Blotter, 1955, party crowd in front of fireplace, Canadian, NM+ ..24.00
Bookmark, 1898, heart shape, celluloid, NM 800.00
Bottle carrier, 1930s, cb box w/cut-out hdl, w/6 full bottles, EX+ ...200.00
Bottle carrier, 1950s, aluminum w/wire hdl, w/6 bottles, VG+ ..230.00
Bottle opener, 1950s, metal bottle shape, flat, EX+ 22.00
Bottle topper, 1926, cb, ice skating couple, 13x13", EX+ 3,600.00
Bowl, 1936, ceramic, gr w/emb logos around fluted rim, M 550.00
Calendar, 1904, incomplete, VG+ 2,300.00
Calendar, 1914, w/bottle, complete, rare, NM+ 1,600.00
Calendar, 1916, complete, EX+ 2,100.00
Calendar, 1922, complete, EX+ 1,000.00
Calendar, 1933, complete, VG+ 350.00
Calendar, 1936, complete, M 1,000.00
Calendar, 1943, complete, VG+ 250.00

Calendar, 1950, complete, EX+ 275.00
Calendar, 1957, complete, NM+ 175.00
Carton display, 1930s, cb, 2-tiered w/marquee, dk gr, 36", G+ ...425.00
Change purse, leather triangle, Drink C-C stamped in gold, NM+ ...490.00
Clock, 1910, Gilbert regulator, Gibson girl decal, VG (EX decal) ..3,700.00
Clock, 1930s-40s, neon, sq w/red octagonal logo on yel dot, 16", VG+ .825.00
Clock, 1950s, mantel, plastic dome/brass base, 4 bottles, 6", EX ..550.00
Clock, 1950s, maroon-pnt metal w/gold numbers, 19" dia, NM ..250.00
Cooler, floor; 1910s-20s, wood, tin sides, 4-legged, 29x32x32", EX ..1,700.00
Cooler, picnic; 1950s, 6-pack, unpnt metal, grip hdl/opener, EX+ 425.00
Dispenser, No Drip Protectors, w/sleeves, rare, 7¾", EX+ 525.00
Dispenser, syrup; 1930s, arched top, red, Drink C-C on sides, NM+ ..1,500.00
Dispenser, syrup; 1960s, red/wht box w/red/wht lettering, Dole, NM .2,100.00
Display, 1950s, cb, clown balancing upside down on bottle, 60", NM .3,300.00
Display bottle, 1960s, gr glass, w/cap, 20", NM+ 100.00
Doll, 1960s, Frozen C-C mascot, stuffed striped cloth, NM+ 145.00
Fan, 1950s, cb w/wooden hdl, Quality Carries On, G+ 40.00
Festoon, 1927, autumn girl, 5-pc, NM 3,500.00
Festoon, 1954, soda jerk/school kids, C-C of Course, complete, VG+ .1,320.00
Game, ca 1964, NFL Football, NM 15.00
Game, 1928, Age Cards, w/orig envelope, NM 700.00
Handkerchief, cloth, Kit Carson, wht/blk print on red, 21x21", EX ..120.00
Ice bucket, waxed cb, striped swag around top, EX+ 50.00
Lighter, 75th Anniversary, flip top, contour logo, M 40.00
Magazine ad, 1904, Lillian Nordica, complete w/coupon, NM ..250.00
Mechanical pencil/fountain pen, stamped advertising, NM 140.00
Menu board/clock, 1960s, fishtail logo/dbl row menu slots, 16x57, NM .1,000.00
Music box, 1950s, floor cooler w/revolving doll, red, EX+ 2,700.00
Notebook, 1903, leather w/gold-stamped lettering, EX 400.00
Pencil holder, 1960s, 1896 dispenser shape, ceramic, 7", EX 150.00
Photo album, 1940 C-C Golden Gate International Expo, NM ..350.00
Pillow, 1970s, print cloth #16 race car w/'Goodyear' tires, 15", NM 100.00
Pin-back button, Member of C-C Bottle Club, 1¼" dia, EX+ 65.00
Pin-back button, 1950s, Member Hi-Fi Club, multicolored, EX ..20.00
Playing cards, 1928, Refresh Yourself!, complete, no box, NM ..2,500.00
Playing cards, 1958, Welcome Friend, complete, M (VG box) ..150.00
Pocket mirror, 1911, VG+ 150.00
Pocket mirror, 1936, CC-/Memos/50th Anniversary, EX+ 120.00
Pocketknife/corkscrew, emb metal, vine design/bottle, 3½ ", EX .70.00
Poster, 1930s, Dancing Lady/J Crawford/C Gable Refresh w/C-C, EX .1,900.00
Push bar, 1930s, porc, Drink C-C, red/wht, zigzag ends, 34", EX ..700.00
Push plate, 1930s, emb tin, Drink C-C, w/bottle, 13", EX 425.00
Radio, 1940s-50s, wood cooler form, red w/blk knobs, EX+ 725.00
Record, 1960s, 45-rpm, Petula Clark, etc, 4 cuts, EX+ 20.00
Saleman's sample, 1939, cooler, closed front, 9x9x11", EX+ ..3,500.00
Sandwich toaster, 1920s, electric, w/orig cord, EX+ 1,800.00
School kit, 1930s, Real Pals, complete, unopened, VG 150.00
Sign, 1907, trolley, Tired?/C-C Relieves Fatigue, soda man, VG ..2,300.00
Sign, 1914, sf tin, Betty, 41x36", EX 10,000.00
Sign, 1920s, celluloid, Drink C-C Highballs, gold/blk, 6x11", EX 6,200.00
Sign, 1920s, celluloid/tin, Refresh Yourself/Drink C-C, 6x12", EX ...1,800.00
Sign, 1920s, paper, man w/bottle, Treat Yourself..., 20x12", EX .550.00
Sign, 1920s, tin, Drink C-C, red, gr rolled rim, 14x42", EX 750.00
Sign, 1920s, tin, Drink C-C/1915 bottle, wht, beveled, 13x26", VG ..1,400.00
Sign, 1920s, tin, lady w/bottle, red, gold rim, oval, 8x11" 4,700.00
Sign, 1920s, tin arrow, Sold Here..., gr/red, 2-sided, 8x30", G+ .300.00
Sign, 1930s, cb, Drink C-C, beach girl in yel suit, 50x30", VG+ .2,100.00
Sign, 1930s, cb, Drink C-C/D&R, girl cyclist, 30x14", EX+ 750.00
Sign, 1930s, cb stand-up, Thirst Asks Nothing More, 16x12", NM ..1,800.00
Sign, 1930s, glass w/chrome, Drink..., Brunoff, rectangle, NM ..3,500.00
Sign, 1930s, paper, 5¢/Drink C-C/5¢, wht on red, wht edge, 6x24", EX ..70.00
Sign, 1930s, rvpt glass light-up on base, Brunoff, 14x12", EX+ ...3,570.00
Sign, 1930s, tin, Drink CC Sold Here Ice Cold, bottle, 54x18", EX .675.00
Sign, 1930s, tin, Gas To-Day, self-fr, 54", EX 1,700.00
Sign, 1930s, tin, triangle hanger w/filigree top, 2-sided, 23", G+ ..675.00
Sign, 1930s, tin bottle shape, 39", G+ 425.00
Sign, 1930s, tin flange, Ice Cold/C-C/Sold Here, 12x16", EX ...850.00
Sign, 1940s, cb, Come Over for Coke, party girl, fr, 21x37", EX .230.00
Sign, 1940s, cb, Drink C-C/D&R, cowboy wiping brow, fr, 27x16", VG ..1,600.00
Sign, 1940s, cb, Mind Reader, sunbather in lounge chair, 30x50", EX ..750.00
Sign, 1940s, cb, Shop Refreshed!, lady shopper, fr, 11x13", NM ..500.00
Sign, 1940s, cb, The Pause That Refreshes, tennis girl, 27x16", EX+ .600.00
Sign, 1940s, cb hanger, B26 Marauder, 13x15", EX+ 55.00
Sign, 1940s, celluloid, Drink C-C/Ask for It..., red/gold, 9" dia, NM ..575.00
Sign, 1940s, masonite, girl tipping bottle, Drink C-C, 12x34", EX+ ...250.00
Sign, 1940s, paper cutout, Home Refreshment/25¢ 6-pack, 16x22", NM .45.00
Sign, 1940s, porc emblem, silhouette carhop/car, 52", NM 1,200.00
Sign, 1940s, tin, Take Home a Carton, 6-pack on yel, 28x20", EX ..550.00
Sign, 1940s, tin flange, Drink C-C, bottle on yel dot, 20x24", EX+ .550.00
Sign, 1940s, wood, Battleship, K Displays, 8½ x25", VG+ 625.00
Sign, 1940s, wood cutout, Stop/Go, cop/traffic, K Displays, EX ..3,500.00
Sign, 1950s, cb, Hospitality, gardening lady/girl, 20x36", VG+ .175.00
Sign, 1950s, cb, Join the Friendly Circle, 1954, horizontal, EX .450.00
Sign, 1950s, cb, Refreshing C-C, teen party, scarce, 27x56" 300.00
Sign, 1950s, cb, Serve Cold, Old Man Winter/6-pack, 21x16", NM 225.00
Sign, 1950s, cb cutout, Drink C-C..., Lionel Hampton, 15x12", NM 975.00
Sign, 1950s, cb cutout, Have a Large Coke, waitress/food, 18x14", NM ..75.00
Sign, 1950s, counter-top motion light-up, Pause, 9x20", VG 850.00
Sign, 1950s, light-up disk on rotating base, Shop Refreshed, NM ..1,100.00
Sign, 1950s, porc button, red, Drink C-C, 24", NM+ 450.00
Sign, 1950s, porc flange, Have a C-C, yel/wht/red, 19x17", EX .400.00
Sign, 1950s, tin flange, fishtail on wht w/gr stripes, 15x18", NM .450.00
Sign, 1960s, cb, Enjoy That..., bongo couple, fr, 39x22", VG 50.00
Sign, 1960s, cb, Things Go Better..., skaters, fr, 24x40", VG 160.00
Sign, 1960s, cb Santa, Santa's Helpers, w/2 bottles, 32x66", VG+ .120.00
Sign, 1960s, porc, fishtail on wht w/gr stripes, 16x44", VG 225.00
Sign, 1970s, tin, Drink/C-C/Trade Mark Reg, wht on red, 12x24", NM+ .25.00
Stamp holder w/calendar, 1900, celluloid, 1½ x2½ ", EX+ 1,200.00
Syrup bottle, 1910, clear glass, gold etched wreath, gold cap, NM ..700.00
Syrup jug, 1950s, paper label w/Coke glass, EX 20.00
Thermometer, 1905, wood, Drink CC/D&R, 21", VG+ 475.00
Thermometer, 1930s, mirror w/gauge, silhouette girl, 14x10", G+ ..325.00
Thermometer, 1930s, tin, gold bottle on red panel, 16", NM 400.00
Thermometer, 1940s, masonite, Thirst Knows No Season, 17", EX .500.00
Thermometer, 1950s, tin bottle shape, 17", VG+ 100.00
Thermometer, 1960s, dial, Things Go Better..., wht, 12" dia, EX+ ..300.00
Tie clip, gold & enameled bar, 5-Year, NM 75.00
Tip tray, 1906, EX+ 725.00
Tip tray, 1907, EX 725.00
Tip tray, 1913, NM+ 1,000.00
Tip tray, 1914, EX+ 330.00
Toy truck, 1950s, Lincoln Toys #809, pressed steel, red, rstr, 16" ...275.00
Toy truck, 1956, Marx, plastic, w/6 plastic cases, EX+ (EX box) ..600.00
Toy truck, 1960s, Buddy L #5426, pressed steel, 15", VG+ 175.00
Watch fob, 1911, Duster Girl, EX+ 900.00

Trays

Values are given for trays in excellent plus condition (C8+). Those that have been reproduced are marked with a (+). The 1934 Weismuller and O'Sullivan tray has been reproduced at least three times. To be original, it will have a black back and must say 'American Artworks, Coshocton, Ohio.' It was not reproduced by Coca-Cola in the 1950s.

All 10½x13½" original serving trays produced from 1910 to 1942 are marked with a date, Made in USA and the American Artworks Inc., Coshocton Ohio. All original trays of this format (1910–40) had REG TM in the tail of the C.

1897, Victorian Lady, 9¼" dia, VG 15,000.00
1901, Hilda Clark, 9¾", VG 4,000.00
1903, Hilda Clark, oval, 18½ x15", EX 6,000.00
1905, Lillian Russell, glass or bottle, 10½ x13¼", EX 3,500.00
1906, Juanita, glass or bottle, oval, 13¼x10½ ", EX 2,200.00
1907, Relieves Fatigue, 10½ x13¼", NM 4,000.00
1907, Relieves Fatigue, 13½ x16½ ", EX 3,600.00
1908, Topless, Wherever Ginger Ale..., 12¼" dia, NM 10,000.00
1909, St Louis Fair, 10½ x13¼", EX 1,800.00
1909, St Louis Fair, 13½ x16½ ", NM 3,000.00
1910, Coca-Cola Girl, Hamilton King, 10½ x13¼", VG 850.00
1914, Betty, oval, 12¼x15¼", EX+ 575.00
1914, Betty, 10½ x13¼", EX 600.00
1916, Elaine, 8½ x19", NM 600.00
1920, Garden Girl, oval, 10½ x13¼", EX+ 800.00
1921, Autumn Girl, oval, 10½ x13¼", EX+ 800.00
1922, Summer Girl, 10½ x13¼", NM 1,100.00
1923, Flapper Girl, 10½ x13¼", NM 400.00
1924, Smiling Girl, brn rim, 10½ x13¼", EX 650.00
1924, Smiling Girl, maroon rim, 10½ x13¼", EX 850.00
1925, Party, 10½ x13¼", NM 500.00

1926, Golfers, 10½x13¼", VG, $700.00.

1927, Curbside Service, 10½ x13¼", EX 750.00
1928, Bobbed Hair, 10½ x13¼", EX+ 650.00
1929, Girl in Swimsuit w/Glass, 10½ x13¼", EX+ 450.00
1930, Swimmer, 10½ x13¼", EX 425.00
1930, Telephone, 10½ x13¼", NM 650.00
1931, Boy w/Sandwich & Dog, 10½ x13¼", NM 1,100.00
1932, Girl in Swimsuit on Beach, Hayden, 10½ x13¼", EX+ ...625.00
1933, Francis Dee, 10½ x13¼", NM 700.00
1934, Weismuller & O'Sullivan, 10½ x13¼", NM 1,000.00
1935, Madge Evans, 10½ x13¼", NM 450.00
1936, Hostess, 10½ x13¼", NM 575.00
1937, Running Girl, 10½ x13¼", NM 350.00
1938, Girl in the Afternoon, 10½ x13¼", NM 300.00
1939, Springboard Girl, 10½ x13¼", NM 350.00
1940, Sailor Girl, 10½ x13¼", NM 350.00
1941, Ice Skater, 10¼x13¼", NM 400.00
1942, Roadster, 10½ x13¼", NM+ 425.00
1950s, Girl w/Wind in Hair, screen bkground, 10½ x13¼", M ..100.00
1950s, Girl w/Wind in Hair, solid bkground, 10½ x13¼", NM .225.00
1955, Menu Girl, 10½ x13¼", M 65.00
1957, Birdhouse, 10½ x13¼", NM 100.00
1957, Rooster, 10½ x13¼", NM 175.00
1957, Umbrella Girl, 10½ x13¼", M 375.00
1961, Pansy Garden, 10½ x13¼", NM 30.00

Machines

Though interest in Coca-Cola machines of the 1949–1959 era rose dramatically over the last few years, values currently seem to have leveled off and actually dropped 15% to 20%. The major manufacturers of these curved-top, 5¢ and 10¢ machines were Vendo (V), Vendorlator (VMC), Cavalier (C or CS), and Jacobs. Prices are for machines in excellent or better condition, complete and working. They vary greatly according to geographical location.

Cavalier, model #CS72, EX orig 1,400.00
Cavalier, model #CS72, M rstr 3,200.00
Cavalier, model #C27, M rstr 2,800.00
Cavalier, model #C27, orig 1,200.00
Cavalier, model #C51, EX orig 850.00
Cavalier, model #C51, M rstr 1,800.00
Jacobs, model #26, EX 1,200.00
Jacobs, model #26, M rstr 2,500.00
Vendo, model #23, EX orig 900.00
Vendo, model #39, EX orig 900.00
Vendo, model #39, M, rstr 2,500.00
Vendo, model #44, EX orig 2,500.00
Vendo, model #44, M rstr 3,750.00
Vendo, model #56, EX orig 1,400.00
Vendo, model #56, M rstr 3,200.00
Vendo, model #80, EX orig 600.00
Vendo, model #80, M rstr 1,250.00
Vendo, model #81, EX orig 1,400.00
Vendo, model #81, M rstr 3,200.00
Vendorlator, model #27, EX orig 1,200.00
Vendorlator, model #27, rstr (w/stand) 2,750.00
Vendorlator, model #27A, EX orig 900.00
Vendorlator, model #27A, M rstr 2,000.00
Vendorlator, model #33, EX orig 1,100.00
Vendorlator, model #33, M rstr 2,250.00
Vendorlator, model #44, EX orig 1,500.00
Vendorlator, model #44, M rstr 3,200.00
Vendorlator, model #72, EX orig 1,000.00
Vendorlator, model #72, M rstr 1,800.00

Coffee Grinders

Coffee mills, also called grinders, are becoming more and more popular with eager collectors and those simply wishing to add to their antique kitchen motif. Coffee mills fall into several basic types and the same mill can sometimes be referred to in various ways. Both mills, also called lap, or table mills are generally made of wood but true wall mills are usually of iron and have a cup or receiver of some kind to catch the ground coffee; side mills; really made to be mounted to a post or the side of a cabinet are usually made completely of iron, or iron with a tin hopper; canister mills have grinding mechanisms made of iron and can have hoppers made of tin, sheet metal, glass, or porcelain. Upright iron mills can have one wheel, two wheels, one wheel and one crank, or just one crank alone and can range in height from around 12 inches up to six or seven feet in height and weigh in excess of 300 lbs. Some mills were made to be calmped to the edge of a table. And of course, the final incarnation came with the advent of electricity in the form of small electric mills available to the homemaker up to the large industrial models for commercial use.

The advent of the Internet and online auctions has brought out both the good and bad among collectible coffee mills. Doing your homework is the most important factor when purchasing coffee mills online. Many reproductions and modern examples are found online that are represented as genuine old coffee mills. It should also be remembered that many companies produced certain models in the hundreds of thousands that still exist in vast numbers and therefore are quite common. Few mills are actually scarce or rare, and there are no known miniature salesmen's samples. Mills most often identified as salesmen's samples are in fact toys. This does not, however, diminish their desirability. Grist mills, for corn or other grains, are often incorrectly identified as coffee mills. While generally not as valuable as coffee mills, they are often found in the collection of coffee mill enthusiasts. Our advisor for this category is Shane Branchcomb; he is listed in the Directory under Virginia.

Key: adj — adjustment

American Beauty, canister, CI/tin, orig cup/papers, NM **135.00**
American Duplex No 47, electric, working, VG **65.00**
Arcade, Favorite No 7, side, CI w/orig lid, grind adj front, VG ...**95.00**
Arcade, Favorite No 27, side, CI w/orig lid, VG/EX **115.00**
Arcade, Favorite No 47, wood box, CI hopper, EX **160.00**
Arcade, Imperial, lap, CI, closed hopper, wood box, EX **110.00**
Arcade, Imperial No 200, lap, CI hopper w/eagle, Pat 88, 89 ....**155.00**
Arcade, IXL, table, ornate CI hopper, hdl on side, 1-lb, EX **325.00**
Arcade, Queen, glass canister & receiver, CI works, EX **295.00**
Arcade, Royal, canister, CI cup, tin hopper, EX **95.00**
Arcade, Telephone, canister, CI front, Pat Sept 25, '88, EX **575.00**
Arcade, Telephone, early motif, CI & wood, EX **575.00**
Arcade, X-Ray, CI works, tin hopper w/glass, EX **175.00**
Arcade Crystal, #9010, CI, Art Deco, glass hopper, EX **175.00**
Arcade Crystal, #9010, CI, w/orig mk cup, NM **285.00**
Arcade No 3, canister, CI w/glass hopper, orig lid, EX **155.00**
Arcade No 4, canister, CI, glass hopper, orig lid, wall mt, EX **175.00**
Arcade No 700, lap, w/dust cover, Sears 1908 catalog, EX **155.00**
Bell, canister, similar to Golden Rule, CI & wood, EX **425.00**
Belmont, Lightning No 23, canister, tin & CI, EX **225.00**
Bronson-Walton, Silver Lake, canister, glass hopper, EX **485.00**
C Ibach stamp on hdl, dvtl walnut, CI hopper, orig drw **165.00**
Cannon No 2, table, CI box & drw, brass hopper, EX **185.00**
Caravan, canister, CI works, tin hopper, ca 1910, VG/EX **165.00**
Cavanaugh Bros, table, front fill, 1-lb, EX **225.00**
Cavanaugh's, table, CI, ornate legs, wood box, EX **525.00**
Chase & Sanborn, coffee bin **175.00**
Clawson & Clark No 1, CI, dbl grind, Pat 1886, 6" wheel **525.00**
Coles, No 00, CI, wall mt w/CI cup, NM **295.00**
Coles Mfg No 7, counter, CI, Pat 1887, 16" wheels, 27", EX **825.00**
Crescent, CI, Rutland VT, orig pnt, 15" wheels, EX **675.00**
Crescent, table, wood, top fill, cylinder, 13", EX **235.00**
DeVe, Holland, lap, copper-plated hopper, decals **85.00**
Elgin Nat'l No 40, counter, CI, red pnt, 2 wheels, orig, VG **575.00**
Elgin Nat'l No 44, CI, red, w/eagle & pan, 15" wheels, 24" **775.00**
Elgin Nat'l No 46, orig pnt/decals, 12" wheels, EX **675.00**
Elma, tin box, EX **55.00**
Elma No 0, CI, single wheel, 9¼" **125.00**
Elma No 1, CI, single wheel, 11" **155.00**
Elma No 3, CI, single Wheel, 15½ " **160.00**
Enterprise, Boss, floor, CI, closed hopper, 1873, 39" wheels ...**3,675.00**
Enterprise No 1, counter, open hopper, hdl, Pat 1873, 11", VG ..**225.00**
Enterprise No 1, counter, orig pnt/decals, side hdl, 1898 ....**235.00**
Enterprise No 7, counter, CI, orig pnt, 17" wheel w/eagle, VG .**825.00**
Enterprise No 9, CI, brass eagle, Pat 1898, 19" wheels, 28", VG .**895.00**
Enterprise No 12, counter, w/eagle/decals, 2 wheels, Pat 1898 ...**895.00**
Enterprise No 16, floor, CI, orig pnt, CI hopper **4,100.00**
Enterprise No 50, single-wheel grist mill, NM **100.00**
Enterprise No 212, floor, CI, 2 wheels, orig pnt, 30½ ", EX ...**3,000.00**
Enterprise No 300, very heavy, wall mt, w/catcher, EX **495.00**
Euclid No 4, counter, aluminum hopper, 10" wheels, VG **395.00**
Golden Rule, canister, w/orig glass, CI front, wood box, EX **425.00**
Grand Union Tea, table, CI sq base, rnd hopper, mfg Griswold .**495.00**
Griswold, counter, CI, 2 wheels, Pat 1897, EX **1,295.00**
Hart, Henry C; Detroit Mich, CI, wall mt, NM **85.00**
Husqvrna No 7, Swedish made, single wheel, 16½ " **525.00**
J Fisher Warranted, lap, dvtl walnut, pewter hopper, unique **265.00**
Japy Freres, ornate wood work, brass hopper, ftd **145.00**
Landers, Frary & Clark, CI, rnd, sq base, ornate, Pat 1875 ....**495.00**
Landers, Frary & Clark, Crown No 11, CI, decals, side crank, EX ..**275.00**
Landers, Frary & Clark, lap, fancy CI top, wood box, VG/EX ...**125.00**
Landers, Frary & Clark, Regal, canister, wall mt **95.00**
Landers, Frary & Clark, Regal No 44, canister, CI/tin, orig **95.00**
Landers, Frary & Clark, table, CI, Pat Feb 14, 1905, EX **125.00**
Landers, Frary & Clark, Universal No 10, table, tin **85.00**
Landers, Frary & Clark, Universal No 14, table, Pat 1905, VG ...**85.00**
Landers, Frary & Clark #24, w/orig mk hopper, NM **155.00**
Landers, Frary & Clark No 50, counter, CI, 12" wheels, EX+ **800.00**
Lightning, canister, CI works, tin hopper, 1-lb, EX **145.00**
Logan & Strobridge, Franco-American, lap, ornate CI hopper ..**125.00**
Luther, side, CI, tin hopper, brass plate, Pat 1843 ....**225.00**
Mimosa, table mt, CI, open hopper, heavy **85.00**
MJB, tin canister, wall mt w/lid & cup, EX **155.00**
Nat'l Specialty, CI, brass hopper, 2 12½ " wheels **1,100.00**
Nat'l Specialty, CI, single crank, 12", EX **375.00**
Nat'l Specialty...Philadelphia, CI, 25" wheels, VG **625.00**
National Specialty No 7, CI, 16½ " wheels, EX **1,000.00**
New Model, lap, CI w/CI drw, bottom open all 4 sides, EX **95.00**
None Such, Bronson Co Cleveland OH, table, tin, pnt, EX **95.00**
Parker, side, CI, grind adj front, Pat 1876, orig brd **75.00**
Parker (mk CPCo) No 1350, CI, wall mt, NM **85.00**
Parker Challenge Fast Grind No 555, table, orig, 1-lb, EX **125.00**
Parker No 49, side, tin hopper w/brass eagle, tin lid **110.00**
Parker No 60, side, tin hopper, brass eagle medallion lid **85.00**
Parker No 340, w/label, tin catcher, 1-lb box, EX **155.00**
Parker No 400 series, lap, split-covered top, ornate **135.00**
Parker No 446, wall mt **185.00**
Parker No 5005, counter, CI, 12½ " wheels, 17", EX **875.00**
Parker Union, side, CI, gear drive, Pat 1855, EX **135.00**
Parker Victor No 535, table, wood/tin hopper, hdl **135.00**
Persepolis, table, CI & brass, unique, rare **700.00**
Primitive, lap, cherry, brass hopper, handmade/unique, 4x4" **195.00**
Primitive, lap, dvtl walnut, wrought iron, brass hopper **175.00**
PS&W Standard No 31, lap, CI open hopper, wood box **125.00**
PSW&Co No 6, side, orig CI lid, EX **75.00**
Queen (toy), CI hopper & drw front, wood box, decal, mini **95.00**
Royal Blue, Supplee Hdwe Co, CI, tin hopper, EX **185.00**
Russell & Erwin, Diamond, CI, bronze finish, rare **350.00**
Russell & Erwin, Diamond, lap, CI, sloped sides, NM **350.00**
Russell & Erwin Mfg Co No 1008, CI hopper, wood box **90.00**
S&H, counter, CI, w/drw, 19" wheels, 21", VG **525.00**
Selsor, Cook & Co, lap, name on hdl, Pat 1859 ....**165.00**
Simmon's Hdwe, Delmar Coffee, table, CI cover **295.00**
Standard Cabinet Co, spice cabinet w/mill built in, EX **600.00**
Star, canister, tin w/CI works, Pat 1910, VG **75.00**
Star, floor, brass hopper, 2 CI wheels **975.00**
Star No 7, counter, CI, w/pan, 2-wheel, VG **475.00**
Steinfield, canister, CI works, glass jar, orig lid, EX **165.00**
Stuttle, Henry; #2, CI, tin hopper, Pat 2/20/77, EX **275.00**
Sun, No 94, side, CI, Greenfield OH, VG **75.00**
Sun No 1050 Improved, lap, wood, tin hopper **85.00**
Sun Success No 25, cylinder, 2 different szs, EX, ea **275.00**
Swift, drug mill, CI, open hopper, Pat June 30, 1874 ....**525.00**
Swift No 12, Lane Brothers, 9" wheel **550.00**
Swift No 13, counter, orig tin drw, red pnt, 12" wheels, 19" **475.00**
Swift No 15, counter, orig decals/pnt, Pat 1875, 19" wheels **875.00**
Swift No 16, counter, red w/lg decal, 2 wheels **795.00**
Swift No 26, Lane Brothers, floor, CI, 2 wheels **2,500.00**

Tillmann's, Hawaiian Coffee, CI, wall mt, EX 195.00
Universal No 109, blk tin w/gr decal, Pat 1905, NM 75.00
Vandergrift, side hinged, CI, ca 1870, complete, EX 185.00
Waddel, A-17, CI, sunflower design, wall mt, EX 250.00
Wilson Increase, side, CI & tin 60.00
Wrightsville Hdwe, Brighton, label, 1-lb box, EX 95.00
Wrightsville Hdwe, CI, eagle pnt on lid, 2 wheels, sm 350.00
Wrightsville Hdwe, Peerless No 200, canister, CI/glass, EX 160.00
WW Weaver Warranted, dvtl walnut, pewter hopper, ca 1830 ..225.00

Coin-Operated Machines

Coin-operated machines may be the fastest-growing area of collector interest in today's market. Many machines are bought, restored, and used for home entertainment. Older examples from the turn of the century and those with especially elaborate decoration and innovative features are most desirable.

The http://www.GameRoomAntiques.com website and *Antique Amusements, Slot Machine, and Jukebox Gazette* are excellent sources of information for those interested in coin-operated machines; see the Clubs, Newsletters, and Catalogs section of the Directory for publishing information. Jackie and Ken Durham are our advisors; they are listed in the Directory under the District of Columbia.

Arcade Machines

Brunswick, pool table, ca 1890, EX orig 4,750.00
Caille Automatic Bowling Alley, ca 1910, EX rstr 1,575.00
Caille Cupid's Post Office, 1905, VG 3,500.00
Caille Electric Wave, ca 1905, EX orig 6,000.00
Caille Happy Home, viewer, 1910, EX 2,250.00
Caille Hermes Grip Test, ca 1905, EX 3,000.00
Caille Supply Love Tester, 1925, EX orig 1,700.00
Exhibit Egyptian Mummy, EX orig 1,750.00
Exhibit Supply Enchantress, 1925, EX orig 3,500.00
Exhibit Supply Whom To Marry, ca 1925, VG orig 3,000.00
Gottlieb Whizz Bang, 1932, EX orig 500.00
Home Billiard Table, ca 1930, EX orig 2,000.00
Kicker & Catcher, 5 balls for 5¢, G 595.00
Mexican 1¢ Baseball, 2-player, metal case, EX orig 500.00
Mills Electricity Is Life, shock machine, early 1900s, rstr 25,000.00
Mills Lifter, strength tester, rstr, from $4,000 to 5,000.00
Mills Lion Lung Tester, 1905, VG 5,000.00
Mills World Horoscope, 1905, EX orig 6,000.00
Mutoscope, Indian front, ca 1900, VG 5,500.00
Mutoscope Clam Shell, ca 1895, CI, EX rstr 4,600.00
Play Football 2¢, Chester-Pollard Amusement Co, electrified, EX ..3,450.00
Rockola World Series, 1937, NM 5,000.00
Roover's Shock Machine, early 1900s, rstr, from $5,000 to 6,000.00
Seeburg Chicken Sam, ca 1931, EX orig 1,000.00

Jukeboxes

The coin-operated phonograph of the early 1900s paved the way for the jukeboxes of the '20s. Seeburg was first on the market with an automatic eight-tune phonograph. By the 1930s Wurlitzer was the top name in the industry with dealerships all over the country. As a result of the growing ranks of competitors, the '40s produced the most beautiful machines made. Wurlitzers from this era are probably the most popularly sought-after models on the market today. The model #1015 of 1946 is considered the all-time classic and often brings prices in excess of $8,000.00.

AMI B, 1947, EX orig 2,250.00
AMI Streamliner, 1938, EX orig 4,000.00
Mills Empress, ca 1939, EX orig 3,000.00
Packard Manhattan, 1946, EX orig 5,500.00
Rockola #1422, rstr 4,000.00
Rockola #1428, Christmas tree, 1948, EX orig 4,000.00
Rockola #1448, 1955, EX orig 2,200.00
Rockola Dialatune, wall type 375.00
Rockola Monarch, 1938, EX 3,200.00
Rockola Premier, 1942, NM 4,500.00
Seeburg #100A, 1950, VG 3,500.00
Seeburg Audiophone Jr, 1928, EX 3,500.00
Seeburg B, 1951, rstr 3,500.00
Seeburg Discotheque, 1965, NM 1,000.00
Seeburg Envoy, 1940, NM 3,500.00
Seeburg R, 1954, EX orig 4,000.00
Wurlitzer #24, 1937, EX orig 3,200.00
Wurlitzer #35, 1936, NM rstr 4,500.00
Wurlitzer #35, 1936, VG 3,500.00
Wurlitzer #600, 1938, EX orig 4,250.00
Wurlitzer #750, NM rstr 9,000.00
Wurlitzer #1015 (Bubbler), rstr 11,000.00
Wurlitzer #2150, 1957, EX orig 1,700.00
Wurlitzer #2500, 1960, M 1,950.00

Pinball Machines

Bally Atlantis #N-16, 1989 ....1,200.00
Bally Flicker #N-13, 1975, EX 695.00
Bally Goofy, 1943, NM 575.00
Bally Spy Hunter #RL-801, 1980s, M 750.00
Bingo, 1931, EX orig 350.00
Mills Redman, w/unusual pay-out mechanism, 1937, 52x45x24", EX ..750.00
Mills Wow, 1932, NM 600.00
Ritz, Stoner Mfg Corp of Aurora IL, floor model, 53", VG 450.00
Rockola, World Series, ca 1934, 40x38", G- 1,900.00
Williams Big Deal #N-10, poker theme, 1977, EX 525.00
Williams Pin Bot #N-7, clean, rubbered, G working 1,250.00

Slot Machines

Jennings Standard Chief 1¢, bronze chief head on chrome body, ca 1946, 27", VG original, $2,800.00.

Buckley Criss Cross 25¢, G orig 1,700.00
Caille, Superior Jackpot Bell, 1928, VG 1,750.00
Caille Busy Bee, EX 9,000.00
Caille Center Pull 5¢, w/vendor, EX orig 4,600.00

Caille Silent Sphinx 5¢, VG 2,500.00
Clawson Carlo, counter-top, 1894, EX orig 3,200.00
Field 4 Jacks 1¢, 1929, EX 1,100.00
Groetchen Twin Falls Bell, console model, 1947, NM 2,200.00
Jennings Bronze Chief 5¢, 1941, EX+ 2,800.00
Jennings Cig-a-Rola 5¢, cigarette vendor, 1937, EX 3,500.00
Jennings New Victoria Bell, 1931, NM 2,900.00
Jennings Prospector $1, rstr, in stand 4,600.00
Jennings Triplex Chief Bell, 1938, EX orig 2,750.00
Jennings Victoria Silent 1932 Peacock, rstr 3,500.00
Mills Dewey Jackpot 5¢, upright, oak case, decals, EX orig 9,000.00
Mills Futurity Bell, 1936, VG 3,500.00
Mills Golden Nugget 5¢ Hi-Top, laminated sides, cast base, EX .2,500.00
Mills Horse Head Bonus 5¢, rstr 3,000.00
Mills Judge, floor wheel, 1899, NM 10,000.00
Mills Liberty Bell, ca 1910, rstr, from $8,000 to 9,000.00
Mills Melon Bell (Bursting Cherry style), 1937, NM 2,800.00
Mills Silent Golden Bell, Roman head front, 1932, EX 2,500.00
Mills Vest Pocket, rstr 750.00
Mills War Eagle, ca 1931, EX orig 2,000.00
Mills 1-Arm Bandit 5¢, laminated & cvd wood, felt hat, EX .6,000.00
OD Jennings Little Duke 1¢, oak w/Deco details, EX 2,700.00
Pace All Star Comet Bell, 1936, NM 2,200.00
Pace Bantam Bell, 1928, EX orig 2,200.00
Pace Kitty 10¢, rstr 4,000.00
Pace Operator's Bell 10¢, 1927, EX orig 2,400.00
Pace Saratoga, console model, 1937, EX orig 1,500.00
Superior Gooseneck Bell, 1934, VG 2,500.00
Watling Jackpot, floor model, 1904, EX 11,000.00
Watling Rol-A-Top Bird 5¢, rstr 4,695.00
Watling Rol-A-Top Coin Front, EX 3,500.00
White Owl, floor model, 1901, EX 8,000.00

Trade Stimulators

Anthony Eclipse, clock, 1893, VG 1,750.00
Bluebird Target, coin drop, 1927, EX orig 500.00
Buckley Horses, 4-reel, horse race, 1935, EX 700.00
Caille Good Luck, 5-reel, 1902, EX orig 1,100.00
Caille Merchant, 3-reel, ca 1905, VG orig 2,900.00
Clawson Automatic Dice, 1890, VG 5,000.00
Daval Ace, 5-reel, 1940, EX orig 300.00
Daval Derby 5¢, horse race, ca 1937, NM 1,250.00
Daval Reel 21, 5-reel, 1936, NM 595.00
Daval Tally, 3-reel, 1938, EX orig 495.00
Exhibit Supply Get A Pack, dice game, w/gumball vendor, NM ..450.00
Fey Midget, 1920, EX orig 1,200.00
Garden City Novelty Gem, 3-reel, 1937, NM 450.00
Gottlieb Indian Dice, ca 1937, EX orig 950.00
Groetchen Gold Rush, 2-reel, ca 1934, EX orig 650.00
Groetchen Klix, 1941, NM 425.00
Groetchen Pok-o-Reel Triplex, 1934, NM 650.00
Groetchen Sparks Champion, 3-reel, 1940, EX orig 395.00
Groetchen 21, 5-reel, w/vendor, 1934, EX+ 750.00
Keeney Steeplechase, ca 1935, EX orig 850.00
Mills Jockey, ca 1901, EX orig 2,000.00
Mills Kounter King, 5-reel, 1938, NM 750.00
Mills Umpire, baseball game, 1905, EX orig 8,000.00
Rockola Hold & Draw, 5-reel, 1934, EX orig 1,000.00
Stephens Magic Beer Barrel, pretzels, 3-reel, EX orig 1,200.00

Vendors

Vending machines sold a product or a service. They were already in common usage by 1900 selling gum, cigars, matches, and a host of other commodities. Peanut and gumball machines are especially popular today. The most valuable are those with their original finish and decals. Older machines made of cast iron are especially desirable, while those with plastic globes have little or no collector value. When buying unrestored peanut machines, beware of salt damage.

Ad Lee Model D, M 600.00
Advance 1¢, matches, glass dome, oak case, 18", G 895.00
Bull Novelty Co Bull's Head 1¢, perfume, EX 6,800.00
Challenger, hot nuts, ca 1947, EX orig, on stand 495.00
Climax, gum, 1920, EX rstr 1,500.00
Columbus Bi-Mor, porc, NM 700.00
Columbus Model 14, gum, w/wall bracket, M 650.00
Cupid, postcards, 1920s, rstr, from $3,000 to 4,000.00
Ford, gum, chrome, orig base, marquee top, rstr 120.00
International Vending, matches, VG 800.00
Italian Balm 1¢, lotion, ca 1935, NM 495.00
Master #2, gum, Pat 1923 & 1924, 16" 395.00
National Hunter, gum, EX orig 495.00
Penny King 4 in 1, 1936, NM 500.00
Premier, cards, 1950s, NM 395.00
Regal, gum, 1935, VG 125.00
Scoopy Gum, clockwork, man drops gum from scoop, 20", EX .1,500.00
Simpson Derby, aluminum, M 2,200.00
Tom Thumb, ca 1920, sm, EX orig 225.00
Victor Vendorama, full globe, EX orig 90.00
White Happy Jap, gum, 1902, NM 3,500.00
Zeno 1¢, gum, CI, clockworks, 17", EX orig 850.00

Cole, A. R.

A second generation North Carolina potter, Arthur Ray Cole opened his own shop in 1926, operating under the name Rainbow Pottery until 1941 when he adopted his own name for the title of his business. He remained active until he died in 1974. He was skilled in modeling the pottery and highly recognized for his fine glazes.

Bowl, Chrome Red, attributed to Jack Kiser, 1930s, NM, 4¼x12½", $150.00. (Photo courtesy Southern Folk Pottery Collectors Society)

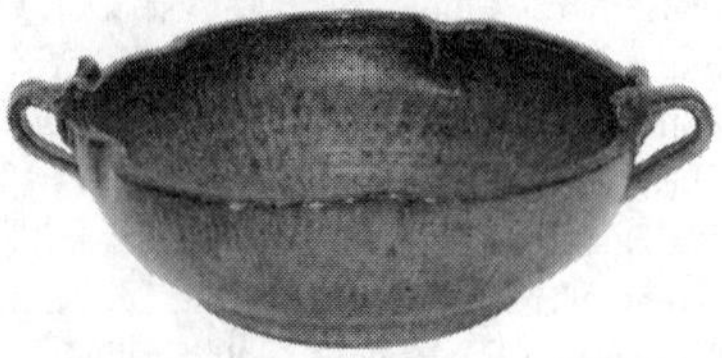

Bowl, fruit; Chrome Red, hdls, att, ca 1930s, 3½ x14" 70.00
Jardiniere/planter, dk gr w/matt gr variations, sgn, 1940s, 10⅞" ..150.00
Jug, chrome red, streaky, att Nel Graves, 5" 40.00
Lemonade set, bl-gray variegated, '60s, 10½ " pitcher+6 tumblers .50.00
Plate, gr matt w/dk gloss, 9½ " 80.00
Vase, red/yel/gr/wht at shoulder over bl, sm hdls, sgn, 1930s, 17⅜" ..140.00
Vase, Spider, brn shiny & matt, 3 long rolled hdls, 13" 350.00

Comic Books

For almost sixty years, the American public has been thrilled by the monthly adventures of everyone's favorite comic book heroes such as Superman, Captain Marvel, and Spider-Man. Each 10¢ comic book issue, featuring a new saga of adventure and mystery, were usually met with excitement and anticipation by the youngsters who eagerly purchased them from their neighborhood candy store or newsstand. Unfortunately, the vast majority of these comic books were eventually discarded in favor of other worldly pursuits. Due to this fact, most comic books from the '30s and '40s did not survive, making them a very scarce and desirable collectible in today's world. Many comic books are worth very little, a few of the better examples are listed here.

Adventures of Mighty Mouse, St John #2, 1952, EX+ 55.00
Adventures of the Fly, Dell #20, NM 30.00
Al Capp's Wolf Gal, Dell #2, 1952, VG+ 40.00
Amazing Spider-Man & Dr Doom, Marvel #5, EX 150.00
Andy Griffith, Dell #1252, EX 75.00
Aquaman, Dell #1, 1962, EX 175.00
Atomic Mouse, #1, VG+ 75.00
Avengers, Marvel #1, 1963, EX 500.00
Bambi's Children, Dell Four-Color #30, VG 145.00
Batman, DC Comics #4, 1940, EX 900.00
Black Rider, Marvel #8, photo cover, VG+ 95.00
Bonanza, Dell #210, 1962, EX 125.00
Brady Bunch, Dell #2, 1970, EX, from $30 to 40.00
Brave & the Bold, Dell #43, EX+ 225.00

Captain America, #100, Marvel Comics Group, NM, $300.00.

Captain Midnight, Dell #37, EX+ 85.00
Conqueror, Dell Four-Color #690, VG+ 40.00
Dale Evans Queen of the West, Dell #479, EX 100.00
Earth Man on Venus, Avon, 1951, EX 325.00
Felix the Cat, Dell #61, 1946, VG 35.00
Flash Gordon, Dell Four-Color #10, 1943, scarce, EX 350.00
Gidget, Dell #1, 1966, EX 35.00
Green Hornet, #1, VG 40.00
Gunsmoke, Dell, Four-Color #0844, EX 45.00
Hunchback of Notre Dame, Dell #854, 1957, EX 40.00
I Dream of Jeannie, Dell #1, 1966, NM, from $40 to 50.00
I Love Lucy, #3, G+ 30.00
Iron Man, Dell #10, NM 25.00
John Carter of Mars, Gold Key #1, 1964, VG 20.00
John Wayne, Toby Press #4, 1950, photo cover, EX 55.00
Justice League of America, Dell #6, VG 50.00
Katzenjammer Kids, Dell #32, 1946, VG 35.00
Lady & the Tramp, Dell #1, 1955, VG 30.00
Lil' Abner, Dell #61, 1947, NM 190.00
Lone Ranger, Dell #37, EX+ 45.00
Lone Ranger Movie, Dell Giant, 1956, EX+ 50.00
Looney Tunes Merrie Melodies, Dell, 1940s, EX, from $50 to 70.00
Marge's Little Lulu, Dell #74, NM 60.00
Marvel Tales, Dell #121, 1954, VG 35.00
Maverick, Dell #980, EX+ 40.00
Mickey Mouse, Dell Four-Color #27, 1943, VG 160.00
Monkees, Dell #1, 1967-68, NM 40.00
Mutt & Jeff, Dell #24, VG+ 30.00
My Favorite Martian, Dell #3, EX 30.00
Mysterious Adventures, Dell #8, 1952, VG 50.00
Mystery in Space, Dell #12, NM 175.00
Nanny & the Professor, Dell #2, EX 25.00
Oswald the Rabbit, Dell #102, EX 30.00
Parent Trap, Dell #1210, VG+ 20.00
Playful Little Audrey, Dell #1, EX 110.00
Pogo Possum, Dell #1, 1949, G 75.00
Rawhide Kid, Dell #12, EX 35.00
Robin Hood, Dell #413, 1952, EX 30.00
Rocky Lane, #5, VG 50.00
Roy Rogers, #10, VG+ 45.00
Savage Tales, Dell #1, EX 50.00
Sheena Queen of the Jungle, Dell #16, EX 35.00
Smilin' Jack, Dell #149, 1947, NM 75.00
Space Ghost, Dell #1, NM 250.00
Spin & Marty, Dell #5, 1958, EX+ 45.00
Star Trek, Dell #3, 1967, EX+ 135.00
Straight Arrow, #1, G+ 55.00
Superboy, Dell #89, VG+ 60.00
Superman, Dell #25, 1941, VG 225.00
Superman's Girlfriend Lois Lane, Dell #13, NM 100.00
Tales to Astonish, Dell #40, NM 245.00
Tarzan, Dell #27, 1951, EX 35.00
Tarzan's Jungle Annual, Dell #2, 1953, EX 40.00
This Is Your Life Donald Duck, Dell #1109, NM 125.00
Tom Mix, Fawcett #2, VG 110.00
Underworld Crime, Dell #3, 1952, EX+ 60.00
Vacation in Disneyland, Dell #1025, NM 140.00
Western Tales, Dell #32, 1956, EX+ 80.00
Wonder Woman, Dell #34, G 30.00
Woody Woodpecker, Dell #350, 1947, EX 25.00
Wyatt Earp, Dell #860, NM 75.00
X-Men, Marvel #60, 1969, EX 15.00
Zorro, Dell #11, 1960, EX 20.00

Compacts

The use of cosmetics before WWI was looked upon with disdain. After the war women became liberated, entered the work force, and started to use makeup. The compact, a portable container for cosmetics, became a necessity. The basic compact contains a mirror and a powder puff.

The vintage compacts were fashioned in a myriad of shapes, styles, materials, and motifs. They were made of precious metals, fabrics, plastics, and in almost any other conceivable medium. Commemorative, premium, patriotic, figural, Art Deco, plastic, and gadgetry compacts are just a few of the most sought-after types available today. Those that are combined with other accessories (music/compact, watch/compact, cane/compact) are also very much in demand. Vintage compacts are an especially desirable collectible since the workmanship, design, techniques, and materials used in their execution would be very expensive and virtually impossible to duplicate today.

Our advisor, Roselyn Gerson, has written four highly informative books: *Vintage Vanity Bags and Purses*; *Vintage and Contemporary Purse Accessories*; and *Vintage Ladies' Compacts*. She is listed in the Directory under the state of New York. See Clubs, Newsletters, and Catalogs for information concerning the compact collectors' club and their periodical publication, *The Powder Puff*.

Basket, K&K, satin brass-tone, engine tooled, swing hdl, 2⅛x1¼" ..120.00

Ball (2" sphere) and chain (with lipstick), Wadsworth, gold-tone, $175.00. (Photo courtesy Roselyn Gerson)

Carryall, Dermay, gold-plate/blk enamel cartouch, mesh strap, 2¾x4" ..250.00
Carryall, Marhill, MOP w/HP peacock & glitter on lid 200.00
Carryall, Volupte, Swinglok, MOP, 1940s-50s 200.00
Cigarette/compact, oblong, plastic w/metal cut-out Scottie, 1940s .110.00
Compass/compact, Elgin Am, rnd w/eng continents, 1950s 175.00
Damascene, Egyptian, sq, gold-tone w/gilt on blk matt 100.00
Damascene, floral, Amita, rnd, gold/silver on blk matt, 1920s ...150.00
Damascene, man & horse, rnd, gilt on blk, 1930s 60.00
Damascene, Mt Fuji, Japan, sq, gold/silver on blk matt, 1920s ..150.00
Damascene, pagoda, gold on blk matt, pendant, bamboo inlay bk, '20s ..300.00
Fan, Japan, MOP w/rhinestones, miniature 60.00
Fan, Wadsworth, gold-tone w/bird & flowers HP on yel enamel, 1940s ..100.00
Half-moon, Rex, lt bl-gr enamel, diagonal gold-tone band, 5x2½" 100.00
Heart, Elgin, Give Me Your Answer Do!, stylized/enameled, 1940s-50s ..120.00
Heart, Evans, pk/yel gold-tone basketweave, 1946 ....225.00
Heart, gold-tone w/brocade lid, 1930s 60.00
Heart, SP w/eng flower, w/carrying chain 100.00
Heart, Zell, emb key w/red enamel, comes w/cb key & tassel, 2¾" .200.00
Horseshoe, bl leather (no design) 60.00
Musical, gold-tone w/silvered music score, 1920s 125.00
Musical, Stratton, gold-tone w/musical notes on MOP, 3¼x2¾" .175.00
Necessaire, blk/ivorene Bakelite w/rhinestones, cord/tassle, 1¾" ..450.00
Oblong, Maxley, MOP w/inlaid diagonal stripes & MOP cameo, 1930s .200.00
Octagonal, Gwenda, pnt foil w/sailing ship motif 80.00
Oval, Avon, gold-tone w/bl & gr emb wavy check design 30.00
Oval, Rex Fifth Ave, gold-tone w/mirror inset on red enamel ...100.00
Picture hat, Dorothy Gray, silver-tone w/emb floral & ribbon design ..175.00
Pocket-watch style, Volupte, MOP, 1940s-50s 75.00
Rnd, Germany, sterling w/3-D Scottie on blk plastic dome, 1920s-30s .200.00
Rnd, Kigu, gold-tone/bl enamel w/heart-shaped flower, 1940s-50s .75.00
Rnd, Norida, hammered gold-tone, emb lady, powder sifter, 1920s .60.00
Rnd, Revlon, brushed gold w/rhinestone & ruby trim, w/puff, 1¾" 45.00
Rnd, Ritz, gold-tone basketweave, orig pouch, 3" 50.00
Rnd, Sabor, gilt/plastic w/poodles kissing on Lucite dome lid, 1930s ..90.00
Rnd, Schildkraut, gold-tone/cloisonne w/2 peacocks on wht 50.00
Sq, blk enamel w/pnt poodle on wht enamel disk, 1930s 60.00
Sq, England, royal bl ribbed silk w/bl stone catch 125.00
Sq, HP enamel Japanese scene on wht ground, 2¾x2½" 75.00
Sq, Marathon, 2-part, gold-tone w/heart & flowers in oval 80.00
Sq, Trifari, brushed gold-tone w/colored stones, 3x3" 200.00
Sq, Volupte, eng gold-tone w/swivel mirror lid 125.00
Sq, Volupte, rigid gold-tone mesh w/buckle closure 100.00
Sq, Wadsworth, gold-tone w/deep-cut plastic crossbar design, 1930s ..150.00
Suitcase, 2-part, yel enamel w/NY stickers, 1940s 150.00
Triangular, Volupte, gr/yel check 80.00
Vanity, heart, gold-tone w/USN insignia in heart on blk enamel, WWII ..100.00
Vanity, Kamra-Pak style, snakeskin, 5-part/manicure, hdl, 1940s-50s ..250.00
Vanity, Kamra-Pak style, 3-part, bl enamel w/girl & lamppost, 1940s .175.00
Vanity, octagonal, RAC, couple on gr enamel, tube on chain, 2" 175.00
Vanity, rnd, R Hudnut, 2-part, gold-tone/blk, dbl cornucopia motif 60.00
Vanity, rnd flapjack, La Mode, cloisonne floral motif 70.00
Vanity, saddlebag, purple/blk lame fabric, 4x3¼" 175.00
Vanity, sq, B Co, 3-part, gr crackle plastic w/floral motif, chain ..125.00
Vanity, sq, 2-part, bl enamel w/Scottie transfer, 1920s-30s 50.00
Vanity, triangle, gr Bakelite, silver leaves/rhinestones, cord/tassel ...225.00
Vanity, w/lipstick, MOP, 1930s 75.00
Watch/compact, Evans, gold-tone trunk shape w/straps, 1940s ..175.00
Watch/compact, Ill Watch Co, yel-enameled bronze clamshell, 1930s ..175.00

Consolidated Lamp and Glass

The Consolidated Lamp and Glass Company of Coraopolis, Pennsylvania, was incorporated in 1894. For many years their primary business was the manufacture of lighting glass such as oil lamps and shades for both gas and electric lighting. The popular 'Cosmos' line of lamps and tableware was produced from 1894 to 1915. (See also Cosmos.) In 1926 Consolidated introduced their Martele line, a type of 'sculptured' ware closely resembling Lalique glassware of France. (Compare Consolidated's 'Lovebirds' vase with the Lalique 'Perruches' vase.) It is this line of vases, lamps, and tableware which is often mistaken for a very similar type of glassware produced by the Phoenix Glass Company, located nearby in Monaca, Pennsylvania. For example, the so-called Phoenix 'Grasshopper' vases are actually Consolidated's 'Katydid' vases.

Items in the Martele line were produced in blue, pink, green, crystal, white, or custard glass decorated with various fired-on color treatments or a satin finish. For the most part, their colors were distinctively different from those used by Phoenix. Although not foolproof, one of the ways of distinguishing Consolidated's wares from those of Phoenix is that most of the time Consolidated applied color to the raised portion of the design, leaving the background plain, while Phoenix usually applied color to the background, leaving the raised surfaces undecorated. This is particularly true of those pieces in white or custard glass.

In 1928 Consolidated introduced their Ruba Rombic line, which was their Art Deco or Art Moderne line of glassware. It was only produced from 1928 to 1932 and is quite scarce. Today it is highly sought after by both Consolidated and Art Deco collectors.

Consolidated closed its doors for good in 1964. Subsequently a few of the molds passed into the hands of other glass companies that later reproduced certain patterns; one such reissue is the 'Chickadee' vase, found in avocado green, satin-finish custard, or milk glass. Our advisor for this category is Jack D. Wilson, author of *Phoenix and Consolidated Art Glass, 1926–1980*; he is listed in the Directory under Illinois.

Key: mg — milk glass

Bird of Paradise, candy box, purple wash, oval 275.00
Bird of Paradise, fan vase, pk wash, 6" 175.00
Bird of Paradise, fan vase, pk wash, 10" 275.00
Bird of Paradise, plate, yel wash, 8¼" 60.00
Bittersweet, lamp, reverse ruby stain on crystal 150.00
Bittersweet, vase, crystal bl, ormolu mts 330.00
Bittersweet, vase, gr cased, 9¾" 275.00
Bittersweet, vase, ruby stain on crystal 150.00
Blackberry, vase umbrella; wht wash 375.00
Catalonian, bowl, Reuben Blue (rare color), 3½x7½" 110.00
Catalonian, plate, russet (rare color), 6" 100.00
Catalonian, vase, gr, triangular, 4" 50.00
Catalonian, vase, Nasturtium, russet (rare color) 250.00
Chickadee, lamp, amber wash w/blk highlighting, 3-way lighting .195.00
Chickadee, vase, irid transparent bl cased 550.00
Chickadee, vase, purple cased 250.00
Chrysanthemum, vase, reverse ruby stain on clear, 12" 200.00
Cockatoo, bowl, console; bl frosted crystal, 13" 395.00

Cockatoo, candlestick, yel wash 250.00
Cockatoo, vase, yel cased 425.00
Dancing Girls, vase, glossy mg, no decor, 12" 400.00
Dancing Girls, vase, straw opal, 12" 750.00
Dancing Nymph, palace platter, amethyst, 18" dia 2,000.00
Dancing Nymph, plate, French crystal, 8¼" dia 125.00
Dancing Nymph, platter, wht wash, 18" dia 800.00
Dancing Nymph, tumbler, ftd, gr frosted, 6½" 105.00
Dogwood, lamp, 3-color on satin mg 125.00
Dogwood, vase, yel cased, 11" 300.00
Dragon & Cattails, vase, yel cased, 5¾" 180.00
Dragon Fly, vase, gold on glossy custard, 7" 175.00
Dragon Fly, vase, 3-color on satin custard, ormolu mt 250.00
Fish, tray, gr wash 150.00
Five Fruits, cocktail, gr wash 15.00
Five Fruits, goblet, purple wash 30.00
Five Fruits, plate, purple wash, 14" 150.00
Five Fruits, plate, salad; yel wash, 8¼" 45.00
Five Fruits, pound box, reverse gold on mg 75.00
Five Fruits, tumbler, gr wash, ftd 30.00
Floral, ruby stain on crystal 125.00
Floral, vase, 3-color on satin mg 125.00
Florette, cookie jar, pk satin 175.00
Foxglove, lamp, bl on satin custard 150.00
Foxglove, vase, 2-color on satin custard 145.00
Hummingbird, compote, yel wash 85.00
Hummingbird, powder jar, amethyst, 3" dia 225.00
Hummingbird, powder jar, purple wash, 5" dia 75.00
Hummingbird, puff box, bl wash on crystal, 5" 110.00
Hummingbird, vase, 3-color on satin mg 110.00
Iris, candlestick, gr wash 75.00
Iris, jug, sepia wash 250.00
Iris, mayonnaise bowl, purple wash 40.00
Iris, plate, gr wash, 6" 45.00
Iris, tumbler, purple wash 35.00
Jonquil, vase, red 350.00
Katydid, ashtray, bl wash, rare 300.00
Katydid, ashtray, purple wash, rare 275.00
Katydid, vase, tumbler shape, purple wash 170.00
Le Fleur, vase, cranberry flash on crystal, 11" 300.00
Line 700, fruit bowl, bl, 10" 175.00
Love Birds, banana boat, bl reverse highlighting on crystal 450.00
Love Birds, banana boat, 3-color on custard, ormolu mt 550.00
Love Birds, glove box, gr wash, w/lid, rare 300.00
Love Birds, powder jar, yel wash 80.00
Love Birds, puff box, gr wash 65.00
Love Birds, vase, ruby stain on crystal, decor surmount, 11" 475.00
Love Birds, vase, sepia cased, 10⅛" 550.00
Nuthatch, planter/vase, purple wash 140.00
Olive, bowl, purple wash, 4" 125.00
Olive, lamp, 3-color, rare 300.00
Olive, plate, yel wash, 8" 35.00
Olive, vase, gold on glossy mg 125.00
Orchids, bowl, console; gray wash, rare 275.00
Orchids, candlestick, yel wash 95.00
Pine Cone, vase, lilac cased (rare color), 7" 355.00
Pine Cone, vase, red 400.00
Pine Cone, vase, reverse rose on glossy custard 150.00
Pine Cone, vase, straw opal, 8½" 185.00
Pond Lily, candy box, purple wash, oval 235.00
Poppy, vase, purple cased 400.00
Poppy, vase, straw opal, ormolu mt 450.00
Regent Line, vase, ash-rose pk over wht opal, #1174-B, 4½" 125.00
Ruba Rombic, bonbon, Smoky Topaz, 8" 310.00
Ruba Rombic, bowl, cupped, Smoky Topaz, 8" 1,425.00
Ruba Rombic, candlesticks, Sunshine, 4½" W, pr 600.00
Ruba Rombic, creamer & sugar bowl, Smoky Topaz, 3½", 2", EX 1,265.00
Ruba Rombic, finger bowl, Smoky Topaz, 4" W 175.00
Ruba Rombic, toilet bottle, Smoky Topaz, 7¾" 1,200.00
Ruba Rombic, tumbler, ftd, Smoky Topaz, chips, 6" 255.00
Ruba Rombic, vase, jade, 9½", NM 2,500.00
Santa Maria, box, cigarette; crystal 130.00
Screech Owl, vase, reverse ruby on crystal 175.00
Screech Owl, vase, sepia wash 250.00
Sea Gull, vase, red w/gold highlights, 11" 750.00
Sea Gull, vase, yel cased 450.00
Tropical Fish, vase, Fr Crystal, 9" 280.00
Tropical Fish, vase, reverse ruby stain on crystal, 9" 225.00
Tropical Fish, vase, straw opal, 9" 480.00

Cookbooks

Cookbooks from the nineteenth century, though often hard to find, are a delight to today's collectors both for their quaint formats and printing methods as well as for their outmoded, often humorous views on nutrition. Recipes required a 'pinch' of salt, butter 'the size of an egg' or a 'walnut,' or a 'handful' of flour. Collectors sometimes specialize in cookbooks issued as advertising premiums. Especially desirable are the figurals that were shaped like a jar, a slice of bread, or some other form relative to the product. Others with unique features such as illustrations by well-known artists or references to famous people or places are priced in accordance. Cookbooks written earlier than 1874 are the most valuable and when found command prices as high as $200.00; figurals usually sell in the $10.00 to $15.00 range.

As is true with all other books, if the original dust jacket is present and in nice condition, a cookbook's value goes up by at least $5.00. Right now, books on Italian cooking from before 1940 are in demand, and bread-baking is important this year. For further information we recommend *A Guide to Collecting Cookbooks* by Col. Bob Allen and *Price Guide to Cookbooks and Recipe Leaflets* by Linda Dickinson. Our advisor for this category is Charlotte Safir; she is listed in the Directory under New York.

Key:
CB — cookbook
dj — dust jacket

Ceresota Cook Book, Northwestern Consolidated Milling Co., Minneapolis, Minn., ca 1880, EX, $30.00. (Photo courtesy Colonel Bob Allen)

Adirondack Country CB, 1987, paperbk, EX 5.00
Am Cookery, James Beard, 1972, hardbk/Fair dj, VG 38.00
American Domestic CB, Herrick, 1870, 32-pg leaflet, VG 8.00
Amish-Dutch CB, Dutch Cupboard Restaurant, 1970, G 5.00
Aunt Jemima's Morning to Midnight CB, Follett, 1969, spiral/dj, G 8.00
Balanced Recipes, Pillsbury Flour Mills ed, 1933, w/metal case, VG 75.00
Basic CB, M Helestine, 1947, G 10.00
Better Homes & Gardens Salad Book, Meredith, 1958, G 3.00

Better Homes & Gardens Soups & Stews CB, 1978, G 3.00
Betty Crocker's Picture CB, McGraw-Hill, 1950, G 50.00
Birches, Beaches & Belches, Phil DeGraff, 1st ed, 1962, spiral, VG .35.00
Bouquet de France, Samuel Chamberlain, 1960, G+ 20.00
Cake Icing & Decoration, Marguerite Patten, 1965, hardbk/dj, EX ...25.00
Chef's Dessert CB, Dominique D'ermo, 1st ed, 1976, hardbk/dj, VG ..15.00
Christmas Cookie Book, Virginia Pasley, 1949, G 15.00
Complete Everday CB, Better Cooking Library, 1971, hardbk/dj, VG ..25.00
Cooking for You, Robert Carrier, Viking ed, 1973, hardbk/dj, VG .18.00
Cooking w/Mickey Around Our World, WD World/Disneyland, EX ...20.00
Craig Clairborne's Kitchen Primer, 1969, hardbk/dj, VG 10.00
Crowley Milner's CB, Mabel Claire, 1932, G 20.00
Daily Dinners, Nancy Lake/Frederick Warne & Co, 1892, G 35.00
Dallas Symphony CB, 1983, G+ 12.00
Desserts for All Occasions, Am Culinary Society, 1974, VG 7.00
Electric Refrigerator Menus, GE, 1927, hardbk, VG 18.00
Everyday Foods, Jessie Harris, 1939, hardbk, G 10.00
Exotic Food, Rupert Croft-Cooke, 1971, hardbk/dj, G 20.00
Famous Kentucky Recipes, Cabbage Patch Circle, 1956, spiral, G .15.00
Fannie Farmer Boston Cooking School CB, 1897, VG 100.00
Fannie Farmer CB, 1968, paperbk, VG 4.00
Fifty Great Buffet Parties, Ruth C Bateman, 1974, hardbk/dj, VG ..6.00
Food in Vogue, Maxime de la Falaise, Doubleday, 1980, hardbk/dj, VG ..20.00
General Foods CB, 1932-34, hardbk/dj, G 8.00
Gold Medal Flour CB, Washburn Crosby Co, 1917, paperbk, VG .16.00
Helen Corbitt's CB, Houghton Mifflin, 1962, hardbk/dj, VG 10.00
Ideal Cookery Book — 1,349 Recipes, 1891, 402 pgs, VG 30.00
Italian CB, M Taglienti, 1955, 309 pgs, VG 10.00
Jell-O Girl Gives a Party, Rose O'Neil illus, leaflet, VG 40.00
Kitchen Treasures, Milwaukee Journal, 1930, 153 pgs, VG 15.00
Lunch & Brunch CB, Barbara Grunes, 1985, hardbk/dj, EX 8.00
Mood Food, Glenn Andrews, 1st ed, 1974, hardbk/dj, VG 10.00
My Favorite Recipes, Melanie DeProft, 1959, G 10.00
New Book of Cake Designs for Bakers, H Heug, 1893, VG 35.00
Old Family Favorites, Eastern Star, 1969, paperbk, VG 10.00
Pickles & Preserves, Marion Brown, 1960, hardbk/dj, G 15.00
Pillsbury Family CB, Houghton Mifflin, 1973, loose-leaf paperbk, EX ..12.00
Pillsbury's Bake Off Cake CB, 1969, VG 10.00
Plaza CB, Eve Brown, 1972, hardbk/dj, G 30.00
Quaker Woman's CB, E Lea, 1982, hardbk, VG 8.00
Royal Baker & Pastry, 1911, paperbk, VG 20.00
Spice CB, Day & Stucky, 1964, hardbk, VG 13.00
Summertime CB, Marian Burros, 1972, hardbk/dj, G 5.00
Sun Maid Raisin Recipes, 1923, VG 7.00
Sunset Chefs of the West, 1st ed, 1951, hardbk, VG 10.00
Text-book Cooking, C Greer, 1915, hardbk, VG 15.00
Trader Vic's Pacific Island CB, Doubleday, 1968, VG 15.00
Twentieth Century CB, H&H Periodical Service Co, 1925, G+ .28.00
Tycoons in the Kitchen, Michael Dorn, 1968, 1st ed, hardbk/dj, VG ..25.00
Universal CB, 1923, 724 pgs, VG 25.00
Victory Garden CB, M Morash, 1982, paperbk, VG 18.00
Virginia Housewife Methodical Cook, Randolph, 1st ed, 1831, VG .300.00
World of Good Eating, Phillips, 1951, box, VG 20.00
Yul Brenner CB, 1983, VG 20.00
Zen Cookery, SHWA, 1966, paperbk, EX 5.00

Cookie Cutters

Early hand-fashioned cookie cutters have recently been commanding stiff prices at country auctions, and the ranks of interested collectors are growing steadily. Especially valuable are the figural cutters; and the more complicated the design, the higher the price. A follow-up of the carved wooden cookie boards, the first cutters were probably made by itinerant tinkers from leftover or recycled pieces of tin. Though most of the eighteenth-century examples are now in museums or collections, it is still possible to find some good cutters from the late 1800s when changes in the manufacture of tin resulted in a thinner, less expensive material. The width of the cutting strip is often a good indicator of age; the wider the strip, the older the cutter. While the very early cutters were 1" to 1½" deep, by the '20s and '30s, many were less than ½" deep. Crude, spotty soldering indicates an older cutter, while a thin line of solder usually tends to suggest a much later manufacture. The shape of the backplate is another clue. Later cutters will have oval, round, or rectangular backs, while on the earlier type the back was cut to follow the lines of the design. Cookie cutters usually vary from 2" to 4" in size, but gingerbread men were often made as tall as 12". Birds, fish, hearts, and tulips are common; simple versions can be purchased for as little as $12.00 to $15.00. The larger figurals, especially those with more imaginative details, often bring $75.00 and up. The cookie cutters listed here are tin and handmade unless noted otherwise.

Angel w/banner standing on cloud, flat bk, 8¼x5" 35.00
Animals, cube form, 1 on ea of 6 sides, 3" 35.00
Bird, flat bk, 19th C, 5¾x4¼x¾" 55.00
Bird w/wings down, flat bk w/hdl, 19th C, 4x3¼x1¼" 35.00
Cat, 3⅛" 20.00
Deer leaping, late, 11¼" 25.00
Distlefink (bird), no hdl, ca 1880s, 3x5" 150.00
Dutch man & woman, 5¼", pr 85.00
Elf w/tall pointed hat, flat bk, 8¼x2⅛" 85.00
Fish, aluminum, 4¾" 8.00
Fish, flat bk, strap hdl, 4x3" 22.00
Heart, flat bk, 3" 35.00
Leaf w/serrated edges, flat bk, sm hdl, 19th C, 2½x¾x⅞" 50.00
Penguin, flat bk, 3¾x2¼" 18.00
Pig, 6" 25.00
Pipe (man's smoking), long stem, flat bk, 8½x5¼" 85.00
Rabbit, birds, bells, etc, rolling type, mk Monopoi Germany 25.00
Rabbit, strap hdl, mk Formay, 6" 25.00
Rabbit leaping, resoldered hdl, 9¾" 25.00
Rocking horse, no hdl, 5¼x3¾" 20.00
Rooster, ornate tail & comb, flat bk, 19th C, 5½x4x½" 75.00
Santa w/gift sack, flat bk, mk S Joseph Co Germany, 7½" 80.00
Snowflake, 5 air holes on bk, curved hdl, early 1900s, 6x6½" 45.00
Tulip w/leaves, 4¾" 35.00

Cookie Jars

The appeal of the cookie jar is universal; folks of all ages, both male and female, love to collect 'em! The early '30s' heavy stoneware jars of a rather nondescript nature quickly gave way to figurals of every type imaginable. Those from the mid to late '30s were often decorated over the glaze with 'cold paint,' but by the early '40s underglaze decorating resulted in cheerful, bright, permanent colors and cookie jars that still have a new look fifty years later.

Stimulated by the high prices commanded by desirable cookie jars, a broad spectrum of 'new' cookie jars are flooding the marketplace in three categories: 1) Manufactures have expanded their lines with exciting new designs specifically geared toward attracting the collector market. 2) Limited editions and artist-designed jars have proliferated. 3) Reproductions, signed and unsigned, have pervaded the market, creating uncertainty among new collectors and inexperienced dealers. One of the most troublesome reproductions is the Little Red Riding Hood jar marked McCoy. Several Brush jars are being reproduced, and because the old molds are being used, these are especially deceptive. In addition to these reproductions, we've also been alerted to watch for cookie jars marked Brush-McCoy made from molds that Brush never used. Remember that none of Brush's cookie jars were marked Brush-McCoy, so any jar bearing the compound name is fraudulent. For more information on cookie jars and reproductions, we recommend *The Collector's Encyclopedia of Cookie Jars, Books I, II,* and *III,* by Fred and Joyce Roerig; they are listed in the Directory under South Carolina. Another good source is *An Illustrated Guide to Cookie Jars, Books I, II,* and *III,* by Ermagene Westfall. Our advisors for this category are Fred and Joyce Roerig; they are listed in the Directory under South Carolina.

The examples listed below were made by companies other than those found elsewhere in this book; see also specific manufacturers.

ABC Bear, Sierra Vista 175.00
Adam & Eve, Fitz & Floyd, minimum value 300.00
Airplane, North American Ceramics, movable propeller 625.00

Airplane with pilot, California Originals, marked 2629 USA, from $100.00 to $125.00. (Photo courtesy Fred and Joyce Roerig)

Balloon Lady, Pottery Guild, unmk 125.00
Bartender, Pan Am Art 300.00
Beaver Fireman, Sigma 275.00
Car w/Flat Tire, Fitz & Floyd 225.00
Checkered Taxi Sedan, Cavanagh 300.00
Chef, Hirsch Mfg Comp 275.00
Christmas Tree Mammy, Erwin Pottery 175.00
City Cab, Japan 225.00
Clown Head, Enesco, #E-5835 ....150.00
Coca-Cola Hollywood Polar Bear, 2nd in series, 1996 ....40.00
Cool Cookie Penguin, Hallmark Cards 275.00
Cream of Wheat Chef, Japan, 10", minimum vlaue 1,500.00
Davy Crockett, Sierra Vista, minimum value 1,500.00
Doctor, Doranne of California, CJ-130 ....275.00
Dorothy & Toto, Star Jars 375.00
Dutch Girl, Delft 55.00
Ernie, blond or blk hair, Newcor 75.00
Famous Amos, Treasure Craft 55.00
Fire Truck, California Originals, #841 ....225.00
Fred & Pebbles (Flintstones), Vandor, paper label 375.00
Frosty the Snowman, Robinson-Ransbottom 650.00
Garfield on Cookies, Enesco 350.00
Giant Panda, Benjamin & Medwin, paper label 50.00
Gone w/the Wind Mammy, Enesco, paper label 300.00
Googly-Eyed Mammy, Japan, 8x6½", minimum value 2,500.00
Grandma w/Child, A Little Company, 13" 160.00
Gulden's Mustard, glass, 12¼" 200.00
Halloween Pumpkin, Lotus International, paper label, 10½" 70.00
Hen w/Chick, FAPCO 55.00
Henny (Dandy Hen), DeForest of California 225.00
Hi Diddle Diddle, Robinson-Ransbottom, gold trim 450.00
Hi Diddle Diddle, Robinson-Ransbottom, plain 300.00
Hippo, Doranne of California 125.00
Holy Devil (Halo Boy), DeForest of California 725.00
Humpty Dumpty, Clay Art, 1991 ....125.00
Jaguar XK-140 Convertible, Appleman, 12 made 2,000.00
James Dean, Happy Memories, bl shirt 400.00
James Dean, Happy Memories, red shirt 350.00
Ken-L-Ration Dog, F&F Mold & Die Works 140.00
King, DeForest of California, 1957, minimum value 800.00
Little Red Riding Hood, California Originals, #320 USA 375.00
M&M Cookie Jar, M&M Mars, Haeger 130.00
Mammy, Artistic Potteries Inc Calif-USA-#31, 9½" 575.00
Man w/Chicken, Animals & Company, minimum value 350.00
Mercedes Benz, Appleman, 1985 ....900.00
MooTown Snackers, Sargento Foods, unmk 175.00
Mother Goose, Gilner #G-720 ....375.00
Mrs Tiggy-Winkle, Sigma 350.00
Noah's Ark, Starnes 250.00
Nun, DeForest of California 275.00
Olympic Torch, Warner Bros 135.00
Peasant Woman, Dept 56 ....125.00
Peter Porker, DeForest of California 275.00
Phantazoom, Appleman, 1981 ....1,000.00
Pig, California Cleminsons 275.00
Pig Head, DeForest of California 90.00
Pinocchio/Court Jester, Doranne of California 300.00
Pirate Bust, Treasure Craft 325.00
Polka Dot Witch, Fitz & Floyd 325.00
Popcorn Vender, Sigma, paper label, minimum value 450.00
Porky Pig, Warner Bros (Duncan mold) 150.00
Potbellied Stove, Treasure Craft 40.00
Rag Doll, Sigma 225.00
Raggedy Andy, California Originals #860 ....150.00
Rocking Horse, Lane 375.00
Sailor Girl Elephant, DeForest of California 125.00
Sea Captain, head, Kreiss 200.00
Sheriff, Fitz & Floyd 300.00
Sid's Taxi, Appleman, 1978, minimum value 700.00
Smokey Bear Head, unknown 675.00
Snoopy Doghouse, Benjamin & Medwin Inc 40.00
Spirit of St Nicholas, Fitz & Floyd 500.00
Sylvester Head w/Tweety, Applause 90.00
The Whistler, New Rose Collection #66 ....125.00
Transformer, Great American Housewares 190.00
Upside Down Turtle, California Originals, #2627 USA 95.00
US Soccer Ball, Procter & Gamble, Friendship Pottery 45.00
4x4 Pickup, Doranne of California 225.00

Cooper, Susie

A twentieth-century ceramic designer whose works are now attracting the attention of collectors, Susie Cooper was first affiliated with the A.E. Gray Pottery in Henley, England, in 1922 where she designed in lustres and painted items with her own ideas as well. (Examples of Gray's lustreware are rare and costly.) By 1930 she and her brother-in-law, Jack Beeson, had established a family business. Her pottery soon became a success, and she was subsequently offered space at Crown Works, Burslem. In 1940 she received the honorary title of Royal Designer for Industry, the only such distinction ever awarded by the Royal Society of Arts solely for pottery design. Miss Cooper received the Order of the British Empire in the New Year's Honors List of 1979. She was the chief designer for the Wedgwood group from 1966 until she resigned in 1972. After 1980 she worked on a free-lance basis until her death in July 1995. Our advisor is J. David Ehrhard; he is listed in the Directory under California.

Bowl, bouillon; red/brn lines w/Xs, 2" H w/plate 48.00
Bowl, mc bands, Gray's period, 9" 150.00

Bowl, wht band, 10" 270.00
Casserole, Wedding Ring, #817, running deer bkstamp, w/lid 90.00
Charger, central leaf, gray & ochre banded rim 450.00
Charger, flowers, pk/bl/gr on shaded bl, #1251, 14" 72.00
Charger, HP leaves, 14" 400.00
Cheese dish, red-brn, slant lid, 4½" H 200.00
Chocolate pot, Patricia Rose, pk wash, 7½" 120.00
Coffeepot, Kestrel, geometric mc decor, lg 120.00
Coffeepot, orange w/blk lines, Kestrel shape, 7¾" 190.00
Cream soup, Wedding Ring, running deer bk stamp 36.00
Creamer, Gardenias, gr & ivory, 1950s 35.00
Cup & saucer, Gardenias, 1960s 25.00
Cup & saucer, Tulip, bone china, gold hdl, 1950s 35.00
Cup & saucer, Wedding Ring 78.00
Egg cup, Printemps, 1936 ....30.00
Grapefruit dish, lime-gr sgraffito panel, mc stripes, 4" dia 66.00
Gravy boat, Gardenias, 1960s 60.00
Jam pot, Nosegay, bl wash, 4" H 84.00
Jug, Cubist, Paris shape, Gray's period, 4¼" 360.00
Pitcher, incised teasel design on lt gr, mk #149, 6¼" 240.00
Plate, Corn Poppy, red/blk/brn, 10½" 36.00
Plate, Leaf & Vine, bl scroll border, 9" 48.00
Plate, stylized animal, sgraffito decor, ca 1935, lg 400.00
Plate, washed red bands, earthenware, 1930s, 10" 34.00
Platter, Wedding Ring, mk, 14" 120.00
Punch bowl, Wedding Ring, gray/brn/turq bands, 12½" 360.00
Teapot, Long Leaf, Kestrel shape, 8½" 200.00
Teapot, orange w/blk lines, 6½" 180.00
Tureen, vegetable; Crayon Loop, w/lid, ladle & tray, Crown Works ..125.00
Vase, pk, appl buttons, 7½" 480.00
Vase, tulips & leaves, olive gr, 4" 420.00

Coors, Rosebud

The firm that became known as Coors Porcelain Company in 1920 was founded in 1908 by John J. Herold, originally of the Roseville Pottery in Zanesville, Ohio. Though still in business today, they are best known for their artware vases and Rosebud dinnerware produced before 1939.

For further information we recommend *Collector's Encyclopedia of Colorado Pottery, Identification and Values,* by Carol and Jim Carlton. Our advisor for this category is Jo Ellen Winther; she is listed in the Directory under Colorado.

Apple baker, w/lid 55.00
Bake pan, 12¼x8¼" 75.00
Bean pot, lg 68.00
Bowl, cream soup; 4" 38.00
Bowl, mixing; 1½-pt, w/hdl 40.00
Bowl, mixing; 3-pt 45.00
Bowl, mixing; 6-pt 65.00
Bowl, mixing; 7-pt, w/hdl 80.00
Bowl, oatmeal 35.00
Bowl, pudding; 3½-pt 45.00
Cake knife 85.00
Casserole, Dutch; lg 95.00
Casserole, Dutch; sm 72.00
Casserole, Fr; 7½" 65.00
Casserole, str sides, 5" 50.00
Casserole, triple service; 3½-pt 65.00
Honey pot, w/spoon 300.00
Muffin set, w/lid, rare 400.00
Plate, cake; 11" 45.00

Pitcher, with lid, large, $150.00.

Plate, 5" 8.00
Platter, 9x12" 48.00
Shirred egg dish, 6½" 42.00
Sugar shaker 80.00
Teapot, 6-cup, from $160 to 185.00
Tumbler, ftd or w/hdl, from $105 to 160.00
Water server, w/stopper 120.00

Copper

Handcrafted copper was made in America from early in the eighteenth century until about 1850, with the center of its production in Pennsylvania. Examples have been found signed by such notable coppersmiths as Kidd, Buchanan, Babb, Bently, and Harbeson. Of the many utilitarian items made, teakettles are the most desirable. Early examples from the eighteenth century were made with a dovetailed joint which was hammered and smoothed to a uniform thickness. Pots from the nineteenth century were seamed. Coffeepots were made in many shapes and sizes and along with mugs, kettles, warming pans, and measures are easiest to find. Stills ranging in sizes of up to fifty-gallon are popular with collectors today. Mary Frank Gaston has compiled a lovely book, *Antique Brass and Copper,* with many full-color photos and current market values.

Coffeepot, Georgian, applewood hdl, 11", VG 350.00
Cook pot, hammered, dvtl seam, iron hdl, 5x8" 150.00
Fish poacher, emb rampant lion/fleur-de-lis, brass ears, 23" L 300.00
Kettle, apple butter; iron straps/hoops, mid-1800s, 20½x30" dia ..450.00
Kettle, iron hdls & brackets, 15x24" dia 400.00
Kettle, JP Schuam, Lancaster PA, 18x29" on 29½" dia stand 500.00
Lavabo, Fr, ca 1830, lg, on pnt pine stand: 73x30x16" 1,980.00
Pitcher, ball shape, 6" 65.00
Plaque, Renaissance Revival, scenic relief, 19" 225.00
Silent butler, scalloped, wood hdl w/copper riveted bands, 12" L ..35.00
Teakettle, dvtl, swivel hdl mk J Grimes Pittsburgh, rpr, 7" 385.00
Teapot, bl & wht porc hdl & finial, 8½" 125.00
Teapot, swivel hdl, mk Volund Hamar, late 1800s 225.00
Wash boiler, metal hdls w/wooden pulls, Behrens Mfg, w/lid, 12x13" ..150.00

Copper Lustre

Copper lustre is a term referring to a type of pottery made in Staffordshire after the turn of the nineteenth century. It is finished in a metallic rusty-brown glaze resembling true copper. Pitchers are found in abundance, ranging from simple styles with dull bands of color to those with fancy handles and bands of embossed, polychromed flowers. Bowls are common; goblets, mugs, teapots, and sugar bowls much less so. It's easy to find, but not in good condition. Pieces with hand-painted decoration and those with historical transfers are the most valuable.

Creamer, tan band w/brn brush strokes, 3½" 35.00
Figurine, dog, EX molded features, lt wear, 7½" 450.00
Pitcher, deer relief & scrolls, 5⅝" 275.00
Pitcher, mask spout, emb mc flowers/fence on bl, 4½" 95.00
Pitcher, mother/daughter reading in landscape transfer, unmk, 4" ..85.00
Pitcher, vintage band/cherubs/eagle, bl band w/wht, 4", EX 165.00
Tumbler, floral decor on wide brn band, 2¾x3" 55.00
Vase, shepherdess w/sheep (purple transfer), hdls, 7" 225.00

Coralene Glass

Coralene is a unique type of art glass easily recognized by the tiny grains of glass that form its decoration. Lacy allover patterns of seaweed, geometrics, and florals were used, as well as solid forms such as fish, plants, and single blossoms. (Seaweed is most commonly found and not as valuable as the other types of decoration.) It was made by several glasshouses both here and abroad. Values are based to a considerable extent on the amount of beading that remains. Our advisors for this category are Betty and Clarence Maier; they are listed in the Directory under Pennsylvania.

Box, powder; allover gr beading w/gold & wht water lilies 165.00
Cracker jar, rose Dmn Quilt w/yel seaweed, silver mts, 7" 800.00
Pitcher, acid peachblow w/seaweed, sqd rim, 8" 350.00
Rose bowl, pk Snowflake MOP w/yel wheat, 3-ftd, 3¾x5" 695.00
Tumbler, peachblow w/yel seaweed 225.00
Vase, bl Dmn Quilt w/pk flowers & gr leaves, 6¾" 225.00
Vase, bl satin w/seaweed, stick neck, 6" 150.00
Vase, peachblow w/yel seaweed, dbl gourd, Webb, 7" 650.00
Vase, pk Herringbone MOP w/allover yel overlapped leaves, 9" .400.00
Vase, pk Snowflake MOP w/yel stars, shouldered, 4" 225.00
Vase, pk/wht/yel w/yel geometrics, 7" 675.00
Vase, wht w/charcoal seaweed, 6" 220.00
Vase, wht w/yel seaweed, pk crimped ruffle w/camphor edge, 8" .140.00

Cordey

The Cordey China Company was founded in 1942 in Trenton, New Jersey, by Boleslaw Cybis. The operation was small with less than a dozen workers. They produced figurines, vases, lamps, and similar wares, much of which was marketed through gift shops both nationwide and abroad. Though the earlier wares were made of plaster, Cybis soon developed his own formula for a porcelain composition which he called 'Papka.' Cordey figurines and busts were characterized by old-world charm, Rococo scrolls, delicate floral appliqués, ruffles, and real lace which was dipped in liquefied clay to add dimension to the work.

Although on rare occasion some items were not numbered or signed, the basic figure was cast both with numbers and the Cordey signature. The molded pieces were then individually decorated and each marked with its own impressed identification number as well as a mark to indicate the artist-decorator. Their numbering system began with 200 and in later years progressed into the 8000s. As can best be established, Cordey continued production until sometime in the mid-1950s. Boleslaw Cybis died in 1957, his wife in 1958.

Due to the increased availability of Cordey on the Internet over the last year, values of the more common pieces have fallen off. Our advisor for this category is Sharon A. Payne; she is listed in the Directory under Washington.

Key: ff — full figure

Poodle, pink, 11" L, $85.00.

#0303, man in plumed hat, 16" 100.00
#0343, pheasant, vibrant mc, very early, scarce, 17" 325.00
#0504, lady in gray & bl dress w/basket of grapes, 16" 150.00
#0627, ginger jar, w/lid, 7½x6" dia 80.00
#0902, wall pocket, lady's face w/ringlets, 10¼" 200.00
#0914, mantel clock, Rococo, Lanshire Electric, 9½" 125.00
#1023, console bowl, lg roses w/gold, oblong, 6x15x8" 85.00
#1027, swan centerpiece planter, lg 200.00
#1028, box, pk & gr flower shape 45.00
#2307, robin on rose branch, 9" 150.00
#3008, Renaissance man, dk gr, 7" 75.00
#3241, Oriental duck, wht, 14½" 250.00
#4001, lady in ruffled cap, 7" 85.00
#4002, man w/ruffles & bow at neck, 7" 85.00
#4004, lamps, bust on metal fr, orig shades, pr 150.00
#4067, Oriental emperor & empress, 8" 175.00
#4077, Oriental emperor & empress, 15" 275.00
#4088, ballet man & lady, 10", pr 205.00
#4129, couple on rnd base, Courting Group, lacy, rare 335.00
#4153, man, much lace, 14" 185.00
#5009, Junior Prom 65.00
#5026, bust of lady w/mantilla, Jr Miss Group 55.00
#5034, bust of Raleigh, Raleigh Group, 7½" 85.00
#5039, Josephine, Raleigh Group 85.00
#5043, man in Colonial attire 175.00
#5045, Neopolitan boy w/basket of breadsticks, 9½" 110.00
#5054, lady w/roses, 9" 95.00
#5064, Caroline, 14" 150.00
#5066, Carmen in Spanish dress & mantilla, 14" 150.00
#5069, lady, pearls, gloves, many roses, 9" 95.00
#5084, lady, Madame w/upswept hair, scrolled base, 11¾" 100.00
#5085, Winter girl, w/lg hat & muff, 11" 120.00
#5097, Oriental emperor, 27¼" 225.00
#6000, box, appl roses on lid, gold trim, 5x7" dia 45.00
#6019, jar, buffalo design on bl, w/lid 95.00
#6029, box, oval 95.00
#6037, box, appl cherubs/roses, cherub finial, ftd, 8x9" 225.00
#6046, ashtray 22.00
#6405, lady in pk & gray dress & flower-trimmed hat, 10½" 110.00
#7000, plaque, primrose, Colonial lady 100.00
#7008, cornucopia, 6½" 95.00
#7026, scent bottle, shades of bl, iris-form stopper, 8" 85.00
#7032, candlesticks, pk roses, 7½", pr 125.00
#7061, vase, birds on leaf, roses appl ea side, 8¾" 90.00
#8002, pin/ashtray, 4" sq 25.00
#8020, Oriental baby, no hat, 15" 200.00
#8308, man's bust, 14¾" 200.00
Lamp, pk roses w/gold on wht 85.00

Corkscrews

The history of the corkscrew dates back to the mid-1600s, when wine makers concluded that the best-aged wine was that stored in smaller containers, either stoneware or glass. Since plugs left unsealed were often damaged by rodents, corks were cut off flush with the bottle top and sealed with wax or a metal cover. Removing the cork cleanly with none left to grasp became a problem. The task was found to be relatively simple using the worm on the end of a flintlock gun rod. So the corkscrew evolved. Endless patents have been issued for mechanized models. Handles range from carved wood, ivory, and bone to porcelain and repousse silver. Exotic materials such as agate, mother-of-pearl, and gold plate were also used on occasion. Celluloid ladies' legs are popular.

For further information, we recommend *The Ultimate Corkscrew Book* and *Bull's Pocket Guide to Corkscrews* by Donald Bull, our advisor for this category. He is listed in the Directory under Virginia. In the following descriptions, values are for examples in excellent condition, unless noted otherwise.

Armor Kissing Couple, celluloid hdls, folding, German 900.00
Art Nouveau Sterling roundlet 250.00
Bar bum w/corkscrew, ice pick & muddler 60.00
Bar mt, mk Champion (1898) 150.00
Bar mt, mk Estate (current) 100.00
Barman Opener, aluminum bartender figure, Italian, 1950s-60s ..60.00
Brass, picnic-type w/cap remover on hexagonal head, tapered sheath .30.00
Bull w/loop opener & folding tail 3.00
Combination, funnel/cap remover/jigger/resealer/corkscrew, Napier ..70.00
Combination cap lifter, mk Nifty 1.00
Figural, birds kissing, metal, Just Anderson/Denmark 90.00
Figural, elephant, cvd wood, wire worm 22.00
Figural, horse heads (2), amber plastic w/metal worm 95.00
Figural, man in vest/bald head, picnic type w/Bakelite sheath ...175.00
Figural, owl, brass, 2-finger pull, English 30.00
Figural, parrot, brass, 6¼" 90.00
Figural, pig, compo in various colors, H Ross, 1949 ....85.00
Fold-up, w/carriage key & foil cutter, metal, Germany 125.00
Frame w/flynut, mk Victor 200.00
Gay '90s folding legs, red & wht stripes, 2⅝" 175.00
Gay '90s folding legs, striped bottom, flesh top, 2⅝" 400.00
Heeley Dbl Lever 175.00
Hollweg, collapsing 60.00
Italian rollover hdl, mk Edwin Jay 30.00
Man w/top hat, 'Old Codger,' Syroco, pnt 90.00
Man w/top hat, 'Old Codger,' Syroco, walnut finish 175.00
Mermaid waiter's friend, celluloid hdls 600.00
Metal T-hdl, clawfoot-type w/bulbous shank 150.00
MOP horn-shaped hdl, sterling trim, metal worm 275.00
Old Snifter, chrome, removable hat, Kirby figure, 6¾" 50.00
Old Snifter, chrome, turning head, 5¾" 140.00
Parrot, chrome, 5¼" 10.00
Pewter, Viking ship form, sail mk Zero 90.00
Silver, cap remover/worm unscrews from bottom 60.00
Spring type, w/T-hdl, steel 75.00
Tip Top, metal fold-up type, Williamson 50.00
Wade Sea Lion 75.00
Waiter w/worm attached to head, Syroco, pnt, 8¼" 90.00
Waiter w/worm attached to head, Syroco, walnut finish 150.00
Wiggle 'N' Twist, w/leather case, England, 1979 ....60.00
Wood T-hdl, w/brush & foil cutter, metal worm 175.00
Wood T-hdl, w/cast metal bell, Anheuser-Busch advertising 30.00
Wood T-hdl, w/finger hole in metal shank, E Wolverson/England .175.00
Zig Zag, multi-lever, concertina action, curved T hdl 60.00

Cosmos

Cosmos, sometimes called Stemless Daisy, is a patterned glass tableware produced from 1894 through 1915 by Consolidated Lamp and Glass Company. Relief-molded flowers on a finely crosscut background were painted in soft colors of pink, blue, and yellow. Though nearly all were made of milk glass, a few items may be found in clear glass with the designs painted on. In addition to the tableware, lamps were also made.

Bottle, cologne; orig stopper, rare 300.00
Butter dish, 6x8" 275.00
Creamer 150.00
Lamp, banquet, kerosene, 24" 575.00
Lamp, banquet, slender base, rnd globe, all orig, 16" 525.00
Lamp, parlour, half-shade on matching base, 8" 375.00
Lamp, 10" 450.00
Lamp, 4" dia half-shade, 7½" 350.00
Pickle castor, mk SP fr 500.00
Pitcher, milk; 5" 250.00
Pitcher, syrup; 6" 300.00

Pitcher, water; 8¾", from $300.00 to $350.00.

Shakers, tall, orig lids, pr 175.00
Spooner 125.00
Sugar bowl, open 150.00
Sugar bowl, w/lid 185.00
Sugar shaker 400.00
Tumbler, 3¾" 75.00

Cottageware

You'll find a varied assortment of novelty dinnerware items, all styled as cozy little English cottages or huts with cone-shaped roofs; some may have a waterwheel or a windmill. Marks will vary. English-made Price Brothers or Beswick pieces are valued in the same range as those marked Occupied Japan, while items marked simply Japan are considerably less pricey. Our advisor for this category is Grace Klender; she is listed in the Directory under Ohio. All of the following examples are Price Brothers/Kensington unless noted otherwise.

Bank, dbl slot, 4½x3½x5" 85.00
Bell, minimum value 150.00
Biscuit jar, wicker hdl, Maruhon Ware, Occupied Japan, 6½" 85.00
Bowl, salad 65.00
Butter dish 60.00
Butter dish, oval, Burlington Ware, 6" 55.00
Butter pat, emb cottage, rectangular, Occupied Japan 18.00
Chocolate pot 135.00
Condiment set, mustard, 2½" s&p on 5" hdld leaf tray 75.00
Condiment set, mustard pot, s&p, row arrangement, 6" 45.00

Condiment set, mustard pot, s&p, tray, row arrangement, 7¾" ...45.00
Condiment set, 3-part cottage on shaped tray w/appl bush, 4½" ...75.00
Cookie jar, pk/brn/gr, sq, Japan, 8½x5½" ...65.00
Cookie jar, windmill, wicker hdl ...150.00
Cookie jar/canister, cylindrical, rare sz, 8x3¾" ...250.00
Cookie jar/canister, cylindrical, 8½x5" ...125.00
Cookie/biscuit jar, Occupied Japan ...85.00
Creamer, windmill, Occupied Japan, 2⅝" ...25.00
Creamer & sugar bowl, 2½x4½" ...45.00
Cup & saucer, chocolate; str-sided cup, 3½x2¾", 5½" ...40.00
Cup & saucer, 2½", 4½" ...45.00
Demitasse pot ...100.00
Dish w/cover, Occupied Japan, sm ...35.00
Egg cup set, 4 on 6" sq tray ...60.00
Gravy boat & tray, rare ...250.00
Grease jar, Occupied Japan, from $25 to ...35.00
Marmalade ...40.00
Mug, 3⅞" ...50.00
Pin tray, 4" dia ...20.00
Pitcher, emb cottage, lg flower on hdl ...135.00
Pitcher, tankard; rnd, 7⅞" ...125.00
Pitcher, water; 8" ...150.00
Platter, oval, 11¾x7½" ...55.00
Reamer, Japan ...60.00
Sugar box, for cubes, 5¾" L ...45.00
Tea set, Japan, child's serves 4, Japan ...150.00
Teapot, Keele Street, w/creamer & sugar ...95.00
Teapot, Occupied Japan, 6½" ...50.00
Teapot, 6¼" ...70.00
Toast rack, 3-slot, 3½" ...65.00
Toast rack, 4-slot, 5½" ...75.00
Tumbler, Occupied Japan, 3½", set of 6 ...60.00

Coverlets

The Jacquard attachment for hand looms represented a culmination of weaving developments made in France. Introduced to America by the early 1820s, it gave professional weavers the ability to easily create complex patterns with curved lines. Those who could afford the new loom adaptation could now use hole-punched pasteboard cards to weave floral patterns that before could only be achieved with intense labor on a draw-loom.

Before the Jacquard mechanism, most weavers made their coverlets in geometric patterns. Use of indigo-blue and brightly colored wools often livened the twills and overshot patterns available to the small-loom home weaver. Those who had larger multiple-harness looms could produce warm double-woven, twill-block, or summer-and-winter designs.

While the new floral and pictorial patterns' popularity had displaced the geometrics in urban areas, the mid-Atlantic, and the Midwest by the 1840s, even factory production of the Jacquard coverlets was disrupted by cotton and wool shortages during the Civil War. A revived production in the 1870s saw a style change to a center-medallion motif, but a new fad for white 'Marseilles' spreads soon halted sales of Jacquard-woven coverlets. Production of Jacquard carpets continued to the turn of the century.

Rural and frontier weavers continued to make geometric-design coverlets through the nineteenth century, and local craft revivals have continued the tradition through this century. All-cotton overshots were factory produced in Kentucky from the 1940s, and factories and professional weavers made cotton-and-wool overshots during the past decade. Many Jacquard-woven coverlets have dates and names of places and people (often the intended owner — not the weaver) woven into corners or borders. In the listings that follow, examples are blue and white unless noted otherwise. When dates are included, they appear on the coverlet itself as part of the woven design.

Key: mdl — medallion

Jacquard

Floral, eagle corners, 3-color, OH, 1850, 2-pc, 75x82" ...660.00
Floral & fruit compotes, 4-color, 1851, 89x92"+fringe ...600.00
Floral mdl, dbl weave, 1849, 81x79", VG ...250.00
Floral mdls, border: houses/sailboats, dtd 1841, 74x91" ...2,420.00
Floral mdls/border, 4-color, minor stains, 1-pc, 73x81" ...400.00
Floral mdls/floral borders, 3-color, 2-pc, 76x92" ...500.00
Floral mdls/stars/birds, 5-color, 1839, 2-pc, 81x96" ...700.00
Floral mdls/stars/etc, Union corners, 3-color, 1839, 70x80" ...1,600.00
Floral w/bird borders, 3-color, OH, 1838, 2-pc, dbl-weave, 83x73" .440.00
Floral w/rose border, red/wht, 1873, wear/stains, 2-pc, 68x80" ...150.00
Flower urns, Christian/Heathen borders, 3-color, 1845, 1-pc, 80x70" .350.00

Geometric floral, navy, persimmon, and olive green against cream background, signed and dated 1838, 72x84", $355.00.

Geometric floral mdls, bl/red/gr/wht, 1-pc, 1847, 76x90", VG ...495.00
Geometric foliage/buildings, 2-pc, 70x80", VG ...330.00
Grape & leaf border (dbl), mustard/red, dbl-weave, fringed, 82x74" ...325.00
Houses/farmer/birds/etc, horse borders, 2-pc, dbl-weave, 70x82", G .6,930.00
Peacocks/turkeys, dbl floral border, 2-pc dbl, 76x82" ...1,980.00
Rose mdls (4), bl/red/wht, 2-pc, single-weave, 72x82" ...385.00
Rose mdls (4), eagle corners, 4-color, 1844, 2-pc, 78x91" ...1,125.00
Rose mdls (4), 4-color, 1840, 2-pc, rpr, 68x86" ...300.00
Rose mdls (4)/flower baskets/birds, 2-pc, 1839, 63x80" ...300.00
Rose mdls (4)/swags & tassles/eagles, 4-color, 1841, 68x88" ...500.00
Rose mdls (4)/vintage/birds, red/wht, 1842, 2-pc, 74x84" ...715.00
Snowflake mdls/stars/grapevines, sgn/1842, 78x88", VG ...650.00
Star mdl w/in sun, eagle corners, red/wht/bl, dbl-weave, 89x82" ...750.00
Star mdls/vintage border, 4-color, OH/1849, 2-pc, 85x76" ...550.00
Star w/florals, Greek fret border, bl/gr/red, 1850s, 84x90" ...400.00
Stars & rose mdls/bird & tree corners, 1845, 2-pc, 80x96" ...800.00
Tulips, Christian/Heathen/bird borders, 4-color, 2-pc, 72x81" ...385.00
Wreath w/leaves, urns & scrolls in corners, red/wht, 2-pc, 89x79", VG ..400.00

Overshot

Optical pattern, 2-color, 2-pc, 94x76" ...240.00
Optical pattern, 5-color, appl fringe 3 sides, 2-pc, 92x78" ...295.00
Optical plaid, mauve/navy/cream, 2-pc, lt wear, 66x92" ...165.00
Sunrise variant, red/wht, 93x69" ...300.00

Cowan

Guy Cowan opened a small pottery near Cleveland, Ohio, circa 1909, where he made tile and artware on a small scale from the natural red clay available there. He developed distinctive glazes — necessary, he felt, to cover the dark red body. After the war and a temporary halt in production, Cowan moved his pottery to Rocky River, where he made a commercial line of artware utilizing a highly-fired white porcelain. Although he acquiesced to the necessity of mass production, every effort was made to insure a product of highest quality. Fine artists, among them Waylande Gregory, Thelma Frazier, and Viktor Schreckengost, designed pieces which were often produced in limited editions, some of which sell today for prices in the thousands. Most of the ware was marked 'Cowan,' except for the 1930 mass-produced line called 'Lakeware.' Falling under the crunch of the Great Depression, the pottery closed in 1931.

The use of an asterisk (*) in the listing below indicates a nonfactory name that is being provided as a suggested name for the convenience of present-day collectors. One example is the glaze *Original Ivory, which is a high-gloss white that resembles undecorated porcelain. It was used on many of Cowan's lady 'flower figures' (Cowan's more graceful term for what some collectors call frogs).

Our advisor for this category is Mark Bassett; he is listed in the Directory under Ohio. With Victoria Naumann, Mark is the author of *Cowan Pottery and the Cleveland School,* a detailed history of Cowan Pottery and of Guy Cowan's students, colleagues, and designers. Prices quoted are for examples in mint condition, unless noted otherwise.

Key: Sp/I — Special Ivory

Bookend #E-2, Elephant, Postgate, Oriental Red, 7½", pr........**1,500.00**
Bowl #733B, October, 9¼" **95.00**
Bowl #733B, April Gr, 9¼" **45.00**
Candlestick #501B, Larkspur, 10¾", pr **95.00**
Comport #779, April, Gregory, 4½" **50.00**
Comport, #736, sea horse base, Apple Blossom, 3¼x6" **25.00**
Decanter #X-12 and X-13, King & Queen, Oriental Red, 12", pr.**1,200.00**
Flower frog #F-8, Awakening, *Orig Ivory, 9" **950.00**
Flower frog #698, Pavlova, *Orig Ivory, 6¼", ...**150.00**
Flower frog #686, Scarf Dancer, Sp/I, 7" **250.00**
Flower frog #717, Triumphant, *Orig Ivory, 15½", ...**2,500.00**
Flower frog, delicate lady flowers on base, Bogatay, 7" **2,500.00**
Sculpture, Bird and Wave, Blazys, Eqyptian Bl, 12" **950.00**
Sculpture, Nautch Dancer, Gregory, Shadow Wht, 18¼", ...**10,000.00**
Sculpture, Spanish Dancers, Anderson, Primrose, 8¾", pr **1,250.00**
Vase #652-B, fluted body, hdls, Marigold, 11½" **150.00**
Vase #747, Chinese Bird, bird in high reliuef, Jade Gr, 11¼" **750.00**
Vase #801, fan shape, Antique Gr, 5¼x8" **95.00**
Vase #822, ribbed body, flared, Russet Brn, 9" **175.00**
Vase #847, ribbed, wisteria decor, 12" **1,250.00**
Vase, Medusa, pk, ivory & blk, sgn Paul Bogatay, 7" **3,500.00**
Vase #V-87, ribbed body, hdls, Peacock, 9" **125.00**

Cracker Jack

Kids have been buying Cracker Jack since it was first introduced in the 1890s. By 1912 it was packaged with a free toy inside. Before the first kernel was crunched, eager fingers had retrieved the surprise from the depth of the box — actually no easy task, considering the care required to keep the contents so swiftly displaced from spilling over the side! Though a little older, perhaps, many of those same kids still are looking — just as eagerly — for the Cracker Jack prizes. Point of sale, company collectibles, and the prizes as well have over the years reflected America's changing culture. Grocer sales and incentives from around the turn of the century — paper dolls, postcards, and song books — were often marked Rueckheim Brothers (the inventors of Cracker Jack) or Reliable Confections. Over the years the company made some changes, leaving a trail of clues that often help collectors date their items. The company's name changed in 1922 from Rueckheim Brothers & Eckstein (who had been made a partner for inventing a method for keeping the caramelized kernels from sticking together) to The Cracker Jack Company. Their Brooklyn office was open from 1914 until it closed in 1923. The first time the sailor Jack logo was used on their packaging was in 1919. The sailor image of a Rueckheim child (with red, white, and blue colors) was introduced by these German immigrants in an attempt to show U.S.A. support during the time of heightened patriotism after WW I. For packages and 'point of sale' dating, note that the word 'prize' was used from 1912 to 1925, 'novelty' from 1925 to 1932, and 'toy' from 1933 on.

The first loose-packed prizes were toys made of wood, clay, tin, metal, and lithographed paper (the reason some early prizes are stained). Plastic toys were introduced in 1946. Paper wrapped for safety purposes in 1948, subjects echo the 'hype' of the day — yo-yos, tops, whistles, and sports cards in the simple, peaceful days of our country, propaganda and war toys in the '40s, games in the '50s, and space toys in the '60s. Few of the estimated 15 billion prizes were marked. Advertising items from Angelus Marshmallow and Checkers Confections (cousins of the Cracker Jack family) are also collectible. When no condition is indicated, the items listed below are assumed to be in excellent to mint condition. 'CJ' indicates that the item is marked. Note: An often-asked question concerns the tin Toonerville Trolley called 'CJ.' No data has been found in the factory archives to authenticate this item; it is assumed that the 'CJ' merely refers to its small size. For further information see *Cracker Jack Toys, The Complete, Unofficial Guide for Collectors,* by Larry White. Our advisor for this category is Wes Johnson; he is listed in the Directory under Kentucky. Also look for *The Prize Insider* newsletter listed in the Directory under Clubs, Newsletters, and Catalogs.

Dealer Incentives and Premiums

Badge, pin-bk, celluloid, lady w/CJ label reverse, 1905, 1¼" **65.00**
Bat, baseball; wood, Hillerich & Bradsby, CJ, full sz **85.00**
Book, pocket; jester on cover, CJ Riddles **65.00**
Book, pocket; riddle/sailor boy/dog on cover, RWB, CJ, 1919 ......**55.00**
Book, recipe; Angelus, 1930s **22.00**
Cart w/2 movable wheels, wood dowel tongue, CJ **50.00**
Corkscrew/opener, metal plated, CJ/Angelus, 3" **85.00**
Harmonica, full scale, emb CJ, early, 5⅛" **365.00**
Jigsaw puzzle, CJ or Checkers, 1 of 4, 7x10", in envelope **35.00**
Marbles, Akro set of 12 in box w/instructions, CJ, 1929 ....**950.00**
Match holder, hinged, eng gold-tone case, CJ, 2½x1⅞" **650.00**
Mirror, oval, Angelus (redhead or blond) on box **89.00**
Pen, ink; w/nib, tin litho bbl, CJ **485.00**
Pencil top clip, metal/celluloid, oval boy & dog logo **220.00**
Pencil top clip, metal/celluloid, tube shape w/package **220.00**
Postcard, bear, 1 of 16, CJ, 1907, ea **35.00**
Riddle card, 2 series of 20, w/package/from factory, CJ, '07, ea **8.00**
Tablet, school; CJ, 1929, 8x10" **195.00**
Thimble, aluminum, CJ Co/Angelus, red pnt, rare, ea **165.00**
Truck, steel, wood wheels for CJ pkg, unmk **85.00**

Packaging

Sleeve for popcorn box (as boost for Christmas sales), For a Cracker Jack Christmas, red and green on white, $225.00. (Photo courtesy Wes Johnson)

Box, popcorn; Question Mark box end for CJ 'Toy,' 1933-34 ....**250.00**
Box, popcorn; red scroll border, CJ 'Prize,' 1912-25, ea **150.00**

Canister, tin, CJ Candy Corn Crisp, 10-oz 75.00
Canister, tin, CJ Coconut Corn Crisp, 1-lb 55.00
Canister, tin, CJ Coconut Corn Crisp, 10-oz 65.00
CJ Commemorative canister, mc scene, 1990s, ea 9.00
CJ Commemorative canister, wht w/red scroll, 1980s, ea 8.00
Crate, shipping; wood, CJ, Rueckheim Bros Eck, 1902-22, lg 165.00

Prizes, Cast Metal

Badge, shield, CJ Jr Detective, silver, 1931, 1¼" 50.00
Button, stud bk, Me for Cracker Jack, boy & dog, oval 55.00
Button, stud bk, Xd bats & ball, CJ pitcher/etc series, 1928 ....130.00
Coins, Presidents, 31 series, CJ, 1933, ea 9.00
Dollhouse items: lantern, mug, candlestick, etc; no mk, ea 6.50
Horse & wagon, CJ, 3-D, silver or gold, early, 2½", ea 250.00
Pistol, soft lead, inked, CJ on bbl, early, rare, 2⅛" 180.00
Ring, alphabet letter setting (series), unmk, ea 4.00
Rocking horse, no rider, 3-D, inked, early, 1⅛" 25.00
Rocking horse w/boy, 3-D, inked, early, 1½" 32.00
Spinner, early pkg in center, 'More You Eat...,' CJ, rare 295.00

Prizes, Paper

Baseball CJ score counter, 3⅜" L 130.00
Book, Bess & Bill on CJ Hill, series of 12, 1937, mini 105.00
Book, Birds We Know, CJ, 1928, mini 105.00
Book, Chaplin flip book, CJ, 1920s, ea 140.00
Book, Twigg & Sprigg, CJ, 1930, mini 105.00
Booklet, stickers/wise cracks/riddles, Borden, CJ, 1965 on 3.00
Decal, cartoon or nursery rhyme figure, 1947-49, CJ 12.00
Disguise, ears, red (still in carrier), CJ, 1950, pr 65.00
Disguise, glasses, hinged, cello lenses, CJ Where Ever..., '33 ....65.00
Disguise, glasses, hinged, w/eyeballs, unmk, 1933 ....6.00
Fan, lady's, folding, mc, unmk 45.00
Fortune Teller, boy/dog on film in envelope, CJ, '20s, 1¾x2½" ...80.00
Fortune wheel, 2-pc litho, turn for fortune, CJ, 1¾" 70.00
Game spinner, ...baseball at home, rectangle, CJ, 2¾" W 125.00
Game spinner, ...baseball at home, unmk, 1946, 1½" dia 60.00
Hat, fold out, More You Eat/More You Want, CJ, early 75.00
Hat, Indian headdress, CJ, 1950s, 5⅝" H 275.00
Hat visor, baseball, tie-on string, red or gr, CJ, 1931 ....120.00
Magic game book, erasable slate, CJ, series of 13, 1946, ea 25.00
Movie, boy at blkboard, turn wheel: draws/erases, CJ, '31, 2" 175.00
Movie, pull tab for 2nd picture, series, CJ, 1943, 1¼", ea 105.00
Paper dolls, Boggie, Betty & Billie 125.00
Sand toy pictures, pours for action, series of 14, 1967, ea 25.00
Top, golf game, wood stick center, CJ, 1933 ....57.00
Top, string; Rainbow Spinner, 2-pc, cb, different designs, ea 45.00
Transfer, iron-on, sport figure or patriotic, unmk, 1939, ea 6.00
Whistle, Blow for More, CJ box/boy/dog, yel, 1931, ea 55.00
Whistle, Blow for More, CJ/Angelus packages, 1928, '31 or '33, ea .45.00
Whistle, Razz Zooka, C Carey Cloud design, CJ, 1949 ....32.00

Prizes, Plastic

Animals, standup, letter on bk, series of 26, Nosco, 1953, ea 4.00
Baseball players, 3-D, bl or gray team, 1948, 1½", ea 8.00
Disc, emb comic character, series of 12, 1954, unmk, 1½" 16.00
Disc, emb fish plaque, oval, series of 10, 1956, unmk, ea 14.00
Figure, circus; stands on base, 1 of 12, Nosco, 1951-54 ....2.50
Figure on rocking base, semi-flat, 1 of 9, Cloud design, '56 ....4.00
Fob, alphabet letter w/loop on top, 1 of 26, 1954, 1½" 4.00
Palm puzzle, ball(s) roll into holes, dome or rnd, from 1966 ....6.00
Palm puzzle, ball(s) roll into holes, rectangle, CJ, 1920s, ea 55.00
Palm puzzle, ball(s) roll into holes, sq, CJ, 1920s, ea 45.00
Ships in a bottle, 6 different, unmk, 1960, ea 6.00
Signs, road; Stop, Caution, etc, yel, series of 10, 1954-60, ea 5.00
Toys, take apart/assemble, variety, from '62, unassembled, ea 5.00
Whistle, tube w/animals on top, CJ, series, 1950-53, 1⅜" 7.00

Prizes, Tin

Badge, boy & dog diecut, complete w/bend-over tab, CJ 150.00
Badge, boy & dog diecut, w/o tab at top, CJ 95.00
Badge, emb/plated CJ officer, 2⅜" or 1⅝", early, ea 110.00
Bank, 3-D book form, red/gr/or blk, CJ Bank, early, 2" 120.00
Bookmark, dogs, 4 different, 1941, 3", ea 25.00
Brooch or pin, various designs on card, CJ/logo, early, ea 125.00
Clicker, 'Noisy CJ Snapper,' pear shape, aluminum, 1949 ....34.00
Clicker, CJ Telegraph, Pat 1897, inked, 1¾" dia, ea 145.00
Doll dishes, tin plated, CJ, '31, 1¾", 1⅞", & 2⅛" dia, ea 35.00
Helicopter, yel propeller, wood stick, unmk, 1937, 2⅝" 27.00
Horse & wagon, litho diecut, CJ & Angelus, 2⅛" 65.00
Horse & wagon, litho diecut, gray/red mks, CJ, 1914-23, 3⅛" ..395.00
Pocket watch, silver or gold, CJ as numerals, 1931, 1½" 55.00
Sled, tin plated, CJ, 1931, 2" L 35.00
Small box shape: Elect Alarm Clock litho, unmk, 1⅛" 75.00
Small box shape: garage litho, unmk, 1⅛" 60.00
Small box shape: radio litho, bl, unmk, 1⅛" 60.00
Soldier, litho, die-cut standup, officer/private/etc, unmk, ea 17.00
Spinner, wood stick, Fortune Teller Game, red/wht/bl, CJ, 1½" ..90.00
Spinner, wood stick, Question Mark Box at center, CJ 50.00
Spinner, wood stick, 2 Toppers, red/wht/bl, Angelus/Jack, 1½" ...85.00
Stand up, oval Am Flag, series of 4, unmk, 1936-45, ea 25.00
Stand up, rectangle litho, boy & dog, ca 1916, lg or sm, ea 155.00
Tall box shape: Frozen Foods locker freezer, '47, unmk, 1¾" 75.00
Tall box shape: radio, Tune in w/CJ, brn/yel, 1939, 1¾" 125.00
Tall box shape: Refrigerator Car, CJ, 1947, 1¾" L 155.00
Train, engine & tender, litho, CJ Line/512 ....125.00
Train, litho engine only, red, 1941, unmk 20.00
Train, Lone Eagle Flyer cars, unmk 65.00
Train, Lone Eagle Flyer engine, unmk 60.00
Tray, emb, litho w/early package, 2¼x1¾" 95.00
Truck, litho, RWB, CJ/Angelus, 1931, ea 65.00
Wagon shape: Caterpillar tractor, unmk, 1931, 1¾" L 35.00
Wagon shape: Circus Wagon, 5 different, ea 150.00
Wagon shape: Playtime Trailer (auto trailer), unmk, 1947 ....50.00
Wagon shape: tank, orange/red/gr camouflage, unmk 65.00
Wagon shape: Tank Corps No 57, gr & blk, 1941 ....30.00

Miscellaneous

Ad, comic book, CJ, ea 14.00
Ad, Saturday Evening Post, mc, CJ, 1919, 11x14" 18.00
Lunch box, tin, 2 hdls, CJ, 1980s, 4½x5x6" 40.00
Lunch box, tin emb, CJ, 1970s, 4x7x9" 30.00
Medal, CJ salesman award, brass, 1939, scarce 125.00
Sign, bathing beauty, 5-color cb, CJ, early, 17x22" 460.00
Sign, boy or girl w/box of CJ, 5-color cb, early, 17x22", ea 460.00
Sign, Jack & Bingo, die-cut litho, easel standup, CJ, early 450.00
Sign, Jack & Bingo, standing on early CJ pkg, mc cb, rare 520.00
Sign, Santa & prizes, mc cb, Angelus, early, lg 220.00
Sign, Santa & prizes, mc cb, CJ, early, lg 265.00

Cranberry Glass

Cranberry glass is named for its resemblance to the color of cranberry juice. It was made by many companies both here and abroad, becoming popular in America soon after the Civil War. It was made in free-blown ware as well as mold-blown. Today cranberry glass is being reproduced, and it is sometimes difficult to distinguish the old from the new. Ask a reputable dealer if you are unsure.

For further information we recommend *American Art Glass* by John A. Shumann III, available from Collector Books or your local bookstore. See also Cruets; Salts; Sugar Shakers; Syrups.

Basket, ruffled, clear hdl, 7x5" ...295.00
Bell, clear rnd hdl, 11", from $85 to ...125.00
Bottle, cherub/lilies of the valley in wht, gold trim, 10x4" ...200.00
Bottle, gold/wht dots & bands, clear cut stopper, 8½x2½" ...175.00
Bottle, scent; brass o/l w/hdl, 2 medallions, Fr, 1875, 7", NM ...575.00
Bowl, appl yel/clear decor, ftd, sq, 5" ...175.00
Bowl, florals/enameling/heavy gold/7 gr jewels, ftd, 4½" ...225.00
Box, mc floral garlands/scrolls, brass hinges, 4x4" ...375.00
Box, yel/gold buds, hinged, 2¾x3½" dia ...150.00
Celery vase, Invt T'print, tapered sides, HP floral, Am, 7" ...100.00
Claret, HP lily-of-valley, ribbed, hollow stopper, 9¾" ...175.00
Cruet, wide-spaced ribs, clear hdl & stopper, 7½", from $90 to ...125.00
Decanter, ducks among rushes in front panel, clear hdl/stopper, 12" ...200.00
Decanter, Invt T'print, HP floral, hollow cut stopper, 10" ...140.00
Decanter, wine; lt ribbing, clear ft/hdl/stopper, 12x3" ...180.00
Finger bowl, Invt T'print, floral coralene & enameling, 4¼" ...225.00
Loving cup, gold threads & decor, crystal base, 11¼" ...200.00
Pitcher, clear rope hdl, 7¼" ...150.00
Pitcher, Dmn Quilt, ruffled, clear hdl, 9" ...350.00
Pitcher, Invt T'print, rippled, clear hdl, milk sz, 6⅛x4½" ...110.00
Shakers, HP daisies, in SP fr ...225.00
Tumbler, HP floral, pinched sides, 4" ...100.00

Creamware

Creamware was a type of earthenware developed by Wedgwood in the 1760s and produced by many other Staffordshire potteries, including Leeds. Since it could be potted cheaply and was light in weight, it became popular abroad as well as in England, due to the lower freight charges involved in its export. It was revived at Leeds in the late nineteenth century, and the type most often reproduced was heavily reticulated or molded in high relief. These later wares are easily distinguished from the originals since they are thicker and tend to craze heavily. See also Leeds; Wedgwood.

Cream jug, pineapple mold, yel/gr, 1765, 5", VG ...650.00
Cream jug, Tea Party, blk transfer, flower knop, 5", EX ...170.00
Cup, stirrup; cow figural, late 18th C, minor rstr, 4⅞" ...345.00
Dish, tortoise-shell glaze, octagonal, ribbed rim, 12", VG ...230.00
Mug, mc floral border at rim, early 1800s, 4½x3" ...250.00
Pitcher, floral swags/wheat sheaf/farm implements, mc, 1793, 8", EX ...1,725.00
Plate, brn mottle, England, late 1700s, 8" ...230.00
Plate, Last Rites, for Dutch market, 10" ...250.00
Tea canister, Tea Party/Shepherd, blk transfer, 1780s, 5" ...635.00
Teapot, bl/gr/brn mottle, crabstock hdl, reeded spout, 1780s, 6" ...500.00
Teapot, fruit/basketweave emb, globular, 1865, rstr, 4½", EX ...980.00
Teapot, gr floral reliefs, crabstock hdl/spout, rstr, 3" ...860.00
Teapot, pineapple mold, yel/gr, 1775, rstr, 5¼", VG ...1,600.00
Teapot, Tea Party, pk lustre trim, early 19th C, 5" ...230.00

Crown Milano

Crown Milano was a line of decorated milk glass (or opal ware) introduced by the Mt. Washington Glass Co. of New Bedford, Massachussetts, in the early 1890s. It had previously been called Albertine Ware. Some pieces are marked with a 'CM,' and many had paper labels. This ware is usually highly decorated and will most likely have a significant amount of gold painted on it. The shiny pieces were recently discovered to have been called 'Colonial Ware' and have a laurel wreath and a crown. This ware was well received in its day, and outstanding pieces bring high prices on today's market. Advisors for this category are Wilfred and Dolli Cohen; they are listed in the Directory under California.

Biscuit jar, allover bamboo on pnt burmese, SP mts, 6" ...875.00
Biscuit jar, Colonial pr blows bubbles, floral/gilt, 7½" dia ...975.00
Biscuit jar, floral/gilt scrolls, sgn/#d SP lid & mts ...750.00
Biscuit jar, gold apple blossom branches, rope hdl ...750.00
Biscuit jar, wild roses reserves, no mk, gold-washed mk lid ...695.00
Bowl, bride's; yel florals & gold; ornate Pairpoint berry fr, 9x7" ...1,700.00
Box, beaded daisies on pnt gold, SP collar/ft, 4x5" dia ...875.00
Cup & saucer, demitasse; floral vines/gilt/blk dots, 2", 5" ...1,750.00
Pickle castor, floral w/emb crosses; SP Knickerbocker fr ...1,000.00
Sugar shaker, floral on yel tint, squat/melon ribbed, 3x4" ...535.00
Sweetmeat, floral, gold on pk to cream, SP lid, 4½" ...1,000.00
Sweetmeat, gold thistles on emb wht/pk swirls, turtle on l ...1,350.00
Vase, allover pastel florals, trumpet form, Colonial, 12" ...1,750.00
Vase, floral, 4-fold neck on swirled bulbous body, 6x5¾" ...1,485.00
Vase, floral/gold shadow branches on wht, Colonial, 9" ...1,000.00
Vase, gold ferns & shadow leaves, bulbous, 4-fold top, 5" ...400.00
Vase, jack-in-pulpit; floral on pnt burmese, crimped, 9¾" ...750.00
Vase, man w/camel, hdld urn form, Albertine, 12¼" ...6,900.00
Vase, mc dots form intricate floral, shadow scrolls, 13x7½" ...1,950.00
Vase, oak leaves, mc on shaded tan, bulbous, petal top, 5¾" ...1,300.00
Vase, pansies, 3 ball ft, thorn rim, #588, 6" ...800.00
Vase, pansies/gilt, petticoat base, lobed rim, long neck, 10½" ...850.00
Vase, petit-point iris/scrolls on lt tan, 8-rib, petal top, 4½" ...850.00
Vase, pk blossoms w/gold, long neck split at rim, 9½" ...865.00
Vase, thistles on shadowed yel, hdls, no mk, 4½x6" ...350.00
Vase, wild roses etc, gold on peach/yel mottle, jewels, 5x7" ...1,150.00
Vase, 6 long-stemmed thistles w/blooms in mc/gold, 15" ...1,950.00

Cruets

Cruets, containers made to hold oil or vinegar, are usually bulbous with tall, narrow throats, a handle, and a stopper. During the nineteenth century and for several years after, they were produced in abundance in virtually every type of glassware available. Those listed below are assumed to be with stopper and mint unless noted otherwise. Our advisor for this category is Elaine Ezell; she is listed in the Directory under Maryland.

See also Specific manufacturers.

Satina Swirl (Swan's Bill), sapphire satin, Hobbs Brockunier, $695.00. (Photo courtesy Neila and Tom Bredehoft)

Alaska, emerald gr ...285.00
Amberina, Invt T'print, trefoil spout, EX color, att Mt WA, 5½" ...435.00
Argonaut Shell, custard w/gold & decor ...800.00

Bagware, vaseline 195.00
Banded Portland, ruby stain 450.00
Beaded Grape, gr 150.00
Big Button, ruby stain 295.00
Bl w/gold scrolls & mc flowers, amber hdl, Moser 350.00
Bl w/HP & gilt lily of the valley, faceted stopper, Moser 450.00
Block & Fan 45.00
Bohemian, amber to clear w/gold, intaglio florals, cut stopper ...200.00
Bohemian, ruby to clear, intricate cutting, star-cut base, 6" 195.00
Burmese, Mt WA, melon ribbed, faceted stopper, 6½ 1,085.00
Burmese, Mt WA, shiny, melon ribbed, mushroom stopper, 7" ...1,250.00
Button Arches, ruby stain 250.00
Challinor, Tree of Life, Nile Green 225.00
Challinor Tree of Life, bl 225.00
Christmas Pearls, gr opal 395.00
Chrysanthemum Base Swirl, wht satin opal 190.00
Chrysanthemum Leaf, chocolate 1,295.00
Chrysanthemum Sprig, custard w/M gold & decor, 6¾" 495.00
Circled Scroll, bl opal 575.00
Cone, pk cased, metal filigree 295.00
Crackle glass, red w/clear stopper, West Virginia Glass, 6½" 25.00
Cranberry, heavy gold o/l, Moser, 5" 525.00
Cranberry crackle w/enameling 190.00
Croesus, gr w/gold, sm 295.00
Cupid & Venus 175.00
Daisy & Button, amber 150.00
Daisy & Fern, Apple Blossom mold, bl opal 195.00
Daisy & Fern, bl opal, Indiana mold, LG Wright 135.00
Dewey, canary 195.00
Dmn & Invt Fan, gr, 7½" 85.00
Dmn Quilt, reverse amberina, reeded hdl, clear stopper, 8" 450.00
Duchess, gr w/gold 395.00
Everglades, custard w/EX gold & decor 1,200.00
Fandango, Heisey 75.00
Feather 50.00
Fine Cut, amber 75.00
Fine Cut, canary, matching stopper 145.00
Florida 60.00
Herringbone, pk, trifold rim, frosted stopper & hdl, 5¼" 375.00
Hobnail, cranberry, bulbous, Hobbs 350.00
Hobnail, vaseline, Hobbs 350.00
Hobnail, 4½" 40.00
Invt Fan & Feather, pk slag, 6¾" 1,950.00
Invt Strawberry, clear faceted stopper 45.00
Invt T'print, amber, pewter ft/hdl/top/stopper, 11x3" 180.00
Invt T'print, amberina, 6" 395.00
Invt T'print, bluerina, clear stopper & hdl, 7½" 300.00
Invt T'print, reverse amberina, amber hdl & stopper, 7½" 400.00
Invt T'print, rubena verde, teepee shape, Hobbs Brockunier, 7" .550.00
IOU, gr, 5½" 95.00
King's 500, cobalt w/M gold, swirl stopper, 8-oz 995.00
Louis XV, custard w/M gold 295.00
Medallion Sprig, gr to clear 350.00
Michigan 60.00
Moon & Star, appl hdl 120.00
Nevada 35.00
Peachblow, New England, shiny, bulbous bottom 1,585.00
Pomona, 1st grind, frosted w/clear stopper 395.00
Portland 65.00
Ranson, vaseline 275.00
Sapphire bl w/flowers, amber hdl/stopper, 8x3" 175.00
Spatter, maroon/wht w/flowers, clear hdl/cut stopper, 5½" 250.00
Swag w/Brackets, deep bl, 7½" 525.00
Texas, rose stain 250.00
Wild Bouquet, bl opal, opal hdl, clear stopper, 7¼" 495.00
Wild Bouquet, custard w/decor 995.00
X-Ray, gr w/gold 250.00
Yeoman, Sahara 75.00

Cup Plates, Glass

Before the middle 1850s, it was socially acceptable to pour hot tea into a deep saucer to cool. The tea was sipped from the saucer rather than the cup, which frequently was handleless and too hot to hold. The cup plate served as a coaster for the cup. It is generally agreed that the first examples of pressed glass cup plates were made about 1826 at the Boston and Sandwich Glass Co. in Sandwich, Cape Cod, Massachusetts. Other glassworks in three major areas (New England, Philadelphia, and the Midwest, especially Pittsburgh) quickly followed suit.

Antique glass cup plates range in size from 2⅝" up to 4¼" in diameter. The earliest plates had simple designs inspired by cut glass patterns, but by 1829 they had become more complex. The span from then until about 1845 is known as the 'Lacy Period,' when cup plate designs and pressing techniques were at their peak. To cover pressing imperfections, the backgrounds of the plates were often covered with fine stippling which endowed them with a glittering brilliance called 'laciness.' They were made in a multitude of designs — some purely decorative, others commemorative. Subjects include the American eagle, hearts, sunbursts, log cabins, ships, George Washington, the political candidates Clay and Harrison, plows, beehives, etc. Of all the patterns, the round George Washington plate is the rarest and most valuable — only four are known to exist today.

Authenticity is most important. Collectors must be aware that contemporary plates which have no antique counterparts and fakes modeled after antique patterns have had wide distribution. Condition is also important, though it is the exceptional plate that does not have some rim roughness. More important considerations are scarcity of design and color.

Our advisor for this category is John Bilane; he is listed in the Directory under New Jersey. The book *American Glass* by George and Helen McKearin has a section on glass cup plates. The definitive book is *American Glass Cup Plates* by Ruth Webb Lee and James H. Rose. Numbers in the listings that follow refer to the latter. When attempting to evaluate a cup plate, remember that minor rim roughness is normal. See also Staffordshire; Pairpoint.

R-20, VG 30.00
R-30, scarce, VG 64.00
R-41, scarce, G+ 38.00
R-47, VG 30.00
R-62-A, VG- 48.00
R-79, G 32.00
R-97, scarce, VG- 48.00
R-99, rare, VG 70.00
R-101, scarce, VG 51.00
R-104, VG 35.00
R-124-A, VG- 37.00
R-151-A, G- 28.00
R-158-B, scarce, EX- 50.00
R-159-A, scarce, G 39.00
R-164-A, EX 40.00
R-169-B, EX 40.00
R-172-A, EX 40.00
R-174, EX 45.00
R-176-A, EX 43.00
R-177, VG 43.00
R-216, G 53.00
R-236, G 28.00
R-245, G- 24.00

R-255, VG ... 20.00
R-257, VG- ... 32.00
R-258, VG ... 30.00
R-269, VG ... 30.00
R-269-B, scarce, G+ ... 34.00
R-271-A, VG ... 30.00
R-285, VG ... 34.00
R-291, VG- ... 26.00
R-311, VG- ... 20.00
R-313, VG ... 21.00
R-323, VG- ... 18.00
R-327, G- ... 12.00
R-332-B, G- ... 12.00
R-334, G+ ... 17.00
R-334-A, G ... 15.00
R-339, VG ... 19.00
R-340, G ... 15.00
R-343-B, scarce, VG ... 35.00
R-367, G- ... 10.00
R-379, VG- ... 12.00
R-390-A, G+ ... 11.00
R-393, G ... 10.00
R-396, VG ... 13.00
R-402, VG ... 14.00
R-425, G ... 21.00
R-447, G ... 22.00
R-465-H, VG ... 23.00
R-465-N, G ... 16.00
R-467-A, G ... 15.00
R-476, G- ... 13.00
R-501, G- ... 10.00
R-508, G+ ... 15.00
R-546, G+ ... 15.00

R-562-A, Henry Clay, 3⅜", EX, $170.00; R-668, Eagle, 3", VG, $150.00.

R-565, G ... 25.00
R-565-A, G+ ... 26.00
R-566-A, scarce, G- ... 33.00
R-590, G ... 28.00
R-593, scarce, G ... 42.00
R-610-A, VG ... 34.00
R-610-C, VG- ... 40.00
R-619, G ... 35.00
R-619-A, G ... 39.00
R-636, VG- ... 42.00
R-637, very rare, VG- ... 260.00
R-661, VG ... 39.00
R-665-A, G+ ... 34.00
R-666, VG ... 35.00
R-670-A, VG ... 39.00
R-670-C, rare, G- ... 55.00
R-676-C, G ... 47.00
R-677, VG ... 38.00
R-677-A, G- ... 24.00
R-679, VG ... 34.00
R-693, G+ ... 75.00
R-695, G- ... 40.00

Cups and Saucers

The earliest utensils for drinking were small porcelain and stoneware bowls imported from China by the East Indian Company in the early seventeenth century. European and English tea bowls and saucers, imitating Chinese and Japanese originals, were produced from the early eighteenth century and often decorated with Chinese-type motifs. By about 1810, handles were fitted to the bowl to form the now familiar teacup, and this form became almost universal. Coffee in England and on the continent was often served in a can — a straight-sided cylinder with a handle. After 1820 the coffee can gave way to the more fanciful form of the coffee cup.

An infinite variety of cups and saucers are available for both the new and experienced collector, and they can be found in all price ranges. There is probably no better way to thoroughly know and understand the various ceramic manufacturers than to study cups and saucers. Our advisors for this category, Susan and Jim Harran, have written two books, entitled *Collectible Cups and Saucers, Identification and Values, Books I* and *II*, published by Collector Books. Over 800 full-color photos fill book II which is divided into six collectible categories: early years (1700 – 1875), cabinet cups, nineteenth and twentieth century dinnerware, English tablewares, miniatures and mustache cups and saucers. The Harrans are listed in the Directory under New Jersey.

Chocolate, emb brn & cream flowers, slim, Doulton Burslem, 1891-1902 ... 115.00
Chocolate, emb harebells & gilt holly leaves & berries, Limoges, 1895 ... 50.00
Coffee, emb shell, pearlized pk & wht on gr w/gold, Meissen, 1860-75 ... 125.00
Coffee can, gilt scrolls on wht, loop hdl, Sevres, ca 1808 ... 325.00
Coffee can, mythological transfer on pk w/gold, Austria, 1890-1918 ... 60.00
Demi, Dr Wall Worcester pattern, fluted, Emile Sampson, ca 1830 ... 400.00
Demi, HP flowers w/gold, scalloped, ftd, Dresden, 1891, from $100 to ... 125.00
Demi, metallic gold, ribbed cup, 'broken' loop hdl, Japan label, 1950s ... 10.00
Demi, Osier molded edge, floral transfer, Royal Copenhagen, ca 1950 ... 35.00
Demi, pastel floral transfer, angle hdl, Steinmann, Silesia, 1900 ... 35.00
Demi, Royal Flute, HP roses, branch hdl, von Schierholz, 1910-20 ... 85.00
Demi, silver o/l flowers on wht, angle hdl, Lenox, 1906-24 ... 160.00
Demi, wht w/pk lustre int, paneled, loop hdl, Ott & Brewer, 1880s ... 125.00
Demi, 16-panel w/printed floral & gold bands, Limoges, 1920s ... 45.00
Tea, bl jasper, classical figures, Wedgwood, 1850-60 ... 600.00
Tea, chinoiserie floral transfer, unmk, Hilditch style, 1815-30, up to ... 200.00
Tea, Du Barry Rose, Tuscan China, 1947-60, from $30 to ... 40.00
Tea, Floret, high 'broken' loop hdl, Gaudy Welsh, 1830-35, from $90 to ... 120.00
Tea, gilt floral band, swirled/fluted/ftd, Aynsley, 1950s ... 45.00
Tea, HP flowers on pear shape, loop hdl, Wedgwood, ca 1935 ... 45.00
Tea, HP scenic/floral medallions on pk & wht, Dresden, 1901-30 ... 115.00
Tea, lav floral on wht w/gold, scalloped, Rosenthal, 1910, from $40 to ... 50.00
Tea, pastel floral, 'broken' loop hdl, Haviland, 1925-45, from $40 to ... 55.00
Tea, pk lustreware grapes & vines, unknown English mk, 1825-35, up to ... 90.00
Tea, rose transfer, 8-flute, Royal Albert, ca 1945+ ... 35.00

Currier & Ives by Royal

During the 1950s dinnerware decorated with transfer-printed scenes taken from prints by Currier and Ives was manufactured by Royal

China and given as premiums through A&P stores. Though it was also made in pink and green, the blue is by far the most popular. Pie plates in black and brown can be found, but no china sets in these colors have been reported. Occasionally pieces are being found that have hand-painted colors on them with the same blue backgrounds. It has become a very popular collectible at malls and flea markets around the country. Included in our listings are pieces from Hostess sets, which should be of great interest to collectors. New pieces which have been added to the price list include the clock, coffee mug with round handle, tall cup, snack plate, spoon rest/wall plaque, second-type gravy and underplate, and third-type sugar bowl with no handles. Also, the 11½" round platter with the 'Rocky Mountains' scene has been added (very rare). Currier and Ives by Royal is one of the fastest growing collectibles on the market today. Our advisors for this category are Treva and Jack Hamlin; they are listed in the Directory under Ohio.

Ashtray, 5½", from $15 to 18.00
Bowl, cereal; tab hdl, 6¼" 48.00
Bowl, cereal; 6¼" 15.00
Bowl, dessert; 5½" 5.00
Bowl, soup; 8" 14.00
Bowl, vegetable, 9" 25.00
Bowl, vegetable; deep, 10" 35.00
Butter dish, Fashionable decal 55.00
Butter dish, Road Winter decal 40.00
Casserole, angle hdls 115.00
Casserole, tab hdls, knob turned 90 degrees 250.00
Clock, 10" plate, bl #s, 2 decals 150.00
Creamer, angle hdl 8.00
Creamer, rnd hdl, tall 48.00
Cup, angle hdl 4.00
Cup, rnd hdl, tall, 9" 10.00
Gravy boat, pour spout 20.00
Gravy boat, tab hdls 50.00
Ladle, gravy; all wht 50.00
Lamp, candle; w/globe 300.00
Mug, coffee; reg 35.00
Mug, coffee; rnd hdl 35.00
Pie baker, 9 decals, 10" 30.00
Plate, bread; 6½" 5.00
Plate, calendar; 10" 20.00
Plate, chop; Getting Ice, 11½" 45.00
Plate, chop; Rocky Mountains, 11½" 65.00
Plate, chop; 12¼" 35.00
Plate, dinner; 10" 7.00
Plate, luncheon; 9" 25.00
Plate, salad; 7¼" 15.00
Plate, snack; w/cup well, 9" 50.00
Platter, oval, 13" 35.00
Platter, tab hdls, 10½" dia 30.00
Platter, 13" dia 75.00
Saucer, 6⅛" 2.00
Shakers, pr 40.00
Spoon rest, wall hanging 75.00
Sugar bowl, hdld, w/lid 18.00
Sugar bowl, no hdls, flared top 48.00
Sugar bowl, no hdls, w/lid 35.00
Teapot 150.00
Tidbit tray, 3-tier, orig only 75.00
Tray, gravy boat; like 7" plate 75.00
Tray, gravy boat; regular 20.00
Tumbler, iced tea; 12-oz, 5½" 17.50
Tumbler, juice; 5-oz, 3½" 17.50
Tumbler, old fashion; 7-oz, 3¼" 17.50
Tumbler, water; 8½-oz, 4¾" 17.50

Hostess Set Pieces

Bowl, candy; 7¾" 25.00
Bowl, dip; 4⅜" 20.00
Pie baker, 11" 45.00
Plate, cake; flat, 10" 45.00
Plate, cake; ftd, 10" 75.00
Plate, serving; 7" 20.00
Tray, deviled egg 150.00

Custard Glass

As early as the 1880s, custard glass was produced in England. Migrating glassmakers brought the formula for the creamy ivory ware to America. One of them was Harry Northwood, who in 1898 founded his company in Indiana, Pennsylvania, and introduced the glassware to the American market. Soon other companies were producing custard, among them Heisey, Tarentum, Fenton, and McKee. Not only dinnerware patterns but souvenir items were made. Today custard is the most expensive of the colored pressed glassware patterns. The formula for producing the luminous glass contains uranium salts which imparts the cream color to the batch and causes it to glow when it is examined under a black light.

Intaglio, master berry bowl, with gold and decor, 9", $250.00.

Argonaut Shell, bowl, master berry; gold & decor, 10½" L 275.00
Argonaut Shell, bowl, sauce; ftd, gold & decor 75.00
Argonaut Shell, butter dish, gold & decor 350.00
Argonaut Shell, butter dish, no gold 300.00
Argonaut Shell, compote, jelly; gold & decor, scarce 165.00
Argonaut Shell, creamer, gold & decor 155.00
Argonaut Shell, creamer, no gold 110.00
Argonaut Shell, cruet, gold & decor 800.00
Argonaut Shell, pitcher, water; gold & decor 475.00
Argonaut Shell, shakers, gold & decor, pr 435.00
Argonaut Shell, spooner, gold & decor 200.00
Argonaut Shell, sugar bowl, w/lid, gold & decor 235.00
Argonaut Shell, tumbler, gold & decor 110.00
Bead Swag, bowl, sauce; floral & gold 50.00
Bead Swag, goblet, floral & gold 65.00
Bead Swag, tray, pickle; floral & gold, rare 300.00
Bead Swag, wine, floral & gold 60.00
Beaded Circle, bowl, master berry; floral & gold 275.00
Beaded Circle, butter dish, floral & gold 500.00
Beaded Circle, creamer, floral & gold 180.00
Beaded Circle, pitcher, water; floral & gold 750.00
Beaded Circle, shakers, floral & gold, pr 1,000.00
Beaded Circle, spooner, floral & gold 185.00

Beaded Circle, tumbler, floral & gold, very rare 150.00
Cane Insert, berry set, 7-pc 450.00
Cane Insert, table set, 4-pc 450.00
Cherry & Scales, bowl, master berry; nutmeg stain 145.00
Cherry & Scales, butter dish, nutmeg stain 250.00
Cherry & Scales, creamer, nutmeg stain 125.00
Cherry & Scales, pitcher, water; nutmeg stain, scarce 350.00
Cherry & Scales, spooner, nutmeg stain, scarce 125.00
Cherry & Scales, sugar bowl, w/lid, nutmeg stain, scarce 150.00
Cherry & Scales, tumbler, nutmeg stain, scarce 75.00
Chrysanthemum Sprig, bowl, master berry; gold & decor 300.00
Chrysanthemum Sprig, bowl, master berry; no gold 175.00
Chrysanthemum Sprig, bowl, sauce; ftd, gold & decor 60.00
Chrysanthemum Sprig, butter dish, gold & decor 375.00
Chrysanthemum Sprig, celery vase, gold & decor, rare 700.00
Chrysanthemum Sprig, compote, jelly; gold & decor 150.00
Chrysanthemum Sprig, compote, jelly; no decor 100.00
Chrysanthemum Sprig, creamer, gold & decor 135.00
Chrysanthemum Sprig, cruet, gold & decor, 6¾" 495.00
Chrysanthemum Sprig, pitcher, water; gold & decor 485.00
Chrysanthemum Sprig, pitcher, water; no decor 350.00
Chrysanthemum Sprig, shakers, gold & decor, pr 300.00
Chrysanthemum Sprig, spooner, gold & decor 135.00
Chrysanthemum Sprig, spooner, no gold 75.00
Chrysanthemum Sprig, sugar bowl, gold & decor 250.00
Chrysanthemum Sprig, toothpick holder, gold & decor 375.00
Chrysanthemum Sprig, toothpick holder, no decor 175.00
Chrysanthemum Sprig, tray, condiment; gold & decor, rare 595.00
Chrysanthemum Sprig, tumbler, gold & decor 80.00
Dandelion, mug, nutmeg stain 175.00
Delaware, bowl, sauce; pk stain 65.00
Delaware, creamer, breakfast; pk stain 75.00
Delaware, tray, pin; gr stain 85.00
Delaware, tumbler, pk stain 65.00
Diamond w/Peg, bowl, master berry; roses & gold 225.00
Diamond w/Peg, bowl, sauce; roses & gold 50.00
Diamond w/Peg, butter dish, roses & gold 275.00
Diamond w/Peg, creamer, ind; no decor 35.00
Diamond w/Peg, creamer, ind; souvenir 50.00
Diamond w/Peg, creamer, roses & gold 85.00
Diamond w/Peg, mug, souvenir 50.00
Diamond w/Peg, napkin ring, roses & gold, rare 175.00
Diamond w/Peg, pitcher, roses & gold, 5½" 275.00
Diamond w/Peg, sugar bowl, w/lid, roses & gold 175.00
Diamond w/Peg, toothpick holder, roses & gold 175.00
Diamond w/Peg, tumbler, roses & gold 75.00
Diamond w/Peg, water set, souvenir, 7-pc 650.00
Diamond w/Peg, wine, roses & gold 65.00
Diamond w/Peg, wine, souvenir 55.00
Everglades, bowl, master berry; gold & decor 215.00
Everglades, bowl, saucer; gold & decor 60.00
Everglades, butter dish, gold & decor 395.00
Everglades, creamer, gold & decor 155.00
Everglades, cruet, EX gold & decor 1,200.00
Everglades, shakers, gold & decor, pr 375.00
Everglades, spooner, gold & decor 160.00
Everglades, sugar bowl, w/lid, gold & decor 235.00
Everglades, tumbler, gold & decor 100.00
Fan, bowl, master berry; good gold 200.00
Fan, bowl, sauce; good gold 60.00
Fan, butter dish, good gold 345.00
Fan, creamer, good gold 110.00
Fan, ice cream set, good gold, 7-pc 500.00
Fan, pitcher, water; good gold 300.00
Fan, spooner, good gold 100.00
Fan, sugar bowl, w/lid, good gold 175.00
Fan, tumbler, good gold 85.00
Fan, water set, good gold, 7-pc 725.00
Fine Cut & Roses, rose bowl, fancy int, nutmeg stain 100.00
Fine Cut & Roses, rose bowl, plain int 85.00
Geneva, bowl, master berry; floral decor, ftd, oval, 9" L 110.00
Geneva, bowl, master berry; floral decor, rnd, 9" 130.00
Geneva, bowl, sauce; floral decor, oval 50.00
Geneva, bowl, sauce; floral decor, rnd 50.00
Geneva, butter dish, floral decor 250.00
Geneva, butter dish, no decor 145.00
Geneva, compote, jelly; floral decor 95.00
Geneva, creamer, floral decor 115.00
Geneva, cruet, floral decor 475.00
Geneva, pitcher, water; floral decor 275.00
Geneva, shakers, floral decor, pr 280.00
Geneva, spooner, floral decor 100.00
Geneva, sugar bowl, open, floral decor 85.00
Geneva, sugar bowl, w/lid, floral decor 175.00
Geneva, syrup, floral decor 500.00
Geneva, toothpick holder, floral w/M gold 375.00
Geneva, tumbler, floral decor 60.00
Georgia Gem, bowl, master berry; good gold 135.00
Georgia Gem, bowl, master berry; gr opaque 115.00
Georgia Gem, butter dish, good gold 200.00
Georgia Gem, celery vase, good gold 145.00
Georgia Gem, creamer, good gold 100.00
Georgia Gem, creamer, no gold 60.00
Georgia Gem, cruet, good gold 395.00
Georgia Gem, mug, good gold 45.00
Georgia Gem, powder jar, w/lid, good gold 80.00
Georgia Gem, shakers, good gold, pr 140.00
Georgia Gem, spooner, souvenir 55.00
Georgia Gem, sugar bowl, w/lid, no gold 95.00
Grape (& Cable), bottle, scent; orig stopper, nutmeg stain 650.00
Grape (& Cable), bowl, banana; ftd, nutmeg stain 350.00
Grape (& Cable), bowl, centerpc; ftd, nutmeg stain 450.00
Grape (& Cable), bowl, master berry; flat, nutmeg stain 200.00
Grape (& Cable), bowl, nutmeg stain, 7½" 60.00
Grape (& Cable), bowl, orange; ftd, flat top, nutmeg stain 400.00
Grape (& Cable), bowl, orange; ftd, nutmeg stain 500.00
Grape (& Cable), bowl, sauce; nutmeg stain, ftd 50.00
Grape (& Cable), butter dish, nutmeg stain 300.00
Grape (& Cable), compote, jelly; open, nutmeg stain 150.00
Grape (& Cable), compote, nutmeg stain, 4½x8" 300.00
Grape (& Cable), cracker jar, nutmeg stain 850.00
Grape (& Cable), creamer, breakfast; nutmeg stain 80.00
Grape (& Cable), humidor, bl stain, rare 950.00
Grape (& Cable), humidor, nutmeg stain, rare 900.00
Grape (& Cable), nappy, nutmet stain, rare 60.00
Grape (& Cable), pitcher, water; nutmeg stain 550.00
Grape (& Cable), plate, nutmeg stain, 7" 50.00
Grape (& Cable), plate, nutmeg stain, 8" 65.00
Grape (& Cable), powder jar, nutmeg stain 350.00
Grape (& Cable), punch bowl, w/base, nutmeg stain 1,900.00
Grape (& Cable), spooner, nutmeg stain 155.00
Grape (& Cable), sugar bowl, breakfast; open, nutmeg stain 85.00
Grape (& Cable), sugar bowl, w/lid, nutmeg stain 225.00
Grape (& Cable), tray, dresser; nutmeg stain, scarce, lg 375.00
Grape (& Cable), tray, pin; nutmeg stain 150.00
Grape (& Cable), tumbler, nutmeg stain 75.00
Grape & Gothic Arches, bowl, master berry; pearl w/gold 200.00
Grape & Gothic Arches, bowl, sauce; pearl w/gold, rare 80.00

Grape & Gothic Arches, butter dish, pearl w/gold 235.00
Grape & Gothic Arches, creamer, pearl w/gold, rare 100.00
Grape & Gothic Arches, favor vase, nutmeg stain 80.00
Grape & Gothic Arches, goblet, pearl w/gold 75.00
Grape & Gothic Arches, pitcher, water; pearl w/gold 300.00
Grape & Gothic Arches, spooner, pearl w/gold 85.00
Grape & Gothic Arches, sugar bowl, w/lid, pearl w/gold 135.00
Grape & Gothic Arches, tumbler, pearl w/gold 65.00
Grape Arbor, vase, hat form 90.00
Heart w/Thumbprint, creamer 90.00
Heart w/Thumbprint, lamp, good pnt, scarce, 8" 450.00
Heart w/Thumbprint, sugar bowl, ind 95.00
Honeycomb, wine 65.00
Horse Medallion, bowl, gr stain, 7" 85.00
Intaglio, bowl, master berry; gold & decor, ftd, 9" 250.00
Intaglio, bowl, sauce; gold & decor 50.00
Intaglio, butter dish, gold & decor, scarce 300.00
Intaglio, compote, jelly; gold & decor 125.00
Intaglio, creamer, gold & decor 125.00
Intaglio, cruet, gold & decor 475.00
Intaglio, pitcher, water; gold & decor 395.00
Intaglio, shakers, gold & decor, pr 250.00
Intaglio, spooner, gold & decor 135.00
Intaglio, sugar bowl, w/lid, gold & decor 180.00
Intaglio, tumbler, gold & decor 95.00
Inverted Fan & Feather, bowl, master berry; gold & decor 275.00
Inverted Fan & Feather, bowl, sauce; gold & decor 75.00
Inverted Fan & Feather, butter dish, gold & decor 400.00
Inverted Fan & Feather, compote, jelly; gold & decor, rare 500.00
Inverted Fan & Feather, creamer, gold & decor 175.00
Inverted Fan & Feather, cruet, gold & decor, scarce, 6½" 1,100.00
Inverted Fan & Feather, pitcher, water; gold & decor 700.00
Inverted Fan & Feather, punch cup, gold & decor 250.00
Inverted Fan & Feather, shakers, gold & decor, pr 750.00
Inverted Fan & Feather, spooner, gold & decor 165.00
Inverted Fan & Feather, sugar bowl, w/lid, gold & decor 250.00
Inverted Fan & Feather, tumbler, gold & decor 115.00
Jackson (Alaska Variant), bowl, master berry; good gold, ftd 150.00
Jackson (Alaska Variant), bowl, sauce; good gold 50.00
Jackson (Alaska Variant), creamer, good gold 85.00
Jackson (Alaska Variant), pitcher, water; good gold 250.00
Jackson (Alaska Variant), pitcher, water; no decor 175.00
Jackson (Alaska Variant), shakers, good gold, pr 195.00
Jackson (Alaska Variant), tumbler, good gold 50.00
Louis XV, bowl, master berry; good gold 250.00
Louis XV, bowl, sauce; good gold, ftd 50.00
Louis XV, butter dish, good gold 250.00
Louis XV, creamer, good gold 85.00
Louis XV, pitcher, water; good gold 250.00
Louis XV, spooner, good gold 110.00
Louis XV, sugar bowl, w/lid, good gold 165.00
Louis XV, tumbler, good gold 65.00
Maple Leaf, bowl, master berry; gold & decor, scarce 350.00
Maple Leaf, bowl, sauce; gold & decor, scarce 50.00
Maple Leaf, butter dish, gold & decor 350.00
Maple Leaf, compote, jelly; gold & decor, rare 475.00
Maple Leaf, creamer, gold & decor 150.00
Maple Leaf, cruet, gold & decor, rare 3,000.00
Maple Leaf, pitcher, water; gold & decor 400.00
Maple Leaf, shakers, gold & decor, very rare, pr 1,000.00
Maple Leaf, spooner, gold & decor 175.00
Maple Leaf, sugar bowl, w/lid, gold & decor 250.00
Maple Leaf, tumbler, gold & decor 100.00
Panelled Poppy, lamp shade, nutmeg stain, scarce 900.00
Peacock & Urn, bowl, ice cream; nutmeg stain, sm 80.00
Peacock & Urn, bowl, ice cream; nutmeg stain, 10" 350.00
Punty Band, shakers, pr 175.00
Punty Band, spooner, floral decor 100.00
Punty Band, tumbler, floral decor, souvenir 65.00
Ribbed Drape, bowl, sauce; roses & gold 45.00
Ribbed Drape, butter dish, scalloped, roses & gold 400.00
Ribbed Drape, compote, jelly; roses & gold, rare 200.00
Ribbed Drape, creamer, roses & gold, scarce 180.00
Ribbed Drape, cruet, roses & gold, rare 700.00
Ribbed Drape, pitcher, water; roses & gold, rare 365.00
Ribbed Drape, shakers, roses & gold, rare, pr 400.00
Ribbed Drape, spooner, roses & gold 195.00
Ribbed Drape, sugar bowl, w/lid, roses & gold 250.00
Ribbed Drape, toothpick holder, roses & gold 475.00
Ribbed Drape, tumbler, roses & gold 75.00
Ribbed Thumbprint, wine, floral decor 80.00
Ring Band, bowl, master berry; roses & gold 200.00
Ring Band, bowl, sauce; roses & gold 50.00
Ring Band, butter dish, roses & gold 300.00
Ring Band, compote, jelly; roses & gold, scarce 195.00
Ring Band, creamer, roses & gold 125.00
Ring Band, cruet, roses & gold, scarce 500.00
Ring Band, cruet, roses decor, clear stopper 175.00
Ring Band, pitcher, roses & gold, 7½" 375.00
Ring Band, shakers, roses & gold, pr 155.00
Ring Band, spooner, roses & gold 125.00
Ring Band, syrup, roses & gold, scarce 475.00
Ring Band, table set, 4-pc 450.00
Ring Band, toothpick holder, roses & gold 155.00
Ring Band, tray, condiment; roses & gold 200.00
Singing Birds, mug, nutmeg stain 85.00
Tarentum's Victoria, bowl, master berry; gold & decor 200.00
Tarentum's Victoria, butter dish, gold & decor, rare 350.00
Tarentum's Victoria, celery vase, gold & decor, rare 300.00
Tarentum's Victoria, creamer, gold & decor, scarce 135.00
Tarentum's Victoria, pitcher, water; gold & decor, rare 375.00
Tarentum's Victoria, spooner, gold & decor 135.00
Tarentum's Victoria, sugar bowl, w/lid, gold & decor 175.00
Tarentum's Victoria, tumbler, gold & decor 75.00
Vermont, butter dish, bl decor 195.00
Vermont, toothpick holder, bl decor 175.00
Vermont, vase, floral decor, jeweled 125.00
Wide Band, bell, roses 195.00
Wild Bouquet, bowl, sauce; gold & decor 60.00
Wild Bouquet, butter dish, gold & decor, rare 750.00
Wild Bouquet, creamer, no gold 145.00
Wild Bouquet, cruet, gold & decor 995.00
Wild Bouquet, spooner, gold & decor 175.00
Wild Bouquet, tumbler, no decor 100.00
Winged Scroll, bowl, master berry; gold & decor, 11" L 250.00
Winged Scroll, bowl, sauce; good gold 50.00
Winged Scroll, butter dish, good gold 235.00
Winged Scroll, butter dish, no decor 175.00
Winged Scroll, celery vase, good gold, rare 400.00
Winged Scroll, cigarette jar, scarce 195.00
Winged Scroll, compote, ruffled, rare, 6¾x10¾" 495.00
Winged Scroll, hair receiver, good gold 135.00
Winged Scroll, pitcher, water; bulbous, good gold 400.00
Winged Scroll, shakers, bulbous, good gold, rare, pr 400.00
Winged Scroll, shakers, str sides, good gold, pr 300.00
Winged Scroll, sugar bowl, w/lid, good gold 175.00
Winged Scroll, syrup, good gold 450.00
Winged Scroll, tumbler, good gold 75.00

Cut Glass

The earliest documented evidence of commercial glass cutting in the United States was in 1810; the producers were Bakewell and Page of Pittsburgh. These first efforts resulted in simple patterns with only a moderate amount of cutting. By the middle of the century, glass cutters began experimenting with a thicker glass which enabled them to use deeper cuttings, though patterns remained much the same. This period is usually referred to as Rich Cut. Using three types of wheels — a flat edge, a mitered edge, and a convex edge — facets, miters, and depressions were combined to produce various designs. In the late 1870s, a curved miter was developed which greatly expanded design potential. Patterns became more elaborate, often covering the entire surface. The brilliant period of cut glass covered a span from about 1880 until 1915. Because of the pressure necessary to achieve the deeply cut patterns, only glass containing a high grade of metal could withstand the process. For this reason and the amount of handwork involved, cut glass has always been expensive. Bowls cut with pinwheels may be either foreign or of a newer vintage, beware! Identifiable patterns and signed pieces that are well cut and in excellent condition bring the higher prices on today's market. For more information we recommend *Evers' Standard Cut Glass Value Guide* (Collector Books). See also Dorflinger; Hawkes; Libbey; Tuthill; Val St. Lambert; other specific manufacturers.

Bonbon, Hiawatha Boat, Pitkins & Brooks, 9", from $50 to 60.00
Bonbon, Juno, JD Bergen, 7", from $80 to 95.00
Bonbon, Manhattan, TB Clark & Co, from $75 to 90.00
Bottle, scent; Prism, JD Bergen, 7", from $60 to 75.00
Bowl, American Beauty, Averbeck, 8", from $85 to 110.00
Bowl, berry; Florida, Higgins & Seiter, 9¼x13½", from $200 to ..225.00
Bowl, Daisy, Averbeck, 8", from $125 to 150.00
Bowl, Desdemona, TB Clark & Co, 9", from $200 to 225.00
Bowl, finger; Cut Star, Higgins & Seiter, from $20 to 25.00
Bowl, finger; Winola, TB Clark & Co, from $35 to 40.00
Bowl, Florence, JD Bergen, 5", from $125 to 150.00
Bowl, grapefruit; Topaz, Pitkins & Brooks, ftd, 7½", from $100 to ...125.00
Bowl, Magnolia, TB Clark & Co, 10", from $150 to 200.00
Bowl, punch; Bedford, Higgins & Seiter, 14", from $400 to 500.00
Bowl, punch; Belmont, ftd, Pitkins & Brooks, 14", from $1,000 to ..1,200.00
Bowl, punch; Corsair, JD Bergen, 14", from $400 to 450.00
Bowl, punch; Keystone, ftd, Pitkins & Brooks, 10", from $600 to .750.00
Bowl, punch; Rajah, ftd, Pitkins & Brooks, 10", from $600 to ...750.00
Box, jewel; Hiawatha, Pitkins & Brooks, from $150 to 200.00
Box, puff; Electra, Pitkins & Brooks, from $150 to 200.00
Box, puff; Teck, Pitkins & Brooks, 5¼", from $150 to 200.00
Butter dish, Orland, JD Bergen, from $250 to 300.00
Butter tub & plate, Ruby, Averbeck, 2-pc set, from $200 to 225.00
Candlestick, Albert, JD Bergen, 10", from $125 to 175.00
Carafe, George, Averbeck, qt, from $75 to 100.00
Carafe, Goldenrod, JD Bergen, qt, from $250 to 300.00
Carafe, Waverly, JD Bergen, qt, from $150 to 175.00
Carafe, Winfield, std grade, Pitkins & Brooks, globe sz, from $100 to ..125.00
Celery tray, Liberty, Averbeck, 11¼", from $150 to 175.00
Celery tray, Sharon, JD Bergen, 4¾x12½", from $225 to 275.00
Celery tray, Venice, Pitkins & Brooks, from $200 to 250.00
Comport, Enterprise, short std, JD Bergen, 8", from $150 to 200.00
Comport, Vienna, ftd, scalloped rim, Averbeck, from $250 to ...300.00
Coport, Huron, Pitkins & Brooks, from $100 to 125.00
Creamer, Glenwood, JD Bergen, from $40 to 50.00
Creamer & sugar bowl, Oriole, Pitkins & Brooks, from $75 to 85.00
Creamer & sugar bowl, Vienna, Averbeck, from $85 to 100.00
Cruet, Florida, Averbeck, 7½", from $85 to 100.00
Cruet, Oregon, JD Bergen, ½-pt, from $75 to 90.00
Cruet, Sunray Globe, std grade, Pitkins & Brooks, from $90 to .100.00
Cup, Garland, Pitkins & Brooks, from $25 to 30.00
Cup, Golf, JD Bergen, from $20 to 22.00
Cup, punch; Progress, JD Bergen, from $22 to 25.00
Cup, Winola, TB Clark & Co, from $20 to 22.00
Decanter, Aladdin, Pitkins & Brooks, from $200 to 250.00
Decanter, Ansonia, JD Bergen, 1-qt, from $225 to 250.00
Decanter, Florentine, Higgins & Seiter, from $175 to 200.00
Decanter, Savoy, JD Bergen, 1-qt, from $150 to 200.00
Decanter, Straw & Fan, w/hdl, TB Clark & Co, qt, from $125 to .150.00
Goblet, Radium, Averbeck, from $40 to 50.00
Goblet, Sunrise, Pitkins & Brooks, from $10 to 12.00
Humidor, Seaside, JD Bergen, holds 25 cigars, from $225 to 250.00
Ice tub, Arlington, w/drainer, Higgins & Seiter, 4¼x7", $150 to .200.00
Jar, horseradish; Renaissance, Higgins & Seiter, 5¼", from $40 to ..50.00
Jug, Arbutus, wide mouth, TB Clark & Co, pt, from $125 to 150.00
Jug, claret: Ivy, JD Bergen, 3-pt, from $250 to 300.00
Jug, Palmetto, TB Clark & Co, depending on sz, from $150 to .250.00
Knife rest, Hexagon, std grade, Pitkins & Brooks, 4", from $12 to .15.00
Ladle, Progress, JD Bergen, from $125 to 150.00

Lamp, Cane and Hobstar, onion dome, prisms, cylindrical column flaring to shaped base edge, flakes, early twentieth century, 29½", $3,500.00.

Lamp, Chrysanthemum, 32 prisms, electric, Pitkins & Brooks, 17", up to .1,500.00
Lamp, Premier, JD Bergen, 14½", from $550 to 750.00
Mustard & underplate, JD Bergen, from $125 to 150.00
Nappy, Canton, Averbeck, 8", from $110 to 150.00
Nappy, Clover, leaf shape, hdl, Higgins & Seiter, from $50 to 60.00
Nappy, Mars, Pitkins & Brooks, 5", from $50 to 65.00
Pickle dish, Marietta, Averbeck, 8", from $90 to 110.00
Pitcher, Colony, JD Bergen, 2-qt, from $350 to 400.00
Pitcher, Naples, Averbeck, 4-pt, 10½", from $225 to 250.00
Pitcher, tankard, Federal, JD Bergen, 2-qt, from $250 to 300.00
Plate, Boston, Averbeck, 7", from $60 to 70.00
Plate, Delaware, JD Bergen, 9" sq, from $250 to 300.00
Shaker, Henry VIII, TB Clark & Co, from $20 to 25.00
Spoon dish, London, ftd, Averbeck, 7½", from $150 to 200.00
Spoon holder, Wheeler, hdls, Hittins & Seiter, from $125 to 150.00
Spooner, Meadville, std grade, Pitkins & Brooks, 7½", from $75 to ...90.00
Spooner, Naples, Averbeck, from $125 to 150.00
Spooner, Vienna, Averbeck, from $90 to 100.00
Sugar bowl, Glenwood, JD Bergen, w/lid, from $65 to 75.00
Syrup, Oregon, JD Bergen, ½-pt, from $125 to 150.00
Tray, Electra, rectangular, Pitkins & Brooks, 11", from $350 to .400.00
Tray, Harvard, 12" dia 350.00
Tray, ice cream; Arabian, JD Bergen, 10x16", from $500 to 550.00
Tray, ice cream; Oak Leaf, Pitkins & Brooks, 13", from $450 to ...500.00
Tray, ice cream; Vienna, Averbeck, 14", from $300 to 350.00
Tumbler, Bedford, JD Bergen, from $22 to 25.00
Tumbler, Florentine, Higgins & Seiter, from $35 to 40.00
Tumbler, Golf, JD Bergen, from $30 to 35.00

Tumbler, Mars, Pitkins & Brooks, from $25 to 30.00
Tumbler, Roland, JD Bergen, from $22 to 25.00
Tumbler, Ruby, Averbeck, from $22 to 25.00
Tumbler, whiskey; Orient, JD Bergen, from $22 to 25.00
Vase, Arans, stick neck, Pitkins & Brooks, 14" from $250 to 300.00
Vase, Aurora Borealis, Pitkins & Brooks, 6½", from $175 to 200.00
Vase, Calumet, waisted, JD Bergen, 9", from $200 to 300.00
Vase, Daisy, slim std, ftd, Averbeck, 8", from $100 to 125.00
Vase, Dixon, JD Bergen, 8", from $150 to 200.00
Vase, Genoa, hdls, Averbeck, 12", from $400 to 500.00
Vase, Heroic, TB Clark & Co, from $100 to 125.00
Vase, Rialto, JD Bergen, 12", from $300 to 400.00
Vase, Rutland, ftd, JD Bergen, 8", from $115 to 200.00
Vase, Sheldon, JD Bergen, 10", from $200 to 300.00
Water set, Newport, JD Bergen, carafe+6 tumblers+tray, from $300 to .350.00
Water set, Ruth, Pitkins & Brooks, pitcher+6 tumblers+tray, $400 to ...450.00
Whiskey flagon, Venus, TB Clark & Co, from $225 to 250.00
Whiskey set, Electric, JD Bergen, decanter/6 whiskeys/tray, $400 to .500.00

Cut Velvet

Cut Velvet glassware was made during the late 1800s. It is characterized by the effect achieved through the execution of relief-molded patterns, often ribbing or diamond quilting, which allows its white inner casing to show through the outer layer.

Bowl, bride's; Dmn Quilt, amber/wht/bl, bamboo cutting/gold, Webb, 11" .900.00
Celery vase, Dmn Quilt, bl, box-pleated top, Mt WA, 6½" 700.00
Tumbler, Dmn Quilt, yel, sqd top, Mt WA, 3¾" 210.00
Vase, Dmn Quilt, bl, daisy-like design to base, att Mt WA, 9" ..385.00
Vase, Dmn Quilt, gr, dbl gourd, 8½" 250.00
Vase, Dmn Quilt, lt gold, dbl gourd, long neck, 13½" 625.00
Vase, Dmn Quilt, orange, flared/ruffled rim, str sides, 9" 650.00
Vase, Dmn Quilt, shaded pk, spherical w/ruffled top, Mt WA, 4" .225.00
Vase, Dmn Quilt, yel, ruffled, 7" 75.00
Vase, Dmn Quilt, yel, ruffled, 9" 125.00
Vase, Dmn Quilt, yel, stick form, appl camphor leaf/nut/stem hdl, 8" .110.00
Vase, Herringbone, bl, gourd shape, hdls, rigaree collar, 7½" 350.00
Vase, vertical threaded ribs, bl, bottle shape, 6" 90.00

Cybis

Boleslaw Cybis was a graduate of the Academy of Fine Arts in Warsaw, Poland, and was well recognized as a fine artist by the time he was commissioned by his government to paint murals in the Polish Pavilion's Hall of Honor at the 1939 World's Fair. Finding themselves stranded in America at the outbreak of WWII, the Cybises founded an artists' studio, first in Astoria, New York, and later in Trenton, New Jersey, where they made fine figurines and plaques with exacting artistry and craftsmanship entailing extensive handwork. The studio still operates today producing exquisite porcelains on a limited edition basis.

Betty, pk 185.00
Boy & girl on sled 275.00
Emily 150.00
Foal, dapple gray 275.00
Funny Face, #34, 9½" 200.00
Goldilocks 375.00
Great Horned Owl, pnt bsk, 17½" 300.00
Heidi 185.00
Lady Macbeth, #104, 13½" 425.00
Oceania the King's Steed, ltd ed 975.00

Othello, #314, 15", $1,000.00.

Peter Pan 575.00
Prince & Princess, 8¼", 7½", pr 200.00
Rebecca 375.00
Springtime 325.00
Sugar Plum carousel pony, ltd ed 885.00
Tinker Bell 525.00
Wendy, w/doll 450.00
Young Eskimo, #292, 9½" 125.00

Czechoslovakian Collectibles

Czechoslovakia came into being as a country in 1918. Located in the heart of Europe, it was a land with the natural resources necessary to support a glass industry that dated back to the mid-fourteenth century. The glass that was produced there has captured the attention of today's collectors, and for good reason. There are beautiful vases — cased, ruffled, applied with rigaree or silver overlay — fine enough to rival those of the best glasshouses. Czechoslovakian art glass baskets are quite as attractive as Victorian America's, and the elegant cut glass perfumes made in colors as well as crystal are unrivaled. There are also pressed glass perfumes, molded in lovely Deco shapes, of various types of art glass. Some are overlaid with gold filigree set with 'jewels.' Jewelry, lamps, porcelains, and fine art pottery are also included in the field.

More than seventy marks have been recorded, including those in the mold, ink stamped, acid etched, or on a small metal nameplate. The newer marks are incised, stamped 'Royal Dux Made in Czechoslovakia' (see Royal Dux), or printed on a paper label which reads 'Bohemian Glass Made in Czechoslovakia.' (Communist controlled from 1948, Czechoslovakia once again was made a free country in December 1989. Today it no longer exists; after 1993 it was divided to form two countries, the Czech Republic and the Slovak Republic.) For a more thorough study of the subject, we recommend *Made in Czechoslovakia* and *Made in Czechoslovakia, Book 2,* by our advisor, Ruth A. Forsythe; she is listed in the Directory under Ohio. Other fine books are *Czechoslovakian Glass & Collectibles*, Volumes I and II, by Dale and Diane Barta and Helen M. Rose; *Czechoslovakian Perfume Bottles and Boudoir Accessories* by Jacquelyne Y. Jones North, and *Czechoslovakian Pottery* by Bowers, Closser, and Ellis. In the listings that follow, when one dimension is given, it refers to height; decoration is enamel unless noted otherwise. See also Amphora; Erphila.

Candy Baskets

Blk w/silver mica, bl int, blk hdl, 8" 350.00
Gr, tangerine & yel mottle, cased, blk hdl & rim, 7" 250.00
Gr varicolored (lt), matching hdl, 8" 190.00
Gr varicolored w/red opaque o/l, gr hdl, 8½" 250.00
Pk varicolored, pk hdl, 8" 190.00
Red & gr mottle, ruffled rim, clear twisted thorn hdl, 6½" 240.00

Red & yel mottle, clear twisted thorn hdl, 7" 220.00
Red & yel mottle, ruffled rim, clear hdl w/str top, 8½" 125.00
Yel w/bl mottling at base, ruffled rim, blk braid hdl, 8" 250.00
Yel w/blk rim, clear arched hdl, 6½" 200.00

Cased Art Glass

Candlesticks, blk w/red flared rim, 3", pr 120.00
Mayonnaise, varicolored bls, knob finial, 5½" 175.00
Pitcher, orange w/mc exotic bird, blk trim & hdl, 11½" 285.00
Vase, bl/gr/blk mottle, stick neck, 8½" 75.00
Vase, cane appl on blk, red int, bulbous, ftd, 6" 200.00
Vase, gr w/appl gr ribbons (2) down trumpet neck, 5½" 85.00
Vase, mottled autumn colors, waisted, ftd, shaped rim, 7⅜" 125.00
Vase, Niagara Falls scene on yel ftd cylinder, 6¼" 75.00
Vase, varicolored w/gr aventurine, trumpet neck w/blk rim, 7" ..150.00
Vase, wht fan form w/red serpentine appl at waist, 6¾" 125.00
Vase, wht w/red opaque overlay, shouldered, can neck, 5½" 110.00
Vase, yel & wht mottle, trumpet form w/blk rim, 6¾" 130.00
Vase, yel w/brn mottling on lower third, shouldered, 6¼" 85.00
Vase, yel w/scalloped rim w/blk trim, slim w/flared ft, 8½" 75.00
Wine, silver bird on orange, clear stem, 3¾" 40.00

Cut Glass Perfume Bottles

Amber, wide shoulders, squat, amber stopper, 3¼" 110.00
Amethyst dome w/sq base, frosted nude stopper, 6⅝" 800.00
Bl w/stepped shoulders, ftd, bl prism stopper, 7½" 150.00
Blk opaque simple shouldered shape w/clear stopper, 4⅝" 165.00
Crystal, shouldered, crystal ring stopper, 6" 95.00
Crystal shouldered, crystal/frost flowers-in-vase stopper, 3⅜" 60.00
Crystal, shouldered, red stopper w/eng figure, 5½" 300.00
Crystal ball on bl ft (2-pc), bl frosted stopper, 5¾" 300.00
Crystal ball w/floral cutting, floral stopper, 5¼" 110.00
For purse, jeweled filigree, 2½" 250.00
Gr w/jeweled ornaments, gr stopper, 4¾" 350.00
Pk, bulbous, rectangular pk stopper, 3⅝" 135.00
Pk arched base w/frosted floral stopper, 7¾" 285.00
Pk frost w/emb figure, matching stopper, 4⅛" 400.00
Pk ftd base, w/clear prism stopper, 7¼" 275.00
Topaz, Art Deco, 5½" 185.00
Topaz arched shape w/frosted horseshoe-shape stopper, 6" 165.00
Vaseline, shouldered, simple matching stopper, 5⅝" 220.00

Lamps

Vanity, white enamel flowers on clear ball form base, brass top, punched floral design on shade, 12", $70.00. (Photo courtesy Barta and Rose)

Boudoir, beaded cylinder form, 7" 950.00
Desk, enameled base, acid-cut shade, 10" 475.00
Perfume, cut bl shade, 4" 350.00
Perfume, mc florals on mushroom shape, 6" 125.00
Shade, mottled autumn colors, cased, 7¼" 200.00
Table, basket form, crystal beads w/glass nuts & fruit, 10¾" ...1,100.00
Table, beads & fruit, 8¾" 750.00
Table, Deco dancer beside bubbly paperweight globe, 9" 800.00
Table, gr & oxblood stepped form, 9½" 200.00
Table, pnt church scene globe, pnt ft, 8¾" 500.00
Vanity, wht cased ball form w/orange rigaree, 4½"+shade 60.00

Mold-Blown and Pressed Bottles

Amethyst & crystal w/pnt daisies, atomizer 175.00
Amethyst w/gold at top, slim ft, flat rnd ft, atomizer, 7" 180.00
Cranberry opal hobnail, bulbous, wht opal stopper, 5½" 225.00
Crystal, orange/blk pnt bands w/geometrics, slim, atomizer, 7¾" ..125.00
Gr, appl serpentine, atomizer, 8" 375.00
Gr w/overall jewels, 2⅜" 200.00
Orange w/blk ft, blk stopper, cased, 6¼" 145.00
Orange w/blk pnt geometric decor, cased, bulbous, atomizer, 5" ..85.00
Topaz (tinted), jeweled lid, 2¼" 100.00

Opaque, Crystal, Colored Transparent Glass

Bowl, King Tut, bl & pk lustre, squat, 3½" 2,500.00
Candlesticks, pk w/gr appl decor, stick form, 8", pr 130.00
Cocktail shaker, violet-pk, flat top, 8¼" 95.00
Vase, bl varicolored ball form, 7¾" 200.00
Vase, blk w/orange spiral decor, cylindrical, 6½" 125.00
Vase, cobalt opaque, trumpet form, 7" 100.00
Vase, crystal w/red & blk o/l, flared rim, ftd, 8¼" 200.00
Vase, crystal w/red threading, ftd, flared rim, 8⅜" 200.00
Vase, dk bl cut to clear w/eng flowers, 10¼" 350.00
Vase, golden topaz w/orange o/l, fan form, 8" 200.00
Vase, pk opaque w/bl streaks, mottled red/bl ft, 9¼" 150.00
Vase, red/bl/yel/blk mottle, blk int, stick neck, 8⅛" 85.00

Pottery and Porcelain

Basket, flower w/leafy vine, blk hdl, 5" 50.00
Candlesticks, orange w/blk & wht bands, 10", pr 65.00
Creamer, moose, open mouth, shaded brown, blk trim, 4" 50.00
Creamer, parrot figural, mc, 4½" 50.00
Figurine, goose, wht w/gold trim, glossy, 5¼" 45.00
Flower arranger, bird on stump, 5¼" 45.00
Lamp, yel w/pnt Deco base, 10" 385.00
Planter, stork figural, pearlescent wht & blk, 7½" 65.00
Toby mug, man w/wht hair, mc clothes, lav hdl/rim, 4" 50.00
Vase, blk w/beige 'crackle,' pierced hdls, 10" 105.00
Vase, blk w/mottled orange lustre stripes & ear hdls, 9½" 95.00
Vase, floral, mc on dk brn, angle hdls, 7" 55.00
Vase, scarlet w/fruit & flowers, ftd, 8½" 250.00
Vase, wedge-cut design w/flared base, orange & blk w/bl ring, 7¾" .95.00
Vase, yel lustre, fluted rim w/blk trim, hdls, 10" 50.00
Wall pocket, bird perched beside house on limb, mc, 5" 65.00

D'Argental

D'Argental cameo glass was produced in France from the 1870s until about 1920 in the Art Nouveau style. Browns and tans were favored colors used to complement floral and scenic designs developed through acid cuttings. Our advisor for this category is Don Williams; he is listed in the Directory under Missouri.

Cameo

Vase, maple leaves and seed pods on branches, cranberry to black overlay on butterscotch to red, Croix de Lorraine mark, 12", $1,500.00.

Vase, berries/vines, brn on citron, ovoid w/sm rim, 8" **900.00**
Vase, castle scene, brn/tan on gold, 10½x4½" **1,500.00**
Vase, lg palm trees/castle, brn on tan, shouldered, 8" **1,100.00**
Vase, morning glories/buds, amber/gr on citron, stick, 10½" **600.00**
Vase, orchids, burgundy on citron, 8" **475.00**
Vase, riverside/mtn landscape, amber/burgundy, ovoid, 8" **865.00**
Vase, woodland scene, forest gr to lime frost, 12" **2,200.00**

Daum Nancy

Daum was an important producer of French cameo glass, operating from the late 1800s until after the turn of the century. They used various techniques — acid cutting, wheel engraving, and handwork — to create beautiful scenic designs and nature subjects in the Art Nouveau manner. Virtually all examples are signed. Daum is still in production, producing many figural items. Our advisor for this category is Don Williams; he is listed in the Directory under Missouri.

Cameo

Bottle, scent; banner/flowers, amethyst on frost w/gold, 8¼" .**1,800.00**
Bottle, scent; floral on shaded amber w/pnt & gold trim, 5½" ..**1,450.00**
Bowl, columbines, cut/pnt on citron to tortoise shell, 4x6" **1,600.00**
Bowl, thistle blossoms, yel opal/cranberry w/gold, 4-fold rim, 3x5" .**900.00**
Box, cherries/leaves, gr/yel on burgundy to yel, 3½x5¾" **2,000.00**
Jar, dresser; thistles/vines, red w/gold on amethyst, stopper, 3" ..**1,350.00**
Lamp, base & ball shade w/riverside scene, gr/blk/turq, 19" ..**12,650.00**
Lamp, base & shade w/leafy trees, purple/gr/wht, bronze base, 14" .**5,175.00**
Lamp base, bell flowers, rust/brn on orange mottle, slim, 24" ..**1,350.00**
Lamp base, magnolia branches, orange/brn on gold mottle, 10" ..**900.00**
Rose bowl, lake scene, blk on amber, int red sunset, X mk, 4" ..**1,565.00**
Salt cellar, church/lake, cut/pnt on texture w/gilt 1¾" dia **1,400.00**
Tray, mistletoe branches, gr to frost w/gold, clover form, 5½" **850.00**
Tumbler, landscape, blk to brn to lt brn, 3½x2" **700.00**
Tumbler, sweet peas, purple/gr on orange/frost, bbl shape **1,600.00**
Vase, autumn branches, mc on orange/yel frost, ftd, 11½" **2,250.00**
Vase, autumn leaves fr landscape on gray to yel, 16" **3,700.00**
Vase, autumn scene, gold mottle & red-amber, ovoid, 14" **4,600.00**
Vase, berries/leaves, dk plum on gray w/lt plum, slender, 24" ..**3,350.00**
Vase, berries/leaves, orange & gr on yel/wht/orange, slim, 15" .**2,600.00**
Vase, berries/leaves, purple/red-orange on gr/orange/yel, 6" **1,650.00**
Vase, blackbirds/winter trees, cut/pnt on bl-gray frost, 6¾" **3,500.00**
Vase, boats/mtn lake/sunset, brn on orange mottle, ftd, 9x9½" .**4,000.00**
Vase, boats/water, brn to orange, 6x4¼" **1,950.00**
Vase, bud; apple blossoms/butterfly, orange/gr on frost w/gold, 4" ..**975.00**
Vase, crocus, lav/gr on gray martele, 16" **6,500.00**
Vase, daisies, yel/gr on mottled yel/pk opal, 7¾" **3,250.00**
Vase, dandelions, gr on martele, cylindrical, 9¾" **3,000.00**
Vase, fleur-de-lis, cut/pnt w/gold, gr on frost, ftd, 6" **1,000.00**
Vase, floral, brns on yel frost, 8½" **1,600.00**
Vase, floral, cut/pnt, purple to frost w/gold, 4-sided, 5" **1,700.00**
Vase, floral, cut/pnt on gray w/mc mottle, sq, 4¾" **1,500.00**
Vase, floral, gr on hammered pk/gr, ftd, 11½" **4,000.00**
Vase, floral, gr on wine, martele base/rim w/fp, 3½" **2,000.00**
Vase, floral, plum on yel martele, fp, bbl shape, 5¾" **2,500.00**
Vase, floral, ruby on lt gr, lobed form, 7" **1,950.00**
Vase, floral, yel on yel/brn mottled frost, 4½" **1,000.00**
Vase, floral/wheat stalks, yel/gr on tan mottle, ftd, 19¾" **4,500.00**
Vase, fuchsia, cut/pnt, red/gr on purple to frost w/gold, 5" **2,000.00**
Vase, iris, gr on clear w/gold, sqd cylinder, 5" **800.00**
Vase, iris, red/yel/gr on gray/yel/red mottle, 21" **4,700.00**
Vase, iris/foliage, cut/pnt, yel/gr/brn on frost, 4⅞" **1,500.00**
Vase, irises/dragonfly on gr mottle, gold outlines, 13¾" **4,500.00**
Vase, landscape, dk gr on orange/yel mottle, bulbous, 7" **4,000.00**
Vase, leaves, wht mottle on brn mottle, cylindrical, 17½" **1,800.00**
Vase, leaves/briars, cut/pnt on yel mottle, conical, 6" **850.00**
Vase, leaves/stems, brn on yel/frost, ftd, 8" **1,100.00**
Vase, mistletoe, cut/pnt w/gold on bl frost, 3½" **600.00**
Vase, orchids/foliage, lemon yel/gr on frost, tubular, 5¾" **1,600.00**
Vase, poppies/butterfly, cut/pnt on emerald gr, 3½" **800.00**
Vase, roses, wht/pk/clear w/gr/rose etching, 13½" **6,500.00**
Vase, seed pods/leaves, red/brn on gr-yel mottle, rectangular, 4x6" ..**1,950.00**
Vase, ships in harbor, blk/dk bl/red/gr/yel, stick neck, 16½" ...**5,000.00**
Vase, spring scene, cut/pnt, pillow form, mini, 1½" **1,800.00**
Vase, sunflowers, yel/gr on pk/yel opal mottle, bbl shape, 4¾" ..**1,750.00**
Vase, tobacco flowers, dk red on yel/red martele, ftd, 8½" **4,000.00**
Vase, tobacco flowers, orange & blk on orange to yel, ftd, 12" ..**4,500.00**
Vase, trees, dk brn on orange/yel mottle, 11½x4¼" **5,500.00**
Vase, trees/lake, cut/pnt on gray/blk/wht, 6" **1,500.00**
Vase, trees/lake, cut/pnt on mottled butterscotch/frost, 14¾" .**4,025.00**
Vase, violets, cut/pnt, violet/gr on purple frost w/gold, 1½x2¼" ..**1,800.00**
Vase, violets, cut/pnt on frost to violet, cylindrical, 4¾x2⅛" .**2,000.00**
Vase, violets, cut/pnt on gr/purple/wht mottle, 5" **2,100.00**
Vase, violets, textured amethyst w/gold on clear, 7" **2,200.00**
Vase, wisteria, purple on purple/frost, slim, 13" **1,200.00**
Vase, woodland scene, brn/gr on frost, slim, 14" **6,000.00**

Enameled Glass

Bottle, scent; daisies etched on red w/gold, silver mts, 5" **1,000.00**
Bottle, scent; floral, mc on textured clear, ornate SP lid, 6" **800.00**
Cruet, etched floral/gold trim, bulbous/ribs, X-cut stopper, 5" ..**1,200.00**
Dish, poppies, gr on gray w/yel, gold trim, ftd, 8" L **1,120.00**
Pin tray, swallow in flight on gray satin w/gilt, 4¾" **650.00**
Pitcher, hops, blk/gold on fiery yel-amber, 3" **2,200.00**
Vase, autumn foliage on yel, swirled ftd baluster, 13" **3,500.00**
Vase, autumnal riverscape, cylindrical, 18¾" **7,750.00**
Vase, fruit, burgundy on mottled purple to yel, pinched, 4" **1,200.00**
Vase, mistletoe on textured rose w/gold, 4¾" **800.00**
Vase, snowy woods, orange sky, flat-sided face, ftd, 5" **1,850.00**
Vase, snowy woods, orange sky, shouldered, 2½" **1,150.00**

Miscellaneous

Bowl, yel, etched ice crystal panels, 3¾x8" **500.00**
Plaque, Ladanse (lady in flowing gown), pate de verre, 11" L **785.00**
Salt cellar, internal streaks of amber/orange/purple, 3" dia **225.00**
Vase, amber/yel mottle, pillow form w/rectangle rim, 4½x7" **250.00**
Vase, bl/purple/gr mottle, spreading sq section, 25½" **1,950.00**
Vase, mottled amber to orange, Marjorelle wrought-iron fr, 12½" ..**1,600.00**
Vase, red/yel/bl/gr mottle, 4-sided slim form, 19½" **1,000.00**

De Vez

De Vez was a type of acid-cut French cameo glass produced by Cristallerie de Pantin in Paris around the turn of the century. Our advisor for this category is Don Williams; he is listed in the Directory under Missouri.

Cameo

Box, sailing ships/floral, bl-gr on golden yel, 3½x5½" 1,100.00
Vase, cottages/mother/child/trees on maroon/amber, 6", EX ...1,200.00
Vase, floral, purple to frost, bulbous, 14x6¼" 865.00
Vase, harbor scene, gr/yel on opal, 7" 1,300.00
Vase, heron/branch/river, wine/dk gr on bl-gray, cylindrical, 10" .1,750.00
Vase, lake scene, bl/yel on frost, 10½" 1,400.00
Vase, trees/villages/mtns, amber/gr/bl on frost, 10" 1,400.00

De Vilbiss

Perfume bottles, atomizers, and dresser accessories marketed by the De Vilbiss Company are appreciated by collectors today for the various types of lovely glassware used in their manufacture as well as for their pleasing shapes. Various companies provided the glass, while De Vilbiss made only the metal tops. They marketed their merchandise not only here but in Paris, England, Canada, and Havana as well. Their marks were acid stamped, ink stamped, in gold script, molded in, or on paper labels. One is no more significant than another. Our advisor for this category is Randy Monsen; he is listed in the Directory under Virginia.

Atomizer, bird & floral on gold, blk finial, mk, 10" 770.00
Atomizer, cranberry w/gold etched/enameled leaves, rpl bulb, 7" .300.00
Atomizer, floral on frost, glass finial, orig bulb, label, 4⅞" 110.00
Atomizer, gr enamel, orig bulb, mk, 6⅜" 100.00
Atomizer, lt bl & gold on crystal, baluster, orig bulb/net, 6¾" ...300.00
Atomizer, penguin, porc, made by Lenox, sprayer in nose, 4⅜" .175.00
Atomizer, pk & gold on crystal baluster, unmk, rpl bulb/tassel, 6¾" ..120.00
Atomizer, porc pk w/draped decor, w/bulb & lid, mk/Lenox, 4¾" 185.00
Atomizer, rose pk, elongated ovoid, rnd ped, orig bulb, unmk, 6¾" ...110.00
Atomizer, tomato red enamel, orig bulb/net, 6⅜" 110.00
Atomizer, yel ovoid w/rnd ped, orig ball, mk, 6¾" 100.00
Atomizer & bottle, allover gold w/orange & blk, dauber/ball, 7", pr ..1,300.00
Atomizer & bottle, gold rings on gr, bulb & dauber, 6⅝", pr, MIB 285.00
Bottle, gold decor on rvpt orange, orig bulb/net, mk, 5½" 300.00
Bottle, lt bl & gold on crystal, glass dropper, 6¼" 250.00
Dresser set, allover gold w/mc flowers, 5 pcs on 10¼x7" tray .1,045.00
Lamp, perfume; fairy & cat among rooftops, glass & metal, 7¼" ..467.50

Decanters

Ceramic whiskey decanters were brought into prominence in 1955 by the James Beam Distilling Company. Few other companies besides Beam produced these decanters during the next ten years or so; however, other companies did eventually follow suit. At its peak in 1975, at least twenty prominent companies and several on a lesser scale made these decanters. Beam stopped making decanters in mid-1992. Now only a couple of companies are still producing these collectibles.

Liquor dealers have told collectors for years that ceramic decanters are not as valuable, and in some cases worthless, if emptied or if the federal tax stamp has been broken. Nothing is further from the truth. Following are but a few of many reasons you should consider emptying ceramic decanters:

1) If the thin glaze on the inside ever cracks (and it does in a small percentage of decanters), the contents will push through to the outside. It is then referred to as a 'leaker' and worth a fraction of its original value.

2) A large number of decanters left full in one area of your house poses a fire hazard.

3) A burglar, after stealing jewelry and electronics, may make off with some of your decanters just to enjoy the contents. If they are empty, chances are they will not be bothered.

4) It is illegal in most states for collectors to sell a full decanter without a liquor license.

Unlike years ago, few collectors now collect all types of decanters. Most now specialize. For example, they may collect trains, cars, owls, Indians, clowns, or any number of different things that have been depicted on or as a decanter. They are finding exceptional quality available at reasonable prices, especially when compared with many other types of collectibles.

We have tried to list those brands that are the most popular with collectors. Likewise, individual decanters listed are the ones (or representative of the ones) most commonly found. The following listing is but a small fraction of the thousands of decanters that have been produced.

These decanters come from all over the world. While Jim Beam owned its own china factory in the U.S., some of the others have been imported from Mexico, Taiwan, Japan, and elsewhere. They vary in size from miniatures (approximately two ounces) to gallons. Values range from a few dollars to more than $3,000.00 per decanter.

Most collectors and dealers define a 'mint' decanter as one with no chips, no cracks, and label intact. A missing federal tax stamp or lack of contents have no bearing on value. All values are given for 'mint' decanters. A 'mini' behind a listing indicates a miniature. All others are fifth or 750 ml unless noted otherwise. Our advisor for this category is Roy Willis; he is listed in the Directory under Kentucky.

Aesthetic Specialties (ASI)

Car, Stanley 1909, blk or gr 65.00
Car, Stanley 1911, blk 75.00
Kentucky Derby 30.00

Ballantine

Fisherman 18.00
Gold Bag 25.00
Knight 10.00

Beam

Statue of Liberty, 1975, 12½", $20.00.

Casino Series, Barney's Slot Machine 25.00
Casino Series, Binion's Horseshoe 10.00
Casino Series, Harold's Club Pinwheel 30.00

Centennial Series, Civil War, North 29.00
Centennial Series, Civil War, South 45.00
Centennial Series, Edison Light Bulb 20.00
Centennial Series, Reno 6.00
Centennial Series, San Diego 5.00
Executive Series, 1958, Gray Cherub 125.00
Executive Series, 1959, Tavern Scene 40.00
Executive Series, 1973, Phoenician 12.00
Executive Series, 1974, Twin Cherubs 18.00
Executive Series, 1987, Twin Doves 18.00
Executive Series, 1988, Holiday Carolers 50.00
Foreign Series, Australia Hobo (Swagman) 20.00
Foreign Series, Australia Magpies 18.00
Foreign Series, Germany, 1970 ....10.00
Foreign Series, Italy, Boys Town 9.00
Foreign Series, Seoul, Korea 20.00
Foreign Series, Thailand 6.00
Organization Series, Ducks Unlimited #11 ....65.00
Organization Series, Ducks Unlimited #12 ....50.00
Organization Series, Ducks Unlimited #13 ....39.00
Organization Series, Ducks Unlimited #14 ....45.00
Organization Series, Ducks Unlimited #15 ....90.00
Organization Series, Homebuilders 25.00
Organization Series, LVNH Owl 18.00
Organization Series, Marine Devil Dog 40.00
Organization Series, Pearl Harbor, 1976 ....12.00
Organization Series, Shrine, Moila w/Camel 19.00
Organization Series, Shrine, Moila w/Sword 22.00
Organization Series, Telephone #1, Wall 25.00
Organization Series, Telephone #3, French Cradle 22.00
Organization Series, Telephone #5, Pay Phone 50.00
People Series, John Henry 35.00
People Series, King Kamehameha 18.00
People Series, Leprechaun 20.00
Political Series, 1968 Clown, Republican or Democrat 12.00
Political Series, 1972 on Football, Republican or Democrat 15.00
Regal China Series, AC Spark Plug 38.00
Regal China Series, Black Canasta, 1957 ....15.00
Regal China Series, Canteen 20.00
Regal China Series, Coffee Mill 15.00
Regal China Series, Franklin Mint 10.00
Regal China Series, Grand Canyon 8.00
Regal China Series, Jug, 1978, brn or oatmeal 6.00
Regal China Series, King Kong 20.00
Regal China Series, London Bridge 6.00
Regal China Series, New York World's Fair, 1964 ....15.00
Regal China Series, Pony Express 10.00
Regal China Series, Redwood 6.00
Regal China Series, Tombstone 10.00
Regal China Series, Yosemite 5.00
Wheel Series, Bass Boat 38.00
Wheel Series, Chevy '57 Belair Hot Rod 110.00
Wheel Series, Corvette, 1968, bl 65.00
Wheel Series, Corvette, 1968, maroon 60.00
Wheel Series, Dodge Challenger, 1970 Hot Rod 60.00
Wheel Series, Dump Truck, Gravel 45.00
Wheel Series, Ford, 1913 Model T, gr or blk 50.00
Wheel Series, Ford, 1929 Phaeton 70.00
Wheel Series, Mercedes, 197r, red 55.00
Wheel Series, Space Shuttle 65.00
Wheel Series, Stutz Bearcat, yel or gray 50.00
Wheel Series, Thomas Flyer, bl or ivory 65.00
Wheel Series, 1934 Fire Chief Car 80.00
Wheel Series, 1956 Thunderbird, blk or gray 100.00

Brooks

American Legion, Hawaii 15.00
Bear, Golden 8.00
Bowler 15.00
Cable Car 6.00
Cannon 9.00
Charolais Bull 15.00
Clown w/Accordion 29.00
Dollar, Silver 9.00
Elephant, Big Bertha 20.00
Greensboro Open, 1972 ....28.00
Hog, Razorback, 1969 ....22.00
Jester 10.00
Liquor Square 7.00
Ontario Racer #10 ....35.00
West Virginia Mountain Lady 22.00
West Virginia Mountain Man 65.00

Double Springs

Cord, 1937 ....35.00
Owl, brn or red 15.00
Peasant, boy or girl 5.00
Tiger on Ball 20.00

Famous Firsts

Hurdy Gurdy 18.00
Phonograph 45.00
Renault Racer #3A 65.00
Riverboat, Robert E Lee 65.00
Telephone, Floral 25.00
Telephone, French 40.00
Telephone, Johnny Reb 35.00

Hoffman

Aesop's Fables, 6 different, ea 25.00
Bird, Turkey, 1980 ....35.00
Dogs, mini, 1978, 6 different, ea 30.00
Dogs, mini, 1981, 6 different, ea 22.00
Generation Gap Pair, mini 15.00
Indy 500 Commemorative, 1972 ....30.00
Indy 500 Commemorative, 1973 ....50.00
Mr Lucky Series, Mr Cobbler 29.00
Mr Lucky Series, Mr Cobbler, mini 15.00
Mr Lucky Series, Mr Doctor 38.00
Mr Lucky Series, Mr Doctor, mini 18.00
Mr Lucky Series, Mr Sandman 25.00
Mr Lucky Series, Mr Sandman, mini 12.00
Russell, CM, Series, Red River Breed 45.00
Russell, CM, Series, Red River Breed, mini 15.00
Wildlife Series, Falcon & Rabbit 65.00
Wildlife Series, Falcon & Rabbit, mini 15.00
Wildlife Series, Owl & Chipmunk 45.00
Wildlife Series, Owl & Chipmunk, mini 15.00

Kontinental

Gandy Dancer 25.00
Homesteader 30.00
Innkeeper 30.00
Medicine Man 50.00

Pharmacist 35.00
Prospector 40.00
Prospector, mini 20.00
Saddle Maker 35.00
Saddle Maker, mini 20.00

Lionstone

Annie Christmas 20.00
Belly Robber 20.00
Betsy Ross 25.00
Blacksmith 29.00
Buccaneer 25.00
Calamity Jane 25.00
Dancehall Girl 50.00
Engineer, Railroad 29.00
Falcon 25.00
Gambler 20.00
Gambler, mini 15.00
Jesse James 22.00
Lonely Luke 25.00
Lonely Luke, mini 18.00
Lucky Buck 25.00
Lucky Buck, mini 18.00
Molly Brown 20.00
Mountain Man 22.00
Paul Revere 30.00
Quail 25.00
Roadrunner 25.00
Roadrunner, mini 15.00
Sheriff 22.00
Sheriff, mini 15.00
Sodbuster 20.00
Stage Driver 25.00
Tinker 25.00
Vigilante 20.00
Woodhawk 25.00

McCormick

Bicentennial Series, Ben Franklin 25.00
Bicentennial Series, Ben Franklin, mini 18.00
Bicentennial Series, John Hancock 25.00
Bicentennial Series, John Hancock, mini 18.00
Bicentennial Series, Thomas Jefferson 25.00
Bicentennial Series, Thomas Jefferson, mini 18.00
Caio Baby 25.00
Carver, George Washington 30.00
Edison, Thomas 25.00
Elvis, Designer I, 750 ml 175.00
Elvis, Designer II, 750 ml 195.00
Elvis, Designer III, 750 ml 250.00
Elvis, Silver Anniversary, 1980, 750 ml 175.00
Ewing, JR 50.00
Gunfighters, 8 different, ea 35.00
Gunfighters, 8 different, mini, ea 25.00
Houston, Sam 35.00
Lobsterman 30.00
Missouri, China 10.00
Missouri, Glass 7.00
Packard, 1937, blk or cream 50.00
Pocahontas 90.00
Shrine, Midian 12.00
Strowger Telephone 45.00

Thelma Lu 35.00
Thelma Lu, mini 18.00
Twain, Mark 30.00

Old Bardstown

Foster Brooks 20.00
Surface Miner 25.00
Tiger 35.00

Old Commonwealth

Coal Miner #3, w/Lump of Coal 40.00
Coal Miner #3, w/Lump of Coal, mini 20.00
Coal Miner #5, Coal Shooter 30.00
Coal Miner #5, Coal Shooter, mini 20.00
Fireman, Volunteer #5 ....75.00
Fireman, Volunteer #5, mini 30.00
Fireman, Volunteer #6 ....75.00
Fireman, Volunteer #6, mini 30.00
Horses of Ireland 30.00
Irish Lore 25.00
Lumberjack 30.00
Oktoberfest 45.00

Old Fitzgerald

Old Ironsides 5.00
Pheasant Rising 7.00
Ram, Bighorn 7.00
Texas 'Hook'em Horns' 20.00
Tree of Life 7.00
Venetian 4.00

Old Mr. Boston

Anthony Wayne 10.00
Molly Pitcher 8.00
Nathan Hale 10.00
Race Car #9, red or yel 48.00

Ski Country

Antelope, Pronghorn 60.00
Basset Hound 55.00
Basset Hound, mini 35.00
Buffalo Stampede 50.00
Buffalo Stampede, mini 20.00
Caveman 28.00
Caveman, mini 18.00
Chicadees 70.00
Chicadees, mini 35.00
Condor 50.00
Condor, mini 30.00
Ducks Unlimited, Bufflehead 58.00
Ducks Unlimited, Bufflehead, mini 35.00
Ducks Unlimited, Oldsquaw 65.00
Ducks Unlimited, Oldsquaw, mini 35.00
Eagle, Easter Seals 60.00
Eagle, Easter Seals, mini 30.00
Falcon, Gyrafalcon 75.00
Falcon, Gyrafalcon, mini 30.00
Falcon, Peregrine 85.00
Falcon, Peregrine, gal 300.00

Falcon, Peregrine, mini 20.00
Fox Family 65.00
Fox Family, mini 40.00
Hawk Eagle 150.00
Hawk Eagle, mini 75.00
Indian, Ceremonial Dancers, #1, Eagle 200.00
Indian, Ceremonial Dancers, #1, Eagle, mini 35.00
Indian, Ceremonial Dancers, #2, Buffalo 180.00
Indian, Ceremonial Dancers, #2, Buffalo, mini 40.00
Kangaroo 35.00
Kangaroo, mini 25.00
Labrador w/Duck 125.00
Labrador w/Duck, mini 40.00
Meadowlark 60.00
Meadowlark, mini 30.00
Owl, Horned 85.00
Owl, Horned, mini 85.00
Peacock 100.00
Peacock, mini 60.00
Penguin Family 60.00
Penguin Family, mini 30.00
Polar Bear 60.00
Polar Bear, mini 30.00
Raccoon 50.00
Raccoon, mini 35.00
Ringmaster 35.00
Ringmaster, mini 25.00
Swan, Black 50.00
Swan, Black, mini 45.00
Woodpecker, Gila 70.00
Woodpecker, Gila, mini 35.00

Wild Turkey

Crystal, Baccarat 225.00
Crystal, Wedgwood 225.00
Flask, silver, plastic-covered 10.00
Flask, stainless steel, leather-covered 20.00
Mack Truck 28.00
Series I, #1, 1971 ....200.00
Series I, #2 ....150.00
Series I, #3 ....65.00
Series I, #4 ....65.00
Series I, #5 ....30.00
Series I, #6 ....30.00
Series I, #7 ....30.00
Series I, #8 ....45.00
Series II, Lore #1 ....25.00
Series II, Lore #2 ....38.00
Series II, Lore #3 ....45.00
Series II, Lore #4 ....50.00
Series III, #7, Turkey & Red Fox, mini 50.00

Decoys

American colonists learned the craft of decoy making from the Indians who used them to lure birds out of the sky as an important food source. Early models were carved from wood such as pine, cedar, balsa, etc., and a few were made of canvas or papier-mache. There are two basic types of decoys: water floaters and shorebirds (also called 'stick-ups'). Within each type are many different species, ducks being the most plentiful since they migrated along all four of America's great waterways. Market hunting became big business around 1880, resulting in large-scale commercial production of decoys which continued until about 1910 when such hunting was outlawed by the Migratory Bird Treaty.

Today decoys are one of the most collectible types of American folk art. The most valuable are those carved by such artists as Laing, Crowell, Ward, and Wheeler, to name only a few. Each area, such as Massachusetts, Connecticut, Maine, the Illinois River, and the Delaware River, produces decoys with distinctive regional characteristics. Examples of commercial decoys produced by well-known factories — among them Mason, Stevens, and Dodge — are also prized by collectors. Though mass produced, these nevertheless required a certain amount of hand carving and decorating. Well-carved examples, especially those of rare species, are appreciating rapidly, and those with original paint are more desirable. In the listings that follow, all decoys are solid-bodied unless noted hollow.

Key:

CG — Challenge Grade	OWP — original working paint
DG — Detroit Grade	PG — Premier Grade
MDF — Mason's Decoy Factory	SG — Standard Grad
OP — original paint	WDF — Wildfowler Decoy Factory
ORP — old repaint	WOP — worn original paint

Canada goose, hollow carved, Ward Brothers, Crisfield, MD, signed by Klem Ward, ca 1931, original paint, old repairs, $2,250.00.

Back Bay Canvasback, MSF, factory rpl eyes, mk WUS, EX OWP .290.00
Black Duck, D Cigar Daisey, glass eyes, cedar, ca 1950s, EX OP ...835.00
Black Duck, Hickman, hollow, pnt tack eyes, 3-pc, ca 1890, WOP .340.00
Black Duck, Ken Anger, owner's name & swing keel on bottom, NM OP .365.00
Black Duck, low head, Tom Chambers, hollow, ca 1905, OWP .515.00
Black Duck, MDF, CG, ca 1910, EX OP 750.00
Black Duck, MDF, DG, glass eyes, ca 1900s, VG OP 340.00
Black Duck, MDF, SG, EX OP 415.00
Bluewing drake & hen, MDF, pnt eyes, EX OP, pr 2,000.00
Bluebill drake, George Peterson Decoy Factory, SG, WOP 240.00
Bluebill drake, Gus Moak, hollow cvd, rpt, prof rpr, 1920s 400.00
Bluebill drake, Tom Collyer, cedar, glass eye, w/weight, sgn, NM ..200.00
Canada Goose, Bradford Salmon, OWP, G 700.00
Canada Goose, Herters, balsa, unmk, EX OP 215.00
Canada Goose, RM Mitchell, sgn, dtd 1969, 25x9½", NM OP .465.00
Canada Goose, RM Mitchell, ½-sz, sgn, mid-1970s, NM+ 400.00
Canvasback drake, MDF, PG, detailed, special order, NM rstr ...315.00
Canvasback drake, MDF, PG, glass eyes, 19½" L 400.00
Canvasback drake, MDF, SG, lt rpr to neck o/w EX OP 380.00
Canvasback drake, MDF, SG, pnt eye, missing weight o/w NM OP ..300.00
Canvasback drake, Morse, juniper, battery-style, 18x10½", NM ..315.00
Canvasback drake, Paul Gibson, EX OP 290.00
Canvasback drake, Ralph Malpage, detailed feathering, NM OP, EX ..150.00
Canvasback hen, MDF, Seneca Model, hollow, 2-pc, WOP, VG ..350.00
Canvasback hen, RM Mitchell, sgn, dtd 1960, NM OP 465.00
Goldeneye, MDF, CG, lt neck filler, VG OP 345.00
Greenwing Teal drake, MDF, 4th Grade, pnt eyes, rstr 290.00

Greenwing Teal drake, WDF, dtd 1939, NM+ OP 265.00
Heron, Grayson Chesser, bill reglued, 1970s, WOP 350.00
Mallard drake, MDF, CG, snakey head, ca 1905, NM OP 585.00
Mallard drake, MDF, PG, glass eyes, ca 1900, WOP 520.00
Mallard drake, MDF, SG, detailed feathers, glass eyes, EX OP ...275.00
Mallard drake, MDF, SG, glass eyes, VG OP 625.00
Mallard drake, Otto Garren, crack in neck, OWP 160.00
Mallard drake, RM Mitchell, sgn, EX OP 275.00
Mallard hen, Carl Koch, sm dents, EX OP 50.00
Mallard hen, Frank Schmidt, EX details, late '60s, NM 600.00
Merganser drake, MDF, PG, H Haertel rstr in 1966 ....820.00
Old Squaw, Bob White, hollow, mk lead keel w/logo, M, pr 700.00
Penguin, Charles Hart, EX OP, 7¼" 725.00
Pintail drake, Doug Jester, sm dents, EX OP 800.00
Pintail drake, Pete Peterson, OWP, EX 215.00
Pintail drake, Phineas Reeves, hollow, branded HL, ORP, 1870s .810.00
Pintail drake, Ward Bros, stamped, sgn, dtd 1963, OP, NM 900.00
Red-Breasted Merganser, Hudson, heartwood, ca 1940s, VG OP .480.00
Redhead drake, Chris Smith, hollow, OWP 200.00
Redhead Drake, MDF, PG, hollow, rstr, EX OP 390.00
Redhead drake, T Chambers, parrot head, hollow, ca 1925, EX OP ..1,250.00
Ruddy Duck, GW Stevens, trn head, eyes missing, WOP 310.00
Ruddy hen, D Cigar Daisey, EX detail, NM+ OP 295.00
Swan, WDF, sgn, ca 1930-40, EX OP 375.00
White-Wing Scoter, Capt W Howard, 1885-1890, EX OP 350.00
White-Wing Scoter, MDF, DG, glass eye, EX OP 800.00
Widgeon drake, Paul Gibson, sgn, ca 1920s, NM OP 430.00
Yellowlegs, Hanford, preening, relief cvd wings, EX OP 300.00

Dedham Pottery

Originally founded in Chelsea, Massachusetts, as the Chelsea Keramic Works, the name was changed to Dedham Pottery in 1895 after the firm relocated in Dedham, near Boston, Massachusetts. The ware utilized a gray stoneware body with a crackle glaze and simple cobalt border designs of flowers, birds, and animals. Decorations were brushed on by hand using an ancient Chinese method which suspended the cobalt within the overall glaze. There were thirteen standard patterns, among them Magnolia, Iris, Butterfly, Duck, Polar Bear, and Rabbit, the latter of which was chosen to represent the company on their logo. On the very early pieces, the rabbits face left; decorators soon found the reverse position easier to paint, and the rabbits were turned to the right. (Earlier examples are worth from 10% to 20% more than identical pieces manufactured in later years.) In addition to the standard patterns, other designs were produced for special orders. These and artist-signed pieces are highly valued by collectors today.

Though their primary product was the blue-printed, crackle-glazed dinnerware, two types of artware were also produced: crackle glaze and flambe. Their notable volcanic ware was a type of the latter. The mark is incised and often accompanies the cipher of Hugh Robertson. The firm was operated by succeeding generations of the Robertson family until it closed in 1943. Our advisor for this category is Dale MacLean; he is listed in the Directory under Massachusetts. See also Chelsea Keramic Art Works.

Bell, Rabbit, 4" 1,200.00
Bootie, bl band & shoelace design on front, 2¼x2" 500.00
Bowl, Elephant & Baby, #3, stamped, 3x7" 1,000.00
Bowl, Elephant & Baby, #5, stamped, 2x5" 800.00
Bowl, lotus; Floral, stamped registered, 2x5" 750.00
Bowl, mayonnaise; Rabbit, stamped, 2⅛x5¼" 350.00
Bowl, nappy; Rabbit, #2 open, stamped registered, 2½x9" 325.00
Bowl, Polar Bear, scalloped rim, imp, 5¾" 600.00
Bowl, Rabbit, #2, stamped, 3½x8¼" 425.00
Bowl, Rabbit, Chinese cut edge, stamped, 3¾x9" 1,800.00
Bowl, Rabbit, stamped, 1¾x4⅛" 350.00
Bowl, Swan, #8, stamped, 3½" 900.00
Bowl, Turkey, #5, stamped, 2⅛x5½" 450.00
Butter pat, Wild Rose, stamped registered, 3½" 350.00
Butter pat, 6-sided star shape, stamped registered, 1931, 3¼" dia .450.00
Candlestick, Horse Chestnut, stamped, 1½x3½" 475.00
Casserole, Rabbit, Davenport rebus, stamped/imp/hand sgn, 3x9" ..800.00
Charger, Azalea, stamped registered/imp, 12" 650.00
Coaster, Swan, stamped registered, 4" 650.00
Coffeepot, Rabbit, w/underliner, stamped/imp, 8¾" 1,200.00
Cookie jar, Rabbit, stamped, 6½x6" 1,500.00
Creamer, Rabbit, #13, stamped, 2¾x3" 350.00
Creamer, Rabbit, stamped, 3½x5¾" 350.00
Cup & saucer, chowder; Rabbit, stamped registered, 2¼x7", 6½" .475.00
Cup & saucer, Duck, stamped registered, 3", 5¾" 400.00
Cup & saucer, Elephant, stamped, 2¼", 6" 700.00
Cup & saucer, Horse Chestnut, 2x4½", 6" 325.00
Cup & saucer, Swan, stamped, 2¼", 6" 425.00
Cup plate, Horse Chestnut, stamped, 4½" 300.00
Egg cup, Elephant, unmk, 2½x2" 600.00
Goblet, Rabbit, superior artwork, hand sgn/stamped, 5⅛x3" 400.00
Jar, marmalade; Grape, stamped, 5x4¼" 550.00
Paperweight, Rabbit, stamped, 2¾" 550.00
Paperweight, Turtle (figural), stamped, 3½" 650.00
Pitcher, Night & Day; Owl & Prey/Rooster & Hen, stamped, 5⅛" .600.00
Pitcher, Rabbit, #3, faint mk, 8½x7⅛" 800.00
Pitcher, Rabbit, #6, stamped, 5x4¼" 450.00
Pitcher, Rabbit, #12, stamped, 4½x5" 450.00

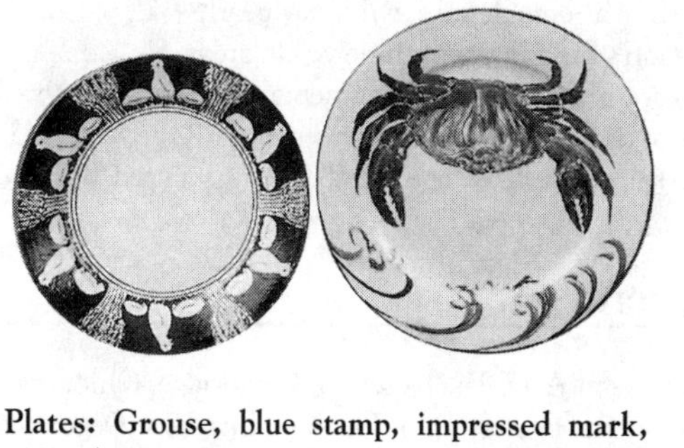

Plates: Grouse, blue stamp, impressed mark, 8¾", $2,875.00; Crab, blue stamp, impressed mark, 10", $900.00.

Plate, Avery Oak, stamped, 8½" 2,900.00
Plate, Azalea, stamped/imp, 6¼" 275.00
Plate, Bird in Potted Orange Tree, imp, 8½" 600.00
Plate, Butterfly & Flower, stamped/imp, 9¾" 700.00
Plate, Cat, child sz, 7½" 4,500.00
Plate, Cosmos, imp, flakes, 6" 1,500.00
Plate, Crab, swirling seaweed border, stamped/imp, 6¼" 600.00
Plate, Dolphin, stamped registered/imp, 8½" 1,200.00
Plate, Double Turtle, stamped/imp, 6⅛" 1,000.00
Plate, Duck, Davenport rebus, stamped/imp, 8½", NM 450.00
Plate, French Mushroom, stamped/imp, rstr flake, 6¼" 800.00
Plate, Grape, stamped/imp, 6" 225.00
Plate, Horse Chestnut, Davenport rebus, stamped/imp, 10" 350.00
Plate, Horse Chestnut, stamped/imp, 6" 250.00
Plate, Iris, stamped, 6¼" 250.00
Plate, Lion Tapestry, hairlines, stamped registered/imp, 9¾" 800.00
Plate, Magnolia, stamped/imp, 6" 250.00
Plate, Magnolia, stamped/imp, 8½" 250.00

Plate, Moth, Davenport rebus, stamped/imp, 6" 650.00
Plate, Mushroom, Davenport rebus, stamped/imp, 8¼" 800.00
Plate, Pineapple, stamped/imp, 9¾" 800.00
Plate, Polar Bear, stamped registered, 8¼" 700.00
Plate, Pond Lily, Davenport rebus, stamped/imp, 8½" 375.00
Plate, Pond Lily, stamped registered/imp, 6" 250.00
Plate, Poppy, Davenport rebus, stamped, 6¼" 800.00
Plate, Poppy, imp, 8½" 850.00
Plate, Rabbit, stamped, 6⅛" 225.00
Plate, Rabbit, stamped registered/imp, 8¾", EX 275.00
Plate, Scottie Dog (portrait), stamped/imp, 9½" 2,500.00
Plate, Snow Tree, Davenport rebus, stamped, 9¾", NM 500.00
Plate, Snow Tree, stamped registered/imp, 7½" 300.00
Plate, Spotted Day Lily, stamped/imp, 8¾" 1,100.00
Plate, Strawberry, faint pitting, imp, 6⅛" 1,500.00
Plate, Swan, stamped registered/imp, 8½" 500.00
Plate, Swan, stamped/imp, 6" 400.00
Plate, Tufted Duck, imp, 10", NM 500.00
Plate, Turkey, Davenport rebus, stamped/imp, 8½" 450.00
Plate, Turkey, Davenport rebus, stamped/imp, 10" 500.00
Plate, Water Lily, stamped/imp, 6" 325.00
Platter, steak; Elephant & Baby, stamped registered, 14x8¼" .2,500.00
Platter, steak; Rabbit, stamped, 14" 1,000.00
Shakers, Rabbit, sgn DP, 3½", pr 375.00
Sherbet, Rabbit, hdls, partial stamp, 3x5½" 400.00
Teapot, Horse Chestnut, stamped, 1931, 7x7¼" 1,500.00
Vase, Rabbit, stamped registered, 5x4¼" 800.00

Miscellaneous

Gin bottle, crackle w/bl G, 4-sided, panels arch at top, 8½" 700.00
Oyster dish, wht crackleware, w/bl-gray pearl, 4½", pr 600.00
Vase, Dragon's Blood w/crystalline & blk areas, 8" 1,100.00
Vase, mirror brn drips on gr, experimental, H Robertson, 9x4¾" .900.00
Vase, mirror oxblood, ovoid, experimental, H Robertson, 8x3" 800.00
Vase, wht 4-sided waisted shape w/emb flowers, stamped, 8½x5¼" .1,200.00

Degenhart

The Crystal Art Glass factory in Cambridge, Ohio, opened in 1947 under the private ownership of John and Elizabeth Degenhart. John had previously worked for the Cambridge Glass Company and was well known for his superior paperweights. After his death in 1964, Elizabeth took over management of the factory, hiring several workers from the defunct Cambridge Company, including Zack Boyd. Boyd was responsible for many unique colors, some of which were named for him. From 1964 to 1974, more than twenty-seven different moulds were created, most of them resulting from Elizabeth Degenhart's work and creativity, and over 145 official colors were developed. Elizabeth died in 1978, requesting that the ten moulds she had built while operating the factory were to be turned over to the Degenhart Museum. The remaining moulds were to be held by the Island Mould and Machine Company, who (complying with her request) removed the familiar 'D in heart' trademark. The factory was eventually bought by Zack's son, Bernard Boyd. He also acquired the remaining Degenhart moulds, to which he added his own logo.

In general, slags and opaques should be valued 15% to 20% higher than crystals in color.

Baby Shoe (Hobo Boot) Toothpick Holder, Rose Marie 15.00
Baby Shoe (Hobo Boot) Toothpick Holder, Toffee Slag 20.00
Basket Toothpick Holder, Amber 12.00
Basket Toothpick Holder, Emerald Green 15.00
Beaded Oval Toothpick Holder, Aqua 20.00
Beaded Oval Toothpick Holder, Bluebell 20.00
Beaded Oval Toothpick Holder, Fog 20.00

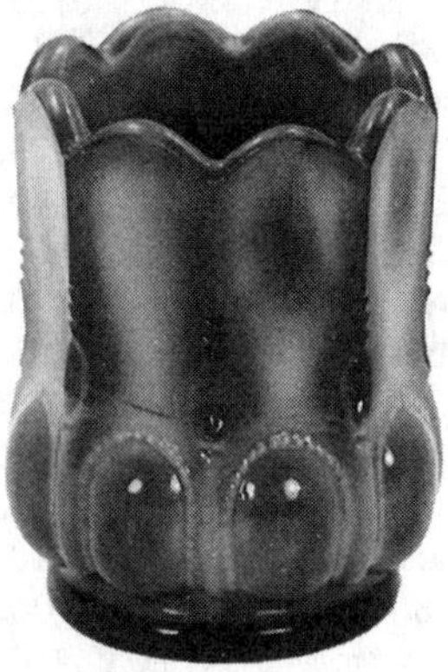

Beaded Oval Toothpick Holder, Mulberry, $20.00.

Bicentennial Bell, Amber 12.00
Bicentennial Bell, Crown Tuscan 13.50
Bird Salt w/Cherry, Bloody Mary 40.00
Bird Salt w/Cherry, Gun Metal 20.00
Bow Slipper, Amberina 25.00
Bow Slipper, Fawn 15.00
Bow Slipper, Olive 25.00
Buzz Saw Wine, Green Carnival 40.00
Buzz Saw Wine, Pistachio 25.00
Colonial Drape Toothpick Holder, Ruby 25.00
Colonial Drape Toothpick Holder, Vaseline 20.00
Daisy & Button Salt, Amberina 15.00
Daisy & Button Salt, Forest Green 12.00
Daisy & Button Toothpick Holder, Bluebell 25.00
Daisy & Button Toothpick Holder, Pink 20.00
Elephant Head Toothpick Holder, Amberina 75.00
Elephant Head Toothpick Holder, Dichromatic 40.00
Forget-Me-Not Toothpick Holder, Blue Jay 20.00
Forget-Me-Not Toothpick Holder, Dogwood 40.00
Forget-Me-Not Toothpick Holder, Gray Slag 20.00
Forget-Me-Not Toothpick Holder, Lemon Opal 20.00
Gypsy Pot Toothpick Holder, Bittersweet 35.00
Gypsy Pot Toothpick Holder, Periwinkle 20.00
Hand, Gray Slag 25.00
Hand, Tomato 25.00
Heart Jewel Box, Antique Blue 25.00
Heart Jewel Box, Ruby 40.00
Heart Toothpick Holder, Blue Marble Slag 25.00
Heart Toothpick Holder, Chartreuse 35.00
Heart Toothpick Holder, Old Lavender 25.00
Hen Covered Dish, Gold, 3" 20.00
High Boot, Crystal 15.00
High Boot, Ruby 40.00
Kat Slipper (Puss & Boots), Light Green 20.00
Lamb Covered Dish, Heliotrope, 5" 90.00
Lamb Covered Dish, Taffeta, 5" 55.00
Mini Slipper w/o Sole, Cobalt Carnival 30.00
Mini Slipper w/o Sole, Forest Green 15.00
Mini Slipper w/Sole, Cobalt 35.00
Mini Slipper w/Sole, Vaseline 35.00
Owl, Baby Green 50.00
Owl, Charcoal 50.00
Owl, Crystal Ice 15.00
Owl, Dichromatic 75.00
Owl, Dickie Bird 150.00

Owl, Just Blue 40.00
Owl, Maverick 200.00
Owl, Rubina 300.00
Owl, Sunset 50.00
Owl, Tangerine 175.00
Owl, Tiger 40.00
Owl, Tomato 100.00
Owl, Willow Green 50.00
Pooch, Autumn 25.00
Pooch, Blue Jay 20.00
Pooch, Daffodil #2 ....15.00
Pooch, Daffodil Slag 60.00
Pooch, Powder Blue Slag 35.00
Pottie Salt, Chocolate Creme Slag 15.00
Pottie Salt, Sunset 12.00
Priscilla, Bittersweet Slag 200.00
Priscilla, Blue Lady 125.00
Priscilla, Green Lavender Slag 150.00
Robin Covered Dish, Bittersweet, 5" 75.00
Robin Covered Dish, Pigeon Blood, 5" 90.00
Skate Shoe, Custard 40.00
Skate Shoe, Milk Blue 35.00
Star & Dewdrop Salt, Custard 20.00
Star & Dewdrop Salt, Lemon Custard 25.00
Stork & Peacock Child's Mug, Apple Green 25.00
Stork & Peacock Child's Mug, Custard 35.00
Texas Creamer & Sugar, Cobalt 50.00
Texas Creamer & Sugar, Opalescent 100.00
Tomahawk, Apple Green 25.00
Tomahawk, Pink Carnival 60.00
Wildflower Candle Holder, Amethyst 25.00
Wildflower Candle Holder, Milk Blue 25.00
Wildflower Candy Dish, Emerald Green 25.00
Wildflower Candy Dish, Sapphire 20.00

Delft

Old Delftware, made as early as the sixteenth century, was originally a low-fired earthenware coated in a thin opaque tin glaze with painted-on blue or polychrome designs. It was not until the last half of the nineteenth century, however, that the ware became commonly referred to as Delft, acquiring the name from the Dutch village that had become the major center of its production. English, German, and French potters also produced Delft, though with noticeable differences both in shape and decorative theme.

In the early part of the eighteenth century, the German potter, Bottger, developed a formula for porcelain; in England, Wedgwood began producing creamware — both of which were much more durable. Unable to compete, one by one the Delft potteries failed. Soon only one remained. In 1876 De Porcelyne Fles reintroduced Delftware on a hard white body with blue and white decorative themes reflecting the Dutch countryside, windmills by the sea, and Dutch children. This manufacturer is the most well known of several operating today. Their products are now produced under the Royal Delft label.

For further information we recommend *Discovering Dutch Delftware, Modern Delft and Makkum Pottery*, by Stephen J. Van Hook (Glen Park Press, Alexandria, Virginia). Examples listed here are blue on white unless noted otherwise. See also specific manufacturers. Our advisor is Ralph Jaarsma; he is listed in the Directory under Iowa.

Bottle, scent; Dutch, floral, silver neck/cap, 1814-1906, 3½" 200.00
Bowl, Dutch, butterfly, 6x13" 1,000.00
Bowl, English, squirrel & flowers, chips, 11⅝" 935.00
Charger, Dutch, bird & landscape, 18th C, 13" 900.00
Charger, Dutch, fern & flower in pot, floral border, 18th C, 13" ..630.00
Charger, Dutch, floral, 14½", EX 300.00
Charger, Dutch, lion figure/columns/flowers, 18th C, 13", EX ...750.00
Charger, English, bird & flowerpots, floral border, 18th C, 13" .500.00
Charger, English, floral, 13", EX 500.00
Charger, English, floral w/X-banded border, 18th C, 13½" 550.00
Charger, English, house & tree w/stylized birds, 13" dia 800.00
Charger, English, man on horsebk w/sword, ca 1700, 12½" 800.00
Ewer, Dutch, windmill scene, elongated neck, 1890s, 10" 235.00
Figurine, Dutch, girl w/basket, 11" 100.00
Jug, man smoking pipe figural, mc, minor rpr, 10" 475.00
Plate, Dutch, landscape w/floral border, 9½", EX 100.00
Plate, Dutch, regal couple, rpr, 8⅞" 770.00
Plate, English, flowers & bird, 8¾", EX 385.00
Plate, Liverpool, floral, scalloped rim, 9", EX 275.00
Tankard, Dutch, floral, rpl pewter base & lid, 5½" 250.00
Tile, Dutch, church/lake/sailboat, 19th C, 5" 50.00

Denver

The Denver China and Pottery Company began production in 1901 in Denver, Colorado. The founder, William A. Long, used materials native to Colorado to produce underglaze-decorated brownware as well as other artware lines. Several marks were used: an impressed 'Denver' (often with the Lonhuda Faience cipher inside a shield), an imprinted 'Denaura,' and an arrow mark.

Vase, gunmetal, three-handled, 1919, 5x7", $650.00.

Bowl vase, plain gr, rnd base, Denaura, 6x7" 250.00
Jug, ear of corn decor on dk brn, sgn, WA Long, 8", minimum value ...350.00
Vase, appl decor around incurvate rim, gr, ovoid, 9½" 195.00
Vase, burro on dk brn, ovoid w/sm rolled rim, 5½x9½" 275.00
Vase, ear of corn on dk brn, integral hdls, sgn Claude L Leffler, 6x9" .650.00
Vase, floral, lt gr matt, Denaura, 6½" 1,000.00
Vase, floral decor on dk brn, 3-ftd, 5" 225.00
Vase, mistletoe, Robin's Egg Blue, Denaura, 6¾x3¼" 1,200.00
Vase, tulips & leaves, gr matt, Denaura, 1903, 9x5" 2,600.00

Denver Terra Cotta Pottery

While on his honeymoon in Colorado, a young chemist by the name of George Frackt became aware of the natural clay deposits there. As an employee of the St. Louis Terra Cotta Company in Missouri, he was impressed with the samples he had analyzed and decided to establish his own terra cotta plant in Denver.

Within a short time, he opened a two-story plant with twelve employees, where he made finished products in high-gloss colors. The company consolidated with Northwestern Terra Cotta Company in 1924. Artificial stone or concrete came into production in 1925 and continued into the late 1920s. The exact date of closing is unknown. Look for pieces of great weight with high-gloss colors and stamped marks.

Ashtray, gargoyle, high-gloss gr, blk or red, minimum value 95.00
Bookends, elephants, charging, 7x8", from $250 to 500.00
Bookends, Liberty Bell, 5x7", pr, minimum value 195.00
Planter, frog w/open mouth, 4x5", minimum value 125.00
Vase, buttressed, clear over yel clay, 6x7" 125.00

Denver White

In 1894 Frederick and Frank White settled in Denver, Colorado, and formed the F.J. White & Son Pottery Company. They located at 1434 Logan Street. After the death of Frederick in 1919, Frank moved the pottery to 1560 South Logan, where he remained until the company closed. He had a kiln set up at home and worked each day on the pottery, often selling his products in his front yard. On many occasions he was commissioned to produce specialty items for customers.

Each piece is hand thrown and many are dated. They are usually incised with the name Denver and the letter 'W' inside the capital 'D.' Many items are decorated with Colorado scenery. Though most pieces are matt glazed with a glossy interior, some later examples were completely glossy. The Whites would also add a small band to some of the ware, similar to what you see on Wedgwood pottery today. They created a line with swirled colors as well. On March 6, 1960, Frank White died at the age of 91.

For more information we recommend *Collector's Encyclopedia of Colorado Pottery* by Jim and Carol Carlton (Collector Books).

Bowl, tree & mnt scene on off wht, sgn CMD, 6x10", minimum value .250.00
Bowl vase, matt gr, 3-hdld, dtd 1917, 5½", from $250 to 350.00
Candlestick, high-gloss turq, minimum value 50.00
Cookie jar, pine cone decor, squirrel finial, 8x6", minimum value ..300.00
Creamer, pine cone decor, minimum value 55.00
Cup & saucer, matt bl, minimum value 35.00
Mug, matt bl, tapers at bottom, minimum value 35.00
Vase, bl, tan & brn matt swirl w/high-gloss int, 6" 150.00
Vase, brn pine cones on wht, brn gloss int, sgn Stabler, 6" 125.00
Vase, glass ivory over tan clay, rnd, 6½" 90.00
Vase, high-gloss cobalt, hdls from rim to shoulder, 10" 125.00
Vase, high-gloss turq, cylindrical w/fluted rim, 10", minimum value .75.00
Vase, lt bl, pot form w/fluted rim, flat bottom, 6" 95.00
Vase, textured drip glaze, cylindrical, 8" 100.00

Depression Glass

Depression glass is defined by Gene Florence, author of several best-selling books on the subject, as 'the inexpensive glassware made primarily during the Depression era in the colors of amber, green, pink, blue, red, yellow, white, and crystal.' This glass was mass produced, sold through five-and-dime stores and mail-order catalogs, and given away as premiums with gas and food products.

The listings in this book are far from being complete. If you want a more thorough presentation of this fascinating glassware, we recommend *The Collector's Encyclopedia of Depression Glass*, *Pocket Guide to Depression Glass*, *Elegant Glassware of the Depression Era*, and *Very Rare Glassware of the Depression Years*, all by Gene Florence, whose address is listed in the Directory under Kentucky. See also McKee; New Martinsville.

Key:
AOP — allover pattern PAT — pattern at top

Adam, ashtray, gr, 4½" 25.00
Adam, bowl, cereal; pk, 5¾" 55.00
Adam, bowl, dessert; pk, 4¾" 20.00
Adam, bowl, gr, w/lid, 9" 90.00
Adam, bowl, pk, oval, 10" 35.00
Adam, butter dish, gr, w/lid 395.00
Adam, candlesticks, pk, 4", pr 95.00
Adam, lamp, gr 325.00
Adam, plate, dinner; gr, sq, 9" 30.00

Adam, plate, salad; pink, 7¾" square, $15.00. (Photo courtesy Gene Florence)

Adam, plate, sherbet; pk, 6" 11.00
Adam, relish dish, pk, divided, 8" 20.00
Adam, sherbet, gr, 3" 38.00
Adam, tumbler, pk, 4½" 40.00
American Pioneer, bowl, gr, w/lid, 9¼" 150.00
American Pioneer, cheese & cracker set, crystal or pk 55.00
American Pioneer, lamp, gr, w/metal pole (9½"), 1¾" 75.00
American Pioneer, pitcher, gr, urn style, w/lid, 5" 225.00
American Pioneer, plate, crystal or pk, hdls, 11½" 30.00
American Pioneer, vase, gr, 4 styles, 7", ea 125.00
American Sweetheart, bowl, console; red, 18" 1,100.00
American Sweetheart, bowl, cream soup; pk, 4½" 95.00
American Sweetheart, bowl, vegetable; monax, oval, 11" 80.00
American Sweetheart, cup, bl 145.00
American Sweetheart, pitcher, pk, 80-oz, 8" 750.00
American Sweetheart, saucer, smoke or other trims 15.00
Aunt Polly, bowl, berry; bl, lg, 7⅞" 45.00
Aunt Polly, bowl, gr or irid, 1-hdl, 5½" 14.00
Aunt Polly, butter dish, gr or irid, w/lid 275.00
Aunt Polly, creamer, gr or irid 55.00
Aunt Polly, plate, sherbet; gr or irid, 6" 6.00
Aunt Polly, sherbet, bl 14.00
Aunt Polly, sugar bowl, gr or irid, w/lid 85.00
Aurora, bowl, cobalt or pk, deep, 4½" 60.00
Aurora, cup, cobalt or pk 15.00
Aurora, saucer, cobalt or pk 6.00
Avocado, bowl, pk, 3¼x9½" 125.00
Avocado, bowl, preserve; crystal, 1-hdl, 7" 8.00
Avocado, cup, gr, ftd, 2 styles, ea 40.00
Avocado, plate, sherbet; pk, 6⅜" 16.00
Avocado, tumbler, pk 175.00
Beaded Block, bowl, crystal, 1-hdl, 5½" 20.00
Beaded Block, bowl, ice bl, 6½" 35.00
Beaded Block, bowl, pk, fluted edges, 7½" 30.00
Beaded Block, creamer, irid 45.00
Beaded Block, sugar bowl, gr or amber 25.00
Block Optic, bowl, pk, 1½x4½" 30.00
Block Optic, butter dish, gr, w/lid, 3x5" 50.00
Block Optic, cup, gr or pk, 4 styles, ea 7.00
Block Optic, goblet, gr, 9-oz, 5¾" 27.00

Block Optic, pitcher, pk, 54-oz, 8½" 50.00
Block Optic, plate, dinner; yel, 9" 45.00
Block Optic, saucer, gr, w/cup ring, 6⅛" 10.00
Block Optic, shakers, yel, ftd, pr 95.00
Block Optic, tumbler, pk, flat, 12-oz, 4⅞" 28.00
Block Optic, tumbler, pk, 3-oz, 2⅝" 28.00
Block Optic, tumbler, yel, ftd, 9-oz 22.00
Block Optic, whiskey, gr or pk, 2-oz, 2¼" 32.00
Bowknot, bowl, berry; gr, 4½" 20.00
Bowknot, cup, gr 9.00
Bowknot, tumbler, gr, 10-oz, 5" 25.00
Cameo, bowl, berry; gr, lg, 8¼" 45.00
Cameo, bowl, cereal; yel, 5½" 33.00
Cameo, cocktail shaker, crystal, metal lid 900.00
Cameo, domino tray, pk, w/no indentation, 7" 250.00
Cameo, pitcher, water; gr, 56-oz, 8½" 60.00
Cameo, plate, sandwich; pk, 10" 55.00
Cameo, tumbler, yel, flat, 11-oz, 5" 60.00
Cameo, Whitehouse vinegar, gr 25.00
Cherry Blossom, bowl, flat soup; pk, 7¾" 90.00
Cherry Blossom, bowl, vegetable; gr, oval, 9" 40.00
Cherry Blossom, cake plate, pk, 3-legged, 10¼" 35.00
Cherry Blossom, creamer, Delphite 20.00
Cherry Blossom, pitcher, pk or gr, PAT, flat, 42-oz, 8" 60.00

Cherry Blossom, plate, dinner; green, 9", $25.00. **(Photo courtesy Gene Florence)**

Cherry Blossom, plate, grill; pk or gr, 9" 32.00
Cherry Blossom, plate, sherbet; pk, 6" 8.00
Cherry Blossom, platter, pk, oval, 9" 950.00
Cherry Blossom, shakers, gr, scalloped bottom, pr 1,100.00
Cherry Blossom, sugar bowl, pk, w/lid 34.50
Cherry Blossom, tray, sandwich; Delphite, 10½" 22.00
Cherry Blossom, tumbler, gr, PAT, flat, 12-oz, 5" 85.00
Cherry Blossom, tumbler, pk or gr, AOP, scalloped ft, 8-oz, 4½" .40.00
Cherryberry, bowl, crystal or irid, 2x6¼" 50.00
Cherryberry, butter dish, crystal or irid, w/lid 145.00
Cherryberry, creamer, pk or gr, lg, 4⅝" 42.50
Cherryberry, pitcher, crystal or irid, 7¾" 175.00
Cherryberry, sugar bowl, pk or gr, open, sm 22.50
Chinex Classic, bowl, soup; brnstone or plain ivory, 7¾" 12.50
Chinex Classic, butter dish, castle decal, w/lid 150.00
Chinex Classic, butter dish, decal decor, w/lid 75.00
Chinex Classic, plate, dinner; brnstone or plain ivory, 9¾" 4.50
Chinex Classic, sherbet, decal decor, low ft 11.00
Circle, bowl, pk or gr, 5¼" 10.00
Circle, decanter, gr, 1-hdl 60.00
Circle, pitcher, gr, 80-oz 35.00
Circle, plate, luncheon; pk, 8¼" 10.00
Circle, saucer, pk, w/cup ring 3.00
Circle, tumbler, juice; gr, 4-oz, 3½" 8.00
Cloverleaf, bowl, dessert; pk, gr or yel, 4" 35.00
Cloverleaf, cup, pk or gr 9.00
Cloverleaf, plate, luncheon; yel, 8" 14.00
Cloverleaf, shakers, blk, pr 100.00
Cloverleaf, sherbet, gr, 3" 12.00
Cloverleaf, tumbler, pk, flat, flared, 10-oz, 3¾" 28.00
Cloverleaf, tumbler, yel, ftd, 10-oz, 5¾" 38.00
Colonial, bowl, berry; crystal, 4½" 10.00
Colonial, butter dish, gr, w/lid 55.00
Colonial, plate, dinner; pk, 10" 55.00
Colonial, saucer/sherbet plate, pk 6.00
Colonial, stem, wine; gr, 2½-oz, 4½" 28.00
Colonial, tumbler, crystal, ftd, 3-oz, 3¼" 13.00
Colonial Block, butter dish, pk or gr, w/lid 45.00
Colonial Block, butter tub, pk or gr 45.00
Colonial Block, pitcher, pk or gr 45.00
Colonial Block, sugar bowl, wht, w/lid 10.00
Colonial Fluted, bowl, berry; gr, 4" 7.50
Colonial Fluted, cup, gr 8.00
Colonial Fluted, sherbet, gr 7.00
Columbia, bowl, crystal, ruffled edge, 10½" 20.00
Columbia, butter dish, crystal, w/lid 20.00
Columbia, plate, luncheon; crystal, 9½" 10.00
Columbia, saucer, pk 10.00
Coronation, bowl, gr, no hdls, 8" 175.00
Coronation, bowl, nappy; Royal Ruby, hdls, 6½" 18.00
Coronation, bowl, pk, no hdls, 4¼" 75.00
Coronation, plate, luncheon; pk, 8½" 4.50
Coronation, tumbler, gr, ftd, 10-oz, 5" 175.00
Cremax, bowl, vegetable; bl or decal decor, 9" 18.00
Cremax, cup, demitasse; cremax 15.00
Cremax, plate, dinner; cremax, 9¾" 4.50
Cremax, saucer, bl or decal decor 3.50
Cube, butter dish, pk or gr, w/lid 70.00
Cube, pitcher, pk, 45-oz, 8¾" 210.00
Cube, shakers, pk or gr, pr 35.00
Cube, tumbler, gr, 9-oz, 4" 75.00
Diamond Quilted, bowl, cereal; bl or blk, 5" 15.00
Diamond Quilted, candlesticks, pk or gr, 2 styles, pr 25.00
Diamond Quilted, creamer, bl or blk 20.00
Diamond Quilted, goblet, wine; pk or gr, 3-oz 12.00
Diamond Quilted, plate, sherbet; bl or blk, 6" 7.00
Diamond Quilted, sandwich server, pk or gr, center hdl 25.00
Diamond Quilted, vase, fan; pk or gr, dolphin hdls 55.00
Diana, bowl, cereal; crystal, 5" 6.00
Diana, bowl, console fruit; pk, 11" 42.50
Diana, cup, amber 9.00
Diana, plate, crystal, 9½" 10.00
Diana, sherbet, amber 10.00
Dogwood, bowl, berry; pk, 8½" 65.00
Dogwood, cake plate, monax or cremax, heavy solid ft, 13" 195.00
Dogwood, cup, pk, thick 18.00
Dogwood, plate, salver; pk, 12" 35.00
Dogwood, tumbler, gr, decor, 10-oz, 4" 97.50
Doric, bowl, cream soup; gr, 5" 450.00
Doric, butter dish, pk, w/lid 70.00
Doric, candy dish, pk, 3-part 12.00
Doric, pitcher, Delphite, flat, 32-oz, 5½" 1,100.00
Doric, plate, salad; pk, 7" 20.00
Doric, relish tray, gr, 4x8" 18.00
Doric, sugar bowl, pk, w/lid 34.00
Doric, tumbler, gr, ftd, 10-oz, 4" 90.00
Doric & Pansy, butter dish, gr or teal, w/lid 450.00
Doric & Pansy, cup, pk or crystal 12.00

Doric & Pansy, plate, dinner; gr or teal, 9" 38.00
Doric & Pansy, plate, sherbet; pk or crystal, 6" 7.50
Doric & Pansy, shakers, gr or teal, pr 400.00
Doric & Pansy, tumbler, gr or teal, 9-oz, 4½" 110.00
English Hobnail, bowl, celery; pk or gr, 12" 35.00
English Hobnail, bowl, nappy; pk or gr, rnd, 6" 16.00
English Hobnail, bowl, rose; pk or gr, 4" 50.00
English Hobnail, bowl, turq or ice bl, hexagonal ft, hdls, 8" 125.00
English Hobnail, candlestick, turq or ice bl, rnd base, 3½" 30.00
English Hobnail, cigarette jar, turq or ice bl, w/lid, rnd 60.00
English Hobnail, compote, sweetmeat; pk or gr, ball stem, 8" 60.00
English Hobnail, ice tub, turq or ice bl, 5½" 120.00
English Hobnail, pitcher, pk or gr, rnd, 60-oz 295.00
English Hobnail, saucer, demitasse; pk or gr, rnd 15.00
English Hobnail, stem, wine; turq or ice bl, sq ft, 2-oz 60.00
English Hobnail, sugar bowl, pk or gr, sq ft 45.00
Fire-King Philbe, bowl, cereal; crystal, 5½" 20.00
Fire-King Philbe, cookie jar, pk or gr, w/lid 950.00
Fire-King Philbe, goblet, bl, thin, 9-oz, 7¼" 235.00
Fire-King Philbe, plate, grill; crystal, 10½" 40.00
Fire-King Philbe, plate, sherbet; crystal, 6" 40.00
Fire-King Philbe, sherbet, pk or gr, 4¾" 450.00
Fire-King Philbe, tumbler, iced tea; crystal, ftd, 15-oz, 6½" 50.00
Fire-King Philbe, tumbler, juice; bl, ftd, 3½" 175.00
Floral, bowl, berry; Delphite, 4" 50.00
Floral, butter dish, pk, w/lid 100.00
Floral, lamp, gr 275.00
Floral, platter, Delphite, oval, 10¾" 150.00
Floral, refrigerator dish, Jade-ite, w/lid, sq, 5" 50.00
Floral, tray, gr, for dresser set, oval, 9¼" 195.00
Floral & Diamond Band, butter dish, gr, w/lid 130.00
Floral & Diamond Band, pitcher, gr, 42-oz, 8" 125.00
Floral & Diamond Band, sherbet, pk 7.00
Floral & Diamond Band, tumbler, iced tea; gr, 5" 50.00
Florentine No 1, bowl, berry; cobalt, 5" 20.00
Florentine No 1, bowl, berry; yel or pk, lg, 8½" 30.00
Florentine No 1, coaster/ashtray, yel, 3¾" 20.00
Florentine No 1, pitcher, crystal or gr, ftd, 36-oz, 6½" 40.00
Florentine No 1, plate, grill; crystal or gr, 10" 12.00
Florentine No 1, shakers, yel or pk, ftd, pr 55.00
Florentine No 1, sherbet, pk, 3-oz 12.00
Florentine No 1, tumbler, pk, ribbed, 9-oz, 4" 22.00
Florentine No 2, bowl, cream soup; crystal or gr, 4¾" 16.00
Florentine No 2, bowl, yel, shallow, 7½" 95.00
Florentine No 2, comport, cobalt, ruffled, 3½" 65.00
Florentine No 2, pitcher, pk, 76-oz, 8¼" 225.00
Florentine No 2, plate, crystal or gr, w/indent, 6¼" 20.00
Florentine No 2, platter, yel, oval, 11" 22.50
Florentine No 2, sugar bowl, crystal or gr, w/lid 25.00
Florentine No 2, tumbler, water; cobalt, 9-oz, 4" 70.00
Flower Garden w/Butterflies, bowl, blk, rolled edge, w/base, 9" .200.00
Flower Garden w/Butterflies, candy box, amber, w/lid, flat, 6" ...130.00
Flower Garden w/Butterflies, compote, amber or crystal, 7¼x8¼" .60.00
Flower Garden w/Butterflies, compote, bl or canary yel, 2⅞" 28.00
Flower Garden w/Butterflies, compote, blk, ftd, 5⅝x10" 225.00
Flower Garden w/Butterflies, plate, pk, gr or bl-gr, 7" 21.00
Flower Garden w/Butterflies, powder jar, crystal, ftd, 6¼" 75.00
Fortune, bowl, berry; pk or crystal, 4" 8.00
Fortune, tumbler, juice; pk or crystal, 5-oz, 3½" 10.00
Fruits, bowl, berry; pk, 8" 45.00
Fruits, saucer, gr 5.50
Fruits, tumbler, gr, 12-oz, 5" 150.00
Georgian, bowl, vegetable; gr, oval, 9" 62.00
Georgian, creamer, gr, ftd, 4" 17.00
Georgian, sugar bowl, gr, ftd, w/lid, 4" 177.00
Hex Optic, bowl, mixing; pk or gr, 10" 25.00
Hex Optic, bowl, mixing; pk or gr, 7¼" 12.00
Hex Optic, butter dish, pk or gr, rectangular, w/lid, 1-lb 90.00
Hex Optic, pitcher, pk or gr, sunflower bottom, 32-oz, 5" 22.00
Hex Optic, refrigerator stack set, pk or gr, 4-pc 65.00
Hex Optic, saucer, pk or gr 2.50
Hex Optic, tumbler, pk or gr, 12-oz, 5" 7.00
Hobnail, cup, crystal 4.50
Hobnail, pitcher, milk; gr, 18-oz 20.00
Hobnail, saucer/sherbet plate, pk 2.50
Homespun, butter dish, pk or crystal, w/lid 60.00
Homespun, plate, sherbet; pk or crystal, 6" 6.00
Homespun, tumbler, pk or crystal, ftd, 5-oz, 4" 7.00
Homespun, tumbler, water; pk or crystal, flared top, 8-oz, 4⅛" 22.00
Indiana Custard, bowl, flat soup; French Ivory, 7½" 35.00
Indiana Custard, cup, French Ivory 37.50
Indiana Custard, plate, luncheon; French Ivory, 8⅞" 18.00
Indiana Custard, sherbet, French Ivory 100.00
Iris, bowl, berry; irid, beaded edge, 4½" 10.00
Iris, bowl, cereal; crystal, 5" 125.00
Iris, bowl, salad; irid, ruffled, 9½" 13.00
Iris, coaster, crystal 110.00
Iris, goblet, irid, 8-oz, 5½" 225.00
Iris, plate, sandwich; crystal, 11¾" 30.00
Iris, sherbet, irid, 2½" 15.00
Iris, sugar bowl, irid, w/lid 23.00
Iris, tumbler, crystal, ftd, 6" 18.00
Jubilee, bowl, fruit; yel, hdls, 9" 125.00
Jubilee, cheese & cracker set, pk 255.00
Jubilee, plate, salad; yel, 7" 14.00
Jubilee, saucer, pk, 2 styles, ea 12.00
Jubilee, tumbler, iced tea; yel, 12½-oz, 6⅛" 150.00
Lace Edge, bonbon, pk, w/lid 67.50
Lace Edge, bowl, pk, plain, 9½" 28.00
Lace Edge, comport, pk, 7" 30.00
Lace Edge, plate, grill; pk, 10½" 25.00
Lace Edge, platter, pk, 5-part, 12¾" 42.00
Laced Edge, bowl, opal, divided, oval, 11" 115.00
Laced Edge, bowl, opal, 5" 37.50
Laced Edge, bowl, soup; opal, 7" 85.00
Laced Edge, creamer, opal 40.00
Laced Edge, saucer, opal 15.00
Lake Como, bowl, flat soup; wht 100.00
Lake Como, cup, St Denis; wht 30.00
Lake Como, platter, wht, 11" 75.00
Lake Como, shakers, wht, pr 45.00
Laurel, bowl, cereal; French Ivory, 6" 12.00
Laurel, bowl, vegetable; wht opal or jade gr, oval, 9¾" 45.00
Laurel, creamer, Poudre Blue, tall 40.00
Laurel, plate, salad; French Ivory, 7½" 10.00
Laurel, plate, sherbet; Poudre Blue, 6" 10.00
Lincoln Inn, bowl, cereal; blk, 6" 9.00
Lincoln Inn, bowl, cobalt or red, ftd, 10½" 75.00
Lincoln Inn, goblet, wine; pk 16.50
Lincoln Inn, vase, cobalt or red, 9¾" 150.00
Lorain, bowl, berry; yel, deep, 8" 175.00
Lorain, cup, crystal or gr 11.00
Lorain, plate, luncheon; yel, 8⅜" 30.00
Lorain, sherbet, crystal or gr 25.00
Madrid, bowl, salad; amber, deep, 9½" 30.00
Madrid, bowl, sauce; gr, 5" 7.00
Madrid, butter dish, gr, w/lid 90.00
Madrid, pitcher, gr, ice lip, 80-oz, 8½" 225.00

Madrid, pitcher, juice; amber, 36-oz, 5½" 40.00
Madrid, plate, cake; amber, rnd, 11¼" 20.00
Madrid, tumbler, amber, ftd, 5-oz, 4" 28.00
Madrid, tumbler, bl, 5-oz, 3⅞" 40.00
Manhattan, bowl, cereal; pk, no hdls, 5¼" 125.00
Manhattan, bowl, salad; crystal, 9" 28.00
Manhattan, cup, pk 225.00
Manhattan, relish tray insert, crystal 5.50
Manhattan, sherbet, pk 18.00
Mayfair (Federal), bowl, cream soup; amber, 5" 20.00
Mayfair (Federal), bowl, vegetable; crystal, oval, 10" 18.00
Mayfair (Federal), plate, salad; gr, 6¾" 9.00
Mayfair (Federal), saucer, crystal 2.50
Mayfair (Federal), tumbler, amber, 9-oz, 4½" 30.00

Mayfair/Open Rose, bowl, pink, 11¾", $60.00.

Mayfair/Open Rose, bowl, cereal; gr or yel, 5½" 85.00
Mayfair/Open Rose, bowl, gr, low/flat, 11¾" 45.00
Mayfair/Open Rose, bowl, vegetable; pk, 10" 35.00
Mayfair/Open Rose, cake plate, bl, ftd, 10" 75.00
Mayfair/Open Rose, celery dish, pk, divided, 10" 265.00
Mayfair/Open Rose, creamer, yel, ftd 225.00
Mayfair/Open Rose, goblet, gr, 2½-oz, 4⅛" 950.00
Mayfair/Open Rose, pitcher, pk, 37-oz, 6" 65.00
Mayfair/Open Rose, plate, grill; bl, 9½" 60.00
Mayfair/Open Rose, platter, gr or yel, open hdls, oval, 12" 165.00
Mayfair/Open Rose, sandwich server, gr, center hdl 40.00
Mayfair/Open Rose, tumbler, juice; bl, 5-oz, 3½" 125.00
Mayfair/Open Rose, vase, sweet pea; pk 145.00
Miss America, bowl, cereal; gr, 6¼" 20.00
Miss America, bowl, Royal Ruby, shallow, 11" 900.00
Miss America, butter dish, pk, w/lid 625.00
Miss America, creamer, crystal, ftd 11.00
Miss America, goblet, juice; Royal Ruby, 5-oz, 4¾" 295.00
Miss America, goblet, wine; pk, 3-oz, 3¾" 110.00
Miss America, plate, dinner; pk, 10¼" 36.00
Miss America, tumbler, water; crystal, 10-oz, 4½" 16.00
Moderntone, ashtray, cobalt, match holder in center, 7¾" 165.00
Moderntone, bowl, soup; amethyst, 7½" 100.00
Moderntone, cheese dish, cobalt, w/metal lid, 7" 495.00
Moderntone, plate, sandwich; amethyst, 10½" 40.00
Moderntone, tumbler, amethyst, 12-oz 90.00
Moondrops, bowl, console; pk, 3-ftd, rnd, 12" 32.00
Moondrops, bowl, divided relish, bl or red, 3-ftd, 8½" 40.00
Moondrops, candles, bl or red, ruffled, 2", pr 45.00
Moondrops, candy dish, gr, ruffled, 8" 20.00
Moondrops, creamer, bl or red, regular, 3¾" 16.00
Moondrops, gravy boat, bl or red 195.00
Moondrops, pitcher, amethyst, w/lip, lg, 50-oz, 8" 115.00
Moondrops, plate, dinner; bl or red, 9½" 30.00
Moondrops, tumbler, shot; crystal, 2-oz, 2¾" 11.00
Mt Pleasant, bowl, pk or gr, 2-hdl, sq, 8" 19.00
Mt Pleasant, bowl, rose; amethyst, blk or cobalt, 4" opening 26.00
Mt Pleasant, candlestick, dbl; amethyst, blk or cobalt, pr 45.00
Mt Pleasant, mint dish, pk or gr, center hdl, 6" 16.00
Mt Pleasant, tumbler, amethyst, blk or cobalt, ftd 25.00
New Century, bowl, berry; gr or crystal, lg, 8" 22.00
New Century, casserole, gr or crystal, w/lid, 9" 75.00
New Century, pitcher, pk, w/ or w/o ice lip, 60-oz, 7¾" 35.00
New Century, plate, sherbet; gr or crystal, 6" 5.00
New Century, platter, gr or crystal, oval, 11" 22.00
New Century, sugar bowl, gr or crystal, w/lid 28.00
New Century, tumbler, gr or crystal, 12-oz, 5¼" 30.00
Newport, bowl, berry; cobalt, 4¾" 22.00
Newport, bowl, cereal; amethyst, 5¼" 35.00
Newport, plate, sherbet; cobalt, 5⅞" 9.00
Newport, platter, cobalt, oval, 11¾" 48.00
Newport, saucer, cobalt or amethyst 5.00
No 610 Pyramid, bowl, berry; yel, 4¾" 40.00
No 610 Pyramid, ice tub, pk or gr 115.00
No 610 Pyramid, relish tray, pk, 4-part, hdls 45.00
No 610 Pyramid, tumbler, crystal, ftd, 11-oz 75.00
No 612 Horseshoe, bowl, berry; yel, lg, 9½" 50.00
No 612 Horseshoe, butter dish, gr w/lid 800.00
No 612 Horseshoe, pitcher, gr, 64-oz, 8½" 275.00
No 612 Horseshoe, plate, sherbet; yel, 6" 9.00
No 612 Horseshoe, relish tray, yel, 3-part, ftd 40.00
No 612 Horseshoe, tumbler, gr, 12-oz, 4¾" 170.00
No 616 Vernon, creamer, gr or yel, ftd 27.50
No 616 Vernon, plate, sandwich; crystal, 11½" 12.00
No 616 Vernon, tumbler, gr or yel, ftd, 5" 40.00
No 618 Pineapple & Floral, bowl, berry; crystal, 4¾" 25.00
No 618 Pineapple & Floral, creamer, amber or red, dmn shape 10.00
No 618 Pineapple & Floral, plate, salad; crystal, 8⅜" 8.50
No 618 Pineapple & Floral, platter, crystal, closed hdls, 11" 17.50
No 618 Pineapple & Floral, vase, crystal, cone shape 55.00
Normandie, bowl, cereal; amber, 6½" 28.00
Normandie, plate, sherbet; pk, 6" 6.00
Normandie, tumbler, iced tea; pk, 12-oz, 5" 110.00
Old Cafe, bowl, berry; crystal or pk, 3¾" 9.00
Old Cafe, bowl, Royal Ruby, closed hdls, 9" 16.00
Old Cafe, olive dish, crystal or pk, oblong, 6" 9.00
Old Cafe, pitcher, crystal or pk, 80-oz 125.00
Old Cafe, tumbler, juice; Royal Ruby, 3" 16.00
Old English, candlesticks, pk, gr or amber, 4", pr 38.00
Old English, fruit stand, pk, gr or amber, ftd, 11" 40.00
Old English, pitcher, pk, gr or amber, w/lid 125.00
Old English, tumbler, pk, gr or amber, ftd, 5½" 35.00
Ovide, candy dish, blk, w/lid 45.00
Ovide, creamer, Art Deco 95.00
Ovide, platter, decor wht, 11" 22.50
Ovide, sugar bowl, gr, open 4.00
Oyster & Pearl, bowl, crystal or pk, heart shape, hdl, 5¼" 14.00
Oyster & Pearl, candle holders, crystal or pk, 3½", pr 35.00
Oyster & Pearl, relish dish, pk, divided, oblong, 10¼" 17.50
Parrot, bowl, berry; amber, lg, 8" 75.00
Parrot, butter dish, gr, w/lid 395.00
Parrot, hot plate, amber, 5" 950.00
Parrot, plate, grill; gr, rnd, 10½" 32.00
Parrot, plate, sherbet; gr, 5¾" 35.00
Parrot, saucer, amber or gr 15.00
Parrot, tumbler, gr, 10-oz, 4¼" 175.00
Patrician, bowl, berry; pk or gr, 5" 12.00
Patrician, bowl, vegetable; amber or crystal, oval, 10" 33.00
Patrician, cookie jar, gr, w/lid 595.00

Patrician, pitcher, amber or crystal, 75-oz, 8" 125.00
Patrician, plate, sherbet; pk or gr, 6" 8.00
Patrician, saucer, amber, crystal, pk or gr 9.50
Patrician, tumbler, gr, 14-oz, 5½" 45.00
Patrick, bowl, fruit; pk, hdls, 9" 175.00
Patrick, goblet, cocktail; pk or yel, 6-oz, 4¾" 80.00
Patrick, plate, luncheon; yel, 8" 27.50
Patrick, tray, pk, center hdl, 11" 155.00
Petalware, bowl, cream soup; monax plain, 4½" 12.00
Petalware, creamer, cremax, monax florette, ftd 12.50
Petalware, plate, salad; red trim floral, 8" 25.00
Petalware, platter, crystal, oval, 13" 8.50
Petalware, sherbet, pk, low ft, 4½" 10.00
Primo, bowl, yel or gr, 3-ftd, 11" 45.00
Primo, creamer, yel or gr 12.00
Primo, plate, dinner; yel or gr, 10" 25.00
Primo, plate, yel or gr, 6¼" 10.00
Primo, sherbet, yel or gr 14.00
Princess, ashtray, topaz or apricot, 4½" 110.00
Princess, bowl, pk, hat shaped, 9½" 50.00
Princess, butter dish, gr, w/lid 100.00
Princess, cookie jar, pk, w/lid 70.00
Princess, plate, grill; gr, closed hdls, 10½" 10.00
Princess, saucer/sherbet plate, bl 60.00
Princess, saucer/sherbet plate, pk 10.00
Princess, tumbler, topaz or apricot, ftd, 12½-oz, 6½" 165.00
Queen Mary, bowl, berry; crystal, 4½" 4.00
Queen Mary, butter dish, crystal, w/lid 25.00
Queen Mary, plate, pk, 6⅝" 6.00
Queen Mary, sherbet, crystal 5.00
Raindrops, bowl, berry; gr, 7½" 50.00
Raindrops, sugar bowl, gr, w/lid 47.50
Raindrops, tumbler, gr, 9½-oz, 4⅛" 9.00
Ribbon, bowl, cereal; gr, 5" 40.00
Ribbon, cup, gr 5.00
Ribbon, shakers, blk, pr 45.00
Ribbon, tumbler, gr, 10-oz, 6" 33.00
Ring, bowl, crystal w/decor or gr, divided, 5¼" 35.00
Ring, cocktail shaker, crystal 20.00
Ring, goblet, wine; crystal w/decor or gr, 3½-oz, 4½" 20.00
Ring, plate, luncheon; crystal, 8" 2.50
Ring, tumbler, iced tea; crystal, ftd, 6½" 8.00
Ring, tumbler, w/decor or gr, 9-oz, 4¼" 10.00
Rock Crystal, bowl, finger; red, plain edge, w/7" plate 85.00
Rock Crystal, bowl, red, scalloped edge, 4" 32.00
Rock Crystal, bowl, roll tray; bl, yel or blk, 13" 60.00
Rock Crystal, bowl, salad; crystal, scalloped edge, 9" 25.00
Rock Crystal, candelabra, bl, yel or blk, 3-light, pr 125.00
Rock Crystal, comport, crystal, 7" 35.00
Rock Crystal, ice dish, crystal, 3 styles, ea 40.00
Rock Crystal, pitcher, bl, yel or blk, w/lid, lg, 9" 330.00
Rock Crystal, plate, red, scalloped edge, 9" 55.00
Rock Crystal, sandwich server, crystal, center hdl 30.00
Rock Crystal, saucer, bl, yel or blk 8.50
Rock Crystal, stem, wine; red, 2-oz 50.00
Rock Crystal, sundae, bl, yel or blk, low ft, 6-oz 18.00
Rock Crystal, vase, red, ftd, 11" 195.00
Rose Cameo, bowl, cereal; gr, 5" 20.00
Rose Cameo, bowl, gr, str sides, 6" 25.00
Rose Cameo, plate, salad; gr, 7" 14.00
Rosemary, bowl, cream soup; pk, 5" 32.00
Rosemary, bowl, vegetable; amber, oval, 10" 17.00
Rosemary, cup, gr 9.50
Rosemary, plate, grill; pk 22.00
Rosemary, tumbler, gr, 9-oz, 4¼" 35.00
Roulette, bowl, fruit; pk or gr, 9" 25.00
Roulette, pitcher, crystal, 65-oz, 8" 30.00
Roulette, plate, sandwich; pk or gr, 12" 16.00
Roulette, tumbler, iced tea; pk or gr, 12-oz, 5½" 33.00
Round Robin, bowl, berry; irid, 4" 9.00
Round Robin, plate, sandwich; irid, 12" 10.00
Roxana, bowl, cereal; yel, 6" 20.00
Roxana, bowl, yel, 4½x2⅜" 15.00
Roxana, plate, sherbet; yel, 6" 10.00
Royal Lace, bowl, berry; gr, rnd, 10" 30.00
Royal Lace, bowl, cream soup; bl, 4¾" 47.00
Royal Lace, bowl, pk, 3-legged, rolled edge, 10" 95.00
Royal Lace, butter dish, crystal, w/lid 75.00
Royal Lace, candlesticks, pk, rolled edge, pr 135.00
Royal Lace, creamer, bl, ftd 60.00
Royal Lace, pitcher, pk, w/o lip, 64-oz, 3" 110.00
Royal Lace, plate, luncheon; crystal, 8½" 8.00
Royal Lace, sugar bowl, gr, w/lid 82.00
Royal Lace, tumbler, crystal, 10-oz, 4⅞" 35.00
S Pattern, pitcher (like American Sweetheart), crystal, 80-oz 75.00
S Pattern, pitcher (like Dogwood), gr or pk, 80-oz 550.00
S Pattern, plate, cake; crystal, heavy, 11¾" 40.00
S Pattern, tumbler, yel, amber or crystal w/trims, 5-oz, 3½" 8.00
Sandwich, basket, amber or crystal, 10" H 35.00
Sandwich, butter dish, teal bl, w/dome lid 155.00
Sandwich, cruet, pk or gr, w/stopper, 6½-oz 175.00
Sandwich, decanter, red, w/stopper 80.00
Sandwich, pitcher, amber or crystal, 68-oz 22.00
Sandwich, sandwich server, red, center hdl 45.00
Sharon, bowl, berry; pk or gr, lg, 8½" 35.00
Sharon, bowl, cream soup; gr, 5" 55.00
Sharon, cheese dish, amber, w/lid 195.00
Sharon, pitcher, amber, w/ice lip, 80-oz 145.00
Sharon, shakers, pk, pr 55.00
Sharon, sugar bowl, gr, w/lid 56.00
Ships, cocktail mixer, bl & wht, w/stirrer 30.00
Ships, plate, sherbet; bl & wht, 5⅞" 30.00
Ships, tumbler, iced tea; bl & wht, 10½-oz, 4⅞" 16.00
Ships, tumbler, roly poly; bl & wht, 6-oz 11.00
Ships, tumbler, shot glass; bl & wht, 2-oz, 2¼" 195.00
Sierra, bowl, berry; pk, lg, 8½" 35.00
Sierra, pitcher, pk, 32-oz, 6½" 115.00
Sierra, serving tray, gr, hdls, 10¼" 20.00
Sierra, shakers, pk or gr, pr 45.00
Spiral, bowl, berry; gr, 4¾" 5.00
Spiral, pitcher, gr, 58-oz, 7⅝" 32.00
Spiral, sandwich server, gr, center hdl 25.00
Spiral, vase, gr, ftd, 5¾" 50.00
Starlight, bowl, cereal; pk, closed hdls, 5½" 12.00
Starlight, plate, bread & butter; crystal or wht, 6" 3.00
Starlight, plate, sandwich; crystal or wht, 13" 15.00
Starlight, sherbet, crystal or wht 15.00
Strawberry, bowl, pk or gr, 2x6¼" 125.00
Strawberry, butter dish, crystal or irid, w/lid 135.00
Strawberry, pitcher, crystal or irid, 7¾" 175.00
Strawberry, sugar bowl, pk or gr, open, sm 22.00
Sunburst, candlesticks, dbl; crystal, pr 30.00
Sunburst, plate, sandwich; crystal, 11¾" 20.00
Sunburst, sherbet, crystal 15.00
Sunflower, cup, pk 16.00
Sunflower, trivet, gr, 3-legged, turned up edges, 7" 335.00
Swirl, bowl, console; ultramarine, ftd, 10½" 30.00
Swirl, bowl, salad; pk, 9" 26.00

Swirl, butter dish, pk, w/lid 210.00
Swirl, cup, Delphite 10.00
Swirl, lug soup, ultramarine, tab hdls 40.00
Swirl, plate, sandwich; pk, 12½" 22.00
Swirl, plate, ultramarine, 7¼" 15.00
Swirl, vase, pk, ruffled, ftd, 6½" 23.00
Tea Room, bowl, banana split; pk, flat, 7½" 115.00
Tea Room, bowl, celery; gr, 8¼" 35.00
Tea Room, creamer, gr or pk, 3¼" 27.50
Tea Room, lamp, electric; gr, 9" 125.00
Tea Room, plate, sherbet; pk, 6½" 30.00
Tea Room, shakers, pk, pr 50.00
Tea Room, sugar bowl, gr, w/lid, 3" 110.00
Tea Room, tumbler, pk, flat, 8-oz, 4¼" 120.00
Thistle, bowl, fruit; gr, lg, 10¼" 250.00
Thistle, plate, grill; gr, 10¼" 30.00
Thistle, plate, luncheon; pk, 8" 20.00
Thistle, saucer, pk or gr 10.00
Tulip, bowl, amber, crystal or gr, oval, oblong, 13¼" 90.00
Tulip, candle holder, amethyst or bl, 3x5¼" 55.00
Tulip, plate, amber, crystal or gr, 6" 9.00
Tulip, sherbet (ivy bowl), amethyst or bl, flat, 3¾" 22.00
Twisted Optic, basket, pk, gr or amber, 10" H 60.00
Twisted Optic, bowl, bl or canary yel, 9" 25.00
Twisted Optic, candy jar, bl, ftd, flanged edge, w/lid 70.00
Twisted Optic, candy jar, pk, gr or amber, flat, w/lid 30.00
Twisted Optic, pitcher, pk, gr or amber, 64-oz 30.00
Twisted Optic, plate, luncheon; bl or canary yel, 8" 8.00
Twisted Optic, sandwich server, bl or canary yel, hdls 18.00
Twisted Optic, tumbler, pk, gr or amber, 9-oz, 4½" 6.00
Twisted Optic, vase, pk, gr or amber, str edge, hdls, 8" 35.00
US Swirl, butter dish, gr or pk, w/lid 120.00
US Swirl, comport, gr 30.00
US Swirl, plate, sherbet; gr or pk, 6⅛" 2.50
US Swirl, sugar bowl, gr or pk, w/lid 35.00
Victory, bowl, cereal; blk or bl, 6½" 40.00
Victory, comport, amber, pk or gr, 6x6¾" 15.00
Victory, plate, bread & butter; amber, pk or gr, 6" 6.00
Victory, plate, luncheon; blk or bl, 8" 30.00
Victory, sherbet, amber, pk or gr, ftd 13.00
Vitrock, bowl, berry; wht, 4" 5.00
Vitrock, cup, wht 4.00
Vitrock, plate, salad; wht, 7¼" 2.50
Vitrock, saucer, wht 2.50
Waterford, butter dish, pk, w/lid 220.00
Waterford, creamer, crystal, Miss America style 35.00
Waterford, goblet, pk, Miss America style, 5½" 110.00
Waterford, pitcher, crystal, tilted, w/ice lip, 80-oz 36.00
Waterford, plate, dinner; pk, 9⅝" 25.00
Waterford, sherbet, crystal 5.00
Waterford, tumbler, pk, ftd, 10-oz, 4⅞" 25.00
Windsor, bowl, berry; pk, lg, 8½" 22.00
Windsor, bowl, cream soup; pk, 5" 24.00
Windsor, butter dish, gr, 2 styles, ea 95.00
Windsor, platter, relish; crystal, divided, 11½" 12.00
Windsor, tray, gr, hdls, sq, 4" 12.00
Windsor, tumbler, crystal, ftd, 11-oz, 5" 11.00

Derby

William Duesbury operated in Derby, England, from about 1755, purchasing a second establishment, The Chelsea Works, in 1769. During this period fine porcelains were produced which so impressed the King that in 1773 he issued the company the Crown Derby patent. In 1810, several years after Duesbury's death, the factory was bought by Robert Bloor. The quality of the ware suffered under the new management, and the main Derby pottery closed in 1848. Within a short time, the work was revived by a dedicated number of former employees who established their own works on King Street in Derby.

The earliest known Derby mark was the crown over a script 'D'; however this mark is rarely found today. Soon after 1782, that mark was augmented with a device of crossed batons and six dots, usually applied in underglaze blue. During the Bloor period, the crown was centered within a ring containing the words 'Bloor' above and 'Derby' below the crown, or with a red printed stamp — the crowned Gothic 'D.' The King Street plant produced figurines that may be distinguished from their earlier counterparts by the presence of an 'S' and 'H' on either side of the crown and crossed batons.

In 1876 a new pottery was constructed in Derby, and the owners revived the earlier company's former standard of excellence. The Queen bestowed the firm the title Royal Crown Derby in 1890; it still operates under that name today. See also Royal Crown Derby.

Platter, cobalt and iron-red floral and foliate design on stoneware, 22½x18½", $935.00.

Figurine, Chas 1, rich colors, ca 1780, rprs, 9" 675.00
Figurine, Dr Syntax riding lady piggy-bk, Debarquant..., 4½" 850.00
Figurine, seated lady (gent), fancy attire, 1810, rstr, 6", pr 800.00
Pitcher & bowl, birds/people/trees, gold on purple, Bloor, mini .850.00
Tea set, Old Avesbury, 9¼" pot+cr/sug 175.00

Desert Sands

As early as the 1850s, the Evans family living in the Ozark Mountains of Missouri produced domestic clay products. Their small pot shop was passed on from one generation to the next. In the 1920s it was moved to North Las Vegas, Nevada, where the name Desert Sands was adopted. Succeeding generations of the family continued to relocate, taking the business with them. From 1937 to 1962 it operated in Boulder City, Nevada; then it was moved to Barstow, California, where it remained until it closed in the late 1970s.

Desert Sands pottery is similar to Mission Ware by Niloak. Various mineral oxides were blended to mimic the naturally occurring sand formations of the American West. A high-gloss glaze was applied to add intensity to the colorful striations that characterize the ware. Not all examples are marked, making it sometimes difficult to attribute. Marked items carry an ink stamp with the Desert Sands designation. Paper labels were also used.

Ashtray, 6½" 25.00
Bowl, console; hand thrown, 9½" 65.00
Bowl, incurvate rim, 3" 18.00
Butter dish 60.00
Candle holder, 3" 18.00

Mug 32.00
Shakers, ftd, pr 30.00
Tumbler 22.00
Vase, bulbous, flared rim, 3½" 35.00
Vase, inverted cylinder, slim, 5" 25.00
Vase, waisted form, flared rim, 2½" 25.00
Vase, 3-color swirl, T Evans, 4¼" 30.00

Devon, Crown Devon

Devon and Crown Devon were trade names of S. Fielding and Company, Ltd., an English firm founded after 1879. They produced majolica, earthenware mugs, vases, and kitchenware. In the 1930s they manufactured an exceptional line of Art Deco vases that have recently been much in demand.

Bowl, galleon/crew, mc/gilt, 2 hdls ea side, '30s, 9½" 425.00
Bowl, wht w/mc roses, gold trim, w/hdls, 3x12½" dia 175.00
Figurine, dancing girl, Art Deco, #172, paper label, 7x4" 240.00
Jug, musical; kangaroo hdl, Cap Cook at Botany Bay 2,130.00
Pitcher, Daisy Bell, #812207, musical, wind-up, sgn, 8x8" 325.00
Pitcher, Scottish couple, emb flowers/figures, musical, 8" 490.00
Tankard, abdication; HM Edward VIII, musical, 6x6", EX 850.00
Vase, galleon, red, gr & yel on cobalt bl, 2 hdls, 8½x16" 360.00
Vase, spider web/flowers, Rouge Royale, V rim w/loop hdls, 9" ..265.00

Dickota

The Dickota Pottery, a name coined from Dickinson, North Dakota, where it was founded as a brickyard, began operations in the early 1930s. In 1934 potters formerly associated with the North Dakota School of Mines and Charles Hyten from Niloak began their own operation there. Hyten developed a line of swirled ware which was marked 'Dickota Badlands.' Vases, bowls, and ashtrays in a mottled glaze were also made. A variety of marks were used, all of which contain the Dickota name. The company closed in the late 1930s. For further information we recommend *Collector's Encyclopedia of the Dakota Potteries, Identification & Values*, by Darlene Hurst Dommel (Collector Books).

Paperweight, shield shape, 2¾", from $35.00 to $45.00. (Photo courtesy Darlene Hurst Dommel)

Ashtray, cowboy hat shape, brn or gr, 4½x5" 50.00
Basket, hanging; matt gold w/molded decor, 5¼" 85.00
Bowl, flower; sundogs in relief, brn gloss, 3x6½" 75.00
Bowl, Peacock Blue, Cableware, 3½x5" 35.00
Creamer & sugar bowl, orange gloss w/gold/blk overglaze, 2½" ...45.00
Dish, blk gloss, Cableware, 1x3½" 25.00
Dish, sea gr, shell form, 1½x7¼" 30.00
Paperweight, Brown Federal House, 4½" 40.00
Pitcher, Peacock Blue, ice lip, 8", +4 4" tumblers 175.00
Pitcher, Peacock Pink, 5" 60.00
Plate, dk bl, Cableware, 8" 30.00
Shakers, maroon red, Cableware, 1½x2½", pr 35.00
Teapot, blk gloss, Cableware, 3¾" 175.00
Teapot, Peacock Blue, 4½x8" 115.00
Vase, bud; Peacock Blue (or Pink), 6½" 30.00
Vase, Dickota Badlands swirl, 6" 175.00
Vase, orange gloss w/gold/blk overglaze, 4" 50.00
Vase, Peacock Pink, 7½" 75.00

Documents

Although the word 'document' is defined in the general sense as 'anything printed or written, etc., relied upon to record or prove something. . .,' in the collectibles market, the term is more diversified with broadsides, billheads, checks, invoices, letters and letterheads, land grants, receipts, and waybills some of the most sought after. Some documents in demand are those related to a specific subject such as advertising, mining, railroads, military, politics, banking, slavery, nautical, or legal (deeds, mortgages, etc.). Other collectors look for examples representing a specific period of time such as colonial documents, Revolutionary or Civil War documents, early western documents, or those from a specific region, state, or city.

Aside from supply and demand, there are five major factors which determine the collector-value of a document. These are:

1) Age — Documents from the eastern half of the country can be found that date back to the 1700s or earlier. Most documents sought by collectors usually date from 1700 to 1900. Those with twentieth-century dates are still abundant and not in demand unless of special significance or beauty.

2) Region of origin — Depending on age, documents from rural and less-populated areas are harder to find than those from major cities and heavily populated states. The colonization of the West and Midwest did not begin until after 1850, so while an 1870s billhead from New York or Chicago is common, one from Albuquerque or Phoenix is not, since most of the Southwest was still unsettled.

3) Attractiveness — Some documents are plain and unadorned, but collectors prefer colorful, profusely illustrated pieces. Additional artwork and engravings add to the value.

4) Historical content — Unusual or interesting content, such as a letter written by a Civil War soldier giving an eye-witness account of the Battle of Gettysburg or a western territorial billhead listing numerous animal hides purchased from a trapper, will sell for more than one with mundane information.

5) Condition — Through neglect or environmental conditions, over many decades paper articles can become stained, torn, or deteriorated. Heavily damaged or stained documents are generally avoided altogether. Those with minor problems are more acceptable, although their value will decrease anywhere from 20% to 50%, depending upon the extent of damage. Avoid attempting to repair tears with tape — sell 'as is' so that the collector can take proper steps toward restoration.

Foreign documents are plentiful; and though some are very attractive, resale may be difficult. The listings that follow are generalized; prices are variable depending entirely upon the five points noted above. Values here are based upon examples with no major damage. Common grade documents without significant content are found in abundance and generally have little collector value. These usually date from the late 1800s to mid-1900s. It should be noted that the items listed below are examples of those that meet the criteria for having collector value. There is little demand for documents worth less than $5.00. For more information we recommend *Owning Western History* by our advisor Warren Anderson. His address and ordering information may be found in the Directory under Utah.

Key:
illus — illustrated vgn — vignette

Captain's log, for Cutter Caroline, 1799, EX 1,095.00
Certification, verifying hospital stay of soldier, 1862 ....45.00
Deed, RI land parcel, printed/filled out in ink, 1808, 13x14" 20.00
Envelope, Confederate Bonds below handcuffs, blk on wht 32.50
Envelope, Major Gen McClellan & portrait, ca 1861, EX 27.50
Envelope, Union, Liberty w/bundle leans on war drum, sword at ft .32.50
Envelope, US flag on pole w/stars & bars shield at base 20.00
General orders, Dept of VA & NC, to Civil War General, 1864 .30.00
Indenture, English, on vellum, 4 wax seals, 1745, VG 70.00
Invoice, articles received by Union officer, handwritten, 1863 ....40.00
Land grant, printed on parchment, sgn Van Buren (by secretary), 1837 ..60.00
Letter, War of 1812, pay schedule for soldiers, 1815, 8x13" 18.00
List of quartermaster's stores, 2-sided, printed/handwritten, 1864 ...55.00
List of stores, received from 2nd OH Heavy Artillery in TN, 1865 ..8.50
Pay voucher, MO officer w/1 servant listed, 1863 ....8.50
Pay voucher, Revolutionary War, pay to captain, handwritten, 1779 ..25.00
Power of attorney, printed/handwritten, legal format, 1864 ....65.00
Printed response, US Treasury Dept, for filing monthly account, 1865 .40.00
Receipt, in-field provisions, handwritten, 1865 ....42.50
Regulations, for admission at Naval academy, 1860s, 4-pg, EX 18.00
Voucher, Treasury Dept, for schooner's services, 1865 ....55.00

Dollhouses and Furnishings

Dollhouses were introduced commercially in this country late in the 1700s by Dutch craftsmen who settled in the East. By the mid-1800s, they had become meticulously detailed, divided into separate rooms, and lavishly furnished to reflect the opulence of the day. Originally intended for the amusement of adults of the household, by the latter 1800s their status had changed to that of a child's toy. Though many early dollhouses were lovingly hand fashioned for a special little girl, those made commercially by such companies as Bliss and Schoenhut are highly valued.

Furniture and furnishings in the Biedermeier style featuring stenciled Victorian decorations often sell for several hundred dollars each. Other early pieces made of pewter, porcelain, or papier-mache are also quite valuable. Certainly less expensive but very collectible, nonetheless, is the quality, hallmarked plastic furniture produced during the '40s by Renwal and Acme, and the 1960s Petite Princess line produced by Ideal. In the listings that follow, dollhouses are litho paper on wood, unless otherwise noted. For more information, see *Schroeder's Collectible Toys, Antique to Modern*. Our advisor for this category is Barbara Rosen; she is listed in the Directory under New Jersey. See also Miniatures.

Furniture

Armoire, Tomy Smaller Homes 10.00
Bathroom set, Arcade, wht-pnt CI, 5-pc, EX 300.00
Bathroom set, Marx, hard plastic, dk ivory, 4-pc 20.00
Bed, Best, pk 5.00
Chair, bedroom; Kilgore, gr-pnt CI 40.00
Chair, living room; Jaydon, reddish brn swirl 15.00
China closet, Renwal, brn w/stenciling 15.00
Dining room set, Marx, hard plastic, brn swirl, 7-pc 30.00
Doll, baby; Renwal 10.00
Doll, mother; Renwal, plastic rivets, pk 25.00
Dresser & lamp, Mattel Littles, MIB 12.00
Dresser w/mirror, Marx, hard plastic, tan 3.00
Hutch, Endeaver, wht w/red 5.00
Ironing board & iron, Renwal, pk or bl, ea 22.00
Living room set, Tootsietoy, complete, MIB 225.00

Parlor Furniture set, paper litho on wood, late nineteenth century, sofa, five chairs, footstool, piano, and table with faux marble top, 1" scale, EXIB, $800.00.

Piano, baby grand; Strombecker, walnut 20.00
Playground set, Kilgore, bl-pnt CI, 3-pc, NM 75.00
Playpen, Wolverine 8.00
Radio, floor; Strombecker, walnut w/etched detail 12.00
Refrigerator, Endeavor, ivory, opening door 5.00
Rocker, Grand Rapids, stained wood 18.00
Rocking horse, Best, pk 12.00
Shopping cart, Ideal, wht w/red basket 40.00
Sink, bathroom; Plasco, pk or turq, ea 4.00
Sink, kitchen; Donna Lee, wht 6.00
Sofa, Ideal Petite Princess, brocade 25.00
Sofa, Superior, brn 5.00
Stove, Donna Lee, wht 6.00
Stove, Marx, hard plastic, ivory or wht, ea 5.00
Stroller, Acme, pk w/bl or wht wheels, ea 6.00
Table, coffee; Marx, hard plastic, lt gr 10.00
Table, dining; Ideal, dk marbleized maroon 20.00
Table, dressing; Blue Box, wht w/pk 4.00
Table, folding; Renwal, copper 18.00
Table, kitchen; Plasco, lt bl 5.00
Toilet, Strombecker, yel, ivory or aqua, ea 10.00
Tub, corner; Ideal, bl w/yel 18.00
Vanity & bench, Plasco, no-mirror style, pk 8.00
Washing machine, Superior, wht 5.00

Houses

Bliss, Rockaway Stable, wood/cb, 2 horses/sled/jockey, 12x10", EX ..800.00
Bliss, 2-story, 2 rooms, yel, red roof, 2 upper windows, 17", VG ...250.00
Carriage house, paper litho, 3-stall w/papier-mache horses, 14", VG .425.00
Fisher-Price, #280, 3-story, battery-operated, 1981-84, M 30.00
Germany, stable, 2-story, 3 stalls w/3 horses, 16", VG 550.00
Germany, 3-story w/8 rooms, wood, cream, red roof, 1920, 23x38", EX .850.00
Marx, Newlyweds' Dining Room, #194, litho tin, 1925, 3x5x3", MIB ..250.00
Marx, split-level, gray siding w/yel brick, w/few accessories, EX ...80.00
Marx, 2-story Colonial w/breezeway, w/54 furniture pcs, 1960s, VG ..150.00
Marx, 2-story w/7 rooms, tin, wht/mc stone, red roof, ¾" scale, VG ..100.00
McLoughlin Bros, Dolly's Playhouse, 1890s, 18½", NMIB 375.00
Paper litho, 2-room, front opens, minor rprs, 14" H, G 450.00
Rich, bungalow, Arts & Crafts style, cb, wht/red, '30s, 32x21", VG ..200.00
Rich, fiberboard, red roof, bl shutters, porch, 1940s, 14x24", VG ..135.00
Schoenhut, 2-room bungalow, wood w/cb roof, electrified, 17x15", EX ..600.00
Schoenhut, 2-story, brick/stone, glass windows, 23x23", VG ..1,100.00
T Cohn, 2-story w/patio, w/50 furniture pcs, 1948, ¾" scale, EX ...335.00
Tommy Smaller Homes, split-level, fiberboard/plastic, 1970s, EX .200.00
Wolverine, Colonial Mansion, no garage, ½" scale, EX 50.00

Wolverine, Grocery Store, tin, separate counter, 1930s, 12x16", G .150.00

Dolls

To learn to invest your money wisely as you enjoy the hobby of doll collecting, you must become aware of defects which may devaluate a doll. In bisque, watch for eye chips, hairline cracks and chips, or breaks on any part of the head. Composition should be clean, not crazed or cracked. Vinyl and plastic should be clean with no pen or crayon marks. Though a quality replacement wig is acceptable for bisque dolls, composition and hard plastics should have their originals in uncut condition. Original clothing is a must except in bisque dolls, since it is unusual to find one in its original costume.

It is important to remember that prices are based on condition and rarity. When no condition is noted, dolls are assumed to be in excellent condition with the exceptions of American Character, Cameo, Celebrity Dolls, Kestner, Madame Alexander, and Shirley Temple, which are generally priced in mint condition. Cabbage Patch values are for dolls mint in the box. In relation to bisque dolls, excellent means having no cracks, chips, or hairlines, being nicely dressed, shoed, wigged, and ready to to be placed into a collection. For a more thorough study of the subject, refer to *Collector's Guide to Dolls of the 1960s and 1970s* by Cindy Sabulis, *Talking Toys of the 20th Century* by Kathy and Don Lewis; *Collector's Encyclopedia of American Composition Dolls, 1900–1950,* by Ursula R. Mertz; and *Modern Collectible Dolls, Vol IV,* and *Doll Values, Antique to Modern, Fourth Edition,* by Patsy Moyer, our advisor for this category. Mrs. Moyer is listed in the Directory under New Mexico. Several other book are referenced throughout this category. All are published by Collector Books.

Key:

bjtd — ball-jointed	OC — original clothes
blb — bent limb body	o/m — open mouth
bsk — bisque	p/e — pierced ears
c/m — closed mouth	pnt — painted
hh — human hair	pwt — paperweight eyes
hp — hard plastic	RpC — replaced clothes
jtd — jointed	ShHd — shoulder head
MIG — Made In Germany	ShPl — shoulder plate
NC — no clothes	SkHd — socket head
o/c/e — open closed eyes	str — straight
o/c/m — open closed mouth	trn — turned

American Character

AC or Petite, baby or mama, compo head & cloth, OC, 14" 175.00
Betsy McCall, all vinyl, rooted hair, mk McCall 1961, OC, 36" ..550.00
Betsy McCall, hp, jtd knees, bathing suit, 1957, EX 100.00
Bottletot, compo head, cryer, o/c/e, pnt hair, OC, 18" 325.00
Campbell Kid, compo, jtd limbs, mk A Petite Doll, OC, 12" 335.00
Carol Ann Berry, compo, o/c/e, c/m, 1935, OC, 13" 400.00
Eloise, cloth, yarn hair, crooked smile, 1950s, OC, 15" 250.00
Ricky Jr, vinyl baby boy, 1955-56, OC, 13" 50.00
Tiny Tears, hp & vinyl, OC, 1955-62, 8" 50.00
Toodles, vinyl, rooted hair, o/c/e, c/m, OC, 14" 125.00

Annalee

Barbara Annalee Davis has been making her dolls since 1950. What began as a hobby, very soon turned into a commercial venture. Her whimsical creations range from tiny angels atop powder puff clouds to funky giant frogs, some 42" in height. In between there are dolls for every occasion (with Christmas being her specialty), all characterized by their unique construction methods (felt over flexible wire framework) and wonderful facial expressions. Naturally, some of the older dolls are the most valuable (though more recent examples are desirable as well, depending on scarcity and demand), and condition, as usual, is very important. To date your doll, look at the tag. If made before 1986, that date is only the copyright date. (Dolls made after 1986 do carry the manufacturing date.) Dolls from the '50s have a long white red-embroidered tag with no date. From 1959 to '64, that same tag had a date in the upper right-hand corner. From 1965 until '70, it was folded in half and sewn into the seam. In 1970, a satiny white tag with a date preceded by a copyright symbol in the upper right-hand corner was used. In '75, the tag was a long white cotton strip with a copyright date. This tag was folded over in 1982, making it shorter. Our advisor for Annalee dolls is Jane Holt; she is listed in the Directory under New Hampshire.

Mouse (painted flat face) holds paint can and brush, 1968, 7", $250.00. (Photo courtesy Jane Holt)

Angel w/instruments, 1982-88, 7" 25.00
Ballerina Pig, 1981, 7" 75.00
Beach girl on towel, 1966, 10" 250.00
Bellhop, 1963, 24" 750.00
Bicentennial Boy & Girl Mice, 1976, 12", pr 300.00
Boy building boat, 1957, 10" 800.00
Bride & Groom, 1984-85, 10", pr 100.00
Bunny w/egg, 1978, 7" 45.00
Cardplayer Mouse, 1978, 7" 45.00
Caroller Mouse, wht, 1979 only, 12" 95.00
Clown, 1981, 42" 450.00
Colonial Boy Mouse, 1975-76, 7" 75.00
Country Cousin Boy & Girl Mice, 1970, 7", pr 250.00
Donkey, 1976, 18" 400.00
Duck, wht, w/raincoat & umbrella, 1985-86, 12" 95.00
Duck head pick, 1973 ....30.00
Easter Parade Boy & Girl Bunnies, 1977, 7", pr 65.00
Easter Parade Boy & Girl Bunnies, 1983, 29", pr 300.00
Easter Parade Goose, 1988, 24" 50.00
Elephant, 1976, 18" 400.00
Elf, red w/blk hair, 1970 10" 40.00
Equestrienne Mouse, 1983, 7" 75.00
Fancy Nancy Cat, yel, wht or hot pk, 1967, ea 450.00
Girl Caroller, 1974, 10" 80.00
Gnome, red, wht or gr, 1978, 12", ea 150.00
Gnome, 1976, 18" 175.00
Honey Pot Bear, 1984, 18" 75.00
Horse, brn w/hearts, 1968, 10" 425.00
Housewife Mouse, 1981, 7" 40.00
Huck Finn, on base w/globe, 1987, 10" 175.00
Jogger Mouse, 1979, 7" 20.00
Logo Kid w/pin, 1986, 7" 250.00
Monk, gr robe, carries sm tree in burlap bag, 1966, 10" 200.00
Nurse Mouse w/needle, 1979, 7" 50.00
Pilgrim Couple, 1978, 10", pr 160.00

Reindeer, flat face, 1966, 36" 575.00
Santa (3") in sleigh, 1989 ....35.00
Santa Frog, 1987, 10" 55.00
Santa in moon, 1983, 7" 50.00
Santa in rocking chair, 1986, 18" 75.00
Santa on Ski-Bob w/sack, 1971, 7" 150.00
Scarecrow, 1976, 10" 100.00
Snowman, 1987, 7" 30.00
Square Dancers, 1957, 10", pr, minimum value 950.00
Uncle Sam, 1976, 18" 500.00
Valentine Bunny, 1984, 7" 75.00
Yum Yum Bunny, 1966, 7" 300.00
Yum Yum Bunny, 1966, 12" 550.00

Armand Marseille

AM, baby, flange neck, 1907, 16" 650.00
AM, Floradora, SkHd, 12" 150.00
AM, Floradora 3748, ShHd, 21" 385.00
AM, Kiddiejoy, ShHd, cloth body, c/m, girl, 20" 1,600.00
AM, Rosebud, ShHd, 1902, 15" 300.00
AM, SkHd, 26" 525.00
AM 248, mk GB (Geo Borgfeldt), o/m, 1912, 10" 325.00
AM 252, SkHd, googly eyes, 10" 1,100.00
AM 253, SkHd, googly eyes, 8" 900.00
AM 300n, adult, SkHd, 15½" 1,200.00
AM 310/7/0 Just Me, SkHd, bl o/c/e to side, c/m, 9" 1,400.00
AM 323, SkHd, googly eyes, 11" 1,200.00
AM 327, SkHd, 1914, 12" 325.00
AM 341, My Dream Baby, flange, c/m, wht, 8" 185.00
AM 341, My Dream Baby, flange, c/m, 21" 625.00
AM 351, My Dream Baby, flange, o/m, wht, 22" 625.00
AM 352, Baby Love, flange, 1914, 19" 675.00
AM 370, 12" 185.00
AM 390, pnt bsk, 9" 145.00
AM 390, SkHd, brn o/c/e, 21" 750.00
AM 390, SKhd, o/m w/4 teeth, jtd compo, orig Scottish outfit, 9" .130.00
AM 390n, nun, SkHd, brn o/c/e, o/m w/teeth, OC, 20" 300.00
AM 390n, 1915, 11" 200.00
AM 500, Infant Berry, molded hair, 1908, 10" 450.00
AM 560a, Dorothy, 1912, 15" 350.00
AM 917, Mobi, baby, Germany, SkHd, 1921, 16" 575.00
AM 975, Sadie, baby, Otto Gans, 1914, 17" 500.00

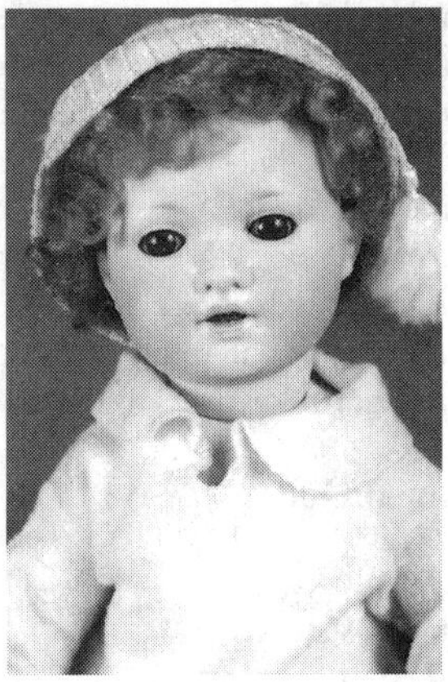

AM 985, bisque socket head, blue sleep eyes, open mouth with two upper teeth, saran wig, five-piece composition toddler body, re-dressed in snow suit, 20", VG+, $300.00. (Photo courtesy McMasters Auctions)

AM 985, baby, SkHd, 13½" 400.00
AM 990, Happy Tot, baby, SkHd, 8" 200.00
AM 992, baby, SkHd, 1914, 22" 700.00
AM 996, baby, SkHd, 15" 425.00
AM 1894, boy, SkHd, brn o/c/e, o/m w/teeth, rprs, RpC, 23" 400.00
AM 1894, ShPl, 26" 650.00
AM 3200, ShHd, some trn, 1898, 14" 265.00
Columbia, ShHd, 1904, 24" 385.00
Mabel, ShHd, 1898, 15" 300.00
Queen Louise, SkHd, 1910, 22" 400.00
Queen Louise, 100, SkHd, 1910, 18½" 425.00

Arranbee

Baby, compo/cloth, OC, 1930s-40s, 16" 125.00
Debu-Teen, compo ShHd, mohair or hh wig, c/m, OC, 1940, 12" ...155.00
Lil' Imp, hp, red hair, freckles, OC, 1960, 10" 75.00
My Angel, hp & vinyl, OC, 1961, 22" 70.00
Nancy, molded hair or wig, o/c/e, o/m, OC, 1930, 17" 300.00
Nancy Lee, compo, o/c/e, c/m, mohair wig, as skater, '49, 21", MIB .650.00
Nancy Lee, hp, o/c/e, c/m, mohair wig, 5-pc body, OC, 16" 350.00
Nanette, hp, o/c/e, c/m, synthetic wig, OC, 1949-59, 14" 250.00

Barbie Dolls and Related Dolls

Allan, 1963, pnt red hair, str legs, MIB 125.00
Allan, 1964, pnt red hair, bendable legs, orig outfit, VG 165.00
Barbie, #1, 1958-59, blond hair, MIB....9,950.00
Barbie, #1 , 1958-59, brunette hair, MIB 1,000.00
Barbie, #2, 1959, brunette hair, MIB....8,500.00
Barbie, #3, 1960, blond hair, orig swimsuit, NM....950.00
Barbie, #4, 1960, brunette hair, MIB....1,500.00
Barbie, #5, 1961, blond hair, orig swimsuit, NM....325.00
Barbie, #6, red hair, replica swimsuit, NM 600.00
Barbie, 1961, Bubble-Cut, jet blk hair, MIB 650.00
Barbie, 1961, Bubble-Cut, red hair, MIB....600.00
Barbie, 1961, Ponytail, blond hair, orig swimsuit, VG....285.00
Barbie, 1964, American Girl, blond hair, orig swimsuit, NM....550.00
Barbie, 1964, Miss, pnt hair, orig swimsuit & hat, 3 wigs & stand, NM .400.00
Barbie, 1964, Swirl Ponytail, blond hair, orig swimsuit, NM....400.00
Barbie, 1970, Standard, blond hair, MIB....700.00
Barbie, 1970, Twist 'N Turn, brunette hair, orig swimsuit & bow, NM .300.00
Barbie, 1971, Live Action, orig outfit, NM....150.00
Barbie, 1971, Talking, M....125.00
Barbie, 1976, Ballerina on Tour, MIB....100.00
Barbie, 1977, Fashion Photo, MIB....85.00
Barbie, 1980, Parisienne, Dolls of the World, MIB....200.00
Barbie, 1985, Greek, Dolls of the World, NRFB....70.00
Ken, 1969, Talking, MIB....275.00
Ken, 1972, Busy Talking, orig outfit, VG 85.00
Ken, 1975, Free Movin', NRFB 100.00
Midge, 1963, bendable legs, MIB....500.00
Midge, 1963, blond hair, str legs, nude, EX 75.00
PJ, 1975, Free Moving, orig swimsuit, NM....85.00
Skipper, 1973-75, Quick Curl, MIB....75.00
Skipper, 1974, Growing Up, NRFB 125.00
Skooter, 1963, brunette hair, orig swimsuit & bows, MIB 175.00
Todd, 1965, NRFB....225.00
Tutti, 1966, brunette hair, orig outfit, NM 85.00

Barbie Gifts Sets and Related Accessories

Case, Barbie Goes Travelin', 1965, EX....195.00
Case, Ken in Rally Days, teal, 1962, EX....20.00
Case, Tutti Play Case, various colors, EX, ea 35.00
Clothes, Barbie's Boudoir Fashion Pak, #1834, MOC 165.00
Clothes, Bride's Dream, Barbie, #947-2, complete, EX 85.00
Clothes, Campus Hero Ken, #770, complete, VG 35.00

Clothes, Cookie Time, Skipper, #1912, MRFB, minimum value..**150.00**
Clothes, First Things First, Francie, #1252-2, complete, NM........**55.00**
Clothes, Fraternity Dance, Barbie, #1638-0, complete, EX.........**225.00**
Clothes, Handsome for School, Todd, #7484, NRFB....................**45.00**
Clothes, Red Sensation, Skipper, #1902, 1964, complete, M........**45.00**
Clothes, Silken Flame, Barbie, #977-0, complete, NM..................**75.00**
Clothes, Tennis Tunic, Francie, #1221-0, complete, NM..............**45.00**
Gift set, Barbie Mix 'N Match Set, 1963, NRFB, from $2,000 to ..**3,000.00**
Gift set, Clowning Around, Tutti, #3606, 1967, complete, M.............**65.00**
Gift set, PJ Swingin' in Silver, Sears, 1970, complete, MIB...............**800.00**
House, Barbie Country Living, 1973-77, complete, EX.........................**75.00**
House, Tutti & Chris, 1967, complete, NM..**125.00**
Shop, Barbie Ice Cream Shoppe, 1987, complete, MIB.........................**50.00**
Vehicle, Barbie Jeep, 1987, MIB...**15.00**
Vehicle, Ken's Hot Rod, Irwin, 1961, NM..**165.00**

Belton

Concave head, 2 or 3 hole, EX bsk, o/c/m or c/m w/wig, 8" **800.00**
Concave head, 2 or 3 hole, EX bsk, o/c/m or c/m w/wig, 10" ...**1,200.00**
Concave head, 2 or 3 hole, EX bsk, o/c/m or c/m w/wig, 13" ...**1,600.00**
Concave head, 2 or 3 hole, EX bsk, o/c/m or c/m w/wig, 15" ...**1,900.00**
Concave head, 2 or 3 hole, EX bsk, o/c/m or c/m w/wig, 16" ...**2,000.00**
Concave head, 2 or 3 hole, EX bsk, o/c/m or c/m w/wig, 17" ...**2,400.00**
Concave head, 2 or 3 hole, EX bsk, o/c/m or c/m w/wig, 20" ...**2,800.00**
Concave head, 2 or 3 hole, EX bsk, o/c/m or c/m w/wig, 22" ...**3,000.00**
Concave head, 2 or 3 hole, EX bsk, o/c/m or c/m w/wig, 23" ...**3,200.00**
Concave head, 2 or 3 hole, EX bsk, o/c/m or c/m w/wig, 26" ...**3,800.00**

Boudoir Dolls

Boudoir dolls, often called bed dolls, French dolls, or flapper dolls, were popular from the late teens through the 1940s. The 1920s and 1930s were the golden age of boudoir dolls!

More common boudoir dolls are usually found with composition heads, arms, and high-heeled feet. Clothes are nailed on (later ones have stapled-on clothes). Wigs are usually mohair, human hair, or silk floss. Smoking boudoir dolls were made in the late teens and early 1920s. More expensive boudoir dolls were made in France, Italy, and Germany, as well as the U.S. Usually they are made entirely of cloth with elaborate sewn or pinned-on costumes and silk, felt, or velvet painted faces. Sizes of boudoir dolls vary, but most are around 30". These dolls were made to adorn a lady's boudoir or sit on a bed. They were not meant as children's playthings! Our advisor for this category is Bonnie Groves; she is listed in the Directory under Texas.

Composition shoulder plate, high-heeled feet, marked WKS Inc., replaced hat, VG clothes, 30", $175.00. (Photo courtesy Bonnie Groves)

Anita, compo head & hands, cloth body, nude, '20s, EX, $50 to .**85.00**
Anita, compo head & hands, silk floss wig, OC/shoes, VG, $150 to .**200.00**
Anita, glass eyes, all orig, EX, from $250 to **450.00**
Anita, nude, 30", VG, from $50 to **135.00**
Anita, sleep eyes, all orig, EX, from $300 to **500.00**
Blossom, lady, all orig, 30", EX, from $300 to **600.00**
Cloth, music box inside, all orig, Fr, 30", EX, minimum value ...**500.00**
Cloth, silk face, mohair wig, nude, shoes & stockings, 30", VG ..**85.00**
Common, std doll mk WKS Inc, crazed, EX clothes, 28" **45.00**
Compo, common carnival type, all orig, 1940s, 28", VG, $95 to .**165.00**
Compo, jtd arms, mk Sterling, all orig, 30", VG **150.00**
Compo, sleep eyes, bald, nude, 30", G **50.00**
Compo ShPl, compo arms/high-heeled ft, WKS Inc, EX clothes, 30" ..**200.00**
Doll head on hat stand, VG, from $65 to **135.00**
Etta, all cloth, all orig, 30", VG, from $200 to **450.00**
Finely pnt features, average clothes & quality, 28", from $85 to ...**125.00**
Finely pnt features, average clothes & quality, 32", from $100 to ..**150.00**
Finely pnt features, EX clothes/quality, glass eyes, 28", $145 to .**200.00**
Finely pnt features, EX clothes/quality, glass eyes, 32", $150 to .**250.00**
Finely pnt features, std quality, dressed, 16" **125.00**
Fr, silk face, bks limbs, OC, 30", VG **200.00**
Fr, silk face & costume, bsk arms & legs, 21", VG, from $150 to .**200.00**
Fr silk ballerina, rare, mini, 16" **500.00**
Fr silk face, bsk arms & legs, mini, 20", EX, from $200 to **350.00**
Glass eyed, 27", EX, from $145 to **200.00**
Lenci, 18-26", from $800 to **1,500.00**
Shoes for doll, EX, from $25 to **45.00**
Silk face, unmk, all orig, EX, 30" **300.00**
Smoker, Anita, head only, VG **50.00**
Smoker, Blossom, Argentine costume, all orig, 30", EX, from $350 to .**650.00**
Smoker, cloth, 16" **285.00**
Smoker, cloth, 25" **475.00**
Smoker, compo, 28" **375.00**
Smoker, jtd compo, all orig, 25", G, from $300 to **600.00**
Smoker, jtd compo, crazed, all orig, VG costume, from $300 to ..**600.00**
Smoker, jtd compo, nude/bald, 15", G-, from $50 to **100.00**
Smoker, Lenci, all orig, moth damage **500.00**
Unmk, silk face, wht mohair, RpC (old pattern), orig shoes, 30", EX .**200.00**
W-K-S, compo head, hands & ft, crazed/cracked, nude **35.00**
W-K-S, Inc, EX orig, from $150 to **275.00**

Bru

Brevete, swivel head, kid body, bsk lower arms, 13" **12,500.00**
Brevete, swivel head, kid body, bsk lower arms, 18" **17,250.00**
Bru Jne, kid over wood, wood legs, bsk lower arms, 12" **11,500.00**
Bru Jne, kid over wood, wood legs, bsk lower arms, 14" **13,500.00**
Bru Jne, kid over wood, wood legs, bsk lower arms, 23" **21,500.00**
Bru Jne R, c/m, 19" **3,850.00**
Bru Jne R, o/m, EX bsk, jtd compo body, 12" **2,000.00**
Bru Jne R, o/m, EX bsk, jtd compo body, 19" **5,000.00**
Circle dot or half circle, kid body, bsk lower arms, 13" **14,500.00**
Circle dot or half circle, kid body, bsk lower arms, 19" **21,500.00**
Nursing, trn key in bk of head, EX quality, 14", minimum **7,000.00**

Cameo Dolls

Annie Rooney, compo, yarn wig, molded shoes, M, minimum value ..**475.00**
Baby Bo Kaye, bsk/compo/cloth, glass eyes, o/m, 1925, 17", EX ..**1,875.00**
Baby Bo Kaye, celluloid, glass eyes, molded hair, 12", M **400.00**
Baby Mine, vinyl/cloth, o/c/e, 1962-64, OC, 16", M **100.00**
Betty Boop, compo/wood, label on torso, 1932, 11", M **650.00**
Giggles, compo, w/molded loop for ribbon, 1946, 14", EX **150.00**
Ho-Ho, plaster, 5½", EX **50.00**
Margie, compo & wood, pnt features, 10", EX **75.00**

Pretty Betsie, compo, pnt eyes, o/c/m, pnt clothes, 18", M 500.00
Scootles, Black compo, eyes pnt to side, 15", EX 200.00
Scootles, compo, eyes pnt to side, 1925+, M w/tag 365.00

China, Unmarked

Adelina Patti, center part, curls at temples, 1860s, 22" 525.00
Biedermeier or Bald head, takes wig, RpC, 14" 575.00
Brn eyes (pnt), any hairstyle or date, 20" 950.00
Common hairdo, blond or blk hair, RpC, after 1905, 23" 285.00
Covered Wagon Style, sausage curls, RpC, 1840s-70s, 24" 900.00
Curly top, loose ringlet curls, RpC, 1845-60s, 20" 700.00
Flat Top, blk hair, mid-part/short curls, RpC, ca 1860, 17" 300.00
Flat Top, blk hair, mid-part/short curls, RpC, ca 1860, 20" 350.00
Japanese, blk or blond hair, mk or unmk, RpC, 1910-20s, 17" ...250.00
Man or Boy, pnt eyes, side part, RpC, 14" 1,200.00
Peg Wood Body, early hairdo, 1840s, 16" 2,800.00
Pet Name, molded shirtwaist w/name on front, RpC, 1905, 8" ..125.00
Snood/Combs, any appl hair decor, RpC, 14" 650.00
Snood/Combs, any appl hair decor, RpC, 17" 800.00
Wood Body, articulated/slim hips, RpC, 1840s-50s, 17" 3,500.00
Wood Body, jtd hips, covered-wagon hairdo, 1840s-50s, 12" ..1,000.00

Cloth

A cloth doll in very good condition will display light wear and soiling, while one assessed as excellent will be clean and bright.

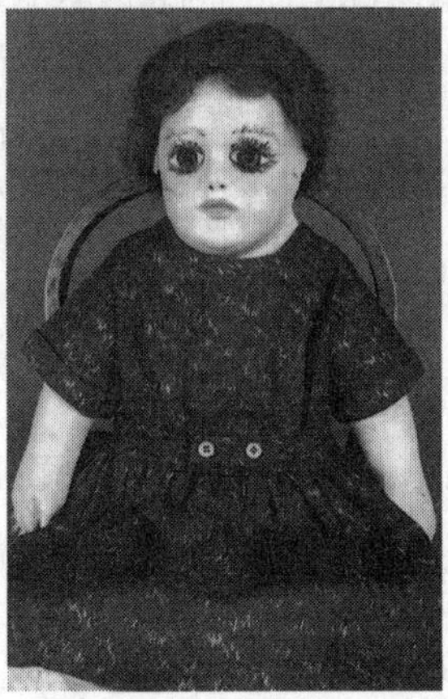

Alabama baby type, painted stockinette head, applied ears, coarse hair wig, cloth body, appropriately clothed, unmarked, 21", EX, $925.00. (Photo courtesy McMasters Auctions)

Alabama Indestructible Doll, baby, 1900-25, 15", VG 850.00
Alabama Indestructible Doll, child, 1900-25, 22" 2,400.00
Art Fabric Mills, Improved Life Sz Doll, printed undies, 20" 275.00
Babyland Rag by Horsman, flat pnt face, 30", VG 810.00
Babyland Rag by Horsman, litho face, 14½", VG 240.00
Babyland Rag by Horsman, molded/pnt face, 13" 700.00
Bing Art, wigged, cloth or felt, 16" 650.00
Black Mammy style, pnt or embr features, 1930s, 15", minimum .165.00
Chad Valley, Bonzo (dog), pnt eyes, 4", VG 65.00
Columbian Doll, Emma E Adams..., HP features, 15" 4,500.00
Mollye, child, 13" 130.00
Mollye, lady, long gown, 16", VG 55.00
Pitty Sing, 4 on uncut litho cloth sheet 300.00
Raggedy Ann & Andy, Mollye Goldman, 1920s, OC, 18", pr ..1,200.00
Wellings, child, pnt eyes, 1926-30, 18" 600.00

Eegee

Andy, vinyl, teen type, pnt/molded hair, pnt eyes, c/m, 1963, M .35.00
Babette, vinyl & cloth, pnt eyes, rooted hair, 1970, 15" 10.00
Baby Luv, vinyl & cloth, rooted hair, pnt eyes, 1973, 14", M 35.00
Barbara Cartland, adult, pnt features, 15", M 52.00
Child, compo, o/m, o/c/e, 14", M 160.00
Flowerkins, hp & vinyl, series of 7, 1973, MIB, ea 60.00
Gigi Perreau, vinyl & hp, o/c smiling mouth, 1951, 17", M 700.00
Miss Charming, compo, Shirley Temple look-alike, 1936, 19", M ..450.00
Shelly, Tammy type w/growing hair, 1964, 12", M 18.00
Tandy Talks, vinyl & hp, pull-string talker, 1961, M 50.00

Effanbee

Bernard Fleischaker and Hugo Baum became business partners in 1910, and after two difficult years of finding toys to buy, they decided to manufacture dolls and toys of their own. The Effanbee trademark is a blending of their names, Eff for Fleischaker and bee for Baum. The company still exists today. For more information we recommend *Effanbee Dolls* by Pat Smith, and *Collector's Encyclopedia of American Composition Dolls, 1900–1950*, by Ursula R. Mertz.

Anne Shirley, compo, 1935-40, 18", M 300.00
Baby Cup Cake, plastic/vinyl, o/c/e, dimples, RpC, 12" 20.00
Baby Dainty, compo/cloth, toddler, 1912+, 12" 80.00
Baby Evelyn, compo/cloth, ca 1925, 17", EX 75.00
Baby Grumpy, compo/cloth, pnt eyes/hair, pouty, 1915+, 11½" ...85.00
Baby Tinyette, compo, str or bent legs, OC, 8" 245.00
Baby Wonder, compo, tin o/c/e, o/c/m, holds bottle, OC, 13" ...165.00
Barbara Joan, compo, o/m, 1936-39, 15", M 700.00
Barbara Lou, compo, 1936-39, 21" 425.00
Button Nose, compo, pnt eyes, molded hair, OC, 8" 185.00
Candy Kid, compo toddler, o/c/e, pnt hair, 1946+, 13½" 75.00
Candy Walker, vinyl/hp, head turns, rooted hair, OC, 24" 200.00
Gumdrop, vinyl, jtd toddler, o/c/e, 1962+, 16", M 35.00
Lil Darlin', vinyl/cloth, cry box, o/c/e, OC, 16" 95.00
Louis Armstrong, vinyl, 1984-85, 11", M 85.00
Marilee, compo ShHd mama, o/c/e, o/m, 1934, 24" 150.00
Mary Ann, compo, o/c/e, o/m, 1932, 19", M 350.00
Patsy, compo/cloth, o/m/teeth, o/c/e, hh wig, 1924, 15", M 300.00
Patsy Ann, jtd vinyl, rooted hair, o/c/e, Scout, 1959, 15", M 350.00
Patsy Baby, compo/cloth/celluloid, o/c/e, OC, 10" 265.00
Patsy Jr, compo, pnt/molded hair, pnt eyes, OC, 11½" 285.00
Patsy Ruth, compo/cloth, brn o/c, hh wig, OC, 27" 850.00
Plymouth Colony Historical, compo, brn pnt eyes, OC, 14" 350.00
Pouting Bess, compo/cloth, pnt eyes, cm, #155 on bk, 1915, 15" .85.00
Precious Baby, Limited Edition Club, 1975, MIB 350.00

Half Dolls

Half dolls were never meant to be objects of play. Most were modeled after the likenesses of lovely ladies, though children and animals were represented as well. Most of the ladies were firmly sewn on to pincushion bases that were beautifully decorated and served as the skirts of their gowns. Other skirts were actually covers for items on milady's dressing table. Some were used for parasol or brush handles or for tops to candy containers or perfume bottles. Most popular from 1900 to about 1930, they will most often be found marked with the country of their origin, especially Bavaria, Germany, France, and Japan. You may also find some fine quality pieces marked Goebel, Dressel and Kester, KPM, and Heubach.

Germany, arms & hands attached, common type, 3" 25.00
Germany, arms & hands attached, common type, 5" 35.00
Germany, arms & hands attached, common type, 8" 55.00
Germany, arms & hands completely away, 3", from $85 to 145.00
Germany, arms & hands completely away, 5", from $100 to 285.00

Germany, girl with hat, hands attached, 3", from $90.00 to $110.00.

Germany, arms & hands completely away, 8", from $165 to 650.00
Germany, arms & hands completely away, 12", from $200 to 950.00
Germany, arms extended, hands attached, 3" 50.00
Germany, arms extended, hands attached, 5" 85.00
Germany, arms extended, hands attached, 8" 125.00
Japan mk, 3" 20.00
Japan mk, 5" 30.00
Japan mk, 8" 50.00

Handwerck, Heinrich

#189, o/m, RpC, 15" 475.00
Bsk ShHd, o/m, kid body, RpC, 18" 350.00
Child, #79 or #89, c/m, RpC, 15" 1,700.00
Child, bsk head, bjtd, set or o/c/e, after 1885, RpC, 15" 375.00
Child, bsk head, bjtd, set or o/c/e, after 1885, RpC, 24" 650.00
Child, bsk head, o/c/e, o/m w/4 teeth, RpC, 21" 425.00
Child, bsk SkHd, bjtd, o/c/e, mold mks, RpC, 31" 1,200.00

Hertel, Schwab and Company

#119, child, bsk head, glass eyes, jtd compo, RpC, 12" 3,100.00
#126, Skippy, bsk head, o/c/m, pnt eyes, 16" 1,500.00
#127, Patsy, bsk head, bent limbs, o/c/e, 15" 1,150.00
#140, bsk head, pnt eyes, jtd compo, RpC, 12" 2,900.00
#152, bsk SkHd, o/c/e, o/m w/2 teeth, mohair wig, RpC, 11" 130.00
#154, character, solid dome, molded hair, glass eyes, o/m, RpC, 20" ..1,900.00
#163, googly eyes, wig or molded hair, c/m, att, RpC, 13" 2,800.00
#167, K&H character, o/c or o/m, RpC, ca 1912, 15" 2,000.00
#169, bsk head, c/m, jtd compo, RpC, 17" 3,200.00
#208, bsk 1-pc body & head, glass eyes, o/ or c/m, 1920s, 6", M ...325.00
#217, googly eyes, c/m, wig, RpC, 7½" 875.00
#222, Our Fairy, molded hair, pnt eyes, RpC, 9" 1,500.00

Heubach, Gebruder

#1017, baby-faced toddler, bsk head, o/m, RpC, 17" 1,500.00
#10633, Dainty Dorothy, ShHd, o/c/e, o/m, Sears Roebuck, 25", MIB ..850.00
#5636, laughing child, 2 teeth, pnt eyes, RpC, 10" 925.00
#6692, bsk ShHd, smiling, intaglio eyes, RpC, 16", minimum value ..1,000.00
#6896, bsk head, pouty, jtd body, RpC, 21" 1,400.00
#7551, squinting eyes, yawning, jtd body, RpC, 16" 3,450.00
#7602, long face pouty, pnt eyes & hair, c/m, RpC, 16" 2,200.00
#7603, bsk head, flocked hair, OC, 17½" 1,950.00
#7711, flapper, glass eyes, o/m, RpC, 13" 900.00
#8197, ShHd, c/m, molded curls, kid body, RpC, 17", minimum value ...8,700.00
Character, bl intaglio eyes, o/c/m w/teeth, hh wig, 16½" 1,400.00

Heubach, Ernstsdorf

#250, jtd body, o/m, o/c or set eyes, after 1888, RpC, 9" 185.00
#300, baby, 5-pc bent limb body, o/m, o/c/e, RpC, 8" 185.00
Child, bsk ShHd, kid or cloth body, bsk lower arms, RpC, 15" ..200.00

Horsman

Angelove, plastic/vinyl, made for Hallmark, 1974, 12", M 25.00
Betty, vinyl, 1-pc body, 1951, 14", MIB 60.00
Bright Star, compo, 1937-46, OC, 19", NM 300.00
Campbell's Kid (boy), compo, pnt eyes, 5-pc body, OC, 12" 200.00
Cindy, hp, jtd waist, 1959, 19", MIB 95.00
Cindy Kay, vinyl child w/long legs, 1950s+, 15", MIB 80.00
Dolly Rosebud, compo/cloth, dimples, sleep eyes, 1926-30 ....50.00
Tinie Baby, vinyl, 1950s, 15", MIB 110.00

Ideal

Two of Ideal's most collectible lines of dolls are Chrisy and Toni. For more information, refer to *Collector's Guide to Ideal Dolls, Second Edition*, by Judith Izen (Collector Books).

Baby Brother Tender Love, 11½", M 38.00
Baby Crissy, jtd vinyl, hair grows, pnt teeth, 1973-76, 24", EX 15.00
Baby Snooks Flexie, wire/compo, OC, 12", EX, minimum value ..285.00
Bamm-Bamm, jtd vinyl, Saran hair, pnt eyes, OC, 12", M 150.00
Betsy Wetsy, vinyl, o/m for bottle, 1983, MIB 35.00
Betty Big Girl, vinyl/plastic, 1968, OC, 30" 245.00
Bizzie-Lizzie, jtd vinyl, o/c/e, blond hair, 1971-72, 18", M 35.00
Bonnie Play Pal, vinyl, bl o/c/e, rooted hair, 1959, 24", M 275.00
Chelsea, posable body, long rooted hair, 1967, 24", M 50.00
Compo baby, cloth body, c/m, o/c/e, 1930s-40s, OC, 16" 200.00
Flexy clown, compo head, wire tubes in legs, OC, 13½", M 225.00
Kissy, vinyl, toddler, Saran hair, o/c/e, 1961-64, 22½", M 155.00
Sara Ann, hp saran wig, 1952 on, OC, 14", minimum value 250.00
Tammy, MIB 65.00
Tammy's Dad, MIB 65.00
Tickletoes, compo/rubber/cloth, crier, o/c/e, 1928-29, 14", EX 40.00

Jumeau

The Jumeau factory became the best known name for dolls during the 1880s and 1890s. Early dolls were works of art with closed mouths and paperweight eyes. When son Emile Jumeau took over, he patented sleep eyes with eyelids that drooped down over the eyes. This model also had flirty (eyes that move from side to side) eyes and is extremely rare. Over 98% of Jumeau dolls have paperweight eyes. The less-expensive German dolls were the downfall of the French doll manufacturers, and in 1899 the Jumeau company had to combine with several others in an effort to save the French doll industry from German competition.

Closed mouth, mk EJ (incised) Jumeau, 14" 5,800.00
Closed mouth, mk Tete Jumeau, 10" 3,000.00
Closed mouth, mk Tete Jumeau, 21" 4,800.00
Closed mouth, mk Tete Jumeau, 30" 6,800.00
Long face, c/m, 21" 23,000.00
Open mouth, mk bebe Jumeau, 27" 2,000.00
Open mouth, mk Jumeau Medaille d'Or, Paris, 20" 1,900.00
Open mouth, mk Tete Jumeau, 10" 2,300.00
Open mouth, mk Tete Jumeau, 21" 3,100.00
Open mouth, mk Tete Jumeau, 30" 4,600.00
Open mouth, mk 1907 Jumeau, 17" 2,500.00
Open mouth, mk 1907 Jumeau, 32" 4,000.00

Portrait Jumeau, c/m, 20" 7,800.00

Kammer and Reinhardt

Max, flirting, sleep eyes, laughing/closed mouth, #123, 16", $14,500.00 at auction. (Photo courtesy McMasters Auctions)

#30, bsk SkHd attached to walking mechanism, bl glass eyes, 11½" ..575.00
#68, boy or girl, bl o/c/e, o/m, wig/, p/e, 27", EX 800.00
#73, SkHd, o/c/e, o/m w/4 teeth, hh wig, jtd compo, RpC, 28" .600.00
#85, SkHd, o/c/e, o/m w/teeth, p/e, wig, jtd compo, RpC, 33" 2,300.00
#100, baby, pnt hair & eyes, o/c/m, 15" 650.00
#101, boy or girl w/pnt eyes, 12" 2,000.00
#101, boy or girl w/pnt eyes, 20" 5,000.00
#109, rare, w/pnt eyes, 18" 22,000.00
#112, rare, w/pnt eyes, 18" 17,000.00
#114, rare, w/pnt eyes, 11" 2,950.00
#114, rare, w/pnt eyes, 18" 5,500.00
#115 or #115a, c/m, 18" 4,900.00
#115 or #115a, o/m, 22" 2,600.00
#116 or #116a, c/m, 18" 3,500.00
#116 or #116a, o/m, 22" 2,600.00
#117a, c/m, 18" 5,400.00
#121, toddler, SkHd, o/c/e, o/m w/teeth, jtd compo, 16" 1,000.00
#192 14, SkHd, o/c/e, o/m w/4 teeth, rpl wig, jtd compo, 27" ..1,100.00
Dolly face, o/m, mold #400-403-102, etc, 24" 850.00
Dolly face, o/m, mold #400-403-109, etc, 38" 2,800.00

Kestner

Johannes D. Kestner made buttons at a lathe in a Waltershausen factory in the early 1800s. When this line of work failed, he used the same lathe to turn doll bodies. Thus the Kestner company began. It was one of the few German manufacturers to make the complete doll. By 1860, with the purchase of a porcelain factory, Kestner made doll heads of china and bisque as well as wax, worked-in-leather, celluloid, and cardboard. In 1895 the Kestner trademark of a crown with streamers was registered in the U.S. and a year later in Germany. Kestner felt the mark was appropriate since he referred to himself as the 'king of German dollmakers.'

B/6, ShHd, kid w/bsk ½-arms, o/m/teeth, o/c/e, 19" 685.00
D/8, SkHd & ShHd, kid w/bsk ½-arms, c/m, 15" 800.00
G/11, Hilda, SkHd, o/c/e, o/m/teeth, 1920s, 15" 3,600.00
G11, SkHd, jtd, bl eyes, o/m, mohair wig, 19" 800.00
Hilda, toddler, jtd body, o/m, o/c/e, 1914, rstr, 15" 4,800.00
JDK, bsk head, glass eyes, c/m, appl ears, OC, 20", EX 4,800.00
JDK 12, SkHd, pwt, o/m, bent limbs, RpC, 15", VG 475.00
JDK/Kestner, Oriental, SkHd, o/m, 14" 4,800.00
L/15, SkHd, bsk ShPl, c/m, 21" 3,000.00
4, SkHd, bl o/c/e, c/m, mohair wig, jtd compo body, 11½" 1,600.00
10, bsk, o/c/e, orig wig, plaster pate, 22" 995.00
10, SkHd, bsk ShPl, c/m, 21" 2,900.00
11, SkHd, pnt eyes to side, o/c/m, JDK/MIG, 11" 550.00
13, bsk SkHd, bl o/c/e, c/m, rpl mohair wig, Germany, 20" 3,100.00
16, SkHd, o/m, JDK/MIG, 21" 65.00
143, ShHd, jtd compo, o/c/e, o/m, mohair wig, 14", EX 850.00
145, SkHd, c/m, 143/4/0/JDK, 11" 325.00
150 4/0, bsk, pnt bl eyes, c/m, wig, pincushion clothing, 5" 135.00
150 5/0, bsk, brn o/c/e, c/m, mohair wig, JDK, 4½", MIB 275.00
150.4 1/2 0, bsk, brn o/c/e, c/m, RpC, 5" 250.00
154, bsk ShHd, brn o/c/e, o/m w/teeth, mohair wig, DEP, 13" ...110.00
155, SkHd, brn o/c/e, o/m w/teeth, wig, jtd compo, K, 6¾" 450.00
167, orig pate & wig, bl eyes, 15" 795.00
171, SkHd, jtd compo, o/c/e, o/m, 'Daisy,' F/M110, 18" 700.00
171, SkHd, jtd compo, o/c/e, o/m, hh wig, RpC, 29" 800.00
201, ShHd, celluloid on kid, o/m, set eyes/lashes, JDK, 19" 685.00
221, jtd compo, googly eyes, c/m, smile, wig, JDK, 12½" 3,500.00
221, jtd compo, googly eyes, c/m, smile, wig, JDK, 15" 5,200.00
245, SkHd, 5-pc baby, G/MIG/11/JDK Jr/1914 Hilda, 14" 3,300.00
245, SkHd, 5-pc baby, H/MIG/12/JDK Jr/1914 Hilda, 16" 3,500.00
257, SkHd, 5-pc baby, o/m, G/JDK, 20" 850.00
260, flirty-eyed toddler, OC, 16" 1,900.00

Lenci

Characteristics of Lenci dolls include seamless, steam-molded felt heads, quality clothing, childishly plump bodies, and painted eyes that glance to the side. Fine mohair wigs were used, and the middle and fourth fingers were sewn together. Look for the factory stamp on the foot, though paper labels were also used. Dolls under 10" are known as mascots and usually sell for $150.00 to $200.00. The Lenci factory continues today, producing dolls of the same high quality. Values are for dolls in near mint condition — no moth holes, very little fading.

Aviator, girl w/felt helmet, all orig, 18", NM, minimum value ..3,200.00
Baby, all orig, 15", NM 2,100.00
Boy, side part, all orig, 17", NM, minimum value 1,900.00
Child, swivel head, c/sm, OC: dress & rain clothes, 16" 800.00

Lady with long limbs, all original, 35", $1,800.00. (Photo courtesy McMasters Auctions)

Lady w/papoose, all orig, 17", NM 4,200.00
Mascotte, all orig, 8", NM 325.00
Shirley Temple type, all orig, 22", NM 1,850.00
Smoking doll, pnt eyes, all orig, 24", NM, minimum value 2,000.00
Teenager, long legs, all orig, 15", NM, minimum value 1,100.00

Liddle Kiddles

From 1966 to 1971, Mattel produced Liddle Kiddle dolls ranging in size from ¾" to 4". They were all poseable and had rooted hair that could be restyled. There were various series of the dolls, among them Animiddles, Zoolery Jewelry Kiddles, extraterrestrials, and Sweet Treats, as well as many accessories. Our advisor for this category is Paris Langford; she is listed in the Directory under Louisiana. Please send a SASE for information or contact Paris by e-mail: bbean415@aol.com.

Babe Biddle, brn hair, yel car, 1966-67, 3", NM complete 65.00
Beach Buggy, pk plastic & vinyl, 1967, 5½x5x6", NM 35.00
Beddy-Bye Biddle, w/robe/bed/etc, Sears, 1967, 3", NM 70.00
Bunson Bernie, fire chief w/engine, 1966-67, 3", NM complete ..65.00
Cherry Blossom Skediddle, blk hair, 1969-70, 4", NM complete .95.00
Cinderella Palace Playset, Sears Exclusive, 1967, NM complete ..175.00
Funny Bunny Kiddle, pk, 1968-69, 3¾", NM complete 30.00
Greta Griddle, blond, w/table & chairs, 1966, 3½", NM complete .65.00
Heart Necklace, 1½" doll on gold-tone chain, NM complete ...125.00
Heart Pin, 1½" doll w/crown in pin, 1968-70, NM complete 25.00
Heather Hiddlehorse, w/horse, 1969-70, 4", NM complete 85.00
Lady Silver, blond w/cup & saucer, 1970-71, 3½", NM complete .100.00
Lenore Limousine, blond w/car, 1969-70, 2⅞", NM complete 55.00
Lickety Spliddle & Her Traveliddles, 1968-69, 4", NM complete 50.00
Liddle Biddle Peep, blond w/sheep, 1967-68, 3½", NM complete .100.00
Liddle Diddle, baby in crib, 1965-67, 2⅞", NM complete 65.00
Liddle Kiddles Club Case, 1966, 12x6x9", NM 25.00
Liddle Kiddles 3-Story House, 1969, 17x11½x7", NM 45.00
Liddle Red Riding Hiddle, w/book, 1967-68, 3½", NM complete .125.00
Lolli-Grape Lollipop, 1969-70, 2", NM complete 40.00
Loretta Locket, gold locket w/bl jewels, 1969, NM complete 25.00
Mattel's Liddle Kiddles Sticker Fun, Whitman, 1966, M 55.00
Nappytime Baby, 1970, 2½", NM complete 50.00
Romeo & Juliet, Storybook Sweethearts, 1969-70, NM complete ..75.00
Shirley Strawberry Kola, w/bottle, 1968-69, 2", NM complete 35.00
Slipsy Sliddle, blond w/slide & tree, 1968, 3½", NM complete ...75.00
Surfy Skiddle, blond w/surfboard/palm/etc, 1963, 3", NM complete .75.00
Tiny Tiger Animiddle, 2-pc tiger suit, 1969-70, NM complete 30.00
Train Case, wht vinyl w/zipper, 1966, 5½x3¼x4", NM 25.00
Tutti Frutti Kone, w/cone, 1969-70, 2", NM complete 40.00
Zoolery Kiddles Frame-Tray Puzzle, Whitman, 1969, 14½x11½", M ..100.00

Madame Alexander

Beatrice Alexander founded the Alexander Doll Company in 1923 by making an all-cloth, oil-painted face, Alice in Wonderland doll. With the help of her three sisters, the company prospered; and by the late 1950s there were over six hundred employees making Madame Alexander dolls. The company still produces these lovely dolls today. For more information, refer to *Collector's Encyclopedia of Madame Alexander Dolls* by Pat Smith; and *Madame Alexander Collector's Doll Price Guide* and *Madame Alexander Store Exclusives and Limited Editions*, both by Linda Crowsey. All are published by Collector Books.

Africa, hp, bend knee, Wendy Ann, #766, 1966-71, 8" 275.00
Alexander-Kin, hp, cotton dress, organdy pinafore, hat, 7½-8" .550.00
Alexander-Kin, str-leg walker, 1954-55, basic doll in undies, MIB .400.00
Alice in Wonderland, compo, Tiny Betty, 1930s, 7" 375.00
Annabelle, hp, Maggie, 1951-52, 14-15" 575.00
Annie Laurie, compo, Wendy Ann, 1937, 14" 650.00
Baby Jane, compo, 1935, 16", minimum value 950.00
Barbara Jane, cloth vinyl, 1952 only, 29" 500.00
Bitsey, compo, 1942-46, 11-12" 250.00
Bride, compo, Wendy Ann, 1935-41, 13-15" 350.00
Bridesmaid, hp, Elise, 1957-59, 16½", minimum value 450.00
Carrot Kate, Ribbons & Bows series, Mary Ann, #25506, 1995, 14" .150.00
Cinderella, Annual Showcase of Dolls, bl gown, 1989, 10" 700.00
Colonial, compo, Tiny Betty, 1937-38, 7" 300.00

Daisy, #1110, Portrette Series, white lace over yellow, 1987 – 88 only, 10", $75.00. (Photo courtesy Pat Smith)

Dearest, vinyl baby, 1962-64, 12" 150.00
Dicksie & Ducksie, cloth/felt, 1930s, minimum value 700.00
Elise, hp/vinyl, 1-pc arms & legs, jtd ankles & knees, 1961-62, 17" .275.00
First Communion, hp, Wendy Ann, #395, 1957 only, 8" 650.00
Funny, cloth 1963-77, 18" 75.00
Gainsborough, Portrette, Cissette, pk gown & hat, 1957, 10" ...600.00
Good Little Girl, cloth, pk dress, 1966 only, 16" 150.00
Harding, Florence; First Ladies Series, Louisa, 1988 ....125.00
Honeyette Baby, comop/cloth, 1941-42, 16" 225.00
India, hp, bend-knee walker, Wendy Ann, #775, 1965, 8" 175.00
Janie, toddler, #1156, 1964-66, 12" 275.00
Karen Ballerina, compo, Margaret, 1946-49, 15", minimum value ...850.00
Lady in Red, Cissy, red taffeta, #1134, 1958 only, 20", minimum value ...1,900.00
Lilibet, compo, Princess Elizabeth, 1938, 16", minimum value ..750.00
Little Genius, compo/cloth, 1935-40, 1942-46, 12-14" 200.00
Madeline, hp, jtd elbows & knees, 1950-53, 17-18", minimum value .800.00
Mambo, hp, Wendy Ann, 1955 only, #481, 8", minimum value ..700.00
Mary, Mary, hp, str leg, mk Alex, 1973-75, 8" 75.00
Michael, plastic/vinyl, Peter Pan set, Janie, 1969 only, 11" 375.00
Mommy & Me, compo, Margaret & Tiny Betty, 1948-49, 14" & 7" .1,700.00
Nina Ballerina, compo, Tiny Betty, 1940, 7" 325.00
Noel, New England Collector Society, porc, Christmas, '89-91, 12" .250.00
O'Brien, Margaret; compo, 1946-48, 14½" 750.00
O'Hara, Scarlett; red gown w/wht lace, #2190, 1969, 21" 650.00
Oliver Twistail, cloth/felt, 1930s 650.00
Peter Pan, hp, Margaret, 1953-54, 15", minimum value 750.00
Pip, cloth, Dicken's character, 1930s 800.00
Princess Elizabeth, compo, 1937-41, 14", minimum value 600.00
Puss'n Boots, Fairy Tales Series, #14552, 8" 65.00
Pussy Cat, FAO Schwarz, bl dress & bonnet, 1987, 18" 150.00
Rebecca, compo, Wendy Ann, 1940-41, 14-17", 21", from $600 to .1,000.00
Renoir Child, plastic/vinyl, Nancy Drew, #1274, 1967 only, 12" ..150.00
Rusty, cloth/vinyl, 1967-68, 20" 300.00
Samantha, hp, From Bewitched TV Series, #15300, 10" 105.00
School Girl, compo, Tiny Betty, 1936-43, 7" 275.00
Sound of Music, Maria, Elise or Polly, sailor suits, 17" 500.00
Sweet Tears, vinyl, 1965-74, 9" 100.00
Tinkerbell, hp, w/magic wand & wings, #140467, 1991-93, 8" 75.00
Tiny Tim, compo, Tiny Betty, 1934-37, 7" 325.00
Victoria, baby, 1967-89, 20" 100.00
Wendy Ann, compo, 1935-48, 11-15", from $350 to 575.00

Mattel

Baby Small Talk, 1968, MIB 75.00
Chatty Baby, early, brunette, brn eyes, M 160.00
Chatty Baby, open speaker, brunette, brn eyes, M 375.00
Chatty Cathy, brunette, bl eyes, M....375.00
Chatty Cathy, later issue, open speaker, brunette, bl eyes, M....750.00
Chatty Cathy, mid-yr or transitional, brunette, brn eyes, M 650.00
Chatty Cathy, pat pending, brunette, bl eyes, M 750.00
Chatty Cathy, soft face, w/pigtails, blond, brunette or redhead, M .550.00
Hi Dottie, complete w/telephone, 17", EX 50.00
Singin Chatty, blond, M 250.00

Papier-Mache

Cloth body, bright coloring, wig, 1920s & later, RpC, 8" 80.00
Cloth body, wooden limbs, glass eyes, RpC, 1840s-60s, 24" 2,200.00
Cloth body, wooden limbs, long curls, RpC, 1840s-60s, 12" 650.00
Cloth body, wooden limbs, pnt eyes, RpC, 1840s-60s, 9" 450.00
Clown, cloth body w/compo pnt features/molded hair, RpC, 8" ..235.00
Clown, pnt features, 5-pc body, o/ or c/m, OC, 9" 265.00
French, solid dome, nailed-on wig, teeth, glass eyes, RpC, 15" ...1,350.00
French/French type, bamboo teeth, glass eyes, RpC, 15" 1,400.00
German, molded hair, pnt eyes, c/m, RpC, 1870-1900, 23" 475.00
German, pnt eyes, c/m, 1870s-90s, EX clothes, 18" 375.00
Kid body, wooden limbs, center part, sausage curls, RpC, 14" 575.00
Kid body, wooden limbs, molded comb, braided coronet, RpC, 16" ..3,300.00
M&S Superior, kid or leather arms/boots, ShHd, RpC, 17" 425.00
M&S Superior, ShHd, glass eyes, kid arms/boots, RpC, 12" 600.00
M&S Superior, ShHd, molded hair, pnt eyes, RpC, 16" 400.00
Motschmann type, wood & twill body, glass eyes, c/m, RpC, 16" ..700.00
Trn ShHd, solid dome, glass eyes, c/m, compo lower arms, RpC, 18" .775.00
Wooden limbs, long curls, 1840s-50s, EX clothes, 14" 650.00

Parian

Alice in Wonderland (head band) style, RpC, 12" 400.00
Bald solid-dome head, ear details, takes wigs, 1850s, RpC, 14" ..775.00
Fancy hairdo w/ribbons/flowers/etc, glass eyes, p/e, RpC, 16" .1,700.00
Man or boy, parted hair, cloth body, shirt & tie, 16" 900.00
Molded hat, blond or blk hair, pnt eyes, 15" 2,200.00
Molded necklace, glass eyes, p/e, RpC, 21", minimum 2,100.00
Plain, no decor in hair or on shoulders, RpC, 10" 175.00

Schoenhut

Albert Schoenhut left Germany in 1866 to go to Pennsylvania to work as a repairman for toy pianos. He eventually applied his skills to wooden toys and later designed an all-wood doll which he patented on January 17, 1911. These uniquely jointed dolls were painted with enamels and came with a metal stand. Some of the later dolls had stuffed bodies, voice boxes, and hollow heads. Due to the changing economy and fierce competition, the company closed in the mid-1930s.

Baby, bent-limb body, pnt hair, decal eyes, OC, 12" 525.00
Baby, cvd & pnt hair, bl pnt eyes, c/m, scuffed, RpC, 17" 2,600.00
Boy, cvd hair, pnt eyes, walker, nude, 16½", VG 2,800.00
Child, cvd hair, molded ribbon, c/m, OC, 14" 2,500.00
Compo, molded curls, Patsy-style body, label, OC, 13" 1,600.00
Dolly face, o/cm w/teeth, pnt eyes, OC, 14" 675.00
Girl, brn decal eyes, o/c/m w/4 teeth, RpC, 17", EX 625.00
Girl, brn pnt eyes, brn hh wig, orig dress, 15", EX 500.00
Girl, intaglio eyes, pouty mouth, rpl wig, rpt, RpC, 21½" 785.00
Girl, pnt eyes, 4 pnt teeth, cvd hair, rpt, RpC, 16" 700.00
Pouty, wooden SkHd, intaglio eyes, c/m, rpl wig, Pat...'11, 16" .750.00
Toddler, OC, 12" 850.00
Tootsie Wootsie, pnt hair, o/m w/tongue/teeth, OC, 14" 2,100.00
Wood & compo, intaglio eyes, fully jtd, OC, 19", EX 1,400.00

SFBJ

By 1895 Germany was producing dolls at much lower prices than the French dollmakers could, so to save the doll industry, several leading French manufacturers united to form one large company. Bru, Raberry and Delphieu, Pintel and Godshaux, Fleischman and Bodel, Jumeau, and many others united to form the company Society Francaise de Fabrication de Bebes et Jouets (SFBJ).

20, molded pnt shoes & eyes, 5-pc body, Paris/12, 10" 365.00
60, French WWI nurse, 5-pc body, SFBJ/13/0, 8½" 475.00
60, o/m w/teeth, o/c/e, hh wig, RpC, 12" 450.00
60, SkHd, compo w/str legs, o/m, curved arms, 15" 650.00
215, bsk swivel head over compo, c/m, inset eyes, 15" 1,800.00
227, bsk swivel closed dome head, animal skin wig, 15" 1,900.00
227, closed dome, o/m, inset eyes, pnt hair, 15" 2,100.00
229, compo w/swivel head, o/c/m, inset eyes, 18" 5,000.00
230, bsk SkHd, pwt, o/m/teeth, jtd wood/compo, wig, RpC, 24" 1,000.00
230, compo walker, p/e, o/m, inset eyes, 16" 1,600.00
235, closed dome, molded hair, o/c/m & eyes, 16" 1,700.00
236, laughing Jumeau, o/m, o/c/e, dbl chin, 13" 1,300.00
236, laughing Jumeau, o/m, o/c/e, dbl chin, 20" 2,200.00
238, compo w/swivel head, o/m, inset eyes, Paris/6, 15" 3,800.00
239, Poulbot, c/m, street urchin, red wig, 17" 9,500.00
245, boy, o/c/m, lg glass googly eyes, pnt shoes, 8" 1,400.00
247, toddler, o/c/m w/2 inset teeth, 20" 2,900.00
247, Twirp, SkHd, o/c/m & eyes, 2 teeth, 21" 3,000.00
252, pouty, c/m, inset eyes, papier-mache body, 11" 2,800.00
252, pouty, c/m, inset eyes, papier-mache body, 22" 7,800.00
266, character, bsk head, closed dome, o/c/m, 20" 4,200.00
301, bsk SkHd on compo, o/m, inset eyes, 22" 1,200.00
301, bsk SkHd on compo, o/m, inset eyes, 28" 1,700.00

Shirley Temple

Prices are suggested for dolls complete and in mint condition. Add up to 25% (depending on her outfit) if mint with box. A played-with doll in only very good condition would be worth only about half of listed values.

Celluloid, 5", Japan 185.00
Celluloid, 8", Japan 245.00
Compo, 11", 1934 to late 1930s 900.00
Compo, 11-18", Ideal, from $875 to 975.00
Compo, 16", Germany, oc/e, o/m smile, 1936, minimum 600.00

Composition, 18", Ideal, 1930s, pink dress with white leaf print, M, from $875.00 to $950.00. (Photo courtesy McMasters Auctions)

Compo, 20" ...1,100.00
Compo, 7-8", Japan ...300.00
Plastic/vinyl, 12", 1982-83 ...40.00
Plastic/vinyl, 8", 1982-83 ...30.00
Vinyl, 15", 1950s ...265.00
Vinyl, 17", 1950s ...325.00
Vinyl, 19", 1950s ...400.00
Vinyl, 36", 1950s ...1,600.00

Simon and Halbig

Simon and Halbig was one of the finest German makers to operate during the 1870s into the 1930s. Due to the high quality of the makers, their dolls still command large prices today. During the 1890s a few Simon & Halbig heads were used by a French maker, but these are extremely rare and well marked S&H.

Handwerck, SkHd, o/m, 1893, 16" ...450.00
50, SkHd, c/m, Simon & Halbig, 16" ...1,800.00
282, SkHd, o/m, S&H, 18" ...650.00
670, SkHd, o/m, Simon & Halbig, 16" ...600.00
729, SkHd, c/m, S&H DEP, 16" ...2,300.00
939, SkHd, c/m, S 11 H DEP, 17" ...2,700.00
940, SkHd, closed dome, o/c/m, S 2 H, 26" ...3,600.00
945, SkHd, o/m, S 2 H DEP, 16" ...2,200.00
949, SkHd, o/c/e, c/m, jtd compo, RpC, 15" ...1,900.00

1079-8½ DEP, bisque socket head, brown sleep eyes, open mouth with teeth, jointed body, in Scottish outfit (possibly original), 21", EX, $800.00. (Photo courtesy McMasters Auctions)

1079, SkHd, o/c/e, o/m w/4 teeth, SH DEP 15, RpC, 32" ...900.00
1159, SkHd, adult, 1905, G/Simon & Halbig/S&H7, 18" ...1,900.00
1249, Santa, bsk head, jtd compo, o/m, o/c/e, p/e, 20" ...1,400.00

Steiner, Jules

Jules Nicholas Steiner established one of the earliest French manufacturing companies (making dishes and clocks) in 1855. He began with mechanical dolls with bisque heads and open mouths with two rows of bamboo teeth; his patents grew to include walking and talking dolls. In 1880 he registered a patent for a doll with sleep eyes. This doll could be put to sleep by turning a rod that operated a wire attached to its eyes.

A Series, Le Parisien, o/m, RpC, 23" ...2,500.00
A Series Child, cb pate, c/m, pwt, jtd, RpC, 29" ...7,500.00
A Series Le Parisien, c/m, 1892, RpC, 10" ...2,600.00
B Series, c/m, pwt, jtd, RpC, 29" ...8,900.00
Bourgoin, wire-eye, c/m, jtd, RpC, 18" ...5,600.00
Infant, bsk head, molded hair, o/c/e, c/m, 9" ...250.00

Vogue

This is the company that made the Ginny doll. Composition was used during the '40s, but vinyl was the preferred material throughout the decade of the '50s. An original mint-condition composition Ginny would be worth a minimum of $450.00 on the market today (played-with about $90.00). The last Ginny came out in 1969. Another Vogue doll that is becoming very collectible is Jill, whose values are steadily climbing. For more information, we recommend *Collector's Guide to Vogue Dolls* by Judith Izen and Carol Stover. Our advisor for Jill dolls is Bonnie Groves; she is listed in the Directory under Texas.

Baby Dear One, 1973, 25", MIB ...175.00
Binny Baby, 20", MIB ...55.00
Boy & Girl Toodles, compo, complete & all orig in trunk ...450.00
Ginny, hp, jtd walker, o/c/e, 1957, 8", M ...150.00
Ginny, hp, molded lashes, walker, 1954-57, OC, minimum value ..300.00
Ginny, hp, pnt lashes, strung, ca 1953, 8", MIB ...325.00
Ginny as Davy Crockett, 1953, 8" ...400.00
Ginny International, vinyl, 1977, OC, minimum value ...45.00
Jan, vinyl, basic bra & girdle, VG ...54.00
Jan/Jill desk & chair, gr, VG, from $50 to ...135.00
Jan/Jill wardrobe, gr, VG, from $50 to ...135.00
Jeff, nude, VG, from $25 to ...45.00
Jeff, vinyl, bl suit 10", VG ...125.00
Jeff, vinyl, in shorts outfit, 10", VG, from $65 to ...85.00
Jill, hp, cotton street dress, all orig, 10½", from $85 to ...135.00
Jill, hp, in formal, 10½", EX, from $150 to ...200.00
Jill, hp, leotard, 1957, 10½", MIB ...250.00
Jill, hp, nude, haircut, 10½", G- ...20.00
Jill, hp, 1957-62, 10½", MIB ...190.00
Jill, in peach flowered formal, all orig, from $135 to ...200.00
Jill, in ribbon hat outfit, complete, 1958 ...175.00
Jill, in 1960 street dress, scarce, incomplete, from $65 to ...80.00
Jill, vinyl, History Land, all orig, from $85 to ...200.00
Jill bed, VG, from $50 to ...85.00
Jill chromium head pendant, MIP, from $50 to ...150.00
Jill coke bottle, accessory to jeans outfits, scarce, from $12 to ...20.00
Jill cotton dress, from $35 to ...50.00
Jill Dream Cozy Bed Set (bedding), MIP, from $35 to ...50.00
Jill dress, semiformal, MIP, from $50 to ...75.00
Jill felt coat, from $45 to ...65.00
Jill jewelry, MIP, from $35 to ...50.00
Jill shoes, MIP ...25.00
Toodles Baby, compo, pnt eyes, OC: dress/coat/bonnet, 7" ...265.00

Wax, Poured Wax

Alice headband hairdo, RpC, 14" ...475.00
Common type, worn wax, RpC, 12" ...150.00
Infant nurser, trn ShHd, set eyes, o/m, wig, RpC, 26" ...1,320.00
Lady, poured head & limbs, glass eyes, cloth body, RpC, 24" .3,600.00
Lever-operated eyes, 1850s, Rpc, 17" ...950.00
Over compo, sleep eyes, cloth body, wood limbs, 1860s, RpC, 16" .850.00
Poured, bl o/c/e, mohair wig, RpC, 15", EX ...400.00
Poured head & limbs, glass eyes, cloth body, RpC, 22" ...1,900.00
Poured ShHd, pnt features, glass eyes, c/m, cloth body, RpC, 17" ..1,500.00
ShHD, inserted hair, glass eyes, wax limbs, cloth body, RpC, 13" ...1,100.00
Wax over compo or papier-mache, inserted hair, RpC, 14" ...1,000.00
Wax over compo ShHd, glass eyes, molded hair/shoes, RpC, 15" ..300.00
2-faced, laughing & crying, Bartenstein, 1890s, RpC, 16" ...950.00

Door Knockers

Door knockers, those charming precursors of the doorbell, come in an intriguing array of shapes and styles. The very rare ones come from England. Cast-iron examples made in this country were often produced in forms similar to the more familiar doorstop figures.

Our listings are prices realized at auction. Most were in exceptional condition. See Doorstops for suggestions on pricing examples in lesser conditions.

Black shoeshine man walking on cobblestone road, brass, 3⅛" ...65.00
Cat w/arched bk, CI, MIB ...275.00
Colonial Man, CI, MIB ...150.00
Dolphin, stylized, hangs from geometric shape, brass, 6½" L ...160.00
Elephant head w/boy sitting atop, brass, mk Africa, 7" ...70.00
Flower basket, mc mixed flowers w/bow, CI, oval bkplate, 4x3" ..85.00
Ivy basket, lt & dk gr in yel basket, wht bkplate, 4½x2½" ...135.00
Lion head, ring in mouth, brass, 6¼" ...95.00
Owl, yel/brn/wht w/blk eyes, cream & gr bkplate, 4¾x3" ...250.00
Parrot, perched on branch, mc pnt on CI, mk Z10, 4¾" ...125.00
Pk zinnias, pnt on CI, Pat Pend mk on bk, 4x2½", EX ...190.00
Pug dog, bronze, mk CB/662, 4¼x1¾" ...235.00
Rooster, mc pnt on CI, 3x2½" ...180.00
Rooster w/branch, yel/brn/red, cream & gr oval bkplate, 4½x3" ...250.00
Samuel Adams (bust), meeting w/Boswell on bkplate, brass, 5¼" ...80.00
Shakespeare bust in wreath w/verse on plaque, brass, 5" ...50.00
Ship & waves, gold w/highlights, oval bkplate w/bl waves, 4x2¾" .250.00
Sir Thomas Wykeham, w/3 children at ft, brass, 19th C, 6x1¾" .55.00
Spur (revolves) & horseshoe, copper, ca 1900, 4¼x9¼", VG ...65.00

Doorstops

Although introduced in England in the mid-1800s, cast-iron doorstops were not made to any great extent in this country until after the Civil War. Once called 'door porters,' their function was to keep doors open to provide better ventilation. They have been produced in many shapes and sizes, both dimensional and flat-backed, and in the past few years have become a popular, yet affordable collectible. While cast-iron examples are the most common, brass, wood, and chalk were also used. An average price is in the $100.00 to $200.00 range, though some are valued at more than $400.00. Doorstops retained their usefulness and appeal well into the '30s.

The prices below reflect market values in the East where doorstops are at a premium. For other areas of the country, it may be necessary to adjust prices down about 25%. When no condition code is present, items are assumed to be in exceptional original condition, flat-backed unless noted full-figured, and cast iron unless another material is mentioned. To evaluate a doorstop in only very good to excellent paint, deduct at least 35%. Values for examples in poor to good paint drop dramatically. For further information we recommend *Doorstops, Identification and Values*, by Jeanne Bertoia.

Key: ff — full figured

Amish Man, ff, 8½x3¾" ...250.00
Ann Hathaway's Cottage, Hubley, 6⅜x8⅜" ...350.00
Beagle Pup, ff, sitting, 8x7½" ...400.00
Bear w/Honey, ff, standing, 15x6½", minimum value ...750.00
Begging Boston Terrier, ff, 8¾x5" ...350.00
Black Man on Cotton Bale, 6⅞x6⅞", minimum value ...750.00
Blowfish, ff, Hubley, 8x7¼" ...400.00
Buster Brown, red, wht & bl outfit, 7¾x5¼" ...450.00
Cape Cod Cottage, Hubley #444, 5½x7¾" ...175.00
Charleston Dancers, Hubley #270, 8⅞x5⅝", minimum value ...750.00
Conestoga Wagon, #100, 8x11" ...175.00
Dachshund, ff, sitting, 8x12" ...400.00
Drum Major, ff, 13½x6½" ...425.00
El Capitan, w/rifle, 7¾x5¼" ...225.00
Fantail Fish, Hubley #464, 9¾x5⅞" ...175.00
French Girl, yel & wht dress, Hubley #23, 9¼x5½" ...275.00
Fruit Basket, Albany Foundry, 10⅛x7½" ...200.00
Giraffe, Hubley, 12½x9", minimum value ...750.00
Grapes & Leaves, Albany Foundry, 7¾x6½" ...175.00
Horse Jumping Fence, Eastern Specialty Co #79, 7⅞x11¾" ...400.00
Humpty Dumpty, ff, #661, 4½x3½" ...350.00

Jungle Boy, yellow clothes with colorful leopard skin, unmarked, 12¾x12", NM, $1,250.00.

Large Frog, ff, standing, 14x7", minimum value ...750.00
Lighthouse, National Foundry #95, 6¼x8" ...275.00
Lil Red Riding Hood, Hubley #95, 9½x5" ...475.00
Lobster, 12½x6½" ...400.00
Mammy, hands on hips, 9", VG ...180.00
Mammy, hands on hips, 13½", VG ...180.00
Mary Quite Contrary, Littco Products, 11⅜x9⅝" ...750.00
Old Fashioned Lady, Hubley #296, 7¾x4" ...350.00
Parrot, glass eye, National Foundry, 10⅜x6¾" ...175.00
Pelican on Dock, Albany Foundry #113, 8x7¼" ...300.00
Persian Cat, ff, Hubley, 8½x6½" ...200.00
Petunias & Asters, Hubley #470, 9½x6½" ...150.00
Popeye, ff, Hubley, 1929, 9x4½", minimum value ...750.00
Poppies & Snapdragons, Hubley #484, 7½x7¼" ...125.00
Rabbit by Fence, Albany Foundry, 6⅞x8⅛" ...375.00
Reclining Kitten, ff, National Foundry, 8⅛x4" ...250.00
Rose Vase, National Foundry #145, 10½x7" ...250.00
Silhouette Girl, Albany Foundry #5, 11¼x10¼" ...550.00
St Bernard, ff, lying down, Hubley, 3½x10½" ...375.00
Stork, wedge, Hubley, 5½x3½" ...275.00
Swan, ff, National Foundry, 5¾x4½" ...250.00
Totem Pole, 12x8½" ...150.00
Tulip Vase, Hubley #443, 10x8" ...175.00
Twin Penguins, 7¼x7½" ...225.00
Woman w/Flowers & Shawl, #42, 11x6¼" ...275.00
Woman w/Muff, ff, 9¼x5" ...275.00

Dorchester Pottery

Taking its name from the town in Massachusetts where it was organized in 1895, the Dorchester Pottery Company made primarily utilitarian wares, though other types of items were made as well. By 1940 a line of decorative pottery was introduced, some of which was painted by hand with scrollwork or themes from nature. The buildings were destroyed by fire in the late 1970s, and the pottery was never rebuilt. In the listings that follow, the decorations described are all in cobalt unless otherwise noted. Our advisor for this category is Dale MacLean; he is listed in the Directory under Massachusetts.

Key: CAH — Charles A. Hill (noted artist)

Bowl, Blueberry, 6" 100.00
Bowl, cereal; Good Morning, pumpkin scene, CH, 2⅛x5¾" 150.00
Bowl, cereal; Poinsettia, unmk, 2¼x5¾" 125.00
Bowl, Pine Cone, lt brn, CAH, 6" 95.00
Candy dish, Grape Leaf, wavy edge, hdls, 7" 150.00
Candy dish, Scroll, hdls, 7" 125.00
Cruet, Pussy Willow, CAH, stamped, 4½x4" 250.00
Cup, All Gone, Peter Pumpkin Eater & wife in pumpkin, Trotter, 3" ..225.00
Cup, Whale & Sea Gulls, mk 1775-1975, CAH & EHH, 3" 75.00
Cup & saucer, Blueberry, 3", 6½" 75.00
Cup & saucer, Whale, deep bl, swirl saucer, CAH, 2¾", 6¼" 125.00
Foot warmer, Henderson; Pat Nov 5, 1912, 6x11", VG 100.00
Jar, jam; Strawberry, K Dennisons, 3¾x3¼" 150.00
Mug, Anchors Aweigh, anchor, K Dennisons, 4¾" 125.00
Mug, Captain Blood, brn w/wht decor, R Blake, 4⅝" 125.00
Mug, geometric design, bl & wht, 4½" 75.00
Mug, Harbor Lights (lighthouse), K Dennisons, 4¾" 100.00
Mug, Pete Black, incised, brn, mk RB, 4⅝" 80.00
Mug, Pine Cone, CAH & EHH, mk 1775-1975, 4½" 80.00
Mug, Sailor's Horn Pipe, K Dennisons, 4¾" 125.00
Mug, Thar She Blows, whale, K Dennisons, 4¾" 125.00
Mug, turkey, K Denison, 4¾", EX 125.00
Mug, Whale & Sea Gulls, CAH & IMEHH, 4½" 85.00
Pitcher, water; Ship & Anchor, K Dennisons, 7¼x8" 300.00
Plaque, I Pray the Lord..., CAH, stamped, 12⅛" dia 400.00
Plate, Blueberry, N Ricci, 10½" 200.00

Dorflinger

Christian Dorflinger was born in Alsace, France, and came to this country when he was ten years old. When still very young, he obtained a job in a glass factory in New Jersey. As a young man, he started his own glassworks in Brooklyn, New York, opening new factories as profits permitted. During that time he made cut glass articles for many famous people including President and Mrs. Lincoln, for whom he produced a complete service of tableware with the United States Coat of Arms. In 1863 he sold the New York factories because of ill health and moved to his farm near White Mills, Pennsylvania. His health returned, and he started a plant near his home. It was there that he did much of his best work, making use of only the very finest materials. Christian died in 1915, and the plant was closed in 1921 by consent of the family.

Dorflinger glass is rare and often hard to identify. Very few pieces were marked. Many only carried a small paper label which was quickly discarded; these are seldom found today. Identification is more accurately made through a study of the patterns, as colors may vary.

Hock goblet, green with etched gold, cut stem, signed Honesdale, 7½", $160.00. (Photo courtesy John A. Shuman III)

Champagne, Kalana, Lilies, 5½" 98.00
Cruet, Renaissance, rpl stopper, 7" 95.00
Cup & saucer, demitasse; Parisian, set of 4 ....1,400.00
Decanter, gr cut to clear, 6-panel neck, 9½", +4 ftd tumblers 395.00
Goblet, gr cut to clear, faceted clear stem, 1930s, 4½" 150.00
Parfait, Renaissance, faceted teardrop stem, 6 for 195.00
Vase, Kalana, poppies w/bands, ftd, 8" 265.00
Vase, sweet pea; Kalana, pansies, 3¼x6" 110.00

Dragon Ware

Dragon ware is fairly accessible and is still being made today. The new Dragon ware is distinguishable by the lack of detail in the dragon. In the older pieces, much care is given to the slipwork dragon's eyes, scales, and wings. In the new ware, the dragon is flat and lacks detail.

Colors are primary, referring to background color, not the color of the dragon. The primary color of a new piece has more shine than that of the older ware. Old colors are vibrant but for the most part not shiny (except for the lustre colors). New colors include green, lavender, yellow, pink, blue, pearlized, and orange as well as the classic blue/black. Old colors include orange, green, yellow, blue, pearlized, and blue/black. In addition to lustre finishes, you will find some background colors that are applied unevenly (and without shine), producing a cloud effect behind the dragon.

Many Dragon ware cups have lithophanes in the bottoms, often the face of a geisha girl. Nude lithophanes are scarcer but can sometimes be found in cups and saki cups. New pieces may also have lithophanes, but they are lacking in detail and tend to be flat.

Items listed below are unmarked unless noted otherwise. (Be sure to examine unmarked items well; in particular, look for good detailing in the dragon. New pieces lack the quality of workmanship evident in items made earlier in the century and should not command the prices of the older ware, so use the low end of the range to evaluate any pieces you feel may be new.) The Internet auction sites are a good place to see different pieces from various eras.

Key:
MIJ — Made in Japan
MIOJ — Made in Occupied Japan

Biscuit jar, orange, w/hdl, Oriental mk, 4", from $15 to 45.00
Bowl, orange, ftd, MIJ, 3½", from $20 to 30.00
Box, cigarette; blk, from $10 to 45.00
Box, dresser; blk, dmn shape, 4½", from $15 to 35.00
Candy dish, brn, w/hdl, HP Japan, 8⅜", from $40 to 55.00
Centerpiece, blk, MIJ, 9", from $45 to 75.00
Child's tea set, Little Hostess, luster, MIJ, 21-pc, +case, from $175 to 200.00
Condiment set, blk, tray w/8 pcs including lids, from $125 to ...175.00
Cup & saucer, blk, MIJ, from $15 to 40.00
Cup & saucer, blk, nude lithophane, MIJ, from $30 to 60.00
Cup & saucer, brn, Satsuma style, from $15 to 45.00
Cup & saucer, demitasse; blk, MIOJ, from $15 to....................20.00
Cup & saucer, demitasse; gold lustre, souvenir from $10 to 15.00
Cup & saucer, demitasse; red cloud, red eyes, from $20 to 40.00
Cup & saucer, orange, chid sz, from $10 to 20.00
Cup & saucer, yel, Nippon, from $25 to 55.00
Ginger Jar, orange, 6", from $25 to 45.00
Glasses, bl cloud, lithophane, 4", set of 4, from $80 to....................125.00
Hatpin holder, gray, Nippon, 5", from $50 to 125.00
Ice bucket, blk, wicker hdl, MIJ, 8", from $100 to 200.00
Incense burner, red, coralene (beaded) dragon, MIJ, 3", from $25 to ..40.00
Lighter, gray, 7¼", from $20 to 50.00
Luncheon set, blk, seashell shape, HP MIJ, plates+c/s, for 8, $75 to..175.00

Mug, bl cloud, MIJ, 3½" from $10 to 25.00
Pitcher, mini, dk bl, 2¼", from $10 to....20.00
Pitcher, mini, 1¾" from $7.50 to 15.00
Sake set, gray, no mk, dispenser w/6 cups w/lithophanes, from $50 to ..80.00
Sake cups, red, coraleme (beaded), MIJ, set of 6, from $30 to 60.00
Sake set, blk, bbl style w/rooster top, 6 cups w/hdl, Nippon, $225 to .275.00
Sake set, gray, bbl style w/elephant top, 6 bbl cups, MIJ, from $150 to ...200.00
Shakers, blk lustre, pr, from $7.50....20.00
Shakers, gr, souvenir, pr, from $5 to 15.00
Shakers, gray, souvenir w/Niagara Falls, 3", pr, from $7.50 to 15.00
Shoe, blk, 2", from $15 to 30.00
Sugar bowl, red, 5", from $15 to 25.00
Tea set, bl, teapot+c/s, child sz, from $20 to 45.00
Tea set, blk, Nippon, teapot+cr/sug+4 c/s, from $125 to 250.00
Tea set, demitasse: blk, MIJ, 17-pc, from $125....150.00
Tea set, gr, MIJ, 7" teapot+cr/sug+6 c/s, from $75 to 150.00
Tea set, pk (newer), paper label, 17-pc, from $50 to 75.00
Tea set, wht/gold, dragon spouts, Kutani, 23-pc, from $125 to 200.00
Teapot, blk, Nippon quality, 7¾", from $30 to....55.00
Teapot, red, 5¾", from $30 to 55.00
Vase, blk, hdl, HP Nippon, 4⅝", from $35 to 55.00
Vase, blk, souvenir, Hinodi, 7" sq, from $25 to 60.00
Vase, bud, bl lustre, MIJ, 7" from $7.50 to 20.00
Vase, yel, w/hdl, 3", from $10 to 25.00
Vases, blk w/gold hdl, 5", pr, from $15 to 30.00
Vases, yel, MIOJ, 2⅜", pr, from $12.50 to 20.00
Wall pocket, brn, Satsuma style, HP Japan, 8½", from $25 to 50.00
Wall pocket, orange, MIJ, 7¼", from $20 to 45.00

Dresden

The term Dresden is used today to indicate the porcelains that were produced in Meissen and Dresden, Germany, from the very early eighteenth century well into the next. John Bottger, a young alchemist, discovered the formula for the first true porcelain in 1708 while being held a virtual prisoner at the palace in Dresden because of the King's determination to produce a superior ware. Two years later a factory was erected in nearby Meissen with Bottger as director. There fine tableware, elaborate centerpieces, and exquisite figurines with applied details were produced. In 1731, to distinguish their product from the wares of such potters as Sevres, Worcester, Chelsea, and Derby, the Meissen company adopted their famous crossed swords trademark. During the next century, several potteries were producing porcelain in the 'Meissen style' in Dresden itself. Their wares were often marked with imitations of Meissen's crossed swords.

The Carl Theime factory produced dinnerware as well as decorative pieces in the Meissen style from 1872 until 1972. Openwork pieces were their specialty. Their mark was an intertwined 'SP' with the word Dresden below. Other companies followed suit, and in 1883 began using the crown mark along with the Dresden indication. There were several variations of this mark employed over the years. Many of these companies produced Meissen-type wares well into the twentieth century. See also Meissen.

Bottle, scent; roses & buds emb/pnt on wht, R Wehsener, mk, 5" ..65.00
Card holders, flower shape, set of 4 ....155.00
Compote, floral relief, mc on wht, rtcl rim, 9x6½", NM 265.00
Figurine, ballerina, seated, ruffled wht/pk dress, 7½ 330.00
Figurine, couple courting beneath trees, suitor spying, late, 17" ..700.00
Figurine, lady w/basket of roses, teal dress, appl roses, 7" 335.00
Figurine, man & lady, standing, lambs at their ft, 7", pr 400.00
Figurine, nude kneeling w/arms outstretched w/shell, 6" 765.00
Salad dish, lobster shape, floral w/gold, 2-part 625.00

Dresser Accessories

Dresser sets, ring trees, figural or satin pincushions, manicure sets — all those lovely items that graced milady's dressing table — were at the same time decorative as well as functional. Today they appeal to collectors for many reasons. The Victorian era is well represented by repousse silver-backed mirrors and brushes and pincushions that were used to display ornamental pins for the hair, hats, and scarves. The hair receiver — similar to a powder jar but with an opening in the lid — was used to hold long strands of hair retrieved from the comb or brush. These were wound around the finger and tucked in the opening to be used later for hair jewelry and pictures, many of which survive to the present day. (See Hair Weaving.)

Celluloid dresser sets were popular during the late 1800s and early 1900s. Some included manicure tools, pill boxes, and buttonhooks, as well as the basic items. Because celluloid tends to break rather easily, a whole set may be hard to find today. (See also Plastics.) With the current interest in anything Art Deco, sets from the '30s and '40s are especially collectible. These may be made of crystal, Bakelite, or silver, and the original boxes just as lavishly appointed as their contents.

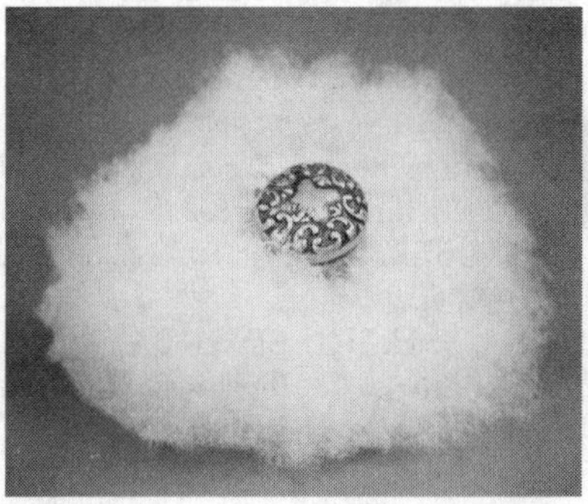

Powder puff, swan's down with sterling top, 3" diameter, $85.00.

Box, collar & cuff; decal on celluloid, 6x6½x6¾", from $225 to ..275.00
Box, handkerchief; children transfer on celluloid, 2½x5½x5¾" ..155.00
Box, powder; butterscotch Catalin & painted glass, Deco style .100.00
Brush & mirror, blk & gold enamel bks, Deco design, M, pr, up to .30.00
Case, glove; birds decal on celluloid, 2½x13x4", from $185 to ..235.00
Case, jewel; children transfer on celluloid, velvet trim, musical, 11" ...275.00
Case, toilet/manicure; children transfer on celluloid, complete, 9" L ..425.00
Hair receiver, HP roses/gold-trimmed cobalt bands on wht, Japan .50.00
Mirror, lady transfer & raised decor on celluloid, 9¾", up to 150.00
Powder box, sterling w/floral enamel, engine trn, F&B, 3" 140.00
Powder jar, lady holding skirt wide, lustre, Japan, 2-pc, 5½" 70.00
Whiskbroom, dog head hdl, blk & wht, Japan, figure, 3¼" 32.00
Whiskbroom, flapper girl hdl, Japan, figure: 3¼" 45.00

Dryden

Dryden Pottery was founded fifty years ago in Ellsworth, Kansas, by Jim Dryden, a WWII veteran with financing from a G.I. loan. A mention on the front page of the Wall Street Journal resulted in substantial orders from Macy's of New York and Fred Harvey Restaurants and gift shops in all the stations of the Santa Fe Railroad.

In the late 1940s and early 1950s, some six hundred stores stocked Dryden pottery. Stiff competition from occupied Japan and Europe forced wholesale prices so low that the only profit from the pottery was from direct sales to the traveling public. Tourists watched potters at work. These sales were profitable, but in 1955 the new transcontinental highway 70 through Kansas missed Ellsworth. The pottery had to move.

Hot Springs, Arkansas, with its hundreds of thousands of tourists was chosen as the new location.

Since 1970 more and more of the production is wheel thrown and hand sculpted in an all-out attempt to follow the example of the world-famous Rookwood Pottery (1880–1967). Beautiful matt and gloss glazes plus one-of-a-kind originals make Dryden Pottery highly collectible.

Kansas pieces have a golden tan clay base. Most are signed and numbered like those made in Arkansas. Rare and specialty pieces have sold for over $200.00. Arkansas pieces have a white clay base. Expect to find molded pieces dating from the 1940s through the 1970s. Pieces from the '70s to the present are primarily wheel thrown, hand-sculpted originals with beautiful matt and gloss glazes. These pieces are often dated. Our advisor for this category is Ralph Winslow; he is listed in the Directory under Missouri.

Kansas Dryden (1946 – 1956)

Ashtray, #17A, Kanopolis Lake 34.00
Ashtray, Lamer Hotels 16.00
Bowl, #7E, 7" 25.00
Creamer/sugar bowl, #108, Lebanon, Kans 35.00
Ewer, yel, #715 ....25.00
Figurine, buffalo, Abilene, Kans 200.00
Figurine, lion, yel 75.00
Figurine, panther, brn 100.00
Figurine, Scottie dog 50.00
Flowerpot, w/liner, 4" 25.00
Jug, bl, Wichita, Kans, #102, 5" 25.00
Jug, KU, 3" 45.00
Juice set, gr, 7-pc 45.00
Pitcher, Black Hills, SD, #180 ....15.00
Pitcher, Brookville Hotel, #98, 5½" 25.00
Pitcher, maroon, #192, 6" 15.00
Shakers, bl & gr, 6", pr 30.00
Spoon holder, yel, Salina, Kans 30.00
Teapot, bl, #108B 30.00
Vase, Bagnall Dam, #7R, pr 75.00
Vase, brn, #106, 3½" 19.00
Vase, brn & pk, 5" 35.00
Vase, bud; yel, #97 ....25.00
Vase, Bull Shoals Dam, sq, #17 ....25.00
Vase, gr, 3½" 26.00
Vase, shamrock, 4-H 30.00
Vase, yel, Sundance, Wyo, #105 ....35.00
Wall pocket, gr, #887 ....28.00
Wall pocket, Grand River, #86 ....50.00

Arkansas Dryden (1956 to Present)

Vase, JK Dryden, Ark., 10", $75.00. (Photo courtesy Ralph Winslow)

Bowl, Ellsworth HS, 1981 ....10.00
Bowl, lobster, 12" 20.00
Bowl, muted, 8½" 10.00
Bowl, sectional 20.00
Coffeepot, 15" 22.00
Mug, face, JK Dryden 10.00
Mug, wheel thrown, snake hdl 35.00
Nude, lady, brn 45.00
Pitcher, folk art, 8½" 15.00
Planter, elephant, brn 10.00
Platter, fish, 14" 25.00
Vase, aqua, 9" 35.00
Vase, wheel thrown, brn, 15" 95.00
Vase, wheel thrown, pk, 6" 45.00
Vase, wheel thrown, sculpted, 6" 50.00
Vase, wheel thrown, 1979, 5" 28.00

Duncan and Miller

The firm that became known as the Duncan and Miller Glass Company in 1900 was organized in 1874 in Pittsburgh, Pennsylvania, a partnership between George Duncan, his sons Harry and James, and his son-in-law Augustus Heisey. John Ernest Miller was hired as their designer. He is credited with creating the most famous of all Duncan's glassware lines, Three Face. (See Pattern Glass.) The George Duncan and Sons Glass Company, as it was titled, was only one of eighteen companies that merged in 1891 with U.S. Glass. Soon after the Pittsburgh factory burned in 1892, the association was dissolved, and Heisey left the firm to set up his own factory in Newark, Ohio. Duncan built his new plant in Washington, Pennsylvania, where he continued to make pressed glassware in such notable patterns as Bagware, Amberette, Duncan Flute, Button Arches, and Zippered Slash. The firm was eventually sold to U.S. Glass in Tiffin, Ohio, and unofficially closed in August 1955.

In addition to the early pressed dinnerware patterns, today's Duncan and Miller collectors enjoy searching for opalescent vases in many patterns and colors, frosted 'Satin Tone' glassware, acid-etched designs, and lovely stemware such as the Rock Crystal cuttings. Milk glass was made in limited quantity and is considered a good investment. Ruby glass, Ebony (a lovely opaque black glass popular during the '20s and '30s), and, of course, the glass animal and bird figurines are all highly valued examples of the art of Duncan and Miller.

Expect to pay at least 25% more than values listed for other colors, for ruby and cobalt, as much as 50% more in the Georgian, Pall Mall, and Sandwich lines. Pink, green, and amber Sandwich is worth approximately 30% more than the same items in crystal. Milk glass examples of American Way are valued up to 30% higher than color, 50% higher in Pall Mall. Chartreuse Canterbury is worth 10% to 20% more than crystal. Add approximately 40% to 50% to listed prices for opalescent items. Etchings, cuttings, and other decorations will increase values by about 50%. For further study we recommend *The Encyclopedia of Duncan Glass*, by Gail Krause; she is listed in the Directory under Pennsylvania. Several Duncan and Miller lines are shown in *Elegant Glassware of the Depression Era* by Gene Florence. Also refer to *Glass Animals and Figural Flower Frogs of the Depression Era* by Lee Garmon and Dick Spencer; they are both listed under Illinois. See also Glass Animals. Our advisor is Roselle Schleifman; she is listed in the Directory under New York.

Byzantine, crystal, cocktail 12.00
Byzantine, crystal, wine 20.00
Cadena, topaz, cordial 80.00
Canterbury, crystal, ashtray, club shape, 5½" 15.00
Canterbury, crystal, basket, oval, 10x4¼x7" 70.00
Canterbury, crystal, bowl, gardenia; 12x2¾" 30.00

Canterbury, crystal, bowl, hdl, 5½x1¾" 7.00
Canterbury, crystal, bowl, 8½x4" 22.00
Canterbury, crystal, candle, low, 3" 12.50
Canterbury, crystal, cheese stand, 5½x3½" 10.00
Canterbury, crystal, crimped, 4" 17.50
Canterbury, crystal, ice bucket or vase, 7" 37.50
Canterbury, crystal, plate, cake; 14" 25.00
Canterbury, crystal, plate, fruit; hdls, 6½" 7.00
Canterbury, crystal, stem, claret or wine; 4-oz, 5" 20.00
Canterbury, crystal, tray, sandwich; center hdl, 12x5¼" 37.50
Canterbury, crystal, tumbler, juice; ftd, 5-oz, 4¼" 10.00
Canterbury, crystal, urn, 4½x4¾" 15.00
Caribbean, bl, bowl, finger; 4½" 32.00
Caribbean, bl, bowl, flower; hdls, oval, 10¾" 90.00
Caribbean, bl, bowl, vegetable; hdls, 9¼" 75.00
Caribbean, bl, creamer 25.00
Caribbean, bl, plate, cheese & cracker liner; hdls, 11" 85.00
Caribbean, bl, salt cellar, 2½" 25.00
Caribbean, bl, stem, wine; ball stem, ftd, 3-oz, 4¾" 45.00
Caribbean, bl, vase, epergne; flared edge, 7¾" 110.00
Caribbean, crystal, bowl, grapefruit; ftd, hdls, 7¼" 20.00
Caribbean, crystal, bowl, hdls, folded side, 5x7" 16.00
Caribbean, crystal, candlestick, 1-light, w/bl prisms, 7¼" 65.00
Caribbean, crystal, ice bucket, hdls, 6½" 75.00
Caribbean, crystal, plate, salad; 7½" 10.00
Caribbean, crystal, relish, 2-part, rnd, 6" 12.00
Caribbean, crystal, stem, wine; ball stem, ftd, 3½-oz, 3½" 20.00
Caribbean, crystal, tumbler, flat, 5-oz, 3½" 20.00
Cerice, crystal, cordial, #15071 ....35.00
First Love, crystal, ashtray, #30, 6½x4¼" 35.00
First Love, crystal, bowl, #111, flared rim, 11x3¼" 62.50
First Love, crystal, bowl, #115, 8½x4" 37.50
First Love, crystal, bowl, #126, oval, 14x7½x6" 75.00
First Love, crystal, cheese stand, #111, 3x5¼" 30.00
First Love, crystal, comport, #115, flat top, 5¼x6¾" 32.00
First Love, crystal, decanter, #5200 or #30, w/stopper, 32-oz 170.00
First Love, crystal, mayonnaise, #115, 5½x2¾" 35.00
First Love, crystal, plate, #111, 11" 47.50
First Love, crystal, plate, lemon; #111, hdls, 6" 15.00
First Love, crystal, relish, #111, hdls, 2-part, 6x1¾" 20.00
First Love, crystal, relish, #111, hdls, 5-part, 12" 55.00
First Love, crystal, stem, iced tea; #5111½, ftd, 12-oz, 6½" 35.00
First Love, crystal, vase, #115, 4½x4¾" 30.00
First Love, crystal, vase, #507, 10" 95.00
Hobnail, bl opal, goblet, 9-oz 45.00
Lily of the Valley, crystal, ashtray, 6" 25.00
Lily of the Valley, crystal, mayonnaise 30.00

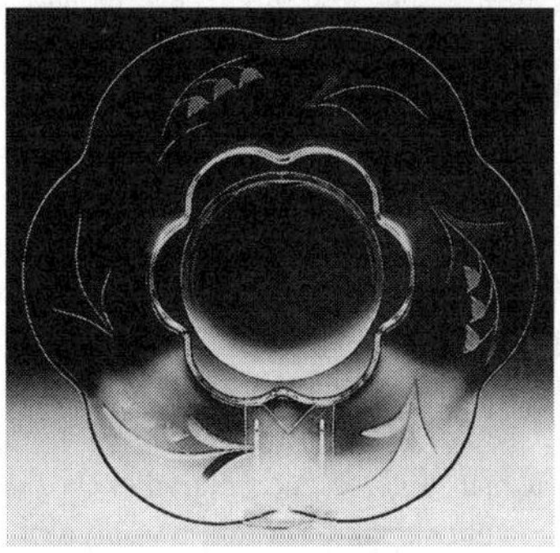

Lily of the Valley, crystal, plate, 9", $40.00 (8", $20.00). (Photo courtesy Gene Florence)

Lily of the Valley, crystal, stem, wine 40.00
Nautical, bl, candy jar, w/lid 500.00
Nautical, bl, plate, 10" 50.00
Nautical, bl, tumbler, orange juice; ftd 25.00
Nautical, crystal, cocktail shaker, fish design 60.00
Nautical, crystal, marmalade 25.00
Nautical, crystal, tumbler, bar; 2-oz 12.50
Nautical, opal, comport, 7" 495.00
Nautical, opal, decanter 550.00
Puritan, crystal, plate, dinner; 10" 25.00
Sandwich, crystal, basket, loop hdl, 6½" 125.00
Sandwich, crystal, bowl, grapefruit; rimmed 17.50
Sandwich, crystal, bowl, nappy; ring hdl, 5" 14.00
Sandwich, crystal, bowl, nut; 3½" 10.00
Sandwich, crystal, bowl, salad; deep, 10" 75.00
Sandwich, crystal, bowl, salad; shallow, 12" 40.00
Sandwich, crystal, candelabra, 1-light, w/bobeche & prisms, 10" ..77.00
Sandwich, crystal, candlestick, 3-light, 5" 45.00
Sandwich, crystal, cigarette holder, ftd, 3" 27.50
Sandwich, crystal, creamer, ftd, 7-oz, 4" 11.00
Sandwich, crystal, cup & saucer 15.00
Sandwich, crystal, plate, deviled egg 70.00
Sandwich, crystal, plate, dinner 40.00
Sandwich, crystal, plate, service; 13" 50.00
Sandwich, crystal, relish, oblong, 3-part, 10" 30.00
Sandwich, crystal, sherbet/ice cream 12.00
Sandwich, crystal, stem, oyster cocktail; ftd, 5-oz, 2¾" 15.00
Sandwich, crystal, tray, celery; oval, 10" 18.00
Sandwich, crystal, tray, for sugar bowl & creamer, oval 10.00
Sandwich, crystal, vase, hat shape, 4" 25.00
Sanibel, bl opal, mint dish, 7" 45.00
Spiral Flutes, amber, gr or pk, bowl, finger; 4⅜" 7.00
Spiral Flutes, amber, gr or pk, bowl, nappy; 7" 15.00
Spiral Flutes, amber, gr or pk, candle, 3½" 15.00
Spiral Flutes, amber, gr or pk, comport, flared, low ft, 9" 55.00
Spiral Flutes, amber, gr or pk, mug, hdl, 9-oz, 7" 35.00
Spiral Flutes, amber, gr or pk, platter, 11" 35.00
Spiral Flutes, amber, gr or pk, stem, water; 7-oz, 6¼" 17.50
Spiral Flutes, amber, gr or pk, vase, 8½" 25.00
Tear Drop, crystal, ashtray, ind, 3" 6.00
Tear Drop, crystal, basket, flower; loop hdl, 12" 130.00
Tear Drop, crystal, bowl, console; crimped, hdls, 10" 30.00
Tear Drop, crystal, butter dish, hdls, w/lid, ¼-lb 25.00
Tear Drop, crystal, candy dish, heart shape, 7½" 25.00
Tear Drop, crystal, comport, ftd, 4¾" 12.00
Tear Drop, crystal, olive dish, 2-part, 6" 14.00
Tear Drop, crystal, plate, salad liner; rolled edge, 13" 35.00
Tear Drop, crystal, shakers, 5", pr 25.00
Tear Drop, crystal, stem, sherry; 1¾-oz, 4½" 30.00
Tear Drop, crystal, stem, 9-oz, 7" 14.00
Tear Drop, crystal, sweetmeat, star shape, hdls, 5½" 35.00
Tear Drop, crystal, tray, cruets; center hdl, 7¾" 12.50
Tear Drop, crystal, tumbler, juice; flat, 3½-oz, 3¼" 6.00
Tear Drop, crystal, tumbler, party; ftd, 8-oz, 5" 9.00
Terrace, cobalt or red, candy urn, w/lid 395.00
Terrace, cobalt or red, plate, sq, 6" 30.00
Terrace, cobalt or red, relish, hdls, 2-part, 6x1¾" 45.00
Terrace, cobalt or red, sugar bowl, w/lid, 10-oz, 3" 100.00
Terrace, crystal or amber, bowl, ftd, 9x4½" 42.00
Terrace, crystal or amber, mayonnaise, crimped, 5½x3½" 32.00
Terrace, crystal or amber, plate, torte; rolled edge, 12" 40.00
Terrace, crystal or amber, stem, ice cream; #5111½, 5-oz, 4" 14.00

Durand

Durand art glass was made by the Vineland Flint Glass Works of

Vineland, New Jersey. Victor Durand Jr. was the sole proprietor. The division called the 'fancy shop' was geared to the production of fine hand-blown art glass in the style of Tiffany and Steuben. Lustered glass and opal glass were used as a base to create such patterns as King Tut, Heart and Vine, Peacock Feather, and Egyptian Crackle. Cased glass was used to produce cut designs. Production of art glass began in 1924 and continued until 1931. Although most of this art glass was unsigned, when it was, it was generally signed within the pontil 'Durand' or 'Durand' written across the top of a large letter V, all in silver script. The numbers that sometimes appear along with the signature indicate the shape and height of the object. Owner Victor Durand employed the owner and several workers from the failed Quezal Art Glass and Decorating Co. This is why early Durand may sometimes look similar to Quezal art glass. In 1926 Durand art glass was awarded a medal of honor at the Sesquicentennial International Exposition in Philadelphia, Pennsylvania. Our advisor for this category is Edward J. Meschi, author of *Durand — The Man and His Glass*, (Antique Publications); he is listed in the Directory under New Jersey.

Vase, blue coil on gold iridescent, 10½", $1,200.00.

Almond dish, gold lustre, fluted top, 2½x5" 295.00
Bowl, ambergris, globular, disk ft, knop stem, 4¾" 400.00
Bowl, buillon; ruby, appl Spanish Yel hdls, ruby ft, 2½x6" 425.00
Bowl, centerpc; marigold, #2605, 2½x14" 350.00
Bowl, finger; ambergris w/gr trim, 2½x5", w/6½" underplate 225.00
Bowl, finger; Optic Rib, bl, 2x4½" 100.00
Bowl, peacock feathers, opal/gr on gr over crystal, 4x9½" 625.00
Bowl, yel lustre, wht-trim ft, bl/wht crisscross bands, 4½x10½" ..725.00
Box, puff; silver bl lustre on bl base, star cutting on lid, 3½x3" ...1,250.00
Candlesticks, peacock feathers, opal/red on red, flared top, 3½", pr ..725.00
Candlesticks, ruby w/Spanish Yel cup/stem, ruby ft, 6", pr 725.00
Champagne, ruby flashed w/Spanish Yel stem & ruby ft, 6" 275.00
Cocktail, peacock feathers, opal/red on red on crystal, 4½" 295.00
Compote, King Tut, bl w/gold irid int, 6½x6" 700.00
Compote, Optic Rib, ruby w/Spanish Yel stem, ruby ft, 4x7½" 625.00
Compote, peacock feathers, opal/gr on gr on clear, ambergris ft, 6" ..525.00
Creamer, peacock feathers, opal/ruby on ruby flashed, crystal hdl/ft ..425.00
Ginger jar, bl irid w/threading, yel reeded florette on lid, 9x8¼" 1,500.00
Goblet, Optic Rib, bl w/Spanish Yel stem, ruby ft, 8½" 375.00
Goblet, peacock feathers, opal/red on red to clear, yel stem/ft, 7" ...325.00
Ice bucket, bl to clear, honeycomb vesicas/X-hatch dmns, SP rim/bail ..650.00
Jar, King Tut, gr w/gold decor, amber prunt on lid, 7" 3,100.00
Nappy, gold lustre, 3x4½" 275.00
Parfait, rose pk, ribbed w/fluted top, ftd base, 5¾" 150.00
Plate, Optic Rib, bl, scalloped rim, 11½" 150.00
Plate, pulled feathers, opal on ruby w/frosted center, 8" 225.00
Plate, salad; Optic Rib, yel lustre w/gr trim, scalloped, 8½" 125.00
Plate, salad; peacock feathers, opal/ruby on gr flashed, 8" 275.00
Plate, salad; yel lustre, 8" dia 75.00
Shade, Egyptian Craquelle, ruby & wht over ambergris base, 5x7" .425.00
Tumbler, iced tea; ambergris w/gr trim, 6" 100.00
Tumbler, lemonade; Optic Rib, ambergris w/gr trim, 5½" 125.00
Tumbler, lemonade; Optic Rib, ruby, 5½" 125.00
Vase, Beehive, bl irid, #20177, 6½" 950.00
Vase, bl irid, amber rim-to-hip hdls, #2010-12", 12" 1,350.00
Vase, bl irid, cylindrical, polished pontil, 1968, 8" 800.00
Vase, bl irid, waisted w/flared rim, 6¼" 850.00
Vase, bl irid w/bl threading overall, #1710-6, 6½" 700.00
Vase, bl w/wht peacock feathers, disk ft, #2028½", 8", NM 800.00
Vase, clear w/controlled air trap, ovoid, #1995, 4x4" 150.00
Vase, coil decor, bl on gold, 10½" 1,000.00
Vase, coils on orange & gold irid, #2011-12, ftd, 12" 1,900.00
Vase, cut o/l, red to clear, 9" 2,250.00
Vase, feathers, gold w/bl tips, allover gold threads, 9½" 1,500.00
Vase, feathers, wht on red, pear shape, #1700, 8¼" 1,350.00
Vase, gold irid, ftd, flared rim, 10½" 400.00
Vase, gold irid, squat w/trumpet neck, #1990-6, 5¾" 300.00
Vase, gold irid w/gold threads, wht-flash gold int, 6½", EX 460.00
Vase, heart & vine, bl irid on orange-gold, #1969-10, 9¾" 1,250.00
Vase, King Tut, bl on gold lustre, #1710, 4¼" 1,150.00
Vase, King Tut, gold on gr, yel int, #1722, 7¾" 1,300.00
Vase, King Tut, gr on gold, #1964, 10" 2,415.00
Vase, King Tut, gr/gold irid, #1717, incurvate rim 1,400.00
Vase, King Tut, wht on gold, 10" 850.00
Vase, Lady Gay Rose w/irid coils, squat/ftd w/long neck, 12½" .2,800.00
Vase, marigold, bulbous, #1977-10, 8x10" 800.00
Vase, marigold lustre w/gold webs, bulbous w/trumpet-form rim, 9" ...700.00

Easter

In the early 1900s to the 1930s, Germany made the first composition candy containers in the shapes of Easter rabbits, ducks, and chicks. A few were also made of molded cardboard. In the 1940s West Germany made candy containers out of molded cardboard. Many of these had spring necks to give a nodding effect. From the 1930s and into the 1950s, United States manufacturers made Easter candy containers out of egg-carton material (pulp) or pressed cardboard. Ducks and chicks are not as high in demand as rabbits. Rabbits with painted-on clothes or attached fabric clothes bring more than the plain brown or white rabbits. When no condition is mentioned in the description, assume that values reflect excellent to near mint condition for all but paper items; those assume to be in near mint to mint condition. Our advisor for this category is Jenny Tarrant; she is listed in the Directory under Missouri.

Note: in the candy container section, measurements given for the rabbit and cart or rabbit and wagon containers indicate the distance to the tip of the rabbits' ears.

Candy Containers

German, begging rabbit, brn w/glass eyes, compo, 1900-1930s, 5" ..85.00
German, begging rabbit, brn w/glass eyes, compo, 1900-1930s, 6" ..95.00
German, begging rabbit, brn w/glass eyes, compo, 1900-1930s, 7" .120.00
German, begging rabbit, brn w/glass eyes, compo, 1900-1930s, 8" .175.00
German, begging rabbit, brn w/glass eyes, compo, 1900-1930s, 9" .250.00
German, begging rabbit, mohair covered, compo, 1900-1930s, 4" .150.00
German, begging rabbit, mohair covered, compo, 1900-1930s, 5" .175.00
German, begging rabbit, mohair covered, compo, 1900-1930s, 6" .200.00
German, begging rabbit, mohair covered, compo, 1900-1930s, 7" .250.00
German, duck, yel w/glass eyes, compo, 1900-1930s, 5" 85.00
German, duck or chick, pnt-on clothes, compo, 1900-1930s, 3-4", $95 to ..100.00
German, duck or chick, pnt-on clothes, compo, 1900-1930s, 5" .145.00
German, duck or chick, pnt-on clothes, compo, 1900-1930s, 6" .185.00
German, duck or chick, pnt-on clothes, compo, 1900-1930s, 7" .200.00
German, egg, molded cb, 1900-1930, 3-7", from $65 to 85.00
German, egg, molded cb, 1900-1930, 8" 100.00

German, egg, tin, 1900-1910, EX, 2-3", from $65 to 75.00
German, rabbit (dressed) in car, compo, 1900-1930s, from $250 to .325.00
German, rabbit (dressed) in shoe, compo, 1900-1930s, from $250 to ...325.00
German, rabbit (dressed) on egg, compo, 1900-1930s, from $250 to .325.00
German, rabbit (dressed) on log, compo, 1900-1930s, from $200 to .250.00
German, rabbit pulling wood cart, mohair covered, 1900-1930s, 4" ..250.00
German, rabbit pulling wood cart, mohair covered, 1900-1930s, 5" ..275.00
German, rabbit pulling wood cart, mohair covered, 1900-1930s, 6" ..300.00
German, rabbit pulling wood cart, mohair covered, 1900-1930s, 7" ..375.00
German, rabbit pulling wood wagon, brn compo, 1900-1930s, 4" 195.00
German, rabbit pulling wood wagon, brn compo, 1900-1930s, 5" 250.00
German, rabbit pulling wood wagon, brn compo, 1900-1930s, 6" .275.00
German, rabbit pulling wood wagon, brn compo, 1900-1930s, 7" .325.00
German, rabbit w/fabric clothes, compo, 1900-1930s, 4" 250.00
German, rabbit w/fabric clothes, compo, 1900-1930s, 5" 300.00
German, rabbit w/fabric clothes, compo, 1900-1930s, 6" 350.00
German, rabbit w/fabric clothes, compo, 1900-1930s, 7" 400.00
German, rabbit w/glass beading, compo, 1900-1930s, 6" 150.00
German, rabbit w/pnt-on clothes, compo, 1900-1930s, 3" 125.00
German, rabbit w/pnt-on clothes, compo, 1900-1930s, 4" 150.00
German, rabbit w/pnt-on clothes, compo, 1900-1930s, 5" 200.00
German, rabbit w/pnt-on clothes, compo, 1900-1930s, 6" 250.00
German, rabbit w/pnt-on clothes, compo, 1900-1930s, 7" 300.00
German, sitting rabbit, brn w/glass eyes, compo, 1900-1930s, 5" .95.00
German, sitting rabbit, brn w/glass eyes, compo, 1900-1930s, 6" ..110.00
German, sitting rabbit, brn w/glass eyes, compo, 1900-1930s, 7" ..125.00
German, sitting rabbit, mohair covered, compo, 1900-1930s, 4" ..150.00
German, sitting rabbit, mohair covered, compo, 1900-1930s, 5" ..175.00
German, sitting rabbit, mohair covered, compo, 1900-1930s, 6" ..225.00
German, walking rabbit, brn w/glass eyes, compo, 1900-1930s, 5" ..110.00
German, walking rabbit, brn w/glass eyes, compo, 1900-1930s, 6" ..125.00
German, walking rabbit, brn w/glass eyes, compo, 1900-1930s, 7" ..150.00
German, walking rabbit, brn w/glass eyes, compo, 1900-1930s, 8" ..175.00
German, walking rabbit, brn w/glass eyes, compo, 1900-1930s, 9" ..250.00
German, walking rabbit, mohair covered, compo, 1900-1930s, 4" ..195.00
German, walking rabbit, mohair covered, compo, 1900-1930s, 5" ..225.00
German, walking rabbit, mohair covered, compo, 1900-1930s, 6" ..250.00
German, walking rabbit, mohair covered, compo, 1900-1930s, 7" ..275.00
German, walking rabbit, wht, compo, 1900-1930s, 6" 125.00
US, begging rabbit, pulp, 1940-1950 ....55.00
US, sitting rabbit, pulp, brn w/glass eyes, Burk Co, 1930 ....140.00
US, sitting rabbit, pulp, no basket, 1940-1950 ....60.00
US, sitting rabbit next to lg basket, pulp, 1930-1950 ....125.00
US, sitting rabbit w/basket on bk, pulp, 1940-1950 ....95.00
W German, egg, molded cb, 1940-1960, 3-8", from $25 to 40.00
W German/US Zone, dressed chick, cb, spring neck, 1940-1950 .65.00
W German/US Zone, dressed duck, cb, spring neck, 1940-1950 ..65.00
W German/US Zone, dressed rabbit, cb, spring neck, 1940-1950 ...75.00
W German/US Zone, plain rabbit, cb, spring neck, 1940-1950 ...65.00

Miscellaneous

Celluloid chick or duck, dressed, 3-5", M 45.00
Celluloid chick or duck, dressed, 6-8", M 65.00
Celluloid chicken pulling wagon w/rabbit, M 80.00
Celluloid rabbit, dressed, 3-5", M 65.00
Celluloid rabbit, dressed, 6-8", M 75.00
Celluloid rabbit, plain, 3-5", M 20.00
Celluloid rabbit, plain, 6-7", M 30.00
Celluloid rabbit & chick in swan boat, M 150.00
Celluloid rabbit driving car, M 150.00
Celluloid rabbit pulling wagon, M 95.00
Celluloid rabbit pushing or pulling cart, lg, M 95.00
Celluloid rabbit pushing or pulling cart, sm, M 60.00
Celluloid windup toy, Japan or Occupied Japan, M 150.00
Celluloid windup toy, Japan or Occupied Japan, MIB 195.00
Rabbit, cotton batten w/paper ears, Japan, 1930-1950, 2-5", $30 to .45.00
Rabbit, cotton batten w/paper ears, Japan, 1930-1950, 6" 85.00

Egg Cups

Egg cups, one of the fastest growing collectibles of the '90s, have been traced back to the ruins of Pompeii. Since then, they have been made in almost every country and in almost every conceivable material (ceramics, glass, metal, papier-mache, plastic, wood, ivory, even rubber and straw). Popular categories include Art Deco, Black Memorabilia, Chintz, Characters/Personalities, Golliwoggs, Railroadiana, Steamship, Souvenir Ware, etc.

Still being produced today in most countries, egg cups appeal to collectors on many levels. Prices can range from quite inexpensive to many thousands of dollars. Those made prior to 1840 are scarce and sought after, as are the character/personality egg cups of the 1930s.

For a more thorough study of egg cups we recommend that you refer to *Egg Cups: An Illustrated History and Price Guide* (Antique Publications) by Brenda Blake, our advisor for this category. You will find her address listed in the Directory under Maine.

Key:
bkt — bucket, a single cup without a foot
dbl — two-sided with small end for eating egg in shell, large end for mixing egg with toast and butter
fig — figural, an egg cup actually molded into the shape of an animal, bird, car, person, etc.
hoop — hoop, a single open cup with waistline
set — tray or cruet (stand, frame or basket) with two to eight cups
sgl — single, with a foot; goblet shaped

Advertising/Souvenir

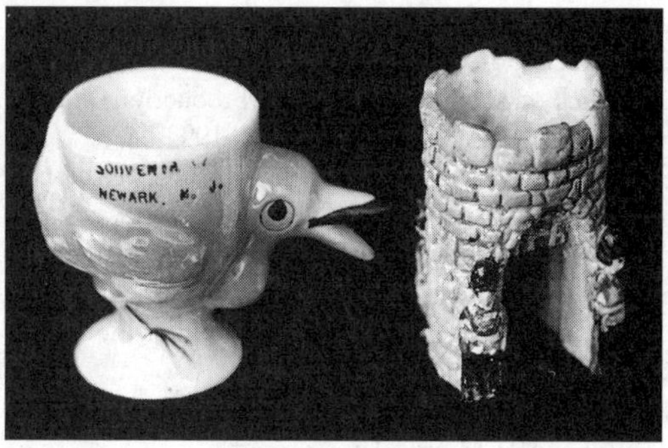

Figural, Duck, Souvenir of Newark, N.J., gold lustre, $25.00; Figural, Tower of London, ca 1928, $95.00. (Photo courtesy Brenda Blake)

Bkt, Western Airlines stamped on bottom 8.00
Dbl, Boston...Hospital, red floral transfer, int seal, mk, 1910s 80.00
Dbl, BPOE #30, gr elk 35.00
Dbl, Caesar's Palace, brn logo, 1990s 12.00
Dbl, Department of Health, gr leaf sprigs 28.00
Dbl, Roger Williams Church 1634, Salem MA, transfer, Germany, ca 1915 ...38.00
Dbl, Sigma Alpha Epsilon, purple Greek letters 22.00
Dbl, Zeppelin Deutsche Aeromail, gold rim, bl stripe, Heinrich ..1,200.00
Sgl, Hermitage, Bauscher Weiden, recent 10.00
Sgl, Howe's Caverns, bl logo & rim 9.00

Sgl, Lancaster PA, Bless This House 8.00
Sgl, Lazarus Stores 89th Anniversary, turq, Fiesta, 1940 ....135.00
Sgl, Plymouth Rock, Plymouth MA, transfer, Germany, ca 1910 ..40.00
Sgl, Souvenir of Indianapolis IN, HP, Japan, 1930s 12.00

American China/Pottery

Bkt, chicks on bl border, Paul Revere Pottery 325.00
Dbl, Ballerina, khaki-gr, Universal 12.00
Dbl, Barkwood, brn on tan, Vernon Kilns, 1953-58 ....16.00
Dbl, bl tall ship, MA Hadley 22.00
Dbl, Brittany, Homer Laughlin 17.00
Dbl, Casual California, Dawn Pk, Vernon Kilns, 1947-56 ....10.00
Dbl, Frost Flowers, Eva Zeisel, Hall, 1950s 28.00
Dbl, Ming, Lenox 45.00
Dbl, Organdie, plaid, Vernon Kilns 22.00
Dbl, Robin Des Bois, Canonsburg Pottery Co, PV in circle 15.00
Dbl, Rooster, Folk Art, Pennsbury 25.00
Dbl, Standing Rabbit, Juvenile, Roseville, ca 1917 ....300.00
Dbls, Bride & Groom, Cleminson, pr 60.00
Sgl, Apple, Franciscan 32.00
Sgl, Lei Lani, maroon printed lotus flower, Vernon Kilns, ca 1940, lg .72.00
Sgl, Tea Leaf, Boston Egg Cup, Buffalo 375.00

Characters/Personalities

Single, Mickey Mouse holding a gun, gold lustre, $125.00. **(Photo courtesy Brenda Blake)**

Bkt, Holly Hobbie, ca 1978 ....13.00
Bkt, Katzenjammer Kids, color illus 100.00
Dbl, Donald Duck, face emb, Walt Disney Productions 45.00
Dbl, Foghorn Leghorn, Acme Home Works, 1992 ....14.00
Fig, Mickey Mouse on scooter, lustre, Walt Disney Productions, Japan ...125.00
Fig, Snoopy, chef's hat 50.00
Fig, Swee' Pea, yel, King Features Syndicate, 1980 ....70.00
Fig set, Snow White & 7 Dwarfs, stand by their cups, Japan, 1937 ..1,450.00
Sgl, Alice in Wonderland, integral saucer, Hammersley 52.00
Sgl, Mickey Mouse, SP, enamel, ca 1950 ....75.00
Sgl, Paddington Bear, taking a walk, Coalport, late 1970s 30.00
Sgl, Prince William, 1982 birthday, Coronet 40.00
Sgl, Queen Elizabeth, 70th Birthday, Coronet, 1996 ....15.00
Sgl, Teletubbies, w/box & chocolate egg 10.00

Chintz

Bkt, Rosalynde, James Kent 45.00
Dbl, Hazel, blk ground, Royal Winton 235.00
Dbl, Sampler pattern, Chintz on bottom half of cup, Masons 32.00
Sgl, Bedale, sq base, Royal Winton 80.00
Sgl, Cheadle, maroon floral, Royal Winton 100.00
Sgl, Julia, Royal Winton 145.00
Sgl, Julia (new), Royal Winton, 1995 ....40.00
Sgl, Marguerite, Royal Winton 70.00
Sgl, Old Cottage, Royal Winton 85.00
Sgl, Welbeck (new), Royal Winton, 1995 ....35.00

Figurals

Bellhop, pillbox hat & cigarette, Art Deco, made in France 75.00
Blk cat, gr eyes, red bow tie 35.00
Blk cat, Shafford, 1950s 100.00
Blk cat sitting on orange lustre boot, Foreign 45.00
Blk male face, Germany, ca 1900 ....100.00
Butler holding cup on tray, Silver Crane Co, 1988 ....60.00
Chicken, wht w/blk trim, Coq Rouge 16.00
Lion, seated, brn pottery 10.00
Miss Cutie Pie, Lefton 35.00
Oriental boy w/dog kissing cheek, Occupied Japan 40.00
Toby Philpot, wht jacket, blk trim, ca 1900 ....58.00
Walking legs, gr shoes, Carlton Ware 40.00
Whistler, bear, lustre 100.00

Foreign

Bkt, Cardinal Tuck, red robe, Goebel 175.00
Dbl, Doll Face, Nippon 200.00
Dbl, Regency, red, Quimper, 1950s 28.00
Dbl, Rooster, Holt Howard, 1961 ....18.00
Hoop, leaves, turq rim, Sarreguemines, ca 1890 ....65.00
Set, 6 pk lustre cups, HP floral rectangular stand w/hdl, Royal Bonn ..80.00
Sgl, cobalt, gilding, integral saucer, rtcl, Limoges 45.00
Sgl, floral mc, gilding, Sevres, ca 1789 ....400.00
Sgl, HP vignettes w/gold, Kunst Palette, Regnitzlosau Bavaria, 1930s .35.00

Glass

Dbl, crackle, vaseline, ca 1890s 75.00
Dbl, English Hobnail, amber, Westmoreland, 1930s-40s 32.00
Dbl, opal, oval silhouette, flared base, Hazel Atlas, 1930s 16.00
Fig, chick, cobalt, hdld, Westmoreland 14.00
Fig, swan, clear, 1930s 12.00
Sgl, blown, opal w/yel opal, appl bl rim, 1790s 285.00
Sgl, Bristol bl, ca 1810-20 ....250.00
Sgl, cobalt, blown, flared rim, 1870s 85.00
Sgl, emb design, bl, scalloped base, Portieux 40.00
Sgl, Hobnail, bl, row of ovals on base, ca 1875 ....65.00
Sgl, lacy glass, leaf pattern, ca 1825-40 ....95.00
Sgl, slag, purple, vertical ribs 75.00
Sgl, Yeoman, marigold, Heisey 60.00

Staffordshire

Bkt, Cornish Kitchen Ware, bl bands, TC Green & Co, 1930s ...16.00
Bkt, Fitzhugh, red rim stripe, Spode 18.00
Dbl, Bristol, red, Crown Ducal, 1931 ....20.00
Dbl, Chinese Bird, Adams, ca 1913 ....35.00
Dbl, Grape, Chelsea Dinnerware 32.00
Dbl, Greydawn, pk, Johnson Bros 10.00
Dbl, Holland, Flow Bl, Johnson Bros, ca 1891 ....52.00
Dbl, Mr Snowman w/dish hat, Royal Doulton 90.00
Dbl, Non-Pareil, Flow Blue, Burgess & Leigh, ca 1891 ....250.00
Dbl, Wicker Lane, Copeland Spode 22.00
Sgl, bl & wht landscape, flared rim, 1850s 130.00
Sgl, British Scenery, Booths 28.00
Sgl, creamware, rtcl, 1770s 800.00
Sgl, Dickensware, Mr Pickwick, Royal Doulton, 1920s 200.00
Sgl, Greenwood Tree, Royal Albert, ca 1932 ....22.00
Sgl, Orange Tree, Art Deco, Crown Ducal 60.00

Sgl, Parian Ware, emb, Minton, ca 1850 ....300.00
Sgl, pastoral scene, red transfer, Wedgwood, ca 1850 ....125.00
Sgl, Tulip, Gaudy Welch, ca 1840 ....250.00

Steamship/Cruiseship

Bkt, Maid Line 20.00
Dbl, Eastern Steamship Lines, bl logo 65.00
Dbl, Red Cross Line, bl & red flag 65.00
Dbl, United Fruit, UFC logo 55.00
Dbl, United States Lines, Lamberton 75.00
Hoop, Cunard, Cunard banner w/lion, bl transfer, ca 1910 ....135.00
Hoop, Dominion Line, bl transfer, ca 1890 ....175.00
Hoop, Union Castle Line, Edinburgh Castle, blk geometric rim, 1930s ..60.00
Hoop, Wht Star Line, turq, repro, 1990s 150.00
Hoop, Wht Star Line, turq, Stoniers, early 1900s 120.00
Sgl, HMS Aquitania, SP, pierced, scalloped rim, enameled crest ..125.00
Sgl, Polska Morska Handlowa, PMH Trident, 1950-70s 20.00
Sgl, Swedish American Lines, bl flag 25.00

Transportation

Fig, airplane, yel, Honiton, 1960s 22.00
Fig, boat, orange, Honiton 22.00
Fig, car, antique model, yel, 1940s 28.00
Fig, car, gr convertible, Honiton 22.00
Fig, car, Volkswagen, Devon Ceramics, 1959 ....20.00
Fig, motorcycle, yel & blk, Carter, ca 1940 ....40.00
Fig, steam roller, yel, 1940s 28.00
Fig, train locomotive, blk & brn, turq cup 14.00
Fig, train locomotive, brn, O'Danaghue's 18.00

Elfinware

Made in Germany from about 1920 until the 1940s, these miniature vases, boxes, salt cellars, and miscellaneous novelty items are characterized by the tiny applied flowers that often cover their entire surface. Pieces with animals and birds are the most valuable, followed by the more interesting examples such as diminutive grand pianos, candle holders, etc. Items covered in 'spinach' (applied green moss) can be valued at 75% to 100% higher than pieces that are not decorated in this manner. See also Salts, Open.

Slippers, applied flowers and green 'spinach,' both approximately 2¼x4¼", from $50.00 to $75.00 each. (Photo courtesy Earlene Wheatley)

Basket, flower encrusted, low hdl, 2x2½x1½" 80.00
Basket, loop hdl, sm 38.50
Boot, flower encrusted 3" L 80.00
Box, oval, 3x4" 75.00
Box, piano form, appl violets & roses, crown mk, 3x5" 195.00
Candlestick, sm ring hdl, 2½" 55.00
Compote, mc florals, mk Germany, 6½x6½x5½" 235.00
Cradle, much spinach, 3½" 82.50
Salt cellar, bl floral on basketweave, hdls 35.00
Salt cellar, floral sprays w/gold on leaf form, 3½" 15.00
Shoe, baby; overall gr spinach & flowers, 4½" L 110.00
Slippers, dbl, lg 110.00
Teapot, spinach & rose on front, Germany, 2" 40.00
Vase, 3" 45.00
Watering can, 6" 60.00

Epergnes

Popular during the Victorian era, epergnes were fancy centerpieces often consisting of several tiers of vases (called lilies), candle holders, dishes, or a combination of components. They were made in all types of art glass, and some were set in ornate plated frames.

Cranberry, 3 rigareed lilies+glass cane; SP 4-arm base, 19" 750.00
Cut crystal bowl, 3-lily, SP griffin & sea horses, 1850s, 20x23x10" ..2,500.00
Cut crystal bowls (5), Georgian Sheffield lion head fr, 14x16x16" ..4,675.00
Peach satin w/flowers, ruffled lily on sm plate, SP ped, 19" 800.00
Pk o/l, 1-pc, mc flowers, 5½x4⅛" 175.00
Pk opal w/3 trumpet flower inserts, gilt cast fr, 29" 550.00
Pk oval cone vases (1 lg/3 sm), on tripod scrolled SP stand, 14" ..300.00
SP, 4-lily w/eng birds/flowers, ca 1910, 11½", in wood box 125.00

Erickson

Carl Erickson of Bremen, Ohio, produced hand-formed glassware from 1943 until 1960 in artistic shapes, no two of which were identical. One of the characteristics of his work was the air bubbles that were captured within the glass. Though most examples are clear, colored items were also made. Rather than to risk compromising his high standards by selling the factory, when Erickson retired, the plant was dismantled and sold.

Bottle, scent; clear w/amethyst-cased int, 3"+clear stopper, pr ...430.00
Bowl, cranberry w/air traps, pinched sides, label, 2x5" 60.00
Bowl, topaz w/swirl center w/bubbles, flat cut top, 13¼" 150.00
Candlesticks, smoke cased in clear, hollow, label, 3½x3", pr 55.00
Compote, gr on pale amber base w/bubbles, 4¼x8¾" 145.00
Decanter, clear, pinched, 11¼" 80.00
Ewer, amber to yel opal, 9⅝" 90.00
Vase, lt amethyst, bubble-ball ft, 13" 130.00

Erphila

The Erphila trademark was used by Ebeling and Ruess Co. of Philadelphia between 1886 and the 1950s. The company imported quality porcelain and pottery from Germany, Czechoslovakia, Italy and France. Pieces more readily found are from Germany and Czechoslovakia. A variety of items can be found and pieces such as figural teapots and larger figurines are moving up in value. There are a variety of marks, but all contain the name Erphila. One of the earlier marks is a green rectangle containing the name Erphila Germany. In general Erphila pieces are scarce, not easily found.

Batter/syrup set, orange & gr on wht, Czech, lids/underplates ...100.00
Creamer, Dutch girl figural, Czech, 4" 55.00
Dresser box, lady in gr w/lav fan in hand, MIG, 6½" 95.00
Dresser box, Madame Pompadour, MIG, 7½" 50.00
Figurine, bear, brn, sitting, MIG, 3½" 45.00

Figurine, bulldog, blk & wht, MIG, 4¼x7½" 125.00
Figurine, dachshund, sitting, MIG, 6¼x9¼" 95.00
Figurine, doves (2), natural color, MIB, 14x10" 245.00
Figurine, G Washington bust, MIG, 3¾" 60.00
Figurine, leopard, natural color, MIB, 2¼x5½" 45.00
Figurine, mountain goats, MIG, 8" 95.00
Figurine, ram's head, wht, Czech, 6x7½" 65.00
Figurine, terrier, blk & wht, crouching, MIG, 5x8½" 65.00
Jug, syrup; Cheery Chintz, 4¼" 130.00
Mug, 2 friars drinking w/Bavarian man, heavy, 4¼" 35.00
Pitcher, batter; poppies, orange & gr on wht, w/lid 55.00
Pitcher, bird figural, tan w/blk & red, #881, Czech, 9⅛" 60.00
Pitcher, milk; rooster figural, Czech, #7457, 7½" 100.00
Pitcher, toucan figural, cream, red & blk, 9" 120.00
Shakers, children figural, wht w/bl hat & scarf, MIG, pr 60.00
Tea/coffeepot, Tartan Plaid, brn/gr/tan/red/blk, 8" 55.00
Teapot, cow figural, brn & wht, pk bow, yel bell, MIG 195.00
Teapot, dachshund figural, beige & brn, MIG, 8" 145.00
Teapot, pig, pk w/blk accents, MIG, 1930s, #722, 7½x7" 145.00
Teapot, poodle, blk/gray, head/lid, paws/spout, tail/hdl, MIG, 8½" 115.00
Teapot, rabbit, brn & wht w/blk accents, head/lid, paws/spout, MIG ..150.00
Vase, face & birds in relief, mc on tan, gr serpent hdls, 9½" 135.00
Vase, floral, tan/brn/gr, rnd, France, 4¼" 48.00
Vase, floral, wht on bl, rnd, France, 4½" 60.00
Vase, girl w/goat, blk silhouette on beige, 7" 65.00
Vase, mc mottle w/orange body center, 3 angle hdls, gr & bl rim, 7" ..175.00
Vase, wht w/bl stars, spherical, Czech 60.00
Watering can, wht w/orange spout & flower w/gr leaves, Czech, 7" ..50.00

Eskimo Artifacts

While ivory carvings made from walrus tusks or whale teeth have been the most emphasized articles of Eskimo art, basketry and woodworking are other areas in which these Alaskan Indians excel. Their designs are effected through the application of simple yet dramatic lines and almost stark decorative devices. Though not pursued to the extent of American Indian art, the unique work of these northern tribes is beginning to attract the serious attention of today's collectors.

Storage basket, alternating crosses and birds, with lid, 1890s, 20x20", rare, $450.00.

Basket, dmn design woven in lt & dk fiber, wear, 3½x7⅛" 200.00
Basket, polychrome, early 1900s, 8¾x10½" dia 95.00
Basket, 2 color bands/mc geometrics, Tlingit, 8x10½" 4,000.00
Bow set, sealskin bow case, sinew-bk bow & 6 arrows, 1870s, 47" ..1,200.00
Carving, fossil ivory walrus tusk, polar bear, 3" 230.00
Carving, ivory, man on sled pulled by reindeer, 1900s, 4x8" 425.00
Carving, serpentine (lt gr), diving polar bear, late 1960s, 6" 475.00
Carving, serpentine & caribou antler, birds on inukshuk, 9¾" ..310.00
Carving, soapstone, figure in parka, traditional style, 1940s, 8½" ..150.00
Carving, soapstone, 2 seals facing opposite directions, mk, 12" .250.00
Carving, walrus penis bone w/baleen, walrus head on end, 15" .485.00
Chess set, mastodon & walrus ivory, ca 1905, w/inlaid brd, EX ...3,180.00
Comb, mammoth ivory, wolf effigies, w/etchings, 2½x1½" 185.00
Cribbage brd, ivory, eng salmon, walrus, 9" 330.00
Cup, cvd from walrus jawbone in natural shape, 19th C, 5½x5" ..350.00
Doll, hide, pnt face, w/fur parka & mukluks, 1930s, 17x7" 375.00
Doll, seal skin mother w/child on bk, seal fur clothes, 1920s, 9" ..65.00
Doll, seal skin pants w/decor, on wooden sled, 1900s, 12x7" 145.00
Ice fishing scoop, caribou antler, laced w/sinew strings, 7" 210.00
Kayak, sealskin covered w/cvd seated figure, 1900s, 33x2" 550.00
Knife, carved fossil ivory, hole for hdl, 12½" 275.00
Lamp, cvd stone, 1880s, 3x13x6" 225.00
Mask, cvd ivory appendages in circular form, 1900s, 5" dia 180.00
Mask, Shaman's; ivory, incised details, bl beaded eyes, 6⅛" ...1,025.00
Mask, snow; seal or walrus skin, long fur trim, ca 1950s, 6x9" ...100.00

Face Jugs, Contemporary

The most recognizable form of Southern folk pottery is the face jug. Rich alkaline glazes (lustrous greens and browns) are typical, and occasionally shards of glass are applied to the surface of the ware which during firing melts to produce opalescent 'glass runs' over the alkaline. In some locations clay deposits contain elements that result in areas of fluorescent blue or rutile; another variation is swirled or striped ware, reminiscent of eighteenth-century agateware from Staffordshire. Collector demand for these unique one-of-a-kind jugs is at an all-time high and is still escalating. Choice examples made by Burlon B. Craig and Lanier Meaders often bring over $1,000.00 on the secondary market. If you're interested in learning more about this type of folk pottery, contact the Southern Folk Pottery Collectors Society; their address is in the Directory under Clubs, Newsletters, and Catalogs. Our advisor for this category is Billy Ray Hussey; he is listed in the Directory under North Carolina.

Appl snake, china teeth, coke glaze, 2-hdl, BB Craig, 12" 2,300.00
Baggy lower eyelids, Xd-eyed, long nose, o-mouth, Hussey, 10" ..250.00
China teeth, incised brows, brn slip, Brown Pottery, 1924-25, 6⅝" .900.00
China teeth, lg nose/lips, bl over cream, L Brown, 7", EX 300.00
China teeth, lt clay eyes w/dk pupils, EX glaze, Reinhardt, 7" .5,250.00
China teeth, nose extends to eyebrows, bl, '77, Craig, 5½" 325.00
China teeth, pierced eyes, 2-pc nose/eyebrows, BB Craig, 10" ...950.00
China teeth, pierced pupils, brn w/melted glass runs, A Teague, 8" .550.00
China teeth, pop eyes, incised lips/brows, BB Craig, 1980s, 19" ..1,050.00
China teeth (sharpened), pop-eyed, 1-pc brows, BB Craig, 9⅝" ..850.00
China teeth (2 rows), Afro-Am influence, J Brown, 6½", EX ...900.00
China teeth & eyes, cobalt lashes/brows, JB Hamilton, 1990, 10" .325.00
Cigar in mouth, lg nose, eyes/ears at shoulder level, R Brown, 7" ..200.00
Devil, china teeth, pop eyes, horns, blk-brn, BB Craig, 6¼" ..1,100.00
Devil, cvd hair, wht teeth, spotted lizard, MG Rogers, 6½" 200.00
Devil, swirlware, cvd brow/mouth, china teeth, C Lisk, 9" 250.00
No teeth, cobalt pupils, cvd brows, dimples, R Meaders, 7" 325.00
Pearl eyes, wht flint teeth, ca 1987, MG Rogers, 3" 90.00
Pop-eyed, 2 rows china teeth, 1-pc brow, BB Craig, 10" 700.00
Self-portrait, unglazed eyes/teeth, full cheeks, L Meaders, 9½" .1,500.00
Wht clay teeth, incised details, AG Meaders, ca 1991, 5⅜" 325.00
Wht clay teeth & eyes, 1-pc brows, Charles Lisk, 11⅝" 120.00
Wht clay teeth & eyes, 2-tone glaze, L Meaders, ca 1987, 8¾" .700.00
2-faced, bald w/beard, cvd hair, deep eyes, 2-hdl, Hussey, 8" 400.00
2-faced (woman/man), wht hair/eyes, Cole Pottery, 8¼" 850.00

Fairings

Fairings are small, brightly colored nineteenth-century hard-paste porcelain objects, largely figural groups and boxes. Most figural fairings portray amusing (if not risque) scenes of courting couples, marital woes, and political satire complete with appropriate base captions.

Fairing boxes, also referred to as trinket boxes, sometimes had captions similar to figural fairings, and often there were similar figures on top. It was originally assumed that fairings were made in the Staffordshire area, and for many years they were referred to as Staffordshire fairings. But soon there were many European makers producing them as well, especially the boxes, since the Europeans could make them more cheaply. England encouraged these makers by not charging import duties. Both the figural fairings and the box fairings (trinket boxes) were made with the same consumers in mind.

Many early fairings were not marked; those that were had only a small incised or painted mark. Before 1850 the makers, especially Conte and Boehme of Possneck, Germany (who became the major maker of the boxes, indicated by 'C&B' in listings), used hand-incised numbers (for one article) and Roman numerals (for the size number). The painter often added his painted-on mark or number. After the 1850s both the article number and the maker's mark were impressed. The Conte and Boehme mark is the most familiar — a bent elbow (arm) holding a sword, laying on a shield. Examples marked 'Conte and Boehme' (words) are post-1890 or newer, possibly even copies.

After 1891 all wares shipped to the U.S. had to be clearly marked by the name of the country. For more information, we recommend *Victorian Trinket Boxes* by Janice and Richard Vogel, published by the authors (see Directory, Florida). Other good references are *Victorian Fairings* by W.S. Bristoe and *Victorian Fairings and Their Value* by Margaret Anderson.

Box, baby in cradle w/kitten, C&B mk, 3¼x2x4¼" 120.00
Box, cat & frog, appl flowers, gold trim, 2¾x2¾" 90.00
Box, cups/saucers/plates/teapots/etc on lid, C&B mk, 4½x7½" .395.00
Box, deer head sticks out of lower front, chickens on lid, 3¾" ..150.00
Box, desk w/shelf of books & clock, mk, 3⅞x3¾x2½" 100.00
Box, lady's hand w/band of flowers, unmk, 1¾x2½" 80.00
Box, organ shape, gold trim, w/orig mirror, 6" 150.00
Box, 3 O'clock in the Morning, husband sneaking in 295.00
Figurine, Let Us Be Friends, 2 children beside bed, unmk, 3x3" ...100.00
Match holder, girl w/shovel, striker on bk of stump, mk #4200, 4½" ..70.00

Fans

The Japanese are said to have invented the fan. From there it went to China, and Portuguese traders took the idea to Europe. Though usually considered milady's accessory, even the gentlemen in seventeenth-century England carried fans! More fashionable than practical, some were of feathers and lovely hand-painted silks with carved ivory or tortoise sticks. Some French fans had peepholes. There are mourning fans, calendar fans, and those with advertising.

Fine antique fans (pre-1900) of ivory or mother-of-pearl are highly desirable. Those from before 1800 often sell for upwards of $1,000.00. Examples with mother-of-pearl sticks are most desirable; least desirable are those with sticks of celluloid. Our advisor for this category is Vicki Flanigan; she is listed in the Directory under Virginia.

Black gauze with velvet and lace mask, wooden sticks, upper guardstick with an etui by W. Thornhill, ca 1900, 13", $400.00.

Brussels lace, pierced MOP sticks w/gold, ca 1900, 10", MIB 400.00
Cabriolet, HP floral on gauze w/bone sticks, 1890s, 12" 300.00
Canton, brise, HP vignette/flowers, cvd ivory sticks, 1790s, 10" ..1,200.00
Canton, ivory brise, cvd/pierced figures/dragons/etc, 1820s, 7" .1,000.00
Canton, MOP brise, etched figures/animals, 1820s, 7" 2,750.00
Feathers, goose; HP roses, cvd ivory sticks, China, 1830s, 9" 700.00
Feathers (wht), tortoise-shell hdl, English, 1890s, 15", NM 200.00
Gauze (blk) w/HP lady by well, tortoise-shell sticks, 1885, 13" .200.00
Gauze, HP florals, sgn Bellini, MOP sticks, 1890s, 13" 250.00
Gauze, HP flowers/butterflies, att Levroyon, bone sticks, 1890s, 13" 225.00
Gauze, HP leaf, embr flower, MOP sticks, 1890s, 8", MIB 300.00
HP litho on paper, cvd/pierced MOP sticks, 1860s, 10" 300.00
HP paper w/3 cartouches, boned stays, Fr, ca 1799, open: 20" ...1,500.00
HP silk w/lovers & putti/flowers/etc, ivory sticks, 1770s, 10" 600.00
HP silk w/Rebecca at Well, bone sticks, Dutch, 1770s, 11" 600.00
HP silk w/sequins & spy holes, cvd ivory sticks, 1770s, 11" 800.00
Lace flowers appl to blk net, tortoise-shell sticks, 1870s, 11" 225.00
Needle lace w/poppies & other flowers, blond sticks, 1890s, 10" 450.00
Pnt figures/landscape, cvd/pierced ivory sticks, Flemish, 1760s, 10" .800.00
Point de gaze w/birds/butterflies/flowers, MOP sticks, 1865, 11" ..750.00
Printed scene w/figures & church, bone sticks, mini, 1780s, 4½" .700.00
Stipple eng w/mc reserves, cvd ivory sticks, English, 1790s, 10" ...700.00

Farm Collectibles

Country living in the nineteenth century entailed plowing, plant ing, and harvesting; gathering eggs and milking; making soap from lard rendered on butchering day; and numerous other tasks performed with primitive tools of which we in the twentieth century have had little first-hand knowledge. Our advisor for this category is Lar Hothem; his address is listed in the Directory under Ohio. See also Cast Iron; Lamps, Lanterns; Woodenware; Wrought Iron.

Corn sheller, Gray Bros, CI, hand held, Pat 1870 ....295.00
Corn sheller, Union FDY Co, Dayton OH, CI, hand held 1,200.00
Corn sheller, 50 Cent, Canton OH, CI, hand held 550.00
Cow bell, w/leather strap, from $55 to 75.00
Dryer, seed corn; handmade, 50" limb w/wire insets, early 1900s .70.00
Emblem, JJ Case, chromed cast metal eagle on globe, 4½", pr 20.00
Harness collar, bentwood w/iron o/l, Norwegian Am, 13", VG 55.00
Horse collar, leather, EX, from $45 to 75.00
Measure, grain; bentwood w/steel bands, CI hdl, 8x14½" 85.00
Measure, grain; staved wood, old sage gr pnt, rpl rings, 11" 100.00
Measure, haystack; copper, dvtl, stamped Gallon, 12" 220.00
Ox yoke, lg, from $175 to 300.00
Ox yoke, wood, New Mexico, ca 1750, 32x6" 50.00
Pump, wood w/old gray pnt, rpl pin at joint, 24" 190.00
Rake, hay; all wood, 4 tines, 64" 275.00
Rake, hay; all wood, 78" 140.00
Shoulder yoke, cvd pine, old patina, 39" 40.00
Single tree, from $15 to 30.00

Fenton

Frank and John Fenton were brothers who founded the Fenton Art Glass Company in 1906 in Martin's Ferry, Ohio. The venture, at first only a decorating shop, began operations in July of 1905 using blanks purchased from other companies. This operation soon proved unsatisfactory, and by 1907 they had constructed their own glass factory in Williamstown, West Virginia. John left the company in 1909 and organized his own firm in Millersburg, Ohio.

The Fenton Company produced over one hundred thirty patterns of carnival glass. They also made custard, chocolate, opalescent, and stretch glass. This company has always been known for its various colors of glass and has continually changed its production to stay attune with current tastes in decorating. In 1925 they produced a line of 'handmade' items that incorporated the techniques of threading and mosaic work. Because the process proved to be unprofitable, the line was discontinued by 1927. Even their glassware made in the past twenty-five years is already regarded as collectible. Various paper labels have been used since the 1920s; only since 1970 has the logo been stamped into the glass. For further information we recommend *Fenton Art Glass, 1907 – 39,* and *Fenton Art Glass Patterns, 1939 – 1980,* by Margaret and Kenn Whitmyer; *Fenton Glass, The Third Twenty-Five Years,* by William Heacock (with 1998 value guide); and *Fenton Glass: The 1980s Decade* by Robert E. Eaton, Jr. (1997 values). For information concerning Fenton Art Glass Collectors of America, Inc., see the Clubs, Newsletters, and Catalogs section of the Directory. See also Carnival Glass; Custard Glass; Stretch Glass.

Aqua Crest, tidbit, 3-tier, #680, 5", 7½", & 9" bowls 65.00
Aqua Crest (dk), basket, aqua hdl, 1940-42, 1948-53 ....85.00
Aventurine Green w/bl vasa murrhina, vase, #6455GB, 5½" 55.00
Aventurine Green w/bl vasa murrhina, vase, #6456GB, 1964-68, 8" ..50.00
Beaded Melon/Ivy, vase, #711GV, 5" 47.00
Bicentennial, plate, Eagle, bl & wht slag, #9418 ....25.00
Black Crest, bowl, #7227B, rare, 7" 80.00
Black Rose, basket, #7237, orig sticker, 7" 225.00
Blue Ridge/Spiral, vase, triangular, #1923, ca 1939, 4½" 65.00
Coin Dot, bowl, French opal, #1522, 10" 45.00
Coin Dot, creamer & sugar bowl, cranberry, #1924 ....120.00
Coin Dot, ewer, cranberry, hdld, 1947-50, 11" 225.00
Coin Dot, top hat, gr opal, #1492LO, 1952 ....110.00
Colonial, Royal Wedding bowl, amber, 1966 ....20.00
Copper Rose, atomizer, 6" 55.00
Crystal Crest, bowl, dbl-crimped, ca 1942, 5½" 25.00
Crystal Crest, cornucopia candle holders, #951, ca 1942, pr 95.00
Crystal Halo, bowl, satin finish, rolled rim, #1800, 12" 55.00
Daisy & Fern, pitcher, topaz opal, 80-oz 165.00
Dancing Ladies, bowl, Pekin Blue, #901, 1932-33, from $245 to .265.00
Dancing Ladies, vase, Mongolian Green, #901, 1934-35 ....595.00
Diamond Lace, epergne, opaline, #4808TG 225.00
Diamond Optic, basket, burmese w/HP roses, CB204RB, 7" 115.00
Diamond Optic, goblet, bridge; Rose, #1502, ca 1928, 9-oz 15.00
Diamond Optic/Dolphin, bowl, gr, cupped, #1502, ca 1921 & 1927, 7" ..50.00
Dogwood, basket, pk on burmese, 7½" 100.00
Dogwood, temple jar, bl, #7488BD 30.00
Dolphin, bowl, aquamarine stretch, ftd, hdls, #1608, 1926 ....200.00
Dolphin, plate, gr, cut decor, hdls, #1521, ca 1921 & 1927 ....55.00
Dolphin, vase, Orchid, fan form, hdls, ca 1928, 5½" 155.00
Dot Optic, decanter, cranberry opal 275.00
Elizabeth, sherbet, blk w/jade ft, #1639, 1930 ....30.00
Empress, vase, burmese 75.00
Fern, fairy light, aqua, #2040, 3-pc 135.00
Flame Crest, cake plate, low ft, #7329, 12¾" 95.00
Florentine, bridge set, gr stretch, 1921-27, 2-pc 50.00
Florentine, cheese & cracker set, gr stretch, 1921-27, 2-pc 45.00
Flute & Dot, vase, bl burmese, #9050, 5½" 45.00
Georgian, mug, beer; pk, #1611, 8-oz 20.00
Goldenrod, vase, #7265GD, ca 1956, 12" 330.00
Grape & Cable, humidor, burmese, #9188BR 85.00
Green, comport/console bowl, etch, #1533, ca 1926 ....55.00
Hanging Vine, vase, turq, #3004, ca 1925, 9" 1,125.00
Historic America, goblet, water; ca 1937, 6" 45.00
Historic America, sherbet, ca 1937, 4½" 35.00

Hobnail, cake plate, milk glass, footed, 12½", from $35.00 to $45.00.

Hobnail, candlestick & bowl, milk glass, #3745MI/#3746MI, 7", 9½" ..50.00
Hobnail, decanter, bl opal w/bl stopper & hdl, +6 wines 400.00
Hobnail, decanter, cranberry opal 525.00
Hobnail, jam set, bl opal, w/spoon 65.00
Hobnail, jug, turq, squat, #3965, 1955-58, 5½" 60.00
Hobnail, lamp, student; cranberry opal w/cranberry font 150.00
Hobnail, pitcher, cranberry opal, #3967, 80-oz 275.00
Hobnail, shakers, French opal, #3806FO, ca 1953-54, pr 30.00
Hobnail, syrup jug, coral, #3752, 12-oz 85.00
Hobnail, vase, cranberry opal, #3859CO, 8" 200.00
Hobnail, vase, swung; topaz opal, #3759TO, 1959-60, 17" 105.00
Hobnail/Melon Rib, lamp, gone-w/the wind; milk glass 150.00
Ivory Crest, tulip vase, #186, 1940-41, 8" 45.00
Ivory Crest, vase, 1940-41, 8" 40.00
Ivy, vase, #1925, 1950s, 6¼" 35.00
Jacqueline, basket, burmese, sample 125.00
Jefferson, comport, wht satin, #8476 ....135.00
Leaf & Orange Tree, bowl, sample color, 3-toe, #8223, 1974 ....45.00
Lily of the Valley, rose bowl, Cameo opal, #8453CO, 1979, 5½" ..17.50
Logo, bl opal 30.00
Love Bird, vase, bl satin, #8258BA, 4¾" 25.00
Mandarin Red, basket, wicker hdl, #1684, 1934 ....150.00
Mandarin Red, bowl, crimped, 1933, 2½x8½" 65.00
Mandarin Red, bowl, crimped, 1934, 5x10" 100.00
Mandarin Red, bowl, salad; #846, ca 1934, 9" 65.00
Mandarin Red, candlestick, #318, ca 1932-35 ....75.00
Mandarin Red, ginger jar, #893, ca 1933 ....300.00
Mandarin Red, vase, fan; 1934, 5x8½" 70.00
Mandarin Red, vase, fan; 1934, 7x10" 100.00
Mandarin Red/Basketweave, bowl, 3-hole edge, #1043, ca 1934, 9" ..110.00
Ming, baby reamer, pk, #1260, ca 1935-36 ....270.00
Ming, bonbon, crystal, w/lid, #846, 1935-36 ....88.00
Ming, bonbon, pk, #1621, 1935-36 ....34.00
Ming, macaroon jar, crystal, wicker hdl, 1935-36 ....95.00
Ming, pitcher, lemonade; pk w/blk, #1352, 1934, w/8 tumblers .380.00
Mongolian Green, bowl, hdls, #950, ca 1935, 12" 100.00
Mosaic, vase, #3000, ca 1926, 11" 2,940.00
Orange Tree, wine sherbet, #1412, 5" 16.50
Orange Tree & Cherry Chain, bowl, burmese satin, #8233BR 30.00
Peach Crest, bowl, #1522, 10" 35.00
Peach Crest, epergne, 1-horn, #345 ....190.00
Peach Crest, shell bowl, #9020 ....95.00
Peach Crest, vase, squat, #192, 5" 45.00
Peach Crest/Wave Crest, vase, #6056, 6" 20.00
Persian Medallion, comport, Independence Blue, #8234 ....30.00
Polka Dot, cruet, cranberry, #2273CR 135.00
Poppy, rose bowl, burmese satin, #9126, w/brass stand 40.00
Rib Optic, iced-tea set, gr opal w/bl, 1926, 6-pc+lid 600.00
Rib Optic, wine bottle, cranberry opal, #1667CO, 13½" 125.00
Rose Crest, top hat, #1924, ca 1945-47, 3½x5" 35.00
Rose Mist, vase, #6459, 14" 210.00
Roses, basket, burmese, 7238RB, 7" deep 185.00
Roses, pitcher, burmese, #7461RB, 5" 55.00

Roses, vase, burmese, #7253RB, 7" 85.00
Silver Crest, tidbit, 2-tier, #7296SC, 1940s, 8x12" 30.00
Silver Crest, torte plate, #7216SC, 1940s, 15½" 35.00
Silver Crest, vanity set, #192A, 3-pc 125.00
Silver Jamestown, basket, 37237SJ, 7" 65.00
Snow Crest/Cranberry, lamp, hurricane; w/base 75.00
Spiral, top hat, Blue Ridge/French opal, #1923, ca 1939 .....75.00
Venetian Red, vase, fan; HP gold leaf, 1932-33, 8" 150.00
Venetian Red, vase, flared, 1932-33, 8½" 150.00
Violets in Snow, cake plate, ftd, #7213 .....110.00
Water Lily, bowl, Rosalene, 3-toed, #8426RE, 1976 .....105.00

Fiesta

Fiesta is a line of dinnerware that was originally produced by the Homer Laughlin China Company of Newell, West Virginia, from 1936 until 1973. It was made in eleven different solid colors with over fifty pieces in the assortment. The pattern was developed by Frederick Rhead, an English Stoke-on-Trent potter who was an important contributor to the art-pottery movement in this country during the early part of the century. The design was carried out through the use of a simple band-of-rings device near the rim. Fiesta Red, a strong red-orange glaze color, was made with depleted uranium oxide. It was more expensive to produce than the other colors and sold at higher prices. During the '50s the color assortment was gray, rose, chartreuse, and dark green. These colors are relatively harder to find and along with medium green (new in 1959) command the highest prices.

Fiesta Kitchen Kraft was introduced in 1939; it consisted of seventeen pieces of kitchenware such as pie plates, refrigerator sets, mixing bowls, and covered jars in four popular Fiesta colors.

As a final attempt to adapt production to modern-day techniques and methods, Fiesta was restyled in 1969. Of the original colors, only Fiesta Red remained. This line, called Fiesta Ironstone, was discontinued in 1973.

Two types of marks were used: an ink stamp on machine-jiggered pieces and an indented mark molded into the hollow ware pieces.

In 1986 HLC reintroduced a line of Fiesta dinnerware in five colors: black, white, pink, apricot, and cobalt (darker and denser than the original shade). Since then yellow, turquoise, seafoam green, 'country' blue, lilac, persimmon, sapphire blue, chartreuse, gray, and juniper have been added. Collectors have found that the new line poses no threat to their investments.

In the listings below, 'original colors' indicates only three of the original six — light green, turquoise, and yellow (or those remaining after specific original colors have been priced). Red, ivory, and cobalt values are listed separately. Turquoise was the last original color to be introduced, so the items that were discontinued in 1946 are harder to find in that color (since it had a shorter production run), and values fall into the price range of red, cobalt, and ivory. These are designated with an asterisk.

For more information we recommend *The Collector's Encyclopedia of Fiesta, Harlequin, and Riviera* by Sharon and Bob Huxford (Collector Books).

Dinnerware

Ashtray, '50s colors 88.00
Ashtray, orig colors 47.00
Ashtray, red, cobalt or ivory 60.00
Bowl, covered onion soup; cobalt or ivory 750.00
Bowl, covered onion soup; red 750.00
Bowl, covered onion soup; turq, minimum value 8,000.00
Bowl, covered onion soup; yel or lt gr 600.00
Bowl, cream soup; '50s colors 72.00
Bowl, cream soup; med gr, minimum value 4,000.00
Bowl, cream soup; orig colors 42.00
Bowl, cream soup; red, cobalt or ivory 60.00
Bowl, dessert; '50s colors, 6" 52.00
Bowl, dessert; med gr, 6" 475.00
Bowl, dessert; orig colors, 6" 38.00
Bowl, dessert; red, cobalt or ivory, 6" 52.00
Bowl, fruit; '50s colors, 4¾" 40.00
Bowl, fruit; '50s colors, 5½" 40.00
Bowl, fruit; med gr, 4¾" 485.00
Bowl, fruit; med gr, 5½" 75.00
Bowl, fruit; orig colors, 4¾" 28.00
Bowl, fruit; orig colors, 5½" 28.00
Bowl, fruit; orig colors, 11¾" 265.00
Bowl, fruit; red, cobalt or ivory, 4¾" 35.00
Bowl, fruit; red, cobalt or ivory, 5½" 35.00
Bowl, fruit; red, cobalt or ivory, 11¾" * 300.00
Bowl, ftd salad; orig colors 300.00
Bowl, ftd salad; red, cobalt or ivory * 350.00
Bowl, ind salad; med gr, 7½" 105.00
Bowl, ind salad; red, turq or yel, 7½" 85.00
Bowl, nappy; '50s colors, 8½" 65.00
Bowl, nappy; med gr, 8½" 140.00
Bowl, nappy; orig colors, 8½" 40.00
Bowl, nappy; orig colors, 9½" 52.00
Bowl, nappy; red, cobalt or ivory, 8½" * 60.00
Bowl, nappy; red, cobalt or ivory, 9½" * 65.00
Bowl, Tom & Jerry; ivory w/gold letters 260.00
Bowl, unlisted salad; red, cobalt, or ivory 500.00
Bowl, unlisted salad; yel 105.00
Candle holders, bulb; orig colors, pr 95.00
Candle holders, bulb; red, cobalt or ivory, pr * 130.00
Candle holders, tripod; orig colors, pr 465.00
Candle holders, tripod; red, cobalt or ivory, pr * 600.00
Carafe, orig colors 250.00
Carafe, red, cobalt or ivory * 300.00
Casserole, '50s colors 300.00
Casserole, French; standard colors other than yel 650.00
Casserole, French; yel 300.00
Casserole, med gr 725.00
Casserole, orig colors 150.00
Casserole, red, cobalt or ivory 200.00
Coffeepot, '50s colors 350.00
Coffeepot, demi; orig colors 340.00
Coffeepot, demi; red, cobalt or ivory * 435.00
Coffeepot, orig colors 195.00
Coffeepot, red, cobalt or ivory 245.00
Compote, orig colors, 12" 148.00
Compote, red, cobalt or ivory, 12" * 185.00
Compote, sweets; orig colors 75.00
Compote, sweets; red, cobalt or ivory * 90.00
Creamer, '50s colors 40.00
Creamer, ind; red 250.00
Creamer, ind; turq or cobalt 345.00
Creamer, ind; yel 70.00
Creamer, med gr 80.00
Creamer, orig colors 22.00
Creamer, red, cobalt or ivory 35.00
Creamer, stick hdld, orig colors 45.00
Creamer, stick hdld, red, cobalt or ivory * 70.00
Cup, demi; '50s colors 350.00
Cup, demi; orig colors 65.00
Cup, demi; red, cobalt or ivory 75.00
Egg cup, '50s colors 160.00

Egg cup, orig colors 58.00
Egg cup, red, cobalt, or ivory 70.00
Lid, for mixing bowl #1-#3, any color, minimum value 785.00
Lid, for mixing bowl #4, any color, minimum value 1,000.00
Marmalade, orig colors 230.00
Marmalade, red, cobalt or ivory * 285.00
Mixing bowl, #1, orig colors 170.00
Mixing bowl, #1, red, cobalt or ivory * 225.00
Mixing bowl, #2, orig colors 110.00
Mixing bowl, #2, red, cobalt or ivory * 125.00
Mixing bowl, #3, orig colors 120.00
Mixing bowl, #3, red, cobalt or ivory * 130.00
Mixing bowl, #4, orig colors 130.00
Mixing bowl, #4, red, cobalt or ivory * 155.00
Mixing bowl, #5, orig colors 155.00
Mixing bowl, #5, red, cobalt or ivory * 185.00
Mixing bowl, #6, orig colors 200.00
Mixing bowl, #6, red, cobalt or ivory * 265.00
Mixing bowl, #7, orig colors 280.00
Mixing bowl, #7, red, cobalt or ivory * 350.00
Mug, Tom & Jerry; '50s colors 100.00
Mug, Tom & Jerry; ivory w/gold letters 65.00
Mug, Tom & Jerry; orig colors 60.00
Mug, Tom & Jerry; red, cobalt or ivory 85.00
Mustard, orig colors 200.00
Mustard, red, cobalt or ivory * 250.00
Pitcher, disk juice; gray, minimum value 2,500.00
Pitcher, disk juice; Harlequin yel 62.00
Pitcher, disk juice; red 450.00
Pitcher, disk juice; yel 45.00
Pitcher, disk water; '50s colors 275.00
Pitcher, disk water; med gr, minimum value 1,150.00
Pitcher, disk water; orig colors 125.00
Pitcher, disk water; red, cobalt or ivory 165.00

Pitcher, ice; red, cobalt, or ivory, $160.00; Original colors, $140.00.

Pitcher, jug, 2-pt; '50s colors 150.00
Pitcher, jug, 2-pt; orig colors 90.00
Pitcher, jug, 2-pt; red, cobalt or ivory 120.00
Plate, '50s colors, 6" 9.00
Plate, '50s colors, 7" 13.00
Plate, '50s colors, 9" 22.00
Plate, '50s colors, 10" 52.00
Plate, cake; orig colors 755.00
Plate, cake; red, cobalt or ivory * 885.00
Plate, calendar; 1954 or 1955, 10" 45.00
Plate, calendar; 1955, 9" 50.00
Plate, chop; '50s colors, 13" 100.00
Plate, chop; '50s colors, 15" 115.00
Plate, chop; med gr, 13" 275.00
Plate, chop; orig colors, 13" 35.00
Plate, chop; orig colors, 15" 48.00
Plate, chop; red, cobalt or ivory, 13" 55.00
Plate, chop; red, cobalt or ivory, 15" 75.00
Plate, compartment; '50s colors, 10½" 75.00
Plate, compartment; orig colors, 10½" 40.00
Plate, compartment; orig colors, 12" 50.00
Plate, compartment; red, cobalt or ivory, 10½" 40.00
Plate, compartment; red, cobalt or ivory, 12" 60.00
Plate, deep; '50s colors 55.00
Plate, deep; med gr 120.00
Plate, deep; orig colors 40.00
Plate, deep; red, cobalt or ivory 60.00
Plate, med gr, 6" 20.00
Plate, med gr, 7" 32.00
Plate, med gr, 9" 45.00
Plate, med gr, 10" 110.00
Plate, orig colors, 6" 5.00
Plate, orig colors, 7" 9.00
Plate, orig colors, 9" 12.00
Plate, orig colors, 10" 32.00
Plate, red, cobalt or ivory, 6" 7.00
Plate, red, cobalt or ivory, 7" 10.00
Plate, red, cobalt or ivory, 9" 18.00
Plate, red, cobalt or ivory, 10" 40.00
Platter, '50s colors 58.00
Platter, med gr 140.00
Platter, orig colors 35.00
Platter, red, cobalt or ivory 45.00
Relish tray, gold decor, complete 250.00
Relish tray base, orig colors 65.00
Relish tray base, red, cobalt or ivory * 85.00
Relish tray center insert, orig colors 42.00
Relish tray center insert, red, cobalt or ivory * 55.00
Relish tray side insert, orig colors 40.00
Relish tray side insert, red, cobalt or ivory * 48.00
Sauce boat, '50s colors 78.00
Sauce boat, med gr 155.00
Sauce boat, orig colors 45.00
Sauce boat, red, cobalt or ivory 75.00
Saucer, '50s colors 6.00
Saucer, demi; '50s colors 95.00
Saucer, demi; orig colors 18.00
Saucer, demi; red, cobalt or ivory 22.00
Saucer, med gr 12.00
Saucer, orig colors 4.00
Saucer, red, cobalt or ivory 5.00
Shakers, '50s colors, pr 45.00
Shakers, med gr, pr 140.00
Shakers, orig colors, pr 22.00
Shakers, red, cobalt or ivory, pr 30.00
Sugar bowl, ind; turq 350.00
Sugar bowl, ind; yel 120.00
Sugar bowl, w/lid, '50s colors, 3¼x3½" 72.00
Sugar bowl, w/lid, med gr, 3¼x3½" 160.00
Sugar bowl, w/lid, orig colors, 3¼x3½" 45.00
Sugar bowl, w/lid, red, cobalt or ivory, 3¼x3½" 55.00
Syrup, orig colors 325.00
Syrup, red, cobalt or ivory * 400.00
Teacup, '50s colors 38.00
Teacup, med gr 58.00
Teacup, orig colors 25.00

Teacup, red, cobalt or ivory ... 35.00
Teapot, lg; orig colors ... 185.00
Teapot, lg; red, cobalt or ivory * ... 220.00
Teapot, med; '50s colors ... 325.00
Teapot, med; med gr, minimum value ... 1,000.00
Teapot, med; orig colors ... 165.00
Teapot, med; red, cobalt or ivory ... 200.00
Tray, figure-8; cobalt ... 90.00
Tray, figure-8; turq or yel ... 350.00
Tray, utility; orig colors ... 38.00
Tray, utility; red, cobalt or ivory * ... 42.00
Tumbler, juice; chartreuse, Harlequin yel or dk gr ... 460.00
Tumbler, juice; orig colors ... 40.00
Tumbler, juice; red, cobalt or ivory ... 45.00
Tumbler, juice; rose ... 65.00
Tumbler, water; orig colors ... 60.00
Tumbler, water; red, cobalt or ivory * ... 85.00
Vase, bud; orig colors ... 80.00
Vase, bud; red, cobalt or ivory * ... 110.00
Vase, orig colors, 8" ... 600.00
Vase, orig colors, 10" ... 750.00
Vase, orig colors, 12", minimum value ... 1,000.00
Vase, red, cobalt or ivory, 8" * ... 700.00
Vase, red, cobalt or ivory, 10" * ... 850.00
Vase, red, cobalt or ivory, 12", minimum value * ... 1,200.00

Kitchen Kraft

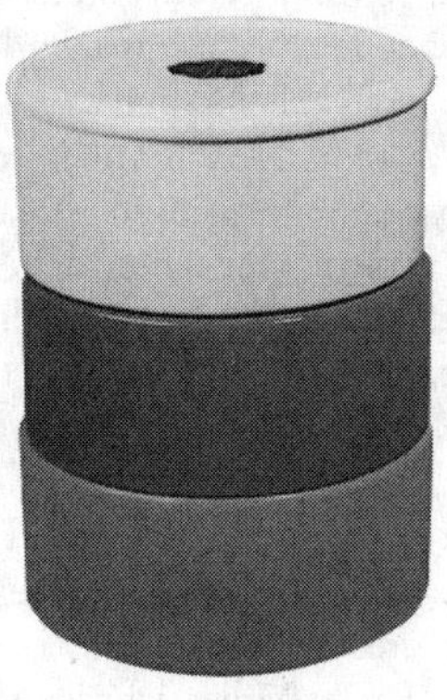

Stacking refrigerator set: Ivory lid, $205.00; Ivory unit, $195.00; Red and cobalt units, $55.00 each. (See listings for other color values.)

Bowl, mixing; lt gr or yel, 6" ... 65.00
Bowl, mixing; lt gr or yel, 8" ... 82.00
Bowl, mixing; lt gr or yel, 10" ... 100.00
Bowl, mixing; red or cobalt, 6" ... 75.00
Bowl, mixing; red or cobalt, 8" ... 92.00
Bowl, mixing; red or cobalt, 10" ... 120.00
Cake plate, lt gr or yel ... 55.00
Cake plate, red or cobalt ... 65.00
Cake server, lt gr or yel ... 130.00
Cake server, red or cobalt ... 140.00
Casserole, ind; lt gr or yel ... 140.00
Casserole, ind; red or cobalt ... 155.00
Casserole, lt gr or yel, 7½" ... 85.00
Casserole, lt gr or yel, 8½" ... 100.00
Casserole, red or cobalt, 7½" ... 90.00
Casserole, red or cobalt, 8½" ... 110.00
Covered jar, lg; lt gr or yel ... 300.00
Covered jar, lg; red or cobalt ... 320.00
Covered jar, med; lt gr or yel ... 260.00
Covered jar, med; red or cobalt ... 280.00
Covered jar, sm; lt gr or yel ... 270.00
Covered jar, sm; red or cobalt ... 290.00
Covered jug, lt gr or yel ... 250.00
Covered jug, red or cobalt ... 275.00
Fork, lt gr or yel ... 100.00
Fork, red or cobalt ... 125.00
Metal frame for platter ... 26.00
Pie plate, lt gr or yel, 9" ... 40.00
Pie plate, lt gr or yel, 10" ... 40.00
Pie plate, red or cobalt, 9" ... 45.00
Pie plate, red or cobalt, 10" ... 45.00
Pie plate, Spruce gr ... 290.00
Platter, lt gr or yel ... 68.00
Platter, red or cobalt ... 78.00
Platter, spruce gr ... 350.00
Shakers, lt gr or yel, pr ... 95.00
Shakers, red or cobalt, pr ... 105.00
Spoon, ivory, 12", minimum value ... 500.00
Spoon, lt gr or yel ... 100.00
Spoon, red or cobalt ... 125.00
Stacking refrigerator lid, lt gr or yel ... 70.00
Stacking refrigerator lid, red or cobalt ... 80.00
Stacking refrigerator unit, lt gr or yel ... 45.00

Fifites Modern

Postwar furniture design is marked by organic shapes and lighter woods and forms. New materials from war research such as molded plywood and fiberglass were used extensively. For the first time, design was extended to the masses and the baby-boomer generation grew up surrounded by modern shape and color, the perfect expression of postwar optimism. The top designers in America worked for Herman Miller and Knoll Furniture Company. These include Charles Eames, George Nelson, and Eero Saarinen.

Unless noted otherwise values are given for furnishings in excellent condition; glassware and ceramic items are assumed to be in mint condition. This information was provided to us by Richard Wright. See also Italian Glass.

Key:
fbrg — fiberglass
lcq — lacquered
uphl — upholstered
vnr — veneer

Armchair, Eames/Aluminum Group, swivels, minor stains/wear ... 225.00
Armchair, Eames/Miller, orange fbrg, Eiffel Tower base, 31" ... 250.00
Armchair, Eames/Miller, Soft Pad, chrome fr, swivels, 33", pr ... 650.00
Armchair, Evans/Directional, abstract molded bronze ext ... 850.00
Armchair, Maloof, walnut, suede uphl, pr ... 4,300.00
Armchair, McArthur, folding, tinted brushed chrome base, 31" ... 250.00
Armchair, Nakashima, walnut, spindle bk, sgn, 30x30x35" ... 2,000.00
Armchair, Wegner, The Chair, caned seat/bk version, 6 for ... 2,100.00
Armchair, Wegner/Hansen, walnut, rope seats/bks, 3 for ... 2,400.00
Bar stool, Chener/Plycraft, funnel-shape bk, reuphl, 38" ... 400.00
Bench, Geo Nelson/Herman Miller, blond wood, slat bk, 14x56⅜" ... 500.00
Bench, Nelson/Miller, multi-slatted, blk lcq, 48" ... 550.00
Bookcase, McCobb, maple, 2-shelf, open, plank stand, 34x60" ... 230.00
Bottle, Fantoni/Raymor, ceramic w/3-color volcanic glaze, 12" ... 225.00
Bowl, Boda (Vallien design), bubble pattern in clear/wht, 4x8" ... 290.00
Bureau, McCobb, maple, 3-drw on platform stand, label, 44x36" ... 290.00
Bureau, McCobb, maple, 6-drw dbl on stand, label, 33x60" ... 430.00
Cabinet, Castelli/Beylerian-Kartell, yel plastic, 17x26" dia ... 225.00
Cabinet, Dux, teak, modular, sliding panel doors, 2-shelf, 38x32" ... 575.00
Cabinet, Frankl, Skyscraper, silver/blk enamel, 86x33", EX ... 7,000.00
Cabinet, Nelson/Miller, birch vnr, 4-drw, SP pulls, 30x36x19" ... 1,500.00

Cabinet, Nelson/Miller, birch vnr, 5-drw, SP pulls, 40x24x19" ..1,300.00
Cabinet, Nelson/Miller Miniature Chest #5211, wht door, 20" L .4,750.00
Cabinet, Rhode, mahog, 2-door w/cvd rnd pulls, 30x33" 650.00
Cabinet, Rhode, walnut, drop-front desk over door+2 drw, 42x36" .300.00
Cabinet, Rhode, 2 open shelves over 2 doors, 42x36" 250.00
Cart, bar; tubular metal fr w/2 rnd ceramic shelves, 30x20" 325.00
Cart, serving; Prober, bleached mahog w/Pyrex top, 32x27" 325.00
Chair, Bertoia/Knoll, Bird, wire grid seat support, 39" 1,200.00
Chair, Bertoia/Knoll, Diamond, blk wire grid seat support 600.00
Chair, Botta/Alias, Seconda, tube-steel fr, sheet steel seat 800.00
Chair, Cantinary; Nelson/Miller, wool uphl, chrome fr, 29x30x28" .2,400.00
Chair, DCM/Miller, walnut bk & seat, chrome fr, 4 for 800.00
Chair, Eames/Miller, bentwood, new ebonized finish, 29" 700.00
Chair, Eames/Miller, red-dyed seat/bk, ebonized fr, early 1,300.00
Chair, Eames/Miller, walnut bentwood, shaped bk/seat, 29x20" ..450.00
Chair, Hovelskov, Harp, rope 'harp' in birch fr 2,600.00
Chair, Iosa-Gihini/Moroso, Numero Uno, all orig, 31x27x32" ..2,600.00
Chair, Jacobsen/Hansen, Oxford, tall bk in blk leather, 4 for .1,800.00
Chair, Knorr, conical metal seat/bk, 4 leg rods, 28x22", EX 2,400.00
Chair, Kramer/Am Desk, Ion, bl fbrg, chrome 3-leg ped, 8 for ..1,300.00
Chair, lounge; Paton design for hotel, tufted bk/scroll seat 350.00
Chair, lounge; Weber, Airlie, maple/ash fr, reuphl 12,000.00
Chair, Panton, wire cone on blk base, new seat/bk rest, 30" ...1,100.00
Chair, Paulin/Artifort, 2 attached pcs: arch bk/sling seat 1,000.00
Chair, Paulin/Hansen, Swan, orig uphl, 30", EX 600.00
Chair, pretzel; Goldman/Plycraft, laminated/bentwood, rfn, 30" ..375.00
Chair, Saarinen/Knoll, Womb, reuphl, 36", +ottoman 1,200.00
Chair, side; Bertoia/Knoll, wire on chrome base, 31", pr 375.00
Chair, side; McArthur, brushed chrome base, uphl bk/seat, 33" .650.00
Chair, side; Stark, mahog, ½-rnd bk, aluminum bk leg, EX 250.00
Chair, side; Wegner/Hansen, walnut, rope seat, 8 for 2,300.00
Chair, van der Rohe/Knoll, Brno, sq bk/seat, 31", 8 for 3,000.00
Chair, Weber/McKaycraft, chrome/blk enamel spring fr, sling seat ...475.00
Chair, Wegner/Hansen, walnut, V-bk, rope seat, 4 for 865.00
Chair, wing-bk; Olsen, teak fr, reuphl, 40x30" 800.00
Chaise, van Keppel-Green, bl enamel fr w/rope support, 70", VG .2,200.00
Chandelier, sunburst, brass rods end in wht wire flowers, 24" 375.00
Chest, Nakashima, walnut, 4-drw, dvtl, cruciform base, 32x36x21" ..5,750.00
Chest, Nakashima, walnut, 5-drw, dvtl, cruciform base, 39x37x20" ..6,300.00
Chest, Nelson/Miller, walnut, 3-drw+drw on end, 56" L 2,000.00
Clock, Nelson, Meridan series, Italian ceramic, 14" dia, VG 170.00
Clock, Nelson, Steering Wheel, 13" dia, VG 500.00
Clock, Nelson, String, wood center w/blk arms, restrung, 18" dia ..1,800.00
Clock, Nelson/Miller, Ball, radiating arms w/wood balls, 14" 750.00
Clock, Nelson/Miller, Starburst, wht enamel w/blk center 550.00
Couch, van der Rohe/Knoll, mahog fr, tubular chromed steel, 79" ..4,890.00
Credenza, Knoll/Knoll, stained ash vnr w/chrome & marble, 75" 1,100.00
Daybed, Maloof, mahog-fr canvas insert over springs, 13x68x30" ..6,000.00
Desk, Heywood-Wakefield, maple, 4 side drw, ca 1955, 30x42" .430.00
Desk, Nakashima, blk walnut wall mt w/2 drw, 1" plank top, 60" .3,000.00
Desk, Rhode/Miller, walnut vnr, free-form top, 3-drw bank, 52" ...2,200.00
Desk, Vodder, teak, 2 3-drw banks, bookshelf on bk, 57" 1,900.00
Dining set, Nakashima/Widdicomb, walnut, dowel seats/bks, 7-pc ..4,500.00
Dresser, Nakashima, walnut w/Free-Edge dvtl top, 32x36" 6,500.00
Jug, Gambone, figural donkey hdl, 7x5x10" 750.00
Lamp, Bubble; Nelson/Miller, plastic/steel wire, 24" dia 200.00
Lamp, floor; Arco, chrome shade & arched std, slate base 550.00
Lamp, floor; chrome w/rnd base & counter-weighted arm 275.00
Lamp, floor; Henningsen/Poulsen, wht saucer shade, aluminum std ..450.00
Lamp, floor; Laurel, wht mushroom shade, bright brass std 425.00
Lamp, floor; Laurel, wht mushroom shade, brushed chrome std .1,250.00
Lamp, floor; shaped as lg light bulb, wht glass, 40" 400.00
Lamp, floor; Weinberg, wrought-iron, glass shelves, 59x14" dia ..700.00
Lamp, hanging; Henningsen, PH-5, bl/wht enamel, 11x21" dia ..400.00
Lamp, hanging; Panton/Poulsen, Flowerpot, enameled aluminum ..110.00
Lamp, table; Jacobsen/Poulsen, AJ Visor, blk enamel, 21" 500.00
Lamp, table; Laurel, wht mushroom shade, wht enamel trumpet std .500.00
Lamp, table; Laurel, wht rnd shade, arched bright chrome base ..225.00
Lamp, table; Laurel, wht rnd shade, brushed chrome trumpet base 275.00
Lounge, Nakashima, walnut/webbing Long Chair, 1 arm, 70", EX ..12,000.00
Love seat, Castle, Dbl Molar, wht molded fbrg, 49" L 2,000.00
Love seat, Nelson/Miller, Marshmallow, 18 vinyl cushions, 52" ..15,000.00
Panels, Strong, 12-tile, Cubist head, bl/gr, 36x12", pr (1 EX) 500.00
Rug, concentric organic forms, peach/bl on ivory, 16x12", G 850.00
Screen, Eames/Evans, molded plywood, 6-panel, 68", MIB ..11,000.00
Screen, Eames/Evans, vnr molded plywood, 10-panel, 68", M ..17,500.00
Sideboard, Nakashima, walnut, 3 sliding doors, 75" L, EX ...69,000.00
Sofa, Aulenti/Knoll, wht enamel fr, 3-seat, 88", EX orig 400.00
Sofa, Nakashima, One-Arm, spindle bk, 1 loose cushion, 78" ...3,250.00
Sofa, Nakashima, 16-spindle bk, no arms, dowel legs, 48" 1,900.00
Sofa, Nelson/Miller, Marshmallow, 51" L, EX 40,000.00
Sofa, Weber, 3-band chrome fr w/reuphl vinyl cushions, 79" ..2,800.00
Stand, McCobb, maple, 2-drw w/46x17" mirror, label, 35x24" ..230.00
Stool, child's, Eames, bent plywood, rfn/touch-up, 9x14x11" ...3,500.00
Stool, Eames, Time-Life, trn walnut w/concave seat, 15x13" ..1,500.00
Stool, Platner/Knoll, corseted wireware base, 21x17" dia, G 325.00
Stool, rocking; Noguchi/Knoll, birch/chromed steel, 16½" 5,750.00
Stool, Saarineen/Knoll, Tulip, ivory enamel base, reuphl, 4 for .600.00
Table, card; Kagan, burlwood, triangular legs, varnished 1,100.00
Table, coffee; Dunbar, 15 olive burl veneer panels, ped base, 16" dia ..350.00
Table, coffee; Kagan, triangular, blk lcq 3-leg base, 34" 500.00
Table, coffee; Knoll/Knoll, 32" dia marble w/chrome legs 250.00
Table, coffee; LaVerne, bronze, lg rnd fluted legs, 65" L 4,000.00
Table, coffee; Nakashima, burled walnut Free-Edge, 40" 8,000.00
Table, coffee; Nakashima, walnut Free-Edge, 53" 4,750.00
Table, coffee; Nelson/Miller, walnut vnr/steel fr, 14x41", VG 700.00
Table, coffee; Noguchi style, mahog & glass free-form, 16x50x37" .575.00
Table, coffee; Noguchi/Miller, free-from top/ebony base, 50" .1,100.00
Table, coffee; Rhode, burl walnut vnr, kidney shape, 41" 1,400.00
Table, coffee; Rhode/Miller, vnr/glass, U-shape ends, 42", VG ..650.00
Table, coffee; Saltman, blk/wht laminate top, walnut fr, 16x41" sq ..500.00
Table, dining; Naksahima, walnut, 48" dia, +4 captain's chairs 3,500.00
Table, dining; Schultz/Knoll, Petal, blk enamel ped, 42" dia 700.00
Table, dining; Wegner, teak, extension, 76", +2 leaves, EX 2,000.00
Table, dressing; Rhode/Miller, rosewood vnr, ½-rnd bank of drw ..600.00
Table, Eames/Miller, wht laminate rnd top, X-leg base, 30" 400.00
Table, folding; Mathsson, walnut, rfn, 36" 850.00
Table, Gehry, corrugated cb, 21x25x17" 1,000.00
Table, lamp; Rhode, burlwood vnr, 2-tier, 27" dia 650.00
Table, lamp; Wright/Modernage, blk-lcq wood, 3 rnd shelves ...400.00
Table, library; McArthur, brushed chrome U-shaped ends, 60" .4,250.00
Table, magazine; Rohsjohn-Gibbings, cherrywood, 21x29" 350.00
Table, Noguchi/Knoll, laminate top/wire struts/birch base, 20x24" ..4,000.00
Table, Risom, blond wood, wht iron base, stacking (4), 21x15" ..700.00
Table, Saarinen/Knoll, 23" marble top, wht enamel ped, 21" .1,000.00
Table, side; Poini (att), blk lcq 3-leg base, 18x25" dia 500.00
Table, side; Stark, punched steel 2-panel base, mahog top 950.00
Table, Weinberg, Giraffe, dk ash top/head, wrought iron legs .1,800.00
Umbrella stand, Peretti/Castelli, Pluvium, plastic, 5-level 150.00
Vase, Beatrice Wood, bl/pk/red irid, ovoid, 6½" 1,000.00
Vase, Beatrice Wood, platinum/purple irid, bottle form, 6" 800.00
Vase, Beatrice Wood, thick platimum/pk/gr irid, ped ft, 6" 950.00
Vase, Beatrice Wood, volcanic bl/gr lustre, 5x4" 1,800.00
Vase, Fantoni, mc abstracts w/cvd outlines, mc, 10x8", EX 275.00
Vase, Friberg, hare's fur bl/gr matt, trumpet neck, 12½" 1,300.00
Vase, Gambone, abstract figures, dk violet on wht crackle, 16" ...1,000.00
Vase, Gambone, abstract panel, primary mc on crackle, 10x8" ..750.00
Vase, Picasso/Madoura, pnt/cvd as owl, blk/brn on wht, 12x7" .2,600.00

Vase, Takaesu, stoneware Moon Pot, dripping dk bl bands, 7x7" ..2,100.00
Vase, Takaesu, stoneware Moon Pot, gray/beige semigloss, 10x9" ...3,250.00
Vase, Voulkos, blk/olive/ivory bands & lines, 8" 2,600.00
Vase, Voulkos, swirls, purple on ivory w/gray patches, 10" 2,400.00
Wall rack, Eames/Rigrett, Hang-it-all, mc wood balls on wire fr ..800.00
Wall sconce shade, Nakashima, semicylinder parchment in walnut fr ...1,400.00
Wastebasket, McArthur, anodized aluminum, sq, 12x13" 1,200.00

Finch, Kay

Kay Finch and her husband, Braden, operated a small pottery in Corona Del Mar, California, from 1939 to 1963. The company remained small, employing from twenty to sixty local residents who Kay trained in all but the most requiring tasks, which she herself performed. The company produced animal and bird figurines, most notably dogs, Kay's favorites. Figures of 'Godey' type couples were also made, as were tableware (consisting of breakfast sets) and other artware. Most pieces were marked, but ink stamps often came off during cleaning.

After Kay's husband, Braden, died in 1962, she closed the business. Some of her molds were sold to Freeman-McFarlin of El Monte, California, who soon contracted with Kay for new designs. Though the realism that is so evident in her original works is still strikingly apparent in these later pieces, none of the vibrant pastels or signature curliques are there.

Kay Finch died on June 21, 1993. Prices for her work have been climbing.

For further information we recommend *Kay Finch Ceramics, Her Enchanted World* (Schiffer), written by our advisors for this category, Mike Nickel and Cynthia Horvath; they are listed in the Directory under Michigan. Another fine reference is *Collectible Kay Finch* by Richard Martinez, Devin Frick, and Jean Frick (Collector Books). *The New Kay Finch Ceramics Identification Guide* (published in 1996), containing many reprints of original catalog pages, is available from Frances Finch Webb; she is listed in the Directory under California. See also Clubs, Newsletters, and Catalogs.

Note: Original model numbers are included in the following descriptions — three-digit numbers indicate pre-1946 models. After 1946 they were assigned four-digit numbers, the first two digits representing the year of initial production. Prices below are for figurines decorated in multiple colors, not solid glazes.

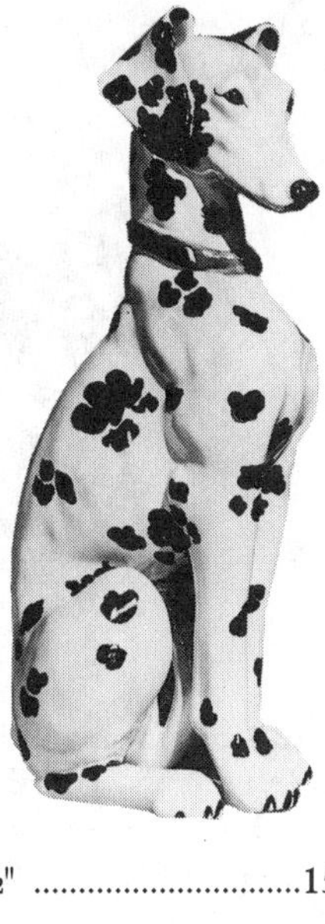

Figurine, Coach Dog, Dalmatian, #159, 17", $1,750.00 minimum value. (Photo courtesy Francis Finch Webb)

Ashtray, Bloodhound head, #4773, 6½x6½" 150.00
Bank, lion, #5921, 8" 500.00
Bank, pig, Winkie, #185, 3¾x5" 150.00
Cookie jar, Cookie Puss, #4614, 11¾", minimum value 2,500.00
Covered dish, swan, #4957, 6" 125.00
Cup, Kitten Face Toby, 3" 150.00
Cup, Missouri Mule, natural colors, 4¼" 125.00
Figurine, Am Indian family, #205/#206/#207, he: 6¾", 3-pc set ...500.00
Figurine, angel, #114a, #114b, or #114c, ea 50.00
Figurine, angel, Little Upside-Down, #140c, 2¾" 150.00
Figurine, bears, Playful, #4848 & #4847, 4¼", pr 400.00
Figurine, birds, Mr & Mrs, pastels, #454 & #453, 4½", 3", pr 175.00
Figurine, bride & groom, #204, he: 6½", pr 450.00
Figurine, camel, #464, 4½x5½" 450.00
Figurine, cat, Ambrosia, pastels, #155, 10½", minimum value ...650.00
Figurine, cat, Baby Ambrosia, #5165, 5½" 200.00
Figurine, cat, Jezebel, #179, 6" 175.00
Figurine, cats, Hear/See/Do No Evil, #4834, #4835, #4836, 3-pc set .375.00
Figurine, cats, Muff & Puff, pastels, #182 & #183, pr 150.00
Figurine, choir boy, #210, 7½" 95.00
Figurine, choir boy, kneeling, #211, 5½" 60.00
Figurine, dog, afghan angel, bl wings, #4911, 2½" 400.00
Figurine, dog, cocker, #5260, blk/wht, 4½" 350.00
Figurine, dog, cocker spaniel, Vickie, pastels, #455, 11" 1,000.00
Figurine, dog, Dog Show Airedale, #4832, 5x5" 450.00
Figurine, dog, Dog Show Poodle, #5024, 5x4½" 550.00
Figurine, dog, Dog Show Yorkshire, #4851, 2½x3" 500.00
Figurine, dog, Pekingese, #154, 14" L 550.00
Figurine, dog, pups, Yorky; #170 & #171, pr 550.00
Figurine, dog, Skye Terrier, Freeman-McFarland, #842, 11" 850.00
Figurine, donkey, Long-Eared w/Basket, #4769, 4" 125.00
Figurine, ducks, Mama & Papa, #471 & #472, pr 500.00
Figurine, ducks, Peep & Jeep, wht or yel, #178a & #178b, 3", pr .80.00
Figurine, elephant, Peanuts, #191, 8½" 350.00
Figurine, elephant, Popcorn, #192, 6¾" 300.00
Figurine, fish, Guppy, #173, 2½" 125.00
Figurine, Goodey Couple, #122, 9½", pr 175.00
Figurine, horse, Armour, #474, 12" 750.00
Figurine, lamb, prancing, #168, 10½", minimum value 750.00
Figurine, lamb, standing, #109, 5½" 95.00
Figurine, monkey, Happy, #4903, 11", minimum value 1,000.00
Figurine, Nativity set, Madonna/Baby/manger, #4900/#4900a, 3-pc ..300.00
Figurine, owl, Hoot, #187, 8½" 150.00
Figurine, owl, Toot, #188, 5¾" 75.00
Figurine, owl, Tootsie, #189, 3¾" 35.00
Figurine, parakeet on perch, #5164, 5¾" 225.00
Figurine, Peasant Boy, #113, 6¾" 60.00
Figurine, pheasant, #5300, 10" 400.00
Figurine, pig, Piggy Wiggy, #5408, 1x1¼" 100.00
Figurine, pig, Sassy, #166, 3¾" 75.00
Figurine, pig, Smiley, 6¾x8" 295.00
Figurine, rabbit, Bunny w/Jacket, #5005, 6" 175.00
Figurine, rabbit, Carrots, #473, 8¾" 495.00
Figurine, rooster, Chanticleer, #129, 11" 400.00
Figurine, rooster & hen, Butch, #177, & Biddy, #178, he: 8½", pr .150.00
Figurine, Scandie Boy & Girl, #126 & #127, 5¼", pr 150.00
Figurine, Seababy, #162, 2½x3½" 175.00
Figurine, squirrel family, Mama, Papa & Baby, #108a/b/c, 3-pc set ...175.00
Planter, Animal Blocks series, ea 75.00
Planter, Animal Books series, ea 75.00
Shaker, Pup, #4617, 6" 595.00
Shaker, Puss, #4615, 6" 395.00
Shakers, stallion head, 5", pr 200.00
String holder, dog head, bow in hair, 4½x4" 400.00
Toby jug, Santa Claus w/cap, scarce #4950, 4" 150.00

Findlay Onyx and Floradine

Findlay, Ohio, was the location of the Dalzell, Gilmore, and Leighton Glass Company, one of at least sixteen companies that flourished there between 1886 and 1901. Their most famous ware, Onyx, is very rare. It was produced for only a short time beginning in 1889 due to the heavy losses incurred in the manufacturing process.

Onyx is layered glass, usually found in creamy white with a dainty floral pattern accented with metallic lustre that has been trapped between the two layers. Other colors found on rare occasions include a light amber (with either no lustre or with gilt flowers), light amethyst (or lavender), and rose. Although old tradepaper articles indicate the company originally intended to produce the line in three distinct colors, long-time Onyx collectors report that aside from the white, production was very limited. Other colors of Onyx are very rare, and the few examples that are found tend to support the theory that production of colored Onyx ware remained for the most part in the experimental stage. Even three-layered items have been found (they are extremely rare) decorated with three-color flowers. As a rule of thumb, using white Onyx prices as a basis for evaluation, expect to pay two to five times more for colored examples.

Floradine is a separate line that was made with the Onyx molds. A single-layer rose satin glassware with white opal flowers, it is usually priced in the general range of colored Onyx.

Chipping around the rims is very common, and price is determined to a great extent by condition. Our advisors for this category are Betty and Clarence Maier; they are listed in the Directory under Pennsylvania.

Floradine

Bowl, fluted, squat bulbous base, 4" 950.00
Celery vase, fluted cylinder neck, bulbous body, 6½", EX 1,000.00
Celery vase, NM 1,800.00
Creamer, bulbous, 4⅝" 950.00
Mustard pot, NM 1,550.00
Spooner, 4¾" 1,285.00
Sugar bowl, bulbous, w/lid, 5½" 1,200.00
Sugar shaker 1,500.00
Syrup pitcher 2,500.00
Toothpick holder, 2½" 1,500.00
Tumbler, slightly bulbous, 3⅝" 1,000.00

Onyx

Syrup, white with silver decor, 7¾", from $850.00 to $1,150.00.

Bowl, wht w/raspberry decor, fluted top, 2½x4½" 2,000.00
Bowl, wht w/silver decor, 2¾x8" 350.00
Butter dish, wht w/silver decor, 3x6" 1,250.00
Covered dish, wht w/silver decor, 5½" 1,000.00
Creamer, wht w/silver decor, 4½" 485.00
Lamp, oil; blk opaque base, sm rpr to collar, 7¼" 6,500.00
Mustard, wht w/raspberry decor, hinged metal lid, 3¼" 2,900.00
Pitcher, water; wht w/silver decor, 8" 1,200.00
Shaker, wht w/silver decor, minor wear, 2¾" 650.00
Shaker, wht w/silver decor, Pat 2/23/1889, 2⅝", NM 800.00
Spooner, wht w/orange decor, 3¾" 950.00
Spooner, wht w/silver decor, 4½x4" 525.00
Sugar bowl, wht w/silver decor, 5½", EX 475.00
Sugar shaker, wht w/silver decor, 5½", from $450 to 550.00
Toothpick holder, wht w/silver decor, from $425 to 500.00
Tumbler, wht w/apricot decor, lt line unseen from w/in, bbl ...2,300.00
Tumbler, wht w/silver decor, bbl shape, 3½", EX 450.00
Tumbler, wht w/silver decor, thin str sides, 3¾", NM 1,000.00

Fire Marks

The earliest American fire marks date back to 1752 when 'The Philadelphia Contributionship for the Insurance of Houses From Loss By Fire' (the official name of this company, who is still in business) used a plaque to identify property they insured. Early fire marks were made of cast iron, sheet brass, lead, copper, tin, and zinc. The insignia of the insurance company appeared on each mark, and they would normally reward the volunteer fire department who managed to be the first on the scene to battle the fire. (Altercations occasionally broke out between firefighting companies vying for the chance to earn the reward!)

Fire marks were first used in Great Britain about 1780 and were more elaborate than U.S. marks. The first English examples were made of lead and carried a policy number. They were used to identify insured property to the fire brigades maintained by the insurance companies. Most copper and brass fire marks are of European origin.

During the latter half of the nineteenth century, municipalities replaced the volunteer fire companies and fire brigades with paid fire departments. No longer was there a need for fire marks, so the companies discontinued their use (though some companies still use fire marks for advertising purposes). See *The Fire Mark Circle of America*, listed under Clubs, Newsletters, and Catalogs in the Directory.

Prices listed are for legitimate fire marks in good to excellent condition. Reproductions are identified when possible. Many fire marks have been and continue to be widely reproduced in cast iron and aluminum. They are sold legitimately as decorator items and collectible reproductions. Fantasy items, on the other hand, are not reproductions, as they depict items that never existed in the first place. They are twentieth century fabrications and never existed in their present form prior to this recent production. They appear in cast iron, aluminum, and other mediums.

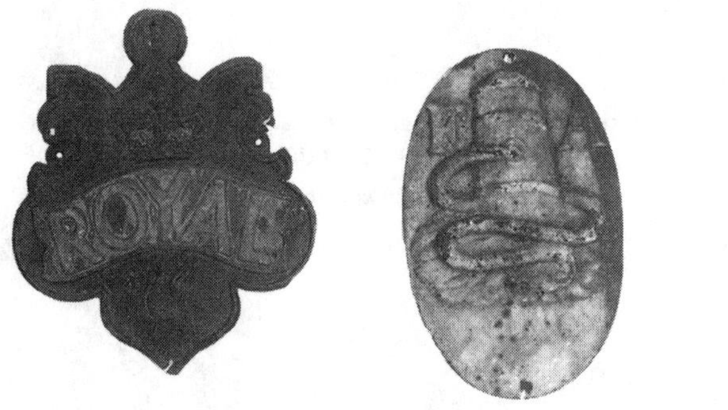

Royal with crown and bird, green and gold traces on stamped copper or brass, British (many varieties, widely reproduced), 12", $120.00; FA (Fire Association) with hydrant and hose, cast iron, 11½", $110.00.

Assoc Fireman's Insurance Co of Baltimore MD, pnt CI, 11¾" .325.00
British, copper on brass, lion & shield, 8" dia 110.00
City Insurance Co Cin, CI, 12½" L 850.00
Fire Assurance of Philadelphia, CI, oval, 11x7½" 85.00
Fireman's Ins Co, Baltimore, red pnt fire wagon, 1855, wear (+) .500.00
German Freeport Ill, pnt tin, 2½x7", EX, from $100 to 150.00
Hands clasped (4) & #906, unmk fantasy item, 7x10½" 15.00
Insured Home New York, tin, 5¼x8⅛", VG 80.00
London Assurance Co AD 1720, tin, British, common, 10x11¾", EX .75.00
PFP Pitman (NJ) Fire Patrol, aluminum, 1920 ....100.00
Phoenix, copper, many varieties, worn 90.00
U (eagle) F, pnt CI oval w/hobnail edge, fantasy item, 11" L 15.00
Valiant Hose No 2, pnt CI, 19th C, fantasy item, 10⅝" 15.00

Firefighting Collectibles

Firefighting collectibles have always been a good investment in terms of value appreciation. Many times the market will be temporarily affected by wild price swings caused by the 'supply and demand principle' as related to a small group of aggressive collectors. These collectors will occasionally pay well over market value for a particular item they need or want. Once their desires are satisfied, prices seem to return to their normal range. It has been noticed that during these periods of high prices, many items enter the marketplace that otherwise would remain in collections. This may (it has in the past) cause a price depression (due again to the 'supply and demand principle' of market behavior).

The recent phenomena of Internet buying and selling has caused wild swings in prices for some fire collectibles. The cause of this is the ability to reach into vast national and international markets. It appears that this has resulted in a significant escalation in prices paid for select items. The everyday, average items have shown an increase in selling price as well. The bottom-line items languish price wise, but at least seem to change hands. This marketplace is growing by leaps and bounds, and many outstanding items have appeared recently in the fire antiques and collectibles field. But when all is said and done, the careful purchase of quality, well-documented firefighting items will continue to be an enjoyable hobby and an excellent investment opportunity.

Today there is a large, active group of collectors for fire department antiques (items over 100 years old) and an even larger group seeking related collectibles (those less than 100 years old). Our advisors for this category (except grenades) are H. Thomas and Patricia Laun; they are listed in the Directory under New York. (SASE required.)

Fire grenades preceded the pressurized metal fire extinguishers used today. They were filled with a mixture of chemicals and water and made of glass thin enough to shatter easily when thrown into the flames. Many varieties of colors and shapes were used. Not all the grenades listed contain salt-brine solution; some, such as the Red Comet, contain carbon tetrachloride, a powerful solvent that is also a health hazard and an environmental threat. (It attacks the ozone layer.) It is best to leave any contents inside the glass balls. The source of grenade prices are mainly auction results; current retail values will fluctuate. Our fire grenades advisor is Larry Meyer; he is listed in the Directory under Illinois.

Key:
ALF — American LaFrance　　s&a — soda & acid
CCL4 — carbon tetrachloride

Alarm, Edwards, red glass w/chain & hammer 20.00
Alarm, electromechanical bell, steel, 8", in oak case, EX 60.00
Ax, Viking type, 18th C, EX 475.00
Badge, Albany FD, silver, horse-head center, 2¼" W 55.00
Badge, Chicago FD Relief Engineer, silver-tone, EX 90.00
Badge, Honorary Lieutenant FD NY, EX 70.00

Badge, Phila Fire Insurance Patrol #195, horse-drawn patrol wagon in center, scarce, $335.00.

Badge, Phoenix 2, brass shield, VG 130.00
Badge, Portland OR Auxillary FD, silver, dtd 1937, EX 35.00
Badge, Rocky Hill NJ FD, silver shield, eagle top, 1¼x⅞" 30.00
Badge, VFA Phila 1875 w/hydrant & hose, silver-tone shield, EX ..170.00
Bed key, CI, early, EX 155.00
Bed key, hand forged, EX 150.00
Bell, muffin type w/trn hdl, 2 3" dia brass bells, EX 275.00
Belt, canvas, Pompier, EX 20.00
Belt, parade; leather, blk w/red & wht, slide mk Vixen, EX 90.00
Belt, parade; leather, brass Old Town buckle, minor pnt flaking .150.00
Belt, parade; leather, 2nd Assistant appl brass, lg 2 by buckle, 48" ...50.00
Belt slide, brass, hose & floral eng, EX 130.00
Belt slide, emb fireman w/child & trumpet, EX 40.00
Book, Black & White & Red All Over, Bartosz, 1971, EX 60.00
Book, History of Fire Dept of Newton MA 1897, 240-pg, scarce .120.00
Boots, salesman's sample, rubber, Woonsocket Rubber Co, pr, EX ..85.00
Box, ballot; wooden, hinged lid, compartment, w/marbles 110.00
Brochure, Gamewell Switchboards, 1906, w/instructions 15.00
Bucket, rubber, old red pnt, metal band at top, Pat 1854, EX 110.00
Cap, bl w/gold embr: Keystone #1 Hook & Ladder, Hortsmann Phila, EX ..50.00
Cap, dress; sq visor w/steel cap badge 45.00
Catalog, Am Fire Engine...NY-Cincinnati, 1902, EX 220.00
Certificate, Friendship Fire Co #3, Baltimore membership, 24x18" .825.00
Extinguisher, Badgers, brass & copper, s&a, EX 40.00
Extinguisher, Carbona label, brn 12-sided bottle w/labels, VG 85.00
Extinguisher, Chief Croker, brass & copper, pony sz 95.00
Extinguisher, Kidde, stainless steel, pressurized water 15.00
Extinguisher, Knight & Thomas, brass & copper, pony sz 110.00
Extinguisher, Minimax, copper, s&a, 2½-gal, VG 50.00
Extinguisher, Minimax 4 AW, cone shape, EX 110.00
Extinguisher, pump; Pyrene, plated brass, 5-gal, M 40.00
Extinguisher, Rameses, tin tube, 22", G 20.00
Extinguisher, Stop-Fire NY, brass 25.00
Extinguisher, Trotex, brass & copper, pony sz 70.00
Extinguisher kit, Shur Stop, 6 grenades in metal case, complete ..135.00
Fire stream table, calculates flows of gallons, Ahrens Fox 25.00
Frontispc, brass, Xd axes/nozzles/hose/etc, Bomberos-Mexico, EX ..60.00
Frontispc, leather, high front, #3, EX 85.00
Gauge, air; General Fire Ext Co, 5½" 20.00
Gavel, wooden, sterling silver band, w/wooden sounder 60.00
Gong, electomechanical, polished brass bell, 10", EX 90.00
Gong, Gamewell, 15" brass bell, in orig Moses Crane case, w/key, EX ...3,450.00
Grenade, Harden's Star, bl, w/contents, EX 120.00
Grenade, Harden's...Pat 31 August 8th 1871...1883, turq, NM .130.00
Grenade, Hayward's Hand Fire...1871, cobalt, crude, NM 210.00
Grenade, Red Comet, ceiling mt, EX 25.00
Grenade, Star Fire, brilliant bl, orig contents, 1875-85, M 180.00
Grenade, Star Fire, sapphire bl, crude, 1875-85, NM 130.00
Grenade, Star Fire, turq, w/contents, 1875-85, NM 110.00
Grenade, Systeme Labbe...Paris, golden amber, 1880-1900, NM ..230.00
Helmet, aluminum, high eagle, Cairns, lacks frontispc, VG 160.00
Helmet, aluminum, leather front, Fire Co-Ord-Rens Co, VG 70.00

Helmet, aluminum, red w/leather front, Engin 4 FFD, EX 100.00
Helmet, blk plastic w/face shield, complete 20.00
Helmet, leather, blk & red front: Torrent 1 FFD, 4-comb, early, EX ..465.00
Helmet, leather, high eagle, FD-NY, Cairns, VG 325.00
Helmet, leather, high eagle, Good Will 1802 GW, EX 2,750.00
Helmet, leather, high eagle, H&L No 1, Cairns/Oak Hall Boston, EX ..465.00
Helmet, leather, high eagle, RFD, Cairns, much wear 275.00
Helmet, leather, high eagle, RS Frost, Olson, rstr brim 350.00
Helmet, leather, high eagle, 32-comb, lacks frontispc, VG 260.00
Helmet, leather, high eagle, 84-comb, Anderson & Jones, 1870s, EX ..850.00
Helmet, leather, high lion, Wm Penn Hose 18, Hortsman, EX 1,400.00
Helmet, leather, New Yorker w/Boston style frontispc, Cairns, EX ..185.00
Helmet, oilcloth, shaped crown, pnt shield, early, EX 775.00
Helmet, solid brass w/leather liner, shield front w/lg R, VG 90.00
Hydrant, APS 1967, Philadelphia, full sz, EX 110.00
Inkwell, Fire Assoc of Philadelphia, wooden hydrant form, EX .375.00
Lantern, chief's style, brass, missing font & globe, EX 170.00
Lantern, Dietz, brass, clear etched globe, last Pat 88, 13½" 325.00
Lantern, Dietz Fire Dept, emb SG&L Co at top, red globe, EX .475.00
Lantern, Dietz Fire King, blk pnt, clear globe, mixed metals, EX .150.00
Lantern, Dietz Fire King, brass & NP, VG 180.00
Lantern, Dietz Fire King, clear globe, mixed metals, EX 150.00
Lantern, Dietz Tubular, clear globe, Pats 1881-1893, EX 265.00
Lantern, hand; chief's, NP brass, Westlake, 1864, EX 325.00
Lantern, wrist; brass, clear globe, stress cracks 100.00
Lantern, wrist; fixed globe, w/burner, New England, 1854, EX ..260.00
Lantern, wrist; SP, eng RAPFD in globe, 13", VG 650.00
Lock, brass, for Gamewell alarm box, 2x2¼", w/key 35.00
Mold, pewter; fireman wearing high-front helmet, Mills, 1866, VG ..325.00
Nozzle, brass, mk Phila, w/Jones coupling, 25" 60.00
Nozzle, brass, shut-off hdl, Rockwood/Bliss-Gamewell, 48" 65.00
Oil can, NP, for engine, EX 180.00
Plaque, Grinnell First Heat, CI 25.00
Play pipe, AJ Morse & Son, brass & copper, 30" 60.00
Play pipe, MFD mk, brass & copper, cord wrapped 60.00
Play pipe, Powhattan, brass & copper, 30" 60.00
Play pipe, WD Allen Co, brass & copper, cord wrapped, 30" 60.00
Print, Great Fire at Boston Nov 9&10 1872, 10x14", EX 35.00
Rattle, alarm; dbl reed, working 80.00
Stamp, Gamewell Excelsior, automatic date & time, w/Chelsea clock, EX .750.00
Telephone handset & cord, for Gamewell boxes w/special jack ...15.00
Trumpet, brass, folded seam, 1850s, scarce, EX 450.00
Trumpet, brass, 17", EX 450.00
Trumpet, brass, made in sections, nonservice type, lg 160.00
Trumpet, NP on brass, old rpr, VG 225.00
Trumpet , presentation; SP, Lafayette Co No 1, 18" 850.00
Trumpet, presentation; SP, Presented to...1873, polished, EX .2,100.00
Trumpet , SP, repousse flowers, 23", EX 400.00
Trumpet, working; SP, missing mouthpc, VG 175.00

Fireglow

Fireglow is a type of art glass that first appears to be an opaque cafe au lait, but glows with rich red 'fire' when held to a strong source of light.

Vase, butterflies/wild flowers, stick neck w/cup rim, 5", pr 180.00
Vase, pk, floral, gourd shape, 13" 150.00
Vase, stylized flowers, stick form, flower-shaped window, 6" 70.00

Fireplace Accessories and Implements

In the colonial days of our country, fireplaces provided heat in the winter and were used year round to cook food in the kitchen. The implements that were a necessary part of these functions were varied and have become treasured collectibles, many put to new use in modern homes as decorative accessories. Gypsy pots may hold magazines; copper and brass kettles, newly polished and gleaming, contain dried flowers or green plants. Firebacks, highly ornamental iron panels that once reflected heat and protected masonry walls, are now sometimes used as wall decorations. By Victorian times the cook stove had replaced the kitchen fireplace, and many of these early utensils were already obsolete; but as a source of heat and comfort, the fireplace continued to be used for several more decades. See also Wrought Iron.

Andirons, cast iron cats with inset glass eyes, PS&W Co., 17½", $1,035.00.

Andirons, brass, Am Classical ball-top, ca 1820, pr 2,500.00
Andirons, brass, dbl-lemon top, hex shafts, ball ft, 19th C, 18" .460.00
Andirons, brass, trn-type post endings, dome top, 18" 500.00
Andirons, iron Renaissance style w/scrollwork, basket top, 37" .350.00
Andirons, wrought iron, gooseneck, Am, 18th C, 15x21" 460.00
Andirons, wrought steel knife-blade style, urn finials, 21" 500.00
Bellows, turtle-bk w/old pnt flowers & stenciling, brass nozzle, rstr 350.00
Bellows, turtle-bk w/orig mc pnt, brass nozzle, worn leather, 18", VG ...150.00
Bellows, turtle-bk w/orig pnt cornucopia, brass nozzle, 18", EX .385.00
Fender, brass & iron wire, serpentine decor, 1790-1830, 12x55x18" ..500.00
Fender, brass Fed style, pierced latticework, 19th C, 43" 350.00
Fender, brass Fed w/pierced leaf band, paw ft, 35" 535.00
Fender, brass Georgian, pierced/eng serpentine style, 19th C, 8x62" ...300.00
Fender, steel & brass w/brass ball ft/finials, 14x37x12" 550.00
Fender, steel & wire w/brass top rail, serpentine, 12x57x19" ..1,200.00
Fender, wire w/brass top rail, 24x36x15" 125.00
Fender, wrought iron w/wire grill, brass top rail, 12x43x12" 275.00
Fire bk, CI, 4 floral panels in cast fr, 19th C, 34x23" 330.00
Insert, CI, molded frieze, fluted pilasters, 19th C, 35x40x10" 400.00
Log fork, worught iron, made from 1 pc of iron, ball finial, 49" .100.00
Mantel, Am Classical King of Prussia marble, fluted supports, 51x67" ..2,000.00
Screen, Biedermeier, cherrywood/ebonized, period embr remnant, 48x28" 2,145.00
Screen, Fr gilt bronze w/mesh inset, 19th C, 39x29" 385.00
Screen, wrought iron, fr fluted circles, scrolled ft, rpr, 29x46" ...500.00
Tongs, ember; wrought iron, spring loaded, EX details, w/tamper, 17" ..400.00

Fishing Collectibles

Collecting old fishing tackle is becoming more popular every year. Though at first most interest was geared toward old lures and some reels, rods, advertising, and miscellaneous items are quickly gaining ground. Values are given for examples in excellent or better condition and should be used only as a guide. For more information we recommend *19th Century Fishing Lures* by Arlan Carter; *The Fishing Lure Collector's Bible* by R.L. Streater with Dudley Murphy and Rick Edmisten; and *Fishing Lure Collectibles* by Dudley Murphy and Rick Edmisten. All are published by

Collector Books. Our advisor for this category is Randy Hilst, an appraiser and collector whose address and phone number are listed in the Directory under Illinois. (SASE required.)

Key:
GE — glass eyes PE — painted eyes

Catalog, Edward Vom Hofe & Co, 1927, 169-pg, EX 110.00
Catalog, Heddon, 1939, w/color chart, 43-pg, M 355.00
Catalog, Heddon-Dowagiac Bait Casting Equipment #19, 1922, 15-pg, VG ..770.00
Catalog, Shakespeare, 1925, 39-pg, VG 275.00
Creel, willow w/leather binding/hinges/strap, lg offset hole, VG ..130.00
Decoy, Menominee, GE, forked tail, Sunny Bashore, 9½", EX+ ..185.00
Decoy, Trout, GE, Dennis Wolf, 12", EX+ 200.00
Fish grabber, Marbles-Gladstone Mich, spring-loaded, NM 100.00
Fly rod, FE Thomas Special, 3-pc, 8½-ft, NM in case 275.00
Fly rod, HL Leonard Tournament, w/extra tip & metal case, 9-ft ...300.00
Gig, 5-prong, blacksmith made, conical hdl receptacle, 17", VG ...30.00
Lure, Creek Chub Lucky Mouse, EX 170.00
Lure, Creek Chub Sucker, yel, GE, produced only 2 yrs, G 245.00
Lure, Creek Chub Wiggler #1000 Trout Size, ⅞", M 550.00
Lure, Heddon #150 Minnow, rare sienna perch finish, G- 660.00
Lure, Heddon Basser, Allen stripe, GE, belly hook, EX 500.00
Lure, Heddon Musky Vamp, shiner scale, GE, 6", EX+ 185.00
Lure, Heddon Shark Mouth Minnow, ca 1935, 3", VG+ 990.00
Lure, Heddon Woodpecker, wht w/orig hdw, red/wht head, 4⅝", EX ...770.00
Lure, K&K Animated Minnow, GE, jtd, 3½", VG 330.00
Lure, Pflueger Dragon Spinner, metal, MOC 225.00
Lure, Pflueger Kent Frog, belly hook, GE, VG+ 475.00
Lure, Pflueger Luminous Crystal Minnow, ca 1883, VG 1,320.00
Lure, Pflueger O-Boy Perch, GE, sm, EX 200.00
Lure, Pflueger Pakron, metal head w/GE, 2¾", EX 110.00
Lure, Shakespeare #33 Rhodes 3-Hook Underwater, GE, 1909, VG+ .325.00
Lure, Shakespeare Egyptian Wobbler, EX 300.00
Lure, Shakespeare Evolution, rubber, 1910, 2¾", VG+ 265.00
Lure, Shakespeare Wooden Minnow #42, GE, 3¾", VG 110.00
Lure, South Bend Minnow, w/2 hooks, GE, 3", EX 165.00
Lure, South Bend Zane Grey Teaser, 11", VG 440.00

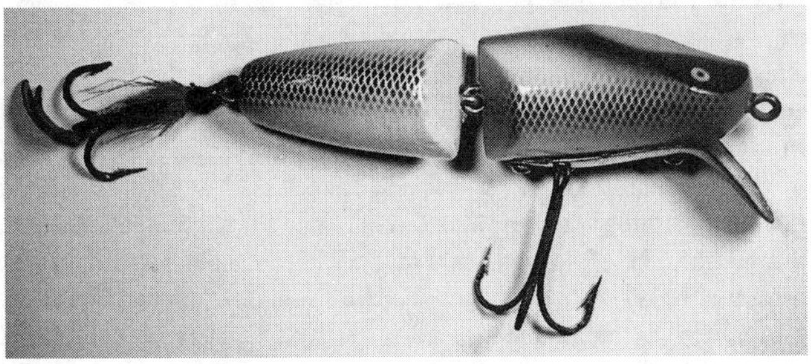

Lure, Wayne Precision Warbler, red head, jointed body, front metal lip, EX, $25.00.

Lure, Wilson Flanged Wobbler, 4", VG 165.00
Minnow bucket, Chief Floating... stenciled on tin, oval, VG 715.00
Minnow trap, CF Orvis, glass w/wire harness, swivel cover, early, EX 385.00
Reel, Abel #2, EX 360.00
Reel, AH Fox, mk Bait Casting..., w/8-sided metal plates, VG 55.00
Reel, Edw Vom Hofe #1, Pat Jan 23 '83, G- 250.00
Reel, Hardy, Longstone 'Center Pin,', 4", VG 110.00
Reel, Hardy, Silex, 1950s, 4", EX 165.00
Reel, Hardy, Silex Superba, 1950s, 4", VG 220.00
Reel, HH Kiffe, mk Non Level Wind 100-yd Bait Casting, VG ...115.00
Reel, Julius Vom Hofe, mk Trout Click Hdl Plate Reel..., VG ...470.00
Reel, Kosmic Black Bass Model #946, mk Quadruple, ca 1890, rare, EX ..636.00
Reel, Meek #2, mk Tournament Casting Reel, EX 1,320.00
Reel, Meek #3, EX 660.00
Reel, Meisselbach, sm fresh-water Neptune Take-Apart, VG 60.00
Reel, Orvus, trout, Pat 1874, w/walnut box, NM 330.00
Reel, Pflueger (1st reel), Pat 1896, wood & brass line winder, EX .770.00
Reel, Seamaster Mark II Anti-Reverse, w/bag & box, NM 880.00
Reel, Seamaster Mark II Single Action, w/zippered case & box, NM ..2,860.00
Reel, Shakespeare Free Spool-1744, mk Model 26-100-yds, VG ..110.00
Reel, Stan Bogdan #300, w/leather case, NM 1,540.00
Reel, Thompson #500, EX+ 440.00
Reel, Westly Richards & Co, Rolo, Pat #20113, 4½", VG 250.00
Rod, Goodwin Granger 9-Ft Champion Trout, w/tube, G 110.00
Rod, James Shaaf Hollow Built 12-93-90-RT Salmon, w/tube, M 550.00
Rod, LL Bean's Atlantic Salmon, w/extra tip/cork hdl, EX in case ..100.00
Rod, Orvis Midge Nymph Combination Trout, w/2 tips, w/tube, M ..470.00
Rod, RL Winston Fly, 2-tip, 2-pc, w/tube, M 770.00
Sign, cb pop-out, Pflueger, 2 anglers in boat w/lg fish, 22x17", EX 330.00
Tackle box, Knickerbocker, leather, 10 cantilevered trays, 16x9", EX ..85.00

Flags of the United States

Over the past few years the popularity of vintage flags has grown dramatically, and prices have risen greatly as a result. The pending restoration of the Fort McHenry Flag (The Star Spangled Banner) has also created greater public interest in flag collecting.

The brevity and imprecise language of the first Flag Act of 1777 allowed great artistic license for America's early flag makers. This resulted in a rich variety of imaginative star formations which coexisted with more conventional row patterns. In 1912 inviolate design standards were established for the new 48-star flag, but the banners of our earlier history continue to survive:

The 'Great Star' pattern — configured from the combined stars of the union, appeared in various star denominations for about 50 years, then gradually disappeared in the post-Civil War years.

The utilitarian 'scatter' pattern — created through the random placement of stars, is traceable to the formative years of our nation and remained a design influence through most of the nineteenth century.

The 'wreath' pattern — first appearing in the form of simple single-wreath formations, eventually evolved into the elegant double- and triple-wreath medallion patterns of the Centennial period.

Acquisition of specific star denominations is also a primary consideration in the collecting process. Pre-Civil War flags of 33 stars or less are very scarce and are typically treated as 'blue chip' items. Civil War-era flags of 34 and 35 stars also stand among the most sought-after denominations. Market demand for 36-, 37- and 38-star flags is strong but less broad-based, while interest in the unofficial 39-, 40-, 41- and 42-star examples is largely confined to flag aficionados. The very rare 43 remains in a class by itself and is guaranteed to attract the attention of the serious collector.

Row-patterned flags of 44, 45, and 46 stars still turn up with some frequency and serve as a source of more modestly priced vintage flags. Ordinary 48-star flags flood the flea markets and are priced accordingly, while the short-lived 49 is regarded as a legitimate collectible. Thirteen-star flags, produced over a period of more than 200 years, surface in many forms and must be assessed on a case-by-case basis.

Many flag buffs favor sizes that are manageable for wall display, while others are attracted to the more monumental proportions. Allowances are typically made for the normal wear and tear — it goes with the territory. But severe fabric deterioration and other forms of excessive physical damage are legitimate points of negotiation.

The dollar value of a flag is by no means based upon age alone. The wide price swings in the listings below have been influenced by a variety of determining factors related to age, scarcity, and aesthetic merit. In fact, almost any special feature that stands out as unusual or distinctive is a potential asset. Imprinted flags and inscribed flags; 8-point stars, gold stars, and added stars; extra stripes, missing stripes, tricolor stripes and war stripes are all part of the pricing equation. And while political and military flags may rank above all others in terms of prestige and price, any flag with a significant and well-documented historical connection has 'star' potential (pardon the pun). Our advisor for this category is Ryan Cooper; he is listed in the Directory under Massachusetts.

13 stars, circular pattern, hand sewn, 1860s, 29x40" 1,800.00
13 stars, hand/machine sewn, Centennial, 60x86" 650.00
13 stars, printed glazed muslin, 1880s, 7x11" 100.00
13 stars, US Naval boat insignia, 1880, 50x96" 750.00
15 stars, Union Jack from War of 1812, rare, 35x62" 23,000.00
15 stars, 15 stripes, all machine sewn, ca 1912, 48x72" 375.00
16 stars, Great Star, hand sewn, 1850s, 54x78" 6,800.00
19 stars, 16 orig+3, sewn scrap fabric, 39x66" 6,500.00
20 stars, oval pattern, ship's flag, 1818, worn, 64x128" 6,500.00
21 stars, Commissioning pennant, ship 'Herald,' 1819, 50-ft ..8,500.00
25 stars, oval pattern w/central star, ship's flag, 96x200" 6,700.00
25 stars, row pattern, Civil War, 90x175" 2,200.00
26 stars, Great Star, embr on sewn silk, 30x43" 7,500.00
29 stars, entirely hand sewn, poor condition, 43x68" 2,500.00
30 stars, gold stars/fringe, silk, delicate, 52x68" 3,500.00
31 stars, Great Star, hand-sewn silk, 14' 2,500.00
31 stars, row pattern, hand-stitched bunting, 104x247" 2,500.00
32 stars, dbl wreath of inset stars, hand sewn, 36x48" 5,200.00
33 stars, Great Star, hand-sewn muslin, 60x96" 4,200.00
33 stars, hand-/machine-sewn wool bunting, 66x92" 2,250.00
33 stars, in rows, printed bunting, 28x44", G- 700.00
34 stars, dbl-wreath pattern, printed silk, 18x28" 900.00
34 stars, Great Star, from Albany RR Depot, 116x175" 4,500.00
34 stars, printed linen, 3 sewn sections, 22x48" 600.00
34 stars, random pattern, hand sewn, 66x140" 1,200.00
35 stars, dbl-wreath pattern, printed, sized muslin, 19x28" 750.00
35 stars, recruiting flag, sewn bunting, 50x116" 1,300.00
35 stars, row pattern, hand/machine sewn, 96x180" 950.00
36 stars, cut-in, in rows, machined stripes, 25x50" 700.00
36 stars, inscr parade flag, muslin print, 6x9" 250.00
36 stars, sailing ship's, inscr & dtd, 75x142" 950.00
37 stars, medallion pattern, printed/sewn muslin, 48x87" 450.00
37 stars, printed silk, 32x40" 225.00
37 stars, row pattern, hand-sewn silk, poor, 60x80" 230.00
37 stars, row pattern, stitched bunting, 30x48" 450.00
38 stars, medallion-wreath pattern, printed cotton, 12x17" 225.00
38 stars, printed silk w/ribbon ties, 30x47" 250.00
38 stars, row pattern, clamp dyed in 3 sections, 60x120" 220.00
38 stars, row pattern, hand/machine-stitched bunting, 71x116" ...250.00
38 stars, unique wreath pattern, sewn, 89x134" 500.00
38 stars, 1776-1876 pattern, printed linen, 27½x46" 1,800.00
39 stars, Centennial 'International Flag,' 16x24" 140.00
39 stars, row pattern, all machine-stitched bunting, 40x84" 350.00
39 stars, row pattern variation, printed silk, 12x24" 125.00
39 stars (6-5 pattern), printed gauze bunting, 19x34" 125.00
40 stars, row pattern, hand-sewn bunting, lg, 98x204" 270.00
40 stars, row pattern, printed/sewn British import, 55x106" 185.00
41 stars (rare), printed cotton sheeting, 15x24" 225.00
42 stars, sewn cotton, from Ft Hamilton NY, 120x177" 275.00
42 stars, 7-row pattern, printed cotton, 12x17" 125.00
43 stars, machine-sewn bunting, extremely rare, 29x70" 1,200.00
44 stars, machine-sewn cotton bunting, 53x82" 200.00
44 stars, triple-wreath pattern, printed cotton, 23x26" 175.00
45 stars, HP w/sewn stripes, 38x70" 120.00
45 stars, machine-sewn cotton bunting, 80x108" 55.00
45 stars, printed silk w/red ribbon ties, 32x46" 45.00
45 stars, row pattern variant, printed muslin, 9x13" 25.00
46 stars, machine-sewn wool bunting, 72x138" 60.00
46 stars, printed silk, GAR Post in gold, 32x45" 350.00
47 stars, unofficial, sewn bunting, 108x137" 350.00
48 stars, all crocheted, dtd 1941, 20x38" 85.00
48 stars, machine-sewn cotton bunting, 60x96" 30.00
48 stars, printed cotton w/GAR surprint, 11x16" 25.00
48 stars, sewn to form 'USA,' unauthorized WWI, 45x69" 300.00
48 stars, USN Union Jack, machine-sewn wool, 23x33" 35.00
48 stars in gold, sewn WWII casket flag, 58x118" 95.00
49 stars, embr, sewn stripes, 36x60" 45.00
49 stars, 3 uncut flags, printed cotton sheet, 37x36" 25.00
50 stars, early prototype 'June 1959,' 52x66" 220.00
50 stars, hand-knitted coverlet w/fringe, 30x51" 30.00
51 stars, printed flaglette for DC statehood, 4x6" 15.00

Florence Ceramics

Figurines marked 'Florence Ceramics' were produced in the '40s and '50s in Pasadena, California. The quality of the ware and the attention given to detail are prompting a growing interest among today's collectors. The names of these lovely ladies, gents, and figural groups are nearly always incised into their bases. The company name is ink stamped. Examples are evaluated by size, rarity, and intricacy of design. For more information we recommend *The Florence Collectibles* by Doug Foland, a co-advisor for this category. You will find him listed in the Directory under Oregon. Another source is *The Collector's Encyclopedia of California Pottery, Second Edition*, by Jack Chipman; he is listed in the Directory under California. Advise also came from Jerry Kline; he is listed in the Directory under Tennessee.

Adeline, fancy, 8¼" 350.00
Amber, 9¼" 700.00
Amelia, 8¼" 275.00
Ann, yel, 6" 150.00
Anna Lisa, 8¼" 275.00
Ava, flower holder, 10½" 225.00
Bea, 7¼" 150.00
Belle, 8" 125.00
Beth, 7½" 125.00
Birthday Girl, rare, 9", from $350 to 950.00
Boy (bust), traditional, 12" 200.00
Bride, 8¾", from $1,000 to 1,200.00
Carmen, rare, 12½", from $1,500 to 1,700.00
Catherine, 6¾x7¾" 700.00
Charles, 8¾" 325.00
Cindy, fancy, 8" 325.00
Claudia, 8¼" 175.00
Colleen, fancy, 8" 285.00
Darleen, rare, 8¼" 650.00
Deborah, rare, 9¼" 750.00
Denise, 10" 500.00
Diana, powder box, 6¼" 400.00
Douglas, 8¼" 175.00
Edward, 7" 450.00
Ellen, 7" 125.00
Emily, flower holder, 8" 60.00
Ethel, plain, 7¼" 125.00
Eugenia, 9" 400.00
Fair Lady, rare, 11½", from $1,500 to 1,700.00
Gary, 8½" 200.00

Georgette, 10" 750.00
Girl (bust), traditional, 12" 200.00
Grace, plain, 7¾" 150.00

Grandmother and I, from $2,500.00 to $3,000.00. (From the collection of Peggy and John Scott)

Halloween Child, 4" 250.00
Her Majesty, 7" 200.00
Irene, 6" 70.00
Jim, 6¼" 80.00
John Alden, 9¼", from $250 to 275.00
Josephine, 9" 250.00
Joyce, 9" 400.00
Judy, 9" 325.00
Julie, flower holder, 7¼" 125.00
Karla (ballerina), 9¾" 325.00
Kiu, 11" 250.00
Lantern Boy, flower holder, 8¼" 100.00
Laura, 7½", from $150 to 190.00
Lavon, rare, 8½" 400.00
Lillian, 7¼" 150.00
Linda Lou, red or teal, 7¾", from $160 to 400.00
Little Don, rare, 5½" 400.00
Louis XVI, 10" 300.00
Louise, 7¼", from $80 to 140.00
Madame Pompadour, 12½" 400.00
Madonna, 10½" 150.00
Margaret, rare, 9¾", from $1,000 to 1,200.00
Margot, rare, 8½" 200.00
Mark Anthony & Cleopatra rare, 13½", pr 3,000.00
Marsie, 8" 275.00
Masquerade, rare, 8¼" 900.00
Master David, 8" 400.00
Melanie, fancy, 7½" 150.00
Mimi, flower holder, 6" 40.00
Nita, 8" 275.00
Pamela (bust), 9½" 175.00
Patsy, flower holder, 6", from $50 to 60.00
Peg, flower holder, 7" 90.00
Pinkie, 12" 350.00
Pompadour (bust) 225.00
Prima Donna, 10" 600.00
Princess, 10¼", from $1,200 to 1,400.00
Priscilla & John Alden, pr 600.00
Richard, rare, 8½" 400.00
Sally, flower holder, 6¾" 40.00
Scarlett, hands away, fancy, 8¾" 300.00
Sherri, 8" 375.00
Sue Ellen, 8¼" 175.00
Susanna, lace & gold, 8¾", from $375 to 400.00
Tess, teenager, 7¼" 275.00
Victor, 9¼", from $325 to 275.00
Vivian, 10" 395.00
Yvonne, plain, 8¾" 350.00

Flow Blue

Flow Blue ware was produced by many Staffordshire potters; among the most familiar were Meigh, Podmore and Walker, Samuel Alcock, Ridgway, John Wedge Wood (who often signed his work Wedgewood), and Davenport. It was popular from about 1825 through 1860 and again from 1880 until the turn of the century. The name describes the blurred or flowing effect of the cobalt decoration, achieved through the introduction of a chemical vapor into the kiln. The body of the ware is ironstone, and Oriental motifs were favored. Later issues were on a lighter body and often decorated with gilt. For further information we recommend *The Collector's Encyclopedia of Flow Blue China* (2nd series) by Mary Frank Gaston (Collector Books).

Albany, platter, Grindley, 16x11¾" 185.00
Alton, relish 125.00
Alton, sauce tureen, w/lid, oval, Grindley 150.00
Amoy, honey dish, Davenport, 5¼" 125.00
Amoy, pitcher, paneled, Davenport, 5¾x6¼" 325.00
Amoy, plate, Davenport, 8¼" 85.00
Amoy, plate, Davenport, 9" 95.00
Amoy, plate, Davenport, 10½" 175.00
Amoy, saucer, paneled, Davenport, 6½", NM 30.00
Arabesque, plate, Mayer, 10½", EX 150.00
Argyle, butter pat 50.00
Athol, egg cup, Burgess & Leigh 150.00
Ayr, bowl, vegetable; W&E Corn, 9½x7" 100.00
Azalea, bowl, potato; J Leigh, 2½x10" 95.00
Blue Danube, plate, 10" 95.00
Blue Ridge, chocolate pot 200.00
Brent, toothbrush holder, standing, Bisto 275.00
Campion, pitcher & bowl, Grindley 1,300.00
Campion, waste jar 500.00
Carlton, plate, 7¼" 80.00
Cashmere, coffeepot, octagonal, sqd/arch hdl, 8¾", VG 1,200.00
Cashmere, plate, 10-sided, FM & Co, 10¾" 175.00
Cavendish, cheese keeper, Keeling, 19th C 450.00
Chen Si, plate, 1812-36, 8" 185.00
Chusan, cup plate, Clementson, 4" 150.00
Chusan, plate, Clementson, 9" 160.00
Coburg, bowl, John Edwards, 2x10¼" 150.00
Coburg, plate, John Edwards, 9", NM 70.00
Conway, platter, New Wharf Pottery, 10" 140.00
Corea, platter, Wedgwood, 16x11¼" 400.00
Dorothy, bone dish 75.00
Douglas, platter, Ford & Sons, 15¼x11¼" 250.00
Formosa, pitcher, TJ&J Mayer, 8¼x7¼" 650.00
Formosa, plate, T&J Mayer, 9¼" 110.00
Formosa, soup, T&J Mayer, 10" 150.00
Garland, chamber pot 195.00
Gilded Floral Design, pitcher, mc details, braided hdl, mk T, 8" 125.00
Gilded Fruit Trees, pitcher, Charles Allerton & Sons, 8x7¾" 126.00
Gothic, bowl, potato; Furnival, 2½x9¾" 200.00
Gothic, bowl, vegetable; w/lid, Furnival, 7x12¼x10" 600.00
Gothic, bowl, 12-paneled rim, Furnival, 1½x10¼" 100.00
Gothic, butter dish, Furnival, 4¼x7¼" 500.00
Gothic, condiment dish, Furnival, 7½x5¼" 125.00
Gothic, pitcher, milk; Furnival, 6" 450.00
Gothic, plate, Furnival, 10¼" 100.00

Gothic, plate, Furnival, 7" 50.00
Gothic, sauce tureen & underplate, unmk, 6½x8x3¾" 650.00
Gothic, sugar bowl, paneled, w/lid, unmk, rpr, 7½x4½" 225.00
Hamilton, teapot 650.00
Hamilton, undertray for gravy, Burgess & Leigh 65.00
Hamilton Spray, soup tureen, Grindley 795.00
Hindustan, plate, Maddock, 8¾" 125.00
Holland, compote, Johnson Bros 350.00
Hong, pitcher, water 1,250.00
Hong Kong, plate, 10" 195.00
Hong Kong, sugar bowl, w/lid, att Meigh, 7¾" 375.00
Hyson, pitcher, milk; Clementson, 6x6" 325.00
Hyson, teapot, Clementson, 9½" 500.00
Ilam, bowl, vegetable; w/lid 225.00
Indian Jar, platter, sm rpr, Pratt, 16" 450.00
Indiana, soup plate, 10½" 125.00
Irene, soup tureen, Wedgwood 750.00
Iris, potty 495.00
Ivanhoe, plate, Wedgwood, 8" 125.00
Japanese, Farmer's saucer, 6¾" 75.00
Japanese, pitcher & bowl 1,295.00
Jeddo, bowl, potato; Adams, 2½x10⅜" 125.00
Jeddo, pitcher & bowl 1,895.00
Jenny Lind, bowl, rare sz, 9½" 145.00
Kaolin, teapot 895.00
Kiota, sauce tureen & ladle, 5x7½x5" 225.00
Knox, plate, New Wharf Pottery, 10" 125.00
Kyber, bowl, Adams, 5" 15.00
Kyber, bowl, Adams, 6" 20.00
Kyber, plate, Adams, 10" 125.00
Kyber, platter, Adams, 17¾" 450.00
Kyber, sugar bowl, 8-sided, ftd, 6½", EX 275.00
Kyber, teapot, squat 1,050.00
La Belle, creamer & sugar bowl, lid rstr 450.00
La Belle, cup & saucer 175.00
La Belle, helmet bowl, 4x8x6" 300.00
La Belle, ice cream tray, 13" 350.00
La Francais, plate, scalloped, 9" 30.00
Libertas, plate, Prussian, 10" 75.00
Lily, chamber pot 195.00

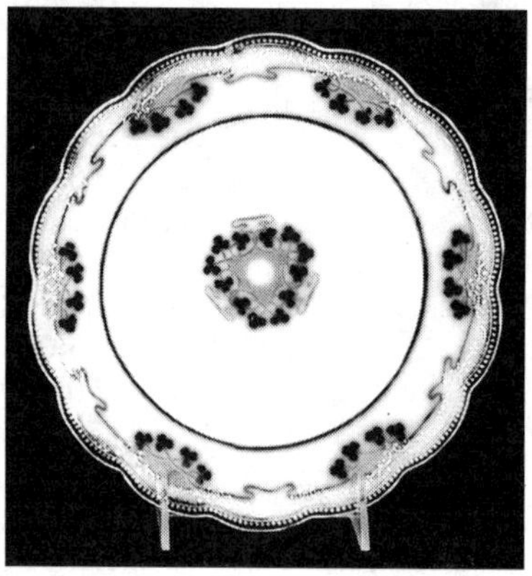

Lorne, soup bowl, clovers at border, 9", $75.00.

Lorne, bowl, vegetable; oval, w/lid, Grindley 295.00
Lorne, cup & saucer 110.00
Lorne, plate, 8¾" 75.00
Lucerne, bowl, vegetable; w/lid 95.00
Madras, bowl, vegetable; Grindley, w/lid 325.00
Madras, egg cup, sm 195.00
Madras, plate, Doulton, 10" 95.00
Madras, plate, rimmed soup; Doulton, 8½" 75.00
Madras, platter, oval, 17¼" 795.00
Manilla, bowl, vegetable; w/lid, Podmore Walker, 6½x12x9¾" .600.00
Manilla, bowl, 8-sided, unmk, 8x10¼" 750.00
Manilla, plate, Podmore Walker, 6", EX 80.00
Manilla, plate, Podmore Walker, 8" 125.00
Manilla, plate, Podmore Walker, 8½" 140.00
Manilla, plate, Podmore Walker, 9½" 185.00
Marechal Neil, bowl, vegetable; w/lid 295.00
Matlock, bowl, vegetable; w/lid, 5½x11½x7" 195.00
Melbourne, gravy boat, w/underplate, Grindley 210.00
Nancy, plate, Grimwades, 10" 55.00
Nankin, bowl, vegetable; w/lid, Davenport 850.00
Ning Po, cup plate 100.00
Non-Pareil, bowl, Burgess & Leigh, 8¾", pr 225.00
Non-Pareil, bowl, vegetable; Burgess & Leigh, w/lid, 5½x12x8¼" .600.00
Non-Pareil, gravy boat, Burgess & Leigh, 4x7½", NM 250.00
Non-Pareil, pitcher, Burgess & Leigh, 6½x8¼" 250.00
Non-Pareil, pitcher, Burgess & Leigh, 7x8½" 450.00
Non-Pareil, plate, Burgess & Leigh, 8¾" 85.00
Non-Pareil, plate, Burgess & Leigh, 9¾" 110.00
Non-Pareil, platter, Burgess & Leigh, 13¼x11" 500.00
Non-Pareil, sugar bowl, w/lid, Burgess & Leigh, 5½" 350.00
Oregon, platter, TJ&J Mayer, 15½x12" 400.00
Oregon, teapot 1,095.00
Oriental, porringer, rosebud finial, G Jones, ca 1878 ....155.00
Osborne, bowl, vegetable; w/lid, Grindley 350.00
Osborne, soup tureen 895.00
Pagoda, cake plate, tab hdls, gold trim, 10" 85.00
Peking, cup, ftd, unmk, ca 1845, 2⅝x3" 125.00
Pelew, plate, Chandler, 9¼" 185.00
Pelew, platter, Challinor, 18x13¾" 1,000.00
Rhone, platter, Furnival, 15x11" 500.00
Rose, bone dish 75.00
Royal, plate, Furnival, 10" 85.00
Scinde, bowl, rectangular, Alcock, 2x10¾x8" 300.00
Scinde, bowl, vegetable; 8-sided, Alcock, 10¾" L 500.00
Scinde, creamer, 8-sided, Alcock, 5½x5" 400.00
Scinde, cup & saucer, handleless; Alcock, EX 125.00
Scinde, gravy boat, ftd, paneled, Alcock, 5½x7¾" 425.00
Scinde, pitcher, Alcock, 12½", EX 750.00
Scinde, plate, Alcock, 7" 90.00
Scinde, plate, Alcock, 9½" 165.00
Scinde, platter, Alcock, 15¾", EX 375.00
Scinde, platter, Alcock, 17½x13¾" 800.00
Scinde, sauce tureen, ped base, w/underplate, Alcock, rpr 950.00
Scinde, sugar bowl, w/lid, Alcock, 8", NM 600.00
Scinde, teapot, Alcock, 8½x8¾" 900.00
Scinde, toothbrush holder, Alcock, 7¾x3⅛", EX 650.00
Scinde, wash bowl, Alcock, 7x13½" 1,100.00
Shanghae, platter, 8-sided, Furnival, 13½x10½" 400.00
Shanghai, bowl, Grindley, 1¼x7¾" 50.00
Shanghai, bowl, Grindley, 2x10x7½" 150.00
Shanghai, butter pat, Grindley 60.00
Shanghai, cup & saucer, Grindley, 2", 6" 75.00
Shanghai, plate, Grindley, 7" 25.00
Shanghai, plate, Grindley, 10" 125.00
Shanghai, gravy boat, Grindley, 8¾" L 125.00
Shanghai, platter, Grindley, 13½x9¾" 300.00
Shanghai, sugar bowl, w/lid, Grindley, 4¼" 300.00
Shell, plate, Challinor, 8½", EX 70.00
Shien-Si, cup & saucer, handleless 150.00
Singan, sauce bowl, T Goodfellow 65.00
Sobraon, bowl, rtcl, ftd, 4x13½x10¼" 1,200.00
Sobraon, bowl, soup; 8¼" 160.00

Sobraon, platter, 15" 475.00
Sobraon, waste bowl 495.00
Sterling, platter, MWP, 16x12" 400.00
Tonquin, bowl, 8-sided, w/lid, Adams, 7½x9¾" 750.00
Tonquin, cup & saucer, handleless; Heath, 3x3⅝", 6" 175.00
Touraine, bone dish, Alcock 85.00
Touraine, bowl, berry; Alcock, 5½" 50.00
Touraine, bowl, oval, scalloped rim, Stanley, 8¾" 110.00
Touraine, bowl, scalloped, hdls, Alcock, 2½x9½" 150.00
Touraine, bowl, vegetable; w/lid, Stanley, 11¼" 375.00
Touraine, butter dish, domed lid, Stanley, 8¼" 275.00
Touraine, butter pat, unmk, 3" 50.00
Touraine, creamer, Alcock, 5½x7¼" 275.00
Touraine, cup & saucer, Alcock 100.00
Touraine, cup & saucer, Stanley, 2¼", 6" 100.00
Touraine, gravy boat, scalloped, ftd, Stanley, 3½x8½" 175.00
Touraine, gravy boat & undertray, Alcock 350.00

Touraine, pitcher, milk; Stanley, large, $1,095.00.

Touraine, pitcher, milk; sm 425.00
Touraine, plate, Alcock, 8" 65.00
Touraine, plate, Alcock, 10" 60.00
Touraine, plate, Alcock, 10½" 110.00
Touraine, plate, Stanley, 6½" 40.00
Touraine, plate, Stanley, 7⅝" 40.00
Touraine, plate, Stanley, 10" 125.00
Touraine, platter, Alcock, 15" 225.00
Touraine, platter, bacon; scalloped rim, Stanley, 10½x7" 100.00
Touraine, platter, Stanley, 15x10½" 275.00
Touraine, sugar bowl, w/lid, Alcock, 6½x8½" 400.00
Touraine, waste bowl, ca 1900, 3¼x5⅞" 175.00
Venice, teapot, Rococo style w/gold, Middler 895.00
Waldorf, creamer, New Wharf Pottery 225.00
Waldorf, cup & saucer, New Wharf Pottery 225.00
Waldorf, plate, New Wharf Pottery, 10" 85.00
Waldorf, plate, 7¾" 65.00
Waldorf, platter, ham/egg 140.00
Waldorf, soup bowl, flanged rim, New Wharf Pottery, 8¾" 85.00
Waldorf, waste bowl, New Wharf Pottery 200.00
Warwick, chamber pot, w/lid 550.00
Warwick, potty, Oriental scene, w/lid, Podmore Walker 595.00
Watteau, biscuit jar, Doulton, 7¼x6¾" 500.00
Watteau, bowl, potato; Doulton, 9⅞x3" 140.00
Watteau, cake set, Royal Doulton, 1890s, lg plate+6 sm 850.00
Watteau, gravy w/attached underplate, Doulton 495.00
Watteau, plate, New Wharf Pottery, 10" 75.00
Watteau, platter, New Wharf Pottery, 10¾x9", NM 150.00
Whampoa, cake stand 895.00
Whampoa, platter, 15½x12¾" 400.00

Flue Covers

When spring housecleaning started and the heating stove was taken down for the warm weather season, the unsightly hole where the stovepipe joined the chimney was hidden with an attractive flue cover. They were made with a colorful litho print behind glass with a chain for hanging. In a 1929 catalog, they were advertised at 16¢ each or six for 80¢. Although scarce today, some scenes were actually reverse painted on the glass itself. The most popular motifs were florals, children, animals, and lovely ladies. Occasionally flue covers were made in sets of three — one served a functional purpose, while the others were added to provide a more attractive wall arrangement. They range in size from 7" to 14", but 9" is the average.

For further information we recommend *Flue Covers, Collector's Value Guide*, by Jim Meckley II, available from Collector Books or your local bookstore.

Dog's portrait, 12x10", $75.00 to $85.00.

Baby Lambs, boy & girl w/3 lambs, 7½", from $85 to 95.00
Blowing Bubbles, blond girl w/bubble pipe, 7¾", from $50 to 60.00
Cherub, winged figure in thoughtful pose, 7½", from $55 to 65.00
Christmas girl, brunette in red cap w/holly, 11¾", from $55 to ...65.00
Collecting Firewood, winter cabin scene, 8½x7", from $50 to 60.00
Dark Town Strutters Ball, Black children in finery, 9½", from $175 to ..200.00
Fall Delight, apples & nuts among greenery, 10", from $65 to 75.00
Feathered Chapeau, girl w/lg feathered hat, 6½x8¼", from $90 to .100.00
Flower Boy, Oriental child w/flowers, 9½", from $50 to 60.00
Kittens Caddy, cat in coat & bonnet, 7¼x9", from $70 to 80.00
Lassie, Collie portrait, 9½", from $75 to 85.00
Maria w/Roses, brunette w/curls & pk roses, 8½", from $85 to 95.00
May Dance, 3 girls dance outdoors, 14", from $90 to 100.00
Olivia, lady w/brn hair in updo, curls fr face, 9½", from $60 to ...70.00
Over the Fence, couple talk at fence, 9½", from $60 to 65.00
Pansies, mc flowers & much greenery, 9½", from $75 to 85.00
Pears on the Tree, deep yel fruit on branch, 9½", from $75 to 85.00
Peri & Pixy, boy & girl w/colored hats, 9½", from $80 to 90.00
Red Roses in Vase, 8¼x7", from $85 to 95.00
Resting w/Storm, lady w/pony, 9¼", from $65 to 75.00
Sabrina's Poppies, brunette w/long hair & poppies, 8", from $75 to 80.00
Springtime, lady in peach dress among many flowers, 8", from $55 to .60.00
Storm, lady & 2 children beneath shawl, 9½", from $85 to 95.00
Swallows, 3 birds on branch, brn tones, 9½", from $85 to 95.00
Tulip Garden, thatched cottage & tulips, 8¼x6¾", from $50 to .60.00
Turban, girl w/curly hair wearing sm turban, 7¾", from $60 to 70.00
Under the Oak Tree, courting couple, 9¼", from $55 to 65.00
Victorian Beauty, lady w/lt brn hair in pk, 9½", from $90 to 110.00
Violet Lady, blond w/violets in hair & hands, 7¾", from $50 to ..60.00

Wintertime, 2 children in hats & coats, 5¾", from $55 to **65.00**
Young Master, boy in wht wig & lace collar, 7¾", from $50 to **60.00**
Zenobia, brunette w/long streaming hair & pk rose, 9½", from $85 to ..**95.00**

Folk Art

That the creative energies of the mind ever spark innovations in functional utilitarian channels as well as toward playful frivolity is well documented in the study of American folk art. While the average early settler rarely had free time to pursue art for its own sake, his creative energy exemplified itself in fashioning useful objects carved or otherwise ornamented beyond the scope of pure practicality. After the advent of the Industrial Revolution, the pace of everyday living became more leisurely, and country folk found they had extra time. Not accustomed to sitting idle, many turned to carving, painting, or weaving. Whirligigs, imaginative toys for the children, and whimsies of all types resulted. Though often rather crude, this type of early art represents a segment of our heritage and as such has become valued by collectors.

Values given for drawings, paintings, and theorems are 'in frame' unless noted otherwise. See also Baskets; Decoys; Frakturs; Samplers; Trade Signs; Weather Vanes; Wood Carvings.

Birdhouse, lighthouse, pnt wood, British flag in distress, 28x25x12" ...**375.00**
Birdhouse, log cabin w/twig-like sides, foiled windows, 9x7x6" .**130.00**
Birdhouse, pnt wood, chimney & decorations, 1930-40s, 23x14x11" .**265.00**
Birdhouse, pnt wood, spool chimney, dowel perch, 1930, 9½x6x5" ..**85.00**
Birdhouse, 3-masted clipper ship form, pnt wood, 1930s, 26" **625.00**
Box, balsawood cat shape w/silver pnt & blk spots, 17" **180.00**

Bust of chieftan with full headdress, polychrome on composition, glass eyes, 29", $1,150.00.

Calligraphic drawing, lion standing, blk & red ink, 1850s, 10x10" .**475.00**
Calligraphic drawing, officer on horse, ink on paper, 21x16"+fr ..**1,495.00**
Calligraphic drawing, Washington on horsebk, mc, SG Hayes, 19x15" ..**1,500.00**
Carnival ball-toss pin, pnt as lady, 4-color, 17", VG **775.00**
Chair, stag horns w/cvd medallions form body, uphl seat, 37" ..**1,750.00**
Charcoal & crayon drawing, girl w/puppies, 11x15"+fr **250.00**
Charcoal drawing, dog seated, gazebo/garden beyond, sgn, 1890s, 14x16" ..**50.00**
Cvg, Indian bust, buff-colored sandstone, Popeye Reed, 9½" **525.00**
Ferris wheel, wood, orig red & blk pnt, 20th C, 19½" **75.00**
Key holder, wooden Black man/lady, stereotypical, 4-hooks, 1930s **65.00**
Oil on board, dog & pups in barn door, 1890s, 18x10" **135.00**
Oil on board, fruit still life w/pitcher, 38x23" **225.00**
Oil on board, identified lady w/hand to ear, 1810s, 21x16"+fr ...**440.00**
Oil on board, portrait of tiger cat, 19th C, 18x12"+fr **7,475.00**
Oil on canvas, New England seascape w/church, 40x22" **350.00**
Spencerian drawing, birds on nest, pen/ink, OH, 1903, 19x26" ..**220.00**
Spencerian drawing, dove on olive branch, mc inks, gold fr, 27x22" ..**225.00**
Theorem on velvet, bee skep w/flowers, sgn, 20th C, 21x20" **525.00**
Theorem on velvet, fruit basket w/bird, D Ellinger, 11x13" **715.00**
Theorem on velvet, roses/foliage, wear, 12½x16½" **100.00**
Theorem on velvet, strawberries/fruit/bird in basket, DYE, 14x16" ..**1,700.00**
Toy, articulated acrobatic man on brd, pnt details, 1900s, 3x1½" **265.00**
Whirligig, man chopping wood, old weathered pnt on wood, 1900s .**220.00**
Whirligig, man dancing & fiddle player, wood/tin/wire, rpr, 35" ..**220.00**
Whirligig, man w/swivel arms (vanes missing), weathered, 44" ..**1,375.00**
Whirligig, Nantucket sailor, cvd/pnt, 15½", EX **575.00**
Whirligig, paddle-arm man, 1-pc wooden body w/pnt, 1930s, 13x8" ..**185.00**
Whirligig, soldier, cvd wood w/mc pnt, 9", pr **1,500.00**
Whirligig, Uncle Sam, wood & sheet metal, MA, ca 1900, 72x48x28" ..**12,650.00**

Fostoria

The Fostoria Glass Company was built in 1887 at Fostoria, Ohio, but by 1891 it had moved to Moundsville, West Virginia. During the next two decades, they produced many lines of pressed patterned tableware and lamps. Their most famous pattern, American, was introduced in 1915 and was produced continuously until 1986 in well over two hundred different pieces. From 1920 to 1925, top artists designed tablewares in colored glass — canary (vaseline), amber, blue, orchid, green, and ebony — in pressed patterns as well as etched designs. By the late '30s, Fostoria was recognized as the largest producer of handmade glassware in the world. The company ceased operations in Moundsville in 1986.

Many items from both the American and Coin Glass lines have been reproduced by Lancaster Colony. In some cases the new glass is superior in quality to the old. Since the 1950s, Indiana Glass has produced a pattern called 'Whitehall' that looks very much like Fostoria's American, though with slight variations. Because Indiana's is not handmade glass, the lines of the 'cube' pattern and the edges of the items are sharp and untapered in comparison to the fire-polished originals. Three-footed pieces lack the 'toe' and instead have a peg-like foot, and the rays on the bottoms of the American examples are narrower than on the Whitehall counterparts. The Home Interiors Company offers several pieces of American look-alikes which were not even produced in the United States. Be sure of your dealer and study the books suggested below to become more familiar with the original line.

Coin Glass reproductions are flooding the market. Among items you may encounter are an 8" round bowl, 9" oval bowl, 8¼" wedding bowl, 4½" candlesticks, urn with lid, 6¼" candy jar with lid, footed comport, sugar, and creamer; there could possibly be others. Colors in production are crystal, green, blue, and red. The red color is very good, but the blue is not the original color, nor is the emerald green. Buyer beware!

For further information see *Elegant Glassware of the Depression Era* by Gene Florence; *Fostoria Glassware, 1887 – 1982,* by Frances Bones; *Fostoria Stemware, The Crystal for America, Fostoria Tableware, 1924 – 1943, Fostoria Tableware, 1944–1986,* and *Fostoria, Useful and Ornamental,* all by Milbra Long and Emily Seate; and *Fostoria, Books I and II,* by Ann Kerr. *Glass Animals and Figural Flower Frogs of the Depression Era* by Lee Garmon and Dick Spencer offers an in-depth look at that particular aspect of Fostoria's production. (See also Glass Animals.) Their addresses are listed in the Directory under Illinois. Items with (+) at the end of the lines have been reproduced; prices are for original issues. Our advisor is Deborah Maggard; she is listed in the Directory under Ohio.

American, crystal, ashtray, oval, 3⅞" **9.00**
American, crystal, bell **395.00**
American, crystal, bonbon, 3-ftd, 6" **15.00**
American, crystal, bottle, water; 44-oz, 9¼" **625.00**
American, crystal, bowl, cupped, 7" **55.00**
American, crystal, bowl, finger; smooth edge, 4½" **40.00**
American, crystal, bowl, fruit; flared, 4¾" **15.00**
American, crystal, bowl, fruit; shallow, 13" **65.00**
American, crystal, bowl, hdls, 4½" **12.00**
American, crystal, bowl, relish/celery; 3-part, 11" **30.00**

American, crystal, bowl, vegetable; oval, 9" 25.00
American, crystal, candlestick, 2-light, rnd ft, 4⅜" 35.00
American, crystal, coaster, 3¾" 9.00
American, crystal, comport, w/lid, 5" 30.00
American, crystal, cup, punch; flared rim 11.00
American, crystal, goblet, claret; #2056, 7-oz, 4⅞" 55.00
American, crystal, goblet, tea; #2056, low ft, 12-oz, 5¾" 14.00
American, crystal, hair receiver, 3x3" 300.00
American, crystal, jar, pickle; w/pointed lid, 6" 350.00
American, crystal, lamp, hurricane; complete, 12" 195.00
American, crystal, pitcher, ice lip, flat bottom, ½-gal, 8¼" 85.00
American, crystal, plate, bread & butter; 6" 10.00
American, crystal, plate, cake; hdls, 10" 27.50
American, crystal, platter, oval, 12" 55.00
American, crystal, sauce boat & liner 60.00
American, crystal, shaker, 3½", ea 10.00
American, crystal, syrup, #2056½, Sani-Cut server, 6½-oz 80.00
American, crystal, tray, rectangular, 5x2½" 80.00
American, crystal, tray, sandwich; w/center hdl, 12" 35.00
American, crystal, tumbler, water; #2056, ftd, 9-oz, 4⅞" 15.00
American, crystal, urn, ped ft, sq, 6" 30.00
American, crystal, vase, str side, 8" 40.00
American, crystal, vase, swung; 10" 200.00

Baroque, Vases: Azure, 7", $145.00; Gold Tint, 8", $140.00. (Photo courtesy Milbra Long and Emily Seate)

Baroque, bl, bowl, celery; 11" 45.00
Baroque, bl, bowl, cereal; 6" 42.00
Baroque, bl, creamer, ind, 3¼" 30.00
Baroque, bl, platter, oval, 12" 65.00
Baroque, bl, tray, for ind creamer & sugar bowl, 6¼" 25.00
Baroque, bl or yel, bowl, 3-ftd, 7" 25.00
Baroque, crystal, bowl, cream soup 35.00
Baroque, crystal, bowl, vegetable; oval, 9½" 25.00
Baroque, crystal, candlestick, 5½" 9.00
Baroque, crystal, plate, 6" 3.00
Baroque, yel, candelabrum, 3-light, 24-lustre, 9½" 175.00
Baroque, yel, mayonnaise, w/liner, 5½" 40.00
Baroque, yel, sherbet, 5-oz, 3¾" 17.50
Baroque, yel, tumbler, tea; ftd, 12-oz, 6" 30.00
Buttercup, crystal, bowl, baked apple; #2364, 6" 18.00
Buttercup, crystal, candlestick, duo; #6023, 5½" 35.00
Buttercup, crystal, mayonnaise, #2364, 5" 25.00
Buttercup, crystal, relish, #2364, 2-part, 6½x5" 22.50
Buttercup, crystal, stem, goblet; #6030, low, 10-oz, 6⅜" 22.50
Camelia, crystal, bowl, triangular, 3-ftd, 7⅛" 18.00
Camelia, crystal, ice bucket 80.00
Camelia, crystal, stem, claret-wine; #6036, 3¼-oz, 4¾" 35.00
Camelia, crystal, vase, bud; 6" 30.00
Century, crystal, bowl, snack; ftd, 6¼" 14.00
Century, crystal, candlestick, triple, 7¾" 40.00
Century, crystal, shakers, ind, 2⅜", pr 15.00

Chintz, crystal, bowl, fruit; #2496, 5" 30.00
Chintz, crystal, jelly, #2496, w/lid, 7½" 85.00
Chintz, crystal, sauce boat, #2496, oval, divided 65.00
Coin, amber, ashtray, #1372/123, 5" 17.50
Coin, amber, candy jar, #1372/347, w/lid, 6⅜" 25.00
Coin, amber, jelly, #1372/448 .....17.50
Coin, amber, lamp, patio; #1372/466, electric, 16⅝" 175.00
Coin, amber, salver, #1372/630, ftd, tall, 6½" 110.00
Coin, amber, urn, #1372/829, ftd, w/lid, 12¾" 85.00
Coin, bl, ashtray, oblong, #1372/115 .....20.00
Coin, bl, creamer, #1372/680 .....16.00
Coin, bl, lamp, coach; #1372/321, electric, 13½" 195.00
Coin, bl, vase, bud; #1372/799, 8" 125.00
Coin, crystal, bowl, #1372/179, rnd, 8" 25.00
Coin, crystal, condiment tray, #1372/738, 9⅝" 40.00
Coin, crystal, nappy, #1372/495, 4½" 22.00
Coin, crystal, stem, wine; #1372/26, 5-oz, 4" 35.00
Coin, crystal, tumbler, iced tea; #1372/58, 14-oz, 5⅛" 35.00
Coin, crystal, vase, #1372/818, ftd, 10" 45.00
Coin, gr, bowl, #1372/189, oval, 9" 75.00
Coin, gr, cigarette holder, #1372/372, w/ashtray lid 90.00
Coin, olive, candle holder, #1372/316, 4½", pr 30.00
Coin, olive, pitcher, #1372/453, 32-oz, 6⅜" 55.00
Coin, ruby, candy box, #1372/354, w/lid, 4⅛" 65.00
Coin, ruby, plate, #1372/550, 8" 40.00
Colony, crystal, ashtray, rnd, 3" 7.00
Colony, crystal, bowl, console; 13" 35.00
Colony, crystal, bowl, cupped, 8" 35.00
Colony, crystal, bowl, finger; 4¾" 45.00
Colony, crystal, bowl, high ft, 10½" 95.00
Colony, crystal, bowl, sq, 5½" 10.00
Colony, crystal, candlestick, w/8 prisms, 7½" 75.00
Colony, crystal, cup, ftd, 6-oz 7.50
Colony, crystal, pitcher, ice lip, 48-oz 200.00
Colony, crystal, plate, cake; hdls, 10" 22.00
Colony, crystal, relish, 3-part, hdls, 10½" 20.00
Colony, crystal, stem, wine; 3½-oz, 4¼" 30.00
Colony, crystal, tumbler, ftd, 5-oz, 4½" 18.00
Corsage, crystal, bowl, #2484, hdls, 10" 60.00
Corsage, crystal, comport, cheese; 3¼" 20.00
Corsage, crystal, stem, wine; #6014, 3-oz, 5¼" 30.00

Fairfax, amber, Butter dish, $115.00; Salad dressing bottle, $125.00. (Photo courtesy Milbra Long and Emily Seate)

Fairfax, amber, bouillon, ftd 10.00
Fairfax, amber, bowl, centerpc; 15" 25.00
Fairfax, amber, creamer, ftd 7.00
Fairfax, amber, plate, salad; 7½" 3.00
Fairfax, amber, platter, oval, 15" 27.00
Fairfax, amber, stem, claret; 4-oz, 6" 25.00
Fairfax, gr or topaz, bowl, cereal; 6" 15.00

Fairfax, gr or topaz, candlestick, 3" 15.00
Fairfax, gr or topaz, grapefruit liner 17.50
Fairfax, gr or topaz, plate, dinner; 10¼" 30.00
Fairfax, gr or topaz, relish, 11½" 13.00
Fairfax, gr or topaz, sugar bowl lid 25.00
Fairfax, rose, bl or orchid, ashtray, 5½" 20.00
Fairfax, rose, bl or orchid, bowl, 12" 45.00
Fairfax, rose, bl or orchid, comport, 7" 35.00
Fairfax, rose, bl or orchid, pickle, 8½" 25.00
Fairfax, rose, bl or orchid, plate, chop; 13" 25.00
Fairfax, rose, bl or orchid, stem, sherbet; low, 6-oz, 4¼" 18.00
Heather, crystal, bowl, flared, 8" 32.50
Heather, crystal, butter dish, w/lid, ¼-lb 75.00
Heather, crystal, saucer 4.50
Heather, crystal, tray, muffin; hdls, 9½" 35.00
Heather, crystal, vase, #4143, ftd, 6" 55.00
Hermitage, amber, gr or topaz, bowl, #2449, ftd, 10" 20.00
Hermitage, amber, gr or topaz, saucer, #2449 ....3.50
Hermitage, Azure, fruit cocktail, #2449, ftd, 5-oz, 2⅜" 12.00
Hermitage, Azure, relish, #2449, 2-part, 6" 15.00
Hermitage, crystal, bowl, finger; #2449½, 4½" 4.00
Hermitage, crystal, tumbler, #2449½, 5-oz, 3⅞" 5.00
Hermitage, Wisteria, plate, #2449, 8" 22.00
Jamestown, amber or brn, bowl, salad; #2719/211, 10" 21.00
Jamestown, amethyst or gr, tray, muffin; #2719/726, hdls, 9⅜" 20.00
Jamestown, bl, pk or ruby, relish, #2719/620, 2-part, 9⅛" 37.50
Jamestown, bl, pk or ruby, tumbler, #2719/64, 12-oz, 5⅛" 26.00
Jamestown, brn, shakers, #2719/653, w/chrome lids, 3½", pr 26.00
Jamestown, crystal or gr, creamer, #2719/681, ftd, 3½" 17.50
June, crystal, bonbon 12.50
June, crystal, candlestick, 2" 14.00
June, crystal, comport, #2375, 7" 25.00
June, crystal, oyster cocktail, 5½-oz 16.00
June, crystal, plate, dinner; 10¼" 37.50
June, crystal, sherbet, low, 6-oz, 4¼" 12.00
June, rose or bl, bowl, mint; 3-ftd, 4½" 40.00
June, rose or bl, candlestick, Grecian; 3" 50.00
June, rose or bl, plate, torte; 14" 100.00
June, rose or bl, sugar pail 225.00
June, rose or pk, creamer, tea 60.00
June, rose or pk, plate, lemon 25.00
June, topaz, bowl, 10" 65.00
June, topaz, comport, #2400, 5" 35.00
June, topaz, goblet, claret; 4-oz, 6" 75.00
June, topaz, plate, cream soup; 7½" 7.50
June, topaz, sauce boat 100.00
June, topaz, tumbler, ftd, 2½-oz 45.00
Kashmir, bl, bowl, centerpc; 12" 50.00
Kashmir, bl, bowl, fruit; 5" 15.00
Kashmir, bl, comport, 6" 45.00
Kashmir, bl, cup, AD; ftd 55.00
Kashmir, bl, plate, salad; rnd, 7" 8.00
Kashmir, bl, sauce boat, w/liner 125.00
Kashmir, bl, stem, ftd, 12-oz 37.00
Kashmir, bl, stem, wine; 2½-oz 42.00
Kashmir, yel or gr, bowl, cream soup 22.00
Kashmir, yel or gr, bowl, soup; 7" 35.00
Kashmir, yel or gr, candlestick, 9½" 40.00
Kashmir, yel or gr, cruet, oil; ftd 275.00
Kashmir, yel or gr, cup 15.00
Kashmir, yel or gr, plate, dinner; 10" 45.00
Kashmir, yel or gr, stem, parfait; 5½-oz 30.00
Lido, crystal, comport, 5¾" 22.50
Lido, crystal, relish, 3-part, 10" 30.00
Lido, crystal, tidbit, flat, 3-ftd, 8¼" 20.00
Mayflower, crystal, bonbon, #2560, 3-ftd, 7¼" 22.50
Mayflower, crystal, creamer, #2560 ....12.00
Mayflower, crystal, plate, #2560, 8½" 15.00
Mayflower, crystal, tumbler, juice; #6020, ftd, 5-oz, 4⅞" 17.50
Meadow Rose, crystal, bottle, salad dressing; #2083, 6½" 235.00
Meadow Rose, crystal, bowl, sweetmeat; sq, 6" 17.50
Meadow Rose, crystal, celery, 11" 37.50
Meadow Rose, crystal, vase, #4128, 5" 75.00
Navarre, bl or pk, dinner bell 85.00
Navarre, bl or pk, stem, claret; #6106, 4½-oz, 6" 85.00
Navarre, bl or pk, stem, water; #6106, 10-oz, 7⅝" 55.00
Navarre, crystal, bonbon, #2496, ftd, 7⅜" 27.50
Navarre, crystal, candlestick, dbl; #2472, 5" 42.50
Navarre, crystal, celery, #2440, 9" 30.00
Navarre, crystal, creamer, #2440, ftd, 4¼" 20.00
Navarre, crystal, mayonnaise, #2496½, 3-pc 67.50
Navarre, crystal, plate, dinner; #2440, 9½" 50.00
Navarre, crystal, relish, #2496, 2-part, sq, 6" 32.50
Navarre, crystal, sauce dish, #2496, 6½x5¼" 125.00
Navarre, crystal, shakers, #2364, flat, 3¼", pr 65.00
Navarre, crystal, stem, sherbet; #6106, low, 6-oz, 4⅜" 24.00
Navarre, crystal, tumbler, water; #6106, ftd, 10-oz, 5⅜" 25.00
New Garland, amber or topaz, bowl, soup; 7" 22.00
New Garland, amber or topaz, creamer, ftd 15.00
New Garland, amber or topaz, mayonnaise, hdls 18.00
New Garland, amber or topaz, platter, 12" 35.00
New Garland, amber or topaz, stem, sherbet; #4120, low, 7-oz 15.00
New Garland, amber or topaz, tumbler, #4120, 5-oz 12.00
New Garland, rose, bowl, finger; #4121 ....15.00
New Garland, rose, candlestick, 2" 20.00
New Garland, rose, pitcher, ftd 250.00
New Garland, rose, sauce boat liner 20.00
New Garland, rose, stem, sherbet; #6002, high 20.00
New Garland, rose, tumbler, #6002, ftd, 5-oz 15.00
Romance, crystal, bowl, #6023, ftd, blown, 9¼" 125.00
Romance, crystal, candlestick, #2594, 3-light, 8" 50.00
Romance, crystal, shakers, #2364, 2⅝", pr 55.00
Romance, crystal, tumbler, #6017, ftd, 12-oz, 6" 27.50
Royal, amber or gr, ashtray, #2350, 3½" 22.50
Royal, amber or gr, bowl, #2324, ftd, 10" 45.00
Royal, amber or gr, bowl, #2367, ftd, 7" 35.00
Royal, amber or gr, bowl, console; #2329, 11" 22.00
Royal, amber or gr, bowl, cream soup; #2350, flat 16.00
Royal, amber or gr, candy, #2331, 3-part, w/lid 75.00
Royal, amber or gr, cologne, #2322, tall 50.00
Royal, amber or gr, creamer, #2315½, ftd, flat 18.00
Royal, amber or gr, ice bucket, #2378 ....60.00
Royal, amber or gr, plate, chop; #2350, 15" 40.00
Royal, amber or gr, plate, salad; #2350, 7½" 4.00
Royal, amber or gr, sauce boat, w/liner 135.00
Royal, amber or gr, stem, sherbet; #869, low, 6-oz 12.50
Royal, amber or gr, stem, wine; #869, 2¾-oz 32.50
Royal, amber or gr, sugar bowl lid, #2350½ 115.00
Royal, amber or gr, tumbler, #5000, ftd, 5-oz 14.00
Seville, amber, bowl, #2297, flared, deep, 12" 30.00
Seville, amber, bowl, baker; #2350, oval, 9" 25.00
Seville, amber, bowl, fruit; #2350, 5½" 10.00
Seville, amber, candlestick, #2324, 2" 18.00
Seville, amber, creamer, #2350½, ftd 12.50
Seville, amber, plate, bread & butter; #2350, 6" 4.00
Seville, amber, platter, #2350, 12" 35.00
Seville, amber, stem, sherbet; #870, low 12.50
Seville, amber, tumbler, #5084, ftd, 2-oz 35.00

Seville, gr, bowl, #2315, low ft, 7" 20.00
Seville, gr, bowl, cream soup; #2350, flat 17.50
Seville, gr, bowl, ftd, 10" 42.50
Seville, gr, celery, #2350, 11" 17.50
Seville, gr, grapefruit, #945½, blown 45.00
Seville, gr, plate, dinner; #2350, 10½" 42.50
Seville, gr, sauce boat, #2350 ....75.00
Seville, gr, stem, water; #870 ....25.00
Sun Ray, crystal, bonbon, hdld 16.00
Sun Ray, crystal, candelabra, 2-light 45.00
Sun Ray, crystal, cup 12.00
Sun Ray, crystal, plate, 16" 70.00
Sun Ray, crystal, stem, fruit cocktail; 3½-oz, 3¼" 12.00
Sun Ray, crystal, tumbler, whiskey; #2510½, 2-oz, 2¼" 12.00
Trojan, rose, ashtray, #2350, sm 30.00
Trojan, rose, bowl, mint; #2394, 3-ftd, 4½" 25.00
Trojan, rose, bowl, scroll; #2395, 10" 75.00
Trojan, rose, candlestick, scroll; #2395½, 5" 65.00
Trojan, rose, plate, canape; #2375 ....30.00
Trojan, rose, relish, #2350, 3-part, rnd, 8¾" 45.00
Trojan, rose, sweetmeat, #2375 ....18.00
Trojan, topaz, bowl, bouillon; #2375, ftd 18.00
Trojan, topaz, bowl, centerpc; #2394, ftd, 12" 45.00
Trojan, topaz, bowl, cereal; #2375, 6½" 37.50
Trojan, topaz, comport, #5299 or #2400, 6" 30.00
Trojan, topaz, goblet, water; #5299, 10-oz, 8¼" 27.50
Trojan, topaz, plate, dinner; #2375, sm, 9½" 20.00
Trojan, topaz, shakers, #2375, pr 80.00
Trojan, topaz, tumbler, #5099, ftd, 12-oz, 6" 30.00
Versailles, bl, bowl, finger; #869/2283, w/6" liner 75.00
Versailles, bl, candlestick, #2395, 3" 35.00
Versailles, bl, goblet, claret; #5098 or #5099, 4-oz, 6" 145.00
Versailles, bl, plate, salad; #2375, 7½" 12.00
Versailles, bl, tray, #2375, center hdl, 11" 65.00

Versailles, blue, Water stem, ten-ounce, 8¼", $40.00. (Photo courtesy Gene Florence)

Versailles, pk, gr or yel, cup, AD; #2375 ....40.00
Versailles, pk or gr, bowl, #2395, ftd, 12" 35.00
Versailles, pk or gr, bowl, baker; #2375, 9" 55.00
Versailles, pk or gr, oyster cocktail, #5098 or #5099 ....22.50
Versailles, pk or gr, sherbet; #5098/5099, high, 6" 20.00
Versailles, yel, bowl, #2395, 3-ftd, 6" 30.00
Versailles, yel, candy, #2394, w/lid, ½-lb 175.00
Versailles, yel, grapefruit, #5082½ 45.00
Versailles, yel, plate, cake; #2375, hdls, 10" 30.00
Versailles, yel, vase, #2417, 8" 165.00
Vesper, amber, bowl, #2350, rnd 50.00
Vesper, amber, ice bucket, #2378 ....70.00
Vesper, amber, stem, cocktail; #5093, 3-oz 27.50
Vesper, bl, candlestick, #2394, 3" 40.00
Vesper, bl, plate, dinner; #2350, sm, 9½" 35.00
Vesper, bl, vase, #2292, 8" 150.00
Vesper, gr, bowl, cream soup; #2350, flat 25.00
Vesper, gr, creamer, #2350½, ftd 14.00
Vesper, gr, sauce boat, #2350, w/liner 135.00

Fostoria Glass Specialty Company

The Fostoria Glass Specialty Company was founded in Fostoria, Ohio, in 1899. In 1910 they were purchased by General Electric. The new owners had an interest in developing a high-quality lustre-type art glass able to complete with the very successful glassware produced by Tiffany. They hired Walter Hicks, who had previously worked for Tiffany, to help develop the line they called Iris. Their efforts were extremely successful. The art glass they developed was cased and iridescent, very similar to Steuben's Aurene. Colors included green, tan, white, blue, yellow, and rose. It was made in several patterns, including Heart and Leaf, Leaf and Tendrils, Heart and Spider Webbing, and Lustred Dot. Although the main thrust of their production was lamp shades, vases and bowls were made as well. Iris was made for only four years, since gold was required in its production and manufacturing costs were very high. It was marked with only a paper label, without which identification is sometimes difficult. Look for a pronounced, well-finished pontil that shows the glass layers represented. Most items show a layer of white, which Fostoria called Calcite, as did Steuben. Very little has been written on the history of this company, but for more information refer to *The Collector's Encyclopedia of Art Glass* by John Shuman (Collector Books), and *Fostoria Ohio Glass, Vol II*, by Melvin L. Murray (self published).

Our advisor for this category is Frank W. Ford; he is listed in the Directory under Massachusetts.

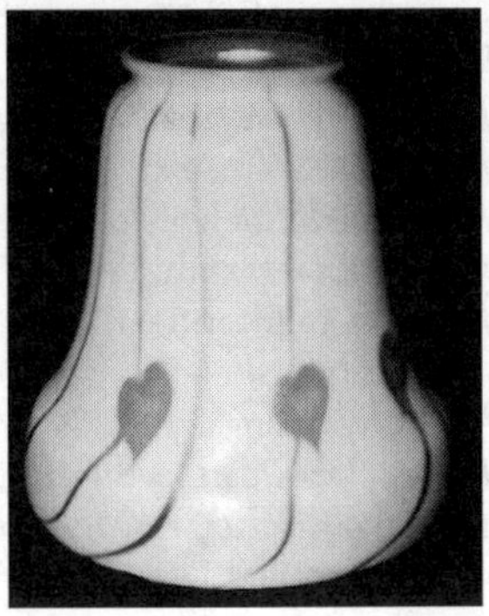

Shade, stylized leaves and vines on pearly white, gold interior, bell form, 4½", $300.00. (Photo courtesy Frank W. Ford)

Rose bowl, Iris, gold lustre leaves on opal, ovoid 500.00
Shade, festoons, gr on opal, 7" 250.00
Shade, leaves & vines, gr & gold on opal, 4-sided 250.00
Vase, Iris, gold lustre, pinched-in sides, narrow neck, ftd, 4½" ..600.00
Vase, Iris, gold lustre w/gr leaves/vines, sq top, 12" 2,000.00

Frakturs

Fraktur is a German style of black letter text type. To collectors the fraktur is a type of hand-lettered document used by the people of German descent who settled in the areas of Pennsylvania, New Jersey, Maryland, Virginia, North and South Carolina, Ohio, Kentucky, and Ontario. These documents recorded births and baptisms and were used as bookplates and as certificates of honor. They were elaborately decorated with colorful folk-art borders of hearts, birds, angels, and flowers. Examples by recognized artists and those with an unusual decorative motif bring prices well into the thousands of dollars; in fact, some have sold at major auction houses well in excess of $5,000.00. Frakturs made in the late 1700s after the invention of the printing press provided the writer with a prepared text that he needed only to fill in at his own discretion. The next step in the evolution of machine-printed frakturs combined woodblock-printed decorations along with the text which the 'artist' sometimes enhanced with color. By the mid-1800s, even the coloring was done by machine. The vorschrift was a handwritten example prepared by a fraktur teacher to demonstrate his skill in lettering and decorating. These are often considered to be the finest of frakturs. Those dated before 1820 are most valuable.

The practice of fraktur art began to diminish after 1830 but hung on even to the early years of this century among the Pennsylvania Germans ingrained with such customs. Our advisor for this category is Frederick S. Weiser; he is listed in the Directory under Pennsylvania. (Mr. Weiser has provided our text, but being unable to physically examine the frakturs listed below cannot vouch for their authenticity, age, or condition. When requesting information, please include a self-addressed stamped evelope.) These prices were realized at various reputable auction galleries in the East and Midwest. Unless otherwise noted, values are for examples in excellent condition. Note: Be careful not to confuse frakturs with prints, calligraphy, English-language marriage certificates, Lord's Prayers, etc.

Key:
lp — laid paper
pr — printed
p/i — pen and ink
wc — watercolored
wp — wove paper

Birth Record

Cut-out/pin-prick design w/wc flowers, 1883, 14x15"+fr 220.00
P/i/wc, heart/birds/flowers/etc, 1886, 6⅜x8"+fr 220.00
P/i/wc, Martin Brechal, G colors, PA, 1808, minor damage, 13x8"+fr ...1,100.00
P/i/wc, tulip/horse head/border, pasted-on paper heart, 10x12" ..415.00
P/i/wc, tulips/hearts/text, PA, 1820, minor damage, 12x14"+fr ..740.00
P/i/wc/lp, blk/brn/olive-yel, flowers, 1808, faded, 13½x12½" 385.00
P/i/wc/lp, floral wreath, PA, 7x9"+mahog veneer fr 525.00
P/i/wc/lp, floral/heart/text, PA, 1782, wear/rpr, 13x15"+fr 385.00
P/i/wc/lp, flowers/tulips verse, Brechal, 1811, 13x16"+rpl fr 770.00
P/i/wc/lp, flying angel, PA, 1795, rebacked on paper, 17x14"+fr ..3,400.00
P/i/wc/wp, heart/parrots/tulips/fans, PA, 1820, 13x16" 2,500.00
Pr/hc, Johann Ritter, PA, 1838, 17x13"+fr 330.00
Pr/wc, Gerburts und Taufschein, OH, 1841, glued on brd, 16x13"+fr ..80.00
Pr/wc, Gerburts und Taufschein, Lang, PA, 1826, 13x14"+fr 330.00
Pr/wc, Gerburts und Taufschein, Ritter, PA, 1798, 16x13"+fr 150.00

Miscellaneous

Bookplate, p/i/wc/wp, 1928, new fr, 5x7⅜" 415.00
House blessing, pr/wc, strong colors, PA, 1785, 17x13"+fr 385.00
Vorschrift, p/i/wc, flowers/border, mc, PA, mid 1800s, 8x12"+fr ..1,200.00

Frames

Styles in picture frames have changed with the fashion of the day, but those that especially interest today's collectors are the deep shadow boxes made of fine woods such as walnut or cherry, those with Art Nouveau influence, and the oak frames decorated with molded gesso and gilt from the Victorian era. Our advisor for this category is Michael Hinton; he is listed in the Directory under Pennsylvania.

Note: Unless another date is given, frames described in the following listings are from the nineteenth century.

Bird's-eye veneer ogee, gilt liner, 33x27" 250.00
Black walnut & gold leaf, oval opening, Pat 1871, 34½x30½" .1,150.00
Brass, oval, convex glass, 14x20" 70.00
Brass & pietra dura, pierced birds/lilies, in wood surround, 10" H .700.00

Brass and pietra dura, pierced foliate standards with engraved florals, Victorian, 18", $2,500.00. (Photo courtesy William Doyle Galleries)

Brass filigree, gilt, 5" dia 150.00
Cast brass, Cupid design, 20x12" 225.00
Cherry, Emp, half-columns & corner blocks, old pnt, 17x13" 425.00
Cherry w/pearl heart at ea cross corner, folky style, 15x11" 75.00
Chip cvd, old red pnt & natural, easel bk, 7x5" 250.00
Copper repousse w/human-head crest w/bat-like wings, 1890s, 50x30" ...2,600.00
Gilt wood, hinged at sides on cvd base, 11¾" H 25.00
Gold-washed metal, Nouveau emb floral, Pat 1897, 8x6" 65.00
Oak, gesso, emb florals 18x24" 125.00
Pine & walnut, 2¾" molding, old finish, 10¾x14½" 125.00
Polychrome w/artificial graining, 1930s, 19x13" 90.00
Poplar, cross corners w/cvd & appl rosettes, 17x15" 110.00
SP, crown/Cupid crest, scroll ft, easel bk, 8½" 275.00
Walnut, oval liner, incised decor, dtd 1871, 20x30" 950.00
Walnut Victorian crisscross, cvd leaves at corners, 22x18" 165.00

Frances Ware

Frances Ware, produced in the 1880s by Hobbs, Brockunier and Company of Wheeling, West Virginia, is a term refering to the decoration or finish used in the production of some of their glassware lines. Hobnail (Dewdrop) is the most commonly found of these lines, though Swirl and on occasion Quartered Block with Stars were also finished with the frosted surface and amber-stained band that defines the Frances Ware indication. Though in general collectors also tend to regard examples in crystal with simply an amber-stained band as Frances Ware, according to *Hobbs, Brockunier & Co. Glass* by Nelia and Tom Bredehoft (Collector Books), this is incorrect. The company called this finish 'decorated #7.' To evaluate examples in crystal with amber stain, deduct 10% from the values given below, which are strictly for the frosted finish. Our advisors for this category are Betty and Clarence Maier; they are listed in the Directory under Pennsylvania.

Hobnail, bowl, ftd, berry pontil, 6x10" 150.00
Hobnail, bowl, no flange, 9" sq 85.00
Hobnail, bowl, oblong, 8" 75.00
Hobnail, bowl, sq, 7½" 70.00
Hobnail, bowl, 2½x5½" 30.00
Hobnail, bowl, 7½", from $65 to 75.00
Hobnail, bowl, 8" dia 75.00
Hobnail, butter dish, from $80 to 120.00
Hobnail, chandelier, amber font, brass fr, 14" dia 950.00
Hobnail, creamer, from $40 to 60.00
Hobnail, cruet, from $425 to 500.00

Hobnail, finger bowl, 4", from $25 to 35.00
Hobnail, pitcher, milk 175.00
Hobnail, pitcher, water; sq top, 8½" 195.00
Hobnail, sauce dish, sq, 4" 28.00
Hobnail, shakers, very rare, pr 300.00
Hobnail, sugar bowl, w/lid, from $65 to 80.00

Hobnail, syrup with pewter lid, $375.00.

Hobnail, toothpick holder/toy tumbler 60.00
Hobnail, tray, cloverleaf, 12", from $90 to 125.00
Hobnail, tumbler, water 45.00
Quartered Block w/Stars, bowl, oval, 10" 65.00
Quartered Block w/Stars, butter dish 95.00
Quartered Block w/Stars, goblet 140.00
Quartered Block w/Stars, sugar bowl, w/lid 75.00
Swirl, bowl, 4" 25.00
Swirl, cruet, from $250 to 295.00
Swirl, mustard jar, from $90 to 125.00
Swirl, pitcher, water 225.00
Swirl, shakers, pr 165.00
Swirl, sugar bowl, w/lid 80.00
Swirl, sugar shaker, orig lid 195.00
Swirl, syrup, Pat dtd 295.00
Swirl, tumbler 45.00

Franciscan

Franciscan is a trade name used by Gladding McBean and Co., founded in northern California in 1875. In 1923 they purchased the Tropico plant in Glendale where they produced sewer pipe, gardenware, and tile. By 1934 the first of their dinnerware lines, El Patio, was produced. It was a plain design made in bright, attractive colors. El Patio Nouveau followed in 1935, glazed in two colors — one tone on the inside, a contrasting hue on the outside. Coronado, a favorite of today's collectors, was introduced in 1936. It was styled with a wide, swirled border and was made in pastels, both satin and glossy. Before 1940 fifteen patterns had been produced. The first hand-decorated lines were introduced in 1937, the ever-popular Apple pattern in 1940, Desert Rose in 1941, and Ivy in 1948. Many other hand-decorated and decaled patterns were produced there from 1934 to 1984.

Dinnerware marks before 1940 include 'GMcB' in an oval, 'F' within a square, or 'Franciscan' with 'Pottery' underneath (which was later changed to 'Ware'). A circular arrangement of 'Franciscan' with 'Made in California USA' in the center was used from 1940 until 1949. At least forty marks were used before 1975; several more were introduced after that. At one time, paper labels were used.

The company merged with Lock Joint Pipe Company in 1963, becoming part of the Interpace Corporation. In July of 1979 Franciscan was purchased by Wedgwood Limited of England, and the Glendale plant closed in October 1984.

Note: Due to limited space, we have used a pricing formula, meant to be only a general guide, not a mechanical ratio on each piece. Rarity varies with pattern, and not all pieces occur in all patterns. Our advisors for this category are Mick and Lorna Chase (Fiesta Plus); they are listed in the Directory under Tennessee. See also Gladding McBean.

Coronado

Both satin (matt) and glossy colors were made including turquoise, coral, celadon, light yellow, ivory, and gray (in satin); and turquoise, coral, apple green, light yellow, white, maroon, and redwood in glossy glazes. High-end values are for maroon, yellow, redwood, and gray. Add 10–15% for gloss.

Bowl, casserole; w/lid, from $85 to 125.00
Bowl, cereal; from $15 to 20.00
Bowl, cream soup; w/underplate, from $40 to 50.00
Bowl, fruit; from $12 to 18.00
Bowl, nut cup; from $16 to 18.00
Bowl, onion soup; w/lid, from $45 to 60.00
Bowl, rim soup; from $28 to 32.00
Bowl, salad; lg, from $35 to 50.00
Bowl, serving; oval, 10½", from $30 to 45.00
Bowl, serving; 7½" dia, from $20 to 25.00
Bowl, serving; 8½" dia, from $18 to 20.00
Bowl, sherbet/egg cup; from $15 to 18.00
Butter dish, from $35 to 45.00
Cigarette box, w/lid, from $75 to 90.00
Creamer, from $12 to 15.00
Cup & saucer, demitasse; from $28 to 45.00
Cup & saucer, jumbo 35.00
Demitasse pot, from $125 to 195.00
Fast-stand gravy, from $28 to 40.00
Jam jar, w/lid, from $65 to 80.00
Pitcher, 1½-qt, from $35 to 60.00
Plate, chop; 12½" dia, from $25 to 35.00
Plate, chop; 14" dia, from $35 to 45.00
Plate, crescent hostess; w/cup well, no established value
Plate, crescent salad; lg, no established value
Plate, ind crescent salad; from $25 to 35.00
Plate, 6½", from $6 to 10.00
Plate, 7½", from $9 to 12.00
Plate, 8½", from $12 to 15.00
Plate, 9½", from $15 to 18.00
Plate, 10½", from $20 to 25.00
Platter, oval, 10", from $20 to 25.00
Platter, oval, 13", from $30 to 45.00
Platter, oval, 15½", from $45 to 60.00
Relish dish, oval, from $20 to 35.00
Shakers, pr, from $20 to 35.00
Sugar bowl, w/lid, from $15 to 25.00
Teacup & saucer, from $12 to 15.00
Teapot, from $65 to 95.00
Tumbler, water; no established value
Vase, 8", no established value

Desert Rose

Ashtray, ind 20.00
Ashtray, oval 125.00
Ashtray, sq 295.00
Bell, Danbury Mint 125.00
Bell, dinner 125.00
Bowl, bouillon; w/lid 395.00

Bowl, cereal; 6" 15.00
Bowl, divided vegetable 45.00
Bowl, fruit 7.00
Bowl, mixing; lg 195.00
Bowl, mixing; med 185.00
Bowl, mixing; sm 175.00
Bowl, porringer 200.00
Bowl, rimmed soup 28.00
Bowl, salad; 10" 115.00
Bowl, soup; ftd 32.00
Bowl, vegetable; 8" 32.00
Bowl, vegetable; 9" 40.00
Box, cigarette 125.00
Box, egg 195.00
Box, heart shape 165.00
Box, rnd 165.00
Butter dish 45.00
Candle holders, pr 145.00
Candy dish, oval 295.00
Casserole, 1½-qt 85.00
Casserole, 2½-qt, minimum value 495.00
Coffeepot 125.00
Coffeepot, ind 395.00
Compote, lg 75.00
Compote, low 125.00
Cookie jar 295.00
Creamer, ind 40.00
Creamer, regular 22.00
Cup & saucer, coffee 85.00
Cup & saucer, demitasse 55.00
Cup & saucer, jumbo 65.00
Cup & saucer, tall 45.00
Cup & saucer, tea 15.00
Egg cup 35.00
Ginger jar 225.00
Goblet, ftd 195.00
Gravy boat 32.00
Heart 145.00
Hurricane lamp 495.00
Jam jar 125.00
Long 'n narrow, 15½x7¾" 495.00
Microwave dish, oblong, 1½-qt 285.00
Microwave dish, sq, 1-qt 215.00
Microwave dish, sq, 8" 245.00
Mug, bbl, 12-oz 50.00
Mug, cocoa; 10-oz 135.00
Mug, 7-oz 32.00
Napkin ring 65.00
Piggy bank 295.00
Pitcher, jug 195.00
Pitcher, milk 75.00
Pitcher, syrup 95.00
Pitcher, water; 2½-qt 125.00
Plate, chop; 12" 75.00
Plate, chop; 14" 175.00
Plate, coupe dessert 65.00
Plate, coupe party 195.00
Plate, coupe steak 195.00
Plate, divided; child's 195.00
Plate, grill 125.00
Plate, side salad 40.00
Plate, TV 175.00
Plate, 6½" 6.00
Plate, 8½" 12.00
Plate, 9½" 20.00
Plate, 10½" 18.00
Platter, turkey; 19" 295.00
Platter, 12¾" 45.00
Platter, 14" 65.00
Relish, oval, 10" 35.00
Relish, 3-section 75.00
Shaker & pepper mill, pr 295.00
Shakers, rose bud, pr 18.00
Shakers, tall, pr 75.00
Sherbet 25.00
Soup ladle 95.00
Sugar bowl, open, ind 125.00
Sugar bowl, regular 32.00
Tea canister 225.00
Teapot 125.00
Thimble 75.00
Tidbit tray, 2-tier 195.00
Tile, in fr 75.00
Tile, sq 45.00
Toast cover 195.00
Trivet, fluted, rnd 325.00
Tumbler, juice; 6-oz 55.00
Tumbler, 10-oz 32.00
Tureen, soup; flat bottom 495.00
Tureen, soup; ftd, either style 695.00
Vase, bud 75.00

Desert Rose, rectangular baking dish, 1½-quart, 13½x8½", $285.00; Bowl, bouillon; with lid, $325.00.

For other hand-painted patterns, we recommend the following general guide for comparable pieces (based on current values):

Cafe Royal	Same as Desert Rose
Daisy	-20%
October	-20%
Forget-Me-Not	Same as Desert Rose
Meadow Rose	Same as Desert Rose
Desert Rose	Base Line Values
Apple	+10%
Ivy	+40%
Strawberry Fair	+20%
Strawberry Time	+20%
Fresh Fruit	+20%
Bountiful	+20%
Poppy	+50%
Original (small) Fruit	+50%
Wild Flower	200% or more!

Apple Pieces Not Available in Desert Rose

There are several Apple items that are so scarce they command higher prices than fit the above formula. The Apple ginger jar is valued at $600.00+, the 4" jug at $195.00+, and any covered box in Apple is at least 50% more than Desert Rose.

There is not an active market in Bouquet, Rosette, or Twilight Rose, as these are scarce, having been produced only a short time. Our estimate would place Bouquet and Rosette in the October range (-20%) and Twilight Rose in the Ivy range (+40%).

Bowl, batter; minimum value 450.00
Bowl, str sides, lg 55.00
Bowl, str sides, med 45.00
Casserole, stick hdl & lid, ind 65.00
Coaster 65.00
Jam jar, redesigned 425.00
Shaker & pepper mill, wooden top, pr 395.00
½-apple baker, from $195 to 225.00

Franciscan Fine China

The main line of fine china was called Masterpiece. There were at least four marks used during its production from 1941 to 1977. Almost every piece is clearly marked. This china is true porcelain, the body having been fired at a very high temperature. Many years of research and experimentation went into this china before it was marketed. Production was temporarily suspended during the war years. More than 170 patterns and many varying shapes were produced. All are valued about the same with the exception of the Renaissance group, which is 25% higher.

Bowl, vegetable; serving, oval 50.00
Cup 20.00
Plate, bread & butter 18.00
Plate, dinner 30.00
Plate, salad 25.00
Saucer 12.00

Starburst

Ashtray, ind 20.00
Ashtray, oval, lg 50.00
Bonbon/jelly dish 35.00
Bowl, crescent salad 40.00
Bowl, divided, 8" 25.00
Bowl, fruit; ind 13.00
Bowl, salad; ind 25.00
Bowl, soup/cereal 13.00
Bowl, vegetable; 8½" 45.00
Butter dish 45.00
Candlesticks, pr, from $175 to 200.00
Casserole, lg 100.00
Coffeepot 150.00
Creamer 15.00
Cup & saucer 25.00
Gravy boat, from $20 to 30.00
Gravy boat, w/attached undertray 40.00
Gravy ladle 30.00
Jug, water; 10" 90.00
Mug, sm 60.00
Mug, tall 95.00
Oil cruet 75.00
Pepper mill 150.00
Pitcher, water; 10" 85.00
Pitcher, 7½", from $50 to 75.00
Plate, chop; from $55 to 65.00
Plate, dinner 12.00
Plate, 6" 6.00
Plate, 8" 8.00
Plate, 11" 45.00
Platter, 15" 80.00
Shakers, bullet shape, lg, pr 50.00
Shakers, sm, pr 20.00
Snack/TV tray w/cup rest, 12½", from $75 to 100.00
Sugar bowl 25.00
Tumbler, 6-oz, from $40 to 50.00
Vinegar cruet 75.00

Frankart

During the 1920s Frankart, Inc., of New York City, produced a line of accessories that included figural nude lamps, bookends, ashtrays, etc. These white metal composition items were offered in several finishes including verde green, jap black, and gunmetal gray. The company also produced a line of caricatured animals, but the stylized nude figurals have proven to be the most collectible today. With few exceptions, all pieces were marked 'Frankart, Inc.' with a patent number or 'pat. appl. for.' All pieces listed are in very good original condition unless otherwise indicated. Our advisor for this category is Walter Glenn; he is listed in the Directory under Georgia.

Silhouette lamp, standing nude figure holds aloft 8½" frosted glass disk, 15", $1,250.00.

Aquarium, nude sits on wrought-iron stand, rectangle tank behind, 42" ..1,350.00
Ashtray, dachshund (stylized) spans 4½" sq ashtray, 5" 275.00
Ashtray, nude dancing, holds tray on hip, box on base, 10" 675.00
Ashtray, nude holds 6" pottery ashbowl over head, 13" 675.00
Ashtray, nude on point, 3 trays form ballerina's tutu, 10" 650.00
Ashtray, nude sits atop column, leg extends over sq tray, 9½" ...650.00
Ashtray, nudes (3) joined at hips hold 6" pottery ball, 25" 1,950.00
Bookends, female heads (futuristic, long-necked), 7", pr 375.00
Bookends, masks (Roman inspired), 7½", pr 475.00
Bookends, nude dancing, frog on base, 10", pr 750.00
Bookends, nude sits atop human skull, 8", pr 750.00
Bookends, nude standing, 'peek-a-boos' around books, 8", pr 550.00
Bookends, nude standing, arms bk to support books, 7½", pr 450.00
Bookends, nudes in headstand, support books, 10", pr 550.00
Bowl, fruit; nudes (2 bk-to-bk) kneeling & holding 8" dish, 6" ...1,150.00
Clock, nudes (2) stand either side rectangular glass clock, 10½" .2,050.00
Lamp, debutante sits/gazes into 3" crackle globe, 8½" 775.00
Lamp, nude, sits/holds 3" crackle globe in lap, 9" 675.00
Lamp, nude (seated) silhouettes against 3 sq glass cylinder, 12" .1,650.00
Lamp, nude kneels before 4" bubble ball, 8" 1,050.00
Lamp, nude sits/extends leg, 3" globes on sides, 7½" 1,250.00
Lamp, nudes (2 bk-to-bk) dancing, hold sq glass cylinder, 13" ..1,950.00
Lamp, nudes (2) sit either side of glass skyscraper, 13" 1,250.00
Lamp, nudes (2) sit either side 5" crackle glass cube, 12" 1,450.00
Mirror, nude kneels & holds 6" gold-bk mirror, 11" 950.00
Smoke set, nude holds rectangular box, tray on base, 12" 650.00

Frankoma

The Frank Pottery, founded in Oklahoma in 1933 by John Frank, became known as Frankoma in 1934. The company produced decorative figurals, vases, and such, marking their ware from 1936 to 1938 with a pacing leopard 'Frankoma' mark. These pieces are highly sought. The entire operation was destroyed by fire in 1938, and new molds were cast — some from surviving pieces — and a similar line of production was pursued. The body of the ware was changed in 1955 from a honey tan (called 'Ada clay,' referring to the name of the town near the area where it was dug) to a red brick clay (known as Sapulpa), and this, along with the color of the glazes (over fifty have been used), helps determine the period of production. A Southwestern theme has always been favored in design as well as in color selection.

In 1965 they began to produce a limited-edition series of Christmas plates, followed by a bottle vase series in 1969. Considered very collectible are their political mugs, bicentennial plates, Teenagers of the Bible plates, and the Wildlife series. Their ceramic Christmas cards are also very popular items with today's collectors.

Frankoma celebrated their 50th Anniversary in 1983. On September 26 of that same year, Frankoma was again destroyed by fire. Because of a fire-proof wall, master molds of all 1983 production items were saved, allowing plans for rebuilding to begin immediately.

Frankoma filed for Chapter 11 in April 1990, and was eventually sold to a Maryland investor in February of 1991, thereby ending the family-ownership era. For a more thorough study of the subject, we recommend that you refer to *Frankoma Treasures* and *Frankoma and Other Oklahoma Potteries* by Phyllis and Tom Bess, our advisors; you will find their address in the Directory under Oklahoma.

Gravy boat and undertray, Plainsman, Prairie Green, $35.00.

Ashtray/candle holder, Wagon Wheel, 6½" dia, from $30 to 35.00
Bookend, Dreamer Girl (Weeping Lady), #427, 5⅝", from $225 to ..275.00
Bookend, Seated Figure, #425, pacing leopard logo, from $450 to 500.00
Candle holders, dbl; #304, Ada clay, 4¼", pr, from $35 to 45.00
Child's serving plate, Mouse, #257, 3-part, +mug, from $15 to 20.00
Christmas card, 1944, from $400 to 500.00
Christmas card, 1947-48, from $95 to 115.00
Christmas card, 1949, from $85 to 95.00
Christmas card, 1950-51, from $125 to 150.00
Christmas card, 1952, Donna Frank, from $150 to 200.00
Christmas card, 1952, from $125 to 140.00
Christmas card, 1953-56, from $90 to 110.00
Christmas card, 1957 ....70.00
Christmas card, 1958-60 ....65.00
Christmas card, 1961-66 ....60.00
Christmas card, 1967-68 ....50.00
Christmas card, 1969-71 ....40.00
Christmas card, 1972 ....35.00
Christmas card, 1973-75 ....30.00
Christmas card, 1976-77 ....25.00
Christmas card, 1980-1982 ....25.00
Christmas plate, 1965, from $275 to 300.00
Christmas plate, 1967 ....70.00
Christmas plate, 1977-82 ....35.00
Earrings, pr, from $20 to 40.00
Flower bowl, ridged shoulder, Frank Potteries, from $300 to 350.00
Mug, Elephant, 1968, from $75 to 95.00
Mug, Elephant, 1969, from $65 to 85.00
Mug, Elephant, 1974, from $35 to 45.00
Mug, Elephant, 1974, Nixon/Ford 500.00
Mug, Elephant or Donkey, 1975-76, from $30 to 40.00
Mug, Elephant or Donkey, 1977-90, from $20 to 30.00
Pitcher, Barrel, #97D, ½-gal, 1950s-60s, from $35 to 45.00
Pitcher, Fireside, #77A, Ada clay, from $100 to 150.00
Planter, Sm Swan, #228, Ada clay, 7½", from $25 to 40.00
Plate, Bicentennial, ea, from $15 to 20.00
Plate, Teenagers of the Bible, 1972, from $35 to 45.00
Plate, Teenagers of the Bible, 1977 through 1982, ea, from $25 to ..35.00
Plate, Wildlife, 1972 through 1975, ea, from $65 to 100.00
Plate, Wildlife, 1977 through 1979, ea, from $55 to 85.00
Sculpture, Coati-Mundi, 4⅜" 3,000.00
Sculpture, Cowboy, no letters on base, 7½" 1,200.00
Sculpture, Elephant, #160, 3", from $90 to 120.00
Sculpture, English Setter, 2⅞", from $100 to 125.00
Sculpture, Fan Dancer, Woodland Moss, pre-1970, from $350 to ..400.00
Sculpture, Gardener Girl, #701, Prairie Green, 5¾", from $100 to ..125.00
Sculpture, Hound Dog, ca 1934-35, 5½", from $650 to 750.00
Sculpture, Indian Bowl Maker, #123, Ada clay, 6", from $350 to ..500.00
Sculpture, Indian Chief, #142, Ada clay, 8", from $200 to 225.00
Sculpture, Rearing Clydesdale, #107, Ada clay, from $250 to 300.00
Sculpture, Two Girls, early 1940s, 5", from $700 to 800.00
Shakers, Elephant, #160H, 3", pr, from $125 to 150.00
Shakers, Guernsey, #93H, pr, from $40 to 50.00
Shakers, Mayan Aztec, #24H (lg), pr, from $15 to 25.00
Shakers, Milk Can, #MC/SP, 1988, pr, from $10 to 15.00
Teapot, ovoid, ca 1934-35, mini, 2", from $125 to 150.00
Teapot, Wagon Wheel, #94T, 6-cup, Sapulpa clay, from $35 to ...45.00
Teapot, 8-cup, #92, 1942 only, from $75 to 100.00
Toby mug, ea, from $20 to 25.00
Trivet, Cattle Brand, from $10 to 15.00
Vase, collector; V-1, from $125 to 150.00
Vase, collector; V-10 & V-11, ea, from $40 to 50.00
Vase, collector; V-12, 13" 65.00
Vase, collector; V-14, from $75 to 85.00
Vase, collector; V-15, 13", from $85 to 100.00
Vase, collector; V-2, 1970, 12", from $80 to 90.00
Vase, collector; V-4, 1972 ....85.00
Vase, collector; V-5, 1973, 13" 85.00
Vase, collector; V-6, from $80 to 90.00
Vase, collector; V-7, 13" 80.00
Vase, collector; V-8, w/stopper, 13" 75.00
Vase, collector; V-9, w/stopper, 13" 75.00
Vase, Fan Shell, #54, Ada clay, 6" 50.00
Vase, Fan Shell, #54, Sapulpa clay, 6", from $15 to 20.00
Vase, Ivy Bowl, #37, 1936 & 1938, 4½", from $125 to 150.00
Vase, shouldered/squat, pacing leopard logo, 4", from $125 to ...175.00
Vase, Tall Cornucopia, #56, Ada clay, 7" 50.00
Vase, Tall Ram's Head, #74, 9¼", from $100 to 150.00
Vase, Wagon Wheel, #94, Ada clay, 7", from $30 to 40.00
Wall pocket, Indian Head, full headdress, 1936-38, 4", from $350 to ..400.00
Wall pocket, Phoebe, #730, bsk w/HP features, 7½", from $175 to 200.00
Wall pocket, Wagon Wheel, 7" 50.00

Fraternal Organizations

Fraternal memorabilia is a vast and varied field. Emblems representing the various organizations have been used to decorate cups, shaving mugs, plates, and glassware. Medals, swords, documents, and other ceremonial paraphernalia from the 1800s and early 1900s are especially prized. Our advisor for Odd Fellows is Greg Spiess; he is listed in the Directory under Illinois. Information on Masonic and Shrine memorabilia has been provided by David Smies, who is listed under Kansas. Assistance concerning Elks collectibles was provided by David Wendel; he is listed in the Directory under Missouri.

Elks

Sugar bowl with lid, BPOE and Elk, Iroquois China, $65.00.

Ashtray, floor; 6-sided w/logo in center, glass w/metal stand 20.00
Badge, ribbon over clock w/sultan, bl & wht enameling, 1906 ....70.00
Badge, 1903 Baltimore Grand Reunion, brass, Charles Vivian bust..55.00
Button, enameled BPOE & star, Atlantic City 1918, VG 25.00
Card case, sterling silver, hand eng, 1½-oz, 4⅛x1½" 80.00
Hat, velvet w/metal decor, purple w/wht tassels, EX 55.00
Match safe, sterling silver, elk w/clock above, EX 250.00
Pendant, elks tooth, 10k gold elks head w/clock in antlers, 1900s .110.00
Pin, flag w/Brooklyn on ribbon w/elk in chair below, enameled ...45.00
Pin, 1912 Portland on ribbon above elks head & clock, EX 45.00
Ring, elk w/antlers around clock, red eyes, 10k gold, EX 150.00

Masons

Banner, HP symbols & earth/moon/stars on cloth, 20th C, 43x40" .190.00
Book, chart of all emblems explained, leather, 172-pg, 1819, EX ..200.00
Medal, De Molay, Legion of Honor 25.00
Mug, china, 3-hdl, Tancred Cmdry #48, Pittsburgh PA, 4x4" 40.00
Needlework panel, Trust in God, Masonic symbols, 1890s, 21x17" .135.00
Print on silk, metallic thread decor w/lodge items, w/fr, 14⅜" ...350.00
Ring, solid 14k gold, emb & eng, 7 grams 155.00
Snuff box, Masonic decor on tortoise shell, 19th C, 3¼" dia 130.00
Watch, pocket; Masonic dial & case, Elgin, 1907, EX 310.00
Watch, pocket; symbols, gold filled/19 jewel/open face, Dudley, '24 ...2,400.00

Odd Fellows

Banner, bl w/gold trim, pnt symbols, w/gold owl & chain, 30x20" ...85.00
Catalog, costume & supplies, #61, CE Ward Comp, 1910 ....70.00
Chain symbol, wrought iron, 3-link w/gold pnt, 19th C, ea link: 5½" .110.00
Match safe, design both sides, NP brass, mk Pat Jan 12 1904 ......80.00
Robe, ceremonial; polished brn cotton, wht skull/Xbones, 20th C ..65.00

Shrine

Belt buckle, silver-tone, w/emblem 25.00
Plate, drunken member in center, porc, Shenango, 10¾" 45.00
Program, Shrine Circus, pics of acts, local adv, 64-pg, 1930, VG+ ...15.00
Toothpick holder, cranberry, souvenir 225.00

Miscellaneous

American Legion, pin, USA in red on wht w/shield in bl, 1" L 8.00
Jordan Lodge, letter opener, blk w/emblem on wht, plastic, 1967 ...25.00
Junior Order of Am Mechanics, bar pin, celluloid 20.00
Knights of Pythias, medal w/bar pin, Conn Lodge 37 ....42.00
Lions, shakers, bl & wht logo, KlayKraft, 1¾", pr 12.00
Modern Woodmen of America, bar pin, celluloid, w/ribbon 20.00
Rotary International, pin-bk ribbon w/medallion, 1925 ....20.00
Salvation Army, medallion, With Heart to God & Hand to Man, 1¼" ..23.00

Fruit Jars

As early as 1829, canning jars were being manufactured for use in the home preservation of foodstuffs. For the past twenty-five years, they have been sought as popular collectibles. At the last estimate, over four thousand fruit jars and variations were known to exist. Some are very rare, perhaps one-of-a-kind examples known to have survived to the present day. Among the most valuable are the black glass jars, the amber Van Vliet, and the cobalt Millville. These often bring prices in excess of $10,000.00 when they can be found. Aside from condition, values are based on age, rarity, color, and special features. Our advisor for this category is John Hathaway; he is listed in the Directory under Maine.

Atlas Strong Shoulder Mason, light cobalt blue (rare color), one-quart, zinc lid, NM, $140.00.

Acme Seal (script), clear, regular mouth, qt 50.00
All Right, reverse: Patd Jan 28th 1868, aqua, qt, repro closure ..118.00
Allen's Patent June 1871 (on base), aqua, qt, w/repro clamps 250.00
Amazon Swift Seal (in circle), bl, pt 22.00
American Fruit Jar (eagle & flag), gr, flaw, qt 125.00
Atlas E-Z Seal, aqua, 48-oz 30.00
Atlas E-Z Seal, clear, ½-pt 3.00
Atlas E-Z Seal, gr, pt, w/gr lid 18.00
Atlas E-Z Seal (in circle), lt bl, aqua lid, qt 27.00
Atlas Mason's Patent, aqua, pt 3.00
Atlas Mason's Patent Nov 30th 1848, aqua, ½-gal 9.00
Atlas Whole Fruit, clear, qt 2.00
Ball (3 L loops) Improved Mason (dropped A), aqua, pt 7.00
Ball Improved, bl, pt 12.00
Ball Improved (dropped A), clear, qt 9.00
Ball Improved Ghost Mason, aqua, pt 20.00
Ball Mason, reverse: Mason's Patent Nov 30th 1858, aqua, ½-gal ..38.00
Ball Mason (dropped A, disconnected underscore), gr, pt 20.00
Ball Mason's Patent 1858, aqua, pt 5.00
Ball Perfect Mason, bl, sq, qt 10.00
Ball Perfection, bl, pt, no closure 100.00
Ball Refrigerator & Freezer Jar, clear, pt 3.00

Ball Special, bl, qt 8.00
Ball Special, bl, shoulder seal, qt 50.00
Ball Standard, aqua, wax sealer, tin lid, ½-gal 20.00
Beaver (beaver chewing log), amber, dk amber insert, qt 700.00
Beaver (beaver chewing log), clear, midget 150.00
Bernardin (script) Underlined Mason, clear, pt 10.00
Best, dk amber, qt 400.00
C Ihmsen & Son Pittsburgh PA (base), aqua, wax sealer, tin lid, qt ..30.00
Canadian Jewel Made in Canada, clear, qt 4.00
Clyde (script), clear, qt 15.00
Conserve Jar, clear, ½-pt 80.00
Crown (crown) Imperial, gr w/clear crown insert, qt 25.00
Crown Cordial & Extract & Co New York, clear, ½-gal 12.00
Crown Crown (ring crown), aqua, qt 17.00
Curtis & Moore Trade (monogram) Mark Boston Mass, clear, ½-gal ..40.00
Drey Improved Ever Seal, clear, glass boss ears, ½-gal 12.00
Excelsior, aqua, ½-gal (unlisted sz) 65.00
Federal (draped flag) Fruit Jar, lt gr, ½-gal 125.00
Franklin Dexter Fruit Jar, aqua, regular zinc lid, qt 30.00
Fruit Keeper GCCo, aqua, orig clamp, ½-gal 75.00
Gem (1 line), aqua, qt 8.00
Geo D Brown, lt aqua, qt, repro clamp 48.00
Gimbel Brothers Pure Food Store Phil, clear, pt 48.00
Green Mountain (in fr), clear, qt 12.00
Hero, aqua, orig 2-pc lid, ½-gal 80.00
Home-Pack, clear, qt 2.00
Howe Jar Scranton PA, aqua, qt 90.00
Ideal, aqua, midget 75.00
Ideal, aqua, qt 25.00
Ivanhoe (base), clear, pt 4.00
Jewel Jar (block letters in fr), clear, qt 15.00
Kerr Economy TM (base: Pat Chicago Ill), lt gr, pt 8.00
Kerr's Self Sealing Mason, amber, qt 30.00
King (on banner below crown), clear, qt 8.00
Lafayette (in script), aqua, qt 150.00
Lamb Mason, clear, zinc lid, qt 3.00
Lockport Mason Improved, clear, ½-gal 15.00
Lustre RE Tongue & Bros Inc Phila (in circle), bl, pt 7.00
Mason's CFJ Patent Nov 30th 1858, aqua, ½-gal 12.00
Mason's Crystal Jar, clear, ½-gal 35.00
Mason's KGBCo Patent Nov 30th 1858, aqua, pt 30.00
Mason's Patent Nov 30th 1858, aquamarine, ½-gal 48.00
Mason's Patent Nov 30th 1858, gr, pt 25.00
Mason's Patent Nov 30th 1858, reverse: hourglass, aqua, qt 15.00
Mason's 16 (underlined) Patent Nov 30th 1858, aqua, ½-gal 28.00
Mason's 3 Patent Nov 30th 1858, aqua, qt 8.00
Mason's 5 Patent Nov 30th 1858, aqua, midget 55.00
Mason's 8 (lg) Patent Nov 30th 1858, swirled glass, gal 30.00
Masons Jar of 1872 (ghost improved), aqua, ground lip chips, qt .58.00
Mid West Canadian Made, clear, qt 14.00
Mrs Chapin's Mayonnaise Boston Mass, clear, pt 6.00
Mrs GE Haller Patd Feb 25 73, aqua, aqua stopper, ½-gal 200.00
Pat'd Feb 9th 1864 WW Lyman, aqua, ½-gal 38.00
Perfection, clear, repro metal, qt 40.00
Presto, glass top, pt 2.00
Putnam (base), amber, qt 45.00
S Mason's Patent 1858, med teal bl, qt 75.00
Safe Seal (in circle), bl, pt 5.00
Silicon (in circle), aqua, pt 18.00
Smalley's (crown) Royal Trade Mark Nu-Seal, clear, pt 9.00
Standard (Mason in flag), lt gr, qt 10.00
Star below Star (str R), clear, ½-gal 58.00
TM Lightning, apple gr, pt 65.00
TM Lightning, dk amber, qt 58.00
Trade Mark Lightning Putnam, aqua, 24-oz 75.00
Trade Mark Masons CFJ Improved, aqua, ½-gal 12.00
Trademark Banner Registered (in banner), clear, qt 10.00
Trademark Lightning (Putnam base only), aqua, ½-pt 35.00
Victory (in shield) on lid, clear, twin side clamps, pt 4.00
Wears Jar (in circle), clear, qt 7.00
Widemouth Telephone Jar, aqua, qt 12.00

Fry

Henry Fry established his glassworks in 1901 in Rochester, Pennsylvania. There, until 1933 when it was sold to the Libbey Company, he produced glassware of the finest quality. In the early years they produced beautiful cut glass; and when it began to wane in popularity, Fry turned to the manufacture of occasional pieces and oven glassware. He is perhaps most famous for the opalescent pearl glass called 'Foval.' It was sometimes made with blue or jade green trim in combination. Because it was in production for only a short time in 1926 and 1927, it is hard to find. Our advisor for this category is Ron Damaska; he is listed in the Directory under Pennsylvania. See also Kitchen Collectibles, Glassware.

Aquarium, amber 95.00
Bean pot set, Pearl Ovenware, set of 4: from ½-pt to 2-pt 215.00
Candlesticks, Foval, wht w/bl threaded stems, 11", pr 550.00
Candy dish, Emerald w/petal ft, crystal swirl connector 145.00
Casserole, Pearl Ovenware, etch lid, silver metal fr, #1954 ....55.00
Coffeepot, Foval, glass works, cylindrical, #3000 ....500.00
Coffeepot, Sylex Vacuumatic, Foval 575.00
Comport, Foval w/Delft Blue stem, trim & festooning, 5½" 350.00
Comport, Foval w/jade gr stem & festooning, #2502, 9" 375.00
Compote, clear w/blk threads at ruffled rim, hollow std, 5" 85.00
Cream soup & underplate, Emerald 40.00
Creamer, blk w/gold trim 50.00
Creamer & sugar bowl, cut, Ivy, sgn 250.00
Creamer & sugar bowl, Foval, #2000 ....245.00
Cruet, cut, Nashville, faceted stopper 200.00
Cruet, Foval, Delft Blue stopper & hdl, 9¾" 150.00
Cup & saucer, China Glass 45.00
Finger bowl, cut, Russian-type pattern 40.00
Goblet, water; Fuchsia (amethyst), crystal swirl ball stem 25.00
Lamp, blk wafer base, 9" 350.00
Muffin pan, Pearl Ovenware, 6-compartment, #1956, 9" 60.00
Pitcher, cut, Leman, sgn hdl 325.00
Pitcher, Foval, Delft Blue finial on lid & hdl, 11" 275.00
Pitcher, lemonade; Foval w/jade gr hdl, flared rim, #9416 ....175.00
Plate, Foval w/jade gr trim, #3101, 7½" 85.00
Plate, grill; Pearl Ovenware w/bl trim, 3-compartment, #1947, 10½" ..55.00
Plate, jade gr w/sterling trim, #3101, 8½" 125.00

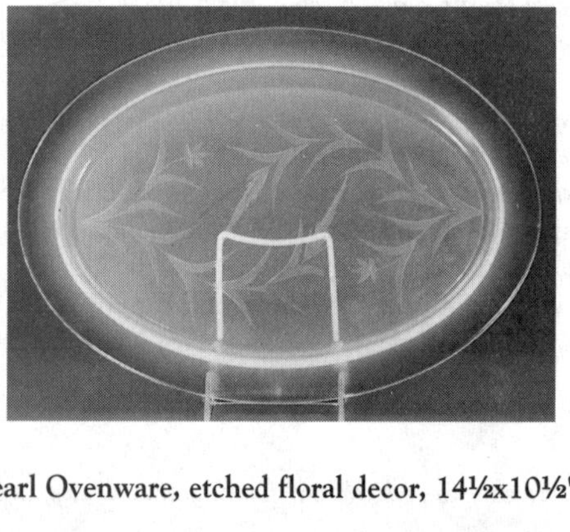

Platter, Pearl Ovenware, etched floral decor, 14½x10½", $65.00.

Relish tray, cut, Thistle, 12" 185.00
Relish tray, Prince, side hdl, 8" 195.00
Sherbet, Foval, jade gr stem 125.00
Snack set, Foval, #1968 ....50.00
Sugar bowl, Foval w/Delft Blue base, hdls, 2½" 125.00
Teacup & saucer, Foval w/silver floral o/l sgn Rockwell, gr hdl, #2000 ..150.00
Teapot, etch, Japanese Maid 350.00
Teapot, Foval w/gold enamel bands, #2000, 6-cup 300.00
Teapot, Foval w/jade gr hdl, spout & finial, #2002, 2-cup 300.00
Vase, bud; Foval w/Delft Blue connector, #831, 6½" 200.00
Vase, cut, Orient w/Buzz Star & Zipper neck, 12" 215.00
Vase, Pearl w/Delft Blue edge & ft, flared rim, #826, 6" 300.00
Whiskey jug, cut, Japan, strap hdl, 7¾" 400.00

Fulper

Throughout the nineteenth century (for perhaps as long as one hundred years) the Fulper pottery in Flemington, New Jersey, produced utilitarian and commercial wares. But it was during the span from 1909 to 1935 (the Arts & Crafts period in particular) that they became prominent producers of beautifully glazed art pottery. Although most pieces were cast and not hand decorated, their graceful, classical shapes combined with their wonderful experimental glaze made each piece a true work of art.

The company also made dolls' heads, Kewpies, figural perfume lamps, and powder boxes. Examples prized most highly by collectors today are those that were produced before the devastating fire of 1929 and the subsequent takeover by Martin Stangl. (See Stangl Pottery.)

Several marks were used: a vertical in-line 'Fulper' being the most common, a horizontal mark, Flemington, Rafco, Prang, and paper labels (on earlier pieces). Most Fulper is marked although unmarked pots that surface can be identified by shape and glaze characteristics. Values are determined by size, desirability of glaze, and rarity of form. Lamps with colored glass inserts are rare and avidly sought by collectors. Our advisor for this category is Douglass White; he is listed in the Directory under Florida.

Basket, bl-gr matt w/openweave design, 5x10" 175.00
Bowl, bl gloss on gr, mk, 4x9½x7½" 230.00
Bowl, bl matt w/Chinese Blue flambe int, rope border, 3x13" 300.00
Bowl, bl-blk gloss flambe over gray & oatmeal matt, 4⅝x12" 250.00
Bowl, caramel & bl flambe, incurvate rim, 2¼x8¾" 150.00
Bowl, Cat's Eye flambe, hdls, 9" 150.00
Bowl, console; Cat's Eye flambe, w/flower frog, 12" 150.00
Bowl, gr matt streaks over gunmetal w/gr/turq irid, 3-ftd, 18¼" .375.00
Bowl, gr mottle w/gold & bl streaks, incurvate rim, 2¾x10½" ..150.00
Bowl, pk & gr matt, 5x7" 175.00
Candle holder, Chinese Blue flambe, hooded, 6⅞" 250.00
Candle sconce, gr crystalline w/3 leaded glass insets, 10½" 2,400.00
Candlestick, speckled butterscotch w/mirror blk, 6" dia 100.00
Chamberstick, dk brn crystalline, 7" 350.00
Cider set, taupe lustre, 9½" pitcher+6 3¼" mugs, NM 250.00
Flower frog, pelican, gunmetal & blk, 7" 175.00
Inkwell/pen tray, ochre matt, Vasekraft, 5x4x4¾" 500.00
Jug, mahog/gr/ivory flambe, 10½x5½" 475.00
Jug, whiskey; Cat's Eye Flambe & silver o/l, musical, 9½" 300.00
Lamp, mushroom shade w/glass inserts, Cat's Eye flambe, 16x13½" ..12,500.00
Lamp, perfume; ballerina, yel, 5¾" 300.00
Lamp, perfume; canary, yel/grey, 8" 375.00
Lamp, perfume; cockatoo, gr & orange plumage, 13" 750.00
Lamp, perfume; Dutch girl in pk, 8" 250.00
Lamp, perfume; girl in bl ball gown w/fan, 7" 250.00
Lamp base, gr to Rose Famille, fluted urn shape, drilled, 12" 175.00
Pilgrim flask, Flemington Green & wht frothy flambe, 10¼" 450.00
Tankard, yel over gray flambe, twist hdl, 10⅝" 475.00
Vase, bl matt, tapered cylinder, hdls, 10½x6" 315.00
Vase, blk, flattened bottom, 5½" 225.00
Vase, blk/bl/caramel drip, 3-hdl, 7" 375.00
Vase, cafe-au-lait, Vasekraft, 4x2¾" 325.00
Vase, Cat's Eye flambe, #26, 1930s, 6½" 225.00
Vase, Celadon crystalline, 4-sided, 8" 400.00
Vase, Chinese Blue flambe, glossy, hdls, 4½" 150.00
Vase, cobalt to Cat's Eye flambe, tapered, 12x8½" 1,400.00
Vase, cucumber crystalline, bulbous, 8x6" 350.00
Vase, cucumber gr matt, classic shape, 12" 375.00
Vase, dk olive-brn w/blk/brn streaks, emb ribs, 11" 300.00
Vase, Elephant's Breath to Leopard Skin Crystalline flambe, 8¼" ..450.00
Vase, Famille Rose (leathery), squat, 5¾x8½" 325.00
Vase, frothy bl on Famille Rose, 3-hdl, #56, 7x8" 230.00
Vase, gr & gunmetal matt, hdls, 5x6½" 250.00
Vase, gr crystalline, cylindrical, 10x5½", NM 350.00
Vase, gr frothy & Rose Famille, ovoid, 7¾" 200.00

Vase, Mirror Black and Flemington Green flambe, shouldered, 16¾x9¼", $2,800.00.

Vase, mirror blk & ivory flambe, buttressed, 8x5¾" 750.00
Vase, multiple grs drip over red, ribbed form, factory plug, 15" ..275.00
Vase, olive-brn flambe, bottle neck, bulbous base, 8x6" 225.00

Furniture

American seventeenth- and eighteenth-century furniture played an important role in our country's environment. Aside from its utility, furniture was a symbol indicating wealth, taste, and station in life of the owner. Each period brought about distinct design changes that created a recognizable form for that particular time frame. Our earliest furniture was handmade by the cabinetmaker with apprentices and journeymen who learned every phase of the craft from the master cabinetmaker. The end of the Civil War brought the Industrial Revolution and mechanization of furniture manufacturing. With it came the ornate Victorian period and the many revival styles. These were followed in the twentieth century by Art Deco and Art Nouveau and more revival of our earliest periods.

It is important for the buyer of antique and collectible furniture to approach each piece from the point of view of the prevailing taste of that particular time frame. Pieces from lesser cabinetmakers should be recognized simply as old furniture, as age alone does not equal value.

Indeed the marketplace has completely recovered from the recession. Equally important is the change in the marketplace. Victorian oak furniture is not as desirable or pricey as it was in years past. Ornate Victorian furniture in dark woods such as rosewood and walnut has not faired as badly and is still being pursued. Prices for case pieces of period furniture in formal and high country styles continue to top most auction houses estimates. Still on the rise are the sound mahogany pieces from the first half of the twentieth century in the traditional styling of Queen Anne, Chippendale, Sheraton, Hepplewhite, and Duncan Phyffe. Enjoying the popularity are English counterparts. Turn of the century European inlaid and carved furniture is still rising in value. Stronger in the marketplace is the 'decorator trade,' who realize this type of furniture is a sound value and can be refinished (without any loss of value) to suit the client's needs. Upholstered pieces that are 'floor ready' are bringing stronger prices at auction. Frames for sofas, chairs, and benches needing new upholstery and some work are being sold reasonably to eager collectors and dealers. They realize that when the work is completed, they have a unique, well made item at a reasonable price.

Items that have sold at auction for at least 25% lower than their normal market values will be designated with (*). Items listed in the lines that are designated with (**) are pieces in the best of form and of museum quality.

Please note: If a piece actually dates to the period of time during which it originated, we will use the name of the style only. For example: 'Hepplewhite' will indicate an American piece from roughly the late 1700s to 1815. The term 'style' will describe a piece that is far removed from the original time frame. 'Hepplewhite style' refers to examples from the turn of the century. When the term 'repro' is used it will mean that the item in question is less than thirty years old and is being sold on a secondary market. When only one dimension is given for blanket chests, dry sinks, tables, settees, sideboards, and sofas, it is length.

Condition is the most important factor to consider in determining value. It is also important to remember that *where* a piece sells has a definite bearing on the price it will realize, due simply to regional preference. Our advisor for this category is Suzy McLennan Anderson, ISA, of Heritage Antiques, whose address is listed in the Directory under New Jersey. (Photo and SASE required; no phone appraisals.) To learn more about furniture, we recommend *The Collector's Encyclopedia of American Furniture* (there are three in the series) and *Furniture of the Depression Era* by Robert and Harriett Swedberg; *Heywood-Wakefield Modern Furniture* by Steve and Roger Rouland; *Antique Oak Furniture* by Conover Hill; *American Oak Furniture, Books I* and *II*, and *Victorian Furniture, Our American Heritage, Books I* and *II*, by Kathryn McNerney; and *Collector's Guide to Oak Furniture* by Jennifer George. See also Art Deco; Art Nouveau; Arts and Crafts; Fifties Modern; Nutting, Wallace; Shaker; Stickley.

Key:

Am — American	Geo — Georgian
bj — bootjack	grpt — grainpainted
brd — board	hdbd — headboard
Chpndl — Chippendale	hdw — hardware
Co — Country	Hplwht — Hepplewhite
cvd — carved	mar — marriage
cvg — carving	NE — New England
c&b — claw and ball	QA — Queen Anne
do — door	rswd — rosewood
drw — drawer	trn — turning, turned
Emp — Empire	uphl — upholstered/upholstery
Fed — Federal	vnr — veneer
Fr — French	Vict — Victorian
ftbd — footboard	W/M — William and Mary
G — good	: — over (example: 1 do:2 drw)

Armoires, See Also Wardrobes

Cherry Fr Provincial, dbl-do, drws, 91x55x24" **2,000.00**
Mahog Am Classical, dbl do, cvd details, 1830s, 86x60" **3,300.00**
Mahog Am Late Classical, scalloped panel dos, 1850s, 86x60" .**2,000.00**
Mahog Am Rococo, dbl mirror do, fruit crest, 1850s, 106x61" ..**550.00**
Walnut Neoclassical style, dbl-do, drw, 19th C, 73x50x22" **1,325.00**
Walnut Vict Renaissance Revival, cvd swags, 1870s, 81x74" .**2,250.00**

Beds

Arts & Crafts, 11 vertical slats, arched apron, 37x42" **800.00**
Bell Epoque in Louis XV style, padded hdbd w/crest, pnt, 49x57" ..**800.00**

Brass bed, scrolled head and foot boards with foliage details, original rails, 64x72x61", EX, $2,200.00. (Photo courtesy Garth's Auctions)

Brass, simple classic design, 59x72x55", EX **400.00**
Butternut Cottage Vict, cvd leaves/flowers on crest, rfn, 77" **300.00**
Cannonball, mahog Emp-style, dk stain, rpl eagle crest, 59x78x54" **1,000.00**
Canopy, mahog Sheraton w/much cvg, sq tester/curtains, 88x73x58" ..**3,200.00**
Canopy, red-pnt Sheraton, reeded ftbd, trn post, ME, 68x52x76" **2,000.00**
Day, cherry Co, scrolled posts, trn spindles, rfn, reuphl, 84" **525.00**
Day, cvd walnut Charles II Cromwellian, reuphl, late 17th C, 78" ..**1,350.00**
Half-tester, walnut Am Renaissance, pierced crest, 1870s, 98x63" ...**3,300.00**
Hired man's, poplar w/red, trn posts/castor ft/rope rails, 20x65x44" **400.00**
Jenny Lind, hardwood w/old dk finish, 50x73x54" **200.00**
Mahog Am Emp w/figure, cvd posts, fitted as daybed **825.00**
Pencil post, cherry Hplwht style, tester fr, 81x76x58" **715.00**
Poplar Co Emp w/worn flame grpt, scrolled posts, 49x73" **200.00**
Rope, hired man's, chestnut, low hdbd, sq posts, scrubbed, 30x68x38" ..**110.00**
Rope, low post, pnt pine, NE, 19th C, 35x76x54" **350.00**
Rope, mahog Emp, trn posts, acorn finials, paneled hd/ftbds, 72" ..**250.00**
Rope, pine/poplar, bold trns/cannonball finials, 39x75x52" **165.00**
Rosewood Rococo, elaborate fruit-cvd crest, cvd ftbd, 1850s, queen sz ..**5,000.00**
Sleigh, mahog, typical form w/horizontal panel, 73x42" * **200.00**
Tall post, cherry Sheraton style w/trn & reeded posts, 20th C ...**300.00**
Tall post, curly maple Emp, poplar hdbd, acorn finials, 89" **1,650.00**
Tall post, cvd mahog Fed, MA, ca 1810-20, 87x79x62" ** ..**10,925.00**
Tall post, maple & cherry, trn posts, much cvg, rstr, 81" **800.00**
Tall post, maple/birch/pine Sheraton, trn posts, rfn, 67x76x75" ..**1,540.00**
Tester, mahog Am w/scroll hdbd, str rails, 1850s, 85x67" **5,000.00**
Walnut Vict, paneled ends w/appl scrolls/fruit, matching crest, 72" * ..**440.00**
Walnut Vict, paneled hdbd, trn posts, old varnish, 75x72" **300.00**
Walnut Vict, paneled hdbd w/crest, trn posts, single sz, 58" **200.00**
4-poster, trn walnut Am, ball finials, 1850s, 77x59" ** **11,000.00**

Benches

Bucket, bl over red pnt, upper shelf w/shaped bkbrd, 43x38x14" **250.00**
Gr pnt Fed w/stencil, ½-spindle bk, plank seat, open arms, 72" ..**1,175.00**
Mahog Classical, uphl slip seat, curled legs, rprs, 1820s, 39x25x15" ..**1,000.00**
Mahog Classical Revival, paw ft, lion heads, velvet cushion, 23x29" ...**575.00**
PA-style Windsor, ½-spindle bk, shaped crest, 8-leg, 70" **1,200.00**
Park, CI & wood, slat bk & seat, scrolled arms, paw ft, 98" **2,000.00**
Pine, orig red pnt, PA, early 19th C, 13x96x18" **750.00**
Pine Co w/red pnt traces, cut-out ft, shaped ends, 37x32x12" ...**500.00**
Pine w/yel comb grpt, bj ends, 17x42x8¾" **190.00**

Poplar Co, gray rpt over weathered surface, 1-brd top, 54" 215.00
Settle, orig gr pnt w/striping & stencil, ½-spindle bk, 69" 1,375.00
Settle, 6 ind crests:spindles:shaped plank seat, scroll arms, 109" ...880.00
Window, mahog Louis XVI style, acanthus cvg, uphl seat, 25x44x16" ..440.00
Work, chestnut w/old patina, drw, disassembles, 39x51x19" 250.00

Blanket Chests, Coffers, Trunks, and Mule Chests

Campaign, mahog w/brass trim, dvtl drw, lift-out tray, 19x32" ...385.00
Cherry Fed, paneled front/sides, 2-drw, PA, 1820s, 49" 500.00
Cvd pine, 6-brd, bl pnt, rope-twist beading, 1790s, 17x44x18" ..2,645.00
Decor PA, pine w/brn grpt & 3-color flowers etc, 50" ** 30,250.00
Dome top, dvtl box w/orig mustard pnt, ca 1800, 12x30x14" 975.00
Dome top, leather covered, brass tacks, dtd 1836, 15x30x15", EX ..1,400.00
Dvtl poplar w/old red, short ft & base, edge molding, 20x31x17" ..500.00
Grpt pine, dvtl case, old rpr, 22x44x21" 275.00
Oak w/relief-cvd geometrics, wrought-iron lock/till, Hadley like, 44" ..350.00
PA German pnt pine w/tulip stencil, lift-lid, 19th C, 54", EX ...2,000.00
Pine, 2 fake:2 drw, lift top, bracket ft, red traces, 45x37x19" ..1,300.00
Pine Co Chpndl, 3 fake drws:3-drw base, red rpt, 2-pc, 48x36x20" ..770.00
Pine Co w/old red, sq corner posts, panel sides/ends, 1-brd top, 39" .495.00
Pine Co w/old red, 6-brd, till w/shelf, old rpl hinges, 56" 550.00
Pine PA Chpndl, rpl bracket ft, old red pnt, bear-trap lock, 33" ...330.00
Poplar, 3 dvtl drw, appl moldings, hinged lid, PA, 30x50x23" ..2,100.00
Walnut Chpndl, dvtl case, ogee ft, bear-trap till lock, 51" 2,200.00
Walnut Chpndl, dvtl case, strap hinges, bracket ft, VA, 48" ..2,500.00
6-brd, red & blk pnt, molded top, side cleats, 22x44x20" 700.00

Bookcases

Walnut Victorian Renaissance Revival three-section bookcase, EX, $11,500.00. (Photo courtesy Jackson's Auctions)

Breakfront, mahog Geo III, 4 do:3-part base w/drws/dos, 93x92" ...15,000.00
Cherry Geo III style, Gothic lattice dos:4 panel do, 84x85x15" 1,680.00
Mahog Am Late Classical, arched dos:2 drw, cvd skirt, 85x48" 1,870.00
Mahog Fed, panel dos:twin panel dos:3 beaded drw, 1830s, 97x43" ...3,150.00
Mahog Geo III style, cvd rosettes, latticed dos:4 panel do, 88x96" ...3,350.00
Mahog Late Vict, egg & dart cornice, Greek Key frieze, 83x86" 1,000.00
Oak, scalloped brass escutcheons, rpl shelves, cvd ft, 62x41x14" ..300.00
On chest, walnut Hplwht w/inlay on base, Fr ft/apron, rfn, 90x39" .3,000.00
Revolving, on 4-leg Vict base, 2 rnd shelves (30"/18"), 40" 145.00
Stacked, quarter-sawn oak w/old varnish, Macey label, 3-part, 47x34" ..330.00
Walnut Am, dbl arch do:4 drw, 1840s, 90x60x12" 4,200.00
Walnut/walnut burl Vict, 2 1-pane do:2 drw, Eastlake details, 64x53" ...1,375.00

Bureaus, See Chests

Cabinets

Breakfront, mahog vnr English style, Kittinger, 78x51x16" 880.00
Cellaret, mahog Classical sarcophagus form, 1815-25, 18x27x16" ..4,600.00
China, cvd oak w/bow-front, cvd lions' heads ft, mirror, 76" ..1,045.00
China, cvd oak w/serpentine glass front, paw ft, 71x49x20" ...2,100.00
China, Golden Oak era, cvd/appl, 4-drw, glass in crest, 76" ...1,500.00
China, hardwood, leaded panels in dos, worn ft, 56x45x14" 440.00
China, mahog vnr, bow-front, dk finish, ca 1900, 62x40x17" 685.00
China, oak, 1 do w/flat glass, curved glass ends, 61x36x13" 420.00
China, oak, 2 curved glass do/glass ends, QA ft, ca 1900, 63x41x16" .850.00
Curio, Golden Oak era, cvd lions on pilasters, paw ft, 65x40" ..1,100.00
Curio, hardwood Fr style w/ormolu, 20th C, 53x23" 495.00
Display case, walnut Gothic Revival, arched cornice, 26x23x14" 865.00
Ebonized Italian Renaissance style, pietra dura inlay, 1790s, 23x40" .4,675.00
Fr-style, figured vnr w/ormolu, porc mts, HP figures, 32x20x14" .495.00
Louis XV style w/open shelves, herringbone inlay, marble top, 39x15" ..770.00
Vitrine, Fr style, gold pnt w/cherubs/flowers, 20th C, 33x19x26" 1,200.00
Vitrine, mahog vnr Hplwht style w/inlay, 20th C, 30x24x17" ...300.00

Candlestands

Mahogany, American Federal tilt-top carved candle stand, early nineteenth century, 30x25x19", $1,100.00.

Mahog Chpndl, tilt-top, tripod w/snake ft, birdcage, 22" dia ..2,750.00
Mahog Hplwht, tilt-top, tripod w/spider legs, 29x27x19" 715.00
Walnut Chpndl, tilt-top, tripod base w/snake ft, rfn, 29x22" dia ..935.00
Walnut PA Chpndl, tilt-top, tripod base w/snake ft, cvd, 20" dia .2,400.00

Chairs

Arm, Biedermeier, finger cvgs, uphl bk/seat/half arms, 38" 350.00
Arm, Co QA, banister-bk, old blk rpt, rpl rush seat, 45" 495.00
Arm, Fr Louis XVI style, cvd fr, reuphl, sm rpr, 37" 250.00
Arm, Fr style, hand-cvd fr w/open arms, reuphl, ca 1900, 40" ...715.00
Arm, hardwood QA, cvd crest/vase splat/Spanish ft/rush seat, rpt, 41" .4,125.00
Arm, high arrow-bk w/rpt grpt/floral crest/yel striping, 45" 275.00
Arm, mahog English style, cabriole legs/paw ft, cvd crest, reuphl, 41" .380.00
Arm, mahog Geo III, bbl bk, uphl leather seat, trn legs, 1800s ..1,500.00
Arm, mahog Hplwht style w/inlay, brocade uphl, 48" 400.00
Arm, mahog/fruitwood Geo III, serpentine ladder-bk, drop-in seat ..300.00
Arm, maple/hardwood QA, Spanish ft, rush seat, 42" 3,500.00
Arm, oak Medieval style, triangular, trn/cvd w/velvet seat, 33" .300.00
Arm, walnut Baroque Revival Flemish scroll, cane bk, uphl seat ..275.00
Arm, walnut Euro Medieval style, leather uphl, 20th C, 36" 100.00
Arm, walnut Jacobean style w/trn/rope-twist detail, rprs, 35" 300.00
Arm, walnut Vict Gothic Revival, worn finish/old uphl seat, 53" ..400.00
Arm, walnut Vict w/finger cvg, brocade reuphl, 39" 440.00
Arm, walnut Vict w/old faded reuphl, 41" 440.00
Campeachy arm, mahog Am Late Classical, flame grpt, uphl, 25" .3,000.00
Corner, mahog Chpndl style, slip seat, old finish, 20th C, 34" ..330.00
Corner, mahog Chpndl style w/hand cvg, slip seat, Fr Korea, 33" ...415.00
Corner, mahog Chpndl w/gilt trim: garlands/eagle, centennial ..470.00
Library, mahog Geo III style, cvd open arms, reuphl 585.00
Lolling, mahog Fed, serpentine crest, uphl seat, 1785-1800, 43" .4,250.00
Recamier, mahog Classical, leaf-cvd scroll, old uphl 8,600.00

Rocker, arm; Adirondack, bentwood seat/bk, twined twig rests .225.00
Rocker, arm; bentwood, tape seat & bk, ca 1900, 37" 230.00
Rocker, arm; oak Japanesque w/quarter-sawn figure & brass, 49" ..715.00
Side, banister-bk, scalloped crest, rush seat, old rfn, 43" 300.00
Side, hardwood QA style, rush seat, some age, 41½" 400.00
Side, mahog Vict w/cvd floral crest/slat, reuphl, 32" 140.00
Side, maple Co QA, vase splat, Spanish ft, old rfn w/red traces, 42" ...1,265.00
Side, oak Renaissance, old needlepoint uphl, 34" 265.00
Side, QA style, red & gold chinoiserie, reuphl seat, 20th C, 42" ..330.00
Side, tiger & bird's eye maple, vase splat, cane seat, 1830s, 32" .750.00
Side, walnut Baroque Revival Flemish scroll, uphl seat, 1900s ..250.00
Side, walnut Chpndl, str crest, shaped splat, 1760-80, 37" 2,600.00
Side, 3-slat ladder-bk w/trns, mushroom arm rests, splint seat ...330.00
Windsor, brace-bk, orig dk finish, Simonds, 20th C, 45" 330.00
Windsor, brace-bk continuous arm, rfn (red traces)/rprs, 37" 715.00
Windsor, Co bow-bk, rfn, 42" 495.00
Windsor, fan-bk, shaped crest, old blk pnt, early 19th C, 36" 315.00
Windsor, 7-spindle fan-bk, splayed base, gr rpt, 38" 1,100.00
Windsor, 7-spindle sack-bk, shaped arms, blk pnt, 1790s, 35" ..2,300.00
Windsor, 8-spindle sack-bk, saddle seat, salmon rpt, 38" 1,850.00
Windsor, 9-spindle brace-bk, continuous arm, rpr/rpl/rfn, 35" ...770.00
Windsor rocker, 7-spindle sack-bk, saddle seat, rfn, 1810s, 37" ..800.00
Wing-bk, birch Co Chpndl, reuphl, rpr, 47½" 1,650.00
Wing-bk, mahog Chpndl, reuphl wool plaid, 44" 1,650.00
Wing-bk, mahog Geo III, ivory reuphl, ca 1760 ....2,800.00
Wing-bk, Sheraton, worn floral tapestry uphl, trn front legs, 45" ...990.00

Chair Sets

Dining, bentwood oak/maple, Heywood-Wakefield, 2 arm+6 side ...2,850.00
Dining, mahog Chpndl style, uphl seats, worn, 38", 2 arm+4 side .890.00
Dining, mahog Chpndl style, vnr splats, cvd rails, 1 arm+5 sides ..1,155.00
Dining, mahog Geo III, rope-trn crest rail, 2 arm+6 side 2,750.00
Dining, mahog Sheraton, shield-bk, cvd corner blocks, 2 arm+8 side .3,000.00
Dining, walnut Jacobean Revival, old finish, 20th C, 2 arm+6 sides ...660.00
Kitchen, Windsor, 5-spindle, saddle seat, rprs, 20th C, 32", 9 for ..350.00
Side, Chpndl style, c&b ft, cvd/pierced splat, 20th C, 6 for ...2,300.00
Side, curly maple saber-leg, detailed, rpl cane, 34", 6 for 2,500.00
Side, mahog Am Late Classical, pierced lyre bks, sabre legs, 7 for ..1,870.00
Side, mahog Am Rococo, balloon bks, pierced crests, 4 for 500.00
Side, mahog Classical, reeded fr w/much cvg, reuhpl seat, 8 for ..2,000.00
Side, tiger maple Am Classical, cvd seats/sabre legs, 1830, 6 for ..2,640.00
Side, vase splat, wide crest, trn legs/posts, grpt w/stripes, 6 for ..1,300.00
Side, Windsor, pnt/decor step-down, all orig, 1820s, 35", 6 for ** ..9,200.00
Side, Windsor, thumb-bk w/orig pnt, J Whitney, 33", EX, 4 for 1,500.00
Side, Windsor, 9-spindle bow-bk, saddle seat, rprs, 37", 6 for .2,145.00
Side, Windsor Co, spindle-bk, plank seat, VA Valley, 33", 9 for ..2,200.00
Side, 3-slat ladder-bk w/worn red rpt, splint seat, 38", 3 for 825.00
Side, 5-splat arrow-bk, old rfn & rprs, 34", 5 for 360.00

Chests (Antique), See Also Dressers

Chest of drawers, mahogany American Federal, carved, reeded outset corners, four drawers with reeded columns, New England, ca 1820, 43x47x25", $2,000.00.

Birch Chpndl serpentine, 4 grad drw, rfn, ca 1780, 37x40x22" .3,750.00
Birch/mahog/curly maple Fed, 4-drw, rope-trn pilasters, rfn, 40x42" ..550.00
Campaign, mahog English Chpndl, 5 dvtl drw, 2-part, 38x38x19" .990.00
Cherry Chpndl, 4 grad dvtl drw, ogee ft, rprs/old rfn, 34x36" .3,600.00
Cherry Co Emp, 2 short:3 grad drw w/beading, rfn, 41x48" 935.00
Cherry Co Sheraton, 4 grad drw, paneled ends, trn ft, 45x40" ...550.00
Cherry Emp w/curly maple vnr/mahog X-banding, 7-drw, 50"+crest ..385.00
Cherry Fed bow-front, 4 dvtl drw, reeded edge top, rpr, 39x43" .1,500.00
Cherry PA Chpndl, 4 grad dvtl drw, rfn/rpl, 38x42" 2,200.00
Cherry Sheraton w/brn grpt, 4 dvtl drw w/beading, rpl pulls, 41x39" .495.00
Cherry/curly maple Hplwht w/inlay, 3-short:3 drw, 40x43" 3,000.00
Curly maple Chpndl, 4 dvtl drw:bracket ft, rpl/rfn, 38x42" 2,400.00
Mahog Emp, 4 dvtl drw, trn ft, molded pilasters, wear/cracks 165.00
Mahog English Chpndl w/pine ends, 4 grad dvtl drw, 39x34" ..1,500.00
Mahog Fed w/satin wood vnr, D-shaped facade w/4 drw, 38x46" .1,750.00
Mahog vnr English Hplwht, bow-front, 2 short:3 grad drw, 43x42" ..1,000.00
Mahog vnr Hplwht w/banding/inlay, 4-drw w/beading, 34x40" ...2,000.00
Maple QA w/figure, 2 short:3 long grad:long:3 sm drw, 2-pc, 69" ** .10,350.00
Oak Jacobean, paneled w/relief cvg, old rstr, 32x45x20" 825.00
On chest, cherry Chpndl, 9 grad drw, rprs/old rfn, 78" ** 13,000.00
On chest, cherry CT Chpndl, bonnet top, shell cvgs, 84" ** ..49,500.00
On chest, cherry QA, 3 short:4 grad long:4 drw, cvgs, 1780s, 48" ** ..9,200.00
On chest, maple Chpndl, 5 grad drw:4, brass pulls, 1770s, 76" ** ...14,950.00
On chest, Walnut PA Chpndl, bold detail, ¼-columns, 65x41" 14,300.00
On fr, English QA style, walnut & burl vnr, cabriole legs, 39" ..825.00
On fr, mahog Emp, 1 long:3 sm:3 grad drw, mahog pulls, 1830s, 53" ..2,900.00
On fr, walnut Co QA, 3 short:4 grad drw, rfn/rprs, 59x40x21" ..1,650.00
Pine English Co, 4 dvtl drw, trn ft, old natural, 32x36" 275.00
Spice, dvtl walnut w/raised panels, PA, 1780-1800, 18x16x11" ..14,950.00
Spice, primitive pine w/old patina, 8-drw, wire nails, 11x12x2⅝" 395.00
Sugar, cherry, breadbrd lid:dvtl drw:trn legs, 1880s, 40x28" 4,675.00
Sugar, cherry Southern, breadbrd lid:dvtl drw:trn ft, rfn, 32x28" ..1,750.00
Tiger maple Chpndl serpentine, 4 grad drw:ogee ft, rstr, 35x35" .16,000.00
Tiger maple Fed, str front, 4 grad drw, ca 1820, 39x42x19" 850.00
Tiger maple W&M, 2:4 drw, old finish, rprs, 48x36x17" 2,950.00
Walnut Chpndl, 4 grad dvtl drw, reeded ¼-columns, rstr, 37x40" ..1,200.00
Walnut Emp, 4-drw, set-bk lower register, pillars, 45x43" * 335.00

Cupboards (See Also Pie Safes)

Corner cupboard, cherry Country, double six-pane doors, dovetailed drawer, raised panel doors, 78x49" (at cornice), $4,675.00.
(Photo courtesy Garth's Auctions)

Ash Co, panel dos, 1 drw, rpl porc knobs, 2-pc, 86x39" 330.00
Cherry Co, dbl do:pie shelf:raised panel dos, rstr, 82x45" 990.00
Cherry Co, 2 6-pane do:2 drw:2 panel do, old rfn, 84x49" 3,950.00
Cherry/poplar/maple Co, 2 8-pane do:2 drw:2 do, rfn, 2-pc, 91x54" ..3,000.00

Corner, cherry Chpndl style, cornice:glazed do:panel do, 83x47" 4,600.00
Corner, cherry Co, 2 8-pane do:3 drw:2 panel do, 1-pc, 87" ...3,400.00
Corner, cherry Hplwht w/figure, 2 8-pane do:3 drw:2 panel do, 86x54" ..3,850.00
Corner, cherry Southern Hplwht, 12-pane do:dbl do, 2-pc, 90x44" .5,225.00
Corner, curly maple architectural 1-pc, panel dos, rstr, 100x45" 10,450.00
Corner, mahog English, curved shelves, 3-drw base, 39x23" 775.00
Corner, mahog English Chpndl style, 2-pc, ca 1900, 73x28" 715.00
Corner, pine Co, 8-pane dbl do:2 dvtl drw:2 panel do, rfn, 89" ...2,900.00
Corner, pine w/glazed panel dos, 2-drw, PA, 1800s, rstr, 78x60" ..2,000.00
Corner, poplar Co, 2 1-pane do:drw:2 panel do, 2-pc, 85x50" ...1,500.00
Corner, poplar Co, 2-tone orange rpt, panel dos, 2-pc, 81x35" ...1,045.00
Corner, walnut, 2 8-pane do:2 panel do, PA, 1-pc, 89x54", VG ..2,750.00
Corner, walnut Co, 2 6-pane do:2 drw:2 do, sq ft, 1-pc, 82x52" ..3,000.00
Corner, walnut Co w/inlay at ft, 4 panel do, KY, 85x44x47" ..2,000.00
Court, olive wood/mahog vnr Euro Renaissance style, 89x72" .2,000.00
Court, walnut Euro Renaissance Revival, moldings/cvgs, 95x62" .1,265.00
Curly maple Hplwht, 3 8-pane do:panel dos, 2-pc, 83x49" 7,900.00
Fr style, pnt w/paneled mirror, oil-on-canvas inset, 19th C, 95x48" .1,650.00
Hardwood Anglo-Indian, sunburst cvd paneled dos, 2-pc, 76x47x18" ..2,100.00
Hoosier, oak w/porc shelf & accessories, rpr/rpl, 72x41x22" 825.00
Jelly, pine w/orig red flame grpt, paneled stiles, 63x45" 4,600.00
Jelly, pine/poplar Co w/grpt, wide brds, brd & batten do, 40x42" ...550.00
Jelly, poplar Co, 3 drw:2 panel dos, paneled ends, rfn, 53" 600.00
Jelly, 2 short:long drw:2 panel do, old rpt grpt, 51x42" 1,700.00
Kitchen, poplar, hutch top:zinc work top:2 drw:dbl do, 62x42" .330.00
Oak Euro, appl moldings/cvd scene on top do, 2-pc, 1900s, 87" ...550.00
Pewter, pine Co, open shelves:top:dbl do, rprs, old finish, 71" ..1,650.00
Pewter, pine w/old rpt, 2-brd dos in base, 1-pc, 75x44" 550.00
Pewter, poplar primitive 1-pc w/open front, 1-brd dos, 72x42" ..1,400.00
Pewter, 2-shelf top:base w/2 drw, shoe-ft, 64x32x11", EX 1,000.00
Pine step-bk, panel dos:shelf:2 drw:panel dos, old rpt, 1-pc, 79x62" 6,000.00
Poplar/walnut Co, 2 8-pane do:3 drw:2 panel do, 2-pc, rfn, 82x51" 825.00
Step-bk, cherry Co, 2 8-pane do:2 panel do, old finish, 1-pc, 81x45" ..2,000.00
Step-bk, pine Co cleaned to red stain, panel dos, 1-pc, rprs, 75" ..660.00
Step-bk, pine w/grpt, 2 panel do:panel do, 1-pc, rprs, 78x41" 880.00
Step-bk, poplar Co 2-pc w/wht traces, dbl do:2 drw:2 panel do, 86x42" ..275.00
Step-bk, walnut, 2 9-pane do:2 drw:2 panel do, 1-pc, 81x46" * 1,980.00
Table-top, poplar, 2 panel do, molded cornice, old red, 22x28x16" ..1,200.00
Walnut Canadian, dbl do:pie shelf:2 drw:2 panel do, rstr, 85x65" 4,400.00
Walnut Co, panel do:panel do, brass thumb latches, 1-pc, 77" 1,375.00
Walnut Co, 2 panel do:2, high tapered ft, CI thumb latch, 84" .1,815.00
Walnut Gothic Revival w/jigsaw work, 4-drw, hangs, 37x16x7" ...385.00
Walnut traditional style, 1-pc, dbl do:3 drw, 20th C, 61x32x16" ..440.00

Desks

Lady's writing desk, bird's-eye maple and faux bamboo, American Aesthetic with carving, three-compartment top with gallery, slant front with fitted interior, New York, 1875 – 85, 52½x32", $6,000.00.

Blond mahog Hplwht style w/inlay, 20th C, 29x48x30" 220.00
Burl walnut Emp style, center drw, tapered legs, 20th C, 51" .1,265.00
Butler's, cherry/curly maple Emp, 3-drw w/beading, paw ft, OH, 58" ..1,925.00
Butler's, curly maple/cherry Fed w/mahog/walnut burl inlay, 54" ...4,600.00
Campaign, camphorwood, brass bound, Ch, 19th C, rfn, 41x36x17" .4,000.00
Cherry Hplwht, slant front, Fr ft, scrolled apron, 8-drw, 46" ..3,000.00
Clerk's, pine Hplwht style, 2-drw top:lift lid:sq legs, rfn, 20th C ..200.00
Clerk's, walnut Vict, high trn legs, 2-drw, attached top, 85" ...1,430.00
Curly cherry Hplwht w/inlay, slant front:4 grad drw, rfn, 44x39" ..3,850.00
Curly maple Hplwht, slant front, 4-drw w/beading, rstr, 42" ...3,300.00
Davenport, mahog Geo III, 4-drw, leather top, EX 1,300.00
Hardwood Euro 2-pc Medieval style, cvd figures/heads, 68x34x15" ..2,100.00
Mahog Chpndl style, slant front, c/b ft, NY, 42" 385.00
Mahog Chpndl-style serpentine, Maddox...NY, 20th C, rfn, 40x29x16" ..440.00
Mahog CT Chpndl w/block front, fitted int, 9-drw, 43x42x22" * 3,850.00
Mahog Fed w/inlay, cove-molded top:3 do:top:4-drw, 1800s, 54x42" ..4,300.00
Partner's, mahog Geo III, leather inset top, ped ends, 71" 5,500.00
Pine Co Emp, 3 dvtl drw, fold-down top, crest missing, 37x37x19" .770.00
Roll-top, cherry, S-curve top w/fitted int, 8-drw, rfn, 45x48" 550.00
Roll-top, oak, C-curve, 8-drw, fitted int, rfn, 46x48" 600.00
Roll-top, oak, S-curve, 8-drw, fitted int, rfn, 54x48" 950.00
Walnut Vict w/burl vnr, slant front, 3-drw, rpr/rfn, 40x42" 600.00
Walnut vnr Sheraton style w/figured vnr on facade/fronts, 30x43" 110.00
Walnut/burl walnut Am, knee-hole, ped, gallery, 1870, 43x51x29" ...1,200.00

Dressers (Machine Age), See Also Chests

Walnut and burl walnut American Victorian dresser with carving, marble tops, drop front, four candle stands, brass pulls, ca 1870, 38x46x23", $1,200.00.

Cherry Vict w/mahog vnr facade, 3-drw/handkerchief drw/mirror, 80" ..360.00
Golden Oak Era, 2 short drw beside do:3 drw, appl cvgs, 48"+crest .330.00
Mahog Chpndl-style serpentine w/figured facade, 4-drw, 20th C, 34x38" ..770.00
Mahog Louis XV style w/inlay, marble top, 5-drw, 20th C, 42" .770.00
Oak Gothic style, relief-cvd panels, rpl legs, CI hinges, 35" 550.00
Walnut Vict, 3 dvtl drw (1 hidden in base), marble top, 32x46" ..440.00

Dry Sinks

Am southern pine, hinged top, 2-do, 19th C, 33x37x19" 330.00
Hutch bk, bl wash, 63x32x18" 550.00
Mahog Am Late Classical, hinged top, trn ft, 1850s, 31x30x17" ..715.00
Maple/poplar Co hutch-top, dbl do in base, 3 drw at right, 51x48" ..800.00
Oak w/yel grpt, panel dos w/scalloped stile/rails, 2 dvtl drw, 45" ..500.00
Poplar, hutch top w/4 drw:shelf:3 drw beside dbl do, rpl knobs ..1,850.00
Poplar Co, high bk w/shelf:shelf:drw:dbl do, gr rpt, 52x43" 770.00
Poplar Co, hutch top w/3 drw:shelf:panel dos, old rpt, 54" 2,000.00
Poplar Co w/old yel-gold rpt, made from cupboard, drw, 37x47x22" .495.00

Hall Piece

Hall stand, walnut and walnut veneer, Renaissance Revival, medallion crest with arched top, mirror, marble top, lower drawer, ca 1875, 101x64", $2,000.00.

Bench, Am Gothic, 3-part crest/quatrefoil spire, uphl, 66x49x23" .**6,000.00**
Bench, walnut Italian w/Renaissance inspiration, uphl, 19th C, 58x54" ..**1,750.00**
Chair, oak Jacoban w/caned bk/seat, eagle crest, 1850s, pr **1,000.00**
Coat rack, twig hooks on barley twist support, ball ft, Vict, 84" ..**1,300.00**
Pier table, mahog Classical w/old Fr polish & cvg, marble top, 42" .**1,750.00**
Rack, chrome frwork w/hat shelf: mirror/shelf, Deco, 27x43" .**3,700.00**
Stand, oak Vict, appl cvgs, stag frieze, shaped seats, 122x68" .**2,750.00**
Stand, rosewood & ebony, trn hooks, Vict, 76" **5,000.00**
Stand, walnut/burl walnut Am Renaissance w/pier mirror, 1865, 126" ..**6,000.00**
Table, Classical style w/mirror top, gilt brass apron, 20th C, 30" **2,600.00**
Tree, blk enameled wood, ball ft, chrome fixtures, drw, mirror, 76" ...**500.00**
Tree, Golden Oak era, appl foliate, CI hooks, mirror bk, pnt, 83" **660.00**
Tree, Golden Oak era, trn/molded details, drw & rack, 74" **340.00**

Highboys

Cherry Chpndl, 3 short:2:4 long:2 short drw, PA, 1760s, 79" ..**11,500.00**
Cherry Co Chpndl, cabriole legs/c&b ft w/cyma cvg, 4 grad drws, 75" ..**4,600.00**
Cherry QA, 4 short drw:4 grad:1 long:3 short:cabriole legs, rfn, 73" **6,000.00**
Cherry/maple MA QA, fan cvgs, 13-drw, rprs/rpl/rfn, 77x36" **8,500.00**
Curly maple QA, 5 grad drw:long:3 short drw, 2-pc, rfn, 73" ..**8,000.00**
Curly maple W&M style, 7 dvtl drw, handmade repro, 66" **5,600.00**
Mahog vnr/oak/pine W&M, 3-part, rfn/rpl, worn finish, 64½" **1,870.00**
Maple QA bonnet-top w/curly facade, 4-drw, cabriole legs, rfn, 86" ..**5,000.00**
QA (NH) walnut/birch, cvd shells, 3 trn finials, 84" **15,400.00**
Walnut Chpndl, 9 grad drw, ogee ft, rpl brasses/rfn, 1800s, 69" **3,000.00**
Walnut PA QA, flame finials, fan cvgs, acorn drops, rstr, 84" ** **18,700.00**
Walnut QA w/figured vnr/X banding, 2 short:3:3 short drw, 64x39" ..**8,000.00**
Walnut/maple QA, 2 short:4 long:3 drw:cabriole legs, 1750s, 72" **17,250.00**

Lowboys

Figured walnut PA QA, cvd shell/foliage columns, 30x28" ** ...**19,800.00**
Mahog English QA, 3 dvtl drw, rnd tapered legs, rpl brasses ..**1,700.00**
Mahog w/inlay, 2 bow-front drw, cabriole legs w/c&b ft, 29x30" ..**330.00**
Oak English Chpndl, 3-drw, sq tapered legs, some age, rfn, 30" .**500.00**
Oak W&M, trn legs w/ball ft, drw, mortised/pinned apron, rstr, 30" ...**440.00**
Walnut Chpndl, 2-brd top:4 drw:cabriole legs:c&b ft, rstr, 29x35" ..**2,475.00**
Walnut QA, molded edge top, central drw/2 sq drw, 28x30x19" **3,000.00**
Walnut QA w/band & compass star inlay, 6-drw, trn drops, 32" ** ..**15,400.00**

Pie Safes

Cherry Co, 12 punched tin panels, dvtl drw in base, gallery, 60x40" ..**1,000.00**
Pine, mortised fr, punched tin panels, old rpr, 45x36" **1,265.00**
Pine Fed w/old red, punched tin panels, sq legs, 19th C **750.00**
Poplar Co, high ft, 1-brd ends, 2 high drw, punched tin, rpt, 58" .**770.00**
Poplar Co, nailed drw, dbl do, 1-brd ends w/cut-out ft, 49x41" ..**1,375.00**
Poplar Co, nailed drw, 12 tin panels, GF Co, rfn, 50x40x14" **850.00**
Walnut & cherry, 3 dvtl drw, punched tin panels, gallery, 55" * ...**900.00**

Secretaries

Golden Oak era, fall-front lid by do, 3-drw, crest, 70" **500.00**
Mahog Chpndl, 4 dvtl drw, slant front, cvg/fretwork, 2-pc, 92" **6,875.00**
Mahog Hplwht style w/inlay, tambour top:drop front:2 do, 2-pc, 75" **1,750.00**
Mahog III mahog w/bookcase, dbl mirror do, late 18th C, 81x39x20½" .**4,300.00**
Oak (quarter-sawn) vnr Vict, slant lid, appl cvgs, paw ft, 78" .**1,100.00**
Poplar Co, 4 dvtl drw, fold-down lid, fitted int, old rpt, 2-pc, 86" ...**2,400.00**
Walnut Hplwht w/figure & inlay, panel dos:drop front:4 drw, 90x40" ** ..**21,000.00**
Walnut Vict Eastlake w/burl vnr, 3 dvtl drw, 2-pc, 90" **1,870.00**
Walnut Vict w/burl vnr & Eastlake detail, 2-pc, 90x39" **1,700.00**
Walnut/burl vnr Vict, arched do:drop front:2 drw:panel dos, 92" ..**1,650.00**

Settees

Barrister's, reclining bk, brass pineapple finials, uphl, 59", pr .**1,100.00**
Fr-style Rococo Revival, cvd, gr w/orig gilt, reuphl, 20th C, 60" ..**750.00**
Hardwood Co, trn legs, plank seat, scrolled arms, spindle bk, 48" .**300.00**
Mahog Adam-style w/cvd urns/swags, caned bk/seat, 39x61x23" ...**880.00**
Mahog Directory-style w/ram's head arm terminals, hoof ft, 48" ..**1,000.00**
Mixed wood Fed, str crest, horizontal splat, plank seat, 19th C, 52" ..**400.00**
Oak Euro Baroque style, oak base (worn), reuphl, 20th C, 60" ..**935.00**
Rswd Rococo Revival cvd in Stanton Hall pattern, att Meeks, 66" ..**5,500.00**
Walnut finger-cvd Vict fr, reuphl in brocade, rpr to fr, 62" **385.00**
Walnut/hardwood Vict w/trn/cvd details, worn uphl, 52" **275.00**

Shelves

Clock, grpt, appl molding, arched bkbrd, 15x18x5" **275.00**
Corner, fretwork w/trn finials, mirrored bk, late, 27" **95.00**
Corner, pine Co, curved front, triangle brackets, 13" **250.00**
Corner, walnut Vict, trn/fretwork details, 6 grad shelves, 67" **160.00**
Corner etagere, walnut, 6 grad shelves, trn posts, 68x27", VG ..**220.00**
Corner etegere, walnut Vict, trn spools, 7-shelf, 77x32" **250.00**
Etagere, Oriental rswd w/cvd birds etc, c/b ft, 60x36" **750.00**
Etagere, Vict walnut, Louis XV, dolphin crest, EX cvg, 89" **2,100.00**
Gothic Revival, reverse-cut mirror insert, hangs, damage, 29" ..**165.00**
Kettle, wrought iron fr w/brass rtcl shelf, trn wood hdl, 13" H ..**200.00**
Mahog Geo III, 4 sq shelves:2 drw:single do, 19th C, 63x21x21" .**1,600.00**
Pine Co, old dk gr pnt, bj ft/chamfered corner top, 25x47x9" ...**450.00**
Pine Co w/old gr, 4 single shelves, cut-out fr, 50x34" **550.00**
Pine Co w/old gray, 2-shelf w/bk, sq nails, 36x35" **525.00**
Pine Euro w/orig rose-mulled decor on red ground, rpr, 59" **495.00**
Pine w/old blk, 3 step-bk shelves, sq nails, 34x29" **1,100.00**
Pine w/old red, 1-brd ends w/cut-out ft, 3 step-bk shelves, 46x43" .**935.00**
Walnut Eastlake Vict, 3-D relief-cvd eagle, old varnish, 20x17" **385.00**
Walnut w/old red stain, scalloped bracket ends, 2 nailed drw, 32" .**550.00**

Sideboards

Cherry Am Fed w/inlay, 2 short drw:bottle drws, gallery, 47x35" ..**1,800.00**
Hunt, walnut Southern, high-trn legs, 3 dvtl drws, rprs, 44x49" ...**2,475.00**
Mahog Am Sheraton style, 3 drw:4 do, fluted pilasters, 50x72x24" .**880.00**
Mahog English Regency, panel dos, ped base, crest, 49x66" ...**1,375.00**
Mahog Fed w/inlay, drw:2 do flanked by dos, NY, 1790s, 37x77" **6,900.00**
Mahog Hplwht style w/inlay, bowed center, rstr/rpl, 38x58x19" **2,200.00**
Mahog Hplwht style w/inlay, 3 dvtl drw:3 do, 19th C, 40x58x25" ...**1,650.00**

Mahog vnr Hplwht-style serpentine w/appl fans, 20th C, 39x68x24" .825.00
Maple/cherrywood Am Late Fed, 3 short:3 long drw, 1820s, 48x48" 1,750.00
Server, Golden Oak era, cvd designs, beveled glass, OH, 79x44x20" ..825.00
Server, mahog Roll-X, brass inlay, marble top, 1825, 47x42" 12,650.00
Server, walnut Eastlake Vict w/burl vnr, marble top, 2-pc, 48x54" ..385.00
Server, walnut Euro Renaissance, drw:2 panel do, marble top, 34x45" .440.00
Walnut/curly maple Co Sheraton w/inlay, 4-drw, rstr/rpr, 43x69" .5,500.00

Sofas

Rosewood sofa, American Late Classical, with distinctive back, scroll arms, S-scroll supports, and feet on brass castors, ca 1835, 40x80", $3,575.00.

Chpndl style, camel-bk, velvet uphl, Ethan Allen, 20th C, 79" ..200.00
Fainting couch, walnut Vict fr w/scroll ft, reuphl, 72" 440.00
Mahog Centennial Emp style, cornucopia supports, uphl, 90" 1,250.00
Mahog Classical, cvd paw ft, acanthus details, old reuphl, 91" ...1,100.00
Mahog Emp w/figure, detailed cvg w/serpents, lyre arms, rstr, 107" ..3,850.00
Mahog Emp w/inlay, paw ft/acanthus/floral cvg, reuphl, 75" 880.00
Mahog Fed, cvd sq bk/curved arms, old reuphl/finish, 1815, 78" .2,400.00
Mahog Hplwht style w/banded inlay, brass rosettes, 79" 1,870.00
Mahog vnr Emp w/brocade reuphl, 92", VG+ 745.00
Mahog vnr Emp w/scroll ft & arms, reuphl, old finish, 82" 850.00
Mahog William IV, cvd crest/rosettes, reuphl, ca 1835, 82" 2,200.00
Mahog/satin wood Sheraton style, old uphl, ca 1900, 66" 1,100.00
Walnut Eastlake Vict w/burl vnr, medallion bk w/crest, reuphl, 66" ..330.00
Walnut Engish Vict w/Renaissance inspiration, uphl, 1850s, 87" 550.00
Walnut Vict medallion-bk w/fruit-cvd crest, reuphl, 59" 220.00

Stands

Bedside, cherry Co, dvtl drw, 2-brd top, old rfn, 30x20x20" 135.00
Bedside, curly & bird's-eye maple Co, dvtl drw, 2-brd top, rfn ...715.00
Bedside, walnut, dvtl drw, alligatored varnish, 29x20x17" 195.00
Bedside, walnut, dvtl drw, trn legs, rfn, rpl top, 29x22x19" 185.00
Birch Co Hplwht, dvtl drw, 2-brd top, old red, 27x17x17" 2,000.00
Canterbury, Fr rswd, trn dividers, shelf, casters, 1850s, 18x17" ..770.00
Cherry Co, dvtl drw, 2-brd top, trn legs, rfn, 29x19x18" 300.00
Cherry Co Hplwht, dvtl/beaded drw, sq legs, rstr top, 21x17" 600.00
Cherry Co Sheraton w/2-brd curly maple top, dvtl drw, rfn, 22x20" .440.00
Cherry Co w/burl & curly maple vnr, appl trns, 2-drw/2-brd top ..385.00
Curly maple Co Hplwht, tripod base, 1-brd top, rpl/rfn, 26x21" dia ..700.00
Curly maple Sheraton, 2 dvtl drw, 2-brd top, rfn 1,150.00
Dictionary, oak Am Late Vict, slant top, shelves, 33x27x13" 165.00
Drop-leaf, walnut, 2 dvtl drw w/inlay, trn legs, rfn, 39x23x15" ..330.00
Fern, cvd & ebonized Am, rouge marble/slate top, 1880s, 34" ...385.00
Hardwood Co Hplwht, tripod base w/chamfered legs, 28x19x15" ..2,000.00
Magazine, Knaus Mfg, vertical slats, 42¼x21x12" 975.00
Magazine, Medina #133, spindle sides, 32x19x12" 375.00
Mahog/curly maple Sheraton, trn/ring legs, 2-drw, rpl pulls 2,400.00
Marjorelle, 3-tier, floral inlay, rpr/wear, 49x22x16" 3,700.00
Pedestal, ebonized hardwood Emp Revival w/scrolls & satyr heads, 48" ..1,100.00
Pedestal, walnut/ebonized/gilded Am Neo-Greco w/much cvg, 1870s, 42" ...3,750.00
Plant, corner style, 4 stepped tiers, 44x44" 300.00
Rswd English Sheraton, 3-tier, trn legs/posts, drw, 42x19x15" ...1,400.00
Telephone, walnut cvd Rococo details, 20th C, 48" 300.00
Tilt-top, pnt papier-mache & pine, CT, 1850s, 17x28" dia 2,600.00
Walnut Co Sheraton w/mahog vnr drw fronts (2), 2-brd top, 28" .250.00
Walnut Emp, scrolled ft, trn columns, dvtl drw, rprs, 30x19x19" ..330.00
Walnut Fr style w/blk marble top, 20th C, 39x11x12" 825.00
Work, pine/poplar Co, 2-drw, hinged top, old rfn, 30x18x14" ...360.00
3-tier, mahog w/trn ft & rope-spiral cvd posts, MIE, 36x15x12", pr ..2,100.00

Stools

Footstool, bamboo Windsor, JC Hubbard Boston stamp, 32", VG ...415.00
Footstool, bamboo Windsor, worn red rpt w/yel striping, 6x12x5" ...165.00
Footstool, birch Biedermeier, ebonized spindles, uphl, 23" L, pr 2,600.00
Footstool, curly & bird's-eye maple Sheraton, cane top, 7x13x8" 440.00
Footstool, mahog base w/sq legs, cvd apron, reuphl top, 9x14x10" ...220.00
Footstool, mahog Hplwht, reuphl brocade top, reeded legs, 20x17x17" ..935.00
Footstool, walnut QA, cabriole legs, slip seat, 18th C, 17x23x17" ...1,950.00
Jacobean-style 'Kittinger', expanding top, cubbyhole, hinged do ..110.00
Joiner's, oak Jacobean style, trn supports, 17x17½x10" 170.00
Ottoman, mahog ogee stepped/molded fr, bracket ft, 1850s 275.00
Piano, cvd oak & gilt-incised, spindle-bk, swivels, Vict 400.00
Piano, trn center post & legs, dk gr pnt, late 1800s, 9¼x7¼" 225.00

Tables

Walnut Renaissance Revival library table, carved, with variegated marble top, ca 1875, 20x38x23", $800.00.

Banquet, cherry Fed w/mahog flame vnr on ogee apron, rfn, 79" ..2,000.00
Banquet, mahog Fed, 2-part, much cvg, ca 1825, rfn, 75" 1,750.00
Boule, cabriole legs, dvtl drw, ormolu trim, ca 1900, 32x58" ..1,300.00
Breakfast, mahog Fed, 2-drw, center cvd ped, paw ft, 49" 900.00
Card, Cherry Hplwht w/inlay, sq legs, stringing on top, 36" ...2,850.00
Card, mahog Fed, folding top, serpentine front, cvgs, 38x37x18" 1,800.00
Card, mahog Geo II, fold-over top, cabriole legs, 1750s, 39x28x14" .1,500.00
Card, mahog Hplwht, D-shape apron, swing-leg supports leaf, 35x17" .1,750.00
Card, mahog Sheraton, reeded edge top, shaped apron 2,600.00
Card, maple/birch/bird's-eye maple Fed, serpentine front, 1820s 1,500.00
Center, rswd Am Aesthetic w/incised gilt, marble top, 30x35x23" ..1,400.00
Coffee, oak/maple Heywood-Wakefield, 2 rectangular tiers 250.00
Console, hardwood English Sheraton-style w/inlay, 20th C, 30x17" .2,100.00
Console, mahog (bleached) Euro, marble top:2 drw:shelf:reeded legs ...275.00
Console, mahog Geo III style w/inlay, demilune, 39x53x26", pr 2,200.00
Corner, mahog w/spider-web inlay top, cabriole legs, rpr, 30" 300.00
Dining, Cherry Co Hplwht, tapered legs, 1-brd, rfn, 36"+leaves ..495.00
Dining, mahog, 2-ped, banded, 2-leaf, Kittinger, 44x68", EX .2,300.00
Dining, mahog Duncan Phyfe style w/brass paw ft, flame vnr band ...800.00

Dining, mahog Geo III-style w/rswd inlay, 168" (w/leaves) **4,675.00**
Dining, mahog Regency, 2-ped, paw ft on casters, rfn, 1812-25, 74" .**1,500.00**
Dining, oak, center leg support, ball ft, 42" sq, +4 leaves **400.00**
Dining, oak Jacobean Revival, trn legs, dbl Y stretcher, open: 114" **500.00**
Dining, walnut, trn/fluted legs, molded apron, 20th C, 48"+leaves **600.00**
Dining/drop-leaf, mahog Am Fed, 2-part, 1820s, 28x48x118" **2,750.00**
Dressing, pine w/flame grpt/striping/gold stencil, dvtl drw, 36x36" ...**3,850.00**
Dressing, walnut QA, 3-drw, cabriole legs, 1760s, 39x31x19" ** ...**16,000.00**
Drop-leaf, birch/maple Co Hplwht w/old red, rpl hinges, 39"+leaves ..**550.00**
Drop-leaf, cherry, dvtl drw, swing-leg, rprs/rfn, 46"+leaves **440.00**
Drop-leaf, cherry, dvtl drw w/curved front, 2-brd top, 19"+leaves ...**330.00**
Drop-leaf, cherry/bird's-eye maple Fed, 2-part, 1820s, 82" **1,725.00**
Drop-leaf, curly maple Sheraton, drw, 3-brd top, rfn, 36"+leaves ..**525.00**
Drop-leaf, ebonized Napoleon w/brass inlay, 1880s, 29x50x26" ..**1,100.00**
Drop-leaf, mahog Chpndl, 8 sq molded/tapered legs, 50"+20" leaves ..**990.00**
Drop-leaf, mahog English Hplwht style, spade ft, drw, 42"+leaves ..**200.00**
Drop-leaf, mahog English QA style, swing legs, 41"+leaves **220.00**
Drop-leaf, mahog Fed, swing-leg, reeded details, VA, 47"+leaves **935.00**
Drop-leaf, mahog Fed, trn legs w/acanthus cvgs, worn, 39"+leaves **440.00**
Drop-leaf, mahog QA, oval top, much rpr, faded finish, 35"+leaves ..**600.00**
Drop-leaf, maple/cherry QA, cabriole legs, 2-brd top, rfn, 27x44x15" .**2,200.00**
Drop-leaf, oak w/old natural finish, rprs/rpl top, 36"+leaves **770.00**
Drop-leaf, tiger maple, 6 ring-trn legs, old rfn, ca 1825, 57" ...**3,335.00**
Drop-leaf, walnut Co, 6 legs (2 swing), 1-brd top, rfn, 46"+leaves **415.00**
Drop-leaf, walnut QA, swing legs, 2-brd top, rprs, 39x50"+leaves .**2,200.00**
Drop-leaf, walnut Southern Sheraton, 6 trn legs, drw, 47"+leaves **500.00**
Drop-leaf breakfast, cherry Fed Pembroke, 1800s, 20" closed **920.00**
Drop-leaf breakfast, mahog vnr Fed, NY, 1810s, 27x32+20" leaves .**1,400.00**
Drop-leaf work, rswd Fr, serpentine top, 2-drw, hinged cupboard bk ...**440.00**
Drum, Classical style w/mc wood vnr, burl top, 20th C, 29x16" ...**195.00**
Drum, mahog Fed, scimitar legs w/brass casters, rprs, 28x36" **880.00**
Farmhouse, cherry Fr Provincial, 1 draw leaf, end drw, open: 110" ..**3,500.00**
Gallery, mahog English, tripod base, trn columns, 1890s, 24" dia ...**330.00**
Hutch, cherry w/old rfn, shoe ft, 3-brd top, 29x43x45½" **5,000.00**
Hutch, hardwood/pine Co w/old red traces, mortised/pinned, 47" ...**880.00**
Library, mahog Chpndl style, c&b ft, cvd knees/apron, rpl top, 24" .**165.00**
Library, rswd William IV, concealed frieze drws, 50" **1,870.00**
Library, walnut QA style, Hickory Chair repro, 29x43x23" **220.00**
Parlor, Louis XVI style, gilt base w/ormolu, onyx top, 20th C, 29x22" **300.00**
Parlor, rswd Vict, turtle top, cvd apron, marble top, 30x42x25" **1,750.00**
Parlor, walnut Vict Gothic Revival w/rswd vnr apron, rpl top, 36" ..**495.00**
Parlor, wlanut Vict Rococo Revival, wht ovolo marble top, rfn, 33" .**660.00**
Sawbuck, old dk finish, 2-brd scrubbed top, 26x19x31" **660.00**
Sawbuck, pine w/old red rpt on base, natural 1-brd top, 29x49x25" .**800.00**
Sawbuck, pnt pine, overhanging top, Xd legs, 1850s, 30x50x28" ..**2,000.00**
Sewing, curly maple, molded edge, folding, 20th C, rfn, 27x34x22" ..**330.00**
Sewing, mahog vnr & grained Classical, drop-leaf, NY, 1840s ..**1,150.00**
Sewing, mahog vnr Fed, 2-drw, sliding bag fr, ca 1805, 29x21x16" .**1,600.00**
Snooker, mahog, Cox & Yemen, English, 1850s, 150x78" **7,150.00**
Sofa, mahog Geo III, 2 frieze drw opposed by sham drws, 19th C, 38" L .**1,600.00**
Sofa, mahog Geo III style w/inlay, 2 drw/2 mock drw, brass pulls, 34" **1,200.00**
Tavern, maple Co QA, splayed base/trn legs/1-brd top, rfn, 29x22" **880.00**
Tavern, walnut QA, 2 dvtl drw, removable 1-brd top, 30x30x17" ** **27,500.00**
Tea, curly maple QA top, cabriole legs, arpon, 30x20" **3,000.00**
Tea, mahog Chpndl, 3-tier, tripod base w/snake ft, rfn, 42x23" ...**990.00**
Tea, mahog English Chpndl style w/tilt top, c&b ft, 19th C ..**1,045.00**
Tilt-top, cherry/mahog Co, tripod w/spider legs, ball ft, 21" dia .**990.00**
Tilt-top, ebonized vnr Emp w/ivory inlay, cvd column, 18½" .**1,400.00**
Tilt-top, mahog Hplwht, trn column:tripod w/spider legs, rprs, 22" L ...**550.00**
Trestle, rfn pine, pins/wedges rpl, 3-brd top, 19th C, 30x55x32" ..**550.00**
Work, cherry Co, dvtl drw, trn legs, 3-brd top, old finish, 47" ...**500.00**
Work, cherry/walnut Co Hplwht, 1-brd top, wear, 39x42x26" ...**825.00**
Work, mahog Classical, trn/reeded legs, 3 dvtl drw w/beading, 24" ..**1,400.00**
Work, walnut PA Co Sheraton, 2 dvtl drw, 2-brd top, rfn, 51" ..**800.00**
Work, walnut/cherry/mahog Sheraton, 3-drw, 1-brd top, rstr, 25x17" ..**1,400.00**
Writing, rswd Regency style w/inlay, trn legs, 26x30x17" **385.00**
Writing, walnut Am Rococo, 2-drw, cabriole legs, 1850s, 51" **1,400.00**
Writing, walnut William IV, leather top, compartments, 39x27x24" ..**770.00**

Wardrobes

Wardrobe, mahogany Victorian double-door, stepped cornice with egg-and-dart frieze, paneled doors with grained veneers, two drawers, plinth base, ca 1850s, 98x64x25", $2,200.00.

Irish pine breakdown, 3 do:2 drw, 3-shelf, rstr, 8x156x24" **750.00**
Kas, cherry Co, dvtl case & drws, rpl ft/rprs, 77x49" **2,800.00**
Linen press, mahog Fed w/inlay, NY, 1820s, 88x48x22" **9,775.00**
Linen press, mahog Geo III, Greek Key cornice:panel dos:drws, 70" ...**3,000.00**
Linen press, mahog Late Georgian, 2-part, later base, 89x49x20" **3,100.00**
Linen press, poplar w/grpt, panel do:3 drw:2 do, 2-pc, 86" **1,550.00**
On fr, burl walnut Vict, panel dos, 3 drw, ca 1870, 81x47" **1,450.00**
Pine, 2 fr-panel do, scroll finial, 79x36" **335.00**
Pine Am, 2-do w/dbl panels, 2 base drw, 83x42" **450.00**
Rswd Neo-Greco, 3 mirror do, appl cvgs, ca 1875, 112x106x23" ..**6,600.00**
Walnut Vict, wide cornice, breakdown base, 86x60" **1,650.00**
Walnut Vict w/Eastlake detail & burl vnr, breakdown, 2-drw, 85x53" ...**990.00**

Washstands

Ash w/trn legs, dvtl drw, towel bars, rfn, 29"+crest **275.00**
Cherry Co Sheraton, low gallery, dvtl drw, 29x20" **300.00**
Cherry Vict, red-brn marble top:do & 3 dvtl drw, rfn, 37x31x16" ..**195.00**
Cherry/walnut Co Sheraton, galleried top:shelf:dvtl drw, 37" **200.00**
Corner, mahog Hplwht, sq legs, 1 dvtl/2 false drw, shelf, 46" **700.00**
Golden Oak era, quarter-sawn figure, 3-drw, panel do, rpl bar, 58" .**300.00**
Mahog Am Fed w/figured vnr, bow-front, trn legs, dvtl drw, 30" .**275.00**
Mahog English Sheraton, dvtl drw/gallery, trn legs **275.00**
Pine English, old putty-colored grpt, dvtl drw, tile top, 43" **400.00**
Walnut Vict, appl moldings/cvgs, dvtl drw, marble top w/crest, 41" ...**550.00**
Walnut Vict, dvtl drw:dbl-do, appl moldings/fruit pulls, crest **525.00**

Miscellaneous

Bedroom suite, Am cvd rswd w/Fr Restauration influence, 1850s, 5-pc ..**35,750.00**
Bedroom suite, burled mahog fronts, Continental, 20th C, 6-pc ..**600.00**
Case of drws, rfn oak, 11 machine-dvtl drws, wire nails, hangs, 22x20" **600.00**
Easel, ebonzied marquetry inlay & burl walnut Am Renaissance, 78" .**2,500.00**
Firescreen, cvd rswd w/leaves/scrolls, 3-ftd, 1860s, 55x28" **1,100.00**
Ice box, pine Co, paneled dos, top lifts, metal lined, rfn, 48" **440.00**
Ice box, poplar Co, trn ft w/castors, worn rfn, 30x34x21" **250.00**
Library steps, mahog Geo II metomorphic, leather treads, 19th C **4,300.00**
Mantel, pine Emp w/worn wht pnt w/gray marbleizing, OH, 54x62" **300.00**

Mantel, pine Fed w/blk pnt, appl moldings, reeded/fluted, 53x58x6" ..1,100.00
Mantel, pine w/old rpt, appl moldings/reeding, 56x54" 688.00
Mantel, wht variegated marble w/shell/flower cvgs, 42x52x16" ..2,000.00
Pole screen, cvd rswd William IV w/embr panel, brass pole, 1835 .475.00
Pole screen, rswd William IV, lotus-cvd base, 54" 880.00
Quilt rack, 5 horizontal slats, putty-colored pnt, pinned, shoe ft ..250.00
Salon suite, walnut Am Egyptian Revival, reuphl, ornate cvgs, 4-pc ..6,000.00
Screen, folding; tromp l'oeil on oak vnr, contemporary, 72" 400.00
Terrarium, walnut, deep cove-molded base, Am, 1860s, 21¾x38x24" .975.00

Galena

Potteries located in Galena, Illinois, area were generally plain utility wares with lead glaze and often found in a pumpkin color with some slip decoration or splashes of other colors. These potteries thrived from the early 1830s until sometime around 1860. In the listings that follow, all items are made of red clay unless noted otherwise.

Jar, gr & orange mottle, flakes, 10" 415.00
Wall pocket vases, mottled gr-amber w/brn flecks, 7¾", pr 220.00

Galle

Emile Galle was one of the most important producers of cameo glass in France. His firm, founded in Nancy in 1874, produced beautiful cameo in the Art Nouveau style during the 1890s, using a variety of techniques. He also produced glassware with enameled decoration, as well as some fine pottery — animal figurines, table services, vases, and other objets d' art. In the mid-1880s he became interested in the various colors and textures of natural woods and as a result began to create furniture which he used as yet another medium for expression of his artistic talent. Marquetry was the primary method Galle used in decorating his furniture, preferring landscapes, Nouveau floral and fruit arrangements, butterflies, squirrels, and other forms from nature. It is for his furniture and his cameo glass that he is best known today. All Galle is signed.

In the listings below, 'fp' indicates items that have been fire polished. Our advisor for this category is Don Williams; he is listed in the Directory under Missouri.

Cameo

Vase, water lilies, citron, brown, and white on frost to teal, carved and mold blown, 10", NM, $12,650.00.

Atomizer, floral, burgundy on yel, orig hardware, 9" 1,800.00
Atomizer, trees/mtns/lake, bl on bl/gr/yel, stick neck, 7" 1,800.00
Bowl, ferns, gr/yel on frost, 5x7½" 1,600.00
Bowl, leaves & pods on branches, dk gr/citron on frost, 4x11" ..1,600.00
Box, floral, purple on burgundy/amber, 2¾x6½" 1,200.00
Box, leaves, gr on bl/lav, 2¼x4½" dia 1,100.00
Box, leaves & berries, purple on frost, 3x7" 2,350.00
Lamp, grapes/leaves on 7" dome shade & base, red on yel, 14" .7,500.00
Lamp base, stylized foliage, frost/lav/gr, 15½" 400.00
Night light, trees, blk on pk/gr frost, slim, metal stand, 9" 3,400.00
Shot glass, leafy sprigs, olive-gr on frost & citron, 1¾" 500.00
Shot glass, leaves, lt/dk gr on pk to frost, 2½" 800.00
Toothpick holder, floral, lav & gr on apricot & frost, 2½" 800.00
Vase, berries, red on yel frost, wood base, 2½x3" 800.00
Vase, berries/leaves on crimson, mold blown, ftd, 9½" 8,400.00
Vase, berries/limbs/leaves, red on red/yel frost, flattened, 12" .1,500.00
Vase, berries/vines, rust on citron, fp, crimped top, 5" 700.00
Vase, birds in landscape, brn on yel & frost, 6" 1,600.00
Vase, boats at sea, cut/pnt on yel/mustard, 4½" 1,300.00
Vase, box elder branches/pods, lime/olive gr on gray to salmon, 13" .1,955.00
Vase, chrysanthemums, butterscotch on wht, fp, 13⅝" 2,000.00
Vase, cineraria blossoms, bl/gr/blk/frost, baluster, 17" 5,000.00
Vase, cyclamen & buds, golden-amber/ruby/maroon, 5¼" 2,000.00
Vase, floral, brn on clear/yel hammered frost, 8" 850.00
Vase, floral, burgundy to pk-red, flattened ovoid, 5x3¼" 1,400.00
Vase, floral, dk/lt gr on frost, 8x5" 1,600.00
Vase, floral, gr on rose & wht, shouldered ovoid, 2¾" 865.00
Vase, floral, gr/wht/purple on purple frost, stick neck, 10" 1,600.00
Vase, floral, purple & gr on purple/frost/pk, stick neck, 17½" ..1,800.00
Vase, floral, purple on gr/purple/frost, 5" 475.00
Vase, floral, purple to lt bl, ovoid, 5x3¼" 1,500.00
Vase, floral, red on rose/frost, bulb w/trumpet neck, 5" 800.00
Vase, foliage, chocolate on citron, invt trumpet form, 5¼" 750.00
Vase, foliage, olive/gr/pk/frost, banjo form, 6½" 1,400.00
Vase, foliage/pods, brn on citron yel, teardrop form, ftd, 9¼" .1,200.00
Vase, fuchsia, purple on frost & yel, bulbous, 6½" 1,250.00
Vase, fuchsia, purple on peach & gr, long neck, 8" 1,100.00
Vase, grapes & vines, brn on yel to wht, flattened sphere, 8" .1,800.00
Vase, irises, dk bl on amber, baluster, 10x3½" 2,500.00
Vase, landscape & village scene, 4-layer, ftd goblet form, 9¾" ..2,300.00
Vase, lily-like flowers/leaves, lt/dk gr on lt pk frost, 12" 1,800.00
Vase, morning glories, dk on lt bl, fp, teardrop form, 8" 1,600.00
Vase, mtn lake, purple on gray to yel, 4" 1,200.00
Vase, orchids, purple on yel, 5½" 1,000.00
Vase, riverscape, rose on pk to wht, flattened ovoid, 13" 3,000.00
Vase, rose hips, bl/brn on citron to lav, mold blown, 9½" 7,000.00
Vase, star/pod branches, red on frost, flat sided, 12¼" 2,250.00
Vase, trees/birds/water, brn on citron frost, banjo form, 6¾" ..1,600.00
Vase, trees/lake, blk on hammered cinnamon, 18" 3,500.00
Vase, trees/lake, brn/gr on yel mottle, bun base, 8½" 1,100.00
Vase, tropical scene w/palms, red/orange on yel/orange, 14" ...4,000.00
Vase, vine/fern, brn/citron on pk, fp, banjo form, label, 6¾" ..1,400.00
Vase, wisteria, purple & gr on apricot, trumpet form, 7¾" 800.00
Vase, wisteria, wht/pk/olive/lav on frost, ovoid, 15¾" 1,955.00

Enameled Glass

Decanter, irises, purple on clear/purple frost, 10" 1,200.00
Sherbet, cherries & leaves on amber, ftd, 3" 325.00
Tray, fish & plants, topaz enamel on clear w/air bubbles, 2¾x15x9" ...1,150.00
Vase, flowers/berries/leaves, mc w/gold on amber, ftd, hdls, 8¾" ..500.00
Vase, hunting/fishing scenes, gray on bl, eng ferns, 5" 900.00
Vase, magnolia, rose on wht to lt rose, bud base, 24" 2,200.00

Marquetry, Wood

Box, country scene inlay, mixed woods, 14x8x5", VG 1,950.00
Cabinet stand, mahog, cvd/inlaid florals & scenic, mk, 36x25" ..4,675.00
Table, butterfly & foliage top, apron, shaped legs, 30x17" dia ..4,000.00

Table, 2-tier, foliate motif on top/stretcher, 20x23", VG 2,600.00
Vitrine, flowers, top/sides/front panel, glass door, 53x24" 6,500.00

Pottery

Inkwell, lg fleur-de-lis shape, mc flowers etc, tin lid 425.00
Plaque, landscape w/4 cows, Limoges style, 12½" dia 800.00
Wall pocket, molded grasshoppers, HP floral/lettering, 9½" ...1,000.00

Gambling Memorabilia

Gambling memorabilia from the infamous casinos of the West and items that were once used on the 'floating palace' riverboats are especially sought after by today's collectors.

Ashtray, Binion's Horseshoe Gambling House, glass w/logo, 1950s .90.00
Ashtray, Railroad Pass Casino, Las Vegas, glass, 1960s, 4½" 160.00
Box of dice, Continental silver & guilloche enamel, mini, 1" ...200.00
Card case, silver & enamel, domino form, Birmingham, 1897, 3½" ..200.00
Card case, snakeskin, holds 2 decks, EX 45.00
Chip, Balinese Room, Galveston TX, red, $100, 1½" dia 100.00
Chip, eng clay compo, clasped hands, ca 1880, VG 35.00
Chip, eng MOP, Ching Dynasty, 1x2½" 65.00
Chip, Hollywood Dinner Club, Galveston TX, $100, 1½" dia ..105.00
Chip, ivory, yel w/eng star motif, 1½" dia 70.00
Chip, ivory, 8-pointed star w/5 in center, ca 1880, 1½" dia 70.00
Chip, MOP, ornate floral w/devil spearing fish, 1x2¾" 75.00
Chip, The Mint, 25¢, bl w/yel edge markings 30.00
Chip rack, Faro; wood w/rpl felt, unmk, EX 620.00
Device, card game, wood case, folding, 12x12" open, EX 475.00
Device, dice in glass dome, wood base, Fr, coin-op, EX 460.00
Device, gamble for cigars, clock shape, Wizard, 1900s, VG 960.00
Device, Kentucky Derby, dice under glass, tin on wood base, VG .170.00
Dice, NYC Stork Club, 1 w/stork logo, 1920s, EX 50.00

Game, arcade; Horse-race Wheel-of-fortune, metal tripod holds painted eglomise panel, $1,200.00.

Game, Chuck-a-Luck, turning 4½" dice cage & 3 dice, 1941, NM .45.00
Game, dice; 2 dice in glass tube w/NP caps, on wood stand, EX ..110.00
Game, horse race, battery-operated, Electrolette Mfg, EX 250.00
Game, roulette, pocket watch shape, Am Pedometer Co, EX 265.00
Gaming/gambling set, 6 games, in case, AP Games, EX 415.00
Lighter, Horseshoe Club, Reno NV, Brother-Lite, Japan, NM 30.00
Machine, 5 Jacks, CI front in wood case, ca 1930-40, EX 310.00
Punch board, Miss Neptune, M (unopened) 100.00
Punch board, New Moon, unused, 16½x10½" 30.00
Punch board, nude drum majorette & slot symbols, 1940s, MIP ..55.00
Punch board, Rapid Play, slot machine look, ca 1930s, unused, 11x16" .110.00
Punch board, Uplift, 1940s, unpunched, EX 50.00
Wheel, roulette; NP steel & wood w/mirrors, tripod base, 50" dia .990.00
Wheel, roulette; wood, table-top type, 16" dia, EX 275.00
Wheel, roulette; wood & plywood w/old pnt, 2-pc (disassembles), 82" ..350.00

Game Calls

Those interested in hunting and fishing collectibles are beginning to take notice of the finer specimens of game calls available on today's market. Our advisor for this category is Randy Hilst; he is listed in the Directory under Illinois.

Duck calls, Reelfoot style: Fay Holt, ebony with metal reed, checkered barrel, 6", M, $160.00; Unknown maker, walnut barrel and stopper, bronze reed, 5½", VG, $70.00; Cochran's, walnut barrel and stopper, metal reed, complete decal, 7", EX, $165.00.

Crow, Charles H Perdew, walnut bbl, silver band, 1909, EX 190.00
Duck, Emory Mitchell, Enticer, walnut bbl, plastic reed, 5½" 45.00
Duck, FA Allen, 5" 90.00
Duck, HW Willis 175.00
Duck, Olt, early Bakelite, D-2 Keyhole 75.00
Duck, Stofer Bean Lake 95.00
Duck, Tom Turpin, Open Water, walnut bbl, 3 stamped ducks, 6¾" ...400.00
Goose, Goosehonker, box call, TN, 1920s 150.00
Goose, Herter's, side blow, MIB 85.00
Goose, Herter's Numara, walnut bbl, plastic stopper, EXIB 25.00
Goose, Johnny Bill Weise, Johnny Bill's IL River, walnut bbl, 7½" ..100.00
Goose/duck, Etherton IL, walnut bbls, 6", matched pr, M 90.00
Squirrel, Herter's No 99, w/instructions, scarce, MIB 30.00
Turkey, Herter's Plantation, scratch type, MIB 50.00
Turkey, Lohman #110, box type, MIB 30.00
Turkey, ML Lynch #102, box type, EX 25.00
Turkey, Quaker Bog Easy Yelper, scratch box type, MIB 15.00

Gameboards

Gameboards, the handmade ones from the eighteenth and nineteenth century, are collected more for their folk art quality than their relation to games. Excellent examples of these handcrafted 'playthings' sell well into the thousands of dollars; even the simple designs are often expensive. If you are interested in this field, you must study it carefully. The market is always full of 'new' examples. Well-established dealers are often your best sources; they are essential if you do not have the expertise to judge the age of the boards yourself. Our advisor for this category is Louis Picek; he is listed in the Directory under Iowa.

Bean bag toss, mc pnt/stencil, sq openings, 19th C, 30x15" 575.00
Checkers, mahog & maple inlaid sqs, 20th C, 14¾" sq 110.00
Checkers, marquetry inlay (mc), inlaid horse on bk, ca 1911, 17x16" ..685.00
Checkers, pine w/alligatored blk & yel pnt, #s on blk sqs, 18x27" .600.00
Checkers, pine w/old red & blk pnt, appl gallery, 27x19" 440.00
Checkers, pine w/stained blk sqs, old patina, gallery, 24x13" 190.00
Checkers, pine w/yel/red/gr/brn pnt, even wear, 17x16½" 900.00
Checkers, poplar w/red & blk pnt, stars at ends, gallery, 19x28" ...545.00
Checkers, poplar w/red & blk sqs, gr/yel striping, appl edge, 20" sq ..1,000.00

Checkers, poplar w/red/yel/blk pnt, EX color, lt wear, 17x16" **1,400.00**
Checkers, red & blk w/yel foliage in corners, gallery, 17" sq **575.00**
Checkers, single drw, on sq base w/grpt, ca 1800s, 29x17x16" ...**700.00**
Checkers, walnut w/blk pnt sqs, fr border, 19th C, 13" sq **165.00**
Checkers/unknown game, mc pnt on wood, ca 1900, 19" sq ..**1,495.00**
Unknown game, pine w/old blk & maroon pnt, wear/touch-up, 14x23" ..**295.00**
Unknown game, pnt rectangles/sqs/stars, mc w/gold/decals, 18" sq ...**460.00**
Unknown game, worn blk & brn pnt w/yel/red/bl, folding box, 24" sq ..**265.00**

Games

Collectors of antique games are finding it more difficult to find their treasures at shows and flea markets. Most of the action these days seems to be through specialty dealers and auctions. The appreciation of the art on the boards and boxes continues to grow. You see many of the early games proudly displayed as art, and they should be. The period from the 1850s to 1910 continues to draw the most interest. Many of the games of that period were executed by well-known artists and illustrators. The quality of their lithography cannot be matched today. The historical value of games made before 1850 has caused interest in this period to increase. While they may not have the graphic quality of the later period, their insights into the social and moral character of the early nineteenth century are interesting.

Twentieth-century games invoke a nostalgic feeling among collectors who recall looking forward to a game under the Christmas tree each year. They search for examples that bring back those Christmas-morning memories. While the quality of their lithography is certainly less than the early games, the introduction of personalities from the comic strips, radio, and later TV created new interest. Every child wanted a game that featured their favorite character. Monopoly, probably the most famous game ever produced, was introduced during the Great Depression.

For further information, we recommend *Baby Boomer Games* by Rick Polizzi; and *Schroeder's Collectible Toys, Antique to Modern;* both are available from Collector Books.

Flying the Beam, Parker Bros., 1941, MIB, $60.00. (Photo courtesy Rick Polizzi)

Across the Continent, Parker Bros, 1952, NM (EX box) **50.00**
Advance to Boardwalk, Parker Bros, 1985, EXIB **20.00**
Aerial Contest, Spear, G (G box) **100.00**
Air Raid Defense Target, Wyandotte, NM (G box) **225.00**
Animal Twister, Milton Bradley, 1967, EXIB **25.00**
Astro Launch, Ohio Art, 1963, EXIB **75.00**
Baseball, Milton Bradley, 1941, EXIB **55.00**
Bash, Milton Bradley, 1965, EXIB **25.00**
Bats in Your Belfry, Mattel, 1964, EXIB **100.00**
Battle-Cry, Milton Bradley, 1961, VG (VG box) **45.00**
Bermuda Triangle, Milton Bradley, 1976, EXIB **35.00**
Bible Game of New Testament Books, David C Cook, 1930s, VG (VG box) .**65.00**
Big Sneeze, Ideal, 1968, EXIB **25.00**
Big Town News Reporting, Lowell, 1950s, rare, NMIB **75.00**
Bob Feller's Big League Baseball, Saalfield, 1950s, EXIB **125.00**
Boom or Bust, Parker Bros, 1951, EXIB **175.00**
Carrier Strike Game of Naval Strategy, 1977, NMIB **40.00**
Challenge of Yankees, Hasbro, 1964, EXIB **165.00**
Chiromagica, McLoughlin Bros, 1870, EX (EX walnut case) **300.00**
Clue, Parker Bros, 1949, orig issue, VG (VG box) **50.00**
Dollar a Second, Lowell, 1956, scarce, unused, MIB **75.00**
Electric Hot Potato, Electric Game, 1960, EXIB **35.00**
Espionage, Transogram, 1963, EXIB **50.00**
Fearless Fireman, Hasbro, 1957, EXIB **85.00**
Flip It Jackpot, Aurora, 1973, EXIB **45.00**
Flip-A-Lid, Hassenfeld Bros, 1950s, VG (VG box) **35.00**
Game of Authors, Russell Mfg, 1920s, VG (VG box) **50.00**
Game of Bagatelle, McLoughlin Bros, 1890s, VG (VG box) **400.00**
Game of Bounce, McLoughlin Bros, late 1800s, EXIB **450.00**
Game of Climbing Monkeys, Spear, VG+ (VG box) **200.00**
Game of Poor Jenny, All-Fair, 1972, EXIB **125.00**
Game of Robbing the Miller, McLoughlin Bros, 1988, VG (VG box) .**375.00**
Game of the District Messenger Boy, McLoughlin Bros, 1886, NMIB .**425.00**
Gang Busters Official Target, Marx, 1940, EXIB **375.00**
Get the Message, Milton Bradley, 1964, VG (VG box) **40.00**
Giant Wheel Hot Rod, Remco, 1960, EXIB **50.00**
Giant Wheels Thrills 'N Spills Horse Race, Remco, 1958, EXIB ..**55.00**
Great American Game of Baseball, Hustler Toys, 1923, NM **400.00**
Hands Down, Ideal, 1964, EXIB **20.00**
Hialeah, Milton Bradley, 1930s, VG (VG box) **75.00**
Hop Off, Parker Bros, 1920, EXIB **250.00**
How To Succeed, Hasbro, 1950s, EXIB **50.00**
Hurdle Races, Milton Bradley, 1920, VG (VG box) **175.00**
Jumpy Tinker, Toy Tinkers, 1920, VG (worn box) **50.00**
Jungle Skittles, American Toy Works, 1950s, EXIB **50.00**
Ker-Plunk, Ideal, 1967, NMIB **25.00**
Knock Your Block Off, Hasbro, 1964, EXIB **35.00**
Knockout, Northwestern, 1950, EXIB **125.00**
League Parlor Baseball, Bliss, 1885, paper on wood, EX (VG box) ..**1,200.00**
Let Them All Come, Spears, 1930s, EXIB **700.00**
Lie Detector, Mattel, 1960, NMIB **50.00**
Mail Express, Milton Bradley, 1920, EXIB **250.00**
Mansion of Happiness, Ives, 1864, VG (VG box) **300.00**
Miss Popularity the True American Teen, Transogram, 1961, EXIB ...**75.00**
Mother's Helper, Milton Bradley, 1969, EXIB **25.00**
Mouse Trap, Ideal, 1963, EXIB **50.00**
Name That Tune, Milton Bradley, 1959, NMIB **50.00**
Operation Orbit, Transogram, 1962, EXIB **125.00**
Parlor Croquet, Bliss, 1890, EXIB **125.00**
Peg Baseball, Parker Bros, 1930s, EXIB **85.00**
Pie in Your Eye, Ideal, 1966, EXIB **30.00**
Pigskin, Parker Bros, 1946, EXIB **64.00**
Pirate Plunder, All-Fair, 1950s, VG (VG box) **50.00**
Pivot Golf, Milton Bradley, MIB **125.00**
Prediction Rod, Parker Bros, 1970, EXIB **35.00**
Radio Amateur Hour, Milton Bradley, 1930s, VG (VG box) **65.00**
Rich Uncle, Parker Bros, 1959, EXIB **40.00**
Robbing the Miller, McLoughlin Bros, 1888, NMIB **225.00**
Rock'Em Sock'Em Robots, Marx, 1966, EXIB **135.00**
Rocket Race to Saturn, Lido, 1950s, NMIB **125.00**
Satellite Space Race, card game, 1957, MIB **75.00**
Scarecrow Target, Ideal, 1965, EXIB **30.00**
Sea Raiders, Parker Bros, 1845, EXIB **45.00**
Shotgun Slade, Milton Bradley, 1960, NMIB **75.00**
Skill-Drive Raceway, Tarco, 1960s, NMIB **45.00**
Slap Stick, Milton Bradley, 1967, MIB **40.00**
Solarquest, Western Publishing, 1986, EXIB **30.00**
Soldiers on Guard, McLoughlin Bros, early 1900s, EXIB **500.00**
Sprint, Holland Crafts, 1930s, EXIB **75.00**
Spy Detector, Mattel, 1960, EXIB **30.00**
Spy's-A-Poppin, Transogram, 1965, EXIB **60.00**

Talking Monday Night Football, Mattel, 1977, MIB 75.00
Think-A-Tron, Hasbro, 1961, EXIB 75.00
Tip-It, Ideal, 1965, MIB 35.00
Trip Trap, Remco, 1969, EXIB 45.00
Tru-Action Electric Football, 1954, EX (VG box) 50.00
Twin Target, Milton Bradley, 1920s, VG (VG box) 225.00
Uranium Rush, Gardner, 1950s, EXIB 100.00
Vegetable Nine Pins, pnt papier-mache, EX 2,300.00
Warrey Marble Game, Warrey, early 1900s, EX 250.00
Western Target, Marx, NM (G box) 100.00
Whirling Jockey Race, McDowell, early 1900s, EX (worn box) .325.00
Whirly Bird Play Catch, Innovation, 1950s, MIB 60.00
Wrestle World, Ideal, 1965, EXIB 18.00
Yacht Race, Parker Bros, 1961, VG (VG box) 85.00
Yankee Trader, Corey Games, 1941, VG (VG box) 75.00

Personalities, Movies, and TV Shows

Adventures of Popeye, Transogram, 1957, EXIB 65.00
Alien, Kenner, 1979, rare, EXIB 50.00
Alvin & the Chipmunks Cross Country, Hasbro, 1960, MIB 70.00
Around the World in 80 Days, Transogram, 1957, EXIB 50.00
Babes in Toyland, Parker Bros, 1961, EXIB 50.00
Batman, marble game, 1966, VG (VG box) 45.00
Batman Pinball, Marx, 1966, EXIB 100.00
Ben-Hur, McLoughlin Bros, 1899, VG (VG box) 1,500.00
Bobbsey Twins, Milton Bradley, 1957, VG (VG box) 50.00
Camelot, Parker Bros, 1931, EX (VG box) 45.00
Captain Video, Milton Bradley, EXIB 125.00
Chubby Checker's Limbo, Wham-O, 1961, EXIB 650.00
Dick Tracy Detective, Whitman, 1937, EX (G box) 125.00
Dick Van Dyke, Standard Toycraft, 1964, EXIB 75.00
Flintstones Brake Ball, 1962, EXIB 100.00
G-Men Clue Games, Whitman, scarce, MIB 175.00
Game of Charlie Brown & His Pals, 1959, EXIB 55.00
Get Smart, card game, Ideal, 1966, unused, NMIB 75.00
Gidget, Standard Toykraft, 1965, NMIB 125.00
Gracie Allen Murder Case, Milton Bradley, 1939, VG (VG box) .350.00
Gray Ghost, Transogram, 1958, VG (VG box) 60.00
Green Hornet Quick Switch, Milton Bradley, 1966, NMIB 250.00
Happy Days, Parker Bros, 1976, EXIB 20.00
Hawaiian Eye, Lowell, 1963, EXIB 80.00
Hopalong Cassidy Lasso, Transogram, 1950, MIB 165.00
Hopalong Cassidy Shooting Gallery, Automatic Toy, 1950, EXIB ..275.00
Humpty Dumpty, Lowell, 1960, EXIB 50.00
Ironside, Ideal, 1967, EXIB 100.00
James Bond, Message From M, Ideal, 1966, unused, MIB 300.00
King Kong, Milton Bradley, 1966, EXIB 150.00
Land of Giants, Ideal, 1968, EXIB 150.00
Legend of Jesse James, Milton Bradley, 1966, EXIB 55.00
Lone Ranger Ring Toss, 1943, NMIB, from $350 to 450.00
Lucy Show, Transogram, 1962, EXIB 175.00
Margie, Milton Bradley, 1961, MIB 60.00
Melvin Purvis' G-Men Detective Game, Parker Bros, 1930s, NM ..250.00
Mickey Mantle Big 6 Sports, Gardner, 1950s, VG (VG box) 150.00
Mickey Mouse Scatter Ball, Marks Bros, 1935, NM (EX box) ...350.00
Mickey Mouse Tiddly Winks, Chad Valley, rare, EXIB 375.00
Mighty Hercules, Hasbro, 1963, EXIB 250.00
Nancy Drew Mystery, Parker Bros, 1957, EXIB 100.00
No Time for Sergeants, Ideal, 1964, EXIB 50.00
Our Gang Tipple-Topple, All Fair, 1930, EXIB 275.00
Perils of Pauline, Marx, 1964, EXIB 65.00
Popeye, card game, Whitman, 1934, EXIB 100.00
Prince Valiant Game of Valor, Transogram, 1955, NMIB 85.00
Raggedy Ann's Magic Pebble, Milton Bradley, 1941, NMIB 85.00
Rat Patrol Spin-To-Win, Pressman, 1967, NMIB 100.00
Skeezyx, Milton Bradley, 1930, EXIB 275.00
Soupy Sales, Ideal, 1965, EXIB 85.00
Steve Allen's Qubila, 1955, scarce, NMIB 100.00
Superboy, 1965, rare, EXIB 150.00
Superman Calling, Transogram, 1954, EXIB 200.00
Tales of Wells Fargo, Milton Bradley, 1959, NMIB 80.00
Terry & the Pirates, Whitman, 1937, NMIB 150.00
That Girl, Remco, 1969, EXIB 70.00
Three Stooges Fun House, Lowell, 1959, EXIB 200.00
Time Tunnel, Ideal, 1966, EXIB 125.00
Tom Mix Circus, Parker Bros, 1930s, EXIB 200.00
Tom Mix in Texas, Klee, scarce, EXIB 350.00
Top Cat, Cadaco, 1961, EXIB 45.00
Twilight Zone, Ideal, 1964, EXIB 140.00
Wackiest Ship in the Army, Standard Toykraft, 1965, EXIB 55.00
Walt Disney's Three Little Pigs, Einson-Freeman, 1933, NMIB ..200.00
Wanted Dead or Alive, Lowell, 1959, EXIB 100.00
White Shadow, Cadaco, 1970s, EXIB 85.00
Wild Wild West, Transogram, 1966, MIB 600.00
Woody Woodpecker Ring Toss, 1958, MIB 100.00
Zorro, WHitman, 1965, NMIB 75.00
12 O'Clock High, Ideal, EXIB 60.00

G. A. R. Memorabilia

The 'Grand Army of the Republic' was first conceived by Chaplain W.J. Rutledge and Major B.J. Stephenson early in 1864 when they were tent-mates during our own Civil War. These men vowed to each other that if they were spared they would establish an organization that would preserve friendships and memories formed during this time. Shortly after the war ended, Rutledge and Stephenson made their desires a reality. The first National Convention of the Grand Army of the Republic was held in Indianapolis, Indiana, on November 20, 1866. The purpose of the organization was to provide aid and assistance to the widows and orphans of the fallen Union dead and to care for the hospitalized veterans as needed. The last comrade of the G.A.R. died in 1949.

Many items are surfacing from the early encampments which were held on both state and national levels and resulted in a wide variety of souvenir items having been made.

Flask, label-under-glass, 29th National Encampment...1895, Louisville, KY, IW Harper's...Whiskey, smooth base, 6", $575.00.

Badge, 1893 Nat'l Encampment Member's, 3-pc, w/ribbon 75.00
Badge, 1916 Nat'l Encampment Representative, Kansas City, 4-pc .125.00
Badge, 1918, Portland 90.00
Badge, 1931 Dept of NY Delegate's, brass, 2-pc, w/red ribbon 45.00
Book, GAR Grand Army Blue Book, RB Heath, hardcover, 168-pg, EX .35.00
Buckle, Vets Star in center w/GAR above, early style 22.50
Flask, label under glass: Nat'l Encampment 1895... on clear, 6" .575.00
Lapel stud, GAR logo, reverse: campfire 6.50

Medal, Ladies of GAR Membership Vets, gold w/red/wht/bl, 2-pc .35.00
Medallion, Am Legion GAR Centennial, NP, PA, 1863-1963 ....20.00
Pamphlet, Rules & Regulations..., 1869, 32-pg, EX 70.00
Paperweight, Soldiers' Monument, glass 20.00
Photo, 1915 Maine reunion 50.00
Postcard, emb gold eagle/flags/wreath/shield, 6-line motto, EX 3.00
Postcard, Soldiers' Monument...Baltimore MD, EX 3.00
Program, 1910 Encampment, Atlantic City, 32 pgs of pictures, 10x8" ..20.00
Ribbon, Dedication of Soldiers' Monument, CT, 1887 ....15.00
Ribbon, Reception 1st Lt Infantry...1886, portrait center, ½x7" ..15.00
Ribbon, 1897 Reunion...Nantasket Beach, wht silk, 2½x6" 15.00
Ribbon, 36th Annual Bridgeport CN Delegate, lady's, red silk, EX .20.00
Rules & Regulations...MA, 1899, 29-pg, 5x6" 12.00
Sword & staff, Model 1860, Boston Regalia, w/NP scabbard 250.00
Tintype, older man w/GAR badge & coat seated w/wife, 6th plate ...95.00

Garden City Pottery

Founded in 1902 in San Jose, California, by the end of the 1920s this pottery had grown to become the largest in Northern California. During that period production focused on stoneware, sewer pipe, and red clay flowerpots. In the late '30s and '40s, the company produced dinnerware in bright solid colors of yellow, green, blue, orange, cobalt, turquoise, white, and black. Royal Arden Hickman, who would later gain fame for the innovative artware he modeled for the Haeger company, designed not only dinnerware but a line of Art Deco vases and bowls as well. The company endured hard times by adapting to the changing needs of the market and during the '50s concentrated on production of garden products. Foreign imports, however, proved to be too competitive, and the company's pottery production ceased in 1979.

Because none of the colored-glazed products were ever marked, to learn to identify the products of this company, you'll need to refer to *Sanford's Guide to Garden City Pottery* by Jim Pasquali, who is listed in the Directory under California. Values apply to items in all colors (except black) and all patterns, unless noted otherwise. Due to relative rarity 20% should be added for any item found in black.

Bean pots, Deco: large, $85.00; small, $35.00. (Photo courtesy Jim Pasquali)

Bowl, mixing; Wide-Ring, solid color, #1 ....20.00
Bowl, str-edge, solid color, 5" 30.00
Candle holders, solid color, 3", pr 45.00
Creamer & sugar bowl, solid color, w/lid, jumbo 65.00
Flowerpot, double rim, solid color, 10" 50.00
Jar, oil; solid color, 9" 150.00
Mug, chowder; solid color, w/lid 45.00
Plate, dinner; solid color; 9" 20.00
Shakers, flared cylinder, solid color, 3", pr 25.00
Teapot, plain, solid color 95.00
Tumbler, solid color 20.00
Water cooler, crockery 75.00

Gas Globes and Panels

Gas globes and panels, once a common sight, have vanished from the countryside but are being sought by collectors as a unique form of advertising memorabilia. Early globes from the 1920s (some date back to as early as 1912), now referred to as 'one-piece globes,' were made of molded milk glass and were globular in shape. The gas company name was etched or painted on the glass. Few of these were ever produced, and this type is valued very highly by collectors today.

A new type of pump was introduced in the early 1930s; the old 'visible' pumps were replaced by 'electric' models. Globes were changing at the same time. By the mid-teens a three-piece globe consisting of a pair of inserts and a metal body was being produced in both 15" and 16½" sizes. Collectors prefer to call globes that are not one-piece or plastic 'three-piece glass' (Type 2) or 'metal body, glass inserts' (Type 3). Though metal-body globes (Type 3) were popular in the 1930s, they were common in the 1920s, and some were actually made as early as 1915. Though rare in numbers, their use spans many years. In the 1930s Type 2 and Type 3 globes became the replacements of the one-piece globe. The most recently manufactured gas globes are made with a plastic body that contains two 13½" glass lenses. These were common in the '50s but were actually used as early as 1932.

Note: Standard Crowns with raised letters are one-piece globes that were made in the 1920s; those made in the 1950s (no raised letters), though one-piece, are not regarded as such by today's collectors. Our advisor for this category is Scott Benjamin; he is listed in the Directory under Ohio.

Type 1, Plastic Body, Glass Inserts (Inserts 13½") — 1931 – 1950s

D-X Marine, rare 850.00
Dixie, plastic band 250.00
DX Lubricating Gasoline, tan body 275.00
Frontier Gas, Rarin' To Go, w/horse 950.00
Kendal Deluxe, Capcolite body w/red pnt, 13½" 325.00
Kendall Polly Power, Capcolite body, 13½", NM 350.00
Marathon, no runner 200.00
Never Nox Ethyl 450.00
Spur, Oval body 350.00
Texaco Diesel Chief, Capcolite body, 13½", NM 1,000.00
Viking, pictures Viking ship 950.00

Type 2, Glass Frame, Glass Inserts (Inserts 13½") — 1926 – 1940s

Aerio, gr gill ripple body, 13½", NM 5,500.00
American, gill body, 12½", NM 400.00
Amoco, gill body, 13½", NM 400.00
Atlantic, glass body, 13½", NM 325.00
Atlantic Imperial, gill body, 13½", EX 400.00
Derby 450.00
Esso 325.00
Frontier Gas, Double Refined 350.00
Guyler Brand, milk glass, EX 850.00
Pitman Streamlined, bl gill rippled body, 13½", NM 5,500.00
Pure 400.00
Sinclair Dino, milk glass, EX 250.00
Sinclair Pennant 850.00
Sky Chief, gill body, 13½", NM 500.00
Standard Crown, gr or orange, ea 900.00
Standard Crown, wht, red or gold, ea 400.00
Standard Flame 400.00
Texaco Ethyl 1,500.00
White Flash, gill body 450.00

WNAX, w/radio station pictured 1,500.00

Type 3, Metal Frame, Glass Inserts (Inserts 15" or 16½") — 1915 – 1930s

Aero Mobilgas, new metal body, rare, 15", NM 2,500.00
Atlantic Ethyl, 16½" 750.00
Atlantic White Flash, 16½" 750.00
General Ethyl, 15" fr, complete 900.00
Kendal Gasoline, airplane, metal body, rare, 15", NM 5,000.00
Oil Creek Gas, drake well & derrick, 15", NM 2,500.00
Phillips Benzo, low profile metal body, 15", NM 3,500.00
Purol Gasoline, w/arrow, porc body 900.00
Red Crown Ethyl 950.00
Signal, old stoplight, 15", VG 4,000.00
Stanolined Aviation, rare, 16½", EX 4,000.00
Texaco Leaded, glass panels, complete globe 4,300.00
White Star, 15" fr, complete 950.00

Type 4, One-Piece Glass Globes, No Inserts, Co. Name Etched, Raised or Enameled — 1912 – 1931

Atlantic, chimney cap 3,000.00
Dixie, etched 1,750.00
Mobil Gargoyle, gargoyle pictured, oval 2,000.00
Pierce Pennant, etched 3,200.00
Republic, 3-sided 2,200.00
Shell, rnd, etched 750.00
Super Shell, clam shape 1,800.00
Super Shell, rnd, etched 3,800.00
Texaco Ethyl 2,100.00
That Good Gulf..., emb, orange & blk letters, EX 1,000.00
White Eagle, some feather detail, 20¾", EX 1,600.00
White Rose, boy pictured, pnt 2,800.00

Gaudy Dutch

Inspired by Oriental Imari wares, Gaudy Dutch was made in England from 1800 to 1820. It was hand decorated on a soft-paste body with rich underglaze blues accented in orange, red, pink, green, and yellow. It differs from Gaudy Welsh in that there is no lustre (except on Water Lily). There are seventeen patterns, some of which are War Bonnet, Grape, Dahlia, Oyster, Urn, Butterfly, Carnation, Single Rose, Double Rose, and Water Lily. For further information we recommend *The Collector's Encyclopedia of Gaudy Dutch & Welsh* by John Shuman, available from Collector Books. Unless otherwise noted, values are given for items with minimal wear and no obvious damage.

Urn, plate, ca 1820, 7½", $550.00.

Butterfly, creamer 990.00
Butterfly, creamer, rare, M 1,650.00
Butterfly, pitcher, milk; 4", M 910.00
Butterfly, plate, butterfly on side, 8", M 880.00
Butterfly, plate, butterfly on side, 8⅜", M 990.00
Butterfly, plate, 6⅜" 630.00
Butterfly, plate, 8⅜", EX 385.00
Butterfly, plate, 9¾" 1,650.00
Butterfly, tea bowl & saucer, butter on the side 825.00
Butterfly, tea bowl & saucer, handleless; close mismatch 300.00
Butterfly, teapot 2,530.00
Butterfly, waste bowl 1,485.00
Carnation, coffeepot 1,430.00
Carnation, cream pitcher, 4⅛" 880.00
Carnation, cup plate 715.00
Carnation, plate, sm feather border, 10" 855.00
Carnation, plate, sm rpr, 8¼" 220.00
Carnation, plate, 8" 660.00
Carnation, plate, 8⅜", M 850.00
Carnation, soup plate, 8½" 770.00
Carnation, sugar bowl 880.00
Carnation, teapot 1,485.00
Cybis, cup plate, butterfly on side, no mk 165.00
Dahlia, creamer 990.00
Dahlia, plate, 8" 880.00
Dahlia, sugar bowl 990.00
Dahlia, tea bowl & saucer 825.00
Double Rose, creamer 660.00
Double Rose, plate, deep, 9¾", M 850.00
Double Rose, plate, 10", M 1,100.00
Double Rose, sugar bowl, w/lid 880.00
Double Rose, tea bowl & saucer 600.00
Double Rose, waste bowl, 6", M 690.00
Dove, creamer 770.00
Dove, plate, plain border, 6¼", M 550.00
Dove, tea bowl & saucer, bl band, M 620.00
Dove, teapot 1,100.00
Dove, waste bowl 700.00
Grape, creamer, M 770.00
Grape, plate, toddy; 4½" 400.00
Grape, plate, 6", M 325.00
Grape, plate, 7", M 440.00
Grape, plate, 8", M 550.00
Grape, plate, 8¼", EX 300.00
Grape, plate, 9¾", M 1,050.00
Grape, platter, 15" 990.00
Grape, tea bowl & saucer 515.00
Grape, tea bowl & saucer, minor flaking 250.00
Leaf, bowl, unusual shape, 8¾" 1,100.00
Leaf, tea bowl & saucer 800.00
Oyster, creamer 440.00
Oyster, plate, 6⅜" 440.00
Oyster, teapot 550.00
Primrose, sugar bowl, w/lid 990.00
Primrose, tea bowl & saucer 770.00
Primrose, waste bowl 825.00
Single Rose, coffeepot 800.00
Single Rose, creamer, M 925.00
Single Rose, plate, 6½", M 500.00
Single Rose, tea bowl & saucer, 2¼x3½", EX+ 500.00
Single Rose, teapot, M 1,650.00
Strawflower, plate, mk Riley, 10", M 2,100.00
Strawflower, plate, 8½" 900.00
Strawflower, soup plate 880.00

Sunflower, creamer 550.00
Sunflower, plate, 8¼", M 700.00
Sunflower, tea bowl & saucer 880.00
Urn, cup plate 465.00
Urn, plate, toddy; rare, 5¼", M 825.00
Urn, plate, 8¼", M 685.00
War Bonnet, creamer 660.00
War Bonnet, cup plate 715.00
War Bonnet, plate, toddy; 6", M 685.00
War Bonnet, soup plate 770.00
War Bonnet, tea bowl & saucer, hairline 250.00
Zinnia, plate, deep, 9¾" 1,245.00
Zinnia, plate, 6⅜" 660.00

Gaudy Welsh

Gaudy Welsh was an inexpensive hand-decorated ware made in both England and Wales from 1820 until 1860. It is characterized by its colors — principally blue, orange-rust, and copper lustre — and by its uninhibited patterns. Accent colors may be yellow and green. (Pink lustre may be present, since lustre applied to the white areas appears pink. A copper tone develops from painting lustre onto the dark colors.) The body of the ware may be heavy ironstone (also called Gaudy Ironstone), creamware, earthenware, or porcelain; even style and shapes vary considerably. Patterns, while usually floral, are also sometimes geometric and may have trees and birds. Beware! The Wagon Wheel pattern has been reproduced.

Our advisor for this category is Cheryl Nelson; she is listed in the Directory under Minnesota. For further information we recommend *The Collector's Encyclopedia of Gaudy Dutch & Welsh* by John Shuman, available from Collector Books.

Note: The Bethedsa pattern is very similar to a Davenport jug pattern. No porcelain Gaudy Welsh was made in Wales.

Asian, creamer & sugar bowl 355.00
Aster, cup & saucer 89.00
Bethesda, jug, 7¾" 750.00
Buckle, plate, 8½" 210.00
Burma, jug, 6" 500.00
Cambrian Rose, jug, 7¼" 530.00
Cherry Tree, cup & saucer 99.00
Chinoiserie, mug, 2¼" 95.00
Chinoiserie, plate, 8" 175.00
Columbine, cup & saucer 80.00
Columbine, waste bowl 90.00
Cosmos, plate, 8" 165.00
Daisy Chain, jug, 6½" 495.00
Dimity, plate, 6" 185.00
Drape, mug, 2" 80.00
Feather, cup & saucer 70.00
Floret, creamer 190.00
Geranium, teapot 480.00
Llangollen, jug, 6" 360.00
Morning Glory, plate 170.00
Nebula, creamer 180.00
Peppermint, plate, 10" 210.00
Pinwheel, teapot 375.00
Pot de Fleurs, plate, rare, 9" 790.00
Sahara, mug, 2" 175.00
Sunbeam, plate, 6" 250.00
Tulip, cup & saucer, porc 100.00
Tulip, jug, mini, 3" 200.00
Tulip, jug, 10" 270.00
Tulip, plate, 10" 130.00
Venus, cup & saucer 135.00
Village, plate, 9" 215.00

Geisha Girl

Geisha Girl Porcelain was one of several key Japanese china production efforts aimed at the booming export markets of the U.S., Canada, England, and other parts of Europe. The wares feature colorful, kimono-clad Japanese ladies in scenes of everyday Japanese life, surrounded by exquisite flora, fauna, and mountain ranges. Nonetheless, the forms in which the wares were produced reflected the late nineteenth- and early twentieth-century Western dining and decorating preferences: tea and coffee services, vases, dresser sets, children's items, planters, etc.

Over a hundred manufacturers were involved in Geisha Girl production. This accounts for the several hundred different patterns, well over a dozen border colors and styles, and several methods of design execution. Geisha Girl Porcelain was produced in wholly hand-painted versions, but most were hand painted over stenciled outlines. Be wary of Geisha ware executed with decals. Very few decaled examples came out of Japan. Rather, most were Czechoslovakian attempts to hone in on the market. Czech pieces have stamped marks in broad, pseudo-Oriental characters. Items with portraits of Oriental ladies in the bottom of tea or sake cups are *not* Geisha Girl Porcelain, unless the outside surface of the wares are decorated as described above. These lovely faces, formed by varying the thickness of the porcelain body, are called lithophanes and are collectible in their own right.

The height of Geisha Girl production was between 1910 and the mid-1930s. Some post-World War II production has been found marked Occupied Japan.

The ware continued in minimal production during the 1960s, but the point of origin of the later pieces was Hong Kong. These productions are discerned by the pure whiteness of the porcelain; even, unemotional borders; lack of background washes and gold enameling; and overall sparseness of detail. A new wave of Nippon-marked reproduction Geisha emerged in 1996. If the Geisha Girl productions of the 1960s–80s were overly plain, the mid-1990s repros are overly ornate. Original Geisha Girl porcelain was enhanced by brush strokes of color over a stenciled design; it was never the 'color perfectly within the lines' type of decoration found on current reproductions. Original Geisha Girl porcelain was decorated with color washes; the reproductions are in heavy enamels. The backdrop decoration of the current reproductions feature solid, thick colors, and the patterns feature too much color; period Geisha ware had a high ratio of white space to color. The new pieces also have bright shiny gold in proportions greater than most period Geisha ware. The Nippon marks on the reproductions are wrong. Some of the Geisha ware created during the Nippon era bore the small precise decaled green M-in-Wreath mark, a Noritake registered trademark. The reproduction items feature an irregular facsimile of this mark. Stamped onto the reproductions is an unrealistically large M-in-Wreath mark in shades of green ranging from an almost neon to pine green with a wreath that looks like it has seen better days, as it does not have the perfect roundness of the original mark. Reproductions of mid-sized trays, chunky hatpin holders, an ornate vase, a covered bottle, and a powder jar are among the current reproductions popping up at flea and antique markets.

Many of our descriptions contain references to border colors and treatments. This information is given immediately preceding the mark and/or size. Our advisor for this category is Elyce Litts; she is listed in the Directory under New Jersey.

Berry set, Parasol C: Parasol, master w/5 ind, red w/gold 40.00
Biscuit jar, Checkerboard, cobalt, 3-ftd 85.00
Biscuit jar, Lady in Rickshaw, melon-ribbed, red-orange w/gold, ftd 65.00
Bonbon dish, Battledore, mum-shaped, olive gr 22.00

Bowl, Cherry Blossoms, red-orange edge, 7½" 30.00
Bowl, Dragon Boat, 6-lobed, bl w/gold, 7" 35.00
Cocoa pot, Basket, conical body, dk apple gr w/gold, 6½" 45.00
Cocoa pot, Battledore, ewer shape, yel-gr, 9" 55.00
Cocoa pot, Courtesan Processional, bl w/gold border, 9" 85.00
Condiment tray, Meeting C, plum blossom form, red-orange, 7½" ...16.00
Creamer, Long-Stemmed Peony, slender, fluted, bl w/gold 12.00
Cup & saucer, child's; Mother & Son, red 12.00
Cup & saucer, tea; Bamboo Trellis, dk gr 10.00
Cup & saucer, tea; Origami, cobalt w/gold 14.00
Dresser box, Garden Bench B, cobalt w/gold, 6" dia 38.00
Dresser tray, Garden Bench D, HP gr & red w/gold 45.00
Egg cup, Cloud A, red 12.00
Hair receiver, Bamboo Trellis, red-orange 20.00
Jug, Torii & Parasol, melon ribs, red-orange w/gr & gold, 5½" 45.00
Lemonade set, Bellflower, brn w/trim, pitcher & 5 mugs 125.00
Match holder, Lantern B, scalloped top/fancy base, red w/gr circles ..45.00
Muffineer, Parasol C: Parasol, bulbous w/fluted base, wavy red 35.00
Mustard jar, Child Reaching for Butterfly, red 20.00
Napkin ring, Flower Gathering C, semicircular, red 28.00
Nappy, Leaving the Teahouse, mc border 25.00
Nut dish, ind; Duck Watching A, red w/gold, ftd 8.00
Nut dish, master; Duck Watching A, red w/gold, ftd 28.00
Olive dish, Mother & Son, oval, red-orange w/gold, 7" 25.00
Pitcher, Garden Bench C, cobalt w/gold & red hdls, mini, 3" 20.00
Plate, Battledore, swirl fluted rim, red w/gold, 8½" 20.00
Plate, Bird Cage, red-orange w/gold, 6" 10.00
Plate, Child's Play, cobalt w/gold buds, 6½" 12.00
Powder jar, Footridge A, red, 3 long legs 28.00
Puff box, Garden Bench C, melon ribs, red-orange w/yel line 16.00
Relish dish, Oxen Song, fluted edge w/cut-out hdls, red, 7" 35.00
Sake cup, Garden Bench B, red rim 6.00
Salt dish, Cloud A, red-orange w/flowers 8.00
Shakers, Blind Man's Bluff, swirl fluted body, lt apple gr, pr 15.00
Shakers, Fan A, bl rim, red top, pr 20.00
Sugar bowl, Boy w/Scythe, cobalt bl w/gold 18.00
Talcum shaker, Parasol L, red-orange w/yel lacing 28.00
Tea caddy, Fan A, modern, red, no inside cover, 3" 15.00
Tea tile, Feather Fan, rnd, Nippon 35.00
Toothpick holder, Court Lady, bl w/gold, 5-sided, ftd 38.00
Vase, Cloud A, cobalt w/gold-drip neck & rim, 5½" 30.00
Vase, Flower Gathering, 3 reserves on ornate ground, 3-ftd, hdls, 3" ..35.00

Georgia Art Pottery

In Cartersville, Georgia, in August 1935, W.J. Gordy first fired pottery turned from regional clays. By 1936 he was marking his wares 'Georgia Pottery' (GP) or 'Georgia Art Pottery' (GAP) and continued to do so until 1950 when he used a 'Hand Made by WJ Gordy' stamp (HM). Since 1970 he has signed his pottery. Known throughout the world for his fine glazes, he won the Georgia Governor's Award in 1983. Examples of his wares are on display in the Smithsonian. His father W.T.B. and brother D.X. are also well-known potters.

Bowl, dk mauve, 2½x3" dia 40.00
Candle holder/bowl, hi-fire copper red/gr, early mk, sgn, 4x7" ...250.00
Flower holder, snow wht, Bill Gordy, ca 1937-39, 4⅞" 50.00
Pitcher, bl mottle, early GAP mk, 12" 250.00
Pitcher, brn-mottled frogskin on buff, w/lid, 5" 145.00
Pitcher, burgundy, Bill Gordy, ca 1940-60, 2" 40.00
Pitcher, cream; pk, 3½" 55.00
Vase, lav-pk, w/hdls, 5x4½" 95.00
Vase, pk mottle, triple hdl, early GAP mk, 5x7" 295.00

Vase, silver-bl, bulbous w/trumpet neck, sticker, 9" 175.00

German Porcelain

Unless otherwise noted, the porcelain listed in this section is marked simply 'Germany.' Products of other German manufactures are listed in specific categories. See also Bisque; Pink Paw Bears; Pink Pigs; Elfinware.

Bottle, scent; cockatoo figural, #9565, metal crown stopper, 3" .110.00
Bottle, scent; Deco lady figural, opens at waist, #2021, 5¼" 175.00
Bottle, scent; lady in bonnet w/flowers, crown stopper, #446, 3¼" ..90.00
Bowl, berry; roses/gilt/emb moldings, IPF, 11", +4 ind 145.00
Bowl, centerpc; classical maiden/verse, Maberei, 1945-55, 11x15" ..1,225.00
Bowl, walls formed by row of parading geese, 6½" 325.00
Charger, floral w/floral relief, mk PF, 13" 85.00
Coffee service, classical scenes w/gold, serves 12, 39-pc 350.00
Compote, cherubs on ft, appl/pnt mc flowers, Schierholz, 8" 175.00
Figurine, baby w/raised hands, wht gloss, 10" 75.00
Figurine, couple in 19th-C attire, w/lace, Muller, 4½" 175.00
Figurine, drunken group at table, 20th C, 9x14" 150.00
Figurine, furniture seller, 20th C, 8" 125.00

Figurine, girl with muff, blue intaglio mouth, painted pastel colors, Made in Germany in circle, 10", $200.00. (Photo courtesy McMasters Auctions)

Figurine, lady dancing in blk gown w/HP flowers, '30s, 9½" 350.00
Figurine, lady dancing in period dress, w/lace, Muller, 7½" 175.00
Figurine, lady seated, w/lace, crown mk, 4½" 70.00
Figurine, lady seated & hound, w/lace, Dresden Art, 7" 100.00
Figurine, lady/2 children/lamb, w/lace, 1902, crown mk, 8", EX ...150.00
Figurine, man, lady & maid in parlor scene, 18th C, rprs, 9x11" ..150.00
Figurine, nude seated, wht gloss, 10" 175.00
Figurine, nude standing, wht gloss, 15½" 175.00
Figurine, Retour Des Champs, woman & wheat, Karl Enz, 20" .260.00
Figurine, washer woman, 20th C, 7⅝" 125.00
Figurine, 2 ladies w/piano & lute, w/lace, crown mk, 6x12" 200.00
Hair receiver, Jasper, bl w/3 ladies in various pursuits, 4x3" 100.00
Jardiniere, floral, mc on ivory, 7" 140.00
Mug, Indian chief portrait 40.00
Plaque, lady w/roses, ornate giltwood fr, oval, 10x7½" 3,450.00
Vase, figures in landscape, tapestry style, 19th C, 14x7" 700.00
Vase, pheasants, HP, 5" 325.00
Vase, Venus & cherubs/Hagar & Ishmael, snake hdls, w/lid, 28½" ..4,300.00

Gladding McBean and Company

This company was established in 1875 in Lincoln, California. They first produced only clay drainage pipes, but in 1883 architectural terra cotta was introduced, which has been used extensively in the United

States as well as abroad. Sometime later a line of garden pottery was added. They soon became the leading producers of tile in the country. In 1923 they purchased the Tropico Pottery in Glendale, California, where in addition to tile they also produced huge garden vases. Their line was expanded in 1934 to included artware and dinnerware.

At least fifteen lines of art pottery were developed between 1934 and 1942. For a short time they stamped their wares with the Tropico Pottery mark; but the majority was signed 'GMcB' in an oval. Later the mark was changed to 'Franciscan' with several variations. After 1937 'Catalina Pottery' was used on some lines. (All items marked 'Catalina Pottery' were made in Glendale.) For further information we recommend *The Collector's Encyclopedia of California Pottery, Second Edition*, by Jack Chipman (Collector Books). See also Franciscan Ware.

Ashtray, cowboy hat, burgundy, Franciscan Ware, 2½x6" 230.00
Bowl, Capistrano Art Ware, coral satin, leaf form, 9¾x14" 240.00
Bowl, Cocinero, yel, #7, 3½x7¼" 60.00
Bowl, flower; wht w/bl int, scalloped/ribbed/flaring, 18" W 175.00
Bowl, mixing; Cocinero, gr, 10" 100.00
Bowl, Oxblood, 2x6" 140.00
Bowl, wht w/pk int, ftd seashell form, Catalina Pottery 75.00
Candlestick, Coronado Art Ware, coral satin, 6½" 20.00
Candlesticks, wht matt, melon ribbed w/flaring petal ft, 3", pr 42.00
Compote, Coronado Art Ware, Swirl, wht, 5x10½" 290.00
Dish, peach on cream, leaf shape, 10x10½" 37.00
Figurine, standing woman holding child, wht matt, 13" 250.00
Mug, coffee; Rancho 10.00
Plate, Rancho, fluted, ivory satin, 14" 65.00
Platter, Montecito, coral, 16" 85.00
Tea set, orange, 3-pc 65.00
Teapot, Metropolitan, bl & wht 125.00
Tray, Capistrano Art Ware, plum & ivory, #411 ....45.00
Vase, Avalon Artware, ivory w/turq int, spherical, 4" 35.00
Vase, bud; Encanto Art Ware, celadon 22.00
Vase, Capistrano Art Ware, plum & ivory, #418 ....135.00
Vase, Celito Art Ware, bl & mauve, flared/ftd, C-304, 6½" 75.00
Vase, Celito Art Ware, periwinkle & plum, C-308, 8" 95.00
Vase, Coronado, swirl, wht matt, flaring w/bulb bottom, 8½" ...115.00
Vase, Garden Ware, bl-gr, bead relief at neck, 35" 550.00
Vase, ivory w/turq int, invt bell w/wide ft, 4¾" 40.00
Vase, orange, oil jar shape, 4" 40.00

Glass Animals and Figurines

These beautiful glass sculptures have been produced by many major companies in America, in fact, some are still being made today. Heisey, Fostoria, Duncan and Miller, Imperial, Paden City, Tiffin, and Cambridge made the vast majority, but there were many others involved on a lesser scale. Some, but not all, marked their animals.

As many of the glass companies went out of business, molds were often sold to others still active who used them to reproduce their own line of animals. While some are easy to recognize, others can be very confusing. For example, Summit Art Glass now owns Cambridge's 6½", 8½", and 10" swan molds. We recommend *Glass Animals of the Depression Era* by Lee Garmon and Dick Spencer, if you're thinking of starting a collection or wanting to identify and evaluate the glass animals you already have. Both are our advisors for this category and are listed in the Directory under Illinois.

Note: Heisey Collectors of America stopped using the plug horse and have adopted the rabbit paperweight as the new yearly mascot.

Cambridge

Bashful Charlotte, flower frog, Dianthus, 6½" 150.00
Bashful Charlotte, flower frog, gr, 11½" 375.00
Bashful Charlotte, flower frog, Moonlight Blue satin, 11½" 800.00
Bird on stump, flower frog, gr, 5¼" 325.00
Blue jay, flower holder, crystal 135.00
Buddha, amber, 5½" 225.00
Draped Lady, flower frog, crystal frost, 13¼" 175.00
Draped Lady, flower frog, Dianthus, 13¼" 225.00
Draped Lady, flower frog, Dianthus, 8½" 175.00
Draped Lady, flower frog, gr frost, 8½" 125.00
Draped Lady, flower frog, ivory, oval base, 8½" 800.00
Draped Lady, flower frog, lt emerald, 8½" 225.00
Frog, crystal satin 25.00
Heron, crystal, lg, 12" 135.00
Mandolin Lady, flower frog, crystal 250.00
Mandolin Lady, flower frog, dk amber 450.00
Melon Boy, flower frog, Dianthus 425.00
Owl, lamp, ivory w/brn enamel, ebony base, 13½" 1,100.00

Rose Lady, flower frog, green, 8½", $250.00. (Photo courtesy Dick Spencer and Lee Garmon)

Rose Lady, flower frog, crystal satin, tall base, 9¾" 225.00
Rose Lady, flower frog, dk amber, tall base, 9¾" 275.00
Scottie, bookends, crystal, hollow, pr 175.00
Swan, amber, #1 style, 10½" 875.00
Swan, Apple Green, #1 style, 13½" 850.00
Swan, Carmen, 6½" 225.00
Swan, Crown Tuscan, 8½" 125.00
Swan, crystal, #1 style, 10½" 180.00
Swan, dk gr, #3 style, 8½" 175.00
Swan, ebony, 12½" 300.00
Swan, ebony, 3" 65.00
Swan, emerald, 3" 40.00
Swan, emerald, 8½" 125.00
Swan, milk glass, 6½" 125.00
Swan, milk glass, 8½" 275.00
Swan, punch bowl, Pearl Mist 2,600.00
Turkey, bl, w/lid 550.00
Turkey, pk, w/lid 400.00
Turtle, flower holder, ebony 225.00
Two Kids, flower frog, amber, oval base, 9¼" 350.00
Two Kids, flower frog, crystal, 9¼" 200.00

Duncan and Miller

Bird of Paradise, crystal 700.00
Donkey, cart & peon, crystal, 3-pc set 475.00
Donkey, crystal 120.00
Dove, crystal, head down, 11½" L 175.00
Duck, ashtray, crystal, 4" 20.00

Duck, ashtray, red, 7" 90.00
Duck, cigarette box, red, 6" 170.00
Heron, crystal 150.00
Heron, crystal satin, 7" 120.00
Swan, bl opal, W&F, spread wings, 10x12½" 245.00
Swan, bowl, dk gr, 10½" 80.00
Swan, chartreuse, open bk, 7" 40.00
Swan, crystal, solid, 5" 35.00
Swan, milk glass w/red neck, 10½" 450.00
Swan, wheat cutting, 11" 200.00
Swordfish, crystal 275.00
Sylvan swan, bl or pk, 5½" 125.00
Sylvan swan, yel opal, 7½" 140.00
Tropical fish, ashtray, pk opal, 3½" 50.00

Fenton

September Morn Nymph, milk glass, with separate flower frog, 1920s, 7", $150.00; Bridesmaid, white iridized, 6¼", 1980s, $55.00. (Photo courtesy Betty and Bill Newbound)

Airedale, Rosalene, 1992 issue for Heisey 125.00
Alley cat, pk carnival, mk, 11" 100.00
Alley cat, Teal Marigold, 11" 85.00
Bear, carnival, sitting 30.00
Bunny, pale yel 25.00
Butterfly, candle holder, ruby carnival, 1989 souvenir, 7½", ea 95.00
Cardinal head, ruby, 6½" 110.00
Elephant, periwinkle, whiskey bottle, 8" 450.00
Filly, Rosalene, head front, 1992 issue for Heisey 125.00
Fish, paperweight, red carnival, ltd ed, 4½" 65.00
Fish, red w/amberina tail & fins, 2½" 55.00
Fish, vase, milk glass w/blk tail & eyes, 7" 425.00
Giraffe, Rosalene 125.00
Hen, Rosalene, 1992 issue for Heisey 125.00
Peacock, bookends, crystal satin, 5¾", pr 175.00
Rabbit, paperweight, Rosalene, 1992 issue for Heisey 65.00
Turtle, flower block, amethyst, 4" L 85.00

Fostoria

Bird, candle holder, crystal, 1½" 20.00
Buddha, bookends, blk, pr 525.00
Cat, lt bl, 3¾" 35.00
Chanticleer, blk, 10¾" 600.00
Colt, Silver Mist, standing 45.00
Deer, bl, sitting or standing, ea 55.00
Dolphin, bl, 4¾" 35.00
Eagle, bookend, crystal, 7½", ea 150.00
Frog, bl, lemon or olive gr, 1⅞", ea from $40 to 50.00
Goldfish, crystal, vertical 110.00
Horse, bookend, crystal, 7¾", ea 45.00
Madonna, Silver Mist, orig issue, 10" (+) 50.00
Madonna, Silver Mist, w/base, orig issue, 11¾" (+) 80.00
Mermaid, crystal, 11½" 125.00
Owl, bl, lemon or olive gr, 2¾", ea from $35 to 50.00
Penguin, crystal, sq base, 4⅝" 75.00
Polar bear, topaz, 4⅝" 125.00
Rebecca at Well, candle holder, crystal frost, ea 125.00
Sea horse, bookend, crystal, 8", ea 125.00
Squirrel, amber, running or sitting, ea 45.00
Squirrel, amber, sitting 45.00
St Francis, Silver Mist, orig issue, 13½" (+) 325.00

Heisey

Airedale, crystal 650.00
Bull, crystal, sgn, 4x7½" 1,800.00
Chick, crystal, head down or up, ea 95.00
Clydesdale, crystal, 7½x7" 450.00
Colt, amber, kicking 650.00
Colt, cobalt, kicking 1,500.00
Colt, cobalt, rearing 1,500.00
Colt, crystal, rearing 200.00

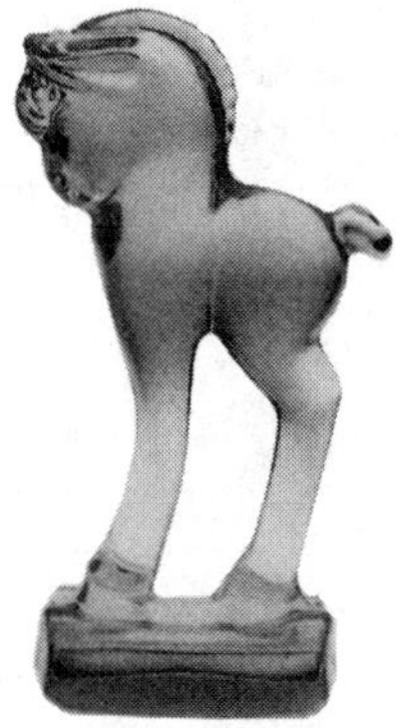

Colt, amber, standing, $650.00. (Photo courtesy Lee Garmon and Dick Spencer)

Colt, crystal, standing 100.00
Cygnet, baby swan, crystal, 2½" 225.00
Doe head, bookend, crystal, 6¼", ea 850.00
Dolphin, candlesticks, Moongleam, #110, pr 800.00
Donkey, crystal 295.00
Duck, ashtray, Marigold 400.00
Duck, flower block, crystal 140.00
Duck, flower block, Hawthorne 295.00
Elephant, amber, sm 1,650.00
Elephant, crystal, lg or med, ea 450.00
Elephant, crystal, sm 225.00
Filly, crystal, head forward 1,000.00
Fish, bookend, crystal, ea 160.00
Fish, bowl, crystal, 9½" 450.00
Fish, match holder, crystal, 3x2¾" 180.00
Frog, cheese plate, Marigold 285.00
Gazelle, crystal, 10¾" 1,200.00
Giraffe, crystal, head to side 275.00
Goose, crystal, wings down 450.00
Goose, crystal, wings up 110.00
Hen, crystal, 4½" 350.00
Horse head, cigarette box, crystal, #1489, 4½x4" 60.00
Horse head, frosted, bookend, ea 140.00
Irish setter, ashtray, Flamingo 45.00
Kingfisher, Moongleam, flower block 250.00
Mallard, crystal, wings down 350.00
Mallard, crystal, wings half 200.00
Piglet, crystal, sitting 100.00
Piglet, crystal, standing 100.00
Plug horse, cobalt 1,200.00
Pouter pigeon, crystal, 7½" L 800.00

Rabbit mother, crystal, 4½x5½" 1,100.00
Ram head, stopper, crystal, 3½" 160.00
Rooster, amber, 5⅜" 2,500.00
Rooster, crystal, 5½x5" 350.00
Rooster, Fighting; crystal frost, 7½x5½" 200.00
Rooster head, cocktail shaker, crystal, 1-qt 75.00
Rooster head, crystal, cocktail 60.00
Rooster head, stopper, crystal, 4½" 45.00
Sea horse, cocktail, crystal 160.00
Show horse, crystal 1,250.00
Sow, crystal, 3x4½" 800.00
Sparrow, crystal 120.00
Swan, crystal, master nut, #1503 ....45.00
Swan, ind nut, crystal, #1503 ....25.00
Tiger, paperweight, crystal, 2¾x8" 900.00
Wood duck, crystal 800.00

Imperial

Phoenix bowl, Dynasty Jade, 1980s issue of Cathay Crystal mold, 5", from $185.00 to $200.00.

Bulldog-type pup, milk glass, 3½", from $45 to 65.00
Chick, milk glass, head down 10.00
Clydesdale, Verde Green 150.00
Colt, amber, standing 125.00
Colt, Horizon Blue, kicking 35.00
Cygnet, blk, 2½" 55.00
Cygnet, Horizon Blue 25.00
Dog, Airedale, Ultra Blue, from $70 to 90.00
Donkey, Meadow Green carnival 90.00
Elephant, caramel slag, sm 85.00
Elephant, Nut Brown, sm 120.00
Fish, candlestick, Sunshine Yellow, 5", from $40 to 50.00
Flying mare, amber, NI mk, extremely rare 1,500.00
Giraffe, amber, ALIG mk, extremely rare 350.00
Mallard, caramel slag, wings down 200.00
Mallard, caramel slag, wings up 40.00
Mallard, lt bl satin, wings down 35.00
Owl, Hootless; caramel slag 50.00
Owl, jar, caramel slag, 16½" 75.00
Owl, purple slag, shiny 95.00
Piglet, amber, standing 40.00
Rabbit, paperweight, Horizon Blue, 2¾", from $80 to 100.00
Rooster, amber 475.00
Scolding bird, Cathay Crystal 175.00
Swan, purple slag, shiny 95.00
Terrier, Parlour Pup, Sunshine Yellow carnival 50.00
Tiger, paperweight, Jade Green slag, 8" L 95.00
Wood duck, Ultra Blue satin 55.00
Wood duckling, standing, Ultra Blue 45.00

L.E. Smith

Camel, cobalt 95.00
Cock, Fighting; bl, 9" 55.00
Elephant, crystal, 1¾" 20.00
Goose Girl, crystal, orig, 6" 25.00
Goose Girl, gr or flame, 6", ea 50.00
Horse, bookend, blk, rearing, ea 65.00
Horse, crystal, bookend, rearing, ea 35.00
King Fish, aquarium, gr, 7¼x15" 265.00
Queen fish, aquarium, gr, 7x15" 225.00
Rooster, butterscotch slag, ltd ed, #208 ....85.00
Sparrow, crystal, head up, 3½" 15.00
Swan, milk glass w/decor, 8½" 45.00
Thrush, bl frost 20.00

New Martinsville

Bear, baby, crystal, head trn or str, 3" 60.00
Bear, papa, crystal frost 225.00
Chick, frosted, 1" 25.00
Chick, orange-red 65.00
Elephant, bookend, crystal, 5½", ea 90.00
German shepherd, lamp base, pk 125.00
Horse, crystal, head up, 8" 95.00
Nautilus shell, bookend, crystal frost, 6", ea 35.00
Pig, mama, crystal 325.00
Piglet, crystal, standing 125.00
Porpoise on wave, orig 750.00
Rabbit, mama, crystal 350.00
Seal, baby w/ball, crystal 60.00
Seal, candlesticks, crystal, lg, pr 150.00
Ship, bookend, crystal, ea 45.00
Starfish, bookends, crystal, pr 170.00
Swan, candle holders, ruby, pr 70.00
Tiger, crystal frost, head down, 7¼" 200.00
Woodsman, crystal, sq base, 7⅜" 135.00

Paden City

Pheasant, Chinese; medium blue, 13¾" long, $175.00. (Photo courtesy Lee Garmon and Dick Spencer)

Bunny, cotton-ball dispenser, bl frost, ears bk 150.00
Bunny, cotton-ball dispenser, crystal frost, ears bk 95.00
Bunny, cotton-ball dispenser, pk frost, ears up 185.00
Dragon swan, crystal, 9¾" L 225.00
Horse, crystal, rearing 150.00
Pelican, crystal 600.00
Pheasant, head bk, crystal, 12" 110.00
Polar bear on ice, crystal, 4½" 65.00
Pony, blk, 12" 350.00
Pony, crystal, 12" 100.00
Pouter pigeon, crystal, bookend, 6¼" 95.00
Rooster, Barnyard; crystal, 8¾" 85.00
Rooster, Chanticleer; crystal, 9½" 95.00

Squirrel on curved log, crystal, 5½" 65.00

Tiffin

Cat, blk satin, raised bumps, #9445, 6¼" 140.00
Cat, Sassy Suzie, blk satin w/pnt decor, #9448, 11" 175.00
Fawn, flower floater, Citron Green 275.00
Fish, crystal, solid, 8¾x9" 350.00
Owl, lamp, cobalt, 1934-29 ....1,250.00

Viking

Angelfish, amber, 7x7" 125.00
Angelfish, milk glass, pr 175.00
Bird, candy dish, med gr, w/lid, 12" 75.00
Bird, med dk bl, 9½" 40.00
Bird, orange, #1311, 10" 35.00
Bird, Orchid, 9½" 45.00
Cat, gr, sitting, 8" 55.00
Dolphin, candle holders, pk, hexagonal ft, 9½", pr 150.00
Duck, dk teal, Viking's Epic Line, 9" 45.00
Duck, orange, rnd, ftd, 5" 35.00
Duck, ruby, rnd, ftd, 5" 40.00
Egret, amber, #1315, 12" 45.00
Horse, aqua bl, 11½" 125.00
Hound dog, crystal, 8" 50.00
Jesus, crystal w/crystal mist, flat bk, 6x5" 65.00
Owl, amber, Viking's Epic Line 45.00
Penguin, crystal, 7" 45.00
Rabbit, amber, 6½" 45.00
Rabbit (Thumper), crystal, 6½" 35.00
Seal, Persimmon, 9¾" L 35.00
Swan, bowl, amber, 6" 45.00
Swan, Yellow Mist, paper label, 6" 50.00

Westmoreland

Bird in flight, Amber Marigold, wings out, 5" W 35.00
Butterfly, Green Mist, 2½" 25.00
Butterfly, pk, 2½" 20.00
Cardinal, Green Mist 20.00
Owl, dk bl, shiny eyes, 5½" 65.00
Penguin on ice floe, Brandywine Blue Mist 45.00
Pig, milk glass, fired pnt, orig label 37.50
Porky Pig, milk glass, hollow, 3" L 25.00
Pouter pigeon, any color, 2½", ea 25.00
Robin, pk, 5⅛" 25.00
Starfish, candle holders, milk glass, 5", pr 45.00
Turtle, cigarette box, crystal 45.00
Turtle, paperweight, Green Mist, no holes, 4" L 25.00
Wren, Crystal Mist, 2½" 20.00
Wren, Pink Mist, 2½" 25.00
Wren, smoke, 2½" 22.50
Wren on perch, lt bl on wht, 2-pc 45.00

Miscellaneous

American Glass Co, horse, crystal, jumping, from $55 to 65.00
Co-Operative Flint, elephant, pk, tusks rpr, 13" 400.00
Federal, Mopey dog, crystal, 3½" 10.00
Haley, horse, crystal, jumping, 9½" L, from $45 to 65.00
Haley, Lady Godiva, bookend, crystal, 1940s, ea 45.00
Haley, thrush, crystal 30.00
Indiana, horse head, bookends, milk glass, 6", pr, from $45 to 65.00
Indiana, panther, amber, walking 300.00
Indiana, pouter pigeon, bookend, crystal frost, ea 40.00
LG Wright, turtle, amber 125.00
New Martinsville by Mirror Images, baby seal, ruby 75.00
New Martinsville by Mirror Images, mama bear, ruby 150.00
New Martinsville by Mirror Images, police dog, ruby 150.00
Unknown, flamenco dancers, crystal frost, mk copyright, 10½" ..225.00

Glass Knives

Glass knives were manufactured from about 1920 to 1950, with distribution at its greatest in the late '30s and early '40s. Colors generally followed Depression glass dinnerware: crystal, light blue, light green, pink (originally called rose), and more rarely amber, forest green, and white (opal). Many glass knives were hand painted in fruit or flower designs. Knife blades were ground to a sharp edge. Today knives are usually found with blades nicked through years of use or bumping in silverware drawers or reground, which is acceptable to collectors as long as the original knife shape is maintained.

Many glass knives were engraved for gift-giving, personalized with the recipient's name and, on occasion, with a greeting. Originally presented in boxes, most glass knives were accompanied by a paper insert extolling the virtues of the knife and describing its care.

Boxes printed with World's Fair logos are fun to find, though not rare. Butter knives, which are smaller than other glass knives, typically were made in Czechoslovakia and sometimes match the handle patterns of glass salad sets. Knife lengths often vary slightly because the knives were snapped off the molded glass and the end ground during manufacture.

Several styles of knives (i.e. Vitex, Dur-X, Cryst-O-Lite) were manufactured by the thousands and are therefore found more often. Prices have become volatile due to the popularity of Internet auctions and the competition that results.

Our advisor for this category is Michele Rosewitz; she is listed in the Directory under California. Values reflect knives with minor blade roughness or resharpening.

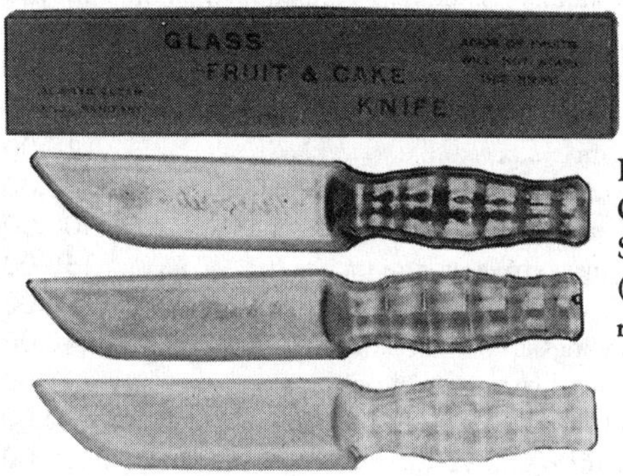

Block: Crystal, $25.00; Green, $35.00; Pink, $40.00; Box, $5.00. (Photo courtesy Gene Florence)

Aer-Flo, amber, 7½" 300.00
Aer-Flo, gr, 7½" 85.00
Buffalo Knife Co, gr, 9¼" 60.00
Dur-X (3-Leaf), bl, 8½ or 9", ea 45.00
Dur-X (3-Leaf), crystal, 8½ or 9", ea 15.00
Dur-X (5-Leaf), crystal, 9" 25.00
Pinwheel, Crystolite 12.00
Plain hdl, gr, 9¼" 40.00
Steel-ite, gr, 8½" 80.00
Steel-ite, pk, 8½" 75.00
Stonex, amber, 8½" 250.00
Stonex, opal, 8½" 350.00

Vitex (Star & Dmn), bl, 8½ or 9" 30.00
Vitex (Star & Dmn), pk, 8½ or 9" 30.00

Glass Shoes

Little shoes made of glass can be found in hundreds of styles, shapes, and colors. They've been made since the early 1800s by nearly every glasshouse, large and small, in America. To learn more about them, we recommend *Shoes of Glass II* (newly updated) by our advisor Libby Yalom, who is listed in the Directory under Maryland. Numbers in the listings refer to her book. Another reference is *Collectible Shoes of Glass* by Earlene Wheatley, published by Collector Books. See also Boyd; Degenhart.

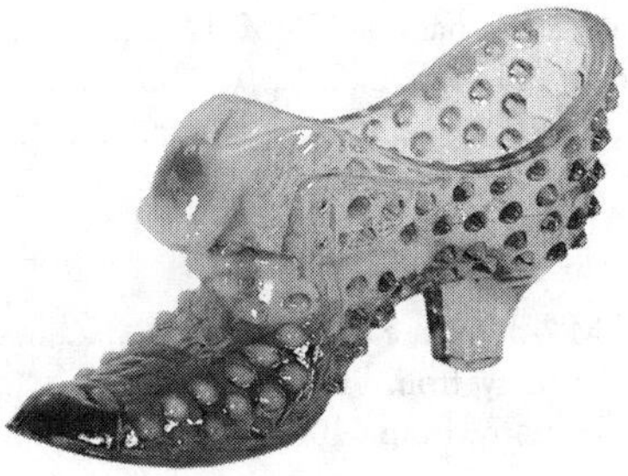

#645, Fenton Hobnail Kitten Slipper, blue opalescent, 3x5⅞", $25.00.

#120, w/bow, purple & wht slag, 4¾" 110.00
#131, boot, Daisy & Button, ruby & crystal, 1880s, 4¼" 150.00
#134, boot, opaque lt bl, ribbed, 4⅜" 135.00
#137, cuffed boot, purple & wht slag, 1890s, 4" 75.00
#171, high-button, crystal w/gold, 4 buttons/solid heel, 4½" 48.00
#243, boot jar, bl w/fine-cut pattern inside lid, 1880s, 2¾" 120.00
#266, man's slipper (pipe holder), amethyst, 1950s, 5⅛" L 25.00
#276, flat bow, crystal w/stippled finish, 4⅜" 30.00
#289, high-button (bouquet holder), amethyst, cane, 5½" 80.00
#385, Dutch style, crystal, 3 ridges on vamp, 3 buttons, 7" 50.00
#432, Dutch style, frosted w/gold-pnt decor, 4⅞" 45.00
#495, thimble holder, bl, emb B&R, ca 1890, 4" L 125.00
#523, bootee, milk glass, knitted look, pk pnt w/gold, 2¾" L 60.00

Glidden

Genius designer Glidden Parker established Glidden Pottery in 1940 in Alfred, New York, having been schooled at the unrivaled New York State College of Ceramics at Alfred University. Glidden pottery is characterized by a fine stoneware body, innovative forms, outstanding hand-milled glazes, and hand decoration which make the pieces individual works of art. Production consisted of casual dinnerware, artware, and accessories that were distributed internationally.

In 1949 Glidden Pottery became the second ceramic plant in the country to utilize the revolutionary Ram pressing machine. This allowed for increased production and for the most part eliminated the previously used slip-casting method. However, Glidden stoneware continued to reflect the same superb quality of craftsmanship until the factory closed in 1957. Although the majority of form and decorative patterns were Mr. Parker's personal designs, Fong Chow and Sergio Dello Strologo also designed award-winning lines.

Glidden will be found marked on the unglazed underside with a signature that is hand incised, mold impressed, or ink stamped. Interest in this unique stoneware is growing as collectors discover that it embodies the very finest of mid-century high style. Our advisor is David Pierce; he is listed in the Directory under Ohio.

Salad bowl, High Tide, #17, $35.00; Platter, High Tide, #28, $40.00. (Photo courtesy David Pierce)

Ashtray, Alfred Stoneware, #821 ....40.00
Ashtray, Gulfstream, #272-U 35.00
Baker, Feather, #22 ....35.00
Boat, Green Mesa, #4033 ....150.00
Bottles, Alfred Stoneware, #813/#814/#815, 3 in basket 200.00
Bowl, Early Pink, oval, #38 ....35.00
Bowl, Sandstone, ped ft, oval, #4041-P 400.00
Bowl, serving; Fish (Fred Press), #622 ....30.00
Bowl, soup; Feather, #270 ....15.00
Candle bench, Afrikans 70.00
Casserole, Pear, #163 ....45.00
Casserole, Sage & Sand, #163 ....35.00
Casserole, Turquoise Matrix, #167 ....15.00
Casserole, Yellowstone, #165 ....30.00
Charger, Leaf, dk bl, #368 ....225.00
Coffee urn, Alfred Stoneware, #816 ....215.00
Creamer & sugar bowl, High Tide, #1430/#1440 ....60.00
Creamer & sugar bowl, Pear, #143/#144 ....65.00
Creamer & sugar bowl, Turquoise Matrix, #1430/#1440 ....45.00
Cup & saucer, Alfred Stoneware, #841/#842 ....35.00
Cup & saucer, Flourish, #141/#142 ....30.00
Cup & saucer, High Tide, #441-A/#442 ....25.00
Cup & saucer, Will o' the Wisp, #141/#142 ....25.00
Flowerpot, Gulfstream, #4031 ....120.00
Flowerpot, Turquoise Matrix, #218 ....35.00
Flowerpot, Yellowstone, #218 ....40.00
Pepper mill, Alfred Stoneware, #801 ....70.00
Pitcher, Feather, #615, 1-qt 50.00
Pitcher, Yellowstone, #617, 3-qt 65.00
Planter, Turquoise Matrix, #104 ....18.00
Plate, chop; High Tide, #608 ....30.00
Plate, dinner; Flourish, #31 ....20.00
Plate, luncheon; Yellowstone, #33 ....12.00
Spice set, Boston Spice, #607-R, 4 jars w/rack 75.00
Tile, serving; Garden, #606 ....60.00
Vase, Early Pink, #87 ....40.00
Vase, Green Mesa, #4019 ....300.00
Vase, Sandstone, #4017 ....350.00

Goebel

F.W. Goebel founded the F&W Goebel Company in 1871, located in Rodental, West Germany. They produced thousands of different decorative and useful items over the years, the most famous of which are the Hummel figurines first produced in 1935 based on the artwork of a Franciscan nun, Sister Maria Innocentia Hummel.

The Goebel trademarks have long been a source of confusion because *all* Goebel products, including Hummels, of any particular time period bear the same trademark, thus leading many to believe all Goebels are Hummels. Always look for the Hummel signature on actual Hummel figurines (these are listed in a separate section).

There are many, many other series — some of which are based on artwork of particular artists such as Disney, Charlot Byj, Janet Robson, Harry Holt, Norman Rockwell, M. Spotl, Lore, Huldah, and Schaubach. Miscellaneous useful items include ashtrays, bookends, salt and pepper shakers, banks, pitchers, inkwells, and perfume bottles. Figurines include birds, animals, and Art Deco pieces. The Friar Tuck monks and the Co-Boy elves are especially popular.

The date of manufacture of a particular piece is determined by the trademark. The incised date found underneath the base on many items is the *mold copyright* date. Actual date of manufacture may vary as much as twenty years or more from the copyright date.

Most Common Goebel Trademarks and Approximate Dates Used:

1.) Crown mark (may be incised or stamped, or both): 1923 – 1950
2.) Full bee (complete bumble bee inside the letter 'V'): 1950 – 1957
3.) Stylized bee (dot with wings inside the letter 'V'): 1957 – 1964
4.) 3-Line (stylized bee with 3 lines of copyright info to the right of the trademark): 1964 – 1972
5.) Goebel bee (word Goebel with stylized bee mark over the last letter 'e'): 1972 – 1979
6.) Goebel (word Goebel only): 1979 – present

Our advisors for this category are Gale and Wayne Bailey; they are listed in the Directory under Georgia.

Cardinal Tuck (Red Monk)

Ashtray, flat, RF142 ....140.00
Bell, 6¼" 115.00
Cigarette holder, RX110, TMK-3, 3" 225.00
Creamer, S141/0, TMK-3 ....175.00
Creamer, S141/1, 5½" 150.00
Mug, T74I, 5¼x5" 260.00
Shakers, TMK-3, 3", pr 145.00
Stein, #74074 13, w/lid, 6½" 215.00
Sugar bowl, Z37, TMK-3, 4" 155.00

Charlot BYJ Redheads and Blonds

Sleepy Head, BYJ 11, $80.00.

Boy sleeping in rowboat w/dog, Goebel BYJ 78, 3¾x5¼" 170.00
Camera Shy, BYJ 79 ....105.00
Cheer Up, BYJ 50, 5", orig box 75.00
Daisies Won't Tell, TMK-4, BYJ 24 ....85.00
Gangway, BYJ 28, TMK-5 ....85.00
Plaque, little redhead stands beside sign, BYJ 47, 4½x6½" 145.00
Roving Eye, BYJ 2, TMK-4, 4¼" 85.00
Sitting Pretty, BYJ 12, 5" 75.00
Spellbound, BYJ 19, TMK-4 ....85.00
Trim Lass, BYJ 49 ....105.00
Trouble Shooter, BYJ 67 ....75.00
Way To Pray, BYJ 46, TMK-5 ....75.00

Co-Boy Figurines

Candy the Confectioner, #523 ....60.00
Chris the Shoemaker, #551, MIP 125.00
Chuck, riding pig w/shamrock in mouth, #17-559-19, 8" 245.00
Chuck the Chimney Sweep, #550 ....155.00
Conny Clock, w/clock 250.00
George the Gourmand, #537 ....125.00
Homer, steering wheel in hand, #17-559-16 ....125.00
Jack the Pharmicist, #517 ....90.00
John the Hunter, #516 ....95.00

Cookie Jars

Cardinal, K 29, TMK-3, from $1,750 to 2,000.00
Cat, Goebel W Germany, from $100 to 125.00
Dog, Goebel W Germany, from $100 to 125.00
Eagle head 130.00
Friar Tuck, K 29 Made in W Germany 1957, from $375 to 475.00
Lion, Goebel W Germany, from $70 to 80.00
Owl, Goebel W Germany, from $70 to 80.00
Panda Bear, Goebel W Germany, from $70 to 80.00
Parrot, Goebel W Germany, from $70 to 80.00

Friar Tuck (Brown Monk)

Ashtray, ZF43/2 ....105.00
Bank, SD29, TMK-2 ....100.00
Cigarette holder, RX110, TMK-3 ....150.00
Creamer & sugar bowl on tray, TMK-4 ....105.00
Decanter, TMK-2 ....85.00
Decanter, KL95, w/4 cups, KL94 ....175.00
Egg timer, TMK-5 ....90.00
Flask/cigarette holder, KL90/B 115.00
Matchbook holder, RX111, TMK-3 ....100.00
Mug, T74/3, lg, 7x5" 150.00
Mustard pot, S183, 3¾" 59.00
Pitcher, M43A 60.00
Pitcher, S141/II, rare 400.00
Shakers, w/Bible, TMK-3, pr, from $100 to 140.00
Sugar bowl, M43B 60.00
Thermometer, KF56 ....115.00
Tobacco jar, RX106/1 ....275.00

Shakers

Bear & beehive, TMK-3, pr 25.00
Duck & drake, P76A/B, TMK-3, pr 25.00
Dutch boy & Breton girl, P449/P450, TMK-1, pr 65.00
Skunks, full bee, WDP mk, 1940, pr 150.00
Thumper (rabbits), TMK-2, pr 150.00

Miscellaneous

Ashtray, Thumper, Disney 8, TMK-2 ....275.00
Beehive Honey Pot, H125/0, TMK-3 ....35.00
Candle holder, Soldier, L314, TMK-1 ....105.00

Figurine, Am eagle, CV104, 9½x20" wingspan 160.00
Figurine, Animal Band, Singing Dog, Amerikids, mk Goebel 55.00
Figurine, Bambi, smoke eater, Disney, 6½" 160.00
Figurine, Bambi standing w/Thumper, TMK-2 mk, 3x4½" 155.00
Figurine, bathing beauty in boat, RF666, 1½x4½" 160.00
Figurine, Benched, Amerikids, mk Goebel 55.00
Figurine, elephant, gray, #3, 15x21½" 185.00
Figurine, Fish for Two, Amerikids #11-609-14, TMK-5 ....75.00
Figurine, gray heron, 7" 260.00
Figurine, Madonna w/Child, HUL10, Huldah series, 6⅜" 175.00
Figurine, Nascha, #7, 7½" 205.00
Figurine, parrot, CV79, TMK-4, 1967, 8½" 210.00
Lamp, scent; Pluto, Disney, Dis 149, TMK-2, 6x3x5" 250.00
Nativity set, Olszewski, 1st ed bkstamp, in glass globe, MIB 375.00
Night light, cat figural, amber eyes, #12171/0, 6¾" 250.00
Pitcher, Harlequin, blk collar, S198 2/0, TMK-3 ....50.00

Goldscheider

The Goldscheider family operated a pottery in Vienna for many generations before seeking refuge in the United States following Hitler's invasion of their country. They settled in Trenton, New Jersey, in the early 1940s where they established a new corporation and began producing objects of art and tableware items. (No mention was made of the company in the Trenton City Directory after 1950, and it is assumed that by this time the influx of foreign imports had taken its toll.) In 1946 Marcel Goldscheider established a pottery in Staffordshire where he manufactured bone china figures, earthenware, etc., marked with a stamp of his signature. Larger artist-signed examples are the most valuable with the Austrian pieces bringing the higher prices.

A wide variety of marks has been found: 1.) Goldscheider USA Fine China; 2.) Original Goldscheider Fine China; 3.) Goldscheider USA; 4.) Goldscheider-Everlast Corp.; 5.) Goldscheider Everlast Corp. in circle; 6.) Goldscheider Inc. in circle; 7.) Goldcrest Ceramics Corp. in circle; 8.) Goldcrest Fine China; 9.) Goldcrest Fine China USA; 10.) A Goldcrest Creation; and 11.) Created by Goldscheider USA.

Our advisors are Randy and Debbie Coe; they are listed in the Directory under Oregon.

Bust, curly hair, hands by face, Austria, #7653, 15½" 1,250.00
Bust, Siamese woman, exotic headdress & jewelry, 12¼x8¼" ...500.00
Figurine, bird on branch, 8" 79.00
Figurine, Boston Terrier, blk & wht, #8, 5" 75.00
Figurine, Cotillion, mk #1611, P Porcher, 6" 90.00
Figurine, dancer on 1 leg w/wrap, 1930s, 20⅝" 1,450.00
Figurine, girl w/dog, lt gr dress, dk skin, #7063, 8" 180.00
Figurine, lady, kneeling, w/fan, gr blouse/pk flowing skirt, 8" 100.00
Figurine, lady at sewing machine, c Singer Mfg Co mk on side, 8x4" .300.00
Figurine, Lady Chrysanthemum, USA, 7" 145.00
Figurine, lady in rose-colored dress, w/bouquet of flowers, 8½" .135.00
Figurine, lady w/hands in muff, fancy hat, #802, 8½" 125.00
Figurine, mother & baby bird on branches, att Jacob, 6" 150.00
Figurine, Old Virginia, USA, 8½" 125.00
Figurine, ringneck pheasant, gr & brn, 14" 125.00
Figurine, sailor playing accordion, #6792/31, 8¼" 175.00
Lamp, Aida, lady by lamppost, Austria, #5981, 21" 2,400.00
Lamp, lady in floral dress w/lute, seated by column, Thomasch, 19" .1,260.00
Powder box, half-doll on lid, 3 ball ft, 6½" dia 195.00

Gonder

Lawton Gonder grew up with clay in his hands and fire in his eyes. Gonder's interest in ceramics was greatly influenced by his parents who worked for Weller and a close family friend and noted ceramic authority, John Herold. In his early teens Gonder launched his ceramic career at the Ohio Pottery Company while working for Herold. He later gained valuable experience at American Encaustic Tile Company, Cherry Art Tile, and the Florence Pottery. Gonder was plant manager at the Florence Pottery until fire destroyed the facility in late 1941.

After years of solid production and management experience, Lawton Gonder established the Gonder Ceramic Art Company, formerly the Peters and Reed plant, in South Zanesville, Ohio. Gonder Ceramic Arts produced quality art pottery with beautiful contemporary designs which included human and animal figures and a complete line of Oriental pottery. Accentuating the beautiful shapes were unique and innovative glazes developed by Gonder such as flambe (flame red with streaks of yellow), 24k gold crackle, antique gold, and Chinese crackle. (These glazes bring premium prices.)

All Gonder is marked with the company name and mold number. They include 'Gonder U.S.A' in block letters, 'Gonder' in script, 'Gonder Original' in script, and 'Gonder Ceramic Art' in block letters. Paper labels were also used. Some of the early Gonder molds closely resemble RumRill designs that had been manufactured at the Florence Pottery; and because some RumRill pieces are found with similar (if not identical) shapes, matching mold numbers, and Gonder glazes, it is speculated that some RumRill was produced at the Gonder plant. In 1946 Gonder started another company which he named Elgee (chosen for his initials LG) where he manufactured lamp bases until a fire in 1954 resulted in his shifting lamp production to the main plant. Operations ceased in 1957.

Our values are for items in mint condition, unless noted otherwise. Our advisor for this category is Ron Hoopes; he is listed in the Directory under Ohio.

Vase, green with brown, cactus-like form, K-26, 12", $65.00.

Basket, brn, L-19, 9x13" 95.00
Bookends, horse head, #582, pr 75.00
Candle holders, crescent moon, gold, J-56, 6½", pr 50.00
Candle holders, starfish, #501, 6", pr 75.00
Conch shell, wht crackle, 16" 225.00
Console, shell form, #505, 16x8" 125.00
Cookie jar, pirate, Gonder Original, 12" 800.00
Cookie jar, sheriff, yel & brn, Gonder Original #950, 12" 800.00
Creamer & sugar bowl, La Gonda, red volcanic glaze, 4" 50.00
Cup & saucer, La Gonda, yel 25.00
Custard dish, gr volcanic glaze, hdld, #952, 7" 10.00
Ewer, cornucopia, starfish base, w/hdl, #508, 14" 150.00
Ewer, gold, J-25, 11" 100.00
Figurine, Chinese coolie, kneeling, #547, 6" 30.00
Figurine, Chinese girl, gr, #763, 13" 50.00
Figurine, gamecock, bl crackle, #525, 11" 175.00
Figurine, horse, paper label, 10" 100.00

Figurine, modern cat, wht crackle glaze, #521, 12" 500.00
Figurine, panther, blk, unmk, 20" 75.00
Figurine, panther, yel or gr, #217, 15" 150.00
Figurine, panther on rocks, unmk, 10" 50.00
Figurine, ram, wht crackle, 6" 75.00
Figurine, 2 deer, stylized, #690, 11" 35.00
Flower holder, swan figural, golden crackle, #E44, 5" 25.00
Head vase, doe, turq, #418, 9¾" 55.00
Lamp, Chinese woman, wht, mk Gonder USA, 18" 300.00
Lamp base, 2 leaping gazelles, yel, 15" 75.00
Lamp base, 2 rearing horses (facing), 13" 75.00
Pitcher, gr & brn, M-9, 13" 75.00
Soap dish, HP/emb flower 35.00
TV lamp, sea gull, 12" 100.00
TV lamp, ship, 14" 50.00
Vase, box w/emb floral, gr & brn, H-76, 8" 50.00
Vase, butterfly, wht, very detailed, #523, 9" 200.00
Vase, Chinese; yel, #535, 12" 125.00
Vase, cornucopia, gr, #691, 8" 35.00
Vase, cornucopia, H-14, 10" 45.00
Vase, Curtain, #605, 10" 75.00
Vase, dolphin on waves, #503, 15" 500.00
Vase, Flame, #510, 11" 75.00
Vase, gr & blk marbleized, pk int, hdls, H-5, 9" 36.00
Vase, horse, yel, #553, 6½" 125.00
Vase, swan shape, gr, J-31, 8" 100.00
Vase, wht crackle, box form, 4 legged, #748, 7" 100.00

Goofus Glass

Goofus glass is American-made pressed glass with designs that are either embossed (blown out) or intaglio (cut in). The decorated colors were aerographed or hand applied and not fired on the pieces. The various patterns exemplify the artistry of the turn-of-the-century glass crafters. The primary production dates were ca 1908 to 1918. Goofus was produced by many well-known manufacturers such as Northwood, Indiana, and Dugan.

When no condition is given, values are for items in mint original paint. Our advisor for this category is Steve Gillespie of the *Goofus Glass Gazette;* he is listed in the Directory under Missouri. See also Clubs, Newsletters, and Catalogs.

Bonbon, strawberry & flower pod, dome ft, 4" dia 42.50
Bowl, Butterfly, pattern decor, Dugan, 9" 65.00
Bowl, Carnation, La Belle & Roses in the Snow, 5½" sq 12.00
Bowl, Carnation, La Belle & Roses in the Snow, 9" 15.00
Bowl, Cupids, 6½" 35.00
Bowl, Dahlia (any of 3 variations), 10" 18.00
Bowl, Daisy & Plume, opal, ruffled edge, 9" 45.00
Bowl, Greek Key & Sunflower, gr glass, Northwood, 9" 65.00
Bowl, nappy; Poppy, pattern decor, Northwood 35.00
Bowl, pears/cherries/plums, crimped rim, EX orig pnt, 4x7" 37.50
Bowl, pine cones & leaves, opal, 10" 45.00
Bowl, Rose, 5-sided (hard to find) 110.00
Bowl, Two Fruits & Olympic Torch, pattern decor, rare, 9" 95.00
Cake plate, Acorn & Leaf, amethyst, 12" 20.00
Cake plate, Acorn & Leaf, 12" 30.00
Cake plate, Carnation, La Belle & Roses in Snow, 9" 15.00
Cake plate, Carnation, La Belle & Roses in Snow, 11" 15.00
Cake plate, Dahlia, 11" 18.00
Cake plate, Wild Flower, crackle glass border, 12" 25.00
Compote, Lightning Flower, clear, unsgn Northwood, clear, 6½" 30.00
Compote, Lightning Flower, gr, unsgn Northwood, 6½" 35.00
Compote, Poppy, 6" 35.00
Compote, Rose, 6" 35.00
Compote, Rose Perfect, 6" 30.00
Compote & saucer set, Poppy, crackle glass, 6" 40.00
Dish, Cupids, heart shape, 6" 90.00
Dish, flowered, heart shape, 6" 50.00
Dish, heart shape, cut or pressed pattern, 6" 70.00
Dish, Rose, heart shape, 6" 60.00
Dresser item, Cabbage Rose powder jar 30.00
Lamp, Cabbage Rose, matching chimney, 12" 150.00
Lamp, oil; Nosegay, #2, EX orig pnt 155.00
Plate, Butterfly, Dugan, rare, 11" 125.00
Plate, Carnation, La Belle & Roses in Snow, 4½" 10.00
Plate, Carnation, La Belle & Roses in Snow, 6" 10.00
Plate, Carnation, La Belle & Roses in Snow, 9" 15.00
Plate, Cupid, 7" 30.00
Plate, Gibson Cameo (series), 8½" 30.00
Plate, Holly, opal, 10½" 70.00
Plate, Latticed Glass Edge Easter Chickens, 7" 60.00
Plate, Latticed Glass Edge St Louis World's Fair, heart shape, 7" 40.00
Plate, Latticed Glass Edge St Louis World's Fair, 7" 35.00
Plate, Lightning Flower, clear, unsgn Northwood, 7" 25.00
Plate, Lightning Flower, gr, unsgn Northwood, 7" 27.00
Plate, monk drinking from tankard, uptrn edges, 7" 32.00
Plate, Poppy, Carnation or Rose, 2 uptrn sides, 7" 30.00
Plate, Poppy, clear, unsgn Northwood, 7" 27.00
Plate, Poppy, gr, unsgn Northwood, 7" 35.00
Plate, Rose & Lattice, 6" 15.00
Plate, Rose Perfect on crackle glass, 7" 12.00
Plate, Roses, Grapes & Apples, w/lattice edge (series), 8½" 23.00
Plate, Roses, Latticed Glass Edge Roses, 7" 25.00
Plate, Wheel & Block, opal, 9½" 45.00
Relish plate, flowered, glass hdls, 7" 45.00
Relish plate, Poppy, glass hdls, 7" 47.00
Relish plate, Rose, glass hdls, 7" 50.00
Sugar shaker, Grape, gold on milk glass, orig pnt/top, 4½" 37.50
Syrup, Cabbage Rose 150.00
Tray, Fruit, 8½" sq 90.00
Tray, Rose, 6" sq 50.00
Tumbler, Grape, gold on crackle, 4", NM 50.00
Vase, Cabbage Rose, 15" 95.00
Vase, Dogwood, baluster, 15" 95.00
Vase, Peacock in a Tree, red/gr/gold, 15" 225.00
Vase, Poppy, 5" 15.00
Water bottle, Grape, on crackle, no pnt, 7½" 35.00

Goss and Crested China

William Henry Goss received his early education at the Government School of Design at Somerset House, London, and as a result of his merit was introduced to Alderman William Copeland, who owned the Copeland Spode Pottery. Under the influence of Copeland from 1852 to 1858, Goss quickly learned the trade and soon became their chief designer. Little is known about this brief association, and in 1858 Goss left to begin his own business. After a short-lived partnership with a Mr. Peake, Goss opened a pottery on John Street, Stoke-on-Trent, but by 1870 he had moved to his business to a location near London Road. This pottery became the famous Falcon Works. Their mark was a spread-wing falcon (goss-hawk) centering a narrow, horizontal bar with 'W.H. Goss' printed below.

Many of the early pieces made by Goss were left unmarked and are difficult to discern from products made by the Copeland factory, but after he had been in business for about fifteen years, all of his wares were marked. Today unmarked items do not command the prices of the later marked wares.

Adolphus William Henry Goss (Goss's eldest son) joined his father's firm in the 1880s. He introduced cheaper lines, though the more expensive lines continued in production. Shortly after his father's death in 1906, Adolphus retired and left the business to his two younger brothers. The business suffered from problems created by a war economy, and in 1936 Goss assets were held by Cauldon Potteries Ltd. These were eventually taken over by the Coalport Group, who retained the right to use the Goss trademark. Messrs. Ridgeway Potteries bought all the assets in 1954 as well as the right to use the Goss trademark and name. In 1964 the group was known as Allied English Potteries Ltd. (A.E.P.), and in 1971 A.E.P. merged with the Doulton Group. Now it remains to be seen if Goss ware will ever be produced again. Our advisor for this category is Patrick Herley; he is listed in the Directory under New York. Values are all for items in mint condition.

Abbots Cup, Fountains Abbey 9.00
Beachy Head Lighthouse, Brighton crest 30.00
Blackgang Cannon 17.00
Canterbury Bottle 6.50
Conical Club Vase 5.50
Jack, Lincoln, Margate 12.50
Jug, Litchfield, St Alban's Abbey 35.00
Kettle, Hastings 7.00
Lamp, Caerleon, Glasgow 9.50
Leather Bottle, Canterbury 18.00
Manx Spirit Measure 14.00
Mather, Irish, Bognor, sm 7.00

Model of Hambledon Cricket Stone, gray, inscribed 'this stone marks the site of the ground of the Hambledon Cricket Club circa 1760 – 1787,' very rare, black printed mark, 3", from $950.00 to $1,000.00.

Mortar, Bideford 15.50
Plymouth Jug 13.00
Portland Lighthouse 75.00
Pot, Guys Porridge, Hurstmonceux 16.00
Queen Victoria's First Shoe, Wembley 27.50
Salt Pot, Carlisle 6.50
Shrewsbury Ewer, Ladysmith crest 9.00
Terra Cotta Kettle, Hereford 22.50
Three Handled Cup 14.20
Tyg, Leeds 8.00
Urn, Laxey 12.50
Vase, Cirencester, Battle Abbey 7.50
Vase, Southwold, 6" 45.00
Waterlooville Bottle 14.00
Windsor Round Tower (Night Light) 245.00

Crested China

Arcadian, Black boy in bed 135.00
Arcadian, bust, Tommy Atkins, Arms of Foefar crest 29.50
Arcadian, vase, Ashover, 2" 8.50
Carlton, bust, Edward VII 75.00
Carlton, HMS Lion (battleship), Burntisland 45.00
Carlton, Winchester Bushel, Winchester 17.00
Chesterfield Parish Church 45.00
Grafton, HMS Landship (tank), Newcastle-on-Tyne 25.00
Snowdon China, Ramshead Vase 7.00
Waterfall, de la Pole Statue 14.95
Willow Art, Burns at the plough 75.00
Willow Art, pig, City of Andrews, 3¼" L 28.00
Willow Art, Windsor Castle, Windsor, 6" L 35.00
Wyknot, A Prehistoric Skull, Cheddar 11.25

Gouda

Gouda is an old Dutch market town in the province of South Holland. Famous for its cheese, Gouda's ceramics industry had its beginnings in the early sixteenth century and was fueled by the growth in the popularity of smoking tobacco. Initially learning their craft from immigrant potters from England who had settled in the area, the clay pipe makers of Gouda were soon regarded as the best. While some authorities give 1898 (the date the Zuid-Holland factory began operations) as the initial date for the manufacturing of decorative pottery in Gouda, C.W. Moody, author of *Gouda Ceramics*, indicates the date was about 1885. Gouda was not the only town in the Netherlands making pottery; Arnhem, Schoonhoven, and Amsterdam also had earthenware factories, but technically the term 'Gouda pottery' refers only to pieces made within the town of Gouda. Today, no Gouda-style factories are active within the city's limits, but in the first quarter of the twentieth century there were several firms producing decorative pottery there — the best known being Zuid, Regina, Zenith, Ivora, and Goedewaagen.

This information was provided to us by Adela Meadows; she is listed in the Directory under California.

For further information we recommend *The World of Gouda Pottery* by Phyllis T. Ritvo (Front & Center Press, Weston, Massachussets).

Bowl, flowers, mc, 8½" 100.00
Candlestick, geometrics/Greek Key bands, #057, Orientale, 8" .325.00
Candlestick, rust/brn/gr decor on blk, w/bobeche, hdl, 11½" 195.00
Clock, wide circular fr w/irises etc on bl & mc, 9" dia, EX 800.00
Compote, gr matt, int w/mc flowers, 5x9½" 175.00
Ink stand, flowers & foliage on cream & blk, #694, mk, 4x9" 200.00
Pitcher, floral, mc on wht gloss, Areo/#3384, 7x7¼" 225.00
Sugar bowl, leaves, gr/wht/bl on blk, CA Lion Cachet, Distel ...200.00
Vase, floral, mc, bulbous, 8" 200.00
Vase, floral, mc on blk, #304, house mk, 12½" 575.00
Vase, fruit compote & village scene, mk, 5½x16½", NM 200.00
Vase, Nouveau design by Zuid, high gloss, ca 1896, 11" 600.00
Vase, Nouveau florals, high gloss, #304, JB, 12½" 800.00
Vase, peasant woman, #7052 RR Holland/#1852R, 12½", NM .350.00
Vase, tulips, mc on gr gloss, rim-to-shoulder hdls, pnt mks, 9" ...375.00

Grand Feu

The Grand Feu Art Pottery existed from 1912 until about 1918 in Los Angeles, California. It was owned and operated by Cornelius Brauckman, who developed a method of producing remarkably artistic glaze effects achieved through extremely high temperatures during the firing process. The body of the ware, as a result of the intense heat (2500 degrees), was vitrified as the glaze matured. Brauckman signed his ware either with his name or 'Grand Feu Pottery, L.A. California.' His work is regarded today as being among the finest art pottery ever produced in the United States. Examples are rare and command high prices on today's market.

Vase, brn crystalline flambe, Brauckman, inscribed, 1917, 7x3¼" ..4,000.00
Vase, gr gloss w/spotty pk/brn crystalline, TT, #154, 10" 4,200.00
Vase, metallic celadon mottle, bulbous, #153, 4¼x4" 4,000.00

Graniteware

Graniteware, made of a variety of metals with enamel coatings, derives its name from its appearance. The speckled, swirled, or mottled effect of the vari-colored enamels may look like granite — but there the resemblance stops. It wasn't especially durable! Expect at least minor chipping if you plan to collect.

Graniteware was featured in 1876 at Phily's Expo. It was mass produced in quantity, and enough of it has survived to make at least the common items easily affordable. Condition, color, shape, and size are important considerations in evaluating an item; cobalt blue and white, green and white, brown and white, and old red and white swirled items are unusual, thus more expensive. Pieces of heavier weight, seam constructed, riveted, and those with wooden handles and tin or matching graniteware lids are usually older. Pieces with matching granite lids demand higher prices than ones with tin lids.

For further study we recommend *The Collector's Encyclopedia of Graniteware, Colors, Shapes, and Values*, Books I and II, by our advisor, Helen Greguire. Both are available from the author and Collector Books. For information on how to order, see her listing in the Directory under South Carolina. For the address of the National Graniteware Society, see the section on Clubs, Newsletters, and Catalogs.

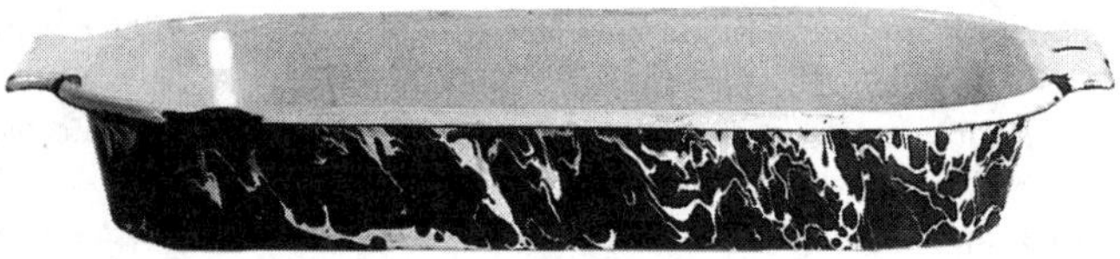

Baking pan, cobalt and white large swirl, oblong with handles and ribbed bottom, G, $225.00.

Baking pan, bl & wht lg swirl, wht int, molded hdls, oblong, EX .115.00
Baking pan, brn & wht lg swirl, corrugated bottom, hdls, oblong, NM ..295.00
Baking pan, cobalt & wht med Snow on Mtn mottle, oblong, Elite, NM .155.00
Batter jug, gray mottle, matching lid, bail hdl, seamed, L&G Mfg, NM .395.00
Biscuit sheet, bl & wht lg swirl w/blk trim, holds 12, 11x8½", NM ...3,550.00
Bowl, dough/salad; bl & wht fine mottle w/blk, wht int, EX 70.00
Bowl, dough/salad; red & wht lg swirl w/cobalt, ltweight, 1960s, NM .65.00
Bowl, mixing; gr-bl & wht lg mottle w/blk trim, NM 95.00
Bowl, mixing/salad; cobalt & wht lg swirl w/blk trim, EX 275.00
Bowl, vegetable; red & wht lg swirl w/blk, oblong, 1950s, M 185.00
Box, salt; wht w/lt bl Chicken Wire veins, rnd, EX 285.00
Bucket, blk & wht lg swirl, tin lid, wooden bail, lg, M 575.00
Bucket, cobalt & wht lg swirl w/blk, w/lid, M 350.00
Bucket, dinner; gray lg mottle, oval, 5-pc, NM 395.00
Bucket, dk gr redipped over orig Chrysolite color, w/lid, NM 185.00
Bucket, gr & wht med mottle w/gr trim, w/lid, Elite Austria, M ...185.00
Bucket, miner's dinner; bl & wht lg swirl, wht int, rnd, seamed, NM .595.00
Bucket, miner's dinner; gray lg mottle, 4-pc, M 355.00
Butter dish, wht w/bl floral decor, rnd, lg, EX 295.00
Butter kettle/carrier, aqua-gr & wht lg swirl w/cobalt, strap hdl, NM ..395.00
Candle holder, solid bl, scalloped style, finger ring, thumb rest, M .185.00
Candle holder, wht w/cobalt decor, ring hdl, M 195.00
Candle holder, wht w/fine bl speckles, ring hdl, EX 95.00
Canister, Meal, solid bl w/wht int, EX 120.00
Chamber pail, wht w/bl lg mottle, wooden bail, NM 575.00
Churn, buttermilk; wht w/cobalt lettering, floor model w/dasher, EX ..1,895.00
Clock, gr & dk gr med mottle, 8-day, Germany, M 395.00
Clothes boiler, wht w/red-brn letters, w/lid, sm, NM 215.00
Cocoa dipper, gray med mottle w/blk trim, wood hdl, 3⅝" opening, EX ...255.00
Coffee biggin, cobalt & wht check w/red trim, 3-pc, M 425.00
Coffee biggin, gray med mottle, 4-pc, welded hdl, M 325.00
Coffee biggin, wht w/bl trim, 4-pc, M 165.00
Coffee biggin, yel w/blk trim, ca 1960s, 5-pc, M 195.00
Coffee boiler, blk & wht fine mottle, gooseneck spout, NM 275.00
Coffee boiler, cobalt & wht lg swirl, M 395.00
Coffee carrier, bl & wht checks w/bl trim, wire ears, tin lid, EX ...395.00
Coffeepot, gr relish, covered spout, wood hdl & knob, M 325.00
Coffeepot, gray lg mottle w/pewter, covered spout, copper bottom, M .295.00
Coffeepot, lav-cobalt & wht lg swirl, tin lid, flared cylinder, M .385.00
Coffeepot, lt bl & wht lg swirl, seamed bottom, EX 295.00
Coffeepot, solid Robin Egg Blue w/pewter, Ideal New England..., M ...325.00
Coffeepot, wht w/gr veins, lg mottle, Elite Austria, EX 200.00
Coffeepot, wht w/gr veins, med mottle, Elite, EX 145.00
Colander, bl & wht lg swirl w/blk trim & hdls, ftd, deep, M 395.00
Colander, cobalt & wht lg swirl w/blk, wht int, ftd, deep, M 395.00
Colander, gr & wht lg swirl w/cobalt, wht int, ftd, EX 395.00

Cream can, medium blue and white large mottle, VG, $265.00.

Cream can, Boston; lt gr & wht relish w/dk bl, NM 295.00
Cream can, Boston; red-brn & wht relish, seamed, EX 325.00
Creamer, bl & wht mottle w/bl strap hdl, squatty, EX 395.00
Cruller/potato fryer, lt gray mottle, w/perforated basket, EX 285.00
Cup, lt bl/cobalt/wht med mottle w/cobalt trim, Granite Steel Ware, EX .125.00
Cup & saucer, lt bl & wht lg mottle w/blk trim, EX 135.00
Dipper, bl & wht lg mottle w/bl trim, flared sides, M 110.00
Dipper, gr & wht lg swirl, brn hollow hdl/trim, flared, EX 125.00
Dipper, Windsor; bl & wht lg swirl w/blk trim & hollow hdl, NM .145.00
Dish pan, wht/bl/gray lg swirl w/blk trim & hdls, NM 155.00
Double boiler, gr & wht lg swirl w/blk, seamless, convex bottom, NM ..525.00
Double boiler, gr & wht lg swirl w/cobalt, Emerald Ware, NM ..575.00
Dustpan, dk bl w/blk appl hdl, seamless, NM 225.00
Fish kettle/poacher, bl & wht fine mottle w/cobalt, wht int, EX ..265.00
Fruit jar filler, bl & wht fine mottle w/cobalt trim, NM 120.00
Fruit jar filler, bl & wht lg mottle, NM 145.00
Fruit jar filler, gray lg mottle, riveted strap hdl, EX 45.00
Fry pan, cobalt & wht lg swirl w/blk hdl, wht int, EX 325.00
Fry pan, dk gr & wht lg swirl w/blk, wht int, Chrysolite, G+ 395.00
Fry pan, gr & wht lg swirl w/wht int, Emerald Ware, EX 495.00
Fry pan, gray-lav & wht lg swirl, wht int, CI, Lava Ware, M 350.00
Fry pan, lav-bl & wht lg swirl w/blk trim & hdl, wht int, EX 325.00
Funnel, cobalt & wht lg swirl w/blk, Azurelite, EX 225.00
Funnel, dk gr & wht fine mottle, wht int, Elite, lg, EX 125.00
Funnel, solid gray, squatty, pierced hanging ear, EX 55.00
Grater, gray fine mottle w/gray specks, revolving, Paris..., sm, M ..295.00
Grater, solid bl, flat hdl, NM 120.00
Gravy boat, wht w/cobalt trim & hdl, ftd, L&G Mfg Co, NM ..185.00

Griddle, gray lg mottle, riveted hdl, L&G Mfg Co, oval, EX 295.00
Honey pot, lt gray w/wht int, insulated tin lid, porc knob, NM .215.00
Kettle, Berlin-style, cobalt & wht lg swirl, seamless, w/lid, M 395.00
Kettle, Maslin-style, bl & wht lg swirl w/blk, Azure Ware, M 275.00
Kettle, preserving; bl & wht lg mottle w/blk, lipped, bail hdl, NM ..265.00
Kettle, preserving; gr & wht lg swirl w/cobalt, lip, Emerald Ware, EX ..385.00
Kettle, stove; bl & wht med mottle w/bl, deep, Solid Steel, M ..265.00
Ladle, cobalt & gray lg mottle, wht int, EX 95.00
Ladle, soup; cream & gr, M 35.00
Lavabo & basin, pk w/gold bands, brass spigot, EX 395.00
Lid, bl & wht med mottle, domed w/vent & top hdl, EX 20.00
Lid, brn & wht lg swirl, domed, wooden knob, EX 35.00
Lid, gray lg mottle, w/handihook, lg, M 75.00
Lid rack, gr & wht speckle, tapered for different szs, EX 195.00
Match box, bl & gray med swirl w/bl trim, fancy bk, NM 285.00
Measure, aqua-gr & wht lg swirl w/cobalt trim, 2-cup, EX 450.00
Measure, bl & wht lg mottle w/cobalt trim, seamed lip, EX 195.00
Measure, brn & wht lg swirl w/cobalt trim, riveted lip, strap hdl, G+ .975.00
Measure, gray lg mottle, Royal Granite 1 Gal Liq'd, M 295.00
Measure, vinegar; gray med mottle, riveted hdl, seamless, ...Nesco, NM ...225.00
Milk can, bl & wht fine mottle w/cobalt, wire ears, seamless, NM .295.00
Milk can, Boston; bl & wht lg mottle w/bl trim, seamed, NM ...525.00
Milk can, Boston; red-brn & wht fine mottle, seamed, 4-pc, EX 185.00
Milk can, dk sea gr to moss gr, lock lid, Shamrock Ware, M 475.00
Milk can, gr & wht lg swirl, seamless, matching lid, Emerald Ware, NM ...1,295.00
Mold, gray lg mottle, ribbed tube style, M 110.00
Mold, gray lg mottle, scalloped, M 95.00
Mold, gray lg mottle, Turk's head, 6½" dia, M 125.00
Mold, lt gr & wht fine mottle, Turk's head, tube style, EX 145.00
Mold, wht, oval, fluted w/emb grapes, ring hanger, EX 165.00
Mug, bl & wht lg swirl w/blk trim, NM 80.00
Mug, cobalt & wht lg swirl w/blk trim, NM 110.00
Mug, dk gr & wht Chrysolite w/blk trim, M 150.00
Mug, gray med mottle, NM 45.00
Mug, mush/camp; bl & wht lg swirl w/blk trim, M 235.00
Pail, bl & wht lg swirl w/blk trim, wooden bail, NM 200.00
Pail, cobalt & wht lg swirl w/blk trim, lg, M 325.00
Pan, bread; gray med mottle, envelope ends, oblong, EX 35.00
Pan, lady finger; cobalt & wht lg swirl w/wht int, extremely rare, M ...4,495.00
Pan, muffin; bl & wht lg swirl, wht int, 6-cup, NM 1,650.00
Pan, muffin; gray lg mottle, deep, 12-cup, NM 75.00
Pan, muffin; gray lg mottle, Turk's head, 9-cup, NM 145.00
Pan, muffin; gray lg mottle, 9-cup, EX 65.00
Pan, muffin; gray med mottle, Turk's head, strapped, 8-cup, EX ..225.00
Pan, muffin; lt bl & wht lg swirl, 8-cup, EX 425.00
Pan, stew; bl & wht lg mottle w/blk, wht int, shallow, EX 210.00
Pan, stew; cobalt & wht lg mottle w/blk trim & hdl, wht int, deep, EX ..235.00
Pan, tube cake; bl & wht lg swirl, Lava Ware, EX 310.00
Pie plate, cobalt & gray lg mottle, solid gray int, NM 75.00
Pie plate, cobalt & wht lg swirl w/blk trim, wht int, deep, EX ...110.00
Pitcher, milk; mc 'End of Day' lg swirl, EX 875.00
Pitcher, molasses; gray lg mottle, thumb lift on lid, EX 225.00
Pitcher, water; bl & wht lg swirl, blk hdl/trim, NM 265.00
Pitcher, water; bl & wht lg swirl w/blk hdl, Columbian, M 1,950.00
Pitcher, water; brn & wht relish w/dk bl trim, NM 250.00
Pitcher, water; lav-bl to lt lav-bl, blk hdl/trim, seamless, M 325.00
Pitcher, water; red & wht 'old' lg swirl w/cobalt, wht int, EX .5,775.00
Pitcher & bowl, red w/blk trim & hdl, squatty, EX 200.00
Pitcher & bowl, wht w/cobalt trim, sm, M 110.00
Plate, red & wht lg swirl (ea side) w/blk trim, 1960s, ltweight, M ..45.00
Plate, red-brn & wht fine mottle, wht inside, 12-sided, EX 65.00
Roaster, brn & wht lg swirl w/blk trim, rnd, 2-pc, NM 525.00
Roaster, cobalt & wht lg swirl, flat top, steam vent, 3-pc, NM ..395.00
Roaster, dk shaded to lt violet, wht int, Thistle Ware, 3-pc, EX ...265.00
Saucer, bl & wht med mottle w/bl trim, NM 60.00
Scoop, grocer's, gray med mottle, semicovered top, seamed/riveted, EX ..225.00
Scoop, spice; gray med mottle, pieced bk, strap hdl, rare, EX 295.00
Shirred egg plate, lt bl & wht lg swirl w/cobalt, ltweight, '60s, M ..65.00
Sink strainer, gray med mottle, seamed, triangular, 3-ftd, NM ...195.00
Skimmer, blk & wht med mottle int/ext, perforated, long hdl, EX .95.00
Skimmer, charcoal gray & wht int/ext, no holes (unusual), NM ..425.00
Skimmer, gray med mottle, perforated, hdld, lg, NM 45.00
Soap dish, lt bl & wht lg swirl, hangs, M 235.00
Soap dish, solid bl, fluted bottom, hangs, EX 95.00
Spatula, gray lg mottle, tapered top, NM 125.00
Spittoon, dk gr & wht lg swirl w/blk, wht int, seamed, Chrysolite, NM ..495.00
Spoon, basting; bl & wht lt mottle w/blk hdl, wht int, EX 85.00
Spoon, brn & wht med mottle w/blk hdl, Onyx Ware, M 65.00
Spoon, ice cream; gray & wht fine mottle, CI base, wood hdl, EX .165.00
Sugar bowl, morning glories on wht, pewter trim & lid 450.00
Syrup, gray lg mottle, pewter trim, squatty, hinged lid, M 1,995.00
Syrup, wht, NP brass lid & thumb rest, EX 195.00
Tea steeper, cobalt & wht lg swirl, riveted strap hdl/spout, NM ..395.00
Tea strainer, wht, screen insert, NM 75.00
Teakettle, bl & wht lg swirl w/blk trim wht int, bail hdl, M 295.00
Teakettle, brn & wht relish on CI, swing lid, EX 295.00
Teakettle, cobalt & wht lg mottle w/blk trim & hdl, EX 425.00
Teakettle, dk lav shaded to lt lav, wooden bail, NM 275.00
Teapot, Blue Willow on wht, cylindrical, EX 165.00
Teapot, calla lilies on wht, pewter trim, 9¾", M 325.00
Teapot, cobalt & wht lg swirl, flared cylinder, NM 425.00
Teapot, floral on solid bl, squatty, Scepter Germany 39, sm, M .185.00
Teapot, heron & rushes, pewter trim, M 550.00
Teapot, red & wht med swirl, flared cylinder, 1960s, M 165.00
Teapot, wildflowers on cream w/brn & wht relish & pewter trim, M ..350.00
Toothbrush holder, solid wht, wall type, holds 3 brushes, EX 145.00
Toothbrush holder, wht w/lt bl lg mottle veins, perforated lid, EX 85.00
Tray, gray med mottle, grooved bottom, NM 145.00
Tray, gray med mottle, oval, NM 165.00
Tray, gray med mottle, sq, NM 165.00
Tray, red & wht mottle w/dk bl trim, rnd, ltweight, 1960s, NM ...85.00
Trivet, aqua bl on CI, 3 molded ft, F&W ETI, M 75.00
Tumbler, cobalt & wht lg swirl w/blk, wht int, M 495.00
Tureen, soup; wht w/bl Chicken Wire veining, ftd, w/lid, EX 325.00
Upcooker, gray lg mottle, ring hdl on perforated lid, Am Gray, NM ...425.00
Utensil rack, bl & wht lg mottle, M 495.00
Utensil rack, lt gray med mottle, EX 295.00
Wash basin, brn & wht lg swirl w/blk trim, eyelet, sm, NM 225.00
Wash basin, gray lg mottle, eyelet, w/label, lg, EX 95.00
Wash basin, lt bl & wht med swirl, eyelet, sm, M 85.00
Washboard, cobalt bl, w/metal soap saver, EX 295.00
Water carrier, dk gr & wht lg swirl w/blk, Crysolite, lg, EX 850.00

Green Opaque

Introduced in 1887 by the New England Glass Company, this ware is very scarce due to the fact that it was produced for less than one year. It is characterized by its soft green color and a wavy band of gold reserving a mottled blue metallic stain. It is usually found in satin; examples with a shiny finish are extremely rare. Values depend to a large extent on the amount of the gold and stain remaining.

Bowl, EX stain, 4x8", NM 985.00
Bowl, M stain & gold, 4x8" 1,150.00
Box, powder; EX stain & gold on bowl & lid, 4x6¼" 1,150.00
Celery vase, worn stain & gold, 6½" 450.00

Cruet, orig stopper, M stain & gold 1,950.00
Cruet, VG stain 1,500.00
Mug, EX stain & gold, 2¼" 500.00
Mug, M stain & gold, 2½" 700.00
Punch cup, M stain & gold 750.00
Punch cup, worn stain & gold, 2½" 225.00
Shaker, M stain & gold, 2½" 400.00
Toothpick holder, EX gold 900.00
Toothpick holder, M gold 1,150.00
Tumbler, lemonade; w/hdl, M stain & gold, 5" 950.00
Tumbler, mint stain & gold, 3½" 800.00
Vase, flared, M stain & gold, 6" 900.00
Vase, 14-rib w/flaring rim, VG stain & gold, 6" 500.00

Greenaway, Kate

Kate Greenaway was an English artist who lived from 1846 to 1901. She gained worldwide fame as an illustrator of children's books, drawing children clothed in the styles worn by proper English and American boys and girls of the very early 1800s. Her book, *Under the Willow Tree*, published in 1878, was the first of many. Her sketches appeared in leading magazines, and her greeting cards were in great demand. Manufacturers of china, pottery, and metal products copied her characters to decorate children's dishes, tiles, and salt and pepper shakers as well as many other items.

What some collectors/dealers call Kate Greenaway items are not actual Kate Greenaway designs but merely look-alikes. Genuine Kate Greenaway items (metal, paper, cloth, etc.) must bear close resemblance to her drawings in books, magazines, and special collections. See also Napkin Rings.

Combination set, Greenaway girl shakers and napkin ring on stand with compartment for the butter plate, Middletown Plate Co. #26, from $350.00 to $500.00. (Photo courtesy Lillian Gottschalk and Sandra Whitson)

Almanac, 1884, London, Routledge, NM 140.00
Almanac, 1892, London, 1st ed, VG 135.00
Biscuit jar, ceramic, boy w/tinted features, w/lid 165.00
Book, A Apple Pie, Warne, 1940, w/dust jacket, VG 28.00
Book, Birthday Book for Children, Greenaway illus, 1880, VG .160.00
Book, Day in a Child's Life, Routledge, 1st ed, VG 150.00
Book, Greenaway's Babies, Saalfield Muslin Book, 1907, G+ 40.00
Book, Kate Greenaway Pictures, London, Warne, 1st ed, 1921, VG .300.00
Book, Kate Greenaway's Alphabet, London, 1880, EX 190.00
Book, Kate Greenaway's Book of Games, Routledge, 1st ed, 1889, NM .475.00
Book, Language of Flowers, Routledge, 1st ed, picture board, VG ..100.00
Book, Marigold Garden, Greenaway illus, London, 1888, VG 60.00
Book, Mother Goose, London, later print of 1st ed, VG 150.00
Book, Pied Piper of Hamlin, Greenaway illus, NM 85.00
Book, Under the Willow, Routledge, 1st ed, orig cloth 165.00
Bowl, Daisy & Button, amber; R&B SP holder w/girl & dog 525.00
Butter pat, children playing transfer, pre-1910 ....40.00
Cup & saucer, pk lustre trim, pre-1910 ....125.00
Engraving, Harper's Bazaar, Jan 1879, full-pg 25.00
Figurine, seated girl tugs on lg hat, bsk, pre-1910, sm 75.00
Hatpin holder, SP, figural girl, Meriden, 4" 125.00
Inkwell, boy & girl, bronze 215.00
Match holder, ornate SP, girl in fancy clothes, Tufts 195.00
Paperweight, CI Victorian girl in lg bonnet, pre-1910, 3x2¾" ..110.00
Pencil holder, pnt porc, pre-1910 ....100.00
Pickle castor, bl; SP fr w/2 girls, blown-out florals 455.00
Plate, ABC, girl in lg hat, Staffordshire, 7" 105.00
Plate, children at play, fruits, birds & flowers, 9" 100.00
Salt cellar, Little People, bsk, arms over basket, 3¾" 110.00
Scarf, Greenaway illus on silk, early, EX 65.00
Tea set, semiporc, floral motif, pre-1910, 3-pc, child sz 95.00
Toothpick holder, bsk, girl sits on stump, basket on bk 40.00
Toothpick holder, clear glass, 2 girls by basket 100.00
Toothpick holder, SP, girl holds amberina cup, ornate base, 5" ..785.00
Wall pocket, ceramic, 6 girls on open book form, 6x9x3" 137.00

Greentown Glass

Greentown glass is a term referring to the product of the Indiana Tumbler and Goblet Company of Greentown, Indiana, ca 1894 to 1903. Their earlier pressed glass patterns were #75 (originally known as #11), a pseudo-cut glass design; #137, Pleat Band; and #200, Austrian. Another line, Dewey, was designed in 1898. Many lovely colors were produced in addition to crystal. Jacob Rosenthal, who was later affiliated with Fenton, developed his famous chocolate glass in 1900. The rich, shaded opaque brown glass was an overnight success. Two new patterns, Leaf Bracket and Cactus, were designed to display the glass to its best advantage, but previously existing molds were also used. In only three years Rosenthal developed yet another important color formula, Golden Agate. The Holly pattern was designed especially for its production. The dolphin covered dish with a fish finial is perhaps the most common and easily recognized piece ever produced. Other animal dishes were also made; all are highly collectible. There have been many repros — not all are marked! The symbol (+) at the end of some of the following lines was used to indicate items that have been reproduced.

Our advisors for this category are Jerry and Sandi Garrett; they are listed in the Directory under Indiana. See the Pattern Glass section for clear pressed glass; only colored items are listed here.

Mug, Serenade, transparent cobalt blue (rare color), 4¾", $450.00.

Animal dish, bird w/berry, Golden Agate 2,000.00
Animal dish, bird w/berry, teal bl 375.00
Animal dish, bird w/berry, wht opaque 425.00
Animal dish, cat on hamper, amber, tall 350.00
Animal dish, cat on hamper, canary, low 850.00
Animal dish, cat on hamper, chocolate, tall 450.00
Animal dish, cat on hamper, cobalt, tall 750.00
Animal dish, cat on hamper, teal bl, tall 425.00
Animal dish, dolphin, canary, sawtooth edge 1,000.00
Animal dish, dolphin, chocolate, beaded edge (+) 350.00

Animal dish, dolphin, chocolate, sawtooth edge (+) 300.00
Animal dish, dolphin, cobalt, beaded edge 1,000.00
Animal dish, dolphin, Nile Green, beaded edge 3,000.00
Animal dish, fighting cocks, amber or emerald gr 1,800.00
Animal dish, fighting cocks, Nile Green or chocolate 2,500.00
Animal dish, fighting cocks, wht opaque 2,000.00
Animal dish, hen on nest, chocolate 850.00
Animal dish, hen on nest, Nile Green 1,500.00
Animal dish, hen on nest, teal bl 275.00
Animal dish, rabbit, chocolate (+) 525.00
Animal dish, rabbit, teal bl 250.00
Austrian, butter dish, canary 425.00
Austrian, cake stand, canary 350.00
Austrian, cordial, amber 250.00
Austrian, punch cup, emerald gr 200.00
Austrian, salt shaker, canary 150.00
Austrian, spooner, chocolate, child sz 250.00
Austrian, wine, amber 350.00
Beaded Panel, syrup jug, wht opaque, metal lid 300.00
Beehive, vase, bud; amber 300.00
Brazen Shield, bowl, bl, 7½" dia 150.00
Brazen Shield, cake stand, bl, 9⅜" dia 250.00
Brazen Shield, compote, bl, w/lid, 6⅜" dia 250.00
Brazen Shield, pitcher, bl 275.00
Brazen Shield, spooner, bl 150.00
Cactus, creamer, Nile Green, w/Dewey lid, 2¼" dia 350.00
Cactus, sugar bowl, canary, w/lid 300.00
Cactus, sugar bowl, clear w/bl-wht opal rim 350.00
Cactus, tumbler, clear, w/bl-wht opal rim 350.00
Cord Drapery, bowl, amber, rectangular 210.00
Cord Drapery, compote, cobalt, w/lid, 8½" dia 350.00
Cord Drapery, cruet, cobalt, w/stopper 625.00
Cord Drapery, sauce, canary, ftd, 4⅛", dia 185.00
Cord Drapery, toothpick, amber 350.00
Cord Drapery, wine, canary 400.00
Cupid, butter dish, chocolate 650.00
Cupid, creamer, Nile Green 425.00
Cupid, sugar bowl, chocolate, w/lid 500.00
Dewey, bowl, amber, 8" dia 90.00
Dewey, bowl, chocolate, 8" dia 285.00
Dewey, creamer, canary, 4" 60.00
Dewey, cruet, emerald gr, w/stopper 175.00
Dewey, serpentine tray, amber, sm 60.00
Dewey, tumbler, Nile Green 650.00
Diamond Prisms, tumbler, chocolate 675.00
Early Diamond, dish, amber, rectangular, 8x5" 175.00
Early Diamond, pitcher, emerald gr 300.00
Early Diamond, tumbler, canary 200.00
Greentown Daisy, butter dish, chocolate 325.00
Greentown Daisy, creamer, frosted emerald gr, w/lid 125.00
Greentown Daisy, mustard pot, wht opaque, w/lid 85.00
Greentown Daisy, sugar bowl, frosted clear, w/lid 60.00
Herringbone Buttress, bowl, amber, 6¼" dia 290.00
Herringbone Buttress, cake stand, emerald gr 500.00
Herringbone Buttress, cracker jar, emerald gr, w/lid 425.00
Herringbone Buttress, nappy, emerald gr 225.00
Herringbone Buttress, spooner, emerald gr 225.00
Herringbone Buttress, syrup jug, emerald gr, metal lid 400.00
Holly, tumbler, wht agate 2,000.00
Holly Amber, bowl, oval 500.00
Holly Amber, bowl, 7½" 650.00
Holly Amber, butter dish 2,100.00
Holly Amber, compote, jelly; w/lid, 4½" dia 1,450.00
Holly Amber, compote, w/lid, 6½" dia 1,625.00
Holly Amber, pitcher 3,000.00
Holly Amber, toothpick (+) 450.00
Leaf Bracket, butter dish, wht opaque 850.00
Leaf Bracket, nappy, wht opaque 190.00
Leaf Bracket, sauce bowl, wht opaque 125.00
Mug, Deer & Child, Nile Green 600.00
Mug, Indoor Drinking Scene, chocolate, w/o pouring lip, 5" 195.00
Mug, Indoor Drinking Scene, chocolate, w/pouring lip, 5" 235.00
Mug, Indoor Drinking Scene, Nile Green or chocolate, 8½" 550.00
Mug, Outdoor Drinking Scene, lt cobalt 350.00
Novelty, buffalo, wht opaque, dtd 1901 ....450.00
Novelty, dustpan, canary 175.00
Novelty, mitted hand, chocolate 1,175.00
Novelty, wheelbarrow, teal bl 175.00
Novely, buffalo, Nile Green, no date (+) 750.00
Pattern #75, vase, emerald gr, 6" 75.00
Pattern #75, vase, emerald gr, 10" 100.00
Pleat Band, cordial, canary 200.00
Pleat Band, wine, canary 200.00
Ruffled Eye, pitcher, water; amber 200.00
Ruffled Eye, pitcher, water; canary 300.00
Scalloped Flange, tumbler, chocolate 165.00
Scalloped Flange, vase, Nile Green 350.00
Shuttle, bowl, chocolate, 8¼" 550.00
Shuttle, creamer, chocolate 650.00
Shuttle, mug, amber 375.00
Shuttle, pitcher, chocolate 3,500.00
Shuttle, spooner, chocolate 500.00
Shuttle, tumbler, canary 400.00
Teardrop & Tassel, bowl, chocolate, 8¼" 650.00
Teardrop & Tassel, creamer, amber 200.00
Teardrop & Tassel, pickle dish, teal bl 150.00
Teardrop & Tassel, tumbler, amber, type 2 ....285.00
Toothpick holder, dog head, frosted amber 325.00
Toothpick holder, dog head, frosted bl 350.00
Toothpick holder, Sheaf of Wheat, cobalt 450.00

Grueby

William Henry Grueby joined the firm of the Low Art Tile Works at the age of fifteen and in 1894, after several years of experience in the production of architectural tiles, founded his own plant, the Grueby Faience Company, in Boston, Massachusetts. Grueby began experimenting with the idea of producing art pottery and had soon perfected a fine glaze (soft and without gloss) in shades of blue, gray, yellow, brown, and his most successful, cucumber green. In 1900 his exhibit at the Paris Exposition Universelle won three gold medals.

Grueby pottery was hand thrown and hand decorated in the Arts and Crafts style. Vertically thrust stylized leaves and flowers in relief were the most common decorative devices. Tiles continued to be an important product, unique (due to the matt glaze decoration) as well as durable. Grueby tiles were often a full inch thick. Obviously incompatible with the Art Nouveau style, the artware was discontinued soon after 1907. The ware is marked in one of several ways: 'Grueby Pottery, Boston, USA'; 'Grueby, Boston, Mass.'; or 'Grueby Faience.' The artware is often artist signed. Our advisor for this category is David Rago; he is listed in the Directory under New Jersey.

Bowl, gr matt, leaves & buds, 2½x8½" 1,265.00
Candlestick, bl-gr, tooled/appl leaves, bulbous top, 8½x4" 1,800.00
Candlestick, dk bl (leathery), tooled leaves, unmk, 8¾x4" 1,500.00
Humidor, gr (curdled), repeating floral band, ER, #3/14, 8" ...1,100.00
Inkwell, bl matt, hammered copper lid & collar, mk, 5x5½" ..1,700.00

Lamp, cobalt (leathery), bronze insert, 12½" slag shade, 11" base ..9,000.00
Paperweight, scarab, lt bl matt, partial label, 4" 450.00
Table, 21 gr/brn/terra-cotta tiles in top; wrought-iron base 1,265.00
Tile, bird, brn tones on bl, 4" sq, +Arts & Crafts fr 500.00
Tile, candle & chamberstick, yel/blk/gr on dk gr matt, 6x4½" ..2,600.00
Tile, fountain & hedgerow, mc, rstr corner, unmk, 4" 300.00
Tile, gr (elephant skin crackle), 1½x6½", in bronze ftd base 500.00
Tile, gulls & waves, wht on bl, 6" 1,400.00
Tile, oak tree & cloudy sky, gr/bl/wht, 6", +new fr 1,800.00
Tile, pines, grs/bls/brn, sm chip, 6", +new fr 2,000.00
Tiles, 2-tile frieze of ship on waves, 4-color, 8x18", +new fr ...2,500.00

Vases: Tooled and applied leaves and buds on blue-green matt, small restoration, Faience stamp, 7½x4½", $1,800.00; Tooled and applied leaves alternating with scrolled handles, green matt, minor chips to handles, Faience mark, 11½x5", $7,250.00. (Photo courtesy Dave Rago)

Vase, bl, vertical leaves, 7x8" 1,600.00
Vase, gr, appl tendril ribs, Post, #156, 5⅞x7" 3,750.00
Vase, gr, leaf blades & yel buds, Post, 9⅞x4¼" 4,900.00
Vase, gr, leaves (incised), faint mk, 3½x5", NM 1,265.00
Vase, gr, leaves (2 tiers, overlapping), Post, #36, 11¾x8" 5,750.00
Vase, gr, leaves (3/broad), bulbous, chips, 7¼x3⅞" 1,380.00
Vase, gr, leaves & stems w/single bud, sm rpr, 8½" 2,100.00
Vase, gr, ovoid, glaze miss, 5½x4" 650.00
Vase, gr, ribbed body, bottle shape, 4½x3", NM 700.00
Vase, gr, ribbed body, bulbous, chips, 4¾x3¼" 750.00
Vase, gr, tooled/appl buds & leaves, closed-in rim, 11¾x5½" .6,500.00
Vase, gr, tooled/appl leaves, gourd shape, 4¾x5" 2,400.00
Vase, gr, tooled/appl leaves, ovoid, sm rstr, unmk, 8¼x5" 1,900.00
Vase, gr, tooled/appl leaves, R Erickson, 9½", NM 3,750.00
Vase, gr, tooled/appl leaves, 3-lobe top, R Erickson, 7½" 3,250.00
Vase, gr, tooled/appl leaves (full length), 5½x4" 1,400.00
Vase, gr, tooled/appl leaves w/buds at 6-sided top, 8½" 4,500.00
Vase, gr (leathery), bottle shape, #166, chip, 13¼x8" 4,250.00
Vase, gr (leathery), cylindrical neck, squat, unmk, 6¼x4½" 900.00
Vase, gr (leathery), ovoid, sm touch-up at rim, 8½x4" 800.00
Vase, gr (leathery), tooled ribbed panels, bulbous, rpr, 3¾x5" ...1,200.00
Vase, gr (mottled), squat, #95-26, 3⅝" 1,200.00
Vase, mauve, bud on stem among low leaves, Priest, 7⅜x4¾" ..2,300.00
Vase, oatmeal, cylindrical, drilled, paper label, 11¼x8" 925.00

Gustavsberg

Gustavsberg Pottery, founded near Stockholm, Sweden, in the late 1700s, manufactured faience, creamware, and porcelain in the English taste until the end of the nineteenth century. During the twentieth century, the factory has produced some inventive modernistic designs, often signed by their artists. Wilhelm Kage (1889–1960) is best remembered for Argenta, a stoneware body decorated in silver overlay, introduced in the 1930s. Usually a mottled green, Argenta can also be found in cobalt blue and white. Other lines included Cintra (an exceptionally translucent porcelain), Farsta (copper-glazed ware), and Farstarust (iron oxide geometric overlay). Designer Stig Lindberg's work, which dates from the 1940s through the early 1970s, includes slab-built figures and a full range of tableware. Some pieces of Gustavsberg are dated.

Bowl, Argenta, bands, Kage, 4x8½" 270.00
Bowl, Argenta, rings, Kage, #1094, 1½x3¾" 60.00
Bowl, Argenta, 4-ftd, 4½x5" dia 200.00
Box, trinket; Argenta, dmns, Kage, w/lid, 3⅝" sq 195.00
Cup & saucer, demi; Argenta, bronze decor at rim 55.00
Cup & saucer, Salix 18.00
Dish, Argenta, sailing ship, WASA 1628, #1225, 3½" sq 65.00
Dish, Stig Lindberg, HP on wht, leaf shape, 12½" 65.00
Figurine, fox, Lisa Larson, w/sticker, 5" 100.00
Figurine, polar bear, Lisa Larson/Nills Kansen, 3½x5½" 70.00
Smoke set, cigarette holder & ashtray, Argenta 85.00
Tray & bowl, fish decor, seafoam/teal w/dk brn, 1950s 100.00
Vase, Argenta, dragon, bulbous, 7", NM 400.00
Vase, Argenta, fish & bubbles, 8x6¾", NM 275.00
Vase, dk bl stylized flowers on lt bl, sgraffito, 1930, 12" 245.00
Vase, floral; Argenta, #978/1, 5¾x5" 85.00
Vase, stylized leaves, bl on turq, bulbous, 1923, 4½" 100.00

Gutta Percha

Gutta percha is the plastic substance from the latex of several types of Malaysian trees. It resembles rubber but contains more resin. A patent for the use of this material in manufacturing an early type of plastic was issued in the 1850s.

Bracelet, love knot center w/crosshatched band 145.00
Brooch, Maltese Cross w/jet ball decor, 2¼x2¼" 115.00
Brooch, open center w/symbolic motif, ca 1860, 1½" dia 90.00
Dresser set, dtd 1879, EX in orig case 150.00
Earrings, horseshoe shape w/sm jet ball decor, ⅝x¾", pr 170.00
Earrings, ornate cvg w/pearl accents, 1" dia drops, pr 190.00
Frame, Pat 1863, opening sz: 6½x4½" 135.00
Locket, cameo of woman w/grapes in hair, ca 1860, oval, 1x1¼" .180.00
Necklace, teardrop-shaped pendant w/grape cluster 140.00
Necklace, 1¼" pendant w/mariner motif on ornate 22" chain ...190.00
Plaque, James Garfield, attached to hinged lidded box, 5x5" 275.00

Hadley, M.A.

Founded by artist-turned-potter Mary Alice Hadley, this Louisville, Tennessee, company has been producing handmade dinnerware and decorative items since 1940. Their work is painted freehand in a folky style with barnyard animals, baskets, whales, and sailing ships in a pastel palette of predominately blues and greens. Each piece is signed with Hadley's first two initials and her last name. She is responsible for creating each design; among collectors, horses and pigs are popular subject matter. Older pieces are generally heavier and along with the more unusual items command the higher prices.

Bowl, salad; sailing ship, 11¼" 48.00
Canister, chicken, The End inside, 6½x6¼" 50.00
Canister, cow, The End inside, 9x6¼" 60.00
Canister set, 8½" w/pig, 7½" w/cow, 5¾" w/horse 180.00
Clock, duck in center, uses 1 'C' battery, 9¼" dia, EX 65.00
Coaster, pig, 4" 35.00
Coaster, stork w/baby, Congratulations, 4" 35.00
Cruets, Oil & Vinegar, w/lids, 6¾", pr 45.00
Dish, cheese; cow on lid, 4x7¾" 50.00

Dish, lamb, 1½x7½" 35.00
Garlic jar, Garlic & bulbs on front, holes for air, w/lid, 4½" 30.00
Honey jar, Sweet to the Sweet, 2 bees w/hive on bk, 4½" 35.00
Pitcher, water; horse, pinched spout, 7¾x6½" 65.00
Plate, dinner; horse, 10¾" 25.00
Plate, dinner; snowman, 11" 20.00
Platter, basket design, sgn, oval, 13½" 60.00
Salt crock, flower on bk lip, Please Fill Me inside, 5x5" dia 55.00
Teapot, house, 2-cup, 4" 38.00

Hagen-Renaker

Best known for their line of miniature animal figures, Hagen-Renaker was founded in Monrovia, California, in 1946. It is estimated that perhaps as many as eighty different dogs were produced. In addition to the animals, they made replicas of characters from several popular Disney films under license from the Disney Studio. The firm relocated in San Dimas in 1960, where they remain active to the present time. Their wares are sometimes marked with an incised 'HR,' a stamped 'Hagen-Renaker' or part of the name, or paper labels. For more information, we recommend *The Collector's Encyclopedia of California Pottery, Second Edition*, by Jack Chipman; *Charlton Standard Catalog of Hagen-Renaker, Second Edition; Disneyana Collector's Guide to Californian Pottery, 1938–1960*, by Devin Frick and Tamara Hodge; and *Hagen-Renaker Pottery: Horses and Other Figurines* by Nancy Kelly (Schiffer). Another source of information is Hagen-Renaker Collectors Club (HRCC), listed in the Directory under Clubs, Newsletters, and Catalogs.

Figurine, Yvonne, French poodle, paper label, $75.00. (Photo courtesy Elaine Butler)

Figurine, Abdullah, Arabian horse, wht matt 400.00
Figurine, Amir, Arabian stallion, wht or gray matt, San Marcos, 9" .200.00
Figurine, calf, recumbent, tan, Monrovia, 1" 10.00
Figurine, Carmencita, begging Chihuahua puppy, Pedigree Dogs, 2" 25.00
Figurine, Champ, seated Boxer puppy, Pedigree Dogs, fawn matt, 5¼" .50.00
Figurine, Cinderella, Disney, on name card, 2½", minimum value 250.00
Figurine, cow, tan, standing, Monrovia, 1949-50, 2" 20.00
Figurine, deer, Patience (1st version), recumbent, 3½x4½" 30.00
Figurine, dodo bird, Black Bisque, 3¼" 45.00
Figurine, Donald Duck, Disney, 1950s, 1½" 140.00
Figurine, Duchess, Boxer, Pedigree Dogs, fawn matt, 5" 55.00
Figurine, duck, swimming, A-218 (decor as mallard), mini, 1¼" .35.00
Figurine, feather-duster bird, Black Bisque, unmk, 5", minimum value .70.00
Figurine, fox, Black Bisque, 4", minimum value 45.00
Figurine, goslings (Mother Goose), Designers Workshop, ea 30.00
Figurine, Honey Girl, Cocker Spaniel, Pedigree Dogs, Monrovia, 5½" .45.00
Figurine, Huey, Dewey or Louie, ducks, Disney, mini, ea 115.00
Figurine, macaw, 1988, 2½" 20.00
Figurine, Malificent, Disney's Sleeping Beauty, 1954, 1½" 600.00
Figurine, Ming Toy, Pekingese, Pedigree Dog, brn, 3" 40.00
Figurine, Miss Pepper, foal, recumbent, Monrovia 125.00
Figurine, Mother Goose, Designers Workshop, 1984, 6½" 75.00
Figurine, Pasha, elephant baby, Designers Workshop, 1955, 3½" .60.00
Figurine, Peter Pan, seated, Disney, mid-1950s, unmk, 2" 125.00
Figurine, Pruneface, Little Horribles, w/card, 1½", minimum value ..55.00
Figurine, Scrooge Duck, Disney, unmk, 1950s, mini 175.00
Figurine, sheep, blk early lamb, ear out, 1949-51, 1⅝" 20.00
Figurine, Silver, sitting cat, wht matt, 9½" 85.00
Figurine, Skunk mama, head trn right & up, 1948, 1⅞" 20.00
Figurine, squirrel baby, brn, buff or gray, sitting, 1948-50, 1⅛" 25.00
Figurine, stallion, rearing, B-535, Monrovia, 5½x5", minimum value .75.00
Figurine, Tramp, dog, from Disney's Lady & Tramp, 1955, 2" 90.00
Figurine, Western horse, palomino w/brn saddle, 1979-85, 2½" ..20.00
Figurines, Three Bears, papa (2"), w/mama & baby, ca 1950, set .90.00
Wall plaque, horses, prancing, 1960, 15x22", minimum value ...200.00
Wall plaque, Siamese cats (2), rock-like decor, unmk, 16", minimum ..125.00

Hair Weaving

A rather unusual craft became popular during the mid-1800s. Human hair was used to make jewelry (rings, bracelets, lockets, etc.) by braiding and interlacing fine strands into hollow forms with pearls and beads added for effect. Wreaths were also made, often using hair from deceased family members as well as the living. They were displayed in deep satin-lined frames along with mementoes of the weaver or her departed kin. The fad was abandoned before the turn of the century. The values suggested below are for mint condition examples. Any fraying of the hair greatly lowers value. For further information, we recommend *Collector's Encyclopedia of Hairwork Jewelry* by C. Jeanenne Bell (Collector Books). See also Mourning Collectibles.

Key:
p-w — palette work t-w — table work

Bracelet, 6-row t-w braid, gold-plated clasp w/onyx & pearl 395.00
Bracelet, snake w/gold emb/eng head, t-w over core, 11" 700.00
Bracelet, t-w w/gold clasp set w/amethyst, ca 1865, 6½" 475.00
Bracelet, t-w w/heart-shaped drop w/braid under glass, 1840s 395.00
Bracelet, 4-row t-w w/o cores, plain gold box clasp, ca 1865 ......365.00
Bracelet, 6-row, t-w w/cypher in p-w, gold clasp, ca 1850, 7" 585.00
Bracelet, 7-row, t-w in 3 weaves, gold locket clasp, ca 1855 ......485.00
Brooch, braided, under beveled glass surrounded w/pearls, ca 1837 ..375.00
Brooch, braided, under crystal surrounded by seed pearls 185.00
Brooch, gold cross w/t-w on core, 2 shades, 2x1⅜" 350.00
Brooch, gold oval p-w curl & flowers on milk glass under glass, 1" .350.00
Brooch, p-w under glass, gold ¼-moon w/seed pearls, 1⅜" 350.00
Brooch, p-w wheat sheaf under crystal, ca 1800 ....575.00
Brooch & earring set, gold-filled settings, 1850-1870 ....220.00
Earrings, p-w flowers on opaline glass, gold & jet mts, ca 1840, pr .775.00
Earrings, t-w, tapered, elongated, gold mts, ca 1855, 2⅝", pr 425.00
Earrings, t-w acorn motif, gold mts, ca 1840, 1¼x⅜", pr 325.00
Necklace, choker; t-w w/gold clasp, ca 1850, 16" 275.00
Necklace, open-weave t-w w/heart drop, gold mts, ca 1865, 17" ...425.00
Necklace, t-w chain w/heart-shaped drop, gold mts, ca 1865, 14" .595.00
Necklace, 5 rows of t-w joined by 4 rods, gold mts, ca 1860, 51" ..350.00
Ring, oval p-w basketweave, gold mt, eng, ca 1780s 500.00
Ring, t-w braid band w/hollow gold emb shield mts, ca 1860 ....275.00

Hall

The Hall China Company of East Liverpool, Ohio, was established in 1903. Their earliest product was whiteware toilet seats, mugs, jugs, etc. By 1920 their restaurant-type dinnerware and cookingware had become so successful that Hall was assured of a solid future. They continue today to be one of the country's largest manufacturers of this type of product.

Hall introduced the first of their famous teapots in 1920; new shapes and colors were added each year until about 1948, making them the largest teapot manufacturer in the world. These and the dinnerware lines of the '30s through the '50s have become popular collectibles. For more thorough study of the subject, we recommend *The Collector's Encyclopedia of Hall China* by Margaret and Kenn Whitmyer; their address may be found in the Directory under Ohio.

Blue Bouquet, bean pot, New England, #4 ....225.00
Blue Bouquet, bowl, cereal; D-style, 6" 18.00
Blue Bouquet, bowl, Radiance, 7½" 18.00
Blue Bouquet, canister, metal 12.00
Blue Bouquet, coffeepot, Terrace 60.00
Blue Bouquet, custard, Thick Rim 20.00
Blue Bouquet, gravy boat, D-style 35.00
Blue Bouquet, leftover, rectangular 50.00
Blue Bouquet, pie baker 32.00
Blue Bouquet, soup tureen 310.00

Blue Crocus, shakers, $60.00 for the pair. (Photo courtesy Margaret and Kenn Whitmyer)

Cameo Rose, bowl, cream soup; 5" 85.00
Cameo Rose, creamer 9.00
Cameo Rose, plate, 9¼" 9.00
Cameo Rose, saucer 1.50
Christmas Tree & Holly, cookie jar, Zeisel 195.00
Christmas Tree & Holly, plate, 10" 25.00
Crocus, bowl, cereal; D-style, 6" 20.00
Crocus, bowl, Radiance, 6" 12.00
Crocus, cake plate 35.00
Crocus, coffeepot, Five Band 60.00
Crocus, creamer, Medallion 16.00
Crocus, custard 35.00
Crocus, jug, Radiance, #4, w/lid 120.00
Crocus, mug, flagon style 60.00
Crocus, plate, D-style, 10" 65.00
Crocus, pretzel jar 225.00
Crocus, soup tureen, clover lid 350.00
Crocus, tidbit, D-style, 3-tier 75.00
Crocus, water bottle, Zephyr style 800.00
Five Band, carafe, red or cobalt 175.00
Five Band, jug, colors other than red or cobalt, 5" 25.00
Game Bird, casserole, china 45.00
Game Bird, creamer 25.00
Game Bird, percolator, electric 90.00
Heather Rose, bowl, salad; 9" 16.00
Heather Rose, cookie jar, Flare shape 45.00
Heather Rose, pie baker 18.00
Heather Rose, sugar bowl, w/lid 16.00
Homewood, bowl, Radiance, 6" 11.00
Homewood, drip jar, Radiance 25.00
Medallion, bowl, Lettuce, #4, 7¼" 15.00
Medallion, casserole, ivory 11.00
Medallion, jug, colors other than Lettuce or ivory, 7" 28.00
Medallion, shaker, ivory 40.00
Mums, bowl, fruit; D-style, 5½" 5.50
Mums, bowl, Radiance, 9" 22.00
Mums, casserole, Medallion 40.00
Mums, coffeepot, Terrace 70.00
Mums, cup, D-style 12.00
Mums, custard, Medallion 18.00
Mums, custard, Radiance 18.00
Mums, mug, beverage 45.00
Mums, platter, oval, D-style, 11¼" 18.00
Mums, shirred egg dish 35.00
Mums, sugar bowl, Medallion, w/lid 30.00
No 488, bean pot, New England, #3 ....185.00
No 488, bowl, flat soup; D-style, 8½" 25.00
No 488, butter dish, Zephyr, 1-lb 500.00
No 488, condiment jar, Radiance 450.00
No 488, cookie jar, Five Band 150.00
No 488, drip jar, #1188, open 32.00
No 488, jug, Medallion 70.00
No 488, mug, Tom & Jerry 25.00
Orange Poppy, canister, Radiance 400.00
Orange Poppy, custard 7.00
Orange Poppy, match safe, metal 85.00
Orange Poppy, mustard, w/liner 120.00
Orange Poppy, plate, C-style, 7¼" 14.00
Orange Poppy, spoon 85.00
Pastel Morning Glory, ball jug, #3 ....110.00
Pastel Morning Glory, creamer, New York 14.00
Pastel Morning Glory, leftover, rectangular 60.00
Pastel Morning Glory, plate, D-style, 9" 14.00
Pastel Morning Glory, shakers, Teardrop, ea 17.00
Primrose, pie baker 22.00
Red Poppy, ball jug, #3 ....120.00
Red Poppy, bowl, D-style, oval, 10¼" 225.00
Red Poppy, coffeepot, Daniel 47.00
Red Poppy, drip jar, Radiance, w/lid 45.00
Red Poppy, dustpan, metal 60.00
Red Poppy, sugar bowl, Daniel, w/lid 25.00
Red Poppy, wax paper dispenser, metal 55.00
Sears' Arlington, gravy boat & underplate 25.00
Sears' Arlington, platter, oval, 15½" 25.00
Sears' Fairfax, cup 5.00
Sears' Fairfax, saucer 2.00
Sears' Monticello, bowl, cereal; 6¼" 7.00
Sears' Monticello, platter, oval, 15½" 25.00
Sears' Mount Vernon, pickle dish, E-style, 9" 12.00
Sears' Richmond/Brown Eyed Susan, bowl, flat soup; 8" 9.00
Sears' Richmond/Brown Eyed Susan, plate, 10" 7.50
Serenade, coffeepot, Terrace 50.00
Serenade, platter, D-style, 11¼" 18.00
Serenade, sugar bowl, Art Deco, w/lid 27.00
Silhouette, bowl, Medallion, 8½" 22.00
Silhouette, clock, electric 125.00
Silhouette, creamer, Medallion 15.00
Silhouette, leftover, rectangular 65.00
Silhouette, mug, beverage 45.00
Silhouette, platter, D-style, oval, 11¼" 22.00
Springtime, bowl, D-style, oval 30.00
Springtime, bowl, Thick Rim, 8½" 17.00
Springtime, jug, Radiance, #6 ....25.00
Teapot, Airflow, Canary, 6-cup 60.00
Teapot, Airflow, Chinese Red, 8-cup 225.00

Teapot, Airflow, Indian Red, 6-cup 250.00
Teapot, Airflow, turq, 8-cup 65.00
Teapot, Aladdin, gold label, rnd opening 100.00
Teapot, Aladdin, red, oval opening 150.00
Teapot, Bellvue, red, 4-cup 60.00
Teapot, Danielle, lt bl, 6-cup 350.00
Teapot, French, common solid colors, 6-cup 32.00
Teapot, French, gold label, 12-cup 85.00
Teapot, Hollywood, gr w/gold 35.00
Teapot, Star, cobalt, no gold, 6-cup 100.00
Teapot, Star, cobalt w/gold, 6-cup 125.00
Teapot, Streamline, bl, blossom, 6-cup 550.00
Teapot, Surfside, Cadet Blue, no gold, 6-cup 275.00
Teapot, Teaball, Emerald, rnd, 6-cup 195.00
Teapot, Windshield, maroon w/gold, 6-cup 95.00
Teapot, Windshield, turq w/gold, 6-cup 85.00
Tulip, coffeepot, Perk 60.00
Tulip, gravy boat, D-style 32.00
Tulip, stack set, Radiance 125.00
Tulip, waffle iron, metal 85.00
Wildfire, bowl, cereal; D-style, 6" 16.00
Wildfire, bowl, Thick Rim, 6" 15.00
Wildfire, drip jar, tab hdl 25.00
Wildfire, sugar bowl, Pert 30.00
Yellow Rose, bowl, flat soup; D-style, 8½" 15.00
Yellow Rose, bowl, salad; 9" 16.00
Yellow Rose, coffeepot, Waverly 55.00
Yellow Rose, onion soup 40.00

Zeisel Designs, Hallcraft

Century Fern, bowl, vegetable; 10½" 20.00
Century Fern, ladle 10.00
Century Fern, saucer 1.50
Century Fern, shaker 12.00
Century Sunglow, butter dish 150.00
Century Sunglow, plate, 6" 3.50
Tomorrow's Classic Arizona, bowl, cereal; 6" 10.00
Tomorrow's Classic Arizona, candlestick, 8" 50.00
Tomorrow's Classic Arizona, jug, 1¼-qt 27.00
Tomorrow's Classic Arizona, platter, 15" 30.00
Tomorrow's Classic Bouquet, bowl, fruit; 5¾" 6.00
Tomorrow's Classic Bouquet, candlestick, 8" 55.00
Tomorrow's Classic Bouquet, egg cup 60.00
Tomorrow's Classic Bouquet, marmite, w/lid 40.00
Tomorrow's Classic Bouquet, saucer 2.50
Tomorrow's Classic Buckingham, bowl, celery; oval 18.00
Tomorrow's Classic Buckingham, creamer, AD 15.00
Tomorrow's Classic Buckingham, onion soup w/lid 45.00
Tomorrow's Classic Buckingham, sugar bowl, w/lid 20.00
Tomorrow's Classic Caprice, ashtray 10.00
Tomorrow's Classic Caprice, creamer, AD 12.00
Tomorrow's Classic Caprice, plate, 8" 6.50
Tomorrow's Classic Caprice, vase 55.00
Tomorrow's Classic Fantasy, bowl, vegetable; open, 8¾" sq 30.00
Tomorrow's Classic Fantasy, egg cup 60.00
Tomorrow's Classic Fantasy, platter, 17" 50.00
Tomorrow's Classic Frost Flowers, ashtray 12.00
Tomorrow's Classic Frost Flowers, casserole, 1¼-qt 55.00
Tomorrow's Classic Frost Flowers, saucer, AD 3.00
Tomorrow's Classic Harlequin, bowl, fruit; 5¾" 5.50
Tomorrow's Classic Harlequin, cookie jar 150.00
Tomorrow's Classic Harlequin, plate, 11" 12.00
Tomorrow's Classic Harlequin, teapot, Thorley 175.00
Tomorrow's Classic Holiday, butter dish 150.00
Tomorrow's Classic Holiday, egg cup 60.00
Tomorrow's Classic Holiday, saucer 1.50
Tomorrow's Classic Lyric/Mulberry, bowl, cereal; 6" 10.00
Tomorrow's Classic Lyric/Mulberry, candlestick, 4½" 45.00
Tomorrow's Classic Lyric/Mulberry, jug, 3-qt 30.00
Tomorrow's Classic Lyric/Mulberry, saucer, AD 2.50
Tomorrow's Classic Peach Blossom, bowl, baker; open, 11-oz 18.00
Tomorrow's Classic Peach Blossom, creamer, AD 15.00
Tomorrow's Classic Peach Blossom, plate, 8" 6.50
Tomorrow's Classic Peach Blossom, vinegar bottle 65.00
Tomorrow's Classic Pinecone, bowl, salad; lg, 14½" 35.00
Tomorrow's Classic Pinecone, ladle 16.00
Tomorrow's Classic Pinecone, plate, 6" 4.00
Tomorrow's Classic Spring, bowl, coupe soup; 9" 14.00
Tomorrow's Classic Spring, egg cup 60.00
Tomorrow's Classic Spring, ladle 12.00
Tomorrow's Classic Spring, vinegar bottle 55.00

Hallmark

Hallmark introduced a line of artplas (molded plastic) ornaments in 1973 which quickly became popular with collectors. The Hallmark Keepsake Ornament Collectors Club was organized in 1987 and offered exclusive limited edition ornaments to club members. Hallmark has produced miniature ornaments since 1988 and added a line of Easter (now known as spring) ornaments beginning in 1991. All these ornaments are very collectible.

Our advice for this category is from the Baggage Car; you will find them listed in the Directory under Iowa. Values are for ornaments in mint condition and with their original boxes unless noted otherwise.

1976, QX 181-1, Yesteryears: Train, MIB, from $170.00 to $175.00.

1973, 250HXD102-2, Manger Ball (red), MIB 95.00
1973, 250HXD110-2, Betsy Clark, 1st ed, glass bell 125.00
1974, 250QX106-1, Tree & Postman, Rockwell, dtd, glass ball, MIB ..95.00
1975, 250QX161-1, Drummer Boy, handcrafted, no box 225.00
1975, 250QX165-1, Raggedy Ann, dtd, satin ball, MIB 59.50
1975, 350QX128-1, Rocking Horse, Nostalgia, handcrafted, MIB .175.00
1976, 225QX205-1, Birds of Winter, Cardinals, glass ball, MIB ...65.00
1976, 300QX177-1, Santa, Tree Treats, dtd, handcrafted, MIB .275.00
1976, 300QX197-1, Currier & Ives, dtd, glass ball, MIB 50.00
1977, 350QX153-5, Charmers, dtd, satin ball, MIB 65.00
1977, 450QX190-2, Snowman, Twirl-About, dtd, handcrafted, MIB ..75.00
1977, 500QX181-5, Nativity, Nostalgia, handcrafted, MIB 165.00
1978, 250QX133-6, Thimble Mouse, 1st ed, handcrafted, MIB .295.00
1978, 350QX267-6, Grandmother, satin ball, MIB 50.00
1978, 600QX146-3, Carousel, 1st ed, dtd, handcrafted, MIB 395.00
1979, 300QX131-9, Christmas Salute, thimble, 2nd ed, handcrafted .175.00
1979, 400QX132-7, A Matchless Christmas, handcrafted, MIB ..85.00
1979, 800QX1419, Snoopy & Friends, 1st ed, panorama ball, MIB .95.00

1979, 900QX155-9, Here Comes Santa, 1st ed, MIB **595.00**
1980, 1200QX143-4, Santa's Express, Here Comes Santa, 2nd ed, MIB ..**275.00**
1980, 400QX132-1, Elf Swinging on Thimble Bell, 3rd ed, MIB .**195.00**
1980, 400QX303-4, Beauty of Friendship, acrylic, dtd, MIB **65.00**
1981, 1300QX438-2, Rooftop Deliveries, Here Comes Santa, MIB .**395.00**
1981, 1500QX441-5, Elf on Candy Cane, Bellringers, 3rd ed, dtd .**95.00**
1981, 800QX433-5, Frosty Friends, 2nd ed, handcrafted, MIB ..**425.00**
1981, 900QX422-2, Rocking Horse, 1st ed, handcrafted, MIB ..**595.00**
1981, 900QX424-2, Kermit the Frog on Sled, handcrafted, MIB .**75.00**
1981, 900QX427-5, Carousel, family ice skating, dtd, MIB **95.00**
1982, 1000QX502-3, Rocking Horse, 2nd ed, handcrafted, MIB .**450.00**
1982, 450QX454-6, Cookie Mouse, dtd, MIB **60.00**
1982, 700QX313-3, Cardinals, Holiday Wildlife, 1st ed, MIB ...**375.00**
1982, 800QX452-3, Frosty Friends, Eskimo on Icycle, 3rd ed, dtd, MIB .**295.00**
1983, 700QX309-9, Chickadees, Holiday Wildlife, 2nd ed, dtd ...**50.00**
1983, 800QX400-7, Frosty Friends, Eskimo & Flocked Seal, 4th ed ...**325.00**
1984, 500QX430-4, Angel w/Thimble of Stars, thimble, 7th ed, MIB ..**60.00**
1984, 900QLX707-1, Brass Carousel, brass, lighted, MIB **95.00**
1985, 1200QX496-2, Santa's Ski Trip, dtd, MIB **60.00**
1985, 1300QX493-5, 1st Christmas, porc bell, dtd, MIB **26.00**
1985, 2750QX405-2, Heavenly Trumpeter, porc, special ed, MIB **75.00**
1985, 550QX471-5, Clothespin Soldier, Scottish Highlander, MIB .**30.00**
1985, 750QX491-5, Snoopy & Woodstock, hockey, MIB **80.00**
1986, 2250QX4296, Jolly St Nick, special ed, MIB **75.00**
1986, 2450QLX7072, Village Express, MIB **125.00**

Halloween

Though the origin of Halloween is steeped in pagan rites and superstitions, today Halloween is strictly a fun time, and Halloween items are fun to collect. Pumpkin-head candy containers of papier-mache or pressed cardboard, noisemakers, postcards with black cats and witches, costumes, and decorations are only a sampling of the variety available.

Here's how you can determine the origin of your jack-o'-lantern:

American
1940 – 1950s

— items are larger
— made of egg-carton material
— bottom and body are one piece

German
1900 – 1930s

— items are generally small
— made of cardboard or composition
— always has a cut-out triangular nose; simple, criss-cross lines in mouth; blue rings in eyes
— have attached cardboard bottoms

For further information we recommend *More Halloween Collectibles, Anthropomorphic Vegetables and Fruits of Halloween,* by Pamela E. Apkarian-Russell (Schiffer). Other good reference books are *Halloween in America* by Stuart Schneider, and *Halloween Collectables* by Dan and Pauline Campanelli.

Our advisor for this category is Jenny Tarrant; she is listed in the Directory under Missouri. See Clubs, Newsletters, and Catalogs for information concerning *Trick or Treat Trader,* a quarterly newsletter. Unless noted otherwise, values are for examples in excellent to near mint condition except for paper items, in which case assume the condition to be near mint to mint.

American

Most American items were made during the 1940s and 1950s, though a few date from the 1930s as well. Lanterns are constructed either of flat cardboard or the pressed cardboard pulp used to make the jack-o-lantern shown on the left.

Bank, devil head, heavy chalkware w/glitter, 1940s, 7" **250.00**
Bridge tally, M **15.00**
Crepe paper roll, illustrations of witches, in pkg **65.00**
Crepe paper roll, plain, in pkg **12.00**
Decoration, Go-Go dancers, cb skeleton & girl, 1960s, 14", MIP ..**55.00**
Decoration, owl, papier-mache, orange/blk w/glass eyes, 11" **225.00**
Dennison Bogie Book, 1920s **145.00**
Dennison envelope of seals or cutouts **25.00**
Diecut, blk cat on jack-o'-lantern, 1930s, 12", EX **125.00**
Jack-o'-lantern, pressed cb pulp w/orig face, 4" **95.00**
Jack-o'-lantern, pressed cb pulp w/orig face, 4½" **125.00**
Jack-o'-lantern, pressed cb pulp w/orig face, 5" **145.00**
Jack-o'-lantern, pressed cb pulp w/orig face, 5½" **165.00**
Jack-o'-lantern, pressed cb pulp w/orig face, 6" **185.00**
Jack-o'-lantern, pressed cb pulp w/orig face, 6½" **195.00**
Jack-o'-lantern, pressed cb pulp w/orig face, 7" **225.00**
Jack-o'-lantern, pressed cb pulp w/orig face, 7½" **245.00**
Jack-o'-lantern, pressed cb pulp w/orig face, 8", minimum value ..**275.00**
Lantern, cat, pressed cb pulp w/orig face **245.00**
Lantern, cat (full body), pressed cb pulp, 7x6½" **350.00**
Lantern, cb w/tab sides, any **95.00**
Lantern, pumpkin man (full body), pressed cb pulp **350.00**
Party invitation, M **15.00**
Place card, M **12.00**
Plastic Halloween car **250.00**
Plastic pumpkin stagecoach, witch & cat **450.00**
Plastic witch holding blk cat w/wobbling head, 7" **150.00**
Plastic witch on rocket, upright, 7" **450.00**
Plastic witch on rocket, 4" **95.00**
Plastic witch on rocket, 5" **350.00**
Tambourine, tin litho/paper, Ohio Art, 1930s, 6" dia **75.00**
Tin noisemaker, bell style **38.00**
Tin noisemaker, can shaker **38.00**
Tin noisemaker, clicker **35.00**
Tin noisemaker, fry pan style **55.00**
Tin noisemaker, horn **55.00**
Tin noisemaker, sq spinner **38.00**
Tin noisemaker, tambourine, Chein **150.00**
Tin noisemaker, tambourine, Kirkoff **95.00**

German

As a general rule, German Halloween collectibles date from 1900 through the early 1930s. They were made either of composition or molded cardboard, and their values are higher than American-made items. In the listings that follow, all candy containers are made of composition unless noted otherwise.

Candy container, blk cat walking, glass eyes, head removes, 3-4" ..**175.00**
Candy container, blk cat walking, glass eyes, head removes, 5-6" ..**250.00**

Candy container, cat, glass eyes, 4-6", from $250 to 325.00
Candy container, cat, w/mohair, 5" 350.00
Candy container, cat, 3-5", from $175 to 285.00

Candy container, lemon-head figure, painted composition, Germany, 7", $575.00. **(Photo courtesy Jenny Tarrant)**

Candy container, pumpkin-head man (or any vegetable), on box, 3" .155.00
Candy container, pumpkin-head man (or any vegetable), on box, 4" .185.00
Candy container, pumpkin-head man (or any vegetable), on box, 5" .225.00
Candy container, pumpkin-head man (or any vegetable), on box, 6" .275.00
Candy container, witch, pumpkin people, devil, ghost, etc, 3" ..225.00
Candy container, witch, pumpkin people, devil, ghost, etc, 4" ..300.00
Candy container, witch, pumpkin people, devil, ghost, etc, 5" ..375.00
Candy container, witch, pumpkin people, devil, ghost, etc, 6" ..425.00
Candy container, witch or pumpkin man, head removes, 4", $225 to .275.00
Candy container, witch or pumpkin man, head removes, 5", $275 to .325.00
Candy container, witch or pumpkin man, head removes, 6", $325 to .365.00
Candy container, witch or pumpkin man, head removes, 7", $375 to .425.00
Diecut, bat, emb cb, from $95 to 125.00
Diecut, cat, emb cb, from $55 to 95.00
Diecut, devil, emb cb, from $95 to 150.00
Diecut, jack-o'-lantern, emb cb 65.00
Diecut, pumpkin lady, emb cb, 7½" 125.00
Jack-o'-lantern, compo w/orig insert, 3" 225.00
Jack-o'-lantern, compo w/orig insert, 3½" 250.00
Jack-o'-lantern, compo w/orig insert, 4" 275.00
Jack-o'-lantern, compo w/orig insert, 4½" 325.00
Jack-o'-lantern, compo w/orig insert, 5" 350.00
Jack-o'-lantern, molded cb w/orig insert, 3" 110.00
Jack-o'-lantern, molded cb w/orig insert, 3½" 120.00
Jack-o'-lantern, molded cb w/orig insert, 4" 155.00
Jack-o'-lantern, molded cb w/orig insert, 4½" 165.00
Jack-o'-lantern, molded cb w/orig insert, 5" 200.00
Jack-o'-lantern, molded cb w/orig insert, 5½" 225.00
Jack-o'-lantern, molded cb w/orig insert, 6" 275.00
Jack-o'-lantern, molded cb w/orig insert, 6½", minimum value .300.00
Lantern, cat, cb, molded nose w/bow under chin, 3-5", from $275 to .375.00
Lantern, cat, cb, simple rnd style 225.00
Lantern (ghost, skull, devil, witch, etc), molded cb, 3-4", minimum .375.00
Lantern (ghost, skull, devil, witch, etc), molded cb, 5"+, minimum ..425.00
Lantern (skull, devil, witch, etc), compo, 3", minimum value ...375.00
Lantern (skull, devil, witch, etc), compo, 4", minimum value ...425.00
Lantern (skull, devil, witch, etc), compo, 5", minimum value ...550.00
Noisemaker, cardboard figure (flat) on rachet 125.00
Noisemaker, cardboard paddle w/diecut face 95.00
Noisemaker, cat (3-D) on wood rachet 150.00
Noisemaker, Devil (3-D) on wood rachet 175.00
Noisemaker, pumpkin head (3-D) on wood ratchet 150.00
Noisemaker, tin frying pan paddle, 5" L 125.00
Noisemaker, tin horn, 3" 65.00
Noisemaker, veggie (3-D) horn (w/pnt face) 150.00
Noisemaker, veggie or fruit (3-D) horn (no face), ea 55.00
Noisemaker, witch (3-D) on wood rachet 175.00
Noisemaker, wood & paper tambourine 250.00

Celluloid (German, Japan, or American)

Blk cat, plain, M 150.00
Egg-shape house, M 400.00
Long-leg veggie rattle, M 300.00
Owl, plain, M 150.00
Owl on pumpkin, M 175.00
Owl on tree, M 200.00
Pumpkin-face man, M 350.00
Pumpkin-face pirate, M 400.00
Scarecrow, M 175.00
Witch, plain, M 300.00
Witch in auto, M 450.00
Witch in corncob car, M 500.00
Witch pulling cart w/ghost, M 400.00
Witch pulling pumpkin cart w/cat, M 400.00
Witch sitting on pumpkin, M 350.00

Hampshire

The Hampshire Pottery Company was established in 1871 in Keene, New Hampshire, by James Scollay Taft. Their earliest products were redware and stoneware utility items such as jugs, churns, crocks, and flowerpots. In 1878 they produced majolica ware which met with such success that they began to experiment with the idea of manufacturing art pottery. By 1883 they had developed a Royal Worcester type of finish which they applied to vases, tea sets, powder boxes, and cookie jars. It was also utilized for souvenir items that were decorated with transfer designs prepared from photographic plates.

Cadmon Robertson, brother-in-law of Taft, joined the company in 1904 and was responsible for developing their famous matt glazes. Colors included shades of green, brown, red, and blue. Early examples were of earthenware, but eventually the body was changed to semiporcelain. Some of his designs were marked with an M in a circle as a tribute to his wife, Emoretta. Robertson died in 1914, leaving a void impossible to fill. Taft sold the business in 1916 to George Morton, who continued to use the matt glazes that Robertson had developed. After a temporary halt in production during WWI, Morton returned to Keene and re-equipped the factory with the machinery needed to manufacture hotel china and floor tile. Because of the expense involved in transporting coal to fire the kilns, Morton found he could not compete with potteries of Ohio and New Jersey who were able to utilize locally available natural gas. He was forced to close the plant in 1923.

Interest is highest in examples with the monochrome glazes, and it is the glaze, not the size or form, that dictates value. The souvenir pieces are not of particularly high quality and tend to be passed over by today's collectors.

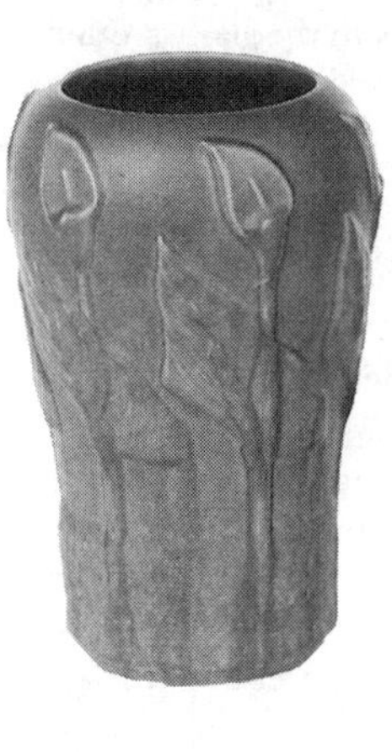

Vase, green matt with embossed stylized flowers, impressed mark, 8¾x6", $800.00.

Bowl, bl & gr matt (leathery), 5½" 400.00
Bowl, cerulean bl matt w/gray & cobalt flecks, #196, 2½x9", NM .225.00
Bowl, gr matt, artichoke form, 2x4" 250.00
Bowl, gr matt, emb flowerheads at shoulder, 2⅝x5½" 225.00
Bowl, gr matt, vertical gray streaks/mottling, 4⅛x12" 400.00
Bowl, gr-brn matt (leathery), lily pads & buds, 3x10" 400.00
Bowl, maroon w/lustre, brn mottle int, Indian Peace symbols, 3x7" .950.00
Ewer, gr matt w/gray mottle, rolled lip, 9½x9½" 550.00
Lamp base, cerulean matt (3-color), electrified, #0021, 9½"+insert ..1,500.00
Lamp base, gr matt, w/hurricane insert, 8½"+15" insert 1,600.00
Lamp base, rose-mauve matt, w/hardware: 11x5" 550.00
Pitcher, gr matt, slim, arched hdl w/emb decor, 11¼x4" 275.00
Vase, bl marbleized matt, stylized leaves, #124, 9½" 985.00
Vase, bl matt (leathery), ovoid, 7" 300.00
Vase, bl matt (2-tone), repeating petals, Robertson, #132, 3x6" ...545.00
Vase, bl matt w/gray mottle at lip to gray on bl mottle, #101, 12" .650.00
Vase, bud; gr matt, Nouveau form w/serpent-head hdl, 6x6" 275.00
Vase, cerulean bl matt w/gray flecks, sgn HK, 8½x6" 550.00
Vase, cerulean bl matt w/wht mottle, shouldered, #136, 7½" 550.00
Vase, cerulean bl matt w/wht mottle, trumpet neck, #116, 5x8" ..450.00
Vase, gr matt, emb dandelion buds at mouth, #64, 6x5" 800.00
Vase, gr matt, flared lip, spherical base, #107, 9¼x6½" 400.00
Vase, gr matt, mottled/dripped, Grecian hdls, 10¾" 700.00
Vase, gr matt, ribbed neck w/pinched waist, 7x5¾" 750.00
Vase, gr matt, shouldered, unmk, 5x8" 325.00
Vase, gr matt, simple Arts & Crafts form, #113, 7x3" 225.00
Vase, gr matt w/cvd geometrics, Robertson, 2½x5½" 345.00
Vase, gr matt w/dk drips, buttressed hdls, 6x7¾" 300.00
Vase, gr matt w/frothy wht highlights, cvd foliage, 6x3½" 400.00
Vase, gr to cream to gray-pk & cerulean bl, shouldered, 9½" .2,500.00
Vase, oatmeal-beige matt w/brn mottle, #107, 9¾x6¾" 450.00
Vase, ochre matt, heart leaves repeat, 3½x3½" 900.00

Handel

Philip Handel was best known for the art glass lamps he produced at the turn of the century. His work is similar to the Tiffany lamps of the same era. Handel made gas and electric lamps with both leaded glass and reverse-painted shades. Chipped ice shades with a texture similar to overshot glass were also produced. Shades signed by artists such as Bailey, Palme, and Parlow are highly valued.

Teroma lamp shades were created from clear blown glass blanks that were painted on the interior (reverse painted), while Teroma art glass (the decorative vases, humidors, etc. in the Handel Ware line) is painted on the exterior. This type of glassware has a 'chipped ice' effect achieved by sand blasting and coating the surface with fish glue. The piece is kiln fired at 800 degrees F. The contraction of the glue during the cooling process gives the glass a frosted, textured effect. Some shades are sand-finished, adding texture and depth.

Both the glassware and chinaware decorated by Handel are rare and command high prices on today's market. Many of Handel's chinaware blanks were supplied by Limoges.

Key:
cb — counterbalance
chp — chipped/lightly sanded

Handel Ware

Box, wht & pk roses, sgn Runge, #4058, hinged lid, 4½x5½" ...150.00
Compote, dragonflies, base: lotus, yel stem w/plants, 7½" 325.00
Fernery, mums, yel/pk on wht opal, 4x9" 1,750.00
Humidor, cancan dancer, spelter pipe lid, #86-199, 6¾x7¼" 300.00
Humidor, deer in mtns, spelter pipe lid, #4060/E, 7x5½" 150.00
Jar, hunting dog w/bird on brn & gr opalware, brass rim, 3½" ...400.00
Vase, Teroma, palm trees, 11" 1,000.00
Vase, Teroma, trees/lake, sgn Gubisch, 8", NM 1,150.00
Vase, Teroma, trees/mtns, sgn Broggi, #4210, 8" 920.00

Lamps

Table lamp, leaded glass 16" #1851-16 shade (EX+) with Nouveau leaves and pods; Hampshire base with complementary embossed design, 21", $3,750.00.

Boudoir, rvpt bamboo shoots & butterflies #6693 shade; gilt std .2,750.00
Boudoir, rvpt 7" palm scenic #6900 shade; bronzed tree std ...2,650.00
Boudoir, rvpt 7" roses #6452 shade; bronzed std 2,200.00
Boudoir, rvpt 7" sunset scenic #5917 shade; ebony stick std, 14" 2,750.00
Boudoir, rvpt 10" roses #7176RG shade; bronzed std, 15" 3,000.00
Boudoir, rvpt 16" windmill #6497 shade; flared/ribbed std 1,350.00
Chandelier, HP scenic on gold irid #7003 6" globe; metal mt, 20" 3,100.00
Chandelier, pk/orange mottled slag w/brass strapping, 6-light, 15x26" .2,200.00
Desk, cased 8" gr to wht opal #6010 shade; adjustable mk std, 15" 1,380.00
Desk, etched 10" geometric-band shade; bronze std, 15" 1,400.00
Desk, etched 10" Mosserine shade; bronze std, 15½" 1,400.00
Desk, HP 10" scrollwork shade; bronze metal #d std, 14" 1,500.00
Desk, slag glass paneled shade; bronze std w/arrow cutouts, 22" ..1,850.00
Desk, slag glass 8" paneled shade; bronze tulip-pattern std, 14" ..2,900.00
Desk, textured 8" caramel to wht opal shade; bronzed std, 16" ..1,500.00
Desk, ½-cylinder 10½" gr shade etch w/pine needles, adjusts ..1,400.00
Desk, 2 ldgl lily shades, lily pad base w/orig verdigris, 16¼x18" .1,700.00
Floor, chp ice 10" shade; bronzed harp std, rfn, 57" 2,300.00
Night light, surface/rvpt 5" floral shade; gilt teakwood std, 7" ...500.00
Table, HP 18" daffodil #5648 shade; tripartite std, 24" 10,350.00
Table, HP 18" scenic #6868 shade; Oriental bronzed std, 23" .8,500.00
Table, ldgl 16" 6-panel shade w/floral band; bronze #5082 std, 23" ..2,500.00
Table, ldgl 20" shade w/overlapped petal tiers, EX; mk std 3,300.00
Table, ldgl 22" tulips & leaves shade; unmk metal std 4,000.00
Table, metal fleur-de-lis o/l 16" bricked slag shade; wood std ..2,000.00
Table, metal goldenrod o/l 7-panel slag shade; bronze std, 22" ..3,350.00
Table, metal palms o/l 20" slag #979554 shade; bronze mk std, 25" ..4,000.00
Table, Prairie-School design w/slag shade; dbl std, 24x20x14" 16,000.00
Table, rvpt 8" floral shade w/3 mc butterflies; sgn/#d std 2,700.00
Table, rvpt 12" evergreen #2957 shade; brass & wht std, 22½" 1,150.00
Table, rvpt 14" birch trees #3718 shade; Prairie-Style std, 24" 11,000.00
Table, rvpt 14" mtn scenic #5800 shade; patinated metal std, 21" ..5,600.00
Table, rvpt 14" mtn scenic #7147 shade; 2-socket std, 20½" ..4,000.00
Table, rvpt 14" raspberry/foliage border #6760 shade; bronzed std ..1,850.00
Table, rvpt 15" tropical fish Bedigie #7538 shade; 2-arm std ..75,000.00
Table, rvpt 15" wild rose #6422 shade; 3-socket mk std, 21½" ..6,900.00
Table, rvpt 16" floral shade; bronze & glass std, 24" 3,250.00
Table, rvpt 16" palms shade w/filigree palm o/l; bronzed std ...4,250.00
Table, rvpt 18" birds in flight #6868 scenic shade; urn-form std .8,500.00
Table, rvpt 18" daffodils #5851 shade; lg bronzed std 13,000.00
Table, rvpt 18" exotic birds sgn Palme #7023 shade; orig std ..12,000.00
Table, rvpt 18" fall scenic #7111 shade; bronze ribbed std, 23" ..6,250.00
Table, rvpt 18" floral panel #7027 shade; mk bronzed metal std .12,500.00

Table, rvpt 18" jungle bird #6874 shade; mk pnt floral std ...16,000.00
Table, rvpt 18" open roses #6941 shade; mk urn-form std 17,000.00
Table, rvpt 18" Oriental pheasant #7021 shade; mk pnt floral std .21,000.00
Table, rvpt 18" parrots among branches shade; bronzed metal std ..16,000.00
Table, rvpt 18" sailing scene shade; #6391 std w/bracket ft, 24" 9,500.00
Table, rvpt 18" temple of Karnac #6825 shade; amphora-form std ...9,500.00
Table, rvpt 18" Treasure Island shade; mk std 9,000.00
Table, rvpt 18" Venetian sailing ships #6757 shade; bronzed std .10,500.00
Table, rvpt 18" wooded landscape #6953 shade; bronzed std ..7,000.00
Table, rvpt 18" woodland 8-lobe #6534 shade; mk baluster std ..7,500.00

Harker

The Harker Pottery was established in East Liverpool, Ohio, in 1840. Their earliest products were yellow ware and Rockingham produced from local clay. After 1900 whiteware was made from imported materials. The plant eventually grew to be a large manufacturer of dinnerware and kitchenware, employing as many as three hundred people. It closed in 1972 after it was purchased by the Jeannette Glass Company. Perhaps their best-known lines were their Cameo wares, decorated with white silhouettes in a cameo effect on contrasting solid colors. Floral silhouettes are standard, but other designs were also used. Blue and pink are the most often found background hues; a few pieces are found in yellow. For further information we recommend *The Collector's Guide to Harker Pottery* by Neva Colbert (Collector Books), and *The Best of Collectible Dinnerware* by Jo Cunningham (Schiffer). Our advisor for this category is Ted Haun; he is listed in the Directory under Indiana.

Amy, hi-rise jug, w/lid 75.00
Amy, rolling pin, 14" 85.00
Amy, sugar bowl, open 10.00
Antique Auto, ashtray, 1903 Cadillac, 5¼" dia 15.00
Basket, creamer 10.00
Becky, bowl, utility 25.00
Blue Blossoms, pitcher, Regal shape 25.00
Brim, plate, snack 8.00
Cameo Rose, platter 25.00
Cameo Rose, rolling pin, pk w/wht hdls, from $130 to 150.00
Cameo Rose, shaker, pk 12.00
Cameo Shellware, cup & saucer 14.00
Cherry, shakers, utility; pr 20.00
Cherry Blossom, platter 15.00
Chesterton, creamer 10.00
Colonial Lady, cookie jar, w/lid 42.00
Cottage, casserole, w/lid 17.00
Countryside, pepper shaker 20.00
Countryside, rolling pin, from $85 to 100.00
Countryside, scoop 40.00

Deco Dahlia, Pie baker, 10", $25.00; Server, $22.00. **(Photo courtesy Jo Cunningham)**

Deco-Dahlia, utility jug, 6" 22.00
Enchantment, sugar bowl, w/lid 12.00
Fruits, pitcher, Regal shape, 7" 45.00
Ivy, platter 25.00
Leaf Swirl, coffee server 37.00
Mallow, lard jar, w/lid 25.00
Mallow, plate, serving/utility; 12" 27.00
Mallow, teapot, 4-cup, 5½" 55.00
Old Vintage, bowl, flat soup; 8" 10.00
Old Vintage, cup & saucer 12.00
Pansy, pepper shaker 18.00
Pastel Tulip, cake plate, 11" 27.00
Pastel Tulip, pie baker, 10" 25.00
Petit Point, pitcher, disk; w/lid 80.00
Red Apple I, server, 12" 25.00
Red Apple II, custard, mk Bakerite 10.00
Red Apple II, pitcher, 64-oz, 8" 75.00
Rose II, bowl, utility; 3¾" 12.00
Rose II, cake server 27.00
Rose Spray, creamer 16.00
Rose Spray, plate, breakfast; 9" 12.00
Ruffled Tulip, tray, serving/utility; 11¾" 30.00
Shellridge sugar bowl, w/lid 12.00
Springtime, saucer 3.00
White Rose, teapot 35.00

Harlequin

Harlequin dinnerware, produced by the Homer Laughlin China Company of Newell, West Virginia, was introduced in 1938. It was a lightweight ware made in maroon, mauve blue, and spruce green, as well as all the Fiesta colors except ivory (see Fiesta). It was marketed exclusively by the Woolworth stores, who considered it to be their all-time bestseller. For this reason they contracted with Homer Laughlin to reissue Harlequin to commemorate their 100th anniversary in 1979. Although three of the original glazes were used in the reissue, the few serving pieces that were made were restyled, and collectors found the new line to be no threat to their investments.

The Harlequin animals, including a fish, lamb, cat, penguin, duck, and donkey, were made during the early 1940s, also for the dime-store trade. Today these are very desirable to collectors of Homer Laughlin china.

In the listings that follow, use the values designated 'high' for all colors other than turquoise and yellow. Unless priced, for medium green, double the 'high' values on all items other than flat items and small bowls. *The Collector's Encyclopedia of Fiesta* (Collector Books, 1998 values) by Sharon and Bob Huxford contains a more thorough study of this subject and includes specific pricing for many medium green examples.

Animals, maverick, gold trim 55.00
Animals, non-standard color 275.00
Animals, standard color 175.00
Ashtray, basketweave, high 58.00
Ashtray, basketweave, low 35.00
Ashtray, regular, high 53.00
Ashtray, regular, low 38.00
Bowl, '36s oatmeal; high 26.00
Bowl, '36s oatmeal; low 16.00
Bowl, '36s; high 40.00
Bowl, '36s; low 26.00
Bowl, cream soup; high 30.00
Bowl, cream soup; low 22.00
Bowl, cream soup; med gr, minimum value 600.00
Bowl, fruit; high, 5½" 11.00
Bowl, fruit; low, 5½" 8.00
Bowl, ind salad; high 42.00
Bowl, ind salad; low 28.00

Bowl, mixing; Kitchen Kraft, mauve bl, 8" 125.00
Bowl, mixing; Kitchen Kraft, red or lt gr, 6", ea 90.00
Bowl, mixing; Kitchen Kraft, yel, 10" 125.00
Bowl, nappy; high, 9" 40.00
Bowl, nappy; low, 9" 26.00
Bowl, oval baker, high 40.00
Bowl, oval baker, low 27.00
Butter dish, cobalt, ½-lb 300.00
Butter dish, high, ½-lb 135.00
Butter dish, low, ½-lb 115.00
Candle holders, high, pr 285.00
Candle holders, low, pr 240.00
Casserole, w/lid, high 160.00
Casserole, w/lid, low 95.00
Creamer, high lip, any color, ea 130.00
Creamer, ind; high 35.00
Creamer, ind; low 20.00
Creamer, novelty, high 40.00
Creamer, novelty, low 28.00

Creamer, regular; high, $20.00; low, $14.00; Sugar bowl with lid, high, $32.00; low, $20.00; Medium green, minimum value, $100.00.

Cup, demitasse; high 110.00
Cup, demitasse; low 42.00
Cup, lg, any color, ea 180.00
Cup, tea; high 11.00
Cup, tea; low 9.00
Egg cup, dbl, high 28.00
Egg cup, dbl, low 20.00
Egg cup, single, high 35.00
Egg cup, single, low 25.00
Marmalade, high 240.00
Marmalade, low 200.00
Nut dish, basketweave, high 18.00
Nut dish, basketweave, low 13.00
Perfume bottle, any color, ea 120.00
Pitcher, service water; high 105.00
Pitcher, service water; low 70.00
Pitcher, 22-oz jug, high 68.00
Pitcher, 22-oz jug, low 40.00
Pitcher, 22-oz jug, med gr, minimum value 250.00
Plate, deep; high 30.00
Plate, deep; low 20.00
Plate, deep; med gr 75.00
Plate, high, 6" 5.50
Plate, high, 7" 8.00
Plate, high, 9" 14.00
Plate, high, 10" 36.00
Plate, low, 6" 4.00
Plate, low, 7" 6.00
Plate, low, 9" 10.00
Plate, low, 10" 24.00
Platter, high, 11" 25.00
Platter, high, 13" 32.00
Platter, low, 11" 18.00
Platter, low, 13" 22.00
Platter, med gr, 11" 200.00
Platter, med gr, 13" 250.00
Sauce boat, high 35.00
Sauce boat, low 22.00
Saucer, demitasse; high 28.00
Saucer, demitasse; low 15.00
Saucer, demitasse; med gr, minimum value 125.00
Saucer, high 4.00
Saucer, low 2.00
Saucer/ashtray, high 63.00
Saucer/ashtray, low 50.00
Shakers, high, pr 26.00
Shakers, low, pr 18.00
Syrup, red or yel 175.00
Syrup, spruce gr or mauve 300.00
Teapot, high 145.00
Teapot, low 85.00
Tray, relish; mixed colors 300.00
Tumbler, car decal 65.00
Tumbler, high 58.00
Tumbler, low 45.00

Hatpin Holders

Most hatpin holders were made from 1860 to 1920 to coincide with the period during which hatpins were popularly in vogue. The taller types were required to house the long hatpins necessary to secure the large hats that were in style from 1890 to 1914. They were usually porcelain, either decorated by hand or by transfer with florals or scenics, although some were clever figurals. Glass examples are rare, and those of slag or carnival glass are especially valuable.

If you are interested in collecting or dealing in hatpins or hatpin holders, you will enjoy *Hatpins and Hatpin Holders* by Lillian Baker, with beautiful color illustrations and current market values. For information concerning the International Club for Collectors of Hatpins and Hatpin Holders, see the Clubs, Newsletters, and Catalogs section of the Directory. Our advisor for this category is Robert Larsen; he is listed in the Directory under Nebraska. (SASE required.)

Bavaria, silver floral o/l on wht, 10 holes, 4¾" 235.00
Carnival glass, Grape & Cable, purple, 7x2½" 375.00
Ceramic, HP lilies of the valley w/gold top, artist sgn 110.00
China, floral decal, pk on cream w/gold, unmk, 4¾" 95.00
Continental silver, bull (charging) figural, 3½" 45.00
Flow blue, Victorian scenes, Watteau 175.00
Germany, mc roses, 7" 150.00
Goss, City of York crest, souvenir, 3½" 110.00
Japan, bl & wht export china, windmill scene, 4" 210.00
Limoges, sm pk flowers, w/ring tray on tray, 3-pc 195.00
Nippon, moriage butterflies, gold on wht, 5⅛x2¾" 130.00
Nippon, pk & wht flowers on swirl 110.00
Nippon, storks around base on turq w/gold top, lg 165.00
Noritake, Arabian scene w/man & camel 150.00
Noritake, geisha girl scene, bulbous 125.00
Pickard, HP Nouveau floral w/much gold, 4¾" 250.00
Pickard-Rosenthal, HP Nouveau floral w/gold, 4¾" 200.00
Pressed glass, Daisy & Button, clear, silver top w/pinholes, rare, 8" ..600.00
Regina, leaves, gr on wht w/tan 85.00
Royal Austria, floral on cream w/gold top 140.00
Royal Bayreuth, lily form, yel & gr, unmk, 4½", from $3,500 to ..3,900.00

Royal Bayreuth, man w/turkey, bl mk 365.00
Royal Bayreuth Sunbonnet Baby, washing, 4½" 1,500.00
Royal Doulton, hunt scene, Lambeth & Burslem, 1902-22, 4¾" ..225.00
RS Germany, pk & yel roses, gr mk 125.00
RS Prussia, pk & wht flowers, red mk 225.00
Schafer & Vater (att), Nouveau portrait, glass beads, 5½" 300.00
Shelley, Heather, 5¾" 115.00
Unmk souvenir, HM King Geo V transfer on pearlized porc, 4½" .95.00
Vienna Austria, Nouveau floral, HP w/gold o/l, 19 holes, 4¾" ..110.00
Willow Art China, transfer, souvenir of Jerusalem, 5½" 110.00

Hatpins

A hatpin was used to securely fasten a hat to the hair and head of the wearer. Hatpins, measuring from 4" to 12" in length, were worn from approximately 1850 to 1920. During the Art Deco period, hatpins became ornaments rather than the decorative functional jewels that they had been. The hatpin period reached its zenith in 1913 just prior to World War I, which brought about a radical change in women's headdress and fashion. About that time, women began to scorn the bonnet and adopt 'the hat' as a symbol of their equality. The hatpin was made of every natural and manufactured element in a myriad of designs that challenge the imagination. They were contrived to serve every fashion need and complement the milliner's art. Collectors often concentrate on a specific type: hand-painted porcelains, sterling silver, commemoratives, sporting activities, carnival glass, Art Nouveau and/or Art Deco designs, Victorian Gothics with mounted stones, exquisite rhinestones, engraved and brass-mounted escutcheon heads, gold and gems, or simply primitive types made in the Victorian parlor. Some collectors prefer the long pin-shanks while others select only those on tremblants or nodder-type pin-shanks.

If you are interested in collecting or dealing in hatpins, see the information in the Hatpin Holders introduction concerning a national collectors' club. For further study we recommend *The Collector's Encyclopedia of Hatpins and Hatpin Holders*, available at your local bookstore or from Collector Books. Our advisor for this category is Robert Larsen; he is listed in the Directory under Nebraska. (SASE required.)

Key: cab — cabochon

Heart-shaped rhinestone hatpin with 10" shank, from $300.00 to $350.00. (Photo courtesy Robert Larsen)

Amethyst stone on 14k gold mt, 6½" pin 195.00
Bakelite, marbled red w/cvd lines/pnt ribbon, fabric flowers, 2¾" .700.00
Brass, 4 bezel-set, faux topaz faceted stones, 2¾", brass pin 95.00
Brass flower w/4 cab sapphires, 8" pin 110.00
Brass heart-shaped fr w/amethyst stone & brilliants, 1905, 1¾"+pin ...110.00
Celluloid, Deco accordion pleats, brass mt, 3¼", steel pin 65.00
Cloisonne, lilies of valley, gilt on silver, ca 1914, 2", steel pin ...110.00
Eastern Star, enameled, 7¾" pin 70.00
Gilt brass w/cab peacock eye glass center, 1", steel pin 95.00
Ivory, hollow-cvd chrysanthemum & flowers, unscrews, 1", steel pin ..145.00
Jet, cut & faceted stones in wire fr, Czech, ca 1875, from $155 to 275.00
Mosaic, dbl fr, metallic mt, granular trim, ca 1875, 1¼", brass pin .95.00
Oxidized silver alloy/amethyst glass, grapes, 1900s, 2¼", steel pin ..85.00
Peacock eye glass oval, ⅞", 7½" steel pin 125.00
Rhinestones set in openwork top, 12½" pin 125.00
Silver, Arts & Crafts, emb floral, ca 1885, 2¾", steel pin 165.00
Silver, figural sweet pea, Delamothe, ca 1900, 1¼", steel pin 155.00
Silver, scarab w/enameled details, Germany, 1½x1¼", 10" pin 95.00
SP Nouveau lady reading book, 8" pin 95.00
Trembler bee, 8" 125.00

Haviland

The Haviland China Company was organized in 1840 by David Haviland, a New York china importer. His search for a pure white, non-porous porcelain led him to Limoges, France, where natural deposits of suitable clay had already attracted numerous china manufacturers. The fine china he produced there was translucent and meticulously decorated, with each piece fired in an individual sagger.

It has been estimated that as many as 60,000 chinaware patterns were designed, each piece marked with one of several company backstamps. 'H. & Co.' was used until 1890 when a law was enacted making it necessary to include the country of origin. Various marks have been used since that time including 'Haviland, France'; 'Haviland & Co. Limoges'; and 'Decorated by Haviland & Co.' Various associations with family members over the years have resulted in changes in management as well as company name. In 1892 Theodore Haviland left the firm to start his own business. Some of his ware was marked 'Mont Mery.' Later logos included a horseshoe, a shield, and various uses of his initials and name. In 1941 this branch moved to the United States. Wares produced here are marked 'Theodore Haviland, N.Y.' or 'Made In America.'

Though it is their dinnerware lines for which they are most famous, during the 1880s and 1890s they also made exquisite art pottery using a technique of underglaze slip decoration called Barbotine, which had been invented by Ernest Chaplet. In 1885 Haviland bought the formula and hired Chaplet to oversee its production. The technique involved mixing heavy white clay slip with pigments to produce a compound of the same consistency as oil paints. The finished product actually resembled oil paintings of the period, the texture achieved through the application of the heavy medium to the clay body in much the same manner as an artist would apply paint to his canvas. Primarily the body used with this method was a low-fired faience, though they also produced stoneware. Numbers in the listings below refer to pattern books by Arlene Schleiger. For further information we recommend Mary Frank Gaston's *Collector's Encyclopedia of Limoges Porcelain*, 3rd edition (the first two editions are out of print), which offers examples and marks of the Haviland Company.

Basket, wht basketweave, floral int, rectangular, H&CO, 7½" L ..300.00
Bowl, roses/gold, ribs/scallops, 9", +underplate, H&CO 550.00
Bowl, wht w/bl bands, gold-trim leaves/acorn finial, H&CO, 12" L ..350.00
Butter pat, wht porc w/pk roses & gr leaves, emb edge, 3⅛" 12.00
Cake tray, gold medallion on beige w/gold rim, Limoges, 10½" ...55.00
Charger, floral w/pk & gold, open hdls, GDA France, 13" 150.00
Charger, ornate roses w/gold, sgn Tatnall, #16975, 13" 95.00
Chocolate pot, Baltimore Rose, gold trim, +4 c/s 765.00
Coffeepot, Princess, 7" 290.00
Creamer & sugar bowl, Baltimore Rose 290.00
Cup & saucer, bouillon; Silver, gold trim, #19 ....15.00
Cup & saucer, demi; delicate bl flowers on wht w/gold, H&CO ..50.00
Dish, roses w/in & w/o, Buxton, scalloped, oval, 7" 65.00
Plate, Autumn Leaf, H&CO, 10" 35.00
Plate, bread & butter; Lancaster, Theo 6.50
Plate, Coromandel, Theo, 8" 12.50
Plate, full-length lady, ornate cobalt/gold border, H&CO, 10" ..1,100.00
Plate, lg roses, scalloped gold border, artist sgn, H&CO, 9½" 350.00

Plate, oyster; pk roses, 6 wells, 1879-89, 8¼" 280.00
Platter, meat; Memphis, w/gravy well, 14x11" 65.00
Ramekin, Miami, Theodore Haviland 15.00
Sandwich set, emb/gilt Nouveau vines on wht, H&CO, cup & plate .225.00
Shaving mug, roses/leaves, simple mold, H&CO, 3¼ 165.00
Soup tureen, Vieux Paris, ftd, hdls, lg, NM 275.00
Teapot, Rosalinde, gold trim, 7½" 360.00
Vase, pillow; HP lake scene, sgn, imp mk, 6½", EX 500.00
Vase, 2 reserves of lady in lg hat w/flowers, Limoges, 5½x3⅝" ..265.00

Hawkes

Thomas Hawkes established his factory in Corning, New York, in 1880. He developed many beautiful patterns of cut glass, two of which were awarded the Grand Prize at the Paris Exposition in 1889. By the end of the century, his company was renowned for the finest in cut glass production. The company logo was a trefoil form enclosing a hawk in each of the two bottom lobes with a fleur-de-lis in the center. With the exception of some of the very early designs, all Hawkes was signed. (Our values are for signed pieces.)

Tray, Pueblo, extremely fine hobstar cuttings between interlocking devices, central mark, 11" diameter, NM, $13,800.00.

Bottle, scent; Florence 250.00
Bottle, vinegar; eng floral, sterling top, Pat 1916, 7½" 50.00
Bottle, Worcestershire; Brunswick, 8" 300.00
Bowl, Carnation, Gravic Glass, 5" 90.00
Bowl, Chrysanthemum, 10x4½" 500.00
Bowl, Crosscut Dmn, birds & dmn border, 4½x9½" 600.00
Bowl, Harvard, 2½x10" 275.00
Bowl, Hobstar, 6-Pointed Star, crimped, 7" 600.00
Bowl, Queens, low, 8" 375.00
Bowl, whipped cream; Jubilee, 3x6" 110.00
Butter pat, Hobstar, set of 6 ....225.00
Butter pat, Hobstar, X-cut Dmn, Strawberry Dmn & Fan, 2¾" ...80.00
Butter pat, Star & T'print 40.00
Champagne, Sheraton, 5¼" 125.00
Compote, Carnation, Gravic Glass, 5½x8" 375.00
Compote, Carnation, Gravic Glass, 6½x10" 500.00
Compote, Classic, 6x8¾" 225.00
Compote, Hobstar, rolled sides, w/hdls, 7x8½" 300.00
Compote, Hobstar, Star, Dmn & Kite, teardrop stem, 9x6½" 375.00
Cordial, Middlesex, 3½" 80.00
Creamer & sugar bowl, Intaglio Strawberry, Gravic Glass 425.00
Cruet, Bullseye & X-hatch, 9" 110.00
Cruet, Hobstar, Strawberry Dmn & Fan, 6" 125.00
Cruet, Hobstar & X-cut Dmn, 6½" 80.00
Doughnut server, Hobstar & Thread, 10" 150.00
Dresser set, Strawberry Dmn & Bullseye, 5-pc 250.00
Nappy, Hobstar & Vesica, flashed, 4-part, w/hdls, 9½" 90.00
Pitcher, Hobstar & Fan, 7½" 200.00
Pitcher, Russian, emb SP spout & hdl, 11" 230.00
Saucer champagne, Marquis, 5", set of 8 ....375.00
Tray, Holland, 13" dia 900.00
Tray, Venetian, oval, 9x7" 275.00
Tumbler, Queens 140.00
Vase, cut/etched flowers/swags/tassels, silver rim, #2262, 9¾" 460.00
Vase, Intaglio Iris, 12x7" 800.00
Vase, Navarre, trumpet form, 10" 400.00
Vase, Queens, trumpet form, 10" 200.00
Vase, Queens, trumpet form, 16" 1,600.00
Violet bowl, Russian & Pillar, 3" dia 700.00
Wine, Russian, pattern-cut/scalloped base, set of 5 ....600.00

Head Vases

Vases modeled as heads of lovely ladies, delightful children, clowns, Madonnas — even some animals — were once popular as flower containers. Today they represent a growing area of collector interest. Most of them were imported from Japan, although some American potteries produced a few as well.

For more information, we recommend *Head Vases, Identification and Values*, by Kathleen Cole; and *The World of Head Vase Planters* by Mike Posgay and Ian Warner.

Baby, Relpo #6744, blond girl in pk/wht dress/bonnet, 5½" 45.00
Baby, Sampson #313A, boy hugging bottle, 5½" 45.00
Baby, unmk, blond girl in ruffled bonnet w/lg bow, 5½" 45.00
Child, Enesco, blond girl holding wht kitten, 5½" 45.00
Child, Inarco #E2965, girl in braids, yel bodice/head scarf, 7" 60.00
Child, Inarco #E3250, boy as soldier, 6" 50.00
Child, Japan, blond curly hair w/pk bow, ruffled collar, 5½" 45.00
Child, Relpo #2010, blond boy w/bl cap, 7" 70.00
Clown, #E92883, red hair w/sm bl hat, lg red nose, 4½" 45.00
Clown, #9115, gr/red hat, smiling, gr/wht ruffle, 6" 45.00
Clown, Inarco, red cone-shaped hat w/bl ball, ruffled collar, 7" ...55.00
Clown, Napcoware #3321, orange hair, gr hat, ruffle at neck, 6" .45.00
Famous People, Benjamin Franklin, 6" 125.00
Famous People, Jackie Kennedy Onassis, Inarco #E1852, 5½" ..500.00
Lady, Ardco, blond updo, blk bodice, pearls, hand up, 7½" 300.00
Lady, Enesco, blond, wht blouse, blk hat w/bow, hand to face, 5" ...55.00
Lady, Ermintrude, Betty Lou Nichols, 6" 350.00
Lady, Inarco #E1610, blond upsweep, gold tiara, brn bodice, 5" ...60.00
Lady, Inarco #E2104, hair over eye, blk bodice, pearls, hand up, 7" .250.00
Lady, Inarco #E3523, blond curls, gr bodice/wht ruffled collar, 7" 250.00
Lady, Inarco #E779, rose in hair, pk bodice, pearls, hand up, 6" ..50.00
Lady, Japan, blond, pk bodice/bonnet w/polka-dot tie, 3" 25.00
Lady, Japan, wht banana curls, ruffled bodice, hand to chin, 5" ...50.00
Lady, Lefton, blond updo, gloved hand to face, pearls, 6" 50.00
Lady, Mary Lou, Betty Lou Nichols, 7½" 600.00
Lady, Napco #3397, frosted blond, lav/wht bodice, 6" 50.00
Lady, Napcoware #C348, blond, blk hat, gloved hand to face, 7" ..125.00
Lady, Napcoware #C7314, blond sidesweep, blk bodice, pearls, 9" ..150.00
Lady, Napcoware #C7471, blond, blk bodice w/leaf pin, 4½" 30.00
Lady, Napcoware #C8501, blond w/bl hair bow/bodice, pearls, 8" 200.00
Lady, Napcoware #36429, 3 flowers at neckline, blk-gloved hand up, 7" ..100.00
Lady, R/B, blond hair, pk bodice w/wht flower, pearls, 5½" 50.00
Lady, Relpo #K1052B, blond, gold-trimmed collar, hat w/flower, 5" ...50.00
Lady, Relpo #K1175L, redhead, pk bodice/hat, pearls, hands folded, 6" ..75.00
Lady, Relpo #K1615, pk head scarf, blk bodice, 5½" 60.00
Lady, Relpo #T961, blond, pk bodice, ruffled hat w/flower, 6" 40.00
Lady, Relpo #1694-L, redhead, peach collar/beret, hand up, 7½" 300.00
Lady, Rubens #R4130, yel bodice/hair bow, pearls, hand to cheek, 6" ...95.00
Lady, Rubens #4107, redhead, yel bodice, blk hat/yel bow, pearls, 6" 45.00

Lady, Rubens #483, blond, pk ruffled collar, pearls, hand up, 6" ..55.00
Lady, unmk, blond, gr shaded bodice/head scarf, 3" 25.00
Lady, unmk, blond curls, ruffled collar & bonnet, 5½" 125.00
Lady, unmk, blond ponytail, brn bodice/top hat, pearls, hand up, 6" ..60.00
Lady, unmk, bright yel hair & hat, bl bodice, 4" 45.00
Lady, unmk, pk fan collar, blond updo, sq base, 6½" 75.00
Lady, Vcagco, frosted hair, peach shaded bodice/head scarf, 5½" .55.00
Religious, nun praying, Napco, 5½" 28.00
Religious, nun praying, Royal Windsor, 8" 48.00
Religious, Virgin Mary w/Baby Jesus, Napcoware #R-7075, 5" 45.00
Teen girl, #4138, blond w/3 yel flowers, gr bodice, 6½" 175.00
Teen girl, #4796, blond braids, wht bodice/hair bow, 6" 60.00
Teen girl, Becky, Betty Lou Nichols, Young Adorables Series, 5½" ...250.00
Teen girl, Enesco, blond ponytails w/daisy berets, ruffled bodice, 4" 40.00
Teen girl, Inarco #E3548, blond w/yel headband holds telephone, 5" ..65.00
Teen girl, Japan, frosted side ponytail, gr bodice/wht collar, 7" ..175.00
Teen girl, Napco #C4072G, graduation cap/gown, w/diploma, 6" ..90.00
Teen girl, Parma #A172, short blond flip, blk bodice, pearls, 5" ..65.00
Teen girl, Relpo #K1694/S, blond w/pk beret/collar, hand up, 5" .75.00
Teen girl, Relpo #2004, blond w/2 orange bows, orange bodice, 7" ..150.00
Teen girl, Relpo #2011, blond, orange bodice/hair bow, pearls, 5½" ...55.00

Heisey

A.H. Heisey began his long career at the King Glass Company of Pittsburgh. He later joined the Ripley Glass Company which soon became Geo. Duncan and Sons. After Duncan's death Heisey became half-owner in partnership with his brother-in-law, James Duncan. In 1895 he built his own factory in Newark, Ohio, initiating production in 1896 and continuing until Christmas of 1957. At that time Imperial Glass Corporation bought some of the molds. After 1968 they removed the old 'Diamond H' from any they put into use. In 1985 HCA purchased all of Imperial's Heisey molds with the exception of the Old Williamsburg line.

During their highly successful period of production, Heisey made fine handcrafted tableware with simple, yet graceful designs. Early pieces were not marked. After November 1901 the glassware was marked either with the 'Diamond H' or a paper label. Blown ware is often marked on the stem, never on the bowl or foot.

For information concerning Heisey Collectors of America, see the Clubs, Newsletters, and Catalogs section of the Directory. See also Glass Animals.

Ipswich, Sahara, candy dish, half-pound, $300.00.

Cabochon, crystal, bowl, dessert; #1951, 5" 5.00
Cabochon, crystal, cake salver, #1951, ftd 65.00
Cabochon, crystal, cup, #1951 ....6.00
Cabochon, crystal, relish, #1951, 3-part, oblong, 9" 22.00
Cabochon, crystal, stem, cocktail; #6091, 4-oz 4.00
Cabochon, crystal, tumbler, juice; #6091, ftd, 5-oz 7.00
Charter Oak, crystal, candle holder, #130 Acorn, 1-light 100.00
Charter Oak, crystal, tumbler, #3362, flat, 10-oz 10.00
Charter Oak, Flamingo, candlestick, #129 Tricorn, 3-light, 5" 90.00
Charter Oak, Flamingo, stem, sherbet; #3362, low ft, 6-oz 15.00
Charter Oak, Hawthorne, plate, salad; #1246 Acorn & Leaves, 6" .20.00
Charter Oak, Hawthorne, stem, parfait; #3362, 4½-oz 60.00
Charter Oak, Marigold, stem, cocktail; #3362, 3-oz 40.00
Charter Oak, Moongleam, comport, #3362, ftd, 7" 60.00
Chintz, crystal, bowl, finger; #4107 ....10.00
Chintz, crystal, bowl, floral; ftd, 2-hdl, 8½" 35.00
Chintz, crystal, grapefruit, #3389, Duquesne, ftd 30.00
Chintz, crystal, shakers, pr 40.00
Chintz, crystal, stem, sherbet; #3389, 5-oz 10.00
Chintz, Sahara, bowl, mint; ftd, 6" 32.00
Chintz, Sahara, comport, oval, 7" 85.00
Chintz, Sahara, plate, salad; sq, 7" 18.00
Chintz, Sahara, stem, cocktail; #3389, 3-oz 35.00
Chintz, Sahara, tumbler, soda; #3389, 8-oz 24.00
Crystolite, crystal, ashtray, sq, 3½" 6.00
Crystolite, crystal, bottle, rye; #107 stopper, 1-qt 300.00
Crystolite, crystal, bowl, dessert; 5½" 14.00
Crystolite, crystal, bowl, punch; 7½-qt 120.00
Crystolite, crystal, bowl, salad; rnd, 10" 50.00
Crystolite, crystal, candy box, w/lid, 7" 60.00
Crystolite, crystal, creamer, ind 20.00
Crystolite, crystal, mustard, w/lid 55.00
Crystolite, crystal, plate, dinner; 10½" 100.00
Crystolite, crystal, plate, salad; 7" 15.00
Crystolite, crystal, plate, sandwich; 14" 55.00
Crystolite, crystal, tray, celery/relish; rectangular, 12" 35.00
Crystolite, crystal, vase, short stem, 3" 45.00
Empress, Alexandrite, bowl, floral; dolphin ft, 11" 500.00
Empress, Alexandrite, plate, sq, 10½" 335.00
Empress, Alexandrite, tray, celery; 10" 150.00
Empress, cobalt, bowl, nasturtium; dolphin ft, 7½" 350.00
Empress, Flamingo, ashtray 175.00
Empress, Flamingo, bowl, floral; rolled edge, 9" 40.00
Empress, Flamingo, marmalade, dolphin ft, w/lid 200.00
Empress, Flamingo, stem, oyster cocktail; 2½-oz 20.00
Empress, Flamingo or Sahara, cup, bouillon; 2-hdl 35.00
Empress, Flamingo or Sahara, tray, buffet relish; 4-part, 16" 75.00
Empress, Moongleam, bowl, mint; dolphin ft, 6" 45.00
Empress, Moongleam, candy, dolphin ft, w/lid, 6" 200.00
Empress, Moongleam, ice tub, w/metal hdls 165.00
Empress, Moongleam, plate, hors d'oeuvre; 2-hdl, 13" 70.00
Empress, Moongleam, plate, 9" 40.00
Empress, Moongleam, tray, relish; 3-part, 10" 65.00
Empress, Sahara, bowl, frappe; w/center 60.00
Empress, Sahara, bowl, vegetable; oval, 10" 55.00
Empress, Sahara, compotier, dolphin ft, 6" 225.00
Empress, Sahara, plate, 6" 14.00
Empress, Sahara, platter, 14" 45.00
Empress, Sahara, stem, sherbet; 4-oz 28.00
Greek Key, crystal, bottle, oil; squat, w/#8 stopper, 4-oz 100.00
Greek Key, crystal, bowl, banana split; ftd, 9" 55.00
Greek Key, crystal, bowl, finger 40.00
Greek Key, crystal, bowl, nappy; plain or scalloped, 4½" 25.00
Greek Key, crystal, bowl, nappy; 5½" 40.00
Greek Key, crystal, bowl, str sides, low ft, 8" 70.00
Greek Key, crystal, candy, w/lid, 2-lb 210.00
Greek Key, crystal, coaster 20.00
Greek Key, crystal, plate, 6" 35.00
Greek Key, crystal, puff box, #3, w/lid 175.00
Greek Key, crystal, sherbet, low ft, 6-oz 35.00

Greek Key, crystal, stem, burgundy; 3½-oz 125.00
Greek Key, crystal, sugar bowl, oval, hotel sz 55.00
Greek Key, crystal, tray, oblong, 15" 300.00
Greek Key, crystal, tumbler, str sides, 10-oz 90.00
Greek Key, Flamingo, bowl, punch; ftd, 12" 750.00
Ipswich, Alexandrite, stem, goblet; knob in stem, 10-oz 750.00
Ipswich, crystal, bowl, finger; w/underplate 40.00
Ipswich, crystal, tumbler, straight rim, flat bottom, 10-oz 70.00
Ipswich, gr, cocktail shaker, w/#86 stopper, strainer, 1-qt 800.00
Ipswich, pk, candlestick, 1-light, 6" 275.00
Ipswich, pk, plate, sq, 8" 65.00
Ipswich, Sahara, stem, oyster cocktail; ftd, 4-oz 50.00
Ipswich, Sahara, tumbler, soda; ftd, 5-oz 40.00
Lariat, crystal, ashtray, 4" 15.00
Lariat, crystal, bottle, oil; oval, 6-oz 75.00
Lariat, crystal, bowl, floral; oval, 13" 35.00
Lariat, crystal, bowl, nappy; 7" 20.00
Lariat, crystal, bowl, punch; 7-qt 130.00
Lariat, crystal, bowl, salad; 10½" 40.00
Lariat, crystal, candy, w/lid, 7" 90.00
Lariat, crystal, cheese dish, w/lid, 8" 60.00
Lariat, crystal, compote, w/lid, 10" 100.00
Lariat, crystal, cup, punch 8.00
Lariat, crystal, plate, deviled egg; rnd, 13" 220.00
Lariat, crystal, plate, salad; 7" 14.00
Lariat, crystal, platter, oval, 15" 60.00
Lariat, crystal, stem, cocktail; pressed, 3½-oz 20.00
Lariat, crystal, stem, fruit or oyster cocktail; 4¼-oz 18.00
Lariat, crystal, stem, sherbet; low, 6-oz 10.00
Lariat, crystal, tumbler, juice; ftd, 5-oz 22.00
Lariat, crystal, vase, fan; ftd, 7" 30.00
Lodestar, Dawn, ashtray 95.00
Lodestar, Dawn, bowl, #1565, 6¾" 60.00
Lodestar, Dawn, bowl, crimped, 11" 100.00
Lodestar, Dawn, candy jar, w/lid, 5" 135.00
Lodestar, Dawn, pitcher, #1626, 1-qt 170.00
Lodestar, Dawn, tumbler, juice; 6-oz 50.00
Minuet, crystal, bowl, finger; #3309 ....50.00
Minuet, crystal, bowl, floral; ftd, 11" 110.00
Minuet, crystal, candlestick, #142 Cascade, 3-light 75.00
Minuet, crystal, creamer, #1511 Toujours, ind 70.00
Minuet, crystal, plate, service; 10½" 190.00
Minuet, crystal, stem, sherbet; #5010, 6-oz 25.00
Minuet, crystal, tumbler, fruit juice; #5010, 5-oz 34.00
Minuet, crystal, vase, #4196, 8" 85.00
New Era, crystal, bottle, rye; w/stopper 120.00
New Era, crystal, cup, AD 62.50
New Era, crystal, plate, dinner; 10x8" 45.00
New Era, crystal, stem, cordial; 1-oz 45.00
New Era, crystal, stem, sherbet; low, 6-oz 12.50
New Era, crystal, tumbler, soda; ftd, 5-oz 8.00
Octagon, crystal, basket, #500, 5" 100.00
Octagon, crystal, tray, celery; 9" 10.00
Octagon, Flamingo, saucer, #1231 ....8.00
Octagon, Flamingo or Moongleam, bowl, jelly; #1229, 5½" 25.00
Octagon, Hawthorne, creamer, hotel sz 50.00
Octagon, Hawthorne, plate, 6" 15.00
Octagon, Marigold, ice tub, #500 ....150.00
Octagon, Moongleam, candlestick, 1-light, 3" 40.00
Octagon, Moongleam, plate, 10½" 35.00
Octagon, Sahara, bowl, grapefruit; 6½" 22.00
Octagon, Sahara, plate, 14" 30.00
Old Colony, crystal, bowl, floral; 2-hdl, ftd, 8½" 30.00
Old Colony, crystal, plate, sandwich; 2-hdl, sq, 13" 25.00
Old Colony, crystal, tumbler, bar; #3380, ftd, 5-oz 6.00
Old Colony, Flamingo, bowl, pickle/olive; 2-part, 13" 21.00
Old Colony, Flamingo, saucer, rnd or sq 9.00
Old Colony, Flamingo, tumbler, iced tea; #3390, ftd, 12-oz 24.00
Old Colony, Marigold, plate, cream soup 15.00
Old Colony, Marigold, stem, water; #3390, low, 11-oz 30.00
Old Colony, Moongleam, cup, bouillon; ftd, 2-hdl 28.00
Old Colony, Moongleam, stem, cocktail; #3380, 3-oz 28.00
Old Colony, Sahara, bowl, nappy; 4½" 14.00
Old Colony, Sahara, cream soup, 2-hdl 22.00
Old Colony, Sahara, decanter, 1-pt 325.00
Old Colony, Sahara, plate, rnd or sq, 6" 15.00
Old Colony, Sahara, plate, rnd or sq, 8" 24.00
Old Colony, Sahara, plate, sq, 10½" 70.00
Old Colony, Sahara, stem, claret; #3390, 4-oz 30.00
Old Colony, Sahara, stem, sherbet; #3380, 6-oz 14.00
Old Colony, Sahara, tray, center hdl, sq, 12" 75.00
Old Colony, Sahara, tumbler, dolphin ft 165.00
Old Sandwich, cobalt, candlestick, 6" 235.00
Old Sandwich, cobalt, tumbler, bar; ground bottom, 1½-oz 100.00
Old Sandwich, crystal, ashtray, ind 9.00
Old Sandwich, crystal, creamer, oval 15.00
Old Sandwich, crystal, pitcher, ice lip, ½-gal 85.00
Old Sandwich, crystal, stem, oyster cocktail; 4-oz 12.00
Old Sandwich, Flamingo, creamer, 14-oz 175.00
Old Sandwich, Flamingo, mug, beer; 18-oz 400.00
Old Sandwich, Flamingo, plate, ground bottom, sq, 6" 20.00
Old Sandwich, Flamingo or Sahara, tumbler, iced tea; ftd, 12-oz .45.00
Old Sandwich, Flamingo or Sahara, tumbler, juice; 5-oz 15.00
Old Sandwich, Moongleam, bowl, floral; ftd, rnd, 11" 100.00
Old Sandwich, Moongleam, parfait, 4½-oz 60.00
Old Sandwich, Moongleam, stem, wine; 2½-oz 55.00
Old Sandwich, Moongleam, tumbler, 10-oz 45.00
Old Sandwich, Sahara, decanter, w/#98 stopper, 1-pt 200.00
Old Sandwich, Sahara, plate, sq, 8" 27.00
Old Sandwich, Sahara or Moongleam, bowl, finger 60.00
Orchid, crystal, ashtray, 3" 30.00
Orchid, crystal, bowl, floral; ftd, 11" 115.00
Orchid, crystal, bowl, floral; Queen Ann, crimped, 9½" 75.00
Orchid, crystal, bowl, floral; Queen Ann, 2-hdl, ftd, 8½" 65.00
Orchid, crystal, bowl, floral; 3 sea horse ft, 11" 150.00
Orchid, crystal, bowl, jelly; Waverly, ftd, 6½" 65.00
Orchid, crystal, bowl, mint; Queen Ann, ftd, 5½" 37.50
Orchid, crystal, bowl, mint; Queen Ann, ftd, 8" 65.00
Orchid, crystal, bowl, relish; 3-part, rnd, 7" 55.00
Orchid, crystal, butter dish, Cabochon, w/lid, ¼-lb 325.00
Orchid, crystal, candlestick, Queen Ann, 1-light, w/prisms 135.00
Orchid, crystal, candy box, low ft, w/lid, 6" 175.00
Orchid, crystal, chocolate box, Waverly, w/lid, 5" 210.00
Orchid, crystal, cocktail icer, #3304 Universal, w/liner 250.00
Orchid, crystal, comport, Waverly, low ft, 6" 55.00
Orchid, crystal, decanter, sherry; oval, 1-pt 250.00
Orchid, crystal, mayonnaise, hdl, 5½" 55.00
Orchid, crystal, mustard, Queen Ann, w/lid 145.00
Orchid, crystal, plate, Queen Ann, 15½" 110.00
Orchid, crystal, plate, salad; Waverly, 8" 24.00
Orchid, crystal, plate, salver; Waverly, ftd, 12" 250.00
Orchid, crystal, stem, water goblet; #5022 or #5025, 10-oz 42.50
Orchid, crystal, stem, wine; #5022 or #5025, 3-oz 80.00
Orchid, crystal, tumbler, iced tea; #5022 or #5025, 12-oz 65.00
Orchid, crystal, vase, bud; ftd, sq, 8" 225.00
Plantation, crystal, bowl, gardenia; ftd, 11½" 140.00
Plantation, crystal, bowl, nappy; 5½" 35.00
Plantation, crystal, bowl, punch; Dr Johnson, 9-qt 600.00

Plantation, crystal, bowl, relish; 4-part, rnd, 8" 70.00
Plantation, crystal, butter dish, oblong, w/lid, ¼-lb 110.00
Plantation, crystal, candle block, hurricane; w/globe 200.00
Plantation, crystal, candy box, flat bottom, w/lid, 7" W 180.00
Plantation, crystal, comport, w/lid, deep, 5" 100.00
Plantation, crystal, cruet, oil; w/#125 stopper, 3-oz 130.00
Plantation, crystal, cup, punch 35.00
Plantation, crystal, plate, demi-torte; 10½" 70.00
Plantation, crystal, plate, punch bowl liner; 18" 120.00
Plantation, crystal, stem, cocktail; pressed, 3½-oz 35.00
Plantation, crystal, stem, oyster cocktail; blown, 4½-oz 40.00
Plantation, crystal, sugar bowl, ftd 40.00
Plantation, crystal, tumbler, water; pressed, 8-oz 125.00
Pleat & Panel, crystal, bowl, chow chow; 4" 6.00
Pleat & Panel, crystal, pitcher, ice lip, 3-pt 45.00
Pleat & Panel, crystal, stem, saucer champagne; 5-oz 5.00
Pleat & Panel, Flamingo, bowl, lemon; w/lid, 5" 45.00
Pleat & Panel, Flamingo, plate, bread; 7" 8.00
Pleat & Panel, Flamingo, tumbler, ground bottom, 8-oz 17.50
Pleat & Panel, Moongleam, compotier, high ft, w/lid, 5" 80.00
Pleat & Panel, Moongleam, plate, sandwich; 14" 40.00
Pleat & Panel, Moongleam, tumbler, tea; ground bottom, 12-oz ..30.00
Provincial, crystal, ashtray, rnd, 4" 22.00
Provincial, crystal, ashtray, sq, 3" 12.50
Provincial, crystal, bowl, gardenia; 13" 40.00
Provincial, crystal, bowl, nappy; hdld, rnd, 5½" 20.00
Provincial, crystal, cigarette box, w/lid 60.00
Provincial, crystal, creamer & sugar bowl, ind, w/tray 80.00
Provincial, crystal, plate, cheese; ftd, 5" 20.00
Provincial, crystal, stem, sherbet/champagne; 5-oz 10.00
Provincial, crystal, vase, violet; 3½" 30.00
Provincial, limelight gr, bowl, candy; ftd, w/lid, 5½" 550.00
Provincial, limelight gr, bowl, nappy; 4½" 70.00
Provincial, limelight gr, bowl, nappy; 4½" 70.00
Provincial, limelight gr, plate, buffet; 18" 175.00
Provincial, limelight gr, tumbler, juice; ftd, 5-oz 60.00
Queen Ann, crystal, bonbon, 6" 12.00
Queen Ann, crystal, bowl, dessert; 2-hdl, oval, 10" 30.00
Queen Ann, crystal, bowl, nappy; 4½" 8.00
Queen Ann, crystal, bowl, relish; 3-part, 7" 18.00
Queen Ann, crystal, candlestick, 3-ftd, 3" 50.00
Queen Ann, crystal, creamer, dolphin ft 30.00
Queen Ann, crystal, plate, sandwich; 2-hdl, 12" 30.00
Queen Ann, crystal, plate, 7" 8.00
Queen Ann, crystal, stem, oyster cocktail; 2½-oz 15.00
Queen Ann, crystal, tray, hors d'oeuvre; 7-part, 10" 60.00
Ridgeleigh, crystal, bowl, floral; cone shape, 13" 65.00
Ridgeleigh, crystal, bowl, jelly; ind, oval 20.00
Ridgeleigh, crystal, bowl, nappy; sq, 8" 55.00
Ridgeleigh, crystal, cigarette box, oval, w/lid 90.00
Ridgeleigh, crystal, creamer, ind 20.00
Ridgeleigh, crystal, plate, rnd, 8" 20.00
Ridgeleigh, crystal, stem, cocktail; pressed 25.00
Ridgeleigh, crystal, stem, oyster cocktail; blown, 4-oz 30.00
Ridgeleigh, crystal, tumbler, soda; pressed, ftd, 5-oz 30.00
Ridgeleigh, crystal, vase, #4 ind, fanned out top 55.00
Rose, crystal, bottle, French dressing; #5031, blown, 8-oz 210.00
Rose, crystal, bowl, lemon; Queen Ann, w/lid, 6½" 250.00
Rose, crystal, bowl, salad dressings; Queen Ann, 7" 60.00
Rose, crystal, bowl, Waverly, 4-ftd, oval, 11" 150.00
Rose, crystal, candlestick, Waverly, 3-light 100.00
Rose, crystal, comport, Waverly, ftd, oval, 7" 145.00
Rose, crystal, ice bucket, Queen Ann, dolphin ft 325.00
Rose, crystal, plate, mayonnaise; Waverly, 7" 20.00
Rose, crystal, plate, torte; Waverly, 14" 90.00
Rose, crystal, stem, oyster cocktail; #5072, ftd, 3½-oz 60.00
Rose, crystal, tray, celery; Waverly, 12" 65.00
Rose, crystal, vase, violet; Waverly, ftd, 3½" 110.00
Saturn, crystal, bottle, bitters; blown, w/short tube 75.00
Saturn, crystal, bowl, nappy; 5" 15.00
Saturn, crystal, comport, 7" 50.00
Saturn, crystal, plate, luncheon; 8" 10.00
Saturn, crystal, sugar shaker (pourer) 80.00
Saturn, limelight gr, bowl, fruit; flared rim, 12" 100.00
Saturn, limelight gr, stem, cocktail; 3-oz 75.00
Saturn, limelight gr, tumbler, 10-oz 80.00
Stanhope, crystal, ashtray, ind 25.00

Stanhope, crystal, candy dish, $180.00. (Photo courtesy Gene Florence)

Stanhope, crystal, plate, 7" 20.00
Stanhope, crystal, saucer 10.00
Stanhope, crystal, stem, oyster champagne; pressed, 5½-oz 20.00
Twist, crystal, bonbon, 2-hdl, 6" 10.00
Twist, crystal, mayonnaise 35.00
Twist, crystal, tumbler, soda; ftd, 9-oz 20.00
Twist, Flamingo, bowl, 2-hdl, 6" 15.00
Twist, Flamingo, cruet, oil; w/#78 stopper, 4-oz 110.00
Twist, Flamingo, Marigold or Sahara, ice tub 125.00
Twist, Flamingo, sugar bowl, zigzag hdls, w/lid 40.00
Twist, Marigold, candlestick, 1-light, 2" 85.00
Twist, Marigold, stem, oyster cocktail; ftd, 3-oz 50.00
Twist, Moongleam, bowl, floral; 9" 50.00
Twist, Moongleam, plate, utility; 3-ftd, 10" 60.00
Victorian, crystal, bottle, rye; 27-oz 180.00
Victorian, crystal, candlestick, 2-light 110.00
Victorian, crystal, cup, punch; 5-oz 10.00
Victorian, crystal, stem, claret; 3-oz 28.00
Victorian, crystal, tray, celery; 12" 40.00
Victorian, crystal, tumbler, w/rim ft, 10-oz 40.00
Waverly, crystal, bowl, fruit; 9" 30.00
Waverly, crystal, candlestick, 3-light 70.00
Waverly, crystal, chocolate box, w/lid, 5" 80.00
Waverly, crystal, comport, low ft, oval, 7" 50.00
Waverly, crystal, plate, luncheon; 8" 10.00
Waverly, crystal, stem, cocktail; #5019, 3½-oz 15.00
Yeoman, crystal, bowl, bouillon; 2-hdl, ftd 10.00
Yeoman, crystal, plate, 10½" 20.00
Yeoman, crystal, plate, 6" 3.00
Yeoman, crystal, tray, hors d'oeuvre; w/covered center, 13" 32.00
Yeoman, Flamingo, bowl, lemon; w/lid, rnd, 5" 20.00
Yeoman, Flamingo, plate, cream soup liner 7.00
Yeoman, Flamingo, stem, champagne; 6-oz 16.00
Yeoman, Hawthorne, bowl, floral; low, 12" 60.00
Yeoman, Hawthorne, cup 50.00

Yeoman, Marigold, comport, shallow, high ft, 5" 70.00
Yeoman, Moongleam, bowl, vegetable; 2-hdl, w/lid, 9" 70.00
Yeoman, Moongleam, grapefruit, ftd 31.00
Yeoman, Sahara, bonbon, hdld, 6½" 14.00
Yeoman, Sahara, parfait, 5-oz 20.00
Yeoman, Sahara or Moongleam, saucer 7.00

Heubach

Gebruder Heubach is a German company that has been in operation since the 1800s, producing quality bisque figurines and novelty items. They are perhaps most famous for their doll heads and piano babies, most of which are marked with the circular rising sun device containing an 'H' superimposed over a 'C.' Items with arms and hands positioned away from the body are more valuable, and color of hair and intaglio eyes affect price as well. Our advisor for this category is Grace Ochsner; she is listed in the Directory under Illinois. See also Dolls, Heubach.

Babies (2) in wht sit in bird's nest, 5" 700.00

Man with walking stick, lady with flowers, each with sunburst marks, minor restorations, 15½", $450.00 for the pair.

Baby (nude) in gr bathtub, 4x5" 600.00
Baby (nude) laughing, knees drawn up/entwined fingers, 9", $500 to .600.00
Baby (nude) sits w/legs curled, finger to mouth, #3903, 5" 450.00
Baby (nude) w/arms out & legs apart, 5", from $400 to 500.00
Baby in bunny costume stands beside pk egg, #10540, 7" 600.00
Baby in wht sits in gr shoe, 4", from $500 to 600.00
Barefoot boy fishing, w/basket & fish, 8" 350.00
Black boy sits w/ear of corn clutched to chest, 3", from $600 to ...700.00
Boy, seated, red coat, yel pants, 1 hand on knee, no mk, 6" 200.00
Boy & girl in Sunday attire on base, intaglio eyes, 14", from $500 to .600.00
Boy in bl sweater/brn leggings w/socker ball, #13530, 6", $400 to ...600.00
Boy in brn cap plays flute, stands before open egg, 7" 500.00
Dog, Spaniel pup on haunches, gray & wht, 4" 350.00
Dog, wht & shaggy, begging, sunburst mk, 5" 650.00
Dove w/tail wide, wht w/maroon talons, open bk, 5" 450.00
Dutch boy & girl flirting, seated, side-glancing eyes, 10", pr 800.00
Dutch boy & girl kissing, bl clothes, 4", NM, pr, from $400 to ..500.00
Dutch boy & girl stand bk to bk, 10", pr, from $400 to 600.00
Dutch boy holding cap to head, unmk, 6", from $300 to 400.00
Dutch girl, seated, hands on knees, no mk, 6½" 200.00
Dutch girl w/Easter egg in arms, #3466, 8", from $400 to 500.00
Girl & boy w/wooden fishing poles, mk, 8½", pr 150.00
Girl in dancing pose, roses & ribbons, sunburst mk, 17" 1,000.00
Girl w/shells at ocean's edge, bl & wht clothes, 7", from $400 to .600.00
Oriental lady w/vase, bl kimono & obi, #3944, 8", from $500 to .600.00
Provincial girl w/sack/shawl/headdress/sandals, #10842, 13", $500 to ..800.00
Tray, pate-sur-pate, maiden on marsh bank relief, wht/mauve, 9¾" ...750.00

Hickman, Royal Arden

Born in Willamette, Oregon, Royal A. Hickman was a genius in all aspects of design interpretation. Mr. Hickman's expertise can be seen in the designs of the lovely Heisey figurines, Kosta crystal, Bruce Fox aluminum, Three Crowns aluminum, Vernon Kilns, and Royal Haeger Pottery, as well as handcrafted silver, furniture, and paintings.

Because Mr. Hickman moved around during much of his lifetime, his influence has been felt in all forms of the media. Designs from his independent companies include 'Royal Hickman Pottery and Lamps' (sold through Ceramic Arts Inc., of Chattanooga, Tennessee), 'Royal Hickman's Paris Ware,' 'Royal Hickman — Florida,' and 'California Designed by Royal Hickman.' The following listings will give examples of pieces bearing the various trademarks. See also Garden City Pottery; Royal Haeger.

Bruce Fox Aluminum

Banana leaf, sgn Royal Hickman-RH6, 22½" L 35.00
Dish, lobster, sgn Bruce For-RH #37, lg 85.00
Dish, 3-point leaf, sgn Royal Hickman, 15½" L 30.00
Ivy tray, #362, 13" 25.00
Platter, fish, EX detail, sgn Royal Hickman-RH 3, 13x9" 85.00
Silent butler, dog's head, sgn, 8x5½" 65.00
2-acorn oak tray, 14½" 30.00
5-point leaf tray, 14" 30.00
7-point leaf tray, sgn Royal Hickman, 14" 35.00

California Designed by Royal Hickman

Bowl, red & blk highlights, #607, 9½" 50.00
Figurine, deer, apple gr w/wht spots, appl eyes, 15" 45.00
Figurine, giraffe w/young, pk w/blk spots 75.00
Gravy boat & leaf tray 75.00
Lamp base, flying geese, 17" 250.00
Punch bowl, Tom & Jerry, w/8 mugs 250.00
Swan, red & blk highlights, #643, 17" 125.00
Vase, fluted, purple, #602, 9¼" 50.00

Miscellaneous Signatures

Vase, figural fish, Petty Crystal Glaze, #467 ....45.00
Vase, figural rooster, Petty Crystal Glaze, #565 ....125.00
Vase, lg heart, sgn Royal Hickman, Italy, #3775 ....95.00
Vase, sea horse shape, sgn Royal Hickman USA, #468, 8" 35.00

Royal Hickman — Florida

Vase, free-form, #578, 14" 50.00
Vase, horse's head, gray w/wht mane, 13¾" 150.00
Vase, leaf, gray, #547, 8½" 45.00
Vase, pouter pigeon, blk cascade, #599, 8½" 60.00
Vase, swan, head down, blk cascade, #3624-R, 14" 75.00

Royal Hickman — Guadallajara, Mexico

Vase, 3 dolphin figures, 14k gold decor, gold crown label, 13" ...200.00

Higgins

Contemporary glass artists Frances and Michael Higgins designed high-quality glassware from the late 1940s until his death on February

13, 1999. (Frances continues with her staff.) Their designs were often created by fusing layers of glass together, though sometimes colored ground glass was used to 'paint' the decoration onto the surface. Molds were used, and through a process called 'slumping,' the glass was fired to a very high temperature, causing it to soften and take on the predetermined shape. Their work is ultramodern and is more readily found in metropolitan areas.

The earliest mark was an engraved signature on the bottom of the glass — either 'Frances Stewart Higgins' or 'Michael Higgins' or both, which was dropped in favor of just 'Higgins' with a raised 'Higgins Man.' From approximately 1957 to 1964, the Higgins signature was embossed in gold on the top. After 1964 the signature again appeared on the bottom and was engraved in the glass. Recent items produced at the Higgins studio in Riverside, Illinois, are marked 'Higgins' and dated (Higgins 99 for example). For more information we recommend *Higgins, Adventures in Glass,* by Donald-Brian Johnson and Leslie Pina (Schiffer). Our advisor is Dennis Hopp; he is listed in the Directory under Illinois.

Ashtray, Inventors, smoky gray w/red, bl & teal, 9x11" 175.00
Ashtray, Sunset, pk, yel-gr & orange w/blk & gold accents, 7x10" .125.00
Ashtray, 5 bl fish & fishing lure, 10x14" 165.00
Bowl, orange/gr vertical stripes on clear, orange circles, 17" 450.00
Bowl, pk & bl w/gold sunbursts, 3 dmn-shaped compartments, 9½" ...245.00
Bowl, wht & brn tortoise-shell design, 8¼" 80.00
Bowl, wht & clear spokes w/bubbles & gold lines, w/underplate ..185.00
Bowl, yel rays from center w/gold rings, 2½x8¼" 85.00
Dish, geometric gr shapes, stepped edge, 5" sq 125.00
Dish, gr, orange & red rays from center, 10x10" 180.00
Dish, mc parallel lines w/sm clear border, 5" sq 140.00
Rondelle, red-orange w/amber center circle, 5⅜x5⅜" 90.00
Tray, aqua teardrop streaks w/gold circles, 2-part, 1¼x14x7" 165.00
Tray, irid bl w/lav dots & beads of aqua bubbles, 7½x7½" 85.00
Tray, radiating spokes w/gold circles, trapezoidal, 9x12" 400.00
Wall pocket, orange & red rays on clear, 10" 325.00

Historical Glass

Glassware commemorating particularly significant historical events became popular in the late 1800s. Bread trays were the most common form, but plates, mugs, pitchers, and other items were also pressed in clear as well as colored glass. It was sold in vast amounts at the 1876 Philadelphia Centennial Exposition by various manufacturers who exhibited their wares on the grounds. It remained popular well into the twentieth century.

In the listings that follow, L numbers refer to a book by Lindsey, a standard guide used by many collectors. Our advisor for this category is Darlene Yohe; she is listed in the Directory under Arkansas. See also Bread Plates; Pattern Glass.

Ale glass, Centennial 60.00
Bank, Liberty Bell 38.00
Bottle, Columbus, milk glass, w/stopper 600.00
Bottle, Grant's Tomb, milk glass, no stopper 250.00
Bottle, Grover Cleveland bust, clear & frosted, L-318, lg 225.00
Bowl, Frosted Eagle (Old Abe), braid trim, w/lid, 8" 395.00
Butter dish, American Shield 195.00
Compote, George Peabody 75.00
Compote, Washington Centennial, ftd, open 40.00
Cup, Harrison & Morton, bl 235.00
Cup plate, Bunker Hill 30.00
Flask, McKinley & Hobart, Distilled Protection, 7" 475.00
Flask, Washington & Jackson, dk amber 495.00
Goblet, Emblem Centennial, L-61 ....45.00
Goblet, Pittsburgh Centennial 95.00
Hat, 1908 Presidental Campaign, milk glass w/red pnt 125.00
Jar, Statue of Liberty, L-530 ....70.00
Lamp, Emblem, L-62 ....195.00
Lamp, Goddess of Liberty, 1887 Centennial 125.00
Mug, Assassination 60.00
Mug, Centennial, waisted 90.00
Mug, Christopher Columbus, L-1 ....45.00
Mug, Columbus/Washington, L-2 ....175.00
Mug, Geo Peabody hdl 35.00
Mug, In Fond Remembrance, Rose-in-Snow 35.00
Mug, Lincoln & Garfield, Our Country's Martyrs, L-272 ....95.00
Mug, Tennessee, L-102 ....55.00
Paperweight, Cleveland sulfide medallion, 3½" 195.00
Paperweight, Geo Washington, frosted center, Gillinder, L-257 ...295.00
Paperweight, Lincoln, L-275 ....175.00
Paperweight, Ruth the Gleaner, frosted, Gillinder 125.00
Pickle dish, E Pluribus Unum 45.00
Pin tray, McKinley bust, frosted base, L-297 ....110.00

Pitcher, Liberty Bell, 6¼", $125.00.

Plate, Atlantic City Lighthouse, Egg & Dart border, 5¼" 22.00
Plate, Battleship Maine, openwork border, 5½" 16.00
Plate, Columbia Shield, sapphire bl 225.00
Plate, Columbus, milk glass, L-7 ....65.00
Plate, Dewey, clear & frosted, sm 15.00
Plate, For President Winfield S Hancock, 8" 110.00
Plate, Grant, Patriot & Soldier, amber, sq, 9½" 50.00
Plate, Mary Had a Little Lamb, Egg & Dart border, 5¼" 25.00
Plate, Old State House, L-32 ....50.00
Plate, Pope Leo, milk glass, L-240 ....40.00
Plate, Present From the Isle of Man, 10" 60.00
Plate, Texas Campaign, lt bl, 9½" 195.00
Plate, US Grant, Peace, clear, gr, vaseline & bl, set of 4 ....295.00
Platter, Carpenter's Hall 65.00
Platter, Washington Centennial, clear & frosted, dtd hdls 95.00
Shot glass, Bryan & McKinley, 1896, NM 130.00
Spooner, Log Cabin, L-184 ....115.00
Statuette, Lincoln, frosted, Gillinder & Sons, L-277 ....385.00
Stein, Centennial, hdld 60.00
Sugar shaker, Proclaim Liberty Throughout the Land 195.00
Toothpick holder, Preparedness, gold on soldier & sailor 225.00
Tumbler, Admiral Dewey, Battle of Manila Bay, 1898 ....50.00
Tumbler, America, L-48 ....25.00
Tumbler, Lincoln Tribute, L-282 ....25.00
Tumbler, Pan American Buffalo Exposition 22.00
Tumbler, Rock of Ages, L-227 ....25.00
Tumbler, whiskey; Union Forever, Bumper to the Flag, flint, 3⅛" ..225.00
Tumbler, 5 stars & flag w/13 stars & rifles 175.00
Wine Washington Centennial 65.00

Hobbs, Brockunier, & Co.

Hobbs and Brockunier's South Wheeling Glass Works was in operation during the last quarter of the nineteenth century. They are most famous for their peachblow, amberina, Daisy and Button, and Hobnail pattern glass. The mainstay of the operation, however, was druggist items and plain glassware — bowls, mugs, and simple footed pitchers with shell handles.

For further information we recommend *Hobbs, Brockunier & Co. Glass, Identification and Value Guide*, by Neila and Tom Bredehoft (Collector Books). See also Frances Ware.

Bar bottle, Polka Dot, rubena, marine gr or sapphire 225.00
Bottle, bitters; Dew Drop/Hobnail, sapphire, marine gr or canary .145.00
Bottle, scent; Daisy & Button, sapphire or marine gr 80.00
Bowl, Craquelle, creamer 45.00
Bowl, Daisy & Button, sapphire or marine gr, sq, 6½" 50.00
Butter dish, Dew Drop/Hobnail, canary, sapphire or marine gr 80.00
Caneo, amber, canary or crystal w/amber stain 80.00
Canoe, Daisy & Button, sapphire or marine gr 100.00
Celery boat, Daisy & Button, amberina, 14" 750.00
Custard cup, pressed shell hdl 10.00
Finger bowl, Spangled 220.00
Flowerpot, emb flower, attached saucer, Russel design, any 250.00
Jug, Venetian, wht loopings w/bl threading, lg, minimum value ..1,800.00
Oil bottle, Craquelle 120.00
Pitcher, tankard; Daisy & Button, qt 125.00
Sugar bowl, Dew Drop/Hobnail, canary, sapphire or marine gr 65.00
Toothpick holder, Daisy & Button, amberina, ftd, 2¾" 175.00
Tray, ice cream; Daisy & Button 80.00
Tumble up, Optic, rubena 155.00
Tumbler, Spangled 140.00

Holt Howard

Novelty ceramics marked Holt Howard represent one of the newest areas of collectibles on today's market, and dealers report a good amount of market activity. Made from the '50s into the '70s, they're not only marked, but most are dated as well. There are several lines to reassemble — the rooster, the white cat, figural banks, Christmas angels and Santas, to name only a few — but the one that most Holt Howard collectors seem to gravitate toward is the Pixie line. For more information see *Garage Sale and Flea Market Annual* (Collector Books). Our advisors for this category are Pat and Ann Duncan; they are listed in the Directory under Missouri.

Kozy Kitten, memo minder, $125.00. **(From the collection of Pat and Ann Duncan)**

Butler, jar, Onions If You Please, minimum value 200.00
Christmas, angel, cardboard cone body w/feathers, cermaic head ..30.00
Christmas, candle huggers, figural snowman, pr, from $20 to 25.00
Christmas, cookie/candy jar, Santa figural, 3-pc 250.00
Christmas, dish, Christmas tree form, divided, 14" 25.00
Christmas, dish, Santa head w/scalloped beard as bowl 25.00
Christmas, hurricane lamp, Santa w/candle holder in hat w/in chimney .35.00
Christmas, planter, candy cane 20.00
Christmas, planter, stylized deer head w/antlers, red nose 25.00
Christmas, shakers, Santa & Rudolph in bed, 3-pc 55.00
Kozy Kitten, bud vase, cat in plaid cap/neckerchief, from $65 to .75.00
Kozy Kitten, cookie jar, head form, from $40 to 50.00
Kozy Kitten, letter holder, cat w/coiled wire bk 75.00
Kozy Kitten, sewing box, figural cat w/tape-measure tongue on lid .100.00
Kozy Kitten, shakers, cat's head, pr 30.00
Kozy Kitten, wall pocket, cat's head 95.00
Pixie, candlesticks, pr 55.00
Pixie, chili sauce, rare, minimum value 300.00
Pixie, creamer 55.00
Pixie, cruets, oil & vinegar, Sally & Sam, pr, minimum value ...200.00
Pixie, dish, flat-head hdl w/X-d eyes, pickle nose, minimum value .100.00
Pixie, instant coffee jar, brn-skinned/blond-head finial, minimum .250.00
Pixie, mustard jar, yel head finial, from $45 to 75.00
Pixie, spice set, stacking 150.00
Pixie, towel hook, flat head w/sm loop hanger, rare, minimum value .200.00
Ponytail Girl, candle holder, from $50 to 60.00
Ponytail Girl, lipstick holder, from $60 to 75.00
Ponytail Girl, shakers, pr 45.00
Rooster, bowl, cereal; 6" 25.00
Rooster, butter dish, emb rooster, ¼-lb 50.00
Rooster, coffeepot, electric 100.00
Rooster, creamer & sugar bowl, emb rooster, pr 75.00
Rooster, jam & jelly jar, emb rooster 75.00
Rooster, mustard jar, emb rooster on front, w/lid 75.00
Rooster, napkin holder 40.00
Rooster, pitcher, cylindrical, rooster on front, no hdl 60.00
Rooster, plate, emb rooster, 8½" 25.00
Rooster, spoon rest, figural rooster, from $30 to 35.00
Rooster, trivet, tile w/rooster in iron fr 50.00

Homer Laughlin

The Homer Laughlin China Company of Newell, West Virginia, was founded in 1871. The superior dinnerware they displayed at the Centennial Exposition in Philadelphia in 1876 won the highest award of excellence. From that time to the present, they have continued to produce quality dinnerware and kitchenware, many lines of which are becoming very popular collectibles. Most of the dinnerware is marked with the name of the pattern and occasionally with the shape name as well. The 'HLC' trademark is usually followed by a number series, the first two digits of which indicate the year of its manufacture. For further information we recommend *The Collector's Encyclopedia of Fiesta, Ninth Edition*, by Sharon and Bob Huxford; *The Collector's Encyclopedia of Homer Laughlin China* by Joanne Jasper; and *Collector's Guide to Homer Laughlin's Virginia Rose* by Richard G. Racheter (all available from Collector Books). Another fine source of information is *Homer Laughlin, A Giant Among Dishes*, by Jo Cunningham (Schiffer). Our advisors for Virginia Rose are Jack and Treva Hamlin; they are listed in the Directory under Ohio.

See also Blue Willow; Fiesta; Harlequin; Riviera.

Dinnerware

Amberstone, casserole 55.00
Amberstone, relish tray, w/center hdl 30.00
Amberstone, sauce boat 22.00

Americana, bowl, dessert/fruit 9.00
Americana, bowl, vegetable; 8" 25.00
Americana, plate, 10" 15.00
Americana, teapot, regular 90.00
Carnival, bowl, fruit; sm 7.00
Carnival, saucer 2.00
Carnival, teacup 6.00
Casualstone, ashtray, rare 15.00
Casualstone, coffee server 45.00
Casualstone, cup & saucer 8.00
Conchita, casserole 135.00
Conchita, cup & saucer 22.00
Conchita, plate, deep, 8" 25.00
Dogwood, bowl, mixing; KK, 10½" 45.00
Dogwood, cup & saucer 12.00
Epicure, gravy boat 40.00
Epicure, nut dish, 4" 35.00
Epicure, plate, 10" 35.00
Epicure, tidbit, 2-tier 65.00
Hacienda, bowl, cream soup; rare 68.00
Hacienda, butter dish, rnd, ½-lb 140.00
Hacienda, sauce boat 35.00
Hacienda, syrup jug, w/lid 425.00
Jubilee, bowl, nappy; 8½" 9.00
Jubilee, egg cup 11.00
Jubilee, platter, 13" 12.00
Max-i-cana, egg cup, rolled edge 45.00
Max-i-cana, platter, oval or sq well, 13½" 50.00
Mexicana, bowl, baker; 9" 32.00
Mexicana, bowl, vegetable; 8½" 30.00
Mexicana, casserole 135.00
Mexicana, sugar bowl, w/lid 32.00
Pastel Nautilus, creamer 8.50
Pastel Nautilus, gravy boat 15.00
Pastel Nautilus, sugar bowl, w/lid 14.00
Priscilla, bowl, soup; gold trim, 8" 15.00
Priscilla, cake plate, KK, gold trim, 11" 25.00
Priscilla, pie plate, KK, gold trim, 9½" 30.00
Priscilla, platter, gold trim, 9" 25.00
Rhythm, plate, 7" 8.00
Rhythm, platter, 11½" 14.00
Rhythm, sauce boat 15.00
Rhythm Rose, cake plate, KK, gold trim, 10½" 22.00
Rhythm Rose, sauce boat, gold trim 14.00
Rhythm Rose, underplate, KK, gold trim, 9" 15.00
Serenade, bowl, lug soup 26.00
Serenade, shakers, pr 18.00
Serenade, teapot 100.00
Skytone, casserole 40.00
Skytone, coffeepot 45.00
Skytone, cupe & saucer 6.50
Suntone, bowl, cereal/soup 8.00
Suntone, plate, 10" 10.00
Suntone, teapot 45.00
Tango, bowl, oval baker; 9" 12.00
Tango, casserole 50.00
Tango, platter, 11¾" 12.00
Virginia Rose, bowl, deep, 5" 22.00
Virginia Rose, bowl, oatmeal, 6" 15.00
Virginia Rose, butter dish, ½-lb 175.00
Virginia Rose, cup & saucer 15.00
Virginia Rose, mug, coffee 65.00
Virginia Rose, pitcher, milk; 5" 80.00
Virginia Rose, plate, deep, 1" flange 20.00

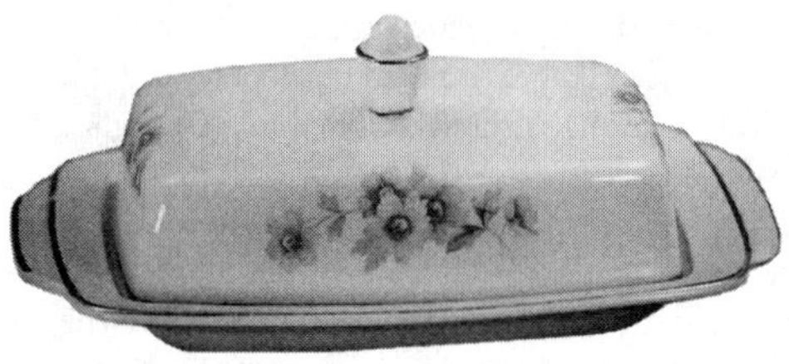

Virginia Rose, butter dish, half-pound, 9⅛", $175.00.

Virginia Rose, tray, w/hdls, 8" 35.00
Wells Art Glaze, coffeepot, ind 120.00
Wells Art Glaze, plate, chop; w/hdls 25.00
Wells Art Glaze, syrup 115.00

Art China

American Beauty, charger, 10" 150.00
American Beauty, mug 125.00
American Beauty, tankard 360.00
American Floral, tankard 360.00
Currant, bread tray, Fe Dora, 12½ 90.00
Currant, chocolate cup & saucer 110.00
Currant, dish, w/lid 210.00
Currant, humidor, w/wooden lid, 5x6" 225.00
Currant, pitcher, str-sided, 6½" 140.00
Currant, plate, 7" 45.00
Currant, sugar basket 200.00
Currant, vase, slim form, 12" 155.00
Dreamland, plaque, 10" 190.00
Dreamland, plate, open hdls, 10" 210.00
Dreamland, stein 185.00
Dreamland, tankard 300.00
Dreamland, vase, 3½" 150.00
Flow Blue, bonbon, gold trim 180.00
Flow Blue, bowl, 17th-C child, gold trim, ruffled 180.00
Flow Blue, chocolate cup & saucer 180.00
Flow Blue, cuspidor, lady's, gold trim, 5½x8" 360.00
Golden Fleece, sugar basket 240.00
White Pets, ewer, 15½" 425.00
White Pets, pitcher, milk 215.00
White Pets, plate, child & donkey 150.00

Hull

The A.E. Hull Pottery was formed in 1905 in Zanesville, Ohio, and in the early years produced stoneware specialities. They expanded in 1907, adding a second plant and employing over two hundred workers. By 1920 they were manufacturing a full line of stoneware, art pottery with both airbrushed and blended glazes, florist pots, and gardenware. They also produced toilet ware and kitchen items with a white semi-porcelain body. Although these continued to be staple products, after the stock market crash of 1929, emphasis was shifted to tile production. By the mid-'30 interest in art pottery production was growing, and over the next fifteen years, several lines of matt pastel floral-decorated patterns were designed, consisting of vases, planters, baskets, ewers, and bowls in various sizes.

The Red Riding Hood cookie jar, patented in 1943, proved so successful that a whole line of figural kitchenware and novelty items was added. They continued to be produced well into the '50s. (See also Little Red Riding Hood.) Through the '40s their floral artware lines flooded the market, due to the restriction of foreign imports. Although best known for their pastel matt-glazed ware, some of the lines were high gloss. Rosella, glossy coral on a pink clay body, was produced for a short time only; and Magnolia, although offered in a matt glaze, was produced in gloss as well.

The plant was destroyed in 1950 by a flood which resulted in a devastating fire when the floodwater caused the kilns to explode. The company rebuilt and equipped their new factory with the most modern machinery. It was soon apparent that the matt glaze could not be duplicated through the more modern processes, however, and soon attention was concentrated on high-gloss artware lines such as Parchment and Pine and Ebb Tide. Figural planters and novelties, piggy banks, and dinnerware were produced in abundance in the late '50s and '60s. By the mid-'70s dinnerware and florist ware were the mainstay of their business. The firm discontinued operations in 1985.

Our advisor, Brenda Roberts, has compiled a lovely book, *The Collector's Encyclopedia of Hull Pottery,* with full-color photos and current values, available from Collector Books. You will find her address in the Directory under Missouri. Another informative book is *Collector's Guide to Hull Pottery, The Dinnerware Lines,* by Barbara Loveless Gick-Burke, available from Collector Books.

Special note to Hull collectors: reproductions are on the market in all categories of Hull pottery — matt florals, Red Riding Hood, and later lines including House 'n Garden dinnerware.

Athena, wall pocket, #611, 8½" **165.00**
Banded, bowl, #A-1, 7½" **35.00**
Blossom, creamer, #28, 4½" **65.00**
Blossom, pitcher, #29, 16-oz **65.00**
Blossom Flite, basket, #T-2, 6" **80.00**
Blossom Flite, basket, #T-9, 10" **215.00**
Blossom Flite, candle holders, #T-11, 3", pr **65.00**
Bouquet, bowl, mixing; #20, 7½" **50.00**
Bouquet, pitcher, #22, 64-oz **150.00**
Bouquet, pitcher, #29, 32-oz **85.00**
Bow-Knot, basket, #B-12, 10½" **850.00**
Bow-Knot, basket, #B-29, 12" **1,800.00**
Bow-Knot, candle holder, #B-17, 4" **165.00**
Bow-Knot, cornucopia, #B-5, 7½" **200.00**
Bow-Knot, jardiniere, #B-18, 5¾" **260.00**
Bow-Knot, vase, #B-11, 10½" **460.00**
Bow-Knot, wall pocket, cup & saucer form; #B-24, 6" **230.00**
Bow-Knot, wall pocket, iron form, unmk, 6¼" **250.00**
Bow-Knot, wall pocket, whisk broom form, #B-27, 8" **230.00**
Butterfly, ashtray, #B-3, 7" **45.00**

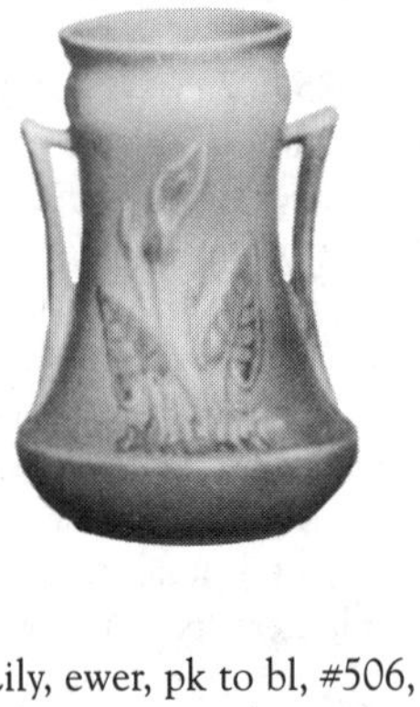

Calla Lily, vase, angle handles, #550/33, 7½", from $165.00 to $200.00. (Photo courtesy Brenda Roberts)

Calla Lily, ewer, pk to bl, #506, 10" **480.00**
Calla Lily, vase, #540/33, 6" **160.00**
Camellia, candle holder, #117, 6½" **215.00**
Camellia, cornucopia, #101, 8½" **200.00**
Camellia, creamer, #111, 5" **135.00**
Camellia, vase, #118, 6½" **195.00**
Camellia, vase, #121, 6¼" **150.00**
Camellia, vase, #123, 6½" **160.00**
Camellia, vase, #136, 6¼" **150.00**
Camellia, wall pocket, #125, 8½" **480.00**
Capri, basket, #70, 6½" **75.00**
Classic, vase, #5, 6" **35.00**
Continental, basket, Mountain Blue & White Haze, #55, 12¾" ... **215.00**
Continental, ewer, #56, 12½" **225.00**
Continental, vase, bud; #66, 9½" **40.00**
Crescent Kitchenware, bowl, #B-1, 9½" **35.00**
Crescent Kitchenware, shaker, #B-4, 3½" **20.00**
Crescent Kitchenware, teapot, #B-13, 7½" **65.00**
Dogwood, basket, #501, 7½" **395.00**
Dogwood, cornucopia, #522, 3¾" **125.00**
Dogwood, ewer, #520, 4¾" **130.00**
Dogwood, vase, #510, 10½" **340.00**
Early Utility, mug, gr, circled H, 4½" **35.00**
Early Utility, mug, gr, Happy Days Are Here Again emb, #497, 5" . **40.00**
Early Utility, salt box, #111, 6" **160.00**
Early Utility, spice jar, block H in dmn, 3½" **95.00**
Ebb Tide, basket, #E-11, 16½" **245.00**
Ebb Tide, candle holder, #E-13, 2¾" **35.00**
Ebb Tide, creamer, #E-15, 4" **100.00**
Fantasy, window box, #74, 12½" **24.00**
Fiesta, basket, #44, 6½" **95.00**
Fiesta, basket, #51, 12½" **155.00**
Fiesta, cornucopia, #49, 8½" **90.00**
Fiesta, flowerpot, #40, 4¼" **30.00**
Figurine, colt, unmk, 5½" **100.00**
Figurine, dancing girl, #955, 7" **75.00**
Floral, bowl, salad; #49, 10" **75.00**
Floral, pitcher, #46, 6" **55.00**
Floral, shakers, #44, 3½", pr **40.00**
Heritageware, cruet, vinegar; mk USA, 6¼" **30.00**
Heritageware, grease jar, #A-3, 5¾" **35.00**
Heritageware, pitcher, #A-6, 7" **45.00**
Imperial, basket, #F-38, 6¾" **35.00**
Imperial, planter, unmk, 6¾" **30.00**
Imperial, vase, carnation pk, #413, 8¾" **24.00**
Imperial, vase, urn shape, #454, 5" **22.00**
Imperial, window box, #82, 12½" **35.00**
Iris, basket, #408, 7" **365.00**
Iris, jardiniere, #413, 5½" **195.00**
Iris, vase, #402, 7" **200.00**
Iris, vase, #403, 4¾" **125.00**
Magnolia, gloss; candle holder, #H-24, 4" **40.00**
Magnolia, gloss; ewer, #H-11, 8½" **130.00**
Magnolia, gloss; ewer, #H-3, 5½" **50.00**
Magnolia, gloss; sugar bowl, w/lid, #H-22, 3¾" **40.00**
Magnolia, gloss; vase, #H-2, 5½" **40.00**
Magnolia, gloss; vase, #H-6, 6½" **55.00**
Magnolia, gloss; vase, #H-9, 8½" **120.00**
Magnolia, matt; basket, #10, 10½" **300.00**
Magnolia, matt; candle holder, #27, 4" **75.00**
Magnolia, matt; creamer, #24, 3¾" **75.00**
Magnolia, matt; ewer, #14, 4¾" **75.00**
Magnolia, matt; vase, #3, 8½" **175.00**
Magnolia, matt; vase, #7, 8½" **195.00**
Magnolia, matt; vase, #11, 6¼" **75.00**
Magnolia, matt; vase, #20, 15" **510.00**
Magnolia, matt; vase, #21, open hdls, 12½" **470.00**
Marcrest, mug, 3¼" **10.00**
Marcrest, pitcher, 7½" **55.00**
Mardi Gras/Granada, ewer, #31, 10" **175.00**

Mardi Gras/Granada, vase, #47, 9" 75.00
Mardi Gras/Granada, vase, #48, 9" 75.00
Mardi Gras/Granada, vase, #216, 9" 65.00
Mayfair, wall pocket, mandolin form, #84, 7" 60.00
Mirror Almond, bowl, divided vegetable; 10⅞x7⅞" 18.00
Mirror Almond, jug, 2-qt 36.00
Mirror Almond, snack set 22.50
Mirror Brown, bean pot, w/lid, 1-qt 40.00
Mirror Brown, bowl, divided vegetable; #542, 7x10⅞" 14.00
Mirror Brown, casserole, oval, w/lid, 2-qt 30.00
Mirror Brown, coffee cup, #597, 7-oz 4.00
Mirror Brown, garlic cellar, #3505, 13-oz 20.00
Mirror Brown, salad server, rectangular, #583, 6½x11" 22.00
Mirror Brown, skillet, #595 .....40.00
Mirror Brown, tidbit tray, 2-tier, #592 .....50.00
Mirror Brown, vase, bud; 9" 30.00

Novelty, planter, cat, #63, 5⅝" H, $75.00.

Novelty, bank, pig form w/floral underglaze, unmk, 14" 200.00
Novelty, dish, leaf form, #85, 13" 45.00
Orchid, candle holder, #315, 4" 155.00
Parchment & Pine, ashtray, #S-14, 14" 185.00
Parchment & Pine, candle holder, unmk, 5" L 35.00
Parchment & Pine, cornucopia, #S-2-R, 7¾" 65.00
Parchment & Pine, ewer, #S-7, 14¼" 240.00
Parchment & Pine, teapot, unmk, 6" 130.00
Planter, goose, #411, 12¼" 80.00
Planter, kitten beside basket, #61, 7½" 45.00
Planter, lovebirds, #93, 6" 60.00
Planter, parrot, #60, 9½x6" 65.00
Planter, pig, #60, 5" 45.00
Planter, poodle, #114, 8" 65.00
Planter, poodle, #38, 6¼" 175.00
Planter, shell form, #203, 5½" 40.00
Poppy, ewer, #610, 4¾" 195.00
Poppy, planter, #602, 6½" 270.00
Poppy, vase, #606, 10½" 500.00
Poppy, vase, #607, 6½" 175.00
Poppy, wall pocket, #609, 9" 450.00
Rainbow, dish, leaf form, 12¼" 40.00
Regal, planter, #301, 3½" 15.00
Regal, planter, parrot, #313, 7¾x12½" 105.00
Rosella, cornucopia, #R-13, 8½" 160.00
Rosella, ewer, #R-7, 9½" 1,500.00
Rosella, lamp base, #L-3, 11" 475.00
Rosella, sugar bowl, #R-4, open, 5½" 65.00
Rosella, vase, #R-2, 5" 75.00
Rosella, vase, #R-5, 6½" 85.00
Royal Ebb Tide, vase, unmk, 7" 40.00
Royal Imperial, jardiniere, #75, 7" 55.00
Royal Woodland, cornucopia, #W-10, 11" 75.00
Royal Woodland, wall pocket, #W-13, 7½" 110.00
Serenade, basket, #S-14, 12x11½" 500.00
Serenade, sugar bowl, w/lid, #S-19, 3¼" 100.00
Serenade, vase, #S-1, 6½" 70.00
Serenade, vase, #S-4, 5¼" 80.00
Sueno Tulip, ewer, pk to bl, #109, 8" 325.00
Sueno Tulip, vase, bud; yel to bl, #104/33, 6" 150.00
Sunglow, casserole, #51, w/lid, 7½" 80.00
Sunglow, flowerpot, #97, 5½" 40.00
Sunglow, flowerpot, #98, 7½" 50.00
Sunglow, vase, #89, 5½" 45.00
Sunglow, vase, dk pk gloss, #100, 6½" 65.00
Sunglow, wall pocket, iron form, unmk, 6" 175.00
Thistle, vase, #52, 6½" 150.00
Tokay/Tuscany, cornucopia, #10, 11" 80.00
Tokay/Tuscany, pitcher, beverage; mk Ovenproof USA, 8½" 140.00
Tokay/Tuscany, plate, dinner; unmk, 10½" 40.00
Tokay/Tuscany, urn, #5, 5½" 60.00
Tokay/Tuscany, vase, #8, 10" 120.00
Tokay/Tuscany, vase, #12, 12" 145.00
Tropicana, basket, #55, 12¾" 600.00
Tropicana, vase, #54, 12½" 525.00
Tulip, jardiniere, #117/30, 5" 155.00
Water Lily, basket, #L-14, 10½" 460.00
Water Lily, candle holder, #L-22, 4½" 75.00
Water Lily, cornucopia, #L-7, 6½" 135.00
Water Lily, creamer, #L-19, 5" 95.00
Water Lily, jardiniere, #L-24, 8½" 390.00
Water Lily, lamp base, unmk, 7½" 350.00
Water Lily, vase, #L-13, 10½" 260.00
Water Lily, vase, #L-15, 12½" 525.00
Wildflower, basket, #W-16, 10½" 410.00
Wildflower, cornucopia, #W-7, 7½" 95.00
Wildflower, ewer, #W-19, 13½" 520.00
Wildflower, vase, #W-1, 5½" 65.00
Wildflower, vase, #W-3, 5½" 65.00
Wildflower, vase, #W-17, 12½" 310.00
Wildflower, vase, #W-20, 15½" 515.00
Wildflower (# series), candle holder, dbl; #69, 4" 195.00
Wildflower (# series), cornucopia, #58, 6¼" 215.00
Wildflower (# series), vase, #59, 10½" 325.00
Wildflower (# series), vase, #67, 8½" 425.00
Wildflower (# series), vase, #78, 8½" 360.00
Woodland, gloss; basket, #W-9, 8¾" 175.00
Woodland, gloss; flowerpot w/attached saucer, #W-11, 5¾" 135.00
Woodland, gloss; vase, #W-4, 6½" 70.00
Woodland, matt; basket, #W-22, 10½" 700.00
Woodland, matt; candle holder, #W-30, 3½" 165.00
Woodland, matt; cornucopia, #W-2, 5½" 100.00
Woodland, matt; ewer, #W-6, 6½" 215.00
Woodland, matt; jardiniere, #W-7, 5½" 225.00
Woodland, matt; vase, #W-16, 8½" 275.00
Woodland, matt; vase, #W-17, 7½" 400.00
Woodland, matt; window box, #W-14, 10" 210.00

Hummel

Hummel figurines were created through the artistry of Berta Hummel, a Franciscan nun called Sister M. Innocentia. The first figures were made about 1935 by Franz Goebel of Goebel Art Inc., Rodental, West Germany. Plates, plaques, and candy dishes are also produced, and the older, discontinued editions are highly sought collectibles. Generally speaking, an issue can be dated by the trademark. The first Hummels, from 1935 to 1949, were either incised or stamped with the 'Crown WG' mark. The 'full bee in V' mark was employed with minor variations until

1959. At that time the bee was stylized and represented by a solid disk with angled symetrical wings completely contained within the confines of the 'V.' The three-line mark, 1964 – 1972, utilized the stylized bee and included a three-line arrangement, 'c by W. Goebel, W. Germany.' Another change in 1972 saw the 'stylized bee in V' suspended between the vertical bars of the 'b' and 'l' of a printed 'Goebel, West Germany.' Collectors refer to this mark as the 'last bee' or 'Goebel bee.' The mark in use from 1979 to 1990 omits the 'bee in V.' The New Crown mark, in use from 1991 to 1999 is a small crown with 'WG' initials, a large 'Goebel,' and a small 'Germany' signifying a united Germany. The current millennium mark came into use in the year 2000. For further study we recommend *Hummel, An Illustrated Handbook and Price Guide*, by Ken Armke; *Hummel Figurines and Plates, A Collector's Identification and Value Guide*, by Carl Luckey; *The No. 1 Price Guide to M.I. Hummel* by Robert L. Miller; and *The Fascinating World of M.I. Hummel* by Goebel. These books are available through your local book dealer. See also Limited Edition Plates.

Key:

ce — closed edition	MM — millennium
CM — crown mark	NC — new crown mark
cn — closed number	oe — open edition
FB — full bee	SB — stylized bee
LB — last bee	tw — temporarily withdrawn
MB — missing bee	3L — three-line mark

#51 3/0, Village Boy, full bee mark, 4", $160.00.

#II/111, Wayside Harmony, table lamp, CM, ce, 7½" 430.00
#II/112, Just Resting, table lamp, FB, ce, 7½" 325.00
#III/110, Let's Sing, box, CM, ce, 6¼" 540.00
#III/38/I, Angel, Joyous News w/Lute, candle holder, CM, ce, 2½" .215.00
#1, Puppy Love, CM, ce, 5" 505.00
#3/I, Book Worm, 3L, ce, 5½" 290.00
#5, Strolling Along, FB, ce, 5¼" 360.00
#6/0, Sensitive Hunter, CM, ce, 4¾" 470.00
#7/I, Merry Wanderer, LB, ce, 7½" 340.00
#9, Begging His Share, LB, ce, 5¾" 215.00
#9, Begging His Share, 3L, ce, 5¾" 235.00
#12/I, Chimney Sweep, SB, ce, 5¾" 305.00
#14 A&B, Boy & Girl Book Worm, bookends, CM, 5½", pr 865.00
#16 2/0, Little Hiker, SB, ce, 4" 125.00
#18, Christ Child, CM, ce, 3¾x6½" 290.00
#20, Prayer Before Battle, FB, ce, 4¼" 250.00
#22/0, Angel w/Bird, font, CM, ce, 3x4" 180.00
#24/I, Lullaby, candle holder, 3L, ce, 3½x5¼" 180.00
#26/0, Child Jesus, font, FB, ce, 2¾x5¼" 90.00
#28/II, Wayside Devotion, LB, ce, 7¼" 360.00
#29, Guardian Angel, font, CM, ce, 2½x5¾" 935.00
#30/0 A&B, Ba-Bee-Ring, SB, ce, 4¾x5", pr 210.00
#32, Little Gabriel, LB, ce, 5" 130.00
#34, Singing Lesson, ashtray, SB, ce, 3½" to 6¼" 160.00
#36, Child w/Flowers, font, CM, ce, 3½x4½" 290.00
#42/0, Good Shepherd, LB, ce, 6¼" 215.00
#44A, Culprits, table lamp, LB, ce, 8½" 250.00
#46/0, Madonna w/o Halo, 3L, wht, ce, 10¼" 36.00
#47, Goose Girl, CM, ce, 5" 575.00
#48/II, Madonna, plaque, CM, ce, 4¾x5¾" 395.00
#50/0, Volunteers, CM, ce, 5¾" 610.00
#52, Going to Grandma's, FB, ce, 6¼" 610.00
#54, Silent Night, candle holder, SB, ce, 3½x4¾" 340.00
#56A, Culprits, CM, ce, 6½" 610.00
#60 A&B, Farm Boy & Goose Girl, bookends, 3L, ce, 4¾", pr .305.00
#63, Singing Lesson, FB, ce, 3" 180.00
#64, Shepherd's Boy, 3L, ce, 5½" 215.00
#67, Doll Mother, SB, ce, 4½" 235.00
#69, Happy Pastime, SB, ce, 3½" 180.00
#70, Holy Child, CM, ce, 7" 540.00
#71, Stormy Weather, CM, ce, 6½" 790.00
#73, Little Helper, SB, ce, 4½" 135.00
#75, White Angel, font, FB, ce, 4" 90.00
#78/VI, Blessed Child (Infant of Krumbad), FB, ce, 10½" 290.00
#80, Little Scholar, FB, ce, 5½" 270.00
#82, School Boy, CM, ce, 5" 450.00
#84, Worship, CM, ce, 5¼" 340.00
#85/II, Serenade, CM, ce, 7¼" 865.00
#87, For Father, CM, ce, 5½" 470.00
#89/I, Little Cellist, SB, ce, 5¾" 235.00
#91 A&B, Angels at Prayer, font, 3L, ce, 3⅜x5" 80.00
#93, Little Fiddler, plaque, SB, ce, 4½x5" 160.00
#94/I, Suprise, CM, ce, 5½" 540.00
#95, Brother, SB, ce, 5½" 215.00
#97, Trumpet Boy, FB, ce, 4¾" 180.00
#98, Sister, CM, ce, 5¾" 395.00
#99, Eventide, FB, ce, 4¼x5" 430.00
#101, To Market, table lamp, plain post, FB, ce, 6½" 4,320.00
#104, Eventide, table lamp, CM, ce, 7½" 6,000.00
#105, Adoration w/Bird, CM, ce, 4¾" 5,040.00
#106, Merry Wanderer, plaque w/wood fr, CM, ce, 6x6" 3,600.00
#109/0, Happy Traveller, SB, ce, 5" 200.00
#114, Let's Sing, ashtray, FB, ce, 3½x6¼" 180.00
#118, Little Thrifty, bank, CM, ce, 5¼" 360.00
#119, Postman, CM, ce, 5¼" 430.00
#124, Hello, FB, ce, 6½" 325.00
#126, Retreat to Safety, plaque, MB, tw, 4¾x4¾" 135.00
#127, Doctor, FB, ce, 5" 215.00
#128, Baker, FB, ce, 5" 250.00
#130, Duet, 3L, ce, 5¼" 240.00
#131, Street Singer, FB, ce, 5¼" 270.00
#132, Star Gazer, FB, ce, 4¾" 290.00
#134, Quartet, plaque, FB, ce, 5½x6¼" 380.00
#136, Friends, CM, ce, 10½" 2,160.00
#138, Tiny Baby in Crib, wall plaque, FB, cn, 2¼x3" 2,160.00
#140, The Mail Is Here, plaque, FB, ce, 4¼x6¾" 325.00
#142, Apple Tree Boy, CM, ce, 6½" 575.00
#142/X, Apple Tree Boy, SB, ce, 30" 12,240.00
#143, Boots, CM, ce, 6¾" 650.00
#145, Little Guardian, FB, ce, 4" 200.00
#147, Angel Shrine, font, SB, ce, 3x5" 60.00
#150 2/0, Happy Days, 3L, ce, 4¼" 160.00
#151, Madonna Holding Child, bl, LB, ce, 12½" 665.00
#152B, Umbrella Girl, CM, ce, 8" 2,880.00
#154, Waiter, CM, ce, 6½" 610.00
#163, Whitsuntide, CM, ce, 7" 720.00
#164, Worship, font, CM, ce, 3¼x5" 180.00
#166, Boy w/Bird, ashtray, FB, ce, 3¼x6" 200.00

#169, Bird Duet, CM, ce, 4" 305.00
#171, Little Sweeper, CM, ce, 4¼" 290.00
#173, Festival Harmony (Flute), flowers at hem, FB, ce, 11" 900.00
#174, She Loves Me, She Loves Me Not, FB, ce, 4¼" 250.00
#175, Mother's Darling, 3L, ce, 5½" 205.00
#177, School Girls, FB, ce, 9½" 2,160.00
#179, Coquettes, CM, ce, 5¼" 575.00
#181, Old Man Reading Newspaper, cn, 6¾" 10,800.00
#183, Forest Shrine, FB, ce, 9" 720.00
#185, Accordion Boy, 3L, ce, 5" 195.00
#187, MI Hummel Plaque (in English), FB, ce, 5½x4" 540.00
#188, Celestial Musician, CM, ce, 7" 1,080.00
#189, Old Woman Knitting, cn, 6¾" 10,800.00
#193, Angel Duet, candle holder, FB, ce, 5" 430.00
#195, Barnyard Hero, CM, ce, 6" 720.00
#196/0, Telling Her Secret, FB, ce, 5¼" 430.00
#197, Be Patient, CM, ce, 6¼" 575.00
#199, Feeding Time, CM, ce, 5¾" 575.00
#201, Retreat to Safety, FB, ce, 6" 470.00
#203, Signs of Spring, FB, ce, 5¼" 395.00
#205, MI Hummel Dealer's Plaque (in German), SB, ce, 5½x4¼" .610.00
#208, MI Hummel Dealer's Plaque (in French), FB, ce, 5½x4" ..2,880.00
#213, MI Hummel Dealer's Plaque (in Spanish), FB, ce, 5¾x4¼" ...5,760.00
#217, Boy w/Toothache, FB, ce, 5½" 305.00
#219, Little Velma, FB, cn, 4" 2,880.00
#221, Happy Pastime, candy jar, cn, factory sample 3,600.00
#224/I, Wayside Harmony, table lamp, FB, ce, 7½" 375.00
#226, The Mail Is Here, SB, ce, 4¼x6" 610.00
#229, Apple Tree Girl, table lamp, FB, ce, 7½" 650.00
#232, Happy Days, table lamp, FB, ce, 9¾" 865.00
#237, Star Gazer, wall plaque, FB, cn, 4¾x5" 7,200.00
#239A, Girl w/Nosegay, SB, ce, 3½" 70.00
#240, Little Drummer, FB, ce, 4" 215.00
#243, Madonna & Child, font, FB, ce, 3⅛x4" 180.00
#247, Standing Madonna w/Child, cn, 13" 7,200.00
#248/0, Guardian Angel, font, SB, ce, 2⅜x5⅜" 145.00
#256, Knitting Lesson, SB, ce, 7½" 630.00
#258, Which Hand?, SB, ce, 5½" 450.00
#261, Angel Duet, 3L, ce, 5" 470.00
#262, Heavenly Lullaby, 3L, ce, 3½x5" 470.00
#266, Globe Trotter, annual plate, 1973, LB, ce, 7½" 145.00
#268, Ride Into Christmas, annual plate, 1975, LB, ce, 7½" 60.00
#278, Chick Girl, annual plate, 1985, MB, ce, 7½" 72.00
#283, Feeding Time, annual plate, 1987, MB, ce, 7½" 250.00
#300, Bird Watcher, SB, early sample, ce, 5" 1,440.00
#301, Christmas Angel, MB, ce, 6" 210.00
#305, The Builder, SB, ce, 5½" 720.00
#308, Little Tailor, 3L, ce, 5½" 720.00
#311, Kiss Me, LB, ce, 6" 250.00
#314, Confidentially, old style, LB, ce, 5½" 575.00
#317, Not for You, SB, ce, 5½" 540.00
#321, Wash Day, SB, ce, 5¾" 540.00
#322, Little Pharmacist, SB, ce, 6" 540.00
#327, The Run-A-Way, 3L, ce, 5¼" 790.00
#330, Baking Day, early sample, FB, ce, 5¼" 2,880.00
#331, Crossroads, 3L, ce, 6¾" 540.00
#334, Homeward Bound, SB, ce, 5¼" 720.00
#337, Cinderella, 3L, ce, 4½" 1,080.00
#342, Mischief Maker, 3L, ce, 5" 540.00
#345, A Fair Measure, 3L, ce, 5½" 720.00
#348, Ring Around the Rosie, SB, ce, 7" 2,880.00
#351, The Botanist, LB, ce, 4" 1,080.00
#353/0, Spring Dance, 3L, ce, 5¼" 1,440.00
#357, Guiding Angel, 3L, ce, 2¾" 125.00
#361, Favorite Pet, SB, ce, 4½" 865.00
#364, Supreme Protection, MB, ce, 9" 360.00
#366, Flying Angel (Nativity set), color, 3L, ce, 3½" 160.00
#369, Follow the Leader, 3L, ce, 7" 1,225.00
#374, Lost Stocking, 3L, ce, 4½" 720.00
#378, Easter Greetings, 3L, ce, 5" 720.00
#382, Visiting an Invalid, NC, oe, 5" 160.00
#386, On Secret Path, 3L, ce, 5¼" 720.00
#389, Girl w/Sheet of Music, 3L, ce, 2½" 125.00
#394, Timid Little Sister, MB, ce, 7" 360.00
#396, Ride Into Christmas, 3L, ce, 5¾" 1,440.00
#399, Valentine Joy, MB, ce, 5¾" 215.00
#406, Pleasant Journey, MB, ce, 7⅛x6½" 1,980.00
#409, Coffee Break, MB, ce, 4" 215.00
#413, Whistler's Duet, MB, ce, 4¼" 360.00
#415, Thoughtful, MB, ce, 4½" 185.00
#418, What's New?, MB, ce, 5¼" 240.00
#420, Is It Raining?, MB, ce, 6" 230.00
#422, What Now?, MB, ce, 5¼" 250.00
#423, Horse Trainer, NC, oe, 4½" 175.00
#429, Hello World, MB, ce, 5½" 250.00
#431, The Suprise, MB, ce 5½" 215.00
#437, Tuba Player, NC, oe, 6¼" 215.00
#440, Birthday Candle, candle holder, MB, ce, 5½" 250.00
#441, Call to Worship, clock, MB, ce, 13" 900.00
#447, Morning Concert, MB, ce, 5¼" 180.00

Hutschenreuther

The Porcelain Factory C.M. Hutschenreuther operated in Bavaria from 1814 to 1969. After the death of the elder Hutschenreuther in 1845, his son Lorenz took over operations, continuing there until 1857 when he left to establish his own company in the nearby city of Selb. The original manufactory became a joint stock company in 1904, absorbing several other potteries. In 1969 both Hutschenreuther firms merged, and that company still operates in Selb. They have distributing centers in both France and the United States.

Candelabrum, dbl; cherub base, rococo, wht, Tutter, 11" 175.00
Figurine, Bremen Town Musicians, 4-animal totem, 7¾" 300.00
Figurine, colt, prancing, H Achtziger, 7½x9" 285.00
Figurine, deer, recumbent, #12, 4" 45.00
Figurine, deer, stag, recumbent, lg 275.00
Figurine, doe, recumbent, sm 95.00
Figurine, hawk landing on log, Achtziger, dtd 1814, 23¼", VG ...365.00
Figurine, lion cub, 8x8½" 230.00
Figurine, Mephistopheles, dressed in red w/blk wrap, 7½" 410.00
Figurine, nude, throwing gold ball, 10" 375.00
Figurine, nude stands on sm gold ball, arms raised, 8½" 290.00
Figurine, nymph w/frolicking goat 325.00
Figurine, Pied Piper, playing flute, 2 mice at ft, 5½x3½" 145.00
Figurine, pointer, gr & brn, Granget, 4½x9¼" 360.00
Figurine, swan landing on water, Achtziger, 8½x12" 545.00
Figurine, Valiant Tailor, Tutter, 6" 200.00

Imari

Imari is a generic term which covers a broad family of wares. It was made in more than a dozen Japanese villages, but the name is that of the port from whence it was shipped to Europe. There are several types of Imari. The most common features a design with panels of birds, florals, or people surrounding a central basket of flowers. The colors used in this type are underglaze blue with overglaze red, gold, and green enamels. The Chinese also made Imari wares which differ from the Japanese type in several ways — the absence of spur marks, a thinner-type body, and a more consistent control of the blue. Imari-type wares were copied on the continent by Meissen and by English potters, among them Worcester, Derby, and Bow. Unless noted otherwise, our values are for Japanese ware.

Bowl, classic palette w/gold, 8-sided, ftd, late 19th C, 4x10" 300.00
Bowl, mc medallion, interlaced phoenixes, late 19th C, 4x9" ...250.00
Bowl, scalloped rim, Meiji (1869-1912), 8¾", EX 180.00

Charger, blue and rust scenic decoration with green and peach accents, blue and white on reverse, ca 1830 – 50, 17½", $495.00.

Charger, deer, mc scenes on gilt, Meiji (1869-1912), rpr, 18" 475.00
Charger, scalloped, late, 12" 225.00
Charger, trees & birds panels, late 19th C, 18" 400.00
Lamp, mc floral w/gold, base vase: 16", 32" overall, late 200.00
Pie plate, 10-sided, 18th C, 1½x9½", VG 225.00
Punch bowl, gold trim, 5x12¼" 1,000.00
Vase, floral panels w/gold, unmk, 19th C, 9" 500.00

Imperial Glass Company

The Imperial Glass Company was organized in 1901 in Bellaire, Ohio, and started manufacturing glassware in 1904. Their early products were jelly glasses, hotel tumblers, etc., but by 1910 they were making a name for themselves by pressing quantities of carnival glass, the iridescent glassware that was popular during that time. In 1914 NuCut was introduced to imitate cut glass. The line was so popular that it was made in crystal and colors and was reintroduced as Collector's Crystal in the 1950s. From 1916 to 1920 they used the lustre process to make a line called Imperial Jewels. Free-Hand ware, art glass made entirely by hand using no molds, was made from 1922 to 1928.

The company entered bankruptcy in 1931 but was able to continue operations and reorganize as the Imperial Glass Corporation. In 1936 Imperial introduced the Candlewick line, for which it is best known. In the late thirties the Vintage Grape milk glass line was added, and in 1951 a major ad campaign was launched, making Imperial one of the leading milk glass manufacturers.

In 1940 Imperial bought the molds and assets of the Central Glass Works of Wheeling, West Virginia; in 1958 they acquired the molds of the Heisey Company; and in 1960 the molds of the Cambridge Glass Company of Cambridge, Ohio. Imperial used these molds, and after 1951 they marked their glassware with an 'I' superimposed over the 'G' trademark. The company was bought by Lenox in 1973; subsequently an 'L' was added to the 'IG' mark. In 1981 Lenox sold Imperial to Arthur Lorch, a private investor (who modified the L by adding a line at the top angled to the left, giving rise to the 'ALIG' mark). He in turn sold the company to Robert F. Stahl, Jr., in 1982. Mr. Stahl filed for Chapter 11 to reorganize, but in mid-1984 liquidation was ordered, and all assets were sold. A few items that had been made in '84 were marked with an 'N' superimposed over the 'I' for 'New Imperial.'

For more information, we recommend *Imperial Glass Encyclopedia, Vols I, II* and *III*, edited by James Measell. Our advisor is Joan Cimini; she is listed in the Directory under Ohio. See also Candlewick; Carnival Glass; Glass Animals and Figurines; Stretch Glass.

Basket, Crocheted Crystal, 6" 27.50
Basket, Crocheted Crystal, 9" 37.50
Basket, Crocheted Crystal, 12" 60.00
Basket, ruby slag, #475, mini 55.00
Basket bowl, Katy, bl opal 225.00
Bottle, cordial; Cape Cod, Ritz Blue, #160/256, 18-oz 250.00
Bowl, berry; Katy, bl opal, flat rim 30.00
Bowl, Cape Cod, crystal, hdls, #160/51F, 6" 33.00
Bowl, cereal; Katy, bl opal, deep 65.00
Bowl, console; Crocheted Crystal, 11" 27.50
Bowl, console; Crocheted Crystal, 12" 30.00
Bowl, Crocheted Crystal, Narcissus, 7" 40.00
Bowl, dessert; Cape Cod, crystal, lug hdl, #160/197, 4½" 40.00
Bowl, Dmn Quilt, blk, crimped, 7" 20.00
Bowl, Grape, caramel slag, #47c, 10" 90.00
Bowl, jelly; Beaded Block, bl opal, hdls 45.00
Bowl, Katy, bl opal, 5⅞" 37.50
Bowl, mayonnaise; Crocheted Crystal, 5¼" 12.50
Bowl, Pillar Flutes, lt bl, 10" 35.00
Bowl, Pipe, ruby slag, #1605, 7½" 40.00
Bowl, punch; Crocheted Crystal, 14" 65.00
Bowl, Rose, jade slag, #52c, 8" 65.00
Bowl, Rose, jade slag, #62c, 9" 75.00
Bowl, salad; Cape Cod, crystal, #7608A, 11" 90.00
Bowl, salad; Crocheted Crystal, 10½" 27.50
Bowl, soup; Katy, gr opal, 7" 80.00
Bowl, vegetable; Katy, bl opal, 9" 95.00
Buffet set, Crocheted Crystal, 14" ftd plate, sauce bowl, ladle 45.00
Cake stand, Crocheted Crystal, ftd, 12" 40.00
Candle holder, Cape Cod, crystal, #160/170, 3" 26.50
Candle holder, Crocheted Crystal, dbl, 4½" 17.50
Candle holder, Crocheted Crystal, Narcissus bowl shape 25.00
Candlestick, Free-Hand, heart/vine, wht on clear, bl cup, 10" ...400.00
Candlesticks, Dolphin, caramel slag, 3779, 5", pr 65.00
Candlesticks, Free-Hand, clear w/red knops & threads, 11", pr .1,400.00
Celery, Crocheted Crystal, oval, 10" 25.00
Champagne, Cape Cod, amber, #1602 .....25.00
Cheese & cracker, Crocheted Crystal, 12" plate, ftd dish 38.00
Claret, Cape Cod, Azalea, #1602 .....20.00
Cocktail, Cape Cod, crystal, #160b 12.00
Cocktail, Cape Cod, ruby, #160 .....27.00
Comport, Cape Cod, crystal, #160F, 5¼" 27.50
Comport, Katy, milk glass, 4¾" 45.00
Cordial, Collector's Crystal, crystal, #612 .....14.00
Cordial, Fancy Colonial, pk, #582, 1-oz 50.00
Creamer, Cape Cod, crystal, #160/30 .....12.00
Creamer, Crocheted Crystal, ftd 18.00
Cruet, Collector's Crystal, caramel slag, #505 .....50.00
Cruet, Octagon, jade, w/stopper, #505 .....80.00
Cup, Katy, bl opal 35.00
Cup, punch; Crocheted Crystal, closed hdl 5.00
Cup, punch; Crocheted Crystal, open hdl 7.00
Cup & saucer, Pillar Flutes, lt bl 25.00
Decanter, bourbon; Cape Cod, crystal, #160/260 .....80.00
Decanter, Cask #1, Antique Blue 55.00
Decanter, Grape, Heather, #8 .....55.00
Epergne, Crocheted Crystal, ftd bowl, center vase, 11" 130.00
Goblet, Cape Cod, Evergreen, #160, 14-oz 55.00

Goblet, Chroma, amber (Maderia), #123 ....24.00
Gravy bowl, Cape Cod, crystal, #160/202, 18-oz 70.00
Hors d'oeuvre dish, Crocheted Crystal, rnd, 4-part, 10½" 30.00
Ivy ball, Reeded (Spun), red, crystal ft, 4" 65.00
Jar, vanity; Reeded (Spun), aquamarine, #701, 7⅝" 40.00
Ladle, mayonnaise; Crocheted Crystal 5.00
Ladle, punch; Cape Cod, crystal 30.00
Lamp, hurricane; Crocheted Crystal, w/shade, 11" 45.00
Mayonnaise, Katy, bl opal, w/underplate 120.00
Mayonnaise, Katy, gr opal, 3-pc 135.00
Mint dish, Cape Cod, crystal, heart shape, #160/49, 5" 25.00
Nappy, Pansy, caramel slag, hdl, 5" 40.00
Pitcher, Cape Cod, crystal, #160/24, 2-qt 125.00
Pitcher, Dew Drop, opal, #624, 56-oz 65.00
Pitcher, Windmill, red slag, satin 55.00
Plate, cheese & cracker; crystal, ftd, 12" 35.00
Plate, Crocheted Crystal, 9½" 12.50
Plate, Crocheted Crystal, 14" 25.00
Plate, Crocheted Crystal, 17" 40.00
Plate, dinner; Cape Cod, crystal, #160/10D, 10" 37.50
Plate, Katy, bl opal, 6" 20.00
Plate, mayonnaise; Crocheted Crystal, 7½" 7.50
Plate, salad bowl liner; Crocheted Crystal, 13" 22.50
Plate, salad; Crocheted Crystal, 8" 7.50
Plate, salad; Katy, bl opal, 8" 32.00
Platter, Katy, gr opal, 13" 175.00
Punch bowl, Crocheted Crystal, 14" 65.00
Punch cup, Crocheted Crystal, closed hdl 5.00
Relish, Cape Cod, crystal, 5-part, #160/102, 11" 75.00
Relish, Crocheted Crystal, 3-part, 11½" 25.00
Rose bowl, Frosted Block, wht carnival 150.00
Rose bowl, Wide Panel, marigold on milk glass 210.00
Shakers, Cape Cod, crystal, #160/109, pr 20.00
Shakers, Cape Cod, Fern Green, #160/117, pr 60.00
Sherbet, Cane #666 ½ (Huckabee), pk, ftd 25.00
Stem, cocktail; Crocheted Crystal, 3½-oz, 4½" 12.50
Stem, cordial; Cape Cod, crystal, #1502, 1½-oz 10.00
Stem, sherbet; Crocheted Crystal, 6-oz, 5" 10.00
Stem, water goblet; Crocheted Crystal, 9-oz, 7⅛" 14.00
Stem, wine; Crocheted Crystal, 4½-oz, 5½" 17.50
Sugar bowl, Crocheted Crystal, ftd 18.00
Sugar bowl, Katy, bl opal 42.50
Toothpick holder, Octagon, caramel slag, #505 ....18.00
Tumbler, fruit juice; Crocheted Crystal, ftd, 6-oz, 6" 10.00
Tumbler, iced tea; ftd, 12-oz, 7⅛" 15.00
Tumbler, Katy, gr opal, 9-oz 55.00
Tumbler, whiskey; Cape Cod, crystal, #160, 2½-oz 12.50
Vase, bud; Free-Hand, hearts/vines, lt gr on opal, 8½" 350.00
Vase, bud; peach & butterscotch w/mirror finish, 10" 225.00
Vase, Cape Cod, crystal, urn form w/hdls, #160/186, 10½" 165.00
Vase, Crocheted Crystal, 8" 20.00
Vase, Free-Hand, cobalt, wht int, bulbous w/trumpet neck, 9½" ..675.00
Vase, Free-Hand, drapes, bl on marigold, 8½" 250.00
Vase, Free-Hand, feathers, bl & gr irid on blk amethyst, 6½" 225.00
Vase, Free-Hand, hearts/vines, bl on marigold irid, ruffled rim, 5x7" .700.00
Vase, Free-Hand, hearts/vines, bl on opal irid, marigold int, 11½" .1,450.00
Vase, Free-Hand, hearts/vines, gr on opal, orange int, cylinder, 9" 550.00
Vase, Free-Hand, hearts/vines, infused opal on cobalt, 10¾" ..1,450.00
Vase, Free-Hand, hearts/vines, lt gr on opal irid, marigold int, 11" ..1,200.00
Vase, Free-Hand, jade gr on opal w/orange lustre lip, beaker form, 8" .425.00
Vase, Free-Hand, marigold irid, tapered w/flared rim, 6½" 175.00
Vase, Free-Hand, orange w/deep orange throat, slender 10" 450.00
Vase, Free-Hand, peacock bl w/folded & stretched top border, 10½" ..450.00
Vase, Free-Hand, swags, bl on opal, orange int, shouldered, 7½" ...550.00
Vase, Katy, bl opal, #743n, 5½" 60.00
Vase, Katy, bl opal, #743x, 4½" 45.00
Vase, Katy, red, #743b, 5¼" 65.00
Vase, Mosaic, cobalt shaded & swirled w/opal, orange int, 6½" ..490.00
Vase, Reeded, cobalt, squat, 5¾" 65.00
Vase, Reeded (Spun), red, 9" 75.00

Imperial Porcelain

The Blue Ridge Mountain Boys were created by cartoonist Paul Webb and translated into three-dimension by the Imperial Porcelain Corporation of Zanesville, Ohio, in 1947. These figurines decorated ashtrays, vases, mugs, bowls, pitchers, planters, and other items. The Mountain Boys series were numbered 92 through 108, each with a different and amusing portrayal of mountain life. Imperial also produced American Folklore miniatures, twenty-three tiny animals one inch or less in size, and the Al Capp Dogpatch series. Because of financial difficulties, the company closed in 1960.

American Folklore Miniatures

Cat, 1½" 50.00
Cow, 1¾" 45.00
Hound dogs 60.00
Plaque, store ad, Am Folklore Porcelain Miniatures, 4½" 450.00
Sow 45.00

Blue Ridge Mountain Boys by Paul Webb

Ashtray, #92, 2 men by tree stump, for pipes 125.00
Ashtray, #101, man w/jug & snake 120.00
Ashtray, #103, hillbilly & skunk 120.00
Ashtray, #105, baby, hound dog, & frog 135.00
Ashtray, #106, Barrel of Wishes, w/hound 115.00
Box, cigarette; #98, dog atop, baby at door, sq 165.00
Dealer's sign, Handcrafted Paul Webb Mtn Boys, rare, 9" 700.00
Decanter, #100, outhouse, man, & bird 125.00
Decanter, #104, Ma leaning over stump, w/baby & skunk 145.00
Decanter, man, jug, snake, & tree stump, Hispch Inc, 1946 ....125.00
Figurine, #101, man leans against tree trunk, 5" 125.00
Figurine, man on hands & knees, 3" 130.00
Figurine, man sitting, 3½" 145.00

Figurine, man sitting with chicken on knee, 3", $130.00.

Jug, #101, Willie & snake 95.00
Mug, #94, Bearing Down, 6" 95.00
Mug, #94, dbl baby hdl, 4¼" 95.00
Mug, #94, ma hdl, 4¼" 95.00
Mug, #94, man w/bl pants hdl, 4¼" 95.00
Mug, #94, man w/yel beard & red pants hdl, 4¼" 95.00
Mug, #99, Target Practice, boy on goat, farmer, 5¾" 95.00
Pitcher, lemonade 200.00

Planter, #81, man drinking from jug, sitting by washtub 95.00
Planter, #100, outhouse, man, & bird 125.00
Planter, #105, man w/chicken on knee, washtub 130.00
Planter, #110, man, w/jug & snake, 4½" 95.00
Shakers, Ma & Old Doc, pr 115.00

Miscellaneous

Items in this section that are designated 'IP' are miscellaneous novelties made by Imperial Porcelain; the remainder are of interest to Paul Webb collectors, though made by an unknown manufacturer. Prints on calendars and playing cards are signed 'Paul Webb.'

Artist board, babies or mtn women, sgn Paul Webb, 30x30" 275.00
Artist board, mtn boys only, sgn Paul Webb, 30x30" 275.00
Calendar, 1954, 12 sgn scenes, Brown & Bigelow, complete 65.00
Figurine, cat in high-heeled shoe, 5½" L 65.00
Hot pad, Dutch boy w/tulips, rnd, IP 30.00
Ink blotters, sgn scenes, ea 15.00
Mug, #29, man hdl, sgn Paul Webb, 4¾" 50.00
Planter, #106, dog sitting by tub, IP 95.00
Playing cards, ad: Rafe Oiling Gun, Brown & Bigelow, MIB 75.00
Shakers, pigs, 5", pr 95.00
Shakers, standing pigs, IP, 8", pr 110.00

Indian Tree

Indian Tree is a popular dinnerware pattern produced by various potteries since the early 1800s to recent times. Although backgrounds and borders vary, the Oriental theme is carried out with the gnarled, brown branch of a pink-blossomed tree. Among the manufacturers' marks, you may find represented such notable firms as Coalport, S. Hancock and Sons, Soho Pottery, and John Maddock and Sons. See also Johnson Brothers.

Bonbon, fluted, Coalport, 6¼" 20.00
Bowl, rim soup; Maddock, 9" 22.00
Bowl, vegetable; oval, Maddock, 9" 25.00
Candy dish, scalloped edge, gr mk, 5¼" L 20.00
Creamer, Johnson Bros 17.00
Cup & saucer, Coalport 20.00
Cup & saucer, Maddock 12.50
Cup & saucer, yel & gold band, Grosvenor Bone 20.00
Gravy boat, Maddock 32.00
Gravy tureen, English, w/lid & ladle 85.00
Pitcher, Coalport, 4¾" 65.00
Plate, cookie; Coalport, 10½" 55.00

Plate, Myott, 9", $9.00.

Plate, dessert; ruffled rim, 8" 30.00
Plate, fluted, Coalport, 5½" 20.00
Plate, Maddock, 8" 8.00
Plate, Staffordshire, 9" 12.00
Platter, Coalport, 18½" 470.00
Platter, Johnson Bros, 12¼" 45.00
Platter, Spode, 15" 165.00
Sugar bowl, Coalport, w/lid, 5¾x4½" 70.00
Sugar bowl, Johnson Bros, w/lid 35.00
Tray, mc w/gold accents, Coalport, 10¾x8½" 85.00
Tray, serving; fluted, w/hdls, 10½", EX 48.00

Inkwells and Inkstands

Receptacles for various writing fluids have been used since ancient times. Through the years they have been made from countless materials — glass, metal, porcelain, pottery, wood, and even papier-mache. During the eighteenth century, gold or silver inkstands were presented to royalty; the well-known silver inkstand by Philip Syng, Jr., was used for the signing of the Declaration of Independence, and impressive brass inkstands with wells and pounce pots (sanders) were proud possessions of men of letters. When literacy vastly increased in the nineteenth century, the dip pen replaced the quill pen, and inkwells and inkstands were widely used and produced in a broad range of sizes in functional and decorative forms from ornate Victorian to flowing Art Nouveau and stylized Art Deco designs. However, the acceptance of the ballpoint pen literally put inkstands and inkwells 'out of business.' But their historical significance and intriguing diversity of form and styling fascinate today's collectors.

For further information we recommend *Collector's Encyclopedia to Inkwells, Books I* and *II*, by Veldon Badders (Collector Books). See also Bottles, Ink.

Abalone, MOP lid, Niagara Falls, 1900-10, 4x5" 90.00
Bakelite, brn cash register, Art Deco style, Am, 1930 ....90.00
Brass, concave, hinged cover, early 1900s, 2½x5" dia 70.00
Brass, cup & saucer w/lid, 1900-10, 2⅝x5" dia 175.00
Brass, Greek Key design, mk Silver Crest..., 1905-10, 3" dia 125.00
Brass, rnd w/concave sides, ornate bands, ca 1910, 2x3" dia 100.00
Brass, urn shape w/garlands/bell flowers, mk Benedict..., 1915-20 ..125.00
Bronze, rooster w/red fabric comb, glass eyes, 1890, 3¾" 200.00
Bronzed CI, Gothic style, mk Bradley & Hubbard, 1880-90 ......400.00
Ceramic, Snoopy figure, 1958-66, 4¼x2½" 45.00
Ceramic, world globe on tiered base, Japan, early 1900s, 3x3⅞" ..125.00
CI, cabinet shape w/triple rest, hinged doors, Am, 1880-90, 3" .350.00
CI, Persian-style base w/sq glass well, mk PRR, 4½" sq base 90.00
Glass, armchair shape w/Daisy & Button design, 1890, 4x½x2½" ..145.00
Glass, bl lighthouse w/brass collar, ball finial, Am, 1890-1900, 4" ..450.00
Glass, bulbous, mushroom-shaped lid, 1910, 4x3" 165.00
Glass, cobalt w/hinged brass lid, 1880-90, 3x3" 150.00
Glass, cylindrical w/swirl design, 1890-1900, 1⅞x2" dia 80.00
Glass, dome shape w/hinged NP cap, ca 1930, 3x3½" dia 85.00
Glass, encased in lead filigree, dome lid, ca 1900, 3x2" sq 100.00
Glass, opaque jade gr, hinged brass lid, 1900-10, 4x3½" dia 600.00
Glass, ruby w/beaded quilt design, rubber funnel top, 1890-1900, 2" ...400.00
Glass, vertical lobed design w/hinged brass cover, ca 1890, 3½" ...125.00
Pnt metal, camel figural, Austria, 6x10" 220.00
Porc, off-wht w/bird & fruit transfer, 6-sided, mk Limoges, 3x2" ..100.00
Porc, rabbit's head cover, orange w/blk trim, German, early 1900s, 5" ..350.00
Porc, Rococo style scrollwork, loose covers, European, 1890-1900 ......150.00
Porc, wht w/floral transfer, dome lid w/finial, 1930, 6x2½" 100.00
Porc, wht w/floral transfer, mk RS Germany, Am, 1900, 5" W 85.00
Porc, wht w/HP gold decor, 6-sided, mk T&V Limoges, ca 1900, 3" .125.00
Soapstone, open type, hand-cvd trees, European, 1900, 2x3" 100.00
Sterling silver, tortoise-shell lid, ca 1900, 2x3¼" dia 350.00
Stoneware, tapered body w/bl HP bands, cork closure, Am, mid-1900s ..100.00

Wood, hand-cvd boat w/glass font, mk Geneve, 1890-1900, 7" L 85.00
Wood, owl on tree stump, glass eyes, 1890-1900, 4½" 175.00

Insulators

The telegraph was invented in 1844. The devices developed to hold the electrical transmission wires to the poles were called insulators. The telephone, invented in 1876, intensified their usefulness; and by the turn of the century, thousands of varieties were being produced in pottery, wood, and glass of various colors. Even though it has been rumored that red glass insulators exist, none have ever been authenticated. There are amber-colored insulators that appear to have a red tint to the amber, and those are called red-amber. Many insulators are embossed with patent dates.

Of the more than 3,000 types known to exist, today's collectors evaluate their worth by age, rarity of color and, of course, condition. Aqua and green are the most common colors in glass, dark brown the most common in porcelain. Threadless insulators (for example, CD #701.1), made between 1850 and 1865, bring prices well into the hundreds, sometimes even the thousands, if in mint condition.

In the listings that follow, the CD numbers are from an identification system developed in the late 1960s by N.R. Woodward.

Those seeking additional information about insulators are encouraged to contact Line Jewels NIA #1380 (whose address may be found in the Directory under Clubs, Newsletters, and Catalogs) or attend a club-endorsed show. (For information see Directory under Florida for Jacqueline Linscott.) In the listings that follow those stating 'no name' have no company identification, but do have embossed numbers, dots, etc. Those stating 'no embossing' are without raised letters, dots, or any other markings.

Key:
* (asterisk) — Canadian
BE — base embossed
CB — corrugated base
CD — Consolidated Design
FDP — flat drip points
RB — rough base
RDP — round drip points
SB — smooth base
SDP — sharp drip points

Threaded Pin-type and Threadless Glass Insulators

CD 105, AM INS CO/PAT SEP 13 1881, BE, aqua 100.00
CD 106, WGM Co, SB, purple 40.00
CD 107, CRISA, SB, purple 40.00
CD 108, dmn-shape mk, RDP, straw 75.00
CD 112, B, SB, lt aqua 5.00
CD 114, Hemingray/No 11, SDP, aqua 10.00
CD 115, Whitall Tatum/No 3, SB, lt peach 5.00
CD 116.5, B, SB, lt aqua 100.00
CD 117, no name, SB, aqua 40.00
CD 120, no emb, SB, teal bl 2,000.00
CD 125, Hemingray-15, RDP, Hemingray Blue 15.00
CD 127, H Brooke's Pat Jan 25th 1870, BE, lt aqua 100.00
CD 128, Hemingray, SB, off-clear 2.00
CD 128, Hemingray E-14-B, SB, opal 150.00
CD 129, Armstrong TS, SB, gr tint 5.00
CD 130.2, Seilers Patent/Feb 6-1877, SB lt gr 10,000.00
CD 131.4, LGT & Co, SB, aqua 125.00
CD 133, BGMC, SB, lt purple 125.00
CD 133, City Fire Alarm, SB, lt aqua 100.00
CD 134, AM Ins Co/Pat Sep 13 1881, BE, lt gr 40.00
CD 134, BGM Co, SB, purple 175.00
CD 134, Fall River, SB, aqua 100.00
CD 134, THE Co, SB, aqua 30.00
CD 135, Chicago Insulating Co/Pat Oct 16 1883, BE, bl 100.00
CD 140, Jumbo, SB, dk aqua 500.00
CD 143, Canadian, RB, lt gr-aqua 5.00
CD 143, Dwight, SB, aqua 5.00
CD 143.5, THE Co, SB, lt gr 60.00
CD 145, EDR, SB, lt bl 20.00
CD 145, KCGW, SB, lt yel-gr 50.00
CD 147, Hemingray Pat Oct 8 1907, SB, aqua 1.00
CD 151, HGCO, SM, ice bl 15.00
CD 153, Gayner, RDP, aqua 15.00
CD 154, Hemingray-42, SB, Hemingray Blue 20.00
CD 154, McLaughlin, RDP, lt gr 2.00
CD 160, California, SB, lt purple 15.00
CD 161, California, SB, sage gr 5.00
CD 162, BGM Co, SB, lt purple 250.00
CD 162, Hemingray-19, SDP, olive-amber 250.00
CD 162, Maydwell-19, RDP, straw 2.00
CD 162, NEGM Co, SB, sapphire bl 250.00
CD 162, THE, SB, bl 10.00
CD 162, Whitall Tatum Co No 4, SB , lt straw 5.00
CD 162.5, PLW, SB, gr 40.00
CD 169.5, Brookfield, SB, gr 30.00
CD 175, Hemingray-25, SB, clear 30.00
CD 183, Hemingray-71, CB, clear 10.00
CD 205, Brookfield, SB, yel-gr 75.00
CD 205, Lynchburg, SB, lt aqua 15.00
CD 208, Brookfield, SM, aqua 30.00
CD 210, Postal, SB, emerald gr 10.00
CD 213, Hemingray-43, RDP, bl 15.00
CD 214, Telegrafos, RDP, dk orange-amber 100.00
CD 232, Hemingray-513, CB, clear 5.00
CD 235, Pyrex-662, SB, carnival 30.00
CD 240, Pyrex-131, SB, clear 15.00
CD 250.2, Telefonos Ericsson-LD-1, SB, celery gr 40.00
CD 251, NEGM Co, SB, ice bl 30.00
CD 252, Gayner, SDP, aqua 50.00
CD 252, Knowles Cable/Insulator, SB, aqua 50.00
CD 252, No 2 Cable, SB, aqua 10.00
CD 253, Knowles Cable/Insulator, SB, milky aqua 300.00
CD 254, No 3 Cable, SB, lt bl-aqua 75.00
CD 256, Manhattan, SB, aqua 35.00

CD 257, Hemingray/No 60-A, SDP, Hemingray Blue, $30.00. (Photo courtesy Jacqueline Linscott)

CD 258, Cable, SDP, dk aqua 200.00
CD 260, Cable, SB, gr 400.00
CD 262, No 2 Columbia, SB, aqua 150.00
CD 263, Columbia, SB, aqua 250.00
CD 263, Pat'd May 12 1891/Columbia, SB, dk aqua 150.00
CD 264, Columbia, SB, lt bl 500.00
CD 266, Patented June 17 1890, SB, dk aqua 1,250.00
CD 267, NEGM, SB, yel-gr 220.00
CD 267, No 4 Cable, SB, emerald gr 600.00
CD 268.5, Standard Glass Insulator Co, BE, aqua 4,000.00
CD 269, Jumbo, SB, dk aqua 500.00

CD 270, no emb, SB, aqua 400.00
CD 272, Whitall Tatum Co No 511-A, SB, root beer amber 10.00
CD 300, Brookfield, SB, dk aqua 50.00
CD 322, Corning Pyrex TM Reg US..., SB, carnival 125.00
CD 325, Pyrex 401, SB, clear 15.00
CD 326, Pyrex TM Reg US Pat Off Made in USA, SB, clear 25.00
CD 724, Chester NY, BE, dk cobalt 5,000.00
CD 728, no emb, SB, lt bl 125.00
CD 728.8, Boston Bottle Works-Oakman's..., BE, lt aqua 4,500.00
CD 729.4, Mulford & Biddle..., SB, emerald gr 3,500.00
CD 742.3, MTCo, BE, teal bl 600.00
CD 1030, no emb, lag screw in base 250.00
CD 1071, Hemingray-110, SB, clear 10.00
CD 1090, B, SB, gr 40.00

Irons

History, geography, art, and cultural diversity are all represented in the collecting of antique pressing irons. The progress of fashion and invention can be traced through the evolution of the pressing iron.

Over seven hundred years ago, implements constructed of stone, bone, wood, glass, and wrought iron were used for pressing fabrics. Early ironing devices were quite primitive in form, and heating techniques included inserting a hot metal slug into a cavity of the iron, adding hot burning coals into a chamber or pan, and placing the iron directly on hot coals or a hot surface.

To the pleasure of today's collectors, some of these early irons, mainly from the period of 1700 to 1850, were decorated by artisans who carved and painted them with regional motifs typical of their natural surroundings and spiritual cultures.

Beginning in the mid-1800s, new cultural demands for fancy wearing apparel initiated a revolution in technology for types of irons and methods to heat them. Typical of this period is the fluter which was essential for producing the ruffles demanded by the nineteenth-century ladies. Hat irons, polishers, and numerous unusual iron forms were also used during this time, and provided a means to produce crimps, curves, curls, and special fabric textures. Irons from this era are characterized by their unique shapes, odd handles, latches, decorations, and even revolving mechanisms.

Also during this time, irons began to be heated by burning liquid and gaseous fuels. Gradually the new technology of the electrically heated iron replaced all other heating methods, except in the more rural areas and undeveloped countries. Even today the Amish communities utilize gasoline fuel irons.

In the listings that follow, prices are given for examples in best possible as-found condition. Damage, repairs, plating, excessive wear, rust, and missing parts can dramatically reduce value. For further information we recommend *Irons by Irons*, *More Irons by Irons*, and *Even More Irons by Irons* by our advisor Dave Irons; his address and information for ordering these books are given in the Directory under Pennsylvania.

Alcohol, revolving, Pat May 4 1875, Crocker & Farnsworth, 7¼" ..650.00
Box, Bless-Drake Salamander, top lifts off, 1890s, 6", from $200 to .300.00
Box, Dutch, brass, openwork at top, 1850s, 8½", from $200 to .300.00
Box, English, #10, brass, lift-up gate, late 1800s, 7¾", $150 to ..200.00
Box, European, CI, dolphin posts, ca 1900, 6⅜", from $100 to ...150.00
Box, Fr, pieced construction, hinged gate, 1700s, 6½", $200 to .300.00
Box, Indian, brass, vents, front latch, bk hinge, 1880s, 8", $100 to ..150.00
Combination, Patented, fluter clamps on sad iron, fluter base, 1890s .400.00
Combination, Pat'd Aug 2 70, Knapp, front latch, 6⅝", $100 to .150.00
Drop-in-bk, European, brass w/eng, mid-1800s, 6⅜", from $300 to ..500.00
Edge/seam, European, narrow base, late 1800s, 5½", from $100 to ...150.00
Egg, Electrical Puff Iron...Calif, Pat 1933, 11", from $150 to 250.00
Electric, Hot Point Edison..., rear rehostat control, 1900s, 10½" .40.00
Flat, cold hdl, coiled hdl, 6⅛", from $200 to 300.00
Flat, cold hdl, Rochester Sad Iron, late 1800s, 6⅝", from $70 to ..100.00
Flat, Loring Patent 1880 #10, CI, 7", from $70 to 100.00
Flat, Russian, H3, Xd hammers, late 1800s, 6½", from $200 to .300.00
Flower, J Alente NY, brass & iron, late 1800s, 9½", from $100 to ..150.00

Fluter rockers, The Lady Friend, 1875, 6"; The Star, ca 1875, 5½"; The (star), ca 1875, 5½", from $150.00 to $250.00 each. (Photo courtesy Dave Irons)

Fluter, rocker, Pat App'd For, brass plates, ca 1875, 5⅜", $200 to ...300.00
Fluter, roller, Am Machine..., hinged plate, yel stripes, '00s, $50 to 70.00
Gas jet, WF Shaw's...Sept 1 1857, holes in top, 6¼", from $150 to .200.00
Gasoline, Comfort...Self Heating, early 1900s, 7", from $70 to .100.00
Glove form, steam-heat press, CI, late 1800s, 15½", from $150 to .200.00
Goffering, English, brass Queen Anne style, late 1800s, 5", $300 to ..500.00
Goffering, European, wrought iron, 4-ftd, 1800s, 5½", minimum ..750.00
Hat, shackle, CI, flat bottom, late 1800s, 5⅛", from $100 to 150.00
Hat, tolliker, solid cast, wood hdl, curved side, late 1800s, 4" 125.00
Little, charcoal, European, jockey head on latch, late 1800s, 5¼" .250.00
Little, hollow grip, Dog Toy, late 1800s, 3¾", from $100 to 150.00
Little, ox tongue, European, brass, w/trivet, 1850s, 4⅞", $200 to .300.00
Little, rnd bk, European, ca 1900, 2⅞", from $400 to 600.00
Little, swan, CI, red w/blk pinstriping, late 1800s, 1⅞", $200 to ..300.00
Little, wrought iron, 1820 (rare date), 3¼", from $150 to 200.00
Machine, Dudley Fluter Patd...1876, red stripes/decals, from $300 to .500.00
Machine, English, fine flutes, gr pnt base, late 1800s, 5", $200 to 300.00
Meta fuel, British Boudoir Iron, ca 1900, 5¼", from $70 to 100.00
Mushroom, European, mid-1800s, 10", from $70 to 100.00
Natural gas, Swing Pat Dec 4 1900, blk enamel, 6½", from $100 to ...150.00
Ox tongue, European, #2, brass, lift-up gate, 1850s, 5½", $200 to 300.00
Ox tongue, European, acorns at hinge/hdl, early 1800s, 8½", $300 to ..500.00
Polisher, English, smooth bottom, late 1800s, 3⅝", from $70 to ...100.00
Polisher, G, dmn grid bottom, late 1800s, 4⅝", from $50 to 70.00
Polisher, GS&Co...8, rnd edges, late 1800s, 5½", from $100 to .150.00
Seam, Lightning...Pat Feb 9 '92...USA, 7", from $200 to 300.00
Sleeve, Pat'd June 15 1897, long flat toe, 9⅞", from $250 to 350.00
Sleeve, Sensible No 1, dtd 1887 on hdl, 6⅞", from $30 to 50.00
Sleeve, Sherman's Improved, mid-1800s, 6⅛", from $100 to 150.00
Slug, European, brass, mid-1800s, 4⅛", from $200 to 300.00
Slug, ox tongue, European, brass, dolphin post, late 1800s, 7¾" ..650.00
Smoother/fluter, NR Streeter, hdl removes, front hinge, 1890s, 6⅞" ...250.00
Steam, Keonig All Steam...1924, thumb valve, 11¾", from $70 to 100.00
Tailor, CI, late 1800s, 9¾", from $50 to 70.00
Tailor, Ober...#20, CI, late 1800s, 9¾", from $100 to 150.00
Tall chimney, charcoal, European, top lifts, 1880s, 6⅜", $150 to ...200.00

Ironstone

During the last quarter of the eighteenth century, English potters began experimenting with a new type of body that contained calcinated flint and a higher china clay content, intent on producing a fine durable whiteware — heavy, yet with a texture that would resemble porcelain. To remove the last trace of yellow, a minute amount of cobalt was added, often resulting in a bluish-white tone. Wm and John Turner of Caughley and Josiah Spode II were the first to manufacture the ware successfully. Others, such as Davenport, Hicks and Meigh, and Ralph and Josiah Wedgwood, followed with their own versions. The latter coined the name 'Pearl' to refer to his product and incorporated the term into his trademark. In 1813 a fourteen-year patent was issued to Charles James Mason, who called his ware Patented Ironstone. Francis Morley, G.L. Asworth, T.J. Mayer, and other Staffordshire potters continued to produce ironstone until the end of the century. While some of these patterns are simple to the extreme, many are decorated with in-mold designs of fruit, grain, and foliage on ribbed or scalloped shapes. In the 1830s transfer-printed designs in blue, mulberry, pink, green, and black became popular; and polychrome versions of Oriental wares were manufactured to compete with the Chinese trade. See also Mason's Ironstone. Our advise for this category comes from Home Place Antiques, whose address is listed in the Directory under Illinois.

Bowl, cereal; White Empress, Wm Adams 12.50
Bowl, soup; plain, J&G Meakins, mk #69, 1½x9" 20.00
Bowl, vegetable; Scalloped Decagon, J Wedgwood, mk 1852, 11" W .150.00
Bowl, vegetable; Sevres, Dean & Stokes, w/lid 110.00
Bowl, vegetable; Wheat & Clover, Turner & Tomkinson, w/lid, 10" W ...210.00
Butter dish, Wheat & Berry, J&C Meakin, w/lid, 5x6¼" dia 75.00
Creamer, Ceres (Wheat), Turner Goddard, 6" 155.00
Creamer, Wheat & Hops, Thos Hughes, 5½" 110.00
Cup & saucer, Wheat & Clover, Turner & Tomkinson 80.00
Ewer, Memmon, J Meir & Sons, mk Feb 4 1857, 12" 185.00
Gravy boat, Ceres (Wheat), Baker & Co, 4¾x9" 50.00
Mug, Ceres (Wheat), 3⅞x4¼" 65.00
Pitcher, Bow & Tassle, Burgess & Goddard, ca 1870, 7" 85.00
Pitcher, Ceres (Wheat), w/melon ribs, Mellor, Taylor & Co, 6" ..80.00
Pitcher, Maple Leaf, J&G Meakin, #33, 8" 55.00
Pitcher, Queens Ware, Meakin, 8" 65.00
Pitcher, Senate, T&R Boote, 7" 65.00
Pitcher, Sydenham, T&R Boote, 12½" 70.00
Pitcher, Wheat (Ceres), Royal Staffordshire, 6" 70.00
Plate, Laurel Wreath, Elsmore & Forster, 8¾" 35.00

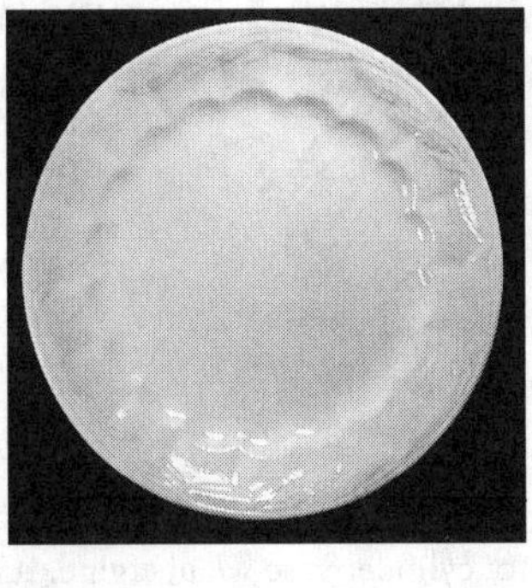

Plate, Wheat, W&E Corn, 9¾", $35.00.

Plate, Wheat & Clover, Turner & Tomkinson, 8¾" 35.00
Plate, Wheat & Flower, Bishop & Stonier, 7¼" 25.00
Plate, Wheat & Husks on Ceres shape, Elsmore & Forster, 8" 45.00
Platter, Curved Gothic, J Edwards, 1840s, 14¾x11¾" 130.00
Platter, Holly Berries, J&G Meakin, 15½x10½" 85.00
Platter, Sydenham, T&R Boote, 8-sided, 16x12½" 110.00
Platter, Wheat & Clover, Turner & Tomkinson, 13¾" 95.00
Relish dish, shell shape, Powell & Bishop, ca 1875 ....90.00
Soap dish, flower finial, w/lid, 3x8" 125.00
Sugar bowl, Ceres (Wheat), Royal Crownford, w/lid, 6" 95.00
Sugar bowl, Ceres (Wheat), Turner & Goddard, w/lid, 8¼" 125.00
Tea set, J&G Meakon, 1850s, child sz, 21-pc 230.00
Teapot, Sydenham, T&R Boote, 9¾" 210.00
Tureen, Fig, Wedgwood, w/lid, 8x13½x9¼" 190.00
Tureen, sauce; Bluet, Hope & Carter, +lid/underplate 90.00
Tureen, soup; Gothic Cameo, James Edwards, ca 1840-50, w/lid, 11" .185.00
Tureen, soup; Hunt Club, TG Green, w/lid 185.00
Tureen, soup; Wheat & Hops, J&G Meakin, w/lid, 6x11" 145.00

Patterned Ironstone

Bowl, punch; red-brn floral transfer, 12¾", EX 475.00
Bowl, vegetable; No 21, purple transfer, 2x9⅜x6⅝" 45.00
Coffeepot, brn floral transfer w/mc, octagonal, 9", EX 210.00
Coffeepot, Cleopatra, bl transfer, 9¼" 195.00
Coffeepot, Cleopatra, bl transfer w/mc accents, octagonal, 9" ...275.00
Cup & saucer, Paradise, purple transfer, Livesley Powell 85.00
Cup plate, Gipsy, bl transfer, 4" 35.00
Pitcher, Eon, red transfer w/mc accents, octagonal, mk, 8¼", EX ..160.00
Plate, Aurora, red transfer w/mc, 16-sided, Morley, 9" 35.00
Plate, Bologna, pk transfer, Adams, 11¾" 90.00
Plate, Cascade, brn transfer, JH Davis, 7¾" 25.00
Plate, Daffodil, brn transfer, WH Grindley & Co, 8" 28.00
Plate, Fern, dk bl transfer, England, 10½" 50.00
Plate, Formosa, blk transfer w/mc accents, Furnival & Sons, 8⅛" ..45.00
Plate, Garfield, brn transfer, LS&S, 8¾" 20.00
Plate, Paradise, purple transfer, Livesley Powell, 8⅝" 100.00
Plate, Spanish Festivities 1798, dk bl transfer, G Jones, 9¼" 65.00
Plate, Summertime, brn transfer, T&R Boote, 7⅞" 25.00
Plate, Tyrol, red transfer, Wedgwood, 12-sided, 10⅜" 35.00
Platter, Gipsy, bl transfer, 15x11¾" 80.00
Platter, Princess Feather, purple transfer, 15¼x11¼", NM 80.00
Platter, Turkey, charcoal gray transfer w/mc accents, 18¾x14¼" ...225.00
Platter, Zamara, gr transfer w/mc accents, 15x11¾", NM 125.00
Soup plate, Aurora, gr transfer w/mc, Morley, 10½" 45.00
Sugar bowl, Cleopatra, bl transfer, w/lid, 7¼" 75.00
Teapot, Hybla, gr transfer, Brougham & Mayer, 8⅞", EX 135.00
Teapot, Washington Vase, brn transfer, Podmore & Walker, 9", EX ...125.00
Waste bowl, Cleopatra, bl transfer, paneled sides, 4x5⅞" 65.00

Italian Glass

Throughout the twentieth century, one of the major glassmaking centers of the world was the island of Murano. From the Stile Liberte work of Artisi Barovier (1890–1920s) to the early work of Ettore Sottsass in the 1970s, they excelled in creativity and craftsmanship. The 1920s to 1940s featured the work of glass designers like Ercole Barovier for Barovier and Toso and Vittorio Zecchin, Napoleone Martinuzzi, and Carlo Scarpa for Venini. Many of these pieces are highly prized by collectors.

The 1950s saw a revival of Italy as a world-renown design center for all of the arts. Glass led the charge with the brightly colored work of Fulvio Bianconi for Venini, Dino Martens for Aureliano Toso, and Ercole Barovier for Barovier and Toso. The best of these pieces are extremely desirable. The '60s and '70s have also seen many innovative designs with work by the Finnish Tapio Wirkkala, the American Thomas Stearns, and many other designers.

Unfortunately, amongst the great glass, there was a plethora of commercial ashtrays, vases, and figurines produced that, though having some value, do not compare in quality and design to the great glass of Murano.

Venini: The Venini company was founded in 1921 by Paolo Venini, and he led the company until his death in 1959. Major Italian designers worked for the firm, including Vittorio Zecchin, Napoleone Martinuzzi, Carlo Scarpa, and Fulvio Bianconi. After his death, his son-in-law, Ludovico de Santillana, ran the factory and employed designers like Toni Zucchieri, Tapio Wirkkala, and Thomas Stearns. The company is known for creative designs and techniques including Inciso (finely etched lines), Battuto (carved facets), Sommerso (controlled bubbles),

Pezzato (patches of fused glass), and Fascie (horizontal colored lines in clear glass). Until the mid-'60s, most pieces were signed with acid-etched 'Venini Murano ITALIA.' In the '60s they started engraving the signatures. The factory still exists.

Barovier: In the late 1920s, Ercole Barovier took over the Artisti Barovier and started designing many different vases. In the 1930s he merged with Ferro Toso and became Barovier and Toso. He designed many different series of glass including the Barbarico (rough, acid-treated brown or deep blue glass), Eugenio (free-blown vases), Efeso, Rotallato, Dorico, Egeo (vases incorporating murrine designs), and Primavera (white etched glass with black bands). He designed until 1974. The company is still in existence. Most pieces were unsigned.

Aureliano Toso: The great glass designer Dino Martens was involved with the company from about 1938 to 1965. It was his work that produced the very desirable Oriente vases. This technique consisted of free-formed patches of green, yellow, blue, purple, black, and white stars and pieces of zanfirico canes fused into brilliantly colored vases and bowls. His El Dorado series was based on the same technique but was not opaque. He also designed pieces with alternating groups of black and white filigrana lines. Pieces are unsigned.

Seguso: Flavio Poli became the artistic director of Seguso in the late 1930s and remained until 1963. He is known for his Corroso (acid-etched glass) and his Valve series (elegant forms of two to three layers of colored glass with a clear glass casing).

Archimede Seguso: In 1946 Archimede Seguso left the Seguso Vetri D'Arte to open a new company and designed many innovative pieces. His Merlatto (thin white filigrana suspended three dimensionally) series is his most famous. The epitome of his work is where a colored glass (yellow or purple) is windowed in the merlotti. His Macchia Ambra Verde is yellow and spots on a gold base encased in clear glass. The A Piume series contained feathers and leaves suspended in glass. Pieces are unsigned.

Alfredo Barbini: Barbini was a designer known for his sculptures of sea subjects and his amorphic-shaped vases with an inner core of red or blue glass with a heavy layer of finely incised outer glass. He worked in the 1950s to 1960s, and some pieces are signed.

Vistosi: Although this glassworks was started in the 1940s, fame came in the 1960s and '70s with the birds designed by Allesandro Pianon and the early work of the Memphis school designer, Ettore Sottsass. Pieces may be signed.

AVEM: This company is known for its work in the 1950s and 1960s. The designer, Ansolo Fuga, did work using a solid white glass with inclusions of multicolored murrines.

Cenedese: This is a postwar company led by Gino Cenedese with Alfredo Barbini as designer. When Barbini left, Cenedese took over the design work and also used the free-lanced designs of Fulvio Bianconi. They are known for their figurines and vases with suspended murrines.

Cappellin: Venini's original partner (1921–25), Giacomo Cappellin, opened a short-lived company (1925–32) that was to become extremely important. His chief designer was the young Carlo Scarpa who was to create many masterpieces in glass both for Cappellin and then Venini.

Ettore Sottsass: Sottass founded the Memphis School of Design in the 1970s. He is an extremely famous modern designer who designed several series of glass for the Vistosi Glass Company. The pieces were created in limited editions, signed and numbered, and each piece was given a name.

Our advisor for this category is Howard Lockwood, publisher of *Vetri: Italian Glass News*. For further information concerning Mr. Lockwood or this publication, see the Directory under New Jersey.

Venini Glass

A Burgne: gr cylindrical vase 6,310.00
Battuto: pale gr vase 13,126.00
Battuto: tall bl vase by T Scarpa 6,199.00
Bird: J shape, bl-gr, copper legs 1,823.00
Bottle, red & gr narrow vertical canes, stopper 1,094.00
Bottle, yel & aubergine vertical canes 948.00
Bottle, yel & bl vertical stripes, stopper 948.00
Cornucopia: pk laguna vase w/gold inclusions 1,536.00
Corroso: red bowl w/appl decor 2,300.00
Fasce, bl bottle w/2 wide yel stripes 802.00
Fasce, Murrine: wht cylinder, murrine bands 9,480.00
Fasce Ritorta: bowl, amethyst, bl & gray 576.00
Fasce Ritorte: cylinder vase, red, bl & turq bands 6,769.00
Fazzoletto: lg, pk & wht zanfirico 3,450.00
Fazzoletto: med sz, yel & wht zanfirico 3,450.00
Fenecio: clear & gr perfume bottle 1,064.00
Figurine, female, wht filigrana 2,875.00
Fish, lav w/yel & mustard decor 1,840.00
Forato: bl & violet single-holed vase 1,750.00
Forato: bl cased w/pk single-holed vase 640.00
Hourglass: gr & red 241.00
Inciso: cylindrical, steel bl w/amber layer 1,056.00
Inciso: flaring vase, clear over gr 690.00
Inciso: triangular bottle, bl, w/stopper 575.00
Latticino: cylinder, pk & wht canes 615.00
Latticino: gray vase w/wht canes 576.00
Murrine: red & blk checkered vase 54,693.00
Murrine: 3-sided vase, gr & blk 8,751.00
Obelisk: 8-sided, smoke-gray 165.00
Occhi: blk & wht, sq 3,646.00
Occhi: red cigar-shaped vase, designed by T Scarpa 8,022.00
Pennalatte: yel & tan stripes, designed by C Scarpa 21,877.00

Pezzato: Bottle, pezzati Arlecchino with transparent and translucent multicolor squares with some patches cased to white, Bianconi design #4319, 14", $10,350.00.

Pezatto: cigar shaped, red, bl, clear & gr patches 6,199.00
Pezzato: cylinder vase w/aubergine, turq, gray & clear 7,475.00
Pezzato: vase, red, bl, beige & gr patches 13,856.00
Pitcher & tumbler, red & bl canes 875.00
Scozzese: cylinder vase, turq vertical stripes 10,560.00
Soffiati: bl compote, ftd 577.00
Soffiati: red Veronese vase 690.00
Tessuto: 2 halfs - red/clear & blk/red 2,552.00
Torso: female torso w/raised arms, amber 6,325.00
Wirkkala Correnno: plate, bl & deep bl 620.00
Wirkkala: bowl, wht mezza filigrana 219.00

Non-Venini Glass

Archimede Seguso, A Piume: teardrop vase, peach w/4 feathers ...4,025.00
Archimede Seguso, Alarante: pierced hdld pitcher, yel w/gr int ...676.00
Archimede Seguso, Losanghe: cylindrical, wht w/caramel sqs ...2,875.00

Archimede Seguso, Merletto: bl w/wht merletto panels 15,314.00
Archimede Seguso, Merletto: purple w/bottom half wht, purple dots ..12,762.00
Archimede Seguso, Sommerso: ribbed vase, amber over deep yel ..747.00
Archimede Seguso, Sommerso: ribbed vase, clear, cranberry & purple ..1,265.00
Artisi Barovier, Mosaic: goblet-shaped ped vase, bl murrines ..28,750.00
Aureliano Toso, A Trina: pigeon, wht, blk & copper aventurine ...747.00
Aureliano Toso, Bianca/Nera: vase, blk & wht spiralling canes .440.00
Aureliano Toso, Eldorado: vase w/appl collar 14,585.00
Aureliano Toso, Mezza Filigrana: lamp base 230.00
Aureliano Toso, Mezza Filigrana: leaf-formed dish 172.00
Aureliano Toso, Oriente: flared vase 9,775.00
AVEM, Anse Volante: irid gr pitcher, flaring hdl 4,084.00
Barbini, Inciso; thick-walled clear bowl w/red int 1,940.00
Barbini, Sasso, ftd w/inciso cut & int red decor 8,022.00
Barbini, Sasso: vase w/inciso cut & red decor 58,340.00
Barbini, Scavo: gray polar bear 952.00
Barovier, Efeso: amber cylindrical vase 93.00
Barovier, figurine: drum major iridized clear w/bl trim 517.00
Barovier, Intarsio: amber & yel patches 5,277.00
Barovier, Intarsio: red, bl, amber, clear triangular patches 7,187.00
Barovier, iridized flared vase w/ribs 2,688.00
Barovier, Rugiadoso: leaf-shaped bowl, clear/wht 230.00
Barovier, Spidereo: waisted vase, windows lined in aubergine ..2,880.00
Barovier, Spina: bowl, mauve & opaline herringboned pattern ..1,840.00
Cenedese, aquarium block w/3 fish 2,415.00
Cenedese, owl, clear & blk sommerso glass 275.00
Cenedese, Scavo: La Fornace: mc, glass workers 5,175.00
Cenedese, Scavo: vase, lt bl 880.00
Cenedese, Scavo: vase w/appl woman carrying fruit 3,450.00
Fratelli Toso, Murrine: bottle vase w/single target murrine 4,609.00
Fratelli Toso, Murrine: mc Kiku vase 13,856.00
Fratelli Toso, Murrine: mc vase of murrines 9,845.00
Fratelli Toso, Nerox: metallic blk vase w/clear glass blobs 9,480.00
Fratelli Toso, Nerox: metallic blk w/blk/red & yel/gr 20,149.00
Salviati, Gasparil Birds, stylized, clear, pr 275.00
Seguso Vetri D'Arte, fish, gray glass on appl ft 676.00
Seguso Vetri D'Arte, Pulegoso, gr leaf bowl 292.00
Seguso Vetri D'Arte, Shell, lt bl amorphic shape 1,458.00
Seguso Vetri D'Arte, Siderale: vase, gr & yel concentric circles 17,500.00
Seguso Vetri D'Arte, Sommerso: flared vase, crimson w/violet int ...1,380.00
Seguso Vetri D'Arte, Sommerso: tall, purple int cased in red .6,760.00
Seguso Vetri D'Arte, Valva: bl int, red & clear layers 8,751.00
Seguso Vetri D'Arte, Valva: gray cased in pale amber 2,300.00
Sottsass, Alcor: vase, clear, wht & bl 3,090.00
Sottsass, Alioth: vase, bl, yel & gr 3,200.00
Sottsass, Altair: vase, bl w/wht appl decor 2,530.00
Tagliapietra, Incalmo: bl top, wht base 862.00
Tagliapietra, Incalmo: turq bl w/folded blk rim 1,725.00
Vistosi, bird, J shape, bl, copper legs 1,035.00
Vistosi, bird, J shape, gr, copper legs 1,350.00
Vistosi, bird, ovoid, bl, copper legs 1,610.00
Vistosi, bird, spherical, red, no protrusions 2,185.00

Ivory

Ivory has been used and appreciated since Neolithic times. It has been a product of every culture and continent. It is the second most valuable organic material after pearls. Ivory is defined as the dentine portion of mammalian teeth. Commercially the most important ivory comes from elephant and mammoth tusks, walrus tusks, hippo teeth, and sperm whale teeth. The smaller tusks of boar and warthog are often used whole.

Ivory has been used for artistic purposes as a palette for oil paints, as inlay on furniture, and especially as a medium for sculptures. Some are in the round, others in the form of plaques. Ivory also has numerous utilitarian uses such as cups and tankards; combs; handles for knives and medical tools; salt and pepper shakers; chess, domino, and checker pieces; billiard balls; jewelry; shoehorns; snuff boxes; brush pots; and fans.

There are a number of laws domestically and internationally to protect endangered animals including the elephant, walrus, and whale. However ivory taken and used before the various enactment dates is legal within the country in which it is located, and can be shipped internationally with a permit. Ivory from mammoths, hippopotamus, wart hog, and boar is excepted from all bans.

Prices have been stable for the last ten years, rising slightly in the last year. Prices are highest for European, Japanese, and Chinese ivories. Prices are lowest for African and Indian ivories. As with all collectibles, the very best pieces will appreciate most in the years to come. Small, poorly carved pieces will not appreciate to any extent. Our advisor for this category is Robert Weisblut; he is listed in the Directory under Maryland.

Figurines and Models

Angelfish (2), fossil walrus ivory, Bali, 1990s, 4" 350.00
Beauty w/flowers, Chinese, 20th C, 13" 775.00

Bust of Voltaire on marble plinth, France, nineteenth century, 10", $7,500.00. (Photo courtesy Robert Weisblut)

Children cvg, Communist Chinese era, 9½" 1,250.00
Grouping of gods & children, Chinese, early 20th C, 10" 2,650.00
Man defeating dragon & taking flaming pearl, Chinese, 9½" 950.00
Sailing vessel w/full sails, walrus ivory, Eskimo, 1950s, 10" 1,500.00
Study of rose branch, Japan, early 20th C, 13" L 1,750.00
Village scene, hippo tooth, Chinese, 1980s, 16" L 325.00
Village scene, Japan, ca 1900, 5½" 2,000.00
Voltaire (bust) on marble plinth, France, 19th C, 10" 7,500.00
Woman w/knitting implements, Chinese, early 20th C, 9" 675.00

Miscellaneous

Ear ornament, hornbill ivory, Borneo, early 20th C, 4" 750.00
Shakers, narwhal tusk, scrimshawed, 2½", pr 350.00
Snuff bottle, deep relief, China, 19th C, 5" 1,250.00

Jack-in-the-Pulpit Vases

Popular novelties at the turn of the century, jack-in-the-pulpit vases were made in every type of art glass produced. Some were simple, others elaborately appliquéd and enameled. They were shaped to resemble the lily for which they were named.

Bl satin, controlled bubbles, 6" 60.00
Butterscotch satin w/crimson int, 7" 125.00
Cranberry, optic ribbed, w/clear ft & rigaree, 13" 280.00
Cranberry, striped, 5 rigaree ft, ruffled rim, 8½" 180.00

Cranberry w/wht opal edge & clear base, Hobbs, 9x5" 300.00
Spangle, bl/yel/brn on wht w/silver, swirled, Mt WA, 5½" 235.00
Spatter, yel/wht, ovoid body, 5x3½" 90.00
Wht opal w/maroon edge, Dmn Quilt/Hobnail, 7¾x6" 115.00
Wht w/aqua opening, HP butterfly/flowers, English, 1890s, 4½" ..235.00

Jervis

W.P. Jervis began his career as a potter in 1898. By 1908 he had his own pottery in Oyster Bay, New York. His shapes were graceful; often he decorated his wares with sgraffito designs over which he applied a matt glaze. Many pieces were incised 'Jervis' in a vertical arrangement. The pottery closed around 1912.

Vase, peacock on railing, blues and greens on Persian blue, unsigned Rhead, marked, kiln scar on side, 10¾x4¼", $8,000.00.

Box, lions/papyrus, bl on gray, Oyster Bay, open, 1½x5" 900.00
Pitcher, hand-cvd/enameled bl flowers & gr foliage on teal, 5½", NM .950.00
Vase, sgraffito trees, denim bl on brn clay, Oyster Bay, 7x3¼" ...950.00

Jewelry

Jewelry as objects of adornment has always been regarded with special affection. Today prices for gems and gemstones crafted into antique and collectible jewelry are based on artistic merit, personal appeal, pure sentimentality, and intrinsic value. Note: In general, diamond prices have gone up more than 20% in the past year, and platinum is becoming popular again, so retail prices are rising. Diamond prices vary greatly depending on cut, color, clarity, etc., and to assess the value of any diamond of more than a carat in weight, you will need to have information about all of these factors. Values given here are for diamond jewelry with a standard commercial grade of diamonds that are most likely to be encountered.

Our advisor for fine jewelry is Rebecca Dodds; her address may be found in the Directory under Florida. Marcia 'Sparkles' Brown is our advisor for costume jewelry and the author of *Unsigned Beauties of Costume Jewelry* (Collector Books); she is also the host of the video *Hidden Treasures, A Collector's Guide to Antique and Vintage Jewelry of the 19th and 20th Centuries*. Mrs. Brown is listed in the Directory under Oregon. Other good references are *Collectible Costume Jewelry* by Cherri Simonds; *Costume Jewelry, A Practical Handbook & Value Guide*, by Fred Rezazadeh; *Collector's Encyclopedia of Hairwork Jewelry, Identification & Values*, by C. Jeanenne Bell; and *Collector's Guide to Hair Combs, Identification and Values*, by Mary Bachman (all available from Collector Books). See also American Painted Porcelain; Hair Weaving.

Key:
cab — cabochon
ct — carat
dmn — diamond
dwt — penny weight
Euro — European cut
g-t — gold-tone
k — karat
plat — platinum
r/stn — rhinestone
stn — stone
fl — filigree
gf — gold filled
gp — gold plated
grad — graduated
gw — gold washed
tw — total weight
wg — white gold
yg — yellow gold
ygf — yellow gold filled

Bar brooch, 14k yg, eng & set w/2 old mine-cut dmns/3 rose-cut dmns ..500.00
Bar pin, plat, 69 old mine cut/single cut dmns, 3.25ct tw 2,400.00
Bar pin, yg, Etruscan Revival w/lion head & ball drop, 19th C .550.00
Bar pin, yg w/emb flower & leaf, 37 sm rose dmns/1 oriental pearl .800.00
Bar pin, 14k pk & gr gold, pine cone & leaves shape 220.00
Bracelet, Geo Jensen, silver, cuff style 500.00
Bracelet, Mary Gage, silver w/free-form moonstone/wht stone, att .350.00
Bracelet, plat, 164 rnd dmns (12.50cts), 4 oval jade stones 7,500.00
Bracelet, plat, 96 rnd dmns (8.50ct tw), 48 sapphires (7ct tw) ...12,000.00
Bracelet, plat w/7 sq dmns (2.5ct), 154 sm rnd dmns, Deco style ..4,000.00
Brooch, cvd angel-skin coral lady's head in nugget gold mt 750.00
Brooch, Geo Jensen, hammered sterling, lapiz cab in flower form .275.00
Brooch, Geo Jensen, silver, stylized flower w/gr stone, 1½" 300.00
Brooch, Mexican, comical sterling cat figural, 2¼" 280.00
Brooch, yg circle w/1 rnd emerald & 4 mine-cut dmns, Continental ..385.00
Brooch, 14k yg & shell cameo, classical lady's profile, fl mt 300.00
Brooch, 14k yg Am Etruscan Revival oblong pendant, fct ball decor .450.00
Brooch, 14k yg sunburst w/9 old mine-cut dmns (.80ct) 1,100.00
Brooch, 18k yg, Nouveau 4-wing dragonfly w/sm ruby eyes 8,000.00
Brooch, 18k yg, stylized leaf w/6 rnd-cut emeralds/13 rnd-cut dmns ..1,265.00
Brooch, 18k yg, 3 oval fct topaz/4 cushion-cut rubies, ball drops 1,265.00
Earrings, yg & agates in dbl-ball drop style, pr 500.00
Earrings, 14k yg w/blk enamel tracery, dbl ball drop, 19th C, pr ...975.00
Earrings, 3-color gold hoop w/pearl & turq, sm, pr 250.00
Necklace, cultured gray & wht pearls, 8.5-9.5mm w/14k yg beads, 30" .330.00
Necklace, cultured pearls, semi-Baroque, 8½-9mm, 52" 3,850.00
Necklace, cultured pearls, strand of 133 6-6.6mm, gold clasp 400.00
Necklace, cultured pearls, 9½-10mm, made in 5 parts, 35" total ..10,450.00
Necklace, Mary Gage, silver cross pendent w/religious figures, 29" 250.00
Neckpc, Alton, silver neck-conforming wire w/leaves at front ..400.00
Pendant, marquise fct smoky quartz topaz in 14k yg mt 135.00
Ring, plat, 10.9mm cultured pearl amid 16 sm dmns/6 sm rubies ..3,000.00
Ring, plat, 6.75 I/J-K emerald-cut dmn+2 baguette dmns 12,000.00
Ring, Van Cleef & Arpels, 18k yg w/solitaire-cut synthetic stone 715.00
Ring, yg w/2ct cat's eye chrysoberyl in mine-cut dmn (1ct) cluster ..3,000.00
Ring, 14k wg, .33ct dmn w/in 32 sm dmns, 1.0ct tw 1,500.00
Ring, 14k yg, .25ct center dmn amid 8 sm dmns/8 sm emeralds ..2,000.00
Ring, 14k yg, 14 mine-cut sm dmns w/9 sm opals in swirl design .750.00
Ring, 14k yg, 16 old mine-cut dmns (1.35cts) on 'Retro' band ..850.00
Ring, 14k yg, 34 full-cut sm dmns in cluster, cocktail style 500.00
Ring, 14k yg w/cushion-cut citrine & half-pearls cluster 275.00
Ring, 18kt yg, cushion-cut 5.50ct emerald+16 mine-cut dmns 2.50 tw ..19,250.00

Costume Jewelry

Rhinestone jewelry has become a very popular field of collecting. Rhinestones are foil-backed leaded crystal stones with a sparkle outshining diamonds. Copyrighting jewelry came into effect in 1955. Pieces bearing a copyright mark (post-1955) are considered 'collectibles,' while pieces (with no copyright) made before then are regarded as 'antiques.' Fur clips are two-pronged, used to anchor fur stoles. Dress clips have a spring clasp and are used at the dress neckline. Look for signed and well-made, unmarked pieces for your collections and preserve this American art form. Our advisor for costume jewelry is Marcia Brown (see introductory paragraphs for information on her books and videos).

Bracelet, Bakelite, Belle Kogan, red w/8 tan ovals, ¾" 550.00
Bracelet, Bakelite, blk hinged cuff w/cvd florals, 1" W 220.00

Bracelet, Bakelite, brn w/2 inlay bands on top, 1" W 325.00
Bracelet, Bakelite, ivory bangle w/12 blk celluloid loops 160.00
Bracelet, Bakelite, mc heart charms on brass chain, 7" 300.00
Bracelet, Bakelite, red clamp type w/cvd flowers, 1" W 475.00
Bracelet, Bakelite, reverse cvd floral, ivory/apple juice, 1" 1,500.00
Bracelet, Bakelite, zigzag ivory & red interlocking sections, 1" W .450.00
Bracelet, celluloid, mc dye/pnt w/bl & red r/stns, ½" 200.00
Bracelet, celluoid, amber w/incised/pnt scrolls, red r/stns, ½" W ..270.00
Bracelet, Ciner, gilt-metal, turq cabs, r/stns, 4 pearl strands, 8" .200.00
Bracelet, Hobe, gilt-metal fl w/topaz/amber r/stns, 1x7" 300.00
Bracelet, KJ Lane, gilt-metal, hinged cuff w/zebra heads, r/stns 90.00
Bracelet, silver-tone, lt bl/moonstone cvd stns/pave r/stns, 7" 325.00
Bracelet, Trifari, gilt metal, bl enameling, red/clear r/stns, 7" 150.00
Brooch, Bakelite, bananas, marbled yel/gr, 4" 325.00
Brooch, Bakelite, bar (red) w/8 cherries/5 gr leaves, 4" 150.00
Brooch, Bakelite, bar (4-color/laminated) w/notch-cvd ends, 2¾" .100.00
Brooch, Bakelite, cherries in wooden bowl, pnt details, 3" 400.00
Brooch, Bakelite, cowboy, articulated, 2-color, pnt, 4" 1,300.00
Brooch, Bakelite, drum major, 4-color, fiber plume, 4" 425.00
Brooch, Bakelite, fishhook, red w/wht string wrap, 3½" 70.00
Brooch, Bakelite, flower, red w/EX details, 3½" 350.00
Brooch, Bakelite, fruit dangles (5) on celluloid chain, 3½" 1,300.00
Brooch, Bakelite, giraffe, hinged neck, string antlers, 3" 2,200.00
Brooch, Bakelite, hand (red) w/cuff holds cherries, 3" hand 100.00
Brooch, Bakelite, hat (red) w/cvd rings, paper flowers, 2½" 475.00
Brooch, Bakelite, lobster, red marbled, string antennae, 4" 1,200.00
Brooch, Bakelite, M Sleeper (att), pony, tan w/leather ears, 3" .500.00
Brooch, Bakelite, racing greyhound pr, red over-dye, 4", VG 650.00
Brooch, Bakelite, rectangle w/cvd/pierced leaves & flowers, 3½" ..160.00
Brooch, Bakelite, stone face w/over-dye, rectangular, 2½" 280.00
Brooch, Bakelite, strawberries (5) & 6 leaves, red & gr, 3½" 330.00
Brooch, Bakelite, swordfish, red marbled, w/appl eye, 4" 900.00
Brooch, Bakelite, toad, gr over-dye, deeply cvd, pnt eyes, 3½" ...1,700.00
Brooch, Bakelite, Uncle Sam Hat, 2-color+red pnt+metal stars ..4,500.00
Brooch, Bakelite/wood, alligator, laminated body, 4½" 375.00
Brooch, Bakelite/wood, cactus & Indian vase, pnt touches, 3½" ..200.00
Brooch, Bakelite/wood, sailor, articulated, 3½" 220.00
Brooch, birds at nest, silver-tone, enamel/r/stns, 3" 1,100.00
Brooch, Boucher, fox face, silver, pave & bl r/stns, 3" 475.00
Brooch, Calvaire, fish, g-t w/pear belly, r/stns, 3" 200.00
Brooch, ceramic/Lucite, Victim of Fashion, 4" 150.00
Brooch, Cini, devil mask, silver, long chain drops, 3½" 150.00
Brooch, Coro, birds, silver-tone w/enamel wings/pave r/stns, 3½" ..70.00
Brooch, Coro, butterfly, silver-tone w/gr/clear r/stns, 3" 150.00
Brooch, Coro, dragonfly, 4 movable wings, r/stns & enamel, 3½" .350.00
Brooch, Coro, fish, sterling w/Lucite body/clear r/stns, 2" 275.00
Brooch, Coro, parrot, silver-tone w/enamel & clear r/stns, 3" 100.00
Brooch, Coro, spider, silver-tone w/enamel & clear r/stns, 3" 290.00
Brooch, CoroCraft, bird, gold-tone w/enamel & r/stns, 3" 200.00
Brooch, CoroCraft, birds/flowers, gilt silver/enamel, 3" 100.00
Brooch, CoroCraft, Chinese water carrier, silver & r/stns, 2" 160.00
Brooch, CoroCraft, fish, Lucite body, red cb eye, r/stns, 3" 300.00
Brooch, CoroCraft, squirrel, gold-ton w/enamel, topaz/clear r/stns, 3" .210.00
Brooch, CoroCraft, 3 owls, gilt silver, r/stns, 2¼" 200.00
Brooch, crown, gilt-sterling w/mc & clear r/stns, 2" 100.00
Brooch, Eisenberg, bow, gilt-sterling w/aqua & clear r/stns, 3½" 500.00
Brooch, Eisenberg, fairy, silver, r/stns, enamel, 2½" 800.00
Brooch, Eisenberg, floral cluster, silver-tone w/clear r/stns, 3" ...110.00
Brooch, Eisenberg, floral spray, silver w/2-color r/stns, 4½" 400.00
Brooch, Eisenberg, flowers, gilt-sterling w/red/clear r/stns, 3½" .350.00
Brooch, Eisenberg, silver w/faux turq cabs & bl r/stns, 3" 230.00
Brooch, Eisenberg Original, bow knot, silver & r/stns, 3" 325.00
Brooch, Eisenberg Original, bow knot, silver metal & r/stns, 4" ...200.00
Brooch, Eisenberg Original, rose/stem/leaves, gilt metal, 4" 150.00

Brooch and earrings, Eisenberg, prong-set red, pink, and clear Austrian crystal rhinestones, rhodium plated, 2¼" wreath pin and 1½" earrings, from $425.00 to $525.00. (Photo courtesy Cherri Simonds)

Brooch, flowers, silver & gilt-metal, red & clear r/stns, 3" 60.00
Brooch, Haskell, butterfly, gilt w/seed pearls/crystals, 2½" 210.00
Brooch, Haskell, butterfly, gold-tone w/coral beads/r/stns, 3½" .200.00
Brooch, Hobe, Chinaman, ivory, brass fl tree, crystals, 3½" 800.00
Brooch, KJ Lane, reclining deer, gilt, sm gr cabs, r/stns, 3½" 60.00
Brooch, Lucite, butterfly, bk cvd, mc pnt, 3½" 140.00
Brooch, Lucite, elephant, bk cvd, 3½", +2 palm trees (3 pcs) ...150.00
Brooch, Lucite, kangaroo, 3-D, laminated, pnt, 4" 170.00
Brooch, Lucite, mallard duck, bk cvd/pnt, 4" 60.00
Brooch, Lucite, owl, googly eyes, bk cvd, pnt, 3½" 250.00
Brooch, Lucite, snowman w/celluloid eyes/broomstick, pnt decor, 2½" ...200.00
Brooch, Lucite, swami, 3-D, w/crystal ball, bk cvd, 3" 160.00
Brooch, Lucite, umbrella, bk cvd, gr pnt, string tie, 3" 90.00
Brooch, Lucite/wood, bee, pnt highlights, 3" 70.00
Brooch, Margot, fish, sterling w/mc mosaic-type enamel, 2½" ...120.00
Brooch, Pennino, floral spray, silver metal+r/stns, 4" 100.00
Brooch, Reja, plant, gilt-sterling w/moonstones/r/stns, 3" 850.00
Brooch, Sandor, potted flowers, crystals, r/stns & enamel, 3" 200.00
Brooch, Spratling, owl (stylized), silver w/amethyst eyes, 3" 800.00
Brooch, Staret, floral spray, red/clear r/stns & enamel, 4" 210.00
Brooch, Staret, jester, gold-tone w/enamel & clear r/stns, 3" 650.00
Brooch, Trifari, ax, gilt-metal w/enameling/faux pearls/r/stns, 3¾" ...450.00
Brooch, Trifari, bird, gilt-sterling w/mc r/stns, 3" 275.00
Brooch, Trifari, sailboat/sailor, r/stns/enameling, 3" 1,200.00
Brooch, Trifari, stork, gilt-silver, Lucite & r/stns, 3½" 600.00
Brooch, Trifari, wheelbarrow, silver metal w/mc r/stns, 3" 475.00
Brooch, Vogue, bow knot, silver w/aqua & clear crystals, 5" 400.00
Brooch, wood, hobo face, w/Bakelite hat/cigarette, 3½" 150.00
Brooch, wood, snow skis w/Bakelite boots, 4" 110.00
Brooch, wood/Lucite, fish, C-shape, pnt highlights, 3" 70.00
Brooch, wood/Lucite/ceramic, flower spray, 5" 90.00
Clip, DeRosa, potted plant, lg/sm clear & red r/stns, 3", VG 400.00
Clip, Eisenberg, flower, silver, lg red/sm clear r/stns, 3" 350.00
Clip, Eisenberg, ribbons, silver-tone w/pk & clear r/stns, 3" 150.00
Clip, Eisenberg Original, Art Deco cascade, silver & r/stns, 3" ..100.00
Clip, Eisenberg Original, floral, silver metal, r/stns, 4½" 170.00
Clip, flowers, gold-tone, crystal beads/drops, 4" 300.00
Clip, scrolls, gilt-sterling, lt topaz r/stn w/mc drops, 5" 600.00
Clip, Trifari, elephant, silver-tone w/enamel & clear r/stns, 2½" ...350.00
Clip, Trifari, flower, gilt-metal w/mc r/stns, 3" 400.00
Clip, Trifari, flowers, silver-tone w/mc enamel, clear r/stns, 3" ..220.00
Clip, Trifari, flowers, silver-tone w/mc enamel, clear r/stns, 4½" ..550.00
Clip, Trifari, lg orchid, clear/mc r/stns, enamel, 4" 1,100.00
Clip, Trifari, poodle, Lucite body, pave r/stns, enamel, 3" 1,200.00
Clip, Trifari, silver-tone flower, mc enameling w/clear r/stns, 3" ...230.00
Clip, Trifari, spider, gilt-sterling w/cvd Lucite & r/stns, 2" 400.00
Earrings, Bakelite, butterscotch disks w/appl mc wedges, 1" 160.00
Earrings, Bakelite, cowboy hats, dangles, 1" 90.00
Earrings, Bakelite, octagonal, mc laminated quarters, ¾" 180.00
Earrings, KJ Lane, rnd w/orange beads, faux pearls, r/stns 30.00
Necklace, Bakelite, rainbow/heart dangles, celluloid chain 260.00
Necklace, Bakelite, strawberries (5 marbled red) & 5 gr leaves, 17" ..500.00

Necklace, Haskell, bib of seed pearl triangles w/pearl centers 130.00
Necklace, Haskell, gold-tone chain w/faux pearls & center medallion ..300.00
Necklace, Trifari, lg central enameled flower, 15", +bracelet 550.00
Pin, See Brooch
Ring, Bakelite, orange w/ivory polka dots, 1" W 200.00

Johnson Brothers

A Staffordshire-based company operating since well before the turn of the century, Johnson Brothers has produced many familiar lines of dinnerware, several of which are becoming very collectible. Some of their patterns were made in both blue and pink transfer as well as in polychrome. One of the more familiar lines is Friendly Village, which is still being produced, though the line is much more limited than it once was.

Values below range from a low base price for lines that are still in production (i.e., Friendly Village) or less collectible to a high that would apply to very desirable patterns such as Old Britain Castles, Wild Turkeys, Strawberry Fair, Historic America, Rose Chintz, Chintz, etc. Mid-range lines include Coaching Scenes, Millsteam, Old English Countryside, Rose Bouquet (and there are others).

For more information on marks, patterns, and pricing, we recommend *Johnson Brothers Dinnerware Pattern Directory and Price Guide* by our advisor, Mary J. Finegan, who is listed in the Directory under North Carolina.

Bowl, berry/fruit; from $8 to 10.00
Bowl, rimmed soup; from $14 to 16.00
Bowl, vegatable; w/lid, minimum value 90.00
Bowl, vegetable; rnd, from $25 to 35.00
Coaster, from $8 to 10.00
Creamer, from $30 to 35.00
Cup & saucer, jumbo, from $30 to 40.00
Egg cup, from $15 to 20.00
Plate, bread & butter; from $6 to 8.00
Plate, luncheon; from $12 to 16.00
Platter, lg, 14"+, minimum value 60.00
Shakers, pr, from $40 to 48.00
Sugar bowl, w/lid, from $40 to 48.00
Tureen, minimum value 200.00

Josef Originals

Figurines of lovely ladies, charming girls, and whimsical animals marked Josef Originals were designed by Muriel Joseph George of Arcadia, California, from 1945 to 1985. Until 1960 they were produced in California, but costs were high and copies of her work were being made in Japan. To remain competitive, she and her partner, George Good, contracted with the Katayama Company in Japan to build a factory to produce her designs to her approval. Muriel retired in 1982; however, George Good continued production of her work as well as new ones of his staff's creation. The company was sold in late 1985; the name is currently owned by Applause, and a limited amount of figurines bear the name. Those made during the ownership of Muriel George are the most collectible. They can be recognized by these characteristics: The girls have a high-gloss finish, black eyes, and most are signed. Brown eyes date from 1982 to 1985. Applause uses a red-brown eye. The animals were mainly done in a matt finish and have labels. Later animals have a flocked coat. Prices are given for figurines (with black eyes unless specified otherwise) in perfect condition. Our advisors, Jim and Kaye Whitaker, are the authors of three books: *Josef Originals, Charming Figurines; Josef Originals, A Second Look;* and *Josef Originals, Figurines of Muriel Joseph George*, an informative book with no repeats of the two previous books. The Whitakers are listed in the Directory under Washington.

Birthstone dolls, Jan through Dec, Japan, 3½", ea 25.00
Boxer Dog, Champions series, Japan, 5" 22.00
Buggy Bugs series, various poses, wire antenna, Japan, 3¼", ea 15.00
Bunny Hutch series, Japan, 4" 15.00

Cat wall plaque, California, 4", from $50.00. **(Photo courtesy Jim and Kaye Whitaker)**

Elephant w/tusks, Japan, 6¾" 50.00
Farmer's Daughter, girl w/hen & basket of eggs, Japan, 5" 50.00
First Love 'Tina,' Japan, 5" 50.00
Happy Home w/Dove Greeting Angel, Japan, 3¾" 45.00
Hawaii, Small World series, brn eyes, Japan, 4½" 40.00
Hunter, beautiful standing horse, Japan, 6" 25.00
It's a Wonderful World series figurines, Japan, 3½", ea 35.00
Jeanne, Colonial Days series, Japan, 9" 135.00
Love Letter, from Love Story-Romance series, Japan, 8" 125.00
Mary Ann & Mama, California, 4" & 7", pr 145.00
Mermaid lipstick holder, wht w/beige trim, Japan, 4" 85.00
Mice, Christmas, Japan, 2¾", ea 12.00
Miss Mary, Nursery Rhymes series, 4" 45.00
Missy, girl in bonnet, several colors, California, 4" 45.00
Monkeys mama & papa, Japan, 3" 15.00
Music box, Christmas, girl decoration tree, 7" 65.00
Music box, Happy Anniversary, Japan, 7¼" 70.00
Nanette, half doll w/jewels, several colors, California, 5½" 65.00
New Hat, from First Time, Japan, 4½" 40.00
Nurse, Career Girls series, in yel, holding baby, Japan, 5¾" 60.00
Pixie, Christmas Helper, pnts toy, Japan, 4¾" 35.00
Pixie, various poses, gr w/red & gold trim, Japan, 2-3¼", ea 30.00
Poodle, from Poodle & Siamese series, 4¼" 30.00
Puerto Rico, Little International series, Japan, 4" 45.00
Rose, Flower Girl series, girl w/flower hat, Japan, 4¼" 40.00
Rose Garden series, brn eyes, Japan, 6 different, 5¼", ea 65.00
Ruby, Little Jewels series, girl w/'ruby' in crown, Japan, 3½" 35.00
Santa, kiss on forehead, Japan, 4¾" 60.00
Secret Pal, girl w/fan, various colors, California, 3½" 40.00
Skunks w/wht hair tuft on head, Japan, 2½" 18.00
Sports Angels series, angels playing various sports, Japan, 2¾", ea .35.00
Tabby cat, orange, I Love My Cat on base, Japan, 3½" 15.00
Three Kings, Japan, 8½-11", set of 3 ....70.00
Wall plaque, gray cat, California 50.00
Warm Hello, Thinking of You series, girl on phone, Japan, 5" 50.00
Wee Ching & Wee Ling, Chinese boy & girl w/dog & cat (much copied), pr ..75.00
Wee Folk, various poses, Japan, 4½", ea 20.00
Yorkshire, Kennel Club series, Japan, 3" 18.00

Judaica

The items listed below are representative of objects used in both the secular and religious life of the Jewish people. They are evident of a culture where silversmiths, painters, engravers, writers, and metal workers were highly gifted and skilled in their art. Most of the treasures shown in recently displayed exhibits of Judaica were confiscated by the Germans during the late 1930s up to 1945; by then eight Jewish synagogues and fifty warehouses had been filled with Hitler's plunder. Judaica is currently available through dealers, from private collections, and the annual auction held in Israel.

Torah shield, Polish parcel-gilt silver, rococo cartouch form, embossed and chased with grapevines and applied flowers, late 1700s, 11", $5,000.00.

Badge, Star of David, blk print on yel cloth, 4x5", EX 635.00
Bezalel chanukah lamp, Palestine, brass triangle, 1920s, 8" 165.00
Bezalel ethrog box, Jerusalem, olive wood, 1930s, 4¼x6½" 200.00
Bezalel tea holder, Jerusalem, silver filigree, ca 1900, 6¾" 525.00
Bezalel vase, Palestine, brass conical form w/etching, 1920s, 7" .450.00
Candy dish, Jerusalem, sterling Bezalel filigree, ftd, 1915, 5" 300.00
Chanukah menorah, European, brass, 8-arm, star finial, 1940s, 26" ..450.00
Dish, Israel, brass, Zion Kislev Tasach, 1948, 7½" dia 165.00
Kiddush cup, Am, eng silver, ftd beaker shape, 20th C, 3⅜" 85.00
Kiddush cup, Coppini & Co (Italy), .800 silver, ca 1880, 4" 300.00
Poem, Italy, on rag paper in Hebrew, ca 1750s, 23x16", EX 450.00
Primer for Hebrew, Warsaw Poland, cloth-covered brds, 1890s, 6", VG ..165.00
Seder plate, Czech, wht porc w/gold, 6-panel, Kuchler, 1920s, 11" 450.00
Shabbos plate, Polish style, brass, stamped lion design, ca 1900 ..300.00
Spice tower, German, gilt silver, openwork/pennant, 1900s, 10½" .980.00
Wedding ring, Keren Heysode & 3 6-pointed stars, bronze 250.00

Jugtown

The Jugtown Pottery was started about 1920 by Juliana and Jacques Busbee, in Moore County, North Carolina. Ben Owen, a young descendant of a Staffordshire potter, was hired in 1923. He was the master potter, while the Busbees experimented with perfecting glazes and supervising design and modeling. Preferred shapes were those reminiscent of traditional country wares and classic Oriental forms. Glazes were various: natural-clay oranges, buffs, 'Tobacco-Spit' Brown, Mirror Black, white, 'Frog Skin' Green, a lovely turquoise called Chinese Blue, and the traditional cobalt-decorated salt glaze. The pottery gained national recognition, and as a result of their success, several other local potteries were established. The pottery closed for a time in the late 1950s due to the ill health of Mrs. Busbee (who had directed the business after her husband died in 1947) but reopened in 1960. Jugtown is still in operation; however, they no longer use their original glaze colors which are now so collectible.

Bean pot, orange w/blk specks, w/lid, '30s, Owen, 5½", NM 120.00
Bowl, brush-appl pastel bl, Oriental Translation, 11½", EX 275.00
Bowl, Chinese Blue, flat rim, 4½x7¼" 750.00
Bowl, Chinese Blue, predominantly turq w/sm red areas, 6" 250.00
Bowl, Frog Skin Green, finger groove at rim, conical, Owen, '30s, 8" .130.00
Bowl, Frog Skin Green, wavy lines, flared rim, 4¾x9½" 375.00
Bowl, Oriental Translation w/incised decor, Mirror Black, 1930s, 4x7" ...250.00
Bowl, salt glaze w/cobalt int & decor, ca 1922-23, 6x9⅞" 2,000.00
Bowl vase, Chinese Blue, Ben Owen, 1930s, 6" H 1,600.00
Chamberstick, orange w/gr spotting, early '60s, 2x8" 325.00
Cracker jar, salt glaze w/heavy pitting, appl rnd hdls, 9" 1,100.00
Jug, Frog Skin Green, w/matt bottom, cvd lines, Owen, 4" 175.00
Jug, Frog Skin Green w/cobalt splotch, Ben Owen, 1930s, 4⅜" ..225.00
Pie plate, med orange w/gr spots & slip chicken, '40s, 10½" 475.00
Pitcher, orange, primitive style, w/lid, Owen, '30s, 6", EX 175.00
Pitcher, pumpkin orange, mk, 10½" 300.00
Teapot, bright orange, earthenware, Ben Owen, 1930s, 6¼x9⅛" ..275.00
Vase, Chinese Blue, corseted, 11x7¾" 3,500.00
Vase, Chinese Blue, experimental turq on blk/wht, 9" 1,700.00
Vase, Chinese Blue, hdls, 8¾x8" 2,200.00
Vase, Chinese Blue, red & turq, incised band at top, 5½x6½" ..2,500.00
Vase, Chinese Blue, tapered shoulder, bulbous, 6x6½" 900.00
Vase, Chinese Blue, 4x3" 750.00
Vase, Chinese Blue drip on brn bsk, 5¾x4½" 1,300.00
Vase, Chinese Blue w/red, urn shape w/hdls, 7x5½" 900.00
Vase, Chinese Blue w/thick/heavy drippings, red int, 4¾x6½" ...2,400.00
Vase, cobalt mottle w/orange clear int, JH Owen, 1923-24, 7⅜" 325.00
Vase, dbl-gourd; Chinese White, late 1950s, 6¾" 550.00
Vase, lt Chinese Blue, classic shape, 9½x7" 1,200.00
Vase, Mirror Black, 7x7" 500.00
Vase, purple & gr drip, glossy, bulbous, 5½x4¼" 1,500.00
Vase, salt glaze w/gray dbl-dip top, Ben Owen, 1930s, 6½" 250.00
Vase, wht drips on brn clay, closed-in rim, ovoid, 6½x4¼" 450.00

K. P. M. Porcelain

The original KPM wares were produced from 1823 until 1847 by the Konigliche Porzellan Manfaktur, located in Berlin, Germany. Meissen used the same letters on some of their porcelains, as did several others in the area. In addition to the initials, the mark sometimes contains a crowned eagle with a scepter. Watch for items currently being imported from China; they are marked KPM with the eagle, but the scepter is not present. Our advisor for this category is Don Williams; he is listed in the Directory under Missouri.

Ashtray, Nouveau grasshopper hdls, slot for matches, #4675 .....290.00
Bowl, centerpc; HP florals w/gold (worn), hdls, 6¼x14x11" 365.00
Cup & saucer, Japanese scene reserved in gold fr 560.00
Egg tray, 12 wells, chicken in center, #4722, 6x9½" dia 370.00
Figurine, bird on tree stump, scepter mk, 10" 420.00
Figurine, nobleman w/bouquet beside tree, 1720-30, 8¾" 825.00
Lobster dish, dbl shell, pk lustre 155.00
Plaque, Eve, sgn L Sibinzel, gilt rococo fr 4,250.00
Plaque, fruits, flowers & bugs, scepter mk, 7½x10" 1,510.00
Plaque, Lady Sheffield, lg red hat, Wagner, giltwood fr, 9x6½" .4,000.00
Plaque, maid, daisies in hair, Wagner, gesso/gilt fr, 9x7" 4,450.00
Plaque, Renaissance lady on balcony, 16½x12½" 7,000.00
Plaque, Ruth, after Landelle, wide gilt fr, 7x5" 2,900.00
Plaque, Slave for Sale, Hock, ornate fr, 7x5" 2,465.00
Tureen, emb roses & leaves, pk, purple & gray on wht, 8½x14" dia ..210.00

Kayserzinn Pewter

J.P. Kayser Sohn produced pewter decorated with relief-molded Art Nouveau motifs in Germany during the late 1800s and into the twentieth century. Examples are marked with 'Kayserzinn' and the mold number within an elongated oval reserve. Items with three-dimensional animals, insects, birds, etc., are valued much higher than bowls, plates, and trays with simple embossed florals, which are usually priced at $100.00 to about $200.00, depending on size.

Ashtray, emb elk, #4797, triangular, 6" 55.00
Basket, floral relief, 9x12", from $260 to 320.00
Dish, emb iris, #4257, 5½" dia 35.00
Flagon, stylized wheat stalks & hops, #4289, 15⅞" 300.00
Inkwell, w/lily pads & leaves, attached to lily pad, 4½x7" 150.00
Knife rest, stylized dachschund, 3½x1¼" 60.00
Lamp, oil; Aladdin style on ped ft, emb floral, 9" 165.00
Pitcher, satyr's face & iris design, #4061, 12½" 430.00
Teapot, emb floral w/flower finial, #4290, 1-cup, 4½" 95.00

Keeler, Brad

Keeler studied art for a time in the 1930s; later he became a modeler for a Los Angeles firm. By 1939 he was working in his own studio where he created naturalistic studies of birds and animals which were marketed through giftware stores. They were decorated by means of an airbrush and enhanced with hand-painted details. His flamingo figures were particularly popular. In the mid-'40s, he developed a successful line of Chinese Modern housewares glazed in Ming Dragon Blood, a red color he personally developed. Keeler died of a heart attack in 1952, and the pottery closed soon thereafter. For more information, we recommend *The Collector's Encyclopedia of California Pottery, Second Edition*, by Jack Chipman (Collector Books).

Dish, gr leaf form w/lobster hdl, divided, stamped mk, 11½" 65.00
Figurine, bluejay, naturalistic, in-mold mk, #735, 9¼" 85.00
Figurine, cocker spaniel pup, begging, in-mold mk, #735, 6" 45.00
Figurine, crested Heron, in-mold mk, #43, 15½", minimum value ...225.00
Figurine, ducks (2) on base, stamped mk, #53, 6" 50.00
Figurine, egret (crane), in-mold mk, 9½" 95.00
Figurine, flamingo, in-mold mk, #903, 6" 85.00
Figurine, peacock, Exotic line, #717, 11½" 165.00
Figurine, pheasant, male, in-mold mk, 9x11" 90.00
Figurine, sea gull, in-mold mk, #29, 10½" 100.00
Figurine, Siamese cat, printed mk, #798 ....100.00
Figurine, Siamese cat on Ming Dragon Blood red pillow, #946, 3x3" ...45.00
Figurine, swan, early stamped mk, #725, 9" 100.00
Figurine, Wee Willie Winkie 100.00
Figurines, canaries (male & female), in-mold mk, 8¼", 6", pr ...100.00
Shakers, lobster form, paper labels, pr 45.00
Vase/planter, circus elephant, Pride & Joy line, #502, 8½" 65.00

Keen Kutter

Keen Kutter was the brand name chosen in 1870 by the Simmons Firm for a line of high-grade tools and cutlery. The trademark was first applied to high-grade axes. A corporation was formed in 1874 called Simmons Hardware Company. In 1922 Winchester merged with Simmons and continued to carry a full line of hardware plus the Winchester brand. The merger terminated in March of 1929 and converted back to the original status of Simmons Hardware Co. It wasn't until July 1, 1950, that Simmons Hardware Co. was purchased by Shapleigh Hardware Company. All Simmons Hardware Co. trademark lines were continued, and the business operated successfully until its closing in 1962. Today the Keen Kutter logo is owned by the Val-Test Company of Chicago, Illinois. For further study we recommend *Keen Kutter Collectibles*, an illustrated price guide by our advisors for this category, Jerry and Elaine Heuring, available at your favorite bookstore or public library. The Heurings are listed in the Directory under Missouri. See also Knives.

Apple parer or peeler, Pat May 24, 1898 ....150.00
Ax, fireman's, pointed end, EX 450.00
Bit, expansive, EX 25.00
Box or crate opener, EX 100.00
Brace, KB, 12", EX 25.00
Calendar, open scissors, scene w/cabin, 1940, EX 225.00
Carving set, knife, fork & steel w/stag hdls, EX 50.00
Catalog, No 476 Specialty Tool Catalog, EX 85.00
Catalog, 1930 No U, paper cover, EX 350.00
Chisel, ¾" socket firmer w/wood hdl, EX 20.00
Display case, Shears & Scissors, oak/etched glass, 31x16x17" ..1,200.00
Fence plier/staple puller, K1946, 2⅝", EX 35.00
Finger nail clippers, EX 55.00
Food chopper, K22, no box 15.00
Fork, baling press; EX 70.00
Gauge, marking; K25, wooden 40.00
Hammer, ball pein; 20-oz, EX 45.00
Hammer, rubber hdl, steel shank, EX 35.00
Hatchet, rubber hdl, steel shank, EX 40.00
Koffee Krusher No 12, 8¾" wheels, EX 1,400.00
Level, KK13, 18", EX 30.00
Nail apron, bib style, EX 100.00
Padlock, Santa Fe, EX 450.00
Pencil, carpenter's, unused 20.00
Plane, cabinet scraper, KK79, EX 60.00
Plane, circular, KK113, EX 360.00
Plane, KK4, iron, Keen Kutter written on lever cap, EX 70.00
Plane, K5, corrugated bottom, adjustable, EX 70.00
Pliers, diagonal cutting, K47, 7", EX 30.00
Plum bob, metal w/logo, 3x1½", EX 175.00
Postcard, The Dog Doesn't Mind, 1912, 4x6", EX 200.00
Rack, pnt; color card holder, tin, 15¼x11¼x4¾", EX 300.00
Razor strop, K94, EX 65.00
Rule, K320, caliper, 4-fold, EX 95.00
Safety razor, K9S, EX 40.00
Saw, hand; w/logo on bottom, K88S, no mk on blade, VG 20.00
Scissors, buttonhole, EX 30.00
Screwdriver, red plastic hdl, EX 10.00

Sign, advertising hardware store location, 9¾x27¾", EX, $125.00. **(Photo courtesy Jerry and Elaine Heuring)**

Spoke pointer, EX 70.00
Thermos, logo on bottom, 1-qt, EX 125.00
Tinner snips, K12, EX 25.00
Tool box, oak w/brass logo, 27x9x5", EX 450.00
Want book, Shapleigh, spiral bound, EX 35.00
Water jug, insulated, faucet type, Shapleigh, EX 75.00
Wrench, adjustable, S w/logo stamped in jaw, EX 175.00

Kellogg Studio

Stanley Kellogg (1908–1972) opened the Kellogg Studio in Petoskey, Michigan, in 1948. It remained in operation until 1976, producing a wide range of both decorative and functional ceramics including dinnerware, vases, and figurines. Most pieces are glazed in rich, solid colors and are marked 'Petoskey' as well as 'S. Kellogg Studio' or 'Kellogg's.' Stanley Kellogg began as a sculptor, and it was while working on an outdoor monument with the great Swedish-American sculptor, Carl Milles, that Stanley suffered the back injury which forced him to turn to studio work. In addition to naturalistic treatments of Michigan wildlife, Kellogg developed some angular, architectural forms in his molded art pottery. Our co-advisors for this category are Walter P. Hogan and Wendy L. Woodworth; they are listed in the Directory under Michigan. See Kellogg Studio website: www.emunix.emich.edu/~whogan/kellogg/index.html

Bowl, burgundy, teardrop shape, sm, +tiny frog insert 15.00
Bowl, tan w/wht int, 1" 7.00
Candle holders, wht, triangular, 1", pr 35.00
Creamer, blk, w/lid, 4" 22.00
Figurine, owl chick, standing, brn, 5" 85.00
Figurines, duck, 5", & 2 ducklings, ea 2", yel, 3-pc set 45.00
Flower frog, bl speckled, spherical w/star top, 3¼" 45.00
Pitcher, blk, rnd w/curved hdl, 7½" 50.00
Plate, gr w/map of Little Traverse Bay, 13" 80.00
Vase, bl, wide cylinder w/vertical grooves, 10" 60.00
Vase, gr, 8-sided irregular rhomboid, 1½" 25.00

Kelva

Kelva was a trademark of the C.F. Monroe Company of Meriden, Connecticut; it was produced for only a few years after the turn of the century. It is distinguished from the Wave Crest and Nakara lines by its unique Batik-like background, probably achieved through the use of a cloth or sponge to apply the color. Large florals are hand painted on the opaque milk glass; and ormolu and brass mounts were used for the boxes, vases, and trays. Most pieces are signed. Our advisors for this category are Dolli and Wilfred Cohen; they are listed in the Directory under California.

Vase, floral on green signed, 12¾", $1,250.00. (Value is more for colors other than green.)

Box, blown-out rose on lid, 3¾x2½" 950.00
Box, floral w/beading, crown mold, ftd, 6½" 1,250.00
Box, metal w/floral glass lid, 3x3¼" 595.00
Box, parrot tulips on gr, 6" dia, NM 850.00
Box, pastoral scenic reserves, crown mold, 6½" dia 1,200.00
Match holder, floral, 1½x2½" 850.00
Napkin ring, floral on peach, bl, gr or red, ea 650.00
Shakers, floral on gr, ftd, 3", pr 550.00
Tray, floral, crown mold, ornate hdls, 6¼" dia 395.00
Tray, floral on gr, SP trim, 6½" dia 450.00
Vase, floral, lg spray on pk & gr, beaded top, 8x3" 945.00
Vase, floral, ornate hdls & ft, 14" 1,500.00
Vase, floral on fuchsia, conical form on 4 gold ft, 6x2" 695.00
Vase, floral on red, beaded pastel ribbons at base, 7¾x2¾" 950.00
Vase, floral on red, shouldered, flared ft, 7¼x3" 950.00

Kentucky Derby Glasses

Kentucky Derby glasses are the official souvenir glasses sold at Churchill Downs filled with mint juleps on Derby Day. Many folks from all over the country who attend the Derby take home the souvenir glass, and thus the collecting begins. The first glass (1938) is said to have either been given away as a souvenir or used for drinks among the elite at the Downs. This one, the 1939 glass, two glasses from 1940, the 1940–41 aluminum tumbler, the 'Beetleware' tumblers from 1941 to 1944, and the 1945 short, tall, and jigger glasses are the rarest, most sought-after, and they command the highest prices. Some 1974 glasses incorrectly listed the 1971 winner Canonero II as just Canonero; as a result, it became the 'mistake' glass for that year. Also, glasses made by the Federal Glass Company (whose logo, found on the bottom of the glass, is a small shield containing an F) were used for extra glasses for the 100th running in 1974. There is also a 'mistake' and a correct Federal glass, making four to collect for that year.

In order to identify the year of a pre-1969 glass, since it did not appear on the front of the glass prior to then, simply add one year to the last date listed on the back of the glass. This may seem to be a confusing practice, but the current year's glass is produced long before the Derby winner is determined. Our advisor for this category is Betty Hornback; she is listed in the Directory under Kentucky.

1940, aluminum 800.00
1940, French Lick, aluminum 800.00
1941-44, Beetleware, from $2,500 to 4,000.00
1945, jigger 1,000.00
1945, regular 1,400.00
1945, tall 425.00
1946-47, ea 100.00
1948, clear bottom 200.00
1948, frosted bottom 225.00
1949 ....200.00
1950 ....425.00
1951 ....550.00
1952 Gold Cup 190.00
1953 ....150.00
1954 ....185.00
1955 ....135.00
1956, 4 variations, ea from $150 to 300.00
1957, gold & blk on frosted 110.00
1958, Gold Bar 175.00
1958, Iron Leige 200.00
1959-60, ea 80.00
1961 ....100.00
1962, Churchill Downs, red, gold & blk on clear 70.00
1963-64, ea 50.00
1965 ....70.00
1966 ....55.00
1967-69, ea 50.00
1970 ....60.00
1971 ....45.00
1972 ....45.00
1973 ....50.00
1974, Federal (ea) 150.00
1974, mistake 18.00
1974, regular 16.00
1975 ....12.00
1976 ....14.00
1976, plastic 12.00

1977 ....12.00
1978-79, ea 14.00
1980 ....18.00
1981 ....14.00
1982 ....12.00
1983 ....10.00
1984-85, ea 10.00
1986 ....12.00
1986 (1985 copy) 20.00
1987-89, ea 9.00
1990-92, ea 8.00
1993-95, ea 6.00
1996-97, ea 5.00
1998 ....4.00
1999 ....3.00
2000 ....3.00

Kew Blas

Kew Blas was a trade name used by the Union Glass Company of Summerville, Massachusetts, for their iridescent, lustered art glass produced from 1893 until about 1920. The glass was made in imitation of Tiffany and achieved notable success. Some items were decorated with pulled leaf and feather designs, while others had a monochrome lustre surface. The mark was an engraved 'Kew Blas' in an arching arrangement.

Bowl, hooked/swirled band, gr/gold on tan, gold int, 3½x5½" ..950.00
Decanter, gold w/pk & purple irid, 14½x4¾" 1,400.00
Finger bowl, gold irid, ribbed 200.00
Goblet, gold irid, 7½" 150.00
Vase, amber, gold stretched int, trumpet form on bulb ft, 12" 865.00
Vase, feathers, gold on gold, waisted w/narrow neck, 8x3¾" 900.00
Vase, swirl stems, gr on caramel, waisted, 4-petal top, 10" 600.00

King's Rose

King's Rose was made in Staffordshire, England, from about 1820 to 1830. It is closely related to Gaudy Dutch in body type as well as the colors used in its decoration. The pattern consists of a full-blown, orange-red rose with green, pink, and yellow leaves and accents. When the rose is in pink, the ware is often referred to as Queen's Rose.

Bowl, int w/wide pk band, deep, 5½" 500.00
Cake plate, Queens' Rose, floral rim band, rose in center, 10" ...200.00
Coffeepot, dome lid, pearlware, 11¼" 650.00
Creamer, Queen's Rose, pearlware, 4½" 230.00
Cup & saucer, handleless; red rose, vine border 245.00
Cup & saucer, Queen's Rose, pearlware, 2⅛x3⅜x5½", EX 150.00
Pitcher, milk; pearlware, 5⅜" 300.00
Plate, orange stripes on rim, 8¼" 250.00
Plate, pk border w/emb dmns, 8⅛" 220.00
Plate, Rogers, 8½" 135.00
Plate, toddy; 4¾" 275.00
Plate, vine border, red rim band, 9¼" 400.00
Plate, wide pk border w/sm floral reserves, 5" 250.00
Plate, wide pk rim band, mk w/asterisk, 6½", EX 200.00
Teapot, Queen's Rose, 6" 400.00

Kitchen Collectibles

During the last half of the 1850s, mass-produced kitchen gadgets were patented at an astonishing rate. Most were ingeniously efficient. Apple peelers, egg beaters, cherry pitters, food choppers, and such were only the most common of hundreds of kitchen tools well designed to perform only specific tasks. Today all are very collectible.

For further information we recommend *Kitchen Glassware of the Depression Years* and *Anchor Hocking's Fire-King & More, Second Edition,* both by Gene Florence; and *Kitchen Antiques, 1790–1940,* by Kathryn McNerney. See also Appliances; Butter Molds and Stamps; Cast Iron; Cookbooks; Copper; Glass Knives; Molds; Pie Birds; Primitives; Reamers; String Holders; Tinware; Trivets; Wooden Ware; Wrought Iron.

Cast Kitchen Ware

Be aware that cast-iron counterfeit production is on the increase. Items with phony production numbers, finishes, etc., are being made at this time. Many of these new pieces are the popular cornstick pans. To command the values given below, examples must be free from damage of any kind or excessive wear. Waffle irons must be complete with all three pieces and the handle. The term 'EPU' in the description lines refers to the Erie PA, USA mark. The term 'block mark' refers to the lettering in the large logo that was used ca 1920 until 1940; 'slant logo' refers to the lettering in the large logo ca 1900 to 1920. Victor was Griswold's first low-budget line (ca 1875). Skillets #5 and #6 are uncommon, while #7, #8, and #9 are easy to find. For further information contact our advisor, Grant S. Windsor (SASE required); he is listed in the Directory under Virginia. See also Keen Kutter; Clubs, Newsletters, and Catalogs.

Skillet, Griswold #4, wood handle, block trademark, no heat ring, Pattern #758, $600.00. (Photo courtesy Grant S. Windsor)

Bacon press, Wagner #1103 ....85.00
Bread stick pan, Wagner #1326 ('E' pan) 35.00
Bundt pan, Frank Hay #965 (made by Griswold) 300.00
Cake mold, lamb, Griswold #866 ....100.00
Cake mold, Santa, Griswold 550.00
Cornstick pan, Griswold #262 ....65.00
Cornstick pan, Griswold #273 ....25.00
Cornstick pan, Wagner #1318 Senior, Krusty Korn Kob 45.00
Dutch oven, Griswold #6 Tite-Top, full writing cover, w/trivet .450.00
Dutch oven, Griswold #9, Erie, rnd bottom 60.00
Dutch oven, Griswold #10 Chuckwagon, 3-leg, lg trade mk 175.00
Gem pan, Griswold #6, full writing 400.00
Gem pan, Wagner #2, hdls, fully mk 700.00
Griddle, Griswold #10, hdl, slant/EPU trade mk 65.00
Kettle, Griswold #8, Erie, regular (3-leg) 65.00
Kettle, Griswold #9, Erie, flat bottom, #812 ....100.00
Loaf pan, Griswold #877 ....400.00
Muffin pan, GF Filley #5, 8-cup 125.00
Muffin pan, Reids Pan Dec 1870, 13-cup, 16¾x9" 200.00
Muffin pan, Wagner, Little Slam Gem Pan (heart/club/dmn/spade) ...275.00
Rack, skillet display; Griswold, all metal 300.00

Roaster (oval), Griswold #3, full writing cover w/trivet 800.00
Roaster (oval), Wagner #7, raised letters, w/trivet 275.00
Skillet, breakfast; Wagner #1101 ....40.00
Skillet, Griswold #2, block trademk, no heat ring 350.00
Skillet, Griswold #3, sm trademk, high-dome smooth-top cover ...200.00
Skillet, Griswold #3, sq, #2103 ....160.00
Skillet, Griswold #4, block trademk, heat ring 600.00
Skillet, Griswold #5, slant EPU trademk, heat ring 40.00
Skillet, Griswold #5, Victor 475.00
Skillet, Griswold #8, slant/EPU trademk, no heat ring 45.00
Skillet, Griswold #10, block trademk, no heat ring 50.00
Skillet, Griswold #10, wood hdl, slant/Erie trademk 200.00
Skillet, Griswold #11, slant/EPU trademk 350.00
Skillet, Griswold #13, block trademk 1,600.00
Skillet, Griswold #15, oval 275.00
Skillet, Griswold Victor #7, fully mk 45.00
Skillet, Wagner #6, Wagner, heat ring 25.00
Skillet, Wagner #8, shallow 85.00
Skillet, Wagner #10, stylized logo, heat ring 50.00
Skillet cover, Griswold #11, low dome, top writing 450.00
Teakettle, Wagner #9 ....75.00
Trivet, coffeepot; Griswold #1738, rnd, sm 250.00
Wafer iron, Wagner Ware Sidney O, #1450, 8½" dia 175.00
Waffle iron, Detroit Iron & Brass Co #7 & 8, Pat...1877 ....100.00
Waffle iron, GF Filley, inside writing, #B&9 ....200.00
Waffle iron, Griswold #8, Pat 1901 ....50.00
Waffle iron, Griswold #13, hotel type 1,000.00
Waffle iron, Wagner, Pat 1925 ....35.00

Egg Beaters

Egg beaters are unbeatable. Ranging from hand-helds, rotary-crank, and squeeze power to Archimedes up-and-down models, egg beaters are America's favorite kitchen gadget. A mainstay of any kitchenware collection, in recent years egg beaters have come into their own — nutmeg graters, spatulas, and can openers will have to scramble to catch up! At the turn of the century, everyone in America owned an egg beater. Every household did its own mixing and baking — there were no pre-processed foods. And every inventor thought he/she could make a better beater. Thus American ingenuity produced more than one thousand egg beater patents, dating back to 1856, with several hundred different models being manufactured over the years. As true examples of Americana, egg beaters have risen in value over the past couple of years, with a half dozen mixers valued at $2,500.00 and more, including the cast-iron, rotary crank 'Dodge Race Course egg beater.' But the vast majority stay under $50.00, while the values of the super rare beaters continue upward. And just when you think you've seen them all, new ones always turn up, usually at flea markets or garage sales. For further information, we recommend our advisor (author of the definitive book on egg beaters) Don Thornton, who is listed in the Directory under California. (SASE required.)

Aluminum Beauty Pat'd April 20, 1920..., rotary crank, 10½" 15.00
Another Androck Product Pat No 2210910, rotary crank, 10¾" .15.00
Biltrite...Pat Stuber & Kuck..., rotary crank, wood hdl, 10½" 30.00
Holt's Improved Dover, CI 55.00
Horlicks, Archimedes, all-wire drink mixer, 9¼" 30.00
Patent No 2906510, hand held, plastic hdl 5.00
Silver No 3, measuring glass w/emb iron top 295.00
Super Speed A&J Spinnit..., rotary turbine, wood hdl, 11½" 30.00
Taplin Light Running, CI w/wood hdl, 1908 Pat, 11½" 45.00
Twin Speed Mixer, rotary crank, plastic hdl, 11½" 20.00
WB-over-W Made in USA, Wallace Bros rotary, wood hdl, 11" ..10.00
Zip Whit S, J&H Dist...Cal, rotary crank, plastic hdl, 13½" 45.00

Glass

Batter bowl, gr, ribbed, Hocking 38.00
Batter jug, clear w/purple lid, Paden City 95.00
Butter dish, cobalt, emb lid, Hazel Atlas, 1-lb 275.00
Butter dish, custard, McKee, 1-lb 45.00
Butter dish, Delphite, emb lid, Jeannette, 1-lb 325.00
Cruet, gr, etched pattern, Cambridge 95.00
Cruet, gr, Imperial 45.00
Cruet, gr, Paden City 75.00
Dispenser, batter; wht w/floral decor, yel lid, Hocking 30.00
Dispenser, custard, McKee 125.00
Ice bucket, ice bl, Cambridge 125.00
Ladle, pk, Cambridge 25.00
Ladle, wht, Imperial 50.00
Measuring cup, bl, 3-spout, Fire-King 30.00
Measuring cup, fired-on red, McKee Glasbake 30.00
Measuring cup, gr, Bunker Hill Coffee 30.00
Measuring cup, gr, Saginaw Milling Co 30.00
Measuring cup, gr, Stickley & Poor Spice Co 30.00
Measuring cup, wht, dry measure, US Glass 200.00
Measuring pitcher, Delphite, McKee, 2-cup 90.00
Measuring pitcher, dk Jade-ite, sunflower in bottom, Jeannette, 2-cup ...90.00
Measuring pitcher, red or blk Dmn Check, McKee, 2-cup 40.00
Measuring pitcher, wht w/floral decal, McKee, 2-cup 40.00
Mixer, yel, Seville, complete 200.00
Mug, cream, Crown Tuscan 75.00
Napkin holder, blk, Paramount 495.00
Napkin holder, crystal, horizontal ribs, LE Smith 55.00
Rolling pin, amethyst, blown, unknown maker 135.00
Rolling pin, custard, shaker end, McKee 350.00
Salad set, blk or lt bl, Cambridge 150.00
Salad set, lt bl, Imperial 85.00
Salt box, gr, emb lid, rnd, Jeannette 250.00
Salt box, Jade-ite, McKee 100.00

Server, Emerald-Glo, metal frame, $50.00. (Photo courtesy Gene Florence)

Shaker, cinnamon; crystal, emb, Jeannette 20.00
Shaker, flour; blk w/wht lettering, Roman Arch, McKee 25.00
Shaker, flour/sugar; Skating Dutch, Hazel Atlas 17.50
Shaker, mouth wash/bicarbonate soda; bl, Jeannette, 8-oz 135.00
Shaker, paprika; bl, Jeannette, 8-oz 125.00
Straw holder, crystal, w/lid, Heisey 300.00
Syrup jug, gr, New Martinsville 75.00
Syrup pitcher, amber, w/lid, Cambridge 70.00
Syrup pitcher, pk, w/slotted lid, Imperial 75.00
Water bottle, Royal Ruby, ribbed bottom, Hocking 250.00

Miscellaneous

Apple peeler, Goodell Bonanza, rpt CI, 23x16½", on brd 182.50
Apple peeler, Goodell Turntable 98, CI 50.00
Apple peeler, RHCo, Pat May 5, 1868 (on turntable) 125.00
Apple peeler, Sargent & Foster, earliest Pat return model (1853) .100.00

Apple peeler, Sinclair Scott, CI heart shape, 1880s 70.00
Apple peeler, SS Hersey Pat June '61/Aug 30 '64, dbl action, NM ..700.00
Apple peeler, Whittemore Bros, CI spiral mechanism, mtd on brd ..700.00
Asparagus buncher, Handy Buncher...Pat 1902, CI 60.00
Beater, Dover Whippo, orig label 550.00
Biscuit cutter, Claro Flour, tin 62.50
Biscuit cutter, Rumford, tin 16.00
Biscuit cutter, tin hexagon, old 9.50
Biscuit/doughnut cutter, gr hdl 10.00
Butter curler, Automatic..., Chadwick-Miller, chrome-plated, MIB ...7.50
Can opener, bronze, greyhound dog figural 26.50
Can opener, CI, bull figural, 1860s, 6" 65.00
Can opener, Dazey, CI, wall mt 50.00
Can opener, Sunbeam, pk, 1950s 27.50
Cherry seeder, Enterprise #16, CI 60.00
Cherry seeder, Goodell Family, CI, dbl 40.00
Cherry seeder, New Standard, CI 110.00
Cherry seeder, Rollman #8, CI & wood, clamps on, 12" 65.00
Chopper, A Freeman, brass w/thin steel blade, wood hdl, 6" W ..55.00
Chopper, Griswold #2, MIB 45.00
Chopper, Universal, CI, pre-1900 ....20.00
Churn, Borden's, glass, 1-qt 60.00
Churn, Dazey #10, beveled edge, 1-qt 1,350.00
Churn, Dazey #10, bull's-eye, 1-qt 1,300.00
Churn, Dazey #20 ....200.00
Churn, Dazey #30, Pat 1922 ....225.00
Churn, Dazey #40 ....140.00
Churn, Dazey #60 ....165.00
Churn, Dazey #80 ....250.00
Churn, Dazey #400, heavy tin, 4-gal 200.00
Churn, syllabub; tin, rnd w/holes in bottom, tall 85.00
Churn, unmk, glass, 1-gal 75.00
Clothesline reel, Lowell Ever Ready, dustless 50.00
Dispenser, Folger's Coffee, glass w/red metal trim, wall type, rare ..50.00
Doughnut lifter, long wooden stick w/hdl 45.00
Egg poacher, dbl; aluminum w/red wooden knob, 4x7" 27.50
Egg timer, bellhop, gr, ceramic, Japan, 4½" 60.00
Egg timer, Black chef stands w/frying pan, chalk, Japan 125.00
Egg timer, boy w/blk cloak & cane, ceramic, Germany, 3¾" 65.00
Egg timer, chicken, wings hold tube, ceramic, Germany, 2¾" 50.00
Egg timer, Dutch boy kneeling, ceramic, Japan, 2½" 40.00
Egg timer, golliwog, bsk, English, 4½" 200.00
Egg timer, Mexican w/guitar, ceramic, Germany, 3½" 65.00
Egg timer, parlor maid w/cat, ceramic, Japan, 4" 65.00
Egg timer, telephone, blk glaze on clay, Japan, 2" 35.00
Egg timer, windmill w/dog on base, Japan, 3¾" 85.00
Egg tongs, heavy wire, egg shape at bottom 45.00
Flour sifter, Androck, pastry pictures on tin, red hdl 22.50
Flour sifter, Androck, red & wht checkerboard, 3-screen, w/lid ...55.00
Flour sifter, Androck Hand-i-Sift, 3-screen, red hdl, 5" 30.00
Flour sifter, Blood's, wooden, Pat Sept Sept 17, 1861 ....350.00
Flour sifter, Bromwell, pnt apples on tin, 1940s-50s, 3-cup, EX ...25.00
Flour sifter, poplar w/old finish, 8x15x10" 350.00
Flour sifter, Savory Sift-Chine, EX 18.00
Flour sifter, tin w/pnt kitchen scene, yel hdl, 1940s-50s, 5½" 32.00
Flour tin, CI loop hdls, japanned/stenciled lid w/wheat, 12x21" .150.00
Food warmer, Clarke's Pat Pyramid, wht ironstone, tin stand, 10½" ...165.00
Grater, cheese; metal grater in wood fr, EX 25.00
Grater, chocolate; Edgar, dk tin, Pat 1891-96 ....275.00
Grater, nutmeg; CI w/brass fittings, wooden hdl, Pat 1870, 4" ...275.00
Grater, nutmeg; Davidson Automatic, Pat 1908 ....660.00
Grater, nutmeg; NP brass, bbl type, 13 star US crest on lid 155.00
Grater, nutmeg; NP CI, Caldwell...NY, early 1900s 82.50
Grater, nutmeg; NP metal, spring loaded, red wood hdl, 4x2½" ..50.00

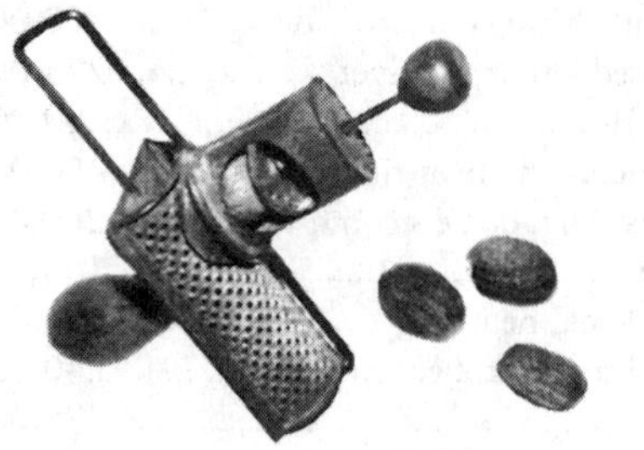

Nutmeg grater, The Edgar, wood, tin, and wire, Patent dated Aug. 18, 1891, $95.00. (Photo courtesy Kathryn McNerney)

Grater, nutmeg; The Rapid, japanned tin, orig label 560.00
Grater, nutmeg; tin & wood, Pat 12-25-1877, 6¼" 165.00
Grater, nutmeg; tin cylinder w/hinged cap, 2⅛x1⅛" dia, EX 65.00
Grater, nutmeg; tin w/bl japanning traces, sliding wooden feeder, 6" ..100.00
Grater, nutmeg; trn mahog w/brass fittings, wear, 7⅝" 285.00
Ice crusher, triple; Dazey, MIB 25.00
Juicer, Columbia...Press, Landers Frary & Clark, CI, 7½" 46.00
Juicer, Juice King, gr & chrome, 1950s, EX 40.00
Juicer, Juice-O-Mat, chrome, Deco style, single action 27.00
Juicer, Juice-O-Mat, chrome, lever action, tilt head 142.50
Kraut cutter/meat slicer, Arcadia 1891, CI/oak, Pat 1885-1891, 21" ..46.00
Lard press, Enterprise, CI, 18x11" 138.00
Lard press, Griswold #2, CI, 4-qt 100.00
Lard press/sausage stuffer, Enterprise #2092, CI, EX 80.00
Lard/fruit press, H Troemner, 1-qt 110.00
Lemon squeezer, Arcade, CI, 8¾" 35.00
Lemon squeezer, burl walnut wood, stainless hinge, 11½" 35.00
Lemon squeezer, Griswold #1, CI 180.00
Lemon squeezer, Sunkist, cast metal, pliers style 65.00
Measure, coffee; Dix Coffee Meater, tin can shape, sm 48.00
Measuring cup, Compliments of Minute Tapoica, tin 35.00
Meat tenderizer, CI axe style w/wood hdl, 1900s, 14¾x5" 26.00
Mixer, Standard Specialty Co 850.00
Mixer churn, Ladd #2 ....450.00
Noodle cutter, roller-like tool w/wire & wood hdl, 3"+6" hdl 16.00
Pie crimper, brass, open heart at end for decorating 135.00
Pie crimper, cast metal 20.00
Pie crimper, solid brass, 6½" 15.00
Pie crimper, wooden, fancy hdl, 2¾" wheel 145.00
Potato baker, Rumford, tin, holds 6 ....70.00
Potato masher, heavy gauge wire, wood hdl, early 20.00
Potato peeler, curved knife blade w/wood hdl, Pat'd Oct 2, 1900 ...10.00
Potato peeler, Devault...Chicago..., 1930s 7.00
Raisin seeder, Everett, Pat Apr '89, May '93 ....22.00
Raisin seeder, Ezy, CI, Pat May 21 1895, table clamp 250.00
Raisin seeder, Ezy, CI, pump hdl, Pat May 21 189 ....200.00
Raisin seeder, The Crown, CI, table clamp, Pat Oct 26, '96 ....95.00
Reamer, lemon; wooden, grooved bottom, pointed end, 6" L 110.00
Rolling pin, milk glass, wooden hdls, 1921 ....40.00
Rolling pin, trn wood, 1-hdl, mortise & tenon joints, 12½" 38.00
Rolling pin, trn wood, 14" 45.00
Slicer, bean; CI, clamp-on style 30.00
Slicer, Enterprise...Vegetable Cutter Pat...1888, CI/tin, 16½" ...200.00
Sprinkler bottle, Chinaman, wht & aqua, Cleminson, from $30 to ..40.00
Sprinkler bottle, clothespin, red, yel & gr plastic, from $20 to 40.00
Sprinkler bottle, elephant, pk & gray, ceramic, from $50 to 75.00
Sprinkler bottle, iron, bl flowers, ceramic, from $100 to 150.00
Sprinkler bottle, Mammy, ceramic (possibly Faltzgraff), from $250 to ..350.00
Sprinkler bottle, peasant lady w/laundry poem on label, from $200 to .300.00
Sprinkler bottle, Sprinkle Plenty, yel & gr, Cardinal China, $20 to 30.00

Knives

Knife collecting as a hobby began in earnest during the 1960s when government regulations required for the first time that knife companies mark their product with the country of origin. The few collectors and dealers cognizant of this change at once began stockpiling the older knives made before this law was enacted. Another impetus to the growing interest in this area came with the Gun Control Act of 1968, which severely restricted gun trading. Frustrated gun dealers transferred their attention to knives. Today there are collectors clubs in many of the states.

The most sought-after pocketknives are those made before WWII. However, Case, Schrade, and Primble knives of a more recent manufacture are also collected. Most collectors prefer knives 'as found.' Do not attempt to clean, sharpen, or in any way 'improve' on an old knife.

The prices quoted here are for knives in mint condition. If a knife has been used, sharpened, or blemished in any way, its value decreases. Knives in excellent condition generally are valued at half the prices listed below. The newer the knife, the greater the reduction in value. For further information refer to *Big Book of Pocket Knives* and *The Standard Knife Collector's Guide, 2nd Edition*, by Ron Stewart and Roy Ritchie (both published by Collector Books); and *Sargent's American Premium Guide to Knives and Razors, Identification and Values, 3rd Edition*, by Jim Sargent. Our advisor for this category is Bill Wright; he is listed in the Directory under Indiana.

Key:
bd — blade
imi — imitation
jack — jackknife
wb — winterbottom

Case, C61050, gr bone hdl, 1-bd, Case Tested XX, 5⅝" 600.00
Case, 04247SP, wht compo hdl, 2-bd, USA, 3⅞" 100.00
Case, 06244, bone stag hdl, 2-bd, 10 Dot, 1970, 3¼" 30.00
Case, 1116SP, walnut hdl, 1-bd, XX, 3½" 45.00
Case, 2137, Sod Buster Jr, blk compo hdl, 1-bd, 7 Dot, 1983, 3⅝" ..16.00
Case, 22028½, slick blk hdl, 2-bd, XX, 3½" 80.00
Case, 2217, slick blk hdl, 2-bd, Tested XX, 3⅞" 250.00
Case, 3201, yel compo hdl, 2-bd, XX, 1940-64, 2⅝" 40.00
Case, 3252, hobo knife, yel compo hdl, 1-bd/1-fork, Tested XX, 3¾" ...450.00
Case, 4200SS, citrus tester, wht compo hdl, 2-bd, USA, 5½" 85.00
Case, 5111½, stag hdl, 1-bd, Case Bros, Little Valley, 4⅜" 700.00
Case, 52042, stag hdl, 2-bd, Tested XX, 1920-40, 3" 150.00
Case, 5254, 2nd cut stag hdl, 2-bd, USA, 4⅛" 550.00
Case, 5287, gunstock, stag hdl, 2-bd, Tested XX, 3½" 550.00
Case, 53131, canoe, stag hdl, 3-bd, Tested XX, 1920-40, 3⅝" 1,000.00
Case, 5364TF, stag hdl, 3-bd, Tested XX, 1920-40, 3⅛" 250.00
Case, 61049LP, gr bone hdl, 1-bd, Case Tested XX, 4⅛" 325.00
Case, 6105LP, gr bone hdl, 1-bd, Tested XX, 3⅞" 300.00
Case, 6106, gr bone hdl, 1-bd, Tested XX, 2⅝" 300.00
Case, 61093, bone hdl, 1-bd, 10 Dot, 1970, 5" 85.00
Case, 61098, gr bone hdl, 1-bd, Tested XX, 5½" 375.00
Case, 62031½, rough blk hdl, 2-bd, Tested XX, 3¾" 140.00
Case, 62048SPLP, gr bone hdl, 2-bd, Tested XX, 4" 250.00
Case, 62052, Congress, bone hdl, 2-bd, XX, 3½" 45.00
Case, 6207, gr bone hdl, 2-bd, Tested XX, 3½" 300.00
Case, 6210½, gr bone hdl, 2-bd, Tested XX, 3⅛" 200.00
Case, 62109X, gr bone hdl, 2-bd, XX, 1940-55, 3⅛" 200.00
Case, 6211LP, gr bone hdl, 2-bd, Tested XX, 4½" 1,200.00
Case, 62131, bone hdl, 2-bd, XX, 1964, 3⅝" 250.00
Case, 6216½, bone hdl, 2-bd, USA, 3⅜" 35.00
Case, 6224½, gr bone hdl, 2-bd, Tested XX, 3" 150.00
Case, 6225LP, gr bone hdl, 2-bd, Tested XX, 3" 250.00
Case, 6228LP, gr bone hdl, easy open, 2-bd, Case Brad, PA, 3⅝" ..200.00
Case, 6247J, gr bone hdl, 2-bd, Tested XX, 1920-40, 3⅞" 800.00
Case, 6296XSS, bone hdl, 2-bd, XX, 4¼" 125.00
Case, 6299SHR, gr bone hdl, 2-bd, Tested XX, 1920-40, 4⅛" ...250.00
Case, 63092, gr bone hdl, 2-bd/1 punch, Tested XX, 1920-40, 4" ..325.00
Case, 6347SHSP, red bone hdl, 3-bd, XX, 1940-64, 3⅞" 85.00
Case, 6400-45R, scout, blk plastic hdl, 4-bd, XX, 1940-50, 3⅝" ..30.00
Case, 6445R, rough blk hdl, 4-bd, Tested XX, 1920-40, 3¾" 200.00
Case, 6488, bone hdl, 4-bd, 10 Dot, 1970, 4⅛" 250.00
Case, 8233, pearl hdl, 1-bd/letter opener, 6¾" 225.00
Case, 8264TF, pearl hdl, 2-bd, Tested XX, 1920-40, 3⅛" 185.00
Case, 8271LP, pearl hdl, 2-bd, XX, 3¼" 225.00
Case, 8279, pearl hdl, 2-bd, Tested XX, 3⅛" 150.00
Case, 92058, bird's eye, Fr pearl hdl, 2-bd, Tested XX, 3¼" 125.00
Case, 9233, cracked ice hdl, 2-bd, XX, 2⅝" 40.00
Case, 9383, cracked ice hdl, 3-bd, XX, 1940-55, 3½" 250.00
Keen Kutter, Coke bottle, ebony hdl, 1-bd, 5¼" 200.00
Keen Kutter, dog-leg jack, walnut hdl, 1-bd, 3⅜" 30.00
Keen Kutter, equal end jack, cocobolo hdl, 1-bd, 3¼" 25.00
Keen Kutter, jack, brn bone hdl, 2-bd, EC Simmons, 3⅞" 45.00
Keen Kutter, jack, coffin, pearl hdl, 2-bd, 3⅝" 150.00
Keen Kutter, jack, metal hdl, 2-bd, EC Simmons, 3½" 30.00
Keen Kutter, K100, Texas toothpick, butter/molasses hdl, 1-bd, 5" ..150.00
Keen Kutter, K345, moose, tan celluloid hdl, 2-bd, 3⅜" 65.00
Keen Kutter, peanut, cracked ice hdl, 2-bd, 2⅞" 35.00
Keen Kutter, peanut dog-leg, pearl hdl, 2-bd, EC Simmons, 3" 50.00
Keen Kutter, senator, pearl hdl, 2-bd, EC Simmons, 3" 40.00
Keen Kutter, senator pen, metal hdl, 2-bd, 3⅛" 20.00
Keen Kutter, trapper, dmn edge, peach seed bone hdl, 2-bd, 3⅞" ..125.00
Keen Kutter, whittler, dmn edge, stag hdl, 3-bd, 3¼" 75.00
Keen Kutter, whittler, pearl hdl, 3-bd, EC Simmons, 3¼" 100.00
Keen Kutter, 1881, barlow, brn bone hdl, 1-bd, 3⅜" 65.00
Keen Kutter, 828, barlow, yel bone hdl, 2-bd, 3⅜" 60.00
Queen, 10, jack, wb bone hdl, 2-bd, 3½" 28.00
Queen, 11, wb bone hdl, 1-bd, Queen Steel, 4⅛" 25.00
Queen, 15, congress, Rogers bone hdl, 2-bd, 3½" 40.00
Queen, 16, wb bone hdl, 3-bd, Queen Steel, 3¼" 30.00
Queen, 18, jack, wb bone hdl, 2-bd, Big Q, 3⅝" 50.00
Queen, 25, barlow, brn bone hdl, 2-bd, Queen Steel, 3½" 60.00
Queen, 29, jack, wb bone hdl, 2-bd, Queen Steel, 4½" 40.00
Queen, 35, serpentine, blk hdl, 3-bd, Queen Stainless, 2⅝" 30.00
Queen, 37, stockman, wb bone hdl, 3-bd, Queen, 4" 60.00
Queen, 49, stockman, wb bone hdl, 3-bd, Queen, 4¼" 40.00
Queen, 54, pearl hdl, 3-bd, Queen Steel, 2⅝" 30.00

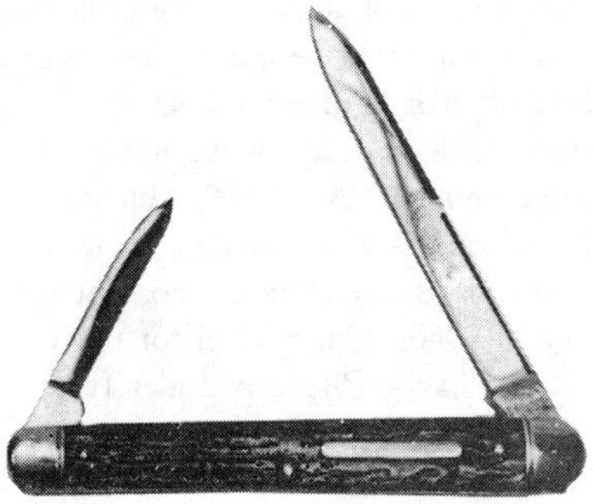

Remington, R6966, stag handle, two-blade, 3¾", $175.00.

Remington, RH73, jack, brn bone hdl, 2-bd, 3⅛" 130.00
Remington, R105A, onyx hdl, 3-bd, 3⅜" 150.00
Remington, R1273, bullet shield, brn bone hdl, 2-bd, 5⅜" 3,500.00
Remington, R1383, fish scaler, lockback, brn bone hdl, 1-bd, 4¼" ..450.00
Remington, R1582, slick blk hdl, 2-bd, 3" 90.00
Remington, R1653, peanut, brn bone hdl, 2-bd, 2⅞" 125.00
Remington, R2095, blk & wht compo hdl, 2-bd, 3⅛" 90.00
Remington, R2605, jack, red scale hdl, 2-bd, 3⅜" 110.00
Remington, R273, Texas jack, acorn shield, brn bone hdl, 2-bd, 4" ..400.00
Remington, R3059, stockman, all metal hdl, 3-bd, 4" 250.00
Remington, R3115, serpentine, imi ivory hdl, 2-bd, 4" 135.00
Remington, R3273, cattle, equal end, brn bone hdl, 3-bd, 3¾" .400.00

Remington, R3424, equal end, slant bolsters, pearl hdl, 3-bd, 3⅜" ..350.00
Remington, R3843, utility, brn bone hdl, 6-bd, 3⅝" 650.00
Remington, R4133, stockman, bone hdl, 3-bd, 3⅜" 175.00
Remington, R4134, stockman, pearl hdl, 3-bd, 3⅜" 250.00
Remington, R563, acorn shield, brn bone hdl, 2-bd, 3¼" 150.00
Remington, R645, switchblade, candy stripe hdl, 1-bd, 4" 500.00
Remington, R698, hawkbill, cocobolo hdl, 2-bd, 4" 110.00
Remington, R708, hawkbill, cocobolo hdl, 1-bd, 3⅝" 125.00
Remington, R71, lobster, redwood hdl, 3-bd, 3⅛" 100.00
Remington, R953, brn bone hdl, 1-bd, 5" 225.00
Remington, R973, jack, imi bone hdl, 2-bd, 4¼" 275.00
Western States, S203B, gr sparkle hdl, 2-bd, bail, 2½" 25.00
Western States, 13228½, dog-leg jack, Christmas tree hdl, 2-bd, 3" ...75.00
Western States, 2106BH, pearl overlay hdl, 1-bd, 5¼" 150.00
Western States, 6100, buffalo skull etched, bone hdl, 1-bd, 5⅝" ...300.00
Western States, 6211½, barlow, bone hdl, 2-bd, 3⅜" 100.00
Winchester, 1938, brn bone hdl, 1-bd, 3⅜" 125.00
Winchester, 2038, jack, pearl celluloid hdl, 1-bd, 3" 170.00
Winchester, 2205, pen, metal hdl, 2-bd, bail, 3¼" 125.00
Winchester, 2303, senator, pearl hdl, 2-bd, 2⅝" 125.00
Winchester, 2608, stabber, cocobolo hdl, 2-bd, 3⅝" 125.00
Winchester, 2612, jack, cocobolo hdl, 2-bd, 3⅝" 190.00
Winchester, 2627, slim jack, cocobolo hdl, 2-bd, 3¼" 125.00
Winchester, 2640, Coke bottle, ebony hdl, 2-bd, 3¾" 250.00
Winchester, 2945, senator, bone hdl, 2-bd, 3⅜" 100.00
Winchester, 2981, pen, brn bone hdl, 2-bd, 3¼" 110.00

Miscellaneous

Bolo US Model 1904, dtd 1913, in Rock Island 1909 scabbard, G ..100.00
Commando, unmk Fairbairn, brass cross guard mk England, EX ..100.00
Dagger, Nazi NSKK, Solingen, complete w/hanger & scabbard .275.00
Fighting, Case, 7½" spear-point bd, iron cross guard, +sheath ...600.00
Hunting, Randall, 6" bd, 10¼" overall, VG in sheath 250.00

Kosta

Kosta glassware has been made in Sweden since 1742. Today they are one of that country's leading producers of quality art glass. Two of their most important designers were Elis Bergh (1929–1950) and Vicke Lindstrand, artistic director from 1950 to 1973. Lindstrand brought to the company knowledge of important techniques such as Graal, fine figural engraving, and Ariel. He influenced new artists to experiment with these techniques and inspired them to create new and innovative designs. Today's collectors are most interested in pieces made during the 1950s and 1960s. Our advisor for this category is Abby Malowanczyk; she is listed in the Directory under Texas.

Bowl, clear w/cut radiating leaves, LS, #5614, 12½" 300.00
Goblet, clear w/etch lion, label Kosta Sweden Bergh Kristall, 9¼" ...65.00
Paperweight, clear w/bl & blk swirls, 2½x2¼" 150.00
Sculpture, egret, eng eyes/ detailed feathers, LF13, 8¼" 195.00
Sculpture, fish, clear w/lg bubble, Lindstrand/91624, 10½" 160.00
Vase, Autumn Leaves, blk trees w/falling leaves, Lindstrand/LU2011 .2,500.00
Vase, blk/wht lines, gourd shape, V Lindstrand, LH1257, 10½x2½" 100.00
Vase, candy red int w/opaque wht stripes, LH 1052, 10½" 175.00
Vase, clear w/inner blk stripe, oval, Lindstrand/LS 606, 5¼" 195.00
Vase, clear w/random wht lines, Lindstrand/LH 1041, 4¾x5¾" ...180.00
Vase, clear w/wht crisscross spirals, Lindstrand/LH 1102, 6¼" ...160.00
Vase, dk purple vertical stripes, Lindstrand/LH 1389, 5" 175.00
Vase, emerald gr sommerso w/bl-gr, Lindstrand/LH 1455, 10¼" ...175.00
Vase, flattened ovoid w/aubergine spirals, LH 1384, 5½" 450.00
Vase, int wht/blk canes, elongated gourd, Lindstrand, 13" 300.00

Kutani

Kutani, named for the Japanese village where it originated, was first produced in the seventeenth century. The early ware, Ko Kutani, was made for only about thirty years. Several types were produced before 1800, but these are rarely encountered. In the nineteenth century, kilns located in several different villages began to copy the old Kutani wares. This later, more familiar type has large areas of red with gold designs on a white ground decorated with warriors, birds, and flowers in controlled colors of red, gold, and black.

Bottle, sake; bell shape, Imperial Army Star in gold w/flag 85.00
Bowl, beach scene w/bird overhead, w/matching lid, 3" 70.00
Bowl, gr birds in mc plum blossoms, 3⅜" dia 45.00
Charger, garden w/birds & florals, Meiji period, 15", EX 125.00
Cup & saucer, bamboo on wht, silver rim, geisha lithopane 30.00
Cup & saucer, temple scene w/mountains, geisha lithopane 35.00
Vase, bud; red flowers, 3½x2" 25.00

Labels

Before the advent of the cardboard box, wooden crates were used for transporting products. Paper labels were attached to the crates to identify the contents and the packer. These labels often had colorful lithographed illustrations covering a broad range of subjects. Eventually the cardboard box replaced the crate, and the artwork was imprinted directly onto the carton. Today these paper labels are becoming collectible — primarily for the art, but also for their advertising appeal. Our advisor for this category is Cerebro; their address is listed in the Directory under Pennsylvania.

Can, Domko's Pride, lg peach/monogram, 1930, EX 6.00
Can, En-Be-Co Syrup, Black boy eating bread, 1914, M 85.00
Can, First Quality Peaches, country scene/peach, 1912, M 25.00
Can, Frontier, hunters over body of slain buck, 1923, EX 35.00
Can, Home Products, woman canning, 1926, VG 25.00
Can, Jack & Jill, tumbling down hill, 1929, EX 30.00
Can, Makepeace Cranberry, Art Deco red/bl rays, 1929, EX 10.00
Can, New Life Malt Syrup, Germans working in forest, 1928, EX .20.00
Can, Peter Piper, farm boy holding pepper, 1940, VG 5.00
Can, Richelieu Clams, clams on shore, 1932, M 15.00
Can, Saazar Malt Syrup, Germans in field/pretty woman, 1929, EX ...15.00
Can, Tri-Som, shrimp/lemon on bed of lettuce, 1929, EX 12.00
Can, Weideman Spaghetti, little baker carring tray, 1927, EX 12.00
Can, Yellowstone Peaches, Indian on buffalo/bowl of peaches, 1923, M ...40.00

Cigar box, outer label, Gold Hunter, 1890s, 5x4½", $200.00. **(Photo courtesy Cerebro)**

Cigar box, inner lid; Aim Hi, bust of Jefferson, 1924, EX 75.00
Cigar box, inner lid; Black Hawk, Indian chief, 1938, M 90.00

Cigar box, inner lid; Companita, angel/nude woman, 1929, EX ..75.00
Cigar box, inner lid; Don Antonio, lion/sun rays/coins, 1933, EX ...25.00
Cigar box, inner lid; Jose Grande, cavalier/coins, 1912, M 75.00
Cigar box, inner lid; Motorist, Mercury driving & AAA, 1922, EX ...125.00
Cigar box, inner lid; Trump, laughing man w/hand of cards, 1876, EX .60.00
Cigar box, outer; Challenge Cup, lg gold trophy, 1883, EX 125.00
Cigar box, outer; David Dudley Field, portrait, 1894, EX 25.00
Cigar box, outer; Garcia Cubans, coins/currency, 1915, M 15.00
Cigar box, outer; Havana Leaf, Cuban vista/newspaper, 1909, M .60.00
Cigar box, outer; Liberty Tie, ribbon/gold bell, 1905, EX 75.00
Cigar box, outer; Mexican Maid, senorita, 1900, EX 17.00
Cigar box, outer; Parole, jockey on horse, oval, 1879, EX 65.00
Crate, apple, Apple Kids, 2 boys pushing/pulling apple, 1940, M ..12.00
Crate, apple, Best Strike, baseball player, 1920, M 45.00
Crate, apple, Lake View, 3 big apples, 1930, M 10.00
Crate, CA Orange, Atlas, Atlas w/globe on bk, 1930, M 45.00
Crate, CA Orange, Indian Belle, couple/orchard/mountains, 1915, M 75.00
Crate, CA Orange, Reindeer, lg buck/mountains/lake, 1920, M ..20.00
Crate, CA Orange, Yo-Semi-Te, forest, 1920, M 85.00
Crate, FL Citrus, Crescent Moon, moonlit orange grove, 1930, EX ...6.00
Crate, FL Citrus, Justice, statue of Lady Justice, 1940, M 4.00
Crate, FL Citrus, Merry Christmas, citrus/blossoms, 1920, M 35.00
Crate, lemon, Basketball, women players, 1920, EX 75.00
Crate, lemon, Onward, rear view of Statue of Liberty, 1930, EX .60.00
Crate, lemon, Tom Cat, cat sitting on red pillow, 1930, EX 75.00
Crate, pear, Buckingham, cowboy riding wild pig, 1920, M 15.00
Crate, pear, Placer, gold mining camp, 1930, M 15.00
Crate, pear, Quercus Ranch, lg tree/lake/orchard, 1927, M 4.00

Labino

Dominick Labino was a glass blower who until mid-1985 worked in his studio in Ohio, blowing and sculpting various items which he signed and dated. A ceramic engineer by trade, he was instrumental in developing the heat-resistant tiles used in space flights. His glassmaking shows his versatility in the art. While some of his designs are free-form and futuristic, others are reminiscent of the products of older glasshouses. Because of problems with his health, Mr. Labino became unable to blow glass himself; he died January, 10, 1987. Work coming from his studio since mid-1985 has been signed 'Labino Studios, Baker,' indicating ware made by his protegee, E. Baker O'Brien. In addition to her own compositions, she continues to use many of the colors developed by Labino.

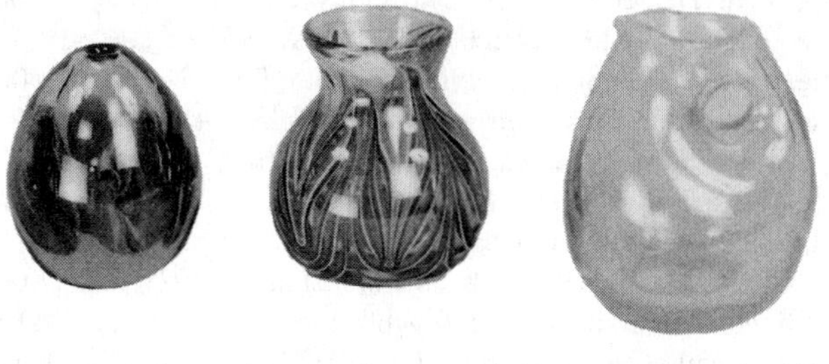

Vases: Egg shape, blue with internal blue, green, and yellow decor, signed, inscribed 'For Alma,' 1969, 4½", $850.00; Globular, clear pulled and trailed with blue, brown, and white, signed, 1968, 4¾", $850.00; Ovoid with circular formed handle, light blue-yellow opalescent, signed, dated 3-1970, 5½", $600.00.

Creamer, #6, 1975, 4⅜" 220.00
Pitcher, gray-amber w/cranberry rim, 1969, 6⅛" 275.00
Sculpture, Emergence, pk/orange int layers+lg & 2 sm bubbles, 7" ..4,890.00
Sculpture, Emergence, pk/orange int layers+4 bubbles, '71, 9" ..6,300.00
Vase, amethyst w/2nd gather in 6 root-like prunts, 1960, 8½" ...440.00
Vase, blk opaque w/subtle ruby swags, 1969, 5" 385.00
Vase, clear w/amber, hourglass opening, red/blk flames, 1974, 5" ...495.00
Vase, gr opaque metallic irid w/purple highlights, 1964, 6" 385.00
Vase, heavy swirled bl cased to red, sm integral hdls, '71, 7" 400.00
Vase, lt gr irid, asymmetrical, 1968, 4¾" 250.00
Vase, owl form, amber on clear w/other colors, 1968, 4½" 250.00
Vase, pk veiling in amber & clear, Labino 12, 1982, 4¾" 495.00
Vase, ruby w/lt irid, urn form w/hdls, 1972, 5" 545.00
Vase, wht opaque w/brn-red flames cased in clear, #11, 1974, 4½" ...275.00
Vase, 4 bubbles in pk veiling & gold flecks in clear, #11, 1978, 5" ...465.00
Wine glass, pale gr w/air-twist stem, 1969, 7" 140.00

Lace, Linens, and Needlework

Two distinct audiences vie for old lace and linens. Collectors seek out exceptional stitchery like philatelists and numismatists seek stamps or coins — simply to marvel at its beauty, rarity, and ties to history. Collectors judge lace and linens like figure skaters and gymnasts are judged: artist impression is half the score, technical merit the other. How complex and difficult are the stitches and how well are they done? The 'users' see lace and linens as recyclables. They seek pretty wearables or decorative materials. They want fashionable things in mint condition, and have little or no interest in technique. Both groups influence price.

Undiscovered and underpriced are the eighteenth-century masterpieces of lace and needle art in techniques which will never be duplicated. Their beauty is subtle. Amazing stitches often are invisible without magnification. To get the best value in any lace, linen, or textile item, learn to look closely at individual stitches, and study the design and technique. The finest pieces are wonderfully constructed. The stitches are beautiful to look at, and they do a good job of holding the item together. Our advisor for this category is Elizabeth M. Kurella; she is listed in the Directory under Michigan.

Key: embr — embroidered

Afghan, crochet, cotton w/mc 1½" dia designs, dainty, 66x48" ...45.00
Bed hanging, crewelwork Tree of Life/birds/flowers on linen, 87x83" ...2,650.00
Bedspread, chenille, 4 floral motifs, flaws, 88x102", EX 65.00
Bedspread, crochet, wht floral design w/knotted fringe, 90x100" 125.00
Bedspread, embr wht linen w/tulip panels, crochet band, 100x80" ...475.00
Collar, bobbin lace, stylized floral, cape-like, 10x50" 400.00
Collar, cotton machine-made floral lace, 2x16", EX 15.00
Collar, tatted lace, V shape, delicate, 15x12" 22.50
Handkerchief, drawnwork, applique & crochet edges 10.00
Handkerchief, drawnwork, wht on lt gr linen, 11" sq 11.50
Handkerchief, drawnwork flowers among scallops at ea corner 13.50
Handkerchief, embr floral corners on wht-on-wht cotton, 1½" ...10.00
Handkerchief, embr flowers w/lace in 1 corner, machine finished, 9" ...7.50
Handkerchief, handmade w/cotton ⅜" tatting around edges 7.50
Handkerchief, linen, handmade in Portugal by DECSCO, 12½" ...10.00
Handkerchief, linen w/bl applique & embr at corners, 12" 7.50
Handkerchief, linen w/crochet edge & butterfly at ea corner, 11½" 15.00
Handkerchief, wht cotton w/embr bl rose, Switzerland, M 8.00
Handkerchiefs, cotton w/embr flowers, Switzerland, boxed set of 3 ..20.00
Handkerchiefs, cotton w/floral embr, 10", boxed set of 3 ....17.50
Handkerchiefs, nylon w/lace edge, Rains, 7½", boxed set of 3 .....17.50
Mat, linen w/cross-stitch border, 16x10" 15.00
Needlework panel, wool/silk on silk, landscape scene, 19x16+fr 1,200.00
Needlework panel, 3-D floral bouquet, wool/chenille on silk, 19x22" ..200.00
Needlework picture, couple, watercolor/sequin details, 1800s, 16" dia ..975.00
Needlework picture, eagle over draped flags & banner, 13x16" .400.00
Needlework picture, Parting of Hector & Romache, 19th C, 20x25" w/mat ..750.00

Needlework picture, USS Franklin commemorative, silk embr, 17x21" ..500.00
Pillowcases, crochet edge, pr 25.00
Pillowcases, embr pre-printed design, crochet edge, M, pr 30.00
Runner, cotton w/pk embr & 3" wide crochet border, 14x41" 37.50
Runner, embr trees in bl on gr, Scotland, 66x16" 600.00
Runner, hand crochet, 44x22½" 40.00
Runner, linen, cross-stitch decor, machine-finished edges, 34x22" ..10.00
Runner, machine rayon embr on chiffon, 20x9" 7.50
Shawl, decor lace net, 24x120", 19th C, EX quality, from $2,000 to .5,000.00
Sheet, bl/wht check homespun linen, rolled hems, 60x72" 110.00
Show towel, embr ABCS & 1821, PA, fringed, 16x67", EX 125.00
Tablecloth, Canton linen, embr trees, 35" sq, w/6 embr napkins .25.00
Tablecloth, cotton w/embr baskets in ea corner (7"), 45x45" 25.00
Tablecloth, cream damask, 90x96", w/8 napkins 200.00
Tablecloth, crochet lace, ecru w/wht embr medallions, 63x107" ..95.00
Tablecloth, floral jacquard, burgundy/natural, 54" sq 250.00
Tablecloth, linen, cutwork/embr panels of Cupid & swans, 48x50" ..85.00
Tablecloth, peach damask, 86x66", w/8 napkins 155.00
Tablecloth, wht linen w/cut-work flowers, machine embr, 80x106" ...165.00

Lacy Glassware

Lacy glass became popular in the late 1820s after the development of the pressing machine. It was decorated with allover patterns — hearts, lyres, sheaves of wheat, etc. — and backgrounds were completely stippled. The designs were intricate and delicate, hence the term 'lacy.' Although Sandwich produced this type of glassware in abundance, it was also made by other eastern glassworks as well as in the Midwest. By 1840, its popularity on the wane and a depressed economy forcing manufacturers to seek less expensive modes of production, lacy glass began to be phased out in favor of pressed pattern glass.

When no condition is indicated, the items listed below are assumed to be without obvious damage; minor roughness is normal.

See also Salts, Open.

Bowl, Rayed Peacock Eye, 1¾x7½" 110.00
Compote, Heart, appl knop stem, 3½x4¾" 400.00
Compote, Roman Rosette (Dmn Rosette), daisy center, 3¾x6" ...375.00
Compote, Shield & Pine Tree, on blown ft, 4¼x6", VG 300.00
Dish, Daisy, 9¼", VG 80.00
Dish, Feather, 9½" 60.00
Dish, Roman Rosette, lt amethyst, 6¼", EX 375.00
Dish, Sheaf of Wheat, oval, 9½" 185.00
Plate, Maple Leaf, sawtooth rim, Gillinder & Sons, 11" 105.00
Plate, Roman Rosette, 9⅜" 165.00
Taster, Sunflower, ftd, 2¼" 150.00

Lalique

Beginning his lengthy career as a designer and maker of fine jewelry, Rene Lalique at first only dabbled in glass, making small panels of cire perdue (wax casting) to use in his jewelry. He also made small flacons of gold and silver with his glass inlays, which attracted the attention of M.F. Coty, who commissioned Lalique to design bottles for his perfume company. The success of this venture resulted in the opening of his own glassworks at Combs-la-Ville in 1909. In 1921 a larger factory was established at Wingen-sur-Moder in Alsace-Lorraine. By the '30s Lalique was world renown as the most important designer of his time.

Lalique glass is lead based, either mold blown or pressed. Favored motifs during the Art Nouveau period were dancing nymphs, fish, dragonflies, and foliage. Characteristically the glass is crystal in combination with acid-etched relief. Later some items were made in as many as ten colors (red, amber, and green among them) and were occasionally accented with enameling. These colored pieces, especially those in black, are highly prized by advanced collectors.

During the '20s and '30s, Lalique designed several vases and bowls reminiscent of American Indian art. He also developed a line in the Art Deco style decorated with stylized birds, florals, and geometrics. In addition to vases, clocks, automobile mascots, stemware, and bottles, many other useful objects were produced. Most items made before his death in 1945 were marked 'R. Lalique'; later the 'R' was deleted even though some of the original molds were still used. Numbers found on the bases of some pieces are catalog numbers. Beware of fraudulent pieces that have began to surface in increasing numbers. Our advisor for this category is John Danis; he is listed in the Directory under Illinois.

Key:
cl/fr — clear and frosted
L — signed Lalique
LF — signed Lalique France
RL — signed R. Lalique
RLF — signed R. Lalique, France

Luminaire, Oiseau de Feau, exotic bird-woman, clear and frosted, R. Lalique France, 17", $15,000.00.

Ashtray, Faune, satyr, cl/fr w/gray stain, ca 1931, 3¾x4⅛" 1,000.00
Ashtray, Sirenes, entwined females, cl/fr w/bl stain, ca 1920, 4½" ..865.00
Atomizer, Figurines No 2, draped nudes, cl/fr, ca 1926, 6" 800.00
Bonbonniere, Cyprins, fish, cl opal w/purple grosgrain, 1921, 10" 1,495.00
Bottle, Camille, sculptured shell, dk bl, RL, 2¼" 4,000.00
Bottle, scent; Calendale, nudes, cl/fr w/peach stain, ca 1937, 4½" ..1,200.00
Bottle, scent; Chypre, cl/fr pyramid w/protrusions, ca 1912, 7½" 750.00
Bottle, scent; dahlia form, cl/fr, RL, 1½x2¾", NM 500.00
Bottle, scent; Dans la Nuite, clear/fr w/dk bl stain, 3" 465.00
Bottle, scent; Faune, faun, pierced flowers, cl/fr, ca 1930, 7½" ..1,500.00
Bottle, scent; Fleurettes, flower heads, cl/fr w/brn stain, 6¼", pr ..500.00
Bottle, scent; Imprudence, circular tiers, cl, Worth, 9" 1,150.00
Bottle, scent; La Renommee, cl/fr w/blk stain, D'Orsay, 8¾" .2,000.00
Bottle, scent; Mimeomai, cl/fr w/brn stain, Volnay, 4½" 1,800.00
Bottle, scent; Sans Adieu, emerald gr, for Worth, 4¼" 865.00
Bottle, scent; Telline, shell, cl/fr, RL, 3¾" 500.00
Bowl, Bulbes, central flower & radiating bulbs, cl/fr, RL, 10" 575.00
Bowl, Chiens No 1, greyhounds, cl/fr w/gr stain, ca 1921 ....800.00
Bowl, finger; Thionvile, fruit, cl/fr w/blk enamel, 4½", pr 115.00
Bowl, ice cream; Fleur, petal rim, cl, ca 1932, 7⅜" 45.00
Bowl, Ondines, nudes, cl/fr opal, ca 1921, 8¼" 2,500.00
Bowl, Perruches, parakeets, cl/fr opal w/gr stain, ca 1931, 9¾" ...3,200.00
Bowl, Tournon, flowers, cl opal, ca 1928, 12" 2,300.00
Box, Figurines et Voiles, cl/fr w/bl stain, ca 1929, 4¼" dia 2,000.00
Box, powder; Compiègne-Faisans, pheasants, fr, RL, 1½x3⅜" ...825.00
Box, powder; rabbits & birds, brn patina, RL, 1½x3½" dia 300.00
Box, Roger, 5 pheasants/11 cabochons/grapevines, opal, RL, 5⅝" ..750.00
Bracelet, Cerisier, cherries/leaves, cl/fr dk bl, ca 1928 ....1,800.00
Chandelier, Feuilles de Charme, 10-panel, cl/fr, RL, 19" dia ..3,450.00
Clock, Marguerites, daisies, fr, ca 1920, 5¾" 2,500.00

Decanter, Reine Marguerite, flower head, cl/fr w/brn enamel, 10¾" ..2,300.00
Figurine, bird, LF, 9" 210.00
Figurine, deer, LF, 3" 60.00
Figurine, elephant, LF, 6" 225.00
Figurine, fish entwined, fr, LF, 11½x11" 1,000.00
Figurine, Pigeon Bruges, pigeon, cl/fr, ca 1931, 10½" L 750.00
Figurine, turtle, amber, LF, 6" 210.00
Lighter, table; fr motif, LF, 4" 90.00
Paperweight, Tete d'Aigle, eagle's head, cl/fr, ca 1928, RL, 4" ...1,725.00
Pendant, Colombes, bust of lady w/2 birds, cl opal, ca 1920, 1⅝" ..1,150.00
Pendant, Serpents, 2 snakes, cl/fr bl, ca 1920, 1¾" 1,800.00
Plate, emb leaf border, LF, 11" 75.00
Platter, leaves emb, FL, 25x14" 500.00
Tray, Galon, cl/fr, ca 1936, 15⅝" L 700.00
Vase, Actinia, stylized wave, cl/fr opal, ca 1934, 8⅝" 1,500.00
Vase, Bacchantes, nudes, cl/fr w/bl stain, ca 1927, 9½" 7,500.00
Vase, Baies, thorny branches, cl/fr w/blk enamel, ca 1924, 10½" ...13,800.00
Vase, Ceylan, parakeets, cl/fr opal w/bl stain, ca 1924, 9½" ...5,000.00
Vase, Champagne, conical projections, cl/satin, ca 1927, 6⅛" ..1,600.00
Vase, Charmilles, leaves, cl/fr w/dk gray stain, ca 1926, 14" ...7,000.00
Vase, Danaides, nudes w/vessels, cl/fr, ca 1926, 7⅛" 5,750.00
Vase, Deauville, vines, cl/fr w/gr stain, ca 1941, 6" 800.00
Vase, Dordogne, spirals, opal fr w/bl stain, ca 1927, 7" 4,600.00
Vase, Esterel, leaves, cl/fr, RL, ca 1932, 6½x6½", NM 500.00
Vase, Formose, fish, cl/fr wht cased, ca 1924, 6⅝" 2,500.00
Vase, grasses in relief, opal, flared top, 6x5" 450.00
Vase, Gui, mistletoe, cl/fr opal w/bl stain, 6⅝" 1,380.00
Vase, Guirlandes, interlacing bands, cl/fr opal, ca 1935, 8⅛" .2,750.00
Vase, Lagamar, geometrics, cl/fr w/blk enamel, ca 1926, 7¼" ..10,000.00
Vase, Martin-Pecheurs, birds & foliage, blk fr, ca 1923, 9½" ...10,000.00
Vase, Mistletoe, yel-gr fr, RLF, 6½" 1,265.00
Vase, Monnaie du Paper, silver dollars, cl/fr dk amber, ca 1914, 9" ..7,500.00
Vase, Ormeaux, leaves, dk amber, ca 1926, 6⅝" 4,000.00
Vase, Ornis, bird hdls, cl/fr dk topaz, ca 1926, 7½" 2,000.00
Vase, Oursin, sea urchin, peach patina, RLF, ca 1935, 7⅛" 2,000.00
Vase, Poissons, fish, cl/fr opal, ca 1921, 9¼" 4,600.00
Vase, Quatre Tete Femmes et Raisins, cl/fr w/bl stain, ca 1939, 5¼" ...1,725.00
Vase, Saint-Emilion, birds, cl/fr w/lt gr stain, ca 1942, 9¾" 2,500.00
Vase, Sophora, leafy branches, cl/fr w/gr stain, ca 1926, 10¼" ...4,600.00

Lamps

The earliest lamps were simple dish containers with a wick that hung over the edge or was supported by a channel or tube. Grease and oil from animal or vegetable sources were the first fuels used. Ancient pottery lamps, crusie, and Betty lamps are examples of these early types. In 1784 Swiss inventor Ami Argand introduced the first major improvement in lamps. His lamp featured a tubular wick and a glass chimney. During the first half of the nineteenth century, whale oil, burning fluid (a highly explosive mixture of turpentine and alcohol), and lard were the most common fuels used in North America. Many lamps were patented for specific use with these fuels.

Kerosene was the first major breakthrough in lighting fuels. It was demonstrated by Canadian geologist Dr. Abraham Gesner in 1846. The discovery and drilling of petroleum in the late 1850s provided an abundant and inexpensive supply of kerosene. It became the main source of light for homes during the balance of the nineteenth century and for remote locations until the 1950s.

Although Thomas A. Edison invented the electric lamp in 1879, it was not until two or three decades later that electric lamps replaced kerosene household lamps. Millions of kerosene lamps were made for every purpose and pocketbook. They ranged in size from tiny night or miniature lamps to tall stand or piano lamps. Hanging varieties for homes commonly had one or two fonts (oil containers), but chandeliers for churches and public buildings often had six or more. Wall or bracket lamps usually had silvered reflectors. Student lamps, parlor lamps (now called Gone-with-the-Wind lamps), and patterned glass lamps were designed to complement the popular furnishing trends of the day. Gaslight, introduced in the early nineteenth century, was used mainly in homes of the wealthy and public places until the early twentieth century. Most fixtures were wall or ceiling mounted, although some table models were also used.

Few of the ordinary early electric lamps have survived. Many lamp manufacturers made the same or similar styles for either kerosene or electricity, sometimes for gas. Top-of-the-line lamps were made by Pairpoint, Phoenix, Tiffany, Bradley and Hubbard, and Handel. See also these specific sections.

When buying lamps that have been converted to electricity, inspect them very carefully for any damage that may have resulted from the alterations; such damage is very common, and when it does occur, the lamp's value may be lessened by as much as 50%. Lamps seem to bring much higher prices in some areas than others, especially the larger cities. Conversely, in rural areas they may bring only half as much as our listed values. One of our advisors for lamps is Carl Heck; he is listed in the Directory under Colorado. Advice for miniature lamps comes from Bob Culver (who is listed in the Directory under Michigan), and Jeff Bradfield (in Virginia) is our advisor for pattern glass lamps. See also Stained Glass.

Key: col — cut overlay

Aladdin Lamps, Electric

From 1908 Aladdin lamps with a mantle became the mainstay of rural America, providing light that compared favorably with the electric light bulb. They were produced by the Mantle Lamp Company of America in over eighteen models and more than one hundred styles. During the 1930s to the 1950s, this company was the leading manufacturer of electric lamps as well. Still in operation today, the company is now known as Aladdin Mantle Lamp Co., located in Clarksville, Tennessee. For those seeking additional information on Aladdin Lamps, we recommend *Aladdin — The Magic Name in Lamps; Aladdin Electric Lamps Collector's Manual & Price Guide #3*, and *Aladdin Collector's Manual and Price Guide #19*, all written by our advisor for Aladdins, J. W. Courter; he is listed in the Directory under Kentucky. Mr. Courter has also published a book called *Angle Lamps, Collector's Manual and Price Guide*.

Lady figure (lamp base, no fixture), crystal, 1930s, $600.00; Alacite version, $500.00.

Bedroom, M-70, metal & ceramic, from $20 to 30.00
Bedroom, P-52, ceramic, from $30 to 40.00
Boudoir, G-1, plain color, 1933 (early), from $40 to 50.00
Boudoir, G-40, Moonstone base, 1935, from $50 to 70.00
Boudoir, New Series; G-15, floral base, crystal, from $125 to 150.00
Boudoir, New Series; G-44, Alacite, from $40 to 50.00
Bridge, #2064, from $250 to 300.00

Bridge, #2079, walnut, from $275 to 350.00
Bridge, #7092, reflector, swing arm, from $125 to 175.00
Bridge, B-135, from $125 to 175.00
Figurine, G-375, Dancing Ladies Urn, glass, from $1,100 to ..1,200.00
Figurine, G-77, Susie, moonstone, from $4,000 to 5,000.00
Floor, #3334, reflector, from $175 to 225.00
Floor, #3579, walnut, from $250 to 275.00
Floor, #3606, reflector, candle arms, from $175 to 250.00
Floor, #3646S, IES reflector, candle arms, from $175 to 250.00
Floor, #3898C, Circline, fluorescent, trigger ring, from $200 to ..250.00
Floor, #3935, night light in base, candle arms, from $200 to 275.00
Floor, #3998, Alacite ring, night light, candle arms, from $250 to ..350.00
Floor, Junior; #1062, candle arms, from $175 to 225.00
Floor, Junior; C-130, Colonial, amber or gr bowl, from $250 to ..300.00
Glass Urn, G-213A, Alacite, closed urn, from $225 to 300.00
Glass Urn, G-379, Alacite tall ribbed urn w/top, from $175 to .225.00
Magic Touch, MT-507, ceramic base, from $300 to 350.00
Magic Touch, MT-520, cherry & brass base, from $400 to 500.00
Ranch House, G-47C, Alacite Bullet, illuminated base, w/shade, up to ...700.00
Shade, Empire, Whip-o-lite, for table lamps, from $125 to 150.00
Shade, pleated, for table lamp, minimum value 300.00
Smoking stand, #7548, from $200 to 300.00
Table, E-305, Vogue Vase, blk, from $550 to 650.00
Table, G-179, opalique glass, from $125 to 175.00
Table, G-263A, Alacite, illuminated base, from $50 to 60.00
Table, G-290D, Alacite, decalcomania, illuminated base, from $60 to ...70.00
Table, G-345R, Alacite, Pineapple, recipe lamp, from $40 to 60.00
Table, G-36, glass, from $80 to 100.00
Table, G-785, Large Vase, gr, from $200 to 250.00
Table, G-85, glass, from $150 to 200.00
Table, M-367, iron base, spun glass shade, from $20 to 30.00
Table, M-93, metal w/Whip-o-lite shade, from $175 to 225.00
Table, P-408, ceramic planter, from $75 to 100.00
Table, P-470, ceramic, from $30 to 50.00
Torchier floor, #4511, wood & metal, from $175 to 225.00
Torchier floor, #4598, from $250 to 300.00
TV, M-367, blk iron base w/shade, from $30 to 40.00
TV, M-469, metal, w/shade, from $25 to 30.00
TV, TV-387, ceramic base, modern design, from $30 to 40.00

Aladdin Lamps, Kerosene

Caboose Model B, B-400, brass font, from $200 to 300.00
Floor Model #12, style #1250, bl & gold, from $200 to 350.00
Floor Model #12, style #1253, Verde Antique, from $175 to 275.00
Floor Model B, B-283, ivory & gold, from $200 to 300.00
Foreign, Super Aladdin, Crown Devon vase, orange or gr, from $350 to ..500.00
Foreign Model #9, table lamp, London, from $85 to 125.00
Hanging Model #3, single chandelier, w/#205 shade, from $3,500 to ...4,500.00
Hanging Model #10, w/#516 shade, from $400 to 500.00
Hanging Model #23, brass w/glass shade (several types), from $60 to 200.00
Shelf Model 23 Lincoln Drape, clear, no oil fill, from $90 to 100.00
Table, Model #9, nickel, 2 knob variations, ea, from $100 to 150.00
Table, Practicus, polished brass, from $300 to 375.00
Table Model #12 Crystal Vase, #1231A, Amber Alpha Art Glass, 10¼" ...300.00
Table Model #12 Crystal Vase, #1241, variegated tan, 12", from $200 to ..250.00
Table Model #23, B-2301, solid brass, from $60 to 80.00
Table Model A, Venetian, #103, rose, from $175 to 275.00
Table Model B, Corinthian, B-114, wht moonstone, brass connector ..200.00
Table Model B, Orientale, B-132, rose gold, EX, from $225 to ..300.00
Table Model B, Solitaire, B-70, wht moonstone, from $3,000 to ..3,500.00
Table Model B, Treasure, B-136, chromium, EX, from $175 to ..225.00
Table Model B, Washington Drape, B-41, amber crystal, rnd base ...150.00
Table Model B, Washington Drape, B-51, gr crystal, filigree stem 150.00
Table Model C, clear glass, ftd, from $700 to 800.00
Table Model 23 Short Lincoln Drape, amber, undtd ('74), from $100 to ...125.00
Wall bracket Model #1, from $550 to 650.00
Wall bracket Model #5, from $250 to 300.00

Angle Lamps

The Angle Lamp Company of New York City developed a unique type of kerosene lamp that was a vast improvement over those already on the market; they were sold from about 1896 until 1929 and were expensive for their time. Nearly all Angle lamps are hanging lamps and wall lamps. Table models are uncommon. Our Angle lamp advisor is J.W. Courter; he is listed in the Directory under Kentucky. See the narrative for Aladdin Lamps for information concerning popular books Mr. Courter has authored.

Note: Old glass pieces for Angle lamps are scarce to rare; the lamp values that follow are for examples with no glass.

Glass, chimney top, clear, petal-top, EX 200.00
Glass, chimney top, ruby (EX color), petal-top, NM 1,200.00
Glass, chimney top, wht, petal-top, EX 85.00
Glass, chimney top, wht, ribbed, EX 75.00
Glass, chimney top, wht opal, petal-top, NM 250.00
Glass, elbow globe, clear, no pattern, EX 75.00
Glass, elbow globe, clear w/birds, NM 275.00
Glass, elbow globe, clear w/floral bouquet band, EX 250.00
Glass, elbow globe, clear w/wreath & torch band, NM 275.00
Hanging, #254, 2-burner, rose floral, polished brass, EX 800.00
Hanging, #283, 2-burner, antique copper, EX 375.00
Hanging, #352, 3-burner, polished brass, EX 625.00
Hanging, Classic, 2-burner, antique gold, NM 1,750.00
Hanging, CW 32 NF, 3-burner, bronze, EX 500.00
Hanging, EG-22, 2-burner, extended grape, EX 375.00
Hanging, MW 5982, 4-burner, nickel, EX 750.00
Table, Classic #1, antique gold, NM 2,000.00
Wall, #101, wall cone, tin, pnt, EX 225.00
Wall, #103, plain can, nickel, EX 275.00
Wall, #104, grape pattern, nickel, EX 325.00
Wall, #182, fleur-de-lis pattern, antique copper, NM 300.00
Wall, #185, pinwheel, antique brass, EX 375.00
Wall, MW 904-NF, leaf & vine, nickel, EX 325.00

Chandeliers

Gilt brass Modern Gothic, three-light gasolier, reticulated band with cast foliage centering three straight arms, 1850s, 36x24", $990.00.

Anglo-Irish crystal, jeweled upper tier, 6-arm, prisms, 48x36" ...2,300.00
Anglo-Irish crystal, swags/pendants/prisms, 7-arm, 50x33" 2,850.00
Baltic gilt bronze & crystal in Emp taste, 12-light, 42x42" ...11,500.00
Brass, 2 tiers of 12 scrolled candle arms, 19th C, 27" H, EX ...1,750.00

Brass, 4 scrolling candle arms, early 1900s, 10½" 250.00
Brass, 6 scrolling candle arms, needs rewiring, 20th C, 21" 440.00
Bronze, 18-light, 2-tier, vintage castings, prisms, 19th C, 42x31" .. 3,000.00
Bronze English Reform Gothic, 4-light, etched glass panels, 37" .. 4,000.00
Cut glass, dmns/florals, central tripartite devices, 12" bowl 575.00
Cut glass, rococo style, 6 scrolling arms, beads/pendants, 34" . 1,600.00
Fr cut crystal & gilt brass, 6 swan-neck candle arms, prisms, 38x26" .. 1,750.00
Gilt bronze & cut glass, leafy frond arms w/pendants, 26" H .. 2,000.00
Glass, S-shaped candle arms (8) w/appl mc flowers, 46" H 3,165.00
Glass & gilt-bronze, rococo style w/foliate casting, 6-light, 48" H 1,500.00
Gr/wht glass w/gold mica, 8-light, bell shades, appl swans, 42x48" ... 3,165.00

Decorated Kerosene Lamps

When only one color is given in a two layer cut overlay lamp description, the second layer is generally clear; in three layer examples, the second will usually be white, the third clear. Exceptions will be noted.

Col (2-layer), cranberry, marble stepped vase, Sandwich, 14" 900.00
Col (2-layer), red, quatrefoil & circles, brass/marble base, 14" ... 400.00
Col (2-layer), wht, reeded brass & marble stepped base, 11½" .. 300.00
Col (2-layer), wht to gr font & std, stepped brass/marble base, 15" 2,300.00
Col (2-layer), wht to red, brass std, marble base, 19th C, 10" 300.00
Col (2-layer), wht to red, wht pressed base, 12" 400.00
Col (3-layer), gr/wht w/gold, brass std, brass/marble base, 11" ... 3,000.00
Jade gr waisted font w/gold on brass stem, marble base, 9" 650.00
Sanded clambroth font w/acanthus decor, marble base, 11½" ... 125.00
Wht font w/gold & gr foliage, marble base, 11½" 400.00
Yel o/l w/mc florals on umbrella shade & ovoid base, 21x10" . 2,000.00

Fairy Lamps

Baby's head, emerald gr frost, pyramid sz, 4½x2⅝" 185.00
Bl MOP Swirl, bl ruffled saucer base (rpl), Stevens & Wms, 6" .. 300.00
Bl Nailsea 8" dome shade, ruffled base, Clarke's cup, 6½" 700.00
Bsk dog/cat/owl faces, glass eyes, 3-sided, 3¼" 375.00
Burmese, berries & vines domed shade, clear pressed base, 5" ... 850.00
Burmese, Clarke's Pyramid pressed glass cup 4" 350.00
Burmese, crimped flaring skirt, Webb, Clarke's cup, 5½x5¾" 950.00
Burmese, flared/pleated skirt, Clarke's cup, 5½x7½" 1,085.00
Burmese, ivy decor, ftd base, crimped rim, Clarke's cup, 5½" 650.00
Burmese, leaves/vines, dome ea side sm bud vase, Clarke's cups .. 1,750.00
Burmese, ruffled base, traditional shade, middle holder, 3-pc, 6x5" .. 1,100.00
Cream to lemon yel top & base, ruffled w/crystal rims, 6x6" 300.00
Custard w/HP floral branch, cup-shaped base, 5" 395.00
Lithophane, children (4 scenes), Clarke's cup, 4¼" 1,750.00
Owl's head, cranberry satin, Clarke's cup 425.00
Pk MOP Dmn Quilt w/clear base, 3½" 450.00
Rubena Dmn Quilt, ruffled, clear Clarke's cup, 6¼x3¾" 225.00
Tapestry w/gilt, lamp on stem above 8" bowl, Doulton Burslem .. 1,950.00
Verre Moire, ruby, fluted bowl base, Clarke's cup, 5x5½" 1,035.00

Gone-With-the-Wind and Banquet Lamps

Banquet, gilt cherub on base holds font, wht shade w/HP cherubs, 34" .. 150.00
Banquet, Nickel Plate 101, wht opal font, 12" 500.00
Cranberry Fern & Daisy shade, satin base, brass fittings, 25½x11" ... 400.00
Gr w/emb leaves/HP florals atop 4 brass ball ft, 27" 500.00
Roses & buds on 9" ball shade & body, ftd ped, 23" 300.00
Roses on butterscotch to white 12" ball shade & body, 26½" 325.00

Hanging Lamps

Cranberry, emb/shaped globe, brass water-lily emb mts 450.00
Cranberry Hobnail 14" shade; ornate fr w/brass font, prisms .. 1,000.00
Harp fr w/conical tin shade 175.00
Lomax, HP conical shade, CI ornate fr, counter-balanced font ... 600.00
Mold-blown opal shade, Lomax font, prisms, ornate fr 1,800.00
Rubena Hobnail shade, gilt brass fr w/jewels/prisms, 40x14" dia .. 1,750.00
Store, B&H #96, brass w/stamped tin shade, smoke bell, 20" dia 175.00
Young's Paraffin Light & Mineral Oil Co, also use on table 200.00

Lanterns

Stonebridge Pat'd Nov 20, 1906 – June 1908, tin, folding type, EX, $60.00.

Barn, cherry wood w/tin heat shield, 11"+bail 300.00
Beaded Bull's Eye Sq globe, pnt/pierced tin fr, glass font, 1850s, 8" .. 900.00
Beehive pear-shaped globe, brass top, bell bottom, tin fr, 12" 450.00
Drapery globe, brass top, bell bottom, pnt tin fr, 1851, 12" 2,875.00
Ferguson Pat Sportsman's, tin/NP brass, worn pnt, 1878, 8½" ... 100.00
Fr Rococo, 4-light, gilt metal, hall type w/chain, 32x16", EX . 2,500.00
Hardwood & pine, old natural patina, old rpr, 10½" 475.00
Lighthouse form, fixed globe, pierced tin fr, wire guard, 1850s, 10" ... 300.00
Lighthouse form (bulging) globe, pierced tin fr, 1850s, 11" 500.00
Onion globe, pierced tin fr, ring hdl, Am, 1850s, 14" 600.00
Onion globe, tin fr w/brass top, Am, 1850s, 9½", pr 925.00
Onion globe (fixed/etched), pierced tin fr, NE, 1850s, 12" 575.00
Onion globe (flattened), pierced tin fr, 1850s, 11¾", VG 635.00
Pear-shaped globe, pierced brass fr, Am, 1850s, 11½" 635.00
Pear-shaped globe, pierced tin fr, NE, 1850s, 9", pr 400.00
Poplar w/old dk gray finish, rprs, 12"+wire hdl 200.00
Red ribbed-swirl globe, pnt/pierced tin fr, no font, 12", VG 175.00
Ribbed globe, pnt pierced tin fr, glass font, Am, 1850s, 10" ... 1,000.00
Shoulder type, pnt tin, single glass lens, 1850s, 6" 250.00
Tin, pyramid shape, hinged base, 2 glass panels, 9x4½x2¾" 525.00
Tin, sq w/glass panels on 3 sides, bk opens, flat top, 11x8" 240.00
Tin cylinder w/cone top, glass door, kerosene burner, 8½" 45.00
Tin w/allover piercing, conical top, 3" ring hdl, 11½", G 275.00

Lard Oil/Grease Lamps

Betty, tin, crimped edge on base & shelf, hinged lid, 10½" 200.00
Betty, tin w/saucer base, hinged lid, wick pick, rpr, 13" 375.00
Betty, wrought & CI, brass heart finial, hinged lid, w/wick pick, 4" ... 385.00
Betty, wrought iron, brass chicken finial (old rpl), 4" 195.00
Betty, wrought iron, cast chicken finial, 6½"+hanger 600.00
Betty, wrought iron, chicken silhouette finial, 7¼" 660.00
Betty, wrought iron, w/wick pick & long hook hanger, hinged lid, 4" . 165.00
Betty, wrought iron/sheet metal/copper, 3-leg, punched/tooled, 26" ... 715.00
Crusie, wrought iron, 3-leg, penny ft, elongated pan w/spout, 8" ... 470.00
Hanging, wrought iron, oblong open pan w/hanger, 17" 915.00
Lace maker's, blown spherical font, hollow stem, appl wafer, 8½" .. 350.00
Rush, wrought iron, w/candle-holder counter-weight, 48" 770.00
Rush, wrought iron, wooden base w/worm holes, 13" 165.00
Tin, cylinder w/sq base, tube shaft, arched/tapered hdl, 6" 130.00

Tin, saucer base, conical font w/stamped bands, 7¾x6½", VG ..**110.00**
Tin, saucer base, cylinder reservoir, hdl, 5½", VG **75.00**

Miniature Lamps, Kerosene

Miniature oil lamps were originally called 'night lamps' by their manufacturers. Early examples were very utilitarian in design — some holding only enough oil to burn through the night. When kerosene replaced whale oil in the second half of the nineteenth century, 'mini' lamps became more decorative and started serving other purposes. While mini lamps continue to be produced today, collectors place special value on the lamps of the kerosene era, roughly 1855 to 1910. Four reference books are especially valuable to collectors as they try to identify and value their collections: *Miniature Lamps* by Frank and Ruth Smith, Schiffer Publishing, 1968 (referred to as SI); *Miniature Lamps II* by Ruth Smith Schiffer Publishing, 1982. (SII); *Miniature Victorian Lamps* by Margorie Hulsebus, Schiffer Publishing, 1996; and *Price Guide for Miniature Lamps* by Marjorie Hulsebus, Schiffer Publishing, 1998 (contains 1998 values for all the above books). References in the following listings correlate with each lamp's plate number in the Smith books. Our advisor is Bob Culver; he is listed in the Directory under Michigan.

Eagle, SI-275, $425.00. (Photo courtesy Bob Culver)

Artichoke, milk glass, pk/gr pnt, SI-Figure III, 8" **300.00**
Beauty Night Lamp, NP w/beehive shade, label, SI-77, 4½" **85.00**
Delft, windmills, ball shade, flaring base, SII-267, 8¾" **750.00**
End-of-day glass in beaded/swirl pattern, SI-369, 8¾" **500.00**
Fishscale, bl or amber, SI-116, 5" **125.00**
Greek Key, w/matching chimney shade, SI-166, 8½" **100.00**
Little Buttercup, emb on sm finger lamp, clear, SI-36, 2¾" **60.00**
Little Buttercup, emb on sm finger lamp, color, SI-36, 2¾" **125.00**
Little Favorite, SI-16, 2½" **150.00**
Log Cabin, amber, SI-50, 3⅝" **700.00**
Milk glass, Acanthus flowers on base/shade, 8¼" **225.00**
Milk glass, Mission style, SI-192, 6½" **85.00**
Moon & Stars, amber, LG Wright, ca 1960, 8" **150.00**
Red satin, emb scrolls & shells, peach or wht satin, 8¼" (+) **65.00**
Red satin, emb scrolls & shells, SI-397, 8¼" **400.00**
Santa Claus, coat & face shade, boots base, SI-Figure VII, 9½" ..**3,000.00**
Twinkle, amethyst, emb base, ball chimney/shade, SI-432, 7" ...**275.00**

Motion Lamps

Animated motion lamps were made as early as 1920 and as late as 1980s. They reached their peak during the 1950s when plastic became widely used. They are characterized by action created by the heat of a light bulb which causes the cylinder to revolve and create the illusion of an animated scene. Some of the better-known manufacturers were Econolite Corp., Scene in Action Corp., and LA Goodman Mfg. Co. As with many collectible items, prices are guided by condition, availability, and collector demand. Collectors should be aware that reproductions of cars, trains, sailing ships, fish, and mill scenes are being made. Values are given for original lamps in mint condition. Any damage or flaws seriously reduce the price. Our advisors for motion lamps are Kaye and Jim Whitaker; they are listed in the Directory under Washington.

Antique Autos, Econolite, 1957, 11" (+) **125.00**
Aquarium, glass bowl for fish motion below in stand, 1931 ....**300.00**
Bar Is Open, Visual Effects, Op Art, 1970s, 13" **35.00**
Davy Crockett **200.00**
Disneyland Express, Econolite, 1955, 11" **155.00**
Elvgrin Pin-Up Girls **300.00**
Firefighters, LA Goodman, 1957, 11" **250.00**
Fireplace, Econolite, 1958, 11" **150.00**
Fish, Fresh Water, Econolite, 1950s, 11" **105.00**
Fish, Salt Water, Econolite, 1950s, 11" (+) **110.00**
Forest Fire, Econolite, 1955, 11" **130.00**
Forest Fire, Rotovue Jr, 1949, 10" **125.00**
Fountain of Youth, Rotovue Jr, 1950, 10" **110.00**
Indian Chief, Gritt Inc, 1920s, 11" **100.00**
Indian Maiden, Gritt Inc, 1920s, 11" **100.00**
Japanese Twilight, Scene in Action, 1931, 13" **185.00**
Jet Planes, Econolite **210.00**
Merry Go Round, Rotovue Jr, 1949, 10" **100.00**
Miss Liberty, Econolite, 1957, 11" **250.00**
Niagara Falls, Econolite, 1955, 11" **95.00**
Niagara Falls, Rotovue Jr, 1949, 10" **75.00**
Niagara Falls, Scene in Action, 1931, 10" **150.00**
Old Mill, Econolite, 1965 (+) **110.00**
Op Art Lamp, Visual Effects, 1970s, 13" **55.00**
Oriental Fantasy, LA Goodman, 1957, 11" **110.00**
Oriental Scene, Econolite, 1959, 11" **165.00**
Sailboats, LA Goodman, 1954, 14" **110.00**
Sailing Ships, Econolite (+) **150.00**
Seattle World's Fair, Econolite **175.00**
Seven Up **75.00**
Snow Scene, LA Goodman **95.00**
Snow Scene (church or cabin), Econolite, 1957, 11" **150.00**
Steamboats, Econolite, 1957, 11" **130.00**
Totville Train, Econolite, 1948, 11" **150.00**
Trains, Econolite, 1956, 11" (+) **125.00**
White Christmas, flat front, Econolite, 11" **190.00**

Pattern Glass Lamps

The letter/number codes in the following descriptions refer to *Oil Lamps, Books I* and *II*, by Catherine Thuro (book, page, item number, or letter). Our advisor for this section is Jeff Bradfield who is listed in the Directory under Virginia.

Atterbury Buckle, stand lamp, CI base, T1-136a, 8" **150.00**
Atterbury Flower Band, stand lamp, T1-141l, 9" **100.00**
Atterbury Loop, stand lamp, T1-141c, 8¾" **85.00**
Bat & Fan, stand lamp, T1-283k, 7¾" **100.00**
Blackberry, cobalt, rnd base, T1-117g, 8" **600.00**
Buckle, stand lamp, brass stem, T1-171f, 10¾" **165.00**
Canadian Drape, stand lamp, T1-271k, 12" **175.00**
Chain w/Star, ftd hand lamp, T1-198c, 3⅞" **125.00**
Cherry Ripe, stand lamp, opaque base, T1-165i, 9" **200.00**
Chester, stand lamp, T1-203g, 7½" **100.00**
Cinderella, stand lamp, T1-275g, 8¼" **150.00**
Cottage w/Fleur-de-Lis, wht base w/gilt, T1-121a, 13" **225.00**
Daisy & Button, Fine Cut base, stand lamp, T1-223i, 10" **125.00**

Diamond Sunburst, stand lamp, emb metal base, T1-173i, 9½" ...100.00
Dorothy, hand lamp, T1-260b, 4¾" ...80.00
Early Moon & Star, stand lamp, T1-113d, 9" ...200.00
Eyewinker, Bubble Base, stand lamp, T1-249k, 7½" ...175.00
Feather Duster w/Sawtooth Band, brass connector, T1-224e, 8½" ...90.00
Feline Fancy, stand lamp, T1-209e, 12" ...125.00
Fishscale w/Panelled Font, hand lamp, T1-252h, 6¼" ...110.00
Flute & Block, stand lamp, T1-263h, 9" ...95.00
Hearts & Stars, stand lamp, opaque base, T1-145g, 10" ...250.00
Hobbs Star Panel, stand lamp, opaque base, T1-154a, 13" ...225.00
Interlocking Diamond Band, hand lamp, T1-197k, 2⅞" ...90.00
Lomax, hand lamp, T1-181e, 5½" ...175.00
Macklin, eng band, opaline base, T1-89d, 12" ...220.00
Panelled Block & Bar, stand lamp, opaque base, T1-167k, 10" ..150.00
Plume, hand lamp, T1-252d, 3⅝" ...125.00
Princess Feather, stand lamp, T1-279f, 8" ...175.00
Queen Heart, stand lamp, T1-251h, 10¾" ...200.00
Rib & Flute, Atterbury, T1-89h, 6" ...95.00
Riverside Rib Band, stand lamp, T1-245f, t8" ...75.00
Scalloped Rib Band, bl-gray slag base, T1-94a, 11" ...350.00
Star Loop & Cable Right, stand lamp, T1-99d, 9" ...150.00
Stippled Daisy & Leaf Band, stand lamp, T1-201l, 8" ...100.00
US Coin, stand lamp, T1-213f, rare, 9¼" ...950.00
Veronica, stand lamp, cloverleaf base, T1-151a, 11" ...300.00
Waffle Cubes, stand lamp, T1-286d, 7½" ...125.00

Perfume Lamps

One catalog from the 1950s states that a perfume lamp 'precipitates and absorbs unpleasant tobacco smoke in closed rooms; freshens air in rooms, and is decorative in every home — can be used as a night lamp or television lamp.' An earlier advertisement reads 'an electric lamp that breathes delightful, delicate fragrance as it burns.' Perfume-burner lamps can be traced back to the earliest times of man. There has always been a desire to change, sweeten, or freshen air. Through the centuries the evolution of the perfume-burner lamp has had many changes in outer form, but very little change in function. Many designs of incense burners were used not only for the reasons mentioned here, but also in various ceremonies — as they still are to this day. Later, very fine perfume burners were designed and produced by the best glasshouses in Europe. Other media such as porcelain and metal also were used. It was not until the early part of the twentieth century that electric perfume lamps came into existence. Many lamps made by both American and European firms during the '20s and '30s are eagerly sought by collectors.

From the mid-1930s to the 1970s, there seems to have been an explosion in both the number of designs and manufacturers. This is especially true in Europe. Nearly every conceivable figure has been seen as a perfume lamp. Animals, buildings, fish, houses, jars, Oriental themes, people, and statuary are just a few examples. American import firms have purchased many different designs from Japan. These lamps range from replicas of earlier European pieces to original works. Except for an occasional article or section in reference books, very little has been written on this subject. The information contained in each of these articles generally covers only a specific designer, manufacturer, or country. To date, no formal group or assocation exists for this area of collecting. Our advisors for this category are Tom and Linda Millman; they are listed in the Directory under Ohio.

Bowler w/cigar & ball, potbelly, 6½" ...235.00
Cat crouching w/tail up, Goebel, ET1217-3/0, 7" ...625.00
Cat sitting w/tail curled to front, 6¼" ...145.00
Cat w/bl glass eyes, pk, sitting, #6006, 3½" ...75.00
Cats (2 playing), Rosenthal, Hamburg, 6" ...165.00
Chimney sweep, Germany #9035, 7¼" ...200.00
Chinese junk, Aerozon #742, 5½" ...195.00
Dancer (Spanish) w/long yel skirt, 8" ...250.00
Fr bulldog, brn/wht w/bl color, Goebel, crown mk, 5" ...300.00
Lady, sitting & reading book, Irice ...35.00
Lady sits on steps w/flower basket, Fr Limoges, 5½" ...275.00
Lady w/Pot-hat, big rose & fur coat, Goebel TMK1, 7½" ...650.00
Man, funny, little & bald, matches lady, Goebel TMK1, 7" ...650.00
Man sitting w/jar on shoulder, Aerozon #286, 5½" ...185.00
Mask, female, (wall mtd), Goebel TMK1 EL111, 7" ...700.00
Monkey climbing (hanging lamp), Goebel TMK1 ET267, 16" ..600.00
Monkeys, 3 Virtues, 4" ...175.00
Owl (red) sitting on 2 books, Goebel TMK 1 ET4/2, 8¼" ...575.00
Penguin sitting on egg, Neuhaus #6073, 8½" ...245.00
Raja sitting, yel coat, Fr, Liane #93P, 8½" ...650.00

Reverse-Painted Lamps

Classique, 8" river scene shade; bronze vasiform std, 14" ...900.00
Jefferson, 14" roses shade; acanthus cast SP Pairpoint std, 22½" ...1,500.00
Jefferson, 14" w/rose sprigs & brn band; Deco std w/leaves, 22" ...1,000.00
Jefferson, 18" scenic sgn shade (worn); gr glass base, EX ...1,800.00
Jefferson, 18" trees shade; bronzed vasiform metal base, 23" ...2,200.00
Jefferson, 18" trees/waterway #1379 shade; Deco floral std, 24" ..2,350.00
Jefferson, 21" scenic flared dome shade #1972; rpl base ...1,265.00
McKenny/Waterbury, 8" daffodils shade; slim metal std, 14" ..1,150.00
Moe Bridges, 7" landscape shade; patinated metal std, 15" ...1,000.00
Moe Bridges, 8" trees shade; bronzed baluster std, 14" ...900.00
Moe Bridges, 17" domed scenic shade; 2-socket std, 23" ...1,035.00
Pittsburgh, 18" autumn leaves shade; urn-form std ...3,250.00
Pittsburgh, 18" Indian scene shade; geometric std ...6,000.00
Pittsburgh, 18" river/trees/moon scenic shade; 3-socket std, 23" .2,000.00
Unmk, bell shade w/sunset lake; pnt metal base, 16" ...200.00
Unmk, 18" floral/pond grasses domed shade; 2-socket std, 24" ..1,800.00

Student Lamps, Kerosene

Brass with cast foliate design, green shades, patented by Wild & Wessel, Berlin, retailed by Shreeve, Crump & Low, 21", $2,570.00 for the pair.

Brass, dbl, cased gr shades, electrified, 22½x27", pr ...400.00
Brass, Miller's Ideal No 0 burner, later milk glass shade ...120.00
NP, Miller syphon-style, wht shade, cut/frosted font, 21" ...1,150.00
NP brass, dbl, GA Kleeman NY, 19½" ...600.00
SP brass, dbl, milk glass shades, Argand/1871, 21x19", EX ...800.00

TV Lamps

When TV viewing became a popular pastime during the 1940s, TV lamps were developed to provide just the right amount of light — not bright enough to compromise the sharpness of the picture, but just enough to prevent the eyestrain it was feared might result from watching TV in a darkened room. Most were made of ceramic, and many were figurals such as cats, owls, ducks, and the like, or made in the shape of

Conestoga wagons, sailing ships, seashells, etc. Some had shades and others were made as planters. Few were marked well enough to identify the maker without some study. *TV Lamps* by Tom Santiso (Collector Books) provides many photos and suggested value ranges for those who want more information.

Our advisors for this category are John and Peggy Scott who are listed in the Directory under Missouri. All lamps listed below are ceramic unless otherwise described. See also Maddux; Morton Pottery; Rosemeade; other specific manufacturers

Bird (exotic), coral w/gold spray & trim, L-701, 13x12", from $75 to ...80.00
Birds on branches, wht w/gold trim, 10" ...35.00
Bluebird, 11" ...30.00
Chinese junk, chartreuse, Corner Creation, 1953, 10" ...20.00
Clam shell, 14" ...20.00
Conch shell, brn & lime gloss, 13" L ...40.00
Deer, spike buck on rocky ledge, naturalistic colors, from $60 to .65.00
Deer, w/twin fawns, leaping in tall grass, Haeger ...70.00
Dove pr, wht w/gold spatter, Royal Fleet CA, 10x13½" ...60.00
Duck, flying, blk gloss, 12½" L ...50.00
English setter, spotted dog on grassy base, 14" ...75.00
Fireplace, fiberglass screen, 10" ...22.00
Fish, stylized, dorsal-fin planter, gold waves, Miller, 1956, 21" ...28.00
Flamingos, Lane, L-26, 1956, 11", minimum value ...150.00
Flowers, mc glass & beads, lg center blossom w/light, plaster base ...35.00
Galleon, brn onyx ...37.50
Horse, blk w/gold mane, planter behind, red shade ...55.00
Horse, rearing, blk w/gold trim, 19" ...90.00
Horse, rearing, little detail, 9" ...18.00
Horses, gold lustre on blk glass base, sm ...35.00
Leaf-mold planter on reticulated brass base, Premco Mfg, 1954, 9" L ..15.00
Lover's Lane, pr on bicycle, Gay Nineties motif, 10" ...30.00
Mallard duck, natural colors, well done, 20" L ...65.00
Nautilus shell, pk glaze, wavy base, 9" L ...16.00
Panther, crouching & stalking, blk, Deco style, 20" L ...35.00
Panther pr prowling atop naturalistic base, 13" L ...30.00
Roman warrior kneeling behind panther, wht foam on brn glaze .35.00
Shell, lg natural conch on rnd fluted plastic base, from $15 to ...25.00
Spanish dancers, avocado gr, 15x12", from $75 to ...80.00
Stagecoach, gr w/much gold detailing, 10" ...22.00

Whale Oil/Burning Fluid Lamps

Coin Spot, bl opal invt pear-form font, milk glass std, 14", pr ...400.00
Coin Spot, clear opal, brass std w/mc opal base, sm chips, 9" ...500.00
Eng elongated free-blown font, wafers in knop stem, step base ..500.00
Paneled font, early rpl burner, Sandwich, mid-19th C, 11x4½" ...150.00
Triple Flute & Bar, marble base, 9¾" ...200.00

Le Verre Francais

Le Verre Francais was produced during the 1920s by Schneider at Epinay-sur-Seine in France. It was a commercial art glass in the cameo style composed of layered glass with the designs engraved by acid. Favored motifs were stylized leaves and flowers or geometric patterns. It was marked with the name in script or with an inlaid filigrane. Our advisor for this category is Don Williams; he is listed in the Directory under Missouri.

Cameo

Bowl, centerpc; 5 scarabs/geometrics, orange/aubergine, 10" ...700.00
Vase, bellflowers, wine on yel/red frost, bulbous w/bun ft, 6" ...600.00
Vase, berries/honeycomb, orange on yel mottle, ovoid, 4⅜" ...800.00
Vase, berries/horse chestnut, pale yel frost, 12x7" ...600.00
Vase, Coque Ret, Art Deco, mc on bubbly yel mottle, 15" ...1,125.00
Vase, Deco flower trees, orange & yel mottle/red/aubergine, 9½x9" ...1,600.00
Vase, ducks in flight, bl/brn on yel/wht, ovoid, 13" ...1,800.00
Vase, floral, red-orange/gr mottle/brn, trumpet, Ovington, 12¼" ..980.00
Vase, floral, trailing, lav/purple on pk, rim hdls, 15x4" ...1,495.00
Vase, floral clusters, opal/lav/lt bl, shouldered, 3 mks, 11¾" ...2,100.00
Vase, floral stems, red/violet on pk, slim/ftd, 10" ...900.00
Vase, floral/neck band, orange/dk bl on yel, bulbous, 8" ...650.00
Vase, grapevines, orange/red/yel mottle/maroon, swollen ovoid, 16" .1,500.00
Vase, hollyhocks, yel/cobalt/orange variegated, trumpet, 19x13½" ...3,750.00
Vase, leaves, brn mottle on lav, trumpet neck, 13x9" ...1,600.00
Vase, ribbons & dots, wht/amber/brns/orange, bulbous, ped ft, 17" ...1,500.00

Leeds, Leeds Type

The Leeds Pottery was established in 1758 in Yorkshire and under varied management produced fine creamware, often highly reticulated and transfer printed, shiny black-glazed Jackfield wares, polychromed pearlware, and figurines similar to those made in the Staffordshire area. Little of the early ware was marked; after 1775 the impressed 'Leeds Pottery' mark was used. From 1781 to 1820, the name 'Hartley Greens & Co.' was added. The pottery closed in 1898.

Today the term 'Leeds' has become generic and is used to encompass all polychromed pearlware and creamware, wherever its origin. Thus similar wares of other potters (Wood for instance) is often incorrectly called 'Leeds.' Unless a piece is marked or can be definitely attributed to Leeds by confirming the pattern to be authentic, 'Leeds-Type' would be a more accurate nomenclature.

Key:
cw — creamware
pw — pearlware

Teapot, creamware, green and yellow stripes, brown dots, leaf-molded spout, entwined handle, minor repairs, ca 1780, 5¾", $2,650.00.

Bowl, pw, Oriental transfer, yel rim, 3⅞x8¾" ...145.00
Bust of Shakespeare, cw, on shaped base, 1800s, 12½", NM ...460.00
Chamber pot, pw, HP & emb Am eagle, 5x9", EX ...450.00
Coffeepot, mc floral, reeded spout, leaf hdl, ca 1775, rstr, 8¾" ..925.00
Creamer & sugar bowl, surface granite, w/lid, ca 1800, rprs ...550.00
Cup & saucer, pw, gaudy floral, Wood & Sons, VG ...260.00
Pitcher, pw, mc floral, stains, 8⅝" ...275.00
Plate, castle scene, blk transfer w/mc, 10", EX ...110.00
Plate, chop; pw, floral w/feather edge, 14¼", EX ...220.00
Plate, cw, emb gr grape center, feather border, 4⅜" ...430.00
Plate, pw, bl & wht Oriental decor, Turner, 7¾" ...165.00
Plate, pw, lg 4-color floral, gr molded edge, 7¾", EX ...430.00
Platter, cobalt leafy rim, emb florals on border, 17x14", NM ...235.00
Platter, pw, bl/wht Oriental decor, bl feather edge, rpr, 21" ...500.00
Teapot, cw, Prince of Orange portraits, ribbed hdl, rstr lid, 5" ...450.00

Lefton China

The Lefton China Company was the creation of Mr. George Zoltan

Lefton who migrated to the United States from Hungary in 1939. In 1941 he embarked on a new career and began shaping a business that sprang from his passion for collecting fine china and porcelains. Though his funds were very limited, his vision was to develop a source from which to obtain fine porcelains by reviving the postwar Japanese ceramic industry, which dated back to antiquity. As a trailblazer, George Zoltan Lefton soon earned the reputation as 'The China King.'

Counted among the most desirable and sought-after collectibles of today, Lefton items such as Bluebirds, Miss Priss, Angels, all types of dinnerware, and tea-related items are eagerly acquired by collectors. As is true with any antique or collectible, prices may vary, dependent on location, condition, and availability. For additional information on the history of Lefton China, its factories, marks, products, and values, readers should consult the *Collector's Encyclopedia of Lefton China, Books I, II,* and *III*, and *Lefton Price Guide* by our advisor, Loretta DeLozier, who is listed in the Directory under Tennessee. All are published by Collector Books.

Angel of the Month, July, #1323 ....18.00
Animal, elephant w/trunk up, #5060, 9½" 150.00
Animal, Wild Hare, on base w/mushrooms, #4493, 9" 125.00
Ashtray, Violet Chintz, #2242, nested set of 4 rnd w/holder 30.00
Bank, Angel, #1588, 7" 55.00
Bell, naughty angel, #8840, 4" 30.00
Bird, bluebird, #4954, 6" 60.00
Bird, parakeet, yel, w/clip, #981, 6½" 35.00
Bird, roosters fighting, #854, 9½", pr 150.00
Bowl, console; Holly w/Candy Cane Red, #032 ....45.00
Coffeepot, Gold Wheat, #20590 ....85.00
Cookie Jar, Country Charm, yel, #4602 ....60.00
Creamer & sugar bowl, Wheat Poppy, #1454 ....28.00
Figurine, farmer & woman w/wheat, #4056, 10", pr 225.00
Figurine, guitar player, #4068, 7" 55.00
Figurine, lady w/lace, bl, #3205, 7¼" 95.00
Figurine, man on homemade boat w/dog, #7120 ....90.00
Figurine, Provincial boy & girl, #4055, 8", pr 130.00
Figurine, Ruffled Charm, lady, #400, 8½" 100.00
Jam jar, Honey Bee, #1280 ....50.00
Mug, Pennsylvania Dutch w/girl for hdl, #3703, 5" 25.00
Nativity set, Christopher Collection, #03224, 3¾", 9-pc 60.00
Pitcher & bowl, Paisley Fantazia, #6806, 3½", 8" 22.00
Plate, Rose Garden, #6574, 7" 12.00
Powder box, hand on cover, bl, #90092, 4" 40.00
Shakers, Dutch boy & girl, #2367, pr 40.00
Snack set, To a Wild Rose, #2580 ....25.00
Soup tureen, Pear 'N Apple, #5197, w/ladle & tray 95.00
Teapot, Lilac Chintz, #693 ....195.00
Wall plaque, baby on leaf, #8145, 3½" 40.00
Wall plaque, ducks in flight, #60310, 11" 32.00
Wall plaque, violin w/pk roses, #703, 5" 45.00

Legras

Legras and Cie was founded in St. Denis, France, in 1864. Production continued until the 1930s. In addition to their enameled wares, they made cameo art glass decorated with outdoor scenes and florals executed by acid cuttings through two to six layers of glass. Their work is signed 'Legras' in relief and in enamel. Our advisor for this category is Don Williams; he is listed in the Directory under Missouri.

Cameo

Box, floral, cut/pnt on textured frost, 3x5" dia 450.00
Compote, foliage, gr on clear, etched ft, 10x16" 1,200.00
Vase, apple blossoms, cut-pnt on frost, ovoid, 8" 325.00
Vase, butterflies/fuchsias/vines, wine on bl opal, stick neck, 10" ...750.00
Vase, florals/ferns, cut/pnt on butterscotch, 13¾" 1,550.00
Vase, grapes (stylized), wht mottle on clear, broad, 6" 300.00
Vase, leaves/berries, gr on red to orange mottle, 8½x3½" 750.00
Vase, maple leaves, cranberry on pk frost, stick neck, 15" 750.00
Vase, mtn scene w/shepherd & flock, mauve on frost, 12½x6½" ..950.00
Vase, pheasant/trees, red/pk on frost, 7" 800.00
Vase, zigzag band of Deco fans on cased wht w/brn mottle, 11" .750.00

Enameled Glass

Vase, autumn leaves/berries, on claret to wht, bun base, 13" 325.00
Vase, floral cascading branches, burgundy on frost, 13½" 500.00
Vase, harbor/sailing scene, metal Depose #357 base, 11½" 260.00
Vase, man & camel/palms/pyramids, mc on orange, 10¼" 225.00
Vase, stylized motif, 3-color on yel mottle, pinched rim, 3½" 280.00
Vase, trees/boats on yel/gr, 15¾x4" 900.00
Vase, winter scene, rnd w/4-lobe rim, 4¾" 400.00

Lenox

Walter Scott Lenox, former art director at Ott and Brewer, and Jonathan Coxon founded The Ceramic Art Company of Trenton, New Jersey, in 1889. By 1906 Cox had left the company, and to reflect the change in ownership, the name was changed to Lenox Inc. Until 1930 when the production of American-made Belleek came to an end, they continued to produce the same type of high-quality ornamental wares that Lenox and Coxon had learned to master while in the employ of Ott and Brewer. Their superior dinnerware made the company famous, and since 1917 Lenox has been chosen the official White House China. Our advisor for this category is Mary Frank Gaston. See also Ceramic Art Company.

Busts, Deco-style man and woman, white glossy porcelain, marked ABCO '35 and green stamped, 8¾x3¾", $500.00.

Bowl, Autumn, w/lid, 5x6" 100.00
Bowl, Autumn, 8-sided, 3½x8" 132.00
Bowl, soup; Abigail 55.00
Bowl, soup; Blue Ridge 45.00
Bowl, soup; Erin 45.00
Bowl, soup; Firelight 60.00
Bowl, vegetable; Caitlin, w/lid 245.00
Bowl, vegetable; Country Tulips, oval 50.00
Candlestick, Autumn 55.00
Candlesticks, wht w/silver o/l, wreath mk, 8½" 125.00
Candy bowl, Christmas, holly leaves on ivory w/gold, 6½x5" 60.00
Cracker barrel, mums encircle shoulder, gold trim, palette mk, 7" ..175.00
Creamer, Autumn 80.00
Creamer, Citation Gold 80.00
Creamer, Country Romance 80.00
Creamer, Erin 70.00

Creamer, Spring Bounty 150.00
Creamer & sugar bowl, brn w/web & scroll silver o/l, wreath mk, w/lid 125.00
Cup, Autumn 30.00
Cup, Ballad 15.00
Cup & saucer, Avanti 55.00
Cup & saucer, Caribbee 40.00
Cup & saucer, Casual Elegance 20.00
Cup & saucer, Citation Lace 45.00
Cup & saucer, cream w/gold Deco hdl & trim, palette mk, 2¾", 4¾" ...40.00
Cup & saucer, Southern Vista 30.00
Dresser set, gold roses on cream, palette mk, 7-pc 300.00
Figurine, African Lion Cubs, Wildlife Collection, 1984, wood base ..200.00
Figurine, Cinderella, Legendary Princesses 150.00
Figurine, girl lifts sides of skirt, faces right, ivory, 14" 350.00
Figurine, girl strokes face of greyhound, ivory, 13½" 425.00
Figurine, Sleeping Beauty 150.00
Figurine, Wind Dancers, swallows on stand, wht w/gold eyes, 7¼" ...90.00
Gravy boat, Bedazzle Citrine 45.00
Gravy boat, Southampton Gardens 225.00
Mug, Avanti 40.00
Mug, bird of paradise, irid, palette mk, 7½" 225.00
Mug, Columbia 45.00
Mug, Diamond Ring 15.00
Mug, golfing theme, gr transfer, silver rim, 5¾" 150.00
Pitcher, cider; raspberries/blossoms & foliage w/gold, palette mk, 6" ...175.00
Pitcher, man & lady portraits w/floral chain & gold, sgn/1903, 6" 100.00
Pitcher, wht w/silver o/l, wreath mk, 8½" 95.00
Plate, bread & butter; Autumn, 6⅜" 15.00
Plate, bread & butter; Eternal 12.00
Plate, bread & butter; Sprite, from $7 to 10.00
Plate, dinner; Abigail 35.00
Plate, dinner; Autumn, 10½" 35.00
Plate, dinner; Belvidere 27.50
Plate, dinner; Blue Breeze 30.00
Plate, dinner; Blue Pinstripes 20.00
Plate, dinner; Blue Ridge, from $35 to 40.00
Plate, dinner; Buchanan 40.00
Plate, dinner; Cafe Java 12.00
Plate, dinner; Charleston 30.00
Plate, dinner; Courtyard 25.00
Plate, dinner; Crossroads 55.00
Plate, dinner; Desert Jewell 25.00
Plate, dinner; Eclipse 55.00
Plate, dinner; Solitaire 30.00
Plate, luncheon; Alyssa 20.00
Plate, salad; Autumn 25.00
Plate, salad; Bricelyn 12.00
Plate, salad; Capitol Gardens 16.00
Plate, salad; Casual Elegance 14.00
Plate, salad; Classic Modern, from $20 to 30.00
Plate, salad; Country Romance 15.00
Plate, salad; Crestwood 15.00
Plate, salad; Dancing Lilies 8.00
Plate, salad; Faith 38.00
Plate, salad; Spring Vista 15.00
Plate, Woodland Wildlife, limited edition, 1974, 10¾" 110.00
Plate, yel w/silver o/l, hexagonal, hdls, wreath mk 160.00
Platter, Autumn, 16" 155.00
Platter, Bedazzle Emerald, med 80.00
Salt & pepper mill set, Lido, enameled colors, 8" 140.00
Sugar bowl, Alyssa, w/lid 90.00
Sugar bowl, Desert Jewell, w/lid 100.00
Sugar bowl, Emma, w/lid 90.00
Tea/coffee set, cream w/gold Deco hdls, palette mks, 2 pots/cr+sug ..175.00
Teapot, Federal Platinum, w/lid 235.00
Teapot, Solitaire, w/lid 200.00
Tumbler, assorted fruit on gold ground, palette mk, 4¾" 45.00
Vase, appl peonies & wildflowers w/gold, baluster, 8¼" 145.00
Vase, Autumn, 4½", from $30 to 45.00
Vase, Autumn, 8", from $45 to 80.00
Vase, daisies, gold trim, stovepipe shape, 4⅝x11⅝" 90.00
Vase, dense floral vines, silver o/l, baluster, 10½" 200.00
Vase, forget-me-nots, HP, palette mk, 8¼" 75.00
Vase, Japanese girl, artist sgn, palette mk, 10¼" 250.00
Vase, ring-neck pheasant, Game Bird Series #57, artist sgn, 12" ..125.00
Vase, rose & bud, pk on ivory w/gold trim, V rim, 8" 60.00
Vase, silver o/l straps over wht, 10½" 250.00
Vase, swan hdls, gr mk, 10½" 75.00
Vase, wht w/silver o/l, Indian on horse, Appeal to God, 11½" ..350.00
Vase, wht w/silver o/l, palette & Rockwell Silver mks, 10½" 150.00

Letter Openers

Made in a wide variety of materials and designs, letter openers make an interesting collection, easy to display and easy on the budget as well. For further information we recommend *Collector's Guide to Letter Openers, Identification & Values*, by Everett Grist (Collector Books); Mr. Grist is listed in the Directory under Tennessee.

Tortoise shell with carved dimensional bird's claw holding moving tortoise marble, Victorian, $125.00. (Photo courtesy Everett Grist)

Aluminum, opener/ruler, Ohio State Fair, ca 1910, 6½" 20.00
Bakelite, Deco design, 8¾" 40.00
Bakelite, simple oblong shape w/pointed end, 7" 30.00
Bone, emblem of Paris, 9½" 20.00
Bone, scimitar form, 6" 20.00
Brass, figural sword, mk Gettysburg PA, 8" 15.00
Brass, pnt dolphins, 7" 10.00
Brass, pnt floral design, China, 9" 15.00
Brass, walnut hdl, Thailand, 6¾" 10.00
Celluloid, figural bird head, 7" 10.00
Celluloid, peapod-shaped hdl, W Atlee Burpee & Co, ca 1905, 8" ..80.00
Celluloid, pnt rooster head, HK Kellogg incised on blade, 8⅝" .120.00
Copper, figure-8 hdl w/filigree trim, blade mk Butte Montana, 9⅜" .25.00
Copper, opener/lighter, ASR, 9½" 45.00
Copper, ship's wheel at top, mk Fort McHenry Baltimore MD, 6¼" ..15.00
Forged nail, Pan-American Souvenir 1901, 5" 25.00
Ivory, cvd Egyptian figure looking sideways, 10¾" 60.00
Ivory, cvd vine design, 9½" 40.00
Mussel shell, simple oblong shape, 4" 10.00
Plastic, Kennedy Will Win!, image of Bobby, red/bl on wht, 8" ...25.00
Plastic, opener/magnifying glass, Masonic lodge advertising, 6¼" 10.00
Plastic, opener/ruler, octagonal hdl w/beach scene, 7⅛" 5.00
Plastic, pinup nude w/lettered advertising disk on head, 8½" 10.00
Plastic, S-form w/Sphinx hdl, Garamycin, 9" 50.00
Steel, bl nautical design on wht curved porc hdl, 8¾" 50.00
Steel, costume-jewelled leaf hdl, 7½" 15.00
Steel, fisherman's fly in Lucite, USA, 9" 30.00
Steel, slim pointed shape w/brn & wht agate hdl, 7⅝" 20.00
Sterling, coat-of-arms w/inset stone, Italy, 5⅝" 40.00

Sterling, horse jockey figure, Tiffany, ca 1938, 7" 200.00
Sterling, MOP hdl, sickle form, 3½" 40.00
Wood, cvd/pnt cloaked woman's profile, 7¼" 15.00
Wood, cvd/pnt gypsy man's profile, 4½" 10.00

Libbey

The New England Glass Company was established in 1818 in Boston, Massachusetts. In 1892 it became known as the Libbey Glass Company. At Chicago's Columbian Expo in 1893, Libbey set up a ten-pot furnace and made glass souvenirs. The display brought them worldwide fame. Between 1878 and 1918, Libbey made exquisite cut and faceted glass, considered today to be the best from the brilliant period. The company is credited for several innovations — the Owens bottle machine that made mass production possible and the Westlake machine which turned out both electric light bulbs and tumblers automatically. They developed a machine to polish the rims of their tumblers in such a way that chipping was unlikely to occur. Their glassware carried the patented Safedge guarantee. Libbey also made glassware in numerous colors, among them cobalt, ruby, pink, green, and amber.

Maize, vase, custard with green husks, 8", $395.00.

Bottle, scent; amberina, 4-fold top, ftd, ball stopper, 8¼" 2,300.00
Bowl, clear w/controlled bubbles & lt gr powders, experimental, 9" ...85.00
Bowl, cut, Hobstar, Cane, Strawberry Dmn & Tusk, shell shape, 10" ...800.00
Bowl, cut, Hobstar, Prism, Nailhead Dmn, Star & Fan, hat shape, 12" ..550.00
Bowl, cut, Hobstar & Zipper border, Snowflake center, 8" 130.00
Bowl, cut, Prism & Fern, rolled rim, 4½x10" 125.00
Candlesticks, eng pattern #019, 10", pr 800.00
Compote, amberina, optic ribs, fuchsia rim, 3¼x7¾" 450.00
Compote, amberina, 4⅛x6" 985.00
Compote, cut, Colonna, 5½x10" 500.00
Compote, cut, Somerset, 11x6" 325.00
Compote, Nailsea-type pk loops in clear, flower top, 11x4" 585.00
Cruet, cut, Hobstar & Prism, 5½" 175.00
Cruet, cut, Hobstar & X-cut Dmn, 6" 150.00
Decanter, cut, Hobstar, Strawberry Dmn, Prism, Vesica & Fan, 13" ..350.00
Ferner, cut, Hobstar & Fan, Dirks, 3-ftd, 7" 50.00
Flower center, cut, Ellsmere, 9½x6½" 1,400.00
Maize, butter dish, bl husks on irid 650.00
Maize, butter dish, gr husks on custard 165.00
Maize, celery vase, clear w/amber & bl stain, 6½" 375.00
Maize, celery vase, clear w/amber stain & bl husks, 6" 235.00
Maize, celery vase, gr husks on custard 200.00
Maize, condiment set, custard, 3 pcs on tray w/metal lid 600.00
Maize, pickle castor, amber stain 595.00
Maize, pickle castor, gr husks on custard, SP fr 550.00
Maize, pitcher, bl husks on clear w/amber irid, clear hdls, 9" 600.00
Maize, pitcher, clear irid w/amber stain, 8½" 550.00
Maize, shakers, gold-edged bl husks on custard, pr 250.00
Maize, sugar shaker, yel/gold husks on custard, 5¾" 345.00
Maize, toothpick holder, gold-edged gr husks on custard 400.00
Maize, tumbler, bl husks on irid 235.00
Maize, vase, yel/gold husks on custard, 6½" 250.00
Pitcher, cut, Hobstar, Cane & Prism, 3-notch hdl, 9" 190.00
Pitcher, tankard; crystal w/embedded ruby dots, att, 8" 250.00
Punch bowl, cut, Hobstar & Geometric, 1-pc, 7½x14½" 550.00
Salt cellar, cut, Hobstar, X-hatch & Fan, ped ft, set of 4 ....325.00
Stem, champagne, squirrel, wht opal, 6" 200.00
Stem, champagne flute, bear stem, wht opal, 5½" 120.00
Stem, claret, bear, blk, 5½" 155.00
Stem, claret, bear, wht opal 165.00
Stem, cordial, kangaroo, blk 110.00
Stem, cordial, monkey, blk 150.00
Stem, cordial, monkey, wht opal, 5" 130.00
Stem, cordial, whippet/greyhound, wht opal 175.00
Stem, goblet, cat, wht opal 200.00
Stem, sherbet, rabbit, wht opal, 2½" 160.00
Stem, sherbet, squirrel, wht opal, 4" 150.00
Stem, wine, giraffe, wht opal, 6" 120.00
Toothpick holder, Little Lobe, floral on wht to bl, ribbed 300.00
Vase, amberina, ribbed bulb on slim stem, 11" 650.00
Vase, amberina, stick neck w/swirls, 11¾" 400.00
Vase, amberina, trumpet form w/petal rim, 11" 875.00
Vase, amberina, very slender, ftd, shape #3004, 11" 1,200.00
Vase, bud; amberina, lt ribbing, 11½" 900.00
Vase, clear w/seafoam gr zippers, trumpet form, K523, 12" 350.00
Vase, jack-in-pulpit; amberina, #3014, rare 1,685.00
Vase, Talisman, clear w/internal gr spiral threads, clear ft, 14" ..230.00
Wine, cut, Hobstar, Strawberry Dmn & Fan, 4½", set of 6 ....70.00
Wine, cut, X-cut Dmn, Strawberry Dmn & Fan, cut stem, no mk, 6 for ..200.00
Wine, eng intricate florals, 4½" 50.00

Lightning Rod Balls

Used as ornaments on lightning rods, the vast majority of these balls were made of glass, but ceramic examples can be found as well. Their average diameter is 4½", but it can vary from 3½" up to 5½". Only a few of the many available pattern and color combinations are listed here. The most common measure 4½" and are found in sun-colored amethyst and milk glass. Our advisor is Rod Krupka, author of a book on this subject. Anyone interested in his book may write to him for more information; he is listed in the Directory under Michigan.

Amber, Hawkeye, 5¼x4½" 175.00
Amber, WC Shinn Mfg Co, aluminum caps, 5x4⅜" 80.00
Amethyst (sun colored), Moon & Star, 5x4½" 80.00
Bl opaque, Diddie Blitze, aluminum caps, 4x3¾" 36.00
Bl opaque, Hawkeye, 5¼x4½" 50.00
Bl opaque, Nat'l, belted, aluminum caps, 5¼x4½" 120.00
Bl opaque, pleat-pointed, aluminum caps, 4½" 45.00
Bl opaque, Shinn-System, aluminum caps, 5¼x4½" 35.00
Blk amethyst, plain, med collars w/aluminum caps, 4½" dia 400.00
Clear, Chestnut pattern 80.00
Clear, Dodd & Struthers, 5¾x5¾" 55.00
Gold mercury, plain, metal tube, 4½" 135.00
Gr transparent, plain, rnd, 4½" 150.00
Lt gr opaque, 10-sided (D&S) 140.00
Milk glass, Electra Cone, boldly emb, 5x4½" 36.00
Milk glass, Maher, heavy, w/aluminum caps, 5¾x5" 65.00
Milk glass, Moon & Star, 4½" 35.00

Orange opaque, plain, rnd, 4½" 400.00
Red, Ribbed Grape, aluminum caps, 5x4⅜" 425.00
Ruby red, Dmn Quilt, 5" 300.00
Ruby red, Electra, cone form, 4⅝" 300.00
Ruby red, Electra, rnd, 4½" 325.00
Ruby red (dk tone), chestnut form, 4" 225.00
Silver mercury, Dmn Quilt, metal tube, 5" 300.00

Limited Edition Plates

Current values of some limited edition plates have risen while others have fallen. Prices charged by plate dealers in the secondary market vary greatly; we have tried to suggest an average.

Since Goebel Hummel plates have been discontinued, values have started to decline. While those who are trying to complete the series continue to buy them, few seem interested in starting a collection. As for the Danish plates, Royal Copenhagen, and Bing and Grondahl, most purchases are for plates that commemorate the birth year of a child or a wedding anniversary, not to add to a collection.

Bing and Grondahl

1895, Behind the Frozen Window 6,250.00
1896, New Moon 2,300.00
1897, Christmas Meal of Sparrows 1,500.00
1898, Roses & Star 850.00
1899, Crows Enjoying Christmas 1,800.00
1900, Church Bells Chiming 1,200.00
1901, 3 Wise Men 495.00
1902, Gothic Church Interior 425.00
1903, Expectant Children 425.00
1904, View of Copenhagen From Fredericksberg Hill 210.00
1905, Anxiety of the Coming Christmas Night 205.00
1906, Sleighing to Church 135.00
1907, Little Match Girl 195.00
1908, St Petri Church 110.00
1909, Yule Tree 125.00
1910, Old Organist 125.00
1911, Angels & Shepherds 110.00
1912, Going to Church 110.00
1913, Bringing Home the Tree 110.00
1914, Amalienborg Castle 105.00
1915, Dog on Chain Outside Window 155.00
1916, Prayer of the Sparrows 105.00
1917, Christmas Boat 105.00
1918, Fishing Boat 105.00
1919, Outside the Lighted Window 95.00
1920, Hare in the Snow 95.00
1921, Pigeons 95.00
1922, Star of Bethlehem 95.00
1923, Hermitage 95.00
1924, Lighthouse 105.00
1925, Child's Christmas 105.00
1926, Churchgoers 105.00
1927, Skating Couple 155.00
1928, Eskimos 95.00
1929, Fox Outside Farm 105.00
1930, Tree in Town Hall Square 115.00
1931, Christmas Train 115.00
1932, Lifeboat at Work 115.00
1933, Korsor-Nyborg Ferry 95.00
1934, Church Bell in Tower 95.00
1935, Lillebelt Bridge 95.00
1936, Royal Guard 95.00
1937, Arrival of Christmas Guests 115.00
1938, Lighting the Candles 175.00
1939, Old Lock-Eye, The Sandman 215.00
1940, Delivering Christmas Letters 265.00
1941, Horses Enjoying Meal 325.00
1942, Danish Farm on Christmas Night 275.00
1943, Ribe Cathedral 235.00
1944, Sorgenfri Castle 145.00
1945, Old Water Mill 165.00
1946, Commemoration Cross 135.00
1947, Dybbol Mill 165.00
1948, Watchman 115.00
1949, Landsoldaten 125.00
1950, Kronborg Castle at Elsinore 155.00
1951, Jens Bang 125.00
1952, Old Copenhagen Canals & Thorsvaldsen Museum 135.00
1953, Royal Boat 135.00
1954, Snowman 145.00
1955, Kaulundborg Church 145.00
1956, Christmas in Copenhagen 175.00
1957, Christmas Candles 175.00
1958, Santa Claus 140.00
1959, Christmas Eve 155.00
1960, Village Church 205.00
1961, Winter Harmony 135.00
1962, Winter Night 125.00
1963, Christmas Elf 145.00
1964, Fir Tree & Hare 65.00
1965, Bringing Home the Tree 55.00
1966, Home for Christmas 45.00

1967, Sharing the Joy, $45.00.

1968, Christmas in Church 35.00
1969, Arrival of Guests 30.00
1970, Pheasants in Snow 27.00
1971, Christmas at Home 27.00
1972, Christmas in Greenland 27.00
1973, Country Christmas 30.00
1974, Christmas in the Village 30.00
1975, The Old Water Mill 30.00
1976, Christmas Welcome 30.00
1977, Copenhagen Christmas 30.00
1978, A Christmas Tale 30.00
1979, White Christmas 40.00
1980, Christmas in the Woods 40.00
1981, Christmas Peace 40.00
1982, The Christmas Tree 57.00
1983, Christmas in Old Town 47.00
1984, Christmas Letter 75.00
1985, Christmas Eve, Farm 65.00
1986, Silent Night 70.00

1987, Snowman's Christmas 55.00
1988, In King's Garden 75.00
1989, Christmas Anchorage 60.00
1990, Changing Guards 65.00
1991, Copenhagen Stock Exchange 65.00
1992, Pastor's Christmas 105.00
1993, Father Christmas in Copenhagen 100.00

M. I. Hummel

The last issue for M.I. Hummel annual plates was made in 1995. Values listed here are for plates in mint condition with original boxes.

1971, Heavenly Angel 395.00
1972, Hear Ye, Hear Ye 40.00
1973, Glober Trotter 60.00
1974, Goose Girl 45.00

1975, Ride Into Christmas, $47.00.

1976, Apple Tree Girl 47.00
1977, Apple Tree Boy 55.00
1978, Happy Pastime 35.00
1979, Singing Lesson 35.00
1980, School Girl 40.00
1981, Umbrella Boy 70.00
1982, Umbrella Girl 85.00
1983, The Postman 125.00
1984, Little Helper 50.00
1985, Chick Girl 60.00
1986, Playmates 100.00
1987, Feeding Time 130.00
1988, Little Goat Herder 85.00
1989, Farm Boy 100.00
1990, Shepherd's Boy 165.00
1991, Just Resting 125.00
1992, Meditation 160.00
1993, Doll Bath 150.00
1994, Doctor 150.00
1995, Come Back Soon 170.00

Royal Copenhagen

1908, Madonna & Child 3,500.00
1909, Danish Landscape 240.00
1910, Magi 185.00
1911, Danish Landscape 185.00
1912, Christmas Tree 185.00
1913, Frederik Church Spire 170.00
1914, Holy Spirit Church 195.00
1915, Danish Landscape 210.00
1916, Shepherd at Christmas 155.00
1917, Our Savior Church 135.00
1918, Sheep & Shepherds 135.00
1919, In the Park 135.00
1920, Mary & Child Jesus 130.00
1921, Aabenraa Marketplace 125.00
1922, 3 Singing Angels 125.00
1923, Danish Landscape 125.00
1924, Sailing Ship 150.00
1925, Christianshavn Street Scene 125.00
1926, Christianshavn Canal 115.00
1927, Ship's Boy at Tiller 175.00
1928, Vicar's Family 125.00
1929, Grundtvig Church 125.00
1930, Fishing Boats 155.00
1931, Mother & Child 150.00
1932, Frederiksberg Gardens 150.00
1933, Ferry & Great Belt 185.00
1934, Hermitage Castle 195.00
1935, Kronborg Castle 275.00
1936, Roskilde Cathedral 240.00
1937, Main Street of Copenhagen 295.00
1938, Round Church of Osterlars 425.00
1939, Greenland Pack Ice 495.00
1940, Good Shepherd 595.00
1941, Danish Village Church 425.00
1942, Bell Tower 495.00
1943, Flight Into Egypt 650.00
1944, Danish Village Scene 395.00
1945, Peaceful Scene 565.00
1946, Zealand Village Church 275.00
1947, Good Shepherd 300.00
1948, Nodebo Church 275.00
1949, Our Lady's Cathedral 295.00
1950, Boeslunde Church 295.00
1951, Christmas Angel 450.00
1952, Christmas in Forest 175.00
1953, Frederiksberg Castle 170.00
1954, Amalienborg Palace 185.00
1955, Fano Girl 230.00
1956, Rosenborg Castle 210.00
1957, Good Shepherd 150.00
1958, Sunshine Over Greenland 155.00
1959, Christmas Night 175.00
1960, Stag 140.00
1961, Training Ship 165.00
1962, Little Mermaid 265.00
1963, Hojsager Mill 75.00
1964, Fetching the Tree 70.00
1965, Little Skaters 70.00

1966, Blackbird, $55.00.

1967, Royal Oak 45.00
1968, Last Umiak 50.00

1969, Old Farmyard 45.00
1970, Christmas Rose & Cat 55.00
1971, Hare in Winter 35.00
1972, In the Desert 27.00
1973, Train Home Bound 37.00
1974, Winter Twilight 36.00
1975, Queens Palace 30.00
1976, Danish Watermill 45.00
1977, Immervad Bridge 30.00
1978, Greenland Scenery 32.00
1979, Choosing Tree 70.00
1980, Bringing Home Tree 35.00
1981, Admiring Tree 45.00
1982, Waiting for Christmas 95.00
1983, Merry Christmas 75.00
1984, Jingle Bells 70.00
1985, Snowman 70.00
1986, Wait for Me 67.00
1987, Winter Birds 80.00
1988, Christmas Eve Copenhagen 82.00
1989, Old Skating Pond 95.00
1990, Christmas in Tivoli 145.00
1991, St Lucia Basilica 75.00
1992, Royal Coach 80.00
1993, Arrival Guests by Train 95.00
1994, Christmas Shopping 90.00

Limoges

From the mid-eighteenth century, Limoges was the center of the porcelain industry of France, where at one time more than forty companies utilized the local kaolin to make a superior quality china, much of which was exported to the United States. Various marks were used; some included the name of the American export company (rather than the manufacturer) and 'Limoges.' After 1891 'France' was added. Pieces signed by factory artists are more valuable than those decorated outside the factory by amateurs. The listings below are hand-painted pieces unless noted otherwise.

For a more thorough study of the subject, we recommend you refer to *The Collector's Encyclopedia of Limoges Porcelain, Third Edition* (with beautiful illustrations and current market values), by our advisor, Mary Frank Gaston.

Candle holders, multicolor roses on white, brushed gold work on base, T&V marks, 6", from $200.00 to $225.00 for the pair. (Photo courtesy Mary Frank Gaston)

Ashtray, 3-masted ship in water, gold trim, mk, 5½" 25.00
Basket, floral, gold rococo hdl & rim, 4½" 50.00
Bottle, scent; floral reserve on yel, metal collar, mk, 4¾" 90.00
Bowl, berry; fruits & berries, 3⅞" 75.00
Bowl, roses, cream/gold border w/bl touches, 11", +undertray ...300.00
Bowl, stylized bird panel in lustre, 5½x8¾" 450.00
Bowl, vegetable; roses w/gold trim, w/lid, mk Elite, 9x6½" 65.00
Chamberstick, floral, sgn ASA, 1½" 50.00
Charger, family w/newborn baby, much gold, late 19th C, 15¾" ..1,400.00
Charger, fruit, scalloped edge, unmk, 12¼" 60.00
Charger, fruit, sgn Goise, gold rococo border, no mk, 12" 225.00
Charger, High Bear Sioux portrait sgn Dubois, 13¼" 1,300.00
Charger, plums & seed pod, Goise, gold rococo, unmk, 12¼" ...225.00
Charger, quail in winter sgn Davas, Coronet, 15½" 950.00
Charger, village scene w/church, fisherman, Conlan, 12" 285.00
Charger, wild boars, sgn Pradet, Coronet, 10½" 100.00
Creamer & sugar bowl, sgn Loh, T&V 160.00
Creamer & sugar bowl, violets/gold on wht, T&V, 3¾", 3½" 120.00
Cup & saucer, bouillon; Martin 24.00
Cup & saucer, mustache; birds & flowers w/gold, unmk 75.00
Egg tray, chickens & chicks, 4-well, mk, ca 1885, 7½" L 55.00
Fish set, fish on pk w/gold, platter/sauce boat/underplate/11 plates ..1,000.00
Goblet, grapes/leaves, HP Metzerott, 9¾" 150.00
Gravy boat, seashells, scalloped gold rim & hdl 95.00
Invalid feeder, holly leaves & red berries, mk, ca 1876-1883 .....200.00
Jar, condensed milk; red roses & daisies, 5¼" 150.00
Mayonnaise, pk & gr on wht w/gold, unmk, w/underplate 90.00
Pitcher, tankard; ears of corn, dragon hdl in gold, JPL, 15" 335.00
Plate, Nouveau lady's portrait, 9¼" 150.00
Plate, oyster; gilt oyster shells & leaves on wht, Ahrenfeldt, 4 for ..525.00
Plate, roses, T&V, scalloped, 9" 50.00
Ramekin, rose garlands w/gold 20.00
Tankard, grapes int/ext, mask spout, dragon hdl, mk 1,150.00
Tureen, lav & wht floral w/gold, 13x8", w/lid & 18" platter ...1,500.00
Vase, roses, Broussillon, Coronet, 5" 60.00

Lithophanes

Lithophanes are porcelain panels with relief designs of varying degrees of thickness and density. Transmitted light brings out the pattern in graduated shading, lighter where the porcelain is thin and darker in the heavy areas. They were cast from wax models prepared by artists and depict views of life from the 1800s, religious themes, or scenes of historical significance. First made in Berlin about 1803, they were used as lamp shade panels, window plaques, and candle shields. Later steins, mugs, and cups were made with lithophanes in their bases. Japanese wares were sometimes made with dragons or geisha lithophanes. See also Dragon Ware; Steins.

Fairy lamp, children (4 scenes), HP/gilt, Clarke cup, 4¼" 1,750.00
Lamp, 3-panel cone shade w/elk hunt, scrollwork, brass stand, 10" ..1,300.00
Shade, peasant couple in woods, Lithophane Francoise, 5x10⅝" 950.00

Little Red Riding Hood

Though usually thought of as a product of the Hull Pottery Company, research has shown that a major part of this line was actually made by Regal China. The idea for this popular line of novelties and kitchenware items was developed and patented by Hull, but records show that to a large extent Hull sent their whiteware to Regal to be decorated. Little Red Riding Hood was produced from 1943 until 1957. For further information we recommend *The Collector's Encyclopedia of Hull Pottery* by Brenda Roberts, and *The Collector's Encyclopedia of Cookie Jars* by Joyce and Fred Roerig. All published by Collector Books. Beware of reproductions.

Bank, standing, from $650 to 850.00
Butter dish, from $400 to 550.00
Canister, coffee, sugar or flour; ea, from $650 to 850.00

Canister, salt; from $1,400 to 1,800.00
Canister, tea; from $650 to 750.00
Clock 375.00
Cookie jar, closed basket, from $375 to 400.00
Cookie jar, full skirt, from $750 to 850.00
Cookie jar, open basket 350.00
Cookie jar, red spray w/gold bows, red shoes, from $700 to 750.00
Cracker jar, unmk, from $700 to 850.00
Creamer, side pour, from $200 to 250.00
Creamer, top pour, no tab hdl, from $425 to 575.00
Creamer, top pour, tab hdl, from $375 to 400.00
Lamp, from $2,200 to 2,450.00
Match holder, wall hanging, from $850 to 1,100.00
Mustard jar, no spoon 350.00
Mustard jar, w/orig spoon 475.00
Pitcher, 7" 500.00
Pitcher, 8" 450.00
Planter, hanging, from $500 to 575.00
Shakers, Pat Design 135889, med sz, pr (+), from $900 to 1,100.00
Shakers, 3¼", pr, from $150 to 195.00
Shakers, 5½", pr 200.00
Spice jar, Ginger, sq base 750.00
String holder, from $2,000 to 3,000.00
Sugar bowl, crawling, no lid, from $200 to 300.00
Sugar, bowl, standing, no lid 175.00
Sugar bowl, w/lid, from $300 to 425.00
Sugar bowl lid, minimum value 175.00
Teapot, from $375 to 400.00
Wolf jar, red base, from $1,000 to 1,400.00
Wolf jar, yel base, from $700 to 900.00

Liverpool

In the late 1700s Liverpool potters produced a creamy ivory ware, sometimes called Queen's Ware, which they decorated by means of the newly perfected transfer print. Made specifically for the American market, patriotic inscriptions, political portraits, or other States themes were applied in black with colors sometimes added by hand. (Obviously their loyalty to the crown did not inhibit the progress of business!) Before it lost favor in about 1825, other English potters made a similar product. Today Liverpool is a generic term used to refer to all ware of this type. In our listings, information following the slash mark describes the transfer on the reverse side.

Jug, The Mercury (three-masted ship) and Masonic symbols, transfer printed, nineteenth century, rim chip and hairline, 9¾", $3,000.00.

Cann, Geo WA General & Commander..., blk transfer, 4⅝", EX ..2,185.00
Creamer, When Brittons Rush On..., blk transfer, rpr, 4½" 100.00
Jug, Am ship & ribbon w/names of 15 states, blk w/mc, 10⅝", VG ...800.00
Jug, British ship/sailor returning, blk, stain/chip, 9" 550.00
Jug, Farmer's Arms/dancing couple, blk, staple rpr, 7" 175.00
Jug, Massacre of Fr King/Marie Anne...LaCorde..., blk transfer, 8" 3,200.00
Jug, Peace Commerce & Honest.../ship & Masonic emblems, 11", EX ..4,000.00
Jug, Peace Plenty.../WA in Glory, blk transfer, rprs, 9" 1,200.00
Jug, Seasons, blk transfer, 7½", EX 635.00
Jug, Telling Fortune in Coffee Grounds, blk, rstr, 5¾" 135.00
Jug, WA in Glory..., blk w/mc, old rpr, 10½" 1,375.00
Jug, WA in Glory..., eagle at spout, blk w/mc, 9" 2,300.00
Jug, WA in Glory.../Mower, blk, Herculaneum, 9", EX 2,000.00
Jug, WA in Glory/Am in Tears, US Seal, blk, 9" 1,300.00
Jug, WA in wreath memorial, blk, Herculaneum, 8", EX 950.00
Jug, Wellington in medallion/English coat of arms, blk transfer, 9" ...880.00
Jug, 3-masted ship & verse: Poor Jack, blk w/mc, 7", EX 450.00
Tea bowl & saucer, Tea Party, blk transfer, ca 1760 ....375.00
Tea canister, Tea Party, blk transfer, canted corners, 6" 450.00

Lladro

Lladro porcelains are currently being produced in Labernes Blanques, Spain. Their retired and limited edition figurines are popular collectibles on the secondary market.

Afternoon Promenade, MIB 300.00
All Aboard, L7617 ....200.00
Angel, lying down, #4541, 3x5" 80.00
Basket of Love, MIB, from $275 to 350.00
Boy Meets Girl, #1188, 8½", from $275 to 350.00
Bull, slate gray on pearlized gray base, 14" L 580.00
Bunny, #F23M, 4½" L 145.00
Butterfly, #4991, 12" 200.00
Caress & Rest, #1246, 8¼" 375.00
Circus Magic, MIB 450.00
Clown, leaning against a domino, #0016, 7¾" 120.00
Curtain Call, MIB 600.00
Destination Big Top, MIB 600.00
Dog & Snail, #1139, 6", from $580 to 680.00
Dressmaker, MIB 450.00
Duck Seller, #1267, 7¾" 260.00
Garden Classic, MIB, from $650 to 700.00
Girl, at sink, #F27, 8" 130.00
Girl, gathering flowers, #4720, matt finish, 8¼" 260.00
Girl, standing in wind carrying flowers, #C160, 6¾" 130.00
Girl w/Doll, #1211, 8¼" 725.00
Girl w/Duck, #1052, 9" 180.00
Girl w/Lamb, #4835, 9¾" 225.00
Girl w/Lantern, #4910, 8½" 280.00
Girl w/Milk Pail, #4682, 9½" 300.00
Girl w/Sparrow, MIB 600.00
Girl w/Turkey, #4569, 5½" 280.00
Heaven & Earth 650.00
Herons (2), by tree stump, 10x6¼" 110.00
Horses, galloping, #4655, 11½x15" 525.00
It Wasn't Me, #07672, 1998 Members Only pc, from $270 to ...315.00
Koala Love, 8" 220.00
Lady w/girl, #1353, 14¼", from $450 to 600.00
Little Friends, sgn, MIB 250.00
Little Red Riding Hood, #4965, 10¼" 600.00
Little Rider, MIB 300.00
Milkmaid, #4939, 11" 250.00
Musical Partners, MIB 650.00
Naughty Girl, #5006, 9¾" 140.00
Nuns in flowing wht robes, #C13E, 13" 150.00
One More Try, MIB 750.00

Pearl Mermaid, L1348 ....750.00
Pensive Clown, MIB 300.00
Physician, #5948, 14" 275.00
Pick of the Litter 270.00
Pierrot w/Concertina, #5279, 5½" 100.00
Polar Bears, #D22N, 4x6" 125.00
Portuguese Helmsman, 18" 200.00
Puppy Love, #1127, matt finish, 1971 ....100.00
Sayonara, #4989, 12" 200.00
Shelly, #1357, 6¼" 160.00
Shepherdess w/Dove, #4660, 6½" 175.00
Shepherdess w/Ducks, #4568, 9½" 275.00
Spring Bouquets, MIB 600.00
Sweety, #1248, 7½" 550.00
Ten & Growing 360.00
Thai Couple, sgn, MIB 1,900.00
Thai Dancers, sgn, MIB 800.00
Trick or Treat, MIB 250.00
Unicorn, 8½" 210.00
Winter Scene, #5287, 10¼x7" 420.00
Wish Come True 300.00

Lobmeyer

J. and L. Lobmeyer, contemporaries of Moser, worked in Vienna, Austria, during the last quarter of the 1800s. Most of the work attributed to them is decorated with distinctive enameling; favored motifs are people in eighteenth-century garb.

Bowl, cranberry to clear w/Nouveau floral, 1910s, 3¾" H 515.00
Creamer & sugar bowl, peasants/castles/etc, 3-ftd, sgn, 3¼"; 2¼" .1,500.00
Goblet, cut floral on boat-shaped bowl, ca 1875, 5" 435.00
Goblet, gent/florals/gilt, unsgn 285.00
Pitcher, clear w/mc Islamic cesign, 11½", +4 4½" beakers 2,500.00
Wine, Colonial man/florals/gilt, sgn, 5⅜" 675.00

Locke Art

By the time he came to America, Joseph Locke had already proven himself many times over as a master glassmaker, having worked in leading English glasshouses for more than seventeen years. Here he joined the New England Glass Company where he invented processes for the manufacture of several types of art glass — amberina, peachblow, pomona, and agata among them. In 1898 he established the Locke Art Glassware Co. in Mt. Oliver, Pittsburgh, Pennsylvania. Locke Art Glass was produced using an acid-etching process by which the most delicate designs were executed on crystal blanks. Most examples are signed simply 'Locke Art,' often placed unobtrusively near a leaf or a stem. Other items are signed 'Jo Locke,' some are dated, and some are unsigned. Most of the work was done by hand. The business continued into the 1920s. For further study we recommend *Locke Art Glass, Guide for Collectors*, by Joseph and Janet Locke, available at your local bookstore.

Our advisor for this category is Richard Haigh; he is listed in the Directory under Virginia.

Bowl, dessert; fish motif, footed, with underplate, signed, $950.00. (Photo courtesy Richard Haigh)

Bowl, dessert; Grape & Vine, ftd 85.00
Cup, punch; Poppy, sgn 90.00
Goblet, Ivy 95.00
Pitcher, Grape & Vine, corset shape, 8¼x6" 350.00
Sherbet, floral, sgn, 3½x3½" 95.00
Sherbet, Ivy 265.00
Tumbler, Grape & Vine 95.00
Vase, Peonies, ruffled rim, 5" 450.00
Vase, sailboat, sgn, 10" 3,500.00

Locks

The earliest type of lock in recorded history was the wooden cross bar used by ancient Egyptians and their contemporaries. The early Romans are credited with making the first key-operated mechanical lock. The ward lock was invented during the Middle Ages by the Etruscans of Northern Italy; the lever tumbler and combination locks followed at various stages of history with varying degrees of effectiveness. In the eighteenth century the first precision lock was constructed. It was a device that utilized a lever-tumbler mechanism. Two of the best-known of the early nineteenth-century American lock manufacturers are Yale and Sargent, and today's collectors value Winchester and Keen Kutter locks very highly. Factors to consider are rarity, condition, and construction. Brass and bronze locks are generally priced higher than those of steel or iron. Our advisor for this section is Joe Tanner; he is listed in the Directory under California.

Key:
bbl — barrel
st — stamped

Brass Lever Tumbler

Ames Sword Co, Perfection st on shackle, 2¾" 65.00
Automatic, emb, flat key, 2⅛" 15.00
Bingham's Best Brand, BBB emb on front, 3¼" 150.00
Blue Grass, emb, 3" 85.00
Cleveland 4 Way, Cleveland 4 Way emb on front, 3⅝" 90.00
Cotterill Birmingham Eng, st, 5⅛" 350.00
Duplex Yale & Towne Mfg Co, st, 2⅞" 125.00
Eagle Lock Co, word Eagle emb on front, scrolled, 3" 60.00
Good Luck, emb, 2¾" 45.00
GW Nock, fancy etch, st, 2⅞" 160.00
Jackson's, st Jackson's on front, 2½" 20.00
Keen Kutter, shape of KK emblem, KK emb on front, 4¾" 125.00
Motor, Motor emb on body, 3¼" 35.00
Our Very Best, OVB emb on body, 2⅞" 150.00
Roeyonoc, Roeyonoc st on body, 3¼" 30.00
Romer & Co, Romer & Co st on dust cover, 3" 55.00
Safe, Safe emb in scroll on front, 2⅜" 20.00
Siberian, Siberian emb on shackle, 2½" 110.00
Sphinx, sphinx & pharaoh head emb on front, 2¾" 35.00
Tower & Lyon NY, st, 3" 25.00
W Bohannan & Co, SW emb in scroll on front, 2⅜" 30.00
Winchester, Winchester emb on front, 3" 160.00
1898, emb, 2¾" 30.00

Combinations

Chicago Combination Lock Co, st on front, brass, 2¾" 60.00
Clark, st, brass, 2¼" 300.00
Corbin Sesamee 4-Dial Brass Lock, st Sesamee, 2¾" 15.00
Junkunc Bros Mfrs, all st on bk, brass, 1⅞" 30.00
Miller Keyless, st, iron, 3¼" 70.00

No Kee, st, brass, 2" 45.00
Number or letter disk, st, 3-disk, brass, 2½" 100.00
Number or letter disk, st, 3-disk, iron, 2" 20.00
Number or letter disk, st, 4-disk, iron, 4½" 275.00
Number or letter disk type (4 disks), brass, 2¾" 130.00
Quaint Mfg Co, st on lock case, 4¼" 200.00
Sorel Limited Canada, st, brass, 3¼" 200.00
Turman's Keyless, st, brass, 2¼" 160.00
Vulcana Push Lock Corp, st on lock case, 3¼" 50.00
Your Own st on body, 3⅞" 325.00

Eight-Lever Type

Blue Chief, st, steel, 4½" 25.00
Excelsior, st, steel, 4¾" 30.00
Goliath, steel, Goliath 8-Lever st on front 25.00
Mastodon, st, steel, 4½" 15.00
Reese, st, steel, 4¾" 15.00
Samson, brass, 8-Lever st on front 18.00

Iron Lever Tumbler

Automobile, st, 2⅞" 35.00
Bear, emb, 2⅝" 25.00
Bull, word Bull emb on front, 2⅝" 30.00
Bulldog, word Bulldog & face of dog emb on front, 2¾" 30.00
Dan Patch, Dan Patch emb on front, horseshoe on bk, 2¾" 130.00
Dragon, word Dragon & dragon emb on front, 2⅞" 25.00
Eagle, 4 dice emb on front, 2¾" 40.00
G Merkel, st, 3" 30.00
Indian Head, Indian head emb on front, 3" 90.00
Karo, word Karo emb on front, CI, 3⅛" 25.00
Lever Buckle Co, emb, 4½" 45.00
Mars, emb, 2¼" 20.00
Moose head, emb, 2¾" 20.00
Owl, emb, 2¼" 30.00
Rough Rider (horse & rider), emb, 3" 50.00
Rugby, football emb on body, 3" 20.00
Star Lock Works, st, 3⅛" 50.00
Thoroughbred, emb, 2⅛" 12.00
Victory, emb, 3⅛" 45.00
W Hall & Co, st, 4½" 300.00
Woodland, emb, 2⅜" 30.00

Lever Push Key

Achilles, emb, iron, 3⅝" 50.00
Aztec, emb 6-lever, 2⅛" 50.00
California, emb, brass, 2½" 20.00
Celtic Cross, emb cross on face, brass, 2¼" 125.00
Cherokee, emb, 6-lever, iron, 2½" 170.00
Climax, emb Climax 6-Lever, iron push-key type, 2¼" 35.00
Crank, emb, iron, 2⅞" 25.00
Dash, emb Dash 6-Lever, iron push-key type, 2¼" 25.00
Duke, emb 6-Lever, 2⅛" 45.00
Eclipse, 4-lever, emb, brass, 2½" 20.00
Elm City 4-Lever, emb, brass, 2" 35.00
Excelsior, emb Excelsior 6-Lever, brass push-key type, 2¼" 25.00
Fordloc, emb, iron, 3¼" 40.00
HS&Co, 6-lever, emb, brass, 2¼" 70.00
IXL, emb IXL on body, 2¼" 75.00
Keystone, emb Keystone 6-Lever, brass push-key type 2¼" 40.00
McIntosh, emb, 6-lever, iron, 2½" 90.00
Morley, emb, iron, 2½" 30.00

National Lock Co, emb, brass, 2½" 120.00
SB Co, emb SB Co on body, 3¼" 60.00
Supplee, emb, iron, 2½" 20.00
Ten Star, emb Ten Star 6-Lever, 2¼" 45.00

Logo — Special Made

Anaconda, st, brass, 2⅞" 60.00
Brass pancake push key emb US Internal Revenue, 2¼" 185.00
City of Boston Dept of Schools, st, brass, 2⅞" 40.00
Coca-Cola, st, brass, 2⅝" 40.00
D&H, emb, brass, 2½" 170.00
Delco Products, st, brass 20.00
Hawaiian Elec, st, brass, 3" 30.00
Heart-shape brass lever type emb Shults Co, bbl key, 2¾" 55.00
International Harvester Co, emb, brass, 2½" 100.00
Lilly, st, brass, 2½" 15.00
Okla State Pen, st, brass, 2⅝" 50.00
Ordinance Dept, st, brass, 2⅞" 20.00
Property of Syracuse Univ, st, brass, 2⅝" 40.00
Sq brass pin-tumbler case st Regd US Mail, int counter, 2¾" 140.00
Sq Yale-type brass pin tumbler, st US/A/tree/Forest Svc, 2⅞" ...125.00
Standard Oil Co, st, brass, 2⅝" 25.00
Texaco, emb, brass, 2¾" 60.00
University of Notre Dame, emb, brass, 2½" 160.00
USBIA, st, brass, 3¾" 80.00
USBIR, st, brass, 3¾" 80.00
USMC, st, brass, 2½" 20.00
West Baking Co, emb, brass, 2½" 90.00
Zoo, st, iron, 2½" 25.00

Pin-Tumbler Type

Corbin, emb, iron, 2¾" 20.00
Eagle, brass, Eagle st on body, 2⅞" 20.00
Fulton, emb Fulton on body, 2⅝" 30.00
Hickory, emb, iron, 2¾" 60.00
Il-A-Noy, emb, iron, 2¾" 35.00
Pearl, brass, emb Pearl on body, 2⅛" 20.00
Rich-Con, emb, iron, 2⅞" 50.00
Sargent, emb, iron, 2¾" 15.00
Segal, iron, emb Segal on shackle, 3¾" 30.00
Yale, brass, emb Yale on body, Made in England on shackle, 3" ...30.00
Yale, emb, iron, 2¼" 70.00

Scandinavian (Jail House) Type

Backalaphknck (Russian), st, iron, 5" 200.00
Bull Dog, emb, brass, 2½" 80.00
Corbin, st, brass, 2½" 50.00
Nrarvck (Russian), st, iron, 4" 160.00
Pear, emb, iron, 3½" 40.00
Romer, st, iron, 4" 70.00
Star, iron, 2½" 70.00
99 Miller, emb 99, brass, 1¾" 80.00

Six-Lever Type

Bon-Ton, st, iron, 3" 15.00
Eagle, brass, Eagle Six-Lever st on body 18.00
Miller Six-Lever, st, brass, 3⅞" 20.00
Olympiad Six-Lever, st, iron, 3¾" 25.00
Safe, brass, Safe st on body 18.00
Yale, brass, Yale emb on front 12.00

Story and Commemorative

AYPEX Seattle (Alaska Yukon Pacific Expo), emb tin/iron, 3" .235.00
Canteen, US emb on lock, lock: canteen shape, 2" 500.00
CI, emb skull/X-bones w/florals, NH Co on bk, 3¼" 200.00
Dan Patch, iron, 1⅞" 125.00

Eagle Liberty, $300.00; NY to Paris, Lindbergh flight commemorative, $150.00. (Photo courtesy Joe Tanner)

Missouri Seal, brass, 2¼" 150.00
National Hardware Co (NHCo), emb, iron, 2½" 200.00
National Hardware Co (NHCo), emb SK, iron, 3½" 425.00
North Pole, brass, 2⅞" 150.00
Russell & Erwin (R&E), emb Aztec figure, iron, 2¼" 200.00
Russell & Erwin (R&E), emb Ganesha form, iron, 3" 325.00
Russell & Erwin (R&E), emb mailbox, iron, 3⅛" 300.00
1901 Pan Am Expo, brass, emb w/buffalo, 2⅝" 175.00

Warded Type

Aetna, emb, brass, 2¼" 35.00
Army, iron pancake ward key, emb letters, 2½" 40.00
Enders, st, brass, 1½" 25.00
Globe, iron sq lock case, emb US on bk, 2⅜" 20.00
Hex, iron, sq lock case, emb US on bk, 2⅛" 95.00
Kirby, emb, brass, 2¼" 20.00
Lucky, emb, brass, 2½" 45.00
Red Cross, brass sq case, emb letters, 2" 10.00
Red Seal, emb, brass, 2" 20.00
Ruby, emb, brass, 2⅛" 20.00
Safety First, brass pancake type, emb letters, 2¾" 15.00
Sampson, emb, iron, 2½" 20.00
Shapleigh, st, brass, 2" 18.00
Sprocket, brass oval shape, emb letters, 2⅛" 50.00
Try Me, iron pancake type, emb letters, 2½" 25.00
Van Guard, emb, iron, 2⅞" 18.00
Winchester, brass sq case, st letters, 2¾" 125.00

Wrought Iron Lever Type (Smokehouse Type)

DM&Co, bbl key, 4¼" 20.00
Improved Warranted, 3½" 35.00
MW&Co, flat key, 3½" 20.00
S&Co, bbl key, 3" 8.00
VR, 3½" 30.00
Waines, 4⅜" 40.00

Loetz

The Loetz Glassworks was established in Klostermule, Austria, in 1840. After Loetz's death the firm was purchased by his grandson, Johann Loetz Witwe. Until WWII the operation continued to produce fine artware, some of which made in the early 1900s bears a striking resemblance to Tiffany's, with whom Loetz was associated at one time. In addition to the iridescent Tiffany-style glass, he also produced threaded glass and some cameo. The majority of Loetz pieces will have a polished pontil. Our advisor for this category is Don Williams; he is listed in the Directory under Missouri.

Basket vase, amber w/oil spots, clear hdl, ca 1910, 12" 295.00
Bowl, amber w/swirls & oil spots, sq; metal fr w/tulips, 9" L ...1,725.00
Bowl, yel w/oil spots, 6 folds in rim, 8" 400.00
Box, silver o/l floral, bl w/oil spots, domed lid, 4x5" 1,250.00
Ewer, silver o/l grapevines, bl w/oil spots, 10½" 800.00
Nautilus shell, amber irid on shiny orange, 4⅜x7½" 900.00
Paperweight, silvery bl w/chartreuse, 4-fold rim, 5¼" 900.00
Shade, amber irid w/gold spots, fluted/scalloped, 6", pr 800.00
Vase, bl irid invt gourd-form body w/gold dome ft, 6" 600.00
Vase, bl oil spots on emerald gr, 'water sprinkler' form, 9½" 450.00
Vase, bl oil spots on gold irid, bl int, ruffled rim, 6¾x2½" 250.00
Vase, bl oil spots on 3-color ground: gr/bl/red irid, ovoid, 6¾" ...1,600.00
Vase, bl-gold irid on gr, ribbed, pinched collar, 5¼" 225.00
Vase, bl-gold oil spots, shouldered, mini, 2" 400.00
Vase, bl-gold w/oil spots, trifold top, 3 lg pinched sides, 9" 800.00
Vase, clear w/olive gr casing, wide oil-spot 'leaves,' 8" 1,265.00
Vase, formosa finish w/bl threads on gr irid, tree trunk form, 8½" ..400.00
Vase, gold, gr-rimmed trefoil top, appl purple flower, 7⅛" 600.00
Vase, gold irid, dimpled, tricorner/fold-out rim, 5¼" 200.00
Vase, gold irid w/dimpled shoulders, flanged rim, combed neck, 4½" .300.00
Vase, gold on bl irid etched to gr, pinch-sided bottle, 7x5½" 150.00
Vase, gold to bl-gold irid, bulbous trumpet form, 9½" 250.00
Vase, gold w/bl/gr/rose irid, dimpled/waisted, 4" 250.00
Vase, gold w/butterfly irid, 3-lobe rim, long dimples, 7" 200.00
Vase, gold w/gr elongated teardrops, gr rim, 8⅝" 750.00
Vase, gold/gr/lav irid w/pnt/scallop rim, tiny dents, 5½" 300.00
Vase, gr, textured surface w/EX irid, 6½" 260.00
Vase, gr cased w/pulled magenta & MOP irid, bulb top, 5", EX ...1,000.00
Vase, gr cylinder w/appl snake decor, 8½x4¾" 450.00
Vase, gr irid w/pulled bl/purple/gr decor, in-body twist, 8" 1,000.00
Vase, gr irid w/purple ribs, 3-hdl, conical, 10x4½" 925.00
Vase, gr satin w/cranberry loops, waisted, 4-fold rim, 6" 140.00
Vase, gr w/bl irid & pulled feathers on crackle, ovoid, 7" 800.00
Vase, gr w/gold irid, ruffled pull-down rim, 7½" 175.00
Vase, gr w/oil spots, bulbous base, cylindrical neck, 9⅛" 300.00
Vase, gr w/random opal threading, 3-petal top, squat, 3¾x5" 150.00
Vase, gr w/ribs, flat flaring top, 7½" 250.00
Vase, King Tut, yel w/gold int, squat, 5¾" 1,300.00
Vase, lt gr irid w/appl bl akimbo hdls, 2 appl bl disks, 6" 300.00
Vase, lt gr irid w/bl coil at long neck, 3 appl bl disks, ...325.00
Vase, maroon w/pk/platinum irid, 6-lobe, crimped top, 4½" 260.00
Vase, mc swirl, unmk, 6" 150.00
Vase, opal irid w/emerald threads at shoulder, fold-down rim, 3¾" ..85.00
Vase, ormolu red-gold insert w/gold feathers, ftd base, 14½" ..1,750.00
Vase, pearl opal w/red & gr threads, floriform mouth, 13" 700.00
Vase, Persian flask; gold, jack-in-pulpit rim, dimpled, 10" 700.00
Vase, purple/brn irid w/lg oil spots, ovoid, 7½x4½" 1,100.00
Vase, rubena verde irid, swirled, 11" 175.00
Vase, salmon w/strong ribs & irid draped threads, 7" 400.00
Vase, silver leaves o/l, bl w/silver, ruffled ovoid, 5¼x3" 1,100.00
Vase, silver lilies o/l, cobalt irid, 5¾" 2,500.00
Vase, silver o/l clovers, gr w/silver-bl oil spots, 4½" 800.00
Vase, silver o/l on gr, 3¾" 700.00
Vase, silver thistles o/l, gold, elongated ovoid, 10" 2,185.00
Vase, silver-bl irid waves on gold, pinched/bulbous, 4⅝" 450.00
Vase, silvery loops & swirls, golden ebony int, pinched, 4¼" 1,200.00

Lomonosov Porcelain

Founded in Leningrad in 1744, the Lomonosov porcelain factory produced exquisite porcelain miniatures for the Czar and other Russian nobility. One of the first factories of its kind, Lomonosov produced mainly vases and delicate sculptures. In the 1800s Lomonosov became closely involved with the Russian Academy of Fine Arts, a connection which has continued to this day as the company continues to supply the world with these fine artistic treasures. In 1992 the backstamp was changed to read 'Made in Russia,' instead of 'Made in USSR.' Some dealers may be pricing items marked 'Made in USSR' at 75% to 100% above prices listed below.

Baby giraffe, #2350 ....31.00
Bear, lying, #6570 ....16.00
Borzoi, #6462 ....34.00
Bullfinch, #9555, mini 5.50
Cat, #6564 ....31.00
Donkey, #6498 ....20.00
Fox, #6541 ....14.00
Hare, #7415, mini 4.50
Lion cub, lying, #6441 ....11.50
Lynx, #6550 ....33.00
Nettle bird, down, #6525 ....5.50
Panda bear, sm, #6531 ....14.50
Rabbit, gray, #9428 ....9.50
Raccoon, #6504 ....14.50
Redstart, #6559 ....10.00
Rock Partridge, #2631 ....9.00
Sea gull, #6579 ....27.50
Seal, #6481 ....16.50
Snow Bunting, turned, #6556 ....8.50
Tiger cub, sm, #9424, mini 9.50
Young elk, #6111 ....82.00

Longwy

The Longwy workshops were founded in 1798 and continue today to produce pottery in the north of France near the Luxembourg-Belgian border under the name 'Societe des Faienceries de Longwy et Senelle.' The ware for which they are best known was produced during the Art Deco period, decorated in bold colors and designs. Earlier wares made during the first quarter of the nineteenth century reflected the popularity of Oriental art, cloisonne enamels in particular. The designs were executed by impressing the pattern into the moist clay and filling in the depressions with enamels. Examples are marked 'Longwy,' either impressed or painted under glaze.

Bowl, dk red w/gold floral int, 5" 45.00
Bowl, floral, mc pks/bls w/turq crackle, ftd, 2¾x10½" 525.00
Box, birds on floral branch, hexagonal, 3½x6" 350.00
Box, floral, mc on turq, 2x7½" dia 425.00
Box, rose medallion on lid, triangular, 1920s, 2x5½" 445.00
Charger, 2 bathers in tropical scene, 1930s, 15" 600.00
Charger, 2 nudes & faun, brn/yel tones, 14" 2,100.00
Humidor, bl Deco motif on wht crackle, Primavera, 6½x4½" ...400.00
Mustard pot, geometric Deco floral on turq, 1870-90, 4x2" 150.00
Plate, bird on floral branch, floral rim, 9" 330.00
Plate, bl spirals w/gold on beige crackle, 1920s, 11" 450.00
Plate, Deco floral w/geometric rim, rectangular, 7½" 300.00
Plate, floral reserve center, wide floral rim w/cobalt, 7½" 300.00
Tea set, Deco floral band on crackle, pot+cr/sug+2 c/s on tray ..650.00
Teapot, floral, mc w/cobalt, Emaux de Longwy, 1920s, 6½" 350.00
Trivet, floral on cobalt, #792, 8" sq 127.50
Vase, bird & flowers on turq, cylindrical, 7¼x3" 225.00
Vase, Deco floral, mc on crackle, bottle neck, 11½x5" 800.00
Vase, Deco fruit on honey crackle, 7¼x7" 325.00
Vase, Deco motif, cobalt on turq crackle, bulbous, Primavera, 6" .250.00
Vase, flowers & vines on pk crackle, #1520, 3¼x4¾" 175.00
Vase, Normandie (ship), Deco style, mc enameling, mks, 10" ...3,200.00

Lonhuda

William Long was a druggist by trade who combined his knowledge of chemistry with his artistic ability in an attempt to produce a type of brown-glazed slip-decorated artware similar to that made by the Rookwood Pottery. He achieved his goal in 1889 after years of long and dedicated study. Three years later he founded his firm, the Lonhuda Pottery Company. The name was coined from the first few letters of the last name of each of his partners, W.H. Hunter and Alfred Day. Laura Fry, formerly of the Rookwood company, joined the firm in 1892, bringing with her a license for Long to use her patented airbrush-blending process. Other artists of note, Sarah McLaughlin, Helen Harper, and Jessie Spaulding, joined the firm and decorated the ware with nature studies, animals, and portraits, often signing their work with their initials. Three types of marks were used on the Steubenville Lonhuda ware. The first was a linear composite of the letters 'LPCO' with the name 'Lonhuda' impressed above it. The second, adopted in 1893, was a die-stamp representing the solid profile of an Indian, used on ware patterned after pottery made by the American Indians. This mark was later replaced with an impressed outline of the Indian head with 'Lonhuda' arching above it. Although the ware was successful, the business floundered due to poor management. In 1895 Long became a partner of Sam Weller and moved to Zanesville where the manufacture of the Lonhuda line continued. Less than a year later, Long left the Weller company. He was associated with J.B. Owens until 1899, at which time he moved to Denver, Colorado, where he established the Denver China and Pottery Company in 1901. His efforts to produce Lonhuda utilizing local clay were highly successful. Examples of Denver Lonhuda are sometimes marked with the LF (Lonhuda Faience) cipher contained within a canted diamond form. For further information we recommend *Collector's Encyclopedia of Colorado Pottery* by Carol and Jim Carlton (Collector Books).

Vase, tulip on brown, 6x9", $650.00. **(Photo courtesy Carol and Jim Carlton)**

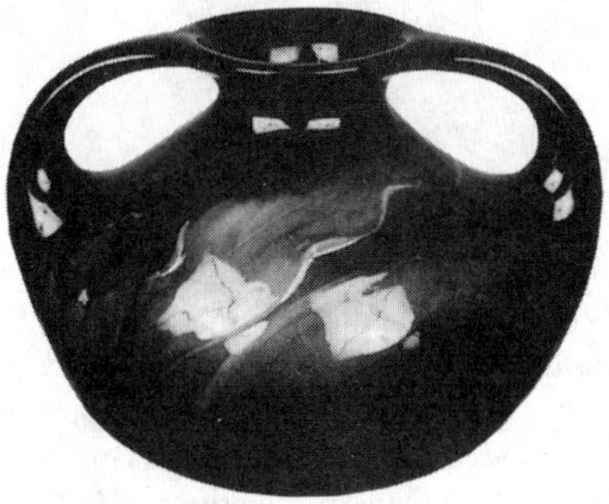

Bowl, floral, sgn Jessie Spaulding, 3-ftd, mk/1899, 7" 275.00
Plaque, lady's profile, ML McLaughlin, oval, #406, 3¼" 435.00
Vase, broad leaves, caramel & brn on dk brn, 14" 225.00
Vase, floral, mc on purple to gray, 8½" 225.00
Vase, pansy cvg, bl on dk brn, sgn MCL, 6x5", NM 3,350.00
Vase, sunset scene in forest glade, lt gr/yel, 8x3¾" 1,100.00

Losanti

Mary Louise McLaughlin, who had previously experimented in trying to reproduced Haviland faience in the 1870s and 'American faience' (a method of inlaying color by painting the inside of the mold before the vessel was cast) in the mid-1890s, developed a type of hard-paste porcelain in which the glaze and the body fused together in a single firing. Her efforts met with success in 1900, and she immediately concentrated on glazing and decorating techniques. The ware she perfected was called Lonsanti, most of which was decorated with Nouveau florals, either carved or modeled. By 1906 she had abanonded her efforts. Examples are marked with several ciphers, one resembling a butterfly, another with the letters MCL superimposed each upon the other, and L. McL in a linear arrangement. Other items were marked Lonsanti, sometimes in the Oriental manner.

Vase, celadon gloss, Chinese shape, #28MCL/8, 6¼x4" 400.00
Vase, gunmetal/gr/bl drips, bulbous, #292, 3½x3¼", NM 650.00

Lotton

Charles Lotton is a contemporary glass artist. He began blowing glass and developing original designs thirty years ago and now has work on display in many major glass museums and collections, among them the Smithsonian, the Art Institute of Chicago, the Museum of Glass, and the Chrysler Museum. He has become famous for his unique lamps. Every piece is signed and dated. His three sons, David, Daniel, and John, each work in their own studios. All four artists produce distinctive work. They sell their glass at antique shows and in their showroom in Lansing, Illinois. For further information read *Lotton Art Glass* by Charles Lotton and Tom O'Conner; see the Directory under Illinois. The values that follow are actual prices realized from a recent auction.

Vase, Multi Flora, signed Charles Lotton, 1984, 9", $500.00 at auction.

Bottle, scent; Multi Flora, pk-amethyst, 11" 750.00
Bottle, scent; orange-gold w/bl leaves & pk flowers, 9" 650.00
Bottle, scent; pk pulled feather bottom trimmed w/gold & bl, 6½" ...250.00
Bottle, scent; red w/silver & bl swirls, 6½" 500.00
Bowl, Multi Flora, pk-amethyst, 5½x9" 900.00
Shade, lily form, gold w/pk & silver highlights, '75, 4½" 60.00
Vase, mc bls w/orange & gold, 6½" 450.00
Vase, pulled decor, silver w/rose & gold on dk bl, Chas, '82, 4½" ..120.00

Lotus Ware

Isaac Knowles and Issac Harvey operated a pottery in East Liverpool, Ohio, in 1853 where they produced both yellow ware and Rockingham. In 1870 Knowles brought Harvey's interests and took as partners John Taylor and Homer Knowles. Their principal product was ironstone china, but Knowles was confident that American potters could produce as fine a ware as the Europeans. To prove his point, he hired Joshua Poole, an artist from the Belleek Works in Ireland. Poole quickly perfected a Belleek-type china, but fire destroyed this portion of the company. Before it could function again, their hotel china business had grown to the point that it required their full attention in order to meet market demands. By 1891 they were able to try again. They developed a bone china, as fine and thin as before, which they called Lotus. Henry Schmidt from the Meissen factory in Germany decorated the ware, often with lacy filigree applications or hand-formed leaves and flowers to which he added further decoration with liquid slip applied by means of a squeeze bag. Due to high production costs resulting from so much of the fragile ware being damaged in firing and because of changes in tastes and styles of decoration, the Lotus Ware line was dropped in 1896. Some of the early ware was marked 'KT&K China'; later marks have a star and a crescent with 'Lotus Ware' added. For further information we recommend *Collector's Encyclopedia of Knowles, Taylor & Knowles China* by Mary Frank Gaston, our advisor for this category.

Bowl, Columbia, filigree medallions, gold trim, 1892-96, 4x6" ..900.00
Bowl, yel flowers, rtcl/gilded bosses ea side, bead rim, 4" H 750.00
Creamer & sugar bowl, gold fishnet, gold twig hdls, w/lid 250.00
Ewer, HP floral sprays, gold trim at top, slim neck, 10" 800.00
Ewer, HP leafy sprigs w/gold, 9½" 600.00
Ewer, pk floral, gold-speckled twig hdl, 6½" 425.00
Pitcher, leaves emb on wht, bulbous/squat, 5" 165.00
Rose jar, floral w/gold, rtcl lid, sgn ASP '97, 7½" 1,000.00
Shell dish, wht w/coral branch ft, 8" 175.00
Teapot, HP bows & gold paste w/appl fishnet, bamboo hdl, 5" ..900.00
Vase, allover appl chains, ruffled bowl, 7½" 1,150.00
Vase, appl floral & leaves, pale gr on wht, scroll hdls, 8½" 1,100.00
Vase, Egyptian, Victorian portraits, hdls, 15" 3,400.00
Vase, HP roses, stick neck, gold hdls, mk KWW 1892, 10" 700.00
Vase, HP violets & gold paste, gold hdls/ft, 8½" 900.00
Vase, lily; appl leaves & stems, gold trim, 8½x7" 1,000.00
Vase, lily; gold flowers, gold branch base w/gr leaves, 9" 900.00
Vase, lily; yel w/mounded leafy base, gold trim, 8" 1,000.00

Lu Ray Pastels

Lu Ray Pastels dinnerware was introduced in the early 1940s by Taylor, Smith, and Taylor of East Liverpool, Ohio. It was offered in assorted colors of Persian Cream, Sharon Pink, Surf Green, Windsor Blue, and Chatham Gray in complete place settings as well as many service pieces. It was a successful line in its day and is once again finding favor with collectors of American dinnerware. For further information we recommend *Collector's Guide to Lu Ray Pastels* by Bill and Kathy Meehan. Our advisor for this category is Shirley Moore; she is listed in the Directory under Oklahoma.

Bowl, '36s oatmeal 60.00
Bowl, coupe soup; flat 15.00
Bowl, cream soup 70.00
Bowl, fruit; Chatham Gray, 5" 16.00
Bowl, fruit; 5" 5.00
Bowl, lug soup; tab hdld 19.00
Bowl, mixing; 10¼" 150.00
Bowl, mixing; 5½" 125.00
Bowl, mixing; 7" 125.00
Bowl, mixing; 8¾" 100.00
Bowl, salad; any color other than yel 65.00
Bowl, salad; yel 55.00
Bowl, vegetable; oval, 9½" 20.00
Butter dish, any color other than Chatham Gray, w/lid 50.00
Butter dish, Chatham Gray, rare color, w/lid 90.00
Calendar plates, 8", 9" & 10", ea 40.00

Casserole 125.00
Chocolate cup, AD; str sides 80.00
Chocolate pot, AD; str sides 400.00
Coaster/nut dish 65.00
Coffee cup, AD 20.00
Coffeepot, AD 200.00
Creamer 8.00
Creamer, AD, ind 40.00
Creamer, AD, ind, from chocolate set 92.00
Egg cup, dbl 24.00
Epergne 110.00
Gravy boat 28.00
Jug, water; ftd 125.00
Muffin cover 125.00
Muffin cover, w/8" underplate 145.00
Nappy, vegetable; rnd, 8½" 20.00
Pitcher, any color other than yel, bulbous w/flat bottom 125.00
Pitcher, juice 200.00
Pitcher, yel, bulbous w/flat bottom 95.00
Plate, cake 70.00
Plate, Chatham Gray, rare color, 7" 16.00
Plate, chop; 15" 38.00
Plate, grill; compartment 35.00
Plate, 10" 20.00
Plate, 6" 3.00
Plate, 7" 12.00
Plate, 8" 20.00
Plate, 9" 10.00
Platter, oval, 11½" 16.00
Platter, oval, 13" 19.00
Relish dish, 4-part 95.00
Sauce boat, any other color than yel, fixed stand 35.00
Sauce boat, yel, fixed stand 22.50
Saucer, coffee; AD 8.50
Saucer, coffee/chocolate 30.00
Saucer, cream soup 28.00
Saucer, tea 3.00
Shakers, pr 16.00
Sugar bowl, AD; w/lid, from chocolate set 92.00
Sugar bowl, AD; w/lid, ind 40.00
Sugar bowl, w/lid 15.00
Teacup 8.00
Teapot, curved spout, w/lid 125.00
Teapot, flat spout, w/lid 160.00
Tray, pickle 28.00
Tumbler, juice 50.00
Tumbler, water 80.00
Vase, bud 400.00

Lunch Boxes

Early twentieth-century tobacco companies such as Union Leader, Tiger, and Dixie sold their products in square, steel containers with flat, metal carrying handles. These were specifically engineered to be used as lunch boxes when they became empty. (See Advertising, specific companies.) By 1930 oval lunch pails with colorful lithographed decorations on tin were being manufactured to appeal directly to children. These were made by Ohio Art, Decoware, and a few other companies. In 1950 Aladdin Industries produced the first 'real' character lunch box — a Hopalong Cassidy decal-decorated steel container now considered the beginning of the kids' lunch box industry. The other big lunch box manufacturer, American Thermos (later King Seely Thermos Company) brought out its 'blockbuster' Roy Rogers box in 1953, the first fully lithographed steel lunch box and matching bottle. Other companies (ADCO Liberty; Landers, Frary & Clark; Ardee Industries; Okay Industries; Universal; Tindco; Cheinco) also produced character pails. Today's collectors often tend to specialize in those boxes dealing with a particular subject. Western, space, TV series, Disney movies, and cartoon characters are the most popular. There are well over five hundred different lunch boxes available to the astute collector. For further information we recommend *The Illustrated Encyclopedia of Metal Lunch Boxes* by Allen Woodall and Sean Brickell. Our advisor for this category is Allan Smith; he is listed in the Directory under Texas. In the following listings, lunch boxes are metal unless noted vinyl or plastic, and values include thermoses only when they are mentioned within the descriptions.

Adam-12, 1972, VG 50.00
Addams Family, 1974, VG+ 75.00
Annie Oakly, 1955, w/thermos, EX 400.00
Archies, 1969, VG+ 85.00
Battlestar Galactica, 1978, w/thermos, EX 85.00

Batman and Robin, 1966, EX, $150.00.

Beatles, 1965, bl, VG 375.00
Benji, 1974, plastic, bl, VG 8.00
Betsy Clark, vinyl, w/thermos, M 90.00
Bobby Sherman, 1972, w/thermos, NM 150.00
Bonanza, 1965, brn rim, VG 65.00
Bullwinkle & Rocky, 1962, w/thermos, EX 700.00
Care Bear Cousins, 1985, w/thermos, M 45.00
Carnival, 1959, VG 400.00
Color Me Happy, 1984, EX 150.00
Davy Crockett at the Alamo, 1955, M 1,000.00
Disneyland Castle, 1957, w/thermos, M 600.00
Dr Seuss, vinyl, rare, EX 150.00
Dr Seuss, 1970, w/thermos, M 300.00
Family Affair, 1969, w/thermos, EX 135.00
Flintstones, 1971, w/thermos, M 300.00
Flying Nun, 1968, EX 150.00
Ghostbusters, 1986, plastic, purple, EX 20.00
Ghostland, 1977, VG 30.00
GI Joe, 1985, plastic, w/thermos, EX 20.00
Goober & the Ghost Chasers, 1974, VG+ 60.00
Hair Bear Bunch, 1971, EX 85.00
Hee-Haw, 1970, EX 100.00
Hong Kong Phooey, 1975, w/thermos, EX 85.00
Hopalong Cassidy, 1954, w/thermos, EX 450.00
Incredible Hulk, 1978, EX 30.00
Jet Patrol, 1957, VG 125.00
Little Dutch Miss, 1959, w/thermos, EX+ 335.00
Ludwig Von Drake, 1962, w/thermos, EX 275.00
Marvel Super Heroes, 1976, EX 45.00
Monroes, 1967, EX 200.00
Mr Merlin, 1981, w/thermos, VG 30.00

New Zoo Revue, 1975, vinyl, w/thermos, EX 225.00
Partridge Family, 1971, EX 85.00
Pathfinder, 1959, VG+ 600.00
Pigs in Space, 1977, VG 25.00
Pink Panther & Sons, 1984, w/thermos, M 85.00
Planet of the Apes, 1974, w/thermos, VG- 60.00
Popeye, 1964, EX 100.00
Pound Puppies, 1986, plastic, red, VG 10.00
Pro Sports, 1962, EX 50.00
Return of the Jedi, 1983, w/thermos, NM 125.00
Rifleman, 1961, w/thermos, EX 450.00
Roy Rogers, 1957, red shirt, G+ 100.00
Satellite, 1958, w/thermos, VG+ 125.00
Shindig, 1960s, vinyl, NM 225.00
Six Million Dollar Man, 1978, w/thermos, EX 100.00
Sleeping Beauty, Canadian, 1960, EX 700.00
Space: 1999, 1975, w/thermos, VG 45.00
Star Wars, 1978, w/thermos, EX 65.00
Supercar, 1962, w/thermos, G 200.00
Swan Lake, 1960, vinyl, VG+ 150.00
SWAT, 1975, plastic, dome top, w/thermos, EX 60.00
Tarzan, 1966, w/thermos, EX+ 200.00
Tom Corbett Space Cadet, 1954, EX 250.00
Underdog, 1974, w/thermos, VG 700.00
Voltron, 1984, plastic, bl, w/thermos, NM 15.00
Wagon Train, 1964, w/thermos, M 600.00
Wonder Woman, 1977, vinyl, w/thermos, VG+ 150.00
Zorro, 1958, G 90.00

Lutz

From 1869 to 1888, Nicholas Lutz worked for the Boston and Sandwich Company where he produced the threaded and striped art glass that was so popular during that era. His works were not marked; and since many other glassmakers of the day made similar wares, the term Lutz has come to refer not only to his original works but to any of this type.

Basket, pk threading, appl pk & clear tooled hdl, 6" 250.00
Goblet, gold/gr aventurine bowl & base, clear stem, 6½" 210.00
Smoke bell, pk/wht/gold striping, ruffled, triangular, iron mt 115.00

Maddux of California

One of the California-made ceramics now so popular with collectors, Maddux was founded in the late 1930s and during the years that followed produced novelty items, TV lamps, figurines, planters, and tableware accessories. Our advisor for this category is Doris Frizzell; she is listed in the Directory under Illinois. (SASE required.)

#0206A, planter, Chinese Bell Tower, 8" 20.00
#0221, vase, swan, wht, 12" 20.00
#0225, vase, horse's head top, str-sided body, aqua, 12" 20.00
#0300, figurine, puppy, 6x5½" 15.00
#0400/401, flamingos, pr 50.00
#0510, planter, swan, blk, 11" 18.00
#0515, planter, flamingo, pk, 10½" 45.00
#0519, TV lamp, rooster, orange, 13" 75.00
#0527, Chinese pheasant, 11½" 20.00
#0528, planter, 2 birds in flight, pk & blk, 10" 20.00
#0529, vase, 2 flamingos, 5" 40.00
#0536, planter, bird in flight, 11½" 20.00
#0612, cockatoo planter, pk & bl 24.00
#0627, TV lamp, stallion, 13" 35.00
#0628, planter, swallow, pk & gray 35.00
#0808, TV lamp, pearl-tone shell, 13" 40.00
#0810, TV lamp, stallion prancing on base, 12" 65.00
#0825, TV lamp, swans, 10x11½x5¾" 55.00
#0826, TV lamp, cockatoos 65.00
#0828, TV lamp, swan planter, wht porc, 12½" 40.00
#0829, TV lamp, deer (2) running, natural, 10½" 45.00
#0839, TV lamp, mallard flying, natural, 11½" 45.00
#0841, TV lamp, head of Christ, 3-D planter 45.00
#0844, TV lamp, prairie schooner (covered wagon), 11" 45.00
#0846, TV lamp, nativity scene, 3-D planter 45.00
#0859, TV lamp, Toro (bull), ft on mound, 11½" 50.00
#0887, TV lamp, Persian Glory (horse head), 11½" 50.00
#0889, TV lamp, Malibu shell, pearl-tone, 10¼" 25.00
#0892, TV lamp, Colonial ship, 10½" 40.00
#0894, TV lamp, Toro (bull) charging, walnut, 11½" 40.00
#0895, TV lamp, dbl swan, 11½" 50.00
#0897, TV lamp, mare & foal, wht porc 60.00

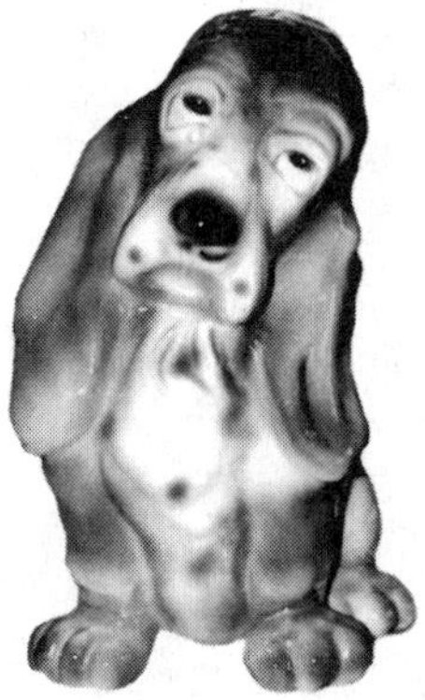

#896, Bassett hound TV lamp, 12", $155.00. (Photo courtesy Lee Garmon)

#0907, doe, walnut, wht porc, tangerine, 12½" 15.00
#0912/913, Chinese pheasants, airbrushed colors, 11", pr 30.00
#0914, stag standing, natural colors, 12½" 20.00
#0923, swans (2), blk matt, 10½" 25.00
#0924, stag standing, natural colors, 12½" 15.00
#0925/926, horses rearing/charging, pr 20.00
#0928/929, mallards, male/female, natural colors, 9½", pr 40.00
#0932, rooster, 10½" 30.00
#0969, Early Birds, blk matt, tangerine, 14½", pr 25.00
#0970, flamingo flying, natural colors, 11" 45.00
#0971, flamingo winging, natural colors, 12" 45.00
#0972/973, bulls, head up/head down, red, 11" L, pr 75.00
#0982, horse prancing 20.00
#0984, elephant sitting, 18" 25.00
#1019, swan console bowl (set), porc wht, 11½" 20.00
#1047, Contempo bowl (set), wht satin, 16½" 20.00
#1050, candlestick, triple 35.00
#1051, candlestick, dbl, 12" 25.00
#1067, shell console bowl (set), pk, 16" 15.00
#2000, snack set, emb grapes, cup & tray 25.00
#2015, Antique Gold, hdls, 12" 15.00
#2102, bowl, ftd 10.00
#2217, cream can, Paul Revere Milc Co, Maddux 75.00
#3006, TV lamp/planter, half-circle 25.00
#3009, serving tray/lazy Susan, pearlized, 2-tiered, 6-pc 25.00
#3017, seashell bowl, wht 15.00
#3051, bowl, red tomato w/gr dbl leaves, w/lid, 16" L 35.00
#3095A, bowl, ped w/6 ind servers 25.00

#3251L, tray, serving; 2-tiered 20.00
#3275, gr pepper relish, w/lid & side bowls 15.00
#3302, bank, cat, yel 25.00
#3304, planter, bird 20.00
#7001, ashtray, 12" dia 10.00
#7134, ashtray, fish, 6" L 20.00
#7204, ashtray, pig form, natural colors, 7" L 12.00
Astray set, yel & red, metal caddy w/6 ind ashtrays 20.00
Bank, smiling pig, red or gr, 12" L 25.00
Bowl, cabbage leaf design, 4x13" L 25.00
Cats, Deco style, blk matt, 12½", facing pr 50.00
Cockatoos on branch w/appl flowers, 11" 40.00
Cookie jar, Baby Birds on Bough, from $45 to 55.00
Cookie jar, Chipmunk on stump, C Romanelli, from $130 to ...145.00
Cookie jar, Don't Let Go, boy & girl on lid, from $75 to 80.00
Cookie jar, Gr Ivy, #2112 ....35.00
Cookie jar, Grapes, purple w/gr leaves on wht, #3112, 10" 55.00
Cookie jar, Koala 60.00
Cookie jar, Queen, #2104, from $150 to 175.00
Cookie jar, Shopping Cat, from $135 to 155.00
Cookie jar, Snowman 75.00
Cookie jar, Strawberry 25.00
Cookie jar, Walrus 50.00
Ducklings, 3 on grassy base 20.00
Flamingo Line, single flamingo planter, 6" 20.00
Planter, horse rearing, 10x7½" 22.00
Wall pocket, bird in metal holder (resembles cage), 7x7"+cage ...35.00

Magazines

Magazines are collected for their cover prints and for the information pertaining to defunct companies and their products that can be gleaned from the old advertisements. In the listings that follow, items are assumed to be in very good condition unless noted otherwise. Our advisor for this category is Charles Zayic; he is listed in the Directory under Maine. See also Movie Memorabilia; Parrish, Maxfield.

Key:
M — mint condition, in original wrapper
EX — excellent condition, spine intact, edges of pages clean and straight
VG — very good condition, the average as-found condition

Agricultural Digest, 1934, November, Parrish cover art, NM 60.00
American Heritage, 1970, December, Parrish cover art, NM 40.00
American Review, 1900, June, VG 15.00
Avante Garde, 1969, #8, VG 35.00
Bachelor, 1937, April, VG 30.00
Baseball Digest, 1951, April, DiMaggio, VG 25.00
Broadway Follies, 1933, October, VG 30.00
Collier's, 1912, May 4, Titanic article, VG 35.00
Collier's, 1945, June, Truman, VG 6.00
Complete Baseball, 1953, December, Campanella, NM 18.00
Cosmopolitan, 1886, June, Buffalo Bill, EX 25.00
Cosmopolitan, 1934, Harrison Fisher, G 18.00
Cosmopolitan, 1955, October, Audrey Hepburn, VG 10.00
Delineator, 1928, May, Rose O'Neill Kewpie pg, VG 20.00
Ebony, 1967, January, Star Trek cover, NM 5.00
Esquire, 1937, April, VG 15.00
Esquire, 1960, November, Lenny Bruce article, EX 6.00
Evergreen, 1969, June, Bobby Kennedy, EX 20.00
Eye, 1951, April, Traffic in Souls, VG 10.00
Family Circle, 1943, June 18, Barbara Stanwyck, VG 8.00
Family Circle, 1945, January 19, Shirley Temple article, VG+ 16.00
Focus, 1953, May, Marylin Monroe, VG 35.00
Fortune, 1948, railroad cover, EX 30.00
Good Housekeeping, 1914, August, M 25.00
Harper's Weekly, 1862, August 30, Stonewall Jackson, EX 35.00
Holiday, 1946, March, VG 20.00
House Beautiful, 1926, February, Horace Shropshire color cover, EX ..12.00
Ice Capades, 1945, Petty cover art, EX 35.00
Jet, 1975, February 20, Florence Ballard (Supremes), EX 20.00
Ladies' Home Journel, 1939, September, VG 12.00
Liberty, 1934, October 27, Dillinger gang article, VG 5.00
Liberty, 1941, September 4, Dionne Quints, EX 10.00
Life, 1938, May 23, Errol Flynn, EX 30.00
Life, 1939, January 23, Bette Davis, EX 25.00
Life, 1942, March 30, Shirley Temple, EX 18.00
Life, 1945, April 23, General Eisenhower, VG 15.00
Life, 1946, January 7, Churchill's paintings, VG 10.00
Life, 1952, April 7, Marilyn Monroe, EX 40.00
Life, 1955, August 8, Ben Hogan, EX 65.00
Life, 1956, June 25, Mickey Mantle, EX 40.00
Life, 1958, December 1, Ricky Nelson, EX 15.00
Life, 1961, January 27, Kennedy Inauguration, EX 12.00
Life, 1964, August 28, Beatles, EX 30.00
Life, 1965, May 7, John Wayne, EX 30.00
Life, 1970, February 27, Daugherty's Spirit of Cinema, VG 6.00
Life, 1981, October, Mania for Marilyn, EX 10.00
Look, 1962, December 4, Grace Kelly, VG 5.00
Look, 1963, December 3, JFK & his son, EX 10.00
Look, 1966, November 5, Honeymooners, NM 16.00

Look, 1971, October 19, White House cover, EX, from $10.00 to $12.00.

Man About Town, 1939, May, EX 28.00
McCall's, 1929, January, Model A ad, VG 25.00
McCall's, 1951, August, VG 12.00
McCall's, 1951, June, Greta Garbo, VG 10.00
Newsweek, 1940, February 19, Disney's Pinocchio article, VG 5.00
Newsweek, 1953, January 19, Lucille Ball, EX+ 25.00
Now, 1953, November, VG 12.00
People Digest, 1951, August 15, Ava Gardner, NM 8.00
Police Gazette, 1940, April, Carol Landis, EX 8.00
Popular Science, 1937, November, EX 8.00
Red Cross, 1918, January, nurse in wht, M 25.00
Redbook, 1955, October, Jackie Gleason, EX 6.00
Rolling Stone, 1967, #1, John Lennon, VG 60.00
Saturday Evening Post, 1946, April 6, Rockwell cover art, VG ...10.00
Saturday Evening Post, 1952, February 16, Rockwell cover art, EX .30.00
Saturday Evening Post, 1963, March 9, Peter O'Toole, VG 5.00
Sports Illustrated, 1974, December 23, Muhammad Ali, EX 20.00
Sports Illustrated, 1974, March 18, Babe Ruth, EX 45.00

Sports Illustrated, 1979, May 28, Pete Rose, VG 8.00
Sports Stars, 1951, November, Jackie Robinson, NM 45.00
Time, 1935, April 15, Dizzy Dean, VG 60.00
Time, 1937, January 4, Woman of the Year/Wallis Simpson, EX .20.00
Time, 1955, Oppenheimer, EX 10.00
True Confessions, 1944, Jeanne Conrad, EX 10.00
True Story, 1938, September, Deanna Durbin, VG 16.00
Vogue, 1924, Brissaud cover art, EX 55.00
Vogue, 1940, January, swimsuit cover, EX 8.00
Wings, 1941, Summer, EX 35.00
Woman's Home Companion, 1955, November, Marlon Brando article, EX 5.00
Yachtman's Magazine, 1942, May, EX 20.00

Majolica

Majolica is a type of heavy earthenware, design-molded and decorated in vivid colors with either a lead or tin type of glaze. It reached its height of popularity in the Victorian era; examples from this period are found in only the lead glazes. Nearly every potter of note, both here and abroad, produced large majolica jardinieres, umbrella stands, pitchers with animal themes, leaf shapes, vegetable forms, and nearly any other design from nature that came to mind. Not all, however, marked their ware. Among those who sometimes did were Minton, Wedgwood, Holdcroft, and George Jones in England; Griffin, Smith, and Hill (Etruscan) in Phoenixville, Pennsylvania; and Chesapeake Pottery (Avalon and Clifton) in Baltimore.

Color and condition are both very important worth-assessing factors. Pieces with cobalt, lavender, and turquoise glazes command the highest prices. For further information we recommend *The Collector's Encyclopedia of Majolica* by Mariann Katz-Marks (see Directory, Pennsylvania). Unless another condition is given, the values that follow are for pieces in mint condition. Our advisor for this category is Hardy Hudson; he is listed in the Directory under Florida.

Biscuit barrel, Daisy & Wheat, Geo Jones 900.00
Bowl, fruit, leaves & berries, Wedgwood, ca 1874, 9⅝" 700.00
Bowl, punch; Water Lily, 15" 850.00
Bowl, salad; crabs/vines/shields, SP trim, Wedgwood, 1869, 7" ..450.00
Bowl, salad; Lily, cobalt, Etruscan 800.00
Bread tray, Bamboo & Fern, cobalt center, Wardles 440.00
Bread tray, Begonia, Eat Thy Bread w/Thankfulness, 13" 375.00
Bread tray, Leaves & Fern, cobalt 400.00
Bread tray, Oak Leaf, Etruscan 400.00
Bread tray, Wheat, 12½" 400.00
Bust, Black man carrying basket, rare, 14" 1,300.00
Butter pat, Blackberry, cobalt 175.00
Butter pat, Fan & Floral 150.00
Butter pat, Geranium, Etruscan 125.00
Butter pat, Pansy, mc, Etruscan 175.00
Butter pat, Pond Lily, Etruscan 150.00
Cake plate, Pond Lily, brn/gr/lav, 12" 400.00
Cake stand, Maple Leaves on pk, Etruscan 350.00
Cake stand, Morning Glory on wht 300.00
Candlestick, frog figural, 8" 300.00
Candlestick, monkey figural, dk gr, Minton's, 8½" 300.00
Card receiver, Blackamoor w/pipe on shell receiver 250.00
Card receiver, fish in basket, Palissy Ware, 7½" 880.00
Card receiver, mermaid figural, 4½x7½" 495.00
Centerpiece, man & dolphin support shell, George Jones, 16" ...2,475.00
Cheese keeper, Blackberry, cow finial 1,000.00
Compote, Chestnut Leaf on Napkin, Geo Jones 650.00
Cup & saucer, Bamboo & Fern, Wardles 250.00
Decanter, Pineapple, 8½" 650.00
Dish, bird atop artichoke, w/lid 500.00
Game dish, pheasant on turq, Geo Jones, 10¼" 3,000.00

Garden seat, relief birds, insects, and water lilies on cobalt, George Jones, 18", EX, $5,175.00. (Photo courtesy Jackson's Auctioneers & Appraisers)

Garden seat, curtain, ribbon, bow & tassel, cobalt, 18" 3,000.00
Garden seat, ears of corn/wheat sheaves, Adams, 1870s, 19" ..2,500.00
Garden seat, flowers, wht/pk/gr on cobalt, English, 18" 2,200.00
Garden seat, stork w/butterflies/fish/cattails, 19½" 2,000.00
Humidor, Black Indian w/turban & tassel, 7" 330.00
Humidor, man w/bl hat & cigar, 5" 195.00
Humidor, Shell & Seaweed, shell lid, Etruscan 1,450.00
Jardiniere, floral & foliate stippled ground, lobed, Minton, 19" ...4,600.00
Jardiniere, Trellis & Floral, turq, Minton, w/underplate, 9½" .3,000.00
Jardiniere & ped, flower panels, Wedgwood, ca 1864, 17" dia, 25" .4,800.00
Jewel stand, child supports 1 end of net, Wedgwood, 1880s, 7" 1,265.00
Jug, fish in relief, bamboo-molded hdl, flat-sided, Holdcroft, 8" 1,300.00
Jug, wine; mermaid, turq, Minton 4,125.00
Match striker, Blackamoor w/hands in pockets, melons behind 440.00
Match striker, Brownie figural, candle holder in hat 600.00
Match striker, dog at doghouse 330.00
Mug, Picket Fence & Floral, Morley & Co 150.00
Mug, Pineapple, Etruscan 250.00
Mug, Pond Lily on cobalt, Holdcroft 275.00
Nut dish, fox at rim, Geo Jones 1,400.00
Nut dish, squirrel on leaf, cobalt ground, American 550.00
Nut dish, squirrel on leaf, Geo Jones 1,900.00
Pitcher, Basket & Floral, cobalt, Geo Jones, 8½" 1,400.00
Pitcher, dog figural, French, 8½" 800.00
Pitcher, Dogwood, ice lip, Holdcroft, 8" 800.00
Pitcher, Fern, Etruscan 500.00
Pitcher, fish, dbl; EX detail, Brownfield & Son, 11½" 1,200.00
Pitcher, honey; bear figural, w/spoon, 10", Holdcroft 1,200.00
Pitcher, monkey figural, St Clement, 10" 500.00
Pitcher, rooster figural, Portugal, 15½" 500.00
Pitcher, squirrel w/nut figural, French, 9" 800.00
Planter, tree trunk w/bird & nest, 10" 400.00
Plate, Asparagus, Luneville, 9" 200.00
Plate, Butterfly & Fan, cobalt, 9" 385.00
Plate, oyster; Fan & Insect, Fielding 1,250.00
Plate, oyster; Shell & Basketweave, Wedgwood 1,250.00
Plate, oyster; w/center shell, turq, Geo Jones, 9" 900.00
Plate, Pineapple, 9" 300.00
Plate, Strawberry & Apple, cobalt, 9" 440.00
Plate, Strawberry & Leaf, 8½" 220.00
Plate, Strawberry & Leaf on shell form, Minton, 1867, 8" 550.00
Plate, 2 lizards/4 frogs/turtle on grass, Palissy, 12" 990.00
Platter, Banana Leaf, yel/gr, 12" dia 375.00
Platter, Pine Cone & Evergreen, Minton, 13½" 1,200.00
Salt cellar, lady w/basket figural, Wedgwood, ca 1865, 7" 750.00

Sardine box, Fish & Seaweed, cobalt, attached underplate, Minton, 8" ..3,500.00
Sardine box, Pineapple, fish on lid 450.00
Sardine box, pointed leaves, turq, Geo Jones 1,800.00
Shaving mug, Pansy, Fielding, rare 375.00
Spittoon, Bamboo & Fern, Wardles 400.00
Sugar bowl, Fan & Bird, butterfly on lid, cobalt 300.00
Sugar bowl, Pineapple, w/lid 300.00
Sweetmeat dish, putti, 2-part, lt wear to flowers, Minton, 15" ..1,800.00
Syrup, Bamboo, pewter lid, Griffin Smith & Hill, 7½" 500.00
Syrup, Sunflower on cobalt, Etruscan 600.00
Teapot, Argenta, florals in arched panels, Wedgwood, ca 1878, 4" ..450.00
Teapot, Chinaman figural, Minton, 6x7" 2,500.00
Teapot, crane, wht on cobalt, English, 5½x8" 500.00
Teapot, emb oriental scene, elephant spout, English, 6¼x9½" ..400.00
Teapot, Fish (form) & Seaweed (hdl), Minton, ca 1878, 7⅛x9" 18,000.00
Toothpick holder, apple figural, Continental 200.00
Tray, ice cream; sea lions & seaweed, Wedgwood, ca 1879, 16" ...1,500.00
Tureen, lobster, w/lid, Minton, rare 16,000.00
Urn, Four Seasons, w/lid, Minton, 14" 2,500.00
Vase, alligator, cobalt, 27" 1,600.00
Vase, Fox & Tree Trunk, Minton, 9" 4,400.00
Vase, lady w/lyre figural, rpr, Eichwald, 13" 350.00
Vase, man w/lantern figural, Continental, 11" 195.00
Vase, spill; monkey figural, English, 8" 440.00
Wall pocket, Swan & Cattail, cobalt, 10" 1,000.00
Wine cooler, paw ft, ring hdls, cobalt, 13½" 1,500.00
Wine cooler, putti on side, lions' heads/oak leaves, Minton, 10½" ...3,575.00

Malachite Glass

Malachite is a type of art glass that exhibits strata-like layerings in shades of green, similar to the mineral in its natural form. Some examples have an acid-etched mark of Moser/Carlsbad, usually on the base. However, it should be noted that in the past fifteen years there have been reproductions from Czechoslovakia with a paper label.

Basket, emb cherubs on sides, 6" 70.00
Bottle, scent; Deco flowers/leaves, floral stopper, Ingrid, 6¾" ..1,250.00
Bottle, scent; elephant stopper on globe of emb birds, 5½" 5,225.00
Bottle, scent; Orientals among trees, glass stopper, Czech, 3" 220.00
Bottle, scent; sq w/emb roses, 6" 150.00
Bottle, scent; 4 tapered sides w/emb scrolls & flowers, 5½" 200.00
Bowl, 2 fish among waves form, oblong, Schlevogt, 2¾x8½x5" ...375.00
Vase, 3 sprites w/vintage, Bohemian, 8½" 330.00

Mantel Lustres

Mantel lustres are decorative vases or candle holders made from all types of glass, often highly decorated, and usually hung with one or more rows of prisms. In the listings that follow, values are given for a pair.

Portrait reserves on clear glass shades, gilt and multicolored jeweled accents, prisms, Bohemia, nineteenth century, 25", $1,550.00 for the pair.

Amber cut to clear w/t'prints & fans, prisms, Bohemian, 11" 300.00
Cobalt w/pnt floral & gold, scallops, prisms, 1850s, 14x7" 550.00
Gr glass w/enamel & gilt, 10 cut glass prisms, 13" 400.00
Ruby bristol w/HP gold rosettes & wht beads, prisms, 14" 650.00

Maps and Atlases

Maps are highly collectible, not only for historical value but also for their sometimes elaborate artwork, legendary information, or data that since they were printed has been proven erroneous. There are many types of maps including geographical, military, celestial, road, and railroad. Nineteenth-century maps, particularly of U.S. areas, are increasing in popularity and price. Rarity, area depicted (i.e. Texas is more sought after than North Dakota), and condition are major price factors. Our advisor for this category is Murray Hudson; he is listed in the Directory under Tennessee.

Key: hc — hand colored

Atlases

Black's General...World New Edition, Edinburgh, 56 maps, 1867, EX ..1,000.00
Carey's Am Pocket, Phila, 20 maps, 1804, 119-pg, orig cover, EX 2,000.00
Century...World, NY, 1st edition, deluxe binding, 382-pg, 1897, EX 275.00
Colton's...Am, GW Colton, 1855, 63 map sheets, EX- 2,250.00
Cram's Unrivaled Family...World, Chicago, 124-pg, 1883, EX ...325.00
Ewings New General, Oliver & Boyd, Edinburgh, hc, 1821, EX ..625.00
Gaskell Family & Business...World, Chicago, bl cloth, 1890, NM ...250.00
Hardesty's Historical & Geographical Encyclopedia, 430-pg, 1884, EX ..550.00
Johnson's New Illus Family, Johnson & Browning, NY, 1861, 99-pg, VG ...1,500.00
McNally Standard...World, Chicago, 192-pg, brn cloth, 1887, EX ..250.00
Peerless...World, Mast, Crowell & Kirpatrick, 128-pg, 1889, VG 125.00
Tunison's Peerless Universal..., NY, brn cloth, 1896, EX 400.00
Winn & Hammond New Family...World, Detroit, orange brds, 1885, VG ..85.00

Maps

Colton's KY & TN, hc litho, lg format, 1862, 14¼x17½", EX+ ...125.00
Eastern US, Hall, Black, Edinburgh, mc litho, 1861, 20x15", VG ..120.00
Harbor of Pensacola FL, Harper's Weekly, newspaper, 1861, 7x9", VG ...90.00
Johnson's CA Territories of NM/UT, hc, forts/etc, 1863, 17x24½", EX .250.00
Johnson's GA & AL, NY, hc, insets, 1861, 15½x22½", EX+ 125.00
Johnson's IL, hc litho, Chicago courthouse view, hc, 1862, 16x12", G ...80.00
KY/TN, Mitchell, hc litho, war sites, 1876, 15¼x22¼", G 75.00
KY/TN Counties, Mitchell, Philadelphia, hc, 1860, 9¼x12¾", VG ..65.00
LA/MS/AR/TX, Smith, Lippincott, hc litho, 1861, 12x10", VG .95.00
MS River from Cairo to Memphis, Wells, NY, mc, 1863, 9½x4½", G .175.00
SW Pass of MS River, Gerdes, gulf entrance, 1862, 18½x14½", G ...100.00
US of N Am, Stanford, London, hc, 1860, 12¼x15", EX 165.00
US Projected by OL Marshfield, pen/ink/hc, 1830, 27x38", unique ..2,500.00

Marblehead

What began as therapy for patients in a sanitarium in Marblehead, Massachusetts, has become recognized as an important part of the Arts and Crafts movement in America. Results of the early experiments under the guidance of Arthur E. Baggs in 1904 met with such success that by 1908 the pottery had been converted to a solely commercial venture. Simple vase shapes were sometimes incised with stylized animal and floral motifs or sailing ships. Some were decorated in low relief; many were plain. Simple matt glazes in soft yellow, gray, wisteria, rose, tobacco brown, and their most popular, Marblehead blue, were used alone or in combination. The Marblehead logo is distinctive — a ship with full sail and the letters 'M' and 'P.' The pottery closed in 1936.

Unless noted otherwise, all items listed below are marked and in the matt glaze.

Vase, fish in beige and blue on gray, cylindrical, 4½x4", $4,500.00.

Bowl, bl, brn int, flat rim, spherical, 3¼x5" 250.00
Bowl, gr, w/flower frog, 1½x3¼" 375.00
Bowl, grapevines, gray/indigo on dk gray, Tutt, 3x6¾" 1,300.00
Bowl, lav, w/flower frog, 4½" 200.00
Bowl, lotus leaves, dk bl w/lt bl int, 3¼x8½" 375.00
Bowl, red metallic (rare glaze), 3x6" 350.00
Creamer, bl, 3½x4" 100.00
Pitcher, ship at sea, waves at rim, gray/yel/bl, 5x6" 700.00
Pitcher, ship at sea cvd on bl gloss, 5" 300.00
Planter, dk bl, melon w/3 hdls, 4¾x6" 250.00
Tile, flowers in basket, mc, kiln pops, 6" 550.00
Tile, ship at sea, wht on bl, 4", EX 210.00
Vase, band at rim, red/purple on pk, 4" 800.00
Vase, bl, pear shape, 6x5" 500.00
Vase, bl, swollen flared body, 6¼x5¼" 460.00
Vase, brn, shouldered, 3½" 350.00
Vase, bud; dk bl matt, corseted, 4½" 200.00
Vase, bud; gray, squat base, 6x3" 125.00
Vase, dk bl, tapered ovoid, 7¾" 800.00
Vase, dk bl matt, flared rim, label, 5½x5" 475.00
Vase, dk gr, cylinder, 7" 525.00
Vase, dove gr w/bl specks, cylinder, 9⅛x5¼" 275.00
Vase, dragonflies at top (4), bl/brn on gr, Tutt, 6" 1,600.00
Vase, flowering trees, bl on gray, Tutt, 5½x3½" 1,600.00
Vase, geometrics, gr on bl, cylinder, 6" 2,500.00
Vase, geometrics, gr on bl, HJH, 4½" 1,600.00
Vase, gr/brn/bl mottle, tapered form, label, 8x4" 1,100.00
Vase, grapes, bl-lav on gray, Tutt, label, 3¾x4½" 2,300.00
Vase, grapevines, mc on mustard, Tutt, rstr, 5x3" 1,300.00
Vase, lav, shouldered, 7½" 650.00
Vase, lav-gr, cylinder, 9x4" 800.00
Vase, ochre over lt beige, ivory int, 3½x2" 225.00
Vase, peacock feathers, brn on dk gr, Tutt, 8½x4" 3,750.00
Vase, purple w/bl highlights, tapered form, 6½" 650.00
Vase, teal to mint w/alligator texturing, 5x4" 275.00
Vase, teal w/blk underglaze at rim, 2¾" 375.00
Vase, trees, blk/bl on gray, Tutt, 3½" 2,400.00
Vase, trees, gr on bl, ovoid, 7x4" 3,250.00
Vase, trees, gr/brn on mustard, Tutt, 3½" 1,700.00
Vase, yel, incurvate rim, 3½x5½" 600.00

Marbles

Marbles have been popular with children since the mid-1800s. They've been made in many types from a variety of materials. Among some of the first glass items to be produced, the earliest marbles were made from a solid glass rod broken into sections of the proper length which were placed in a tray of sand and charcoal and returned to the fire. As they were reheated, the trays were constantly agitated until the marbles were completely round. Other marbles were made of china, pottery, steel, and natural stones. Below is a listing of the various types, along with a brief description of each.

Agates: stone marbles of many different colors — bands of color alternating with white usually encircle the marble; most are translucent.

Ballot Box: handmade (with pontils), opaque white or black, used in lodge elections.

Bloodstone: green chalcedony with red spots, a type of quartz.

China: with or without glaze, in a variety of hand-painted designs — parallel bands or bull's-eye designs most common.

Clambroth: opaque glass with outer evenly spaced swirls of one or alternating colors.

Clay: one of the most common older types; some are painted while others are not.

Comic Strip: a series of twelve machine-made marbles with faces of comic strip characters, Peltier Glass Factory, Illinois.

Crockery: sometimes referred to as Benningtons; most are either blue or brown, although some are speckled. The clay is shaped into a sphere, then coated with glaze and fired.

End of the Day: single-pontil glass marbles — the colored part often appears as a multicolored blob or mushroom cloud.

Goldstone: clear glass completely filled with copper flakes that have turned gold-colored from the heat of the manufacturing process.

Indian Swirls: usually black glass with a colored swirl appearing on the outside next to the surface, often irregular.

Latticinio Core Swirls: double-pontil marble with an inner area with net-like effects of swirls coming up around the center.

Lutz Type: glass with colored or clear bands alternating with bands which contain copper flecks.

Micas: clear or colored glass with mica flecks which reflect as silver dots when marble is turned. Red is rare.

Onionskin: spiral types which are solidly colored instead of having individual ribbons or threads, multicolored.

Peppermint Swirls: made of white opaque glass with alternating blue and red outer swirls.

Ribbon Core Swirls: double-pontil marble — center shaped like a ribbon with swirls that come up around the middle.

Rose Quartz: stone marble, usually pink in color, often with fractures inside and on outer surface.

Solid Core Swirls: double-pontil marble — middle is solid with swirls coming up around the core.

Steelies: hollow steel spheres marked with a cross where the steel was bent together to form the ball.

Sulfides: generally made of clear glass with figures inside. Rarer types have colored figures or colored glass.

Tiger Eye: stone marble of golden quartz with inclusions of asbestos, dark brown with gold highlights.

Vaseline: machine-made of yellowish-green glass with small bubbles.

Prices listed below are for marbles in near-mint condition unless noted otherwise. When size is not indicated, assume them to be of average size, ½" to 1". Polished marbles have greatly reduced values. (We do not list tinted marbles because there is no way of knowing how much color the tinting has, and intensity of color is an important worth-assessing factor.)

For a more thorough study of the subject, we recommend *Antique and Collectible Marbles, 3rd Edition; Machine-Made and Contemporary Marbles, 2nd Edition;* and *Big Book of Marbles, Second Edition,* all by our advisor, Everett Grist (published by Collector Books); you will find his address in the Directory under Tennessee.

Agate, contemporary, carnelian, 1¾" 160.00
Banded Opaque, gr & wht, 2" 1,200.00
Banded Opaque, red & wht, 1¾" 1,200.00
Banded Opaque, red & wht, ¾" 95.00
Banded Transparent Swirl, bl, ¾" 75.00
Banded Transparent Swirl, lt gr, 1¾" 750.00
Bennington, bl, 1¾" 40.00
Bennington, bl, ¾" 5.00
Bennington, brn, 1¾" 30.00
Bennington, fancy, 1¾" 80.00
Bennington, fancy, ¾" 10.00
China, decorated, glazed, apple, 1¾" 1,200.00
China, decorated, glazed, rose, 1¾" 2,000.00
China, decorated, glazed, wht w/geometrics, 1¾" 125.00
China, decorated, unglazed, geometrics & flowers, ¾" 300.00
Clambroth, opaque, bl & wht, 1¾" 2,600.00
Clambroth, opaque, bl & wht, ¾" 300.00
Clambroth Swirl, red/wht, Germany, 1900, ⅞" 475.00
Comic, Andy Gump 125.00
Comic, Betty Boop 200.00
Comic, Cotes Bakery, advertising 900.00
Comic, Kayo, rare 450.00
Comic, Little Orphan Annie 150.00
Comic, Moon Mullins 300.00
Comic, set of 12 ....1,500.00
Comic, Skeezix 150.00
Cork Screw, machine-made, common, ⅝" 5.00
End of Day, bl & wht, 1¾" 400.00
Goldstone, ¾" 35.00
Indian Swirl, 1¾" 2,500.00
Indian Swirl Lutz-type, gold flakes, ¾" 600.00
Line Crockery, clay, 1¾" 75.00
Mica, bl, ¾" 35.00
Mica, gr, 1¾" 800.00

Onionskin, red, yellow, and green, 1¾", $175.00. (From the collection of Brian Estepp/ Courtesy Everett Grist)

Onionskin, w/mica, 1¾" 1,500.00
Onionskin, w/mica, ¾" 110.00
Onionskin, 16-lobe, unusual, 1¾" 1,800.00
Onionskin, ¾" 90.00
Onionskin, 4-lobe, 1¼" 450.00
Opaque Swirl, gr, ¾" 75.00
Opaque Swirl Lutz-type, bl, yel, gr, ¾" 325.00
Peppermint Swirl, opaque, red, wht, & bl, 1¾" 2,000.00
Peppermint Swirl, opaque, red, wht, & bl, ¾" 125.00
Pottery, 1¾" 75.00
Ribbon Core Lutz-type, red, 1¾" 1,800.00
Slag, bl, machine-made, sm 3.00
Slag, bl, machine-made, 1½" 150.00
Solid Opaque, gr, 1¾" 800.00
Solid Opaque, ¾" 75.00
Sulfide, angel face w/wings, 1¾", M 1,000.00
Sulfide, baboon playing bass fiddle, 2⅛" 1,200.00
Sulfide, bear cub on all 4s, detailed, 1¼", NM+ 400.00
Sulfide, billy goat, 1½" 100.00
Sulfide, bird, 2", EX 150.00
Sulfide, boar, 1⅞" 165.00
Sulfide, camel, 1-hump, on grassy mound, 1½" 200.00
Sulfide, child sitting, 1¾", M 600.00
Sulfide, circus bear, 2" 140.00
Sulfide, crane w/fish, 1¾" 600.00
Sulfide, crucifix, 1¾", M 600.00
Sulfide, deer, 1¼" 175.00
Sulfide, dog howling, 1⅜", M 140.00
Sulfide, dog on grass mound, HP/3-color, pontil, 1¼" 3,500.00
Sulfide, dog w/bird in mouth, 1¾", M 900.00
Sulfide, dove, 1⅝", M 165.00
Sulfide, eagle w/closed wings, 1⅞" 200.00
Sulfide, elephant standing, sea gr glass, 1¾" 900.00
Sulfide, elephant w/long trunk, 1¼" 140.00
Sulfide, fish, 1¾", M 175.00
Sulfide, fox, 1½", EX 130.00
Sulfide, George Washington, bust, 2⅜" 650.00
Sulfide, hen, 1⅛", M 150.00
Sulfide, horse rearing, 1⅞" 175.00
Sulfide, horse standing, 2", EX 130.00
Sulfide, lamb, 1¾" 125.00
Sulfide, lion standing, male, 1½" 125.00
Sulfide, Little Boy Blue, 1¾", M 700.00
Sulfide, monkey seated on drum, 1⅜", M 200.00
Sulfide, Nipper dog, 1¾", EX 350.00
Sulfide, owl w/closed wings, 1¾" 150.00
Sulfide, papoose, 1¾", M 700.00
Sulfide, parrot, 1½", EX 100.00
Sulfide, poodle on hind legs, 1⅛" 100.00
Sulfide, rabbit running, lg/offset/sm bubble, 1½", M- 110.00
Sulfide, razor-bk hog, 1½" 150.00
Sulfide, rooster, 1¾" 150.00
Sulfide, sheep grazing, 1¼" 150.00
Sulfide, squirrel standing, 1¾", EX 170.00
Sulfide, woman (Kate Greenaway), 1½" 650.00

Marine Collectibles

Vintage tools used on sea-going vessels, lanterns, clocks, and memorabilia of all types are sought out by those who are interested in preserving the romantic genre that revolves around the life of the sea captains, their boats and their crews; ports of call; and the lure of far away islands. See also Steamship Collectibles; Telescopes; Scrimshaw; Tools.

Axe, naval boarding; long hdl, well made, 27" overall 575.00
Beckets, sailor-made-sea-chest lift hdls, orig pnt, pr 300.00
Bell, ship's; brass, Belvoir 1954, 9", VG 400.00
Binnacle, lifeboat; copper, lacks compass, VG 110.00
Book, Navigating Instruments, Brewington 1963, 1st edition, EX ..175.00
Boot, sea diver's; canvas & brass, VG 160.00
Cannon, Lt Snow-Strong Cannon Mfg, 14" brass bbl, mahog carriage .2,500.00
Chronometer, Thomas Mercer, 56-hr, working 1,450.00
Clock, bulkhead; M Low NY, US Govt on 12-hr face, VG, w/key ..175.00
Clock, lighthouse; w/baromoter/thermometers, directional vane, 35", VG 2,750.00
Clock, ship's bell; Seth Thomas, NP brass, working 400.00
Clock, US Maritime Commission, quartz, 7½", in brass case 100.00
Clock, waterboy ship's bell; #10, Pat 1910, 8¼" dia 285.00
Compass, Nickerson & Baxter Boston, brass, w/gimbal, 3" dia, EXIB ..135.00
Fog horn, brass, working, 14½" 90.00
Gauge, Watson-Stillman, registers up to 2000, brass, 7" dia 50.00
Harpoon, LB&CO, dbl flue, iron, 39½", VG 1,150.00

Harpoon, dbl swivel head, iron, 23", EX 275.00
Harpoon gun, Norwegian bolt action, 19th C, 42", VG in case ...500.00
Journal, Howard of Nantucket whaling history, 1841-45, EX .1,300.00
Lamp, ship's salon; brass, gimbaled on top, 32", EX 825.00
Lantern, fixed onion globe, bronze fr, 2 tie-down rings, 19th C, 11" ...600.00
Lantern, wrist; brass w/clear globe, w/burner, early, 12"+hdl 180.00
Light, Perco, red/bl lenses, 10½", port/starboard pr, EX 150.00
Model, USN Civil War ship, 17x30" in cased shadow box 1,200.00
Octant, Chrichton & Son London, ebony, ivory scale, EX in case 800.00
Octant, Spencer Browning & Co, San Francisco, ebony/ivory/brass ...375.00
Portholes, matched pr 375.00
Sextant, A Hurlimann's Paris, silver arc, w/accessories, EXIB 800.00
Sextant, I Macrow London, brass, 4 shades, detachable sight, 12" 920.00
Ship's log, Cherub Mark III, Thomas Walker & Son, w/spinner, G ...250.00
Timer, sand/glass, 4 trn wood columns, 2-pc glass, 10½", VG 725.00
Trophy, yachting; Gorham, sterling silver, Pequoit, 1933, EX 150.00
Wheel, brass w/wooden spokes, brass shaft, 24" dia 300.00

Martin Bros.

The Martin Bros. were studio potters who worked from 1873 until 1914, first at Fulham and later at London and Southall. There were four brothers, each of whom excelled in their particular area. Robert, known as Wallace, was an experienced stonecarver. He modeled a series of grotesque bird and animal figural caricatures. Walter was the potter, responsible for throwing the larger vases on the wheel, firing the kiln, and mixing the clay. Edwin, an artist of stature, preferred more naturalistic forms of decoration. His work was often incised or had relief designs of seaweed, florals, fish, and birds. The fourth brother, Charles, was their business manager. Their work was incised with their names, place of production, and letters and numbers indicating month and year.

Though figural jars continue to command the higher prices, decorated vases and bowls have increased a great deal in value. Our advisor for this category is David Rago; he is listed in the Directory under New Jersey.

Bird jar, brn, aventurine, gr & beige feathers, lg flat beak, 7¼" ..9,750.00
Bird jar, droopy beak, sleepy eyes, 11½x5½" 9,500.00
Bird jar, kingfisher, lt gr chest & head, mustard beak, 1898, 11" 16,250.00
Bird jar, tobacco, dk gr & brn feathers, lg beak, w/lid, 1907, 10" 9,750.00
Dog jar, eyes shifted, tongue out, brn/orange/gray, 1895, 12x6" 32,500.00
Double-faced jug, opal faces, caramel spout, 5½x6¼" 4,200.00
Face jug, bearded man, bl, dimpled, mk, 1879, 8x6½" 3,900.00
Face jug, face w/berries & leaves, brn glaze, bulbous, 1910, 7x5" ..4,550.00
Gargoyle dish, finely cvd, unglazed, 1894, 2¾x5½" 1,700.00
Imp jar, rnd brn scales, 5¾x3" 12,000.00
Pen stand, man's head wearing hat, 3x3½" 1,600.00
Pen stand, turtle w/gaping mouth, 1910, 5x3½" 3,900.00
Pitcher, iguanas/lizards, brn/blk on mottled apple gr, 1875, 7½" ..2,300.00
Toby jug, seated male, blk & caramel brn glaze, 1903, 10x5½" 4,900.00
Vase, bud; 2 storks in brn & ivory on ivory, 4-sided, 1904, 5½" ...1,300.00
Vase, bud; 3 storks, brn on orange, cylindrical, 1903, 2x5" 1,300.00
Vase, crab/lobster/etc, brn on bl, dtd 1903, 9", pr 1,700.00
Vase, eels/fish in brn on mottled pk & brn-gr, cylindrical, 2¾x8" ..2,300.00
Vase, red/gr lustre crystalline, squat/faceted, 1900, 5x7" 475.00

Mary Gregory

Mary Gregory glass, for reasons that remain obscure, is the namesake of a Boston and Sandwich Glass Company employee who worked for the company for only two years in the mid-1800s. Although no evidence actually exists to indicate that glass of this type was even produced there, the fine colored or crystal ware decorated with figures of children in white enamel is commonly referred to as Mary Gregory. The glass, in fact, originated in Europe and was imported into this country where it was copied by several eastern glasshouses. It was popular from the mid-1800s until the turn of the century. It is generally accepted that examples with all-white figures were made in the U.S.A., while gold-trimmed items and those with children having tinted faces or a small amount of color on their clothing are European. Though amethyst is rare, examples in cranberry command the higher prices. Blue ranks next; and green, amber, and clear items are worth the least. Watch for new glass decorated with screen-printed children and a minimum of hand painting. The screen effect is easily detected with a magnifying glass.

Vase, rubena satin, Inverted Thumbprint, girl within floral frame, gold trim at ruffled rim, 9¼", $250.00. (Photo courtesy John A. Schuman III)

Bottle, sapphire bl, boy, w/matching stopper, 10¼x3¼" 195.00
Bottle, sapphire bl, girl, shouldered w/cut stopper, 8½x3½" 200.00
Box, amber, boy w/bird, 3¾" dia 250.00
Box, bl, lady w/parrot on perch, scroll hdls/ft, 6½" 675.00
Box, blk amethyst, boy/trees/grassy mound, oval, 3x2¼x3¾" 375.00
Calling card tray, lt bl, girl among foliage, 8" dia 250.00
Carafe, cranberry, lady in shawl, 11" 300.00
Cordial, bl, boy w/rifle 115.00
Pitcher, gr, boy in apple tree, fluted, 10½" 280.00
Stein, clear w/eng floral, amber lid w/boy, 8" 150.00
Tumbler, cranberry, girl 40.00
Vase, bud; amber/wht spatter, boy/girl, 7x2½", pr 550.00
Vase, cobalt, boy in foliage, gold trim, mini, 2½" 300.00
Vase, cobalt, boys & lilies of valley, 7x2⅞" 145.00
Vase, cranberry, boy walking, 4½" 145.00
Vase, cranberry, girl/tree, paneled int, 10x5" 285.00
Vase, dk amethyst, boy & bird, spiked rim, Bohemian, 1890, 10½", EX ...300.00
Vase, gr, boy, shell trim down sides, 6½x3¼" 145.00
Vase, gr opaque, boy w/tray of flowers, 11x4" 235.00
Vase, lt amber, girl in forest/bk: flowers, 6¾" 225.00
Vase, olive-amber, boy & girl, 13½x5¾" 395.00
Vase, sapphire bl, boy, cylindrical, 8" 180.00

Mason's Ironstone

In 1813 Charles J. Mason was granted a patent for a process said to 'improve the quality of English porcelain.' The new type of ware was in fact ironstone which Mason decorated with colorful florals and scenics, some of which reflected the Oriental taste. Although his business failed for a short time in the late 1840s, Mason re-established himself and continued to produce dinnerware, tea services, and ornamental pieces until about 1852, at which time the pottery was sold to Francis Morley. Ten years later, Geo. L. and Taylor Ashworth became owners. Both Morley and the Ashworths not only used Mason's molds and patterns but often his mark as well. Because the quality and the workmanship of the later wares do not compare with Mason's earlier product, collectors should take care to distinguish one from the other. Consult a good book on marks to be sure. The Wedgwood Company now owns the rights to the Mason patterns and is reproducing Vista. Note: Blue Vista is generally valued at 15% to 20% above prices for pink/red.

Beaker, Persiana, HP mc o/l on mauve transfer, 1830s mk, 5¾" ...125.00
Bowl, fruit; Vista, red, scalloped, ftd, 1890-1900, 4¼x10¼" 300.00
Bowl, Mogul, mc on bl-tinged, rectangular, 1818, 9" L 275.00
Bowl, nesting; Vista, red, 8-sided, 1890-1900, 3¾x7½" 275.00
Bowl, nesting; Vista, red, 8-sided, 1925-30, 3¼x6½" 125.00
Bowl, Table & Flower Pot, mc on gray-wht, 1813-25, 11¼x7½" ...400.00
Bowl, Vista, red, oval, 1925-30, 10¾x6½" 150.00
Cake plate, Vista, red, sq, 1925-30, 11" 100.00
Coffeepot, Bandana, mc on wht w/lustre overglaze, 1890, 9¼" .350.00
Coffeepot, Vista, red, 1925-30, 9" 350.00
Coffeepot & trivet, Vista, brn, 1925-30, 9x8", 6" dia 150.00
Creamer, Bible, sq, 1925-30, 3¼x4" 40.00
Creamer, Vista, red, sq, 1925-30 mk, crazing, 3½x4" 70.00
Creamer, Vista, red, 1890-1900, 3¼x4½" 100.00
Cup & saucer, chowder; Vista, red, 1890-1900, 3¼x6", 8½" 150.00
Cup & saucer, demitasse; Vista, red, 1890-1900, 2¼", 5", ea 30.00
Egg cup, Vista, red, 1890-1900, 2¼x2" 100.00
Egg cups, Floral & Bird, blk transfer w/mc, 1890-1900, 5 for 225.00
Jar, Fruit Basket, 6-sided, 1925-30, 6¼x3½" 100.00
Jug, Dragon motif, patterned hdl, 8-sided, early, 6¼" 195.00
Jug, Fruit Basket, 8-sided, 1890-1900, 6¼x6½" 175.00
Jug, Japan, 8-sided, serpent hdl, 1813-25, 4¼x3½" 175.00

Jug, Japan, multicolor, octagonal body, 1840+, 6½x5½", $225.00.

Jug, Red Scale, blk transfer w/mc, 8-sided, 5¼x4½" 175.00
Jug, Red Scale, mc on wht, serpent hdl, 1840, 5¼" 200.00
Jug, Red Scale, 8-sided, branch hdl, 1818 mk, 4¼x4" 200.00
Jug, Vista, red, bulbous, 1890-1900, 4¾x5" 80.00
Jug, Vista, red, 1925-30, 6¼x6½" 150.00
Jug, Vista, red, 8-sided, 1925-30, 4½x4" 125.00
Jug, Willow, blk w/mc, 8-sided, serpent hdl, 1840, 5¼x4¾" 125.00
Plaque, Double Landscape, rolled rim, Ashworth, 9" 125.00
Plate, American Marine, brn, Ashworth, 7", 6 for 125.00
Plate, Temple & Bridge, 1890-1900, 8" dia, 6 for 125.00
Plate, Vista, brn, 1890-1900, 7¾", 4 for 100.00
Plate, Vista, red, 1890-1900, 9", 5 for 150.00
Plate, Wood Pigeon, 1890-1900, 9¼", 5 for 250.00
Platter, American Marine, brn, Ashworth, 14¾x12" 200.00
Platter, Vista, red, 1925-30, 11¼x9" 125.00
Platter, Vista, red, 1925-30, 15½x12½" 200.00
Relish tray, Vista, red, rectangular, 1925-30, 8½" 90.00
Shakers, Vista, red, 1890-1900, 3¼", pr 100.00
Shakers, Vista, red, 8-sided, 1890s-1900, 3¼", 4", pr 90.00
Soap dish, Willow, blk w/mc, w/drainer & lid, 1840, 3¾x5" 100.00
Soup, Floral Design, Imari colors, 1813-35, 1¼x9½" 175.00
Soup, Mogul, mc on bl-tinged, scalloped, 1818, 1½x9½" 225.00
Sugar bowl, Vista, red, 1925-30, 6x6½" 100.00
Teapot, Vista, red, bulbous, 1890-1900, 6¾x9" 300.00
Teapot, Willow, blk w/mc, 1840s, 6¼x8¾" 225.00
Trivet, Vista, red, 1925-30, 6x6" 150.00

Massier

Clement Massier was a French artist-potter who in 1881 established a workshop at Golfe Juan, France, where he experimented with metallic lustre glazes. (One of his pupils was Jacques Sicardo, who brought the knowledge he had gained through his association with Massier to the Weller Pottery Company in Zanesville, Ohio.) The lustre lines developed by Massier incorporated nature themes with allover decorations of foliage or flowers on shapes modeled in the Art Nouveau style. The ware was usually incised with the Massier name, his initials, or the location of the pottery. Massier died in 1917.

Bud vase, mistletoe, red/gold/gr irid, no mk, 6¾x2½" 200.00
Pitcher, satyr face under spout, nude hdl, Vallauris, 10" 1,495.00
Vase, Nouveau swirls, dbl gourd w/4 lg dimples at base, 6½" 750.00

Match Holders

John Walker, an English chemist, invented the match more than one hundred years ago, quite by accident. Walker was working with a mixture of potash and antimony, hoping to make a combustible that could be used to fire guns. The mixture adhered to the end of the wooden stick he had used for stirring. As he tried to remove it by scraping the stick on the stone floor, it burst into flames. The invention of the match was only a step away! From that time to the present, match holders have been made in amusing figural forms as well as simple utilitarian styles and in a wide range of materials. Both table-top and wall-hanging models were made — all designed to keep matches conveniently at hand. The prices in this category are very volatile due to increased interest in this field and the fact that so many can be classified as a cross or dual collectible.

Caution: as prices for originals continue to climb, so do the number of reproductions. Know your dealer. Our advisor for this category is Ron Damaska; he is listed in the Directory under Pennsylvania. See also Advertising.

Bakelite, mc cvd bird w/glass eyes, sanded striker 200.00
Brass, devil figure, scrolled wall mt, early 55.00
Brass, man swinging on fence, desk type, lg 250.00
Bronze, bear on stump, mk Dodge Inc 85.00
Bronzed cast metal, Nouveau lady, 3 flower compartments 175.00
Bsk, bathing beauty stands by pond, 2 compartments/striker, German, 9" 595.00
Bsk, girl w/NY paper & lg pipe, 3 compartments, German/R in dmn, 9" ..595.00

Cast iron with gold paint, double box with one lid, key-hole top, 7", $125.00.

China, chamberstick w/matchbox holder, Dresden 110.00

China, saucer type, box holder, Mayer 25.00
CI, frog figural, hinged lid w/striker, stove advertising 150.00
CI, grapes/leaves, lacy openwork, old 55.00
CI, lady's shoe, old mc pnt w/G color, 5⅜" 100.00
CI, mechanical house, mk Match Safe Pat Dated 1883 ....450.00
CI, rtcl bkplate, 2-compartment, 7" 45.00
CI, urn pockets (2), hangs, dtd 1867, w/striker, 5x7½" 70.00
Coon Chicken Inn, Black smiling face figural, M 325.00
E Bohne Sohne, bsk, Am Indian head, Germany 175.00
E Bohne Sohne, devil's head figural, HP 150.00
Goebel, blk cat w/glass eyes, sanded striker 150.00
Majolica, Am Indian, 2 compartments & tray striker on front, 7" ..425.00
Majolica, Black man w/bales of cigars, 2 compartments, 7" 595.00
Majolica, monkey on log, 3 compartments+smoking ashtray, 7" ..595.00
Majolica, Nouveau lady's head on lily pad tray, 5½" 200.00
Manning-Bowman, chrome, light-up, Pull Quick, Art Deco, w/orig refill 125.00
Porc, artist at easel figural, HP, Germany 200.00
Porc, girls playing near fence, Germany 125.00
Porc, vulture tobacco jar w/match holder & tray, Austria 3,950.00
Pottery, saucer base on low stem, unglazed sides, 3½" 25.00
Schafer & Vater, bsk, bulldog & man, Scratch My Back 225.00
Schafer & Vater, bsk, cats, Don't Scratch Me Scratch Mother ..150.00
Schafer & Vater, bsk, man, Scratch My Bald Head 175.00
Schafer & Vater, bsk, thin man & woman in chairs, pr 395.00
SP, antique auto form, flip lid, WB Mfg Co Pat 1907 ....250.00
Stoneware, dog's head figural, Guinness advertising, Read Bros London ..375.00
Stoneware, Ushers man in Kharki, Kipling ball shape, Tuck & Sons ...250.00
Tin, crest w/crimped & cut-out decor, pnt traces, 4x7", EX 32.00
Vaseline glass, PA Rubber Co, Jeannette PA, tire-shape box holder ..250.00
Victoria Austria, bulldog head figural, sgn 150.00
Victoria Austria, lion's head figural, sgn 165.00
Victoria Austria, Nubian head figural 175.00
Wht metal, pnt Oriental man on flying carpet 225.00

Match Safes

Before the invention of the safety match in 1855, matches were carried in small pocket-sized containers because they ignited so easily. Aptly called match safes, these containers were used extensively until about 1920, when cigarette lighters became widely availabe. Some incorporated added features (hidden compartments, cigar cutters, etc.), some were figural, and others were used by retail companies as advertising giveaways. They were made from every type of material, but silverplated styles abound. Both the advertising and common silverplated cases generally fall in the $50.00 to $100.00 price range.

Beware of reproductions and fakes; there are many currently on the market. Know your dealer. Our advisor for this category is Ron Damaska; he is listed in the Directory under Pennsylvania. See also Advertising.

Advertising, Collins & Co. Liquor Dealers, Steubenville, O., Xmas 1904, minor wear and dents, ½x1½x2½", $125.00.

Brass, dragon figural, Japan 200.00
Brass, United Machine & Supply Co, knapsack form 45.00
Brass w/emb horse head & horseshoe, 2⅝x1½x2½" 45.00
Fonerden & Bell Corn cure advertising tin w/striker 45.00
German silver, Art Nouveau flowers, 1½x2¾x½" 50.00
Nazi 830 Silver, SS Troops, pocket safe insert for striker, 1944 ..350.00
NP brass, turtle form w/button latch, 2⅞x1⅝" 175.00
Plated brass, violin bottle shape 175.00
Sterling, Art Nouveau Cupid kissing sleeping maiden, ca 1900 .225.00
Sterling silver, gambling decor, w/cigar cutter/knife, 3-pc in box ..2,500.00
Tin & NP brass, Art Nouveau reserves of deer & Gibson girl, 2¼" 65.00
United States, Vulcanite, Arm & Hammer advertising 100.00
Whitehead & Hoag, celluloid, advertising, hinged lid 65.00

Mauchline Ware

Mauchline ware is the generic name for small, well-made, and useful wooden souvenirs and giftware from Mauchline, Scotland, and nearby locations. It was made from the early nineteenth century into the 1930s. Snuff boxes were among the earliest items, and tea caddies soon followed. From the 1830s on, needlework, stationery, domestic, and cosmetic items were made by the thousands. Today, needlework items are the most plentiful and range from boxes of all sizes made to hold supplies to tiny bodkins and buttons. Napkin rings, egg cups, vases, and bowls are just a few of the domestic items available.

The wood most commonly used in the production of Mauchline ware was sycamore. Finishes vary. Early items were hand decorated with colored paints or pen and ink. By the 1850s, perhaps even earlier, transfer ware was produced, decorated with views associated with the place of purchase. These souvenir items were avidly bought by travelers for themselves as well as for gifts. Major exhibitions and royal occasions were also represented on transferware. An alternative decorating process was initiated during the mid-1860s whereby actual photos replaced the transfers. Because they were finished with multiple layers of varnish, many examples found today are still in excellent condition.

Tartan ware's distinctive decoration was originally hand painted directly on the wood with inks, but in the 1840s machine-made paper in authentic Tartan designs became available. Except for the smallest items, each piece was stamped with the Tartan name. The Tartan decoration was applied to virtually the entire range of Mauchline ware, and because it was favored by Queen Victoria, it became widely popular. Collectors still value Tartan ware above other types of decoration, with transferware being their second choice. Other types of Mauchline decorations include Fern ware and Black Lacquer with floral or transfer decorations.

When cleaning any Mauchline item, extreme care should be used to avoid damaging the finish! Mauchline ware has been reproduced for at least twenty-five years, especially some of the more popular pieces and finishes. Collectors should study the older items for comparison and to learn about the decorating and manufacturing processes.

Box, Lyme from the Holmes Bush, 2x5x7" 100.00
Box, pill; Margate & Sands Resort, EX 70.00
Box, Queen Victoria's Jubilee 1887/castle, 3x3" dia 80.00
Box, sewing; decoupage lid, w/orig tray/latch, 2½x7x5½" 110.00
Box, sewing; Stanley/Livingston pics on lid, 6 bone eyelets, 4x3x2" ...135.00
Box, sewing; Whirlpool Rapids, 1 thread hole, 2½x2¾" 75.00
Crochet thread ball, floral decor, EX 120.00
Darning egg, Watermouth Cave, EX 90.00
Knitting case, blk, Winchester Cathedral w/florals, EX 160.00
Knitting case, St Alban's Abbey, EX 140.00
Letter opener, Robert Burn's Monument souvenir, EX 110.00
Match holder, College Church in St Andrews, 1½x1½" dia 75.00
Notebook, Congress Park, Saratoga NY, wood w/orig clasp, 2x3" 115.00
Notebook, mc ferns/2 views, leather binding w/emb brass, 2¼x1⅝" ...150.00
Thimble holder, Isle of Wight/Needles, beehive style, EX 170.00

McCoy

The third generation McCoy potter in the Roseville, Ohio, area was Nelson, who with the aid of his father, J.W., established the Nelson McCoy Sanitary Stoneware Company in 1910. They manufactured churns, jars, jugs, poultry fountains, and foot warmers. By 1925 they had expanded their wares to include majolica jardinieres and pedestals, umbrella stands and cuspidors, and an embossed line of vases and small jardinieres in a blended brown and green matt glaze. From the late '20s through the mid-'40s, a utilitarian stoneware was produced, some of which was glazed in the soft blue and white so popular with collectors today. They also used a dark brown mahogany color and a medium to dark green, both in a high gloss. In 1933 the firm became known as the Nelson McCoy Pottery Company. They expanded their facilities in 1940 and began to make the novelty artware, cookie jars, and dinnerware that today are synonomous with 'McCoy.' More than two hundred cookie jars of every theme and description were produced.

More than a dozen different marks have been used by the company; nearly all incorporate the name 'McCoy,' although some of the older items were marked 'NM USA.' For further information consult *The Collector's Encyclopedia of McCoy Pottery* (with recently updated values) by Sharon and Bob Huxford; or *McCoy Pottery Collector's Reference & Value Guide, Vol. I* and *II*, by Margaret Hanson, Craig Nissen, and Bob Hanson (all published by Collector Books). Also available is *Sanfords Guide to McCoy Pottery* by Martha and Steve Sanford. (Mr. Sanford is listed in the Directory under California.)

Alert! Stimulated by the high prices commanded by desirable cookie jars, a broad spectrum of 'new' cookie jars are flooding the marketplace in three categories: 1) Manufacturers have expanded their lines with exciting new designs to attract the collector market. 2) Limited editions and artist-designed jars have proliferated. 3) Reproductions, signed and unsigned, have pervaded the market, creating uncertainty among new collectors and inexperienced dealers. After McCoy closed its doors in the late 1980s, an entrepreneur in Tennessee tried (and succeeded for nearly a decade) to adopt the McCoy Pottery name and mark. This company reproduced old McCoy designs as well as some classic designs of other defunct American potteries, signing their wares 'McCoy' with a mark which very closely approximated the old McCoy mark. Legal action finally put a stop to this practice, though since then this company has used other fradulent marks as well: Brush-McCoy (the compound name was never used on Brush cookie jars) and B.J. Hull.

Note: At the present time, the cookie jar market is somewhat soft, so consider our values to be high end.

Cookie Jars

Picnic Basket, from $65.00 to $75.00.

Animal Crackers	100.00
Apollo Age, minimum value	1,000.00
Apple, 1950-64	50.00
Apple, 1967	60.00
Apple on Basketweave	70.00
Asparagus	50.00
Astronauts, from $750 to	850.00
Bananas	140.00
Barnum's Animals, from $350 to	400.00
Barrel, Cookies sign on lid	125.00
Baseball Boy, from $250 to	250.00
Basket of Eggs	40.00
Basket of Potatoes	40.00
Bear, cookie in vest, no 'Cookies', from $75 to	85.00
Betsy Baker (+), from $250 to	300.00
Black Kettle, w/immovable bail, HP flowers	40.00
Blue Willow Pitcher	50.00
Bobby Baker	65.00
Bugs Bunny, cylinder, from $165 to	200.00
Burlap Bag, redbird on lid, from $50	70.00
Caboose, from $200 to	250.00
Cat on Coal Scuttle	250.00
Chairman of the Board (+)	550.00
Chef (+)	110.00
Chilly Willy	50.00
Chipmunk	125.00
Christmas Tree, minimum value	800.00
Churn, 2 bands	35.00
Circus Horse, blk	250.00
Clown Bust (+)	75.00
Clown in Barrel, yel, bl or gr	85.00
Clyde Dog	250.00
Coalby Cat	375.00
Coca-Cola Can	100.00
Coca-Cola Jug	85.00
Coffee Grinder	45.00
Coffee Mug	45.00
Colonial Fireplace	85.00
Cookie Bank, 1961	165.00
Cookie Boy	225.00
Cookie Cabin	80.00
Cookie Jug, dbl loop	35.00
Cookie Jug, single loop, 2-tone gr rope	35.00
Cookie Jug, w/cork stopper, brn & wht	40.00
Cookie Log, squirrel finial, from $35 to	45.00
Cookie Mug	45.00
Cookie Pot, 1964	40.00
Cookie Safe	65.00
Cookstove, blk or wht	35.00
Corn, row of standing ears, yel or wht, 1977	85.00
Corn, single ear	175.00
Covered Wagon	95.00
Cylinder, w/red flowers	45.00
Dalmatians in Rocking Chair (+)	375.00
Davy Crockett (+)	600.00
Dog on Basketweave, from $75 to	90.00
Drum, red	90.00
Duck on Basketweave, from $75 to	90.00
Dutch Boy	45.00
Dutch Girl, boy on reverse, rare	250.00
Dutch Treat Barn	50.00
Eagle on Basket, from $35 to	50.00
Early American Chest (Chiffoniere)	85.00
Elephant	200.00
Elephant w/Split Trunk, rare, minimum value	300.00
Engine, blk	175.00
Flowerpot, plastic flower on top	500.00
Football Boy (+), from $245 to	275.00
Forbidden Fruit, from $65 to	90.00

Freddy Gleep (+), minimum value 500.00
Friendship 7 .....200.00
Frog on Stump 75.00
Frontier Family 55.00
Fruit in Bushel Basket, from $65 to 80.00
Gingerbread Boy 75.00
Globe, from $300 to 375.00
Grandfather Clock 90.00
Granny 120.00
Hamm's Bear (+) 225.00
Happy Face 80.00
Hen on Nest, from $85 to 95.00
Hillbilly Bear, rare, minimum value (+) 900.00
Hobby Horse (+), from $125 to 150.00
Hocus Rabbit 45.00
Honey Bear, rustic glaze, from $65 to 80.00
Hot Air Balloon 40.00
Ice Cream Cone 45.00
Indian, brn (+) 350.00
Indian, majolica 400.00
Jack-O'-Lantern 600.00
Kangaroo, bl 300.00
Keebler Tree House 70.00
Kettle, bronze, 1961 .....40.00
Kissing Penguins, from $100 to 125.00
Kitten on Basketweave 90.00
Kittens (2) on Low Basket, minimum value 600.00
Kittens on Ball of Yarn 85.00
Koala Bear 85.00
Kookie Kettle, blk 35.00
Lamb on Basketweave 90.00
Leprechaun, minimum value (+) 1,800.00
Liberty Bell 75.00
Little Clown 75.00
Lollipops 80.00
Mac Dog 95.00
Mammy, Cookies on base, wht (+) 150.00
Mammy w/Cauliflower, G pnt, minimum value (+) 1,100.00
Milk Can, Spirit of '76 .....45.00
Modern 65.00
Monk 50.00
Mother Goose 175.00
Mouse on Clock 40.00
Mr & Mrs Owl, from $75 to 90.00
Mushroom on Stump 55.00
Nursery, decal of Humpty Dumpty, from $70 to 80.00
Oaken Bucket, from $25 to 30.00
Orange 55.00
Owl 50.00
Pear, 1952 .....85.00
Pears on Basketweave 70.00
Penguin, yel or aqua, from $175 to 200.00
Pepper, yel 40.00
Pig, winking 300.00
Pineapple 80.00
Pineapple, Modern 90.00
Pirate's Chest, from $125 to 145.00
Popeye Cylinder 200.00
Potbelly Stove, blk 30.00
Puppy, w/sign 60.00
Quaker Oats, rare, minimum value 500.00
Raggedy Ann 110.00
Red Barn, cow in door, rare, minimum value 350.00
Rooster, wht, 1970-1974 .....60.00
Rooster, 1955-1957 .....95.00
Round w/HP Leaves 45.00
Sad Clown 85.00
Snoopy on Doghouse (+), mk United Features Syndicate 200.00
Snow Bear, from $65 to 75.00
Spaniel in Doghouse, bird finial 250.00
Stagecoach, minimum value 800.00
Strawberry, 1955-57 .....65.00
Strawberry, 1971-75 .....45.00
Teapot, 1972 .....60.00
Tepee, slat top 350.00
Tepee, str top (+) 300.00
Tilt Pitcher, blk w/roses 50.00
Timmy Tortoise 45.00
Tomato 60.00
Touring Car 100.00
Traffic Light 50.00
Tudor Cookie House 125.00
Tulip on Flowerpot 225.00
Turkey, gr, rare color 300.00
Turkey, natural colors 250.00
Upside Down Bear, panda 50.00
WC Fields 200.00
Wedding Jar 90.00
Windmill 100.00
Wishing Well 40.00
Woodsy Owl, from $250 to 300.00
Wren House, side lid 175.00
Yosemite Sam, cylinder, from $150 to 200.00

Miscellaneous

Planter, hunting dog with bird in mouth, ca 1955, 12½" long, from $150.00 to $175.00.

Bank, Liberty Bell, bronze color 50.00
Basket, hanging; pipe form, 1970s 50.00
Caddy, buffalo figural, Swank 50.00
Caddy, dresser; Am Eagle, Swank 55.00
Cat dish, emb letters on yel, late 1930s 50.00
Creamer, dog, tail forms hdl, mk, 1950s 150.00
Dog dish, emb bird dog on brn, 1940s, lg 95.00
Jar, strawberry; quail on top, mk, 1950 .....40.00
Novelty, birdbath, w/pk bird, mk, 1950 .....40.00
Pencil holder, cowboy boot form, 1973 .....50.00
Planter, Basketweave, dbl, 1953 .....25.00
Planter, bunny w/carrot, mk, rare 100.00
Planter, carriage, blk w/wht & orange wheels & separate umbrella ..200.00
Planter, cradle, unmk 30.00
Planter, fish, pk w/gr fins, mk, 1955, lg 500.00
Planter, goose w/cart, mk, 1943 .....30.00
Planter, lamb, wht w/big bl bow, mk, 1953 .....50.00
Planter, lamb w/lg bl bow, mk, 1953 .....50.00

Planter, pear form on leaf base, mk, 1957 ....65.00
Planter, quail family among leaves, mk, 1955 ....55.00
Planter, rooster, mk, 1951 ....30.00
Planter, stork beside basket, 1956 ....50.00
Planter, triple-lily, 1950 ....60.00
Planter/bookends, hunting dog w/bird in mouth, mk, 1955, pr ..130.00
Spoon rest, penguin, gr, mk, 1953 ....100.00
Tankard, wht w/hunting scene, mk, 1970 ....50.00
Teapot, Sunburst Gold, mk, w/lid, 1957 ....85.00
Violet pot & saucer, dk gr, 1961 ....16.00
Violet pot & saucer, emb decor, 1950, lg 30.00
Wall pocket, bellows, 1956 ....90.00
Wall pocket, bird on birdbath, 1949, 8" 100.00
Wall pocket, grape cluster on leaves, 7x6" 85.00
Wall pocket, iron on trivet 75.00
Wall pocket, leaf, ivory to red, 1950 ....50.00
Wall pocket, lily, mk, 7½" 65.00
Wall pocket, Mexican emb on gr conical form, 1941 ....60.00
Wall pocket, owls on trivet, 1953 ....75.00
Wall pocket, pear on leaves, 1953 ....60.00
Wall pocket, umbrella form, yel, mk, 1955 ....75.00
Window box, gr, resembles stone wall, rectangular, 1954, lg 20.00

McCoy, J. W.

The J.W. McCoy Pottery Company was incorporated in 1899. It operated under that name in Roseville, Ohio, until 1911 when McCoy entered into a partnership with George Brush, forming the Brush-McCoy Company. During the early years, McCoy produced kitchenware, majolica jardinieres and pedestals, umbrella stands, and cuspidors. By 1903 they had begun to experiment in the field of art pottery and, though never involved to the extent of some of their contemporaries, nevertheless produced several art lines of merit. Their first line was Mt. Pelee, examples of which are very rare today. Two types of glazes were used, matt green and an iridescent charcoal gray. Though the line was primarily mold formed, some pieces evidence the fact that while the clay remained wet and pliable it was pulled and pinched with the fingers to form crests and peaks in a style not unlike George Ohr.

The company rebuilt in 1904 after being destroyed by fire, and other artware was designed. Loy-Nel Art and Renaissance were standard brown lines, hand decorated under the glaze with colored slip. Shapes and artwork were usually simple but effective. Olympia and Rosewood were relief-molded brown-glaze lines decorated in natural colors with wreaths of leaves and berries or simple floral sprays. Although much of this ware was not marked, you will find examples with the die-stamped 'Loy-Nel Art, McCoy,' or an incised line identification.

Corn Line, mug, unmk, from $50 to 70.00
Corn Line, tankard, unmk, 1910, from $300 to 350.00
Loy-Nel-Art, bowl, floral, hdls, mk, 1905, 2", from $150 to 200.00
Loy-Nel-Art, spittoon, floral on brn, mk, 1905, 4½", from $200 to ...300.00
Loy-Nel-Art, vase, floral, integral hdls, mk, 11", from $350 to ..400.00
Loy-Nel-Art, vase, rim-to-hip hdls, unmk, 1905, 8", from $250 to ..300.00
Olympia, jug vase, floral, ftd, 1-hdl, unmk, 1905, sm, from $225 to .275.00
Olympia, punch bowl, mk, 1905, from $500 to 600.00
Rosewood, vase, floral, mk, #41, 1905, 5", from $200 to 250.00
Rosewood, vase, trumpet neck, unmk, pre-1903, 6", from $200 to ...300.00

McKee

McKee Glass was founded in 1853 in Pittsburgh, Pennsylvania. Among their early products were tableware of both the flint and nonflint varieties. In 1888 the company relocated to avail themselves of a source of natural gas, thereby founding the town of Jeannette, Pennsylvania. One of their most famous colored dinnerware lines, Rock Crystal, was manufactured in the 1920s. Production during the '30s and '40s included colored opaque dinnerware, Sunkist reamers, and 'bottoms up' cocktail tumblers as well as a line of black glass vases, bowls, and novelty items. All are popular items with today's collectors, but watch for reproductions. The mark of an authentic 'bottoms up' tumbler is the patent number 77725 embossed beneath the feet. The company was purchased in 1916 by Jeannette Glass, under which name it continues to operate. Our advisor for this category is Lisa Rastello; she is listed in the directory under Illinois. See also Animal Dishes with Covers; Depression Glass; Kitchen Collectibles; Reamers.

Lamp, Danse de Lumiere, in green, $650.00; in pink, $600.00. (Photo courtesy Margaret and Kenn Whitmyer)

Bottoms Down, ale glass, Jade-ite, 5½" 355.00
Bottoms Up, coaster, cream ivory (custard), from $50 to 60.00
Bottoms Up, coaster, Jade-ite 225.00
Bottoms Up, tumbler, butterscotch opal 125.00
Bottoms Up, tumbler, cream ivory (custard), from $90 to 100.00
Bottoms Up, tumbler, Jade-ite, from $125 to 150.00
Bottoms Up, tumbler, lt opal, from $50 to 75.00
Bottoms Up, tumbler, split legs, Jade-ite 285.00
Butter dish, Aztec, NM 35.00
Pitcher, Toltec, tankard, 8½" 110.00
Punch bowl, Aztec, w/stand & 2 cups 60.00
Punch bowl, Tom & Jerry; Jade-ite, w/6 matching mugs 430.00
Vase, Chalaine Blue, shouldered, scalloped rim, 11½" 110.00
Vase, nudes (3 in panels), Jade-ite, 9½" 125.00
Window box, blk, 3¼x9x5" 100.00

Medical Collectibles

The field of medical-related items encompasses a wide area from the primitive bleeding bowl to the X-ray machines of the early 1900s. Other closely related collectibles include apothecary and dental items. Many tools that were originally intended for the pharmacist found their way to the doctor's office, and dentists often used surgical tools when no suitable dental instrument was available. A trend in the late 1700s toward self-medication brought a whole new wave of home-care manuals and 'patent' medical machines for home use. Commonly referred to as 'quack' medical gimmicks, these machines were usually ineffective and occasionally dangerous. Our advisor for this category is Jim Calison; he is listed in the Directory under New York.

Apothecary jar, pressed dmns, frosted lid, 15" 65.00
Bag, doctor's; brn alligator leather 200.00
Book, Changes of Blood in Disease, M Gilbert/Dix translation, 1841 ..66.00
Book, Diseases of Females..., F Churchill, 1950, 632-pg, EX 80.00
Book, Lectures on Diseases in Children, Henoch, NY, 1882, 357-pg ...75.00

Book, Practice of Medicine, J Tyson, leather bound, 1898, EX 34.00
Bowl, bleeding; CI, flat hdl mk WT, 1850s, 5¼" dia 150.00
Bowl, bleeding; tin, oval, scalloped rim, cutout on front, 1850s, 12" ..1,100.00
Brush, bone; neurosurgery, horn hdl, 1860s, 2⅝x1¼" at bristles ..135.00
Case, lancet; fishskin on wood, w/complete contents, 1800s 240.00
Catheter, urinary; Blackwell London, telescopic, 1850s, 4¼" 30.00
Curette, Collin, unplated steel shaft w/ebony hdl, 8-sided, 9⅛" ..60.00

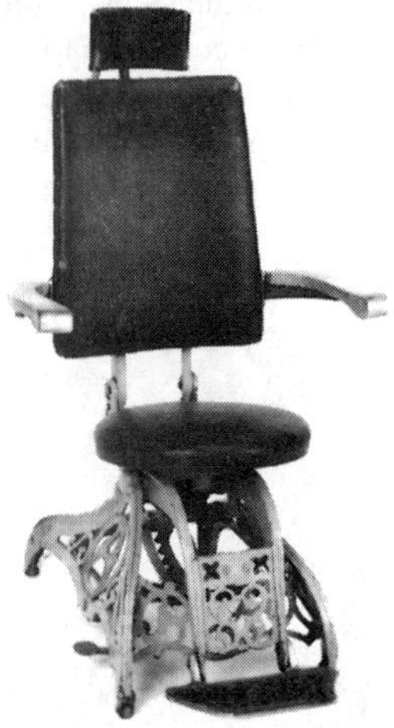

Dental chair, leather and cast iron, 41", EX original condition, $225.00.

Ear trumpet, tin, oval acoustic pc, 5-pc curved shaft, 10" 425.00
Elevator, dental; unplated steel shaft, 8-sided ebony hdl, 1850s, 6" ...90.00
Elevator, dental; unplated steel shaft, 8-sided horn hdl, 1830s, 4" ..115.00
Extractor, comedo; Arnold & Son, sm scoops w/perforations, 5½" ...24.00
Extractor, Couranjou, unplated steel, scissors type, 1850s, 7" 34.00
Extractor, dental; pediatric, unplated steel, checked hdls, 1860s, 5" ...66.00
Extractor, dental; Weiss London, unplated steel, checkered hdls, 6" ..30.00
Fleam, Borwick Cast Steel, folds, 3-blade, brass casing, 1850s, 6" ...68.00
Forceps, arterial; JW Wood, unplated steel, central clamp, 1860s, 5" ...65.00
Forceps, Coxeter's, mk Milliken & Down, unplated steel, 4⅞" 44.00
Forceps, Ferguson London, unplated steel, 1860s, 4⅝" 60.00
Forceps, Levret type, Paris, steel, hdls w/curved ends, 1750, 16" ..2,250.00
Forceps, needle; unplated steel, str hdls, curved tips, 1850s, 4" 38.00
Forceps, unplated steel, ribbed mid-shaft, CW era, 4⅝" 50.00
Knife, amputation; Leiter in Wein, checkered ebony hd, 1860s, 7" ..68.00
Knife, hernia; Arnold & Son London, ebony hdl, 7" 34.00
Lancet, gum; unplated steel, 8-sided shaft, 1860s, 5¼" 45.00
Lancet, phlebotomy; tortoise shell cover, folding, 1830s, EX in case ..65.00
Machine, pill; hardwood w/brass fr, 24 grooves, #3059, 12x5½" .245.00
Mirror, dental; ivory fr, oval, 1850s, 4½" 260.00
Mold, suppository; S Maw, Son & Thompson, 2 brass plates, 5¾" ..70.00
Perforator, unplated steel, scissors type, spear-like tip, 1860s, 10" ..145.00
Probe, bullet; silver, sm knob at 1 end, eye of needle at other, 5" ..60.00
Pump, breast; blown glass, globular reservoir, 1850s, 9½" 145.00
Quack device, produces mild shock to sooth muscles, lg battery/box .120.00
Retinoscope, Hamblin, brass-fr dbl mirror w/central openings, 1⅝" 24.00
Retractor, eye lid; ivory hdl, metal shaft, 1860s, 5½" 65.00
Saw, amputation; Gangeret a Paris, 1820s, 2½" blade+ebony hdl ...345.00
Scalpel, Boyals a Toulouse, ebony hdl, curved blade, 1860s, 7" 36.00
Scalpel, smooth ivory hdl, 1860s, 5⅜" 50.00
Scissors, surgical; unplated steel, triangular hdls w/loops, 1860s, 5" 40.00
Screw, bullet; bulbous, ebony hdl, steel shaft, screw-like tip, 12" 725.00
Stethoscope, monaural, blk wood w/ring on shaft, flared chestpc, 7" .235.00
Stethoscope, monaural, dk fruitwood, flat chestpc, 7" 285.00
Stethoscope, monaural, hard rubber, flat removable earpc, 7" ...210.00
Syringe, ear; S Maw Son on bubber bulb, brass clamp, ivory guard ...44.00
Syringe, lachrimal duct; silver, loop-hdl plunger, 1800s, EXIB ...515.00
Tenaculum, Baker, unplated steel shaft, smooth ebony hdl, 1860s, 6" ...34.00
Test tube holder, steel, baluster finial support, 1860s 65.00
Tongue depressor, silver-tone metal, pseudo hallmks, 5" 34.00
Tooth key, rosewood hdl w/knobs, steel str shaft, 1800s, 5½" 215.00
Tooth key, steel angulated shaft, ivory hdl, 1840s, 5⅞" 335.00
Vaccinator, A Hanbury's, brass, pencil-like, ends remove, 5-prong, 5" ...315.00

Meissen

The Royal Saxon Porcelain Works was established in 1710 in Meissen, Saxony. Under the direction of Johann Frederick Bottger, who in 1708 had developed the formula for the first true porcelain body, fine ceramic figurines with exquisite detail and tableware of the highest quality were produced. Although every effort was made to insure the secrecy of Bottger's discovery, others soon began to copy his ware; and in 1731 Meissen adopted the famous crossed swords trademark to identify their own work. The term 'Dresden ware' is often used to refer to Meissen porcelain, since Bottger's discovery and first potting efforts were in nearby Dresden. See also Onion Pattern.

Candelabrum, Cupid on std, 4 scrolling candle arms, 20" 1,500.00
Compote, floral reserve, turq ribbon border, rtcl rim, 5½x8" 155.00
Cup & saucer, floral, tripod cup, late 19th C, 4" H 125.00
Figurine, Africa allegorical, female on camel, 7" 700.00
Figurine, boy w/eggs in his hat, 7⅛", EX 925.00
Figurine, cherub w/horn & 1 w/music book, 5½" 1,375.00
Figurine, child in night dress w/newspaper hat, on toy horse, 7" ..1,725.00
Figurine, child reading floral-printed book, 2¾" 1,150.00
Figurine, Cupid piercing heart w/arrow, Xd swords, 7¼" 925.00
Figurine, eagle on rocky outcrop, wht porc, 10½" 460.00
Figurine, girl w/flower basket, rprs, 5⅜" 335.00
Figurine, girl w/grapes in apron, J84/124, Xd swords, 7" 415.00
Figurine, lady in struggle w/captor, rprs, 8¾" 1,120.00
Figurine, lady w/bird, Xd swords & star, late 19th C, 6x4" 865.00
Figurine, lady w/flower basket, rprs, 7½" 1,000.00
Figurine, putto catching fish, late 19th C, 4¼x5" 865.00
Figurine, Spring allegorical, lady w/putto & flower basket, 10¼" ..1,550.00
Figurine, Venus w/attendants & infant mermaid, 17½" 3,000.00
Figurine, warrior king w/cherubs, Xd swords, 9½x9¼" 3,450.00
Figurines, lady w/flower basket (he picks roses), 5", pr 650.00
Sculpture, eagle, wht porc, wood base, pnt mk, 16½" 750.00
Tea service, cobalt w/mc flowers & gold, pot+cr/sug+12 c/s+12 plates ..1,100.00
Tea set, Kakiemon, butterfly & flowering shrubs, 20-pc 15,850.00
Vase, cobalt w/gold, snake hdls, wide base, 19¼" 1,150.00
Vase, courting scene on cobalt w/gilt, floral medallions, 9" 350.00

Mercury Glass

Silvered glass, commonly called mercury glass, was a major scientific achievement of the nineteenth century. It was developed by the glass industry, who was searching for an inexpensive substitute for silver. Though very fragile, it was lightweight and would not tarnish. Mercury glass was made with two thin layers, either blown with a double wall or joined in sections, with the space between the walls of the vessel filled with a silvering compound, the perfecting of which involved much experimentation. Colored glass was also silvered. Green, blue, and amber were favored. Occasionally, colors were achieved using clear glass by adding certain chemicals to the compound. Besides hollow ware items, flat surfaces were silvered as well, through a process whereby small facets were cut on the underneath side, then treated with the silvering compound. Sometimes mercury glass was decorated by engraving; it was also hand painted. Besides decorative items such as vases and candlesticks, for instance, utilitarian items — doorknobs, curtain tiebacks, and reflectors for lamps — were also popular. Silvered Christmas ornaments were produced in large quantities.

Condition is an issue, though opinions are divided. While some prefer their acquisitions to be in mint condition, others accept items with flaked silvering. Watch for reproductions marked Made in China. In the listings that follow, all examples are silver unless noted another color.

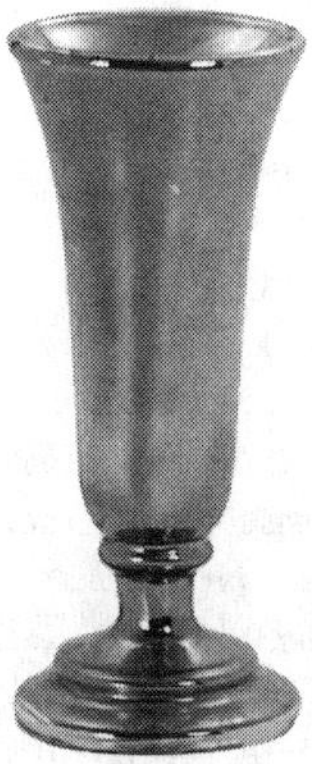

Vase, gold, footed, 8¼", $50.00.

Candlestick, grape leaves w/wreath & Gothic etchings, 7¾" 240.00
Candy container, gun form, 7½" L 28.50
Chalice, 5¾x4" 120.00
Compote, gilt int, wht leaf decor, 6x6⅜" 95.00
Curtain pins, eng vintage, pewter collars, NE Glass, 3½", pr 300.00
Ornament, organ grinder monkey 30.00
Rose bowl, Czechoslovakia, 10" 200.00
Salt cellar, ftd 20.00
Salt cellar, ped ft, 2¾" 46.00
Shade, dmn pattern, bl, 5" dia 300.00
Tie backs, 2½x4", pr 85.00
Vase, HP floral sprays in panel, 10", pr 225.00

Merrimac

Founded in 1897 in Newburyport, Massachusetts, the Merrimac Pottery Company primarily produced gardenware. In 1901, however, they introduced a line of artware that is now attracting the interest of collectors. Marked examples carry an impressed die-stamp or a paper label, each with the firm name and the outline of a sturgeon, the Indian word for Merrimac.

Bud vase, curdled jade/dk gr w/blk accents, trumpet neck, 4" 400.00
Jar, brn speckled, w/lid, paper label, 5¼x3¼" 450.00
Umbrella stand, leaves, tooled/appl on leathery gr label, 23x8½", EX 3,750.00
Vase, dogwood, tooled/appl on leathery gr matt, 7½", EX 1,800.00
Vase, gr & mirrored blk mottle, cylindrical neck, unmk, 10x5" 1,500.00
Vase, gr matt, squat, fleck to rim, 4x9" 1,200.00
Vase, gr/blk speckled semimatte, hdls, 3¼" 375.00

Metlox

Metlox Potteries was founded in 1927 in Manhattan Beach, California. Before 1934 when they began producing the ceramic housewares for which they have become famous, they made ceramic and neon outdoor advertising signs. The company went out of business in 1989.

Well-known sculptor Carl Romanelli designed artware in the late 1930s and early 1940s (and again briefly in the 1950s). His work is especially sought after today.

Some Provincial dinnerware lines can be confusing. There are two 'rooster' lines, Red Rooster (red, orange, and brown) and California Provincial (dark green and burgundy), and there are three 'homestead' lines, Colonial Heritage (red, orange, and brown like the Red Rooster pieces), Homestead Provincial (dark green and burgundy like California Provincial), and Provincial Blue (blue and white). For further information we recommend *Collector's Encyclopedia of Metlox Potteries* by our advisor Carl Gibbs, Jr.; he is listed in the Directory under Texas.

Cookie Jars

Bear, Teddy, w/red heart 250.00
Bear, Uncle Sam, minimum value 950.00
Blue Bird on Pine Cone, glazed, 3-qt 175.00
Blue Bird on Pine Cone, stained, 3-qt 75.00
Calf, says 'Moo,' 3½-qt, 10½", from $300 to 375.00
Cat, Calico, cream w/bl ribbon 150.00
Chickadee, Cookie Creations Series, 2-qt 85.00
Chicken, Mother Hen, wht 150.00
Clown, yel, 3-qt 150.00
Cookie Girl, color glazed 80.00
Cow, purple w/wht flowers, yel butterfly & bell 600.00
Daisy Cookie Canister, 3½-qt 45.00
Dina-Stegosaurus, rose 175.00
Dog, bl gingham 225.00
Dog, wht 225.00
Drummer Boy, 2½-qt, minimum value 500.00
Duck, Francine 275.00
Dutch Girl, minimum value 350.00
Easter Bunny, solid chocolate, minimum value 350.00
Elephant, 11", minimum value 750.00
Feathered Friends, Cookie Creations Series 85.00
Gingerbread, bsk, 3½-qt 125.00
Gingerbread, glazed, 3½-qt 175.00
Hen & Chick, minimum value 350.00
Humpty Dumpty, no ft , 11", minimum value 500.00
Jolly Chef, bl or blk eyes, 11", ea 425.00
Lamb, says 'Baa,' 3½-qt 125.00
Lamb w/Flowers, 2½-qt 325.00
Little Piggy, decorated 175.00
Little Red Riding Hood, minimum value 1,250.00
Mammy, Cook, red 850.00
Mammy, Scrub Woman, minimum value 2,000.00
Miller's Sack 75.00
Mona-Monoclonius, French Blue 175.00
Mother Goose, 2-qt 325.00
Mushroom Cottage 350.00
Nun, minimum value 1,000.00
Owl, bl, 2½-qt 75.00
Owls on Stump, bsk, 2½-qt 55.00
Parrot, minimum value 300.00
Pelican, Salty 250.00
Pig, Slenderella 150.00
Pineapple, 3¾-qt 125.00
Pumpkin, stem on lid 175.00
Rabbit on Cabbage, 3-qt, 10" 150.00
Raccoon Cookie Bandit, color-glazed 150.00
Rex-Tyrannosaurus Rex, aqua 175.00
Rocking Horse, 11", minimum value 650.00
Sammy Seal, minimum value 500.00
Santa, standing 750.00
Santa, standing, Black, minimum value 750.00
Santa Head, minimum value 400.00
Squirrel on Pine Cone, stained, 3-qt, 11" 95.00
Squirrel w/Acorn, glazed 425.00

Topsy, bl polka-dots 575.00
Tulip Time, Cookie Creations Series, 2-qt 85.00
Wally Walrus, cream w/bl tie & hat 250.00
Whale, bl 450.00
Wheat Shock, 4-qt 125.00

Dinnerware

Antique Grape, creamer, 10-oz 28.00
Antique Grape, cup, 7-oz 12.00
Antique Grape, saucer, 6⅛" 4.00
Antique Grape, sugar bowl, w/lid, 10-oz 30.00
Autumn Berry, bowl, fruit; 5½" 12.00
Autumn Berry, butter dish, w/lid 55.00
Autumn Berry, shakers, ea 12.00
California Aztec, bowl, salad; minimum value 300.00
California Aztec, bowl, twin vegetable 200.00
California Aztec, mug, cocoa 40.00
California Confetti, bowl, fruit; 5¼" 15.00
California Confetti, bowl, vegetable; 9¼" 50.00
California Confetti, coaster 25.00
California Confetti, creamer 30.00
California Confetti, jam & jelly 55.00
California Confetti, tumbler 38.00
California Freeform, cup 18.00
California Freeform, plate, dinner 25.00
California Freeform, saucer 5.00

California Ivy, bowl, divided vegetable; $50.00.

California Ivy, bowl, salad; 11¼" 90.00
California Ivy, butter dish, w/lid 60.00
California Ivy, celery dish 45.00
California Ivy, cup, 6-oz 12.00
California Ivy, plate, bread & butter; 6½" 9.00
California Ivy, plate, luncheon; 9¼" 13.00
California Ivy, tidbit tray, 2-tier 50.00
California Peach Blossom, celery dish 45.00
California Peach Blossom, chop plate 75.00
California Peach Blossom, lug soup 25.00
California Peach Blossom, plate, dinner 15.00
California Provincial, bowl, med vegetable; 10" 55.00
California Provincial, coffee crafe, w/lid, 44-oz (7-cup) 140.00
California Provincial, creamer, 6-oz 32.00
California Provincial, pepper mill 65.00
California Provincial, plate, salad; 7½" 15.00
California Provincial, platter, oval, 11" 50.00
California Provincial, teapot, w/lid, 42-oz (7-cup) 135.00
California Provincial, tumbler, 11-oz 45.00
Colorstax, bowl, cereal; 6½" 14.00
Colorstax, bowl, salad; 13" 65.00
Colorstax, butter dish 50.00
Colorstax, pitcher, water; 2-qt 55.00
Colorstax, plate, dinner; 10½" 13.00
Colorstax, platter, oval, 16" 50.00
Homestead Provincial, bowl, salad; 11⅛" 95.00
Homestead Provincial, creamer, 6-oz 32.00
Homestead Provincial, cup, 6-oz 13.00
Homestead Provincial, gravy boat, 1-pt 50.00
Homestead Provincial, saucer, 6⅛" 5.00
Homestead Provincial, soup tureen, w/lid 450.00
Lotus, bowl, salad; 13½" 95.00
Lotus, chip & dip, shell 60.00
Lotus, chop plate, extra lg, 17" 75.00
Lotus, cup, demitasse 25.00
Lotus, gravy 40.00
Lotus, platter, banana leaf, 20" 65.00
Navajo, bowl, cereal; 7¼" 16.00
Navajo, lug soup 22.00
Navajo, plate, bread & butter; 6½" 9.00
Provincial Blue, casserole, w/chicken lid, 1-qt 10-oz 155.00
Provincial Blue, jam jar 75.00
Provincial Blue, lug soup, 5" 28.00
Provincial Blue, pitcher, water; 2¼-qt 95.00
Provincial Blue, plate, dinner; 10" 20.00
Provincial Blue, platter, oval, 13½" 65.00
Provincial Blue, shakers, ea 16.00
Red Rooster Provincial, bowl, fruit; 6" 15.00
Red Rooster Provincial, bowl soup; 8" 24.00
Red Rooster Provincial, buffet server, 12¼" 75.00
Red Rooster Provincial, cruet, vinegar; w/lid, 7-oz 35.00
Red Rooster Provincial, cup, 7-oz 12.00
Red Rooster Provincial, platter, oval, 16" 80.00
Red Rooster Provincial, saucer, 6⅛" 4.00
Red Rooster Provincial, tumbler, 11-oz 40.00
San Fernando (Vernonware), bowl, salad; 12½" 65.00
San Fernando (Vernonware), coffeepot, w/lid, 8-cup 90.00
San Fernando (Vernonware), gravy boat, w/attached stand, ¾-pt ..35.00
Sculptured Daisy, bowl, vegetable; divided, 7" dia 40.00
Sculptured Daisy, buffet server, 12¼" dia 65.00
Sculptured Daisy, pitcher, 2-qt 70.00
Sculptured Daisy, platter, oval, 11" 40.00
Sculptured Grape, baker, oval, 10¼" 55.00
Sculptured Grape, pitcher, 2¼-qt 75.00
Tickled Pink (Vernonware), chop plate, 13" 35.00
Tickled Pink (Vernonware), cup 9.00
Tickled Pink (Vernonware), plate, bread & butter; 6¼" 7.00
Tickled Pink (Vernonware), sugar bowl, w/lid 25.00
True Blue (Vernonware), bowl, rim soup; 8⅛" 18.00
True Blue (Vernonware), cheese server, w/lid 65.00
True Blue (Vernonware), plate, salad; 7½" 10.00
True Blue (Vernonware), salad fork & spoon 55.00
True Blue (Vernonware), sugar bowl, w/lid, 8-oz 28.00
True Blue (Vernonware), tureen, soup; w/lid, 3-qt 165.00
Vernon Antiqua (Vernonware), baker, oval, 12⅛" 50.00
Vernon Antiqua (Vernonware), casserole w/lid, 2-qt 95.00
Vernon Antiqua (Vernonware), mug, 10-oz 22.00
Vernon Antiqua (Vernonware), platter, med, oval, 11⅛" 45.00
Vernon Antiqua (Vernonware), teapot, 4½-cup 110.00
Woodland Gold, bowl, vegetable; 8⅛" 35.00
Woodland Gold, coffeepot, w/lid, 8-cup 95.00
Woodland Gold, mug, 8-oz 22.00
Woodland Gold, platter, oval, 11" 35.00

Disney Figurines

Alice in Wonderland 400.00
Baby Mouse (Cinderella) 500.00

Bambi, looking left, lg 165.00
Bambi, miniature, 2½" 265.00
Bashful (Snow White) 250.00
Cinderella, as peasant girl 500.00
Donald Duck, w/guitar 300.00
Donald Duck (Three Caballeros) 350.00
Dumbo, miniature, 1¾" 200.00
Dumbo, seated w/bonnet, front legs up 225.00
Figaro (Pinocchio), standing w/1 ft up 225.00
Gus (Cinderella) 250.00
Happy (Snow White) 250.00
Huey, Dewey & Louie (Donald's nephews), baseball, miniature, ea ...275.00
Huey, Dewey & Louie (Donald's nephews), waving, ea 175.00
Jiminy Cricket, miniature, 1¼" 225.00
Lady (Lady & the Tramp), sitting, miniature, 1¾" 125.00
March Hare (Alice in Wonderland) 350.00
Mickey Mouse, waving, miniature, 2½" 300.00
Minnie Mouse 300.00
Owl (Bambi) 200.00
Peter Pan, standing 450.00
Pinocchio, miniature, 2" 250.00
Pluto, sitting 250.00
Sneezy (Snow White) 250.00
Sprite (Fantasia) 250.00
Three Little Pigs, miniature, 1¼", ea 200.00
Thumper, thumping w/eyes closed 125.00
Thumper's Girlfriend, sm 125.00
Timothy Mouse (Dumbo) 250.00
Tinker Bell (Peter Pan) 500.00
Trusty (Lady & the Tramp), miniature, 3" 250.00
Tweedle Dee or Tweedle Dum, ea 250.00
Unicorn (Fantasia) 325.00
Walrus (Alice in Wonderland) 325.00
Wendy (Peter Pan) 400.00

Miniatures

Bird, on branch, 4⅝" 70.00
Bird, sitting w/tail up, 6¼" 35.00
Burro, sitting or standing, 3", ea 45.00
Circus Horse, front legs raised, 6" 100.00
Dinosaur, 4½" 195.00
Duck, head down, 3" 35.00
Fawn, 5½" 50.00
Flamingo, head down, 6¼" 50.00
Lizard, 9½" 120.00
Otter 115.00
Sea Horse, 4½" 75.00
Squirrel, 2" 35.00
Terrier, 12½" 95.00

Nostalgia Line

Reminiscent of the late 1800s and early 1900s, the Nostalgia line contained models of locomotives, gramaphones, early autos, stage coaches, and baby carriages. There were also wagons and carts pulled by horses or donkeys, sometimes with separate drivers and passengers. The line was produced from the late 1940s through the 1960s.

American Royal Horse, Arabian, 7¾x8¾" 115.00
American Royal Horse, Dobbin, 9x11" 105.00
American Royal Horse, Pony, 6x7½" 95.00
American Royal Horse, Thoroughbred, lg, 8¾x8½" 115.00
Amish Father, Mother or Child, ea 75.00
Chevrolet 85.00
Delivery Wagon 85.00
Grandmother Clock 60.00
Ice Wagon 80.00
Locomotive 65.00
Powder Horn w/Strap 50.00
Santa 105.00
Stagecoach 100.00
Train set, 3-pc 165.00
Trolley Car 95.00
Wagon Master 70.00

Poppets

From the mid-'60s through the mid-'70s, Metlox produced a line of 'Poppets,' eighty-eight in all, representing characters ranging from royalty and professionals to a Salvation Army group. They came with a name tag; some had paper labels, others backstamps.

Alaskan Girl, 5" 35.00
Angelina, angel, 7⅝" 55.00
Casey, policeman 45.00
Cigar Store Indian, 8¾" 55.00
Dutch Girl, 5" 35.00
Emma the Cook, 8" 45.00
Friar Tuck, 6½" 45.00
Jackie, choir boy #3 ....45.00
Minnie, mermaid 55.00
Molly, Salvation Army tambourine girl, 6⅜" 35.00
Mother Goose, w/4" bowl 65.00
Mother Nature, 6¾" 60.00
Myra & Mattie, mother & daughter, 8¼" 60.00

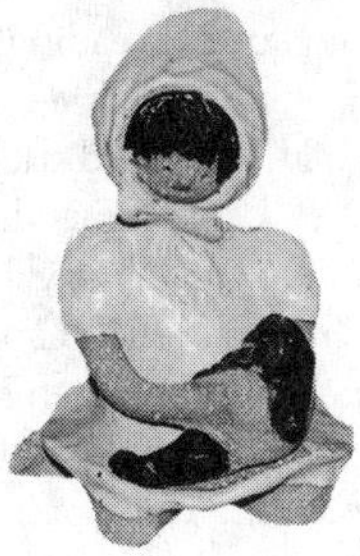

Nancy, girl with dog, 6¾", $35.00.

Pamela, girl in gown 45.00
St Francis, 7¾" 60.00
Tina, costumed girl, 8½" 55.00

Mettlach

In 1836 Nicholas Villeroy and Eugene Francis Boch, both of whom were already involved in the potting industry, formed a partnership and established a stoneware factory in an old restored abbey in Mettlach, Germany. Decorative stoneware with in-mold relief was their specialty, steins in particular. Through constant experimentation, they developed innovative methods of decoration. One process, called chromolith, involved inlaying colorful mosaic designs into the body of the ware. Later underglaze printing from copper plates was used. Their stoneware was of high quality, and their steins won many medals at the St. Louis Expo and early world's fairs. Most examples are marked with an incised castle and the name 'Mettlach.' The numbering system indicates size, date, stock number, and decorator. Production was halted by a fire in 1921; the factory was not rebuilt.

Key:
L — liter PUG — print under glaze
POG — print over glaze tl — thumb lift

#24, stein, relief: hunting scenes, dog head finial, rpl tl, 1L 200.00
#32, stein, relief: Gambrinus scene, keyhole base, tower hdl, .5L ..150.00
#64, stein, HP: family crest, pewter lid, 2L 450.00
#171, stein, relief: tan/cream/bl, .25L 150.00
#235, stein, etch: people dancing, inlaid lid, .5L 330.00
#285, stein, transfer/HP: eagle, St Louis World's Fair, .5L, NM .375.00
#485, stein, relief: musicians in vines, inlaid lid, .5L 250.00
#675, stein, bbl w/marble finish, inlaid lid, .5L 115.00
#1005, stein, relief: 3 drinking scenes, brns, inlaid lid, .5L 220.00
#1044-102A, plaque, PUG: ducks & flowers, stain, 12" 120.00
#1044-291, plaque, PUG: Stadtthor Esslingen, 12" 245.00
#1044-484, plaque, PUG: Manderscheid, 12" 350.00
#1124, stein, etch/glazed: man & lady portraits, Warth, rpr, 2L .485.00
#1161, stein, etch: ladies/Prussian eagle/state shields, Warth, 7L ..4,800.00
#1266, stein, relief: 3 drinking scenes, inlaid lid, .25L 140.00
#1365, plaque, etch: castle, M gold, 17" 1,400.00
#1384/#1385, plaque, etch: warrior & cavalier, 14½", pr 2,550.00
#1440, vase, relief: appl floral, 2½" 140.00
#1477, stein, etch: dwarfs w/grapes, inlaid lid, .5L 400.00
#1525-1077, stein, PUG: man w/trumpet, pewter lid, Schlitt, .5L ..175.00
#1526, stein, HP: man shooting rifle/verse, pewter lid, 1L 300.00
#1526, stein, HP: Student Society crest, pewter lid, .5L 230.00
#1526, stein, HP: 3 blk cats by stein, pewter lid, .5L, NM 500.00
#1526, stein, transfer: Staten Island Quartet, 1861-1911, .4L 80.00
#1526-1101, stein, PUG: barmaid w/animals, pewter lid, .5L 280.00
#1526-1272, stein, PUG: night watchman & student, no lid, .5L ..110.00
#1561, stein, etch/relief: dog portrait, boar inlay lid, .5L, EX 300.00
#1577, stein, etch: Gasthaus scene, pewter lid, 4.5L 2,000.00
#1629, vase, etch/glazed: repeating design, flaw, 4" 100.00
#1794, stein, etch: Bismark, inlaid lid, sm rpr, .5L, NM 425.00
#1801, stein, glazed threading, repeating design, inlaid lid, .5L .345.00
#1818, stein, etch/relief: drinking scene, pewter lid, Gorig, 6.2L .1,275.00
#1909, stein, HJP: billiard sticks/balls/bowling pins, rpr, .35L 175.00
#1914, stein, etch: 4F Turner design, eagle tl, inlaid lid, .5L, NM ..400.00
#1999, stein, etch/relief: cavaliers & vine, inlaid lid, .5L, EX 120.00
#2001K, stein, etch/relief: Commerce, inlaid lid, .5L 885.00
#2002, stein, etch: Munchen skyline & verse, inlaid lid, .5L 425.00
#2005, stein, etch: people dining, inlaid lid, .5L 450.00
#2008, stein, etch: Trumpeter of Sackingen, inlaid lid, rpr, .5L .350.00
#2009, stein, etch: lovers, inlaid lid, line, .5L 330.00
#2033, stein, relief: Tree of Life w/deer, inlaid lid, .5L, NM 465.00
#2035, stein, etch: festive scene, inlaid lid, .3L 350.00
#2082, stein, etch: Wilhelm Tell & son, inlaid lid, .5L 1,275.00
#2091, stein, etch: St Florian puts out fire, inlaid lid, .5L, EX ...500.00
#2092, stein, etch: dwarf adjusts clock, inlaid lid, Schlitt, .5L, NM ...500.00
#2093, stein, etch: cards, inlaid lid, .5L 835.00
#2099, stein, etch: Diogenes, inlaid lid, rpr, 3L 1,155.00
#2100, stein, etch: Germans meet Romans, inlaid lid, Schlitt, .3L ...575.00
#2130, stein, cameo/relief: Gambrinus, inlaid lid, .5L, EX 575.00
#2134, stein, etch: dwarf in nest, inlaid lid, Schlitt, .3L, NM 450.00
#2134, stein, etch: dwarf in nest, inlaid lid, Schlitt, .5L 2,000.00
#2140, stein, PUG: Newport, inlaid lid, rare, .5L, NM 925.00
#2181-957, stein, PUG: barmaid, pewter lid, Schlitt, .25L 175.00
#2204, stein, etch/relief: Prussian eagle, inlaid lid, .5L 685.00
#2204, stein, etch/relief: Prussian eagle, inlaid lid, 1L 1,200.00
#2235, stein, etch: barmaid w/target, targets by hdl, 1L 995.00
#2236, pass cup, etch/relief: couples, Schlitt, rpr, 6" 330.00
#2327-1414, beaker, PUG: Snow White & 7 Dwarfs, .25L, EX .120.00
#2358, stein, relief: drinking scene, cob finial, .5L 350.00
#2362, plaque, etch: Heidelburg Castle, 17½", NM 700.00
#2479, stein, cameo: castle scenes, tower body, inlaid lid, .5L ...550.00
#2580, stein, etch: activities at castle, tower body, 1L 1,045.00
#2602, punch bowl, cameo/relief: women & children/grapes, rpr, 5.75L ...925.00
#2690, stein, etched/relief: cavaliers, inlaid lid, Quidenus, 1.4L .1,675.00
#2765, stein, etch: knight on horse, figural tower roof lid, 1L ..3,250.00
#2796, stein, etch: Heidelberg, inlaid lid, rpr, 3L, EX 1,445.00

#2814, punch bowl, Nouveau maidens among grapevines, paneled lower half, handles, ca 1905, 9¾x11", $1,265.00.

#2833A, stein, etch: man & linden tree, inlaid lid, .3L 335.00
#2833A, stein, etch: man holding hat by trees, inlaid lid, .5L ...440.00
#2833B, stein, etch: men rest under tree, inlaid lid, .3L 330.00
#2833B, stein, etch: men rest under tree, inlaid lid, .5L 360.00
#2833C, stein, etch: river scene, inlaid lid, .3L 445.00
#2833E, stein, etch: soldiers, inlaid lid, .3L 445.00
#2856 I, vase, ethed/glazed: repeating design, 10" 430.00
#2857, vase, etch/glazed: repeating design, 10½" 330.00
#2921, stein, etch: hunters at campfire, inlaid lid, 2.4L 800.00
#2962, cup & saucer, gold/cream/bl, 2¼", 6" 175.00
#2974, punch bowl, etch: Art Nouveau, w/lid/underplate, 4.5L, EX ..1,000.00
#3001, stein, etch: man w/beer glass, pewter lid, rpr, .5L 220.00
#3073-419, stein, transfer/HP: Bavaria, owl inlaid lid, .5L 600.00
#3170, stein, etch: people in snowy night, Hohlwein, .5L, EX ..275.00
#3183, plaque, etch: Burg Nurnberg, lt wear, 17" 1,050.00
#3220, stein, etch: couple dancing, rpr, .5L 385.00
#3248, stein, etch/relief: Art Nouveau, pewter lid, .5L 425.00
#3364, bowl, salad; etch: Art Nouveau design, 4x8½", NM 435.00
#7032, plaque, cameo of lady on gr, dtd 1900, 7½x8¾" 350.00

Microscopes

The microscope has taken on many forms during its 250-year evolutionary period. The current collectors' market primarily includes examples from England, those surplused from institutions, and continental beginner and intermediate forms which sold through Sears Roebuck & Company and other retailers of technical instruments. Earlier examples have brass maintubes which are unpainted. Later, more common examples are all black with brass or silver knobs and horseshoe-shaped bases. Early and more complex forms are the most valuable; these always had hardwood cases to house the delicate instruments and their accessories. Instruments were never polished during use, and those that have been polished to use as decorator pieces are of little interest to most avid collectors. Our advisor for this category is Dale Beeks; he is listed in the Directory under Iowa.

B Pike & Sons, NY, Barlimb, w/optics, 1870s, EX 550.00
French student's, brass, ivory slides, 1880s, 9¾-10¾", G 450.00
Gundlach, #582, 10", ca 1865, EX in old (not orig) case 900.00
Hartnack, Paris, brass, ca 1860s, mahog case, EX 900.00
Henry Crouch, brass, 1800s, 14", w/case/accessories 500.00
John W Sidle, Bausch & Lomb, japanned, 1880s, w/mahog box, EX ...750.00
Leitz, fish-eye condenser, #82146, 1900s, EX w/case 450.00
Leitz, metallurgical polarizing, w/case/attachments, G 450.00

Leitz Wetzlar, brass, 3-turret, 1899, EX in case 400.00
Martin drum type, brass, rack & pinion, unmk, 1800s, w/case, EX ..1,100.00
R&J Beck, top-mtd botanical, brass, 3 magnifiers, 19th C, EXIB 400.00
RB Tolles Boston, student's, brass w/CI stand, 15", w/case, EX 1,000.00
Schrauer of NY, homeopathic, brass, 3 lenses, tools, 19th C ..1,200.00
Smith Beck & Beck, brass, chain-drive focus, ca 1855, EX 775.00
W Watson Edinburgh student's, brass, tripod base, ca 1910s, NMIB .1,150.00
Zeiss, w/reflected bright/dark field, w/stage, complete 1,000.00

Midwestern Glass

As early as 1814, blown glass was made in Ohio. By 1835 glasshouses in Michigan were producing similar pattern-molded types that have long been highly regarded by collectors. During the latter part of the nineteenth century, all six of the states of the Northwest Territory were mass producing the pressed-glass tableware patterns that were then in vogue. Various types of art glass were produced in the area until after the turn of the century. Items listed here are attributed to the Midwest by certain physical characteristics known to be indigenous to that part of the country. See also Findlay Onyx; Greentown Glass; Libbey; Mantua; Zanesville Glass. Our advisor for this category is Mark Vuono; he is listed in the Directory under Connecticut.

Bottle, club; dk bl-aqua, 16 left-swirl ribs, appl mouth, 8" 210.00
Bottle, club; yel-olive, 24 right-swirl ribs, pontil, 8¾" 4,800.00
Bottle, dk red-amber, globular, 24 left-swirl ribs, 8¼" 500.00
Bottle, golden yel-amber, globular, 24 right-swirl ribs, 7¾" 550.00
Bottle, med amber, globular, rolled rim, pontil, 11½" 575.00
Bottle, nursing; aqua, faint broken swirl, wear, 6⅜" 50.00
Bottle, yel-amber w/olive tone, 24 left-swirl ribs, 7⅝" 375.00
Chestnut flask, amber, 15-Dmn, wear, 7⅜" 1,485.00
Chestnut flask, golden amber, 24 left-swirl ribs, pontil, 5" 425.00
Chestnut flask, yel-amber, 24 vertical ribs, pontil, 4¾" 275.00
Compote, med amber, appl ft & knob stem, pontil, 3⅞" 3,500.00
Fish bowl, pressed flared base, scratches, 16⅜" 195.00
Flip, dk bl-aqua, 24 broken left-swirl ribs, 4⅝" 1,450.00
Mug, dk red-amber, appl hdl, tooled rim, pontil, 4¼" 4,100.00
Pan, med amber, folded rim, pontil, 1820-30, 6¼" 1,100.00
Pitkin flask, lt apple gr, 14 right-swirl pattern, 4½" 650.00
Salt cellar, dk bl-aqua, 24 vertical ribs, dbl ogee, 3½" 4,500.00

Militaria

Because of the wide and varied scope of items available to collectors of militaria, most tend to concentrate mainly on the area or areas that interest them most or that they can afford to buy. Some items represent a major investment and because of their value have been reproduced. Extreme caution should be used when purchasing Nazi items. Every badge, medal, cap, uniform, dagger, and sword that Nazi Germany issued is being reproduced today. Some repros are crude and easily identified as fakes, while others are very well done and difficult to recognize as reproductions. Purchases from WWII veterans are usually your safest buys. Reputable dealers or collectors will normally offer a money-back guarantee on Nazi items purchased from them. There are a number of excellent Third Reich reference books available in bookstores at very reasonable prices. Study them to avoid losing a much larger sum spent on a reproduction. Our advisor for this category is Ron L. Willis; he is listed in the Directory under Florida.

Key: insg — insignia

Imperial German

Badge, wound; gold wash, NM 75.00
Buckle, Enlisted, NP inset on brass, Gott Mit Uns, EX 25.00
Canteen, gray wool cover, leather harness 25.00
Helmet, spiked, steel, eagle hat plate, lobster tail bk, G- 275.00

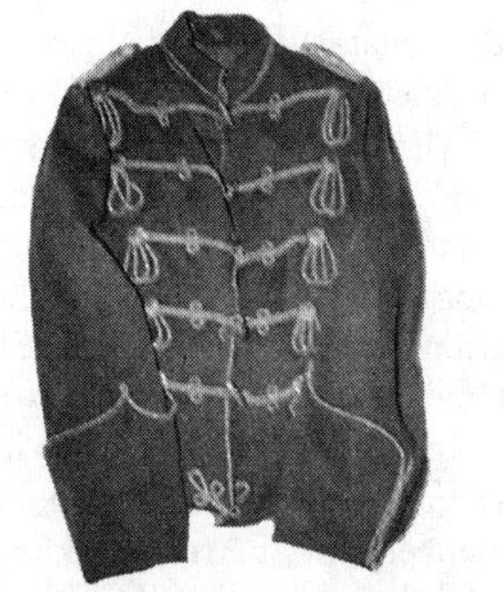

Hussar tunic, Lieutenant rank shoulder boards, medium blue wool, EX, $185.00.

Knapsack, WWI Army, field gray canvas w/leather straps 75.00
Medal, Braunsweig Waterloo, bronze, dtd 1815, rare 375.00
Medal, Franco-Prussian War Commemorative, bronze, lacks ribbon ...30.00
Medal, Kaiser Wilhelm I Veterans Assoc, emb portrait on brass ..25.00
Medal, Life Saving, silver, w/ribbon, M 150.00
Medal, Order of Military Merit, 4th Class, silver/bl enamel/gold ..185.00
Medal, 12 Military Long Service, gilt bronze, w/ribbon 25.00
Medal, 1915 War Service Cross, gray metal, w/ribbon 25.00
Spike helmet cover, Enlisted, field gray cotton, attached spike cover ...130.00
Tunic, dress; dk bl wool w/red accents, cotton lined, EX 80.00

Third Reich

Armband, SA Sports, embr/sewn composite on red cotton 60.00
Badge, Infantry assault, bronze, stamped construction 55.00
Badge, Navy Blockade Runner Combat, SP, solid bk, hallmk 165.00
Badge, Navy Patrol/Torpedo Boat War, 1st pattern, silver/gilt ...285.00
Badge, SA Sports, bronze, hallmk 27.50
Badge, Silesian Eagle, 1st class, silver eagle w/blk enamel 95.00
Bar, Army Close Combat, gray metal, hallmk 85.00
Buckle, belt; Army Enlisted, steel w/field gray, brn leather tab 25.00
Buckle, belt; Luftwaffe Officer, aluminum w/gilt eagle 75.00
Cap, Luftwaffe, folding side, gray wool w/embr eagle/cockade insg 120.00
Dagger, Hitler Youth Leader, silvered furniture, dmn insgn, w/scabbard ..2,500.00
Flight suit, Luftwaffe, blk leather w/zippers, EX 375.00
Gaiters, Army, gray canvas w/leather straps, VG 20.00
Goggles, Army Ski Troop, slotted metal eye covers, flannel mask ..35.00
Greatcoat, Army General, gray wool w/gr & red, shoulder boards, EX ..850.00
Grenade, Army practice stick, trn wood shafts w/metal collars 35.00
Hat, Nazi N Africa campaign, gr w/red liner, VG 125.00
Hat, Police, gray wool w/fur flaps, eagle front plate, 1943 ....135.00
Helmet, Army Chicken Wire M35, gray camo, w/liner, EX 435.00
Helmet, Luftschutz M34 Square Dip, dk bl, winged insg, w/liner 265.00
Helmet, Waffen SS M35, field gray w/SS runics/swastika, w/liner ...2,500.00
Helmet, Waffen SS M42, field gray, runics decal, complete 550.00
Insignia, Army Breast Eagle, enlisted, flat silver on gray wool 20.00
Insignia, Luftwaffe Eagle, enlisted, gray embr on gray wool 20.00
Knife, Hitler Youth, gray metal hilt, compo grips w/dmn insg ...100.00
Leaflet, propaganda; Sucker You Believed It..., dropped on Am troops ...45.00
Log book, Luftwaffe Official Pilot's, many entries, 1944 ....285.00
Medal, Mother's Cross, silver, w/bowed ribbon 45.00
Photo, Hitler in open car, blk & wht, 3x2" 20.00
Plate, mess; Luftwaffe Officer, wht porc w/eagle, 9¾" 40.00
Shorts, Army Tropical, olive cotton twill 125.00
Shoulder boards, Army Transport Hauptmann, silver trees on bl wool ...20.00
Stickpin, Hitler Youth, red/wht/blk enameling 15.00

Japanese

Banner, WWII Military Youth Group, rising sun, 34x26", EX ...175.00
Bayonet frog, WWII, brn leather, brass rail buckle 35.00
Belt, dress sword; WWII Navy Officer, dk bl leather, brass buckle ..175.00
Binoculars, WWII, 7x50 power, lg fr, tube covers, strap, w/case ...90.00
Booklet, identity; WWII, Japanese character inscription, EX 25.00
Bowl, mess; WWII Army, wht porc w/star, 7" 35.00
Bugle, WWII Army, brass, complete w/mouthpc 130.00
Coat, WWII Army, khaki twill w/fur lining, gr compo buttons ...85.00
Goggles, WWII Pilot's, aluminum fr, elastic strap, VG 200.00
Grenade, hand; WWII, pottery, brn mat w/rubber collar insert ...75.00
Grenade, rifle; WWII, hollow charge style w/tail stabilizer 165.00
Helmet, flight; WWII, brn leather, hard ear flaps, star insg, VG .80.00
Helmet, WWII Army, brn khaki, lacking front star, VG 115.00
Helmet, WWII Army, khaki canvas, 5-pointed star insg 200.00
Medallion, table; WWII China War, bronze, officer w/field glasses ...180.00
Tray, rising sun flag/cherry blossoms, lacquerware, 8½" 15.00

Russia/Soviet

Badge, hat; Imperial Era, bronze w/eagle, St Geo & dragon shield ..25.00
Badge, hat; Imperial Militia, cross w/Nicholas II, prong bk 70.00
Badge, Imperial Era Tercentenary Cross, gilt w/mc enamel, rare ..350.00
Binoculars, brass w/blk lacquer, clear optics, ca 1915 ....95.00
Book, identification; red cover w/emb gilt, 1980s, M 25.00
Breast star, Order of Bogdan Khmelnitsky, 3rd class, silver star .300.00
Buckle, belt; Imperial Era Artillery, eagle/artillery tubes 60.00
Cap, side; Marine Enlisted, blk wool, star insg, 1990 ....20.00
Hat, Army Officer Papakha, gray fur, star insg, gold trim, 1980s ..55.00
Hat, visor; Army, khaki twill, bl wool piping, 1980s 50.00
Helmet, Army, gr finish, compo fabric liner, ca 1960, EX 35.00
Helmet, pilot; blk leather w/cushion top, pile lining, 1963, EX ...90.00
Helmet, Tank Crew, gray cotton w/cushion top, chin strap, 1961 .125.00
Helmet, WWII Model 1936, old khaki finish, sm top comb, EX ...150.00
Insignia, Imperial Era Starburst, gilt brass w/eagle/wreath 125.00
Jetton, Imperial Era, crown & pierced rnd silver plancet w/enameling ...90.00
Medal, Imperial Era Campaigns in Central Asia, bronze, w/ribbon ..110.00
Medal, Imperial Era Crimean War, bronze, w/ribbon 85.00
Medal, Imperial Era War w/Turkey, bronze, dk patina, lacks ribbon ...80.00
Medal, Imperial Era 200 Anniversary of St Petersburg, bronze 30.00
Medal, Imperial Order of Compassionate Heart, gilt/enamel cross/eagle ...120.00
Medal, Imperial Red Cross for Russo-Japanese War, SP w/enamel ...40.00
Medal, Order of Glory, 3rd class, WWII era, SP w/red, w/ribbon ..100.00
Medal, Order of Lenin, w/ribbon 600.00
Medal, Order of Red Banner of Labor, gilt/silver/enameled 35.00
Medal, St George Cross, WWI Era, hallmk 90.00
Medallion, Imperial Era Commemorative, Nicholas I, bl jasper ...50.00
Shoulder boards, KGB Intelligence Officer, bl flecks on gray, 1984, M .20.00
Tunic, Navy Officer, bl cotton, gilt buttons, 1990 ....30.00

United States

Drum, Civil War era, patriotic eagle, sunburst, and flowing ribbon painted 'REG' and 'INFANTRY,' 11½x16½", EX, $325.00.

Badge, WWII Army Glider, wreath & star device, mk Sterling ...65.00
Blanket, WWII Army, khaki wool, EX 20.00
Boots, Korean War Model 1944, winter combat, blk rubber, MIB ...60.00
Boots, WWII Army Paratrooper, brn leather, unissued 150.00
Breeches, WWI Army, khaki wool, EX 20.00
Canteen, Civil War, cedarwood w/iron bands, cvd w/name & 1863 .3,000.00
Canteen, Spanish-Am War Era, canvas over tin, cork stopper 60.00
Chevrons, Marine Corps 1st Sergeant, gold stripes on red, 1890s ...40.00
Coat, trench; WWII Army Officer, khaki cotton twill, dbl breasted, EX ..20.00
Drum, Civil War Era, pnt eagle (flaking), E Baack NY label, EX ..800.00
Gas mask, WWII Mark V, complete w/carrier, unissued, M 75.00
Handcuffs, Indian War Era Marine Corps, Western pattern, 1880s ..95.00
Hat, Hardee, bugle insg/brass eagle/shield plate, EX 1,500.00
Hat, Vietnam War tropical combat, camo cotton, ca 1968, M 20.00
Hat, visor; Army Signal Troups M1902, dk bl wool, eagle buttons, EX ..65.00
Hat cord, Civil War Union Officer, gold bullion/blk silk 85.00
Helmet, pith; US Model 1892 w/blk plume & braid, Horstmann Bros, G ..350.00
Helmet, pith; US Model 1892 w/gold plume & braid, G 700.00
Helmet, pith; US Model 1892 w/red plume & braid, VG 450.00
Helmet, US Model 1884 Artillery, red plume & aigullett, EX ...700.00
Helmet, WWI Anti-Aircraft Unit, dk khaki sand, red front, EX .50.00
Helmet, WWI Army Medical Corps, camo, w/oilcloth liner 245.00
Insignia, Civil War, Corp of Engineers, brass, 1½x1¾", EX 220.00
Insignia, Civil War, emb Xd sabres, 2⅞", EX 55.00
Insignia, Civil War, Infantry bugle, brass, VG 70.00
Jacket, Indian Wars Period Infantry, VG 100.00
Jacket, Post Civil War, red w/brass buttons, rprs to lining, VG ..400.00
Kepi, Civil War Era, red wool w/wht piping & blk band, eagle buttons 600.00
Kepi, Civil War musician's, hard style, VG 350.00
Leggings, WWII Army, khaki canvas, w/leggings, EX 20.00
Medal, WWII Marine Corps Good Conduct, bronze, w/ribbon ...45.00
Oxygen mask, WWII AAF Type A-10A, gr rubber w/hose, complete ..65.00
Plate, mess; Navy Commodore, wht porc w/pennant border, ca 1912 ...35.00
Saddle, McClellan, w/saddlebags/stirrups/girth, EX 500.00
Shako, Indian War Era Militia Bandman, bl wool/gold bullion, EX ..190.00
Sleeping bag, WWII Army, khaki wool mummy style, dtd 1944, EX ...25.00
Trousers, WWII Army, fall camo cotton, unissued 170.00
Tunic, field; WWII Marine Corps, camo cotton, emb bronze buttons, NM ..165.00

Miscellaneous

Austrian, Cross of Merit, silver cross w/enameling, 1849 ....125.00
British, beret, Lancer, khaki wool w/badge on blk leather disk, 1951 ...22.50
British, busby, blk bear fur, wicker fr, rpr leather lining, 1900s ...170.00
British, helmet, Army, desert camo, w/liner, ca 1950s, EX 25.00
British, helmet, combat; WWII, khaki camo, complete 120.00
British, helmet, WWII Motorcycle Driver, camo netting, complete, EX ...30.00
British, plaque, Commander Montgomery in relief, cast brass, 4½" 50.00
British, swagger stick, WWII Army Air Corps Officer, blk pnt wood 40.00
British, War Metal, 1914-20, silver, member of Canadian Infantry Rgt ..20.00
Chinese, WWII Pilot Wings, brass, clutch bk 125.00
French, cap, folding side; WWII Artillery Bugler, bl wool w/red .55.00
Hungarian, WWI Service Medal, Pro Deo Et Patria 1914-18, bronze ...20.00
Italian, helmet, combat; WWII, field grey w/leather liner, EX 85.00
Italian, WWII Fascist Militia Long Service Cross, bronze, w/ribbon ..27.50
Italian, WWII Mussolini medallion, bronze, helmeted portrait 55.00
North Vietnamese, cap, visor; Army, cotton twill, star/wreath insg ..75.00
Yugoslavian, badge, WWII Pilot Wings, bronze, w/eagle & wreath ..90.00

Milk Glass

Milk glass is the current collector's name for milk-white opaque glass. The early glassmaker's term was Opal Ware. Originally attempted in

England in the eighteenth century with the intention of imitating china, milk glass was not commercially successful until the mid-1800s. Pieces produced in the U.S.A., England, and France during the 1870–1900 period are highly prized for their intricate detail and fiery, opalescent edges.

For further information we recommend *Collector's Encyclopedia of Milk Glass, An Identification & Value Guide*, by Betty and Bill Newbound. (CE numbers in our listings refer to this publication.) Another highly recommended book is *The Milk Glass Book* by Frank Chiarenza and James Slater. Our advisor for this category is Rod Dockery; he is listed in the Directory under Texas. See also Animal Dishes with Covers; Bread Plates; Historical Glass; Westmoreland.

Key:
B — Belknap
CE — Newbound
F — Ferson
MGB — Milk Glass Book

Platter, The Retriever, B-53, 9¾x13¼", $135.00.

Bottle, dresser; Draped Leaf, pk roses decor, CE-2f, 10½" 35.00
Bottle, dresser; Father's, CE-10/F-508, rare, 11½" 175.00
Bowl, Daisy, pnt, Challinor Tayler, F-165, 8¼" 90.00
Bowl, fruit; Monroe, Fostoria, CE-24, 1960s, 10⅝" 30.00
Bowl, Rib & Scroll, ftd, w/lid, Vallerysthal, CE-44a/F-443, 7" 75.00
Box, cuff; Three Kittens, gold trim, w/lid, CE-39b, 4½" 50.00
Butter dish, Wild Rose, w/lid, CE-82 ....75.00
Candle holder, lady holding urn, MGB-63, 8¼" 165.00
Candle holders, Lace & Dewdrop, Kemple, CE-98b, 4½", pr 25.00
Compote, Doric Border, 3-column stem, Westmoreland, CE-93b, 11" ...40.00
Covered dish, Crown, Vallerysthal, F-636/MGB-169, 5¾x4⅝" .200.00
Covered dish, Dewey on Battleship Base, F-555, 4½x5½" L, NM ..200.00
Creamer, Grape w/overlapping foliage, F-310 ....55.00
Creamer, Roman Cross, sq w/4 ft, F-239, M 65.00
Creamer, Tomato, CE-298F, ca 1910, 3⅞" 30.00
Decanter, wine; Grape, Imperial, CE-13a, 1950-68, 11½" 45.00
Figurine, rabbit, solid, heavy, CE-198a, Mosser Glass, 6" 25.00
Figurine, young Victoria Statuette, MGB-52, 9x4½" 250.00
Goblet, Dewberry, Kemple, CE-218a, 6" 15.00
Honey jar, Beehive, pk, Jeannette, CE-52b, w/lid, 4⅛" 35.00
Lamp, banquet; HP flower trim, lacy base, CE-237, 17" 120.00
Lamp, electric; Dancing Couple, CE-229, 1940s, 7⅝" 80.00
Lamp, Nellie Bly, 1-pc chimney & shade, CE-236a, 9" 140.00
Lamp, oil; Cosmos Variant, CE-227, 1940s, 6¼" 75.00
Mug, Bleeding Heart, CE-212b, 3¼" 35.00
Mustard jar, Log Cabin, orig labels, Westmoreland, F-644, 3¾" ...130.00
Plaque, coupe; Eagle & Shield, mk MarCor, CE-251, 15" 50.00
Plaque, Lincoln, Kemple, CE-273/F-560, 6⅜x8¼" 150.00
Plate, Closed Lattice Edge, Challinor Taylor, CE-261a, 10½" 40.00
Plate, Club & Shell border, Audubon decal, Kemple, CE-260, 9½" ...35.00
Plate, dogs & cats, He's All Right, B-20d, 6" 150.00
Plate, Easter Sermon, B-7C, 7½" 95.00
Plate, No Easter Without Us, Dithridge, CE-268c/F-592, ca 1900, 6¼" ..55.00
Plate, Pan-American Exposition, 1901, MGB-197 ....150.00
Plate, Rabbit & Horseshoe, Westmoreland, B-7a, 7½" 55.00
Plate, Roses, both sides emb, Imperial, CE-275-76, 12" 30.00
Plate, Woof-Woof, Westmoreland, CE-274b, 6" 60.00
Rolling pin, wooden hdls, mk Cambridge, CE-224a, 20½" 55.00
Shaker, John Bull, Atterbury, F-340, 6" 150.00
Sugar bowl, Betsy Ross, Fostoria, open, CE-294b, 3⅝" 12.00
Sugar bowl, Cactus, Fenton, w/lid, 6⅛" 25.00
Tray, apple form, Imperial, 2-section, CE-335a, 9½x9" 30.00
Tray, pin; Versailles, Dithridge, CE-344a, 9⅜x5" 22.00
Urn, Betsy Ross, Tiffin Glass, CE-306b, 7½" 30.00
Vase, hand-holding Hobnail cornucopia, Fenton, CE-371b, 6½" ..35.00
Vase, Mephistopheles, sq, emb roses, Vallerysthal, CE-368, 9½" ...80.00

Millefiori

Millefiori was a type of art glass produced during the 1800s. Literally the term means 'thousand flowers,' an accurate description of its appearance. Canes, fused bundles of multicolored glass threads such as are often used in paperweights were cut into small cross sections, arranged in the desired pattern, refired, and shaped into articles such as cruets, lamps, and novelty items. It is still being produced, and many examples found on the market today are fairly recent in manufacture. See also Paperweights.

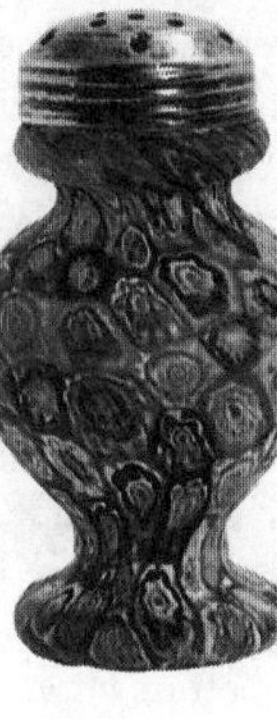

Sugar shaker, 5", $250.00.

Bottle, scent; pk dominate in stopper & base, 4½x3¼" 325.00
Bottle, scent; 5-color, 3-color stopper, Perthshire, 5½x2½" 325.00
Decanter, gr dominant, pre-WWII, matching stopper, 11" 395.00
Lamp, bl dominate, pre-WWII, 20", w/10" dome shade 995.00
Vase, ruffled edge, 4⅝" 85.00

Miniatures

There is some confusion as to what should be included in a listing of miniature collectibles. Some feel the only true miniature is the salesman's sample; other collectors consider certain small-scale children's toys to be appropriately referred to as miniatures, while yet others believe a miniature to be any small-scale item that gives evidence to the craftsmanship of its creator. For salesman's samples, see specific category; other types are listed below. See also Dollhouses and Furnishings; Children's Things.

Armoire, Rococo rosewood, mirror door, molded crest, drw, 17x10x5" ..660.00
Bed warmer, brass, emb lid, trn wood hdl, 10", EX 430.00
Blanket chest, cherry, appl molding, brass mts, 10x17x10" 400.00
Blanket chest, cherry & walnut, dvtl case, scroll apron, rfn, 20" ...880.00
Bureau, grpt Emp, sleigh-front, 4-drw, rfn, 1830s, 12x10x7" 430.00
Bureau, mahog, 3-drw, shaped skirt, paneled sides, 17x15x13", VG ..450.00
Chest, cherry & curly maple w/inlay, 2 short drw over 4, rfn, 26" ..2,300.00
Chest, cherry Country, 4 dvtl drw, paneled ends, 25x20" 3,500.00

Chest, cherry Fed, 4-drw, cvd ft/trn pilasters, rstr, 26" **2,950.00**
Chest, cherry Hplwht w/inlay, 4-drw, Fr ft, apron, 19" **3,950.00**
Chest, cherry/curly maple Country Emp, 3-drw, walnut pulls, 20x21" ...**2,000.00**
Chest, mahog & cherry, 4-drw, appl beading, rfn, 16⅜x12x8" ...**495.00**
Chest, mahog Hplwht, 5 dvtl drw w/inlay, 21x34" **2,100.00**
Chest, mahog serpentine case w/scrolled apron, 3 dvtl drw, 8½" ...**550.00**
Chest, poplar w/orig grpt/striping/decals, 3-drw, porc knobs, 20" ...**300.00**
Chest, walnut w/porc hdls, 3-drw, appl cvgs, 15x18x12", VG **425.00**
Chest on fr, walnut QA style, 4-drw, wire nails, 18" **500.00**
Corner cupboard, cherry, Am, ca 1880s, 32" **1,495.00**
Dry sink, pine w/pnt traces, scalloped base/paneled doors, rfn, 25" **330.00**
Fire dogs, wrought iron, penny feet, gooseneck finials, 7", pr **700.00**
Table, tilt top, brass, 4½" **250.00**

Minton

Thomas Minton established his firm in 1793 at Stoke on Trent and within a few years began producing earthenware with blue-printed patterns similar to the ware he had learned to decorate while employed by the Caughley Porcelain Factory. The Willow pattern was one of his most popular. Neither this nor the porcelain made from 1798 to 1805 was marked (except for an occasional number series), making identification often impossible.

After 1805 until about 1816, fine tea services, beehive-shaped honey pots, trays, etc., were hand decorated with florals, landscapes, Imari-type designs, and neoclassic devices. These were often marked with crossed 'L's. It was Minton that invented the acid gold process of decorating (1863), which is now used by a number of different companies. From 1816 until 1823, no porcelain was made. Through the '20s and '30s, the ornamental wares with colorful decoration of applied fruits and florals and figurines in both bisque and enamel were usually left unmarked. As a result, they have been erroneously attributed to other potters. Some of the ware that was marked bears a deliberate imitation of Meissen's crossed swords. From the late '20s through the '40s, Minton made a molded stoneware line (mugs, jugs, teapots, etc.) with florals or figures in high relief. These were marked with an embossed scroll with an 'M' in the bottom curve. Fine parian ware was made in the late 1840s, and in the '50s Minton experimented with and perfected a line of quality majolica which they produced from 1860 until it was discontinued in 1908. Their slogan was 'Majolica for the Millions,' and for it they gained widespread recognition. Leadership of the firm was assumed by Minton's son Herbert sometime around the middle of the nineteenth century. Working hand in hand with Leon Arnoux, who was both a chemist and an artist, he managed to secure the company's financial future through constant, successful experimentation with both materials and decorating methods. During the Victorian era, M.L. Solon decorated pieces in the pate-sur-pate style, often signing his work; these examples are considered to be the finest of their type. After 1862 all wares were marked 'Minton' or 'Mintons,' with an impressed year cipher.

Many collectors today reassemble the lovely dinnerware patterns that have been made by Minton. Perhaps one of their most popular lines was Minton Rose, introduced in 1854. The company itself once counted forty-seven versions of this pattern being made by other potteries around the world. In addition to less expensive copies, elaborate hand-enameled pieces were also made by Aynsley, Crown Staffordshire, and Paragon China. Solando Ware (1937) and Byzantine Range (1938) were designed by John Wadsworth. Minton ceased all earthenware production in 1939.

Dinnerware values given in the following listings are for items that were produced from 1870–1950. Current production pieces bring lower prices on the resale market. See also Majolica; Pate-Sur-Pate.

Bowl, vegetable; Ancestral, oval, 10¼" **95.00**
Bowl, vegetable; Dainty Sprays, oval, 10¼x7½" **90.00**
Bowl, waste; Rose, mk, 4¼" **30.00**
Candy dish, Rose, mk, 6½" **45.00**
Creamer, Ancestral **55.00**
Creamer, Spring Bouquet **30.00**
Cup & saucer, Rose, demi **30.00**
Egg cup, Ancestral, 1½x2" dia **25.00**
Figurine, Cowslip, girl w/wings, bone china & bronze, 7" **210.00**
Gravy boat, Dainty Sprays, w/underplate **125.00**
Platter, Ancestral, oval, 15¼" **80.00**
Teapot, Buckingham, wht w/gold band/hdl/spout/finial, 5x5½" .**200.00**
Toast rack, sm pk rose sprays, ca 1914, 2½x8¼x4⅛" **225.00**
Vase, floral transfer in bl & yel on ivory, stick neck, 25x12" **500.00**
Vase, poppies, mc, 4x3" **375.00**
Vase, stylized plants, 4-color, hdls, #108, 10x5" **1,000.00**
Vase, stylized plants & swags, red/olive/gold/wht, hdls, 11¾x5½" ...**1,250.00**

Mirrors

The first mirrors were made in England in the thirteenth century of very thin glass backed with lead. Reverse-painted glass mirrors were made in this country as early as the late 1700s and remained popular throughout the next century. The simple hand-painted panel was separated from the mirrored section by a narrow slat, and the frame was either the dark-finished Federal style or the more elegant, often-gilded Sheraton.

Mirrors changed with the style of other furnishings; but whatever type you purchase, as long as the glass sections remain solid, even broken or flaking mirrors are more valued than replaced glass. Careful resilvering is acceptable if excessive deterioration has taken place. In the listings that follow, items are from the nineteenth century unless noted otherwise. The term 'style' (example: Federal style) is used to indicate a mirror reminiscent of but made well after the period indicated. Obviously these retro styles will be valued much lower than their original counterparts. Our advisor for this category is Michael Hinton; he is listed in the Directory under Pennsylvania.

Key:

Chpndl — Chippendale	QA — Queen Anne
Emp — Empire	Vict — Victorian
Fed — Federal	vnr — veneer

Shaving mirror, cast iron with original polychrome paint, Victorian ladies hold ornate frame, monument, shield, flag and arrows at base, late 1800s, 21x14x6½", $650.00.

Blk lacquered Geo III w/penwork, ca 1800, 28x35" **825.00**
CI fr on stand, old gold pnt w/mc floral detail, 14" **250.00**
Curly maple Chpndl style, 19th C, rstr, 18x12" **275.00**
Gilt gesso cvd girandole, appl spherules/eagle crest, 1810, 33x20" ...**9,200.00**
Gilt gesso Fed, appl spherules, vintage relief, 1825, 44x27" **1,035.00**

Giltwood Chpndl style in Rococo taste, pierced foliage, 57x33" .450.00
Giltwood Continental Louis XVI taste, bird/trophies crest, 68x40" 1,750.00
Giltwood Regency, cvd horse w/dragon tail on cliff/lion's head, 38" 8,000.00
Mahog & giltwood Am Classical by H Strauff, ornate crest, 42x25" ..4,800.00
Mahog Am Late Classical, molded flame-grained fr, 1840s, 38x24" 300.00
Mahog Chpndl scroll, molded fr, rstr, 20x12", from $220 to 300.00
Mahog Chpndl scroll, parcel-gilt, shell in crest, 1790s, 28x15" .630.00
Mahog Chpndl scroll w/compo eagle crest, gilt traces, rfn, 30x15" ..550.00
Mahog Chpndl scroll w/gilt, Prince of Wales feather, rstr, 29x18" ...350.00
Mahog Chpndl w/appl moldings, crest missing, old rfn, 54x29" 990.00
Mahog Chpndl-style scroll, old repro, 22x13" 300.00
Mahog Emp, wide ogee fr w/pressed decor, rfn, 33x22" 200.00
Mahog Fed w/vnr crest/gilt moldings, 1800s, rstr, 48x19" 2,400.00
Mahog scroll, rfn/rpr, late 19th C, 26x16" 165.00
Mahog vnr Emp, half-columns, gold stencil, 2-part, 26x14" 220.00
Maple QA scroll, eng swan/sunbursts/etc on glass, rprs, 16x10" ..1,485.00
Oak English QA, old glass & finish, 21x13" 200.00
Over-mantel, gilt gesso Classical, 3-part, 1830s, 60x22" 900.00
Over-mantel, giltwood & gesso Am Neo-Greco, ornate crest, 68x50" ..1,900.00
Over-mantel, giltwood & gesso cvd w/rocaille crest, 19th C, 55x65" 1,750.00
Over-mantel, giltwood & gesso Vict, foliage/swags, 64x56" 1,500.00
Over-mantel, giltwood Louis XV style, rocaille crest, 1850s, 60x44" ..2,200.00
Pier, giltwood Neoclassical style, 19th C, 87x32" 1,900.00
Pier, Rococo Revival w/EX cvg, minor rprs, regilding, 94" 1,155.00
Pier, walnut Eastlake Vict, trn/reeded, surface cvg, 88x35" 750.00
Pine Continental Rococo, vines/leaves/scrolls w/mc traces on gray, 60" 1,750.00
Shaving, mahog bowfront, 3-drw, oval miror, rpr/rpl, 25x21" 495.00
Shaving, mahog/vrn w/figure Hplwht, serpentine front, 23x17" ..1,000.00
Trumeau, cvd/pnt, 2 molded panels w/foliate swags, 59x27" 550.00
Walnut Eastlake, cvd crest/marble shelf/pillars, 103x24" 565.00
Walnut Eastlake, sm crest, wht marble shelf, 92x24" 500.00
Walnut QA scroll, crests & fretwork, gilt liner, rprs, 39x24" ..3,750.00
Walnut vnr English QA, scrolled crest, 2-part, 40x15" 4,400.00
Walnut vnr English QA-style, gilt garlands/phoenix, 38" 550.00
Walnut vnr QA w/old alligatored varnish, appl ornaments, 25x11" ..600.00

Mocha

Mochaware is utilitarian pottery made principally in England (and to a lesser extent in France) between 1780 and 1840 on the then prevalent creamware and pearlware bodies. Initially, only those pieces decorated in the seaweed pattern were called 'Mocha,' while geometrically decorated pieces were referred to as 'Banded Creamware.' Other types of decorations were called 'Dipped Ware.' During the last thirty to forty years the term 'Mocha' has been applied to the entire realm of 'Industrialized Slipware' — pottery decorated by the turner on his lathe using coggle wheels and slip cups.

Mocha was made in numerous patterns — Tree, Seaweed or Dandelion, Rope (also called Worm or Loop), Cat's-eye, Tobacco Leaf, Lollypop or Balloon, Marbled, Marbled and Combed, Twig, Geometric or Checkered, Banded, and slip decorations of rings, dots, flags, tulips, wavy lines, etc. It came into its own as a collectible in the latter half of the 1940s and has become increasingly popular as more and more people are exposed to the rich colorings and artistic appeal of its varied forms of abstract decoration.

The collector should take care not to confuse the early pearlware and creamware Mocha with the later kitchen yellow ware, graniteware, and ironstone sporting mocha-type decoration that was produced in America by such potters as J. Vodrey, George S. Harker, Edwin Bennett, and John Bell. This type was also produced in Scotland and Wales and was marketed well into the twentieth century.

Bowl, earthworm, gray-gr band, 3½x7¼", VG 175.00
Mug, cat's eye, bl/brn on wht, brn lines, mustard bands, 4" 800.00
Mug, cream band w/mc splashes, leaf hdl, chips, 5" 750.00
Mug, earthworm & cat's eye, 4-color on tan, wht bands, 3⅝", NM ...400.00
Mug, herringbone, dk brn/orange-brn/lt bl stripes, 4⅝" 500.00
Mug, machined/molded bands, 3-color, 5⅛" 375.00
Mug, marbled red/pumpkin/bl/lt/bl w/scattered mc seaweed, 3¾" ...975.00
Mug, seaweed, bl/brn/blk bands, 4⅜" 110.00
Mug, seaweed, brn on orange, 2 gray bands, 3x3" 200.00
Mug, seaweed, gray band & 2 sm bl bands, 6¼" 400.00
Pepper pot, 4 bl/5 brn bands, bulbous, dome top, 4¾" 200.00
Pitcher, blk bands, w/dots & flowers, bl & brn stripes, 7", EX ...425.00
Pitcher, cat's eye, blk on gr band w/mc, 7½", EX 1,750.00
Pitcher, cat's eye, wht/brn/bl, brn stripes, wear/line, 8" 1,200.00
Pitcher, earthworm, bl & brn on wht w/bl/brn bands, 4¾" 700.00
Pitcher, earthworm/polka dots, 6-color, rprs, 8" 880.00
Pitcher, marbled bl/brn/blk/wht w/bl band at rim, rpr hdl, 7¾" ..2,400.00

Molds

Food molds have become popular as collectibles — not only for their value as antiques, but because they also revive childhood memories of elaborate ice cream Santas with candy trim or barley sugar figurals adorning a Christmas tree. Ice cream molds were made of pewter and came in a wide variety of shapes and styles. Chocolate molds were made in fewer shapes but were more detailed. They were usually made of tin, copper, and occasionally of pewter. Hard candy molds were usually metal, although primitive maple sugar molds (usually simple hearts, rabbits, and other animals) were carved from wood. (Unless otherwise indicated, the hard candy molds in our listings are cast aluminum or stainless steel.) Cake molds were made of cast iron or cast aluminum and were most common in the shape of a lamb, a rabbit, or Santa Claus. Our advisors for this category are Dale and Jean Van Kuren; they are listed in the Directory under New York.

Chocolate Molds

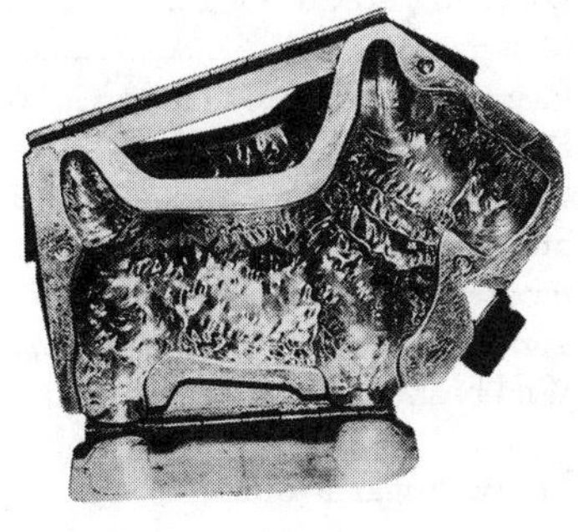

Scottie dog, tin, hinged, 1940s, 7x4x8", $150.00. (Photo courtesy Candace Sten Davis and Patricia Baugh)

Basket, Made in USA, clips missing, 3" 45.00
Boxer dog, 2-pc, 12¼x10½" 50.00
Boy, MIG, clips missing, 5½" 45.00
Bryant 1896 campaign, 16-1, metal, EX 36.00
Bugs Bunny, Warner Bros Productions, 3-part, 11¼x7¾" 85.00
Chick, 2-pc, Germany, #4302/#19, 3½x3¾" 35.00
Cigar, 2-part, 12¼" L 65.00
Dog, LeTang Fils, #3693 ....40.00
Elephant, 2-pc, hinged, #28, 4x6" 60.00
Flower bouquet, 2-pc, hinged, pewter, 3½" 70.00
French bulldog, 11" 55.00
Hen on nest, removable base, clipped top, K&M, 7x7" 300.00
Horses (3), 2-part, heavy pewter, #163, 6½" L 75.00
Rabbit, copper w/tin lining, 5" 50.00

Rabbit, seated, tinned steel, 11" 125.00
Rabbit w/egg cart, 2-pc, clips missing, 1920s, 4x8" 90.00
Rabbits (2), 2-pc, hinged, Germany 40.00
Rabbits (4), standing, Germany, 6" 40.00
Rabbits (8), early metal, 2-pc, w/clamps, 8½x10" 80.00
Rooster, clips missing, 4⅝" 60.00
Sailing ships (3), 2-part, 3x8" 94.00
Santa, 2-pc, hinged, Germany, 6⅛x3¾" 55.00
Squirrel Nutkin, ca 1900s, 9x8" 100.00
St Nicholas on horsebk over rooftop, Holland, #15930 ....75.00
St Nicholas/Santa, 2-pc (clips missing), #4175, 4¾" 67.50
Swan boat, MIG, 8¼" L 40.00
Tractor & wagon, EX details, 2-pc, 10¾x6¾" 100.00
Turkeys (4), 10½" 100.00
Volkswagon, Made in Germany, #4225, 2-pc, 4" 45.00
Witch, Eppelsheimer, 2-pc, 1940s, 4¼" 75.00

Ice Cream Molds

Asparagus bunch, CC, 9½" 55.00
Bell, E&Co, 3¼x3½" 50.00
Bonnet, E&Co, #1989, 3x4" 50.00
Bride, E&Co, 4½" 75.00
Carnation, #554, 3x3½" 50.00
Christmas tree, E&Co, #1154 ....125.00
Cupid, E&Co 125.00
Daisies (3), 5" L 75.00
Deer head, 3" 25.00
Ear of corn, E&Co, #219, 5" 42.50
Ear of corn, 7" 65.00
Floral wreath, 4" dia 40.00
Flower & strawberries, E&Co 35.00
Fruit pie, CC Brenette 35.00
Grapes cluster, 4-part, 8 hinges, unmk, 19th C, lg 150.00
Heart, E&Co, 3x3¾" 35.00
Lemon, E&Co, #115, 3x2½" 38.00
Lily, 3-pc, E&Co, #354, 5½x4" 80.00
Lovebirds, E&Co, #565 ....75.00
Melon, 2-part, 6½" 55.00
Pig, 2-part, 3 hinges, #1149 CC, 19th C, 10¼" 395.00
Puss 'n Boots, E&Co, #657, 4¾" 65.00
Ship, #513, from $85 to 110.00
Snowman, #601, 5" 172.50
Swan, S&Co, #167, 4x4" 55.00
Turkey, E&Co, #650, 3x3½" 50.00
Wild boar, E&Co, #647, 3½x4" 100.00

Maple Sugar Molds

Elephant, dog & goat, cvd hardwood, early 1900s, 3½x12", pr 70.00
Fish (4), cvd walnut, lollipop style, 19th C, 2½x13¾" 55.00
Floral & bee designs, cvd wood, 5x10" 36.00
Flowers (5), cvd hardwood, ca 1900s, 2¼x13½" 45.00
Fluted sides, cvd hardwood, ca 1880s, 7¾x3¾x1¾" 125.00
Heart shape w/cvd house-like design, pine, old patina, 6" 140.00

Monart

Scottish glassmaker, John Moncrief was fascinated by the technique of suspending colored enamels within the molten glass during the glassmaking process. Recognizing the potential of the process (which he had observed while in France), he began his own business in Perth, Scotland, in 1924. The glassware he created was called Monart. Several commercial lines were along the fine artware pieces designed with scrolls or feathers suspended within the glass. Nearly all examples are unmarked, most having originally carried a paper label.

Bowl, bl to blk w/gold aventurine, 3⅞x7¾" 225.00
Vase, blk w/gold flecks, 12" 105.00
Vase, Cluthra, cherry red & gr opaque, unmk, 5½" 260.00

Monmouth

The Monmouth Pottery Company was established in 1892 in Monmouth, Illinois. It was touted as the largest pottery in the world. Their primary products were utilitarian: stoneware crocks, churns, jugs, water coolers, etc. — in salt glaze, bristol, spongeware, and Albany brown. In 1906 they were absorbed by a conglomerate called the Western Stoneware Company. Monmouth became their #1 plant and until 1930 continued to produce stoneware marked with their maple leaf logo. Items marked 'Monmouth Pottery Co.' were made before 1906. Western Stoneware Co. introduced a line of artware in 1926. The name chosen for the artware was Monmouth Pottery. Some stamps and paper labels add ILL to the name. Our advisor for this category is Jim Martin; he is listed in the Directory under Illinois.

Stenciled stoneware: #3 crock, $150.00; #2 churn, no mark, $75.00; #2 crock, no mark, $60.00. (Photo courtesy Jim Martin)

Churn, salt glaze, mini, 4" 1,200.00
Churn, 2 Men in a Crock stencil, 5-gal 600.00
Crock, Bristol, mini, 2½" 600.00
Crock, salt glaze, 3-gal 150.00
Crock, stencil, bl on dk brn Albany, 3-gal 300.00
Crock, stencil, bl on dk brn Albany, 6-gal 400.00
Crock, 2 Men in a Crock stencil, 10-gal 300.00
Hen on nest, bl/wht spongeware 1,200.00
Jug, Bristol w/Albany top, mini, 2½" 500.00
Tobacco jar, monk, brn Albany 300.00
Water cooler, bl/wht spongeware, mini 1,000.00

Mont Joye

Mont Joye was a type of acid-cut French cameo glass produced by Cristallerie de Pantin in Paris around the turn of the century. It is accented by enamels. Our advisor for this category is Don Williams; he is listed in the Directory under Missouri.

Bowl, iris int, incurvate rim, ftd, 3½x9¾x7" 435.00
Ewer, violets on clear, sgn STV, emb SP hdl/spout/lid 700.00
Vase, floral, red/yel/gr/wht/tan, stick neck, 15½" 1,450.00
Vase, floral on purple, 7¾x3¼" 700.00
Vase, floral on purple w/gold, trumpet form, 10x3" 800.00
Vase, floral w/spider & web, on fr, 9½" 550.00
Vase, hollyhock w/gr leaves on golden-brn frost, 10" 1,200.00

Vase, lg irises, lav/gold on clear, low width, 13" 850.00
Vase, violets on textured frost, gold collar/base tint, 7½" 275.00

Moon and Star

Moon and Star was originally produced in the 1880s by John Adams & Company of Pittsburgh. In the 1960s, Joseph Weishar of Wheeling, West Virginia, owner of the Island Mould & Machine Company, reproduced some of the original molds and incorporated the pattern into approximately forty new and different items. Two of the largest distributors of this line were L.E. Smith of Mt. Pleasant, Pennsylvania, who pressed their own glass, and L.G. Wright of New Martinsville, West Virginia, who had theirs pressed by Fostoria, Fenton, and Westmoreland. Both companies carried a large and varied assortment of shapes and colors. Several other companies were involved in its manufacture as well, especially of the smaller items.

Over the years the glassware has been pressed in amberina (yellow shading to orange- or ruby-red), green, amber, crystal, light blue, and ruby. Pieces in ruby and light blue are most collectible and harder to find than the other colors, which seem to be abundant. Purple, pink, cobalt, amethyst, tan slag, and light green and blue opalescent were made, too, but on a lesser scale.

Current L.E. Smith catalogs contain a small assortment of pieces that are still available in crystal, pink, cobalt (lighter than the old shade), and these colors with an iridized finish. A new color, teal green, was introduced in 1992, a water set in sapphire blue opalescent was pressed in 1993, and the new color in 1994 was cranberry ice. Items are currently being pressed in various colors by the Weishar Company, who add their mark to the new glassware which is made primarily for collectors. Our values are given for ruby and light blue. For amberina, green, and amber, deduct 20%.

Ashtray, allover pattern, scalloped rim, 4 rests, 8" dia 25.00
Banana boat, allover pattern, scalloped rim, 9" 35.00
Basket, allover pattern, scalloped rim, ftd, upright hdls, 4" 22.00
Bell, pattern along sides, plain rim & hdl, from $35 to 45.00
Bowl, allover pattern, ftd, crimped rim, 7½" 35.00
Butter/cheese dish, patterned lid, plain base, 7" dia 65.00
Cake stand, allover pattern, removable plate, 11" dia 75.00
Candle bowl, allover pattern, ftd, 8", from $28 to 32.00
Candle lamp, patterned shade, clear base, 2-pc, 7½" 25.00
Candy dish, allover pattern on base & lid, ftd ball shape, 6" 25.00
Chandelier, ruffled shade w/allover pattern, w/'font,' amber, 14" ...265.00
Compote, allover pattern, w/lid, 12" 75.00
Creamer, allover pattern, raised ft, scalloped rim, 5¾x3" 35.00
Cruet, vinegar; 6¾", from $65 to 75.00
Epergne, allover pattern, 2-pc, 9" 65.00
Goblet, wine; plain rim & ft, 4½", from $12 to 15.00
Jardiniere, allover pattern, patterned lid & finial, 9¾" 85.00
Jelly dish, allover pattern, stemmed ft, w/lid, 10½" 65.00
Lamp, miniature; bl, from $185 to 225.00
Lamp, miniature; milk glass 245.00
Lighter, patterned body, metal fittings, from $40 to 60.00
Plate, patterned body & center, smooth rim, 8" 35.00
Relish bowl, 6 lg scallops form allover pattern, 1½x8" 35.00
Sugar bowl, allover pattern, w/lid, sm flat ft, 5¼x4" 40.00

Moorcroft

William Moorcroft began to work for MacIntyre Potteries in 1897. At first he was the chief designer but very soon took over their newly created art pottery department. His first important design was the Aurelian Ware, part transfer and part hand painted. Very shortly thereafter, around the turn of the century, he developed his famous Florian Ware, with heavy slip, done in mostly blue and white. Since the early 1900s there has been a succession of designs, most of them very characteristic of the company. Moorcroft left MacIntyre in 1913 and went out on his own. He had already established his name, having won prizes and gold medals at the St. Louis World's Fair as well as in Paris. In 1929 Queen Mary, who had been collecting his pottery, made him 'Potter to the Queen,' and the pottery was so stamped up until 1949. William Moorcroft died in 1945, and his son Walter ran the company until recent years. The factory is still in existence. They now produce different designs but continue to use the characteristic slipwork. Moorcroft pottery was sold abroad in Canada, the United States, Australia, and Europe as well as in specialty areas such as the island of Bermuda.

Moorcroft went through a 'Japanese' stage in the early teens with his lovely lustre glazes, Oriental shapes, and decorations. During the mid-teens he began to produce his most popular Pomegranate Ware, and Wisteria (often called 'Fruit'). Around that time he also designed the popular Pansy line as well as Leaves and Grapes. Soon he introduced a beautiful landscape series called variously Hazeldine, Moonlit Blue, Eventide, and Dawn. These wonderful designs along with Claremont (Mushrooms) seem to be the most sought after by collectors today. It would be possible to add many other designs to this list.

During the 1920s and 1930s, Moorcroft became very interested in highly fired Flambe (red) glazes. These could only be achieved through a very difficult procedure which he himself perfected in secret. He later passed the knowledge on to his son.

Dating of this pottery is done by knowledge of the designs, shapes, signatures, and marks on the bottom of each piece; an experienced person can usually narrow it down to a short time frame. Prices escalated for this 'rediscovered' pottery in the late 1980s but has now leveled off. This is true mainly of the pre-1935 designs of William Moorcroft, as it is items from that era that attract the most collector interest. Prices in the listings below are for pieces in mint condition unless noted otherwise; no reproductions are listed here. Advisors for this category are Wilfred and Dolli Cohen; they are listed in the Directory under California.

Humidor, Spanish-style floral on green to blue, early MacIntyre Burslem-England mark, initialed W.M., 4½x5", $2,950.00.

Bottle, scent; pansies on cobalt, silver cap, unmk, 2x1¼" 600.00
Bowl, anemones on bl-gr, ftd base, script mk, 1½x3" 90.00
Bowl, clematis on cobalt, mks/paper label, 1½x8¾" 225.00
Bowl, clematis on maroon & gr, By Appointment..., 2x5⅝" 125.00
Bowl, Dawn, bl matt, 1928, 4" 795.00
Bowl, hibiscus, 10½" 275.00
Bowl, hibiscus on cobalt, MIE, 1⅞x9" 150.00
Bowl, hibiscus on gr, MIE/label/script mk, 2¾x6¼" 225.00
Bowl, poppies on bl, 11" 950.00
Bowl, waving corn on celadon, ftd, 4x9", NM 650.00
Box, hibiscus, w/lid, 3½x5" 175.00
Creamer & sugar bowl, Florian, MacIntyre, 2½" 950.00
Creamer & sugar bowl, pomegranates on celadon, 5½", 4½", NM ..1,250.00

Humidor, pomegranates on cobalt, pewter rim, ca 1912, 7x5" ..1,500.00
Jam jar, pomegranates, Duchese, SP rim 475.00
Jardiniere, tulips on cream, Liberty, ca 1907-10, 6x8" 925.00
Lamp, berries & leaves on flambe, rewired, 1930s, 10¾x6½" .1,500.00
Lamp, leaves & fruit on flambe, MIE, 11⅛"+fittings 1,500.00
Lamp base, orchids, mc on bl to crimson, 9", +brass fixtures 300.00
Pitcher, orchid, 3¼" 125.00
Plate, pomegranates, 8½" 550.00
Vase, anemones on cobalt, MIE, 3x2" (opening) 125.00
Vase, anemones on cobalt to gr, MIE, 8x3½" 500.00
Vase, anenomes on lt bl, ca 1945-49, 6x3½" 500.00
Vase, Claremont, mushrooms, red/gr/yel on bl, 8½" 2,900.00
Vase, Claremont, mushrooms on gr, 1914, 12x6½" 3,500.00
Vase, clematis on cobalt, bulbous, 4⅝" 275.00
Vase, clematis on flambe, mk, 7¼x5" 835.00
Vase, cornflowers on yel, hdls, MacIntyre, 1912, w/lid, 8½" ...3,500.00
Vase, Florian, anemones, bl & yel on wht, hdls, 10x7" 2,250.00
Vase, Florian, bl poppies, MacIntyre, ca 1903-04, 8", NM 1,000.00
Vase, Florian, jonquils on bl, 6¾x3" 1,250.00
Vase, hibiscus, gold/tan on sage gr, F Deep, 7x5" 375.00
Vase, hibiscus, 3" 150.00
Vase, Moonlit Blue, landscape on cobalt, ca 1925, 6" 1,600.00
Vase, Moonlit Blue, trees on cobalt, w/copper liner, 19½x8", NM ...7,000.00
Vase, orchids on cobalt, sgn WM, Royal Warrant label, 5⅝" 250.00
Vase, orchids on cobalt, 3½" 150.00
Vase, orchids on flambe, bulbous, 3¾" 450.00
Vase, pansies, mini, 2" 295.00
Vase, pansies on cobalt, baluster, 13x7¼" 1,250.00
Vase, pansies on cobalt, bulbous, 1918-24, 10" 950.00
Vase, pansies on cobalt, Tudric pewter base, 6¼" 800.00
Vase, pansies on wht, mk, 1916, 10¼x4¼" 1,750.00
Vase, pomegranates, 5½x5" 695.00
Vase, pomegranates on bl to brn, 12¾x8" 1,350.00
Vase, pomegranates on cobalt, classic form, 9½x6" 925.00
Vase, pomegranates on cobalt, shouldered, ca 1925, 10" 1,100.00
Vase, pomegranates on cobalt, trumpet form, ca 1915, 14x4¾" ...1,450.00
Vase, pomegranates on yel-gr, hdls, #1396, 1913, 3½" 650.00
Vase, poppies on shaded wht to bl, ca 1935, 8½x5" 850.00
Vase, poppies on turq/cobalt flambe, early, 7x5" 950.00
Vase, tulips, Katherine Keeling, 7¾x5¾" 475.00

Moravian Pottery and Tile Works

The Moravian Pottery and Tile Works, Doylestown, Pennsylvania, was founded by Dr. Henry Chapman Mercer in 1898. He discovered the art and science of tile making on his own, without training from the existing American or European tile industry. This, along with his diverse talents as an author, anthropologist, historian, and artist, led Dr. Mercer to create something very unique. He approached tile design with an historic point of view, and he created totally new production methods that ultimately became widely accepted by manufacturers of handcrafted tile. The subject matter for the designs he preferred included nature and the arts, colonial tools and artifacts, storytelling, and medieval themes. Both of these 'new' approaches (to design and production) allowed Dr. Mercer to become extremely influential in the development of pottery and tile in the Arts & Crafts movement in America.

After Mercer's death in 1930, the Tile Works was managed by Frank Swain until 1954. In 1967 it was purchased by the Bucks County Dept. of Parks & Recreation. Tiles are being produced there today in the handmade tradition of Mercer; they are marked with a conjoined MOR and dated. Collectors look for the early tiles (mostly pre-1940), the preponderance of which bear no backstamps. These tiles were made using both red and white clays and are also referred to as 'Mercer' tiles. Our advisor for this category is Karen Guido; she is listed in the Directory under Connecticut.

Tile, Flying Dutchman, blue and cream with red flush, 4x4", $110.00.

Bee, from Season Animals, bl/cream w/red flush high glaze, 4" 95.00
Bounty, filigree border, dk gr/blk, 4" 60.00
Foliate Circle of Castle Acre Priory, bl w/red flush high glaze, 4" ..36.00
Goat, gr/cream w/red flush high glaze, 4" 70.00
Grapes, blk/wht, 2¾" 25.00
Grapes, gr/cream w/red flush high glaze, 3" 35.00
Harp brocade musician, mc, 6x4" 250.00
Knight of Margham, bl/cream w/red flush, 4½x7½" 300.00
Libra, from Zodiac Series, bl/cream w/red flush high glaze, 4" 70.00
Lions of Bedwyn Magna, cream/gr w/red flush high glaze, 5" 90.00
Priscilla, filigree border, bl/wht matt glaze, 4" 68.00
Santa Maria, 2-line border, bl/wht matt glaze, 4" 70.00
Sconce, 2 robins encircled, bl w/red flush high glaze, 11x5x3" ..400.00
Wife of Bath, Canterbury Tales, gr/cream w/red flush high glaze, 4" ...95.00

Morgantown Glass

Incorporated in 1899, the Morgantown Glass Works experienced many name changes over the years. Today 'Morgantown Glass' is a generic term used to identify all glass produced there. Purchased by Fostoria in 1965, the factory was permanently closed in 1971.

Adam etch, crystal; stem, champagne; #7810 Monaco, 5-oz 38.00
Am Beauty etch, crystal; stem, champagne; #7695 Trumpet, 6-oz ..48.00
Am Beauty etch, crystal; stem, wine; #7695 Trumpet, 2½-oz 70.00
Am Beauty etch, crystal; tumbler, water; #9715 Calhoun, 10-oz ..45.00
Aquaria etch, crystal; stem, goblet; #7640 Art Moderne 145.00
Art Moderne, crystal/frost; stem, icer; sgn DC Thorpe, 2-pc 250.00
Barry #37, crystal/rose; jug, hdld/ftd, Palm Optic, 48-oz 500.00
Bramble Rose etch, crystal; stem, champagne; #7577 Venus, 5½-oz ...58.00
Carlton, platinum Marco; stem, goblet; #7653 Cantata, 9-oz 82.00
Cathay etch, crystal; stem, champagne; #7711 Callahan, 5½-oz 50.00
Courtney #7637, crystal/DC Thorpe decor; stem, claret; 4½-oz ...280.00
Crinkle, lt bl frosted; tumbler, flat, #1962, 20-oz 38.00
Crinkle, ruby; Ockner jug, 1962, 54-oz 145.00
Elizabeth, crystal; stem, wine; #7630 Ballerina, 2¾-oz 95.00
Fernlee, crystal/blk; stem, goblet; #7640 Art Moderne, 9-oz 145.00
Golf Ball, cobalt/crystal; candlesticks, 2 styles, #7643, 4", pr 265.00
Golf Ball, ruby/crystal; candy dish, flat, #1212 Michael, 7" 525.00
Guest set, Azure; Festoon optic, #25 Trudy, 2-pc 135.00
Hollywood, blk band; tumbler, highball; flat, #8701, 12-oz 56.00
Lace Bouquet etch, crystal; stem, goblet, #7668 Galaxy, 10-oz 42.00
LMX (El Mexicano), Ice; candle holders, bulbous, #1933, 4", pr ...325.00
Maytime etch, topaz; stem, champagne; #7664½ Vernon, 5½-oz ...42.00
Monroe #7690, cobalt or ruby/crystal; stem, champagne; 6-oz 75.00
Nantucket etch, crystal/gr; stem, goblet; #7654 Lorna, 9-oz 85.00
Old English #7678, cobalt/crystal; stem, champagne; 6½-oz 50.00
Palm Optic, Anna Rose; stem, goblet; #7477 Venus, 9-oz 95.00
Palm Optic, Azure; stem, parfait; #7536, #7536 Alycia, 5½-oz 50.00
Paragon #7624, crystal/blk; stem, sherbet; 5½-oz 110.00
Persian etch, crystal; marmalade jar, glass lid, #106 Willett 175.00
Prairie Rose, crystal/gr; stem, goblet; #6046 Kirby 65.00

Pygon #7623, frosted; wine, Thorpe HP bird decor, 3½-oz 265.00
Rosalie etch, crystal; bowl, console; #4355 Janice, 13" 260.00
Sea Gulls enamel decor, jug, #545 Pickford, 60-oz 475.00
Sonoma etch, crystal; stem, goblet; #7659 Cynthia, 10-oz 68.00
Superba, blk filament; champagne, #7664 Queen Anne, 3½-oz .195.00
Toulon gold stencil, rose; stem, goblet; #7604½, 10-oz 225.00
Virginia etch, amber; stem, goblet; #7614 Hampton, 9-oz 55.00

Mortens Studio

Oscar Mortens was already established as a fine sculptural artist when he left his native Sweden to take up residency in Arizona. During the 1940s he developed a line of detailed animal figures which were distributed through the Mortens Studios, a firm he co-founded with Gunnar Thelin. Thelin hired and trained artists to produce Mortens' line, which he called Royal Designs. More than two hundred dogs were modeled and over one hundred horses. Cats and wild animals such as elephants, panthers, deer, and elk were made, but on a much smaller scale. Bookends with sculptured dog heads were shown in their catalogs, and collectors report finding wall plaques on rare occasions. The material they used was a plaster-type composition with wires embedded to support the weight. Examples were marked 'Copyright by the Mortens Studio' either in ink or decal. Watch for flaking, cracks, and separations. Crazing seems to be present in some degree in many examples. When no condition is indicated, the items listed below are assumed to be in near-mint condition, allowing for minor crazing.

Beagle, lying down, #554 ....55.00
Bloodhound, #877 ....150.00
Boston Terrier, sitting, #793 ....70.00
Boxer, #556, mini 65.00
Chow pup, brn, #816, 3" 50.00
Cocker Spaniel, brn, #786 ....75.00
Collie pup, #818, mini 55.00
Colt, standing, #714 ....65.00
Dachshund head plaque, lg, pr 475.00
Dalmatian, #854, 7½" 95.00
Doberman, #785 ....95.00
Filly, chestnut brn, #716, 8½" 95.00
Fox Terrier, blk, #766 ....95.00
German Shepherd, #556, mini 70.00
German Shorthair Pointer, #849 ....175.00
Greyhound, gray, #747, 6¾" 100.00
Irish Setter, standing, #856, 5½x7¼" 95.00
Norwegian Elkhound, gray, #764, 5⅛" 110.00
Palomino, rearing, 9" 110.00
Pekingese, #553, mini 65.00
Pointer, tail to leg, #851 ....95.00
Pointer pup, recumbent, #503, 5" L 75.00
Pomeranian, #739 ....95.00
Poodle, gray, 4" 85.00
Pug, #738, 4x5" 125.00
Springer Spaniel, #745, 5¾x4¾" 95.00
Stag, 7½x7" 150.00
Stallion, rearing, blk, #662 ....95.00

Morton Pottery

Six potteries operated in Morton, Illinois, at various times from 1877 to 1976. Each traced its origin to six brothers who immigrated to America to avoid military service in Germany. The Rapp brothers established their first pottery near clay deposits on the south side of town where they made field tile and bricks. Within a few years, they branched out to include utility wares such as jugs, bowls, jars, pitchers, etc. During the ninety-nine years of pottery operations in Morton, the original factory was expanded by some of the sons and nephews of the Rapps. Other family members started their own potteries where artware, gift-store items, and special-order goods were produced. The Cliftwood Art Pottery and the Morton Pottery Company had showrooms in Chicago and New York City during the 1930s. All of Morton's potteries were relatively short-lived operations with the Morton Pottery Company being the last to shut down on September 8, 1976. For a more thorough study of the subject, we recommend *Morton's Potteries: 99 Years, Vols. I and II,* by Doris and Burdell Hall; their address can be found in the Directory under Illinois.

Morton Pottery Works — Morton Earthenware Co. (1877 – 1917)

Jug, yellow ware with brown and green spatter, #245, three-pint, $150.00. (Photo courtesy Doris and Burdell Hall)

Chamber pot, yel ware, w/lid, 10" dia 90.00
Churn, brn Rockingham, mk, 4-gal 180.00
Crock, brn Rockingham, mk, 2-gal 60.00
Milk boiler, brn Rockingham, 3½-pt 60.00
Milk jug, cobalt, fancy appl hdl, #36s, 1-pt 50.00
Miniature, chamber pot, yel ware, w/lid, 3" dia 100.00
Miniature, jug, brn Rockingham, 1½" 50.00
Rice nappy, yel ware, fluted, 7" dia 70.00
Stein, brn Rockingham, German motto top/bottom, 1-pt 80.00
Teapot, brn Rockingham, pineapple shape, 7-pt 110.00

Cliftwood Art Potteries, Inc. (1920 – 1940)

Figurine, Bald Eagle, yel/brn/gr/wht spray glaze, 8½" 100.00
Figurine, cat, reclining, cobalt, 7x10¾" 55.00
Figurine, cat, sitting, cobalt, 5¾" 40.00
Figurine, elephant, gray, 13½x7¼" 125.00
Figurine, frog, gr & wht, lg glass eyes, 3¼x4½" 60.00
Figurine, lion, brn & lt tan spray glaze, 9¼x16" 200.00
Figurine, tiger, dk tan w/HP brn stripes, 5x16" 150.00
Miniature, chamber pot, yel clay, transparent glaze, 3" dia 30.00
Miniature, flower bowl, shallow, brn drip glaze, 4", +2" disk 25.00
Miniature, stein, brn drip glaze, barrel shape, 2½" 40.00
Wall pocket, bl & mulberry, cone shape, #123, 6x2¾" 55.00
Wall pocket, gr matt, teardrop shape, #216, 7½x5¾" 50.00
Wall pocket, Herbage Green, tree trunk shape, 8x3" 70.00
Wall pocket, turq & ivory matt, teardrop shape w/hdl, 7¾x5¼" ..65.00

Midwest Potteries, Inc. (1940 – 1944)

Miniature, goose, head bent, wht & yel w/gold, 1½" 20.00
Miniature, goose, head up, wht & yel w/gold, 2¼" 20.00
Miniature, hen & rooster, brn & yel on wht, 2", pr 24.00
Miniature, rabbits kissing, wht w/gold, 2½x3¼" 30.00
Miniature, sailboat, bl & tan on wht, 2x2" 15.00

Miniature, squirrel, wht & brn w/yel acorn, 2¼" 18.00
Planter, elephant, bl & yel drip, 4½x6¾" 20.00
Planter, fawn, lt brn drip, 6½x7" 18.00
Planter, fox, brn, 5¾x7" 18.00
Planter, lion, lt gr, 3¼x6½" 16.00
Planter, lioness, yel, 3¼x6½" 14.00
Wall mask, African female, ebony & gold w/15 neck rings, 8¼x5" .. 55.00
Wall mask, African male, blk matt, w/headband, 9x4" 40.00
Wall mask, man's head caricature, Classical Greek style, wht, 5x4½" ... 35.00
Wall mask, man's head caricature, pouting, tears in eyes, bl, 5x3¾" 30.00
Wall mask, man's head caricature, short hair, winking, yel, 5x3¼" 30.00
Wall mask, man's head caricature, 18th-C English monk, gr, 5x6" .. 40.00

Morton Pottery Company (1922 – 1976)

Bank, acorn, wht w/HP blossoms, gold decor, 3½" 50.00
Bank, bulldog, brn, 4" 20.00
Bank, cat sitting, yel w/bl bow & bell, 8½" 40.00
Bank, church, brn, 3½x4x2" 24.00
Bank, country schoolhouse, brn, 3x4x2½" 30.00
Bank, hen on nest, wht/blk/red cold pnt, 4" 50.00
Bank, kitten reclining, gray, 4x6" 25.00
Bank, pig, blk w/gr base, 5x7½" 45.00
Bank, pig, Skeedaddle, bl, #671, 6x6" 50.00
Bank, pig, Skeedoodle, pk, #672, 5x6" 50.00
Bank, shoe house, yel w/red roof, 6½" 30.00
Christmas planter, Santa on chimney, red & wht, #870 .... 30.00
Christmas planter, Santa's boot, red & wht, #676 .... 24.00
Christmas planter, Santa stands by blk cauldron holding gold bell .. 35.00
Christmas planter, Santa stands by chimney, red & wht, gold bell .. 30.00
Christmas planter, sleigh, wht w/HP holly & berries, #3015 .... 24.00
Cookie jar, Basket, w/fruit cluster lid 50.00
Cookie jar, Bluebird, top of head is lid 50.00
Cookie jar, Clown, straw hat lid 75.00
Cookie jar, Hen, chick finial 130.00
Cookie jar, Panda, head is lid 95.00
Cookie jar, sq w/harlequin design, mc 40.00
Cookie jar, Turkey, brn, w/chick finial 150.00
Cookie jar, Turkey, wht w/chick finial 225.00
Easter planter, bunny creeping, wht & pk, 4½x7½" 18.00
Easter planter, bunny w/carrot stands by basket, HP decor, 5¾" .. 20.00
Easter planter, chick sitting on egg, HP decor, 4½" 15.00
Easter planter, hen w/bonnet, yel & bl, 4¾" 16.00
Easter planter, rabbit, female w/umbrella & bonnet beside egg, HP, 10" ... 30.00
Easter planter, rabbit, male, pushing egg-shape cart, HP decor, 9¾" ... 30.00
Easter planter, rabbit, male in top hat beside egg, HP decor, 10" ... 30.00
Miniature, bear, leg Xd, brn, 2½" 12.00
Miniature, elphant trumpeting, bl, 2½" 10.00
Miniature, horse, maroon, 2½" 10.00
Miniature, kangaroo, pk, 2¼" 10.00
Miniature, squirrel, brn, 2½" 12.00
Miniature, turkey, brn w/HP decor, 2½" 12.00
Political figurine, donkey, gray, mk Tawes, 2¼x2¼" 25.00
Political figurine, elephant, cobalt, mk D'Ewart, 2½x2¼" 24.00
Political figurine, elephant, gr, mk Schoeppel, 2½x2¼" 20.00
Political figurine, JFK Jr saluting father's casket, gray & lt tan, 7" .. 50.00

American Art Potteries (1947 – 1963)

Bowl, gr, flat leaf shape, #351, 1½x7" 10.00
Bowl, grey & yel, butterfly, #135, 7x6½" 18.00
Bowl, wht, octagonal, #18, 2½x11" 12.00
Figurine, deer, brn & gr, #502, 11½" 35.00
Figurine, frog, gr & yel, #400, 3x7" 18.00
Figurine, hen, gray & blk spray, #304, 6½" 18.00
Figurine, rooster, gray & blk spray, #305, 8" 24.00
Figurine, turtle, gr & yel, #412, 2½x7" 18.00
Planter, bunny reclining, wht & pk, #309, 6x6½" 25.00
Planter, conch shell, orchid & lt gray, #131, 7½x6" 24.00
Planter, kitten sitting, gray, #314, 6x6½" 24.00
Planter, pk & gray, oval w/under tray, #62, 3x7x3½" 18.00
Planter, squirrel sitting, brn, #311, 6½x6" 20.00
Planter, winged horse, pk, #49, 5x5" 18.00
Planter (windowsill box), HP leaves, wht & gr, #25, 4x13x2½" .. 30.00
Vase, cowboy boot, gray & pk, #312, 5½" 15.00
Vase, emb leaves, brn & yel, bulbous w/long neck, #128 .... 20.00
Vase, mauve & gray, 6-sided, #214, 12" 24.00
Vase/cornucopia, rose & gray, #204, 7½" 18.00

Moser

Ludwig Moser began his career as a struggling glass artist, catering to the rich who visited the famous Austrian health spas. His talent and popularity grew and in 1857 the first of his three studios opened in Karlsbad, Czechoslovakia. The styles developed there were entirely his own; no copies of other artists have ever been found. Some of his original designs include grapes with trailing vines, acorns and oak leaves, and richly enameled, deeply cut or carved floral pieces. Sometimes jewels were applied to the glass as well. Moser's animal scenes reflect his careful attention to detail. Famed for his birds in flight, he also designed stalking tigers and large, detailed elephants, all created in fine enameling.

Moser died in 1916, but the business was continued by his two sons who had been personally and carefully trained by their father. The Moser company bought the Meyr's Neffe Glassworks in 1922 and continued to produce quality glassware.

When identifying Moser, look for great clarity in the glass; deeply carved, continuous engravings; perfect coloration; finely applied enameling (often covered with thin gold leaf); and well-polished pontils. Our advisor for this category is Don Williams; he is listed in the Directory under Missouri. Items described below are enameled unless noted otherwise. If no color is mentioned in the line, the glass is clear.

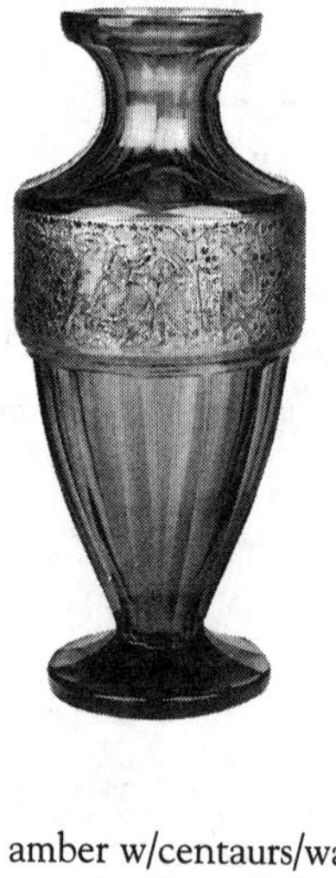

Vase, amber with acid-cut and gold enameled female warrior band, engraved mark, 13¾", $900.00.

Bottle, amber w/centaurs/warriors frieze, 8½", +9" tray 357.50
Bottle, scent; amber w/gilt Amazon warriors frieze, 6" 357.50
Bottle, scent; amethyst w/Amazon women band, missing bulb, 10½" .. 325.00
Bottle, scent; cranberry w/aquatic scene, appl fish, pr 350.00
Bowl, purple opal w/gold ivy & red jewels, 4-fold rim, 10½" 865.00
Box, cranberry, lady & floral w/gold, hinged lid, 1857, 5" dia 650.00
Box, cranberry w/allover floral, ribbed, metal mts, 4" dia 350.00
Compote, pk opaline, oak leaves, amber tree branch ft, 7½" . 1,725.00

Cruet, amethyst to clear, mc floral, 7¾" 500.00
Cruet, cranberry, heavy gold o/l, 5" 400.00
Cruet, deep bl w/gold scrolls & mc flowers, amber hdl 175.00
Cruet, sapphire bl w/gold/jeweled bands, flat sided, sm 1,100.00
Cup & saucer, cobalt, allover gold/wht florals, 3", 5⅜" 400.00
Cup & saucer, cranberry w/heavy gold intricate floral 350.00
Decanter, alexandrite, allover facet cut, 10", +6 cordials 635.00
Ewer, cranberry, bugs/dragonfly/ferns, bulb w/angle rim, sm 425.00
Goblet, amber w/wht & gold floral, Venetian style, 1900s, 6½" ...145.00
Goblet, bowl w/fluted int & floral, amber stem, 1890s, 7", NM ...115.00
Goblet, cobalt cut to clear w/gold rims, cut stem, 1930s, 7¼" ...300.00
Goblet, cranberry, gold floral, clear stem, 1890s, 6¼" 200.00
Goblet, cranberry, w/gold floral, blown-out ft, 1890s, 4¾" 150.00
Goblet, gr to clear w/trees/rabbit/stag/doe, cut stem, 5x3½" 400.00
Goblet, marriage; cranberry w/allover decor & gold 500.00
Goblet, Middle Eastern design, mc w/gold & wht border, 5¾" ..350.00
Jewelry casket, bl opaline egg, floral band w/gold, 13" L 500.00
Pitcher, bird decor, Celeste Blue legs/eyes/wings/hdl, 4¼" 275.00
Pitcher, pk w/gold floral, int fluted body, 1890s, 12¾" 665.00
Pokal, blk, acid-etched/gold tiger-hunt scene, 1920s, 12½" 400.00
Tumbler, cranberry, heavy gold/flowers, 3¾" 290.00
Tumbler, nudes at water in reserve, 4" 800.00
Tumbler, rainbow w/dogwood on diagonal ribs, 1890s, 4½", NM ..575.00
Vase, alexandrite frost w/cherubs, 3⅛x2¼" 150.00
Vase, allover mc flowers, gold rings on ft, 7½" 200.00
Vase, amethyst w/gold elephants & palms, triple signature, 8x7" ..1,600.00
Vase, amethyst w/platinum & gold floral, 5¼" 185.00
Vase, bl cased, mc floral, appl elephant hdls w/gold, 13", pr ...3,500.00
Vase, bl w/wht floral w/gold, scalloped rim, 15" 600.00
Vase, bright bl, heavy gold enamel, 11" 300.00
Vase, cranberry, floral, appl/HP buds, att, 10½", pr 300.00
Vase, cranberry, floral & gold, 6-sided, bulbous, 13½" 600.00
Vase, cranberry, flower w/in dmns w/gold, 8¾" 100.00
Vase, gr opal w/8 appl gold acorns & insect, 4 gold ft, 4¾" 1,050.00
Vase, gr to clear w/HP florals/web leaves/etc, sq, 9" 400.00
Vase, gr w/gold & yel floral, ruffled trumpet form, 16" 165.00
Vase, lt to dk bl w/5 oak leaves & appl acorn, 2" 450.00
Vase, pk opaline, oak leaves/acorns, 4-ftd, 1890s, 6" 1,035.00
Vase, vaseline to gr opal w/florals & scrolls, ruffled, 7x10" 365.00

Moss Rose

Moss Rose was a favorite dinnerware pattern of many Staffordshire and American potters of the mid-1800s. In America the Wheeling Pottery of West Virginia produced the ware in large quantities, and it became one of their bestsellers, remaining popular well into the '90s. The pattern was colored by hand; this type is designated 'old' in our listings to distinguish it from the more modern Moss Rose design of the twentieth century, which we've also included. It's not hard to distinguish between the two. The later ware you'll recognize immediately, since the pattern is applied by decalcomania on stark white backgrounds. It has been made in Japan to a large extent, but companies in Germany and Bavaria have produced it as well. Today, there is more interest in the twentieth-century items than in the older ware.

Bell, Japan 10.00
Bowl, HP, gold rim, ped ft, unmk, old, 5x9¾" 35.00
Bowl, serving; Johann Haviland Bavaria, 2½x10½x7½" 35.00
Bowl, soup; Rosenthal, US Zone 42.00
Bowl, soup; Wardel, Poland, 8 for 65.00
Bowl, sterling base, 4½x9½" 195.00
Casserole, hdls, ftd, w/lid, Pompadour shape, Rosenthal, 11½" .250.00
Child's set, 6 5-pc settings+9 serving pcs, Japan, 39 pcs, MIB ...200.00
Coffee set, pk striping, unmk, old, 9" pot+cr/sug+6 c&s, EX 175.00
Coffeepot, Johann Haviland Bavaria Germany, 11¼" 75.00
Coffeepot, Pompadour shape, Rosenthal, 11" 197.50
Cruets, oil & vinegar; Japan sticker, pr 25.00
Cup & saucer, demi; Japan 8.00
Cup & saucer, ped ft, scalloped saucer, gold trim, old 12.00
Cup & saucer, Pompadour shape, Rosenthal 45.00
Egg coddler, Apco, Japan, paper labels, w/clamp & lid, 3½" 32.00
Fairy lamp, Japan 18.00
Gravy boat, Pompadour shape, Rosenthal, 4½x9½x6½" 65.00

Gravy tureen with lid and undertray, old, H&Co, Limoges, $375.00.

Mirror on stand, Japan 15.00
Plate, dinner; Johann Haviland Bavaria, 10", from $12 to 20.00
Plate, dinner; Wardel, Poland, 8 for 65.00
Plate, Powell Bishop, old, 9" 25.00
Platter, Wardel, Poland, 13x9" 35.00
Shakers, Johann Haviland Bavaria, 4¼", pr 30.00
Tea set, Japan, child sz, 27-pc, MIB 155.00
Tea set, Japan, 7½" pot+cr/sug+4 plates+4 c/s, 15-pc 70.00
Toothbrush holder, w/drain, old 75.00

Mother-of-Pearl Glass

Mother-of-Pearl glass was a type of mold-blown satin art glass popular during the last half of the nineteenth century. A patent for its manufacture was issued in 1886 to Frederick S. Shirley, and one of the companies who produced it was the Mt. Washington Glass Company of New Bedford, Massachusetts. Another was the English firm of Stevens and Williams. Its delicate patterns were developed by blowing the gather into a mold with inside projections that left an intaglio design on the surface of the glass, then sealing the first layer with a second, trapping air in the recesses. Most common are the Diamond Quilted, Raindrop, and Herringbone patterns. It was made in several soft colors, the most rare and valuable is rainbow — a blend of rose, light blue, yellow, and white. Occasionally it may be decorated with coralene, enameling, or gilt. Watch for twentieth-century reproductions, especially in the Diamond Quilted pattern. Our advisors for this category are Betty and Clarence Maier; they are listed in the Directory under Pennsylvania. See also Coralene.

Bottle, scent; Peacock Eye, yel, sphere w/stick neck, 7½" 750.00
Bottle, scent; Ribbon, wht, flip-top eng sterling cap, 4" dia 400.00
Bowl, bride's; Dmn Quilt, pk w/stork decor, Webb, 5x9" 1,300.00
Bowl vase, Flower & Acorn, wht w/gold flowers etc, Webb, 3½x5½" ..650.00
Creamer, Raindrop, bl, reeded hdl, bulbous, 4½" 195.00
Creamer & sugar bowl, Ribbon, bl, 3-lobe rim, 2⅛", 2⅜" 335.00
Cruet, Herringbone, bl, ruffled top, frosted hdl/stopper, 6" 500.00
Cruet, Raindrop, bl, reeded frosted hdl & stopper 350.00
Cup & saucer, Raindrop, pk to wht, 3", 5" dia 385.00
Ewer, Dmn Quilt, pk, melon ribs, ruffled rim, thorn hdl, 11" 350.00
Ewer, Dmn Quilt, pk, ruffled, thorn hdl, 7" 200.00
Ewer, Herringbone, rainbow, trefoil rim, camphor hdl, 6½" 700.00

Ewer, Herringbone, shaded rose, thorn hdl, ruffled, Mt WA, 9" ..435.00
Ewer, Herringbone, yel, sm neck w/flared ruffled rim, amber hdl, 7" ...200.00
Mustard pot, Raindrop, pk, SP lid & hdl, 3" 275.00
Nappy, Dmn Quilt, wht w/gold trim, 3-lobed/crimped, hdl, 6" ..400.00
Pitcher, Dmn Quilt, apricot, folded/ruffled rim, water sz 500.00
Pitcher, Herringbone, bl, melon shape, frosted hdl, 5" 150.00
Pitcher, Herringbone, pk, melon shape, frost hdl, SP collar, 8½" ..350.00
Rose bowl, Dmn Quilt, bl, ground pontil, 2¾x3½" 385.00
Rose bowl, Dmn Quilt, rose, 6-petal top, mk Pat, 2¾x3½" 385.00
Rose bowl, Swirl, bl, 7-crimp top, 2¾x3¼" 265.00
Shade, Dmn Quilt, cranberry, sqd w/fluted rim, 4½", pr 725.00
Shade, Swirl, yel, emb ribs, 5x8" dia base 295.00
Tumbler, Dmn Quilt, bl w/floral, Mt WA, 3¾" 275.00
Vase, Basketweave, shaded bl, Webb, 7x5" 750.00
Vase, Basketweave, tan to brn to gold, Webb, 8x7" 365.00
Vase, Bridal (rare pattern), wht, trifold top w/gold trim, 6¾" 175.00
Vase, Dmn Quilt, apricot, stick neck, melon ribs, 8" 100.00
Vase, Dmn Quilt, bl, frosted 3-petal rim, 7¾x4" 225.00
Vase, Dmn Quilt, pk w/wildflowers, pulled/crimped rim, 5½" 200.00
Vase, Dmn Quilt, rainbow, mk Pat, 7x4" 1,200.00
Vase, Dmn Quilt, rainbow, 3 emb neck rings, lobed rim, 6" 375.00
Vase, Dmn Quilt, shaded bl, ruffled, Mt WA, 5x3" 235.00
Vase, Dmn Quilt, shaded rose, ruffled, ftd, Mt WA, 9", pr 850.00
Vase, Drape, yel, long neck, ruffled top, Mt WA, 7¾x5" 485.00
Vase, Frederzeichnung, gold on brn, can neck, minor wear, 11x5" ...1,950.00
Vase, Frederzeichnung, gold on brn, 7x4½", M 2,500.00
Vase, Frederzeichnung, mahog brn w/gold tracery, stick neck, 12¾" ...1,750.00
Vase, Herringbone, bl w/gold leaves, shouldered, 6½x4" 235.00
Vase, Hobnail, shaded bl, 4-fold top, Mt WA, 5¾x4" 650.00
Vase, Hobnail, shaded pk, ovoid w/4-fold rim, 5¾" 500.00
Vase, Muslin, bl, 3-petal top, bulbous, Mt WA, 8x7" 650.00
Vase, Raindrop, butterscotch w/camphor edge, slender, 8" 365.00
Vase, Raindrop, gold w/crimped camphor rim, Mt WA, 9x3½" .265.00
Vase, Raindrop, wht w/frosted edge, 6½x3" 260.00
Vase, Ribbon, bl, fluted/ruffled, Mt WA, 8x4" 300.00
Vase, Ribbon, chartreuse, wide boxy top, 2½x2¾" 190.00
Vase, Swirl, gold to lt pk, Mt WA, 9x3½" 400.00

Mountainside

John Kovaks operated a ceramic studio from the late 1920s until about 1939 in Mountainside, New Jersey, where through extensive experimentation he produced stoneware and earthenware items glazed with colors of his own formulation.

Lamp, ivory gloss, ribbed dbl-gourd shape, MP, 11" 70.00
Vase, frothy gr matt, bulbous w/3 ring hdls, MP, 6" 75.00

Mourning Collectibles

During the eighteenth and early nineteenth centuries, ladies made needlework pictures, samplers, painting on ivory plaques, watercolor drawings, etc., to commemorate the death of a loved one. Elements contained in nearly all examples are the tomb, mourners, a weeping willow tree, and data relating to the deceased. Often plaits of hair were included. Today these are recognized and valued as a valid form of folk art.

Needlework memorial, girl at 3 urn-form monuments, Am, 1850s, 18x21" 5,175.00
Needlework memorial, lady & urn, Werter, early 1800s, 12½" dia 700.00
Needlework memorial, lady at grave of Washington, ca 1800, 14x12" ...1,000.00
Needlework memorial, pnt/emb silk, lady at monument, 18th C, 22x20" ...1,000.00
Oil on artist's board, primitive scene, 10x14"+fr 440.00
Pen & ink on paper, willow/verse, 1823, 10x7"+fr 545.00
Scroll, pen/ink/watercolor on paper, lady at tomb, 1929, 6x4" ...190.00
Watercolor & pencil on paper, lady at tomb/willow, 1825, 12x13" ..1,900.00
Watercolor on ivory, memorial of baby, 2½", in case, G 800.00
Watercolor on paper, lady beside tomb & willow, ca 1807, 12x11"+fr ..1,075.00
Watercolor on paper, Memorial to Miss..., tomb scene, 14x18½"+fr 600.00
Watercolor on paper, parents at tomb, willow, 1794, 19x15"+fr ...485.00
Waxwork floral arrangement on lyre, 19th C, 17x11", EX 200.00

Movie Memorabilia

Movie memorabilia covers a broad range of collectibles, from books and magazines dealing with the industry in general to the various promotional materials which were distributed to arouse interest in a particular film. Many collectors specialize in a specific area — posters, pressbooks, stills, lobby cards, or souvenir programs (also referred to as premiere booklets). In the listings below, a one-sheet poster measures approximately 27" x 41", three-sheet: 41" x 81", and six-sheet: 81" x 81". Window cards measure 14" x 22". Values are for examples in NM condition unless noted otherwise. See also Autographs; Cartoon Art; Magazines; Paper Dolls; Personalities; Rock 'n Roll Memorabilia; Sheet Music.

Poster, *Coquette,* Mary Pickford, United Artists, 1929, 28x22", NM, $485.00.

Insert card, Born Yesterday, W Holden/J Holliday, 1951 ....65.00
Insert card, Christopher Columbus, Fredric March, 1949 ....40.00
Insert card, Cinderella, Disney artwork, 1957 (re-release) 65.00
Insert card, Desire Under the Elms, Sophia Loren, 1958 ....35.00
Insert card, Double Trouble, Elvis Presley, 1967, rolled 40.00
Insert card, Ebb Tide, Francis Farmer/Ray Milland, 1937 ....75.00
Insert card, Forever Darling, Lucille Ball/Desi Arnez, 1956 ....75.00
Insert card, Harum Scarum, Elvis Presley, 1965, rolled 50.00
Insert card, Here We Go Again, E Bergman/Charlie McCarthy, 1942 ..85.00
Insert card, Hollywood & Vine, Jimmy Ellison/Wanda McKay, 1944 ....65.00
Insert card, Island in the Sky, John Wayne, 1953 ....45.00
Insert card, Johnny Belinda, Jane Wyman, 1948 ....65.00
Insert card, King of Kings, Jeffery Hunter, 1961 ....50.00
Insert card, Ma Barker's Killer Brood, Lurene Tuttle, 1959 ....50.00
Insert card, Machine Gun Kelly, Charles Bronson, 1958, AIP artwork .55.00
Insert card, Our Man in Havana, Alec Guiness/Noel Coward, 1960 ....35.00
Insert card, Paris When It Sizzles, A Hepburn/W Holden, 1964 ..50.00
Insert card, Red River Range, John Wayne, 1953 (re-release) 65.00
Insert card, Saratoga, Jean Harlow/Clark Gable, 1937, rolled 750.00
Insert card, Stalag 17, William Holden, 1953, rare 65.00
Insert card, To the Shores of Tripoli, R Scott/M O'Hara, 1943 ....85.00
Insert card, Tropic Zone, Ronald Reagan/Rhonda Flemming, 1953 ...50.00
Insert card, War & Peace, Audrey Hepburn/Henry Fonda, 1956 .65.00
Lobby card, Beau Brummel, Elizabeth Taylor/Stewart Granger, 1954 ..15.00
Lobby card, Boom Town, C Gable/S Tracy, 1946 ....15.00
Lobby card, Funny Face, Fred Astaire/Audrey Hepburn, 1957 .....18.00
Lobby card, Hour Before Dawn, Veronica Lake, 1944 ....24.00
Lobby card, House of the Seven Gables, G Sanders/V Price, 1940 ..25.00
Lobby card, Sabrina, Audrey Hepburn/William Holden, 1954 .....35.00
Lobby card, Wrong Man, Henry Fonda, 1957 ....30.00

Lobby card set, Betrayed, C Gable/L Turner/V Mature, 1954 ......50.00
Lobby card set, Bridges of Toko-Ri, Wm Holden/Gene Kelly, 1955 ...50.00
Lobby card set, Cheyenne Autumn, J Ford/R Widmark/J Stewart, 1964 ...50.00
Lobby card set, Follow the Sun, Ben Hogan biography, 1951 ....100.00
Lobby card set, Fuller Brush Man, Red Skelton, 1948 ....50.00
Lobby card set, Gunfight at the OK Corral, Douglas/Lancaster, 1941 ...50.00
Lobby card set, Guys & Dolls, Brando/J Simmons/Sinatra, 1955 .75.00
Lobby card set, Hole in the Head, Sinatra/EG Robinson/E Parker, 1959 ..50.00
Lobby card set, Houseboat, Cary Grant/Sophia Loren, 1958 ....45.00
Lobby card set, Pat & Mike, Spencer Tracy/Kathyrn Hepburn, 1952 ....65.00
Lobby card set, Rally Round the Flag Boys, Newman/Woodward, 1959 ..35.00
Poster, A Very Private Affair, B Bardot/M Mastroianni, 1962, 1-sheet 45.00
Poster, Adventures of Mark Twian, F March/A Smith, 1944, 3-sheet 45.00
Poster, Asphalt Jungle, M Monroe (not pictured), 1950, 1-sheet .65.00
Poster, Barbarella, Jane Fonda, 1966, 60x40" (rolled) 65.00
Poster, Betrayal, E Jannings/G Cooper, 1929, silent film, 1-sheet ..750.00
Poster, Breakfast at Tiffany's, Audrey Hepburn, 1961, 3-sheet ...950.00
Poster, Bridge on the River Kwai, W Holden, 1958, style B 1-sheet ...300.00
Poster, Butch Cassidy & Sundance Kid, Redford/Newman, 1973, 1-sheet ...50.00
Poster, Captain Lightfoot, Rock Hudson, 1955, 1-sheet 45.00
Poster, Cinderella, Disney artwork, 1950, 3-sheet 750.00
Poster, Cyclops, Lon Chaney Jr, 1956, 1-sheet 225.00
Poster, Dial M for Murder, Grace Kelly/Ray Milland, 1954, 1-sheet 385.00
Poster, Fantastic Voyage, Raquel Welch, 1966, 3-sheet 65.00
Poster, Gene Krupa Story, Sal Mineo, 1960, 3-sheet 50.00
Poster, Girl Can't Help It, J Mansfield/T Ewell, 1957, 1-sheet ..185.00
Poster, Godzilla King of the Monsters, Raymond Burr, 1956, 1-sheet ..1,500.00
Poster, Guess Who's Coming to Dinner?, Tracy/Hepburn, 1967, 1-sheet ..25.00
Poster, Honeymoon, Shirley Temple/Guy Madison, 1947, 3-sheet 100.00
Poster, Hush, Hush, Sweet Charlotte, Bette Davis, 1965, 3-sheet ..65.00
Poster, In This Our Life, Bette Davis & others, 1942, 1-sheet ...500.00
Poster, It's a Mad, Mad, Mad, World, 1963, Jack Davis art, 6-sheet ...100.00
Poster, Last Time I Saw Paris, Elizabeth Taylor, 1954, 6-sheet ...150.00
Poster, Life Begins at 40, Will Rogers portrait, 1934, ½-sheet ...150.00
Poster, Lone Wolf's Daughter (silent), Bert Lytell, 1928, 1-sheet 350.00
Poster, Long, Long Trailer, Lucille Ball/Desi Arnez, 1954, 1-sheet ..375.00
Poster, Man Who Came to Dinner, B Davis/J Durante, 1941, 1-sheet 400.00
Poster, Man Who Shot Liberty Valance, Wayne/Stewart, 1962, 3-sheet ..250.00
Poster, Marine, Sean Connery/Tippi Hedren, 1964, 1-sheet 80.00
Poster, Never Say Goodbye, Errol Flynn, 1946, 3-sheet 65.00
Poster, Night Walker, R Taylor/B Stanwyck, 1965, 1-sheet 40.00
Poster, No Time for Love, C Colbert/F McMurray, 1943, 1-sheet ...75.00
Poster, Painted Hills/MGM, Lassie artwork, 1951, 1-sheet 50.00
Poster, Sandpiper, Elizabeth Taylor/Richard Burton, 1965, ½-sheet ..65.00
Poster, Searchers, John Wayne/Natalie Wood, 1956, ½-sheet ...400.00
Poster, Shane, Alan Ladd, 1959 (re-release), 1-sheet 65.00
Poster, Some Like It Hot, M Monroe/T Curtis/J Lemmon, 1958, 1-sheet ...400.00
Poster, Stagecoach, B Crosby/A-Margaret, 1966, Rockwell art, 60x40" ..100.00
Poster, Stagecoach, John Wayne, 1943 (re-release), 1-sheet 550.00
Poster, Tap Roots, S Hayward/B Karloff/Van Helfin, 1948, ½-sheet .50.00
Poster, That Touch of Mink, Cary Grant/Doris Day, 1962, ½-sheet .50.00
Poster, Trouble in Sundown, George O'Brien, 1939, 1-sheet 65.00
Poster, War of the Wildcats, John Wayne, 1943, 1-sheet 185.00
Poster, We're Not Married, Marilyn Monroe, 1952, ½-sheet 100.00
Poster, While Satan Sleeps (silent), Jack Holt, 1922, 1-sheet 600.00
Pressbook, Black Raven, George Zucco, 1943 ....20.00
Statue, King Kong, compo w/plaque on marble-like base, 1972, 23", NM ...1,100.00
Window card, An Affair To Remember, Cary Grant/Deborah Kerr, 1957 ...65.00
Window card, Band Wagon, Fred Astaire, 1953 ....85.00
Window card, Cat on a Hot Tin Roof, E Taylor/P Newman, 1958 ...100.00
Window card, Conquest of Space, George Pal classic, 1954 ....75.00
Window card, David & Bathsheba, Gregory Peck/Susan Hayward, 1951 ...25.00
Window card, From the Earth to the Moon, J Cotton, 1958 ....25.00
Window card, Hustler, P Newman/J Gleason/Geo C Scott/P Laurie, 1961 ...65.00
Window card, I'll Give a Million, Warner Baxter, 1938, 22x28" ...85.00
Window card, King Creole, Elvis Presley, 1958 ....150.00
Window card, Lawrence of Arabia, Peter O'Toole, 1971 (re-release) 35.00
Window card, Lonely Wives, EE Horton, 1930, Art Deco artwork 50.00
Window card, M*A*S*H, Donald Sutherland, 1970 ....25.00
Window card, Men Are Such Fools, H Bogart/P Lane/W Morris, 1938 ...300.00
Window card, Nun's Story, Audrey Hepburn, 1958 ....40.00
Window card, Teenage Millionaire, Chubby Checker, 1961 ....25.00
Window card, War & Peace, Audrey Hepburn/Henry Fonda, 1956 ..60.00

Mt. Washington

The Mt. Washington Glass Works was founded in 1837 in South Boston, Massachusetts, but moved to New Bedford in 1869 after purchasing the facilities of the New Bedford Glass Company. Frederick S. Shirley became associated with the firm in 1874. Two years later the company reorganized and became known as the Mt. Washington Glass Company. In 1894 it merged with the Pairpoint Manufacturing Company, a small Brittania works nearby, but continued to conduct business under its own title until after the turn of the century. The combined plants were equipped with the most modern and varied machinery available and boasted a working force with experience and expertise rival to none in the art of blowing and cutting glass. In addition to their fine cut glass, they are recognized as the first American company to make cameo glass, an effect they achieved through acid-cutting methods. In 1885 Shirley was issued a patent to make Burmese, pale yellow glassware tinged with a delicate pink blush. Another patent issued in 1886 allowed them the rights to produce Rose Amber, or amberina, a transparent ware shading from ruby to amber. Pearl Satin Ware and Peachblow, so named for its resemblance to a rosy peach skin, were patented the same year. One of their most famous lines, Crown Milano, was introduced in 1893. It was an opal glass either free-blown or pattern-molded, tinted a delicate color and decorated with enameling and gilt. Royal Flemish was patented in 1894 and is considered the rarest of the Mt. Washington art glass lines. It was decorated with raised, gold-enameled lines dividing the surface of the ware in much the same way as lead lines divide a stained glass window. The sections were filled in with one or several transparent colors and further decorated in gold enamel with florals, foliage, beading, and medallions.

Our advisors for this category are Betty and Clarence Maier; they are listed in the Directory under Pennsylvania. See also Amberina; Cranberry; Salt Shakers; Burmese; Crown Milano; Mother of Pearl; Royal Flemish; etc.

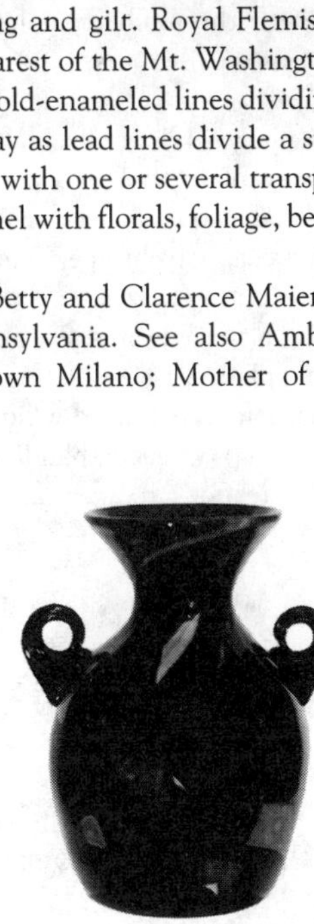

Vase, Lava, multicolor flux on glossy black, 5¾", $2,250.00. (Photo courtesy Clarence and Betty Maier)

Atomizer, opalware w/mc flowers/cobalt band/gilt buttons, att, 6½" ...300.00
Bottle, scent; floral on gr-brn pnt opal, spherical, 5" 365.00
Bowl, bride's; cameo, griffins/urn/floral, yel on wht, SP fr, 10" ...850.00
Bowl, cameo, griffins/scroll, bl on wht, fluted, 8" 1,400.00
Box, dresser; dk bl Xs on wht, sgn portrait lid, 3x4¾" 750.00
Box, florals/gilt on gr-pnt opal, emb floral/ribbon, 6½" L 1,700.00

Condiment set, mums & asters on pk to almond, s&p+mustard+tray ...1,200.00
Cracker jar, pansies on pnt peach to yel, 7½x6" 635.00
Cracker jar, poppies on yel-pnt opal, blown-out/squat, 7½" dia .500.00
Humidor, Delft, windmill etc, emb scrolls, SP mts, 5½" 900.00
Humidor, Delft, windmill etc in lacy reserve, SP rim/ft, 7½" .1,800.00
Muffineer, pansy sprays on opal to yel, egg shape, 4" 350.00
Shaker, Fig, florals/tan wash on wht, 3" 185.00
Shakers, Lobe 4, floral on cream, pr 265.00
Sugar shaker, cut, Fan, egg shape, 4½" 950.00
Sugar shaker, ferns on opal, egg shape, 4½" 300.00
Sugar shaker, floral on bl to wht, tomato form, 2¾x4" 450.00
Sugar shaker, flowers & foliage on yel to wht, fig shape, 3¾" .2,160.00
Sugar shaker, mums on wht to bl, egg shape, 4¼" 445.00
Sugar shaker, vines/violets on gr tint, egg shape, 4½" 385.00
Sweetmeat, gold roses & jewels on yel to wht, 4", NM 450.00
Syrup pitcher, violets on wht w/cream wash, SP mts, 7½" 1,250.00
Vase, Lava, mc patches on mirror blk, curlicue hdls, 5¾" 2,250.00
Vase, Lava, mc patches on mirror blk, flared rim, 5" 800.00
Vase, Napoli, chicks in rain (gold drops), rim hdls, 8½", NM .1,700.00
Vase, Napoli, spider mums, 8-rib, long trumpet neck, 10" 1,450.00

Mulberry China

Mulberry china was made by many of the Staffordshire area potters from about 1830 until the 1850s. It is a transfer-printed earthenware or ironstone named for the color of its decorations, a purplish-brown resembling the juice of the mulberry. Some pieces may have faded out over the years and today look almost gray with only a hint of purple. (Transfer printing was done in many colors; technically only those in the mauve tones are 'mulberry'; color variations have little effect on value.) Some of the patterns (Corean, Jeddo, Pelew, and Formosa, for instance) were also produced in Flow Blue ware. Others seem to have been used exclusively with the mulberry color. Our advisor for this category is Mary Frank Gaston.

Abbey, platter, 12" 165.00
Alleghany, plate, 9¼" 75.00
Alleghany, teapot 295.00
Argyle, tazza, polychrome, Dimmock 325.00
Avon, teapot, lg 385.00
Bochara, plate, Edwards, 9" 75.00
Bochara, platter, 14" 110.00
Bryonia, soup tureen, rnd w/lid 110.00
Calcutta, cup & suacer, handleless 175.00
Calcutta, teapot 275.00

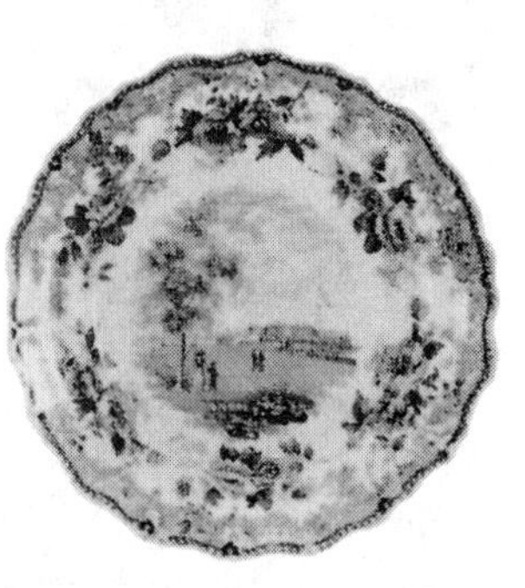

Castle Garden, plate, four-medallion floral-border series, Wood, 7⅞", NM, $60.00.

Castle Scenery, sugar bowl, w/lid, Furnival 275.00
Chusan, cup & saucer, Peter Holdcroft, 2¾", 5¾" 60.00
Corburg, shaving mug, Edwards 250.00
Corea, plate, 7¼" 55.00
Corean, creamer, att Podmore Walker, 5x4½", NM 175.00
Corean, cup, handleless; unmk, 3x3¼" 40.00
Corean, cup plate 65.00
Corean (similar), sugar bowl, lion-head hdls, 7½x4½" 125.00
Cyprus, cup & saucer, handleless 125.00
Cyprus, plate, Davenport, 9¼" 45.00
Delhi, plate, Clementson, 9¾" 75.00
Delhi, plate, 9½", NM 50.00
Delhi, platter, unmk, 11x8¼", NM 150.00
Delhi, soap box, w/lid 140.00
Foliage, cup & saucer 95.00
Foliage, cup & saucer, handleless 95.00
Foliage, plate, 9" 30.00
Heath's Flower, soup plate, 10½" 75.00
Hyson, sugar bowl 165.00
Jeddo, creamer 215.00
Jeddo, gravy boat, Adams 175.00
Jeddo, platter, 13½" 180.00
Jeddo, platter, 15½" 245.00
Jeddo, teapot 415.00
Lozere, cup & saucer, handleless 55.00
Madras, plate, 10" 145.00
Marble, pitcher, 8" 325.00
Medina, sugar bowl, Furnival 195.00
Medina, teapot, coxcomb hdl, Furnival, 10¼x9¼" 700.00
Nankin, creamer, Davenport 225.00
Ning-Po, pitcher, ca 1850, 8" 195.00
Panama, plate, 7¼" 35.00
Pelew, pitcher, water 195.00
Pelew, sauce plate, 4¼" 55.00
Rhone Scenery, cup & saucer, TJ&J Mayer, 3", 6" 40.00
Rhone Scenery, platter, 13½" 175.00
Rhone Scenery, teapot 275.00
Savoy, teapot 275.00
Seaweed, potty 270.00
Shapoo, platter, 14x10" 225.00
Strawberry Brushstroke, chamber pot, w/lid, mk Best, 8½x10" ..900.00
Tonquin, cup & saucer 95.00
Tonquin, sauce bowl 50.00
Tulip & Fern, tea set, Brushstroke, child sz, 14-pc 2,100.00
Udina, cup & saucer, Clementson 80.00
Vincennes, creamer 225.00
Vincennes, plate, 10", EX 65.00
Washington Vase, pitcher, Podmore Walker, 12x7" 375.00
Washington Vase, plate, Podmore Walker, 7½" 70.00
Washington Vase, teapot 475.00
Whampoa, sugar bowl 225.00
Wreath, cup & saucer, handleless 75.00

Muller Freres

Henri Muller established a factory in 1900 at Croismare, France. He produced fine cameo art glass decorated with florals, birds, and insects in the Art Nouveau style. The work was accomplished by acid engraving and hand finishing. Usual marks were 'Muller,' 'Muller Croismare,' or 'Croismare, Nancy.' In 1910 Henri and his brother Deseri formed a glassworks at Luneville. The cameo art glass made there was nearly all produced by acid cuttings of up to four layers with motifs similar to those favored at Croismare. A good range of colors was used, and some later pieces were gold flecked. Handles and decorative devices were sometimes applied by hand. In addition to the cameo glass, they also produced an acid-finished glass of bold mottled colors in the Deco style. Examples were signed 'Muller Freres' or 'Luneville.'

Our advisor for this category is Don Williams; he is listed in the Directory under Missouri.

Cameo

Box, raspberries/flowers, maroon on dusty pk, 2¾" H 900.00
Vase, aquatic plants/seashells, red on frost, 6" 1,650.00
Vase, fish, aqua irid on textured crystal, squatty, 7x8½" 3,700.00
Vase, fuchsia, cut/pnt on yel/orange mottle, 7¾" 980.00
Vase, gazelles on yel frost to lemon yel w/silver flecks, 7½x6½" ..3,000.00
Vase, lilies, cut/polished, caramel on lt bl opal, 9" 900.00
Vase, peonies w/stems/leaves, golden red/blk on yel frost, 5" ..1,300.00
Vase, poppies/scroll leaves, dk/lt purple on gray w/mc, 16" 5,700.00

Muncie

The Muncie Pottery was established in Muncie, Indiana, by Charles O. Grafton; it operated there from 1922 until about 1935. The pottery they produced is made of a heavier clay than most of its contemporaries; the styles are sturdy and simple. Early glazes were bright and colorful. In fact, Muncie was advertised as the 'rainbow pottery.' Later most of the ware was finished in a matt glaze. The more collectible examples are those modeled after Consolidated Glass vases — sculptured with lovebirds, grasshoppers, and goldfish. Their line of Art Deco-style vases bear a remarkable resemblance to the Consolidated Glass Company's Ruba Rombic line. Vases, candlesticks, bookends, ashtrays, bowls, lamp bases, and luncheon sets were made. A line of garden pottery was manufactured for a short time. Items were frequently impressed with MUNCIE in block letters. Letters such as A, K, E, or D and the numbers 1, 2, 3, 4, or 5 often found scratched into the base are finishers' marks.

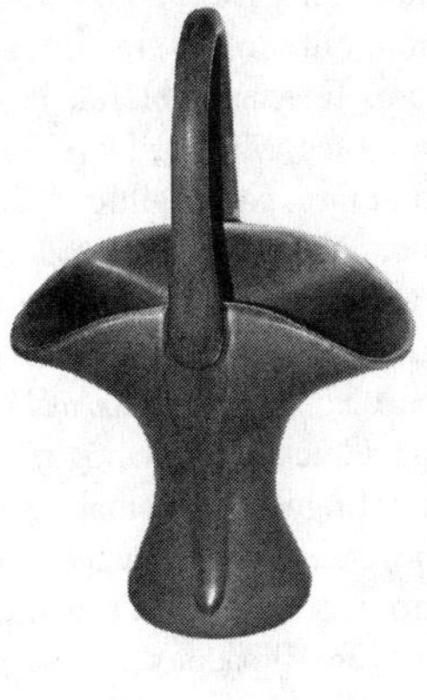

Basket, #174, green drip on rose matt, oval with handle, 12", $650.00. **(Photo courtesy Virginia Heiss)**

Bookends, #257, owls, gr/peachskin gloss, 5x6½", pr 350.00
Bookends, Leda & Swan, bl/gr gloss, 5x7", pr 375.00
Bowl, bulb; #306, Rhombic, gr matt/rust, 9" 375.00
Bowl, console; #276, gr matt, 4-hdl, 6x10" 235.00
Ewer, #136, bl/rose matt, bulb bottom, 12" 150.00
Flowerpot, #G4, gr matt/rust, 6" 185.00
Vase, #119, gr matt/rust, corseted, 9" 135.00
Vase, #129, gr matt/lav, corseted, w/hdls, 11" 200.00
Vase, #186, gr matt, fan shape, 7" 135.00
Vase, #278, Aorta, blk gloss, 5" 285.00
Vase, #312, Rhomic Star, bittersweet, 4x5" 425.00
Vase, #413, gr matt/lav, 4" 65.00
Vase, #485, Morning Glory, gr matt/rose, 5x6" 110.00
Vase, bud; #108, cobalt gloss, 1½" sq base, 6" 75.00
Vase, gate; #262, dk gr/peachskin gloss, 4½" 135.00
Wall pocket, #252, dk bl/wht gloss, 4x8½" 300.00

Musical Instruments

The field of automatic musical instruments covers many different categories ranging from watches and tiny seals concealing fine early musical movements to huge organs and orchestrions which weigh many hundreds of pounds and are equivalent to small orchestras. Music boxes, first made in the early nineteenth century by Swiss watchmakers, were produced in both disc and cylinder models. The latter type employs a cylinder with tiny pins that lift the teeth in the comb of the music box (producing a sound much like many individual tuning forks), and music results. The value of a cylinder music box depends on the length and diameter of the cylinder, the date of its manufacture, the number of tunes it plays (four or six is usually better than ten or twelve), and its manufacturer. Nicole Freres, Henri Capt, LeCoultre, and Bremond are among the most highly regarded, and the larger boxes made by Mermod Freres are also popular. Examples with multiple cylinders, extra instruments (such as bells or an organ section), and those in particularly ornate cabinets or with matching tables bring significantly higher prices. While smaller cylinder boxes are still being made, the larger ones (over 10" cylinders) typically date from before 1900. Disc music boxes were introduced about 1890 but were replaced by the phonograph only twenty-five years later. However, during that time hundreds of thousands were made. Their great advantage was in playing inexpensive interchangeable discs, a factor that remains an attraction for today's collector as well. Among the most popular disc boxes are those made by Regina (USA), Polyphon, Mira, Stella, and Symphonion. Relative values are determined by the size of the discs they play, whether they have single or double combs, if they are upright or table models, and how ornate their cases are. Especially valuable are those that play multiple discs at the same time or are incorporated into tall case clocks.

Player pianos were made in a wide variety of styles. Early varieties consisted of a mechanism which pushed up to a piano and played on the keyboard by means of felt-tipped fingers. These use sixty-five note rolls. Later models have the playing mechanism built in, and most use eighty-eight note rolls. Upright pump player pianos have little value in unrestored condition because the cost of restoration is so high. 'Reproducing' pianos, especially the 'grand' format, can be quite valuable, depending on the make, the size, the condition, and the ornateness of the case. 'Reproducing' pianos have very sophisticated mechanisms and are much more realistic in the reproduction of piano music. They were made in relatively limited quantities. Better manufacturers include Steinway and Mason & Hamlin. Popular roll mechanism makers include Ampico, Duo-Art, and Welte. The market for all types of player pianos has been weak for several years.

Coin-operated pianos (Orchestrions) were used commercially and typically incorporate extra instruments in addition to the piano action. These can be very large and complex, incorporating drums, cymbals, xylophones, bells, and hundreds of pipes. Both American and European coin pianos are very popular, especially the larger and more complex models made by Wurlitzer, Seeburg, Cremona, Weber, Welte, Hupfeld, and many others. These companies also made automatically playing violins (Mills Violin Virtuoso, Hupfeld), banjos (Encore), and harps (Whitlock); these are quite valuable.

Collecting player organettes is a fun endeavor. Roller ograns, organettes, player organs, grind organs, hand organs — whatever the name — are a fascinating group of music makers. Some used wooden barrels or cobs to operate the valves, or metal and cardboard discs or paper strips, paper rolls, metal donuts or metal strips. They usually played from 14 to 20 keys or notes. Some were presser operated or vacuum type. Their heyday lasted from the 1870s to the turn of the century. Most were reed organs, but a few had pipes. Many were made in either America or Germany. They lost favor with the advent of the phonograph, as did the music box. Some music boxes were built with little player organs in them.

Any player organette in good working condition with some music and in their original finish should be worth from $300.00 to $1,200.00, depending on the model. Generally the more keying it has and the larger and fancier the case, the more desirable it is. Rarity plays a part too. There are a handfull of individuals who make new music rolls for these player organs. Some machines are very rare, and music for them is nearly impossible to find. For further information on player organs we recommend *Encyclopedia of Musical Instruments* by Bowers. Our advisor for player organs is James R. Wilkins; he is listed in the Directory under Texas.

Unless noted, prices given are for instruments in fine condition, playing properly, with cabinets or cases in well-preserved or refinished condition. In all instances, unrestored instruments sell for much less, as do those with broken or missing parts, damaged cases, and the like. On the other hand, particularly superb examples in especially ornate case designs and those that have been particularly well kept will often command more. Our advisor for mechanical instruments (other than player organs) is Martin Roenigk; he is listed in the Directory under Arkansas.

Key:
c — cylinder
d — disc

Regina music box, pressed-design mahogany case, double comb, 12¼" disc, 9x15x14", with crank and seven discs, $3,850.00.

Box, Criterion 15½", dbl combs, w/matching base, EX 5,800.00
Box, Ideal Sublime Harmonie/Orpheus, 12" d, Switzerland, 1880s ..5,225.00
Box, Imperial Symphonion, 17⅝" upright, 2 c, EX 7,000.00
Box, Mandoline Quatour, 17¼" c, ornate 28" case 4,500.00
Box, Mermod Freres, 17½" c, 8-tune, 35" case 3,200.00
Box, Mira, 18½" d, console w/decal case, rstr 11,000.00
Box, Mira, 18½" d, mahog table model, rstr 6,800.00
Box, Polyphone, upright, 19⅝" d, G 5,700.00
Box, Regina, oak upright, 27" d, gallery, single play 13,500.00
Box, Regina, oak w/gallery, 27" d, autochanger 21,000.00
Box, Regina, upright, 12¼" d, rstr 3,800.00
Box, Regina, 11" d, oak case, VG, 16" d 1,300.00
Box, Regina, 15½" d, dbl c, zither attachment, 1880s, 21" L ..3,800.00
Box, Regina, 15½" d, single c, mahog case, EX 2,700.00
Box, Regina Sublima Corona Style #31, auto changer, 20¾" d, EX ...21,000.00
Box, Stella, 15½" d, mahog case w/decor top, 13x25x19", VG 4,200.00
Box, Stella, 17¼" d, console w/cvd cabinet, G 6,000.00
Box, Stella, 17¼" d, table model, G 4,000.00
Box, Swiss, pnt decor, 5½" c w/zither attachment, 8-tune, 17½" L ...500.00
Box, Swiss, 11⅛" c, 4-tune, key wind, 1850s 1,700.00
Box, Symphonion, 11⅞" d, dbl comb, G 1,650.00
Box, Symphonion Eroica, 3 d, upright, +15 d sets 28,500.00
Box, Symphonium, 17⅝" d, dbl comb, mahog table model 5,800.00
Caliola, Wurlitzer, Clancy O'Toole front, rare, EX 14,500.00
Nickelodeon, Peerless, beveled glass front, 1902, rstr 10,500.00
Nickelodeon, Seeburg A, w/xylophone, rstr 6,900.00
Nickelodeon, Seeburg F, w/xylophone, rstr 8,000.00
Nickelodeon, Wurlitzer IX-B, bells/auto roll changer, rstr 12,500.00
Orchestrelle, Aeolian V, oak, EX orig 3,500.00
Orchestrion, Coinola C-2, EX 27,000.00
Orchestrion, Western Electric, 10-tune, G roll, 1920s, rstr 7,500.00
Organ, band; Wurlitzer #125, partially rstr 20,000.00
Organ, band; Wurlitzer #146, rstr 18,000.00
Organ, bbl; Bacigalupo, 38-key, 90 pipes, G 6,600.00
Organ, bbl; Molinari, 20-key, G 3,800.00
Organ, Concert Roller, 12 6½" wooden cobs, G 800.00
Organ, Dutch street; Limonaire, 34-key, w/music book/1 figure ...22,000.00
Organ, fairground; Gasparini, 52-key, early 1900s, rstr 16,000.00
Organ, military band; Artisan A-1, 1920s, 76", G- 16,000.00
Organ, pump; Aeolian Orchestrelle Reed, mahog, '03, EX+, +rolls ..4,000.00
Organette, Celestina, 20-note, G, +10 rolls 850.00
Piano, baby grand; Chickering Ampico, 65x59", w/200 rolls ..5,000.00
Piano, grand; Knabe Ampico, art case, 68", EX orig 9,500.00
Piano, grand; Mason & Hamlin, 1982, 68", M 8,500.00
Piano, grand; Weber #77755 Model FR Duo-Art, mahog, 1922, 71½", EX 5,000.00
Piano, Steinway Duo Art, walnut, 79", rstr 17,500.00
Piano, upright; Charles Steiff Welte, M orig 1,200.00
Piano, upright; Duo-Art, ft pump, walnut, 1922, EX orig 1,250.00
Piano, upright; Stroud Duo-Art Style #593, walnut, 1938, rstr ..3,800.00
Rollmonica, toy player harmonica, Bakelite, G, +6 rolls 125.00
Violano, Mills Dbl, EX 60,000.00
Violano, Mills Virtuoso, single violin & piano, oak, G 24,000.00

Non-Mechanical

Bagpipes, Scottish, w/Stewart bag, EX 250.00
Banjo, Vega Senator, 5-string, 1929, 11" rim, EX 770.00
Drum, Excelsior, wood, gut snares, rope tension, 16x10", G 90.00
Flute, Firth Hall & Pond, coccuswood, ivory mts & cap, 21" 600.00
Guitar, Chet Atkins CE, rosewood brd, 1982-92, any color, M ...1,000.00
Guitar, Fender 'slab brd,' ca 1960, EX orig (+), from $8,000 to .10,000.00
Guitar, Fender Stratocaster, 1962 ....4,500.00
Guitar, Gibson ES-335N, 1982 ....1,650.00
Guitar, Gibson L-3, reddish sunburst w/inlay, 1930s, EX 2,000.00
Guitar, Telecaster, blond, 1980, NM, from $800 to 900.00
Harmonica, Magnus Duo-Tone Giant, 1950s, 9½" 15.00
Harp, Erard, parcel-gilt cvd Gothic-style capital w/figures, 71" ..2,000.00
Piano, Am, rosewood, scrolled lyre music rest, 1860s, 38x80⅝" .1,650.00
Piano, baby grand; Chickering, walnut, lyre-form ped support ..1,000.00
Piano, baby grand; Kranich & Bach NY, mahog Rococo style, 1889 ....3,000.00
Piano, CFI Albrecht Phila, mahog cvd/mahog veneer w/gilt, 1825, 68" ..700.00
Piano, Chickering, mahog w/late Classical influence, lg ivories .1,250.00
Piano, Eng Regency, mahog w/ebony bands, 1815, 66" 1,500.00
Piano, grand; J Strohmenger London, ebonized/parcel-silver, 54" ..5,750.00
Piano, H&W Geib NY, mahog w/inlay, 7 trn legs, 68" W, VG ..600.00
Piano, John Broadmore...London, mahog Geo III, 1796, 33x63x21" ..800.00
Piano, Robert Fearn Jr, London, 1810, on stand, 32x65x23" ..2,300.00
Piano, Robt & Wm Nuns NY, rosewood-banded mahog, 1830s, 33x67x27" ...700.00
Piano, upright; French, Henri Herz model B, walnut, 1880s, 47x48" ..925.00
Violin, Am, baroque neck, pnt-on stars, early 1800s, child sz 325.00
Zither, Am Concert, floral marquetry, ca 1890s 365.00

Mustache Cups

Mustache cups were popular items during the late Victorian period, designed specifically for the man with the mustache! They were made in silverplate as well as china and ironstone. Decorations ranged from simple transfers to elaborately applied and gilded florals. To properly position the 'mustache bar,' special cups were designed for the 'lefties.' These are the rare ones!

Blue Onion, 1800s 95.00

Floral, bl on wht w/gold trim, Germany 60.00
Floral, emb, gold trim, mc beadwork, lt wear 30.00
Floral, mc w/emb decor, Germany, w/saucer 60.00
Floral, RS Germany, mold 26, gr mk, w/saucer 90.00
Flowers & bird on pk, Limoges, 3⅜", 6⅝" saucer 90.00
Knights & angels, gold trim, Royal Bavaria, w/saucer 70.00
Landscape w/sheep & buildings, worn gold trim, 4½" dia 70.00
Oriental motif, HP, 2¾x3", w/saucer 65.00
Roses on wht w/gold, w/saucer 65.00
Violets on turq w/gold swirls, left-handed, Germany, w/saucer 70.00

Nailsea

Nailsea is a term referring to clear or colored glass decorated in contrasting spatters, swirls, or loops. These are usually white but may also be pink, red, or blue. It was first produced in Nailsea, England, during the late 1700s but was made in other parts of Britain and Scotland as well. During the mid-1800s a similar type of glass was produced in this country. Originally used for decorative novelties only, by that time tumblers and other practical items were being made from Nailsea-type glass. See also Lamps; Witch Balls.

Atomizer, red w/wht loopings, egg shape, orig hardware, 7¾" ...180.00
Creamer, aqua w/red & wht spatter, appl hdl, 4", NM 110.00
Cruet, clear w/wht opal loopings, appl ring & hdl, pontil, 8", EX ..100.00
Flask, cased milk glass w/red loopings, pontil scar, 9" 210.00
Flask, clear w/pk & wht herringbone, pontil scar, 7⅞" 175.00
Flask, clear w/red & wht loopings, pontil scar, 8¾" 230.00
Flask, clear w/wht loopings, pontil scar, 8¾" 125.00
Flask, clear w/wht loopings, tooled lip, pontil scar, 6¼" 75.00
Flask, cranberry w/tight wht herringbone, 7⅛" 925.00
Flask, cranberry w/wht swirls, pontil scar, 7⅜" 375.00
Flask, dk amber w/wht loopings, pontil scar, 4⅝" 350.00
Flask, Gemel; clear, red/wht loops alternate, pontil scar, 8¼" 160.00
Flask, Gemel; clear w/heavy wht loopings, pontil scar, 7¾" 130.00
Flask, Gemel; milk glass w/red loopings, pontil scar, 8¾" 190.00
Flask, milk glass w/pk & wht loopings, 8¾" 220.00
Flask, milk glass w/red & bl alternating loopings, 7¼" 475.00
Flask, milk glass w/red herringbone, tooled mouth, 8" 200.00
Flask, milk glass w/red loopings, pontil scar, 7¾" 220.00
Flask, milk glass w/red loopings, pontil scar, 9¼" 275.00
Flask, olive gr w/wht loopings, pontil scar, 6½" 400.00
Rolling pin, clear w/cobalt loopings, plaster filled, 13¼" 325.00
Rolling pin, clear w/pk & wht loopings, 16¼" 200.00
Vase, clear w/wht loopings, rolled rim, ftd, 11½" 550.00

Nakara

Nakara was a line of decorated opaque milk glass produced by the C.F. Monroe Company of Meriden, Connecticut, for a few years after the turn of the century. It differs from their Wave Crest line in several ways. The shapes were simpler; pastel colors were deeper and covered more of the surface; more beading was present; flowers were larger; and large transfer prints of figures, Victorian ladies, cherubs, etc., were used as well. Ormolu and brass collars and mounts complemented these opulent pieces. Most items were signed; however, this is not important since the ware was never reproduced. Our advisors for this category are Dolli and Wilfred R. Cohen; their address is listed in the Directory under California.

Ashtray, floral, pk on gr, ornate rim, 6" 300.00
Box, blown-out pansy on bl, 3¼" dia 950.00
Box, cherubs transfer on bl, 8" dia 1,950.00
Box, floral & cross, lt pk, mirror in lid, clip missing, 5" 650.00
Box, floral on bl, hexagonal, 3x3¼" 495.00
Box, floral on bl, 2¼x3¾" dia 450.00
Box, floral on bl w/wht beading, oval, 2¾x5¼" 650.00
Box, floral on gr, crown mold, 8½" dia 1,750.00
Box, floral on rare burmese coloring, ftd, lg 1,950.00
Box, lady's portrait in reserve on bl w/wht enamel, 5" dia 900.00

Box, portrait transfer on blue, 8" diameter, $2,750.00. (Photo courtesy Wilfred and Dolli Cohen)

Box, portrait transfer, Collars & Cuffs on bl 2,250.00
Box, portrait transfer on pk, bishop's hat mold, 4½" dia 695.00
Box, Spindrift, floral on cream to bl, 8" dia 2,250.00
Card holder, floral on gr, rectangular 650.00
Cracker jar, floral on rose w/gold, gold metal hdl & lid 750.00
Humidor, Cigars & flowers on bl 1,250.00
Humidor, The Old Sport, bulldog, 7" 750.00
Match holder, floral on pk, 1½x2½" 850.00
Mirror tray, floral, pastel int, 3¾" dia 695.00
Pin receiver, floral on gr, beaded rim, 1x2½" 250.00
Pin tray, floral on cream, ornate rim & hdl, color-washed int 275.00
Smoke set, 4-pc on metal base, floral on gr w/beaded rims 800.00
Vase, floral, stick neck, 8" 995.00

Napkin Rings

Napkin rings became popular during the late 1800s. They were made from various materials. Among the most popular and collectible today are the large group of varied silverplated figurals made by American manufacturers. Recently the larger figurals in excellent condition have appreciated considerably. Only those with a blackened finish, corrosion, or broken and/or missing parts have maintained their earlier price levels. When no condition is indicated, the items listed below are assumed to be all original and in very good to excellent condition. Check very carefully for missing parts, solder repairs, marriages, and reproductions.

A timely warning: inexperienced buyers should be aware of excellent reproductions on the market, especially the wheeled pieces and cherubs. However, these do not have the fine detail and patina of the originals and tend to have a more consistent, soft pewter-like finish. These are appearing at the large, quality shows at top prices, being shown along with authentic antique merchandise. Beware! For further information we recommend *Figural Napkin Rings* (Collector Books) by Lillian Gottschalk and Sandra Whitson. Our advisor for this category is Deborah Maggard; she is listed in the Directory under Ohio.

Key:
gw — gold washed
R&B — Reed & Barton
SH&M — Simpson, Hall, & Miller

Acorns at side of ring, rnd base, Meriden #163 ....65.00
Billiken seated beside ring, unmk, less than 200.00

Bird on leaf, Meriden #202, 3¼x3½" 295.00
Bird w/wings wide beside ring on tiered base, Derby #365 ....295.00
Birds (2 sm) flank SP bud vase atop ring on ped, Wilcox #1899 ..275.00
Boy pulls sled on which ring rests, Wilcox #01576, minimum ...595.00
Boy removing socks sits beside ring, Derby #341 ....375.00
Bull stands by bright-cut ring, fancy cast base, Knickerbocker #1250 ...275.00
Calla lily beside ring, acanthus-leaf ftd base, Barbour Bros #9 ...275.00
Chair of tree limbs holds ring, rstr 125.00
Cherries (3) drape over side of ring, Toronto #1173 ....200.00
Cherub (nude) up on 1 ft stands by ring, Middletown #73 ....275.00
Cherub w/drum stick raised to strike drum ring, Meriden #232 .275.00
Cherubs (2) support filigree ring on bks, Toronto #273 ....295.00
Chick on wishbone by beaded ring, Sincere Wishes, SH&M #2361, under ...150.00
Cockatoo on sunflower stem beside book-shape holder, Derby #370 ..275.00
Cockatoo w/glass eyes on C-scroll support for ring, Rogers Smith & Co ..275.00
Crane w/stick in beak stands beside ring on stump, unmk 400.00
Croquet mallets (4) & flowers, holder simulates wicket, Derby #302 ...275.00
Cupid w/quiver behind bk stands beside ring, Tufts #1546 ....425.00
Dog on hind legs w/bk against narrow ring, R&B #1425, under ...225.00
Dolphins (2) hold ring w/tails, knife rest at heads, Pairpoint #30 .275.00
Eagle atop ring on ped w/domed base, Meriden Britannia #167 ..275.00
Elegant lady w/spyglass beside ring, Southingham Cutlery #39 ..275.00
Elephant w/raised trunk beside ring on oval base, Knickerbocker #1249 ..275.00
Fawn flower garland around neck, angel emb on ring, R&B #1807 .275.00
Flower bud vase atop ring flanked by 2 sm rearing horses, unmk .450.00
Fox on ea side of ring, Rockford #174 ....275.00
Game bird & branch beside spool-shaped ring, Aurora #17 ....275.00

Girl with begging dog stands before ring, Meriden #199, 3⅜", $395.00.

Girl w/long braid & apron pushes ring, Meriden Britannia #280 .275.00
Greenaway boy sitting on fence (forming holder), unmk 295.00
Greenaway boy w/whistle, Tufts #1622 ....400.00
Greenaway girl in dress & bonnet touches ring, Middletown #25 ..425.00
Greenaway girl teaches ABCs to poodle, blkboard holder, Tufts #1669 ..550.00
Horse prances w/ring on bk, leafy base, ftd 225.00
Horse pulls ring on wheels, Meriden Britannia #214 ....275.00
Horseshoe emb Bonheur on oval ftd fr, Tufts #1540 ....275.00
Lady on toboggan grasps ring, West Silver #273 ....425.00
Lizard on base, 2nd draped over top of ring, Southington #33 ...275.00
Monkey playing cymbals beside emb ring, #066 (maker unknown) ...275.00
Oriental fans form ring, raised tiered base, Derby #335 ....275.00
Owl on leaf before ring on ftd base, Rogers #257 ....275.00
Palmer Cox Brownie on raised base w/hands on ring, Pairpoint #37 .275.00
Palmer Cox Brownie w/rifle by ring w/emerging rabbit, unmk ...425.00
Poodle on hind legs beside ring on plain base, Tufts #1616 ....275.00
Rabbit peers over scalloped-edged ring, Derby #547 ....425.00
Rifles (4 crossed) support rtcl ring, Meriden Britannia #335 ....275.00
Rooster stands on shovel that supports ring, Meriden Britannia #181 ...275.00
Rustic chair w/bentwood bk supports ring, SH&M #18, under ..200.00
Sailor boy w/rope & anchor by pitcher bud vase atop ring, R&B #1357 ..550.00
Squirrel w/glass eyes blows horn 250.00
Squirrel w/nut faces away from ring, SH&M #09 ....275.00
Sunflower base, octagonal, Meriden #37 ....75.00
Wheelbarrow holds ring, shield-shaped base, Tufts #1537 ....225.00

Nash

A. Douglas Nash founded the Corona Art Glass Company in Long Island, New York. He produced tableware, vases, flasks, etc. using delicate artistic shapes and forms. After 1933 he worked for the Libbey Glass Company.

Bowl, Chintz, 8" 150.00
Bowl, console; Chintz, violet/lime decor, #501 DD, 12" 300.00
Vase, chartreuse & opal pulls on golden-brn, #94-11, 11" 600.00
Vase, Chintz, brn/yel/rust 'zippers,' tan int, spherical, 6" 230.00
Vase, clear w/orange stripes, unsgn, 5½" 100.00

Natzler, Gertrude and Otto

The Natzlers came to the United States from Vienna in the late 1930s. They settled in Los Angeles where they continued their work in ceramics, for which they were already internationally recognized. Gertrude created the forms; Otto formulated a variety of interesting glazes, among them volcanic, crystalline, and lustre. Our advisor for this category is Abby Malowanczyk; she is listed in the Directory under Texas.

Bottle, bl/gr/yel mottled gloss w/melt fissures, 5x10" 4,500.00
Bottle, turq crystalline semigloss, paneled, 8½x4½" 2,400.00
Bowl, blk to dk brn, wide mouth, 8⅛" 1,725.00
Bowl, blk w/bl crystals, oval, 2x6" 1,600.00
Bowl, chartreuse semigloss, flaring/shallow, 2½x8½" 3,500.00
Bowl, hare's fur bl & gr w/melt fissures, 2x5½" 5,000.00
Bowl, hare's fur bright yel w/rust rim, dimpled/sqd, 3½x5" 2,600.00
Bowl, hare's fur cobalt gloss, flat bottom, str sides, 3x5" 2,100.00
Bowl, hare's fur frothy bl, M994 tag, 4x5" 2,300.00
Bowl, lime gr, oval, 2x5½" 1,000.00
Bowl, lt bl semigloss, flared, 2½x6¼", NM 1,200.00
Bowl, red/blk reduction, ftd, 2½x6½" 1,800.00
Bowl, tomato red w/crystals at bottom, mk/label, 7" 1,100.00
Bowl, volcanic, gr & brn, spherical, N129 tag, 5x5" 6,000.00
Bowl, volcanic cream & yel, hemispherical, L610 tag, 4½x6" .5,000.00
Bowl, volcanic verdigris, 1½x5½" 1,600.00
Bowl/vase, volcanic, brn & yel, M288 tag, 4¾x6½" 5,500.00
Plate, volcanic turq, 5½" dia 1,000.00
Sculpture, 2 disk shapes on cylindrical post, 21" 1,700.00
Teapot, orange crystalline uranium, +trivet, bowl, 4 c/s 14,000.00
Vase, beige w/melt fissures, str walls, K986 tag, 4¾x3¾" 2,600.00
Vase, bl/turq/brn flambe crystalline, bulbous, L254 tag, 4x3" ..4,500.00
Vase, hare's fur chartreuse, U-form, sm ft, 6x5½" 2,600.00
Vase, lt bl gloss, 2½" 950.00
Vase, thick bl & rose, flaring/ftd, 5½" dia 2,400.00
Vase, volcanic sea gr flowing over gray-gr, 1960, 13" 8,000.00
Vessel, semi-volcanic brn/gold/orange, teardrop form, M444, 10x7" .11,000.00
Vessel, turq/bl/brn flambe crystalline, bottle shape, N828 tag, 13x4" ..8,000.00

New Martinsville

The New Martinsville Glass Company took its name from the town in West Virginia where it began operations in 1901. In the beginning years, pressed tablewares were made in crystal as well as colored and opalescent glass. Considered an innovator, the company was known for their imaginative applications of the medium in creating lamps made entirely of glass, vanity sets, figural decanters, and models of animals and birds. In 1944 the company was purchased by Viking Glass, who continued to use many of the old molds, the animals molds included. They marked their wares 'Viking' or 'Rainbow Art.' Viking recently ceased operations and has been purchased by Kenneth Dalzell, president of the Fostoria Company. They, too, are making the bird and animal models. Although at first they were not marked, future productions are to be marked with an acid stamp. Dalzell/Viking animals are in the $50.00 to $60.00 range. Values for cobalt and red items are two to three times higher than for the same item in clear. See also Depression Glass; Glass Animals and Figurines.

Bedside set, cobalt or red, four-piece, $175.00.

Basket, Janice, crystal, 11" 85.00
Bowl, celery; Radiance, red or bl, 10" 35.00
Bowl, fruit; Janice, red or bl, ruffled top, 12" 95.00
Bowl, Janice, crystal, flared, 3-toed, 10½" 45.00
Bowl, Janice, red or bl, cupped, 9½" 55.00
Bowl, Prelude, crystal, cupped, 7" 25.00
Bowl, Prelude, crystal, shallow, 10" 35.00
Bowl, Prelude, crystal, 3-ftd, 15" 70.00
Bowl, Radiance, amber, flared, 12" 30.00
Bowl, Radiance, amber, ftd, 6" 17.50
Bowl, soup; Moondrops, red or bl, 6¾" 90.00
Candlestick, Prelude, crystal, 4½" 20.00
Candy box, Prelude, crystal, w/lid, 3-ftd, 7" 65.00
Comport, cracker; Janice, crystal, for cheese plate 16.00
Creamer, Prelude, crystal, 4-ftd 15.00
Creamer, Radiance, red or bl 25.00
Decanter, Michael, red, w/hdl 145.00
Decanter, Moondrops, colors other than red or bl, sm, 7¾" 40.00
Goblet, Moondrops, red or bl, 5-oz, 4¾" 25.00
Ice pail, Janice, red or bl, hdl, 10" 170.00
Jam jar, Janice, crystal, w/lid, 6" 20.00
Lamp, Radiance, amber, 12" 65.00
Lazy susan, Prelude, crystal, 3-pc set, 18" 165.00
Pitcher, berry cream; Janice, red or bl, 15-oz 110.00
Plate, dinner; Prelude, crystal, 10" 37.50
Plate, Janice, crystal, 13" 30.00
Plate, Prelude, crystal, hdls, 6½" 12.50
Plate, Prelude, crystal, 18" 90.00
Platter, Janice, red or bl, oval, 13" 75.00
Punch bowl, Radiance, red or bl 225.00
Relish, Prelude, crystal, hdls, 3-part, 10", from $30 to 40.00
Saucer, Radiance, amber 6.00
Stem, water; Prelude, crystal, 9-oz 27.00
Stem, wine; Prelude, crystal, 3-oz 22.50
Syrup, Janice, crystal, w/dripcut top 55.00
Treasure jar, Prelude, crystal, w/lid, 8" 110.00
Tumbler, shot; Moondrops, colors other than red or bl, 2-oz, 2¾" ..10.00
Vase, ball; Janice, crystal, 9" 55.00
Vase, bud; Moondrops, red or bl, Rocket style, 8½" 275.00
Vase, Janice, red or bl, ftd, 7" 70.00
Vase, Prelude, crystal, crimped, 11" 65.00
Vase, Radiance, red or bl, flared, 10" 80.00

Newcomb

The Newcomb College of New Orleans, Louisiana, established a pottery in 1895 to provide the students with first-hand experience in the fields of art and ceramics. Using locally dug clays — red and buff in the early years, white-burning by the turn of the century — potters were employed to throw the ware which the ladies of the college decorated. Until about 1910 a glossy glaze was used on ware decorated by slip painting or incising. After that a matt glaze was favored. Soft blues and greens were used almost exclusively, and decorative themes were chosen to reflect the beauty of the South. The year 1930 marked the end of the matt-glaze period and the art-pottery era.

Various marks used by the pottery include an 'N' within a 'C,' sometimes with 'HB' added to indicate a 'hand-built' piece. The potter often incised his initials into the ware, and the artists were encouraged to sign their work. Among the most well-known artists were Sadie Irvine, Henrietta Bailey, and Fannie Simpson.

Newcomb pottery is evaluated to a large extent by two factors: design and condition. In the following listings, items are assumed matt unless noted otherwise. Our advisor for this category is David Rago; he is listed in the Directory under New Jersey.

Note: In the following descriptions, the decoration is slip painted unless noted carved within the line. The term 'transitional' defines a period of two to three years between earlier and later work, and signifies changes to the glazes, colors, and style of decoration.

Bowl, centerpc; floral on bl, AF Simpson, 4x11¼"+frog 1,600.00
Bowl, crocus, bl/gr/lav, sgn, 2¼x8" 250.00
Bowl, floral, gr/wht on bl, A Simpson, #ND25, 7" dia 1,600.00
Bowl, gr & brn hare's fur glaze, NC/MF/F/D, 2½x4¾" 450.00
Candlestick, freesia, bl/gr/yel, AF Simpson, #232, 1919, 7¼" .7,150.00
Candlestick, spring flowers, bl/yel/gr, Sadie Irvine, #232, 7¼" ..4,400.00
Candlesticks, spiderwort on bl, S Irvine, 1923, 7¼x4¼", pr ...1,700.00
Mug, floral band, cobalt & gr on denim bl, SE Wells, 1911, 4x5" ...1,500.00
Pitcher, daffodils, glossy, Harriet Joor, 1905, 8x6½", NM 8,500.00
Pitcher, floral emb band, bl on gr/cream, ca 1929, #RP42, 5" .1,600.00
Pitcher, milk; leaves, gr on bl, Aurelia Arbo, 1933, 4x4" 1,200.00
Pitcher, roses, yel on bl-gr gloss, H Bailey, 1903, 2½x3¼" 1,600.00
Plaque, satyr & musical instruments below moon & star, 7x8½" .2,000.00
Plate, chrysanthemums, AF Simpson, Transitional, 1913, 8¾" 1,600.00
Plate, clover leaves, gr on gr & ivory, H Joor, 1898, 10¼" 1,600.00
Plate, floral, mc on aqua, Haviland blank, att, 8½" 500.00
Tile, freesia & vine, bl/gr/yel, May Louise Dunn, 1911, 4¾" 525.00
Trivet, floral, bl & gr on ivory, Mary Butler, 1906, 6" dia 1,400.00
Vase, bats & crescent moons, bl & gr borders, #AQ47, 6½" ..9,000.00
Vase, camellias, CP Littlejohn, #260, ca 1914, 2¾x5½" 935.00
Vase, crocus on H Bailey, Transitional, 1916, 3¼x6" 1,300.00
Vase, dogs' heads, amber/cobalt/ivory, S Wells, 1902, 4¾x2¾" ..3,500.00
Vase, dogwood, C Littlejohn, Transitional, 1914, 5½x3" 1,600.00
Vase, floral, mc on purple, Henrietta Bailey, 1918, 4¼x3" 1,800.00
Vase, floral, Sadie Irvine, 1925, 6x3¼" 1,400.00
Vase, floral on bl-gr, AF Simpson, Transitional, 1914, 3x5½", NM ...850.00
Vase, freesia, mc on dk bl, Leona Nicholson, 1909, 8¼x6¼" ...24,000.00
Vase, geese (6), cream & bl on bl/gr/cream, Richardson, #V12, 6½" .12,000.00
Vase, geometrics at rim, mc on bl, S Irvine, #UQ37, 3" 900.00
Vase, gr mottle on neutral opaque, J Meyer potter, 1907, 4x4¼" 385.00
Vase, grapevines, cobalt/bl-gr on bl gloss, RB Kennon, 1902, 6x7½" ..7,500.00
Vase, horizontal lines, turq/cranberry/mushroom, ca 1910-27, 3½" ..385.00
Vase, irises, mc on bl, Sadie Irvine, Transitional, 1915, 11¾", NM ...4,000.00

Vase, lilies (cvd), wht/gr/bl, AF Simpson, 1916, 4¼x5¾" 2,800.00
Vase, magnolias, MM 15, 1903, 6x4" 6,000.00
Vase, moon/moss, bl & gr, F Ford/Aurelia Arbo, ZB7, 4¾x5" ...1,875.00
Vase, moon/moss, Henrietta Bailey, 1933, 6⅜x6½" 5,000.00
Vase, moon/moss/trees, H Bailey, #330, 1931, 9x4" 5,400.00
Vase, moonlit barn/trees/moss, S Irvine, 1925, drilled, 11¼" ..3,750.00
Vase, moss/moon/oaks, on gr matt, AF Simpson, 5" 2,900.00
Vase, moss/oaks, bl/gr/pk, illegible mk, #49, 1923, 6x8½" 5,500.00
Vase, moss/oaks, Sadie Irvine, 1930s, 9x3½", NM 4,500.00
Vase, moss/trees relief, ML Dunn (Joseph Meyer), 1913, 9⅜x3" 2,100.00
Vase, narcissus (cvd), 4-color, A Mason, Transitional, 1914, 7x9" ...2,400.00
Vase, narcissus on bl, AF Simpson, #223, 1924, 8½x3¼" 3,250.00
Vase, pine needles, mc on gr matt, #314, ca 1915, 4¾x5⅛" 635.00
Vase, raspberry w/periwinkle bl int, bulbous, 5¼x4½" 400.00
Vase, repeating curvilinear decor, Sadie Irvine, 1932, 6x5" 2,300.00
Vase, roses & leaves, mc on bl, S Irvine, #OF70, 10½" 6,000.00
Vase, teal lustre over gr, bottle shape, L Nicholson, 1918, 7½" ..1,300.00
Vase, thistles, gr & bl on cream & dk bl, MW Butler, 4" 4,750.00
Wall pocket, cockatoos, bl/gr/wht, Irvine, ca 1930, 8¼x4½" .7,480.00
Wall pocket, stylized trees, cobalt & gr, L Nicholson, 1904, 11x4" ...8,500.00

Newspapers

People do not collect newspapers simply because they are old. Age has absolutely nothing to do with value — it does not hold true that the older the newspaper, the higher the value. Instead, most of the value is determined by the historic event content. In most cases, the more important to American history the event is, the higher the value. In over two hundred years of American history, perhaps as many as 98% of all newspapers ever published *do not* contain news of a significant historic event. Newspapers not having news of major events in history are called 'atmosphere.' Atmosphere papers have little collector value. (See price guide below.)

To learn more about the hobby of collecting old and historic newspapers, be sure to visit our mega-web sight on the Internet at www.historybuff.com/. The e-mail address for the NCSA is help@historybuff.com/. See Newspaper Collector's Society of America in Clubs, Newsletters, and Catalogs for more information.

Charleston Courier.

1818, June, First Seminole War News (Jackson hangs two chiefs), Charleston Courier, four pages, with editor's marks, EX, $690.00.

1800-1820, Atmosphere editions 7.00
1821-1859, Atmosphere editions 5.00
1836, Texas declares independence 60.00
1845, Annexation of Texas 35.00
1846, Start of Mexican War 30.00
1846-1847, Major battles of Mexican War 20.00
1847, End of Mexican War 30.00
1848, Gold discovered in California 60.00
1859, John Brown's raid on Harper's Ferry 45.00
1860, Lincoln elected 1st term 150.00
1861, Lincoln's inaugural address 175.00
1861-1865, Atmosphere editions: Confederate titles 50.00
1861-1865, Atmosphere editions: Union titles 7.00
1861-1865, Major battles of Civil War 75.00
1862, Emancipation Proclamation 135.00
1863, Gettysburg Address 250.00
1865, April 29 edition of Frank Leslie's 350.00
1865, April 29 edition of Harper's Weekly 300.00
1865, Capture & death of J Wilkes Booth 100.00
1865, Fall of Richmond 100.00
1865, NY Herald, Apr 15 (Beware: reprints abound) 900.00
1865, Titles other than NY Herald, Apr 15 ......400.00
1866-1900, Atmosphere editions 4.00
1876, Custer's Last Stand 150.00
1881, Billy the Kid killed 200.00
1881, Garfield assassinated 50.00
1881, Gunfight at OK Corral 225.00
1882, Jesse James killed 200.00
1898, Sinking of Maine 40.00
1901, McKinley assassinated 60.00
1903, Wright Brother's flight 300.00
1906, San Francisco earthquake, other titles 30.00
1906, San Francisco earthquake, San Francisco title 500.00
1912, Sinking of Titanic 250.00
1915, Sinking of Lusitania 125.00
1927, Babe Ruth hits 60th home run 70.00
1927, Lindbergh arrives in Paris 75.00
1929, St Valentine's Day Massacre 150.00
1929, Stock market crash 90.00
1931, Al Capone found guilty 35.00
1931, Jack 'Legs' Diamond killed 35.00
1933, Machine Gun Kelley captured 35.00
1934, Baby Face Nelson killed 40.00
1934, Bonnie & Clyde killed 125.00
1934, Dillinger killed 150.00
1934, Pretty Boy Floyd killed 35.00
1937, Hindenbergh explodes 65.00
1941, Honolulu Star-Bulletin, Dec 7, 1st extra (+) 600.00
1941, Other titles, Dec 7, w/Pearl Harbor news 35.00
1948, Chicago Daily Tribune, Nov 3, Dewey Defeats Truman ...900.00
1961, Alan Shephard 1st astronaut in space 20.00
1961, Roger Maris hits 61st home run 25.00
1962, Death of Marilyn Monroe 30.00
1962, John Glenn orbits Earth 18.00
1963, JFK assassination, Nov 22, Dallas title 60.00
1963, JFK assassination, Nov 22, titles other than Dallas 8.00
1968, Assassination of Martin Luther King 7.00
1968, Assassination of Robert Kennedy 7.00
1969, Moon landing 10.00
1974, Nixon resigns 5.00

Nicodemus

Chester Nicodemus moved from Dayton, Ohio, to Columbus in 1930 and started teaching at the Columbus Art School. During this time he made vases and commissioned sculptures, water fountains, and limestone and wood carvings. In 1941 Chester left the field of teaching to pursue pottery making full time, using local red clay containing a large amount of iron. Known for its durability, he called the ware Ferro-stone. He made teapots and other utility wares, but these goods lost favor, so he started producing animal and bird sculptures, nativity sets, and Christmas ornaments, some bearing Chester's and Florine's names as personalized cards for his customers and friends. Chester died in 1990.

His glaze colors were turquoise or aqua, ivory, green mottle, pussy willow (pink), and golden yellow. The glaze was applied so that the color of the warm red clay would show through, adding an extra dimension to each piece. Examples are usually marked with his name incised in the clay, but paper labels were also used. For more information, we recommend *Sanford Guide to Nicodemus, His Pottery and His Art*, by our advisor for this category, James Riebel; he is listed in the Directory under Ohio.

Bottle, turquoise, $275.00.

Figurine, Great Dane, #12, 14" 800.00
Figurine, knight 6¼", on 4¾x2½" base 225.00
Figurine, pelican, #255, 8" 475.00
Flower frog/arranger, St Francis Feeding the Birds, #212, 16" 900.00
Fountain, baby w/frog, 18½", on 9" base 3,250.00
Planter, elephant, #137, 4" L 130.00
Teapot, yel w/brn edges, dripless, #224, 1¼-qt 225.00
Vase, mustard, #70 ....190.00
Vase, yel, #70 ....150.00

Niloak

During the latter part of the 1800s, there were many small utilitarian potteries in Benton, Arkansas. By 1900 only the Hyten Brothers Pottery remained. Charles Hyten, a second generation potter, took control of the family business around 1902. Shortly thereafter he renamed it the Eagle Pottery Company. In 1909 Hyten and former Rookwood potter Arthur Dovey began experimentation on a new swirl pottery. Dovey previously worked for the Ouachita Pottery Company of Hot Springs and produced a swirl pottery there as early as 1906. In March 1910 the Eagle Pottery Company introduced Niloak, kaolin spelled backwards. During 1911 Benton businessmen formed the Niloak Pottery corporation. Niloak, connected to the Arts and Crafts Movement and known as 'mission' ware, had a national representative in New York by 1913. Niloak's production centered on art pottery characterized by accidental, swirling patterns of natural and artificially colored clays. Many companies through the years have produced swirl pottery, yet none achieved the technical and aesthetic qualities of Niloak. Hyten received a patent in 1928 for the swirl technique. Although most examples have an interior glaze, some early Mission Ware pieces have an exterior glaze as well; these are extremely rare. Swirl/Mission Ware production continued steadily until the Depression when hard times and sagging sales caused Hyten to produce more traditional wares. In 1931 Niloak introduced Hywood Art Pottery, a glazed ware (sometimes similar in shape to Weller's Nile) of mostly hand-thrown vases. Soon thereafter, Niloak introduced castware as its primary production and renamed the line Hywood by Niloak. Throughout its existence, the company produced utilitarian items as well as artware.

In 1934 Hyten's company found itself facing bankruptcy. Hardy L. Winburn, Jr., along with other Little Rock businessmen, raised the necessary capital and were able to provide the kind of leadership needed to make the business profitable once again. Both lines (Eagle and Hywood) were renamed 'Niloak' in 1937 to capitalize on this well-known name. The pottery continued in production until 1947 when it was converted to the Winburn Tile Company, which exists to this day in Little Rock.

Be careful not to confuse the swirl production of the Evans Pottery of Missouri with Niloak. The significant difference is the dark brown matt interior glaze of Evans pottery. For further information we recommend *Collector's Encyclopedia of Niloak Pottery* by David Edwin Gifford (Collector Books). Our advisors for this category are Lila and Fred Shrader; they are listed in the Directory under California.

Mission Ware

Key

N — N Mark	NI — Niloak (impressed) mark
NB — Niloak (block letters) mark	NL — Niloak (in low relief)

Ashtray, rolled rim w/3 rests, 1½x5" dia 200.00
Ashtray, w/secured match holder, 3 rests, 5" dia 185.00
Bowl, flat w/str sides, 2½x7" 155.00
Bowl, fruit; rolled rim, 4x11" 580.00
Bowl, powder; ball-shaped finial, 3x4½" dia 290.00
Bowl, punch; 2½" ped base, 10x14" 1,200.00
Bowl, w/secured 3" dia flower frog, 1st art mk, 6" 300.00
Box, ball-shaped finial, 2½x4½x3½" 275.00
Candlestick, flared base, 8" 210.00
Carafe, w/cork-wrapped stopper, 8" 355.00
Chamberstick w/finger ring, 5½" dia 268.00
Compote, ped ft, flared base, 6½x8" 310.00
Cup, punch; no hdl, bbl shape, 3" 65.00
Flower frog, unmk, 1½x3" 75.00
Jar, cigarette; str sides, w/lid, 4½x3½" 245.00
Jar, rose; w/lid & perforated insert, 8½" 550.00
Jardiniere, bulbous, rolled rim, 13" 675.00
Jug, whiskey; mini, 3" 260.00
Lamp base, factory drilled, no hardware, 8½" 290.00
Tankard, 5", 3½" dia rim, 4½" dia base 185.00
Tray, rolled edge, cut-out hdls, 7x9" 385.00
Tumbler, shot glass sz, 2" 95.00
Tumbler, 3½" 82.00
Vase, bbl-shape w/perforations at opening, 6½" 285.00
Vase, brn/tan/cream tones, early, 1st art mk, 8" 265.00
Vase, bud; stick neck, flared base, 6¾" 135.00
Vase, bulbous w/high shoulders, 6" 165.00
Vase, bulbous w/long neck, blk matt, 1st art mk 278.00
Vase, bulbous w/rolled rim, 1st art mk, 2¾x4" 145.00
Vase, bulbous w/slight flare at base, narrow neck, 7" 278.00
Vase, cone shape, flared base, 9½" 275.00
Vase, elongated teardrop form, 7" 200.00
Vase, fan shape, flared base, 7½" 265.00
Vase, rose bowl, 4x6" 155.00
Vase, simple shape & lines, 4", from $70 to 90.00
Vase, simple shape & lines, 6", from $85 to 150.00
Vase, simple shapes & lines, mini (under 2"), from $100 to 150.00
Vase, violet; rolled rim, 3½" 185.00
Wall pocket, rolled rim, 8½" 295.00

Miscellaneous

Ashtray, duck, matt, NL, 2¾", from $11 to 22.00
Basket, angular, Hywood by Niloak, 6" H 85.00
Basket, hanging w/3 sm loops, NB, 4½" dia 37.00
Basket, upright hdl, N, 3½" H, from $11 to 21.00
Bowl, attached 7" child figure peering into bowl, 9½" 72.00

Bowl, float; oblong w/tiny scroll hdls, NI, 3x14x8" 80.00
Bowl, scalloped petals, NB, 3x10½" 35.00
Candle holder, flat, hand thrown, 1½x5" 35.00
Candlesticks, wht gloss, flared base, Hywood, 7", pr 55.00
Cookie jar, tab hdls, Hywood by Niloak, 10½" 145.00
Creamer, cow figural, 4½x6" 68.00
Creamer, Hywood by Niloak, 4" 40.00
Cup & saucer, petal design, N 42.00
Ewer, braided hdl, extended lip, ped ft, NI, 8" 77.00
Ewer, cameo-like profiles emb on ea side, 10" 45.00
Ewer, elongated hdl, extended spout, NI, 6", from $12 to 25.00
Ewer, extended lip & flared base, NI, 16½" 110.00
Figurine, camel, resting, N, 4", from $25 to 35.00
Figurine, dog, seated retriever, 3-4", from $25 to 45.00
Figurine, donkey, stubborn, head turned, facial features, 3½" 95.00
Figurine, polar bear on ice floe, NL, 5½" L 55.00
Figurine, rabbits (2), ears up, NB, 5½" 50.00
Figurine, razorback hog, w/or w/o 'U of A,' matt, NB, 4½" 135.00
Figurine, Trojan Horse, Hywood by Niloak, 8½" 80.00
Flowerpot, attached saucer, NB, 3½", from $12 to 25.00
Jar, strawberry; 4 openings, matt, mini, 4½", from $12 to 22.00
Jar, strawberry; 6 tulip-shaped openings, matt, NL, 8" 24.00
Match holder, open-mouth frog, N, 3" 20.00
Mug, Hywood by Niloak, 4¼" 29.00
Pin dish, open flower shape, matt, 3½" 22.00
Pitcher, Art Deco, angular hdl, NB, 7½" 85.00
Pitcher, emb flowers, squarish, 7", from $16 to 26.00
Planter, bunnies (2) w/ears up & alert, 4½" 35.00
Planter, dog, wht matt, 3½x4½" 28.00
Planter, frog atop lily pad, matt, 4", from $27 to 38.00
Planter, kangaroo wearing boxing gloves, 5½" 37.00
Planter, pelican w/open mouth, matt, NB, 5½", from $80 to 95.00
Planter, rabbit w/ears up, glossy, 4x4½" 16.00
Planter, rocking horse, NL, 6½" 75.00
Planter, Southern Belle (head vase type), unmk, 7" 85.00
Plate, petal design, NB, 10" 65.00
Shakers, various shapes, 2-3", pr, from $18 to 35.00
Shakers, WWII tanks, pr 44.00
Teapot, Aladdin-like style, 6½" 60.00
Tumbler, emb flowers, squarish, N, 3¾", from $12 to 18.00
Vase, cornucopia; nicely detailed, Hywood by Niloak, 7" 40.00
Vase, high shoulders & hdls, Hywood by Niloak, 6" 55.00
Vase, intricate swirling & curved hdls, sticker, 11" 40.00
Vase, ribbed fan w/flared base, NI, 14" 110.00
Vase, 3 appl hdls, Hywood by Niloak, 10" 125.00
Wall pocket, cup & saucer, emb flowers, NI, 5x5" 65.00

Nippon

Nippon generally refers to Japanese wares made during the period from 1891 to 1921, although the Nippon mark was also used to a limited extent on later wares (accompanied by 'Japan'). Nippon, meaning Japan, identified the country of origin to comply with American importation restrictions. After 1921 'Japan' was the acceptable alternative. The term does not imply a specific type of product and may be found on items other than porcelains. For further information we recommend *The Collector's Encyclopedias of Nippon Porcelain* (there are five in the series) by our advisor, Joan Van Patten; you will find her address in the Directory under New York. In the following listings, items are assumed hand painted unless noted otherwise. Numbers included in the descriptions refer to these specific marks:

Key:
#1 — China E-OH
#2 — M in Wreath
#3 — Cherry Blossom
#4 — Double T Diamond in Circle
#5 — Rising Sun
#6 — Royal Kinran
#7 — Maple Leaf
#8 — Royal Nippon, Nishiki
#9 — Royal Moriye Nippon

Ashtray, dog seated at side of tray w/pastoral scenic, #2, 7" 850.00
Ashtray, Sitting Bull portrait, 3-rest, #2, 5½" 500.00
Basket vase, moriage flying geese on lt bl, unmk, 8½" 700.00
Berry set, berries on wht w/gold, gr border, lg bowl+6 sm+tray ..300.00
Bottle, scent; pastoral scene, ball stopper, #2, 4½" 175.00
Bowl, moriage birds in mc landscape, ruffled rim, ftd, #7, 4¾" ..400.00
Cake set, roses on wht w/gold, RC mk, lg+6 sm plates 500.00
Chocolate set, pastoral scenic band on cobalt w/gold, #7, pot+4 cups ...2,000.00
Chocolate set, pk mums on wht w/gold, #7, pot+8 c/s 925.00
Chocolate set, roses, mc on wht w/much gold, #7, pot+6 c/s 900.00
Coffeepot, river scenic in earth tones, stick hdl, #7, 6" 150.00
Compote, river scenic reserve on cobalt w/gold, tall ft, #7, 8½" ...425.00
Condensed milk container, moriage dragon, #2 ....450.00
Cracker jar, gold floral decor on wht, #7, 8" 465.00
Cracker jar, roses (lg) w/much gold, ftd, #7, 8" 500.00
Demitasse set, sampan scenic, #2, 6½" pot+cr/sug+2 c/s+tray ...650.00
Ewer, lady's portrait on pk & wht w/much gold, ornate hdl, unmk, 9" ..1,500.00
Ewer, Madame Recamier portrait on gr w/gold, #7, 12" 1,600.00
Figurine, bird on brn base, #2, 4" 275.00
Humidor, cards on brn, dice & suits symbols form band, #2, 7" ..800.00
Humidor, Chief Red Cloud portrait, #7, 7½" 1,400.00
Humidor, coaching reserve on gr, 8-sided, #7, 7¾" 1,200.00
Humidor, dogs in relief, brn tones, gr #2, 6" 1,100.00
Humidor, floral w/moriage decor, squirrel finial, unmk, 7½" 750.00
Humidor, gargoyles in relief, brn tones, #2, 6½" 3,350.00
Humidor, horse at open window of stall, #2, 7¼" 1,000.00
Humidor, monk sniffing flower reserve, moriage trim, #7, 8" ..2,400.00
Humidor, sampan scenic, gold trim, #2, 7" 650.00
Humidor, swans in river scenic tapestry, #7, 6½" 2,200.00
Loving cup, Wedgwood, bl w/river scenic reserve, 32, 7¾" 550.00
Mug, owl on branch on yel to bl, brn hdl, #2, 5" 350.00
Pitcher, Dutch lady & child looking to sea, #2, 4½" 350.00
Pitcher, fox hunt scene, Greek Key trim, #7, 7" 465.00
Pitcher, geishas in garden w/gold, #2, 7½" 325.00
Pitcher, woodland scene, brn hdl, #7, 5¼" 425.00
Plaque, coaching scene, gr #2, 11" 500.00
Plaque, lady w/horse portrait, geometric border, #2, 10" 925.00
Plaque, lion portrait, #2, 12¼" 1,900.00
Plaque, lobster & wine bottle, #2, 12¼" 465.00
Plaque, portrait w/coralene, ornate border w/gold, Kinran mk, 7½" ..1,800.00
Plaque, swan scenic, #2, 10" 3.65

Plate, roses tapestry, gold trim along rim, 12", $2,800.00. (Photo courtesy Jackson's Auctions)

Plate, lady's portrait reserve on wht, ornate rim w/gold, unmk, 10" ..850.00
Plate, moriage flying geese in colorful river scenic, #7, 11" 650.00

Shaving mug, roses on wht w/gold, mk, 3½" 350.00
Tankard, gold leaves on wht, slim waisted form, mk, 16" 800.00
Tankard, irises, ivory & lt brn on bl to dk brn, #6, 12¼" 700.00
Tankard, ladies in reserve w/flowers & gold on cobalt, #7, 14½" ..2,300.00
Tankard, roses (lg) on wht w/much gold, lobed sides, unmk, 12½" ..800.00
Tankard set, moriage dragon, #2, 14", w/6 mugs 2,700.00
Tea set, woodland scene, brn hdls, #2, pot+cr/sug+4 c/s 700.00
Urn, floral w/coralene, ornate gold hdls, US Pat mk, 14½" 2,100.00
Urn, Madame Lebrun reserve w/gold & red on turq, bolted, #7, 15" ..2,300.00
Urn, pastoral scenic band on cobalt w/gold, bolted, #2, 15½" ...2,200.00
Urn, Queen Louise portrait w/gold on turq, #7, 14½" 2,400.00
Urn, river scenic on cobalt w/gold, bolted, #7, 21" 3,400.00
Urn, scenic reserve on cobalt w/gold o/l, #7, bolted, 14½" 2,200.00
Urn, sheep by river scene, much gold, bolted, #2, 28" 9,500.00
Vase, autumn river scene, gold hdls, #2, 15" 2,000.00
Vase, bird on floral branch, waisted, #2, 9" 425.00
Vase, Capital Building, Washington DC souvenir, hdls, #7, 11½" ..400.00
Vase, coralene flowers, integral hdls, stick neck, mk, 8" 700.00
Vase, Deco-style geometric decor, gold ring hdls, SK mk, 15½" ..900.00
Vase, Deco-style tapestry, mc on wht w/gold, bulbous, #7, 5½" .725.00
Vase, floral reserve on cobalt w/much gold, hdls, #7, 12¼" 900.00
Vase, flowers w/moriage trim, integral hdls, unmk, 7¾" 300.00
Vase, freesia on wht, bulbous, gold hdls, #7, 8¼" 225.00
Vase, grapes tapestry w/gold, shouldered, #7, 8" 875.00
Vase, horse & driver w/carriage & figures, elephant-head hdls, #2, 7" ...700.00
Vase, irises in shaded brn tones, floral hdls, #6, 9" 425.00
Vase, irises on yel to gr, angle hdls, ftd, #2, 12" 325.00
Vase, lady's portrait reserve on cobalt w/gold, ring hdls, #7, 7¾" ...950.00
Vase, lady's portrait reserve on wht w/gold, hdls, #7, 8" 900.00
Vase, man on camel in desert scene, hdls, #2, 9¼" 550.00
Vase, moriage birds & branches, ring hdls, unmk, 12½" 365.00
Vase, moriage dragon, ornate hdls, #7, 9½" 725.00
Vase, moriage flying geese, bulbous, hdls, #7, 5½" 440.00
Vase, moriage sea life & sea horse hdls, bl #7, 11" 1,700.00
Vase, moriage woodland pattern, angle hdls, ftd, #2, 8¼" 500.00
Vase, ocean scenic w/gulls & whitecaps, gold angle hdls, #2, 8½" ..600.00
Vase, Oriental-style poppy on gold, bottle neck, hdls, #2, 13" ...465.00
Vase, pastoral scene, gold at top, angle hdls, #2, 9" 275.00
Vase, Queen Louise reserve w/gold on turq, sm hdls, #7, 9¼" ...1,500.00
Vase, river scenic, sq sides, angle hdls, #7, 5¾", pr 250.00
Vase, river tapestry, bottle neck, #7, 6" 700.00
Vase, roses, pk on shaded bl, gold ring hdls, scalloped top, #7, 13" ...625.00
Vase, roses & much gold beadwork, slim w/sm hdls, #6, 4½" 325.00
Vase, roses reserve on red w/gold, hdls, #7, 10½" 400.00
Vase, roses/berries reserve on gold, gold ring hdls, #7, 13½" ...1,600.00
Vase, sampan scenic, gold at top, ring hdls, #2, 8" 400.00
Vase, scenic band on cobalt w/gold, sm hdls, ftd, #7, 7¾" 350.00
Vase, scenic reserve on cobalt w/gold o/l, sm hdls, #7, 5" 365.00
Vase, swans scenic, leafy borders, sm hdls, #7, 10" 400.00
Vase, Wedgwood, bird on floral branch, mc on bl, hdls, #2, 7" ..550.00
Vase, windmill scenic band, geometric borders, 6-sided, #2, 15" ..1,200.00
Vase, winter scenic w/silver o/l, angle hdls, RC mk, 9½" 1,500.00
Vase, woodland scene, shouldered, hdls, #2, 10½" 750.00
Whiskey jug, moriage wht woodland pattern, #2, 7½" 950.00
Wine jug, monk drinking, moriage trim, #7, 9½" 2,400.00
Wine jug, windmill scenic, brn hdl, gr #2, 11" 1,000.00

Nodders

So called because of the nodding action of their heads and hands, nodders originated in China where they were used in temple rituals to represent deity. At first they were made of brass and were actually a type of bell; when these bells were rung, the heads of the figures would nod. In the eighteenth century, the idea was adopted by Meissen and by French manufacturers who produced not only china nodders but bisque as well. Most nodders are individual; couples are unusual. The idea remained popular until the end of the nineteenth century and was used during the Victorian era by toy manufacturers. For further information we recommend *Figural Nodders, Identification & Value Guide,* by Hilma R. Irtz, available from Collector Books or your local bookstore. Our advisor for non-German nodders is Barry Larkins; he is listed in the Directory under Florida.

Twins molded together in fancy blankets, painted bisque, Germany, late 1800s, 3½x2½", $500.00. (Photo courtesy Hilma R. Irtz)

Basketball player, Portland Trailblazer, papier-mache, 1967-71, 6½" ...100.00
Black mandarin sits, tongue wags/hands wave, unmk Conta & Boehme, 6" ..450.00
Blackamore w/long pole, pnt pewter, 1880s, 3", VG, minimum value ..250.00
Canadian Mountie, spring neck, Canada souvenir, Japan, 5¼" ...35.00
Canaries swing from banches, Japan 15.00
Chicks rock on broken eggshells, ceramic, China, from $65 to 100.00
Chinese lady w/umbrella, pnt bsk, unmk Sohne, 4¾", up to 200.00
Comic character w/banjo, pnt/fired bsk, Japan, 3½" 45.00
Donkey, celluloid, head hanger, Occupied Japan, lg, from $75 to ..100.00
Japanese actor w/mask on top of head, pnt bsk, unmk, 4" 275.00
Japanese man w/lg fan, pnt bsk, Germany, 6½" 150.00
Kissing Eskimo children, compo, mk Foreign or Japan, from $40 to ...60.00
Kitten, flocked papier-mache, pearls, spring in neck, Japan, 7¾" ...50.00
Lady at piano/man w/harpsicord, Germany, 1940s, minimum value ..275.00
Monk, pnt bsk, post nodder, Germany, 5½", minimum value 140.00
Pig dressed as Buddha, glazed ceramic, unmk (China?), 5", from $35 to ..45.00
Rabbit, chalkware, coiled spring neck, post WWII, 5", VG 30.00
Santa, flocked cb, fur beard, Western Germany, 6¼" 85.00
Skulls (2) w/gold eyes on 1 sq base w/bottom teeth, wht, Pat TT, up to ..65.00
Twin babies in blanket, pnt bsk, Germany, late 1800s, 3½x3½" 500.00

German Comic Characters

During the early 1930s, Germany produced a collection of small figure dolls, approximately 2" to 4" high, representing the most popular comic strip and cartoon characters of that time. They were made of bisque with brightly painted details and clearly stamped with their appropriate names and 'Germany' on their backs. Generally, their movable heads were attached with an elastic string going through their bodies, hence the name 'nodders,' but there were some characters produced earlier that were frozen with no movable parts. The most popular ones came in boxed sets, but the lesser-known characters were sold separately, making them rarer and harder to find today. We have listed the most valuable characters from the series here; those not mentioned below are valued at $125.00 and under. Our advisor for German character nodders is Doug Dezso; he is listed in the Directory under New Jersey. He will answer questions (as long as an SASE is included) on German character nodders only.

Ambrose Potts 350.00
Auntie Blossom 150.00
Auntie Mamie & Uncle Willie, ea 250.00
Bill, Dock, Avery, Max or Pop Jenks, ea 200.00

Buttercup 250.00
Chubby Chaney 250.00
Corky 475.00
Dinty Moor (frozen) 500.00
Fanny or Rudy Nebbs, ea 250.00
Ferina 350.00
Grandpa Teen 350.00
Happy Hooligan 625.00
Harold Teen 150.00
Jeff Regus, med or lg, ea 250.00
Jeff Regus, sm 175.00
Josie 425.00
Junior Nebbs 625.00
Lilacs 425.00
Lillums 150.00
Little Annie Rooney, movable arms, complete 300.00
Little Egypt 350.00
Lord Plushbottom 150.00
Ma & Pa Winkle, ea 350.00
Marjorie 425.00
Mary Ann Jackson 250.00
Min Gump 150.00
Mr Bailey 150.00
Mr Bibb 400.00
Mushmouth 175.00
Mutt, med or lg, NM, ea 250.00
Mutt, sm 175.00
Nicodemus 350.00
Old Timer 350.00
Our Gang, 6-pc set, MIB 1,400.00
Pat Finnegan 400.00
Patsy 425.00
Pete the Dog 250.00
Pop Jenks 200.00
Rudy Nebs 250.00
Scraps 250.00
Widow Zandor 400.00
Winnie Winkle 150.00

Noritake

The Noritake Company was first registered in 1904 as Nippon Gomei Kaisha. In 1917 the name became Nippon Toki Kabushiki Toki. The 'M in wreath' mark is that of the Morimura Brothers, distributors with offices in New York. It was used until 1941. The 'tree crest' mark is the crest of the Morimura family.

The Noritake Company has produced fine porcelain dinnerware sets and occasional pieces decorated in the delicate manner for which the Japanese are noted. (Two dinnerware patterns are featured below, and a general range is suggested for others.)

Authority Joan Van Patten has compiled two lovely books, *The Collector's Encyclopedia of Noritake, Vols. I* and *II*, with many full-color photos and current prices; you will find her address in the Directory under New York. In the following listings, examples are hand painted unless noted otherwise. Numbers refer to these specific marks:

Key:
#1 — Komaru
#2 — M in Wreath
#3 — N in Wreath

Azalea

The Azalea pattern was produced exclusively for the Larkin Company, who gave the lovely ware away as premiums to club members and their home agents. From 1916 through the 1930s, Larkin distributed fine china which was decorated in pink azaleas on white with gold tracing along edges and handles. Early in the '30s, six pieces of crystal hand painted with the same design were offered: candle holders, a compote, a tray with handles, a scalloped fruit bowl, a cheese and cracker set, and a cake plate. All in all, seventy different pieces of Azalea were produced. Some, such as the fifteen-piece child's set, bulbous vase, china ashtray, and the pancake jug, are quite rare. One of the earliest marks was the Noritake 'M in wreath' with variations. Later the ware was marked 'Noritake, Azalea, Hand Painted, Japan.'

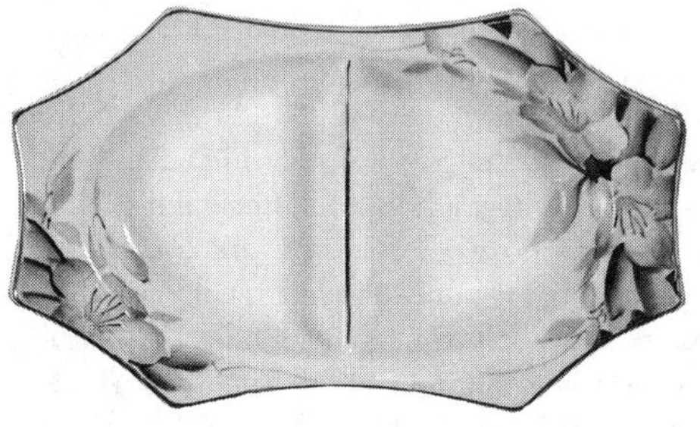

Relish, two-compartment, #171, $58.00.

Basket, mint; Dolly Varden, #193 ....195.00
Bonbon, #184, 6¼" 50.00
Bowl, #12, 10" 42.50
Bowl, candy/grapefruit; #185 ....195.00
Bowl, deep, #310 ....68.00
Bowl, fruit; shell form, #188, 7¾" 385.00
Bowl, oatmeal; #55, 5½" 28.00
Bowl, vegetable; divided, #439, 9½" 295.00
Bowl, vegetable; oval, #101, 10½" 60.00
Bowl, vegetable; oval, #172, 9¼" 58.00
Butter chip, #312, 3¼" 145.00
Butter tub, w/insert, #54 ....48.00
Cake plate, #10, 9¾" 40.00
Candy jar, w/lid, #313 ....695.00
Casserole, gold finial, w/lid, #372 ....540.00
Casserole, w/lid, #16 ....115.00
Celery/roll tray, #99, 12" 55.00
Cheese/butter dish, #314 ....135.00
Child's set, #253, 15-pc 2,500.00
Coffeepot, AD; #182 ....595.00
Compote, #170 ....98.00
Condiment set, #14, 5-pc 65.00
Creamer & sugar bowl, #7 ....45.00
Creamer & sugar bowl, AD; open, #123 ....140.00
Creamer & sugar bowl, gold finial, #401 ....155.00
Creamer & sugar bowl, ind, #449 ....395.00
Creamer & sugar shaker, #122 ....158.00
Cruet, #190 ....195.00
Cup & saucer, #2 ....20.00
Cup & saucer, AD; #183 ....150.00
Cup & saucer, bouillon; #124, 3½" 24.50
Egg cup, #120 ....30.00
Gravy boat, #40 ....48.00
Jam jar set, #125, 4-pc 155.00
Mayonnaise set, scalloped, #453, 3-pc 495.00
Mustard jar, #191, 3-pc 60.00
Pickle/lemon set, #121 ....24.50
Pitcher, milk jug; #100, 1-qt 195.00

Plate, #4, 7½" 10.00
Plate, bread & butter; #8, 6½" 10.00
Plate, breakfast; #98 ....28.00
Plate, cream soup; #363 ....175.00
Plate, dinner; #13, 9¾" 28.00
Plate, grill; 3-compartment, #38, 10¼" 165.00
Plate, scalloped sq, salesman's sample 950.00
Plate, soup; #19, 7⅛" 25.00
Platter, #17, 14" 60.00
Platter, #186, 16" 475.00
Platter, #56, 12" 58.00
Platter, cold meat/bacon; #311, 10¼" 215.00
Refreshment set, #39, 2-pc 48.00
Relish, #194, 7⅛" 85.00
Relish, oval, #18, 8½" 20.00
Relish, 2-part, #171 ....58.00
Relish, 2-part, loop hdl, #450 ....425.00
Relish, 4-section, #119, rare, 10" 150.00
Saucer, fruit; #9, 5¼" 10.00
Shakers, bell form, #11, pr 30.00
Shakers, bulbous, #189, 8" 115.00
Shakers, ind, #126, pr 27.50
Spoon holder, #189, 8" 115.00
Syrup, #97, w/underplate & ladle 135.00
Tea tile 40.00
Teapot, #15 ....110.00
Teapot, gold finial, #400 ....495.00
Toothpick holder, #192 ....135.00
Vase, bulbous, #452 ....1,150.00
Vase, fan form, ftd, #187 ....185.00
Whipped cream/mayonnaise set, #3, 3-pc 38.50

Tree in the Meadow

Another of their dinnerware lines has become a favorite of many collectors. Tree in the Meadow features a hand-painted scene with a large dark tree in the foreground, growing near a lake. There is usually a cottage in the distance. Sometimes referred to as Tree by the Lake, this line was made during the 1920s and 1930s and seems today to be in good supply. Various interesting forms are seen, and reassembling a complete set should be an enjoyable undertaking.

Candy dish, 5½", $400.00.

Ashtray, 5" 55.00
Basket, Dolly Varden 125.00
Bowl, cream soup; 2-hdl 35.00
Bowl, fruit; shell form, #210 ....300.00
Bowl, oatmeal 15.00
Bowl, soup 20.00
Bowl, vegetable; 9" 35.00
Butter pat 15.00
Butter tub, open, w/drainer 35.00
Cake plate 35.00
Celery dish 35.00
Cheese dish 45.00
Coffeepot 200.00
Compote 50.00
Condiment set, 5-pc 45.00
Creamer & sugar bowl, demitasse 40.00
Cruets, vinegar & oil; cojoined, #319 ....360.00
Cup & saucer, breakfast 25.00
Cup & saucer, demitasse 35.00
Egg cup 30.00
Gravy boat 50.00
Jam jar/dish, 4-pc 70.00
Lemon dish 15.00
Mayonnaise set, 3-pc 50.00
Platter, 11¾x9" 50.00
Platter, 13¾x10¼" 60.00
Relish, divided 35.00
Sugar bowl, #204 ....25.00
Tea set, 3-pc 100.00

Miscellaneous

Ashtray, flowers on shaded cream, 4 rests, #2, 5¾" 50.00
Ashtray, Indian chief portrait, geometric rim, 6-sided, #2, 6½" .160.00
Bowl, exotic birds on wht, Deco-style band, #2, 7¼" 90.00
Bowl, floral reserve w/orange lustre, bl rim, hdls, #2, 9¼" 65.00
Bowl, irises on wht, bl rim w/gold hdls, #2, 10½" 85.00
Bowl, river scenic, 8-sided, red #2, 6½" 35.00
Bowl, roses, pk on wht w/gold border & hdls, gr #2, 11" W 150.00
Bowl, 3 floral reserves w/gold on wht, 3 pierced hdls, #2, 6¼" 30.00
Candlesticks, exotic bird on branch, bl rims & ft, #2, 8¼", pr ...240.00
Candy jar, river reserve & band on gold lustre, #2, 6½" 225.00
Celery tray, celery stalks on cream, #2, 12", +6 3¾" salts 140.00
Cheese dish, yel band w/Deco flowers on wht, slant lid, #2, 8" L ..100.00
Chocolate pot, gold o/l on wht, 32, 9" 140.00
Chocolate set, exotic birds on wht w/gold, #2, 9½" pot+5 c/s ...300.00
Cigarette holder, flowers on bell shape, bird finial, #2, 5" 200.00
Compote, floral on cream w/gold hdls, ftd, #2, 9¾" 80.00
Compote, swans in river scenic, hdls, #2, 9" W 85.00
Condensed milk container, Deco floral on wht w/gold, #2, 5¼" ..160.00
Condiment set, exotic birds on red, #2, 3 pcs on 6¾" tray 150.00
Egg cup, windmill & river scenic, earth tones, #2, 3½" 40.00
Humidor, camel scene at sunset, gr #2, 5¾" 375.00
Humidor, owl on branch in relief, #2, 7" 575.00
Jam jar, bl & gold lustre, rose finial, #2, w/spoon & tray, 5¼" 80.00
Lemon dish, flowering branch on yel, red #2, 6½" L 40.00
Lemon dish, lemons & leaves, tan lustre rim, #2, 5¾" 40.00
Mantel set, Deco floral on cream w/gold, #2, 9" bowl+pr sticks .425.00
Mustard set, roses, pk & yel on wht, #2, 3", 4-pc 35.00
Napkin ring, mc roses, #2, 2¼" W 45.00
Nappy, roses, pastels on cream, 1-hdl, #2, 5" 40.00
Night light, lady praying figural, lustre dress, #2, 9¾" 2,400.00
Plaque, river scenic w/swans, earth tones, #2, 6½" 115.00
Plate, windmill & river landscape, bright colors, #2, 7½" 65.00
Playing card holder, horse on tan lustre, ftd, #2, 3¾" 150.00
Sauce dish, flowers & bird on wht w/tan lustre, #2, 4½", +spoon ...50.00
Sauce dish, roses on tan w/orange lustre, #2, 5", +ladle & tray 80.00
Shakers, river scenic, earth tones, #2, 2½", pr 16.00
Shaving mug, river scenic, earth tones w/gold, #2, 3¾" 120.00
Spooner, river scenic w/red-roofed cottage, #2, 8" L 70.00
Sugar shaker, floral band on wht, gold top, #2, 6½" 30.00
Syrup, trees, river & red-roofed cottage scene, #2, 4¼"+tray 85.00
Tea set, river scenic, #2, child sz, 3½" pot+8 pcs 225.00

Tile, river scenic, canted corners, #2, 5" 55.00
Toast rack, bl lustre w/bird finial, #2, 5½" L 125.00
Tray, river scenic w/swans, bl #1, 12" 80.00
Vase, lg open roses, pastel tones w/gold, hdls, #2, 11¼" 250.00
Vase, peacock feathers on tan, ruffled rim, slim, #1, 8", pr 180.00
Vase, river scenic, jack-in-pulpit shape, #2, 7¾" 200.00
Vase, roses on long stems on wht, hdls, #2, 8½" 165.00
Vase, tulip figural, purple & gr, #2, 5¼" 250.00
Vase, Wedgwood type, wht flowers on bl, hdls, #1, 9½" 475.00
Wall pocket, butterflies on tan lustre, red #2, 9" 125.00

Various Dinnerware Patterns, ca. 1933 to Present

So many lines of dinnerware have been produced by the Noritake company that to list them all would require a volume in itself. In fact, just such a book is available — *The Collector's Encyclopedia of Early Noritake* by Aimee Neff Alden (Collector Books). And while many patterns had specific names, others did not, so you'll probably need the photographs the book contains to help you identify your pattern. Outlined below is a general guide for the more common pieces and patterns. The high side of the range will represent lines from about 1933 until the mid-1960s (including those marked 'Occupied Japan'), while the lower side should be used to evaluate lines made after that period.

Bowl, berry; ind, from $8 to 12.00
Bowl, soup; 7½", from $12 to 16.00
Bowl, vegetable; rnd or oval, ca 1945 to present, from $28 to 38.00
Butter dish, 3-pc, ca 1933-64, from $40 to 50.00
Creamer, from $18 to 28.00
Cup & saucer, demi; from $12 to 17.50
Gravy boat, from $35 to 45.00
Pickle or relish dish, from $18 to 28.00
Plate, bread & butter; from $8 to 12.00
Plate, dinner; from $15 to 30.00
Plate, luncheon; from $10 to 18.00
Plate, salad; from $10 to 15.00
Platter, 12", from $25 to 40.00
Platter, 16" (or larger), from $40 to 60.00
Shakers, pr, from $15 to 25.00
Sugar bowl, w/lid, from $18 to 30.00
Tea & toast set (sm cup & tray), from $18 to 28.00
Teapot, demi pot, chocolate pot, or coffeepot, ea, from $45 to 60.00

Norse

The Norse Pottery was established in 1903 in Edgerton, Wisconsin, by Thorwald Sampson and Louis Ipson. A year later it was purchased by A.W. Wheelock and moved to Rockford, Illinois. The ware they produced was inspired by ancient bronze vessels of the Norsemen. Designs were often incised into the red clay body. Dragon handles and feet were favored decorative devices, and they achieved a semblance of patina through the application of metallic glazes. The ware was marked with model numbers and a stylized 'N' containing a vertical arrangement of the remaining letters of the name. Production ceased after 1913. Our advisor for this category is John Danis; he is listed in the Directory under Illinois.

Bowl, band of lines & dots, 1 w/zigzags, cvd lines on hdls, #4, 7" ..225.00
Bowl, bands of cvd waves, 3 dragon-head ft, sm rpr, 4x7½" 325.00
Bowl, chain-like band under rim, looping band above ft (3), #55, 5" ...225.00
Bowl, 3 ft w/facial features, #55, 2½x4½", EX 60.00
Mug, gold & gr trim, bands of zigzags/circles, #64, 5x4" 195.00
Toothpick holder, hammered/riveted look, 4-sided, #87 ....145.00
Urn, tribal cvgs, open hdls, #14, 5½x12" 250.00

Vase, band of circles at top, gold band below, 1½x5", NM 190.00
Vase, bud; faces at bottom, gold wash, 7" 130.00

North Dakota School of Mines

The School of Mines of the University of North Dakota was established in 1890, but due to a lack of funding it was not until 1898 that Earle J. Babcock was appointed as director, and efforts were made to produce ware from the native clay he had discovered several years earlier. The first pieces were made by firms in the East from the clay Babcock sent them. Some of the ware was decorated by the manufacturer; some was shipped back to North Dakota to be decorated by native artists. By 1909 students at the University of North Dakota were producing utilitarian items such as tile, brick, shingles, etc., in conjunction with a ceramic course offered through the chemistry department. By 1910 a ceramic department had been established, supervised by Margaret Kelly Cable. Under her leadership, fine artware was produced. Native flowers, grains, buffalo, cowboys, and other subjects indigenous to the state were incorporated into the decorations. Some pieces have an Art Nouveau–Art Deco style easily attributed to her association with Frederick H. Rhead, with whom she studied in 1911. During the '20s the pottery was marketed on a limited scale through gift and jewelry stores in the state. From 1927 until 1949 when Miss Cable announced her retirement, a more widespread distribution was maintained with sales branching out into other states. The ware was marked in cobalt with the official seal — 'Made at School of Mines, N.D. Clay, University of North Dakota, Grand Forks, N.D.' in a circle. Very early ware was sometimes marked 'U.N.D.' in cobalt by hand. For more information refer to *Collector's Encyclopedia of Dakota Potteries* by Darlene Hurst Dommel (Collector Books). Our advisor for this category is William M. Bilsland III; he is listed in the Directory under Iowa.

Vases: Viking ships among waves and gulls, carved, teal and dark blue on gray, incised 'Viking Ship,' Mattson '49A, 5", $1,200.00; Triangular geometric band at shoulder, green, cornflower blue, and light blue with black accents, signed HO, B.D. 16, 8", $750.00.

Bowl, Red River Ox Cart, brn & gr, Margaret Cable, 3½x6½" ..1,400.00
Bowl vase, band w/wagon train/oxen, brn tones, Cable, 6x7" .2,300.00
Bust, Mary, Queen of Scots, Esther Shabert, 1942, 5¾" 175.00
Figurine, horse, brn matt, Julia Mattson, 1948, 6" 350.00
Humidor, berries, brn & gr on mustard, Margaret Cable, 1917, 6x6¼" ..4,750.00
Pitcher, Red River Ox Carts, ivory on buff clay, Cable, 5x8½" .900.00
Trivet, eagle, blk on brick, J Mattson, Bentonite, 1958, 4¾" 250.00
Vase, band of stylized bison, brn/ochre matt, Cable, 5x6" 1,800.00
Vase, bl shaded to burgundy gloss, bulbous, XX/1933, 5" 500.00
Vase, cowboys emb in brn on gr, Julia Mattson, 7x4¾" 2,900.00
Vase, daffodils, gr semimatt, Margaret Cable, ink stamp, 7¼x5" ...2,600.00
Vase, evergreens & deer, brn/yel/red, J Mattson, Bentonite, 3x3½" .750.00
Vase, floral, red/bl/gr on bl, Reinert, 1938, 7½x3¼" 1,800.00
Vase, floral band (cvd), cream w/bl tint on red clay, Cable, 8" ..550.00
Vase, floral emb on gr matt, buff clay, Cable, #167, 3x2" 300.00
Vase, lattice emb in cobalt over ivory, ovoid, XX, 6½" 400.00
Vase, mushrooms, bl & turq on wht, experimental, 1949, 6¼x7½" ..1,500.00

Vase, ND Sioux, Indians on horsebk, dk brn, Huckfield, 5¾x5½" 1,800.00
Vase, Plowman scenes (cvd) on brn matt, F Huckfield, 5x6½" ..1,700.00
Vase, Plowman scenes (repeating), Huckfield, #119, 4¾x6¼" ..1,100.00
Vase, Praire Roses (cvd) on pk gloss, Julia Mattson, 8½x5¼" ...600.00
Vase, Prairie Rose on gr, F Huckfield, 1931, 3x3½" 450.00
Vase, Trees/Thorne, trees on gr, F Huckfield, classic shape, 11" ...4,500.00
Vase, turkeys on gr, Julia Mattson, #170, 3¼x3¾" 500.00
Vase, Viking ships, bl & gr on lt bl, J Mattson, 4x4½" 700.00

North State

In 1924 the North State Pottery of Sanford, North Carolina, began small-scale production, the result of the extreme fondness Mrs. Rebecca Copper had for potting. With the help of her husband Henry and the abundance of suitable local clay, the pottery flourished and became well known for lovely shapes and beautiful glazes. They shared the knowledge they gained from their glaze experiments with the ceramic engineering department of North Carolina University; and during summer vacation, they often employeed some of the university students. Salt glazed stoneware was produced in the early years but was quickly abandoned in favor of Henry's vibrant glazes. Colors of copper red, Chinese red, moss green, and turquoise blue were used alone and in combination, producing bands of blending colors. Some swirl ware was made as well. The pottery was in business for thirty-five years; most of its ware was sold in gift and craft shops throughout North Carolina.

Hurricane lamp, crimson/aqua, ca 1930s, section of jug, 9" 110.00
Jar, Chinese Red matt flambe, hdls, w/lid, no mk, 9", NM 150.00
Jug, pansy; Chrome Red, Walter Owens, 1950s, 4½" 50.00
Vase, Chinese Red, 4-fold flared rim, 1930s-40s, att, 4¼x5½" 60.00
Vase, frothy periwinkle-bl matt, urn shape, mk, 8½" 150.00
Vase, mint gr w/violet at neck, Walter Owens, 1930s, 6⅝" 70.00

Northwood

The Northwood Company was founded in 1896 in Indiana, Pennsylvania, by Harry Northwood, whose father, John, was the art director for Stevens and Williams, an English glassworks. Northwood joined the National Glass Company in 1899 but in 1901 again became an independent contractor and formed the Harry Northwood Glass Company of Wheeling, West Virginia. He marketed his first carnival glass in 1908, and it became his most popular product. His company was also famous for its custard, goofus, and pressed glass. Northwood died in 1923, and the company closed. See also Carnival; Custard; Goofus; Opalescent; Pattern Glass.

Cup and plate with cup well, coral with gold trim, #722, very rare, $150.00. (Photo courtesy Ferill Jean Rice)

Bowl, berry; Royal Oak, crystal & frosted, 7½" 60.00
Bowl, sauce; Leaf Umbrella, mauve 45.00
Butter dish, Cherry T'print, crystal w/ruby & gold 125.00
Butter dish, Royal Oak, crystal & frosted, w/lid 60.00
Butter dish, Royal Oak, frosted rubena 425.00
Butter dish, Royal Oak, rubena 375.00
Condiment set, Zippered Corners, pk cased, 4-bottle, glass holder ...850.00
Creamer, Leaf Medallion, gr w/gold 85.00
Creamer, Peach, gr w/gold 80.00
Creamer, Royal Oak, crystal & frosted 75.00
Creamer, Royal Oak, frosted rubena 235.00
Cruet, Leaf Umbrella, bl o/l, clear faceted stopper, 7" 250.00
Cruet, Royal Ivy, cased rainbow spatter 700.00
Cruet, Royal Ivy, frosted rubena, ca 1889, 4⅞" 500.00
Cruet, Royal Ivy, rubena 300.00
Cruet, Royal Oak, frosted rubena 500.00
Pickle castor, Royal Ivy, crystal & frosted, SP fr 155.00
Pickle castor, Royal Ivy, rubena, SP Acme SP fr 475.00
Pitcher, Leaf Medallion, amethyst w/gold, water sz 495.00
Pitcher, Leaf Umbrella, bl cased, water sz 525.00
Pitcher, Memphis, gr w/gold, water sz 200.00
Pitcher, Oriental Poppy, gr, water sz 275.00
Pitcher, Royal Ivy, cased rainbow spatter, water sz 475.00
Pitcher, Royal Ivy, frosted rubena, water sz 395.00
Pitcher, Royal Oak, crystal & frosted, water sz 85.00
Pitcher, Royal Oak, rubena, water sz 325.00
Rose bowl, Fine Cut & Roses, amethyst 170.00
Rose bowl, Royal Ivy, cased rainbow spatter 200.00
Shakers, Cactus, amethyst, pr 155.00
Shakers, Flat Flower, rubena, 1894-96, 4", pr 700.00
Shakers, Jewel, rubena, 3", pr 300.00
Shakers, Leaf Medallion, cobalt w/gold, 3⅛", pr 435.00
Shakers, Nestor, amethyst w/HP lace enamel, 3⅛", pr 225.00
Shakers, Parian Swirl, bl satin opaque, 2⅜", pr 250.00
Shakers, Quilted Phlox, lav, rare color, 3", pr 400.00
Shakers, Venetian, gr w/HP floral, 3x2⅛", pr 300.00
Spooner, Royal Ivy, crystal & frosted 35.00
Spooner, Royal Oak, crystal & frosted 45.00
Sugar bowl, Memphis, gr w/gold, w/lid 85.00
Sugar shaker, Royal Oak, crystal & frosted 90.00
Sugar shaker, Royal Oak, rubena 315.00
Syrup, Leaf Mold, vaseline spatter 465.00
Syrup, Royal Ivy, frosted rubena 500.00
Table set, Memphis, gr w/gold, 4-pc 300.00
Table set, Peach, gr w/gold, 4-pc 350.00
Toothpick holder, Royal Ivy, rubena, from $80 to 95.00
Toothpick holder, Royal Oak, crystal & frosted 55.00
Toothpick holder, Royal Oak, frosted rubena 165.00
Tumbler, Cherry & Plum, crystal w/ruby & gold 32.50
Tumbler, Leaf Umbrella, bl cased 90.00
Tumbler, Oriental Poppy, gr w/gold 50.00

Nutcrackers

The nutcracker, though a strictly functional tool, is a good example of one to which man has applied ingenuity, imagination, and engineering skills. Though all were designed to accomplish the same end, hundreds of types exist in almost every material sturdy enough to withstand sufficient pressure to crack the nut. Figurals are popular collectibles, as are those with unusual design and construction. Patented examples are also desirable. Our advisor for this category is Earl MacSorley; he is listed in the Directory under Connecticut. For more information, we recommend *Ornamental and Figural Nutcrackers* by Judith A. Rittenhouse.

Alligator, brass, 1-pc, 14" 65.00

Dog, CI, Harper's dog tray, 13" 125.00
Eagle, brass plier 25.00
Eagle head w/feather hdl, CI, Pat 1860, 10¼" 300.00
Lawrence, knee type, CI 125.00
Mermaid, brass plier 125.00
Parrot, CI 80.00
Perfection, screw type, clamps to table 15.00
Pliers type, hand-held, CI, from $3 to 17.50
Rabbit's head, wooden w/glass eyes 150.00
Rooster, brass plier 25.00
Squirrel, CI 22.00
Woman's legs, cast brass, from $30 to 60.00

Nutting, Wallace

Wallace Nutting (1861–1941) was America's most famous photographer of the early twentieth century. A retired minister, Nutting took more than 50,000 pictures, keeping 10,000 of his best and destroying the rest. His popular and bestselling scenes included *exterior scenes* (apple blossoms, country lanes, orchards, calm streams, and rural American countrysides), *interior scenes* (usually featuring a colonial woman working near a hearth), and *foreign scenes* (typically thatch-roofed cottages). His poorest selling pictures, which have become today's rarest and most highly collectible, are classified as *miscellaneous unusual scenes* and include categories not mentioned above: animals, architecturals, children, florals, men, seascapes, and snow scenes. *Process prints* are 1930s machine-produced reprints of twelve of Nutting's most popular pictures. These have minimal value and can be detected by using a magnifying glass.

Nutting sold literally millions of his hand-colored platinotype pictures between 1900 and his death in 1941. He started in Southbury, Connecticut, and later moved his business to Framingham, Massachusetts. The peak of Wallace Nutting picture production was 1915–25. During this period Nutting employed nearly two hundred people, including colorists, darkroom staff, salesmen, and assorted office personnel. Wallace Nutting pictures proved to be a huge commercial success and scarcely an American household was without one by 1925.

While attempting to seek out the finest and best early American furniture as props for his colonial interior scenes, Nutting became an expert in early American antiques. He published nearly twenty books in his lifetime, including his 10-volume *State Beautiful* series and various other books on furniture, photography, clocks, stools, chairs, settles, settees, tables, stands, desks, mirrors, beds, chests of drawers, cabinet pieces, and treenware. He made furniture as well, which he clearly marked with a distinctive paper label that was glued directly onto the piece, or a block or script signature brand which was literally branded into the furniture.

The overall synergy of the Wallace Nutting name — on pictures, books, and furniture — has made anything 'Wallace Nutting' quite collectible.

Our advisor for this category is Michael Ivankovich, author of many books concerning Nutting. Those currently available are *The Collector's Guide to Wallace Nutting Pictures; The Wallace Nutting Expansible Catalog; The Alphabetical and Numerical Index to Wallace Nutting Pictures; The Guide to Wallace Nutting Furniture*, *Wallace Nutting General Catalog, Supreme Edition; Wallace Nutting: A Great American Idea; Wallace Nutting's Windsors: Correct Windsor Furniture;* and *The Guide to Wallace Nutting-Like Photographers of the Early 20th Century*. Also available through Mr. Ivankovich is *The History of The Sawyer Pictures* by Carol Begley Gray. Mr Ivankovich's address and ordering information are listed in the Directory under Pennsylvania.

Prices below are for pictures in good to excellent condition. Mat stains or blemishes, poor picture color or frame damage can decrease value significantly.

Wallace Nutting Pictures

An Eventful Journey, 14x17", $650.00. (Photo courtesy Michael Ivankovich)

All the Comforts of Home, 13x15" 130.00
Apple Tree by the Stream, 10x13" 90.00
At Paul Revere's, 13x17" 25.00
Autumn Grotto, 14x17" 140.00
Berkshire Spring, 7x13" 70.00
Between Cloud Crested Hills, 13x22" 200.00
Blossom Cove, 12x15" 100.00
Blossom Pasture, 9x15" 240.00
Blossom Point, 14x17" 140.00
Braiding a Rag Rug, 16x20" 150.00
Canopied Road, 14x17" 80.00
Cathedral Brook, 9x11" 75.00
Checkered Road, 9x11" 305.00
Confluence, 13x16" 150.00
Cottage on the Floss, 11x14" 50.00
Daisy Lawn, 13x16" 210.00
Dividing Path, 11x17" 170.00
Dykeside Blossoms, 11x17" 90.00
Envangeline Lane, 9x11" 140.00
From Berkshire Crests, 13x16" 160.00
From the Mountain, 11x17" 60.00
Fruit Luncheon, 14x17" 220.00
Gorgeous May, 11x14" 75.00
Grandmother's Parlor, 10x12" 60.00
Heart of Maine, 16x20" 110.00
Hollycock Cottage, 12x14" 110.00
Home Under Thatch, 11x14" 350.00
Honeymoon Cottage, 12x16" 85.00
Hope, 16x20" 120.00
Indian Summer Haze, 11x17" 95.00
Informal Call, 11x14" 120.00
Ladies in White Satin, 16x20" 130.00
Light on a Dark Subject, 7½x9½" 950.00
Listless Day, 14x17" 110.00
Litchfield Minister, 14x17" 170.00
Masque Pitcher, 16x20" 250.00
Meadow Blossoms, 12x14" 140.00
Meeting of the Ways, 14x17" 170.00
Natural Bridge, 9x12" 160.00
New Market Belle, 11x17" 110.00
Notch Mountain, 13x16" 220.00
October Bank, 11x17" 50.00
Old Back Door, 11x14" 90.00
Old Drawing Room, 10x13" 45.00
Orchard Shadows, 14x17" 35.00
Original Dennison House, 14x17" 250.00

Overflowing Cup, 9x11" 160.00
Pennsylvania Hillside, 13x16" 440.00
Petersham Banks, 13x16" 140.00
Pine Landing, 14x17" 290.00
Porch Door, 11x14" 90.00
Portsmouth Roadside, 9x11" 120.00
Preparing an 'At Home,' 11x17" 115.00
Ready for Callers, 14x17" 260.00
River Song, 15x22" 190.00
Rose Standish, 12x14" 150.00
Rug Pattern, 13x16" 350.00
San Gabriel Stair, 11x14" 350.00
Sea Ledges, 13x16" 220.00
Shadow Road, 14x17" 80.00
Shadows in the Dell, 16x20" 110.00
Sip of Tea, 11x14" 120.00
Skirting Profile Lake, 9x11" 50.00
Stone Churn, 11x17" 230.00
Sudbury in October, 13x16" 130.00
Swirling Seas, 10x12" 160.00
Tea for Yorktown Parlor, 13x15" 260.00
Tranquil Vale, 11x17" 50.00
Under Curving Hills, 13x16" 75.00
Undulating Reflections, 9x19" 210.00
Vico Esquene, 10x13" 600.00
Village Vale, 8x12" 120.00
Warm Spring Day, 11x14" 175.00
Water Loving Blooms, 12x15" 440.00
Whirling Candlestand, 11x14" 45.00
Woodstock Arch, 12x15" 100.00

Wallace Nutting Furniture

Bow-back armchair, #420 ....500.00
Carver armchair, #464 ....650.00
Fan-back chair w/comb, #311 ....1,100.00
Hanging wall shelf, #907 ....1,300.00
Maple drop-front desk, #701 ....1,100.00
Maple tuckaway table, #616 ....1,900.00
Oak chest, 1-drw, #909 ....1,600.00
Tavern table, #660 ....600.00

Major Wallace Nutting-Like Photographers

Although Wallace Nutting was widely recognized as the country's leading producer of hand-colored photographs during the early twentieth century, he was by no means the only photographer selling this style of picture. Throughout the country literally hundreds of regional photographers were selling hand-colored photographs from their home regions or travels. The subject matters of these photographers was very comparable to Nutting's, including interior, exterior, foreign, and miscellaneous unusual scenes. The key determinants of value include the collectibility of the particular photographer, subject matter, condition, and size. Keep in mind that only the rarest pictures in the best condition will bring top prices. Discoloration and/or damage to the picture or matting can reduce value significantly.

Several photographers operated large businesses, and although not as large or well known as Wallace Nutting, they sold a substantial volume of pictures which can still be readily found today. The vast majority of their work was photographed in their home regions and sold primarily to local residents or visiting tourists. It should come as little surprise that three of the major Wallace Nutting-like photographers — David Davidson, Fred Thompson, and the Sawyer Art Co. — each had ties to Wallace Nutting.

David Davidson: Second to Nutting in overall production, Davidson worked primarily in the Rhode Island and Southern Massachusetts area. While a student at Brown University around 1900, Davidson learned the art of hand-colored photography from Wallace Nutting, who happened to be the minister at Davidson's church. After Nutting moved to Southbury in 1905, Davidson graduated from Brown and started a successful photography business in Providence, Rhode Island, which he operated until his death in 1967.

Sawyer: A father and son team, Charles H. Sawyer and Harold B. Sawyer, operated the very successful Sawyer Art Company from 1903 into the 1970s. Beginning in Maine, the Sawyer Art Company moved to Concord, New Hampshire, in 1920 to be nearer their primary market of New Hampshire's White Mountains. Charles H. Sawyer briefly worked for Nutting in 1902–03 while living in southern Maine. Sawyer's production volume ranks #3 behind Wallace Nutting and David Davidson.

Fred Thompson: Frederick H. Thompson and Frederick M. Thompson were another father and son team that operated the Thompson Art Company (TACO) from 1908 to 1923, working primarily in the Portland, Maine, area. We know that Thompson and Nutting had collaborated because Thompson widely marketed an interior scene he had taken in Nutting's Southbury home. The production volume of the Thompson Art Company ranks #4 behind Nutting, Davidson, and Sawyer.

Charles Higgins: Working out of Bath, Maine, some of Higgins's finest pictures rivaled Nutting's best. No firm connection has been found between Higgins and Wallace Nutting.

Carlock, Washington Monument, 7x11" 20.00
Davidson, Arboretum Jewels, 13x16" 55.00
Davidson, Berkshire Sunset, 8x11" 55.00
Davidson, Contentment, 8x10" 55.00
Davidson, Four O'Clock Tea, 13x16" 65.00
Davidson, Her House in Order, 12x15" 80.00
Davidson, Mt Washington Goblet, 7x9" 45.00
Davidson, Promise of Harvest, 7x9" 50.00
Davidson, Red Parasol, 5x7" 110.00
Davidson, Road Home, 5x7" 45.00
Davidson, Sunset Point, 12x16" 35.00
Davidson, Three Arches, Mohawk Trail, 10x12" 50.00
Gibson, Back Road, 7x9" 10.00
Harris, Charlotte Street, Saint Augustine, 13x20" 225.00
Haynes, Untitled Old Faithful, 6x9" 45.00
Sankaty, 9x11" 425.00
Sawyer, Among the New England Hills, 11x20" 330.00
Sawyer, Country Highway, 10x16" 40.00
Sawyer, Elephant's Head, 6x9" 35.00
Sawyer, Joseph Lincoln's Garden, 8x10" 120.00
Sawyer, Lake Louise, 8x10" 90.00
Sawyer, Mt Chocorua, 11x14" 45.00
Sawyer, Plymouth Birches, 8x10" 150.00
Thompson, Birchland, 10x16" 70.00
Thompson, Calm of Fall, 7x9" 35.00
Thompson, Flower Maid, 7x15" 40.00
Thompson, Foot Hills, 13x16" 45.00
Thompson, Golden Trail, 7x11" 25.00
Thompson, Mountains From Intervale, 14x16" 90.00
Thompson, Old Mill Dam, 7x9" 60.00
Thompson, Pepperell Hall, 5x11" 75.00
Thompson, Quiet Autumn Road, 10x16" 40.00
Thompson, Rail Fence, 5x7" 50.00
Thompson, Roller, 11x22" 110.00
Thompson, Spinning Days, 10x13" 55.00
Thompson, Tranquil Stream, 7x12" 35.00

Minor Wallace Nutting-Like Photographers

Hundreds of other smaller local and regional photographers attempted to market hand-colored pictures comparable to Nutting's during the 1900–30s time period. Although quite attractive, most were not as appealing to the general public as Wallace Nutting pictures. However, as the price of Wallace Nutting pictures has escalated, the work of these lesser-known Wallace Nutting-like photographers have become increasingly collectible.

A partial listing of some of these minor Wallace Nutting-like photographers include Babcock; J.C. Bicknell; Blair; Ralph Blood (Portland, Maine); Bragg; Brehmer; Brooks; Burrowes; Busch; Carlock; Pedro Cacciola; Croft; Currier; Depue Bros; Derek; Dowly; Eddy; May Farini (hand-colored colonial lithographs); Geo. Forest; Gandara; Gardner (Nantucket, Bermuda, Florida); Gibson; Gideon; Gunn; Bessie Pease Gutmann (hand-colored colonial lithographs); Edward Guy; Harris; C Hazen; Knoffe; Haynes (Yellowstone Park); Margaret Hennesey; Hodges; Homer; Krabel; Kattleman; La Bushe; Lake; Lamson (Portland, Maine); M. Lightstrum; Machering; Rossiler Mackinae; Merrill; Meyers; William Moehring; Moran; Murrey; Lyman Nelson; J. Robinson Neville (New England); Patterson; Owen Perry; Phelps; Phinney; Reynolds; F. Robbins; Royce; Fred'k Scheetz (Phila...Pennsylvania); Shelton; Standley (Colorado); Stott; Summers; Esther Svenson; Florence Thompson; Thomas Thompson; M.A. Trott; Sanford Tull; Underhill; Villar; Ward; Wilmot; Edith Wilson; and Wright.

A very general breakdown of prices for works by these minor Wallace Nutting-like photographers would be as follows: Larger pictures, greater than 14" x 17", from $75.00 to over $200.00. Medium pictures, from 11" x 14" to 14" x 17", from $50.00 to $200.00. Smaller pictures, 5" x 7" to 10" x 12", from $10.00 to $75.00.

The same pricing guidelines that apply to Wallace Nutting pictures typically apply to Wallace Nutting-like pictures

1.) Exterior scenes are the most common.

2.) Some photographers sold colonial interior scenes as well.

3.) Subject, matter, condition, and size are all important determinants of value.

Miscellaneous Nutting Memorabilia

Advertising sign, paper, 11x16" 125.00
Book, England Beautiful, gr cover, 1st edition 55.00
Book, Furniture of the Pilgrim Century, 1st edition 140.00
Book, Ireland Beautiful, gr cover, 1st edition 50.00
Book, Photographic Art Secrets 28.00
Book, Wallace Nutting Biography, w/dust jacket 140.00
Catalog, furniture, 1927-28 .....65.00
Christmas card, 4x5" 150.00
Miniature exterior scene, 5x6" 65.00
Pirate print, Swimming Pool, unsgn 10.00
Silhouette, Girl Sits at Vanity, 4x4" 45.00
Silhouette, Girl w/Powder Puff, 4x4" 70.00
Treenware salt dish 105.00

Occupied Japan

Items marked 'Occupied Japan' have become popular collectibles in the last few years. They were produced during the period from the end of World War II until April 18, 1952, when the occupation ended. By no means was all of the ware exported during that time marked 'Occupied Japan'; some was marked 'Japan' or 'Made In Japan.' It is thought that because of the natural resentment felt by the Japanese toward the occupation, only a fraction of these wares carried the 'Occupied' mark. Even though you may find identical 'Japan'-marked items, because of its limited use, only those with the 'Occupied Japan' mark are being collected to any great extent. Values vary considerably, based on the quality of workmanship. Generally, bisque figures command much higher prices than porcelain, since on the whole they are of a finer quality.

For those wanting more information, we recommend *The Collector's Encyclopedia of Occupied Japan Collectibles* (there are six in the series) by Gene Florence; he is listed in the Directory under Kentucky. Our advisor for this category is Florence Archambault; she is listed in the Directory under Rhode Island. She represents the Occupied Japan Club, whose mailing address may be found in the Directory under Clubs, Newsletters, and Catalogs. All items described in the following listings are assumed ceramic unless noted otherwise.

Ashtray, alligator form w/tail curled up & mouth open 15.00
Ashtray, horse standing on horseshoe tray, silver-tone metal 20.00
Bank, elephant trumpeting, floral design on wht 35.00
Biscuit jar, tomato form w/rattan-type hdl, mk Maruhon Ware .100.00
Book, Japanese Cook Book, Japan Tourist Bureau 40.00
Book, Suggested Motor Tours Around Tokyo 15.00
Bookends, masted ships supporting 2 books on bases, wood, pr ...75.00
Boot, cowboy, wht/tan w/emb scrolls & bl florals, 6½" 15.00
Box, piano form, silver-tone metal w/red velvet liner 25.00
Butter dish, basketweave pattern, stick sz, mk T in circle 20.00
Butter pat, peaches w/leaves, gold band, lt bl scalloped edge, 3½" ...12.00
Candle holders, cups on ftd & hdld trays, silver-tone metal, pr ...30.00
Cigarette box, Chinese man w/dragon box, gold trim, glossy, 6⅜" ...30.00
Cigarette box, w/2 ashtrays, wht w/violets, gold trim, set 35.00
Coasters, papier-mache, floral, 8-pc set w/box 35.00
Condiment set, jar/shakers/tray, wht w/mc Colonial scene, gold trim 35.00
Creamer & sugar bowl, strawberry form, w/tray, Maruhon Ware ..30.00
Crumb pan, emb swan, metal 20.00
Cup & saucer, demi; blk w/wht lacy floral band, gold trim 15.00
Cup & saucer, demi; lg emb dragon, gold trim, bl mk 20.00
Dinner set, Livonia (Dogwood), w/sm platter, serves 8 .....300.00
Doll, baby in red snowsuit w/bl trim, celluloid, jtd 50.00
Figurine, ballerina, 4¾" 45.00
Figurine, boy & girl dancing w/heads bk, on oval base, mc 25.00
Figurine, boy & girl under umbrella on oval base (Hummel type) ...45.00
Figurine, boy & girl w/dogs, she w/closed umbrella, sq bases, 8", pr .90.00
Figurine, boy musician serenading dog on oval base, mc 20.00
Figurine, Colonial couple courting on oval base w/gold trim, 6¼" .65.00
Figurine, Colonial couple playing instruments, 10⅛", pr 100.00
Figurine, cowboy w/rope, 6½" 20.00

Figurines, dancing couple, cobalt blue, white, and gold, marked SGK, 8¾", $175.00 for the pair. (Photo courtesy Florence Archambault)

Figurine, dog seated w/hat, pipe & bow tie, brn/wht gloss, 3½" ...12.50
Figurine, donkey w/prospecting gear 12.50
Figurine, fishing couple seated, bsk, 4" 20.00
Figurine, flutist standing w/legs crossed, gold trim, 6" 20.00
Figurine, girl dancing w/arms behind head, 5" 20.00
Figurine, Mexican lady, mk Ucagco China, 7¼" 40.00
Figurine, Mexican man on donkey on wht base w/gold trim, 8¼" ..40.00

Figurine, old woman seated w/mc balloons & basket by side 25.00
Figurine, Oriental lady in skirt w/basket on head, gold trim, 8" ...30.00
Figurine, Oriental musician, mc, 10" 65.00
Figurine, peacock, head up w/tail curved under, mc gloss, 5" 25.00
Figurine, villain in blk w/captive lady, bl mk, 7½" 55.00
Fishbowl ornament, mermaid sitting upright, gold trim 35.00
Incense burner, ftd pot w/emb dragon, gold trim 20.00
Jewelry box, silver-tone metal, emb scrolls, ftd, 3½x4½" 20.00
Lamp base, Colonial couple, bsk, gold trim, red mk, 7¼" 65.00
Leaf dish, floral on dbl overlapped wht leaves, gold trim, 6" 10.00
Leaf dish, wht w/mc fruit decal in center, gold trim 17.50
Match holder, coal hod form, blk w/floral, gold trim 15.00
Picnic basket, rectangular 2-tone bamboo w/dbl swing hdls 75.00
Pitcher, chicken form, wht w/red, blk & yel trim, red mk 25.00
Planter, cat (Figarro type) next to pot, blk/wht, 3⅝" 12.00
Planter, circular w/mc parrot & floral, w/chain hanger, Maruhon ...65.00
Planter, cornucopia, wht w/pk appl roses, ftd, Lamore China 40.00
Planter, cucumber form 15.00
Planter, elf w/tulip pot 20.00
Planter, mallard duck (mc) next to sq wht stone pot 15.00
Planter, Nubian type holding basket, gold trim, 7⅛" 30.00
Plate, floral, sgn Ito, Gold China, 7" 40.00
Plate, lacquerware, pagoda scene, sq w/canted corners, Maruni ...40.00
Plate, wht w/violets, open lattice rim, med 20.00
Relish dish, bee in center of wht 2-part honeycomb, mk T 35.00
Salt box, wooden lid, mk Ucagco, 5x5" 50.00
Shakers, bees on wht honeycomb domes w/hdld tray, 3-pc 20.00
Shakers, Dutch couple, mc, red mk, pr 15.00
Shakers, fruit forms on basket, 3-pc 20.00
Shoe, lady's; bl/wht w/bow & ruffle trim w/floral, red cross mk 20.00
Shoe, lady's; rust w/wht dots & emb florals, 2⅜" 10.00
Snack set, plate w/fluted edge, wht w/pk floral, gold trim 20.00
Sugar bowl, blk/wht birds & flowers on tan lustre, w/lid 25.00
Teapot, ribbed ball shape w/knob on flat lid, bamboo hdl, stoneware ..40.00
Tray, serving; lacquerware, 5-part w/hdls, florals on brn 100.00
Tray, serving; papier-mache, ornate florals, rectangular 20.00
Vase, ballerina figure against urn on ftd base, gold trim, 8¼" 60.00
Vase, cornucopia, vertical, silver-tone metal, 8", pr 40.00
Vase, iris on wht urn w/open lattice top, hdld, gold trim 60.00
Vase, lacquerware, Maruni, 13" 150.00
Vase, stylized mc swan, 5" 12.50
Vase, w/cherub, bsk, gold trim, 3⅜" 15.00
Wall figure, Dutch boy w/flower baskets, chalkware, Yomaka, 7½" 22.50
Wall figures, Oriental couple, flowers & baskets, red mk Yamaka, pr 50.00
Wall plaques, Colonial couple/trees/grass emb on oval plates, bsk, pr 50.00
Wall pockets, Colonial couple, fr ½-figures, bsk, 3⅝", pr 25.00
Wind chimes, geometric glass shapes w/pnt decor 35.00

Ohr, George

George Ohr established his pottery in the 1880s in Biloxi, Mississippi. The first pottery burned down and was subsequently rebuilt. Ohr, among other things, was a master of the wheel. This mastery enabled him to create unique forms of unbelievable thinness, verging at times on Abstraction and looking far ahead toward many art movements of the twentieth century. In addition to Abstraction, by studying Ohr, one can discover elements of Expressionism and Fauvism (the wild use of color often seemingly at odds with the piece being glazed) and Dada (meaning shock the bourgeosie). An Ohr piece may be rooted in the functional form of a teapot, but following his manipulation it becomes a sculpture for which the functional form serves only as a take-off point for the finished piece. Ohr was also a master of glazes. Highly esteemed are his volcanic and gunmetal glazes. He was not well received in his day and sold few pieces of his art pottery — a van Gogh-like tale. Ohr decorated his pieces with snakes and lizards and sometimes with asymmetrical handles. He believed that like all things on earth, no two things should be alike. This dictum was applied to his pottery making. He signed his pieces either in impressed letters or florid script. In the early 1900s Ohr ceased making pottery and became a motorcycle dealer and ultimately sold automobiles. His pottery was stored away to be rediscovered many years later. Ohr died in 1918.

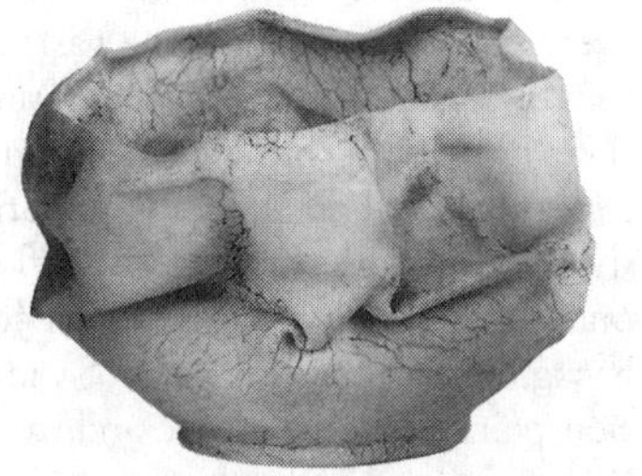

Vase, red and tan bisque with black highlights, numerous pinches and folds, 5x7", $3,750.00.

Bowl, aventurine, horizontal dimples/folds, 3x4" 2,100.00
Bowl, brn-blk speckled, folded rim, dimpled, 2½x4" 1,200.00
Bowl, dk gr/raspberry, in-body twist, folded, rstr, 1903, 4x6" ..3,500.00
Bowl, gr drip on purple, free-form, collapsed rim, sm rstr, 2x4¼" ..1,100.00
Bowl, gunmetal/gr/ochre, raspberry int, free-form, 2x5" 4,250.00
Bowl, scroddled bsk, free-form, pinched/folded, 4x6" 2,900.00
Chamberstick, gunmetal, dimpled base, ribbed neck, 5x3¾" ..1,500.00
Chamberstick, gunmetal/gr, in-body twist, ribbon hdl, 4x3½" ..2,100.00
Chamberstick, raspberry/gr, dimpled base, ribbon hdl, 6x4" ...2,600.00
Cup, brn gunmetal, lg triangular pinched/cut-out hdl, 3½" 1,900.00
Cup, gr/purple gloss, red int, 5-lobe body, 3x4¾" 2,600.00
Dish, gr/gunmetal, crumpled, 1897, 1½x4¼" 1,700.00
Jug, puzzle; brn/gr, incised wheat & landscape, 1899, 8x6¾" ..1,400.00
Mug, olive gr, pierced rim, modeled hdl, mk, 3½" 770.00
Pitcher, gunmetal, leaf shape, 1¾x4¾" 1,300.00
Pitcher, gunmetal blk, asymmetrical, deeply folded/pinched, 3¾" ..1,600.00
Pitcher, pk/gr/red/wht sponged matt, scrolled ribbon hdl, 6½" ...7,000.00
Pitcher, umber/gr sponged bands under glossy clear, 8¾x4" 5,000.00
Vase, bright red mottle, free-form, pinched/flared, 3¾" 375.00
Vase, bsk, bulbous w/deep in-body twist & folds, 6x4¾" 1,500.00
Vase, bsk, folded & dimpled, 5¼x4" 1,200.00
Vase, bsk, pinched/folded, dendrite pattern, firing tear, 5x7½" ...5,000.00
Vase, bsk, red clay, folded/collapsed in 3 lobes, 5x5½" 1,800.00
Vase, deep purple gloss, in-body twist, folded rim, 3¾x4½" ...4,750.00
Vase, dk bl, pinched/twisted neck, shouldered, ped ft, 9¾" 2,500.00
Vase, dk bl drip gloss, bulbous w/twisted top, 4½x4½" 2,000.00
Vase, dk brn, ochre int, corseted/pinched, in-body twist, 3½" ...1,100.00
Vase, dk brn granular lustre, tightly folded rim, 3¾x3¾" 700.00
Vase, dk gr, bulbous, folded rim, 4x2¾" 1,500.00
Vase, gr mottle, asymmetrical, folded/twisted rim, 3¾x4½", NM ..2,300.00
Vase, gr mottled gloss, folded labial rim, 4½x4¾" 3,000.00
Vase, gr speckled, 2 rows of dimples, bulbous, 4½x4½" 1,900.00
Vase, gr/bl matt, cobalt/gr int, in-body twist, 4¼x4" 3,750.00
Vase, gr/brn/gunmetal sponging, ruffled rim, 4¾x2½", NM 2,100.00
Vase, gr/brn/ochre sponging, teardrop w/cupped rim, 5½x3" ..2,800.00
Vase, gr/gunmetal, dbl-lobed top, pear-shaped body, 5x2½" ...3,250.00
Vase, gr/mahog/gunmetal/ochre speckled, torn rim/slumped, 5x4" .5,000.00
Vase, gunmetal, raspberry & gr froth, bottle shape, 4x3¾" 2,500.00
Vase, gunmetal drip over bright gr, blk/coffee int, 6⅝" 1,600.00
Vase, khaki to brn, twisted/pinched flowerpot form, 4¼", NM 1,725.00
Vase, mirror blk speckled, dimpled/pinched, 4-lobe top, 3x4½" 3,500.00
Vase, mirrored brn mottle, ruffled, in-body twist, 6¼x5¾", NM ...6,000.00
Vase, mirrored gr/amber/red mottle, twisted, bulbous, 1895, 8x4½" ...5,500.00
Vase, pk/gr mottle, cupped/ruffled bottle form, JHP, 7x3¼" 400.00

Vase, purple/gr, dimpled/pinched, 3-sided opening, 3x4¼" **5,000.00**
Vase, raspberry/gr/bl/gray sponging, folded/pinched rim, 6", NM ..**4,000.00**
Vase, scroddled dk brn & red bsk, folded/pinched/dimpled, 3¼" ..**550.00**

Old Ivory

Old Ivory dinnerware was produced during the late 1800s by Herman Ohme, of Lower Salzbrunn in Silesia. The patterns are referred to by the numbers stamped on the bottom of many items. (Though not every piece is numbered, the vast majority bears the tiny blue fleur-de-lis/crown mark with Silesia or Germany beneath. Handwritten numbers signify something other than pattern.) Patterns #16 and #84 are the easiest to find and come in a wide variety of table items. Values are about the same for both patterns. Other floral designs include pink, yellow, and orange roses; holly; and lavender flowers — all on the same soft ivory background. The ware was not widely marketed; its two main distribution points were in Maine and, to a lesser extent, Chicago. Our price ranges are intended to represent a nationwide average, though you may have to pay a little more in some areas. Minor damage and gold wear can lower these prices by as much as 25%. Holly pieces command from 25% to 50% more. Novice collectors should be aware of copy-cat versions from the turn of the century that are much heavier and of a coarser material. They are marked 'Old Ivory' without the blue trademark. They are not included in this listing.

In the past year prices for Old Ivory have skyrocketed. Record prices were set when a well-known collection crossed the auction block, and prices realized on the Internet now rival RS Prussia. Another area gaining in popularity is the vases from Ohme usually featuring portraits of Edwardian children. There are few other forms with portraits, and these are very pricey, with 4" to 5" vases going in the range of $250.00 to $400.00, and 8" and 9" vases about $500.00 to $900.00.

For further information we recommend *Collector's Encyclopedia of Old Ivory China, The Mystery Explored*, by Alma Hillman (our advisor), David Goldschmitt, and Adam Szynkiewicz (Collector Books). Ms. Hillman is listed in the Directory under Maine.

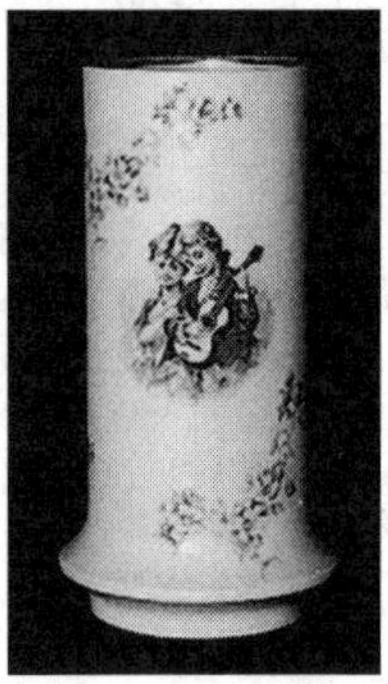

Vase, portrait, 9", from $500.00 to $900.00. (Photo courtesy Alma Hillman)

Basket, oblong, hdld, 8", from $200 to **400.00**
Bowl, ice cream; #4, 10", from $250 to **450.00**
Bowl, oatmeal; 6½", from $55 to **95.00**
Bowl, oyster/waste; 5", from $175 to **225.00**
Bowl, soup; 7½", from $125 to **225.00**
Bowl, vegetable; #84, rnd, w/lid, 10½", from $600 to **1,000.00**
Bowl, vegetable; oval, 9½", from $125 to **185.00**
Bun tray, #121, oblong, 10", from $200 to **300.00**
Butter dish, #16, w/lid & insert, 7½", from $700 to **900.00**
Butter pat, 3¼", from $100 to **150.00**
Candy dish, #84, bow-tie shape, 8", from $125 to **225.00**
Celery dish, #15, oblong, 11¼", from $100 to **195.00**
Charger, #82, Empire, 13", from $400 to **600.00**
Charger/chop plate, #11, 13", from $200 to **400.00**
Chocolate pot, #15, 9½", from $400 to **600.00**
Compote, 9", from $400 to **600.00**
Cracker jar, #22, Holly, Clarion, from $1,000 to **1,500.00**
Cracker/biscuit jar, #16, 8", from $400 to **600.00**
Creamer, service; 5½", from $150 to **325.00**
Cup & saucer, chocolate; #7, 2¼", from $95 to **145.00**
Cup & saucer, cider; 3", from $250 to **350.00**
Cup & saucer, coffee; 3½", from $70 to **90.00**
Cup & saucer, demi; #122, Carmen, from $125 to **200.00**
Cup & saucer, tea; #63, Clarion, from $100 to **150.00**
Cup & saucer, 5-o'clock tea; 3", from $65 to **85.00**
Dish, #200, 3-lobed, 7¼", from $95 to **200.00**
Dresser tray, 11½", from $100 to **200.00**
Gravy boat, 8½", from $800 to **1,000.00**
Hair receiver, from $300 to **500.00**
Jam jar, #200, 3½", from $300 to **400.00**
Ladle holder, oblong, 6½", from $200 to **300.00**
Muffineer/sugar shaker, from $300 to **400.00**
Olive dish, oblong, 6½", from $65 to **85.00**
Plate, coupe; 6¼", from $50 to **75.00**
Plate, coupe; 8½", from $100 to **200.00**
Plate, dessert; #62, Florette, 6½", from $100 to **150.00**
Plate, dessert; 6", from $25 to **55.00**
Plate, dinner; 9½" or 10", from $200 to **300.00**
Plate, salad; 7½", from $40 to **85.00**
Platter, fish; 23", from $800 to **1,000.00**
Platter, 11½", from $100 to **200.00**
Platter, 16½", from $400 to **500.00**
Powder jar, w/lid, from $300 to **500.00**
Ramekin & underplate, #11, 4¼", 5", from $400 to **600.00**
Shaving mug, 3¼", from $550 to **1,200.00**
Soup tureen, 13", from $1,800 to **2,500.00**
Spooner, lay down; oblong, 8¼", from $100 to **150.00**
Sugar bowl, service; 6", from $175 to **350.00**
Tea tile, 6", from $150 to **250.00**
Teapot, 8½", from $500 to **700.00**
Vase, many szs, from $300 to **1,000.00**

Old Paris

Old Paris porcelains were made from the mid-1700s until about 1900. Seldom marked, the term refers to the area of manufacture rather than a specific company. In general, the ware was of high quality, characterized by classic shapes, colorful decoration, and gold application.

Bottle, scent; bird & scroll decor, sq, w/stopper, 3x3" **110.00**
Bottle, scent; medieval knight (& lady) on base, 10½", pr **600.00**
Bowl, centerpc; floral reserve w/cobalt & gold, rstr, 19th C, 9x14" .**450.00**
Bowl, vegetable; gilt melon finial, scroll hdls, 1860, 7x12" **175.00**
Censers, period couple on floral scrolled bases, 10", pr **385.00**
Creamer, HP shells/swans/mythical fish on gold, ca 1800, 4½" .**385.00**
Cup & saucer, Napoleonic general w/gold, gilt paw ft, early 19th C ...**770.00**
Cup & saucer, scenic panels w/cobalt & gold decor **1,100.00**
Figurines, lady & gentleman, ornate costumes, 1850s, 9", pr **250.00**
Figurines, lady reads (he w/flute), high ornate base, 11", pr **600.00**
Fruit stand, rtcl, scalloped border, gilt paw ft, 4½x9" **250.00**
Pitcher, floral panel, pk lustre, repousse lid, 4", pr **660.00**
Pitcher, pk bands w/gold highlights on wht, 9" **100.00**
Platter, floral w/gold, 20" **500.00**
Soup tureen, floral w/gold, oval, w/lid, 9½x13" L **600.00**
Sweetmeat stand, gr w/gold on wht, paw ft, 3-tier, 1820-30, 16x10" .**1,045.00**
Tazza, gilt-metal foliate mts, 19th C, 7x7", pr **330.00**
Urn, Campagna; courting scene, mask hdls, 1840s, 9", pr **2,300.00**

Vase, bird & flower reserves on bl & puce w/gold, hdls, 17", pr ..1,000.00
Vase, cornucopia; mc floral w/gold, bsk appl figure, rpr, 12" 450.00
Vase, garniture; courting scenes on puce w/gold, 19", pr 2,100.00
Vase, ladies in landscape, vine hdls, ruffled, 19½x11", pr 1,200.00
Vase, mc floral w/gold, 13x9" 300.00

Old Sleepy Eye

Old Sleepy Eye was a Sioux Indian chief who was born in Minnesota in 1780. His name was used for the name of a town as well as a flour mill. In 1903 the Sleepy Eye Milling Company of Sleepy Eye, Minnesota, contracted the Weir Pottery Company of Monmouth, Illinois, to make steins, vases, salt crocks, and butter tubs which the company gave away to their customers. A bust profile of the old Indian and his name decorated each piece of the blue and gray stoneware. In addition to these four items, the Minnesota Stoneware Company of Red Wing made a mug with a verse which is very scarce today.

In 1906 Weir Pottery merged with six others to form the Western Stoneware Company in Monmouth. They produced a line of blue and white ware using a lighter body, but these pieces were never given as flour premiums. This line consisted of pitchers (five sizes), steins, mugs, sugar bowls, vases, trivets, and mustache cups. These pieces turn up only rarely in other colors and are highly prized by advanced collectors. Advertising items such as trade cards, pillow tops, thermometers, paperweights, letter openers, postcards, cookbooks, and thimbles are considered very valuable. The original ware was made sporadically until 1937. Brown steins and mugs were produced in 1952. Our advisor for this category is Jim Martin; he is listed in the Directory under Illinois.

Banner, center portrait & western scenes, 22" sq, EX 1,450.00
Barrel, flour; orig paper label, 1920s 1,800.00
Barrel, grapevine-effect banding 3,500.00
Barrel, oak w/brass bands 4,500.00
Barrel label, Chief Strong Bakers..., 16", EX+ 170.00
Blanket, horse; w/logo, EX 2,500.00
Butter crock, Flemish bl & gray 750.00
Cabinet, bread display; Old Sleepy Eye etched in glass 950.00
Calendar, 1904, NM 375.00
Cookbook, Indian on cover, Sleepy Eye Milling Co, 4¾x4" 300.00
Cookbook, loaf of bread shape, NM 210.00
Coupon, for ordering cookbook 250.00
Dough scraper, tin/wood, To Be Sure, EX 435.00
Fan, diecut image of Old Sleepy Eye, EX+ 200.00
Flour sack, cloth, mc Indian, red letters 345.00
Flour sack, paper, Indian in blk, blk lettering, NM 125.00
Hot plate/trivet, bl & wht 4,500.00
Ink blotter 125.00
Letter opener, bronze 900.00
Match holder, pnt 1,000.00
Match holder, wht 1,050.00
Mug, bl & gray, 4¼" 360.00
Mug, bl & wht, 4¼" 220.00
Mug, verse, Red Wing, EX 1,625.00
Paperweight, bronzed company trademk 560.00
Pillow cover, Sleepy Eye & tribe meet President Monroe 750.00
Pillow cover, trademk center w/various scenes, 22", NM 1,800.00
Pin-bk button, Indian, rnd face 350.00
Pitcher, #1, 4" 300.00
Pitcher, #2 ....350.00
Pitcher, #3 ....315.00
Pitcher, #3, w/bl rim 1,375.00
Pitcher, #4 ....400.00
Pitcher, #5 ....435.00
Pitcher, bl & gray, 5" 400.00
Pitcher, bl on cream, 8", M 345.00
Pitcher, brn on yel, Sesquicentennial, 1981, from $100 to 125.00
Pitcher, standing Indian, good color, #5 size 1,560.00
Postcard, colorful trademk, 1904 Expo Winner 185.00
Ruler, wooden, 15" 700.00
Salt crock, Flemish bl & gray, 4x6½" 700.00
Sheet music, in fr 300.00
Sign, self-fr tin, Old Sleepy Eye Flour, 20x24" 3,000.00
Sign, tin litho die-cut Indian, ...Flour & Cereals, 13½" 1,650.00
Spoon, demitasse; emb roses in bowl, Unity SP 105.00
Spoon, Indian-head hdl 125.00
Stein, bl & wht, 7¾" 800.00
Stein, Board of Directors, all yrs, 40-oz 265.00
Stein, Board of Directors, 1969, 22-oz 550.00
Stein, brn, 1952, 22-oz 300.00
Stein, brn & wht 1,500.00
Stein, brn & yel, Western Stoneware 1,500.00
Stein, chestnut, 40-oz, 1952 ....325.00
Stein, cobalt 1,250.00
Stein, Flemish, bl on gray 700.00
Stein, ltd edition, 1979-84, ea 125.00
Sugar bowl, bl & wht, 3" 750.00
Thermometer, front rpl 800.00
Vase, cattails, all cobalt 1,450.00
Vase, cattails, bl & wht, good color, 9" 800.00
Vase, cattails, brn on yel, rare color 1,500.00
Vase, cattails, gr & wht, rare 5,000.00
Vase, Indian & cattails, Flemish, 8½" 470.00

O'Neill, Rose

Rose O'Neill's Kewpies were introduced in 1909 when they were used to conclude a story in the December issue of *Ladies' Home Journal*. They were an immediate success, and soon Kewpie dolls were being produced worldwide. German manufacturers were among the earliest and also used the Kewpie motif to decorate chinaware as well as other items. The Kewpie is still popular today and can be found on products ranging from Christmas cards and cake ornaments to fabrics, wallpaper, and metal items.

For further information we recommend *Doll Values, Antique to Modern*, by Patsy Moyer (Collector Books). In the following listings, 'sgn' indicates that the item is signed Rose O'Neill. Doll values are for examples in mint condition. Look also for the © mark on items. Unsigned items can be of interest to collectors; many are authentic and collectible, some are too small to sign.

Kewpie bisque, seated with book, Germany, 4", $850.00.

Ad, Hendler Ice Cream Co, Kewpie waitress, ca 1940, 5x12", EX .25.00

Book, Master-Mistress, poems & drawings, 227-pg, 1922, VG ...110.00
Book, The 1 Rose, biography, R Godding, sgn, 2nd ed, 1972 ....55.00
Booklet, Jell-O Ice Cream Powder, 10-pg, w/insert, ca 1910 ....55.00
Clock, bl w/2 wht Kewpies, Jasperware, Germany, 3¾x4¾" 410.00
Creamer, lustreware, 2 Kewpies & foliage, Germany, 2½" 220.00
Crib, Kewpie decals on all sides, wooden, Gem Mfg Co, 31x36x19" ..300.00
Cup & saucer, Bavaria 165.00
Kewpie, bsk, American Doughboy, WWI, sticker, sgn ft, 5½" ...900.00
Kewpie, bsk, Bell Hop, molded gr jacket & hat, sgn, 4", minimum ..950.00
Kewpie, bsk, Blunderboo, falling, sgn, 1¾", from $395 to 525.00
Kewpie, bsk, Doodle Dog, molded into bathtub, sgn, 1¾x3¼" ...2,700.00
Kewpie, bsk, Farmer by vase, sgn, 6½", minimum value 950.00
Kewpie, bsk, ghost, Enesco, mk Jesco, 1993, MIB 80.00
Kewpie, bsk, Huggers, 2½" 125.00
Kewpie, bsk, jtd hips & shoulders, sgn, 5" 525.00
Kewpie, bsk, jtd shoulders, pnt/molded hair, sgn, 2" 95.00
Kewpie, bsk, kneeling, sgn, 4" 900.00
Kewpie, bsk, nonjtd, pnt/molded hair, sgn, 2" 110.00
Kewpie, bsk, reclining, w/dog on bk, 3" L, EX 1,600.00
Kewpie, bsk, sitting, heart label, sgn, 3½" 525.00
Kewpie, bsk, straddling goose, sgn/#d, rare, 3½", from $5,500 to .6,200.00
Kewpie, bsk, thumbsucker, mk Lefton's Japan, KW228, 5", EX 30.00
Kewpie, bsk, w/baby bottle & baby Kewpie, sgn, 3½" 2,900.00
Kewpie, bsk, w/rabbit, sgn, 2½" 400.00
Kewpie, celluloid, Bride & Groom, sgn, Germany, 3", M 150.00
Kewpie, celluloid, jtd arms, heart label, Germany, sgn, 12", minimum ...325.00
Kewpie, compo, Hottentot, jtd arms, red wings, decal, 1946, 11" ..575.00
Kewpie, compo, jtd arms, sgn, 9" 185.00
Kewpie, compo & cloth, jtd forearms, tagged dress, 11" 875.00
Kewpie, hard plastic, jtd, neck/shoulders/hips, sleep eyes, sgn, 12" 435.00
Kewpie, papier-mache (compo type), Twin Children's Shoes, 32" ..1,000.00
Kewpie, plush, stockinette face, tagged, 8", M 225.00
Kewpie, vinyl, Black, striped pajamas, 11", MIB 100.00
Kewpie, vinyl, jtd neck, shoulders & hips, sgn, 14" 170.00
Kewpie, vinyl, Ragsy, 1-pc w/molded clothes, sgn, 8", minimum .85.00
Kewpie, vinyl head & limbs, cloth body, sgn, 16" 185.00
Magazine, illus for story, Harper's Bazaar, Nov 1906, VG 24.00
Magazine, Ladies' Home Journal, Jell-O illus, 1919, VG 48.00
Magazine page, LHJ, Kewpies & Little German Girl, 1913, EX ...35.00
Pin-bk, Kewpie w/horn, Saturday Chicago Am paper, 1930s, EX ...48.00
Plaque, bl bsk, Joe Kallus, oval, c 1973, 7x5" 15.00
Plate, Kewpie, Love to You, World Wide Arts, 1973, 8¼", M (VG box) 14.00
Plate, Kewpie in flower w/verse, porc, gold trim, 1973, 8" 22.00
Plate, Time To Be Happy Is Now, collectors ed, 1973, EX 50.00
Plate, 3 Kewpies, Bavaria, 5" 145.00
Postcard, Kewpie mermaids, sgn, (+) from 1973 watercolor 18.00
Postcard, Kewpie on mother blbird w/young, postmk 1918, G 25.00
Postcard, 3 Kewpies in heart, Gibson Art Comp, sgn, EX 35.00
Postcard, 5 Kewpies/4 birds on branch, sgn, postmk 1918, EX 28.00
Print, Kewpie w/ball cap eats ice cream, sgn/c, 12x9" 30.00
Soap figure, Kewpie bathing Kewpie doll, mk, ca 1917, 4", G 50.00
Sugar bowl, lustreware, 2 Kewpies (1 more on bk), sgn, 3" 110.00
Tobacco felt, Kewpie chasing frog, sgn, 1914, 6x4¾", EX 50.00
Tobacco felt, Kewpie cuts hair of another, sgn, 1914, 6x4¾" 55.00
Tobacco felt, Kewpie soldier, sgn, 1914, 6x4¾", EX 45.00
Tobacco felt, 2 Kewpies, sgn, 1914, 6x4¾", VG 28.00
Toothpick holder, Kewpie, glass 65.00
Tray, Kewpies making lemonade, tin litho, 10x13", EX+ 720.00
Valentine, 2 Kewpies w/verse, 2½x3¾", VG 28.00

Onion Pattern

The familiar pattern known to collectors as Onion acquired its name through a case of mistaken identity. Designed in the early 1700s by Johann Haroldt of the Meissen factory in Germany, the pattern was a mixture of earlier Oriental designs. One of its components was a stylized peach, which was mistaken for an onion; as a result, the pattern became known by that name. Usually found in blue, an occasional piece may also be found in pink and red. The pattern is commonly associated with Meissen, but it has been reproduced by many others including Villeroy and Boch and Royal Copenhagen.

Many marks have been used, some of them fraudulent Meissen marks. Study a marks book to become more familiar with them. In our listings, 'Xd swords' indicates first-quality old Meissen ware. Meissen in an oval over a star was a mark of C. Teichert Stove and Porcelain Factory of Meissen; it was used from 1882 until about 1930. Items marked simply Meissen were produced by the State's Porcelain Manufactory VEB after 1972. The crossed swords indication was sometimes added. Today's market abounds with quality reproductions.

Blue Danube is a modern line of Onion-patterned dinnerware produced in Japan and distributed by Lipper International of Wallingford, Connecticut. At least one hundred items are available in porcelain; it is sold in most large stores with china departments.

Plate, openwork woven rim, crossed swords, 8", $100.00. (Photo courtesy 'At Merri's House')

Basket, rtcl, shallow, Xd swords, 1890s, 7", from $300 to 350.00
Bone dish, Xd swords, 7" 60.00
Bowl, berry; Meissen w/star, 5½" 15.00
Bowl, fruit; Meissen, England, 5" 7.50
Bowl, lattice edge, Blue Danube, 9", from $50 to 60.00
Bowl, soup; Bilton's England, 6¾" 6.50
Butter dish, stick type, Blue Danube, ¼-lb, from $25 to 35.00
Butter pat, Xd swords, 3¼" 45.00
Candlestick, Xd swords, 9", from $300 to 350.00
Candlesticks, Blue Danube, 6½", pr, from $40 to 50.00
Candy dish, rolled hdl, Xd swords, 4¾" 85.00
Canister, bbl shape, Germany, 3" 85.00
Canister, bbl shape, Germany, 4" 135.00
Canister, bbl shape, Germany, 6" 150.00
Casserole, Blue Danube, 5½x10½" 65.00
Casserole (open), MIG, 8½" 65.00
Charger, Xd swords (late), 16" dia 300.00
Coffeepot, GMT & Bro Germany, 8¼", EX 225.00
Cookie jar, GMT & Bro Germany, 7½", NM 250.00
Creamer, Meissen w/star (ca 1910), 6" 45.00
Creamer, str sides, Homer Laughlin 14.00
Cup & saucer, 'y' hdl, scalloped rims, Blue Danube, from $6 to 8.00
Cup & saucer, demitasse; mk: lg X+2 sm, Germany 50.00
Cutting brd, flow bl, 7¾x4¾", EX 110.00
Dish, scalloped 4-lobe rim, Xd swords, 6x6" 85.00
Egg cup, dbl, Meissen, 3½" 75.00
Knifes (8) w/brass blades, in floriate brass holder, no mk 200.00
Knives, Steelbronce blades, Meissen, set of 2 (ea 7½"), MIB 125.00
Plate, Cauldon England, 7½", EX 20.00
Plate, Cauldon England, 9" 32.00

Plate, deep; Meissen, MIG, 1½x10", from $75 to 85.00
Plate, gold trim, Xd swords, lt wear, 9¾", set of 8 ....475.00
Plate, lattice rim, Blue Danube, 8" 15.00
Plate, lt bl, Meissen w/star, 1⅜x10" 40.00
Plate, MPM, E&A Muller Prozellanfabrik, ca 1900-1920, 8" 25.00
Plate, soup; faux Meissen Xd swords mk 45.00
Plate, Staffordshire England Tableware, 10" 12.00
Platter, amber/gold trim, 4 leafy stations in rim, Xd swords, 18" ...350.00
Platter, flow bl, LS&S, 12" 50.00
Platter, Meissen w/star, 10½" 65.00
Platter, Meissen w/star, 20x10" 170.00
Salt box, German, 6x6", NM 85.00
Salt box, wooden lid, Blue Danube, 4¾x4¾" 50.00
Salt box, ½-cylinder w/high bk crest, wood lid, German, 8", EX ...200.00
Shell dish, Germany w/Xd swords, #54-275, 5" 60.00
Stein, str sides, pewter lid, Xd swords, 6" 275.00
Tidbit tray, 2-tier, Blue Danube 35.00
Tureen, Meissen, dome lid, 9x13" 425.00

Opalescent Glass

First made in England in 1870, opalescent glass became popular in America around the turn of the century. Its name comes from the milky-white opalescent trim that defines the lines of the pattern. It was produced in table sets, novelties, toothpick holders, vases, and lamps. Note that American-made sugar bowls have lids; sugar bowls of British origin are considered to be complete without lids. For further information we recommend *The Standard Encyclopedia of Opalescent Glass, Third Edition*, by Bill Edwards and Mike Carwile (Collector Books).

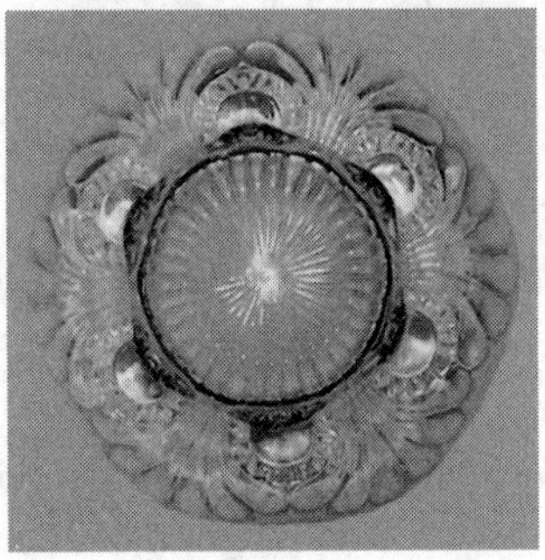

Tokyo, footed plate, blue opalescent, $55.00. (Photo courtesy Bill Edwards)

Abalone, bowl, bl 35.00
Ala-Bock, pitcher, vaseline 250.00
Arabian Nights, tumbler, cranberry 125.00
Argonaut Shell (Nautilus), jelly compote, bl 100.00
Ascot, creamer, canary 60.00
Autumn Leaves, bowl, banana; gr 70.00
Barbells, bowl, gr 50.00
Beaded Fan, bowl, wht, ftd 35.00
Beaded Ovals in Sand, bowl, sauce; gr 30.00
Beads & Bark, vase, gr, ftd 70.00
Beatty Rib, salt dip, wht 45.00
Beatty Swirl, mug, vaseline 85.00
Berry Patch, plate, bl or gr 75.00
Blackberry Spray, hat, amethyst 100.00
Blown Twist, sugar shaker, canary 200.00
Brideshead, tray, vaseline, oval 120.00
Bull's Eye, shade, bl 50.00
Button Panels, bowl, wht 35.00
Carousel, bowl, gr 50.00
Chippendale, basket, canary 65.00
Chippendale, ice cream dish, vaseline, 6" 68.00
Christmas Pearls, cruet, gr 280.00
Chrysanthemum Base Swirl, butter dish, wht 300.00
Chrysanthemum Base Swirl, straw holder, cranberry, w/lid 1,200.00
Chrysanthemum Swirl VT, pitcher, teal, rare 400.00
Circled Scroll, jelly compote, gr 140.00
Coin Dot Chevron Base, oil lamp, wht 225.00
Coinspot, tumbler, rubena 90.00
Colonial Stairsteps, toothpick holder, bl 200.00
Compass, bowl, bl or gr, scarce 150.00
Consolidated Crisscross, sugar shaker, rubena 600.00
Consolidated Crisscross, vase, celery; cranberry 175.00
Contessa, pitcher, amber 325.00
Corolla, vase, wht 175.00
Crocus, vase, bl, rare 350.00
Curtain Call, castor set, cobalt, rare 550.00
Daffodils, oil lamp, gr 300.00
Dahlia Twist, vase, wht, scarce 50.00
Daisy & Greek Key, bowl, sauce; gr, ftd 60.00
Daisy & Plume, bowl, gr, ftd 45.00
Diamond Point, vase, gr 50.00
Dolly Madison, bowl, sauce; gr 35.00
Double Greek Key, tray, pickle; bl 150.00
Dragon & Lotus, bowl, wht, rare 325.00
Dragon Lady, bowl, novelty; bl 140.00
Duchess, bowl, master; vaseline 80.00
Duchess, toothpick holder, bl 250.00
Dugan Intaglio Grape, compote, wht 85.00
Dugan Strawberry Intaglio, bowl, fruit; wht, stemmed 65.00
Ellipse & Diamond, pitcher, cranberry 400.00
Elson Dew Drop, mug, wht 50.00
English Duck, novelty dish, canary 150.00
Everglades, butter dish, bl 325.00
Fan, bowl, master; gr 70.00
Fancy Fantails, bowl, gr 45.00
Fancy Fantails, rose bowl, wht w/cranberry rim 85.00
Fenton #220 (Stripe), pitcher, vaseline, w/lid 225.00
Fenton #370, nappy, amber 55.00
Fern, bottle, barber; cranberry 300.00
Finecut & Roses, rose bowl, gr 45.00
Fishscale & Beads, bowl, wht 30.00
Flora, vase, celery; bl 130.00
Fluted Bars & Beads, tumbler, bl 100.00
Fluted Scroll w/Vine, vase, wht, ftd 50.00
Four Pillars, vase, bl 75.00
Gonterman (Adonis) Swirl, pitcher, amber 400.00
Greek Key & Ribs, bowl, bl 65.00
Harrow, creamer, bl 75.00
Hearts & Flowers, compote, bl 350.00
Herringbone, cruet, wht 225.00
Hobnail, Hobbs, bride's basket, rubena 500.00
Hobnail, Hobbs, shakers, wht, pr 400.00
Hobnail, Northwood's, spooner, bl 75.00
Hobnail in Square (Vesta), butter dish, wht 200.00
Hobnail 4-Footed, butter dish, cobalt 225.00
Holly, bowl, wht 175.00
Honeycomb (Beatty), mustard pot, bl 100.00
Honeycomb & Clover, creamer, gr 140.00
Horse Chestnut, vase, canary, blown 100.00
Idyll, bowl, master; gr 60.00
Inside Rubbing, creamer, bl 75.00
Inside Rubbing, cruet, vaseline 150.00
Intaglio, bowl, master; bl, ftd 115.00
Intaglio, spooner, bl 60.00
Interior Panel, vase, fan; amethyst 100.00

Inverted Coindot, tumbler, gr 60.00
Inverted Fan & Feather, bowl, sauce; gr 100.00
Inverted Fan & Feather, pitcher, wht 625.00
Iris w/Meander, butter dish, gr 275.00
Iris w/Meander, spooner, gr 80.00
Jackson, candy dish, wht 35.00
Jackson, tumbler, bl 80.00
Jazz, vase, bl 50.00
Jefferson Spool, vase, gr 45.00
Jewelled Heart, bowl, master; bl 65.00
Lady Caroline, basket, vaseline 60.00
Late Coinspot, tumbler, gr 35.00
Lattice (Bubble), bride's basket, cranberry 225.00
Lattice (Bubble), spooner, bl 60.00
Lattice & Points, vase, wht 75.00
Leaf & Beads, rose bowl, gr 50.00
Leaf & Diamonds, bowl, bl 50.00
Leaf Molds, bowl, master; cranberry 140.00
Lily Pool, epergne, bl 300.00
Lined Heart, vase, gr 40.00
Little Nell, vase, wht 20.00
Lorna, vase, bl 40.00
Lustre Flute, custard cup, wht 30.00
Many Loops, bowl, gr, ruffled 45.00
Mary Ann, vase, bl, rare 300.00
Melon Swirl, tumbler, bl 75.00
Monkey (Under a Tree), pitcher, wht, rare 1,000.00
Netted Cherries, plate, wht 65.00
Northern Star, bowl, banana; gr 70.00
Northwood Block, vase, celery; vaseline 55.00
Old Man Winter, basket, gr, sm 65.00
Opal Loops, decanter, wht 160.00
Opal Urn, vase, bl 80.00
Orange Tree, vase, custard opal, rare 250.00
Palm & Scroll, bowl, gr, ftd 45.00
Palm Beach, jelly compote, canary 200.00
Panelled Sprig, cruet, wht 150.00
Pearls & Scales, compote, emerald gr 60.00
Picket, planter, bl 75.00
Plain Panels, vase, gr 40.00
Poinsettia, bowl, fruit; bl 125.00
Polka Dot, bowl, bl, lg 75.00
Popsicle Sticks, bowl, wht, ftd 35.00
Prince William, creamer, bl 65.00
Princess Diana, butter dish, vaseline 110.00
Pussy Willow, vase, canary, 4½" 50.00
Question Mark, tray, card; bl 75.00
Quilted Pillow Sham, butter dish, canary, oval 100.00
Reflecting Diamonds, bowl, wht 40.00
Regal (Northwood's), creamer, bl 60.00
Reverse Drapery, bowl, gr 45.00
Reverse Swirl, toothpick holder, cranberry 275.00
Reverse Swirl, water bottle, bl 150.00
Ribbed Lattice, cruet, wht 175.00
Ribbed Oval Rings, tumbler, cranberry 125.00
Ribbed Spiral, cup & saucer, canary 100.00
Ric-Rac, jar, vaseline 100.00
Richelieu, basket, bl, hdld 65.00
Rippled Rib, vase, wht 40.00
Roulette, plate, gr 100.00
Ruffles & Rings, bowl, nut; wht 30.00
S-Repeat, tumbler, bl 65.00
Scroll w/Acanthus, bowl, sauce; canary 25.00
Sea Scroll, compote, gr 145.00
Seaweed, vase, celery; cranberry 175.00
Serpent Threads, epergne, vaseline, 23" 300.00
Shell Beaded, pitcher, gr (+) 625.00
Shells & Dots, rose bowl, bl 45.00
Sir Lancelot, bowl, bl, ftd 65.00
Somerset, dish, bl, sq 50.00
Spanish Lace, spooner, cranberry 175.00
Spatter, tumbler, bl 35.00
Speckled Stripe, bottle, barber; wht 265.00
Spool, compote, gr 50.00
Stars & Stripes, lamp shade, wht 65.00
Stripe, tumbler, bl 55.00
Sunburst on Shield (Diadem), bowl, sauce; bl 40.00
Sunk Hollyhock, bowl, canary, rare 100.00
Swag w/Brackets, creamer, vaseline 65.00
Swastika, pitcher, bl or gr 700.00
Swirl, butter dish, gr 125.00
Swirl, mustard jar, wht 60.00
Swirl, toothpick holder, cranberry 150.00
Target, vase, bl 65.00
Thousand Eye, creamer, wht 40.00
Tokyo, bowl, master; gr 40.00
Trailing Vine, bowl, novelty; wht 40.00
Trellis, tumbler, canary 65.00
Twist (Miniatures), spooner, bl 65.00
Twister, plate, bl 60.00
Victoria & Albert, biscuit jar, vaseline 150.00
Vintage, Northwood/Dugan, plate, gr 45.00
War of the Roses, bowl, bl 75.00
Waterlily & Cattails, gravy boat, gr, hdld 55.00
Waterlily & Cattails, spooner, amethyst 75.00
White Chapel, creamer, canary 30.00
Wild Bouquet, pitcher, gr 300.00
Wild Daffodils, mug, amethyst 45.00
Wild Rose, bowl, amethyst 75.00
William & Mary, plate, canary 60.00
Window Stripe, vase, cranberry 125.00
Windows (Plain), bowl, finger; bl 50.00
Windows (Swirled), bowl, master; wht 40.00
Winter Cabbage, bowl, bl, ftd 50.00
Woven Wonder, bowl, novelty; wht 40.00
Wreath & Scroll, bowl, sauce; bl 35.00
Wreath & Scroll, spittoon, lady's; bl 100.00
Zipper & Loops, vase, gr, ftd 70.00

Opaline

A type of semiopaque opal glass, opaline was made in white as well as pastel shades and is often enameled. It is similar in appearance to English bristol glass, though its enamel or gilt decorative devices tend to exhibit a French influence.

Jewelry box, pink opaline, round with brass hinge and footed frame, 2⅞x3¼", $195.00.

Bottle, scent; bl, Islamic HP floral, Bohemian, ca 1850, 10", NM ..575.00
Bottle, scent; gr w/gold, Fr, 1860s, chip on stopper, 7½" 500.00
Bottle, scent; turq serpent encircles, gold decor, stopper, 7" 135.00
Bottle holder, rose pk in branch fr, w/wht 2" bottle, 4" overall ..525.00
Box, pasty HP floral, Bohemian, ca 1850, 4¾x3", NM 800.00
Condiment set, open salt & 2 w/lids, rstr fr, 6½x5" 225.00
Vase, wht, slim urn form, ormolu rim & ft, 9", pr 400.00

Orientalia

The art of the Orient is an area of collecting currently enjoying strong collector interest, not only in those examples that are truly 'antique' but in the twentieth-century items as well. Because of the many aspects involved in a study of Orientalia, we can only try through brief comments to acquaint the reader with some of the more readily available examples. We suggest you refer to specialized reference sources for more detailed information. See also specific categories.

Key:

Ch — Chinese	hdwd — hardwood
cvg — carving	Jp — Japan
drw — drawer	Ko — Korean
Dy — Dynasty	lcq — lacquer
E — export	mdl — medallion
FR — Famille Rose	rswd — rosewood
FV — Famille Verte	tkwd — teakwood

Blue and White Porcelain

Bowl, chrysanthemum sprays in panels, ca 1800, 7x14", EX, $715.00.

Bottle, sake; globular, rolled mouth, Ko-Imari, 17th C, 10½" 230.00
Bowl, asymmetrical crane & sea turtle design, Edo, 19th C, 8¼" ..200.00
Bowl, E, 7 robed men among bamboo, 5x13½" dia 600.00
Charger, E, cottage among pines, diapering/scrolls, 21½" 400.00
Garniture set, chicken skin decor w/gold, 19th C, 3-pc 1,265.00
Ginger jar, landscape scene, Ming Dy, 6", EX 150.00
Ladle, Sanskrit inscription, peonies, Wanli, 13⅛" 2,000.00
Lamp, ginger jar; figures & horse, not drilled, 19th C, 14" 300.00

Bronze

Avalokitesvara seated on dbl lotus, Ming Dy, 11⅝" 575.00
Buddha sits beneath canopy of cobras, Cambodia, ca 1800, 12½" ..525.00
Censer, flattened form on rnd ft, well hdls, rosewood lid, Ch, 1800s ..100.00
Censer, phoenix birds/dragon & cloud, ring neck, 19th C, 9¾" ...300.00
Elephant w/raised trunk, ivory tusks, Jp, 20½" L 800.00
Guanyn in flowing robes, silver inlay, Ch, 19th C, 9¾" 1,850.00
Hand mirror, nature scenes of Ibis & turtle, silvered bk, 1790s, 11" ...400.00
Jar, 2 shore birds among flowers, gold/silver/brn, Meiji, 6¼" 170.00
Letter opener, molded cranes (4), appl silver, Meiji, 12¼" 225.00
Sadaskari on dbl lotus, Nepal, ca 1500, 4¾" 575.00
Temple lions, worn dk patina, 42½", pr 2,400.00
Vishnu, 4-armed diety, Chola, 10th/11th C, 9⅜" 2,300.00

Celadon

Bottle, bbl form w/slim neck, uptrn rim, Ko, ca 1400, 7¾" 300.00
Bottle, globular w/scrolling florals, 14th C, 4" 335.00
Bottle, gray stoneware w/thick glaze, short neck/loop hdls, 1300s, 4" ..600.00
Bowl, cranes amid clouds, allover crackle, 19th C, 5⅞" 300.00
Bowl, Longquan, 6 sections, even sea-gr, early Ming Dy, 7¼" ...600.00

Furniture

Armchair, horseshoe-shaped bk, cvgs/details, Ch, 40", EX 330.00
Cabinet, pacouk & elm, 2 short/1 long drw/2 door, Ch, 1820, 32x35" ...1,500.00
Cupboard, clothes storage, mixed woods/cvd panels, Ch, 74x46x20" ...400.00
Cupboard, elm w/blk lcq/red on fretwork, 3-drw base, Ch, 68x52" 500.00
Cupboard, Wan Li, open top over 2 doors, cvd panels in base, Ch, 71" ..990.00
Desk, cvd rswd, dragon/cherry blossom cvgs, 47x36x24" 565.00
Screen, cvd tkwd w/2 cloisonne mdls in ea panel, 6-part, 72x96" ...770.00
Screen, pnt paper wildlife scenes, 6-fold, ca 1700, Jp, 63x112" 1,725.00
Screen, wood w/mc lcq decor/relief cvgs, 4-part, 78" H 600.00
Shelves, rfn hdwd, 3 scalloped shelves, triangular, 56x42x22" ...350.00
Stand, cvd rswd, marble insert, fish on skirt, 32x14" dia 535.00
Stand, cvd tkwd w/soapstone insert top, Ch, 17¾" 250.00
Stand, hdwd, cvd/pierced florals, marble top, Ch, 32x18" 250.00
Stand, scenic scrolls/palace scenes decor, Ch, nesting set of 4 ...1,250.00
Table, alter; hdwd, pierced dragon cvgs, scroll ends, Ch, 80" .1,000.00
Table, cvd hdwd w/marble top, dragon claw ft, Ch, 19th C, 18x20" ...250.00
Table, hdwd, cvd aprons, shelf, marble top, Ch, 32", pr 365.00
Table, side; hdwd w/cvd rope aprons/scrolls, Ch, 1900s, 46" 475.00
Table, tkwd w/floral nacre inlay, 3 dvtl drws, Ch, 15x56x14" 165.00
Table, writing; cvd wood, lion mask pulls, Ch, 20th C, 32x37x24" ..350.00
Trunk, leather w/brass studs, bail hdls, 20", on repro stand 400.00

Hardstones

Jade, bowl, lt celadon, cvd dragons, on wood stand, 8x21" 1,850.00
Jade, brushwasher jar, wht, 2 boys cling to sides, 4¼" 1,375.00
Jade, dish, gr mottle, grapes & leaves form, w/wood stand, 5" L ...350.00
Jade, incense burner, fu dog hdls, ox head on lid, Ch, 1900s, 11" ..400.00
Jade, lotus root, wht, 3 nodules/seed pod/foliate, 5¾" 1,725.00
Jade, plaque, lt celadon, mtn scene w/figures, 22x13" 1,265.00
Jade, vase, gr, cvd bird among foliage, w/lid & chain, 8⅞" 8,000.00
Jade, veiled goddess, gr w/brn specks, Ch, 1900, 11½" 750.00
Malachite, mtn w/pavilion & lone pine, 6⅝" 350.00
Moss agate, match safe, late 1800s, 2¾x1¼x½" 160.00
Serpentine, incense burner, bearded wise man w/open mouth, 8" ...150.00

Lacquer

Lacquerware is found in several colors, but the one most likely to be encountered is cinnabar. It is often intricately carved, sometimes involving hundreds of layers built one at a time on a metal or wooden base. Later pieces remain red, while older examples tend to darken.

Box, phoenix & flowers MOP inlay, 2 compartments, Ko, 4⅝x9x7" ..115.00
Jar, EX cvg/detail, over bronze, enamel int, 5", pr 90.00
Pipe case, flame pattern, Meiji, 8⅝" 1,200.00
Tea safe, E, w/pewter canisters, Ch, 1800s, 11x8" 325.00
Trunk, pagodas cvd on hinged top, cvd panel, Ch, 20th C, 21x26x17" ..200.00

Netsukes

A netsuke is a miniature Japanese carving made with two holes called the Himitoshi, either channeled or within the carved design. As kimonos (the outer garment of the time) had no pockets, the Japanese man hung his pipe, tobacco pouch, or other daily necessities from his waist sash. The most highly valued accessory was a nest of little drawers called an Inro, in which they carried snuff or sometimes opium. The netsuke was the toggle that secured them. Although most are of ivory, others were made of bone, wood, metal, porcelain, or semiprecious stones. Some were inlaid or lacquered. They are found in many forms — figurals the most common, mythological beasts the most desirable. They range in size from 1" up to 3", which was the maximum size allowed by law. Many netsukes represented the owner's profession, religion, or hobbies. Scenes from the daily life of Japan at that time were often depicted in the tiny carvings. The more detailed the carving, the greater the value.

Careful study is required to recognize the quality of the netsuke. Many have been made in Hong Kong in recent years; and even though some are very well carved, these are considered copies and avoided by the serious collector. There are many books that will help you learn to recognize quality netsukes, and most reputable dealers are glad to assist you. Use your magnifying glass to check for repairs. In the listings that follow, netsukes are ivory unless noted otherwise; 'stain' indicates a color wash.

Boy & girl on horse, 4⅜x1½" 475.00
Bull, recumbent, Matsubi, 20th C 1,000.00
Cats (2) in short jackets dancing, wood w/shell inlay, 19th C, 2" ...3,165.00
Chinese sage resting beard on fan, ca 1800 ....1,000.00
Cluster of persimmons, Meiji, sgn Gyokuyusai 1,000.00
Fish, red inlay eyes, 2½x1¼" 820.00
Fisherman seated, ebony w/coral inlay, gilt decor, Norimitsu, 19th C ...575.00
Frog on roof tile, boxwood, Masanao of Ise, 19th C, ¾x1⅜x1⅜" 1,680.00
Man seated by armrest, 18th C 800.00
Manzai entertainers (2), elephant ivory, ca 1875, 2¼" 500.00
Mask group, 4 faces, dk brn stain on boxwood, 19th C, 1¾x1¼" ..410.00
Monkey, wood, 18th C, 2x1" 480.00
Oni cowering under hat, wood, sgn Shogyoku, 19th C 1,250.00
Oni w/drum on bk, stain, 19th C, 1¼" 400.00
Oni weeping over severed arm, 19th C, 1¼" 200.00
Puppy playing w/ball, inlay/stain, Gyokko, 19th C, 1⅛" 315.00
Rakkan bathing, wood, Sozan, 19th C 1,375.00
Shishi w/ball, dk boxwood, sgn Yoshikazu 1,250.00
Skull group (8), mammoth ivory, sgn, 1⅜x1⅜x1" 335.00

Porcelain

Chinese export ware was designed to appeal to Western tastes and was often made to order. During the eighteenth century, vast amounts were shipped to Europe and on westward. Much of this fine porcelain consisted of dinnerware lines that were given specific pattern names. Rose Mandarin, Fitzhugh, Armorial, Rose Medallion, and Canton are but a few of the more familiar.

Bowl, berry; E, floral, Imari palette early 18th C, 6¼", pr 400.00
Bowl, E, Chrysanthemum, Imari palette, early 18th C, 10" 420.00
Bowl, E, FR, gilt-bronze mts, foliate hdls, 20" 1,000.00
Bowl, E, Rose Canton, cut corners, 19th C, 10½" 1,100.00
Bowl, fruit; E, floral mdl in well, ca 1780s, 7¾", EX 215.00
Bowl, punch; E, court figures on dragon boat, 19th C, 15⅝" ..2,650.00
Bowl, punch; E, FV, exotic birds, 19th C, 14¾" 1,725.00
Bowl, punch; E, Samson style w/crest & floral panels, 11¼" 275.00
Box, FV, 4-tier, phoenix/clouds/rondels, Kangxi, 7½" 2,875.00
Charger, E, FV, deer & crane beneath pine, rpr, 19th C, 12½" ..275.00
Charger, E, foliage/floral mdl, Imari palette Kangxi, 14" 1,000.00
Hat stand, E, FR, house furnishings, mid 19th C, 11¼", NM 250.00
Mug, E, FR florets, red diapering, C-hdl, early 18th C, 6¼" 850.00
Plate, E, shore scene, Imari palette, ca 1700, 9⅛", EX, 4 for 750.00
Platter, Blue Fitzhugh w/gold, lion crest on rim, 19th C, 12x9" .350.00
Platter, E, bl & gold vintage border, pierced insert, 17½" 1,265.00
Tankard, E, buildings/fishermen, Imari palette, early 18th C, 6½" 675.00
Tea caddy, E, FV, phoenix decor, early 18th C, 4⅜" 425.00
Tea set, Rose Canton, 2 sm teapots+4 handleless c/s 200.00
Teapot stand, E, floral decor, rtcl hdl, rstr, 18th C 150.00
Vase, E, FR, foo-lion hdls, scenic panels, Ch, 19th C, 17½", VG ...1,000.00
Vase, Mirror Black, narrow neck, cylindrical, 19th C, 15⅜" 120.00
Watch hutch, E, cylinder w/mc appl flowers & foo dog, rpr, 6½" ..800.00

Pottery

Bowl, Junyao, lt gr-bl w/crazing, shallow, Yuan Dy, 8" 1,150.00
Bowl, Oribe Yaki, gr & brn decor, ped ft, 19th C, 6¾" 200.00
Model, horse & female rider, pnt decor, Tang Dy, 16" 1,380.00
Mud figure, Aesthete man, bl robe, EX detail/form, 12½", EX 50.00
Tokuri, Kyoto Yaki, ovoid w/slim neck, Kiku mon decor, Edo, 4" ...35.00
Vase, bl w/silver Ho-o & floral band decor, Meiji, 11½" 150.00
Vase, clair-de-lune; bl w/rtcl bird & dragon panels, Kangxi, 11⅝" ..6,000.00
Vase, Kenzan, red irises, 4 dimples, 19th C, 7½" 170.00
Vase, Oribe Yaki, gr drips over iron brn pattern, Meiji, 12¼" 300.00
Water pot, stylized dragon rondels, mottled peachbloom, Kangxi, 5" .2,300.00

Rugs

The 'Oriental' or Eastern rug market has enjoyed a renewal of interest as collectors have become aware of the fact that some of the semiantique rugs (those sixty to one hundred years old) may be had at a price within the range of the average buyer.

South Caucasian rug, Memling guls, brown field, ivory border, late 1800s, 108x44", $1,100.00.

Adghan, red w/gr/bl/ivory/brn/orange, 84x103" 1,155.00
Anatolian, mc floral panel w/corner pockets on red, 130x69" ...785.00
Bijar, dk bl ground w/rust & red border, 29x53" 550.00
Bijar, dk bl spandrells & border w/roses on red, 106x138" 4,950.00
Ch, dragons, tan/turq on blk, blk border, 1930, 50x83" 500.00
Dergizene, red w/dk bl (blk) border, 33x216" 2,600.00
Ersari, 4 rows of Golli gulls, rebound sides, 1890s, 94x140" 2,600.00
Fetti, ivory/bl/pk on lt brn, sm reweave, ca 1910, 184x211" ...4,000.00
Heriz, ivory spandrels on red-brn w/dk bl border, rstr, 114x148" ...500.00
Heriz, mc goemetrics on brick red, blk border, 132x91" 1,120.00
Heriz, midnight bl/salmon spandrels on burgundy, 138x210" ..2,500.00
Ingrain, dmn latice, floral border, 1900, 84x144", VG 1,200.00
Karaja, brn w/dk bl border, lt wear, 36x125" 715.00
Karaja, geometric mdls on rust, 1930s, 38x166" 3,750.00
Kashan, dk bl w/rust red border, 101x142" 3,200.00
Kashan, Marquise silk mdls on flat-weave ground, 1930s, 81x125" ..3,500.00
Kashan, mc floral mdl w/mc florals & vines on ivory, 120x98" ..1,065.00
Kashan, red ground w/dk bl border & spandrels, lt wear, 40x60" ..825.00
Kashan, red w/dk bl border & spandrels, rstr, 96x139" 900.00
Kashan, rust-red w/dk bl border, fringe, 123x166" 8,500.00
Kashan, wine red borders & spandrels w/bl on ivory, 107x144" ...5,235.00
Kerman, dense floral on ivory w/lt pk border, lt wear, 117x204" ..2,000.00

Kerman, pastel floral mdl w/mc floral on ivory, 142x103" 950.00
Khamseh, stepped diagonal mdls, ca 1910, 40x106" 2,500.00
Kuba, dk bl & ivory w/mc border, rprs, 48x73" 770.00
Meshed, burgundy spandrels on taupe, w/bl border, 126x184" ...2,200.00
Meshed, burgundy spandrels on taupe, w/bl border, 132x195" ...2,750.00
Meshed, mc floral mdl over floral wine-red, 140x104" 3,450.00
NW Persia, mc border w/bl & charcoal ground, minor losses, 45x143" ..990.00
Oushak, pk & gold floral border on lt gold, 120x144" 300.00
Peking, salmon w/dragon mdl, brn/bl borders, 128x151", VG ...1,850.00
Persian Najatabad, floral w/red border on ivory, 92x136" 1,400.00
Qum, silk faced, Persian hunt scene, prayer mdls, 60x73" 535.00
Sarouk, allover floral, 7 borders, red/bl, 1950s, 12x18" 4,000.00
Sarouk, allover floral/borders, rust/bl, 63x78" 1,120.00
Sarouk, blk border on red, 25x48" 300.00
Sarouk, burgundy w/dk bl & camel borders, 108x135" 2,300.00
Sarouk, burgundy w/dk bl border, 33x240" 2,000.00
Sarouk, dk bl w/pk spandrels & border, EX sheen, 54x85" 1,650.00
Sparta, mc bird/flowers on burgundy, 117x93" 1,065.00
Tabriz, midnight bl w/ivory & lt pk borders, 111x156" 3,300.00
Turkoman, geometric floral w/mdls & pyramid border, 129x88" ...250.00
Vis, red w/dk bl spandrels & lt bl border, 53x72" 1,595.00
Zenjan, allover floral w/3 mdls, reds/bl, 1910, 90x63" 600.00

Snuff Bottles

The Chinese were introduced to snuff in the seventeenth century, and their carved and painted snuff bottles typify their exquisite taste and workmanship. These small bottles, seldom measuring over 2½", were made of amber, jade, ivory, and cinnabar; tiny spoons were often attached to their stoppers. By the eighteenth century, some were being made of porcelain, others were of glass with delicate interior designs tediously reverse painted with minuscule brushes sometimes containing a single hair. Copper and brass were used but to no great extent.

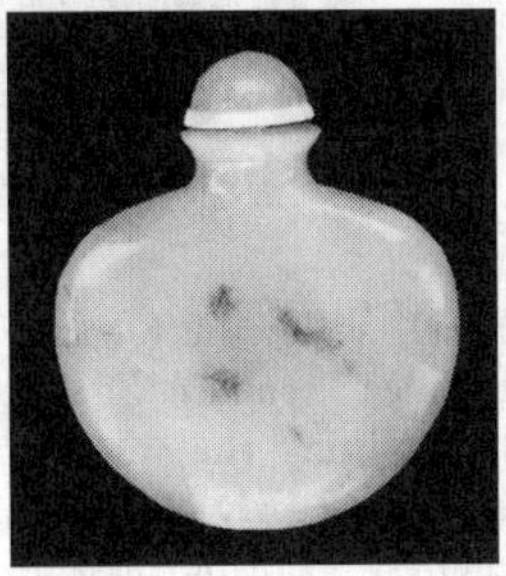

Jade, mottled green with coral stopper, flattened baluster form, $575.00.

Amethyst glass, lion mask hdls, silver stopper, ca 1800, 3" 125.00
Blk lcq w/silver jacket/ft/stopper, ca 1800, 2¾", EX 115.00
Cinnabar lcq, scholars in garden/scrolls, w/stopper, 2½" 155.00
Coral w/cvd bird & flower, 19th C, 2⅛" 750.00
Ivory, cvd figures in garden, floral shoulder band, 2⅝" 145.00
Jade, etched gold prunus branch/verse, w/stopper, 1800s, 2¾" ...150.00
Jade, russet & gr w/cvd floral, 19th C, 3⅛" 400.00
Overlay glass, gr on cafe-au-lait glass, 19th C 450.00
Overlay glass, 4-color, no stopper 800.00
Porc, pnt to resemble cinnabar lcq, silver ft, Ming Dy, 2¾" 300.00
Porc, wht lotus-leaf form, 19th C 350.00
Ruby glass, cut facets, Quianlong Period 925.00
Ruby glass, vase form w/cvd seals & poem, 19th C 375.00
Ruby glass, 18th C 285.00

Textiles

Kimono, wedding; peacocks, w/floral obi, 20th C, NM 880.00
Robe, embr flowers & birds on ivory silk, red lining, Jp, NM 300.00

Woodblock Prints, Japanese

Framed prints are of less value than those not framed, since it is impossible to inspect their condition or determined whether or not they have borders or have been trimmed.

Amuro, Hiroshi Yoshida (1876-1950), temple scene, 9¾x14¾" ..450.00
Cherry Tree in Kawagae, H Yoshida, 9½x14¾"+fr 450.00
Courtesan & man w/pipe, Utamaro, hashira, mtd as scroll 460.00
Hirasaki Castle, H Yoshida, 14¾x9½"+fr 550.00
In a Temple Yard, H Yoshida, 9½x14¾"+fr 450.00
Ogura-100 Poet Series, Utagawa Kuniyoshi, 19th C 360.00
Old Palace of Idaipur, Hiroshi Yoshida, Indian scene, 1931, 15x10" ..400.00
Women w/Servants, Yeizan, 19th C, 9½x14½" 300.00

Miscellaneous

Brush, cvd yel glass hdl, dragons among clouds, 7½" 920.00
Cricket cage, molded gourd, ivory/articulated tortoise shell, 5½" ...1,725.00
Cvg, buddha head, stone, Thailand, ca 1690s, 12" 175.00
Cvg, coral figure, elderman in flowing robe, EX detail, 4½" 265.00
Cvg, coral figures, 2 women w/lantern & instrument, ornate cvg, 11" ..1,440.00
Cvg, foo dog w/2 pups, hdwd/lcq, Ch, 19th C, 15" 550.00
Cvg, noble woman & attendant, wood/polychrome, 32", VG ...925.00
Fan, cvd ivory w/figures in landscapes, Ch trade, 1850s, 10" 575.00
Figure, bronze frog w/2 cvd wooden coy w/glass eyes, 12" 165.00
Figure, elephant, bronzed cast metal, ivory tusks, 1900, 20" 335.00
Shrine, traveling; 7 gods of Felicity, Jp, ca 1800, 11½" 1,150.00
Tsuba, copper, Mokume Sakashu, rnded hexagon, 19th C 425.00
Tsuba, iron, Kaneie Hamadashi, cvd/molded sage & moon, 17th C ..120.00
Tsuba, iron, Shoami style, lg ryu-hitsu, cvd dragon guard, 18th C 500.00
Tsuba, silver, Omori School, pierced/cvd dragons 750.00
Watercolor, riverscape, Ch trade, unsgn, 1850s, 8x11" 230.00

Orrefors

Orrefors Glassworks was founded in 1898 in the Swedish province of Smaaland. Utilizing the expertise of designers such as Simon Gate, Edward Hald, Vicke Lindstrand, and Edwin Ohrstrom, it produced art glass of the highest quality. Various techniques were used in achieving the decoration. Some were wheel engraved; others were blown through a unique process that formed controlled bubbles or air pockets resulting in unusual patterns and shapes. Our advisor for this category is Abby Malowanczyk; she is listed in the Directory under Texas.

Bowl, Ariel, cobalt/clear, #167H/Ingeborg/Lunden, 5½x6½" .1,250.00
Bowl, Graal, bl w/clear loops, disk ft, #2109-E6 Hald, 2¼x6" ...1,380.00
Bowl, Graal, brn/wht cased clear cut w/circles, Hald, #1862 ......800.00
Bowl, Slipgraal, int bl swirl lines, Hald, #870, 3x8" 500.00
Vase, Ariel, vertical bubbles in blood red, 3½" 280.00
Vase, clear w/eng nude & snake, Gate, #128J 03 XR, 7" 375.00
Vase, Graal, aquatic scene, #558N Hald, 4¾", NM 750.00
Vase, Graal, clear w/gr fish/plants, #259F Hald, ca 1950, 6¼x5" ..750.00
Vase, Ravenna, int red/bl layers w/bl rim, Palmquist, '57, 5" ..2,000.00
Vase, tear-shape 4-sided sommerso w/gr int, #N U 3538-2, 10x5" ..200.00
Vase, 3-sided sommerso w/gr int, #N U 35381/label, 15¼x3½" .450.00

Ott and Brewer

The partnership of Ott and Brewer began in 1865 in Trenton, New

Jersey. By 1876 they were making decorated graniteware, parian, and 'ivory porcelain' — similar to Irish belleek though not as fine and of different composition. In 1883, however, experiments toward that end had reached a successful conclusion, and a true belleek body was introduced. It came to be regarded as the finest china ever produced by an American firm. The ware was decorated by various means such as hand painting, transfer printing, gilding, and lustre glazing. The company closed in 1893, one of many that failed during that depression. In the listings below, the ware is belleek unless noted otherwise. Our advisor for this category is Mary Frank Gaston.

Basket, HP flowers, gold cactus hdl w/appl blooms, 7½x9" 1,000.00
Bowl, gold paste florals, scalloped border, 2x4¾" 475.00
Compote, shell w/branch support base, pale bl lustre, 3½x5¾" .500.00
Creamer & sugar bowl, pk & bl floral, scalloped rim, 3¼", 2" ...550.00
Cup & saucer, bouillon; gold acorns on branch & rim 250.00
Cup & saucer, red flowers & gold-paste leaves, unmk, 1¾", 5½" ..175.00
Cup & saucer, shell surface w/gold flower branches, 2", 5½" 125.00
Ewer, gold-paste floral & leaf decor, curved body, 5¼" 600.00
Ewer, gold-paste leaves, cactus-shaped hdl, 8½" 1,000.00
Jardiniere, gold-paste leaves, gold-sponged hdls, bulbous, 4½" ..600.00
Plate, pk lustre w/gold, 6¾" 100.00
Teapot, Irish Tridacna body w/gold-paste florals, unmk, 4½" 500.00
Tray, wild duck scenic HP on wht, scalloped border, 8" sq 800.00
Vase, gold-paste floral, dbl neck, twig hdls, 6½" 700.00
Vase, gr w/gold bands, wht center w/gold clouds, 9¾" 600.00

Overbeck

The Overbeck Studio was established in 1911 in Cambridge City, Indiana, by four Overbeck sisters. It survived until the last sister died in 1955. Early wares were often decorated with carved designs of stylized animals, birds, or florals with the designs colored to contrast with the background. Others had tooled designs filled in with various colors for a mosaic effect. After 1937, Mary Frances, the last remaining sister, favored handmade figurines with somewhat bizarre features in fanciful combinations of color. Overbeck ware is signed 'OBK,' frequently with the designer's and potter's initials under the stylized 'OBK.'

Figurine, couple in Southern 19th-C attire, 5", pr, NM 400.00
Figurine, dog, gr w/blk polka-dots & pk webbed ft, 2¼x3¼" 375.00
Figurine, dog (Spaniel), OBK, 1½" 225.00
Figurine, frog, OBK, 1¼x2¼" 275.00
Figurine, lady in 19th-C attire, appl bow/bouquet, 4" 450.00
Figurine, woodpecker, OBK, 2½" 350.00
Pin, bluebird in flowering tree, mc, metal bk, 1½" 325.00
Pin, flower form, pk w/gr, metal bk, 1⅞" 300.00
Vase, hummingbirds (16), brn/gr, cut-out hdls, EF, 6x5" 5,500.00

Overlay Glass

Art glass having layers of more than one type or color of glass is sometimes called overlay or cased glass. Very often glassware of this type has applied decorations such as fruit, flowers, leaves, or ruffles (rigaree), such as is commonly identified with Stevens and Williams. See also Stevens and Williams.

Candlestick, pk w/wht, clear rigaree & looped branch std, 6" 580.00
Vase, apricot satin w/bird & flowers, gilt ring hdls, 13" 175.00
Vase, pk w/appl clear protruding leaves & ft, 3¼x3" 125.00
Vase, shaded pk w/wht int, lg amber hdls, ruffled neck, 7x3¾" .135.00
Vase, Swirl, rainbow colors, wht int, str sides, 13x4" 235.00

Overshot

Overshot glass is characterized by the beaded or craggy appearance of its surface. Earlier ware was irregularly textured, while twentieth-century examples tend to be more uniform.

Basket, cranberry to crystal, thorn hdl, rectangular, 10x7½" 225.00
Bowl, lt bl w/appl rigaree & flower, 4x6" 225.00
Compote, cranberry to clear, ruffled rim, ormolu fr, 4⅞x6" 135.00
Ice pail, cranberry w/emb decor, brass rim & hdl, 5¾x5" 145.00
Mug, rubena w/emb pattern, clear ft & hdl, 4⅛x2¾" 95.00
Pitcher, clear, rope twist hdl, ice bladder, 10½" 80.00
Pitcher, clear, Sandwich, 4½" 75.00
Pitcher, tankard, cranberry, lg ice bladder, 9½", from $400 to ...450.00
Vase, rubena w/appl flowers & leaves, ruffled hdls, 10x7" 200.00

Owen, Ben

Ben Owen worked at the Jugtown Pottery of North Carolina from 1923 until it temporarily closed in 1959. He continued in the business in his own Plank Road Pottery, stamping his ware 'Ben Owen, Master Potter,' with many forms made by Lester Fanell Craven in the late 1960s. His pottery closed in 1972. He died in 1983 at the age of 81.

The pottery was reopened in 1981 under the supervision of Benjamin Wade Owen II. One of the principal potters was David Garner who worked there until about 1985. This pottery is still in operation today with Ben II as the main potter.

Bowl, yellow-buff earthenware, double-corded style handle, Premiere glaze example with fly ash drools highlighting the interior, signed Ben Owen Master Potter, ca early 1960s, 3½x10½x9", $225.00. (Photo courtesy Southern Folk Pottery Collectors Society)

Bean pot, Tobacco Spit Brown, earthenware, 1960s, 7⅝x8⅜" ...100.00
Bowl, Korean, brush-appl wht dogwood, conical, mid-'60s, 3x9" ...450.00
Bowl, salt glaze w/cobalt int, early 1960s, 2¾x5¾" 100.00
Candlesticks, bright orange, cupped drip pans, Craven, 9", pr ...275.00
Candlesticks, orange lead glaze, earthenware, 1960s, 8½", pr 275.00
Candlesticks, Tobacco Spit Brown, Ben, early '60s, perfect, 12", pr ...600.00
Creamer & sugar bowl, orange, dome lid, Craven, 1960s, 4", 4¾" 100.00
Jug, Frogskin Green, cvd shoulder lines, Craven, 1960s, 5" 80.00
Jug, orange peel, ovoid w/hdl, 1960s, 4⅜" 175.00
Jug, salt glaze (straw color), ovoid, Ben, 24" circumference 400.00
Pie pan, warm orange w/subtle spotting, early '60s, 2½x10½" 70.00
Pitcher, cobalt decor, glazed lining, 1960s, 4" 100.00
Pitcher, Frogskin Green, EX details, Ben, early '60s, 9¾" 275.00
Platter, warm orange w/subtle spotting, bent sides, 11" 80.00
Soup tureen, orange lead glaze, earthenware, w/lid, 1960s, 8½x11" ...550.00
Teapot, salt glaze, ovoid w/dome lid, att Ben, 7x9½" 425.00
Tray, Tobacco Spit Brown, 2 sides bent up, early '60s, 7" L 40.00
Vase, Chinese Blue type, appl bosses ea side, Garner, 9½" 225.00

Vase, Chinese Blue type, aqua w/blackened area (rare glaze), 4" ..275.00
Vase, Frogskin Green, shouldered ovoid, F Craven, 1965, 4½" 70.00
Vase, salt glaze over wht, att Craven, 5x5" 150.00
Vase/lamp, pumpkin lead glaze, Oriental translation, '60s, 14" ..375.00
Vase/lamp, Tobacco Spit Brown, shouldered, Ben, 14" 225.00

Owens Pottery

J.B. Owens founded his company in Zanesville, Ohio, in 1891, and until 1907, when the company decided to exert most of its energies in the area of tile production, made several quality lines of art pottery. His first line, Utopian, was a standard brown ware with underglaze slip decoration of nature studies, animals, and portraits. A similar line, Lotus, utilized lighter background colors. Henri Deux, introduced in 1900, featured incised Art Nouveau forms inlaid with color. (Be aware that the Brush McCoy Pottery acquired many of Owens' molds and reproduced a line similar to Henri Deux, which they called Navarre.) Other important lines were Opalesce, Rustic, Feroza, Cyrano, and Mission, examples of which are rare today. The factory burned in 1928, and the company closed shortly thereafter. Values vary according to the quality of the artwork and subject matter. Examples signed by the artist bring higher prices than those that are not signed. For further information we recommend *Owens Pottery Unearthed* by Kristy and Rick McKibben and Jeanette and Marvin Stofft. Mrs. Stofft is listed in the Directory under Indiana.

Henri Deux, jardiniere & ped, Nouveau decor w/gold, #10, 26½", NM ...1,200.00
Incised Matt, vase, cvd tulips/leaves, 7" 550.00
Lotus, pitcher, 2 floating blossoms, #1, 8⅝" 350.00
Matt Utopian, vase, H Eberlein, #112, 6" 225.00
Mission, vase, mission scene, 9", in oak stand 1,800.00
Opalesce, vase, nasturtium, bottle shape, Owenzart, 13" 800.00
Tile, oak leaves & acorns, brn/bl/gr/cream, 6", EX 275.00
Tile, rose & leaves, pk on gr matt, 5½" sq, EX 275.00
Utopian, ewer, roses, ST (S Timberlake), 9⅜" 375.00
Utopian, jug, ear of corn, #1266, 7½x5" 325.00
Utopian, letter holder, daisies, pillow form w/4 toes, 5x4½" 250.00
Utopian, vase, apple blossoms, twisted form, #117, 4½" 175.00
Utopian, vase, berries & leaves, 12x8¼" 500.00
Utopian, vase, clover blossoms, bottle shape, 15" 425.00
Utopian, vase, daffodils, tan gloss to brn, long neck, unmk, 13¼" ..375.00
Utopian, vase, daisies on bottle shape, mk, 7¼" 200.00
Venetian, mug, irid, paper label, 4½" 450.00

Pacific Clay Products

The Pacific Clay Products Company got its start in the 1920s as a consolidation of several smaller southern California potteries. The main Los Angeles plant had been founded in 1890 to make kitchen stoneware, ollas, and similar items. Terra cotta and brick were later produced.

In 1932 Hostess Ware, a vividly colored line of dinnerware, was introduced to compete with Bauer's Ring Ware. Coralitos, a lighter-weight, pastel-hued dinnerware line was first marketed in 1937, and a similar but less expensive line called Arcadia soon followed. Art ware including vases, figurines, candlesticks, etc., was produced from 1932 to 1942, at which time the company went into war-related work and pottery manufacture ceased. A limited amount of hand-decorated dinnerware was also made. For further information we recommend *The Collector's Encyclopedia of California Pottery, 2nd Edition,* by Jack Chipman; he is listed in the Directory under California.

Bowl, punch; Pacific Blue, unmk, 14", minimum value 300.00
Bust, Madonna, pastel gr, #902, 8" 90.00

Batter pitcher, Delphinium Blue, 8x10", NM, from $150.00 to $200.00.
(Photo courtesy calpots.com)

Coaster, Hostessware, 4" 10.00
Cocktail mixer, w/chrome-plated spoon, emb mk #630, 10½", minimum ...350.00
Creamer & sugar bowl (open), Hostessware, sm 40.00
Cup & saucer, coffee/tea; Hostessware 25.00
Egg cup, later design, in-mold mk 35.00
Figurine, deer, Deco, HP, 7" 75.00
Figurine, fan dancer, ivory, stamped mk, 15½", minimum value ...500.00
Flower holder, cockatoo shape, canary yel, #3802 ....200.00
Jar, cookie/pretzel; jade gr, Hostessware, rare, minimum value ...500.00
Jug, ball shape, early 100.00
Pitcher, Hostessware, 2-qt 150.00
Planter, Jill, pastel gr, #906, 5" 45.00
Plate, dinner; Plaid 85.00
Plate, dinner; Wave 100.00
Plate, salad; Spiral 85.00
Shaker, Hostessware 10.00
Tureen, soup; Delphinium Blue, Hostessware, rare, minimum value 500.00
Vase, bl, spittoon shape, hand-thrown, ca 1930s, 8", minimum value ..500.00
Vase, maroon, hand-thrown, ca 1930, 10", minimum value 500.00
Vase, mc blends, stoneware, 10½", minimum value 250.00
Vase, rose; blended brn, yel & blk, stoneware, #520, 7", minimum ..200.00

Paden City

The Paden City Glass Company began operations in 1916 in Paden City, West Virginia. The company's early lines consisted largely of the usual pressed tablewares, but by the 1920s production had expanded to include colored wares in translucent as well as opaque glass in a variety of patterns and styles. The company maintained its high standards of handmade perfection until 1949, when under new management much of the work formerly done by hand was replaced by automation. The Paden City Glass Company closed in 1951; its earlier wares, the colored patterns in particular, are becoming very collectible.

Paden City Glass is not always easily recognized by collectors or dealers, as it was almost never marked. It is believed this was so the glass could be sold to decorating companies. The company assigned both line numbers and names to many of its blanks or sets of glassware. Colors were sometimes given more than one name, and etchings were named as well. All this makes identification of items offered for sale through mail order difficult, and labels prepared by dealers are often confusing.

A review of literature available on Paden City reveals the following names for the company's plate etchings: Ardith; California Poppy; Cupid; Delilah Bird (Peacock Reverse); Eden Rose; Frost; Gazebo; Gothic Garden; Lela Bird; Nora Bird; Orchid (three variations); Peacock and Rose (Peacock and Wild Rose); Samarkand; Trumpet Flower; Utopia. Names given to cuttings made on Paden City blanks are Yorktown and Lazy Daisy. It is not clear whether the names originated with Paden City or with secondary decorating companies.

Our advisors for this category are George and Mary Hurney; they are listed in the Directory under Illinois. (Note: Their interest is only in

Paden City glassware, not the pottery.) See also Glass Animals and Figurines; Kitchen Collectibles, Glass.

This list gives company line numbers with corresponding line names. This information was obtained from Hazel Marie Weatherman's *Price Trends 2*, Jerry Barnett's *Paden City: The Color Company*, and from Michael Krumme, long-time collector and student of Paden City.

#69, #69½ — Georgian, Aristocrat
#90 — Breton, Chevalier
#154 — Rena
#191 — Party Line
#198 — Ross
#199 — Inna
#202 — Virginia
#203 — Webb
#204 — Etta
#205 — Estelle
#206 — Pineapple
#209 — Edna
#210 — Skidoo, Spire
#215 — Hotcha, Glades
#220 — Cantina, Largo
#221 — S.S. Dreamship, Maya
#300 — Archaic
#330 — Luli, Cavendish
#400 — City Lights
#411 — Vaara, Mrs B
#412 — Crow's Foot (Square)
#440 — Nerva
#444 — Vale
#555 — Vermillion
#700 — Simplicity
#701 — Lazy Daisy
#777 — Secrets
#836 — Future
#881 — Wotta Line, Gadroon
#890 — Crow's Foot (Round)
#895 — Lucy
#900 — Nadja
#991 — Penny Line
#994 — Popeye and Olive
#1503 — Trance
#1504 — Chaucer
#2000 — Mystic

And, finally, a listing of colors with alternate names or descriptive phrases:

Amber — (dull)	Mulberry — amethyst
Cheriglo — (delicate) pink	Opal — opaque white
Cobalt Blue — Royal Blue	Primrose — (amber with reddish tint)
Crystal — (clear, no tint)	Red — ruby
Dark Green — forest green	Rose — (dark pink)
Dark Amber — (honey color)	Yellow — (pale, soft)
Light Blue — Copen, Neptune	

Ardith, candy dish, yel, 2-part, w/lid, sq 75.00
Ardith, cup & saucer, yel 48.00
Ardith, plate, yel, 8" sq 20.00
Ardith, vase, red, on Crow's Foot blank, 11½" 175.00
Black Forest, batter jug, crystal 150.00
Black Forest, bowl, console; amber, 11" 50.00
Black Forest, candlestick, blk, mushroom style 40.00
Black Forest, comport, pk, 6½" 100.00
Black Forest, cup & saucer, red, 3 styles, ea 110.00
Black Forest, ice tub, pk, 2-hdl 150.00
Black Forest, pitcher, gr, 72-oz, 10½" 500.00
Black Forest, tumbler, old fashion; pk, 8-oz, 3⅞" 40.00
Chaucer, server, crystal, center hdl 35.00
Crow's Foot, bowl, colors other than red or bl, ftd, 10" 32.50
Crow's Foot, bowl, console; colors other than red or bl, 11½" 37.50
Crow's Foot, bowl, red or bl, sq, 11" 60.00
Crow's Foot, bowl, red or bl, 6" 30.00
Crow's Foot, candlestick, red or bl, rnd base, tall 75.00
Crow's Foot, cheese stand, colors other than red or bl, 5" 12.50
Crow's Foot, cup, red or bl, ftd or flat, ea 10.00
Crow's Foot, mayonnaise, colors other than red or bl, 3-ftd 22.50
Crow's Foot, plate, red or bl, rnd, 8" 9.00
Crow's Foot, plate, red or bl, 2-hdl, rnd, 10⅜" 50.00
Crow's Foot, platter, colors other than red or bl, 12" 15.00
Crow's Foot, sandwich server, red or bl, center hdl, sq 45.00
Crow's Foot, tumbler, colors other than red or bl, 4¼" 37.50
Crow's Foot, vase, colors other than red or bl, flared, 11¾" 65.00
Cupid, bowl, fruit; gr or pk, 10¼" 200.00
Cupid, cake stand, gr or pk, ftd, 2" 195.00
Cupid, creamer, gr or pk, ftd, 5" 135.00
Cupid, ice tub, gr or pk, 4¾" 295.00
Cupid, tray, gr or pk, ftd, oval, 10⅞" 225.00
Emerald Glo, bottle, oil; Emerald Green 30.00
Emerald Glo, bowl, salad; Emerald Green, 10" 30.00
Emerald Glo, casserole, Emerald Green, w/metal lid 40.00
Emerald Glo, cruet, Emerald Green 30.00
Emerald Glo, relish tray, Emerald Green, heart shape 25.00
Emerald Glo, syrup, Emerald Green, w/metal lid & liner 45.00
Future, cup, cobalt 9.00
Gazebo, cake salver, crystal, #555 ....125.00
Gazebo, plate, crystal, #555, 11" 50.00

Glades #215 vanity set with ruby stoppers, lid and tray, $90.00. (Photo courtesy Margaret and Kenn Whitmyer)

Orchid, bowl, red or bl, ftd, 10" 195.00
Orchid, bowl, red or bl, sq, 4⅞" 50.00
Orchid, bowl, red or bl, 2-hdl, 8½" 135.00
Orchid, candlesticks, red or bl, 5¾", pr 195.00
Orchid, comport, red or bl, 6¼x3¼" 50.00
Orchid, ice bucket, red or bl, 6" 195.00
Orchid, mayonnaise, red or bl, 3-pc 165.00
Orchid, plate, red or bl, sq, 8½" 75.00
Orchid, vase, red or bl, 10" 295.00
Orchid, vase, red or bl, 8" 275.00
Peacock & Wild Rose, bowl, any color, center hdl, 10½" 125.00
Peacock & Wild Rose, bowl, any color, ftd, 8¾" 175.00
Peacock & Wild Rose, bowl, fruit; any color, 10½" 185.00
Peacock & Wild Rose, candlesticks, any color, 5", pr 165.00
Peacock & Wild Rose, candy dish, any color, w/lid, 7" 225.00
Peacock & Wild Rose, creamer, any color, pointed hdl, 5" 55.00
Peacock & Wild Rose, ice tub, any color, 6" 175.00
Peacock & Wild Rose, plate, any color, 8" 25.00
Peacock & Wild Rose, tumbler, any color, ftd, 4¾" 75.00
Peacock & Wild Rose, tumbler, any color, 3" 55.00
Peacock & Wild Rose, vase, any color, 12" 295.00

Peacock Reverse, bowl, any color, sq, 8¾" 110.00
Peacock Reverse, bowl, console; any color, 11¾" 125.00
Peacock Reverse, candy dish, any color, sq, 6½" 175.00
Peacock Reverse, creamer, any color, flat, 2¾" 85.00
Peacock Reverse, plate, luncheon; any color, 8½" 60.00
Peacock Reverse, sherbet, any color, 2 szs, ea 65.00
Peacock Reverse, tumbler, any color, flat, 10-oz, 4" 85.00
Skidoo, tumbler, crystal, 5-oz 3.00
Vermillion, punch bowl, crystal, 7-cup 75.00

Paintings on Ivory

Miniature works of art executed on ivory from the 1800s are assessed by the finesse of the artist, as is any fine painting. Signed examples and portraits with identifiable subjects are usually preferred.

Memorial portrait of child, American school, nineteenth century, 2x2½", G, in leather case, $800.00.

Child w/blond hair & bl eyes, modern fr: 4¼x3⅝" 385.00
Jenny Lind, sgn March, 3⅜" 110.00
Lady (East Indian), fine attire & jewels, Bender, 3¼"+fr 325.00
Lady (identified), Am school, 19th C, 2¾x2¼"+fr 600.00
Lady (identified) of Providence RI, Am school, 19th C, 3⅛x2½" ...1,600.00
Lady (matron) in lace bonnet, dtd 1778, 3¼x2¾" 465.00
Lady & floral garland, classical, sgn Plahant, 2½"+fr 300.00
Lady in elegant 18th-C attire, sgn, ormolu fr, 4½" 335.00
Lady in wht w/bl accessories, sgn Rd Mills...1829, brass fr: 4⅜" 385.00
Lady in wht w/red sash, 3⅛", in leatherized case 200.00
Lady w/dog, artist sgn, in gilt fr w/easel bk, 4x3⅜" 440.00
Lady w/fancy hairdo, wht dress, fr, 5½x5" 275.00
Lady w/lace bonnet & collar, sgn, dtd 1839, 2¼" dia 200.00
Lady w/ornate hairdo at instrument, Bouillard, 7x5" 850.00
Lady w/shawl, minute pigment loss, Am school, 19th C, 3⅝x2¾" ...900.00
Man, late 18th C, in later oval pendant fr, 1⅝x1⅜" 745.00
Man, mid-1800s, in oval brooch fr, 2½x2" 600.00
Man (identified), in blk fr w/brass trim, 6½" 165.00
Man & lady, well dressed, pr in leatherized case, 3⅞" 1,300.00
Man in bl, lady w/feather hat, 2¼", pr 200.00
Man in frock coat, Am school, 19th C, 3½x2½" 345.00
Military officer of the 18th C, 8-sided gilt fr 165.00
Napoleon & Josephine, 3¾x3", in brass frs, pr 465.00
Youth in frock coat, blk fr w/brass trim, 4⅜" 165.00

Pairpoint

The Pairpoint Manufacturing Company was built in 1880 in New Bedford, Massachusetts. It was primarily a metalworks whose chief product was coffin fittings. Next door, the Mt. Washington Glassworks made quality glasswares of many varieties. (See Mt. Washington for more information concerning their artware lines.) By 1894 it became apparent to both companies that a merger would be to their best interest.

From the late 1890s until the 1930s, lamps and lamp accessories were an important part of Pairpoint's production. There were three main types of shades, all of which were blown: puffy — blown-out reverse-painted shades (usually floral designs); ribbed — also reverse painted; and scenic — reverse painted with scenes of land or seascapes (usually executed on smooth surfaces, although ribbed scenics may be found occasionally). Cut glass lamps and those with metal overlay panels were also made. Scenic shades were sometimes artist signed. Every shade was stamped on the lower inside or outside edge with 1) The Pairpoint Corp., 2) Patent Pending, 3) Patented July 9, 1907, or 4) Patent Applied For. Bases were made of bronze, copper, brass, silver, or wood and are always signed.

Because they produced only fancy, handmade artware, the company's sales lagged seriously during the Depression, and as time and tastes changed, their style of product was less in demand. As a result, they never fully recovered; consequently part of the buildings and equipment was sold in 1938. The company reorganized in 1939 under the direction of Robert Gundersen and again specialized in quality hand-blown glassware. Isaac Babbit regained possession of the silver departments, and together they established Gundersen Glassworks, Inc. After WWII, because of a sharp decline in sales, it again became necessary to reorganize. The Gundersen-Pairpoint Glassworks was formed, and the old line of cut, engraved artware was reintroduced. The company moved to East Wareham, Massachusetts, in 1957. But business continued to suffer, and the firm closed only one year later. In 1970, however, new facilities were constructed in Sagamore under the direction of Robert Bryden, sales manager for the company since the 1950s.

In 1974 the company began to produce lead glass cup plates which were made on commission as fund-raisers for various churches and organizations. These are signed with a 'P' in diamond and are becoming quite collectible. See also Burmese; Napkin Rings; Peachblow.

Glass

Bottle, scent; Nevada, sterling eng stopper, sm 295.00
Bowl, blk amethyst w/clear bubble-ball connector, att, 12" 200.00
Bowl, Potato Glass, floral on clear, 12", +pr candlesticks 550.00
Box, cut, Murillo, SP mts, 6" W 400.00
Carafe, cut, Beatrice 250.00
Centerpiece, allover dmns w/SP putto support, #C1413, 9¼" ...230.00
Compote, ice bl w/bubbles/threading, bell-shape ped ft, 13¾" ..300.00
Compote, rvpt florals w/gilt, in SP base, ca 1915, 7½x11½" ..1,100.00
Cracker jar, roses, wht/pk on gold & tan, paneled, 6½x6" 550.00
Cracker jar, 2 reserves w/peonies, #3912-10, mk lid 300.00
Ewer, ruby, classical form w/tricon rim, clear hdl, disk ft, 13½" .200.00
Jug & tumbler set, Colias, etched butterflies/flowers/webs, 5-pc ...300.00
Syrup pitcher, cut, Elena, 6" 300.00
Vase, cut, Adelaide, cobalt to clear, trumpet form, 13", EX 1,200.00
Vase, cut, Auroria, amber, polished/satin eng, 12x5" 425.00
Vase, Dmn Quilt, amethyst w/clear controlled-bubble stem, 12" ..325.00
Vase, flip; Tavern Glass, random bubbles, HP flowers, 8x6" 265.00
Vase, ruby w/clear bubble-ball connector, att, 13½", NM 175.00

Lamps

Mantel, 2-arm candelabrum form, SP mts, ball stems/finials, 14", pr ...700.00
Pnt 10" butterflies/trees shade w/flaring rim; #C3064 std 1,265.00
Puffy 5" dogwood shade; brass urn-shaped mk base 4,300.00
Puffy 5" grapes shade; shouldered std 3,500.00
Puffy 5" pansy shade; brass urn-form mk std 4,250.00
Puffy 8" apple blossom/roses Stratford shade; #C3064 std, 14½" 2,875.00
Puffy 8" dogwood Stratford shade; #C3084 std, 15" 3,450.00
Puffy 8" floral/lattice Stratford shade; Pat Appl 1907 std 2,500.00
Puffy 8" rose tree shade; metal #C3057 std, 14" 4,000.00
Puffy 9" roses Stratford shade; organic #C3064 std, 19" 3,500.00

Puffy 10" peony Torino shade; Pat Appl orig std 9,000.00
Puffy 12" floral San Remo shade; mk std 15,000.00
Puffy 12" lotus shade; Nouveau-style mk std 16,000.00
Puffy 12" rose bouquet shade; SP emb grape std 12,000.00
Puffy 12" roses/butterfly Albermarl shade; mk std 12,000.00
Puffy 14" gladioli Stratford shade; mk columnar std 12,000.00
Puffy 14" hummingbird/roses Stratford shade; SP mk std 7,500.00
Puffy 14" rvpt vintage shade; #3089 vintage std, 19½" 20,700.00
Puffy 15" floral Marlborough shade; #3099 NM orig base 7,950.00
Puffy 16" bumblebees/butterflies/flowers shade; #3093 std, 26" ...32,000.00
Rvpt 7" red poppy on frosted ground shade; SP std 1,300.00
Rvpt 9" floral Portsmouth shade; gilt-finish std, 16" 4,000.00
Rvpt 9" rose/foliage shade; berries/vines #3047½ std, 15" 2,100.00
Rvpt 9" shade w/Deco flowers; NP slim std, 13½" 950.00
Rvpt 10" garden scene Directoire shade; silvered 3-arm std, 26" ...4,000.00
Rvpt 10" meadow scenic shade; slim step base, 15" 2,500.00
Rvpt 13" butterfly/roses shade; rtcl/4-sided std #3086 ....1,500.00
Rvpt 14" seascape/village scene shade; SP mk std w/planter ...4,500.00
Rvpt 14" Venetian scene Torino shade; bronze sgn std 9,000.00
Rvpt 15" castle scene Carlise shade; mahog mk std, 20" 3,165.00
Rvpt 15" Exeter shade; 2-socket mk/#d baluster std, 20¼" 1,150.00
Rvpt 15" rider & castle Carlisle conical shade; #D3225 std, 22" ...2,800.00
Rvpt 16" floral Berkely shade; mk shouldered std 3,250.00
Rvpt 16" floral Tivoli shade; bronze std 8,000.00
Rvpt 16" Garden of Allah Chesterfield shade; SP sq-ftd std ...15,000.00
Rvpt 16" landscape shade; 2-hdl patinated metal std, 22" 2,875.00
Rvpt 16" scenic woodland Directoire shade; 3-light std 3,000.00
Rvpt 17" floral/urns on textured tan shade, EX; urn std 2,300.00
Rvpt 17" landscape Exeter shade; #D2342 std, 23" 2,600.00
Rvpt 17" tapestry Directoire shade; metal/crystal marble std, 28" ...2,400.00
Rvpt 18" windmill scenic shade; obverse-pnt windmill std, 26" 9,500.00
Rvpt 18" windmills Touraine shade (Schultz); mk bronze std .2,350.00
Rvpt 20" forest scene Berkley shade; silvered mk std, 24" 4,000.00
Rvpt 20" harbor scene Bombay shade (Durand); mk std 6,500.00
Rvpt 22" floral shade; silvered tripod std on marble base, 22" ...4,600.00

Pairpoint Limoges

Limoges china blanks were imported from France in strict accordance with Pairpoint specifications. They were decorated by Pairpoint in designs that ranged from simple to elaborate florals and scenics. Called Crown Point French China in old Pairpoint and Mt. Washington catalogs, these are easily identified. Look for the Pairpoint name over a crown with the Limoges name below. You may also find similar ware marked 'Pairpoint Minton.'

Gravy boat, Dresden, mc flowers on wht, +underplate 165.00
Plate, harbor scene w/ship, sgn Tripp, fuchsia trim/gilt, 8" 485.00
Vase, little girl on dk red (EX art), ftd, worn gold, 14" 585.00
Vase, mums/gilt, petal top, widely flaring w/Nouveau hdls, 9" ...625.00

Paper Dolls

No one knows quite how or when paper dolls originated. One belief is that they began in Europe as 'pantins' (jumping jacks). During the nineteenth century, most paper dolls portrayed famous dancers and opera stars such as Fanny Elssler and Jenny Lind. In the late 1800s, the Raphael Tuck Publishers of England produced many series of beautiful paper dolls; retail companies used them as advertisements to further the sale of their products. Around the turn of the century, many popular women's magazines began featuring a page of paper dolls.

Most familiar to today's collectors are the books with dolls on cardboard covers and clothes on the inside pages. These made their appearance in the late 1920s and early '30s. The most collectible (and the most valuable) are those representing celebrities, movie stars, and comic-strip characters of the '30s and '40s.

When no condition is indicated, the dolls listed below are assumed to be in mint, uncut, original condition. Cut sets will be worth about half price if all dolls and outfits are included and pieces are in very good condition. If dolls were produced in die-cut form, these prices reflect such a set in mint condition with all costumes and accessories.

For further information we recommend *A Collector's Guide to Magazine Paper Dolls* (Collector Books) and *Tomart's Price Guide to Lowe and Whitman Paper Dolls*, both by Mary Young, our advisor for this category; she is listed in the Directory under Ohio. We also recommend *Schroeder's Collectible Toys, Antique to Modern* (Collector Books).

I Love Lucy Packaway Kit, #5624, 1953, EX, $125.00. (Photo courtesy Bill Bruegman)

Angel Baby Dolls, Merrill #4853, 1943, uncut, M 95.00
Ann Sothern, Saalfield #2438, 1943, uncut, M 100.00
Annette Stand-Up Cut-Out Doll, Whitman #1971, 1960, uncut, M ..60.00
Baby Sue, Whitman #972, 1944, uncut, M 40.00
Barbie, Midge, Skipper, Whitman #4793, 1965, uncut, M 50.00
Bette Davis, Merrill #4816, 1942, uncut, M 175.00
Bob Hope & Dorothy Lamour, Whitman #976, 1942, uncut, M ..250.00
Brenda Lee, Lowe #2785, 1961, uncut, M 60.00
Bridal Party, Whitman #4625, 1957, uncut, M 45.00
Career Girls, Lowe #1045, 1942, uncut, M 75.00
Cindy & Mindy, Whitman #1974, 1960, uncut, M 30.00
Deanna Durbin, Merrill #4804, 1941, uncut, M 175.00
Diana Lynn, Saalfield #2732, 1953, uncut, M 75.00
Doris Day, Whitman #2103, 1952, uncut, M 100.00
Dr Kildare, Lowe #2740, 1962, uncut, M 65.00
Fashion Previews, Lowe #1246, 1949, uncut, M 45.00
Flapper Fanny, Whitman #957, 1938, uncut, M 200.00
Girl Pilots of the Ferry Command, Merrill #4852, 1943, uncut, M ..100.00
Girls in Uniform, Lowe #1048, 1942, uncut, M 100.00
Giselle MacKenzie, Saalfield #4421, 1957, uncut, M 85.00
Glamour Girl, Whitman #973, 1942, uncut, M 50.00
Gulliver's Travels, Saalfield #1261, 1939, uncut, M 125.00
Heidi, Whitman #4601, 1967, uncut, M 26.00
Hi Gals!, Whitman #974, 1953, uncut, M 35.00
It's a Date, Whitman #1976, 1956, uncut, M 40.00
Jill & Her Trunk Full of Clothes, Merrill #4828, 1943, uncut, M ...35.00
Joan Caulfield, Saalfield #2725, 1953, uncut, M 85.00
Julie Andrews, Saalfield #4424, 1958, uncut, M 85.00
June & Stew Erwin, Saalfield #2735, 1954, uncut, M 85.00
Life Size Doll, Whitman #4770, 1959, uncut, M 50.00
Lollypop Crowd, Lowe #1049, 1945, uncut, M 40.00
Lydia, Whitman #1970, 1977, uncut, M 20.00
Mary Hartline, Whitman #2104, 1952, uncut, M 75.00
Me & Mimi, Lowe #1044, 1942, uncut, M 40.00
Miss Teen Cut Outs, Whitman #4607, 1960, uncut, M, ea 30.00
Mousketeers, Whitman #1974, 1964, uncut, M 60.00
Nancy, Whitman #1971, 1971, uncut, M 25.00

Paper Doll Family & Their House, Saalfield #2094, 1934, uncut, M ...**75.00**
Peter & Pam, Whitman #1974, 1961, uncut, M **30.00**
Peter Rabbit, Whitman #955, 1939-40, uncut, M **90.00**
Photo Fashions, Whitman #973, 1953, uncut, M **35.00**
Playmate, Whitman #4415, 1965, uncut, M **12.00**
Quiz Kids, Saalfield #2430, 1942, uncut, M **100.00**
Shirley Temple, Saalfield #5110, 1958, uncut, M **75.00**
Slumber Party, Merrill #4854, 1943, uncut, M **65.00**
This Is Pennie, Whitman #4795, 1962, uncut, M **35.00**
Tiny Tots, Whitman #4412, 1959, uncut, M **25.00**
Tom Aviator/Dick Sailor/Harry Soldier, Lowe #1074, 1941, uncut, M, ea **75.00**
Trudy Phillips & Her Crowd, Whitman #2104, 1954, uncut, M ..**45.00**
Virginia Mayo, Saalfield #4422, 1957, uncut, M **100.00**
Wonderful World of the Bros Grimm, Saalfield #1336, 1963, uncut, M ..**45.00**

Paperweights

Glass paperweight collecting has become a feverish passion, growing in intensity in the past few years. Perhaps it is because there many glass artists in the marketplace today who are creating beautiful examples, and a beginning collector can pick up these lovely objects d'art for under $100.00. Hundreds of glass artisans in the U.S. and factories in China, Italy, and Scotland produce 'gift range' paperweights. Collectors have the choice of forming their collections strictly from that price range, or they can choose to select pieces that can run into the thousands of dollars — or anywhere in between. Additionally, astute collectors are beginning to piece together collections of the old Chinese paperweights that were imported into this country during the 1930s. These were basically unrefined imitations of the lovely and unique French weights of the mid 1800s. When viewed some seventy years later, however, one can appreciate the beauty and craftsmanship these weights exhibit. Murano weights, especially those from the 1960s and 1970s, represent another area of concentrated interest. Prices are beginning to escalate in both categories. Collectors who have a larger budget for these exquisite 'glass balls' may form their collection with only antique French paperweights from the classic period (1845–1860), the wonderful English or American weights from the 1850s, or choose to collect the high quality contemporary artistry of master glass artists such as Ayotte, the Banfords, Buzzini, Ebelhare, Grubb, Kontes, S. Lundberg, Rosenfeld, G. Smith, Tarsitano, the Trabuccos or Stankard. The door is wide open for everyone to begin collecting in whatever price range they can afford, and the Paperweight Collector's Association, Inc. with chapters in many states can be of great assistance to collectors at all levels.

Baccarat, St. Louis, and Clichy (names synonymous with classic French paperweights) as well as some American factories stopped making paperweights between the 1880s and 1910 due to a decline in their popularity. In the 1950s Baccarat and St. Louis resumed their production. Other factories producing high quality millefiori and lampworked weights today include Perthshire and Caithness/Whitefriars (Scotland). In the 1960s smaller furnaces were developed that allowed more freedom for the individual glassmaker to design and fabricate a piece from the fire to the annealing kiln. As a result, many new studios began to spring up. The success of these ventures are evident in the creative glass produced by Lundberg Studios, Orient & Flume, and Correia Studios, to name only a few.

Books on paperweights abound, but *The Encyclopedia of Glass Paperweights* (Hollister) and *Paperweights of the World, 2nd Edition, With Updated Value Guide* (Flemming & Pommerencke) are two excellent selections for the beginning collector.

Many factors determine value, particularly of antique weights, and auction-realized prices of contemporary weights usually differ from issue price. Competition among new collectors entering the field has greatly influenced prices. As the number of collectors increases, available antique weights decrease per capita, forcing prices upwards. Antique paperweights have steadily increased in value as has the work of many now-deceased glass artists (i.e., Paul Ysart, Joe St. Clair, Charles Kazian, Del Tarsitano).

In the listings that follow, the dimension given at the end of the line is diameter. Prices are for weights in perfect or near-perfect conditon and our values should be considered maximum retail. Our advisors for this category are Betty and Larry Schwab, The Paperweight Shoppe; they are listed in the Directory under Illinois.

Key:

con — concentric	jsp — jasper
(d) — deceased	latt — latticinio
fct — faceted	mill — millefiori
gar — garland	o/l — overlay
grd — ground	sil — silhouette

Ayotte, Rick

Blk-capped tan bird on floral branches, yel to wht grd, 3½" ...**1,200.00**
Meadowlark, 5 blk-eyed-susans, 2 pk buds, 1985, 3¼" **1,300.00**
Oriole w/3 babies in nest on soft bl grd, 1984, 3½" **1,200.00**
Yel rose, ltd ed of 50, 1995, 3¾" **1,500.00**

Baccarat, Antique

Close-pack mill, lightly polished, 1¾" **800.00**
Close-pack mill intricate canes including B1846, 3", NM **2,200.00**
Con arrowhead & star canes, 3 gridel animal sil, 3⅛" **1,375.00**

Faceted sulfide of Joan of Arc on green flashed ground, 3½", NM, from $2,000.00 to $2,200.00.

Macedoine, colorful twists, 2⅝" **700.00**
Pansy, stardust center cane, gr leaves, star-cut base, 1¾" **750.00**
Purple striped dahlia on bl & wht grd, 3" **900.00**
Red & wht primrose w/stardust central cane, gr leaves, 2¼" ..**1,400.00**
Scattered mc mill, B 1848 cane, polished, 3⅛" **2,500.00**
2 red/lilac clematis on upset wht muslin, 3¼" **1,000.00**

Baccarat, Modern

Blk center cane w/wht squirrel, gridel sil cane circle, 3⅛" **600.00**
Dahlia w/bud on bl grd, B1970 cane, 3⅜" **500.00**
Deer sil cane on swirled gr/yel carpet, 17 gridel canes, 3¼" **600.00**
Geo Washington sulfide, gr grd, X-hatch base, 6/1 fct, 1957, 2⅝" ..**250.00**
Water lily on gr, 1977, 3¼" **600.00**
3 strawberries/wht flower/gr leaves on bl grd, 1974, 3" **500.00**

Banford, Bob

Bl cornflower w/yel centers, pk/wht twisted torsade, 3" **525.00**
Bouquet w/6 different flowers/4 buds/gr leaves, grid-cut base, 3¼" ..**500.00**
Dahlia surrounded by dk gr leaves, grid-cut base, 3¼" **550.00**
Pk flowers & buds w/yel centers/gr leaves on bl grd, 3¼" **450.00**

Red flowers (5) on stems, B cane, dmn-cut base, 3¼" 500.00
Rose & 3 irises, dmn-cut base, B cane at stem, 3" 500.00
Wht clematis on bl grd, 3" 450.00
Yel/wht/clear fct o/l w/2 purple asters/2 buds/gr leaves, 3" 600.00

Clichy, Antique

Chequer, mc canes w/gr & pk rose, polished, 3⅛" 3,000.00
Pk & gr rose, open con mill, 5/1 fcts, 2⅛" 800.00
Pk/wht rose, open con mill, mini, 1⅞" 800.00
6-pointed mill scatter w/pk rose in center, wht rose aside, 3" 865.00

New England Glass, Antique

Bl clematis, wht central cane, gr leaves, in gar, 2¾" 900.00
Bl poinsettia, waffle central cane, gr leaves, 2⅞" 1,000.00
Close con canes w/crude row of running rabbits (31), polished .800.00
Fruit set on swirling latt grd, 2¾" 1,000.00
Lg central cane w/wht/gr canes on swirl latt grd, 2½" 400.00
Nosegay w/gar, 11 bl rabbit canes alternate w/red, 2⅜", EX 650.00
Scramble, 12 running rabbit canes, cane w/star center, 2¾" 450.00

Perthshire

Butterfly w/cane wings on clear, gr/wht dbl o/l, 2", MIB 450.00
Pk flower w/brn buds/gr leaves on latt, red/wht/clear o/l, fct, 3" ...500.00
Wht & orange flowers w/gr leaves on bl grd, 1986, 3" 400.00

Rosenfeld, Ken

Pk flowers & buds w/gr leaves, 1992, 3¼" 500.00
Yel flowers & striped buds w/gr leaves on bl grd, 1990, 2¼" 250.00
5 flowers & 4 buds on stems on bl, 1993, 3¼" 600.00

Sandwich Glass

Bl poinsettia w/gr leaves, swirling latt grd, 2¾" 800.00
Pk blossom w/dewdrop bubbles at petals, bl/wht jsp grd, att, 3" .700.00
Red cross flower w/gr leaves on wht & bl jsp grd, 2⅞" 700.00
Red poinsettia w/bl/goldstone dots central cane, gr leaves, 3⅛" ..600.00

St. Louis, Antique

Panel weight on JSP grd, 3" 1,000.00
Pk Dahlia, star-cut base 2⁷⁄₁₆" 2,500.00

St. Louis, Modern

Bl/wht/clear o/l, mc mill mushroom, star-cut base, 5/2 fct, 1953, 3" ...600.00
Eagle sulfide, red/wht/clear o/l, 5/1 fct, 3" 450.00
Gr/wht/clear ol w/mc mill mushroom, star-cut base, 1953, 3" 700.00
Pk/wht/bl flowers close packed, multi-fct, 1993, ltd ed, 3¾" 850.00
Red dahlia w/star center cane/gr leaves, 1996, ltd ed, 3¼" 400.00
Red/wht/yel mill central star on wht grd, 6/1 fct, 1971, 3¼" 400.00
2 pk Clichy-type rose/bud/thorns/gr leaves, 6/1 fct, 1976, 3¼" ..450.00

Tarsitano, Debbie

Dahlia & 2 sm blossoms, spotted bug on gr leaf, 3¼" 1,200.00
Pk tulips & bud held by hand on clear grd, 3¼" 500.00
Purple dahlia w/yel center & gr leaves, 3" 900.00
2 pk & bl/1 purple flower w/4 lily-of-the-valley sprays, 3" 700.00
2 pk & wht flowers w/yel centers, bl bud, gr leaves, 2¾" 400.00
5-petal flower & bud on bl scrambled cane grd, flat top, 3½" 500.00
6-petal flower & bud on clear, DT cane on reverse, 2½" 450.00

Trabucco, Victor

Bouquet of flowers, fct, 2¾" 400.00
Pears (2) on branch w/buds, 1995, 3¼" 635.00
Pk/yel/wht/purple flower bouquet, fct, 1983, 2⅞" 400.00
4 pk morning glories/3 buds/5 leaves, 1983, 3¾" 900.00

Miscellaneous

Bagwell, orange sea plant & striped fish, mc mill canes, 5¼" 110.00
Banford, Ray; pk & wht iris w/gr leaves, bl opaque grd, 2¾" 450.00
Banford, Ray; 6 flowers, yel centers/gr leaves, grid-cut base, 3¼" ...600.00
Bohemian, mc con mill, honeycomb fct, magnum, 4", NM 500.00
Bohemian, scrambled mc canes on gr speckled grd, 2¾" 200.00
Cathiness, 5-petal pk flower w/gar of mill cane on lt amber, 2⅝" .200.00
D'Albert, Prince Charles sulfide on dk violet grid-cut grd, fct, 3" ..100.00
D'Albert, Shepard/Armstrong/Collins/Aldrin in spacesuits on bl, 1971 ...85.00
Deacons, John; fantasy floral on blk, 6/1 fcts, 3" 400.00
Deacons, John; bl/wht o/l, mill butterfly on wht latt cushion, 3⅛" 300.00
Donofrio, gnome/2 Indian pots/sm orange flowers on earth, 1992, 3⅜" ...375.00
Donofrio, Jim; frog & blossom on sand grd, 3½" 500.00
Glass, J; 3 clematis w/mill centers on yel/pk swirl grd, '81, 2⅜" .250.00
Lundberg, heron/full moon on cobalt, 1983, 2¾" 300.00
Lundberg, jonquil on coablt, 1983, 2¾" 300.00
Millville NJ, orange rose w/3 gr leaves, clover pontil, 3⅝" 250.00
Nailsea, flowerpot w/2 flowers in gr bottle glass, pontil, 3½" 150.00
Schmid, Sister Berta Hummel sulfide on cobalt, 1973, 2⅞", MIB ..50.00
Simpson, Josh; spaceship in orbit over lt bl, dtd 1989, 3" 175.00
Tarsitano, Delmo; peach branch on cobalt, 3" 850.00
Whitefriars, Christmas 1976, 3 wise men mosaic 700.00
Ysart, Paul; butterfly, bl & turq on latt grd, fct, 2¾" 1,200.00
Ysart, Paul; red & bl flowers in latt basket, 2¾" 1,000.00

Papier-Mache

The art of papier-mache was mainly European. It originated in Paris around the middle of the eighteenth century and became popular in America during Victorian times. Small items such as boxes, trays, inkwells, frames, etc., as well as extensive ceiling moldings and larger articles of furniture were made. The process involved building layer upon layer of paper soaked in glue, then coaxed into shape over a wood or wire form. When dry it was painted or decorated with gilt or inlays. Inexpensive twentieth-century 'notions' were machine processed and mold pressed. See also Christmas; Candy Containers.

Tray, black lacquer with floral design, mid-nineteenth century, stamped Jennens and Bettridge, 31x24" on later ebonized faux-bamboo 19¾" stand, $1,400.00.

Cat, gray & natural wht, red ribbon w/bell, glass eyes, 7½", VG ..100.00
Cat, gray pnt w/mc details, dressed as girl in cloth costume, 6½" ...600.00
Cat, seated, gray & wht pnt, glass eyes, 7", EX 140.00
Hen on nest, mc pnt, glass bead eyes, Pat 1919/c 1924, 7" 165.00
Inkstand, blk pnt petal form w/MOP inlay on tray 250.00

Snuff box, Andrew Jackson litho on lid, 3½" dia 1,400.00
Writing stand, MOP inlay & gilt decor, drw, 19th C, 13" W 300.00

Parian Ware

Parian is hard-paste unglazed porcelain made to resemble marble. First made in the mid-1800s by Staffordshire potters, it was soon after produced in the United States by the U.S. Pottery at Bennington, Vermont. Busts and statuary were favored, but plaques, vases, mugs, and pitchers were also made.

Bust, Cenone, on base, Copeland/Crystal Palace/1860, 12", NM .750.00
Bust, Music, Copeland, 1874, 13½", NM 500.00
Figurine, classical lady on naturalistic base, 19th C, 13x7½" 450.00
Figurine, Dorthea, seated upon rock, John Bell, 1850, 14", EX ..500.00
Group, Naomi & 2 daughters-in-law, att Bell, rstr, 13", VG 575.00
Group, 3 Graces, nude figures on base, ca 1880, 19" 2,300.00
Jug, Grecian figures/trees & columns, bl on wht, head on hdl, 7½" ...175.00
Vase, wht ram-head hdls & floral designs, Bevington, ca 1870, 23" ...800.00

Parrish, Maxfield

Maxfield Parrish (1870–1966), with his unique abilities in architecture, illustrations, and landscapes, was the most prolific artist during 'The Golden Years of Illustrators.' He produced art for more than one hundred magazines, painted girls on rocks for the Edison-Mazda division of General Electric, and landscapes for Brown & Bigelow. His most recognized work was 'Daybreak' that was published in 1923 by House of Art and sold nearly two million prints. Parrish began early training with his father who was a recognized artist, studied architecture at Dartmouth, and became an active participant in the Cornish artist colony in New Hampshire where he resided. Due to his increasing popularity, reproductions are now being marketed.

In our listings, values for prints apply to those that are in their original frames (or very nice and appropriate replacement frames) unless noted otherwise. For further information we recommend *Collector's Value Guide to Early 20th Century American Prints* by Michael Ivankovich. Bobby Babcock, our advisor for this category, is listed in the Directory under Texas.

Print, Air Castles, 12x16", $325.00.

Book, Dream Days & Golden Age (2-pc set), 2nd edition 250.00
Book, Early Years, Skeeter's, 1973 ....300.00
Book, Maxfield Parrish, Coy Ludwig, 1st edition, 1973 ....150.00
Book, Mother Goose in Prose, 2nd edition, 1901 ....600.00
Bookplate, Villa Bella, Italian Villas & Their Gardens, new matt & fr ..40.00
Check, sgn Parrish...350.00
Frontispiece, Bellerophon, Collier's 5-15-09, new matt & fr 125.00
Frontispiece, Story of King's Son, Collier's 10-13-06, new matt & fr ...125.00
Magazine cover, Balloon Man, Collier's 12-26-08 ....150.00
Magazine insert, Aucassin Seeks for Nicolette, Scribner's 7-03 ....75.00
Playing cards, Ecstasy, Edison-Mazda, 1930, M 325.00
Playing cards, Waterfall, Edison-Mazda, 1931, NM 325.00
Poster, Nat'l Authority on Amateur Sports, museum-quality fr, rare ..5,000.00
Poster, New Hampshire, Winter, 1939, 24x29" 850.00
Poster stamp, Brill Bros, 1915, 1½x2½" 75.00
Print, A Perfect Day, Brown & Bigelow, 1943, 9x10", new mat & fr ..100.00
Print, Air Castles, 1904, 12x16" 325.00
Print, Atlas, 1908, 9½x11½" 225.00
Print, Canyon, 1924, 12x15" 325.00
Print, Cassim, 1909, 11x9" 225.00
Print, Centaur, 1910, 9x11" 225.00
Print, Circe's Palace, 1908, 9x11" 250.00
Print, Contentment, Edison-Mazda, 1928, lg, cropped: 14x23" .950.00
Print, Dawn, Edison-Mazda, rare, 1918, 19x8½", w/pad 3,500.00
Print, Daybreak, 1922, 6x10" 150.00
Print, Daybreak, 1922, 10x18" 275.00
Print, Dinkey Bird, 1905, 11x16" 300.00
Print, Dreaming, 1928, lg, 18x30" 1,750.00
Print, Dreamlight, Edison-Mazda, 1925, lg, cropped: 14x23" ..1,250.00
Print, Dreamlight, Edison-Mazda, 1925, sm, cropped: 10x6¼" ..460.00
Print, Ecstasy, Edison-Mazda, 1930, sm, cropped: 9x6⅜" 450.00
Print, Enchantment, Edison-Mazda, 1926, lg, cropped: 14⅝x23¼" ...1,500.00
Print, Evening Shadows, Brown & Bigelow, 1940, 13x17½" 550.00
Print, Evening Shadows, 9x10" 250.00
Print, Eventide, Brown & Bigelow, 1944, 13¾x9½" 300.00
Print, Garden of Allah, 1918, 15x30" 350.00
Print, Golden Hours, Edison-Mazda, 1929, sm, cropped: 12x7¼" ...265.00
Print, Golden Hours, lg, cropped: 14½x22⅝" 300.00
Print, Hilltop, med, 1927, 12x20" 550.00
Print, King of the Black Isles, 1907, 9x11" 250.00
Print, Lampseller of Bagdad, Edison-Mazda, sm, cropped: 10⅝x6⅜" ...495.00
Print, Landing of the Brazen Boatsman, 1907, 9x11" 225.00
Print, Lute Players, 1924, 10x18" 350.00
Print, New Hampshire, Land of Scenic, Summer Poster, 1936, 24x29" ..750.00
Print, Peaceful Valley, Brown & Bigelow, 18x22" 350.00
Print, Peaceful Valley, Brown & Bigelow, 1936, 13x17½" 290.00
Print, Queen Gulnare, 1907, 9x11" 250.00
Print, Reveries, Edison-Mazda, 1927, lg, cropped: 22⅛x14½" ...900.00
Print, Romance, 1925, 12x24" 1,500.00
Print, Stars, 1927, 6x10" 350.00
Print, Sunrise, Edison-Mazda, 1933, sm, cropped: 9¾x7" 330.00
Print, Thy Templed Hill, 1942, med, 9x10" 195.00
Print, Tranquility, Brown & Bigelow, 1936, jumbo, 24x29½" 585.00
Print, Twilight, 1937, 9x10" 195.00
Print, Valley of Enchantment, Brown & Bigelow, 1946, 14x22" ..310.00
Print, Village Brook, 1941, 10x12" 250.00
Print, Village Church, Brown & Bigelow, 1949, lg, 11¼x22", EX ..350.00
Print, Wild Geese, 1924, 12x15" 325.00
Triptych, Buds Below Roses, Love's Pilgrimage, Garden of Opportunity ..1,500.00

Pate-De-Verre

Simply translated, pate-d-verre means paste of glass. In the manufacturing process, lead glass is first ground, then mixed with sodium silicate solution to form a paste which can be molded and refired. Some of the most prominent artisans to use this procedure were Almaric Walter, Daum, Argy-Rouseau, and Decorchemont. See also specific manufacturers.

Paperweight, frog on lily pad, blk-gr on bl, 5¼" dia 3,500.00
Tray, summer leaves & red fruit on gr frost, Decorchemont, 6½" ...2,500.00

Pattern Glass

Pattern Glass was the first mass-produced fancy tableware in America and was much prized by our ancestors. From the 1840s to the Civil War, it contained a high lead content and is known as 'Flint Glass.' It is exceptionally clear and resonant. Later glass was made with soda lime and is known as non-flint. By the 1890s pattern glass was produced in great volume in thousands of patterns, and colored glass came into vogue. Today the highest prices are often paid for these later patterns flashed with rose, amber, canary, and vaseline; stained ruby; or made in colors of cobalt, green, yellow, amethyst, etc. Demand for pattern glass declined by 1915, and glass fanciers were collecting it by 1930. No other field of antiques offers more diversity in patterns, prices, or pieces than this unique and historical glass that represents the Victorian era in America.

Our advisor for this category is Darlene Yohe; she is listed in the Directory under Arkansas. For a more thorough study on the subject, we recommend *Field Guide to Pattern Glass* and *The Collector's Encyclopedia of Pattern Glass*, both by Mollie Helen McCain; *Standard Encyclopedia of Pressed Glass, 1860–1930, Identification & Values*, by Bill Edwards and Mike Carwile; and *Early American Pattern Glass* and *Much More Early American Pattern Glass* by Alice Hulett Metz. All are available from Collector Books. See also Bread Plates; Cruets; Historical Glass; Salt and Pepper Shakers; Salts, Open; Sugar Shakers; Syrups; specific manufacturers such as Northwood.

Note: Values are given for open sugar bowls and compotes unless noted 'w/lid.'

Actress, tray, dresser 65.00
Admiral Dewey, See Dewey; See Also Greentown Dewey
Alabama, creamer, ruby stain 65.00
Alabama, jelly compote 65.00
Alabama, tray, water; 10½" 115.00
Alaska, celery tray 70.00
Allover Diamond, cordial 50.00
Allover Diamond, egg cup 22.00
Almond Thumbprint, cordial, flint 42.50
Almond Thumbprint, creamer, non-flint 42.00
Almond Thumbprint, tumbler, flint, ftd 40.00
Amazon, butter dish 75.00
Amazon, creamer 40.00
Amberette, See Klondike
Apollo, sugar bowl, plain, w/lid 55.00
Apollo, syrup 80.00
Arched Ovals, butter dish, gr 48.00
Arched Ovals, pitcher, water; gr 45.00
Argus, compote, high std, w/lid, flint, 12" 180.00
Argus, whiskey, appl hdld 72.00
Art, biscuit jar, ruby stain 165.00
Art, bowl, flared rim, ftd, 7" 28.00
Ashburton, carafe 178.00
Ashburton, egg cup, flint 32.00
Ashburton, tumbler, lemonade 62.00
Atlas, cordial 36.00
Atlas, goblet, ruby stain 70.00
Atlas, molasses can 65.00
Atlas, syrup 67.50
Aurora, mug, ruby stain 65.00
Aurora, waste bowl 30.00
Austrian, butter dish, canary 325.00
Austrian, goblet 37.50
Austrian, wine 32.00
Aztec, claret 42.50
Aztec, pitcher, tankard 55.00
Aztec, syrup 80.00
Balder, See Pennsylvania
Baltimore Pear, bowl, 9" 37.50
Baltimore Pear, creamer 30.00
Baltimore Pear, goblet 35.00
Baltimore Pear, plate, 10" 42.50
Bar & Diamonds, shakers, pr 55.00
Bar & Diamonds, tumbler 24.00
Barberry, egg cup....24.00
Barberry, plate, bl, 6" 48.00
Barberry, salt cellar, master 15.00
Barley, bowl, oval, 10" 35.00
Barley, creamer 25.00
Barley, wine, 3¾" 28.00
Barrel Huber, See Huber
Basket Weave, creamer, amber 32.50
Basket Weave, pitcher, milk; bl 47.50
Basket Weave, wine 20.00
Beaded Band, goblet 34.00
Beaded Grape, olive dish, hdl 22.50
Beaded Grape, pitcher, water; gr 125.00
Beaded Grape, wine 32.00
Beaded Grape Medallion, compote, collared base, w/lid 90.00
Beaded Grape Medallion, goblet, buttermilk 34.00
Beaded Medallion, sugar bowl 32.00
Beaded Medallion, tumbler 48.00
Beaded Mirror, See Beaded Medallion
Beaded Swirl, compote, high std, gr 50.00
Beaded Tulip, wine 32.00
Bearded Head, See Viking
Bellflower, bowl, scalloped rim, 4½x8" 78.00
Bigler, cordial 48.00
Bigler, salt cellar, master 65.00
Bigler, tumbler 67.50
Bird & Strawberry, pitcher, water 275.00
Bird & Strawberry, plate, 12" 75.00
Bird & Strawberry, wine 70.00
Bleeding Heart, cake stand, 10" 85.00
Bleeding Heart, egg cup 42.50

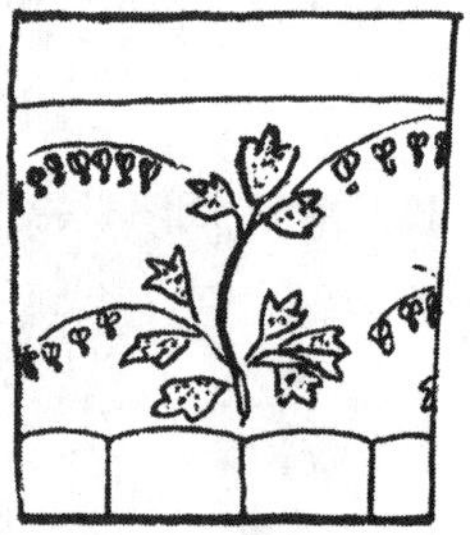

Bleeding Heart

Block & Fan, cake stand, 10" 45.00
Block & Fan, finger bowl 45.00
Block & Fan, goblet, ruby stain 125.00
Blue Jay, See Cardinal Bird
Bohemian, mug, rose stain & gold 75.00
Bohemian, tumbler, rose stain 50.00
Bohemian, wine 17.50
Bow Tie, bowl, 5x10" 55.00
Bow Tie, butter pat 28.00
Bow Tie, goblet 65.00
Bridal Rosette, bowl, 9" 22.50
Bridal Rosette, pitcher, water 37.50
Broken Column, cake stand 80.00
Broken Column, punch cup 15.00

Broken Column, vase, 6½" 30.00
Buckle, creamer, flint 100.00
Buckle, syrup, spring lid 125.00
Buckle w/Star, syrup 80.00
Buckle w/Star, whiskey 150.00
Bull's Eye, carafe 50.00
Bull's Eye, sweetmeat, w/lid 120.00
Bull's Eye & Diamond Point, egg cup 185.00
Bull's Eye & Diamond Point, tumbler 130.00
Bull's Eye & Diamond Point, whiskey 150.00
Bull's Eye & Fan, relish 24.00
Bull's Eye & Fan, wine, emerald gr 45.00
Bull's Eye Band, See Reverse Torpedo
Bull's Eye in Heart, See Heart w/Thumbprint
Button Arches, banana dish 20.00
Button Arches, butter dish, ruby stain 100.00
Button Arches, sugar bowl, w/lid 48.50
Button Arches, tumbler, frosted band 25.00
Button Band, bowl, 10" 32.00
Cabbage Rose, basket, 12" 130.00
Cabbage Rose, butter dish 55.00
Cabbage Rose, tumbler, bar 40.00
Cable, bowl, 9" 55.00
Cable, honey dish, 3½" 17.50
Cable, syrup 450.00
Cable, wine 215.00
California, See Beaded Grape
Cane, celery vase, gr 35.00
Cane, relish, amber 25.00
Cane, wine, bl 38.00
Cape Cod, compote, 5½x8" 45.00
Cape Cod, goblet 48.00
Cape Cod, pitcher, water 100.00
Cardinal Bird, goblet 40.00
Cardinal Bird, sugar bowl, w/lid 60.00
Cathedral, bowl, berry; amethyst, 8" 55.00
Cathedral, butter dish 45.00
Cathedral, pitcher, water; amber 75.00
Chain w/Diamonds, See Washington Centennial
Chain w/Star, jelly compote 20.00
Chain w/Star, pickle dish, oval 15.00
Chandelier, celery vase 22.00
Chandelier, creamer 40.00
Chandelier, sugar bowl, w/lid 500.00
Classic, butter dish, collared base 135.00
Classic, pitcher, water; open log ft, 9½" 375.00
Classic, spooner, log ft 115.00
Classic, sugar bowl, log ft, w/lid 175.00
Coin, See US Coin
Colorado, banana stand 36.00
Colorado, creamer, bl, ind 35.00
Colorado, wine, gr 42.50
Columbian Coin, goblet, gold coins 65.00
Columbian Coin, tumbler, clear coins 28.00
Comet, butter dish 195.00
Comet, pitcher, water 550.00
Connecticut, biscuit jar 27.50
Connecticut, tumbler, lemonade; w/hdl 22.50
Connecticut, wine 37.50
Cord & Tassel, compote, low, 8" 32.50
Cord & Tassel, egg cup 42.00
Cord Drapery, butter dish 80.00
Cord Drapery, mug 40.00
Cord Drapery, sugar bowl 60.00
Cord Drapery, wine 90.00
Cordova, bowl, berry; w/lid 35.00
Cordova, compote, high std, w/lid 45.00
Cottage, plate, 7" 24.00
Cottage, sauce bowl 12.50
Cottage, tumbler 20.00
Croesus, bowl, gr, ftd, w/lid, 8" 125.00
Croesus, bowl, gr w/gold, 8" 125.00
Croesus, creamer & sugar bowl, purple, pr 265.00
Croesus, sauce bowl 25.00
Crow's Foot, See Yale
Crown Jewels, See Chandelier
Crystal Wedding, cake plate, sq 47.50
Crystal Wedding, relish, 7½" L 25.00
Crystal Wedding, syrup 185.00
Crystal Wedding, syrup, ruby stain 400.00
Crystal Wedding, wine, ruby stain 65.00
Cube & Fan, See Pineapple & Fan
Cupid & Venus, bread plate 45.00
Cupid & Venus, cake plate, bl, 11" 125.00
Cupid & Venus, goblet 78.00
Cupid & Venus, wine 90.00
Currant, relish 20.00
Currant, wine 45.00
Currier & Ives, bowl, oval, 10" 36.00
Curtain, spooner 25.00
Curtain, sugar bowl, w/lid 45.00
Curtain Tieback, creamer 35.00
Curtain Tieback, pitcher, water 50.00
Cut Log, cake stand, high std, 10½" 80.00
Cut Log, sugar bowl, w/lid 60.00
Dahlia, cake stand, bl, 9½" 60.00
Dahlia, mug, canary 60.00
Dahlia, tankard 75.00
Daisy & Button, bowl, flat, 8" 17.50
Daisy & Button, butter pat, bl 32.00
Daisy & Button, dessert tray, canary w/8 wedges in various colors ..325.00
Daisy & Button, plate, bl, scalloped rim, 10" 40.00
Daisy & Button w/Crossbars, butter dish, amber 65.00
Daisy & Button w/Crossbars, creamer, ind 22.00
Daisy & Button w/Crossbars, syrup 85.00
Daisy & Button w/Crossbars, wine 27.50
Daisy & Button w/Narcissus, goblet 22.00
Daisy & Button w/Narcissus, tumbler 17.50
Daisy & Button w/Thumbprint Panels, butter dish 195.00
Daisy & Button w/Thumbprint Panels, cake stand 55.00
Daisy & Button w/V Ornament, butter pat 8.50
Daisy & Button w/V Ornament, mug 25.00
Daisy & Button w/V Ornament, tumbler, amber 25.00
Dakota, basket, etched, 10" 210.00
Dakota, cake stand, etched, 10½" 275.00
Dakota, creamer, plain 32.00

Deer & Pine Tree

Deer & Pine Tree, bowl, 5½x8" 55.00

Deer & Pine Tree, marmalade 235.00
Deer & Pine Tree, sugar bowl, w/lid 85.00
Delaware, bowl, 9" 25.00
Delaware, butter dish 135.00
Delaware, pin tray, gr w/gold 50.00
Delaware, sugar bowl, rose w/gold, w/lid 95.00
Dew & Raindrop, pitcher, water 55.00
Dew & Raindrop, punch cup 10.00
Dewey, butter dish 55.00
Dewey, parfait 45.00
Dewey, See Also Greentown, Dewey
Diagonal Band, creamer 35.00
Diagonal Band, pitcher, water 45.00
Diagonal Band, plate, 7" 15.00
Diamond Horseshoe, See Aurora
Diamond Medallion, See Grand
Diamond Point, cake stand, nonflint, 9" 85.00
Diamond Point, compote, nonflint, w/lid, 8" 60.00
Diamond Point, egg cup, canary, flint 365.00
Diamond Quilted, bowl, vaseline, 7" 25.00
Diamond Quilted, tumbler, amber 32.50
Diamond Thumbprint, butter dish 215.00
Diamond Thumbprint, compote, low std, 8" 90.00
Diamond Thumbprint, goblet 465.00
Dinner Bell, See Cottage
Doric, See Feather
Double Leaf & Dart, See Leaf & Dart
Drapery, egg cup 30.00
Drapery, goblet 27.50
Drapery, tumbler 38.00
Egg in Sand, creamer 28.00
Egg in Sand, pitcher, water 45.00
Egg in Sand, sugar bowl, amber, w/lid 70.00
Egyptian, butter dish 90.00
Egyptian, spooner 20.00
Egyptian, sugar bowl 35.00
Elephant, See Jumbo
Emerald Green Herringbone, See Florida
Empress, creamer, gr w/gold, 5¼" 45.00
Empress, tumbler, gr w/gold 55.00
Esther, bowl, gr w/gold, 8" 75.00
Esther, creamer, ind 175.00
Esther, pitcher, water; gr 350.00
Esther, relish, gr, 4½x8½" 40.00
Etched Dakota, See Dakota
Excelsior, champagne 95.00
Excelsior, creamer 95.00
Excelsior, egg cup, dbl 65.00
Eyewinker, banana stand 130.00
Eyewinker, butter dish 85.00
Eyewinker, creamer 75.00
Feather, sugar bowl, gr 55.00
Feather, tumbler, gr 95.00
Festoon, bowl, berry; rectangular, 8" L 24.00
Festoon, cake stand, high std, 9" dia 50.00
Festoon, waste bowl 55.00
Fine Cut, finger bowl, canary 32.50
Fine Cut, pitcher, water; bl 95.00
Fine Cut, plate, amber, 10" 42.50
Fine Cut & Block, champagne, amber 68.00
Fine Cut & Block, cordial 70.00
Fine Cut & Diamond, See Grand
Fine Cut & Feather, See Feather
Fine Cut & Panel, goblet, amber 35.00
Fine Cut & Panel, plate, amber, 6" 28.00
Fine Cut & Panel, plate, 7" 12.50
Fine Cut & Panel, wine, bl 40.00
Fine Rib, egg cup, dbl, flint 38.00
Fine Rib, spoon holder 57.00
Fingerprint, See Almond Thumbprint
Fishscale, creamer 27.50
Fishscale, tumbler 90.00

Flamingo

Flamingo Habitat, butter dish 60.00
Flamingo Habitat, celery vase 50.00
Flamingo Habitat, creamer 38.00
Florida, mustard pot, w/lid & attached underplate 27.50
Florida, pitcher, water; gr 82.50
Florida, spooner 18.00
Flower Pot, butter dish 55.00
Flower Pot, cake stand, 10¼" 45.00
Flower Pot, sugar bowl, w/lid 42.50
Frosted Circle, champagne 50.00
Frosted Circle, goblet 37.50
Frosted Circle, tumbler 27.50
Frosted Leaf, celery vase 125.00
Frosted Leaf, egg cup 100.00
Frosted Leaf, wine 175.00
Frosted Lion, See Lion
Frosted Roman Key, champagne 80.00
Frosted Roman Key, sugar bowl, w/lid 88.00
Frosted Stork, platter, oval, 11½" 78.00
Frosted Stork, sauce bowl 32.00
Galloway, creamer, rose stain 95.00
Galloway, mug, 4½" 38.00
Galloway, pitcher, milk 72.50
Galloway, sherbet, 3¼" 25.00
Garfield Drape, bowl, 6" 45.00
Garfield Drape, compote, w/lid, 9½" 150.00
Garfield Drape, spooner 32.50
Gem, See Nailhead
Georgia, butter dish 45.00
Georgia, compote, 6" dia 20.00
Georgia, plate, 5¼" 17.50
Georgia, tumbler 40.00
Good Luck, See Horseshoe
Gothic, butter dish 125.00
Gothic, compote, 3½x7" 65.00
Gothic, tumbler 145.00
Grand, butter dish 45.00
Grand, celery vase 22.50
Grand, cordial 50.00
Grand, wine 32.00
Grape & Festoon, pitcher, water; stippled leaf 95.00
Grape & Festoon, sugar bowl, stippled leaf, w/lid 60.00

Grape & Festoon w/Shield, pitcher, water 75.00
Grasshopper, bowl, w/lid, ftd, 7" 60.00
Grasshopper, butter dish, amber 100.00
Grasshopper, honey dish w/lid, 3-ftd, no insect, from $150 to ...175.00
Greek Key, goblet, buttermilk 55.00
Greek Key, sardine box 38.00
Guardian Angel, See Cupid & Venus
Hairpin, champagne, flint 75.00
Hairpin, goblet 42.50
Halley's Comet, wine 18.00
Hamilton, butter dish 70.00
Hamilton, goblet 42.50
Hand, tumbler, water 95.00
Harp, pitcher, water 50.00
Harp, relish, gr 25.00
Harp, salt cellar, master 50.00
Hawaiian Lei, cake stand, 9¼" 40.00
Hawaiian Lei, cup & saucer 40.00
Heart w/Thumbprint, banana boat, ruby stain 150.00
Heart w/Thumbprint, bowl, finger; emerald gr 75.00
Heart w/Thumbprint, goblet 62.00
Herringbone Buttress, See Greentown, Herringbone Buttress
Hickman, goblet 42.50
Hickman, wine 28.00
Hidalgo, butter dish 55.00
Hidalgo, celery vase, amber stain 30.00
Hinoto, egg cup 40.00
Hinoto, tumbler, ftd 50.00
Holly, cake stand, 11" 135.00
Holly, goblet 125.00
Holly, spooner 65.00
Holly, sugar bowl, w/lid 135.00
Holly Amber, See Greentown, Holly Amber
Honeycomb, champagne, flint 60.00
Honeycomb, decanter, flint, pt 90.00
Honeycomb, plate, nonflint, 6" 15.00
Honeycomb, tumbler, ftd, flint 38.00
Hops & Barley, See Wheat & Barley
Horn of Plenty, bottle, bar; orig stopper, qt 140.00
Horn of Plenty, egg cup 45.00
Horn of Plenty, honey dish 20.00
Horseshoe, bowl, oval, 9x6" 32.00
Horseshoe, bowl, 3-horseshoe finial, 5x8" 315.00
Horseshoe, butter dish 115.00
Horseshoe, plate, 10" 90.00
Huber, champagne, flint 34.00
Huber, egg cup 32.50
Hummingbird, creamer 48.00
Hummingbird, wine 100.00
Illinois, basket, 11½" 120.00
Illinois, pitcher, milk; SP rim 185.00
Illinois, pitcher, tankard, SP trim 90.00
Iowa, cup 17.50
Iowa, decanter 38.00
Iowa, olive dish 18.00
Iris w/Meander, See Opalescent Glass
Ivy in Snow, cordial, ruby stain 95.00
Ivy in Snow, tumbler 25.00
Ivy in Snow, tumbler, ruby stain 38.50
Ivy in Snow, wine 37.50
Jacob's Ladder, cake stand, 12" 55.00
Jacob's Ladder, compote, 5x10" 45.00
Jacob's Ladder, plate, amber, 6" 95.00
Jacob's Ladder, sauce bowl, bl, ftd 22.50
Jersey Swirl, marmalade 60.00
Jersey Swirl, pitcher, water; bl 60.00
Jersey Swirl, plate, 10" 32.50
Jewel Band, compote, w/lid, 12x8¼" 50.00
Jewel Band, creamer 25.00
Jewel Band, goblet 37.50
Jewel w/Dewdrop, cake stand, 8" 47.50
Jewel w/Dewdrop, relish, oval, 8½" 22.00
Jeweled Moon & Star, butter dish 70.00
Jeweled Moon & Star, carafe 40.00
Jeweled Moon & Star, wine 32.50
Job's Tears, See Art
Jumbo, butter dish, frosted elephant finial 725.00
Jumbo, goblet 695.00
Jumbo, marmalade, frosted elephant finial, head hdls 465.00
Jumbo, spooner 100.00
Kentucky, celery tray 27.50
Kentucky, cup, gr 22.50
Kentucky, tumbler, gr 55.00
Kentucky, wine 32.50
King's Crown, banana stand, ftd, ruby stain 150.00
King's Crown, cake stand, 9" 60.00
King's Crown, champagne, ruby stain 30.00
Klondike, goblet 100.00
La Clede, See Hickman
Lace, See Drapery
Lawrence, See Bull's Eye
Leaf & Dart, egg cup 22.50
Leaf & Dart, pitcher, milk 140.00
Leaf & Dart, wine 35.00
Leaf Bracket, See Greentown, Leaf Bracket
Leaf Medallion, See Northwood, Leaf Medallion
Liberty Bell, creamer, mini 85.00
Liberty Bell, mug, snake hdl 475.00
Liberty Bell, pitcher, water 800.00
Liberty Bell, sugar bowl, w/lid 115.00
Lily of the Valley, butter dish 100.00
Lily of the Valley, celery vase 65.00
Lily of the Valley, pitcher, milk 235.00
Lincoln Drape, creamer, flint 190.00
Lincoln Drape, goblet 150.00
Lion, butter dish, frosted lion head finial 95.00
Lion, celery vase 75.00
Lion, compote, low std, 5" dia 60.00
Lion, marmalade, frosted lion finial 145.00
Log Cabin, bowl, w/lid, 3⅝x8x5¼" 130.00
Log Cabin, spooner 125.00
Log Cabin, spooner, sapphire bl 400.00
Long Spear, See Grasshopper
Loop, compote, flint, 8x8" 92.50
Loop, creamer, flint 75.00
Loop, pitcher, water; flint 195.00
Loop, vase, flint, 9⅜" 80.00
Loop & Dart, butter dish, rnd ornaments, flint 90.00

Loop & Dart

Loop & Dart, compote, low std, rnd ornaments, w/lid, 8" dia 80.00
Loop & Dart, goblet 35.00
Loop w/Stippled Panels, See Texas
Maine, bowl, 8" 27.50
Maine, creamer 32.00
Maine, mug 37.50
Maine, wine, gr 75.00
Manhattan, bowl, 9" 22.50
Manhattan, marmalade 37.50
Manhattan, tumbler, gold trim 27.50
Maryland, banana bowl, flat, 11¼" L 40.00
Maryland, goblet 27.50
Maryland, tumbler 30.00
Mascotte, cake stand, 10" dia 50.00
Mascotte, celery vase 37.50
Mascotte, goblet, etched 42.50
Massachusetts, creamer & sugar bowl, breakfast sz 32.50
Massachusetts, plate, 8" sq 35.00
Massachusetts, vase, trumpet shape, 9" 35.00
Medallion, goblet, amber 48.00
Medallion, sugar bowl, amber, w/lid 48.00
Melrose, compote, 5¾x7½" 27.50
Melrose, pitcher, milk 55.00
Michigan, crushed fruit bowl 70.00
Michigan, mug, lemonade; rose stain 35.00
Michigan, sugar bowl, w/lid 70.00
Minerva, compote, 8½x8" 90.00
Minerva, goblet 90.00
Minerva, platter, 13" L 55.00
Minnesota, bowl, 8" sq 30.00
Minnesota, cracker jar 92.50
Minnesota, tumbler 20.00
Minor Block, See Mascotte
Mirror, See Galloway
Missouri, jelly compote 30.00
Missouri, sauce bowl, gr 12.50
Missouri, spooner 25.00
Missouri, tumbler, gr 32.50
Moon & Star, cake stand, 10" 90.00
Moon & Star, champagne 70.00
Moon & Star, compote, 7½x7" 45.00
Nail, tumbler, ruby stain 60.00
Nailhead, bowl, 6" 18.00
Nailhead, butter dish 47.50
Nailhead, sauce bowl, rose stain, 4" dia 12.50
Nailhead, sugar bowl, w/lid 32.50
Nestor, tumbler, gr 34.00
New England Pineapple, bar tumbler, flint 130.00
New England Pineapple, goblet, flint 75.00
New Jersey, creamer, ruby stain 60.00
New Jersey, vase, gr, 10" 45.00
New Jersey, wine 38.00
O'Hara Diamond, bowl, berry; sm 12.00
O'Hara Diamond, plate, 7" 22.50
Oaken Bucket, See Wooden Pail
One Hundred & One, relish 20.00
One Hundred & One, sugar bowl, w/lid 48.00
One-O-One, See One Hundred & One
Open Rose, egg cup 22.50
Open Rose, salt cellar 25.00
Oregon #1, bowl, 3½" 8.00
Oregon #1, butter dish, flanged 55.00
Oregon #1, butter dish, flat 42.00
Oregon #1, wine 48.00
Orion, See Cathedral
Palmette, bottle, vinegar 95.00
Palmette, cup plate 60.00
Palmette, goblet 38.00
Palmette, wine 115.00
Panelled Forget-Me-Not, butter dish, w/lid 65.00
Panelled Forget-Me-Not, cake stand 47.50
Panelled Forget-Me-Not, pitcher, water 75.00
Panelled Thistle, plate, w/bee, 7" sq 28.00
Panelled Thistle, sugar bowl, w/lid 42.50

Pavonia

Pavonia, butter dish, eng 88.00
Pavonia, pitcher, water 60.00
Pavonia, spooner 40.00
Pavonia, sugar bowl, ruby stain, w/lid 80.00
Pennsylvania, creamer 30.00
Pennsylvania, molasses can 80.00
Pennsylvania, tumbler, water 22.50
Pigmy, See Torpedo
Pillow Encircled, creamer 27.50
Pillow Encircled, tumbler, ruby stain 42.50
Pineapple & Fan, pitcher, water 82.00
Pineapple & Fan, vase, trumpet form, 10" 35.00
Pineapple Stem, See Pavonia
Pioneer, See Westward Ho
Pleat & Panel, bowl, flat, 8" sq 47.50
Pleat & Panel, plate, 7" sq 20.00
Pleat & Panel, sugar bowl, w/lid 88.00
Plume, butter dish 47.50
Plume, cake stand, high std, 9" 48.00
Plume, tumbler, ruby-stained souvenir 42.50
Polar Bear, goblet 110.00
Polar Bear, tray, water; frosted 230.00
Popcorn, butter dish 58.00
Popcorn, pitcher, water 90.00
Portland, cake stand, 10½" 60.00
Portland, creamer 45.00
Portland, creamer, in SP fr 75.00
Portland, goblet 40.00
Portland, pitcher, water 35.00
Powder & Shot, creamer, flint 110.00
Powder & Shot, egg cup, flint 62.50
Prayer Rug, See Horseshoe
Primrose, pitcher, milk; bl 22.50
Primrose, plate, amber, 7" 22.00
Princess Feather, goblet, flint 45.00
Princess Feather, plate, nonflint, 8" 25.00
Priscilla, butter dish 90.00
Priscilla, creamer, ind 25.00
Priscilla, sugar bowl, w/lid 48.00
Psyche & Cupid, celery vase 50.00
Psyche & Cupid, goblet 55.00
Psyche & Cupid, spooner 45.00

Recessed Pillared Red Top, See Nail
Red Block, banana boat, ruby stain 80.00
Red Block, mug 47.50
Red Block, tumbler 32.00
Red Top, See Button Arches
Reverse Torpedo, butter dish 75.00
Reverse Torpedo, celery vase 65.00
Reverse Torpedo, syrup 200.00
Reverse Torpedo, tumbler 48.00
Ribbed Palm, honey dish, flint 17.00
Ribbed Palm, wine, flint 75.00
Ribbon, celery vase 37.50
Ribbon, compote, w/lid, 8" 95.00
Ribbon, sugar bowl, w/lid, 7¾" 70.00
Ribbon Candy, cordial 58.00
Ribbon Candy, wine 98.00
Rochelle, See Princess Feather
Roman Rosette, cordial 50.00
Roman Rosette, goblet 50.00
Roman Rosette, plate, 7" 37.50
Rose in the Snow, platter 135.00
Rose in the Snow, sugar bowl, amber, w/lid, rnd 58.00
Rose in the Snow, tumbler, bl 110.00
Rose Sprig, cake stand, 8-sided, 10" 75.00
Rose Sprig, pitcher, milk; bl 90.00
Rosette, goblet 30.00
Rosette, jelly compote 20.00
Rosette, plate, hdls, 9" 22.50
Royal Ivy, See Northwood
Royal Oak, See Northwood
Ruby Thumbprint, See King's Crown
S-Repeat, butter dish 125.00
S-Repeat, carafe, water 525.00
Sandwich Star, butter dish 180.00
Sandwich Star, compote, low std, 8½" 62.50
Sawtooth, butter dish, nonflint 45.00
Sawtooth, champagne, knob stem, flint 60.00
Sawtooth, sauce bowl 8.00
Sawtooth Band, See Amazon
Scalloped, Daisy Red Top, See Button Arches
Scroll w/Flowers, mustard jar 55.00
Scroll w/Flowers, sugar bowl, w/lid 55.00
Seneca Loop, See Loop
Shell & Jewel, creamer 25.00
Shell & Jewel, tumbler, amber 25.00
Shell & Tassel, creamer, sq 60.00
Shell & Tassel, oyster dish 235.00
Shell & Tassel, tumbler, gr 40.00
Sheraton, plate, 8½" sq 15.00
Sheraton, relish, bl, hdl 22.50
Shoshone, cake stand, gr 45.00
Shoshone, tumbler, gold trim 75.00
Shoshone, wine 22.50
Shuttle, cordial, sm 20.00
Shuttle, mug 25.00
Shuttle, tumbler 47.50
Skilton, compote, low std, 8½" 22.50
Skilton, pitcher, water tankard; ruby stain 120.00
Skilton, wine 32.00
Spades, See Medallion
Sprig, bowl, oval, 7" 27.50
Sprig, butter dish 62.50
Star & Feather, creamer 35.00
Star & Feather, plate, amber, 7" 20.00
Star Rosetted, compate, 7½" 20.00
Star Rosetted, plate, 7" 12.00
Stars & Stripes, cordial 20.00
Stars & Stripes, wine 20.00
States, punch cup 12.50
States, sauce dish 8.00
States, tumbler, ...27.50
Stedman, champagne 42.00
Stedman, spooner 18.00
Stippled Chain, cake stand 55.00
Stippled Chain, egg cup 30.00
Stippled Forget-Me-Not, butter dish 50.00
Stippled Forget-Me-Not, plate, stork center, 11" 85.00
Stippled Forget-Me-Not, sugar bowl, w/lid 42.50
Stippled Grape & Festoon, goblet 35.00
Stippled Grape & Festoon, pitcher, water 110.00
Stippled Ivy, egg cup 28.00
Stippled Ivy, spooner 30.00
Stippled Panelled Flower, See Maine
Strigil, plate, 11" 28.00
Strigil, punch cup 16.00
Sunk Honeycomb, cake stand, ruby stain 115.00
Sunk Honeycomb, cup & saucer, ruby stain 40.00
Sunk Honeycomb, tumbler, eng 22.00
Sunken Primrose, See Florida
Swan, compote, 7½x10" 150.00
Swan, marmalade jar 120.00
Swan, spooner 50.00
Teardrop & Tassel, goblet 30.00
Teardrop & Tassel, See Also Greentown, Teardrop & Tassel
Teardrop & Tassel, tumbler 36.00
Tennessee, butter dish 58.00
Tennessee, creamer 40.00
Tennessee, goblet, ruby stain 95.00
Tennessee, relish tray 17.50

Texas

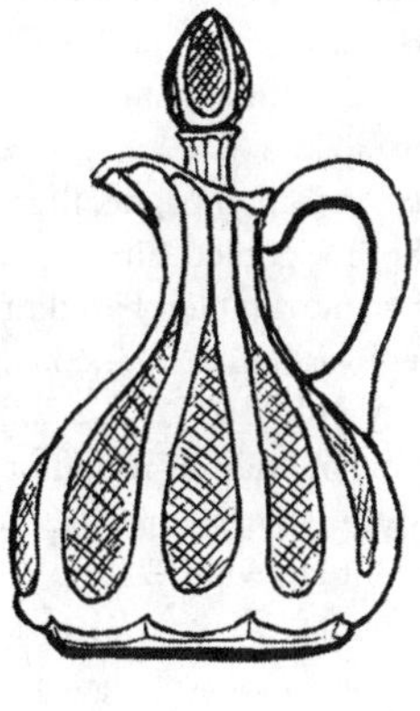

Texas, creamer 48.00
Texas, goblet 95.00
Texas, spooner, ruby stain 85.00
Texas, wine 80.00
Theatrical, See Actress
Thousand Eye, cologne bottle, gr 55.00
Thousand Eye, cordial, bl 42.50
Thousand Eye, platter, 8x11" 35.00
Three Face, champagne 150.00
Three Face, compote, high std, w/lid, 8" dia 300.00
Three Face, goblet 55.00
Three Face, goblet, eng 100.00
Three Face, salt cellar 40.00

Three Panel, creamer, bl 45.00
Three Panel, sugar bowl, vaseline, w/lid 67.50
Thumbprint, See Argus
Thumbprint Band, See Dakota
Thunderbird, See Hummingbird
Torpedo, banana stand 60.00
Tree of Life, See Portland
Tree of Life w/Hand, cake stand, frosted base, 11½" 130.00
Tree of Life w/Hand, mug, 3" 120.00
Tulip w/Sawtooth, champagne, flint 150.00
Tulip w/Sawtooth, creamer, flint 88.00
Two Panel, creamer 20.00
Two Panel, goblet 22.00
Two Panel, pitcher, water; bl 75.00
US Coin, bread tray, frosted coins, 10" 350.00
US Coin, butter dish, clear coins 500.00
US Coin, champagne, frosted coins, flared rim 750.00
US Coin, compote, frosted coins, high std, str rim, 8½" dia 500.00
US Coin, compote, frosted coins, 6" dia, NM 275.00
US Coin, goblet, frosted coins 425.00
US Coin, sauce bowl, frosted coins 105.00
US Coin, sauce bowl, frosted coins, plain rim, flat, 3¾" 115.00
US Coin, spooner, clear coins 200.00
US Coin, sugar bowl, frosted coins, w/lid 450.00
US Coin, syrup pitcher, frosted coins 600.00
US Coin, toothpick holder, frosted coins, ftd, sq 100.00
Utah, sugar bowl, w/lid 40.00
Utah, tumbler 37.50
Valencia Waffle, basket, clear w/gold 38.00
Valencia Waffle, butter dish, gr 58.00
Valencia Waffle, relish, amber, 9x5⅜" 22.50
Vermont, creamer, gr w/gold 65.00
Vermont, pitcher, water; gr w/gold 130.00
Vermont, tumbler, clear w/gold 25.00
Viking, bowl, 8" sq 48.00
Viking, butter dish, frosted 75.00
Viking relish 20.00
Waffle, celery vase 75.00
Waffle, goblet 85.00
Waffle, wine, flint 130.00
Waffle & Thumbprint, champagne, flint 120.00
Waffle & Thumbprint, goblet, flint 95.00
Waffle & Thumbprint, tumbler, bar; flint 95.00
Washington, celery vase, flint 125.00
Washington, honey dish, 3½" 32.00
Washington, salt cellar, master; rnd, flint 37.50
Washington Centennial, egg cup 42.50
Washington Centennial, wine 48.00
Westward Ho, bowl, ftd, 5" 140.00
Westward Ho, creamer 125.00
Westward Ho, pickle dish, oval 68.00
Westward Ho, sugar bowl, w/lid 195.00
Wheat & Barley, mug, amber 30.00
Wheat & Barley, spooner 25.00
Wheat & Barley, tumbler 22.50
Wildflower, champagne, bl 80.00
Wildflower, creamer, bl 37.50
Willow Oak, celery vase, amber 38.00
Willow Oak, creamer, bl 55.00
Willow Oak, tumbler 38.00
Willow Oak, tumbler, bl 62.50
Windflower, creamer 38.00
Wisconsin, banana stand 72.50
Wisconsin, bowl, 6½" 30.00
Wisconsin, compote, tricornered, ftd, 4x7" 25.00
Wisconsin, tumbler 40.00
Wooden Pail, pitcher 100.00
Wooden Pail, sugar bowl, amethyst, mini 25.00
Wyoming, cake stand, high std, 9" 55.00
Wyoming, relish tray 25.00
Wyoming, tumbler, water 27.50
X-Ray, compote, jelly; gr 45.00
X-Ray, goblet 22.50
X-Ray, tumbler 20.00
X-Ray, tumbler, amethyst 45.00
Yale, bowl, 10" 34.00
Yale, butter dish 55.00
Yale, creamer 70.00
Yale, tumbler 28.00
Zipper, compote, w/lid, 8" dia 48.00
Zipper, goblet 25.00
Zipper, pitcher, water 55.00
Zipper, sugar bowl, w/lid 55.00

Paul Revere Pottery

The Saturday Evening Girls were a social group of young Boston ladies who met to pursue various activities, among them pottery making. Their first kiln was bought in 1906, and within a few years it became necessary to move to a larger location. Because their new quarters were near the historical Old North Church, they chose the name Paul Revere Pottery. With very little training, the girls produced only simple ware. Until 1915 the pottery operated at a deficit, then a new building with four kilns was constructed on Nottingham Road. Vases, miniature jugs, children's tea sets, tiles, dinnerware, and lamps were produced, usually in soft matt glazes often decorated with incised, hand-painted designs from nature. Examples in a dark high gloss may also be found on occasion.

Several marks were used: 'P.R.P.'; 'S.E.G.'; or the circular device, 'Boston, Paul Revere Pottery' with the horse and rider.

The pottery continued to operate; and even though their product sold well, the high production costs of the handmade ware caused the pottery to fail in 1946.

Ashtray, 1897 EHS 1937 commemorative, bls, PRP/5-37, 5¼" dia ..100.00
Bowl, buttercup yel & chicory bl runs on dk bl, logo, 3x7½" 225.00
Bowl, centerpc; geometric border, SEG/12-11/TB, 4x10" 550.00
Bowl, cereal; hens & chicks, yel & wht, 241-4-09/FL, 1¾x6", EX ..750.00
Bowl, chicks trio on ivory ground, PRP/10-34, 2x4¼" 550.00
Bowl, gr gloss w/red tinted rim, SEG 323/SJM, 3⅜x4½" 165.00
Bowl, lotus on yel, SEG/TM, 1½x5" 225.00
Bowl, maroon-mauve w/lustre, flared mouth, Revere logo, 3¼x5¾" ...150.00
Bowl, porridge; dancing rabbits, bl band, SEG/3-1-11/TB, 5½" ...2,400.00

Bowl, white rabbits on yellow, 265-3-11/IG/SEG, 1911, 2¼x5½", repair, $700.00.

Breakfast set, crouching rabbit, SEG/7-22/L?, 3-pc 1,300.00
Cup & saucer, landscapes, Eva Geneco, SEG/12-19/EG/6-17 ....250.00
Inkwell, sailing ships on bl w/wht sky, SEG/3-14/SG, 2x4" 1,600.00
Inkwell, trees landscape, brn & bl, paper label, 2x2½x2¾" 850.00
Mug, Benjamin His Mug, swan scene, PRP/6-1934, 3⅛x4¼" 475.00
Nut dish, landscape, dk bl sky, SEG/2-12-14/JG, ¾x3" dia 250.00
Paperweight, Revere on horse, mc w/gr field/bl sky, SEG/5-14/FL, 3" ..900.00
Pitcher, chicks trio, PRP/10-34, 3⅛x3¾" 550.00
Plate, chicks trio, yel border, ivory ground, SEG/3-21/RB, 6½" .600.00
Plate, cottage & lansdscape, S/1922, 6½" 500.00
Plate, ducks, wht on bl band, logo/2-26/JMD, 6¼" 500.00
Plate, goose, Sara Galner, SEG/3-14/EG, 7½" 1,300.00
Plate, landscape amid bl borders, SEG/4-21/FL, 8", NM 425.00
Plate, pigs border, mc on ivory, SEG/241-4-09/FL, 8½" 2,700.00
Plate, pine cones & pine needles on rope bkground, SEG/2-17/EG, 7¾" ...225.00
Plate, rabbit in dress, sm rstr, PRP logo, 6½" 1,600.00
Plate, stylized rooster, bl & wht bands, PRP logo/12-29/LS/EB, 7¾" ...425.00
Plate, trees, gr/brn on dk bl, SEG/7-14/AM, 7½" 350.00
Tankard, bl-gr matt, 7½x9½"+6 mugs 550.00
Tea caddy, bl semi-matt, flared lid, stamped, 4" 150.00
Tea caddy, iris band, mc on brn & gr, SEG/11-14, 4x3½", EX ..1,200.00
Tile, windmill scene, 8-sided, SEG/8-14/SG, 2½" dia 900.00
Vase, abstract landscape, gr/wht/gray, 3-22/SEG/EG, 5¼x4½" ..1,400.00
Vase, daffodils & long gr leaves, bl sky, cream band, 4-24, 10" ...3,500.00
Vase, lt bl matt, SEG 7-26, 9⅞" 400.00
Vase, robin's egg bl, swirling form, PRP/11-20, 8¾x7¼" 400.00
Vase, robin's egg bl matt, bulbous, SEG, 1919, 7½" 200.00
Vase, tulips on bl band, imp logo/EB/10-23, 4½x3¾" 1,000.00
Wall pocket, dk sage gr pocket form, SEG, paper label, 4x6" 300.00

Pauline Pottery

Pauline Pottery was made from 1883 to 1888 in Chicago, Illinois, from clay imported from the Ohio area. The company's founder was Mrs. Pauline Jacobus, who had learned the trade at the Rookwood Pottery. Mrs. Jacobus moved to Edgerton, Wisconsin, to be near a source of suitable clay, thus eliminating shipping expenses. Until 1905 she produced high-quality wares, able to imitate with ease designs and styles of such masters as Wedgwood and Meissen. Her products were sold through leading department stores, and the names of some of these firms may appear on the ware. Not all are marked; unless signed by a noted local artist, positive identification is often impossible. Marked examples carry a variety of stamps and signatures: 'Trade Mark' with a crown, 'Pauline Pottery,' and 'Edgerton Art Pottery' are but a few.

Vase, applied flowers and leaves, gold on mottled brown, stick neck, 10½", EX, $600.00.

Vase, HP floral swags on ochre/yel gloss, 4-lobe rim, 8x7" 425.00
Vase, 3 panels w/HP flowers, cream/brn/gold outlines, 9", EX 170.00

Peachblow

Peachblow, made to imitate the colors of the Chinese Peachbloom porcelain, was made by several glasshouses in the late 1800s. Among them were New England Glass, Mt. Washington, Webb, and Hobbs, Brockunier and Company (Wheeling). Its pink shading was achieved through action of the heat on the gold content of the glass. While New England's peachblow shades from deep crimson to white, Mt. Washington's tends to shade from pink to blue-gray. Many pieces were enameled and gilded. While by far the majority of the pieces made by New England had a satin (acid) finish, they made shiny peachblow as well. Wheeling glass, on the other hand, is rarely found in satin. In the 1950s Gundersen-Pairpoint Glassworks initiated the reproduction of Mt. Washington peachblow, using an exact duplication of the original formula. Though of recent manufacture, this glass is very collectible. Our advisors for this category are Betty and Clarence Maier; they are listed in the Directory under Pennsylvania.

Bottle, scent; Webb, floral/butterfly/insect, 5½x4" dia 850.00
Bowl, bride's; crimped rim; ornate Manhattan SP fr, 11½x10½" ...800.00
Candlestick, Gundersen, rolled socket edge, 8" 365.00
Celery, NE Glass, shiny, sq/scalloped rim, 6½" 650.00
Celery, NE Glass, thin walls, EX color, 7" 750.00
Compote, Gundersen, swirled stem, flared rim, 7½" 250.00
Cracker barrel, Webb, gold peacock on floral vine, rope hdl, SP trim .525.00
Creamer, NE Glass, World's Fair 1893 in gold, 2½" 500.00
Cruet, Gundersen, ribbed hdl, 8" 850.00
Cruet, NE Glass, EX color (shiny), wht stopper, bulbous body ...1,585.00
Cruet, NE Glass, 3-lobe top, petticoat form, 6¾" 1,800.00
Cruet, Wheeling, cut amber stopper 1,250.00
Cup, punch; Wheeling, appl amber hdl, 2½" 300.00
Decanter, Gundersen, spherical w/long neck, 10" 645.00
Decanter, Wheeling, faceted stopper, twist hdl, rnd body, 9½" ..2,500.00
Finger bowl, Wheeling, 4½" 200.00
Goblet, Gundersen, Burmese base, 7" 275.00
Pear, NE Glass, full stem, World's Fair 175.00
Pear, NE Glass, shiny, 5" 150.00
Pear, Wheeling, stem nearly intact, 4¾" 850.00
Pitcher, lemonade; Wheeling, satin (rare), tankard, 11" 3,450.00
Pitcher, Wheeling, Drape, ruffled rim, clear reeded hdl, 5¼" 475.00
Pitcher, Wheeling, sq mouth, amber hdl, 4" 450.00
Pitcher, Wheeling, 7½" 1,400.00
Rose bowl, Webb, bulbous, rigaree collar, wishbone base, 6" 200.00
Spooner, NE Glass, sqd top 800.00
Sugar shaker, Wheeling, shiny, 5" 2,500.00
Toothpick holder, NE Glass, tricon rim 375.00
Toothpick holder, Wheeling 1,150.00
Tumbler, NE Glass, EX color, 3¾" 400.00
Tumbler, Wheeling, Drape, 3½" 250.00
Tumbler, Wheeling, 3⅞" 385.00
Vase, Gundersen, urn form w/M hdls, sq ped ft, 9" 535.00
Vase, Gundersen, wide/flaring rim, pinched body, 5x6" 500.00
Vase, lily; Gundersen, EX color, 9" 400.00
Vase, lily; NE Glass, scarce sz, 6½" 635.00
Vase, lily; NE Glass, shiny, 8¼" 575.00
Vase, lily; NE Glass, wht wafer base, EX color, 7" 945.00
Vase, lily; NE Glass, 12" 985.00
Vase, lily; NE Glass, 19" 1,200.00
Vase, Morgan; Hobbs Brockunier, plastic griffin stand, 9" 1,450.00
Vase, Morgan; Wheeling, orig griffin holder, 10x3½", NM 2,800.00
Vase, NE Glass, bulbous w/long neck & cup lip, 10½" 1,200.00
Vase, NE Glass, long neck, dimpled body, 10½" 1,400.00
Vase, Webb, gold prunus, long neck, bulbous base, 10" 875.00

Vase, Webb, gold prunus/butterflies, gourd shape, 11" 745.00
Vase, Webb, shiny, irregular crimped rim, 3-ftd, 4¾" 125.00
Vase, Webb, tapered, 6" 125.00
Vase, Wheeling, bulbous, sm neck, 3½" 400.00
Vase, Wheeling, dbl-gourd form, 7½" 900.00
Vase, Wheeling, shouldered, 13" 1,750.00
Vase, Wheeling, stick neck, 8" 875.00
Wine, Gundersen, shiny, 5" 165.00

Peloton

Peloton glass was first made by Wilhelm Kralik in Bohemia in 1880. This unusual art glass was produced by rolling colored threads onto the transparent or opaque glass gather as it was removed from the furnace. Usually more than one color of threading was used, and some items were further decorated with enameling. It was made with both shiny and acid finishes.

Pitcher, clear with multicolor strings, 9", from $350.00 to $400.00.

Biscuit jar, wht/yel/bl/pk strings, HP bird, ribbed, 7x6½" 785.00
Bowl, brn/yel strings, ribbed, 3 clear ft, 8-point top, 6x6½" 300.00
Bowl, mc strings on wht, clear petal ft & 4-peak rim, 3¾" 285.00
Bowl, pastel strings on shaded bl, clear ft, pulled rim, 4" 385.00
Lamp, banquet; rainbow, mc strings, marble base, 17½" 450.00
Lamp, banquet; ribbed font w/mc strings, brass stem, marble base, 19" 500.00
Rose bowl, variegated brn strings, ribbed/swirled, 6x5½" 300.00
Vase, mc strings on pk to wht, pinched top, ribbed, 2¾x3" 400.00
Vase, mc strings on wht, bulbous, tricorner top, 4x4¾" 275.00

Pennsbury

Established in the 1950s in Morrisville, Pennsylvania, by Henry Below, the Pennsbury Pottery produced dinnerware and novelty items, much of which was sold in gift shops along the Pennsylvania Turnpike. Henry and his wife, Lee, worked for years at the Stangl Pottery before striking out on their own. Lee and her daughter were the artists responsible for many of the early pieces, the bird figures among them. Pennsbury pottery was hand painted, some in blue on white, some in multicolor on caramel. Pennsylvania Dutch motifs, Amish couples, and barbershop singers were among their most popular decorative themes. Sgraffito (hand incising), was used extensively. The company marked their wares 'Pennsbury Pottery' or 'Pennsbury Pottery, Morrisville, PA.'

In October of 1969 the company closed. Contents of the pottery were sold in December of the following year, and in April of 1971, the buildings burned to the ground. Items marked Pennsbury Glenview or Stumar Pottery (or these marks in combination) were made by Glenview after 1969. Pieces manufactured after 1976 were made by the Pennington Pottery. Several of the old molds still exist, and the original Pennsbury Caramel process is still being used on novelty items, some of which are produced by Lewis Brothers, New Jersey. Production of Pennsbury dinnerware was not resumed after the closing. Our advisor for this category is Shirley Graff; she is listed in the Directory under Ohio. Note: Prices may be higher in some areas of the country — particularly on the East Coast, the southern states, and Texas. Values for examples in the Rooster pattern apply to both black and red variations.

Ashtray, Pennsbury Inn, 8" 45.00
Ashtray, Summerseat, commemorative pc, 5" dia 30.00
Bank, jug shape, Stuff Me, pig decor, 7" 150.00
Bowl, Dutch Talk, 9" 90.00
Bowl, pretzel; Amish, 12x8" 85.00
Butter dish, Hex, 5x4" 45.00
Candle holder, Holly, 5½" 45.00
Coaster, Quartet, face of Shultz, 5" 20.00
Coffeepot, Rooster, 2-cup, 6" 55.00
Compote, Holly, 5" 45.00
Cup & saucer, Hex 30.00
Desk basket, National Exchange Club, 5" 40.00
Dispensers, vinegar & oil; Amish, 7", pr 150.00
Display sign, Pennsbury Pottery, bird on top, 5x4½" 175.00
Egg cup, Rooster, 4" 20.00
Figurine, Barn Swallow, #123, 6¼" 185.00
Figurine, Blue Bird, #103, sgn, 4" 150.00
Figurine, Cardinal, #120, sgn, 6½" 375.00
Figurine, Chickadee, #111, sgn, 3½" 110.00
Figurine, Gold Finch, #102, sgn 150.00
Figurine, Marsh Wren, #106, sgn, 6½" 120.00
Figurine, Wren, #109, 3" 150.00
Letter holder, Neshaminy Woods 55.00
Mug, beer; Eagle, 5" 35.00
Mug, coffee; Amish, 3¼" 30.00
Mug, coffee; Quartet, face of Olson, 3¼" 35.00
Mug, coffee; Red Barn, 3¼" 35.00
Pie pan, boy & girl, 9" 85.00
Pie pan, mother serving pie, 9" 85.00
Pie pan, Rooster, 9" 55.00
Pitcher, Folkart, mini, 2½" 30.00
Pitcher, Hex, 6¼" 65.00
Plaque, Groundhog Lodge #9 on the Deep Run, commemorative, 5" ...35.00
Plaque, Mercury Dime, 8" dia 65.00
Plaque, River Steamboat, 13½x10¼" 95.00
Plaque, Swallow the Insult, 6" dia 50.00
Plaque, The Flying Cloud, dtd 1851, 9½x7" 75.00
Plaque, Walking to Homestead, 6" 40.00
Plaque, Washington Cossing the Delaware, 5" 25.00
Plate, Bible Reading, w/o primary colors, 9" 75.00
Plate, Blue Dowery, 10" 35.00
Plate, Chatting, 8" 65.00
Plate, Christmas 1961, Treetops 45.00
Plate, Rooster, 10" 35.00
Plate, Two Birds Over Heart, 11" 85.00
Platter, Rooster, oval, 11" 48.00
Sugar bowl, Rooster, w/lid 40.00
Tray, cigarette; Eagle, sculptured in relief, 7½x5" 40.00
Tray, Laurel Ridge, 8½x5¼" 40.00
Tray, novelty; Colt 31 Caliber, 7½x5" 50.00
Tray, relish; Tulips, triangular, 3-section, 14½x11½" 95.00
Wall pocket, sailing ship w/brn border, 6½" 65.00

Pens and Pencils

The first metallic writing pen was patented in 1809, and soon machine-produced pens with steel nibs gradually began replacing the quill. The first fountain pen was invented in 1830, but due to the fact that the ink flow was not consistent (though leakage was), they were not manufactured commercially until the 1880s. The first successful commercial producers were Waterman in 1884 and Parker with the Lucky Curve in 1888.

The self-filling pen of the early 1900s featured the soft, interior sack which filled with ink as the metal bar on the outside of the pen was raised and lowered. Variations of the pumping mechanism were tried until 1932 when Parker introduced the Vacumatic, a sackless pen with an internal pump.

For more information we recommend *Fountain Pens, Past & Present,* by Paul Erano (Collector Books). Our advisor for this category is Gary Lehrer; he is listed in the Directory under Connecticut. For those seeking additional information, catalogs are published by our advisor as well as the Pen Fanciers, whose address can be found in the Directory under Clubs, Newsletters, and Catalogs.

Key:

AF — aeromatic filler	GPT — gold-plated trim
BF — button filler	HR — hard rubber
CF — capillary filler	LF — lever filler
CPT — chrome-plated trim	NPT — nickel-plated trim
ED — eyedropper filler	PF — plunger filler
GFM — gold-filled metal	TD — touchdown filler
GFT — gold-filled trim	VF — vacumatic filler

Fountain Pens

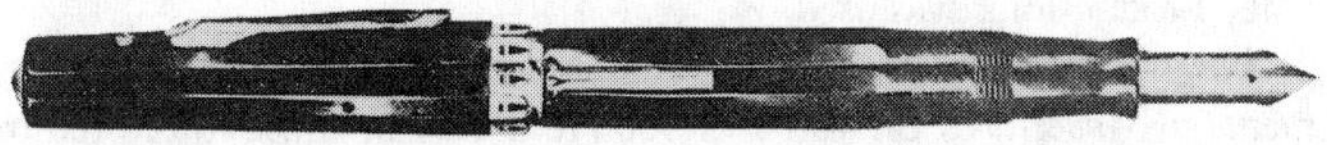

Eversharp Gold Seal Doric pen, 1940, black with gold-filled trim, lever filler, EX, $350.00. **(Photo courtesy Judy and Cliff Lawrence)**

Conklin #3, 1915, blk HR, GF 4-leaf clover o/l, crescent filler, NM 1,100.00
Conklin #25P, 1918, blk chased HR, GFT, crescent filler, EX ...175.00
Conklin Nozac, 1931, silver pearl stripes, 14 sides, wht GFT, LF, EX ...200.00
Conklin Nozac, 1934, 7M Word Gauge, blk, LF, GFT, NM 400.00
Conklin Nozac, 1934, 7M Word Gauge, red/silver herringbone, LF/GFT, NM .1,000.00
Conklin Sr Endura, 1929, blk, GFT, LF, NM 400.00
Conklin Sr Endura, 1929, sapphire bl, GFT, LF, NM 650.00
Conway Stewart, 1948, emerald marble, GFT, LF, G 65.00
Diamond Point #8, 1931, gold marble, GFT, LF, EX 125.00
Eversharp Bantam, 1932, gr swirl marble, GFT, AF, EX 50.00
Gold Medal #8, 1925, red mottle, HR, GFT, LF, NM 175.00
Moore L-79, 1923, blk chased HR, GFT, LF, MIB 125.00
Moore L-93, 1929, burgundy, GFT, LF, NM 200.00
Moore L-96, 1929, burgundy, GFT, LF, NM 550.00
Parker Duofold Jr, 1927, red, GFT, BF, NM 125.00
Parker Duofold Jr, 1927, yel, GFT, BF, NM 350.00
Parker Duofold Jr, 1929, blk, GFT, BF, EX 125.00
Parker Duofold Jr, 1933, burgundy red & blk marble, GFT, BF, EX ..120.00
Parker Duofold Jr, 1941, gold, gr & blk stripes, GFT, VF, EX 85.00
Parker Duofold Jr, 1942, red, pearl & blk, GFT, VF, EX 85.00
Parker Duofold Sr, 1927, red, GFT, BF, NM 225.00
Parker Duofold Sr, 1927, yel, GFT, BF, NM 1,500.00
Parker Duofold Sr, 1928, blk, GFT, BF, EX 300.00
Parker Duofold Sr, 1928, red, GFT, BF, slight wear, o/w EX 250.00
Parker Lady Duofold, 1923, blk HR, GFT, lg imprint, BF, EX 150.00
Parker Lady Duofold, 1926, Mandarin Yel, GFT, BF, EX 250.00
Parker Lady Duofold, 1926, red, GFT, BF, EX 100.00
Parker Lady Duofold, 1927, red, GFT, BF, NM 100.00
Parker Lady Duofold, 1927, yel, GFT, BF, NM 200.00
Parker Lady Duofold, 1929, Gr Jade, GFT, BF, M 125.00
Parker Lady Duofold, 1929, red, GFT, BF, EX 100.00
Parker Lucky Curve #12, 1904, blk HR w/MOP & gold bands, EX ...2,000.00
Parker Lucky Curve #16, 1907, GFM filigree over blk HR, ED, EX 750.00
Parker Lucky Curve #41, 1906, GFM filigree over blk HR, ED, EX ...1,800.00
Parker Lucky Curve Blk Giant, 1916, blk HR, GFT, ED, EX .2,000.00
Parker Vacumatic, silver pearl stripes, wht GFT, VF, EX 85.00
Parker Vacumatic, 1937, brn stripes, GFT, oversz, NM 450.00
Parker Vacumatic, 1940, brn stripes, GFT, std sz, NM 100.00
Parker Vacumatic (Canadian), silver pearl stripes, wht GFT, VF, EX ...85.00
Parker Vacumatic Debutante, 1940, brn stripes, GFT, NM 100.00
Parker Vacumatic Jr, 1934, red marbleized, GFT, VF, EX 150.00
Parker Vacumatic Jr, 1947, silver pearl stripes, wht GFT, VF, NM 85.00
Parker Vacumatic Major, 1937, blk, GFT, VF, EX 125.00
Parker Vacumatic Slender Maxima, 1940, brn stripes, GFT, NM ...300.00
Parker Vacumatic Sr Maxima, 1940, brn stripes, GFT, NM 400.00
Parker 51, 1942, Cordovan Brn w/sterling caps, GFT, VF, EX ...200.00
Parker 51, 1946, blk, w/GFM cap, GFT, VF, EX 125.00
Parker 51, 1947, gray, Lustraloy cap, wht GFT, VF, G 60.00
Parker 51 Demonstrator, 1947, transparent bbl/shell, GFT, M ...300.00
Parker 51 Special, 1954, bl w/Lustraloy cap, wht GFT, AF, EX 45.00
Parker 51 Vac-Fill, 1942, blk, dbl-jeweled, GF cap, NM 225.00
Parker 51 Vac-Fill, 1942, Yellowstone, dbl-jeweled, GF cap, NM ..450.00
Parker 75, 1965, sterling, GFT, AF, M 200.00
Parker 75, 1975, sterling, GFT, AF, M 150.00
Parker 75, 1977, vermeil, GFT, AF, M 275.00
Postal Reservoir, 1928, brn marble, GFT, AF, EX 125.00
Reynolds #400 Ballpoint, 1946, blk & silver, GFT, dried up M in pkg ..100.00
Sheaffer #2, 1919, self-filling, blk HR, GFM, GFT, LF, clip, NM 275.00
Sheaffer #2, 1919, self-filling, blk HR, GFM, GFT, LF, ring top, NM ..125.00
Sheaffer #3, 1935, ebonized pearl marbleized, GFT, LF, EX 75.00
Sheaffer #350, 1949, red stripes, GFT, LF, EX 80.00
Sheaffer Feathertouch, 1940, red stripes, GFT, LF, EX 50.00
Sheaffer Lifetime Balance, 1929, blk, GFT, LF, lg, NM 175.00
Sheaffer Lifetime Balance, 1929, blk, GFT, LF, std sz, NM 100.00
Sheaffer Lifetime Balance, 1929, blk & pearl, GFT, LF, lg, NM ...375.00
Sheaffer Lifetime Balance, 1929, blk & pearl, GFT, LF, std sz, NM ...175.00
Sheaffer Lifetime Flat Top, 1927, blk, GFT, LF, lg, NM 175.00
Sheaffer Lifetime Flat Top, 1927, blk, GFT, LF, std sz, NM 100.00
Sheaffer Lifetime Vigilant, 1942, gold pearl stripes, GFT, LF, EX ..100.00
Sheaffer Masterpiece Triumph, 1942, solid 14k, LF, M 450.00
Sheaffer PFM I Snorkel, 1959, maroon, CPT, NM 150.00
Sheaffer PFM II Snorkel, 1959, maroon, brushed steel cap, NM ..200.00
Sheaffer PFM III Snorkel, 1959, maroon, GFT, NM 225.00
Sheaffer PFM IV Snorkel, 1959, polished chrome cap, NM 375.00
Sheaffer PFM V Snorkel, 1959, maroon, GFM cap, NM 325.00
Sheaffer Targa Ballpoint, 1976, GFM, GFT, M 35.00
Sheaffer Triumph TM, 1951, gr, GFT, TD, EX 50.00
Wahl Deco-Band, 1927, gr & bronze, GFT, LF, oversz, NM 700.00
Wahl Deco-Band, 1927, Jade, GFT, LF, oversz, NM 800.00
Wahl Gold Seal Personal Point, 1927, Lapis, GFT, LF, NM 450.00
Wahl Gold Seal Personal Point, 1927, Rosewood, GFT, LF, NM ..300.00
Wahl-Eversharp Gold Seal Doric, 1940, blk, GFT, LF, oversz, EX 600.00
Wahl-Eversharp Skyline Presentation, 1946, gray, GFM/GFT, LF, EX ...125.00
Wahl-Eversharp 1928, desk, brn woodgrain HR, GFT, LF, EX ...100.00
Waterman, 1941, pearl marble, NPT, LF, G 45.00
Waterman, 1942, gold marble, NPT, LF, G 45.00
Waterman #52, 1923, red ripple, GFT, LF, NM 150.00
Waterman #54, 1923, red ripple, GFT, LF, NM 175.00
Waterman #56, 1923, red ripple, GFT, LF, NM 375.00
Waterman #58, 1923, red ripple, GFT, LF, NM 1,750.00
Waterman #452, 1915, blk HR, sterling silver filigree o/l, lg, NM ..450.00
Waterman Ideal #7, 1927, red ripple, HR, GFT, purple nib/band, LF, NM 300.00

Waterman Ideal #12 SF, 1908, sleeve fill, blk HR, AF, rare 250.00
Waterman Ideal #514S Safety, 1908, solid 14k filigree, ED, M 1,100.00
Waterman Ideal #52, 1923, blk chased HR, NPT, LF, EX 85.00
Waterman Ideal #52½V, 1925, red mottle, HR, GFT, LF, ring top, G 50.00
Waterman Ideal #52V, 1925, blk chased HR, NPT, LF, EX 85.00
Waterman Ideal #52V, 1926, red ripple, clip, HR, GFT, LF, EX .125.00
Waterman Ideal Lady Patricia, 1932, Nacre, wht GFT, LF, EX ..135.00
Waterman Patrician, 1931, Onyx (red cream), GFT, LF, NM ...1,000.00
Waterman Patrician, 1931, turq, GFT, LF, NM 1,750.00
Waterman 100 Year, 1939, red, GFT, LF, military clip, NM 600.00
Waterman 100 Year, 1941, blk, GFT, LF, std sz, EX 135.00

Mechanical Pencils

Conklin Endura, 1927, sapphire marble, GFT, lg, EX 180.00
Eversharp, 1925, GFM, GFT, EX 30.00
Eversharp, 1925, sterling, EX 75.00
Eversharp, 1927, woodgrain HR, GFT, EX 35.00
Eversharp Coronet Repeater, 1936, gr marble, chrome top, CPT, G ..45.00
Eversharp Repeater, 1936, bl striped w/chrome top, CPT, G 25.00
Eversharp Repeater, 1943, maroon w/red striped top, GFT, EX 25.00
Eversharp Repeater, 1944, brn, GFT, EX 22.00
Eversharp Repeater, 1944, brn or gr, GFT, M 25.00
Parker, 1924, red enameled metal, GFT, NM 35.00
Parker Duofold, 1930, Gr Jade marble, GFT, EX 50.00
Parker Duofold Deluxe, 1929, Modern Blk & pearl marble, GFT, EX ...75.00
Parker Duofold Jr, 1924, blk HR, GFT, perfect crown, NM 60.00
Parker Duofold Jr, 1930, burgundy & blk marble, GFT, EX 90.00
Parker Duofold Sr, 1928, Mandarin Yel, GFT, perfect color/crown, NM ..350.00
Parker Duofold Sr, 1930, Gr Jade marble, GFT, EX 150.00
Parker Pastel, 1927, Naples Bl, GFT, EX 65.00
Parker Vacumatic, 1935, burgundy red & blk marble, GFT, EX ...90.00
Parker Vacumatic, 1941, gold stripes, GFT, EX 65.00
Parker Vacumatic, 1942, emerald stripes, GFT, EX 65.00
Parker 51, 1942, blk w/16k GFM top, solid 14k clip & point, M ...175.00
Parker 51, 1946, blk w/GFM, GFT, price sticker, M 100.00
Parker 51, 1946, blk w/GFM top, GFT, M 50.00
Parker 51, 1946, Cordovan Brn w/16k GFM top, GFT, M 50.00
Parker 51, 1949, blk, GFM cap, GFT, AF, G 50.00
Parker 51 Repeater, 1949, bl, Lustraloy top, wht GFT, sticker, M ...35.00
Sheaffer, 1934, blk, wht GFT, EX 20.00
Sheaffer, 1934, gold stripes, GFT, EX 30.00
Sheaffer, 1934, silver pearl stripes, wht GFT, EX 30.00
Sheaffer Sr Balance, 1930, pearl & blk marble, GFT, EX 100.00
Sheaffer Sr Balance, 1932, emerald marble, GFT, EX 150.00
Sheaffer Targa, 1976, sterling, M 90.00
Waterman, 1934, red streaked pearl marble, GFT, M 35.00
Waterman Crusader Repeater, bl w/gold-silver top, NPT, M 30.00
Waterman Ideal #0721 VN, 1920, blk HR, GFT, M 72.00
Waterman Patrician, 1933, turq (bl-gr marble), GFT, M 275.00
Waterman 100 Year, 1940, red, GFT, EX 150.00

Personalities, Fact and Fiction

One of the largest and most popular areas of collecting today is character-related memorabilia. Everyone has favorites, whether they be comic-strip personalities or true-life heroes. The earliest comic strip dealt with the adventures of the Yellow Kid, the smiling, bald-headed Oriental boy always in a nightshirt. He was introduced in 1895, a product of the imagination of Richard Fenton Outcault. Today, though very hard to come by, items relating to the Yellow Kid bring premium prices.

Though her 1923 introduction was unobtrusively made through only one newspaper, New York's *Daily News*, Little Orphan Annie, the vacant-eyed redhead in the inevitable red dress, was quickly adopted by hordes of readers nationwide, and before the demise of her creator, Harold Gray, in 1968, she had starred in her own radio show. She made two feature films, and in 1977 'Annie' was launched on Broadway.

Other early comic figures were Moon Mullins, created in 1923 by Frank Willard; Buck Rogers by Philip Nowlan in 1928; and Betty Boop, the round-faced, innocent-eyed, chubby-cheeked Boop-Boop-a-Doop girl of the early 1930s. Bimbo was her dog and KoKo her clown friend.

Popeye made his debut in 1929 as the spinach-eating sailor with the spindly-limbed girlfriend, Olive Oyl, in the comic strip *Thimble Theatre*, created by Elzie Segar. He became a film star in 1933 and had his own radio show that during 1936 played three times a week on CBS. He obligingly modeled for scores of toys, dolls, and figurines, and especially those from the '30s are very collectible.

Tarzan, created around 1930 by Edgar Rice Burroughs, and Captain Midnight, by Robert Burtt and Willfred G. Moore, are popular heroes with today's collectors. During the days of radio, Sky King of the Flying Crown Ranch (also created by Burtt and Moore) thrilled boys and girls of the mid-1940s. Hopalong Cassidy, Red Rider, Tom Mix, and the Lone Ranger were only a few of the other 'good guys' always on the side of law and order.

But of all the fictional heroes and comic characters collected today, probably the best loved and most well known is Mickey Mouse. Created in the late 1920s by Walt Disney, Micky (as his name was first spelled) became an instant success with his film debut, Steamboat Willie. His popularity was parlayed through wind-up toys, watches, figurines, cookie jars, puppets, clothing, and numerous other products. Items from the 1930s are usually copyrighted 'Walt Disney Enterprises'; thereafter, 'Walt Disney Productions' was used.

For more information we recommend *Schroeder's Collectible Toys, Antique to Modern,* by Sharon and Bob Huxford. For those interested in Disneyana, we recommend *Stern's Guide to Disney Collectibles* (there are three in the series), and *The Collector's Encyclopedia of Disneyana* by David Longest and Michael Stern. *Cartoon Toys & Collectibles* by David Longest; *Collector's Guide to TV Toys & Memorabilia, Second Edition,* by Greg Davis and Bill Morgan; *Roy Rogers and Dale Evans Toys and Memorabilia* by P. Allan Coyle; *Collector's Reference & Value Guide to the Lone Ranger* by Lee Felbinger; and *G-Men and FBI Toys and Collectibles* by Harry and Jody Whitworth are other great publications. All are available from Collector Books.

See also Autographs; Banks; Big Little Books; Children's Books; Comic Books; Cookie Jars; Dolls; Games; Lunch Boxes; Movie Memorabilia; Paper Dolls; Pin-Back Buttons; Posters; Puzzles; Rock 'N Roll Memorabilia; Toys.

Cinderella wristwatch, US Time, 1951, MIB, from $250.00 to $300.00. (Photo courtesy Dunbar Gallery)

Addams Family, gumball machine, w/1" plastic figures/photos, M .25.00
Addams Family, hand puppet, Gomez, cloth/vinyl, Ideal, 1964, EX ..75.00
Alice in Wonderland, tea set, china, 11-pc, Plasco, MIB 150.00
Alice in Wonderland, wristwatch, pk fabric strap, Ingersoll, EXIB ...250.00
Alvin & the Chipmunks, bank, Alvin, plastic, NM 12.00
Alvin & the Chipmunks, kite, Roalex, 1960s, MIP 65.00
Annie Oakley, doll, plastic w/outfit, Kellogg's, 1955, 8", EX 25.00

Annie Oakley, wristwatch, blk leather strap, New Haven, 1951, EX ..200.00
Archies, ring, sterling silver, MIB (w/certificate) 185.00
Bambi, push-button puppet, Kohner, 1960s, NM 40.00
Banana Splits, harmonica, Larami, 1973, MOC 45.00
Batman, bank, ceramic figure, NPPI, 1966, NM 90.00
Batman, bank, vinyl figure, Transogram, 1966, 20", VG 45.00
Batman, banner, Batman Vs the Riddler, cloth, 1966, 27", EX ..100.00
Batman, belt, blk vinyl w/brass buckle, Morris Belt, 1966, MOC ..50.00
Batman, bicycle ornament, plastic figure, Empire, 1966, MOC ...50.00
Batman, figure set, plastic, 3-pc, Ideal, 1966, 3", NMIP 125.00
Batman, helmet & cape, plastic/vinyl, Ideal, 1966, MIB 250.00
Batman, kite, inflatable vinyl, Sky, 1974, 45", MIP 45.00
Batman, pencil sharpener, plastic figure, 1975, 3", EX 15.00
Batman, pin, Zonk!, purple border, 1966, MOC 45.00
Batman, sunglasses, blk plastic bat design w/sticker, 1966, EX 25.00
Batman, wallet, yel vinyl/color image, Standard Plastics, 1966, NM 50.00
Batman & Robin, figure set, hard rubber/bat bases, 1960s-70s, 4", EX ..45.00
Battlestar Galactica, wallet, silver vinyl, Larami, 1978, MOC 20.00
Beany & Cecil, Cartoon Kit, Colorforms, 1960s, complete, EXIB ..125.00
Ben Casey, bobbin' head, NM 125.00
Betty Boop, figure, chalkware, 14", NM 275.00
Betty Boop, figure, jtd wood, Jaymar, 1930s, 4", M 100.00
Betty Boop, ukelele, wood w/silkscreened image, 21", NM 250.00
Bionic Woman, bank, plastic, BW on rock pile, Animals Plus, 1970, NM ..45.00
Bionic Woman, tattoos & stickers, Kenner, 1976, MIP 20.00
Blondie & Dagwood, blocks, paper on wood, Gaston, 1950s, VG (G box) ...25.00
Blondie & Dagwood, marionette, Dagwood, Hazelle's, 1950s, MIB 250.00
Bozo the Clown, alarm clock, Larry Harmon/French, 1960s, rare, EX 150.00
Bozo the Clown, bank, plastic, 1972, lg, NM 35.00
Bozo the Clown, Decal Decorator Kit, Meyercord, 1950s, EXIB ..40.00
Bozo the Clown, wristwatch, Bradley, 1960s, EX 75.00
Brady Bunch, Fan Club Kit, Tiger Beat, 1972, MIB, from $150 to ...200.00
Buck Rogers, badge, Solar Scout, 1930s, NM 115.00
Buck Rogers, figures, lead, set of 3, Cocomalt, 1932, 3", VG 650.00
Buck Rogers, map of solar system, fr, Cocomalt, 1933, EX 935.00
Buck Rogers, Midget Caster Set, 1934, rare, VG (VG box) 750.00
Bugs Bunny, alarm clock, Ingraham, 4" sq, EX, from $150 to 200.00
Bugs Bunny, bank, pnt metal, Bugs w/carrot by tree, 6", EX 135.00
Bugs Bunny, doll, dressed as Davy Crockett, 1950s, EX 325.00
Bugs Bunny, Magic Rub-Off Pictures, Whitman, complete, EXIB .100.00
Bugs Bunny, pull toy, Bugs on trike, paper on wood w/bells, NM ..350.00
Captain America, bicycle license plate, tin, Marx, 1967, NM 50.00
Captain America, doll, Super Baby series, Amsco, 1970s, 8", NMIB ...45.00
Captain America, kite, Pressman, 1966, MIP 65.00
Captain Marvel, key chain, Captain Marvel Club, plastic, 1940s, EX ...75.00
Captain Marvel, Magic Whistle, litho cb, 1947, NM 165.00
Captain Midnight, Detect-O-Scope (5-Way), 1941, M (w/mailing tube) ...200.00
Captain Midnight, ring, Flight Commander, NM 550.00
Casper the Ghost, toss-up balloon, Pioneer Rubber, 1950s, MOC ...70.00
Charlie McCarthy, figure, jtd wood, Jaymar, rare, 5½", NM 675.00
Charlie McCarthy, ventriloquist doll, Effanbee, 15½", M 575.00
Charlie McCarthy, ventriloquist doll, Effanbee, 18", EX 425.00
Charlie's Angels, backpack, vinyl w/photo, Travel Toys, 1977, M ..75.00
Charlie's Angels, magic slate, Whitman, 1977, M, from $25 to ...30.00
CHiPs, bicycle siren, 1970s, EX 20.00
Cinderella, wastebasket, metal, story w/graphics, 1950s, 19", EX .50.00
Cisco Kid, mask, Pancho, Tip Top Bread, 1953, VG+ 25.00
Cisco Kid, ring, Club Member, gold-tone, Cisco on horse, VG .125.00
Daffy Duck, doll, stuffed plush, Mighty Star, 1971, 19", NM 25.00
Davy Crockett, boots, leather/suede fringe/picture, 1950s, EX ...250.00
Davy Crockett, charm bracelet, gold-tone metal, 7 charms, 1950s, NM ...35.00
Davy Crockett, sunglasses, wht plastic/gr lenses/rifles & image, EX ..65.00
Davy Crockett, wallet, raised image of Davy in profile, 1950s, EX 65.00
Dennis the Mennace, phonograph, Hank Ketcham, 1960s, NM ..150.00
Deputy Dawg, doll, stuffed cloth w/vinyl head, Ideal, 1960s, EX ..100.00
Dick Tracy, Crimestopper Play Set, Hubley, MIB 200.00
Dick Tracy, doll, pnt compo/cloth clothes, movable mouth, 15", EX ..250.00
Dick Tracy, Junior Detective Kit, Golden Press, 1962, NMIB 40.00
Dick Tracy, Secret Service Phone, Lan-Dee, 1930s, VG 100.00
Dick Tracy, wristwatch, New Haven, 1930s, NMIB 400.00
Donald Duck, doll, drum major, felt, Knickerbocker, 1930s, 9", NM ..1,400.00
Donald Duck, hand puppet, cloth/vinyl, Gund, 1960s, MIP 25.00
Donald Duck, pnt box, litho tin, Transogram, 1948, EX 50.00
Donald Duck, telephone/bank, red-pnt metal, 1930s, EX 500.00
Donald Duck, wristwatch, Ingersoll/US Time, EXIB 635.00
Dr Dolittle, jack-in-the-box, Giraffe, 1967, NM 40.00
Dr Dolittle, Mystery Chamber Magic Set, Remco, 1939, NMIB ..30.00
Dr Kildare, scrapbook, 1962, unused, 14x11", NM 65.00
Dumbo, doll, compo w/cloth ears, Cameo Doll Prods, 1941, 8", EX ...300.00
Elmer Fudd, mask, cb, Warner Bros, NM, from $60 to 90.00
Emmett Kelly, doll, vinyl/cloth clothes, 1960s, 13", EX 50.00
Fanny Brice, doll, Ideal, 12½", EX 150.00
Felix the Cat, figure, celluloid, jtd arms, Japan, 1920s, 5", EX ...300.00
Felix the Cat, figure, wood, jtd, Schoenhut, 5½", EX 1,200.00
Felix the Cat, tea set, lustreware, service for 6, Germany, 1920s, M ..900.00
Felix the Cat, TV Color Set, Lido, 1950s, NMIB 175.00
Ferdinand the Bull, figure, bsk, Japan, 1930s, 3", VG 45.00
Flash Gordon, space outfit, Esquire Novelty, 1950s, EXIB 425.00
Flintstones, alarm clock, ceramic Fred figure, Sheffield, 1960s, EX ..185.00
Flintstones, bank, Fred, hard plastic, Homecraft, 14", M 75.00
Flintstones, doll, Barney, plush/vinyl, Knickerbocker, 1960s, 12", NM ..85.00
Flintstones, figure set, Flintstone Circus, Kohner, 1960s, NMIB ..85.00
Flintstones, Play Fun Set, Whitman, 1965, EXIB 65.00
Flintstones, push-button puppet, Dino, plastic, Kohner, 1960s, M 65.00
Flintstones, ramp walker, Fred & Wilma on Dino, plastic, Marx, EX .60.00
Flipper, bank, plastic figure, 1960s, 17½", NM 70.00
G-Men, Secret Communucation Set, NY Toy & Game, 1936, EXIB .375.00
Gabby Hayes, sheriff's set, 1950s, unused, MOC, from $75 to ...100.00
Garfield, bank, Garfield bowling, Enesco, NM, from $35 to 45.00
Gene Autry, vest/chaps, brn suede, Leslie-Henry, 1940s, NMIB ...250.00
Gilligan's Island, doll, Gilligan, vinyl, Turner, 9", M 20.00
Goofy, ramp walker, riding hippo, plastic, Marx, EX 45.00
Green Hornet, Black Beauty balloon, 1966, MIP 100.00
Green Hornet, wrist radios, gr plastic, Remco, 1966, 4", NMIB ...200.00
Green Hornet & Kato, flasher ring, Vari-Vue, 1960s, NM 70.00
Gumby & Poky, hand puppets, cloth/vinyl, EX, ea 30.00
Gumby & Poky, Lolly Pop-Up Puppet, unused, 1967, MIB 65.00
Gunsmoke, pencil case, bl cb, Matt Dillon image, Hasbro, 1961, EX ..30.00
Hansel & Gretel, marionettes, Hazelle's, M, pr 175.00
Happy Days, doll, Fonzie, stuffed cloth, 1976, 16", NM 25.00
Hogan's Heroes, writing tablet, unused, 1965, NM 30.00
Hoot Gibson, boy's shirt, plaid w/Universal Jewel Ranch patch, VG+ ..150.00

Hopalong Cassidy, silk tie and handkerchief set, Glick, NMIB, $400.00. (Photo courtesy Phil Helley)

Hopalong Cassidy, barrette, silver-tone metal w/emb image, unmk, NM ..25.00

Hopalong Cassidy, figure, chalkware, 14", NM 450.00
Hopalong Cassidy, key chain w/TV viewer, Plastic Novelties, 1950, NM ...75.00
Hopalong Cassidy, necktie, child's clip-on, image, Gluck, 1950s, NM ...125.00
Hopalong Cassidy, sparkler, plastic Hoppy bust, 1950s, 4", EX+ ...300.00
Hopalong Cassidy, transfers, various images, 4 on sheet, 8x3", NM ..50.00
Horace Horsecollar, figure, bsk, Japan, 1930s, 3½", VG 110.00
Horace Horsecollar, figure, wood/rope tail, Fun-E-Flex, rare, EX ..1,000.00
Howdy Doody, alarm clock, Western Clock/Kagran, 5", EX 450.00
Howdy Doody, Bee-Nee Kit, 1950s, NMIB 65.00
Howdy Doody, Circus Wagon, plastic, 1950s, 5", EX 300.00
Howdy Doody, doctor kit, Ja-Ru, 1987, MOC 15.00
Howdy Doody, film, Trip to Fun Land, 8mm, Castle Films, 1950s, NMIB ...65.00
Howdy Doody, hand puppet, Flub-A-Dub, cloth/rubber, 1950s, EX ..70.00
Howdy Doody, hand puppets, Howdy/Clarabelle/Dilly/Buster, 5", set ...100.00
Howdy Doody, Magic Piano, Kagran, 15x10", EXIB 575.00
Howdy Doody, marionette, Mr Bluster, Peter Puppet, 14", MIB ...500.00
Howdy Doody, ventriloquist doll, Ideal, 1950s, 18", EX 200.00
Huckleberry Hound, chalkboard, diecut image, Pressman, 1960s, EX ..50.00
Huckleberry Hound, doll, plush/vinyl, Knickerbocker, 20", EX ...55.00
Huckleberry Hound, Flip Show, 1961, EXIB 40.00
Huckleberry Hound, marionette, Pelham, 1960s, 9", NMIB 450.00
Incredible Hulk, bank, plastic bust, Renzi, 1979, 15", NM 15.00
Jackie Coogan, figure, celluloid, Japan, prewar, 5", NM 100.00
Junior G-Men, Fingerprint Set, Hale-Nass Corp, early 1940s, EXIB ...200.00
King Kong, bank, pnt plaster, Universal Statuary, 1952, 11", M ...100.00
Krazy Kat, doll, stuffed felt w/appl face, Averill, 18", VG 500.00
Lady & the Tramp, wallet, red vinyl, 1950s, NM, from $30 to 40.00
Lassie, Day in the Life of Lassie Play Kit, Plas-Trix, 1956, NMIB ...200.00
Lassie, doll, plush/vinyl/glass eyes, Knickerbocker, 1960s, 12", VG ...15.00
Little Lulu, doll, stuffed cloth/red dress/yarn hair, 1944, 15", EX 200.00
Little Lulu, perfume set, NMOC 60.00
Little Orphan Annie, figure, pnt celluloid, Harold Gray, 7½", M 300.00
Little Orphan Annie (Radio), brooch, Girl Alone, M (EX mailer) ...400.00
Little Orphan Annie & Sandy, figures, jtd wood, Jaymar, 5", EX, pr .165.00
Little Red Riding Hood, tea set, litho tin, 8-pc, early 1900s, EX ...375.00

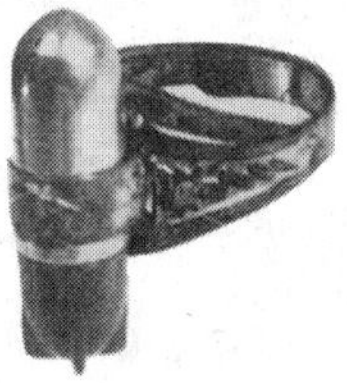

Lone Ranger, Atom Bomb ring, brass with gilt bomb on red plastic fins, 1947, NM, from $125.00 to $145.00.

Lone Ranger, beanie, wht image on blk felt w/red trim, 1940, NM .85.00
Lone Ranger, binoculars, red & blk plastic w/decals, 1950, EX ..125.00
Lone Ranger, harmonica, SP, 1947, NMIB, from $75 to 125.00
Lone Ranger, hat, gr felt/yel band, repeated image, 1950s, EX 65.00
Lone Ranger, magic slate, Whitman, 1978, EX, from $55 to 75.00
Lone Ranger, mask, cb, Buchan's Bread premium, 1940, NM, from $75 to .150.00
Lone Ranger, Picture Printing Set, 1938, complete, NMIB 225.00
Lone Ranger, poster, General Mills, 1957, 6", rare, EX (EX mailer) ..200.00
Lone Ranger, Tattoo Picture Book, 1950, MIP, from $65 to 85.00
Maggie & Jiggs, comb, mechanical Maggie figure, celluloid, M .150.00
Maggie & Jiggs, figures, jtd wood, Schoenhut, 8" & 6", EX, pr ...1,200.00
Magilla Gorilla, squeeze toy, vinyl, Screen Gems, 1967, 6", VG ..125.00
Mama Katzenjammer/Hans/Fitz, figure set, bsk, German, 1920s, 3", NM .465.00
Man From UNCLE, Secret Print Putty, Colorforms, 1965, NMOC ...80.00
Marvel Super Heroes, Deluxe Sparkle Paints, Kenner, 1967, MIB ...150.00
Marvel Super Heroes, record case, 1977, 18x15", EX 25.00
Mary Poppins, tea set, plastic, 1964, MIB 100.00
Maverick, coin, Kaiser Foil premium, 1950s, NM 25.00
Mickey Mouse, alarm clock, Bayard, 1964, NM 300.00
Mickey Mouse, bank, Mickey waving, ceramic, Japan, 1960s, 6", M ..50.00
Mickey Mouse, bobbin' head, yel shirt/red pants, rnd gr base, NM 75.00
Mickey Mouse, camera, box type, Ensign, 1930s, VG (G box) ..325.00
Mickey Mouse, doll, band leader, Knickerbocker, 1930s, EX ..2,000.00
Mickey Mouse, doll, Sun Rubber, 1950s, 10", VG 65.00
Mickey Mouse, dominoes, Halsam/WDE, 1935, EXIB, from $275 to ...375.00
Mickey Mouse, figure, bsk, movable arms, Japan, 1930s, 8½", NM ...3,500.00
Mickey Mouse, figure, wood, Fun-E-Flex, 5", NM 525.00
Mickey Mouse, push-button puppet, wood/plastic, Kohner, 1948, 7", NM ..150.00
Mickey Mouse, saxophone, WDE, 1930s, NM, from $450 to 650.00
Mickey Mouse, tool chest, litho metal box, 1930s, EX 275.00
Mickey Mouse, wristwatch, Ingersoll/US Time, 1947, NM (EX box) ...350.00
Mickey Mouse & Minnie, party horn, cb, Marks Bros/WDE, 1935, 7", EX 165.00
Mickey Mouse & Minnie, scrapbook, 1930s, 11x15", EX 145.00
Mickey Mouse Club, stamp book, Kathleen Daly/Golden Press, 1956, EX ..40.00
Mighty Mouse, charm bracelet, 6 charms, House of Charms, 1950s, EX ...50.00
Mighty Mouse, magic slate, Lowe, 1950s, NM 50.00
Mighty Mouse, squeeze toy, pnt vinyl, Terrytoons, 1950s, 10", EX ...75.00
Minnie Mouse, bank, compo, Minnie in House, WDE/Japan, NM .20.00
Minnie Mouse, doll, cowgirl, Knickerbocker, 1930s, EX 3,000.00
Minnie Mouse, figure, bsk, in nightshirt, Japan, 1930s, 4", EX ..150.00
Minnie Mouse, figure, wood, Fun-E-Flex, 7", EX 450.00
Minnie Mouse, wristwatch, Timex, 1958, NM 225.00
Moon Mullins, ventriloquist doll, Pure Oil Co premium, 1938, EX 65.00
Moon Mullins & Kayo, figures, jtd wood, Jaymar, 5½" & 4", EX, pr ...200.00
Mork & Mindy, gumball machine, Hasbro, 1980, EX 25.00
Mother Goose, Nursery Pianette, Schoenhut, 1940s, VG (VG box) ..125.00
Mr Ed, puppet, pull-string talker, Mattel, 1962, MIB 200.00
Muppets, wristwatch, Miss Piggy, digital, Timex, 1982, MIB 65.00
Mutt & Jeff, figures, celluloid, HC Fisher/US-Stasco, 4" & 5", EX ...275.00
Peanuts, alarm clock, Charlie Brown/Snoopy sleeping, Janex, 1974, EX ...45.00
Peanuts, bank, Snoopy, chalkware, Lego, 1950s, 8", VG 45.00
Peanuts, bobbin' head, Lucy, ceramic, gr baseball cap/bat, Japan, NM ..60.00
Peanuts, bobbin' head, Snoopy, sq blk base, Lego, NM 95.00
Peanuts, doll, Charlie Brown, vinyl, 1950s, 9", VG 75.00
Peanuts, tea set, litho tin, Chein, complete, MIB 50.00
Peter Pan, hand puppet, cloth/vinyl, Gund, EX 35.00
Peter Pan, hatbox, flocked cb, Ne Evel/WDP, 1950s, NM 175.00
Phantom of the Opera, bobbin' head, sq base, NM 500.00
Pinky Lee, party packet, 1950s, M (NM mailer) 100.00
Pinocchio, clicker, yel plastic Jiminy Cricket head, NM 20.00
Pinocchio, marionette, Pelham, 1960s-70s, MIB 135.00
Pinocchio, mask, Figaro, paper, Gillette premium, 1939, EX 35.00
Pinocchio, Pinocchio Circus, punch-out set, 1939 premium, EX .75.00
Pinocchio, ramp walker, Figaro w/ball, plastic, Marx, EX 30.00
Pinocchio, ramp walker, Jiminy Cricket, plastic, Marx, EX 30.00
Pinocchio, roly poly, celluloid, 5", EX 175.00
Pinocchio, tea set, litho tin, Ohio Art, 18-pc, EX, minimum value ...150.00
Pluto, alarm clock, Bayard, 1964, NM 250.00
Pluto, figure, bsk, Pluto sitting, Japan, 1930s, 2½", EX 85.00
Pluto, wristwatch, Ingersoll, 1948, VG 165.00
Popeye, alarm clock, KFS, EX 500.00
Popeye, Bifbat paddle, wood, no ball, 1929, 11", EX 15.00
Popeye, figure, Olive Oyl, jtd wood, KFS/USA, 5", EX 85.00
Popeye, figure, Popeye, jtd wood/compo, Chein, 1931, 8", EX ..400.00
Popeye, flasher ring, silver plastic, Vari-Vue, 1960s, NM 30.00
Popeye, Magic Play Around, Amsco, NMIB 300.00
Popeye, pencil-by-number, unused, 1959, MIB 35.00
Porky Pig, bobbin' head, NM, from $100 to 175.00
Porky Pig, wristwatch, Sheffield, 1960s, NMIB 150.00
Raggedy Andy, bulletin board, diecut, Manton Cork Corp, 23", MIP ...30.00
Raggedy Ann, bank, ceramic/yarn hair, seated w/puppy, 1981, 6", M .25.00
Raggedy Ann, jump rope, plastic hdls, Hallmark, 1968, MOC 22.00
Red Ryder, token, target design/Red Ryder, 1938, 2", EX 25.00

Ricochet Rabbit, push-button puppet, Kohner, NM 45.00
Rocky & Bullwinkle, blackboard, Frolic Toys, 1970s, 12x16", VG ..50.00
Rocky & Bullwinkle, dish set, Melmac, EX 65.00
Roy Rogers, bank, litho tin, Roy & Trigger, Ohio Art, 8", MIP .250.00
Roy Rogers, banner, gr felt w/wht lettering, 1950s, 28", EX 185.00
Roy Rogers, hand puppet, cloth/rubber, 1950s, VG 100.00
Roy Rogers, pencil box, cb, 2 pull-out drws/tray, 1950s, EX 100.00
Roy Rogers, wallet, brn leather/emb lettering/mc image, 1950s, EXIB ..150.00
Roy Rogers, wristwatch, w/Trigger, brn strap, Ingraham, 1951, NMIB ..400.00
Sgt Preston, trail goggles, cb, Quaker Oats, 1952, EX 15.00
Sgt Preston, 10-in-1 Trail Kit, Quaker Oats, 1956, 6", EX 800.00
Shmoo, alarm clock, figural w/dial in middle, Lux, 1950, 8", EXIB ..200.00
Simpsons, poster book, Button-Up, complete, NM 8.00
Simpsons, slide-tile puzzles, set of 4, Jaru, NM 15.00
Six Million Dollar Man, fan club kit, 1970s, NM 85.00
Sleeping Beauty, Dress Designer Kit, Colorforms, 1959, MIB 65.00
Sleeping Beauty, ring, silver plastic w/bl shield & sword, EX 45.00
Smurfs, Fun Club Packet, w/newsletters & stickers, EX 45.00
Snow White, alarm clock, Bayard, 1960, 4½", NM 300.00
Snow White, coloring set, Whitman, 1930s, EXIB 200.00
Snow White, doll, dwarfs, Knickerbocker, 1938, NM, ea from $300 to ..500.00
Snow White, doll, Knickerbocker, 1938, MIB, from $750 to .1,000.00
Snow White, tea set, 10-pc, Aluminum Goods Mfg, 1937, MIB ..300.00
Soupy Sales, doll, Sunshine Dolls, 1956, 6", MIB 235.00

Spark Plug, wooden ride-on horse, 36x36x8", EX, from $685.00 to $750.00. (Photo courtesy Dunbar Gallery)

Spider-Man, bank, plastic bust, Renzi, 1979, 15", EX 25.00
Spider-Man, bicycle license plate, litho tin, Marx, 1967, NM 50.00
Spider-Man, poster, glossy, Hudson Pharmaceutical, 1975, 30x20", EX ..50.00
Starksy & Hutch, handcuffs & wallet, Fleetwood, 1976, MOC ...25.00
Superman, comic book, Duel in Space, Kellogg's 1955, NM 100.00
Superman, Krypton Rocket, plastic, Kellogg's, 1950, complete, MIB ..285.00
Superman, membership kit, 1942, complete, NM 400.00
Superman, scrapbook, 50 pgs, Saalfield, 1940, NM 200.00
Superman, wallet w/magic pad & pencil set, yel vinyl, 1966, NM 85.00
Tarzan, Magic Rub-Off Picture Set, Whitman, 1966, VG (VG box) ...25.00
Tasmanian Devil, doll, stuffed cloth, Mighty Star, 1970s, EX 40.00
Thor, pillow, inflatable plastic, Marvel Comics, 1968, 12x12", MIP 100.00
Three Little Pigs, figure set, wood, Fun-E-Flex, EX 400.00
Three Little Pigs, tea set, gr litho tin, Ohio Art/WDE, 1935, NM 350.00
Three Stooges, Slap-Stick-On, Colorforms, 1959, MIB 300.00
Tom Corbett Space Cadet, ID bracelet, premium, M 135.00
Tom Corbett Space Cadet, membership card, Rocket Light, EX ..50.00
Tom Mix, badge, Ranch Boss, premium, 1938, M 375.00
Tom Mix, bird call/telescope, EX 85.00
Tom Mix, spinner, Good Luck, EX 75.00
Topo Gigio, puppet, Am Character, 1960s, 12", MIB 125.00
Tweety Bird, lantern, battery, tin/glass, Amico, 1950s, 5½", EX ..85.00
Universal Monsters, pencil sharpener, Mummy, plastic, 1960s, 3", EX ..40.00
Welcome Back Kotter, chalkboard, Board King, 1976, M 45.00
Winnie the Pooh, doll, Gund, 1960s, 9", EX 225.00
Wizard of Oz, figure, Lion, rubber, Multiple, 1960s, 6", EX 55.00
Wizard of Oz, toy watch, Scarecrow/Tin Man, Occupied Japan, 1940s, M ...50.00
Wolfman, bobbin' head, sq base, NM 500.00
Wonder Woman, slide-tile puzzle, 1978, EX 30.00
Woody Woodpecker, alarm clock, Woody's Cafe, Westclox, 5½", EX ..175.00
Woody Woodpecker, kazoo, red plstic figure, Linden, 1960s, 7", EX 25.00
Woody Woodpecker, wristwatch, Ingraham, EX 325.00
Yogi Bear, bubble pipe, red plastic figure, Hanna-Barbera, 1960s, NM ...25.00
Yogi Bear, camera, 1960s, MIB 65.00
Yogi Bear, doll, plush/felt, Playtime, 1960s, 17", EX 50.00
Zorro, keychain, flasher, WDP, 1966, EX 35.00
Zorro, pinwheel, plastic 8-point star/wood stick, 1950s, rare, EX 150.00
Zorro, wristwatch, blk strap/silver-stamped designs, US Time, EXIB ...400.00

Peters and Reed

John Peters and Adam Reed founded their pottery in Zanesville, Ohio, just before the turn of the century, using the local red clay to produce a variety of wares. Moss Aztec, introduced about 1912, has an unglazed exterior with designs molded in high relief and the recesses highlighted with a green wash. Only the interior is glazed to hold water. Pereco (named for Peters, Reed and Company) is glazed in semi-matt blue, maroon, cream, and other colors. Orange was also used very early, but such examples are rare. Shapes are simple with in-mold decoration sometimes borrowed from the Moss Aztec line. Wilse Blue is a line of high-gloss medium blue with dark specks on simple shapes. Landsun, characterized by its soft matt multicolor or blue and gray combinations, is decorated either by dripping or by hand brushing in an effect sometimes called Flame or Herringbone. Chromal, in much the same colors as Landsun, may be decorated with a realistic scenic, or the swirling application of colors may merely suggest one. Vivid, realistic Chromal scenics command much higher prices than weak, poorly drawn examples. (Brush-McCoy made a very similar line called Chromart. Neither will be marked; and due to the lack of documented background material available, it may be impossible make a positive identification. Collectors nearly always attribute this type of decoration to Peters and Reed.) Shadow Ware is usually a glossy, multicolor drip over a harmonious base color but occasionally seen in overall matt glaze. When the base is black, the effect is often iridescent.

Perhaps the most familiar line is the brown high-glaze artware with the 'sprigged'-type designs. Although research has uncovered no positive proof, it is generally accepted as having been made by Peters and Reed. It is interesting to note that many of the artistic shapes in this line are recognizable as those made by Weller, Roseville, and other Zanesville area companies. Several other lines were produced including Mirror Black, Persian, Egyptian, Florentine, Marbleized, etc., and an unidentified line which collectors call Mottled-Marbleized Colors. In this high-gloss line, the red clay body often shows through the splashed-on multicolors.

In 1922 the company became known as the Zane Pottery. Peters and Reed retired, and Harry McClelland became president. Charles Chilcote designed new lines, and production of many of the old lines continued. The body of the ware after 1922 was light in color. Marks include the impressed logo or ink stamp 'Zaneware' in a rectangle. See also Zaneware.

Basket, hanging; Moss Aztec, 2½x5½" 85.00
Bowl, gr matt, 8½" 50.00
Bowl, Moss Aztec, 2¼x10½" dia, NM 125.00
Dish, gr matt w/red-brn highlights, 2x4⅞" 60.00
Jardiniere, Chromal, scenic (realistic), 7x10" 800.00
Jardiniere, Florentine, majolica glaze, 6½x7½" 175.00
Jardiniere, Moss Aztec, emb roses, Frank Ferrell, 6" 150.00
Vase, Brown Ware, 4 figure heads, bulbous bottom w/trumpet neck, 8" 125.00
Vase, bud; Landsun, feathered bl & ivory matt, 8" 95.00

Vase, Chromal, mountains/river/forest (realistic), 11½" 1,200.00
Vase, Chromal, scenic (realistic), unmk, 3¾" 425.00
Vase, Chromal, scenic (realistic), 7¾" 700.00
Vase, Chromal (impressionistic), 11½" 600.00
Vase, floral, brn on cream matt, 18" 425.00
Vase, gr dripping matt, bbl shape, unmk, 10½" 325.00
Vase, Marbleized, blk, bl & yel on terra cotta, 11" 250.00
Vase, Moss Aztec, emb floral, incurvate cylinder, 10" 225.00
Vase, Moss Aztec, emb floral, red clay w/gr highlights, 12" 275.00
Vase, Pereco, gr matt, emb berries, 13x8½", NM 250.00
Vase, Shadow Ware, dripping yel over mirror blk, classic shape, 9" ...275.00
Vase, Shadow Ware, mc, 7" 195.00
Vase, Shadow Ware, mc, 9" 275.00

Pewabic

The Pewabic Pottery was formally established in Detroit, Michigan, in 1907 by Mary Chase Perry Stratton and Horace James Caulkins. The two had worked together since 1903, firing their ware in a small kiln Caulkins had designed especially for use by the dental trade. Always a small operation which relied upon basic equipment and the skill of the workers, they took pride in being commissioned for several important architectural tile installations.

Some of the early artware was glazed a simple matt green; occasionally other colors were added, sometimes in combination, one over the other in a drip effect. Later Stratton developed a lustrous crystalline glaze. (Today's values are determined to a great extent by the artistic merit of the glaze.) The body of the ware was highly fired and extremely hard. Shapes were basic, and decorative modeling, if used at all, was in low relief. Mary Stratton kept the pottery open until her death in 1961. In 1968 it was purchased and reopened by Michigan State University; it is still producing today. Several marks were used over the years: a triangle with 'Revelation Pottery' (for a short time only); 'Pewabic' with five maple leaves; and the impressed circle mark.

Plate, dragonflies, bl on wht crackle, flakes, 10¾" 1,000.00
Vase, bl/gr/gunmetal metallic, bulbous w/trumpet neck, 8" 550.00
Vase, blk/gr/lav lustres, 3½x5¼" 450.00
Vase, celadon & lav lustre, unmk, 2¼x2¼" 350.00
Vase, celadon & oxblood lustre, 2½x2" 350.00
Vase, celadon & purple lustre, bulbous, mk/label, 4¾x4" 300.00
Vase, cobalt w/gr flecks, mk, 10¼" 1,300.00
Vase, dk bl lustre, 8x6" 750.00
Vase, gold & mauve lustre, ovoid, 4¾x3½" 650.00
Vase, gr/gold/ivory lustre, paper label, 2½x3¼" 550.00
Vase, mirror gold on bl gloss, bulbous, 4¾x4", NM 1,100.00
Vase, Persian Blue crackle, #40B, 2x2½" 275.00
Vase, pk/gold/bl lustre drips, 2½x2¾" 1,200.00
Vase, platinum & multi-tone bl metallic, bulbous, rstr, 10x9" ...2,300.00
Vase, purple mirror glaze, trumpet neck on angle shoulder, 5x5" ..700.00
Vase, taupe w/turq patches, mottled lustre, 5½x5½" 650.00
Vase, turq & purple dripping lustre, bulbous, 3¾x3¾" 600.00
Vase, turq/gr/bl lustre drips, 2½x2" 425.00

Pewter

Pewter is a metal alloy of tin, copper, very small parts of bismuth and/or antimony, and sometimes lead. Very little American pewter contained lead, however, because much of the ware was designed to be used as tableware, and makers were aware that the use of lead could result in poisoning. (Pieces that do contain lead are usually darker in color and heavier than those that have no lead.) Most of the fine examples of American pewter date from 1700 to the 1840s. Many pieces were melted down and recast into bullets during the American Revolution in 1775; this accounts to some extent why examples from this period are quite difficult to find. The pieces that did survive may include buttons, buckles, and writing equipment as well as the tableware we generally think of.

After the Revolution makers began using antimony as the major alloy with the tin in an effort to regain the popularity of pewter, which glassware and china was beginning to replace in the home. The resulting product, known as britannia, had a lustrous silver-like appearance and was far more durable. While closely related, britannia is a collectible in its own right and should not be confused with pewter.

Key: tm — touch mark

Basin, Compton tm, 2x8" 220.00
Basin, Compton...London tm, dk patina, 3½x14" 425.00
Bowl, B Barns Philda eagle tm, shallow, wear, 11⅛" 355.00
Bowl, baptismal; unmk (att Boardman family), polished, 7⅞", pr ...880.00
Bowl, Townsend & Compton tm, shallow, wear/scratches, 13" ..195.00
Candlesticks, Sellew & Co Cincinnati tm, 8", pr 550.00
Candlesticks, unmk, Neoclassical style w/pushups, rpr, 7¼", pr .246.00
Candlesticks, unmk Am, sm rpr, 9¾", pr 200.00
Candlesticks, unmk Am, 9¾", pr 300.00
Chalice, unmk (att Israel Trask), polished, 5¾" 140.00
Charger, crowned rose tm, lt wear, 14¼" dia 220.00
Charger, Edward Toms tm, wear/scratches, 14¾" 330.00
Charger, illegible tm, wear, 12" 130.00
Charger, Robert Bush & Co tm, wear/scratches, 14⅞" 220.00
Charger, unmk, pitted, 14" 195.00

Coffeepot, James Putnam touch mark, Malden, Massachusetts, pear shape, 1830 – 35, 11", NM, $350.00; Ale pitcher, resoldered lid, English, early nineteenth century, two-quart, EX, $350.00.

Coffeepot, Homan & Co tm, cast flower finial, sm dents, 8¾" ..125.00
Coffeepot, unmk but att to Hall & Cotton, pinpoint hole, 11⅜" ...220.00
Commode, unmk Am, cylindrical w/flared sides, flattened rim, 11¾" ..80.00
Funnel, unmk Am, rnd w/long spout, wire loop, late 1880s, 9x6" ...150.00
Ice bucket, Liberty & Co tm, foliate design, 6x8½" 750.00
Lamp, chamber; R Gleason tm, orig whale-oil burner, lemon font, 5" ..200.00
Lamp, unmk Am, old rpr, single spout burner, 5⅝" 155.00
Pitcher, att Boardman & Hart, globular, domed lid, 1850s, 10" .350.00
Plate, Jacob Whitmore crowned rose tm, wear, 8" 220.00
Plate, love tm, 7⅞" 300.00
Plate, TD Boardman, eagle tm, worn/battered, 7⅝" 195.00
Plate, unmk Am, minor wear, polished, 8⅛" 100.00
Plate, Wm Danforth eagle tm, wear/scratches, polished, 8" 200.00
Porringer, unmk, cast flower hdl, sm crack, 5½" 275.00
Soup plate, Boardman lion tm w/dbl X, 9½", EX 385.00
Spoons, John Yates tm, 5¼", set of 6 ....120.00
Spoons, unmk, rnd bowl w/rectangular hdls, 6¾", pr 80.00

Sugar bowl, Sheldon & Feltman tm, 7⅝" 95.00
Tall pot, F Porter Westbrook No 1 tm, finial wafer missing, 11" ...300.00
Tall pot, G Richardson tm, 10½" 300.00
Tall pot, Simpson & Benham NY tm, old soldered rpr, 11" 385.00
Tall pot, TS Derby tm, corrosion/soldering, 11" 220.00
Tall pot, unmk Am, minor rprs, rpl finial, 12" 190.00
Tall pot, Whitlock Troy NY tm, lt wear/pitting, 10¾" 250.00
Teapot, B&P tm, rprs, rare, 6½" 415.00
Teapot, Geo Richardson tm, pear shape, pnt metal hdl, 11", EX ..350.00
Teapot, Putnum tm, sm holes in hdl, 8¾" 250.00
Teapot, R Gleason tm, battered, 9" 110.00
Teapot, Roswell Gleason tm, pnt metal hdl, wood finial, 8", VG ..250.00
Teapot, Savage #6 tm, some battering, 6¾" 110.00
Teapot, Smith & Co tm, rprs, 8½" 165.00
Teapot, unmk Am, 8" 110.00
Teapot, unmk Continental, C-shaped hdl, removeable lid, 4½" ...340.00

Pfaltzgraff

Pfaltzgraff has operated in Pennsylvania since the early 1800s making redware at first, then stoneware crocks and jugs, yellow ware and spongeware in the '20s, artware and kitchenware in the '30s, and stoneware kitchen items through the '40s. To collectors, they're best known for their Gourmet Royal (circa 1950s), a high-gloss dinnerware line of solid brown with frothy white drip glaze around the rims, and their giftware line called Muggsy, comic-character mugs, ashtrays, bottle stoppers, children's dishes, pretzel jars, cookie jars, etc. It was designed in the late 1940s and continued in production until 1960. The older versions have protruding features, while the features of later examples were simply painted on.

Their popular Village line, an almond-glazed pattern with a brown-stenciled folk-art tulip design, was discontinued a few years ago, and is today becomming very collectible. Yorktown and Folk Art are manufactured today only on a very limited basis, so discontinued items in those lines are attracting much interest as well. (In general, use Village prices to help you evaluate those two lines.) For more information on their dinnerware, we recommend *The Flea Market Trader* and *The Garage Sale and Flea Market Annual*, both by Collector Books.

Village, soup tureen, with lid and ladle, #160, from $40.00 to $45.00; underplate (dinner plate) from $3.50 to $4.00.

Christmas Heritage, beverage server, 48-oz 17.50
Christmas Heritage, bowl, vegetable; oval, 2⅞x10¾x8½" 22.50
Christmas Heritage, cup & saucer 3.00
Christmas Heritage, ginger jar 10.00
Christmas Heritage, gravy pitcher, 5", from $15 to 20.00
Christmas Heritage, napkin rings, 4 for 16.00
Christmas Heritage, plate, salad; 7" 5.00
Christmas Heritage, platter, 14" 17.50
Christmas Heritage, relish, oval, 8¼x6⅛" 12.00
Gourmet Royale, ashtray, #AT32, skillet shape, 9", from $10 to ..15.00
Gourmet Royale, ashtray, 12", from $15 to 18.00
Gourmet Royale, baker, #321, oval, 7½", from $18 to 20.00
Gourmet Royale, baker, #323, 9½", from $20 to 24.00
Gourmet Royale, bean pot, #11-2, 2-qt, from $28 to 30.00
Gourmet Royale, bean pot, #11-3, 3-qt 35.00
Gourmet Royale, bean pot, #11-4, 4-qt 45.00
Gourmet Royale, bean pot, #30, w/lip, lg, from $45 to 50.00
Gourmet Royale, bean pot warming stand 12.00
Gourmet Royale, bowl, #241, oval, 7x10", from $15 to 18.00
Gourmet Royale, bowl, cereal; #934SR, 5½", from $6 to 8.00
Gourmet Royale, bowl, mixing; 6", from $8 to 14.00
Gourmet Royale, bowl, mixing; 8", from $12 to 14.00
Gourmet Royale, bowl, salad; tapered sides, 10", from $25 to 28.00
Gourmet Royale, bowl, soup; 2¼x7¼", from $6 to 8.00
Gourmet Royale, bowl, vegetable; #341, divided, from $20 to 24.00
Gourmet Royale, bowl, vegetable; 9¾" 15.00
Gourmet Royale, butter dish, #394, ¼-lb stick type, from $12 to ...14.00
Gourmet Royale, candle holders, tall, w/finger ring, 6", pr, $25 to ...35.00
Gourmet Royale, casserole, hen on nest, 2-qt, from $75 to 95.00
Gourmet Royale, casserole, ind; #399, stick hdl, 12-oz, from $10 to ...12.00
Gourmet Royale, casserole, stick hdl, 1-qt 18.00
Gourmet Royale, casserole, stick hdl, 3-qt 30.00
Gourmet Royale, casserole, stick hdl, 4-qt 40.00
Gourmet Royale, casserole, 2-qt, from $20 to 22.00
Gourmet Royale, chafing dish, w/hdls, lid & stand, 8x9", from $30 to ...35.00
Gourmet Royale, cheese shaker, bulbous, 5¾", from $18 to 22.00
Gourmet Royale, chip 'n dip, #306, 2-pc set, w/stand, from $28 to ...30.00
Gourmet Royale, coffee server, on metal & wood stand, 10¾", $100 to ...125.00
Gourmet Royale, coffeepot, #303, 10-cup, from $30 to 35.00
Gourmet Royale, creamer, #382, from $5 to 7.00
Gourmet Royale, cruet, coffeepot shape, fill through spuot, 5" 22.00
Gourmet Royale, cup, from $2 to 3.00
Gourmet Royale, flour scoop, sm, from $12 to 15.00
Gourmet Royale, gravy boat, #426, 2-spout, lg, +underplate, $14 to ..16.00
Gourmet Royale, gravy boat, w stick hdl, 2-spout, from $15 to ...20.00
Gourmet Royale, jug, #384, 32-oz, from $32 to 36.00
Gourmet Royale, jug, #386, ice lip, from $40 to 48.00
Gourmet Royale, ladle, sm, from $12 to 15.00
Gourmet Royale, ladle, 3½" dia bowl w/11" hdl, from $18 to 20.00
Gourmet Royale, Lazy Susan, #220, 5-part, molded in 1-pc, 11", $22 to ...28.00
Gourmet Royale, mug, #391, 12-oz, from $6 to 8.00
Gourmet Royale, mug, #392, 16-oz, from $12 to 14.00
Gourmet Royale, pie plate, #7016, 9½", from $14 to 18.00
Gourmet Royale, plate, egg; holds 12 halves, 7¾x12½", $20 to ..22.00
Gourmet Royale, plate, grill; #87, 3-section, 11", from $18 to 20.00
Gourmet Royale, plate, salad; 6¾", from $3 to 4.00
Gourmet Royale, plate, steak; 12", from $15 to 20.00
Gourmet Royale, platter, #320, 14", from $20 to 25.00
Gourmet Royale, platter, #337, 16", from $25 to 30.00
Gourmet Royale, rarebit, #330, w/lug hdls, oval, 11", from $15 to ..18.00
Gourmet Royale, rarebit, w/lug hdls, oval, 8½", from $10 to 12.00
Gourmet Royale, relish dish, #265, 5x10", from $15 to 17.00
Gourmet Royale, roaster, #326, oval, 16", from $50 to 60.00
Gourmet Royale, serving tray, rnd, 4-section, upright hdl in center ..20.00
Gourmet Royale, shakers, #317/318, 4½", pr, from $12 to 14.00
Gourmet Royale, shakers, bell shape, pr, from $25 to 35.00
Gourmet Royale, shirred egg dish, #360, 6", from $10 to 12.00
Gourmet Royale, souffle dish, #393, 5-qt +underplate, from $65 to ..70.00
Gourmet Royale, sugar bowl, from $5 to 7.00
Gourmet Royale, teapot, #381, 6-cup, from $18 to 22.00
Gourmet Royale, tray, tidbit; 2-tier, from $15 to 18.00
Heritage, butter dish, #002-028, from $6 to 8.00
Heritage, cake/serving plate, #002-529, 11¼" dia, from $9 to 12.00
Heritage, cup & saucer, #002-002, 9-oz 3.00
Heritage, soup tureen, #002-160, 3½-qt 35.00
Planter, donkey, brn drip glaze, common, 10", from $15 to 20.00

Planter, elephant, brn drip glaze, scarce, from $90 to 110.00
Village, baker, #237, sq, tab hdls, 9", from $10 to 14.00
Village, baker, #24, oval, 10¼", from $8 to 10.00
Village, baker, #240, oval, 7¾", from $6 to 8.00
Village, bowl, batter; w/spout & hdl, 8", from $35 to 42.00
Village, bowl, mixing; #453, 1-qt, 2-qt, 3-qt, 3-pc set, $40 to 50.00
Village, bowl, rim soup; #012, 8½" 6.00
Village, bowl, serving; #010, 7", from $8 to 12.00
Village, bowl, soup/cereal; #009, 6" 4.50
Village, bowl, vegetable; #011, 8¾", from $12 to 15.00
Village, bread tray, 12", from $18 to 25.00
Village, butter dish, #028 ....8.00
Village, canisters, #520, 4-pc set, from $50 to 60.00
Village, casserole, w/lid, #315, 2-qt 25.00
Village, coffee mug, #89F, 10-oz, from $6 to 8.50
Village, coffeepot, lighthouse shape, 48-oz, from $30 to 35.00
Village, cookie jar, #540, 3-qt, from $18 to 25.00
Village, creamer & sugar bowl, #020, from $9 to 12.00
Village, cup & saucer, #001 & #002 ....3.50
Village, flowerpot, 4½", from $15 to 20.00
Village, gravy boat, #443, w/saucer, 16-oz, from $12 to 15.00
Village, onion soup crock, #295, stick hdl, sm, from $6 to 8.50
Village, pitcher, #416, 2-qt, from $20 to 25.00
Village, plate, dinner; #004, 10¼", from $3 to 4.50
Village, platter, #016, 14", from $18 to 22.00
Village, spoon rest, #515, 9" L, from $6 to 7.50

Muggsy Line

Ashtray 125.00
Bottle stopper, head, ball shape 85.00
Canape holder, Carrie, lift-off hat, from $125 to 150.00
Cigarette server 125.00
Clothes sprinkler bottle, Myrtle, Black, from $225 to 260.00
Clothes sprinkler bottle, Myrtle, wht, from $195 to 225.00
Cookie jar, character face, minimum value 250.00
Jar, utility; Handy Harry, hat forms lid 200.00
Mug, action figure, Black 125.00
Mug, action figure (golfer, etc), ea from $65 to 85.00
Mug, character face, ea 38.00
Shot mug, character face 50.00
Tumbler 60.00

Phoenix Bird

Blue and white Phoenix Bird china has been produced by various Japanese potteries from the early 1900s. With slight variations the design features the Japanese bird of paradise and scroll-like vines of Kara-Kusa, or Chinese grass. Although some of their earlier ware is unmarked, the majority is marked in some fashion. More than one hundred different stamps have been reported, with 'Made in Japan' the one most often found. Coming in second is Morimura's wreath and/or crossed stems (both having the letter 'M' within). The cloverleaf with 'Japan' below very often indicates an item having a high-quality transfer-printed design. Among the many categories in the Phoenix Bird pattern are several shapes; therefore (for identification purposes), each has been given a number, i.e. #1, #2, etc. Newer items, if marked at all, carry a paper label. Compared to the older ware, the coloring of the new is whiter and the blue more harsh; the design is sparse with more ground area showing. Although collectors buy even 'new' pieces, the older is, of course, more highly prized and valued.

For further information we recommend *Phoenix Bird Chinaware, Books I – IV,* written and privately published by our advisor, Joan Oates; her address is in the Directory under Michigan. Join Phoenix Bird Collectors of America (PBCA) and receive the *Phoenix Bird Discoveries* newsletter, an informative publication that will further your appreciation of this chinaware. See Clubs, Newsletters, and Catalogs for ordering information.

Bowl, berry, #3, 5-scallop top, 2¼x9" 85.00
Bowl, cereal; 6" 15.00
Bowl, serving (oval vegetable); 10" 65.00
Butter dish, #3, w/lid, w/o drain, 5x7¼" dia 95.00
Butter pat, single phoenix, 3¼" dia 20.00
Chocolate pot, #2, scalloped base, 6¾x9" 190.00
Coffeepot, #7, str hdl, 5½x3" 155.00

Chop plate/charger, superior quality, 11½", $175.00. (Photo courtesy Joan Oates)

Glass, lemonade; flared top, 3¾" 75.00
Gravy ladle, #2, 6" 85.00
Gravy tureen, #2, lid w/ladle hole, on attached stand 175.00
Marmalade, lid w/spoon hole, 4½x5¼" at hdls 75.00
Muffineer (sugar shaker), 4" 95.00
Nut cup, ftd, scalloped, 2x3" 35.00
Pitcher, milk; #3, 4½x4¼" 65.00
Pitcher, water tankard; 6½x6" 175.00
Platter, scalloped, oval, 12½" 70.00
Platter, scalloped, oval, 17" 280.00
Ramekin, style B, white int w/rim design 30.00
Salt dip, #3, oval, 3⅝x2¼" 35.00
Tea strainer, #5, scalloped, w/underpot, 6" L 140.00
Teapot, #19, Myott & Son (English) 135.00
Teapot, #27 (mk 56), 5x7" 135.00
Tumbler/custard cup, w/border inside, 2¾x2¾" 18.00
Tureen, vegetable; oval, 11" including hdls 195.00

Phoenix Glass

Founded in 1880 in Monaca, Pennsylvania, the Phoenix Glass Company became one of the country's foremost manufacturers of lighting glass by the early 1900s. They also produced a wide variety of utilitarian and decorative glassware, including art glass by Joseph Webb, colored cut glass, Gone-with-the-Wind style oil lamps, hotel and barware, and pharmaceutical glassware. Today, however, collectors are primarily interested in the 'Sculptured Artware' produced in the 1930s and 1940s. These beautiful pressed and mold-blown pieces are most often found in white milk glass or crystal with various color treatments or a satin finish.

Phoenix did not mark their 'Sculptured Artware' line on the glass; instead, a silver and black (earliest) or gold and black (later) foil label in the shape of the mythical phoenix bird was used.

Quite often glassware made by the Consolidated Lamp and Glass Company of nearby Coraopolis, Pennsylvania, is mistaken for Phoenix's 'Sculptured Artware.' Though the style of the glass is very similar, one distinguishing characteristic is that perhaps 80% of the time Phoenix applied color to the background leaving the raised design plain in contrast, while Consolidated generally applied color to the raised design and left the background plain. Also, for the most part, the patterns and colors used by Phoenix were distinctively different from those used by Consolidated.

In 1970 Phoenix Glass became a division of Anchor Hocking which in turn was acquired by the Newell Group in 1987. Phoenix has the distinction of being one of the oldest continuously operating glass factories in the United States. For more information refer to *Phoenix and Consolidated Art Glass, 1926–1980,* written by our advisor, Jack D. Wilson, who is listed in the Directory under Illinois. See also Consolidated Glass.

Key: mg — milk glass

Dancing Girl, red with pearlized design, 12", $625.00. (Photo courtesy Jack D. Wilson)

Aster, vase, burgundy w/pearlized design, 7" 125.00
Aster, vase, lt tan w/pearlized design, 7" 85.00
Bicentennial, vase, machine made, spray pnt, 11½" 65.00
Bluebell, vase, deep burgundy w/pearlized design, 7" 125.00
Bluebell, vase, florist gr finish, KR Haley, 1948, 7" 250.00
Bluebell, vase, reverse decorated, bl/gr on wht, 7" 325.00
Cosmos, vase, gr w/mg design, 7½" 145.00
Cosmos, vase, lt gr w/pearlized design, 7½" 175.00
Cosmos, vase, pk w/pearlized design, 7½" 175.00
Cosmos, vase, purple w/pearlized design, 7½" 185.00
Daisy, vase, bl w/mg design, 9x9" 425.00
Daisy, vase, frosted w/tan design, 9x9" 325.00
Dancing Girl, vase, custard w/brn/tan/lt orange design, 12" 550.00
Dancing Girl, vase, pk w/mg design, 12" 500.00
Dancing Nymph, platter, palace sz, Rueben Blue, 18" dia 2,000.00
Diving Girl, oblong bowl, lt bl-purple w/frosted design, 14" L 375.00
Diving Girl, oblong bowl, slate bl shadow w/mg design, 14" L 400.00
Fern, vase, burgundy w/pearlized design, 7" 155.00
Fern, vase, deep brn w/brn overwiped wht design, 7" 145.00
Fern, vase, slate gray w/pearlized design, 7" 155.00
Freesia, vase, brn w/mg design, fan shape, 8" 175.00
Jewel, vase, lt gr w/pearlized design, 4¾" 125.00
Jewel, vase, wht w/lt bl design, 4¾" 85.00
Lily, console bowl, gr wash w/frosted design 425.00
Lily, vase, aqua wash (rare color), str sides, 8" 225.00
Lily, vase, yel wash (scarce color), tri-crimped, 10" 295.00
Madonna, vase, burgundy red w/pearlized design, 10" 250.00
Madonna, vase, florist gr finish, KR Haley, 1948, 10" 350.00
Madonna, vase, pk w/pearlized design, 10" 200.00
Madonna, vase, wht w/pearlized design, 10" 200.00
Philodendron, vase, burgundy w/pearlized design, 11½" 185.00
Phlox, ashtray, aqua wash 85.00
Phlox, candy dish, rose w/pearlized design, w/lid 225.00
Phlox, cigarette box, deep burgundy w/pearlized design, w/lid 180.00
Phlox, cigarette box, gr w/mg design, w/lid 120.00
Pine Cone, vase, frosted w/soft yel design, rare, 6¼" 425.00
Star Flower, vase, reverse decorated, bl/gr on wht, 7" 285.00
Star Flower, vase, rose w/mg design, 7" 145.00
Star Flower, vase, very lt bl w/frosted design, 7" 120.00
Strawberry, console bowl+ pr sticks, milk glass w/lav design, 3-pc set 535.00
Thistle, vase, med gr w/pearlized design, 18" 550.00
Wild Geese, vase, amber w/frosted design, 9" 275.00
Wild Geese, vase, bl frost, 9x12" 225.00
Wild Geese, vase, burgundy w/mg design, 8" 160.00
Wild Geese, vase, gr w/mg design, 9" 175.00
Wild Geese, vase, tan w/tan shadowed design, 9x12" 175.00
Wild Rose, vase, burgundy-red w/pearlized design, 10½" 250.00
Wild Rose, vase, slate bl w/bl-shadowed wht design, 10½" 200.00
Zodiac, vase, med bl w/frosted design, 10½" 875.00
Zodiac, vase, mg w/slate bl design, rare, 10½" 950.00

Phonographs

The phonograph, invented by Thomas Edison in 1877, was the first practical instrument for recording and reproducing sound. Sound wave vibrations were recorded on a tinfoil-covered cylinder and played back with a needle that ran along the grooves made from the recording, thus reproducing the sound. Very little changed to this art of record making until 1885, when the first replayable and removable wax cylinders were developed by the American Graphaphone Company. These records were made from 1885 until 1894 and are rare today. Edison began to offer musically recorded wax cylinders in 1889. They continued to be made until 1902. Today they are known as brown wax records. Black wax cylinders were offered in 1902, and the earlier brown wax cylinders were discontinued. These wax two-minute records were sold until 1912. From 1912 until 1929, only four-minute celluloid blue amberol record cylinders were made. The first disc records and disc machines were offered by the inventor Berliner in 1894. They were sold in America until 1900, when the Victor company took over. In the 1890s, all machines played 7" diameter disc records; the 10" size was developed in 1901. By the early 1900s there existed many disc and cylinder phonograph companies, all offering their improvements. Among them were Berliner, Columbia, Zonophone, United States Phono, Wizard, Vitaphone, Amet, and others.

All Victor I's through VI's originally came with a choice of either brass bell, morning-glory, or wooden horns. Wood horns are the most valuable, adding $1,000.00 (or more) to the machine. Spring models were produced until 1929 (and even later). After 1929 most were electric (though some electric-motor models were produced as early as 1910). Unless another condition is noted, prices are for complete, original phonographs in at least fine to excellent condition. Note: Edison coin-operated cylinder players start at $7,000.00 and may go up to $20,000.00 each. All outside-horn Victor phonographs are worth at *least* $1,000.00 or more, if in excellent original condition. Machines that are complete, still retaining all their original parts, and with the original finish still in good condition are the most sought after, but those that have been carefully restored with their original finishes, decals, etc., are bringing high prices as well. Our advisor for this category is J.R. Wilkins; he is listed in the Directory under Texas. Unless noted, values are for examples in excellent condition, sold at popular, repeated buying prices.

Key:
cyl — cylinder
mg — morning glory
NP — nickel plated
rpd — reproducer

Aretino, disc, orig gr mg horn, 3" center spindle 750.00
Berliner Trade Mark, disc, Clark-Johnson rpd, brass horn 5,000.00
Bing Kiddyphone, disc, Bing rpd, cone horn, circular base 250.00
Bing Pigmyphone, disc, orig rpd, cone horn 400.00
Brunswick, cvd upright case w/moldings, lg 350.00
Busy Bee Grand, disc, orig rpd red mg horn, w/decal 700.00

Cameraphone, disc, orig rpd, tortoise-shell resonator, oak 550.00
Colibri, disc, box camera type, Colibri rpd, sound box, w/case ..350.00
Columbia AA, cyl, eagle rpd, blk horn, oak 1,000.00
Columbia AB (McDonald), cyl, eagle rpd, brass horn, 2 mandrels ..1,400.00
Columbia AH, disc, Columbia rpd, brass bell horn, no decal .1,000.00
Columbia AJ, disc, Columbia rpd, blk/brass bell horn, top crank ...1,200.00
Columbia AK, disc, orig rpd, brass bell horn, 7¼" turntable 800.00
Columbia AO, cyl, D rpd, brass bell horn 500.00
Columbia AQ, cyl, D type, blk cone horn, trivet base 400.00
Columbia AZ, cyl, Lyric rpd, repro blk/brass horn 500.00
Columbia BE Leader, cyl, Lyric rpd, mg 6" mandrel , serpentine .650.00
Columbia BF Peerless, cyl, Lyric rpd, NP horn, M case 800.00
Columbia BI Sterling, disc, Columbia rpd, oak horn 2,250.00
Columbia BK Jewel, cyl, Lyric rpd, orig horn, striping 450.00
Columbia BKT (New Leader), cyl, Columbia rpd, maroon mg horn ...2,400.00
Columbia Grafonola, disc, orig rpd, inside horn, mahog, upright ..200.00
Columbia Grafonola Mignon, disc, inside horn, floor model 200.00
Columbia K, disc, orig rpd, front mt 1,000.00
Columbia P Premium, disc, orig rpd, red horn 625.00
Columbia Q, cyl, Q rpd, repro cone horn, oak w/banner 350.00
Columbia Q Busy Bee, D rpd, 14" blk cone horn, keywind 300.00
Columbia Regent Desk, disc, Columbia rpd, inside horn, mahog ..400.00
Edison Amberola VI, cyl, Dmn B rpd/inside horn, oak table top ...450.00
Edison Amberola VIII, cyl, Dmn B rpd, internal horn, oak table model ..400.00
Edison Amberola X, cyl, Dmn B rpd, inside horn, NM 400.00
Edison Amberola 30, cyl, Dmn C rpd, inside horn, oak, NM 375.00
Edison Business Phono D, cyl, Spectacle rpd, speaking tube, oak ..335.00
Edison Concert, cyl, D rpd, brass horn/stand, 5" mandrel 2,500.00
Edison Concert A, cyl, automatic, rpr, 36" brass horn, w/stand ..3,000.00
Edison Concert C, cyl, R rpd, 30" brass bell, floor stand, M ...2,500.00
Edison Dmn Disc Army-Navy, DD rpd, inside horn, olive drab ..650.00
Edison Dmn Disc A100, DD rpd, inside horn, Moderne golden oak ..350.00
Edison Dmn Disc B-250, disc, DD+78rpm rpd, inside horn, dolphin key ...900.00
Edison Dmn Disc B80, DD rpd, inside horn, table model 350.00
Edison Dmn Disc S19, DD rpd, inside horn, oak, upright 250.00
Edison Fireside A, cyl, Dmn B rpd, oak Music Master horn ...2,250.00
Edison Fireside A, cyl, K rpd, maroon horn/crane 1,000.00
Edison Fireside B, cyl, Dmn B rpd, blk cygnet horn, 4-min 1,000.00
Edison Gem D Maroon, cyl, K rpd, maroon Fireside horn, w/crane ..1,800.00
Edison Gem D Maroon, cyl, K rpd, 20" maroon horn 1,800.00
Edison Gem E Maroon, cyl, all orig 2,000.00
Edison Home, cyl, H rpd, metal cygnet horn, 2/4-min 675.00
Edison Home A, cyl, C rpd, 14" blk/brass horn, gr oak/banner ..500.00
Edison Home A Suitcase, cyl, C rpd, 14" repro horn, decal 550.00
Edison Home E, cyl, O rpd, oak cygnet horn, oak case 1,800.00
Edison Opera, cyl, Dmn A rpd, Music Master horn, mahog, rstr ..5,000.00
Edison Opera A, cyl, L rpd, mahog Music Master horn, mahog 5,000.00
Edison Standard, cyl, C rpd, brass bell horn 475.00
Edison Standard, cyl, Y rpd, brass bell horn, 2/4-min 400.00
Edison Standard A Suitcase, cyl, old-style rpd, 14" brass bell 550.00
Edison Standard C, cyl, C rpd, mg horn, repeating attachment .700.00
Edison Standard D, cyl, K rpd, blk cygnet horn 1,000.00
Edison Triumph, cyl, O rpd, oak cygnet horn, NM 2,500.00
Edison Triumph, cyl, O rpd, wood cygnet, 2/4-min repeater ...2,800.00
Edison Triumph A, cyl, O rpd, Music Master cygnet, striping ...2,850.00
Edison Triumph D, cyl, H rpd, 23" bell horn, 2/4-min 1,000.00
Edison Triumph G, cyl, opera case 7,500.00
Fren-O-Grand Baby Grand, disc, inside horn, piano shape 950.00
Kalamazoo Duplex, disc, Kalamazoo rpd, 2 blk/brass horns, rare ..4,300.00
Kalamazoo Duplex, disc, Kalamazoo rpd, 2 lg horns 3,300.00
Klingsor, disc, Klingsor rpd, inside horn, stained glass doors ...2,000.00
Mignonphone camera type, disc, Mignonphone rpd, cb horn in cover ...175.00
Mikiphone pocketwatch type, disc, blk resonator, circular NP case ...525.00
Nirona box type, disc, Nirona rpd, sound reflector, red metal case, sm ..550.00
Pathe Actuelle, disc, cone horn, mahog console 1,000.00
Pathe Coq, cyl, ebonite rpd, aluminum horn, walnut cover 425.00
Puck Lyre, cyl, floating rpd, red mg horn 400.00
Puck Lyre, cyl, floating rpd, sm Puck horn 450.00
Regina Hexaphone #102, cyl, Hexaphone rpd, oak horn, rstr ...7,500.00
Regina Hexaphone #103, cyl, Hexaphone rpd, oak horn, rstr ...7,500.00
Regina Hexaphone #104, cyl, Hexaphone rpd, oak horn, rstr ...8,500.00
Standard A, disc, Standard rpd, bl mg horn, decal 650.00
Standard X, disc, Standard rpd, front mt brass bell w/support 600.00
Talk-O-Phone Brook, disc, Exhibition rpd, 16" brass bell 525.00
Thorens Excelda, disc, Excelda rpd, internal horn, camera type ...265.00
United Symphony, disc, United rpd, inside horn, table model ..250.00
Victor I, disc, Exhibition rpd, repro brass bell, oak case 1,000.00
Victor II, disc, Exhibition rpd, metal horn 1,200.00
Victor II, disc, Exhibition rpd, oak horn & case 2,500.00
Victor IV, disc, Exhibition rpd, mahog horn & case 2,200.00
Victor M Monarch, disc, Exhibition rpd, 11" horn, oak/composite ...1,500.00
Victor MS Monarch Specialty, disc, Exhibition rpd, oak horn ..2,500.00
Victor R Royal, disc, Exhibition rpd, 9½" brass bell, oak 1,000.00
Victor Schoolhouse XXF, disc, orig oak horn, oak upright 3,000.00
Victor Schoolhouse XXV, disc, oak schoolhouse horn, oak upright ..4,500.00
Victor Type Z, disc, Exhibition rpd, brass bell horn 1,400.00
Victor VI, disc, Exhibition rpd, mahog horn & case 5,000.00
Victor VV-VI, disc, Exhibition rpd, inside horn, oak table top ..200.00
Victor VV-X, disc, Exhibition rpd, inside horn, table top 500.00
Victor VV-50, disc, #2 rpd, inside horn, oak portable 150.00
Victor VV-70, disc, #4 rpd, inside horn, table top 325.00
Victor VV-8-30, disc, Orthophonic rpd, inside horn, credenza 1,000.00
Vitaphone, disc, w/horn, minimum value 1,000.00
Zonophone, disc, front mt w/horn, from $1,000 to 3,000.00
Zonophone A, disc, Concert rpd, brass horn, glass sides 2,500.00
Zonophone Grand Opera, brass horn, rear mt 2,000.00
Zonophone Parlor, disc, brass bell horn, rear crank 1,100.00

Photographica

Photographic collectibles include not only the cameras and equipment used to 'freeze' special moments in time but also the photographic images produced by a great variety of processes that have evolved since the daguerrean era of the mid-1800s. For the most part, good quality images have either maintained or increased in value. Poor quality examples (regardless of rarity) are not selling well. Interest in cameras and stereo equipment is down, and dealers report that average-priced items that were moving well are often completely overlooked. Though rare items always have a market, collectors seem to be buying only if they are bargain priced.

Our advisor for this category is John Hess; he is listed in the Directory under Massachusetts.

Albumens

Harvard-Yale football game, Jarvis Field, November 29, 1890, 9¾x13½", EX, $575.00 at auction.

Ann Pixley, Am actress seated at base of tree in tattered dress, VG 25.00
Band of 9th Veteran Reserve Corps at Washington DC, 1865, 7x9" ..350.00
Barnum's Midgets, 3 in living room scene w/gas lamp on table 35.00
Bearded Navy officer, seated w/elbows on table, ca 1870 ....45.00
Black soldiers stand in front of 3 shacks, 6x8½" on 10x12" mt .475.00
Defenders of the Union, 42 Union Generals, 1862, 8½x10", VG ..100.00
John Hayes, Civil War Soldier Killed at Murfreesboro TN, 8x10" ..250.00
Woman w/hand-held stereo viewer on ornate Belter-style marble table ..30.00

Ambrotypes

An ambrotype is a type of photograph produced by an early wet-plate process whereby a faint negative image on glass is seen as positive when held against a dark background.

Full-plate, Niagara Falls, couple in foreground, 1850s, in fr, $500 to ...700.00
Half-plate, Abraham Lincoln portrait, in Geometric Union case, G ..2,000.00
Half-plate, family grouping of 10 people, VG in full leather case ..100.00
Half-plate, lady w/birds, no case 700.00
Half-plate, lady w/brooch, HP, McClees of Philadelphia, in case ...400.00
Half-plate, Niagara Falls, 2 man in foreground, in leather case ..200.00
4th-plate, Civil War drummer by seashore, in case 1,000.00
4th-plate, Confederate soldier w/bayonett scabbard & musket ..550.00
6th-plate, Black man w/hand-rolled cigars, occupational, WP Beck, G ...550.00
6th-plate, Confederate private seated, dbl-breasted coat, in case ...275.00
6th-plate, Confederate soldier, identified, EX in case 795.00
6th-plate, Confederate soldier sitting in spindle-bk chair, in case ...440.00
6th-plate, Confederate soldier w/revolver, in case 660.00
6th-plate, infantryman w/forage cap/bowie knife/revolver ea hand ..400.00
6th-plate, infantryman w/musket, wearing kepi/X belts/eagle plate ..400.00
6th-plate, Union soldier, ruby, in Xd Cannons Union case, G ..225.00
6th-plate, wht dog smoking pipe (most unusual), in case 850.00
9th-plate, Confederate in battle shirt w/red trim, EX 385.00
9th-plate, Confederate w/musket, EX in case 275.00
9th-plate, VA Confederate private, identified, EX+ in case 550.00

Cabinet Photos

Annie Jones, The Bearded Girl, by Eisenmann, full figure, 1860s ..40.00
Colorado Springs & Pikes Peak, panoramic scene, VG+ 25.00
Drummer w/Quartermaster sword, 5th New York on cap, 1870s, VG ..45.00
Eugene Barry, Big-foot Man, sits w/pants rolled, Wendt, 1900 .....50.00
High-wheel bike & rider, who is holding it up, studio pose, VG ..35.00
John L Sullivan, boxer, in suit coat, 1890s 30.00
Little girl w/doll, dressed alike, Freeman's, MA 25.00
Man w/dog in lap, sits in wicker chair, 1880s 12.00
Midget Major Atom, age 18, stands beside stump, Eisenmann, VG ..35.00
Mille Clifford, Champion Sword Swallower, full view 35.00
Mobile Alabama Militiaman, by Reed & Wallace, full view 30.00
Mount Washington Railroad, locomotive & passenger car 15.00
Woman on bicycle w/bellringer, studio shot w/outdoor bkdrop 35.00

Cameras

Most pre-1900 cameras are large format view cameras or studio camera types. Many are well worn, and there is a large difference in value between an average-wear item and an excellent or mint-condition camera. It is rare indeed to find one of these early cameras in mint condition.

Cameras are generally classified into large format, medium format, early folding and box types, 35 mm single-lens-reflex (SLR), 35mm rangefinders, twin-lens reflex (TLR), miniature or subminiature, novelty, and even a few other types. Collectors may specialize in a type, a style, a time period, or even in high-quality examples of the same camera.

In the 1900 to 1940 period, large quantities of various makes of box cameras and folding bellows type cameras were produced by many manufacturers, and the popular 35mm camera was introduced in the 1930s. Most have low values because they were made in vast numbers, but mint-condition cameras are prized by collectors. In the 1930 to 1955 period, the 35mm rangefinders and the SLR's and TLR's became the cameras of choice. The most prized of these are the early German or Japanese rangefinders such as the Leica, Canon, or Nikon. Earlier, German optics were favored, but after WWII, Japanese cameras and optics rivaled and/or even exceeded the quality of many German optics.

Now there are thousands of different cameras to choose from, and collectors have many options when selecting categories. Quality is the major factor. This brief list suggests average prices for good working cameras with average wear. The same camera in mint condition will be valued much higher, while one with excessive wear (scratches, dents, corrosion, poor optics, nonworking meters or rangefinders) may have little value.

Buying, selling, and trading of old and late vintage cameras on the Internet, both in direct transactions and e-mail auctions, has affected the number of cameras available and their values. Large numbers of old mass-produced box cameras and folding cameras have been offered for sale on the Internet in hopes that a rare one will turn up and reap high rewards. Many are in poor condition or are offered by persons unknowledgeable about quality, so prices have dropped except for the *mint* quality offerings. Many common models in poor to average condition can be bought for $1.00 to $10.00. The collector is advised to purchase only those of a quality that will enhance his collection.

Note: To date, no appreciable collector's market has developed for most old movie cameras or projectors. The Polaroid type of camera has little value, although a few models are gaining in popularity among collectors, and values are expected to increase. Note that there are many fakes and copies of several classic cameras such as the German Leica, and caution is advised in purchasing one of these at a price too good to be true. Consult a specialist on high-priced classics if good reference material is not available. Our advisor for this category is Gene Cataldo; he is listed in the Directory under Alabama (e-mail: genecams@aol.com). SASE required for information by mail.

Wizard, Manhattan Optical Co., polished wood, brass lens, red bellows, ca 1900, from $150.00 to $200.00. (Photo courtesy C. E. Cataldo)

Argus A, early model, 35mm Bakelite, 1936-41, from $20 to 30.00
Cannon III, 1952 ....295.00
Canon IIB, 1949-52 ....275.00
Canon J-II, Rangefinder, rare, 1945, from $4,500 to 6,000.00
Canon S, 1938-46 (usually Nikkor Lenses), from $3,000 to ...4,500.00
Canon 7s Rangefinder, w/F1.2 lens, 1964-67, from $450 to 600.00
Conley 5x7, folding plate, 1908-17, from $175 to 250.00
Eastman Baby Brownie Special, 1939-54, from $1 to 10.00
Eastman Kodak No 2C Brownie Box, 1917-34, from $7 to 15.00
Edinex, by Wirgen, Germany, 1930s-50s 50.00
FED, 35mm, Russian made, various models, from $50 to 200.00
Foth Derby II, German, 1931-36, from $50 to 85.00
Kine Exakta 1, Ihagee, Dresden, 35mm Rangefinder, from $175 to ...250.00
Kodak, vest pocket folding automatic, 1912-14, from $40 to 60.00

Kodak Brownie Target Six-20, 1952, from $1 to 10.00
Kodak Medalist 1, 1941-48, from $175 to 250.00
Kodak Nr 2 Folding Pocket Brownie, horizontal/red bellows, '05, $50 to 75.00
Kodak Retina 1a, Type (015), 1952, from $50 to 75.00
Kodak Tourist II, 1951-58, from $12 to 15.00
Leica II, 1934-48, from $250 to 400.00
Leica IIIa, 1935-50, from $200 to 350.00
Leica IIIc, gray (ball-bearing model), 1942, from $2,500 to 4,500.00
Leica M3 Rangefinder, dbl-stroke advance, 1954-66, from $700 to ...1,000.00
Linex Stereo, by Lionel, 1954, from $100 to 150.00
Minox B, chrome, 1958-71, from $100 to 125.00
Minox II, made in Wetzlar, Germany, from $250 to 400.00
Nikon F, SLR, w/finder & lens, 1960s, from $150 to 450.00
Nr3A Folding Pocket Kodak, ModB-4, red bellows, 1903-15, from $40 to ...70.00
Olympus OM Series, many models, from $75 to 325.00
Olympus Pen, half-fr, many models, from $50 to 225.00
Olympus Pen EED, 33mm half-fr, 1967-72, from $80 to 120.00
Olympus-35, many models, from $30 to 100.00
Orion Works 6x9 Plate, 1921-28, from $60 to 100.00
Voigtlander Prominent 1, 35mm Rangefinder, 1952-58, from $200 to ..300.00
Yashicaflex TLR, Yashikor 80mm lens, from $175 to 250.00
Zeiss Contax III, 1936-42, from $175 to 350.00

Carte De Visites

Among the many types of images collectible today are carte de visites, known as CDVs, which are 2¼" x 4" portraits printed on paper and produced in quantity. The CDV fad of the 1800s enticed the famous and the unknown alike to pose for these cards, which were circulated among the public to the extent that they became known as 'publics.' When the popularity of CDVs began to wane, a new fascination developed for the cabinet photo, a larger version measuring about 4½" x 6½". Note: A common portrait CDV is worth only about 50¢ unless it carries a revenue stamp on the back; those that do are valued at about $2.00 each.

Abraham Lincoln seated at Brady's DC gallery, Feb 9, 1864, VG 145.00
Battle flag of 11th New Hampshire Volunteer Infantry (in studio) ..150.00
Calvary soldier w/revolver in belt, pnt camp scene (in studio), 1860s .180.00
Central City CO scene, att Wm Chamberlain, ca 1867, horizontal .125.00
Chief Justice Roger B Tanney, decided Dred Scott case, oval 80.00
Children of the Battlefield of Gettysburg, EX 40.00
Chinese boy in robe by lg ornate vase, John Thomson, ca 1865 ..50.00
Denver w/Cherry Creek flooded in bkground, att Chamberlain, 1864 ...125.00
Edwin Booth, brother of John Wilkes Booth, seated looking right, VG ...25.00
Gen Charles Devens Jr in civilian coat, ca 1870, VG 30.00
Gen John F Miller, vignette bust shot, revenue stamp on bk, VG ..60.00
Girl depicting Old Lady in the Shoe w/12 dolls, EX 25.00
Infantryman stands before tents,'71 NY' on haversack, from $75 to 150.00
Jenny Lind & her husband, by M Ormsbee, NYC, unpublished, rare 50.00
Military cadets w/12-lb artillery pc disassembled, 1870s, EX 80.00
Navy surgeon wearing Lincoln mourning armband, EX 150.00
Negro soldier holding bayonetted M1863 Springfield rifle, rare ...500.00
Pauline Cushman, Civil War Union spy in officer's uniform, VG ..90.00
President Andrew Johnson, Gardner 350.00
Rutherford Birchard Hayes as Brigadier General, 4x5½" 70.00
Union Major in staff frock w/Rhode Island logo, vignette, VG ...30.00
Union Medical Dept Lieutenant, vignetted pose, VG+ 40.00
Union soldier holding crutches wearing 9-button frock coat 195.00
Union soldier w/16th NHV Co E kepi ID, G 50.00

Daguerreotypes

Among the many processes used to produce photographic images are the daguerreotypes (made on a plate of chemically treated silver-plated copper) — the most-valued examples being the 'whole' plate which measures 6½" x 8½". Other sizes include the 'half' plate, measuring 4½" x 5½", the 'quarter' plate at 3¼" x 4¼", the 'sixth' plate at 2¾" x 3¼", the 'ninth' at 2" x 2½", and the 'sixteenth' at 1⅜" x 1⅝". (Sizes may vary slightly, and some may have been altered by the photographer.)

Half-plate, graduating class of 20 men, in poor leather case 900.00
Half-plate, man & lady w/parasol, in half leather case 550.00
Half-plate, NY or NY winter scene, tinted, Anson on matt ...4,400.00

Sixth-plate, two men seated, one with fur hat, hand resting on his friend's knee, ca 1850, EX, $150.00.

6th-plate, child w/doll, tinted cheeks, in full leather case 850.00
6th-plate, harness maker, in split-leather case 1,000.00
6th-plate, lady reading book, mk Plumbe, in full leather case 465.00
6th-plate, man in Masonic apron, EX in leather case 550.00
6th-plate, mother & child, bl tinted dress, Williamson NY 300.00
6th-plate, mother & child, Fredericks, in full leather case 1,150.00
6th-plate, 2 houses in middle of woods, G in leather case 450.00
9th-plate, lady in purple-tinted dress, G Ruff, England 175.00

Photos

Blk/wht, Jersey City baseball player, youth in knickers, 1890s, 6x4" ...25.00
Blk/wht, 3 early autos at hotel, all ID/dtd 1915, 10x14", +fr 70.00
Goldtone, ES Curtis, Prayer to the Stars, lg Indian, 14x10" ...2,500.00
Photogravure, ES Curtis, Maiden Jicarialla, 1904, 17x12½", EX ...800.00
Photogravure, ES Curtis, Middle Calf-Piegan, #202, 11½x15½" ...500.00
Sepia, Blind Mammy w/bonnet in garden, ca 1910, 3½x5½" 12.00
Sepia, young boy on tricycle w/iron wheels, JW Beaner 35.00

Stereoscopic Views

Stereo cards are photos made to be viewed through a device called a stereoscope. The glass stereo plates of the mid-1800s and photo prints produced in the darkroom are among the most valuable. In evaluating stereo views, the subject, date, and condition are all-important. Some views were printed over a thirty- to forty-year period; 'first generation' prices are far higher than later copies, made on cheap card stock with reprints or lithographs, rather than actual original photographs.

It is relatively easy to date an American stereo view by the color of the mount that was used, the style of the corners, etc. From about 1854 until the early 1860s, cards were either white, cream-colored, or glossy gray; shades of yellow and a dull gray followed. While the dull gray was used for a very short time, the yellow tones continued in use until the late 1860s. Red, green, violet, or blue cards are from the period between 1865 until about 1870. Until the late '70s, corners were square; after that they were rounded off to prevent damage. Right now, quality stereo views are at a premium.

Alaska, Through Fields of Ice & Snow, ...to the Klondyke, Kilburn ...35.00
Camping on the Boulder, view of area, Martin, VG 35.00
Decoration Day Parade, St Paul MN, yel mat, G+ 20.00

Fighting From Stone Wall Defences, Washington Volunteers, 1899, VG ..35.00
Flathead Indian Ponies, F Jay Haynes, beige mat, VG+ 70.00
From Hayden's Survey #131, Navajo Indian Hunter, gray mat ..180.00
Giantess Geyser, Yellowstone, Ingersoll, beige mt, VG 20.00
Great Chicago Fire, view of burned-out bldg, 1871, yel mat 20.00
Libby Prison, flat mt 80.00
Martyred Presidents, Lincoln, McKinley & Garfield, Graves, 1902 ..25.00
Old Fort San Marco, FL, orange mat, VG 10.00
President Teddy Roosevelt's Inaugural Address, 1905, Keystone, VG ..35.00
Sentiment Rock, Yellowstone, Lovejoy & Foster, lg orange mt, VG 25.00
Soldiers launch military balloons to locate enemy, 1905 ....35.00
Span Am War, US Battleship Indiana, side view 5.00
Splendid Geyser in Eruption, 1886, Ingersoll, beige mt, VG 20.00
The Lake, Spanish Fort, LA, orange mat, EX 30.00
US Monitor Terror, CH Graves, ca 1910, VG+ 15.00
WWI French field kitchen w/equipment & soldiers w/mess gear ...3.00
WWI French sharpshooters in trenches, EX 3.00
Zepplin Flying Over German Town, Lower Valley of Rhine, WWI, Keystone ..55.00

Tintypes

Tintypes, contemporaries of ambrotypes, were produced on japanned iron and were not as easily damaged.

Half-plate, Artillery private, waist-up view, in G- Union case ...175.00
4th-plate, Cavalry soldier on horse, epaulets/sword, in case 350.00
4th-plate, Civil War captain w/sword, Eagle belt buckle, in Union case ...400.00
4th-plate, infantry officer, holding Hardee hat, in case 330.00
4th-plate, privates (4) from Lt Artillery unit, in case 250.00
4th-plate, Union private w/arm on table, in Roger deCoverly case ..275.00
4th-plate, Union sergeant w/sword, kepi w/red sash 385.00
6th-plate, enlisted man w/forage cap/sack coat, in case 110.00
6th-plate, infantryman stands w/musket/bayonet/revolvers 385.00
6th-plate, Naval officers (3) standing, in thermoplastic case 330.00
6th-plate, outdoor view of 2 Union soldiers w/muskets, in Union case ...525.00
6th-plate, seargent in striped pants, star on jacket 250.00
6th-plate, solder wearing kepi/holding telescope 250.00
6th-plate, Union officer w/Hardee hat/holster/drawn sword, in case ...500.00
6th-plate, Union sergeant, gilded button, EX in worn case 165.00
6th-plate, Union soldier holding kepi, gloves & sash, VG in case ..275.00
9th-plate, Confederate holding slouch hat 225.00
9th-plate, infantryman & wife, fine tinting on faces, in case 275.00

Union Cases

From the mid-1850s until about 1880, cases designed to house these early images were produced from a material known as thermoplastic, a man-made material with an appearance much like gutta percha. Its innovator was Samuel Peck, who used shellac and wood fibers to create a composition he called Union. Peck was part owner of the Scoville Company, makers of both papier-mache and molded leather cases, and he used the company's existing dies to create his new line. Other companies (among them A.P. Critchlow & Company; Littlefield, Parsons & Company; and Holmes, Booth & Hayden) soon duplicated his material and produced their own designs. Today's collectors may refer to cases made of this material as 'thermoplastic,' 'composition,' or 'hard cases,' but the term most often used is 'Union.' It is incorrect to refer to them as gutta percha cases.

Sizes may vary somewhat, but generally a 'whole' plate case measures 7" x 9⅛" to the outside edges, a 'half' plate 4⅞" x 6", a 'quarter' plate 3¾" x 4¾", a 'sixth' 3⅛" x 3⅝", a 'ninth' 2⅜" x 2⅞", and a 'sixteenth' 1¾" x 2". Clifford and Michele Krainik and Carl Walvoord have written a book, *Union Cases*, which we recommend for further study. Another source of information is *Nineteenth Century Photographic Cases and Wall Frames* by Paul Berg. Values are for examples in excellent condition unless noted otherwise.

Half-plate, Washington Monument, K-4, with child ambrotype, EX, $475.00.

Half-plate, American Country Life, VG 310.00
Half-plate, geometrics, w/velvet pad, mat & glass, EX 175.00
Half-plate, The Wedding Procession, ambrotype of couple, M ..495.00
Half-plate, Washington Monument, w/poor ambrotype, EX 350.00
1¾" cookie shape, 2 rnd pcs, w/tintype of sm boy, EX 270.00
4th-plate, Angel w/Stag, G- 100.00
4th-plate, Roger deCoverly, w/tintype, VG 150.00
4th-plate, Washington Monument, w/ambrotype of man, EX 200.00
6th-plate, G Washington on both sides, mk S Peck 160.00
9th-plate, Civil War soldier, mk Union Now & Forever, K-370 ...180.00
9th-plate, geometric scrolls, w/ambrotype of man, EX 85.00
9th-plate, Moses in Bulrushes, w/tintype of seated man, oval 80.00
9th-plate, Twice Armed, Civil War infantryman w/Warner pistol ..380.00

Miscellaneous

Stanhope, Civil War bullet, Gettysburg views 50.00
Stanhope, pipe, wooden, 6 views of Niagara Falls 100.00
Stanhope, telescope, Grant view by Joseph Ward 250.00
Stanhope, telescope, Stanton Secretary of War 400.00
Stanhope, umbrella, ivory, Buffalo Bill portrait, ca 1920 ....450.00
Stereopticon, Am Novelty Co, metal/CI/pnt enamel, 14" 195.00

Piano Babies

A familiar sight in Victorian parlors, piano babies languished atop shawl-covered pianos in a variety of poses: crawling, sitting, on their tummies, or on their backs playing with their toes. Some babies were nude, and some wore gowns. Sizes ranged from about 3" up to 12". The most famous manufacturer of these bisque darlings was the Heubach Brothers of Germany, who nearly always marked their product; see Heubach for listings. Watch for reproductions. These guidelines are excerpted from one of a series of informative doll books by Patsy Moyer, published by Collector Books. Values are for examples in excellent condition.

Blk, bsk, 5", EX quality 525.00
Blk, bsk, 9", EX quality 500.00
Blk, bsk, 14", EX quality 900.00
Bsk, w/animal, pot, flowers, chair, etc, 5", EX quality, ea 360.00
Bsk, w/animal, pot, flowers, chair, etc, 8", EX quality, ea 425.00
Bsk, w/animal, pot, flowers, chair, etc, 10", EX quality, ea 525.00
Bsk, w/animal, pot, flowers, chair, etc, 15", EX quality, ea 1,000.00
Bsk, 4", EX quality 325.00
Bsk, 4", med quality, unmk 100.00
Bsk, 6", EX quality 475.00
Bsk, 8", med quality 200.00
Bsk, 9", EX quality 700.00
Bsk, 12", med quality 400.00

Bsk, 16", EX quality 1,225.00

Pickard

Founded in 1895 in Chicago, Illinois, the Pickard China Company was originally a decorating studio, importing china blanks from European manufacturers. Some of these early pieces bear the name of those companies as well as Pickard's. Trained artists decorated the wares with hand-painted studies of fruit, florals, birds, and scenics and often signed their work. In 1915 Pickard introduced a line of 23k gold over a dainty floral-etched ground design. In the 1930s they began to experiment with the idea of making their own ware and by 1938 had succeeded in developing a formula for fine translucent china. Since 1976 they have issued an annual limited edition Christmas plate. They are now located in Antioch, Illinois.

The company has used various marks. The earliest (1893–1894) was a double-circle mark, 'Edgerton Hand Painted' with 'Pickard' in the center. Variations of the double-circle mark (with 'Hand Painted China' replacing the Edgerton designation) were employed until 1915, each differing enough that collectors can usually pinpoint the date of manufacture within five years. Later marks included the crown mark, 'Pickard' on a gold maple leaf, and the current mark, the lion and shield. Work signed by Challinor, Marker, and Yeschek is especially valued by today's collectors. For further information we recommend *Collector's Encyclopedia of Pickard China* by Alan B. Reed, available from Collector Books.

Pitchers, lemonade; Classic Ruins by Moonlight, signed Marker, 1912 – 18 mark, 6¼", $550.00; Carnations on gold, signed Fisher, 1905 – 10, 6¼", $450.00; Goosberries Conventional pattern, signed N.R. Gifford, 1903 – 05 mark, 6½", $700.00. (Photo courtesy Joy Luke Fine Arts Brokers and Auctioneers)

Berry set, apples/blossoms, gilt border, Leon, 1903-04, 7-pc 1,050.00
Bonbon, allover gold, central hdl, 9¾" 75.00
Bottle, scent; violets, Marker, 1912-18 ....200.00
Bowl, nuts/leaves on brn, hexagonal, Challinor, 1912-18, 8¾" .300.00
Bowl, strawberries, C Hahn, 1903-05, 9¾" 300.00
Cake plate, allover gold, hdls, 10" 170.00
Candlesticks, Antique Chinese Enamel, Eldon, 1912-18, 9", pr ...350.00
Candlesticks, oval panel w/basket of flowers on pk, 8", pr 375.00
Charger, Golden Pheasant, E Challinor, 1912-22, 12½" 500.00
Chocolate pot, grapes/leaves on blk & red, Gibson, 1898-03, 12" ...1,050.00
Chocolate pot, Raised Gold Daisy, 1905-10, 10¾" 300.00
Chocolate set, platinum o/l, pot, creamer & sugar w/lid 275.00
Coffeepot, Poppy Conventional (red), Fox, 1905-10, 10" 400.00
Cracker jar, Twin Poppies, F Loba, 1905-1910, 5x7½" 325.00
Creamer & sugar bowl, currants, JN (Nessey, 1903-05) 425.00
Creamer & sugar bowl, Rose & Daisy, allover platinum/gold 75.00
Creamer & sugar bowl on tray, allover gold 90.00
Cruet, Crocus Conventional, 1903-05, 6¾" 350.00
Cup & saucer, floral, gold on teal, 1912-18 ....80.00
Dish, bird & butterflies, 1925-30, 7" 70.00
Dish, Deserted Garden, hdls, Vokral, 1919-22, 12" L 275.00
Dish, Walled Garden, Alex, hdls, 1912-18, 6½" L 200.00
Ginger jar, oval panel w/flowers on bl mottle, 1925-39, 12" 600.00
Hatpin holder, irises, Beutlich, 1905-10, 5" 300.00
Jam jar, Deserted Garden, J Nessy, 1912-18, hdls/lid 320.00
Jardiniere, lily pads on gold border, Schoner, 1905-10, 5x5" 325.00
Jug, Alexander, strawberries, Beitler, 1903-05, 8" 1,000.00
Mayonnaise, allover gold, flower shaped, +tray & spoon 140.00
Pin tray, flowers, Beutlich, 1905-10, 5¾" 30.00
Pitcher, cider; Arabian, 1903-05, 8" 1,600.00
Pitcher, Dorique, Poppy & Black, 1903-05, 8" 750.00
Pitcher, lemonade; Hops in Lustre & Matt Gr, Lind, 1905-10, 6½" ..550.00
Pitcher, lemonade; purple plums, LeRoy, 1903-05, 6½", NM 650.00
Pitcher, Moorish Design, Kriesche, 1905-10, 5¾" 525.00
Pitcher, tankard; Pond Lily, heavy gold, sgn Firchs, 5" 210.00
Plate, apples, Rean (Maxwell Klipphahn), 1903-05, 8½" 160.00
Plate, Aura Argenta Linear, Hessler, 1905-10, 8" 150.00
Plate, Cherries & Gold, Beitler, 1903-05, 7½" 70.00
Plate, ears of corn, Vokral, 1905-10, 8½" 250.00
Plate, strawberries, Fisher, 1903-05, 7½" 70.00
Plate, trees/lake/snow-cap mtns, Challinor, 1918-19, 8¾" 250.00
Plate, Walled Garden, Challinor, hdls, sq, 1912-18, 7½" 250.00
Plate, Wildwood, roses/birch trees, Wagner, 1912-18, 8½" 275.00
Punch bowl, currants/leaves, Vokral, 1905-1910, 6x13" 3,600.00
Shakers, allover gold, pr 20.00
Sugar cube holder, reversed scrolls/pk leaves, 1912-18, 8" L 150.00
Syrup jug, Easter Lily, OS (Schoner), 1903-05, 6", +tray 575.00
Tankard, blackberries/flowers, gilt rim, Reury, 6" 100.00
Tankard, grapes/leaves, Coufall, 1905-10, 14" 2,250.00
Tankard, Metallic Grapes, Hessler 1903-05, 15" 1,100.00
Tankard, monk peeling turnip, Gasper, 1905-10, 14" 2,900.00
Teapot, Classic Ruins by Moonlight, Marker, 1912-18, 6½" 375.00
Trivet, Aura Argenta Linear, OP, 1905-10, 6½" dia 75.00
Vase, allover gold, hdls, 9¾" 120.00
Vase, Aura Mosaic, Hess, 1905-10, 6" 275.00
Vase, Classic Ruins by Moonlight, HLC (Corey), 1912-18, 7" ..450.00
Vase, daffodil, Motzfeldt, 1898-1903, 8½" 1,250.00
Vase, Encrusted Fruit on gold, Rean (Klipphahn), 1912-18, 8" .250.00
Vase, Encrusted Linear, sgn RH, 1912-18, 6½" 140.00
Vase, Florida Lagoon/palm tree, F Cernct (Cirnacty), 7½" 350.00
Vase, Fruits Linear, Tolpin, 1912-18, 10" 450.00
Vase, geraniums, Challinor, 1903-05, 10" 900.00
Vase, haystacks by moonlight, Alex, 1912-18, 6¾" 400.00
Vase, landscape/highland cattle, Kubash, 1903-05, 7" 3,500.00
Vase, palm trees, 1918-1919, 8" 400.00
Vase, pine trees by moonlight, Challinor, 1912018, 7" 850.00
Vase, Poppy, sgn PG, 1905-10, 14" 1,500.00
Vase, Poppy & Black, Loh, 1903-05, 13½" 850.00
Vase, Walled Garden, gilt hdls, Challinor, 1912-18, 10" 1,800.00
Vase, White Poppy & Daisy, Gasper, hdls, 1905-10, 9¾" 700.00
Whiskey jug, hops/leaves outlined in gold, Lind, 1903-05, 11" ..850.00

Pickle Castors

Pickle castors, which were both functional and decorative, became popular after the Civil War, reaching their peak about 1885. By 1900 they had virtually disappeared from factory catalogs. Numerous styles were available. They consisted of a decorated, silverplated frame that held either a fancy clear pressed-glass insert or one of decorated colored art glass — the latter being popular in the more affluent Victorian households and more desirable with collectors today.

In the listings below, the description prior to the semicolon refers to the jar (insert), and the remainder of the line describes the frame. Unless a color is mentioned, all glassware is clear. When no condition is indicated, the silverplate is assumed to be in very good to excellent condition, with the fork or tongs present. Glass jars are assumed near mint. Our advisor for this category is Deborah Maggard; she is listed in the Directory under Ohio.

Warning: Watch for reproduction frames from Taiwan!

Key: rsl — resilvered

Albertine, tiny emb triangles/mc florals on lav; mk SP fr 2,800.00
Albertine w/caladium leaf, Mt WA; ornate Tufts fr 1,100.00
Balder; SP fr 90.00
Bridal Rosette, ruby stain; SP fr 425.00
Butterfly & Fan; SP fr & lid 85.00
Cone, pk cased; ornate pierced SP fr, 10" 400.00
Cranberry w/floral, ribbed; simple eng SP fr 400.00
Cranberry w/floral; ornate SP fr 500.00
Cupid & Venus; rstr SP fr 195.00
Daisy & Button, amber; Webster fr w/emb faces on ft 400.00
Daisy & Button, bl canoe insert; 4-wheeled Holman carriage fr 400.00
Daisy & Button, sapphire bl; SP fr 250.00
Daisy & Button, vaseline; ornate Tufts fr 475.00
Dmn Point, bl, nonflint; orig SP fr & lid 175.00
Dmn T'print, cranberry; ornate SP fr w/ball & claw ft 350.00
Frosted w/emb/pnt wild rose wreath, 4¾" bbl; SP fr, 11" 450.00
Hobnail, cranberry, str sides; mk SP ftd fr 500.00
Invt T'print, amberina, belled body; ornate ornament on SP fr ..500.00
Invt T'print, cranberry vase shape w/gold floral; Tufts fr 600.00
Invt T'print, cranberry w/floral; Holman Eastlake-style fr 600.00
Invt T'print, cranberry w/floral; ornate SP fr, 10" 400.00
Invt T'print, cranberry w/floral; ornate SP fr, 11½" 900.00
Jersey Swirl; SP fr & lid 135.00
Optic Panel, pk opal, Mt WA; ornate Pairpoint fr 395.00
Royal Oak, rubena frost; fr needs rsl 375.00
Rubena, crystal ribs w/gold; R&B fr, 14", +shell tongs 750.00
Sapphire bl pressed glass; Simpson Hall Miller fr, 11¾" 350.00
Spangle, yel/wht w/mica, swirled, flared at base; ornate SP fr 325.00
Spanish Lace, cranberry opal; Meriden fr, 12¼" 400.00
Swirl bbl, cranberry opal; ornate eng SP fr w/top ornament 650.00
Vaseline; orig Meriden fr, 12" 375.00
Wht w/red rose buds, red int; ornate fr, 11" 375.00
Yel-orange mottle w/opal gray, pinched; ornate SP fr, 10" 600.00

Pie Birds

A pie bird or pie funnel (pie vent) is generally made of pottery, glazed inside and out. Most are 3" to 5" in height with arches at the base to allow steam to enter. The steam is then released through an exit hole at the top.

The English pie funnel was as tall as the special baking dish was deep and held the crust even with the dish's rim, thereby lifting the crust above the filling so it would stay crisp and firm. These dishes came in several different sizes, which accounts for the variances in the heights of the pie birds.

The first deviations from the basic funnels were produced in the mid-1930s to late 1940s: the Clarice Cliff (signed Midwinter or Newport) pie bird (reg. no. on white base) and the signed Nutbrown elephant. Shortly thereafter (1940s–1960s), figures of bakers and colorful birds were created for additional visual baking fun. From the 1980s to present, many novelty pie vents have been added to the market for the enjoyment of both the baker and collector. These have been made by commercial (including Far East importers) and local enterprises in Canada, England, and the United States. A new category for the 1990s includes an array of holiday-related pie vents. Basic tip: Older pie vents were air-brushed, not hand-painted.

Incense burners (i.e., elephants and Oriental people), one-hole pepper shakers, dated brass toy bird whistle, egg timers (missing glass timer), and ring holders (i.e., elephant with clover on his tummy) should not be mistaken for pie vents. Our advisor for this category is Linda Fields; she is listed in the Directory under Tennessee.

The Arnel Mold Company (Portland, OR) has sold this three-pie-bird mold from 1977 to the present. They are painted in a solid color or with good feather detail. These 4¼" pie birds are valued at $10.00 to $25.00 each. (Photo courtesy Lillian Cole)

Benny the Baker, w/pie crimper & cake tester, Cardinal, from $125 to ...135.00
Bird on nest, Artesian Galleries, copyright mk, 1950s, from $200 to ..250.00
Bl & wht bird on wht base, Royal Worcester, 2-pc (ea mk), from $130 to 150.00
Blackbird, thin neck, mk Scotland, from $60 to 75.00
Blackbird, wht head, teardrop eyes, Australia, from $40 to 60.00
Blackbird on wht base, orange beak, Clarice Cliff, from $45 to ...50.00
Chef, The Servex; from $150 to 175.00
Chick, Josef Original, 1950s-70s, from $45 to 50.00
Cutie Pie, Josef (or Lorrie Design), hen in bonnet, from $125 to ..150.00
Duck (or swan) head, brn w/yel beak, from $150 to 175.00
Dutch girl, multipurpose kitchen tool, from $150 to 195.00
Eagle, mk Sunglow, golden color, from $75 to 85.00
Elephant, mk Nutbrown, wht, tan or gray, respectively, from $75 to ..175.00
Elephant on drum, mk CCC (Cardinal), solid pk base 120.00
Elephant on drum, mk CCC (Cardinal), XXX base 200.00
Fred the Flour Grater, (orig has) dots for eyes, from $65 to 75.00
Fruit (apple, peach or cherries), import, ea, from $350 to 400.00
Funnel, aluminum, England 25.00
Funnel, aluminum, plain, from $10 to 15.00
Funnel, Grimwade Perfection 110.00
Funnel, pagoda, Gourmet Pie Cup, Reg No 369793 ....75.00
Funnel, pagoda, Nutbrown 95.00
Funnel, wht w/rosebud on top, from $150 to 175.00
Half-bird, blk, w/scalloped or triangular bottom, from $75 to 100.00
Long-neck Pie Duckling, American Pottery, 1940s, from $50 to .75.00
Mammy, multipurpose kitchen tool, outstretched arms, from $125 to 150.00
Pie Boy, gr sombreros on outfit, from $350 to 400.00
Rooster, Cleminson Pottery, mk 'C' encircling a 'b,' from $45 to .50.00
Songbird, Chic Pottery (Le Pere), cream or blk w/gold, from $125 to ..150.00
Welsh Lady, Cymru, from $75 to 95.00

Pierce, Howard

Collectors of Howard Pierce's work have witnessed new trends and higher prices this year. Values are topping the scales on almost all his work, due in part, perhaps, because of his death on February 28, 1994. Pierce designed a line of pins which he first produced in 1941. The originals were in pewter, but a short time later, he made them in a copper finish. Some painted pins and figurines were created as well. These items bear the early 'Howard Pierce' mark. While most researchers believed just last year that examples of this jewelry would be in the $100.00 to $175.00 range, dealers and collectors thought differently; and it has not been uncommon to find the gavel dropping at about $200.00 for most examples. (If any pin is more plentiful than any other, it would be the lamb.) Almost all animals have seen a substantial rise in value. The vases with bisque inserts, even though they have increased about 10% over last year's values, have not seen the growth one would expect, given the few that were produced.

Howard Pierce and his wife Ellen (Van Voorhis) opened his Claremont, California, studio in 1941, where they worked side by side. Howard was one of few artists who attempted to work with so many varied materials: polyurethane, Wedgwood-type Jasperware, ash from Mt. St. Helens' eruption, gold leaf and a gold leaf-type (the latter being created for Sears, Roebuck & Company), rough-textured as well as high-gloss porcelain, cement, pewter, copper, aluminum, bronze, and hydrocal.

Pierce had ambivalent feelings about experimental glazes. He tested glazes on a large scale, especially during the later years of his career, but most of the time he did not like what he had created. Today's collectors actively seek them out. Some of these glazes are deep purple, pale blue, iridescent pink, green, and a very dark cobalt that sometimes appears ebony in recessed details. Scratched-in numbers sometimes found on these items correspond to Howard's formula book. Howard preferred gray, white, or brown glazes. Though he liked the leopards and tigers with hand-painted stripes and spots, because they were so time consuming, less than a dozen of each were ever produced. His porcelain angels, though popular sellers (especially those with a Black face), also had a short production run, due to the fact that their wings were often damaged in the kiln.

Because of his poor health, in 1992 Howard and Ellen destroyed all the molds they had ever created. Still the artist in Howard needed to create, so in 1993 (only a year before he died) they purchased a small kiln and began making miniature versions of their original products. These pieces are simply stamped 'Pierce.' Some collectors are speculating that in a short time, these miniature pieces will be more costly than their larger counterparts, since their production time was so limited.

For further information we recommend *Collector's Encyclopedia of Howard Pierce Porcelain* by Darlene Hurst Dommell (Collector Books). Our advisor for this category is Susan Cox; she is listed in the Directory under California.

Figurine, pelican, bill away from body, brown and white, 8½x6", rare, $155.00. (Photo courtesy Susan Cox)

Ashtray, experimental gr, trefoil, 1950s mk, 25X, 5" 65.00
Bowl, gondola shape, brn on wht, 5x9½" 70.00
Bowl, Lava, brn & wht, 2½x9" 115.00
Creche, Joseph, Mary w/Jesus & lamb, bl, mk, 7½", 4½", 2" 175.00
Figurine, cat, stylized, brn & wht, 8" 100.00
Figurine, chickadee, bl, 3¾", 2½", pr 38.00
Figurine, dove, 6" 75.00
Figurine, duck, Sears gold, mk, 7¾" 48.00
Figurine, elephant, trunk up, rare pk glaze, 4½" 275.00
Figurine, ermine, standing, 1950s, 9" 195.00
Figurine, Eskimo, brn & wht, #206P, 7" 95.00
Figurine, horned owl, 8" 110.00
Figurine, horse, dk brn w/beige-tipped mane & tale, 1950s, 9" ..185.00
Figurine, panther, dk brn, 11½" 190.00
Figurine, raccoon, brn, tail w/4 stripes, 9" 135.00
Figurine, rooster & hen, brn & wht, 1950s, 9¼", 7¾", pr 220.00
Figurine, water bird, gr & wht, 5½" 60.00
Figurine, water bird, 14" 125.00
Magnet, coyote, brn, no mk, 4¼" 95.00
Pencil holder, lg nude woman, brn, 4¼" 170.00
Pin, lamb, pewter, mk Howard Pierce, 2¾" 195.00
Vase, bud; brn, stamp mk, 3½" 45.00
Vase, gondola style, oval, 7½x5" 85.00
Wall plaque, 2 raccoons on branch, brn cement, 16" 490.00
Whistle, bird shape, brn, 3½" 115.00

Pigeon Blood

Pigeon blood glass, produced in the late 1800s, may be distinguished from other dark red glass by its distinctive orange tint.

Salt shaker, Torquay, 3⅛", from $110.00 to $125.00. (Photo courtesy Mildred and Ralph Lechner)

Biscuit jar, Florette, metal lid 325.00
Bisquit jar, Little Shrimp 325.00
Bowl, berry; Open Heart Arches 225.00
Butter dish, Coreopsis 275.00
Creamer, Beaded Drape 150.00
Creamer, Coreopsis 125.00
Cruet, Torquay, shiny 795.00
Cup, 4" 65.00
Mustard pot, Torquay, w/hinged lid 110.00
Rose bowl, HP flowers w/gilt, 5" dia 70.00
Spooner, Torquay, all glass 150.00
Sugar bowl, Torquay, glass lid 165.00
Wine, 6" 42.00

Pigeon Forge

Douglas J. Ferguson and Ernest Wilson started their small pottery in Pigeon Forge, Tennessee, in 1946. Using red-brown and gray locally dug clay and glazes which they themselves formulate, bowls, vases, and sculptures are produced there. Their primary target is the tourist trade.

Bowl, dk red & gr curdled volcanic glaze, Ferguson, mk, 2¾x5⅛" ...300.00
Figurine, bear, sitting up, Ferguson, 4½" 38.00
Figurine, owl, Ferguson, 6½" 42.00
Teapot, off-wht w/umber drips, crystalline glaze, w/lid 60.00

Vase, red speckles on blk, 4½" 50.00

Pillin

Polia Pillin was born in Poland in 1909. She came to the U.S. as a teenager and showed an interest and talent for art, which she studied in Chicago. She married William Pillin, who was a poet and potter. They ultimately combined their talents and produced her very distinctive pottery from the 1950s to the mid-1980s. She died in 1993.

Polia Pillin won many prizes for her work, which is always signed Pillin with the loop of the 'P' over the full name. Some undecorated pieces are signed W&P, due to her husband's collaboration.

Her work is prized for its art, not for the shape of her pots, which for the most part are simple vases, dishes, bowl, and boxes. Wall plaques are rare. She pictured women with hair reminiscent of halos, girls, an occasional boy, horses, birds, and fish. After viewing a few of her pieces, her style is unmistakable. Some of her early work is very much like that of Picasso.

Her pieces are somewhat difficult to find, as all the work was done without outside help, and therefore limited in quantity. In the last few years, more and more people have become interested in her work, resulting in escalating prices. Our advisors for this category are Dolli and Wilfred Cohen; they are listed in the Directory under California.

Bowl, lady w/bl hair, bird in hand, 2x7½" 900.00
Bust, lady w/2 stylized birds, mc 425.00
Dish, harlequins (2) dancing on brn, 6" dia 650.00
Dish, horses (pr), sq, 9" 1,100.00
Dish, lady w/mandolin, mc on shaded bl, w/lid, 2x4" dia 375.00
Dish, nudes bathing, oyster shape, rstr chips, 4x6½" 450.00
Oil on paper, Yellow Bird, Polla Pillin, sight: 12¾x11¾" in fr ..850.00
Plate, lady & bird, 7¾" 850.00
Ring tray, mother & daughter on orange & blk, 7" 550.00
Vase, birds, 5" 595.00
Vase, bud; cobalt bl over snowy wht, 7" 230.00
Vase, chickens (3) on bl-gray, bottle shape, 4½x3½" 375.00
Vase, dk gr/bl crystalline, 1950s, 9¾" 395.00
Vase, gr/olive matt texture, wide gourd w/tiny neck, 13" 375.00
Vase, horses (2) frolicking, mk, 4¾" 450.00
Vase, ivory w/bright irid highlights, rnd w/stick neck, 8½" 750.00
Vase, ladies, mc on bl, rectangular, 9", NM 850.00
Vase, ladies (2) seining for fish, bulbous, 4¼" 475.00
Vase, ladies dancing, mc on mottled pk & yel, 7½" 750.00
Vase, lady & birds/lady w/horse, bottle shape, 6½x2½" 550.00
Vase, lady & horse, 6" 625.00
Vase, lady & horses, brn on blk, bottle shape, 11¾x5", NM ..1,500.00
Vase, lady in ermine cap w/chicken, bottle form, 5¾x3½" 325.00
Vase, lady w/bird, 2 ladies dance, mc on bl, 4½x5" 495.00
Vase, lady/horse/rooster, flared rim, 7" 650.00
Vase, nudes, 6" 750.00
Vase, Oriental-look bl & gr gloss w/red highlights, 11½x12" .1,000.00
Vase, rooster on bl, cylindrical, 7" 495.00
Vase, suspended charcoal/yel gloss, rnd w/sm neck, 8½" 750.00
Wine cup, rooster, mc on gr, 2½" 325.00

Pin-Back Buttons

Buttons produced up to the early 1920s were made of a celluloid covering held in place by a ring (or collet) to the back of which a pin was secured. Manufacturers used these 'cellos' to advertise their products. Many were of exceptional quality in both color and design. Buttons were produced in sets featuring a variety of subjects. These were given away by tobacco, chewing gum, and candy manufacturers, who often packed them with their product as premiums. Usually the name of the button maker or the product manufacturer was printed on a paper placed in the back of the button. Often these 'back papers' are still in place today. Much of the time the button maker's name was printed on the button's perimeter, and sometimes the copyright was added. Beginning in the 1920s, a large number of buttons were lithographed on tin; these are referred to as tin 'lithos.' Nearly all pin-back buttons are collected today for their advertising appeal or graphic design. There are countless categories to base a collection on.

The following listing contains non-political buttons representative of the many varieties you may find. Our advisor for this category is Michael J. McQuillen; he is listed in the Directory under Indiana. See also Political.

Rainbow Fire Company Outing, fireman's portrait, multicolor on white, 1928, EX, $20.00.

Always Shoot Winchester, target w/W in inner circle, 1", NM ...32.00
America's First Orbital Spaceman, John Glenn, 1962, 3½", NM ..30.00
Another Nash, auto fr by tire, 1¼" dia, VG+ 500.00
Buster Brown Walking Club, 1920s, oval, EX 25.00
Buy American, flag on bl/wht, 1930s, ⅞", EX 20.00
Casper the Friendly Ghost, 1950s 20.00
Charge, Bring Back the Bullmoose Party!..., Bullwinkle yelling, EX ..20.00
Dale Evans, blk/wht photo on gr, 1950s, 1½", EX 25.00
Davy Crockett King of the Frontier, blk/wht photo on yel, 1¼", EX ...35.00
Elsie the Cow for President, red/wht/bl, 1960s, 3" 25.00
Frankenstein, name under bust image, 1960s, EX 10.00
Green Hornet Agent, 1960s, 4", EX 15.00
I Go Pogo, 1956, ⅞", NM 22.00
I'm Bugs About You, 3½", EX 15.00
Jackie Gleason Fan Club/And Awa-a-ay We Go!!!, tin, bl/wht, 1½", EX ...35.00
Joe DiMaggio, NY Yankees, blk/wht photo, 1¾", EX 20.00
John Wayne Western Saddle Kings Series, blk/gr, 1¾", M 12.00
Johnston Fudge Sundae, red/wht/bl, 1940s, 2¼", EX 15.00
Life Bread Radio Club, yel/red/bl, 1930s, 1", EX 15.00
Lindbergh, red/wht/bl, St Louis, rare, 1½", EX 175.00
Mummy, name under bust image, EX 10.00
Philadelphia Phillies 1950 Champs, 1¾", EX 15.00
Red Comb Poultry Foods, rooster's head, blk/wht/red, 1910s, 1¼", EX ..18.00
Red Goose Club Member, red on wht, 1940s, 1¼", EX 15.00
Remember Pearl Harbor, shows American flag, red/wht/bl, 1¼", EX ...20.00
Remington-UMC, wht on red, VG 15.00
Rin-Tin-Tin, Screen Gems, head shot, 1956, NM 20.00
Snow White Jingle Club, red/wht/bl, 1938, 3", EX 150.00
Stanley Steamer, auto/dealer, bl/blk/wht, 1", EX 825.00
Vote for Philip Morris, bellhop yelling, 1930s, EX 18.00
Wolf Man, name under bust image, 1960s, EX 10.00

Pine Ridge

In the mid-1930s, the Indian Bureau of Affairs and the Work Progress Administration offered the Native Americans living on the Pine Ridge Indian Reservation in South Dakota a class in pottery making. Originally, Margaret Cable (director of the University of North Dakota ceramics department) was the instructor and Bruce Doyle was director. By the early 1950s, pottery production at the school was abandoned. In 1955 the equipment was purchased by Ella Irving, a student who had been highly involved with the class since the late 1930s. From then until 1980 when it closed, Ella virtually ran the pot shop by herself.

The clay used in Pine Ridge pottery was red and the decoration reminiscent of early Indian pottery and beadwork designs. A variety of marks and labels were used. For more information we recommend *Collector's Encyclopedia of the Dakota Potteries* by Darlene Hurst Dommel (Collector Books).

Basket, hanging; geometric motif, 5x7½" 275.00
Bowl, geometric motif, sgn N Firethunder, 2x10" 325.00
Bowl, incised geometrics under milky transparent glaze, 3x6" ...325.00
Bowl, triangular devices, beige on brick red, 3x4½" 125.00
Cup & saucer, bl-gr, 2", 5½" 65.00
Jardiniere, flowing glaze, mk Sioux Indian, 4¾x9¼" 450.00
Mug, gray drip over red clay w/turq int, restaurant ware, 3" 65.00
Pitcher, rust gloss, 4½" 55.00
Shakers, geometric star motif, 2x2¾", pr 85.00
Vase, Cottier; sgraffito cream geometric motifs on red, 7¼x5" ..375.00

Pink Lustre Ware

Pink lustre was produced by nearly every potter in the Staffordshire district in the late 1700s and first half of the 1800s. The application of gold lustre on white or light-colored backgrounds produced pinks, while the same over dark colors developed copper. The wares ranged from hand-painted plaques to transfer-printed dinnerware. Design features in the phrase immediately following the item (i.e. cup, plate, etc.) are in pink lustre unless otherwise specifically described within the line.

Bust, John Wesley, enameled decor, ca 1825, 10½" 1,035.00
Cup plate, House pattern, 4" dia 50.00
Pitcher, Lord Brougham Vaix/Lord High Chancellor, blk stransfer, 7" ...400.00
Pitcher, Protestant Ascendancy/Let Brother Love..., 19th C, 5¼" ...230.00
Pitcher, Queen Caroline, emb/pnt floral border, 1820, 5¼" 625.00
Pitcher, 1812 war-hero commemorative magenta transfers, 6½", NM ...1,700.00
Plaque, Prepare To Meet Thy God, early 19th C, 6⅝x7¾" 145.00
Punch bowl, Scotch Drink, hunting scenes, 4 transfers, Moore, 10½" ..1,400.00
Sugar bowl, purple transfer genre scene, hdls, w/lid, 4½" 45.00
Vase, peasant scene/bird in flight, rstr, 7½", pr 700.00

Pink Paw Bears

These charming figural pieces are very similar to the Pink Pigs described in the following category. They were made in Germany during the same time frame. The cabbage green is identical; the bears themselves are whitish-gray with pink foot pads. You'll find some that are unmarked while others are marked 'Germany' or 'Made in Germany.' In theory, the unmarked bears are the oldest, made prior to 1890 when the McKinley Tariff Act required imports to be marked with the country of origin. Those marked 'Made In' were probably produced after the revision of the Act in 1914.

1 by bean pot 135.00
1 by graphophone 150.00
1 by honey pot 145.00
1 by top hat 125.00
1 in front of basket 135.00
1 in roadster (car identical to pk pig car) 185.00
1 on binoculars 150.00
1 peaking out of basket 135.00
1 sitting in wicker chair 150.00
2 in hot air balloon 150.00
2 in purse 165.00
2 in roadster 165.00
2 on pin dish 120.00
2 on pin dish w/bag of coins 145.00
2 peering in floor mirror 150.00
2 sitting by mushroom 125.00
2 standing in wash tub 135.00
3 in roadster 190.00
3 on pin dish 145.00

Pink Pigs

Pink Pigs on cabbage green were made in Germany around the turn of the century. They were sold as souvenirs in train depots, amusement parks, and gift shops. 'Action pigs' (those involved in some amusing activity) are the most valuable, and prices increase with the number of pigs. Though a similar type of figurine was made in white bisque, most serious collectors prefer only the pink ones. They are marked in two ways: 'Germany' in incised letters, and a black ink stamp 'Made in Germany' in a circle. The unmarked pigs are the oldest, made prior to 1890 when the McKinley Tariff Act required imports to be marked with the country of origin. Those marked 'Made In' were probably produced after the revision of the Act in 1914.

1 beside gr drum, wall-mt match holder 95.00
1 beside purse 115.00
1 beside shoe 115.00
1 beside stump, camera around neck, toothpick holder 185.00

One beside wastebasket, $95.00.

1 coming out of cup 95.00
1 coming out of suitcase 95.00
1 coming through gr fence, post at sides, open for flowers 125.00
1 driving touring car 185.00
1 going through purse 90.00
1 holding cup by fence 140.00
1 in case looking through binoculars 165.00
1 in gr Dutch shoe 75.00
1 in gr suitcase bank, head 1 side, bk other, gold trim 110.00
1 in Japanese submarine, Japan imp on both sides 125.00
1 in money sack bank 95.00
1 in roadster 150.00
1 lg pig sitting behind 3" trough 95.00
1 on binoculars, gold trim 150.00
1 on chair 125.00
1 on gr trinket dish, leg caught in lobster claw 125.00

1 on horseshoe-shaped dish w/raised 4-leaf clover 110.00
1 on keg playing piano 185.00
1 on shoulder of gr ink bottle 115.00
1 playing accordion on side of tray, wht bear ea side 185.00
1 pushing head through wooden gate 115.00
1 putting letter in mailbox 125.00
1 reclining on horseshoe ashtray 85.00
1 riding train, 4½" 190.00
1 sits, holds orange Boston Baked Beans pot match holder 125.00
1 sits by high-top boot 110.00
1 sitting in bathtub 135.00
1 sitting on log, mk Germany 110.00
1 standing in front of cracked open egg 110.00
1 standing in gr tub 95.00
1 w/attached toothpick holder 95.00
1 w/bean pot 85.00
1 w/front ft in 3-part dish containing 3 dice, 1 ft on dice 125.00
1 w/tennis racket stands beside vase, Lawn Tennis, 3¾" 150.00
1 wearing chef's costume, holds frypan, w/basket 150.00
2, mother & baby in bl blanket in tub, rabbit on board atop 150.00
2, mother in tub gives baby a bottle, lamb looks on, 4x3½" 125.00
2, 1 at telephone booth, 1 inside, 4½" 165.00
2 at confession, 4½" 125.00
2 at wishing well 130.00
2 behind trough, unmk 95.00
2 by eggshell 95.00
2 dancing, in top hat, tux & cane 135.00
2 in basket, Merry Squeelers, 3½x3" 135.00
2 in bed, Good Night on footboard, 4x3x2½" 145.00
2 in carriage 150.00
2 in open car 165.00
2 in open trunk, 3¾" 125.00
2 in purse 115.00
2 on basket, head raising lid, plaque on front 110.00
2 on cotton bale, 1 peers from hole, 1 over top 135.00
2 on seesaw on top of pouch bank 135.00
2 on top hat 125.00
2 on tray hugging, 3x4½" 125.00
2 sitting at table playing card game 'Hearts' 190.00
2 under toadstool 125.00
3, 1 on lg slipper playing banjo, 2 dancing on side 165.00
3, 2 sit in front of coal bucket, 3rd inside 125.00
3 at trough, 4½" L 110.00
3 dressed up on edge of dish 125.00
3 sm pigs behind oval trough, mk, 2¾x2½x1¾" 115.00
3 w/baby carriage, father & 2 babies, Wheeling His Own 145.00
3 w/carriage, mother & 2 babies, Germany 145.00

Pisgah Forest

The Pisgah Forest Pottery was established in 1920 near Mount Pisgah in Arden, North Carolina, by Walter B. Stephen, who had worked in previous years at other locations in the state — Nonconnah and Skyland (the latter from 1913 until 1916). Stephen, who was born in the mountain region near Asheville, was known for his work in the Southern tradition. He produced skillfully executed wares exhibiting an amazing variety of techniques. He operated his business with only two helpers. Recognized today as his most outstanding accomplishment, his Cameo line was decorated by hand in the pate-sur-pate style (similar to Wedgwood Jasper) in such designs as Fiddler and Dog, Spinning Wheel, Covered Wagon, Buffalo Hunt, Mountain Cabin, Square Dancers, Indian Campfire, and Plowman. Stephen is known for other types of wares as well. His crystalline glaze is highly regarded by today's collectors.

At least nine different stamps mark his wares, several of which contain the outline of the potter at the wheel and 'Pisgah Forest.' Cameo is sometimes marked with a circle containing the line name and 'Long Pine, Arden, NC.' Two other marks may be more difficult to recognize: 1) a circle containing the outline of a pine tree, 'N.C.' to the left of the trunk and 'Pine Tree' on the other side; and 2) the letter 'P' with short uprights in the middle of the top and lower curves. Stephen died in 1961, but the work was continued by his associates. Our advisor for this category is R.J. Sayers; he is listed in the Directory under North Carolina.

Teapot, Cameo, musician and inscription 'To Stephen From Lucia,' white on blue, repair, $495.00.

Tea set, Cameo, wagons in prairie landscapes on gr, Stephen, 3-pc ..1,100.00
Vase, amber flambe w/a few bl crystals, baluster, 7½x4¾" 475.00
Vase, aqua w/gr mottling, potter at wheel mk, ca 1942, 6¾" 90.00
Vase, aqua w/turq, glossy, 3-hdl, ca 1930, 5¼", pr 250.00
Vase, Cameo, Christmas Carol figures on bl, sgn, ca 1953, 6" ...450.00
Vase, crystalline, amber flambe w/celadon, Stephen, 3¾x4½" ..275.00
Vase, crystalline, amber w/bl, bulbous, 1940, 5x4¾" 325.00
Vase, crystalline, amber w/wht & bl, bulbous, 5¼x3½" 275.00
Vase, crystalline, amber w/wht & bl, classic shape, 1940, 6½x4" ...600.00
Vase, crystalline, amber w/wht & bl, spherical, 1947, 5x5¾" 350.00
Vase, crystalline, bl & wht, classic shape, Stephen, 7¾x4¾" 500.00
Vase, crystalline, bl & wht, classic shape, 1940, 6¾x4" 425.00
Vase, crystalline, bl & wht, classic shape, 1950, 6x5½" 225.00
Vase, crystalline, bl on mustard, wide shoulders, 7¼" 550.00
Vase, crystalline, bl over tan w/long gr-blk drippings, 7" 750.00
Vase, crystalline, brn & amber flambe w/bl, bulbous, 7x4", NM ...400.00
Vase, crystalline, gr over cream, gold flecks, Stephen, 9" 800.00
Vase, crystalline, gr-bl over camel, rose int, 6" 275.00
Vase, crystalline, med brn over gr-camel, 8¼" 225.00
Vase, crystalline, wht, bottle shape, 1941, mk, 8" 500.00
Vase, crystalline, wht, bottle shape, 1941, 8x5¼" 650.00
Vase, crystalline, wht, spherical, 1951, 3¾x5¾" 275.00
Vase, crystalline, wht w/tan drips over bl, rose int, 6" 750.00
Vase, lt bl mottled gloss, squat w/raised rim, 1934, 4" 125.00
Vase, turq crackle, celadon int, red decor at lip, 7¼x5" 200.00

Pittsburgh Glass

As early as 1797, utility window glass and hollow ware were being produced in the Pittsburgh area. Coal had been found in abundance, and it was there that it was first used instead of wood to fuel the glass furnaces. Because of this, as many as 150 glass companies operated there at one time. However, most failed due to the economically disastrous effects of the War of 1812. By the mid-1850s those that remained were producing a wide range of flint glass items including pattern-molded and free-blown glass, cut and engraved wares, and pressed tableware patterns. Our advisor for this category is Mark Vuono; he is listed in the Directory under Connecticut.

Candlestick, dolphin std, att, 7", EX 130.00
Candlesticks, Pillar mold, 8-rib hollow stem, pewter insert, 12", pr .3,685.00
Compote, cut ovals/strawberry dmns/fans, 6⅞x8", NM 190.00
Compote, folded lip, wafer stem, appl ft, ground top of finial, 6x7" ...200.00
Decanter, strawberry dmns & fans, 3 appl rings, 8¼" 135.00
Lamp, HP 12" landscape domed shade; CI foliate mk std, 18" ...800.00
Tumbler, amethyst, 8-panel, 3¼" 150.00
Vase, cut, strawberry/fans/dmns, rnd star-cut base, 7½", EX 175.00
Vase, cut panels & daisy dmns, cut flutes on lip, appl ft, 8¾" 165.00

Plastics

Synthetic plastic were invented in 1868. Since then, many types have been developed, each with unique characteristics and uses. Among the earliest, those most familar to us today are celluloid and French ivory; they were commonly used to make toiletry articles. In the early years of the century, buttons were made from Casein plastics, which could be made in a wide variety of colors and easily laminated and carved. The plastic jewelry that is so popular today had its heyday in the 1930s. The material used for its production was phenol formaldehyde. Two of the more recognizable tradenames for cast phenolics are Bakelite and Catalin. Buckles, buttons, radio and clock cases, cutlery handles, desk sets, and novelties were also made from this type of plastic. (Vinyl and Lucite, acrylic resins, were used during the period between the two World Wars. There were many applications for vinyl, which is still commonly used. Lucite items that are particular interesting to todays collectors are purses and jewelry. See also Purses; Jewelry.

For more information we recommend *Celluloid Treasures of the Victorian Era* by Joan Van Patten and Elmer and Peggy Williams; *Celluloid Collectibles* by Shirley Dunn; and *Celluloid Collector's Reference and Value Guide* by Keith Lauer and Julie Robinson. All are published by Collector Books.

Bakelite

Cigarette box, half-cylinder, rotates open, dk brn 45.00
Clock, mantel; wind-up alarm, Deco design, dk brn 60.00
Penholder, streamlined, blk 22.50

Catalin

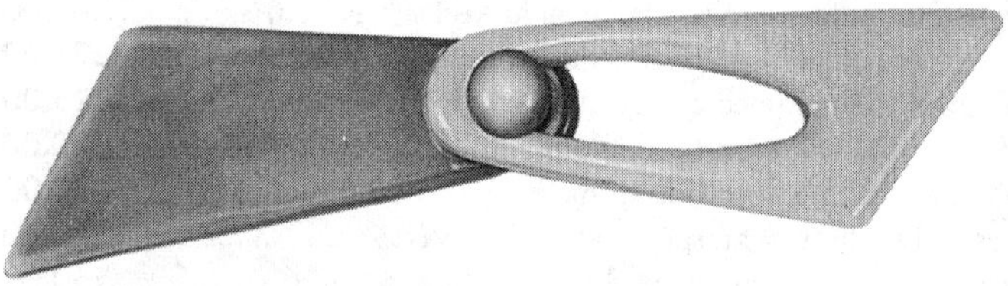

Belt buckle, beige and taupe, two-piece, ca 1935, $45.00. (Photo courtesy Lillian Baker)

Buckle, latch type, mc, uncvd 25.00
Buckle, latch type, 1-color, stylized floral or geometric 30.00
Buttons, card of 6, uncvd octagonal, amber, 1" dia 10.00
Carving set, knife, fork, steel 30.00
Checkers, red & blk, full set, in box 35.00
Cigarette box, chrome inserts, cylindrical, 4½" 45.00
Corkscrew, chrome, red, gr or amber hdl, ea 12.50
Crib toy, Tykie Toy, boy, girl, clown, kitten, etc, ea 195.00
Flatware, chrome plate, 1-color hdl 3.00
Flatware, stainless, 1-color hdl 4.00
Gavel, lathe trn, ivory 25.00
Inkwell, Carvacraft Great Britain, amber, dbl well 115.00
Letter opener, chrome/Catalin, Deco design 20.00
Pencil sharpener, Bambi, Walt Disney Productions, 1" dia 55.00
Pencil sharpener, Goofy, rnd & fluted, 1½" 50.00
Pencil sharpener, mantel clock, Germany 2" 50.00
Pencil sharpener, USA Army plane 80.00
Pencil sharpener, Walt Disney's train, figural, 1¾" 85.00
Picture frame, red, gr or amber, 6" sq 35.00
Powder box, amber & blk fluted cylinder, 2½" 50.00
Shaving brush, red, gr or amber, w/holder 40.00
Spoon, iced tea; chrome, w/Catalin knob, 6-pc set 25.00

Celluloid

Autograph album, Victorian lady, 4½x6", from $175 to 225.00
Box, collar & cuff; lady's portrait, 6x6¼x6¼", from $300 to 350.00
Box, handkerchief; Mucha print, 3x5½x5½", from $175 to 225.00
Box, letter; Victorian girls, 2x5x7½", from $100 to 150.00
Box, sewing; harvest scene, 4x9x7½", from $175 to 200.00
Brush, Victorian lady bk, ornate hdl, 8½", from $90 to 125.00
Glove case, Victorian scene, 3¼x11¼x3½", from $250 to 300.00
Jewel case, mother/child reserve, gilt lock, 3x8x5", from $185 to ..250.00
Jewel case, Victorian children, velvet trim, musical, 4x10x6" 250.00
Manicure set, Victorian scene, 9-pc in 4x13x11" case, from $325 to ..400.00
Mirror, hand; ornate bk, 9¾x4", from $100 to 150.00
Mirror, shaving; emb classic figures, trifold, 12¼x20½" 500.00
Photo album, Victorian child, musical, 12x9½", from $600 to ..700.00
Photo album, Victorian scene, upright, 8½x10½", from $450 to ...525.00
Shaving set, ivoroid, 5-pc in 3½x9x7" box, from $350 to 400.00
Whisk broom holder, lady in plumed hat, from $125 to 175.00

Playing Cards

Playing cards can be an enjoyable way to trace the course of history. Knowledge of the art, literature, and politics of an era can be gleaned from a study of its playing cards. When royalty lost favor with the people, kings and queens were replaced by common people. During the periods of war, generals, officers, and soldiers were favored. In the United States, early examples had portraits of Washington and Adams as opposed to kings, Indian chiefs instead of jacks, and goddesses for queens.

Tarot cards were used in Europe during the 1300s as a game of chance, but in the eighteenth century they were used to predict the future and were regarded with great reverence.

The backs of cards were of no particular consequence until the 1890s. The marble design used by the French during the late 1800s and the colored wood-cut patterns of the Italians in the nineteenth century are among the first attempts at decoration. Later the English used cards printed with portraits of royalty. Eventually cards were decorated with a broad range of subjects from reproductions of fine art to advertising.

Although playing cards are becoming popular collectibles, prices are still relatively low. Complete decks of cards printed earlier than the first postage stamp can still be purchased for less than $100.00. In the listings below decks are without boxes unless the box is specifically mentioned. Information concerning the American Antique Deck Collectors Club, 52 Plus Joker, may be found in the Directory under Clubs, Newsletters, and Catalogs.

Key:

AC — ad card	SC — score card
C — complete	std — standard
cts — courts	ws — wide scenic
J — joker	XC — extra card

Advertising

Murphy Varnish, Andrew Dougherty, NY, transformation deck, 1883, fifty-two cards and Joker, M in NM box, $2,900.00.

Atkins Saws-Std of World, euchre, 1910, 52+special J, VG-/poor box ...**33.00**
Eagle-Picher Lead Co, eagle bk, narrow, 1929, 104+2J+2SC, MIB .**112.00**
English Ovals Cigarettes, Std PCC, narrow, 1925, 52 no J, EXIB ...**20.00**
Famous-Barr Co, St Louis MO, 1924-29 tax stamp, MIB, sealed .**96.00**
Ford, car drawings & info, 1968, 52, no J, EXIB **25.00**
Green River Whiskey, pinochle, 1894 tax stamp, 48C, NM/torn box ..**48.00**
Helmsley Hotels, nonstd pictorial, 1986, 52+4XC, MIB **63.00**
Lyon & Healy Pianos, 1920s, 52+2J, VG/NM box **136.00**
Masonic Zembro, Shriners sphinx bk, Brn & Bigelow, 1930s, MIB ..**33.00**
Page Dairy, Toledo OH, narrow, 1920s, 52 no J, VG/no box **10.00**
Pep Boys, Deluxe Pinochle H-A11, 1940, MIB (sealed) **42.00**
Rockwell Int'l, nonstd astronaut courts, 1980, 52+robot J, NMIB **55.00**
United Drug Co (Rexall), Country Club PC, lady bk, '20s, 52+J+SC, NMIB ...**44.00**
Winchester Firearms, narrow, 52+SC, EXIB **45.00**

Foreign Manufacturers

Austria, Dante & Beatrice, Piatnik, 1923, 52+J, NM/no box **138.00**
Belgium, Great Mogul, L Biermans, Turnhout, 1880, M (sealed) ...**50.00**
England, Bezique by Thos deLa Rue, 64C+J+markers+booklet, EXIB ..**28.00**
England, Goodall & Son, For King & Co, WWI era, 52+J, EX/partial box ..**57.00**
England, Goodall & Son, Queen Victoria Dmn Jubilee, 1897, 52C, EX- ...**85.00**
England, Hunt & Sons, Geo III ace of spades, 1813, EX+/no box **110.00**
England, Worshipful 1911 Coronation, bl edge bks, worn gold, VGIB .**85.00**
France, Le Florentin, nonstd cts, 1955, dbl deck, 104+2J+XC, NMIB ..**85.00**
Germany, 4 Continents, Dondorf, floral bk, late 19th C, 52C, EX/no box ..**310.00**
Iceland, History of Iceland, Magnusson, 1930, 52 no J, EX+/no box ..**27.50**
Netherlands, Hollandia Whist, scenic Aces, 1924-29, 52, NM/broken box ..**83.00**
Portugal, nonstd, Alacantara, costumed cts, 1930s, 52+donkey J, NMIB ...**58.00**
Spain, Naypes Refinos SH, mk RLF Dem, 1850, 48, NM/no box ...**170.00**
Switzerland, Historic & Popular Cards, Muller & Co, dbl deck, MIB ...**50.00**

Odd Sizes

Buster Brown, USPC, cartoon ea card, 1906, 1¾x2½", VG+/no box ...**40.00**
Cadets Playing Cards #343, USPC, 50+Cadet J+XC, NM/partial box .**40.00**
Colonial Art, Morgan Press, nonstd, 1980s, 3¼x4⅞", EXIB **22.00**
Elf #93, NYCC, 1900, 52+Best Bower, 2x2¾", EXIB **15.00**
Fauntleroy Miniature, USPC, gold edge, 1930, 5J+2XC, NMIB ..**10.00**
Little Duke #24, USPC, 1898, 52 no J, EX in celluloid box **50.00**
Personalities, photos bk, 1970, 52 on cheap paper, 1½x2¼", EX .**13.00**
Pigmy, Thos de la Rue, London, 1890, 30x40mm, 52, EXIB **20.00**
Zulu, African shield shape, Waddington, 1960s?, 52+J, NMIB **20.00**

Older Narrow Decks

Carnival Cards, New Orleans, Mardi Gras cts, 1925, M/no box ...**144.00**
Celluloid, Whitehead & Hoag, 1920s, 52+J, VG/leather case ...**155.00**
Comet, narrow, gold edge, 1910, 52+2J, NMIB **52.00**
Congress #606, Delores, Deco bk, 1930s, MIB (sealed) **35.00**
Congress #606, Mildred, gold edge, 1930s, MIB (sealed) **40.00**
Marguerite, Sailing, Doughtery, narrow, dbl deck, 1920s, MIB (sealed) ..**60.00**
Royal Coach, 5-suit bridge, Arrco, dbl deck, 65+J+XC+booklet, MIB ...**27.00**
Samuel Hart, floral bk, 1925, 52+J, NM/no box **16.00**
Submarine, Brn & Bigelow, 1941, dbl deck, EXIB **165.00**

Older Wide Decks

Automobile #192, auto bk, NYCC, 1901, 52+special J, VGIB ..**150.00**
Bicycle #808, Acorn red bk, 52 no J, MIB **40.00**
Bicycle #808, lantern bl bk, 51 no J (lacks 9 hearts), VGIB **35.00**
Bicycle #808, league bl bk, 1924, 52 no J, MIB **30.00**
Bicycle #808, Model 2, 52+J, VG, no box **20.00**
Congress #606, Airedale, unbroken Canadian 15¢ stamp, MIB (sealed) ...**75.00**
Congress #606, Mill, worn gold, 52+J, 1899, VGIB **32.00**
Congress #606, Pocahontas, worn gold, 1906, 52+J, EXIB **77.00**
Congress #606, Rookwood, worn gold, 51+J (no 5 spades), VG in case ..**55.00**
Congress #606, Shooting the Rapids, 1915, 52+J, VG/partial box **44.00**
Congress #606, The Hunt, rare, 52 no J, 1901, MIB **80.00**
Democracy Playing Cards, biplane bks, 1918, 52+J, VG/poor box .**480.00**
Dougherty Excelsior, 1-way cts, ca 1860, 52C, EX+/no box **145.00**
Dougherty Polo...#80, red bks, 1910, 52+special J, EX/broken box **80.00**
Dougherty Triplicate #19, triplicate-style indices, 1876, G+/no box ..**195.00**
Hart Faro, sq corners/no indices/1-way cts, 1890, 52C, EX/no box **115.00**
Nile Fortune Cards #68X, 52+Life C+SC+booklet, 1922, NMIB ..**42.00**
Pinochle #48, USPC, Russell & Morgan, 1898, 48C, VG/no box ..**17.00**
Rambler #22, ca 1910, 52+J+XC, broken Canadian 8¢ war tax stamp, MIB **28.00**
Tiffany Transformation, red bks, 1879, 52C, VG+ (no box) **900.00**

Souvenir

Alaska Yukon Pacific, fair scenes, 1909, VGIB **88.00**
Country Music Playing Cards, country stars, 1950s, NMIB **100.00**
Forbidden City, Boxer Rebellion, 1901, 52+J+XC, EXIB **395.00**
Great Southwest, photos in oval, 1901, 52+J+XC, EX/no box **78.00**
Hawaiian, Wall Nichols Co, 1901, 52+J+XC, M/EX box **68.00**
Los Leones Naipes #71, Spanish suits, EX/no box **35.00**
Midwinter Expo, CA & Pacific Coast, pk bk, 1894, 52+J, NM/torn box .**445.00**
Montreal & Quebec, oval scenes, Canadian PCC, 52+J+map, MIB ..**50.00**
Olympic & Movie Star, Xth Olympiad/Los Angeles, 1932, 52+J, NMIB .**138.00**
Paris, Philibert, gold fr scenes, 1957, 52+2J, NM/plastic box **45.00**
Paris Expo, Tom Jones, 1900, 52 no J, NM/poor box **45.00**
Pittsburgh, scenic views, Gilmore & Co, 52+Father Pitt J, EXIB ..**75.00**
Royal Playing Cards, European rulers cts, NYCC, 1895, 52+J, VG/no box ...**250.00**
Stage Playing Cards #65X, star cts, USPC, 1896, 52+J, EXIB **55.00**
Texas, Van Noy-Interstate Co, 1900, 52+J, M/poor box **125.00**
Vermont, Chisholm Bros, gold edge, 1910, 52+J+2XC, MIB **65.00**
WA State/Pacific Northwest, oval photos, 1895 tax stamp, 52+J, NMIB ...**128.00**

Transportation

B&O, bl border, 1953, MIB **26.00**
Canadian National, scenic photos, 1900s, 52+J, VGIB **130.00**
Denver & Rio Grande, photos, gold edge, 1915, 52+J, MIB **40.00**
Denver & Salt Lake, Moffat Line, 1914, 52+J+booklet, MIB **195.00**
Leyland Line, narrow, 1920s, 52+special J+SC+map, VG/rpl poor box ...**78.00**
London & North Eastern, Edinburgh bk, 1925, 52+J+XC, NMIB ..**40.00**

Political

The most valuable political items are those from any period which relate to a political figure whose term was especially significant or marked by an important event or one whose personality was particularly colorful. Posters, ribbons, badges, photographs, and pin-back buttons are but a few examples of the items popular with collectors of political memorabilia.

Political campaign pin-back buttons were first mass produced and widely distributed in 1896 for the president-to-be William McKinley and for the first of three unsuccessful attempts by William Jennings Bryan. Pin-back buttons have been used during each presidential campaign ever since and are collected by many people. The scarcest are those used in the presidential campaigns of John W. Davis in 1924 and James Cox in 1920.

Contributions to this category were made by Michael J. McQuillen, monthly columnist of *Political Parade,* which appears in *AntiqueWeek* newspapers; he is listed in the Directory under Indiana. Our advisor for this category is Paul J. Longo; he is listed under Massachusetts. See also Autographs; Broadsides; Historical Glass; Watch Fobs.

Badge, 1908 Republican Nat'l Convention, metal top, ribbon, EX+ ...80.00
Badge, 1944 IN Republican State Convention, plastic, EX+ 20.00
Balloon, 1888 Harrison/Morton rally, 8 panels, wire form, EX ...350.00
Ballot, Fremont-Dayton, OH, gr paper, 3½x10" 100.00
Bandana, Harrison/Reid jugate, wht bkground, 1892, EX 275.00
Bandana, Parker/Davis jugate, blk/wht, EX 250.00
Bell, She Shall Have Votes/Votes for Women, young/old woman, porc, 4" ...600.00
Book, Barry Goldwater, Mr Conservative, 1964, 159-pg, 9x11" ...12.00
Book, Life & Public Career of Gen James A Garfield, 1880, EX .25.00
Book, McKinley Memorial edition, 1902, 296-pg, G 25.00
Bookmark, Hawthorne for Ike, silk, 1956, VG 40.00
Bookmark, Willkie/McNary, aluminum, 1940, 6", EX 155.00
Bust, Abraham Lincoln, plaster, LW Volk, 1860, 13" 700.00
Cane, bust of McKinley finial (worn SP), Protection 1896, 33" ...150.00
Cane, James Blaine pewter hdl, malacca shaft, brass ferrule, 1884 .....350.00
Cane, McKinley pewter hdl, hardwood shaft, dtd 1896, from $285 to ...300.00
Envelope, cachet; Grant/Colfax jugate, 1860s 75.00
Envelope, cachet; Jefferson Davis on 11 star CSA flag, 1860s ...125.00
Envelope, cachet; Lincoln (beardless), People's Candidate..., 1860s 125.00
Envelope, cachet; Votes for Women, NJ Next, 1915, M 75.00
Ferrotype, Lincoln/Hamlin, Constitution & Laws..., EX 650.00
Figurine, Uncle Sam, HP string-jtd plaster compo, 9", EX+ 150.00
Fob, Debs/Siedel jugate, portraits in relief, NP 250.00
License plate, Reagan Inaugural, 1981, NM 30.00
License plate attachment, All the Way w/LBJ, metal, 1964, EX ..30.00
Medal, Dewey portrait, reverse: Battle of Manilla scene 25.00
Napkin, Welcome Adm Dewey, red/wht/bl paper, 14", NM 35.00
Necktie, FDR/Garner jugate, mc, EX 100.00
Pamphlet, Cass & Taylor on Slavery Questions, 23-pg, EX 75.00
Pamphlet, FDR Round Up Rally, red/wht/bl trim, 1936, open: 10x36" ..20.00
Pennant, Vote Dewey, Republican, gr felt, 1958, 13", VG 35.00
Pincushion, Hitler bent forward w/cushion on rear, plaster, 5", EX ..100.00
Pipe, clay, bust of Harrison, Protection for Am Labor, 5¼" 100.00
Plate, JFK & RFK, America's Martyrs, 1968, 8", EX+ 24.00
Plate, Wm H Taft President...1909-1913, blk transfer w/gr rim, 7½" ...50.00
Postcard, Eugene V Debs Workers' Candidate, brn/wht, 1908, VG ...250.00
Postcard, Nixon's the One w/photo, 1968, unused, VG+ 6.00
Postcard, Taft Speaking on Podium, real photo card, used, VG+ .20.00
Postcard, Wilson, Stand Behind Our..., red/wht/bl, 1916, used, EX ..12.00
Poster, Hoover/Curtis/Reed & PA locals, blk/wht, 22x28", NM ...200.00
Poster, Re-Elect Gov Franklin D Roosevelt..., Hayes, 14x22", VG ..135.00
Poster, Teddy Roosevelt, Republican meeting, 1904, 17x11", EX ...75.00
Poster, Truman for President, portrait, 1948, 13x17", NM 65.00
Program, 1961 John F Kennedy Inaugural, NM 75.00
Razor, Taft/Sherman jugate, EX 150.00
Record album, JFK on civil rights, 7 speeches, EX 35.00
Sheet music, Good-Bye Teddy You Must March March March, 1904 ..75.00
Sheet music, Hail Prosperity, FDR portrait cover, 1936 ....40.00
Sheet music, Nat'l Whig Song, WH Harrison portrait, 1840 ....85.00
Sheet music, President Lincoln's Grand March, portrait, 1865 ..200.00
Sheet music, Roosevelt, Garner & Me, Irving Berlin, Cantor cover, 1932 ..40.00
Sheet music, Teddy Come Back, 1912 ....75.00
Silk, Douglas/Johnson, Union Now & Forever, bl, NM 1,750.00
Silk, Harrison/Tyler VA Convention, rare, NM 285.00
Soap doll, McKinley, Clean Up..., w/tag, 1896, 4½", NM 75.00
Stud, Cox in emb letters on rooster, 1920, 1x1" 30.00
Textile, Wilson/Pershing, Miss Liberty w/banner, 17", NM in fr ..200.00
Ticket, Nixon inaugural, January 20, 1973, encased in Lucite fr ..20.00
Tie bar, Landon w/sunflower, Deco design, metal, 1936, 4", EX ...35.00
Token, Grant/Colfax portraits, wht metal, EX 45.00
Token, Lincoln/Johnson jugate, wht metal, 'Man for the Union' ...550.00
Token, McClellan People's Choice for President, wht metal 65.00
Watch fob, Dewey bust amid brass cross shape, M 25.00
Water squirter, McKinley/Hobart jugate, fits in lapel, EX 85.00

Pin-back Buttons

Clinton for Ex-President, caricature picture, 1996, 2¼", EX 5.00
Coolidge, blk/wht litho, portrait, 1924, ⅞", VG 24.00
Cox-Roosevelt, names, red/wht/bl, 1920, ⅝", EX 45.00
Cox-Roosevelt, portraits, blk/wht, 1920, 1", EX, minimum value ...20,000.00
Harding for President, red rim, 1920, ⅝", NM 20.00
Hoover, 100% for Hoover, 1932, ⅞", EX 28.00
Ike, I like Ike & Dick, 1956, ⅞", NM 5.00
Kennedy-Johnson, American Needs, 1960, 3", EX 35.00
McGovern, dove, Vote McGovern, 1972, 1¼", EX 5.00
McKinley-Roosevelt jugate, gold bkground, 1900, 1¼", NM 35.00
Roosevelt, Happy Birthday, portrait, 1936, 1¼", EX 45.00
Taft, sepia portrait w/name, 1908, 1", EX 25.00
Teddy Roosevelt on bronco, Our Teddy Never Pulls Leather, 1¼" ..1,700.00
Truman-Barkley, names w/Capitol Dome, 1948, ⅞", EX 28.00
Votes for Women, mc, NM 115.00
Willkie, Wings for Willkie, plane pictured, 1940, 1¼", EX 12.00
Willkie Lumbermen, red/wht/bl cello, rare, EX 150.00
Wilson, 8 Hour Day, 1912, ⅞", EX 40.00
WPA Worker's Assoc, red/wht/bl cello, EX 50.00

Pomona

Pomona glass was patented in 1885 by the New England Glass Works. Its characteristics are an etched background of crystal lead glass often decorated with simple designs painted with metallic stains of amber or blue. The etching was first achieved by hand cutting through an acid resist. This method, called first ground, resulted in an uneven feather-like frost effect. Later, to cut production costs, the hand-cut process was discontinued in favor of an acid bath which effected an even frosting. This method is called second ground. Our advisors for this category are Betty and Clarence Maier; they are listed in the Directory under Pennsylvania.

Bowl, 1st ground, NM stain, 4½" dia 265.00
Champagne, 2nd ground, EX amber stain, 5" 245.00
Cruet, Cornflower, 2nd ground, spherical w/petal base, 7" 335.00
Cruet, frosted, 1st ground, w/clear stopper, 6½" 100.00
Cup, punch; 2nd ground, 2¾" 75.00
Mustard pot, 2nd ground, scalloped, metal lid, 2x3½" 230.00
Pitcher, Honeycomb, 1st ground, HP floral, twist hdl, 7½" 700.00
Punch cup, Cornflower, 1st ground, EX color/stain 145.00
Punch cup, Cornflower, 2nd ground, EX color/stain 110.00
Punch cup, lt T'print, 1st ground, w/amber stain 100.00
Tumbler, Cornflower, 2nd ground, 3⅝" 145.00
Tumbler, Dmn Quilt, Cornflower, 2nd ground, 4" 165.00

Vase, Baby T'print, 2nd ground, fan shape w/crimped rim, 3x5¾" ..185.00
Vase, Cornflower, 1st ground, amber stain, ftd planter form, 5½" 545.00
Vase, lily; Optic Rib w/Dmn Quilt mouth, 2nd ground, 10" 385.00

Porcelier

The Porcelier Manufacturing Company, originally from East Liverpool, Ohio, started business in the late 1920s and moved to Greensburg, Pennsylvania, in the early 1930s. The company flourished until the late 1940s and finally closed its doors in 1954.

They produced an endless line of vitrified porcelain products including furniture coasters, electric appliances, coffee makers, and light fixtures. These products were sold in many stores under a variety of names and carried over ten different types of marks and labels.

The prices below are for items in excellent condition with no chips, cracks or excessive wear. To learn more about this subject, we recommend *Collector's Guide to Porcelier China* by our advisor, Susan E. Grindberg. If you have any questions or information regarding Porcelier, please contact her; she is listed in the Directory under Nevada. (Queries require a SASE.)

Boiler, Oriental Deco, 8-cup 65.00
Bowl, spaghetti; floral decal 125.00
Canisters, Country Life, ea 90.00
Casserole, Country Life, w/lid, 9½" 110.00
Coffeepot, Diamond Leaf, 2-cup 32.00
Coffeepot, Dutch Boy & Girl, gold trim, 8-cup 85.00
Coffeepot, Serv-All Line, platinum, gold, or red/blk, #576-D 65.00
Cookie jar, Barock-Colonial, ivory, red, or bl, #2015 ....150.00
Creamer & sugar bowl, Medallion, ea 25.00
Creamer & sugar bowl, Scalloped Wild Flowers, ea 15.00
Cup, coffee; US Dept of Defense Ware, decorated 10.00
Decanter, Oriental Deco 85.00
Drip coffe maker, Pears, 6-cup 30.00
Egg cooker, electric, blk/gold trim 35.00
Egg cup, blk trim 10.00
Gravy boat, US Dept of Defense Ware, plain wht 25.00
Grease catcher, Barock-Colonial, ivory only 50.00
Lamp, dresser; cobblestone w/emb flowers 50.00
Light fixture, ceiling; Basketweave Wild Flowers 40.00
Light fixture, wall; w/shade, floral decor w/yel & gold trim 40.00
Percolator, Antique Rose Deco Set 85.00
Percolator, Field Flowers 60.00
Percolator, Pink Flower Hostess Set 75.00
Percolator, Pink Flower Platinum Set 60.00
Pitcher, ball form, Mexican (Santa Fe) 80.00
Pitcher, disc form, 1939 New York World's Fair, 7", from $175 to ..250.00
Pitcher, hexagonal, Field Flowers 55.00
Sandwich grill, Serv-All Line, gold or red/blk, #3004, from $175 to ...250.00
Shakers, Oriental Deco, ea 35.00
Syrup jar, Serv-All Line, gold or red/blk, #3012 ....45.00
Teapot, Latticework, pale gr or yel, 4-cup 45.00
Toaster, Scalloped Wild Flowers, from $1,500 to 1,900.00
Urn, Antique Rose Platinum Set 115.00
Waffle iron, Barock-Colonial, gold, #461, from $150 to 225.00

Postcards

Postcards are often very difficult to evaluate, since so many factors must be considered — for instance the subject matter or the field of interest they represent. For example: a 1905 postcard of the White House in Washington D.C. may seem like a desirable card, but thousands were produced and sold to tourists who visited there, thus the market is saturated with this card, and there are few collectors to buy it. Value: less than $1.00. However, a particular view of small town of which only five hundred were printed could sell for far more, provided you find someone interested in the subject matter pictured on that card. Take as an example a view of the courthouse in Hillsville, Virginia. This card would appeal to those focusing on that locality or county as well as courthouse collectors. Value: $3.00.

The ability of the subject to withstand time is also a key factor when evaluating postcards. Again using the courthouse as an example, one built in 1900 and still standing in the 1950s has been photographed for fifty years, from possibly a hundred different angles. Compare that with one built in 1900 and replaced in 1908 due to a fire, and you can see how much more desirable a view of the latter would be. But only a specialist would be aware of the differences between these two examples.

Postcard dealers can very easily build up stocks numbering in the 100,000s. Greeting and holiday cards are common and represent another area of collecting that appeals to an entirely different following than the view card. These types of cards range from heavily embossed designs to floral greetings and, of course, include the ever popular Santa Claus card. These were very popular from about 1900 until the 1920s, when postcard communication was the equivalent of today's quick phone call or e-mail. Because of the vast number of them printed, many have little if any value to a collector. For instance, a 1909 Easter card with tiny images or a common floral card of the same vintage, though almost one hundred years old, are virtually worthless. It's the cards with appeal and zest that command the higher prices. One with a beautiful Victorian woman in period clothing, her image filling up the entire card, could easily be worth $3.00 and up. Holiday cards designed for Easter, Valentines Day, Thanksgiving and Christmas are much more common than those for New Year's, St. Patrick's Day, the 4th of July, and Halloween. Generally, then, they're worth less, but depending on the artist, graphics, desirability, and eye appeal, this may not always be true. The signature of a famous artist will add significant value — conversely, an unknown artist's signature adds none.

In summary, the best way to evaluate your cards is to have a knowledgeable dealer look at them. For a list of dealers, send a SASE to the International Federation of Postcard Dealers, P.O. Box 1765, Manassas, VA 20108. *Do not* expect a dealer to price cards from a list or written description as this is not possible. For individual questions or evaluation by photocopy (front and back), you may contact our advisor, Jeff Bradfield, 90 Main St., Dayton, VA 22821. You *must* include a SASE for a reply.

Posters

Advertising posters by such French artists as Cheret and Toulouse-Lautrec were used as early as the mid-1800s. Color lithography spurred their popularity. Circus posters by the Strobridge Lithograph Co. are considered to be the finest in their field, though Gibson and Co. Litho, Erie Litho, and Enquirer Job Printing Co. printed fine examples as well. Posters by noted artists such as Mucha, Parrish, and Hohlwein bring high prices. Other considerations are good color, interesting subject matter and, of course, condition. The WWII posters listed below are among the more expensive examples; 70% of those on the market bring less than $65.00. See also Movie Memorabilia; Rock 'N Roll.

Advertising

Bal de la Grande Ourse, red/blk design, Paris, 1925, 47x31", NM 2,750.00
Bianca, toothpaste/brush in glass, N Stoecklin, 1941, 50x36", EX+ .2,300.00
Cognac Albert Robin, bird on keg, Paris, 62x45", NM 1,265.00
Hires Root Beer, Special Sale, 1950s, 16x14" 35.00
Manufacture Royal de Corsets, Privat Livemont, 1897, 26x14" ...4,600.00
Pabst Famous BR Beer/Quality Yes-Suh-h, Blk waiter, fr, 40x30", EX ...275.00

Southwestern Bell Telephone Booth, Holiday Calls, 1954 ....15.00
Stetson Hat, The Last Drop From His Stetson, 23x30" 85.00
TWA New York, Statue of Liberty & other bldgs, sgn D Klein, 40x25" ...150.00

Circus

Ringling Bros. and Barnum & Bailey, Gargantua the Great, 17x24½", EX, $200.00.

Barnum & Bailey Big Free Street Parade..., 24½x16¾", EX 300.00
Barnum & Bailey/...Zoological Features, 4 giraffes, 36x24", VG ...300.00
Barnum & Bailey/Greatest Show on Earth, lg tiger head, 25x17", EX 75.00
Barnum & Bailey/Greatest Show on Earth, 2 portraits, 25x17", VG 200.00
Big John A Strong & Son Circus, red/yel/bl/wht, 28x14", VG 75.00
BPO Elks Circus/A Show for Your Money, red/yel on wht, 22x14", EX 30.00
Carson & Barnes Wild Animal Circus, tiger on elephant, 28x21", VG ..125.00
Circus Vargas, Burbank..., performers in brn tones, 22x14", G ..100.00
Elks Circus, Santa Ana Municipal Stadium, clown/elephant, 22x14", EX 25.00
Elks Circus, Santa Ana Municipal Stadium, lg clown face, 42x28", EX ...30.00
Hubert Castle International Circus, elephant/girl on bl, 22x14", G ..100.00
Las Vegas International Circus, bl/wht scenes on red/wht, 28x22", G .75.00
Miller-Johnson Circus, San Bernadino, performers/animals, 22x14", VG ...75.00
Paul Eagles Circus, Long Beach, 12-12 1972, performers, 22x14", VG ...100.00
Ringling Bros & B&B Circus, mc bkside view of 6 clowns, 17x24", EX ...500.00
Ringling Bros & B&B Combined Shows, 8 horses/2 riders, 17x25", VG ...300.00
Ringling Bros/Proprietors & Managers, 5 sepia portraits, 17x25", VG 300.00
Rudy Bros Circus/Elks Circus, 3 trapeze artists, 35x14", Fair 75.00
Shrine Circus, clown/tiger/lion heads on bl, 22x14", VG 75.00

Magic

Alexander, The Man Who Knows, red litho, ca 1920s, 28x40" .350.00
Carter the Great, Modern Princess of Delphi, Otis Litho, 76x40" ..765.00
Great Virgil, full color, 3-sheet, 80x40", 2-pc, VG 375.00
Love Moods, Lili St Cyr, burlesque, 3-color, 1940s, 41x28", VG ..200.00
Nostradamus Jr, Argentina, ca 1940, 29x43" 245.00

Theatrical

Black Patti's Troubadours, man's portrait, fr, 31x21", EX 75.00
Casino de Paris, Camille Stefani, Cheret, 32x23", EX 525.00
Casino de Paris, Nouveau Theatre..., Jean de Palèologue, 48x32", EX ...700.00
Folies-Bergère, Phryne, Charles Lucas, 63x24", EX 1,000.00
Hurly Burly (burlesque), red/blk, 1940, 41x28", EX 150.00
Pantomimes Lumineuses, lady holds skirt wide, Cheret, 37x33", EX 2,000.00
Parisiana Mam'zell 5 Louis, 49x32", VG 500.00
Queen of Burlesque, full color, 1940s, 39x14", VG 125.00
Uncle Tom's Cabin/Topsy's Recreation, paper, fr, 83x46", VG ...700.00

Travel

Again to Austria, mother/son anticipating a day of skiing, 37x25", EX ..375.00
Air France World Air Services, world view, 1956, 39x24", EX ..430.00
Baignade de St Maurice, activities along Seine, 1890, 23x31", NM ..545.00
Findland Winter Sports, train/skiers/lg snowman, OK Oksanen, 39x25" ..360.00
Lagos de Chile, mother & daughter lakeside, 1930, 39x42", EX+ 575.00
Polska, mtn scene, Pruszynski, 1930, 39½x27¼", EX 260.00
Union Pacific's Sun Valley, dancer/ski parade/etc, 38x25", NM ..635.00
Venezia, gondolier, AM Cassandre, 1951, 38¾x24", EX 1,800.00
Winter Sports in Carinthia, shadowed face of skier, 1947, 33x23", EX ..400.00

War

WWI, I Want You for Navy, Wave in uniform, Christy, 42x28", VG 900.00
WWI, Spirit of the Red Cross, nurse on battlefield, 1918, 41x28", M 920.00
WWI, The Motor Corps of America, circular image, 1918, 40x30", M ...550.00
WWI, US Marines.../Enlist At, soldier, Riesenberg, 1917, 42x28", EX 430.00
WWI, Women of Britain Say Go!, figures at window, E Keakey, 29x19", M 350.00
WWII, Four Freedoms, Norman Rockwell, 1943, 40x30", EX+, set of 4 ....1,035.00
WWII, Get in the Scrap..., cartoon image, W Steig, 1941, 57x40", M 600.00
WWII, I Want You...US Army/Enlist Now, Uncle Sam, 1940, 38x25", EX 865.00
WWII, Production/America's Answer!, hand w/wrench, Carlu, 40x30", EX ...1,380.00
WWII, This Is the Enemy, hanging reflected in monocle, 35x25", NM ...2,300.00

Miscellaneous

Buffalo Bill's Wild West, North Platte NB, 22x14", VG 100.00
Fiesta de Los Angeles, street fair, 3-color cb, 1930s, 26x22" 175.00
Harper's May, lady & sheep, 1895, 16½x13¼" 300.00
Harper's September, color litho on paper, 1895, 13⅜x9¼" 250.00
Internat'l Air Races, St Louis, 4-color, 1923, 22x14", NM 350.00
Minnesota State Fair & Expo, red/blk, 1915, 41x28", VG 250.00
Montana Frank Shows, Indians attacking settlers, 1929, 28x20", EX+ 425.00

Pot Lids

Pot lids were pottery covers for containers that were used for hair dressing, potted meats, etc. The most common were decorated with colorful transfer prints under the glaze in a variety of themes, animal and scenic. The first and probably the largest company to manufacture these lids was F. & R. Pratt of Fenton, Staffordshire, established in the early 1800s. The name or initials of Jesse Austin, their designer, may sometimes be found on exceptional designs. Although few pot lids were made after the 1880s, the firm continued into the twentieth century.

American pot lids are very rare. Most have been dug up by collectors searching through sites of early gold rush mining towns in California. Minor rim chips are expected and normally do not detract from listed values. When no condition is given, assume that the value is based on an example in such condition.

American

Bazin's Unrivaled Premium..., red transfer, 3⅛", M 110.00
Cold Cream of Roses...Newport, red transfer, 2½", M 155.00
General Depot in Phila...Chestnut St, blk transfer, 2¾" sq 100.00
Genuine Beef Marrow Pomatum..., blk transfer, 3", EX 110.00
Genuine Beef Marrow X Bazin..., blk transfer, 3⅛" 130.00
Hardy's Scurf Pomatum..., red transfer, 3⅛", EX 65.00
HP & W Taylor's New Sz Saponaceous..., blk transfer, 4⅛", EX 110.00
HP Wakelee Druggist...Bear's Grease..., mc transfer, 3", EX 1,400.00
HP Wakelee Druggist...Odonto, mc transfer, 3⅛", NM 1,050.00
HP Wakelee Druggist...Philicome, mc transfer, 3⅛", NM 1,100.00
Jules Hauel Perfumer... (bust of Franklin), purple transfer, 2¾" .475.00
Jules Hauel Saponaceous..., red transfer, 4⅛", EX 130.00
Occidental Tooth...Vennard & Co NY, blk transfer, 3¼", VG ..140.00
Odonto Oak Bark Orris Tooth Paste..., orange transfer, 3¼", NM ...425.00
Odonto Oak Bark Orris Tooth Paste..., purple transfer, 3¼", NM 165.00
Prepared by X Bazin Perfumer..., blk transfer, 4⅜", VG 140.00
Taylor's Saponaceous Compound..., blk transfer, 3¾", M 375.00

Taylor's Saponaceous Compound..., purple transfer, 3⅜", NM ...350.00
Taylor's Saponaceous...in 1820, bl transfer, 3¾", NM 350.00
Whorsley Wholesale...Washington, blk transfer, 3½", NM 550.00
Whorsley Wholesale...Washington, purple transfer, 3½", NM ...475.00
Wright's Gold Medal Saponaceous..., blk transfer, 3⅝", M 800.00
Wright's Gold Medal Saponaceous..., blk transfer, 4¼", NM 925.00
X Bazin Succor...Chapped Hands, blk transfer, 2⅞", NM 150.00

English

Children sailing boat in tub, multicolor transfer, 3", painted wood frame, EX, $120.00.

Bear Pit, mc transfer, chip, 3½" 45.00
Cherry Tooth Paste...Registered, blk transfer, 2⅞", EX 130.00
Crosse & Blackwell's, Anchovy Paste..., brn transfer, 3⅜" 80.00
Genuine Russian Bears Grease..., blk transfer, 3¼", EX 110.00
I Consent She Replied If You Promise..., mc transfer, 4⅛", EX .110.00
Improved Cold Cream of Roses..., bl transfer, 2⅜", EX 60.00
Landing Fare Pegwell Bay, mc transfer, 4", EX 110.00
Mrs Terry's Analeptic Pomade..., blk transfer, 3¼", EX 65.00
Russian Bear's Grease..., blk transfer, 2½", M 350.00
Swinton's English Primrose Tooth Paste..., cobalt transfer, 2¾", M ...130.00

Powder Horns and Shot Flasks

Though powder horns had already been in use for hundreds of years, collectors usually focus on those made after the expansion of the United States westward in the very early 1800s. While some are basic and very simple, others were scrimshawed and highly polished. Especially nice carvings can quickly escalate the value of a horn that has survived intact to as high as $400.00. Those with detailed maps, historical scenes, etc., bring even higher prices.

Metal flasks were introduced in the 1830s; by the middle of the century they were produced in quantity and at prices low enough that they became a viable alternative to the powder horn. Today's collector regards the smaller flasks as the more desirable and valuable, and those made for specific companies bring premium prices.

Flask, brass, German writing/boar & dog scene, 5", VG 300.00
Flask, brass disk form w/silver inlay, Morocco, 6½" 275.00
Flask, brass w/stamped cannon/anchors/pistols/etc, 7¾" 175.00
Flask, copper, rococo shell decor, brass spout 45.00
Flask, copper, USLSS, brass spout mk Walton Bros NY, 1890s, 10½" 1,250.00
Flask, copper, USLSS, fitted top, wells Pat Aug 24 188?, 12" .1,285.00
Flask, glass w/emb game scene, wire hanger, old stopper, 7" 50.00
Flask, iron w/leather cover/brass top, G&W Hawksley Sheffield, 1860s ..95.00
Flask, leather, emb hunter medallion on bag form, brass top, 1850s ...65.00
Flask, leather, tear shape, brass bands/top, ca 1800, 9" dia 135.00
Flask, leather, 2-pc body w/iron ring, bag shape, 1850s 50.00
Flask, leather/brass w/emb dog, Am Flask & Cap Co 3#, 8½" 25.00
Horn, cvd, African buffalo horn, 3-ring brass nozzle, EX 300.00
Horn, cvd animals/boats, dtd 1812, 6", VG 125.00
Horn, cvd bands, wood plug w/cvd face, 1870s, 9½" 35.00
Horn, cvd coat of arms/dragons/crowns/soldier, EX patina, 17" .660.00
Horn, cvd date: 1888, flattened shape, plain spout, 6½" 85.00
Horn, cvd hunters w/deer on horsebk, 14" 120.00
Horn, cvd Revolutionary war inscriptions, dtd 1779, 10", VG ..350.00
Horn, cvd ship/heart/house/trees/dtd 1871, worn plug, 9" 135.00
Horn, cvd squirrel/rabbit/deer/horse/etc, orig brass collar, 13¼" ...130.00
Horn, deeply cvd figures w/crowns, Scandinavian, 7", VG 450.00
Horn, spout w/cvd flange, wood plug, cord tacks, 1870s, 6" 30.00
Horn, wood butt secured w/sm iron tacks, 13" 425.00

Pratt

Prattware has become a generic reference for a type of relief-molded earthenware with polychrome decoration. Scenic motifs with figures were popular; sometimes captions were added. Jugs are most common, but teapots, tableware, even figurines were made. The term 'Pratt' refers to Wm. Pratt of Lane Delph, who is credited with making the first examples of this type, though similar wares were made later by other Staffordshire potters. Pot lids and other transfer wares marked Pratt were made in Fenton, Staffordshire, by F. & R. Pratt & Co. See Pot Lids.

Figurine, cat w/farmer, Yorkshire-type palette, 1810s, 6" 1,700.00
Figurine, cradle, pearlware, typical palette, 11¾", EX 2,415.00
Figurine, man w/2 sheep & treen, mc, ca 1790, minor rstr, 4" ...500.00
Figurine, peasant lady w/basket, pearlware w/mc, sm flakes, 3½" 475.00
Figurine, ram & lady gardener on oval base, rstr, 6x5½" 1,725.00
Pitcher, children in heart reserves, 5" 375.00
Pitcher, portrait medallions, mc, 19th C, rpr, 7¼" 250.00
Plate, children w/dog, animals in border, mc w/brn stripe rim, 5¾" ...160.00
Sauce boat, fish form, orange & gr, ca 1790, 6", EX 375.00
Toby jug, underglaze palette, minor hat rstr, 1790s, 8¼" 1,000.00

Precious Moments

Known as 'America's Hummels,' Precious Moments® are a line of well-known collectibles created by Samuel J. Butcher and produced by Enesco, Inc. These pieces have endeared themselves to many because of the inspirational messages they portray. Over 300,000 club members have joined the national club since 1982.

The collection is twenty-one years old as of 1999. Each piece is produced with a different mark each year. This mark, not the date, is usually the link to the value of the piece. Most mold changes result in increased values, and when a piece is retired or suspended, its price increases as well. As an example, 'God Loveth a Cheerful Giver' retailed for $9.50 in 1980; it was retired in 1981 and has a secondary market price now of $850.00 to $950.00. The majority of the collection has increased in value from its original retail. Items listed below are assumed to be in mint condition with the original box.

E-1377B, He Careth For You, no mark, $140.00; Triangle mark, $120.00; Hourglass mark, $110.00; Fish mark, $98.00; Cross mark, $90.00.

#104035, Cheers to the Leader, cheerleader, Bow/Arrow mk 35.00
#104035, Cheers to the Leader, cheerleader, Cedar Tree mk 45.00
#12211, Baby's First Haircut, Cedar Tree mk 125.00
#12211, Baby's First Haircut, Dove mk 145.00
#12300, Love Never Fails, teacher w/report card, Dove mk 60.00
#12300, Love Never Fails, teacher w/report card, Ship mk 40.00
#521175, Hello World!, kangaroo w/baby, Flower mk 30.00
#521175, Hello World!, kangaroo w/baby, Heart mk 17.50
E-0513, Boy w/Wreath, ornament, dtd 1983, Fish mk 60.00
E-0517, The Perfect Grandpa, ornament, Bow/Arrow mk 30.00
E-0517, The Perfect Grandpa, ornament, Fish mk 45.00
E-0539, Katie Lynne, doll, Cross mk 180.00
E-0539, Katie Lynne, doll, Flower mk 180.00
E-2344, Angel w/Trumpet, candle climbers, suspended 1985, Crow mk, pr ...95.00
E-2344, Angel w/Trumpet, candle climbers, suspended 1985, no mk ...120.00
E-2347, Let Heaven & Nature Sing, plate, Dove mk 45.00
E-2347, Let Heaven & Nature Sing, plate, missing mk 50.00
E-2355, I'll Play My Drum for Him, musical, Hourglass mk 185.00
E-2355, I'll Play My Drum for Him, musical, suspended 1984, Fish mk ...175.00
E-5620, We Have Seen His Star, shepherd bell, Dove mk 40.00
E-5620, We Have Seen His Star, shepherd bell, missing mk 50.00
E-7166, The Lord Bless You & Keep You, bride & groom fr, Butterfly mk ...40.00
E-7166, The Lord Bless You & Keep You, bride & groom fr, Hourglass mk .65.00
E-9265, Press On, girl ironing, Heart mk 65.00
E-9265, Press On, girl ironing, Hourglass mk 120.00

Primitives

Like the mouse that ate the grindstone, so has collectible interest in primitives increased, a little bit at a time, until demand is taking bites instead of nibbles into their availability. Although the term 'primitives' once referred to those survival essentials contrived by our American settlers, it has recently been expanded to include objects needed or desired by succeeding generations — items representing the cabin-'n-cornpatch existence as well as examples of life on larger farms and in towns. Through popular usage, it also respectfully covers what are actually 'country collectibles.'

From the 1600s into the latter 1800s, factories employed carvers, blacksmiths, and other artisans whose handwork contributed to turning out quality items. When buying, 'touchmarks,' a company's name and/or location and maker's or owner's initials, are exciting discoveries.

Primitives are uniquely individual. Following identical forms, results more often than not show typically personal ideas. Using this as a guide (combined with circumstances of age, condition, desire to own, etc.) should lead to a reasonably accurate evaluation. For items not listed, consult comparable examples. Authority Kathryn McNerney has compiled several lovely books on primitives and related topics: *Primitives, Our American Heritage; Collectible Blue and White Stoneware*; and *Antique Tools, Our American Heritage*. You will find her address in the Directory under Florida. See also Butter Molds and Stamps; Boxes; Copper; Farm Collectibles; Fireplace Implements; Kitchen Collectibles; Molds; Tinware; Weaving; Woodenware; and Wrought Iron.

Bed warmer, brass, eng floral lid, trn maple hdl, 43" 470.00
Bed warmer, brass, punched lid, wood hdl, 20th C, 27" 150.00
Bed warmer, brass, tooled starflower lid, trn wood hdl, 42" 275.00
Bed warmer, brass, tooled starflower/X lid, trn brass hdl, 42" 525.00
Bed warmer, copper, eng floral lid, trn wood hdl, 43" 220.00
Bed warmer, copper, eng sunburst, turn walnut hdl, early 1800s ...340.00
Bellows, relief-cvd ship & anchor, poor leather, 22x8" 150.00
Candle dryer, pnt wood, stand w/2 cvd arms, rnd base, 19th C, 22" ..575.00
Candle mold, 3-tube, arch ribbon hdl to top of mold, 11" 120.00
Candle mold, 5-tube, tin, mini, 4¼x4½x3½", EX 1,150.00
Candle mold, 6-tube, gallery top/base, 1-row, 11x9x3" 150.00
Candle mold, 8-tube, gallery top/ft, ribbon hdl, 6x5½x2¾" 675.00
Candle mold, 8-tube, 2 rows of 4, lg ribbon hdl, 11" 150.00
Candle mold, 12-tube, poplar fr, rpl wire rods, old patina, 16x18x6" ...700.00
Candle mold, 16-tube, step-like sides, ribbon hdl, 10½", VG 265.00
Candle mold, 36-tube, dvtl cherry case, 15x18x7" 1,200.00
Cheese mold, pierced tin, dmn shape w/flat bottom, 3x7¾x5⅜" ...250.00
Cheese mold, pierced tin, ring-shaped ft, 4x4¼" 70.00
Cheese sieve, woven splint, 9" 350.00

Churn, Buffton Mfg. Co, Buffton, Indiana, six-gallon, 26x17x16", EX, $375.00.

Churn, staved wood, old red pnt, rpr, 24"+hdl & dasher 525.00
Cookie board, cast aluminum, 12 segments w/berries/flowers/etc, 8x5" ...165.00
Cookie board, cast aluminum, 12 segments: different occupations, 8x5" ..190.00
Corn cutter, maple w/wrought iron blade, 1⅝x20x3" 25.00
Dough box, poplar w/cherry finish, splayed legs, 37x36x21" 400.00
Dough box, poplar w/early-style base, trn legs, dvtl, PA, 43" L ..675.00
Dough box, red pnt wood, canted sides, on stand, EX patina, 27x36x15" ...250.00
Dough scraper, wrought iron, heart-shaped cutout in center of blade ...300.00
Dough scraper, wrought iron, str blade, 3" hdl 65.00
Dough tray, lift-off lid, batten hdls, dvtl, 30" L 180.00
Foot warmer, dvtl walnut, pierced circle, 1814 on lid, 7x9x8" ...300.00
Foot warmer, pine w/old red pnt, star cvg, rpl sliding door, 9" L ...165.00
Foot warmer, punched tin, rpl wood base & top, 12" 250.00
Foot warmer, punched tin in mortised hardwood fr, old patina, 9" ...195.00
Foot warmer, rectangular copper box w/drw, 10x18¾" 55.00
Quilting frame, pine w/old bl, mortised & pinned, 100" rods 195.00
Rack, drying; hardwood, tripod base w/trn legs, top revolves, 39" ...200.00
Rack, drying; pine, mortised, steel hinges, 43x24" 88.00
Rack, drying; pine European w/dvtl ends, traces of finish, 42x30" ..525.00
Rack, drying; pine w/med gr rpt, 2 mortised bars, 34x25" 110.00
Rack, drying; pine w/old gray, shoe ft, mortised/pinned, 28x19" 400.00
Rack, drying; pine w/old patina, canvas hinge, 31x40" 60.00
Smoothing board, chip-cvd w/horse hdl, dtd 1787 ....1,400.00
Smoothing board, old red pnt w/some gr, horse hdl, 24¾" 330.00
Sugar hammer, brass/steel w/curly maple hdl, EX detail, 8" 1,155.00
Sugar nippers, steel, ca 1845, 3¼x9" 130.00
Wick trimmers, brass, scrolled edge pan, battered, 9½" 130.00

Prints

The term 'print' may be defined today as almost any image printed on paper by any available method. Examples of collectible old 'prints' are Norman Rockwell magazine covers and Maxfield Parrish posters and calendars. 'Original print' refers to one achieved through the efforts of the artist or under his direct supervision. A 'reproduction' is a print produced by an accomplished print maker who reproduces another artist's print or original work. Thorough study is required on the part of the collector to recognize and appreciate the many variable factors to be considered in evaluating a print. Prices vary from one area of the country to another and are dependent upon new findings regarding the scarcity or abundance of prints as such information may arise. Although each collector of old prints may have their own varying criteria by which to judge condition, for those who deal only rarely in this area or newer collectors, a few guidelines may prove helpful. Staining, though unquestionably detrimental, is nearly always present in some degree and should be weighed against the rarity of the print. Professional cleaning should improve its appearance and at the same time help preserve it. Avoid tears that affect the image; minor margin tears are another matter, especially if the print is a rare one. Moderate 'foxing' (brown spots caused by mold or the fermentation of the rag content of old paper) and light stains from the old frames are not serious unless present in excess. Margin trimming was a common practice; but look for at least ½" to 1½" margins, depending on print size.

When no condition is indicated, the items listed below are assumed to be in very good to excellent condition. See also Nutting, Wallace; Parrish, Maxfield.

Audubon, John J.

Audubon is the best known of American and European wildlife artists. His first series of prints, 'Birds of America,' was produced by Robert Havell of London. They were printed on Whitman watermarked paper bearing dates of 1826 to 1838. The octavo edition of the same series was printed in seven editions, the first by J.T. Bowen under Audubon's direction. There were seven volumes of text and prints, each 10" x 7", the first five bearing the J.J. Audubon and J.B. Chevalier mark, the last two, J.J. Audubon. They were produced from 1840 through 1844. The second and other editions were printed up to 1871. The bien edition prints were full size, made under the direction of Audubon's sons in the late 1850s. Due to the onset of the Civil War, only 105 plates were finished. These are considered to be the most valuable of the reprints of the 'Birds of America Series.'

In 1971 the complete set was reprinted by Johnson Reprint Corp. of New York and Theaturm Orbis Terrarum of Amsterdam. Examples of the latter bear the watermark G. Schut and Zonen. In 1985 a second reprint was done by Abbeville Press for the National Audubon Society.

Although Audubon is best known for his portrayal of birds, one of his less-familiar series, 'Vivaparous Quadrupeds of North America,' portrayed various species of animals. Assembled in corroboration with John Bachman from 1839 until 1851, these prints are 28" x 22" in size. Several octavo editions were published in the 1850s. In the following listing, all measurements are actual print size unless stated otherwise.

Canada Jay, hand colored, Havell, Plate CVII, 1831, 26x20½", EX, $3,000.00.

Am Sparrow Hawk, #142, Havell, 1829, 25¾x20½" 5,175.00
Barnacle Goose, Plate CCXCVI, Amsterdam, 1972, 24x36½" ..550.00
Black or Surf Duck, Plate CCCXVII, Amsterdam, 1972, 24¼x34¼" ...400.00
Bluebird, Plate CXIII, Havell, 1831, sight: 29¾x21" 1,250.00
Canada Jay, Plate CVII, 26x20½"+fr 800.00
Grafs Finch or Way-Winged Bunting, Plate XCIV, Havell, sight: 30x22" ..1,500.00
Green Heron, #323, 1836, 20½x22¼" 18,400.00
Hudsonian Godwit, Plate CCLVIII, Havell, 1835, sight: 21¼x34½" ...2,000.00
Little Sandpiper, J Bien, 1860, 16x21" 400.00
Louisiana Heron, Plate CCXVII, Havell, 1834, 13x16" 195.00
Mallard Duck, Amsterdam edition, 22½x34¾"+fr 750.00
Rocky Mountain Plover, #350, Havell, 1836, 12¼x19½" 500.00
White-Fronted Goose, Julius Bien, 1860, 25¼x37¼" 1,400.00

Boileau, Philip

Anticipation, 13x20" 260.00
Mother's Love, 10x16" 100.00
Twins, 4x6" 50.00
Untitled Mother & Daughter, 6x8" 135.00

Currier and Ives

Nathaniel Currier was in business by himself until the late 1850s when he formed a partnership with James Merrit Ives. Currier is given credit for being the first to use the medium to portray newsworthy subjects, and the Currier and Ives views of nineteenth-century American culture are familiar to us all. In the following listings, 'C' numbers correspond with a standard reference book by Conningham. Values are given for prints in very good condition; all are colored unless indicated black and white. Unless noted 'NC' (Nathaniel Currier), all prints are published by Currier and Ives. Our advisors for this category are John and Barbara Rudisill (Rudisill's Alt Print Haus); they are listed in the Directory under Maryland.

Alnwick Castle, Scotland; undtd, C-87, med folio 175.00
Am Country Life, Pleasures of Winter; NC, 1855, C-123, lg folio ...2,300.00
Am Farm Scenes/No 2 (summer), NC, C-135, 1853, C-135, lg folio ..3,000.00
Am Fireman, Facing Enemy; 1858, C-153, med folio 1,300.00
Battle of Gettysburg, undtd, C-407, sm folio 300.00
Bear Hunting, Close Quarters (summer); undtd, C-447, sm folio ..750.00
Beautiful Blonde, undtd, C-452, med folio 90.00
Belle of New York, undtd, C-490, sm folio 75.00
Black-Eyed Susan, NC, 1848, C-551, sm folio 300.00
Blue Fishing, undtd, C-578, sm folio 950.00
Brook Trout Fishing, 1872, C-704, sm folio 900.00
Camping Out, Some of Right Sort; NC, 1856, C-777, lg folio ...3,500.00
Celebrated Trotting Mare Lady Thorn, 1866, C-918, lg folio .1,500.00
Central Park NY, the Bridge; undtd, C-950, sm folio 300.00
Children in the Woods, undtd, C-1033, sm folio 150.00
Clipper Ship in a Hurricane, 1855, C-1154, med folio 2,000.00
Clipper Ship in a Snow Squall, undtd, C-1157, sm folio 900.00
Cork Castle & Black Rock Castle, undtd, C-1253, sm folio 125.00
Cozzen's Dock, West Point; undtd, C-1277, med folio 800.00
Destruction of Rebel Monster Merrimac, undtd, C-1572, sm folio ...500.00
Distanced, 1878, C-1589, sm folio 225.00
Dude Belle, 1883, C-1634, sm folio 230.00
Easter Offering, 1871, C-1659, sm folio 30.00
Enchanted Isle, 1869, C-1740, sm folio 100.00
Family Pets, NC, undtd, C-1840, sm folio 125.00
Farmer's Home - Harvest, C-1890, 1864, lg folio 2,300.00
Fiend of the Road, 1881, C-1945, lg folio 1,400.00
First Ride, NC, 1849, C-1987, sm folio 130.00
Flower Vase, NC, 1848, C-2047, sm folio 150.00
Fruits of Temperance, 1870, C-2195, sm folio 200.00
General Shields at the Battle..., 1862, C-2294, sm folio 195.00
Georgie, Quite Tired; undtd, C-2359, sm folio 100.00
Good Times on the Old Plantation, undtd, C-2451, sm folio 700.00

Got the Drop on Him, 1881, C-2455, sm folio 250.00
Grand Pacer Richball, 1890, C-2519, sm folio 300.00
Grandest Palace Drawing Room..., 1878, C-2541, lg folio 1,500.00
Great Fire at Boston, 1872, C-2614, sm folio 350.00
Harbor for the Night, undtd, C-2724, sm folio 300.00
Henry Clay of Kentucky, NC, undtd, C-2791, sm folio 120.00
Homeward Bound, NC, 1845, C-2885, sm folio 750.00
Hudson From West Point, 1862, C-2972, med folio 1,050.00
In the Harbor, undtd, C-3069, sm folio 425.00
Inviting Dish, 1870, C-3124, sm folio 175.00
Italian Landscape, undtd, C-3139, sm folio 100.00
Just Married, undtd, C-3321, sm folio 100.00
Life in the Woods - Returning, 1860, C-3513, lg folio 3,500.00
Life in Woods - Starting Out, 1860, C-3514, lg folio 3,500.00
Life of a Fireman, Ruin; NC, 1854, C-3520, lg folio 2,500.00
Lincoln Family, 1867, C-3546, sm folio 100.00
Little Mary & Lamb, 1877, C-3670, sm folio 175.00
Little May Blossom, 1874, C-3671, sm folio 95.00
Maggie, undtd, C-3864, sm folio 95.00
May Queen, NC, undtd, C-4089, sm folio 90.00
Mink Trapping, 1862, C-4139, lg folio 9,500.00
Mother's Pet, NC, undtd, C-4237, sm folio 100.00
Mountain Rumble, undtd, C-4244, sm folio 175.00
Mrs Lucretia R Garfield, undtd, C-4263, med folio 95.00
My Little White Kitties Playing Dominoes, undtd, C-4336, sm folio 190.00
My Pet Bird, undtd, C-4348, med folio 175.00
My Three White Kitties..., Their ABC's; undtd, C-4357, sm folio 190.00
New Suspension Bridge, Niagara Falls; undtd, C-4432, sm folio 300.00
Nosegay, 1870, C-4512, sm folio 150.00
Old Ford Bridge, undtd, C-4559, sm folio 225.00
Old Mill in Summer, undtd, C-4571, sm folio 300.00
Old Oaken Bucket, 1872, C-4577, sm folio 225.00
On the Coast of California, undtd, C-4598, sm folio 350.00
On the Owago, undtd, C-4608, sm folio 200.00
Peaceful River, undtd, C-4736, sm folio 175.00
Perry's Victory on Lake Erie, NC, undtd, C-4754, sm folio 650.00
Pigeon Shooting, Playing the Decoy; 1862, C-4780, lg folio 3,000.00
Prince & Princess of Wales, undtd, C-4926, sm folio 90.00
Providence & Stonington Steamship..., 1877, C-4969, lg folio 1,500.00
Quails, NC, undtd, C-4992, sm folio 350.00
Queen of Beauty, undtd, C-4997, sm folio 75.00
Race on Mississippi, 1870, C-5042, sm folio 650.00
Renowned Trotter Prince Wilkes, 1889, C-5113, lg folio 1,400.00
Residence of Lord Byron, Diodati, Italy; undtd, C-5118, sm folio 90.00
Roadside Mill, 1870, C-5175, sm folio 350.00
Royal Mail Steamship Persia, NC, 1856, C-5240, lg folio 1,100.00
Siege & Capture of Vicksburg MS..., undtd, C-5507, sm folio 250.00
Silver Cascade, White Mountains; undtd, C-5521, sm folio 275.00
Soldier's Adieu, NC, 1847, C-5593, sm folio 125.00
Soldier's Home, 1862, C-5599, sm folio 125.00
Spring, NC, 1849, C-5671, sm folio 225.00
Staten Island & Narrows, 1861, C-5715, lg folio 1,700.00
Summer Evening, undtd, C-5853, sm folio 175.00
Summer Ramble, undtd, C-5874, med folio 350.00
Sunny Side Residence...Irving...NY, undtd, C-5892, lg folio 800.00
Through the Pacific, 1870, C-6051, sm folio 1,200.00
Tomb of Kosciusko, West Point; undtd, C-6103, sm folio 125.00
Tomb of Washington, Mt Vernon VA, undtd, C-6110, med folio 175.00
Tomb of Washington, Mt Vernon VA; undtd, C-6112, sm folio 125.00
Trolling for Bluefish, 1866, C-6158, lg folio 10,000.00
Trotting Cracks on the Snow, 1858, C-6170, lg folio 6,500.00
US Frigate Independence, 64 Guns; NC, 1841, C-6307, sm folio 465.00
Valley Forge VA, undtd, C-6355, sm folio 250.00
View of Astoria LI, 1862, C-6388, med folio 1,250.00
View of Roundout, undtd, C-6451, med folio 600.00
Village Blacksmith, 1864, C-6462, lg folio 3,000.00
Washington as a Mason, undtd, C-6512, sm folio 175.00
Washington at Trenton NJ, NC, 1845, C-6555, sm folio 150.00
Washington's Entry Into NY, 1857, C-6549, med folio 750.00
Water Jump at Jerome Park, undtd, C-6564, sm folio 465.00
Water Rail Shooting, NC, 1855, C-6567, sm folio 800.00
Why Don't He Come..., undtd, C-6653, sm folio 125.00
Wild Duck Shooting, Good Day's Sport; NC, 1854, C-6670, lg folio 6,000.00
Woodlands in Summer, undtd, C-6778, sm folio 250.00
Wreck of the Atlantic, 1873, C-6787, sm folio 290.00
Zachary Taylor, Nation's..., NC, 1847, C-6874, sm folio 175.00

Fox, R. Atkinson

A Canadian who worked as an artist in the 1880s, R. Atkinson Fox moved to New York about ten years later, where his original oils were widely sold at auction and through exhibitions. Today he is best known, however, for his prints, published by as many as twenty printmakers. More than thirty examples of his work appeared on Brown and Bigelow calendars, and it was used in many other forms of advertising as well. Though he was an accomplished artist able to interpret any subject well, he is today best known for his landscapes. Fox died in 1935. Our advisor for Fox prints is Pat Gibson whose address is listed in the Directory under California.

Ready for Market, #903, 9x12", $225.00.
(Photo courtesy Pat Gibson)

After the Storm, #103, 10x16" 75.00
An Old Fashion Garden, #12, 14x18" 145.00
An Old Oak, #211, 10x16" 95.00
Approaching Storm, #85, 4x9" 55.00
At the Foothills of Pike's Peak, #332, 9x7" 95.00
Battle of the Wild, #109, 10x8" 175.00
Clipper Ship, #75, 12x16" 95.00
Dawn, #1, 8x14" 125.00
Garden of Contentment, #78, 10x18" 135.00
Garden of Hope Puzzle, #20, 9x15" 85.00
Garden of Love, #42, 10x18" 145.00
Garden of Romance, #40, 12x19" 120.00
Glorious Vista, #6, 14x10" 90.00
Going to the Sun Mountain, #142, 7x5" 85.00
Good Guide, #632, 12x7" 245.00
Grandeur of Nature, #390, 4x5" 95.00
Great Falls of Yellowstone, #134, 9x7" 75.00
Heart's Desire, #55, 14x22" 195.00
In Green Pastures, #122, 4x10" 225.00
In Meditation Fancy Free, #101, 14x11" 475.00
Inspiration Inlet, #58, 18x10" 85.00
Journey's End - Oregon, #702, 10x14" 225.00

Love's Paradise, #13, 8x14" 125.00
Magic Pool, #74, 10x15" 125.00
Memories of Childhood Days, #305, 14x18" 165.00
Music of the Waters, #218, 4x3" 80.00
Nature's Grandeur, #22, 8x6" 55.00
Nature's Grandeur, #22, 14x22" 170.00
Nature's Charms, #88, 14x22" 250.00
Neath Sunset Skies, Turner, 8x6" 70.00
Old Mill, #538, 10x7" 135.00
Out of the Sky He Comes, #736, 7x10" 235.00
Paradise, Wainwright, 9x7" 65.00
Poppies, #45, 14x20" 180.00
Poppies, #45, 18x30" 235.00
Prides of the West, #426, 8x11" 235.00
Romance Canyon, #32, 15x12" 145.00
Rose Bower, #46, 16x10" 135.00
Russet Gems, #72, 12x9" 140.00
Sheltering Bower, #96, 5x4" 85.00
Sheltering Bower, #96, 20x12" 150.00
Silent Rockies, #318, 8x6" 85.00
Snow-Capped Mountain, #281, 10x7" 100.00
Supremacy, #139, 16x20" 245.00
Taking a Trench, #644, 16x20" 295.00
Thoroughbreds, #282, 6x8" 225.00
Two Medicine River Falls, Wainright, 9x7" 55.00
Where Nature Beats in Perfect Tune, #155, 12x10" 135.00

Fox, G. B.

Awaiting the Call, 7x5" 15.00
Champion, 9x12" 20.00
Majestic Mountains, 10x7" 10.00
Majestic Nature, 9x7" 25.00
So Sweet the Dreams, 9x7" 25.00

Gutmann, Bessie Pease

Delicately tinted prints of appealing children sometimes accompanied by their pets, sometimes asleep, often captured at some childhood activity are typical of the work of Gutmann; she painted lovely ladies as well and was a successful illustrator of children's books. Her career spanned the earlier decades of this century. Our advisor for this category is Earl MacSorley; he is listed in the Directory under Connecticut.

A Little Bit of Heaven, #650 ....75.00
Asking for Trouble, #820 ....150.00
Awakening, #664 ....75.00
Butterfly, The; #632 ....150.00
Dreams Come True, #636 ....500.00
Fairest of the Flowers, #659 ....350.00
Happy Dreams, #800 ....200.00
His Majesty, #793 ....200.00
Home Builders, The; #655 ....175.00
In Disgrace, #792 ....175.00
Introducing Baby, #646 ....400.00
Kitty's Breakfast, #805 ....175.00
Messages of the Roses, The; #641 ....350.00
On Dreamland's Border, #692 ....125.00
Reward, The; #794 ....175.00
Rosebud, #780 ....350.00
Sonny Boy, #784 ....225.00
Thank You God, #822 ....125.00
To Love & To Cherish, #615 ....275.00
Tom Tom the Piper's Son, #219 ....225.00

Winged Aureole, The; #700 ....275.00
Wood Magic, #703 ....400.00

Icart, Louis

Louis Icart (1888 – 1950) was a Parisian artist best known for his boudoir etchings in the '20s and '30s. In the '80s prices soared, primarily due to Japanese buying. The market began to readjust in 1990, and most etchings now sell at retail between $1,400.00 and $2,500.00. Value is determined by popularity and condition, more than by rarity. Original frames and matting are not important, as most collectors want the etchings restored to their original condition and protected with acid-free mats.

Beware of the following repro and knock-off items: 1. Pseudo engravings on white plastic with the Icart 'signature.' 2. Any bronzes with the Icart signature. 3. Most watercolors, especially if they look similar in subject matter to a popular etching. 4. Lithographs where the dot-matrix printing is visible under magnification. Some even have phony embossed seals or rubber stamp markings. Items listed below are in excellent condition unless noted otherwise. Our advisor is William Holland, author of *Louis Icart: The Complete Etchings*, and *The Collectible Maxfield Parrish*; he is listed in the Directory under Pennsylvania.

At the Urn, 1948, 12⅞x18⅛" 1,600.00
Bare Bottom, erotic etching, 8x5¾" 400.00
Belle Rose, 1933, 16¾x21¼", VG 1,500.00
Blue Bracelets, 1924, 17¼x13¼", VG 1,250.00
Bubbles, 1930, 17¼x13" 5,750.00
Coach, 1926, sheet: 35½x24¾", VG 925.00
Delilah, 1929, 20½x13", VG 985.00
Faust, bookplate litho, 7½x5½" 200.00
Favorite, 1936, 14½x14½", VG 1,725.00
Four Dears, 1929, sheet: 30⅝x21", rprs 1,000.00
Gay Senorita, 1939, 18½x22", VG 1,600.00
Grand Eve, 1934, 31x20¼" 15,000.00
Guardians, 1936, 14½x14½", VG 1,950.00
Lady of the Camelias, 1927, 17x21" 1,450.00

Lilies, 1934, touches of hand coloring, full margins, framed: 28½x19½", EX, $3,600.00.

Love's Blossom, 1937, 17½x25¼", VG 3,000.00
Mealtime, 1927, 18¼x14" 2,400.00
Mignon 1928, sheet: 25½x18", VG 800.00
Miss America, 1927, sheet: 28¼x22¼" 2,300.00
On the Beach, 1925, 11x16" 1,375.00
Orchids, 1937, 28x19½", VG 4,800.00
Poem, 1928, 19x22¾", rprs 1,725.00
Rainbow, 1930, 25⅛x17¼" 2,600.00
Repose, 1934, 19½x46", VG 11,500.00
Salome, 1928 20½x13⅝" 1,250.00
Seduction Le Faune, 1921, 14⅜x19" 1,600.00
Sulking, 1930, 12x17", VG 1,250.00
Two Beauties, 1931, rare, 17½x25½" 19,550.00

Wisteria, 1940, 18x21¾", VG 2,400.00
Youth, 1930, 24¼x15⅞", VG 3,500.00

Kurz and Allison

Louis Kurz founded the Chicago Lithograph Company in 1833. Among his most notable works were a series of thirty-six Civil War scenes and one hundred illustrations of Chicago architecture. His company was destroyed in the Great Fire of 1871, and in 1880 Kurz formed a partnership with Alexander Allison, an engraver. Until both retired in 1903, they produced hundreds of lithographs in color as well as black and white.

Values in our listings are for large folio prints (image size 17½" x 25") in excellent condition. Our advisor for these prints is Robert Wieland; he is listed in the Directory under Florida.

Battle of Antietam, Gen McClellan vs Gen Pleasonton 325.00
Battle of Atlanta, Gen McPherson Killed... ....395.00
Battle of Bull Run, Gen McDowell vs Gen Beaureguard 425.00
Battle of Champion Hills, MI, Rear Attack by Gen Logan 395.00
Battle of Corinth MS, 63rd Ohio & 2nd Texas Banners Shown ..395.00
Battle of Five Forks, VA, Gen Sheridan's Cavalry Charge 395.00
Battle of Ft Donelson TN, Grant to left, Gen Buckner & Army captured 395.00
Battle of Gettysburg, 1884, full margins 400.00
Battle of Kenesaw Mtn, Sherman vs Johnson 395.00
Battle of Quingua, Phillipine Isles, April 23, 1899 ....295.00
Battle of Wilson's Creek MO, Gen Lyon killed in battle 395.00
De Soto's Discovery of Mississippi 295.00
Declaration of Independence, after Trumbull's painting, in old fr ...325.00
Entrance of Cortez Into Mexico, full margins 300.00
Geo Washington at Mt Vernon w/Wife & 2 Grandchildren, blk & wht ..95.00
Geo Washington Enters Trenton...to Inauguration, med folio, 16x20" ...89.00
Perry's Victory on Lake Erie, Perry in longboat 495.00
Storming Stony Point, blk & wht, 12x18" 55.00
Wm Penn's Treaty w/Indians, 1621 ....345.00

McKenney and Hall

Unless otherwise noted, values are for 18x13" prints in excellent condition. Our advisor for McKenney and Hall prints is Robert Wieland; he is listed in the Directory under Florida.

Ne-sou-a-quoit, Fox Chief, hand colored, folio edition, 1836, 21¾x15½", unframed, $985.00.

Ap-Pa-Noo-Se, hand colored, 1838-41, Greenough & Bowen, 18x12⅞" ...495.00
Catahacassa, Shawnee, Greenough 345.00
Chippewa Widow, Chippewa, Biddle 355.00
Hoe Wan Ne Ka, Winnebago, Bowen 1,985.00
Jakopa, Chippewa, Rice & Clark 325.00
John Ross, Cherokee, Rice & Clark 355.00
Meetakoosega, Chippewa, Biddle 255.00
Misstippi, Creek, Greenough 795.00
Nehetluchopie, Muskogee, Rice & Clark 395.00
Ohyaminceekee, Chippewa, Rice & Clark 450.00
Pah She Pa Haw, Sauk-Fox, Greenough 325.00
Quataqapea, Shawnee, Greenough 395.00
Rant Che Wai Me, hand colored, sight: 15x13" 495.00
Shau Hau Napo Tinia, Iowa, Greenough 695.00
Stumanu, Flathead, Greenough 250.00
Timpoochee Barnard, Uchee, Greenough 395.00
Wabishkepeenas, Chippewa, Greenough 195.00
Wanata the Charger, Sioux, Biddle 1,385.00

Mucha, Alphonse

Mucha became famous for his beautiful Art Nouveau lithographs featuring Sarah Bernhardt and Job cigarette papers, which he issued in the 1890s. Born in Prague in 1860, he studied there as well as in Paris and for a time taught at the New York School of Applied Design for women before returning to Prague.

Flirt-Biscuits Lefever-utile, 1899, 23¼x10", EX 3,165.00
Lorenzaccio, 1896, 40x14½", VG 2,875.00
Maid picking berries in forest, 1896, 33½x18½" 3,750.00
Maid w/flowing hair, 5 birds & harp, 1896, 33½x18½" 3,500.00

Yard Longs

Values for yard-long prints are given for examples in *near mint* condition, full length, nicely framed, and with the original glass. To learn more about this popular area of collector interest, we recommend *Those Wonderful Yard-Long Prints and More, More Wonderful Yard-Long Prints*, Book 2, and *Yard-Long Prints*, Book 3, by our advisors Bill and June Keagy, and Charles and Joan Rhoden. They are listed in the Directory under Indiana and Illinois respectively. A word of caution: watch for reproductions; *know your dealer.*

A Happy Family, 9 monkeys, #1037, 3rd in series, c 1904 ....400.00
Cats & kittens on seesaw, c 1893 ....300.00
Diamond Crystal Salt Co, lady in gray dress & fox fur, c 1913 ..400.00
Favorites, Am Beauty Roses, A Romes 250.00
Hula girl, girl on surfboard, sgn Gene Pressler 400.00
Indian maiden w/basket of flowers, river beyond, ca 1918 ....350.00
Lady in gray & yel dress w/parasol & flower basket, Lister, 1918 ..350.00
Last Rose of Summer, Paul DeLongpre 300.00
Metropolitan Life Ins Co, 4 stages of life shown, c 1907 ....400.00
Pabst by CW Henning, lady in red, blk sash w/purple flowers, 1907 ...400.00
Pabst Extract, American Girl, CW Henning, 1911 ....400.00
Pabst Malt Extract, Oriental lady w/bottle, The Best Tonic, 1903 ..450.00
Pabst Malt Extract, Rose Girl, c 1909 ....400.00
Pompeian, blond w/young man, grandfather clock beyond, 1915 ..350.00
Pompeian, lady & man on balcony, eye-mask on wrist, G Pressler, 1926 ...300.00
Pompeian, Mary Pickford in bl dress, seated/holding daisy, 1916 ...400.00
Schlitz Malt Extract, Priscilla, c 1910 ....450.00
Selz Good Shoes, lady in bl dress holds walking stick, c 1925 ...450.00
Selz Good Shoes, lady in blk dress holds long-stem rose, c 1918 ..400.00
Spring Is Here, Cambril, c 1907 ....250.00
Spring's Message, Paul DeLongpre 300.00
Walk-Over Shoe, calendar at bottom, c 1917 ....400.00
Yard of Pansies, Heinmuller 200.00

Purinton

Founded in 1936 in Wellsville, Ohio, Purinton Pottery relocated in 1941 in Shippenville, Pennsylvania, and began producing hand-painted wares that are today attracting the interest of collectors of 'country-type' dinnerware. Using bold brush strokes of vivid color, simple yet attractive patterns such as Apple, Fruit, Tea Rose, and Pennsylvania Dutch were manufactured in tableware sets and accessory pieces. For more information we recommend *Purinton Pottery* by Susan Morris, our advisor for this category; she is listed in the Directory under Oregon.

Baker, Pennsylvania Dutch, 7" 45.00
Baker, Turquoise, 7" dia 45.00
Bean pot, Mountain Rose, 4½" 65.00
Bottle, vinegar; Fruit, cobalt trim, 1-pt, 9½" 35.00
Bottles, oil & vinegar; Apple, 1-pt, 9½", pr 95.00
Bowl, fruit; Apple, plain border, 12" 35.00
Bowl, fruit; Normandy Plaid, 12" 35.00
Bowl, fruit; Petals, 12" 50.00
Bowl, vegetable; Apple, open, 8½" dia 30.00
Bowl, vegetable; Chartreuse, open, 8½" 30.00
Butter dish, Intaglio, 6½" 55.00
Candle holder, Peasant Lady, sgn, minimum value 500.00
Candy dish, Pennsylvania Dutch, 6¼" 65.00
Canister, Apple, half-oval, 5½" 65.00
Canister, Ming Tree, variation of orig pattern, 7½" 65.00
Canister, tea; Daisy, red trim, 9" 60.00
Coaster, Crescent Flower, 3½" dia 40.00
Cocktail dish, Desert Flower, 3-D sea horse, bowl ea side, 12" 75.00
Coffee server, Seaform, 9" 125.00
Coffeepot, Apple, 8-cup, 8" 90.00
Coffeepot, Fruit, 8-cup, 8" 65.00
Coffeepot, Ivy — Red Blossom, 8" 65.00
Cookie jar, Apple, w/wooden lid, sq, 9½" 90.00
Cookie jar, Normandy Plaid, oval, 9½" 60.00
Cookie jar, Saraband, oval, w/lid, 9½" 50.00
Creamer & sugar bowl, Chartreuse, mini 40.00
Cruets, oil & vinegar; Saraband, sq, 5", pr 25.00
Decanter, Intaglio, mini, 5" 35.00
Decanter, Mountain Rose, 5" 45.00
Dish, Apple, w/lid, 9" 65.00
Ewer, souvenir, Cook Forest, 9" 150.00
Grease jar, Normandy Plaid, w/lid, 5½" 60.00
Grease jar, Provincial Fruit, 5" 30.00
Honey jug, Petals, 6¼" 45.00

Jam and Jelly dish, Apple, 5½", $45.00.
(Photo courtesy Susan Morris)

Jar, biscuit; Ivy — Red Blossom, w/lid, 8" 55.00
Jardiniere, Leaves, 5" 25.00
Jug, Dutch; Crescent Flower, 2-pt, 5¾" 75.00
Jug, honey; Petals, 6¼" 45.00
Jug, Intaglio, 5-pt, 8" 75.00
Jug, Kent; Fruit, 1-pt, 4½" 30.00
Jug, oasis; Fruit, 9½", minimum value 500.00
Mug, Apple, 8-oz, 4" 35.00
Mug, beer; Intaglio, 16-oz, 4¾" 40.00
Mug, beer; Palm Tree, 16-oz, 4¾" 85.00
Mug, Heather Plaid, 8-oz, 4" 25.00
Mug, Kent; Normandy Plaid, 1-pt, 4½" 30.00
Pickle dish, Pineapple, unusual sponged edge, 6" dia 35.00
Pitcher, beverage; Ivy — Red Blossom, 2-pt, 6¼" 55.00
Pitcher, beverage; Normandy Plaid, 2-pt, 6¼" 55.00
Pitcher, beverage; Petals, 2-pt, 6¼" 75.00
Pitcher, Peasant Garden, Rubel mold, 5" 150.00
Planter, basket; Blue Pansy, 6¼" 65.00
Planter, Tea Rose, 5" 65.00
Plate, breakfast; Apple, 8½" 20.00
Plate, breakfast; Peasant Garden, 8½" 100.00
Plate, chop; Fruit, 12" 45.00
Plate, chop; Heather Plaid, 12" 35.00
Plate, chop; Intaglio, 12" 30.00
Plate, chop; Ming Tree, 12" 75.00
Plate, dinner; Intaglio, 9¾" 15.00
Plate, dinner; Palm Tree, 9¾" 125.00
Plate, dinner; Turquoise, 9¾" 50.00
Plate, lap; Fruit, 8½" 30.00
Platter, grill; Maywood, 12" 45.00
Platter, meat; Apple, 12" 55.00
Platter, meat; Ming Tree, 12" 65.00
Platter, meat; Pennsylvania Dutch, 12" 85.00
Platter, meat; Seaform, 12" 50.00
Relish, Fruit, wood hdl, solid apple/purple grapes, 3-part, 10" 45.00
Shakers, Apple, range style, 4", pr 50.00
Shakers, Fruit, range style, red trim, 4", pr 40.00
Shakers, Ivy — Red Blossom, jug style, 2½", pr 20.00
Shakers, pour 'n shake; Heather Plaid, 4¼", pr 60.00
Sugar bowl, Pennsylvania Dutch, w/lid, 5" 50.00
Tea & toast set, Intaglio, cup, 2½", & lap plate, 8½" 25.00
Teapot, Crescent Flower, 6-cup, 6" 85.00
Teapot, Maywood, 6-cup, 6½" 45.00
Teapot, Mountain Rose, 4-cup, 5" 75.00
Teapot, Petals, 8-cup, 8" 75.00
Tray, roll; Apple, 11" 35.00
Tray, roll; Intaglio, 11" 35.00
Tray, roll; Tea Rose, 11" 50.00
Tray, tidbit; Intaglio, metal hdl, 2-tier, 10" 45.00
Tumbler, Mountain Rose, 12-oz, 5" 35.00
Tumbler, Pennsylvania Dutch, 12-oz, 5" 35.00
TV lamp, Red Feather, 8½" 75.00
Vase, cornucopia; Ivy — Yellow Blossom, 6" 25.00
Wall pocket, Apple, 3½" 50.00
Wall pocket, Chartreuse, 3½" 35.00
Wall pocket, Heather Plaid, 3½" 35.00

Purses

Purses from the early 1800s are often decorated with small, brightly colored glass beads. Cut steel beads were popular in the 1840s and remained stylish until about 1930. Purses made of woven mesh date back to the 1820s. Chain-link mesh came into usage in the 1890s, followed by the enamel mesh bags carried by the flappers in the 1920s. Purses are divided into several categories by (a) construction techniques — whether beaded, embroidered, or a type of needlework; (b) material — fabric or metal; and (c) design and style. Condition is very important. Watch for dry, brittle leather or fragile material. For those interested in learning more, we recommend *Antique Purses, A History, Identification, and Value Guide, Second Edition*, by Richard Holiner; *More Beautiful Purses*, and *Combs and Purses*, both by Evelyn Haertigi of Carmel, California; and *Vintage Vanity Bags & Purses* by Roselyn Gerson. An interesting related book is *Vintage Contemporary Purse Accessories*, also by Roselyn Gerson. Our advisor for this category is Veronica Trainer; she is listed in the Directory under Ohio.

Key: W&D — Whiting & Davis

Beaded, butterflies, blk & silver 350.00
Beaded, butterflies/rose, w/fringe & tassel hdl, gold/red on blk, 11" ...150.00
Beaded, castle scene, mc, w/fringe, mc metal fr, 10¾x7" 165.00
Beaded, checked, wht/gr/blk, blk & wht fringe, metal fr, Czech, 9x7" ...65.00
Beaded, clamshell shape, blk, silver fr, Germany, 4x3¾" 45.00
Beaded, cottage scene w/lake, mc, metal fr, 8½x6½" 95.00
Beaded, Deco style, silver & blk, 7x8" 175.00
Beaded, floral, mc, w/fringe, rhinestone/metal fr, 12¾x8½" 225.00
Beaded, geometric, blk/silver/gold, fringe, metal fr, Fr, 4½x7½" ..60.00
Beaded, geometric, blk/silver/gold, w/fringe/drawstring, 12x7¼" .85.00
Beaded, geometric on oval shape, mc, w/fringe, sterling fr, 13¾x11" ..275.00
Beaded, gondola scene, mc, w/fringe, beaded metal fr, 12¼x7½" ...175.00
Beaded, leaves, mc, Indian style, beaded hdl, 6½x12½" 375.00
Beaded, peacock & red roses, ornate SP fr, 8x12" 400.00
Beaded, robin on blk, lg Bakelite fr, 7x12" 350.00
Beaded, romance scene tapestry, gold fr 75.00
Beaded, rose, mc on gold, blk crochet top/bottom tassel, 8¾x6" .60.00
Beaded, roses, blk w/pk, 8x10" 300.00
Beaded, roses on tan, ornate SP fr, 6½x9" 300.00
Celluloid/suede, tortoise-color elephants as hdl terminals 260.00
Leather, peacock decor, Meeker, 6x6½" 125.00
Leather, tooled geometric on brn, strap hdl, metal fr, Jemco, 9x7½" 85.00
Lucite vanity, burl-like, envelope closure, swing hdl, Wilardy, 8x8x4" ..400.00

Mesh, blue, gold, and white geometric design, Gold Mandalain frame, fringe, 7", from $110.00 to $160.00.

Mesh, birds on branch, zigzag bottom, Mandalain fr, 8x5" 125.00
Mesh, chrome, W&D, 4x5½" 125.00
Mesh, clutch, metallic gold-tone, W&D, w/box, 4¾x8¾" 85.00
Mesh, dmns pattern, bl/yel/wht, w/fringe, fold-over top, W&D, 9x5½" 135.00
Mesh, floral, zigzag bottom, metal fr, W&D, 8¾x6" 110.00
Mesh, floral on chevron shape, pk, w/fringe, Mandalain, 7x3¾" .65.00
Mesh, floral/geometric, mc, 1 tassel bottom, fold-over, W&D, 8½x5" ...105.00
Mesh, necessaire, 6-sided, gold/pearls/bl stones, tassel/chain, 3x2" .300.00
Mesh, silver-tone, beaded bottom, silver fr, Germany, 6½x7¾" ...65.00
Mesh, spider web, blk on wht/silver/gold, W&D fr, 6¾x5½" 95.00
Mesh, vanity, geometric, brn/tan/gold, rnd lid/tassel/chain, 5½x3" ..450.00
Mesh, vanity, gold-tone, flat engine-turned lid, chain, 4x3x2" ..250.00
Silk, blk, silver fr w/emb harvest design, chain, 9x10" 150.00

Puzzles

'Jigsaw' puzzles have been around almost as long as games. The first examples were handcrafted from wood, and they are extremely difficult to find. Most of the early examples featured moral subjects just as the board games did. By the 1890s jigsaw puzzles had become a major form of home entertainment. During the Depression years jigsaw puzzles were set up on card tables in almost every home. The early wood examples are the most valuable.

Cube puzzles, or blocks, were often made by the same companies as the board games. Again, early examples display the finest quality lithography. While all subjects are collectible, some (such as Santa blocks) often command prices higher than games from the same period. In the listings all items are jigsaw puzzles unless noted otherwise.

Personalities, Movies, and TV Shows

Aquaman, jigsaw, Whitman, 1968, 100 pcs, MIB 40.00
Batman at the Docks, fr-tray, Whitman, 1966, EX 35.00
Beatles Yellow Submarine, jigsaw, Jaymar, 650 pcs, NMIB 150.00
Bonny Braids Dick Tracy's New Daughter, fr-tray, Saalfield, 1950s, NM ...20.00
Captain America, fr-tray, Whitman, 1966, M 50.00
Cinderella, jigsaw, 1950s, EX (EX canister) 30.00
Davy Crockett, fr-tray, Jaymar, 1950s, EX 75.00
Dilly Dally the Human Bullet, fr-tray, Whitman, 1950s, EX 40.00
Flintstones, fr-tray, Whitman, 1964, NM 45.00
Goldfinger, jigsaw, Milton Bradley, VG (VG box) 35.00
Goofy, fr-tray, Whitman, 1940s, set of 2, NMIB 85.00
Gunsmoke, fr-tray, Whitman, 1958, EX 30.00
Howdy Goes West, fr-tray, Whitman, 1953, EX 40.00
Jetsons, fr-tray, Whitman, 1960s, NM, from $35 to 45.00
Land of the Giants, jigsaw, Whitman Jr, 1960s, rnd, EXIB 35.00
Lassie, jigsaw, Whitman Big Little Book Series, 1960s, NMIB 50.00
Lone Ranger, fr-tray, Puzzle Craft Industries, 1945, set of 3, NMIB ..200.00
Mighty Mouse, fr-tray, Jaymar, 1950s, NM 15.00
Mighty Mouse Playhouse, jigsaw, Fairchild, 1956, MIB 20.00
Mod Squad, jigsaw, Milton Bradley, 1969, MIB 35.00
Monkees, jigsaw, Fairchild, 1967, MIB 45.00
Patty Duke, jigsaw, Whitman Jr, 1963, 100 pcs, EXIB 45.00
Pinky Lee, fr-tray, Gabriel, 1950s, set of 4, EX (VG box) 85.00
Planet of the Apes, jigsaw, HG Toys, 1967, EX (EX canister) 40.00
Quick Draw McGraw, fr-tray, Whitman, 1960, EX 25.00
Raggedy Ann Picture..., jigsaw, Milton Bradley, 1940, set of 4, MIB ..95.00
Roger Ramjet, fr-tray, Whitman, 1966, NM 75.00
Sleeping Beauty, jigsaw, Jaymar, 1960s, NMIB 20.00
Story Book Puzzles, USA, 1945, set of 4, unused, MIB 100.00
Tom & Jerry, fr-tray, Whitman, 1959, NM 25.00
Top Cat, fr-tray, Whitman, 1960s, MIP, from $20 to 25.00
Wild Bill Hickok, jigsaw, Built Rite, 1956, 100 pcs, EXIB 25.00
Woody Woodpecker, fr-tray, Whitman, 1954, VG 25.00
Wyatt Earp, jigsaw, Whitman, 1960s, NMIB 25.00
Zorro, fr-tray, 1957, EX 35.00

Miscellaneous

Approving the Vintage, plywood, J Straus, 1930s, 300 pcs, EXIB ...40.00
Autumn, plywood, 150 pcs, Parker Bros, 1909, EXIB 50.00
Blocks, paper litho on wood, 6 puzzles, wood box, 12" L, VG 65.00
Columbus Blocks, McLoughlin Bros, early 1900s, EXIB 700.00
Cut Up Birds Scroll Picture Puzzle, Parker Bros, early 1900s, EXIB ...250.00
Fire Engine Picture Puzzle, McLoughlin Bros, 1887, EXIB 700.00
Flying Steamship (Untitled), McLoughlin Bros, early 1900s, EXIB ...375.00
Home Scroll Puzzle, McLoughlin Bros, complete, G in box 110.00

In Full Sail, Chad Valley, 1930s, plywood, 258 pcs, EXIB **65.00**
Mallards, plywood, J Straus, 1930s, 100 pcs, EXIB **20.00**
Natures Splendor, plywood, Galles, 1930s, 100 pcs, EXIB **75.00**
Old Tow Path, cb, Tuco/Deluxe, 1940-50, 350 pcs, EXIB **15.00**
Over Field & Fence, masonite, Leisure Moment, 1930s, 329 pcs, EXIB ..**50.00**
Quai Vert, plywood, Parker Bros, 1920-30, 350 pcs, EXIB **125.00**
Rounding the Cape, plywood, Glengarry, 1930s, 300 pcs, EXIB ..**65.00**
Santa blocks, 6-sided paper lithos, w/matching lithos on linen sheets ..**650.00**
Winter, plywood, Parker Bros, 1938, 509 pcs, EXIB **200.00**
Young Folks Cube Puzzle, Little Bo Peep, paper litho, w/linen sheet, G ...**275.00**

Pyrography

Pyrography, also known as wood burning, Flemish art, or poker work, is the art of burning designs into wood or leather and has been practiced over the centuries in many countries.

In the late 1800s pyrography became the hot new hobby for thousands of Americans who burned designs inspired by the popular artists of the day including Mucha, Gibson, Fisher, and Corbett. Thousands of wooden boxes, wall plaques, novelties, and pieces of furniture that they purchased from local general stores or from mail-order catalogs were burned and painted. These pieces were manufactured by companies such as The Flemish Art Company of New York and Thayer & Chandler of Chicago, who printed the designs on wood for the pyrographers to burn.

This Victorian fad developed into a new form of artistic expression as the individually burned and painted pieces reflected the personality of the pyrographers. The more adventurous started to burn between the lines and developed a style of 'all-over burning' that today is known as pyromania. Others not only created their own designs but even made the pieces to be decorated. Both these developments are particularly valued today as true examples of American folk art.

By the 1930s its popularity had declined. Like Mission furniture, it was neglected by generations of collectors and dealers. The recent appreciation of Victoriana, the Arts and Crafts Movement, the American West, and the popularity of turn-of-the-century graphic art has rekindled interest in pyrography which embraces all these styles.

An informative book, *The Burning Passion — Antique and Collectible Pyrography*, by Carole and Richard Smyth, our advisors for this category, is currently available from the authors; they are listed in the Directory under New York.

Key: hb — hand burned

Extending book rack, hand-burned and painted girl with book, 5¾x15¾" closed (25¼" when extended), $150.00. (Photo courtesy Carole and Richard Smyth)

Bedroom set, hb/pnt, Wm Rogers/Forusville PA, 1905-07, 3-pc ..**4,000.00**
Box, flatware; factory burned/pnt poinsettias, Rogers, 9x11x5" .**195.00**
Box, floral decor, stamped design, 14½" sq **40.00**
Box, lady w/flowing hair, Flemish Art Co, 1909, 11¾x4¼" **120.00**
Chair-table, hb/pnt poinsettias, Rest-Ye... on chair bk, EX **950.00**
Checker/backgammon brd, red & gr decor/glass bead insets, 30x15" **1,550.00**
Chest, blanket; hb/pnt swans/lady's head/flowers/etc, ca 1890 ...**850.00**
Chest, medicine; hb/pnt Nouveau lady & vines, wall mt **450.00**
Coat hanger, hb/pnt poppies & leaves, Mother Dearest **80.00**
Cue holder, hb pool-hall scene, folk art, unique **650.00**
Egg cup, hb/pnt, pr **60.00**
Etching set, Snow White, Disney/Marks, 1938, electric pen, complete ...**175.00**
Footstool, hb/pnt allover w/owl/branches/leaves **125.00**
Frame, hb/pnt cherries, standing type, 7½x6", EX **85.00**
Frame, hb/pnt chrysanthemums, Thayer-Chandler, 10½x8", EX .**85.00**
Frame, hb/pnt flower garland, Thayer-Chandler, 8" dia **85.00**
Frame, owls in tree, 2 Is Company, 2 oval cutouts **145.00**
Gameboard, hb/pnt ea side/edges, Flemish Art, 15" sq (open) ...**200.00**
Knife rack, hb Lizzie Borden w/axe, 5 hooks below, rare **550.00**
Magazine stand, 4-shelf, burned/pnt florals, Thayer-Chandler, 48" **800.00**
Mirror, hand; hb/pnt lady's head w/flowing hair, 13¼x6¾" **180.00**
Nut bowl, hb/pnt squirrel on branch, Flemish Art Co #816, 5" ...**65.00**
Panel, basswood, burned/pnt orange, Thayer-Chandler, 16x30" **465.00**
Panel, hb after painting: To the Feast, minor gold, 9x34" **500.00**
Pedestal, hb/pnt Nouveau flowers & vines, 45" **400.00**
Plaque, cvd/burned/pnt strawberry basket, 3-ply, 12" dia **70.00**
Plaque, girl bathing puppies, #854, 14½" **125.00**
Plaque, hb orange cat w/bow, paper 1912 calendar, 5¾" dia **50.00**
Plaque, Nouveau lady w/cherries, 19½" **150.00**
Plaque, Victorian couple, Parting by a Wall & flowers **145.00**
Ribbon holder, hb/pnt Sunbonnet babies (3), 5x12" **160.00**
Spoon holder, geometric florals, wall hanging, 1915, 10x8" **45.00**
Tie rack, factory stamp, HP solider/nurse/sailor, WWI motto **125.00**

Quezal

The Quezal Art Glass and Decorating Company of Brooklyn, New York, was founded in 1901 by Martin Bach. A former Tiffany employee, Bach's glass closely resembled that of his former employer. Most pieces were signed 'Quezal,' a name taken from a Central American bird. After Bach's death in 1920, his son-in-law, Conrad Vohlsing, continued to produce a Quezal-type glass in Elmhurst, New York, which he marked 'Lustre Art Glass.' Examples listed here are signed unless noted otherwise.

Lamp base, feathers, gold on gr, cream feathered neck, 12" **750.00**
Shade, feather edge, gr on gold to wht opal, 5½", pr **350.00**
Shade, feathers, gold w/gr outlines on wht, 6" **150.00**
Shade, feathers, gr w/gold on opal irid, gold int, 4¼x8" **425.00**
Shade, feathers, opal on gold irid, cylindrical, 6", pr **300.00**
Shade, gold, ribbed/flaring, 6" **250.00**
Shade, heart leaves, gold/gr, gold threading/int, 5½" **250.00**
Shade, leaves, gold on opal irid, morning-glory shape, 6" **200.00**
Shade, opal irid w/golden int, bell form, 5" **100.00**
Vase, bl irid, slender classic form, 10½" **1,000.00**
Vase, bl irid, wide flared neck, 10½" **1,100.00**
Vase, feathers, gold on yel opal, gourd shape w/stick neck, 6" ...**1,900.00**
Vase, feathers, silver-bl on gr to opal, baluster, 7½" **865.00**
Vase, feathers & wide gold neck band on gr, gourd shape, 9" ...**4,600.00**
Vase, floriform; feathers, gr on wht, gold int, #838, 5" **1,000.00**
Vase, gold, bulbous w/flared neck, lt ribbing, #I-866, 3" **690.00**
Vase, gold irid, flared rim, 8" **525.00**
Vase, gold irid, squatty, 3¾" **400.00**
Vase, gold w/pk & bl irid, trumpet form w/wide cupped rim, 5½" ...**375.00**
Vase, jack-in-pulpit; feathers, gr w/gold stretch, gold int, 11" .**3,000.00**
Vase, leaves, gr on wht, gold int, 5" **1,200.00**
Vase, leaves, gr w/amethyst gold veins, threading, petal rim, 6" ...**3,500.00**
Vase, wht w/gold int, flared top, 6½" **225.00**

Vase, yel transparent w/purple-yel base, stick neck, 10" 150.00

Quilts

Quilts, while made of necessity, nevertheless represent an art form which expresses the character and the personality of the designer. During the seventeenth and eighteenth centuries, quilts were considered a necessary part of a bride's hope chest; the traditional number required to be properly endowed for marriage was a 'baker's dozen'! American Colonial quilts reflect the English and French taste of our ancestors. They would include the classifications known as Lindsey-Woolsey and the central medallion appliqué quilts fashioned from imported copper-plate printed fabrics.

By 1829 spare time was slightly more available, so women gathered in quilting bees. This not only was a way of sharing the work but also gave them the opportunity to show off their best handiwork. The hand-dyed and pieced quilts emerged, and they are now known as sampler, album, and friendship quilts. By 1845 American printed fabric was available.

In 1793 Eli Whitney developed the cotton gin; as a result, textile production in America became industrialized. Soon inexpensive fabrics were readily available, and ladies were able to choose from colorful prints and solids to add contrast to their work. Both pieced and appliquéd work became popular.

Pieced quilts were considered utilitarian, while appliquéd quilts were shown with pride of accomplishment at the fair or used when itinerant preachers traveled through and stayed for a visit. Today many collectors prize pieced quilts and their intricate geometric patterns above all other types. Many of these designs were given names: Daisy and Oak Leaf, Grandmother's Flower Garden, Log Cabin, and Ocean Wave are only a few. Appliquéd quilts involved stitching one piece — carefully cut into a specific form such as a leaf, a flower, or a stylized device — onto either a large one-piece ground fabric or an individual block. Often the background fabric was quilted in a decorative pattern such as a wreath or medallions.

Amish women scorned printed calicos as 'worldly' and instead used colorful blocks set with black fabrics to produce a stunning pieced effect. To show their reverence for God, the Amish would often include a 'superstition' block which represented the 'imperfection' of Man!

One of the most valuable quilts in existence is the Baltimore album quilt. Made between 1840 – 1860 only three hundred or so still exist today. They have been known to fetch over $100,000.00 at prominent auction houses in New York City. Usually each block features elaborate appliqué work such as a basket of flowers, patriotic flags and eagles, the Oddfellow's heart in hand, etc. The border can be sawtooth, meandering, or swags and tassels.

During the Victorian period the crazy quilt emerged. This style became the most popular quilt ever in terms of sheer numbers produced and popularity. The crazy quilt was formed by random pieces put together following no organized lines and was usually embellished by elaborate embroidery stitches. Fabrics of choice were brocades, silks, and velvets.

Another type of quilting, highly prized and rare today, is trapunto. These quilts were made by first stitching the outline of the design onto a solid sheet of fabric which was backed with a second having a much looser weave. White was often favored, but color was sometimes used for accent. The design (grapes, flowers, leaves, etc.) was padded through openings made by separating the loose weave of the underneath fabric; a backing was added and the three layers quilted as one.

Besides condition, value is judged on intricacy of pattern, color effect, and craftsmanship. Examine the stitching. Quality quilts have from ten to twelve stitches to the inch. A stitch is defined as any time a needle pierces through the fabric. So you may see five threads but ten (stitches) have been used. In the listings that follow, examples rated excellent have minor defects, otherwise assume them to be free of any damage, soil, or wear. Values given here are auction results; retail may be somewhat higher. Our advisor is Craig Ambrose; he is listed in the Directory under Iowa.

Key:
hs — hand sewn, sewing
hq — hand quilted, quilting
mp — machine pieced
ms — machine sewn

Amish

Bars, two-color, intricate hand quilting, early, full size, EX, $575.00. (Photo courtesy Aston Macek Auctioneers and Appraisers)

Dmn in Square, mc cottons, fine hq, late 19th C, 108x108" 925.00
Dmn in Square, 5-color crepe, floral hq, wear/patches, 82x84" .300.00
Flower Garden, dk prints & solid on blk, 19th C, 67x78" 350.00
Grandmother's Flower Garden, prints/solids on wht, 109x119" .350.00
Rob Peter To Pay Paul, orange/burgundy/brn, reverse: stripes, 86x90" ..750.00
Stars, mc solids on beige w/bl border, red binding, 75x82" 330.00
Sunshine & Shadow, mc wools/knits, ca 1930, 80x80", VG 350.00
4 geometric designs, blk/bl/beige/brn, 1946, some fading, 84x72" ..650.00

Appliquéd

Butterflies, 1930s prints on wht, unused, 60x72", M 250.00
Floral medallions, bl/red/orange, minor stains, 86x90" 700.00
Floral medallions (6) & vintage border, red/gr/bl on wht, 74x89" ...200.00
Floral medallions & 3-D trapunto on wht, 87" sq 2,400.00
Flower baskets & vining border, red/gr/gold on wht, fine hq, 89x88" ...850.00
Geometric designs, pk calico & wht, EX hq, minor stains, 85x68" .275.00
Oak leaves, gr on wht, fading, 1850s, 81x61" 300.00
Rose of Sharon floral medallions, mc on wht, fine hq, 68x83" ..770.00
Rose wreaths w/similar border, red/teal/wht, 1850s, 84x82" 450.00
Sunburst & eagle, gr/tan/red/wht, fading/stain, 1850s, 88x90" ...400.00
Tulip, yel/gr on wht, hs, fine hq, 72x84", EX 300.00

Pieced

Basket, mc on wht w/red Greek key border, 1850s, 71x72" 350.00
Baskets of flowers, beige & red on wht, hs, feather border, 82x85" ...350.00
Blocks, red & beige on wht, late 1800s, rprs/fading, 71x78" 300.00
Bow Tie, mc on wht sqs, pk calico grid, 78x78", EX 250.00
Broken Star, bl/tan/off-wht cottons, 67x83" 350.00
Courthouse Steps, mc cottons, late 19th C, 67x80" 300.00
Crazy, silk/satin/cotton/wool w/appliques & embr, ca 1900, 68x81" ...200.00
Crazy, velvets/silks/rayons, sateen lining, 72x58", EX 295.00
Delectable Mountain, red/bl/blk/wht ginghams, 1920s, 68x80", EX .325.00
Double Irish Chain, dk red/bleached muslin, 1930s, 80x90", EX 350.00
Dresden Plate, pastels/wht, red binding, 1930s, 78x90", EX 295.00
Flower Garden, bright mc w/gr binding, hs/hq, 1940s, 88x102", EX ...400.00
Flower Garden, pastel prints/solids/yel/wht, 1930s, 70x88", VG ...225.00
Flying Geese, red & wht, frayed edges, 74x80" 330.00
Goblet, homespun, dk bl & blk w/mc prints, 1850s, 68x66", EX ...400.00
Ice cream cone-like medallions, 4-color on wht, sawtooth edge, 81x72" 200.00

Irish Chain, gr calico & solid red, hs, 63x80", EX 440.00
LeMoyne Star, pastels, pk & wht binding, 1930s, 70x85", M 295.00
Log Cabin, ginghams/dk red/wht, 1920s, 62x74", NM 425.00
Log Cabin, silk & satin, late 19th C, 84x73", EX 250.00
Lone Star, bright pastels/lav binding, 1930s, 80x94", EX 300.00
Lone Star, pastels & solids, peach binding, hs/hq, 1930s, 84x94", M ..375.00
Mariner's Compass, gr/red/wht w/applique work, 1850s, 68x94" .350.00
Mosaic Design, aqua/wht, triangles form border, 1930s, 78" sq, EX 300.00
Occupational, Irish chain, red on wht w/mc embr, dtd 1885, 97x79" ...1,600.00
Old Scraps (patchwork), red/wht, EX red hq, 1930s(?), 72x88", EX 300.00
Patchwork Sofa, pk/wht, EX hq, 1930s, 62x70", EX 295.00
Pineapple medallions, pk calico & wht, EX hq, 94x77" 400.00
Railroad, red/bl ginghams/muslin, hs, 1920s, 72x88", EX 300.00

Sampler with collage of patterns: Bowtie, Log Cabin, Chimney Sweep, Pinwheel, Four-Patch, Nine-Patch, and Postage Stamp; fabric colors: shades of Turkey red, blue, burgundy, gray, black, and white; ca 1860 – 1880, $2,500.00. (Photo courtesy Craig Ambrose)

Snowball, bleached muslin/pastels, gr binding, 1930s, 66x75" ...300.00
Star & Hexagons, bls/pks, fine hq, 1930s, 72x74", EX 300.00
Star medallions (9) w/trapunto between, mc on wht, full sz 600.00
Star of Bethlehem, red/saffron/gr on lt bl, 19th C, 79x80" 1,725.00
Stars, polished cottons/ginghams/checks, some age, unused, 82x82" ...325.00
Stars (12) mc on wht, ms binding, youth sz, 64x48" 270.00
Triangles, mc cottons/wht muslin, ms binding, EX hq, 1930s, 76x78", EX ..300.00
Trip Around World, prints/solid (some feed sacks), hq, 78x92", EX ..225.00
Tumbling Block, red/yel/blk/wht, PA, ca 1900, 70x80" 285.00
Wedding Ring, pastels/pk/bl, pk binding, hq, 1930s, 78x94", EX 400.00
Wedding Ring, pastels/yel/bleached muslin, 1930s, hs, 68x82", EX ...300.00
Yo-Yo, pastels/solids, summer weight, 1930s, 88x88", EX 200.00
Yo-Yo, solids/prints, 1930s, hs/hq, 76x96", M 250.00
8-Point design, pk/bl/bleached muslin, 1930s, 63x80", M 295.00
9-Patch, red/brn/gr/bl/beige, late 19th C, 71x87", EX 300.00

Quimper

Quimper pottery bears the name of the Breton town in northwestern France where it has been made for over three hundred years. Production began in 1690 when Jean-Baptiste Bousquet settled into a small workshop in the suburbs of Quimper, at Locmaria. There he bagan to make the hand-painted, tin enamel-glazed earthenware which we know today as faience. By the last quarter of the nineteenth century, there were three factories working concurrently: Porquier, de la Hubaudiere (the Grand Maison), and Henriot. All three houses produced similar wares which were decorated with scenes from the everyday life of the peasant folk of the region. Their respective marks are an AP or a P with an intersecting B (similar to a clover), an HB, and an HR (which became HenRiot after litigation in 1922).

The most desirable pieces were produced during the last quarter of the nineteenth century through the first quarter of the twentieth century. These are considered to be artistically superior to the examples made after World War I and II with the exception of the Odetta line, which is now experiencing a renaissance among collectors here and abroad.

Most of what was made was faience, but there was also a history of utilitarian gres ware (stoneware) having been produced there. In 1922 the Grande Maison HB revitalized this ware and introduced the line called Odetta, examples of which seemed to embody the bold spirit of the Art Deco style. The companion faience pieces of this period and genre are classified as Modern Movement examples and frequently bear the name of the artist who designed the mold.

Currently there are two factories still producing Quimper pottery. La Societe Nouvelle des Faienceries de Quimper is owned by Sarah and Paul Jenessens along with a group of American investors. Their mark is a stamped HB-Henriot logo. The other, La Faiencerie d'art Breton, is operated by the direct descendents of the HB and Henriot families. Their pieces are marked with an interlocked F and A conjoined with an inverted B. Other marks include HQF which is the Henriot Quimper France mark and HBQ, the HB Quimper mark. If you care to learn more about Quimper, we recommend *Quimper Pottery: A French Folk Art Faience* by Sandra V. Bondhus, our advisor for this category, whose address can be found in the Directory under Connecticut.

Bell, peasant man/lady/flowers, biniou form, HRQ, 3½" 60.00
Bell, peasant man/lady/flowers/bluets, animal head hdl, HRQ, 4¼" 65.00
Bonboniere, Decor Riche peasant man w/flute, HBQx501bis, 3x5" ..275.00
Bowl, roosters, 3-part molded leaf shape w/hdl, HBQF, 13½", MM ...200.00
Bowl, salad; peasant man/flowers, cut corners, HQF123, 6½" sq .75.00
Box, bonboniere; Decor Riche man w/bagpipes, HBQ, 6" L 450.00
Box, Crosille, man w/flute, detailed border, HQF163, 3½", NM ..350.00
Box, Decor Riche, peasant w/bagpipes, heart shape, HBQ143, 3" ..350.00
Box, peasant man/floral garland band, HQF107, 2¼x5x4" 200.00
Box, Rouenesque, flower swags, cut corners, PB, 6" 825.00
Bucket, naive peasant man/flowers/fir tree, w/lid, HBQ, 5" 350.00
Candlestick, peasant lady & florals, soleil yel, HBQFxx, 7¼" ...175.00
Candlestick, peasant lady & gr fir tree/flower sprays, HBQ222, 9" 250.00
Chamberstick, man w/pipe/flowers, leaf form, HB, 19th C, rstr, 6" L ..325.00
Charger, Decor Riche, grandfather w/grandchildren, HQ139, 13¼" ...1,900.00
Cheese dish, peasant lady & garland, HBQ, 6½x10", NM 235.00
Cigarette holder, Camel cigarette logo, HQF96, 3x3½" 275.00
Coffeepot, peasant couple/florals/dots, Macy, 8" 250.00
Coffeepot, peasant man/lady/florals, HBQ470, rprs, 9½" 65.00
Condiment jar, man w/flute, HBQ Loc-Maria Cream, 3" 185.00
Creamer, lattice dmns/floral, 2 thumb rests on hdl, HQ, 3½", NM ..100.00
Creamer, peasant lady & garland, HQF96, 4", EX 60.00
Doll's dish, Mayflower in full sail, bl/red border, 4¼" 125.00
Doll's tea service, dancing children, unmk, 11-pc 275.00
Egg cup, peasant lady/floral spray/dots, HQF121, 2½", EX 20.00
Egg dish, peasant man & lady/florals, 12-section, hdl, HQF101, 10½" ...350.00
Figurine, 3 ladies w/banner, HQJE Sevellec, 6½" 350.00
Inkwell, floral geometric, HBQ, 3½" sq 275.00
Inkwell, lady w/basket/floral/lattice, w/inset/lid, HQF71, 4" 425.00
Inkwell, peasant couple/a la touche floral, heart shape, HQ, 3", NM 200.00
Inkwell, seated peasant man w/flute, hat form, HRQ, 6x5¼" 475.00
Jardiniere, Botanique, blackberries, branch hdls, PB, 6x15x11¼" ...2,500.00
Knife rest, peasant/floral sprays/bluets, HRQ, 3¼", NM, pr 60.00
Liqueur set, peasants & flowers, soleil yel, HBQF, complete 275.00
Match holder, Lys, bl w/blk ermine tails, HBQ, 3½", EX 160.00
Match holder, peasant lady/lattice, HRQ, 3x3¼" 160.00
Match holder, peasant man/florals, AP mk, 19th C, 4¼" 200.00
Menu card holder, peasant lady, easel form, HRQ, 4x3" 300.00
Menu card holder, peasant lady & easel, unsgn AP, 19th C, 3" .250.00
Nut dish, peasant man/florals/bluets, 4-lobe, pk clay, HQ, 3" dia 120.00

Pitcher, baby's feeding; Naive a la touche garland, HB, 4½", EX ...160.00
Pitcher, Biberon, peasant man/flowers, HQ, glaze skips, 5" 160.00
Pitcher, peasant lady/florals/dots, HRQ, 8", EX 130.00
Pitcher, peasant man w/walking stick, flower garland, HBQF, 5½", NM ...150.00
Pitcher, peasant man/florals, HQF, 7½", EX 120.00
Pitcher, Tennis Ball, EX color, red clay, HQ, 6½", EX 240.00
Plate, Botanique, rose canes, PB, 9¼", NM 1,250.00
Plate, Bretonne lady at holy water font, PB, prof rstr, 9½" 1,050.00
Plate, bride & groom at gate posts, HBQ, 10" 240.00
Plate, concentric bands in yel/bl, bl a la touche border, HBQ, 6" ...50.00
Plate, Crosille, lady w/walking stick, HQF100, 8" 225.00
Plate, Demi Fantasie man w/pipe, lattice/flower rim, HQ159, 10" ..240.00
Plate, Demi Fantasie peasant man/garlands, HRQ, 10½x6¾" ...300.00
Plate, Faience Populaire hen w/garland, HR, 9¼" 200.00
Plate, flower sprays, flower shape, HQF77, 5" 25.00
Plate, geometric w/a la touch border, unmk (but HR), 8¾" 90.00
Plate, lady w/laundry basket, floral sprays, HB, prof rpr, 9¾" 275.00
Plate, lattice & dots w/a la touche buds, red clay, HRQ, 9¼" 275.00
Plate, lattice center w/6-pointed star, HBQ, 9" 175.00
Plate, Malicorne, Breton cottage w/mother & daughter, PBx, 9½" ..575.00
Plate, Malicorne, man looks over shoulder, PBx, 4¾" 200.00
Plate, Malicorne, man smoking near farmhouse/dog beside, unmk, 9½" ...400.00
Plate, Malicorne, peasant man by wall, girl in window, unmk, 9½" ...350.00
Plate, Naive lady w/tall coiffure, florals, HB, 19th C, 9¾", NM ...325.00
Plate, peasant lady on rock w/tree, HBQ, 9", NM 150.00
Plate, peasant lady w/flower & fir tree, early, unmk, 9", NM 275.00
Plate, peasant lady w/flowers, scalloped flower rim, HQ, 9½" 135.00
Plate, peasant man, red/gr border, HRQ, 19th C, 9¼" 190.00
Plate, peasant w/ax toasting w/glass, HQF, 8½", EX 100.00
Plate, Porquier Beau, flower chain on cobalt, PB, 5¼x6" 450.00
Plate, Rouen, parrots on branches, PB, 10", NM 675.00
Plate, star center w/lattice & dots, HBQ, 6", NM 90.00
Plate, Sunflower center w/lattice/bands, bl/red/gr/yel, unmk, 6" ..90.00
Plate, Tennis Ball, scalloped, HQ23, 5½" 35.00

Platter, Bretonne scene (payment to the lawyer), green on yellow acanthus border, rolled rims, PB mark and Rosporden, 11x11", $1,800.00.

Platter, Broderie Breton, Danse au Puits, HBQ, 24x14¼" 1,750.00
Platter, Decor Riche peasant couple, HBQ, 14x10½" 1,000.00
Platter, Malicorne, peasant man in field/lady w/flowers, PBx, 15¾" ...1,250.00
Platter, oyster; Fruits de la Mer, sea life on blk, HQ, 21" 425.00
Platter, peasant man on stomach w/flute, hdls, HBQ1171ox, rstr, 15" 285.00
Platter, Porquier Beau, peasants dancing, PBQ130, 19½x13¾", NM ...2,450.00
Porringer, Ivoire Corbeille, bl/red/yel, HQ, mini, 1¼x3½" 75.00
Porringer, Tennis Ball w/lattice, pierced, HQ14, 2½x7¼", NM ...70.00
Pot de creme set, Fleuri Royal, HBQCP199, 4 pots on 11½" tray 300.00
Salt cellar, dbl sabots (shoes) w/ring hdl, peasant couple, HBQ, 3" 45.00
Salt cellar, Ivoire Corbelle, sabot (shoe) shape, HQ, 3½" 50.00
Saucer, croisille w/flower sprigs/lattice, HQF161, 5⅛" 15.00
Saucer, croisille w/4 lattice patterns, HRQ, 5" 25.00
Snuff bottle, donut shape, 8-pointed star, unsgn AP, 19th C, NM ...400.00
Snuff bottle, heart shape, w/pansy & lady, HB Quimper, 3", NM 350.00
Snuff bottle, Malicorne, biniou shape w/peasant man, 19th C, 3", NM ..210.00
Soap dish, bl fleur-de-lis & ermine tails, HB, 4½x3½" 90.00
Soup, man w/flute, yel blossoms/panels/lattice, HQQ222, 9½" ..200.00
Spoon rest, peasant lady in fish form, HQF596, 4½", EX 50.00
Teacup & saucer, flower sprig/dots, HGF, doll sz, 1¾", 3" 95.00
Tray, Demi Fantasie man & flowers, hdls, HRQ, 9x4" 230.00
Tray, Demi Fantasie man w/flute, chain border, HQ, 9x4" 210.00
Trivet, peasant man & florals, chain border, Macy, 5¾" sq 85.00
Tureen, Ivoire Corbelle, peasant medallion, w/lid, HQ116, 5x9½", EX ..325.00
Vase, bud; Malicorne, Breton pr/crest/flowers, 5 opening, mk, 8" ..375.00
Vase, bud; Mayflower in full sail, 5 openings, HQF70, 3½", EX 135.00
Vase, bud; peasant couple on 3 shoes joined at toes, HBQ, 3½x4" ..120.00
Vase, Decor Riche peasant man w/flute, HQ102, prof rpr, 8" 240.00
Vase, demi Fantasie lady w/hand in apron pocket, HQF71, 7" ...200.00
Vase, Demifantasie peasant spinning, trumpet form, HQF96, 11" ...450.00
Vase, lady w/basket in medallion, 5-opening, HQF73, 5½" 175.00
Vase, Malicorne, peasant/fleur-de-lis, dolphin hdls, 19th C, 6", pr 725.00
Vase, man w/flowers, butterfly ft, fan shape, HQF82, 8x4¾" 275.00
Vase, peasant couple/a la touche sprays, fan shape, HQF80, 5x7½" ...250.00
Wall pocket, Malicorne, peasant lady w/fluffy coif, unmk, 11" ..240.00
Wall pocket, peasant lady/fleur-de-lis, cone shaped, PBx, 4¼" ..110.00
Watering can, peasant lady/flowers, soleil yel, HB1F, 6x9" 300.00

Radford

Pottery associated with Albert Radford (1882–1904) can be categorized by three periods of production. Pottery produced in Tiffin, Ohio (1896–1899), consists of bone china (no marked examples known) and high-quality jasperware with applied Wedgwood-like cameos. Tiffin jasperware is often impressed 'Radford Jasper' in small block letters. At Zanesville, Ohio, Radford jasperware was marked only with an incised, two-digit shape number, and the cameos were not applied but rather formed within the mold and filled with a white slip. Zanesville Radford ware was produced for only a few months before the Radford pottery was acquired by the Arc-en-Ciel company in 1903. Production in Zanesville was handled by Radford's father, Edward (1840–1910), who remained in Zanesville after Albert moved to Clarksburg, West Virginia, where the Radford Pottery Co. was completed shortly before Albert's death in 1904. Jasperware was not produced in Clarksburg, and the molds appear to have been left in Zanesville, where some were subsequently used by the Arc-en-Ciel pottery. The Clarksburg, West Virginia, pottery produced a standard glaze, slip-decorated ware, Ruko; Thera and Velvety, matt glazed ware often signed by Albert Haubrich, Alice Bloomer, and other artists; and Radura, a semimatt green glaze developed by Albert Radford's son, Edward. The Clarksburg plant closed in 1912.

Pottery marked 'E. Radford, Burslem,' or 'E. Radford, England,' includes a variety of earthenware designed by Edward Radford (1883–1968), first for H.J. Wood and later for himself in Burslem (production ending in 1948). A variety of floral patterns, cottage or tavern scenes, and Art Deco motifs distinguish this ware. His father, Edward Thomas Radford, worked at the Pilkington Tile and Pottery Co. in Manchester, England, and appears to have been a brother of Albert Radford. Our advisor for this category is James L. Murphy; he is listed in the Directory under Ohio.

Jasper

Bowl, muses & vintage, fluted rim, imp mk 295.00
Box, figure w/cornucopia on lid, prof rpr, ca 1896, 5⅝" H 500.00
Ewer, appl grapes/raspberries, Old Man Winter hdl, #17, 9" 350.00
Letter holder, lady w/bow & target scene, bark trim, #61 ....500.00
Mug, floral, 4½" 165.00
Mug, vintage, gray, #25, 5" 165.00
Pitcher, tankard, vintage, lt bl, #26, 12" 200.00

Vase, bust of Gladstone ea side, twisted form, 3" 125.00
Vase, bust of Lincoln, eagle on reverse, bark trim, #12, 7" 350.00
Vase, bust of Washington, eagle on reverse, bark trim, #12, 7" ..265.00
Vase, cherubs & lion, #15, 6½" 325.00
Vase, lady by fire, grapes on reverse, #55, 3½" 100.00
Vase, lady kneeling w/bird, gray, #24, 10½x4½" 250.00
Vase, lady w/dog, #22, 10x6" 250.00
Vase, lady w/flowers, grapes on reverse, #59, 4" 165.00
Vase, running girl, flat & twisted, #53, 3½" 100.00

Miscellaneous

Jardiniere, Ruko, tulips, 8½x9" 250.00
Pitcher, dog & goose scenic panels, pine tree hdl, 10½" 160.00
Plate, E Radford, HP floral, gr matt, 5x9" 27.50
Teapot, E Radford, HP floral, gr matt, 4½" 75.00
Umbrella stand, Ruko, tulips, red & yel on gr to brn, 23", NM ..500.00
Vase, Radura, 4-hdl, scalloped rim, 10" 400.00
Vase, Ruko, floral, standard glaze, 15" 325.00
Vase, Thera, floral, mc on gr, #1453, 12½" 700.00
Vase, Velvety, mums, mc on gr matt, sgn, bottle form, 10½x3" .550.00

Radios

Vintage radios are very collectible. There were thousands of styles and types produced, the most popular of which today are the breadboard and the cathedral. Consoles are usually considered less marketable, since their size makes them hard to display and store. For those wishing to learn more about antique radios, we recommend *The Collector's Guide to Antique Radios, Volumes I* through *IV*, by Sue and Marty Bunis, available from your local bookstore or Collector Books. They are also the authors of *A Collector's Guide to Transistor Radios, Second Edition*. For information on novelty radios, refer to *Collector's Guide to Novelty Radios, Books I and II*, by Marty Bunis and Robert Breed. Unless otherwise noted in the descriptions, values are given for radios in near mint to mint condition. Our advisor for this category is James Fred; he is listed in the Directory under Indiana.

Key:
BC — broadcast
pb — push button
phono — phonograph
R/P — radio-phonograph
s/r — slide rule
SW — short wave
tbl/m — table model

Silvertone 1660, wooden cathedral case, lower window dial with escutcheon, upper grill with cutouts, five tubes, three knobs, from $160.00 to $180.00. (Photo courtesy Sue and Marty Bunis)

Adler, #199 (Royal), tbl/m, wood, 3-dial front panel, battery, 1924 .150.00
Admiral, #AM786, console, wood, 4-band dial, AC, 1936 ....135.00
Admiral, #7C60M, console, R/P, wood, lift-top, s/r dial, BC, AC, 1948 ..60.00
Admiral, #21-A6, tbl/m, ivory plastic streamline, AC/DC, 1940 ..110.00
Aetna, #255, tbl/m, wood, 1937 ....65.00
Air Castle, #106B, tbl/m, plastic, streamline, BC, AC/DC, 1947 ..125.00
Air Castle, #9904, tombstone tbl/m, wood, BC, SW, AC, 1934 .140.00
Air King, #4603, tbl/m, wood, s/r dial, BC, AC/DC, 1946 ....35.00
Airline, #04BR-514B, tbl/m, plastic Deco style, s/r dial, BC, 1940 .....90.00
Airline, #84WG-2712A, console, R/P, wood, BC, SW, FM, AC, 1948 ...60.00
American Bosch, #200-A, tbl/m, wood treasure chest style, AC, 1932 .275.00
American Bosch, #5C, console, wood, bowed front legs, 1931 ..125.00
Amrad, #81, console, walnut, AC, 1929 ....175.00
Apex, #89, tbl/m, metal, AC, 1929 ....60.00
Arvin, #444A, tbl/m, metal midget, BC, 1946 ....85.00
Arvin, #665, console, R/P, wood, BC, AC, 1947 ....50.00
Atwater Kent, #435, console, wood, airplane dial, BC, SW, AC, 1935 ...160.00
Atwater Kent, #82D, tbl/m, wood cathedral, DC, 1931 ....450.00
Belmont, #575, tbl/m, wood tombstone, rnd dial, AC, 1934 .....110.00
Bendix, #95M9 (Wayne), console, R/P, mahog, BC, FM, AC, 1949 ..70.00
Brunswick, #T-2580, tbl/m, wood, dbl doors, AC, 1939 ....75.00
Bulova, #M-701, tbl/m, wood cathedral w/clock, 1932 ....425.00
Capehart, #1P55, portable, plastic, BC, AC/DC/battery, 1955 ....35.00
Case, #1017, console, wood, Tell-Time Jumbo Dial, 1935 ....175.00
Clarion, #61, tbl/m, wood cathedral, window dial, AC, 1931 ....200.00
Cleartone, #80 (Super Clear-O-Dyne), tbl/m, wood, battery, 1925 ..135.00
Coronado, #43-7601, console, R/P, wood, s/r dial, BC, SW, AC, 1946 ...70.00
Crosley, #E15WE, tbl/m, plastic, BC, AC/DC, 1953 ....100.00
Crosley, #1-N (Litlfella), tbl/m, wood cathedral, AC, 1932 ....200.00
Crosley, #11-119U, tbl/m, plastic, BC, AC/DC, 1951 ....110.00
Crosley, #48 (Johnny Smoke), console, repwood 400.00
Crosley, #899, console, wood, BC, SW, AC, 1936 ....125.00
DeForest, #D-4 (Radiophone), tbl/m, wood, battery, 1923 ....500.00
Delco, #1106, tbl/m, wood tombstone, BC, SW, AC, 1935 ....125.00
Dewald, #548 (Organ-Tone), tbl/m, plastic, s/r dial, 1940 ....110.00
Dewald, #802, tbl/m, wood tombstone, BC, 3 SW, AC, 1934 ....125.00
Elgin, #77 (Tiny-Toy Air Roamer), tbl/m, wood midget, AC/DC, 1939 ...65.00
Emerson, #AX-219, tbl/m, R/P, wood, BC, AC, 1938 ....30.00
Emerson, #CV-298, tbl/m, wood violin shape, BC, AC/DC, 1939 .450.00
Emerson, #L-559, tbl/m, wood chest type, AC, 1932 ....225.00
Emerson, #35, tbl/m, walnut Sheraton design, AC/DC, 1933 ....250.00
Emerson, #321-AW, tbl/m, blk/gold Chinese lacquer design, AC, 1933 ...225.00
Emerson, #400 (Aristocrat), tbl/m, Catalin, AC, 1940, minimum value ..400.00
Emerson, #414, tbl/m, pressed wood, AC, 1933 ....175.00
Emerson, #553, portable, leatherette, BC, AC/DC/battery, 1947 .35.00
Emerson, #747, portable, plastic, BC, battery, 1954 ....175.00
Fada, #30, console, wood highboy, AC, 1928 ....140.00
Fada, #160-A (One-Sixty), tbl/m, wood, battery, 1925 ....140.00
Federal, #A-10 (Orthosonic), tbl/m, wood, battery, 1925 ....125.00
Firestone, #4-A-42 (Georgian), console, R/P, wood, BC, FM, AC, 1947 ..70.00
Garod, #1B55L, tbl/m, Catalin, 1940, minimum value 900.00
GE, #A-64, tbl/m, wood tombstone, 1935 ....100.00
GE, #E-62, tbl/m, wood, BC, SW, 1936 ....50.00
GE, #G-76 (Radiogrande), console, wood, BC, SW, AC, 1938 .200.00
GE, #H-500, tbl/m, plastic Deco style, AC, 1939 ....130.00
GE, #K-51-P, tbl/m, wood, dbl sliding doors, AC, 1932 ....200.00
Gilfillan, #66B, portable, leatherette, BC, AC/DC/battery, 1946 ..40.00
Grantline, #5610, end table, wood, s/r dial, BC, AC/DC, 1948 ...90.00
Grebe, #CR12, tbl/m, wood w/Bakelite front panel, battery, 1923 ..800.00
Grunow, #1541, console, wood, Tele-dial, BC, SW, AC, 1936 ..300.00
Hoffman, #MP-402 (Nugget), portable, plastic, BC 150.00
Howard, #225, tbl/m, wood, BC, SW, AC, 1937 ....65.00
Jackson-Bell, #25AV (Pandora), tbl/m, wood chest style, AC, 1932 ...300.00
Kadette, #24 (Clockette/Futura), tbl/m, wood, AC, 1937 ....125.00
Kingston, #600B, console, wood Deco style, 1934 ....150.00
Knight, #11C-300, console, R/P, wood, BC, FM, AC, 1947 ....60.00
Lafayette, #BE-79, tbl/m, plastic walnut-look, BC, AC/DC, 1940 ..125.00
Lafayette, #EB65, chairside, R/P, wood Deco style, AC, 1938 ...175.00
Magnavox, #TRF-50, tbl/m, wood, dbl doors, battery, 1924 ....255.00
Majestic, #7P420, portable, leatherette, BC, AC/DC/battery, 1947 ..45.00

Motorola, #5P23WB-1, portable, leatherette/plastic, BC, AC/DC/battery ..40.00
Motorola, #53H, tbl/m, plastic, BC, AC, 1954 ....75.00
Motorola, #61K23, console, wood, BC, SW, AC, 1942 ....110.00
Olympic, #7-925, console, R/P, wood, BC, FM, AC, 1948 ....60.00
Packard-Bell, tbl/m, plastic, BC, AC/DC, 1948 ....45.00
Philco, #38-7, chairside, wood Deco style, BC, SW, AC, 1938 ..150.00
Philco, #39-7, tbl/m, walnut, BC, AC, 1939 ....60.00
Philco, #42-390, console, wood, BC, SW, AC, 1942 ....120.00
Philco, #144B, tbl/m, wood cathedral, BC, SW, AC, 1934 ....225.00
RCA, #R-4 (Superette), wood cathedral, AC, 1932 ....300.00
RCA, #8BX5, portable, plastic/snakeskin, BC, AC/DC/battery, 1947 ...40.00
RCA, #9SX1 (Little Nipper), plastic walnut-look, BC, SW, AC/DC, 1939 .160.00
RCA, #28 (Carryette), tbl/m, wood, 1933 ....100.00
RCA, #813K, console, wood, BC, SW, AC, 1937 ....175.00
Silvertone, #6177-A, tbl/m, plastic Deco style, BC, AC/DC 150.00
Sonora, #TW-49, tbl/m, plastic Deco style, BC, 1939 ....150.00
Sparton, #71, tbl/m, wood tombstone, AC, 1933 ....125.00
Stewart Warner, #A51T4 (Air Pal), tbl/m, plastic, BC, AC/DC, 1947 .125.00
Stromberg-Carlson, #500-J, tbl/m, 2-tone wood, AC/DC, 1940 ..55.00
Trav-ler, #5049, portable, alligator-look finish, BC, battery, 1948 .30.00
Truetone, #D2018, tbl/m, plastic modern style, BC, AC/DC, 1950 ...175.00
US Radio, #9-A, tbl/m, wood tombstone, 1932 ....165.00
Viking, #599, tbl/m, 2-tone cb/leatherette, 1926 ....175.00
Zenith, #4-B-422, tbl/m, plastic, BC, battery, 1940 ....75.00
Zenith, #5-G-403, portable, 2-tone wood, BC, AC/DC/battery, 1940 ...85.00

Novelty Radios

Batman, AM/FM, yellow neon light at edge of clock, Popworks for DC Comics, 1989, 12½x12¼", M, from $250.00 to $300.00. (Photo courtesy Marty Bunis and Robert F. Breed)

A&W Music Boat, EX 50.00
Ballantine Ale/Beer, brn keg form, EX 65.00
Batman, AM, w/belt clip & swing hdl, DC Comics, 1989, 5½x3", EX ..85.00
Blizzard/Oreo, 2-sided, NM, from $25 to 35.00
Bob Hope the Golfer, figure on rnd stepped base, National, 11", EX ..175.00
Chicken & Egg, figural plastic quartz clock/radio, 6x9" L, EX 50.00
Coca-Cola Classic, Isis billboard, EX 85.00
Crayola Crayons, box form w/clock, EX 130.00
Duracell D-Cell Alkaline Battery, China, EX 50.00
Huffy Radio Bike, ...For Parts & Service Call..., figural, EX 45.00
Hunt's Whole Tomatoes, can shape, EX 55.00
Jewelry Box, wooden chest w/3 drws, grill door, ftd, EX 40.00
Kangaroo Boxer, plush w/gloves, Korea, 1987, 11" 100.00
Keebler Animal Crackers, braided hdl, EX 70.00
Kennedy 1964 Liberty Silver Dollar, clock/radio, 6¼" dia, EX ..140.00
Kent King Size Cigarettes, pack form, transistor, Japan, EX 250.00
KFC, Isis Model 103 or 39, EX, ea 30.00
Nestle Nesquik Milk Shake Mix, can form, EX 45.00
Nixon, figure in victory pose on rectangular base, EX 65.00
Old Spice FM Radio, aerosol can form, Isis model #105, EX 85.00
Paper Towel Holder/Radio, plastic, fold-out ends, EX 15.00
Pepperidge Farm Distinctive Stuffing/Tony's Pizza, 2-sided, EX ...50.00
Swinger, girl doll w/guitar at microphone, Juliette #1026, 12", EX ...165.00
Tide Detergent, box form w/NASCAR info on bottom, EX 40.00
Weight Watchers Ice Cream Sandwich, w/headphones, EX 55.00
7-Up Cherry, jukebox form, Popworks, EX 60.00
9 Lives Crunchy Meals, Isis block radio, EX 60.00

Transistor Radios

Post-World War II baby boomers, now approaching their fiftieth year, are rediscovering prized possessions of youth, their pocket radios. The transistor wonders, born with rock 'n roll, were at the vanguard of miniaturization and futuristic design in the decade which followed their introduction to Christmas shoppers in 1954. The tiny receiving sets launched the growth of Texas Instruments and shortly to follow abroad, Sony and other Japanese giants.

The most desirable sets include the 1954 four-transistor Regency TR-1 and colorful early Sony and Toshiba models. Certain pre-1960 models by Hoffman and Admiral represented the earliest practical use of solar technology and are also highly valued. To avoid high tariffs, scores of two-transistor sets, boys' radios, were imported from Japan with names like Pet and Charmy. Many early inexpensive transistor sets could be heard only with an earphone. The smallest sets are known as shirt-pocket models while those slightly larger are called coat-pockets. Early collectible transistor radios all have civil defense triangle markings at 640 and 1240 on the frequency dial and nine or fewer transistors. Very few desirable sets were made after 1963. Model numbers are most commonly found inside. Our advisor for this category is Mike Brooks; he is listed in the Directory under California and welcomes questions. (Please include a SASE.)

Admiral, #Y2009, 7 transistors, AM, battery, 1960 ....25.00
Arrow, 2 transistors, boy's radio 80.00
Arvin, #61R13, 6 transistors, AM, battery, 1961 ....35.00
Bulova, #250, leather case w/strap, AM, battery 450.00
Bulova, #620, horizontal 90.00
Channel Master Signal Seeker, #6459, 10 transistors, battery 30.00
Continental, #TR-150, horizontal 60.00
Dewald, #K-544, horizontal, 4 transistors, AM, battery, 1957 ....125.00
Emerson, #856, horizontal/hybrid, tubes & transistors, AM, battery ...125.00
Emerson Explorer, #888, vertical 90.00
Falcon, #8THK (DeLuxe), vertical, 8 transistors, AM, battery 25.00
GE, #P-805D, vertical, 6 transistors, AM, battery, 1964 ....30.00
GE, #675, horizontal, 5 transistors, AM, battery, 1956 ....100.00
GE, #678, horizontal, 1959 ....110.00
Hi-Delity, #6T-330 ....130.00
Hitachi, #TH-600, vertical, 6 transistors, AM, battery 60.00
Hitachi, #TH-666, vertical, 1959 ....110.00
Hoffman, #OP706, horizontal, 6 transistors, AM, battery 175.00
Itt, #628, horizontal, 6 transistors, AM, battery, 1963 ....35.00
Juliette, #SH-516, vertical, 16 transistors, AM, battery 20.00
Kobe Kogyo, #KF75 ....80.00
Kowa, #KT-91, vertical, 9 transistors, AM, battery 40.00
Linmark, #T-62, vertical, 6 transistors, AM, battery, 1960 ....35.00
Magnavox, #AM-22, horizontal, 6 transistors, AM, battery, 1960 ..35.00
Magnavox, #AM-5, horizontal 80.00
Mantola, #MDA, vertical, 1957 ....450.00
Motorola, #6X39A-2, horizontal, 6 transistors, AM, battery, 1958 ...80.00
Motorola, #56T1, horizontal, 1956 ....200.00
Nec NT-61, horizontal, 1960 ....90.00
Norelco, #L4X05T, horizontal, 7 transistors, 3SW, AM, battery, 1964 ...35.00
Olympic, #447, horizontal, 4 transistors, AM, battery, 1957 ....160.00
Panasonic, #T-92 (Portalarm), vertical, 6 transistors, AM, battery ...80.00
Philco, #T-7-126, horizontal, 7 transistors, AM, battery, 1956 ....65.00
Raytheon, #T-150-4, horizontal, AM, battery, 1956 ....200.00
RCA, #8-BT-7LE, horizontal, 4 transistors, AM, battery, 1957 ....65.00

Realtone, #TR-561, vertical, 4 transistors, AM, battery, 1962 .....45.00
Realtone, #TR-1088, vertical, 1962 .....175.00
Regency, #TR-6, horizontal, 6 transistors, AM, battery, 1957 ......55.00
Silvertone, #211, vertical, 6 transistors, AM, battery, 1959 ....30.00
Sony, #TR-8, horizontal, micro, 1967 .....250.00
Sony, #TR-65, vertical, damaged 560.00
Sony, #TR-610, vertical, 6 transistors, AM, battery, 1959 ....100.00
Sony, #2F-23W, vertical, 9 transistors, AM/FM, battery 45.00
Sylvania, #2808 (Golden Shield), AM, battery, 1960 ....25.00
Toshiba, #TR-193 Lace, vertical, 1959 .....400.00
Toshiba, #6TP-31A, vertical, 1963 .....185.00
Toshiba, #7TH-425, rnd, 7 transistors, AM, battery, 1961 ....300.00
Toshiba, #7TM-312S, horizontal, 7 transistors, SW, AM, battery, 1961 ..50.00
Trav-Ler, #TR-283, vertical, 6 transistors, AM, battery, 1959 ......45.00
Universal, #PTR-62B, vertical, 6 transistors, AM, battery, 1963 .25.00
Viscount, #6TP-103, vertical, 6 transistors, AM, battery 35.00
Westinghouse, #H-699P7, vertical, 7 transistors, AM, battery 30.00
Yaecon, #YTR-58, vertical, 6 transistors, AM, battery, 1960 ....40.00
Zenith, Royal 500D, vertical, 8 transistors, AM, battery, 1959 ....75.00
Zephyr ZR-620, vertical, 1961 .....100.00

Railroadiana

Collecting railroad-related memorabilia has become one of America's most popular hobbies. The range of collectible items available is almost endless; not surprising, considering the fact that more than 175 different railroad lines are represented. Some collectors prefer to specialize in only one railroad, while others attempt to collect at least one item from every railway line known to have existed. For the advanced collector, there is the challenge of locating rarities from short-lived railroads; for the novice, there are abundant keys, buttons, and passes. Among the most popular specializations are dining-car collectibles — flatware, glassware, dinnerware, etc., in a wide variety of patterns and styles. Railroad blankets are also collectible. Most common are Pullman blankets. The early ones had a cross-stitch pattern; these were followed by one in a solid cinnamon color; both are marked clearly with the Pullman name. These are now valued at $125.00 up to $175.00 in good condition. Pullman, in the 1920s, put out a blue blanket, marked Pullman, specifically for ethnic use. There is one in the Sacramento railroad museum. Other railroads had their own 'marked' blankets that are even more desirable, such as the Soo line, the Chessie, and one marked 'Pheasant' (which was a private car on the Milwaukee Line that was reserved to carry special parties for hunting trips).

As is true in most collecting fields, scarcity and condition determine value. There is more interest in some railway lines than in others; generally speaking, it is greater in the region serviced by the particular railroad. Reproductions abound in railroadiana collectibles — from dinnerware and glassware to lanterns, keys, badges, belt buckles, timetables, and much more. Repro hand-executed, reverse-painted glass signs have been abundant throughout the country, most of them read 'Santa Fe,' but some say 'Whites Only.' Beware! Also railroad drumheads are coming out of collections. A drumhead is a large (approximately 24" diameter) glass sign in a metal case. They were used on the back end of all railroad observation cars to advertise a special train or a presidential foray, etc. They're now beginning to surface, and a good one like the Flying Crow from the Kansas City Southern Railroad will go for $2,500.00, as will many others. When items of this value come out, the counterfeiters are right there. It is important to 'Know Thy Dealer.' For a more thorough study, we recommend *Railroad Collectibles, Third Revised Edition,* by Stanley L. Baker. The values noted for most of our dinnerware, glassware, linen, silverplate, and timetables are actual selling prices. However, because prices are so volatile, the best pricing sources are often monthly or quarterly 'For Sale' lists. Two you may find helpful may be ordered from Golden Spike, P.O. Box 422, Williamsville, NY 14221, and Grandpa's Depot, 6720 E. Mississippi Ave., Unit B, Denver, CO 80224. Our co-advisors for this category are Fred and Lila Shrader (See Directory, California), and John White (Grandpa's Depot, see Colorado).

Key:

BL — bottom logo	SL — side logo
BS — bottom stamped	SM — side mark
FBS — full back stamp	TL — top logo
NBS — no back stamp	TM — top mark
NTL — no top logo	

Dinnerware

Many railroads designed their own china for use in their dining cars or company-owned hotels or stations. Some railroads chose to use stock patterns to which they added their name or logo; others used the same stock patterns without the added identification.

Bowl, Thomas Viaduct 1835, various engines along border, Shenango China, 1937, 7", $95.00.

Ashtray, GN, Mountains & Flowers, BS, 2 rests, 4½" 67.00
Ashtray/matchbox holder, MKT, Blue Bonnet, BS, 5" 595.00
Bowl, berry; FH, Webster, NBS, 4½" 8.00
Bowl, berry; UP, Corporate, TL, 4½" 44.00
Bowl, oatmeal; N&W, Cavalier, TM, 6" 52.00
Bowl, salad; WP, Feather River, TL, 7" w/undulating top rim 375.00
Butter pat, ATSF, Black Chain, 3½" 25.00
Butter pat, ATSF, California Poppy, NBS, 3½" 26.00
Butter pat, B&O, Centenary (Shenango), NBS, 3" to 3⅜" 27.00
Butter pat, CB&Q, Violets & Daisies, NBS, 3½" 25.00
Butter pat, CRI&P, LaSalle, TL, 3½" 100.00
Butter pat, SAL, Hamlet, NBS, 3½" 56.00
Butter pat, SR, Peach Blossom, TL, 3½" 345.00
Butter pat, UP, Historical, TL & BS, 3¼" 340.00
Chocolate pot, B&O, Centenary, FBS, 5½" 480.00
Coffeepot, IC, Louisane, SL, 5¼" 655.00
Creamer, ATSF, Mimbreno, BS, 3" 225.00
Creamer, FH, Blue Chain, no hdl, NBS, ind, 2" 28.00
Creamer, GN, Spokane, hdl, NBS, 2½" 93.00
Cup, bouillon; ATSF, Mimbreno, BS, 4"+hdls 320.00
Cup, bouillon; CMStP&P, Traveler, no hdls, NBS, 4" 54.00
Cup, bouillon; UP, Harriman Blue, no hdls, BS, 4" 45.00
Cup & saucer, demitasse; ATSF, Mimbreno, both BS 690.00
Cup & saucer, GN, Oriental, NBS 175.00
Cup & saucer, KCS, Roxbury, NBS 11.00
Cup & saucer, SP, Prairie Mountain Wildflower, both BS, from $85 to ...125.00
Cup & saucer, UP, Challenger, TL & SL, NBS 68.00
Cup & saucer, Y&MV, Vicksburg, cup: SL, saucer: TL 585.00
Egg cup, CMStP&P, Traveler, NBS, 2¼" 210.00
Egg cup, SP, Prairie Mountain Wildflowers, NBS, 3¾" 285.00
Gravy/sauce boat, SP, Sunset, SL 265.00
Hot food cover, SRR, Peach Blossom, SL, 6½" 258.00
Ice cream shell, ATSF, Mimbreno, BS, 6" (includes tab hdl) 238.00
Mug, coffee; CB&Q, Violets & Daisies, NBS 32.00

Plate, ATSF, Adobe, BS, TL, 9¾" 62.00
Plate, CMStP&P, Traveler, FBS, 9¾" 235.00
Plate, CN, Ottowa, TL, 10" 55.00
Plate, GM&O, Rose, TM, 7¼" 68.00
Plate, GN, Glory of the West, BS, 9½" 205.00
Plate, grill; CRI&P, El Reno, TL, 10¼" 425.00
Plate, IC, Magnolia Star, NBS, 10½" 80.00
Plate, N&W, Pine Hurst, NBS, 8½" 36.00
Plate, NP, Monad, TL, 9¼" 134.00
Plate, PRR, Gotham, BS & TL, 10½" 65.00
Plate, service; C&NW, Flambeau '400,' BS, 10½" 595.00
Plate, service; MP, State Flowers/Stream, NBS, 10½" 222.00
Platter, C&S, Pueblo, TL, 11½x8" 420.00
Platter, GN, Glory of the West, BS, 7x5¾" 155.00
Platter, Harriman Blue, BS, 11x7½" 67.00
Platter, Maine Central, Poland Spring, TL, 19½x7½" 90.00
Platter, Richmond, Fredricksburg & Potomac, Fredricksburg, TL, 9½" 247.00
Platter, UP, Winged Streamliner, TL, 6½x8½" 22.00
Relish, ATSF, California Poppy, NBS, 10x5" 78.00
Soup plate, B&O, Scarab, TL, 9" 80.00
Sugar bowl, GN, Oriental, w/lid, NBS 200.00
Teapot, B&O, Centenary, BS 598.00

Glass

Ashtray, Alaska RR, ARR over Mt McKinley Park Hotel, 3½" ...49.00
Ashtray, ATSF, Santa Fe logo, silkscreen, 5¼x3½" 30.00
Ashtray, ATSF, Turquoise Room, silkscreen turq & blk, 4¾x3¾" ..25.00
Ashtray, McCloud RR, logo in red, 3½" dia 16.00
Ashtray, NP/Yelloswtone..., blk & red TL, 4½" sq 25.00
Bottle, medicine; SP Co Hospital Dept (emb), 5½" 42.00
Bottle, milk; StLSW, Cotton Belt logo (bl) 2 sides, ½-pt 38.00
Cordial, ATSF, cut Santa Fe in script+lines, 3¼" 85.00
Cordial, ATSF, Santa Fe in script, 3½" 40.00
Cordial, stem; B&O, SL, 4" 35.00
Cruet, SP, Daylight w/ball & wing logo 175.00
Goblet, Amptrak Pioneer, train in oval, twisted stem, 6⅞" 45.00
Goblet, CN, etched logo, 5½" 35.00
Goblet, UP, etched logo in shield, 5½" 20.00
Goblet, UP, wht enamel shield, SM, ftd, 5½" 15.00
Mug, ATSF, Santa Fe in wht script, 3½" 15.00
Mug, coffee; BN in gr w/logo, 1972 ....15.00
Pilsner, CRI&P, etched Rock Island logo, 7" 45.00
Roly-poly, PRR, SM w/red & wht enamel, 2¼" 15.00
Shot glass, D&H in shield, 2¾" 20.00
Shot glass, Erie in bl & wht dmn logo, 2½" 20.00
Tumbler, ATSF, SM Santa Fe cross logo, 4½" 19.00
Tumbler, CRI&P, Golden State Route+3 oranges, hi-ball sz, 2¾" ..23.00
Tumbler, D&H, cut D&H in shield logo, 4½" 18.00
Tumbler, juice; NYC, wht enameling, 3" 28.00
Tumbler, PRR, Army Navy games 1890-1961, frosted, 4" 76.00
Tumbler, PRR, gold keystone w/blk & gold locomotives, 3½" 25.00
Tumbler, PRR, logo cast in base, 3½" 48.00
Wine, ATSF, wht enamel Santa Fe in script+stripes, 4¾" 13.00
Wine, CN, etched logo, 4½" 25.00
Wine, NYC, gold logo, 4½" 27.00
Wine, NYC, 20th C Ltd, 4" 75.00
Wine, stem; CP script logo w/ornate facets, 4" 39.00
Wine, stem; Fred Harvey, amber, Heisey, 6" 145.00

Keys

Switch keys are brass with hollow barrels and round heads with holes for attaching to a key ring. They were used to unlock the padlocks on track-side switches when the course of the tracks had to be changed. (Switches were padlocked to prevent them from being thrown by accident or vandals, a situation that could result in a train wreck.) A car key used to open padlocks on freight cars and the like is very similar to the switch key, except the bit is straighter instead of being specifically curved for a particular railroad and its accompanying switch locks. A second type of 'car' key was used for door locks on passenger cars, Pullmans, etc.; this type was usually of brass, but instead of having a hollow barrel, they were shaped like an old-fashioned hotel door key. In order for a key to be collectible, the head must be marked with a name, initials, or a railroad identification, with 'switch' generally designated by 'S' and 'car' by 'C' markings. Railroad, patina 'not polished,' and the presence of a manufacturer's mark other than Adlake all have a positive affect on pricing and collectibility.

A new precedent was set in 1995 when a Denver and South Park 'car' key went at a Missouri auction for $2,500.00. The key was marked DSP&P (an early Colorado road that stopped running in 1898); it was brass and had a hollow barrel and straight bit. Switch keys that only recently brought $15.00 to $17.00 are now bringing $35.00.

Switch, B&M, brass, Slaymaker, hollow bbl 25.00
Switch, C&NW RR, brass, Adlake, lt wear 20.00
Switch, CI&S, brass, sm hilt, tapered hollow bbl 40.00
Switch, CM&StP, brass, hollow bbl 20.00
Switch, CRI&P, brass, Adlake, unused 17.50
Switch, CRR, brass 17.50
Switch, CStPM&O, brass, Adlake, hollow bbl 25.00
Switch, CStPM&O, brass, hollow bbl 25.00
Switch, Frisco, brass, Adlake, hollow bbl 20.00
Switch, L&N RR, brass, fat hollow bbl, old, much use 20.00
Switch, M&C RR, brass, ornate bbl 45.00
Switch, MOPAC, brass, hollow bbl 17.50
Switch, NNG, steel, Adlake, worn 15.00
Switch, NP RR, brass, Adams & Westlake 23.50
Switch, Soo Line, brass, Adlake, hollow bbl 25.00
Switch, SPTCo, brass, Adlake, unused 15.00

Lamps

Backhead gauge, N&W, Dietz, ca 1930, M 45.00
Desk, Handlan, steel top, CI base (fancy), 8-sided base, EX 95.00
Hand, Dew-Light (Dewar), carbide burning, unmk, 10x5¾" dia .55.00
Hand, unmk, Adams & Westlake Queen variant, screw-off pot holder, 10" ...80.00
Inspector's, Star Headlight & Lantern Co, ornate, NM 65.00
Spare, N&W, brass, Adams & Westlake, EX 75.00
Wall, caboose; UPRR, Aladdin, brass, steel mt, EX 55.00
Wall, NYCL, kerosene burner, steel w/copper trim, 5¾" ring holder ...100.00
Wall candle, Adams & Westlake 1907P, older style w/drilled top .55.00

Lanterns

Before 1920 kerosene brakemen's lanterns were made with tall globes, usually 5⅜" high. These are most desirable to collectors and are usually found at the top of the price scale. Short globes from 1921 through 1940 normally measure 3½" in height, except for those manufactured by Dietz, which are 4" tall. (Soon thereafter, battery brakemen's lanterns came into widespread usage; these are not highly regarded by collectors and are generally not railroad marked.)

All lanterns should be marked with the name or initials of the railroad — look on the top, the top apron, or the bell base (if it has one). Globes may be found in these colors (listed in order of popularity): clear, red, amber, aqua, cobalt, and two-color.

BR&P, Dietz #39 Standard, clear mk globe, Pat 1910 ....150.00

C&C, Armspear, pot insert, clear unmk globe, Pat 1913, NM ..100.00
CH&D, Adlake, insert pot/burner, red globe, 1909, EX 145.00
CTA, Adlake Kero, red unmk globe, dtd 4-49, NM 75.00
DL&W, Dietz Vesta, unmk red globe, 1951, EX 60.00
Hand, Burlington Route, The Buck, E&WVRR globe, EX fr 195.00
IC, Adlake Reliable, clear mk 5⅜" globe, #300 burner, EX 125.00
MOPAC, Handlan, flat top, twist-off pot, short clear mk globe, EX ..100.00
MOPAC, Handlan, mk bell & panel, bell bottom, twist-off pot, VG ..75.00
MP, Handlan-Buck, bell bottom, clear globe, lg, M 195.00
P&R, Armspear, twist-off pot, clear unmk 5½" globe, EX 75.00
PA Lines, Adams & Westlake Reliable, Pat 1913, VG 65.00

Linens and Uniforms

Blanket, C&O, Chessie stamped in blk on 100% wool, 50x60" ...255.00
Cap, B&N Conductor, old style, blk w/gold-tone badge, NM 125.00
Coat, conductor's, D&H on lapels & silver button, 1960s 92.00
Hat, C&O Baggageman, dome-style badge 100.00
Hat, cook's; NP Monad/Northcoast Ltd logo on band, paper 7.00
Head rest, ACL RR FL Vacationland, purple on gray 15.00
Head rest, CA Zephyr & observation car w/mtns, brn on tan 25.00
Head rest, L&N The Dixie Line, red on wht, used, G 15.00
Head rest, Milwaukee Rd Domeliners, brn on tan 15.00
Head rest, N&W, red on tan, ticket pocket, VG 15.00
Head rest, PRR (keystone) & passenger train, brn on tan 15.00
Head rest, Santa Fe, Please Do Not Sit..., bl & wht, 16x20" 15.00
Head rest, UP Streamliner (winged train logo), red/gray/yel 20.00
Head rest cover, C&O for Progress, gray on lt gray, 19x15" 39.00
Laundry bag, GN goat, canvas w/grommets & cord at top, 28x36" ..29.00
Napkin, CRI&P, Rock Island logo, wht-on-wht damask, 17" sq ..23.00
Pillowcase, CMStP&P, printed on wht, 23x35", VG 10.00
Tablecloth, Amtrak, wht w/stamped NRPC, 32x45" 10.00
Tablecloth, CRI&P, Rock Island logo, wht-on-wht damask, 42x50" ..32.00
Towel, hand; Fred Harvey, wht-on-wht, woven both ends, 16x28" 52.00
Towel, hand; Pullman, bl on wht, 23x16" 17.50

Locks

Brass switch locks (pre-1920) were made in two styles: heart-shaped and Keen Kutter style. Values for the heart-shaped locks are determined to a great extent by the railroad they represent and just how its name appears on the lock. Most in demand are locks with large embossed letters; if the letters are small and incised, demand for that lock is minimal. For instance, one from the Union Pacific line (even with heavily embossed letters) may go for only $45.00, while the same from the D&RG railroad could go easily sell for $250.00. Old Keen Kutter styles (brass with a 'pointy' base) from Colorado & Southern and Denver & Rio Grande could range from $600.00 to $1,200.00.

Steel switch locks (circa 1920 on) with the initials of the railroad incised in small letters — for example BN, L&H, and PRR — are usually valued at $20.00 to $28.00.

Switch lock, brass heart shapes: PRR, Fraim 1911, Keystone hallmark on shackle, $100.00; N&W Ry Co, 1924, $50.00. (Photo courtesy Stanley Baker)

Signal, CB&Q, RACO emb on side, brass, takes wrench-type key ..15.00
Signal, GN Ry Signal, Slaymaker, rnd bottom, steel shackle 28.00
Switch, B&O, Slaymaker, steel w/brass rivets 17.00
Switch, C&NW, Slaymaker, brass heart shape 45.00
Switch, Frisco, Pat 2040482 on bk, Adlake on drop, steel 15.00
Switch, M&I, Slaymaker, brass, heart shape 75.00
Switch, MHC&W RR, Bohannan...Pat June 25, 79, brass, heart shape ...300.00

Silverplate

The value of silverplate, hollow ware or flatware, is influenced by the location of the logo or railroad name and, of course, by condition. A side- or top-marked piece is preferable to one with a bottom mark. Examine a prospective purchase carefully. Some unmarked flatware has been 'enhanced' with a rather crude stamping of the railroad's name. Authentic railway markings were done at the time of manufacture and were generally executed in a flawless manner.

Basket, bread; MP, BS, 1924, 9", EX 70.00
Bowl, grapefruit; Pullman, 1925, 2½x6½" 92.00
Butter pat, CRI&P, BS, Gorham, 3¼" 19.00
Butter pat, UP, BS, Internat'l, 3½" 15.00
Butter pat, UP, BS, 1914, 3½" 34.00
Butter pat, UP, Internat'l Silver, 1918, 3½" dia 25.00
Coffee server, Am President Lines w/eagle, Reed & Barton, 8½" ...45.00
Coffeepot, CA Zephyr, BM, worn, 14-oz 100.00
Coffeepot, NYNH&H, BS, Reed & Barton, 6¼" 75.00
Coffeepot, Rio Grande, Curecanti logo, SM, 12-oz 280.00
Coffeepot, UP, Internat'l, BS, 1947, 8-oz, VG 90.00
Cream soup stand, NP, BS, Internat'l, 5" excluding tab hdls 65.00
Creamer, NYK Line, 2½x2½" 18.00
Crumber, Canadian Pacific, oval, Elkington, TM, NM 92.50
Finger bowl, Rio Grande, 'speed' letters, BM, 1941, 3" 45.00
Fork, cocktail; UP, Zephyr, BS, Internat'l, 5¾" 12.00
Fork, dinner; UP, Savoy, BS, Internat'l, 7½" 20.00
Fork, pickle; Fred Harvey, Albany, early 22.50
Fork cocktail; SRR, Sierra, TM, Reed & Barton, 5½" 20.00
Horseradish holder, NYC, complete w/glass jar, BM 95.00
Knife, dinner; ATSF, Albany, SM, Internat'l, 9½" 15.00
Knife, steak; ATSF, Cromwell, 1912 ....20.00
Mustard, UP, TM: Overland Route, BS: System, +spoon & insert ...190.00
Platter, RI, dome cover, 1929, 10", EX 205.00
Sauce boat, RI, BM, Wallace, 1921, 3-oz, NM 125.00
Spoon, bouillon; FH, Albany, BS, Internat'l, 5½" 24.00
Spoon, cream soup; SP&S Ry, Winthrop, GMCo, 1895 ....18.00
Spoon, fruit; GN, Hutton, TM, Internat'l Silver 15.00
Spoon, grapefruit; MP, Devon, TM, Wallace 16.00
Spoon, iced tea; Paisley, BS 20.00
Spoon, place; NP Monad, Rte of...Big Baked Potato, NM 75.00
Sugar bowl, D&RG, w/lid, SL w/Curecanti Needle, Internat'l, 9-oz ...498.00
Sugar bowl, Santa Fe, hinged lid, Gorham, SM, BS, 10-oz 55.00
Sugar tongs, SP, TM: SPCo, Meridian, 4" 165.00
Sugar tongs, SRR, spoon shape, SM, Internat'l 75.00
Tablespoon, Fred Harvey, Cromwell, Internat'l, 1912 ....18.00
Teapot, C&NW, pagoda style, Internat'l, BS, 1925, 8-oz 82.50
Teapot, D&RG, SL w/Curecanti Needle, Internat'l, 12-oz 400.00
Teaspoon, D&RG, Belmont, TM, Reed & Barton 27.00
Teaspoon, SP, Modern, TM w/winged logo, Reed & Barton, 5½" ..22.00
Tray, bread; CP, TM, Elkington, 11¼x6" 55.00
Tray, UP, TM w/Wing Streamliner, BS: UPRR, Internat'l, 6" dia ...65.00
Tureen, soup; B&O, TM, Reed & Barton, 1-pt, 3-pc 235.00
Vase, bud; WAB, BS, 1948 ....150.00
Wine cooler, CI&L (Monon), BS, Reed & Barton, 7¾" 200.00

Miscellaneous

Annual passes continue to be favored over trip and one-time passes. Their value is contingent upon the specific railroad, its length of run, and the appearance of the pass itself. Many were tiny works of art enhanced with fancy calligraphy and decorated with unique vignettes.

Timetables continue to gain in popularity and offer the collector vast information about the glory days of railroading. Pins and badges bearing the name or logo of a railroad are also popular collectibles. The novice needs to be cautious about signs (metal as well as cardboard) and belt buckles. Reproductions flourish in these areas.

Handkerchief, Chessie and kittens in corners with Peake (proud father) in center, made for Chesapeake & Ohio Railway, 8x8", $25.00.

Ashtray, Mississippi Central, blk on SP, 3½" dia 35.00
Ashtray, UP RR shield logo on glass, red/wht/bl, 4½" dia 12.50
Badge, ACL Police Department Patrolman, silver-tone, 1920s, 1⅞" .145.00
Badge, C&O Ry Brakeman, silver w/much emb, 1½x4¼" 65.00
Badge, Canadian Pacific Hotels, domed, silver-tone w/bl & blk, sm ..12.50
Badge, Canadian Pacific News Agent, silver w/blk & yel, 2x1½" ..35.00
Badge, Canadian Pacific Special Service, silver-tone, 2⅝x1⅞" .200.00
Badge, cap; Amtrak Trainman, blk on gold w/bl & red, 1⅞x3" ...28.00
Badge, cap; Boston & Maine Trainman, blk on silver, 1⅛x3⅝", NM ...35.00
Badge, cap; Brakeman (cut-out letters), silver-tone, 3" W 18.00
Badge, cap; Conrail (logo) Conductor, gold w/bl & blk, 1⅞x2⅝" ...30.00
Badge, cap; Dining Car Steward, polished brass & blk, 3¼" 25.00
Badge, cap; Expressman, SP, blk traces, ⅝x3" 45.00
Badge, cap; Foreman Baggage Department, blk on silver, 3¼" 50.00
Badge, cap; LI RR Conductor, blk on silver, ⅞x3¼" 24.00
Badge, cap; MCRR Conductor, incised but no color markings, 3¼" W ...25.00
Badge, cap; Penn Central Conductor, gold w/red & blk enamel ..27.50
Badge, cap; Santa Fe Conductor, silver w/blk & bl, circle cross logo ..65.00
Badge, cap; Trainman, blk on silver-tone, 3" 28.00
Badge, CMStP&P Waiter, silver w/blk, flat, 1¾x1⅜" 17.50
Badge, DL&W RR Police, silver, Clover hallmk, 2¼" W 75.00
Badge, DL&W RRCo Ry Police, silver-tone, 2⅜x1⅝" 140.00
Badge, DM&N Ry Employee, blk on silver-tone, 1¼x1¼", EX ...20.00
Badge, Erie RR Police, silver, Am Ry Sup Co, EX 80.00
Badge, PRRCo Ry Police, silvered, Am Ry Sup Co, 2⅜" 75.00
Badge, Railway Watchman PRRCo, blk on silver, 1¾" W 60.00
Badge, SAL Ry Co Special Agent Chief, blk on gold finish, 1¾", NM ...165.00
Badge, UP Waiter, shield shape, Whitehead & Hoag, 1⅜" 12.50
Badge, Virginian Ry Special Agent, eagle top, SP, 1910s 165.00
Bell, cast bronze w/iron clapper, 192C-71, gr patina, ca 1871, 10" 200.00
Bell, engine room; NP, mtd on base, 15½" at yoke, from $1,200 to ...1,500.00
Beverage list, D&RGW, 1950s, 5x7" 8.00
Blotter, C&NW New 5400-Series Freight Diesel, 3⅜x9", M 15.00
Book, Methods of the Santa Fe..., Going, 1909 ....130.00
Book, WP RR From San Francisco to Salt Lake City, 1944, 40-pg, VG ..25.00
Book matches, UP, gold on red, unopened, 6 packs 8.00
Booklet, SP, descriptive of Coast Route+steamship info, 96-pg, 1905 ..14.00
Booklet, WP&Y Route, Gold Rush Trail, blk on gr, 44-pg 10.00
Box, cigarette; N Am Car Corp, tooled leather cover, 4", VG 40.00
Box, NY System First Aid, pnt metal, fold-down hdls, 8¼x5" 25.00
Brochure, M&PP, blk & wht pictures on most, 1920s, 8¾x7¾", EX ..15.00
Builder's plate, NYC, Alco & GE, pnt gone, 1952, 12x6" 110.00
Button, AC&S RR Shore Fast Line, silver, 6 sm 25.00
Button, Boston & Maine, silver, vest sz, pr 15.00
Button, Canadian Pacific Rys, silver, sew-on, 4 jacket/5 vest 16.00
Button, Clinton Street Ry Co, silver, fancy, 3 lg 17.50
Button, CT Co & monogram, silver, Superior 4.00
Button, CTA, descending slant, gold, Waterbury, 3 lg 9.00
Button, D&RG, silver, fancy, Waterbury, lg 8.00
Button, Motorman, silver, Burton Pierce, sew-on, jacket sz 4.00
Button, pin-bk; C&WI Construction, blk & wht, domed 25.00
Button, pin-bk; White Pass & Yukon Rte, 5-color tin, 2¼" 16.00
Button, Rock Island Lines around star, silver, sm 4.00
Button, uniform; Wabash, Waterbury Button Co, ⅞", set of 4 ....9.00
Button, Wabash, fancy trim, gold, Waterbury, lg 7.50
Calendar, C&O, 1937, baby/Chessie graphics, 16x14", NM+ 60.00
Calendar, D&RGW, mtn & springs/train, 1952, 25½x15", NM ..55.00
Calendar, GN, long train/campers, 1968, unused, 26x16¼", NM ...20.00
Calendar, GN RR, Angry Bull, 1951, EX+ 120.00
Calendar, GN RR, Clears-Up, 1939, NM 145.00
Calendar, GN RR, Julia-Wades-In-Water, 1946, M 130.00
Calendar, GN RR, Many Guns, 1955, EX 100.00
Calendar, GN RR, Takes-The-Gun-Strong, 1943, EX+ 120.00
Calendar, pocket; SRR, showing diesel engine 4221, 1954 ....30.00
Call box, Western Union Everywhere, fancy front, 4⅛x2¼" 37.00
Cigarette lighter, Bro of Loco Engineers, 3-color logo, EX 12.50
Coaster, Air Express RY EX AGY Division, Coffee Break, cardstock ..2.00
Comic book, Soo Line...Thrill of Power, safety theme, 1953, VG ..7.00
Gauge, steam; Am Steam Gauge Co, blk-on-silver dial, 5" 36.00
Hard hat, Amtrak, complete w/inner head band 22.00
Herald, Post Sugar Crisp, approximately 3", from $5 to 18.00
Ice scraper, NYC logo, plastic, for car window 15.00
Magazine, Brotherhood of Locomotive Firemen, 170-pg, 1903 ....15.00
Matchbook, LV route of the Black Dmn, 1950s, unused 9.00
Oiler, GT Ry, teapot style, 14x6" dia, VG 55.00
Oiler, Rock Island Lines, teapot type, 10½x6", EX 30.00
Paperweight, Soo Line 75th Anniversary, magnifying, 1958, 3¾" ..30.00
Pass, C&NW Ry, 1927, EX 6.50
Pass, CMStP&P, 1937-38 ....6.50
Pencil, mechanical; UP Route of Streamliners/Challenger, 4" 14.00
Photo, OW RR&N turntable & lg crew, on cardstock mt, 14x12" ...30.00
Pin, lapel; Algoma Central Ry, bear logo, brn & wht w/gold 10.00
Pin, lapel; B of LF&E 20 Years Service, gold w/mc enamel, ⅝" dia .12.50
Pin, lapel; BN Service by Design, gold in blk, sq, ½" 8.50
Pin, lapel; Burlington Rte, blk & red on gold-tone, ¾x⅞" 16.50
Pin, lapel; Milwaukee Road Service Club, emb dk gold, ⅝" dia ..15.00
Pin, lapel; Nat'l Ry Appliance Assn, blk/red on gold, worn, 1950 ..12.00
Pin, lapel; NYC Honorably Retired, gold & wht, oval, ⅝" 12.50
Pin, lapel; PA RR 25 Service Years, bronze, cast steamer 22.50
Pin, lapel; PC, gold w/blk, Metal Arts, ⅝x1⅛" 12.50
Pin, lapel; SP Safety, dk bl on silver wreathed circle, ½" dia 15.00
Pin, necktie; Milwaukee Road Hiawatha Tribe Member, blk/wht/yel ..7.50
Pin, necktie; UP, shield logo, blk & gold on wht w/red jewels 15.00
Plate, Mfg for Baldwin Locomotive Works, brass, 1½x3¾" 20.00
Postcard, ATSF roundhouse at Emporia KS, blk & wht, 1900s 22.00
Postcard, D&RGW, scenery, unused, 5 for 10.00
Postcard, real photo of train wreck, unidentified, from 3.00
Print, Chessie & Kittens (cropped calendar top), 8½x11"+fr 23.00
Print, MP, Route of Eagles, full color, 20x31"+fr 147.00
Rule book, IC, 1959, 141-pg, unused 16.00
Ruler, CNW System, wooden, 2 lg trains, 15", EX 20.00
Ruler, D&RGW & passenger train, plastic, blk & yel on clear, 12" ..30.00

Seat, locomotive cab; IC, folds down, leatherette cover 88.00
Sign, Restroom, lt magnetic metal, 2⅝x10⅝", EX 17.50
Sign, SCL RR, pnt metal, name around initials, blk/yel, 22" dia, EX ...70.00
Sign, Telephone, blk on silvered metal, 1x6", M 45.00
Sign, Trains, wht porc block letters, ea letter 15", EX+ 235.00
Sign, Western Union, yel on blk enameled metal, grommets, 48x24" ...135.00
Signal relay, WUTCo, single coil, silvered brass, VG 22.50
Tag, GN Ry, brass, raised dot border, 1¼" dia 25.00
Tag, luggage; Lufthansa, leather, 2¼x4"+strap 12.50
Tag, shipping; MStP&SSteM RR Co, blk on tan cardstock, M 2.00
Telegraph key, Electric Specialty, pre-logo version, VG 45.00
Telegraph key, Vibroplex, oval bug logo, EX 60.00
Timetable, employee; CN, British Columbia, 1966 ....15.00
Timetable, employee; GN, Kalispell Division, 1964 ....20.00
Timetable, employee; KCS, Northern Terminal Division, 1945 ...20.00
Timetable, employee; White Pass & Yukon System, 1958 ....25.00
Timetable, public; ACL, full system, 1932 ....25.00
Timetable, public; C&O System, map, 1914 ....45.00
Timetable, public; D&RGW, 1927 ....35.00
Timetable, public; DRGW, Rio Grand System, 1939 ....25.00
Timetable, public; SP System, 4 Great Routes, 1932 ....25.00
Timetable, public; UP System, maps, 1917 ....35.00
Tool check, LA&AR Ry, brass, 1⅛" dia 17.50
Wax sealer, Adams Express Co, brass toadstool type, 2½" 125.00
Wax sealer, ATSF OK Agent, rope-trimmed head, NP steel hdl .350.00
Wax sealer, CM&StP, CB Division, Tama City IA, brass head, enamel hdl ...300.00
Wax sealer, CRI&P IA Agent, rope-trimmed brass oval, fancy wood hdl ...300.00
Wax sealer, Nat'l Express Co, 2-tone wooden bulb on oval head, 3½" ...215.00
Wax sealer, Ry EX Agy Inc Messenger, oval head, hardwood hdl, 4" ...68.00
Wax sealer, Southern Ex Co, brass w/rope border, CI hdl 200.00
Wax sealer, Wells Fargo & Co Express, NPCI bulb hdl, EX 225.00
Whistle, caboose back-up; GN Ry, brass, 1910P Sherburne, 8" 75.00
Whistle, exhaust; Fulton No 1 Aermore, brass, 4-tube, 1912, 15" ...150.00

Razors

As straight razors gain in popularity, prices of those razors also increase. This carries with it a lure of investment possibilities which can encourage the novice or speculator to make purchases that may later prove to be unwise. We recommend that before investing serious money in razors, you become familiar with the elements which make a razor valuable. As with other collectibles, there are specific traits which are desirable and which have a major impact on the price of a piece.

The following information is based on the second edition of *The Standard Guide to Razors* by Roy Richie and Ron Stewart (available from R&C Books, P.O. Box 151, Combs, KY 41729, $9.95 +$2.50 S&H, autographed). Their book is a valuable reference guide to both the casual and serious collector of razors. Other books by these authors include *Cattraugus Cutlery, Identification and Values* and the *Big Book of Pocket Knives*.

There are four major factors which determine a razor's collector value. These are the brand and country of origin, the handle material, the art work found on the handles or blades, and the condition of the razor. Ritchie and Stewart freely admit that there are other factors that may come into play with some collectors, but these are the major players in determining value. They have devised a system of evaluation which is based on these four factors.

The most important factor is the value placed on the brand and country of origin. This is the price of a common razor made by (or for) a particular company. It has plain handles, probably made of plastic, no art work, and is in collectible condition. It is the beginning value. Hundreds (thousands?) of these values are provided in the 'Listings of Companies and Base Values' chapter in the book.

The second category is that of handle material. This covers a wide range of materials, from fiber on the low end to ivory on the high end. The collector needs to be able to identify the different handle materials when he sees them. This often takes some practice, since there are some very good plastics that can mimic ivory quite successfully. Also, the difference between genuine celluloid and plastic can become significant when determining value. A detailed chart of these values is supplied in the book. The listing below can be used as a general guide.

The third category is the most subjective. Nevertheless, it is an extremely important factor in determining value. This category is artwork, which can include everything from logo art to carving and sculpture. It may range from highly ornate to tastefully correct. Blade etching as well as handle artistry are to be considered. Perhaps what some call the 'gotta have it' or the 'neatness' factors properly fall into this category. You must accurately determine the artistic merits of your razor when you evaluate it relative to this factor. Again, the book we referenced earlier provides a more complete listing of considerations than is used here.

Finally, the condition is factored in. The book's scales run from 'parts' (10% +/-) to 'Good' (150% +/-) Good should be rated as mint in the box — blemish free. Average (100% +/-) is classified as 'Collectible.'

Samplings from charts:

Chart A: Companies and Base Values:

Abercrombie & Finch, NY 14.00
Aerial, USA 24.00
Boker, Henri & Co, Germany 14.00
Brick, F, England 10.00
Case Mfg Co, Spring Valley, NY 40.00
Chores, James 9.00
Dahlgren, CW; Sweden 14.00
Diane, Japan 10.00
Electric Co, NY 15.00
ERN, Germany 12.00
Fautless, Germany 11.00
Fox Cutlery, Germany 11.00
Griffon XX, Germany 11.00
Henckels, Germany 15.00
Holly Mft Co CT 27.00
International Cutlery Co NY/Germany 11.00
IXL, Germany 12.00
Jay, John; NY 12.00
KaBar, Union Cut Co, USA 28.00
Kanner, J; Germany 11.00
Kern, R&W; Canada/England 12.00
LeCocltre, Jacque; Switzerland 12.00
Levering Razor Co, NY/Germany 18.00
McIntosh & Heather, OH 12.00
Merit Import Co, Germany 10.00
National Cut Co, OH 11.00
Oxford Razor Co, Germany 10.00
Palmer Brothers, Savannah, GA 20.00
Primble, John; Indian Steel Works, Louisville, KY 24.00
Queen City, NY 30.00
Quigley, Germany 12.00
Rattler Razor Co 10.00
Robeson Cut Co, USA 28.00
Salamander Works, Germany 11.00
Soderein, Ekilstuna, Sweden 11.00
Taylor, LM; Cincinnati OH 14.00
Tower Brand, Germany 16.00
Ulmer, Germany 11.00
US Barber Supply, TX 12.00
Vinnegut Hdw Co, IN 11.00
Vogel, Ed; PA 10.00

Wade & Butcher, England 24.00
Weis, JH; Supply House, Louisville, KY 15.00
Yankee Cutlery Co, Germany 11.00
Yazbek, Lahod, OH 10.00
Zacour Bros, Germany 10.00
Zepp Germany 10.00

Chart B, as described below, is an abbreviated version of the handle materials list in *The Standard Guide to Razors*. It is an essential category in the use of the appraisal system developed by the authors.

Ivory	550%
Tortoise Shell	500%
Pearl	400%
Stag	400%
Bone	300%
Celluloid	250%
Composition	150%
Plastic	100%

Chart C deals with the artistic value of the razor. As pointed out earlier, this is a very subjective area. It takes study to determine what is good and what is not. Taste can also play a significant role in determining the value placed on the artistic merit of a razor. The range is from superior to nonexistent. Categories generally are divided as follows:

Exceptional	650%
Superior	550%
Good	400%
Average	300%
Minimal	200%
Plain	100%
Nonexistant	0%

Chart D is also very subjective. It determines the condition of the razor. You must judge accurately if the appraisal system is to work for you.

Good 150%

Does not have to be factory mint to fall within this category. However, there can be no visible flaws if it is to be calculated at 150%.

Collectible 100%

May have some flaws that do not greatly detract from the artwork or finish.

Parts 10%

Unrepairable, valuable as salvageable parts.

Razors may fall within any of these categories, ie. collectible + 112%.

Now to determine the value of your razor, multiply A times B, then multiply A times C. Add your two answers and multiply this sum times D. The answer you get is your collector value. See the example below.

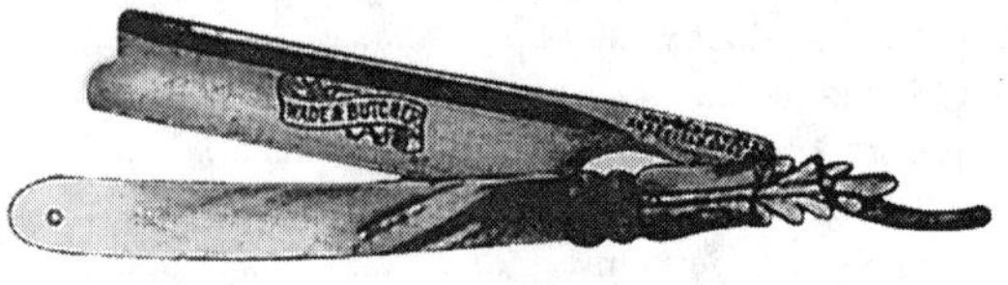

(a) Brand and Origin Base Value	(b) Handle Material % Value	(c) Artwork % Value	(d) Condition % Value	(e) Collector Value
Wade & Butcher England **$24.00**	Iridescent Pearl Handles 24 x400% **$96.00**	Carved handles 24 x 500% **$120.00**	Cracked handle at pin Collectible- 80%	$96+$84=$180 $180 x 80%= **$230.00**

Reamers

The reamer market is very active right now, and prices are escalating rapidly. They have been made in hundreds of styles and colors and by as many manufacturers. Their purpose is to extract the juices from lemons, oranges, and grapefruits. The largest producer of glass reamers was McKee, who pressed their products from many types of glass — custard; Delphite and Chalaine Blue; opaque white; Skokie Green; black; caramel and white opalescent; Seville Yellow; and transparent pink, green, and clear. Among these, the black and the caramel opalescents are the most valuable.

The Fry Glass Company also made reamers that are today very collectible. The Hazel Atlas Crisscross orange reamer in pink is valued at $275.00 to $300.00 or more — the same in blue, $375.00. Hocking produced a light blue orange reamer and, in the same soft hue, a two-piece reamer and measuring cup combination. Both are considered rare and very valuable with currently quoted estimates at $400.00 and up for the former and $800.00 and up for the latter. In addition to the colors mentioned, red glass examples — transparent or slag — are rare and costly. Prices vary greatly according to color and rarity. The same reamer in crystal may be worth three times as much in a more desirable color.

Among the most valuable ceramic reamers are those made by American potteries. The Spongeband reamer by Red Wing is valued in excess of $500.00; Coorsite reamers with gold or silver trim are worth $300.00 and up. Figurals are popular — Mickey Mouse and John Bull may bring $600.00 to $1,000.00. Others range from $55.00 to $350.00. Fine china one- and two-piece reamers are also very desirable and command very respectable prices.

A word about reproductions: A series of limited edition reamers is being made by Edna Barnes of Uniontown, Ohio. These are all marked with a 'B' in a circle. Other repoductions have been made from old molds. The most important of these are Anchor Hocking two-piece two-cup measure and top, Gillespie one-cup measure with reamer top, Westmoreland with flattened handle, Westmoreland four-cup measure embossed with orange and lemons, Duboe (hand-held darning egg), and Easley's Diamonds one-piece.

Our advisor for this category is Dee Long; she is listed in the Directory under Illinois. For more information concerning reamers and reproductions, contact our advisor or the National Reamer Collectors Association (see Clubs, Newsletters, and Catalogs). Be sure to include a SASE when requesting information.

Ceramic

Clown, multicolor, Japan, two-piece, 6½", from $65.00 to $70.00; Lotus, multicolored shiny and lustre glazes, Japan, 5", from $50.00 to $65.00. (Photo courtesy Carole Bess White)

Baby's, Baby's Orange, red & wht 60.00
Baby's, Jack & Jill, boy & girl, mc, angle hdls, 2-pc 85.00
Baby's, Kiddie's Orange Juice, orange figural, 2-pc 55.00
Baby's, Noah's Ark, ark & animals scene, mc on wht, 2-pc 90.00
Clown, brn body & hat, bl button & collar, 6", from $95 to 125.00
Clown, dk gr, 5½", from $95 to 125.00
Clown, gr ruffle, mc base, 4¾" 95.00
Clown, orange textured body, hands on stomach, 6¼" 150.00

Clown, Sourpuss, w/saucer, 4¾", from $115 to 135.00
Clown, teal gr/wht/yel, 2-pc, Japan, 6½" 95.00
Duck, wht lustre w/orange/gr/yel, 3x5½x3¼" 75.00
Floral w/gold, Royal Rudolstadt, 2-pc 250.00
Lemon, yel w/gr leaves, gold trim, 2-pc, Japan, 4", from $60 to ...75.00
Old Charley, toby-style figure, 1-pc, 4¾" 175.00
Pitcher, blk w/gold wheat, 2-pc, 8" 45.00
Rose, pk w/gr leaves, Germany, 1¾" 225.00
Teapot, yel, tan & wht, 2-pc, England/Shelley, 3½" 200.00
Teapot style, emb floral, Japan, 5½" 45.00
Teapot style, pnt floral, Japan, 6" 50.00
Teapot style, tomato base, wht cone, Japan 45.00
Teapot style, various contemporary designs, Japan, 4½" 25.00
Universal Cambridge, Cattail 200.00
USA, Jiffy Juicer, US Pat 2,130,755, Sept 2, 1928, yel, 5¼" 85.00

Glass

Anchor Hocking, gr, w/pitcher, 2-cup 45.00
Anchor Hocking, Vitrock, tab hdl 45.00
Cambridge, gr w/silver Rockwell decor 300.00
Federal, gr, paneled, loop hdl 35.00
Federal, gr, tab hdl, seed dam, ribbed 28.00
Fenton, blk, w/pitcher 1,350.00
Fenton, jade, w/pitcher 1,000.00
Fleur-de-Lis, red-orange slag 550.00
Fleur-de-Lis, wht 95.00
Fry, Pearl, str sides 45.00
Fry, vaseline, str sides 75.00
Hazel Atlas, Crisscross, cobalt, loop hdl 325.00
Hazel Atlas, Crisscross, pk 345.00
Hazel Atlas, gr, w/pitcher, mk A&J, 4-cup 45.00
Hazel Atlas, red, fired-on, w/pitcher, 2-cup 45.00
Hazel Atlas, yel, w/pitcher, 2-cup 375.00
Indiana Glass, amber, 6-sided cone 350.00
Jeannette, crystal, Jennyware 120.00
Jeannette, lt Jadite, w/pitcher, 2-cup 40.00
Jeannette, pk, Hex Optic, bucket form 45.00
Jeannette, pk, panelled, Jennyware, lg, 5½" 130.00
Jeannette, ultramarine, paneled, Jennyware, 5½" 130.00
Jenkins, gr, 2-pc, baby sz, tall, 3½" 175.00
McKee, butterscotch, emb Sunkist 850.00
McKee, Chalaine Blue, grapefruit sz 750.00
McKee, chocolate, emb Sunkist 850.00
McKee, custard, emb McK 35.00
McKee, gr 225.00
McKee, wht, Sunkist name in box 120.00
Morgantown, crystal pitcher w/blk hdl & reamer lid 350.00
Paden City, blk, Party Line 650.00
Saunders, blk 1,500.00
Sunkist, blk 750.00
Sunkist, caramel 400.00
Sunkist, Chalaine Blue 225.00
Sunkist, Crown Tuscan 400.00
Sunkist, wht opal (depending on opalescence), from $65 to 175.00
US Glass, amber, w/pitcher, 4-cup 600.00
US Glass, lt honey amber, w/pitcher, 2-cup 350.00
US Glass, pk, w/pitcher & lid (+) 295.00
Westmoreland, crystal w/oranges decor, flattened loop hdl 65.00
Westmoreland, gr, 2-pc, baby sz 225.00

Miscellaneous

Aluminum, mechanical press, from $10 to 25.00
Aluminum, scissors style, from $5 to 15.00
Silverplate cocktail shaker, 8¾", from $75 to 100.00
Sterling silver, 2-pc, 4-5", ea 150.00
Sterling silver saucer, 4" 125.00
Sterling w/glass cone, 3-4", ea 175.00

Records

Records of interest to collectors are often not the million-selling hits by 'superstars.' Very few records by Bing Crosby, for example, are of any more than nominal value, and those that are valuable usually don't even have his name on the label! Collectors today are most interested in records that were made in limited quantities, early works of a performer who later became famous, and those issued in special series or aimed at a limited market. Vintage records are judged desirable by their recorded content as well; those that lack the quality of music that makes a record collectible will always be 'junk' records in spite of their age, scarcity, or the obsolescence of their technology.

Records are usually graded visually rather than aurally, since it is seldom if ever possible to first play the records you buy at shows, by mail, at flea markets, etc. Condition is one of the most important determinants of value. For example, a nearly mint-condition Elvis Presley 45 of 'Milk Cow Blues' (Sun 215) has a potential value of over $1,500.00. A small sticker on the label could cut its value in half; noticeable wear could reduce its value by 80%. A mint record must show no evidence of use (record jackets, in the case of EPs and LPs, must be equally choice). Excellent condition denotes a record showing only slight signs of use with no audible defects. A very good record has noticeable wear but still plays well. Records of lesser grades may be unsaleable, unless very scarce and/or highly sought-after.

While the value of most 78s does not depend upon their being in appropriate sleeves (although a sleeveless existence certainly contributes to damage and deterioration!), this is not the case with most EPs (extended play 45s) and LPs (long-playing 33⅓ rpm 'albums'), which *must* have their jackets (cardboard sleeves), in nice condition, free of disfiguring damage, such as writing, stickers or tape. Often, common and minimally valued 45s might be collectible if they are in appropriate 'picture sleeves' (special sleeves that depict the artist/group or other fanciful or symbolic graphic and identify the song titles, record label and number), e.g. many common records by Elvis Presley, The Beatles, and The Beach Boys.

Promotional copies (DJ copies) supplied to radio stations often have labels different in designs and/or colors from their commercially issued counterparts. Labels usually bear a designation 'Not for Sale,' 'Audition Copy,' 'Sample Copy,' or the like. Records may be pressed of translucent vinyl; while most promos are not particularly collectible, those by certain 'hot' artists, such as Elvis Presley, The Beach Boys, and The Beatles are usually premium disks.

Many of the most desirable and valuable 45s have been 'bootlegged' (counterfeited). For example, there are probably more fake Elvis Presley *Sun* records in circulation than authentic copies — certainly in higher grades! Collectors should be alert for these often deceptive counterfeits.

Our advisor for this category is L.R. Docks, author of *American Premium Record Guide*, which lists 60,000 records by over 7,000 artists, now in its fifth edition. He is listed in the Directory under Texas. In the listings that follow, prices are suggested for records that are in excellent condition; worn or abused records may be worth only a small fraction of the values quoted, and may not be saleable at all.

Blues, Rhythm and Blues, Rock 'N Roll, Rockabilly

Adams, Art; Rock Crazy Baby, Cherry 1005, 45 rpm 50.00
Adventurers, Rock & Roll Uprising, Columbia 42227, 45 rpm ...10.00
Aladdins, Cry Cry Baby, Aladdin 3275, 45 rpm 30.00
Armstrong, Shelly; Chain Gang Bound, Champion 50024, 78 rpm 30.00
Avalon, Frankie; De De Dinah, Chancellor 1011, 78 rpm 20.00
Baker, Katherine; Chicago Fire Blues, Gennett 6157, 78 rpm ...200.00
Beale Street Sheiks, Half Cup of Tea, Paramount 12518, 78 rpm ...200.00
Big Bopper, Chantilly Lace, Mercury 71343, 45 rpm 8.00
Big Bopper, Chantilly Lace, Mercury 71343, 78 rpm 100.00

Black Birds of Paradise, Muddy Water, Gennett 6211-A, $200.00. (Photo courtesy Les Docks)

Buccaneers, The Stars Will Remember, Rama 21, 45 rpm 200.00
Cadillacs, Gloria, Capitol 765, 45 rpm 75.00
Capris, It Was Moonglow, Gotham 7306, 45 rpm 40.00
Channel, Bruce; Hey! Baby, Le Cam 953, 45 rpm 20.00
Charles, Ray; What'd I Say, Atlantic 2031, 78 rpm 30.00
Clanton, Jimmy; Just a Dream, Ace 546, LP 40.00
Cochran, Eddie; Sittin' in the Balcony, Liberty 55056, 78 rpm ...30.00
Collins, Sam; Hesitation Blues, Gennett 6379, 78 rpm 400.00
Crawford, Roberta; Down on the Levee Blues, Okeh 8096, 78 rpm ...75.00
Cuff Links, Only One Love, Gait 543, 45 rpm 20.00
Danny & the Juniors, At the Hop, ABC Paramount 9871, 45 rpm ..8.00
Danny & the Juniors, At the Hop, ABC Paramount 9871, 78 rpm ..30.00
Day, Bobby; Rockin' Robin, Class 229, 78 rpm 30.00
Deep River Boys, Midnight Magic, Que 104, LP 100.00
Del (Dell) Vikings, Come Go w/Me, Fee Bee 205, 45 rpm 30.00
Diddley, Bo; Crackin' Up, Checker 924, 78 rpm 20.00
Domino, Fats; Boogie Woogie Baby, Imperial 5065, 78 rpm 20.00
Domino, Fats; Rose Marie, Imperial 5251, 45 rpm 150.00
Down Home Boys, It's All Gone Now, Victor V38567, 78 rpm .200.00
Duke, Bernice; Back Door Blues, Broadway 5038, 78 rpm 120.00
Duprees, You Belong to Me, Coed 905, LP 75.00
Ebbtones, I've Got a Feeling, Ebb 100, 45 rpm 20.00
Eddy, Duane; Rebel-'Rouser, Jamie 1104, 78 rpm 15.00
Elegants, Little Star, Apt 25005, 78 rpm 30.00
Elegants, Little Star, Apt 25005 (blk label), 45 rpm 12.00
Erby, John; Lonesome Jimmy Blues, Columbia 14151-D, 78 rpm .50.00
Everetts, Macon Blues, Columbia 14444-D, 78 rpm 80.00
Everly Bros, Songs Our Daddy Taught Us, Cadence 3016, LP 30.00
Everson, Lottie; Lost Lover Blues, Champion 15591, 78 rpm 175.00
Feathers, Charlie; I've Been Deceived, Flip 503, 45 rpm 150.00
Five Keys, With a Broken Heart, Aladdin 3085, 45 rpm 200.00
Foster, Jim; Riverside Blues, Champion 15301, 78 rpm 250.00
Four Tops, Could It Be You, Chess 1623, 45 rpm 30.00
Framer, Eli; Framer's Blues, Victor 23409, 78 rpm 200.00
Fuller, Johnny; Train Train Blues, Hollywood 1043, 45 rpm 18.00
Gallahads, Keeper of Dreams, Starla 15, 45 rpm 12.00
Gibson, Clifford; Old Timer Rider, Victor 23255, 78 rpm 250.00
Gilley, Mickey; Lonely Wine, Astro 101, LP 175.00
Goosby, Fannie Mae; Fortune Teller Blues, Brunswick 7030, 78 rpm ...100.00
Green, Ruby; Cool Lovin' Mama, Excello 2074, 45 rpm 30.00
Griffin, Buck; Ballin' & Squalin', Lin 1015, 45 rpm 40.00
Hall Brothers, My White Convertible, Arc 4444, 45 rpm 12.00
Halos, The Halos, Warwick 2046, LP 50.00
Harrie, Willie, West Side Blues, Brunswick 7092, 78 rpm 200.00
Harum Scarums, Alabama Scratch, Paramount 13054, 78 rpm .300.00
Holly, Buddy; Peggy Sue, Coral 61885, 45 rpm 10.00
Holly, Buddy; Peggy Sue, Coral 61885, 78 rpm 75.00
Hooker, John Lee; Boogie Rambler, JVB 30, 78 rpm 30.00
Horton, Johnny; The Fantastic Johnny Horton, Mercury, 20478, LP ..50.00
Hunter, Alberta; I'm Hard To Satisfy, Okeh 8294, 78 rpm 75.00
Husky, Ferlin; Ferlin's Favorites, Capitol 1280, LP 150.00
Imperials, You'll Never Walk Alone, Great Lakes 1212, 45 rpm ..100.00
Ink Spots, Ebb Tide, King 1297, LP 15.00
Inspirations, Raindrops, Apollo 494, 45 rpm 30.00
Jackson, Lulu; Careless Love Blues, Vocalion 1193, 78 rpm 75.00
James, Elmore & Broomdusters; Country Boogie, Checker 777, 45 rpm ..150.00
James, Etta; Good Rockin' Daddy, Modern 962, 45 rpm 10.00
James, Sunny; Excuse Me Baby, Down Town 2010, 78 rpm 20.00
Johnny Burnette Trio, Tear It Up, Coral 61651, 45 rpm 30.00
Kansas City Kitty, Scronchin', Vocalion 1632, 78 rpm 100.00
King, BB; BB King Wails, Crown 5115, LP 40.00
King, BB; Got the Blues, Bullett 315, 78 rpm 12.00
Knickerbockers, You Must Know, Natural 3000, 45 rpm 200.00
Lampkin, Tommy; Eternal Love, Imperial 5361, 45 rpm 30.00
Lamplighters, Tell Me You Care, Federal 12176, 45 rpm 35.00
Little Brother, Crescent City Blues, Bluebird 6733, 78 rpm 40.00
Little Richard, Long Tall Sally, Specialty 572, 78 rpm 15.00
Lottie & Winston, Wayward Girl Blues, Superior 2717, 78 rpm ..300.00
Lymon, Frankie & the Teenagers; Rock & Roll, Roulette 25036, 45 rpm ...30.00
Mack, Alura; Old Fashioned Blues, Gennett 6767, 78 rpm 150.00
Marquees, The Bells, Grand 141, 45 rpm 75.00
Martin, Sara; Jug Band Blues, Okeh 8166, 78 rpm 125.00
Mayfield, Percy; Lonesome Highway, Specialty 439, 45 rpm 12.00
McTell, Kate, Dying Gambler, Decca 7093, 78 rpm 75.00
Miles, Jose; Picnic Time, Ajax 17083, 78 rpm 50.00
Miracles, Your Love, Fury 1002/1003, 45 rpm 75.00
Moonglows, I Just Can't Tell a Lie, Champagne 7500, 45 rpm ..150.00
Muddy Waters, Screamin' & Cryin', Aristocrat 406, 78 rpm 100.00
Nelson, Ricky; Ricky Sings Again, Imperial 9061, LP 40.00
Nighthawks, Jackson Town Gal, Aristocrat 413, 78 rpm 50.00
Noble, George; Bed Spring Blues, Vocalion 02923, 78 rpm 200.00
Old Man Oden, Thick & Thin, Decca 7545, 78 rpm 40.00
One String Sam, I Need a Hundred Dollars, JVB 40, 78 rpm 50.00
Orioles, I Miss You So, Jubilee 5051, 45 rpm 150.00
Papa Too Sweet, Big Fat Mama, Okeh 8651, 78 rpm 100.00
Patton, Charley; It Won't Be Long, Paramount 12854, 78 rpm .300.00
Perkins, Carl; Whole Lotta Shakin', Columbia 12441, EP 100.00
Pete & Repeat, Toodle-Oodle-Oo, Brunswick 7104, 78 rpm ...100.00
Platters, Give Thanks, Federal 12153, 45 rpm 75.00
Quander, Sis; Black Snake Blues, Pathe-Actuelle 7530, 78 rpm ..30.00
Rafferty, Carl; Mr Carl's Blues, Bluebird, 5429, 78 rpm 100.00
Reed, Willie; Dreaming Blues, Columbia 14407-D, 78 rpm 100.00
Rivieras, Moonlight Serenade, Coed 508, 45 rpm 12.00
Robbins, Marty; Rock'n Roll'n Robbins, Columbia 2601, LP, 10" ..250.00
Rose, Lucy; Papa You're Too Slow, Champion 15471, 78 rpm ...100.00
Rucker, Laura; I'm the Lonesome One, Paramount 13030, 78 rpm ..200.00
Shirelles, Tonight's the Night, Scepter 501, LP 75.00
Smith, Bessie; Sobbin' Hearted Blues, Columbia 14056-D, 78 rpm ..50.00
Solitaires, If I Loved You, Old Town, 1003, 45 rpm 75.00
Superiors, Lost Love, Main Line 104, 45 rpm 100.00
Sweet Papa Tadpole, Black Spider Blues, Vocalion 1592, 78 rpm ...150.00

Sykes, Roosevelt & Honeydrippers; Stop Her Papa, RCA 50-0025, 45 rpm .50.00
Sykes, Roosevelt; Highway 61 Blues, Champion 16586, 78 rpm ..200.00
Tarter & Gay, Brownie Blues, Victor V38017, 78 rpm 150.00
Taylor, Eva & Her Boyfriends; Farewell Blues, Okeh 3055, 78 rpm, 12" ...100.00
Teardrops, My Heart, Josie 771, 45 rpm 75.00
Thunderbirds, Baby Let's Play House, De Luxe 6075, 45 rpm 50.00
Uncle Skipper, Look What Shape I'm In, Decca 7455, 78 rpm ...30.00
Valens, Ritchie; In Concert at Pacoima Jr High, Del-Fi 1214, LP ...40.00
Vassar, Callie; Original Stomps, Gennett 5173, 78 rpm 75.00
Vaughn, Edith; Mad Mama's Blues, Oriole 298, 78 rpm 15.00
Velours, My Love Come Back, Onyx 501, 45 rpm 40.00
Vincent, Walter; Overtime Blues, Brunswick 7141, 78 rpm 150.00
Walker, T-Bone; Cold Cold Boogie, Imperial 5171 (bl label), 45 rpm ..40.00
Washington, Lizzie; East Coast Blues, Champion 15303, 78 rpm ..150.00
Wheelers, Once I Had a Girl, Cenco 107, 45 rpm 40.00
White Mountain Orchestra, Leather Britches, Victor V40185, 78 rpm .30.00
Young, Billie; You Done Played Out Blues, Victor 23339, 78 rpm ..350.00
Zircons, Return My Love, Winston 1022, 45 rpm 20.00

Country and Western

Allen Bros, Moonshine Bill, Victor 23631, 78 rpm 50.00
Arkansas Charlie, Goodbye Old Paint, Vocalion 5270, 78 rpm ...15.00
Blue Ridge Highballers, Round Town Girls, Columbia 15089-D, 78 rpm ...25.00
Carolina Twins, Since My Baby's Gone Away, Victor 23502, 78 rpm ...40.00
Cobb & Underwood, Black Sheep Blues, Gennett 7311, 78 rpm ...60.00
Davis, Jimmie; Lonely Hobo, Victor 23648, 78 rpm 100.00
Delmore Bros, Smoky Mountain Bill, Bluebird 5589, 78 rpm 12.00
East Texas Serenaders, Ozark Rag, Brunswick 538, 78 rpm 20.00
Fleming & Townsend, Sweet Daddy From Tennessee, Victor 23575, 78 rpm ...50.00
Floyd County Ramblers, Barn Dance, Victor 23759, 78 rpm 75.00
Four Virginians, Swing Your Partner, Okeh 45181, 78 rpm 20.00
Fruit Jar Guzzlers, Kentucky Bootlegger, Paramount 3113, 78 rpm ..50.00
Grinnell Giggers, Plow Boy Hop, Victor 23675, 78 rpm 100.00
Harmonica Jim, The Prisoner's Radio, Superior 2789, 78 rpm 35.00
Humphries Bros, What Made the Wild Cat Wild, Okeh 45501, 78 rpm ..50.00
Jimmy Yate's Boll Weevils, Bloody War, Victor V40065, 78 rpm .40.00
Jones, Carl; My Tennessee Girl, Okeh 45540, 78 rpm 30.00
Kid Smith's Family, Little Bessie, Victor 23576, 78 rpm 50.00
Lonesome Cowgirl, My Mother Was a Lady, Superior 2652, 78 rpm 75.00
Lullaby Larkers, Shine on Harvest Moon, Champion 16257, 78 rpm ...30.00
Martin, Dan; The Cross-Eyed Butcher, Superior 2824, 78 rpm 20.00
Moore, Byrd & Hot Shots; Oh Take Me Back, Champion 16498, 78 rpm ..75.00
Narmour & Smith, Texas Breakdown, Okeh 45492, 78 rpm 80.00
Oaks, Charlie; Poor Little Joe, Vocalion 15103, 78 rpm 10.00
Ozark Rambler, The Wreck of the 1262, Paramount 3322, 78 rpm ..20.00
Parker, Chubby; Down on the Farm, Columbia 15296-D, 78 rpm ..20.00
Porter, Royce; Yes I Do, Look 1001, 45 rpm 50.00
Prairie Ramblers, Kentucky Blues, Victor 23859, 78 rpm 100.00
Quadrillers, Cumberland Blues, Paramount 3009, 78 rpm 20.00
Ray Bros, Mississippi Echoes, Victor 23552, 78 rpm 75.00
Ritter, Tex; Bill the Bar Fly, Decca 5305, 78 rpm 12.00
Rodgers, Jimmie; My Good Gal's Gone, Bluebird 5942, 78 rpm ..40.00
Rogers, Roy; When a Cowboy Sings a Song, Vocalion 04050, 78 rpm ...12.00
Scottsdale String Band, Charleston Wobble, Okeh 45527, 78 rpm ..50.00
Snow, Hank; Country Classics, RCA 1233, LP 20.00
Sons of the Pioneers, Ridin' Home, Decca 5013, 78 rpm 12.00
Sprague, Carl T; Cowboy Love Song, Aurora 418, 78 rpm 30.00
Stripling Bros, Wolves Howling, Vocalion 5412, 78 rpm 40.00
Tennessee Drifters, Boogie Woogie Baby, Dot 1166, 45 rpm 50.00
Tennessee Travelers, Forked Deer, Champion 15300, 78 rpm 40.00
Texas Drifter, Cowboy's Lullaby, Decca 5021, 78 rpm 12.00
Thompson, Ernest E; Medley, Gennett 7139, 78 rpm 30.00
Tubb, Ernest; Favorites, Decca 5301, LP 30.00
Vagabonds, Ninety-Nine Years, Victor 23820, 78 rpm 50.00
Virginia Mtn Boomers, Cousin Sally Brown, Gennett 6687, 78 rpm ...30.00
Virginia Ramblers, Rag Time Annie, Timely Tunes 1561, 78 rpm ..20.00
Wallace, Jerry; O Jailer Bring Back That Key, Superior 2643, 78 rpm ...20.00
Wallace, Sippie; Up the Country Blues, Okeh 8106, 78 rpm 60.00
Williams, Hank; Pan American, Sterling 210, 78 rpm 100.00
Wills, Bob & Texas Playboys; Blue River, Vocalion 03230, 78 rpm ..12.00
Young, Clarence; Little Pal, Champion 15924, 78 rpm 15.00
Young, Faron; Sweethearts or Strangers, Capitol 778, LP 30.00
Zack & Glenn, The Gambler's Lament, Okeh 45212, 78 rpm 10.00

Jazz, Dance Bands, Personalities

Abbott, Larry & Orch; I'm More Than Satisfied, Okeh 41044, 78 rpm ...40.00
Alabama Fuzzy Wuzzies, Congo Stomp, Champion 15415, 78 rpm ...200.00
Alberts, Al & Orch; Building a Nest, Cameo 9142, 78 rpm 15.00
Armstrong, Louis; I'm Gonna Gitcha, Okeh 8343, 78 rpm 75.00
Banks, Billy & Orch; Mighty Sweet, Victor 23399, 78 rpm 125.00
Barrel House Five Orch, Endurance Stomp, Paramount 12875, 78 rpm ..150.00
Blythe's Blue Boys, My Baby, Champion 15528, 78 rpm 200.00
Bryant, Laura; Saturday Night Jag, Paramount 12870, 78 rpm ...150.00
California Poppies, What a Wonderful Time, Sunset 506/507, 78 rpm ...500.00
Cannon's Jug Stomper, Goin' to Germany, Bluebird, 5413, 78 rpm ...100.00
Carter, Benny; Devil's Holiday, Columbia 2898-D, 78 rpm 30.00
Charleston Chasers, Delirium, Columbia 1076-D, 78 rmp 20.00
Chicago Hot Five, Oh! What a Thrill, Victor 23326, 78 rpm 40.00
Count Basie, Pennies From Heaven, Decca 1121, 78 rpm 10.00
Cox, Ida; I Ain't Got Nobody, Paramount 12334, 78 rpm 100.00
Crosby, Bing; Star Dust, Brunswick 6169, 78 rpm 12.00
Dedroit, Johnny; The Swing, Okeh 40090, 78 rpm 40.00
Dixieland Jug Blowers, Carpet Alley, Victor 20480, 78 rpm 60.00
Dixon's Jazz Duo/Maniacs, Crazy Quilt, Paramount 12446, 78 rpm ..75.00
Dorsey Bros, Mary Ann, Okeh 40995, 78 rpm 20.00
Dudley, Roberta; Krooked Blues, Nordskog 3007, 78 rpm 300.00
Elger's Creole Orch, Brotherly Love, Vocalion 15478, 78 rpm ...100.00
Ellington, Duke; Rose Marie, Blu-Disc 1004, 78 rpm 60.00
Frenchy's String Band, Sunshine Special, Columbia 14387-D, 78 rpm ...120.00
Fuller, Bob; Spread Yo' Stuff, Ajax 17091, 78 rpm 25.00
Garland, Judy; Stompin' at the Sovy, Decca 848, 78 rpm 10.00
Glenn Oswald's Serenader's, Bucktown Blues, Victor 19733, 78 rpm ..20.00
Goodman, Benny; A Jazz Holiday, Vocalion 15656, 78 rpm 200.00
Goodman, Benny; Ain'tcha Glad?, Columbia 2835-D, 78 rpm 25.00
Gulf Coast Trio, Grand Opera Blues, Buddy 8041, 78 rpm 100.00
Happy Harmonists, Steady Steppin' Papa, Gennett 5518, 78 rpm ..100.00
Harlem Trio, Fuzzy Wuzzy, Herwin 93012, 78 rpm 200.00
Hayes, Nap; Somethin' Doin', Okeh 45231, 78 rpm 100.00
Herman, Woody; The Goose Hangs High, Decca 1056, 78 rpm ..12.00
Holiday, Billy; Practice Makes Perfect, Okeh 5806, 78 rpm 10.00
Hottentots, Pensacola, Vocalion 15209, 78 rpm 50.00
James, Billy; Sweet Child, Oriole 565, 78 rpm 20.00
James, Harry; From the Bottom of My Heart, Brunswick 8443, 78 rpm 100.00
Jazz Harmonists, Riverboat Shuffle, Claxtonola 40339, 78 rpm .150.00
Jolson, Al; Pullman Porter's Parade, Columbia A-1374, 78 rpm ..40.00
Kay, Dolly; A Good Man Is Hard To Find, Vocalion 15664, 78 rpm ...40.00
Kentucky Jug Band, Walkin' Cane Stop, Vocalion 1564, 78 rpm ..150.00
Keppard, Freddie; Stock Yards Strut, Paramount 12399, 78 rpm ..300.00
Leslie, Nate & His Orch; Shake Yo' Bones, Vocalion 3584, 78 rpm ...20.00
Louisana Rhythm Kings, Little By Little, Vocalion 15841, 78 rpm ..150.00
Mapp, Eddie; Riding the Blues, QRS-7078, 78 rpm 200.00
McKinney's Cotton Pickers, Plain Dirt, V-38097, 78 rpm 40.00
Memphis Jug Band, Boodle Bum Bum, Okeh 8956, 78 rpm 120.00
Miller, Glenn; A Blues Serenade, Columbia 3052-D, 78 rpm 50.00
Mills Bros, Doin' the New Low-Down, Brunswick 6517, 78 rpm .15.00
Missourians, Vine Street Drag, Victor V-38103, 78 rpm 100.00

Nelson, Ozzie & His Orch; Tiger Rag, Bruswick 7523, 78 rpm 10.00
New Orleans Wild Cats...Dancing Joe, Baby Mine, 14662-D, 78 rpm ...100.00
Northwest Melody Boys, Sugar Foot Strut, Champion 15363, 78 rpm ...75.00
Original Indiana Five, Sugar, Banner 6008, 78 rpm 12.00
Pacific Coast Players, Jazzing Around, Radiex 1326, 78 rpm 12.00
Pichon, Walter; Yo Yo, Victor V38544, 78 rpm 75.00
Prima, Louie & New Orleans Gang; Star Dust, Brunswick 7320, 78 rpm 12.00
Rainey, Ma & Georgia Band; Bad Luck Blues, Paramount 12081, 78 rpm ..100.00
Red Devils, Tiger Rag, Columbia 14586-D, 78 rpm 75.00
Rhythm Kings, You Rascal You, Victor 23279, 78 rpm 60.00
Rocky Mountain Trio, Blowin' Off Steam, Gennett 3288, 78 rpm 15.00
Rogers, Ike; It Hurts So Good, Broadway 5081, 78 rpm 200.00
Sammy Smith's Stompers, Blues in My Heart, Clarion 5417-C, 78 rpm ...30.00
Skillet, Dick & Frying Pans; Asphalt Walk, Champion 15883, 78 rpm ..175.00
Smith, Kate; Moon Song, Brunswick 6497, 78 rpm 12.00
State Street Ramblers, Tiger Moan, Champion 16247, 78 rpm .250.00
Sullivan, Joe; Onyx Bringdown, Columbia 2876-D, 78 rpm 40.00
Thomas, Hociel; I Must Have It, Buddy 8020, 78 rpm 150.00
Tin Pan Paraders, Puttin' on the Ritz, Gennett 7148, 78 rpm 20.00
Travelers, I Apologize, Melotone 12227, 78 rpm 10.00
Tucker, Sophie; I've Got a Cross-Eyed Papa, Okeh 40068, 78 rpm ..25.00
University Six, The Camel Walk, Harmony 36-H, 78 rpm 10.00
Vagabonds, You Gotta Be Good to Me, Gennett 6398, 78 rpm ...15.00
Vallee, Rudy; Strange Interlude, Columbia 2702-D, 78 rpm 15.00
Wally Spencer's Georgians, Gold Digger, Champion 15366, 78 rpm ..250.00
Walter Page's Blue Devils, Blue Devil Blues, Vocalion 1463 ......250.00
Waters, Ethel; Jazzin' Babies Blues, Black Swan 14117, 78 rpm ...75.00
Williams, Clarence; Squeeze Me, Broadway 1348, 78 rpm 125.00
Wolverine Orch, Copenhagen, Gennett 5454, 78 rpm 150.00
Young's Creole Jazz Band, Tin Roof Blues, Claxtonola 40272, 78 rpm ...150.00
Zenith Knights, Keep on the Sunny Side, QRS 1039, 78 rpm 25.00

Red Wing

The Red Wing Stoneware Company, founded in 1878, took its name from its location in Red Wing, Minnesota. In 1906 the name was changed to the Red Wing Union Stoneware Company after a merger with several of the other local potteries. For the most part they produced utilitarian wares such as flowerpots, crocks, and jugs. Their early 1930s catalogs offered a line of art pottery vases in colored glazes, some of which featured handles modeled after swan's necks, snakes, or female nudes. Other examples were quite simple, often with classic styling. After the addition of their dinnerware lines in 1935, 'Stoneware' was dropped from the name, and the company became known as Red Wing Potteries, Inc. They closed in 1967.

The pottery was reopened several years ago, and handmade and decorated salt-glazed stoneware is again being produced. Each piece is stamped with the potters' initials and the year of production.

Our artware advisors are Wendy and Leo Frese (Three Rivers Collectibles); they are listed under Texas. For further study we recommend *Red Wing Stoneware, An Identification and Value Guide*, and *Red Wing Collectibles* by Dan DePasquale, Gail Peck, and Larry Peterson; and *Red Wing Art Pottery, Books I and II*, by B.L. Dollen. All are published by Collector Books. Another good reference is *Red Wing Art Pottery* by Ray Reiss (privately published).

Commercial Art Ware and Miscellaneous

Ashtray, book form, w/3 center rests, Radiant Orange 20.00
Ashtray, leaf form, contoured, Silver Gr, #828, 9½" 20.00
Ashtray, leaf form, Fleck Orchid, #739, 5" 28.00
Ashtray, sq w/center rests, gold/brn, #M3005, 11" 36.00
Ashtray, tri-circle w/9 center rests, wht, #742, 9" 60.00
Bowl, Aladdin shape w/scroll hdl, Fleck Zepher Pk, #M1572, 10x7" ...30.00
Bowl, Belle, wht w/orange int, #881, 8" oval 40.00
Bowl, boat shape, pk, #H18, 11½" L 36.00
Bowl, contoured shape, wht, #M1447, 12½" 26.00
Bowl, curled rim, Garden Club, Fleck Nile Bl, #M1463, 12" 48.00
Bowl, fluted, Salmon, #1620, 10" 56.00
Bowl, fluted triangular shape w/ped ft, Cinnamon, #M1485, 8" ...42.00
Bowl, Mandarin, matt gr, #331, 11" L 52.00
Bowl, shell form, Fleck Nile Bl, #M1567, 6" 56.00
Bowl, teardrop shape, gray w/Coral int, #B2108, 11½" 42.00
Candle holder, Deluxe/ivy design, Fleck Gr, #B2504, 14½" 40.00
Candle holder, English Garden, ivory w/brn wipe, #1190, 6" 28.00
Candle holder, fluted, Salmon, #1619, 4½" 20.00
Candle holder, Renaissance, ivory w/brn wipe, #529, 6" 28.00
Candle holder, Sylvan, dbl cup, ivory w/brn wipe, #397, 5½" 28.00
Candle holder, teardrop shape, wht w/gr int, #B1409, 5" 24.00
Centerpiece, bird in center, Lustre Bl w/Coral int, #1037, 8" 72.00
Compote, fluted bowl w/cherubs on ped ft, Cypress Gr/yel, #761, 6" ..100.00
Compote, ribbed w/fluted rim, wht w/gr int, #690, 1960s, 9" 38.00
Compote, Stereoline, Butterscotch, #764, 13" 42.00
Console set, bowl/candle holders, scalloped, wht, #1620/#1619, 3-pc ...55.00
Figurine, bird perched on branch w/tail up, dk forest gr, 10" 22.00
Figurine, Oriental woman, yel, #1308, 10" 130.00
Figurine, swans (2) w/necks twisted, Fleck Gr, #B2506, 9" 165.00
Flowerpot, aqua, w/underplate, #970, 3½" 36.00
Jardiniere, emb vertical leaf design, Walnut Gr, 9x10" dia 130.00
Jardiniere, ped ft, Cypress Gr w/lt yel int, #110, 10" 70.00
Lamp, covered wagons emb on brn/gr crystalline, base: 7¾" 300.00
Leaf dish, dk gr w/yel int, #1429, 10" 40.00
Leaf dish, Lustre Bl w/Coral int, #1251, 12" L 54.00
Leaf dish, Pea Gr w/Caramel int, #428, 14x8" 32.00
Planter, basketweave, yel w/brn int, #431, 10" 32.00
Planter, boat, contour, Cinnamon, #1582, 10" 36.00
Planter, cart (2-wheeled), Celadon Yel, brass hdl, #M1531, 9x7" ...70.00
Planter, deer resting, turq, #1338, 5½" 38.00
Planter, emb gridwork, gr, #1616, 7½" 26.00
Planter, lamb, bl, 6½" 145.00
Planter, shoe, wht w/lt gr int, #651, 6" 80.00
Planter, sq w/emb sqs, gray w/Coral int, #1378, 5½" 45.00
Planter, tulip, yel w/turq int, #896, 7" 40.00
Planter, violin, blk, #1484, 13" 58.00
Urn, wht w/gr int, w/lid, #1056, 9½" 98.00
Vase, acanthus leaf/flower emb on turq, clay exposed, 11½" 70.00
Vase, ball shape w/emb design, wht w/gr int, #1245, 5½" 56.00
Vase, bamboo, wht w/lt gr int, #1400, 8" 42.00
Vase, bud shape, contoured, Fleck Gr, Colonial Buff int, #437, 8" ...28.00
Vase, cattails, Lemon Yel w/gray int, 7½" 36.00
Vase, cloverleaf style, Fleck Zephyr Pk, #1556, 6" 44.00
Vase, cornucopia style, gr w/wht int, hdls, #1356, 7½" 30.00
Vase, cup style w/hdl, Bronze w/Tahitian Gold int, #847, 5½" 58.00
Vase, fan, fluted w/leaf-trimmed hdls, bl w/Coral int, #1102, 8" ..75.00
Vase, fan, Neoclassic, w/beaded hdls, ivory w/gr int, #668, 10" ..225.00
Vase, fan, wht w/gr int, #892, 1950s-60s, 7½" 42.00
Vase, flared rim, lt pk w/wht int, #887, 7½" 67.00
Vase, gladiolus, Cinnamon w/lt gr int, #416, 12" 75.00
Vase, leaf-trimmed hdls & base, brn/tan w/gr int, #1103, 8¼" 62.00
Vase, leaves emb on pk w/wht int, fancy hdls, #1174, 7" 62.00
Vase, magnolias on ivory w/brn wipe, ruffled rim, #975, 6" 42.00
Vase, Medallion/English Garden, turq w/wht int, #1183, 6" 68.00
Vase, oil lamp style w/emb vertical leaves, maroon, #1377, 10" .110.00
Vase, pitcher; English Garden, ivory w/brn wipe, #1187, 12½" ...85.00
Vase, pitcher; fish hdl, yel w/gray int, #220, 10" 120.00
Vase, Prismatique, Persian Bl w/wht int, #797, 11" 82.00
Vase, ribbon, lt pk w/wht int, #1169, 7½" 42.00

Vase, Shell, scrolled hdls, ivory w/pk int, #432, 7¾" 82.00
Vase, snifter, Fleck Yel, #M1442, 8½" 38.00
Vase, stacked cups, w/hdls, Cocoa Brn w/Sagebrush int, #1359, 8" ...35.00
Vase, Sylvan, Coral w/tan int, #445, 8" 78.00
Vase, Tropicana/Desert Flower, gr w/yel int, #B2004, 10" 46.00
Wall pocket, funnel shape, Cypress Gr, #M1630, 10" 110.00
Wall pocket, Magnolia, ivory w/brn wipe, #1630, 7" 175.00

Cookie Jars

Be aware that there is a very good reproduction of the King of Tarts. Except for the fact that the new jars are slightly smaller, they are sometime difficult to distinguish from the old.

Pineapple, yellow, $135.00. (Photo courtesy Ermagene Westfall)

Bob White, unmk 250.00
Carousel, unmk 750.00
Crock, wht 80.00
Dutch Girl (Katrina), yel w/brn trim 175.00
Friar Tuck, cream w/brn, mk 250.00
Friar Tuck, gr, mk 175.00
Friar Tuck, yel, unmk 150.00
Grapes, cobalt or dk purple, ea 275.00
Grapes, gr 135.00
Jack Frost, unmk, short 250.00
Jack Frost, unmk, tall 450.00
King of Tarts, mc, mk (+) 900.00
King of Tarts, pk w/bl & blk trim, mk 600.00
King of Tarts, wht, unmk 250.00
Peasant design, emb/pnt figures on aqua 110.00
Peasant design, emb/pnt figures on brn 120.00
Pierre (chef), bl, unmk 150.00
Pierre (chef), brn, unmk 150.00
Pierre (chef), pk, mk 150.00

Dinnerware

Dinnerware lines were added in 1935, and today collectors scramble to rebuild extensive table services. Although interest is obvious, right now the market is so volatile, it is often difficult to establish a price scale with any degree of accuracy. Asking prices may vary from $50.00 to $200.00 on some items, which indicates instability and a collector market trying to find its way. (One guide currently on the market, for instance, lists Midnight Rose dinner plates at $15.00 to $20.00, while another terms them 'rare,' and values them at $145.00 each.) Sellers seem to be unfamiliar with pattern names and proper identification of the various pieces that each line consists of. There were many hand-decorated lines; among the most popular are Bob White, Tropicana, and Round-Up. But there are other patterns that are just as attractive and deserving of attention. The Dollen books referenced above both have dinnerware sections, and Ray Reiss has published a book called *Red Wing Dinnerware, Price and Identification Guide*, which shows nearly one hundred patterns on its back cover alone.

Town and Country, designed by Eva Zeisel, was made for only one year in the late 1940s. Today many collectors regard Zeisel as one of the most gifted designers of that era and actively seek examples of her work. Town and Country was a versatile line, adaptable to both informal and semiformal use. It is characterized by irregular, often eccentric shapes, and handles of pitchers and serving pieces are usually extensions of the rim. Bowls and platters are free-form comma shapes or appear tilted, with one side slightly higher than the other. Although the ware is unmarked, it is recognizable by its distinctive shapes and glazes. White (often used to complement interiors of bowls and cups), though an original color, is actually more rare than Bronze (metallic brown, also called gunmetal), which enjoys favored status; Gray is unusual. Other colors include Rust, Dusk Blue, Sand, Chartreuse, Peach and Forest Green. Pieces have also shown up in Mulberry and Ming Green and are considered quite rare. (These are Red Wing Quartelle colors!) Note: Eva Zeisel recently gave permission to reissue a few select pieces of Town and Country; these are being made by World of Ceramics. In 1996 salt and pepper shakers were reproduced in *new* colors not resembling Red Wing colors. In 1997 the mixing bowl and syrup were reissued. All new pieces are stamped EZ96 or EZ97 and are visibly different from the old, as far as glaze, pottery base and weight.

Our advisor for this category is Brenda Dollen; she is listed in the Directory under Minnesota. Karen Silvermintz (see Texas) and Charles Alexander (see Indiana) advise on the Town and Country dinnerware.

Bob White, dinner plate, $20.00.

Ardennes, casserole, grip hdl, w/lid 60.00
Ardennes, creamer 25.00
Ardennes, plate, 10" 30.00
Ardennes, shakers, pr 22.00
Bob White, bowl, cereal 22.00
Bob White, casserole, 2-qt 75.00
Bob White, hors d'oeuvres bird 50.00
Bob White, mug 40.00
Bob White, plate, 6" 15.00
Bob White, platter, 13" 75.00
Bob White, relish, 3-part 50.00
Bob White, teapot, w/stand 125.00
Chrysanthemum, bowl, sauce 6.00
Chrysanthemum, butter dish 45.00
Chrysanthemum, creamer 25.00
Chrysanthemum, egg plate, w/lid 75.00
Chrysanthemum, sugar bowl, w/lid 30.00
Crocus, bowl, salad, lg 48.00
Crocus, bowl, vegetable; divided 36.00
Crocus, bread tray 50.00
Crocus, plate, 7½" 20.00
Crocus, relish dish, 6-part 60.00
Desert Sun, plate, 10" 20.00
Desert Sun, platter, 13" 35.00
Desert Sun, relish dish, 3-part 40.00
Desert Sun, teapot, w/lid 75.00

Driftwood, platter, 15" 40.00
Fantasy, chop plate 40.00
Fantasy, cup & saucer 16.00
Fantasy, plate, 6½" 10.00
Fantasy, shakers, pr 25.00
Gypsy Trail, bowls, mixing; assorted colors, 5" to 10", 5-pc set ..135.00
Iris, bowl, rim soup 12.00
Iris, chop plate 40.00
Iris, coffee cup 15.00
Lotus, beverage server 45.00
Lotus, butter dish 40.00
Lotus, cup & saucer 18.00
Morning Glory, bowl, cereal 10.00
Morning Glory, celery tray 20.00
Morning Glory, creamer 12.50
Nassau, coffee cup 25.00
Nassau, gravy boat, w/underplate 80.00
Nassau, plate, 7½" 75.00
Normandy, bowl, cream soup; w/lid 36.00
Normandy, chop plate, 14" 55.00
Normandy, plate, 7" 25.00
Orleans, cup & saucer 22.00
Orleans, gravy boat 50.00
Orleans, nappy 35.00
Orleans, plate, 10" 22.00
Orleans, water jug 80.00
Pink Spice, bowl, buffet; 10½" 54.00
Provincial Oomph, bowls, mixing; brn/aqua, 6", 8", 10", 3-pc set ...80.00
Provincial Oomph, plate, 10" 20.00
Random Harvest, bowl, cereal 17.50
Random Harvest, bowl, dessert; 6¾" 10.00
Random Harvest, bowl, salad; 8½" 30.00
Random Harvest, bowl, sauce; 5" 10.00
Random Harvest, bowl, soup 10.00
Random Harvest, bowl, vegetable; oval 35.00
Random Harvest, cup & saucer 15.00
Random Harvest, plate, 10¾" 25.00
Random Harvest, plate, 8½" 20.00
Random Harvest, teapot 85.00
Round-Up, beverage server 225.00
Round-Up, bowl, salad; 10" 95.00
Round-Up, butter dish 90.00
Round-Up, casserole, 2-pt 95.00
Round-Up, creamer 50.00
Round-Up, plate, 10½" 55.00
Round-Up, plate, 7½" 30.00
Round-Up, relish dish, 3-part 125.00
Round-Up, sugar bowl 20.00
Smart Set, bowl, soup 17.50
Smart Set, creamer 17.50
Smart Set, plate, 6½" 7.50
Smart Set, relish, 3-part 45.00
Tampico, beverage server, w/lid 90.00
Tampico, bowl, fruit; sm 15.00
Tampico, cake stand 80.00
Tampico, mug, coffee, from $40 to 50.00
Tampico, plate, 10½" 35.00
Tampico, trivet, 6½" 75.00
Town & Country, bean pot, Rust, w/lid, minimum value 400.00
Town & Country, bowl, mixing; Dusk Bl 125.00
Town & Country, bowl, vegetable; Sand, 8" 35.00
Town & Country, bowl, 5" 15.00
Town & Country, coaster 18.00
Town & Country, creamer & sugar bowl, w/lid, minimum value .60.00
Town & Country, cruets, mixed colors, orig stoppers, pr 160.00
Town & Country, mug, Coffee 75.00
Town & Country, pitcher, Peach, 3-pt 150.00
Town & Country, plate, Bronze, 10½" 45.00
Town & Country, plate, 10½" 30.00
Town & Country, shakers, Shmoo shape, mixed colors, pr 75.00
Town & Country, teapot, Sand 275.00
Turtle Dove, bowl, cereal 15.00
Turtle Dove, bread tray 55.00
Turtle Dove, shakers, pr 22.00
Vintage, ashtray 30.00
Vintage, butter dish 35.00
Vintage, cup & saucer 26.00
Vintage, platter, sm 30.00
Zinnia, creamer 25.00
Zinnia, cup & saucer 20.00
Zinnia, plate, 6½" 20.00

Stoneware

Key:

c/s — cobalt on stoneware
MN — Minnesota
NS — North Star
RW — Red Wing
RWUS — Red Wing Union Stoneware

Beehive jug, #5/elephant-ear leaves on white, Union Oval, five-gallon, $1,500.00. (Photo courtesy DePasquale and Peterson)

Bean pot, Albany slip, Boston style, RW, 1-gal 250.00
Bean pot, brn & wht, bail hdl, RWUS, 1-qt 95.00
Bowl, batter; Sponge Band, pour spout/bail hdl, RWUS 1,200.00
Bowl, red & bl spatter on wht, 5" 450.00
Bowl, Sponge Band on wht, RWUS, 4" 375.00
Butter crock, Albany slip, low style, MN, 2-lb 50.00
Butter crock, salt glaze, low style, RW, 10-lb 80.00
Butter crock, wht, low style, MN, 10-lb 50.00
Casserole, Sponge Band, RWUS, sm 400.00
Chamber pot, wht, fancy hdl, RW 125.00
Churn, #4/P, c/s, RW, 4-gal 950.00
Churn, #6/butterfly, c/s, RW, 6-gal 1,500.00
Churn, #8/2 birch leaves, c/s, unmk, 8-gal 800.00
Cooler, #25/Ice Water/birch leaves, c/s, RWUS, 25-gal 600.00
Cooler, #4/2 birch leaves, c/s, RW, 4-gal 2,400.00
Cooler, #8/daisy, c/s, RW, 8-gal 2,000.00
Crock, #2/dbl P, c/s, MN, 2-gal 200.00
Crock, #30/lily, c/s, stenciling, RW, 30-gal 2,400.00
Crock, #5/leaf, c/s, RW, 5-gal 500.00
Cuspidor, brn & wht, fancy style, MN, lg 450.00
Cuspidor, brn & wht, molded seam, unmk 200.00
Custard cup, bl shading to wht, unmk 175.00
Jar, butter; Albany slip, high style, MN, 1-gal 70.00
Jar, butter; Albany slip, low style, RW, 1-lb 80.00

Jar, packing; wht, bail hdl, RW, 5-lb 75.00
Jar, preserve/snuff; Albany slip, RW, 2-gal 150.00
Jar, refrigerator; name outlined in rectangle, w/lid & bail hdl, 5-lb ..300.00
Jug, beehive threshing; #5/red wing/oval, c/s, RWUS, 5-gal ...1,000.00
Jug, beehive; #3/birch leaves, c/s, RW oval, 3-gal 350.00
Jug, beehive; Albany slip, #5 etched in glaze, RW, 5-gal 900.00
Jug, common; Albany slip, dome top, MN, 1-gal 75.00
Jug, common; Albany slip, std top, MN, 1-qt 100.00
Jug, fancy; wht w/brn ball top, RW, ½-pt 175.00
Jug, molded seam; wht, bail hdl, MN, 1-gal 125.00
Jug, molded seam; wht, bail hdl, RW, 1-qt 125.00
Jug, shoulder; #3/birch leaves, c/s, standard top, MN, 3-gal 175.00
Jug, shoulder; brn & salt glaze, ball top, RW, 1-gal 225.00
Jug, shoulder; brn & salt glaze, dome top, MN, ½-gal 200.00
Jug, shoulder; brn & salt glaze, pear top, NS, 1-gal 375.00
Jug, shoulder; red wing on wht, brn top, 2-gal 500.00
Jug, shoulder; wht, funnel top, MN, 2-gal 75.00
Jug, shoulder; wht, std top, MN, 1-pt 90.00
Jug, shoulder; wht, std top, RW, 2-gal 75.00
Pipkin, Albany slip, unmk, 2-pt 85.00
Pitcher, Albany slip w/emb irises, RW 175.00
Pitcher & bowl, emb lily on wht w/pale bl at top & rim, RW ...850.00
Spittoon, bl sponging on wht, unmk 550.00
Syrup, wht, cone top, MN, 1-gal 70.00
Umbrella stand, red & bl sponging on wht, unmk 1,300.00
Water bottle, leaf motif, bl & wht, RWUS 1,400.00

Redware

The term redware refers to a type of simple earthenware produced by the Colonists as early as the 1600s. The red clay used in its production was abundant throughout the country, and during the eighteenth and nineteenth centuries redware was made in great quantities. Intended for utilitarian purposes such as everyday tableware or use in the dairy, redware was simple in design and decoration. Glazes of various colors were used, and a liquid clay referred to as 'slip' was sometimes applied in patterns such as zigzag lines, daisies, or stars. Plates often have a 'coggled' edge, similar to the way a pie is crimped or jagged, which is done with a special tool. In the following listings, EX (excellent condition) indicates only minor damage. Our advisor for this category is Barbara Rosen; she is listed in the Directory under New Jersey.

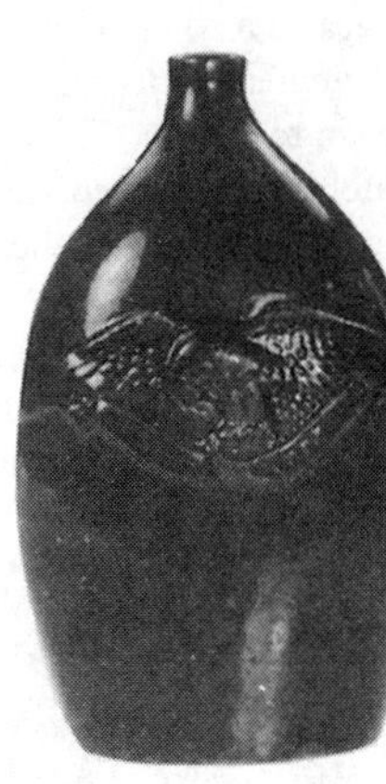

Flask, Eagle - Eagle/Pluribus Unum (in banner), Albany slip, minor chipping at lip, 1850 – 1870, 7¼", $400.00.

Bank, spool shape w/emb ribs, 4x2½", EX 70.00
Bowl, brn & orange 2-tone, rim hdls, pouring spout, 6½x9¾" 50.00
Bowl, dk brn, tapered collar, 3½x5", NM 100.00
Bowl, dk brn w/manganese splotches, 3⅜x8¾" 95.00
Bowl, gr mottle w/amber spots, 3x6¾" 275.00
Bowl, gr-brn mottle, flat bottom, flared sides, 2⅞x6⅝" 65.00
Bowl, milk; brn & yel slip in str & wavy lines, 3x11", VG 385.00
Bowl, milk; yel slip border stripe on rim, rpr chip, 5¼x12" 50.00
Bowl, orange, flared sides, flattened rim, 3¾x11", EX 70.00
Bowl, vegetable; dk brn sponging, beaded rim, 8¼" 585.00
Bowl, yel slip in str & wavy lines, 8⅝" 275.00
Cheese bowl/cup, gr/orange mottle, flared sides, 2⅝x4¼" 60.00
Cheese bowl/cup, orange-brn w/yel slip decor, 1½x2" 225.00
Cream pot, dk brn mottle w/incised decor, strap hdl, 4¾x4⅜" 90.00
Creamer, yel/gr/gold mottle, globular, pinched spout, C hdl, 3⅜" ...330.00
Crock, apple butter; dk brn, flared/flattened rim, 4x4⅜", EX 65.00
Crock, brn mottling, 5⅜x6⅛" 45.00
Cup, stirrup; hound figural, late 18th C, chips, 4½" 288.00
Egg cup, blk sponging, sm flakes, 3" 465.00
Flowerpot & saucer, dk brn, flared sides, 6x6¾", 1x6", EX 90.00
Foot warmer, ram figural, minor chips, 19th C, 6¾x13½" 500.00
Jar, brn splotches on burnt orange, wear/sm chips, ovoid, w/lid, 8" ..110.00
Jar, lt brn w/dk brn slip at shoulder, 1850s, 8½" 350.00
Jar, storage; dk brn w/incised decor, knob finial, 7x5" 150.00
Jar, storage; orange-brn w/manganese splotches, ear hdls, 9x7¼" ...140.00
Jug, dk brn, ovoid, strap hdl, 10x7" dia, EX 75.00
Jug, dk brn w/some mottling, ½-gal, 8¾x5", EX 95.00
Jug, gr mottle, ribbed strap hdl, 8½", EX 85.00
Jug, olive gr w/brn & orange mottle, ovoid, 9½" 700.00
Lion, yel slip w/spaghetti mane, brn highights, 9¼" 500.00
Lion on rectangular base, mottled tan & cream, 8¾" L 385.00
Loaf pan, yel slip w/polka-dot bird/foliage, coggled rim, 16" 550.00
Loaf pan, 3-line yel slip, coggled rim, wear/hairline/chips, 17" ..700.00
Mold, Turk's head, brn sponging, fluted, sm chips, 8" 85.00
Mold, Turk's head, brn w/splotches, vertical ribs, 3½x10" 110.00
Mold, Turk's head, dk brn, fluted body, scalloped rim, 2x7¼", EX ...60.00
Mold, Turk's head, manganese, emb swirls, 2⅛x6⅛" dia 50.00
Mold, Turk's head, orange-brn w/manganese splotches, 2¾x9½", EX ...65.00
Mold, yel-gr mottle, int vertical fluting, 2⅜x3⅞", EX 130.00
Mug, milk; gray-gr w/orange mottling, 5¾" 1,500.00
Pie plate, brn splotches on salmon, old patina, 8⅛" 220.00
Pie plate, brn sponging, hairline, 8¼" 135.00
Pie plate, dk brn w/triple yel slip crow's ft designs, 1¼x7¼" 150.00
Pie plate, orange-brn w/yel slip linear decor, 1¾x7½" 120.00
Pie plate, 3-line yel slip, coggled rim, chips, 10" 450.00
Pie plate, 3-line yel slip, coggled rim, 8" 195.00
Pitcher, brn mottle, w/lid & offset hdl, 5¼" 450.00
Pitcher, brn sponging on red, strap hdl, w/lid, 9" 525.00
Pitcher, milk; brn mottled, pinched spout, C hdl, 8⅛", EX 160.00
Pitcher, milk; brn w/manganese splotches, globular, 6¾", NM ..100.00
Plate, orange-brn w/yel slip entwined lines & dots, coggled rim, 9" ...200.00
Plate, orange-brn w/yel slip squiggles, coggled rim, 10", EX 250.00
Plate, slip stylized leaves (4), crimped edge, 9¾" 485.00
Pot, dk brn sponging, strap hdl, mismatched lid, 5", EX 110.00
Pot, 4 yel slip bands, bulbous, appl hdl, 6½x5½", EX+ 400.00
Sugar bowl, dk brn, globular w/arched hdls, w/lid, 5x5", EX 925.00
Whistle, dk brn, vasiform, unglazed spout, 19th C, 3¾" 485.00

Regal China

Located in Antioch, Illinois, the Regal China Company opened for business in 1938. Products of interest to collectors are James Beam decanters, cookie jars, salt and pepper shakers, and similar novelty items. The company closed its doors sometime in 1993. The Old MacDonald Farm series listed below is especially collectible, so are the salt and pepper shakers.

Note: Where applicable, prices are based on excellent gold trim.

(Gold trim must be 90% intact or deductions should be made for wear.) See also Decanters.

Alice in Wonderland

Cookie jar, from $3,000.00 to $3,200.00. (Photo courtesy Fred and Joyce Roerig)

Creamer, White Rabbit, from $625 to 650.00
Pitcher, King of Hearts, milk sz 650.00
Shakers, matching colors, rare, pr, from $600 to 675.00
Shakers, Tweedledee & Tweedledum, pr 850.00
Shakers, wht w/gold trim, pr 675.00
Sugar bowl, White Rabbit, w/lid 600.00
Teapot, Mad Hatter 2,500.00

Cookie Jars

Cat, from $375 to 425.00
Churn Boy 275.00
Clown, gr collar, from $700 to 750.00
Davy Crockett, from $500 to 550.00
Dutch Girl, from $675 to 725.00
Dutch Girl, peach trim 800.00
FiFi Poodle, from $675 to 725.00
Fisherman, from $700 to 800.00
French Chef, from $400 to 450.00
Goldilocks (+) 375.00
Harpo Marx 1,200.00
Hobby Horse, from $275 to 300.00
Hubert Lion, $800 to 950.00
Humpty Dumpty, red 325.00
Little Miss Muffett, from $350 to 385.00
Majorette, from $425 to 675.00
Oriental Lady w/Baskets, from $650 to 700.00
Peek-a-Boo (+), from $1,400 to 1,500.00
Quaker Oats 125.00
Three Bears 285.00
Toby Cookies, unmk, from $750 to 775.00
Tulip 300.00
Uncle Mistletoe 850.00

Old McDonald's Farm

Butter dish, cow's head 220.00
Canister, flour, cereal, coffee; med, ea, from $225 to 275.00
Canister, pretzels, peanuts, popcorn, chips, tidbits; lg, ea, $325 to ..375.00
Canister, salt, sugar, tea; med, ea, from $225 to 275.00
Canister, soap, cookies, lg, ea, from $350 to 425.00
Cookie barn, from $275 to 300.00
Creamer, rooster, from $110 to 125.00
Grease jar, pig, from $200 to 250.00
Pitcher, milk, from $425 to 500.00
Shakers, boy & girl, pr 75.00
Shakers, churn, gold trim, pr, from $75 to 90.00
Shakers, feed sacks w/sheep, pr 195.00
Spice jar, assorted lids, sm, ea, from $100 to 150.00
Sugar bowl, hen 125.00
Teapot, duck's head, from $275 to 350.00

Shakers

A Nod to Abe, 3-pc nodder 300.00
Bendel, bears, wht w/pk & brn trim, pr 100.00
Bendel, bunnies, wht w/blk & pk trim, pr, from $150 to 200.00
Bendel, kissing pigs, gray w/pk trim, lg, pr, from $400 to 450.00
Bendel, love bugs, burgundy, lg, pr, from $175 to 225.00
Bendel, love bugs, gr, sm, pr 65.00
Cat, sitting w/eyes closed, wht w/hat & gold bow, pr 225.00
Clown, pr 450.00
Dutch Girl, pr 275.00
Fifi, pr 450.00
Fish, mk C Miller, 1-pc 55.00
French Chef, wht w/gold trim, pr, from $250 to 350.00
Humpty Dumpty, pr 140.00
Peek-a-Boo, red dots, lg, pr (+), from $450 to 500.00
Peek-a-Boo, red dots, sm, pr, from $250 to 275.00
Peek-a-Boo, wht solid, sm, pr 200.00
Pig, pk, mk C Miller, 1-pc 95.00
Tulip, pr 50.00
Van Telligen, bears, brn, pr, from $25 to 28.00
Van Telligen, boy & dog, wht, pr 65.00
Van Telligen, bunnies, solid colors, pr, from $25 to 28.00
Van Telligen, ducks, pr 35.00
Van Telligen, Dutch boy & girl, pr, from $40 to 45.00
Van Telligen, Mary & lamb, pr 55.00
Van Telligen, sailor & mermaid, pr, from $200 to 250.00

Relief-Molded Jugs

Early relief-molded pitchers (ca 1830s – 40s) were made in two-piece molds into which sheets of clay were pressed. The relief decoration was deep and well defined, usually of animal or human subjects. Most of these pitchers were designed with a flaring lip and substantial footing. Gradually styles changed, and by the 1860s the rim had become flatter and the foot less pronounced. The relief decoration was not as deep, and foliage became a common design. By the turn of the century, many other types of pitchers had been introduced, and the market for these early styles began to wane.

Watch for recent reproductions; these have been made by the slip-casting method. Unlike relief-molded ware which is relatively smooth inside, slip-cast pitchers will have interior indentations that follow the irregularities of the relief decoration. Values below are for pieces in excellent condition. Our advisor for this category is Kathy Hughes; she is listed in the Directory under North Carolina.

Cup Tosser or Reading the Tea Leaves by Worthing and Green, ca 1855, 8½", $250.00. (Photo courtesy Kathy Hughes)

Key: Reg — Registered

Apostle, wht, Meigh, 1842, 9⅞" 565.00
Ariadne, Samuel Alcock & Co, ca 1850, 9" 550.00
Bacchanalian Dance loving cup, bl/wht parian, Meigh, 6½" 675.00
Barley, gr, Dudson, April 25, 1861, 8" 175.00
Beaded Medallions, parian, unmk, 19th C, 7" 125.00
Bullrushes on bl-gray, Ridgway & Abington, Reg Mar 7, 1848, 9" 200.00
Dancers, George Ray of Longton, Reg April 21, 1852, 6" 250.00
Eglington Tournament, buff, Ridgway, 1840, 7¼" 375.00
Equestrian Hunters, grapevines, lt gr, branch hdl, unmk, 6" 150.00
Gipsy (sic), lav on parian, Alcock, Reg July 1, 1842, 4¾" 350.00
Gleaner, Edward Walley, Reg Nov 11, 1858, 10¾" 550.00
Gothic Floral, bl/brn/wht, Beech & Hancock, 7/14/1862, 8" 250.00
Hunters & Hounds, gray-gr w/wht vintage, Wedgwood, 1810, 6⅞" 500.00
Ivy, creamer w/mc enameled trim, S Alcock, 5½" 625.00
Jousting Jug, Ridgway, Reg Sept 1, 1840, 7¼" 375.00
Moses & the Rock, Ridgway & Abington, Jan 1, 1859, 5½" 275.00
Musical Instruments, WT Copeland, ca 1855, 10" 550.00
Nineveh, Ridgway & Abington, Reg August 15, 1851 ....800.00
Nymphea, WT Copeland, May 30, 1861, 6" 300.00
Pan, buff, w/lid, Ridgway, 1830s, 7¼" 275.00
Pansies & Leaves, wht on bl, hinged lid, Dixon & Sons on lid, 8" .185.00
Prince Consort, Old Hall Earthenware Co, Apr 9, 1862, 8" 750.00
Rose, parian, unmk, ca 1850, 6½" 175.00
Silenus, gr, Minton, 1845, 9" 425.00
Sleeping Beauty, teal & wht, Dudson, ca 1860, 5¼" 185.00
Tam-O'-Shanter, glazed bl, Ridgeway, 1835, 8¼" 295.00
Two Drivers, gray, Minton, ca 1849, 7⅞" 750.00
Victoria Regina, Sanford Pottery, July 6, 1860, 9¾" 750.00

Restraints

Since the beginning of time, many things from animals to treasures have been held in bondage by hemp, bamboo, chests, chains, shackles, and other constructed devices. Many of these devices were used to hold captives who awaited further torture, as if the restraint wasn't torturous enough. The study and collecting of restraints enables one to learn much about the advancement of civilization in the country or region from which they originated. Such devices at various times in history were made of very heavy metals — so heavy that the wearer could scarcely move about. It has only been in the last sixty years that vast improvements have been made in design and construction that afford the captive some degree of comfort. Our advisor for this category is Joseph Tanner; he is listed in the Directory under California.

Key:
bbl — barrel
d-lb — double lock button
K — key
Kd — keyed
lc — lock case
NST — non-swing through
ST — swing through
stp — stamped

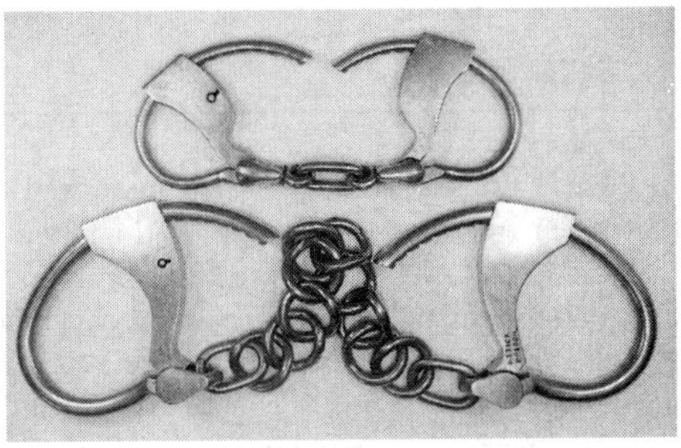

Tower Double Lock handcuffs, non-swing through, takes barrel-bitted key, $60.00; Tower Double Lock leg irons, $100.00.

Foreign Handcuffs

Australian, Saf Lock, ST, takes pin-tumbler K in side, stp 160.00
Czechalaviak, ST, Ralken flat key, modern ST 100.00
Deutsche Polizei, ST, middle hinge, folds, takes bbl-bit K 80.00
East German, aluminum, single lg hinge, ST, bbl key 60.00
East German, heavy steel, NP single lg hinge, NST, bbl key 90.00
English, Chubb, NST, hi-security 10-slider lock mechanism 300.00
English, Chubb Arrest, steel, ST, multi-bit solid K 250.00
English, Latrobe, aluminum alloy, center chain, ST, dbl-bit K ...160.00
French Lapegy, ST, aluminum alloys, takes flat bitted K 75.00
French Revolved, oval, ST, takes 2 Ks: bbl & pin tumbler 150.00
German, Swartiger, steel, NST, bbl K goes in at end of cuffs 400.00
German, 3-lb steel set, 2⅝" thick, center chain, bbl K 175.00
German Clejuso, oval design, ST, dbl-cuff weight, 22-oz 100.00
German Clejuso, sq lc, adjusts/NST, d-lb on side, bbl K 100.00
German Darby, adjusts, well finished, NST, sm 120.00
German Hamburg 8, non-adjust NST, center bar/post w/K-way ...250.00
Hiatt, English Darby, like US CW Darby, stp Hiatt & #d 75.00
Hiatt, solid state, 2 separate cuffs joined bk to bk, stp/#d 165.00
Hiatt English non-adjust screw K Darby style, uses screw K 100.00
Hiatt Figure 8, swings open to insert/withdraw wrists 125.00
Italian, stp New Police, modern Peerless type, ST, sm bbl K 35.00
Plug 8, remove plug before inserting external threaded K 200.00
Russian modern ST, blued bbl key, unmk, crude 80.00
Spanish, stp Alcyon/Star, modern Peerless type, flat K 65.00
Spanish, stp Alcyon/Star, modern Peerless type, ST, sm bbl K 45.00

Foreign Leg Shackles

East German, aluminum, lg hinge, cable amid 4 cuffs, bbl key 80.00
German Clejuso, sq lc, adjusts/NST, d-bl on side, bbl K 125.00
German Clejuso Darby type, adjusts/NST/plated, uses screw K .160.00
Hiatt English combo manacles, handcuff/leg irons w/chain 275.00
Hiatt English non-adjust screw K Darby style, uses screw K 100.00
Hiatt Plug leg irons, same K-ing as Plug-8 cuffs, w/chain 225.00

U.S. Handcuffs

Adams, teardrop lc, bbl Kd, NST, usually not stp 170.00
American Munitions, modern/rnd, sm bbl Kd, ST bow, stp 45.00
Bean Giant, sideways figure-8, solid center lc, dbl-bit K 450.00
Bean Patrolman, kidney-bean form, d-lb on lc, NST, stp T 100.00
Bean-Cobb, sm rnd lc, removable cylinder, d-lb, NST, 1899 ....90.00
Cavenay, looks like Marlin Daley but w/screw K, NST 160.00
Civil War padlocking type, various designs w/loop for lock 200.00
Colt, modern ST bow, sm bbl Kd, stp w/Colt & Co name 160.00
Flash Action Manacle, like Bean Giant w/ST, K-way center 250.00
Flexibles, steel segmented bows, NST Darby type, screw K 150.00
Guardian, modern ST, NP steel, bbl K 60.00
H&R Super, ST, shaft-hinge connector takes hollow titted K ...100.00
Harvard, takes sm bbl K, ST, stp Harvard Lock Co 65.00
Judd, NST, used rnd/internally triangular K, stp Mattatuck 120.00
Lilly Hand Iron, 2" strap iron (8" L), oval bands, NST, sq K 500.00
Marlin Daley, NST, bottle-neck form, neck stp, dbl-titted K 200.00
Mattatuck, NST, propeller-like K-way, stp Mattatuck/etc 90.00
Palmer, 2" steel bands, 2 K-ways (top & center), NST stp 300.00
Peerless, ST, takes sm bbl K, stp Mfg'ered by Peerless Co 40.00
Peerless, ST, takes sm bbl K, stp Mfg'ered by S&W Co 75.00
Peerless Big Guy, modern ST, bbl key 50.00
Phelps, NST, twist chain between cuffs, Tower look-alike 250.00
Pratt combo, 1 cuff connnects w/nipper/claw, ST, mk Pratt 275.00
Providence Tool Co, stp, NST, Darby screw K style 120.00
Rankin, steel NST, mk screw K 225.00

Romer, NST, takes flat K, resembles padlock, stp Romer Co 250.00
S&W 94 Maximum Security, ST, takes Ace-type K, stp S&W 90.00
Strauss, ST, takes lg solid bitted K, stp Strauss Eng Co 85.00
Tower, NST, bottom K, solid/flat-fitted K goes in cuff edge 100.00
Tower bar cuffs, cuffs separate by 10-12" steel bar 120.00
Tower Detective Pinkerton, NST, sq lc, bbl-bitted K, no stp 120.00
Tower Single Lock, NST, bbl-bit K, K-way slanted on lc, sm 70.00
Tower-Bean, NST, sm rnd lc, takes tiny bbl-bitted K, stp 75.00
Tri-lock, heavy polymer & stainless steel, ST, triple lock 200.00
Walden 'Lady Cuff,' NST, takes sm bbl K, lightweight, stp 300.00

U.S. Leg Shackles

American Munitions, as handcuffs 55.00
Civil War or prison ball & chain, padlocking or rivet type 300.00
Cloc spike, 30" L opening for ankle w/padlock & 2 spikes 500.00
H&R Supers, as handcuffs 400.00
Harvard, as handcuffs 75.00
Judd, as handcuffs 135.00
Leg lock brace, metal brace, ankle to knee, lever locked 225.00
Oregon boot, break-apart shackle on above ankle support 700.00
Palmer, as handcuffs but w/detachable chain, NST 425.00
Peerless Big Guy, modern ST, bbl key 60.00
Providence Tool Co, stp, NST 150.00
Strauss, as handcuffs 125.00
Tower, bottom K, as handcuffs 100.00
Tower ball & chain, leg iron w/chain & 6-lb to 50-lb ball 250.00
Tower Detective, as handcuffs 150.00

Various Other Restraining Devices

African slave Darby-style cuffs, heavy iron/chain, handmade 130.00
African slave Darby-style leg shackles, heavy/hand forged 160.00
African slave padlocking or riveted forged iron shackles 135.00
Argus iron claw, twist T to open & close 40.00
Darby neck collar, rnd steel loop opens w/screw K 200.00
English figure-8 nipper, claws open by lifting top lock tab 80.00
Gale finger cuff, knuckle duster, non-K, mk GFC 125.00
German nipper, twist hdl opens/closes cuff, stp Germany/etc 75.00
Jay Pee, thumb cuffs, mk solid body, bbl K 15.00
Mighty-Mite, thumb cuffs, solid body, ST, mk, bbl K 75.00
Phillips nipper, claw, flip lever on top to open 80.00
Thomas Nipper, claw, push button top to open 80.00
Tower Lyon, thumb cuffs, solid body, NST, dbl-bit center K 170.00

Reverse Painting on Glass

Verre eglomise is the technique of painting on the underside of glass. Dating back to the early 1700s, this art became popular in the nineteenth century when German immigrants chose historical figures and beautiful women as subjects for their reverse glass paintings. Advertising mirrors of this type came into vogue at the turn of the century.

George and Martha Washington portraits, original frames, 22x20", $2,400.00 for the pair. (Photo courtesy Garth's Auctions)

Lady in bl dress w/wht collar on gr ground, 15x11⅝"+fr 550.00
Sinking of Titanic w/rafts in water, dark, 15½x19½", EX 150.00
Victorian seated at table w/book, 13½x10½"+fr 135.00

Richard

Richard, who at one time worked for Galle, made cameo art glass in France during the 1920s. His work was often multilayered and acid cut with florals and scenics in lovely colors. The ware was marked with his name in relief. Our advisor for this category is Don Williams; he is listed in the Directory under Missouri.

Cameo

Chandelier, pine cones/butterfly, brn on yel mottle, 15" dia ...3,250.00
Lamp, 7½" dome shade w/mtns/castle; 3-D bird on metal base ..2,500.00
Vase, floral stalks, bl-blk on gold-yel, ftd, slim, 6½" 525.00
Vase, scenic, lt on dk purple, 18¼" 2,000.00
Vase, trees/sailboats/mtns, bl on dk red, ftd, crimped rim, 6" 850.00

Ridgway

As early as 1792, the Ridgway brothers, Job and George, produced fine quality earthenwares in Shelton, Staffordshire, marking their products 'Ridgway, Smith, & Ridgway,' and later 'Job & George Ridgway.' Around 1800 the brothers split, and each had his own firm, both at Shelton. They were joined in the business by various members of the Ridgway family, and, in fact, their descendants still operate there today.

The two firms created by the split were the Bell Works and the Cauldon Pottery. Bell produced stone china and earthenware decorated with blue transfer printing. Their mark was 'J. & W. Ridgway' or J. & W.R.' (John and William) until 1848 when 'William Ridgway' was used. The Cauldon Pottery made earthenware, stone china, and high quality porcelains fine enough to win them the distinction of being appointed potters to the Queen. From 1830 their wares attest to this fact, bearing the Royal Arms mark with 'J.R.' within the crest. In 1940 '& Co.' was added. Most examples of Ridgway's wares found today are transfer-printed historical scenes. See also Staffordshire, Historical; and Flow Blue.

Baking dish, Coaching Days, 11¼x6¼" 75.00
Bowl, Coaching Days, w/silver trim, 9½" dia 75.00
Creamer & sugar bowl, Coaching Days, w/tray 210.00
Cup & saucer, Coaching Days 40.00
Hot plate, Coaching Days, 6" dia 125.00
Pitcher, Coaching Days, 8" 95.00
Plate, Coaching Days, 9" 35.00
Plate, Coaching Days, 6" 27.50
Plate, Coaching Days, 8" 30.00
Plate, cup; giraffes w/floral & scroll border, 3¾" dia 210.00
Plate, Indus, crane & bamboo floral border w/birds, lt brn, 9¼" ..60.00
Tankard, Coaching Days, 5" 50.00

Rie, Lucie

Lucie Rie was born in 1902. She moved to London in 1938 and shared her studio with Hans Coper from 1946 to 1958. Her ceramics look modern; however they are based on shapes from many world cultures dating back to Roman times. Lucie Rie is best known for the use of metallic oxides in her clay and glazes. She specializes in the hand throwing of thin porcelain bowls, which is a very difficult process. Her works are in the world's best museums. All of her ceramics are impressed with a seal mark on the bottom, a cojoined 'L & R' within a rectangular reserve. Recently when her work is offered at auction, it has been bringing prices that are sometimes double the presale estimates.

Bowl, wht w/bronze band at rim w/runs along body, ftd, 7¼" 8,000.00
Vase, beige w/brn, cylindrical w/diagonal fluting, invt rim, 6" ..3,165.00
Vase, pitted wht w/brn speckles, long neck, flared rim, 14½" .10,925.00
Vase, tan & cream w/diagonal brn sgraffito lines, mk, 7⅛" 5,750.00
Vase, wht w/brn spots, tall neck, flattened shoulder, 17" 9,775.00

Riviera

Riviera was a line of dinnerware introduced by the Homer Laughlin China Company in 1938. It was sold exclusively by the Murphy Company through their nationwide chain of dime stores. Riviera was unmarked, lightweight, and inexpensive. It was discontinued sometime prior to 1950. Colors are mauve blue, red, yellow, light green, and ivory. On rare occasions, dark blue pieces are found, but this was not a standard color. For further information we recommend *The Collector's Encyclopedia of Fiesta* by Sharon and Bob Huxford, available from Collector Books.

Teacup and saucer, $15.00.

Batter set, complete 285.00
Batter set, ivory, w/decals, complete 170.00
Bowl, baker; 9" 28.00
Bowl, cream soup; w/liner, ivory 95.00
Bowl, fruit; 5½" 12.00
Bowl, nappy; 7¼" 28.00
Bowl, oatmeal; 6" 40.00
Bowl, utility; ivory 50.00
Butter dish, cobalt, ¼-lb 250.00
Butter dish, colors other than cobalt or turq, ¼-lb 135.00
Butter dish, turq, ¼-lb 290.00
Butter dish, ½-lb 140.00
Casserole 110.00
Creamer 12.00
Cup & saucer, demitasse; ivory 80.00
Jug, open, ivory, 4½" 95.00
Jug, w/lid 130.00
Pitcher, juice; mauve bl 210.00
Pitcher, juice; yel 120.00
Plate, deep 24.00
Plate, 10" 55.00
Plate, 6" 8.00
Plate, 7" 12.00
Plate, 9" 18.00
Platter, closed hdls, 11¼" 28.00
Platter, cobalt, 12" 70.00
Platter, 11½" 25.00
Platter, 15" 60.00
Sauce boat 27.00
Shakers, pr 20.00
Sugar bowl, w/lid 20.00
Teapot 145.00
Tidbit, ivory, 2-tier 75.00
Tumbler, hdl 75.00
Tumbler, hdl, ivory 145.00
Tumbler, juice 52.00

Robineau

After short-term training in ceramics in 1903, Adelaide Robineau (with the help of her husband Samuel) built a small pottery studio at her home in Syracuse, New York. She was adept in mixing the clay and throwing the ware, which she often decorated by incising designs into the unfired clay. Samuel developed many of the glazes and took charge of the firing process. In 1910 she joined the staff of the American Women's League Pottery at St. Louis, where she designed the famous Scarab Vase. After this pottery failed, she served on the faculty of Syracuse University. Her work was and is today highly acclaimed for the standards of excellence to which she aspired.

Bowl, celadon & amber crystalline, incurvate rim, #260, 4x6" ...7,500.00
Vase, bright gr mottle, AR mk, 2x1¾" 600.00
Vase, gr/bl/taupe/brn hi-glaze, #627, 5½" W 3,500.00

Robj

Robj was the name of a retail store that operated in Paris for only a few years, from about 1925 to 1931. Robj solicited designs from the best French artisans of the period to produce decorative objects for the home. These were executed mostly in porcelain but there were glass and earthenware pieces as well. The most well known are the figural bottles which were particularly popular in the United States. However, Robj also promoted tea sets, perfume lamps, chess sets, ashtrays, bookends, humidors, powder jars, cigarette boxes, figurines, lamps, and milk pitchers. Robj objects tend to be whimsical, and all embody the Art Deco style. Items listed below are ceramic unless noted otherwise. Our advisors for this category are Randall Monsen and Rod Baer; their address is listed in the Directory under Virginia.

Set of five decanters: Lady in blue, Scottish man with bag pipes, Man in green double-breasted jacket, Napoleon, Man in blue with pipe, all with hat stoppers, marked, 10" to 10½", $1,150.00 for the set. (If sold separately values would be from $250.00 to $300.00 each.)

Decanter, bearded man in orange robe w/blk cuffs, mk, 10½" ...250.00
Jar, Fr policeman, blk w/yel & wht, ca 1920, 9½" 635.00

Lamp, perfume; Oriental medallions, flattened oval, mk, 5½" ...330.00

Rock 'N Roll Memorabilia

Memorabilia from the early days of rock 'n roll recalls an era that many of us experienced firsthand; these listings are offered to demonstrate the many and various aspects of this area of collecting. Beware of reproductions! Many are so well done even a knowledgeable collector will sometimes be fooled.

Our advisor for Elvis memorabilia is Rosalind Cranor, author of *Elvis Collectibles* and *Best of Elvis Collectibles* (Overmountain Press); she is listed in the Directory under Virginia. The remainder is under the advisement of Bob Gottuso, author of Beatles and Kiss sections in *Garage Sale Gold* by Tomart; see Pennsylvania. For more information we recommend *Rock-N-Roll Treasures* by Joe Hilton and Greg Moore (Collector Books).

Beatles, Remco vinyl figures, 4", complete with instruments, M, set of four, $425.00. (Photo courtesy June Moon)

Allman Brothers, poster, Gardens Auditorium, 1972, 17x11" 800.00
Beatles, bag, vinyl, hang tags, Japan, 1966, EX 125.00
Beatles, blow-up dolls, 1 ea member, US, 14", set of 4 ....150.00
Beatles, book, Out of the Mouths..., softcover, 1964, VG 15.00
Beatles, cake decorations, swingers, bl, 1964, 2", sealed 90.00
Beatles, charm, from gumball machine, record shape w/images, NM ...10.00
Beatles, doll, Ringo, rubber, King Features, 1964, 6" 450.00
Beatles, dolls, Sgt Pepper, Applause, '88, 22", M w/stands, 4 for ...385.00
Beatles, flasher rings, set of 4, EX 60.00
Beatles, Flip Your Wig Game, Milton Bradley, 1964, EX, from $180 to ..200.00
Beatles, handbag, vinyl w/brass hdls, Dame, 1964, 10x10" 500.00
Beatles, harmonica, Hohner, 1964, MOC 600.00
Beatles, hummer, Louis F Dow, cb w/head shots, 1960s, NM 150.00
Beatles, key ring, Apple Records, apple shape 125.00
Beatles, mobile, Sunshine Art Studios, cb pop-outs, unused, MIP ...140.00
Beatles, money clip, Apple Records, apple shape 175.00
Beatles, pen, faces on shirt clip, Randall, 1964 ....80.00
Beatles, poster, Ringo For President, blk & wht, 1964 ....175.00
Beatles, punch-out portraits, Whitman, cb, unpunched, 1964, NM ..200.00
Beatles, sticker from gumball machine, gold & blk w/faces & names, EX ...25.00
Beatles, wig, Lowell, MIP 135.00
Bee Gees, mirror, picture & logo, EX 25.00
Bee Gees, patch, wht w/blk & red letters, fan club issue, 1979 ....35.00
Bee Gees, school folder, by Rock On, 1979 ....25.00
Bob Dylan, Gerdes Folk City handbill, Sept 26-Oct 28, 1961, M ..2,500.00
Buddy Holly & the Crickets, sheet music, Oh Boy!, 1957 ....150.00
Cat Stevens, frisbee, yel, promo, 1980s 12.50
Chubby Checker, concert program, United Kingdom, 1962 ....95.00
Chubby Checker/4 Seasons/Platters, poster, Philadelphia, 1972 ...300.00
Chuck Berry, sheet music, School Day, 1957 ....100.00
Creedence Clearwater Revival, poster, July 10, 1970 ....350.00
Dick Clark, cuff links, on orig American Bandstand card, 1958 ..85.00
Dick Clark Show, program, various performers, 1950s, EX 125.00

Elvis Presley, karate gi, white cotton with red satin trim, embroidered initials on the back, EX, $500.00.

Elvis Presley, board game, The EP Game, 1956, MIB 1,350.00
Elvis Presley, card set, Golden Boys, A&BC Gum, 1958, 36 cards ..80.00
Elvis Presley, clock, Love Me Tender, Unique Time Co, 1977 ....80.00
Elvis Presley, concert pin, laughing portrait, 3⅜" 12.00
Elvis Presley, fan club publication, Elvis for Everyone, 1967, M ..18.00
Elvis Presley, flipbook, Jailhouse Rock, EX 100.00
Elvis Presley, fold-over carry-all bag, red vinyl, 1956, M, minimum ...750.00
Elvis Presley, game, Elvis Welcomes You to His World, Duff, 1978, NMIB ...125.00
Elvis Presley, handkerchief, bl border, EPE 1956, M 450.00
Elvis Presley, King Galahad punching bag balloon, EX 65.00
Elvis Presley, lobby cards, Jailhouse Rock, set 825.00
Elvis Presley, mobile, cb, hangs, RCA, in wht jumpsuit, 18x24", M 40.00
Elvis Presley, pencils, Sincerely Yours..., 1956, set of 12, MIP 250.00
Elvis Presley, pennant, Birthplace Tupelo..., EPE 1962, M 30.00
Elvis Presley, pocket calendar, gold suit, 1969, M, from $15 to 20.00
Elvis Presley, postcard, West Germany, color, M, from $10 to 12.00
Elvis Presley, print, portrait by June Kelly, 1960s, 20x16", M 50.00
Elvis Presley, promotional photo, blk/wht, 1956, 8x10", M 50.00
Elvis Presley, record catalog, full color, 1973, M 20.00
Elvis Presley, scarf, concert give-away, silky, M 40.00
Elvis Presley, sheet music, Don't Be Cruel, M 40.00
Elvis Presley, Tickle Me feather pen, EX 35.00
Elvis Presley, tour photo, singing, down on 1 knee, mc, 8x10" 25.00
Grateful Dead, poster, Dante's Inferno, creased, 1967, 21x13½" .550.00
Heart, music box, Dog & Butterfly, wooden, 1978 ....175.00
Heart, perfume, All I Want To Do, rare 65.00
Janis Joplin/Big Brother/Holding Co, poster, November 30, 1968 ....1,200.00
Jethro Tull, sticker, Too Old To Rock 'n Roll..., 1976, EX 12.00
Jimi Hendrix, unused concert ticket, Muncie IN, 1968 ....1,250.00
Jimi Hendrix/The Who/Pink Floyd, poster, United Kingdom, 1967 ..3,000.00
KISS, Army Fan Club kit, EX 70.00
KISS, belt buckle, face picture, EX 60.00
KISS, Custom Chevy KISS Van, AMT, 1977, sealed 175.00
KISS, Halloween costumes, 1978, boxed, ea 175.00
KISS, make-up kit, Remco, 1978 ....150.00
KISS, song book, Unmasked, rare 125.00
Led Zeppelin, handbill, Memorial Coliseum, March 23, 1970 ...300.00
Led Zeppelin, inflatable blimp, promotional 150.00
Led Zeppelin, patch, blk w/gold-trimmed bl letters, sew-on 7.00
Lynyrd Skynrd, handbill, Antioch CA, February 8, 1974 ....95.00
Madonna, book, The Girlie Show, hardcover, 1994 ....55.00
Madonna, Cosmetic Glamour set, Cosrich, Dick Tracy movie, 1990 ...50.00
Madonna, pillow, from Desperately Seeking Susan movie, 1986 ..65.00
Madonna, sports bottle, Express Yourself, Boy Toy, 1990 ....30.00
Madonna, View-Master gift set, Dick Tracy movie, Tyco, 1990 ...22.50
Madonna, wristbands, bl & wht, pr 35.00

Madonna, wristwatch, Dick Tracy movie, Timex, 1990 ....45.00
MC Hammer, doll, w/cassette, Mattel, 1991, MIB 50.00
MC Hammer, school folder, by Bustin' Productions, 1991 ....12.50
Michael Jackson, doll, American Music Awards, LJN, 12" 50.00
Michael Jackson, electric microphone, LJN, 1984, boxed 40.00
Michael Jackson, Sing-A-Long Sound Machine, LJN, 1984 ....45.00
Monkees, book, Monkees Go Mad/Mod, Raybert..., paperbk, 1967, EX ..12.00
Monkees, Monkeemobile, Corgi, 1967-68, 5" 175.00
Monkees, Monkeemobile, Corgi, 1967-68, 5", MIB 400.00
Monkees, pen, wht w/blk faces & names, Raybert, 1967, EX 27.50
Monkees, record carrying case for 45s, Raybert, 1966, EX 325.00
Monkees, thermos, photos on bl, TM Screen Gems, 1967, EX 50.00
New Kids on the Block, bkpack, purple & blk, Big Step Prom, 1990 ..15.00
New Kids on the Block, card game, Milton Bradley, 1990 ....15.00
Peter Paul & Mary, program, mid-1960s 95.00
Rolling Stones, ad for Chicago concert, 1972 ....125.00
Rolling Stones, clock, Mick Jagger in red, wht & bl outfit, 1980 .55.00
Rolling Stones, phone, lip & tongue logo shape, Musidor, 1983 ..100.00
Rolling Stones, program, Pontiac Silverdome, 1981 ....125.00
Rolling Stones, puzzle, Shmuzzle, Musidor, 1983 ....65.00
Rolling Stones, tie, blk w/red lips & tongue logo, Brockman, 1994 .35.00
Vanilla Ice, doll, THQ, 1991, 12" 40.00
Vanilla Ice, Electronic Rap Game, Internat'l Games, 1991 ....75.00

Rockingham

In the early part of the nineteenth century, American potters began to prefer brown- and buff-burning clays over red because of their durability. The glaze favored by many was Rockingham, which varied from a dark brown mottle to a sponged effect sometimes called tortoise shell. It consisted in part of manganese and various metallic salts and was used by many potters until well into the twentieth century. Over the past two years, demand and prices have risen sharply, especially in the East. For further information we recommend *Collector's Guide to Rockingham, The Enduring Ware*, by Mary Brewer. See also Bennington.

Spaniel, inverted bowl-shaped base with molded Gothic arches and pointed stars, incised scrolls simulate fur, 12x12x8½", repair, $450.00.

Boiler, milk; emb bands, curved hdl, 3¾x4½", from $40 to 55.00
Bowl, mixing; molded Gothic arches, wear, 6x13" 195.00
Bowl, mixing; plain, 10½", from $75 to 95.00
Bowl, mush; flared rnded rim, 1¾x5⅝" 150.00
Box, Toby, dk brn, Am, 19th C, 4¼", NM 250.00
Creamer, cow figural, gilt detail, 8¼" 350.00
Creamer, emb acanthus leaf on spout, arched hdl, 4½" 175.00
Crock, butter; str sides, gallery rim, knob finial, 4¼x7⅛" 150.00
Crock, lambrequin borders below plain band, ear hdls, 1870-84, 7x9" ..150.00
Crock (fruit jar), ca 1848-61, 5-cup, 5½", from $12 to 22.00
Custard, heavy glaze on thick body, 3" 45.00
Figurine, dog, seated, free-standing front legs, 10½" 440.00
Figurine, lion on rectangular base, 9⅜" L 880.00
Figurine, lion w/paw on ball, lg teeth, on base, 9x11½", pr 3,000.00
Flask, hunting dogs in relief, hairline, 7¼" 330.00
Loving cup, emb drinking scenes & dog fight, 6⅞", EX 250.00
Mug, emb scenes of dressed monkeys drinking, PA mk, 4¼" 600.00
Sugar bowl, scalloped panels, rpr/wear, 8¾" 95.00
Teapot, ribbed panels, simple geometrics, scroll hdl dome lid, 7" 130.00

Rockwell, Norman

Norman Rockwell began his career in 1911 at the age of seventeen doing illustrations for a children's book entitled *Tell Me Why Stories*. Within a few years he had produced the *Saturday Evening Post* cover that made him one of America's most beloved artists. Though not well accepted by the professional critics of his day who did not consider his work to be art but 'merely' commercial illustration, Rockwell's popularity grew to the extent that today there is an overwhelming abundance of examples of his work or those related to the theme of one of his illustrations.

The figurines described below were issued by Gorham. Our advisor for this category is Barb Putratz; she is listed in the Directory under Minnesota.

A Tough One, 1983 ....95.00
Adventures Between Adventures, 1972 ....300.00
Antique Dealer, 1983 ....195.00
At the Vets, Gorham Miniature, 1981 ....55.00
At the Vets, 1974 ....110.00
Baby Sitter, Gorham Miniature, 1987 ....90.00
Batter Up, Gorham Miniature, 1984 ....76.00
Beguiling Buttercup, 1977 ....115.00
Best Friends, Gorham Miniature, 1986 ....45.00
Blasting Out, 1983 ....95.00
Boy & His Dog, 4 seasons set, complete 1,200.00
Boy Meets His Dog, Gorham Miniature, 1981 ....180.00
Canine Solo, 1982 ....100.00
Captain, 1974 ....115.00
Careful Aim, Gorham Miniature, 1984 ....80.00
Careful Aim, 1981 ....300.00
Checking Good Deeds, 1982, 3½" 25.00
Choosing Up, 1978 ....175.00
Christmas Goose (ltd ed of 7,500) 150.00
Closed for Business, 1980 ....240.00
Coal Seasons Coming, 1980 ....240.00
Confrontation, Gorham Miniature, 1988 ....90.00
Cool Aid, 1979 ....260.00
Country Pedlar, 1985 ....100.00
Dad's Boy, 4 seasons set, complete 1,050.00
Day Dreamers, 1975 ....175.00
Day in the Life of a Boy I, 1980 ....115.00
Day in the Life of a Boy III, 1982 ....120.00
Day in the Life of a Girl II, 1981 ....115.00
Diary, Gorham Miniature, 1988 ....95.00
Disastrous Daring, 1976 ....275.00
Downhill Daring, Gorham Miniature, 1981 ....80.00
Downhill Daring, 1973 ....250.00
Drum for Tommy, ltd ed of 7,500, 1986 ....100.00
Expert Salesman, ltd ed of 1,500, 1983 ....225.00
Final Speech, 1984 ....100.00
First Annual Visit, 1980 ....185.00
Fishing, Gorham Miniature, 1984 ....80.00
Flying High, 1973 ....250.00
Football Season, Gorham Miniature, 1986 ....70.00
Four Ages of Love, 4 seasons set, complete 900.00
Gaily Sharing Vintage Times, 1977 ....130.00
Gay Blades, Gorham Miniature, 1981 ....75.00
Ghostly Gourds, 1977 ....300.00
God Rest Ye Merry Gentlemen, 1976 ....1,400.00

Goin' Fishing, Gorham Miniature, 1984 ....70.00
Going on Sixteen, 4 seasons set, complete 750.00
Grand Pals, 4 seasons set, complete 1,050.00
Grandpa & Me, 4 seasons set, complete 700.00
Helping Hand, 4 seasons set, complete 950.00
Home for the Holidays, 1988 ....140.00
Horse Trader, 1985 ....100.00
In His Spirit, 1981 ....250.00
In His Spirit, Gorham Miniature, 1984 ....70.00
Jolly Coachman, Gorham Miniature, 1984 ....45.00
Jolly Coachman, ltd ed of 7,500, 1980 ....175.00
Lazy Days, 1982 ....100.00
Life w/Father, 4 seasons set, complete 380.00
Little Angel, Gorham Miniature, 1986 ....70.00
Marriage License, Gorham Miniature 85.00
Marriage License, 1976, 6¼" 310.00
Me & My Pal, 4 seasons set, complete 1,100.00
Missed, 1978 ....245.00
Morning Walk, Gorham Miniature, 1986 ....75.00
New Arrival, Gorham Miniature, 1985 ....50.00
New Year Look, 1979 ....260.00
No Swimming, 1974 ....160.00
Oh Yeah, 1978 ....245.00
Old Sign Painter, Gorham Miniature, 1986 ....90.00
Old Sign Painter, ltd ed of #7,500, 1984 ....120.00
Pensive Pals, 1975 ....175.00
Pilgrimage, 1978 ....190.00
Pride of Parenthood, 1972 ....300.00
Prom Dress, Gorham Miniature, 1987 ....90.00
Puppet Maker, 1985 ....195.00
Runaway, 1978 ....105.00
Santa's Friend, ltd ed of 7,500, 1985 ....150.00
Santa's Friend, 1983, 3½" 25.00
Season's Greetings, Gorham Miniature, 1986 ....60.00
Serenade, 1983 ....170.00
Shared Success, 1984 ....100.00
Shoulder Ride, Gorham Miniature, 1986 ....65.00
Snow Sculpture, Gorham Miniature, 1981 ....80.00
Soaring Spirits, 1977 ....250.00
Springtime, Gorham Miniature, 1987 ....85.00
Summer, Vacation, pewter, 1980 ....105.00
Sweet Serenade, Gorham Miniature, 1981 ....60.00
Sweet Serenade, 1978 ....190.00
Sweet Song So Young, 1974 ....225.00
Tackled, 1976 ....110.00
To Love & To Cherish, Gorham Miniature, 1985 ....50.00
Traveling Salesman (ltd ed of #1,500, issued at $175), 1981 ....210.00
Triple Self Portrait, 1980, 10½" 620.00
Trout Dinner, Gorham Miniature, 1983 ....80.00
Weighing In, 1974 ....150.00
Welcome Mat, Gorham Miniature, 1986 ....90.00
Winter, Bringing Home the Tree, pewter, 1980 ....105.00
Young Man's Fancy, Gorham Miniature, 1981 ....75.00
Young Man's Fancy, 1976 ....275.00
Yuletide Reckoning, ltd ed of 7,500, 1984 ....100.00
Yuletide Reckoning, 1981, 3½" 25.00

Rogers, John

John Rogers (1829 – 1904) was a machinist from Manchester, New Hampshire, who turned his hobby of sculpting into a financially successful venture. From the originals he meticulously fashioned of red clay, he had bronze master molds made from which plaster copies were cast. He specialized in five different categories: theatrical, Shakespeare, Civil War, everyday life, and horses. His large detailed groupings portrayed the life and times of the period between 1859 and 1892. In the following listings, examples are assumed to be in very good to excellent condition. Our advisor for this category is George Humphrey; he is listed in the Directory under Maryland.

The Favored Scholar, 21x16x11", $425.00.

Balcony 1,500.00
Bubbles 2,000.00
Bushwacker 2,000.00
Checker Players, sm 1,200.00
Chess 1,200.00
Council of War 1,100.00
Country Post Office 750.00
Fairy's Whisper, ca 1881 ....1,400.00
Fetching the Doctor 750.00
Fighting Bob, ca 1889 ....1,100.00
Frolic at the Old Homestead, 1887, 22½" 800.00
Madam, Your Mother Craves a Word w/You 700.00
Mail Day 2,000.00
Neighboring Pews 475.00
Parting Promise 475.00
Peddler at the Fair 800.00
Referee 600.00
Rip Van Winkle on the Mountain 425.00
Rip Van Winkle—At Home 325.00
Shaughraun & Tatters 700.00
Speak for Yourself John 500.00
Tap on the Window 525.00
Washington 1,250.00
Watch on the Santa Maria 1,000.00
Weighing the Baby, 20½" 600.00

Rookwood

The Rookwood Pottery Company was established in 1879 in Cincinnati, Ohio. Its founder was Maria Longworth Nichols Storer, daughter of a wealthy family who provided the backing necessary to make such an enterprise possible. Mrs. Storer hired competent ceramic artisans and artists of note, who through constant experimentation developed many lines of superior art pottery. While in her employ, Laura Fry invented the airbrush-blending process for which she was issued a patent in 1884. From this, several lines were designed that utilized blended backgrounds. One of their earlier lines, Standard, was a brown ware decorated with underglaze slip-painted nature studies, animals, portraits, etc. Iris and Sea Green were introduced in 1894 and Vellum, a transparent mat-glaze line, in 1904. Other lines followed: Ombroso in 1910 and Soft Porcelain in 1915. Many of the early artware lines were signed by the artist. Soon after the turn of the twentieth century, Rookwood manufactured 'production' pieces that relied mainly on molded designs and forms rather than freehand decoration for their esthetic appeal. The Depression brought on financial difficulties from which the pottery never recovered. Though it continued to operate, the quality of the ware deteriorated, and the pottery was forced to close in 1967.

Unmarked Rookwood is only rarely encountered. Many marks may be found, but the most familiar is the reverse 'RP' monogram. First used in 1886, a flame point was added above it for each succeeding year until 1900. After that a Roman numeral added below indicated the year of manufacture. Impressed letters that related to the type of clay utilized for the body were also used — G for ginger, O for olive, R for red, S for sage green, W for white, and Y for yellow. Artware must be judged on an individual basis. Quality of the artwork is a prime factor to consider. Portraits, animals, and birds are worth more than florals; and pieces signed by a particularly renowned artist are highly prized.

Black Opal

Bowl, butterflies, Sara Sax, 1926, #2813C, 2½x13" 2,600.00
Vase, floral, Sara Sax, 1927, #2996, 9" 1,200.00
Vase, pansies, Harriet Wilcox, 1924, #2105, 4⅝", NM 700.00

Cameo

Pitcher, white narcissus on salmon pink, A.M. Valentien, 1890, 8¾", $400.00.

Cup & saucer, pansies, H Straffer, 1890 ....375.00
Pitcher, floral branches, Anna M Valentien, 1890, #487B, 7", NM ...210.00

Iris

Teapot, roses & buds, Irene Bishop, 1905, #404 X, rpr, 4" 400.00
Vase, apple blossom branches, Laura E Lindeman, 1906, #30F, 6½" 700.00
Vase, bl-gray iris on gray to celadon, SE Coyne, #907D, 1905, 11¼" 2,600.00
Vase, dandelions on blk, John D Wareham, 1899, #732A, 13" 20,000.00
Vase, fish (realistic), Edward T Hurley, 1905, #950C, 10" 3,500.00
Vase, fish in underwater scene, ET Hurley, 1903, #745C/#222, 5½" ...850.00
Vase, floral (delicate), Constance A Baker, 1901, #30E, 8" 750.00
Vase, floral (delicate), Irene Bishop, 1906, #904B, 7" 650.00
Vase, floral (EX art), Ed Diers, 1911, #1654D, 9½" 3,250.00
Vase, floral (EX art), Lenore Asbury, 1904, #909C, 8½" 1,500.00
Vase, heron (unusual), Carl Schmidt, 1905, #941C X, 9½" ...1,200.00
Vase, honeysuckle on gray, Ed Diers, #604D, 1905, 6¾x5½" .1,000.00
Vase, hyacinths (EX art), Sara Sax, 1904, #935C, 9" 4,000.00
Vase, iris on blk to ivory, L Asbury, #939B, 1907, 10x4¾" 2,600.00
Vase, iris on gray, SE Coyne, #907D, 1907, 10¾x4" 1,800.00
Vase, lilies of the valley, Laura E Lindeman, 1906, #952F, 5½" .700.00
Vase, lily pads, Matt Daly, 1901, illegible #, 6", NM 950.00
Vase, mums (bold), Rose Fechheimer, 1901, #925C X, 9½" ...2,000.00
Vase, orchid (detailed), Carl Schmidt, 1902, #939B, 10" 3,750.00
Vase, poppies (detailed), Caroline Steinle, 1911, #943E, 7" ...1,200.00
Vase, poppy (cvd/pnt), John D Wareham, 1897, #614E X, 8" ..2,500.00
Vase, swallows in flight, ET Hurley, 1905, #951B, 12", NM ...2,600.00
Vase, swans (5) on blk, K Shirayamadani, 1899, #786C X, 10" 9,000.00
Vase, swans (5) on blk, K Shirayamadani, 1909, #1654C, 11½" ..20,000.00
Vase, tropical leaves, Ed Diers, 1907, #1126C, 9" 650.00
Vase, tulips (cvd/pnt), Olga Geneva Reed, 1910, #30E, 8" 2,400.00
Vase, tulips (cvd/pnt), SE Coyne/JD Wareham, 1901, #732B X, 10" ...4,750.00
Vase, violets, Constance A Baker, 1902, #922E, 5½" 550.00
Vase, violets (vivid colors), Constance A Baker, 1903, #916C, 7½" ...6,000.00
Vase, violets on gray, ED Diers, #914E, 1902, 5¼x4½" 1,400.00
Vase, water lilies, Constance Baker, #935C, 1902, 8¾x5" 2,100.00

Limoges

Jug, bamboo/swallow on beige, Rettig, 1884, 4¾" 350.00
Jug, sprigged-on tree-like decor, unsgn, ca 1883, 2⅜" 425.00
Jug, water; birds fly among rushes, AR Valentien, 1886, #41, 9½" ...1,100.00
Vase, bats (9) among flowers, ML Nichols, 1882, 11", NM 650.00
Vase, trees & river, Matthew A Daly, 1884, #49B, 11x2x10", NM ..1,100.00
Vase, 3 Oriental scenic panels, ML Nichols, 1883, rstr, 23" ...3,250.00

Mat

Note: Both incised mat and painted mat are listed here. Incised mat descriptions are indicated by the term 'cvd' within the line; the others are for the hand-painted mat ware.

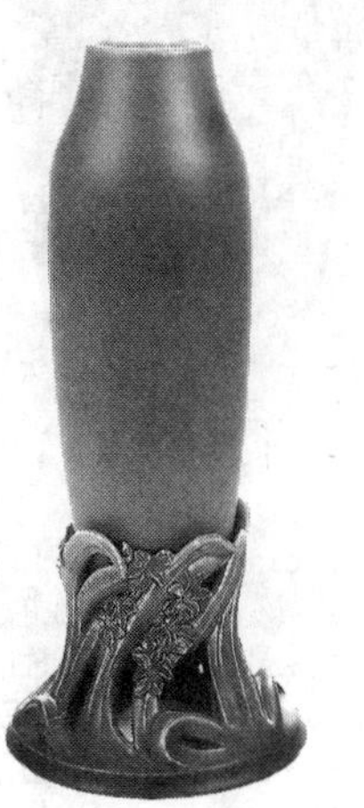

Vase, reticulated green leaves entwined with lavender flowers, Kataro Shirayamadani, #932C, 1904, 15", professional repair, $2,600.00.

Bowl, foliage, Vera Tischler, 1922, #214E, 2x5" dia 275.00
Dish, lizard (cvd/modeled), K Shirayamadani, 1907, #1080E, 1x3½" ...500.00
Plaque, landscape (cvd/pnt/bold), Sallie Toohey, 9x7"+orig fr ..4,750.00
Plaque, rooks on branch, Sallie Toohey, 1900s, 6x8"+orig fr ...17,000.00
Vase, berries & leaves (EX art), Elizabeth Barrett, 1927, #1348, 5" ..1,800.00
Vase, berries on branch, Katherine Jones, 1930, #2721, 6½" 425.00
Vase, berry branches, Anna M Valentien, 1901, #3EZ, 6" 850.00
Vase, butterflies, Sallie E Coyne, 1925, #1369F, 6" 900.00
Vase, butterflies (cvd/pnt), Wm E Hentschel, 1911, #614E, 8½" ...750.00
Vase, crocus, K Shirayamadani, 1934, S, 5½" 1,000.00
Vase, crocus on curdled wht, Margaret H McDonald, 1938, 7" ..700.00
Vase, dogwood blossoms, Margaret H McDonald, 1921, #2102, 7½" 500.00
Vase, ferns (Modernistic), Elizabeth Barrett, 1927, #324, 17" .2,100.00
Vase, ferns (stylized), Wm E Hentschel, 1927, #915D, 7½" ...1,800.00
Vase, fish & plants, K Shirayamadani, 1929, #6091, 11¼x8" .1,200.00
Vase, floral, Louise Abel, 1927, #2905, 9½" 375.00
Vase, floral, Margaret H McDonald, 1928, #2724, 6" 350.00
Vase, floral, Sallie E Coyne, 1927, #951E, 7½" 850.00

Vase, floral (cvd/inlaid), Wm E Hentschel, 1914, #2100, 5" 700.00
Vase, floral (cvd/pnt/EX art), Wm E Hentschel, 1926, #2903, 10" ..1,100.00
Vase, floral (cvd/pnt/ornate), K Shirayamadani, 1904, #276CZ, 9" .9,000.00
Vase, floral (EX art/color), EN Lincoln, 1927, #1918, 9" 800.00
Vase, floral (EX art/color), K Shirayamadani, 1935, 5" 700.00
Vase, floral (EX art/color), K Shirayamadani, 1936, #6600, 7" ..2,200.00
Vase, floral (EX color), Katherine Jones, 1927, #551, 7" 800.00
Vase, floral (impressionistic), EN Lincoln, 1925, #2040C, 12" ..850.00
Vase, floral (stylized), Louise Abel, 1922, #2305, 7" 850.00
Vase, floral (unusual colors), Jens Jensen, 1931, #927E, 7½" ..1,100.00
Vase, florals/lg leaves, pk w/gr overspray, Shirayamadani, 14" 675.00
Vase, geometrics, bottle form, Rose Fechheimer, 1904, #299 ..1,000.00
Vase, leaves (stylized), E Barret, 1930, #614D X, 10½" 475.00
Vase, leaves (stylized), Wm E Hentschel, 1926, #1929, 4½x6½" 800.00
Vase, leaves & berries (cvd/pnt), Sallie Toohey, 1905, 3½x6½" ...1,000.00
Vase, mums, Albert R Valentien, 1901, #189AZ, 14½" 4,750.00
Vase, mushrooms (cvd/rtcl), John D Wareham, 1901, #909 X, 9" ..1,500.00
Vase, roses on stems, Harriet E Wilcox, 1902, #35D, 4½" 2,400.00
Vase, stripes & circles (cvd/pnt), CS Todd, 1916, #214C, 3x5½" ...240.00
Vase, swirled decor, Cecil A Duell, 1908, #1124E, 6½", NM 425.00
Vase, tulips, ET Hurley, 1905, #950D, 8½" 450.00
Vase, violets (cvd/pnt), Sallie E Coyne, 1905, #1124E X, 7" ..1,000.00

Porcelain

Vase, bleeding hearts on violet and purple Chinese Plum high glaze, Kataro Shirayamadani, 1926, 10", $7,000.00.

Bowl, cockatoo on branch, Lois Furukawa, 1946, #6313/#60, 8½" ..550.00
Bowl, floral (Deco style), Lorinda Epply, 1929, #2258X, 2¼x13" 650.00
Bowl, floral (detailed), Sara Sax, 1921, #2287, 4x8" 1,300.00
Bowl, floral int, Lorinda Epply, 1929, #2574C, 2¾x12" 850.00
Lamp base, magnolias, initialed, 1950, #6920, 13" 550.00
Vase, boats in harbor, Carl Schmidt, 1921, #808, 8" 3,000.00
Vase, boats in harbor, Carl Schmidt, 1923, #357F X, 6½" 1,100.00
Vase, dove among flowers, Jens Jensen, 1945, #6873/#8149, 7" ..1,400.00
Vase, fish, (EX art), Jens Jensen, 1945, #6184E/#50, 6½" 850.00
Vase, floral, Lorinda Epply, 1927, #2077, 6½" 650.00
Vase, floral (EX art), K Shirayamadani, 1939, #6735, 6½" 950.00
Vase, floral (EX art), Margaret H McDonald, 1940, #S2139, 12" ...6,000.00
Vase, floral bands, Key Ley, 1946, #778/#4443, 10", NM 275.00
Vase, flowing mc drips & runs, Sallie Toohey, 1920, #S2009, 16" ..2,700.00
Vase, fruit & leaves, EN Barrett, 1944, #6305, 5" 325.00
Vase, irises (EX art), L Holtkamp, 1951, #6933, drilled, 11½" ..700.00
Vase, orchids (ornate), K Shirayamadani, 1930, #1065B, 10½" ..2,600.00
Vase, parrots/flowers/leaves, Edward T Hurley, 1924, #2640C, 13", NM ..1,800.00
Vase, snails (unusual), John D Wareham, 1952, 6½" 1,200.00
Vase, storks (incised/pnt), Kay Ley, 1946, #778/#4308, 10" 450.00
Vase, tulips, Margaret H McDonald, 1946, #6659, 7½", NM 400.00

Sea Green

Ewer, fish (over 30), Albert R Valentien, 1894, #T976, rpr, 13" ..2,900.00
Vase, crocus, Sallie Coyne, 1904, #922 C, X, 5½" 700.00
Vase, fish & water lilies, Rose Fechheimer, 1901, #786D X, 8¼" ...9,500.00
Vase, hydrangea, wht on opal bl/gr, Sara Sax, 1902, 6¾x4¾" 4,750.00
Vase, jonquils, Matt Daly, 1895, S #1175, 9⅛" 1,100.00
Vase, jonquils (EX art/color), Sallie E Coyne, 1901, #562, 10" .2,900.00
Vase, turtles (cvd/pnt) in sea, ET Hurley, 1900, #80B G, 6¾", NM 3,000.00

Standard

Basket, orange blossoms, Grace Young, 1887, #45D, 4½x7" 325.00
Bowl, floral (delicate), Albert Pons, 1906, #1142, 1½x3½" 225.00
Bowl, poppies, Jeanette Swing, 1903, #923, 2½x6½", NM 700.00
Chocolate pot, floral branches, Shiraymadani, 1891, #T589W, 10½" ..850.00
Chocolate pot, roses/thorny stems, L Asbury, 1900, #772, 10", NM 425.00
Creamer & sugar bowl, crocus, Ed Diers, 1898, #330, 2½x4" 500.00
Cup, flower blossoms, Sallie Toohey, 1889, 2x4½" 400.00
Ewer, floral, Albert R Valentien, 1881, #101A, 11½" 750.00
Ewer, floral, Matthew A Daly, 1886, #101C, 8" 400.00
Ewer, roses & buds (detailed), AM Valentien, 1891, #387C, 11" ...850.00
Jug, clover & leaves, silver wire mesh, M Daly, 1893, #512W, 9½" ..2,100.00
Mug, gnome in cemetery, Grace Young, 1897, #587C, 5" 1,200.00
Mug, mail bag w/laurel, Edith Noonan, 1905, 4¾" 300.00
Mug, man w/jug, att Grace Young, 1891, #587W, 4½" 600.00
Mug, Standing Bear portrait, Sadie Markland, 1897, #837, 5" ..2,000.00
Pitcher, berry branches, Sara Sax, 1899, #564D, 9" 750.00
Stein, Black boy w/cap, Bruce Horsfall, 1895, #656, 7" 5,500.00
Stein, man in wide-brim hat, MA Daly, 1896, #775, bird hdl, 8½" ..2,400.00
Vase, acorns, cut-out silver o/l, J Zettel, 1903, #925C, 9½" 5,800.00
Vase, Am Indian Chief, Eagle Deer Soiux, A Sehon, 1901, #604D, 7" .4,750.00
Vase, birds on floral branch, F Rothenbusch, 1896, #712, 5x4½" ...400.00
Vase, bleeding hearts, Frances Vreeland, 1901, #913 X, 5½" 350.00
Vase, clover blossoms, Constance A Baker, 1894, #566D W, 7" ...425.00
Vase, curled leaves (EX art), Van Briggle, 1900, #866, 6½" 425.00
Vase, dandelions, Jeannette Swing, 1903, #906E, 4" 450.00
Vase, dogwood branches, silver o/l, E Fortmeyer, 1903, #900C, 8" ...2,700.00
Vase, elk, R Bruce Horsfall, 1895, #707A, 8x7½", NM 1,900.00
Vase, floral, Caroline Steinle, hdls, 1901, #911, 4x5" 250.00
Vase, floral, Mary L Perkins, 1898, #848, 6½" 325.00
Vase, floral (EX color), Josephine E Zettel, 1892, #654D, 3½" ..600.00
Vase, floral (feathery), Lenore Asbury, 1898, #725C, 7" 500.00
Vase, Ho-Wear Comanche portrait, S Laurence, 1898, #829, 9¼" ..4,000.00
Vase, irises, (EX detail), Carl Schmidt, 1900, #639, 9" 700.00
Vase, Joe Jefferson portrait, ER Felton, 3-hdl, 1903, #659C, 6", NM .1,000.00
Vase, lily of valley (EX art), Irene Bishop, 1901, #534D, 6" 700.00
Vase, man's portrait, Artus Van Briggle, 1899, #604C, 9⅛x7" ..1,800.00
Vase, monkey on branch, S Laurence, 1897, #707B, 5½" 1,500.00
Vase, orange blossoms, EN Lincoln, 1904, #735DD, 7½" 600.00
Vase, peach blossoms (EX art), K Shirayamadani, 1887, #344B, 6x12" ...900.00
Vase, poppies, Edith R Felton, 1901, #734D, 6½" 550.00
Vase, poppies, silver o/l, Irene Bishop, 1900, #654C, 5" 2,300.00
Vase, roses on ribbed body, Laura A Fray, 1886, #269A, 15" ..2,400.00
Vase, violets, K Hickman, slim neck, 1897, #765, 5¾" 225.00

Vellum

Box, floral (delicate), Elizabeth Lincoln, 1908, #622C X, 4" ..1,500.00
Jar, boats in harbor, Carl Schmidt, 1922, #834, 6½" 2,500.00
Plaque, birches along riverbank, Edward T Hurley, 1919, 8½x11" ...3,000.00
Plaque, boats in harbor, Sara Sax, 1912, 8½x10½" +fr 3,250.00
Plaque, evergreens & country road, Sara Sax, 11x9"+oak fr ...4,500.00
Plaque, mtns & evergreens, Lenore Asbury, 4x8"+fr 1,300.00
Plaque, river landscape w/birches, ET Hurley, 10½x8½"+fr ...4,750.00
Plaque, sunset w/trees & water, Sallie E Coyne, 1924, 7x9" ...4,500.00
Plaque, trees & hills (EX art), Fred Rothenbusch, 11x8½" 4,000.00

Plaque, trees on grassy knoll, Ed Diers, 1924, 8½x5" +fr **4,250.00**
Plaque, trees reflecting in water, Ed Diers, 1920, 6x8"+fr **3,750.00**
Plaque, trees/stream/sunset, Fred Rothenbusch, label, 14½x9" **9,500.00**
Vase, bell flowers (EX art), Charles S Todd, 1916, #1929, 4½x7" ...**500.00**

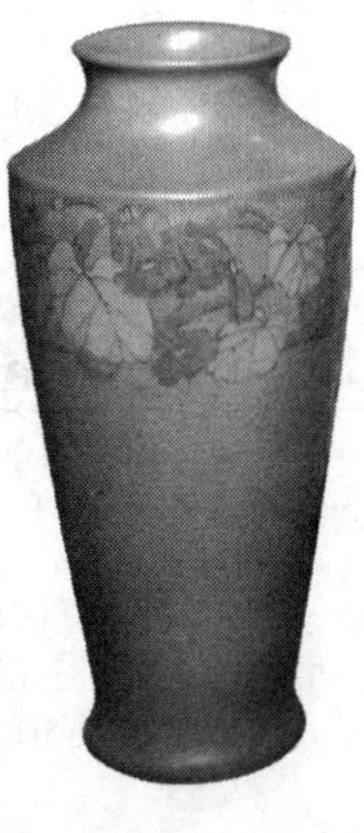

Vase, red trumpet creepers with brown vines and green leaves at shoulder, Sara Sax, 1918, 9⅝", minor repair, $500.00.

Vase, berries & leaves, Lenore Asbury, 1922, #604F, 6½", NM .**500.00**
Vase, berry branches, Ed Diers, 1931, #2918E, flake, 6½" **800.00**
Vase, birch trees/grasses/sunset, L Asbury, 1920, #1660D, 9½" **2,400.00**
Vase, birches at river bank, Edward T Hurley, 1946, #5322 S, 8" ..**2,600.00**
Vase, boats in harbor, Carl Schmidt, 1925, #2544, 8½" **3,500.00**
Vase, butterflies (3/unusual), Lorinda Epply, 1911, #1369E, 7" ..**750.00**
Vase, carnations (delicate), Fred Rothenbusch, 1905, #943D, 8" **900.00**
Vase, cherry blossoms, Edward T Hurley, 1910, #942D, 6" **650.00**
Vase, circles & lines (stylized), Charles S Todd, 1921, #3105, 5" **375.00**
Vase, daisies, Ed Diers, 1925, #356F, 5½" **800.00**
Vase, dogwood, Ed Diers, 1926, #568C, 7" **1,200.00**
Vase, fish (5) & undercurrents, Edward T Hurley, 1906, #604D, 7" ..**1,100.00**
Vase, fish swim among plants, Edward T Hurley, 1910, #679, 7½" ...**2,500.00**
Vase, floral, Fred Rothenbusch, 1919, #1278F, 7½" **400.00**
Vase, floral (colorful), Harriet E Wilcox, 1923, #614E, 8½" ...**1,100.00**
Vase, floral (cvd/pnt), Edith F McDermott, 1918, #295E, 7½" ...**1,900.00**
Vase, floral (delicate), Ed Diers, 1924, #2463, 8" **1,100.00**
Vase, floral (delicate), Fred Rothenbusch, 1919, #2033E, 8" **425.00**
Vase, floral (EX art), Margaret H McDonald, 1938, S, 6" **1,100.00**
Vase, floral (EX art), Sallie E Coyne, 1905, #977, 10½" **2,100.00**
Vase, floral band, Katherine Van Horne, 1926, #1778 E XII, 7½" ..**750.00**
Vase, floral branches, Ed Diers, 1923, #1926, 6½" **1,500.00**
Vase, floral branches, Edward T Hurley, 1928, #764C, 5½" **700.00**
Vase, floral branches, Edward T Hurley, 1930, #914E, 5½" **1,000.00**
Vase, floral branches, Lenore Asbury, 1923, #2547, 9½" **1,400.00**
Vase, floral branches, unknown artist, 1930, #892B, 11½" **1,100.00**
Vase, floral panels (Oriental style), Sara Sax, 1913, #392C, 9½" ..**1,300.00**
Vase, flower band, Edward T Hurley, 1917, #937, 10" **800.00**
Vase, forest & mtns, F Rothenbusch, 1923, #1045, 5½" **900.00**
Vase, geese (5) in flight, Edward T Hurley, 1907, #943G, 10½" .**2,600.00**
Vase, geese in landscape, K Shirayamadani, 1910, #951C, 11" ...**7,000.00**
Vase, grape branches, Sallie E Coyne, 1904, #915D, 7½" **1,100.00**
Vase, jonquils (lifelike), Irene Bishop, 1905, #30E, 8" **1,500.00**
Vase, leaves (encircling), Caroline Steinle, 1914, #1357, 7" ..**1,200.00**
Vase, lilies (cvd/pnt), Sara Sax, 1914, #1661, 8½" **750.00**
Vase, lilies of the valley, EN Lincoln, 1911, #233, 8" **550.00**
Vase, mtns (unusual), Ed Diers, 1908, #1369D X, 9" **1,400.00**
Vase, Oriental boats, Sallie E Coyne, 1914, #1343, 5" **800.00**
Vase, palm trees (unusual), Edward T Hurley, 1910s, rpr, 8½" .**1,200.00**
Vase, peach blossoms, Ed Diers, 1929, #1120, 4½" **700.00**
Vase, poppies (EX art), Elizabeth M McDermott, 1915, #943E, 7" **650.00**
Vase, Queen Anne's Lace blossoms, Lenore Asbury, 1914, #904, 11" ...**1,500.00**
Vase, roses (EX detail), Ed Diers, 1926, #907D, 12" **3,250.00**
Vase, roses & buds on shoulder, Edward T Hurley, 1942, #932E, 8" .**1,500.00**
Vase, sampan scenic, Carl Schmidt, #1358D, 1925, 8¾x4¾" .**5,500.00**
Vase, sea horses (EX detail), Edward T Hurley, 1904, #166Z, 5" ...**2,500.00**
Vase, swans on lake, Edward T Hurley, 1909, #904D, 8½" **2,500.00**
Vase, trees & hills (EX art), F Rothenbusch, 1923, #1779, 7½" ...**1,500.00**
Vase, trees & water, Sallie E Coyne, 1921, #1660, 9½" **2,100.00**
Vase, trees landscape (bold), Ed Diers, 1915, #328B, 6½" **2,000.00**
Vase, trees/mtn, Fred Rothenbusch, 1918, #2069, 8" **1,100.00**
Vase, winter landscape w/trees, F Rothenbusch, 1914, #922E, 11" ...**1,500.00**
Vase, wisteria, Ed Diers, 1906, #932E, 8" **1,000.00**
Vase, wisteria, salmon int, Diers, #900A, 1926, 13½" **4,450.00**

Wax Mat

Bud vase, floral, bl/gr on burgundy butterfat, HM, 7x2½" **650.00**
Planter, cobalt flowers, Louise Abel, 1925, #2000, 6x6½" **700.00**
Vase, berries & leaves, Katherine Jones, 1930, 8¾x4½" **1,200.00**
Vase, cherry blossoms, faceted, E Lincoln, 1922, #2577, 3½x6" ...**600.00**
Vase, Deco gazelles/mtns, Wm Hentschel, 1931, #619 F, 4⅝" ...**1,600.00**
Vase, dogwood blossoms, Louise Abel, 1927, #2969, 7½x6½" ..**1,500.00**
Vase, elm trees, Mary Helen McDonald, #892C, 1938, 10x5¾" ..**3,500.00**
Vase, floral, red on pk, Catherine Covalenco, 1925, 7x3¼" **700.00**
Vase, floral (heavy slip), Jens Jensen, 1943, #6197 F, 4¾" **450.00**
Vase, irises, bl/gr on pk, Sallie Coyne, #1369, 1925, 15x7½" ...**3,250.00**
Vase, Picasso-style Anniversary, MH McDonald, 1930, #654C, 5¾" ...**800.00**
Vase, pine cones, E Lincoln, 1927, #546C, 9½x4¾" **1,100.00**
Vase, trefoils, wht on bl to yel, K Shirayamadani, 1938, 7x4½" ..**1,300.00**
Vase, tulips (EX art), K Shirayamadani, 1936, 8x6¾" **1,700.00**
Vase, tulips on yel to gr, MH McDonald, 1937, 9x4¾", pr **2,200.00**
Vase, wild roses, C Steinle, 1923, #514F, 7x3¾" **800.00**

Miscellaneous

Vase, #339B, 1910, mustard microcrystalline, 12¾x9½", $1,300.00.

Ashtray, #6329/#95-L-3, 1944, fish, wht mat, 5½" dia **60.00**
Bookends, #2446, 1921, girl on bench w/book, bl mat, 5½", EX, pr **200.00**
Bookends, #2565, 1921, owls, brn mat, MH McDonald, 6½", NM, pr ..**350.00**
Bookends, #2837, 1927, flower baskets, mc on bl to gr, rpr, 6½", pr **160.00**
Bowl, #2051, 1913, rabbit (cvd), bl/gr/brn mat, hdls, 2¾x3" **400.00**
Bowl, #2179, 1931, floral, bl mat, X, 4½x6" **120.00**
Bowl, #928E, 1021, navy hi-glaze w/yel int, 4x8½" **160.00**
Bowl, #974D, 1915, burgundy mat w/gr mottling, 2x4" **200.00**
Candlesticks, #1636, 1921, floral, yel mat, 7", NM, pr **270.00**
Candlesticks, #822D, 1921, pk mat w/gr tint, 6½", pr **160.00**
Dish, #1139, 1900, rook perched on edge, brn hi-glaze, 4½x8" ...**80.00**
Dish, #2765, 1928, frog on rim, gr/brn mottle, tricorner, 5½" ...**200.00**
Jar, #622C, 1920, pk mat, w/lid, 3½x4½" **200.00**
Mug, #587G, 1909, geometrics, gr to bl mat, 5" **150.00**
Paperweight, #2747, 1924, foo dog, dk bl, 4" **275.00**
Paperweight/match holder, #6404, 1938, donkey, ochre, 4" **275.00**
Pitcher, #2568, 1900, lav/brn/gr mottled hi-glaze, 3½" **90.00**

Pitcher, Made for...Laurence A Horan..., 1949, rose hi-glaze, 4½" 50.00
Tile, #1683, 1930, grapes & leaves, 5½" 150.00
Tile, #3069, 1919, lady, purple/bl/wht/yel, 5½", NM 200.00
Tile, #3069, 1921, Victorian lady w/umbrella, 5½" 200.00
Tile, #3077, 1930, parrot w/flowers, 5½" 260.00
Tile, #3204, 1925, leaves, gr & dk bl, 5½" 250.00
Tile, #3207, 1926, geese in landscape, mc, 6" in fr 400.00
Trivet, #3091, 1919, leaves/berries, lt & dk bl on tan mat, 6" dia 200.00
Trivet, #3969, 1922, lady w/umbrella & hoop skirt, mc on bl, 6" dia ..230.00
Vase, #1188, 1914, geometrics, yel mat, 2½x5" 180.00
Vase, #1308, 1922, purple mat, 4 buttressed ft, 2½x6½", NM ...200.00
Vase, #1349, 1908, lt to dk bl mat, 4-ftd, 3x5½" 90.00
Vase, #1681, 1929, lily of the valley, bl mat, 4½" 150.00
Vase, #1747, 1914, floral, gr to pk matt, 6½", NM 200.00
Vase, #1795, 1922, rooks, rose mat, 4¾" 250.00
Vase, #1903, 1921, emb leaves at top, yel mat, 5¼" 250.00
Vase, #2076, 1928, pk & gr mat, hdls, 6½" 130.00
Vase, #2090, 1937, panel design, yel mat, 4½" 160.00
Vase, #2097, 1920, swans circle top, yel mat, 3½" 225.00
Vase, #2111, 1927, floral band, pk & gr mat, 6½" 110.00
Vase, #2139, 1923, berries, gr mat, 4½" 110.00
Vase, #2141, 1927, 3-panel floral, plum mat, 6¾" 250.00
Vase, #2218, 1920, gr & bl mottle hi-glaze, 5½" 200.00
Vase, #2224, 1928, geometrics, gr crystalline, 3-hdl, 6" 220.00
Vase, #2359, 1918, birds in flight, lt bl mat, 4-ftd, 3x6½" 100.00
Vase, #2413, 1931, Arts & Crafts floral, bl mat, 7½" 750.00
Vase, #2420, 1924, blk hi-glaze, 9½", NM 200.00
Vase, #2434, 1921, lt bl mat, 5½", NM 120.00
Vase, #2435, 1919, geometrics, bl mat, 7" 140.00
Vase, #2484, 1920, floral, lt brn mat, 9" 180.00
Vase, #2545F, 1923, rose mat, classic shape w/flared rim, 7" 100.00
Vase, #2591, 1929, sunflower, gr mat, 5½" 170.00
Vase, #2593, 1922, berries & leaves, pk & gr mat, 7" 150.00
Vase, #2604, 1922, vintage, pk & gr mat, 6½" 120.00
Vase, #2815, 1925, teal mat, hdls, 7" 260.00
Vase, #2870, 1928, yel mat, flakes, 5" 120.00
Vase, #2951, 1946, daisies, gr hi-glaze, 5½" 100.00
Vase, #2989, 1945, floral, bl mat, 7" 90.00
Vase, #6006, 1930, poppies, bl mat, 11" 550.00
Vase, #614F, 1909, geometrics, dk red mat, 6" 230.00
Vase, #6147, 1930, leaves & berries, gr mat, 6½" 200.00
Vase, #6214, 1938, deer & shrubs, gr hi-glaze, 4½" 110.00
Vase, #6230, 1931, floral (molded), bl mat, 4½" 180.00
Vase, #6363, 1956, floral, gr hi-glaze, 5½" 90.00
Vase, #6474, 1938, floral, gr mat, flattened form, 4x4" 60.00
Vase, #6548, 1938, bird, yel mat, 3½" 160.00
Vase, #6818, 1945, broad leaves, ivory hi-glaze, 6" 90.00
Vase, #6833, 1957, floral, bl hi-glaze, 6½" 100.00
Vase, #696, 1916, lt bl mat, 9½" 175.00
Vase, #7075, 1955, geometrics, gr hi-glaze, 7" 100.00
Vase, #9602 X, 1908, monk, red to brn mat, 6" 750.00

Rorstrand

The Rorstrand Pottery was established in Sweden in 1726 and is today Sweden's oldest existing pottery. The earliest ware, now mostly displayed in Swedish museums, was much like old Delft. Later types were hard-paste porcelains that were enameled and decorated in a peasant style. Contemporary pieces are often described as Swedish Modern. Rorstrand is also famous for their Christmas plates.

Bowl, lt gr crystalline leaf shape, 3x17" 100.00
Bowl, slate gray matt, sunburst pattern, H Bengtson, 2x7" 100.00
Plate, Christmas, child in sled pulled by reindeer, 1971 ....45.00
Plate, Mother's Day, mk Mors Dag, 1974, 8" 40.00
Vase, bl/brn/ivory, irregular fine vertical ribs, 6½" 170.00
Vase, brn matt, tear shape, w/certificate, 19½x12" 2,800.00
Vase, emb nubs under brilliant cobalt, cylindrical, 12x5½" 200.00
Vase, leafy trails form hearts at base, 4 hdls, bl/wht, 9½" 120.00
Vase, lg daisies, bl on wht, integral hdls, 8½" 200.00
Vase, mottled wht w/gray, cvd stripes/zigzag, Nylund, 7½" 245.00
Vase, nasturtium, violet/gr on wht, porc, 5¼x3¼", NM 325.00

Rose Mandarin

Similar in design to Rose Medallion, this Chinese Export porcelain features the pattern of a robed mandarin, often separated by florals, ladies, genre scenes, or butterflies in polychrome enamels. It is sometimes trimmed in gold. Elaborate in decoration, this pattern was popular from the late 1700s until the early 1840s.

Wash basin, ornate rim with birds, butterflies, hunters, and animals on gold ground above base cameo of seven figures in a garden, 5x16¼", $1,870.00.

Garden seat, 19" H, pr 4,600.00
Jug, cider; woven dbl strap hdl, foo dog finial, 9½" 3,000.00
Pitcher, water; paneled form w/scalloped rim, 7¾" 1,400.00
Pitcher, water; 9½" 1,750.00
Platter, 14¾x12" 900.00
Pot, bough; hexagonal, appl squirrels/berries, 9", EX 1,400.00
Punch bowl, 13½", NM 1,500.00
Punch bowl, 14¾" 2,300.00
Shrimp dish, 9¾" 500.00
Soup plate, court scene, 10", 7 for 600.00
Teacup & saucer, rstr, 12 for 1,000.00
Teapot, dome lid, gilt on spout & hdl, 8½" 1,200.00
Vase, bottle form, appl kylins & foo dogs, 9⅞x3½" 375.00
Vase, w/lid, 10¾x7", pr 3,200.00

Rose Medallion

Rose Medallion is one of the patterns of Chinese export porcelain produced from before 1850 until the second decade of the twentieth century. It is decorated in rose colors with panels of florals, birds, and butterflies that form reserves containing Chinese figures. Pre-1850 ware is unmarked and is characterized by quality workmanship and gold trim. From about 1850 until circa 1860, the kilns in Canton did not operate, and no Rose Medallion was made. Post-1860 examples (still unmarked) can often be recognized by the poor quality of the gold trim or its absence. In the 1890s the ware was often marked 'China'; 'Made in China' was used from 1910 through the 1930s.

Basket, fruit; rtcl, w/undertray 750.00

Bin, rectangular, rare, 1¾x13½x7" 800.00
Bottle, water; 19th C, 14½" 650.00
Bough pot, appl squirrel & berry devices, 8-sided, 9" 4,850.00

Bough pots, court figures in panels, square with foliate handles, nineteenth century, 9", $4,300.00 for the pair.

Bowl, centerpc; scalloped, ftd, 19th C, 6½x10⅜" 2,875.00
Bowl, rectangular w/cut corners, w/lid, 9½" L, pr 865.00
Bowl, shaped rim, 2¾x9¾x8½", EX 200.00
Bowl, w/lid, 19th C, 10" 400.00
Bowl, 3½x9½" 175.00
Box, brush; rectangular, divided int, 2¾x7x3½" 475.00
Brush pot, cylindrical, 4¾x3" 450.00
Brush pot, cylindrical, 5¾x5" 550.00
Charger, 19th C, 21½" 1,100.00
Charger, 20th C, 18" dia, pr 300.00
Compote, rtcl, 19th C, 3⅝x7⅝", pr 700.00
Creamer, curved spout, 4½x7" 225.00
Creamer & sugar bowl, w/lid, 3½" 350.00
Ewer & bowl, bottle shape w/dome stopper, wide rim, 15", 16" ..1,800.00
Garden seat, hexagonal, 19th C, 19x12x10" 2,185.00
Jar, 20th C, 12½" 150.00
Plate, 3-lobe, 10" 350.00
Platter, cabbage leaf center, 16½x13¼", EX 625.00
Platter, well & tree; flower/butterfly panels, 18¾x13¼", EX 800.00
Platter, 11¾x9", EX 200.00
Platter, 14½x11¾" 300.00
Platter, 15½x11½" 350.00
Platter, 16x13" 600.00
Platter, 18" 500.00
Punch bowl, elegant figures/birds/butterflies w/gold, 19th C, 16" ..4,000.00
Punch bowl, 19th C, 14½" 1,550.00
Sauce tureen, w/lid, 6" H 500.00
Shrimp dish, 9½" 350.00
Soap dish, rectangular, w/insert & lid, 3x6x5" 250.00
Sugar bowl, strap hdl, w/lid, 5x6" 200.00
Tazza, 19th C, 3½x14⅛" 800.00
Tazza, 4½x10½" 545.00
Tea set, 20th C, 5" pot+cr/sug 400.00
Teapot, dome lid, rstr hdl, 9½" 1,000.00
Teapot, urn form, landscape reserves, 9½x7" 550.00
Tray, dresser; ingot shape, ca 1890s, 10⅛" 280.00
Tureen, soup; w/lid & underplate, 10", 15" 3,100.00
Tureen, strapped hdls, ped base, mushroom finial, 11½x14½" L 1,450.00
Umbrella stand, 12 panels w/people/birds/butterflies, 24x9½", EX ...1,650.00
Vase, appl kylins & foo dogs, 19th C, 14" on wood stand, pr .2,300.00
Vase, baluster, 13x6½", EX 1,400.00
Vase, baluster, 20th C, 14" 375.00
Vase, baluster w/appl kylins & foo dogs, 19th C, 9¼", pr 635.00
Vase, baluster w/emb kylins & foo dogs at neck, 24", pr 3,000.00
Vase, bottle form, 19th C, 13½x8" 1,100.00
Vase, Ku form, 20th C, 13¾x8¾", NM 435.00
Vase, roses, appl flower hdls, flared rim, 20th C, 12" 200.00
Wash basin & pitcher, 19th C, 14¼", 16" dia 800.00

Roselane

As collectors begin considering California pottery, many turn their attention toward the products created by William 'Dock' Fields and his wife, Georgia. In 1938 they started Roselane Pottery which they operated together from their home. Less than two years later they had moved the operation to Pasedena, California, and then onto Baldwin Park, California, where it remained for six years. William died in 1973. Georgia sold the company to Prather Engineering Corporation, and they moved it to Long Beach, California. By 1977 Roselane no longer existed.

Various items were created over the years such as candlesticks, ashtrays, bowls, wall pockets, and sculptured high-gloss animals on wooden bases. Lines included the Sparkler series, Aqua Marine, and Chinese Modern. Collectors today are looking for the sculptured high-glazed animals on walnut bases. Being stylistic in nature, this series was not well received by the public, and it was soon discontinued. Roselane surpassed many companies with their deer groups. These lightweight deer, extremely fragile, have become regarded as masterpieces. Many have multiple figures one one base. The glazes are usually muted, and the deer can most often be found in pale blue, ivory, brown, or pale green. Paper labels as well as a variety of other marks were used. Even if the label is missing and there is no other mark, experience and a well-trained eye will make it easily possible to distinguish Roselane creations from those of other companies. Our advisor for this category is Susan Cox; she is listed in the Directory under California.

Bowl, Chinese Key design, sq, ped ft, 6¼" 25.00
Bowl, console; pk w/blk swirls w/3 fish, wooden legs, 4x13" 110.00
Dealer sign, deep aqua high glaze, 3x12½", minimum value 350.00
Figurine, angelfish, Aqua Marine line, in-mold mk #20, 7½" 85.00
Figurine, angelfish, Sparkler, 4½" 25.00
Figurine, Bali dancer, male & female, 11", 11½", pr 135.00
Figurine, Basset Hound pup, Sparkler, 2" 18.00
Figurine, cat, abstract, wht, wood base, mid-50s, burned-in mk, 10" ...175.00
Figurine, cocker spaniel, Sparkler, 4½" 20.00
Figurine, deer, pk w/head up, 10" 65.00
Figurine, dog, stylized, wht on wooden base, 9½" 145.00
Figurine, elephant, sitting on hind quarters, Sparkler, 6" 25.00
Figurine, fawn, legs folded under body, Sparkler, 4x3½" 25.00
Figurine, fawn, Sparkler, 4½x1½" 20.00
Figurine, frog, Sparkler, 2½", from $25 to 30.00
Figurine, giraffe, brn w/blk horns, lying down w/head up, 5½" 55.00
Figurine, horse, wht, on wood base, burned-in mk, 9", minimum value 175.00
Figurine, kangaroo, mama w/babies, Sparkler 40.00
Figurine, kitten, sitting, Sparkler, 1¾" 12.00
Figurine, owl, Sparkler, 5¼" 25.00
Figurine, pouter pigeon, Sparkler, 3½" 20.00
Figurine, Whippet, sitting, Sparkler, 7½" 28.00
Incense burner, fawn w/dk brn accents, #11, 6½" 50.00

Rosemeade

Rosemeade was the name chosen by Wahpeton Pottery Company of Wahpeton, North Dakota, to represent their product. The founders of the company were Laura A. Taylor and R.J. Hughes, who organized the firm in 1940. It is most noted for small bird and animal figurals, either in high gloss or a Van Briggle-like matt glaze. The ware was marked 'Rosemeade' with an ink stamp or carried a 'Prairie Rose' sticker. The pottery closed in 1961. Our advisor for this category is Bryce L. Farnsworth; he is listed in the Directory under North Dakota. For more information we recommend *Collector's Encyclopedia of Rosemeade Pottery* by Darlene Hurst Dommel (Collector Books).

Bank, bear, 3" 450.00
Bank, buffalo, World's Largest - Jamestown, ND 400.00

Bell, peacock figural, with sticker, 5", $400.00.

Bell, tea; Art Nouveau tulip, various colors, 3¾" 150.00
Bookends, wolfhound, Art Deco, 6½x7½", pr 325.00
Cotton dispenser, wht rabbit w/pk HP eyes & inner ears 185.00
Cranberry dish, turkey, w/spoon notch, 4½" 150.00
Figurine, buffalo, bronze, 6½x8½" 325.00
Figurine, Chinese ring-neck pheasant, cock, med, 7x12½" 250.00
Figurine, Chinese ring-neck pheasant, hen, 3½x11½" 400.00
Figurine, dog, begging Cocker Spaniel, 2¾" 85.00
Figurine, God of Peace, St Paul City Hall & Courthouse 300.00
Figurine, horse, Palomino, w/cut-out foliage, 9½" 500.00
Figurine, Rocky Mountain goat on base, wht, 2¾x2¾" 200.00
Figurines, cats, wht, 2x2", pr 90.00
Figurines, seals, blk, set of 3 ....50.00
Moccasin, bsk w/HP details 50.00
Mug, Minnesota Centennial, brn, 3" 90.00
Pin, Prairie Rose, 2x2" 500.00
Pitcher, 2-color swirl, 3¼" 250.00
Planter, deer on log, 4x5¼" 60.00
Planter, dove, 4¼x5¼" 150.00
Planter, swan, 4¾x5¼" 50.00
Shakers, buffalo, pr 175.00
Shakers, cucumbers, 1½", pr 50.00
Shakers, deer, fawns, recumbent, pr 95.00
Shakers, deer, leaping, pr 125.00
Shakers, dog heads, Chihuahuas, pr 500.00
Shakers, dog heads, Dalmatians, pr 135.00
Shakers, dog heads, English Setters, pr 60.00
Shakers, dog heads, Greyhounds, pr 110.00
Shakers, elephants, various colors, pr 120.00
Shakers, fish w/tails up, pr 75.00
Shakers, gophers, upright, lg, pr 150.00
Shakers, mallard drake & hen, pr 100.00
Shakers, Paul Bunyan & Babe the Blue Ox, 2¼", pr 150.00
Shakers, quail w/feather topknots, male & female, 2¼", pr 100.00
Shakers, raccoons, pr 175.00
Shakers, rooster & hen, brn, 2½", pr 125.00
Shakers, skunks, lg, pr 60.00
Shakers, swans, various colors, pr 100.00
Shakers, turkeys, lg, pr 75.00
Spoon rest, flying cock pheasant, 3¼x5½" 55.00
Spoon rest, Minnesota Centennial, spoon, dk gr, 8" 80.00
Spoon rest, pansy, 3¾" 150.00
Spoon rest, tulip, 5½" 100.00
Spoon rest, wild rose (prairie rose), 4" 65.00
Tv lamp, Palomino horse, 9½" 600.00
Vase, deer, standing, 8" 50.00
Vase, gr, textured, 9½" 80.00
Vase, peacock, 7½" 275.00
Vase, 2-color swirl, 4" 125.00
Wall plaque, fish, bass, 3½x6" 300.00
Wall plaque, fish, blue gill, 3½x6" 365.00
Wall plaque, fish, northern pike, 3½x6" 375.00

Rosenthal

In 1879 Phillip Rosenthal established the Rosenthal Porcelain Factory in Selb, Bavaria. Its earliest products were figurines and fine tablewares. The company has continued to operate to the present decade, manufacturing limited edition plates. Our advisor for this category is Raphael Wise; he is listed in the Directory under Florida.

Bowl, sauce; Gwendolyn 15.00
Bowl, vegetable; Gwendolyn, w/lid 140.00
Cake plate, Gwendolyn 60.00
Cup & saucer, Gwendolyn 33.00
Cup & saucer, hummingbird of the world, set of 6 different 150.00
Ewer, lav floral, 6" 395.00
Figurine, bunny, laughing, 5" 70.00
Figurine, cat, sgn Karner 150.00

Figurine, lady with swirling skirt, bare midrift, 10", $850.00.

Figurine, rabbit, wht, laughing, sm 57.00
Gravy, Gwendolyn 75.00
Pitcher, floral w/gold, lt wear on hdl, 15" 495.00
Plaque, snow-covered mtn peak & lake, orig fr, 10x12" 700.00
Plate, dinner; Gwendolyn 20.00
Plate, mc roses w/much gold, 1890s, 8½" 95.00
Platter, Gwendolyn, 11" 55.00
Sculpture, fish & seaweed, F Heidenreich, 9" base, 16" overall .200.00
Sculpture, recessed hemispheres on circular form, gilt porc, 1971, 12" ...150.00
Teapot, Gwendolyn 85.00
Vase, nude at cliff w/flowers & doves, pate-sur-pate, wht/gr, 11" ...1,500.00
Vase, silver o/l florals, cream bosses on rust, paneled, 7" 290.00

Roseville

The Roseville Pottery Company was established in 1892 by George F. Young in Roseville, Ohio. Finding their facilities inadequate, the company moved to Zanesville in 1898, erected a new building, and installed the most modern equipment available. By 1900 Young felt ready to enter into the stiffly competitive art pottery market. Roseville's first art line was called Rozane. Similar to Rookwood's Standard, Rozane featured dark blended backgrounds with slip-painted underglaze artwork of nature studies, portraits, birds, and animals. Azurean, developed in 1902, was a blue and white underglaze art line on a blue blended background. Egypto (1904) featured a matt glaze in a soft shade of old green and was modeled in low relief after examples of ancient Egyptian pottery. Mongol (1904) was a high-gloss oxblood red line after the fashion of the Chinese Sang de Boeuf. Mara (1904), an iridescent lustre line of magenta and rose with intricate patterns developed on the surface or in low relief, successfully duplicated Sicardo's work. These early lines were followed by many others of highest quality: Fudjiyama and Woodland (1905 – 06) reflected an Oriental theme; Crystalis (1906) was covered with beautiful frost-like crystals. Della Robbia, their most famous line (introduced in 1906), was decorated with designs ranging from florals, animals, and birds to scenes of Viking warriors and Roman gladiators. These designs were worked in sgraffito with slip-painted details. Very limited but of great importance to collectors today, Rozane Olympic (1905) was decorated with scenes of Greek mythology on a red ground. Pauleo (1914) was the last of the artware lines. It was varied — over two hundred glazes were recorded — and some pieces were decorated by hand, usually with florals.

During the second decade of the century until the plant closed forty years later, new lines were continually added. Some of the more popular of the middle-period lines were Donatello, 1915; Futura, 1928; Pine Cone, 1931; and Blackberry, 1933. The floral lines of the later years have become highly collectible. Pottery from every era of Roseville production — even its utility ware — attest to an unwavering dedication to quality and artistic merit.

Examples of the fine art pottery lines present the greatest challenge to evaluate. Scarcity is a prime consideration. The quality of artwork varied from one artist to another. Some pieces show fine detail and good color, and naturally this influences their values. Studies of animals and portraits bring higher prices than the floral designs. An artist's signature often increases the value of any item, especially if the artist is one who is well recognized.

The market is literally flooded with imposter Roseville that is coming into the country from China. An experienced eye can easily detect these fakes, but to a novice collector, they may pass for old Roseville. Study the marks. If the 'USA' is missing or appears only faintly, the piece is most definitely a reproduction. Also watch for lines with a mark that is not correct for its time frame; for example, Luffa with the script mark, and Woodland with the round Rozane stamp from the 1917 line.

For further information consult *The Collector's Encyclopedia of Roseville Pottery, First* and *Second Series*, by Sharon and Bob Huxford (Collector Books); *Collector's Compendium of Roseville Pottery, Volumes I, II*, and *III*, by R.B. Monsen (see Directory, Virginia); and *Roseville in All Its Splendor with Price Guide* by Jack and Nancy Bomm (self-published). Note: Reference names in the Futura descriptions that follow have developed via communication among collectors (Monsen follows up on this in Volume I). The values we list for this very popular line were prices realized at auction. Futura prices tend to be volatile, and only when there were multiple sales for a particular piece did we choose to include it here.

Apple Blossom, jardiniere, #342-6, 6" 140.00
Apple Blossom, vase, #390-12, 12½" 250.00
Apple Blossom, window box, #368-8, 2½x10½" 95.00
Aztec, lamp base, 11" 325.00
Aztec, pitcher, bulbous, sgn L, 5½" 325.00
Azurean, candlestick, floral, 9" 575.00
Azurean, vase, #822/7, floral, 15½" 1,150.00
Baneda, candle holder, red, 5½" 275.00
Baneda, console bowl, red, 13" 450.00
Baneda, vase, gr, 12" 1,250.00
Baneda, vase, red, 4½" 325.00
Bittersweet, bowl vase, #842-7, 7" 150.00
Bittersweet, cornucopia, #857-4, 4½" 95.00
Bittersweet, planter, #828-10, 10½" 120.00
Blackberry, console bowl, 13" 400.00
Blackberry, jardiniere, 6" 400.00
Blackberry, vase, 12½" 1,000.00
Blackberry, wall pocket 850.00
Bleeding Heart, bowl vase, #651-3, 3½" 95.00
Bleeding Heart, console bowl/frog, #384-14/#40, 17" 250.00
Bleeding Heart, hanging basket, 8" 300.00
Burmese, planter, #908-10, 10" 60.00
Bushberry, candlestick, #144-7-CS, 2" 70.00
Bushberry, cornucopia, dbl, #155-8, 6" 150.00
Bushberry, hanging basket, 7" 375.00
Bushberry, vase, #32-7, 7" 125.00
Capri, Late Line; basket, #510-10, 9" 150.00
Capri, Late Line; leaf dish, #532-16, 16" 35.00
Capri, Late Line; window box, #569-10, 3x10" 45.00
Carnelian, bowl, flared rim, drip glaze, 5x12½" 300.00
Carnelian, candle holder, drip glaze, hdls, 3" 75.00
Carnelian, fan vase, textured, hdls, 8" 125.00
Carnelian, fan vase, textured, 6½" 100.00
Carnelian, flower frog, textured, 4x6" 150.00
Carnelian, vase, textured, 8" 225.00
Ceramic Design, pitcher, geometrics on cream, 6½" 250.00
Ceramic Design, tumber, geometrics on cream, 4" 125.00
Cherry Blossom, candle holders, 4", pr 450.00
Cherry Blossom, jardiniere, 10" 800.00
Cherry Blossom, jug vase, 7" 400.00
Chloron, bud vase, dbl, gate type, 5x8" 50.00
Chloron, vase, cone shape, 6½" 250.00
Clemana, bowl, #281-5, 4½x6½" 225.00
Clemana, flower frog, #23, 4" 175.00
Clemana, vase, #750-6, 6½" 250.00
Clematis, candle holder, #1155-2, 2½" 60.00
Clematis, console bowl, #456-6, 9" 75.00
Clematis, vase, #102-6, 6½" 85.00
Colonial, pitcher, 7½" 125.00
Colonial, soap dish, w/lid, 4" 90.00
Columbine, bookend planter, #8, 5" 175.00
Columbine, cornucopia, #149-6, 5½" 95.00
Columbine, hanging basket, 8½" 250.00
Cornelian (spongeware), pitcher, corn, 6" 150.00
Cornelian (spongeware), pitcher, 4" 60.00
Cornelian (spongeware), shaving mug, 4" 75.00
Cosmos, flower frog, 3½" 125.00
Cosmos, vase, #905-8, 8" 150.00
Cosmos, vase, #956-12, 12½" 550.00
Cremona, bowl, 9" 125.00
Cremona, vase, 10" 175.00
Cremona, vase, 8" 150.00
Dahlrose, bowl, oval, 10" 200.00
Dahlrose, bud vase, triple, 6" 150.00
Dahlrose, vase, 4-sided, 10" 250.00
Decorated Utility Ware, pitcher, center band, 6" 75.00
Della Robbia, vase, arrow leaves/florettes, 6-color, 11", rstr 9,500.00
Dogwood I, hanging basket, 7" 150.00
Dogwood I, jardiniere, 6" 115.00
Dogwood II, basket, 6" 150.00
Dogwood II, bowl, 2" 75.00
Dogwood II, bud vase, 9" 85.00
Donatello, bud vase, dbl; 5" 75.00
Donatello, compote, 4" 100.00
Donatello, jardiniere, 8½" 150.00

Dutch, soap dish, w/lid, 3" 225.00
Dutch, tankard, rnd or angled hdl, 5", ea 95.00
Earlam, bowl, hdls, 3x11½" 160.00
Earlam, candle holders, 6", pr 175.00
Earlam, vase, hdls, 4" 110.00
Earlam, vase, 6" 175.00
Earlam, vase, 9" 375.00
Egypto, compote, Egypto seal mk, 5" 450.00
Egypto, oil lamp, Egypto seal mk, 5" 450.00

Falline vases: Flared body, loop handles, unmarked, 8¼", $750.00; Bulbous with upturned handles, foil label, 6", $700.00.

Falline, bowl, 11" 250.00
Falline, candle holder, 4" 200.00
Falline, vase, 12½" 900.00
Ferella, candlesticks, 4½", pr 500.00
Ferella, lamp base, hdls, blended bl & gr, 10½" 800.00
Ferella, vase, hdls, 6" 275.00
Florane, bowl, hdls, 5" 50.00
Florane, bud vase, dbl, gate type, 5" 60.00
Florane, bud vases, 8", pr 125.00
Florentine, basket, 8" 200.00
Florentine, bud vase, dbl, gate type, 6" 110.00
Florentine, vase, 6½" 100.00
Foxglove, bud vase, dbl, #160, 4½" 135.00
Foxglove, cornucopia, #164, 8" 140.00
Foxglove, flower frog, #46, 4" 135.00
Foxglove, tray, 15" 160.00
Foxglove, vase, #52-12, 12½" 350.00
Freesia, basket, #390-7 ....150.00
Freesia, console bowl, #469-14, 16½" 175.00
Freesia, window box, #1392-8, 10½" 95.00
Fuchsia, candlesticks, #1132, 2", pr 150.00
Fuchsia, console bowl/frog, #353-14/#37 ....325.00
Fuchsia, vase, #898-8 ....275.00
Fudji, jardiniere, 9" 1,350.00
Fudji, vase, 4-sided w/twisted rim, 10" 1,450.00
Futura, bowl, Balloons, #187-8, from $300 to 350.00
Futura, bowl, Flying Saucer, #195-10, from $1,000 to 1,200.00
Futura, hanging basket, #344, 6x8¾" 375.00
Futura, jardiniere, leaves, hdls, 14" dia, from $350 to 400.00
Futura, jardiniere, leaves, hdls, 9" dia, from $275 to 325.00
Futura, vase, Balloons Globe, #404-8, from $1,000 to 1,300.00
Futura, vase, Bamboo Leaf Ball, #387-7, from $650 to 850.00
Futura, vase, Beehive, #406-8, from $600 to 700.00
Futura, vase, Beer Mug, #381-6, from $250 to 325.00
Futura, vase, Big Blue Triangle, #388-9, from $450 to 600.00
Futura, vase, Black Flame, #391-10, from $850 to 1,100.00
Futura, vase, Blue Sunray, #81-5x1½x5 ....350.00
Futura, vase, Bomb, #394-12, from $1,000 to 1,100.00
Futura, vase, Bottle, #348-8, from $350 to 425.00
Futura, vase, Brown Stump, #421-5, from $275 to 325.00
Futura, vase, Chinese Pillow, #430-9, from $850 to 1,000.00
Futura, vase, Christmas Tree, #390-10, from $500 to 650.00
Futura, vase, Cone, #401-8, from $450 to 550.00
Futura, vase, Egg w/Leaves, #428-8, from $400 to 500.00
Futura, vase, Emerald Urn, #398-9 ....600.00
Futura, vase, Football Urn, #409-9, from $1,000 to 1,200.00
Futura, vase, Half-Egg or 3-Leg Bowl, #197-6, from $600 to 650.00
Futura, vase, Jukebox, #386-8 ....600.00
Futura, vase, Little Blue Triangle, #383-8, from $300 to 375.00
Futura, vase, Mauve Thistle, #427-8, from $850 to 1,000.00
Futura, vase, Milk Carton, #402-8, from $600 to 650.00
Futura, vase, Pink Twist, #425-8, from $450 to 550.00
Futura, vase, Pleated Star, #358-8 ....450.00
Futura, vase, Red V (Victory), #399-7, from $350 to 400.00
Futura, vase, Sand Toy, #189-4-6, from #400 to 500.00
Futura, vase, Sea Gull, #408-10, from $1,000 to 1,200.00
Futura, vase, Shooting Star, #392-10, from $800 to 1,100.00
Futura, vase, Space Capsule, #432-10, from $600 to 650.00
Futura, vase, Spaceship, #405-7½, from $600 to 650.00
Futura, vase, Spittoon, #403-7, from $800 to 1,000.00
Futura, vase, Square Box, #191-8 ....375.00
Futura, vase, Square Cone, #397-6, from $325 to 365.00
Futura, vase, Stepped Egg, #424-7, from $600 to 750.00
Futura, vase, Table Leg, #410-12, from $1,200 to 1,400.00
Futura, vase, Tall Thistle, 15½", from $1,200 ....1,500.00
Futura, vase, Telescope, #382-7, from $250 to 325.00
Futura, vase, Tombstone, #423-6, from $250 to 350.00
Futura, vase, Twist, #398-6½, from $300 to 350.00
Futura, vase, 2-Pole Pink Bud, #84-4, from $300 to 400.00
Futura, vase, 4-Ball, #393-12, from $1,000 to 1,200.00
Futura, wall pocket, 8", from $475 to 550.00
Gardenia, hanging basket, 6" 225.00
Gardenia, tray, #631-14, 15" 165.00
Gardenia, vase, #610-12 ....225.00
Gardenia, window box, #658-8, 3x8½" 95.00
Holland, mug, 4" 75.00
Holland, pitcher, #1, 6½" 200.00
Imperial I, basket, 6" 150.00
Imperial I, basket, 8" 225.00
Imperial I, bud vase, triple; 8" 175.00
Imperial II, bowl, cone shape, 4½" 350.00
Imperial II, bowl, flared rim, 5x12½" 425.00
Imperial II, wall pocket 275.00
Iris, basket, #355-10, 9½" 300.00
Iris, console bowl, #361-8, 3x10" 125.00
Iris, planter, #364, 14" 250.00
Iris, vase, #924-9, 10" 250.00
Ivory II, candlestick, #1122-5, 5½" 40.00
Ivory II, hanging basket, 7" 100.00
Ivory II, jardiniere, #574-4, 4" 50.00
Ixia, bowl, #326, 4" 125.00
Ixia, candle holder/bud vase, #1128, 5" 150.00
Ixia, vase, #856-8, 8½" 150.00
Jonquil, basket, ped ft, 9" 450.00
Jonquil, bud vase, hdls, 7" 150.00
Jonquil, crocus pot, 1-pc w/underplate, 7" 400.00
Jonquil, pot/frog, 1-pc, 5½" 300.00
Juvenile, mug, standing rabbit, 3" 120.00
Juvenile, pitcher w/saucer, ind; chicks 175.00
Juvenile, plate, chicks, 7" 150.00
La Rose, bowl, 6" 75.00
La Rose, candle holders, 4", pr 225.00
La Rose, vases, 10", pr 350.00
Laurel, bowl, 3½" 225.00
Laurel, bowl, 7" 200.00
Laurel, vase, 10" 400.00

Lombardy, jardiniere, 6½" 200.00
Lombardy, vase, 6" 200.00
Lotus, bowl, #L6-9, 3x9" 135.00
Lotus, pillow vase, #L4-10, 10½" 200.00
Lotus, planter, #L9-4, 3½x4" 100.00
Luffa, candlestick, 9½" 650.00
Luffa, lamp, bl/gr, 9½" 600.00
Luffa, lamp, bl/rose, 9½" 650.00
Lustre, candle holder, 6" 55.00
Lustre, vase, 10" 75.00
Magnolia, ashtray, #28, 7" 125.00
Magnolia, basket, #386-12, 12" 225.00
Magnolia, candlestick, #1157-4½, 5" 85.00
Magnolia, cornucopia, #184-6, 6" 95.00
Magnolia, planter, #183-6, 6" 110.00
Magnolia, planter, #388-6, 8½" 95.00
Mara, filigree design, 13" 2,000.00
Mara, vase, 5½" 1,650.00
Matt Green, jardiniere, 6" 125.00
Matt Green, pot/frog, ftd, 2½" 50.00
Matt Green, tobacco jar, w/lid, 6" 200.00
Mayfair, bowl, #1119-9, 10" 60.00
Mayfair, flowerpot, #71-4, 4½" 45.00
Mayfair, planter, #1113-8, 3½x8½" 60.00
Mayfair, teapot, #1121, 5" 110.00
Mayfair, vase, #1104-9, 9" 110.00
Mock Orange, planter, #931-8, 3½x9" 125.00
Mock Orange, vase, #985-12, 13" 175.00
Mock Orange, window box, #956-8, 8½x4½" 95.00
Moderne, candle holder, triple, #1112, 6" 225.00
Moderne, comport, #297-6, 6" 150.00
Moderne, vase, #299, 6½" 175.00
Mongol, mug, 3-hdl, 6" 850.00
Mongol, pitcher, 6½" 950.00
Mongol, vase, 2½" 500.00
Monticello, vase, hdld jar shape, 5" 300.00
Monticello, vase, low hdls, 10½" 500.00
Morning Glory, console bowl, 4½x11½" 350.00
Morning Glory, pillow vase, 7" 275.00
Moss, bud vase, triple, #1108, 7" 400.00
Moss, candlestick, triple, #1104, 2" 85.00
Moss, urn, #290-6, 6" 225.00
Mostique, bowl, mottled, geometrics, 2½" 75.00
Mostique, jardiniere, mottled, geometrics, 10" 300.00
Normandy, hanging basket, 7" 300.00
Olympic, tankard, Triptalemos & a Grain of Wheat, 11" 2,400.00
Orian, candle holder, 4½" 95.00
Orian, console bowl, ped ft, 5" 200.00
Orian, vase, 9" 165.00
Panel, bud vase, dbl, gate type 150.00
Panel, candle holder, 2" 70.00
Panel, vase, 8" 200.00
Pasadena, flowerpot, #L-36, 4" 60.00
Pasadena, planter, #L-17, 9x3½" 45.00
Pauleo, vase, #11, 16½" 1,150.00
Pauleo, vase, #340, 19" 1,300.00
Peony, bookends, #11, 5½", ea 110.00
Peony, pitcher, #1326, 7½" 325.00
Peony, planter, #387-8, 10" 95.00
Peony, tray, 8" 100.00
Peony, wall pocket, #1293, 8" 250.00
Persian, candlestick, 8½" 150.00
Persian, hanging basket, 9" 250.00
Persian, jardiniere, 8" 250.00
Pine Cone, boat dish, #427-8, 9" 250.00
Pine Cone, centerpiece/candle holder, #324, 6" 750.00
Pine Cone, planter, #124, 5" 225.00
Pine Cone, tumbler, #414, 5" 200.00
Pine Cone, window box, #431-15, 3½x15½" 400.00
Poppy, bowl, #336-10, 12" 175.00
Poppy, ewer, #880-18, 18½" 750.00
Poppy, vase, #642-4, 5" 95.00
Primrose, vase, #760-6, 7" 150.00
Primrose, vase, #767, 8" 250.00
Raymor, casserole, ind; #199, 7½" 45.00
Raymor, casserole/hot plate, #198/#84-198 ....85.00
Raymor, gravy boat, #190, 9½" 30.00
Raymor, shirred egg, #200, 10" 60.00
Raymor, vegetable bowl, #160, 9" 30.00
Rosecraft Black & Colors, bud vase, dbl, gate type, 5" 95.00
Rosecraft Black & Colors, ginger jar, 8" 250.00
Rosecraft Blended, vase, #35, 10" 125.00
Rosecraft Blended, window box/frog, 2-pc, 5x8" 100.00
Rosecraft Hexagon, bud vase, dbl, gate type 250.00
Rosecraft Hexagon, candlestick, 8" 250.00
Rosecraft Hexagon, vase, 6" 300.00
Rosecraft Vintage, jardiniere, 5" 150.00
Rosecraft Vintage, vase, 10" 350.00
Rosecraft Vintage, vase, 12" 300.00
Rosecraft Vintage, window box, 6x11½" 275.00
Rozane Light, bowl, floral, sgn WM, ornate hdls, ftd, 5" 200.00
Rozane Light, mug, berries, sgn Timberlake, 5" 350.00
Rozane Light, vase, floral, sgn Walter Myers, 8½" 325.00
Rozane Royal, jug, cherries, sgn J Imlay, 7" 275.00
Rozane Royal, mug, floral, sgn Harry Rhead, #886, 4½" 200.00
Rozane Royal, vase, dog portrait, sgn Dunlavy, 8" 2,250.00
Rozane Royal, vase, floral, #901, w/lid, 7½" 550.00
Rozane Royal, vase, floral, artist sgn, #853, 5½" 200.00
Rozane 1917, basket, gr, 8" 175.00
Rozane 1917, candlestick, ivory, 6" 125.00
Rozane 1917, spittoon, ivory, 5" 200.00
Russco, cornucopia, triple, 8x12½" 250.00
Russco, vase, ped ft, hdls, 8" 175.00
Silhouette, basket, #710, 10" 250.00
Silhouette, box, #740, w/lid, 4½" 125.00
Silhouette, cornucopia, #721, 8" 85.00
Silhouette, planter, #731, 14" L 150.00
Snowberry, ashtray 85.00
Snowberry, candlesticks, #1CS-2, 4½", pr 150.00
Snowberry, console bowl, #1BL-8, 11" 110.00
Snowberry, ewer, #1TK-15, 16" 400.00
Snowberry, pillow vase, #1FH-6, 6½" 110.00
Sunflower, candlesticks, 4", pr 450.00
Sunflower, jardiniere, 9" 700.00

Sunflower, umbrella stand, 20½x11½", $4,000.00.

Sunflower, vase, 5" 375.00
Sunflower, window box, 3½x11" 450.00
Teasel, bowl, #342, 4" 150.00
Teasel, ewer, #890, 18" 500.00
Teasel, vase, 5" 135.00
Thorn Apple, bowl vase #305-6, 6½" 175.00
Thorn Apple, bud vase, dbl, #1119 ....125.00
Thorn Apple, bud vase, triple, #1120 ....200.00
Thorn Apple, candle holders, #1117, 2½", pr 150.00
Topeo, bowl, 4x13" 250.00
Topeo, vase, 14" 550.00
Topeo, vase, 7" 200.00
Tourmaline, candlesticks, 5", pr 200.00
Tourmaline, ginger jar, w/lid 175.00
Tourmaline, planter, 5x12½" 300.00
Tourmaline, vase, twisted hexagon, 8" 125.00
Tuscany, candle holders, 3", pr 150.00
Tuscany, console bowl, 11" W 150.00
Tuscany, flower-arranger vase, 5" 100.00
Velmoss, bowl, 3x11" 200.00
Velmoss, vase, angled hdls, 8" 225.00
Velmoss II, bud vase, dbl, 8" 175.00
Velmoss II, vase, 6" 175.00
Velmoss Scroll, bowl, #C7, 3" 100.00
Velmoss Scroll, bowl, 2½x9" 100.00
Velmoss Scroll, candlestick, 8" 200.00
Velmoss Scroll, vase, 10" 200.00
Velmoss Scroll, vase, 12" 300.00
Velmoss Scroll, vase, 6" 120.00
Vista (Forest), basket, 8x5½" 550.00
Vista (Forest), vase, angle hdls, EX mold/color, 12x6" 950.00
Vista (Forest), vase, 10" 375.00
Water Lily, basket, #380, 8" 175.00
Water Lily, candlesticks, #1155-4½", 5", pr 175.00
Water Lily, cornucopia, #178, 8" 135.00
Water Lily, ewer, #11, 10" 200.00
Water Lily, flower frog, #48, 4½" 95.00
White Rose, bud vase, dbl, #148, 4½" 95.00
White Rose, console bowl/frog, #3393-12/#41, 16½" 200.00
White Rose, pitcher, #1324 ....250.00
White Rose, vase, #980-6, 5" 110.00
Wincraft, bookends, #259, 6½", pr 175.00
Wincraft, cornucopia, #221-8, 9x5" 95.00
Wincraft, planter, #231, 10" 125.00
Wincraft, planter set, #1051/1050, 6" 160.00
Windsor, basket, fan shape, ped ft, 4½" 350.00
Windsor, bowl, angled hdls, 3½x10½" 175.00
Windsor, lamp base, ball shape, 7" 600.00
Wisteria, bowl vase, 5" 350.00
Wisteria, hanging basket, 7½" 550.00
Wisteria, vase, 10" 550.00
Woodland, vase, orange poppy/gr stem, Rozane Ware seal mk, 10" ...1,200.00
Zephyr Lily, console bowl, #479-14, 16½" 200.00
Zephyr Lily, fan vase, #205-6, 6½" 115.00
Zephyr Lily, hanging basket, 7½" 175.00
Zephyr Lily, pillow vase, #206-7, 7" 125.00

Rowland and Marsellus

Though the impressive back stamp seems to suggest otherwise, Rowland and Marsellus were not Staffordshire potters but American importers who commissioned various English companies to supply them with the transfer-printed crockery and historical ware that had been a popular import commodity since the early 1800s. Plates (both flat and with a rolled edge), cups and saucers, pitchers, and platters were sold as souvenirs from 1890 through the 1930s. Though other importers — Bawo & Dotter and A. C. Bosselman & Co., both of New York City — commissioned the manufacture of similar souvenir items, by far the largest volume carries the R. & M. mark, and Rowland and Marcellus has become a generic term that covers all twentieth-century souvenir china of this type. Their mark may be in full or 'R. & M.' in a diamond. Though primarily made with blue transfers on white, other colors may occasionally be found as well. Our advisor for this category is David Ringering; he is listed in the Directory under Oregon.

Key:
r/e — rolled edge
s/o — souvenir of
v/o — view of

Plate, Souvenir of Lookout Mountain, Tennessee, rolled edge, 10", $70.00.

Creamer, Plymouth, mk as Burbank 35.00
Cup & saucer, Am Poets 95.00
Cup & saucer, Brooklyn, s/o 95.00
Cup & saucer, Lewis & Clarke Expo 175.00
Cup & saucer, mush; Take ye a cupp o'kindnesse..., gr 45.00
Cup & saucer, Pittsburgh, s/o 95.00
Cup & saucer, Yale, s/o 95.00
Fern pot, w/stand, lady's portrait by British artist, 11½" 460.00
Plate, Asbury Park NJ, v/o, 9" 35.00
Plate, Battle of Lake Erie, fruit & flower border 50.00
Plate, Boston MA, v/o, 9" 35.00
Plate, Bunker Hill Monument, fruit & flower border 50.00
Plate, Butte MT, s/o, r/e 70.00
Plate, Cape Cod, fisherman's portrait, 9" 35.00
Plate, coupe; American Poets, 7 portraits, 10" 50.00
Plate, coupe; Cooperstown NY, s/o, 6" 40.00
Plate, coupe; Fresno CA, 5 scenes, 6" 40.00
Plate, coupe; Harrisburg, s/o, 10" 50.00
Plate, coupe; Minneapolis MN, s/o, 10" 50.00
Plate, coupe; New Bedford MA, s/o, 5 scenes, 6" 35.00
Plate, coupe; Salem MA, witch & 5 scenes, v/o, 6" 45.00
Plate, coupe; Tucson AZ, 5 scenes, v/o, 6" 40.00
Plate, coupe; Washington DC, v/o, 6" 35.00
Plate, coupe; Yale, s/o, 10" 50.00
Plate, Decator IL, s/o, r/e 65.00
Plate, Flint MI, v/o, 9" 35.00
Plate, Haverhill (MA), s/o, r/e 60.00
Plate, Horseshoe Curve, fruit & flower border 50.00
Plate, Lynn MA, 9" 35.00
Plate, New Library at Boston, fruit & flower border 50.00
Plate, Omaha NE, v/o, 9" 35.00
Plate, Pilgrim Hall, fruit & flower border 50.00
Plate, Portland OR, s/o, r/e 70.00

Plate, Ride of Paul Revere, fruit & flower border 50.00
Plate, Sacramento CA, v/o, 9" 35.00
Plate, Valley Forge (PA), 1777-78, r/e 55.00
Plate, Whirlpool Rapids, fruit & flower border 50.00
Plate, Zanesville OH, s/e, r/e 60.00
Sugar bowl, Plymouth, Am pilgrims 55.00
Tumbler, Ashville, mc, s/o 85.00
Tumbler, Ottawa Canada 75.00
Tumbler, Tacoma WA, s/o 75.00
Tumbler, Thousand Islands, v/o 75.00

Royal Bayreuth

Founded in 1794 in Tettau, Bavaria, the Royal Bayreuth firm originally manufactured fine dinnerware of superior quality. Their figural items, produced from before the turn of the century until the onset of WWI, are highly sought after by today's collectors. Perhaps the most abundantly produced and easily recognized of these are the tomato and lobster pieces. Fruits, flowers, people, animals, birds, and vegetables shapes were also made. Aside from figural items, pitchers, toothpick holders, cups and saucers, humidors, and the like were decorated in florals and scenic motifs. Some, such as the very popular Rose Tapestry line, utilized a cloth-like tapestry background. Transfer prints were used as well. Two of the most popular are Sunbonnet Babies and Nursery Rhymes (in particular, those decorated with the complete verse).

Caution: Many pieces were not marked; some were marked 'Deponiert' or 'Registered' only. While marked pieces are the most valued, unmarked items are still very worthwhile. Our advisors for this category are Larry Brenner from New Hampshire and Dee Hooks from Illinois; they are listed in the Directory under their home states.

Figurals

Ashtray, court jester, Welcome Is the Best Cheer, bl mk, 5" 225.00
Ashtray, Devil & Cards, bl mk 250.00
Ashtray, duck (mallard), bl mk, 2½x6" 1,009.00
Ashtray, elk, bl mk 375.00
Bowl, grapes, MOP, bl mk, 5½" 75.00
Bowl, poppy, apricot, open hdls, bl mk, 9½" 725.00
Box, card; Devil & Cards, bl mk 550.00
Candlestick, clown, sitting, bl mk, #832 ....675.00
Candlestick, clown w/match holder, red, bl mk, 6¾" 2,400.00
Candy dish, grape, MOP, bl mk 100.00
Candy dish, lobster, bl mk, 5½" 195.00
Celery tray, lobster, bl mk 225.00
Compote, poppy, wht or orchid MOP, bl mk 595.00
Compote, shells, bl mk 325.00
Cracker jar, shells, bl mk 725.00
Cup, Devil & Dice, bl mk, 3" 280.00
Cup & saucer, demi; rose, bl mk 550.00
Gravy boat & ladle, shells, bl mk 425.00
Hair receiver, cows, bl mk, 4" 200.00
Hatpin holder, poppy, bl mk, 4" 625.00
Humidor, Devil & Cards, bl mk, 7¾" 1,150.00
Humidor, red lady clown, bl mk, 5" 1,750.00
Match holder, clown, sitting, bl mk, 2½" 620.00
Match holder, clown, wall hanging, 5x3½" 675.00
Mustard, poppy, red, bl mk 275.00
Mustard, tomato on lettuce leaf, bl mk, 3½x5½" 170.00
Nappy, poppy, red, bl mk 175.00
Nut set, pansy, pk lustre, bl mk, 5-pc 1,100.00
Pitcher, alligator, gr, unmk, cream sz 350.00
Pitcher, bear, brn, bl mk, milk sz 850.00
Pitcher, beetle, red, cut-out under eyes, bl mk, milk sz 1,700.00
Pitcher, cat hdl, bl & brn, bl mk, 4" 500.00
Pitcher, clown, red, bl mk, cream sz 375.00
Pitcher, coachman, bl mk, milk sz 350.00
Pitcher, Devil & Cards, bl mk, water sz, 7½", NM 700.00
Pitcher, Devil & Cards, face cards, bl mk, cream sz 300.00
Pitcher, duck, bl mk, cream sz 350.00
Pitcher, eagle, bl mk, cream sz 400.00
Pitcher, eagle, bl mk, milk sz 500.00
Pitcher, elk, bl mk, cream sz 250.00
Pitcher, fish head, unmk, lemonade sz 1,250.00
Pitcher, frog, unmk, cream sz 250.00
Pitcher, grapes, wht MOP, unmk, cream sz 250.00
Pitcher, hawk, unmk, cream sz 650.00
Pitcher, lemon, bl mk, cream sz 275.00
Pitcher, lemon, bl mk, milk sz 350.00
Pitcher, lobster, bl mk, milk sz 350.00
Pitcher, maple leaf, bl mk, cream sz 385.00
Pitcher, melon, bl mk, cream sz 425.00
Pitcher, monk, bl mk, cream sz 825.00

Pitcher, monkey, blue mark, cream size, $525.00.

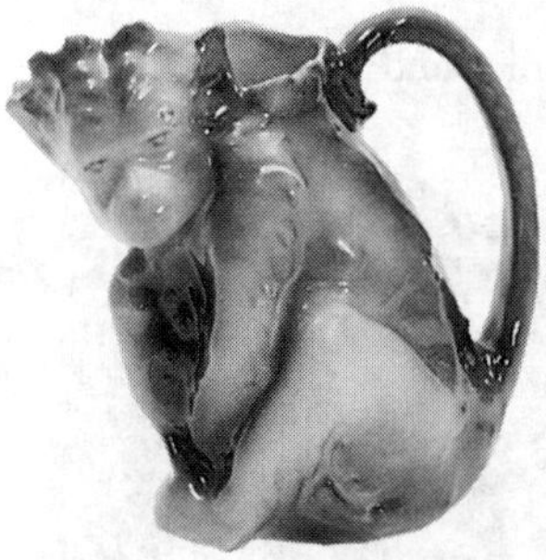

Pitcher, mtn goat, bl mk, cream sz 525.00
Pitcher, oak leaf, bl mk, cream sz 395.00
Pitcher, orchid, red base, bl mk, cream sz 1,200.00
Pitcher, owl, bl mk, cream sz 650.00
Pitcher, pansy, pk & yel, bl mk, cream sz 350.00
Pitcher, parakeet, red, unmk, cream sz 375.00
Pitcher, pig, red, bl mk, cream sz 650.00
Pitcher, platypus, bl mk, cream sz 1,275.00
Pitcher, poodle, gray, bl mk, cream sz 400.00
Pitcher, rabbit, brn, registered mk, cream sz, M 6,000.00
Pitcher, robin, bl mk, cream sz 250.00
Pitcher, Santa, red, bl mk, cream sz 2,700.00
Pitcher, seal, gray, bl mk, cream sz 350.00
Pitcher, snake, amethyst tones, bl mk, water sz 7,200.00
Pitcher, spiky shell, boot shape, bl mk, water sz 800.00
Pitcher, spiky shell, wht MOP, bl mk, cream sz, 4x5" 300.00
Pitcher, squirrel, bl mk, water sz (rare) 6,500.00
Pitcher, St Bernard, unmk, cream sz 300.00
Pitcher, strawberry, bl mk, water sz 975.00
Pitcher, tomato, bl mk, water sz 610.00
Pitcher, turtle, bl mk, cream sz 800.00
Pitcher, turtle, bl mk, lemonade sz 8,750.00
Pitcher, water buffalo, bl mk, cream sz 300.00
Shakers, coachman, 3", NM, pr 1,110.00
Shakers, corn, bl mk, pr 800.00
Shakers, nautilus shells, bl mk, pr 210.00
Shakers, oak leaf, bl mk, pr 800.00
Shaving mug, elk, bl mk 650.00
Stein, elk, bl mk, 6" 625.00
Sugar & cream pitcher, pansy, purple, bl mk 550.00
Sugar bowl, pansy, purple, bl mk 550.00

Tea strainer, flower, unmk 440.00
Teapot, poppy, red, bl mk 400.00
Teapot, shells, bl mk 475.00
Teapot, spikey shell, bl mk, 4½" 475.00
Toothpick holder, Art Nouveau, bl mk, M 1,200.00
Toothpick holder, clown, red, bl mk, 3" 550.00
Toothpick holder, Devil & Cards, bl mk 800.00
Toothpick holder, rose, pk, bl mk, 2½" 550.00
Tray, Devil & Cards, bl mk, 9½x7" 700.00

Nursery Rhymes

Bell, Jack & Beanstalk, w/verse & clapper, bl mk 350.00
Cauldron, Jack & the Beanstalk, bl mk, 3-ftd, 3" 275.00
Coffeepot, Jack & Jill, bl mk 475.00
Mug, Jack & Beanstalk, w/verse, bl mk, lg 200.00
Pitcher, Jack & Jill, w/verse, bl mk, cream sz 275.00
Pitcher, Little Boy Blue, w/verse, bl mk, 3½" 275.00
Pitcher, Little Miss Muffet, bl mk, milk sz 300.00
Pitcher, Little Miss Muffet, w/verse, dbl hdl, bl mk, cream sz 300.00
Plate, Little Bo Peep, bl mk, 6¼" 200.00

Scenics and Action Portraits

Pitcher, man with turkeys, blue mark, water size, 6", $450.00.

Bell, monastery in mtns, orig wood clapper, unmk, 3¼" 325.00
Bottle, cologne; turkey farmer, bl mk, w/stopper, 6½" 275.00
Bowl, Dogs in Tree, Hunt Scene, ftd, ruffled, bl mk, 9½" 275.00
Bowl, Snow Baby, ruffled rim, bl mk 250.00
Box, peacock scene, bl mk 200.00
Box, pin; 2 cows in pasture, bl mk, 1½x4" 225.00
Chocolate pot, 2 donkeys w/boy sitting on log, bl mk, 8½" 375.00
Cup & saucer, Beach Baby, bl mk 250.00
Cup & saucer, Brittany girl, bl mk 175.00
Hair receiver, deer in woodland scene, 3-ftd, bl mk, 3¾" 225.00
Hair receiver, hunter w/gun & dog, 3-ftd, bl mk, 3⅜" 250.00
Hair receiver, mtn goats in meadow, bl mk, lg 250.00
Hatpin holder, musicians, bl mk, 4⅜" 375.00
Inkwell, Corinthian, blk & wht, w/lid, bl mk 200.00
Match holder, elk, bl mk, 1¾x3¾x2⅛" box 200.00
Match striker, Shadow Trees, boat in water, no mk, 2½x3" 150.00
Pitcher, Babes in the Woods, flow bl, bl mk, cream sz 450.00
Pitcher, Beach Baby, bl mk, cream sz 250.00
Pitcher, birds of paradise, bl mk, cream sz 175.00
Pitcher, cockfight, bl mk, milk sz, 6" 200.00
Pitcher, musicians, bl mk, lemonade sz, 6½x7¼" 450.00
Pitcher, musicians, no mk, 3½" 150.00
Plate, boy w/2 donkeys, bl mk, 7½" 125.00
Plate, Dutch boy & girl ice skating, bl mk, 8½" 195.00
Plate, hunter w/gun & dog, bl mk, 9" 225.00
Plate, man w/turkeys, bl mk, 7" 125.00
Teapot, Babes in Woods, girls w/elf, flow bl, 3¾" 1,283.00
Teapot, woman hunter, 2 farmers & dogs, bl mk 350.00
Toothpick holder, musicians on brn, 4-ftd, bl mk 250.00
Toothpick holder, Ring Around the Rosie, 2-hdl, ftd, bl mk 350.00
Toothpick holder, roses (lg), 3-hdl, bl mk 275.00
Toothpick holder, woman w/horse & dogs, 2-hdl 350.00
Vase, Babes in Woods, bl mk, 4" 550.00
Vase, goats, bl mk, 7" 260.00
Vase, highland sheep, hdls, bl mk, 4" 250.00
Vase, pastoral scene, bl mk, 7" 275.00
Vase, 2 horses, 1 w/Arabian rider, 4-ftd, bl mk, 2¾x2½" 250.00

Sunbonnet Babies

Bowl, ironing, gold trim, 6-sided, unmk, 8" 275.00
Bowl, sweeping, ruffled edge, bl mk, 6" 200.00
Candle holder, fishing, shield bk, bl mk 775.00
Candle holder, washing, low, ring hdl, bl mk 350.00
Hair receiver, sewing, 3-leg, bl mk 550.00
Pitcher, sweeping, bl mk, cream sz 275.00
Plate, cake; folding & ironing clothes, 2 open hdls, bl mk, 10½" ...350.00
Plate, ironing, bl mk, 6" 200.00
Sugar bowl, fishing, w/lid, bl mk 350.00
Toothpick holder, fishing, lay down, oval, bl mk 600.00
Vase, fishing, 3-hdl, unmk, 3" 450.00

Tapestries

Box, dresser; Rose Tapestry, 3-color, bl mk 450.00
Chocolate set, Rose Tapestry, pot +6 c/s, bl mk 9,000.00
Creamer & sugar bowl, Rose Tapestry, bulbous, w/lid 550.00
Hair receiver, Rose Tapestry, bl mk 375.00
Hatpin holder, Bathers, castle in bkground, rtcl base, 4½" 575.00
Hatpin holder, Rose Tapestry, bl mk 500.00
Hatpin holder, violets, bl mk 600.00
Mug, Rose Tapestry, 3-color, gold hdl, bl mk, 3⅜" 450.00
Pitcher, nudes in river, bl mk, cream sz 595.00
Pitcher, Rose Tapestry, pinched spout, bright gold, unmk, 3½" .250.00
Pitcher, Rose Tapestry, pk, pinched spout, bl mk, cream sz 400.00
Pitcher, sheep scene, bl mk, 4" 400.00
Shoe, chrysanthemum, low cut, orig lace, bl mk 920.00
Shoe, Dutch style, cottage in winter, gr mk 450.00
Tray, Colonial Curtsy, bl mk, 11¾x8¼" 600.00
Tray, dresser; cottage by waterfall, bl mk, 8x11" 975.00
Vase, Bathers, castle in bkground, stick neck, 4" 400.00
Vase, Victorian lady's portrait, bk: landscape, bl mk, 7" 750.00

Royal Bonn

Royal Bonn is a fine-paste porcelain, ornately decorated with scenes, portraits, or florals. The factory was established in the mid-1800s in Bonn, Germany; however, most pieces found today are from the latter part of the century.

Clock, Agate, turq w/red flowers, 30-hr movement, 7¼x5¼" 255.00
Clock, La Cette, mc w/gold trim, sgn, #807, 12x12" 925.00
Clock, La Cheze, cast bezel w/beveled glass, Ansonia, 10x8x4¾" ...510.00
Clock, La Sharpe, mc floral w/gold trim, Ansonia, 11x9x4" 760.00
Umbrella stand, roses spray, cylindrical, 19½", EX 250.00
Vase, floral, mc w/gold, dolphin hdls, bulbous, mk, 12½" 235.00
Vase, floral, wht w/purple leaves on lav, ca 1900, 13" 110.00
Vase, orchids, mc w/much ornate goldwork, 11x7½" 475.00

Royal Copenhagen

The Royal Copenhagen Manufactory was established in Denmark in about 1775 by Frantz Henrich Muller. When bankruptcy threatened in 1779, the Crown took charge. The fine dinnerware and objects of art produced after that time carry the familiar logo, the crown over three wavy lines. For further information we recommend *Royal Copenhagen Porcelain, Animals and Figurines*, by Robert J. Heritage (Schiffer). See also Limited Edition Plates.

Bowl, lt gr, triangular, #2762, 2½x5" dia 130.00
Bowl, mottled mahog, bl & gray matt, A Boesen, 1920s, 4¼x15½" 650.00
Bowl, salad; Flora Danica, #3510, sq, 8¾" 1,480.00
Bowl, serving; Blue Fluted, full open lace, #1018, 2x8¼" 230.00
Bowl, stylized trees on mustard matt, G Bogelund, 6x7" 250.00
Bowl, vegetable; Flora Danica, #3582, w/lid, 8" 2,330.00
Bowl, Viking Dragon Ship form, Viking w/ships in bkground, #187 ...260.00
Box, Flora Danica, branch hdls & lid, rnd 385.00
Cache pot, Blue Fluted, plain, #264, oval, 4" 210.00
Cup, Flora Danica, #3597, 6-oz 255.00
Dish, lobster on 1 side, gray on pearl gray, 2x7½" dia 200.00
Figurine, boy, sitting cross-legged, #2859, 2¾" 110.00
Figurine, boy w/beach ball, #3542, 6½" 115.00
Figurine, boy w/calf, #772, 6½x7" 290.00
Figurine, boy whittling on pole, #905 ....210.00
Figurine, bulldog, sitting, #3169, 3" 140.00
Figurine, cat sleeping, porc, 8½" 260.00
Figurine, dachshund, #3140, 3x4¼" 165.00
Figurine, dachshund, chasing tail, #1407, 4½" L 100.00
Figurine, dachshund puppy, playing on bk, #1408, 5" L 105.00
Figurine, elephant, raised trunk, #21517, 7½x7" 160.00
Figurine, farmer w/sickle standing by haystack, #685, 10¼" 195.00
Figurine, girl holding puppy, #253, 6" 210.00
Figurine, girl sitting w/apron on, #1315, 5¼x5" 155.00
Figurine, girl w/calf, #779, 6½x6½" 190.00
Figurine, girl w/duck, #528 ....125.00
Figurine, girl w/goose, #527, 9½x4½" 140.00
Figurine, Great Dane, lying down, #1679, 4½x9" 225.00
Figurine, kingfishers (2), #1769, 7" 160.00
Figurine, lady knitting, #1314, 6x4" 145.00
Figurine, man w/2 sheep, #627, 11" 260.00
Figurine, mermaid on rock, #4431, 8½x6¾" 265.00
Figurine, mother w/2 children, #12159, 6" 185.00
Figurine, Pan holding bl macaw, #752, 7¼" 230.00
Figurine, Pan holding rabbit, #439, 5½" 270.00
Figurine, Pan riding goat, #737, 8x8" 390.00
Figurine, Pan sitting on stump, #1738, 3½" 145.00
Figurine, Pan w/crow, #2113, 6½" 340.00
Figurine, Pan wrestling bear, #648, 6¼" 255.00
Figurine, parrots on branches, #649, 7½" 150.00
Figurine, pointer dog, lying down, #1635, 5x9½" 245.00
Figurine, polar bear, roaring, #502, 12¾" 270.00
Figurine, pug puppy, #3169, 3x3" 150.00
Figurine, puppies (2), playing, #453, 2½x3½" 100.00
Figurine, raccoon, 1 paw up, #5401, 4x8" 290.00
Figurine, Schoolboy, #4528, 6¾" 110.00
Figurine, Scottie, #3161, 4x5" 155.00
Figurine, Snowy Owl, #1829, 15¾", from $675 to 825.00
Figurine, swan, #755, 4¼x6½" 135.00
Figurine, Tawney Owl, #1304, pre-1923 mk, 8½x8½" 335.00
Figurine, The Couple, #1783, 9¼x6" 560.00
Figurine, turkey, #4784, 3" 105.00
Figurine, 2 children w/dachshund puppy, #707, 5¾" 265.00
Gravy boat, Blue Fluted, full open lace, w/attached underplate .205.00
Jar, Paaske (Easter) 1918, bird on tree in reserve, 6" 200.00
Plate, bread & butter; Blue Fluted, full open lace, 6" 60.00
Plate, bread & butter; Flora Danica, #3552, 5½" 310.00
Plate, dinner; Flora Danica, #3553, 10" 710.00
Plate, salad; Blue Fluted, full open lace, 8" 75.00
Platter, Blue Fluted, full open lace, 14¼" 275.00
Salt cellar, Flora Dancia, #3557, 4¼" 325.00

Vases: blue and white jonquils on gray, Paaske (Easter) 1926, #135, green stamp and blue wave mark, 7¼", $100.00; Birds in tree, two in flight, blue, white, and gray, Jul (Christmas) 1920, #199, green stamp and blue wave logo, 8", $125.00.

Vase, gray mottle, classic shape, #26-12, 1924, 10x6½" 175.00

Royal Copley

Royal Copley is a decorative type of pottery made by the Spaulding China Company in Sebring, Ohio, from 1942 to 1957. They also produced two other major lines — Royal Windsor and Spaulding. Royal Copley was primarily marketed through five-and-ten cent stores; Royal Windsor and Spaulding were sold through department stores, gift shops, and jobbers. Items trimmed in gold are worth 25% to 50% more than the same item with no gold trim.

For more information we recommend *Collector's Guide to Royal Copley Plus Royal Windsor & Spaulding, Books I and II*, by our advisor for this category, Joe Devine; he is listed in the Directory under Iowa.

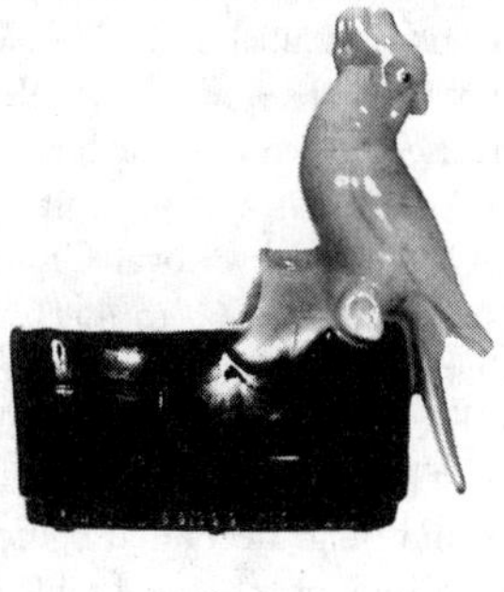

Planter, Cockatiel, 8½", from $40.00 to $45.00. (Photo courtesy Glenn Hovinga)

Ashtray, abstract butterfly shape, 4 rests, label, 5x9" 25.00
Ashtray, abstract sq shape, 2 rests, label, 4½x5¾" 16.00
Ashtray, heart shape w/bird, emb mk, 5½", from $50 to 60.00
Bank, teddy bear, blk/wht, 8", from $150 to 170.00
Candle holder/planter/vase, star shape, ribbed, label, 6¾" 25.00
Candy dish, various leaf shapes, speckled, USA, ea 25.00
Coaster, hunting dog, from $35 to 40.00
Figurine, canary, paper label, 5½", from $55 to 60.00
Figurine, cocker spaniel, sitting up, mouth open, 8", from $30 to ...35.00
Figurine, cocker spaniel sitting up, dk brn, 6¼", from $30 to 35.00
Figurine, mallard drake & hen, sgn, RW label, 8½", 6¼", pr 250.00
Figurine, nuthatch, label, 4½", from $16 to 18.00

Figurine, pouter pigeon, brn or gray, label, 5¾", from $20 to 25.00
Figurine, rooster, blk/wht, gr base, label, lg, from $100 to 110.00
Figurine, sea gull, wht w/gold trim, 8", from $50 to 55.00
Lamp base, Birds in the Bower, label, 8", from $50 to 60.00
Lamp base, cocker spaniel, 10", from $100 to 125.00
Pitcher, Floral Beauty, 8", from $45 to 50.00
Planter, Big Blossom, gr stamp, rectangular, 3", from $10 to 12.00
Planter, birdhouse w/bird, 8", from $100 to 110.00
Planter, cat w/ball of yarn, 8¼", from $35 to 40.00
Planter, dog by mailbox, blk/wht (blk ears), 8½", from $110 to ...125.00
Planter, dog in picnic basket, label, 7¾", from $70 to 75.00
Planter, dogwood plaque, w/verse, 4½", from $18 to 20.00
Planter, elephant (Stuffed Animal Series), label, 6½" 65.00
Planter, Oriental boy or girl w/basket on ground, 7¾", from $20 to ..25.00
Planter, Oriental girl w/sq bamboo pot, label, 7¾" 65.00
Planter, palomino horse head, label/gr stamp, 6", from $35 to 40.00
Planter, poodle (wht) sitting by blk pot, label, 7", from $45 to 50.00
Planter, rooster, stylized, speckled, USA, 7½x9¼" 45.00
Razor blade receptacle, barber pole, gold top, label, 6¼" 60.00
Vase, bamboo decor, paper label, cylindrical, 8", from $18 to 20.00
Vase, Carol's Corsage, cobalt, gr stamp, 7", from $25 to 30.00
Vase, Congratulations (baby) decal, flared at top, 6x8", from $55 to ...60.00

Royal Crown Derby

The Royal Crown Derby company can trace its origin back to 1848. It first operated under the name of Locker & Co. but by 1859 had became Stevenson, Sharp & Co. Several changes in ownership occurred until 1866 when it became known as the Sampson Hancock Co. The Derby Crown Porcelain Co. Ltd. was formed in 1876, and these companies soon merged. In 1890 they were appointed as a manufacturer for the Queen and began using the name Royal Crown Derby.

In the early years, considerable 'Japan ware' decorated in Imari style, using red, blue, and gold in Oriental patterns was popular. The company excelled in their ability to use gold in the decoration, and some of the best flower painters of all time were employed. Nice vases or plaques signed by any of these artists will bring thousands of dollars: Gregory, Mosley, Rouse, Gresley, and D'esir'e Leroy. We have observed porcelain plaques decorated with flowers signed by Gregory selling at auction for as much as $12,000.00. If you find a signed piece and are not sure of its value, if at all possible, it would be best to have it appraised by someone very knowledgeable regarding current market values.

As is usual among most other English factories, nearly all of the vases produced by Royal Crown Derby came with covers. If they are missing, deduct 40% to 45%. There are several well illustrated books available from antique booksellers to help you learn to identify this ware. The back stamps used after 1891 will date every piece except dinnerware. The company is still in business, producing outstanding dinnerware and Imari-decorated figures and serving pieces. They also produce custom (one only) sets of table service for the wealthy of the world.

Bowl, console; Imari, ftd, acorn hdls, 1900s, 2x11½x10½" 400.00
Bowl, Imari, mid-1800s, 9½" 325.00
Bowl, Pattern #1128, hdls, ped ft, ca 1920, 2¼x11x7" 500.00
Candle holder, Imari, old, 11" 175.00
Compote, Imari #2451, 3x6⅝" 250.00
Creamer, cow figural, enamel & gilt decor, w/lid, 19th C, 4" 920.00
Cup & saucer, demitasse; Chinese Birds, 1940 ....35.00
Dinnerware, Border, service for 8, 69 pcs 2,000.00
Dinnerware, Lombardy, 1959, service for 12, 60 pcs 1,800.00
Figurine, Irish setter on grassy base, 2¾x6" 400.00
Ginger jar, Red Aves, 1949, 4½" 215.00
Paperweight, elephant baby, sgn Gumps, Imari colors 600.00
Paperweight, fox, bl w/gold, 2¼x4¼", NM 455.00
Plates, Mikado, bl & wht, 10½", 4 for 285.00

Soup tureen, Imari-style pattern, 15", with lid and 16½" underplate, late 1800s, $1,200.00.

Teapot, Imari #2451, 1930, 4x8½" 250.00
Vase, floral, mc/gilt on cream, teardrop w/flaring neck, 11" 285.00

Royal Doulton, Doulton

The range of wares produced by the Doulton Company since its inception in 1815 has been vast and varied. The earliest wares produced in the tiny pottery in Lambeth, England, were salt-glazed pitchers, plain and fancy figural bottles, etc. — all utility-type stoneware geared to the practical needs of everyday living. The original partners, John Doulton and John Watts, saw the potential for success in the manufacture of drain and sewage pipes and during the 1840s concentrated on these highly lucrative types of commercial wares. Watts retired from the company in 1854, and Doulton began experimenting with a more decorative product line. As time went by, many glazes and decorative effects were developed, among them Faience, Impasto, Silicon, Carrara, Marqueterie, Chine, and Rouge Flambe. Tiles and architectural terra cotta were an important part of their manufacture. Late in the nineteenth century at the original Lambeth location, fine artware was decorated by such notable artists as Hannah and Arthur Barlow, George Tinworth, and J.H. McLennan. Stoneware vases with incised animal drawings, gracefully shaped urns with painted scenes, and cleverly modeled figurines rivaled the best of any competitor.

In 1882 a second factory was built in Burslem which continues even yet to produce the famous figurines, character jugs, series ware, and table services so popular with collectors today. Their Kingsware line, made from 1899 to 1946, featured flasks and flagons with drinking scenes, usually on a brown-glazed ground. Some were limited editions, while others were commemorative and advertising items. The Gibson Girl series, twenty-four plates in all, was introduced in 1901. It was drawn by Charles Dana Gibson and is recognized by its blue and white borders and central illustrations, each scene depicting a humorous or poignant episode in the life of 'The Widow and Her Friends.' Dickensware, produced from 1911 through the early 1940s, featured illustrations by Charles Dickens, with many of his famous characters. The Robin Hood series was introduced in 1914; the Shakespeare series #1, portraying scenes from the Bard's plays, was made from 1914 until World War II. The Shakespeare series #2 ran from 1906 until 1974 and was decorated with featured characters. Nursery Rhymes was a series that was first produced in earthenware in 1930 and later in bone china. In 1933 a line of decorated children's ware, the Bunnykin series, was introduced; it continues to be made to the present day. About 150 'bunny' scenes have been devised, the earliest and most desirable being those signed by the artist Barbara Vernon. Most pieces range in value from $60.00 to $120.00.

Factors contributing to the value of a figurine are age, demand, color, and detail. Those with a limited production run and those signed by the artist or marked 'Potted' (indicating a pre-1939 origin) are also more valuable. After 1920 wares were marked with a lion — with or without a crown — over a circular 'Royal Doulton.' Our advisor for this category is Nicki Budin; she is listed in the Directory under Ohio.

Animals and Birds

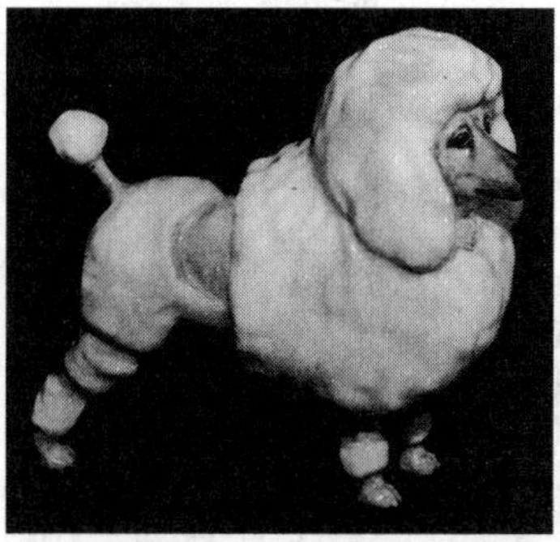

Poodle, HN2631, 1952 – 85, from $140.00 to $160.00.

Cairn, begging, HN2589 ....95.00
Collie, Ashstead Applause, HN1057, 7¼" 400.00
Dachshund, K-17 ....95.00
Dalmatian, HN1116 ....250.00
English Setter, HN2529, blk & wht, pheasant in mouth, 8½" 450.00
Fox, sitting, HN2634, 12" 1,000.00
Pekinese, HN1012 ....195.00
Penguin, K22, 1¾" 225.00
Scottie, HN1016 ....195.00
Sealyham, HN1032 ....275.00
Spaniel w/pheasant in mouth, HN1062 ....165.00
St Bernard, K-19 ....85.00
Terrier, K-3 ....95.00

Bunnykins

Figurine, Artist, DB13 ....325.00
Figurine, Australian, DB58 ....750.00
Figurine, Bathtime, DB148 ....45.00
Figurine, Bedtime, DB55 ....45.00
Figurine, Birthday, DB21 ....40.00
Figurine, Bride & Groom, DB101/DB102, pr 90.00
Figurine, Christmas Surprise, DB146 ....50.00
Figurine, Collector, DB54 ....775.00
Figurine, Cooling Off, DB3 ....150.00
Figurine, Halloween, DB132 ....75.00
Figurine, Helping Mother, DB2 ....45.00
Figurine, Jogging 75.00
Figurine, Jubilee Bunnykin Band, set of 5 pcs 525.00
Figurine, Mountie, DB135 ....750.00
Figurine, Olympic, DB28B 475.00
Figurine, Rainy Day, DB147 ....45.00
Figurine, Sleepytime, DB15 ....45.00
Figurine, Soccer Player, DB123 ....200.00
Toothpick holder, bunny reading book, 2" 100.00

Character Jugs

'Ard of 'Earing, D6588, lg 1,250.00
'Arriet, D6250, mini 65.00
'Arriet, D6526, tiny 195.00
'Arry, D6255, tiny 195.00
Airman, sm 65.00
Angler, sm 65.00
Anne Boleyn, D6644, lg 125.00
Apothecary, D6574, sm 65.00
Aramis, D6454, sm 65.00
Bacchus, D6505, sm 65.00
Beefeater, pk, D6251, mini 45.00
Captain Henry Morgan, D6467, lg 125.00
Captain Henry Morgan, D6469, sm 65.00
Cavalier, D6114, lg 150.00
Churchill, wht, D6170, lg 7,800.00
Clark Gable, D6709 ....4,200.00
Clown, wht hair, D6322, lg 1,500.00
Collector, D6796, lg 175.00
Count Dracula, lg 175.00
Davy Crocket/Santa Anna, D6729, lg 195.00
Dealer, lg 145.00
Dick Turpin, gun hdl, D6128, mini 45.00
Dick Turpin, horse hdl, D6528, lg 125.00
Dick Turpin, horse hdl, D6542, mini 40.00
Dick Whittington, D6375, lg 350.00
Dick Whittington, D6846, 1989 ....150.00
Don Quixote, D6455, lg 95.00
Don Quixote, D6460, sm 65.00
Drake, D6115, lg 125.00
Falconer, D6533, lg 125.00
Falconer, D6540, sm 65.00
Falstaff, D6287, lg 125.00
Falstaff, yel, D6287, lg 115.00
Farmer John, D5788, lg 150.00
Fortune Teller, D6503, sm 325.00
Gardener, D6630, lg 125.00
General Eisenhower, lg 295.00
Gladiator, D6550, lg 600.00
Gladiator, D6556, mini 325.00
Golfer, D6623, lg 100.00
Gondolier, D6589, lg 525.00
Gone Away, D6531, lg 125.00
Gone Away, D6538, sm 65.00
Gone Away, D6545, mini 45.00
Granny, D5521, lg 115.00
Grant & Lee/Civil War, D6698, lg 295.00
Gulliver, D6560, lg 595.00
Gunsmith, D6573, lg 115.00
Isaac Walton, D6404, lg 115.00
John Barleycorn, D5327, lg 150.00
King Charles I, lg 295.00
Leprechaun, lg 150.00
Liverpool Soccer, sm 120.00
Lobsterman, D6652, mini 45.00
London Bobby, D6744, lg 150.00
London Bobby, D6762, sm 65.00
Lumberjack, D6610, lg 125.00
Mephistopheles, D5757, lg 2,000.00
Merlin, D6536, sm 65.00
Mine Host, D6488, lg 125.00
Mine Host, D6513, mini 50.00
Monty (Field Marshal Montgomery), D6202, lg 180.00
Mr Micawber, D6143, tiny 95.00
Mr Pickwick, D6060, lg 165.00
Napoleon & Josephine, D6750, lg 135.00
Old Charley, D6046, mini 45.00
Old Salt, D6551, lg 115.00
Paddy, D6145, tiny 95.00
Parson Brown, D5486, lg 145.00

Pied Piper, D6403, lg 145.00
Poacher, D6515, mini 45.00
Rip Van Winkle, D6438, lg 115.00
Robin Hood, 1st version, D6205, lg 150.00
Robinson Crusoe, D6533, lg 115.00
Robinson Crusoe, D6534, sm 65.00
Robinson Crusoe, D6546, mini 45.00
Sam Weller, D5841, sm 80.00
Sam Weller, D6064, lg 150.00
Sam Weller, D6140, mini 45.00
Sam Weller, D6147, tiny 95.00
Sampson & Delilah, lg 150.00
Sancho Panza, D6518, mini 60.00
Santa Claus, plain hdl or red & wht hdl, D6706, mini, ea 55.00
Shakespeare, sm 65.00
Sleuth, D6635, sm 65.00
Sleuth, D6639, mini 45.00
Smuggler, D6616, lg 125.00
Tam O' Shanter, D6636, sm 65.00
Tam O'Shanter, D6632, lg 125.00
Tony Weller, D5531, lg 135.00
Town Crier, D6530, lg 150.00

Veteran Motorist, Doulton & Co Limited 1972 Made in England, 7½", $150.00.

Vicar of Bray, D5615, lg 225.00
Viking, D6526, mini....140.00
Walrus & Carpenter, D6608, mini 65.00
Washington, sm 65.00
Yachtsman, D6622, lg 150.00
Yeoman of the Guard, lg 135.00

Figurines

Afternoon Tea, HN1747 ....450.00
All Aboard, HN2940 ....180.00
Anna (Kate Greenaway), HN2802 ....150.00
Ascot, HN2356 ....175.00
Autumn, 2nd version, HN2087 ....450.00
Autumn Breezes, HN1911, pk 175.00
Autumn Breezes, HN1934 ....175.00
Autumn Breezes, HN2148, blk & wht 395.00
Babie, HN1679 ....90.00
Ballerina, HN2116 ....235.00
Balloon Girl, HN2618, 6½" 175.00
Balloon Man, HN1954 ....175.00
Beggar, HN2175 ....325.00
Belle of the Ball, HN1997, 6x8½x4" 325.00
Blacksmith, HN2782 ....200.00
Blithe Morning, HN2065, red 200.00
Bo-Peep, HN1811 ....125.00
Boatman, HN2417 ....180.00
Bonnie Lassie, HN1626, 5½" 450.00
Camellia, HN2222 ....260.00
Captain, 2nd version, HN2260 ....225.00
Carolyn, HN2112 ....300.00
Carpenter, HN2678 ....250.00
Cavalier, 2nd version, HN2716 ....195.00
Centurian, HN2726 ....175.00
China Repairer, HN2943, 6½" 225.00
Christine, HN2792 ....225.00
Christmas Time, HN2110 ....350.00
Cinderella, HN3677, Disney, ltd ed 350.00
Clarinda, HN2724 ....175.00
Clarissa, 2nd version, HN2345 ....155.00
Clown, HN2890 had at 175 & 275 ....185.00
Daffy-Down-Dilly, HN1712 ....375.00
Damaris, HN2079, 7½" 1,800.00
Debbie, HN2385 ....90.00
Diana, HN1986 ....150.00
Easter Day, HN1976 ....495.00
Easter Day, HN2039, 7¼" 350.00
Emma, HN2834 ....250.00
Enchantment, HN2178 ....175.00
Ermine Coat, HN1981 ....250.00
Eventide, HN2814 ....150.00
Faith, HN3082 ....175.00
Falstaff, 2nd version, HN2054 ....165.00
Fat Boy, 3rd version, HN2096, 7¼" 425.00
Favorite, HN2249 ....195.00
Foaming Quart, HN2162 ....165.00
Fragrance, HN2334 ....175.00
Francine, HN2422 ....95.00
Gaffer, HN2053, 8" 350.00
Genevieve, HN1962 ....250.00
Giselle, HN2139, 6¼x5⅞" 375.00
Goody Two Shoes, 2nd version, M80, 4" 750.00
Gossips, HN2025, 5½x7" 350.00
Grand Manner, HN2723 ....195.00
Griselda, HN1993, 5¾" 395.00
Groucho Marx, HN2777, 9" 350.00
Hazel, HN1796, 5¼" 395.00
HRH Prince of Wales, HN2883 ....395.00
HRH Prince Philip Duke of Edinburgh, HN2386 ....350.00
Invitation, HN2170 ....125.00
Ivy, HN1768 ....95.00
Janine, HN2461 ....175.00
Jester, HN2016 ....295.00
Julia, HN2705 ....165.00
Lady Fayre, HN1557, 5¼" 650.00
Laird, HN2361 ....175.00
Lily, HN1798 ....125.00
Lisa, HN2310 ....165.00
Lobster Man, HN2323, wht 175.00
Loretta, HN2337 ....165.00
Love Letter, HN2149 ....375.00
Lunchtime, HN2485 ....165.00
Lydia (child), HN1908 ....125.00
Marie, 2nd version, HN1370 ....125.00
Marjorie, HN2788 ....225.00
Mask Seller, HN2103 ....175.00
Masque, HN2554 ....250.00
Master, HN2325 ....175.00
Maureen, HN1770, 7¾" 350.00
Melanie, HN2271 ....150.00
Milkmaid, HN2057 ....195.00

Modesty, HN2744 ....150.00
Monica (child), HN1467 ....150.00
Moor, HN2082, 16½" 1,500.00
Old Balloon Seller, HN1315 ....175.00
Old King, HN2134 ....450.00
Owd Willum, HN2042 ....200.00
Penelope, HN1901 ....375.00
Piper, HN2907 ....250.00

The Potter, HN14937, $450.00; Bluebeard, HN2105, $450.00.

Prized Possession, HN2942 ....450.00
Professor, HN2281 ....150.00
Prue, HN1996, 6¾" 325.00
Punch & Judy Man, HN2765 ....225.00
Rest Awhile, HN2728 ....165.00
Reverie, HN2306 ....195.00
Robin Hood, HN2773 ....185.00
Romance, HN2430 ....155.00
Roseanna, HN1926 ....425.00
Rosemary, HN2091 ....425.00
Rowena, HN2077 ....550.00
Royal Governor's Cook, HN2233 ....450.00
Ruby, HN1724, 5¼" 395.00
Silks & Ribbons, HN2017 ....200.00
Silversmith of Williamsburg, HN2208 ....200.00
Simone, HN2378 ....165.00
Sleepyhead, HN2114 ....2,050.00
Southern Belle, HN2229 ....250.00
Stephanie, HN2807 ....150.00
Stitch in Time, HN2352 ....155.00
Stop Press, HN2683 ....165.00
Suzette, HN2026 ....325.00
Sweet & Twenty, HN1298 ....325.00
Taking Things Easy, HN2677 ....175.00
This Little Pig, HN1793, red 125.00
This Little Pig, HN1794 ....395.00
Tootles, HN1680 ....125.00
Top o' the Hill, HN1834, red 260.00
Town Crier, HN2119 ....250.00
Toymaker, HN2250 ....375.00
Tuppence a Bag, HN2320 ....175.00
Uncle Ned, HN2094 ....450.00
Veneta, HN2722 ....155.00
Victorian Lady, HN728 ....300.00
Votes for Women, HN2816 ....250.00
Windflower, HN1763 ....400.00
Winter, HN2088 ....350.00
Wizard, HN2877 ....175.00

Flambe

Charger, Pansy, 13" dia 130.00
Dish, hallmk Sterling Silver rim, #926, oval, 2¼x3½" 120.00
Figurine, cat, seated, 11" 175.00
Figurine, cat, seated, 4½" 265.00
Figurine, dog, sitting, #116, 4" 965.00
Figurine, Dog of Fo, #2957 ....225.00
Figurine, Dog of Fo, #3819, 1982, 4¾" 185.00
Figurine, drake, resting, #112 ....90.00
Figurine, drake, standing, #395 ....85.00
Figurine, elephant, med, #489A 300.00
Figurine, Emperor penguin, #84 ....160.00
Figurine, fox, seated, #14 ....160.00
Figurine, fox, stalking, #29B 200.00
Figurine, Geisha, HN3229 ....375.00
Figurine, Gift of Life, mare & colt lying down, 9" 910.00
Figurine, guinea fowl, #69 ....425.00
Figurine, owl, ca 1970, 12¼" 600.00
Figurine, rabbit, ears tucked, #113, 2½" 100.00
Figurine, tiger, stalking, Noke, 6x14" 750.00
Pin tray, wood cut, 4½" dia 110.00
Thimble 40.00
Vase, country scene w/daisy field, Noke, dtd 1922, 7¾" 240.00
Vase, red, bl & yel, Noke, #1304, 6" 380.00
Vase, Sung, Moore, 4" 125.00
Vase, Sung, red/bl flambe, ovoid, Noke, 6x3" 225.00
Vase, Veined, #1605, 4½" 160.00
Vase, Veined, #1612, 8½" 200.00
Vase, Veined, #1613, 6½" 175.00
Vase, wood cut, 4½" 150.00

Series Ware

Whiskey jug, Kingsware, Bonnie Prince Charlie, Dewars Scotch Whiskey, ca 1910 – 30, 7⅛", $250.00.

Ashtray, Ships, Trading Ketch, mc, 5¼" sq 78.00
Bowl, Gallant Fishers, 8½" 225.00
Candlestick, Fishermen, Noke, Izaac Walton Ware, 6⅝" 275.00
Candlesticks, Woodlands, 7", pr 85.00
Chamberstick, Fisherman, Izaac Walton Ware, 2x5¾" 300.00
Creamer, Coaching Days, 3¼x3¾" 50.00
Fern pot, Dutch People, 5" 110.00
Matchstand, Mr Pickwick, D2973, 3x6½" 340.00
Mug, Golfers, 5⅞" 490.00
Pitcher, Babes in Woods, girl, winter scene, flow bl, 9" 1,250.00
Plaque, Babes in Woods, girl w/basket, P Jones, 9¾x7¾" 1,525.00
Plate, bunnies & floral, bl & wht, 1902-27 mk, 10" 350.00
Plate, Canadian Views, Vermillion Lake & Mt Rundle, 10½" 60.00
Plate, Dickensware, Cap'n Cuttle, 10" 125.00
Plate, Fisherman, Jedo border, scalloped, Burslem, 10¼" 225.00
Plate, Gibson Girl, And Here Winning New Friends..., 10½" 155.00
Plate, Gibson Girl, dressed as nun, 10" 100.00
Plate, Golf, All Fools Are Not..., 1911-32, 10½" 300.00
Plate, Gondoliers, lady w/fan & gentleman, D3039, 10½" 165.00

Plate, Historical England, Francis Drake at Plymouth, D5940 .....85.00
Plate, landscape & cows, floral border, Burslem, 1891-1902, 11" 175.00
Plate, Professionals, The Falconer, D3756 ....95.00
Plate, Robin Hood & Friar Tuck, sq, 7½" 90.00
Stein, Night Watchman, front view, D4746, 5" 95.00
Sugar bowl, Coaching Days, w/lid, 4¾x5½" 110.00
Tankard, Cavaliers, D4749, 5⅝" 110.00
Teapot, Coaching Days, coach & 4 horses, 5⅜" 195.00
Toothpick holder, Woodland, mc transfer, D5815, 1938, 2½" ...110.00
Tray, Dickensware, Cap'n Cuttle, 10½x5⅝" 125.00
Vase, Babes in Woods, children in garden, 5½" 650.00
Vase, Blue Children, 3 girls outdoors, 8x8½" 675.00

Stoneware

Bottle, Victoria figural, brn salt glaze, att, ca 1840, 12" 575.00
Jar, incised floral band, hdls, Lambeth, 19th C, 30" 500.00
Jardiniere, bl floral w/brn ornate band, mk RB3, #6941, 7½" 520.00
Pitcher, hunt scene/3 men/2 windmills, Lambeth, #6266, 8¼" ..175.00

Vase, incised frieze of stags escaping wolves, Hannah Barlow, ca 1888, 21½", EX, $2,250.00.

Vase, emb floral, wht on brn, bulbous, Lambeth, 3¼" 125.00
Vase, relief outline, Arts & Crafts flowers & vines, FJ, 7¾" 255.00

Toby Jugs

Best Is Not Too Good, D6107 ....445.00
Capt Cuttle, D6266 ....165.00
Double XX, D6088 ....365.00
Fat Boy, D6264 ....250.00
Happy John, D6070 ....100.00
Huntsman, D6320 ....100.00
Mr Micawber, D6262 ....185.00
Mr Pickwick, D6261 ....250.00
Sairey Gamp, D6263 ....185.00
Sam Weller, D6265 ....165.00
Sherlock Holmes, D6661 ....135.00
Sir Winston Churchill, D6171, lg 115.00

Miscellaneous

Bowl, Titanian, stork in flight on bl to wht, H Allen, #134, 2¼x4" ..400.00
Chocolate pot, iris & bee, w/gold, Burslem, 1880 mk, 10¼" 450.00
Cracker jar, florals HP on tapestry, Slater's Pat, 7½" 200.00
Jug, bl w/gilt o/l Persian spray design, Burslem, 1885-1902, 6" ...200.00
Jug, florals & geometrics, blk transfer, Burslem, 1885-1902, 4¾" 150.00
Jug, Galleon, bl ship on waves, Burslem, 1892-1902, 6¾" 150.00
Jug, wht w/bl to blk roses ea side, Burslem, 1892-1900, 7x6" 200.00
Loving cup, winged dragon hdls, emb scrolls, Burslem, 7" 100.00
Pitcher, flower designs w/gilt Persian spray, 1879 mk, 10x4¼" ...350.00
Plaque, jackals & lion w/carcass, HB Barlow, 9x9" 1,150.00
Plaque, Ye Fable of Ye Proud Horse, HB Barlow, 9x9" 865.00
Vase, aventurine on porc, shouldered, mk, 5¼x3" 700.00
Vase, bud; Stratford Church, 1885-1902 Burslem, 5¾" 275.00
Vase, crystalline, wht ground, mk, ca 1910, 8⅝" 920.00
Vase, daffodils, wht w/bl on lt olive, sgn MW, 1898, 6¾" 175.00
Vase, fish/kelp, celadon slip on dk brn, Lambeth, 1883, 5¾" 400.00
Vase, Floral & Leaf, bl sprigs w/gold, Burslem/Slater's Pat, 5½" .125.00
Vase, Titanian, swan on gr to bl, #1048, 2½x2" 400.00

Royal Dux

The Duxer Porzellan Manufactur was established by E. Eichler in 1860. Located in what is now Duchcov, Czechoslovakia, the area was known as Dux, Bohemia, until WWI. The war brought about changes in both the style of the ware as well as the mark. Prewar pieces were modeled in the Art Nouveau or Greek Classical manner and marked with 'Bohemia' and a pink triangle containing the letter 'E.' They were usually matt glazed in green, brown, and gold. Better pieces were made of porcelain, while the larger items were of pottery. After the war the ware was marked with the small pink triangle but without the Bohemia designation; 'Made in Czechoslovakia' was added. The style became Art Deco, with cobalt blue a dominant color.

Figurine, boy on urn, #1304, #55, 7" 150.00
Figurine, cockatoo, pk crest, on limb w/sea-foam gr leaves, 16" .235.00
Figurine, fox, sleeping, #847, 2½x3¼" 55.00
Figurine, kingfisher, bl on wht base, Cernoch, 1970s, 9x7" 145.00
Figurine, lady in royal coach w/attendants, Czech, 15x14" 675.00
Figurine, lady w/fan, pk triangle mk, 10" 375.00
Figurine, man in long-tail coat & tricorner hat w/cane on stump, 10" ..350.00
Figurine, man w/dog, mk, 21½x8" 260.00
Figurine, Nouveau maiden on wave crest w/net, shell bowl, 17" ...1,950.00
Figurine, setter retrieving pheasant, 7x14½" 95.00
Figurine, tiger, prowling, 15½" L 105.00
Tazza, 3 diaphanously clad maidens surround std, mk, 20½" ..1,000.00

Royal Flemish

Royal Flemish was introduced in the late 1880s and was patented in 1894 by the Mt. Washington Glass Company. Transparent glass was enameled with one or several colors and the surface divided by a network of raised lines suggesting leaded glasswork. Some pieces were further decorated with enameled florals, birds, or Roman coins. Our advisors for this category are Betty and Clarence Maier; they are listed in the Directory under Pennsylvania.

Vase, gold and silver metallic coin medallions with raised gold enamel lines and decor, raised rim, angular handles, 4½x5½", $2,650.00.

Cracker jar, gold coins, section lines, blown-out, 7¾x5½" 2,000.00
Cracker jar, gold griffin on window panels, SP mts 1,700.00
Pickle castor, HP mums w/gold on frost; ornate gold Pairpoint fr, 10" ..2,000.00
Tankard, band w/leaves & jewel berries, lines/circles below, 7" 3,050.00

Tumbler, scrolls, pk on wht, gold wild roses, 4¼" 2,200.00
Vase, coins on sectioned ground, bun base, cup neck, 7½" 5,500.00
Vase, floral on swirl ribs, rococo borders, wide flat rim, 7" 1,475.00
Vase, pansies/4 suns in gold, gold tracery, neck hdls, 6½x6" ...2,200.00
Vase, rose vines/sections, ovoid w/cup & bulb neck, 9½" 3,335.00
Vase, violets on frost w/gold outlines & daubs, hdls, 6½x6" ...2,200.00
Vase, 3 gold disks (1 w/dragon), sectioned, long neck, 11x7" .4,500.00
Vase, 5 snow geese fly over sun on bl/gr/tan, gold stars, 14" ...9,000.00

Royal Haeger, Haeger

In 1871 David Henry Haeger, a young son of German immigrants, purchased a brick factory at Dundee, Illinois. David's bricks rebuilt Chicago after their great fire in 1871. Many generations of the Haeger family have been associated with the ceramic industry that his descendants have pursued to the present time. Haeger progressed to include artware in their production as early as 1914. That was only the beginning. In the '30s they began to make a line of commercial dinnerware that was marketed through Marshall Field's. Not long after, Haeger's artware was successful enough that a second plant in Macomb, Illinois, was built.

Royal Haeger was their premium line beginning in 1938 and continued in to modern-day production. The chief designer in the '40s was Royal Arden Hickman, a talented artist and sculptor who also worked in mediums other than pottery. For Haeger he designed a line of wonderfully stylized animals, birds, high-style vases, and human figures, all with extremely fine details. His designs are highly regarded by collectors today.

Paper labels have been used throughout Haeger's production. Some items from the teens, '20s, and '30s will be found with 'Haeger' in a diamond shape in-mold script mark. Items with 'RG' (Royal Garden) are part of their Flower-Ware line (also called Regular Haeger or Genuine Haeger). Haeger has produced a premium line (Royal Haeger) as well as a regular line for many years, it just has changed names over the years.

Collectors need to be aware that a certain glaze can bring two to three times more than others. Items that have Royal Hickman in the mold mark or on the label are usually higher valued than without his mark. The current collector trend has leaned more towards the mid-century modern styled pieces of artware. The most desired items are ones done by glaze designers Helmut Bruchman and Alrun Osterberg Guest (presently employed by Haeger). These items are from the late '60s into the very early '80s.

For those wanting to learn more about this pottery, we recommend *Haeger Potteries Through the Years* by our advisor for this category, David Dilley (L-W Books); he is listed in the Directory under Indiana.

#7, cockatoo, pk, 1933, no mk, 3x4" 20.00
#33, dbl-leaf vase, 13" 100.00
#86, mermaid & child flower frog, jade gr matt, no mk, 7" 200.00
#109-S, ashtray, Gold Tweed, 2¼x7x7" 10.00
#120, candle holders, spiral stems, yel, no mk, ca 1917, 10", pr ...75.00
#141, ginger jar lamp base, purple, no mk, ca 1914, 9¾" 60.00
#177, leaf dish, 1950s, 5" 8.00
#329-H, pheasant bowl, 7¼" 50.00
#342, compote, hexagonal, 6x7x7" 20.00
#394, pilgrim hat planter, 4⅝" 15.00
#495, panther, ebony, 24½" L 75.00
#502-H, matador planter, 13" 125.00
#508, laughing donkey planter, 9½x7½" 40.00
#612-613, rooster & hen, 11", 10", pr 50.00
#616, teddy bear w/drum planter, ca 1938, 4¾x7" 15.00
#702, ashtray/cigarette holder, 3¼x10¼x6⅜" 20.00
#776, goblet planter, Aqua Tweed, 9" 15.00
#812-H, fish table lighter, 1960s, 10" 40.00
#815-H, compote/candle holder, Gold Tweed, 15¼" 75.00
#863, bowl, emb dmn pattern, 2¾x9¾" 10.00
#889, table lighter, ribbed cylinder, 1950s-60s, 3" dia 15.00
#917-A, rocking cradle wall pocket, ca 1939, 3x5" 10.00
#3003, compote, 4½x12" 15.00
#3178, planter, upside hat shape, lemon peel (rarest peel), 6½" ...175.00
#3248, fat rabbit, bl, no mk, 1940s, 5x4x4" 20.00
#3277, bow candle holder, ca 1947, 7½" 75.00
#3622, planter/bookends, ball shape, 7x4¾", pr 40.00
#4160X, vase, cylinder, other than Seminole Orange, 12" 37.50
#4160X, vase, cylinder, Seminole Orange (squiggles), 12" 150.00
#4162X, vase, cylinder, lemon peel (rarest peel glaze), 7" 95.00
#4171X, vase, other than Seminole Orange, 15" 56.00
#4171X, vase, Seminole Orange (squiggles), 15" 225.00
#4194, bamboo vase, 10¾" 25.00
#4208X, vase, lg hdls, lemon peel (rarest peel glaze), 15" 275.00
#5015-H, owl hanging basket, Bennington Brn Foam, 7x8½" 75.00
#5190, bucking bronco w/rider & cactus lamp base, 26" 250.00
#5202, parrot on tree branch lamp base, no mk, ca 1947, 17" ...250.00
#6202, greyhound TV lamp/planter, brn, no mk, 6¼x11½" 75.00
#8010-8011, tidbit tray, 2-tier, 10½" 20.00
#8034, dog bank, 8½" 40.00
#8167, table lighter, ball shape, no mk, 3½" 15.00
#8170, box w/rooster emb on lid, mk Haeger/Sascha B, 3x5x9" ...150.00
#8186-8187, lavabo, 2-pc set, 14¼", 5¼" 75.00
#8188, pitcher, Brn Earth Graphic Wrap, 9" 50.00
#8229, bean bot, 8" 35.00
#8294-8300, figures w/instruments (Toe Tappers), 8"-12", ea, $50 to ..75.00
R-31, peacock planter, 14½" 75.00
R-115, gazelle head lamp, ebony, 12½" 100.00
R-138, flying fish (3/attached), teal/yel, paper tag, 9x4x8" 200.00
R-189, sitting nude flower frog, Peach Agate 150.00
R-203, dbl-fish candle holder, 5" 35.00
R-277, spiral plume dish, ca 1942, 7" 35.00
R-284, trout planter, MOP w/gold fin & tail, 9¼" 75.00
R-297, shell bowl, 14" L 25.00
R-298, cornucopia shell vase, ca 1948, 9x11" 75.00
R-333, bowl, ftd, 4½x16x7" 25.00

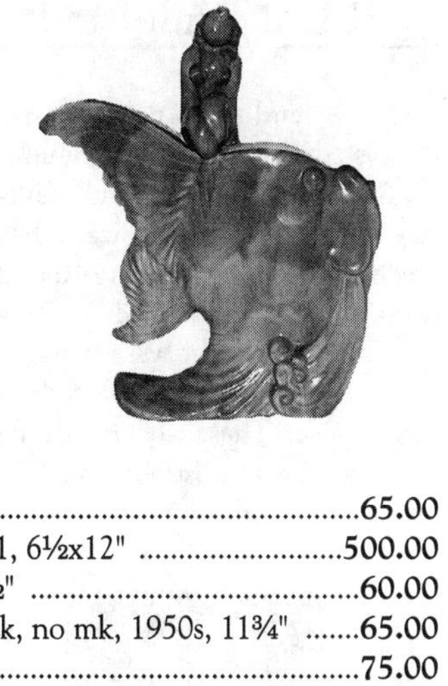

R-347, fish vase with mermaid, Mauve Agate, 13", minimum value, $500.00. (Photo courtesy David Dilley)

R-370, Dutch cup bowl, 3½x18½" 65.00
R-379, bull, no base, Mallow, ca 1941, 6½x12" 500.00
R-386, basket w/flowers, ca 1943, 8½" 60.00
R-412, fawn standing on oval base, pk, no mk, 1950s, 11¾" 65.00
R-419, pitcher vase, 14⅜" 75.00
R-422, butterfly vase, ca 1940, 5½x9" 40.00
R-424, bucking bronco w/rider & cactus, amber, 1940s, 13" 200.00
R-431, lily candy dish, w/lid, 6x7½" dia 50.00
R-433, triple-plume candle holder, 5x11" 30.00
R-434, hen pheasant, 5¼x15" 40.00
R-441, 4-circle vase, Deco, no mk, 1940s, 11½" 150.00
R-451, mare & foal, ca 1943, 11x13" 200.00
R-455, vase w/figural bow, ca 1936, 14" 75.00

R-459, triple-shell dish w/fish finial, ca 1946, 8½" 40.00
R-479, prospector, 7x11¼" 175.00
R-482, 3-feather/plume vase, 14½" 75.00
R-523, fan vase, 10x16" 65.00
R-525, dbl-tulip planter, ca 1947, 4¼x9¾" 90.00
R-540, turtle planter, 4x13½" 60.00
R-575, Rose of Sharon basket, ca 1948, 8x7" 75.00
R-596, barnyard riders planter, silver spray/yel, chartreuse base, 13" 500.00
R-631, leopard cigarette box, 5x6½x4" 50.00
R-638, panther planter/bookends, blk, 1950s, 7¾", 4", pr 200.00
R-648, panther sitting on ped base, ebony, no mk, 1950s, 6" 50.00
R-649, panther resting, 2⅝x7¼" 40.00
R-685, cigarette box, 5x6¾x4" 75.00
R-697, starfish bowl, 2⅜x14½" 75.00
R-706, running deer vase, 15¼" 40.00
R-718, ram's head bookends, 5¾", pr 65.00
R-721, Indian on horse, Desert Red, minimum value 750.00
R-745, grape cluster wall pocket 65.00
R-777, cocker spaniel on belly w/legs spread, brn, 1950s, 5½" 75.00
R-838, frog flower frog, 4½" 75.00
R-975, deer running, stylized, ebony, no mk, 5¾x11¾" 45.00
R-1135, flower wall pocket 50.00
R-1144, water lily bookends, ca 1952, 7½", pr 75.00
R-1146, running deer planter, 6½x11¼" 50.00
R-1170, Comedy & Tragedy masks planter, 7¼x11" 65.00
R-1191, sailfish planter bowl, Briar Agate, no mk, 7½x11" 45.00
R-1224, gypsy girl w/2 baskets, brn/gr, no mk, 16½" 65.00
R-1265, colt w/leg up, oval base, brn, 6½x7½" 50.00
R-1285, lily candle holders, 5", pr 20.00
R-1460, dbl-leaf vase, scrolled ft, antiqued coloring, no mk, 10¾" ...25.00
R-1585SS, coffeepot, ca 1957, 10½" 45.00
R-1602, horseshoe ashtray, 8" 15.00
R-1639-S, basket w/metal bracket, 14½" 30.00
R-1679-S, pitcher, 10¼" 65.00
R-1761, turkey planter, 12x14" 150.00
R-1787, egg-shaped ashtray, 4x6¼" 20.00
R-1844, duck planter, 6½x8" L 25.00

Royal Rudolstadt

The hard-paste porcelain that has come to be known as Royal Rudolstadt was produced in Thuringia, Germany, in the early eighteenth century. Various names and marks have been associated with this pottery. One of the earliest was a hay-fork symbol associated with Johann Frederich von Schwarzburg-Rudolstadt, one of the first founders. Variations, some that included an 'R,' were also used. In 1854 Earnst Bohne produced wares that were marked with an anchor and the letters 'EB.' Examples commonly found today were made during the late 1800s and early 1900s. These are usually marked with an 'RW' within a shield under a crown and the words 'Crown Rudolstadt.' Items marked 'Germany' were made after 1890.

Bust, fanciful girl holding (separate) fan $850.00.

Bowl, mc floral w/gold rim, sgn Hut, 9½" 65.00
Bowl, pk roses w/gr leaves, 3 gold ft, Beyer, 8" 85.00
Cake plate, lilies, Deco form, w/hdls, 11" 85.00
Celery dish, pk roses, pierced hdls, mk 55.00
Dresser set, pk roses, tray/hair receiver/box/pin tray 225.00
Hatpin holder, pk, cream & yel roses on wht, 8" 120.00
Plate, St Bernard, gold trim, gr mk, sgn, 8½" 50.00
Plate, 3 roses, gold trim, 6¼" 25.00
Tea set, Happifats, pot+cr/sug+4 c/s+4 sm plates, child sz 350.00
Vase, floral on lt gr w/gold trim, #37, 12x6½" 220.00

Royal Vienna

In 1719 Claude Innocentius de Paquier established a hard-paste porcelain factory in Vienna where he made highly ornamental wares similar to the type produced at Meissen. Early wares were usually unmarked; but after 1744, when the factory was purchased by the Empress, the Austrian shield (often called 'beehive') was stamped on under the glaze. In the following listings, values are for hand-painted items unless noted otherwise. Decal-decorated items would be considerably lower.

Note: An influx of Japanese reproductions on the market have influenced values to decline on genuine old Royal Vienna. Buyer beware! On new items the beehive mark is over the glaze, the weight of the porcelain is heavier, and the decoration is obviously decaled. Our advisor for this category is Madeleine France; she is listed in the Directory under Florida.

Bottle, scent; boy pulls goat among grapes, 1744-1820 mk, 2½" 770.00
Bowl, wht snowflake carnations on bl-gr w/gold, 10" 150.00
Box, Victorian scenes, gold borders, rose finial, beehive mk, 4x5½" 200.00
Cup & saucer, rooster in landscape w/gold, 3½", 5½" 150.00
Plate, lady & flowers, cobalt w/gold, beehive mk, 15", pr 3,200.00
Plate, lady in rose sgn Wagner, heavy gold border, 9½" 900.00
Plate, Lassitude, Wagner, cobalt w/emb gold edge, 9½" 650.00
Teapot, lovers in reverse on bl w/gold, hdls, late, 7" 525.00
Vase, Diana the Huntress on cobalt w/gold, 7x5" 520.00
Vase, lady on maroon w/gold, turq beading, 9¾" 895.00
Vase, Ruth portrait sgn Wagner, heavy gold, 6" 750.00

Roycroft

Near the turn of the century, Elbert Hubbard established the Roycroft Printing Shop in East Aurora, New York. Named in honor of two seventeenth-century printer-bookbinders, the print shop was just the beginning of a community called Roycroft, which came to be known worldwide. Hubbard became a popular personality of the early 1900s, known for his talents in a variety of areas from writing and lecturing to manufacturing. The Roycroft community became a meeting place for people of various capabilities and included shops for the production of furniture, copper, leather items, and a multitude of other wares which were marked with the Roycroft symbol, an 'R' within a circle below a double-barred cross. Hubbard lost his life on the Lusitania in 1915; production in the community continued until the Depression.

Interest is strong in the field of Arts and Crafts in general and in Roycroft items in particular. Copper items are evaluated to a large extent by the condition and type of the original patina. The most desirable patina is either the dark or medium brown; brass-wash, gunmetal, and silver-wash patinas follow in desirability. The acid-etched patina and the smooth (unhammered) surfaced Roycroft pieces are later (after 1925) developments and tend not to be attractive to collectors. Furniture was manufactured in oak, mahogany, bird's-eye maple, and occasionally walnut or ash; collectors prefer oak. Books with Levant binding, tooled leather covers, Japan vellum, or hand illumining are especially collectible; suede cover and parchment paper books are of less interest to collectors as they are fairly common. In the listings that follow, values reflect the worth of items in excellent original condition unless noted to the contrary. Our advisor for this category is Bruce Austin; he is listed in the Directory under New York.

Key: h/cp — hammered copper

Pedestal, mahogany, four shelves supported by splayed slab sides, double-keyed tenons, incised orb each side, 50x29x18", $4,750.00.

Armchair, 2-slat ladder-bk, apron, rpl leather seat, 38" 2,600.00
Bench, 'Ali Baba', half log, keyed-thru tenon trestle base, 42" ..6,500.00
Book, An American Bible, Alice Hubbard, emb gilt/leather 40.00
Book, Book of Songs, H Heine, Levant binding, 1903, VG 175.00
Book, Dreams, Olive Schreiner, 1901, sgn Hubbard, w/slip case ..250.00
Book, Friendship, Henry Thoreau, Levant binding, 1903 ....400.00
Book, Garnett & Brindled Cow..., Alice Hubbard, 1913, VG ...100.00
Book, Intellectual Life, PG Hammerton, suede binding, 1899 .....75.00
Book, Justinian & Theodora, Alice & Elbert Hubbard, 1906 ......75.00
Book, Law of Love, WM Reedy, red suede binding, 1905, EXIB ..75.00
Book, Life Lessons, Alice Hubbard, suede binding, 1909 ....50.00
Book, Little Journeys/Famous Women, author sgn, 1900 reprint .50.00
Book, Message to Garcia & 13 Other Things, Levant binding, 1901 ..150.00
Book, Nature, RW Emerson, gr suede cover by Hunter, 1905, VG 100.00
Book, Ruskin & Turner, sgn E Hubbard, c Putnam, 1895 ....150.00
Book trough, hand-cut dvtl wood, curved sides, 4½x18x5¾" ...900.00
Bookcase, 5-shelf, low drw, overhanging top, chamfered bk, 65x34" ...4,000.00
Bookends, h/cp, emb poppies, 5½x5", pr 700.00
Bookends, h/cp, emb 4-leaf clover on verdigris sq, 5x4¼", pr 400.00
Bookends, h/cp, incised floral border, 8½x5¾", pr 400.00
Bookends, h/cp, rose garlands, 3-sided, 5x3¾", pr 300.00
Bookends, h/cp w/brass wash, open hemipsheres, 3½x6", pr 200.00
Bookends, h/cp w/brass wash, stylized dogwood, 4½x5", pr 250.00
Bowl, h/cp, incised lotus, new patina, 3x3¾" 350.00
Bowl, h/cp, squat w/closed-in rim, heavy, 3x11" 450.00
Bowl, nut; h/cp, closed-in rim, 3-ftd, new dk patina, 2¾x10¼" ..400.00
Box, cigar; Elbert Hubbard inside label, John Merriam & Co, 10" L ...325.00
Box, Goodie, mahog w/h/cp latch/trim/hdls, mk, 26" L, VG 700.00
Box, h/c, floral repousse, deep patina, orb mk, 1½x3¼x3¼" 400.00
Box, jewelry; tooled leather w/birds, suede lined, 8¼" L 4,000.00
Candelabra, h/cp w/brass wash, 5-light, lt wear, 13½x13½" 350.00
Candle sconces, h/cp, flame covers, 9x2½", pr 600.00
Candlesticks, h/cp, cylindrical shafts, dk patina, 9¾", pr 750.00
Candy dish, h/cp, emb trefoil & starburst, unmk, 4½x5½" 350.00
Chair, desk; mahog, hourglass bk-slat, leather seat, 44" 1,400.00
Chair, dining side; hourglass bk-slats, leather seats, 40", 6 for ..8,000.00
Chair, mahog, 4 vertical slats, child sz 2,000.00
Chair, Meditation, broad/flat crest rail, new leather/rfn 2,400.00
Chair, side; 2-slat ladder-bk, rpl leather seat, 38" 1,300.00
Chair, side; 3-slat ladder-bk, leather seat, rfn, 37", pr 1,200.00
Clock, mantel; tooled leather case w/floral decor, mini, 4½x6x2" 5,000.00
Console set, h/cp w/brass wash, hdld 9" bowl+2 candlesticks 550.00
Footstool, inset gr vinyl (rpl) seat, rfn, 14½x17x12" 900.00
Frame, holds 6 images, orb mk, 11x36½" 2,500.00
Frame, tooled leather w/emb daisy, lt wear, 9x6½" 1,500.00
Hatpin, h/cp, sq head w/emb quatrefoil, 1¼" sq 375.00
Hatpin, h/cp, sq head w/incised orb/cross mk, 1½" 750.00
Humidor, h/cp, 4-pointed arrow on lid, 5½x4½" 750.00
Lamp, h/cp, 4 riveted ribs over mica shade, new patina, 14x10" .2,600.00
Lamp, h/cp base & dome shade, 14½" 2,500.00
Magazine stand, solid sides, rnded top, 3-shelf, 37x14x12" 5,500.00
Mirror, hall; wood w/6 hammered hooks, orig chains, unmk, 30x56" ...2,000.00
Motto sign, gray oak brd, Self Reliance/symbol, 10x42" 1,700.00
Nut set, h/cp, bowl w/center funnel, 5 picks/spoon, rfn 425.00
Nut set, h/cp, 6 6" trays, ladle & 3-ftd 7½" bowl 1,200.00
Plate, h/cp, trefoils against verdigris panels, heavy, 10" 300.00
Poker chip holder, h/c w/brass wash, w/orig chips, 6½x4½" 475.00
Settle, even-arm, 2-slat sides & bk, tapered posts, rfn, 79" 3,000.00
Sidebrd, plate rack, drw, 2 glass doors, rfn, 45x42" 12,000.00
Sidebrd, 3 sm drws amid doors over linen drw, mirrored, 55x60" 12,000.00
Stand, Little Journey's; 2-shelf, shoe ft, metal tag, 26" 600.00
Table, library; Mackmurdo ft, apron, low shelf, 28x30x22" 2,000.00
Table, library; stretcher w/dbl-keyed tenons, mk/#072, 50" 3,500.00
Table, library; 1-drw, plank sides w/cutouts, 30x60x30" 7,500.00
Table, tacked leather top, apron, mk legs, rfn, 16" sq 2,100.00
Table, writing; mahog, slatted sides, 2-drw, shelf, 30x48x30" ..5,000.00
Table, 36" dia top over wide apron, X-stretcher, 30" 5,000.00
Table mat, tooled leather w/Trillium & Celtic rose, 17½" dia ...1,700.00
Tray, card; h/cp w/silver wash, W Jennings, lt wear, 7" 375.00
Tray, h/cp w/brass wash, emb flower on verdigris panel, 22" 500.00
Vase, Am Beauty, h/cp, rstr patina, 19½" 1,600.00
Vase, bud; h/cp, emb dogwood blossoms, glass liner, 8x3" sq 200.00
Vase, h/cp, closed-in rim, 5x4½" 400.00
Vase, h/cp, cylindrical, unmk, 9¼x3¾" 1,000.00
Vase, h/cp, cylindrical w/riveted flared base, 10½x6" 2,500.00
Vase, h/cp, dmn-pattern band, some pitting, unmk, 12x4¼" ..1,100.00
Vase, h/cp, shouldered, flared rim, 8½" 575.00
Vase, h/cp, tooled floral stems, worn orig patina, 10", EX 900.00
Vase, h/cp w/brass wash, stylized band, cylindrical, 4¾x2¼" 300.00
Vase, h/cp w/etched decor, dk patina, cylindrical, 7x2½" 2,000.00
Waste basket, slatted, ebonized finish, 14" sq 2,100.00

Rozenburg

Some of the most innovative and original Art Nouveau ceramics were created by the Rozenburg factory at the Hague in The Netherlands between 1883 and 1914, when production was ceased. (Several of their better painters continued to work in Gouda, which accounts for some pieces being similar to Gouda.) Rozenburg also made highly prized eggshell ware, so called because of its very thin walls; this is eagerly sought after by collectors. T.A.C. Colenbrander was their artistic leader, with Samuel Schellink and J. Kok designing many of the eggshell pieces. The company liquidated in 1917. Most pieces carry a date code. Our advisor for this category is Ralph Jaarsma; he is listed in the Directory under Iowa.

Plaque, scenic, 19x8", in old wood fr 3,250.00
Plaque, 3-figure indoor scene, sgn Neuhys, 14x10" +fr 3,500.00
Vase, abstract foliage, mc on dk gr speckled, #401, mk, 12x8" ..1,800.00

Vase, Nouveau floral & butterflies, 1896, 15x9½" 1,750.00

Rubena

Rubena glass was made by several firms in the late 1800s. It is a blown art glass that shades from clear to red. See also Art Glass Baskets; Cruets; Sugar Shakers; Salts; specific manufacturers.

Celery vase, bird & floral, SP holder, 8" 750.00
Pitcher, Coin Spot, sq top, gr hdl, water sz 220.00
Pitcher, Hobnail, sq rim, camphor hdl, 7" 285.00
Rose bowl, Herringbone, irid, 3x4" 70.00
Vase, floral w/gold, trumpet form in brass stand, 16½x6" 225.00
Vase, florals, appl ft, 10" 210.00

Rubena Verde

Rubena Verde glass was introduced in the late 1800s by Hobbs, Brockunier, and Company of Wheeling, West Virginia. Its transparent colors shade from red to green. See also Art Glass Baskets; Cruets; Sugar Shakers; Salts.

Pitcher, Inverted Thumbprint with enameled butterfly and flowers, 6¾", $400.00. (Photo courtesy John A. Shuman III)

Bowl, Hobnail, trefoil mouth, acid etched, 2½x4½" 125.00
Cheese dish, Coin Spot lid on gr Daisy & Button base, 7" dia ..250.00
Cruet, Invt T'print, teepee shape, Hobbs Brockunier, 7" 550.00
Pitcher, Invt T'print, vaseline gr hdl, Hobbs, 7¼" 250.00
Pitcher, pk opal at top, gr reeded hdl, 8½" 350.00
Vase, jack-in-pulpit; 12" 200.00
Vase, opal Dmn Quilt, appl gr/clear florals & petal ft, 11", NM ...300.00

Ruby Glass

Produced for over one hundred years by every glasshouse of note in this country, ruby glass has been used to create decorative items such as one might find in gift shops, utilitarian bottles and kitchenware, figurines, and dinnerware lines such as were popular in the Depression era. For further information and study, we recommend *Ruby Glass of the 20th Century* by our advisor, Naomi Over; she is listed in the Directory under Colorado.

Ashtray/match holder, rnd dish w/metal holder, Gilco Prod, 5" ...35.00
Bottle, barber; Victorian, sq w/rnd stopper, early 1900s, 6¾" 25.00
Bottle, medicine; Pyrex/Corning, ca 1920, 1-qt 35.00
Bottles, vinegar/oil; Victorian, silver tags/castors, 1910s, 6", pr 60.00
Bowl, salad; plain, France, early 1900s, 5¾" 10.00
Candlesticks, Dmn T'print, crimped base, Viking, 1986, 5", pr ...65.00
Candy dish, bail finial on peaked lid, clear stem/ft, att Louie, 11" 25.00
Candy dish, Epic, 3-legged, Viking, 5¼x7½" 30.00
Candy dish, Eyewinker, ped ft, w/lid, LG Wright, 1960s, 6" 35.00
Cigarette box, Royal Ruby lid w/roses, crystal box, Anchor Hocking ..20.00
Compote, Blenko, 1930-50, 8½" W 20.00
Compote, clear twisted stem, Italy, 10¼x10⅜" 32.00
Cornucopia nut dish, 3¾" 25.00
Creamer, Eyewinker, LG Wright, 1960s, 3¾" 25.00
Creamer, ruby insert in ftd/hdld silver holder, England, 1970s, 3¾" ...15.00
Dish, Daisy & Button, Am Flint Glass Works, 5½" sq 20.00
Jug, molasses, crystal hdl, Blenko, 1980, 5½" 20.00
Knife sharpener, ruby marbles in silver holder 10.00
Lamp, satin, ball shade/base, fabric-like panels, LG Wright, 21½" ...850.00
Pickle jar, w/silver castor & tongs, AA Imports/Poland, 12½" 75.00
Pitcher, Eyewinker, LG Wright, 1960s, 1-qt 100.00
Pitcher vase, Venetian, crystal hdl, Kanawha/USA, 5" 20.00
Plate, Epic, free-form, Viking, 17" 55.00
Punch bowl, Royal Ruby, Anchor Hocking, 1940s 35.00
Punch bowl stand, Royal Ruby, Anchor Hocking, 1940s 20.00
Relish tray, Old Cafe, crystal w/5 ruby inserts, Anchor Hocking 60.00
Shakers, Viking, 1980s, 3½", pr 20.00
Spittoon, Mexico, ca 1970, 6x7¾" 75.00
Tumbler, juice; Standard (Anchor Hocking), 1940s, 6-oz 6.00
Tumbler, water; Rosette patterned base, Blenko, 1930-50, 8-oz ...10.00
Vase, air-twist stem, Blenko, 1950, 12" 20.00
Vase, goblet form w/clear stem, Italy, ca 1950, 15½" 35.00

Ruby-Stained Glass

Ruby-flashed or ruby-stained glass was made through the application of a thin layer of color over clear. It was used in the manufacture of some early pressed tableware and from the Victorian era well into the twentieth century. These items were often engraved on the spot with the date, location, and buyer's name.

Butter dish, Nat'l Star 145.00
Celery vase, Pioneer's Victoria 135.00
Compote, jelly; Bar & Flute 95.00
Creamer, Beaded Thumbprint Block, eng 95.00
Creamer, Royal Crystal 65.00
Mug, Scalloped Daisy, eng, 2½" 28.00
Spooner, Beaded Thumbprint Block 85.00
Tankard, Bracelet, 12" 175.00
Toothpick holder, Button Arches, eng 26.00
Tumbler, Leaf & Star 75.00
Tumbler, Skilton 20.00

Rugs, Hooked

Hooked rugs are treasured today for their folk-art appeal. Rug making was a craft that was introduced to this country in about 1830 and flourished its best in the New England states. The prime consideration when evaluating one of these rugs is not age but artistic appeal. Scenes with animals, buildings, and people; patriotic designs; or whimsical themes are preferred. Those with finely conceived designs, great imagination, interesting color use, etc., demand higher prices. Condition is, of course, also a factor. Marked examples bearing the stamps of 'Frost and Co.,' 'Abenakee,' 'C.R.,' and 'Ouia' are highly prized. Note: The rugs listed here are made of rag unless noted otherwise. See also Orientalia, Rugs.

Cats (3) w/yarn, mc on magenta, 21x33½" 465.00
Checkerboard pattern, grs/grays/blk/wht, mc zigzag border, 35x20" ..110.00
Dog, blk on gray w/mc borders, 30x54" 700.00
Dog & flowers w/in leafy border, mc, minor rprs, 39x66" 700.00
Eagle w/wings wide among thistles/shamrocks/roses, 20th C, 42x61" ..975.00

Eagle reserve on gray and green with star and oak-leaf border, twentieth century, 72x47½", $2,400.00.

Floral, mc on gray w/red & brn border, 37x78" 200.00
Geometric center w/scrolling leaf border, mc, ca 1900, 61" sq .2,500.00
Moose reserve w/swag & foliate border, ca 1900s, 32x44" 1,600.00
Owl on branch in moonlight, mc on gray w/bl border, 19x33½" ...250.00
Penny, mc wool circles embr on tan twill, 23x43", EX 330.00
Potted plant & floral border on homespun ground, 1850s, 49x48" ..2,000.00
Rooster, blk w/mc arabesque stripes, loss, 22x39" 150.00
Roosters (2) w/in geometric border, bright mc, 20th C, 32x51" 2,185.00
Sailor's Homecoming, J Moshimer/Forestine Heath, 1879, 58", EX ..1,500.00
Santa in sleigh w/toys on rooftop, mistletoe border, Heath, 27x42" 275.00
Skunk in landscape, minor fading/rprs, 20x33½" 925.00
Stag among flowers, mc on brn, 37x37" 800.00

RumRill

George Rumrill designed and marketed his pottery designs from 1933 until his death in 1942. During this period of time, four different companies produced his works. Today the most popular designs are those made by the Red Wing Stoneware Company from 1933 until 1936 and Red Wing Potteries from 1936 until early 1938. Some of these lines include Trumpet Flower, Classic, Manhattan, and Athena, the Nudes.

For a period of months in 1938, Shawnee took over the production of RumRill pottery. This relationship ended abruptly, and the Florence Pottery took over and produced his wares until the plant burned down. The final producer was Gonder. Pieces from each individual pottery are easily recognized by their designs, glazes, and/or signatures. It is interesting to note that the same designs were produced by all three companies. They may be marked RumRill or with the name of the specific company that made them. You will find information on RumRill in these books: *Red Wing Art Pottery, Books I* and *II*, by B.L. and R.L. Dollen (Collector Books). Our advisors for this category are Wendy and Leo Frese; they are listed in the Directory under Texas.

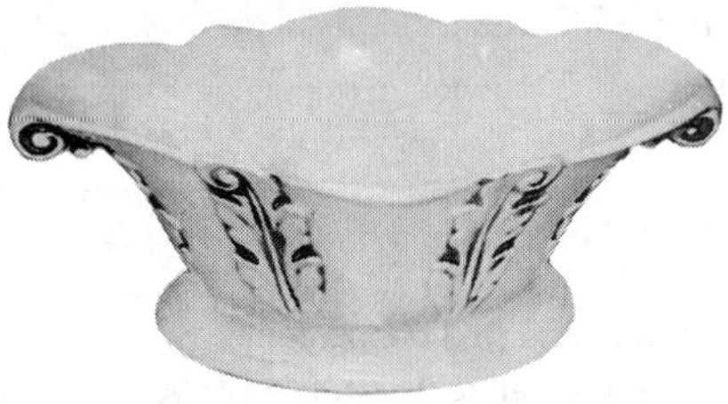

Bowl, #530, Renaissance Group, matt ivory with brown stain, 10½", from $62.00 to $78.00. (Photo courtesy B.L. and R.L. Dollen)

Athena Dbl Nude, #568, Seashell, 11" 685.00
Basket, #615, Vintage Group, 12½" 125.00
Basket, #619, Vintage, dbl hdls 110.00
Bowl, #E-12, lt gr, OH 25.00
Bowl, #274, pk, 6½" 35.00
Bowl, #302, Dutch Blue, dbl hdls, 6" 55.00
Bowl, #509, Seafoam, 5" 27.50
Bowl, console; #571, Athena, dk bl 1,350.00
Ewer, #616L, Vintage Group, 11" 110.00
Flower frog, #563, Athena, Eggshell 1,350.00
Ivy ball, #601-6, Suntan w/gr int, 'bowling ball' shape 85.00
Ivy ball, #601-6, Suntan w/lt gr int, triangular openings 85.00
Jug, #547, Scarlet & Bay, ball from 40.00
Vase, #T-1, Dutch Blue, swirl design, OH, floor sz 625.00
Vase, #249, Transition Dbl Nude, lilac 825.00
Vase, #302, Fluted, Dutch Blue, 11" 350.00
Vase, #364, Dutch Blue, Grecian Group, 7" 80.00
Vase, #570, Triple Nude Athena, Seafoam 1,500.00
Vase, #686, Riviera, 11" 75.00
Vase, bud; #290, Dutch Blue, 9½" 85.00
Vase, bud; #510, #510, Scarlet & Bay, 8" 50.00

Rushmore

Ivan House studied sculpture and fine arts at the University of Oregon. He gained valuable experience in the potting field, first by producing terra cotta architectural sculptures and later through the work he did with the carvers on Mt. Rushmore. In 1933 he purchased a tract of land near Mt. Rushmore where he built his own pottery. Using the especially adaptable clay he found there, he produced a line of decorative items until 1941, after which he went into the teaching field. His wares are characterized by the natural shading of the clay which he allowed to show through the glazes.

Ashtray, relief pine cones, bl, 3½x4½" 85.00
Creamer & sugar bowl, Permaclay, 2¼" 275.00
Dealer sign, gr-gold, 3½x8½", minimum value 500.00
Dish, slip-pnt cattails on gr-wht, 11" 85.00
Paperweight, molded animal & star, maroon, 2¼" 85.00
Pitcher, pale bl, striation, 4½" 75.00
Pitcher, swirl, gr w/bl highlights, dk gr or yel, 7" 115.00
Pitcher, swirl, Uranium orange, 7" 135.00
Trivet, stylized Art Deco floral, mint gr or maroon, 5" 135.00
Vase, gr, striation, 3¾" 65.00

Ruskin

This English pottery operated near Birmingham from 1889 until 1935. Its founder was W. Howson Taylor, and it was named in honor of the renowned author and critic, John Ruskin. The earliest marks were 'Taylor' in block letters and the initials 'WHT,' the smaller W and H superimposed over the larger T. Later marks included the Ruskin name.

Vase, apple gr lustre w/ice crackle, 1919, 6¾" 300.00
Vase, blk w/silver o/l floral, 1917, 4" 360.00
Vase, crystalline, gr, closed-in rim, corseted, unmk, 8x4¼" 80.00
Vase, crystalline, gr/pk/lav/gray, 1920, 10¼" 345.00
Vase, crystalline, ivory/bl-gray, teardrop shape, 4½" 150.00
Vase, crystalline brn-maroon w/lt bl highlights, 1923, 10¼" 945.00
Vase, crystalline sang-de-boeuf, bulbous, stovepipe neck, 1922, 9x4" ..950.00
Vase, dk bl, slender w/str neck, 1916, 7¾" 285.00
Vase, lt bl lustre, bulbous, 6" 175.00
Vase, orange/gr/yel flambe, bottle shape, 8" 225.00
Vase, reactive yel-gray w/bl-gr overglaze, 7x5¾" 350.00

Russel Wright Dinnerware

Russel Wright, one of America's foremost industrial designers, also designed several lines of ceramic dinnerware, glassware, and aluminum ware that are now highly sought-after collectibles. His most popular dinnerware then and with today's collectors, American Modern, was manufactured by the Steubenville Pottery Company from 1939 until 1959. It was produced in a variety of solid colors in assortments chosen to stay attune with the times. Casual (his first line sturdy enough to be guaranteed against breakage for ten years from date of purchase) is relatively easy to find today — simply because it has held up so well. During the years of its production, the Casual line was constantly being restyled, some items as many as five times. Early examples were heavily mottled, while later pieces were smoothly glazed and sometimes patterned. The ware was marked with Wright's signature and 'China by Iroquois.' It was marketed in fine department stores throughout the country. After 1950 the line was marked 'Iroquois China by Russel Wright.' For those wanting to learn more about the subject, we recommend *The Collector's Encyclopedia of Russel Wright, Second Edition*, by our advisor, Ann Kerr. She is listed in the Directory under Ohio.

American Modern

To calculate values for American Modern, double the values listed for these colors: Canteloupe, Glacier Blue, Bean Brown, and White. Chartreuse is represented by the low end of our range; Cedar, Black Chutney, and Seafoam by the high end; and Coral and Gray near the middle.

Baker, sm, scarce, from $30 to 40.00
Bowl, lug fruit; from $15 to 20.00
Bowl, salad, from $75 to 100.00
Bowl, vegetable; w/lid, from $60 to 80.00
Carafe (jug), from $185 to 225.00
Casserole, w/lid, from $40 to 60.00
Celery, from $22 to 30.00
Coaster, scarce, from $15 to 20.00
Cup, from $8 to 10.00
Gravy boat, 10½", from $20 to 30.00
Pitcher, water; from $100 to 135.00
Plate, dinner; 10", from $10 to 12.00
Plate, 6", from $5 to 8.00
Platter, 13½", from $25 to 40.00
Sauce boat, from $40 to 50.00

Casual

To price Brick Red, Aqua, and Canteloupe, double our values; for Avacado, use the low end of the range. Oyster and Charcoal are valued at 50% more than the prices listed.

Bowl, fruit; 5½", from $12 to 14.00
Bowl, salad; 10", from $30 to 40.00
Bowl, vegetable; divided, from $40 to 50.00
Butter dish, ½-lb, from $85 to 100.00
Chop plate, 13⅞", from $30 to 50.00
Creamer, redesigned, from $20 to 25.00
Cup & saucer, redesigned, from $18 to 22.00
Gravy, 12-oz, 5¼", from $15 to 18.00
Mug, redesigned, from $100 to 150.00
Pitcher, w/lid, 1½-qt, from $150 to 200.00
Plate, luncheon; 9½", from $8 to 10.00
Plate, salad; 7½", from $9 to 12.00
Platter, oval, 14½", from $40 to 50.00

Glass

Unless otherwise described, values are given for glassware in Coral and Seafoam; other colors are 10% to 15% less.

Bartlett Collins, highball, 5", from $16 to 18.00
Bartlett Collins, ice tub, from $40 to 45.00
Bartlett Collins, juice, from $10 to 15.00
Bartlett Collins, old fashioned, dbl; from $20 to 25.00
Imperial Flair, tumbler, iced tea; 14-oz, from $65 to 70.00
Imperial Flair, tumbler, juice; 6-oz, from $50 to 75.00
Imperial Flair, tumbler, water; 11-oz, from $65 to 70.00
Imperial Pinch, tumbler, iced tea; 14-oz, from $50 to 75.00
Imperial Pinch, tumbler, juice; 6-oz, from $45 to 60.00
Imperial Pinch, tumbler, water; 11-oz, from $50 to 65.00
Imperial Twist, old fashioned; from $65 to 85.00
Imperial Twist, tumbler, iced tea; from $60 to 75.00
Imperial Twist, tumbler, juice; from $45 to 60.00
Oceana serving item, candy box, shell covered, from $1,000 to ..2,000.00
Oceana serving item, flat shell salad bowl, from $800 to 1,500.00
Oceana serving item, leaf relish tray, from $800 to 1,500.00
Oceana serving item, salad fork & spoon, from $275 to 350.00
Old Morgantown/Modern, goblet, 4½", from $35 to 40.00
Old Morgantown/Modern, pilsner, 7", from $125 to 150.00
Old Morgantown/Modern, sherbet, 2¾", from $25 to 30.00
Old Morgantown/Modern, tumbler, iced tea; 5¼", from $40 to ...60.00
Old Morgantown/Modern, tumbler, water; 4½", from $40 to 50.00
Theme Formal, cordial, from $250 to 300.00
Theme Formal, highball, 7", from $200 to 250.00

Highlight

Bowl, salad or vegetable; rnd, from $65 to 75.00
Bowl, soup/cereal; 2 szs, ea, from $35 to 40.00
Bowl, vegetable; oval, from $65 to 75.00
Creamer, from $50 to 60.00
Cup, from $25 to 30.00
Plate, bread & butter; from $8 to 10.00
Shakers, 2 szs, pr, from $50 to 60.00
Sugar bowl, from $50 to 60.00

Spun Aluminum

Russel Wright's aluminum ware may not have been especially well accepted in its day — it tended to damage easily and seems to have had only limited market appeal — but today's collectors feel quite differently about it, as is apparent in the suggested values noted in the following listings.

Beverage set, from $500 to 600.00
Candelabra, from $300 to 350.00
Casserole, from $150 to 200.00
Cheeseboard, from $75 to 100.00
Gravy boat, from $150 to 200.00
Ice bucket, from $75 to 100.00
Pitcher, sherry; from $250 to 300.00
Relish server (hot), w/ceramic insert, from $350 to 400.00
Spaghetti set, from $700 to 800.00
Vase, 12", from $150 to 175.00
Wastebasket, from $125 to 150.00

Sterling

Bowl, soup; 6½-oz, from $20 to 30.00
Coffee bottle, scarce, from $150 to 200.00

Cream pitcher, 9-oz, from $16 to 18.00
Creamer, ind; 1-oz, from $10 to 15.00
Cup, 7-oz, from $10 to 15.00
Plate, bread & butter; 6", from $5 to 10.00
Plate, dinner; 10¼", from $10 to 15.00
Platter, oval, 7½", from $15 to 20.00
Saucer, 6¼", from $5 to 7.00
Teapot, 10-oz, from $150 to 225.00

Miscellaneous

Bauer, flowerpot, 7", from $600 to 800.00
Bauer, mantel bowl, 24", from $850 to 1,000.00
Bauer, Pinch ashtray, 6½", from $400 to 500.00
Bauer, vase, oval, 12", from $750 to 850.00
Country Garden, bowl, serving; lg, from $150 to 200.00
Country Garden, casserole, w/hinged lid, from $300 to 350.00
Country Garden, cruet, from $200 to 250.00
Country Garden, cup & saucer, from $100 to 125.00
Country Garden, plate, 8", from $100 to 125.00
Country Garden, relish, divided, from $150 to 200.00
Country Garden, sauce boat, deep, from $150 to 200.00

Flair, cup and saucer in Arabesque pattern, $11.00.

Flair, plate, dinner; from $8 to 10.00
Flair, sugar bowl, w/lid, from $12 to 15.00
Harker White Clover, bowl, vegetable; 7½", from $25 to 30.00
Harker White Clover, creamer, clover, from $18 to 20.00
Harker White Clover, plate, barbecue; color only, 11", from $30 to 50.00
Harker White Clover, saucer, clover, from $3 to 4.00
Harker White Clover, shakers, 2 szs, pr, from $30 to 35.00
Home Decorator, lug soup, from $10 to 12.00
Home Decorator, platter, from $20 to 25.00
Home Decorator, saucer, from $20 to 3.00
Home Decorator, tumbler, from $15 to 18.00
Ideal Adult Kitchen Ware, juice decanter, from $30 to 40.00
Ideal Adult Kitchen Ware, salad servers (fork & spoon), from $40 to 50.00
Ideal Adult Kitchen Ware, water jug, lg, from $55 to 65.00
Ideal Children's Toy Dishes, boxed set, from $150 to 200.00
Ideal Children's Toy Dishes, place setting item, ea, from $10 to 15.00
Ideal Children's Toy Dishes, serving pc, ea, from $25 to 30.00
Knowles Esquire, plate, bread & butter; 6", from $5 to 6.00
Knowles Esquire, plate, salad; 8½", from $8 to 10.00
Knowles Esquire, sauce boat, from $25 to 40.00
Knowles Esquire, sugar bowl, w/lid, from $25 to 40.00
Meladur, cup, from $7 to 10.00
Meladur, plate, dinner; 9", from $8 to 10.00
Meladur, saucer, from $3 to 5.00
Pinch cutlery, butter speader, from $100 to 125.00
Pinch cutlery, fork, salad; from $75 to 85.00
Pinch cutlery, spoon, from $75 to 88.00
Pinch cutlery, spoon, soup; from $100 to 120.00
Residential, cup, from $6 to 8.00
Residential, platter, from $20 to 25.00
Residential, saucer, from $2 to 3.00
Theme Formal, cup & saucer, from $100 to 125.00
Theme Formal, plate, bread & butter; from $50 to 75.00
Theme Formal, plate, salad; from $75 to 100.00
Theme Formal lacquerware, bowl, rice; from $350 to 400.00
Theme Formal lacquerware, plate, from $175 to 200.00
Theme Informal, bowl, soup; from $75 to 100.00
Theme Informal, cup & saucer, from $100 to 150.00
Theme Informal, plate, dinner; 10", from $100 to 150.00
Theme Informal, platter, oval, from $200 to 300.00

Russian Art

Before the Revolution in 1917, many jewelers and craftsmen created exquisite marvels of their arts, distinctive in the extravagant detail of their enamel work, jeweled inlays, and use of precious metals. These treasures aptly symbolized the glitter and the romance of the glorious days under the reign of the tsars of Imperial Russia. The most famous of these master jewelers was Carl Faberge (1852 – 1920), goldsmith to the Romanovs. Following the tradition of his father, he took over the Faberge workshop in 1870. Eventually Faberge employed more than five hundred assistants and set up workshops in Moscow, Kiev, and London as well as in St. Petersburg. His specialties were enamel work, clockwork automated figures, carved animal and human figures of precious or semiprecious stones, cigarette cases, small boxes, scent flasks, and his best-known creations, the Imperial Easter Eggs — each of an entirely different design. By the turn of the century, his influence had spread to other countries, and his work was revered by royalty and the very wealthy. The onset of the war marked the end of the era. Very little of his work remains on the market, and items that are available are very expensive. But several of his contemporaries were goldsmiths whose work can be equally enchanting. Among them are Klingert, Ovchinnikov, Smirnov, Ruckert, Loriye, Cheryatov, Kuzmichev, Nevalainen, Adler, Sbitnev, Third Artel, Wakewa, Holmstrom, Britzin, Wigstrom, Orlov, Nichols, and Plincke. Most of them produced excellent pieces similar to those made by Faberge between 1880 and 1910.

Perhaps the most important bronze Russian artist was Eugenie Alexandrovich Lanceray (1847 – 87). From 1875 until 1887, he modeled many equestrian groups of falconers and soldiers ranging in height from about 20" to 30". Some of them bear the Chopin foundry mark; they are presently worth from $4,000.00 up. Other excellent artists were Schmidt Felling (nineteenth century), who specialized in mounted figures of cossacks wearing military uniforms, and Nicholas Leiberich (late nineteenth century), who also specialized in equestrian groups. Most of the pieces made by the above artists were signed and had the foundry mark (Chopin, Woerfell, etc.)

Russian porcelain is another field where Imperial connections have undoubtedly added to the interest of collectors and museums worldwide. The most important factories were: Imperial Russian Porcelain, St. Petersburg (or Petrograd or Leningrad, 1744 – 1917); Gardner, Moscow (1765 – 1872); Kuznetsoff, St. Petersburg and Moscow (1800 – 1900); Korniloff, St. Petersburg (1800 – 1900); and Babunin, St. Petersburg (1800 – 1900).

Altar cross, silver, eng w/cross, hollow, Moscow, 1910, 10" 675.00
Angel, cvd gilt/polychrome, 18th C, 8x8" 650.00
Beaker, burnt wood simulating tree bark/pnt Troika, 1900, 3" 110.00
Beaker, silver-gilt/bees & dragonflies, Faberge, 1908, 4" 3,350.00
Beaker, silver-gilt/neillo, att Semenov, ca 1865, 3½x3" 375.00
Bowl, porc, Catherine II Everyday Service, 1770, 10" 500.00
Box, lacquer, court scene w/Tsar, Vishiakov, 3x9½" 2,000.00

Box, presentation; silver, Faberge, 1899-, 4x6" 4,750.00
Box, silver/neillo geometrics, Ivanov, 1869, 3x2" 280.00
Box, wood, pnt w/Krestianka in garden, 1920, 8¾x6" 140.00
Buckle, silver filigree, Tiflis, 1899-1907, 3½" 100.00
Candlesticks, silver, 3 grape cluster legs, Minsk, 1886, 12", pr ...985.00
Case, cigarette; silver, Psyche & Cupid, pre-revolutionary, 4x3" .450.00
Case, cigarette; silver, Psyche & Cupid eng, KC/84, 4x3" 350.00
Case, cigarette; silver/enamel, Tillander, 1900, 3" 2,000.00
Case, sterling, repousse elephants, gr stone latch, 6¾" L 400.00
Chalice, silver-gilt w/eng wheat etc, AD, 1819, 10¼" 1,400.00
Charka, silver-gilt enamel flowers, Khlebnikov, 1896, 3" 585.00
Cream jug, silver, milk can form, Grachev Bros, 1885, 4½" 450.00
Cream spoon, enameled wood, 1800s, 7¼" 165.00
Cross, bronze, 19th C, 15x7¾" 280.00
Cross, bronze w/enamel & side panels, 1800s, 6½x4¼" 135.00

Cuff links, center rose-cut diamond, chased gold foliate mounts over oyster moire guilloche ground, gilt and white enameled borders, Peter Carl Faberge, St. Petersburg, 1903 – 1917, $7,500.00.

Cup, silver w/heavy eng, ftd, Ivanov, 1880, 6" 450.00
Cup holder, enamel on silver, KC/84, 4¾", EX 775.00
Desk tray, silver/champleve florals, AP, pre-1896, 3" L 225.00
Easter egg, blown cased glass, 1800s, 3" 165.00
Easter egg, porc w/HP florals & gilt, 1890s, 2¾" 165.00
Easter egg, silver, gilt int, 2-pc, Moscow, 1900s, 3" 675.00
Figurine, porc, bearded man in robe, Gardner, late 19th C, 9" ..975.00
Figurine, porc, lady w/drunk, child at side, Gardner, late 19th C, 7" ..1,495.00
Figurine, porc, peasant man drinking, Gardner, late 19th C, 6" 925.00
Icon, Blessed Silence, bronze, 1800, rare, 5¾x4¾" 165.00
Icon, Iverskaya Mother of God, egg tempera on gold leaf, 14x12" ...2,000.00
Icon, Kazan Mother of God, silver-gilt eng riza, 1900s, 12x10" ...1,600.00
Icon, Lampada, rtcl silver w/red glass insert, DM, 1890s, 17" 675.00
Icon, Lord Almighty, gilt ground/highlights, Palekh School, 12x10" ..200.00
Icon, Lord Almighty, 7-pc riza, champleve, DLS, 1880, 9x7" .5,800.00
Icon, Maxim the Greek, holds inscr book, 1800, 13x12" 2,350.00
Icon, Selected Saints, gilt/faux enamel, 1890s, 9x7" 450.00
Icon, St Ermogen, gilt w/faux enamel, 1900, 3½x2" 300.00
Icon, St Nicholas, cvd ivory, ca 19th/20th C, 2x1¾" 290.00
Icon, St Nicholas, emb/eng riza w/gilt halo, Orlov, 1858, 5x7" ..500.00
Icon, St Nicholas/saints, bronze/enamel w/gilt, 19th C, 5¾x5" .200.00
Icon, St Nil Stolbenskiy, gold leaf/enamel, 1890, 7x5¾" 400.00
Icon, St Pateleimon, pnt on gilt, 19th C, 7x5½" 425.00
Icon, Trinity, silver/gold-plated metal riza, SG, 8x9" 785.00
Icon, Unburnt Thornbush Mother of God, Palekh, 19th C, 10x12" ..1,795.00
Icon, Vladimir Mother of God, cvd/enameled, 1900, 12x10" .2,000.00
Icon triptych, Deisis, bronze, 19th C, as pendant, 8x3" (open) .250.00
Inkwell, wood, cvd/pnt landscape, porc insert, 5½" dia 200.00
Jardiniere, porc, turkeys scene, St Petersburg, ca 1895, 17" 9,775.00
Kovsh, enameling on silver, eng initials MC, mk 84, 4½" 1,380.00
Kovsh, silver-gilt/enamel foliage, Nikola, Zreve, 1908-, 3" 1,400.00
Kovsh, silver/enamel florals etc, Saltykov, 1899-, 4" 1,000.00
Locket/compact, silver, bl enamel over sunburst, DK, 1908, 1¾" ..400.00
Matchbox holder, silver-gilt/enamel swan, Agafonov, 1899, 2½" ..500.00
Medallion, silver, St Nicholas/inscription, Moscow, 1890, 2½" .165.00
Napkin ring, silver w/eng foliage, Khlebrikov, 1899-, 1¾" 100.00
Napkin ring, silver-gilt/enamel scrolls etc, Spitnev, 1908, 2¼" ..225.00
Paper knife, silver/enamel w/onyx blade, CK, 1908-, 9" 1,000.00
Pencil holder, wood bbl form w/cvd & pnt Kremlin walls decor ..100.00
Pitcher, water; hand-hammered brass, baluster, Moscow, 19th C, 9" ...150.00
Plaque, Virgin, porc in bronze fr w/stand, after Murillo, 2½" 650.00
Plate, lacquered metal, peasant girl/musician, Vishiakov, 6" 140.00
Salt cellar, enamel on silver, ca 1889, mk 84, 1½", +spoon 150.00
Salt cellar, silver, lines at rim, ftd, Faberge, 1½" 400.00
Salt celler, silver, Baroque style, CM Stahle, 1841, 3½" 140.00
Silhouette toy of a Prince, wooden, pnt ea side, 1915, 7½" 200.00
Spoon, enamel on silver, mk 84, ca 1886, 4¼", pr 185.00
Spoon, enamel on silver, mk 88, ca 1891, 5" 125.00
Spoon, silver-gilt/neillo w/floral, Astrakhantsev, 1833, 5¼" 865.00
Spoon, silver/plique-a-jour, butterfly on hdl, Ovchinnikov, 7" ..1,400.00
Sugar sifter, silver/enamel, florals, 11th Artel, '08, 6½" 1,000.00
Tea caddy, burntwood/polychrome rural scene, 1900, 7½" 225.00
Tea caddy, lacquer, horse-drawn cart/hound, att Vishiakov, 4" dia ..180.00
Tea glass holder, silver, rtcl/eng, SK, Moscow, 1908-1917, 4" 200.00
Toasting cup, silver, 2 eng cherubs, Mishukova, 1891, 5½" 336.00
Tray, lacquer, family scene, Visnrikov, 1890, 5¾x7" 200.00
Tumbler, silver/enamel, ftd, Ovchinnikov, 1786, 3" 450.00
Vase, silver-gilt/enamel, cloisonne foliage, Alekseev, 1899-, 4" 1,850.00

Sabino

Sabino art glass was produced by Marius-Ernest Sabino in France during the 1920s and 1930s. It was made in opalescent, frosted, and colored glass and was designed to reflect the Art Deco style of that era. In 1960, using molds he modeled by hand, Sabino once again began to produce art glass using a special formula he himself developed that was characterized by a golden opalescence. Although the family continued to produce glassware for export after his death in 1971, they were never able to duplicate Sabino's formula.

Blotter, dealer's gift, 1930s 450.00
Bottle, scent; nude bathers/swans, 4¼" 120.00
Bottle, scent; nudes w/garlands frieze, 6" 120.00
Bottle, scent; 4 nudes, 5½" 120.00
Bottle, scent; 4 nudes/swans/fishes emb, opal frost, 6x2⅜" 180.00
Box, dresser; emb flower motif, w/lid 95.00
Dish, clam shell shape, 7x4" 60.00
Figurine, butterfly, 2¾x1½" 50.00
Figurine, cat, sitting, 3¾" 100.00
Figurine, cherub, kneeling holding flowers, 1¾" on ⅞" base 80.00
Figurine, Egyptian Goddess, 5" on ⅞" base 200.00
Figurine, gazelle, 5x6" on 2" base 175.00
Figurine, Pekinese dog, 3½" L on rectangular base 75.00
Figurine, pig, 2x3" 100.00
Figurine, porcupine, standing on head, 3x3¼" 105.00
Plaque, nymphs among foliage, lime gr, oval, 7¾x12", NM 250.00
Vase, lattimo emb w/sqs & X-hatching, trapezoidal, 6" 250.00
Vase, Les Ondes, stylized flowers, 5-sided, 6¾x3" 235.00

Salesman's Samples and Patent Models

Salesman's samples and patent models are often mistaken for toys or homemade folk art pieces. They are instead actual working models made by very skilled craftsmen who worked as model-makers. Patent models were made until the early 1900s. After that, the patent office no longer required a model to grant a patent. The name of the inventor or the model-maker and the date it was built is sometimes noted on the patent model. Salesman's samples were occasionally made by model-makers, but often they were assembled by an employee of the company. These usually carried advertising messages to boost the sale of the product. Though they are still in use today, the most desirable examples date from the 1800s to about 1945.

Many small stoves are incorrectly termed a 'salesman's sample'; remember that no matter how detailed one may be, it must be considered a toy unless accompanied by a carrying case, the indisputable mark of a salesman's sample.

Columbian washer, wooden machine with cast-iron grearing, wooden handles, stenciled on sides, Pat. Dec. 3, 1895, 20", EX, $1,300.00.

Boiler, Round Oak..., cast metal, Doe-Wah-Jack image, w/case, 18" **275.00**
Bottle, Parker Quick Ink **50.00**
Kettle, CI, Bean Hot Pot, w/lid **125.00**
Lawn jockey, CI Black figure on base, wht w/red vest, 11", G ...**300.00**
Rake, Horton's Pat Improved Horse Rake & Seed Sower, 12½" ..**1,265.00**
Sadiron, Dover **75.00**
Sled, wood platform, curved runners, mc pnt, 4¾x15¾x6", NM **1,100.00**
Stove, blk & wht porc over CI, w/case, Universal, 16x7x18", NM ..**7,000.00**
Tractor, aluminum, clockwork, Unique..., 27" **2,700.00**

Salt Shakers

The screw-top salt shaker was invented by John Mason in 1858. Around 1871 when salt became more refined, some ceramic shakers were molded with perforated tops.

Today's Victorian glass shalt shaker collectors' interests primarily encompass art glass of all types and colored glass, with preference given to hand-painted cranberry and ruby glass forms. Also, examples in rubena, opalescent, and custard glass are very desirable in both decorated and undecorated styles.

If you would like to learn more about Victorian glass salt shakers, we recommend *The World of Salt Shakers*, *Second* and *Third Editions*, written by Mildred and Ralph Lechner; their address may be found in the Directory under Virginia. (Mildred and Ralph deal only in Victorian glass shakers. Please do not contact them with questions pertaining to novelty types; *written queries require a long self-addressed stamped envelope.*) Values listed are for old, original shakers in excellent condition unless otherwise noted in the description.

Acanthus, Stippled; lt gr translucent, 1891-99, 2⅝" **85.00**
Annie (Actress), amber, 1879-1883, 2⅞x1⅝" **225.00**
Artichoke, Fostoria's (Valencia); clear & frost, 1891, 2⅝" **75.00**
Aster & Leaf, bl, bulbous, Beaumont, ca 1895, 3" **110.00**
Baby Optic Rib, clear w/HP floral, 1893-97, 2" **90.00**
Barrel, Challinor 14 Variant; HP opaque opalware, 1888-91, 2¾" ...**30.00**
Barrel, Christmas; sepia winter scene **300.00**
Barrel, Sm Block; cranberry, 10 rows, 1986-91, 2½", pr **20.00**
Barrel, Sm Bull's Eye, orange, 2-pc lid, NE Glass, 1886-88, 3¼" ..**165.00**
Barrel, Windows; bl opal, windows molded inside, 1896-99, 3x2¾" ..**165.00**
Bead & Panel, gr opal, Jefferson, 1901-03, 3" **100.00**
Beaded Square, dk amethyst w/HP decor, Tarentum, 1898-1904, 2¼" ..**55.00**
Belladonna Variant, cranberry w/HP decor, 1887-91, 3¼" **200.00**
Bohemian (Florador), rose flashed, US Glass, 1899-1901, 3¼" .**165.00**
Brilliant, Riverside's; ruby stain, 1895, 2⅞" **60.00**
Bulbous Base Variant, clear w/amber stain, Hobbs Brockunier, 2⅞" **80.00**
Butterfly & Tassel, bl opaque, 1894-1900, 3" **40.00**
Cactus, Fenton's; vaseline, 1959-63, 2⅞" **32.00**
Cambridge #1207, ruby red, allover Dmn Point pattern, 1918-25, 2⅞" ...**35.00**
Cartouche, floral panel on opalware, Helmschmeid, 1904-07, 2⅝" ...**100.00**
Champion (Fan w/Cross Bars), ruby stain, McKee, 1894-1917, 2⅞" ...**75.00**
Chick on Pedestal, wht opal w/metal head, CF Monroe, 3" (+) .**285.00**
Chrysanthemum Base Variant, cranberry opal, emb ribs, 1888-91, 3⅛" **125.00**
Clover, Duncan's; vaseline, pillar w/panels, 1890, 3⅛" **70.00**
Co-op's #1901, clear, ca 1901, 3x2¾" **25.00**
Coin Dot, Phoenix; apricot opal, 2-pc lid, 1884-87, 2¾" **195.00**
Cone, Thin Footed; dk red, Paden City, 1928-36, 3½", pr **125.00**
Cord & Pleat, cobalt, 1896-99, 2½" **70.00**
Corn, pk opaque, triple cased, Dithridge & Co, 1894-1901, 3⅛" ..**145.00**
Cotton Bale, butterscotch (variegated) translucent, 1894-95, 2⅝" ..**175.00**
Curved Ribbing, amberina, 2-pc lid, NE Glass, 1883-86, 1⅞" ...**950.00**
Daisy & Button, Footed; vaseline, 1878-1885, 2⅞" **30.00**
Dbl Bubble Invt T'print, amber w/HP floral, 1885-90, 3¼" **185.00**
Dewdrop, vaseline opal, bulbous, Imperial, 1965-69, 2¾" **25.00**

Diamond Panels, blue opaque with four large embossed diamonds, ca 1885 – 1890, 2¾", from $60.00 to $70.00. (Photo courtesy Mildred and Ralph Lechner)

Eye-Winker Variant, cranberry, 1985-93, Dalzell-Viking, 3⅝" **18.00**
Fleur-de-Lis, Arched (Higbee's); ruby stain, 1895-1906, 2⅝" **75.00**
Fleur-De-Lis, Skirted; bl opaque, 18-rib base, 1894-1900, 2¾" **40.00**
Florentine (Single Rose), dk gr, Riverside, 1906, 2¾" **70.00**
Flower & Leaf, Flair; opalware w/goofus decor, 1900-04 ....**20.00**
Flower in Teardrop, opalware, 1901-12, 3⅛" **12.00**
Flower Tracery, opalware w/red & bl goofus decor, 1899-1905, 2⅜" .**30.00**
Forget-Me-Not, butterscotch (variegated) opaque, 1887-91, 2" .**110.00**
Globule, pigeon blood, pr **160.00**
Honeycomb, rubena opal, 2-pc lid, Hobbs Brockunier, 1886-88, 2⅝" **175.00**
Invt t'print, Sm; dk bl (not cobalt), 1881-89, 2⅝" **45.00**
Isabella, gr opaque, Novelty Glass, 1891-92, pr **1,700.00**
Leaning, pk & wht variegated opaque, Consolidated, 3¼" **60.00**
Louisiana, clear, US Glass, 1898, 2⅝" **35.00**
Marble Shaped, wht opalware w/HP winter scene, ca 1780, 1¾" **145.00**
Mary Ann, cobalt w/HP Cupid scene, 1897-1905, 2½" **85.00**
Multiple Ring, Hawkes'; amber stain, 1940, 2¾" **30.00**
Net & Scroll, gr opaque, Dithridge, 1894-1900, 2⅞" **50.00**
Paneled Icicle, bl, 4-panel, McKee, 1900-10, 3¼" **35.00**
Plain Joe, opalware w/HP floral, 1897-1903, 2⅝" **35.00**
Reverse Swirl, Tall; bl opaque & wht spatter, bulbous, 1887-90, 3" ..**85.00**
Rib, Triple; gr (variegated) opaque, cased, 1894-1900, 3¼" **175.00**
Ring Neck Variant, bl opal swirls, Hobbs Brockunier, 1887-90, 3" **85.00**
Rose, Colonial Amber, 8-scallop ft, Fenton, 1962-80, 3⅜" **22.00**
Scroll, Gaudy; gr opaque, Gillinder, 2½" **32.00**

Swag w/Brackets Variant, gr opal, Jefferson, 3" 90.00
Swirl, Dainty; reverse rubena, cylindrical, 1889-94, 3⅜" 145.00
Swirl, Multi; bl opaque, grooved emb swirls, 1894-1900, 2⅝" 45.00
Tapered Rib, Optic; electric bl w/HP roses, 1884-87, 2⅜" 195.00
Tube, Ringed Base; red, Paden City, 1927-37, 2⅛", pr 115.00
Washington (Beaded Base), ruby stain, US Glass, 1901, 3¾" 25.00
Wellington (Staple), ruby stain, Westmoreland, 1903-12, 2⅜" ...70.00
Yarn, brn & wht spatter, blown cylinder w/reverse swirls, 1895-96, 3" 130.00
Zipper, aqua, patterned corners, Belmont, 1888-90, 3⅞" 75.00
Zippered Corner, Ring (Zippered Borders); ruby stain, 1905, 3x1⅝" ..45.00

Novelty Salt Shakers

Those interested in novelty shakers will enjoy *Salt and Pepper Shakers, Volumes I, II, III,* and *IV,* by Helene Guarnaccia; and *The Collector's Encyclopedia of Salt and Pepper Shakers, Figural and Novelty, Volumes I* and *II,* by Melva Davern. All are available at your local library or from Collector Books. Note: 'Mini' shakers are no taller than 2". Instead of having a cork, the user was directed to 'use tape to cover hole.' Our advisor for novelty salt shakers is Judy Posner; she is listed in the Directory under Pennsylvania. See also Regal; Rosemeade; Occupied Japan; Shawnee; other specific manufacturers.

Advertising, Campbell Soup cans, barbecue sz, pr 35.00
Advertising, Cities Service gas pump, plastic, 1970s, pr 75.00
Advertising, Diamond Crystal Shaker Salt, cb, pr 10.00
Advertising, French's pepper & Sterling salt, picnic sz, pr 8.00
Advertising, Hamm's Bear bears, ceramic, Ceramarte, 5", pr 150.00
Advertising, Nabisco Blue Bonnet Sue, pr 45.00
Advertising, Philgas tanks, plastic, pr 35.00
Advertising, Sinclair Power-X gas pump, red plastic w/decal, pr ..75.00
Advertising, Stroh's Beer bottles, glass w/metal lids (older), pr 25.00
Animals, antelopes, realistic, bone china, sm, pr 26.00
Animals, cat sitting on block of ice (2nd shaker), ceramic, pr 22.00
Animals, cats w/rhinestone eyes, comic, ceramic, pr 18.00
Animals, Collies, realistic appearance, ceramic, pr 22.00
Animals, cow ladies w/parasols, ceramic, pr 35.00
Animals, dinosaurs w/twisted necks, gr, ceramic, pr 25.00
Animals, dogs, Deco style, mc on wht, ceramic, pr 18.00
Animals, dogs on bar stools, ceramic, Enesco, pr 28.00
Animals, fish (Northern Pike), realistic, Enesco, pr 18.00
Animals, giraffe heads, 1 up/1 down, ceramic, pr 18.00
Animals, goats, realistic appearance, ceramic, pr 26.00
Animals, mermaid & starfish, ceramic, pr 25.00
Animals, mermaids w/ball, ceramic Norcrest, pr 35.00
Animals, penguins, silver-colored metal, pr 22.00
Animals, pigs, silver-colored metal, pr 18.00
Animals, Scotties begging, 1 blk/1 wht, ceramic, gold trim, pr 10.00
Animals, snails on tray, bl & wht, bone china, pr 10.00
Animals, toucans, bright mc, ceramic, Germany, pr 35.00
Anthropomorphic, bowling-pin people, plastic, pr 15.00
Anthropomorphic, cacti (boy & girl w/hats), ceramic, pr 45.00
Anthropomorphic, fish w/child-like faces, ceramic, pr 35.00
Anthropomorphic, girls w/corn bodies, ceramic, pr 15.00
Anthropomorphic, potato pancakes w/fork & spoon arms, ceramic, pr ..22.00
Anthropomorphic, vegetable head people w/hats, ceramic, pr 22.00
Anthropomorphic, vegetable head sports figures, ceramic, pr 55.00
Anthropomorphic, vegetable heads w/gold, ceramic, Vallona Star, pr ...65.00
Character, Astro Boy & sister in rocket, ceramic, 3-pc set 100.00
Character, Barney Google & Snuffy Smith, chalkware, pr 45.00
Character, Felix the cat, ceramic, 1930s, sm, pr 125.00
Character, Fred & Wilma Flintstone, ceramic, Vandor, pr 40.00
Character, Garfield (head only), ceramic, pr 50.00
Character, Genie & lamp, ceramic, Poinsettia Studio, pr 45.00
Character, hare & tortoise, ceramic, Vallona Star, pr 50.00
Character, Humpty Dumpty, nodders, Norcrest, pr 35.00
Character, Little Miss Muffet, Vallona Star, pr 65.00
Character, Little Miss Muffet & spider, ceramic, pr 48.00
Character, Mickey Mouse, pyro on glass, plastic lids, 1930s, pr .300.00
Character, Moon Mullins, blk face, ceramic, pr 45.00
Character, Mr & Mrs Santa, ceramic, Poinsettia Studio, pr 30.00
Character, Paul Bunyan & Blue Babe, ceramic, G Nov Co Japan, pr ..30.00
Character, Shmoo, Al Capp, ceramic, 1940s, pr 125.00
Character, Smokey Bear (heads only), ceramic, unmk, pr 75.00
Character, Woody Woodpecker & girlfriend, Walter Lantz 1990, pr ...75.00

Barney Google and Snuffy Smith, Comic, painted chalkware, WWII era, 2⅞", $45.00 for the pair.

Holiday, Christmas, Santas w/candy canes, Fitz & Floyd, pr 35.00
Inanimate objects, cigarettes in pack w/lighter, ceramic, pr 18.00
Inanimate objects, cookies (Oreo type), ceramic, pr 22.00
Inanimate objects, golf balls on tees, ceramic, pr 18.00
Inanimate objects, gumball machines, plastic, pr 20.00
Inanimate objects, guns in holsters, ceramic, pr 18.00
Inanimate objects, oil lamps, clear glass w/red chimneys, pr 18.00
Inanimate objects, pretzels, ceramic, J Rayton California, pr 15.00
Inanimate objects, radio & clock, wood w/decals, pr 14.00
Inanimate objects, shoes, cvd wood, much detail, pr 50.00
Inanimate objects, telephone (receiver 2nd shaker), ceramic, pr ..18.00
Inanimate objects, telephone & directory, ceramic, sm, pr 12.00
People, cartoon sports players, Napco, 1958, pr 30.00
People, Chinese boy & girl, Josef Originals Japan, pr 24.00
People, clowns w/huge shoes & sm top hats, Napco, 1957, pr 24.00
People, drunk & lamppost, ceramic, pr 16.00
People, Eskimo couple, ceramic, pr 12.00
People, farm boy & girl, Enesco Imports Japan, pr 80.00
People, Mexican boy & girl, red sombreros, Elbee Art, pr 18.00
People, Native boy w/alligator, ceramic, pr 75.00
People, sailor in boat, Elbee Art, pr 24.00
Skunk & flower, Poinsettia Studio, pr 45.00
Souvenir, Bonneville Dam, Oregon, scene on cubes, pr 22.00
Souvenir, Long Island, Milford Pottery State series, pr 15.00
Souvenir, Loretta Lynn Dude Ranch, western hats, ceramic, pr ...20.00

Salts, Open

Before salt became refined, processed, and free-flowing as we know it today, it was necessary to serve it in a salt cellar. An innovation of the early 1800s, the master salt was placed by the host and passed from person to person. Smaller individual salts were a part of each place setting. A small silver spoon was used to sprinkle it onto the food.

If you would like to learn more about the subject of salts, we recommend *5,000 Open Salts,* written by William Heacock and Patricia Johnson, with many full-color illustrations and current values. Our advisor for this category is Chris Christensen; he is listed in the Directory under California. In the listings below, the numbers refer to *Open Salts* by Johnson and Heacock and *Pressed Glass Salt Dishes* by L.W. and D.B. Neal. Lines with 'repro' within the description reflect values for reproduced salts.

Key:
EPNS — electroplated nickel silver HM — hallmarked

Animals, Figurals, and Novelties

Bird & Berry, amber, bl or vaseline, McKee, HJ-997 ....55.00
Bird & Berry, colors, mk Degenhart, HJ-932, up from 25.00
Bird & Berry, colors, unmk Degenhart, HJ-933, up from 15.00
Chicken, covered, milk glass, Westmoreland, HJ-949, from $18 to ..25.00
Pilgrim shoes, pressed, milk glass, HJ-3736 ....45.00
Sleigh, clear or milk glass, Fostoria, HJ-3735, ca 1940 ....60.00
Squirrel on stump, various colors, sgn Boyd, HJ-929, repro, from $8 to ..10.00
Swan, Crown Tuscan, Cambridge, HJ-935 ....110.00
Swan, Crown Tuscan, unsgn, repro 15.00

Cameo, Art Glass, and Miscellaneous

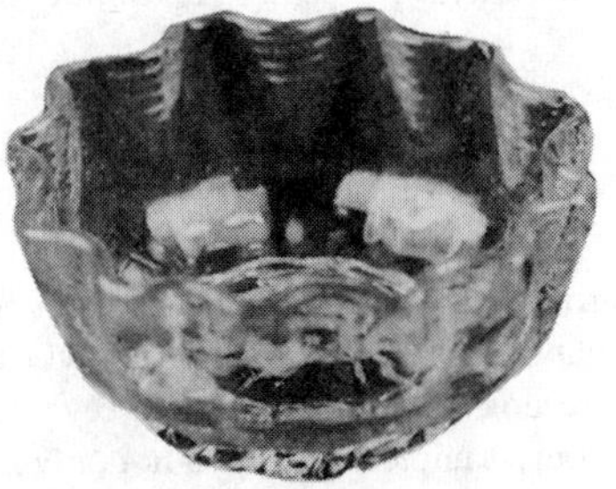

Venetian glass, light green, ruffled, with clear base, ca 1900, 3", $75.00.

Crown Milano, HJ-46 ....175.00
Daum Nancy, flowers, mk, HJ-11, from $900 to 1,200.00
Daum Nancy, windmill scene, HJ-10, from $900 to 1,200.00
Daum Nancy, winter scene, sgn 1,500.00
Doulton, Lambeth, sterling HM rim, HJ-1851, ca 1900 ....65.00
Intaglio, animals or butterfly HP, sgn, HJ-159 ....60.00
Intaglio, bl, gr, etc..., unsgn, HJ-215 ....15.00
Intaglio, jeweled ormolu holder, HJ-90 ....125.00
LeGras, sterling base, sgn, HJ-12 ....900.00
Millefiori: European, HJ-609, ca 1900, 2" dia 350.00
Monot Stumpf, HJ-19 to HJ-22, ea 100.00
Monot Stumpf, jeweled ormolu holder 325.00
Moorcroft, sterling HM rim, London, HJ-1762, ca 1920 ....65.00
Mt Washington, HJ-35 to HJ-44, unsgn 110.00
Plique-a-jour, Viking boat, Norway 930S, HJ-83, 2½" 750.00
Quezal, sgn, HJ-18, 1" dia 250.00
Royal Doulton, sterling HM rim, HJ-1870, ca 1873 ....125.00
Sowerby, HJ-385 to HJ-2090, sgn & #d 55.00
Steuben, Calcite, ped ft, HJ-34 ....295.00
Steuben, clear w/blk threading, HJ-113 ....225.00
Stevens & Williams, opal w/vaseline ruffled, HJ-72 ....125.00
Tiffany, bl, ruffled top, sgn, HJ-30 ....475.00
Tiffany, pulled ears, sgn, HJ-3 ....300.00
Tiffany, ruffled, sgn LCT Favrile, HJ-32 ....200.00
Tiffany, witch's pot, sgn, HJ-1 ....300.00
Victorian, bl, rigaree, berry pontil, SP holder, HJ-96 ....225.00
Webb, Burmese, HJ-75, ca 1890, 1¾" dia 650.00
Webb, 2-color, sgn, HJ-84 ....1,100.00
Webb, 3-color, HJ-27 ....1,200.00
Wedgwood, sterling rim, sgn, HJ-1850, ca 1897 ....160.00

China and Porcelain

Austria, HP, mk, HJ-1272, rnd, ind 15.00
Belleek, HP, ruffled top, mk, HJ-1310, rnd, ind 35.00
Celery salt, HP, HJ-1720, ind 12.00
Dresden, attached flowers, HJ-1689, ind 45.00
Elfinware, heavy decor, sgn Germany, HJ-1270, ind 30.00
Elfinware, Japan, HJ-1222, ind 12.00

Elfinware, multicolor flowers on white, 2¼", $50.00.

Elfinware, tub, sgn Germany, HJ-1250, ind 25.00
Elfinware, wheelbarrow, sgn Germany, HJ-1244, ind 65.00
Haviland, HJ-1400, ind 35.00
HP, artist sgn, scalloped ft, HJ-1390, ind 20.00
Limoges, HP, mk, HJ-1275, rnd, ind 12.00
Meissen, HJ-1595, sq, ind 60.00
Nippon, celery salt, HJ-1714, ind 10.00
Nippon, HP, HJ-1365, ind 12.00
Nippon, HP, ped ft, HJ-1495, ind 24.00
Nippon, HP floral tub, HJ-1454, ind 20.00
Pickard, HJ-1569, sq, ind 45.00
Royal Bayreuth, animal decor, ped ft, HJ-1666, ind 135.00
Royal Bayreuth, figural claw, HJ-1667, ind 95.00
Royal Copenhagen, HJ-1332, ind 25.00
Royal Worcester, HJ-1861, ca 1862, ind 120.00
Satsuma, HJ-1931, ca 1940-60, ind 25.00

Cut Glass

Hawkes, sgn, HJ-3064 ....60.00
Heart, spade, diamond, club, HJ-3034 to HJ-3035, 4 for 200.00
J Hoare, sgn, HJ-3166 ....45.00
Waterford, ped ft, sgn, HJ-3698, ca 1970 ....35.00
Waterford type, gr, ped gt, HJ-601, ca 1860 ....125.00
Waterford type, ped ft, HJ-3699, ca 1860 ....75.00
Zippered, HJ-3088 ....12.00

Doubles

Austria Hungary, HM sterling, w/mustard, HJ-751, 1850s 350.00
Automobile, pressed glass, mk Pontieux, HJ-3764 ....55.00
European, pressed glass, plain, HJ-3976 to HJ-3978 ....25.00
European, 800 sterling, figural, cobalt inserts, HJ-2062 ....125.00
French, cobalt pressed glass, HJ-2087 ....65.00
French, pressed glass, figural, HJ-3777 ....45.00
French, sterling HM, cobalt inserts, HJ-761, ca 1845 ....150.00
German, HP porc, HJ-1150 ....45.00
KPM, figural, porc, HJ-1155 to HJ-1156, ca 1860 ....295.00
KPM, porc, wht w/gold border, HJ-1142 ....35.00
Meissen, porc, w/hdl, HJ-1169 ....125.00
Quimper, porc, sgn, old, HJ-1135 ....65.00
Venetian swans, cranberry or gold, ea 125.00

Lacy Glass

Neal BF-1A, violet bl, 2" H, EX 425.00
Neal BS-3, lt opal, 2", NM 180.00
Neal CD-2b, Sandwich, EX 500.00
Neal CN-1A, fiery opal, line in base, 2" 155.00

Neal CT-1A, 1¾", EX 50.00
Neal DI-12 variant, cobalt, att Pittsburgh 500.00
Neal DI-4, bl, rectangular, ftd, 1½", NM 500.00
Neal GA-2, opaque fiery bl, Gothic arches, 1¾" 700.00
Neal JY-2b, med gr, 3", EX 190.00
Neal MV-I, Mt Vernon, blk olive, 1¾x2⅞x2⅛" 800.00
Neal MV-1, pk tint, 1¾", EX 90.00
Neal OO-12, amethyst, canted corners, 1¼" 800.00
Neal OP-1, Sandwich, NM 140.00
Neal OP-4, gr, extremely rare, 3⅝" 500.00
Neal PE-1, Flint Glass, EX 450.00
Neal PO-4, bl opal, 1¼", EX 550.00
Neal SC-5, pk tint, heavy mold roughness, 1¾", VG 300.00
Neal SD-7, bl, 2", VG 130.00
Neal SD-12, purple-bl, Sandwich, sm chips 375.00
Neal SD-15, purple-bl, Sandwich, EX 275.00
Neal SL-11, peacock bl, heavy mold roughness, 1¾" 700.00
Neal SN-1B, clambroth, 1½" 205.00

Pottery and Faience

Adams, HM, HJ-1849, ca 1902 ....140.00
Niloak, rnd, mk, HJ-1735, 1½" 65.00
Quimper, dbl, pr of shoes, HJ-1162 ....45.00
Quimper, dbl, w/dog or pig, HJ-1134 ....115.00
Royal Doulton, HM, emb animals, HJ-1859 ....75.00
Royal Doulton, pyramid shape, HJ-1870, ca 1873 ....125.00
Staffordshire, bl on tan, ped ft, HJ-4577, ca 1850 ....65.00
Staffordshire, Elfinware decor, ca 1840 ....125.00
Staffordshire, Toby, w/pepper, mc, old, (+), 5¼", set 350.00
Wedgwood, bl & wht, sgn HM, HJ-1871, ca 1900 ....165.00
Wedgwood, chariots, gr & wht, sgn HM 225.00
Wedgwood, 3-pc condiment w/worn EPNS holder, HJ-4762 ....225.00

Silverplate

American, cobalt liner, mk W&S, HJ-653 ....20.00
American, ruby liner, mk Derby, HJ-319 ....65.00
American, Victorian, crackle glass liner, Meriden, HJ-4215 ....85.00
English, ornate, w/babies, gold wash, ca 1880 ....150.00
English, ruby liner, paw ft, ca 1900 ....75.00
English, set of 4 w/spoons, ca 1880, MIB 175.00
English, vaseline ruffled Webb insert, HJ-95, ca 1880 ....225.00
European, vaseline ruffled liner, HJ-91, ca 1880 ....125.00

Sterling and Continental Silver

Ball Black & Co, New York, #420, sleigh with butterfly at top, 2¾x3½", $65.00; Unmarked, mermaid on base holds salt cellar with glass insert, 4x3", $150.00.

Albert Cole, medallion, HJ-4028, ca 1860 ....20.00
American, ped ft, HJ-4034, ca 1930 ....35.00
Dutch, cobalt liner, HM, HJ-713, ca 1880, 4-pc set 300.00
English, gr liner, HJ-379, ind 75.00
English, ornate, HM, HJ-4164, ca 1899 ....45.00
French, cobalt liner, HM, HJ-720, ca 1845, master 155.00
French, liner & spoon, HJ-3937, ind 135.00
German, HJ-4286, ca 1800, master, pr 500.00
German 800, HJ-3983 ....45.00
Gorham, medallion, ped ft, HJ-3976, ca 1860 ....175.00
Gorham, plain, HJ-3992, ca 1920 ....25.00
Gorham, ruby liner, HJ-323, ca 1890 ....150.00
Russian, chair, HM, HJ-4735, ca 1890 ....450.00
Swan, cut glass w/835 sterling wings, old, HJ-4287 ....55.00

Other Types

Abalone shell over copper, w/spoon, Mexico, HJ-2011 ....20.00
Celadon, silver o/l, HJ-1427 ....30.00
Celluloid, Viking salt & horn pepper, w/spoon, HJ-207, set 55.00
Cloisonne, w/pepper, HJ-1995, not old, set 25.00

Samplers

American samplers were made as early as the colonial days; even earlier examples from seventeenth-century England still exist today. Changes in style and design are evident down through the years. Verses were not added until the late seventeenth century. By the eighteenth century, samplers were used not only for sewing experience but also as an educational tool. Young ladies, who often signed and dated their work, embroidered numbers and letters of the alphabet and practiced fancy stitches as well. Fruits and flowers were added for borders; birds, animals, and Adam and Eve became popular subjects. Later houses and other buildings were included. By the nineteenth century, the American Eagle and the little red schoolhouse had made their appearances.

Many factors bear on value: design and workmanship, strength of color, the presence of a signature and/or a date (both being preferred over only one or the other, and earlier is better), and, of course, condition.

ABC panels/verses/florals/house/birds, 1833, 17x15" 1,375.00
ABCs, homespun, sgn, 1836, lt stains, 25x20" in modern fr 550.00
ABCs (3 styles)/verse/trees/birds/flowers, homespun, 1797, 19x18" 2,000.00
ABCs/#s/flower basket/stars, linen, New England, 1835, 18x15", EX ..1,100.00
ABCs/#s/flowers/birds/trees, linen, OH, 1842, 17x17" 3,165.00
ABCs/#s/verse about nature & mental health, homespun, 1817, 15x23" ...465.00
ABCs/#s/verse/flowers, canvas, 1854, 22x16"+fr 300.00
ABCs/acorns/dancers/flowers, homespun, 1698, 35x8½"+fr ...8,000.00
ABCs/birds/flowers/trees, homespun, 1826, 19x15", EX 600.00
ABCs/birds/fruit/flowers/verse, homespun, 1833, 18x18", VG ...1,800.00
ABCs/birds/trees/flowers, mtd on fabric, stain, 11½x8¾" 700.00
ABCs/family genealogy/flowers/birds/etc, homespun, 19th C, 16x14" ..975.00
ABCs/flower border/house/verse/etc, homespun, 1833, 13x14"+fr ..520.00
ABCs/flower vases/animals/verse/Adam & Eve, 1741, 7⅜x9⅝" ..8,000.00
ABCs/flowers/couple/stag, homespun, sgn, 13x23"+fr 275.00
ABCs/flowers/turkey/dog, needlepoint canvas, 1842, 18x23" 440.00
ABCs/geometrics/verses, sgn, 1733, 16x7", VG 1,600.00
ABCs/ivy, linen canvas, 1870s, 14x14", EX 350.00
ABCs/name, homespun, fading, 9x7" in fr 165.00
ABCs/scenic panel/animals/florals, homespun, 15x17" 1,700.00
ABCs/stars/flowers/etc, homespun, 1814, wear, 20x11¼" in fr ...935.00
ABCs/stylized flower/birds/fruit basket, losses, 10½x8" 150.00
ABCs/verse/floral border, homespun, sgn, 20x20" in gilt fr 440.00
ABCs/verse/florals, signed, unknown age, stain, 16x11" 400.00
ABCs/verse/geometrics/flowers, MA, early 1800s, 19x17"+fr .4,850.00
ABCs/verse/trees/flowers, homespun, 174, 16x22" 1,375.00
ABCs/verse/trees/flowers, homespun, 1812, losses, 16x17" 575.00

ABCs/verse/vines, homespun, 1814, OH, fr: 15½x13½" 1,600.00
ABCs/verse/4-bay house/flowers, homespun, sgn, 1814, 20x15" ...800.00
Adam & Eve/animals/birds/flower border, homespun, 1823, 20x15" .7,400.00
Flowers/animals/geometrics, linen, ca 1835, 13x13"+fr 990.00
Lord's Prayer/verse/hearts/crowns/animals, homespun, 1736, 16x8" .1,350.00
Shepherds in landscape/verse/floral border, 1821, 14x14"+gilt fr 935.00

Sandwich Glass

The Boston and Sandwich Glass Company was founded in 1820 by Deming Jarves in Sandwich, Massachusetts. Their first products were simple cruets, salts, half-pint jugs, and lamps. They were attributed with being one of the first to perfect a method for pressing glass, a step toward the manufacture of the 'lacy' glass which they made until about 1840. Many other types of glass were made there — cut, colored, snakeskin, hobnail, and opalescent among them. After the Civil War, profits began to dwindle due to the keen competition of the Western factories which were situated in areas rich in natural gas and easily accessible sand and coal deposits. The end came with an unreconcilable wage dispute between the workers and the company, and the factory closed in 1888.

In 1907 the vacant glasshouse was purchased and refurbished by the Alton Manufacturing Company. They specialized in lighting fixtures, but under the direction of an ex-Tiffany glassblower and former Sandwich resident James H. Grady, they also produced a line of iridescent art glass called Trevaise, examples of which are very rare today. It was often decorated with pulled feathers, whorls, leaves, and vines similar to the glassware produced by Tiffany, Quezal, and Durand. Examples that surface on today's market range in price from $1,500.00 to $2,000.00. Trevaise was made for less than one year. Due to financial problems, the company closed in 1908. (This information was provided by the Sandwich Glass Museum.) See also Cup Plates; Lacy Glass; Salts, Open; other specific types of glass.

Basket, Tomato, yel exterior, thorn hdl, 5½" 250.00
Bottle, bar; canary, 8-panel, long neck, att, 11½" 600.00
Bottle, scent; amethyst, waisted, 8-sided, smooth base, 4" 200.00
Bottle, scent; amethyst, 12-panel tapered form, 6½" 155.00
Bottle, scent; Baby T'print, canary, orig stopper 395.00
Bottle, scent; cobalt, 12-sided, sloped shoulders, 7¼" 150.00
Bottle, scent; dk amethyst, waisted form, pewter cap, 2½" 45.00
Bottle, scent; fiery opal, waisted, smooth base, att, 4½" 600.00
Bottle, scent; Loop, electric bl, flower stopper, 5" 1,100.00
Bottle, scent; Pillar mold, canary, 1865075, 5", NM 240.00
Bottle, scent; wht fiery opal, clear rigaree, ftd, stopper, 6½" 550.00
Bowl, free-blown opal center w/gr threading at ruffle, 8" 295.00
Bowl, Princess Feather, lacy, 7¼" 160.00
Candlestick, amethyst, hex socket/stem/base, 8⅜", NM 600.00
Candlestick, bl opaque socket, wht dolphin stem, hex base, 9½" ...1,900.00
Candlestick, canary socket on canary dolphin base, 10½" 425.00
Candlestick, clambroth, petal socket, dolphin base, 10¼", EX ..300.00
Candlestick, clambroth columnar base, bl opaque socket, 9¼" ..1,300.00
Candlestick, violet bl, hexagonal, att, 7½" 350.00
Candlestick, wht opaque, petal & loop variant, 7½" 100.00
Candlesticks, bl opaque socket on gray opaque dolphin base, 11", pr ...4,500.00
Candlesticks, canary, dbl-step dolphin base, 9¼", pr 1,300.00
Candlesticks , canary, hexagonal, 7¼", pr 450.00
Candlesticks, canary, Petal & Loop, 6¾", NM, pr 225.00
Cigar holder, pk to wht to clear, rare, 2¾" 60.00
Creamer, GI-29, sapphire bl, appl base & hdl, 4⅜" 1,800.00
Decanter, bk bar; canary, pontiled, 10" 725.00
Decanter, bk bar; emerald gr, 8-panel, pontiled, 11", NM 3,600.00
Dish, Roman Rosette/Dmn Rosette, fiery opal, 5½" 180.00
Hat whimsey, cobalt, BIII-23, blown 3-mold, att, 2¼", EX 225.00
Jar, clambroth, overall dmns, bl stem, 5¾" 85.00
Lamp, canary, Loop, made in 1 pc, pewter collars, 9½" 457.00
Lamp, canary, 8-panel font, monument base, brass collar, 10" ...550.00
Lamp, sapphire bl, Loop, 8-sided std, sq base, 9½" 850.00
Nappie, Bigler (Flute & Soplit), canary, Loop ft, 5¾x7¼" 1,600.00
Spoon holder, Punty & Ellipse (Monroe), cobalt, 5" 1,300.00
Sugar bowl, bl opaque, Gothic Arch, sm chips, 5¼" 1,375.00
Syrup, Chrysanthemum Leaf, heavy hdl, orig dtd lid 75.00
Toddy, lacy, lt amethyst, att, 5" 500.00
Toothpick holder, threaded & rainbow swirled, blown, 2" 325.00
Tumbler, lemonade; appl pk threading & hdl, 5½", 6 for 200.00
Vase, Arch, sapphire bl, ribbed wafer to waterfall base, att, 11" ...1,300.00
Vase, Bigler, canary, tooled/ruffled rim, 9¾", pr 1,200.00
Vase, emerald gr (brilliant), tulip form, att, 9½", NM 3,500.00
Vase, gr, flared rim, polished pontil, wafer connector, att, 4½" 85.00
Vase, Loop, amethyst, made in 1 pc, ruffled rim, att, 11" 800.00
Vase, spill; dk electric bl, hexagonal body & base, 4⅞", NM 275.00
Vase, tulip; emerald gr, 10" 2,750.00
Vase, tulip; yel-emerald gr, 8-sided base, 10" 2,750.00

Sarreguemines

Sarreguemines, France, is the location of Utzschneider and Company, founded in 1770, producers of majolica, transfer-printed dinnerware, figurines, and novelties which are usually marked 'Sarreguemines.'

Pitchers: Man with black beard and mustache, purple hat, 7½", $350.00; Man with smiling face, 5¼", from $160.00 to $175.00.

Box, wicker basket w/oranges, spoon slot, #5143 ....75.00
Ewer, gold crystalline on mauve, slim, angle hdl, mk, 12" 200.00
Jardiniere, oak leaves/acorns, boar's head hdls, 2-pc, 27x24", EX ..1,650.00
Pitcher, dbl-face, 9" 440.00
Pitcher, man's face, blk beard, 9", NM 275.00
Pitcher, man's face, Night Watchman, #653A, 7½" 415.00
Pitcher, man's face, upturned eyebrows & grin, #652, 7½" 195.00
Pitcher, man's face, winking, showing teeth, rosy cheeks, 8" 200.00
Pitcher, man's face w/beard, Christian Michelsen, 6½" 770.00
Pitcher, soldier's face, rare 990.00
Plate, grapes w/spoked edge, 11" 70.00
Plate, oyster; star in center, pk-sage gr w/dk gr, brn & bl, 9½" ...420.00
Platter, snowball fight, flower border w/ribbons/bows, 17x6" 125.00
Sauce dish, winged cherubs, 1800, 3¼" 100.00
Stein, airbrushed/HP: mother & fawn, pewter lid, 1-litre, rare ..325.00
Tray, dancers in street, flower/bow border, #5G, 8x4½" 100.00
Tray, peddlers cart w/villagers, imp Hz, oval, 10x5¾" 110.00
Vase, lilies/leaves/stems cvg, yel on brn, cylinder, 17", NM 250.00
Vase, monkey playing organ figural, earthenware, 8" 635.00

Satin Glass

Satin glass is simply glassware with a velvety matt finish achieved through the application of an acid bath. This procedure has been used by many companies since the twentieth century, both here and abroad, on many types of colored and art glass. See also Mother-of-Pearl; Webb.

Biscuit jar, pk, lg shells in relief on lower half, HP floral 235.00
Ewer, pk w/HP floral, 9¾" 130.00
Mug, loopings, pk & gold on wht, frosted hdl, 3½" 175.00
Rose bowl, bl w/birds & floral, camphor hdls, 4½" 100.00
Vase, yel w/wht int, bulbous w/stick neck, pontil, 7½" 145.00

Satsuma

Satsuma is a type of fine cream crackle-glaze pottery or earthenware made in Japan as early as the seventeenth century. The earliest wares, made at the original kiln in the Satsuma province, were enameled with only simple florals. By the late eighteenth century, a floral brocade (or nishikide design) was favored, and similar wares were being made at other kilns under the direction of the Lord of Satsuma. In the early part of the nineteenth century, a diaper pattern was added to the florals. Gold and silver enamels were used for accents by the latter years of the century. During the 1850s, as the quality of goods made for export to the Western world increased and the style of decoration began to evolve toward becoming more appealing to the Westerners, human forms such as Arhats, Kannon, geisha girls, and samurai warriors were added. Today the most valuable pieces are those marked 'Kinkozan,' 'Shuzan,' 'Ryuzan,' and 'Kozan.' The genuine Satsuma 'mon' or mark is a cross within a circle — usually in gold on the body or lid, or in red on the base of the ware. Character marks may be included.

Caution: Much of what is termed 'Satsuma' comes from the Showa Period (1926 to the present); it is not true Satsuma but a simulated type, a cheaper pottery with heavy enamel. Collectors need to be aware that much of the of the 'Satsuma' today is really Satsuma style and should not carry the values of true Satsuma.

Vase, ovoid with four figures, rim repair, nineteenth century, 15½", $600.00.

Ewer, dragon, blk w/red on dk brn w/flowers, mk, 13x10½" 500.00
Figurine, girl in gold brocade robe, w/dog, 7" 200.00
Teapot, ca 1930s, 4½", +cup & saucer 55.00
Vase, hawk & pine, Meiji period, slim baluster, 9⅝" 300.00
Vase, mc & gilt decor on cream, baluster, Meiji period, 10" 375.00
Vase, Samurai in battle, gourd hdls, Meiji period, 18½", pr 1,100.00

Scales

In today's world of pre-measured and pre-packaged goods, it is difficult to imagine the days when such products as sugar, flour, soap, and candy first had to be weighed by the grocer. The variety of scales used at the turn of the century was highly diverse; at the Philadelphia Exposition in 1876, one company alone displayed over three hundred different weighing devices. Among those found today, brass, cast-iron, and plastic models are the most common. Fancy postal scales in decorative wood, silver, marble, bronze, and mosaic are also to be found.

A word of caution on the values listed: these values range from a low for those items in fair to good condition to the upper values for items in excellent condition. Naturally, items in mint condition could command even higher prices, and they often do. Also, these are *retail* prices that suggest what a collector will pay for the object. When you sell to a dealer, expect to get much less. The values noted are averages taken from various auction and other catalogs in the possession of the society members. Among these, but not limited to, are the following: Joel L. Malter & Co., Inc., Encino, CA; *Auktion Alt Technic*, Auction Team, Koln, Germany.

For those seeking additional information concerning antique scales we recommend *Scales, A Collector's Guide*, by Bill and Jan Berning (Schiffer). You are also encouraged to contact the International Society of Antique Scale Collectors, whose address can be found in the Directory under Clubs, Newsletters, and Catalogs.

Key:
ap — arrow pointer
bal — balance
bm — base metal
br — brass
Brit — British
Can — Canadian
Col — Colonial
CW — Civil War
cwt — counterweight
Engl — English
eq — equal arm
Euro — European
FIS — Fairbanks Infallible Scale Co.
h — hanging
hcp — hanging counterpoise
hh — hand held
l+ — label with foreign coin values
lb w/i — labeled box with instructions
lph — letter plate or holder
pend — pendulum
PP — Patent Pending
st — sterling
tt — torsion type
ua — unequal arm
wt — weight

Salter's Improved Family scale, heavy brass stand with clock-like face, tin receptacle, ca 1900, 12", EX, $150.00.

Analytical (Scientific)

Am, eq, mahog w/br & ivory, late 1800s, 14x16x8", $200 to 400.00

Assay

Am, eq, mahog box w/br & ivory, plaque/drw, 1890s, $400 to 1,000.00

Coin: Equal Arm Balance, American

Blk japanned metal, eagle on lid, late 19th C, $125 to 225.00
Col, oak 6-part box, Col moneys, Boston, 1720-75, $600 to 1,200.00
Post Col to CW, oak 6-part box, l+, 1843, $400 to 1,000.00

Coin: Equal Arm Balance, English

Charles I, wooden box w/11 Brit wts, 1640s, $900 to 1,500.00
1-pc wood box, rnd wts, label, Freeman, 1760s, $250 to 450.00

6-pc oak box, coin wts label, Thos Harrison, 1750s, $200 to 450.00

Coin: Equal Arm Balance, French

Solid wood box, 12 sq wts, J Reyne, Bourdeau, 1694, $400 to .1,000.00
Solid wood box w/recesses, 5 sq wts, A Gardes, 1800s, $250 to .800.00
1-pc oval box, nested/fractional wts, label, 18th C, $250 to 400.00
1-pc oval box, no wts, label of Fr/Euro coins, 18th C, $150 to ..250.00
1-pc walnut box, nested wts, Charpentier label, 1810, $275 to .675.00

Coin: Equal Arm Balance, Miscellaneous

Amsterdam, 1-pc box, 32 sq wts, label, late 1600s, $850 to 2,500.00
Cologne, full set of wts & full label, late 1600s, $1,200 to 2,800.00
German, wood box, 13+ wts beneath main wts, label, 1795, $650 to .900.00

Counterfeit Coin Detectors, American

Allender Pat, lb w/i, cwt, Nov 22, 1855, 8½", $350 to 650.00
Allender PP, rocker, labeled box, cwt, 1850s, 8½", $450 to 750.00
Allender PP, rocker, no box or cwt, 1850s, 8½", $250 to 375.00
Allender PP, space for $3 gold pc, lb w/i, cwt, 1855, $350 to 750.00
Allender PP, space for $3 gold pc, no box or cwt, 1855, $275 to ...375.00
Allender Warranted, rocker, no box or cwt, 1850s, 8½", $350 to ..475.00
McNally-Harrison Pat 1882, rocker, cwt, JT McNally, $275 to .500.00
McNally-Harrison Pat 1882, rocker, cwt & box, FIS, $400 to ...750.00
McNally-Harrison...1882, rocker, CI base, no cwt/box, $250 to 400.00
Thompson, Z-formed rocker, Berrian Mfg, 1877 Pat, $175 to 350.00

Counterfeit Coin Detectors, Dutch

Rocker, Ellinckhuysen, brass, +copy of 1829 Patent, $150 to 165.00

Counterfeit Coin Detectors, English

Folding, Guinea, self-rising, labeled box, 1850s, $175 to 225.00
Folding, Guinea, self-rising, wood box/label, ca 1890s, $125 to .175.00
Folding, Guinea, self-rising, wooden box, pre-1800, $175 to 275.00
Rocker, simple, no maker's name or cb, end-cap box, $85 to 125.00
Rocker, w/maker's name & cb, end-cap box, $120 to 150.00

Postal

In the listings below an asterisk (*) was used to indicate that any one of several manufacturers' or brand names might be found on that particular set of scales. Some of the American-made pieces could be marked Pelouze, Lorraine, Hanson, Kingsbury, Fairbanks, Troemner, IDL, Newman, Accurate, Ideal, B-T, Marvel, Reliance, Howe, Landers-Frary-Clark, Chatillon, Triner, American Bank Service, or Weiss. European/U.S.-made scales marked with an asterisk (*) could be marked Salter, Peerless, Pelouze, Sturgis, L.F.&C., Alderman, G. Little, or S&D. English-made scales with the asterisk (*) could be marked Josh. & Edmd. Ratcliff, R.W. Winfield, S. Mordan, STS (Samuel Turner, Sr.), W.&T. Avery, Parnall & Sons, S&P, or H.B. Wright. There may be other manufacturers as well.

Brit/Can Bal, eq, br or CI on base, *, 4"-15", $100 to 750.00
Engl Bal, eq/Roberval, gilt or st, on stand, *, 3"-8", $500 to ...2,500.00
Engl Bal, eq/Roberval, plain to ornate, *, 3"-8", $100 to 2,500.00
Engl Spring, candlestick, br or st, *, 3½"-15", $100 to 500.00
Engl Spring, CI, br or NP fr, Salter, ozs/lbs, 7"-10", $25 to 200.00
Engl Steelyard, ua, 1- or 2-beam, h lph, *, 4"-15", $100 to 1,500.00
Euro pend, gravity, br, CI or NP fr on base, oz/grams, $75 to 350.00
Euro pend, gravity, 2-arm, bm, br or NP, *, 6"-9", $50 to 300.00
Euro/US Spring, br or NP, pence/etc, h or hh, *, 4"-17", $10 to .100.00
US Pend, gravity, metal, pnt face, ap, hcp, sm, $20 to 100.00
US Spring, pnt base metal, *, 2½"-8", $10 to 80.00
US Spring, pnt bm, *, mtd on inkstand, 2½"-8", $75 to 250.00
US Spring, pnt bm, rnd glass-covered face, *, 8"-10", $25 to 100.00
US Spring, SP, oblong base, *, 2½"-8", $100 to 200.00
US Spring, st, oblong base, *, 2½"-8", $200 to 500.00
US Steelyard, ua, CI, *, 5"-13" beam, 4½"-12" base, $25 to 100.00

Schafer and Vater

Established in 1890 by Gustav Schafer and Gunther Vater in the Thuringia region of southwest Germany, by 1913 this firm employed over two hundred workers. The original factory burned in 1918 but was restarted and production continued until WWII. In 1972 the East German government took possession of the building and destroyed all of the molds and the records that were left.

You will find pieces with the impressed mark of a nine-point star with a script 'R' inside the star. On rare occasions you will find this mark in blue ink under glaze. The items are sometimes marked with a four-digit design number and a two-digit artist mark. In addition or instead, pieces may have 'Made in Germany' or in the case of the Kewpies, 'Rose O'Neil copyright.' The company also manufactured items for sale under store names, and those would not have the impressed mark.

Schafer and Vater used various types of clays. Items made of hard-paste porcelain, soft-paste porcelain, jasper, bisque, and majolica can be found. The glazed bisque pieces may be multicolored or have an applied colored slip wash that highlights the intricate details of the modeling. Gold accents were used as well as spots of high-gloss color called jewels. Metallic glazes are coveted. You can find the jasper in green, blue, pink, lavender, and white. New collectors gravitate toward the pink and lavender shades.

Since Schafer and Vater made such a multitude of items, collectors have to compete with many cross-over collections. These include shaving mugs, hatpin holders, match holders, figurines, figural pitchers, Kewpies, tea sets, bottles, naughties, etc.

Reproduction alert: In addition to the crudely made Japanese copies, some English firms are beginning to make figural reproductions. These seem to be well marked and easy to spot. Our advisor for this category is Joanne M. Koehn; she is listed in the Directory under Minnesota.

Pitcher, clown with mandolin, marked, 5½", $185.00. (Photo courtesy Joanne M. Koehn)

Ashtray, Happy & Sad Black Man, unmk, 3" 265.00
Box, Peter & Paul in washtub, unmk, 3" 200.00
Figurine, baby w/big mouth, unmk, 3" 230.00
Figurine, Cassandra, Paul & puppy, mk, 3¾" 200.00
Figurine, Castle Walk, mk, 5½" 240.00
Figurine, Don't Tell Anyone, #8055, mk, 4" 175.00
Figurine, egg lady w/big mouth, unmk, 4" 275.00

Figurine, egg man waiter, unmk, 3" 100.00
Figurine, In Love, couple dancing, #4565, unmk, 6" 195.00
Figurine, Kewpie angel, #9202, mk, 3", NM 150.00
Figurine, monk w/big mouth, unmk, 4" 60.00
Figurine, Mr Adam, Black man w/lg leaf, unmk, 7½" 325.00
Figurine, organ grinder w/big mouth, #20, mk, 4", NM 300.00
Figurine, Present for You, #9410, mk, 6", NM 300.00
Figurine, Sailor Dreadnought, #7278, mk, 7", NM 255.00
Figurine, Tango, #9271, mk, 6" 195.00
Flask, Bowling Man, mk, 5¼" 150.00
Flask, Devil, MIG, 6½" 275.00
Flask, Everybody's Doing It, mk, 4" 80.00
Flask, Just a Little Nip, dog biting lady, unmk, 4¾" 185.00
Flask, One of the Boys, mk, 6¾" 175.00
Flask, What a Night, MIG, 5¼" 160.00
Match holder, dog, #8499, mk, 3¼" 140.00
Match holder, Get Your Hair Cut, smiling man, mk, 4" 200.00
Match holder, Hand It Over, mk, 3½" 265.00
Match holder, man w/open mouth, #7214, mk, 3¼", NM 100.00
Match holder, sailor & woman, #7127, mk, 4" 240.00
Match holder, smiling boy w/happy-face ft, #8198, mk, 3¼" 185.00
Match holder, smiling man, mk, 3¼" 200.00
Match holder, Weather Forecast Partly Cloudy..., #9625, mk, 4" ...185.00
Match holder, What a Night, unmk, 5" 335.00
Match holder/ashtray, thin man, #9091, unmk, 3¼" 140.00
Match holder/striker, Don't Scratch Me..., cats, mk, 3¾" 300.00
Match holder/striker, Dutch boy & girl, #7891, mk, 3¾" 200.00
Match holder/striker, jackass, We Are Two, #8206, mk, 4⅛" 250.00
Match holder/striker, Scratch Your Match on My Patch, mk, 3½" ..250.00
Nodder, Waiting for the Tide, ft swing, #7986, mk, 4¼" 95.00
Nodder, What I Am?, mk, rpl wire, 4¾" 300.00
Nodder/match holder, Hookums, unmk, 4¼" 335.00
Nodder/pincushion, Oriental lady, #1357, mk, 3½" 400.00
Pitcher, elf on pig, mk, 4½" 325.00
Toothpick holder, baseball player, unmk, 2" 115.00

Scheier

The Scheiers began their ceramics careers in the late 1930s and soon thereafter began to teach their craft at the University of New Hampshire. After WWII they cooperated with the Puerto Rican government in establishing a native ceramic industry, an involvement which would continue to influence their designs. In the '50s they retired and moved to Mexico; they currently reside in Arizona.

Bottle, child-like animals/people, unglazed stoneware, 18" 900.00
Bowl, bl-lav w/brn sections, ftd, 4½x6" 200.00
Bowl, buff cornmeal yel w/lt gr speckles, thin walls, 9" 200.00
Bowl, cobalt w/shaded aqua & ochre, 4x5" 200.00
Bowl, mahog flambe w/ocher & dk brn accents, 3½x7" 250.00
Bowl, metallic silver on tan to khaki, 3¼x5½" 200.00
bowl, multi-brns bleed together w/ochre, #6, 4¼x5" 125.00
Bowl, rich brn w/mirror accents, mc abstracts/streaks, ftd, 9" 325.00
Bowl, sgraffito horse on bl, ribbed, wht-beige/bl, 4½" 100.00
Bowl, yel/brn mottled matt, 9" 175.00
Creamer & sugar bowl, red-brn on ochre gloss, 4x3½", pr 100.00
Cup, prancing horse, brn on beige, 5½", 3½", pr 100.00
Lamp base, cvd/protruding face design, brns/chartreuse/olive-brn, 19" ...700.00
Tea set, sage gr drip, teal/brn accents, glossy, pot+5 demi c/s 250.00
Vase, band w/stylized heads, bl on cratered blk, rpr, 17" 1,200.00
Vase, primitive figures reserves, gunmetal, ftd bowl form, 8" 550.00
Vase, tan w/brn-over-khaki sections, pinched fan form, 5¼x7¼" 250.00

Schlegelmilch Porcelain

For information about Schlegelmilch Porcelain, see Mary Frank Gaston's books: *R. S. Prussia Popular Lines,* which addresses R. S. Prussia molds and decorations, and *The Collector's Encyclopedia of R. S. Prussia, Fourth Series,* which contains information on the other Schlegelmilch marks, such as Erdman Schlegelmilch (E. S.), Oscar Schlegelmilch (O. S.), and the other R. S. marks (R. S. Germany, R. S. Suhl, R. S. Poland, and R. S. Tillowitz). Both books contain full-color illustrations and current values. Mold numbers appearing in some of the listings refer to these books. Assume that all items described below are marked unless noted otherwise.

Key:

BM — blue mark	SM — steeple mark
GM — green mark	RM — red mark

E.S. Germany

Fine chinaware marked 'E.S. Germany' or 'E.S. Prov. Saxe' was produced by the E.S. Schlegelmilch factory in Suhl in the Thuringia region of Prussia from sometime after 1861 until about 1925.

Bowl, bird on limb, Prov Saxe, GM, sq, 6" 60.00
Bowl, bird/berry tree, mc on yel/gr, Prov Saxe GM, hdls, 13x8" ..75.00
Bowl, boat scene, sq w/hdls, 6½" 30.00
Bowl, divided; Hortense & Josephine 150.00
Bowl, hunter w/dogs on gr 90.00
Bowl, pansies & flowers, steeple mold #3, circle mk 125.00
Chocolate pot, Napoleon portrait 375.00
Cup & saucer, demitasse; Madam Lebrun portrait 125.00
Cup & saucer, demitasse; woman & roses, MOP lustre, ornate ..175.00
Flower/candle holder, violets, GM, 4½", pr 115.00
Lobster dish, tail forms hdl, florals/gilt, BM, 10" 85.00
Nappy, 3-D parrot in recess, florals, heart shape, 6½" 115.00
Plate, bird on limb, rtcl hdls, GM, 10" 50.00
Plate, High Hawk Indian chief portrait, orange border, 6½" 50.00
Plate, robin in mulberry tree, red/gr, Prov Saxe GM, hdls, 8" 65.00
Vase, classical scene, gold/enamel jewels, Royal, 8" 300.00
Vase, lady w/doves, much gold/turq beads, Tiffany finish, hdls, 6½" ..425.00

R.S. Germany

In 1869 Reinhold Schlegelmilch began to manufacture porcelain in Suhl in the German province of Thuringia. In 1894 he established another factory in Tillowitz in upper Silesia. Both areas were rich in resources necessary for the production of hard-paste porcelain. Wares marked with the name 'Tillowitz' and the accompanying 'R.S. Germany' phrase are attributed to Reinhold. The most common mark is a wreath and star in a solid color under the glaze. Items marked 'R.S. Germany' are usually more simply decorated than R.S. Prussia. Some reflect the Art Deco trend of the 1920s. Certain hand-painted floral decorations and themes such as 'Sheepherder,' 'Man With Horses,' and 'Cottage' are especially valued by collectors — those with a high-gloss finish or on Art Deco shapes in particular. Not all hand-painted items were painted at the factory. Those with an artist's signature but no 'Hand Painted' mark indicate that the blank was decorated outside the factory.

Basket, pheasants on yel, Deco mold, GM, 5" 250.00
Bowl, bluebird on cherry tree, gold ground, rtcl, BM, 6" 70.00

Bowl, Iris mold, Summer Season portrait on white satin, handles, marked, 8½x13", from $1,600.00 to $1,800.00. (Photo courtesy Mary Frank Gaston)

Bowl, roses, Deco mold, hdls, GM, 10" 95.00
Bowl, roses, hdls, BM, sq, 8½" 55.00
Cake plate, roses/gold, Nouveau mold, 10" 125.00
Chocolate set, tulips/gold on cream, Deco mold, BM, 10-pc 365.00
Coffeepot, roses, gold trim, BM, 8½" 95.00
Condensed milk holder, roses/gold, w/lid, BM, 4¾" 100.00
Cup, floral on pearlized ground, emb swirls, BM, 3½" 40.00
Ewer, floral, mold #640, GM, 5" 165.00
Fernery, florals, ftd, SM, 3½x6½" dia 180.00
Hatpin holder, floral, mold #656, GM, 4½" 90.00
Hatpin holder, roses, mold #77, BM, 4¾" 130.00
Mustache cup & saucer, floral, mold #26, GM 90.00
Night light, owl, brn/yel, BM, 5½" 900.00
Pin tray, roses on pearlized finish, mold #327, GM, 5½" 40.00
Pitcher, milk; roses, GM, 5½" 140.00
Pitcher, tankard; roses, pk on wht, mold #584, GM, 10" 280.00
Plate, cottage scene, 6" 95.00
Relish, bird of paradise, hdls 250.00
Ring tree, pointed scallops w/gold accents, RM, 4½" 45.00
Shaving mug, floral, Steeple mold, unmk 115.00
Teapot, roses, locking lid, BM w/red script, 5½" 70.00
Toothpick holder, lilies, RM, 2¼" 75.00
Toothpick holder, roses, 3 hdls/ft, mold #362, RM, 2" 90.00
Tray, bun; medieval castle scene on lake w/sailboat, 13" 500.00
Tray, bun; woman w/oxen, Deco mold, 13" 275.00
Tray, bun; woman w/oxen at country house, purple/pk/yel, 13" .300.00
Trivet, heart shape w/parrot hdl 110.00
Vase, roses, hdls, GM, 5½" 60.00

R.S. Poland

'R.S. Poland' is a mark attributed to Reinhold Schlegelmilch's factory in Tillowitz, Silesia. It was in use for a few years after 1945.

Bowl, crowned cranes, 5¾" 465.00
Cup & saucer, pk flowers on wht, swirled body 55.00
Muffineer, roses, Made in Germany Poland RM, 4½" 95.00
Relish, mc roses w/gold, 4½x9" 35.00
Shaving mug, daffodils & tulips 150.00
Vase, lg peach roses on shaded brn, Nouveau hdls, mold #956, 12" ...550.00
Vase, pastoral scene w/cobalt & gold, mold #3, 8½" 1,400.00

R.S. Prussia

Art porcelain bearing the mark 'R.S. Prussia' was manufactured by Reinhold Schlegelmilch in the early 1900s in a Germanic area known until the end of WWI as Prussia. The vast array of mold shapes in combination with a wide variety of decorations is the basis for R.S. Prussia's appeal. Themes can be categorized as figural (usually based on a famous artist's work), birds, florals, portraits, scenics, and animals.

Bowl, berry; poppies, shell shape, unmk, set of 4 .....35.00
Bowl, berry; roses, gold stencil, mold #29, set of 6 .....120.00
Bowl, blueberries & blossoms on satin, 10" 120.00
Bowl, cottage scene, 10½" 700.00
Bowl, Lady Recamier portrait on gr, mold #29, unmk, 8½" 900.00
Bowl, lilies on gr lustre, 11" 175.00
Bowl, nasturtiums w/gold, bowl-in-bowl mold #211A 175.00
Bowl, peacock & bluebird, fancy mold, EX colors, 11" 950.00
Bowl, poppies on satin, mold #204, 8" 90.00
Bowl, Potocka portrait, Tiffany finish, mold #29, unmk, 10½" ...5,400.00
Bowl, roses, mc w/lav & bl border, ftd, unmk, 10" 120.00
Bowl, roses, pk & wht on satin, 10" 150.00
Bowl, roses, pk on wht, mold #327, 9½" 70.00
Bowl, roses & Tiffany carnations on wht to peach, RM, 10½" ..595.00
Bowl, roses in center, scalloped mold, RM, 10" 170.00
Bowl, swans on satin, 11" 300.00
Bowl, Winter Season, satin, iris mold, 9½" 1,100.00
Bowl, 3 scenes: turkeys/ducks/etc; mold #77 variant, RM, 11" ..1,550.00
Cake plate, floral on pk & yel, gold trim, hdls, 9¾" 195.00
Cake plate, florals on satin, mold #301, 10" 80.00
Cake plate, Melon Eaters on brn/yel/gr, 11" 400.00
Cake plate, poppies, pk on yel & gr, 11½" 125.00
Cake plate, roses, pk & wht on wht & lav satin, mold #82, 11" ...200.00
Cake plate, roses on gr w/tan border, mold #9, 11" 175.00
Cake plate, roses on white & gr, mold #324, 11" 110.00
Cake plate, spilled basket on lustre, medallion mold, 10" 175.00
Cake plate, tulips on lustre, 9¾" 70.00
Celery tray, carnations & roses on wht to peach, RM, 9" 375.00
Celery tray, fruit on yel, iris mold, 12" 175.00
Celery tray, roses w/gold & lav, RM, 9" 350.00
Chocolate pot, floral, wht on wht, mold #509A, 9" 165.00
Chocolate pot, lilies on lustre, 10" 175.00
Chocolate pot, poppies, pk on yel & gr, mold #644, 9½" 225.00
Coffeepot, poppies, Tiffany finish, mold #643, unmk, 9" 300.00
Compote, floral w/in swags w/jewels, mold #157, RM, 4½" 180.00
Compote, rose garlands, wht w/heavy gold, 4½x7" 225.00
Cracker jar, leaves & gold accents, mold #878, RM, 5½" 260.00
Cracker jar, poppies, Tiffany finish, mold #643, unmk 275.00
Cracker jar, swan & castle, bluebird lid, w/hdls 500.00
Creamer & sugar bowl, mill & cottage scenes, mold #576 .....300.00
Creamer & sugar bowl, Old Man in the Mountain 350.00
Creamer & sugar bowl, poppies, Tiffany finish, mold #643, unmk ..225.00
Creamer & sugar bowl, roses, pk on gr 175.00
Creamer & sugar bowl, roses, pk on wht/lav/gr satin 200.00
Cup & saucer, roses & shadow leaves, gilt, unmk, 2½", 5½" 80.00
Hatpin holder, Swan in Evergreen, mold #728, unmk 225.00
Muffineer, roses, mold #781, hdls, RM, 5" 280.00
Mug, scuttle; swans on lake, satin, mold #577, unmk 350.00
Mustard pot, mc roses on wht, RM 150.00
Mustard pot, snowballs & roses, mold #643 .....175.00
Pitcher, cider; ornate dbl images, star mk, 9x9" 1,200.00
Pitcher, tankard; poppies, red on cream, mold #586, RM, 11½" ..565.00
Pitcher, tankard; poppies & Tiffany carnations on wht, RM, 11" ..1,100.00
Plate, daisies & roses, gr & Tiffany border, 8½" 90.00
Plate, floral on cream satin, 8¾" 50.00
Plate, Melon Eaters, mold #300, RM, 10½" 675.00
Plate, mill scene, mold #300, brn mk, 8½" 425.00
Plate, pine & blossom on satin, 8¾" 60.00
Plate, roses/gilt, mold #156, RM, 8½" 140.00
Plate, wild flowers, bl border, mold #258, unmk, 9½" 60.00
Shaving mug, roses, pk on wht & pk 80.00
Syrup, calla lilies on wht, EX gold 125.00
Syrup, swans on pearlized finish, mold #577, RM, 5½" 235.00
Teapot, carnations on gr lustre, 6½" 100.00
Teapot, wild roses, wht on 'watered silk,' molded base, 5½" 165.00

Toothpick holder, snowball floral, swirl mold, RM 125.00
Tray, bun; roses & snowballs w/cobalt, mold #56, RM 200.00
Tray, dresser; Diana the Huntress, much gold, unmk, 12x9" 575.00
Tray, dresser; poppies on gr & tan satin, 11½" 375.00
Vase, castle scene, bulbous, 4" 225.00
Vase, mill & cottage scenes on cobalt, mold #907, red mk 400.00

R.S. Suhl, Suhl

Porcelains marked with this designation are attributed to Reinhold Schlegelmilch's Suhl factory.

Bowl, lav & wht flowers w/gold, hdls, 8⅛" 150.00
Box, Night Watch, brn to tan w/Musketeers, w/lid, 3½" dia 50.00
Box, Night Watch, brn to tan w/Musketeers, w/lid, 4½" dia 75.00
Box, pk roses w/gold, egg shape, mk, 3½x5⅞x4" 1,100.00
Cup & saucer, couple scene, flower hdl, gold trim 125.00
Cup & saucer, Night Watch, 2¼", 5" 100.00
Vase, floral on dk gr, ornate gold hdls, mold #12, 13½" 650.00
Vase, lilac clematis, gold hdls, mold #9, 7⅜" 250.00
Vase, Melon Eaters, 9" 660.00
Vase, pk flowers/wht snowflakes on blk, RSP mold #907, 5" 200.00
Vase, seaside scene w/bk views of figures, mold #7, 8⅝" 1,200.00

R.S. Tillowitz

R.S. Tillowitz-marked porcelains are attributed to Reinhold Schlegelmilch's factory in Tillowitz, Silesia.

Bowl, pheasants, scalloped rim, open hdls, oval, 10" 265.00
Cake plate, pears & grapes, pierced hdls, 10⅞" 90.00
Coffeepot, China Blau (china bl), 8¾" 250.00
Dessert set, birds & floral on wht w/gold, lg+6 sm bowls 165.00
Gravy boat, pk roses in int, wht ext, gold trim, 6½" L 35.00
Pitcher, floral garland at neck on wht, 8½" 80.00
Plate, peafowl, 8" 125.00
Toothpick holder, wht w/silver trim 55.00
Vase, pheasants, 6" 250.00

Schneider

The Schneider Glass Company was founded in 1914 at Epinay-sur-Seine, France. They made many types of art glass, some of which sandwiched designs between layers. Other decorative devices were appliqué and carved work. These were marked 'Charder' or 'Schneider.' During the '20s commercial artware was produced with Deco motifs cut by acid through two or three layers and signed 'LeVerre Francais' in script or with a section of inlaid filigrane. Our advisor for this category is Don Williams; he is listed in the Directory under Missouri. See also Le Verre Francais.

Vase, mottled tomato red shading to green, cameo cut with honeycomb band at neck above maple seed pods rising from leaves at lower half, signed, 17½", $2,500.00.

Bowl, att, burgundy/opal mottle to pk/frosty mottle, blk ft, 14" .225.00
Bowl, gr/wht mottled, in metal grape/leaves 3-leg stand, 10x8" ...1,200.00
Bowl, mottled orange to pk swirl, incurvate rim, '20s, 2½x4½" ...260.00
Bowl, mottled swirl rose on blk ft, flaring rim, ca 1925, 4¾x12" ..420.00
Bowl, yel to orange-red w/maroon streaks, Ovington, 3½x12" ..375.00
Compote, rose w/wine mottle, flaring rim, stem ft, 7½" 490.00
Compote, wht mottle w/blk amethyst columns on wrought base, 8½x9" ...950.00
Inkwell, red-orange sq w/lid on burgundy tray, glass insert 650.00
Vase, amber marbleized w/amethyst base, ribbon hdls, 1930s, 14" ..600.00
Vase, att, amber/gr/wht mottle, encased in Deco iron frwork, 9" .1,800.00
Vase, dk amber w/yel-striped amethyst stem/ft, goblet form, 15" ..600.00
Vase, pk/red/wht/clear swirls w/bubbles, urn form, 12" 980.00
Vase, rust w/dk veins, bulbous tapering to 1¾" top, 17" 400.00
Vase, wine/gr w/drip of orange/yel/gray at rim, slender, 17" 1,100.00

Schoolhouse Collectibles

Schoolhouse collectibles bring to mind memories of a bygone era when the teacher rang her bell to call the youngsters to class in a one-room schoolhouse where often both the 'hickory stick' and an apple occupied a prominent position on her desk. Our advisor for this category is Kenn Norris; he is listed in the Directory under Texas.

Slate, laced padded edges, 9½x13½", VG, $22.00. (Photo courtesy Kenn Norris)

Bell, teacher's; brass w/wood hdl, brass cap, 1800s, 6x3" dia 150.00
Book, Art Stories...Children, Foresman, 1933, w/dust jacket, EX ...80.00
Book, Dick & Jane, advanced reading, 1st ed, Elson Reader, 1930 ..235.00
Book, Dick & Jane, Friends & Neighbors, 1956, EX 110.00
Book, Dick & Jane, Fun w/Our Family, VG 70.00
Book, Dick & Jane, Guess Who, Foresman, 1951, 95-pg, EX+ ..120.00
Book, Dick & Jane, New Friends & Neighbors, 1952, NM 110.00
Book, Dick & Jane, Our New Friends, 1940, EX 80.00
Book, Dick & Jane, We Look & See, 1946-47 ed, 48-pg, 8x6, VG ...65.00
Book, Dick & Jane, We Work & Play, 1951, EX 85.00
Book, Dick & Jane Bigbook, teacher's aide, EX 350.00
Book, Morse's School Geography, Harper & Brothers, 1847, G ...60.00
Book, NJ School for the Deaf, Trenton, 32-pg, 1905, 6½x5", EX .50.00
Book, Smith's Geography, Cady & Burgess, NY, 1858, 8x5", EX .45.00
Book carrier, metal & wood w/strap winders, ca 1840, VG 100.00
Desk, master's; pine w/old yel grpt, dvtl drw, lift lid, 36", EX 550.00
Desk, master's; rfn pine w/old gr int, dvtl drw, slant top, 42x32x21" 400.00
Desk, student's; seat w/desk on bk, ornate wrought-iron fr, 1880s 180.00
Desk, student's; walnut w/ornate wrought-iron, Andrews, 1880, EX ...160.00
Inkwell (for desk), Am Seating Comp #60, Bakelite/glass, VG+ ..45.00
Pencil sharpener, Bakelite, Donald Duck decal, 1" dia, EX 35.00
Pencil sharpener, Bakelite, paneled cylinder, 2½" 12.00
Pencil sharpener, Bakelite, USA Army plane 80.00
Pencil sharpener, celluloid, pelican, Japan, 3" 130.00
Pencil sharpener, metal, rifle, Japan, 3½" 75.00
Pencil sharpener, pan-style, nickel, mtd on wood base, 1800s ...660.00
Pencil sharpener, plastic, Sunbeam Bread, 1" 15.00
Slate, 2-section, hinged cherry fr, ruled slates, 15x11", EX 165.00

Yearbook, Oracle, Lansing MI, pub by Senior class 1902, vol 11, EX ..25.00

Pencil Boxes

Among the most common of school-related collectibles are the many classes of pencil boxes. Generally from the period of the 1870s to the 1940s, these boxes were made in hundreds of different styles. Materials included tin, wood (thin frame and solid hardwood), and leather; fabric and plastics were later used. Most pencil boxes were in a basic, rectangular configuration, though rare examples were made to resemble other objects such as rolling pins, ball bats, nightsticks, etc. They may still be found at reasonable prices, even though collectors have recently taken a keen interest in them. All boxes listed below are in very good to near mint condition. Our advisors for pencil boxes are Sue and Lar Hothem, authors of *School Collectibles of the Past;* they are listed in the Directory under Ohio.

Advertising giveaway, Security Shoes, tin, sliding lid, 8" 38.00
Butternut w/orig orange-red pnt, dvtl, sliding lid 140.00
Fabric, slide drw, Am, 1940s, 8¼x5x⅞" 15.00
Hardwood, 2-level, roses lid decal, lock on lower compartment, 9½" ..40.00
Store display, Ti-Con-Der-Oga, cb, Dixon, partial contents, 7¾" ...20.00
Tin, Jackie Coogan, smiling face, 7⅞x2¼x1⅝" 55.00
Tin, Scholar's Companion, Pat 1874, 7¼x3x1" 85.00
Tin, sliding lid, 1-compartment, dk bl w/sm pnt flowers, 7⅝" 30.00
Wood fr, School Companion, Octagon Soap premium, 7⅞" 40.00
Wooden, 4-level, 1 compartment per level, floral decal, 9¼" 95.00

Schoop, Hedi

Swiss-born Hedi Schoop started her ceramics business in North Hollywood in 1940. With a talented crew of about twenty decorators, she produced figurines, figure-vases, console sets, TV lamps, and other decorative housewares — much of which was accented with gold or platinum trim. Schoop's pottery closed after a fire destroyed the building in 1958. Marks are impressed or printed. For further information we recommend *The Collector's Encyclopedia of California Pottery, Second Edition*, by Jack Chipman; he is listed in the Directory under California.

Bookends, poodle, sitting, gray w/blk highlights, on base, 12", pr ..170.00
Box, butterfly finial, maroon/pk/gray-gr, mk #218, 3½x5½" 30.00
Box, poodle (pk/wht) on lid, blk base, triangular, 1¾x8" 155.00

Candle holder, mermaid holds two shell cups aloft, ca 1950, 13½", rare, $500.00 minimum value.

Candle holder, swirled free-form, gr & wht w/gold, 11½" 30.00
Cookie jar, Darner Doll, wht w/bl & gr apron, mk, 12" 375.00
Figurine, dancing girl, bl dress w/HP florals, wht basket, 12" 165.00
Figurine, Dutch lady in gr w/wht flower vase, 9½" 50.00
Figurine, fan dancer, in wht w/teal trim, HP yel-brn roses, 13" ..120.00
Figurine, gypsy dancer, yel dress & scarf w/gold trim, 10" 200.00
Figurine, lady, bowl overhead, in wht w/bl appl flowers/apron, 13" ..140.00
Figurine, lady, hat w/bow, plaid shawl on shoulders, head up, 13" 135.00
Figurine, lady in cream dress w/appl flowers, holds 2 baskets, 12" 150.00
Figurine, lady in wht & gr w/appl flowers in hair & on dress, 9" ..55.00
Figurine, lady w/flowers on chest, 2 flowerpots in bk, 11½" 65.00
Figurine, senorita w/basket on head, mk #100, 12½" 210.00
Plate, Old Crow mascot, blk/wht/gray, mk Hedi Scoop orig, 11x7½" ..90.00
Plate, poodle (blk/wht) w/flower on head/tail, gold edge, 7½" sq ..75.00
Tray, lady figural, skirt forms tray 185.00
Vase, butterfly, brn/lav/pk w/gold, 6x9" 50.00

Schramberg

The Schramberg factory was founded in the early nineteenth century in Schramberg Wuttemberg, Germany. The pieces most commonly seen are those made by Schramberger Majolika Fabrik (SMF) dating from 1912 until 1989.

Pieces are stamped with the pattern name (i.e. Gobelin) and the number of the painter who executed it. The imprinted number identifies the shape. Marks may also include these names: Wheelock, Black Forest, and Mepoco.

Perhaps the most popular examples with collectors are those from the Gobelin line. Such pieces have a gray background with as many as ten other colors used to create that design. For example, Gobelin 3 pieces will be painted with green and orange leaves and yellow eyes along with other colors specific to that design.

Little is known of the designers who worked for Schramberg; however, Eva Zeisel was employed at the factory for nearly two years starting in the fall of 1928. Her duties included design, production, and merchandising. Our advisor is Ralph Winslow; he is listed in the Directory under Missouri

Ashtray, G5 ....45.00
Basket, G5, 4" 50.00
Bowl, ftd, G6, 10½" 61.00
Lamp, G6 ....125.00
Luncheon set, 18-pc 76.00
Planter, Wheelock, G6, 10" 52.00
Plate, country scene 30.00
Tea set, Deco, 23-pc 160.00
Vase, abstract 25.00
Vase, blk & orange, 4¼" 41.00
Vase, country scene, 5" 25.00
Vase, floral, 7¼" 25.00
Vase, G1, 7" 85.00
Vase, G7, 8" 75.00
Vase, w/frog, G5, 4" 75.00

Scouting Collectibles

Boy Scouts

Scouting was founded in England in 1907 by a retired Major General, Lord Robert Baden-Powell. Its purpose is the same today as it was then — to help develop physically strong, mentally alert boys and to teach them basic fundamentals of survival and leadership. The movement soon spread to the United States, and in 1910 a Chicago publisher, William Boyce, set out to establish scouting in America. The first World Scout Jamboree was held in 1911 in England. Baden-Powell was honored as the Chief Scout of the World. In 1926 he was awarded the Silver Buffalo Award in the United States. He was knighted in 1929 for distinguished military service and for his scouting efforts. Baden-Powell died in 1941.

For more information you may contact our advisor, R.J. Sayers, author of *Guide to Scouting Collectibles*, whose address (and ordering information regarding his book) may be found in the Directory under North Carolina. (Correspondence other than book orders requires SASE please.)

Armband, Explorer Emergency Service, red twill, lightning bolt, 1950 ..10.00
Ashtray, Special Philmont Souvenir, w/logo, tin 5.00
Bank, young scout w/hands on waist, metal, slot in bk 75.00
Belt buckle, Nat'l Jamboree, sold at Trading Post, 1989 ....10.00
Belt buckle, 1983 World Jamboree, Max Silber, 1,100 made 50.00
Blotter, 1937 Nat'l Jamboree, NY Council issue, w/section #s 10.00
Book, BS w/the Allies, Maj R Maitland, 167-pg, Saafield, 1915, VG ...5.00
Book, Handbook for Boys, N Rockwell cover, 1945, VG 14.00
Book, Nat'l Jamboree Insigna Checklist, Ellis, 1981 ....6.00
Book, Scoutmaster's Handbook, 512-pg, 1956, VG 6.00
Book, The Merit Badge Chronicle, Hubbard, 1986 ....2.00
Bookends, shape of emblem w/Be Prepared inscr, CI, pr 90.00
Box, BSA emblem on lid, dvtl corners, 12½x8½x2½" 35.00
Box, Official Firemaking Equipment, complete contents, 1950s, 25" L ..40.00
Camera, Official Seneca #3 type, in box 30.00
Canteen, 1970 issue, plastic, w/plastic screw top 4.00
Card, membership; 3-fold, mc scout scene, 1922 ....3.00
Cards, cigarette; scout scenes, Ogdens Tobacco Co, 1911, set of 48 ..150.00
Cards, Scout Gum; 1930s, set of 25 ....50.00
Catalog, equipment; Rockwell cover, 76-pg, 1938, 8½x11" 22.00
Compact, Cub Scout den mother, 1950s, M 20.00
Compass, 1935 issue, blk plastic 11.00
Decal, Historic Trails Award, red border 2.00
Decal, Nat'l Issue Region 1, orig set of 13 ....40.00
Diary, maroon w/gold letters, 266-pg w/gold edges, 1920, EX 85.00

Drum, tin with japanned band, Boy Scout Band, repairs, 12" dia, $150.00.

Figurine, Scoutmaster, 6½" 12.00
First-aid kit, Bauer & Black, rectangular, in khaki case 15.00
Flag, Local Cub Pack, bl wool, pack #s sewn on, 1940 ....12.00
Flint & Steel Fire Starting kit, in pouch 5.00
Game, The Game of Boy Scouts, Parker Bros, 1912, VG 40.00
Handkerchief, scout w/camp scene, sm cotton sq, 1930 ....6.00
Hatchet, Plumb, Voyager, 1970 ....20.00
Medal, God & Country Award, ca 1971, NM 30.00
Mug/stein, 1973 Nat'l Jamboree, w/logo 5.00
Neckerchief, Nat'l Staff, sq w/emblems, 1937 ....50.00
Pamphlet, Fun Around the Campfire, BSA 4.00
Pamphlet, Troop Committee, BSA, 1946 ....2.00
Patch, 1937 World Jamboree in Washington DC, 3" 80.00
Pencil box, mc scene of camp activities, 1930 ....25.00
Pennant, 1963 World Jamboree, bl woven w/logo 15.00
Pin, stick-bk; Strengthen the Arm of Liberty 3.00
Plate, Young Doctor, Rockwell-Gorham, ceramic 45.00
Postcard, Christmas Greetings, Scout Band, mc, 1912 ....6.00
Postcard, The Hero of the Day, scout w/flag, 1920 ....7.00
Postcard, 1947 World Jamboree Official; w/logo 10.00
Poster, Boy Scout Week, Breakthrough for Youth, mc 10.00
Poster, 50th Anniversary, heavy poster brd 10.00
Record, Morse Code Made Easy, 1950, 78-rpm 15.00
Ring, full First Class, sterling 10.00
Ring, 1957 Nat'l Jamboree, souvenir, sterling, w/logo 25.00
Signal set, Official Scout Field, telephone-telegraph, #1091 ....100.00
Tie bar, Nat'l Staff, gold bar, w/logo, clip-on 6.00
Tie holder, laminated wood, w/foldable metal loops, logo 10.00
Wallet, camp craft, leather, sewn, 1940s 7.00
Watch, Official BSA, Daynite, sterling silver, #1379, 1919 ....75.00
Watch, Official BSA, Imperial, #1547, 1941 ....30.00
Watch fob, Offical BSA, Nat'l Councilman, purple & gold, #311 ..300.00
Watch fob, scout w/crossed rifles, 1920 ....45.00
Wood-burning kit, w/wood & cord 20.00

Girl Scouts

Collecting Girl Scout memorabilia is a hobby that is growing nationwide. When Sir Baden-Powell founded the Boy Scout Movement in England, it proved to be too attractive and too well adapted to youth to limit its great opportunities to boys alone. The sister organization, known in England as the Girl Guides, quickly followed and was equally successful. Mrs. Juliette Low, an American visitor to England and a personal friend of the father of scouting, realized the tremendous future of the movement for her own country, and with the active and friendly cooperation of the Baden-Powells, she founded the Girl Guides in America, enrolling the first patrols in Savannah, Georgia, in March 1912. In 1915 National Headquarters were established in Washington, D.C., and the name was changed to Girl Scouts. The first national convention was held in 1914. Each succeeding year has shown growth and increased enthusiasm in this steadily growing army of girls and young women who are learning in the happiest ways to combine patriotism, outdoor activities of every kind, skill in every branch of domestic science, and high standards of community service. Today there are over 400,000 Girl Scouts and more than 22,000 leaders. Mr. Sayers is also our Girl Scout advisor.

Ad, GS & Brownie shoes, 4-panel fold-out, ca 1930-40, 6x13½" ...30.00
Armband, Senior Service Scout 20.00
Badge, GSA Collar emblem, brass, 1918 ....10.00
Badge, Life Saving Cross, cloverleaf type, Maltese cross, 1917 ..150.00
Badge, patrol; Corporal, on bar, khaki twill 15.00
Book, Brownie Scout Mystery, Sterling, Doubleday, 190-pg, 1955, VG .10.00
Book, The Girl Scouts Nature; for leaders 5.00
Bookends, GS emblem, 5¾x5" 40.00
Booklet, info/training tips, dues/achievement record, 1923, VG ..20.00
Bracelet, interlocking silver-tone sq links, GSA emblem, 1930s, 6" .50.00
Calender, 1920 ....100.00
Camera, Kodak Vest Pocket, gr w/blk bellows, 1929-34, w/case, NM ...160.00
Camera, Official Girl Scout Falcon, 1940 ....30.00
Cap, uniform; bl, burlap-like, 1930s, EX 15.00
Card, registration; Brownies, 1921 ....10.00
Catalog, equipment; Spring 1937, 45-pg, 8½x11", EX 30.00
Catalog, uniforms & equipment, Fall 1929, EX 30.00
Compass, jeweled pivot point, brass case, US Gauge Co, 2" dia ..45.00
Cookie cutters, gr hdls, 1950, set 20.00
Cuff links, wht enamel on gold, 1960s, NM 35.00
Diary, gr cover, 1930 ....10.00
Diary, GSA, 1936-37 calender, unused, EX 20.00
Doll, Bluebird Girl Scout, Effanbee, 1965, 8½" 60.00
Doll, uniform; gr shorts, Uneeda, 1960-64, 15" 30.00
Emblem, Girl Scout Hospital Aide 20.00
Flag, Official Brownie; 1930, sm 25.00
Handbook, Official; c 1916, Juliette Low, EX 140.00
Handbook, Official; tan cover, 1920 ....25.00
Magazine, Girl Scout Leader; 1922-30, ea 7.00
Patch, GS Scribe, gr twill, 1933 ....10.00

Patch, Senior Service, orange logo w/orange & wht border, 1943, EX ..35.00
Pin, Brownie, shape like elf, plastic & metal, 1920 ....20.00
Pin, GSA Tenderfoot, 1918-23 ....6.00
Pin, hat; lg GS, 1917 ....30.00
Pin, Mariner's Program, sm anchor guard, 1940 ....15.00
Pin, Wing; 1941 ....35.00
Pin, 50 year commemorative, wht & gr w/gold lettering, 1962 ....20.00
Poster, scout in uniform, 1st issue, 1917 ....75.00
Printer's block, scout w/logo, wood w/metal top, 1⅜x1¾" 30.00
Ring, gold-tone w/gr stone 10.00
Sewing kit, Official; gr w/gold, tin, Boye Needle Co, 4x2½" 35.00
Song book, leader's copy, gr, hardbk, 130-pg, 1929, VG 20.00
Uniform, Official GSA, full dress, w/badges/pins/labels, 1940s, EX ...75.00
Whistle, cylinder; Official GSA, 1920s 20.00

Scrimshaw

The most desirable examples of the art of scrimshaw can be traced back to the first half of the nineteenth century to the heyday of the whaling industry. Some voyages lasted for several years, and conditions on board were often dismal. Sailors filled the long hours by using the tools of their trade to engrave whale teeth and make boxes, pie crimpers (jagging wheels), etc., from the bone and teeth of captured whales. Eskimos also made scrimshaw, sometimes borrowing designs from the sailors who traded with them.

Beware of fraudulent pieces; fakery is prevalent in this field. Many carved teeth are of recent synthetic manufacture (examples engraved with information such as ship's or captain's names, dates, places, etc., should be treated with extreme caution) and have no antique or collectible value. A listing of most of these plastic items has been published by the Kendall Whaling Museum in Sharon, Massachusetts. If you're in doubt or a novice collector, it's best to deal with reputable people who *guarantee* the items they sell. Our advisor for this category is John Rinaldi; he is listed in the Directory under Maine. See also Powder Horns.

Whalebone and walrus tusk double jagging wheel, with three-tined crimper, baleen spacers, nineteenth century, 7¾", $1,850.00.

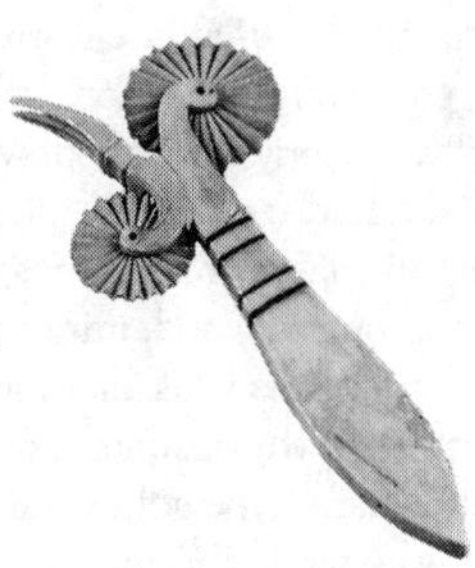

Busk, 6 lg scenes, flowers/tree/ship/horse, well cvd, 13¼" 1,975.00
Cane, 2-pc twist-cvd whalebone shaft, ivory monkey-fist knob, 1850s ..2,650.00
Clock tower, 2 4¾" teeth, tortoise-shell inlay, 19th C, 6x8" ..2,450.00
Crimper, whale ivory, hand & w/extended fingers & thumb, 1840-50, 6" ...3,750.00
Fid, whale bone, EX patina, 11" 190.00
Shoehorn, walrus ivory, Turk's head knot, twist rope shaft, 1860s, 7" 1,790.00
Tooth, Alwilda (lady pirate)/male pirate, red details, 1840s, 7x2¾" ..5,875.00
Tooth, Am eagle/arrows/shield/stars, mc, 1850-60, 5¾x2¾" ..3,200.00
Tooth, couple/flowers/stars/house/flag/etc, att W Hill, ca 1820, 6" ...2,150.00
Tooth, girl in fancy dress, boots & bonnet, 19th C, 5½x2¾" 895.00
Tooth, God Protect Us All, soldier on horsebk/flags/etc, 1860s, 7" ..2,175.00
Tooth, Lady Liberty w/pole & shield, old chip, 19th C, 4½" 695.00
Tooth, lady's portrait/Sarah in leaf border, mc, 19th C, 6½" ..1,295.00
Tooth, Neptune w/King of the Sea motto on flag/ship, 19th C, 5½x2" ...2,175.00
Tooth, port view of Am ship, bk: Am eagle, mc flags, 1840-50, 4⅝" 1,925.00
Tooth, ship portraits (EX cvg), 19th C, w/iron stand, 7¾x2¾" 3,950.00

Sebastians

Sebastian miniatures were first produced in 1938 by Prescott W. Baston in Marblehead, Massachusetts. Since then more than six hundred have been modeled. These figurines have been sold through gift shops all over the country, primarily in the New England states. In 1976 Baston withdrew his Sebastians from production. Under an agreement with the Lance Corporation of Hudson, Massachusetts, one hundred designs were selected to be produced by that company under Baston's supervision. Those remaining were discontinued. In the time since then, the older figurines have become very collectible. Price is determined by three factors: 1) in production/out of production; 2) labels — color of oval label, i.e. red, blue, green, etc.; Marblehead label, a green and silver palette-shaped label used until 1977; or no label; 3) condition. If there is no label and the varnish coat is quite yellowed, then it is considered to be of the Marblehead era. Dates are merely copyright dates and have no particular significance in regard to value. (Signed) 'P.W. Baston' should only have impact on price when the signature is an actual autograph. Most pieces are manufactured with an imprinted 'P.W. Baston' on the base. Baston died in 1984; the miniatures are now being done by P.W. Baston, Jr. Our advisor for this category is Jim Waite; he is listed in the Directory under Illinois.

Adams Academy, w/steeple 100.00
Andrew Jackson 35.00
Becky Thatcher 23.00
Betsy Ross 23.00
Calvary 500.00
Candy Store 80.00
Christmas Morning 30.00
Clown 50.00
Darned Well He Can 275.00
Doctor 75.00
Elizabeth Monroe 65.00
Farmer 35.00
Gathering Tulips 100.00
George Washington w/cannon 35.00
Grocery Store, Marblehead era 65.00
Hanna Dustin, pen stand 300.00
Jack & Jill, bl label 35.00
JF Kennedy 60.00
Little Sister, bl label 40.00
Mrs Obocell 400.00
Old North Church, autographed Woody Baston, bl 45.00
Paul Revere 45.00
Prince Philip 200.00
Ronald Reagan, Young Republican 85.00
Sam Weller 60.00
Shoemaker, gr label 70.00
Skipping Rope 35.00
Son of the Desert 225.00
Swanboat, Masons 200.00
Weaver & Loom, Marblehead era 65.00
White House, gold 100.00

Sevres

Fine-quality porcelains have been made in Sevres, France, since the early 1700s. Rich ground colors were often hand painted with portraits, scenics, and florals. Some pieces were decorated with transfer prints and decalcomania; many were embellished with heavy gold. These wares are the most respected of all French porcelains. Their style and designs have been widely copied, and some of the items listed below are Sevres-type wares.

Bleu Celeste dresser box, couple in floral-framed reserve, scrolling foliate feet, 6x14x9", $1,300.00.

Bowl, exotic birds & flower swags, mk, 18th C, 3¼x8¾" **500.00**
Bowl, floral sprays/cherubs/Louis Philip seal, 4½x11¼" **400.00**
Bowl, landscape reserves on cobalt w/gold, gilt-bronze mts, 7" ..**635.00**
Bowl, 18th-C courting scene, floral rim/scrolls, ca 1900, 13" **925.00**
Bust, Napoleon (youthful) on plinth, 9" **440.00**
Candelabra, Cupid figural, floral base, gilt-bronze mts, 16", pr ...**1,150.00**
Chandelier, gilt-bronze, pnt porc reserves, 22" dia **1,265.00**
Charger, Napoleon on horsebk, gilt rococo border, 1804, 12" ..**1,195.00**
Cup, Roi De Rome portrait, burgundy & gold decor, 1804-14, mk **660.00**
Sweetmeat dish, cobalt bands & gold, navette shape, 1804-14, 10½" ..**395.00**
Tazza, Mme Lefevre portrait w/cobalt & gold, 5½x8½" dia **350.00**
Urn, lady in garden, ornate ormolu mts w/champleve enamel, 9" ...**250.00**
Urn, maid/cherub in garden, sgn Roche, ormolu mts, 11" **400.00**
Urn, Nouveau lady's portrait amid flowers, bronze mts, mk, w/lid, 26" ..**8,000.00**
Vase, bud; lady in garden, sgn Carree, ormolu/champleve std, 7" **125.00**
Vase, continuous garden scene, foliate hdls, mtd as lamp, 22" ...**2,185.00**
Vase, Europa, sgn Hendrik van Balen, 10¼" **385.00**
Vase, floral reserves on pk w/gold, mtd as lamp, 11", pr **1,725.00**
Vase, thistle, mc on wht, classic form, 1907, 9¼x4¾" **1,600.00**
Vase, turq & gr crystalline, bottle shape, 1902, 5¼x3" **850.00**
Vase, Venus, sgn Angelica Kaufmann, 10¼" **385.00**

Sewer Tile

Whimsies, advertising novelties, and other ornamental items were sometimes made in potteries where the primary product was simply tile.

Ashtray, lion head at side, Carl Vera, 4x5" **120.00**
Bank, pig form, hand molded, incised details, gr-amber, 9" **600.00**
Figurine, Basset hound, hand molded, incised details, 14" **1,500.00**
Figurine, cowboy boot, 4½" **25.00**
Figurine, dog, free-standing front legs, tooling, dk pnt, rpr, 12" ..**1,300.00**
Figurine, dog, seated, free-standing front legs, hand tooling, 10" ...**275.00**
Figurine, dog, seated, Super Clay...OH/Walter Smith, 12½" **330.00**
Figurine, lion, molded w/hand detail, OH 7-16-52, 8½" **220.00**
Figurine, lion on rectangular base, tooled detail, 6¼x9¼" **385.00**
Figurine, squirrel w/nut, 6" **215.00**
Lamp base, owl figural, hollow w/open top, 17" **600.00**
Lamp base, tree-trunk form, OH, 14" **495.00**
Pitcher, tooled bark, face on spout, Stasser, 6½" **150.00**
Pitcher, tooled tree bark w/knots, 7¾" **120.00**
Planter, tree stump w/vines, open bottom, chips, 17½" **250.00**
Vase, tree trunk, cvd sides, 2¾x5¼" **50.00**

Sewing Items

Sewing collectibles continue to intrigue collectors, and fine nineteenth-century and earlier pieces are commanding higher prices due to increased demand and scarcity. Complete needlework boxes and chatelaines in original condition are rare, but even incomplete examples can be considered prime additions to any collection, as long as they meet certain criteria: boxes should contain fittings of the period; the chains of the chatelaine should be intact and contemporary with the style; and the individual holders should be original and match the brooch. As nineteenth-century items become harder to find, new trends in collecting develop. Needle books, many of which were decorated with horses, children, beautiful ladies, etc., have become very popular. Some were giveaways printed with advertisements of products and businesses. Even early pins are collectible; the first ones were made in two parts with the round head attached separately. Pin disks, pin cubes, and other pin holders also make interesting additions to a sewing collection.

Tape measures are very popular — especially Victorian figurals. These command premium prices. Early wooden examples of transferware and Tunbridge ware have gained in popularity, as have figurals of vegetable ivory, celluloid, and other early plastics. From the twentieth century, tatting shuttles made of plastics, bone, brass, sterling, and wood decorated with Art Nouveau, Art Deco, and more modern designs are in demand — so are darning eggs, stilettos, and thimbles. Because of the decline in the popularity of needlework after the 1920s (due to increased production of machine-made items), novelty items were made in an attempt to regain consumer interest, and many collectors today also find these appealing.

Watch for reproductions. Sterling thimbles are being made in Holland and the U.S. and are available in many Victorian-era designs. But the originals are usually plainly marked, either in the inside apex or outside on the band. Avoid testing gold and silver thimbles for content; this often destroys the inside marks. Instead, research the manufacturer's mark; this will often denote the material as well. Even though the reproductions are well finished, they do not have manufacturers' marks. Many thimbles are being made specifically for the collectible market; reproductions of porcelain thimbles are also found. Prices should reflect the age and availability of these thimbles. Our advisor for this category is Kathy Goldsworthy; she is listed in the Directory under Washington.

Button, gray MOP w/fine lustre, 1¾" **4.00**
Caddy, grpt, cvd/galleried top, 16 spool holders, drw, 1800s, 8x8x6" ...**230.00**
Caddy, thread: orig worn gr pnt w/yel striping, metal rods, 13" L **350.00**
Caddy, walnut, trn details, spire finial, varnish, 9x8½" **260.00**
Darner, blk glass w/red & yel splotches, 7½" **160.00**
Darner, ebonized wood, minor pnt loss, 6¼" **15.00**
Darner, milk glass w/dk maroon splotches cased in clear, 6" **130.00**
Darner, pk to wht opaque, sheared end, 5⅝" **125.00**
Darner, Tiffany-type gold w/rainbow colorations in glass, 7⅜" **80.00**
Darner, wooden egg form, unscrews for thread (gone) & thimble ..**35.00**
Darner, wooden wheel w/clip holder, convex top & bottom, 1900s, 4" ..**17.50**
Dress form, adjustable, w/iron claw-ft base, 60" **70.00**
Dress form, cloth-covered form on CI base, Wolf...1939, 61" **190.00**
Dress form, formed cb, brass neck, full body, 60" **45.00**
Magazine, Needlecraft, July 1921, EX **14.00**
Measure, advertising General Electric Refrigerators, 1920s **40.00**
Measure, celluloid, basket of flowers **110.00**
Measure, ceramic, lion, HP, Ries, w/scissors, 6" **30.00**
Needle book, Crystal White Laundry Soap, 1916-17 calendar, VG ..**12.50**
Needle book, Lady Betty, w/needle threader & many needles, EX .**7.00**
Needle book, Liberty, w/West Germany needles, G **8.50**
Needle book, Old Safeway, Cragmont soft drinks ad, VG **7.00**
Needle book, Rose, Made in West Germany for Stanley Home Products, M ...**13.50**
Needle book, S&H Green Stamps, Queen Victoria...Needles, Germany **7.50**
Needle book, Sweetheart, missing threader & some needles, MIJ ..**6.00**
Needle box, Sewing Susan, gold-eye needles, w/threader, NM **5.00**
Needle case, wooden, Boye, Pat Jan 26, '28, EX **3.00**

Needle holder, trn, sponge pnt, ftd, ball finial, 4½x1½" 400.00
Needle threader, Singer, w/instructions, 1926-27, EX in worn pkg ...10.00
Oil can, brass, long tube w/slanted tip, Japan 7.50
Oil can, Singer, red/wht/bl, 5¼", EX 15.00
Pattern, Advance, sheath silhouette dress, 1950s 7.00
Pattern, Du Barry Perfect..., lady's housecoat, 1942, EX in pkg 12.50
Pattern, McCall's, slim 3-gore skirt, 1959, M 5.00
Pincushion, ceramic, nodder poodle w/jewel eyes, Florenza, 3¼" ..60.00
Pincushion, pine, cvd shoe w/tack eyelets, cushion top, 20th C, 5" 65.00
Pincushion, porc, figure stands by basket cushion, Occupied Japan, 3" ..40.00
Pincushion, silver, bear figural, jtd 150.00
Pincushion, velvet, cat on pillow, glass eyes, 4½" 220.00
Scissors, buttonhole cutting 15.00
Scissors, pinking, hand-operated wheel, steel 45.00
Spool, wood w/bone ends, ca 1900, 1⅜" 35.00
Thimble, bone china, HP cottage scene, Royal Worcester 30.00
Thimble, cloisonne bird scene, unmk 12.50
Thimble, Jasperware, bl, lady in bed by spinning wheel, Wedgwood ..30.00
Thimble, Mason's Ironstone, HP floral 15.00
Thimble, porc, Simm's Roasted Coffee, att MSR Imports, 1982 ....7.50
Thimble, porc, tiger cub, Lenox Endangered Species series 15.00
Thimble, porc w/HP floral, Caversall England 15.00
Tracing wheel, Bakelite, Dritz, EX 12.50

Sewing Machines

The fact that Thomas Saint, an English cabinetmaker, invented the first sewing machine in 1790 was unknown until 1874 when Newton Wilson, an English sewing machine manufacturer and patentee, chanced upon the drawings included in a patent specification describing methods of making boots and shoes. By the middle of the nineteenth century, several patents were granted to American inventors, among them Isaac M. Singer, whose machine used a treadle. These machines were ruggedly built, usually of cast iron. By the 1860s and 1870s, the sewing machine had become a popular commodity, and the ironwork became more detailed and ornate.

Though rare machines are costly, many of the old oak treadle machines (especially these brands: Davis, Home, Household, National, New Home, Singer, Weed, Wheeler & Wilson, and Willcox & Gibbs) have only nominal value. Machines manufactured after 1875 are generally very common as most were mass produced. Values for these later sewing machines range from $50.00 to $100.00. Refer to *Toy and Miniature Sewing Machines (Books I* and *II)* by Glenda Thomas for more information. Our advisor for this category is Peter Frei; he is listed in the Directory under Massachusetts. In the listings that follow, unless noted otherwise, values are suggested for machines in excellent working order.

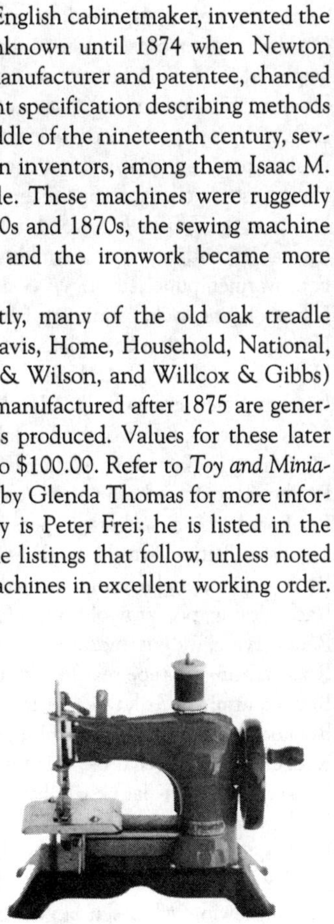

Child's, Little Princess Sewing Machine, Hoge Mfg. Co. NY, all metal, ca 1937, 7x4¼x8¾", $185.00. (Photo courtesy Glenda Thomas)

Child's, Betsy Ross, 1949 ....100.00
Child's, Casige Our Pet, sheet metal, pre WWII 135.00
Child's, Cornet, heavy metal, wht rabbit in circle, 9" 170.00
Child's, FW Muller #12, CI 225.00
Child's, Gateway, red-pnt lightweight steel 50.00
Child's, Holly Hobbie, manual or battery-op, 1977-82 ....25.00
Child's, KAYanEE Sew Master, hand-op, wood base 50.00
Child's, Little Mary Mix Up, sheet metal, 1930s 75.00
Child's, Little Modiste, red metal, battery-op, Japan 75.00
Child's, Little Mother, Artcraft, 1940s 85.00
Child's, Muller #19, CI, floral trim, pre WWII 225.00
Child's, Olympia, manual or battery-op, Japan 35.00
Child's, Peerless Automatic, CI 495.00
Child's, Princess, belt drive, Japan 175.00
Child's, Sew-n-Play, plastic, manual or battery-op 25.00
Eldredge Automatic, 1880s, complete, EX 145.00
Florence, CI, belt driven, Pat Nov 12, 1850, fancy stand, EX 750.00
Florence, CI, belt driven, Pat Nov 12, 1850, plain stand, EX 260.00
General Electric Featherweight, gr, 1949, EX 40.00
Goodrich, treadle, quarter-sawn oak cabinet, EX 195.00
New Home, Orange MA, 1903, EX 185.00
Singer Featherweight Convertible Model 222K, w/accessories & case, NM .1,300.00
Singer Featherweight Model 221, blk case, NM 385.00
Singer Portable #3, hand-crank, dome case, 1898, NM 150.00
Wheeler & Wilson, 625 Broadway, EX 200.00
Willcox & Gibbs, early, sm 200.00

Shaker Items

The Shaker community was founded in America in 1776 at Niskeyuna, New York, by a small group of English 'Shaking Quakers.' The name referred to a group dance which was part of their religious rites. Their leader was Mother Ann Lee. By 1815 their membership had grown to more than one thousand in eighteen communities as far west as Indiana and Kentucky. But in less than a decade, their numbers began to decline until today only a handful remain. Their furniture is prized for its originality, simplicity, workmanship, and practicality. Few pieces were signed. Some were carefully finished to enhance the natural wood; a few were painted.

Although other methods were used earlier, most Shaker boxes were of oval construction with overlapping 'fingers' at the seams to prevent buckling as the wood aged. Boxes with original paint fetch triple the price of an unpainted box; number of fingers and overall size should also be considered.

Although the Shakers were responsible for weaving a great number of baskets, their methods are not easily distinguished from those of their outside neighbors, and it is nearly impossible without first-hand knowledge to positively attribute a specific example to their manufacture. They were involved in various commercial efforts other than woodworking — among them sheep and dairy farming, sawmilling, and pipe and brick making. They were the first to raise crops specifically for seed and to market their product commercially. They perfected a method to recycle paper and were able to produce wrinkle-free fabrics. Our advisor for this category is Nancy Winston; she is listed in the Directory under New Hampshire. Standard two-letter state abbreviations have been used throughout the following listings.

Key:

bj — bootjack	PH — Pleasant Hill
CB — Canterbury	ML — Mt. Lebanon
EF — Enfield	SDL — Sabbathday Lake
NL — New Lebanon	WV — Watervliet

Apple peeler & slicer w/floor stand, minor damage, 34" 220.00
Basket, sewing; 3-finger, stain lined, old rfn, 4¼x12x8½" 460.00
Bed, maple/pine w/salmon wash, trn posts, NL, 36x81x36", EX 3,000.00
Blanket, natural wool w/bl & brn edge, machine-sewn binding, 74" sq .100.00
Bonnet, woven poplar splint w/blk & beige ribbons, #5 label, 9½" 250.00

Box, bentwood, copper tacks, swivel hdl, old varnish, 7x14" 300.00
Box, blanket; dvtl cherry, 2 short drws, ML, ca 1840, 26x44x17" ...1,400.00
Box, finger, steel tacks, old gr rpt, MA, 6⅝" 715.00
Box, interlocking wooden bands, copper tacks, 12½" dia, VG ..220.00
Box, knife; walnut, shaped divider, worn finish, 4½x15x10" 100.00
Box, lapped seams, steel tacks, gray rpt, 10½" dia 275.00
Box, pine w/orig gr pnt, dvtl, NH, rprs, 11x20x12" 715.00
Box, red stain, steel tacks, age cracks in lid, 8½x15" 220.00
Box, seed; orig finish, paper label: Shaker's...ML NY, 3x24x12" ..1,200.00
Box, seed; pine & poplar w/OH stencil, incomplete hinges, 4x27x11" 770.00
Box, sewing; cherry/curly maple/mahog, drw, 2-tier, 6", EX 250.00
Box, sewing; cherry/maple/walnut, tiered, cushion finial, 6¾" ...250.00
Box, sewing; lapped seams, copper tacks, swivel hdl, rfn, 7" 185.00
Box, sewing; mahog & maple, 2-tier, pincushion finial, 1900s, 7" ..230.00
Box, sewing; 4-finger, copper tacks, old varnish, sm rpr, 8¼" 400.00
Box, sewing; 5-finger, copper tacks, cushion top, ML, 11½" 880.00
Box, 3-finger, copper tacks, old varnish, 6" 385.00
Box, 3-finger, copper tacks, old wht rpt over gray, 12", EX 495.00
Box, 3-finger, copper tacks, red stain, 6¼" 700.00
Box, 3-finger, copper tacks, worn bl-gr pnt over lt bl, 7¼" 715.00
Box, 3-finger, pincushion lid, old varnish, CB, 3¾" 1,000.00
Box, 4-finger, copper tacks, old gr pnt, SDL, 10¾" 2,000.00
Box, 4-finger, copper tacks, old natural patina, CB, 5½" 440.00
Box, 4-finger, copper tacks, old red rpt, 12¼" 1,000.00
Box, 4-finger, copper tacks, old yel pnt, 8¾" 800.00
Box, 4-finger, copper tacks, worn bl pnt, SDL, 10¾" 1,500.00
Box, 4-finger, copper tacks, worn lt bl pnt, 11¾" 2,950.00
Box, 4-finger, copper/steel tacks, red stain, SDL, 10½" 800.00
Box, 4-finger (left-hand), copper tacks, EX dk patina, 9" 525.00
Box, 5-finger, copper tacks, dtd 1784 on top, old varnish, 13" ...500.00
Box, 5-finger, copper tacks, old red, EF, 11½" 800.00
Broom, cobweb; incomplete stitching, wear, OH, 94" 150.00
Brush, hearth; worn finish, blk bristles incomplete, 22" 72.00
Buck saw, old patina, OH, 26" 330.00
Bucket, staved, old bl w/blk on metal bands, w/lid, 11" 700.00
Bucket, staved, old gray pnt, metal bands, wire bail, 12x14" 165.00
Bucket, staved, old yel pnt, steel bands, 13x12", EX 200.00
Cabinet, cloak; walnut, paneled doors, shelves, rprs/rfn, OH, 77" ..2,750.00

Cabinet, painted pine and poplar, paneled doors, one interior shelf, two drawers with turned pulls, original red wash, wall hanging, Mt. Lebanon or Watervliet, New York, 1835 – 45, 23½x16x7", EX, $3,225.00.

Candlestand, cherry w/old dk red, tripod base, 1-brd top, ML .3,000.00
Carpet, mc rags, PA, unused, 39x506" 330.00
Carrier, chip; pine w/tin corner braces, dvtl, worn finish, 7x19x12" ..330.00
Carrier, chip; poplar, bentwood hdl (split), dvtl, 9x16x10" 250.00
Carrier, sewing; 4-finger, copper tacks, orig varnish, 3x9x6¼" ...240.00
Carrier, 3-finger, swivel hdl, old varnish, 12" 230.00
Carry-all, walnut, 6 compartments/divider, old dk finish, OH, 15" L ..440.00
Case, leather, satin-lined, spools/scissors, busk, rolls up, 7" 250.00
Case, sewing; blk leather w/purple knit binding, ribbon tie, 7½" .60.00
Case of drws, dvtl, 8-drw, old mellow finish, 16x25x9½" 1,375.00
Chair, dining; 2-slat bk, woven splint seat, rfn, OH, 28" 825.00
Chair, revolving, maple w/pine seat, CI swivel, NL, 1860s, 30" 6,300.00
Chair, side; #3, 3-slat bk, orig tape seat, ML, 34" 385.00
Chair, side; 3 arched slats, cloth seat, trn legs, rfn, EF, 41" 700.00
Chair, side; 3-slat bk, rpl cane seat, dk varnish, 39" 440.00
Chair, side; 3-slat bk, tape seat, CB, 41" 1,300.00
Chair, side; 3-slat bk, tilters on bk legs, rprs, 39" 715.00
Chair, side; 3-slat bk, trn finials, rpl tape seat, ML, 41" 770.00
Cheese ladder, old patina & worn wht pnt, 25" 575.00
Chest, blanket; poplar w/old grpt & stencil, PA, 1857, 39x47x21" ..3,000.00
Chest, blanket; walnut, dvtl, varnished, rprs, OH, 22x39x18" ..1,100.00
Chest, cherry, 6-brd, old pnt, PH, 24x46x17" 575.00
Chest, tool; cherry dvtl case, 9 drws, old varnish, rprs, OH, 24" ...1,100.00
Chest, walnut, 2 short:3 graduated drws, rfn, OH, 50x40x24" ...1,650.00
Cloak, bl wool, minor moth damage/soiling, child sz, 25" 465.00
Coffeepot, tin, side spout, pewter finial, att, 12" 100.00
Colander, cheese; tin w/rim hdls, sm split, 22" dia 75.00
Cradle, butternut & poplar, old red, 36" 440.00
Crutches, oak & ash, late 1800s, EX 300.00
Cupboard, chimney; pine w/old wht rpt over orig orange, EF, 87x21" ...5,280.00
Cupboard, cloak; walnut, dbl doors, paneled base, att, 77x47" ..935.00
Cupboard, pine, paneled doors in reeded frs, dvtl, rfn, 20x48x12" ..990.00
Cupboard, poplar, 4-pane door, rprs/rpl hinges, hangs, 26x22" ..385.00
Cupboard, walnut, paneled doors, scalloped apron, 1-pc, OH, 87x50" 4,000.00
Cupboard chest, pine, 3 doors over 6 graduated drws, rfn, CB, 72" ..17,600.00
Darner, cvd/trn wood, EX patina, 6" 60.00
Desk, curly maple, panel door/compartments/drop front/door, 55x24" ..20,000.00
Desk, lap; pine/poplar/walnut, drw for inkwell, hinged lid 935.00
Desk, trustee's, cherry, compartmented int, 1-drw, 1830s, 51x31" ...2,500.00
Dustpan, floor; tin w/trn wood hdl, 34½" L 300.00
Egg carrier, bird's-eye maple w/old patina, wire fasteners, EF, 13" 500.00
Foot warmer, punched tin w/wood, EF, 11" 795.00
Footstool, pine w/old patina, orig fabric cover, wire nails, 9x14x10" ...195.00
Hanger, cloak; pine & poplar, MA, 37" 195.00
Hanger, dbl; cherry, ML, 15½" 300.00
Jug, brn-glazed stoneware, Corbett's Shakers' Syrup..., 1890s, 7" ..115.00
Measure, grain; bentwood, SDL label, 7½", EX 160.00
Measuring stick, walnut w/old patina, 39" 165.00
Peg board, pine & hardwood w/old yel pnt, 6-peg, 101" 770.00
Peg board, poplar w/7 maple pegs, old natural patina, 46" 220.00
Pie basket, lattice, swivel hdls/plywood bottom, shelf removes, 16" ...465.00
Rack, drying; poplar w/old red, ladder-style w/X fr, 43x30x16" ..350.00
Rack, drying; poplar w/old rpt, 3 folding sections, ea: 35x56" 200.00
Rack, drying; walnut, mortised, shoe ft, old finish, rpl ft, 39x28" ...165.00
Rocker, arm; #0, tape seat/bk, trn posts/finials, ML, 24" 2,000.00
Rocker, arm; #0, 3-slat bk, rpl tape seat, rprs/rfn, 23" 600.00
Rocker, arm; #1, shawl bar, rpl tape seat, rfn/rprs, 27½" 650.00
Rocker, arm; #1, 3-slat bk, orig tape seat (worn), 29" 798.00
Rocker, arm; #6, 4-slat bk w/rpl shawl bar, old dk finish, ML, 40" ..450.00
Rocker, arm; #7, rpl tape seat/bk, trn posts, rfn, 41" 300.00
Rocker, arm; #7, 4-slat, worn rpt down to orig finish, ML, 40" ..825.00
Rocker, arm; 4-slat bk, orig seat, EF, 45x15½" 3,750.00
Rocker, sewing; #3, 3-slat bk, trn finials, rpl tape seat, ML, 34" .600.00
Rocker, sewing; #4, tape seat, old dk finish, ML label, 35" 500.00
Rug, mc rags w/bl border, 34x20" 385.00
Rug, mc rags; buggy robe binding, sewn rpr, 53x33" 140.00
Rug, shaped braid, 3 rnd attached centers form scallop, 57x36" 200.00
Scarf, sister's, bl/wht homespun w/woven border pattern, 29x30" ..300.00
Shawl, gray & wht wool w/fringe, shoulder fitted, SDL, 24" L 95.00
Shawl, plaid wool w/fringe, CB, 36x74" 65.00

Shelves, walnut, 4-tier, trn posts, rprs/rfn, att, 20x24" **495.00**
Sieve, bentwood w/woven horsehair, att PH, 9" **200.00**
Stand, cherry, curved shoe ft, mid shelf, 1 dvtl drw, att, 25x18x9" .**880.00**
Stand, cherry, dvtl drw, 2-brd top, old varnish, rpr, 27x19x19" ..**400.00**
Stand, cherry Hplwht, dvtl drw, 2-brd top, ML, rprs, 17" sq **550.00**
Stool, cricket; orig dk finish, traces of label, ML, 7x11x12" **200.00**
Stool, pine/ash/maple/iron, revolves, NL, 1860s, 17x15" **1,150.00**
Stool/armrest, birch w/old red, shaped ends/cut-out ft, dvtl top, 14" ...**1,250.00**
Swift, maple & birch w/yel wash, MA, 1850s, 25x29" dia, EX ..**400.00**
Table, cherry Hplwht w/old red & poplar top, drw, OH, 39" ..**1,100.00**
Table, harvest; walnut, sq tapered legs, 2-brd top, apron, OH, 77" ...**2,500.00**
Table, poplar cleaned to pnt traces, 3-brd top, trn legs, OH, 61" **2,200.00**
Table, tilt-top; maple, tripod base w/snake ft, rfn, WV, 36" dia **2,300.00**
Table, walnut Country Hplwht, dvtl drw, 1-brd top, OH, 37" ...**770.00**
Washstand, cherry, dvtl drw in bottom shelf, breadbrd top, 29" **440.00**
Washtub, bl & ivory pnt, iron staves, pierced hdls, 28x20" **3,680.00**

Shaving Mugs

Between 1865 and 1920, owning a personalized shaving mug was the order of the day, and the 'occupationals' were the most prestigious. The majority of men having occupational mugs would often frequent the barber shop several times a week, where their mugs were clearly visible for all to see in the barber's rack. As a matter of fact, this display was in many ways the index of the individual town or neighborhood.

During the first twenty years, blank mugs were almost entirely imported from France, Germany, and Austria and were hand painted in this country. Later on, some china was produced by local companies. It is noteworthy that American vitreous china is inferior to the imported Limoges and is subject to extreme crazing.

Artists employed by the American barber supply companies were for the most part extremely talented and capable of executing any design the owner required, depicting his occupation, fraternal affiliation, or preferred sport. When the mug was completed, the name and the gold trim were always added in varying degrees, depending on the price paid by the customer. This price was determined by the barber who added his markup to that of the barber-supply company. As mentioned above, the popularity of the occupational shaving mug diminished with the advent of World War I and the introduction by Gillette of the safety razor. Later followed the blue laws forcing barber shops to close on Sundays, thereby eliminating the political and social discussions for which they were so well noted.

Occupational shaving mugs are the most sought after of the group which would also include those with sport affiliations. Fraternal mugs, although desirable, do not command the same price as the occupationals. Occasionally, you will find the owner's occupation together with his fraternal affiliation. This combination could add anywhere between 25% to 50% to the price, which is dependent on the execution of the painting, rarity of the subject, and detail. Some subjects can be done very simply; others can be done in extreme detail, commanding substantially higher prices. It is fair to say, however, that the rarity of the occupation will dictate the price. Mugs with heavily worn gold lose between 20% and 30% of their value immediately. This would not apply to the gold trim around the rim, but to the loss of the name itself. Our advisor for this category is Burton Handelsman; he is listed in the Directory under New York.

Character, Black face w/red hat, Bavaria, 3¾" **400.00**
Character, dog, Bavaria, 3½" **200.00**
Character, monkey, Bavaria, 3½", NM **200.00**
Character, Oriental man, Bavaria, 3¾", NM **200.00**
Character, skull, Bavaria, 3½" **185.00**
Decorative, urn w/vines, MIG, 3¼" **110.00**
Fraternal, FCB in triangle, T&V Limoges, 3½" **110.00**

Occupational, blacksmith shoeing horse, name at top, T&V Limoges France, 1885–1925, M, $300.00.

Occupational, butcher, steer's head, Limoges France, 3¾", EX ..**140.00**
Occupational, butcher at block cutting meat, 3⅝" **325.00**
Occupational, carpenter's tools, name in gold, V&D Austria **210.00**
Occupational, farmer plowing his field, 3½" **230.00**
Occupational, horse running in field, 3⅝" **100.00**
Occupational, horse-drawn wagon w/bbls, MIG, 3¼" **475.00**
Occupational, ice wagon delivery man, T&V Limoges, NM **500.00**
Occupational, jockey on running horse, T&V Limoges France, 3⅝" ...**400.00**
Occupational, livery stable, gold name, 3½", NM **300.00**
Occupational, locomotive & tender, T&V Limoges **140.00**
Occupational, lumberjack, w/gold, Vienna Austria, 3½", $700 to ..**1,000.00**
Occupational, machine lathe operator, rpr, 3½" **350.00**
Occupational, man driving stake-body Mack truck, 3⅝" **2,600.00**
Occupational, man driving touring car, maroon wrap, Germany, 4" ...**1,150.00**
Occupational, metal worker, 3½" **250.00**
Occupational, miner's tools, Germany, 3⅞", $300 to **400.00**
Occupational, sheared sheep, 3¾", $250 to **350.00**
Occupational, steer, (full body) name in gold, flower sprigs, 3½", $250 to ...**350.00**
Occupational, violin w/bow, name in gold, T&V Limoges, 3⅝" **130.00**
Occupational, 2 bucking goats, name in gold, minor pnt rstr, 3⅜" ..**160.00**
Patriotic, eagle w/Xd Am flags, 4" **250.00**
Sportsman's, 2 hunting dogs on point, 3¾" **150.00**

Shawnee

The Shawnee Pottery Company operated in Zanesville, Ohio, from 1937 to 1961. They produced inexpensive novelty ware (vases, flowerpots, and figurines) as well as a very successful line of figural cookie jars, creamers, and salt and pepper shakers.

They also produced three dinnerware lines, the first of which, Valencia, was designed by Louise Bauer in 1937 for Sears & Roebuck. A starter set was given away with the purchase of one of their refrigerators. Second and most popular was the Corn line. The original design was called White Corn. In 1946 the line was expanded and the color changed to a more natural yellow hue. It was marketed under the name Corn King, and it was produced from 1946 to 1954. Then the colors were changed again. Kernels became a lighter yellow and shucks a darker green. This variation was called Corn Queen. Their third dinnerware line, produced after 1954, was called Lobsterware. It was made in either black, brown, or gray; lobsters were usually applied to serving pieces and accessory items.

For further study we recommend these books: *The Collector's Guide to Shawnee Pottery* by Janice and Duane Vanderbilt, who are listed in the Directory under Indiana; and *Shawnee Pottery, An Identification and Value Guide*, by Jim and Bev Mangus, who are listed in Ohio.

Cookie Jars

Note: The prices in the following listings should be considered minimum values.

Basketweave, bl w/floral decals, gold trim, mk USA **175.00**

Basketweave, hexagon, yel or bl, mk USA 70.00
Bean pot, Snowflake, yel, bl or gr, mk USA 70.00
Dutch Boy (Jack), bl pants w/patches, gold trim, mk USA 525.00
Dutch Boy (Jack), wht pnts w/decals, gold trim, mk USA 385.00
Dutch Girl (Jill), bl & wht dress w/tulips, decals & gold, mk USA 455.00
Dutch Girl (Jill), cream dress, decals, gold trim, mk USA 385.00
Dutch Girl (Jill), gr dress, mk Great Northern #1026, from $425 to 475.00
Fruit Basket, mc, mk Shawnee #84, from $175 to 225.00

Jill (name Cooky in gold), blue and white dress with gold flowers and trim, marked USA, minimum value $400.00. (Photo courtesy Ermagene Westfall)

Jo Jo the Clown, gold trim, mk Shawnee #12 ....500.00
Jug, bl w/cold pnt flowers, mk USA 105.00
Little Chef, wht, yel or bl, mk USA 105.00
Muggsy, no decals, gold trim, mk Pat Muggsy USA 910.00
Puss'n Boots, decals, gold trim, mk Pat Puss'n Boots, from $575 to 625.00
Puss'n Boots, short tail, mk Pat Puss'n Boots 215.00
Sitting Elephant, cold pnt, mk USA, from $100 to 125.00
Smiley the Pig, gold & decals, mk USA 460.00
Smiley the Pig, plums on chest, mk USA 560.00
Smiley the Pig, strawberries on chest, gold trim, mk USA 700.00
Smiley the Pig, tulips on chest, gold trim, mk USA, $475 to 525.00
Winnie the Pig, apples, gold trim, mk USA 910.00
Winnie the Pig, red collar, gold trim, mk USA 595.00

Corn Line

Bowl, cereal; King or Queen, mk #94 ....55.00
Bowl, fruit; King or Queen, mk #92 ....48.00
Bowl, vegetable; King or Queen, mk #95 ....42.00
Bowl mixing; King or Queen, mk #8, 8" 42.00
Butter dish, King or Queen, w/lid, mk #72 ....60.00
Casserole, King, mk #74 ....45.00
Casserole, King or Queen, mk #73 ....60.00
Casserole, Queen, mk #74 ....48.00
Cookie jar, mk #66, from $260 to 300.00
Corn roast set, Queen, #108 ....165.00
Creamer, King, w/gold, mk #70 ....95.00
Creamer, King or Queen, mk #70 ....30.00
Creamer, White, mk USA 32.00
Cup, King or Queen, mk #69 ....35.00
Mug, King or Queen, mk #90 ....55.00
Pitcher, King or Queen, mk #71 ....80.00
Pitcher, White, mk USA 85.00
Pitcher, White, w/gold, mk USA 120.00
Popcorn set, Queen, mk #100 ....275.00
Relish, King or Queen, mk #79 ....20.00
Shakers, King Indian, pr 80.00
Shakers, King or Queen, lg, pr 30.00
Shakers, King or Queen, sm, pr 20.00
Shakers, White, lg, pr 35.00
Shakers, White, w/gold, sm 42.00
Sugar bowl, White, w/lid 35.00
Sugar shaker, White 70.00
Sugar shaker, White, w/gold 110.00
Table set, Queen, mk #102 ....55.00
Teapot, King or Queen, mk #65, 10-oz 210.00
Teapot, King or Queen, mk #75, 30-oz 85.00
Teapot, White, gold trim, mk USA, 30-oz 145.00
Town & country snack set, King, mk #101 ....275.00

Kitchenware

Bowl, mixing; w/Medallion lid, mk Kenwood #940 ....48.00
Bowl, nesting; Snowflake, mk USA, 5" 15.00
Bowl, nesting; Snowflake, mk USA, 7" 20.00
Bowl, pig; mk USA 100.00
Casserole, fruit, mk Shawnee #83 ....85.00
Coffeepot, Sunflower, mk USA 270.00
Creamer, elephant, gold trim, mk Pat USA 210.00
Creamer, Puss'n Boots, cream, mk Pat Puss'n Boots 55.00
Creamer, Puss'n Boots, decals, gold trim, mk Pat Puss'n Boots 360.00
Creamer, Smiley, bl & yel, gold trim, mk Shawnee #86 ....195.00
Creamer, Smiley, clover bud, mk Pat Smiley 100.00
Creamer, Smiley, peach flower, mk Pat Smiley 60.00
Creamer, tilt; yel, mk USA #10 ....50.00
Fondue pot, Sundial, turq, w/stand & candle cup, mk #902, med 48.00
Jar, utility; basketweave, bl, mk USA 115.00
Jug, ball; Pennsylvania Dutch, mk USA #12 ....95.00
Jug, ball; Quill, mk USA #12 ....135.00
Jug, Fernware, octagon shape, mk USA 60.00
Pitcher, Bo Peep, bl or lav bonnet, mk Pat Bo Peep 110.00
Pitcher, Bo Peep, decals &/or gold trim, mk Pat Bo Peep 300.00
Pitcher, Bo Peep, gold trim, mk Shawnee #47, sm 240.00
Pitcher, Bo Peep, mk Shawnee #47, sm 95.00
Pitcher, Boy Blue, gold trim, mk Shawnee #46 ....240.00
Pitcher, Boy Blue, mk Shawnee #46 ....115.00
Pitcher, Charlie Chicken, decals &/or gold trim, mk Chanticleer 360.00
Pitcher, Charlie Chicken, plain, mk Pat Chanticleer 90.00
Pitcher, fruit, mk Shawnee #80 ....90.00
Pitcher, Smiley, clover bud on side, mk Pat Smiley USA 225.00
Pitcher, Smiley, peach flowers on chest, mk Pat Smiley 160.00
Pitcher, Smiley, red flower on chest, gold trim, mk Pat Smiley 345.00
Pitcher, sunflower, mk USA 95.00
Salt box, Fernware, mk USA 95.00

Shakers, Dutch Boy and Girl, large, $75.00 for the pair.

Shakers, Charlie Chickens, plain, lg, pr 36.00
Shakers, Charlie Chickens, plain, sm, pr 25.00
Shakers, Dutch Boy & Girl, Great Northern, lg, pr 330.00
Shakers, fruit, gold trim, mk USA, lg, pr 36.00
Shakers, fruit, gold trim, sm, pr 50.00
Shakers, jugs, bl, lg, pr 36.00
Shakers, milk cans, plain, sm, pr 18.00
Shakers, Muggsy, gold trim, lg, pr, from $250 to 265.00
Shakers, owls, plain, gr eyes, sm, pr 35.00

Shakers, Puss'n Boots, gold trim, sm, pr 165.00
Shakers, Smiley, any color bibs, decals, gold trim, lg, pr 300.00
Shakers, Smiley, gr bib, lg, pr 155.00
Shakers, Swiss Boy & Girl, gold trim, lg, pr 60.00
Shakers, wheelbarrows, plain, sm, pr 18.00
Shakers, Winnie & Smiley, clover bud, pr, from $190 to 200.00
Shakers, Winnie & Smiley, gold trim, sm, pr 120.00
Sugar bowl, bucket style, w/lid, mk USA 50.00
Sugar bowl, Cottage, mk USA #8 ....240.00
Sugar bowl, fruit, mc, mk Shawnee #83 ....65.00
Sugar jug, Pennsylvania Dutch, mk USA 115.00
Tankard, medallion finish, mk Shawnee USA #990 Pat Pen 30.00
Teapot, ball shape, red flowers, mk USA 50.00
Teapot, Cottage, mk USA #7 ....360.00
Teapot, elephant, bl, gr or yel, mk USA 180.00
Teapot, Granny Ann, mk Pat Granny Ann or USA 130.00
Teapot, Tom Tom, mk Tom the Piper's Son Pat USA 120.00
Toastie susan, pk or turq 110.00

Lobsterware

Baker/mixing bowl, open, #917, 7" 55.00
Baker/mixing bowl set, #920, 3-pc 138.00
Bowl, batter; w/hdl, #928 ....100.00
Bowl, salad/spaghetti; #922 ....80.00
Casserole, Fr; #900, 10-oz 19.00
Casserole; Fr; #902, 16-oz 31.00
Plate, compartment; #912 ....188.00
Relish pot, w/lid, #926 ....100.00
Salad set, #924, 9-pc 345.00
Shakers, claw form, #905, pr 25.00
Shakers, full body, #933, pr 280.00
Sugar bowl/utility jar, w/lid, #907 ....31.00

Valencia

Baking pie plate, 9¼" or 10½" 30.00
Bowl, dessert; 6" 17.00
Bowl, mixing; 10" 35.00
Bowl, mixing; 12" 38.00
Bowl, mixing; 5" 24.00
Bowl, mixing; 8" 28.00
Bowl, onion soup; w/lid 30.00
Bowl, vegetable; w/lid, 9½" 75.00
Candle holders, tripod, pr 75.00
Carafe, 3-pt 75.00
Casserole, w/lid, 7½" or 8½" 75.00
Coaster 17.00
Coffeepot, regular or AD 80.00
Comport, sweets; 7" 30.00
Cookie jar 140.00
Creamer 17.00
Egg cup 17.00
Marmite, w/lid, 4½" 30.00
Mustard jar, w/lid 24.00
Nappy, 8½" or 9½" 25.00
Pie server, 9" 85.00
Pitcher, ice; 2-qt 40.00
Plate, chop; 13" 45.00
Plate, compartment; 11½" 45.00
Plate, deep, 8" 24.00
Plate, 10¾" 21.00
Saucer, chocolate; 8" 31.00
Saucer, coffee; AD 17.00
Spoon, 9½" 65.00
Teacup 24.00
Vase, bud 24.00
Vase, flower; 10" 28.00

Miscellaneous

Bank, Howdy Doody, mk USA Bob Smith 510.00
Clock, pyramid; Medallion finish 195.00
Clock, Trellis 120.00
Figurine, deer, plain, sm 130.00
Figurine, Oriental playing mandolin, lg, from $35 to 50.00
Figurine, pekingese, plain, sm 95.00
Figurine, puppy dog, plain, sm 95.00
Figurine, rabbit, decals, gold trim 240.00
Figurine, raccoon, plain 95.00
Figurine, squirrel, plain, sm 95.00
Figurine, tumbling bear, decals & gold trim 240.00
Figurines, dk natives, gold trim, pr 155.00
Figurines, Spanish dancers, pr 48.00
Flower frog, dolphin on low base, unmk, 3½" 35.00
Flower frog, turtle figural, gr, unmk, 4x5" 35.00
Flowerpot, gr w/emb flowers, w/saucer, mk USA #454, 3" 8.00
Flowerpot, ribbed duotone, mk USA #494, 4" 12.00
Flowerpot, yel, emb goemetrics, mk USA #484, 4" 8.00
Jardiniere, pk w/emb tulips, mk USA, 3½" 10.00
Lamp base, Champ the Dog 25.00
Match holder, Fernware, mk USA 95.00

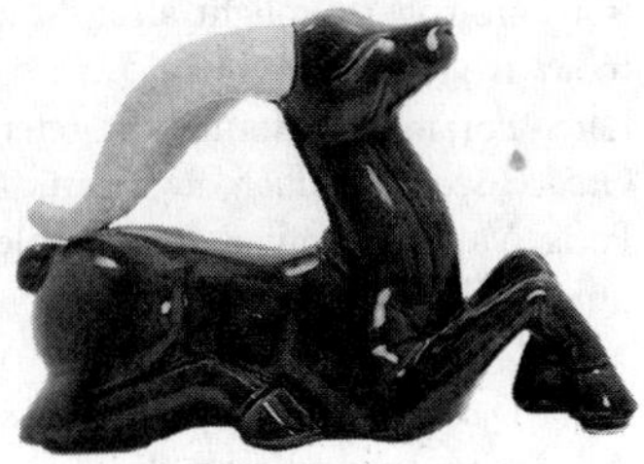

Planter, gazelle, turquoise and white, USA #614, $25.00.

Planter, bl w/emb daisy-like flowers, mk USA #152, 9½" 12.00
Planter, Chinese girl w/book, gold trim, mk USA #574 ....16.00
Planter, kitten & basket, mk Shawnee USA #2026 ....30.00
Planter, pig & basket, mk USA 10.00
Planter, poodle on bicycle, mk USA #712 ....32.00
Planter, shells form sides, bl, mk USA #154, 6" 10.00
Planter, Southern Girl, mk USA, 8½" 10.00
Vase, emb ribs, trumpet neck, hdls, mk USA, 5" 10.00
Vase, flowers emb on wht, hdls, mk USA, 6" 10.00
Vase, wheat on wht w/bl & gold trim, mk USA, 5" 22.00
Wall pocket, cornucopia w/bird, lt bl, unmk 25.00
Wall pocket, Little Jack Horner, mk USA #585 ....30.00
Wall pocket, star, mk USA 24.00

Shearwater

Since 1928 generations of the Peter, Walter, and James McConnell Anderson families have been producing figurines and artwares in their studio at Ocean Springs, Mississippi. Their work is difficult to date. Figures from the '20s and '30s won critical acclaim and have continued to be made to the present time. Early marks include a die-stamped 'Shearwater' in a dime-sized circle, a similar ink stamp, and a half-circle mark.

Any older item may still be ordered in the same glazes as it was originally produced, so many pieces on the market today may be relatively new. However, the older marks are not currently in use. Currently produced Black and pirate figurines are marked with a hand-incised 'Shearwater' and/or a cipher formed with an 'S' whose bottom curve doubles as the top loop of a 'P' formed by the addition of an upright placed below and to the left of the S. Many are dated, '93, for example. These figures are generally valued at $35.00 to $50.00 and are available at the pottery or by mail order. New decorated and carved pieces are very expensive, starting at $400.00 to $500.00 for a 6" pot.

Bowl, blk metallic over gr matt, ftd, mk, 1940s, 3⅝x8¾" 70.00
Figurine, Androcales & the Lion, WI Anderson, 5½" 300.00
Pitcher, blk over gr matt, stoneware, 1940s, 7" 50.00
Pitcher, Blue Rain, wheel thrown, thin-walled, 6" 90.00
Teapot, comical rooster form, 6-color, ca 1991 ....275.00
Vase, dancers/grapevines emb, crystalline bl on gunmetal, 11x10" ...4,000.00
Vase, gr lustred crystalline, bottle-neck top, squat, 6" 100.00
Vase, gr/brn concentric circles, squat, 3¾x4¼" 35.00
Vase, molded fish/birds/pelican/horse w/rider on lt bl, 3½" 450.00
Vase, spring gr, melon shape, Peter Anderson, ca 1945, 6x3¼" .300.00
Vase, spring gr, Peter Anderson, ca 1970, 8x4½" 250.00

Sheet Music

Sheet music is often collected more for its colorful lithographed covers, rather than for the music itself. Transportation songs (which have pictures or illustrations of trains, ships, and planes), ragtime and blues, comic characters (especially Disney), sports, political, and expositions are eagerly sought after. Much of the sheet music on the market today is valued at under $5.00; some of the better examples are listed here. For more information refer to *Sheet Music Reference and Price Guide®, Second Edition,* by Anna Marie Guiheen and Marie-Reine A. Pafik. Values are given for examples in excellent to near-mint condition unless otherwise noted.

Ain't Dat Scan'lous?, Bob Cole & Billy Johnson, 1901 ....10.00
All Alone, Irving Berlin, 1924 ....10.00
Amapola, Joseph M Lacalle, Jimmy Dorsey photo, 1924 ....5.00
Angel's Dream, Gustav Lange 5.00
Arabian Ooze, Duffy, Pfeiffer cover artist, 1911 ....15.00
Automobile Honeymoon, Norris, 1902 ....15.00
Ballad of John & Yoko, John Lennon & Paul McCartney, 1969 ..25.00
Beau James, Baker, Movie: Beau James, Hope & Miles photo, 1957 ...5.00
Bianca, Cole Porter, Musical: Kiss Me Kate, 1948 ....5.00

Bill Bailey, Won't You Please Come Home?, Hughie Cannon, photo cover, 1902, EX, $35.00 (Photo courtesy Anna Marie Guiheen and Marie-Reine A. Pafik)

Blue Orchids, Hoagy Carmichael, 1939 ....5.00
Breeze From Alabama, Scott Joplin, 1902 ....50.00
By Candle Light, Cole Porter, Movie: You Never Know 5.00
Caravan of Dreams, Fred Ahlert, Bing Crosby photo, 1947 ....5.00
Carlotta, Bacher, Pfeiffer cover artist, 1914 ....10.00
Chicka Boom, Bob Merrill, 1953 ....5.00
Cohen Owes Me $97, Irving Berlin, 1915 ....15.00
Cool, Sondheim/Bernstein, Movie: West Side Story, 1957 ....5.00
Cossack Love Song, G Gershwin, 1926 ....10.00
Cutey Boy, Williams & Greenberg, Pfeiffer cover artist, 1913 .....10.00
Dawn, David & Livingston, Jaye P Morgan photo 5.00
Dill Pickles, Charles L Johnson, 1906 ....20.00
Don't Forget Me When You're Gone, West & Redding, 1922 ....5.00
Down in the Depths, Cole Porter, Movie: Red, Hot & Blue, 1936 .5.00
Driftwood, Gus Kahn & Lew Gold, Perret cover artist, 1926 ....10.00
Encore, Cherie, J Fred Coots, Eddy Howard photo, 1947 ....5.00
Entertainer, Scott Joplin, 1903 ....50.00
Extra, Extra, Irving Berlin, Musical: Miss Liberty, 1949 ....5.00
Faithful Forever, Robin/Rainger, Movie: Gulliver's Travels, 1939 ..5.00
For the Good Times, Kris Kristofferson, 1968 ....5.00
Galveston, Webb, Glen Campbell photo, 1968 ....5.00
Gangster's Warning, Gene Autry, Curt Poulton photo, 1932 ....5.00
Girl on the Magazine Cover, Irving Berlin, 1916 ....10.00
Golden Years, Movie: Houdini, Curtis & Leigh photo, 1953 ....5.00
Good Night Boat, Caldwell & Kern, Musical: The Night Boat, 1920 ..10.00
Gypsy in Me, Cole Porter, Movie: Anything Goes, 1934 ....5.00
Have a Heart, Buck & Kern, Musical: Zeigfeld Follies, 1916 ....10.00
Heigh-Ho, Morey & Churchill, Movie: Snow White, Disney, 1938 ..10.00
Hesitation Blues, WC Handy, 1915 ....5.00
Home on the Range, Nick Manoloff, Jackie Heller photo, 1935 ....5.00
How Do You Do?, McGimsey, Movie: Song of the South, Disney, 1946 .10.00
I'd Like to Find Another Girl Like Mary, Pfeiffer cover artist 10.00
I Dreamt My Daddy Came Home, Joe Darcey & Lew Porter, 1919 ..15.00
I Hear a Dream, Robin & Rainger, Movie: Gulliver's Travel, 1939 ..5.00
I'll Know, Swerling/Burrows/Loesser, Musical: Guys & Dolls, 1950 ..5.00
I Love You, Thompson & Archer, Musical: Little Jessie James, 1923 ..10.00
I'm Awfully Strong for You, George M Cohan 10.00
I'm Going Back to Dixie, Irving Berlin, 1912 ....10.00
I'm Not Your Steppin' Stone, Monkees, 1966 ....5.00
I Sing a Little Tenor, Linton & Gilroy, 1902 ....5.00
I've Got a Right To Sing the Blues, Hoagy Carmichael, 1932 ....5.00
I Was So Young, George Gershwin, 1919 ....5.00
If I Had You, Irving Berlin, 1914 ....10.00
If You'll Smile, Fahey, Pfeiffer cover artist, 1919 ....10.00
In a Garden of Roses w/You, Davidson & Whipple, 1926 ....35.00
It Was Written in the Stars, Robin & Arlen, Movie: Casbah, 1948 ...5.00
Johnny Q Public, George M Cohan 10.00
Katie, Cole Porter, Movie: DuBarry Was a Lady, 1943 ....10.00
La Cucaracha, Carl Field, Don Pedro photo, 1935 ....5.00
Let Your Love Walk In, Joe Greene, De Castro Sisters photo, 1955 .....5.00
Little Bit Independent, Leslie & Burke, Ozzie & Harriet photo, 1935 .5.00
Love & a Dime, Brooks Bowman, Musical: Stags at Bay, 1935 ......8.00
Magna Carta, John Phillip Sousa, 1927 ....20.00
Merry Madness, Thomas S Allen, Starmer cover artist, 1914 ......15.00
Moonlight Waltz, Victor LaSalle, Indian, 1912 ....20.00
My Honolulu Bride, Harold Weeks, Dember cover artist, 1915 .....5.00
My Way, Frank Sinatra & Paul Anka, signed 50.00
On the Sidewalks of Berlin, Clinton Keithley, WWI, 1918 ....10.00
Ring Out Wild Bells, ET Paull, ET Paull cover artist, 1912 ....35.00
She Knows It, Al Jolson, 1921 ....10.00
Sleep, Earl Liebieg, PM Griffith cover artist, 1923 ....5.00
Son of the Sheik, Rudolph Valentino photo, 1926 ....15.00
Sooner or Later, Wolcott & Gilbert, Movie: Song of the South, 1946 ..10.00
Thumper Song, Bliss, Sour & Manners, Movie: Bambi, 1942 ......10.00
Voice in My Heart, George M Cohan 10.00
YMCA, Irving Berlin, 1917 ....10.00
You Can't Walk Back From an Aeroplane, 1927 ....20.00

Shell-Work Collectibles

Not long after the natural beauty of the shell was discovered, man began to use them for decorative purposes of many types. Shells were used to decorate clothing and household items as well as jewelry, personal gifts, and souvenirs. Remains of shell necklaces have been found that date to a time prior to the great flood!

During Victorian times shell work became a hobby for the middle class. Shell-work jewelry became popular at that time, but very little has survived due to its delicate nature. Examples of love tokens, souvenirs, and whimsies from that era are listed below. For further information we recommend *Neptune's Treasures, A Study and Value Guide*, available from our advisors, Carole and Richard Smyth (see their listing in the Directory under New York for ordering information).

Victorian dresser-shaped box, lift-top with mirror, shell back, litho paper resembles flame mahogany at front, faux drawers, $250.00 to $385.00. (Photo courtesy Carole and Richard Smyth)

Bank, doghouse w/bsk dog peering out, litho paper, English Vict, EX ..**400.00**
Box, shoe shape, litho scene around heel, English Vict, EX **385.00**
Desk letter holder, shells & litho, young woman, Vict, EX **375.00**
Dollhouse, garden of shells, 1930s Am folk art, VG **1,200.00**
Dresser, w/mirror, 2 silk pincushions & drw, English Vict, EX ...**300.00**
Inkwell/letter holder, 3 lg shells, pnt ship, Fr Vict, EX **185.00**
Mirror, hand; lady's, shells on bk & hdl, Vict, EX **200.00**
Necklace, feather/shell, on animal sinew, Am Indian, late 1800s, G ..**385.00**
Obelisks, shell encrusted, 19th C, pr **4,500.00**
Pie safe, hearts motif, 19th C Am folk art **3,500.00**
Pincushion, crown shape, shell & silk, Vict, EX, from $125 to ..**200.00**
Pincushion, heart shape, 1-sided litho, pins at edge, Vict, EX ...**185.00**
Roundel, layered shells around bubble glass w/seascape litho, EX **450.00**
Shadow box, house scene, papier-mache/wire/grasses, Vict English .**7,000.00**
Thimble holder, sailboat shape, MOP, bsk sailor boy, Vict, EX ..**375.00**
TV lamp, bsk mermaid w/shells & coral, 1950s, EX **55.00**
TV lamp, 3 conch shells w/2 flamingos, 1950s, EX **45.00**
West Indies Sailor's Valentine, dbl mahog hex fr w/glass, G- .**8,000.00**

Shelley

In 1872 Joseph Shelley became partners with James Wileman, owner of Foley China Works, thus creating Wileman & Co. in Stoke-on-Trent. Twelve years later James Wileman withdrew from the company, though the firm continued to use his name until 1925 when it became known as Shelley Potteries, Ltd. Like many successful nineteenth-century English potteries, this firm continued to produce useful household wares as well as dinnerware of considerable note. In 1896 the beautiful Dainty White shape was introduced, and it is regarded by many as synonymous with the name Shelley. In addition to the original Dainty (6-flute) design, other lovely shapes were produced: Ludlow (14-flute), Oleander (petal shape), Stratford (12-flute), Queen Anne (with 8 angular panels), Ripon (with its distinctive pedestal), and the 1930s shapes of Vogue, Eve, and Regent.

Though often overlooked, striking earthenware was produced under the direction of Frederick Rhead and later Walter Slater and his son Eric. Many notable artists contributed their talents in designing unusual, attractive wares: Rowland Morris, Mabel Lucie Attwell, and Hilda Cowham, to name but a few.

In 1966 Allied English Potteries acquired control of the Shelley Company, and by 1967 the last of the exquisite Shelley China had been produced to honor remaining overseas orders. In 1971 Allied English Potteries merged with the Doulton group.

It had to happen: Shelley forgeries! Chris Davenport, author of *Shelly Pottery, The Later Years*, reports seeing Mocha-shape cups and saucers with the Shelley mark. However, on close examination it is evident that the mark has been applied to previously unmarked wares too poorly done to have ever left the Shelley Pottery. This Shelley mark can actually be 'felt,' as the refiring is not done at the correct temperature to allow it to be fully incorporated into the glaze. (Beware! These items are often seen on Internet auction sites.)

Some Shelley patterns (Dainty Blue, Bridal Rose, Blue Rock) have been seen on Royal Albert and Queensware pieces. These companies are part of the Royal Doulton Group. Our advisors for this category are Lila and Fred Shrader; they are listed in the Directory under California.

Key:
MLA — Mabel Lucie Attwell

Ashtray, Blue Rock, Rosebud, Bridal Rose, 3½" dia, up to **29.00**
Ashtray, various dog breeds, 3 rests, 3½" dia, from $24 to **48.00**
Bowl, cream soup; Wildflower, hdls, #13668, +liner **75.00**
Bowl, flat soup; Bridal Rose, Oleander shape, no rim, 7½" **72.00**
Bowl, fruit; Summer Glory, #13381, 5½" **48.00**
Bowl, rim soup; Lilac Time, Dainty Shape, 8¾" **135.00**
Bowl, vegetable; Sheraton, #13291, 8¾" **50.00**
Butter dish, Rose, Pansy, Forget-Me-Not, Dainty shape, w/lid, 7¼" ...**160.00**
Butter pat, Dainty Blue, 3¾" **105.00**
Butter pat, Pansy Chintz w/lav border, 3¼" **82.00**
Cake plate, Blue Iris, Queen Anne w/tab hdls, 9½x8¼" **45.00**
Cake plate, Ferndown, tab hdls, #14131, 9" **75.00**
Cake plate, Regency, Dainty shape, ped ft, 8¾" **175.00**
Candlestick, Cloisello, #7919, 6½" **126.00**
Children's ware, cup (Mocha shape), MLA, 3", 5½" dia **205.00**
Children's ware, heated feeding dish, MLA, 7¼" **325.00**
Children's ware, plate, MLA, '...little man...caravan,' 8" **154.00**
Chop plate, Golden Harvest, #13685, 14" **66.00**
Coffeepot, Begonia, Dainty shape, 8½" **280.00**
Coffeepot, Morning Glory, Dainty shape, #13885, 7½" **479.00**
Coffeepot, Regency, Dainty shape, 7½" **120.00**
Condiment set, Blue Rock, shakers+mustard & lid on clover-shaped tray ..**174.00**
Coronation ware, mug, King George V, 6/22/11, Late Foley, 2¾" ...**55.00**
Coronation ware, plate, Princess Elizabeth & Margaret, 9" **75.00**
Creamer, Primrose, Dainty shape, ind, 2½" **34.00**
Creamer & sugar bowl, Pansy, Dainty shape, #13823 ....**77.00**
Crested ware, pin tray, Crest of Scarborough, 5½" **11.00**
Cup & saucer, Dainty Blue, #051/28, demi **68.00**
Cup & saucer, Duchess, #13410, demi **50.00**
Cup & saucer, floral transfer, Alexandra, Wileman, pre 1910, $48 to ...**65.00**
Cup & saucer, Fruit Centre, Boston Shape, #14208 ....**37.00**
Cup & saucer, Georgian, Gainsborough shape, #13361 ....**61.00**
Cup & saucer, Morning Glory, Dainty shape, #13885 ....**68.00**
Cup & saucer, Ning Poo, Mocha shape, #11259, demi **63.00**
Cup & saucer, Violets, Canterbury shape, mini, 1½" **160.00**
Cup & saucer, Woodland, Dorothy shape, #13348, 2¾" **55.00**
Dinner service, Regency, 43-pc service for 8, 5-pc place set+bowls ..**885.00**
Dinner service, Serenity, 6 5-pc place settings+cr/sug **285.00**
Egg cup, Blue Rock, Bridal Rose, Rosebud, Dainty shape, lg, 3⅝" **85.00**

Egg cup set, Regency, dainty shape, 4 sm 1¾" cups on stand 195.00
Figurine, bird study, Fly Catcher, 4¼" 182.00
Figurine, bird study, King Fisher, 7¾" 485.00
Figurine, I's Shy, MLA, child w/basket & beribboned puppy, 4½" ...389.00
Flower bouquet, all shells, 19th C England, in glass dome, 23x17x10" 7,500.00
Flower bouquet, in Samson bowl, ca 1830, 25x23" 1,200.00
Gravy boat & liner, Blue Rock, Rosebud, Dainty shape 195.00
Gravy boat & liner, Heavenly Blue, Dainty shape 295.00
Gravy bowl & attached liner, Sheraton, 6¼" 110.00
Jam pot, w/slotted lid, Celandine, Dainty shape, 4¼" 56.00
Menu plaque, Mallards in Flight, 4x6" 625.00
Mustard pot, Dainty Green, w/slotted lid, 2½" 165.00
Mustard pot, Ferndown, w/slotted, 2½" 54.00
Napkin ring, Dainty Blue, unmk (Royal Albert?) 45.00
Place setting, Begonia, Regency, Begonia Dainty shape, 5-pc 140.00
Place setting, Dainty White, 5-pc: 10½", 8", 6" plates+c/s 80.00
Place setting, Rosebud, Blue Rock, Dainty shape, 5-pc, up to 180.00
Plate, bread & butter; Crochet, #13371, 6¼" 24.00
Plate, Daffodil Time, #13370, 8" 32.00
Plate, dinner; Georgian, #13360, 10½" 52.00
Plate, luncheon; Dainty Blue, #051, 9½" 65.00
Plate, Rosebud, Dainty shape, 6" 35.00
Plate, Thistle, Dainty shape, #13820, 8" 71.00
Platter, Crochet, #13371, 12x10" 136.00
Platter, Stocks, Dainty shape, oval, 14½" 288.00
Relish, Bridal Rose, Dainty shape, oval, 9x5" 125.00
Relish, Campanula, Daisy shape, oval, 7x4" 62.00
Shakers, Rosebud, Dainty shape, pear shape, unmk, 3¾", pr 112.00
Smoking set, Blue Rock, 2" cigar holder, 2 3" ashtrays 75.00
Sugar bowl, Green Daisy Chintz, band on outside, #13205, 4¼" ..32.00
Sugar bowl, Rose & Red Daisy, Dainty shape, hdls, w/lid, 3¾" 76.00
Sugar bowl, Rosebud, Dainty shape, ind, 1¾" 45.00
Tea & toast set, Rosebud, Dainty shape, plate: 4x6½" 78.00
Tea & toast set, Wild Anemone, Richmond shape, #13978, 5½x8" 88.00
Teapot, Dainty Blue, #051/28, 5½" 480.00
Teapot, Dainty White, 5½" 162.00
Teapot, Harebell, Oleander shape, 6½" 290.00
Teapot, Regency, Dainty shape, 4¾" 183.00
Teapot, Shamrocks, Dainty shape, 6¼" 285.00
Teapot, various pastels, Dainty shape, 5½" 225.00
Teapot, various patterns, Henley shape, 5¼", from $90 to 150.00
Tray, sandwich; Chrysanthemum, tab hdls, #2377, 12x4½" 135.00
Tray, triple, Blue Rock, Dainty shape, long leaf hdl, 12" 265.00
Trio, Balloon Tree, Queen Anne shape, #11624, c/s+7" plate ...165.00
Trio, Dainty Blue, c/s+6" plate 89.00
Trio, Dainty Blue, c/s+8" plate 135.00
Trio, pastel flowers (#12293) on Eve shape, c/s+6" plate 52.00
Trio, Primrose Chintz, New Cambridge shape, 5½" sq plate 121.00
Trio, Surrey Scenery, Oleander shape, #13623, 8" plate 135.00

Silhouettes

Silhouette portraits were made by positioning the subject between a bright light and a sheet of white drawing paper. The resulting shadow was then traced and cut out, the paper mounted over a contrasting color and framed. The hollow-cut process was simplified by an invention called the Physiognotrace, a device that allowed tracing and cutting to be done in one operation. Experienced silhouette artists could do full-length figures, scenics, ships, or trains freehand. Some of the most famous of these artists were Charles Peale Polk, Charles Wilson Peale, William Bache, Doyle, Edouart, Chamberlain, Brown, and William King. Though not often seen, some silhouettes were completely painted or executed in wax. Examples listed here are hollow-cut unless another type is described and assumed to be in excellent condition unless noted otherwise.

Key:
c/p — cut and pasted
fl — full length
p — profile
wc — watercolor

Lt. Edward M. Yard, US Navy, Boston...1842 on John Adams Sloop of War, cut and pasted, unsigned (Auguste Edouart), framed, 11¾x5¼", $600.00.

Brothers (2 identified), p, c/p, in later 5¼x7⅜" fr 110.00
Lady, p, c/p, identified, 3½x2¾" in brass fr, VG 100.00
Lady, p, cut detail at collar, stains, 6⅜x5¾" fr 190.00
Lady w/ornate hat, p, c/p, 5¾x4⅞" fr 195.00
Man, fl p w/wc detail, c/p, in 10x8" rosewood fr 330.00
Man, p, c/p, gilt details, 5½x4¾" fr 165.00
Man (youthful), p to waist, German inscription, 5⅝x4½"+fr 115.00
Man & lady, p, c/p, pencil details, 3½x2¾", pr 200.00
Man & wife, p, ink detail, in 6⅝x5½" rosewood frs, pr 575.00
Man in top hat, fl, c/p, in 8⅛x5⅛" pine fr 165.00
Man w/top hat & walking stick, fl, initialed WHB, in 12x10" fr 365.00

Silver

Coin Silver

During colonial times in America, the average household could not afford items made of silver, but those fortunate enough to have accumulations of silver coins (900 parts silver/100 parts alloy) took them to the local silversmith who melted them down and made the desired household article as requested. These pieces bore the owner's monogram and often the maker's mark, but the words 'Coin Silver' did not come into use until 1830. By 1860 the standard was raised to 925 parts silver/75 parts alloy and the word 'Sterling' was added.

Key:
gw — gold washed
t-oz — troy ounce

A Himmel for Hyde & Goodrich, New Orleans; presentation cup, 1850s ...600.00
Bailey & Co, fish slice, 1846-78 .....275.00
Ball Tompkins & Blk, NY; presentation pitcher, flower-like bands, 13" ..1,750.00
C Kuchler, New Orleans; trowel, hollow hdl, eng blade, 6" 550.00
C Wiltberger, Philadelphia; sugar tongs, bright-cut, ca 1800 .....300.00
Francis Bassett, bowl, ped ft, flared rim, 5½x7" 650.00
Henry Salisbury, NY; baby cup, 8-sided, faceted, domed hdl, ped ft 600.00
Holland...Baltimore, soup ladle, Fiddle, 1820-30 .....276.00
J Clark, NY; soup ladle, Fiddle, monogram, 14⅜" 285.00
J&I Cox, NY; tea set, flower-like borders, flower finials, 3-pc 3,000.00
J&S Franks, Philadelphia; master butter knife, ca 1850 .....55.00
John B Ginochio, NY; soup ladle, Fiddle & Thread, 1837-54 ....330.00
John B Jones, Boston; salver, foliate rim/ft, 1816-37, 10" dia 635.00
JT Young, Petersburg (VA); fiddle-bk spoons, 9", set of 4 .....285.00
JW Cortelyou, NJ; tablespoons, w/monogram, 1805, lg, 5 for 110.00
Lincoln & Reed, Boston; salver, pie-crust border, 1835-46, 31-t-oz ...3,300.00
Lincoln & Reed, Boston; salver, rococo form, scrolled border, 30-t-oz ...865.00
Low, Ball & Co, Boston; teapot, whippet finial, scroll hdl, 6½" .935.00

R&A Campbell, Baltimore; sugar tongs, shell-shaped tips, 1840s ...470.00
R&W Wilson, Philadelphia; cream pitcher, acanthus decor, 1830s, 7" ...300.00
R&W Wilson, Philadelphia; cream pitcher, bead decor, ftd, 6" .250.00
S Hoyt & Co, presentation chalice, dtd 1852, 8x4¼" 700.00
S Kirk & Son, pitcher, bird & floral, 1880-90, 30-t-oz 2,600.00
Wendell & Fettman, sugar sifting spoon, Fiddle Thread, rtcl 250.00
WG Forbes (NY), spoons, bright-cut hdls, 8⅞", set of 5 ....285.00
Wm Gale & Son, NY; tea set, 5-pc set on SP tray 6,250.00
Wm I Tenney, NY City; pitcher, repousse/chased decor, 1840s, 11¼" 1,150.00
Wood & Hughes, NY; fish knife & fork, scrolls/florals, 1866-70 ...360.00

Flatware

Silver flatware is being collected today either to replace missing pieces of heirloom sets or in lieu of buying new patterns, by those who admire and appreciate the style and quality of the older ware. Prices vary from dealer to dealer; some pieces are harder to find and are therefore more expensive. Items such as olive spoons, cream ladles, lemon forks, etc., once thought a necessary part of a silver service, may today be slow to sell; as a result, dealers may price them low and make up the difference on items that sell more readily. Many factors enter into evaluation. Popular patterns may be high due to demand though easily found, while scarce patterns may be passed over by collectors who find them difficult to reassemble. If pieces are monogrammed, deduct 20% (for rare, ornate patterns) to 30% (for common, plain pieces). Place settings generally come in three sizes: dinner, place, and luncheon, with the dinner size generally more expensive. In general, dinner knives are 9½" long, place knives, 9" to 9⅛", and luncheon knives, 8¾" to 8⅞". Dinner forks measure 7⅜" to 7½", place forks, 7¼" to 7⅜", and luncheon forks, 6⅞" to 7⅛". Our advisor for this category is Rick Spencer; he is listed in the Directory under Utah.

Francis I service by Reed and Barton, 122 pieces in case (selected pieces shown), $5,225.00 at auction.

Alexandra, Lunt, butter spreader, hollow hdl 32.00
Alexandra, Lunt, pierced serving spoon 85.00
Alexandra, Lunt, place setting, 4-pc 145.00
American Classic, Easterling, grapefruit spoon 32.00
American Classic, Easterling, ice cream fork 22.00
American Classic, Easterling, teaspoon 18.00
American Classic, Easterling, wooden salad set 50.00
Bell Rose, Oneida, jelly server 35.00
Blossom, Geo Jensen, gravy ladle 395.00
Blossom, Geo Jensen, mayonnaise ladle 200.00
Bridal Bouquet, Alvin, gumbo soup spoon 30.00
Bridal Bouquet, Alvin, luncheon setting, 4-pc 75.00
Bridal Bouquet, Alvin, nut spoon 35.00
Bridal Bouquet, Alvin, poultry shears 85.00
Calvert, Kirk, bonbon server 40.00
Calvert, Kirk, lemon fork 28.00
Carnation, Wallace, dinner fork 58.00
Carnation, Wallace, dinner knife 58.00
Carnation, Wallace, twisted butter pick 40.00
Carpenter, Hall-Towle, place setting, 4-pc 130.00
Castle Rose, Royal Crest, cheese scoop 24.00
Castle Rose, Royal Crest, grill setting, 4-pc 55.00
Castle Rose, Royal Crest, roast carving set, 2-pc 85.00
Chapel Bells, Alvin, ind butter spreader, flat hdl 12.00
Chapel Bells, Alvin, olive spoon 32.00
Chapel Bells, Alvin, salad fork 25.00
Decor, Gorham, cocktail fork 30.00
Decor, Gorham, demitasse spoon 27.00
Decor, Gorham, iced teaspoon 40.00
Decor, Gorham, place setting, 4-pc 135.00
Della Robia, Alvin, bouillon spoon 26.00
Della Robia, Alvin, tablespoon 35.00
Dorothy Manners, Towle, gravy ladle 55.00
Edgewood, International, berry spoon, 9" 200.00
Edgewood, International, dinner knife 60.00
Edgewood, International, fruit spoon 40.00
Edgewood, International, soup ladle, 10" 375.00
Edgewood, International, sugar spoon 40.00
Eighteenth Century, Reed & Barton, cold meat fork 65.00
Eighteenth Century, Reed & Barton, horseradish spoon 44.00
Eighteenth Century, Reed & Barton, tomato server 120.00
Empire, Buccellati, oval soup spoon 75.00
Empire, Buccellati, salad fork 75.00
Empire, Whiting, asparagus fork 295.00
Etruscan, Gorham, jelly server 29.00
Etruscan, Gorham, luncheon setting, 4-pc 90.00
Etruscan, Gorham, salt spoon 15.00
Etruscan, Gorham, tablespoon 55.00
Faneuil, Tiffany, demitasse spoon 29.00
Faneuil, Tiffany, ice tongs 375.00
Faneuil, Tiffany, ind butter spreader, hollow hdl 35.00
Faneuil, Tiffany, luncheon fork 48.00
Faneuil, Tiffany, pastry tongs 250.00
Faneuil, Tiffany, waffle server 375.00
Feather Edge, Tuttle, luncheon setting, 4-pc 120.00
Fiddle, Porter Blanchard, cold meat fork 125.00
Fiddle, Porter Blanchard, pie server, all silver, 9¼" 220.00
Fiddle, Porter Blanchard, teaspoon 45.00
Georgian Maid, International, cheese server 24.00
Georgian Maid, International, luncheon setting, 4-pc 55.00
Georgian Maid, International, sugar tongs 24.00
Golden Aegean Weave, Wallace, cold meat fork 65.00
Gramercy, Tiffany, bouillon spoon 45.00
Gramercy, Tiffany, dinner fork 65.00
Gramercy, Tiffany, dinner knife 65.00
Grand Baroque, Wallace, asparagus server, hooded 250.00
Grand Baroque, Wallace, chocolate spoon 36.00
Grand Baroque, Wallace, dinner setting, 4-pc 150.00
Grand Baroque, Wallace, place setting, 4-pc 125.00
Grand Baroque, Wallace, salad serving set, all silver 285.00
Grand Baroque, Wallace, steak knife 45.00
Grand Baroque, Wallace, strawberry fork 29.00
Hamilton, Tiffany, iced teaspoon 65.00
Hampton, Tiffany, pie server, hollow hdl 85.00
Hampton, Tiffany, serving spoon 120.00
Homewood, Stieff, bonbon server 30.00
Homewood, Stieff, lobster pick 34.00
Inaugural, State House, cream soup 16.00
Inaugural, State House, grill setting, 4-pc 52.00
Irion, Wallace, berry spoon, lg 325.00
Irion, Wallace, fish server, 11¼" 525.00
Irion, Wallace, soup ladle 775.00
Kirk Rose, Kirk, luncheon setting, 4-pc 105.00

Kirk Rose, Kirk, place setting, 4-pc 110.00
Lady Hilton, Westmoreland, pierced tablespoon 40.00
Lady Hilton, Westmoreland, salad fork 20.00
Lady Hilton, Westmoreland, sugar spoon 15.00
Landsdowne, Gorham, dinner setting, 4-pc 140.00
Landsdowne, Gorham, lettuce fork 125.00
Legato, Wallace, berry server 75.00
Legato, Wallace, lemon fork 24.00
Legato, Wallace, strawberry fork 25.00
Lily of the Valley, Whiting, ind asparagus tongs 375.00
Lily of the Valley, Whiting, salad fork 120.00
Lily of the Valley, Whiting, tea strainer 475.00
Love Disarmed, Reed & Barton, sardine server 199.00
Love Disarmed, Reed & Barton, waffle server 325.00
Madame Royale, Durgin, preserve spoon 100.00
Madame Royale, Durgin, roast carving set, 3-pc 295.00
Madame Royale, Durgin, sauce ladle 65.00
Marie Antoinette, Dominick & Haff, serving spoon 65.00
Marie Antoinette, Dominick & Haff, teaspoon 24.00
Marquis, Tiffany, egg spoon 45.00
Marquis, Tiffany, fried oyster server 350.00
Marquis, Tiffany, stuffing spoon 575.00
Marquis, Tiffany, terrapin fork 65.00
Marquis, Tiffany, tomato server 400.00
Mary Chilton, Towle, beef fork 32.00
Mary Chilton, Towle, butter pick 26.00
Mary Chilton, Towle, luncheon setting, 4-pc 75.00
Mary Chilton, Towle, relish scoop 27.00
Mythologique, Gorham, breakfast knife, 7¾" 63.00
Mythologique, Gorham, dinner fork 80.00
Mythologique, Gorham, dinner knife 80.00
Mythologique, Gorham, ice cream fork 75.00
Narcissus, National, cream soup spoon 30.00
Narcissus, National, teaspoon 18.00
Normandie, Wallace, cocktail fork 15.00
Normandie, Wallace, demitasse spoon 12.00
Normandie, Wallace, dinner setting, 4-pc 69.00
Normandie, Wallace, service for 12 w/monogram, 102-pc set 850.00
Old Charleston, Rogers, place setting, 4-pc 69.00
Poppy, Gorham, cucumber server 150.00
Poppy, Gorham, lettuce spoon 150.00
Processional, Fine Arts, ice cream fork 24.00
Processional, Fine Arts, lobster pick 29.00
Provence, Tiffany, gumbo soup spoon 65.00
Pyramid, Jensen, dinner fork 125.00
Pyramid, Jensen, salad fork 85.00
Quintessence, Lunt, place setting, 4-pc 125.00
Quintessence, Lunt, salad set, all silver 245.00
Quintessence, Lunt, soup ladle 175.00
Raphael, Alvin, berry spoon 850.00
Raphael, Alvin, cold meat fork 575.00
Raphael, Alvin, jam server, 6" 575.00
Raphael, Alvin, jelly cake server 1,200.00
Raphael, Alvin, sugar spoon 120.00
Raphael, Alvin, teaspoon 75.00
Renaissance, Tiffany, gravy ladle 395.00
Renaissance, Tiffany, ice spoon 595.00
Renaissance, Tiffany, master salt spoon 80.00
Renaissance, Tiffany, pierced cracker scoop 995.00
Renaissance, Tiffany, salad serving set 995.00
Ribbon Rose, Hallmark, cream soup spoon 36.00
Ribbon Rose, Hallmark, place setting, 4-pc 100.00
Richelieu, Tiffany, cheese knife 275.00
Richelieu, Tiffany, conch spoon 475.00
Richelieu, Tiffany, ice cream fork 75.00
Richelieu, Tiffany, soup ladle 750.00
Richelieu, Tiffany, sugar sifter 325.00
Saint Cloud, Gorham, cake breaker 225.00
Saint Cloud, Gorham, fish fork 145.00
Saint Cloud, Gorham, salad fork 145.00
San Lorenzo, Tiffany, iced teaspoon 55.00
San Lorenzo, Tiffany, mustard ladle 110.00
Southern Rose, Manchester, pie server 45.00
Southern Rose, Manchester, serving spoon 59.00
Strasbourg, Gorham, dinner setting, 4-pc 125.00
Strasbourg, Gorham, luncheon setting, 4-pc 95.00
Strasbourg, Gorham, place setting, 4-pc 110.00
Trojan, Reed & Barton, dinner fork 60.00
Trojan, Reed & Barton, dinner knife 110.00
Trojan, Reed & Barton, lettuce fork 150.00
Trojan, Reed & Barton, stuffing spoon 475.00
Versailles, Gorham, bouillon spoon 48.00
Versailles, Gorham, crumber, 11½" 425.00
Versailles, Gorham, nut spoon 70.00
Versailles, Gorham, strawberry fork 85.00
Vine, Tiffany, conch spoon 520.00
Vine, Tiffany, grapefruit spoon 99.00
Vine, Tiffany, ice cream spoon 85.00
Vine, Tiffany, sugar sifter 325.00
Vine, Tiffany, teaspoon 75.00
Waltz of Spring, Wallace, baked potato fork 58.00
Waltz of Spring, Wallace, cream soup spoon 40.00
Waltz of Spring, Wallace, dinner setting, 4-pc 155.00
Waltz of Spring, Wallace, pierced serving spoon 70.00
Wave Edge, Tiffany, asparagus fork 895.00
Wave Edge, Tiffany, bouillon ladle 695.00
Wave Edge, Tiffany, punch ladle 1,350.00
Wave Edge, Tiffany, sardine fork 295.00
Wave Edge, Tiffany, stuffing spoon 695.00
Windham, Tiffany, gumbo soup spoon 80.00
Windham, Tiffany, ice tongs 450.00
Windham, Tiffany, pastry fork 70.00
Windham, Tiffany, sherbet spoon 58.00
Windham, Tiffany, steak knife 75.00

Hollow Ware

Until the middle of the nineteenth century, the silverware produced in America was custom made on order of the buyer directly from the silversmith. With the rise of industrialization, factories sprung up that manufactured silverware for retailers who often added their trademark to the ware. Silver ore was mined in abundance, and demand spurred production. Changes in style occurred at the whim of fashion. Repousse decoration (relief work) became popular about 1885, reflecting the ostentatious preference of the Victorian era. Later in the century, Greek, Etruscan, and several classic styles found favor. Today the Art Deco styles of this century are very popular with collectors.

In the listings that follow, manufacturer's name or trademark is noted first; in lieu of that information, listings are by country or item. Weight is given in troy ounces. See also Tiffany, Silver.

Key: t-oz — troy ounce

Abraham Carlisle, creamer, urn form w/beaded edge, loop hdl, 1795 ...865.00
Am, ladle, scrolling foliate terminal, 11½", 6-t-oz 145.00
Am, sugar bowl, twin hdls, flame finial, faded monogram, ca 1845 ...335.00
Arthur Stone, bowl, eng names, dtd 1926, 4¼x9½", 25-t-oz 460.00
Aytoun, Edinburgh; teapot, skittle ball; ornate spout, 1725, 20-t-oz ..2,750.00

Barbour, chocolate pot, ribbons at base/hdl/spout, 7", EX **375.00**
Bateman, London; sugar basket, hinged hdl, eng crest, 3x6" ..**1,100.00**
Bateman, London; vase, floral/bird/scroll, 1806, 13", 40-t-oz ..**2,950.00**
Birmingham, bud vase, trumpet shape, 5½" **90.00**
Birmingham, salver, pie-crust edge, floral eng, 8" dia, 7.2-t-oz ...**300.00**
Cartier, sweetmeat, hammered body, pierced foliate base, 2¾" ..**175.00**
Cellini Craft, bowl, openwork foliage, fluted, 2¾x5½", 4-t-oz ..**450.00**
Cellini Shop, bowl, serving, emb foliage, scroll hdls, 2x8½" **400.00**
Continental, cake basket, chased scrolls, central scene, rtcl, 18" dia **990.00**
Continental, cream pitcher, helmet, strap hdl, appl decor, 7-t-oz ...**330.00**
Continental, pill box, hinged lid, cherubs in relief **130.00**
Continental, pitcher, baluster w/foliate hdl, 9¾", 40-t-oz **635.00**
Continental, shakers, urn shape w/leaf decor, ca 1880, pr **200.00**
Continental 800, sugar shaker, ram's head w/wreaths, Fr, 1900s ..**235.00**
Edwardian, muffineer, spreading cylindrical form, ca 1910, 5½" .**200.00**
Erickson, bowl, fluted, 7-rib, ftd, 1970, 3x12", 43-t-oz **1,050.00**
Fisher, pitcher, water; classical shape, 9", 21-t-oz **385.00**
Frank M Whiting, cup & saucer, demitasse; floral eng, 12 for ...**300.00**
Friedel, tray, rectangular w/rnded corners, 14½", 27-t-oz **975.00**
Geo I style, teapot, domed lid, treen hdl, 10" **430.00**
Georg Jensen, bowl, openwork vintage, 6x7¾", 20-t-oz **2,400.00**
Georg Jensen, bowl, pierced foliate std, belled ft, 10-t-oz **1,725.00**
Georg Jensen, sauce boat & tray, openwork berries, 16-t-oz ...**2,875.00**
Gorham, basket, rtcl oval, 12x9½", 12-t-oz **300.00**
Gorham, cake basket/tray, openwork border/hdl, 11½", 19.5-t-oz ...**400.00**
Gorham, coddling cup, lobed baluster, 3 horn hdls, 7¾", 29-t-oz ..**865.00**
Gorham, fruit compote, rosette repousse, 16.5-t-oz **300.00**
Gorham, hot water urn, Cupid finial, twin hdls, 18", 105-t-oz ...**7,800.00**
Gorham, pitcher, water; Buttercup, 1908 ....**935.00**
Gorham, pitcher, water; hammered, bulbous, ear hdl, 27-t-oz **500.00**
Gorham, sauce ladle, Buttercup, gw, sm **100.00**
Gorham, tea set, 10" & 7" pots+cr/sug **600.00**
Gorham, waste bowl, Zodiac, 2½x5" **150.00**
Gyllenberg, FJR; bowl, hammered, flared rim, 2x5¾" **145.00**
H Woodward, Birmingham; mustard pot, bl liner, w/spoon, 1876 ..**155.00**
Handicraft Shop, plate, punched/emb floral rim band, '04, 10" .**430.00**
Hencho En Mexico, tray, acanthus border & hdls, 50-t-oz, 22½" ...**300.00**
Henry Vincent, London; pitcher, milk; urn form w/strap hdl, 1800, 4" ...**200.00**
Hester Bateman, shaker, bulbous, domed top, twist finial, 1780s, 6" ...**325.00**
Hester Bateman, toast rack, 10 half-circle wires on base, 1783-84 ..**350.00**
International, candlesticks, Neoclassical scroll/floral, 14", pr **700.00**
International, julep cup, 4", set of 8, 30-t-oz **990.00**
IW (crowned harp/Hibernia figure), creamer, lion's head ft, 4" .**125.00**
JE Caldwell, bowl, centerpc; boat shape, repousse/swags, 17" L **2,500.00**
John McMullin, Philadelphia; teapot & sugar bowl, 1830s, 42-t-oz ...**980.00**
Kalo, bowl, floriform w/5 petal-like panels, hammered, 7" **400.00**
Kalo, bowl, simple flared form, ftd, hammered, 10" dia, 23-t-oz .**750.00**
Kalo, bowl, 7-sided rolled rim, hammered, ftd, 2x9" **345.00**
Katherine Pratt, bowl, hammered, notched rim, 3¼x5¾", 9-t-oz ..**300.00**
Katherine Pratt, bowl, hammered floriform, 2x4" **200.00**
Katherine Pratt, tea strainer, pierced hdls, 6" L **260.00**
LeBolt, hammered, hexagonal w/glass bottom, hdl, 5x10" **325.00**
LeBolt, tray, hammered, detailed decor at edge, 11" dia **160.00**
London, dresser box, Geo IV, eng crest on lid, 1825, 3¼" dia **220.00**
London, mustard pot, hinged lid, strap hdl, ribbed middle, 1811 ...**250.00**
London, pastry tongs, pierced/eng ends, 1894 ....**440.00**
London, pitcher, Geo III, fluted w/eng floral swag, 1796, 4¼" ...**200.00**
London, teapot, Wm IV, fluted melon shape, wood hdl, 1837 ...**450.00**
London, wine funnel, Geo III, 1787 ....**550.00**
M Boulton, candelabra, Georgian, 1830s, 21x18", pr **2,970.00**
Mary P Winlock, ladle, pierced hdl, champleve floral, 5" **350.00**
MFME Sterling 76, dessert plate, w/monogram, set of 8, 20-t-oz ..**100.00**
Paul Revere Jr, beaker, everted lip, bowed sides, ca 1800, 3¾" ..**8,000.00**
Randahl B32, plate, emb berry border, 12-t-oz, 10½" **135.00**
Randahl B68, fruit bowl, emb berry border, 9" dia, pr **200.00**
Reed & Barton, centerpc, Neoclassical emb, 8x11" **700.00**
Reed & Barton, centerpc on ped, eng decor, 13" dia, 33-t-oz **300.00**
Reed & Barton, salad servers, muse & putto terminals, pr **520.00**
S Kirk, tea/coffee set, allover repousse, ftd, 11" pot, 5-pc **2,520.00**
S Kirk & Son, soup ladle, floral repousse **300.00**
SB Star, NY: salver, pierced scrolls/florals, 1900s, 20-t-oz **250.00**
Schofield, Baltimore; salt & pepper castors, baluster, paw ft, pr .**100.00**
Shreve, Crump & Low; bowl, 8", 12½-t-oz **150.00**
Spratling, chocolate pot, wood finial & low wood hdl, 7" **900.00**
Stieu, teapot, hammered, spherical w/swing hdl, hinged lid, 23-t-oz ...**300.00**
Suzuyo 950, plate, scalloped/molded rim, 25-t-oz **90.00**
T Robins, London; box, Geo III, crested/hinged lid, 1812, 5x3½" **880.00**
Tea urn, Georgian, lion medallions, dolphins, serpent hdls, 1810, 17" ..**385.00**
Thomas Bradbury & Son, bowl, Edwardian, ftd, 1903, 4x6½" ...**300.00**
Towle, tray, Louis XIV, rose medallion rim, #6617, 14" dia **700.00**
W Wilson, Philadelphia; cream pitcher, acanthus hdl, repousse, 6½" ..**500.00**
Wallace, coffee service, AD; pot+cr/sug+tray, 32-t-oz **700.00**
Warner, Baltimore; tea strainer, floral repousse, 19th C **165.00**
WB (Wm Breed), candlesticks, eng floral, 10", 10-t-oz, pr **600.00**
WF Marquand, NY; tea set, fruit finials, gadrooning, 1823, 3-pc **2,100.00**
Whitney, tea/coffee, allover floral repousse, pot: 8x9", 5-pc ...**3,000.00**
Woodside, pitcher, water; & salver, ornate roses, 34-t-oz **1,045.00**
Woolley, bowl, scalloped rolled rim, 2½x6", 5-t-oz **315.00**

Silver Overlay

The silver overlay glass made since the 1880s was decorated with a cut-out pattern of sterling silver applied to the surface of the ware.

Vase, blue iridescent with Nouveau floral overlay, 5", $435.00.

Bottle, scent; cranberry cased, allover o/l & HP, metal lid, 3¼" ...**450.00**
Bottle, scent; crystal, allover o/l, bulbous, o/l stopper, 4¼" **130.00**
Bottle, scent; gr, allover o/l, onion form, 4½" **600.00**
Shot glass, red, elaborate vintage o/l, 2½" **190.00**
Trivet, clear, scrolling wide o/l border, 6" dia **80.00**
Vase, cranberry, elaborate rim/base o/l bands, waisted, 6½" **425.00**
Vase, purple, Nouveau o/l, 4" **475.00**

Silverplate

Silverplated flatware is fast becoming the focus of attention for many of today's collectors. Silver prices rose to over $7.00 an ounce in 1998, causing a slight increase in both sterling and silverplate prices on the secondary market. Demand is strong for early, ornate pieces, and prices have continued to rise steadily over the past five years. Our values are based on pieces in excellent or restored/resilvered condition. Serving pieces are priced to reflect the values of examples in complete original condition, with knives retaining their original blades. If pieces are monogrammed, deduct from 20% (for rare, ornate patterns) to 30% (for common, plain pieces). Our advisor for this category is Rick Spencer; he is listed in the Directory under Utah. See also Railroadiana, Silverplate.

Key:

CF — cocktail/seafood fork	ITS — iced tea spoon
DF — dinner/luncheon fork	OS — oval soup spoon
DK — dinner/luncheon knife	RS — round cream soup spoon
FS — fruit/citrus spoon	SF — salad/dessert fork
IB — individual butter spreader	TS — teaspoon

Flatware

Adam, 1917, Oneida Community, fruit spoon 6.50
Adam, 1917, Oneida Community, soup ladle 50.00
Adoration, 1930, 1847 Rogers, carving set, 2-pc, lg 80.00
Aria, current, Christofle, 12 ea: DF, SF, TS, DK, OS, +4 pcs .1,750.00
Arundel, 1899, Wm A Rogers, DK 18.00
Arundel, 1899, Wm A rogers, luncheon fork 5.00
Avon, 1901, 1847 Rogers, chopped beef fork 18.00
Berkshire, 1897, 1847 Rogers, jelly slice 24.00
Berkshire, 1897, 1847 rogers, sugar spoon 7.00
Beswick/Diana, 1904, Rogers, nut pick 12.00
Betsy Ross, 1919, International, SF 5.00
Betsy Ross, 1919, International, tablespoon 7.00
Carnation, 19??, punch ladle 158.50
Coronation, 1936, Community, bonbon spoon 24.00
Coronation, 1936, Community, CF 8.50
Coronation, 1936, Community, gravy ladle 24.00
Coronation, 1936, Community, pierced pie server 34.00
Croydon, 1932, Oneida, berry spoon 8.50
Daffodil, 1950, 1847 Rogers, carving set, 2-pc, lg 80.00
Daffodil, 1950, 1847 Rogers, slotted tablespoon 24.00
Danish Princess, 1938, Holmes & Edwards, CF 7.50
Distinction, 1951, Prestige, CF 5.00
Distinction, 1951, Prestige, IB 5.00
Evening Star, 1950, Community, ITS 7.50
Flair, 1956, 1847 Rogers, cold meat fork 18.00
Flair, 1956, 1847 Rogers, gravy ladle 20.00
Florette, 1909, Rogers, pickle/olive spoon 12.00
Florette, 1909, Rogers, tomato server 24.00
Gloria Grenoble, 1906, Oneida, bouillon soup 12.00
Grenoble, 1938, Heirloom, cream soup 5.00
Grenoble, 1938, Heirloom, sugar tongs 30.00
Hampton Court, 1926, Community, cake-serving fork 16.00
Hampton Court, 1926, Community, TS 3.00
Holly, 1904, Simmons, berry spoon 225.00
Holly, 1904, Simmons, TS 26.00
Hollywood, 1937, Wallace, cream soup 5.00
Hollywood, 1937, Wallace, master butter spreader 5.00
Imperial, 1904, Holmes & Edwards, DF 7.00
Imperial, 1928, Oneida, ITS 6.00
Imperial, 1928, Oneida, SF 5.00
Inheritance, 1941, Rogers, pierced pastry server 15.00
Joan, 1896, Wallace, fish-serving fork 29.00
Joan, 1896, Wallace, horseradish spoon 26.00
Joan, 1896, Wallace, ice cream fork 14.00
June, 1915, Pas Plate, DF 5.00
King Cedric, 1933, Community, grill fork 4.00
King Cedric, 1933, Community, grill knife 5.00
Kings, 1800s, Gorham, IBS 8.00
Kings, 1800s, Reed & Barton, luncheon fork 6.00
La Concorde, 1910, Rogers, fish fork 24.00
La Concorde, 1910, Rogers, TS 6.50
Lafayette, 1908, sugar shell 8.00
Love Lace, 1936, 1847 Rogers, berry spoon 25.00
Love Lace, 1936, 1847 Rogers, ITS 9.00
Magic Rose, 1963, 1847 Rogers, pickle fork 6.00
Magic Rose, 1963, 1847 Rogers, tomato server 16.00
May Queen, 1951, Holmes & Edwards, fish fork 12.00
May Queen, 1951, Holmes & Edwards, fish knife 14.00
Newport/Chicago, 1879, 1847 Rogers, sugar tongs 26.00
Noblesse, 1930, Oneida, demitasse spoon 7.00
Old Colony, 1911, 1847 Rogers, coffee spoon 8.00
Old Colony, 1911, 1847 Rogers, fruit knife, flat hdl 9.00
Old Colony, 1911, 1847 Rogers, ice cream slice, hollow hdl 35.00
Old Colony, 1911, 1847 Rogers, SF 10.00
Patrician, 1914, Oneida, lemon fork 24.00
Persian, 1871, 1947 Rogers, twisted butter 16.00
Presentation, 1948, Oneida, cream ladle 10.00
Queen Bess, 1924, Tudor, gravy ladle 12.00
Queen Bess, 1924, Tudor, OS 5.00
Renaissance, 18??, fish knife 67.00
Royal Rose, 1939, Oneida, IBS 5.00
Royal Rose, 1939, Oneida, sugar tongs 27.00
Royal Rose, 1939, Oneida, TS 4.00
Savoy, 1892, 1847 Rogers, fish-serving set 65.00
Savoy, 1892, 1847 Rogers, FS 5.00
Savoy, 1892, 1847 Rogers, SF 12.00
Savoy, 1892, 1847 Rogers, soup ladle 45.00
Silver Lace, 1968, 1847 Rogers, berry spoon 20.00
Silver Lace, 1968, 1847 Rogers, pickle fork 8.00
Talisman, 1938, Rogers, demitasse spoon 6.00
Talisman, 1938, Rogers, pierced pastry server 10.00
Tower, 1932, Stratford International, grill fork 6.00
Tower, 1932, Stratford International, grill knife 6.00
Tudor, 1904, Rogers & Hamilton, ice cream spoon 10.00
Tudor, 1904, Rogers & Hamilton, salad-serving set 60.00
Vanity Fair, 1924, Gorham, jelly server 7.00
Vanity Fair, 1924, Gorham, master butter spreader 4.00
Vanity Fair, 1924, Gorham, salad fork 5.00
Vesta, 1895, 1847 Rogers, youth fork 9.00
Vesta, 1895, 1847 Rogers, youth knife 9.00
White Orchid, 1952, gravy ladle 12.00
White Orchid, 1953, cold meat 12.00
Woodland Rose, 1955, demitasse spoon 4.00
Woodland Rose, 1955, Rogers, TS 4.00
Yale, 1894, Wm Rogers, beef fork 10.00
Yale, 1894, Wm Rogers, ice cream fork 18.00
Yale, 1894, Wm Rogers, soup ladle 75.00

Hollow Ware

Hot water urn, American Aesthetic, with lamp, engraved presentation date: June 1, 1881, 15¼", $300.00.

Am, dbl entree dish on warming stand, gadroon border, ftd, hdls ...150.00
Am, lazy Susan, 2-tier, scrolled border, scroll chasing 175.00
Am, meat dome, typical form, loop hdl, monogram, 18" 175.00
Am, wine cooler, classical form, scroll borders, sq base, 11" 200.00
Chrichton, London; bachelor coffeepot, 1928, 6½" 385.00
Crispin Fuller, London; pepper castor, baluster, 1795, 6" 500.00
English, tea/coffee set, eng, 2 pots+kettle+stand+lamp+cr/sug, 1850s 2,000.00
English, tea/coffee set, Georgian style, 2 pots+cr/sug+waste bowl ...550.00
Geo III style, entree dish, chased florals, foliate scrolls, 12", pr .350.00
Georgian style, standish, foliate hdl, hinged compartments, 7" .260.00
Gorham, meat platter, gadrooned border, oval, 23x17" 165.00
Mappin & Webb, tea urn, w/int heating element, urn finial, 1850s, 19" ..500.00
Marquise, 1933, 1847 Rogers, serving dish, 14x10" 85.00
Marquise, 1933, 1847 Rogers, water pitcher 130.00
Oneida, Paul Revere, platter, well-&-tree, 1927 ....50.00
Oneida, Paul Revere, shakers, 1927, pr 29.00
Reed & Barton, tazzas, Buffalo & Indian, frosted liners, 8½x9", pr ..650.00
Reed & Barton, tea/coffee set, Regent, 5-pc w/serving tray 275.00
Regency Geo III style, columns, 8¾", pr 300.00
T Bradbury & Sons, garnitures, palm-tree form, scrolled base, 12", pr ...1,400.00
Towle, tea/coffee set, Scroll, 2 pots+tray+kettle+cr/sug+bowl ...650.00
Unmk, sweetmeat basket, rtcl/emb flowers, cobalt glass int, 7x7" 180.00
Unmk, tea service, 3 pots (2 w/stand), cr/sug+waste bowl+30" tray ..550.00
Wilcox, syrup pitcher, heavy emb flowers, emb lid, 4½" 100.00
1847 Rogers, Ambassador, coffee set, 1919, 4-pc 395.00
1847 Rogers, Marquise, coffeepot, 1933 ....195.00
1847 Rogers, Reflection, covered dish, 1959, 8x13" 45.00

Sheffield

Basket, bread; wirework, swing hdl, gadroon border, 1800s, 9x11" ...150.00
Biscuit box, gadrooned borders, 6½" 175.00
Bowl, fruit; vintage on 6-lobed form 125.00
Cake basket, openwork twisted ribbon design, swing hdl, 1800s, 13" 250.00
Candelabra, crested w/gadroon borders, 3-light, 19th C, 17x15", pr ...2,500.00
Candelabra, Louis XVI taste, acanthus, bobeches, 3-light, 22", pr 2,400.00
Candelabrum, 'Fr' gadroon banding, 3-light, 1820s, 19½x19" ...600.00
Candle snuffer, scissors type, shell hdl, 1810-20 ....165.00
Candle snuffer, scissors type, spring action, 19th C 135.00
Candlesticks, acanthus, scroll & floral decor, 1820-30, 12", pr ..600.00
Candlesticks, baluster shaft, floral bobeches, 7", pr 330.00
Candlesticks, Georgian, trumpet form, orig bobeches, 11", pr ...415.00
Castor set, Georgian, floral decor/paw ft, 4 bottles/2 shakers/pot 880.00
Centerpice, Georgian, Irish cut crystal fitted bowl, 16x10" dia ..600.00
Coaster, decanter; gadroon & shell border, trn wood base, 7" dia, pr ...600.00
Coaster, wine; Georgian, gadroon rim, trn hardwood base, 1810s, pr ..600.00
Coffeepot, baluster, pineapple finial, pearwood hdl, 1800s 715.00
Coffeepot, Georgian, ped base, urn shape w/crest, wood hdl 250.00
Entree dish & lid on stand, scrolls/florals, 1830s, 7x14x9" 600.00
Epergne, sphinx surmounts, cut glass center bowl, 28" 3,575.00
Hot water urn, gadroon border, flower finial, 1820s, 12" 715.00
Hot water urn, Georgian, dolphin spout, scroll hdls, w/liner, 16x14" ...1,980.00
Hot water urn, sq base w/ball ft, 18x10" 450.00
Meat dome, Georgian, crested, w/gadroon & shell border, 10x17" 880.00
Platter, crest, gadroon border, 1820s, 19x15", pr 1,750.00
Platter, meat warming; well-&-tree, domed lid, 26" L 1,700.00
Shakers, eng, England, 3⅞", pr 220.00
Souffle dish, Georgian in Neoclassical taste, ca 1880, pr 1,750.00
Tea caddy, beaded decor, urn finial on hinged lid, 19th C, 4¼" 300.00
Teakettle, Regency style, ebony hdl/finial, Walker & Hall, 9" ...125.00
Tray, Regency style, pierced galleried border, 24" L 800.00
Tureen, sauce; gadrooned/foliage/paw ft, crest, w/lid, 6x8x5" ..1,750.00
Tureen, soup; Georgian, armorial crest, scroll hdls, 1820s, 10x16" ...2,500.00
Vegetable stand, bead borders, wreath hdls, w/lid, 14½" L 500.00
Venison dish w/hot-water compartment & lid, 1920s, 15x25x17" ...2,300.00
Wine coasters, floral border, 6¼" dia, pr 200.00
Wine cooler, Georgian, floral borders, ped ft, 1820s, 10½x9" .1,650.00

Cases

Plastic/Bakelite, fancy, minimum value 35.00
Pre-1920s, fancy wood, minimum value 50.00
Silver cloth pocket protector, from $2 to 6.00
1920s-50s, wooden, dbl drw, from $35 to 45.00
1920s-50s, wooden, single drw, from $25 to 35.00

Sinclaire

In 1904 H.P. Sinclaire and Company was founded in Corning, New York. For the first sixteen years of production, Sinclaire used blanks from other glassworks for his cut and engraved designs. In 1920 he established his own glassblowing factory in Bath, New York. His most popular designs utilize fruits, flowers, and other forms from nature. Most of Sinclaire's glass is unmarked; items that are carry his logo: an 'S' within a wreath with two shields.

Tray, Plaid and Thistle, cut and engraved, signed, 14½x11½", $4,200.00.

Bowl, canoe w/eng flowers, 11x7½" 185.00
Compote, Hobstar & Honeycomb, 8½x10" 600.00
Creamer & sugar bowl, Hobstar & eng floral 575.00
Teapot, Silver Thread/Adam #2, rare, 10x6½" 4,850.00
Tumbler, iced tea; eng thistles 40.00
Vase, eng bulbous bowl on pencil stem, 12" 465.00

Sitzendorf

The Sitzendorf factory began operations in East Germany in the mid-1800s, adopting the name of the city as the name of their company. They produced fine porcelain groups, figurines, etc., in much the same style and quality as Meissen and the Dresden factories. Much of their ware was marked with a crown over the letter 'S' and a horizontal line with two slash marks.

Centerpc, floral basketweave bowl, couple at base, 2-pc, 18" 550.00
Figurine, cupid clinging to bk of leaping donkey, 1890s, 6x7½" ...325.00
Vase, jack-in-pulpit; gray pearlized w/emb floral, appl lady, 12" 350.00

Skookum Dolls

Representing real Indians of various tribes, stern-faced Skookum dolls were designed by Mary McAboy of Missoula, Montana, in the early 1900s. The earliest of McAboy's creations were made with air-dried apple faces that bore a resemblance to the neighboring Chinook Indian tribe. The name Skookum is derived from the Chinook/Siwash term for large or excellent (aka Bully Good) and appears as part of the oval paper labels often attached to the feet of the dolls.

In 1913 McAboy applied for a patent that described her dolls in three styles: a female doll, a female doll with a baby, and a male doll. In 1916 George Borgman and Co. partnered with McAboy, registered the Skookum trademark, and manufactured these dolls which were distributed by the Arrow Novelty Co. of New York and the HH Tammen Co. of Denver. The Skookum (Apple) Packers Association of Washington state produced similar 'friendly faced' dolls as did Louis Ambery for the National Fruit exchange.

The dried apple faces of the first dolls were replaced by those made of a composition material. Plastic faces were introduced in the 1940s, and these continued to be used until production ended in 1959. Skookum dolls were produced in a variety of styles, with the most collectible having stern, lined faces with small painted eyes glancing to the right, colorful Indian blankets pulled tightly across the straw- or paper-filled body to form hidden arms, felt pants or skirts over wooden legs, and wooden feet covered with decorated felt suede or masking tape.

Skookums were produced in sizes ranging from a 2" souvenir mailer with a cardboard address tag to 36" novelty and advertising dolls. Collectors highly prize 21" to 26" dolls as well as dolls that glance to their left. Felt or suede feet predate the less desirable brown plastic feet of the late 1940s and '50s. Our advisor is Glen Rairigh; he is listed in the Directory under Michigan.

Male, suede feet, 24", $3,100.00. (Photo courtesy Glen Rairigh)

Baby, looks left, cradle brd, beaded body/head covering, 10½" 1,100.00
Baby, mc blanket, leather headband w/pnt decor, 4" 30.00
Baby, wrapped in mc blanket, feather in headband, 3½x3" 200.00
Baby mailer, 1½¢ postcard attached, feather/ribbon binding, 4" ...100.00
Baby mailer, 1½¢ postcard attached, rattan binding, 4" 105.00
Baby/child in loop basket, blanket wrap, necklace, 14" 200.00
Baby/child in loop basket, blanket wrap, unbraided hair, 12" 225.00
Boy, brn ft w/pnt decor, Bully Good label, 6½" 100.00
Boy, brn suede ft w/decor, headband, 10" 150.00
Boy, mc blanket, felt pants, leather shoes, 6½", VG 50.00
Boy, w/blanket/felt pants, brn plastic ft w/mk, wood beads, 9½" ..85.00
Chief, w/headdress, paper shoes w/decor, 12½" 250.00
Family, chief w/mc feathers, 15", female w/baby, clothes match, 14" ..600.00
Family, man w/exposed right arm, 13½", female w/baby, 12½" ..900.00
Family, w/blanket/clothes/beads, 35", 33" w/10" baby in arms ...5,900.00
Female w/baby, floral skirt, glass bead necklace, 11½" 300.00
Female w/baby, w/blanket, purple felt ft/skirt, necklace, 11½" ...200.00
Female w/baby, w/blanket, worn paper ft, 12½", VG 150.00
Girl, cotton-wrapped legs, beaded ft decor, headband, 9½" 150.00
Girl, cotton-wrapped legs, pnt suede ft covers, Bully Good, 6½" ...100.00
Girl, w/blanket, felt skirt, decor felt ft, bandana, 10" 85.00
Girl, w/blanket/skirt, leather shoes, feather, label, 6½" 125.00
Mailer, baby in bl & yel cotton, Grand Canyon 10-1-52 ....25.00
Mailer, baby in patterned cotton on yel cb 25.00
Mailer, baby in red bandana on yel cb 55.00
Mailer, clay child in leather pouch, Yel Stone Park 6-22-39 ....35.00

Slag Glass

Slag glass is a marbleized opaque glassware made by several companies from about 1870 until the turn of the century. It is usually found in purple or caramel (see Chocolate Glass), though other colors were also made. Pink is rare and very expensive. It was revived in recent years by several American glassmakers, L.E. Smith, Westmoreland, and Imperial among them.

For more information refer to *American Slag Glass* by Ruth Grizel (Collector Books.) The listings below reflect values for items with excellent color. Our advisor for this category is Sharon Thoerner; she is listed in the Directory under California.

Almond, coal bucket, LE Smith, #125A, 5" 25.00
Caramel, Cherry, butter dish, LG Wright Glass #7-2 ....110.00
Caramel, Herringbone, basket, Imperial #156, 5½" 35.00
Caramel, pie wagon, Imperial #43890CS 300.00
Green, pitcher, Imperial #104, mini 25.00
Jade Green, Poppy, nappy, hdl, Imperial #478, 5½" 45.00
Pastel Blue, Hobnail, bowl, Kanawah #2980ED, ca 1973, 6" 40.00
Pastel Blue, Thumbprint, pitcher, Kanawha #204ED, 4½" 35.00
Pink, Invt Fan & Feather, creamer 500.00
Pink, Invt Fan & Feather, cruet 900.00
Pink, Invt Fan & Feather, pitcher, 7½" 1,200.00
Pink, Invt Fan & Feather, punch cup, from $285 to 315.00
Pink, Invt Fan & Feather, sauce dish, ball ft, 2½x4⅝" 165.00
Pink, Invt Fan & Feather, shakers, rare, pr 1,200.00
Pink, Invt Fan & Feather, spooner, 4¼" 425.00
Pink, Invt Fan & Feather, toothpick holder 500.00
Pink, Invt Fan & Feather, toothpick holder, ftd, 2⅜" 1,500.00
Pink, Invt Fan & Feather, tumbler, 4" 300.00
Purple, baker's cake stand, Imperial #98, 10" 25.00
Purple, Dewdrop, bowl, Imperial #641, 8½" 65.00
Purple, Hobnail, bell, Fenton #3667PS, 5½" 50.00
Purple, Orange Tree & Cherry, basket, Fenton #9136PS, minimum value 150.00
Purple, Orange Tree & Cherry, bowl, Fenton #8233PS 95.00
Purple, Peacock, vase, Fenton #8257PS, 8", from $95 to 110.00
Purple, syrup, Imperial #981 ....45.00
Red, Dmn Dot, basket, Kanawha #324ED, 8¼" 65.00
Red, Eagle, mug, Imperial #154 ....40.00
Red, Grape, nappy, hdl, Imperial #851, 5" 45.00
Red, vase, burgundy & wine swirls, bulbous, 7½x9" 150.00
Red Marble, English Hobnail, basket, Westmoreland #555, tall ..75.00
Ruby, Cherry, sugar bowl, LG Wright #7-5 ....50.00
Ruby, vase, tricorn, Imperial #192, 8½" 125.00

Smith Bros.

Alfred and Harry Smith founded their glassmaking firm in New Bedford, Massachusetts. They had been formerly associated with the Mt. Washington Glass Works, working there from 1871 to 1875 to aid in establishing a decorating department. Smith glass is valued for its excellent enameled decoration on satin or opalescent glass. Pieces were often marked with a lion in a red shield. Our advisors for this category are Betty and Clarence Maier; they are listed in the Directory under Pennsylvania.

Biscuit jar, daisies/ferns on lt yel, bbl shape, 4¾" 250.00
Biscuit jar, ivy on cream, melon ribbed, gilt mts, 7" dia 885.00
Biscuit jar, pansies, brn/maroon/gold on beige, metal lid 735.00

Biscuit jar, wheat, gold on cream, melon ribbed, 6½" dia 575.00
Bowl, daisies, yel & gr on ivory, lion trademk, 3¾x5½" 250.00
Bowl, gold prunus allover, beaded wht rim, melon ribbed, 6" 365.00
Box, daisies on tan, melon ribbed, 3x4" 375.00
Creamer & sugar bowl, violets on bl to tan, SP mts, 4", 3½" 695.00
Humidor, pansies, bl on cream, melon-ribbed lid, 6½x4" 800.00
Jar, daisies/leaves, melon ribbed, w/lid, lion mk 450.00
Plate, Santa Maria, 1893 World's Fair souvenir, 8" 550.00
Rose bowl, daisies on tan, melon ribbed, 2½x3" 325.00
Rose bowl, gold prunus/jewels/beaded top on cream, 2¼x3" 275.00
Sugar shaker, daisies on pnt burmese, ribbed, 5¾" 400.00
Sugar shaker, florals on wht, ribbed cylinder, 6x2½" 575.00
Sweetmeat jar, lilies on beige, melon ribbed, rstr mk mts 750.00
Toothpick holder, violets on wht, pillar ribbed, 2" 275.00
Toothpick holder, wild roses on wht, pillar ribbed, 2½" 235.00
Vase, daisies & dots, mc on ivory base, pinched sides, 4½" 325.00
Vase, floral on beige, bulbous, 4½" 300.00
Vase, mums on cream & gr, melon ribbed, bowl neck w/decor, 8½" ..1,150.00
Vase, orchids, int ribs, cylinder w/lobed rim, 8½" 475.00
Vase, orchids/traceries/gilt on tan, rnd flask form, 8½" 1,800.00
Vase, pond lily/leaves, mc on lt pk, 7" 175.00
Vase, sm flowers on lt yel, 3-sided, tiny neck, 5¼x4" 400.00
Vase, wisteria on pnt burmese w/gold, swirled, 7x4½" 1,100.00

Snow Babies

During the last quarter of the nineteenth century, snow babies — little figurals in white snowsuits — originated in Germany. They were made of sugar candy and were often as decoration for Christmas cakes. Later on they were made of marzipan, a confection of crushed almonds, sugar, and egg whites. Eventually procelain manufacturers began making them in bisque. They were popular until WWII. These tiny bisque figures range in size from 1" up to 7" tall. Quality German pieces bring very respectable prices on the market today. Beware of reproductions. Our advisor for this category is Linda Vines; she is listed in the Directory under New Jersey.

Baby riding polar bear, 1930s, Germany, 2½", $175.00. (Photo courtesy Linda Vines)

Babies (2) sliding down brick wall, Germany, 2½" 175.00
Babies (3) caroling, holding yel song book, Germany, 2" 265.00
Babies climbing on world, flag on top, open bk, Germany, 3".....250.00
Baby crawling, pointed hood, very early face, Germany, 5".........350.00
Baby inside glass snow dome, USA, 4" 95.00
Baby pulling 3 penguins on sled, Germany, 2" 285.00
Baby riding sled, blk 'chimney sweep' outfit, Germany, 3" 325.00
Baby skier, wooden skis & pole, very early face, Germany, 5" 375.00
Baby standing on lg snowball, Japan, 2½" 45.00
Baby w/seal & red ball, B Shackman, recent, 2" 35.00
Baby w/seal & red ball, Germany, 2" 195.00
Child on skates, snowed hat & sweater, pastel pants, Germany, 2"..110.00
Santa at chimney, hanging stocking on mantel, Germany, 2" 135.00
Santa in boat beside snow-topped lighthouse; Germany, 3" 165.00
Santa in silver car, toys in bk, Germany, 1½" 125.00
Santa sitting, candle holder at bk, Germany, 1" 95.00
Santa standing w/sleeping children, Germany, 2" 175.00
Snow bear, comic eyes, astride yel sled, Germany, 2" 165.00
Snow bear on hind legs, lifelike, Germany, 5½" 375.00
Snowman, British 'Bobby' hat, arm raised, Germany, 2" 120.00

Snuff Boxes

As early as the seventeenth century, the Chinese began using snuff. By the early nineteenth century, the practice had spread to Europe and America. It was used by both the gentlemen and the ladies alike, and expensive snuff boxes and bottles were the earmark of the genteel. Some were of silver or gold set with precious stones or pearls, while others contained music boxes. In the following listings, the dimension noted is length. See also Orientalia, Snuff Bottles.

Antler, SP top w/initials, European, early 19th C, 2½x2¼" 75.00
Bone, inscr name, 19th C, 3x1⅛" 200.00
Brass coffin shape w/tack decor, English, 19th C, 4⅛x1⅝", VG .200.00
Burl, Lafayette gilt medallion under glass, tortoise-shell lined, 3" ...245.00
Burl & tortoise shell, pressed decor, 19th C, 3⅛" dia, VG 300.00
Burl walnut, men w/musical instruments cvg, English, 19th C, 3¼" ...250.00
Coquilla nut w/cvd figures/flowers/angel, 19th C, 3½x2" 600.00
Enameled copper, shoe form, 2¼", EX 185.00
French enamel, boats & floral sprays, late 18th C, 2¾" 260.00
Horn w/red & gr wax inlay, English, late 18th C, 3¾x2½" 300.00
Ivory w/copper inlay, pnt cards on lid, European, 1780s, 1¼" dia 475.00
Papier-mache, 2 men using snuff scene, European, 19th C, 4⅞" dia ...450.00
Silver, set w/oyster shell, eng decor, 2½" 115.00
Silver, striated polished stone on lid, English, 2⅝" L 265.00
Tortoise shell, cvd Chinese figures, early 1800s, ⅞x2½x1½" 375.00
Tortoise shell w/gold inlay, 3¾", EX 425.00
Tortoise shell w/pressed decor: man/bicycles, 19th C, 3" dia, VG ..275.00

Soap Hollow Furniture

In the Mennonite community of Soap Hollow, Pennsylvania, the women made and sold soap; the men made handcrafted furniture. Rare today, this furniture was stenciled, grain painted, and beautifully decorated with inlaid escutcheons. These pieces are becoming very sought after. When well kept, they are very distinctive and beautiful. The items described in these listings were recently sold through Merle S. Mishlers Auctions, RD 2, Hollsopple, Pennsylvania. All are in excellent condition unless otherwise noted. Our advisor for this category is Anita Levi; she is listed in the Directory under Pennsylvania.

Chest, blanket; feathers on mustard & brn, MB/1897 ....1,400.00
Chest, blanket; grpt w/blk lid, fruit/florals w/gold, 1882 ....2,900.00
Chest, blanket; maroon w/gold stencil, rnd escutcheon, 1856 ...2,000.00
Chest, blanket; poplar, orig red pnt w/blk/gold, att, 22x42" 3,850.00
Chest, blanket; red & blk, gold stencil, CW/1874, 25x18x45" 6,700.00
Chest, blanket; red & blk, gold stencil, MH/1871, 25x15x10", VG ...6,200.00
Chest, blanket; red w/floral stencils, rpl hinges, FJ/1892, VG .3,800.00
Chest, blanket; rose decals, blk & brn grpt, LK/1890 ....5,000.00
Chest, 4 lg/2 sm drws w/decor, enamel pulls, sgn, 1851, EX+ .4,600.00
Chest, 4 lg/3 sm drws, stencil, enamel pulls, sgn, 1883, EX+ ..5,400.00
Chest, 6-drw, brn w/mustard & decals, blk top & sides, Sala ..1,900.00
Chest, 6-drw, no pnt or decor, EX wood, G 475.00
Chest, 7-drw, grpt w/blk, gold stencil, MH 1887, 47½x39½" 14,500.00
Chest, 7-drw, maroon w/blk top & sides, rpt CKM/1879, G 550.00

Chest of drws, bk brd, hidden lock, stencil, HS/1879 ....5,500.00
Chest of drws, brn grpt w/stencil, pnt pulls, 1883, EX+ 5,400.00
Chest of drws, floral decals/fruit gilt stencil/grpt, MH/1879 ....2,750.00
Chest of drws, rosewood, 1841 ....750.00
Chest of drws, stenciling w/decals, dk brn, fancy bk brd 7,200.00
Cradle, gilt stencils, mustard trim, maroon grpt 1,100.00
Cupboard, corner; maroon w/blk, stencil, 1856 ....11,500.00
Cupboard, Dutch; 4 doors/2 drws, stencil/old rpt, 1875, 84x65" ...8,000.00
Cupboard, step-bk; 3 glass doors/2 solid, 3-drw, no decor, 87½x64" 20,000.00
Cupboard top only, 2 glass doors, no decor, 40x42x13" 3,500.00
Dresser, Emp style, columns on 3 drws, HF/1874 ....2,200.00
Frame, cross pcs, gr/yel striping, 15½x19¾" 1,000.00
Frame, gilt edges, stenciled, blk 1,050.00
Rope bed, cherry, red & brn finish, rare 2,300.00
Stand, bedside; rpt mustard brn 400.00

Soapstone

Soapstone is a soft talc in rock form with a smooth, greasy feel from whence comes its name. (It is also called Soo Chow Jade.) It is composed basically of talc, chlorite, and magnetite. In colonial times it was extracted from out-croppings in large sections with hand saws, carted by oxen to mills, and fashioned into useful domestic articles such as footwarmers, cooking utensils, inkwells, etc. During the early 1800s, it was used to make heating stoves and kitchen sinks. Most familiar today are the carved vases, bookends, and boxes made in China during the Victorian era. For further information we recommend *Collector's Digest Soapstone* by L-W Book Sales.

Ashtray, vining floral, 3x4¾" 27.50
Censor, foo dogs, 3-ftd ped on rnd plinth, 9½" 125.00
Figure, Hotei Buddha, w/bats/coins/floral, 4½x6x3" 160.00
Figure, Inuit mother holding child, 6x3¼" 65.00
Figure, Shao Lu, ca 19th C, mtd as lamp: 28" 200.00
Figure, water buffalo, 1½x3" 17.50
Incense burner, Foo Dog w/pup, blk & brn, 1920s, 7x7x4", EX .250.00
Vase, dbl; bird among floral vine, 8x6¼x3¼" 125.00
Vase, grapevines & fruit, 9", pr 125.00
Vase, monkey & bird at sides, 3x5¼x1⅜" 40.00

Soda Fountain Collectibles

The first soda water sales in the United States occurred in the very late 1790s in New York and New Haven, Connecticut. By the 1830s soda water was being sold in drug stores as a medicinal item, especially the effervescent mineral waters from various springs around the country. By this time the first flavored soda water appeared at an apothecary shop in Philadelphia.

The 1830s also saw the first manufacturer (John Matthews) of devices to make soda water. The first marble soda fountain made its appearance in 1857 as a combination ice shaver and flavor-dispensing apparatus. By the 1870s the soda fountain was an established feature of the neighborhood drug store.

The fountains of this period were large, elaborate marble devices with druggists competing with each other for business by having fountains decorated with choice marbles, statues, mirrors, water fountains, and gas lamps.

In 1903 the fountain completed its last major evolution with the introduction of the 'front' counter service we know today. (The soda clerk faced the customer when drawing soda.)

By this time ice cream was a standard feature being served as sundaes, ice cream sodas, and milk shakes. Syrup dispensers were just being introduced as 'point-of-sale' devices to sell various flavorings from many different companies. Straws were commonplace, especially those made from paper. Fancy and unusual ice cream dippers were in daily use, and they continued to evolve, reaching their pinnacle with the introduction of the heart-shaped dipper in 1927.

This American business has provided collectors today with an almost endless supply of interesting and different articles of commerce. One can collect dippers, syrup dispensers, glassware, straw dispensers, milk shakers, advertising, and trade catalogs. (Note: The presence of a 'correct' pump enhances the value of a syrup dispenser by 25%.)

Collectors need to be made aware of decorating pieces that are actually fantasy items: copper ice cream cones, a large copper ice cream dipper, and a copper ice cream soda glass. These items have no resale value. Our advisors for this category are Joyce and Harold Screen; they are listed in the Directory under Maryland. See also Advertising; Coca-Cola.

Dispensers: Ward's Lemon Crush, porcelain, lemon shape, original metal pump, 12¾x9", EX, $1,500.00; Howel's Orange Julep, ceramic with metal top, orange shape with base, 15x9", VG, $1,600.00.

Banana split bowl, Heisey #412 pattern, ftd, 8" 35.00
Banana split dishes, milk glass, set of 4, 4x9" 50.00
Bowl, Bardwell's Root Beer, Whites Utica pottery, 20" 3,000.00
Bowl, crushed fruit; American pattern, Fostoria, 2-qt 2,000.00
Bowl, crushed fruit; Greek Key, Heisey, 2-qt 350.00
Canteen, Bardwell's Root Beer, Whites Utica pottery, orig 750.00
Catalog, Liquid Carbonic, 1899, full sz 400.00
Catalog, Matthews, 1868 ....500.00
Cone holder, Crisp Cone Cabinet Co, glass w/warming light, 18" ...450.00
Cone holder, glass tube w/metal base, 31", EX 450.00
Cone holder, ind; heavy clear glass, Heisey, 5x2½", EX 100.00
Cone holder, plain glass w/metal lid & insert, 6x15", EX 450.00
Dipper, AJ Daniel, parachute shape, wood hdl, Pat 1910, 12", EX ...5,250.00
Dipper, banana split; Gilchrist, 11", M 650.00
Dipper, Bohlig, squeeze hdl & bowl divides in half, 10", EX ...2,000.00
Dipper, Clipper Disher/Geer Mfg, lg sz 6, 10" L 300.00
Dipper, Gilchrist, #33, cone shape, lg sz 6, 11", EX 150.00
Dipper, Hamilton Beach #50 ....30.00
Dipper, heart shape, wood hdl, 11", MIB 6,000.00
Dipper, IcyPi Scoop, Automatic Cone Co, 10", NMIB 450.00
Dipper, Kingery, squeeze hdl, rotating bowl, Pat 1894, 8½", EX ...1,500.00
Dipper, Mosteller, press lever & bowl flips over, 11", EX 2,000.00
Dipper, saucer-shaped bowl, wood hdl, 1932, 10", EX 1,650.00
Dipper, slicer; Dover, 11", EX 600.00
Dispenser, Brazilla, ceramic bbl form, rpl pump, 15", VG 1,250.00
Dispenser, Cherry Chic, emb ceramic ball form, no pump, 10", VG+ .6,000.00
Dispenser, Cherry Smash, red glass bowl, metal clamp, 1930s, EX 475.00
Dispenser, Fowler's Root Beer, ceramic ball form, w/spigot, 14", EX+ ..1,500.00
Dispenser, Grape Julep, ceramic ball form, bl/wht, VG 1,500.00
Dispenser, Grape Kola 5¢, wht 3-pc ceramic urn w/pnt decor, 21", EX ...3,100.00
Dispenser, Howel's Cherry Julep, ceramic ball, w/orig pump, VG+ ...2,500.00
Dispenser, Jersey Cream, wht ceramic urn, gold trim, EX 2,000.00
Dispenser, Johnston's Cold Fudge, chrome top, Bakelite knob 90.00
Dispenser, Lash's Orangeade, metal canister w/fruit topper, 22", VG ..500.00

Dispenser, Lash's Orangeade, textured vaseline glass globe, VG ...300.00
Dispenser, Liberty Root Beer, wooden bbl, 1920s, 27", EX+ 300.00
Dispenser, Middleby Root Beer, amber mug, chrome lid, 16", NM ..600.00
Dispenser, Mission Beverages, glass bottle, metal base, 28", EX .372.00
Dispenser, Mission Beverages, glass goblet, chrome top/bottom, NMIB 275.00
Dispenser, Mission Beverages, orange/brn cylinder, porc base, 26", VG+ 190.00
Dispenser, Mission Beverages, vaseline bbl, Bakelite base, VG ..225.00
Dispenser, Murray's Root Beer, ceramic bbl on stump, no lid, NM+ 400.00
Dispenser, Orange-Crush, clear glass bowl, clamp base, 1930s-40s, NM 325.00
Dispenser, Orange-Crush, ribbed glass, aluminum base, porc top, EX ..350.00
Dispenser, Rochester Root Beer, metal box, 12x19x21", VG 90.00
Dispenser, Rochester Root Beer, wooden bbl, claw ft, 13", VG .500.00
Dispenser, syrup; Hires Root Beer, Little Boy, Mettlach 50,000.00
Dispenser, Vola, ceramic urn on base, emb decor, 17", VG 2,000.00
Dispenser, Ward's Lemon-Crush, ceramic lemon, new pump, M 1,200.00
Dispenser, Ward's Orange-Crush, ceramic orange, 1920, no pump o/w NM ...800.00
Display, cone, Peerless, light-up, 12x6", G 350.00
Display, cones, papier-mache, 20" to 26", EX, ea 125.00
Flavor board, Dairy Made Ice Cream, tin, wht on bl, 40x11", NM ..4,600.00
Flavor board, Klover Ice Cream, diecut cb, 21x10", EX 450.00
Flavor board, Sealtest, 10 flavor/price inserts, metal fr, 22x10", NM ...100.00
Fountain backbar, Lippincott, dtd 1893, 118x27x85", EX 1,000.00
Fountain glass, Allen's Red Tame Cherry, flared, etched, 5" 150.00
Fountain glass, California Grapine 5¢, flared, etched, 5½" 175.00
Fountain glass, Green River, flared, etched, 4" 100.00
Fountain glass, Orange-Crush, flared, etched, waisted, 5½" 225.00
Fountain glass, Orange-Crush, flared, etched, 5" 120.00
Fountain glass, Richard's Liberty Drinks, flared, syrup line, 5½" ...120.00
Fountain glass, Richardson's Drinks, flared, etched, syrup line, 6" 120.00
Fountain glass, Zipp's Cherri-O, flared, etched, waisted, 5½" 150.00
Fountain glasses, glass, mk Mondae Siren, set of 4, 7½" 180.00
Ice-cream dish, glass heart shape w/bird motif (for heart scoop), 3" ...700.00
Ice-cream dishes, glass, dbl scoop, ped ft, set of 6, 3" 100.00
Ice-cream dishes, glass, 3-leaf clover shape, ped ft, set of 6, 3" ...100.00
Ice-cream dishes, NP, ruffled edge, ped ft, set of 6, 2" 50.00
Ice-cream sandwich maker, Sanisco, 1917, EX 1,500.00
Match striker, Orange-Crush, porc, 1930s, rare 1,250.00
Mixer, milk shake; Hamilton Beach, wht porc, light-up, 20", EX ...350.00
Mixer, milk shake; Hires Root Beer, mechanical, w/can & lid ..3,000.00
Mixer, milk shake; Hires The Flavor For Milk Drinks, 13", EX .4,250.00
Mixer, milk shake; Horlick's, wht porc, iron base, 20", EX 850.00
Mixer, milk shake; Kwikmix, hand crank, wood base, 10", EX ..450.00
Mixer, milk shake; Walker's Quick & Easy, floor model, 60" ..4,000.00
Mug, bouillon; OXO, maroon letters 15.00
Mug, hot soda; Armour's Vigoral Bouillon Cubes 35.00
Mug, hot soda; Bovox, monk, brn 25.00
Photo, orig inside view of old soda fountain, blk/wht, ca 1900, 5x8" ..150.00
Pitcher, Bardwell's Root Beer, Whites Utica pottery 2,000.00
Printer's block, Kewpie eating ice cream, 1¾x2" 20.00
Sign, Hendlers Ice Cream, neon, working, ca 1950, 30x18" 450.00
Sign, Ice Cream/Sundaes, glass, silver on bl, rstr, 26x7" fr 550.00
Sign, Soda Fountain & Confections, glass, gold leaf, fr, 20x56", EX 600.00
Soda fountain, Tufts 'Canadian' model, marble counter top ...5,000.00
Straw holder, frosted glass w/pnt flowers, 4-ftd, open, 9x4", EX 1,000.00
Straw holder, Manhattan pattern glass, gold top/bottom, 11", EX 700.00
Straw holder, milk glass, copper top, fluted, 12", EX 1,650.00
Straw holder, Orange Julep, pressed-glass box, VG 425.00
Straw holder, San-I-Straw, paneled, mechanical chrome top, 12", EX ...250.00
Syrup bottle, Gay-Ola/It's Better label, w/cap, 12" 400.00
Syrup bottle, Grapefruitola label, dtd 1912, 12" 300.00
Syrup bottle, Pepsinade gold label, w/gold cap, 12" 400.00
Syrup jug holder, Hires metal counter-top w/clamp base, 12x5", EX ...200.00
Table w/2 connected chairs, wood top/seats, 35x25x38", EX ..1,300.00
Table w/4 swing-out stools, glass display-case top, 27" sq 1,750.00

Spangle Glass

Spangle glass, also known as Vasa Murrhina, is cased art glass characterized by the metallic flakes embedded in its top layer. It was made both abroad and in the United States during the latter years of the 1800s, and it was reproduced in the 1960s by the Fenton Art Glass Company.

Vasa Murrhina was a New England distributor who sold glassware of this type manufactured by a Dr. Flower of Sandwich, Massachusetts. Flower had purchased the defunct Cape Cod Glassworks in 1885 and used the facilities to operate his own company. Since none of the ware was marked, it is very difficult to attribute specific examples to his manufacture. See also Art Glass Baskets; Fenton.

Bowl, amethyst w/goldstone flakes, 3 folded-in sides, 8" W 185.00
Ewer, pk mottle, ruffled rim, clear branch hdl, 9" 125.00
Pitcher, rainbow on wht w/silver, swirled ribs, ruffled, Mt WA, 8" ..575.00
Rose bowl, pk opal & amber stripes w/mica, broken pontil 195.00
Rose bowl, rose w/mica coral branches, 8-crimp, 3¾x3⅜" 120.00
Tumbler, Dmn Quilt, orange/wht spatter w/mica, 3¾" 40.00
Vase, butterscotch to yel to wht w/silver mica, stick neck, 10" ..135.00
Vase, cranberry/wht/tan, gold mica, ruffled rim, 4¼" 165.00

Spatter Glass

Spatter glass, characterized by its multicolor 'spatters,' has been made from the late nineteenth century to the present by American glasshouses as well as those abroad. Although it was once thought to have been made entirely by workers at the 'end of the day' from bits and pieces of leftover scrap, it is now known that it was a standard line of production. See also Art Glass Baskets.

Pitcher, pink and white, cylindrical neck, clear handle, 9¼, $175.00.

Bowl, centerpc; pk frost & wht; fancy SP figural base, 21x13" ...795.00
Cruet, cranberry & wht, ruffled top, clear stopper, 5¾" 75.00
Cruet, maroon/wht w/floral, clear hdl/cut stopper, 5½" 250.00
Muffineer, wht & purple, ring in mold, metal lid, 4¾" 135.00
Vase, mc on wht, wht int, 7½x3⅜" 110.00

Spatterware

Spatterware is a general term referring to a type of decoration used by English potters as early as the late 1700s. Using a brush or a stick, brightly colored paint was dabbed onto the soft-paste earthenware items, achieving a spattered effect which was often used as a border. Because much of this type of ware was made for export to the United States, some of the subjects in the central design — the schoolhouse and the eagle patterns, for instance — reflect American tastes. Yellow, green, and black spatterware is scarce and highly valued by collectors.

In the descriptions that follow, the color listed after the item indicates the color of the spatter. The central design is identified next, and the color description that follows that refers to the design. Our advisor is Diane Patalano; she is listed in the Directory under New Jersey.

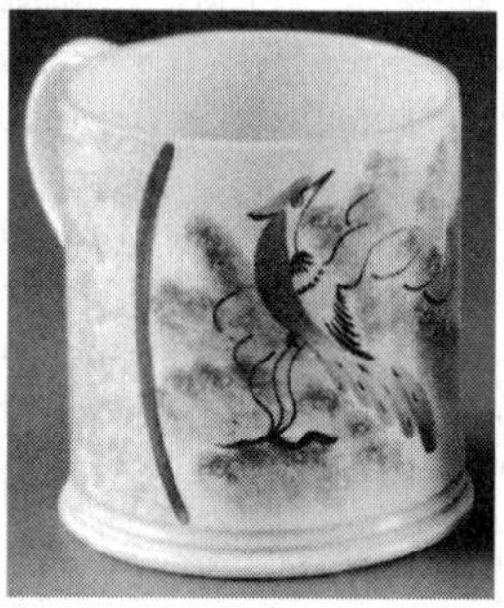

Mug, Peafowl, red, yellow, and blue in green spatter tree with blue spatter panels and yellow rim, 6⅛", from $600.00 to $700.00.

Bowl, brn/yel/gr, Rainbow, ftd base, 2¼x4⅛", NM 900.00
Bowl, vegetable; yel, Thistle, 2-color, 2⅛x10½x7¾", NM 2,000.00
Bowl, waste; red, Peafowl, 3-color, 3x5⅝", EX 950.00
Coffeepot, red, Peafowl, 3-color, domed lid, rprs, 8¾" 800.00
Creamer, bl, House, 3-color, w/lid, rprs 650.00
Creamer, bl, Memorial Tulip, 3-color, globular, 4⅜", NM 400.00
Creamer, bl, overall spatter, 8-sided, arched hdl, 5¾", NM 360.00
Creamer, bl, Peafowl, 3-color, 8-sided, 6", EX 875.00
Creamer, bl, Thistle, 2-color, 4½", NM 330.00
Creamer, bl/purple, Rainbow, hexagonal, 4½", EX 220.00
Creamer, yel, Thistle, 2-color, waisted, 4⅛", NM 500.00
Pitcher, bl, Peafowl, 3-color, acanthus hdl, 7½", EX+ 6,700.00
Pitcher, cranberry w/wht, ribbed, sqd rim, 9", NM 200.00
Pitcher, milk; red/bl/gr rainbow (vertical bands), bbl shape, 5", NM ..4,200.00
Pitcher, water; 4-color, clear hdl, pinched spout, 9⅜", NM 110.00
Plate, bl, Acorn, 3-color, 12-sided, 9½", NM 1,150.00
Plate, bl, Fort, 3-color, 8¾", EX 275.00
Plate, bl, Holly Berry, 3-color, 12-sided, 6½", NM 175.00
Plate, bl, Peafowl, 3-color, 12-sided, 8⅝", EX 375.00
Plate, bl, Star, 3-color, hairline, 8½" 275.00
Plate, bl, Star, 3-color, 14-sided, 9⅜", NM 950.00
Plate, bl, Willow Tree, 3-color, Adams & Son, 9⅛", EX 240.00
Plate, gr, Peafowl, 4-color, 8", NM 350.00
Plate, red, Acorn, 4-color, 12-sided, 8½", NM 3,100.00
Plate, red, Memorial Tulip, 4-color, 10-sided, 8¾", NM 700.00
Plate, red, Peafowl, 3-color, plain rim, 9", EX+ 650.00
Plate, red, Peafowl, 4-color, 7⅜", NM 415.00
Plate, red, Peafowl, 4-color, 8⅜", NM 685.00
Plate, red, Reafowl, 3-color, 8", NM 425.00
Plate, red, Wigwam, 1-color, scalloped rim, 8⅜", NM 425.00
Plate, red & yel, Rainbow, flake, 8¼" 1,375.00
Plate, red/bl/gr, Rainbow, Adams, 9⅜", NM 475.00
Plate, toddy; bl/gr, Tulip, red/gr/blk, 6½", NM 195.00
Plate, toddy; red, Peafowl, 4-color, chip, 5¼" 100.00
Platter, red/gr, Rainbow, 12¼x9½", NM 2,600.00
Soup plate, red, Open Tulip, 3-color, 12-sided, 9¼", NM 1,350.00
Sugar bowl, bl, Fort, 4-color, w/lid, 4", EX 275.00
Sugar bowl, bl, Peafowl, 4-color, stains/line, 4⅝" 220.00
Sugar bowl, bl, Willow Tree, 3-color, w/lid, NM 1,350.00
Sugar bowl, gr, Peafowl, 3-color, globular, w/lid, 5" 975.00
Sugar bowl, purple/blk, Rainbow, w/lid, 4¼", NM 1,000.00
Tea bowl & saucer, bl, Cockscomb, red/gr, NM 625.00
Tea bowl & saucer, bl, Fort, 3-color, child sz, NM 800.00
Tea bowl & saucer, bl, Memorial Tulip, EX 250.00
Tea bowl & saucer, bl, Peafowl, 3-color, G 220.00
Tea bowl & saucer, bl, Rooster, 4-color, 2¾x3¾", 6", EX 1,350.00
Tea bowl & saucer, gr, Deer, 2-color, EX 1,800.00
Tea bowl & saucer, gr, House, 3-color, NM 1,000.00
Tea bowl & saucer, gr, House, 4-color, EX 400.00
Tea bowl & saucer, purple, Adams Rose, oversz, NM 525.00
Tea bowl & saucer, purple, Adams Rose, 3-color, NM 375.00
Tea bowl & saucer, red, Bull's Eye, 2¼x4", 5⅝", EX 90.00
Tea bowl & saucer, red, flower, 4-color, EX 300.00
Tea bowl & saucer, red, Peafowl, 4-color, 2¾x4", 5⅞", EX 375.00
Tea bowl & saucer, red, Shed, 3-color, 2⅜x4", 5⅝", NM 800.00
Tea bowl & saucer, red, Wigwam, 1-color, 2¼x3¾", 5⅝", NM .450.00
Tea bowl & saucer, red (coarse), Guinea Hen, 3-color, G 350.00
Tea bowl & saucer, yel, Thistle, 2-color, 2½x4", 5¾", EX 450.00
Tea bowl & saucer, yel, wide bands, 2½x4¼", NM 775.00
Teapot, purple, Rooster, 4-color, prof rpr, 6⅛" 1,600.00
Teapot, red, Peafowl, 3-color, C-hdl, 3¾", EX 800.00

Design Spatter

Creamer, bl, Snowflake, 4", NM 200.00
Cup & saucer, blk stars on bl band w/red stripes, child sz 170.00
Cup & saucer, Pansy, bl floret border w/red stripes, EX+ 350.00
Cup & saucer, Pansy, red bowknot border w/bl stripes, VG 325.00
Plate, Columbine, gr daisies/red stripe border, 9", NM 260.00
Plate, Dogwood, bl border w/stars, red stripes, 14-side, 10", NM 275.00
Plate, flowers: HP/cut-sponge, border w/blk flowers, Adams, 9", NM ..200.00
Plate, Pansy, bl florets border w/red stripes, 14-side, 8½", NM ..325.00
Plate, Pansy, gr floret border w/red stripes, 8½", EX 225.00
Plate, Thistle, red smoke rings/lt bl stripes, 14-side, 9", EX 290.00
Platter, Columbine, purple daisies/red stripe border, 12", VG 400.00
Soup plate, Dogwood, purple star border, bl stripes, 14-side, EX ...300.00

Spelter

Spelter items are cast from commercial zinc and coated with a metallic patina. The result is a product very similar to bronze in appearance, yet much less expensive

Card holder, exotic lady figure holds tray on sq base, 1890s, 44" ..400.00
Figurine, draped warrior w/ax & fallen prey, Picault, 37" 1,150.00
Figurine, young man stands by rearing horse, on base, 12½", EX 100.00

Spode-Copeland

The Spode Works was established in 1770 in England by Josiah Spode I and continued to operate under that title until 1843. Their earliest products were typical underglaze blue-printed patterns. After 1790 a translucent porcelain body was the basis for a line of fine enamel-decorated dinnerware. Stone China was introduced in 1805, often in patterns reflecting an Oriental influence. In 1833 William Taylor Copeland purchased the company, having been Spode's business partner. Copeland continued the business in much the same tradition as the Spode-Copeland partnership. Spode was the Royal Potter for years, providing many exquisite items for the Royal Families. They employed paintresses to decorate the merchandise by hand. Most of the Spode-Copeland wares were marked with one of several variations that incorporate the firm's name, making identification possible. The Spode Company merged with Worcester Royal Porcelain Company in 1976 and became Royal Worcester Spode Limited. This company was then purchased by Derby International in 1988. The two firms separated in 1989. The holding company is the Porcelain and Fine China Companies Limited, a division of Derby International. Spode china is still being manufactured today at exactly the same location where Josiah Spode I began in 1770. Robert Copeland, a descendent of William Taylor Copeland, resides in England. He writes books and gives lectures on Spode. Our advisor for this category is Don Haase; he is listed in the Directory under Washington.

The price quotes listed in these three categories of Spode are for twentieth-century pre-1965 dinnerware in pristine condition — no cracks, chips, crazing, or stains. Minor knife cuts do not constitute damage unless extreme.

The patterns in the first group are the most common and popular earthenware lines. The second group contains the rarer and higher priced patterns; they are both earthenware and stoneware. Bone china patterns comprise the third group.

First Group:

Ann Hathaway, Billingsley Rose, Buttercup, Byron, Camilla Pink, Chelsea Wicker, Chinese Rose, Christmas Tree (green), Cowslip, Fairy Dell, Fleur de Lis (blue/brown), Florence, Gadroon, Gainsborough, Hazel Dell, Indian Tree, Jewel, Moss Rose, Old Salem, Raeburn, Reynolds, Romney, Rosalie, Rose Brier, Rosebud Chintz, Tower Blue, Valencia, Wickerdale, Wickerdell, Wickerlane

Bowl, cereal; 6½" **32.00**
Bowl, fruit; 5¼" **28.00**
Bowl, waste; 6" **35.00**
Coffeepot, 8-cup **265.00**
Creamer, lg **75.00**
Creamer, sm **65.00**
Cup & saucer, demitasse **45.00**
Cup & saucer, low/tall **39.00**
Plate, bread & butter; 6¼" **28.00**
Plate, butter pat **28.00**
Plate, chop; rnd, 13" **185.00**
Plate, dinner; 10½" **39.00**
Plate, luncheon; rnd, 8-9" **35.00**
Plate, luncheon; sq, 8½" **45.00**
Plate, salad; 7½" **32.00**
Platter, oval, 13" **140.00**
Platter, oval, 15" **160.00**
Platter, oval, 17" **180.00**
Sauce boat, w/liner **145.00**
Soup, cream; w/liner **55.00**
Soup, rim, 7½" **35.00**
Soup, rim, 8½" **45.00**
Sugar bowl, w/lid, lg **75.00**
Sugar bowl, w/lid, sm **65.00**
Teapot, 8-cup **265.00**
Vegetable, oval, 10-11" **165.00**
Vegetable, oval, 9-10" **155.00**
Vegetable, sq, 8" **145.00**
Vegetable, sq, 9" **155.00**
Vegetable, w/lid **265.00**

Second Group:

Aster, Buchart, Christmas Tree (magenta), Italian, Mayflower, Herring Hunt (green/magenta), Patricia, Tower Pink, Wildflower (blue/red), Delhi, Fitzhugh (blue/red/green), Gloucester (blue/red), Ruins (blue/pink/brown), Tradewinds (blue/red).

Herring Hunt, demitasse cup with magenta rim, $55.00. (Photo courtesy Don Haase)

Bowl, cereal; 6¼" **39.00**
Bowl, fruit; 5½" **35.00**
Bowl, waste; 6" **45.00**
Coffeepot, 8-cup **375.00**
Creamer, lg **95.00**
Creamer, sm **85.00**
Cup & saucer, demitasse **55.00**
Cup & saucer, low/high **65.00**
Plate, bread & butter; 6¼" **35.00**
Plate, butter pat **35.00**
Plate, chop; rnd, 13" **295.00**
Plate, dinner; 10½" **65.00**
Plate, luncheon; rnd, 8-9" **49.00**
Plate, luncheon; sq, 8½" **65.00**
Plate, salad; 7½" **39.00**
Platter, oval, 13" **165.00**
Platter, oval, 15" **180.00**
Platter, oval, 17" **225.00**
Sauce boat, w/liner **185.00**
Soup, cream; w/liner **75.00**
Soup, rim, 7½" **45.00**
Soup, rim, 8½" **55.00**
Sugar bowl, w/lid, lg **95.00**
Sugar bowl, w/lid, sm **85.00**
Teapot, 8-cup **395.00**
Vegetable, oval, 10-11" **195.00**
Vegetable, oval, 9-10" **175.00**
Vegetable, sq, 8" **165.00**
Vegetable, sq, 9" **185.00**
Vegetable, w/lid **395.00**

Third Group:

Billingsley Rose Savoy, Bridal Rose, Carolyn, Chelsea Garden, Christine, Claudia, Colonel, Dimity, Dresden, Rose Savoy, Fleur de Lis (gray/red/blue), Geisha (blue/pink/white), Irene, Maritime Rose, Primrose (pink), Shanghi, Savoy.

Bowl, cereal; 6¼" **45.00**
Bowl, fruit; 5½" **42.00**
Bowl, waste; 6" **55.00**
Coffeepot, 8-cup **445.00**
Creamer, lg **120.00**
Creamer, sm **110.00**
Cup & saucer, demitasse **65.00**
Cup & saucer, low/tall **75.00**
Plate, bread & butter; 6¼" **45.00**
Plate, butter pat **39.00**
Plate, chop; rnd, 13" **315.00**
Plate, dessert; 8" **55.00**
Plate, dinner; 10½" **69.00**
Plate, luncheon; rnd, 9" **59.00**
Plate, luncheon; sq, 8½" **69.00**
Plate, salad; 7½" **49.00**
Platter, oval, 13" **195.00**
Platter, oval, 15" **225.00**
Platter, oval, 17" **295.00**
Sauce boat, w/liner **215.00**
Soup, cream; w/liner **145.00**
Soup, rim, 7½" **65.00**
Soup, rim, 8½" **75.00**
Sugar bowl, w/lid, lg **120.00**
Sugar bowl, w/lid, sm **115.00**
Teapot, 8-cup **445.00**

Vegetable, oval, 10-11" 235.00
Vegetable, oval, 9-10" 215.00
Vegetable, sq, 8" 245.00
Vegetable, sq, 9" 275.00
Vegetable, w/lid 425.00

Spongeware

Spongeware is a type of factory-made earthenware that was popular during the last quarter of the nineteenth century and into the first quarter of the twentieth century. It was decorated by dabbing color onto the drying ware with a sponge, leaving a splotched design at random or in simple patterns. Sometimes a solid band of color was added. The vessel was then covered with a clear glaze and fired at a high temperature. Blue on white is the most preferred combination, but green on ivory, orange on white, or those colors in combination may also occasionally be found. For further information we recommend *Collector's Encyclopedia of Salt Glaze Stoneware* by Terry Taylor, our advisor for this category, and Terry and Kay Lowrance, available from Collector Books.

Batter jug, pawprint bl sponging, thumb-pinched rim lip, open, 6" 165.00
Bean pot, mc/wht allover overlapping rings, single hdl, 5¾" 200.00
Bowl, berry/mixing; brush-appl color, flat bottom, 2¼x6½" 175.00
Bowl, brn specks on yel w/yel int, 5x9" 75.00
Bowl, custard; bl & orange brushed decor, wide bl band, 3½x4" 120.00
Bowl, paneled pattern, bl on wht, 3½x9" 225.00
Bowl, random bl dashes, dk bl rim, 2½x5½" 125.00
Bowl, soup; heavy dk bl/wht, 1¾x9" dia 150.00
Butter crock, bl/wht, stenciled name, repeated rings, w/lid, 5x7" 375.00
Chamber pot, lt bl/wht, appl hdl, 4½x8" dia 200.00
Crock, bl/wht, 6x5¼", from $125 to 135.00
Cuspidor, bl 75.00
Jardiniere, bl/wht, w/banded rim, bulbous, 6" 375.00
Mug, bl rings on wht (primitive), brush decor, 6x6", from $185 to 215.00
Mug, bl/wht, 4½" 175.00
Pie plate, bl on gray, emb grooves on bottom, 10½" 165.00
Pitcher, bl/wht, leaf & flower emb decor, 10x5" 300.00
Pitcher, bl/wht pattern sponging, bulbous, 12" 375.00
Pitcher, brn/gr/wht, bbl form, 7" 100.00
Pitcher, girl & dog, allover sponging, 8½" 500.00
Pitcher, Indian Good Luck Sign, bl on wht, rim chip, 6" 200.00
Pitcher, tankard; bl/wht top & bottom, bl bands at mid-point, 7" 250.00
Plate, heavy bl/wht, scalloped/emb rim, 8½" 125.00
Platter, bl/wht, 13x9" 175.00
Salt box, bl/wht, wooden lid, 3⅜x3" dia, EX 325.00
Soap dish, bl/wht, plain center, emb bars for drainage, 6x4" 110.00
Spittoon, bl/wht, brass lid, 4x10½" 220.00
Teapot, bl, w/lid, 4" 550.00
Teapot, brn/gr/cream, horizontal ribbing, 5½" 175.00
Umbrella stand 500.00

Spoons

Souvenir spoons have been popular remembrances since the 1890s. The early hand-wrought examples of the silversmith's art are especially sought and appreciated for their fine craftsmanship. Commemorative, personality-related, advertising, and those with Indian busts or floral designs are only a few of the many types of collectible spoons. In the following listings, spoons are sorted by city, character, or occasion. For further information we recommend *Collectible Souvenir Spoons, Identification & Values*, by Wayne Bednersh (Collector Books).

Key:
B — bowl
BR — bowl reverse
emb — embossed
eng — engraved
ff — full figure
GW — gold wash
H — handle
HR — handle reverse

New Casino, Santa Cruz Cal., Irving pattern, Wallace, from $35.00 to $60.00. (Photo courtesy Wayne Bednersh)

Bryce Canyon & cut-out scene on H; sunburst-style B; Robbins, $20 to 40.00
Chick emerging from egg eng in B; Easter on H; demi, from $15 to 20.00
Cincinnati Bridge eng in B; bridge ff H; Paye & Baker, from $50 to 75.00
Cincinnati OH & suspension bridge in B; Floral Lily H; Whiting, $25 to 40.00
Cleveland & Soldier/Sailor Monument in B; Georgian, Towle, 1905 ....35.00
Compliments of R Wallace & Sons Mfg in B; Wallace, from $10 to 20.00
Coon River Dam IA eng in B; Virginia pattern H; Lunt, from $40 to 60.00
Denver capitol emb in B; Colorado/miner/seal on H; from $15 to 25.00
DeWitt Clinton steamer eng/pnt B; Schenectady NY H; Shepard, up to 140.00
Dr FE Townsend portrait finial H; Shepard, from $5 to 15.00
Eagle Grove IA high school eng in B; Gorham, from $15 to 40.00
Eskimo ice fishing ff H; emb B; Meyer Bros, from $125 to 200.00
Farmer ff H; plain B; Meyer Bros, from $75 to 125.00
Female graduate ff H; generic type, Mechanics, from $30 to 70.00
Fort Wayne IN Courthouse in B; wavy H; Shepard, from $40 to 60.00
Hawaiian fisherman w/surfboard ff H; Mechanics, demi, from $25 to 50.00
Hebron NE & courthouse in B; La Viola pattern H; Watson, from $30 to 50.00
Kansas City MO & scene in B; state seal finial H; Watson, from $15 to 30.00
Layton Art Gallery Milwaukee eng in B; from $25 to 50.00
Long Beach CA auditorium eng in B; fish finial; Mechanic, 1894, up to 80.00
Los Angeles City of Angels & cut-out angel H; plain B; 1904, $40 to 75.00
Marseilles Dam eng in B; state H; Paye & Baker, from $30 to 45.00
Mt Baker eng in B; totem pole H; Joseph Meyer & Bros, from $40 to 60.00
Nathaniel Hawthorne (1804-1864) on H; Durgin & Low, from $40 to 60.00
Niagara Falls scene & name on H; Watson, from $20 to 25.00
Norma Talmadge reserve on H; plain B; Oneida, from $8 to 15.00
Oklahoma Newest Star enameled in B; state H; Shiebler, from $50 to 95.00
Old Point Comfort on H; eng scene in B; Durgin, from $30 to 50.00
President Wm McKinley eng in B; wavy H; GW, Shepard, from $40 to 65.00
Rawlings WY State Penetenionary (sic) eng in B; Watson, from $40 to 80.00
Robert Ingersol finial H; plain B; unmk, from $35 to 60.00
Ropin' cowboy ff H; plain B; Watson, from $150 to 200.00
San Juan Capistrano CA & mission on H; plain B; Robbins, $20 to 40.00
Santa Barbara Mission eng in B; GW, from $25 to 50.00
Selma AL & bridge eng in B; Shepard, from $30 to 50.00
Ski Jumping Ishpeming MI & scene eng in B; Watson, from $75 to 100.00
Spokane in B; Indian maiden FF H; Meuer Bros, from $80 to 125.00
Stanford University Gate, Palo Alto CA in B; J Mayer Bros, $25 to 50.00
State Hospital Massillon OH eng in B; Shepard, from $30 to 50.00
State Normal School, Dekalb IL in B; Codding Bros, from $15 to 40.00
Steam shovel eng in B; coal mining H; from $25 to 40.00
Toledo OH library in B; Majestic pattern H; Alvin, 1900, from $30 to 50.00
Train scene (copper insert on silver) eng B; J Mayer Bros, $40 to 90.00
Virgin & Child ff H: Ramona's Marriage Place San Diego CA H; up to 75.00
Washington Monument ff H; Capitol building in B; Pat 11/18/90 ....50.00
Wells Building Milwaukee WI eng in B; Strousberg H; Gorham, $30 to 50.00

White Horse VT eng in B; dog sled ff H; Joseph Meyer, from $75 to ..125.00
Williamsport PA post office in B; Louis XV H; Whiting, 1891, up to ...50.00
Woolworth Building NY eng in B; (depending on H) from $35 to 75.00

Sporting Goods

When sports cards became so widely collectible several years ago, other types of related memorabilia started to interest sports fans. Now they search for baseball uniforms, autographed baseballs, game-used bats and gloves, and all sorts of ephemera. Although baseball is America's all-time favorite, other sports have their own groups of interested collectors. Our advice for this category comes from Paul Longo Americana. Mr. Longo is listed in the Directory under Massachusetts. See also Target Balls; Tennis Rackets.

Key: sig — signature

Andirons, cast-iron batter and pitcher, EX detail, 20", $1,000.00 for the pair.

Ball, golf; tethered for practice, ca 1950 ....30.00
Bank, ball-in-glove shape, chalkware w/appropriate pnt, '70s, 7" ..40.00
Baseball, Babe Ruth/Lou Gerig sigs, Barnard AI Official, VG .1,100.00
Baseball, Brooklyn Dodgers, team autographed, 1938-40, Frick, EX+ ..200.00
Baseball, Joe DiMaggio sig, American League ball, M 250.00
Baseball, Mickey Mantle sig in bl ink, Am League ball, M 175.00
Baseball, NY Giants, team autographed, 1942, Frick NI, EX+ ...400.00
Baseball, NY Yankees, team autographed, 1942, Harridge, EX+ .650.00
Baseball, NY Yankees, team autographed, 1975, MacPhail, EX .225.00
Baseball, Pepper Martin sig, Official League, VG 350.00
Baseball, Phila Athletic, team autographed, Harridge, '53, EX+ ..200.00
Bat, Adirondack Big Stick, sgn Harmon Killebrew 100.00
Bat, child's, Mickey Mantle, 12K model, 28", EX+ 50.00
Bat, commemorating Steve Carlton's 329 wins, ltd ed, NM 150.00
Bat, commemorative, NY Mets, sgn by 17 players, 1969, EX 200.00
Bat, Jackie Robinson, Hillerich & Bradsby store model 100.00
Book, Great Outdoors, leather-bound, 1947 1st ed, EX 50.00
Candy dish, Los Angeles Rams, pottery, stadium shape, 1960, 8" ..60.00
Cigar box, City Sports, mahog w/int lid label, early 1900s, EX 60.00
Cigar box, Harvard, bust of student in athletic sweater, '20s, EX .50.00
Cigar box, Joe Tinker, int/ext labels, 1926 tax stamp, 10" L 500.00
Desk calendar, brass-plated baseball on cone base, 1930, 5" 300.00
Doll, Detroit Tigers, celluloid w/stadium button, '40s, 7", EX 65.00
Doll, Twistum, football, compo, ca 1930-40, EXIB 125.00
Figurine, football player in bl jersey, German bsk, 1890, 10" 450.00
Football inflator, red pnt w/2 game scenes, 1910-20, EX 125.00
Game, Aydelott's Baseball, 1910, EX 150.00
Game, Base Hit (baseball), Games Inc NY, 1944, NM 175.00
Game, Baseball, Milton Bradley, 1941, EX 60.00
Game, Bob Feller's Big League Baseball, 1949, EX 100.00
Game, Diceball (baseball), Ray-Fair Co, 1938, EX 45.00
Golf club, spliced head, hickory shaft, 1890s, EX 350.00
Hat, Baltimore Orioles, World Series souvenir, styrofoam, '66 ....50.00
Jersey, Bill Russell (sgn in silver ink), Boston Celtics (road), NM 250.00
Magazine, Boy's Life, Mickey Mantle on cover, Aug 1959, EX 35.00
Pennant, Baltimore Orioles, blk w/orange letters, 1960s, EX 50.00
Pennant, Brooklyn Dodgers, bl w/wht letters, 1940s, EX 125.00
Pennant, Brooklyn Dodgers, Dem Bums, logo on left, '50s, EX .175.00
Pennant, Fightin' Phillies, red w/facsimile sigs, 1950s, EX+ 250.00
Pennant, Joe DiMaggio, bust picture/facsimile sigs, '40s, EX 450.00
Pennant, Notre Dame, pictures football player, 1940s, EX+ 75.00
Pennant, NY Yankees, facsimile sigs on wht, 1970s, VG+ 45.00
Pennant, NY Yankees AL Champions, 1956, EX+ 120.00
Pennant, Oberlin College, maroon w/red letters, '20s, EX 50.00
Pennant, Phila Athletics, elephant on left, '40s, faded, VG+ 85.00
Pennant, Phila Phillies, bl w/wht letters, 1940s, EX+ 95.00
Pennant, Phila Phillies, NL Champion, Go - Go... on red, 1964 ...100.00
Pennant, Phila Phillies, purple w/wht letters, '30s, 25", EX+ 330.00
Pennant, Phila Phillies, yel w/bl letters, bl jay/sigs, '40s, EX 400.00
Pennant, Univ of PA, mc player running w/early ball, 1900s, NM ..250.00
Pennant, WA Senators, gr w/wht lettering, '40s, EX+ 130.00
Pennant, World Series 1915, hand sewn, game used, 34", EX+ ..2,200.00
Photo, Babe Ruth, published by Baseball Magazine, '30s, 9x12" ..40.00
Photo, Phils, 1950s Whiz Kids, panoramic, from Sunday paper .175.00
Photograph, Babe Ruth w/11 lovely ladies, sepia-tone, 8x10"+fr 120.00
Pin, stadium; Phila Phillies, w/ribbon, ball & bat charms, '50s 85.00
Poem board, mc illus at top, Play Up!, by Lampada, 1910, 10x12" ..100.00
Program, 1958 World Series, Braves at Yankees 65.00
Program, 1970 World Series, at Baltimore, EX 50.00
Silk, Pittsburgh vs St Louis, 1984 opening game, NM 300.00
Sweater, football, heavy wool knit, Lowe & Campbell, '20s 135.00
Uniform, basketball, Clarion, Lowe & Campbell, 1930s, EX 85.00
Uniform, gray & red, Champion Baseball, child's, '40s, MIB 75.00
Yearbook, Boston Red Sox, 1973 ....25.00
Yearbook, Brooklyn Dodgers, 1957 ....125.00
Yearbook, NY Mets, 1966 ....50.00
Yearbook, NY Yankees, 1953 ....125.00

St. Clair

The St. Clair Glass Company began as a small family-oriented operation in Elwood, Indiana, in 1941. Most famous for their lamps, the family made numerous small items of carnival, pink and caramel slag, and custard glass as well. Later, paperweights became popular production pieces; many command relatively high prices on today's market. Weights are stamped and usually dated, while small production pieces are often unmarked. Lamps are in big demand (prices depend on size and whether or not they are signed) as are items signed by Paul or Ed St. Clair. For further information we recommend *St. Clair Glass Collector's Book* by Bonnie Pruitt, available from our advisor, Ted Pruitt, who is listed in the Directory under Indiana.

Animal dish, reclining colt, cobalt custard, from $135 to 160.00
Ashtray, bowl shape w/3 rests, brns, from $85 to 95.00
Bell, Bicentennial, various colors, sm, from $20 to 25.00
Bell, fruit pattern, bl carnival, from $90 to 100.00
Bottle, Grape & Gable, w/stopper, bl or red carnival, ea from $125 to ..135.00
Compote, ruffled rim, low ped base, pk slag, from $150 to 175.00
Cruet, bulbous w/2 loop hdls, stopper, bl, from $125 to 150.00
Figurine, owl on rnd base, various colors, from $100 to 125.00
Figurine, Southern Belle, various colors, from $30 to 40.00
Goblet, Fruit Pattern, wht carnival, from $35 to 50.00
Mug, Holly Band, caramel slag, from $90 to 95.00
Paperweight, apple form w/stem & leaf, bl carnival, blown 100.00
Paperweight, egg on base (yel flowers/grass) 55.00
Paperweight, pear form, bl carnival 100.00
Paperweight, sulfide, cameo, windowed/etched, from $300 to ...350.00

Paperweight, sulfide, elephant, wht, mk Ford, from $140 to **165.00**
Paperweight, sulfide, kitten, from $140 to **165.00**
Paperweight, turtle form, from $150 to **175.00**
Pen holder, red flowers, from $90 to **100.00**
Perfume bottle, bulbous w/ball stopper, gold/brn/bl carnival **100.00**
Pitcher, Hollyband, caramel slag, from $90 to **95.00**
Plate, John F Kennedy, from $75 to **100.00**
Ring holder, ball form w/stem, flowers **55.00**
Ring holder, teapot form w/spout, from $75 to **85.00**
Salt cellar, swan form, wht carnival or red, rare, ea, from $100 to ..**125.00**
Salt cellar, wheelbarrow form, various colors, from $25 to **30.00**
Sauce dish, Paneled Grape, ice bl carnival, from $35 to **40.00**
Sugar bowl, Hollyband, wht carnival or amber Tiffany, ea from $85 to ...**100.00**
Toothpick holder, Argonaut Shell, various colors, from $25 to **30.00**
Toothpick holder, dog heads, gr opaque, from $60 to **75.00**
Toothpick holder, flowers, bl, ruffled rim, from $65 to **75.00**
Toothpick holder, Indian, various colors, from $20 to **45.00**
Toothpick holder, owl, various colors, from $35 to **45.00**
Toothpick holder, sheaf of wheat, various colors, from $30 to **45.00**
Toothpick holder, Star 'N Shuttle, various colors, from $25 to **30.00**
Toothpick holder, swans, various colors, from $35 to **45.00**
Toothpick holder, witch head, Nile Green, from $85 to **100.00**
Toothpick holder, 3-Face Bicentennial, pk slag, from $35 to **50.00**
Tumbler, Cactus, various colors, from $30 to **35.00**
Vase, bulbous, trumpet neck w/wide flat rim, pk slag, from $100 to ...**125.00**
Wine glass, Paneled Grape, cobalt, from $50 to **65.00**

Staffordshire

Scores of potteries sprang up in England's Staffordshire district in the early eighteenth century; several remain to the present time. (See also specific companies.) Figurines and groups were made in great numbers; dogs were favorite subjects. Often they were made in pairs, each a mirror image of the other. They varied in heights from 3" or 4" to the largest, measuring 16" to 18". From 1840 until about 1900, portrait figures were produced to represent specific characters, both real and fictional. As a rule these were never marked.

The Historical Ware listed here was made throughout the district; some collectors refer to it as Staffordshire Blue Ware. It was produced as early as 1820, and because much was exported to America, it was very often decorated with transfers depicting scenic views of well-known American landmarks. Early examples were printed in a deep cobalt. By 1830 a softer blue was favored, and within the next decade black, pink, red, and green prints were used. Although sometimes careless about adding their trademark, many companies used their own border designs that were as individual as their names.

This ware should not be confused with the vast amounts of modern china (mostly plates) made from early in the century to the present. These souvenir or commemorative items are usually marketed through gift stores and the like. (See Rowland and Marcellus.) See also specific manufacturers. Our advisors for this category are Dave and Anne Middleton; they are listed in the Directory under New Jersey.

Key:

blk — black	l/b — light blue
gr — green	m/b — medium blue
d/b — dark blue	m-d/b — medium dark blue

Figures and Groups

Birds in branches, nest w/3 eggs, Wood, ca 1760, 7¾", NM ...**3,200.00**
Calf, brush-stroked orange spots, gr-brn base, 2½x3", EX **275.00**
Camel, recumbent, brn-tan w/red, 3¼x3¼" **550.00**
Castle, bl roofs, 2 chimneys, Gothic windows, coleslaw, 10¾" ..**425.00**
Castle w/turret & stairs to rock cropping, trinket holder, 2-part, 8" ...**150.00**
Cat, blk sponging over yel, some red on emb base, 2¾x3½", NM **400.00**
Cat, seated, blk & yel sponging on wht, wear, 4¼" **275.00**
Cat, seated, sponged blk & brn on wht, sm crack, 4½" **300.00**
Couple stand w/basket of fish, 19th C, 7¾", from $450 to **550.00**
Cow w/calf, vase, mc, lt wear, 12" **275.00**
Dog, seated, red & wht w/yel & blk, sm chips, 3⅜" **110.00**
Duke of Wellington, standing on marbleized plinth, w/gilt, 13", VG ..**345.00**
Esmeralda & Gringoire, mc details, 10", EX **160.00**
Fox, hollow, gr/brn/wht, att Wood, ca 1770-1780, 2¾" **400.00**
Fox w/swan in mouth, spill/match holder, 9¾" **600.00**
Girl sits beside oversz dog, red & wht w/mc details, 6½" **1,595.00**
Goat, mc pnt, flat bk, 3⅝" **220.00**
Holy Family w/donkey, mc, early 1800s, rprs, 9x9¾" **250.00**
Horse, mc pnt, flat bk, 4" **125.00**
Hunter, rstr gun, 19th C, 7⅛" **175.00**
King William III on horse, gold trim, 11" **195.00**
Lady weaping at funerary urn, hollow, mc, 9¼" **475.00**
Lion, recumbent, on oval free-form base, no color, 4", EX **865.00**
Lute player, 19th C, rstr/chip, 5⅛" **115.00**
Man puts shoe on lady's ft, rstr bocage, 9x6¼" **700.00**
Man w/egg basket, hollow, mc, pearlware, flakes, 3¾" **150.00**
Peter Restoring the Lame Man, mc w/pk lustre, 1810s, 6¾" **440.00**
Rabbit, blk sponging w/blk & gr, 3¾x2½" **425.00**
Rooster, red/yel/gr on wht, chip, early, 4" **245.00**
Sailor w/bottle & cup stands near bbl, 19th C, 10" **485.00**
Scotsman in kilt, EX color, rpr to bagpipes, 13" **150.00**
Scottish couple, 19th C, 7⅞", EX **230.00**
Spaniel, recumbent, on base, mc details, pearlware, 4x6½" **750.00**
Spaniels, blk & wht w/gilt chain & leash, 9¾", pr **895.00**
Squirrel perched on branch, vase, mc details, 1850-70, 6" **450.00**
Stag, recumbent, bocage, cole slaw decor, pearlware, 3¼x3", VG **200.00**
Stag & doe, mc, molded X on bottom, chips, 3¼" **220.00**
Swan beside tree trunk w/egg nearby, pastille burner, 4" **110.00**
Wounded Soldier, 2 sailors w/hats, capes/walking stick, 12¾" ...**485.00**

Historical

Pitcher, Boston State House, medium blue, 10¼", repaired, $1,200.00.

Bowl, Arms of MD, d/b, Mayer, 4½x12½", NM **3,750.00**
Bowl, Franklin (flying kite), red, lt wear, 3¼x11⅛" **500.00**
Bowl, fruit; Acropolis, pk, scalloped ft, 5½x11½x8" **400.00**
Bowl, Landscape w/Cows & Figures, d/b, unmk, 1950s, 1x10" ...**150.00**
Bowl, vegetable; Arms of MA, d/b, Mayer, 1½x8½x7" **1,265.00**
Bowl, vegetable; Hanover Terrace Regents Park, d/b, Adams, 8¼" ..**385.00**
Bowl, vegetable; Landscape Designs, pk, w/lid, 6¼x12¾x10" **375.00**
Bowl, vegetable; Quebec, Wood, w/lid, 5½x10x10" **1,100.00**
Bowl, vegetable; Tappan Zee From Greenburg, d/b, Wood, 9x7" ..**3,350.00**
Bowl, vegetable; Undercliff Near..., l/b, Ridgeway, 7⅝" **200.00**
Bowl, vegetable; Washington, l/b w/red on lid, 6½x12½", EX ..**300.00**
Bowl, waste; Boston Harbor, d/b, unmk, 3⅝x7", NM **825.00**
Bowl, waste; Residence of Late...Jordan, blk, 3⅛x6⅜", EX **110.00**
Cake stand, Capital Washington, d/b, Ridgway, rare, 2½x10½" ..**2,750.00**
Coffeepot, Residence of Late Richard Jordan, l/b, 11¾", NM ...**1,200.00**

Coffeepot, Wadsworth Tower, d/b, dome top, 11" 2,365.00
Compote, Landscape Designs, pk, feather hdls, ftd, 6x10¾" 550.00
Cup & saucer, handleless; Floral, Bird & Fruits, d/b, unmk 150.00
Cup & saucer, handleless; flowers/birds/shells, d/b, Clews, EX ...290.00
Cup & saucer, handleless; Lafayette at Franklin's tomb, d/b, Wood, EX ..190.00
Cup & saucer, handleless; Moses in Bulrushes, d/b, unmk 450.00
Cup & saucer, handleless; Sleigh Ride, d/b, Wood 550.00
Cup & saucer, handleless; Wadsworth Tower, d/b, Wood's shell border ...425.00
Cup & saucer, handleless; 2 men by river, d/b, Clews, NM 110.00
Cup plate, Belzoni, l/b, scalloped, E Wood & Sons, 4¾", NM 50.00
Cup plate, California, d/b/blk, Podmore Walker, 4", EX 60.00
Cup plate, Castle Garden Battery NY, d/b, Wood, lt stain, 3¾" ...350.00
Cup plate, English brick bridge, d/b, Wood, 3⅝" 150.00
Cup plate, Stone Bridge w/1 Arched Section, d/b, French Views, 3⅝" ...110.00
Fruit stand/compote, Country Church, m-d/b, unmk, rstr, 5x12" 450.00
Gravy boat, Pass in Catskill Mtns, d/b, Wood's shell border, 7", EX 400.00
Gravy boat, W Penn's Treaty, brn, Thomas Green, 4x7" dia 425.00
Gravy tureen, Landing of Lafayette, d/b, 9⅞" 275.00
Mug, Residence of Late Richard Jordan, purple, 4⅛", EX 375.00
Mustard pot, Catskill Mtns Hudson River, d/b, Wood, w/lid, 2½" ...900.00
Pickle dish, Trinity College Oxford, d/b, Ridgway, 9" 1,300.00
Pitcher, Boston From Dorchester Heights, l/b, Meigh, 8", EX 110.00
Pitcher, Boston State House/City Hall NY, d/b, Stubbs, 6½", EX 800.00
Pitcher, City of Dublin Steam Packet Co, gr, Cauldon, 8½" 975.00
Pitcher, Entrance of Erie Canal...Rochester, d/b, Wood, 6" 650.00
Pitcher, Landing of Lafayette, d/b, Clews, hairline, 7⅞" 1,100.00
Pitcher, Seal of US w/Eagle, d/b, wear/stain, 7⅜" 1,300.00
Pitcher, wash; Chinoiserie, m/b, old prof rstr, 9½" 110.00
Plate, Albany, d/b, Wood's shell border, 9⅞" 450.00
Plate, Am & Independence, d/b, Clews, line, 5⅝" 110.00
Plate, Am & Independence, d/b, Clews States border, 10½" 400.00
Plate, Am & Independence, d/b, Clews States border, 8¾" 300.00
Plate, Am Villa, d/b, fruit & flower border, lt stain, 8½" 150.00
Plate, antelope, d/b, Hall's Quadruped series, 8" 225.00
Plate, Arms of Rhode Island, d/b, Mayer, 8½" 600.00
Plate, B&O Railroad, d/b, Wood's shell border, 9¼", EX 550.00
Plate, Bakers Falls, Hudson River; brn, 9" 100.00
Plate, Baltimore & OH RR (level), d/b, lt wear, 10⅛" 950.00
Plate, Battle of Chapultepec, gr, Shaw, 9¼" 475.00
Plate, Battle of Palo Alto, gr, Shaw, 10½" 475.00
Plate, Boston State House, d/b, Rogers, 9½", NM 130.00
Plate, Boston State House, d/b, unmk, 8½" 200.00
Plate, Caldwell Lake George, l/b, Ridgeway, 7¾", NM 60.00
Plate, Capital Washington, d/b, Stevenson, 10" 425.00
Plate, Castle Scenery, m-d/b, Mayer, 9¾", EX 300.00
Plate, Chief Justice Marshall, d/b, Wood, 10" 850.00
Plate, Christ Church Oxford, d/b, scalloped, Ridgway, 10" 125.00
Plate, City Hall NY, d/b, lt wear, 9¾" 275.00
Plate, City Hall NY, m-d/b, Ridgway's Beauties of Am, 9¾" 300.00
Plate, City Hall NY, m/b, Stubbs' eagle border, 6⅝", EX 300.00
Plate, City of Albany, d/b, Wood's shell border, 10¼", EX 375.00
Plate, Commodore MacDonnough's Victory, d/b, Wood, 10⅛", EX 385.00
Plate, Constitution & the Guerriere, d/b, Wood's shell border, 10" .1,200.00
Plate, Dam & Waterworks... (side-wheeler), d/b, Henshall, 10" ...500.00
Plate, Dam & Waterworks... (stern-wheeler), d/b, Henshall, 10", EX ...440.00
Plate, Erie Canal Inscription... (Governor), d/b, unmk, 10¼" ...400.00
Plate, Fair Mount Near Philadelphia, d/b, Stubbs, 10¼" 275.00
Plate, Fisherman's Hut, d/b, scalloped, mid-1800s, 6¾" 150.00
Plate, Floral, d/b, Riley's, 9⅞" 150.00
Plate, Fonthill Abbey Wiltshire, d/b, Clews, 10" 300.00
Plate, Hamden Mortally Wounded, m/b, Jones & Son, 6½", NM ..225.00
Plate, Hancock House Boston, purple, Jackson, 7⅞" 120.00
Plate, Harvard College, m-d/b, Stevenson & Williams, 10", EX .300.00
Plate, Hoboken in NJ, d/b, Stubbs' eagle border, 7¾" 275.00
Plate, Hospital Boston, d/b, Stevenson, 9" 180.00
Plate, Hudson River, d/b, Wood, 5¾", EX 225.00
Plate, Insane Hospital Boston, m-d/b, Ridgway, 7⅛" 350.00
Plate, La Grange...Lafayette, d/b, French Views, 10¼" 350.00
Plate, Landing of Fathers at Plymouth, m-d/b, Wood, 10¼", EX ...250.00
Plate, Landing of Fathers at Plymouth, m/b, Wood, 8⅝" 135.00
Plate, Landing of Lafayette, d/b, Clews, 10⅛" 450.00
Plate, Landing of Lafayette, d/b, Clews, 5½" 400.00
Plate, Landing of Lafayette, d/b, Clews, 9" 330.00
Plate, Landing of Lafayette, d/b, 6¾" 200.00
Plate, Landscape w/Animals, l/b, roses/shamrocks border, unmk, 10" ..125.00
Plate, Lion, d/b, Hall's Quadrupeds border, 10" 325.00
Plate, Marine Hospital Louisville KY, d/b, Wood, 9¼" 400.00
Plate, Nahant Hotel Near Boston, d/b, Stubbs, 9" 400.00
Plate, Near Fort Miller..., blk, 10¾", NM 225.00
Plate, NY Battery, d/b, stain, 7" 110.00
Plate, NY From Brooklyn Heights, d/b, Stevenson, 10" 750.00
Plate, Oriental, med bl, scalloped, Ridgway, 9½", EX 50.00
Plate, Park Theatre NY, d/b, Stevenson, 10", NM 400.00
Plate, Peace Plenty, d/b, Clews, scratches/flake, 8¾" 220.00
Plate, Peace Plenty, d/b, Clews, 10¼", NM 500.00
Plate, Pittsfield Elm, d/b, Clews, 10½", EX 300.00
Plate, President's House Washington, purple, Jackson, 10½" 280.00
Plate, Race Bridge Philadelphia, purple, Jackson, 9" 130.00
Plate, Residence of Late Richard Jordan, l/b, 6¾", NM 110.00
Plate, Residence of Late Richard Jordan, l/b, 9⅛" 130.00
Plate, Residence of Late Richard Jordan, red, 7⅞" 110.00
Plate, Sheltered Peasants, d/b, Hall, ca 1822-49, 10" 175.00
Plate, Sheltered Peasants, d/b, Hall, 7½", NM, pr 400.00
Plate, St Catherine's Hill, d/b, 10⅛" 160.00
Plate, St Paul's School London, d/b, Adams, 7¾" 165.00
Plate, Stratford on Avon..., b/d, Clew's Bluebell border, 9" 200.00
Plate, Table Rock Niagara, d/b, Wood, 10" 700.00
Plate, Transylvania University..., d/b, Wood, 9¼" 300.00
Plate, Trenton Falls, d/b, Wood's shell border, 7½" 350.00
Plate, Upper Ferry Bridge...Schuylkill, d/b, Stubbs, 8¾" 145.00
Plate, Valley of Shenandoah..., l/b, Ridgway, 5¾" 80.00
Plate, View From Ruggles House..., l/b, Ridgway, 10⅜", EX 250.00
Plate, View of Greenwich, d/b, Clews foliage & scroll border, 8¾" ...125.00
Plate, View of Mt Vernon, red, Mellor Venables & Co, 8¼" 170.00
Plate, View of Trenton Falls, d/b, Wood, 7⅝" 300.00
Plate, Warleigh House, d/b, Hall's Select Views, 8⅛" 190.00
Plate, West Point Hudson River, blk, nick, 8" 60.00
Plate, Winter View of Pittsfield, d/b, 6" 230.00
Plate, Yale Collage, l/b, Meigh, chip, 9½" 100.00
Platter, Almshouse Boston, d/b, Stevenson, 16¼x13" 950.00
Platter, Am Marine, brn, GL Ashworth & Bro, 15" 150.00
Platter, Boston State House, d/b, Stubbs eagle border, rstr, 14½" ...900.00
Platter, Castle Garden Battery NY, d/b, Wood, 18½x14½" 2,750.00
Platter, Castle Garden Battery NY, d/b, Wood's shell border, 18¾" ...2,600.00
Platter, Christianburg...Africa, d/b, Wood, 10½x16", NM 3,700.00
Platter, Columbus, brn, Adams, 11" 275.00
Platter, Family & Mule, d/b, 15½" 375.00
Platter, Fishkill, Hudson River; blk, 15½", NM 400.00
Platter, game birds, d/b, wear, 16½" 935.00
Platter, India Temple, d/b, Ridgway, 21¼x18¼", EX 400.00
Platter, Jedburgh Abbey Roxburghshire, d/b, Adams, 17", NM .355.00
Platter, Ladies' Cabin Boston Mails, l/b, 16" 260.00
Platter, Landing of Lafayette, d/b, Clews, 12½" 1,350.00
Platter, Landing of Lafayette, d/b, Clews, 17x13", EX 1,300.00
Platter, Landing of Lafayette, d/b, Clews, 18⅞", NM 1,500.00
Platter, Narrows From Fort Hamilton, blk, Ridgway, 17½" 275.00
Platter, Newburg, Hudson River, blk, 15½", NM 400.00
Platter, NY From Weehawk, d/b, Stevenson, 18¾", NM 1,200.00

Platter, Picturesque View Little Falls..., blk, Clews, 17½", EX ...440.00
Platter, Pittfield Elm, d/b, Clews, 18½x15½" ...1,300.00
Platter, St Peters College Cambridge, d/b, 14¾" ...650.00
Platter, View From Fort Putnam, l/b, Ridgeway, 15¼" ...250.00
Platter, View of Capitol at Washington, l/b, Ridgeway, 19" ...950.00
Platter, well & tree; Death of Gen Wolfe, m/b, Jones & Son, 20" ...1,800.00
Sauce tureen, Boston Mails, brn, 3-pc, 6½x8x5¾", EX ...450.00
Soup, Am Marine, brn, GL Ashworth & Bro, 8¼" ...35.00
Soup, Harvard College, d/b, acorn & leaf border, 9⅞" ...250.00
Soup, Near Jessups Landing..., blk, 10½", NM ...275.00
Soup, Sun of Righteousness, red, Wood, 10½" ...200.00
Soup, Winter View of Pittsfield..., d/b, 8¾" ...400.00
Spittoon, lady's; Priory, l/b, Alcock, 3½x7½", NM ...150.00
Sugar bowl, Gun Dogs, m-d/b, unmk, 5¼", NM ...275.00
Sugar bowl, Landing of Lafayette, d/b, w/lid, 6", EX ...925.00
Sugar bowl, Mount Vernon, d/b, floral border, 6" ...800.00
Teapot, Eagle & Banner, d/b, 6", VG ...200.00
Teapot, Gun Dogs, m-d/b, unmk, rstr spout, 5½x9" ...375.00
Tile, Boston State House, d/b, Mintons, 6", NM ...325.00
Tray, Landing of Gen Lafayette, d/b, Clews, 9¾" ...960.00
Tray, Windsor Castle, d/b, Clews' foliage & scroll border, 15½" ...900.00

Miscellaneous

Coffeepot, redware, engine trn, pear shape, 1770, 8½", VG ...750.00
Jug, puzzle; bl transfer floral, rtcl neck, 1830, rpr, 7", VG ...175.00
Plate, Cabbage Rose, red w/yel & red sm flowers, scalloped, 8" .250.00
Teapot, bl/gr/brn mottle, crabstock hdl, 1780s, rstr, 6" ...235.00
Teapot, HP floral (style of Rhodes), spherical, 1774, 5½", G ...230.00

Stained Glass

There are many factors to consider in evaluating a window or panel of stained glass art. Besides the obvious factor of condition, intricacy, jeweling, beveling, and the amount of selenium (red, orange, and yellow) present should all be taken into account. Remember, repair work is itself an art and can be very expensive. Our advisor for this category is Carl Heck; he is listed in the Directory under Colorado.

Lamps

Wilkinson, 19" dragonfly shade, embossed floral standard, 25", from $8,500.00. (Photo courtesy Carl Heck)

Best, 14" floral-&-geometric panel shade; ornate std, 20" ...2,400.00
Bigelow & Kennard, allover roses, irregular border, ceiling, 22" ..17,500.00
Bigelow & Kennard, 14" gr brickwork shade, slim std ...5,000.00
Bigelow & Kennard, 18" stylized leaves domical shade; bronze std, 23" ...5,000.00
Duffner Kimberly, 20" geometric shade w/tuck-under apron; EX ..3,500.00
Miller, 21" bent-panel shade w/scalloped floral band; 59" H ..1,150.00
Morgan, 24" grapes/jewel clusters shade; tree/tendril std, 65" H ...23,000.00
Suess, 18" stylized flowers shade; slim std w/lg flat ft ...6,000.00
Wilkinson, 18" caramel/gr conical shade w/jewels; bronzed std ...3,000.00
Wilkinson, 20" cattails/water lilies shade (sm rstr); bronze std ..2,500.00

Windows

Floral, lime gr/red/bl/orange, ca 1900, 27x48" ...500.00
Flower garland w/glass jewels & jeweled ripple edge, 30x70" w/fr ...2,800.00
Hansel & Gretal in woods scene, flower border, 64x42" ...3,500.00
Owl on branch/moon/stars w/tied-bk curtains, 32x19", EX ...4,500.00
Prairie School, floral, clear/gr, copper caming, 23x25½" ...1,500.00
Prairie School, floral, clear/wht/gr/violet slag, 36x16", 5 for ...4,500.00
Prairie School, geometrics in amethyst/tile border, 66x21" 4 for ...2,500.00
Trees & meadow w/twilight sky, 45x30" in fr, VG ...3,000.00
Triptych, grapevines fr 1 side of 2/top of 3rd, ea 34x28", VG .1,500.00

Stanford

The Stanford Pottery Co. was founded in 1945 in Sebring, Ohio. One of the founders was George Stanford, a former manager at Spaulding China (Royal Copley). They continued in operations until the factory was destroyed by a fire about 1961. They produced a Corn Line, similar to that of the Shawnee Company, that is today very collectible. Most examples are marked (either Stanford Sebring Ohio or with a paper label), so there should be no difficulty in distinguishing one line from the other.

In addition to their Corn Line, they produced planters and figurines, many of which were black trimmed with gold, made to be sold as pairs or sets. Wall pockets and vases were made as well. In 1949 they introduced a line called Tomato Ware, consisting of a cookie jar, grease jar, salt and pepper shakers, creamer and sugar bowl, mustard jar, marmalade jar, etc. These were shaped as bright red tomatoes with green leaves and stems (often used as lid finials), and were marketed under the name 'The Pantry Parade.' Our advisor for this category is Joe Devine; he is listed in the Directory under Iowa.

Ashtray, free-form, orange w/wht 'stucco,' #270-D, mk, 10x7" ...12.00
Corn Line, butter dish ...60.00
Corn Line, casserole, 8" L ...50.00
Corn Line, cookie jar ...100.00
Corn Line, creamer & sugar bowl ...60.00
Corn Line, cup ...20.00
Corn Line, pitcher, 7½" ...65.00
Corn Line, plate, 9" L ...35.00
Corn Line, relish tray ...45.00
Corn Line, shakers, sm, pr ...30.00
Corn Line, shakers, 4", pr ...35.00
Corn Line, spoon rest ...30.00
Corn Line, teapot ...75.00
Corn Line, tumbler ...35.00
Planter, Dutch boy or girl by tulip, blk w/gold trim, ea ...20.00
Planter, marching drummer, boy or girl, 7", ea ...22.00
Planter, teddy bear, wht w/pk & bl trim, paper label, 7" ...35.00
Tomato Ware, casserole, w/lid, 6x9" ...60.00
Tomato Ware, cookie jar, 8" ...80.00
Tomato Ware, creamer ...30.00
Tomato Ware, grease jar, w/lid ...38.00
Tomato Ware, marmalade jar ...35.00
Tomato Ware, mustard jar ...35.00
Tomato Ware, pitcher, 6½" ...65.00
Tomato Ware, sugar bowl ...30.00
Wall pocket, bird, bl & cobalt w/gold trim, 7", from $40 to ...45.00

Wall pocket, cherry branch, red pie-crust edge, #299, mk, 6¼" ...28.00

Stangl

Stangl Pottery was one of the longest existing potteries in the United States, having as its beginning in 1814 the Sam Hill Pottery, becoming the Fulper Pottery which gained eminence in the field of art pottery (ca 1860), and then coming under the aegis of Johann Martin Stangl. The German-born Stangl joined Fulper in 1910 as chemical engineer, left for a brief stint at Haeger in Dundee, Illinois, and rejoined Fulper as general manager in 1920. He became president of the firm in 1928. Although Stangl's name was on much of the ware from the late '20s onward, the company's name was not changed officially until 1955. J.M. Stangl died in 1972; the pottery continued under the ownership of Wheaton Industries until 1978, then closed. Stangl is best known for its extensive Birds of America line, styled after Audubon; its brightly colored, hand-carved, hand-painted dinnerware; and its great variety of giftware, including its dry-brushed gold lines. For more information we recommend *Collector's Encyclopedia of Stangl Dinnerware* by Robert Runge, Jr. (Collector Books). Another good reference is *Stangl Pottery* by Harvey Duke; for ordering information refer to the listing for Nancy and Robert Perzel, Popkorn Antiques (our advisors for this category), in the Directory under New Jersey.

Animals

#3243, dog, Wire-Haired Terrier, 3¼" ...350.00
#3244, draft horse, 3" ...200.00
#3245, rabbit, 2" ...350.00
#3246, buffalo, 2½" ...325.00
#3247, gazelle, 3¾" ...400.00
#3248, giraffe, 2½" ...650.00
#3249, elephant, Antique Gold, 5" ...125.00
#3249, elephant, 3" ...350.00
#3277, colt, 5" ...1,500.00
#3278, goat, 5" ...1,500.00
#3279, calf, 3½" ...1,000.00
#3280, dog, sitting, 5¼" ...350.00
Cat, Siamese, sitting, decor, 8½" ...500.00
Cat, sitting, Granada Gold, 8½" ...300.00

Birds

#3250A, Standing Duck, 3¼" ...115.00
#3250B, Preening Duck, 2¾" ...115.00
#3250D, Gazing Duck, 3¾" ...115.00
#3250F, Quacking Duck, 3¼" ...115.00
#3273, Rooster, 5¾" ...250.00
#3274, Penguin, 6" ...475.00
#3275, Turkey, 3½" ...375.00
#3276D, Bluebird pr, 8½" ...200.00
#3281, Duck, mother, 6" ...650.00
#3285, Rooster, early, 4½" ...100.00
#3286, Hen, late, 3¼" ...50.00
#3400, Lovebird, old version, 4" ...100.00
#3400, Lovebird, revised, 4" ...60.00
#3401, Wren, dk brn, revised, 3½" ...50.00
#3401D, Wren pr, tan, old version ...500.00
#3402, Oriole, beak down, 3¼" ...150.00
#3402, Oriole, revised, 3¼" ...65.00
#3402D, Oriole pr, revised, w/leaves, 5½" ...125.00
#3404D, Lovebirds pr, kissing, old version, 4½" ...400.00
#3405, Cockatoo, 6" ...65.00
#3405D, Cockatoo pr, revised, 9½" ...175.00
#3406, Kingfisher, 3½" ...75.00
#3406D, Kingfisher pr, 5" ...150.00
#3407, Owl, 5½x2½" ...350.00
#3408, Bird of Paradise, 5½" ...125.00
#3432, Duck, running, brn/grayish wht w/blk spots, 5" ...650.00
#3433, Rooster, 16", minimum value ...3,000.00

#3443, Flying Duck, teal, 9½x12", $325.00.

#3444, Cardinal, revised, glossy pk, 7" ...100.00
#3445, Rooster, gray, 10" ...275.00
#3445, Rooster, yel, 10" ...200.00
#3446, Hen, yel, 7" ...175.00
#3448, Blue-Headed Vireo, 4¼" ...85.00
#3449, Parrot, 5½" ...175.00
#3450, Passenger Pigeon, 9x18" ...1,500.00
#3452, Painted Bunting, 5" ...125.00
#3453, Mountain Bluebird, 6⅛" ...1,250.00
#3454, Key West Quail Dove, wings spread ...1,250.00
#3455, Shoveler Duck, 12¼x14", minimum value ...2,500.00
#3457, Pheasant, walking, 7¼x15" ...2,500.00
#3458, Quail, 7½" ...1,200.00
#3490D, Redstart pr, 9" ...225.00
#3491, Hen Pheasant, 6¼x11" ...225.00
#3518D, White-Crowned Pigeon pr, bl w/wht heads, 8x14" ...850.00
#3580, Cockatoo, med, 8⅞" ...165.00
#3581, Chickadees, blk/wht, group of 3, 5½x8½" ...300.00
#3581, Chickadees, brn/wht, group of 3, 5½x8½" ...200.00
#3582D, Parakeet pr, bl, 7" ...275.00
#3583, Parula Warbler, 4¼" ...65.00
#3584, Cockatoo, sgn Jacob, lg, 11⅜" ...275.00
#3585, Rufous Hummingbird, 3" ...75.00
#3586, Pheasant (Della Ware), natural colors, 9x15½", minimum value ...1,200.00
#3586, Pheasant (Della Ware), terra rose, gr ...500.00
#3590, Carolina Wren, 4½" ...165.00
#3591, Brewer's Blackbird, 3½" ...175.00
#3593, Nuthatch, 2½" ...65.00
#3595, Bobolink, 4¾" ...150.00
#3596, Gray Cardinal, 5" ...85.00
#3598, Kentucky Warbler, 3" ...60.00
#3599D, Hummingbird pr ...350.00
#3626, Broadtail Hummingbird w/bl flower ...65.00
#3627, Rivoli Hummingbird, pk flower, 6" ...175.00
#3628, Rieffer's Hummingbird ...150.00
#3629, Broadbill Hummingbird, 4½" ...150.00
#3634, Allen Hummingbird, 3½" ...85.00
#3715, Blue Jay, w/peanut, 10¼" ...675.00
#3716, Blue Jay, w/leaf, 10¼" ...675.00
#3746, Canary (right), rose flower, 6¼" ...225.00
#3747, Canary (left), bl flower, 6¼" ...225.00
#3749, Western Tanager, red matt, 4¾" ...375.00
#3750D, Western Tanager pr, pk, 8" ...600.00
#3751, Red-Headed Woodpecker, glossy pk, 6¼" ...345.00
#3751, Red-Headed Woodpecker, red matt, 6¼" ...400.00
#3752D, Red-Headed Woodpecker pr, glossy pk, 7¼" ...525.00

#3754, White Wing Crossbill (single), minimum value 2,500.00
#3754D, White-Wing Crossbill pr, glossy pk, 9x8" 450.00
#3755, Audubon Warbler, 4¼" 400.00
#3755D, Audubon Warbler pr, 7¼" 650.00
#3758, Magpie-Jay, 10¾" 1,350.00
#3810, Blackpoll Warbler, 3½" 175.00
#3811, Chestnut-Backed Chickadee, 5" 165.00
#3813, Evening Grosbeak, 5" 165.00
#3814, Black-Throated Green Warbler, 3" 165.00
#3815, Western Bluebird, 7" 450.00
#3821, Yellow-Headed Verdin, 4½" 1,500.00
#3848, Golden-Crowned Kinglet, 4¼" 110.00
#3850, Yellow Warbler, 4" 150.00
#3851, Red-Breasted Nuthatch, 3¾" 85.00
#3852, Cliff Swallow, 3½" 150.00
#3868, Summer Tanager, 4" 600.00
#3923, Vermillion Fly-Catcher, 5¾" 2,000.00
#3924, Yellow-Throated Warbler, 6" 450.00
#3925, Magnolia Warbler 2,500.00

Dinnerware

Magnolia, dinner plate, 10", $15.00.

Amber Glo, egg cup 15.00
Amber Glo, tray, condiment 20.00
Apple Delight, ashtray, fluted 12.00
Apple Delight, gravy liner 10.00
Apple Delight, mug, 2-cup 35.00
Apple Delight, plate, picnic; 8" 4.00
Apple Delight, plate, 6" 5.00
Apple Delight, server, 2-tier 20.00
Apple Delight, tile 20.00
Apple Delight, tile, Wentzel 15.00
Blueberry, bowl, salad; 12" 100.00
Blueberry, butter dish 55.00
Blueberry, coaster/ashtray 30.00
Blueberry, coffeepot, 8-cup 100.00
Blueberry, creamer 20.00
Blueberry, pitcher, 1-pt 40.00
Blueberry, plate, 11" 35.00
Blueberry, plate, 9" 22.00
Blueberry, platter, oval, 14¾" 75.00
Blueberry, relish dish 30.00
Blueberry, tray, bread 30.00
Chicory, bowl, lug soup; 5½" 20.00
Chicory, bowl, salad; 12" 100.00
Chicory, cup 15.00
Chicory, gravy boat 25.00
Chicory, pitcher, 1-qt 50.00
Chicory, skillet, w/hdl, 8" 50.00
Country Garden, bowl, salad; 10" 65.00
Country Garden, cake stand 30.00
Country Garden, cigarette box, 3¾x4½" 100.00
Country Garden, coffeepot, 8-cup 100.00
Country Garden, cruet 40.00
Country Garden, mug, coffee; low 25.00
Country Garden, pitcher, 2-qt 75.00
Country Garden, plate, chop; 14½" 90.00
Country Garden, plate, 9" 30.00
Country Garden, server, 3-tier 35.00
Country Garden, teapot 100.00
Country Life, bowl, fruit; rooster, 5½" 35.00
Country Life, bowl, salad; pig at fence, rnd, 10" 175.00
Country Life, coaster, duckling 45.00
Country Life, plate, chop; farmhouse & garden, 12½" 400.00
Country Life, plate, chop; farmhouse & lane, 12½" 250.00
Country Life, plate, cow standing in grass, 8" 100.00
Country Life, saucer, 3 little eggs 15.00
Country Life, sugar bowl, rooster 60.00
Cranberry, bowl, salad; 10" 50.00
Cranberry, pitcher, 1-qt 35.00
Festival, butter dish, ¼-lb 45.00
Festival, plate, 9" 20.00
Flora, casserole, 8" 50.00
Flora, plate, chop; 14½" 75.00
Fruit, ashtray, fluted, 5" 15.00
Fruit, bowl, coupe soup; 7½" 30.00
Fruit, bowl, mixing; 5½" 45.00
Fruit, bowl, vegetable; divided, rnd, 10" 60.00
Fruit, clock 45.00
Fruit, cup, peach decor 12.00
Fruit, pitcher, ½-pt 30.00
Fruit, plate, 6" 9.00
Fruit, saucer, jumbo 25.00
Fruit, sherbet 30.00
Fruit, tray, sq, 7½" 35.00
Fruit & Flowers, bowl, soup; lug hdl, 5½" 20.00
Fruit & Flowers, coffee warmer 30.00
Fruit & Flowers, gravy boat stand 20.00
Fruit & Flowers, plate, grill; 9" 35.00
Fruit & Flowers, sugar bowl, w/lid 20.00
Garden Flower, bowl, salad; Campanula, rnd, 10" 55.00
Garden Flower, casserole, Balloon Flower, 8" 60.00
Garden Flower, creamer, Calendula & Morning Glory 18.00
Garden Flower, pitcher, Rose, 1-pt 35.00
Garden Flower, plate, Tiger Lily, 9" 18.00
Garden Flower, teapot, Sunflower 85.00
Golden Harvest, bowl, salad; 10" 35.00
Golden Harvest, coffeepot, ind 65.00
Golden Harvest, gravy boat 15.00
Golden Harvest, plate, 10" 13.00
Kiddieware, plate, Old Woman, late 175.00
Kiddieware, plate & cup, Peter Rabbit 245.00
Kiddieware, set, Little Quackers, 3-pc 300.00
Kiddieware, set, Mother Hubbard, 3-pc 400.00
Lyric, bowl, soup; lug hdl, 5½" 20.00
Lyric, coaster/ashtray 30.00
Lyric, mug, coffee; low 40.00
Lyric, plate, chop; 12½" 100.00
Magnolia, bowl, vegetable; divided 35.00
Magnolia, cruet 35.00
Magnolia, pitcher, 1-qt 45.00
Magnolia, sugar bowl, ind 20.00
Orchid Song, casserole, skillet shape, 8" 25.00
Provincial, creamer 12.00
Rooster, bowl, salad; 10" 55.00
Rooster, cake stand 35.00
Rooster, plate, 8" 22.00
Rooster, server, center hdl 15.00

Thistle, bowl, mixing; 4" 45.00
Thistle, bowl, salad; 12" 160.00
Thistle, butter dish 45.00
Thistle, chip & dip 125.00
Thistle, coffee warmer 35.00
Thistle, pitcher, 1-qt 50.00
Thistle, plate, chop; 12½" 40.00
Thistle, platter, oval, 14¾" 75.00
Town & Country, beanpot, bl, 3-qt 125.00
Town & Country, bowl, soup/cereal; bl, 15-oz 30.00
Town & Country, clock, bl, skillet shape, battery powered 75.00
Town & Country, spoon rest, bl, 8¾" 50.00
Water Lily, egg cup 30.00
Wild Rose, bowl, salad; 12" 75.00
Wild Rose, casserole, w/hdls, 6" 30.00
Wild Rose, coffee warmer 30.00
Wild Rose, pitcher, 1-pt 30.00
Wild Rose, saucer 7.00
Yellow Tulip, bowl, fruit; 5½" 15.00
Yellow Tulip, bowl, salad; 10" 50.00
Yellow Tulip, casserole, 8" 75.00
Yellow Tulip, plate, 10" 25.00

Stanley Tools

The Stanley company was founded in Connecticut in 1854, and over the years has absorbed more than a score of tool companies already in existence. By the second decade of the twentieth century, having long since solidified their position as *the* source for tools of the highest grade, the company enjoyed worldwide prestige. Through both World Wars, they were recognized as one of the nation's premier producers of wartime goods. Industrial arts classes introduced baby boomers to Stanley tools and provided yet another impetus to expansion and recognition. Overall, the company's growth and development has kept an easy pace along with the economy of the nation, and it continues today as a leader in the field of tool production.

Three factors to consider when evaluating a tool are age, completeness, and condition. One of their earliest trademarks (1854 – 1857) is 'A. Stanley,' found only on rulers. In the early '20s, their now-familiar 'sweetheart' trademark, the letters SW and a heart shape within the confines of a modified rectangle, was adopted. They continued to use this trademark until it was discontinued in 1936. Many other variations were used as well, some of which contain a patent date. A study of these marks will help you determine the vintage of your tools. Condition is extremely important, and though a light cleaning is acceptable, you should never attempt to 'restore' a tool by sanding, repainting, or replacing parts that may be damaged or missing. Tools listed below are for those in average 'as found' condition, ranging from very good to excellent. Note: Any common number $20.00 rule with the A. Stanley trademark is easily worth $500.00 plus!

For more information, we recommend *Antique and Collectible Stanley Tools*, written by our advisor, John Walter, who is listed in the Directory under Ohio.

Bevel, #43, single brass blade, rosewood hdl, 12", from $300 to 600.00
Chisel, everlasting; #50, hickory hdl, ¼-1½" W, $20 to 100.00
Dividers, #58, NP steel, 6-8", from $25 to 50.00
Drill, hand; #617, NP steel fr, cocobolo hdls, 11" L, $10 to 40.00
Grasping fork & ladle, polished steel, 14", from $50 to 100.00
Hand beader, #66, CI w/NP, 2 fences, w/7 cutters, 10", $100 to 225.00
Hatchet, lathing; #10, hickory hdl, 12" L, from $5 to 50.00
Knife, shop; #299, polished aluminum, 6", from $2 to 5.00
Level, carpenter's; #1040, maple & brass, 18" or 24", from $25 to 125.00
Level, hexagon pocket; #31, NP brass or steel, 2-4½", $10 to 40.00
Level, Mason's; #48, 6 vials, 48", from $5 to 50.00
Level sights, #2, japanned CI, 1¾", from $30 to 50.00
Mallet, #14½, hickory w/iron rings, 10½" L, from $5 to 35.00
Marking gauge, #62, laquered wood, adjustable point, 8", $5 to 40.00
Marking gauge, #90, NP CI, 6½", from $5 to 25.00
Meter stick, boxwood, 1 meter x¾"x¾", from $200 to 400.00
Plane, block; #101, CI, 1" cutter, 3½", from $20 to 45.00
Plane, block; #19, type #1, japanned CI, NP trim, 7", from $75 to 150.00
Plane, block; japanned CI, NP trim, 6", from $20 to 40.00
Plane, butcher's block; #64, CI & beech, 12½", from $1,500 to 2,500.00
Plane, circular; #113, type #1, CI w/NP trim, 10", from $100 to 250.00
Plane, core box; #56, CI & wood, ⅜" cutter, 6" L, $1,000 to 1,650.00
Plane, jack; #A5, aluminum & wood, 2" cutter, 14", from $100 to 300.00
Plane, jack; #27, type #1, CI & wood, 15", from $150 to 250.00
Plane, match; #146, NP CI, ⅛" cutter, 9", from $100 to 300.00
Plane, plow; #248A, CI w/NP trim, 7 cutters, 9½", from $100 to 200.00
Plane, rabbet; #192, type #1, CI, 1" cutter, 8", from $50 to 100.00
Plane, rabbet; #90A, NP CI, 1" cutter, 4", from $1,000 to 2,500.00
Plane, scrub; #40½, CI, 1½" cutter, 10½" L, from $75 to 150.00
Plane, smooth; #2, type 2, CI, rosewood hdl & knob, 7", $400 to 800.00
Plumb & level, Mason's; #7½, brass & wood, 36", from $10 to 50.00
Plumb bob, #1, brass w/steel point, ⅝-lb, 3½", from $100 to 300.00
Putty knife, 4 sq; wood hdl, 3¾" L, from $5 to 35.00
Rule, bench; #34VR, maple w/brass trim, 12", from $5 to 25.00
Rule, blacksmith's; #17, type #1, brass, 2-fold, 24", from $50 to 100.00
Rule, caliper; #83½, boxwood w/brass trim, 4-fold, 24", $300 to 750.00
Rule, carpenter's; #3, boxwood w/brass trim, 2-fold, 24", $400 to 800.00
Rule, 4-sq zigzag; #1156, wood w/yel enamel, 48", from $50 to 125.00
Scraper, cabinet; #80M, malleable CI, 2¾" cutter, 11", $20 to 60.00
Scraper, venner; #12½, CI, wood hdl & bottom, 6¼", $50 to 150.00
Screwdriver, handy; Victor, palm grip, 5½", from $5 to 50.00
Spoke shave, #51, japanned CI, 2⅛" cutter, 10", from $5 to 25.00
Square, mitre; dbl brass plated hdl, rosewood, 8", 10", 12", $50 to 150.00
Yard stick, #41, maple w/brass trim, 36", from $10 to 50.00

Statue of Liberty

Long before she began greeting immigrants in 1886, the Statue of Liberty was being honored by craftsmen both here and abroad. Her likeness was etched on blades of the finest straight razors from England, captured in finely detailed busts sold as souvenirs to Paris fairgoers in 1878, and presented on colorfully lithographed trade cards, usually satirical, to American shoppers. Perhaps no other object has been represented in more forms or with such frequency as the universal symbol of America. Liberty's keepsakes are also universally accessible. Delightful souvenir models created in 1885 to raise funds for Liberty's pedestal are frequently found at flea markets, while earlier French bronze and terra cotta Liberties have been auctioned for over $100,000.00. Some collectors hunt for the countless forms of nineteenth-century Liberty memorabilia, while many collections were begun in anticipation of the 1986 Centennial with concentration on modern depictions. Our advisor for this category is Mike Brooks; he is listed in the Directory under California.

Antenna, figural, CI, Pal Radio Comp, 18½" 400.00
Bank, Kenton, 1920s, 9⅝" 280.00
Booklet, Rays From Liberty's Torch, 1890 ....30.00
Bookmark, fabric, Bartholdi Souvenir, 1886 ....25.00
Bottle, seltzer; etched Liberty, A Doeink, Liberty, NY 35.00
Box, Liberty Hair Clipper, 1930s 25.00
Card, admission to inauguration, 1886 ....70.00
Charm bracelet, NY World's Fair 40.00
Cigar box label, Victory Day, WWII 6.00

Clock, figural, United, animated, very rare, 1955 ....350.00
Container, Yourex Silver Saver, rnd, cb, ca 1930 ....27.00
Cup, pewter, Germany, ca 1904 ....60.00
Cup, sterling, Windsor Club, 1907, 2" 22.00
Damask runner, ca 1890 ....85.00
Flyer, Statue of Liberty steamboat excursions, 1890s 25.00
Hanukkah memorah, Liberty-featured candle holders, M Anson ...1,800.00
Harper's Weekly, various litho prints, 1880s, ea, from $10 to 25.00
Invitation to inauguration, by President Cleveland 200.00
Lamp, figural, bronze-tone metal, electric, 11" 130.00
Letter, by Bartholdi, 1866 ....225.00
Letter, teen to military father re: parade on Broadway, 1886 ....95.00
Magic lantern side, harbor scene 30.00
Medal, Central Valley Nat'l Bank 18.00
Medal, Democratic National Convention, NY, 1924 ....30.00
Napkin holder, sterling 15.00
Paperweight, rnd, ca 1880s 100.00
Pennant, felt, 1930s 25.00
Photo album, celluloid image on front, velvet bk, 10x8" 275.00
Pin, enamel, 77th Div, WWI 12.00
Pin-bk, No Beer, No Work, prohibition 15.00
Pipe, glazed clay, 1880s 90.00
Plate, glass, eng statue, heart shape 22.00
Plates, various makers, 1980s, ea, from $10 to 20.00
Playing cards, Allied Nations, WWI, complete deck 20.00
Pocketwatch, Elgin, 1890s 175.00
Postcard, hold-to-light, night scene 45.00
Poster, DeLand, WWI 150.00
Puzzle, America, Ellis Island scene, Tuco, 320-pcs, 1940s, 16x20" ..85.00
Radio speaker stand, wht metal casting, Palcone, 17" 175.00
Runner, damask, ca 1890 ....85.00
Snow dome, figural, Atlas Crystal Works, 1920s 55.00
Spoon, figural stem, sterling, Shiebler 75.00
Statue, cast metal on marble base, June 13, 1885 ....1,000.00
Statue, fund-raising, 1885, 6" 200.00
Statue, Wenck perfume, 1908 ....325.00
Stereo card, head of Liberty, Paris, 1878 ....80.00
Straight razor, Liberty-etched blade, Sheffield, ca 1880 ....75.00
Thermometer, key form, Liberty coin at top, solid brass, 8½" 50.00
Ticket, lg souvenir of Gauthier et Cie (Liberty foundry), 1883 ..105.00
Tin, William's American Chewing Nuts, oval, British, 1930s, lg .65.00
Trade card, satirical, A&C Hams 70.00
Trade card, satirical, Moline Plow 30.00
Vase, frosted Liberty hand, Gillinder, 1876 Centennial 70.00
Watch fob, 1919 ....25.00

Steamship Collectibles

For centuries, ocean-going vessels with their venturesome officers and crews were the catalyst that changed the unknown aspects of our world to the known. Changing economic conditions, unfortunately, have now placed the North American shipping industry in the same jeopardy as the American passenger train. They are becoming a memory. The surge of interest in railroad collectibles and the railroad-related steamship lines has lead collectors to examine the whole spectrum of steamship collectibles.

Reproduction (sometimes called 'Replica') and fantasy dinnerware has been creeping into the steamship dinnerware collecting field. Some of the 'replica' ware is quite well done so one should practice caution and... 'Know Thy Dealer.' Our advisors for this category are Lila and Fred Shrader; they are listed in the Directory under California.

Key:
BS — back stamped
SM — side mark
NBS — no back stamp
R&B — Reed & Barton
SL — side logo
TL — top logo
TM — top mark

Broadside, Memphis and Cincinnati Packet Co., 1890 seasonal schedule, steamboat vignette in center, EX, $350.00.

Dinnerware

Ashtray, Orient Line, TL&BS, Doulton, cigar-sz, 6½" 59.00
Bowl, fruit; Bibby Line, TM: Bibby Line ribbon+hand, 5¼" 21.00
Bowl, oatmeal; Luckenbach Line, TL: house flag, 6½" dia 32.00
Butter pat, Clipper Line (Sweden), Stella Polaris, 3½" 16.00
Butter pat, Knutsen, TL house flag w/red stripes, 3½" 48.00
Butter pat, Merchants & Miners Transp Co house flag TL 194.00
Butter pat, Pickand-Mathers, Pegasus, 3½" 26.00
Butter pat, Red Star Line, Brownfield, 3x3½" 285.00
Butter pat, United States Lines, Chapman, TL, 3½" 44.00
Butter pat, White Star Line, Brownfield, 3x3½" 700.00
Compote, United Fruit Co, TL, 4x7½" 225.00
Creamer, Ocean SS Co, house flag w/'Savanna Line' beneath, 3" ..105.00
Cup & saucer, Am President Lines, APL Eagle, c-SL/s-TL, demi ...49.00
Cup & saucer, Cunard, TM+kosher mk for meat+BM 45.00
Cup & saucer, Farrell Lines, c-SL/S-TL: African Enterprise 66.00
Cup & saucer, Italian Line, Oriental, BM w/name & logo 93.00
Cup & saucer, Italian Line, Roma (in bl), cup SM, saucer NBS ..55.00
Cup & saucer, Mallory Line, San Marcos, cup SL, saucer TS 58.00
Cup & saucer, White Star, Brownfield, cup SL, saucer TS, demi ..800.00
Egg cup, Hamburg-Atlantic Line, Hanseatic TL, 3½" 24.00
Egg cup, Knutsen Line, TL: house flag, 2¼" 67.00
Egg cup, United Fruit Lines, Castilla, 2½" 55.00
Egg cup, White Star, Brownfield, SL, 3/1912, Rd No 117214, 2¼" ...1,345.00
Egg cup, White Star, Brownfield (replica), same as above, 2¾" ...92.00
Hot food cover, Am Mail Line, SL, 7" dia 184.00
Oyster plate, SP SS, Harriman Blue w/TL, 9" 370.00
Pitcher, Pere Marquette, AutoFerry, w/ice lip, 7" 1,010.00
Pitcher, States Lines, California, TL w/bl stripes, 6½" 76.00
Plate, Alaska SS, Yukon, Shenango, TL, 5½" 48.00
Plate, Am Export-Isbrandtsen, Constitution, TL, 7½" 30.00
Plate, Italian Line, Roma, TM, 9½" 307.00
Plate, Mississippi & Dominion SS Co, LTD, TL of flags, wreath, 9+" 292.00
Plate, Nippon Yusen Kaisha, Kamakaura Maru w/o floral border, 9" 32.00
Plate, rim soup; Am-Hawaiian SS Co, TM, 9" 71.00
Plate, rim soup; Goodrich Line Steamers TM, 9" 316.00
Plate, rim soup; Merchants & Miners, TM w/rope logo, 9½" 96.00
Plate, rim soup; White Star, BS, TM: OSNC, 7¾" 238.00
Plate, Vaccaro Line (Standard Fruit & SS Co), TL: Altantida, 9" ..92.00
Plate, White Star, Brownfield, TL, BS, 7¾" 700.00
Platter, Eastern SS Lines, TM house flag inside ring, 8x5" 22.00
Platter, Los Angeles SS Co, TM house flag inside ring, BS, 8x6" ..135.00
Relish, Matson, TL w/ripple edge, rectangular, 9x5" 195.00
Relish, Texaco, TL: house flag, 8x5" 145.00
Relish, United States Lines, Chapman, TL, 10x7" 26.00

Teapot, Am Mail Line, SL w/house flag, ind sz 195.00

Glassware

Ashtray, French Line, Deco style, wht opaque glass, 3" sq 26.00
Ashtray, Grace Lines, TM w/Grace encircled, 4½" 11.00
Ashtray, Matson, SS Lurline/Matson Lines, triangular, 3½" 14.00
Ashtray, Swedish-Am Line, triple crown molded BM, 3" sq 6.00
Decanter, Red Star Line, SL, cut glass, prof rstr, +stopper 388.00
Souvenir, pin tray, United States Lines, emb stars, 3½x5¼" 36.00
Souvenir, shot glass, Starlight Cruises, SL: Pacific Star, 2½" 7.00
Souvenir, tray, Eastern, map of routes, blk & gold, 7x9" 22.00
Stem, cocktail; Matson, LS in wht enamel, 4¼" 21.00
Stem, cordial; Cunard, full etched SL w/garter & crown, 3¾" 49.00
Stem, cordial; Union Castle Line enclosed in garter, SL, 3½" 29.00
Stem, wine; Italian Lines, SL, 3½" 49.00
Stir rod, Grace Line w/Grace on flat globe, cobalt, 6" 16.00
Stir rod, New England SS Co in gold on blk, spoon-tip, 6" 12.00
Tumbler, Alaska SS Co, SL, 4" 33.00
Tumbler, Matson Lines, SL, 4½" 12.00
Tumbler, old-fashioned; Am President Lines, SL, 4" 16.00

Linens and Uniforms

Bath mat, United States Lines, heavy toweling, lg woven logo, 18x24" 157.00
Blanket, P&O SS Co, wool, 54x84" 67.00
Napkin, Alaska SS, full logo, wht on wht, 23" sq 48.00
Napking, CPSS, Empress of Canada woven on border, wht on wht ...36.00
Place mat, Am President Lines, APL embr corner, wht on wht, 12x18" ...26.00
Tablecloth, Cunard woven on 2 sides, wht damask, 54x82" 41.00
Towel, bath; French Line, CGT, woven, 24x48" 82.00
Towel, bath; SP SS, woven both ends: Southern Pacific SS, 24x40" ..110.00
Towel, hand; Canadian Steamship Lines on red stripe, 15x26" 14.00

Paper

Baggage sticker, Pacific Mail SS Co, 5½" dia 17.00
Baggage sticker, United States Lines, 1st class, 3½" dia 4.00
Baggage tag, NY & Puerto Rico SS Co, oval, 1934, 4½x3" 4.00
Book, The Other Titanic, sinking of Oceanic, dust jacket, 1958 .47.00
Booklet, Cunard's RMS Berengaria, photos, 1925, 24-pg, 8½x11" 31.00
Booklet, Queen Mary, Guide to Accomodations, 1st class, 1936, 36-pg ...117.00
Bookmark, Canada SS Lines, diecut ship, freight info, 1930s, 2x7" ..7.00
Bridge pad, P&O, TM, cover has bridge info, 4x6" 23.00
Brochure, Cuba Mail Line, 4-panel, schedules+hotel info, 2½x5" ...29.00
Brochure, Fall River Line, schedules/map, 1891, 3½x7½" 41.00
Brochure, OR-WA RR & Nav Co, SF to Portland, views, early 1900s ..65.00
Brochure, Red Collar SS Line, afternoon cruises, early 1900s 32.00
Brochure ToyoKisen-Kaisha, Orient/San Francisco, 1920, 30-pg, 8x9" ..26.00
Calendar, Moore-McCormack Lines, 13 sheets, 1958, 12x16" 27.00
Coaster, w/ship's logo, flag, name, from $1 to 8.00
Deck plans, Moore-McCormack, 1950s, 10x24", folds to 5x3" 18.00
Menu, CP the Princess, cover scene ship in Aleutian inlet, 1925 ..22.00
Menu, Cunard's RMS Queen Mary+passenger list, 1937, 5x6" 51.00
Menu, Flandre, Jean Mercier cover, 1958, 9x13" 10.00
Menu, P&O, Deco-like style, blk & wht, 1920s, 8x4" 10.00
Note pad, French Line, CGT in gold on wht cover, unused, 2x3½" ..18.00
Pamphlet, Duchess of Bedford, 1929-30 cruise schedule, 3x6" 5.00
Pass, annual; New England Fuel & Transp Co, Mr Jas Thoms, 1924 .....32.00
Pass, annual; Pacific Coast SS Co, Mr Harrison, family & maid, 1911 .48.00
Passenger list booklet, Alaska SS, Mt McKinley, 1939, 7x5" 39.00
Passenger list folder, White Star Line, Britanic II, 1957, 5x7" 7.00
Photograph, P&O SS, SS Florida departing Miami, 1960s, 5x7" ...5.00
Place mat, Bull Lines, Caribbean scene, 12x18" 11.00
Playing cards, Alaska SS, 52+2 in plastic case 28.00
Playing cards, Eastern SS Lines, dbl deck in plastic case, ea: 52+2 ...22.00
Postcard, Olympic, int views of 1st-class lounge, unused 38.00
Postcard, White Star's Finland painting, mailed, 1906 ....11.00
Sheet music, Just as the Ship Went Down, Titanic sinking illus, 1912 ...23.00

Silverplate

Bowl, North German Lloyd, BM, scallop tab hdls, 6¾" 36.00
Bowl, United States Lines, str-sided, BM, 3½x8½" 305.00
Champagne cooler, French Lines, SL & BS, 2 bail hdls 705.00
Child's feeding dish, Grace Lines, TL, compartments, Dixon, 6½" ...24.00
Cocktail shaker, Holland America, SL, 10½" 55.00
Coffee service, ind; Matson, pot+cr/sug w/lid, 5½" 195.00
Coffeepot, Am Export Lines, TM & BS, 6½" 67.00
Coffeepot, Holland America, SM w/NASM dmn logo, 5½" 42.00
Creamer, Cunard, BM, Four Star, 2½" 26.00
Creamer, Grace Lines, SL Grace encircled, R&B, 4" 46.00
Fork, Luckenbach Lines TL, Rogers 17.00
Fork, salad; Grand Trunk Pacific SS, TL house flag, Elkington 21.00
Knife, butter; North German Lloyd, TM: Bremen, R&B, 8¼" 29.00
Knife, Cunard White Star TL, Gladwin 38.00
Knife, fruit; Italian Line, TM: Italia, 7½" 26.00
Napkin ring, Alfred Holt Line, house flag SL 38.00
Napkin ring, Canadian Pacific SS, SL 35.00
Napkin ring, Royal Mail Lines, Ltd, house flag/RMS Andes 42.00
Napkin ring, Royal Mail Steamer/Royal George, enamel SL 114.00
Spoon, soup; Goodrich SS Lines TL in rectangular box 27.00
Teaspoon, Matson, TL, International 16.00
Teaspoon, Pacific Coast SS, TM w/house flag, Wallace 24.00
Teaspoon, White Star, TM w/house flag, Elkington, 5¾" 182.00
Tray, Am Export Lines, TM & BS, hdls, 6x11" 91.00
Tray, Nippon Yusen Kaisha, TM w/house flag, 5" dia 41.00

Miscellaneous

Advertising, US Lines fr in ship's wheel, 1920s, 32" 228.00
Ashtray, US Lines, vertical anchor on 5" tray w/3 rests 55.00
Button, Am Mail Line, house flag, brass color, ⅞" 12.00
Button, Baltimore Steam Packet Co, BPS w/S superimposed, ⅝" ..28.00
Button, Dollar SS Line, house flag TL, ⅝" 14.00
Canape stick, French Line, CGT in bubble in 3½" stick 15.00
Chamber pot, French Line, CGT SL, Limoges 385.00
Compass, Ritchie & Sons, Boston, mid-1800s, 11" dia 185.00
Flag, travel agency; French Line, 3½x5" 49.00
Lamp, anchor; 360 degree ribbed lens, no reservoir, 21" 138.00
Lamp, passageway; brass wall mt w/gr frensel lens, oil, 9" 34.00
Lamp, signal; copper/brass, orig burner, clear frensel lens, 19" ...216.00
Life jacket, RMS Queen Elizabeth, person 70 lbs or more, 1966 ..187.00
Lighter, Moore-McCormick Lines, Zippo, in orig box 23.00
Lighter, SS America, picture of ship passing Statue of Liberty 54.00
Matchbook, Fjell-Oranje Lines, full, house flag on cover & matches ...8.00
Matchbook, French Line, Normandie, full, 2¼x6" 14.00
Matchbook, SS Res, '30s gambling ship off Santa Monica, CA, empty 10.00
Medallion, Queen Elizabeth II World Cruise 1977, orig felt-covered box ...33.00
Mirror, Am Line, celluloid w/sketch of ship, 2¼" 19.00
Mirror, DeWitt Clinton Lake Steamer, celluloid, 3¾" dia 25.00
Mirror, signaling; opening+cross-hairs, GE, mfgr, instructions 22.00
Napkin Ring, Matson, Bakelite w/appl metal logo 48.00
Passenger list, SS Matsonia, Hula girl cover, September 1939, M ...40.00
Pocketknife, emb Bremen pictured on brass case, w/cigar cutter ..115.00
Pocketknife, RMS Scythia on silver, detailed ship illus, 3½" 100.00
Porthole, brass, operable, 10" 98.00
Porthole w/aluminum cover plate, USS Wilson, decommissioned, 12" dia ..82.00

Sextant, Husun, 9" long arc, 1944, orig mahog case 405.00
Sign, Canadian Nat'l Steamships, fr brass, 17¼x26¼" 300.00
Soap, various '30-'50s, guest sz, wrapped, ea, from $2 to 8.00
Speaker tube, mouthpc & whistle attachment, brass 55.00
Stationery, Delta Line, sheet & envelope, 1930s 3.00
Swizzle stick, Andrea Doria figural, plastic 86.00
Wall hanging, SS Normandy, woven, hemmed for rods, 84x48" ..226.00
Wheel, John Hastie & Co Ltd, teak w/brass rim & hub, 36" 550.00

Steins

Steins have been made from pottery, pewter, glass, stoneware, and porcelain, from very small up to the four-liter size. They may be decorated by etching, in-mold relief, decals, and occasionally they may be hand painted. Some porcelain steins have lithophane bases. Collectors often specialize in a particular type — faience, regimental, or figural, for example — while others limit themselves to the products of only one manufacturer. See also Mettlach.

Key:
L — liter
lith — lithophane
POG — print over glaze
PUG — print under glaze
tl — thumb lift

Character steins, E. Bohne Sohne, three-liter: Apple and Snake, NM, $1,725.00; Fisherman, hairline crack, $1,095.00.

Anheuser-Busch, Germany, Osprey, w/lid, 1L, rare 825.00
Anheuser-Busch, Thewalt, Brvo Vox, w/lid, .5L 175.00
Anheuser-Busch by Ceramarte, Americana, .5L 495.00
Anheuser-Busch by Ceramarte, Bud Man, solid head, .5L 450.00
Anheuser-Busch by Ceramarte, Grant's Farm, wht hoofs, .5L 155.00
Anheuser-Busch by Ceramarte, USA 200 Years, w/lid, 1L 365.00
Character, alligator, porc, Musterschutz by Schierholz, rpr, .5L .575.00
Character, artillery shell, stoneware, inlaid lid dtd 1914, .5L, NM ...150.00
Character, bear, pottery, #1455, .5L 750.00
Character, bell, pottery, Merkelbach & Wick, ca 1910, .5L 1,150.00
Character, Bismark retired, porc, porc lid, Schierholz, .5L, NM ...500.00
Character, Bustle Lady, stoneware, R Hanke, #895, rpr, .5L ...1,600.00
Character, clown, stoneware/bl salt glaze, #987, .5L 775.00
Character, drunken monkey, inlaid lid, Schierholz, .5L, NM 350.00
Character, East Berlin Town Hall, porc, .5L 2,995.00
Character, Feurer Thurm (Bad Killingen), pottery, .5L 5,750.00
Character, globe w/Captain Cook finial, pottery, rpr, .5L 800.00
Character, Hops Lady, porc, Musterschutz by Schierholz, .5L 635.00
Character, Iron Maiden, stoneware, mk TW, rpr, .5L 300.00
Character, money bag, porc, E Bohne Sohne, flake, .5L 1,900.00
Character, Munich Child on Bbl, porc, 1899 roster, .5L 925.00
Character, nun, pottery, #8671, .5L 160.00
Character, nun in blk robe, porc, lith, .5L 175.00
Character, Nurnberg Tower, pewter, mk F&MN, .5L 400.00
Character, Nurnberg Tower, pottery, pewter lid, #129, .25L 155.00
Character, Oriental man, pottery, inlaid lid, .5L 400.00
Character, owl, porc, E Bohne Sohne, .5L 1,785.00
Character, pickle, porc, E Bohne Sohne; rpr hdl, .5L 725.00
Character, rook, stoneware, mk J Reinemann, rare, .5L 1,550.00
Character, skull, porc inlaid lid, student assoc, E Bohne Sohne, .5L ...1,065.00
Character, skull on book, porc, E Bohne Sohne, .5L 600.00
Character, St Peter's Church, stoneware, rpl tl, rpr tang, 1L ..1,000.00
Character, stag, porc, Musterschutz by Schierholz, .5L, NM ...2,400.00
Character, Student Fox, porc, lith, unmk, .5L, NM 660.00
Character, Student Frog, porc, mk Bauer, pewter rpr, .5L 865.00
Character, Uncle Sam, porc, Musterschutz by Schierholz, .5L, EX 980.00
Character, 4F Man, stoneware, R Hanke, .5-L 430.00
Glass, blown, amber, t'print design, pewter o/l & lid, 1.5L 350.00
Glass, blown, bl, HP floral, pewter lid, .5L 85.00
Glass, blown, clear, cut decor, pewter lid, .5L 85.00
Glass, blown, clear, faceted, SP lid w/helmet, .5L 235.00
Glass, blown, clear, Hobnail, porc lid w/man fishing, .5L 100.00
Glass, blown, clear, HP lion & shield, Nouveau pewter lid, .5L ...330.00
Glass, pressed, clear, Am flag in shield, porc lid, .5L 290.00
Glass, pressed, clear, Faust transfer, porc inlaid lid, .5L 195.00
Glass, pressed, clear, Lake Side Casino, porc inlaid lid, .5L 140.00
Military, glass, blown, helmet/leaf finial on SP lid, .5L 90.00
Military, stoneware, transfer/HP: soldiers, cross finial, .5L 275.00
Occupational, porc, farming transfer, pewter lid, lith, .5L 450.00
Occupational, porc, transfer/HP: butcher, pewter lid, lith, .5L ..300.00
Occupational, porc, transfer/HP: cabinetmaker, pewter lid, .5L, EX ..375.00
Occupational, porc, transfer/HP: carpenter, lion tl, lith, .5L 400.00
Occupational, porc, transfer/HP: carpenter, pewter lid, lith, .5L ..575.00
Occupational, porc, transfer/HP: coach driver, rpr lid, .5L 575.00
Occupational, porc, transfer/HP: saw operator, flakes, .5L 600.00
Occupational, porc, transfer/HP: wagon driver, pewter lid, lith, .5L 450.00
Occupational, pottery, transfer/HP: beer brewer, pewter lid, .5L, NM ...357.00
Pewter, relief: Founders of German Reich, military scenes, .5L 90.00
Pewter, relief: Nouveau leaves & berries w/wheat, pewter lid, .5L 140.00
Porc, transfer/HP: Dom zu Ulm, pewter lid, lith, .3L 150.00
Porc, transfer/HP: King Ludwig, dented pewter lid, lith, .5L 80.00
Pottery, etch: lady soldier/men at table, Thewalt #407, 1L 100.00
Pottery, HP: monks drinking, Hauber & Reuther, .5L 230.00
Pottery, relief/HP: souvenir of Florida, inlaid lid, #6049, .5L 135.00
Pottery, relief/HP: St Louis Cathedral, #6041, .5L 175.00
Pottery, relief: dancing scene w/color, pewter lid, #1305, 3L 265.00
Pottery, relief: 3 women in oval, #780B, stain, 2L 120.00
Pottery, transfer/HP: edelweiss around castle, pewter lid, .5L 185.00
Pottery, transfer/HP: monks drinking, Hauber & Reuther, rpr, 1L ...200.00
Pottery, transfer/HP: Trumpeter of Sackingen, pewter lid, 2L 235.00
Pottery, transfer/HP: Voigt's...Michigan, .3L 425.00
Pottery, transfer: Pabst...WI, .5L 295.00
Regimental, porc, 6 Dragoon...1895-98, rpl lid, .5L, 10¼" 225.00
Regimental, porc, 6 Ulannen Hanau 1904-07, 2 scenes, eagle tl, .5L ...635.00
Regimental, porc, 7 Ulan...1896-99, eagle tl, poor lith, .5L, EX ...200.00
Regimental, porc, 9 Bavarian Infantry...1905-07, lion tl, .5L 550.00
Regimental, porc, 12 Infantry...1897-99, lion tl, .5L 440.00
Regimental, porc, 22 Field Artillery...1910-11, eagle tl, .5L 475.00
Regimental, porc, 23 Garde Dragoon...1899-1902, lion tl, .5L ..550.00
Regimental, porc, 115 Garde...1888-91, inlaid lid, lith, .5L 575.00
Regimental, porc, 127 Infantry Ulm 1900-02, Wurttemberg tl, .5L ...330.00
Regimental, pottery, SMS Gneisenau...1906-09, eagle tl, 1L, NM ..965.00
Stoneware, transfer/HP: barmaid on bbl, pewter lid, 1L, NM 325.00
Stoneware, transfer/HP: Brauerei Karg..., pewter lid, .5L 375.00
Stoneware, transfer/HP: XII Deutsches...1913, rpr, 1L 120.00
Stoneware, transfer: Schlossbrauerei Odelahausen, pewter lid, .5L ...250.00
Third Reich, pottery, transfer/HP: UFFZ Korp..., rpl lid, .5L 235.00
Third Reich, stoneware, transfer/HP: 5 Battr AR 7..., helmet lid, .5L 1,000.00

Steuben

Carder Steuben glass was made by the Steuben Glass Works in

Corning, New York, while under the direction of Frederick Carder from 1903 to 1932. Perhaps the most popular types of Carder Steuben glass are Gold Aurene which was introduced in 1904 and Blue Aurene, introduced in 1905. Gold and Blue Aurene objects shimmer with the lustrous beauty of their metallic iridescence. Carder also produced other types of 'Aurenes' including Red, Green, Yellow, Brown, and Decorated, all of which are very rare. Aurene also was cased with Calcite glass. Some pieces had paper labels.

Other types of Carder Steuben include Cluthra, Cintra, Florentia, Rosaline, Ivory, Ivrene, Jades, Verre de Soie; there are many more.

Frederick Carder's leadership of Steuben ended in 1932, and the production of colored glassware soon ceased. Since 1932 the tradition of fine Steuben art glass has been continued in crystal.

Our advisor for this category is Thomas P. Dimitroff; he is in the Directory under New York. In the following listings, examples are signed unless noted otherwise.

Key: ACB — acid cut back

Bowl, Amethyst Quartz, applied and etched leafing branches connect to branching feet, #6856, 6x7¼", $4,000.00.

Basket, Blue Aurene, ruffled, coiled prunt, #5069, 7" 2,100.00
Basket, Verre-de-Soie, berry prunt at hdl, #5069, 14¼" 950.00
Bottle, atomizer; Blue Aurene, #5612, 7" 900.00
Bottle, scent; aquamarine cylinder w/flame stopper, #1988, 8" ..400.00
Bottle, scent; Blue Aurene, #2853, 3¼" 950.00
Bottle, scent; Green Jade, Alabaster stopper, melon ribs, #1455, 5" 600.00
Bottle, scent; off-wht rising to Black Cluthra, faceted, #7327, 6" 1,200.00
Bottle, scent; Pomona Green, ftd, flame stopper, #1988, 8" 450.00
Bottle, scent; Rosaline w/Alabaster stopper & ft, #1988, 8" 550.00
Bottle, scent; Verre D'Soie, Celeste Blue flame stopper, #1455, 5" 500.00
Bottle, scent; Verre D'Soie, Celeste Blue flame stopper, #1988, 8" 500.00
Bowl, amethyst, ribbed center, #3314, 2x16½" 275.00
Bowl, Blue Jade, #5019, 10" 1,200.00
Bowl, clear w/gr threading, 3½x12" 400.00
Bowl, console; Gold Aurene, 3 punty ft, #2586, 10" 500.00
Bowl, console; Mirror Black, similar to #5019, 12" 350.00
Bowl, Gold Aurene, #2889, 4¾"; w/underplate #2025 ....500.00
Bowl, Grotesque, clear, floriform, #7534, 6¾" 350.00
Bowl, Grotesque, Ivrene, undulating rim, #7449, 7x12x7½" 800.00
Bowl, Grotesque, Pomona Green to clear, #7535, 6½x12" 375.00
Bowl, Ivrene, ruffled rim, #7423, 4¾x12" 350.00
Bowl, Rosaline, shouldered, #2687, 6x11½" 275.00
Bowl, topaz pear shape on Pomona Green ft, #1311 (similar), 6¼" ..250.00
Bowl, Verre-de-Soie, EX irid, gr edge, 12" 275.00
Bowl, Yellow Jade, #5019, 10" 900.00
Box, Blue Aurene, #1515, 3½x5" 900.00
Candelabrum, Cyprian, aqua verre-de-soie w/Celeste Bl rims, 3-arm, 19" ..5,500.00
Candle holders, Grotesque, Ivrene, folded cups, #7564, 3¼", pr ..550.00
Candlestick, Aurene w/fold-over Calcite top, #3581, 6½" 500.00
Candlestick, Celeste Blue, 4-leaf bobeche, bulbed std, 12" 950.00
Candlestick, clear w/Pomona Green Cintra rim wraps, berry prunts, 10" ..350.00
Candlestick, Gold Aurene, button pontil, #2329 (similar), 4¾" ..400.00
Candlesticks, Amber, baluster w/wide disk ft, #2956, 12", pr 750.00
Candlesticks, Gold Aurene, twisted stem, #686, 10", pr 1,500.00
Candlesticks, Wisteria w/Pillar eng, #7093, 8", pr 1,850.00
Ceiling light, Calcite w/etched foliage, 3-socket, 15¾" dia 950.00
Compote, Gold Aurene, twisted shaft, #2604, 5¾x6½" 800.00
Compote, Gold Aurene, 5¼x5¼" 550.00
Compote, Gold Calcite, ped ft, #2942 (similar), 8¾x10" 500.00
Compote, Green Jade & Alabaster, #3234, 3x7", pr 500.00
Cruet, clear, needle nose, gooseneck spout, #2720, 5" 1,000.00
Epergne, Ivrene, triple jack-in-pulpit style, #7566, 12¼" 1,500.00
Figurine, Quan Yan (goddess), Alabaster, w/flower arranger, 9" .600.00
Goblet, Alabaster & Rosaline, twisted stem, 8" 275.00
Goblet, Gold Aurene, twist stem, #4231, 6½" 375.00
Goblet, Wisteria w/Pillar eng, dots on base, bell shape, 9" 350.00
Jar, Blue Aurene w/intense irid, #1616, w/lid, 5" 1,200.00
Jar, potpourri; Gold Aurene, 3-hole top, #2812, 5¾" 900.00
Lamp base, Alabaster w/ACB grapes, stick neck, #8006, 14"; +mts ...1,150.00
Lamp base, Belgrade ACB on Plum Jade, 12", EX; +gilded mts 2,400.00
Lamp base, Cluthra, wht w/ACB flowers, bulbous, 12½"; +mts 2,000.00
Lamp base, Oriental Jade, vasiform, #8412, 10½" 1,000.00
Pitcher, Spanish Green, ribbed/ftd sphere, #6665, 9" 460.00
Potpourri urn, Alabaster, hooded mc design w/gold, acorn finial, 7" ...2,200.00
Salt cellar, Gold Aurene on Calcite, ped ft, 1½x2½" 450.00
Shade, Gold Aurene, ribbed, 5½" 200.00
Sherbet, Gold Aurene, +undertray 500.00
Sherbet, Oriental Poppy, pk opal swirled optic ribs, 3-ftd, 2¾" .350.00
Toothpick holder, gold w/Calcite, cup shape w/flared rim 250.00
Tumbler, Gold Aurene, #2361, 4½" 250.00
Tumbler, juice; Gold Calcite 225.00
Tumbler, Verre-de-Soie, flared rim, 4x3¼" 275.00
Vase, ACB Green Jade over Alabaster (sculptured), 8¾" 1,450.00
Vase, Alabaster, gold irid veins & 5 strewn leaves, #429, 6¼" ...1,100.00
Vase, Aquamarine, stump form, 3 branches, 6" 450.00
Vase, Black Matsu-no-ke, ming trees, #6391, foiled label, 12" ...1,100.00
Vase, Blue Aurene, classical form, #5133, 9" 1,100.00
Vase, Blue Aurene, melon shape w/short neck, #2653, 10¼x9" 1,265.00
Vase, Blue Aurene, stump form, 3 branches, #2744, 6½" W 900.00
Vase, Blue Aurene, 10-sided, flared rim, #913, 5½" 850.00
Vase, Blue Aurene w/purple irid, 10-rib, 5" 1,095.00
Vase, Bristol Dmn Quilt w/blk threading, #6813 (similar), 7x7" ..500.00
Vase, Celeste Blue, urn form w/disk ft, 7" 450.00
Vase, Cluthra, gr to wht w/clear base, 9¾" 800.00
Vase, Cluthra, Rose Pink, flared rim, #2683, 10½" 1,375.00
Vase, Cluthra, royal bl/wht, urn form, #2683, 6" 1,000.00
Vase, floriform; Gold Aurene, #346, 10x6¼" 1,200.00
Vase, French Blue, 2-prong triangular form, #6874, 9" 550.00
Vase, Gold Aurene, classic form, 5x5½" 650.00
Vase, Gold Aurene, ribbed neck, #240, 5¾" 1,000.00
Vase, Gold Aurene, ruffled trumpet form, #723, 8" 750.00
Vase, Gold Aurene, stump form, 3 branches, #2744, 6" 800.00
Vase, Gold Aurene, 6-sided rim, disk ft, #6241, 8¼" 700.00
Vase, Gold Aurene on Calcite, scalloped rim, 2" 250.00
Vase, Gold Aurene on Calcite, 6-scallop trumpet form, #346, 8¼" ...575.00
Vase, Gold Aurene w/bl peacock feathers, #261, 8" 4,500.00
Vase, Gold Aurene w/gr hearts & vines, baluster, 5" 3,200.00
Vase, Gold Aurene w/gr pulled loops, #209, 4¾" 1,500.00
Vase, gr & frosted gr w/ACB mums, minor flakes, 7" 750.00
Vase, Green Jade, Alabaster knob stem & base, fan form, 10½" ..400.00
Vase, Green Jade & Alabaster Matsu-no-ke, bonsai trees, #6078, 7x8" ..1,035.00
Vase, Grotesque, Dark Blue Jade, pillar ribs, 6½x12½x6¼" ...3,500.00
Vase, Grotesque, Ivory, ftd, #7090, 12" 400.00
Vase, Grotesque, Pomona Green to clear, ftd, #7090, 9" 275.00
Vase, Ivrene, morning-glory form, #913, 5½" 250.00
Vase, Ivrene, 3 aqua cintra hdls, #7568, 11¼" 1,380.00

Vase, Ivrene, flared ruffled rim, #2934, 7¾x10" 300.00
Vase, lt amethyst w/molded swirls, flared, 10" 500.00
Vase, Mansion, flared rim, sq ped, M hdls, #7389, 12x9" 1,000.00
Vase, Pomona Green, shaded ribs, wht int, fleur-de-lis mk, 9" ...275.00
Vase, Pomona Green w/air traps, 4-pillar w/5 openings, 5¼" 275.00
Vase, Rosalene, pk & ivory, bottle shape, 7½" 325.00
Vase, Spanish Green on appl oval base, 3-prong, #6873, 10" 175.00
Wall pocket, Cluthra, blk/wht, conical w/ormolu bands, 8x16" .490.00

Stevengraphs

A Stevengraph is a small picture made of woven silk resembling an elaborate ribbon, created by Thomas Stevens in England in the latter half of the 1800s. They were matted and framed by Stevens, usually with his name appearing on the mat or often with the trade announcement on the back of the mat. He also produced silk postcards and bookmarks, all of which have 'Stevens' woven in silk on one of the mitered corners. Anyone wishing to learn more about Stevengraphs is encouraged to contact the Stevengraph Collectors' Association, whose address can be found in the Directory under Clubs, Newsletters, and Catalogs.

Are You Ready?, EX 300.00
Columbus Leaving Spain, G 225.00
Coventry, 2 blk & wht scenes, fr, pr 110.00
Death of Nelson, G 195.00
Declaration of Independence, woven at Columbian Exhibition ...225.00
First Innings, G 325.00
First Train Built by Geo Stephenson in 1825, 8⅞x11⅝" 150.00
Full Cry, w/mat 120.00
God Speed the Plow, G 220.00
Kenilworth Castle, orig matt & fr, 15½x22½" 175.00
Landing of Columbus, NM 250.00
Meet, orig matt, old fr, NM 250.00
Mrs Cleveland, VG 135.00
Present Time, 60 Miles an Hour, Lord Howe, orig mat, EX 175.00
Queen Victoria Jubilee, 1837-1887, unfr 55.00
Victoria, Queen of Empire on Which the Sun Never Sets, unfr, EX ...195.00
Water Jump, fr, EX 225.00
Wellington & Blugher, EX 300.00

Miscellaneous

Bookmark, Behold the man, blk fr, G 50.00
Bookmark, Dr Guthrie 50.00
Bookmark, Garibaldi, United Italy 50.00
Bookmark, Home Sweet Home, VG 65.00
Bookmark, Love's Remembrance, VG 75.00
Bookmark, Remember Me, VG 65.00
Bookmark, To My Dear Sister 60.00
Postcard, Ann Hathaway's Cottage 40.00
Postcard, Shakespeare's Birthday 45.00

Stevens and Williams

Stevens and Williams glass was produced at the Brierly Hill Glassworks in Stourbridge, England, for nearly a century, beginning in the 1830s. They were credited with being among the first to develop a method of manufacturing a more affordable type of cameo glass. Other lines were also made — silver deposit, alexandrite, and engraved rock crystal, to name but a few. Our advisor for this category is Don Williams; he is listed in the Directory under Missouri.

Vase, dogwood cameo, white on turquoise, bulbous flask form, signed, 8", $1,900.00.

Basket, bl opal o/l w/amber ruffle & hdl, appl oak leaves, 10" ...150.00
Basket, pk o/l, amber ft, cranberry rigaree, mc leaves, 10" 400.00
Basket, rose/ol w/appl flowers, amber ft & hdl, 13½x7" 850.00
Bowl, bl to clear, amber rigaree & rim, sq, 4¼" 150.00
Bowl, Matsu-no-ke, appl on yel, 3 florets ft, 3x6", NM 1,250.00
Goblet, gr to clear, wheel-cut floral, ca 1900, 7" 200.00
Lamp, Matsu-no-ke, pk w/crystal, ruffled bowl shade, 17" 3,000.00
Pitcher, gr/bl cased, appl 3-blossom branch, tendril hdl, 7", NM 385.00
Pitcher, yel/pk opal stripes on clear, ribbed, 6" 225.00
Rose bowl, Jewel, lt rose w/zipper-like airtrap ribs, 5" dia 215.00
Vase, bl o/l w/intaglio ferns, bl ft w/stripes, 6½x3¾" 225.00
Vase, cameo, apple blossoms, wht on pk, 4½" 1,050.00
Vase, cream opaque o/l, appl flower w/mc leaves, amber ft, 6½" 295.00
Vase, cut o/l, bl/wht/red, circles/oval panels, petal top, 12" 1,000.00
Vase, Matsu-no-ke, bl satin Hobnail w/camphor, 5" 625.00
Vase, Matsu-no-ke, turq/cream int, str sides, pinched rim, 4½" .785.00
Vase, MOP Swirl, lav, bulbous w/gourd neck, 9¾" 750.00
Vase, pk o/l, indaglio daisy ea side & corner cuttings, 4" 225.00
Vase, pk o/l w/lacy intaglio cuttings, clear opal ft, 4¼" 195.00
Vase, Pompeian Swirl, bl w/pk, bulbous bottom, 7½" 545.00
Vase, Pompeian Swirl, lime gr, bulbous w/ped ft, 11" 835.00
Vase, Pompeian Swirl, rose satin, wht int, dbl gourd, 8" 550.00
Vase, Swirl, dk rose/yel on frost, ribbed, 7½x5" 400.00

Stickley

Among the leading proponents of the Arts and Crafts Movement, the Stickley brothers — Gustav, Leopold, Charles, Albert, and John George — were at various times and locations separately involved in designing and producing furniture as well as decorative items for the home. (See Arts and Crafts for further information.) The oldest of the five Stickley brothers was Gustav; his work is the most highly regarded of all. He developed the style of furniture referred to as Mission. It was strongly influenced by the type of furnishings found in the Spanish missions of California — utilitarian, squarely built, and simple. It was made most often of oak, and decoration was very limited or non-existent. The work of his brothers display adaptations of many of Gustav's ideas and designs. His factory, the Craftsman Workshop, operated in Eastwood, New York, from the late 1890s until 1915, when he was forced out of business by larger companies who copied his work and sold it at much lower prices. Among his shop marks are the early red decal containing a joiner's compass and the words 'Als Ik Kan,' the branded mark with very similar components, and paper labels.

The firm known as Stickley Brothers was located first in Binghamton, New York, and then Grand Rapids, Michigan. Albert and John George made the move to Michigan, leaving Charles in Binghamton (where he and an uncle continued the operation under a different name). After several years John George left the company to rejoin Leopold in New York. (These two later formed their own firm called L. & J.G. Stickley.) The Stickley Brothers Company's early work produced furniture featuring fine inlay work, decorative cutouts, and leaned strongly toward a style of Arts and Crafts with an English influence. It was tagged with a paper label 'Made by Stickley Brothers, Grand Rapids,' or with a brass plate or decal with the words 'Quaint Furniture,' an English term chosen to refer to their product. In addition to furniture, they made metal accessories as well.

The workshops of the L. & J.G. Stickley Company first operated under the name 'Onondaga Shops.' Located in Fayetteville, New York, their designs were often all but copies of Gustav's work. Their products were well made and marketed, and their business was very successful. Their decal labels contained all or a combination of the words 'Handcraft' or 'Onondaga Shops,' along with the brothers' initials and last name. The firm continues in business today. Our advisor for this category is Bruce Austin; he is listed in the Directory under New York. Note: When only one dimension is given for tables, it is length. Cleaning diminishes values; ours are for furniture and metals with excellent original finishes unless noted otherwise.

Key:
b — brand
brd — board
d — red decal
h/cp — hammered copper
hdw — hardware
n — no mark
p — paper label
t — Quaint metal tag
vnr — veneer
w — work of...

Gustav Stickley

Andirons, #102, curled straps, wrought iron, sgn, 19", pr 3,750.00
Armchair, #310½, 3-slat bk, leatherette seat w/tacks, d, 36", pr ..1,000.00
Armchair, #324, 5 slats under ea arm, altered seat, 40", VG ...1,600.00
Armchair, #353A, 3 vertical slats, arched seat rail, rush seat ..2,000.00
Bed, Harvey Ellis form, paneled head/ft brds, 50x58", VG 9,000.00
Bed, 12 vertical spindles, b, 50½x57½" 1,600.00
Bed, 5 wide vertical slats in head/ft brd, b, 48x59x78" 8,000.00
Bookcase, #717, 2 8-pane doors, b/p, rfn, 56x48", VG 4,750.00
Bookcase, #718, 2 8-pane doors, keyed tenons, 56x47", VG ..6,000.00
Bookcase, like #716, gallery over 2 8-pane doors, d, 56x42" ...6,000.00
Bowl, floral on cream & gr, Onandaga Pottery/logo, 7½x12½" ..1,300.00
Cabinet, china; #803, arched door & toe brd, d/p, 60x33x16" .8,000.00
Cabinet, china; #815, 2 8-pane doors/thru tenons, b/p, 64x42", VG ..8,000.00
Cabinet, magazine; #72, 3-shelf, arched aprons, p, 42x22x13" .2,500.00
Cabinet, sewing; #630, drop leaf w/2 drws, some rstr, VG 1,100.00
Chair, desk; #39h, H-bk, rstr leather seat, 33" 500.00
Chair, Morris; #336, bow arm, rstr spring cushion, d, EX 12,000.00
Chair, Morris; #369, 5-slat arms, 4-slat bk, rpl seat, 40", VG ..7,500.00
Chair, side; #1301, 3 horizontal slats, rush seat, d, pr 750.00
Chair, side; #349, heavy ladderbk, rush seats, VG, set of 4 .....3,000.00
Chair, side; #353, 3 bk slats, rush slip seat, d, 30", G 450.00
Chair, side; Thornden #1299, 2-slat bk, rush seat, 36", VG 800.00
Chandelier, #670, 4 wrought iron & glass lanterns on chains ..32,000.00
Chandelier, willow w/center glass globe, h/cp cap, 86x37" dia .9,500.00
Chest, #906, 2 half drws/4 long drws, copper pulls, b, 48x41x21", VG ..8,500.00
Chest, #909, 2 short drws over 3 long, 42x36x20", VG 2,700.00
Chest, #913, 6 half drws over 3 long, wooden pulls, 47x36x20" ..1,200.00
Coat stand, d, 70¾x22" 1,500.00
Compote, pine needles & cones, Onandaga Pottery/logo, 4½x9" 1,000.00
Costumer, #53, dbl posts, iron hooks, shoe-ft base, 72x22x13", VG ..2,000.00
Desk, #550, slant front over 3 drws+2 doors, d, 48x33" 10,000.00
Desk, #708, 2-drw, postcard top, orig finish, 36x40x22" 1,725.00
Desk, #720, pigeonhole organizer, 2-drw, p, rfn, 37x38", VG .1,250.00
Desk, oak vnr drop front, 2 half drws/2 long, att, 43x32x14" 900.00
Dresser, #905, 2 drws over 3, d, 33x48x23", VG 2,000.00
Dresser, #911, w/mirror, 2 half drws/2 long, 67x48x23" 7,000.00
Dresser, #913, Ellis design, 6 sm drw over 3, d, 51x36", VG ...7,000.00
Footstool, #300, arched seat rail, new leather, 20x16", VG 1,200.00
Footstool, #302, b, orig tacks, rpl cover, 4½x12½" sq 250.00
Gong, arched top rail, 5-ftd base, rpl 1928 gong, 36x23x11" ..5,500.00
Hall seat, #224, panel bk, lift seat, thru tenons, 42x48", VG .5,000.00

Jardiniere, #275, hammered copper with embossed decor, applied handles, rare form, EX, $4,000.00.

Lamp, #608, 7" sq hammered glass shade; h/cp std on oak base, 18" ...8,500.00
Lamp, #609, 4 h/cp straps on oak base, 12" wicker shade, 20" 8,000.00
Lamp, h/cp canister std on oak ped, 15" wicker shade, 22", VG ..8,500.00
Magazine stand, #506, beveled top, 4-shelf, rfn, 39x16", VG .4,000.00
Magazine stand, #79, 4-shelf, arched toe brd, thru tenons, 40", VG ...1,600.00
Magazine stand, like #514, 3-shelf, paneled sides, 35x15", VG 3,500.00
Mirror, cheval; #918, dbl-arch stretchers, 1904 mk, 70" 17,000.00
Plant, stand, #604, b, 26x20" dia 1,300.00
Rocker, #309, 3-slat ladder-bk, rush seat, d, 32", VG 650.00
Rocker, #313, H-bk, orig leather seat, d, cleaned, 37", VG 700.00
Rocker, #323, bk w/4 horizontal slats, 5 slats under arm, b, VG ..1,700.00
Rug, Drugget; honeycomb pattern, gr on oatmeal, 72x38", VG .550.00
Sconce, #830, hammered iron w/6 cutouts over glass, 12x6x11" ...3,000.00
Server, #802, inset bksplash, 2 short drw, arched apron, 1907, 39x42" ...3,000.00
Settle, #208, even arm, 8-slat bk, 3-slat sides, d, 76" 8,000.00
Sideboard, #814½, door ea side 3 drws over 1 long, d, 54", VG ..1,900.00
Somno, drw over panel door, 38x16x16" 5,000.00
Table, #603, notched stretchers, b/p, 20x18" dia 1,000.00
Table, #644, 4 cut-in leg posts, p, rfn/stained, 29x30" dia 2,000.00
Table, #655, 13-spindle sides, rfn, 36", VG 3,750.00
Table, chest; #419, leather top, keyed tonons, 39" 10,000.00
Table, dining; #632, 48" dia top, 5 legs, 4 leaves, p, VG 3,500.00
Table, dining; #634, w/6 leaves, b/p, 30x54" extends to 120" .8,000.00
Table, dressing; #907, d/p, rfn, 29¾x48x22" 2,300.00
Table, hexagonal leather top 6-leg, rfn, 29x48" 3,750.00
Table, library, #653, drw, iron hdw, d, rstr top, 48", VG 1,800.00
Table, library; #456, 2 hidden drws, low shelf, 29x36x24", VG ..7,500.00
Table, library; #524, 3-drw, 3 side slats, d, worn finish, 54" 1,800.00
Table, library; #617, 2-drw w/copper pulls, b, 54", VG 2,500.00
Table, library; #652, overhang top, drw, rfn/rpl drw, 36", VG 750.00
Table, tea; #604, arched stretcher, d, 25x20", VG 1,600.00
Table, trestle; #637, dbl keyed tenons, rfn, 38x48x30", VG 1,400.00
Table, trestle; thick shelf w/keyed tenons, b, 48", VG 1,400.00
Table, writing; #720, divided bk, 2-drw, copper pulls, d, 37x38", VG 1,500.00
Umbrella stand, #100, flared/slatted, no pan, cleaned, 24" 1,600.00
Umbrella stand, #55, 4 tapered posts, divided top, rfn, 34", VG ...850.00
Umbrella stand, like #54, sq fr w/sq finials, copper liner, 33" 500.00
Vanity, #919, swivel mirror, 2 drws, b, 55½x36" 3,500.00
Vanity stool, #301, rush seat, tapered legs, b, 20x16x18" 800.00
Wardrobe, #920, 2 panel doors, copper pulls, Eastwood p, 60x33x16" ...23,000.00
Wine cooler, #553, circular form w/copper bands, 15x13" dia ..8,500.00

L. & J.G. Stickley

Armchair, #422, V-bk over 6 vertical slats, d, 38x28x21" 400.00

Armchair, #810, 5 bk slats/peaked rail, w, rfn/new leather 400.00
Bookcase, #643, narrow dbl-door style, copper hdw, 55x39" ...6,000.00
Bookcase, #647, 9 stationary shelves, 3 12-pane doors, 55x72" ...16,000.00
Bookcase, 2 12-pane doors, h/cp hdw, 55x53x12" 7,000.00
Chafing dish stand, low shelf, 28x18x12" 2,700.00
Chair, #820, Handcraft d, 36x19½x17", pr 400.00
Chair, desk; 3-slat bk, recovered seat, b, 36", VG 375.00
Chiffonier, #90, 2 over 4 drws, b, 49¾x42x18¼" 4,000.00
Desk, #501, drw w/2 drw ea side, b, 48" 1,900.00
Desk, gallery top over 2 drw, gate leg, b, 35x32x10", VG 1,800.00
Footstool, #394, new leather, 19x15x16" 500.00
Magazine stand, #46, 4-shelf, 3 slats ea side, Handcraft d, 42x21" 1,900.00
Rocker, #413, w/arms, rpl seat covers, 37x34x37" 2,500.00
Rocker, #451, 6-slat bk, flat arms w/corbels, b, 39x28x32" 1,400.00
Rocker, #781½, flat 5-slat arms, orig leather seat, 38", VG 3,000.00
Rocker, bk w/6 vertical slats, open arms, uphl seat, 35", VG 500.00
Rocker, like #819, w/arms, 3-slat bk, leather seat 700.00
Rocker, like #859, 6-slat, sq stiles, drop-in seat, b 550.00
Settle, #281, cube style, 16-slat bk, w, reuphl, 77" 10,000.00
Settle, att Onondaga Shop, 22-slat bk/7 ea side, 4-post, 77", VG ...6,000.00
Settle, drop-arm, 12-slat bk, drop-in rstr cushion, 65x36x25", VG ..2,800.00
Sideboard, #734, 3 drw amid 2 drws, rfn, 44x48", VG 2,100.00
Stool, #399, folds, rpl leather seat, orig tacks, 15x18x16" 2,600.00
Table, #22, copper-sheathed top, X stretcher, p, 28x17¾" dia ...3,750.00
Table, #541, 30" dia top, shelf, Handcraft d, VG 1,600.00
Table, #558, octagonal top, X stretchers, b, 20x18", VG 1,100.00
Table, #558, 8-side top w/exposed leg joints, d, 17", VG 400.00
Table, work; #530, frieze drw, sq legs, platform stretcher, 36" .1,200.00

Stickley Bros.

Armchair, 3 short slats to bk, bk/seat leather, rfn, 40", VG 450.00
Armchair, 4 bk slats, spring seats, rfn/reuphl, 48" 375.00
Bookcase, 3 doors, ea w/ldgl sqs in top panel, 60x59" 4,750.00
Cabinet, bar/liquor; 4-door, drw, pull-out copper tray, 51x27" ...2,700.00
Cabinet, china; #8644, 3 pulls missing, rfn, 68x48x17½" 4,000.00
Cabinet, china; pr 8-pane doors, 4-pane sides, plate rail, 64" .3,250.00
Chair, side; #312½, 3-slat bk, plank seat, 38", VG 300.00
Chamberstick, #178, h/cp, appl/curled hdl, 12" 650.00
Costumer, #188, dbl posts, shoe-ft base, orig hooks, 69" 1,200.00
Desk, #6516, slant front over drw on shoe-ft base, 47x30", VG ...1,900.00
Footstool, p, new leather, 8x8½x12" 250.00
Hall chair, 5-sided bk w/floral inlay, trapezoidal seat, att, 40" 800.00
Hall tree, dbl costumer w/iron hooks, shoe-ft base, no pan, VG ...550.00
Magazine rack, spindle sides, 4-shelf, 39x26x12" 1,100.00
Plate rail, #903, arched top, slatted bk, d, 24x48", VG 5,000.00
Rocker, #298, 4 vertical bk slats, saddle seat, w/arms, 39" 325.00
Rocker, concave crest rail, uphl panel, t, 42x27x29" 175.00
Server, arched bksplash, 1 drw over lower shelf, 42" 225.00
Server, rectangular top w/bksplash, low shelf, recoated, 36" 800.00
Settle, att; 9 vertical slats, 3 vertical side slats, no seat, 65" ...2,000.00
Sideboard, plate rack, 4-drw/2-door, 66" L 2,100.00
Smoking stand, flaring legs, spindle lower shelf, 27x10" sq 100.00
Table, dining; corbeled ped base, rfn, 54" dia; +5 leaves 4,000.00
Table, game; #324, hexagonal top, arched apron, 41" dia, +6 chairs ...3,250.00
Table, lamp; #926, 26x28" dia 925.00
Vase, #20, h/cp, appl 'horn' hdls, 3 emb hemispheres, rfn, 10" ..850.00

Stocks and Bonds

Scripophily (scrip-awfully), the collecting of 'worthless' old stocks and bonds, gained recognition as an area of serious interest around the mid-1970s. Today there are an estimated 5,000 collectors in the United States and 15,000 worldwide. Collectors who come from numerous business fields mainly enjoy its hobby aspect, though there are those who consider scripophily an investment. Some collectors like the historical significance that certain certificates have. Others prefer the beauty of older stocks and bonds that were printed in various colors with fancy artwork and ornate engravings. Even autograph collectors are found in this field, on the lookout for signed certificates.

Many factors help determine the collector value: autograph value, age of the certificate, the industry represented, whether it is issued or not, its attractiveness, condition, and collector demand. Certificates from the mining, energy, and railroad industries are the most popular with collectors. Other industries or special collecting fields include banking, automobiles, aircraft, and territorials. Serious collectors usually prefer only issued certificates that date from before 1910. Unissued certificates are usually worth one-fourth to one-tenth the value of one that has been issued. Inexpensive issued common stocks and bonds dated between the 1930s and 1980s usually retail between $1.00 to $10.00. Those dating between 1890 and 1930 usually sell for $10.00 to $50.00. Those over one hundred years old retail between $25.00 and $100.00 or more, depending on the quantity found and the industry represented. Some stocks are one of a kind while others are found by the hundreds or even thousands, especially railroad certificates. Autographed stocks normally sell anywhere from $50.00 to $1,000.00 or more. A formal collecting organization for scripophilists is known as The Bond and Share Society with an American chapter located in New York City.

Our advisor for this category is Warren Anderson; he is listed in the Directory under Utah. In many of the following listings, two-letter state abbreviations immediately follow company name. All are in fine condition unless noted otherwise.

Key:
cp — coupon
I/C — issued/cancelled
I/U — issued/uncancelled
U — unissued
vgn — vignette

Tonawanda Valley & Cuba R.R., $1,000 bond, train at station vignette, New York, 1881, EX, $65.00 at auction.

Anglo-Am Oil, TX/1902, Spindletop, train vgn, I/U 30.00
AX-Mexican Mining & Smelting Co, AZ Territory/1905, 3 vgns, I/C ...25.00
Baldwin & Northrup Co, ME/1902, Geo Washington portrait/banner, I/U ..15.00
Bankers & Merchants Petroleum, TX/1919, Lone Star vgn, I/U ..15.00
Big Five Mining Co, WY/1912, Big 5 in corners, blk/wht, 5x9", I/C ..20.00
Branch Mint Mining & Milling Co, SD/1907, eagle vgn/art/banner, I/U ...25.00
Buffalo & Susquehanna Railway, NY/1907, train vgn, ABNCo, I/U ...25.00
Butte Electric Railway, WV/190-, trolley vgn, ABNCo, U 20.00
Chicago Railway's Co, IL/1911, city & goddess vgns, $100 bond, I/U 25.00
Cleveland Gold Mining & Milling, CO/1896, miners vgn/artwork, I/U .50.00
CO City & Manitou Prospecting & Mining, CO/1901, vgn, much gold, I/U 40.00
Comet Placer Mining Co, NV/1912, 3 vgns, blk/wht, seal, I/U ...40.00
Congressional Oil Corp, NV/1920, capitol building vgn, I/U 20.00
Consolidated Mining & Development, WA/1902, bl paper, red seal, I/U ...20.00
Copper-Gold Mining/Milling Syndicate, WY/1926, goddess vgn, 5x9", I/U .15.00
Dennos Food Co of Portland, OR/1913, child vgn, gold seal, I/U ...15.00
Erie Mining Co, CA/1895, bold title, blk/wht, 6x9", I/C 40.00

First State Savings Bank of West Frankfort, IL/1929, eagle vgn, I/U ..15.00
Francisco Mining & Milling Co, OR/1904, miners vgn, orange border, I/U ..30.00
Haynes Copper Mining Co, AZ Territory/1910, unusual print, I/C ..20.00
Land Co of Florida, MD/1925, bold title, orange border, ABNCo, I/U ..20.00
Lawrence Petroleum, OK/1921, train/oil field vgn, gr print, I/U ..15.00
Manhattan Mascot Gold Mining Co, AZ Territory/1907, 3 vgns, 6x9", I/U .30.00
Mines Securities Corp, ME/1906, bold title, gold border/seal, I/U ..20.00
Nat'l Coal Railway, UT/1925, capitol building vgn, I/C 45.00
Oil Fields Corp, AR/1925, oil well vgn, artwork, brn border, I/U 15.00
Portland Coal & Development Co, OR/1905, mining vgn, gr border, I/U ..30.00
Republican Valley Railroad, NB/1880s, arch title, bl paper, U 15.00
Silver Cliff Gold & Mining Co, ID/1917, Miss Liberty vgn, I/U .20.00
Spanish Mining & Milling Co, UT/1911, miners vgn/artwork, I/U ..25.00
Steger-Mexia Oil, TX/1922, gusher vgn/banner, blk/brn, brn seal, I/U ...15.00
Studebaker Corp, DE1953, ABNCo, blksmith shop vgn, I/C 40.00
Texas Ranger Producing & Refining, TX/1920, oil field vgn, I/U ...20.00
Thunder Mtn Syndicate, WA/1903, blk on yel, red seal, I/U 20.00
Tideman Electric Mfg Co, IL/1919, title on banner, brn border, I/U ..10.00
Tintic Zenith Mining Co, UT/1919, 3 vgns, blk/wht, gr border, I/C ..25.00
Triangle Mining & Development To, MT/1922, angel vgn, I/C ..25.00
Utah (Coal) Railway Co, UT/1915, miners vgn/banner, I/C 45.00

Stoneware

There are three broad periods of time that collectors of American pottery can look to in evaluating and dating the stoneware and earthenware in their collections. Among the first permanent settlers in America were English and German potters who found a great demand for their individually turned wares. The early pottery was produced from red and yellow clays scraped from the ground at surface levels. The earthenware made in these potteries was fragile and coated with lead glazes that periodically created health problems for the people who ate or drank from it. There was little stoneware available for sale until the early 1800s, because the clays used in its production were not readily available in many areas and transportation was prohibitively expensive. The opening of the Erie Canal and improved roads brought about a dramatic increase in the accessibility of stoneware clay, and many new potteries began to open in New York and New England.

Collectors have difficulty today locating earthenware and stoneware jugs produced prior to 1840, because few have survived intact. These ovoid or pear-shaped jugs were designed to be used on a daily basis. When cracked or severely chipped, they were quickly discarded. The value of handcrafted pottery is often determined by the cobalt decoration it carries. Pieces with elaborate scenes (a chicken pecking corn, a bluebird on a branch, a stag standing near a pine tree, a sailing ship, or people) may easily bring $1,000.00 to $12,000.00 at auction.

After the Civil War there was a need and a national demand for stoneware jugs, crocks, canning jars, churns, spittoons, and a wide variety of other pottery items. The competition among the many potteries reached the point where only the largest could survive. To cut costs, most potteries did away with all but the simplest kinds of decoration on their wares. Time-consuming brush-painted birds or flowers quickly gave way to more quickly executed swirls or numbers and stenciled designs. The coming of home refrigeration and Prohibition in 1919 effectively destroyed the American stoneware industry.

Investment possibilities: 1) Early nineteenth-century stoneware with elaborate decorations and a potter's mark is expensive and will continue to rise in price. 2) Late nineteenth-century hand-thrown stoneware with simple cobalt swirls or numbers is still reasonably priced and a good investment. 3) Mass-produced stoneware (ca. 1890 – 1920) is available in large quantities, inexpensive, and slowly increases in price over the years.

Skillfully repaired pieces often surface; their prices should reflect their condition. Look for a slight change in color and texture. The use of a black light is also useful in exposing some repairs. Buyer beware! Hint: Buy only from reputable dealers who will guarantee their merchandise.

In the following listings, 'c/s' means 'cobalt on salt glaze'; all decoration described before this abbreviation is in cobalt. See also Bennington, Stoneware. Assume that values are for examples in near mint condition with only minimal damage unless another condition code is given in the description.

Churn, #6/bird on tree trunk, professional restoration, T. Harrington Lyons, ca 1855, 19½", $5,775.00.

Batter pail, #8/accents, c/s, tin lid, 8-qt, 1860s, 10", EX 220.00
Bowl, #3/plume, c/s, unmk, att Hudson Valley, 1840s, 11" 275.00
Churn, #2/flower basket, c/s, West Troy Pottery, 1880s, 13", EX .715.00
Churn, #5/bird (paddletail), c/s, NA White & Son, chip, ca 1885, 17" ..1,700.00
Churn, #6/flower (dbl), c/s, AO Whittemore...NY, 1870s, 18", EX ...990.00
Crock, #1/accents, c/s, T Goodwin, 1830s, chips, 8" 80.00
Crock, #1/dbl scallop, c/s, tooled decor, S Amboy NJ, ca 1805, 9½" .2,500.00
Crock, #1/simple brush design, c/s, M Tyler Albany, 1840s, 9", EX 100.00
Crock, #1/Village Store...Conn, c/s, stain/flaking, 1880s, 7½" ...145.00
Crock, #2/bird on plume, c/s, Fulper Bros...NJ, 1870s, 9¼" 635.00
Crock, #2/tulip, c/s, WH Farrar...NY, 1850s, 10" 360.00
Crock, #2/wreath & plume, c/s, Smith & Day Norwalk, ca 1845, 12", VG ...80.00
Crock, #3/bird (running), c/s, Whites Utica NY, ca 1865, 10½", EX ...440.00
Crock, #3/butterfly, c/s, John Schmidt...NY, 1890s, 10¼", EX .1,375.00
Crock, #3/flower, c/s, CW Braun...NY, sm line/chips, ca 1870, 9½" 135.00
Crock, #3/plume, c/s, N Clark...Mt Morris, chip/stain, 1840s, 12½" ...300.00
Crock, #4/bird (dbl), c/s, S Hart Fulton, line, ca 1875, 11" 525.00
Crock, #4/bird on plume (facing left), c/s, Haxstun & Ottman, 11½" ...495.00
Crock, #4/hops vine, c/s, J Fisher & Co Lyons NY, 1880s, 11½" ..450.00
Crock, #4/pear on branch, c/s, AO Whittmore...NY, chip, 1870s, 10½" ..550.00
Crock, #5/flower basket, c/s, FT Wright...Mass, crack, 1870s, 12" 385.00
Crock, #6/birds on floral branches (ornate), c/s, Whites Utica NY, 13" ..3,100.00
Crock, #6/lovebirds, c/s, Whites Utica, prof rstr, ca 1865, 13½" 2,400.00
Crock, cake; #2/swags, c/s, John Bell Waynesboro, ca 1860, 7x12" 550.00
Crock, cake; flower, c/s, Edmands & Co, 1870s, about 2-gal, rstr 200.00
Jar, #1/plume, c/s, Lyons, 1870s, 10" 175.00
Jar, #2/bird & flower, cs, WH Farrar...NY, stain/chip, 1850s, 11" ..1,980.00
Jar, #2/bird on plume, c/s, Whites Utica, line, ca 1865, 11" 440.00
Jar, #2/flower (simple), c/s, Edmands & Co, ca 1870, 12½" 200.00
Jar, #2/vine & floral, c/s, NA White...NY, 1870s, 11" 470.00
Jar, #3/dove on fern branch, c/s, FB Norton...Mass, rstr, 1870s, 14" ...450.00
Jar, oyster; T Downing's Pickled...NY, c/s, sm chip, 1850s, 6" 550.00
Jar, preserve; #1/flower, c/s, Penn Yan, rpl lid, 1860s, 9½" 330.00
Jar, preserve; #2/plume, c/s, T Harrington Lyons, lines, 1860s, 12" ...130.00
Jar, preserve; pears, c/s, Hamilton & Jones, tin lid, 8⅜" 495.00
Jar, preserving; GW Roberts..Elizabeth WV, c/s, ca 1860, ½-gal ...120.00
Jug, #1/accent, c/s, SS Perry West Troy, ca 1833, 10½" 300.00
Jug, #1/bird on triple flower, c/s, Roberts Binghamton NY, 11", EX ...880.00
Jug, #1/flower, c/s, incised dbl snake, H&G Nash Utica NY, 1830s, 11" ...1,100.00
Jug, #1/man's profile against vine, c/s, Jordan, rstr, 1850s, 12" ...1,300.00
Jug, #1/plume, c/s, FB Norton...Mass, chip, 1870s, 11½" 150.00
Jug, #2 (lg/dotted), c/s, Troy NY, 2 sm pings, ca 1885, 13½" 360.00

Jug, #2/bird (paddle tail)/floral plume, c/s, NA White..., 1870s, 14" ..3,400.00
Jug, #2/bird on plume, c/s, Troy NY, 1870s, 13½" 360.00
Jug, #2/cabbage flower, c/s, John Burger Jr, rstr hdl, ca 1865, 15" ...220.00
Jug, #2/eagle w/banner, c/s, Wm Warner West Troy, 1850s, 13" ...700.00
Jug, #2/flower, c/s, C Hart...Ogdensburgh, lines, ca 1855, 14" 155.00
Jug, #2/flower, c/s, John Burger Rochester, ca 1865, 14" 580.00
Jug, #2/flower (bold), c/s, Lyons, ca 1870, 13½" 360.00
Jug, #2/flower compote, c/s, Whites Utica, ca 1865, 13" 635.00
Jug, #2/plume, c/s, Satterlee & Morey, stain/ping, 1870s, 14" 200.00
Jug, #2/snake, c/s, Whites Utica, ping/stain, ca 1865, 13" 200.00
Jug, #2/swimming turtle, c/s, West Troy, 1880s, 16½" 635.00
Jug, #2/tulip, c/s, Burger Bros...NY, ca 1868, 15" 500.00
Jug, #3/leaf & vine, Edmands & Co, ping/spider, 1870s, 15" 220.00
Jug, #4/vine, c/s, NA White...NY, ca 1885, 16½" 300.00
Jug, syrup; #2/plume, c/s, NY Stoneware, chipped spout, 1880s, 14" ...110.00
Pail, #2/wreath, c/s, S Hart Oswego Falls, 1860s, 9" 250.00
Pitcher, #1/roses (3), c/s, att Pottery Works NY, 1870s, 11" ...2,500.00
Pitcher, One/accent, c/s, N Clark Mt Morris, 1840s, 11½" 855.00
Pot, cream; #2/floral vine, c/s, N Clark Jr...NY, hairline, 1850s, 9" ...190.00
Spittoon, swags/accents, c/s, Cowden & Wilcox, 1870s, 6x10" ..715.00

Store

Perhaps more so than any other yesteryear establishment, the country store evokes feelings of nostalgia for folks old enough to remember its charms — barrels for coffee, crackers, and big green pickles; candy in a jar for the grocer to weigh on shiny brass scales; beheaded chickens in the meat case outwardly devoid of nothing but feathers. Today mementos from this segment of Americana are being collected by those who 'lived it' as well as those less fortunate! Our advisor for this category is Charles Reynolds; he is listed in the Directory under Virginia. See also Advertising; Scales.

Bolt cabinet, top swivels, 1880s, 65", EX, $2,000.00.

Bag holder, heavy wire, folds up 140.00
Bag sorter, poplar w/orig varnish & stenciled details, 16" 550.00
Butcher block, 16x19x33" 395.00
Cabinet, bk wall; 3 bases, 1 long top 4,500.00
Candy jar, clear glass, known as 'Columbia' jar, ca 1900, 8" 800.00
Candy jar, HD Foss & Co...Boston, clear glass, w/stopper, 7⅝" .100.00
Case, bread; oak & glass 650.00
Case, cheese; counter-top style 500.00
Case, pipe; wood w/glass front, wall mount, holds 48 pipes, 40x30", G 450.00
Case, wood/glass, dbl cathedral, Quincy Showcase Works, 39x96", VG ..4,250.00
Case of drws, rfn pine & walnut, 44-drw, wire nails, 22x37" ..1,375.00
Coffee bin, pine w/orig stencil, 33" H 550.00
Dispenser, spice; orig blk pnt w/mc & gilt, Pure Spices, 21x28x12" ...825.00
Dispenser, spice; tin w/rolled front, 12 drws & mirror, 28x32", VG ...800.00
Display, twisted wire tree w/wooden base, holds 12 lures, 11" 195.00
Dolly, worn red rpt, railroad track wheels, 22x24", VG 220.00
Flour sifter, general store sz, Pat 1892 and 1893, 28x13" 300.00
Fly paper holder, counter mdoel, CI/steel 265.00
Mannequin, child's torso & legs (made w/no head/arms), compo, 33" ...435.00
Mannequin, Wolfform Garment Co, NY, 44x10", VG 75.00
Paper cutter/string holder, counter-top; CI, 23x29", G 150.00
Paper holder, w/string dispenser 150.00
Rack, broom display; CI, on casters, Pat 1885, 28x12", EX 245.00
Rack, paper bags 300.00
Scale, butcher's; porc, filigree trim/mirror, Toledo, 33", rstr 400.00
String/bag holder, Tulip Soap, 12x15", G+ 2,000.00
Sugar nippers, wrought steel & brass, trn wood hdl, 11" 165.00

Stoves

Antique stoves' desirability is based on two criteria: their utility and their decorative merit. It's the latter that adds an 'antique' premium to the basic functional value that could be served just as well by a modern stove. Sheer age is usually irrelevant. Decorative features that enhance desirability include fancy, embossed ornamentation, nickel-plated trim, mica windows, ceramic tiles, and (in cooking stoves) water reservoirs and high warming closets rather than mere high shelves. The less sheet metal and the more cast iron, the better. Look for crisp, sharp designs in preference to those made from worn or damaged and repaired foundry patterns. Stoves with a pastel porcelain finish can be very attractive; blue is a favorite, white is least desirable. Chrome trim, rather than nickel, dates a stove to circa 1933 or later and is a good indicator of a post-antique stove. Though purists prefer the earlier models trimmed in nickel rather than chrome, there is now considerable public interest in these post-antique stoves as well, and some people are willing to pay a good price for these appliance-era 'classics.' (Note: Not all bright metal trim is chrome; it is important to learn to distinguish chrome from the earlier, more desirable nickel plate.)

Among stove types, base burners (with self-feeding coal magazines) are the most desirable. Then come the upright, cylindrical 'oak' stoves, kitchen ranges, and wood parlors. Cannon stoves approach the margin of undesirability; laundries and gasoline stoves plunge through it.

There's a thin but continuing stream of desirable antique stoves going to the high-priced Pacific Coast market. Interest in antique stoves is least in the Deep South. Demand for wood/coal stoves is strongest in areas where firewood is affordable and storage of it is practical. Demand for antique gas ranges has become strong, especially in metropolitan markets, and interest in antique electric ranges is starting to surface. The market for antique stoves is so limited and the variety so bewildering that a consensus on a going price can hardly emerge. They are only worth something to the right individual, and prices realized depend very greatly on who happens to be in the auction crowd. Even an expert's appraisal will usually miss the realized price by a substantial percent.

In judging condition look out for deep rust pits, warped or burnt-out parts, unsound fire bricks, poorly fitting parts, poor repairs, and empty mounting holes indicating missing trim. Search meticulously for cracks in the cast iron. Our listings reflect auction prices of completely restored, safe, and functional stoves, unless indicated otherwise.

Base Burners

Art Garland 250, Michigan Stove Co, 1920, rstr 1,250.00

Art Garland 58, Michigan Stove Co, ca 1910, rstr 8,000.00
Ideal Garland 200, wood/coal, no urn ca 1898, rstr 1,300.00
Imperial Universal 50, Cribben & Sexton, Chicago, 1913, rstr ...4,000.00
Noble Crown, ca 1920, dismounted from base, rstr 1,300.00
Radiant Stewart 34, Fuller & Warren, Milwaukee, ca 1900, rstr ...5,000.00
Retort 218, Marion IN, soft coal, 3 mica doors, 1914, rstr 2,400.00
Wehrle 100, Wehrle Co Newark OH, 1911, 14", rpl parts/rstr ..4,000.00
Wehrle 100, Wehrle Co Newark OH, 1911, 18", rstr 9,000.00

Parlor

The term 'parlor stove' as we use it here is very general and encompasses at least eight distinct types recognized by the stove industry: cottage parlor, double-cased airtight, circulator, cylinder, oak, base burner, Franklin, and the fireplace heater.

Estate Oak F-316, no urn, ca 1915, G 425.00
Fr enamel, Neoclassical ormolu mts, ca 1880s, 30½x22½" 500.00
Ideal Garland 220, wood/coal, no urn, ca 1898, rstr 1,300.00
Ideal Heater 417, Gem City Stove Mfg...IL, oak stove, 1925, G ..175.00
Peoria Oak, Culter & Proctor, oak stove, 1920, unrstr 25.00
Retort 218, cased oak, 3 mica doors, ca 1905, rstr 2,400.00
Round Oak D-18, 1901, complete, unrstr 300.00
Round Oak D-18, 1904, complete, unrstr 300.00
Round Oak 18-T-31, 1940, G 225.00
Round Oak 18-0-2, 1916, unrstr 100.00

Ranges (Gas)

Alcazar, Milwaukee, pk & wht w/wood side, ca 1927, unrstr 40.00
Alcazar, Milwaukee, 4-burner/1-oven, 1928, G 50.00
Detroit Jewel, 4-burner/1-oven, 1928, unrstr 15.00
Magic Chef, wht, 6-burner/2-oven, high closet, 1938, rstr, up to ...12,000.00
Magic Chef, wht, 6-burner/2-oven, high closet, 1938, unrstr .1,000.00
O'Keefe & Merritt, 4-burner, cabinet base, ca 1929, G 110.00
Prosperity, Wehrle/Sears, 4-burner/1-oven, 1929, G 35.00
Quick Meal, 4-burner, bl, cabinet style, 1919, G 925.00
Quick Meal, 4-burner, gray, canopy/high closet, 1924, unrstr 375.00
Quick Meal, 4-burner/1-oven, 1928, unrstr 10.00
Roper, 4-burner/1-oven, 1929, unrstr 20.00
White Star, Detroit Vapor Stove Co, 4-burner/1-oven, 1929, unrstr ...10.00

Ranges (Wood and Coal)

Alpine Bride, CI, blk, ca 1920, rstr 300.00
Brilliant Universal, bl, high closet, no reservoir, 1917, G 200.00
Chambers, wht, 4-burner, ca 1949, G 250.00
Garland 1925, CI, Pat 1876, EX 4,000.00
Glenwood F 107, high shelf, 1910, rstr 1,100.00
Globe, Kokomo IN, gray, ca 1925, G 150.00
Kalamazoo Peerless, gray & wht, wood/coal/gas, G 875.00
Magee 88, 2-oven/8-hole, CI, high closet/no reservoir, 1880, rstr ...5,500.00

Stove Manufacturers' Toy Stoves

Buck's Jr Range, St Louis MO, new body/pnt/recast parts, 26" ..850.00
Charter Oak #503, GF Filley, St Louis MO, 14x12x25", EX ..2,050.00
Dainty, Reading Stove Works, PA, 7x13x8", VG 150.00
Estate Fresh Air Oven, blk/wht enamel, NP, working gas range, 15" 2,400.00
Karr, Qualified, bl porc w/NP, Belleville IL, 1925, EX 2,500.00
Karr Range, Belleville IL, bl porc, older model, 21½x13x9" ...3,000.00
Little Eva T Southard, NYC, 8½x14x11", G 350.00
Little Fanny, CI, minor rust, EX 300.00
Qualified Range, aluminum/tin, dial on door, 21½x13", EX 775.00
Royal American, Bridgeford, Louisville KY, 14x12x10", G 950.00

Toy Manufacturers' Toy Stoves

Arcade Hotpoint Range, pnt CI, tan & gr, VG 150.00
Arcade Roper Range, pnt CI, gas type, door opens, 4½", EX 70.00
Bing, cookstove, bl steel, brass trim, 16½", VG 600.00
Crescent, cookstove, plated CI & steel, 4-burner, 11½", EX 230.00
Eagle, Hubley, Lancaster PA, NP, recast parts 450.00
Eagle, Kenton, CI, heavily scrolled, 4-ft, 11½x10", G 125.00
Eclipse, CI, EX 175.00
Kenton Royal, CI & steel, 4-burner, ornate, 10", VG 100.00
Lionel, porc & CI, cream & gr, 4-leg, 32x26", EX 550.00
Little Giant, unmk/unidentified, 7½x8½x11", EX orig 675.00
Novelty, Kenton Hdwe, bl pnt/NP trim, rfn, 13x6½x8½" 600.00
Pet, The Young Bros, Albany NY, 10½x6x8½" 165.00
Rival, J&E Stevens, Cromwell CT, 14x9x16", M, +2 kettles ..1,350.00
Rival, no shelves, 12" L, EX 900.00
Royal, Kenton, CI & steel, 4-burner/working grates, rpt, 10", G .50.00
Royal, plated CI, stovepipe, shield shape, 16", G 85.00
Triumph, Kenton Hdwe, OH, 14x8½x19", G 195.00

Stretch Glass

Stretch glass, produced from circa 1916 through 1935, was made in an effort to emulate the fine art glass of Tiffany and Carder. The pressed or blown glassware was sprayed with a metallic salts mix while hot, then reshaped, causing a stretch effect in the iridescent finish. Pieces which were not reshaped had the iridized finish without the stretch, as seen on Fenton's #222 lemonade set and #401 guest set. Northwood, Imperial, Fenton, Diamond, Lancaster, Jeannette, Central, Vineland Flint, and the United States Glass Company were the manufacturers of this type of glass. See also specific companies.

Compote, topaz, #314, U.S. Glass, 5x9½", $60.00.

Bonbon, Jade Blue, Northwood #643, w/lid 80.00
Bowl, amber, 3-ftd, Jeannette, 3x9⅛" 45.00
Bowl, bl, crimped edge, Diamond, 2⅞x7½" 80.00
Bowl, bl, Northwood #642, 2½x7⅛" 40.00
Bowl, Green Ice, wide panel, Imperial, 3¼x10½" 75.00
Bowl, pk, US Glass #310, 2¾x9⅞" 65.00
Bowl, Russet, Optic Rays, ftd, Northwood #682 ....135.00
Bread tray, topaz w/blk trim, US Glass, 7x12" 50.00
Candlestick/bowl, amethyst, Imperial, 8x10⅛" 200.00
Candlesticks, bl, Vineland, 9⅞", pr 120.00
Candlesticks, gr, Central, 7", pr 70.00
Candlesticks, topaz w/blk trim, twist bobeche, US Glass, 9⅜", pr 130.00
Candlesticks, Velva Rose, Fenton #316, 4½", pr 45.00
Candy dish, Iris Ice, 3-ftd, Lancaster, w/lid 100.00
Candy dish, topaz, Fenton, 9¼", w/lid 50.00

Cheese & cracker, Iris Ice, decor, Lancaster 95.00
Comport, Blue Ice, Imperial #44/48, 7x8" 125.00
Comport, crystal, low ft, US Glass, 5x5⅝" 40.00
Comport, red, Optic Rays, Imperial #44/50, 7½" 300.00
Comport, topaz, ribbed, Northwood #637 ....65.00
Guest set, Velva Rose, Fenton #200 ....400.00
Lemon tray, topaz, printed decor, Fenton #66 ....45.00
Mayonnaise plate, Rose Ice, Imperial #725 ....80.00
Night set, topaz, Diamond Optic, Northwood #559 ....500.00
Plate, cake; pk w/gold decor, Imperial #7257 ....80.00
Plate, Florentine Green, Decor 2, Fenton #682 ....100.00
Plate, gr, panels, US Glass, 9" 25.00
Plate, ruby, Fenton, 8" 125.00
Server, aquamarine, center hdl, Fenton #1502 ....400.00
Server, bl, center hdl, Northwood #698 ....55.00
Sherbet, gr, Diamond, 3⅜x3¾" 20.00
Vase, gr, ribbed, Diamond, 8" 48.00
Vase, Iris Ice, Imperial #692, 4½x4" 40.00
Vase, Old Rose (opaque), US Glass, 8¾" 150.00

String Holders

Today, if you want to wrap and secure a package, you have a variety of products to choose from: cellophane tape, staples, etc. But in the 1800s, string was about the only available binder; thus the string holder, either the hanging or counter type, was a common and practical item found in most homes and businesses. Chalkware and ceramic figurals from the 1930s and '40s contrast with the cast and wrought-iron examples from the 1800s to make for an interesting collection. Our advisor for this category is Charles Reynolds; he is listed in the Directory under Virginia. See also Advertising.

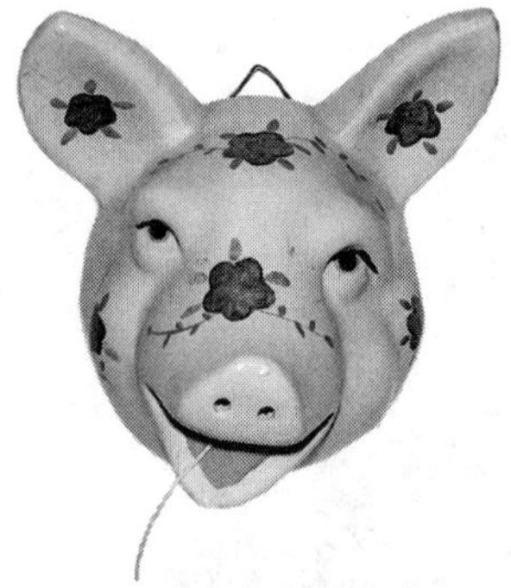

Pig with flowers, ceramic, $130.00. (Photo courtesy Ellen Bercovici)

Apple w/berries, ceramic, 8" 45.00
Baby face, chalkware, mk Toronto Canada, 4x3", EX 165.00
Ball shaped open-work cage, CI, on open-work ped base, 6½" 80.00
Betty Boop, string comes out mouth, chalkware, 1930s, 10x9" ..255.00
Bird, ceramic, String Nest Pull 65.00
Black child's face, chalkware, EX 125.00
Boy fishes through whale's mouth, F&F, NM 40.00
Campbell's Soup Kid, chalkware, orig pnt, ca 1940, 6½" 365.00
Child sits on globe on beast-head base, brass, 1870s, 14" 350.00
Clown w/stubby cigar in mouth, top holds matches, chalkware, '20s ..100.00
Counter type, CI, Pat Feb 16, 1880, 6" on 6½" base 110.00
Girl w/bl ribbon in hair, chalkware, 8x7" 185.00
Heinz Pickle, metal ceiling type for cone string 2,500.00
I Hate Housework, ceramic 160.00
Little Chef, Rice Crispy Guy, chalkware, ca 1950s, 7" 170.00
Mammy, smiling, w/wht handkerchief on head, ceramic, 6x6" ..155.00
Mammy w/laundry, chalkware, EX 125.00
Monkey on string ball 200.00
Pear 55.00
Sailor boy, w/pipe, chalkware 150.00
Snip, cat w/yarn ball, Fitz & Floyd 60.00
Southern belle, ceramic, Japan, 6" 50.00
SSS for the Blood, CI w/top 500.00

Sugar Shakers

Sugar shakers (or muffineers, as they were also called) were used during the Victorian era to sprinkle sugar and spice onto breakfast muffins, toast, etc. They were made of art glass, in pressed patterns, and in china. See also specific types and manufacturers (such as Northwood). Our coadvisors for this category are Jeff Bradfield and Dale MacAllister; they are listed in the Directory under Virginia.

Criss-Cross Bubble Lattice, blue opal, $450.00.

Acorn, gr w/decor 275.00
Argus Swirl, pk (Peach Bloom), scarce 260.00
Beatty Honeycomb, wht opal 200.00
Block & Fan 50.00
Bridal Rosette 160.00
Bridal Rosette, ruby stain 195.00
Bubble Lattice, bl, tapered 395.00
Bubble Lattice, wht opal 225.00
Chrysanthemum Swirl, bl opal 325.00
Chrysanthemum Swirl, cranberry opal 395.00
Coin Spot, bl opal 180.00
Cone, bl opaque 135.00
Connecticut 35.00
Cranberry, 12-panel cylinder, sterling top, 6¼" 250.00
Creased Teardrop, bl slag 160.00
Daisy & Fern, bl opal, wide waist 275.00
Daisy & Fern, cranberry opal, bulbous 375.00
Daisy & Fern, wht opal, wide waisted 150.00
Daisy & Fern/Parian Swirl Mold, cranberry opal 395.00
Fern, bl opal 350.00
Gillinder Melon 225.00
Guttate, cranberry (+) 495.00
Guttate, pk satin 280.00
Hobbs Polka Dot, cranberry 550.00
Hobbs Swirl, cranberry opal 450.00
Illinois 75.00
Inverted Thumbprint, cranberry 190.00
Late Block, Duncan 50.00
Medallion Sprig, bl to clear 500.00

Melon, yel floral-decor top, Smith Bros 375.00
Netted Oak, milk glass, decor, Northwood 155.00
Panelled Sprig, milk glass, decor 75.00
Parian Mold, cranberry 295.00
Parian Swirl, gr opaque, decor 185.00
Quilted Phlox, pk, 4¾" 225.00
Ribbed Lattice, bl opal 265.00
Ribbed Lattice, cranberry opal 350.00
Ribbed Lattice, wht opal 135.00
Ring Neck Optic, cranberry 175.00
Ruby cased w/clear, 12 cut panels, sterling top, 6" 335.00
Scrolled Rib, bl opaque 125.00
Short Ribbed Lattice, wht 275.00
Snail 120.00
Spanish Lace, bl opal, bulbous 250.00
Swirl, cranberry opal 395.00
Swirl, 9-panel, cranberry opal (reproduced in 1960s) 125.00
Venetian Diamond, cranberry 225.00

Sunderland Lustre

Sunderland lustre was made by various potters in the Sunderland district of England during the eighteenth and nineteenth centuries. It is often characterized by a splashed-on application of the pink lustre, which results in an effect sometimes referred to as the 'cloud' pattern. Some pieces are transfer printed with scenes, ships, florals, or portraits.

Bowl, Lady Liberty sailing ship, 10" 485.00
Creamer, cow figural, w/red & gr enameling, w/lid, 1850s, 5" 485.00
Pitcher, Battle of Wasp & Reindeer/Constitution, 6½", VG 350.00
Plaque, ship/May Peace & Plenty..., blk transfer, 7x8½" 175.00
Puzzle jug, pk lustre, house & landscape, ca 1820, 6½" 285.00
Salt cellar, lt wear, 2" 50.00

Surveying Instruments

The practice of surveying offers a wide variety of precision instruments primarily for field use, most of which are associated with the recording of distance and angular measurements. These instruments were primarily made from brass; the larger examples were fitted with tripods and protective cases. These cases also held accessories for the instruments, and these can sometimes play a key part in their evaluation. Instruments in complete condition and showing little use will have much greater values than those that appear to have had moderate or heavy use. Instruments were never polished during use, and those that have been polished as decorator pieces are of little interest to most avid collectors. Our advisor for this category is Dale Beeks; he is listed in the Directory under Iowa.

Alidade, folding sights, military, 20th C, EX 75.00
Alidade, telescopic Gurley; exploration sz 350.00
Alidade, K&E, 1915, EX in case 250.00
Aneroid, Short & Mason, w/barometer pressure scale, 2x4⅞" ...110.00
Chain, brazed, mk, complete 450.00
Chain, Gurley, link-type, 4-pole, 66-ft, dirty 250.00
Compass, Baher, Melrose, MA; monochrome rose brass case, 8½" ...230.00
Compass, French, hand-held, 1920s, EX 32.00
Compass, Gurley or K&E, 4" pocket, wooden case 100.00
Compass, plane; Gurley, 1880s, VG in case 900.00
Compass, solar; Gurley, incomplete, G- 1,450.00
Compass, staff type, 4", EX in leather case 250.00
Compass, telescopic; Randolph, unusual, EX 1,800.00

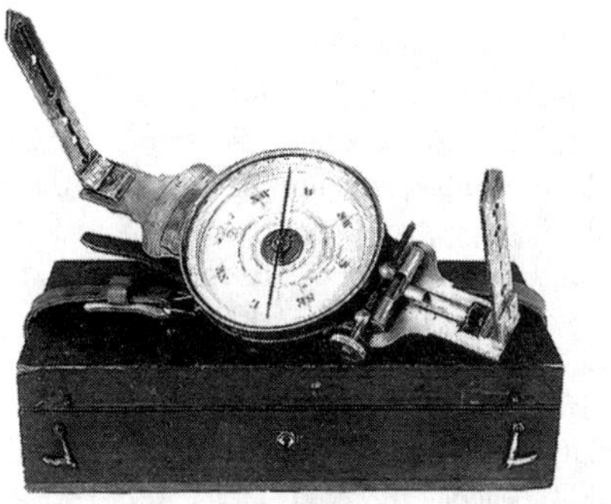

Large American surveying compass, Benj Pike's Son, New York, ca 1880, some repairs, with box, $1,200.00. (Photo courtesy Dale Beeks)

Compass, vernier; Gurley, 1880s, VG, w/case staff 1,100.00
Compass/inclinometer, K&E, geologist's, aluminum, EX 350.00
Level, farm; Bostrom Brady, EXIB 120.00
Level, Gurley, brass, w/leather strap, orig wood case, EX 620.00
Transit, astronomical, 10" telescope, sm, EX 1,600.00
Transit, Gurley, Solar Burt type, no case, G 1,650.00
Transit, Pool NY, 1870s, VG in case 1,400.00
Transit, Roach SF, 1890s, VG in case 1,200.00
Transit, W&LE Gurley, 7" scope, orig leather case, EX 1,200.00
Transit, Wurdemann, DC, VG in case 2,500.00
Transit level, surveyor's; W&LE Gurley...NY, brass, 12½", +case 450.00

Swarovski Crystal

The Swarovski family has been perfecting the glassmaker's art in Wattens, Austria, since 1895. Collectible figurines and desk items were introduced in 1977, and the Swarovski Collectors Society (SCS) was created in 1987. Featuring lead content of 30%+, these 'Silver Crystal' limited edition decorative accessories have attracted a following of over 500,000 dedicated collectors worldwide. Some designs were distributed regionally, making pursuit of retired items an interesting challenge that spans the globe. Most items have an etched mark on the underside. The first mark was a block-style SC. In 1989 the mark was changed to a Swan. Marks on larger items also include the name Swarovski. SCS figurines are further identified with the year and designer's initials. As the vigilance of Swarovski collectors has grown, their interest in all items of Swarovski manufactures has increased. In addition to Swarovski Silver Crystal, collectors also seek Trimlite, Giftware Suite, Swarovski Selections, Ebeling & Reuss, and private label productions by the Swarovski company. Prices listed below reflect the presence of complete original packing and enclosures, without which prices are compromised 10% to 35%.

DO1X861, lovebirds #1, from $5,400 to 5,500.00
DO1X891, turtledoves, #3, from #1,000 to 1,055.00
DO1X891S, turtledoves, #3, sgn, from #1,380 to 1,435.00
DO1X951, lion, #9, from $480 to 495.00
DO1X961S, unicorn, #10, sgn, from $900 to 935.00
DO1X971, dragon, #11, from $435 to 445.00
SDW001W/S, Mickey Mosue, jeweled, w/stand, from $695 to ..720.00
7463NR062, cigarette holder, from $175 to 220.00
7465NR52/100, treasure box, heart & butterfly, from $330 to ...350.00
7470NR50, bird's nest, from $175 to 195.00
7474NR000027, Town Hall, from $235 to 265.00
7475NR001, Nativity, Holy Family w/arch, from $365 to 375.00

7476NR000001, apple, from $280 to 300.00
7505NR75G, picture fr, oval, from $465 to 515.00
7505NR76G, beetle bottle opener, gold, from $2,250 to 2,600.00
7507NR60002, pineapple, rhodium, sm, from $170 to 200.00
7550NR02209G, grapes, gold, med, from $465 to 485.00
7551NR100, butterfly, gold, from $1,125 to 1,375.00
7600NR119P, candle holder, from $400 to 450.00
7600NR121V1, candle holder, Baroque Diamond, cut, from $425 to ..500.00
7600NR134-1, candle holder, Global, lg, from $110 to 140.00
7600NR144090, candle holder, Neo Classic, lg, from $265 to ...300.00
7607NR000002, peacock, ltd ed, from $5,500 to 5,575.00
7621NR000003, owl, from $265 to 275.00
7621NR000004, parrot, from $195 to 205.00
7624NR072000, south sea shell, from $150 to 165.00
7629NR70V2, fox, blk nose, from $105 to 110.00
7631NR40V3, mouse, med, from $125 to 135.00
7637NR92, bear, king sz, from $2,500 to 2,565.00
7640NR55, elephant, lg, from $275 to 285.00
7642NR48B, Prince Frog, blk eyes, from $145 to 170.00
7644NR077000, butterfly fish, from $170 to 200.00
7645NR100V2, falcon head, lg, from $2,435 to 3,250.00
7645NR85V4, seal, facing left, lg, from $180 to 235.00
9280NR4035, Hong Kong commemorative, ltd ed, from $2,365 to ..2,500.00
950NR000011, Julia, from $85 to 95.00

Syracuse

Syracuse was a line of fine dinnerware and casual ware which was made for nearly a century by the Onondaga Pottery Company of Syracuse, New York. Early patterns were marked O.P. Company. Collectors of American dinnerware are focusing their attention on reassembling some of their many lovely patterns. In 1966 the firm became officially known as the Syracuse China Company in order to better identify with the name of their popular chinaware. Many of the patterns were marked with the shape and color names (Old Ivory, Federal, etc.), not the pattern names. By 1971 dinnerware geared for use in the home was discontinued, and the company turned to the manufacture of hotel, restaurant, and other types of commercial tableware.

Cup and saucer, demitasse; red silhouettes on white, from $15.00 to $18.00.

Allandale, plate, dinner 30.00
Alpine, creamer 20.00
Apple Blossom, platter, sm 40.00
Arcadia, cup & saucer 40.00
Arcadia, gravy boat 100.00
Arcadia, platter, med 65.00
Barbados, shakers, pr 25.00
Baroque, plate, dinner 35.00
Beloved, sugar bowl, w/lid 30.00
Bracelet, bowl, vegetable; w/lid 160.00
Bracelet, cream soup & saucer 55.00
Bridal Rose, bowl, soup 25.00
Candlelight, cup & saucer 40.00
Celeste, creamer 25.00
Celeste, sugar bowl, w/lid 35.00
Coralbel, creamer 50.00
Coralbel, plate, dinner 35.00
Coventry, platter, sm 40.00
Debonair, cup & saucer 20.00
Eggnog set, Tom & Jerry, serves 6 ....40.00
Elizabeth, gravy boat 45.00
Finesse, bowl, vegetable; divided 20.00
Forget Me Not, platter, lg 65.00
Gardenia, plate, luncheon 30.00
Gold Riviera, plate, dinner 25.00
Greek K9, plate, salad 12.00
Jefferson, bowl, fruit/dessert 24.00
Jefferson, teapot, w/lid 125.00
Lynnfield, bowl, soup 12.00
Lynnfield, butter dish, w/lid 20.00
Lyric, cup & saucer 35.00
Lyric, platter, lg 90.00
Marietta, plate, dinner 20.00
Mayflower, shakers, pr 20.00
Meadow Breeze, cup & saucer 50.00
Melodie, plate, dinner 12.00
Monticello, bowl, rimmed soup 20.00
Old Ivory Kent, plate, salad 15.00
Portland, platter, sm 60.00
Rosalie, sugar bowl, w/lid 30.00
Santa Rosa, bowl, vegetable; w/lid 100.00
Santa Rosa, creamer 45.00
Selma, plate, dinner 30.00
Selma, plate, salad 18.00
Sharon, creamer 35.00
Sharon, sugar bowl, w/lid 42.00
Shell Edge (White), bowl, fruit/dessert 8.00
Sherwood, cream soup & saucer 30.00
Sherwood, platter, lg 70.00
Stansbury, gravy boat 85.00
Stansbury, plate, bread & butter 20.00
Vintage, creamer 12.00
Wayside, bowl, vegetable; divided 25.00
Westvale, sugar bowl, w/lid 30.00
Windswept, bowl, divided, oval 65.00
Windswept, bowl, salad; 5½" 35.00
Windswept, bowl, soup 30.00
Windswept, bowl, vegetable; 8" 55.00
Windswept, butter dish 60.00
Windswept, coffee server, copper lid 85.00
Windswept, creamer & sugar bowl 50.00
Windswept, cup & saucer 25.00
Windswept, gravy boat 45.00
Windswept, plate, bread & butter; 6½" 12.00
Windswept, plate, dinner; 10½" 18.00
Windswept, plate, luncheon; 8" 15.00
Windswept, shakers, pr 28.00
Woodbine, gravy boat 25.00
Yorktown, plate, salad 10.00

Syrups

Values are for old, original syrups. Beware of reproductions and watch handle area for cracks! See also various manufacturers (such as

Northwood) and specific types of glass. Our coadvisors are Jeff Bradfield and Dale MacAllister; they are listed in the Directory under Virginia. See also Pattern Glass.

Acorn, Peach Bloom 300.00
Alba, bl milk glass 200.00
Apple Blossom, milk glass, decor 250.00
Big Windows, wht opal 250.00
Bohemian, amber & clear, etched floral, flat sided 225.00
Britannic 85.00
Button Arches, ruby stain 325.00
Challinor's #313, bl opaque 125.00
Coinspot, gr, 9-panel 350.00
Cosmos, milk glass, decor 275.00
Empress, clear w/gold 225.00
Galloway, rose stain 225.00
Guttate, cased glossy pk 300.00
Guttate, shiny Peach Bloom 225.00
Hobb's Hexagonal Block, yel stain, etch 195.00
Hobb's Hobnail, cranberry, shiny 325.00
Honeycomb, bl, pewter lid 450.00
Invt T'print, amber, pinched base 125.00
Jeweled Heart, bl 350.00
Leaf & Flower, clear w/amber stain, Hobbs, 1899 ....275.00
Medallion Sprig, amethyst to clear 500.00
Paneled Herringbone, gr 195.00
Ribbed Lattice, wht opal 265.00
Ring Neck, pk & wht spatter 300.00
Roman Rosette, ruby stain 225.00
Royal Oak, frosted rubena 375.00
Scroll & Net, flower decor 125.00
Sunset, bl opaque 300.00
Tall Cone, pk cased 325.00
Thousand Eye, bl 225.00
Torpedo, ruby stain 225.00
US Coin, frosted 600.00
West Virginia Optic Mold/Daisy & Fern 250.00
Wild Iris, colored milk glass 175.00
X-Ray, clear w/gold 275.00

Target Balls

Prior to 1880 when the clay pigeon was invented, blown glass target balls were used extensively for shotgun competitions. Approximately 2¾" in diameter, these balls were hand blown into a three-piece mold. All have a ragged hole where the blowpipe was twisted free. Target balls date from approximately 1840 (English) to World War I, although they were most widely used in the 1870 – 1880 period. Common examples are unmarked except for the blower's code — dots, crude numerals, etc. Some balls were embossed in a dot or diamond pattern so they were more likely to shatter when struck by shot, and some have names and/or patent dates. When evaluating condition, bubbles and other minor manufacturing imperfections are acceptable; cracks are not. The prices below are for mint condition examples.

Boers & CR Delft Flesschen Fabriek, lt gr, rare, 2⅝" 500.00
Bogardus' Glass Ball Pat'd April 10 1877, amber, Am 350.00
Bogardus' Glass Ball Pat'd April 10 1877, cobalt, 2¾" 800.00
Bogardus' Glass Ball Pat'd April 10 1877, olive gr, 2⅝" 1,150.00
C Newman, Dmn Quilt, amber, rare, 2⅝" 825.00
CTB Co, blk pitch, Pat dates on bottom, Am 250.00
Dmn Quilt w/o center band, yel-amber, 2¾" 250.00
Dmn Quilt w/plain center band, clear ground top, Am 150.00
Dmn Quilt w/plain center band, cobalt, 2⅝" 250.00
Dmn Quilt w/shooter emb in 2 panels, clear, English 300.00
Dmn Quilt w/shooter emb in 2 panels, cobalt, English 725.00
Dmn Quilt w/shooter emb in 2 panels, deep moss gr, English 575.00
Dmn Quilt w/shooter emb in 2 panels, gr or purple, English 500.00
EE Eaton Guns & C 53 State St Chicago, golden yel-amber, 2⅝" ..1,000.00
For Hockey's Pat Trap, gr, English 850.00
Glashutten Dr A Frank Charlottenburg, yel-olive, 2⅝" 1,200.00
Glashuttenewotte Un Charlottenburg, clear, emb dmns, 2⅝" ...700.00
Glashuttenewotte Un Charlottenburg, med yel-olive, 2⅝" 1,000.00
Great Western Gun Works, Pittsburgh, amber, Am 900.00
Gurd & Son, London, Ontario, amber, Canadian 500.00
Hobnail w/horizontal ribs along seams, yel-amber, 2¾" 800.00
Horizontal or vertical ribs, amber, either style 150.00
Horizontal ribs (2) intersect w/2 vertical, cobalt, 2⅝" 120.00
Horizontal ribs (7), root beer amber, 3-pc mold, 2⅝" 725.00
Ilmenau (Thur) Sophiehutte, amber, Dmn Quilt, Germany 425.00
Ira Paine's Filled Ball Pat Oct 23 1877, amber, Am 250.00
Ira Paine's Filled Ball Pat Oct 23 1877, other than amber, Am .800.00
NB Glass Works Perth, other than pale gr, English 200.00
NB Glass Works Perth, pale gr, English 100.00
Plain, amber w/mold mks 65.00

Plain center band and horizontal ribs, amber, either style, $150.00.

Plain, clear w/mold mks 1,000.00
Plain, cobalt w/mold mks 150.00
Plain, dk grape amethyst w/mold mks, 2¾" dia 250.00
Plain, dk teal gr w/mold mks, 2¾" 300.00
T Jones, Gunmaker, Blackburn, pale bl, English 150.00
Van Cutsem A St Quentin, cobalt, 2¾" dia 100.00
WW Greener, St Mary's Works, various colors, English, ea 350.00

Related Memorabilia

Ball thrower, dbl; old red pnt, ME Card, Pat...78, 79, VG 900.00
Clay birds, Winchester, Pat May 29 1917, 1 flight in box 100.00
Pitch bird, blk DUVROCK 1.00
Shell, dummy, w/single window, any brand 35.00
Shell, dummy shotgun, Winchester, window w/powder, 6" 125.00
Shell set, dummy, Gamble Stores, 2 window shells, 3 cut out 125.00
Shell set, dummy, Winchester, 5 window shells 175.00
Shell set, dummy shotgun, Peters, 6 window shells+full box 175.00
Shotshell loader, rosewood/brass, Parker Bros, Pat 1884 ....50.00
Target, Am, sheet metal, rod ends mk Pat Feb 8 '21, set 25.00
Target, blk japanned sheet metal, Bussey Patentee, London 50.00
Target, BUST-O, blk or wht breakable wafer 20.00
Trap, DUVROCK, w/blk pitch birds 250.00
Trap, MO-SKEET-O, w/birds 150.00

Tartan Glass

Tartan glass is accredited to Henry G. Richardson at Wordsley Flint Glass Works near Stourbridge, England. Glass threads were arranged to form a plaid similar to Tartan. Tartan glass was registered February 24, 1886.

Base for fairy lamp, bl/wht/pk plaid w/swirled center, 8", NM **950.00**
Shade/vase, yel/wht/pk plaid, 1½" base dia, 3¼" fitter **285.00**

Tea Caddies

Because tea was once regarded as a precious commodity, special boxes called caddies were used to store the tea leaves. They were made from various materials: porcelain, carved and inlaid woods, and metals ranging from painted tin or tole to engraved silver. Our advisor for this category is Tina Carter; she is listed in the Directory under California.

Tortoise shell, ivory-inlaid panel on lid, fitted compartments with lids, crystal mixing bowl, England, 1850s, 5x12x5¾", $1,000.00.

Blk lacquer w/gilt, nacre inlay, HP lily of the valley, 6½" **385.00**
Bronze w/gold & silver, bullfighting scenes in relief, 6¼" **440.00**
Burlwood, inlaid top & band on sides, late 18th C, 4½x5x3½" ...**850.00**
Cherry Chpndl w/mahog X-banding, ogee ft, 10", EX **2,750.00**
Figured mahog/veneer w/inlay, ball ft, ring hdls, 8¾", EX **470.00**
Fruitwood, trn pear form, England, late 1700s, 6¼" **5,750.00**
Inlaid wooden casket w/twin tin compartments, English, 19th C ..**365.00**
Mahog Chpndl, dvtl case, orig bail hdl, 8x12x7" **1,650.00**
Mahog English Regency sarcophagus, brass ball ft, 1830s **250.00**
Mahog veneer Fed, edge inlay, brass lion/ring hdls, 12", EX **580.00**
Mahog Wm IV w/lift-lid, ca 1835, EX **500.00**
Quillwork w/inlaid mahog fr, dtd 1804, English, 8½x5x4¾" ..**2,750.00**
Regency, brass ball ft, compartments, w/ivory finials, 5x8x5" **250.00**
Rosewood veneer w/inlay Fed, brass rings w/cornucopias, 12" L .**990.00**
Rosewood veneer w/ivory inlay, English, 12¼" **350.00**
Silver, monogram, Wm B Kerr & Co...NJ, 19th C **135.00**

Tea Leaf Ironstone

Tea Leaf Ironstone became popular in the 1880s when middle-class American housewives became bored with the plain white stone china that English potters had been exporting to this country for nearly a century. The original design has been credited to Anthony Shaw of Longport, who decorated the plain ironstone with a hand-painted copper lustre design of bands and leaves. Originally known as Lustre Band and Sprig, the pattern has since come to be known as Tea Leaf Lustre. It was produced with minor variations by many different firms both in England and the United States. By the early 1900s, it had become so commonplace that it had lost much of its appeal.

Items marked Red Cliff are reproductions made from 1950 until 1980 for this distributing and decorating company of Chicago, Illinois. Hall China provided many of the blanks.

Our advice for this category comes from Home Place Antiques, whose address is listed in the Directory under Illinois.

Bone dish, scalloped, Meakin **75.00**
Bowl, high crimped rim, Wilkinson, 3⅜x9½" **75.00**
Bowl, vegetable; Fish Hook, w/lid, Meakin, 10½x6½" **195.00**
Bowl, vegetable; gold trim, Powell Bishop, 9½x6" **135.00**
Bowl, vegetable; Pagoda, sq, Burgess, w/lid **265.00**
Bowl, vegetable; Sunburst, ftd, w/lid, Shaw, 11½x5½", EX **225.00**
Bowl, waste; Rondeau, Davenport **145.00**
Butter dish, sq, leaf finial, vertical ribs, w/drain, Mellor-Taylor .**195.00**
Butter pat, Anthony Shaw & Sons, VG **16.00**
Butter pat, scalloped edge, ribbed, sq, Mellor-Taylor **16.00**
Chamber pot, Square Ridged, Mellor-Taylor, EX **325.00**
Coffeepot, Basketweave, Shaw, 1887 ....**295.00**
Coffeepot, Favorite, paneled sides, rope hdl, Grindley **300.00**
Coffeepot, Fish Hook, 1880s **225.00**
Coffeepot, Lily of the Valley, Shaw, 1860s **425.00**
Compote, fruit; ped ft, Royal Ironstone, Meakin, 5½x8½", NM ..**375.00**
Cup & saucer, Adams Microtex **35.00**
Cup & saucer, Chelsea type, Johnson Bros, 2⅝", 3½" **85.00**
Cup & saucer, Pomegranate **85.00**
Cup & saucer, ribbed below waist & around saucer, Wedgwood ..**75.00**
Cup plate, unmk, 3½" **60.00**
Doughnut stand, Alfred Meakin, 4½x8" **395.00**
Egg cup, Boston, wide mouth, ftd **325.00**
Egg cup, regular, unmk **350.00**
Gravy boat, Bamboo, Alfred Meakin **75.00**
Gravy boat, simple sq, unmk **75.00**
Mug, Maidenhair Fern, Wilkinson, 1890s **245.00**
Nappy, Red Cliff **18.00**
Pitcher, hot water; jug type, Mayer **250.00**
Plate, gold lustre, Bridgewood, 7" **12.00**
Plate, Meakin, 7⅞" **14.00**
Plate, Red Cliff, 8¼" **18.00**
Plate, Teaberry, 8" **35.00**
Platter, Brocade, Meakin, 12¾x9⅛" **75.00**
Platter, Red Cliff, 11x8¾" **40.00**
Relish, Lily of the Valley, Shaw **245.00**
Sauce dish, rnd, Meakin, 4¾" **18.00**
Shaving mug, leaf at hdl, Shaw **225.00**
Soap dish, Bamboo, w/lid & drainer, Meakin, 1870s **250.00**
Soap dish, gold lustre, Powell & Bishop **110.00**
Soap dish, Lily of the Valley, Shaw, w/liner **425.00**
Sugar bowl, Bamboo, Meakin **65.00**
Sugar bowl, Crystal Shape, unmk, 1870s **225.00**
Sugar bowl, Gentle Square, animal hdls, Furnival, 1870s, w/lid ...**175.00**
Sugar bowl, Morning Glory, Portland shape, Elsmore & Forster ...**225.00**
Sugar bowl, Pagoda, Burgess **85.00**
Teapot, Fish Hook, Meakin, 8½" **225.00**
Wash bowl, Meakin, 14¾" **200.00**

Teapots

Teapots have become popular collectibles in recent years with a surge in tea shops featuring tea and teapots and serving afternoon tea. Collectors should be aware of modern teapots which imitate older, similar versions. Study the types of pottery, porcelain, and china, as well as the marks. Multicolored, detailed marks over the glaze represent modern pieces. Teapots made in the last thirty years are quite collectible but generally don't demand the same prices as their antique counterparts.

A wide range of teapots can be found by the avid collector. Those from before 1880 are more apt to be found in museums or sold at quality auction houses. Almost every pottery and porcelain manufacturer in Asia, Europe, and America have produced teapots. Some are purely decorative and whimsical, while others are perfect for brewing a pot of tea. Tea drinkers should beware of odd-shaped spouts which sputter and drip. Reproductions to be aware of: majolica styles with modern marks, Blue Willow which has been made continuously for almost two centuries, and those marked Made in China (older teapots have 'chop marks' in Chinese).

Refer to various manufacturers' names for further listings. Our advisor for this category is Tina M. Carter, listed in the Directory under California. Her book, *Teapots*, is available at bookstores or direct from the author.

Ellgreave, Marked Div of Wood & Sons England, floral on white with gold trim: Large (four-cup), $30.00; two-cup, $25.00. (Photo courtesy Tina Carter)

ALB, dripless, mottled, England, ca 1920 ....52.00
Automobile, silver lustre, Carlton Ware, England 495.00
Barge, brn, emb mk, Derbyshire, England, lg 75.00
Basket, picnic teapot & 2 cups, hinged lid, padded, China 100.00
Ben Franklin figural, ceramic w/metal hdl 65.00
Boston Tea Party, commemorative, Davison Newman, +cr/sug 45.00
Charles & Diana, brn pottery, Wales CM, 2½" 78.00
Cloisonne, animal or designs, China, mini 35.00
Copper, Art Deco style, enamel decor, ball ft, China 38.00
Crinoline Lady (Cinderella), Sadler, England, ca 1930 ....65.00
Cube, HP, Made in Japan, ca 1940 ....20.00
Dickens Christmas scenes from Christmas Carol, Sadler, up to ...80.00
Ebeling & Reuss, Santa, musical, from $75 to 125.00
Fitz & Floyd, King Wenceslas & forest creatures, from $80 to ...135.00
Floral, mc on majolica-like bark, blk Japan mk, 4½" 35.00
Floral band at top & rim of lid on shiny wht, Noritake, 5½" 45.00
Floral, yel & gold trim, Sadler 30.00
Folklore, Robin Hood/King Arthur/etc, ca 1990, Sadler 35.00
Gold dragon, gr Japan mk, 5" 35.00
Goldcastle, floral yel & mc lustre, red mk, 6½" 50.00
Granny, Queensware, modern 35.00
Lefton, cozy set, violets, ca 1950 ....32.00
Lipton's, rnd, various colors, Hall China Co 30.00
Lipton's, tan lustre w/blk hdl & finial, Noritake, ind, 3¼" 250.00
Lustreware, amber mottled, blk Japan mk, 4¾" 65.00
Man in tux forms hdl, lady forms pot, ceramic, unmk, modern 35.00
Meakin, Alfred; blk trim, china relief, England 38.00
Meito, floral reserve on tan lustre, blk hdl, red mk, w/matching tile ..65.00
Nippon, floral tapestry w/beadwork, 6⅛" 525.00
Pewter, New Amsterdam Silver Co, USA 35.00
Pottery, pk, mk Ford, USA, 1-cup 25.00
Quimper-style couple among red & gr florals, shiny, Japan, 7¼" .55.00
Racing car, silver trim Sadler 140.00
Rough glaze, buff sharkskin, tan, slip decor, Japan, 1920s 28.00
RS Prussia, scalloped hdl/edge, HP decor, unmk 75.00
Salada Tea, promotional item, USA, 1-cup 25.00
Sigma, Kliban Cat Tastesetter, hat & bow tie 125.00
Sigma, Star Wars, rare 215.00
Silverplate, Rococo style, Community 70.00
Snow White w/Dwarfs, musical, Walt Disney Prod 75.00
Spode's Tower, bl/wht transfer, London shape, England, VG 58.00
Sylvestri, Victorian Skating Couple, from $125 to 200.00
Tepco, Western Traveler, Brands pattern, 3" 130.00
Tiffin, tea liqueur, depot decanter, Germany, 1960 ....95.00
Violets on wht, ZS & Co Bavaria, 3½x5" 300.00
WWII, Esc to US by Royal Navy or Allied Fleets, brn, England .45.00
Yxing, padded box, chop mk, China repro 45.00

Teco

Teco artware was made by the American Terra Cotta and Ceramic Company, located near Chicago, Illinois. The firm was established in 1886 and until 1901 produced only brick, sewer tile, and other redware. Their early glaze was inspired by the matt green made popular by Grueby. 'Teco Green' was made for nearly ten years. It was similar to Grueby's, yet with a subtle silver-gray cast. The company was one of the first in the United States to perfect a true crystalline glaze. The only decoration used was through the modeling and glazing techniques; no hand painting was attempted. Favored motifs were naturalistic leaves and flowers. The company broadened their lines to include garden pottery and faience tiles and panels. New matt glazes (browns, yellows, blue, and rose) were added to the green in 1910. By 1922 the artware lines were discontinued; the company was sold in 1930.

Values are dictated by size and shape, with architectural and organic forms being more desirable. Teco is usually marked with a vertical impressed device comprised of a large 'T' to the left of the remaining three letters.

Jardiniere, gr & charcoal, closed-in rim, 4x7" 600.00
Pitcher, gr, waisted, 9" 1,000.00
Vase, bl-gray on brn, buttress hdls, rpr, 7x4" 600.00
Vase, cobalt, tulip-shaped top, Moreau design, 11½x5" 3,250.00
Vase, gr, amphora form, 9x5" 900.00
Vase, gr, beaker shape w/2 buttress hdls, 8x5¾" 2,300.00
Vase, gr, bulbous, 4¼x3½" 350.00
Vase, gr, cylindrical w/emb ribs, 5x4" 450.00
Vase, gr, dbl gourd w/dbl buttresses, 6½" 2,900.00
Vase, gr, leaf buttresses surround base, rstr, 11½x4¾" 7,000.00
Vase, gr, ovoid w/4 lobes, 5½x3½" 950.00
Vase, gr, ribbed, #51, 4x4" 350.00
Vase, gr, 2 buttresses, label, rpr, 11" 1,100.00
Vase, gr, 2 closed buttresses, heavy charcoaling, 9" 1,500.00
Vase, gr, 4-ftd, rstr, 18½" 400.00
Vase, gr & charcoal, bulbous, 4x3¾" 425.00
Vase, gr & charcoal, cylindrical, 6¼x3¼" 375.00
Vase, gr & charcoal, flared neck, bulbous base, 5x4½" 400.00
Vase, gr & charcoal, tall neck, squat base, rstr, 16½x8" 1,200.00
Vase, mirror black/gold/amber microcrystalline flambe, 10½x3¾" ...2,700.00
Wall pocket, gr, emb stylized leaves, #156A, 16¾x6½" 1,900.00

Teddy Bear Collectibles

The story of Teddy Roosevelt's encounter with the bear cub has been oft recounted with varying degrees of accuracy, so it will suffice to say that it was as a result of this incident in 1902 that the teddy bear got his name. These appealing little creatures are enjoying renewed popularity with collectors today. To one who has not yet succumbed to their obvious charms, one bear seems to look very much like another. How to tell the older ones? Look for long snouts, jointed limbs, large feet and felt paws, long curving arms, and glass or shoe-button eyes. Most old bears have a humped back and are made of mohair stuffed with straw or excelsior. Cute expressions, original clothes, a nice personality, and, of course, good condition add to their value. Early Steiff bears in mint condition may go for a minimum of $100.00 per inch (for a small bear) up to $200.00 per inch (for one 20" high or larger). These are easily recognized by the trademark button within the ear. Our advisor for this category is Candace Gunther; she is listed in the Directory under California. For further information we recommend *Teddy Bear Treasury* by Ken Yenke; and *Teddy Bears, Annalee's & Steiff Animals,* by Margaret Fox Mandel. Both are available from Collector Books. See also Toys, Steiff.

Key: jtd — jointed

Bears

Am, brn mohair w/glass eyes, 1920s, 18", EX 300.00
Am, gold mohair w/glass eyes, straw-filled, jtd, 1920-30, 12", EX ..500.00
Am, gold mohair w/glass eyes, straw-filled, 1920-30, 17", EX 465.00
Chad Valley, gold mohair, rexine pads, 14", M 375.00
East Germany, brn mohair w/glass eyes, paper label, 1950s, 10", NM ...100.00
East Germany, tan plush w/glass eyes, pk ribbon, 1950s, 4¼", NM ...25.00
Germany, brn mohair w/glass eyes, pnt details, 1927, 15", EX ...350.00
Germany, tan mohair w/amber glass eyes, 1940-50, 6¾", VG 150.00
Ideal, blond mohair w/glass eyes, emb, jtd, 1919, 34", NM 2,500.00
Ideal, ginger mohair w/shoe-button eyes, emb, jtd, 1919, 20", EX ..450.00
Ideal, gold mohair w/glass eyes, emb, jtd, 1920s, 25", EX 450.00
Ideal, yel mohair w/emb features, jtd, 12", VG 485.00
Original Teddy, gold mohair, 1950s, NM, 3½" 250.00
Ride-on, brn mohair w/glass eyes, metal fr w/CI wheels, 1913, 21", EX ...250.00
Schuco, brn w/cinnamon ears, orig ribbon, 1950, 3½", M 200.00
Schuco, brn w/metal eyes, orig paper label, 1950s, 2½", M 265.00
Schuco, champagne, 1950s, 2½", NM 150.00
Schuco, compo head w/tan mohair, blk & red felt w/aqua buttons, 3½" ...60.00
Schuco, gold w/metal bead eyes, 1950s, 2½", NM 165.00
Schuco, in soccer outfit, 1960, 3½", MIB 325.00
Schuco, orange w/metal eyes, shaved muzzle, 1950s, 3½", NM .300.00
Schuco, pale gold, orig gr ribbon, 3½", EX 150.00
Schuco, pale gold w/metal eyes, orig paper label, 1950s, 2½", NM ..265.00
Schuco, red mohair, Germany stamped on felt ft, 1920, 2½", minimum ..500.00
Schuco, tan, orig red ribbon, 1950s, 3½", NM 150.00
Schuco, Yes/No Bear, blk w/glass eyes, 1950s, rare, 5", EX 1,100.00
Schuco, Yes/No Bear, caramel w/glass eyes, 1950, 5", NM 550.00
Schuco, Yes/No Bear, dk brn w/glass eyes, 1950, 5", NM 865.00
Schuco, Yes/No Bear, gold w/faceted jewel eyes, 1920s, 9", EX 1,950.00
Unmk, brn mohair w/shoe-button eyes, embr nose/mouth, jtd, 11", G ...125.00
Unmk, frosted hair, open mouth, 1940s, 21", NM 275.00
Unmk, gold mohair w/glass eyes, straw-filled, 1930, 2½", M 75.00
Unmk, gold mohair w/glass eyes, 1940s, 4½", EX 75.00
Unmk, wht mohair, plastic braids on outside, 5", EX 75.00

Miscellaneous

Book, The Three Bears, die-cut, McLoughlin Bros, 1892, EX, minimum ..150.00
Bugle, Teddy B & Teddy G on pnt glass, 1907 ....200.00
Figurine, US Guard House, Teddy R & bear meet at outhouse, MIG, 1908 ...250.00
Mug, bl B & 1907 on wht w/wht teddy bear inside, 2", minimum ..75.00
Plate, Busy Bear Christmas, pnt scene/pine boughs, 1907, NM .250.00

Telephones

Since Alexander Graham Bell's first successful telephone communication, the phone itself has undergone a complete evolution in style as well as efficiency. Early models, especially those wall types with ornately carved oak boxes, are of special interest to collectors. Also of value are the candlestick phones from the early part of the century and any related memorabilia.

Western Electric Company oak wall telephone, 1920s, 19x9x5", $225.00.

Am Electric, str shaft desk stand, 1903, 11", VG 135.00
Automatic Electric, chrome payphone, wired for noncoin use, 1960s ..285.00
Automatic Electric, dial, 1950s 15.00
Automatic Electric, str-shaft upright desk stand, dial, NM 250.00
Cracraft, oak, wall type, complete 250.00
Danish Fr, Bakelite, 1913, EX 75.00
Fr, w/eavesdropper 60.00
Gray #50, pay phone, blk 400.00
Kellogg, walnut, wall mt w/orig finish, 32", EX 350.00
Kellogg, wood, oak mt, Pat'd Nov 26, 1901 on speaker, 23", EX ..290.00
Kellogg Redbar 50.00
Leich Magneto 25.00
Manhattan Electric Intercom, walnut, 1899, 5¾x5x3½" 150.00
North Electric H-6, blk, 'Bogart' phone, EX 85.00
Pay phone, chrome, Western Electric 250.00
Stromberg-Carlson, candlestick, NP head 125.00
Stromberg-Carlson, candlestick type 110.00
Stromberg-Carlson, desk type, 1930s, EX 40.00
Stromberg-Carlson, oak wall type/crank hdl/Bakelite mouthpc & receiver .200.00
Table model, oak, metal plate: Long Distance, 40", EX 2,650.00
Viaduct Mfg, 3-box wall type, Blake transmitter, 1883, EX 1,800.00
Western Electric, dial, desk stand, 1920s, 12", EX 250.00
Western Electric, oak, wall type, complete, EX 300.00
Western Electric #202, blk metal cradle type, dial, 1931, EX 125.00
Western Electric #300, red, cradle type, NM 265.00
Western Electric Interphone, wall type, watch case receiver 95.00

Blue Bell Paperweights

First issued in the early 1900s, bell-shaped glass paperweights were used as 'give-aways' and/or presented to telephone company executives as tokens of appreciation. The paperweights were used to prevent stacks of papers from blowing off the desks in the days of overhead fans. Over the years they have all but vanished — some taken by retiring employees, others accidentally broken. The weights came to be widely used for advertising by individual telephone companies; and as the smaller companies merged to form larger companies, more and more new paperweights were created. They were widely distributed with the opening of the first transcontinental telephone line in 1915. The bell-shaped paperweight embossed 'Opening of Trans-Pacific Service, Dec. 23, 1931,' in peacock blue glass is very rare, and the price is negotiable. (Weights with 'open' in the price field are also rare and impossible to accurately evaluate.) In 1972 the first Pioneer bell paperweights were made to sell to raise funds for the charities the Pioneers support. This has continued to the present day. These bell paperweights have also become 'collectibles.' For further study we recommend *Blue Bell Paperweights,*

1992 Revised Edition, and its accompanying *1995 Addendum* by Jacqueline C. Linscott; she is listed in the Directory under Florida.

Bell System (front/bk), Region 12 (base emb), ruby red 40.00
Bell System (front/bk), Region 15 (base emb), cobalt 50.00
Bell System (front/bk), TPA Region 12 (base emb), carnival ruby red ...60.00
Bell System C&P Telephone Company & Associated Companies, ice bl 250.00
Bell System New York Telephone Company, ice bl 150.00
Bell System/Michigan Bell Telephone Company, Ocean Blue 65.00
Bell Telephone Company, cobalt 175.00
Break-Up of the Bell System, opaline bl swirl 65.00
Commemorating Florida's 1,000,000 Telephone, cobalt 200.00
Compliments of Clarion Kiwanis Club, ice bl.................................open
Compliments of Millville Kiwanis Club, ice bl 900.00
Diamond Jubilee 1911-1986 - 75 Years of..., opaline gold swirl.......open
Missouri & Kansas Telephone Company, cobalt 225.00
Nebraska Telephone Company, peacock 325.00
Nevada Bell, blk glass (etched in silver) 75.00
Save Time—Telephone/Save Steps—Telephone, cobalt 100.00
The Creamer Glass Works, ice bl ....open
1973 Telephone Pioneers of America, amber.................................open

Novelty Telephones

Bart Simpson, Columbia Tel-Com, 1990s, MIB 35.00
Batmobile (Batman Forever), MIB, from $35 to 50.00
Bugs Bunny, Warner Exclusive, MIB 100.00
Darth Vader, 1983, MIB 195.00
Ghostbusters, M 100.00
Gumball Machine, 1980s, rare, NM 95.00
Little Orphan Annie & Sandy, Columbia Pictures, 1982, 11", EX ...100.00
Mickey Mouse, Western Electric, 1976, EX 175.00
New Kids on the Block, Big Step Products, 1990, MIB 25.00
Raggedy Ann & Andy, Pan Phone, 1983, plastic, 7½", EX 40.00
Sly Dog, 1986, MIB, from $85 to 110.00
Spider-Man Climbing Down Chimney, NM, from $165 to 200.00
Strawberry Shortcake, M 55.00

Telescopes

Antique telescopes were sold in large quantities to sailors, astronomers, voyeurs, and the military but survive in relatively few numbers because their glass lenses and brass tubes were easily damaged. Even scarcer are antique reflecting telescopes, which use a polished metal mirror to magnify the world. Telescopes used for astronomy give an inverted image, but most old telescopes were used for marine purposes and have more complicated optics that show the world right-side up. Spyglasses are smaller, hand-held telescopes that collapse into their tube and focus by drawing out the tube to the correct length. A more compact instrument, with three or four sections, is also more delicate, and sailors usually preferred a single-draw spyglass. They are almost always of brass, occasionally of nickel silver or silver plate, and usually covered with leather, or sometimes a beautiful rosewood veneer. Solid wood barrel spyglasses (with a brass draw tube) tend to be early and rare. Before the middle of the 1800s, makers put their names in elaborate script on the smallest draw tube, but as 1900 approached, most switched to plain block printing. From the WWII era, British instruments by a variety of makers are commonly found, sharing a format of a 2" objective, 30" long with three draws extended, a tapered main tube, and sometimes having low- and high-power oculars and beautiful leather cases. U.S. Navy WWII spyglasses are quite common but have outstanding optics and focus by twisting the eyepiece, which makes them weather-proof. The Quartermaster (Q.M.) 16x spyglass is 31" long, with a tapered barrel and a 2½" objective. The Officer of the Deck (O.D.D.) is a 23" cylinder with a 1½" objective. Very massive, short, brass telescopes are usually gun sights or ship equipment and have little interest to most collectors. World War II marked the first widespread use of coated optics, which can be recognized by a colored film on the objective lens. Collectible post-WWII telescopes include early refractors by Unitron or Fecker and reflectors by Cave or Questar. Modern spotting scopes often use a prism to erect the image and are of great interest if made by the best makers, including Nikon and Zeiss. Several modern makers still use lacquered brass, and many replica instruments have been produced.

A telescope with no maker's name is much less interesting than a signed instrument, and 'Made in France' is the most common mark on old spyglasses. Dollond of London made instruments for two hundred years and this is probably the most common name on antiques; but because of their important technical innovations and very high quality, Dollond telescopes are always valuable. Bardou, Paris, telescopes are also of very high quality. Bardou is another relatively common name, since they were a prolific maker for many years, and their spyglasses were sold by Sears. Alvin Clark and Sons were the most prolific early American makers, in operation from the 1850s to the 1920s, and their astronomical telescopes are of great historical import.

Spyglasses are delicate instruments that were subject to severe use under all weather conditions. Cracked or deeply scratched optics are impossible to repair and lower the value considerably. Most lenses are doublets, two lenses glued together, and deteriorated cement is common. This looks like crazed glaze and is fairly difficult to repair. Dents in the tube and damaged or missing leather covering can usually be fixed. The best test of a telescope is to use it, and the image should be sharp and clear. Any accessories, eyepieces, erecting prisms, or quality cases can add significantly to value. The following prices assume that the telescope is in very good to fine condition and give the objective lens (obj.) diameter, which is the most important measurement of a telescope.

Our advisor for this category is Peter Abrahams, who studies and collects telescopes and other optics. Please contact him, especially to exchange reference material. (See his comments concerning online auctions under Binoculars; they are applicable to telescopes as well.) Mr. Abrahams is listed in the Directory under Oregon. (Please include SASE with questions.)

Key:
obj — objective lens
ODD — Officer of the Deck

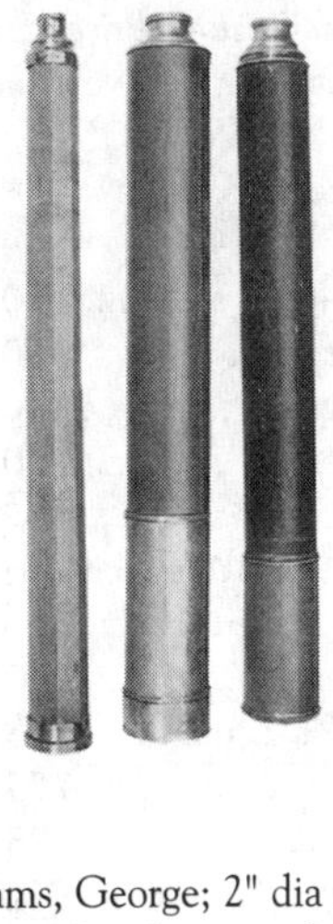

Brass, one-draw, probably England, nineteenth century, original leather casing, extends to 26⅝", EX, $300.00; Brass and leather, one-draw, G Young & Co. London Day & Night, replaced leather, 20¼", EX, $400.00; Brass and wood, eighteenth century, replaced objective lens, 20¼", $350.00.

Adams, George; 2" dia reflecting, brass cabriole tripod 3,200.00
Adams, London, wooden bbl, rack & pinion fine focus, cased ..1,800.00
Bardou & Son, Paris, 4-draw, 50mm obj, leather, 36" 270.00
Bardou Rue St Marton...Paris, wood w/brass ends, extends: 52" ...350.00
Bausch & Lomb, 1-draw, 45mm obj, wrinkled pnt, 17" 90.00
Brashear, 3½" obj, brass, tripod, w/eyepcs 5,000.00

Cary, London (script), 2" obj, tripod, w/3 eyepcs 2,500.00
Chapman-London, 1-draw, 10-sided, 18th C, extends to 31", EX ..1,200.00
Clark, Alvan; 4" obj, 48", iron mt on wooden legs 5,000.00
Criterion RV-6 Dynascope, 6" reflector, 1960s 500.00
Dallmeyer, London (script), 5-draw, 2½" obj, SP, 49" 450.00
Dollond, London, captain's spy glass, 1-draw, SP, early, 29" 800.00
Dollond, London (block), 2-draw, 2" obj, leather cover 270.00
Dollond, London (script), 2-draw, 2" obj, leather cover 340.00
Dollond, London (script), 3" obj, brass, 40", on tripod 2,500.00
France or Made in France, 3-draw, 30mm obj, lens cap 80.00
McAlister (script), brass, 3½" obj, 45", tripod 3,000.00
Mogey, 3" obj, brass, 40", on tripod, w/4 eyepcs 2,800.00
Negretti & Zambra, 2½" obj, 36", equatorial mt, tripod 2,200.00
Plossl, Wien, 2½" obj, 24", tabletop tripod, Dialytic optics 3,000.00
Queen & Co (script), 6-draw, wood veneer, 50", 70mm obj 750.00
Questar, 3½" dia reflecting on astro mt, 1950s 2,400.00
R&J Beck, 2" obj, 24", table-top tripod, cabriole legs 2,000.00
Short, James; 3" dia reflecting, brass cabriole tripod 3,300.00
T Cook & Sons, York & London, 5" main obj lens, 80", EX ..4,000.00
Tel Sct Rgt Mk 2 S (many maker's names), UK, WWI 120.00
Unitron, 4" obj, wht, 60", on tripod, w/many accessories 1,800.00
Unmk, brass, 2" obj, spyglass, leather cover, from $150 to 300.00
Unmk, brass, 2" obj, stand w/cabriole legs 1,200.00
Unmk night & day, 2-draw, brass & leather, fine optics, 19" 150.00
US military, brass, very heavy, complex housing, from $100 to .300.00
US Navy, Bu Ships, Mk II, 10-Power, ODD, 1943 ....150.00
Vion, Paris, 40 Power, 3-draw, 21", 40mm obj, leather 110.00
Wollensak Mirroscope, 1950s, 2" dia, 12" L, leather case 250.00
Wood bbl, rnd taper, 1½" obj, sgn, 1800s 350.00
Wood bbl, 8-sided, 1½" obj, 1700s, 30" 1,500.00
Zeiss, 60mm obj, brass w/eps & porro prism, tripod 1,600.00
Zeiss Asiola, 60mm obj prism spotting scope, pre-WWII 450.00

Televisions

Many early TVs have escalated in value over the last few years. Pre-1943 sets (usually with only one to five channels) are often worth $500.00 to $5,000.00. Unusually styled small-screen wooden 1940s TVs are 'hot'; but most metal, Bakelite, and large-screen sets are still shunned by collectors. Color TVs from the 1950s with 16" or smaller tubes are valuable; larger color sets are not. One of our advisors for this category is Harry Poster, author of *Poster's Radio & Television Price Guide 1920–1990, 2nd Edition;* he is listed in the Directory under New Jersey. Another source of information is *Collector's Guide to Vintage Televisions* by Bryan Durbal and Glenn Bubenheimer (Collector Books).

Admiral, #17T12, table-top, mahog Bakelite, 1948, 7" screen ...150.00
Admiral, #20X122, console, Bakelite, 1950, 10" screen 350.00
Admiral, #24A12, console, Bakelite, 1948, 12" screen 40.00
Air King, #A-1000, table-top, wood, 1948, 10" screen 100.00
Arvin, #4080T, table-top, metal w/mahog front, 1950, 8" screen 150.00
Bendix, #235M1, table-top, mahog, push-button, 1949, 10" screen ..75.00
CBS-Columbia, #RX90, color console, 1954, 15" screen 150.00
Coronado, #FA43-8965, table-top, 1949, 7" screen 200.00
Crosley, #AC10, console, wood, 4-legged, 1965, 21" screen 15.00
Crosley, #9-425, portable, 1949, 7" screen 175.00
DuMont, #RA-103D, table-top, 1949, 12" screen 75.00
DuMont, #RA-119, Royal Sovereign, w/FM radio, 1951, 30" screen ..300.00
DuMont, #183X, console, 1941, 14" screen, minimum value .3,500.00
GE, #HM-225, console, 1939, 9" screen, minimum value 3,500.00
GE, #17T027, portable, metal, 1956, 17" screen 75.00
GE, #800, portable, Bakelite, 1948, 10" screen 200.00
GE, #811, console, 1949, 10" screen 125.00
Hallicrafters, #505, table-top, wood w/metal front, 1947, 7" screen ...300.00
Hallicrafters, #509, portable, 1948, 10" screen 150.00
Hallicrafters, #716, table-top, leatherette, 1950, 12" screen 150.00
HMV, #904, table-top w/radio, 1938, 5" screen, minimum value ..3,000.00
Meck, #XA-701, table-top, mahog, 1949, 7" screen 200.00
Meck, #XC-703, portable, leatherette, w/lid & hdl, 7" screen ...175.00
Motorola, #TS-902, color console, 1954, 15" screen, mimimum value ...1,000.00
Motorola, #VT-105, table-top, wood, 1947, 10" screen 200.00
Motorola, #VT71, table-top, 1947, 7" screen 175.00
Motorola, #17T32BZ, portable, metal, 1958, 17" screen 75.00
Motorola, #7VT5, portable w/lid, 7" rnd screen 100.00
Motorola, #9L1, portable, leatherette, 1950, 8" screen 150.00
National, #TV7W, table-top, mahog, 1949, 7" screen 200.00
Olympic, #TV-104, table-top, wood, 1948, 10" screen 75.00
Pilot, #TV-37, table-top, 1949, 3" screen w/magnifier 250.00
RCA, #621-TS, table-top, blond, 1946, 7" screen, minimum value ..700.00
RCA, #621-TS, table-top, mahog, 1946, 7" screen 400.00
RCA, #721-TCS, console, 1947, 10" screen 200.00
RCA, #721-TS, table-top, wood, 1947, 10" octagonal screen 125.00
Sentinel, #400, portable, 1949, 7" screen 175.00
Silvertone, #9115, portable, leatherette, 8" screen 150.00
Stromberg Carlson, #TC-10H, table-top, 1958, 10" rnd screen .175.00
Teletone, #TV-208, portable, 1949, 7" rnd screen 175.00
Zenith, #28T925E, table-top, blond, 1948, 10" screen 225.00

Philco Predictas and Related Items

Made in the years between 1958 and 1960, Philco Predictas have become one of the most sought after lines of televisions in the post-war era. Predictas are now over forty years old, yet their atomic-age styling is just as futuristic today as it was in 1958. As we move into the new millennium, the Predicta line will continue to be highly collectible. Philco Predictas feature a swivel or separate enclosed picture tube and radical cabinet designs.

The values given here are for as-found, average, clean, complete, unrestored sets, running or not, that have good picture tubes. Predictas that are missing parts or have damaged viewing screens will have a lower value. Above average Predictas will have much higher values. Please keep in mind that Predictas that have been completely professionally restored to as new in appearance as well as electronically can easily bring four to five times the stated values. Our advisor for Predicta televisions is David Weddington; he is listed in the Directory under Tennessee.

G4710 'Tandem,' 21" separate screen with 25-foot cable, mahogany finish, $625.00. (Photo courtesy David Weddington)

G4242 Holiday 21" table-top, wood cabinet, blond finish 455.00
G4242 Holiday 21" table-top, wood cabinet, mahog finish 400.00
G4654 Barber-Pole 21" console, boomerang front leg, blond 725.00
G4654 Barber-Pole 21" console, boomerang front leg, mahog ...650.00

G4710 Tandem 21" separate screen w/25' cable, mahog finish ..625.00
G4720 Stereo Tandem w/matching 1606S phono/amp, mahog 1,100.00
G64720 Stereo Tandem 21" separate screen, 4 brass legs, mahog 900.00
H3406 Motel 17" table-top, metal cabinet, cloth grill, no antenna .275.00
H3408 Debutante 17" table-top, cloth grill, w/antenna, charcoal 375.00
H3410 Princess 17" table top, w/orig metal stand, red finish 500.00
H3410 Princess 17" table-top, metal grill, plastic tuner window 400.00
H3412 Siesta 17" table-top, w/clock-timer above tuner, gold finish 550.00
H4730 Danish Modern 21" console, 4 fin-shaped legs, mahog finish ..950.00
H4744 Townhouse 21" room-divider, walnut shelves, brass finish 1,400.00
17DRP4 picture tube, MIB, replacement for all 17" T/T Predictas 175.00
21EAP4 or 21FDP4 picture tube, MIB, replacement for all 21" Predictas ...275.00

Tennis Rackets

Early tennis rackets (pre-1940) generally exhibit these characteristics: head shape — may be oval, flat-top, transitional flat-top, triangular (or other); throat wedge — the triangular section of wood at the junction of the head and the handle may be concave, convex, solid or laminated; handle — most from this era are not covered by leather and are either combed (grooved) or checkered wood, and some may have cork handles or enlargements at the butt end. Values vary, dependent on age, rarity, style, and condition. Brand and model are important, and all identifying decals should be legible and in good condition. Rackets from 1880 – 1940 range in price from $300.00 to $600.00 for rare models like the Hazel's Streamline down to $10.00 to $20.00 for more common models.

Our advisor for this category is Donald Jones; he is listed in the Directory under Georgia. In the listings that follow, values apply to examples in excellent condition.

Key:
cx-lam — convex laminated tran — transitional
cx-s — convex solid

AJ Reach, Driver, concave wedge, combed hdl, over head, 1920 ...75.00
E Kent, Duchess, concave wedge, bulbous hdl, over head, 1930 ...120.00
Hazel's, Streamline, branched wedge, leather hdl, over head, 1935 .....500.00
Horsman, Elberton, concave wedge, smooth hdl, flat-top head, 1885 .350.00
Iver Johnson, Special, cx-s wedge, bulbous hdl, tran head, 1900 ..175.00
Magnon, Superior, concave wedge, combed hdl, over head, 1928 ..75.00
Slazenger, Demon, cx-lam wedge, fishtail hdl, oval head, 1910 .250.00
Spaulding, Park, cx-s wedge, combed hdl, flat-top head, 1895 ...450.00
Wright-Ditson, Hub, cx-s wedge, checkered hdl, oval head, 1890 ...175.00
Wright-Ditson, Octagon, concave head, combed hdl, oval head, 1895 ...120.00
Wright-Ditson, Star, cx-s wedge, combed hdl, oval head, 1904 .135.00

Teplitz

Teplitz, in Bohemia, was an active art pottery center at the turn of the century. The Amphora Pottery Works was only one of the firms that operated there. (See Amphora.) Art Nouveau and Art Deco styles were favored, and much of the ware was hand decorated with the primary emphasis on vases and figurines. Items listed here are marked 'Teplitz' or 'Turn,' a nearby city. Our advisor for this category is Jack Gunsaulus; he is listed in the Directory under Michigan.

Bowl, figural bears fight for seal above rim, blk matt, 8x11" 225.00
Bowl, gargoyle birds astride pk rim, bl body w/cobalt & gold, 7x8½" ..500.00
Bust, Nouveau maiden w/grapes in hair, Stellmacher, 1910s, 22" 925.00
Creamer, child & dog, Stellmacher, lg 65.00
Pitcher, fish figural w/open mouth, RS&K..., 12" 325.00
Vase, floral on beige, gold winged creature coils neck, rpr, 15" ..160.00
Vase, lady's head/flowers, stems form asymetric hdls, 13x5" 400.00
Vase, Secessionist style, roses, wht w/gold on bl-gray, corseted, 14" ...375.00
Vase, 2 dancers emb, mc matt, flaring w/5 openings, 11" 250.00

Terra Cotta

Terra cotta is a type of earthenware or clay used for statuary, architectural facings, or domestic articles. It is unglazed, baked to durable hardness, and characterized by the color of the body which may range from brick red to buff.

Group, satyr with grape-filled tambourine and two young satyrs, after Clodion, 17", $2,185.00.

Bust, Moroccan boy w/fez, red/brn/blk/gr, 20th C, 15⅝" 700.00
Corbels, acanthus decor, 18x30x9½", pr 165.00
Group, satyr w/grape-filled tambourine & 2 young satyrs, 17" ...2,185.00
Lamp, Aladdin style, lt orange buff, EX fluting & decor, 1¾x4" ..80.00

Thermometers

Few objects man has invented have been so eloquently expressed both functionally and artistically as the ubiquitous thermometer. Developed initially by Galileo as a scientific device, thermometers slowly evolved into decorative objet d'art, functional household utensils, and eye-catching advertising specialties. Most American thermometers manufactured early in the twentieth century were produced by Taylor (Tycos), and today their thermometers remain the most plentiful on the market. Decorative thermometers manufactured before 1800 are now ensconced in the permanent collections of approximately a dozen European museums. Because of their fragility, few devices of this era have survived in private collections. Nowadays most antique thermometers find their way to market through estate sales.

Insofar as sheer beauty, uniqueness, and scientific accuracy, decorative thermometers are far superior to the ordinary and inexpensive versions which carry advertising. Decorative thermometers run the gamut from plain tin household varieties to the highly ornate creations of Tiffany and Bradley and Hubbard. They have been manufactured from nearly every conceivable material — oak, sterling, brass, and glass being the favorites — and have tested the artistry and technical skills of some of America's finest craftsmen. Ornamental models can be found in free-hanging, wall-mounted, or desk/mantel versions.

Since 1994 instrument prices have been escalating at a rate of 35% annually. This is due to their relative scarcity, infrequent trading and absence of a 'knock-off' (retro) market. Look for this trend to continue indefinitely.

Thermometer prices are based on age, ornateness, and whether mercury or alcohol is used as the filler in the tube. A broken or missing tube will cut at least 40% off the value. Virtually all American-made thermometers available today as collectors' items were made between 1875 and 1940. The golden age of decoratives ended in the early 1940s as modern manufacturing processes and materials robbed them of their natural distinctiveness.

Key:
br — brass
Cen — Centigrade
Fah — Fahrenheit
mrc — mercury in tube
pmc — permacolor
R — rare
Rea — Reaumer
sc — scale
stl — stainless
strl — sterling
VR — very rare

French, Greenaway girl on ladder figural, bronze, 7", $525.00.

Alexandre, desk, scimitar figural, br sc, mrc, 9" 430.00
Anonymous, cvd wood squirrel, glass Rea sc, mrc, 1905, 10" 800.00
Anonymous, desk, br conquistador figural, br sc, mrc 650.00
Anonymous, Fr, desk, alabaster fr/sterling Rea sc/mrc, 1885, 6x3" ..920.00
Anonymous, wall, giltwood fr, ivory, Fah sc, mrc, 1790, 10x3½" ..3,100.00
Bearskin Ltd, wall, metal clip, rnd mrc, 1930, 3x4" 750.00
Blk/Starr/Frost, desk, barometer, stl, Fah/Cen, mrc, '10, 11" ...2,200.00
Bradley & Hubbard, desk, br fr & Fah sc, mrc, 1895, 13x6" ...2,800.00
Brn & Bigelow, novelty desk, pot-metal fr/Fah sc/spirit, 1906, 6x1" ...375.00
Capendium, desk, handmade br/porc fr, Fah/Cen sc, rnd mrc, 4" ..850.00
Casella London, wall, maxi/minimum, 2 units, wood, plastic sc ...430.00
Cheshire Silversmiths, desk, br candelabra, mrc, 1875, 10" 4,500.00
Chevallier, L'ingre, wall, ivory/mahog, Rea/Cen sc, 1880, 11x3" ...2,350.00
Cloister, inkwell, stl bk & base w/angels at side, 1901 ....1,050.00
Creswel, travel, ivory case/mirror, removable sc, mrc, 2½" 2,800.00
CW Wilder...NH, bear & billboard br figural, mrc, 6½" 300.00
Diamond, wall, br Fah sc on wood, R, 7½x1½" 525.00
Dixie, W (London); desk, gilt/br, Gothic, SP sc, mrc, 8" 790.00
Dollard London, desk, strl, br sc, mrc, 1908, R, 6" 750.00
Dollard London, hanging, mahog fr, strl sc, mrc, 1810, 18" 4,600.00
Dring & Fage, desk, marble, ivory sc, mrc, 1880, 6" 1,500.00
Freeborn, desk, bronze w/3 lead decor, br sc, mrc, 8" 180.00
G Cooper, desk, bell shape w/cupola, strl, dial, 2x3" 400.00
G Strait, London, desk, tower br fr/ivory Rea/Fah, mrc, 1890, 6x2" ...850.00
Gilbert & Co, travel, silver eng sc, mrc, 1850, 8" 630.00
Heath & Wing, figural calendar, br w/porc sc, mrc, 1870 ....930.00
Hohmann Maurer Co, steel Fah/Cen sc & bk, mrc, 12" 80.00
J Waldstein, wall, br Rea sc on wood, mrc, 1900s, VR, 10½" 920.00
M Comyns, Chelsea, desk, wood/ivory, Rea/Fah sc, mrc, 1880, 7x3" 890.00
Moreau, desk, mahog, Rea/Cen, spiral tube, mrc, 1860, 6½x5½" ...1,725.00
Negretti & Zambra, England, desk, wood w/ivory Fah sc, 1900, 7x2" ...650.00
Nova, desk, br/glass hex fr/br Fah sc/dial, 1925, R 450.00
Pairpoint, desk, strl picture fr, mrc, 1907, 5" 650.00
Phila Therm Co, hygrometer, br sc, rotating wheel, 1928 ....30.00
Rowley & Sons, travel, ivory sc, mrc, 1894, 4", +case 350.00
Seavers, English, desk, ivory fr, compass, Rea/Fah sc, mrc, 1890, 6x2" 1,750.00
Slouche, desk, alabaster ped, paper sc insert, mrc, 8x2½" 95.00
Standard, wall, ivory Fah sc on ebony, mrc, 9" 750.00
Standard..., wall, br fr, enamel dial Fah sc, 1885, 9" dia 950.00
T Barton, desk, Tunbridge, wood fr, ivory Fah sc, mrc, 1875, 5x2" ...1,350.00
Thermindex Switzerland, desk, Bakelite stand, Fah sc, 5" 725.00
Tiffany, desk, strl tetrahedron fr & Fah sc, mrc, 1910, 2x4" 4,000.00
Tiffany, gr glass w/pine needles, br sc/mrc, 1902, 8x12" 2,800.00
Unknown, cvd wood squirrel, glass Rea sc, mrc, 1905, 10", VR ...800.00
Unknown, desk, alabaster w/eagle, Rea/Cen sc, mrc, 1895 ....875.00
Unknown, desk, love scene, silver metal, br Rea/Cen sc, mrc, 8" ...830.00
Unknown, England, desk, glass obelisk/8-sided, br Fah sc, mrc, 1880 ..1,259.99
Unknown, England, desk, marble ped fr, Cen, mrc, 1885, 6½" .930.00
Unknown, England, wall, br game bag fr, Fah sc, mrc, 1890, 9x5" 1,650.00
Unknown, England, wall, rect wood fr, porc Cen sc, mrc, 1905, 5" ..1,350.00
Unknown, wall, giltwood fr, ivory Fah sc, 1790, 10x3½" 3,100.00
VJD Inc, wall, clip Fah br sc, mrc, VR, 4" 1,650.00
W Dixey, London, desk, br figural fr, Fah sc, mrc, 1865, 8x3" ...930.00
W Pratt, desk, wood inlays, ivory sc, mrc, 1900, 6" 350.00
Warren Foundries, wall, umbrella w/dragon hdl, br sc, mrc, 12" ...220.00
West, desk, Gothic design, br, 1900, 12" 1,360.00
WG Loveday, wall, Clearside, Fah sc, 5" dia 725.00
Whitehead & Hoag, Lambrecht's Polymeter, mrc, 9" 1,200.00
Wise, desk, Tunbridge, twin columns, mrc, 1870, 5" 2,750.00

1000 Faces China

So named because of its many hand-painted faces, much of this chinaware was made during the '30s through the '50s (some even earlier). Though many pieces are unmarked, others are marked 'Made in Japan.' There are two primary patterns, 'Black Face' and the 'Gold' pattern, and variations exist. Both designs employ many colors. Dinner plates usually are decorated with an outer-most 'ring of color' (two or three hues) containing a simple design which is often flowers. The inner ring is usually comprised of many colors radiating from the center circle which may be done in a primary color (red, for instance) with a design such as a dragon or clouds painted in gold. 'Black Face' is distinguishable by its range of colors — primarily red, white, and yellow with some green and blue — and the black hand-painted faces. The 'Gold' pattern is also multicolored but is dominated by the gold throughout the design, and the faces themselves are gold as well. Other variations include '1000 Men in Robes' and '1000 Faces' with black or blue rims on the saucers and cups. These pieces seem to be very scarce. In the listings that follow, all items are marked 'Made in Japan' (MIJ) unless noted otherwise. Our advisor for this category is Suzi Hibbard; she is listed in the Directory under California.

Bowl, gold faces, petal shape, 6" 20.00
Cup & saucer, blk, MIJ, from $30 to 55.00
Cup & saucer, blk faces 40.00
Cup & saucer, demitasse; gold faces 25.00
Cup & saucer, gold faces, from $30 to 50.00
Cup & saucer, 1000 Geishas 40.00
Egg cup, bl faces, from $15 to 30.00
Ginger jar, gold faces, from $75 to 100.00
Incense burner, gold, MIJ, from $25 to 40.00
Lamp, gold faces, 8" vase base, from $100 to 150.00
Nappy, gold, 6¾", from $10 to 35.00
Plate, blk, MIJ, 8½", from $15 to 45.00
Plate, blk, 10", from $30 to 50.00
Plate, blk/gold, 6", from $7.50 to 15.00
Salt cellar, bl faces, from $5 to 12.50
Shakers, bl faces, pr, from $10 to 25.00
Snack set, blk faces, kidney shape, from $20 to 50.00
Soup set, blk faces, 3-pc, from $50 to 80.00
Sweetmeat, blk faces, 9-pc set in lacquer box, from $150 to 200.00
Tea set, blk, blk rim, 23-pc, from $200 to 300.00
Tea set, demitasse; bl faces, 15-pc, from $150 to 200.00
Tea set, gold, MIJ, teapot+cr/sug, from $40 to 75.00
Tea set, gold faces, 21-pc, from $175 to 250.00
Teapot, blk faces, dragon spout, 7", from $50 to 75.00
Teapot, gold, HP Nippon, from $40 to 55.00

Teapot, gold faces, dragon spout, 7", from $30 to 75.00
Teapot, Men in Robes, 6-sided, Japanese mk, from $40 to 75.00
Teapot, 1000 Geishas, dragon spout, from $50 to 75.00
Vase, blk faces, 8", from $50 to 75.00
Vase, gold, 8", from $50 to 100.00

Threaded Glass

Threaded glass has been made both here and abroad since the 1870s. The procedure was done entirely by hand until about 1876 when a machine was developed to apply the fine threads to the glass automatically.

Finger bowl, Dmn Quilt, cranberry, 2¾", 7" 285.00
Stein, bl to clear, emb pewter hinged top & ft, 7½" 175.00

Tiffany

Louis Comfort Tiffany was born in 1848 to Charles Lewis and Harriet Young Tiffany of New York. By the time he was eighteen, his father's small dry goods and stationery store had grown and developed into the world-renowned Tiffany and Company. Preferring the study of art to joining his father in the family business, Louis spent the next six years under the tutelage of noted artists. He returned to America in 1870 and until 1875 painted canvases that focused on European and North African scenes. Deciding the more lucrative approach was in the application of industrial arts and crafts, he opened a decorating studio called Louis C. Tiffany and Co., Associated Artists. He began seriously experimenting with glass, and eschewing traditionally painted-on details, he instead learned to produce glass with qualities that could suggest natural textures and effects. His experiments broadened, and he soon concentrated his efforts on vases, bowls, etc., that came to be considered the highest achievements of the art. Peacock feathers, leaves and vines, flowers and abstracts were developed within the plane of the glass as it was blown. Opalescent and metallic lustres were combined with transparent color to produce stunning effects. Tiffany called his glass Favrile, meaning handmade.

In 1900 he established Tiffany Studios and turned his attention full time to producing art glass, leaded-glass lamp shades and windows, and household wares with metal components. He also designed a complete line of jewelry which was sold through his father's store. He became proficiently accomplished in silverwork and produced such articles as hand mirrors embellished with peacock feather designs set with gems and candlesticks with Favrile glass inserts.

Tiffany's work exemplified the Art Nouveau style of design and decoration, and through his own flamboyant personality and business acumen he perpetrated his tastes onto the American market to the extent that his name became a household word. Tiffany Studios continued to prosper until the second decade of this century when due to changing tastes his influence began to diminish. By the early 1930s the company had closed.

Serial numbers were assigned to much of Tiffany's work, and letter prefixes indicated the year of manufacture: A–N for 1896–1900, P–Z for 1901–1905. After that, the letter followed the numbers with A–N in use from 1906–1912; P–Z from 1913–1920. O-marked pieces were made especially for friends and relatives; X indicated pieces not made for sale.

Our listings are primarily from the auction houses in the East where Tiffany sells at a premium. All pieces are signed unless noted otherwise.

Glass

Bottle, scent; bl irid, bulbous w/long neck, button-top stopper, 6" ..900.00
Bowl, bl irid, 10-rib w/ruffled rim, 2x6" 700.00
Bowl, console; gold irid, optic ribs/rolled rim, #1883, 2½x8" 515.00
Bowl, console; gold irid w/rolled rim, 2¼x9⅝" 350.00
Bowl, dessert; Dmn Optic, clear to wht w/gr irid, #1701 ....700.00
Bowl, dessert; gold irid, scalloped rim, ca 1900, 2½x6" 1,150.00
Bowl, gold irid, ribbed, bronze multi-leaf form base, #500, 5x12" ...1,600.00
Bowl, gold spotted opal w/gr & bl at rim, shell ft, 6" 900.00
Bowl, leaf & vine border eng on gold irid, ribbed, crimped, 2¾x6" ...635.00
Bowl, peacock bl, folded/ruffled top, shallow, 4" 500.00
Bowl, vines eng on pendant, amber w/fuchsia irid, 10⅜" 1,950.00
Bowl, yel & wht w/rainbow irid, #1898, label, 8½" 550.00
Candlesticks, gold w/amethyst irid, #1817, 4", pr 1,150.00
Candlesticks, pk irid, opal disk stem, #1846, 3½", pr 1,600.00
Candlesticks, Pk Pastel, #1927, 4", pr 1,500.00
Candlesticks, red w/gold dore cups, enamel trim, #41, 12", pr .4,750.00
Candy dish, bl irid, petal top, 6" 600.00
Champagne, gold irid, #5, 6x3¼", 7 for 1,150.00
Compote, amber w/violet irid, stretched rim, ftd, 4¼" 750.00
Compote, butterflies (2) eng on gold irid, folded ped ft, 4" 1,150.00
Compote, Dmn Optic, gold irid, bronze mtd #492 base, 4½x10¼" ..975.00
Compote, feathers, wht on clear opal, gr rim, ftd, #1952, 8" ..1,150.00
Compote, feathers (5), gr on wht opal, gold irid int, #590E, 4½" ...1,500.00
Cordial, bl-gold irid, 4 pinched sides, 1¾" 300.00
Finger bowl, red-gold irid, 2½x3" 225.00
Goblet, gold irid, 5½" 100.00
Loving cup, leaves/vines, gr on gold irid, wafer pontil, 3-hdl ..2,500.00
Nut dish, gold irid, 8-rib, ruffled, 1¼x4⅛" 385.00
Rose bowl, leaves & vines, gr on gold irid, #1036-6525M, 2½x3" ...2,150.00
Salt cellar, gold irid, sm scrolled hdls, 2¼", pr 460.00
Salt cellar, gold irid, 3½" dia 160.00
Salt cellar, tan to gr irid w/prunts 1,250.00
Sherbet, gold irid, 4¾" 375.00
Tazza, gold irid w/amethyst hues, ribbed, scalloped, 4x8" 825.00
Tumbler, bl-gold irid, bulbous w/flared top, 3¾" 225.00
Vase, bl irid, flared/ruffled, 10-rib gourd form, disk ft, 10" 1,495.00
Vase, bl irid, ruffled rim, ribbed, #X919, 9" 1,400.00
Vase, bl w/fuchsia & gold irid, slim, #5935D, 14¾" 2,000.00
Vase, bl-gold irid, trumpet form w/ball stem, #5519K, 12" 925.00
Vase, cobalt irid w/bl enameled metal base, #156A, 17" 3,000.00
Vase, feathers, gr on gold irid, #4453B, 6" 650.00
Vase, feathers, gr on opal & crystal, triangle top, #1026G, 6¼" ..3,000.00
Vase, feathers, gr on opal irid, #04483, 4¾x4" 1,200.00
Vase, feathers, silver-bl on yel opal, #41529, 6x3½" 1,265.00
Vase, floriform; bl w/violet irid, #1526 37N, 12⅜" 2,185.00
Vase, floriform; feathers, gr on crystal, amber ft, #8194M, 12" 4,600.00
Vase, floriform; gr & wht leaf tips on wht opal, #7831, 12⅛" .3,750.00
Vase, floriform; gr & wht leaves on wht opal, #Y8257, 9¾" ...1,850.00
Vase, gold irid, baluster w/ribs & dimples, V9945, 4⅞" 650.00
Vase, gold irid, spittoon shape, #W-378, 2½" 450.00
Vase, gold irid w/enameled gr & gold circular base, 13x3¼" 900.00
Vase, gold irid w/ruffled top, #7294G, 9½x6" 800.00
Vase, gold irid w/shell hdls, #1063-8984, 4½" 1,265.00
Vase, gold irid w/triangular rim, #3517D, 4½" 700.00
Vase, gold phantom lustre, 6½x3½" 700.00
Vase, gold w/silver-violet irid, bulbous, 6¾" 1,100.00
Vase, gold w/violet irid, dimpled & ribbed, #U6534, 3¾" 750.00
Vase, gold w/violet irid, flattened triangle, 4 prongs, #7687, 5½" ...750.00
Vase, gold w/violet irid, teardrop form, ribbed, #841E, 2⅞" 750.00
Vase, hearts & vines, fuchsia/bl on irid, #1539G, 7½" 1,500.00
Vase, hearts & vines, opal-gr on cobalt w/irid, long neck, 6" ..2,185.00
Vase, hooks, gr & gold on opal, gold int, Corona, label, 6¼" 950.00
Vase, leaf tips, gr on gold irid, bronze base, #715, 24⅞" 4,000.00
Vase, leaves, gold on blk sand-finish, #0559, 7" 7,500.00
Vase, leaves, gold on wht, #7493J, 8" 900.00
Vase, leaves (5, coiled/pulled), gold on gr, 4¾" 2,400.00

Vase, leaves intaglio on gold irid, #424M, 9" 4,300.00
Vase, lily pads, gr on gold irid, #5431, 5½" 1,600.00
Vase, Merovingian, gold swollen cylinder, ruffled rim, #4392B, 8" ...800.00
Vase, peacock bl w/silver dots, ambergris int, 18-rib, #R812, 5" 2,875.00
Vase, red w/clear ft & amber top, textured int, #370T, 8" 2,100.00
Vase, ruby red, bulbous, ftd, wide neck, #5949, 5½" 3,700.00
Vase, swirls, amber w/pk & gr irid, #7592C, 1¾" 1,400.00
Vase, tadpoles appl on gold irid, #8132, 3¼" 400.00
Vase, turq cased, ovoid, #6467, 4¼" 1,600.00
Vase, wreaths & festoons, pk on opal amber, yel opal ft, 9¾" .1,900.00

Lamps

Lamp prices seem to be getting stronger, especially for leaded lamps with brighter colors (red, blue, purples). Bases that are unusual or rare have brought good prices and added to the value of the more common shades that sold on them. Bases with enamel or glass inserts are very much in demand. Our advisor for Tiffany lamps is Carl Heck; he is listed in the Directory under Colorado.

Key: c-b — counterbalance

Table lamp, leaded glass 16" pansy shade signed Tiffany Studios; three-arm bronze base with naturalized tobacco-leaf pedestal, signed, #26530, 19", from $33,350.00 to $37,500.00.

Base, leaf motif, spun bronze w/wht int, swing socket, #42S ...3,250.00
Base, 6-socket, trumpet form w/artichoke leaves, #542, 27" .54,625.00
Bridge, kapa shell bell-shape shade; 5-leg #468 std adjusts 2,990.00
Bridge, 12" ldgl acorn #1410 shade; 5-leg spade-form #423 std, 58" ...18,500.00
Candle, gold irid ruffled shade; swirled ribbed std, 12" 1,500.00
Ceiling, 12" feathered shade; rtcl bronze surround, EX 10,000.00
Desk, glass scarab on bronze harp base #2238, early, 8½x7½" ...6,500.00
Desk, 3 upright lilies, gold sgn shades; #S1447 std 5,000.00
Desk, 4-panel caramel slag shade w/Deco fretwork; #556 std ..4,250.00
Desk, 6" bell shade w/pulled feathers; 2-arm c-b #417 std, 14" ..5,500.00
Desk, 6" gold dome shade; gold dore Zodiac #661 std, 13" 3,600.00
Desk, 7" gold damascene shade; c-b #416 base 6,500.00
Desk, 7" gold dome shade; 3-arm std #322, 15" 5,500.00
Desk, 7" shade w/mc damascene trailings; 1-arm c-b #1077 std, 14" ...6,500.00
Floor, 7½" Calcite w/gr & gold shade; pod-ftd #468 std 1,900.00
Floor, 8" linenfold mk shade; bronze c-b #468 std, 53½" 11,000.00
Lily, 3-light, bronze cushion #320 std, 8½" 4,000.00
Lily, 3-light, wht opal shades; ribbed #319 circular std 4,500.00
Lily, 6-light, gold rib shades; overlapped leaves on bronzed std, 22" ...10,000.00
Lily, 7-light, gold sgn shades; #385 gold dore base, 22" 14,000.00
Lily, 12-light, feathered shades, lily pad base, 21", EX 33,000.00
Piano, linenfold border shade #1928 w/amber/gold tiles; #2113 std, 11" ..5,000.00
Shade, gold irid bell form w/pulled/swirled opal designs, 4" 450.00
Shade, ldgl, acorn, domical, 1899-1920, 16x22" 8,500.00
Shade, ldgl, hydrangeas, bronze beaded borders, 11½x28½" 68,500.00
Shade, ldgl, pomegranate & fruit pattern, #57-109, 16" 9,500.00
Shade, linenfold, 12 amber panels, bronze fr, Pat...1927, 19¼", EX ..9,500.00
Student, 10" damascene mk dome shades, 2-arm Manhattan Brass std, 29" ...20,000.00
Table, ribbons, gr on gold 10" dome shade; simple std, 17" 5,500.00
Table, 12" opal shade w/gold pulled feathers; #S508/24 std, 16" ..6,500.00
Table, 14" ldgl acorn shade; Greek urn #D548 std, 20", EX 7,500.00
Table, 14" ldgl jonquil shade; bronze std w/floral std, #26350 font .31,000.00
Table, 15" ldgl mottled leaves bell-shaped #D804 shade, mk std 16,500.00
Table, 16" glass/bronze turtle-bk tile shade; Rookwood std, 20½" ..14,500.00
Table, 16" ldgl shade w/oval panels & dmn shapes; #444 std ..10,500.00
Table, 16" linenfold 10-sided amber shade; gold dore 24" std .4,500.00
Table, 18" ldgl geometric shade; tree-shaped bronze std, 28" ...21,000.00
Table, 19" linenfold paneled gold shade; gold dore std 22,500.00
Table, 20" ldgl pond-lily shade; petal form #359 std, 26½" ...39,000.00
Table, 22" ldgl brickwork shade; #532 std, 28½" 21,500.00
Table, 22" ldgl geometric #1501 shade; #443 std, EX 32,000.00
Table, 24" silk fringed/pleated shade; pottery vase, 32" 6,000.00

Metal Work

Items are bronze unless noted otherwise.

Bookends, Zodiac, #1091, 5x6", pr 950.00
Box, cigar; Zodiac, #1655, 2½x6½x6" 1,600.00
Box, cigarette; enamel band at edges, #130, 2x6x3¾" 750.00
Box, turtle-bk w/gr glass top, 1½x8x6" 2,300.00
Box, Zodiac, gold dore, #166, 2x4½x3½" 900.00
Calendar, Zodiac, gold dore, 4½" 110.00
Candlestick, slim shaft, 3 arms support bobeches, 17½" 1,600.00
Candlestick, 7 gr/gold jewels, 3-leg plant-form base, 9¾" 1,600.00
Candlesticks, beading/reeding, tapered shafts, #740, 8x3¾", pr ..825.00
Candlesticks, blown-in glass, pencil stds, 17½", VG 2,600.00
Candlesticks, gold dore, lily-pad form, #1243, 10", pr 525.00
Casket, Cobweb, gold dore, rectangular, ball ft, 6¾" 450.00
Compote, Abalone, decor rim, #1668, 5x9" 650.00
Compote, classical border w/gr enameling, shallow, low, #506 ...980.00
Compote, Greek Key pattern, #1/24, 3¾x6¼" 260.00
Desk set, Chinese, blotter ends/letter opener/inkwell/pen holder/rack ...1,000.00
Desk set, Graduate, inkwell/tray/blotter/fr/bookends 1,000.00
Desk set, Pine Needle, lg & sm inkwells/letter rack/box+4 pcs ..3,000.00
Desk set, Zodiac, inkwell/blotter & blotter ends 635.00
Desk set, Zodiac, pen tray #1000, box #802, file #962, inkstand #842 ...700.00
Desk set, Zodiac, 8-pc 1,850.00
Dish, gold dore, etched border, #1707, 9" dia 250.00
Frame, etched, gr slag inserts, #948, 7½x6½" 3,250.00
Frame, etched/textured w/gr enamel inserts, #600, 5½x4" 1,800.00
Frame, Heraldic, brn patina, easel bk, 12x10" 1,000.00
Frame, narrow w/zigzag relief, easel bk, 10x8" 750.00
Frame, Zodiac, 8x7" 1,500.00
Inkstand, pierced w/gr opaque blown glass, glass insert, #849, 4x7" ..2,500.00
Inkstand, SP w/bl decor, hinged lid, #354, 2x2¾x2¾" 300.00
Inkstand, Zodiac, hinged lid, #1072 ....430.00
Inkwell, Pine Needle, gold dore w/caramel slag glass, #845 ....350.00
Letter rack, gold dore, 3-compartment, 11½" 530.00
Letter rack, Zodiac, 3-compartment, #1090, 12½" W 600.00
Paperweight, dog holding toy, 1½x2½" 250.00
Paperweight, lion, recumbent, #932, polished gilt, 1¾x4¾" 450.00
Paperweight, Shandu (bust of dog), brn/gr patina, #889 ....750.00
Paperweight, sphinx, some gilt to patina, 1½x2¼" 275.00
Pen tray, Nautical, seashell & seaweed decor, #1843, 9½" L ..1,100.00
Planter, mixed metal, distressed silver/etched decor, 3½x10½" .575.00
Plaque, classical scene, stamped mk, 14½" dia 400.00
Roundel, relief flowers w/radiating floral/leaves, pnt, 13" 2,300.00
Smoking stand, gold dore, ceramic bowl, #1649, 26½" 700.00
Thermometer, Bookmark pattern, fruiting trees, #1018 13280, 8½" ...865.00
Tray, Abalone, gold dore, #1730, 12" dia 300.00
Tray, Abalone, gold dore, #1738, 9" dia 175.00
Tray, gold dore w/floral cloisonne hdls, #512, 10" 460.00

Tray, gold dore w/HP flowers, #313, 4¾x2½" 400.00
Tray, gold dore w/random fire-polishing, #9064, 14¾" dia 980.00

Pottery

Vase, molded and reticulated arrowroot plants under blue and green lustre, 8¾x3¼", NM, $14,000.00.

Vase, floral vines, tan matt, spherical, 9¼" 865.00
Vase, Gothic scene emb on bsk, 6-sided, early mk, 3" 300.00
Vase, narcissus, brn to bl to khaki matt, bulbous, ftd, 14½" ...1,400.00
Vase, streaky amber/brn/olive, cylindrical, #P312, 11½" 725.00
Vase, unglazed wht bsk, classic shape, 20x10½" 500.00
Vase, wisteria pods under apple gr/turq, rstr, 6½x4" 900.00
Vase, yel-ochre/amber/brn/cream crystalline mottle, #P666, 8" ..1,035.00

Silver

Key: t-oz — troy ounces

Bowl, funnel shape, disk ft, monogram, 3x5½", 10-t-oz 150.00
Candelabra, 2-arm w/center candle holder, mk, 16x12", pr 2,200.00
Cocktail shaker, entwined leaves, ovoid, 9¼", 24-t-oz 1,265.00
Compote, shallow bowl on wide circular ft, 3¼" H, 8-t-oz 160.00
Cutter, cigar; basketweave decor, 14k gold trim 115.00
Fish slice, medallion/foliage/fiddle/shell/thread decor, 19th C, 12" ...400.00
Hot water kettle on burner stand, eng fruit, 52-t-oz 1,150.00
Ornament, flower-in-basket form, gilt, 7" 175.00
Pen set, rectangular form w/2 winged pen wells, 7¼" L 150.00
Pill box, apple form, 1¾" 110.00
Porringer, foliate hdl, typical form, 6½" 150.00
Spoon, serving; vintage, scalloped shell-shaped gold-wash bowl, 9" ...635.00
Sweetmeat basket, cartouche form, pierced foliate band, 7", pr .525.00
Tazza, emb scrolls & florals, ca 1920, 4½x6" dia, pr 1,045.00
Tea service, 6-sided 8½" pot+cr/sug on 13½" tray, 80-t-oz 1,850.00
Tea/coffee set, AD; cupids decor, 2 pots+cr/sug+tray, 77-t-oz .5,750.00
Tea/coffee set, 2 pots+cr/sug+waste bowl w/liner, 1855, 126-t-oz ..3,950.00
Teapot, faceted baluster w/appl trefoil border, 1907-38, 8" 865.00
Tray, monogram, open hdls, ca 1898, 26x18" 3,750.00
Tray, ridged trefoil border, 1907-38, 12¾" dia, 33-t-oz 800.00
Trophy, Brooklyn Eagle...Best Gig Horse, horse-head mts, 1907, 20" ...1,000.00
Vase, ped form w/scrollwork, shell ft & lip, #18027, 14" 1,100.00
Vase, trumpet form, flared, 8-sided, 11⅝", 13-oz 425.00

Tiffin Glass

The Tiffin Glass Company was founded in 1887 in Tiffin, Ohio, one of the many factories composing the U.S. Glass Company. Its early wares consisted of tablewares and decorative items such as lamps and globes. Among the most popular of all Tiffin products was the black satin glass produced there during the 1920s. In 1959 U.S. Glass was sold, and in 1962 the factories closed. The plant was re-opened in 1963 as the Tiffin Art Glass Company. Products from this period were tableware, hand-blown stemware, and other decorative items.

Those interested in learning more about Tiffin glass are encouraged to contact the Tiffin Glass Collectors' Club, whose address can be found in the Directory under Clubs, Newsletters, and Catalogs. See also Black Glass; Glass Animals.

Ashtray, Twilight, cloverleaf form, #9123/97, 5" 55.00
Basket, Empress, Killarney Green, 13" 400.00
Bonbon, Twilight, center hdl, #5480, 6" 95.00
Bottle, bitters; Fuchsia, crystal 325.00
Bowl, bouillon; Flanders, crystal, 2-hdl 40.00
Bowl, centerpc; Cherokee Rose, crystal, flared, 12½" 50.00
Bowl, centerpc; June Night, crystal, crimped, 12" 75.00
Bowl, Classic, crystal, 2-hdl, 8x9½" 110.00
Bowl, console; amber, #15328, w/pr 8" candlesticks 100.00
Bowl, console; Flanders, pk, ftd, 11" 95.00
Bowl, console; Fuchsia, crystal, flared, #5902, 11⅞" 80.00
Bowl, cream soup; Cadena, pk or yel 30.00
Bowl, finger; Cherokee Rose, crystal, 5" 25.00
Bowl, finger; June Night, crystal, 5" 17.00
Bowl, nappy, Cadena, crystal, hdld, 6" 25.00
Bowl, Optic, Copen Blue, #583, on stem w/bubble 195.00
Bowl, salad; Cherokee Rose, crystal, deep, 10" 55.00
Bowl, salad; Fuchsia, crystal, #5902, 7¼" 40.00
Bowl, whipped cream; Fuchsia, crystal, 3-ftd, #310 ....40.00
Candlestick, Cadena, pk or yel 35.00
Candlestick, Fuchsia, crystal, ball center, 2-light, #5902, 5⅝" 75.00
Candlestick, Twilight, #6554, 7" 135.00
Candlesticks, amberina satin, twisted stem, 8", pr 110.00
Candy jar, Flanders, yel, flat, w/lid 225.00
Celery, June Night, crystal, oblong, 10½" 35.00
Cocktail shaker, Fuchsia, crystal, w/metal lid, 8" 235.00
Compote, Cherokee Rose, crystal, 6" 35.00
Compote, Flanders, crystal, 3½" 25.00
Compote, Palace of Versailles, #5501 ....150.00
Creamer, Classic, pk, flat 60.00
Creamer, Flanders, pk, ftd 115.00
Creamer, Flanders, yel, flat 80.00
Cup, Classic, crystal 50.00
Decanter, crystal, cvd roses, globe stopper, #3700 ....260.00
Decanter, Flanders, yel 225.00
Jug, martini; Twilight, 11½" 350.00
Lamp, electric; Fuchsia, crystal 300.00
Mayonnaise, Cadena, crystal, ftd, w/liner 30.00
Mayonnaise, Cherokee Rose, crystal, w/liner & ladle 55.00
Nut cup, Flanders, crystal, ftd, blown 30.00
Nut dish, Fuchsia, crystal, 6¼" 35.00
Pitcher, Cadena, pk or yel, ftd, w/lid 350.00
Pitcher, Classic, pk, w/lid, 61-oz 495.00
Pitcher, Enchanted, #17477, water sz 18.00
Pitcher, Flanders, pk, w/lid 350.00
Plate, Byzantine, yel, 7½" 15.00
Plate, Cadena, crystal, 9¼" 30.00
Plate, cracker; Deerwood, blk, gold edge 225.00
Plate, dinner; Classic, crystal, 10" 85.00
Plate, Fuchsia, crystal, 2-hdl, #5831, 6⅜" 12.50
Plate, luncheon; Cherokee Rose, crystal, 8" 18.50
Plate, Mystic, #17378, 8" 20.00
Plate, Sandcarved, ruby stain, 8" 125.00
Plate, sherbet; June Night, crystal, 6" 18.00
Plate, Williamsburg, crystal, #17301, 8" 15.00
Relish, Cherokee Rose, crystal, 3-part, 6½" 35.00
Relish, Flanders, yel, 3-part 50.00
Relish, Fuchsia, crystal, 3-part, sq, 9¼" 40.00

Relish, June Night, crystal, 3-part, 12½" 65.00
Rose bowl, Royale Line, crystal, #6805 .....85.00
Rose bowl, Sandcarved, #525 .....75.00
Rose bowl, Twilight, ftd 225.00
Saucer, Flanders, crystal 8.00
Stem, champagne; Cherokee Rose, crystal, #17403 .....20.00
Stem, champagne; Fontaine, Twilight, lav bowl w/clear stem 45.00
Stem, claret; Flanders, pk 135.00
Stem, cocktail; Adam, crystal 17.00
Stem, cocktail; Byzantine, crystal 18.00
Stem, cocktail; Byzantine, yel, #15048 .....25.00
Stem, cocktail; Cadena, pk or yel, 5¼" 25.00
Stem, cocktail; Cordella, crystal 15.00
Stem, cocktail; June Night, crystal, 3½-oz 27.00
Stem, cordial; Cherokee Rose, crystal, 1-oz 50.00
Stem, cordial; Flanders, yel, 5" 75.00
Stem, cordial; Fuchsia, #15083, 1-oz 40.00
Stem, cordial; Mystic, crystal, #17378 .....40.00
Stem, cordial; Persian Pheasant, crystal 65.00
Stem, cordial; Royal Splendor, crystal 55.00
Stem, goblet; Mystic, #17378, crystal 35.00
Stem, goblet; Royal Splendor, crystal 35.00
Stem, goblet; Westchester, #17679, crystal 64.00
Stem, goblet; Williamsburg, #17301, crystal 23.00
Stem, iced tea; Royal Splendor, crystal 35.00
Stem, iced tea; Westchester, crystal, #17679 .....64.00
Stem, juice; Westchester, crystal #17679 .....45.00
Stem, juice; Williamsburg, crystal, #17301 .....23.00
Stem, oyster cocktail; Flanders, yel, 4½" 65.00
Stem, parfait; Cadena, pk or yel, 8-oz, 6⅜" 35.00
Stem, parfait; June Night, crystal, 4½-oz 35.00
Stem, saucer champagne; Fuchsia, crystal, #15083, 5⅜" 18.00
Stem, sherbet; Byzantine, crystal, low 12.00
Stem, sherbet; Cherokee Rose, crystal, #17399, 5½-oz 18.00
Stem, sherbet; Cordella, crystal, 3¾" 12.00
Stem, sherbet; Fuchsia, crystal, #15083, 4⅛" 18.00
Stem, sherbet; Mystic, #17378, crystal 23.00
Stem, sherbet; Royal Splendor, crystal 25.00
Stem, sherbet; Westchester, #17679, crystal 35.00
Stem, sherbet; Williamsburg, #17301, crystal 20.00
Stem, sherbet/champagne; Cherokee Rose, crystal, 5½-oz 20.00
Stem, sherry; June Night, crystal, 2-oz 35.00
Stem, water; Cherokee Rose, crystal, 9-oz 28.00
Stem, water; Classic, crystal, 9-oz, 7¼" 30.00
Stem, water; Fuchsia, crystal, 'S' stem, #17457, 7⅝" 60.00
Stem, wine; Byzantine, crystal 18.00
Stem, wine; Cherokee Rose, crystal, 3½-oz 35.00
Stem, wine; Classic, pk, 3-oz, 4⅞" 47.50
Stem, wine; Fuchsia, crystal, #15083, 5⅛" 30.00
Stem, wine; Mystic, crystal, #17378 .....35.00
Stem, wine; Royal Splendor, crystal 35.00
Stem, wine; Westchester, #17679, crystal 45.00
Stem, wine; Williamsburg, #17301, crystal 23.00
Table bell, Cherokee Rose, crystal 50.00
Table bell, June Night, crystal 50.00
Tray, Fuchsia, crystal, for creamer & sugar bowl 50.00
Tumbler, iced tea; Classic, pk, ftd, 13-oz, 6" 47.50
Tumbler, juice; Cadena, crystal, ftd, 4¼" 17.50
Tumbler, pilsner; Classic, crystal, ftd, 6½-oz 32.50
Tumbler, water; Cherokee Rose, crystal, ftd, 8-oz 22.50
Tumbler, water; Classic, pk, ftd, 8½-oz, 4½" 37.50
Tumbler, water; Flanders, yel, ftd, 10-oz, 4¾" 28.00
Tumbler, water; Fuchsia, crystal, flat, #517, 5⅛" 27.50
Tumbler, water; June Night, crystal, ftd, 8-oz 22.00
Tumbler, whiskey; Classic, crystal, ftd, #185, 2-oz 75.00
Vase, bud; Cherokee Rose, crystal, 10" 40.00
Vase, bud; Cherokee Rose, crystal, 8" 35.00
Vase, bud; Classic, crystal, 10½" 42.50
Vase, bud; Fuchsia, crystal, beaded stem, #15082, 11" 100.00
Vase, bud; June Night, crystal, 10" 40.00
Vase, Cadena, pk or yel, 9" 90.00
Vase, Cherokee Rose, crystal, flared, 12" 125.00
Vase, Coralene Poppy, blk satin, 5½" 75.00
Vase, fan; sapphire bl w/yel, unmk, 9½" 75.00
Vase, Flanders, pk, ftd 225.00
Vase, Fuchsia, crystal, flared, crimped, 8⅞" 35.00
Vase, lily; blk w/gold cattails decor, 1930s, 8¼" 75.00
Vase, lily; Twilight, #85, 13" 275.00
Vase, Sandcarved, crystal, #17430, 11" 150.00
Vase, Sweet Pea, Copen Blue, Sandcarved, #17430 .....150.00

Tiles

The history of tile making dates back to ancient Egypt and Assyria. For centuries tiles have played an important role as a decorative art form, as well as having a utilitarian function. Places such as palace walls, Islamic mosques, Roman floors, and medieval English churches were all adorned with tiles or glazed ceramic surfaces. Remnants of these tile installations can still be seen throughout the world.

The heyday of tile making in England and the United States dates back to circa 1860 through 1930 and envelops the Victorian, Art Nouveau, and Arts & Crafts Movements in both countries. These tiles comprise most of those seen on today's market.

Tiles are being collected today as individual art objects and are increasingly used as decorative accessories. They are also sought in order to restore homes, buildings, and furniture to original period condition. Many people are now incorporating antique and collectible tiles into their home-rebuilding projects for gardens, kitchens, bathrooms, fireplaces, stair risers, and floors.

Tiles must be judged on an individual basis. The condition of the tile face; the quality of the design; the rarity of the artist, company, or series; and the size of the tile or tile panel are just some of the factors to consider when assessing value. People, animals, and scenes are generally more desirable than florals and geometrics. Some glaze colors, such as true pale pink or bright red majolica, add value to Victorian tiles. Tiles may be more difficult to find than many other antiques or collectibles, partly because many were permanently installed. Unfortunately many installations have been destroyed. These factors all have influence on the tile market, and it is not unusual for prices to vary greatly. See also American Encaustic Tiling Co.; Batchelder; Moravian; Grueby; Rookwood; other specific manufacturers. Our advisor for this category is Karen Guido; she is listed in the Directory under Connecticut.

Key:

bkg — background	pr mld — press molded
geo — geometric	srs — series
hrz — horizontal	tbld — tube lined
maj — majolica glaze	tp — transfer printed
plych — polychrome	vrt — vertical

American

AETCO, elephant, cuerda seca brn/gr/cream, 4½" 245.00
AETCO, fox head, olive gr maj pr mld, 6" 295.00
AETCO, man w/hat portrait, dk brn maj pr mld, 6" 235.00
AETCO, rampant lion, bl/ochre pr mld, self-fr, 3" 125.00
Batchelder, peacock, Pasadena, bl engobe incised, 6" 450.00

Batchelder, pomegranate, dk red/brn engobe, 2¾" 80.00
Batchelder, 3 tulips, Pasadena, bl engobe, 6" 275.00
Beaver Falls, girl w/feather in hat, gr maj pr mld stove tile, 3½" ..120.00
Byrdcliff, basket of flowers, HP mc, self-fr, 5¾", G 455.00
Claycraft, flower basket, mc high glaze, self-fr, 8" 300.00
Claycraft, geometric wave, rtcl, mc matt, 6" 200.00
Empire, Dutch man & scene, cuerda seca, mc, 6", VG 550.00
Enfield, urn w/cacti, bl w/gold overglaze, pr mld, 6" 60.00
Franklin, lion in shield, bl/blk pr mld, self-fr, 6" 125.00
Handcraft, floral, unglazed red clay, 4" 40.00
Harris Strong, pr 2-tile vrt panels fr, HP mc house scene, ea 18x6" .350.00
Harris Strong, pr 3-tile hrz panels fr, tbld mc farm scene, ea 24x6" ..495.00
ITT, female portrait, gr maj pr mld, 6" , G 200.00
Kaospar, goemetric Hispano Moresque style, mc pr mld, 6" 150.00
Kensington, floral, brn maj pr mld, 6" 45.00
Low, geometric, bl maj pr mld, 4" 30.00
Low, Hic Haec Hoc & profile, gold maj, sgn Osborne, 6" 370.00
Mosaic, goemetric A & C motif, bl/cream semimatt, 3" 45.00
Mosaic, Hercules & the Waggonner, tp mc, 6" 185.00
Mosaic, rabbit, incised mc, 6" 195.00

Mueller (attributed), twelve-tile scenic frieze, cuerda seca, brown trees, green river, and multicolor sky, 18x24", $1,400.00.

Mueller, stylized geometric, deeply incised bl/yel/wht, 6" 135.00
Providential, pr 3-tile vrt panels, hunters gold maj pr mld, ea 24x6" ..450.00
Providential, woman w/4 angels, lt br maj pr mld, 6" dia 325.00
Solon & Larkin, leaves & geometric, cream/gr/bl pr mld, 4" 35.00
Taylor, man on horse, Santa Monica line, brn/wht tp, 6" 55.00
Trent, celtic knot, brn maj pr mld, 2" 18.00
Trent, male profile, gold-gr maj pr mld, stove tile, 4½" 150.00
Tropico, brn/gr mottled glaze, 3" 25.00
Wheatley, geometric, mc semimatt, 4" 200.00
Woolenius, geometric, cuenca, mc, 6", G 135.00

English

E Smith & Co, woman w/urn & 'Fire,' tp brn on buff, 6" 115.00
English, Red Riding Hood & wolf, tp brn on buff, 6" 200.00
English, sailing ship, tbld mc, 6", G 150.00
Maw, Gothic arches, C Dresser design, tp brn on cream, 6" 125.00
Maw, man at desk, gold/gr maj pr mld, 6", G 195.00
Minton & Co, encaustic geometric, bl/terra cotta/cream, 6" 150.00
Minton Hollins, flowers & vines, mauve maj pr mld, 6", 2 for ..170.00
Mintons Ch Wks, Aesop's Fbl srs Eagle & Tortoise, brn on buff tp, 6" ..135.00
Mintons Ch Wks, Shakespeare srs King Lear, bl/wht tp, 6" 125.00
Mintons Ch Wks, Shakespeare srs Troilus & Cressia, bl/wht tp, 6" ...125.00
Pilkington, Art Nouveau tulip, gr maj, 6" 80.00
Sadler, girl in field, tin glazed red/wht, 5", VG 350.00
Sherwin & Cotton, apple, photographic, caramel glaze, 6", G ..115.00
Wedgwood, Helena, brn/cream tp, 8" 225.00
Wedgwood, maiden w/tambourine, W Crane design, HP mc, 6" ..250.00

Other Countries

Germany, duck in grass, mc maj pr mld, wire fr, 6", VG 70.00
Germany, Dutch boy & girl, tbld mc, 8" 275.00
Holland, Royal Delft, baker baking, mc pr mld, 11½x8" 225.00
Spain, Ramos Rehanos warrier, cuerda seca mc, 10x6" 135.00
Spain, Spanish dancers, 3-tile panel, cuerda seca mc, 18x12" 285.00

Tinware

In the American household of the seventeenth and eighteenth centuries, tinware items could be found in abundance, from food containers to foot warmers and mirror frames. Although the first settlers brought much of their tinware with them from Europe, by 1798 sheets of tin plate were being imported from England for use by the growing number of American tinsmiths. Tinwares were often decorated either by piercing or painted designs which were both freehand and stenciled. (See Toleware.) By the early 1900s, many homes had replaced their old tinware with the more attractive aluminum and graniteware.

In the nineteenth century, tenth wedding anniversaries were traditionally celebrated by gifts of tin. Couples gave big parties, dressed in their wedding clothes, and reaffirmed their vows before their friends and families who arrived bearing (and often wearing) tin gifts, most of which were quite humorous. Anniversary tin items may include hats, cradles, slippers and shoes, rolling pins, etc. See also Primitives and Kitchen Collectibles.

Bathtub, rnd back & armrests, 1800s, 31x39x23" 150.00
Cheese mold, heart-shape, 3 ring ft, rolled rim, hdl, 4x5½" 300.00
Cheese sieve, 3 ring ft, dbl hdls, 4¼x4½" dia 110.00
Coffeepot, pressed spout, cast Gothic arch finial, 11½" 300.00
Colander, heart shape, 4½" 230.00
Downspout, appl cast stars & eagle, Am, dtd 1830, 23x25½" 460.00
Pail, emb bands, wire bail at rounded shoulder, ftd, w/lid, 7" 130.00
Rolling pin, tin cylinder, wood hdls, 16½", dents o/w VG 400.00
Tinder lighter w/candle socket, missing hdl, 3¼" H 175.00
Watering pot, squat/conical, curved spout, ribbon hdl, 3½" 65.00

Tobacciana

Tobacciana is the generally accepted term used to cover a field of collecting that includes smoking pipes, cigar molds, cigarette lighters, humidors — in short, any article having to do with the practice of using tobacco in any form. Perhaps the most valuable variety of pipes is the meerschaum, hand carved from hydrous magnesium, an opaque white-gray or cream-colored mineral of the soapstone family. (Much of this is today mined in Turkey which has the largest meerschaum deposit in the world, though there are other deposits of lesser significance around the globe.) These figural bowls often portray an elaborately carved mythological character, an animal, or a historical scene. Amber is sometimes used for the stem. Other collectible pipes are corn cob (Missouri Meerschaum) and Indian peace pipes of clay or catlinite. (See American Indian Art.)

Chosen because it was the Indians who first introduced the white man to smoking, the cigar store Indian was a symbol used to identify tobacco stores in the nineteenth century. The majority of them were hand carved between 1830 and 1900 and are today recognized as some of the finest examples of early wood sculptures. When found they command very high prices.

For further information on lighters, refer to *Collector's Guide to Cigarette Lighters* by James Flanagan. Ashtray collectors will enjoy *Collector's Guide to Ashtrays* by Nancy Wanvig. See also Advertising; Snuff Boxes.

Art plate, El Gallo Cigars, strutting cock, ornate fr, 20½" 800.00
Ashtray, brass cat figure w/umbrella in center, 3 rests, 4" 21.00
Ashtray, brass tray w/dragonfly in relief, 6 rests, 1880s, 7" dia ...135.00

Ashtray, bronze figural girl seated w/matchbox holder, 4½" 295.00
Ashtray, ceramic pig face in hat smoking pipe, 1880s, 3¾" 75.00
Ashtray, ceramic pipe form, HP, hdl is rest, France, 1911, 5⅜" 35.00
Ashtray, ceramic w/bsk nude reclining, HP flowers on rise, 6¼" .78.00
Ashtray, ceramic w/dancing monkeys on bottom, hollow match holder, 6" ...75.00
Ashtray, china, HP, raised rest, Pickard, mk #5 1905-12, 4½" ...160.00
Ashtray, glass (frosted) head w/streaming hair, chrome base, 7" ...135.00
Ashtray, glass clown seated w/hands as rests, bowl in lap, Murano, 5" 90.00
Ashtray, metal & wood bellhop form w/2 suitcase ashtrays, 7" ..195.00
Ashtray, stacked seashells w/ornate brass cigar cutter, 1 rest, 6" ...95.00
Ashtray, sterling silver, coupe shape, ball ft, Spratling, 2x3½" ...200.00
Cheroot holder, meerschaum, Zouave w/musket, amber stem, 5" .600.00

Cigar boxes: Casino Bell, 1926 tax stamp, VG, $40.00; El Mascotte Tampa, EX, $60.00.

Cigar case, burl walnut w/gilt-metal mts, rectangular, 6" 175.00
Cigar cutter, brass, key-wind mechanism, Erie...1888, 3½x6½x5" ..100.00
Cigar cutter, Above the Average cigar atop world, copper-plated, 8" .1,050.00
Cigar cutter, B-Y's & Buy Y-B's, rvpt front, 5" 450.00
Cigar cutter, Betsy Ross 5¢ Cigar on shield, 8" 900.00
Cigar cutter, Declarencia Havana Cigars, NP CI, 8¾", VG 900.00
Cigar cutter, Dunhill & France Depose, circular, 1940-50s 300.00
Cigar cutter, figure of portly man on stepped base, pot metal/CI, 8" ...1,300.00
Cigar cutter, HA Schneck Cigars... emb on ornate fr, 7½" 1,050.00
Cigar cutter, Havana Cigars... on oval marquee w/portrait, CI, 9" 750.00
Cigar cutter, JJ Astor 5¢ Cigar on rnd clock marquee, ornate, 13½" ...2,400.00
Cigar cutter, Lillian Russell...5¢, cast metal, 8½" L, VG 275.00
Cigar cutter, New York Specials... eng on oval marquee, 7½" ...750.00
Cigar cutter, rvpt w/key-wind mechanism, Kohler, 8¼x6½x4½" 1,600.00
Cigar cutter, stylized parrot shape w/brass wings on 4-ftd base, 11" 350.00
Cigar cutter, Waitt & Bond's Blackstone... emb on marquee, rstr, 5" ..300.00
Cigar cutter/lighter, lamppost w/mailbox & fence, CI/brass, 19½" 375.00
Cigar cutter/match dispenser, Havana High Grade Cigars, pictorial, 6" ..850.00
Cigar cutter/match holder, giraffe figure on tray, brass, 10" 225.00
Cigar cutter/match holder, The Yankee, shield-shaped top, 7" ..700.00
Cigar dispenser, rosewood & gilt brass, early 1900s, 13½x7x5" .150.00
Cigar holder, Bakelite & meerschaum, ca 1920, in orig leather case ..75.00
Cigar jar, faceted glass w/3-D elk on Art Nouveau metal lid, 10" 100.00
Cigar mold, cvd wood, Am, ca 1900, 11⅞x4⅞", VG 75.00
Cigar piercer, Dunhill, 14k gold 150.00
Cigar vendor, CI, wall mt, Automatic Vending Machine Co, 1910, 21" ..1,100.00
Cigarette case, Am sterling silver quadruple foldout, Dreicer 650.00
Cigarette case, Lucite blk w/pearl chips 38.00
Cigarette case, MOP lid w/gold leaves, appl turtle 85.00
Cigarette case, 14k yel gold mesh, fitted int, 100 dwt 880.00
Cigarette dispenser, bird on log, plastic, 1950s-60s 65.00
Cigarette dispenser, camel figural, plastic, 1960s 65.00
Cigarette dispenser, donkey figural, plastic, 1960s 65.00
Cigarette dispenser, donkey figural, tin, 10", NM 195.00
Cigarette holder, 18k gold w/3 rnd dmns/3 sm sapphires, Dunhill ..265.00
Cigarette papers, City Club, NM 33.00
Cigarette papers, Golden Grain, gummed, NM 16.00
Cigarette papers, Queen Quality, NM 108.00
Cigarette papers, Wind Mill, NM 33.00
Figure, bust of woman, bandanna/pipe in hair, 19th C, 16x11" .200.00
Figure, Indian, cvd wood, EX cvg & rpt, 65" 2,600.00
Figure, Scotsman, cvd wood, mc pnt over gesso, 19th C, 38½", EX 3,600.00
Figure, Turk w/pipe, cvd wood w/orig mc pnt, 19th C, 19", VG 2,000.00
Figure, Wm Penn w/cigar box & scroll, papier-mache, 65" 2,850.00
Humidor, ebonized, marble-inlay top, dbl hinged, 5½x14x9" 275.00
Humidor, hunter, terra cotta, mk BB, #8351, 11½" 1,375.00
Humidor, Indian head, porc, Tobacco lettered on head band, 7", NM ..155.00
Humidor, lady smoking, porc, #2532, 10½" 625.00
Humidor, mahog w/brass corners, central plaque, tin lined 150.00
Humidor, man in lav bathrobe & gr nightcap, 8¾" 85.00
Humidor, man smokes/drinks, acanthus leaves, cast lead, 19th C ...175.00
Humidor, Munich Child on barrel, terra cotta, mk JM, #3464, 8", EX ..325.00
Humidor, Scottish man, terra cotta, #939, 5¾" 300.00
Humidor, skull, terra cotta, #3386, 4½" 300.00
Humidor, walnut w/ivory bands/patera inlay, Continental 965.00
Lighter, cigar; bl globe w/spiraled CI legs, 2 wick holders, 11½" ...750.00
Lighter, cigar; brass jester w/cigar (lighter), mc pnt, wall mt 200.00
Lighter, cigar; brass Punch figural, 19th C, 8½", EX 400.00
Lighter, cigar; brass Punch figure, wall mt, 5½" 275.00
Lighter, cigar; brass/copper dome w/center burner, 1890s, 4¾" ..100.00
Lighter, cigar; pot metal man w/cigar (lighter), Woodward, 4¼" 250.00
Lighter, cigar; silver w/cvd jade hdl, Gump, 8½" 330.00
Lighter, cigar; wht globe atop figural bust of Victorian lady, 12" ...650.00
Lighter, cigarette; Dunhill, crocodile covering, 1930s-40s, NM .350.00
Lighter, cigarette; Electro Match, blk w/gold, Korex, Pat Pend, #4234 ...20.00
Lighter, cigarette; Kaschie, etched hunting dogs, US Zone Germany 70.00
Lighter/case combo, Mastercase, Ronson, Deco chrome 20.00
Pipe holder, cvd snake decor, 18th C, 11" L, VG 250.00
Pipe holder, cvd wood w/animals/figures/flowers/etc, 18th C, 7¼" L ..1,600.00
Pipe holder, wood w/brass inlay & appl decor, 18th C, 11½" L .400.00
Snuff mull, horn & pewter, ca 1800, 6x11", VG 475.00
Snuff mull, horn w/brass-mtd horn top, Scotland, 4½", VG 125.00
Snuff mull, horn w/cvd animal head & inlaid eyes, silver mts, 4½" ...650.00
Snuff mull, horn w/silver top, eng thistles, inset crystal, 4½" 650.00
Spittoon, copper w/CI liner, stepped rnd base, 19th C, 7x14" ...225.00
Tamper, silvered copper, Victorian man's bust shape, 2¾" 50.00
Tobacco box, brass, domestic scenes, Dutch, 18th C, 5⅛x3" ..1,100.00
Tobacco box, brass, domestic scenes, English, 17th C, 3½" dia .400.00
Tobacco box, brass, eng Biblical scenes, Dutch, 18th C, 4½x2½" ..300.00
Tobacco box, brass/copper, eng Biblical scenes, Dutch, 18th C, 7x2" ...750.00
Tobacco box, hardwood w/ivory inlay, English, 19th C, 5x2", EX ..525.00
Tobacco pouch, Choice Tobacco/Ogburn, Hill & Co, leather, EX ..40.00
Tobacco tag, Catcher, EX 20.00
Tobacco tag, Hot Stuff, EX 30.00
Tobacco tag, Old Joe, EX 55.00
Tobacco tag, Truthful James, EX 25.00

Pipes

China, man polishing lady's boots, skirt raised, Holland, 19th C, EX ..65.00
Chinese, sea captain form, E Bohne Sohne, 2½" 500.00
Clay, Black man's head, detailed, 19th C, 6½", VG 100.00
Cvd wood, Black man w/cap, mc pnt, glass eyes, 2¾x5½" 225.00
Cvd wood, hunter & hounds w/stag/trees, 19th C, 5½x11", VG ...225.00
Cvd wood, Nubian head w/glass eyes, ivory-colored teeth, 19th C, EX ...300.00
Cvd wood, peasant man's head, stocking hat, 19th C, 5x11" 300.00
Meerschaum, helmeted warrior w/MOP & gold, amber stem, 27", EX ..650.00
Meerschaum, Leda & swan, 5½", in case 110.00
Meerschaum, sailor cvg, EX patina, 1880s, 7½x2¾" 750.00
Meerschaum, seated man w/ax, cottage on bk, wood stem, 4x11", VG ...100.00
Meerschaum, tavern scene relief, wood shaft, ca 1800, 19", VG 400.00

Smoking Sets with Compartments for Cigars or Tobacco, Matches and Spent Matches

Austria porc, vulture tobacco jar w/match holder & tray figurine ...395.00

Bronzed cast metal, Nouveau lady w/3 flower compartments 175.00
German bsk, bathing beauty by pond, 2 compartments, side striker, 9" 595.00
German bsk, girl w/NY Herald paper, lg pipe, HP R-in-Dmn striker, 9" ..595.00
Majolica, Am Indian, 2 compartments & tray striker on front, 7" 425.00
Majolica, Black Americana man w/bales of cigars, 2 compartments, 7" ...595.00
Majolica, monkey on log, 4 compartments (1 ashtray), 7" 595.00

Toby Jugs

The delightful jug known as the Toby dates back to the eighteenth century, when factories in England produced them for export to the American colonies. Named for the character Toby Philpots in the song *The Little Brown Jug*, the Toby was fashioned in the form of a jolly fellow, usually holding a jug of beer and a glass. The earlier examples were made with strict attention to details such as fingernails and teeth. Originally representing only a non-entity, a trend developed to portray well-known individuals such as George II, Napoleon, and Ben Franklin. Among the most-valued Tobies are those produced by Ralph Wood I in the late 1700s. By the mid-1830s Tobies were being made in America. See also Doulton; Occupied Japan.

Man in chair w/keg between ft holds jug of ale, sm chip, sgn RB, 10" ...450.00
Man seated w/jug & pipe, England, 8" 160.00
Man w/pitcher, mc florals/bl spongework, Delft, 1700s, 10" 560.00
Snuff Taker, Allerton, 7" 125.00
Snuff Taker, mc w/gold, sm rpr, early 19th C, 9" 400.00

Toleware

The term 'toleware' originally came from a French term meaning 'sheet iron.' Today it is used to refer to paint-decorated tin items, most popular from 1800 to 1850s. The craft flourished in Pennsylvania, Connecticut, Maine, and New York state. Early toleware has a very distinctive look. The surface is dull and unvarnished; background colors range from black to cream. Geometrics are quite common, but florals and fruits were also favored. Items made after 1850 were often stenciled, and gold trim was sometimes added.

American toleware is usually found in practical, everyday forms — trays, boxes, and coffeepots are most common — while French examples might include candlesticks, wine coolers, jardinieres, etc. Be sure to note color and design when determining date and value, but condition of the paint is the most important worth-assessing factor. In the listings that follow, the dimension given for boxes and trays indicates length. Unless noted otherwise, values are for very good examples with average wear.

Bowl, stylized flowers, red, yellow, blue, and green on brown, shallow, early, 12", $1,000.00.

Bank, conical, trace of brn w/gold stripes, 1800s, 3½" 160.00
Box, deed; floral, mc on blk, incomplete hasp, dome top, 7" 330.00
Box, deed; floral, mc on blk japanning, loose seam, 8¾" 825.00
Box, deed; fruit & floral on blk japanning, dome top, 19th C, 7x9x6" ..500.00
Bucket, Davies Welsh candy in wreath, gold on bl, w/lid, 3½" ..200.00
Cheese rack, floral w/gold on boat form, early 19th C, 13" 225.00
Coffeepot, floral, mc on blk japanning, pnt touchup, 9½" 850.00
Coffeepot, floral, mc on blk japanning, touchup, rprs, 10" 495.00
Coffeepot, floral, red on blk japanning, lighthouse form, 10" 750.00
Creamer, floral, mc on blk japanning, hinged lid, 4" 500.00
Lamp, worn gray w/gold, saucer base w/hdl, brass/copper burner, 6" ..110.00
Lamps, scroll & floral, decoupage battle scenes, 19th C, 33", pr 5,000.00
Sugar bowl, floral, mc on dk japanning, 3¾" 275.00
Tea caddy, fruit, mc on blk w/gold, dome top, 3x6x4" 400.00
Teapot, floral, mc on dk gr, rpr hdl, 8¼" 335.00
Tray, bread; floral, red on blk, sloped ends, 19th C, 13x8" 575.00
Tray, compass star & pinwheels, mc on blk, wear, sm hole in rim, 27" ...220.00
Water cooler, floral, red & gold on bl, 23" 280.00

Tools

Before the Civil War, tools for the most part were handmade. Some were primitive to the point of crudeness, while others reflected the skill of those who took pride in their trade. Increasing demand for quality tools and the dawning of the age of industrialization resulted in tools that were mass produced. Factors important in evaluating antique tools are scarcity, usefulness, and portability. Those with a manufacturer's mark are worth more than unmarked items. When no condition is indicated, the items listed here are assumed to be in excellent condition. Our advisor for this category is Jim Calison; he is listed in the Directory under New York. See also Keen Kutter; Stanley; Winchester.

Adze, carpenter's 75.00
Anvil, slater's roofing 36.00
Awl, cobbler's, thumb screw allows for varied points 18.00
Axe, felling; Kelly, minimum value 95.00
Beck iron, cooper's, to splay & rivet hoops, minimum value 125.00
Broadaxe, goosewing; Pennsylvania, 1700s, minimum value 475.00
Broadaxe, Pennsylvania New Orleans pattern, minimum value ..145.00
Chalk-line reel, mortised well-balanced hickory, freely spins 110.00
Chisel, peeling; 1-pc wrapped top iron, early 1800s, minimum value ..95.00
Divider, measuring/scribing; metal, factory-made 45.00
Hacksaw, iron w/brass collar, wood hdl 68.00
Hammer, bricklayer's, wood hdl, VG 18.00
Hayfork, wood w/long metal prongs, Pennsylvania origin 475.00
Jack, for Conestoga wagon, wrought iron & wood, dtd 1758, weathered ..75.00
Knife, corn cutting 25.00
Knife, field; iron hdl w/wood extension, 21½" L 22.00
Knife, hay; wood hdl, factory-made 35.00
Knife, hoof; imp horse outline, Heller 35.00
Ladle, lead pouring; str-sided cup w/single spout, long hdl 45.00
Mallet, stonecutter's, slash-pegged hdl in burled wood, 1700s, minimum ...95.00
Maul, 1-pc hickory wood w/some bark 15.00
Oilstone, w/walnut box 75.00
Pick, slater's 28.00
Pulley block, cypress w/iron fixtures 42.00
Router, cvd-out hdl 45.00
Ruler, 4-fold, wood w/brass fixtures 50.00
Sander, cabinetmaker's, maple, folds for toolbox storage 35.00
Saw, Buhl; fine-toothed fret, cherry hdl, ornamental lines, sgn 85.00
Scythe, cradle; 4-finger bow, metal blade, w/handhold, minimum ..175.00
Scythe, mowing; minimum value 75.00
Stitcher's horse, hickory wood, used in leather shops/farms, scarce 225.00
Trammel, mechanical drawing tool for scribing ovals, wood/brass, 1890 ...100.00
Witchet, hardwoods w/brass-lined throat, dbl blades, 1840, minimum 225.00

Toothbrush Holders

Most of the collectible toothbrush holders were made in prewar

Japan and were modeled after popular comic strip, Disney, and nursery rhyme characters. Since many were made of bisque and decorated with unfired paint, it's not uncommon to find them in less-than-perfect paint, a factor you must consider when attempting to assess their values. Our advisor for this category is Marilyn Cooper, author of *Pictorial Guide to Toothbrush Holders*; she is listed in the Directory under Texas.

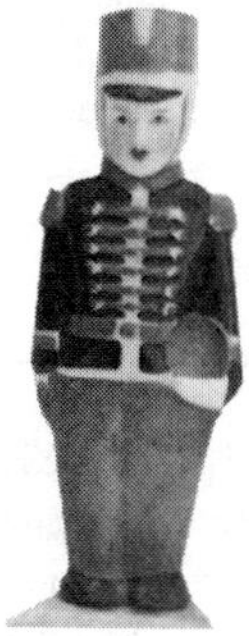

Soldier, one hole, tray at feet, wall mount, 6¾", $80.00. (Photo courtesy Marilyn Cooper)

Bear w/Scarf & Hat, bsk, Japan, 5½", from $85 to **110.00**
Betty Boop w/Toothbrush, KFS, 4¾", from $85 to **100.00**
Big Bird, Taiwan (RCC), 4½", from $85 to **90.00**
Bonzo, Japan, 6", from $80 to **95.00**
Candlestick Maker, Japan (Goldcastle), 5", from $80 to **90.00**
Cat, Japan (Goldcastle), 6", from $70 to **95.00**
Cat on Pedestal, Japan (Diamond T), 6", from $150 to **175.00**
Circus Elephant, Japan, 5", from $85 to **100.00**
Clown Head w/Bug on Nose, Japan, 5", from $160 to **195.00**
Dalmatian, Germany, 4", from $170 to **190.00**
Donald Duck, bsk, WDE, 5", from $250 to **300.00**
Dutch Boy & Girl Kissing, Japan, 6", from $55 to **65.00**
Dwarfs in Front of Fence (Sleepy & Dopey), bsk, WDE/Japan, 3½" ...**1,275.00**
Humpty Dumpty, bsk, Pat Pending, 5½", from $200 to **225.00**
Little Red Riding Hood, Germany (DRGM), 5½", from $200 to ...**250.00**
Mary Poppins, Japan, 6" **200.00**
Mickey Mouse & Pluto, WDE, 4½", from $250 to **325.00**
Old Mother Hubbard, Germany, 6", from $350 to **410.00**
Penguin, Japan, 5½", from $125 to **175.00**
Pinocchio & Figaro, Shafford, 5", from $500 to **525.00**
Snow White, WD, foreign copyright, 6", from $225 to **250.00**
Three Bears w/Bowls, Japan (KIM USUI), 4", from $100 to **150.00**
Three Little Pigs w/Piano, bsk, WDE, 5", from $150 to **175.00**
Traffic Cop, Don't Forget the Teeth, Germany, 5", from $350 to **375.00**
Uncle Willie, Japan/FAS, 5", from $110 to **140.00**

Toothpick Holders

Once common on every table, the toothpick holder was relegated to the china cabinet near the turn of the century. Fortunately, this contributed to their survival. As a result, many are available to collectors today. Because they are small and easily displayed, they are very popular collectibles. They come in a wide range of prices to fit every budget. Many have been reproduced and, unfortunately, are being offered for sale right along with the originals. These 'repros' should be priced in the $10.00 to $30.00 range. Unless you're sure of what you're buying, choose a reputable dealer. In addition to pattern glass, you'll find examples in china, bisque, art glass, and various metals. For further information we recommend *Glass Toothpick Holders, Identification & Values*, by Neila and Tom Bredehoft and Jo and Bob Sanford.

Toothpick holders in the listings that follow are glass unless noted otherwise. Values here are for originals. Our advisor for this category is Judy A. Knauer; she is listed in the Directory under Pennsylvania.

See also specific companies (such as Northwood) and types of glassware (such as Burmese, cranberry, etc.)

Klondyke, frosted with amber stain, 2⅜", $395.00.

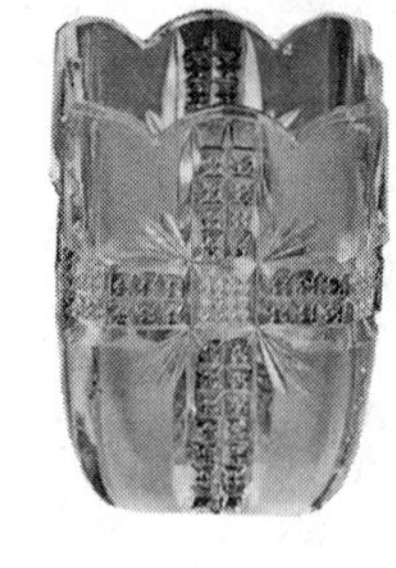

Acorn, pk & wht, w/decor, Challinor, Taylor & Co, 2¼" **135.00**
Alfa/Rexford, John B Higbee, 1908, 2¼" **32.00**
American, Fostoria, 1915, 2¼" (+) **35.00**
Anvil, Daisy & Button, Co-operative Flint Glass, 1880s, 2"(+) ..**35.00**
Arched Ovals/Concave Almond, clear w/gold band, US Glass, 1905, 2⅛" ...**38.00**
Atlanta/Royal Crystal, Tarentum, 1894, 2½" **85.00**
Atlas, Bryce Bros, 1889, 2⅛" **20.00**
Atlas, ruby stain, Bryce Bros, 1889, 2⅛" **85.00**
Banded Flute, Heisey, 1907, 2⅜" **80.00**
Beatty Waffle/Beatty Honeycomb, bl opal, AJ Beatty & Sons, 2⅜" ..**55.00**
Block & Double Bar, Findlay Flint Glass Co, 1889, 2¼" **160.00**
Block & Rosette, Duncan & Miller, 1902, 2⅜" **110.00**
Brilliant, amber stain, Riverside, 1895, 2½" **145.00**
Butterfly, wht opal, Eagle Glass, 1899, 2¾" **48.00**
Button Arches, ruby stain, Jefferson Glass, 1910, 2¼" **25.00**
Cadmus, Beaumont Glass Co, 1902, 2⅜" **48.00**
Carnation, ruby stain, New Martinsville, 1906, 2⅝" **250.00**
Chair, Daisy & Button; amber, Canton Glass Co, 1880s, 4½" **85.00**
Colonial, Cambridge, #2750 ....**28.00**
Colonial Prism, Fostoria, 1918, 2¼" **38.00**
Column Block/Panel & Star, amber, O'Hara, 1888, 3⅛" **150.00**
Cone, bl opaque, Consolidated Lamp & Glass, 1894, 2⅜" **80.00**
Continental, Heisey, 1903, 2⅜" **135.00**
Dew Drop/Hobnail, marine gr, Hobbs, Brockunier & Co, 1885, 2⅜" ..**65.00**
Diana, satin & enamel decor, Fostoria, 1898, 2⅜" **55.00**
Dog's Head, frosted clear, Indiana Tumbler & Goblet Co, 2⅜" (+) ...**350.00**
Doric/Feather, ruby stain, McKee, 1896, 2¾" **250.00**
Fandango, Heisey, 1896, 2½" **90.00**
Flemish, Fostoria, 1913, 2⅛" **42.00**
Florida, ruby & amber stain, Greensburg, 1893, 2¼" **325.00**
Flute, Imperial Glass, 1913, 2½" **35.00**
Forget Me Not, turq opaque, Challinor, Taylor & Co, 1885, 1⅞" ..**85.00**
Georgia Gem, gr opaque, Tarentum, 1900, 2¾" **58.00**
Heart, bl opaque, Dithridge & Co, 1894, 2½" **85.00**
Honeycomb, Doyle's; canary, Doyle & Co, 2¼" **48.00**
Iris w/Meander, bl, Jefferson Glass, 1904, 2½" **135.00**
Jefferson Optic, HP decor, Jefferson Glass, 1910, 2¼" **42.00**
Josephine's Fan, Robinson, 1896, 2½" **45.00**
King Arthur, clear w/gold trim, Duncan & Miller, 1908, 2" **90.00**
Kitten on a Pillow, amber, Richards & Hartley, 1880s, 3½" (+) ..**75.00**
Long Buttress, Fostoria, 1904, 2¼" **32.00**
Oneata/Chimo, clear w/gold, Riverside, 2" (+) **45.00**
Oval Basket, amber, Adams & Co, 1892, 2¾x2¼" **55.00**
Paneled Cane, Heisey, 1901, 2¼" **110.00**
Persian/Crown & Shield, Fostoria, 1897, 2⅝" **65.00**
Pointed Gothic, Indiana Glass, 1920s, 2⅜" **28.00**
Polished Mirrors, clear w/silver o/l, Duncan & Miller, 1907, 2⅜" ..**50.00**
Polka Dot Hat, amber, Geo Duncan & Sons, 2¼" **125.00**
Pride/Beveled Star, amber, Model Flint Glass Co, 1899, 2½" **135.00**

Priscilla, clear w/cut decor, Heisey, 1907, 2¼" 60.00
Punty Band, ivorina verde (custard), Heisey, 1897, 2¼" 75.00
Queen's Necklace, Bellaire Goblet Co, 1890, 4½" 65.00
Regina/Reeding, clear w/gold, Co-operative Flint Glass, 1902, 2½" 52.00
Sovereign, clear w/gold, Fostoria, 1909, 2⅛" 52.00
St Regis/Beveled Windows, US Glass, 1909, 2⅜" 45.00
Star in Square, ruby stain, Duncan & Miller, 1909, 2¼" 225.00
Sunbeam, bl, McKee, 1898, 2½" 75.00
Swirl, sapphire opal, Hobbs, Brockunier & Co, 1889, 2½" 365.00
Tennessee, US Glass, 1900, 2⅝" 45.00
Thumbnail, Duncan & Miller, 1909, 2⅜" 50.00
Truncated Cube, ruby stain, Thompson, 1894, 2⅝" 75.00
Tuxedo, Fostoria, 1908, 3" 48.00
Virginia, Fostoria, 1906, 2⅛" 42.00
Vogue/Scalloped Skirt, bl w/HP decor, Jefferson Glass, 1904, 2½" ...125.00
Widmer, ruby stain, Beaumont Glass Co, ca 1902, 2¾" 140.00
Zipper & Diamonds, Federal Glass Co, 1913, 1¾" 35.00

Torquay Pottery

Torquay is a unique type of pottery made in the South Devon area of England as early as 1867. At the height of productivity, at least a dozen companies flourished there, producing simple folk pottery from the area's natural red clay. The ware was both wheel-turned and molded and decorated under the glaze with heavy slip resulting in low-relief nature subjects or simple scrollwork. Three of the best-known of these potteries were Watcombe (1867 – 1962); Aller Vale (in operation from the mid-1800s, producing domestic ware and architectural products); and Longpark (1890 until 1957). Watcombe and Aller Vale merged in 1901 and operated until 1962 under the name of Royal Aller Vale and Watcombe Art Pottery.

A decline in the popularity of the early classical terra-cotta styles (urns, busts, figures, etc.) lead to the introduction of painted and glazed terra-cotta wares. During the late 1880s, white clay wares, both turned and molded, were decorated with colored glazes (Stapleton ware, grotesque molded figures, ornamental vases, large jardiniers, etc.). By the turn of the century, the market for art pottery was diminishing, so the potteries turned to wares decorated in colored slips (Barbotine, Persian, Scrolls, etc.).

Motto wares were introduced in the late nineteenth century by Aller Vale and taken up in the present century by the other Torquay potteries. This eventually became the 'bread and butter' product of the local industry. This was perhaps the most famous type of ware potted in this area because of the verses, proverbs, and quotations that decorated it. This was achieved by the sgraffito technique — scratching the letters through the slip to expose the red clay underneath. The most popular patterns were Cottage, Black Cockerel, Multi-Cockerel, and a scrollwork design called Scandy. Other popular decorations were Kerswell Daisy, ships, kingfishers, applied bird decorations, Art Deco styles, Egyptian ware, and many others. Aller Vale ware may sometimes be found marked 'H.H. and Company,' a firm who assumed ownership from 1897 to 1901. 'Watcombe Torquay' was an impressed mark used from 1884 to 1927.

Our advisors for this category are Jerry and Gerry Kline; they are listed in the Directory under Ohio. If you're interested in joining a Torquay club, you'll find the address of The North American Torquay Society under Clubs, Newsletters, and Catalogs.

Art Pottery

Biscuit barrel, apple blossoms, porc, SP lid & hdl, 6½" 295.00
Biscuit barrel, cherries on bl, Royal Torquay, 6½x5¾" 230.00
Bottle, scent; Sweet Lavender, Longpark, pine-cone top, 3¼" 97.50
Bottle, scent; Violet, Bathe's Orig, unmk, 3" 65.00
Bottle, scent; 3 dimples on purple, crown top, 1924-40 mk, 3½" ...70.00
Butter dish, apples, 'Duee Ave Zum...,' 7⅜x5¼" 122.00
Candlestick, Kerswell Daisy, Aller Vale, 'I Slept & Dreamed...,' 10" ...210.00
Cat, gr, Aller vale, rpr, 9" 490.00
Chamberstick, Persian Aladdin Lamp, Aller Vale, wht clay 250.00
Creamer & sugar bowl, Scrolls, Aller Vale, 2½", 2½" 97.00
Hot water jug, Sandringham, Aller Vale, 6½" 198.00
Humidor, Tintern Abbey, Longpark, 1904-18 ....230.00
Jardiniere, Scrolls, HM Exeter, 1910, 5½" 250.00
Jug, Aladdin Lamp, Aller Vale, no motto, wht clay, bl flower, mini ...75.00
Jug, Marbleized, Watcombe, 1884-1901, mini, 2¼" 65.00
Jug, Persian, Aller Vale, bl flower, S-shape hdl, 4½" 125.00
Jug, Persian, Aller Vale, wht clay, 4½" 85.00
Jug, Terra Cotta, Aller Vale, wht flower, 2¼" 65.00
Jug, Tintern, Longpark, ruins/water/grasses, 4¾" 95.00
Pitcher, Wadecombe Fair, Royal Torquay, names listed, 3¾" 65.00
Pitcher, Windmill, Aller Vale, motto, 11⅝" 375.00
Plate, Sandringham, Aller Vale, wht clay, bl scrolls, 6½" 75.00
Plate, Terra Cotta, Watcombe, dog w/butterfly, 1900s, 3" 74.00
Serving dish, Jazz pattern, single hdl, 'Enoughs As Good...,' 11¾" ...67.00
Stile, gr, Watcombe, 1884-01, 7¾x4⅞" 150.00
Vase, Dorset Cottage, Lest We Forget, mini, 2¼" 60.00
Vase, Old Rhodian, Aller Vale, no motto, 3¾" 155.00
Watering pot, Honeysuckle, amber bkground 175.00

Devon Motto Ware

Basket, Ribbon & Bows, unmk Exeter, 'Toom Shalls...,' rstr, mini ..70.00
Bottle, scent; Violet, 'Kind Words Are Music...,' crown top, 4½" 115.00
Bowl, Black Cockerel, 'Be Aisy w/That Sugar,' 4¼x5¼" 135.00
Butter dish, Cottage, 'Help Yourself...,' 3½x4¼" dia 70.00
Candlestick, Black Cockerel, Longpark, 'Night Is Long...,' 2½" ..85.00
Candlestick, Scandy, Longpark, 'Last in Bed...,' 1903-14, 2½" 65.00
Chamberstick, Scandy, Aller Vale, 'I Have Slept...,' 4" 175.00
Chamberstick, 2 men in sailboat, 'Great Yarmouth, Last in ...,' 3½" ..65.00
Cheese dish, Scandy, Longpark, no motto, 6½" base 195.00
Cup, Forget Me Not, Aller Vale, 1900s, mini, 1¼" 30.00
Cup & saucer, 'Have Another Cup Full,' 3x3⅜"; 5⅝" 80.00
Cup & saucer, 'The Cup That Cheers,' 2½", 4½" 45.00
Cup & saucer, Cottage, 'Make Hay While...,' 2½", 5¼" 55.00
Cup & saucer, Kerswell Daisy, Aller Vale, 'Jist a Teeny...,' sm 85.00
Egg cup, Black Cockerel, 'Just Laid,' 1¾x1½" 45.00
Egg cup, Cottage, 'Laid To Day,' 3¼x3½" 37.00
Fish, Shamrock, Longpark, 'Chosen Leaf of Bard & Chief,' 6" L .75.00
Inkwell, Shamrock, Aller Vale, 'Chosen Leaf of Bard & Chief,' 3" ...85.00
Jardiniere, Passion Flower, HM Exeter, 'For Every Ill...,' 6¼" 310.00
Jug, Half Scandy, Royal Watcombe, 'Thumbs Ups,' mini, 2" 55.00
Jug, Kerswell Daisy, Aller Vale, 'Take a Little Cream,' mini, 2½" 87.00
Jug, Multi-Cockerel, Aller Vale, 'Be Canny Wi'...,' mini, 2½" 85.00
Jug, Multi-Cockerel, Aller Vale, 'Stracht Fre the Coo...,' 2½" 85.00
Jug, Multi-Cockerel, Aller Vale, 'Wa'al Us Be Main...,' mini, 2½" ...125.00
Jug, puzzle-liquor; Scandy, Aller Vale, 'Come Fill Me...,' 1900s, 6" ...240.00
Jug, Scandy, Aller Vale, 'Be Canny Wi'...,' mini, 2½" 75.00
Jug, Scandy, Aller Vale, 'Ca' Yer Ain Girr Neer...,' 1900s, 4¼" ...75.00
Jug, Scandy, Aller Vale, 'Demsher Craim Yak...,' mini, 2½" 60.00
Match holder/striker, Scandy, 'I'll Help Console Ye,' 2¾" 90.00
Mustard, Cottage, 'Few Words Are Best,' 2½", w/spoon 65.00
Mustard pot, 'Soft Words Win Hard Hearts,' 3" 60.00
Pin dish, Scandy, Longpark, 'Dawntee Vall Be Vore...,' 3¼" 42.50
Pin dish, Scandy, unmk Longpark, 'If You Can't Fly...,' 3¼", EX .40.00
Pinch pot, Double Sandy, Aller Vale, no motto, mini, 2" 75.00
Pitcher, 'Help Yourself Don't Be Shy,' 5¼" 110.00
Pitcher, 'If You Can't Be Aisy...,' 5x4" 110.00
Pitcher, Cottage, 'Help Yoursel...,' 5¼x4½" 110.00
Pitcher, Cottage, 'If You Can't Be Aisy...,' 5x4" 110.00
Plate, Cockerel, Aller Vale, 'Tiz an Ill Wind...,' 6½" 150.00

Plate, Double Scandy, unmk, 'Gude Folks...,' 4¼" 65.00
Plate, Longpark, 'Always Help a Lame Dog...,' 3¾" 75.00
Plate, Longpark, 'Dawnt'ee Vall Be Vore...,' 3¾" 75.00
Plate, Scandy, Longpark, 'Reeky House & Grinnin' Wife,' 6" 80.00
Plate, Scandy, unmk, 'Rolling Stone Gathers...,' 4" 50.00
Plate, Shamrock, Longpark, 'Chosen Leaf of Bard & Chief,' 8" .120.00
Plate, Ship, Royal Watcombe, 'A Thing of Beauty...,' mini, 4½" .70.00
Salt tub, Scandy, Aller Vale, 'Tak a Little Saut,' hdls, 1¼" 67.50
Sugar bowl, Black Cockerel, 'Be Aisy w/the...,' 4¼x5¼" 85.00
Sugar bowl, Black Cockerel, 'Be Asy w/tha Sugar,' 3¼" W 55.00
Sugar bowl, Forget Me Not, Aller Vale, no motto, mini, 1½" 55.00
Teapot, Cottage, 'Du-ee Drink a Cup a Tay,' 3¾x4½" 110.00
Tile, Cottage, 'Except the Kettle Boiling...,' 5½" dia 75.00
Vase, Crocus, 'Gather the Roses...,' 3¾x3" 70.00
Vase, Scandy, Aller Vale, 'Have Courage Boys...,' 10⅛" 450.00

Toys

Toys can be classified into at least two categories: early collectible toys with an established history, and the newer toys. The antique toys are easier to evaluate. A great deal of research has been done on them, and much data is available. The newer toys are just beginning to be studied; relative information is only now being published, and the lack of production records makes it difficult to know how many may be available. Often warehouse finds of these newer toys can change the market. This has happened with battery-operated toys and to some extent with robots. Review past issues of this guide. You will see the changing trends for the newer toys. All toys become more important as collectibles when a fixed period of manufacture is known. When we know the numbers produced and documentation of the makers is established, the prices become more predictable.

The best way to learn about toys is to attend toy shows and auctions. This will give you the opportunity to compare prices and condition. The more collectors and dealers you meet, the more you will learn. There is no substitute for holding a toy in your hand and seeing for yourself what they are. If you are going to be a serious collector, buy all the books you can find. Read every article you see. Knowledge is vital to building a good collection. Study all books that are available. These are some of the most helpful: *Collecting Toys*, *Collecting Toy Soldiers*, and *Collecting Toy Trains, An Identification & Value Guide #3*, by Richard O'Brien; and *Toys of the Sixties, A Pictorial Guide*, by Bill Bruegman. Other informative books (published by Collector Books) are *Schroeder's Collectible Toys, Antique to Modern*, by Sharon and Bob Huxford; *Collector's Guide to Tinker Toys* by Craig Strange; *Classic Plastic Model Kits* by Rick Polizzi; *The Golden Age of Automotive Toys, 1925–1941*, by Ken Hutchinson and Greg Johnson; *Motorcycle Toys, Antique & Contemporary*, by Sally Gibson-Downs and Christine Gentry; *Collector's Encyclopedia of Disneyana* by David Longest and Michael Stern; *Stern's Guide to Disney Collectibles, Vol I–3*, by Michael Stern; *Modern Toys, American Toys, 1830–1980*, by Linda Baker; *Antique and Collectible Toys, 1970–1950*, *Toys, Antique & Collectible*, and *Cartoon Toys & Collectibles* all by David Longest; *Collectible Male Action Figures* by Paris and Susan Manos; *Collector's Guide to Bubble Bath Containers* by Greg Moore and Joe Pizzo; *G-Men and FBI Toys and Collectibles* by Harry and Jody Whitworth; *Breyer Animal Collector's Guide* by Felicia Browell; *Collector's Guide to Battery Toys, Identification & Values*, by Don Hultzman; *Collector's Guide to TV Memorabilia, 1960s & 1970s, Second Edition*, by Greg Davis and Bill Morgan; and *Matchbox Toys, 1948–1993*, *Matchbox Toys, 1974–1996, Second Edition*, and *Diecast Toys and Scale Models*, all by Dana Johnson.

In the listings that follow, toys are listed by manufacturer's name if possible, otherwise by type. Measurements are given when appropriate and available; if only one dimension is noted, it is the greater one — height if the toy is vertical, length if it is horizontal. See also Children's Things; Personalities. For toy stoves, see Stoves.

Key:
b/o — battery operated
cl — celluloid
jtd — jointed
NP — nickel plated
w/up — wind-up

Toys by Various Manufacturers

Alps, Batman Batmobile, friction, litho tin, 1966, 8", EX 900.00
Alps, Bozo the Clown, w/up, litho tin, 8½", NMIB 1,000.00
Alps, Chippy the Chipmunk, b/o, 1950s, MIB 225.00
Alps, Clown Magician, b/o, tin/vinyl/cloth clothes, 1950s, 12", MIB ..475.00
Alps, French Cat, b/o, 1950s, 10", EX 100.00
Arcade, Steamboat, CI, gold w/red detail, 7½", EX 285.00
Arcade, 1929 Caterpiller Tractor, CI, 6½", VG 700.00
Arcade, 1941 Ford Pumper Truck, CI, w/6 figures, 13", VG 450.00
Aurora AFX, '55 Chevy Bel Air #1913, yel, VG 16.00
Aurora AFX, Corvette #7, 1927, red, wht & bl, VG+ 20.00
Aurora AFX, Dodge Fever Dragster, wht & yel, EX 15.00
Aurora Cigarbox, Ford J Car, diecast, yel, MIB 35.00
Aurora G-Plus, Amrac Can Am, yel & blk stripe, EX 15.00
Aurora G-Plus, Lotus F1 #1783, blk & gold, EX 20.00
Aurora Thunderjet, Cougar #1389, wht, EX 40.00
Aurora Thunderjet, Ferrari GTO Flamethrower #1493, lt bl & wht, EX ..30.00
Automatic Toy, Capt Marvel Car, w/up, litho tin, 1947, 4", NM ...250.00
Automatic Toy, Magic Crossroads, w/up, litho tin, 19" base, MIB ..265.00
Bandai, Comic Road Roller, b/o, 1960s, 9", EX 150.00
Bandai, Flipper the Spouting Dolphin, b/o, MIB 125.00
Bandai, Old Fashioned Police Car, friction, litho tin, 7", EXIB .200.00
Bandai, Oldsmobile Toronado, b/o, red w/blk tires, 11", NM 200.00
Bandai, Pete the Indian, b/o, MIB 175.00
Bandai, Rolls Royce Silver Cloud, friction, bl/wht/chrome, 12", NMIB ...350.00
Bing, Battleship, clockwork, pnt tin, 2-tone gray, 12", EX 1,000.00
Bing, Ocean Liner, clockwork, pnt tin, 12½", EX 1,000.00
Bliss, Battleship Maine, paper litho on wood, rare, EX 1,600.00
Borgfeldt, Donald Duck Waddler, w/up, celluloid, 5½", NMIB ...2,400.00
Breyer, Indian Pony, buckskin, 1970-72 ....250.00
Breyer, Lying Foal, blk blanket appaloosa, 1969-84 ....30.00
Breyer, Morgan, woodgrain, 1963-85 ....750.00
Breyer, Silky Sullivan, matt brn, 1975-90 ....25.00
Buddy L, Ford Model T #210B, EX 500.00
Buddy L, Hook & Ladder Truck #205, EX, from, $1,400 to 1,500.00
Buddy L, Pile Driver #260, 23", EX 2,500.00
Buddy L, Pumper Truck #29, rider, rstr, 26" 1,200.00
Buddy L, Steam Shovel #220, 24", VG 275.00
Chein, Aquaplane, 1939, 8½", EXIB 500.00

Chein, Barnacle Bill, tin windup walker, 1930s, 6½", NM, $400.00. (Photo courtesy Dunbar Gallery)

Chein, Fancy Groceries Truck, 6", EX 350.00

Chein, Happy Hooligan, 1932, 6", NM, from $1,400 to **1,500.00**
Chemtoy, Superman Movie Viewer, 1965, MOC **50.00**
Corgi, Air Canada Concorde, #653, MIB **325.00**
Corgi, Austin A-40, w/motor, #216m, MIB **300.00**
Corgi, Beast Carrier, #58, MIB **40.00**
Corgi, Ford Consul, dual colors, #200, MIB **200.00**
Corgi, Mini-Cooper Rally, #227, MIB **275.00**
Corgi, Rambler Marlin, #263, MIB **75.00**
Corgi, Simca Sports Car, #315, MIB **65.00**
Cragstan, Nautilus Periscope, b/o, MIB **225.00**
Cragstan, Shuttling Freight Train, b/o, litho tin, 1950, MIB **225.00**
Daiya, Smoking Bulldozer, b/o, 1960s, 9½", EX **225.00**
Dakin, Baby Puss, Hanna-Barbera, 1971, EX+ **100.00**
Dakin, Deputy Dawg, Terrytoons, 1977, EX **50.00**
Dakin, Foghorn Leghorn, Warner Bros, 1970, EX+ **75.00**
Dakin, Goofy, Disney, cloth clothes, EX **20.00**
Dakin, Hokey Wolf, Hanna-Barbera, 1971, EX **100.00**
Dakin, Kernal Renk, American Seeds, 1970, rare, EX+ **300.00**
Dakin, Scooby Doo, Hanna-Barbera, 1980, EX **75.00**
Dayton, Hillclimber Roadster, pressed steel, friction, 12", VG+ ...**330.00**
Dent, American Oil Co Truck, CI w/NP wheels, w/driver, 10½", EX ..**2,300.00**
Dinky, Austin Taxi #254, yel, MIB **120.00**
Dinky, DeSoto Fireflite #192, MIB **165.00**
Dinky, DH Comet Jet #999, MIB **225.00**
Dinky, Esso Petro Tanker #442, MIB **175.00**
Dinky, Ford Thunderbird #555, MIB **200.00**
Dinky, Maserati 2000 #505, MIB **135.00**
Dinky, Military Gift Set #699, MIB **400.00**
Distler, Clowns on Seewsaw, w/up, litho tin, 10½" L, VG+ **500.00**
Fisher-Price, Bunny Cart, #10, 1940, EX **75.00**
Fisher-Price, Cartoon Viewer, 1986, M **15.00**
Fisher-Price, Donald & Donna Duck, #160, 1937, EX **700.00**
Fisher-Price, Jingle Giraffe, #472, 1956, EX **225.00**
Fisher-Price, Running Bunny Cart, #312, 1960-64, EX **45.00**
Fisher-Price, Tuggy Turtle, #139, 1959, EX **100.00**
Gilbert, Mysto Magic Exhibition Set, 1920s, EXIB **450.00**
Gunthermann, Lady Chasing Mouse, w/up, pnt tin, 7½", EX ...**1,100.00**
Gunthermann, Monoplane, w/up, litho tin, 7½" W, EX **250.00**
Gunthermann, Vis-A-Vis, w/up, litho tin/rubber tires, 6½", NM ...**3,200.00**
Hartland Plastics, Alkine Ike, NM **150.00**
Hartland Plastics, Bullet, w/tag, NM **100.00**
Hartland Plastics, Cochise, NM **150.00**
Hartland Plastics, General Custer, NMIB **250.00**
Hartland Plastics, Jim Bowie, w/tag, NM **250.00**
Hubley, Bremen Airplane, CI, gr, 6½", VG **525.00**
Hubley, Royal Circus Cage Wagon, CI, driver/bear/2 horses, 16", EX ...**1,200.00**
Hubley, Static Speedboat w/Johnson Seahorse Motor, CI, 9½", EX **4,500.00**
Ideal, Clancy the Great, b/o, 1960s, MIB **375.00**
Ideal, Old West Playset, EXIB, from $50 to **75.00**
Ives, Woman Churning Butter, w/up, wood/tin/cloth clothes, 9", NM **4,500.00**
Kenner, Easy-Show Movie Projector, Marvel Super Heroes, 1966, MIB **175.00**
Kenton, Car Carrier, CI w/wht rubber tires, 3 roadsters, 18", EX **2,400.00**
Kenton, Overland Circus Band Wagon, w/7 figures & 2 horses, 15", EX ...**800.00**
Keystone, Airmail Plane #NX-265, pressed steel, 23", VG **550.00**
Keystone, Fire Truck, pressed steel, 4 ladders, crank-op, 25", EX **550.00**
Keystone, Railroad Wrecking Car #6600, pressed steel, 20", EX ..**475.00**
Keystone, Rapid-Fire Tri-Motor Plane, pressed steel, 24", EX .**1,700.00**
Keystone, Truck Loader #44, pressed steel, 18", EX **650.00**
Kingsbury, Bluebird Racer #335, pressed steel, 19", G+ **990.00**
Kingsbury, Fire Pumper, pressed steel, w/up, 10", EX **275.00**
Kingsbury, Golden Arrow #337, pressed steel, 21", VG+ **715.00**
Kingsbury, Monocoupe, pnt pressed steel, clockwork, 10" W, VG **150.00**
Kingsbury, Sedan w/Boat & Trailer, pressed steel, clockwork, 22", EX ..**1,400.00**
Lehmann, AHA Delivery Van, litho tin, 8", EX **700.00**
Lehmann, Anxious Bride, pnt & litho tin, 4½", VG+ **500.00**
Lehmann, Performing Sea Lion, litho tin, 7", VG **200.00**
Lehmann, UHU Amphibious Car, litho tin, 9", EX **650.00**
Lehmann, Wild West Bucking Bronco, litho tin, 7", NMIB ...**1,600.00**
Lido, Hanna-Barbera Television Viewer, 1960, VG **55.00**
Lindstrom, Mammy Dancing, w/up, litho tin, 7½", VG **250.00**
Lindstrom, Mammy Sweeping, w/up, litho tin, 8", NM (EX box) ..**500.00**
Linemar, Circus Truck, friction, litho tin, 5½", EXIB **175.00**
Linemar, College Jalopy, remote control, litho tin, 9½", EXIB ..**450.00**
Linemar, Dick Tracy Police Car, remote control, litho tin, 8", EXIB ...**475.00**
Linemar, Disney Acrobats (Mickey/Donald/Pluto), b/o, 10", NMIB, ea ...**400.00**
Linemar, Disney Airplane, friction, litho tin, 1950s, 8" W, EXIB **1,600.00**
Linemar, Hopping Astro, w/up, litho tin, 4", EXIB **3,300.00**
Linemar, Tin Lizzy w/Driver, friction, tin/celluloid, 5", NMIB ...**500.00**
Linemar, Vacationer 22 Cabin Cruiser, b/o, litho tin, 1950s, 12", EX ..**275.00**
Lionel, Santa Car, w/up, compo, 1935, 11", NM (EX box) **3,400.00**
Marklin, Railcar Plane, pnt tin, 8", VG **60.00**
Marusan, Lucky Baby Machine, w/up, tin/celluloid, 1950s, 6", NMIB ...**575.00**
Marx, Aircraft Carrier, b/o, 20", EX **250.00**
Marx, Battleground Playset #4749, 1958, EXIB **250.00**
Marx, BO Plenty, w/up, litho tin, 8", NMIB **385.00**
Marx, Colonel Hap Hazard, b/o, 1968, 11", EX **700.00**
Marx, George Jetson, w/up, litho tin, 4", NM **300.00**
Marx, History of the Pacific Playset #4164, 1972, MIB **350.00**
Marx, Honeymoon Express, w/up, litho tin, 1940, EXIB **200.00**
Marx, Lazy Day Farms Stake Truck, pressed steel w/tin bed, 18", NMIB ...**400.00**
Marx, Lizzy of the Valley Jalopy, w/up, litho tin, 7", EX **300.00**
Marx, Marx-A-Serve Table Tennis, b/o, rare, MIB **200.00**
Marx, Motor Market Grocery Truck, pressed steel, 14", NMIB .**500.00**
Marx, Pathe Camera, w/tripod, 1930s, 6", EX **500.00**
Marx, Roadside Rest Service Station, litho tin, 10x14" base, EX ..**800.00**
Marx, Top Cat Viewer, plastic, 1962, EXIB **100.00**
Matchbox, Federal Express Lear Jet, #SB-01A, 1973, MIB **10.00**
Matchbox, Long Distance Coach, #21-A, 1-75 series, reg, 1956, M ...**60.00**
Matchbox, Massey Harris Tractor, #4-B, 1-75 series, 1957, M **80.00**
Matchbox, Peterbilt Refrigerator Truck, #K-31B, 1978, M (NM box) ..**31.00**
Matchbox, Y-02B, 1911 Renault 2-Seater, type-2 radiator, 1963, MIB .**15.00**
Mattel, Dareplane Wingwalker Stunt Set, 1978, MIB (sealed) ..**175.00**
Mattel, Godzilla, b/o, plastic, 1977, 19", NMIB **250.00**
Mattel, Twirl-A-Tune, litho tin w/wood hdl, 1951, 8", EX **45.00**
Mattel Hot Wheels, Alive '55, 1973, red line, plum, EX+ **120.00**
Mattel Hot Wheels, Live Wire Sizzler, 1971, chrome, M **35.00**
Mattel Hot Wheels, Prowler, 1978, blk walls, Super Chrome, NM **16.00**
Mattel Hot Wheels, Road Hog Rumbler, 1971, NM **20.00**
Mattel Hot Wheels, Rock Buster, 1977, blk walls, Super Chrome, NM ..**20.00**
Mattel Hot Wheels, S'Cool Bus, 1971, red line, yel, NM **120.00**
Mego, Wizard of Oz Munchkinland, 1976, MIB **450.00**
Metalcraft, Sand & Gravel Truck, pressed steel, 10½", VG **225.00**
Metalcraft, Shell Motor Oil Stake Truck, pressed steel, 12", EX ...**1,100.00**
MT, Make-Up Bear, b/o, tin/plush, 9", NM, minimum value .**1,000.00**
Nifty, Jiggs Jazz Car, w/up, litho tin, 1920s, NM **2,400.00**
Nifty, Mickey Mouse Jazz Drummer, plunger activated, tin, 7", VG ..**2,300.00**
Nifty, Rudy the Ostrich, w/up, litho tin, 1924, 8½", EX **575.00**
Ohio Art, Merry-Go-Round Music Box, crank-op, litho tin, 6", NMIB ...**185.00**
Ohio Art, Toyland Band, tin drum set, 1950s, 8", EXIB **55.00**
Orkin, Speedboat, w/up, pnt steel, compass/driver/hatch, 27", G+ ..**500.00**
Remco, Firebird Dashmobile, b/o, litho tin, 1960s, 13", EX **225.00**
Remco, Flintstone Yacht, b/o, mostly plastic, 17", EX **200.00**
Remco, Voyage to the Bottom of the Sea Seaview Sub Set, MIB ...**1,500.00**
Rich Toys, Davy Crockett Rocking Horse, 1950s, pressed wood, 24", EX **250.00**
Schuco, BMW 535 Doctor's Car, 1976, M **25.00**
Schuco, Motodrill, w/up, litho tin/cloth clothes, 5", NMIB ...**2,600.00**
Schuco, Mouse in Open Roadster, w/up, litho tin, 6", EX **250.00**
Schuco, Santa Claus, w/up, litho tin/felt suit/fur beard, 5", NM ..**1,000.00**

Schuco, Volkswagen Micro Racer, w/up, litho tin, 4", MIB 200.00
Smith-Miller, Mack Custom Union 76 Tanker Truck, pressed steel, NM ..600.00
Smith-Miller, Silver Steak Trailer, pressed steel, EX 450.00
Smith-Miller, West Coast Fast Freight, pressed steel, EX 1,000.00
Strauss, Air Devil, w/up, litho tin, 8½", EX, from $500 to 600.00
Strauss, Chicago Zeplin, w/up, litho tin, 9", G 275.00
Strauss, Jazzbo Jim, w/up, litho tin, 10", EXIB, from $700 to 800.00
Structo, Army Ambulance #416, pressed steel, 17", EX 275.00
Structo, Cement Mixer, pressed steel, 1950s, 20", EX 175.00
Structo, Truck Fleet Set #725, pressed steel, NMIB 600.00
Sturditoy, Ambulance, pressed steel, open cab/closed van, 27", NM ...12,000.00
Sturditoy, Dairy Truck, pressed steel, 2-pc, rstr, 34" 4,000.00
Sturditoy, Fire Water Tower Truck, pressed steel, 11", VG 1,020.00
Sturditoy, Oil Truck, pressed steel, rstr, 26" 1,800.00
TN, Buzzy Bee, w/up, litho tin/plush, MIB 150.00
TN, Cragstan Biplane, b/o, litho tin w/plastic prop, 11½", NMIB ..600.00
TN, Dog Sled, b/o, litho tin, 1950s, 14", NM 600.00
TN, Firebug, b/o, litho tin, 1950s, 9", MIB 150.00
TN, Little Indian, b/o, litho tin, 1960s, 9", EX 165.00
TN, TWA Passenger Jet, b/o, litho tin/plastic, 14" W, NM 100.00
TN, US Air Force/Navy Helicopter, friction, litho tin, 10" L, NMIB .175.00
TN, 1958 Ford Skyliner, b/o, red/chrome, retractable roof, NMIB 300.00
Tonka, Allied Van Lines Truck #1089, 1962, 16", NMIB 150.00
Tonka, Army Tractor #250, 1964, EX 75.00
Tonka, Dump Truck #180, 1949-53, NM 275.00
Tonka, State Highway Dept Dump Truck, 1956, NM 275.00
Tonka, Thunderbird Express Semi #37, 1960, MIB 600.00
Tootsietoy, Aero-Dawn #4660, 1934, red, NM 70.00
Tootsietoy, Biplane #4650, 1926, NM 115.00
Tootsietoy, Chevy Coupe #231, 1940-41, med aqua, NM 40.00
Tootsietoy, Greyhound Bus #1045, 1942-46, bl & silver, NM 55.00
Tootsietoy, Insurance Patrol Car #104, 1932-34, red, NM 35.00
Tootsietoy, Motors Set #7200, 9-pc, MIB 900.00
Tootsietoy, Police Van #1299, 1976-79, NM 10.00
Tootsietoy, Station Wagon #239, 1940-41, gr & cream, NM 45.00
Tootsietoy, US Army Plane #119, 1936, NM 75.00
TPS, Cleo Clown, w/up, litho tin, 5", NM (EX box) 275.00
TPS, Dune Buggy, b/o, plastic, 1960s, 11", EX 100.00
TPS, Monkey Basketball Player, w/up, litho tin, 7½", NMIB 475.00
TT, Jaguar E-Type, friction, red w/chrome detail, 11", NMIB 475.00
Tyco, A-Team Van, diecast, blk w/red stripe, EX 40.00
Tyco, Firebird #6914, diecast, cream & red, VG 12.00
Tyco, Hardee's Ford Car #28, diecast, red & wht, G 12.00
Tyco, Indy Pennzoil Car, diecast, yel, EX 15.00
Unique Art, Hee-Haw the Balky Mule, w/up, tin, 1930, 10", NMIB 500.00
Unique Art, Hott & Tott, 2 Black minstrels, w/up, litho tin, 8", EXIB ..1,400.00
Unique Art, Lincoln Tunnel, w/up, litho tin, 24", MIB 600.00
Unique Art, Sky Rangers Tower, w/up, litho tin, 9", EX 800.00
Wolverine, Action Ski Jumper, w/up, litho tin, 26" ramp, MIB .300.00
Wolverine, Dandy Andy Rooster, w/up, litho tin, 10", NMIB ...850.00
Wolverine, Luxury Liner, w/up, litho tin, 14", EXIB 200.00
Wolverine, Over & Under Race Car, w/up, litho tin, 2½" car, EXIB ...300.00
Wyandotte, Acrobatic Monkeys, w/up, litho tin, 10" base, NM (VG box) ...600.00
Wyandotte, Hoky & Poky, w/up, litho tin, 6", NM (EX box) 400.00
Wyandotte, SS America Boat, w/up, litho tin, 12", EX 150.00
Y, Happy 'N Sad Magic Face Clown, b/o, 1960s, 10", MIB 300.00
Y, Playful Pup in Shoe, b/o, 1960s, 10", EX 100.00

Farm Toys

Bale processor, Massey-Ferguson, Ertl, #1093, 1/64th scale, MIB ...3.00
Bale throw wagon, John Deere, Ertl, #5755, 1/64th scale, MIB 4.00
Barge wagon, Duetz Allis, Ertl, #2241, 1/64th scale, MIB 3.00
Combine, Agco R-52, Ertl, #1282, 1/64th scale, MIB 10.00
Combine, John Deere 12-A, Ertl, #5601, 1/16th scale, MIB 45.00

Combine, Oliver, SLIK 1952, painted metal, 5¼x12", $200.00.

Corn harvester, Arcade #702, CI, rubber tires, 5½", MIB 950.00
Fertilizer spreader, John Deere, Ertl, #5558, 1/64th scale, MIB 3.00
Forge harvester, New Holland, Ertl, #372, 1/64th scale, MIB 4.00
Four-row planter, John Deere 494-A, Ertl, #5838, 1/16th scale, MIB ...125.00
Grain cart, Brent Dual-Wheel, Ertl, red or gr, 1/64th scale, MIB, ea 20.00
Gravity wagon, John Deere, Ertl, #5552, 1/64th scale, MIB 3.00
Hay rake, Case IH, #210, 1/64th scale, MIB 3.00
Mixer mill, Case IH, #480, 1/64th scale, MIB 3.00
Mower conditioner, John Deere, Ertl, #5657, 1/64th scale, MIB 3.00
Planter, Case IH, #478, 1/64th scale, MIB 3.00
Rotary cutter, John Deere, Ertl, #5600, 1/64th scale, MIB 4.00
Skid loader, John Deere, Ertl, #5536, 1/64th scale, MIB 5.00
Thresher, McCormick-Deering, Arcade, CI, 10", MIB 2,500.00
Tractor, Allis Chalmers, Ertl, 1/16th scale, MIB 30.00
Tractor, Case, Vindex, EX 2,450.00
Tractor, Farmall Model A, Arcade, CI, 7½", MIB 2,500.00
Tractor, Farmall 140, Ertl, 1/16th scale, MIB 35.00
Tractor, Ford F, Ertl Collector's Edition, #872, 1/16th scale, MIB ..45.00
Tractor, Oliver 1555 Diesel, Ertl, #2223, 1/16th scale, MIB 22.00
Truck, Caterpiller 32 Ford Panel, Ertl, #7707, 1/43rd scale, MIB ...6.00
Wagon, Tru Scale, red-pnt tin, 7½", EX 20.00

Guns: Cast-Iron Cap Guns (Caution: Some reproductions exist.)

In years past, virtually every child played with toy guns, and the survival rate of these toys is minimal, at best. The interest in these charming toy guns has recently increased considerably, especially those with western character examples, as collectors discover their scarcity, quality, and value. Toy gun collectibles encompass the early and the very ornate figural toy guns and bombs through the more realistic ones with recognizable character names, gleaming finishes, faux jewels, dummy bullets, engraving and colorful grips. This section will cover some of the most popular cast-iron and diecast toy guns from the past one hundred years. Recent market trends have witnessed a decline of interest in the earlier (1900 – 40) single-shot cast-iron pistols. The higher collector interest is for known western characters and cap pistols from the 1960 – 65 era. Generic toy guns such as, Deputy, Pony Boy, Marshal, Ranger, Sheriff, Pirate, Cowboy, Dick, Western, Army, etc., generate only minimal collector interest.

Our advisor is James Schleyer, internationally recognized collector and appraiser of toy guns. He has authored numerous books, articles, and newsletters on antique toy guns and holsters. He is the former editor for *Toy Gun Purveyors*, an international newsletter that fostered the collecting of these valuable and rare toys. His current book, *Backyard Buckaroos — Collecting Western Toy Guns*, contains nearly 2,500 photographs. Toy gun inquiries that include a SASE will be gracious answered. Send to: Jim Schleyer, Box 243-M, Burke, VA 22015.

In the listings below (*) designates a classic example.

American, cylinder revolves, Kilgore, 1940, 9⅜", EX (*) 550.00
Army 45 Auto, Hubley, 1945, 6½", M (*) 150.00

Atta Boy, single shot, Hubley, 1935, 4", Fair 35.00
Bango, eng, jewels, Stevens, 1940, 7½", VG 90.00
Big Bill, single shot, Kilgore, 1935, 4⅞", M 35.00
Big Horn, cylinder revolves, Kilgore, 1940, 8⅝", M (*) 600.00
Big Scout, single shot, Stevens, 1930, 9⅜", Fair 100.00
Billy the Kid, single shot, Stevens, 1950s, 6¾", Fair 100.00
Border Patrol, automatic, Kilgore, 1935, 4½", VG 65.00
Buc-A-Roo, single shot, Kilgore, 1940, 7¾", M 100.00
Buffalo Bill, single shot, Kenton, 1930, 13½", rare, VG 550.00
Buffalo Bill, single shot, Stevens, 1890, 11¾", rare, Fair 225.00
Bull's Eye, eng, Kenton, 1940, 6½", M 250.00
Bulldog, single shot, Hubley, 1935, 6", G 35.00
Bunker Hill, single shot, National, 1925, 5¼", M 90.00
Captain, automatic, Kilgore, 1940, 4¼", VG 85.00
Champ, automatic, star medallion, Hubley, 1940, 5", EX 100.00
Chief, single shot, Dent, 1935, 7½", VG 65.00
Colt, single shot, Stevens, 1900, 5½", EX 55.00
Cowboy, Hubley, 1940, 8", VG 100.00
Cowboy King, Stevens, 1940, 9", M (*) 300.00
Dick, automatic, Hubley, 1930, 4⅛", VG 40.00
Doughboy, automatic, Kilgore, 1920, 4⅞", VG 125.00
Eagle, single shot, Hubley, 1935, 8½", VG 150.00
Federal, automatic, clip, polished, 1940, 4⅞", M 145.00
G-Man, automatic, Kilgore, 1935, 6", rare, M (*) 185.00
Gene Autry, dummy, Kenton, 1940, 8⅜", rare, M 260.00
Gene Autry, eng, Kenton, 1951, 6½", rare, VG 450.00
Gene Autry, eng, Kenton, 1951, 8⅜", rare, M 550.00
Gene Autry, repeater, nickel, Kenton, 1940, 8⅜", EX (*) 250.00
Guard, bl finish, Kilgore, 1935, 6¼", EX 100.00
Invincible, Kilgore, 1935, 5¼", Fair 45.00
Lasso 'Em Bill, cylinder revolves, Kilgore, 1930, 9", EX 225.00
Lawmaker, nickel, Kenton, 1940, 8⅜", rare, M (*) 350.00
Lone Eagle, cylinder revolves, Kilgore, 1930, 5¼", EX 130.00
Lone Ranger, nickel, Kenton, 1940, 8¼", rare, M (*) 325.00
Long Boy, single shot, Kilgore, 1920, 11⅛", VG 135.00
Long Tom, cylinder revolves, Kilgore, 1940, 10⅜", M (*) 650.00
Mohican, single shot, Dent, 1930, 6¼", EX 60.00
National Automatic, National, 1915, 3¾", Fair 25.00
Officer's Pistol, automatic, Kilgore, 1940, 6", rare, M (*) 400.00
Patrol, Hubley, 1935-40, 6", M 75.00
Pawnee Bill, Stevens, 1940, 7⅝", VG (*) 235.00
Peacemaker, gold, Stevens, 1940, 8½", M 155.00
Pirate, dbl bbl, Hubley, 1940, 9⅜", M (*) 125.00
Police Chief, plastic grip, Kenton, 1940, 4⅝", EX 135.00
Presto, automatic, Kilgore, 1940, 5⅛", VG 65.00
Rodeo, single shot, Hubley, 1940, 7", EX 45.00
Roy Rogers, CI, polished, 10¼", rare, EX (*) 1,250.00
Scout, single shot, Stevens, 1890, 7", VG 75.00
Six Shooter, cylinder revolves, Kilgore, 1940, 6½", VG 100.00
Spitfire, automatic, Kilgore, 1940, 4⅝", EX 90.00
Texan, cylinder revolves, nickel, dummy model, Hubley, M (*) ...200.00
Texan, cylinder revolves, NP on CI, Hubley, 1940, 9¼", M (*) ...175.00
Texan Jr, CI, Hubley, 1940, 8⅛", VG (*) 100.00
Trooper Safety, repeater, Kilgore, 1925, 10¼", M 145.00
Two Time, rubber band, Kenton, 1929, 9¼", VG 155.00
Warrior, repeater, nickel, Kilgore, 1920s, 9", EX 175.00
Wild West, single shot, Kenton, 1920s, 11½", rare, M 275.00
101 Ranch, single shot, Hubley, 1930, 11½", VG 245.00
2 in 1, rubber band, Stevens, 1930, 9¼", VG 150.00
49-er Stevens, 1940, 9", M (*) 325.00

Guns: Diecast and Miscellaneous Toy Guns

Alan Ladd, Geo Schmidt, 10¼", rare, EX 325.00
Annie Oakley, gold, Leslie-Henry, 9", very rare 850.00
Army 45 Auto, compo, Hubley, 1940, nonworking 75.00
Army 45 Auto, dull gray finish, Hubley, 6½", M 95.00
Atomic Disintegrator, space gun, Hubley, 8", VG 445.00
Bonanza, cylinder revolves, Leslie-Henry 44, 10¼", M 185.00
Bronco, cylinder revolves, Kilgore, 9¼", VG 75.00
Buck'n Bronc, Geo Schmidt, 10½", EX 115.00
Buckle Gun, derringer, Mattel, 3", VG 75.00
Burke's Law Snub Nose, blk, Lone Star, 5", M 85.00
Champion, Leslie-Henry, 9", VG 125.00
Colt, Snub Nose Detective, Hubley, mini, M 30.00
Colt .45, cylinder revolves, bullets, Hubley, 14", VG 135.00
Cowboy, cylinder revolves, gold, Hubley, 12", rare, EX 250.00
Cowboy, cylinder revolves, Hubley, 12", M 165.00
Cowhand 250, Nichols, 8½", VG 70.00
Coyote, Hubley, 8¼", M 65.00
Dale Evans, jewels, Geo Schmidt, 10¼", rare, VG 400.00
Davy Crockett, Flintlock Buffalo Rifle, Hubley, 25", EX 175.00
Deputy, BB, copper grips, Schmidt, sm, 8½", EX 75.00
Dick Tracy, steel clicker, blk w/decal, Marx, EX 100.00
Dick Tracy Siren Pistol, red finish, Marx, VG 100.00
Dick Tracy Squad Shotgun, cap & water, pump, Mattel 125.00
Eagle, cylinder revolves, nickel, Kilgore, 8", M 100.00
Fanner 'Shootin' Shell,' bullets, Mattel, 9", M 150.00
Fanner 45 'Shootin' Shell,' Mattel, 11¼", rare, EX 350.00
Fanner 50, nickel, non-revolving cylinder, nickel, 10⅝", M 130.00
Fanner 50, revolving cylinder, nickel, Mattel, 10⅝", EX 165.00
Flip Rifleman Ring Rifle, Hubley, 32", VG 300.00
G-Boy, pressed steel, Acme Novelty Co, 7", M 65.00
G-Man, tin clicker pistol w/jewel, Marx, 1935, M 85.00
G-Man Sparking Machine Gun, tin, Marx, 26", VG 225.00
G-Man Sparking Wind-Up, steel pistol, Marx, 5", VG 75.00
Gene Autry, nickel, Leslie-Henry, 9", M 175.00
Gene Autry 44, cylinder revolves, bullets, Leslie-Henry, 11", EX ..185.00
Gray Ghost, nickel, silver grips, Lone Star, 9", rare, EX 550.00
Grizzly, cylinder revolves, gold, Kilgore, 10¼", M 350.00
Hawk, automatic, amber grips, Hubley, 5", VG 35.00
Hawkeye, automatic, Kilgore, 4¼", M 45.00
Hopalong Cassidy, cameo grips, Geo Schmidt, 9", EX 325.00
Hopalong Cassidy, gold, Wyandotte, 9", M 550.00
Hopalong Cassidy, nickel, Wyandotte, 9", VG 325.00
Indian Scout Rifle, bullets, Mattel, 30", M 200.00
Lone Ranger, antique bronze, Actoy, 10", VG 175.00
Lone Ranger, tin clicker w/jewel, Marx, 8", M 95.00
Maire's Leg, Winchester Lever-Pistol, Marx, 14", EX 135.00
Marshal, cylinder revolves, bullets, Halco, 10½", M 150.00
Mattel Snub-Nosed Detective, chrome, shootin' shell, EX 90.00
Maverick, Leslie-Henry, 10½", VG 130.00
Maverick 45, cylinder revolves, Halco, 11", M 325.00
Me & My Buddy, tin clicker, Wyandotte, 1935-40, VG 100.00
Model 61, cylinder revolves, chrome finish, Nichols, rare, M 450.00
Model 61, cylinder revolves, steel-bl finish, Nichols, rare, M 365.00
Mountie, automatic, blk finish, Kilgore, 6", M 45.00
Mustang 500, nickel, Nichols, 12¼", EX 175.00
Pal, single shot, nickel, Kilgore, 1945-60, sm, M 5.00
Paladin, repeater, nickel, Leslie-Henry, 9", rare, EX 285.00
Pet, nickel, Hubley, 1945-60, M 5.00
Pioneer, blk grips w/compass, Hubley, 10¼", EX 130.00
Pioneer, nickel, amber grips, Hubley, 10½", M 100.00
Pirate, over-under bbls, Hubley, 1960, VG 45.00
Pony Boy, nickel, Exquire-Actoy, 10", EX 65.00
Rebel Scattergun, dbl bbl, Marx, 21", rare, M 800.00
Red Ranger, Wyandotte, 7¾", VG 45.00
Remington 36, cylinder revolves, bullets, Hubley, 8¼", EX 85.00

Ric-O-Shay, cylinder revolves, bullets, 12¼", M 125.00
Roy Rogers, copper grips, Geo Schmidt, 10¼", EX 225.00
Roy Rogers, cylinder revolves, eng, diecast, Kilgore, 10", M 385.00
Roy Rogers, gold, Leslie-Henry, 9", EX 375.00
Roy Rogers, nickel, diecast, Kilgore, 8", M 185.00
Scout Rifle, lever, nickel, Hubley, 1960, EX 125.00
Sharps Carbine Civil War Model, Marx, 1960, rare, EX 250.00
Stallion .32, Nichols, 8", VG 35.00
Stallion 38, cylinder revolves, bullets, Nichols, 9½", EX 115.00
Stallion 45 Mk II, cylinder revolves, bullets, Nichols, 12", M ...300.00
Stallion 45 Mk II, cylinder revolves, gold, Nichols, 12", rare, EX ...1,500.00
Star, single shot, nickel, Hubley, 7", MIB 25.00
Sure Shot, nickel, Hubley, 8", EX 30.00
Tex, single shot, Hubley, sm, M 5.00
Texan, cylinder revolves, gold finish, diecast, Hubley, 9½", M ..175.00
Texan Jr, break action, diecast, Hubley, 9", VG 65.00
Texan Jr, side opener, diecast, Hubley, 9½", M 65.00
Thundergun, eng, nickel, Marx, 12½", M 200.00
Tightrope Snub Nose, nickel, Lone Star, EX 85.00
Trooper, snub nose, nickel, Hubley, 1950-60, EX 25.00
US Marshall, cylinder turns, antique bronze, Leslie-Henry, 11¼", VG 130.00
Wagon Train 44, antique bronze, Leslie-Henry, 11¼", VG 135.00
Wells Fargo, nickel, Actoy, 11", M 155.00
Western, nickel, Hubley, 9", M 55.00
Wild Bill Hickok, Leslie-Henry, 9", VG 150.00
Wild Bill Hickok 44, Leslie-Henry, 11¼", EX 165.00
Winchester Carbine, shootin' shell, Mattel, 26", M 165.00
Winchester Saddle Gun, Mattel, 33", M 185.00
Wyatt Earp, Buntline Special, Actoy, 11", M 150.00
Wyatt Earp, nickel, long bbl, Hubley, 11", M 165.00
2 in 1, 2 interchanging bbls, Hubley, 6", EX 45.00
44 Colt 1860, cylinder revolves, ivory grips, Hubley, 14", M 225.00
45 Colt, cylinder revolves, nickel, ivory grips, Hubley, 14", VG ...135.00

Guns: Early-Style Figural Guns and Bombs (Caution: Reproductions exist.)

Admiral Dewey Bomb, CI, Grey Iron, 1900, 1¾", VG 250.00
Butting Match, CI, Ives, 1885, 5", EX 350.00
Cannon, CI, Kenton, 1900, 4⅞", VG 400.00
Chinese Must Go, CI, Ives, 1880, 4¾", EX 350.00
Clown on Powder Keg, CI, Ives, 1890s, 3¾", VG 400.00
Devil's Head Bomb, CI, .22 blank, Ives, 1880, 2¼", VG 300.00
Dog's Head Bomb, CI, Ives, 1880, 2⅛", EX 265.00
Double-Face Man, CI, Ives, 1890, 1⅝", VG 125.00
George Washington Bomb, CI, 1900, 1¼", EX 300.00
Hobo Bomb, CI, Ideal, 1890s, 2", Fair 100.00
Liberty Bell Bomb, CI, 1876, 2⅜", EX 200.00
Lightning Express, CI, Kenton, 1900, 5", EX 650.00
Punch & Judy, CI, Ives, 1880s, 5¼", EX 750.00
Sea Serpent, CI, Stevens, 1890, 3½", Fair 775.00
Yellow Kid Bomb, CI, Grey Iron, 1900, 1½", VG 170.00

Model Kits

Adams, Hawk Missle Battery, 1958, MIB 70.00
Addar, Planet of the Apes, General Ursus, 1973-74, MIB 50.00
Addar, Super Scenes, Jaws, 1975, NM (VG+ box) 30.00
Airfix, Apollo Saturn V, MIB (sealed) 30.00
Airfix, Skeleton, 1970, MIB 20.00
AMT, Flintstone's Family Sedan, 1974, MIB 90.00
AMT, Girl From UNCLE Car, 1967, MIB 250.00
AMT, Sonny & Cher Mustang, 1960s, MIB 250.00
Arii, Regult Missile Carrier, MIB 25.00
Aurora, Adventure Series, Spartacus, 1964, MIB 275.00
Aurora, Batman, 1964, MIB 225.00
Aurora, Castle Creatures, Vampire, 1966, MIB 175.00
Aurora, Comic Scenes, Superman, 1974, MIB 50.00
Aurora, Dracula, 1969, glow-in-the-dark, MIB 100.00
Aurora, Mad Dentist, 1972, MIB 375.00
Aurora, Monster Scenes, Pendulum, 1971, MIB 140.00
Aurora, Mummy, 1963, MIB 250.00
Aurora, Spider-Man, 1966, MIB 250.00
Aurora, Witch, 1969, glow-in-the-dark, MIB 125.00
Bachmann, Birds of the World, Screech Owl, 1950s, MIB 45.00
Bachmann, Fisher Boy, 1962, MIB 80.00
Bandai, UFO, SHADO Intercepter, MIB 80.00
Hawk, Explorer, 18 Satellite, 1960, MIB 70.00
Hawk, Weird-Ohs, Huey's Hut Rod, 1969, MIB 50.00
ITC, Explorer Satellite I, 1959, MIB 250.00
ITC, Tyrannosaurus Rex Skeleton, 1950s, MIB 60.00
Lindberg, Flying Saucer, 1952, MIB 200.00
Lindberg, Krimson Monster, 1974, MIB 50.00
Lindberg, Wells Fargo Overland Stagecoach, 1960s, MIB 50.00
Monogram, Bad Medicine, 1970s, MIB 60.00
Monogram, Bathtub Buggy, 1960s, MIB 90.00
Monogram, Tijuana Taxi, 1960s, MIB 85.00
MPC, Beatles Yellow Submarine, 1968, MIB (sealed) 300.00
MPC, Star Wars, R2-D2, 1978, MIB 50.00
Pyro, Wyatt Earp, 1958, MIB 100.00
Revell, Apollo Lunar Spacecraft, 1969, MIB (sealed) 175.00
Revell, Beatles, John Lennon, 1964, MIB 225.00
Revell, Gemini Astronaut, 1967, MIB 55.00
Revell, Gemini Capsule, 1967, MIB 75.00
Strombecker, Interplanetary Vehicle, 1959, MIB 175.00
Superior, Seeing Eye, 1959, MIB 35.00

Pedal Cars and Ride-On Toys

BMC Racer, 1950s, M, from $1,500.00 to $1,750.00. (Photo courtesy Nate Stoller)

Ace roadster, Am National, wood w/metal spoke wheels, 33", G ...750.00
Air Pilot airplane, Am National, rstr, 50" 2,300.00
Bel Air Chevy convertible, 1955 model, rstr, 38" 2,400.00
Bugatti, Eureka, uphl seat, chrome trim, rstr, 46" 2,200.00
Caterpiller Diesel Tractor, New London Metal Products, 1950s, rstr ..6,000.00
Chrysler roadster, Steelcraft, side spare, disk wheels, 52", NM ..5,200.00
Earth mover, Murray, 1961, w/Playload Dump, rstr, from $1,000 to ..1,500.00
FBI Radio Cruiser, 1950s, orig condition, 37", EX 700.00
Fire truck, Am National, mk AFD, wooden ladders, rstr, 63" .8,000.00
Fire truck #B640, Steelcraft, 1941, wooden ladders, rstr 2,500.00
Gilmore Speedway Special Racer #8, BMC, 1950s, rstr 2,500.00
Graham-Bradley Jr Tractor, rubber tires, rstr, 41" 700.00

John Deere tractor, Ertl, cast aluminum/rubber tires, rstr, 37" 450.00
Packard, Am National, working steering, rstr, 29" 3,300.00
Roamer, Am National, w/tonneau, rstr, from $3,000 to 5,000.00
Spirit of America airplane, Steelcraft, mk NC 66, 53", EX 1,000.00
Super Sonic Jet, 3-wheeled, EX, from $800 to 1,200.00
Tee-Bird, Murry, VG, from $300 to 700.00
Torpedo convertible, Murray, 1949, side vents, chrome trim, rstr ...3,000.00
US Navy Patrol airplane, Steelcraft, 3-wheeled, 48", EX 3,000.00

Penny Toys

Airplane & hangar, Distler, 3", EX 350.00
Armored gun car, Germany, inertia mechanism, 3", EX 300.00
Baby in rolling chair w/nanny, Meier, 3¼", EX 385.00
Biplane, Distler, figure seated on wing, NM 1,500.00
Boat, Gely, sleek, 2 stacks & flag, 10", VG 900.00
Boy at school desk, Meier, top slides out, 2½", EX 800.00
Cat w/dog in doghouse, Meier, lever action, 4", EX 650.00
Chinese man on cart w/rotating parasol, Distler, 3¾", EX 465.00
Christmas tree, Distler, 3½", EX 125.00
Clown in barrel, Stock, 2½", VG+ 400.00
Delivery truck #245 w/driver, Fischer, 3½", EX 175.00
Dirigible in hangar, Meier, spring-loaded action, 2¾", EX 2,300.00
Dustpan, pictures children at play, 4", EX 150.00
Elephant cart, Fischer, nodding head, 5", VG+ 100.00
Fat man tipping hat, Kellerman, pull-string action, 3½", EX 150.00
Flying swing ride, Germany, 4½", EX 125.00
Garage w/2 sedans, Germany, 2½", EX 225.00
Gnome seated on egg, Meier, rectangular base, EX 1,200.00
Gondola on swinging platform, Meier, 2¾", EX 325.00
Horse & jockey on platform, Germany, 3¼", EX 175.00
Horse-drawn cab, Meier, dapple-gray horse, 4¼", EX 325.00
Horse-drawn sulky, Distler, w/driver, spoke wheels, NM 600.00
Horse-drawn water wagon, Meier, 5", VG+ 275.00
Jigger on horn, Germany, 5", VG 300.00
Ocean liner, Fischer, 2 stacks, 4¼", EX 275.00
Race car #32, Germany, 4½", VG 250.00
Roosters pecking, Meier, 4", VG+ 150.00
Trolley, Kellerman, 3", EX 300.00

Pipsqueaks

Pipsqueak toys were popular among the Pennsylvania Germans. The earliest had bellows made from sheepskin. Later cloth replaced the sheepskin, and finally paper bellows were used.

Cat w/kitten, pnt papier-mache, cloth bellows, late 19th C 325.00
Chickens in coop, pnt cb & papier-mache, 1880s, 6x4x5", G ...550.00
Goose, papier-mache, mc pnt, spring legs, squeaks, rprs, 6" 165.00
Rabbit (furry) in wood cage w/red & blk paper litho, 7x7¾", G ..110.00
Rooster (felt/feathers) in wood cage w/red & blk paper litho, 7", EX ...275.00

Pull Toys

George Brown horse-drawn express wagon, white horse, red cart, 1870s, 11" long, EX, $1,000.00. (Photo courtesy Dunbar Gallery)

Baby Haymaker, Animated Toy Co, litho tin tractor, EXIB 220.00
Bull on platform, Shimer, CI w/4 spoke wheels, 7", EX 200.00
Buttercup & Spareribs, Nifty, litho tin, 7½", VG (w/box) 1,760.00
Cable car, 1920s, litho tin w/emb images of Santa/reindeer, 4x7", EX ..100.00
Charlie Chaplin bell toy, Watrous, NP CI, EX 550.00
Donald Duck in boat, Chad Valley England, 1930s, paper/wood, 12", NM 575.00
Elephant on wheels, Bing, mohair/felt blanket, 9½", G 200.00
Felix the Cat in roadster, Nifty, 1920s, 12", EX 300.00
Fisherman on platform, J&E Stevens, CI, daisy-spoke wheels, 8", EX ..660.00
Happy Hooligan on platform, 1920s, pnt wood, 4½x6", EX+ 120.00
Horse on platform, hide-covered w/reins, saddle, blanket, 15", EX ..385.00
Horse-drawn surrey, pnt & stenciled w/CI spoke wheels, 9", G .230.00
Horse-drawn 8th Ave & Central Park Trolley, litho tin, 12", EX ...3,000.00
Krazy Kat chasing mice on platform, Nifty, litho tin, 7½", EX ..660.00
Krazy Kat, Chein, 7", EX 700.00
Mickey McGuire & mouse on platform, Performance Toys, 12", VG ..145.00
Milk truck, Gong Bell, litho tin/wood, MIB 400.00
Patriotic Boy bell ringer, Bergmann, 1880, pnt tin, 8½", EX ..5,000.00
Rowing team in boat, Hustler, 1930s, wood/metal, 14", EX 125.00
Sunny Andy Street Railway, litho tin, 21½", G+ 200.00
Trick Pony bell toy, Gong Bell, pnt CI, 8", VG 580.00

Robots and Space Toys

Apollo II Lunar Module, Japan, b/o, litho tin/plastic, 9", MIB ..250.00
Atomic Robot, Japan, w/up, litho tin, 5", NM 750.00
Billy Blastoff Space Scout, Eldon, 1968, b/o, complete, 4½", EX ...200.00
Cragstan Satellite, 1950s, b/o, litho tin, 5½", VG 175.00
Esso Energy Rocket, b/o, MIB 375.00
Flashy Jim, SNK, remote control, tin, 8", NM (EX box) 1,400.00
Jupiter Jyro Set, Tomy, 1970s, b/o, mostly plastic, 13", EX 125.00
King Ding Robot, b/o, litho tin, EX 225.00
Lunar Captain, TN, 1960s, b/o, 13½", EX 225.00
Man in Space, Alps, 1960s, b/o, litho tin, rare, 7", NM 825.00
Mighty Robot, MT, w/up, litho tin, 6", MIB 300.00
Moon Explorer, KO, crank action, tin/plastic, 7", NMIB 850.00
NASA New Flying Saucer, KO, 1960s, b/o, 7½", NM 250.00
Planet Explorer X-80, MT, 1960s, b/o, litho tin, 8" dia, EX 185.00
Robot Car, Yonezawa, 1950s, b/o, litho tin, scarce, 9", NM 200.00
Robotank TR-2, TN, 1950s, b/o, 5", EX 275.00
Rocket Ranger, Japan, 1950s, friction, litho tin, 7", NM (EX box) ..650.00
Space Conquerer, Daiya, 1960s, b/o, litho tin, 14", NM 800.00
Space Explorer S-61, Japan, friction, litho tin, 13", EX 65.00
Space Patrol 2019, b/o, MIB 300.00
Space Rocket Blue Eagle, b/o, MIB 475.00
Space Tank X-4, TN, friction, litho tin, 7", MIB 175.00
Spaceship Jupiter, K, w/up, litho tin/plastic dome, 5" dia, NMIB 150.00
Spaceship X-8, Tada, 1960s, b/o, litho tin, 8", EX 200.00
Swinging Baby Robot, Yone, w/up, litho tin, 6", MIB 575.00
Thunder Robot, b/o, litho tin, scarce, 11", NMIB 6,500.00
Twikki Robot (Buck Rogers), w/up, plastic, 7", NM 75.00
Winky Robot, Y, w/up, litho tin, 9½", NMIB 2,000.00

Schoenhut

Our advisor for Schoenhut toys is Keith Kaonis, who has collected these toys for over twenty years. Because of his involvement with the publishing industry (currently *Collectors' Eye*, *Antique DOLL Collector*, and during the '80s, *Collectors' SHOWCASE*), he has visited collections across the United States, produced several articles on Schoenhut toys, and served a term as president of the Schoenhut Collectors' Club. Keith is listed in the Directory under New York.

The listings below are for Humpty Dumpty Circus pieces. All values are based on rating conditions of good to very good, i.e., very minor scratches and wear, good original finish, no splits, chips, no excessive paint wear or cracked eyes, and of course completeness and condition of clothes (if dressed figures).

Clowns with two-part heads (a cast face applied to a wooden head) were made from 1903 to 1915 and are most desirable — condition always is important. There have been nine distinct styles in fourteen different costumes recorded. Only eight costume styles apply to the two-part headed clowns. The later clowns had one-part heads whose features were pressed wood, and the costumes on the later ones, circa 1920+, were no longer tied at the wrists and ankles.

Humpty Dumpty Circus Clowns and Other Personel

Black Dude, reduced sz, from $100 to 375.00
Black Dude, 1-part head, purple coat, from $250 to 700.00
Black Dude, 2-part head, blk coat, from $400 to 850.00
Chinese Acrobat, 1-part head, from $400 to 800.00
Chinese Acrobat, 2-part head, rare, from $400 to 1,200.00
Clown, early, G, from $150 to 600.00
Clown, reduced sz, 1925-53, from $75 to 125.00
Gent Acrobat, bsk head, rare, from $300 to 750.00
Gent Acrobat, 2-part head, very rare, from $600 to 1,800.00
Hobo, reduced sz, from $200 to 375.00
Hobo, 1-part head, from $200 to 400.00
Hobo, 2-part head, curved-up toes, blk coat, from $500 to 1,200.00
Hobo, 2-part head, facet toe ft, from $400 to 900.00
Lady Acrobat, bsk head, from $400 to 750.00
Lady Acrobat, 1-part head, from $200 to 400.00
Lady Rider, bsk head, from $250 to 500.00
Lady Rider, 1-part head, from $200 to 400.00
Lady Rider, 2-part head, very rare, from $700 to 1,800.00
Lion Tamer, bsk head, rare, from $500 to 850.00
Lion Tamer, 1-part head, from $400 to 750.00
Lion Tamer, 2-part head, early, very rare, from $700 to 1,500.00
Ring Master, bsk, ca 1912-14, from $400 to 700.00
Ring Master, 1-part head, from $200 to 450.00
Ring Master, 2-part head, early, very rare, from $800 to 1,800.00

Humpty Dumpty Circus Animals

Humpty Dumpty Circus animals with glass eyes, ca. 1903 – 1914, are more desirable and can demand much higher prices than the later painted-eye versions. As a general rule, a glass-eye version is 30% to 40% more than a painted-eye version. (There are exceptions.) The following list suggests values for both GE (glass-eye) and PE (painted-eye) versions and reflects a *low PE price* to a *high GE price*.

There are other variations and nuances of certain figures: Bulldog — white with black spots or brindle (brown); open- and closed-mouth zebras and giraffes; ball necks and hemispherical necks on some animals such as the pig, leopard, and tiger, to name a few. These points can affect the price and should be judged individually. Condition and rarity affect the price most significantly and the presence of an original box virtually doubles the price.

Alligator, GE/PE, from $200 to 600.00
Arabian Camel, 1 hump, GE/PE, from $250 to 750.00
Bactrian Camel, 2 humps, GE/PE, from $200 to 1,200.00
Brown Bear, GE/PE, from $200 to 800.00
Buffalo, cloth mane, GE/PE, from $300 to 900.00
Buffalo, cvd mane, GE/PE, from $200 to 1,200.00
Bulldog, GE/PE, from $400 to 1,500.00
Burro (made to go w/chariot & clown), GE/PE, from $200 to ...700.00
Cat, GE/PE, rare, from $600 to 3,000.00
Cow, GE/PE, from $300 to 1,200.00
Deer, GE/PE, from $300 to 1,400.00
Donkey, GE/PE, from $75 to 300.00
Donkey w/blanket, GE/PE, from $100 to 600.00
Elephant, GE/PE, from $75 to 300.00
Elephant w/blanket, GE/PE, from $200 to 600.00
Gazelle, GE/PE, rare, from $500 to 2,750.00
Giraffe, GE/PE, from $200 to 900.00
Goat, GE/PE, from $150 to 400.00
Goose, PE only, from $200 to 600.00
Gorilla, PE only, from $1,500 to 3,750.00
Hippo, GE/PE, from $250 to 900.00
Horse, brn, saddle & stirrups, GE/PE, from $200 to 500.00
Horse, wht, platform, GE/PE, from $190 to 450.00
Hyena, GE/PE, very rare, from $1,000 to 6,000.00
Kangaroo, GE/PE, from $300 to 1,800.00
Leopard, GE/PE, from $300 to 1,200.00
Lion, cloth mane, GE, from $500 to 1,000.00
Lion, cvd mane, GE/PE, from $250 to 1,200.00
Monkey, 1-part head, PE only, from $250 to 600.00
Monkey, 2-part head, wht face, from $300 to 900.00
Ostrich, GE/PE, from $250 to 900.00
Pig, 5 versions, GE/PE, from $200 to 800.00
Polar Bear, GE/PE, from $400 to 2,000.00
Poodle, cloth mane, GE only, from $150 to 450.00
Poodle, GE/PE, from $100 to 300.00
Rabbit, GE/PE, very rare, from $700 to 3,500.00
Rhino, GE/PE, from $250 to 800.00
Sea Lion, GE/PE, from $400 to 1,500.00
Sheep (lamb) w/bell, GE/PE, from $200 to 700.00
Tiger, GE/PE, from $250 to 1,200.00
Wolf, GE/PE, very rare, from $500 to 5,000.00
Zebra, GE/PE, from $250 to 1,200.00
Zebu, GE/PE, rare, from $600 to 3,000.00

Humpty Dumpty Circus Accessories

There are many accessories: wagons, tents, ladders, chairs, pedestals, tight rope, weights, and more.

Menagerie, later, ca 1914-20, from $1,200 to 2,000.00
Menagerie tent, early, ca 1904, from $1,500 to 2,500.00
Oval litho tent, 1926, from $4,000 to 10,000.00
Sideshow panels, 1926, pr, from $2,000 to 5,000.00

Steiff

Margaret Steiff began making her stuffed felt toys in Germany in the late 1800s. The animals she made were tagged with an elephant in a circle. Her first teddy bear, made in 1903, became such a popular seller that she changed her tag to a bear. Felt stuffing was replaced with excelsior and wool; when it became available, foam was used. In addition to the tag, look for the 'Steiff' ribbon and the button inside the ear. For further information we recommend *Teddy Bears and Steiff Animals*, a full-color identification and value guide by Margaret Fox Mandel, available from Collector Books or your public library. See also Teddy Bears.

Dog, Revue Susi, long and short blond mohair, straw stuffed, jointed head, glass eyes, squeaker, ca 1960 – 1970, 11" (scarce size), $200.00.

Bazi Dog, orig bl collar, chest tag, 1960s, 4", NM 110.00
Bendy Panda, all ID, 1960s, 3", NM 200.00
Biggie Beagle, orig red collar, all ID, 1960s, 7½", M 185.00
Clownie Clown, orig outfit, chest tag, 5", M 100.00
Coco Monkey, orig red leather collar, all ID, 5½", M 225.00
Floppy Beagle, sleeping, orig ribbon, chest tag, 8", NM 125.00
Gaty Alligator, all ID, 1968, 14", NM 150.00
Gaty Alligator, puppet, all ID, 1950s, 9", NM 135.00
Gogo Chinchilla, Dralon & felt, all ID, 5½", M 200.00
Goldy Hamster, all ID, 4", NM 100.00
Hucky Raven, all ID, 1960, 7", M 300.00
Jumbo Elephant, all ID, 1968, 9", M 385.00
Kid, all ID, 1950s, 4", M 125.00
Lama Llama, raised script button & chest tag, 1957, 17½", M ..600.00
Lizzy Lizard, complete ID, 1959-61, 12", EX 475.00
Maxi Mole, all ID, 1964, 4", M 135.00
Moosy Moose, all ID, 5", NM 425.00
Nagy Beaver, all ID, 1958, 7", M 165.00
Nelly Snail, chest tag, 6½", NM 400.00
Ossi Rabbit, incised button, 6", NM 85.00
Pieps Mouse, all ID, M 100.00
Raccy Raccoon, stock tag, 6", EX 100.00
Richard Bear, 1983, 12", MIB 350.00
Siamy Cat, complete ID, 1950s, 5", NM 300.00
Snaky Snake, puppet, raised script button, 1966-67, 13", EX 450.00
Sonny Rabbit, orig ribbon/bell, raised script button & tag, 3", EX ..100.00
Susi Cat, orig pk ribbon, all ID, 1960s, 5", NM 200.00
Tessie Schnauzer, chest tag, 4½", NM 150.00
Tucky Turkey, all ID, 1952, 4¼", M 365.00
Vario Rabbit, raised script button & stock tag, 5", EX 100.00
Waldili Dog, all ID, 1968, 8½", NM 450.00
Woolie Owl, 2 real feathers for tufts, rare, 2", NM 250.00
Xorry Fox, chest tag, 1950s, 4½", EX 135.00
Zooby Bear, raised script button, rare, 11", M 950.00

Toy Soldiers and Accessories

Among the better-known manufacturers of 'dimestore' soldiers are Barclay, Manoil, and Jones, all of whom made hollow cast-lead figures; Grey Iron, who used cast iron; and Auburn, who made figures of rubber. They all measured about 3" to 3½" tall, and often accessories such as trucks, tanks, and airplanes were designed to add to the enjoyment of staging mock battles, parades, encampments, etc.

Britains is a very popular line, smaller and usually more detailed than the 'dimestores.' They've been made in England since 1893, and most of their boxed sets sell for a minimum of $100.00.

Some examples are very rare and therefore expensive, but condition is the driving force in making a value assessment. Percentages in the description lines refer to the amount of original paint remaining. Our advisors for this category are Stan and Sally Alekna; they are listed in the Directory under Pennsylvania. To learn more about this subject, we recommend *Collecting Toy Soldiers* by Richard O'Brien (Krause).

Barclay, Naval officers in blue: short stride, very scarce 75%, $250.00; short stride, tin top to cap, 98% (one known), $450.00; long stride, very scarce, 95%, $350.00. (Photo courtesy Stan and Sally Alekna)

American Metal Toys, doctor, wht, scarce, 98%, scarce 175.00
American Metal Toys, farmer, 99% 19.00
American Metal Toys, horse, gray, 98% 11.00
Auburn Rubber, baseball batter, wht w/bl trim, 98%, scarce 59.00
Auburn Rubber, doctor in wht, 99%, scarce 47.00
Auburn Rubber, howitzer, red, 98% 45.00
Auburn Rubber, sound detector, 97% 38.00
Auburn Rubber, US Infantry private, 97% 13.00
Barcay, soldier, marching, shoulder arms, long stride, tin helmet, 95% ...20.00
Barclay, airplane mechanic, 95%, scarce 65.00
Barclay, boy skater, 98% 17.00
Barclay, cow, grazing, 98% 16.00
Barclay, cowboy, masked, w/pistol, on horse, 99% 48.00
Barclay, cowboy, tin hat brim, 97% 26.00
Barclay, girl on sled, 99% 22.00
Barclay, HO scale, hobo, 99% 11.00
Barclay, HO scale, train conductor, NM 12.00
Barclay, Indian chief w/tomahawk & shield, 96" 21.00
Barclay, jockey on silver horse, #4, 97% 31.00
Barclay, knight w/pennant, 99% 24.00
Barclay, knight w/sword overhead, 98% 38.00
Barclay, mailman, 99% 20.00
Barclay, man on sled, 97% 19.00
Barclay, marine, 95% 18.00
Barclay, officer's car w/megaphone, very scarce, 95% 300.00
Barclay, old man w/cane, 93% 17.00
Barclay, parachute jumper, 98% 34.00
Barclay, pirate, red outfit, 97% 33.00
Barclay, policeman, figure-8 base, 97% 21.00
Barclay, policeman on motorcycle, scarce, 94% 50.00
Barclay, porter, w/whisk broom, 98% 25.00
Barclay, sailor in bl, 98% 24.00
Barclay, sailor in puttees, short stride, bl, 97% 22.00
Barclay, Santa on sled, 99% 50.00
Barclay, sharpshooter, standing/firing, long stride, tin helmet, 98% ...25.00
Barclay, soldier bomb thrower, khaki, 98% 22.00
Barclay, soldier marching, khaki, 99% 16.00
Barclay, soldier running w/rifle, cast helmet, 98% 31.00
Barclay, soldier standing firing rifle, khaki, NM 18.00
Barclay, train passenger, girl, 93% 10.00
Barclay, train passenger, woman w/dog, pk or bl, NM, ea 16.00
Britains, #006 Middlesex Regiment, dtd 1905, 8-pc, G 200.00
Britains, #019 West India Regiment, ca 1930, 9-pc, G-EX 275.00
Britains, #032 Royal Scots Greys, 5-pc, M (M box) 140.00
Britains, #033 16th Queen's Lancers, 5-pc, EX 185.00
Britains, #075 Scots Guards, ca 1935, 8-pc, G-EX 75.00
Britains, #092 Spanish Infantry, 8-pc, EX-M (EX box) 1,150.00
Britains, #117 Egyptain Infantry, standing at attention, 8-pc, EXIB 200.00
Britains, #147 Zulus of Africa, 8-pc, M (EX box) 220.00
Britains, #164 Arabs of the Desert, M (EX Britains Ltd box) 115.00
Britains, #173 Serbian Infantry, charging, 8-pc, EX 175.00
Britains, #228 US Marines, 8-pc, EX-M (G Whisstock box) 160.00
Britains, #230 US Navy Blue Jackets, ca 1935, 8-pc, G-EX 100.00
Courtenay, King of Scotland, position 6, VG 300.00
Courtenay, Thibaud de Scey, position 2, VG 450.00
Elastolin, Knights in Armour, 22-pc, Fair-G 520.00
Grey Iron, cadet, right shoulder arms, prewar, 94% 29.00
Grey Iron, colonial officer, 97% 28.00
Grey Iron, farm cow, brn & yel, 98% 15.00
Grey Iron, farm hand digging, 98%, scarce 20.00
Grey Iron, farm wife, 97% 16.00
Grey Iron, farmer, 98% 17.00
Grey Iron, Greyklip Company B, drummer, EX+ 7.00
Grey Iron, Greyklip Company B, officer, EX+ 7.00

Grey Iron, holdup man in grey, prewar, scarce, 96% 38.00
Grey Iron, Indian chief w/knife, 98% 32.00
Grey Iron, Legion drummer, prewar, 96% 26.00
Grey Iron, lifeguard, very scarce 70.00
Grey Iron, mailman, 99% 16.00
Grey Iron, old woman sitting, prewar, 95% 11.00
Grey Iron, sailor in wht, prewar, 92% 18.00
Grey Iron, ski trooper, 97%, scarce 55.00
Grey Iron, train conductor, 99% 13.00
Grey Iron, train porter, 97%, scarce 19.00
Grey Iron, US doughboy, charging, prewar, 98% 23.00
Grey Iron, US Doughboy, officer, 95% 19.00
Grey Iron, US Infantry, port arms, prewar, 99% 24.00
Grey Iron, US Navy Officer in bl, postwar, 98% 24.00
Imperial, #14 65th Foot Regiment, 6-pc, MIB 75.00
Jones, calf, #236, 93% 10.00
Jones, mule, 99% 12.00
Jones, Scot Highlander of 1814, 54 mm, 98%, scarce 28.00
Lineol, Swiss Army Band, 10-pc, G 160.00
Manoil, Black man eating watermelon, 99%, scarce 99.00
Manoil, blacksmith making horseshoes, 97% 27.00
Manoil, colt, maroon, 99%, scarce 29.00
Manoil, cowgirl, no horse, 98% 29.00
Manoil, doctor, wht, red cross on cap, 95% 28.00
Manoil, ensign in wht, 93% 25.00
Manoil, farm woman picking berries, 94%, scarce 51.00
Manoil, farmer pitching sheaves, NM 29.00
Manoil, flagbearer, hollow base, very scarce, 94% 93.00
Manoil, hound dog, tan w/brn spots 98% 28.00
Manoil, man in gray w/barrel of apples, scarce, 97% 70.00
Manoil, mason laying bricks, 98%, scarce 41.00
Manoil, Naval gunner, bare ft, 98% 40.00
Manoil, policeman, 95% 25.00
Manoil, pontoon boat on wheels, 92%, scarce 51.00
Manoil, scarecrow in top hat, 95% 28.00
Manoil, shoe cobbler, 90%, scarce 25.00
Manoil, soldier, trench mortar, 99% 35.00
Manoil, soldier in poncho w/slung rifle, 97% 47.00
Manoil, soldier kneeling w/bayonet, 95%, scarce 72.00
Manoil, soldier marching, w/pack & slung rifle, 97% 29.00
Manoil, soldier standing firing rifle, 98% 31.00
Mignot, Ancient Gaul Archers, 12-pc, M (EX box) 150.00
Mignot, French Cuirassiers (1890-1914), ca 1950, 12-pc, G (G box) ..175.00
Mignot, Infantry of the Line, 12-pc, M (EX box) 290.00
Mignot, Saracen Warriors, 8-pc, G-EX (EX repro box) 165.00
Mignot, Volontaires, #25, 12-pc, M (Fair box) 290.00
Tradition, #83 Royal Scots Fusiliers (1895), EX (G box) 100.00
Tradition, #88 Scots Guards (1895), 6-pc, M (EX box) 75.00

Trains

Electric trains were produced as early as the late nineteenth century. Names to look for are Lionel, Ives, and American Flyer. Identification numbers given in the listings below actually appear on the item.

Am Flyer, Burlington Zephyr Set #9900, locomotive/4 cars, VG 225.00
Am Flyer, Comet Set, locomotive/3 cars, VG 450.00
Am Flyer, DC Northern, locomotive/tender #332, G 250.00
Am Flyer, passenger station #102, EXIB 350.00
Am Flyer, Potomac Set, locomotive/3 cars, VG 400.00
Bing, Station, 0 gauge, emb tin, 15", EX 575.00
Carlisle & Finch, Railway Trolley #1, w/track & ties, VG (G box) .2,700.00
Fandor, Station, litho tin, w/electric light, VG 325.00
Girard, Cars #424, #425, #426, 2-tone gr, EX (EX boxes) 2,000.00
Hafner, Century of Progress Set, clockwork, G 200.00
Hafner, Set #1010, w/Pennsylvania RR caboose, EXIB 300.00
Hornby, Platform Crane #42330, EXIB 200.00
Hornby, Ripon Station, litho tin, G 175.00
Ives, Locomotive & Tender #1125, VG 250.00
Ives, Pennsylvannia RR Caboose #67, VG 375.00
Ives, Set #11, complete, EX 1,100.00
Ives, Set #258, locomotive/3 cars, EX 1,500.00
Ives, Tank Car #66, red or gray, VG, ea 250.00
Lionel, Chesapeake Flyer Set #1865, EX 150.00
Lionel, Control Tower #12702, EX 75.00
Lionel, Freight Special Set #51001, MIB 500.00
Lionel, Hiawatha Set #51000, MIB 825.00
Lionel, Illinois Central Baggage Car #7220, MIB 100.00
Lionel, New Englander Set #1050, NM 200.00
Marklin, Locomotive & Tender #12910, VG 750.00
MTH, Hellgate Bridge, early colors, EX 500.00
Williams, Amtrak Amfleet Set, MIB 225.00
Williams, NYC Drefuss Hudson Set #4001, w/5 cars, EX (EX boxes) ..550.00
Williams, Pennsylvania RR E62-4-4-2 Locomotive & Tender, MIB 350.00

Trade Signs

Trade signs were popular during the 1800s. They were usually made in an easily recognizable shape that one could mentally associate with the particular type of business it was to represent, especially appropriate in the days when many customers could not read!

Jeweler's, pocket watch form, wood with gold paint and white faces, 19½" diameter, some repaint, $550.00.

Arm w/pointing finger, cut-out pnt wood, Delightful in script ..600.00
Beauty Shoppe, 2-sided porc flange, Deco lady/lettering, 12x24", G ...275.00
Choice Perfumes, rvpt glass, MOP/glitter on lettering, 16x54", VG 400.00
Drugs, rvpt glass w/fancy filigree ground, copper fr, 7½x47" 400.00
Drugs & Soda, rvpt, blk on crinkled gold/silver, trapezoidal, fr ..725.00
Fish, cvd/5-color pnt, iron loops/chain, 1890s, 21" L 1,250.00
Fish lure, worn/weatherized wood w/old pnt, gr glass eyes, 25" L 600.00
Horseshoes & lettering w/anvil & horse above, CI, 1890s, 23x20" ..460.00
Law Office, worn gold & blk on wood (old rpt), 2-sided, 18x24" 165.00
Mortar & pestle form, mc jeweled copper light-up, 30", VG ..2,000.00
Pocket watch shape, pnt zinc, pnt losses, ca 1890s, 20½" dia 485.00
Tavern, pine w/mc pnt: eagle/shield/1824, self-fr, 30x22" 5,225.00

Tramp Art

'Tramp' is considered a type of folk art. In America it was primarily made from the end of the Civil War through the 1930s, though it employs carving and decorating methods which are much older, originating mostly in Germany and Scandinavia. 'Trampen' probably refers to the itinerant stages of Middle Ages craft apprenticeship. The carving techniques were also used for practice. Tramp art was spread by soldiers in the Civil War and primarily practiced where there was a plentiful and free supply of materials such as cigar boxes and fruit crates. The belief that this work was done by tramps and hobos as payment for room or meals is generally incorrect. The larger pieces especially would have required a lengthy stay in one place.

There is a great variety of tramp art, from boxes and frames which are most common to large pieces of furniture and intricate objects. The most common method of decoration is chip carving with several layers built one on top of another. There are several variations of that form as well as others such as 'Crown of Thorns,' an interlocking method, which are completely different. The most common finishes were lacquer or stain, although paints were also used. The value of tramp art varies according to size, detail, surface, and complexity. The new collector should be aware that tramp art is being made today. While some sell it as new, others are offering it as old. In addition, many people mistakenly use the term as a catchall phrase to refer to other forms of construction — especially things they are uncertain about.

For further information we recommend *Tramp Art: A Folk Art Phenomenon* by Helaine Fendelmam, Jonathan Taylor (Photographer)/ Stewart Tabori & Chang; and *Hobo & Tramp Art Carving: An Authentic American Folk Tradition* by Adolph Vandertie, Patrick Spielman/Sterling Publications. Our advisors are Matt Lippa and Elizabeth Schaaf; they are listed in the Directory under Alabama.

Basket, burnt/cvd/stained, Indian design, 4-panel, sign/dtd, 17¾" ..490.00
Box, chip-cvd, hidden compartments, 6½x8½x8½" 375.00
Box, chip-cvd, lid w/5 pyramids, 2 sides w/2, 2 w/1, ftd, 6x11" ..185.00
Box, chip-cvd (5 to 10 layers), appl dmns, ftd, lt/dk wood, 8x10x7" ...160.00
Box, chip-cvd borders, 'AJ' & 1906 in brass, 7x9x7½" 210.00
Cross, Crown of Thorns, 13½x10x3" 190.00
Frame, chip-cvd, sqs on corners, dmns on sides, 1900s, 21x17½" ..460.00
Frame, chip-cvd, 2 sides ea of hearts/dmns, 5-tier, 11¼" sq 315.00
Frame, chip-cvd, 2-layer, appl elements, ocher pnt w/varnish, 23x19" ..335.00
Frame, chip-cvd, 4-layer, old wht pnt, orig mirror, 15x11x1½" .125.00
Frame, chip-cvd, 6-layer w/rectangle corner pcs, dk varnish, 16x20" ..260.00
Frame, chip-cvd discs on corners, orig varnish & pnt, 27½x23" .615.00
Frame, dmn-shaped chip cvgs, 5-layer, 18x16", EX 235.00
Frame, 6-tiered notched pyramids on corners, 14-layer sides, 15x12" ...590.00

Traps

Though of interest to collectors for many years, trap collecting has gained in popularity over the past ten years in particular, causing prices to appreciate rapidly. Traps are usually marked on the pan as to manufacturer, and the condition of these trademarks are important when determining their value. Grading is as follows:

Good: one-half of pan legible.
Very Good: legible in entirety, but light.
Fine: legible in entirety, with strong lettering.
Mint: in like-new, shiny condition.

Our advisor for this category is Boyd Nedry; he is listed in the Directory under Michigan. Prices listed here are for traps in fine condition.

Hand-forged bear trap, light rust, EX, $400.00. (Photo courtesy Russ Trading Post)

Abbey Mcleod, #4 rnd base, Pat Oct 5 97 ....450.00
Alaxander, clutch trap, Pat Oct 18 1887, sz A 550.00
All Steel, #3, dbl long spring 150.00
Alligator #1 ....100.00
Arrow, #1½, single under spring 35.00
Austin Humane, killer #1 ....50.00
Auto-set Mouse, wood snap 10.00
Automatic Trap Co, steel rat trap 30.00
Beaten Path, GOMBER metal mousetrap 35.00
Bell Spring, #1¼, single long spring 195.00
Big Bear, #115, killer 30.00
Bigglow, coil spring, sm 20.00
Blake-Lamb, #3, dbl long spring 15.00
Buffalo Bill, wood snap, rat trap 35.00
Cinch mole trap 18.00
Crago, #7, clutch trap, Missoula MT 650.00
Curry, metal & screen, fly trap, Pat Jan 4 1916 ....35.00
Cyclone, metal, mousetrap 25.00
Dalgrim, sure pelt, 7" sz 22.00
Dearborn, #3, dbl long spring, dish-eye springs 950.00
Delusion, self-setting, tin & wood, mousetrap 60.00
Diamond, #H22 Hi Grip, dbl long spring, dbl jaw 160.00
Diamond, #15, dbl long spring 180.00
Dodd Safe-t-set, wood snap, mousetrap 35.00
Elgin, metal, mousetrap 35.00
End-o-mice, snap trap, cb base 22.00
Evans, brass claw, mousetrap 675.00
Faltless, metal snap, rat trap 40.00
Fary, mousetrap w/exercise wheel 85.00
French Marty, wire cage, live mousetrap 55.00
Funsten, float trap 565.00
Gabriel Fish & Game 525.00
Gibbs, 2-trigger 18.00
Gibbs Dope, #4 ....575.00
Good, Stilson Spec Co, wood snap, rat trap 32.00
Half Moon, tin killer, mousetrap 75.00
Hawley Norton, #1, single long spring 20.00
Helfrich, #550, coil spring 20.00
Herters, #4, dbl coil spring, US Government on base 125.00
Herters, #41AX, bear trap 575.00
IT, metal choker, mousetrap 40.00
Jack Frost, killer, brass trigger 20.00
Jack Frost, Never Lose, #1, coil spring 40.00
Jillson, spear type, rat trap 400.00
JVJ Gopher, Crete NE 45.00
Katch-N-Kary, wood & screen, Jackson TN, roach trap 38.00
Ketchem Tile Trap 45.00
Kitty Got Cha, plastic, mousetrap 60.00
Knapp, #1½ coil spring, Belknap Hdw, KY 15.00
Kriket, #1 single under spring 9.00
Little Champ, plastic choker, mousetrap 30.00
Little Samson, iron, rat trap 135.00
Lomar, #4, dbl coil spring 40.00
Macabee, gopher trap 5.00
Mackenzy Dist Fur Co, #15, bear trap, not old 200.00
Manning, #9, dbl coil spring, Fairbanks AK, wolf trap 95.00
McGill, metal, self-setting, mousetrap 15.00
Michigan Wire Goods, gopher trap 40.00
Mockba, CCCP (Russia), wood snap, rat trap 20.00
Montgomery Digger, coil spring 165.00
Nash, 2-loop choker, CI base, mole trap 30.00
Nelson Boode, 'trailsend' #1 single long spring 95.00
Newhouse, #2½, single long spring 75.00
Newhouse, #4½, dbl long spring, wolf trap 195.00

Newhouse, #48, dbl long spring 50.00
Oberto, #400 ....40.00
OK, wood choker, Abingdon IL, gopher trap 45.00
Olmsteds, spear type, mole trap 38.00
Peacock, wire choker 85.00
Pines, 'ketch the flies/save the babies,' tin & screen, fly trap 95.00
Pioneer, #2, single long spring 8.00
PS Mfg Co, #2, dbl long spring 40.00
PS&Co, #0 jumper 140.00
Push & Set, plastic snap, mousetrap 35.00
Quigley Van Camp, wood snap, mousetrap 18.00
Rev-O-Noc, #101, single long spring 155.00
Rice copy of Jackson otter dog, single long spring 235.00
Roto, plastic PVC pipe, mousetrap 25.00
Runway, tin, mousetrap 35.00
Sabo, cast jaw, den trap 115.00
Snappy, metal mousetrap 20.00
Special, St Paul MN, mousetrap 30.00
Standish, hand forged, beaver trap 325.00
Sure Catch, roach trap 55.00
Sure Hold, wooden cone, w/spikes, sm 80.00
Taylor, Ketchem, #1½, single long spring 45.00
Teeter, gopher trap 40.00
The Baby Superior, tin & screen, fly trap 100.00
Tom Cat, wood snap, rat trap 40.00
Tree Trap, #1, Pat 1907 ....35.00
Triumph, #0, w/Triumph crossed on pan 55.00
Typhoon, by McGill, wood snap, mousetrap 35.00
U-Neek, glass poison holder, for mice 35.00
Verbail, chin trap, leg hold 125.00
Victor, two, trigger 20.00
Victoria, #0, single long spring 90.00
Webley, #1½, dish-eye spring 20.00
Woods & Waters, killer 12.00
Woodward Death Clamp 65.00
Zip, metal, mousetrap 20.00

Trenton

The Trenton, New Jersey, was an area that supported several pottery companies from the mid-1800s until the late 1960s. A consolidation of several smaller companies that occurred in the 1890s was called Trenton Potteries Company. Each company produced their own types of wares independent of the others.

Bowl, turquoise, inverted rim, 10", $45.00.

Planter, frog w/whimsical face, gr w/yel throat, mk, 7½x6" 155.00
Vase, blk gloss, bulbous shoulders, mk TEPECO #P12/SKR, 9¼" ...160.00
Vase, maroon, emb columns, sq, 7" 185.00
Vase, sky bl gloss, bulbous bottom w/long tapered neck, 8" 75.00
Vase, wht, flying saucer shape, 10½" dia 100.00
Vase, wht, trumpet form w/wing hdls, 8x5½" 80.00
Vase, yel gloss, ball shape, 3 rings around center, 6" dia 60.00

Trivets

Although strictly a decorative item today, the original purpose of the trivet was much more practical. They were used to protect table tops from hot serving dishes, and irons heated on the kitchen range were placed on trivets during use to protect work surfaces. The first patent date was 1869; many of the earliest trivets bore portraits of famous people or patriotic designs. Florals, birds, animals, and fruit were other favored motifs. Watch for remakes of early original designs. Some of these are marked Wilton, Emig, Wright, Iron Art, and V.M. for Virginia Metalcrafters. However, many of these reproductions are becoming collectible. Expect to pay considerably less for these than for the originals, since they are abundant.

Brass

Horse design, hand-tooled, early, 6¼x3¾" 85.00
Horseshoe w/1888 in center, w/hdl 95.00
Rtcl scrolls, kettle style, 3-ftd, 1780s, 13x11½x13" 155.00
Rtcl scrolls, trn ft, 6½" 190.00
Rtcl w/gallery, trn hdl, 14" 275.00
6-pointed star in hexagon, 3-ftd, 8½" 85.00

Cast Iron

Arrowhead w/scrollwork, center plaque, for iron, Am Butt Co, ftd ..60.00
Butterfly, 9½" 80.00
Football shape, letters JOHNSON, EX patina, 4⅛x7¾x¾" 80.00
Ober, sq grid, Chagrin Falls, O, NP, 4½" 35.00
Star & braid, buffed, 8" 80.00
Strause Gas Iron Co, 3-leg, gallery 45.00
Uneedit, ornate, 7" 50.00

Wrought Iron

Circular w/twisted & tooled details, folding spit rest, 18" L 260.00
Dbl heart, shoe ft, blk pnt, 4½" 175.00
Foot shape, 4-ftd, 1700s, 3½x9x6" 90.00
Round, 3 penny ft, 3¼x4½" dia 70.00
Tooled leaf detail, turned-up ft, 10½" L 330.00
Triangular, high legs w/paw-like ft, 9" 55.00
5-bar rectangle, 16x13x15" 120.00

Trunks

The first use of the term 'trunk' can be traced back to Egyptian times, when hollowed-out tree sections were used to transport goods of commerce. In the the days of steamboat voyages, stagecoach journeys, and railroad travel, trunks were used to transport clothing and personal belongings.

The most desirable trunks are flat-tops, 24" to 38" long, from the late 1800s, preferably in restored condition. Embossed dome-tops (rounded on top to better accommodate milady's finery) from the 1880s, 24" to 38" long, in complete original condition are very desirable as well. On the other hand, ca 1870s flush tin trunks, even in mint condition, inspire very little collector interest.

Unless the trunk is complete (retaining all original trays and compartments), its value is considerably lessened. If parts are absent or broken, the trunk is judged incomplete. All interiors differ; some had upper-lid compartments, others did not. Our advisor is Doris Harroff; she is listed in the Directory under Indiana.

Dome-top, emb decor, 1880s, 24" to 38", complete, from $75 to ...175.00

Dome-top, top & front pnt w/mc flowers on blk, mid-1800s, complete ...2,000.00
Flat-top, orig, 1880-1890, complete, rstr, from $300 to 425.00
Flat-top, orig, 1880-1890, 24" to 38", complete, from $75 to 125.00
Leather trim, flat ot dome, pre-1860s, 24" to 38", rstr, up to 475.00
Leather trim w/brass tacks on pine, 19x10x9" 110.00
Stagecoach, flat or dome, pre-1860s, 24" to 38", rstr, up to 475.00

Tuthill

The Tuthill Glass Company operated in Middletown, New York, from 1902 to 1923. Collectors look for signed pieces and those in an identifiable pattern. Condition is of utmost importance, and examples with brilliant cutting and intaglio (natural flowers and fruits) combined fetch the highest prices.

Basket, Hobstar, Prism, Strawberry Dmn, Fan & step cutting, 13½" ...3,200.00
Basket, Wild Rose, rope twist hdl, 5x6" 2,100.00
Bowl, Reverse Gothic Arch, cluster of hobs, low, 10" 800.00
Box, powder; +hair receiver, Strawberry Dmn, Beaded Vesica & Fan ..325.00
Creamer & sugar bowl, Rosaceae 550.00
Pitcher, eng floral, prisms, 9½" 190.00
Pitcher, milk; eng vintage, 8" 375.00
Rose bowl, Primrose, deeply cut, 7x8" 1,600.00
Tray, bread; Primrose, Fan, Hobstar & Strawberry Dmn, 13x6" .600.00
Tray, cut flowers & leaves w/frosted ovals, sawtooth rim, 10x4¼" 295.00
Vase, sweet pea; Lillium, 8x6" 300.00

Twin Winton

Twin brothers Don and Ross Winton started this California-based company during the mid-1930s while still in high school. In the mid-1940s they shut it down while in the armed forces and started up again in the late 1940s, when older brother Bruce Winton joined them and bought them out in the early 1950s. The company became a major producer of cookie jars, kitchenware, and household items sold nationally until it closed its San Juan Capistrano location in 1977.

Beside their extensive line of very collectible cookie jars, they're also well known for their Hillbilly line — mugs, pitchers, bowls, lamps, ashtrays, decanters, and other novelty items, which evolved from the late 1940s through the early 1970s with a variety of decorating methods still being discovered. Don Winton was the only designer for Twin Winton and created literally thousands of designs for them and hundreds of other companies. He is still sculpting in Corona del Mar, California, and collectors and dealers are continuing to find and document new pieces daily. To learn more about this subject, we recommend *Collector's Guide to Don Winton Designs* (Collector Books) by our advisor, Mike Ellis; he is listed in the Directory under California or visit the collector club website at www.twinwinton.com.

Ashtray, Bambi, deer lying on base, 6x8" 100.00
Ashtray, Bronco Group, cowboy sits beside saddle, B-208, 5½" ...75.00
Ashtray, Elf, sits on base, 8x8" 100.00
Bank, Cop, dress in 'Keystone Cop' era uniform, 8" 65.00
Bank, Dobbin, donkey wearing hat, 8" 70.00
Bank, Friar Tuck, Thou Shall Not Steal on robe, 8" 40.00
Bank, Hotei, lg Oriental man, 8" 50.00
Bank, Lamb, sits wearing bow tie, holds purse, 8" 40.00
Bank, Pirate Fox, patch on 1 eye, sword in belt, 8" 65.00
Bank, Ranger Bear, holds money bag, 8" 50.00
Bank, Shack, lg dollar sgn on chimney, 8" 50.00
Bank, Wooly Mammoth, made for Ford dealership, 5" 75.00
Candle holder, Verdi (long), 4x9½" 15.00
Candy jar, Ranger Bear, sits on stump licking lollipop, 8x10½" ...85.00
Candy jar, Sailor Elephant, holds lollipop, 6x9" 65.00
Candy jar, Shoe, boy on roof, girl in window, 10x10" 75.00
Candy jar, Turtle, turtle w/rabbit on bk, 8x10" 85.00
Canister, Coffee Bucket, 5x6" 30.00
Canister, Coffee Coop, Canister Farm set, 4x6" 40.00
Canister, Cookie Barn, Canister Farm set, 8x12" 60.00
Canister, House (Coffee), Canisterville, 4x8" 75.00
Canister, House (Cookies), Canisterville, 8x12" 175.00
Canister, Sugar Bucket, 6x7" 40.00
Cookie jar, Baker, man w/spatula & plate of cookies, 7x11" 400.00
Cookie jar, Cookie Barn, red roof, Collector's Series 175.00
Cookie jar, Cookie Elf, sitting on stump, 8½x12" 65.00
Cookie jar, Cookie Nut, nut w/squirrel on lid, 9x10" 65.00
Cookie jar, Cookie Time, clock w/mouse sitting on top, 7½x14" ...45.00
Cookie jar, Dog in Basket, 8½x10" 85.00
Cookie jar, Dutch Girl, hands on hips, 8½x12½" 85.00
Cookie jar, Flopsy, Raggedy Andy sits on drum, Collector's Series ..300.00
Cookie jar, Friar Tuck, Thou Shall Not Steal on robe, 7x12" 65.00
Cookie jar, Grandma, holding bowl of cookies, 7x10" 200.00
Cookie jar, Gunfighter Rabbit, w/gun in holster & scarf, 8x13" ..75.00
Cookie jar, Little Lamb, For Good Little Lambs Only on apron, 8x13" ...40.00
Cookie jar, Persian Kitten, 1 front paw raised, 8x12" 140.00
Cookie jar, Pot of Cookies, flowers on body & lid, 8x10" 40.00
Cookie jar, Potbellied Stove, 7x12" 85.00

Cookie jar, Raggedy Ann (has been reproduced), fully painted, $250.00. (Photo courtesy Fred and Joyce Roerig)

Cookie jar, Ranger Bear, 7x12" 50.00
Cookie jar, Sailor Elephant, sitting, 9½x12" 40.00
Cookie jar, Sailor Mouse, sitting, 7x12" 75.00
Cookie jar, Shaggy Pup, sits, wears bow tie, 8x11" 300.00
Cookie jar, Sheriff, sitting bear wearing hat & badge, 8x11" 75.00
Cookie jar, Walrus, in clown outfit, 10x11" 375.00
Creamer & sugar bowl, Hen & Rooster, 5x6" 250.00
Decanter, Robin Hood, stands beside tree, 10½x4⅜" 50.00
Expanimals, Poodle, 7½" 200.00
Figurine, boy shot putting w/Yale logo on shirt, on base, 3" 150.00
Figurine, boy w/airplane & hot dog wearing Mickey Mouse ears, 5½" ...150.00
Figurine, collie, sitting, 7½" 65.00
Figurine, deer laying down, dtd 1940-43, 3x5" 75.00
Figurine, girl holding bird to nest, 5½" 175.00
Figurine, Yogi Bear sitting on a stump, 5" 150.00
Lamp, Monkey, hugging tree, 13" 275.00
Lamp, Squirrel, on top of stump, 12" 275.00
Men of the Mountains, bank, Mtn Dew Loot, 7" 75.00
Men of the Mountains, bowl, pretzel; #H-104, 4½" 40.00
Men of the Mountains, cigarette box, outhouse, #H-109, 7" 75.00
Men of the Mountains, pitcher, #H-101, 7½" 85.00
Men of the Mountains, pouring spout, man's head, #H-104, 6½" ...30.00
Men of the Mountains, punch cup, #H-111, 3" 15.00
Mug, ABC & flowers, squirrel hdl, 5" 100.00
Mug, Bear, smiling face, 3¼" 85.00

Mug, Lamb, smiling face, 3¼" 85.00
Mug, Owl, wearing spectacles, 3¼" 85.00
Mug, Woodgrain (BK Bar) line, rope & spur hdl, 4" 40.00
Napkin holder, Horse, sits on base, 4x6" 150.00
Napkin holder, Rabbit, sits on base, 4x6" 150.00
Napkin holder, Rooster, head up & crowing, 6x7" 75.00
Napkin holder, Squirrel, standing holding acorn, 4x8" 65.00
Planter, Cat, wearing Sailor suit playing w/boat, 8" 80.00
Planter, Circus Elephant, plays hollow drum, 8" 80.00
Planter, Fisherman's Basket, 6" 80.00
Planter, Golf Bag, 7" 80.00
Planter, Ranger Bear, stands beside hollow stump, 8" 80.00
Shakers, Bull, sits w/flowers around neck, pr 40.00
Shakers, Chipmunk, sack of acorns over shoulder, pr 40.00
Shakers, Churn, 2 cats play around churn, pr 40.00
Shakers, Cow, brn w/wht spots, wearing bell around neck, pr 50.00
Shakers, Dutch Girl, hands on hips, pr 35.00
Shakers, Jack-in-the-Box, pr 125.00
Shakers, Kangaroo, mother in bonnet w/joey in pouch, pr 85.00
Shakers, Lamb, wearing apron, pr 30.00
Shakers, Lion, wearing King's crown, pr 45.00
Shakers, Mother Goose, wearing bonnet, pr 45.00
Shakers, Mr Garlic, garlic bulb w/face, 3", pr 40.00
Shakers, Nut, squirrel w/hammer on top, pr 75.00
Shakers, Pirate Fox, patch on 1 eye & sword in belt, pr 45.00
Shakers, Ranger Bear, sitting in Ranger suit, pr 40.00
Shakers, Sailor Elephant, in bibs & wht hat, pr 35.00
Shakers, Snail, elf riding snail, pr 125.00
Shakers, Tommy Turtle, in hat & tie, pr 40.00
Spoon rest, Ranger Bear, sits holding spoon, 5x10" 40.00
Spoon rest, Sailor Elephant, sits holding spoon, 5x10" 40.00
Stein, Bamboo line, 8" 35.00
Toothpick dispenser, Pig, flowers on bk, chin down, 5" 60.00

Typewriters

The first commercially successful typewriter was the Sholes and Glidden, introduced in 1874. By 1882 other models appeared, and by the 1890s dozens were on the market. At the time of World War I, the ranks of typewriter-makers thinned, and by the 1920s only a few survived.

Collectors informally divide typewriter history into the pioneering period, up to about 1890; the classic period, from 1890 to 1920; and the modern period, since 1920. There are two broad classifications of early typewriters: (1) Keyboard machines, in which depression of a key prints a character and via a shift key prints up to three different characters per key; (2) Index machines, in which a chart of all the characters appears on the typewriter; the character is selected by a pointer or dial and is printed by operation of a lever or other device. Even though index typewriters were simpler and more primitive than keyboard machines, they were none-the-less a later development, designed to provide a cheaper alternative to the standard keyboard models that were selling for upwards of $100.00. Eventually second-hand keyboard typewriters supplied the low-price customer, and index typewriters vanished except as toys. Both classes of typewriters appeared in a great many designs.

It is difficult, if not impossible, to assign standard market prices to early typewriters. During the past decade, competition from a handful of wealthy overseas collectors has drastically affected the American market, and prices have become inflated on the rarer models. Some auction-realized prices have been astronomical. It is predicted that the market will drop again when this small group of collectors are satisfied and this atypical activity subsides. For now, we have updated values to reflect current market activity. Also, condition is a very important factor, and typewriters can vary infinitely in condition. A third factor to consider is that an early typewriter achieves its value mainly through the skill, effort, and patience of the collector who restores it to its original condition, in which case its purchase price is insignificant. Some unusual-looking early typewriters are not at all rare or valuable, while some very ordinary-looking ones are scarce and could be quite valuable. No general rules apply.

For further information we recommend *Antique Typewriters & Office Collectibles* by Darryl Rehr (Collector Books). When no condition is indicated, the items listed below are assumed to be in excellent, unrestored condition. Our advisor for this category is Mike Brooks; he is listed in the Directory under California.

Allen, NP 150.00
Anderson Shorthand 125.00
Bar-Lock #2-3, fancy iron front 825.00
Bennet, 1910 ....60.00
Bing #2 ....75.00
Blickensderfer, Blick Oriental 150.00
Burnett 1,100.00
Burroughs Electric 50.00
Caligraph #2 ....300.00
Carissima 200.00
Columbia Index 1,350.00
Commercial Visible, blk 350.00
Corona, folding, w/tripod stand 100.00
Crandall 1,000.00
Daugherty 350.00
Densmore, #1 or 2, ea 200.00
Dollar 300.00
Edelmann 200.00
Edland 800.00
Elliot-Fisher 150.00
Famos 500.00
Fay-Sholes, blk/brn, upstrike 50.00
Fox Sterling 150.00
Franklin, Type I 500.00
Garbell 200.00
Graphic 1,000.00
Hall, New York 200.00
Hammond #1, curved or straight 500.00
Hammonia, minimum value 2,000.00
Herrington 250.00
Imperial Model D 550.00
Jewett #4 ....400.00
Kanzler #3 ....900.00
Keaton Music Typewriter 300.00
Liliput 1,000.00
Masspro 50.00
Mignon #2, red 350.00
National #5 ....200.00
Oliver, #2, nickel base 125.00
Olivetti Lettera #22, turq enameled, 1950s, +case 350.00
Pearl (Searling) 1,100.00
Picht 250.00
Postal, #7 ....750.00
Remington Streamline, portable, Model 5/5T, manual, +case 50.00
Rofa, curved keyboard 125.00
Royal #1 ....95.00
Salter, #5 ....1,100.00
Sampo 700.00
Shimer 1,000.00
Sholes Visible 400.00
Smith Premier, #1 ....250.00
Standard Folding 75.00
Underwood, brass 75.00

Volksschreibmaschine 2,000.00
Wellington 100.00
Williams, curved keyboard 750.00
Williams Junior 200.00
Yankee 250.00
Yost #1 ....250.00

Uhl Pottery

Founded in Evansville, Indiana, in 1849 by German immigrants, the Uhl Pottery was moved to Huntingburg, Indiana, in 1908 because of the more suitable clay available there. They produced stoneware — Acorn Ware jugs, crocks, and bowls — which were marked with the acorn logo and 'Uhl Pottery.' They also made mugs, pitchers, and vases in simple shapes and solid glazes marked with a circular ink stamp containing the name of the pottery and 'Huntingburg, Indiana.' The pottery closed in the mid-1940s. Those seeking additional information about Uhl pottery are encouraged to contact the Uhl Collectors' Society, whose address is listed in the Directory under Clubs, Newsletters, and Catalogs.

Bowl, emb tulips, bl, #119, 3x6" dia 85.00
Bowl, mixing; Reverse Picket Fence, bl, 6" 55.00
Chicken feeder, wht, bl acorn logo, 10" 65.00
Cookie jar, gr, sm emb rib in center, w/lid, unmk, 8¾" 75.00
Cookie jar, red, rnd w/2 sm tab hdls, rnd knob on lid, 5x5½" dia .55.00
Crock, wht, bl acorn logo, 1-gal 55.00
Jug, blk top w/wht bottom, rnd, hdl, mk, 3½" 60.00
Jug, brn, football shape, Meier's Port Wine label, mini 55.00
Jug, brn top w/wht bottom, bl acorn logo, 5-gal 50.00
Jug, Christmas 1941, salmon top w/gr bottom, 2-hdl, mk, 3¼" ...225.00
Mug, bbl shape, bl, wht int, 2½" 115.00
Mug, wht, Yes We Have No Bananas, We Have No Bananas Today ...85.00
Pitcher, yel, #28, 3x2½" dia 55.00
Planter, bl, trumpet form, 5x4½" 50.00
Urn, Grecian; rose gloss, #162, w/stopper, 12¾" 40.00
Vase, bud; dk gr, bulbous bottom w/long trumpet neck, 5" 65.00

Unger Brothers

Art Nouveau silver items of the highest quality were produced by the Unger Brothers, who operated in Newark, New Jersey, from the early 1880s until 1909. In addition to tableware, they also made brushes, mirrors, powder boxes, and the like for milady's dressing table as well as jewelry and small personal accessories such as match safes and flasks. They often marked their products with a circle seal containing an intertwined 'UB' and '925 fine sterling.' In addition to sterling, a very limited amount of gold was also used. Note: This company made no pewter items; Unger designs may occasionally be found in pewter, but these are copies. Items dated in the mark or signed 'Birmingham' are English (not Unger).

Ashtray, smoking lady 375.00
Bowl, Floral, rnd, 8" or larger 475.00
Box, hinged lid, Unger/#B-2649, 1x4½", EX 180.00
Box, powder; cut w/hobstars, dmns & fan, angels/dolphins on lid ..245.00
Brooch, silver, veiled head of lady in plumed hat, att, 2½" 900.00
Buttonhook, retractable, for lady's gloves, 3" 150.00
Coffee set, demitasse; Floral, 3-pc, from $900 to 1,000.00
Cuff links, lady figural, pr 195.00
Dresser set, Love's Dream, 5-pc 950.00
Flask, knight's head 795.00
Hatpin, sterling, Art Nouveau, 8¾" 225.00
Thread case, ornate, mk 275.00
Tray, bread; Floral, oval 450.00
Vanity set, Love's Dream, 1904, 5-pc 950.00

Universal

Universal Potteries Incorporated operated in Cambridge, Ohio, from 1934 to 1956. Many lines of dinnerware and kitchen items were produced in both earthenware and semiporcelain. In 1956 the emphasis was shifted to the manufacture of floor and wall tiles, and the name was changed to the Oxford Tile Company, Division of Universal Potteries. The plant closed in 1976. Our advisor for this category is Ted Haun; he is listed in the Directory under Indiana.

Cattail, teapot, from $40.00 to $50.00. (Photo courtesy Jo Cunningham)

Blue & White, coffee server 25.00
Blue & White, jug, canteen 25.00
Calico Fruit, shakers, 3¾", pr 25.00
Cattail, bowl, oval, 9" 29.00
Cattail, bowl, serving; 8½" 35.00
Cattail, custard 10.00
Cattail, jug, batter; 6" 55.00
Cattail, pie plate 35.00
Cattail, pitcher, 5½" 28.00
Cattail, plate, dinner; 10" 17.50
Cattail, plate, sq, 7¼" 8.00
Cattail, platter, 11½x11" 20.00
Cattail, shakers, glass, made by Tipp, pr 50.00
Cattail, sugar bowl, w/lid 25.00
Fruit & Flowers, tray, utility 17.00
Hollyhock, bean pot, w/lid, 2-hdl, 5¾" 60.00
Iris, canteen refrigerator jug 22.00
Iris, casserole, w/lid 25.00
Iris, pie baker, 10" dia 28.00
Iris, stack set, w/lids 30.00
Largo, creamer 7.00
Largo, pie baker, 10" 15.00
Largo, plate, dessert; 6" 3.00
Largo, plate, luncheon 5.00
Largo, shakers, pr 8.00
Rambler Rose, bowl, flat, sm 6.00
Rambler Rose, gravy boat 12.00
Rambler Rose, milk pitcher 25.00
Rambler Rose, plate, 9" 6.00
Rambler Rose, utility shaker 8.00
Red Poppy, plate, utility; 11½" 15.00
Windmill, bowl, utility; w/lid 10.00
Woodvine, bowl, soup; flat 4.00
Woodvine, bowl, vegetable; oval 10.00
Woodvine, creamer 10.00
Woodvine, cup & saucer 8.00
Woodvine, gravy boat 14.00
Woodvine, jar, utility; w/lid 20.00

Woodvine, plate, luncheon 4.00
Woodvine, plate, 6" 3.00
Woodvine, plate, 9" 8.00
Woodvine, relish dish 10.00
Woodvine, shakers, pr 12.00
Woodvine, sugar bowl, w/lid 14.00
Woodvine, tray, utility 20.00

University City

Located in University City, Missouri, this pottery opened for only five years (1910 – 1915), but because of the outstanding potters associated with it, produced notable artware. The company's founder was Edward Gardner Lewis, and among the well-known artists he employed were Adelaide Robineau, Fredrick Rhead, Taxile Doat, and Julian Zsolnay.

Jardiniere, sytlized plants, periwinkle bl, #5122, 8¼x9¼" 400.00
Paperweight, cameo of 2 twined carp/waves on bl & gray, Doat, 2½" ..900.00
Vase, ivory crystalline (resembling MOP), bottle shape, 1913, 9¼" ..4,000.00
Vase, pea gr mottled crystalline, bottle shape, 1912, 7½x3¾" ...1,400.00

Val St. Lambert

Since its inception in Belgium at the turn of the nineteenth century, the Val St. Lambert Cristalleries has been involved in the production of high-quality glass, producing some cameo. The factory is still in production.

Bowl, ruby cut to clear, repeated bull's eyes & bars, 5½x12" 315.00
Compote, cranberry cut to clear, 6x8" 250.00
Sherbet, cameo, children & animals, gold & bl on clear 225.00
Tumbler, classic figures, cranberry on clear w/gold, 5½" 250.00
Vase, cameo, fishing scene, dk/lt bl on frost, sgn, 7¾" 1,250.00
Vase, flowering trees (3 repeats), ruby to clear, 7" 575.00
Vase, pk w/int free-form bands & trailings, 14" 600.00

Valentines

These valentine listings have been separated into the following styles of cards: dimensional, flat, greeting card, mechanical, mechanical-flat, folded-flat, honeycomb paper puff, and novelty.

The number preceding the dimensional cards refers to the number of layers each of these cards have. This is very important along with height, width, and depth when determining the value of this style of card.

As always, please remember the six specifications when evaluating your card: age, condition, category, manufacturer, size, and your location. Our advisor for this category is Katherine Kreider, author of *Valentines With Values*, *One Hundred Years of Valentines*, and *Valentines For the Eclectic Collector*; she is listed in the Directory under Pennsylvania.

Key:
dim — dimension/dimensional HCPP — honeycomb paper puff
mech — mechanical

Dim, 1D, gondola, PIG, 1900s, 7x8x2", EX 125.00
Dim, 2D, baseball catcher, USA, 1930s, 6½x4x2½", EX 35.00
Dim, 2D, Kewpie look-alike, MIG, 1940s, 6x4x2", EX 35.00
Dim, 2D, Kewpie w/violin, PIG, 1930s, 5½x3½x2", EX 20.00
Dim, 2D, water mill, MIG, 1940s, 8½x5¾x2", EX 50.00
Dim, 4D, cherub orchestra, MIG, 1900s, 11x11x3", EX 225.00
Dim, 4D, garden, MIG, 1900s, 8x4x5½", EX 125.00
Dressed or paper doll valentine, early 1900s, EX 225.00
Flat, boy in bbl, CT, USA, 1920s, 8x5", EX 15.00
Flat, children & dog, JG Scott, USA, 12x6", EX 25.00
Flat, dog, JG Scott, USA, 4x3", EX 5.00
Flat, gondola w/easel bk, PIG, 1900s, 5x6", EX 50.00
Flat, hanging; heart w/Dutch children, Tuck, 8x7", EX 125.00
Flat, Kewpie, PIG, 1920s, 5½x3", EX 10.00
Flat, Scottish bagpipe player, USA, 1920s, 5x5½", EX 10.00
Flat, stick cowboy, USA, 1940s, 5½x4¾", EX 15.00
Flat, Winnie the Pooh, USA, 1960s, 5½x3", EX 15.00
Flat/folded, Dachshund, USA, 1940s, 5x4", EX 10.00
Flat/folded, oyster, hand-colored, 1900s, 7x5", EX 40.00
Flat/folded, Popeye, 1930s, 5½x3", EX 50.00
Flat/folded, top, 1940s, 4x5", EX 5.00
Greeting card, football player, Tuck, 1900s, 7x5", EX 75.00
Greeting card, heart w/dim, PIG, 1900s, 4½x4x4½", EX 45.00
Greeting card, Howland, 1850s, 6x4¾", EX 75.00
Greeting card, Scottie Dog ACE, USA, 4½x3½", EX 10.00
Greeting card, Whitney, 1850s, 6x3¾", EX 75.00
Greeting card, Whitney, 5 snow angels spell Love, USA, 1930s, 5x5", EX ..10.00
HCPP, cherubs fishing, bl base, PIG, 1900s, 5½x4x4", EX 50.00
HCPP, dove cote, PIG, 1900s, 9x6½x3", EX 75.00
HCPP, sailboat, gr base, PIG, 1900s, 6¾x6x6", EX 50.00
HCPP, vase, PIG, 1920s, 9x6½x3", EX 75.00
Hold-to-light, fountain, PIG, 1900s, 10x8x3", EX 275.00

Mechanical-flat, cigar-smoking man with top hat, early 1900s, Germany, 6½x3¾", EX $45.00. (Photo courtesy Katherine Kreider)

Mech-flat, African Americans & rooster, 6x11", EX 75.00
Mech-flat, bear playing drum, PIG, 1920s, 5x2½", EX 10.00
Mech-flat, crystal ball, USA, 1940s, 7x4½", EX 35.00
Mech-flat, owl, PIG, 1940s, 6x4½", EX 5.00
Mech-flat, roadster, PIG, 1940s, 8¾x7", EX 15.00
Mech-flat, scissors, USA, 1930s, 4x4½", EX 10.00
Novelty, boy w/plastic eyes on hobby horse, MIG, 7x4", EX 45.00
Novelty, favor cups, USA, 1920s, 5x2x2", EX 10.00
Novelty, flirt fan, USA, 1870s, 5x8" opened, EX 200.00
Novelty, HCPP fan, Beistle, USA, 1920s, 8½x2" closed, EX 75.00
Novelty, paper doll heart, USA, 1940s, 4½x5", EX 45.00
Novelty greeting card, Bo Peep, USA, 6½x3½", EX 25.00
Paper cut valentine, 1800s, 6x4", EX 125.00
Valentine's Day Book, Happy Times, 1930s, EX 75.00
Valentine Writer, 1800s, EX 200.00
Watch paper token of love, 1800s, USA, 2x2", EX 200.00

Vallerysthal

Fine glassware has been produced in Vallerysthal, France, since the middle of the nineteenth century.

Candle holder, pk, beading on tapered stem & rim, 9" 65.00
Jug, mc pnt grasshoppers, gr serpentine hdl, ribbed, 10" 2,600.00

Vase, dahlias, mc/etched on olive gr, appl centers, 9" 1,100.00
Vase, orchids cameo, mc on frost, appl raindrops on stick neck, 13" ...3,500.00

Van Briggle

The Van Briggle Pottery of Colorado Springs, Colorado, was established in 1901 by Artus Van Briggle, whose early career had been shaped by such notables as Karl Langenbeck and Maria Nichols Storer. His quest for several years had been to perfect a completely flat matt glaze, and upon accomplishing his goal, he opened his pottery. His wife, Anne, worked with him, and they, along with George Young, were responsible for the modeling of the wares. Their work typified the flow and form of the Art Nouveau movement, and the shapes they designed played as important a part in their success as their glazes. Some of their most famous pieces were Despondency, Lorelei, and Toast Cup. Increasing demand for their work soon made it necessary to add to their quarters as well as their staff. Although much of the ware was eventually made from molds, each piece was carefully trimmed and refined before the glaze was sprayed on. Their most popular colors were Persian Rose, Ming Blue, and Mustard Yellow.

Van Briggle died in 1904, but the work was continued by his wife. New facilities were built; and by 1908, in addition to their artware, tiles, gardenware, and commercial lines were added. By the '20s the emphasis had shifted from art pottery to novelties and commercial wares. Reproductions of some of the early designs continue to be made. The double AA mark has always been in use, but after 1920 the dates and/or shape numbers were dropped. Mention should be made here as well that the Anna Van Briggle glaze is a later line which was made between 1956 and 1968. Our advisor for this category is Michelle Ross; she is listed in the Directory under Michigan.

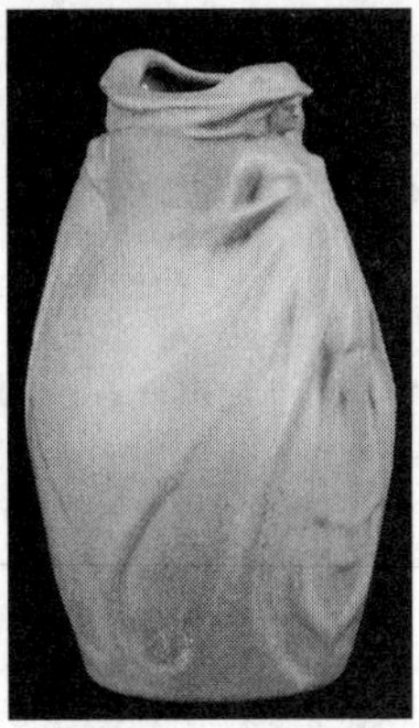

Vase, Dos Cabezas, two embossed Nouveau ladies with flowing hair and garments under light green matt, marked AA/Van Briggle/1902/III, firing lines in base, 7½x5", $19,000.00.

Bookend, ram, copper brn w/soft blk, late 1910s, 5x5" 225.00
Bowl, rose, leaf shape, 14½" 60.00
Bowl & flower frog, mauve/teal, 1914, 12" dia 450.00
Candlestick, Persian Rose, #26, 10" 60.00
Dish, woman grinding corn, turq, 6½" 125.00
Flower frog, frog figural, Mountain Craig Brown, 2⅜x5" 175.00
Mug, eagle in flight, leathery gr, 1906, 5x5" 400.00
Paperweight, horned toad, amber on gr base, no mk, 1914 ....900.00
Plate, grapes/leaves, burgundy/bl, 1907-12, 8½" 210.00
Scarab, peppered mustard, souvenir, 1928, 2⅝" 600.00
Tile, scenic, cream/mustard/gr/lt bl/bl, 6⅛" 1,380.00
Vase, bl (curdled), bulbous, 1905, 6x4½" 425.00
Vase, bl (2 tone) w/emb daffodils on stems, 1919, 9½" 550.00
Vase, bud; floral (3-leaf), mulberry, 5¾x2⅛" 200.00
Vase, crocuses, dk red/bl, squat, 1920s, 7½" 350.00
Vase, desert flowers, gr/burgundy, hdls, 1904, 10x8" 2,250.00
Vase, Despondency, bl/turq, ca '20s, 13½" 2,600.00
Vase, dk red/bl, tapered, 1920s, 8" 225.00
Vase, dogwood blossoms, dk gr, 1906, 8¼x5" 2,200.00
Vase, dragonflies, gr/mahog, incurvate, 7" 300.00
Vase, dragonflies (3), mustard, 1907-12, 3x2½" 800.00
Vase, dragonfly, maroon on mulberry, late 1910s, 6¾x3" 400.00
Vase, floral, dk red/bl, spherical, 1925, 3¾" 125.00
Vase, floral, gr/rose, dtd 1905, 10½" 1,100.00
Vase, floral buds, cobalt on teal, #20, ca 1920, 5½" 250.00
Vase, floral buds, maroon on mulberry, late 1910s, 5½" 175.00
Vase, floral stems/leaves, 2-tone gr/bl, 1907-12, 9" 700.00
Vase, gooseberries, gr on raspberry, hdls, 1905, 7½x9½" 2,500.00
Vase, Indian faces (3), mahog/bl, ftd, 11" 400.00
Vase, irises, dk red/bl, drilled, 1920s, 14¼" 325.00
Vase, jonquils, bl over turq, corseted, 10" 150.00
Vase, jonquils, maroon to mulberry w/bl spray, baluster, 1918, 9½" ...425.00
Vase, jonquils on long stems, dk gr, 1902, 7x3½" 2,500.00
Vase, Lady of the Lily, lt gr, 1902, 11x9½" 37,500.00
Vase, leaves, amber clay under gunmetal-brn, #849, 1913, 4¾x3½" ...1,100.00
Vase, leaves, bl/turq, ftd cylinder, 8" 200.00
Vase, leaves, dk red/bl, squat, ca 1925, 3¾" 150.00
Vase, leaves, turq w/cobalt spray, 1915, 8½x6" 375.00
Vase, leaves (4/lg), gr on brn, ca 1910, 5½" 260.00
Vase, leaves (4/lg), yel-gr, tapered ovoid, dtd 1902, 8" 2,400.00
Vase, leaves at angle shoulder, maroon/bl, post-1920s, 5x10" 300.00
Vase, leaves/berries, raspberry, 1904, 8½x7" 3,000.00
Vase, Lorelei, bl/turq, 1920-25, 9½x4" 1,300.00
Vase, Lorelei, burgundy/turq, late, 11x4½" 300.00
Vase, Lorelei, wht dead-matt, recent, 10½" 200.00
Vase, lt bl, waisted, 4" 250.00
Vase, maroon, elongated teardrop form, ca 1914, 7" 300.00
Vase, peacock feathers, gr on bl, 1904, 11x4" 3,000.00
Vase, peacock feathers, yel/turq/butterfat on burgundy, 1905, 12x4" .1,800.00
Vase, poppies, dk bl, spherical, pre-1912, 5½x6½" 900.00
Vase, poppies, gr, #218, 1915, 7⅜" 750.00
Vase, poppies, gr/bl, 1907-12, 6½" 1,400.00
Vase, poppies, gr & brn, 1920s, 3½" 300.00
Vase, poppies, mulberry w/bl spray, 1920s-40s, 8⅛x4" 175.00
Vase, poppies, turq, 1916, 7½x4" 850.00
Vase, poppy pods on stems, sheer frothy ivory, 1907, 6½x5¼" ..3,500.00
Vase, stylized feathers, leathery dk gr, bulbous, 1907-12, 7x6" ...1,100.00
Vase, stylized trefoils w/long stems, bl, 5½" 525.00
Vase, sunflowers, maroon/bl, 1916, 9½" 800.00
Vase, trefoils on gr, 1904, 7¼x4¾" 1,100.00
Vase, vertical ribs, brn clay under lt bl microcrystalline, 5½x4" ..950.00
Vase, yucca leaves, curdled brn, 1907-11, #162, 5x3½" 900.00
Vase, yucca leaves, purple on gr, tapering, 1915, 15½x7" 4,750.00
Vase, 2 ladies heads w/flowing hair, charcoal/brn/gr, 7½x13" .6,500.00

Vaseline

Vaseline, a greenish-yellow colored glass produced by adding uranium oxide to the batch, was produced during the Victorian era. It was made in smaller quantities than other colors and lost much of its popularity with the advent of the electric light. It was used for pressed tablewares, vases, whimseys, souvenir items, oil lamps, perfume bottles, drawer pulls, and doorknobs. Pieces have been reproduced, and some factories still make it today in small batches. Vaseline glass will fluoresce under an ultraviolet light.

Bottle, scent; Star & Punty, orig stopper, 6½" 350.00
Candelabrum, 3-light, child sz, 4½x4½" 225.00
Compote, fiery opal rim, dolphin stem, 5½", pr 400.00
Compote, Sawtooth, scalloped rim, att Sandwich, 10" 2,000.00

Goblet, Flute, flared rim, 4" 70.00
Paperweight, owl, 4½" 60.00
Paperweight, rabbit, 5x6" 75.00
Rose bowl, Wreath & Shell 100.00
Spill holder, Prism Panel Rosette, flint, 4¾" 85.00
Tumblers, Daisy & Button pattern on lower half, 4", set of 6 ....250.00
Vase, Pressed Loop, appl to marble base, 10¾" 140.00

Verlys

Verlys art glass, produced in France after 1931 by the Holophane Company of Verlys, was made in crystal with acid-finished relief work in the Art Deco style. Colored and opalescent glass was also used. In 1935 an American branch was opened in Newark, Ohio, where very similar wares were produced until the factory ceased production in 1951. French Verlys was signed with one of three mold-impressed script signatures, all containing the company name and country of origin. The American-made glassware was signed 'Verlys' only, either scratched with a diamond-tipped pen or impressed in the mold. There is very little if any difference in value between items produced in France and America. Though some seem to feel that the French should be higher priced (assuming it to be scarce), many prefer the American-made product.

In June of 1955, about sixteen Verlys molds were leased to the A.H. Heisey Company. Heisey's versions were not signed with the Verlys name, so if an item is unsigned it is almost certainly a Heisey piece. The molds were returned to Verlys of America in July 1957. Fenton now owns all Verlys molds, but all issues are marked Fenton. Our advisor for this category is Don Frost; he is listed in the Directory under Washington.

Vase, Lance, Dusty Rose 8", $345.00. (Note: Dusty Rose is a sprayed-on color that is applied over the glassware; it is considered rare.)

Bowl, Alpine Thistle, frosted, 8½" 135.00
Bowl, Butterfly (moths w/flower sprays), opal, 2½x13½" 650.00
Candle holders, Water Lily, clear & frosted, 5½x2½", pr 125.00
Vase, Alpine Thistle, fiery opal, script mk, 9" 750.00
Vase, butterfly (actually moths), clear & frosted, oval, 4½x5" ...165.00
Vase, Grasshopper (actually moths) w/grass, bulbous, 4½x5¼" .450.00
Vase, Lovebirds, clear & frosted, script mk, 4½x6½" 175.00
Vase, mermaids/fish etched/emb in amber, baluster shape, 10" ..1,130.00

Vernon Kilns

Vernon Potteries Ltd. was established by Faye G. Bennison in Vernon, California, in 1931. The name was later changed to Vernon Kilns; until it closed in 1958, dinnerware, specialty plates, artware, and figurines were their primary products. Among its wares most sought after by collectors today are items designed by such famous artists as Rockwell Kent, Walt Disney, Don Blanding, Jane Bennison, and May and Vieve Hamilton. Our advisor is Maxine Nelson, author of *Collectible Vernon Kilns* (now out of print); you will find her listed in the Directory under Arizona.

Anytime Shape

Patterns you will find on this shape include Tickled Pink, Heavenly Days, Anytime, Imperial, Sherwood, Frolic, Young in Heart, Rose-A-Day, and Dis 'N Dot.

Bowl, fruit; 5½", from $4 to 6.00
Bowl, vegetable; divided, 9", from $15 to 20.00
Butter dish, w/lid, from $25 to 30.00
Coffeepot, w/lid, 8-cup, from $30 to 45.00
Gravy boat, from $15 to 18.00
Mug, from $12 to 20.00
Pitcher, 1-qt, from $20 to 25.00
Platter, 9½", from $9 to 12.00
Shakers, pr, from $10 to 15.00
Syrup, drip-cut top, from $45 to 65.00
Tumbler, 14-oz, from $12 to 22.00

Chatelaine Shape

This designer pattern by Sharon Merrill was made in four color combinations: Topaz, Bronze, Platinum, and Jade.

Bowl, chowder; Topaz & Bronze, 9", from $15 to 25.00
Creamer, Topaz & Bronze, from $20 to 25.00
Cup & saucer, tea; ped ft, decor Platinum & Jade, from $25 to ...30.00
Plate, chop; Topaz & Bronze, 14", from $45 to 50.00
Plate, salad; decor Platinum & Jade, 7½", from $15 to 18.00
Sugar bowl, decor Platinum & Jade, w/lid, from $30 to 35.00

Lotus and Pan American Lei Shape

Patterns on this shape include Lotus, Chinling, and Vintage. Pan American Lei was a variation with flatware from the San Marino line. To evaluate Lotus, use the low end of our range as the minimum value; the high end of values apply to Pan American Lei.

Ashtray, Pan American Lei, 5½" 25.00
Bowl, chowder, 6", from $11 to 18.00
Bowl, mixing; Pan American Lei only, 7" 40.00
Bowl, salad; Lotus only, 12½", from $35 to 45.00
Bowl, salad; Pan American Lei only, 10½" 95.00
Creamer, from $15 to 27.00
Pitcher, jug; 2-qt, from $30 to 95.00
Plate, coupe; Pan American only, 10" 25.00
Plate, offset; Lotus only, 6½", from $6 to 8.00
Shakers, pr, from $15 to 50.00
Sugar bowl, w/lid, from $16 to 35.00

Melinda Shape

Patterns found on this shape are: Arcadia, Beverly, Blossom Time, Chintz, Cosmos, Dolores, Fruitdale, Hawaii (Lei Lani on Melinda is priced at two times base value), May Flower, Monterey, Native California, Philodendron. The more elaborate the pattern, the higher the value.

Bowl, lug chowder; 6", from $12 to 25.00
Bowl, serving; oval, 10", from $15 to 25.00
Butter dish, w/lid, oblong, from $30 to 45.00
Creamer, short or tall, from $10 to 18.00
Egg cup, from $18 to 30.00
Pitcher, 2-qt, from $40 to 60.00
Plate, dinner; 10½", from $12 to 18.00

Platter, salad; 7½", from $7 to 12.00
Platter, 14", from $20 to 35.00
Relish, leaf shape, 2-part, 11", from $35 to 45.00
Sauce boat, from $20 to 30.00
Teapot, w/lid, 6-cup, from $45 to 85.00
Tidbit, wooden fixture, 2-tier, from $20 to 30.00

Montecito Shape (and Coronado)

This was one of the company's most utilized shapes — well over two hundred patterns have been documented. Among the most popular are the solid colors, plaids, the florals, westernware, and the Bird and Turnbull series. Bird, Turnbull, and Winchester 73 (Frontier Days) are two to four times base values. Disney hollow ware is seven to eight times base values. Plaids (except Tweed and Calico), solid colors, Brown-eyed Susan are represented by the lower range.

Ashtray, ind, 3" sq, from $8 to 12.00
Bowl, chowder; angular, appl pierced hdls, open, 6", from $20 to 30.00
Bowl, fruit; 5½", from $6 to 8.00
Bowl, lug chowder; tab hdls, 6" dia, from $12 to 25.00
Bowl, mixing; 5", from $15 to 20.00
Bowl, mixing; 8", from $35 to 45.00
Bowl, salad; 13", from $45 to 65.00
Bowl, serving; oval, 10", from $18 to 22.00
Bowl, serving; 7½" dia, from $12 to 15.00
Butter tray, oblong, w/lid, from $25 to 45.00
Carafe, angular or rnd, w/stopper, 10-cup, from $30 to 45.00
Casserole, 2-hdl, angular, w/lid, from $45 to 50.00
Coaster/cup warmer, 4½", from $18 to 25.00
Comport, ftd, early, scarce, 9½" dia, from $45 to 65.00
Cup & saucer, colossal; 4-qt, 9⅜", 15" dia saucer, $125 to 150.00
Flowerpot, 4", from $35 to 45.00
Jam jar, notched lid, 5", from $55 to 65.00
Mug, bulbous, appl hdl, 8-oz, 3¾", from $20 to 25.00
Pitcher, jug; bulbous bottom, 1-qt, from $30 to 35.00
Pitcher, streamlined, 1-pt, 6", from $20 to 24.00
Plate, bread & butter; 6½", from $5 to 8.00
Plate, grill; 11", from $18 to 25.00
Platter, 12", from $17 to 25.00
Sauce/gravy boat, fast-stand, dbl spout, from $20 to 30.00
Shaker, pepper; regular, ea, from $7.50 to 10.00
Spoon holder, from $45 to 65.00
Teapot, rnd, w/lid, from $35 to 65.00
Tidbit, wooden fixture, 3-tier, from $25 to 40.00
Tumbler, str sides, #5, 14-oz, from $18 to 25.00

San Fernando Shape

Known patterns for this shape are Desert Bloom, Early Days, Hibiscus, R.F.D., Vernon's 1860, and Vernon Rose.

Bowl, fruit; 5½", from $8 to 10.00
Bowl, lug chowder; tab hdls, 6" dia, from $12 to 25.00
Bowl, rim soup; 8", from $12 to 20.00
Coffeepot, 8-cup, from $35 to 65.00
Cup & saucer, tea; from $12 to 16.00
Mug, red only, 9-oz, from $16 to 22.00
Olive dish, oval, 10", from $20 to 25.00
Plate, dinner; 10½", from $12 to 18.00
Platter, 12", from $18 to 25.00
Sauce boat, fast-stand, from $25 to 30.00
Shakers, pr, from $18 to 25.00
Sugar bowl, w/lid, from $15 to 20.00

San Marino Shape

Known patterns for this shape are Barkwood, Bel Air, California Originals, Casual California, Gayety, Hawaiian Coral, Heyday, Lei Lani (two times base values), Mexicana, Pan American Lei (two times base values), Raffia, Shadow Leaf, Shantung, Sun Garden, and Trade Winds.

Ashtray, 5½", from $15 to 25.00
Bowl, chowder; 6", from $12 to 20.00
Bowl, coupe soup; 8½", from $15 to 25.00
Bowl, mixing; 8", from $25 to 35.00
Bowl, salad; 10½", from $30 to 45.00
Casserole, ind; w/lid, 4", from $15 to 20.00
Coffee server, w/stopper, 10-oz, from $25 to 30.00
Cup & saucer, tea; from $8 to 12.00
Custard, 3", from $20 to 25.00
Flowerpot, w/saucer, 5", from $45 to 55.00
Pepper mill, wood encased, 4½", from $40 to 60.00
Pitcher, 1-qt, from $20 to 25.00
Plate, bread & butter; 6", from $4 to 7.00
Plate, chop; 13", from $15 to 30.00
Platter, 9½", from $10 to 15.00
Shakers, gourd shape, pr, from $15 to 20.00
Tumbler, style #5, 14-oz, from $15 to 22.00

Ultra Shape

More than fifty patterns were issued on this shape. Nearly all the artist-designed lines (Rockwell Kent, Don Blanding, and Disney) utilized Ultra. The shape was developed by Gale Turnbull, and many of the elaborate flower and fruit patterns can be credited to him as well; use the high end of our range as a minimum value for his work. For Frederick Lunning, use the mid range. For other artist patterns, use these formulae based on the high end: Blanding — 2X (Aquarium 3X); Disney, 7–8X; Kent — Moby Dick and Our America, 2½X, Salamina, 5–7X.

Bowl, chowder; from $12 to 25.00
Bowl, fruit; 5½", from $6 to 12.00
Bowl, mixing; 6", from $20 to 25.00
Bowl, mixing; 9", from $35 to 45.00
Bowl, serving; 9" dia, from $15 to 30.00
Coffeepot, AD; 2-cup, from $60 to 70.00
Creamer, open, regular, short or tall, from $12 to 18.00
Cup & saucer, AD; from $19 to 30.00
Mug, 8-oz, 3½", from $18 to 30.00
Pitcher, disk; from $35 to 70.00
Pitcher, jug; w/lid, 1-pt, from $35 to 50.00
Plate, chop; 12", from $20 to 50.00
Plate, luncheon; 8½", from $12 to 15.00
Shakers, pr, from $12 to 18.00
Sugar bowl, regular, w/lid, short or tall, from $15 to 25.00
Tureen, notched lid, sm, 7", from $60 to 85.00

Year 'Round Shape

Patterns on this shape include Country Cousin and Lollipop Tree.

Bowl, vegetable; 9" dia, from $10 to 14.00
Coffeepot, w/lid, 6-cup, from $25 to 45.00
Gravy boat, from $12 to 22.00
Plate, bread & butter; 6", from $4 to 6.00
Platter, 13½", from $15 to 25.00
Teapot, w/lid, from $25 to 45.00

Fantasia

Fantasia, figurine, Dumbo, #41, $200.00.

Bowl, goldfish, #121 ....375.00
Bowl, mushroom, HP decor, rectangular, #120 ....295.00
Bowl, satyr, #124 ....250.00
Cup & saucer, demi 225.00
Figurine, dancing hippo, arms out, #32 ....350.00
Figurine, ostrich ballerina, #29 ....2,000.00
Vase, Pegasus, bl, #127 ....700.00

Souvenir Plates

Alaska, Scrimshaw, artist sgn, 10½" 45.00
Bits of the Old South, Down on the Levee, 14" 95.00
El Camino Real, CA Missions, 14" 65.00
Gen Douglas MacArthur, brn 12.00
Grand Canyon Nat'l Park, red, 10½" 15.00
Historic Baltimore, Johns Hopkins Hospital, 8½" 20.00
Marineland, FL, bl 18.00
North Carolina State, mc 10.00
Statue of Liberty, bl 25.00

Villeroy and Boch

The firm of Villeroy and Boch, located in Mettlach, Germany, was brought into being by the 1841 merger of three German factories — the Wallerfangen factory, founded by Nicholas Villeroy in 1787; and Boch's father's factory in Septfontaines, established in 1767. Villeroy and Boch produced many varieties of wares, including earthenware with printed under-glaze designs which carried the well-known castle mark with the name 'Mettlach.' See also Mettlach.

Candy box, Le Ballon, lg 65.00
Candy box, Le Ballon, sm 45.00
Dinnerware, Vieux Luxembourg, bl & wht, service for 8, +5-pc tea set ..385.00
Pitcher, water; butterflies on sq body, 11" 135.00
Tray, rtcl brass, inlaid Secessionist-motif ceramic, +coasters 325.00
Turkey set, bl transfer, 22½" platter+10 10" plates 1,100.00
Vase, dripping blk/gr matt, hdls, spherical, V&B, 8" 125.00

Vistosa

Vistosa was produced from about 1938 through the early 1940s. It was Taylor, Smith, and Taylor's answer to the very successful Fiesta line of their nearby competitor, Homer Laughlin. Vistosa was made in four solid colors: mango red, cobalt blue, light green, and deep yellow. 'Pie crust' edges and a dainty five-petal flower molded into handles and lid finials made for a very attractive yet nevertheless commercially unsuccessful product. For further information, we recommend *Collector's Guide to Lu-Ray Pastels* by Kathy and Bill Meehan (Collector Books). Our advisor for this category is Ted Haun; he is listed in the Directory under Indiana.

Bowl, cream soup; from $20 to 25.00
Bowl, fruit; from $10 to 15.00
Bowl, nappy; from $40 to 50.00
Bowl, salad; ftd, 12", from $175 to 200.00
Bowl, soup; lug hdld, from $25 to 30.00
Chop plate, 12" 40.00
Chop plate, 15", from $40 to 50.00
Coffee cup, AD; from $30 to 35.00
Coffee saucer, AD; from $15 to 20.00
Creamer 20.00
Egg cup, ftd, from $25 to 35.00
Jug, water; 2-qt 85.00
Plate, 6", from $10 to 15.00
Plate, 7", from $12 to 18.00
Plate, 9", from $15 to 20.00
Plate, 10", from $50 to 60.00
Sauce boat, from $150 to 175.00
Shakers, pr 32.00
Sugar bowl, w/lid 25.00
Teacup, from $10 to 15.00
Teapot, 6-cup, from $150 to 175.00

Volkmar

Charles Volkmar established a workshop in Tremont, New York, in 1882. He produced artware decorated under the glaze in the manner of the early barbotine work done at the Haviland factory in Limoges, France. He relocated in 1888 in Menlo Park, New Jersey, and together with J.T. Smith established the Menlo Park Ceramic Company for the production of art tile. The partnership was dissolved in 1893. From 1895 until 1902, Volkmar located in Corona, New York, first under the name Volkmar Ceramic Company, later as Volkmar and Cory, and for the final six years as Crown Point. During the latter period he made art tile, blue under-glaze Delft-type wares, colorful polychrome vases, etc. The Volkmar Kilns were established in 1903 in Metuchen, New Jersey, by Volkmar and his son. Wares were marked with various devices consisting of the Volkmar name, initials, or 'Crown Point Ware.'

Bowl, centerpc; Persian Blue crackle, turq bl, 1928, 6½x13½" ..700.00
Charger, WA Headquarters Tappan NY, bl on wht, Delft style, 11" ..225.00
Cider set, gr mottle w/mustard to brn int, 9" pitcher+4 3¾" mugs 600.00
Vase, cvd panels w/dbl outline & arched top, rust/gr, 8", EX 180.00
Vase, gr matt, bulbous, mk V, 5½" 225.00
Vase, leathery gr matt, 4-sided base, squat, 3¾" 200.00
Vase, mottled/frothy purple, 1929, 6½x4" 400.00
Vase, teal gr matt, faceted, squat, mk V, 3" 150.00

Vontury

Located in New Jersey, F.J. Von Tury is primarily a designer of architectural artware, tile and murals in particular, but he also produces a line of vases, bowls, and other decorative items. These are signed 'Vontury' in script. Impressionistic florals are favored.

Platter, leaves, bl/brn on lt gr, scalloped edge, 12¾x9½" 30.00
Vase, floral, gr & brn, mk, 8⅞" 75.00
Vase, leaves & vines, brn & yel on soft bl-gray, mk, 14⅜" 175.00

Wade

The Wade Potteries was established in 1867 by George Wade and his partner, a man by the name of Myatt. It was located in Burslem, England, the center of that country's pottery industry. In 1882 George Wade bought out his partner, and the name of the pottery was changed to Wade and Sons. In 1919 the pottery underwent yet another name change and became known as George Wade & Son Ltd. The year 1891 saw the establishment of another Wade Pottery — J & W Wade & Co., which in turn changed its name to A.J. Wade & Co. in 1927. At this time (1927) Wade Heath & Co. Ltd. was also formed.

The three pottries plus a new Irish pottery named Wade (Ireland) Ltd. were incorporated into one company in 1958 and given the name The Wade Group of Potteries. In 1990 the group was taken over by Beauford plc. and became Wade Ceramics Ltd. It sold again in early 1999 to Wade Management and is now a private company.

For those interested in learning more about Wade pottery, we recommend *The World of Wade* and *The World of Wade Book 2* by Ian Warner and Mike Posgay; Mr. Warner is listed in the Directory under Canada.

Viking Ship Posey Bowl, ca 1959 – 65, 7⅜" long, $25.00.

Animal Figurine, Playful Lamb 155.00
Basket Ware 2 Butter Dish, 3¼x4½" dia 40.00
Bud Vase Souvenirs 1950s-1961, HP floral decor, 4½" 15.00
Candleholder, Flowerlight, 1x4" dia 14.00
Candleholder, Mayfair, 3⅛" 12.00
Cellulose Figurine, Jeanette, 6½" 285.00
Championship Dogs, English Setter, 2¾" 100.00
Circus Animal Set, Poodle, 1¾" 10.00
Connoisseur's Collection, Nuthatch, 5½" 450.00
Cranky Tankards, The Miasma, 5" 75.00
Disney Blow Ups 1961-1965, Scamp, 4⅛" 235.00
Disney Hat Box Series 1956-1965, Baby Pegsus, 1¾" 75.00
Disney 1981-1987 (Lady & the Tramp), Chief, 1⅞" 26.00
Dog Pipe Rests, Corgi 40.00
Dogs & Puppies Series, Alsatian (Adult), 2½" 25.00
Dogs & Puppies Series, Corgi (Adult), 2¼" 40.00
Farmyard Set, Duck, 1" 20.00
Golf Bag Jug, 3½" 35.00
Gothic Basket, 7" 160.00
Happy Family, Owl (Parent), 1¾" 15.00
Honey Pot, Beehive, 4x3" dia 45.00
Irish Ware Preserve Jar, 4x2¾" dia 30.00
KP Foods Potato Chip Promotion, Brother Francis, 1⅝" 40.00
Lady & the Tramp Disneys 1981-1987, Big Mama, 1¾" 37.00
Mabel Lucie Attwell Character, Sam, 3⅛" 220.00
Man in Boat, 1⅝x6" 105.00
Nursery Rhyme Figurine, Blynken, 2" 195.00
Nursery Rhyme Figurine, Little Jack Horner, 2½" 260.00
Painted Ladies, Pink Lady, 2¼" 75.00
Posy Vase, Viking Ship, 7⅜" 25.00
Red Rose Tea Promotion (Canada), Hedgehog 8.00
Red Rose Tea Promotion (Canada), Queen of Hearts, 1¾" 15.00
Red Rose Tea Promotion (USA), Beaver, 1¼" 6.00
Romance Range Trinket Box, 1⅞x2⅝x2¼" 15.00
Safari Set, Polar Bear, 1⅛" 14.00
Spirit Containers, Baby Chick, 3⅜" 45.00
Spirit Containers, Cockatoo, 5" 120.00
Survival Set, Golden Eagle, 1¾" 16.00
Tom & Jerry, 3⅝" & 1⅞", ea 75.00
Tortoise Family, Slow Fe Baby Tortoise 60.00
TV Pet Series, Droopy Jr, 2¼" 90.00
TV Pet Series, Fifi, 2⅝" 45.00
Wall Plates, Niagara Falls, 9½" dia 15.00
Whimsey-On-Why Village Sets 1980, Doctor Healer's House, 1¾" ...20.00
Whimsie-Land Series, Rabbit, 2" 20.00
Whimsies 1953-1959, Crocodile, ¾x1⅝" 65.00
Whimsies 1953-1959, Leaping Fawn, 1⅞" 45.00
Whimsies 1971-1984, Corgi, 1½" 8.00
Whimsies 1971-1984, Rabbit, ears apart, 1⅛" 9.00
Whimtray, Lion Cub 30.00
Whoppas, Otter, 1¼" 40.00
World of Survival Series, African Elephant, 6x10" 500.00
Zamba Ware Ashtray, 4¼" sq 20.00

Wallace China

Dinnerware with a Western theme was produced by the Wallace China Company, who operated in California from 1931 until 1964. Artist Till Goodan designed three lines, Rodeo, Pioneer Trails, and Boots and Saddle, which they marketed under the package name Westward Ho. When dinnerware with a western theme became so popular just a few years ago, Rodeo was reproduced, but the new trademark includes neither 'California' or 'Wallace China.'

This ware is very heavy and not prone to chip but be sure to examine it under a strong light to look for knife scratches, which will lessen its value to a considerable extent when excessive. Our advisor for this category is Marv Fogleman; he is listed in the Directory under California. If you'd like to learn more about this company, we recommend *The Collector's Encyclopedia of California Pottery* by Jack Chipman.

Aztec, platter, 13½x9" 30.00
Boots & Saddle, ashtray, 5½" 60.00
Boots & Saddle, plate, bread & butter 45.00
Boots & Saddle, plate, dinner, 10⅝" 130.00
Boots & Saddle, plate, 7" 50.00
Boots & Saddle, sugar bowl, w/lid 125.00
Chuck Wagon, bowl, soup; 3x6¾" 50.00
Chuck Wagon, creamer, 3" 75.00
Chuck Wagon, cup, Coffee Pot Cafe advertising, mk 110.00
Chuck Wagon, cup & saucer, demitasse 70.00
Chuck Wagon, saucer, 6¼" 30.00
Desert Ware, plate, lunch; Mrs Gray's Inn pattern 45.00
El Rancho, bowl, sauce 35.00
El Rancho, coffee mug 20.00
El Rancho, cup & saucer 50.00
El Rancho, platter, oval, 11½" 95.00
Plate, Yellowstone Nat'l Park, bear/waterfalls/geyser, 9¾" 70.00
Rodeo, ashtray 55.00
Rodeo, bowl, serving; 9" 220.00
Rodeo, chop plate, 13" 220.00
Rodeo, creamer, from $60 to 70.00
Rodeo, cup & saucer, demitasse 100.00
Rodeo, mug, coffee; 3¾" 100.00
Rodeo, plate, dinner; 10½" 100.00
Rodeo, plate, 7", from $50 to 65.00
Rodeo, platter, oval, 15x10" 250.00
Rodeo, shakers, 5", pr 125.00
Westward Ho, ashtray, Pioneer Trails 50.00
Westward Ho, bread tray, oval 125.00
Westward Ho, creamer, Longhorn 85.00

Westward Ho, cup & saucer, stacking 50.00
Westward Ho, pitcher, cowboy on bucking bull, 3½" 75.00
Westward Ho, plate, child's; 9" 165.00
Westward Ho, plate, Little Buckaroo, 9" 180.00
Westward Ho, platter, 49ers, oval, 12" 65.00
Westward Ho, shakers, 4", pr 100.00

Walley

The Walley Pottery operated in West Sterling, Massachusetts, from 1898 to 1919. Never more than a one-man operation, Walley himself handcrafted all his wares from local clay. The majority of his pottery was simple and unadorned and usually glazed in matt green. On occasion, however, you may find high- and semi-gloss green, as well as matt glazes in blue, cream, brown, and red. The rarest and most desirable examples of his work are those with applied or relief-carved decorations. Some pieces are marked 'WJW.'

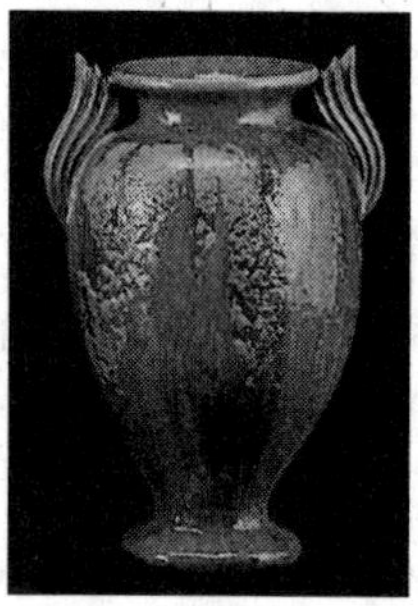

Vase, frothy multi-toned green gloss, 9½x6¾", $1,100.00.

Vase, brn & gr flambe, bulbous, 5½x5½" 400.00
Vase, dk bl (leathery) over dk bl semimatt, WJW mk, 4½x6½", NM ..200.00
Vase, gr over brn w/sections of bsk, WSH, 3¾" 150.00
Vase, mahog flambe, collar rim, WJW mk, 6¾x6¾" 1,500.00
Vase, periwinkle w/lt lustre, curdling & lg specks, rnd 4" 275.00
Vase, vertical leaves, gr & brn matt, 6½" 2,900.00

Walrath

Frederick Walrath was a studio potter who worked from around the turn of the century until his death in 1920. He was located in Rochester, New York, until 1918 when he became associated with the Newcomb Pottery in New Orleans, Louisiana.

Bowl, gray matt, 8" 110.00
Flower frog/centerpc, seated nude w/vase on shoulder, 9x6", $800 to ...1,100.00
Paperweight, scarab, French Blue, 3½x2¼" 600.00
Sculpture, nude picking rose, gr sheer matt w/yel details, 4x6" ..300.00
Vase, cypress trees, ochre/red on bl-gray, bell shape, 5¼x3¾" ..5,000.00
Vase, floral, purple/gr on lt gray-gr (rare colors), 6¼x4" 4,000.00

Walter, A.

Almaric Walter was employed from 1904 through 1914 at Verreries Artistiques des Freres Daum in Nancy, France. After 1919 he opened his own business where he continued to make the same type of quality objets d'art in pate-de-verre glass as he had earlier. His pieces are signed A. Walter, Nancy H. Berge Sc.

Paperweight, swan, brn on gr opal base, 2x3½" 150.00
Tray, amber beetle on bl, 9½" L 3,000.00
Tray, beetle on rim, brn/blk/dk gr etc, 5" dia, NM 900.00
Vase, floral border, maroon on amber, dk gr ft, 4x4½" 1,495.00
Vase, tree & flowers, gr & red on yel, 8¼x3½" 900.00
Vase, trees & flowers, bl & yel on gr, 6x3" 850.00

Wannopee

The Wannopee Pottery, established in 1892, developed from the reorganization of the financially insecure New Milford Pottery Company of New Milford, Connecticut. They produced a line of mottled-glazed pottery called 'Duchess' and a similar line in porcelain. Both were marked with the impressed sunburst 'W' with 'porcelain' added to indicate that particular body type.

In 1895 semiporcelain pitchers in three sizes were decorated with relief medallion cameos of Beethoven, Mozart, and Napoleon. Lettuce-leaf ware was first produced in 1901 and used actual leaves in the modeling. Scarabronze, made in 1895, was their finest artware. It featured simple Egyptian shapes with a coppery glaze. It was marked with a scarab, either impressed or applied. Production ceased in 1903.

Bowl, Lettuce Leaf, mk/#219, 1¾x9½" 410.00
Pedestal, vine/scroll decor on majolica gr, buttresses, 5½x6½" 75.00
Pitcher, gr & tan mottle, squat, 4½" 200.00
Umbrella stand, Dutchess, mc w/mottled glaze, 24" 510.00

Warwick

The Warwick China Company operated in Wheeling, West Virginia, from 1887 until 1951. They produced both hand-painted and decaled plates, vases, teapots, coffeepots, pitchers, bowls, and jardinieres featuring lovely florals or portraits of beautiful ladies done in luscious colors. Backgrounds were usually blendings of brown and beige, but ivory was also used as well as greens and pinks. Various marks were employed, all of which incorporate the Warwick name. For a more thorough study of the subject, we recommend *Warwick, A to W,* a supplement to *Why Not Warwick* by our advisor, Donald C. Hoffmann, Sr.; his address can be found in the Directory under Illinois. In an effort to inform the collector/dealer, Mr. Hoffmann now has a video available that identifies the company's decals and their variations by number.

Vase, A-Beauty, brn w/floral decor, A-27, 15" 325.00
Vase, A-Beauty, wht w/rose decor, D-2, 15" 450.00
Vase, Albany, brn matt w/floral decor, A-40, 7" 270.00
Vase, Albany, brn w/floral decor, A-27, 7" 260.00
Vase, Alexandria, brn w/portrait, A-17, 12½" 315.00
Vase, Bonnie, brn w/floral decor, A-23, 10½" 280.00
Vase, Bonnie, wht w/bird decal, D-1, 10½" 325.00
Vase, Carol, brn matt w/nut decor, M-64, 8" 290.00
Vase, Carol, brn w/floral decor, A-27, 8" 285.00
Vase, Carol, gr w/roses decor, F-2, 8" 280.00
Vase, Chrys, brn w/floral decor, A-40, 13½" 200.00
Vase, Chrys, red w/floral decor, E-2, 13½" 210.00
Vase, Clytie, red w/floral decor, E-2, 6¼" 285.00
Vase, Clytie, red w/portrait decal, E-1, 6¼" 295.00
Vase, Dahlia, brn to tan matt, nut decor, M-64, 8½" 210.00
Vase, Dahlia, brn w/floral decor, A-27, 8½" 195.00
Vase, Den, red w/portrait, E-1, 6x10" 425.00
Vase, Favorite, brn w/floral decor, A-6, 10½" 260.00
Vase, Favorite, pk w/portrait, H-1, 10½" 465.00
Vase, Favorite, tan to gr matt w/portrait, M-1, 10½" 350.00
Vase, Grecian, brn w/floral decor, A-27, 8" 150.00

Vase, Grecian, brn w/portrait, A-17, 8" 200.00
Vase, Iris, brn w/floral decor, A-6, 9¾" 160.00
Vase, Iris, brn w/floral decor, E-2, 9¾" 170.00
Vase, Lemonade, brn w/floral decor, A-27, 6½" 150.00
Vase, Lemonade, brn w/fruit decor, A-26, 6½" 165.00
Vase, Lemonade, red w/floral decor, E-2, 6½" 170.00
Vase, Lily, brn w/floral decor, A-21, 9½" 245.00
Vase, Lily, red w/portrait, E-1, 9½" 320.00
Vase, Lily, wht w/bird decal, D-1, 9½" 340.00
Vase, Maria, pk w/portrait, H-1, 10½" 425.00
Vase, Maria, red w/portrait, E-1, 10½" 225.00
Vase, Penn, brn w/floral decor, A-40, 9½" 200.00
Vase, Penn, brn w/nut decor, A-64, 9½" 225.00
Vase, Penn, pk w/portrait, H-1, 9½" 425.00
Vase, Royal, brn w/floral decor, A-16, 10" 290.00
Vase, Royal, brn w/floral decor, A-27, 10" 285.00
Vase, Victoria, brn w/floral decor, A-26, 8½" 225.00
Vase, Windsor, brn w/floral decor, A-40, 9½" 300.00
Vase, Windsor, pk w/portrait, H-1, 9½" 500.00

Wash Sets

Before the days of running water, bedrooms were standardly equipped with a wash bowl and pitcher as a matter of necessity. A 'toilet set' was comprised of the pitcher and bowl, toothbrush holder, covered commode, soap dish, shaving dish, and mug. Some sets were even more elaborate. Through everyday usage, the smaller items were often broken, and today it is unusual to find a complete set.

Porcelain sets decorated with florals, fruits, or scenics were produced abroad by Limoges in France; some were imported from Germany and England. During the last quarter of the 1800s and until after the turn of the century, American-made toilet sets were manufactured in abundance. Tin and graniteware sets were also made.

Bl & wht stoneware, rose in relief, 1880s, 13", 15" dia, from $300 to ...425.00
Earthenware w/gaudy decor & lustre, 10½" pitcher only 475.00
Ironstone, Etruscan vase decor, England, 1865, 13½", 16" dia ...400.00
Ironstone, red rose transfer, strapwork design, English 200.00
Porc, wht w/gold trim, child's, +chamber pot/soap dish, MIG, NMIB ...170.00
Staffordshire, floral, brn on wht, ca 1900, 10", 16" dia 125.00

Watch Fobs

Watch fobs have been popular since the last quarter of the nineteenth century. They were often made by retail companies to feature their products. Souvenir, commemorative, and political fobs were also produced. Of special interest today are those with advertising, heavy equipment in particular. Some of the more pricey fobs are listed here, but most of those currently available were produced in such quantities that they are relatively common and should fall within a price range of $3.00 to $10.00. Our advisor for this category is Tony George; he is listed in the Directory under California. When no material is mentioned in the descripition, assume the fob is made of metal.

Acme Cement 40.00
Alaska Yukon Pacific Expo 55.00
Allis-Chalmers TS-360, cut-out bottom, bronze, 1950s 8.00
Avery Dog 80.00
Avery Tractor 115.00
Case Cross Engine 125.00
Caterpillar DW2 ....12.00
Clark, bronze w/yel enamel machine, blank bk, 1960s, lg 12.00
Detroit Diesel, cutout of motor, Great Lakes Diesel Co, bronze 8.00
Dodge Bros Motor Vehicles, bl/wht/blk enamel 75.00
Dynahoe, cut-out bottom of backhoe, silver, 1970, blank bk 7.00
Elmco Rocker Shovel, silver, 1960s 6.00
Euclid Equipment 15.00
Fordson Tractor 80.00
Gisholt, 3 emb work scenes, silver, 1930s 35.00
Heider Tractor 110.00
Hupmobile, bl & wht enamel, tiny edge chips, scarce 75.00
IHC 50.00
IHC, celluloid 150.00
International Harvester, dozer, bronze, Metal Arts, 1970s, ...8.00
John Deere, JD 570 Motor Grader, bronze, full cutout, 1970 ....6.00
Joliet Corn Shellers 125.00
Kalamazoo Railway Supply 90.00
Kellog Switchboard, stick telephone, NP 185.00
Kress Corp, Brimfield IL, cement truck, bronze, 1960s, lg 15.00
Lawson Engines 125.00
Litchfield Mfg 90.00
Lorain, shovels, draglines & cranes, bronze, 1950s 30.00
Manitowoc Speedshovel, 8-sided, bronze, 1960s 12.00
Mueller Values 90.00
Northwest, crane, silver, Mark Tractor & Equipment, 1960s 6.00
NY to Paris, w/compass 95.00
Our Next President WH Taft 50.00
Peter Weatherbird Shoes 225.00
Ram-Joy-VCR 260 ....6.00
Rock Island Plows 110.00

Watch Stands

Watch stands were decorative articles designed with a hook from which to hang a watch. Some displayed the watch as the face of a grandfather clock or as part of an interior scene with figures in period costumes and contemporary furnishings. They were popular products of Staffordshire potters and silver companies as well.

Cherubs on front of watch tower, Staffordshire, 10", $450.00.

Cvd wood w/scrimshaw inlay, compass rose on top, 8½x6x1½" ..1,000.00
Hutch, red pnt/glazed pine, Europe, 19th C, 16x8¼x5⅝" 230.00
Pine, rectangular w/lollipop-shape bk-board, red/blk trim, 1800s, 16" ...3,750.00
Prisoner of War, cvd bone w/mc stain, clock form w/drw, 19th C, 10" 300.00

Watches

First made in the 1500s in Germany, early watches were actually small clocks, suspended from the neck or belt. By 1700 they had become the approximate shape and size we know today. The first watches produced in America were made in 1810. The well-known Waltham Watch

Company was established in 1850. Later, Waterbury produced inexpensive watches which they sold by the thousands.

Open-face and hunting-case watches of the 1890s were often solid gold or gold-filled and were often elaborately decorated in several colors of gold. Gold watches became a status symbol in this decade and were worn by both men and women on chains with fobs or jeweled slides. Ladies sometimes fastened them to their clothing with pins often set with jewels. The chatelaine watch was worn at the waist, only one of several items such as scissors, coin purses, or needle cases, each attached by small chains.

Most turn-of-the-century watch cases were gold-filled; these are plentiful today. Sterling cases, though interest in them is on the increase, are not in great demand. For more information we recommend *Complete Price Guide to Watches, No. 20,* by Cooksey Shugart, Richard E. Gilbert, and Tom Engle (Collector Books).

Our advice for this category comes from Maundy International Watches, Antiquarian Horologists, price consultants, and researchers for many watch reference guides and books on Horology. Their firm is a leading purveyor of antique watches of all kinds. They are listed in the Directory under Kansas. For character-related watches, see Personalities.

Key:

adj — adjusted
brg — bridge plate design
d/s — double sunk dial
fbd — finger bridge design
g/f — gold-filled
g/j/s — gold jewel setting
h/c — hunter case
HCI#P — heat, cold, isochronism & position adjusted
j — jewel
k — karat
k/s — key set
k/w — key wind
l/s — lever set
mvt — movement
o/f — open face
p/s — pendant set
r/g/p — rolled gold plate
s — size
s/s — single sunk dial
s/w — stem wind
w/g/f — white gold-filled
y/g/f — yellow gold-filled

Swiss, 18 size captain's pocketwatch, keywind key set from back, two time zones, sweep seconds hand, two-train keywind movement, silver hunter case, ca 1855, EX, $725.00. (Photo courtesy Maundy International Watches)

Am Watch Co, 0s, 7j, #1891, 14k, h/c, Am Watch Co, M 400.00
Am Watch Co, 6s, 7j, #1873, y/g/f, h/c, Am Watch Co, M 95.00
Am Watch Co, 12s, 17j, #1894, 14k, o/f, Royal, M 300.00
Am Watch Co, 12s, 21j, #1894, 14k, h/c, M 600.00
Am Watch Co, 16s, 11j, #1872, p/s, silver h/c, Park Road, M ...400.00
Am Watch Co, 16s, 15j, #1899, y/g/f, h/c, M 250.00
Am Watch Co, 16s, 16j, #1884, 5-min, 14k, Repeater, M 5,500.00
Am Watch Co, 16s, 17j, #1888, Railroader, M 1,400.00
Am Watch Co, 16s, 19j, #1872, 14k, h/c, Am Watch Woerd's Pat, M ...5,500.00
Am Watch Co, 16s, 21j, #1888, h/c, 14k, Riverside Maximus, M ...1,700.00
Am Watch Co, 16s, 21j, #1899, y/g/f, l/s, o/f, Crescent St, M ...400.00
Am Watch Co, 16s, 21j, #1908, y/g/f, o/f, Grade #645, M 350.00
Am Watch Co, 16s, 23j, #1908, o/f, 18k, Premier Maximus, MIB ...12,000.00
Am Watch Co, 16s, 23j, #1908, y/g/f, o/f, adj, RR, Vanguard, M 450.00
Am Watch Co, 16s, 23j, #1908, y/g/f, o/f, Vanguard Up/Down, EX .650.00
Am Watch Co, 18s, #1857, silver h/c, Samuel Curtiss k/w, M ..4,500.00
Am Watch Co, 18s, 11j, #1857, k/w, 1st run, PS Barlett, M ..5,000.00
Am Watch Co, 18s, 11j, #1857, silver h/c, k/w, DH&D, EX ..1,300.00
Am Watch Co, 18s, 11j, #1857, silver h/c, k/w, s/s, Wm Ellery, EX ...300.00
Am Watch Co, 18s, 15j, #1877, k/w, RE Robbins, M 550.00
Am Watch Co, 18s, 15j, #1883, y/g/f, 2-tone, Railroad King, EX ...500.00
Am Watch Co, 18s, 17j, #1883, y/g/f, o/f, Crescent Street, M ...175.00
Am Watch Co, 18s, 17j, #1892, HC, Canadian Pacific Railway, M ..950.00
Am Watch Co, 18s, 17j, #1892, y/g/f, o/f, Sidereal, rare, M ...2,400.00
Am Watch Co, 18s, 17j, 25-yr, y/g/f, o/f, s/s, PS Bartlett, M 150.00
Am Watch Co, 18s, 21j, #1892, y/g/f, o/f, d/s, Crescent St, M ...450.00
Am Watch Co, 18s, 21j, #1892, y/g/f, o/f, Grade #845, EX 200.00
Am Watch Co, 18s, 21j, #1892, y/g/f, o/f, Pennsylvania Special, M 3,000.00
Am Watch Co, 18s, 7j, #1857, silver case, k/w, CT Parker, M .3,200.00
Auburndale Watch Co, 18s, 7j, k/w, l/s, Lincoln, M 1,500.00
Aurora Watch Co, 18s, 11j, k/w, silver h/c, M 300.00
Aurora Watch Co, 18s, 15 ruby j, y/g/f, s/w, 5th pinion, M 1,500.00
Ball (Elgin), 18s, 17j, o/f, silver, Official RR Standard, M 450.00
Ball (Hamilton), 16s, 21j, #999, g/f, o/f, l/s, M 500.00
Ball (Hamilton), 16s, 23j, #998, y/g/f, o/f, Elinvar, M 1,650.00
Ball (Hamilton), 18s, 19j, #999, g/f, o/f, l/s, EX 450.00
Ball (Hampden), 18s, 17j, o/f, adj, RR, Superior Grade, M 1,800.00
Ball (Illinois), 12s, 19j, w/g/f, o/f, M 300.00
Ball (Waltham), 16s, 17j, y/g/f, o/f, RR, Commercial Std, M 300.00
Ball (Waltham), 16s, 21j, o/f, Official RR Standard, M 550.00
Columbus, 6s, 11j, y/g/f hc, M 185.00
Columbus, 18s, 11-15j, k/w, k/s, M 500.00
Columbus, 18s, 15j, o/f, l/s, M 200.00
Columbus, 18s, 15j, y/g/f, o/f, Jay Gould on dial, G 800.00
Columbus, 18s, 21j, y/g/f, h/c, train on dial, Railway King, M ...700.00
Columbus, 18s, 23j, y/g/f, h/c, Columbus King, M 1,800.00
Cornell, 18s, 15j, s/w, JC Adams, EX 350.00
Cornell, 18s, 15j, silver h/c, k/w, John Evans, EX 350.00
Dudley, 12s, #1, 14k, o/f, flip-bk case, Masonic, G 2,600.00
Elgin, 6s, 11j, 14k, h/c, M 350.00
Elgin, 6s, 15j, 20-yr, y/g/f, h/c, s/s, EX 80.00
Elgin, 10s, 18k, h/c, k/w, k/s, s/s, Gail Borden, M 500.00
Elgin, 12s, 15j, 14k, h/c, EX 275.00
Elgin, 12s, 17j, 14k, h/c, GM Wheeler, M 400.00
Elgin, 16s, 15j, doctor's, 4th model, 18k, 2nd sweep hand, h/c, M ...1,800.00
Elgin, 16s, 15j, 14k, h/c, EX 550.00
Elgin, 16s, 21j, y/g/f, g/j/s, o/f, BW Raymond, EX 250.00
Elgin, 16s, 21j, y/g/f, g/j/s, 3 fbd, M 450.00
Elgin, 16s, 21j, y/g/f, o/f, l/s, RR, Father Time, M 400.00
Elgin, 16s, 21j, 14k, 3 fbd, grade #91, scarce, M 3,700.00
Elgin, 16s, 23j, up/down indicator, BW Raymond, EX 1,100.00
Elgin, 17s, 7j, k/w, orig silver case, Leader, M 150.00
Elgin, 18s, 11j, silver, h/c, k/w, gilded, MG Odgen, M 225.00
Elgin, 18s, 15j, o/f, d/s, k/w, silveroid, RR, BW Raymond 1st run, M ...1,500.00
Elgin, 18s, 15j, silver, k/w, k/s, h/c, HL Culver, M 300.00
Elgin, 18s, 15j, silver h/c, Penn RR dial, BW Raymond k/w mvt, M ...5,500.00
Elgin, 18s, 17j, silveroid h/c, BW Raymond, M 300.00
Elgin, 18s, 21j, y/g/f, o/f, Father Time, G 225.00
Elgin, 18s, 23j, y/g/f, o/f, 5-position, RR, Veritas, M 600.00
Fredonia, 18s, 11j, y/g/f, h/c, k/w, M 450.00
Hamilton, #910, 12s, 17j, 20-yr, y/g/f, o/f, s/s, EX 70.00
Hamilton, #912, 12s, 17j, y/g/f, o/f, adj, EX 60.00
Hamilton, #920, 12s, 23j, 14k, o/f, M 600.00
Hamilton, #922MP, 12s, 18k case, Masterpiece (sgn), M 1,200.00
Hamilton, #925, 18s, 17j, y/g/f, h/c, s/s, l/s, M 300.00
Hamilton, #928, 18s, 15j, y/g/f, o/f, s/s, EX 175.00
Hamilton, #933, 18s, 16j, h/c, nickel plate, low serial #, M 800.00
Hamilton, #938, 18s, 17j, y/g/f, adj, M 700.00
Hamilton, #940, 18s, 21j, nickel plate, coin silver, o/f, M 400.00
Hamilton, #946, 18s, 23j, y/g/f, o/f, g/j/s, M 1,200.00

Hamilton, #947 (mk), 18s, 23j, 14k, h/c, orig/sgn, EX 4,500.00
Hamilton, #950, 16s, 23j, y/g/f, o/f, l/s, sgn d/s, M 1,500.00
Hamilton, #965, 16s, 17j, 14k, p/s, h/c, brg, scarce, M 1,350.00
Hamilton, #972, 16s, 17j, y/g/f, g/j/s, o/f, d/s, l/s, adj, EX 150.00
Hamilton, #974, 16s, 17j, 20-yr, y/g/f, o/f, s/s, EX 80.00
Hamilton, #992, 16s, 21j, y/g/f, o/f, adj, d/s, dbl roller, M 350.00
Hamilton, #992B, 16s, 21j, y/g/f, o/f, l/s, Bar/Crown, M 500.00
Hamilton, #4992B, 16s, 22j, o/f, steel case, G 200.00
Hampden, 12s, 17j, w/g/f, o/f, thin model, Aviator, M 150.00
Hampden, 16s, 17j, o/f, adj, EX 60.00
Hampden, 16s, 17j, y/g/f, h/c, s/w, M 150.00
Hampden, 16s, 21j, g/j/s, y/g/f, NP, h/c, Dueber, ¾-mvt, M 400.00
Hampden, 16s, 23j, o/f, adj, dbl roller, Special Railway, M 600.00
Hampden, 16s, 7j, gilded, nickel plate, o/f, ¾-mvt, EX 60.00
Hampden, 18s, 15j, k/w, mk on mvt, Railway, M 1,200.00
Hampden, 18s, 15j, s/w, gilded, JC Perry, M 175.00
Hampden, 18s, 15j, silver, k/w, h/c, Hayward, M 225.00
Hampden, 18s, 15j, y/g/f, damascened, h/c, Dueber, M 200.00
Hampden, 18s, 21j, y/g/f, g/j/s, h/c, New Railway, M 400.00
Hampden, 18s, 21j, y/g/f, o/f, d/s, l/s, N Am Railway, M 450.00
Hampden, 18s, 23j, y/g/f, o/f, d/s, adj, New Railway, M 425.00
Hampden, 18s, 23j, 14k, h/c, Special Railway, M 1,100.00
Hampden, 18s, 7-11j, k/w, gilded, Springfield Mass 200.00
Howard, E; 6s, 15j, s/w, 18k h/c, Series VIII, G sz, M 1,475.00
Howard, E; 16s, 15j, s/w, 14k h/c, L sz, M 1,400.00
Howard, E; 18s, 15j, h/c, silver case, k/w, Series I, N sz, M 4,000.00
Howard, E; 18s, 15j, 18k h/c, k/w, Series II, N sz, M 4,500.00
Howard, E; 18s, 17j, 25-yr, y/g/f, o/f, orig case, split plate 800.00
Howard (Keystone), 12s, 23j, 14k, h/c, brg, Series 8, M 700.00
Howard (Keystone), 16s, 17j, y/g/f, o/f, Series 9, M 225.00
Howard (Keystone), 16s, 21j, y/g/f, o/f, RR Chronometer II, M ...675.00
Howard (Keystone), 16s, 23j, y/g/f, o/f, Series 0, jeweled bbl, M ..800.00
Illinois, 0s, 7j, 14k, l/s, h/c, EX 250.00
Illinois, 8s, 13j, ¾-mvt, Rose LeLand, scarce, EX 275.00
Illinois, 12s, 17j, y/g/f, o/f, d/s dial, EX 50.00
Illinois, 16s, 17j, y/g/f, o/f, d/s, Bunn, EX 200.00
Illinois, 16s, 21j, g/j/s, h/c, Burlington, M 295.00
Illinois, 16s, 21j, o/f, d/s, Santa Fe Special, M 600.00
Illinois, 16s, 21j, y/g/f, o/f, d/s, Bunn Special, M 425.00
Illinois, 16s, 23j, y/g/f, o/f, d/s, 60-hr, Sangamo Special, mk, M ...2,400.00
Illinois, 16s, 23j, y/g/f, stiff bow, o/f, Sangamo Special, EX 900.00
Illinois, 18s, 11j, #1, silver, k/w, Alleghany, EX 100.00
Illinois, 18s, 11j, #3, o/f, s/w, l/s, Comet, G 100.00
Illinois, 18s, 11j, Forest City, G 100.00
Illinois, 18s, 15j, #1, adj, y/g/f, k/w, h/c, gilt, Bunn, M 775.00
Illinois, 18s, 15j, #1, k/w, k/s, silver hunter, Stuart, G 500.00
Illinois, 18s, 15j, k/w, k/s, gilt, Railway Regulator, M 900.00
Illinois, 18s, 15j, s/w, silveroid, G 50.00
Illinois, 18s, 17j, g/j/s, adj, B&O RR Special (Hunter), h/c, M 2,200.00
Illinois, 18s, 17j, h/c, s/w, nickel plate, coin silver, Bunn, M 400.00
Illinois, 18s, 17j, o/f, d/s, adj, silveroid case, Lakeshore, G 100.00
Illinois, 18s, 17j, o/f, s/w, 5th pinion, Miller, EX 175.00
Illinois, 18s, 21j, g/j/s, g/f, o/f, A Lincoln, M 425.00
Illinois, 18s, 21j, g/j/s, o/f, adj, B&O RR Special, EX 1,500.00
Illinois, 18s, 21j, 14k, g/j/s, h/c, Bunn Special, M 1,100.00
Illinois, 18s, 23j, g/j/s, Bunn Special, EX 625.00
Illinois, 18s, 24j, g/j/s, adj, o/f, Chesapeake & Ohio, M 3,000.00
Illinois, 18s, 24j, g/j/s, o/f, Bunn Special, EX 650.00
Illinois, 18s, 26j, g/j/s, o/f, Ben Franklin USA, G 5,000.00
Illinois, 18s, 26j, 14k, Penn Special, M 8,000.00
Illinois, 18s, 7j, #3, o/f, Interior, G 65.00
Illinois, 18s, 7j, #3, silveroid, America, G 65.00
Illinois, 18s, 9-11j, o/f, k/w, s/s, silveroid case, Hoyt, M 150.00
Ingersoll, 16s, 7j, wht base metal, Reliance, G 30.00
Lancaster, 18s, 7j, o/f, k/w, k/s, eng silver case, EX 150.00
Marion US, 18s, h/c, k/w, k/s, ¾-plate, Asa Fuller, M 450.00
Marion US, 18s, 15j, nickel plate, h/c, s/w, Henry Randel, M ...450.00
Melrose Watch Co, 18s, 7j, k/w, k/s, G 250.00
New York Watch Co, 18s, 7j, silver, h/c, k/w, Geo Sam Rice, EX ...200.00
New York Watch Co, 19j, low sz #, wolf's teeth wind, M 1,850.00
Patek Philippe, 12s, 18j, 18k, o/f, M 2,500.00
Patek Philippe, 16s, 20j, 18k, h/c, M 3,500.00
Rockford, 16s, 17j, y/g/f, h/c, brg, dbl roller, EX 100.00
Rockford, 16s, 21j, #515, y/g/f, M 550.00
Rockford, 16s, 21j, g/j/s, o/f, grade #537, rare, M 1,500.00
Rockford, 16s, 23j, 14k, o/f, mk Doll on dial/mvt, M 2,900.00
Rockford, 18s, 15j, o/f, k/w, silver case, EX 450.00
Rockford, 18s, 17j, silveroid w/M mc dial, fancy mvt/hands, M .700.00
Rockford, 18s, 17j, y/g/f, o/f, Winnebago, M 300.00
Rockford, 18s, 21j, o/f, King Edward, M 600.00
Seth Thomas, 18s, 17j, #2, g/j/s, adj, Henry Molineux, EX 625.00
Seth Thomas, 18s, 17j, Edgemere, G 50.00
Seth Thomas, 18s, 25j, g/j/s, g/f, Maiden Lane, EX 2,450.00
Seth Thomas, 18s, 7j, ¾-mvt, bk: eagle/Liberty model, M 250.00
South Bend, 12s, 21j, dbl roller, Grade #431, M 250.00
South Bend, 12s, 21j, orig o/f, d/s, Studebaker, M 300.00
South Bend, 18s, 21j, g/j/s, h/c, Studebaker, M 1,200.00
South Bend, 18s, 21j, 14k, h/c, M 1,000.00
Swiss, 18s, 18k, h/c, 1-min, Repeater, High Grade, M 4,000.00

Waterford

The Waterford Glass Company operated in Ireland from the late 1700s until 1851 when the factory closed. One hundred years later (in 1951) another Waterford glassworks was instituted that produced glass similar to the eighteenth-century wares — crystal, usually with cut decoration. Today Waterford is a generic term referring to the type of glass first produced there.

Bowl, centerpc; Master Cutter, 10" 800.00
Clock, oval, swirl bevels, lg 175.00
Cocktail, Colleen, 3½" 85.00
Cocktail, Colleen, 4⅞" 85.00
Comport, Lismore, ftd, 6¼" 150.00
Creamer, Glengariff 85.00
Decanter, Alana, ships 298.00
Decanter, Lismore, 13" 295.00
Iced tea, Colleen, 12-oz 75.00
Lamp, knopped form, dmn-shaped cuttings, 19", pr 950.00
Liqueur, Alana 55.00
Liqueur, Colleen, 1-oz 70.00
Marmalade, Comeragh 85.00
Marmalade, Glengariff 85.00
Saucer champagne, Colleen 85.00
Tumbler, Colleen, 9-oz 85.00
Vase, Lismore, heavy, 9" 200.00
Wine, Colleen, 3-oz 85.00
Wine, Colleen, 6-oz 85.00

Watt Pottery

The Watt Pottery Company was established in Crooksville, Ohio, on July 5, 1922. From approximately 1922 until 1935, they manufactured hand-turned stone containers — jars, jugs, milk pans, preserve jars, and various sizes of mixing bowls, usually marked with a cobalt blue acorn stamp. In 1936 production of these items was discontinued, and the company began to produce kitchen utility ware and ovenware such as mixing bowls, spaghetti bowls and plates, canister sets, covered casseroles, salt and pepper shakers, cookie jars, ice buckets, pitchers, bean pots, and salad and dinnerware sets. Most Watt ware is individually hand painted with bold brush strokes of red, green, or blue contrasting with the natural buff color of the glazed body. Several patterns were produced: Apple, Autumn Foliage, Cherry, Dutch Tulip, Morning Glory, Rio Rose, Rooster, Tear Drop, Starflower, and Tulip, to name a few. Much of the ware was made for advertising premiums and is often found stamped with the name of the retail company.

Tragedy struck the Watt Pottery Company on October 4, 1965, when fire completely destroyed the factory and warehouse. Production never resumed, but the ware they made has withstood many years of service in American kitchens and is today highly regarded and prized by collectors. The vivid colors and folk art-like execution of each cheerful pattern create a homespun ambiance that will make Watt pottery a treasure for years to come.

For further study we recommend *Watt Pottery, An Identification and Price Guide*, by our advisors for this category, Sue and Dave Morris; they are listed in the Directory under Oregon. For the address of the *Watt's News* newsletter, see the section on Clubs, Newsletters, and Catalogs.

Apple, baker on wire stand, #96, w/lid 175.00
Apple, bowl, cereal; #94 ....50.00
Apple, bowl, mixing; #9 ....85.00
Apple, bowl, spaghetti; #39 ....175.00
Apple, canister, #72 ....500.00
Apple, cheese crock, #80, w/lid 1,500.00
Apple, grease jar, #01, rare 375.00
Apple, mug, #501 ....350.00
Apple, pitcher, refrigerator; #69, rare 550.00
Apple, platter, #31 ....350.00
Apple, shakers, hourglass shape, 4", pr 275.00
Apple, sugar bowl, #98, w/lid 400.00
Autumn Foliage, baker, #96, w/lid 90.00
Autumn Foliage, fondue, w/hdl & lid, 3x9" 275.00
Autumn Foliage, oil & vinegar set, #126, w/lids 550.00
Banded, casserole, bl & wht, w/lid, 8¾" 45.00
Banded, cookie jar, bl & wht, 7½" 100.00
Banded, pitcher, bl & wht, 7" 95.00
Basketweave, bean pot, #76, brn, w/lid 40.00
Basketweave, pitcher, #810, brn 55.00
Cherry, bowl, #4 ....45.00
Cherry, platter, #31 ....145.00
Cherry, shaker (salt only), bbl shape, 4" 90.00
Dutch Tulip, bean pot, #76, w/lid 350.00
Dutch Tulip, bowl, #05, w/lid 250.00
Dutch Tulip, bowl, spaghetti; #39 ....400.00
Kitch-N-Queen, bowl, #8 ....40.00
Kitch-N-Queen, bowl, mixing; #12 ....60.00
Kitch-N-Queen, cookie jar, #503 ....225.00
Kla Ham'rd, casserole, #43-18, w/lid 60.00
Kla Ham'rd, pitcher, #43-14 ....55.00
Morning Glory, cookie jar, brn tones, #95 ....400.00
Morning Glory, creamer, #97 ....500.00
Morning Glory, pitcher, #96, w/ice lip 375.00
Morning Glory, sugar bowl (open), #98, ...250.00
Pansy (Cut-Leaf), creamer & sugar bowl, 2¾", pr 175.00
Pansy (Cut-Leaf), platter, 15" dia 110.00
Pansy (Old), bowl, spaghetti; #39 ....80.00
Pansy (Old), casserole, #2/48 ....55.00
Rooster, bean pot, #76, w/lid 350.00
Rooster, bowl, #05, w/lid 190.00
Rooster, bowl, #73 ....145.00
Rooster, casserole, ind; #18, w/lid 245.00
Rooster, pitcher, #15 ....145.00
Starflower, bean pot, #76, w/lid 175.00
Starflower, bowl, berry; 5¾" dia 35.00
Starflower, casserole, ind; stick hdl, #18, w/lid 125.00
Starflower, cookie jar, #21 ....185.00
Starflower, grease jar, #47 ....250.00
Starflower, ice bucket, w/lid, 7¼" 185.00
Starflower, mug, #121 ....275.00
Starflower, pitcher, refrigerator; #69 ....700.00
Starflower, platter, #31 ....110.00
Starflower (Green-on-Brown), casserole, ind; #18, w/lid 45.00
Starflower (Green-on-Brown), tumbler, #56 ....175.00
Tear Drop, bowl, mixing, #07 ....40.00
Tear Drop, bowl, mixing; #63 ....45.00
Tear Drop, casserole, #86, w/lid, rare 750.00
Tulip, bowl, mixing; #603 ....150.00
Tulip, cookie jar, #503 ....375.00
Tulip, pitcher, #15 ....550.00
White Daisy, bowl, mixing; #9 ....65.00
White Daisy, casserole, w/lid, 8¾" dia 165.00

Wave Crest

Wave Crest is a line of decorated opal ware (milk glass) patented in 1892 by the C.F. Monroe Co. of Meriden, Connecticut. They made a full line of items for every room of the house, but they are probably best known for their boxes and vases. Most items were hand painted with various levels of decoration, but more transfers were used in the later years prior to the company's demise in 1916. Floral themes are common; items with the scenics and portraits are rarer and more highly prized. Many pieces have ornately scrolled ormolu and brass handles, feet, and rims. Early pieces were unsigned (though they may have had paper labels); later, about 1898, a red banner mark was used. The black mark is probably from about 1902 – 03. However, the glass is quite distinctive and has not been reproduced, so even unmarked items are easy to recognize. Our advisors for this category are Dolli and Wilfred Cohen; they are listed in the Directory under California. Note: There is no premium for signatures on Wave Crest. Values are given for hand-decorated pieces (unless noted 'transfer') that are *not* worn.

Box, pink floral on white with gilt-metal rim, scroll molded, 6", $650.00.

Ash receiver, floral, bowl on ormolu ped ft, hdld ormolu rim 125.00
Atomizer, floral on ball shape, orig hardware 350.00
Blotter, floral on pastel yel, rare 1,750.00
Box, blown-out aster lid, florals on bl, 3x4½", from $1,000 to ..1,200.00
Box, cherubs & mtn scenic transfer, oval, 5" 495.00
Box, cigar; Egg Crate, strawflowers, 6½" sq 700.00
Box, Egg Crate, daisies, 6" sq 425.00
Box, glove; roses/scrolls, pk & wht on chartreuse, 3x8½" L ...1,250.00
Box, handkerchief; wild roses/emb scrolls, ormolu ft, 9½" L ...1,250.00
Box, Lg Baroque Shell, Moorish Fantasy on wht, no lining, 7" dia 1,450.00
Box, Swirl, floral, 4½x7" dia 750.00

Box, Swirl, floral/foliage allover on tan, 3½x5½" dia 535.00
Box, Swirl, lily of the valley on lt bl, 2¾x3" dia 145.00
Cigarette urn, floral, cylinder on ftd ormolu base, 3¾" 200.00
Clock, easel bk, cobalt border, ornate gilt fr, 8¾" 1,950.00
Clock box, floral on ivory, 3x5" 1,500.00
Cracker jar, emb scroll reserve w/wild roses, str sides 650.00
Creamer & sugar bowl, Swirl, mc floral, SP trim 500.00
Cruet, floral, pk on wht, gold top & stopper, 6" 600.00
Ewer, floral, ornate gilt-metal top w/figural hdl, 6½" 750.00
Fernery, floral, bl on ivory, w/liner, 3½x7¾" 450.00
Hair receiver, roses on wht w/cobalt 500.00
Humidor, Indian on horsebk w/bow down, 6½x5" 975.00
Jam jar, berry branches transfer, w/lid & spoon, 3½x3½" 400.00
Jardiniere, lg bl flowers (decal), 7¾x10" 450.00
Mirror tray, floral on cream, 9¾x7½" 1,250.00
Paperweight, gilt cherub on floral dome shape, gilt ft 995.00
Planter, HP floral (most are transfers), 7½" 650.00
Shaker, Erie Twist, florals, 2½" 150.00
Shakers, Billow, floral branch on bl, pr 295.00
Shakers, Creased Neck, floral on ivory to bl, pr 225.00
Shakers, Tulip, floral, pr 125.00
Syrup, Swirl, violets on shaded pk, hinged lid, 3" 400.00
Vase, asters, wht/gold on pk/tan, cylinder, ormolu ft, 6½" 475.00
Vase, bud; floral on ivory, flattened bulb w/stick neck, 4½" 450.00
Vase, floral, acorn body w/long neck, lg ormolu hdls/ft, 6¾" 465.00
Vase, floral, egg shape w/long neck, lg ormolu hdls/base, 7½" 650.00
Vase, floral, ornate ormolu: rim w/ear hdls & ftd holder, 5" 465.00
Vase, floral, squatty, beaded rim, 3¾x4¼" 450.00
Vase, floral panels, ornate ormolu hdls & ft, 9x6½" 850.00
Vase, lady & cherubs, ornate ormolu hdls & ft, 12x8½" 1,795.00
Whisk broom holder, asters cartouch on pk, ornate metal, 10" ..2,395.00

Weapons

Among the varied areas of specialization within the broad category of weapons, guns are by far the most popular. Muskets are among the earliest firearms; they were large-bore shoulder arms, usually firing black powder with separate loading of powder and shot. Some ignited the charge by flintlock or caplock, while later types used a firing pin with a metallic cartridge. Side arms, referred to as such because they were worn at the side, include pistols and revolvers. Pistols range from early single-shot and multiple barrels to modern types with cartridges held in the handle. Revolvers were supplied with a cylinder that turned to feed a fresh round in front of the barrel breech. Other firearms include shotguns, which fired round or conical bullets and had a smooth inner barrel surface, and rifles, so named because the interior of the barrel contained spiral grooves (rifling) which increased accuracy. For further study we recommend *Modern Guns, Twelfth Edition;* by Russell Quertermous and Steve Quertermous, available at your local bookstore. All weapons are under the advisement of Steve Howard, see the Directory under California. See also Militaria.

Key:

bbl — barrel	mag — magazine
cal — caliber	mgn — magnum
conv — conversion	mod — modified
cyl — cylinder	oct — octagon
f/l — flintlock	o/u — over/under
f/s — full stock	p/b — patch box
ga — gauge	perc — percussion
hdw — hardware	/s — stock
h/s — half stock	

Carbines

JH Merrill Breechloader (2nd type), 54 cal, 22⅛" bbl, G 1,350.00
Spencer M1865 Post War Alteration, 50 cal, rimfire, 20" bbl, G 950.00
US Springfield (Krag) M1898, 30 US cal, 22" bbl, G 225.00
US Springfield M1863 w/Robert conv, 58 cal, 24½" bbl, G 500.00
US Springfield M1879 Trapdoor, 45/70 cal, 22" bbl, G 475.00
Winchester M1892, 38/40 cal, button mag, str/s, 20" bbl, G ..1,250.00
Winchester M1892, 44/40 cal, 20" bbl, full mag, saddle ring, EX+ ..1,300.00
Winchester M1894, 30/30 cal, full mag, 20" bbl, w/saddle ring, G 575.00
Winchester M94, 30/30 cal, 20" bbl, full mag, str/s, saddle ring, G 300.00
Winchester M94, 32 Win special cal, full mag, saddle ring, G ...400.00
Winchester M94 Eastern, 30/30 cal, full mag, hooded front sight, EX ...425.00

Muskets

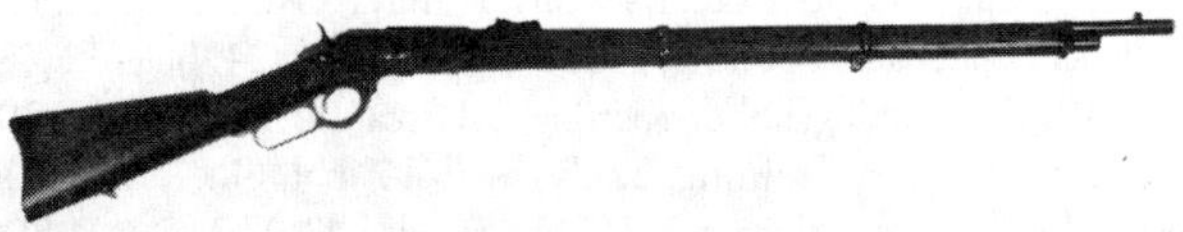

Winchester Model 73 musket, 44/40 caliber, military sights, 30" barrel, full-length military stock with sling swivels, NM, $3,200.00.

European f/l (reconverted), 69 cal, 42" bbl, military/s, G 475.00
Springfield M 1816 f/l, perc conv, 69 cal, dtd 1829, 42" bbl, G .475.00
Springfield M1795, perc conv, 69 cal, dtd 1809, 44½" bbl, G- ..400.00
Springfield M1795, perc conv, 69 cal, dtd 1812, 44½" bbl, G- ..475.00
Springfield M1830, f/l, 69 cal, dtd 1834, 42" bbl, G 700.00
Springfield M1861, 58 cal, 40" rifled bbl, dtd 1862 on hammer, VG 850.00
US Bridesburg Civil War w/Meadham conv, 58 cal, 57" bbl, VG 750.00
US Civil War w/Phoenix conv, 58 cal, 32" rifled bbl, dtd 1878, G ...550.00
Winchester M1873, 44WCF cal, std sights, angular bayonet, VG 900.00
Winchester M1873 Lever-Action, 44 WCF cal, 30" rnd bbl, ⅞ mag, G ...900.00

Pistols

Allen & Thurber Pepperbox, 31 cal, 4½" bbls, eng iron fr, G ...375.00
Beretta Model 948, 22LR cal, w/6" & 3¼" bbls, compo grips, VG 250.00
Browning Inglis Military, 9mm cal, 4¾" bbl, shoulder/s, VG 950.00
Japanese Nambu Military, 8mm cal, 4½" bbl, wood grips, EX 400.00
Mauser HSc Pocket, 32 ACP cal, 3¼" bbl, wood grips, VG 300.00
Mortimer Dueling, f/l converted to perc, 55 cal, 10½" oct bbls, VG ...3,400.00
Philadelphia-Type Derringer, 44 cal, 2⅝" oct bbl, VG 500.00
Remington Dbl Derringer, 41 cal, ivory grips, 3" bbl, G 450.00
Remington Elliot Derringer, 22 cal rimfire, 5-shot, 3" bbls, G ...375.00
Remington Elliot Derringer, 32 cal, rimfire, 4-shot, 3¼" bbls, VG ...280.00
Remington Elliot SS Derringer, 41 cal, 2½" bbl, G 275.00
Remington Vest Pocket, 22 cal, wood grips, 3½" bbl, G 325.00
Remington Vest Pocket, 42 cal rimfire, wood grips, 4" bbl, G ...400.00
W Parker, center hammer f/l blunderbuss, 50 cal, brass bbl, VG ...1,000.00
Walther P38 Military, 9mm cal, 5" bbl, compo grips, EX 500.00

Revolvers

Adams Pat Perc, 45 cal, 6" oct bbl, bag-type grips, VG 800.00
Colt M1877 Dbl-Action, 38L Colt cal, 4½" bbl w/rod, VG 725.00
Colt Single-Action 1st Generation, 357 mag cal, 4¾" bbl, EX ...3,100.00
Colt 1849 Pocket (London Model), 31 cal, 5-shot, 5" bbl, VG in case ..2,600.00
English Perc, 45 cal, 5" oct bbl, eng fr, bag-ty-en grips, G 425.00
Remington Beal's Navy, 36 cal, wood grips, 7½" bbl, VG 750.00
Remington M1890, 44 cal, wood grips, 5¼" bbl (shortened), G ...1,150.00
Remington New Model #4, 41 cal rimfire, 2½" bbl, G 200.00

Remington New Model Army, 44 cal, wood grips, 8" oct bbl, VG ..1,500.00
Remington Rider Dbl-Action New Model Belt, 36 cal, 6½" bbl, G ...675.00
Remington Rider Pocket, cartridge conv, 32 cal, 3" oct bbl, VG 325.00
Remington Single-Action M 1875, 44 cal, wood grips, 7½" bbl, VG ..1,900.00
Ruger Bearcat, 22 cal, wood grips, brass trigger guard, 4" bbl, NM 225.00
Trantors Pat Perc, 36 cal, 4½" oct bbl, cases, w/accessories 1,800.00

Rifles

CG Hafnel Sporting, 8mm cal, pistol-grip/s, 23" bbl, VG 475.00
Green Breechloader, 54 cal, 55" bbl, military/s, G 1,100.00
Hall M1819 Breechloader, f/l, 52 cal, 33" bbl, dtd 1837, VG .1,700.00
Hammerli M300 Olympic Target, 30/06, 30" heavy bbl, EX 900.00
JW Wilkinson...NY, perc, 45 cal, 36½" oct bbl, h/s, VG 425.00
KY perc, T Davidson...OH, 36 cal, 38" oct bbl, tiger-maple/s, G 250.00
KY perc, 32 cal, 40" ltweight oct bbl, tiger-maple/s, G 350.00
KY perc, 45 cal, 36½" oct bbl, f/s w/silver inlays, G 550.00
Mannlicher Schoenauer Sporting, 7x64 cal, pistol-grip/s, 24" bbl, G ...450.00
Mauser Bolt-Action Single Shot Sporting, 22LR cal, 26½" bbl, VG ...300.00
Mauser M62 Military Training, 22LR cal, 26½" bbl, G 300.00
Mauser M98 Military, 8mm cal, 24" bbl, f/s, dtd 42, VG 800.00
N Beyer KY f/l, curly maple/s w/cvg, 46⅝" oct-to-rnd bbl, 62" 7,200.00
N Kendall, 45 cal, 29" oct bbl, blade front, rear sights, h/s, G ...375.00
NS (N Shenafelt) KY, perc, curly maple/s, 40" oct bbl, 55" 4,500.00
Remington Lee Model Sporting, 30/40 US cal, 25" bbl, VG 700.00
Remington M14 D Grade, factory eng, 35 Rem cal, 22" bbl, EX 2,100.00
Remington M14 Premiere F-Grade, eng game, 32 Rem cal, 22" rnd bbl, EX ...3,100.00
Remington M141 Premiere F-Grade, eng game, 35 Rem cal, 24" bbl, EX+ 2,300.00
Springfield M1903 Military, 30/06 cal, 24" bbl, f/s, w/swivels, G ...325.00
Springfield M1903 Military, 30/06 cal, 24" bbl, f/s w/no lugs, G 525.00
US M1917 Army (Eddy Stone), 30/06 cal, 26" bbl, f/s, w/swivels, VG ...175.00
US Rock Island Arsenal M1903, 30/06 cal, 24" bbl, f/s, 1918, G ...475.00
US Rock Island Arsenal M1903 Military, 30/06 cal, 24" bbl, f/s, VG ...400.00
US Rock Island M1903 Military, 30/06 cal, military/s, 24" bbl, VG 375.00
US Springfield (Krag) Army M1896, 30 US cal, 30" bbl, f/s, G ...700.00
US Springfield M1866 w/Allin conv, 50 cal, 40" bbl, dtd 1864, VG ..500.00
US Springfield M1879, 45/70, military/s, 32⅝" bbl, G- 300.00
US Springfield M1884, 45/70 cal, military/s dtd 1886, 32⅝" bbl, EX 900.00
US Springfield M1888, 45/70 cal, military/s dtd 1890, 32⅝" bbl, VG ...775.00
US Springfield M1903, 30/06 cal, 24" bbl, f/s, single lug, VG ...850.00
US Springfield M1903 (Nat'l Match), 30/06 cal, 24" star gauge bbl, VG 1,400.00
US Springfield M1903 Hoffer-Thompson Gallery Practice, 22 cal, VG ...1,750.00
US Springfield M1903 Military, 30/06 cal, military/s, 24" bbl, VG ..600.00
US Springfield Trapdoor M1873, 45/70 cal, 32⅝" bbl, G 450.00
Winchester M1873, 44/40 cal, full mag, 24" rnd bbl, EX 2,100.00
Winchester M1892 Take-Down, 44/40 cal, half mag, 24" bbl, EX ...2,500.00
Winchester M1894, 38/55 cal, full mag, 26" rnd/oct bbl, G 600.00
Winchester M1895, 35 Win cal, 24" rnd bbl, rpl sight, VG 850.00

Shotguns

Browning M12, 28 ga, 26" ventilated ribbed bbl/mod choke/gold inlay, M ...600.00
DH Hilliard perc fowler, 12-ga, 42" military bbl, h/s, single shot, G ..225.00
J Woodward Perc, 12 ga, 31" Damascus bbls, eng locks/hammers, VG+case 3,000.00
Lane & Reed perc fowler, 12-ga, 42" single bbl, h/s, 1838, G 150.00
Oates f/l blunderbuss, 12 ga, 14½" brass bbl w/cannon muzzle, VG ..2,400.00
Simon Deluxe, f/l, 20 ga, 32" bbls, relief-cvd/s, VG 3,000.00
Stevens M620 Trench, 12 ga, 20" bbl, w/hand guard, G 650.00
Twigg f/l blunderbuss, 12 ga, 17" steel bbl, full length/s, VG 850.00
US Springfield Trapdoor M1881, 20 ga, half/s, 26" bbl, G 1,500.00
W&C Scott, 12 ga, 30" Damascus steel bbls, full/mod choke, G ..600.00
Ward Dbl-Bbl Perc, 12 ga, 30" twist steel bbls, h/s, G 150.00
Webley & Scott, 12 ga, 20" dbl bbls, full/mod choke, str/s, G ...500.00
Winchester Delux Eng M42 Pump, 410 cal, 16" choked skeet bbl, EX ..1,350.00
Winchester M101 Dmn Grade, 20 ga, 27½" o/u bbls, EX+ 1,000.00
Winchester M1893 Riot Gun, 12 ga, 20" bbl, pistol-grip/s, G ...250.00
Winchester M1897 Riot Gun, 12 ga, 20" bbl, pistol-grip/s, VG .500.00
Winchester M1897 Trench, 12 ga, 20" bbl, pistol-grip/s, G 1,300.00
Winchester M42, 410-3" ga, 26" ventilated ribbed bbl, mod choke, EX ..1,550.00
Winchester M42, 410-3" ga, 28" ventilated ribbed bbl, much eng, EX 1,350.00
WW Greener Empire, 12 ga, 32" dbl bbls, full chokes, pistol-grip/s, M 1,000.00

Weather Vanes

The earliest weather vanes were of handmade wrought iron and were generally simple angular silhouettes with a small hole suggesting an eye. Later copper, zinc, and polychromed wood with features in relief were fashioned into more realistic forms. Ships, horses, fish, Indians, roosters, and angels were popular motifs. In the nineteenth century, silhouettes were often made from sheet metal. Wooden figures became highly carved and were painted in vivid colors. E.G. Washburne and Company in New York was one of the most prominent manufacturers of weather vanes during the last half of the century. Two-dimensional sheet metal weather vanes are increasing in value due to the already heady prices of the full-bodied variety. Originality, strength of line, and patination help to determine value. When no condition is indicated, the items listed below are assumed to be in excellent condition.

Rooster, cast and sheet iron, minor pitting, late 1800s, 32x34", $4,850.00.

Arrow w/pierced feathers in bk, steel, uniform rust, 74" L 1,900.00
Bull, molded/appl copper, fine verdigris, ca 1880s, 30x42" ...34,500.00
Cow, galvanized sheet tin, punched-out eye, no pnt, 31x22" 135.00
Cow, molded copper, gilt w/verdigris traces, 1890s, 28" 2,185.00
Cow, molded copper w/EX gilt/verdigris, late 19th C, 21x33" ...23,000.00
Eagle, molded copper, on earlier arrow/copper stand, 104" overall ...1,725.00
Eagle, molded copper, wings wide, regilded, ca 1900, 28x30" 600.00
Eagle, molded copper w/gilt & EX verdigris, 20th C, 9x17" 230.00
Elephant, cut sheet-steel silhouette, old bl pnt, arrows, 28" H ...200.00
Fish, cvd wood, EX folky details, wire nails hold fins, 40" 600.00
Fox running, copper, LW Cushing...MA, ca 1883, gilt traces, 22" ..5,750.00
Horse, copper/zinc, full bodied, JW Fiske, 31x33" on plinth ...7,000.00
Horse jumping, molded/appl copper, gilded, old rprs, 18x37" ..23,000.00
Horse running, copper, late 19th C, rpr holes/rfn, 25½" 400.00
Horse running, molded copper & zinc, gilded, 1890s, 25½" ...1,500.00
Horse trotting, molded copper w/gilt, EX verdigris, 1880s, 17x25" ..3,000.00
Horse-drawn fire-hose wagon, zinc & copper, 25x49" 3,450.00
Jockey on horse, copper & zinc, full bodied, Cushing & Wht, 28" L ...7,000.00
NATCO on arrow, worn silver pnt, early 20th C, 24¼x5" on cone 185.00
Peacock, sheet iron, paint losses, 19th C, 64" on stand 2,300.00
Pig, tin & CI, aged unpnt surface, 9x5x½" on 22" arrow 345.00
Rooster, cast zinc/sheet steel w/old blk pnt, 24"+base 1,125.00
Rooster, galvanized sheet silhouette, old rpt, 24"+stand 600.00
Rooster, molded copper, verdigris, dents/rprs, 1890s, 22" 1,100.00
Rooster, sheet iron, stylized, simple arrow, 11x13" 200.00
Schooner, copper w/gilt, 2-masted sailing ship, MA, 59x64", EX ...4,500.00

Whale, wood w/worn pnt & gilt traces, hinged tail, ca 1900, 30" ..1,650.00

Weaving

Early Americans used a variety of tools and a great amount of time to produce the material from which their clothing was made. Soaked and dried flax was broken on a flax brake to remove waste material. It was then tapped and stroked with a scutching knife. Hackles further removed waste and separated the short fibers from the longer ones. Unspun fibers were placed on the distaff on the spinning wheel for processing into yarn. The yarn was then wound around a reel for measuring. Three tools used for this purpose were the niddy-noddy, the reel yarn winder, and the click reel. After it was washed and dyed, the yarn was transferred to a barrel-cage or squirrel-cage swift and fed onto a bobbin winder.

Today flax wheels are more plentiful than the large wool wheels since they were small and could be more easily stored and preserved. The distaff, an often-discarded or misplaced part of the wheel, is very scarce. French spinners from the Quebec area painted their wheels. Many have been stripped and refinished by those unaware of this fact. Wheels may be very simple or have a great amount of detail, depending upon the owner's ethnic background and the maker's skill.

Flax wheel, blk w/salmon red & bl pnt wood, PA-German, 1859, 38" ..350.00
Reel, mortised hardwood, old red-brn finish, ME, 20" dia 140.00
Reel, pine & hardwood, floor standing, rpr, 32" 330.00
Reel, 4 spider legs, 2 Xd arms w/6 peg holders, primitive 35.00
Spinning wheel, oak/hardwoods, trn detail, dk finish, 34", VG .100.00
Spinning wheel w/ivory decor, dtd 1860, 12" dia wheel, 26" 550.00
Swift, old dk patina, wrought-iron thumb screw, 20" 195.00

Webb

Thomas Webb and Sons have been glassmakers in Stourbridge, England, since 1837. Besides their fine cameo glass, they have also made enameled ware and pieces heavily decorated with applied glass ornaments. The butterfly is a motif that has been so often featured that it tends to suggest Webb as the manufacturer. Our advisor for this category is Don Williams; he is listed in the Directory under Missouri. See also specific types of glass such as Alexandrite, Burmese, Mother of Pearl, and Peachblow.

Cameo

Bonbon, morning glories, red/yel/wht, SP lid & dome ft, 7½" ..2,500.00
Bottle, lay-down scent; duck head, wht on yel, EX detail, 9" 7,000.00
Bottle, scent; fantasy scene w/boy, turq on wht, teardrop, 4¼" ...4,000.00
Bottle, scent; floral, wht on red, 3-ftd, dbl SP cap, 5" 1,840.00
Bottle, scent; floral branches, wht on yel, SP lid/rim, 2⅜" 1,700.00
Bottle, scent; ivy, feather border, wht on turq, SP rim/lid, 3½" ..1,800.00
Bottle, scent; snowdrop floral, gr to wht, teardrop, 4" 1,375.00
Bottle, scent; wild roses allover, wht on citron, sq, 2¾" 1,850.00
Rose bowl, wild rose/buds, wht on citron, 2½" H 1,200.00
Vase, blackberry branches/bee, citron & opal on wht, 8½" 3,500.00
Vase, chrysanthemums/bumblebee/butterfly, citron/wht/red, 10" ..1,955.00
Vase, daisies/stalks, wht/red on citron, stick neck, 8" 3,200.00
Vase, floral (mixed), wht on bl, ovoid, 5" 1,600.00
Vase, floral medallions (6) on lattice, cobalt to lt bl, 4" 7,000.00
Vase, floral vines/borders, brn on wht, squat, 3x3¼" 700.00
Vase, flowering plant, 4-color, ovoid, Gem mk, 7" 4,850.00
Vase, foxglove plants/insects, wht on bl, att, 5¼" 3,675.00
Vase, geraniums/seed pods, wht on peachblow, 6¼" 2,500.00
Vase, Ivory, bird/floral reserves w/gold, dbl-gourd, 9" 3,500.00
Vase, Ivory, mythological creatures, urn form, 8½" 5,175.00
Vase, oak leaves, bl on wht, trumpet form, 8" 1,725.00
Vase, orchids/daisies, amber/red/wht opal, flattened oval, 5¾" ...5,175.00
Vase, Persian scrolling reserves, amber-brn to yel-ivory, att, 8" ..865.00
Vase, sunflowers/butterfly, wht on raisin brn, shouldered, 6" ..3,750.00
Vase, wild roses/butterfly, wht on bright bl, 7½x6½" 2,700.00

Miscellaneous

Bottle, egg shape w/appl legs & bronze rooster head, pk cased ...400.00
Creamer, gold prunus/butterfly on shaded tan, ovoid, 3¼" 385.00
Rose bowl, cranberry w/crystal petal rim, amber leafy base, 4" ...450.00
Vase, azaleas on citron satin, hdld banjo form, 20x7" 875.00
Vase, bronze, lustre finish, 6½" 200.00
Vase, gold prunus on brn to gold satin, wht int, 10½x4" 650.00
Vase, gold prunus on shaded brn satin, bulbous, collar rim, 5½" ..450.00
Vase, pk/wht satin, bulbous w/ruffled top, 8x4" 400.00
Vase, rose shaded satin, ruffled, sm pulled hdls at rim, 10" 275.00
Vase, yel shaded satin, wht int, gourd shape w/base, 10½" 275.00

Wedgwood

Josiah Wedgwood established his pottery in Burslem, England, in 1759. He produced only molded utilitarian earthenwares until 1770 when new facilities were opened at Etruria for the production of ornamental wares. It was there he introduced his famous Basalt and Jasperware. Jasperware, an unglazed fine stoneware decorated with classic figures in white relief, was usually produced in blues, but it was also made in ground colors of green, lilac, yellow, black, or white. Occasionally three or more colors were used in combination. It has been in continuous production to the present day and is the most easily recognized of all the Wedgwood lines. Jasper-dip is a ware with a solid-color body or a white body that has been dipped in an overlay color. It was introduced in the late 1700s and is the type most often encountered on today's market.

Though Wedgwood's Jasperware was highly acclaimed, on a more practical basis his improved creamware was his greatest success. Due to the ease with which it could be potted and because its lighter weight significantly reduced transportation expenses, Wedgwood was able to offer 'chinaware' at affordable prices. Queen Charlotte was so pleased with the ware that she allowed it to be called 'Queen's Ware.' Most creamware was marked simply 'WEDGWOOD.' ('Wedgwood & Co.' and 'Wedgewood' are marks of other potters.) From 1769 to 1780, Wedgwood was in partnership with Thomas Bentley; artwares of the highest quality may bear the 'Wedgwood & Bentley' mark indicating this partnership. Moonlight Lustre, an allover splashed-on effect of pink intermingling with gray, brown, or yellow, was made from 1805 to 1815. Porcelain was made, though not to any great extent, from 1812 to 1822. Bone china was produced before 1822 and after 1872. These types of wares were marked 'WEDGWOOD' (with a printed 'Portland Vase' mark after 1872). Stone china and Pearlware were made from about 1820 to 1875. Examples of either may be found with a printed or impressed mark to indicate their body type. During the late 1800s, Wedgwood produced some fine parian and majolica. Creamware, hand painted by Emile Lessore, was sold from about 1860 to 1875. From the twentieth century, several lines of lustre wares — Butterfly, Dragon, and Fairyland (designed by Daisy Makeig-Jones) — have attracted the collector and, as their prices suggest, are highly sought after and admired.

Nearly all of Wedgwood's wares are clearly marked. 'WEDGWOOD' was used before 1891, after which time 'ENGLAND' was added. Most examples marked 'MADE IN ENGLAND' were made after 1905. A detailed study of all marks is recommended for accurate dating. See also Majolica.

Key:
WW — WEDGWOOD
WWE — WEDGWOOD England
WWMIE — WEDGWOOD Made in England

Atomizer, Jasper, dk bl, classical figures, WW, 2⅝" 350.00
Bookends, girl, seated/reclining, moonstoon/wht, D Linder, 6½" ...1,265.00
Bowl, Daventry; Fairyland Lustre, Nizami, WWE, 7⅞" 5,465.00
Bowl, Jasper, blk, Dancing Hours, WWE, 10" 650.00
Bowl, Jasper, blk, Dancing Hours, WWE, 9" 375.00
Bowl, K'ang Hsi; Butterfly Lustre, MOP, Z4842, WWE, 8" 500.00
Bowl, orange; Queen's Ware, floral festoons/scalloped/pierced, WW, 12" ..975.00
Bowl, salad; Jasper, 3-color, SP rim, WW, 8" 750.00
Box, Jasper, crimson, classical figures, WWE, rstr, 5" 1,500.00
Box, Keith Murray, gr matt, ribbed sides, 3½x7" L 285.00
Brooch, Jasper, 3-color, classical portrait, WW, 1" dia 450.00
Bust, Byron, Basalt, WW, 8" 630.00
Bust, John Locke, Rosso Antico, WW, 8" 850.00
Bust, Joseph Addison, Basalt, WW, 10" 700.00
Bust, Mercury, Carrara, WW, 17" 2,300.00
Bust, Milton, Basalt, WW, 13" 745.00
Bust, Paul Bunyon, Carrara, WW, 14" 460.00
Bust, Shakespeare, Carrara, WW, 12" 545.00
Bust, Sir Isaac Newton, Basalt, WW, 9" 485.00
Bust, Stephenson, Carrara, WW, 14" 600.00
Bust, Virgil, Basalt, WW, 12" 800.00
Candlesticks, Jasper, dk bl, classical figures, WW, 6", pr 800.00
Candlesticks, Jasper, dk bl, classical figures, WWE, 6", pr 750.00
Candlesticks, Rosso Antico & Basalt, WW, 3", pr 545.00
Cheese dish, Jasper, lilac, classical figures/oak leaves, WW, 7" ..1,265.00
Coffee biggin, Caneware, florals on orange peel, dog finial, WW, 6" 700.00
Coffee can & saucer, Jasper, crimson, classical figures, WWE, 5⅛" ...1,265.00
Coffeepot, Drabware, arabesque, dog finial, smear glaze, WW, 9" ...450.00
Coffeepot, Queen's Ware, blk transfer, flower finial, WW, 7" 460.00
Cooler, fruit; Queen's Ware, floral bands, w/lid & stand, WW, 12" ...650.00
Cooler, wine; Caneware, fruiting vintage, WW 1,380.00
Cup & saucer, Caneware, Bacchanalian boys, WW, 5" saucer ...460.00
Desk accessories, Jasper, dk bl, SP mts, WWE, 6-pc 500.00
Ewer, Jasper, blk, classical figure, WWE, ltd ed, 16" 1,950.00
Flower holder, Jasper, dk bl, hdls, w/lid, WW, 5" dia 500.00
Game dish, Caneware, cauliflower finial, vintage relief, WW, 7" ..400.00
Game dish, Caneware, rabbit finial, emb game/vines, WW, 8" ..545.00
Girandoles, Jasper, blk, brass mts, crystal drops, WWE, 11", pr ..1,250.00
Group, Finding of Moses, Carrara, unmk, ca 1860, 20" 5,450.00
Jar, canopic; Jasper, dk bl, hieroglyphs/zodiac signs, WW, 10" ...6,325.00
Jar, Jasper, yel, appl blk classical relief, WWE, 4", NM 575.00
Jar, potpourri; Basalt, festoons, dolphin supports, WW, 15" 8,000.00
Jar, potpourri; Stoneware, wht smear glaze w/gr/lilac flowers, WW, 10" ..1,265.00
Jug, club; Rosso Antico, blk enamel grapevine band, WW, 7" ...900.00
Jug, Egyptian; Rosso Antico, Basalt hieroglyph band, WW, 3" ..575.00
Lamp, vestal/reading; Basalt, blk, female figure at top, WW, 8", pr ...1,800.00
Letter box, Jasper, lt bl, medallions, brass & wood mts, WW, 8" ..700.00
Medallion, Jasper, bl, Garrick portrait, WW & Bentley, 3x3⅞" ..1,725.00
Medallion, Jasper, lt bl, Gassendi portrait, WW & Bentley, 3⅜x3" ..1,265.00
Mold, jelly; Pearlware, enameled fruits, WW, 8" 1,150.00
Pedestal base, Jasper, dk bl, Achilles Dragging...Hector, WW, 10" ..575.00
Pitcher, Jasper, dk bl, str sides, metal lid, WW, 6½x3¾" 225.00
Plaque, Bacchus, Jasper, gr, WW, 8" dia 1,150.00
Plaque, Cupid, Jasper, lt bl, WW, 3x5", pr in dbl fr 550.00
Plaque, Dancing Hours, Jasper, lt bl, WW, 6x18"+gilt wood fr ...1,150.00
Plaque, Dancing Hours figures, Jasper, gr, WW, 4x11"+fr 485.00
Plaque, George Washington, Jasper, lt bl, WW, 4⅜x6" 625.00
Plaque, hunt scene w/4 horsemen, emb/mc, 1930, 6½x15" 860.00
Plaque, Jasper, gr, cherubs as seasons, WW, 6x18"+fr 1,500.00
Plaque, Judgment of Hercules, Jasper, blk, WW, 5x17" 1,500.00
Plaque, Muse, Basalt, WW, 6x8", pr 630.00
Plate, Jasper Diceware, 3-color, WWE, ltd ed, 9" 550.00
Pot, bough; Pearlware, floral festoons/brn slip, w/lid, WW, 5" ...900.00
Root pot, Basalt, cherubs/laurel wreaths, WW, w/lids, 6", pr ..4,000.00
Sconces, Jasper, lt bl medallions, ormolu, WW, 22", pr 1,950.00
Servers, salad; Jasper, yel, appl blk acanthus/etc, SP trim, WWE, 11" ..285.00
Shell dish, Bone China, mc enamel w/gilt, WW, 12⅜" 150.00
Soup tureen, Jasper, dk bl, w/lid & stand, WW, 11" L 2,500.00
Tea bowl & saucer, Jasper, blk, floral, ram medallion, WW 1,000.00
Tea set, Drabware, bl grapevines, WW, 3-pc 600.00
Teacup & saucer, Jasper, gr, classical figures, WW, 5" 700.00
Teapot, Rosso Antico, Basalt grapevine banding, WW, 9⅝" 700.00
Teapot, Rosso Antico, Sybil finial, basketweave body, WW, 8" .700.00
Urn, crater; Caneware, Rosso Antico grapevines, pierced top, WW, 10" ...700.00
Vase, Agateware, on sq Basalt plinth, WW & Bentley, 6" 700.00
Vase, Basalt, Bacchus-head hdls, laurel swags, WW/Bentley, 10" 700.00
Vase, Basalt, classical medallion, WW & Bentley, 5" 800.00
Vase, Basalt, classical reliefs, scrolled hdls, WW, 10" 1,750.00
Vase, Bone China, foliate designs, mc on ivory, hdls, WW, 8" ...630.00
Vase, Caneware, blk foliate & Greek Key decor, WW, 5" 750.00
Vase, canopic; Basalt, gilt decor, WWE, ltd ed, 9" 3,100.00
Vase, Dragon Lustre, bl mottle w/MOP int, Z4829, #2351, WWE, 9" ...700.00
Vase, Fairyland Lustre, Firbolgs, gr, Z5247, WWE, 8" 2,200.00
Vase, Jasper, blk, undraped, ca 1870, 10¼" 3,000.00
Vase, Jasper, crimson, classical figures, WW, 5" 1,100.00
Vase, Jasper, dk bl, neck hdls, WWI, 4" 170.00
Vase, Jasper, lt bl, swags & foliage, WW, 8" 1,265.00
Vase, Jasper, Portland Blue, classical figure, WW, 10" 3,100.00
Vase, Jasper, Portland Blue, classical figures, WW, 4", pr 975.00
Vase, Keith Murray, gr-gray glaze, U-form, ftd, 8½" 175.00
Vase, Keith Murray, wide banded shoulder, gr, 6x7½" 865.00
Vase, Lindsay Ware, butterflies, hdls, 7" 1,350.00
Vase, Queen's Ware, lizard/bamboo w/gold on ivory, w/lid, WW, 9" ..250.00
Vase, Rosso Antico, Basalt acanthus & bellflowers, WW, 7" ..2,300.00

Weil Ware

Max Weil came to the United States in the 1940s, settling in California. There he began manufacturing dinnerware, figurines, cookie jars, and wall pockets. American clays were used, and the dinnerware was all hand decorated. Weil died in 1954; the company closed two years later. The last backstamp to be used was the outline of a burro with the words 'Weil Ware — Made in California.' Many unmarked pieces found today originally carried a silver foil label; but you'll often find a four-digit handwritten number series, especially on figurines. For further study we recommend *The Collector's Encyclopedia of California Pottery* by Jack Chipman (Collector Books).

Vases: lady in rose dress with flower decor and lady in green with black lace fan, from $50.00 to $60.00 each.

Bowl, fruit; Malay Blossom, sq 10.00
Bowl, lug soup; Malay Blossom, sq 25.00
Bowl, vegetable; Malay Bambu, dbl hdls, burro mk, 8x10" 35.00
Candy dish, Malay Blossom, pedestal, 3½x7" sq top 50.00
Casserole, Malay Bambu, w/lid 45.00

Casserole, Malay Blossom, gr, w/lid, 10x5¼" 45.00
Compote, Malay Blossom, bl, ped ft, 3½x6½" sq top 25.00
Creamer & sugar bowl, Malay Bambu, burro mk 40.00
Creamer & sugar bowl, Malay Blossom 40.00
Cup, Malay Blossom, sq 10.00
Figurine, little girl in pk, flowers in hand, 11½" 70.00
Figurines, Asian children, boy, #3051, #3053, 9", 7", pr 70.00
Flower holder, blonde lady holding parasol, unmk, 10" 65.00
Flower holder, brunette in bl w/bonnet, hole in muff, unmk, 10½" ..65.00
Flower holder, Dutch boy or girl, #3040, #3041, 7¼", ea, $35 to .45.00
Flower holder, sailor boy, stamped mk, ca 1943, 10¾", $50 to 65.00
Pitcher, iced tea; Malay Bambu, 9" 60.00
Plate, chop; Malay Bambu, 13" dia 45.00
Plate, dinner; Malay Blossom, sq, 9¾", from $10 to 15.00
Teapot, brn roses/gr leaves on yel bkground, burro mk, 7" 60.00
Vase, Ming Tree, #1924, 8½x4½" 35.00
Vase, Ming Tree, burro mk, 6¾x3⅞x5¼" 32.00
Wall pocket, lady w/horn of plenty, stamped mk, 9" 75.00
Wall pocket, Oriental lady on bench w/bowl ea side, 10½x7" 45.00

Weller

The Weller Pottery Company was established in Zanesville, Ohio, in 1882, the outgrowth of a small one-kiln log cabin works Sam Weller had operated in Fultonham. Through an association with Wm. Long, he entered the art pottery field in 1895, producing the Lonhuda Ware Long had perfected in Steubenville six years earlier. His famous Louwelsa line was merely a continuation of Lonhuda and was made in at least five hundred different shapes until 1924. Many fine lines of artware followed under the direction of Charles Babcock Upjohn, art director from 1895 to 1904: Dickens Ware (1st Line), under-glaze slip decorations on dark backgrounds; Turada, featuring applied ivory bands of delicate openwork on solid dark brown backgrounds; and Aurelian, similar to Louwelsa, but with a brushed-on rather than blended ground. One of their most famous lines was 2nd Line Dickens, introduced in 1900. Backgrounds, characteristically caramel shading to turquoise matt, were decorated by sgraffito with animals, golfers, monks, Indians, and scenes from Dickens novels. The work is often artist signed. Sicardo, 1903, was a metallic lustre line in tones of rose, blue, green, or purple with flowing Art Nouveau patterns developed within the glaze.

Frederick Hurten Rhead, who worked for Weller from 1903 to 1904, created the prestigious Jap Birdimal line decorated with geisha girls, landscapes, storks, etc., accomplished through application of heavy slip forced through the tiny nozzle of a squeeze bag. Other lines to his credit are L'Art Nouveau, produced in both high-gloss brown and matt pastels, and 3rd Line Dickens, often decorated with Cruikshank's illustrations in relief. Other early artware lines were Eocean, Floretta, Hunter, Perfecto, Dresden, Etched Matt, and Etna.

In 1920 John Lessel was hired as art director, and under his supervision several new lines were created. LaSa, LaMar, Marengo, and Besline attest to his expertise with metallic lustres. The last of the artware lines and one of the most sought after by collectors today is Hudson, first made during the early 1920s. Hudson, a semimatt glazed ware, was beautifully artist decorated on shaded backgrounds with florals, animals, birds, and scenics. Notable artists often signed their work, among them Hester Pillsbury, Dorothy England Laughead, Ruth Axline, Claude Leffler, Sarah Reid McLaughlin, E.L. Pickens, and Mae Timberlake.

During the '30s Weller produced a line of gardenware and naturalistic life-sized figures of dogs, cats, swans, geese, and playful gnomes. The Depression brought a slow, steady decline in sales, and by 1948 the pottery was closed. For a more thorough study we recommend *The Collector's Encyclopedia of Weller Pottery* by Sharon and Bob Huxford, available at your local library or from Collector Books.

Mammy Line, teapot, Weller Pottery since 1872 on bottom, ca 1938, 8", $825.00.

Alvin, bud vase, dbl; V-shaped tree trunk w/connecting branch, 6" 80.00
Ansonia, batter jug, brn matt, ring pattern, 14½" 250.00
Ansonia, strawberry pot, tan matt, ring pattern, 10" 125.00
Arcadia, bud vase, leaf form, 7½" 30.00
Arcadia, fan vase, flared leaves, 8x15" 100.00
Ardsley, bud vase, cattails w/flowers around base, 7½" 95.00
Ardsley, console bowl w/fish frog, 12", 6½" 550.00
Ardsley, pillow vase, iris, 7" 300.00
Athens, vase, cat heads on matt brn, 10½" 700.00
Aurelian, ewer, floral, squatty w/long neck, ruffled rim, 6" 275.00
Aurelian, tankard, corn, 12½" 1,350.00
Aurelian, tankard, dog scene, w/silver lid, sgn K, 7" 1,750.00
Aurelian, vase, Black man in fez, cylindrical, sgn Fouts, 18" ..3,500.00
Aurelian, vase, branches/leaves, silver overlay top, sgn, HM, 11½" ..1,500.00
Baldin, bowl, red apples on bl, 4" 200.00
Baldin, vase, bulbous, yel apples on branch, branch hdls, 9½" ..325.00
Barcelona, candle holder, stylized floral, 2x5" 100.00
Barcelona, oil jar, stylized floral, hdld, 25½" 1,750.00
Barcelona, vase, stylized floral, tapered cylinder, rolled rim, 7" ..200.00
Besline, vase, berries & leaves, tapered cylinder, 11" 550.00
Blo' Red, vase, 7" 95.00
Blossom, planter, 4" 125.00
Blossom, vase, dbl; #G-24, 12½" 150.00
Blue & Decorated, bud vase, floral, 10" 150.00
Blue & Decorated, vase, banded floral rim, cylindrical, 8½" 225.00
Blue Drapery, candlestick/lamp base, roses on bl, 9½" 145.00
Blue Drapery, planter, roses on bl, 4" 75.00
Blue Drapery, wall pocket, roses on bl, 9" 250.00
Blue Ware, lamp base, band of fruit, 9" 175.00
Bonito, bowl, stylized floral, sgn CF, 3½" 135.00
Bonito, candle holders, stylized floral, 1½", pr 125.00
Bonito, vase, stylized floral, scrolled shoulder hdls, sgn NC, 10" ..400.00
Bouquet, bowl, floral, #B-8, 4" 45.00
Bouquet, pillow vase, floral, #B-5, 5½" 50.00
Bouquet, pitcher, floral, #B-18, 9½" 150.00
Breton, vase, emb floral band, 6" 75.00
Brighton, kingfisher on stump, 9" 350.00
Brighton, parakeets (2) on perch, 9" 1,350.00
Brighton, parrot on perch, 7½" 700.00
Brighton, penguins (2), 5" 800.00
Brighton, pheasant, 7x11½" 750.00
Brighton, rooster, 9½" 1,400.00
Burntwood, vase, birds & flowers, 8½" 250.00
Burntwood, vase, pine cones, incurvate rim, 5½" 100.00
Cactus, cat, 5½" 125.00
Cameo, bowl, wht floral on bl, 3-ftd, 4" 40.00
Cameo, hanging basket, wht floral on bl, 5" 110.00
Cameo Jewel, jardiniere & ped, portrait cameos & jewels, 34" ...1,500.00
Candis, candle holders, scrolls & flowers, 1½", pr 75.00
Candis, ewer, scrolls & flowers, 11" 110.00
Candis, hanging basket, scrolls & flowers, 5½" 125.00
Chase, fan vase, wht hunt scene on bl, 8½" 350.00
Chase, vase, mc hunt scene on lt bl, sgn DE, 7½" 1,250.00

Chengtu, jar, uptrn hdls, w/lid, 8" 250.00
Chengtu, vase, hexagonal, 8" 125.00
Classic, bowl, 11" 70.00
Classic, window box, 4" 85.00
Claywood, mug, floral, 5" 125.00
Claywood, plate, floral, 7" 150.00
Claywood, vase, floral, 3½" 100.00
Claywood, vase, spider web, cylindrical, 5½" 110.00
Coppertone, ashtray, w/frog, 6½" 225.00
Coppertone, fan vase, 2 frogs on base, 8" 750.00
Coppertone, figurine, frog, 4x4" 550.00
Coppertone, figurine, frog w/banjo, 7½" 1,700.00
Coppertone, pillow vase, emb branches, ftd, 7" 200.00
Coppertone, vase, frog hdls, 8" 1,000.00
Copra, jardiniere, tulips, ring hdls, 8" 200.00
Cornish, jardiniere, berries & leaves, 5" 60.00
Creamware, comport, rtcl pattern, hdls, 6" 200.00
Creamware, match holder, roses, 6½" 150.00
Darsie, pot, 3" 45.00
Darsie, vase, cylindrical w/scalloped rim, 7½" 60.00
Dickens I, jug, corn, 6½" 450.00
Dickens I, lamp, owl, squatty base w/long str neck, sgn EA, 14" ..1,625.00
Dickens I, mug, banded design top/bottom, 6" 175.00
Dickens I, mug, floral, 7" 225.00
Dickens I, pillow vase, lady's portrait, ftd, 7" 2,500.00
Dickens II, ewer, mermaid, shell-formed lip, 10½" 700.00
Dickens II, fish, ball form/short str neck/shoulder hdls, 9½" 2,000.00
Dickens II, mug, Prost, high-gloss, 5½" 900.00
Dickens II, tobacco jar, The Captain (head form), 7" 1,750.00
Dickens II, vase, Black Bear, sgn Anna Dautherty, 10" 2,250.00
Dickens II, vase, Dombey & Son, sgn W Gibson, 10½" 1,250.00
Dickens II, vase, dueling fencers, shoulder hdls, sgn LJB, 5½" ...600.00
Dickens II, vase, knights in forest, high-gloss, sgn Upjohn, 14" ...2,750.00
Dickens III, carafe w/cup, David Copperfield, #0002, 14½" ...1,600.00
Dickens III, flask vase, Dombey & Son, #0021, 7½" 700.00
Dickens III, vase, lady in bonnet, sm high hdls, 6" 300.00
Dickens III, vase, Mr Weller Sr Pickwick Papers, #15, 8" 1,000.00
Dickens III, vase, owls, brn, sgn LP, 8" 900.00
Dresden, mug, windmills, cylindrical w/angled hdl, sgn LJB, 5½" ...450.00
Dupont, bowl, flower baskets, incurvate rim, 2½" 45.00
Dynasty, vase, gr drip glaze over bl, urn w/ring hdls, 4" 35.00
Elberta, console bowl, uptrn boat shape w/hdls, 6x11½" 115.00
Eocean, candlestick, floral, sgn LJB, 9" 450.00
Eocean, flask vase, poodle head, ftd/hdld, sgn L Blake, 7½" ...1,600.00
Eocean, floral, tapered urn w/trumpet neck, sgn M Rauchfuss, 12½" ..1,100.00
Eocean, vase, carnations, red/bl on shaded gr, 8½x4" 450.00
Eocean, vase, cherries, cylindrical w/4 sm hdls at rim, 16" 900.00
Eocean, vase, owl, sgn EB, 10½" 2,000.00
Eocean, vase, wild roses, pk/wht on shaded gr & pk, 10½" 550.00
Etna, bowl, mouse on rim, 2½" 850.00
Etna, vase, floral, pk on shaded bl-gray, thick shoulder hdls, 11" ...325.00
Etna, vase, frog & snake, 6½" 900.00
Etna, vase, pansies, 6½" 175.00
Evergreen, candle holder, triple; fluted cups on scrolled base, 7½" ...115.00
Evergreen, console bowl, flared scalloped rim, 5" 95.00
Fairfield, bowl, band of cherubs w/fluted bottom, 4½" 80.00
Flemish, basket tub, roses, 3½" 95.00
Flemish, comport, roses, w/lid, 8½" 350.00
Flemish, jardiniere, floral, ftd, 6" 150.00
Flemish, umbrella stand, apples/trees, 22" 1,250.00
Floral, console bowl, floral swag, #F9, 4½x10" 60.00
Florala, candle holders, mc flowers on flared hexagonal panels, 5", pr ...175.00
Florala, console bowl, mc floral rim, 11" 125.00
Florenzo, basket, floral, vertical ribbing, 4" 140.00
Florenzo, fan vase, 5½" 65.00
Floretta, ewer, emb grapes, brn, 10½" 275.00
Floretta, vase, emb grapes, cylindrical w/bulbous bottom, brn, 17" ...350.00
Forest, basket, 8½" 275.00
Forest, bowl, #3, 2½" 75.00
Forest, hanging basket, 8" 225.00
Forest, teapot, glossy, 4½" 275.00
Fruitone, vase, shoulder hdls, 4½" 75.00
Fruitone, wall pocket, 5½" 200.00
Glendale, bowl/frog/candle holders, bird scenes, 16", 5½", 4-pc set ...725.00
Glendale, bud vase, dbl; bird scene between 2 tree trunks, 7" 300.00
Glendale, vase, 2 birds on a branch, 8½" 700.00
Glendale, wall pocket, emb mc birds, no mk, 12" 600.00
Goldenglow, ginger jar, leaves, 8" 275.00
Greenbriar, ewer, 2-loop hdl, 11½" 300.00
Greenbriar, vase, 6" 85.00
Greora, strawberry pot, marbleized, 5" 150.00
Greora, vase, marbleized, 3-sided/ftd, 4½" 85.00
Hobart, bowl, ftd, 3x9½" 85.00
Hobart, console bowl w/flower frog, 2 nudes, 2½x12", 7½" 450.00
Hobart, nude flower frog, wht, 8½" 325.00
Hobart, nude seated on oval base, bl, 4½" 250.00
Hudson, cottage scene w/tall tree, cylindrical, sgn Timberlake, 8½" ..800.00
Hudson, figurines, parrots, 7½x11" or 12", ea 4,000.00
Hudson, vase, fall scene w/pumpkins & cornstalks, sgn Pillsbury, 8" ..3,000.00
Hudson, vase, floral (wht/pk on leafy branches), hdls, 13½" ..1,750.00
Hudson, vase, iris on bl, sgn MT, 15½" 1,600.00
Hudson, vase, Mt Fuji scene on bl, sgn Pillsbury, 12" 3,000.00
Hudson, vase, Wise Men following star, tapered cylinder, 13½" ..2,500.00
Hudson-Light, vase, floral, rnd w/sm bottle neck, 4½" 175.00
Hudson-Light, vase, wisteria, hexagonal, 11x5" 275.00
Hudson-Perfecto, vase, acorns & leaves around top, sgn HP, 4½" ..175.00
Hudson-Perfecto, vase, iris, shouldered cylinder w/rolled rim, 9" 400.00
Hudson-Perfecto, vase, pine cones & branches, sgn Leffler, 10" ..1,250.00
Hunter, ewer, bird, 4-sided, tapered, mk x357, 11" 850.00
Hunter, pillow vase, butterflies, sgn UJ, 5x3½" 425.00
Ivoris, basket, floral, 5" 95.00
Ivoris, ginger jar, floral, w/lid, 8½" 125.00
Ivory (Clinton Ivory), pillow vase, swag design, ftd, 5" 100.00
Ivory (Clinton Ivory), window planter, berries & leaves, 6x15½" ..225.00
Jap Birdimal, oil pitcher, sgn HMR, 10½" 1,100.00
Jap Birdimal, vase, flying ducks, twisted form, fluted rim, 11" 800.00
Jap Birdimal, vase, flying ducks, 6-sided squat form, 4" 500.00
Jap Birdimal, vase, landscape w/tall trees, incurvate rim, 14" .1,100.00
Klyro, basket, flowers & berries, ftd, 7" 150.00
Klyro, candle holder, flowers & berries, tower shape, ftd, 9½" ...125.00
Klyro, circle vase, flowers & swag, ftd, 8" 150.00
Knifewood, tobacco box, fox/chickens, w/lid, 3½" 400.00
Knifewood, vase, squirrel, cylindrical w/slightly curved sides, 11" ...650.00
L'Art Nouveau, ewer, floral, 4-sided, 14½" 550.00
L'Art Nouveau, mug, floral, 5" 225.00
L'Art Nouveau, vase, grapes, 4-sided, 16" 600.00
L'Art Nouveau-Glossy, console bowl, emb grapes, hdls, 6x12" ...500.00
La Sa, bud vase, slim cone form, incurvate rim, 5½" 250.00
La Sa, lamp, palm trees, 14½" 650.00
Lamar, lamp, scenic, 16" 500.00
Lavonia, vase, emb thistles, 10" 200.00
Lido, basket, swirled w/ruffled rim, 8½" 95.00
Lido, ewer, swirled, 10½" 115.00
Lonhuda, ewer, bulbous, #215, sgn JRS, 7" 450.00
Lonhuda, ewer, floral, bulbous w/scroll hdl, 6" 300.00
Lonhuda, vase, squat/long trumpet neck, brns, sgn McLaughlin, 5½" .325.00
Lorbeek, console bowl & flower frog, 3x14", 5" 200.00
Lorbeek, wall pocket, 8½" 200.00

Loru, bowl, 3-leaf decor, fluted rim, 2½x8" 45.00
Louella, basket, 6½" 145.00
Louella, powder jar, w/lid, 4" 125.00
Louwelsa, candle holder, pansies, sgn HL, 9" 275.00
Louwelsa, ewer, floral, bulbous w/long neck, ruffled lip, 10" 350.00
Louwelsa, lamp, roses, ftd squat form, sgn MM, 6½" 1,250.00
Louwelsa, mug, man's portrait, sgn Ferrell, 6½" 1,000.00
Louwelsa, pillow vase, hawk, ftd, 9½x9½" 800.00
Louwelsa, pitcher vase, floral, sgn AC, 3" 150.00
Louwelsa, tankard, grapes, sgn E Roberts, 16½" 1,100.00
Louwelsa, tobacco jar, wooden top, sgn CA, 5½" 500.00
Louwelsa, vase, berries, shoulder hdls, 13" 365.00
Louwelsa, vase, dog in profile, sgn A Wilson, 10½" 1,700.00
Louwelsa, vase, exotic leaves, lion head hdls w/rings, sgn AH, 11" 2,750.00
Louwelsa, vase, floral, 4-sided, ftd, sgn CJ Dibowski, 12" 750.00
Louwelsa, vase, grapes & leaves, sgn CJ Dibowsky, 25" 2,250.00
Louwelsa, vase, man's portrait, sgn RGT, 11" 1,500.00
Louwelsa, vase, poppies, by Chilcote, 19x8" 1,850.00
Lustre, bud vase, 4-sided cone shape, 6" 35.00
Malverne, circle vase, floral, 8" 200.00
Malverne, wall pocket, floral, 11" 250.00
Mammy Line, creamer, 3½" 350.00
Mammy Line, sugar bowl, w/lid, 3½" 375.00
Mammy Line, teapot, 8" 825.00
Manhattan, vase, emb lily pad decor around bulbous bottom, 8½" 75.00
Marbleized, bowl, incurvate rim, 1½x5½" 50.00
Marbleized, vase, hexagonal, tapered, rolled rim, 10½" 175.00
Marbleized, vase, trumpet form, 7½" 150.00
Marengo, wall pocket, trees & mountains, 8½" 350.00
Marvo, hanging basket, emb floral, 5" 150.00
Marvo, pitcher, emb floral, 8" 150.00
Matt Green, poppy pods emb, cylindrical, 10½x4¾" 700.00
Melrose, console bowl, roses, fluted rim, branch hdls, 5x8½" 150.00
Melrose, vase, berries & leaves, twisted form w/branch hdls, 8½" 125.00
Mi-Flo, bowl, floral, uptrn hdls, 4" 60.00
Minerva, planter, mythical figures, 12x16" 1,250.00
Minerva, vase, stylized forest scene on textured ground, 13½" 800.00
Mirror Black, bowl, 11" 60.00
Mirror Black, strawberry jar, 6½" 75.00
Modeled Etched Matt, vase, berries & branches, concave sides, 10½" 400.00
Modeled Etched Matt, vase, roses on thorny stems, tower form, 10" 400.00
Monochrome, bowl, pk, incurvate rim, ftd, 1½x8" 35.00
Montego, vase, gr drip glaze over brn, ribbed center band, 9½" 300.00
Muskota, bowl w/goose, 4½" 450.00
Muskota, dogs (2) pointing, 7½" 800.00
Muskota, gate w/pots & cats, 7" 550.00
Muskota, girl w/doll seated by tree trunk, 8" 475.00
Neiska, bowl, textured, 3-ftd, 4" 35.00
Noval, bowl, apple hdls on blk/wht panels, 3½x9½" 95.00
Noval, comport, apple hdls, w/lid, 9½" 150.00
Novelty, dish, monkey sitting on edge of peanut, 5x8" 125.00
Novelty, planter, kangaroo w/open pouch, 5½" 125.00
Oak Leaf, planter, 6" 100.00
Oak Leaf, wall pocket, 8½" 150.00
Panella, cornucopia, pansy decor, 5½" 55.00
Panella, wall pocket, pansy decor, 8" 150.00
Paragon, candle holders, floral, 2", pr 150.00
Paragon, vase, floral, 6½" 325.00
Parian, vase, floral tile-like design, 8½" 125.00
Pastel, vase, #P-14, 6½" 25.00
Patra, jardiniere, 6" 250.00
Patra, nut dish, #2, 3" 85.00
Patricia, planter, pelican, wht, 5" 110.00
Pearl, basket, roses & pearls on cream, ftd, 6½" 225.00
Pearl, bud vase, roses & pearls on cream, cylindrical, 7" 125.00
Pearl, candle holders, roses & pearls on cream, 8½", pr 225.00
Perfecto (Matt Louwelsa), ewer, thorny flowers, #436, sgn HP, 17" 1,000.00
Perfecto (Matt Louwelsa), vase, roses, cylindrical, sgn MH, 14" 1,000.00
Pumila, candle holder, flower petals form cup on base, 3" 85.00
Roba, planter, floral, ftd, 4½" 90.00
Roba, vase, floral, #R-20, 13" 225.00
Roma, bud vase, dbl; V-shape w/center ring hdl, ftd, 8" 120.00
Roma, candlestick, grapes, 11½" 130.00
Roma, planter, floral, log form, 3x10½" 150.00
Roma, wall pocket, roses & bl ribbon, fan shape, 7" 300.00
Rudlor, console bowl, flower branch, bead-like hdls, 4½x17½" .125.00
Rudlor, vase, floral, angled hdls, 8" 35.00
Sabrinian, ewer, 9" 400.00
Sabrinian, planter, 4½" 175.00
Sabrinian, window box, 3½x9" 225.00
Scandia, bowl, 3" 75.00
Senic, pillow vase, river scene, #S-11, 7½" 95.00
Senic, vase, river scene, ruffled rim, 3-ftd, #S-1, 5" 60.00
Sicardo, pillow vase, 3-scallop rim, wavy hdls, 6½x10" 1,100.00

Sicardo, Vases: grape clusters and foliage, green and burgundy, 15½x4", $2,600.00; spider mums and foliage, green, purple and gold, X-492, 11x6½", $1,500.00.

Sicardo, vase, bulbous base w/long thick trumpet neck, sgn, 15½" 1,750.00
Sicardo, vase, fanned plumes/dots, curved sides, 4½" 400.00
Sicardo, vase, irregular form, 5" 425.00
Sicardo, vase, 4-sided, flared ftd base, shouldered, sgn, 12½" .2,500.00
Silvertone, vase, floral, plain rim, thick twisted hdls, 11½" 325.00
Silvertone, vase, floral, ruffled rim, thick hdls, 11½" 500.00
Softone, hanging basket, yel, 10" 125.00
Souevo, bowl, band of swastikas, rolled rim, 2½x6½" 100.00
Sydonia, console bowl, 6x17" 125.00
Sydonia, cornucopia, slim, 8" 80.00
Tivoli, bowl, floral-banded rim, 2½" 115.00
Tivoli, vase, goblet form w/mc floral band on 4-ftd base, #2, 6" .115.00
Turada, lamp base, appl filigree on brn, bulbous, ftd, 8" 1,000.00
Turada, tobacco jar, appl filigree on brn, 5½" 350.00
Turada, umbrella stand, appl filigree, 21" 1,500.00
Turkis, bowl vase, hdld, 5" 85.00
Tutone, planter, floral, 5½" 125.00
Tutone, wall pocket, floral, 10½" 275.00
Velva, vase, flower & leaf panels, bulbous, uptrn hdls, 9" 125.00
Velvetone, vase, tricolor, ring pattern w/ruffled rim, hdls 9½" 200.00
Voile, fan vase, fruit tree, 7" 100.00
Voile, vase, fruit tree, scalloped rim, 9" 150.00
Warwick, basket, branch hdl, 9" 225.00
Warwick, bud vase, flower vine on tree trunk, 7" 75.00
Warwick, planter, 3½" 120.00
White & Decorated, bowl, floral rim, 4" 200.00
White & Decorated, vase, birds on berry branch, 15" 1,800.00

Wild Rose, basket, floral, ball shape, 5½" 60.00
Wild Rose, vase, floral, cylindrical w/dbl-loop hdls, 10½" 75.00
Woodcraft, basket, acorn form w/branch hdl, 9½" 450.00
Woodcraft, bowl, cherries, 3" 125.00
Woodcraft, fan vase, fruit tree, 8" 125.00
Woodcraft, tankard, fox family in tree trunk, 12½" 1,150.00
Woodcraft, vase, owl on trunk of apple tree, 16" 1,150.00
Woodrose, jardiniere, roses on wooden bucket, hdls, 7" 175.00
Woodrose, vase, roses on wooden bucket, cylindrical, no hdls, 7" ..85.00
Zona, bowl, rabbit/bird on branch, 5½" 110.00
Zona, comport, floral, 5½" 125.00
Zona, cream pitcher, duck on wht, 3½" 100.00
Zona, mug, duck, 3" 95.00

Western Americana

The collecting of Western Americana encompasses a broad spectrum of memorabilia. Examples of various areas within the mainstream would include the following fields: weapons, bottles, photographs, mining/railroad artifacts, cowboy paraphernalia, farm and ranch implements, maps, barbed wire, tokens, Indian relics, saloon/gambling items, and branding irons. Some of these areas have their own separate listings in this book. Western Americana is not only a collecting field but is also a collecting *era* with specific boundries. Depending upon which field the collector decides to specialize in, prices can start at a few dollars and run into the thousands.

Our advisor for this category is Bill Mackin, author of *Cowboy and Gunfighter Collectibles* (order from the author); he is listed in the Directory under Colorado.

Bit, basic port-mouth, from $40 to 65.00
Bit, Garcia, silver mts w/eagle ea side, 1940s, 10x5" 425.00
Bit, jtd mouth w/twist, from $15 to 20.00
Bit, silver on brass, CA type, from $950 to 1,250.00
Bridle, braided horsehair, ca 1900, from $1,425 to 2,000.00
Bridle, mc horsehair, prison made, 1920s, 27" 300.00
Buffalo horns, set on tooled brass base w/tooled brass caps, 1880s ..180.00
Hat, blk Stetson, 1930s, MIB 295.00
Poke, gold; buckskin w/drawstrings, ca 1850, from $110 to 135.00
Saddle, CA style, leather/wood/metal, basket stamped, w/bags, up to 2,250.00
Saddle, lady's side; leather, from $375 to 550.00
Saddle, parade; stamped leather w/silver decor, from $3,500 to ..6,500.00
Spurs, silver inlaid Charro type, pr, from $375 to 700.00
Spurs, spoke rowels, Mexican, pr, from $175 to 325.00
Stirrups, cvd wood, pr, from $45 to 75.00

Western Pottery Manufacturing Company

This pottery was originally founded as the Denver China and Pottery Company; William Long was the owner. The company's assets were sold to a group who in 1905 formed the Western Pottery Manufacturing Company, located at 16th Street and Alcott in Denver, Colorado. By 1926, 186 different items were being produced, including crocks, flowerpots, kitchen items, and other stoneware. The company dissolved in 1936.

Seven various marks were used during the years, and values may be higher for items that carry a rare mark. Numbers within the descriptions refer to specific marks, see the line drawings. Prices may vary depending on demand and locale. Our advisors for this category are Cathy Segelke and Pat James; they are listed in the Directory under Colorado.

Churn, #2, hdl, 4-gal, M 75.00
Churn, #2, hdl, 5-gal, M 65.00
Churn, #2, no lid, 5-gal, G 80.00
Crock, #4, bail lip, 4-gal, G 55.00
Crock, #4, hdl, no lid, 8-gal, M 90.00
Crock, #4, ice water; bl/wht sponge pnt, 3-gal, NM 30.00
Crock, #4, 6-gal, EX 72.00
Crock, #4b, 20-gal, M 200.00
Crock, #4b, 22x17½", 15-gal, NM 150.00
Crock, #5, bail lip, 1½-gal, M 45.00
Crock, #5, no lid, 6-gal, M 70.00
Crock, #6, wire hdl, 10-gal, NM 100.00
Crock, #6, 3-gal, M 40.00
Crock, #6, 4-gal, M 50.00
Crock, #6, 5-gal, NM 60.00
Foot warmer, #6, M 60.00
Jug, #6, brn/wht, 1-gal, EX 25.00
Jug, #6, brn/wht, 5-gal, M 75.00
Rabbit feeder, #1, EX 25.00
Rabbit waterer, #1, M 25.00

Western Stoneware Co.

The Western Stoneware Co., Monmouth, Illinois, was formed in 1906 as a merger of seven potteries: Monmouth Pottery Co., Monmouth, IL; Weir Pottery Co., Monmouth, IL; Macomb Pottery Co. and Macomb Stoneware Co., Macomb, IL; D. Culbertson Stoneware Co., Whitehall, IL; Clinton Stoneware Co., Clinton, MO; and Fort Dodge Stoneware Co., Fort Dodge, IA.

Western Stoneware Co. manufactured stoneware, gardenware, flowerpots, artware, and dinnerware. Some early crocks, jugs, and churns are found with a plant number in the Maple Leaf logo. Plants 1 through 7 turn up. In 1926 an artware line was introduced as the Monmouth Pottery Artware. One by one each branch of the operation closed and today one branch remains. Western Stoneware Co. is still in operation in Monmouth on the site of the Weir Pottery Co. Our advisor for this category is Jim Martin; he is listed in the Directory under Illinois. See also Old Sleepy Eye.

Bowl, bl banded, w/advertising 85.00
Chicken waterer, complete, 1-gal 95.00
Churn, flowers on side, 3-gal 200.00
Churn, Maple Leaf mk, mini 600.00
Churn, Maple Leaf mk, oval, 2-gal 135.00
Combinet, w/lid & hdl, mini 350.00
Crock, Maple Leaf mk, 60-gal 600.00
Custard cup, Colonial 125.00

Hot water bottle, pig, bl tint 225.00
Jar, Maple Leaf & oval mk, 2-gal 50.00
Jardiniere, Egret pattern, brushed gr 75.00
Jardiniere, Egyptian motif, brn-glazed int, 7" 75.00
Jug, Monmouth advertising, 1-qt 125.00
Pitcher, Cattail, bl & wht, 1-qt 150.00
Shakers, 2nd Nat'l Bank, pr 30.00
Vase, Etruscan pattern, gr & wht 45.00
Wall pocket, Egyptian, Burntwood, #312 ....60.00
Water cooler, Cupid, wht w/advertising 500.00
Water cooler, Egyptian, 9¼x11", M 450.00
Water cooler, Maple Leaf mk, no lid or spigot, 2-gal 400.00

Westmoreland

Originally titled the Specialty Glass Company, Westmoreland began operations in East Liverpool, Ohio, producing utility items as well as tableware in milk glass and crystal. When the company moved to Grapeville, Pennsylvania, in 1890, lamps, vases, covered animal dishes, and decorative plates were introduced. Prior to 1920 Westmoreland was a major manufacturer of carnival glass and soon thereafter added a line of lovely reproduction art glass items. High-quality milk glass became their speciality, accounting for about 90% of their production. Black glass was introduced in the 1940s, and later in the decade ruby-stained pieces and items decorated in the Mary Gregory style became fashionable. By the 1960s colored glassware was being produced, examples of which are very popular with collectors today. Early pieces were marked with a paper label; by the 1960s the ware was embossed with a superimposed 'WG.' The last mark was a circle containing 'Westmoreland' around the perimeter and a large 'W' in the center. The company closed in 1985, and on February 28, 1996, the factory burned to the ground.

Note: Though you may find pieces very similar to Westmoreland's, their Della Robbia has no bananas among the fruits relief. In the descriptions, items in this pattern listed as 'crystal with trim' refers to those prices with the colored lustre stains. Our advisors for this category are Philip J. Rosso and Philip Rosso Jr. They are listed in the Directory under Pennsylvania. See also Animal Dishes with Covers; Carnival Glass.

Plates, Della Robbia, crystal with lustre colors: Torte, 14", $150.00; Dinner, 10½", $65.00; Salad, 7¼", from $22.00 to $30.00.

Ashtray, English Hobnail, pk or gr, several shapes, ea 15.00
Ashtray/pipe holder, bird, pk mist 15.00
Basket, Della Robbia, crystal w/trim, 9" 195.00
Basket, English Hobnail, amber or crystal, hdld, 5" 20.00
Bottle, toilet; Paneled Grape, milk glass w/decor, 5-oz 62.50
Bowl, banana; Old Quilt #500, milk glass, ftd, 11" 125.00
Bowl, banana; Paneled Grape, Electric Blue Carnival, ftd, 12" ..150.00
Bowl, banana; Paneled Grape, milk glass w/decor, ftd, 12" 125.00
Bowl, Della Robbia, crystal w/trim, rolled edge, 13" 125.00
Bowl, Paneled Grape, milk glass, cupped, 8" 45.00
Bowl, Paneled Grape, milk glass w/decor, ruffled edge, stemmed, 6" ..30.00
Cake salver, Old Quilt, milk glass, skirted, bell ftd, 12" 125.00
Candlesticks, English Hobnail, pk or gr, 8½", pr, from $50 to 75.00
Candy container, mantel clock, Brandywine Blue, hollow, unmk ...35.00
Candy dish, English Hobnail, amber or crystal, 3-ftd 20.00
Candy jar, Paneled Grape, milk glass w/decor, w/lid, ftd 32.50
Canister, Paneled Grape, milk glass, ftd, w/lid, 11½x6¾" 400.00
Cheese/butter dish, Old Quilt, purple marble, w/lid, 7" 75.00
Cigarette box, English Hobnail, pk or gr 35.00
Compote, Della Robbia, crystal w/trim, bell shape, ftd, 12", from $75 to ..100.00
Compote, English Hobnail, amber or crystal, bell shape, 5½" 15.00
Compote, Paneled Grape, milk glass w/decor, ftd, crimped, 9" 80.00
Creamer, Beaded Edge, milk glass, plain, ftd 11.00
Cup & saucer, Paneled Grape, milk glass 15.00
Decanter, English Hobnail, amber or crystal, 20-oz, from $65 to .75.00
Egg tray, Paneled Grape, milk glass, w/center hdl, 10" 90.00
Epergne, Paneled Grape, milk glass, lipped, 3-pc, 12" 275.00
Flowerpot, Paneled Grape, milk glass w/decor 47.50
Goblet, English Hobnail, pk or gr, 8-oz, 6¼", from $15 to 20.00
Goblet, wine; Paneled Grape, milk glass, ftd, 2-oz, from $15 to ...18.00
Jelly/puff box, Paneled Grape, milk glass w/decor, w/lid 27.50
Lamp, any child's decor, w/shade, electric, mini, from $50 to 75.00
Lamp, candle; crystal w/decal, w/shade, mini 30.00
Lamp, dolphin; pk, electric 175.00
Lamp, fairy; almond w/HP flowers, ftd, 2-pc 65.00
Napkin ring holder, milk glass w/holly decor, 6-sided, from $30 to ...40.00
Nappy, Beaded Edge, milk glass w/decor, 5" 16.00
Nappy, Della Robbia, crystal w/trim, hdld, 6½" 35.00
Novelty, egg on ped, any color, blown, 1-pc, from $75 to 100.00
Novelty, Grandma's slipper, honey, from $25 to 30.00
Novelty, revolver, blk milk glass, solid 65.00
Paperweight, turtle, milk glass, no holes, from $35 to 45.00
Parfait, Paneled Grape, wht w/decor, 6" 25.00
Plate, Beaded Edge, milk glass, plain, 15" 35.00
Plate, Beaded Edge, milk glass w/red edge, 6" 7.00
Plate, Beaded Edge, milk glass w/red edge, 7" 8.00
Plate, Della Robbia, crystal 15.00
Plate, Della Robbia, crystal w/trim, 18" 185.00
Plate, Della Robbia, crystal w/trim, 6⅛", from $22 to 30.00
Plate, English Hobnail, amber or crystal, sq, 6" 5.00
Plate, Paneled Grape, milk glass or mint gr, 10½", from $30 to ...35.00
Plate, Paneled Grape #1881, milk glass w/decor, 8½" 40.00
Punch bowl set, Fruits, lilac opal, 15-pc 350.00
Relish, Beaded Edge, milk glass, plain, 3-part 22.50
Rose bowl, English Hobnail, amber or crystal, 6" 17.50
Rose bowl, Wildflower & Lace, ice bl 28.00
Salt dip, duck, apricot 25.00
Sauce boat, Paneled Grape, milk glass, w/tray 50.00
Saucer, English Hobnail, pk or gr 4.00
Shakers, Beaded Edge, milk glass w/red edge, pr 35.00
Shakers, English Hobnail, amber or crystal, ftd, rnd, pr 20.00
Stem, wine; Della Robbia, crystal w/trim, 3-oz 25.00
Toothpick holder, owl, crystal, 3" 15.00
Toothpick holder, Paneled Grape, milk glass w/decor 24.00
Tray, tidbit; Beaded Grape, milk glass, 2-tier 75.00
Tray, tidbit; Paneled Grape, milk glass, 1-tier, 10½" 50.00
Trinket box, egg shape, cameo, w/lid 40.00
Tumbler, ginger ale; English Hobnail, amber or crystal, 5-oz 8.00
Tumbler, iced tea; Della Robbia, crystal w/trim, ftd, 11-oz 45.00
Tumbler, iced tea; English Hobnail, pk or gr, 10-oz, 4" 25.00
Tumbler, juice; Old Quilt, milk glass, 5-oz 15.00
Tumbler, water; Beaded Edge, milk glass w/decor, ftd, 8-oz 18.00
Tumbler, water; Della Robbia, crystal w/trim, 8-oz 40.00
Vase, epergne; Paneled Grape, milk glass w/decor, bell shape, 8½" ...60.00
Vase, flip; English Hobnail, amber or crystal, 7½" 30.00

Vase, Paneled Grape, milk glass w/decor, bell shape, 9" 25.00
Vase, Paneled Grape, milk glass w/decor, 15" 40.00
Water set, Old Quilt, purple slag, 3-pt pitcher+6 8-oz tumblers ...280.00

Wheatley, T. J.

In 1880 after a brief association with the Coultry Works, Thomas J. Wheatley opened his own studio in Cincinnati, Ohio, claiming to have been the first to discover the secret of under-glaze slip decoration on an unbaked clay vessel. He applied for and was granted a patent for his process. Demand for his ware increased to the point that several artists were hired to decorate the ware. The company incorporated in 1880 as the Cincinnati Art Pottery, but until 1882 it continued to operate under Wheatley's name. Ware from this period is marked 'T.J. Wheatley' or 'T.J.W. and Co.,' and it may be dated.

Matt green pieces dominate today's marketplace and will bring much more than the decorated pieces. The matt green pieces are seldom, if ever, marked or dated.

Bowl, embossed dogwood blossoms and leaves under thick green matt, #642, 3x7½", $500.00.

Chamberstick, leaves on gr matt, scroll hdl, unmk, 4x6", EX 550.00
Jardiniere, vertical leaves, gr matt, 11½x8½", EX 1,600.00
Lamp, gr matt, gourd shape w/leaded slag-glass floral shade, 22x18" ...5,500.00
Planter, woven design on buff terra cotta, 8-sided, 14x24" 700.00
Stein, emb shield, gr matt, pretzel hdl, Compliments of..., 7" 150.00
Vase, apple blossoms, wht on dk bl, Limoges style, 6½", NM 145.00
Vase, gr matt, rib at shouldered, broad form, 9" W 1,200.00
Vase, gr matt, 4 lg buttresses ea w/stems & buds, 13", EX 3,250.00

Whieldon

Thomas Whieldon was regarded as the finest of the Staffordshire potters of the mid-1700s. He produced marbled and black Egyptian wares as well as tortoise shell, a mottled brown-glazed earthenware accented with touches of blue and yellow. In 1754 he became a partner of Josiah Wedgwood. Other potters produced similar wares, and today the term Whieldon is used generically.

Figurine, cat on pillow, brn w/some gr & yel, 4", EX 600.00
Jug, sporting dogs, bk: long-haired dog, mixed colors, 5" 450.00
Plate, tortoise shell, scalloped/emb rim, 9", NM 300.00
Plate, tortoise shell, 8-sided, rprs, 11½" 165.00
Teapot, serpent spout, 3¾", G 345.00

Wicker

Wicker is the basket-like material used in many types of furniture and accessories. It may be made from bamboo cane, rattan, reed, or artificial fibers. It is airy, lightweight, and very popular in hot regions. Imported from the Orient in the eighteenth century, it was first manufactured in the United States in about 1850. The elaborate, closely woven Victorian designs belong to the mid- to late 1800s, and the simple styles with coarse reedings usually indicate a post-1900 production. Art Deco styles followed in the '20s and '30s. The most important consideration in buying wicker is condition — it can be restored, but only by a professional. Age is an important factor, but be aware that 'Victorian-style' furniture is being manufactured today.

Key:
HB — Heywood Bros. H/W — Heywood Wakefield

Chair, corner; fancy scrollwork, cane seat, HB, 1890s, EX 765.00
Chair, corner; much scrollwork at bk & skirt, 29" 250.00
Chair, dmn weave, continuous arm, 6-leg, cane seat, 34x23" 250.00
Chair, fan bk w/arms, natural & blk, 68", +matching stool 385.00
Chair, side; ornate curliques & scrolls, padded seat, 43" 250.00
Chair, side; tight weave, Deco dmn-design bk, skirt, 37", EX 175.00
Cradle, swings in fr, tight weave, ca 1900, EX 1,300.00
Cradle, tight weave, wht pnt, ca 1920, doll sz, 20x10x18", EX ..325.00
Desk, wooden shelved framework, 1-drw, H/W, 43x75", EX 850.00
Jardiniere, w/suspended birdcage, Am, late 1800s, 63x29" 400.00
Porch swing, tight weave along top of str bk, uphl seat, 54" 500.00
Rocker, continuous arm, tight weave, uphl seat, Lloyd, 32", EX ...200.00
Rocker, dmn weave w/curliques, platform type, 36" 575.00
Rocker, openweave bk, sm arms, pressed cane seat, platform style, 35" ...375.00
Rocker, ornate pattern to bk, platform type, H/W, 48" 1,000.00
Rocker, rolled arms & bk w/curliques, cane seat, 42" 295.00
Rocker, tight-weave fiber, continuous arm, 1930s, child sz, 23" .150.00
Rocker, w/arms, gr pnt, rpl cane seat, child sz, 24" 110.00
Rocker, wicker decor-bk & apron, wooden fr, 39" 225.00
Set: 30" table w/glass top, 41x41" settee, 4 side chairs, 1890s .1,650.00
Settee, heart shapes w/curliques, woven seat, 1950s, 33x57" 400.00
Settee, tight machine weave, 2 cushions, no arms, 37" 275.00
Settee, tight weave & curliques, pressed cane seat, 31x48" 450.00
Settee, tight weave w/dmn in skirt, lift seat, 39x42x18" 475.00
Settee, tight-weave fiber, 1-pc cushion, 1930s, 60" 300.00
Sewing stand, lift top, D-hdl, shelf, HB/Wakefield, 27x17x14" .150.00
Sofa, tight weave w/2 dmns in bk, continuous arms, 1920s, child sz 200.00
Table, braided edge, tight-weave apron, shelf, 39x31" dia 175.00
Table, tight-weave apron, wooden top, X-stretchers, 24x36" L ..125.00
Table, tight-weave top, magazine shelf, 25x24x16" 200.00
Table, wooden top, apron, woven shelf, 30x42x26" 215.00
Table, wooden top, 2-tier w/apron, 30x30" dia 200.00
Table, wooden top w/tight-weave apron, sm shelf, 39x35x18" ...185.00
Tea cart, rpl glass in tray, old finish, 32x30x18", EX 175.00

Will-George

In 1934, after years of working in the family garage, the Will-George company was founded by William and George Climes in Los Angeles, California. They manufactured high-quality art china of porcelain and earthenware. Both brothers, motivated by their love of art pottery, had extensive education and training in manufacturing and decoration. In 1940 actor Edgar Bergen, a collector of pottery, developed a relationship with the brothers and invested in their business. With this new influx of funds, the company relocated to Pasadena. There they produced an extensive line of art pottery, but they excelled in their creation of bird and animal figurines. In addition they molded a large line of human figurines similar to Royal Doulton. The brothers, now with a staff of decorators, precisely molded their pieces with great care and emphasis on originality and detail, creating high quality works of art that were only carried by exclusive gift stores.

In the late 1940s after a split with Bergen, the company moved to San Gabriel to a larger, more modern location and renamed themselves The Claysmiths. There they mass produced many items, but due to the cheap, postwar imports from Italy and Japan that were then flooding the market, they liquidated the business in 1956. Our advisor for this category is Marty Webster. He is listed in the Directory under Michigan.

Bird figure, eagle on a rock, white and brown, 10", $150.00. (Photo courtesy Marty Webster)

Bird figurine, Baltimore Oriole 155.00
Bird figurine, cardinal on branch, 10" 75.00
Bird figurine, cardinal on branch, 12½" 150.00
Bird figurine, cockatoo, pk, late 1940s, sm 85.00
Bird figurine, eagle on rock, wht/brn, 10" 150.00
Bird figurine, female pheasant 110.00
Bird figurine, flamingo, female, head down, 6½" 150.00
Bird figurine, flamingo, head up, looking bk, 7½" 150.00
Bird figurine, flamingo, preening, 10" 200.00
Bird figurine, flamingo, wings spread, 15½" 275.00
Bird figurine, Mallard duck w/spread wings, 7x11" 95.00
Bird figurine, parrot (mc) on branch, 15" 200.00
Bowl, flower; low, 15" L 60.00
Candle holders, lily design, pr 120.00
Figurine, artist holding a palette, mc, 8" 95.00
Figurine, boy holding frog, on base, mc, 9" 95.00
Figurine, child-like artist & model, ca 1939, set 200.00
Figurine, dachshund, 6½x9" 200.00
Figurine, giraffe, 14½" 150.00
Figurine, girl holding doll, mc, on base, 9" 125.00
Figurine, hula dancer, wht skirt, 12" 155.00
Figurine, monk, brn bsk, 4½" 50.00
Figurine, monk, brn bsk, 5½" 75.00
Figurine, Polynesian female, seated, 5½" 80.00
Figurine, young Pan, w/attendant forest creatures, 7" 85.00
Glass, wine-cordial; rooster-shaped ceramic base, 5" 55.00
Pitcher, chicken figural, mc, 7" 125.00
Tumbler, chicken figural, mc, 4½" 50.00
Vase, Chinese girl seated in front, pillow form 85.00
Wine glass, chicken figural, mc, 5" 55.00

Willets

The Willets Manufacturing Company of Trenton, New Jersey, produced a type of belleek porcelain during the late 1880s and 1890s. Examples were often marked with a coiled snake that formed a 'W' with 'Willets' below and 'Belleek' above. Not all Willet's is factory decorated. Items painted by amateurs outside the factory are worth considerably less. High prices usually equate with fine artwork. In the listings below, all items are belleek unless noted otherwise. Our advisor for this category is Mary Frank Gaston; she is listed in the Directory under Texas.

Bowl, blackberries w/gold, dragon hdls, 11" 500.00
Bowl, red & pk roses, gold dragon hdls, 4" H 200.00
Bowl, roses reserve, much gold, ftd, 2x6" L 140.00
Bowl, thistles on creamy texture, gold twig hdls, 5x6½" 300.00
Chamberstick, appl flowers & spaghetti work in Irish Belleek style, 5" 400.00
Creamer & sugar bowl, floral sprays, gold dragon hdls, 4" 175.00
Creamer & sugar bowl, gold lacy decor rim, gold hdls, 3", 3¾" .125.00
Jar, peacocks, w/lid, 10" 200.00
Mug, Dutch figures on blk, 7¼" 100.00
Mug, lady's portrait w/gold trim & hdl, sgn Nosek, 5¾" 1,200.00
Mug, monk drinking on dk gr, 5¾" 120.00
Mug, Oriental lady on bl to gray, 4½" 150.00
Mug, red currants w/gr leaves, 5½" 90.00
Mug, sleeping girl on brn, left-handed hdl, 3½" 175.00
Pitcher, birds on gray, 10½" 200.00
Pitcher, cider; water lilies/buds/pods, gold hdl, sgn Darcy, 7" 350.00
Pitcher, gargoyle, ornate hdl & decor, pierced mask spout 750.00
Pitcher, pk floral branch w/gold paste, branch hdl, 5¼" 250.00
Plate, lav & bl pansies w/gold leaves, gold leaf border, 7" 25.00
Salt cellar, wht heart shape w/scallped rim, no decor, 1¾" H 25.00
Stein, landscape/pelican, gold dragon hdl, 5¾" 300.00
Sugar shaker, wht w/no decor, 4½" 100.00
Tankard, troubadour & girl, HP D'Aarcy Decorators, 15" 675.00
Vase, child's portrait reserve, gold trim, sgn Nosek, 18½" 2,200.00
Vase, floral silver o/l, angle hdls, 12¾" 425.00
Vase, lg mc roses, gold uptrn hdls, prof decor/rstr, 14" 1,000.00
Vase, pk orchid, artist sgn, 8½" 350.00
Vase, poppies, artist sgn, 8" 100.00
Vase, red poinsettia w/gold & blk, 8½" 125.00
Vase, red poppies on gold, Pickard decor, 13" 600.00
Vase, roses, yel on brn & gr w/gold, 15½" 400.00
Vase, wht bamboo on gold, 8¼" 125.00
Vase, yel roses & lilacs, 14" 425.00

Winchester

The Winchester Repeating Arms Company lost their important government contract after WWI and of necessity turned to the manufacture of sporting goods, hardware items, tools, etc., to augment their gun production. Between 1920 and 1931, over 7,500 different items, each marked 'Winchester Trademark U.S.A.,' were offered for sale by thousands of Winchester Hardware stores throughout the country. After 1931 the firm became Winchester-Western. Collectors prefer the prewar items such as we have listed below. Concerning current collecting trends: Oil cans that a short time ago could be purchased for $2.00 to $5.00 now often sell for $25.00, some over $50.00, and demand is high. Good examples of advertising posters and calendars seem to have no upper limits and are difficult to find. Winchester fishing lures are strong, and the presence of an original box increases values by 25% to 40%. Unless noted otherwise, values are for examples in excellent condition.

Our advisor for this category is James Anderson; he is listed in the Directory under Minnesota. See also Knives.

Advertising envelope, dbl-side, mc, WWI era, unused, M 125.00
Baseball bat, Model #2310, 35" 250.00
Batteries, 6-volt, dry cell, 6x2½" dia, pr 95.00
Bayonet, for Model 1895 musket, w/orig cosmoline 190.00
Bore scope, brass, mk Model 1892, 1⅜" 130.00
Bullet mold, 44WCF, EX (VG box) 140.00
Calendar, 1897, AB Frost art, 26½x14½", VG+ 825.00
Calendar, 1915, eagle attacking mtn goats, Forbes, fr, 30x15", G 1,500.00
Calendar, 1921, 2 men/dog on hillside, PR Goodwin art, 30x15", EX+ 1,750.00
Cartridge, for 45-125 cal, brass, primed, never loaded 25.00
Cartridge box, 45-70 cal, holds 500-grain rounds, pre-1900 ....100.00
Catalog, fishing tackle, ca 1920s, VG+ 110.00
Cotter pin puller, mk #2795, 8½" 165.00

Cover, bearded hunter, 3½x6½" 80.00
Cover, hunter tracking wolves in snow, 3½x6½", EX 130.00
Cover, hunter w/dead game & gun on shoulder, 1915, 3½x6½", NM ..200.00
Cover, Repeating Shotguns, game/gun, 3½x6½", EX+ 100.00
Drill bit case, canvas, buckle mk Pat 10/7/15, VG 190.00
Fishing reel, #1218 ....210.00
Fishing reel, #2242 ....125.00
Fly rod, mk Winchester Hop Brook, split bamboo, 4-pc, 108" ...200.00
Fly rod, steel w/cork hdl, #5130, in orig bag (w/tie strings) 80.00
Football, VG 300.00
Golf club, Niblick, Jock Hutchinson, leather grip, #6640 ....195.00
Golf club, Spade Mashie, Jock Hutchinson, leather grip, #6631 ..160.00
Hatchet, logo on head, 12" hdl, w/leather sheath 95.00
Hockey puck, ca 1920s, ⅞x2¾" 110.00
Lawn mower, VG 450.00
Level, 3 vials, CI, #9864, 18" 250.00
Lure, 5-hook, EX 1,100.00
Meat grinder, EX 65.00
Medal, Winchester Jr Rifle Corp, Expert Rifleman, 10k gold 360.00
Padlock, EX 125.00
Paint brush, G 90.00
Pamphlet, .22 Leader ammo, mc, fold-out, 3½x6¼" 45.00
Pamphlet, Shoot Winchester Lublack, bird graphics, 7x6", unused, NM ...350.00
Plane, #W120, 70% orig blk pnt, mk blade, 7", VG 90.00
Plane, block; #3055, 24" 155.00
Plane, smooth; #3006, CI, 95% japanning, 10" 120.00
Pliers, needle nose; EX 110.00
Poster, rabbit & hunter, 1955, AS Weimer Pursell, 25½x39", NM 105.00
Razor, straight; gold celluloid hdl, #8520 ....110.00
Reloading tool, for Winchester 45-60, CI, mk 9/14/1880, 9¼" ..140.00
Roller skates, VG 45.00
Saw, key-hole; G 125.00
Scraper, cabinet; mk W79 ....105.00
Sign, cb, close-up of dogs, wood fr, 35x26", EX 4,000.00
Sign, cb, stand-up, blk duck on yel ground, 1952, 8x5", NM+ 50.00
Sign, cb, stand-up, red beaver on yel ground, 1952, 8x5", EX+ 50.00
Sign, linen, They Are Hitters, wood fr, c 1904, 36x26", VG ..1,500.00
Sign, paper, snow scene w/hunter & wolves, fr, c 1906, 29x14", VG ...3,300.00
Sign, tin, 1892, VG+ 2,200.00
Sign, tin-on-wood plaque, ...Gun Advisory Center, 1950s, 20", NM+ ..100.00
Spool of braided silk line, EX 135.00
Stock certificate, 100 shares, Class A, #TA-44, issued 1929 ....100.00
Talcum tin, Winchester After Shave Talc, red w/scene, 4¾", EX+ ...75.00
Thermos set, 2 thermoses/sandwich box/case, red w/blk sqs, NM ...100.00
Wagon, steel, VG 850.00

Windmill Weights

Windmill weights made of cast iron were used to protect the windmill's plunger rod from damage during high winds by adding weight that slowed down the speed of the blades.

Bull, Fairbury, cast tail lines, blk pnt, 24½x18x½" 750.00
Bull, Fairbury, wht over gray, late 19th C, 24½", VG 465.00
Crescent, Eclipse A13, Fairbanks Morse & Co, no pnt, 10½" ...165.00
Crescent, Elipse A13, Fairbanks Morse & Co, w/pnt, 10½" 415.00
Horse, bobtail, pnt losses, emb 586, ca 1900, 16½x17" 600.00
Horse, bobtail, rpt, emb 58, ca 1900, 21½x17½" 350.00
Horse, Dempster bobtail, old pnt, 17½x16½x¾" 385.00
Horse on plinth, pnt traces, emb 58, ca 1900, 19x18" 350.00
Rooster, Elgin, old wht & red pnt, 18"+modern base 1,000.00
Rooster, full tail, 2-color pnt, ca 1900, 16x17", from $750 to 975.00
Rooster, rainbow tail, pnt traces, ca 1900, 19x17" 1,380.00
Rooster, rpt, ca 1900, 19x17" 575.00
Squirrel, Elgin Co, worn pnt, 60-lb 2,500.00

Winfield

The Winfield Pottery was founded in 1929 in Pasadena, California. The artware and giftware items they made were marked Winfield, Pasadena, sometimes with the date added. In 1946 the line of more than four hundred shapes was licensed to the American Ceramic Products Company of Santa Monica who began using the Winfield trade name on their semiporcelain dinnerware. The Winfield Pottery from then on marked their output 'Gabriel.' Both companies closed during the early 1960s.

Gravy boat, Passion Flower, bl bkstamp, w/underplate 30.00
Pitcher, Passion Flower, bl bkstamp, 8½", from $40 to 50.00
Plate, deep yel, underside w/sage gr border, mk #227, 10" 30.00
Plate, salad; Blue Bamboo, 7½" 12.00
Platter, Bird of Paradise, 14½x10¼" 25.00
Shakers, cats (stylized), blk & wht, 6", pr 20.00
Teapot, fruit, elephant head on top, mk #302 ....22.00
Teapot, Passion Flower, 8", from $25 to 35.00

Wire Ware

Very primitive wire was first made by cutting sheet metal into strips which were shaped with mallet and file. By the late thirteenth century, craftsmen in Europe had developed a method of pulling these strips through progressively smaller holes until the desired gauge was obtained. During the Industrial Revolution of the late 1800s, machinery was developed that could produce wire cheaply and easily; and it became a popular commercial commodity. It was used to produce large items such as garden benches and fencing as well as innumerable small pieces for use in the kitchen or on the farm. Beware of reproductions. Our advisor for this category is Rosella Tinsley; she is listed in the Directory under Kansas.

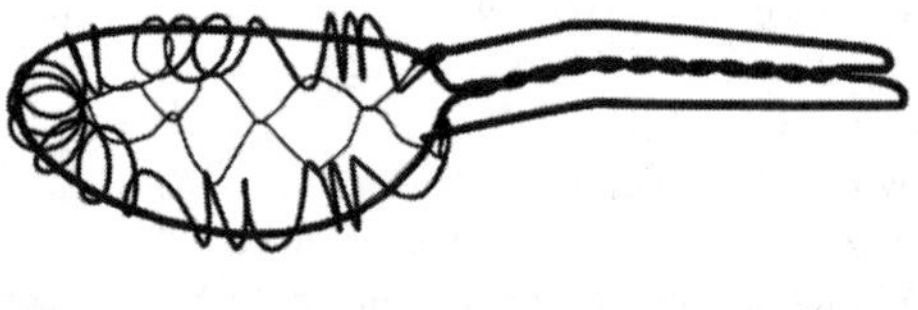

Whisk/whip, tinned wire, double handle with center twist, 10½", $25.00. (Photo courtesy Kathryn McNerney)

Basket, bread; wire in sm sqs, oval, 2-hdl 75.00
Basket, calling card; heart-shaped hdls, w/majolica plate, 3x8½" ..105.00
Basket, globular w/inverted bottom, scalloped rim, hdls, 7x10" ...30.00
Basket, petal-shaped sides, scalloped bottom, folding, 4½x7" 55.00
Basket, potato; sm dmn designs, bail hdl, ½-bushel 50.00
Bottle carrier, holds 6, twisted hdl, 4x9x14" 50.00
Carpet beater, single loop w/woven design, wood hdl 50.00
Compote, twisted wire, ped base 150.00
Egg basket, rnd, folds 48.00
Egg cooker, 6-part, simple style 35.00
Fly trap, globe shape, screenwire w/tin base 65.00
Fork, meat; heavy wire, 3 sharp prongs, loop hdl, 1800s, 15" 20.00
Hanger, heavy wire & wood, PA advertising 50.00
Napkin ring, twisted wire, fancy design, pr 115.00
Pie rack, 4-tier 75.00

Pillow fluffer, filigree w/twisted neck, wood handgrip 25.00
Postcard holder, twisted wire, 2 rows of circles 110.00
Scrubber, wire ringlets, twisted wire hdl 45.00
Soap dish, twisted wire, fancy wire bk w/hanging loop 75.00
Soap saver, oblong screen-wire shape, wire & wood hdl 18.00
Spoon holder, twisted wire, ftd goblet shape 95.00
Tea ball, egg shape, ½" tin band ea side, 2¾" 28.00
Toaster, Maltese cross design, wood hdl 55.00
Tongs, egg; heavy wire, egg-shaped ends 50.00
Tray, bakery display; oval, rare type, 14x9" 185.00
Trivet, triangular, dbl wire at sides, loop hdl, 3-ftd 40.00
Trivet, twisted wire, rnd, 5½" 45.00
Whisk, tined loops w/twisted hdl, German, 8", EX 25.00

Witch Balls

Witch balls were a Victorian fad touted to be meritorious toward ridding the house of evil spirits, thus warding off sickness and bad luck. Folklore would have it that by wiping the dust and soot from the ball, the spirits were exorcised. It is much more probable, however, considering the fact that such beautiful art glass was used in their making, that the ostensive Victorians perpetrated the myth rather tongue-in-cheek while enjoying them as lovely decorations for their homes.

Blk amethyst, sm sheared opening on 1 end, 1970-90, 4¼" 85.00
Clear w/opal loopings, on matching base, 11¼" 600.00
Clear w/wht loopings, sheared ends, 1860-80s, 3¾" dia 90.00
Cobalt, open pontil 1 end, many bubbles, 1860-90, 8" 150.00
Dk amber, sheared open end, 6⅝", on wood stand 200.00
Dk chocolate-amber, sheared opening, 4⅛" 60.00
Milk glass w/red & bl loopings, sheared end, Am, 3¼" 400.00
Red honey-amber, open pontil, 4" 250.00
Ruby flashed in striated ruby-flashed bowl, clear ft, 4" dia 850.00
Smoky sapphire bl, sheared end, Am, 4⅝" 160.00

Wood Carvings

Wood sculptures represent an important section of American folk art. Wood carvings were made not only by skilled woodworkers such as cabinetmakers, carpenters, etc., but by amateur 'whittlers' as well. They take the form of circus-wagon figures, carousel animals, decoys, busts, figurines, and cigar store Indians. Oriental artists show themselves to have been as proficient with the medium of wood as they were with ivory or hardstone. See also Carousel Animals; Decoys; Tobacciana.

Angel kneels on base, curly hair, mc pnt, 21x19x10", EX, pr .1,450.00
Bird, orig mc pnt, 2½" 95.00
Birds, burl root, cvd heads, old brn finish, 2¾", 3¼", pr 360.00
Dog, cvg simulates fur, arched tail, yel glass eyes, 9x6" 200.00
Dog, cvg simulates fur, tail glued, 5½x6½" 50.00
Eagle, EX detail, gilt & mc rpt over weathered surface, 20th C, 72" 3,400.00
Eagle, mc & gilt pnt, 20th C, 42" 1,200.00
Eagle, mc pnt, att JH Bellamy (Am, 1836-1914), 24¼", VG .1,265.00
Eagle, mc pnt on pine, minor rstr, att Bellamy, 30½" 5,225.00
Eagle, oak, natural finish, ca 1900, old rpr, 25" 400.00
Eagle, walnut & natural finish, artist sgn, PA, 30½" 250.00
Eagle, wings spread, rock base, sgn Carl Snavely, 7½", VG 250.00
Eagle, 3-pc w/attached wings, late 1800s, 9½" 850.00
Eagle & flag, old mc rpt, old rprs, dtd 1819, 22x29" 5,900.00
Eagle on branches, wht head, gilt decor, 23x69", VG 1,600.00
Lady's head, brn pnt hair/eyes, some age, 4¾" 185.00
Polar bear w/open mouth, old wht/blk/red pnt, ca 1940s, 6½" 85.00
Rooster, EX cvg, fine mc pnt, PA, 17½x11½" 2,150.00
Rooster, poplar w/lt varnish, 14" 165.00
Rooster, X-hatched cvg w/mc pnt & stain, 20th C, 13" 190.00

Woodenware

Woodenware (or treenware, as it is sometimes called) generally refers to those wooden items such as spoons, bowls, food molds, etc., that were used in the preparation of food. Common during the eighteenth and nineteenth centuries, these wares were designed from a strictly functional viewpoint and were used on a day-to-day basis. With the advent of the Industrial Revolution which brought with it new materials and products, much of the old woodenware was simply discarded. Today original handcrafted American woodenwares are extremely difficult to find. See also Primitives.

Cake board, walnut with carving of mounted soldier within a foliate border, stamped J.L. Watkins, N.Y., ca 1850, 10¾" diameter, $825.00.

Bowl, ash burl, old scrubbed finish, 6x16½" 1,100.00
Bowl, ash burl, protruding rim hdls, EX patina, 5x13½" 935.00
Bowl, ash burl, rfn, old rpr, 5¼x12" 300.00
Bowl, ash burl, scrubbed finish, edge damage, 3¾x14½x12" 825.00
Bowl, ash burl, soft finish, cvd ft, 1½x3¾" 220.00
Bowl, ash burl, soft finish & good color, lt wear, 4⅜x11" 880.00
Bowl, ash burl, soft warm finish, 6x14" 1,500.00
Bowl, ash burl (dense), sm hole, rfn, 5x11" 550.00
Bowl, ash burl w/EX figure, trn details, sm crack, 6½x15½" ...2,900.00
Bowl, ash burl w/fissures that are part of figure, 6x16" 1,210.00
Bowl, ash burl w/G figure & detail, 2½x6½" 525.00
Bowl, dk rubbed finish, 3¾x9" 330.00
Bowl, EX old patina w/gray pnt traces, cvd hdls, 5x19x12" 230.00
Bowl, flared sides, gr pnt w/later red trim, 19th C, 3¼x10½" 700.00
Bowl, maple, ivory pnt (lt wear), trn, 18th C, 9¼x25" 1,955.00
Bowl, maple w/mc feather decor, trn, lt wear/sm rpr, 1830s, 7x6" ...2,645.00
Bowl, old gray, 5¾x19x19¼" 400.00
Bowl, old red, incised rim, beaded body, 19th C, 4¼x12¾" 920.00
Bowl, poplar, red-brn stain, trn, wear, PA, 8½x27" 500.00
Bowl, poplar, worn finish, NE, 5x16½x15½" 140.00
Bowl, trn, lt bl pnt, worn, 5¾x17½x16¾" 465.00
Bowl, trn, stabilized crack, gray pnt, worn, 6x19x20" 300.00
Bowl, trn, worn lt bl pnt, 5¾x17½x16¾" 350.00
Bowl, wood, red w/natural int, trn, old patina, 2¼x7½" 250.00
Bucket, pine & walnut staves, metal bands, worn blk pnt, 3½x4½" 385.00
Bucket, staved, metal bands, old brn-red stain, 4½x5⅝" 400.00
Bucket, staved, metal bands, old gray-bl rpt, 4¼x5¾" 220.00
Churn, worn bl pnt, ca 1800, 26x8¾" 500.00
Compote, ash burl w/G figure, old shellac, 4¼x9" 800.00
Cookie board, bear cvg, cherry w/old patina, 5x7⅞" 190.00
Cookie board, poplar w/old patina, 19x24" 200.00
Crimper, cvd oak, serrated edges, 19th C, 7¾x3" dia 65.00
Cup, ash burl, minor damage, 4¾" 195.00
Cup, bird's-eye, natural shape, w/hdl, 5¼" 385.00
Cup, maple w/old brn-amber finish, cvd 1-pc hdl, 6¼" 140.00

Cup, saffron; stained maple, acorn shape, ivory finial, 3¼" 165.00
Dipper, ash burl, figured bowl, plain hdl, varnish, 11¾" 700.00
Dipper, hardwood w/natural burl-growth bowl, natural finish, 12" ...175.00
Firkin, staved, copper tacks, old brn finish, 9¾" 165.00
Firkin, staved, copper tcks/staples, old red pnt, 12x12" 465.00
Firkin, staved, old bl rpt, branded name, 12x12" 745.00
Firkin, staved, old worn finish, 13" 140.00
Firkin, staved, red pnt int, minor damage to lid, RFN, 13" 165.00
Firkin, staved w/wooden bands, old red rpt over brn, 14" 385.00
Jar, maple, ring-trn base, trn finial, brn patina, 4¼" 100.00
Jar, Pease ware, old varnish, 4", pr 660.00
Jar, Pease ware, wire bail w/wood hdl, 9½" 965.00
Jar, poplar w/red sponging, worn, no lid, 5⅜" 140.00
Paddle, butter; maple w/burl bowl, primitive, 8½" 165.00
Paddle, curly maple w/bird's-head hdl, rfn, 10" 250.00
Paddle, oak burl, worm holes, rfn, 8¾" 90.00
Pie board, softwood, oval hdl, worn, 28x18" 60.00
Rolling pin, poplar w/old dk patina, 1 loose end, 12" 190.00
Salt cellar, red/gr/wht stripes, trn, ftd, 19th C, 2½x3" 300.00
Snuff box, ash burl, metal hinge, soft finish, 2⅛x3⅜" 125.00
Spoon, mahog, chip-cvd details, worn patina, 13¾" 100.00
Trencher, pine, Am, early 19th C, 17" 300.00
Tub, staved w/wooden bands, old gr pnt, 6x17" 300.00

Woodworking Machinery

Vintage cast-iron woodworking machines are monuments to the highly skilled engineers, foundrymen, and machinists who devised them, thus making possible the mass production of items ranging from clothespins, boxes, and barrels to decorative moldings and furniture. Though attractive from a nostalgic viewpoint, many of these machines are bought by the hobbyist and professional alike, to be put into actual use — at far less cost than new equipment. Many worth-assessing factors must be considered; but as a general rule, a machine in good condition is worth about 65¢ a pound (excluding motors). A machine needing a lot of restoration is not worth more than 35¢ a pound, while one professionally rebuilt and with a warranty can be calculated at $1.10 a pound. Modern, new machinery averages over $3.00 a pound. Two of the best sources of information on purchasing or selling such machines are *Vintage Machines — Searching for the Cast Iron Classics,* by Tom Howell, and *Used Machines and Abused Buyers* by Chuck Seidel from *Fine Woodworking,* November/December 1984. Prices quoted are for machines in good condition, less motors and accessories. Our advisor for this category is Mr. Dana Martin Batory, author of *Vintage Woodworking Machinery, An Illustrated Guide to Four Manufacturers.* See his listing in the Directory under Ohio for further information. No phone calls, please.

American Saw Mill Machinery Company, 1931

Jointer, Monarch Line, #XII, ball-bearing, 16" 1,200.00
Planer, Monarch Line, single surface, 30" 2,600.00
Table saw, Monarch Line, #X24, tilting arbor, 16" 425.00

Blue Star Products, 1939

Band saw, #1200, 12" floor model 85.00
Lathe, #1001, 72" bed, 12" swing 60.00
Table saw, #800, 8" 95.00

Boice-Crane Power Tools, 1937

Drill press, #1600, 15" 75.00
Scroll saw, #900, 24" 75.00

Crescent Machine Company, 1921

Band saw, 36" 975.00
Mortiser, hollow chisel 525.00
Universal Wood-Worker, #59, 5 machines in 1 ....2,050.00

Defiance Machine Works, 1910

Band saw, 28" 520.00
Table saw, #2, hand feed, 20" 650.00
Table saw, #2, power feed, 20" 1,100.00

Delta Manufacturing Company, 1939

Band saw, #768, 10" 50.00
Disk sander, belt drive, #1425, 12" 35.00
Drill press, floor, #1370, 17" 200.00
Drill press, floor, #989, 14" 70.00
Jointer, ball-bearing, #654, 6" 50.00
Lathe, ball-bearing, #1460, 12" 60.00
Lathe, timken bearing, #930, 11" 45.00
Scroll saw, multi-speed, #1440, 24" 50.00
Table saw, tilt top, #1160, 10" 95.00
Table saw, tilt top, #860, 8" 35.00

F.H. Clement Co., 1896

Band saw, 30" 555.00
Band saw, 36", Patent Improved 815.00
Boring Machine, Post, #2 ....325.00
Jointer, Perfection, 30" 1,690.00
Mortising & boring machine, No 1 ....520.00
Planer, #3, dbl belted, Improved, 20" 2,015.00
Ripsaw, #2, iron fr, 16" 585.00
Sand-papering machine, #2, Universal 585.00
Sander, #3, dbl spindle 585.00
Shaper, variety, #3, heavy, dbl spindle 1,300.00
Splitting saw, #1, iron fr, wood top, 12" 325.00
Table saw, variety, #1, 15" 585.00

Gallmeyer & Livingston Company, 1927

Band saw, Union, 20" 390.00
Jointer, Union, motor on arbor, 8" 370.00
Table saw, Union #7, 7" 210.00

G.N. Goodspeed Company, 1876

Boring machine, upright 225.00
Planer, New & Improved, Pony, 24" 900.00
Table saw, 12" 200.00

Greenlee Bros. & Company, 1925

Tenoner, #530, sash, door & cabinet, ball-bearing 1,530.00

Hoyt & Brother Company, 1888

Cut-off saw, overhung, traversing, 14" 650.00
Mortiser & borer, #2 ....780.00
Planing & matching machine, #7, 13" 3,250.00
Scroll saw, #1 ....300.00
Table saw, #2, 14" 800.00
Wood shaper, dbl spindle 850.00

J.A. Fay & Egan Company, 1900

Jointer, New #2, 16" 1,550.00
Jointer, New #2, 20" 1,625.00
Jointer, New #2, 24" 1,700.00
Jointer, New #2, 30" 1,820.00
Jointer, New #4, extra heavy, 16" 1,625.00
Jointer, New #4, extra heavy, 20" 1,690.00
Jointer, New #4, extra heavy, 24" 1,885.00
Jointer, New #4, extra heavy, 30" 2,275.00
Molder, #1½, 4-sided, 4" 1,050.00
Molder, #2, 4-sided, 6" 1,500.00
Molder, #2½, 4-sided, 7" 2,100.00
Mortiser, #2, hollow chisel, automatic horizontal 1,500.00
Mortiser, #5, dbl hollow chisel, horizontal 1,100.00
Planer, #2½, dbl-belted surface, med sz, 26" 1,850.00
Ripsaw, #2, Improved Standard 1,175.00
Ripsaw, #2, self feed, lg 1,775.00
Ripsaw, #3, self feed, X-lg 2,400.00

J.D. Wallace Company, 1940s

Band saw, 16" 210.00
Jointer, 4" 15.00
Saw, circular (table saw); Universal, 7" 75.00

L. Power & Co., 1888

Mortiser & borer, #2 ....780.00
Shaper, single spindle, reversible 585.00
Table saw, self feed, 14" 715.00

Levi Houston Co., 1897

Dovetailing machine, #2, sash 520.00
Moulder, new 4", 4-sided 650.00
Moulding machine, 4-headed, 10" 2,400.00
Panel raising machine, Pat Improved 650.00
Saw, heavy swing 910.00
Saw, new combination, bench 910.00
Sticker, open-sided, door 500.00
Sticker, special, door 520.00
Tenoning machine, new stile, #3 ....585.00

Ober Manufacturing Company, 1889

Rip saw, self feed, 14" 725.00
Saw, swing cut-off, 18" 275.00
Shaper, saw & jointer combination 400.00

Oliver Machinery Company, 1922

Band saw, #17, 30" 925.00
Shaper, #483, high speed, dbl spindle 1,300.00
Table saw, #32, Variety, 12" 500.00

Parks Ball Bearing Machine Company, 1925

Jointer, H-133, Ideal, 12" 400.00
Sanding machine, H-165, Economy, 24" 230.00

P.B. Yates Machine Company, 1917

Planer, #160, dbl surface, 20" 1,235.00
Saw, #232, swing cut-off, 16" 260.00

Powermatic, Inc., 1965

Band saw, #81, 20" 500.00
Jointer, #60, 8" 170.00
Lathe, #90, 12" 360.00
Mortiser, #15, chain saw 390.00
Planer, #160, 16" 650.00
Planer, #221, 20" 725.00
Sander, #300-01, 12" disk & 6" belt combination 95.00
Sander, #35, 12" disk 55.00
Shaper, #26, single spindle 240.00
Table saw, #66, 10" 230.00
Tenoner, #2-A, single end 620.00

S.A. Woods Machine Company, 1876

Circular resawing machine, Joslin's Improved, 50" 2,275.00
Planer, panel; Improved, 20" 520.00
Planer, surface; Pat Improved, 30" 1,430.00

Sprunger Power Tools, 1950s

Band saw, 14" 60.00
Lathe, gap bed, 10" 50.00
Table saw, tilt arbor, 10¼" 75.00

Worcester Porcelain Company

The Worcester Porcelain Company was deeded in 1751. During the first or Dr. Wall period (so called for one of its proprietors), porcelain with an Oriental influence was decorated in underglaze blue. Useful tablewares represented the largest portion of production, but figurines and decorative items were also made. Very little of the earliest wares were marked and can only be identified by a study of forms, glazes, and the porcelain body, which tends to transmit a greenish cast when held to light. Late in the '50s, a crescent mark was in general use, and rare examples bear a facsimile of the Meissen crossed swords. The first period ended in 1783, and the company went through several changes in ownership during the next eighty years. The years from 1783 to 1792 are referred to as the Flight period. Marks were a small crescent, a crown with 'Royal,' or an impressed 'Flight.' From 1792 to 1807 the company was known as Flight and Barr and used the trademark 'F&B' or 'B,' with or without a small cross. From 1807 to 1813 the company was under the Barr, Flight, and Barr management; this era is recognized as having produced porcelain with the highest quality of artistic decoration. Their mark was 'B.F.B.' From 1813 to 1840 many marks were used, but the most usual was 'F.B.B.' under a crown to indicate Flight, Barr, and Barr. In 1840 the firm merged with Chamberlain, and in 1852 they were succeeded by Kerr and Binns. The firm became known as Royal Worcester in 1862. The production was then marked with a circle with '51' within and a crown on top. The date of manufacture was incised into the bottom or stamped with a letter of the alphabet, just under the circle. In 1891 Royal Worcester England was added to the circle and crown. From that point on, each piece is dated with a code of dots or other symbols. After 1891 most wares had a blush-color ground. Prior to that date it was ivory. Most shapes were marked with a unique number.

During the early years they produced considerable ornamental wares with a Persian influence. This gave way to a Japanesque influence. James Hadley is most responsible for the Victorian look. He is considered the 'best ever' designer and modeller. He was joined by the finest porcelain painters. Together they produced pieces with very fine detail and exquisite painting and decoration. Figures, vases, and tableware were produced in great volume and are highly collectible. During the 1890s they allowed the artists to sign some of their work. Pieces signed on the face by the Stintons, Baldwyn, Davis, Raby, Austin, Powell, Sedgley, and Rushton (not a complete list) are in great demand. The company is still in production. There is an outstanding museum on the company grounds in Worcester, England.

Note: Most pieces had lids or tops (if there is a flat area on the top lip, chances are it had one), if missing deduct 30% to 40%.

Key:
BFB — Barr, Flight and Barr FBB — Flight, Barr and Barr

Bowl, floral, mc on tan, gilt hdls, 1903, 4x8½x7½" ...300.00
Bowl, floral on ivory/peach, shell form, rolled hdls, 9½" ...225.00
Cake plate, Tea Party variation, dk gray transfer, ca 1765, 6" ...630.00
Candlestick, woodsman stands on base by basket, #1793, 12" ...635.00
Creamer, Tea Party, blk transfer, pear shape, ca 1760, 3" ...400.00
Ewer, ferns/gilt/mc on ivory, ornate hdl, #1309, 10½" ...635.00
Ewer, floral, mc/gilt on ivory, satyr mask at hdl, #1144, 11" ...575.00
Ewer, Palmer Cox Brownie carpenters on ivory, 1884, 10" ...750.00
Ewer, pheasant, sgn Jarman, 8" ...280.00
Figural vase, boy/girl w/waterpot before lg urn, Hadley, 7" ...500.00
Figurine, Duke of Marlborough on horse ...2,495.00
Figurine, Elf Owl & Saguaro, Doughty, 12¾", on stand ...475.00
Figurine, Exmoor Pony ...1,095.00
Figurine, Fr fisher boy w/basket in hand, Hadley, ca 1893, 17" ...1,380.00
Figurine, girl tiptoes w/skirt held up, #23325, late 19th C, 9" ...180.00
Figurine, Hide & Seek, boy/girl/tree trunks, #825, 1881, 6", EX ...485.00
Figurine, Princess Anne Doublet on horse ...2,295.00
Figurine, Royal Canadian horse ...1,195.00
Figurine, Shire horse ...1,295.00
Figurine, Trooper Papal guard on horse ...895.00
Figurine, Vermillion Flycatcher/Pussy Willow, Doughty, #64A, 10" ...895.00
Flask, pilgrim; Chinese figures & decor, 2-hdl, ca 1878, 10" ...1,400.00
Inkstand, 3 shells alternate w/3 female sphinx, rstr, 7", EX ...900.00
Jardiniere, emb lotus leaves, bronze/gilt, faux cvd base, 6½" ...375.00
Jardiniere, floral on gr & cream, 8½" ...325.00
Jug, chocolate; floral/gilt, mask under spout, w/lid, #934, 10" ...690.00
Jug, webbed melon body w/lg gold/red leaf spray, 1886, 7", EX ...345.00
Pitcher, floral on tan, gold hdl, ca 1899, 8¾" ...260.00
Plate, Exotic Birds, G Davis, BFB, 1807-13, 8" ...350.00
Platter, detailed scene, cherubs reserves in border, FBB, 16" ...3,100.00
Shell dish, ca 1907, 4½x4" ...50.00
Soup plate, armorial w/gilt, 1800s, 10½", EX, set of 10 ...865.00
Soup plate, scenic, lt bl shaped border w/gilt, FBB, 9½" ...400.00
Spoon tray, Tea Party, blk transfer, ca 1760, 5⅞" ...485.00
Tea bowl & saucer, Tea Party, blk transfer, ca 1760, 4⅞" ...300.00
Tea canister, Tea Party, blk transfer, 5" ...375.00
Teacup & saucer, Tea Party, blk transfer, twig hdl ...350.00
Teapot, Tea Party, blk transfer, loop hdl, chip, 5⅝" ...1,150.00
Vase, basketweave w/gilt/red leafy twig, twig ft, #357, 8" ...235.00
Vase, bears/mtns sgn Davis, creature hdls, #1764, no lid, 14" ...16,100.00
Vase, bud; floral on ivory w/gilt, #854, 1888, 6", pr ...300.00
Vase, bud; floral on pk to yel, petal rim, gilt hdls, 1900, 7" ...350.00
Vase, dbl walls: allover rtcl, int w/gilt scenes, 1887, 3¼" ...1,150.00
Vase, ferns, gilt/mc on cream, lg gold hdls, 1891, 9", EX ...375.00
Vase, ferns etc, bulbous w/cup neck, sm hdls, ftd, #1109, 12" ...635.00
Vase, floral, gilt creature hdls, w/lid, ftd, #1764, 16", EX ...1,265.00
Vase, floral, gilt hdls, bowl body/trumpet neck/ftd, #1491, 10" ..635.00
Vase, floral, Oriental form, hdls, ca 1879, 10½" ...300.00
Vase, irises & dragonfly, hdls, Hadley, 7¾" ...200.00
Vase, Sabrina Ware, bl/iron red/wht mottle, 1902, 9" ...235.00
Vase, Sabrina Ware, fish & seaweed, dk/lt bl, '09, 4", pr ...385.00
Vase, Sabrina Ware, game birds on med bl, 5½" ...150.00
Vase, spill; stork & vegetation in relief, mk, ca 1876, 6" ...625.00
Vase, swag relief/gilt, satyr heads on shoulder, rtcl lid, 13" ...1,000.00

World's Fairs and Expos

Since 1851 and the Crystal Palace Exhibition in London, World's Fairs and Expositions have taken place at a steady pace. Many of them commemorate historical events. The 1904 Louisiana Purchase Exposition, commonly known as the St. Louis World's Fair, celebrated the 100th anniversary of the Louisiana Purchase agreement between Thomas Jefferson and Napoleon in 1803. The 1893 Columbian Exposition commemorated the 400th anniversary of the discovery of America by Columbus in 1492. (Both of these fairs were held one year later than originally scheduled.) The multitude of souvenirs from these and similar events have become a growing area of interest to collectors in recent years. Many items have a 'crossover' interest into other fields: i.e., collectors of postcards and souvenir spoons eagerly search for those from various fairs and expositions. For additional information collectors may contact World's Fairs Collectors Society (WFCS), whose address is in the Directory under Clubs, Newsletters, and Catalogs, or our advisor, Herbert Rolfes. His address is listed in the Directory under Florida.

Key:
T&P — Trylon & Perisphere WF — World's Fair

1876 Centennial, Philadelphia

Book, Illus History...Exposition, leather spine, 874-pg, 9x6" ...70.00
Guide, red cloth w/blk design, JB Lippincott, c 1875, 48-pg, EX .50.00
Print, Corliss, steel eng, Lowell & Co, 7½x10", EX ...25.00
Stereoview, Agriculture Hall, Centennial Photographic Co #603 ..22.00
Stereoview, main entrance, EX ...25.00
Stereoview, Memorial Hall, Centennial Photographic Co #1017, EX ..25.00
Ticket, admission; eng, EX ...13.00

1893 Columbian, Chicago

Admission tickets, facsimile signatures of Treasurer and President, printed by American Bank Note Co., EX, fom $15.00 to $20.00 each.

Bell, dinner; acid-etched glass: ...Exposition, 5¾" ...125.00
Fan, folding; wood & paper, map/Am eagle w/shield & people, VG ...155.00
Miniature, china urn, Gov't Bldg, w/gold, Germany, 3½" ...125.00
Paperweight, blk & wht view of Women's Bldg, 2½x4" ...75.00
Paperweight, Ferris wheel w/wheel info on bk, ¾x2½x4" ...80.00
Tray, card; china, mc Machinery Hall transfer, 4½x4¾" ...65.00

1901 Pan American

Book, Glimpses of Pan-Am Expo, die-cut buffalo head, 80-pg, VG+ ..35.00
Booklet, official; pics/etc of bands at fair, 48-pg, EX ...35.00
Buttonhook, blk metal, eng floral/Pan Am 1901, 6⅝" ...50.00

Change receiver, glass, fair scene, 3½x7" 80.00
Elongated cent, Geronimo/Indian Congress PAE 200.00
Fan, folding; paper, aerial view/map w/ads, EX 100.00
Fork, Niagara Falls & buffalo on shank, made from 5" nail 28.00
Handkerchief, cotton, wht w/mc embr logo, 17½x17½" 30.00
Medal, brass, Buffalo NY, buffalo on bk, 1¼" dia 30.00
Paperweight, litho of North & South Am w/2 ladies holding hands ...40.00
Pincushion, trn maple w/orig silk covering & varnish, 4" 40.00
Shot glass, acid etch buffalo & verse, 2½", w/orig cb box 55.00
Spoon, Indian/Pan w/fife on hdl, Niagara Falls/buffalo in bowl, 6" ...20.00

1904 St. Louis

Axe, glass, emblem of Peace & Prosperity, 9½" 150.00
Cup, collapsible, Palace of Mines & Metallurgy, Pat 1897 ....60.00
Match safe, Palace of Manufacturing/Palace of Mines & Metallurgy ...65.00
Pin-bk, Liberty Bell, celluloid, EX 25.00
Pin-bk, Miss Columbia portrait, bright mc, EX 45.00
Pin-bk, Transportation Bldg, mc on celluloid, EX 45.00
Plate, glass, festival Hall & Cascade Gardens 50.00
Postcard, wooden, postmk 1904, EX 25.00
Vase, Palace of Machinery, bl transfer w/gold on wht, 6" 250.00

1905 Lewis and Clark

Cup, porc, Liberal Arts Bldg, MIG #135, 2⅝" 55.00
Guide, official; info/fold-out map, 112-pg, 5x8", VG 40.00
Pin-bk button, L&C w/Miss Liberty, celluloid, 1½" 45.00
Spoon, L&C w/salmon/totem pole/etc on hdl, US Govt Bldg in bowl ..75.00
Textile, 6 sq & 1 rnd photographic transfers, 18x19" 70.00
Watch fob, 5 links w/Expo scenes, 5" 100.00

1907 Jamestown

Elongated cent, Jamestown Expo 1907/Pocahontas, 1907 Indian head cent ...30.00
Postcard, USS Kentucky, #82, EX 5.00
Postcard, USS Porpoise & Shark, #84, EX 5.00
Tray, bronze & gilt on tin, 5 fair views, 7" dia, EX 25.00

1909 Alaska Yukon Pacific

Plate, Oregon State Bldg, 8" 90.00
Plate, Territory of Hawaii, gold trim, 8¾" 80.00
Plate, 6 Seattle bldgs w/3 women in center, 9¼" 70.00
Ribbon, Grand Champion Horse, w/badge 170.00
Spoon, gold miner on hdl, dog sled team & driver in bowl 40.00

1915 Panama Pacific

Cloth, woven silk, Tower of Jewels, 12x14", EX 30.00
Folder, Painted Desert Exhibit, illus, 3x6", EX 10.00
Lucky penny, Indian on front, Souvenir...Expo on bk 35.00
Match safe, Tower of Jewels 100.00
Skillet, copper, California Bldg, 2" hdl, 2½" 30.00
Tip tray, Buffalo Brewing Co 110.00

1926 Sesquicentennial

Book, cb cover, Liberty Bell in oval on front, 8x5" 45.00
Coin, gold; commemorative, $2.50 pc, NM 275.00
Letter opener, heavy dk metal, serpent from, 7" 45.00
Paperweight, hollow pot-metal Liberty Bell, 3" 20.00
Spoon, sterling, gold-washed bowl, Independence Hall hdl, 6" 50.00
Tray, brass, emb Independence Hall/Liberty Bell/City Hall, 13x6" ..12.00

1933 Chicago

Book, Official View; c 1933, 30-pg, 12x9¼" 35.00
Book, Official..., views/info, 266-pg, fair brd issue, 8x11" 25.00
Bookends, metal, Travel Bldg/Carillon Hall of Science, pr 35.00
Bookmark, brass, Chicago scene & WF logo, 4½" 30.00
Bottle opener, blk w/silvered logo, pen-knife style, 2⅜" closed 35.00
Coasters, brass, eng, in wooden box w/cvd Indian head, set of 6 .30.00
Hat, red felt w/Adm Bldg/Science Bldg/Fort Dearborn, VG 35.00
Letter opener/bookmk, metal, A Lincoln pic, red/gold, 4½", MOC ...40.00
Lucky penny, w/Indian head on front, WF Pavillion on bk, 2¼" .15.00
Medal, Fort Dearborn eng on plaque w/eagle on banner, 1½" W ...25.00
Paperweight, Travel/Transportation Bldg on card, mc, 2½x4" 50.00
Pennant, felt, gr w/pnt image of Travel Bldg & letters, 28" 35.00
Pennant, felt, Hall of Science/Ave of Flags, VG 33.00
Playing cards, Hall of Science/Ave of Flags, EXIB 35.00
Postcard, Am Legion Band Champions, unused, 5½x3½" 8.00
Printer's block, Chicago scene w/Century of Progress/WF/1933, 1x2" ...50.00
Replica, Hall of Science, metal, hollow, 3¼" on 2¾" dia base ...210.00
Tapestry, aerial view of fair, 42x24½" 125.00
Thermometer, CI, Havoline Tower shape, 5" 45.00

1939 New York

Cuff links, T&P 75.00
Drinking glass, fair scene (color varies), ea 25.00
Guard doll, celluloid head, cloth body, 12", NM, minimum value ...225.00
Key ring, brass w/attached seashell, M on card 35.00
Map, Offical WF Pictorial, Tony Sarg, NM 45.00
Pin-bk, Asbury Park Day at WF, May 18, 1939, EX 100.00
Pin-bk, China Day, Am & Chinese flags, Whitehead & Hoag, 2" ...115.00
Program, opening day; T&P, orange & bl, April 30, NM 190.00
Thermometer, syrocco wood w/T&P emb, 3¼x3" 50.00

1939 San Francisco

Ashtray, Bakelite, pnt fair bldgs, horseshoe shape, 3x2¾", NMIB ..30.00
Ashtray, tire; Firestone, Golden Gate Bridge & bear, 1½x6" dia ...100.00
Book, Official Guide; photos/maps/ads, c 1939, 117-pg, 8x5½" ...17.00
Brochure, photos/etc, 8x3½" closed, folds out to 14" W 30.00
Sticker, Tower of Sun, SF Bay w/sun/rays w/orange sky, sq 17.00

1962 Seattle

Bank, Coliseum; Century 21, EXIB 70.00
Bottle cap opener, silver w/rhinestones, center logo, NM 25.00
Bracelet, goldplate w/mc enameled charms of fair bldgs, 6½" 25.00
Glasses, different bldgs/scenes, 8 in all, set 45.00
Replica, metal, Seattle Space Needle, 6" 20.00
Spoon, Space Needle hdl, Century 21 Exposition in bowl, 5¾" ..10.00
Tie clip, SP, Alweg Monorail, MOC 15.00
Trinket dish, amber smoked glass w/US Science Pavillion, 4x4¼" ...23.00

1964 New York

Ashtray, brass w/eng floral, shoe shape, 3½x1⅜" 25.00
Key ring, Unisphere on chain, MOC 20.00
License plate, blk w/orange letters/#s, validation sticker, NM 35.00
License plate, NY State, orange & blk, 1964, 5¾x12" 75.00
Map, Official; printed by Time Inc, EX 45.00
Matches, fair sponsors, gold-tipped, 7 books, MIP 65.00
Patch, Police, orange w/bl letters, globe in center, NM 75.00
Pennant, felt, orange & bl w/wht lettering, 27", M 35.00
Pin-bk, I Was There NY WF, mc litho tin 15.00

T-shirt, Unisphere/flags/fireworks/date, mc on wht, child's **45.00**
Tablecloth, Official; Unisphere Globe, fair scenes, MIP, minimum value **120.00**
Tray, plastic, fair scene on blk, Peace Through Understanding, 10½" ...**35.00**

Wright, Frank Lloyd

Born in Richland Center, Wisconsin, in 1869, Wright became a pioneer in architectural expression, developing a style referred to as 'prairie.' From early in the century until he died in 1959, he designed houses with rooms that were open, rather than divided by walls in the traditional manner. They exhibited low, horizontal lines and strongly projecting eaves, and he filled them with furnishings whose radical aesthetics complemented the structures to perfection. Several of his homes have been preserved to the present day, and collectors who admire his ideas and the unique, striking look he achieved treasure the stained glass windows, furniture, chinaware, lamps, and other decorative accessories made by Wright.

Key:
drw — drawer
H — Heritage Henredon

Window, geometric design in white, red, and clear, with provenance, ca 1900, 33x16", minor damage, $2,900.00.

Armchair, cherry finish, rfn/reuphl, 29x33x22" **2,100.00**
Blueprint, Executive Chair, 1955, 25x25", fr **2,000.00**
Buffet, H #200 w/#2006 utility rack, mahog, 85x66" **4,000.00**
Cabinet, H #2005 w/cradle base #200, mahog, 26x34" **6,000.00**
Carpet from hotel, 9' sq, NM **3,250.00**
Chair, dining; H #2002, mahog, 4 for **1,100.00**
Chair, side; cherry finish, rfn, reuphl, 2924x22" **3,500.00**
Chair, Tower, uphl hex seat & bk on rhombic ped, EX orig ...**6,500.00**
Chest, H #2000, mahog, 6 drw+2 cabinet drws, 53" **2,500.00**
Dresser, dual, H #2000, 29x62x20" **2,600.00**
Headboard, H #2004, mahog, 3-compartment, king sz **4,750.00**
Mirror, H #2000, mahog, 35x47" **600.00**
Photo, Frank Lloyd Wright, by P Guerrero, blk/wht, 8x10" **200.00**
Sculptures, Nakomis & Nakoma, unglazed terra cotta, 12", 15", pr ..**4,000.00**
Table, coffee; H, cruciform base, 16x33x33" **1,200.00**
Table, coffee; H #450C, mahog, 14x60x20" **4,750.00**
Table, dining; H #2002, mahog, V-base, w/leaves **2,500.00**
Table, end; H #450E, mahog, shelf & drw, 23x27x21" **1,000.00**
Theatre seats from Dallas Theatre, steel & formica, 4 for **2,100.00**
Window, Luxter Prism Co, 10 prisms flank 20, leaded casement, 20x24" **900.00**

Wrought Iron

Until the middle of the nineteenth century, almost all the metal hand forged in America was made from a material called wrought iron. When wrought iron rusts it appears grainy, while the mild steel that was used later shows no grain but pits to an orange-peel surface. This is an important aid in determining the age of an ironwork piece. See also Fireplace Implements.

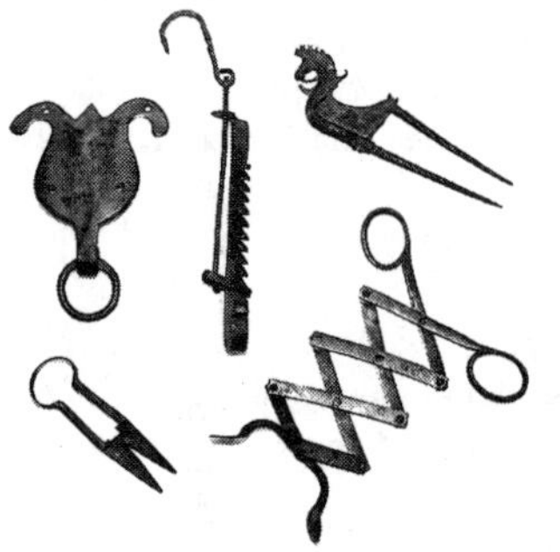

Conestoga wagon toolbox hasp plate, $260.00; Miniature sawtooth ratchet-style trammel, $280.00; Figural sea horse cutter, $55.00; Weaver's shears, small, $65.00; Extending toggle ember tongs, $410.00. (Photo courtesy Aston Macek Auctioneers & Appraisers)

Brazier, wear & edge damage, old rpl trn wood hdl, 9x10" **220.00**
Candlestand, tripod base, arm adjusts, 2 candle sockets, 46" **855.00**
Candlestand, tripod base w/penny ft, twist post, 56" **1,375.00**
Cresset, floor standing, 3-leg, twisted stem, rnd top, 82" **450.00**
Cresset, hanging, 22" **200.00**
Fish broiler, ca 1800, 18", EX **300.00**
Fork, meat; 2-tine, dbl-scroll design, 1800s, 20" **190.00**
Fork, roasting; w/drip pan, penny ft, pitted, 19" **250.00**
Kettle shelf, brass trim, rtcl, trn wood hdl, 13x12" **330.00**
Knuckles, rich old patina, pre-1900, EX **65.00**
Pipe tongs, detailed, 21" **1,155.00**
Pipe tongs, 18th C, 16½", EX **635.00**
Rack, utensil; scrolled detail, 5 hooks, 16" L **485.00**
Rack, utensil; scrolls & 2 birds, 5 hooks, pitted, 15" L **385.00**
Rush light holder, w/candle socket counterbalance, 15½" **250.00**
Skewer holder, RE mk, 18th C, 12¾", +6 flat skewers **500.00**
Spatula, flared blade w/rnded top, tapered hdl, 16½" **85.00**
Table, demilune w/grey stone top, 32x28x15" **525.00**
Toaster, penny ft, tooled details, 19x17" **330.00**
Trammel, sawtooth, old dk patina, adjusts from 39" **500.00**
Trammel, sawtooth, 2 candle sockets, rush-light holder, 27" **495.00**
Trammel, 2 bars (1 rnd/1 flat) w/hooks & holes, adjusts from 44" ..**65.00**

Yellow Ware

Ranging in color from buff to deep mustard, yellow ware which almost always has a clear glaze can be slip banded, plain, Rockingham decorated, flint enamel glazed, or mocha decorated. Black or red mocha decorated pieces are the most desirable. Although blue mocha decorated pieces are the most common, green decorated pieces command the lowest prices. Pieces having a combination of two colors are the rarest. The majority of pieces are plain and do not bear a manufacture's mark. Primarily produced in the United States, England, and Canada this utilitarin ware was popular from the mid-nineteenth century until the early twentieth century. Yellow ware was first produced in New York, Pennsylvania, and Vermont. However, the center for yellow ware production was East Liverpool, Ohio, a town which once supported more than thirty potters. Yellow ware is still being produced today in both the United States and England. Because of websites and Internet auctions, prices have tended to become uniform throughout the United States. The use of this pottery as accessories in decorating and its exposure in country magazines has caused prices to rise, especially for the more utilitarian forms such as plates and bowls. Note: Because this is a utilitarian ware, it is often found with damage and heavy wear. Damage does have a negative impact on price, especially for the common forms. For further information we recommend *Collecting Yellow Ware: An Identification and Value Guide* written by our advisor John Michel and Lisa McAllister, and *Collector's Guide to Yellow Ware* by Lisa McAllister. Mr. Michel's address is in the Directory under New York. See also Rockingham.

Bowl, Earthworm on cream with blue rings, nineteenth century, possibly American, 6½" diameter, $1,000.00 and up. (Photo courtesy Lisa S. McAllister)

Bowl, batter; banded w/looped earthworm decor, 11", minimum ..2,000.00
Bowl, brn-wht-brn bands w/bl seaweed, 6x12½" 950.00
Bowl, 1 wide wht band, rolled lip, 4¼x9" 225.00
Bowl, 3 thin bl bands, 2¼x4" 150.00
Bowl, 3 wht bands, 5x9¾" 115.00
Bowl, 4 thin wht wavy bands between 2 brn bands, 14", minimum ..1,000.00
Canning jar, wax sealer, bbl shape w/staves, 6¼" 175.00
Canning jar, wax sealer, w/scalloped rim, 7¼" 180.00
Colander, thin brn/wht bands, mk Jefford's Pottery, 13", minimum ..1,200.00
Cup, custard; plain, cone shape, 4" 40.00
Cup, custard; ribbed, 3 bl bands, H in circle (Hull) mk 45.00
Flower frog, plain, mushroom shape, 3¼" 45.00
Milk pan, plain, 9½" 265.00
Mold, rectangular w/pear & leaf design, 4x5" 425.00
Mold, rectangular w/rose & leaf design, 5¾x4¼" 385.00
Mold, scalloped oval w/parrot, 7¼x6" 675.00
Mug, wide brn-wht-brn bands w/gr seaweed, 4¾" 350.00
Mug, wide brn-wht-brn bands w/sparce bl seaweed, 4½" 475.00
Mug, 2 sets of 2 bl bands, mk Buckeye 65.00
Mug, 3 thin wht bands, 3½x3½" 270.00
Nappy, plain, heart-shaped ft, 9¾" 250.00
Pepper pot, 2 brn-wht-2 brn bands w/gr seaweed, 5¼" 900.00
Pepper pot, 3 brn-3 wht-3 brn bands w/bl seaweed, 5¼" 975.00
Pepper pot, 5 bl-5 wht-5 bl bands, 5½" 875.00
Pie plate, plain, 11" 225.00
Pie plate colander, plain, dtd October 8, 1861 ....525.00
Pitcher, 2 brn-wht-2 brn bands w/bl seaweed, 5¼" 575.00
Pitcher, 2 brn-wht-2 brn bands w/gr seaweed, 4" 415.00
Pitcher, 2 brn-wht-2 brn bands w/gr seaweed, 5½" 475.00
Pitcher, 2 sets of 2 bl bands, mk Buckeye, 7½" 225.00
Salt box, 5 bl bands, Hull Zane Gray, 5½" 225.00
Salt cellar, wht band w/bl seaweed, master sz, 2½" 525.00
Salt cellar, 2 wht-3 bl-2 wht bands, master sz, 2¼" 350.00
Tea bowl, 2 wide wht bands, ftd, 6" 170.00
Tea bowl, 8 thin wht bands, ftd, 6¼" 290.00

Zanesville Glass

Glassware was produced in Zanesville, Ohio, from as early as 1815 until 1851. Two companies produced clear and colored hollow ware pieces in five characteristic patterns: 1) diamond faceted, 2) broken swirls, 3) vertical swirls, 4) perpendicular fluting, 5) plain, with scalloped or fluted rims and strap handles. The most readily identified product is perhaps the whiskey bottles made in the vertical swirl pattern, often called globular swirls because of their full, round bodies. Their necks vary in width; some have a ringed rim and some are collared. They were made in several colors; amber, light green, and light aquamarine are the most common. Our advisor for this category is Mark Vuono; he is listed in the Directory under Connecticut.

Bottle, globular; medium amber, 24 left-swirled ribs, rolled rim, 8¼", $575.00.

Bottle, globular; amber, 24 swirled ribs, 7½" 550.00
Bottle, globular; golden amber, 24 swirled ribs, 9" 1,155.00
Flask, chestnut; amber, 24 vertical ribs, lg bubbles, 5" 220.00
Flask, chestnut; dk golden amber, wear/flake, 5½" 935.00
Flask, GIV-32, Masonic, amber, flake, 6¾" 330.00
Flask, grandfather's; amber, 24 vertical ribs, stain/wear, 9" 500.00
Flask, GXV-28, Zanesville City Glass Works, 7⅜" 575.00
Hat whimsey, bl-aqua, trn rim, rough pontil, att, 3x7" 110.00
Pitcher, golden amber, free-blown, flared rim, solid ft, 5¾x7¼" ...400.00

Zaneware

In 1922, the Peters and Reed pottery company of Zanesville, Ohio, reorganized under the name Zane Pottery. Charles Chilcote designed new lines, and production of many of the old lines continued. The body of the ware was light in color. Marks include the impressed logo or ink stamp 'Zaneware' in a rectangle.

Bowl, gr matt, leaves/vines emb, 9", NM 200.00
Vase, brn/gr matt over cream, 6" 200.00
Vase, vines/leaves in heavy relief, ivory w/brn wash, 12" 160.00

Zark

Vase, lt bl-gray matt, shouldered, 10x4½" 500.00
Vase, stylized bows on bl & gr matt, buttressed ft, 4½x3¼" 700.00

Zell

The Georg Schmider United Zell Ceramic Factories has a long and colorful history. Affectionately called 'Zell' by those who are attracted to this charming German-Dutch type tin-glazed earthenware, this type of ware came into production in the latter part of the last century.

While Zell has created some lovely majolica-like examples (which are beginning to attract their own following), it is the German-Dutch scenes that are collected with such enthusiasm.

Typical scenes are set against a lush green background with windmills on the distant horizon. Into the scenes appear typically garbed girls (long dresses with long white aprons and lowland bonnet head-gear) being teased or admired by little boys attired in pantaloon-type trousers and short rust-colored jackets, all wearing wooden shoes. There are variations on this theme, and occasionally a collector may find an animal theme or even a Kate Greenaway-like scene.

A similar ware in both theme, technique and quality but bearing the mark Haag or Made in Austria is included in this listing.

While Zell produced a wide range of wares and even quite recently (1970s) introduced an entirely hand-painted hen/rooster line, it is this early charming German-Dutch theme pottery that is coveted by increasing numbers of devoted collectors. Our advisors for this category are Fred and Lila Shrader; they are listed in the Directory under California.

Key: MIA — Made in Austria

Bowl, mixing; boy & man w/pipe, mid sz, 9" 79.00
Bowl, rim soup; Kate Greenaway-like scene in garden, Baden, 8½" .82.00
Butter pat, boy & girl strolling, Baden, 2½" 77.00
Candlestick, boy strolling, Baden, 2½" drip-guard top, 7" 179.00
Child's warmer feeding dish, '70s chicken decor, 8½" 103.00
Chocolate pot, boy on path w/dog, w/lid, 5" 170.00
Chocolate pot, girl walking w/geese, Haag, Germany, 7" 82.00
Creamer, '70s chicken decor, str-sided, 3½" 27.00
Creamer, boy & dog on path, hdl right angle to spout, Baden, 3" ..31.00
Creamer, chickens pecking at ground, MIA, 3½" 35.00
Creamer, girl chasing chicken, hdl right angle to spout, MIA, 3" ...49.00
Creamer & sugar bowl, aproned girl doing chores, w/lid, MIA ..175.00
Cup, woman/cats/table/abundant food, Baden, 3¾" 78.00
Cup & saucer, boy & girl strolling, harbor bkground, Germany ...42.00
Cup & saucer, girl feeds lamb on cup, landscape on saucer 35.00
Mug, girl walking chickens, str-sided, Germany, 3½" 75.00
Pitcher, boys walking on path, str-sided, Germany, 5" 39.00
Plaque, boy & girl kissing, copper rtcl fr, 6" dia 110.00
Plate, birds & leaves on smooth ground, majolica-like, 7" 45.00
Plate, father w/son on path, tab hdls, 9" 40.00
Plate, fruit on basketweave, majolica-like, 6½" 28.00
Plate, girl feeds fish to cat, ships/windmill bkground, 9" 70.00
Plate, grapevine border, majolica-like, 11" 70.00
Plate, proverb: 'Every Good Cook Praises His...,' Haag, 8½" 70.00
Plate, rimless; boy/man at harbor, Germany, 8½" 32.00
Plate, rooster/chicken, 9½" 45.00
Plate, strawberries on smooth bkground, majolica-like, 7" 33.00
Plate, strawberries/leaves/flowers, #50, 9¼" 55.00
Porringer, girl playing w/dog, w/hdl, Haag, MIA, bowl: 4" dia 64.00
Powder jar, Poudre in fancy cursive on lid, Germany, 4" dia 110.00
Shakers, boy & girl strolling, Baden, 3¼", pr 165.00
Teakettle, whistling; '70s chicken decor, metal, 7½" w/hdl 49.00
Teapot, basketweave w/flowers & leaves, majolica-like, 5½" 67.00
Teapot, girl raking garden, Baden, 5½" to finial 268.00
Trivet, boy & girl strolling, Baden, 6¼" dia 75.00
Tumbler, boy & girl arm-in-arm, Baden, 4¾" 52.00
Vase, children strolling, windmill bkground, Haag, 7½" 46.00
Vase, rooster, blk on ivory, dk/lt gr borders, 3¾" 30.00

Zsolnay

Only until the past decade has the production of the Zsolnay factory become more correctly understood. In the beginning they produced only cement; industrial and kitchen ware manufacture began in the 1850s, and in the early 1870s a line of decorative architectural and art pottery was initiated which has continued to the present time.

The city of Pecs (pronounced Paach) is the major provincial city of southwest Hungary close to the Yugoslav border. The old German name for the city was Funfkirchen, meaning 'Five Churches.' (The 'five-steeple' mark became the factory's logo in 1878.)

Although most Americans only think of Zsolnay in terms of the bizarre, reticulated examples of the 1880s and 1890s and the small 'Eosine' green figures of animals and children that have been produced since the 1920s, the factory went through all the art trends of major international art potteries and produced various types of forms and decorations. The 'golden period,' circa 1895 – 1920, is when its Art Nouveau (Sezession in Austro-Hungarian terms) examples were unequaled. Vilmos Zsolnay was a Renaissance man devoted to innovation, and his children carried on the tradition after his death in 1900. Important sculptors and artists of the day were employed (usually anonymously) and married into the family, creating a dynasty.

Nearly all Zsolnay is marked, either impressed 'Zsolnay Pecs' or with the 'five steeple' stamp. Variations and form numbers can date a piece fairly accurately. For the most part, the earlier ethnic historical-revival pieces do not bring the prices that the later Sezession and second Sezession (Deco) examples do. Our advisor for this category is John Gacher; he is listed in the Directory under Rhode Island.

Fish vessel, carp leaping from waves, opaque rosin glazes, iridescent lustre details, Pecs, 14¾x14", NM, $6,000.00.

Bowl, garden party transfer, cobalt w/gold, boat shape, 21" L 450.00
Figurine, buffalo, EX detail, Eocine gr, #1868, 9½", EX 200.00
Figurine, cello player, Art Deco, Eocine gr, on base, 8½" 140.00
Figurine, girl w/basket, Eocine gr, 3x4½" 50.00
Figurine, hedgehog smelling flowers, Eocine gr, 2½" 90.00
Figurine, nude, kneeling on 1 knee, Eocine gr, 9" 130.00
Figurine, owl on book, Eocine gr, 5 steeple mk, 6¼" 145.00
Figurine, partially clad lady, reclining, gr/gold/pk lustres, 10" 900.00
Figurine, polar bear pr, Eocine gr, glacier base, 5x7½" 125.00
Tile, lady slipper orchid on bl, 6" sq 175.00
Vase, allover flowers, red/tan gold irid, wafer mk, 8x8" 1,100.00
Vase, draped lady on shoulder, gr/bl metallic, 9" 600.00
Vase, Eosine bl/gr/gold, ovoid, ca 1900, 12½x7½" 575.00
Vase, moth conforms to rim, mc on red gloss, #6383, ca 1901, 3" ..1,600.00
Vase, nude, scroll design sides, Eocine mc, 1883, 5" 100.00
Vase, peacock/bees/flowers, tan w/much mc/gold decor, #531, 8" ..350.00
Vase, peacock/florals in high relief, #991, 1800s, bl mk, 14" ...2,000.00
Vase, red pomegranate on Eocine MOP, Pecs castle mk, 10x5" ..1,600.00
Vase, red w/10 gold recesses along base, #5595, 4" 200.00
Vase, sunset scene, floral/leaf motif, w/hdl, #5572 M 23, 10" ...1,600.00

Advisory Board

The editors and staff take this opportunity to express our sincere gratitude and appreciation to each person who has in any way contributed to the preparation of this guide. We believe the credibility of our book is greatly enhanced through their efforts. See each advisor's Directory listing for information concerning their specific areas of expertise.

You will notice that at the conclusion of some of the narratives the advisor's name is given. This is optional and up to the discretion of each individual. Simply because no name is mentioned does not indicate that we have no advisor for that subject. Our board grows with each issue and now numbers nearly 450; if you care to correspond with any of them or anyone listed in our Directory, you must send a SASE with your letter. If you are seeking an appraisal, first ask about their fee, since many of these people are professionals who must naturally charge for their services. Because of our huge circulation, every person who allows us to publish their name runs the risk of their privacy being invaded by too many phone calls and letters. We are indebted to every advisor and very much regret losing any one of them. By far, the majority of those we lose give that reason. Please help us retain them on our board by observing the simple rules of common courtesy. Take the differences in time zones into consideration; some of our advisors tell us they often get phone calls in the middle of the night. For suggestions that may help you evaluate your holdings, see the Introduction.

AAA Antique Shop
Nappanee, Indiana

Peter Abrahams
Lake Oswego, Oregon

Charles and Barbara Adams
South Yarmouth, Massachusetts

Geneva D. Addy
Winterset, Iowa

Stan and Sally Alekna
Lebanon, Pennsylvania

Charles Alexander
Indianapolis, Indiana

Craig Ambrose
Des Moines, Iowa

James Anderson
New Brighton, Minnesota

Suzy McLennan Anderson
Holmdel, New Jersey

Tim Anderson
Provo, Utah

Warren R. Anderson
Cedar City, Utah

Dan Andrews
Rancho Palos Verdes, California

Dorothy Malone Anthony
Fort Scott, Kansas

Una Arnbal
Ames, Iowa

Bruce A. Austin
Pittsford, New York

Bobby Babcock
Austin, Texas

Veldon Badders
Hamlin, New York

Rod Baer
Vienna, Virginia

Wayne and Gale Bailey
Dacula, Georgia

Jim Barker
Allentown, Pennsylvania

Kit Barry
Brattleboro, Vermont

Henry Bartsch
Rockaway, Oregon

Mark Bassett
Lakewood, Ohio

Dana Martin Batory
Crestline, Ohio

D.R. Beeks
Mt. Vernon, Iowa

Scott Benjamin
LaGrange, Ohio

Phyllis and Tom Bess
Tulsa, Oklahoma

Robert Bettinger
Mt. Dora, Florida

John E. Bilane
Union, New Jersey

William M. Bilsland III
Cedar Rapids, Iowa

Brenda Blake
York Harbor, Maine

Clarence H. Bodine, Jr.
New Hope, Pennsylvania

Sandra V. Bondhus
Unionville, Connecticut

Clifford Boram
Monticello, Indiana

Jeff Bradfield
Dayton, Virginia

Shane Branchcomb
Fairfax, Virginia

Larry Brenner
Manchester, New Hampshire

Mike Brooks
Oakland, California

Jim Broom
Effingham, Illinois

David L. Brown
Victoria, British Columbia, Canada

Marcia Brown
White City, Oregon

Rick Brown
Newspaper Collector's Society of America
Lansing, Michigan

Nicki Budin
Worthington, Ohio

Donald A. Bull
Wirtz, Virginia

Robert C. Butz
Newbury Park, California

Jim Calison
Wallkill, New York

Tina M. Carter
El Cajon, California

Gene Cataldo
Huntsville, Alabama

Cerebro
East Prospect, Pennsylvania

Mick and Lorna Chase
Cookeville, Tennessee

Pat and Chris Christensen
Costa Mesa, California

Joan Cimini
Belmont, Ohio

Debbie and Randy Coe
Lafayette, Oregon

Wilfred and Dolli Cohen
Santa Ana, California

Marilyn Cooper
Houston, Texas

Ryan Cooper
Yarmouthport, Massachusetts

J.W. Courter
Kevil, Kentucky

Susan N. Cox
El Cajon, California

Rosalind Cranor
Blacksburg, Virginia

Bob Culver
Northville, Michigan

Ron Damaska
New Brighton, Pennsylvania

John Danis
Rockford, Illinois

Patricia M. Davis
Portland, Oregon

Hal & Meredith DeGood
Des Moines, Iowa

Loretta DeLozier
Knoxville, Tennessee

Joe Devine
Council Bluffs, Iowa

Doug Dezso
Maywood, New Jersey

David Dilley
Indianapolis, Indiana

Thomas P. Dimitroff
Corning, New York

Ginny Distel
Tiffin, Ohio

Rod Dockery
Ft. Worth, Texas

L.R. 'Les' Docks
San Antonio, Texas

Rebecca Dodds
Coral Springs, Florida

Brenda Dollen
Council Bluffs, Iowa

Ron Donnelly
Tuscaloosa, Alabama

Robert A. Doyle, C.A.I., I.S.A.
Pleasant Valley, New York

James Dryden
Hot Springs National Park, Arkansas

Louise Dumont
Leesburg, Florida

Pat and Ann Duncan
Cape Fair, Missouri

Ken and Jackie Durham
Washington, DC

William Durham
Belvidere, Illinois

Rita and John Ebner
Columbus, Ohio

Bill Edwards
Madison, Indiana

Larry Egelhoff
Indianapolis, Indiana

J. David Ehrhard
Tujunga, California

Michael L. Ellis
Costa Mesa, California

Dr. Robert Elsner
Boynton Beach, Florida

Barbara Endter
Rochester, New York

Elaine Ezell
Pasadena, Maryland

Bryce Farnsworth
Fargo, North Dakota

Arthur M. Feldman
Highland Park, Illinois

Linda Fields
Dover, Tennessee

Mary J. Finegan
Boone, North Carolina

Paul Fink
Kent, Connecticut

Vicki Flanigan
Winchester, Virginia

Gene Florence
Lexington, Kentucky

Marv Fogleman
Santa Ana, California

Doug Foland
Portland, Oregon

Frank W. Ford
Shrewsbury, Massachusetts

Ruth Forsythe
Galena, Ohio

Madeleine France
Ft. Lauderdale, Florida

James Fred
Cutler, Indiana

Peter Frei
Brimfield, Massachusetts

Wendy and Leo Frese
Dallas, Texas

Tony Freyaldenhoven
Conway, Arkansas

Doris Frizzell
Springfield, Illinois

Donald M. Frost
Vancouver, Washington

John Gacher
Newport, Rhode Island

William Galaway
Belvidere, Illinois

Lee Garmon
Springfield, Illinois

Sandi and Jerry Garrett
Kokomo, Indiana

Mary Frank Gaston
Bryan, Texas

Dr. Joan M. George
Old Bridge, New Jersey

Tony George
Rancho Santa Margarita, California

Roselyn Gerson
Lynbrook, New York

Carl Gibbs, Jr.
Houston, Texas

Pat Gibson
Newark, California

Steve Gillespie
Village of the Oaks, Missouri

Walter Glenn
Atlanta, Georgia

Kathy Goldsworthy
Bothell, Washington

Bob Gottuso
Cranberry Township, Pennsylvania

Shirley Graff
Brunswick, Ohio

Helen Greguire
Landrum, South Carolina

Woody Griffith
Chicago, Illinois

Susan Grindberg
Henderson, Nevada

Everett Grist
East Ridge, Tennessee

Bonnie Groves
Elgin, Texas

Tom Guenin
Chardon, Ohio

Karen Guido
Bridgewater, Connecticut

Jack Gunsaulus
Plymouth, Michigan

Candace Gunther
Pasadena, California

Norman Haas
Quincy, Michigan

Don Haase
Mukilteo, Washington

Richard Haigh
Richmond, Virginia

Doris and Burdell Hall
Morton, Illinois

Jack and Treva Hamlin
Proctorville, Ohio

Burton Handelsman
White Plains, New York

Don and Barbara Hardisty
Las Cruces, New Mexico

Jim and Susan Harran
Neptune, New Jersey

John Harrigan
Minneapolis, Minnesota

Gwynneth M. Harrison
Mira Loma, California

Mary Jane Hastings
Mt. Olive, Illinois

John Hathaway
Bryant Pond, Maine

Ted Haun
Kokomo, Indiana

Carl Heck
Aspen, Colorado

Virginia Heiss
Indianapolis, Indiana

Patrick J. Herley
Long Island, New York

John Hess
Andover, Massachusetts

Jerry Heuring
Scott City, Missouri

Suzi Hibbard
Fairfield, California

James Highfield
South Bend, Indiana

Alma Hillman
Searsport, Maine

Randy Hilst
Pekin, Illinois

Michael C. Hinton
Doylestown, Pennsylvania

Susan and Larry Hirshman
Medford, Oregon

Pat and Don Hoffmann, Sr.
Aurora, Illinois

Walter P. Hogan
Ann Arbor, Michigan

William Holland
West Chester, Pennsylvania

Jane Holt
Derry, New Hampshire

Dee Hooks
Percy, Illinois

Dennis Hopp
Chicago, Illinois

Betty Hornback
Elizabethtown, Kentucky

Cindy Horvath
Portland, Michigan

Lar Hothem
Lancaster, Ohio

Steve Howard
San Ramon, California

Hardy Hudson
Winter Park, Florida

Murray Hudson
Halls, Tennessee

Kathy Hughes (Mrs. Paul)
Charlotte, North Carolina

George C. Humphrey
Beltsville, Maryland

Mary and George Hurney
Palatine, Illinois

Billy Ray and Susan Hussey
Robins, North Carolina

Dan Iannotti
Bloomfield Hills, Michigan

Dave Irons
Northampton, Pennsylvania

Michael Ivankovich
Doylestown, Pennsylvania

Ralph Jaarsma
Pella, Iowa

Denis C. Jackson
Sequim, Washington

Pat James
Hillrose, Colorado

Wes Johnson
Louisville, Kentucky

John R. Joiner
Newnan, Georgia

Donald Jones
Savannah, Georgia

Dorothy Kamm
Port St. Lucie, Florida

Fern Kao
Bowling Green, Ohio

Keith Kaonis
Northport, New York

Jerome R. Katz, Vice President
International Society of Antique Scale Collectors
Frederick, Maryland

William and June Keagy
Bloomfield, Indiana

Ed Kenney
Vienna, Virginia

Ann Kerr
Sidney, Ohio

Steve Ketcham
Edina, Minnesota

Anne Kier
Toledo, Ohio

Lorrie Kitchen
Toledo, Ohio

Dondee and Bob Klein
Guthrie, Oklahoma

Grace and James Klender
Pioneer, Ohio

Jerry Kline
Kodak, Tennessee

Mr. and Mrs. Jerry and Gerry Kline
Maumee, Ohio

Judy A. Knauer
National Toothpick Holder Collectors Society
West Chester, Pennsylvania

Suzanne Knight
Abilene, Texas

Joanne M. Koehn
Eden Prairie, Minnesota

Terry Krause
Zanesville, Ohio

Katherine Kreider
Lancaster, Pennsylvania

Rod Krupka
Ortonville, Michigan

Elizabeth M. Kurella
Whiting, Indiana

Louis Kuritzky
Gainesville, Florida

Paris Langford
Jefferson, Louisiana

Robert V. Larsen
Columbus, Nebraska

Patricia and H. Thomas Laun
Syracuse, New York

Mildred and Ralph Lechner
Mechanicsville, Virginia

Gary Lehrer
Woodbridge, Connecticut

Beverly Leslie
Boonville, Indiana

Anita Levi
Allegheny Mountain Antique Gallery
Windber, Pennsylvania

Ralph Lindsay
New Holland, Pennsylvania

Jacqueline Linscott (in memory of Len Linscott)
Titusville, Florida

Matt Lippa
Mentone, Alabama

Elyce Litts
Morris Planes, New Jersey

Howard J. Lockwood
Fort Lee, New Jersey

Dee Long
Lacon, Illinois

Paul J. Longo
Magnolia, Massachusetts

James Lewis Lowe
Norwood, Pennsylvania

Dale MacAllister
Singers Glen, Virginia

Bill Mackin
Craig, Colorado

Dale MacLean
Dedham, Massachusetts

Earl MacSorley
Orange, Connecticut

Deborah Maggard
Chagrin Falls, Ohio

Betty and Clarence Maier
The Burmese Cruet
Montgomeryville, Pennsylvania

Lucille Malitz
Scarsdale, New York

Abby and Wlodek Malowanczyk
Dallas, Texas

William Manns
Santa Fe, New Mexico

Linda K. Marsh
Lansing, Michigan

Betty O. Martin
Santa Ynez, California

Jim Martin
Monmouth, Illinois

Richard Mathes
Springfield, Ohio

Gene Matzke
Hancock, Wisconsin

Maundy International
Shawnee Mission, Kansas

Oveda L. Maurer
San Anselmo, California

Michael J. McQuillen
Indianapolis, Indiana

John, Jean and Michael Meadows
Baltimore, Maryland

Mirko Melis
Mississauga, Ontario, Canada

Edward J. Meschi
Monroeville, New Jersey

Larry Meyer
Stickney, Illinois

Barbara and John Michel
New York, New York

Dave and Anne Middleton
Allenwood, New Jersey

Clark Miller
Minneapolis, Minnesota

Larry Miller
East Peoria, Illinois

Tom and Linda Millman
Bethel, Ohio

Randall B. Monsen
Vienna, Virginia

Carolyn Moore
Bowling Green, Ohio

Shirley Suber Moore
Tulsa, Oklahoma

Albert Morin
Dracut, Massachusetts

Susan and David Morris
Merlin, Oregon

Thomas G. Morris
Medford, Oregon

Patsy Moyer
Deming, New Mexico

James L. Murphy
Columbus, Ohio

Marge Musgrave
Salesville, Arkansas

Boyd W. Nedry
Comstock Park, Michigan

Leonard Needham
Bernicia, California

Nancee P. Neely
Omaha, Nebraska

C.L. Nelson
Spring Park, Minnesota

Maxine Nelson
Scottsdale, Arizona

Scott H. Nelson
Santa Fe, New Mexico

Betty Newbound
Sanford, North Carolina

George Newhouse
Pasadena, Maryland

Mike Nickel
Portland, Michigan

Kenn Norris
Sanderson, Texas

Joan Oates
Constantine, Michigan

The Occupied Japan Club
c/o Florence Archambault
Newport, Rhode Island

Grace Ochsner
Niota, Illinois

Old World Antiques
Kansas City, Kansas

Naomi Over
Arvada, Colorado

Sally and Larry Owen
Illinois

Dick Pardini
Stockton, California

Jim Pasquali
San Francisco, California

Diane Patalano, I.S.A.
Upper Saddle River, New Jersey

Sharon A. Payne
Granite Falls, Washington

Nancy and Robert Perzel
Flemington, New Jersey

Louis Picek
West Branch, Iowa

David Pierce
Danville, Ohio

Judy Posner
Effort, Pennsylvania;
Englewood, Florida

Harry Poster
S. Hackensack, New Jersey

Joyce M. Pringle
Arlington, Texas

Ted Pruitt
Anderson, Indiana

Barb Putratz
Spring Lake Park, Minnesota

David Rago
Lambertville, New Jersey

Glen Rairigh
Sunfield, Michigan

Jim Rash
Egg Harbor Township, New Jersey

Lisa Rastello
St. Charles, Illinois

Debbie Rees
Zanesville, Ohio

Leon Reimert
Coatesville, Pennsylvania

Charles Reynolds
Falls Church, Virginia

Joan and Charles Rhoden
Georgetown, Illinois

Ferill J. Rice
Kaukauna, Wisconsin

James Riebel
Zanesville, Ohio

Blume Rifken
New York

John F. Rinaldi
Kennebunkport, Maine

David Ringering
Salem, Oregon

Roy B. Ritchie
Hindman, Kentucky

Brenda Roberts
Marshall, Missouri

Fred and Marilyn Roberts
Medford, Oregon

Joanne Rodgers
Stretch Glass Society
Hampshire, Illinois

Martin Roenigk
Eureka Springs, Arkansas

Joyce and Fred Roerig
Walterboro, South Carolina

Herbert Rolfes
Mt. Dora, Florida

Gayle Roller
San Marcos, California

Barbara Rosen
Wayne, New Jersey

Kenna Rosen
Dallas, Texas

Michelle Rosewitz
San Bernardino, California

Michelle Ross
Berrien Center, Michigan

Philip J. and Philip Rosso, Jr.
Port Vue, Pennsylvania

Peggy E. Roush
Ocala, Florida

John and Barbara Rudisill
Worton, Maryland

Charlotte Safir
New York, New York

Martha and Steve Sanford
Campbell, California

R.J. Sayers
Brevard, North Carolina

Elizabeth Schaaf
Mentone, Alabama

Roselle Schleifman
Spring Valley, New York

Jim Schleyer
Burke, Virginia

Betty and Larry Schwab
Bloomington, Illinois

Roger R. Scott
Tulsa, Oklahoma

Virgil Scowden
Williamsport, Indiana

Joyce and Harold Screen
Baltimore, Maryland

Cathy Segelke
Merino, Colorado

Lila and Fred Shrader
Crescent City, California

Brenda and Jerry Siegel
St. Louis, Missouri

Karen Silvermintz
Dallas, Texas

David Smies
Manhattan, Kansas

Allan Smith
Sherman, Texas

Carole and Richard Smyth
Huntington, New York

Charlie and Rose Snyder
Independence, Kansas

Diane Snyder-Haug
St. Petersburg, Florida

Dick Spencer
O'Fallon, Illinois

Rick Spencer
Salt Lake City, Utah

Greg Spiess
Joliet, Illinois

Nancy Steinbock
Chestnut Hill, Massachusetts

Stella's Collectibles
Torrance, California

Ron Stewart
Combs, Kentucky

Craig Stifter
Naperville, Illinois

Liz Stillwell
Pico Rivera, California

Dick Strickfaden
Pekin, Illinois

Pamela and Joseph Tanner
Elk Grove, California

Jenny Tarrant
St. Peters, Missouri

Terry Taylor
East Bend, North Carolina

Bruce Thalberg
Weston, Connecticut

Sharon Thoerner
Bellflower, California

Chuck Thompson
Houston, Texas

Don Thornton
Moss Beach, California

Rosella Tinsley
Osawatomie, Kansas

Marlena Toohey
Longmont, Colorado

Veronica Trainer
Cleveland, Ohio

Dan Tucker
Toledo, Ohio

Valerie and Richard Tucker
Argyle, Texas

Robert Tuggle
New York, New York

Hobart D. Van Deusen
Watertown, Connecticut

Jean and Dale Van Kuren
Clarence Center, New York

Joan F. Van Patten
Rexford, New York

Linda L. Vines
Upper Montclair, New Jersey

Stephen Visakay
West Caldwell, New Jersey

Mark Vuono
Stamford, Connecticut

John W. Waddell
Mineral Wells, Texas

Jim Waite
Farmer City, Illinois

John Walter
Marietta, Ohio

Judith and Robert Walthall
Huntsville, Alabama

Ian Warner
Brampton, Ontario, Canada

Maret Webb
Phoenix, Arizona

Marty Webster
Saline, Michigan

David Weddington
Murfreesboro, Tennessee

Robert Weisblut
Wheaton, Maryland

Pastor Frederick S. Weiser
New Oxford, Pennsylvania

BA Wellman
Westminster, Massachusetts

David Wendel
Poplar Bluff, Missouri

Kaye and Jim Whitaker
Lynnwood, Washington

Douglass White
Orlando, Florida

John 'Grandpa' White
Denver, Colorado

Margaret and Kenn Whitmyer
Gahanna, Ohio

Steven Whysel
Plantation, Florida

Robert Wieland
Ormond Beach, Florida

Doug Wiesehan
St. Charles, Missouri

James R. Wilkins
Duncanville, Texas

Don Williams
Kirksville, Missouri

Ron L. Willis
Matlacha, Florida

Roy M. Willis
Lebanon Junction, Kentucky

Jack D. Wilson
Chicago, Illinois

Grant S. Windsor
Richmond, Virginia

Ralph Winslow
Laurie, Missouri

Nancy Winston
Northwood, New Hampshire

Jo Ellen Winther
Arvada, Colorado

Raphael C. Wise
West Palm Beach, Florida

Bill Wright
New Albany, Indiana

Libby Yalom
Adelphi, Maryland

Darlene Yohe
Stuttgart, Arkansas

Mary Young
Kettering, Ohio

Charles S. Zayic
Ellsworth, Maine

Audrey Zeder
North Bend, Washington

Auction Houses

We wish to thank the following auction houses whose catalogs have been used as sources for pricing information. Many have granted us permission to reproduce their photographs as well.

A-1 Auction Service
2042 N. Rio Grande Ave., Suite 'E,' Orlando, FL 32804; 407-839-0004. Specializing in American antique sales

A&B Auctions, Inc.
Marlboro, MA; 508-480-0006 or fax 508-460-6101. Specializing in English ceramics, flow blue, pottery and Mason's Ironstone

Absolute Auction & Realty, Inc./Pleasant Valley Auction Hall
Robert Doyle
PO Box 1739, Pleasant Valley, NY 12569; website: www.auctionweb.com/aar-ny and absoluteauctionrealty.com
Antique and estate auctions twice a month at Pleasant Valley Auction Hall; Free calendar of auctions

Alex G. Malloy, Inc.
PO Box 38, South Salem, NY 10590; 203-438-0396. Specializing in ancient and medieval coins, antiquities, numismatic literature; 4 mail bid auctions per year

Allard Auctions Inc.
Col. Doug Allard
PO Box 460, St. Ignatius, MT 59865-0460; 406-745-2951 or fax 406-745-2961

America West Archives
Anderson, Warren
PO Box 100, Cedar City, UT 84721; 435-586-9497; e-mail: warren@americawestarchives.com. Publishes 26-page illustrated catalog 6 times a year that includes auction section of scarce and historical early western documents, letters, autographs, stock certificates, and other important ephemera, Subscription: $15 per year

Americana Auctions
c/o Glen Rairigh
12633 Sandborn, Sunfield, MI 48890. Specializing in Skookum dolls and antique auctions

Anderson Auctions/Heritage Antiques & Appraisal Services
Suzy McLennan Anderson
65 E. Main St., Holmdel, NJ 07733; 908-946-8801 or fax 908-946-1036. Specializing in American furniture and decorative accessories

Andre Ammelounx
The Stein Company
PO Box 136, Palatine, IL 60078; 847-991-5927 or fax 847-991-5947. Specializing in steins, catalogs available

Anthony J. Nard & Co.
U.S. Rt. 220, Milan, PA 18831; 717-888-9404 or fax 717-888-7723

Aston Macek Auctioneers and Appraisers
2825 Country Club Rd., Endwell, NY 13760-3349; phone/fax: 607-785-6598. Also have auctions on the internet: ebay (folkman 2) and ehammer (folkman@stnylrun.com); specializing in and appraisers of Americana, folk art, other primitives, furniture, Shaker, fine art, porcelain, and china

Bill Bertoia Auctions
2413 Madison Ave., Vineland, NJ 08360; 609-692-4092 or fax 609-692-8697. Specializing in toys, dolls, advertising, and related items

Bider's
241 S. Union St., Lawrence, MA 01843; 508-688-4347 or 508-683-3944. Antiques appraised, purchased, and sold on consignment

Brian Riba Auctions Inc.
PO Box 53, Main St., S. Glastonbury, CT 06073; 203-633-3076

Buffalo Bay Auction Co.
5244 Quam Circle, Rogers, MN 55374; 612-428-8480; or fax 612-428-8879; e-mail: buffalobay@aol.com. Specializing in advertising, tins and country store items

Butterfield & Butterfield
220 San Bruno Ave., San Francisco, CA 94103; 415-861-7500 or fax 415-861-8951. Also located at: 7601 Sunset Blvd., Los Angeles, CA 90046; 213-850-7500 or fax 213-850-5843 and 441 West Huron St., Chicago, IL 60610; 312-377-7500 or fax 312-377-7501; e-mail: info@butterfields.com or website: www.butterfields.com. Fine Art Auctioneers and Appraisers since 1865

Butterfield & Dunning
441 W. Huron St., Chicago, IL 60610; 312-664-8400; www.butterfields.com

Cerebro
PO Box 327, E. Prospect, PA 17317-0327; 717-252-2400 or 800-69-LABEL: fax: 717-252-3685; e-mail: Cerebro@Cerebro.com. Specializing in antique advertising labels, especially cigar box labels, cigar bands, food labels, firecracker labels; Holds semi-annual auction on tobacco ephemera; Consignments accepted

Charles E. Kirtley
PO Box 2273, Elizabeth City, NC 27096; 919-335-1262. Specializing in World's Fair, Civil War, political, advertising and other American collectibles

Cincinnati Art Gallery
225 E. Sixth St, Cincinnati, OH 45202; 513-381-2128. Specializing in American art pottery, American and European fine paintings, watercolors

Collector's Auction Services
R.D. 2, Box 431, Oil City, PA 16301; 814-677-6070. Specializing in advertising, oil and gas, toys, rare museum and investment-quality antiques

Collector's Sales & Service
PO Box 4037, Middletown, RI 02842; 401-849-5012 or fax 401-846-6156

Country Girls Estate & Appraisal Service
Diane Patalano
PO Box 144, Saddle River, NJ 07458

Dargate Auction Galleries
5607 Baum Boulevard, Pittsburgh, PA 15206; 412-362-3558. Specializing in estate auctions featuring fine art, antiques, and collectibles

David Rago
20th Century Design
Auction hall: 333 N. Main, Lambertville, NJ 08530; 609-397-6780 or fax: 609-397-6790; www.ragoarts.com or ragoarts@ragoarts.com. Specializing in American art pottery and Arts and Crafts

Du Mouchelles
409 Jefferson Ave., Detroit, MI 48226

Dunbar's Gallery
Leila and Howard Dunbar
76 Haven St., Milford, MA 01757; 508-634-8697 or fax 508-634-8698; e-mail: Dunbars@mediaone.net or website: dunbarsgallery.com

Early American Numismatics
Dana Linett, President
PO Box 2442, La Jolla, CA 92038

Early Auction Co.
123 Main St., Milford, OH 45150

Flying Deuce Auctions & Antiques
1224 Yellowstone Ave., Pocatello, ID 83201; 208-237-2002 or fax: 208-237-4544; e-mail: flying2@nicoh.com or website: www.flying2.com

Frank's Antiques & Auctions
2405 N. Kings Rd., Hilliard, FL 32046; 904-845-2870 or fax 904-845-4000. Specializing in antique advertising, country store items, rec room and restaurant decor as well as sporting collectibles, pottery and stoneware; catalogs issued

Freeman Fine Arts
1808 Chestnut St., Philadelphia, PA 19103; 215-563-9275 or fax 215-563-8236

Full House
Gene Willett
9090 Cherokee, Clarkston, MI 48348; 248-394-0313. Specializing in mail-bid playing card auctions

Garth's Auctions Inc.
2690 Stratford Rd., Box 369, Delaware, OH 43015; 740-362-4771; e-mail: info@garths.com or website: www.garths.com

Glass-Works Auctions
102 Jefferson, East Greenville, PA 18041; 215-679-5849 or fax: 215-679-3068; e-mail: glswrk@enter.net. America's leading auction company in early American bottles and glass and barber shop memorabilia

Hanna-Whysel Auctioneers & Appraisers
Steven Whysel
3403 Bella Vista Way, Bella Vista, AR, 72714; 501-855-9600. Antiques and art auctions

Harmer Rooke Galleries
32 E. 57th St, 11th Floor, New York, NY 10022; 212-751-1900 or fax 212-758-1713

Henry/Pierce Auctioneers
1456 Carson Court, Homewood, IL 60430; 708-798-7508. Specializing in bank auctions

High Noon
9929 Venice Blvd., Los Angeles, CA 90034; 310-202-9010 or fax: 310-202-9011. Specialing in cowboy and western collectibles

History Buff's Auctions
www/historybuff.com. Specializing in paper collectibles spanning 5 centuries

Horst Auctioneers
Horst Auction Center
50 Durlach Rd. (corner of Rt. 322 & Durlach Rd., West of Ephrata), Ephrata, Lancaster County, PA 17522; 717-859-1331 or 717-738-3080. Voices of Experience

Jack Sellner
Sellner Marketing of California
PO Box 308, Fremont, CA 94537; 510-792-9463

Jackson's, Auctioneers & Appraisers of Fine Art
2229 Lincoln St., Cedar Falls, IA 50613; 319-277-2256 or fax 319-277-1252; online auctions homepage: jacksons@jacksonsauction.com; and website: www.jacksonsauction.com. Specializing in American and European art pottery and art glass, American and European paintings, Russian works of art, decorative arts, toys and jewelry

James D. Julia
PO Box 830, Rt. 201, Skowhegan Rd., Fairfield, ME 04937; 207-453-7125 or fax 207-453-2502; e-mail: jjulia@juliaauctions.com or website: www.juliaauctions.com

James R. Bakker Antiques, Inc.
James R. Bakker
370 Broadway, Cambridge, MA 02139; 617-864-7067. Specializing in American paintings, prints and decorative arts

James J. Reeves
PO Box 219, 328 Allegheny St., Huntingdon, PA 16652; 814-643-5497 or fax 814-641-2600; e-mail: Reeves5@vicon.net or website: www.JamesJReeves.com. Monthly mail-bid catalog dealing with stamps, coins, railroadiana, sports cards, comics, and all shippable antiques/ collectibles

John Toomey Gallery
818 North Blvd., Oak Park, IL 60301; 708-383-5234 or fax 708-383-4828. Specializing in furniture and decorative arts of the Arts & Crafts, Art Deco and Modern Design movements; Modern Design Expert: Richard Wright

Joy Luke Auctioneers & Appraisers
The Gallery
300 East Grove St., Bloomington, IL 61701; 309-828-5533 or fax 309-829-2266; website: www.joyluke.com or e-mail: joyluke@aol.com

Kerry & Judy's Toys
7370 Eggleston Rd., Memphis, TN 31825-2112; 901-757-1722. Specializing in toys, 1920s-1960s; Consignments always welcome

Kit Barry Ephemera Auctions
136 High St., Brattleboro, VT 05301; 802-254-3634. Tradecard and ephemera auctions, fully illustrated catalogs with prices realized; Consignment inquiries welcome

Kurt R. Krueger
160 N. Washington St., PO Box 275, Iola, WI 54945-0275

L.R. 'Les' Docks
Box 691035, San Antonio, TX 78269-1035. Providing occasional mail-order record auctions, rarely consigned; only consignments considered are exceptionally scarce and unusual records

Lloyd Ralston Toys
400 Long Beach Blvd., Stratford, CT 06615; 203-386-9399 or fax 203-386-9519

Lowe, James Lewis
PO Box 8, Norwood, PA 19074; e-bay: JLewisLowe@juno.com. Specializing in Kate Greenaway, postcards

Majolica Auctions
Michael G. Strawser
200 North Main, PO Box 332, Wolcottville, IN 46795; 219-854-2859 or fax 219-854-3979. Issues color catalogs

Manion's International Auction House, Inc.
PO Box 12214, Kansas City, KS 66112; 913-299-6692 or fax 913-299-6792; e-mail: manions@qni.com; www.manions.com. Specializing in international militaria, particularly the US, Germany and Japan. Extensive catalogs in antiques and collectibles, sports, transportation, political and advertising memorabilia and vintage clothing and denim. Publishes 9 catalogs for each of the 5 categories per year. Request a free sample of past auctions, 1 issue of current auction for $7 or a 6-catalog subscription for $35.

Maritime Auctions
935 US Rt. 1, PO Box 322, York, ME 03909-0322; 207-363-4247 or fax 353-1415; website: www.maritiques.com or Auction: www.eswap.com

McMasters Doll Auctions
PO Box 1755, 5855 Glenn Highway, Cambridge, OH 43725; 740-432-4419 or fax 740-432-3191; or 800-842-3526; e-mail mcmasters@jadeinc.com or website: angelfire.com/oh/mcmastersauctions

Michael Ivankovich Auctions, Inc.
PO Box 1536, Doylestown, PA, 18901; 215-345-6094. Specializing in early hand-colored photography and prints. Auction held 4 times each year, providing opportunity for collectors and dealers to compete for the largest variety of Wallace Nutting, Wallace Nutting-like pictures, Bessie Pease Gutmann, R. Atkinson Fox, Philip Boileau, Harrison Fisher, etc., available anywhere.

Michael John Verlangieri
PO Box 844, Cambria, CA 93428; 805-927-4428; www.calpots.com. Specializing in fine California pottery; cataloged auctions (video tapes available)

Monsen & Baer, Annual Perfume Bottle Auction
Monsen, Randall; and Baer, Rod
Box 529, Vienna, VA 22183; 703-938-2129 or fax 703-242-1357. Cataloged auctions of perfume bottles; will purchase, sell, and accept consignments; specializing in commercial, Czechoslovakian, Lalique, Baccarat, Victorian, crown top, factices, miniatures

Neal Auction Company
4038 Magazine St., New Orleans, LA 70115; 504-899-5329 or 1-800-467-5329; fax: 504-897-3803; website: www.nealauction.com

New England Absentee Auctions
16 6th St., Stamford, CT 06905; 203-975-9055. Specializing in Quimper pottery

Noel Barrett Antiques & Auctions
PO Box 1001, Carversville, PA 18913; 215-297-5109 or fax 215-297-0457

Norman C. Heckler & Company
79 Bradford Corner Rd., Woodstock Valley, CT 06282; 860-974-1634 or fax 860-974-2003. Auctioneers and appraisers specializing in early glass and bottles

Nostalgia Co.
21 S. Lake Dr., Hackensack, NJ 07601; 201-488-4536; www.nostalgiapubs.com

Past Tyme Pleasures
Steve Howard
PMB #204, 2491 San Ramon Blvd., Ste. #1, San Ramon, CA 94583; 925-484-4488 or fax 925-484-2551. Offers 2 absentee auction catalogs per year pertaining to old advertising items

Phillips
406 E. 79th St., New York, NY 10021

Postcards International
Martin J. Shapiro
2321 Whitney Ave., Suite 102, PO Box 185398; Hamden, CT 06518; 203-248-6621 or fax 203-248-6628; www.vintagepostcards.com

Rafael Osona, Auctioneer & Appraiser
PO Box 2607, Nantucket, MA 02584; 508-228-3942. Specializing in Americana, fine arts, continental & marine antiques, Nantucket baskets, art, and memorabilia

Refinders
737 Barberry Rd., Highland Park, IL 60035; 708-831-1102 or 708-831-1160. Refinders will find your wants from 1860 to 1960

Richard Opfer Auctioneering, Inc.
1919 Greenspring Dr., Timonium, MD 21093; 410-252-5035; fax: 410-252-5863; website: www.opferauction.com or e-mail: info@opferauction.com

Roan, Inc.
R.R. 4, Box 118, Cogan Station, PA 17728-9334

Schoolmaster Auctions and Real Estate
Kenn Norris
PO Box 4830; 513 N. 2nd St., Sanderson, TX 79848; 915-345-2640. Specializing in school-related items, barbed wire and related literature, and L'il Abner

Shot Glass Exchange
PO Box 219, Western Springs, IL, 60558; 706-246-1559. Publishes mail-auction catalog twice yearly

Skinner, Inc.
Auctioneers & Appraisers of Antiques and Fine Arts
The Heritage on the Garden, 63 Park Plaza, Boston, MA 02116; 617-350-5400 or fax 617-350-5429. Second address: 357 Main Street, Bolton, MA 01740; 978-779-6241 or fax 978-779-5144; website: www.skinnerinc.com

Smith & Jones, Inc.
12 Clark Lane, Sudbury, MA 01776; 508-443-5517 or fax 508-443-8045. Specializing in Dedham dinnerware, Buffalo china and important American art pottery; Full-color catalogs available

Soldiers Trunk
60 Craigs Rd., Windsor, CT 06095; 203-688-0580. Specializing in American and foreign military items; 4 catalog issues for $20

SOLDUSA.COM (formerly Dixie Sporting Collectibles)
1206 Rama Rd., Charlotte, NC 28211; 704-364-2900 or 877-SoldUSA; fax 704-364-2322; e-mail: gun1898@aol.com or website: www.sportauction.com. Specializing in fine sporting collectibles

Sotheby's
1334 York Ave., New York, NY 10021

Stanton's Auctioneers & Realtors
144 S. Main St., PO Box 146, Vermontville, MI 49096; 517-726-0181 or fax 517-726-0060. Specializing in all types of property, at auction, anywhere

Steffen Historical Militaria
Roger S. Steffen
14 Murnan Rd., Cold Springs, KY 41076; 606-431-4499. Specializing in quality militaria, military art, rare books, antique firearms

Superior Galleries
9478 West Olympic Boulevard, Beverly Hills, CA 90212-4246; 310-203-9855 or fax: 310-203-0496; website: www.superiorsc.com. Specializing in manuscripts, decorative and fine arts, Hollywood memorabilia, sports memorabilia, stamps and coins

Swann Galleries, Inc.
104 E. 25th St., New York, NY 10010; 312-254-4710 or fax: 212-979-1017; website: www.swanngalleries.com

Three Rivers Collectibles
Wendy and Leo Frese
PO Box 551542, Dallas, TX 75355; 214-341-5165. Annual Red Wing and Rum-Rill pottery and stoneware auctions

Toy Scouts, Inc.
137 Casterton Ave., Akron, OH 44303; 330-836-0668 or fax: 330-869-8668; e-mail: toyscouts@toyscouts.com or website: www.toyscouts.com. Specializing in baby-boom era collectibles

Tradewinds Auctions
Henry Taron
PO Box 249, Manchester-By-The-Sea, MA 01944-0249; 508-768-3327

Treadway Gallery, Inc.
2029 Madison Rd., Cincinnati, OH 45208; 513-321-6742 or fax 513-871-7722; website: www.treadwaygallery.com. Specializing in American Art Pottery; American and European art glass; European ceramics; Italian glass; fine American and European paintings and graphics; and furniture and decorative arts of the Arts & Crafts, Art Nouveau, Art Deco and Modern Design Movements. Modern Design expert: Thierry Lorthioir. Members: National Antique Dealers Association, American Art Pottery Association, International Society of Appraisers, American Ceramic Arts Society, Ohio Decorative Arts Society, Art Gallery Association of Cincinnati

Vogel Auction
4720 S.E. Fort King St., Ocala, FL 34470-1501; 352-694-5776; e-mail: Vogels@atlantic.net. Specializing in souvenir china

Vicki and Bruce Waasdorp
PO Box 434; 10931 Main St.; Clarence, NY 14031; 716-759-2361; www.antiques-stoneware.com. Specializing in decorated stoneware

Weschler's
Adam A. Weschler & Son
905 E. St. N.W., Washington, DC 20004

William Doyle Galleries
Auctioneers & Appraisers
175 East 87th St., New York, NY 10128; 212-427-2730 or fax: 212-369-0892; e-mail: info@doylegalleries.com or website: www.doylegalleries.com

Willis Henry Auctions
22 Main St., Marshfield, MA 02050

Yorktown Auction Inc.
1625 Haviland Rd. York , PA 17404; 717-751-0211; fax 717-767-7729; e-mail: yorktownauction @cyberia.com. Fine antiques, art, real estate

Directory of Contributors

When contacting any of the buyers/sellers listed in this part of the Directory by mail, you must include a SASE (stamped, self-addressed envelope) if you expect a reply. As hectic as our lifestyles are, the time it saves them is probably worth more to them than the price of a stamp. Not only that, but trying to decipher someone's handwritten name and address can be very frustrating. Sometimes even zip codes are unreadable, and even more time is required to double check zip code numbers. And in the end, if 'Rosen' becomes 'Rirer' and 'Ave. 5' becomes 'Ave. S,' even if the person you contacted was gracious enough to answer you, you probably won't ever know he did. Many of these people are professional appraisers and there will be a fee for their time and service. Find out up front. Include a clear photo if you want an item identified. Most items cannot be described clearly enough to make an identification without a photo.

If you call and get their answering machine, when you leave your number so that they can return your call, tell them to call back collect. And please take the differences in time zones into consideration. 7:00 AM in the Midwest is only 4:00 AM in California! And if you're in California, remember that even 7:00 PM is too late to call the East Coast. Most people work and are gone during the daytime. Even some of our antique dealers say they prefer after-work phone calls. Don't assume that a person who deals in a particular field will be able to help you with related items. They may seem related to you when they are not.

Please, we need your help. This book sells in such great numbers that allowing their names to be published can create a potential nightmare for each advisor and contributor. Please do your part to help us minimize this, so that we can retain them on our board and in turn pass their experience and knowledge on to you through our book. Their only obligation is to advise us, not to evaluate your holdings. Many of our people tell us that even with the occasional problem, they feel that the good outweighs the bad and makes all their hard work worthwhile.

Alabama

Cataldo, Gene
C.E. Cataldo
4726 Panorama Dr., S.E., Huntsville, 35801; 256-536-6893; e-mail: genecams@aol.com. Specializing in classic and used cameras

Donnelly, Ron
Saturday Heroes
6302 Championship Dr., Tuscaloosa, 35405. Specializing in Big Little Books, movie posters, premiums, western heroes, Gone With the Wind, character collectibles, early Disney; Inquiries require SASE; No free appraisals

Lippa, Matt; and Schaaf, Elizabeth
Artisans
PO Box 256, Mentone, 35984; 256-634-4037; website: www.folkartisans.com or e-mail: artisans@folkartisans.com. Specializing in folk art, quilts, painted and folky furniture, tramp art, whirligigs, windmill weights

Walthall, Judith and Robert
PO Box 4465, Huntsville, 35815; 256-881-9198. Judith founded Peanut Pals in 1978. Robert is serving second term as president of Peanut Pals. Specializing in Planters Peanuts memorabilia; also Old Crow collectibles

Arizona

Nelson, Maxine
7657 E. Hazelwood St., Scottsdale, 85251. Specializing in Vernon Kilns; Author of *Collectible Vernon Kilns* (out of print). SASE appreciated for inquiries.

Webb, Maret
Vehr/Webb Studio Architects
4118 E. Vernon Ave., Phoenix, 85008-2333; 602-957-0653 or fax 602-957-1631. Specializing in Swarovski crystal; Founder of Swan Seekers Network

Arkansas

Dryden, James
Dryden Pottery
PO Box 603, Hot Springs National Park, 71902; 501-627-4201. Specializing in hand-thrown artware vases, mugs, ovenware, etc.

Freyaldenhoven, Tony
PO Box 1295, Conway, 72033; 501-329-0628 or e-mail: camarket@cyber-back.com. Specializing in Camark pottery

Musgrave, Marge
Look Nook Antiques
10757 Hwy. 5-S, Salesville, 72653-9698; 870-499-5283. Specializing in colored Victorian and art glass

Roenigk, Martin
Crescent Hotel & Spa
75 Prospect St., Eureka Springs, 72632; 800-671-6333; e-mail: mroenigk@aol.com. Specializing in mechanical musical instruments, music boxes, band organs, musical clocks and watches, coin pianos, orchestrions, monkey organs, automata, mechanical birds and dolls, etc.

Yohe, Darlene
Timberview Antiques
PO Box 343, Stuttgart, 72160; 870-673-3437. Specializing in American pattern glass, historical glass, Victorian pattern glass, carnival glass, and custard glass

California

Andrews, Dan
27105 Shorewood Rd., Rancho Palos Verdes, 90275; 310-541-5149 or e-mail: brewpub@earthlink.net. Specializing in beer cans, breweriana

At Merri's House
74300 Highway 111
Palm Desert, 92260

Berg, Paul
PO Box 8895, Newport Beach, 92620. Author of *Nineteenth Century Photographica Cases and Wall Frames*

Brooks, Mike
7355 Skyline, Oakland, 94611; 510-339-1751 (evenings). Specializing in typewriters, transistor radios, early televisions, Statue of Liberty

Butz, Robert C.
Collector's Wedgwood
PO Box 462, Newbury Park, 91319. Specializing in Wedgwood (**no dinnerware**); SASE required for reply

Carter, Tina M.
882 S. Mollison, El Cajon, 92020; 619-440-5043. Specializing in teapots, tea-related items, tea tins, children's and toy tea sets, plastic cookie cutters, etc.; Book on teapots available; send $16 (includes postage) or $17 for CA residents, Canada: add $5, to above address.

Chipman, Jack
California Spectrum
PO Box 1079, Venice, 90294-1079. Specializing in California ceramics; author of *Collector's Encyclopedia of California Pottery*, and *Collector's Encyclopedia of Bauer Pottery*, autographed copies available from author; either book: $28.45 ppd., +(CA) tax of $2.35

Christensen, Pat and Chris
1067 Salvador St., Costa Mesa, 92626. Specializing in open salts

Cohen, Wilfred and Dolli
Antiques & Art Glass
PO Box 27151, Santa Ana, 92799; 714-545-5673; e-mail: antsandartglass@aol.com. Specializing in Wave Crest (C.F. Monroe); French cameo glass; Victorian-era art and pattern glass (salt shakers, toothpick holders, syrups, cruets, sugar shakers, tumblers, biscuit jars, table and pitcher sets); art glass and cameo glass open salts; custard and ruby-stained glass; burmese, peachblow and amberina glass; pottery by Moorcroft (pre-1935 only); Buffalo (Deldare and Emerald ware); Polia Pillin; Shelley China; Chintz China; and Clarice Cliff. Please include SASE for reply; a photo is very helpful for identification.

Conroy, Barbara J.
PO Box 2369, Santa Clara, 95055-2369; e-mail: restaurantchina@earthlink.net. Specializing in Commercial China; author and historian

Cox, Susan N.
800 Murray Drive, El Cajon, 92020; 619-697-5922; e-mail: antiqfever@aol.com. Specializing in California pottery and Frankoma

Ehrhard, J. David
Psycho-Ceramic Restorations
7212 Valmont St., Tujunga, 91042. Specializing in restoration of ceramics, collects Susie Cooper and other British pottery, Mabel Lucie Attwell, 'Old Bill' china by Grimades, etc., Artist: Bruce Bairnsfather

Ellis, Michael L.
266 Rose Ln., Costa Mesa, 92627; 949-646-7112; fax: 949-645-4919; Toll free (book orders): 877-646-7119. Author (Collector Books) of *Collector's Guide to Don Winton Designs, Identification & Values*; Specializing in Twin Winton

Enge, Delleen
Franciscan Dinnerware Matching Service
323 E. Matilija, Ste. 112, Ojai, 93023

Fogleman, Marv
Marv's Memories
1814 W. Carriage Dr., Santa Ana, 92704. Specializing in Western Dinnerware, Metlox, Mikasa, and Franciscan

George, Tony
22431-B160 Antonio Pkwy., #252, Rancho Santa Margarita, 92688; 714-589-6075. Specializing in watch fobs

Gibson, Pat
38280 Guava Dr., Newark, 94560; 510-792-0586. Specializing in R.A. Fox

Gunther, Candace (Candelaine)
Phone: 626-796-4568; fax: 626-796-7172; e-mail: candelaine@aol.com. Specializing in Steiff and Schuco bears and animals; send SASE for list

Harrison, Gwynne
PO Box 1, Mira Loma, 91752-0001; 951-685-5434; e-mail: morgan99@pe.net. Specializing in Autumn Leaf (Jewel Tea)

Hibbard, Suzi
WanderWares
E-mail: SRHACS@Pacbell.net. Specializing in Dragon ware and 1000 Faces china

Howard, Steve
Past Tyme Pleasures
PMB #204, 2491 San Ramon Valley Blvd., Suite #1, San Ramon, 94583; 925-484-4488 or fax 925-484-2551. Specializing in antique American firearms, bowie knives, Western Americana, old advertising, vintage gambling items, barber and saloon items

Main Street Antique Mall
237 E Main St., El Cajon, 92020; 619-447-0800

Martin, Betty
PO Box 1616; Santa Ynez, CA 93460. Collector of Borsato figures

Maurer, Oveda L.
Oveda Maurer Antiques
34 Greenfield Ave., San Anselmo, 94960; 415-454-6439. Specializing in 18th-century and early 19th-century American furniture, lighting, pewter, hearthware, glass, folk art, and paintings

The Meadows Collection
Mark and Adela Meadows
PO Box 819, Carnelian Bay, 96104; 530-546-5516; e-mail: meadows@cwo.com. Specializing in Gouda and Quimper; lecturers, authors of *Quimper Pottery, A guide to Origins, Styles, and Values*, serving on the board of directors of the Associated Antiques Dealers of America. Please include SASE for inquiries.

Needham, Leonard
118 Warwick Dr. #48
Benicia, 94510; 707-748-4286; website: www.tias.com/stores/macadams. Specializing in automobiles

Pardini, Dick
3107 N. El Dorado St., Dept. SAPG, Stockton, 95204-3412; 209-466-5550 (recorder may answer). Specializing in California Perfume Company items dating from 1886 to 1928 and 'go-with' related companies: buyer and information center. Not interested in items that have Avon, Perfection, or Anniversary Keepsake markings. California Perfume Company offerings must be accompanied by a photo, photocopy, or sketching along with a condition report and, most importantly, price wanted. Inquiries require large SASE and must state what information you are seeking; not necessary if offering items for sale.

Pasquali, Jim
479 Church #4, San Francisco, 94114; 415-861-4184. Author of *Sanfords Guide to Garden City Pottery, A Hidden Treasure of Northern California*

Roller, Gayle
PO Box 222, San Marcos, 92079-0222. Specializing in Hagen-Renaker

Rosewitz, Michele
3165 McKinley, San Bernardino, 92404; 909-862-8534; e-mail: rosetree@sprintmail.com. Specializing in glass knives manufactured in the USA during the 1920s through the 1950s. All requests for information should include a SASE.

Sanford, Steve and Martha
230 Harrison Ave., Campbell, 95008; 408-978-8408. Authors of 2 books on Brush-McCoy and *Sanford's Guide to McCoy Pottery* (available from the authors)

Shrader, Fred and Lila
Shrader Antiques
2025 Hwy. 199, Crescent City, 95531; 707-458-3525. Specializing in railroad, steamship and other transportation memorabilia; Shelley china (and its predecessor, Foley China); Buffalo china and Buffalo Pottery including Deldare; Niloak, and Zell (and Haag)

Stella's Collectibles
Pieces of the Past
19032 S. Vermont Ave., Gardena, (Space 11), 90248; 310-316-7198; Julie's Antiques, Long Beach (Space 24); Westchester Faire Mall (Space 320); Enchanted Treasures, Lake Elsinore (Space 25); Collector's Corral, Lake Elsinore. Specializing in quality glass and china

Stillwell, Liz
Our Attic Antiques & Belleek
PO Box 1074, Pico Rivera, 90660; 323-257-3879 or 562-949-0592. Specializing in Irish and American Belleek

Tanner, Joseph and Pamela
Wheeler-Tanner Escapes
6442 Canyon Creek Way, Elk Grove, 95758-5431; 916-684-4006. Specializing in handcuffs, leg shackles, balls and chains, restraints, and non-lockng devices; also Houdini memborabilia, autographs, photos, books, letters, etc.

Thoerner, Sharon
15549 Ryon Ave., Bellflower, 90706; 562-866-1555. Specializing in covered animal dishes, powder jars with animal and human figures, slag glass

Thornton, Don
271 California Ave., Moss Beach, 94038; 650-728-7978; e-mail: THORNTON-HOUSE.COM. Specializing in egg beaters and apple parers; author of *The Eggbeater Chronicles, 2nd Edition* ($50.45 ppd.); and *Apple Parers* ($59 ppd.)

Webb, Frances Finch
1589 Gretel Lane, Mountain View, 94040. Specializing in Kay Finch ceramics

Canada

Brown, David L.
Stevengraph Collectors Assn.
2103-2829 Arbutus Rd., Victoria, British Columbia, V8N 5X5; 250-477-9896. Specializing in Stevengraphs

Melis, Mirko
Marcelle Antiques
PO Box 53039, 5100 Erin Mills Pkwy., Mississauga, Ontario, L5M 4Z5; 905-689-1648. Specializing in American and European art glass, Russian works of art (enamels, porcelains, silver, etc.), English and Continental glass and china; Member of Antique Appraisal Association of America, Inc., and AADA (Associated Antique Dealers of America, Inc.)

Warner, Ian
PO Box 93022, 499 Main St. S., Brampton, Ontario, L6Y 4V8; 905-453-9074 or fax: 905-453-2931. Specializing in Wade porcelain and Swankyswigs, author of *The World of Wade, The World of Wade Book 2, Wade Price Trends*, and *The World of Head Vase Planters*, Co-author: Mike Posgay

Colorado

Heck, Carl
Carl Heck Decorative Arts
Box 8416, Aspen, 81612; Phone/fax: 970-925-8011; www.carlheck.com. Specializing in original Tiffany lamps, art glass, windows and chandeliers; Also reverse-painted and leaded-glass table lamps, stained and beveled glass windows, bronzes, paintings, etc.; Buy and sell; Fee for written appraisals. Please include SASE for reply.

Mackin, Bill
Author of *Cowboy and Gunfighter Collectibles;* available from author: 1137 Washington St., Craig, 81625; 970-824-6717. Paperback: $25; Other titles available; Specializing in old and fine spurs, guns, gun leather, cowboy gear, Western Americana (Collection in the Museum of Northwest Colorado, Craig)

Over, Naomi L.
8909 Sharon Lane, Arvada, 80002; 303-424-5922. Specializing in ruby glassware, author of *Ruby Glass of the 20th Century, Book I*, autographed copies available from author for $25.00 softbound or $32.50 hardbound, ppd.; Book II available (1999 values) for $32.50 softbound or $42.50 hardbound, ppd. Naomi will attempt to make photo identifications for all who include a SASE with correspondence.

Segelke, Cathy; and James, Pat
970-847-3759 (Pat). Specializing in crocks, Western Pottery Mfg. Co. (Denver, CO)

Toohey, Marlena
703 S. Pratt Pky., Longmont, 80501; 303-678-9726. Specializing in black glass (buy, sell, or trade); Books available from author: Book 1 (over 600 colored pictures, descriptions and price guide), $23 ppd.; Book 2 (over 1,200 colored pictures, descriptions and price guide), $33 ppd

White, John 'Grandpa'
Grandpa's Depot
6720 E. Mississippi Ave., Unit B, Denver, 80224; 303-300-3984 or 303-758-8540. Specializing in railroad-related items; Catalogs available

Winther, Jo Ellen
8449 W. 75th Way, Arvada, 80005; 800-872-2345 or 303-421-2371. Specializing in Coors

Connecticut

Bondhus, Sandra V.
Box 100, Unionville, 06085; 860-678-1808. Author of *Quimper Pottery: A French Folk Art Faience;* Specializing in Quimper pottery

FDS Antiques, Inc.
62 Blue Ridge Dr., Stamford, 06903-4923. Publishes *The 'No Nonsense' Antique Mall Directory*, a directory of antique malls, centers, and multi-dealer co-ops; Over 4,700 listings listed according to state

Fink, Paul
Fun & Games
PO Box 488, Kent, 06757; 860-927-4001. Specializing in board games

Guido, Karen M.
Karen Michelle
PO Box 489, Bridgewater, 06752. Specializing in tiles; Buy & sell; Books on tiles available, many out of print. Fee for written appraisal; please include SASE for inquiries.

Kilbride, Mrs. Richard J.
81 Willard Terrace, Stamford, 06903; 203-322-0568. Has available for sale: *Art Deco Chrome, The Chase Era*, and *Art Deco Chrome, Book 2, A Collector's Guide, Industrial Design in the Chase Era*

Lehrer, Gary
16 Mulberry Road
Woodbridge 06525-1717; 203-389-5295. Specializing in pens and pencils. Catalog available

MacSorley, Earl
823 Indian Hill Rd., Orange, 06477; 203-387-1793 (after 7:00 p.m.). Specializing in nutcrackers, Bessie Pease Gutmann prints, figural lift-top spittoons

Postcards International
Martin J. Shapiro
2321 Whitney Ave., Suite 102, PO Box 185398, Hamden, 06518;203-248-6621 or fax 203-248-6628; www.vintagepostcards.com. Specializing in vintage picture postcards

Thalberg, Bruce
Mountain View Dr., Weston, 06883; 203-227-8175. Specializing in canes and walking sticks: novelty, carved, and Black

Van Deusen, Hobart D.
28 The Green, Watertown, 06795; 860-945-3456. Specializing in Canton, SASE required when requesting information

Vuono, Mark
16 6th St., Stamford, 06905; 203-357-0892 (10 a.m. to 5:30 p.m. E.S.T.). Specializing in historical flasks, blown 3-mold glass, blown American glass

District of Columbia

Durham, Ken & Jackie (By appointment)
909 26 St. N.W., Suite 502, Washington, D.C. 20037; website: www.GameRoomAntiques.com. Specializing in slot machines, jukeboxes, arcade machines, trade stimulators, vending machines and service manuals

Florida

Bettinger, Robert
PO Box 333, Mt. Dora, 32756; 352-735-3575. Specializing in American art pottery

Dumont, Louise
318 Palo Verde Dr., Leesburg 34748. Specializing in cookie jars, Abingdon

Dodds, Rebecca
Silver Flute
PO Box 670664, Coral Springs, 33067. Specializing in jewelry

Elsner, Dr. Robert
29 Clubhouse Lane, Boynton Beach, 33436; 561-736-1362. Specializing in antique barometers and nautical instruments

France, Madeleine
PO Box 15555, Ft. Lauderdale, 33318; 305-584-0009. Specializing in top-quality perfume bottles: Rene Lalique, Steuben, Czechoslovakian, DeVilbiss, Baccarat, Commercials; French dore bronze and decorative arts

Hudson, Hardy
Our Antiques Market
5453 Lake Howell Rd., Winter Park, 32792; 407-657-2100 from 11:00 a.m. to 6:00 p.m. or (Home) 407-647-3454; todiefor@mindspring.com. Specializing in majolica, American art pottery (buying one piece or entire collections); Also buying Weller (garden ornaments, birds, Hudson, Sicard, Sabrinian, Glendale, or animal related), Roseville, Grueby, Newcomb, Overbeck, Kay Finch, Clewell, Tiffany, etc.

Kamm, Dorothy
PO Box 7460, Port St. Lucie, 34985-7460; 561-465-4008 or fax 561-460-9050. Specializing in American painted porcelain; Author of *American Painted Porcelain: Identification & Value Guide* (Collector Books), and *Comprehensive Guide to American Painted Porcelain* (Antique Trader Books). Publishes *Dorothy Kamm's Porcelain Collector's Companion*, bimonthly newsletter, subscription: $28 per year

Kuritzky, Louis
4510 NW 17th Place, Gainesville, 32605; 352-377-3193. Author (Collector Books) of *Collector's Guide to Bookends*

Lawrence, Judy and Cliff
1169 Overcash Dr., Dunedin, 34698. Specializing in fountain pens and mechanical pencils

Linscott, Jacqueline C.
Line Jewels
3557 Nicklaus Dr., Titusville, 32780. Specializing in glass insulators and other telephone items. Distributor of the only known set of books dealing with insulators, *North American Glass Insulators* (2 volumes), and accompanying Price Guide; LSASE required for information

McNerny, Kathryn
118 Creek Hollow Lane, Middleburg, 32068. Author (Collector Books) on blue and white stoneware, primitives, tools

Posner, Judy
October - May: PO Box 2194 SC, Englewood, 34295, fax: 941-475-2645; e-mail: judyandjef@aol.com or www.judyposner.com. Specializing in Disneyana, Black memorabilia, salt and pepper shakers, souvenirs of the USA, character and advertising memorabilia, figural pottery; Buy, sell, collect; Informal appraisals: $5+LSASE and photo of item

Rolfes, Herbert
Yesterday's World
PO Box 398, Mt. Dora, 32756; 352-735-3947; e-mail: NY1939@aol.com. Specializing in World's Fairs and Expositions

Roush, Peggy E.
Peggy's Matching Service
PO Box 476, Ocala, 34478; 352-629-3954; e-mail: PegsMatch@worldnet.att.net. Specializing in discontinued Noritake patterns

Snyder-Haug, Diane
PO Box 815, St. Petersburg, 33731. Specializing in women's clothing, 1850–1940

Supnick, Mark
2771 Oakbrook Manor, Ft. Lauderdale, 33332. Author of *Collecting Hull Pottery's Little Red Riding Hood* ($12.95 ppd.); Specializing in American pottery

Vogel, Janice and Richard
4720 S.E. Fort King St., Ocala, 34470-1501. Authors of *Victorian Trinket Boxes*

White, Douglass
Classic Interiors & Antiques
2042 N. Rio Grande Ave., Suite E, Orlando, 32804; 407-839-0004. Specializing in Fulper, Arts & Crafts furniture (photos helpful)

Whysel, Steven
7867 N.W. 11th St., Plantation, 33322; 954-382-0008. Specializing in Art Nouveau, 19th- and 20th-century art

Wieland, Robert
American Antique Prints
33 South St. Andrews Drive, Ormond Beach, 32174; 904-672-9972. Specializing in early American prints: Currier & Ives, Kurz & Allison, and McKenny & Hall

Willis, Ron L.
PO Box 278, Matlacha, 33993; 941-282-5567. Specializing in military collectibles

Wise, Raphael C.
The Collector's Stop
12018 Suellen Circle, West Palm Beach, 33414; 561-793-0986. Specializing in Wedgwood Jasper Ware, Rosenthal (dogs & cats only), Moorcroft, Buffalo Deldare and Emerald Ware, Heisey, contemporary paperweights, English porcelains

Georgia

Bailey, Wayne and Gale
PO Box 173, Dacula, 30019; 770-963-5736. Specializing in Goebels (Friar Tuck)

Glenn, Walter
Geode Ltd.
3393 Peachtree Rd., Atlanta, 30326. Specializing in Frankart

Joiner, John R.
Aviation Collectors
173 Green Tree Dr., Newnan, 30265; 770-502-9565. Specializing in commercial aviation collectibles

Jones, Donald
107 Rivers Edge Dr., Savannah, 31406; 912-354-2133. Specializing in vintage tennis collectibles; SASE with inquiries please

Illinois

Ammelounx, Andre
The Stein Auction Company
PO Box 136, Palatine, 60078; 847-991-5927 or fax 847-991-5947. Specializing in steins, catalogs available

The Barrel Antique Mall
5850 S. St. Road, I-55 Exit 90, Springfield, 62707; 217-585-1438

Broom, Jim
Box 65, Effingham, 62401. Specializing in opalescent pattern glassware

Danis, John
11028 Raleigh Ct., Rockford, 61115; 815-877-2410 or fax: 815-877-6042; e-mail: danis6033@aol.com. Specializing in R. Lalique and Norse pottery

Feldman, Arthur M.
Arthur M. Feldman Gallery
1815 St. Johns Ave., Highland Park, 60035; 847-432-8858 or fax: 847-266-1199; website: judaicaconnection.com. Specializing in Judaica, fine art, and antiques

Frizzell, Doris
5687 Oakdale Dr., Springfield, 62707; 217-529-3873. Specializing in Royal Haeger and Maddux of California. Co-author (Collector Books) of Royal Haeger book. SASE required when requesting information.

Garmon, Lee
1529 Whittier St., Springfield, 62704; 217-789-9574. Specializing in Royal Haeger, Royal Hickman, glass animals; Co-author (Collector Books) of *Glass Animals and Figural Flower Frogs of the Depression Era*

Griffith, Woody
PO Box 408277, Chicago, 60640. Specializing in De Vilbiss perfumes and perfume lamps

Hall, Doris and Burdell
B&B Antiques
210 W. Sassafras Dr., Morton, 61550-1245. Authors of *Morton's Potteries: 99 Years* (Vols. I and II); Specializing in Morton pottery, American dinnerware, early American pattern glass, historical items

Hastings, Mary Jane
310 West 1st South, Mt. Olive, 62069; Phone/fax: 217-999-1222. Specializing in Chintz dinnerware

Hilst, Randy
1221 Florence #4, Pekin, 61554; 309-346-2710. Specializing in general line including fishing and hunting collectibles

Hoffmann, Pat and Don, Sr.
1291 N. Elmwood Dr., Aurora, 60506-1309; 630-859-3435; www.skognet.com/~warwick/. Authors of *Warwick, A to W*, a supplement to *Why Not Warwick?*; video regarding Warwick decals currently available

The Home Place Antiques
Durham, William; Galaway, William
615 S. State St., Belvidiere, 61008; 815-544-0577. Specializing in Tea Leaf ironstone and white ironstone

Hooks, Dee
Dee's China Shop
13050 Blackstump Rd., Percy, 62272; 618-965-3832. Specializing in R.S. Prussia, Royal Bayreuth, Haviland, other fine china

Hopp, Dennis Carl
Midcentury
Chicago, 773-935-7872. Specializing in 20th-century design, glass, pottery, metal, art

Hurney, George and Mary
Glass Connection (Mail-order only)
312 Babcock Dr., Palatine, 50067; 847-359-3839; website: www.dealersdirect.com/ or e-mail: glasscon@voyager.net. Specializing in Depression Glass and Paden City glass (not advising on pottery)

The Illinois Antique Center
320 S.W. Commercial St., Peoria, IL 61602

John Toomey Gallery
818 N. Blvd, Oak Park, 60301

Long, Dee
112 S. Center, Lacon, 61540. Specializing in reamers

Lubliner, Larry
Refinders mail/telephone auction
737 Barberry Rd., Highland Park, 60035; 708-831-1102 or 708-831-1160. Refinders will find your wants from 1860 – 1960

Martin, Jim
R.R. 1, 1091 215th Ave., Monmouth, 61462; 309-734-2703. Specializing in Old Sleepy Eye, Monmouth pottery, Western Stoneware

Meyer, Larry
4001 Elmwood, Stickney, 60402; 708-749-1564; e-mail: lmeyer1212@aol.com. Specializing in fire grenades and extinguishers

Miller, Larry; and Strickfaden, Dick
218 Devron Circle, E. Peoria, 61611-1605. Specializing in German and Czechoslovakian Erphila

Ochsner, Grace
Grace Ochsner Doll House
1636 E. County Rd. 2700, Niota, 62358; 217-755-4362. Specializing in piano babies, bisque German dolls

Owen, Larry and Sally
Specializing in Morten Studio dogs, etc.

Randy's Ol' Time Collectibles
Illinois Antique Center
308 S.W. Commercial, Peoria, 61602; 309-346-2710. Specializing in general line, including hunting and fishing collectibles

Rastello, Lisa
Milkweed Antiques
5N531 Ancient Oak Lane, St. Charles, 60175; 630-377-4612. Specializing in Depression-Era collectibles

Rhoden, Joan and Charles
Rhoden Books & Publishing
8693 N. 1950 East Rd., Georgetown, 61846-6264; 217-662-8046; e-mail: rhoden@soltec.net or website: www/antiqueref.com. Specializing in new reference books on antiques and collectibles, Heisey and other Elegant Glassware, spice tins, lard tins and Yard-Long Prints. Co-authors of *Those Wonderful Yard-Long Prints and More*, and *More Wonderful Yard-Long Prints, Book II*, and *Yard-Long Prints, Book III*, illustrated value guides.

Rodgers, Joanne
Stretch Glass Society
PO Box 573, Hampshire, 60140. Membership: $22 per year; Quarterly newsletter with color photos; Annual Spring convention

Schwab, Betty and Larry
The Paperweight Shoppe
2507 Newport Dr., Bloomington, 61704; 309-662-1956; e-mail: PAPERWGT1@aol.com. Specializing in glass paperweights

Spencer, Dick
Glass and More (Shows only)
1203 N. Yale, O'Fallon, 62269; 618-632-9067. Specializing in Cambridge, Fenton, Fostoria, Heisey, etc.

Spiess, Greg
230 E. Washington, Joliet, 60433; 815-722-5639; e-mail: spiessantq@aol.com. Specializing in Odd Fellows lodge items

Stifter, Craig
PO Box 6514, Naperville, 60540; 630-789-5780; Mobile phone: 630-939-7479; e-mail: cocacola@enteract.com. Specializing in Coca-Cola, Pepsi-Cola, Orange Crush, Dr. Pepper, Hires and other soda-pop brand collectibles

TV Guide Specialists
Box 20, Macomb 61455; 309-833-1809

Waite, Jim
112 N. Main St., Farmer City, 61842; 800-842-2593. Specializing in Sebastians

Wilson, Jack D.
3926 N. Keeler, Chicago, 60641-2915; 773-282-9553; e-mail: jdwilson1@earthlink.net; website: home.earthlink.net/~jdwilson1/. Specializing in Phoenix and Consolidated glass; Buying Ruba Rombic; Author of *Phoenix & Consolidated Art Glass: 1926 – 1980*

Yester-Daze Glass
c/o Illinois Antique Center
320 S.W. Commercial St., Peoria, 61604; 309-347-1679. Specializing in glass from the 1920s, '30s and '40s; Fiesta; Hall; Pie Birds; Sprinkler Bottles; and Florence figurines

Indiana

AAA Antique Shop
US 6 West, Nappanee, 46550; 219-773-4912. Specializing in trunks

Alexander, Charles
221 E. 34th St., Indianapolis, 46205; 317-924-9665. Specializing in American dinnerware

Boram, Clifford
Antique Stove Information Clearinghouse
Monticello; Free consultation by phone only: 219-583-6465

Crossroads Antique Mall
311 Holiday Square, Seymour, 47274; 812-522-5675. Open 7 days a week

Dilley, David
PO Box 225, Indianapolis, 46206; 317-251-0575; e-mail: glazebears@aol.com or bearpots@aol.com. Specializing in Royal Haeger and Royal Hickman

Edwards, Bill
620 W. 2nd, Madison, 47250. Author (Collector Books) on carnival glass

Egelhoff, Larry
Still Bank Collectors Club of America
4175 Millersville Rd., Indianapolis, 46205; 317-846-7228. Specializing in still banks, safe banks, antique safes

Freese, Carol and Warner
House With the Lions Antiques
On the Square; Covington, 47932. General line

Fred, James A.
Antique Radio Labs
5355 So. 275W, Cutler, 46920; 765-268-2214. Specializing in radios made from 1922 to 1950

Garrett, Jerry and Sandi
Jerry's Antiques (Shows only)
1807 W. Madison St., Kokomo, 46901; 765-457-5256. Specializing in Greentown glass, old postcards

Gilley's Antique Mall and Collectibles
1209 W. Main (US 40), Plainfield, 46168; 317-839-8779. Open daily from 10 a.m. to 5 p.m., features booths with over 250 dealers; Outdoor summer weekend flea market

Haun, Ted
2426 N. 700 East, Kokomo, 46901; 765-628-7028; e-mail: Sam17@webtv.net. Specializing in American pottery and china, '50s items, Russel Wright designs

Highfield, James
6301-D University Commons, South Bend, 46635; 219-272-4200. Specializing in relief-style Capo-di-Monte-style porcelain (Doccia, Ginori and Royal Naples)

Heiss, Virginia
7777 N. Alton Ave., Indianapolis, 46268; 317-875-6797. Specializing in Muncie, AMACO, Brandt Steele, Marblehead, Kenton Hills

Keagy, William and June
PO Box 106, Bloomfield, 47424; 812-384-3471. Co-authors of *Those Wonderful Yard-Long Prints and More*, *More Wonderful Yard-Long Prints, Book II*, and *Yard-Long Prints, Book III*, illustrated value guides

Kurella, Elizabeth
Box 244, Whiting, 46394; 219-659-1124; e-mail: ekurella@home.com. Specializing in lace, linens and needlework; Author of *The Complete Guide to Vintage Textiles* (Krause) and The Guide to Lace and Linens (Antique Trader, acquired by Krause)

Leslie, Beverly
Secretary/Treasurer of Uhl Collectors Society
801 Poplar St., Boonville, 47601; 812-897-3681. Contact for newsletter and membership information

McQuillen, Michael J. and Polly
McQuillen's Collectibles
PO Box 50022, Indianapolis, 46250-0022; 317-845-1721; e-mail: buttons@oaktree.net or website: www.politicalparade.com. Writer of column, *Political Parade*, which appears monthly in *AntiqueWeek* other newspapers; Specializing in political memorabilia, Kentucky Derby items and sports memorabilia; Buys and sells

Pruitt, Ted
3350 W. 700 N., Anderson, 46011. *St. Clair Glass Collector's Book*, available ($15 ea) from Ted at above address

Ricketts, Vicki
Covington Antique Company
6431 W US Highway 136
Covington 47932. General line

Scowden, Virgil
Williamsport, 47993; 317-762-3408 or 317-762-3178. Antiques museum, general line, tours

Slater, Thomas D.
Slater's Americana
1325 W. 86th St., Indianapolis, 46260; 317-257-0863. Specializing in political and sports memorabilia

Stofft, Jeanette
Marnette Antiques
Tell City, 47586; 812-547-5707. Specializing in Ohio art pottery, buy and sell; No phone appraisals; SASE required

Swayzee Antique Mall
115 N. Washington St., Swayzee, 46986; 317-922-7903

Webb's Antique Mall
over 400 Quality Dealers
200 W. Union St., Centerville, 47330

Wright, Bill
325 Shady Dr., New Albany, 47150. Specializing in knives: Bowie, hunting, military, and pocketknives

Iowa

Addy, Geneva D.
PO Box 124, Winterset, 50273; 515-462-3027

Ambrose, Craig
3717 6th Ave., Apt. 244, Des Moines, 50313; 515-288-4595. Specializing in quilts; Author of *Picture Book and Price Guide to Antique Quilts*, available from author for $45 +postage

Arnbal, Una
Woodland Antiques
242 Trail Ridge Rd., Ames, 50014; 515-292-1005. Specializing in Lomonosov figurines, Danish collector plates

The Baggage Car
Hal and Meredith DeGood
3100 Justin Dr., Ste. B; Des Moines 50322; 515-270-9080; e-mail: baggagecar@aol.com. Specializing in Hallmark ornaments, cookie cutters, etc.; Publishes Hallmark newsletter and list

Beeks, Dale
PO Box 117, Mt. Vernon, 52314; 319-895-0506; e-mail: dbeeksci@aol.com. Specializing in instruments of science technology and medicine, also surveying instruments and microscopes

Bilsland, William M., III
PO Box 2671, Cedar Rapids, 52406-2671; 319-368-0658. Specializing in American art pottery

Devine, Dennis, Norman, and Joe
D & D Antique Mall
1411 3rd St., Council Bluffs, 51503; 712-323-5233 or 712-328-7305. Specializing in furniture, phonographs, collectibles, general line; Joe Devine: Royal Copley and other types of pottery (collector), author of *Collector's Guide to Royal Copley Plus Royal Windsor & Spauldins*, Books I and II

Dollen, Brenda
210 Benton St., Council Bluffs, 51503. Specializing in Red Wing pottery; Co-author (with R.L. Dollen) of *Red Wing Art Pottery*, Books I and II (Collector Books)

Jaarsma, Ralph
De Pelikaan Antieks
812 Washington St., c/o Red Ribbon Antique Mall, Pella, 50219. Specializing in Dutch antiques; SASE required when requesting information

Picek, Louis
Main Street Antiques
110 W. Main St., Box 340, West Branch, 52358. Specializing in folk art, country Americana, the unusual

Westmoreland Glass Society
Jim Fisher, President
513 5th Ave., Coralville, 52241; 319-354-5011. Membership: $15 (single) or $25 (household)

Kansas

Anthony, Dorothy Malone
World of Bells Publications
2401 S. Horton, Fort Scott, 66701; 316-223-3404. Specializing in publishing and selling books on all types of small bells

Maundy International
PO Box 13028-GG, Shawnee Mission, 66282; 1-800-235-2866. Specializing in watches — antique pocket and vintage wristwatches

Old World Antiques
4436 State Line Rd., Kansas City, 66103; 913-677-4744 or fax 913-677-4879. Specializing in 18th- and 19th-century furniture, paintings, accessories, clocks, chandeliers, sconces, and much more

Smies, David
Pops Collectibles
Box 522, 315 So. 4th, Manhattan, 66502; 913-776-1433. Specializing in coins, stamps, cards, tokens, Masonic collectibles

Street, Patti
Currier & Ives (China) Quarterly Newsletter
PO Box 504, Riverton, 66770; 316-848-3529. Subscription: $12 per year (includes 2 free ads)

Tinsley, Rosella
105 15th St., Osawatomie, 66064; 913-755-3237. Specializing in primitives, kitchen, woodenware, and miscellaneous (phone calls only, no letters please)

Kentucky

Courter, J.W.
3935 Kelley Rd., Kevil, 42053; 270-488-2116. Specializing in Aladdin lamps; Author of *Aladdin — The Magic Name in Lamps, Revised Edition*, hardbound, 304 pages; *Aladdin Electric Lamps*, softbound, 229 pages; and *Angle Lamps Collectors Manual & Price Guide*, softbound, 48 pages

Florence, Gene
Box 7186H, Lexington, 40522. Author (Collector Books) on Depression Glass, Occupied Japan; Elegant Glass, Kitchen Glassware

Hornback, Betty
Betty's Antiques
707 Sunrise Lane, Elizabethtown, 42701. Specializing in Kentucky Derby glasses

Johnson, Wes, Sr.
3606 Glenview Ave., Glenview, 40025. Specializing in Cracker Jack: toys, point of sale, packages, etc.; Checkers Confection, Schoenhut toys, Victor Toy Oats, Universal Theatre (Chicago), old toys; Please include SASE

Ritchie, Roy B.
PO Box 384, Hindman, 41822; 606-785-5796. Co-author of *Standard Knife Collector's Guide* and *Standard Guide to Razors;* Specializing in razors and knives, all types of cutlery

Stewart, Ron
PO Box 151, Combs, 41729; 606-435-2412. Co-author of *Standard Knife Collector's Guide* and *Standard Guide to Razors;* Specializing in razors and knives, all types of cutlery

Willis, Roy M.
Heartland of Kentucky Decanters and Steins
PO Box 428, Lebanon Jct., 40150; website: www.ka.net/heartlandky. Huge selection of limited edition decanters and beer steins — open showroom. Include large self-addressed envelope (two stamps) with correspondence. Fee for appraisals. Decanter price guide (listings only, no pictures, information on marketing decanters): $9.50 ppd

Louisiana

Langford, Paris
Kollecting Kiddles
415 Dodge Ave., Jefferson, 70121; 504-733-0667; e-mail: BBEAN415@AOL.COM. Specializing in all small vinyl dolls of the '60s and '70s; Author of *Liddle Kiddles Identification and Value Guide* (now out of print). Please include SASE when requesting information. Contact for information concerning Liddle Kiddle convention to be held in Atlanta in the fall of 2000.

Maine

Blake, Brenda
Box 555, York Harbor, 03911; 207-363-6566; e-mail: Eggcentric@AOL.com. Specializing in egg cups

Hathaway, John
Hathaway's Antiques
3 Mills Rd., Bryant Pond, 04219; 207-665-2214. Specializing in fruit jars; Mail order a specialty

Hillman, Alma
Antiques at the Hillman's
362 E. Main St., Searsport, 04974; 207-548-6658. Co-author (Collector Books) of *Collector's Encyclopedia of Old Ivory China, the Mystery Explored, Identification & Values;* Specializing in Old Ivory China

Rinaldi, John
Nautical Antiques and Related Items
Box 765, Dock Square, Kennebunkport, 04046; 207-967-3218. Specializing in nautical antiques, scrimshaw, naval items, marine paintings, naval items, etc.; Fully illustrated catalog: $5

Zayic, Charles S.
Americana Advertising Art
PO Box 57, Ellsworth, 04605; 207-667-7342. Specializing in early magazines, early advertising art, illustrators

Maryland

Ezell, Elaine; & Newhouse, George
Cruets Cruets Cruets
PO Box 1609, Pasadena, 21123-1609; 410-551-4101 (daytime) or 410-255-6777. Specializing in cruets and glass

Humphrey, George C.
4932 Prince George Ave., Beltsville, 20705; 301-937-7899. Specializing in John Rogers groups

Katz, Jerome R.
Katz Collectibles
Antique Station, Frederick, 21702; 301-695-0888. Specializing in technological artifacts; Please include SASE when requesting information.

Meadows, John, Jean and Michael
Meadows House Antiques
919 Stiles St., Baltimore, 21202; 410-837-5427. Specializing in antique wicker furniture (rustic, twig, and old hickory), quilts and tramp art

Rudisill's Alt Print Haus
Rudisill, John and Barbara
PO Box 199, Worton, 21678; 410-778-9290; e-mail: Rudi@dmv.com or website: chesapeake-bay.com/altprinthaus. Specializing in Currier & Ives. Calls for information will be taken in return for a contribution (honor system) to the American Heart Association.

Screen, Harold and Joyce
2804 Munster Rd., Baltimore, 21234; 410-661-6765; e-mail: hscreen@home.com. Specializing in soda fountain 'tools of the trade' and paper: catalogs, 'Soda Fountain' magazines, etc.

Weisblut, Robert
International Ivory Society
11109 Nicholas Dr., Wheaton, 20902; 301-649-4002. Specializing in ivory carvings and utilitarian objects

Welsh, Joan
7015 Partridge Pl., Hyattsville, 20782; 301-779-6181. Specializing in Chintz; Author of *Chintz Ceramics*

Yalom, Libby
The Shoe Lady
PO Box 7146, Adelphi, 20783-2758; 301-422-2026. Specializing in glass and china shoes; Author of book

Massachusetts

Adams, Charles and Barbara
South Yarmouth, 02664; 508-760-3290 or (business) 508-587-5640. Specializing in Bennington (brown only)

Cooper, Ryan
205 White Rock Rd., Yarmouthport, 02675; 508-362-1604; e-mail: rcmaritime@capecod.net. Specializing in flags of historical significance and exceptional design

Dunbar's Gallery
Leila and Howard Dunbar
76 Haven St., Milford, 01757; 508-634-8697 or fax 508-634-8698; e-mail: Dunbars@mediaone.net or website: www.dumbarsgallery.com/. Specializing in advertising and toys

Ford, Frank W.
237-26 South Street; Shrewsbury, 01545. Specializing in Fostoria Specialty Company glassware

Frei, Peter
PO Box 500, Brimfield, 01010; 1-800-942-8968. Specializing in sewing machines (pre-1875, non-electric only), adding machines, typewriters, and hand-powered vacuum cleaners; SASE required with correspondence

Hess, John A.
Fine Photographic Americana
PO Box 3062, Andover, 01810. Specializing in 19th-century photography

Longo, Paul J.
Paul Longo Americana
Box 5510, Magnolia, 01930; 978-525-2290. Specializing in political pins, ribbons, banners, autographs, old stocks and bonds, baseball and sports memorabilia of all types

MacLean, Dale
183 Robert Rd., Dedham, 02026; 781-326-3010 or 781-329-1303 (evenings). Specializing in Dedham and Dorchester potteries

Morin, Albert
668 Robbins Ave. #23, Dracut, 01826; 978-454-7907. Specializing in miscellaneous Akro Agate and Westite

Steinbock, Nancy
Nancy Steinbock Posters
800-438-1577. Specializing in posters: travel, literary, advertising; Charter member of the IVPDA (International Vintage Poster Dealers Association)

Wellman, BA
PO Box 673, Westminster, 01473-0673; e-mail: bawellman@net1plus.com. Specializing in **all** areas of American ceramics, dinnerware, figurines, and art pottery

Michigan

Brown, Rick
Newspaper Collector's Society of America
Lansing, 517-887-1255; www.historybuff.com or e-mail: help@historybuff.com. Specializing in newspapers

Culver, Bob
Night Light Club
38619 Wakefield Ct., Northville, 48167; 248-473-8575. Specializing in miniature oil lamps

Gunsaulus, Jack
Gray's Gallery/Jack's Corner Bookstore
583 W. Ann Arbor Trail, Plymouth, 48170. Specializing in porcelain, books, jewelry, glass

Haas, Norman
264 Clizbe Rd., Quincy 49802; 517-639-8537. Specializing in American art pottery

Hogan & Woodworth
Walter P. Hogan and Wendy L. Woodworth
520 N. State, Ann Arbor, 48104; 313-930-1913; www.emunix.emich.edu~whogan/kellogg/index.html. Specializing in Kellogg Studio

Iannotti, Dan
212 W. Hickory Grove Rd., Bloomfield Hills, 48302-1127S. 248-335-5042; e-mail: modernbanks@ameritech.net. Specializing in modern mechanical cast-iron banks; Member of The Mechanical Bank Collectors of America

Krupka, Rod
2615 Echo Lane, Ortonville, 48462; 248-627-6351. Specializing in lightning rod balls

Marsh, Linda K.
1229 Gould Rd., Lansing, 48917. Specializing in Degenhart glass

Nedry, Boyd W.
728 Buth Dr., Comstock Park, 49321; 616-784-1513. Specializing in traps (including mice, rat, and fly traps) and trap-related items

Nickel, Mike
A Nickel's Worth
PO Box 456, Portland, 48875; 517-647-7646. Specializing in American Art Pottery: Roseville/Rozane, Weller, Rookwood, Kay Finch, Stangl and Pennsbury birds, Ceramic Art Studio, Josef and Florence figurines

Oates, Joan
685 S. Washington, Constantine, 49042; 616-435-8353; e-mail: koates@remc12.k12.mi.us. Specializing in Phoenix Bird chinaware

Rairigh, Glen
Americana Auctions
12633 Sandborn, Sunfield, 48990; 800-919-1950. Specializing in Skookum dolls and antique auctions

Ross, Michelle
PO Box 94, Berrien Center, 49102; 616-925-1604. Specializing in Van Briggle and American pottery

Webster, Marty
6943 Suncrest Drive, Saline, 48176; 313-944-1188. Specializing in California porcelain and pottery, Orientalia

Minnesota

Anderson, James
Box 120704, New Brighton, 55112; 651-484-3198. Specializing in old fishing lures and reels, also tackle catalogs, posters, calendars, Winchester items

Harrigan, John
1900 Hennepin, Minneapolis, 55403; 612-660-2794 or (in winter) 561-732-0525. Specializing in Battersea (English enamel) boxes, Moorcroft, and Toby jugs

Ketcham, Steve
Steve Ketcham Antiques (Shows and mail order only)
Box 24114, Edina, 55424; 952-920-4205; e-mail: s.ketcham@unique-software.com. Specializing in and buying early American bottles; Red Wing stoneware (no dinnerware); advertising signs, trays, trade cards, pocket mirrors, etched beer and shot glasses. Please include SASE for reply.

Koehn, Joanne M.
Temple's Antiques
PO Box 46237, Eden Prairie, 55344; 612-941-7641. Specializing in Victorian glass and china

Miller, Clark
4444 Garfield Ave., Minneapolis, 55409-1847; 612-827-6062. Specializing in Anton Lang pottery, American art pottery, Scandinavian glass and pottery

Nelson, C.L.
Box 222, Spring Park, 55384; 612-473-5625. Specializing in 18th-, 19th-, and 20th-century English pottery and porcelain, among others: Gaudy Welsh, ABC plates, relief-molded jugs, Staffordshire transfer ware

Putratz, Barb
Spring Lake Park, 612-784-0422. Specializing in Norman Rockwell

Schoneck, Steve
HG Handicraft Guild, Minneapolis
PO Box 56, Newport, 55055; 651-459-2980; Specializing in American art pottery, Arts & Crafts, HG Handicraft Guild Minneapolis

Missouri

Duncan, Pat and Ann
Box 175, Cape Fair, 65624; 417-538-2311. Specializing in Holt Howard, Lefton, Roseville, etc.

Gillespie, Steve, Publisher
Goofus Glass Gazette
400 Martin Blvd, Village of the Oaks, 64118; 888-452-5554 or fax 816-452-554; e-mail: goofus@mid-west.net. Specializing in Goofus Glass, curator of 'Goofus Glass Museum,' had 4,000+ piece collection of Goofus Glass; Buy, sell & collect Goofus for 30+ years; Expert contributor to forums on Goofus Glass; Contributor to website for Goofus Glass

Heuring, Jerry
28450 US Highway 61, Scott City, 63780; 573-264-3947. Specializing in Keen Kutter

International Rose O'Neill Club
Contact Karen Stewart
PO Box 668, Branson, 65616. Dues: $7 (single) or $10 (family) includes newsletter *Kewpiesta Kourier*, published quarterly

Roberts, Brenda
Country Side Antiques
906 South Ann Dr., Marshall, 65340. Specializing in Hull pottery and general line. Author of *Collectors Encyclopedia of Hull Pottery, Roberts' Ultimate Encyclopedia of Hull Pottery* and *The Companion Guide to Robert's Ultimate Encyclopedia of Hull Pottery*, all with accompanying price guides; SASE required

Siegel, Brenda and Jerry
Tower Grove Antiques
3308 Meramec, St. Louis, 63118; 314-352-9020. Specializing in Ungemach pottery

Scott, John and Peggy
Scotty's Antiques
4640 S. Leroy, Springfield, 65810; 417-887-2191. Specializing in Depression-era glassware and pottery, Florence Ceramics

Tarrant, Jenny
Holly Daze Antiques
4 Gardenview, St. Peters, 63376; e-mail: JennyJOL@aol.com or website: business.fortunecity.com/JV/712/index.htm. Specializing in early holiday items, Halloween, Christmas, Easter, etc.; Always buying Halloween collectibles (except masks and costumes) and German holiday candy containers

Wendel, David
F.E.I., Inc.
PO Box 1187, Poplar Bluff, 63902-1187; 573-686-1926. Specializing in Fraternal Elks collectibles

Wiesehan, Doug
D & R Farm Antiques
4535 Hwy. H, St. Charles, 63301. Specializing in salesman's samples and patent models, antique toys, farm toys, metal farm signs

Williams, Don
PO Box 147, Kirksville 63501; 660-627-8009 (between 8 a.m. and 6 p.m. only). Specializing in art glass; SASE required with all correspondence

Winslow, Ralph
Box 1175, Laurie, 65038. Specializing in Dryden Pottery

Nebraska

Larsen, Robert V.
3214 19th St., Columbus, 68601. Specializing in old hatpins and hatpin holders; Please include SASE when requesting information

Neely, Nancee P.
16592 Hascall, Omaha, 68130; 402-330-7033. Specializing in Fairing boxes

Nevada

Grindberg, Susan
1412 Pathfinder Rd., Henderson, 89014; 702-898-7535; e-mail: sue@porcelierconnection.com; or website: www.porcelierconnection.com. Collector book author of *Collector's Guide to Porcelier China, Identification and Values*

New Hampshire

Apakarian-Russell, Pamela
Halloween Queen Antiques
PO Box 499, Winchester, 03470. Specializing in Halloween (and other holidays) and postcards

Brenner, Larry
Brenner Antiques
1005 Chestnut St., Manchester, 03104; 603-625-8203; e-mail: elberenee@aol.com. Specializing in Royal Bayreuth

Holt, Jane
Jane's Collectibles
PO Box 115, Derry, 03038. Specializing in Annalee Mobilitee Dolls

Winston, Nancy
Willow Hollow Antiques
648 1st N.H. Turnpike, Northwood, 03261; 603-942-5739. Specializing in Shaker smalls, primitives, iron, copper, stoneware, and baskets

New Jersey

Anderson, Suzy McLennan
Heritage Antiques & Appraisal Services
65 E. Main St., Holmdel, 07733; 908-946-8801 or fax 908-946-1036. Specializing in American furniture and decorative accessories. Please include photo and SASE when requesting information. Appraisals and identification are impossible to do over the phone.

Bilane, John E. (Mail order only)
2065 Morris Ave., Apt. 109, Union, 07083. Specializing in antique glass cup plates

Dezso, Doug
864 Paterson Ave., Maywood, 07607-2119; 201-488-1311. Specializing in nodders (comic German), glass candy containers, Tonka; SASE required for information

Doorstop Collectors of America
Doorstopper Newsletter
Jeanie Bertoia
2413 Madison Ave., Vineland, 08630; 609-692-4092. Membership: $20 per year, includes 2 newsletters and convention. Send 2-stamp SASE for sample.

George, Dr. Joan M.
ABC Collector's Circle Newsletter
67 Stevens Ave., Old Bridge, 08857; fax: 732-679-6102 or e-mail: drgeorge@nac.net. Specializing in educational china (particularly ABC plates and mugs)

Harran, Jim and Susan
208 Hemlock Dr., Neptune, 07753; 732-922-2825; www.tias.com/stores/amit. Specializing in English and Continental porcelains with emphasis on antique cups and saucers; Author of *Collectible Cups and Saucers, Identification and Values, Book I & II* (Collector Books); Available for $20.95 ppd

Litts, Elyce
PO Box 394, Morris Plains, 07950; 973-361-4087; e-mail: happy-memories@worldnet.att.net. Author (Collector Books) of *Collector's Encyclopedia of Geisha Girl Porcelain* (Out of print. Ask your reference librarian or used bookstore to secure you a copy.)

Lockwood, Howard J.; Publisher
Vetri: Italian Glass News
Box 191, Fort Lee, 07024; 201-969-0373. Specializing in Italian glass of the 20th century

Meschi, Edward J.
129 Pinyard Rd., Monroeville, 08343; Phone/fax: 609-358-7293. Specializing in Durand art glass, Icart etchings, Maxfield Parrish prints, Rookwood pottery, occupational shaving mugs, oil paintings, and other fine arts; Author of *Durand — The Man and His Glass*, available from author for $43 ppd

Middleton, Dave and Anne
Pot O' Gold Antiques
PO Box 124, Allenwood, 08720; 732-528-6648. Specializing in epergnes, historical and figural Staffordshire, Flow Blue, fine glass

Patalano, Diane. I.S.A.
Appraisals, Liquidations and Auctions
PO Box 144, Saddle River, 07458. Specializing in banks, Black Americana, furniture, spatterware, various antiques and collectibles

Perzel, Robert and Nancy
Popkorn
3 Mine St. (near Main St.), PO Box 1057, Flemington, 08822; 908-782-9631. Specializing in Stangl dinnerware, birds, and artware; American pottery and dinnerware

Poster, Harry
Vintage TVs
Box 1883, S. Hackensack, 07606; Days: 201-794-9606; 24-Hour fax: 201-794-9553; www.harryposter.com. Writes *Poster's Radio and Television Price Guide*; Specializes in vintage televisions, transistor radios, 3-D stereo cameras; Catalog available online

Rago, David
333 N. Main St., Lambertville, 08530; 609-397-6780 or fax: 609-397-6790; website: www.ragoarts.com or e-mail: ragoarts@ragoarts.com. Specializing in Arts & Crafts, art pottery

Rash, Jim
135 Alder Ave., Egg Harbor Township, 08234; 609-646-4125. Specializing in advertising dolls

Rosen, Barbara
6 Shoshone Trail, Wayne, 07470. Specializing in figural bottle openers and antique dollhouses

Vines, Linda L.
Yesterday Once More
PO Box 43721, Upper Montclair, 07043; 973-748-4990; e-mail: lja@viconet.com. Specializing in Snow Babies, all holidays (Christmas, Easter, Halloween), dolls, toys, and Steiff

Visakay, Stephen
Vintage Cocktail Shakers (By appointment)
PO Box 1517, W. Caldwell, 07007-1517; e-mail: SVisakay@aol.com. Author of book and specializing in vintage cocktail shakers and bar ware

New Mexico

Hardisty, Don
Artistic Restorations
3020 E. Majestic Ridge, Las Cruces, 88011; For information and questions: 505-522-3721; fax: 505-522-7909; e-mail: donsbossons@zianet.com or visit Don's web page: www.zianet.com/donsbossons. Specializing in Bossons, Hummels, postcards, rare coins. Don's Collectibles carries a full line of current issues and most discontinued Bossons and Hummel figurines of all marks. Postcard inventory inclues over 500,000 with many original photo cards and all current issues of Legend (lot purchase offers now being accepted). When mail ordering Bossons and Hummels, you may dial toll free 800-267-7667. The book *The Imagical World of Bossons* (there are 2 volumes) is also available; call for further information.

Manns, William
PO Box 6459, Santa Fe, 87502; 505-995-0102; e-mail: zon@nets.com. Co-author of *Painted Ponies*, hardbound (226 pages), available from author for $40+$6 shipping; Specializing in carousel art and cowboy antiques

Moyer, Patsy
PO Box 311, Deming, 88031; 505-546-4019; fax: 505-546-5360; e-mail: sctrading@zianet.com. Collector Books author on dolls

Nelson, Scott H.
PO Box 6081, Santa Fe, 87502. Specializing in African art

New York

Austin, Bruce A.
1 Hardwood Hill Rd., Pittsford, 14534; 716-387-9820 (evenings); 716-475-2879 (week days); e-mail: bssgll@rit.edu. Specializing in clocks and Arts & Crafts furnishings and accessories including medalware, pottery, and lighting

Badders, Veldon
692 Martin Rd., Hamlin, 14464; 716-964-3360. Author (Collector Books) of *Collector's Guide to Inkwells, Identification & Values*; Specializing in inkwells

Calison, Jim
Tools of Distinction
Wallkill, 12589; 914-895-8035. Specializing in antique and collectible tools, buying and selling

Dimitroff, Thomas P.
Dimitroff's Antiques (Appointment only)
140 E. First St., Corning, 14830; 607-962-6745; e-mail: tdimi1@aol.com. Specializing in Steuben and cut glass

Doyle, Robert A.
Absolute Auction & Realty, Inc./ Pleasant Valley Auction Hall
PO Box 1739, Pleasant Valley, 12569; website: www.auctionweb.com/aar-ny. Antique and estate auctions twice a month at Pleasant Valley Auction Hall; Free calendar of auctions available

Endter, Barbara
29 Sandalwood Dr., Rochester, 14616-1513; 716-621-1433. Specializing in Chase Brass & Copper Company

Gerson, Roselyn
PO Box 40, Lynbrook, 11563; 516-593-8746. Author/collector specializing in unusual, gadgetry, figural compacts, vanity bags and purses, solid perfumes and lipsticks

Handelsman, Burton
18 Hotel Dr., White Plains, 10605; 914-428-4480 (home) and 914-761-8880 (office). Specializing in occupational shaving mugs, accessories

Herley, Patrick J.
PO Box 606, E. Setauket, Long Island, 11733; 631-928-6052; e-mail: pherley@ms.cc.sunysb.edu. Specializing in Goss china

Kaonis, Keith; Manager
Collectors Eye and *Antique Doll Collector* Magazines
6 Woodside Ave., Suite 300, Northport, 11768 or PO Box 344, Center Port, NY 11721-0344; 631-261-4100 or 631-361-0982 (evenings). Specializing in Schoenhut toys

Laun, H. Thomas and Patricia
Little Century
215 Paul Ave., Syracuse, 13206; 315-437-4156. Summer residence: 35109 Country Rte. 7, Cape Vincent, 13618; 315-654-3244. Specializing in firefighting collectibles. All appraisals are free, but we will respond only to those who include a self-addressed stamped envelope (photograph is requested for accuracy).

Malitz, Lucille
Lucid Antiques
Box KH, Scarsdale, 10583; 914-636-7825. Specializing in lithophanes, kaleidoscopes, stereoscopes, medical and dental antiques

Malloy, Alex G.
Alex G. Malloy, Inc.
PO Box 38, South Salem, 10590; 203-438-0396. Specializing in ancient and medieval coins; antiquities, numismatic literature

Michel, John and Barbara
Iron Star Antiques
200 E. 78th St., 18E, New York City, 10021; 212-861-6094. Specializing in yellow ware, cast iron, tramp art, shooting gallery targets, and blue feather-edge

Rifken, Blume J.
Author of *Silhouettes in America — 1790 – 1840 — A Collector's Guide*. Specializing in American antique silhouettes from 1790 to 1840

Russ, William A.
Russ Trading Post
23 William St., Addison 14801-1326. Animal lure manufacture; hunting and trapping supply; catalog $1.00

Safir, Charlotte F.
1349 Lexington Ave., 9-B, New York City, 10128-1513; 212-534-7933. Specializing in cookbooks, children's books (out-of-print only)

Schleifman, Roselle
Ed's Collectibles/The Rage
16 Vincent Rd., Spring Valley, 10977; 914-356-2121. Specializing in Duncan & Miller, Elegant Glass, Depression Glass

Smyth, Carole and Richard
Carole Smyth Antiques
PO Box 2068, Huntington, 11743. Authors of *The Burning Passion — Antique and Collectible Pyrography*, available from authors at above address for $22.95 ppd. (New York: add $1.74 state sales tax), and Neptune's Treasures, A Study & Value Guide on Antique Shell Decorated Love Tokens, Souvenirs, Whimsie. Call for price

Tuggle, Robert
105 W. St., New York City, 10023; 212-595-0514. Specializing in John Bennett, Anglo-Japanese china

Van Kuren, Jean and Dale
Ruth's Antiques, Inc.
PO Box 152, Clarence Center, 14032; 716-741-8001; e-mail: ruthsantq@aol.com. Specializing chocolate molds, Buffalo pottery, Deldare ware

Van Patten, Joan F.
Box 102, Rexford, 12148. Author (Collector Books) of books on Nippon and Noritake

North Carolina

Finegan, Mary
Marfine Antiques
PO Box 3618; Boone 28607; 828-262-3441; e-mail: marfine@boone.net. Specializing in Johnson Brothers dinnerware; replacement service; author of book ($14 +postage and handling)

Hughes, Kathy (Mrs. Paul)
Tudor House Galleries
4126 Park Road, Suite E, Charlotte, 28209; 704-676-4871; fax: 704-676-5197; e-mail: paulh65304@aol.com or website: www.tudorhouse.com. Specializing in relief-molded jugs, 18th- and 19th-century English pottery and 19th-century oil paintings

Iannantuoni, Jean-Paul
4179 Brownwood Lane, Concord, 28027-4501; website: www.freeyellow.com/members/royaldoulton/home. Discontinued Dinnerware Shopping Service; send $2 for Royal Doulton list; Appraisals $2 each

Kirtley, Charles E.
PO Box 2273, Elizabeth City, 27096; 919-335-1262. Specializing in monthly auctions and bid sales dealing with World's Fair, Civil War, political, advertising, and other American collectibles

Newbound, Betty
2206 Nob Hill Dr., Sanford, 27330. Author (Collector Books) on Blue Ridge dinnerware, milk glass, wall pockets and figural planters and vases; Specializing in collectible china and glass

Sayers, R.J.
Southeastern Antiques & Appraisals
PO Box 629, Brevard, 28712. Specializing in Boy Scout collectibles, Pisgah Forest pottery, primitive American furniture; Author of *Guide to Scouting Collectibles, Revised 1996 Edition*, available from author for $32.95 ppd.; Member NEAA Appraisers

Southern Folk Pottery Collector's Society, Shop, and Museum
1828 N. Howard Mill Rd., Robbins, 27325; 910-464-3961 or fax: 910-464-2530. Specializing in historical research and documentation, education and promotion of the traditional folk potter (past and present) to a modern collecting audience

Taylor, Terry
3648 Prides Rd., East Bend, 27018. Co-author of *Collector's Encyclopedia of Salt Glaze Stoneware* (Collector Books). Specializing in salt glaze stoneware

North Dakota

Farnsworth, Bryce
1334 14½ St. South, Fargo, 58103; 701-237-3597. Specializing in Rosemeade pottery; If writing for information, please send a picture if possible, also phone number and best time to call

Ohio

Bassett, Mark
PO Box 771233, Lakewood, 44107; 216-221-6025. Specializing in Ohio art pottery (including Roseville, Cowan, Weller, Rookwood, others), Cleveland arts and crafts, Art Deco, and other 20th century design movements; Author of *Introducing Roseville Pottery* (1999), *Cowan Pottery and the Cleveland School* (1997), and *Bassett's Roseville Prices* (2000), all published by Schiffer

Batory, Mr. Dana Martin
402 E. Bucyrus St., Crestline, 44827. Specializing in antique woodworking machinery, old and new woodworking machinery catalogs; Author of *Vintage Woodworking Machinery, an Illustrated Guide to Four Manufacturers*, currently available from Astragal Press, PO Box 239, Mendham, NJ 07945 for $25.45 ppd. In order to prepare a definitive history on American manufacturers of woodworking machinery, Dana is interested in acquiring (by loan, gift, or photocopy) catalogs, manuals, photos, personal reminiscences, etc., pertaining to woodworking machinery and/or their manufacturers. Also available for $7.50 money order: 30+ page list of catalogs, owner's manuals, parts lists, company publications, etc. (updated quarterly). NO phone calls please.

Benjamin, Scott
PO Box 556, LaGrange, 44050-0556; 440-355-6608; www.oilcollectibles.com (visit website or call). Specializing in gas globes; Co-author of *Gas Pump Globes* and several other related books, listing nearly 4,000 gas globes with over 1,800 photos, prices, rarity guide, histories, and reproduction information (currently available from author); Also available: *Petroleum Collectibles Monthly* Magazine; Please inquire

Blair, Betty
Golden Apple Antiques
216 Bridge St., Jackson, 45640; 614-286-4817. Specializing in art pottery, Watt, cookie jars, chocolate molds, Beanie Babies, general line

Budin, Nicki
Curio Cabinet
679 High St., Worthington, 43085; 614-885-1986. Specializing in Royal Doulton

Business Recollections, Antiques and Collectibles
Nada Sue Knauss
1211 Potter Rd., Weston, 43569; 419-669-4735. Specializing in pottery, postcards

China Specialties, Inc.
Box 471, Valley City, 44280. Specializing in Autumn Leaf

Cimini, Joan
67183 Stein Rd., Belmont, 43718-9715. Specializing in Imperial glass; Candlewick matching service

Cincinnati Auction Gallery
225 E. 6th St., Cincinnati, 45202; 513-381-2128. Specializing in American art pottery (especially Rookwood), American and European fine paintings, watercolors

Collectors of Findlay Glass
PO Box 256, Findlay, 45840. An organization dedicated to the study and recognition of Findlay glass; *The Melting Pot* Newsletter published quarterly; Convention held annually; Membership: $10 per year

Distel, Ginny
Distel's Antiques
4041 S.C.R. 22, Tiffin, 44883; 419-447-5832. Specializing in Tiffin glass

Ebner, Rita and John
Columbus. Specializing in door knockers, cast-iron bottle openers, Griswold

Forsythe, Ruth A.
Box 327, Galena, 43021. Author of *Made in Czechoslovakia*, books I and II; SASE required

Graff, Shirley
4515 Grafton Rd., Brunswick, 44212. Specializing in Pennsbury pottery

Guenin, Tom
Box 454, Chardon, 44024. Specializing in antique telephones and antique telephone restoration

Hamlin, Jack and Treva
145 Township Rd. 1088, Proctorville, 45669; 740-886-7644; e-mail: trevajo@ezwv.com. Specializing in Currier and Ives by Royal China Co. and Homer Laughlin China

Hothem, Lar
Hothem House
Box 458, Lancaster, 43130. Specializing in books about Indians and artifacts

Kao, Fern Larking
PO Box 312, Bowling Green, 43402; 419-352-5928. Specializing in jewelry, sewing implements, ladies' accessories

Kerr, Ann
PO 437, Sidney, 45365; 937-492-6369. Author (Collector Books) of *Collector's Encyclopedia of Russel Wright Designs;* Specializing in work of Wright; Interested in 20th-century decorative arts

Kitchen, Lorrie
Toledo, 419-475-1759. Specializing in Depression-era glass, Hall china, Fiesta, Blue Ridge, Shawnee

Klender, James and Grace
Town & Country Antiques & Collectibles
PO Box 447, Pioneer, 43554; 419-737-2880. Specializing in pattern glass, and general line

Kline, Mr. and Mrs. Jerry and Gerry
The Founding Members of North American Torquay Society and Members of Torquay Pottery Collectors' Society
604 Orchard View Dr., Maumee, 43537; 419-893-1226. Specializing in collecting Torquay pottery

Maggard, Deborah
P.O Box 211, Chagrin Falls, 44022; e-mail: debmaggard@worldnet.att.net. Specializing in elegant glassware, china, Victorian art glass and Victorian silver plate

Mathes, Richard
PO Box 1408, Springfield, 45501-1408; 513-324-6917. Specializing in buttonhooks

Millman, Tom and Linda
231 S. Main St., Bethel, 45106; Phone/fax: 513-734-6884 (after 9 p.m.). Specializing in perfume lamps, other antique and unique lighting

Moore, Carolyn
445 N. Prospect, Bowling Green, 43402. Specializing in primitives, yellow ware, graniteware, collecting stoneware

Murphy, James L.
1023 Neil Ave., Columbus, 43201; 614-297-0746. Specializing in Radford, Vance Avon

National Imperial Glass Collectors' Society, Inc.
PO Box 534, Bellaire 43906. Dues: $15 per year (plus $1 for each additional member in the same household); Quarterly newsletter; Convention every June

Otto, Susan; Editor
Nutcracker Collectors' Club and Newsletter
12204 Fox Run Dr., Chesterland, 44026

Pierce, David
PO Box 248, Danville, 43014; 614-599-6394. Specializing in Glidden pottery; Fee for appraisals

Rees, Debbie
Zanesville. Specializing in Watt, Roseville juvenile and other Roseville pottery, Zanesville area pottery, cookie jars, and Steiff

Riebel, James; Krause, Terry
Pottery Peregrinators
Zanesville, 740-452-7687. James is author of *Sanford's Guide to Nicodemus*, available from the author; Specializing in American art pottery, Nicodemus, and Carnival glass and Millersburg glass; Promoter Zanesville's Voyage through the Past, Antique Pottery and Dinnerware Show & Sale, 14th and 15th of July

Shields, Lorne
PO Box 211, Chagrin Falls, 44022-0211; 440-247-5632; e-mail: vintage@globalserve.net. Specializing in bicycles

Trainer, Veronica
Bayhouse
Box 40443, Cleveland, 44140; 440-871-8584. Specializing in beaded and enamelled mesh purses

Tucker, Dan
Toledo, 419-478-3815. Specializing in Depression-era glass, Hall china, Fiesta, Blue Ridge, Shawnee

Walter, John
The Old Tool Shop
208 Front St., Marietta, 45750; 740-373-9973; fax: 740-373-9059; e-mail: toolmerchant@sprynet.com (Coming soon: www.stanleytoolcollectors.org). Specializing in all types of antique tools; For detailed information on Stanley tools, John Walter's *Antique & Collectible Stanley Tools Guide to Identity and Value* is highly recommended, 885 pages, over 1500 crisp photos and engravings, current values, Softcover: $35 ppd., Hardcover: $45 ppd.; *2000 Stanley Pocket Price Guide*: $12 ppd

Whitmyer, Margaret and Kenn
Box 30806, Gahanna, 43230. Author (Collector Books) on children's dishes. Specializing in Depression-era collectibles

Wilkins, Juanita
The Bird of Paradise
Wapakoneta. Specializing in R.S. china, Old Ivory china, colored pattern glass, lamps, and jewelry

Young, Mary
Box 9244, Wright Brothers Branch, Dayton, 45409; 937-298-4838. Specializing in paper dolls; Author of several books

Oklahoma

Bess, Phyllis and Tom
14535 E. 13th St., Tulsa, 74108; 918-437-7776. Authors of *Frankoma Treasures*, and *Frankoma and Other Oklahoma Potteries*. Specializing in Frankoma and Oklahoma pottery

Moore, Art and Shirley
4423 E. 31st St., Tulsa, 74135; 918-747-4164 or 918-744-8020. Specializing in Lu Ray Pastels, Depression Glass

Scott, Roger R.
4250 S. Oswego, Tulsa, 74135; 918-742-8710 or fax 918-583-1226. Specializing in Victor and RCA Victor trademark items along with Nipper

Oregon

Abrahams, Peter
1948 Mapleleaf Rd., Lake Oswego, 97034; 503-636-2988; e-mail: telscope@europa.com. Specializing in telescopes, binoculars, microscopes. Peter studies and collects optics: telescopes, binoculars, hand magnifiers, and microscopes and especially seeks reference material on these subjects, including books, catalogs, repair manuals, and histories

Bartsch, Henry
Antique Registers
Box 444, Rockaway, 97136; 503-355-2932. Specializing in servicing antique cash registers (by appointment)

Brown, Marcia
Sparkles
PO Box 2314, White City, 97503; 541-826-3039 or fax 541-830-5385. Author of *Unsigned Beauties of Costume Jewelry* (Collector Books); Co-author and host of 6 volumes: *Hidden Treasures* videos; Specializing in rhinestone jewelry; Please include SASE if requesting information

Coe, Debbie and Randy
Coe's Mercantile
Lafayette School House Mall #2, 748 3rd (Hwy. 99W), Lafayette, 97127. Specializing in Elegant and Depression Glass, art pottery

Davis, Patricia M.
Antique and personal property appraisals
4326 N.W. Tam-O-Shanter Way, Portland, 97229-8738; 503-645-3084

Foland, Doug
1811 N.W. Couch #303, Portland, 97209. Author of *The Florence Collectibles, an Era of Elegance*, available at your local bookstore or from Schiffer publishers.

Hirshman, Susan and Larry
Everyday Antiques
2011 E. Main St., Medford, 97504. Specializing in china, glassware, kitchenware

Main Antique Mall
30 N. Riverside, Medford, 97501. Quality products and services for the serious collector, dealer, or those just browsing

Medford Antique Mall
Jim & Eileen Pearson, Owners
1 West 6th St., Medford 97501

Miller, Don and Robbie
541-535-1231. Specializing in milk bottles, TV Siamese cat lamps, seltzer bottles, red cocktail shakers

Morris, Sue and Dave
PO Box 1519, Merlin, 97532. Specializing in Watt pottery and Purinton pottery; Author of *Watt Pottery — An Identification and Value Guide*, and *Purinton Pottery — An Identification and Value Guide*

Morris, Thomas G.
Prize Publishers
PO Box 8307, Medford, 97504; e-mail: chalkman@cdsnet.net. Author of *The Carnival Chalk Prize*, Books I and II, pictorial price guides on carnival chalkware figures with brief histories and values for each

Ringering, David
Kay Ring Antiques
4063 Durbin Ave., S.E., Salem, 97301; 503-364-0464 or pager: 503-588-3747; e-mail: DRinge1023@aol.com. Specializing in Rowland & Marsellus and other souvenir/historical china with scenes of buildings, parks, and other tourist attractions of the 1890s-1930s. Feel free to contact David if you have any questions about Rowland and Marsellus or other souvenir china. He will be happy to answer questions about souvenir china.

Roberts, Fred and Marilyn
Bah Humbug Collectibles
890 Biddle Road, PMB-265, Medford, 97504; fax: 541-776-0641; e-mail: bahhumbug@juno.com. Specializing in Hummel figurines

Pennsylvania

Alekna, Stan and Sally
732 Aspen Lane, Lebanon, 17042-9073; 717-228-2361 or fax: 717-228-2362. Specializing in Toy Soldiers

Barker, Jim
Toastermaster Antique Appliances
PO Box 746, Allentown, 18105; 610-439-0751; e-mail: jbar@enter.net. Specializing in early electric toasters and fans, Porcelier and Royal Rochester; Unusual electric toasters always wanted

Barrett, Noel
Rosebud Antiques
PO Box 1001, Carversville, 18913; 215-297-5109. Specializing in toys

Bodine, Clarence H., Jr., Proprietor
East/West Gallery
41B Ferry St., New Hope, 18938. Specializing in antique Japanese woodblock prints, netsuke, inro, porcelains

Cerebro
PO Box 327, E. Prospect, 17317-0327; 717-252-2400 or 800-69-LABEL; fax: 717-252-3685; e-mail: Cerebro@Cerebro.com. Specializing in antique advertising labels, especially cigar box labels, cigar bands, food labels, firecracker labels

Christie, Dr. Victor J.W.; Author/Appraiser/Broker
1050 West Main St., Ephrata, 17522; 717-738-4032; e-mail: smiller1@redrose.net. Specializing in Bessie Pease Gutmann & other Gutmann artists

Damaska, Ron
738 9th Ave., New Brighton, 15066; 724-843-1393. Specializing in Fry cut glass, match holders; SASE required when requesting information

Gottuso, Bob
Bojo
PO Box 1403, Cranberry Township, 16066-0403; phone/fax: 724-776-0621. Specializing in Beatles, Elvis, KISS, Monkees, licensed Rock 'n Roll memorabilia

Hagenbuch, James
Glass-Works Auction
102 Jefferson, East Greenville, 18041; 215-679-5849. America's leading auction company in early American bottles, glass, and barbershop memorabilia

Hain, Henry F., III
Antiques & Collectibles
2623 N. Second St., Harrisburg, 17110; 717-238-0534. Lists available of items for sale

Hinton, Michael C.
246 W. Ashland St., Doylestown, 18901; 215-345-0892; e-mail: old stuff@worldnet.att.net . Owns/operates Bucks County Art & Antiques Company and Chem-Clean Furniture Restoration Company; Specializing in quality restorations of a wide range of art and antiques from colonial to contemporary; Also owns Trading Post Antiques, 532 Durham Rd., Wrightstown, PA, 18940, a 60-dealer antiques co-op with 15,000 square feet — something for everyone in antiques and collectibles

Holland, William
William Holland Fine Arts
1554 Paoli Pike, PMB #300, West Chester, 19380; 610-344-9848 or fax 610-344-0651; bill@hollandarts.com or website: www.hollandarts.com. Specializing in Louis Icart etchings and oils, Art Nouveau and Art Deco items; Author of *Louis Icart: The Complete Etchings*, *The Collectible Maxfield Parrish*, and *Louis Icart Erotica*

Irons, Dave
Dave Irons Antiques
223 Covered Bridge Rd., Northampton, 18067; 610-262-9335 or fax 610-262-2853; www.ironsantiques.com. Author of *Irons By Irons*, *More Irons By Irons*, and *Even More Irons by Irons*, available from author, (each contains pictures of over 1,600 irons, current information and price ranges, collecting hints, news of trends, and information for proper care of irons); Specializing in pressing irons, country furniture, primitives, quilts, accessories

Ivankovich, Michael
Michael Ivankovich Auctions, Inc.
PO Box 1536, Doylestown, 18901. Specializing in early 20th-century hand-colored photography and prints; Author of *The Collector's Value Guide to Popular Early 20th Century American Prints*, (1998) $19.95; *The Collector's Guide to Wallace Nutting Pictures*, $17.95; *The Wallace Nutting Expansible Catalog*, $14.95; *The Alphabetical and Numerical Index to Wallace Nutting Pictures*, $14.95; and *The Guide to Wallace Nutting Furniture*, $14.95. Also available: *Wallace Nutting General Catalog, Supreme Edition* (reprint), $13.95; *Wallace Nutting: A Great American Idea* (reprint), $13.95; and *Wallace Nutting's Windsor's: Correct Windsor Furniture* (reprint), $13.95. Related books available are *The Guide to Wallace Nutting-Like Photographers of the Early 20th Century*, $13.95; and *The History of Sawyer Pictures* by Carol Begley Gray, $14.95. All these books are currently available at the above address. Shipping is $3.75 for the first item ordered and $1.50 for each additional item

Knauer, Judy A.
National Toothpick Holder Collectors Society
1224 Spring Valley Lane, West Chester, 19380-5112; 610-431-3477. Specializing in toothpick holders and Victorian glass

The Krauses
Krause, Gail
97 W. Wheeling St., Washington, 15301; 412-228-5034. Author of book on Duncan glass

Kreider, Katherine
Kingsbury Antiques
PO Box 7957, Lancaster, 17604-7957; 717-892-3001; e-mail: Kingsbry@aol.com. Author of *Valentines With Values*, available for $22.90 ppd. ($24.09 PA residents); *One Hundred Years of Valentines*, available for $28.90 ppd. ($30.40 PA residents); and *Valentines for the Eclectic Collector* ($28.90 ppd. ($30.40 PA residents; No free appraisals. Stop by Booth #315 in Stroudtburg Antique Center (formerly Black Angus), in Adamstown, PA, Sundays only

Levi, Anita
Allegheny Mountain Antique Gallery
5151 Clear Shade Dr., Windber, 15963; 814-467-8539. Specializing in novelty clocks, advertising tins, primitives, holiday decorations, quilts, purses, Black memorabilia, linens, stoneware, Roseville, kitchenware, Art Deco

Lindsay, Ralph
PO Box 21, New Holland, 17557. Specializing in target balls. SASE required with correspondence.

Lowe, James Lewis
Kate Greenaway Society
PO Box 8, Norwood, 19074; e-mail: JLewisLowe@juno.com. Specializing in Kate Greenaway

Maier, Clarence and Betty
Mail order: The Burmese Cruet
Box 432, Montgomeryville, 18936; 215-855-5388; burmesecruet@erols.com or burmesecruet.com. Specializing in Victorian art glass.

Merchants Square Mall
Jim & Annetta Vitez, Managers
1901 S. 12th St., Allentown, 18103; 610-797-7743

Posner, Judy
June - September: R.D. 1 Box 273 SC, Effort 18330, fax: 717-629-0521; e-mail: judyandjef@aol.com. Specializing in Disneyana, Black memorabilia, salt and pepper shakers, souvenirs of the USA., character and advertising memorabilia, figural pottery; Buy, sell, collect; Informal appraisals, $5 LSASE and photo of item

Reimert, Leon
121 Highland Dr., Coatesville, 19320; 610-383-6969. Specializing in Boehm porcelain

Rosso, Philip J. and Philip Jr.
Wholesale Glass Dealers
1815 Trimble Ave., Port Vue, 15133; 412-678-7352. Specializing in Westmoreland glass

Weiser, Pastor Frederick S.
55 Kohler School Rd., New Oxford, 17350-9210; 717-624-4106. Specializing in frakturs and other Pennsylvania German documents; SASE required when requesting information; No telephone appraisals/ Must see original or clear colored photocopy

Rhode Island

Gacher, John
The Zsolnay Store
152 Spring St., Newport, 02840; 401-841-5060; website: www.drawrm.com. Specializing in Zsolnay, Fischer, Amphora, and Austro-Hungarian art pottery;

The Occupied Japan Club
c/o Florence Archambault
29 Freeborn St., Newport, 02840-1821; e-mail: florence@aiconnect.com. Publishes bimonthly newsletter, *The Upside Down World of an O.J. Collector;* SASE required when requesting information

South Carolina

Greguire, Helen
Helen's Antiques
216 Mountain View Rd, Landrum, 29356; 864-457-7340. Specializing in graniteware (any color), carnival glass lamps and shades, carnival glass lighting of all kinds; Author (Collector Books) of *The Collector's Encyclopedia of Graniteware, Colors, Shapes & Values* (updated values $28.45 ppd.); Second book on graniteware now available with prices updated to 2000 (same price); Also available is *Carnival in Lights*, featuring carnival glass, lamps, shades, etc. ($13.45 ppd.); and *Collector's Guide to Toasters and Accessories, Identification & Values*, ($21.95 ppd.); All available from author; Please include SASE when requesting information; Looking for people interested in collecting toasters to form a national club

Roerig, Fred and Joyce
1501 Maple Ridge Rd., Walterboro, 29488; 843-538-2487. Specializing in cookie jars; Authors of *Collector's Encyclopedia of Cookie Jars, An Illustrated Value Guide*, (three in the series), publishers of *Cookie Jarrin' with Joyce: The Cookie Jar Newsletter*

Tennessee

Chase, Mick and Lorna
Fiesta Plus
380 Hawkins Crawford Rd., Cookeville, 38501; 931-372-8333. Specializing in Fiesta, Harlequin, Riviera, Franciscan, Metlox, Lu Ray, Bauer, Vernon, other American dinnerware

DeLozier, Loretta
PO Box 50201, Knoxville, 37950-0201; e-mail: Leftonlady@AOL.com. Author (Collector Books) of *Collector's Encyclopedia of Lefton China, Identification & Values*, Books I, II, III, and Price Guide. Specializing in Lefton China; Buy, sell, and consign; Fee for written appraisals; Price list available for each pattern or series

Fields, Linda
158 Bagsby Hill Lane, Dover, 37058; 931-232-5099 after 6 p.m.; e-mail: Fpiebird@compu.net. Specializing in pie birds

Foil, Richard and Sue
Serendipity Antiques
at Antiques Unlimited; State St. Birstol; 540-628-8315; Authors of book on Cumbow China

Grist, Everett
PO Box 91375, Chattanooga, 37412-3955; 423-510-8052. Specializing in covered animal dishes and marbles

Hudson, Murray
Murray Hudson Antiquarian Books & Maps
109 S. Church St., Box 163, Halls, 38040; 901-836-9057 or 800-748-9946; fax: 901-836-9017. Specializing in antique maps, globes and books with maps, atlases, explorations, travel guides, geographies, surveys, etc.

Kline, Jerry
Florence Showcase
PO Box 937, Kodak, 37764; 423-933-9060; fax: 423-933-4492. Specializing in Florence Ceramics of California, Rookwood pottery, Shelley English china, English chintz

Weddington, David
Predicta Sales & Service
2702 Albany Ct., Murfreesboro, 37129; 615-890-7498. Specializing in vintage Philco Predicta TVs

Texas

Babcock, Bobby
Jubilation Antiques
5108 Saddleridge Cove, Austin, 78759; 512-418-9373. Specializing in Maxfield Parrish, Black memorabilia, and brown Roseville Pine Cone

Cooper, Marilyn
8408 Lofland Dr., Houston, 77055-4811; 713-465-7773 or Summer address: PO Box 755, Douglas, MI 49406. Specializing in figural toothbrush holders, Pez, candy containers

Dockery, Rod
4600 Kemble St., Ft. Worth, 76103; 817-536-2168. Specializing in milk glass; SASE required with correspondence

Docks, L.R. 'Les'
Shellac Shack; Discollector
Box 691035, San Antonio, 78269-1035. Author of *American Premium Record Guide*. Specializing in vintage records

Frese, Leo and Wendy
Three Rivers Collectibles
Box 551542, Dallas, 75355; 214-341-5165. Specializing in RumRill, Red Wing pottery and stoneware

Gibbs, Carl, Jr.
PO Box 131584, Houston, 77219-1584; 713-521-9661. Author of *Collector's Encyclopedia of Metlox Potteries*, autographed copies available from author for $27.95 ppd.; Specializing in American ceramic dinnerware

Groves, Bonnie
402 North Ave. A, Elgin, 78621. Specializing in boudoir dolls

Knight, Suzanne
Abilene, 79602-4634; 915-673-9115; e-mail: knight@camalott.com. Specializing in Alamo and Gilmer potteries

Malowanczyk, Abby and Wlodek
Collage-20th Century Classics
2820 N. Henderson, Dallas, 75206; Phone/fax: 214-828-9888; 214-880-0020; e-mail: txcollage@aol.com and website: www.collageclassics.com. Specializing in architect-designed furniture and decorative arts from the modern movement

Norris, Kenn
Schoolmaster Auctions and Real Estate
PO Box 4830, 513 N. 2nd St., Sanderson, 79848-4830; 915-345-2640. Specializing in school-related items, barbed wire, related literature, and L'il Abner (antique shop in downtown Sanderson)

Pringle, Joyce M.
Antiques and Moore
3708 W. Pioneer Pkwy., Arlington, 76013; www.Antiquesandmoore.com/glas/ or e-mail: chip@antiquesandmoore.com. Specializing in Boyd, Summit, and Mosser glass

Rosen, Kenna
Rosen Estate Sales & Appraisals, Inc.
9138 Loma Vista, Dallas, 75243; 972-503-1436; e-mail: ke-rosen@swbell.net. Specializing in Bluebird china, quality estate sales

Silvermintz, Karen
6164 Ravendale Lane, Dallas, 75214; 214-826-1107. Specializing in American dinnerware

Smith, Allan
1806 Shields Dr., Sherman, 75092; 903-893-3626. Specializing in children's lunch boxes, Coca-Cola, Dr. Pepper, Pepsi Cola, RC Cola, western stars' items, character tin windup toys, and most character collectibles.

Thompson, Chuck
Chuck Thompson & Associates
10802 Greencreek Dr., Suite 703, Houston, 77070. Chucks *Fables for Collectors*, a column of stories with proverbs, is featured each month in *Collectors News* magazine. He also writes *Antiques and Prayers*, a monthly syndicated column for antique collectors.

Tucker, Richard and Valerie
Argyle Antiques
PO Box 262, Argyle, 76226; 940-464-3752; e-mail: lead1234@gte.net or rtucker@jw.com. Specializing in windmill weights, shooting gallery targets, figural lawn sprinklers, cast-iron advertising paperweights and other unusual figural cast iron

Turner, Danny and Gretchen
Running Rabbit Video Auctions
PO Box 701, Waverly, 37185; 615-296-3600. Specializing in marbles

Waddell, John
2903 Stan Terrace, Mineral Wells, 76067. Specializing in buggy steps

Wilkins, James R.
Olden Year Musical Museum
Box 381951, Duncanville, 75138-1951; 972-298-5587; e-mail: museum1@airmail.net. Specializing in music boxes, phonographs, grind organs, nickelodeons

Woodard, Dannie; Publisher
The Aluminist
PO Box 1345; Weatherford, 76086. Annual subscription: $20 (includes membership); Second book available concerning aluminum for $24.95+shipping & handling

Utah

Anderson, Tim
Box 461, Provo, 84603; website: www.AutographsOfAmerica.com. Specializing in autographs; Buys single items or collections — historical, movie stars, US Presidents, sports figures, and pre-1860 correspondence. Autograph questions? Please include photocopies of your autographs if possible and enclose a SASE for guaranteed reply.

Anderson, Warren R.
America West Archives
PO Box 100, Cedar City, 84721; 435-586-9497; e-mail: warren@americawestarchives.com. Specializing in old stock certificates and bonds, western documents and books, financial ephemera, autographs, maps, photos; Author of *Owning Western History*, with 75+ photos of old documents and recommended reference guide available ($20 ppd., soft cover) from author at the above address

Spencer, Rick
Salt Lake City, 801-973-0805. Specializing in American silverplate and sterling flatware, hollowware, Shawnee, Van Telligen, salt and pepper shakers. Appraisals available at reasonable cost.

Vermont

Barry, Kit
136 High St., Brattleboro, 05301; 802-254-3634. Author of *Reflections 1* and *Reflections 2*, reference books on ephemera; Specializing in advertising trade cards and ephemera in general

Virginia

Bradfield, Jeff
Jeff's Antiques
90 Main St., Dayton, 22821; 540-879-9961. Also located in Pat's Antique Mall (I-81), Exit 227, Verona, and Rolling Hills Antique Mall, I-81, Exit 247B, Harrisonburg. Specializing in candy containers, toys, postcards, sugar shakers, lamps, furniture, pottery, and advertising items

Branchcomb, Shane
5523 Sideburn Rd., Fairvax, 22032; e-mail: acmeman@erols.com. Specializing in antique coffee mills, send SASE for reply

Bull, Donald A.
PO Box 596, Wirtz, 24184; 540-721-1128. Author of *The Ultimate Corkscrew Book, Bull's Pocket Guide to Corkscrews, Just for Openers* (with John Stanley) and *Soda Advertising Openers;* Specializing in corkscrews

Cranor, Rosalind
PO Box 859, Blacksburg, 24063. Specializing in Elvis collectibles; Author of *Elvis Collectibles* (out of print) and *Best of Elvis Collectibles*, available from author for $21.70 ppd

Flanigan, Vicki
Flanigan's Antiques
PO Box 1662, Winchester, 22604. Specializing in antique dolls, hand fans, and Hawaiian dolls. Please include SASE with correspondence. Fee for appraisals, thank you.

Haigh, Richard
PO Box 29562, Richmond 23242; 804-741-5770. Specializing in Locke Art, Steuben, Loetz, Fry, Italian; SASE required for reply

Lechner, Mildred and Ralph
Box 554, Mechanicsville, 23111; 804-737-3347. Author (Collector Books) on glass salt shakers; Specializing in art and pattern glass salt shakers circa 1870 – 1940; Directors of Antique and Art Glass Salt Shakers Collectors Society Club, 1991-92. Please note: Mildred and Ralph have absolutely NO involvement or dealings concerning novelty salt shakers or their values.

MacAllister, Dale
PO Box 46, Singers Glen, 22850. Specializing in sugar shakers and syrups

Monsen, Randall; and Baer, Rod
Monsen & Baer
Box 529, Vienna, 22183; 703-938-2129. Specializing in perfume bottles, Roseville pottery, Art Deco

Reynolds, Charles
Reynolds Toys
2836 Monroe St., Falls Church, 22042; 703-533-1322; e-mail: reynoldstoys@erols.com. Specializing in limited-edition mechanical and still banks, figural bottle openers

Schleyer, Jim
Box 243-M, Burke, 22015. Former editor of the newsletter, *Toy Gun Purveyors* and author of *Backyard Buckaroos — Collecting Western Toy Guns*, which contains nearly 2,500 photographs and value guide. Toy gun inquiries that include a SASE will be graciously answered.

Windsor, Grant S.
PO Box 72606, Richmond, 23235-2606; 804-320-0386. Specializing in Griswold cast-iron cookware. SASE required for inquiries. Grant currently has a reprint of Griswold Catalog S, dated November 1, 1895, 20 pages. It contains much information and illustrations of several items not seen in catalogs previously known. Information is revealed which specifically dates the 'World's Fair' griddle. Currently available for $11.50 each (ppd.); For orders of 10 or more: $7.50 each (ppd)

Washington

Frost, Donald M.
Country Estate Antiques (Appointment only)
14800 N.E. 8th St., Vancouver, 98684; 360-604-8434. Specializing in art glass and earlier 20th-century American glass

Goldsworthy, Kathy
Past Glories, Bothell; 425-806-2077 Specializing in sewing items; www.tias.com/stores/pastglories/

Haase, Don (Mr. Spode)
D&D Antiques
PO Box 818, Mukilteo, 98275; 425-348-7443; e-mail: mrspode@aol.com or Don@mrspode.com. or www.mrspode.com. Specializing in Spode-Copeland China

Jackson, Denis C., Editor
The Illustrator Collector's News
PO Box 1958, Sequim, 98382; 360-452-3810; e-mail: ticn@olypen.com. Copy of recent sample: $3. Specializing in old magazines & illustrations such as Rose O'Neill, Maxfield Parrish, pinups, Marilyn Monroe, Norman Rockwell, etc.

Payne, Sharon A.
Antiquities & Art
9104 163rd Ave. NE, Granite Falls, 98252; e-mail: hotel_california94546@yahoo.com. Specializing in Cordey

Weldin, Bob
Miner's Quest
W. 3015 Weile, Spokane, WA 99208; 509-327-2897. Specializing in mining antiques and collectibles (mail-order business)

Whitaker, Jim and Kaye
Eclectic Antiques
PO Box 475 Dept. S, Lynnwood, 98046; www.eclecticantiques.com. Specializing in Josef Originals and motion lamps; SASE required.

Zeder, Audrey
1320 S.W. 10th Street #S, North Bend, 98045 (Appointment only). Specializing in British Royalty Commemorative souvenirs (mail-order catalog available); Author (Wallace Homestead) of *British Royalty Commemoratives*

West Virginia

Fostoria Glass Society of America, Inc.
Box 826, Moundsville, 26041. Specializing in Fostoria glass

Wisconsin

Antique Associates Mall
220 Walnut St.; Suite #1, Spooner, 54801; 715-635-6666. Furniture, glassware & china, quilts, dolls, toys, books, pottery, primitives, lamps; Open: Mon. – Sat. 10 a.m. – 5 p.m.; Sunday by chance

Helley, Phil
Old Kilbourne Antiques
629 Indiana Ave., Wisconsin Dells, 53965; 608-254-8770. Specializing in premiums, German and Japanese tin toys, Cracker Jack, toothbrush holders, radio premiums, pencil sharpeners and comic strip toys

Knapper, Mary
Phoneco, Inc.
207 E. Mill Rd., PO Box 70, Galesville, 54630; 608-582-4124. Specializing in telephones, antique to modern

Matzke, Gene
Gene's Badges & Emblems
455 Big Horn Ct., Hancock, 54943; phone/fax: 715-249-5695. Specializing in police badges, leg irons, old police photos, fire badges (old), patches, old handcuffs, and memorabilia

Rice, Ferill J.
302 Pheasant Run, Kaukauna, 54130. Specializing in Fenton art glass

Clubs, Newsletters, and Catalogs

ABC Collectors' Circle (16-page newsletter, published 3 times a year)
Dr. Joan M. George
67 Stevens Ave., Old Bridge, NJ 08857; e-mail: drjgeorge@nac.net or fax 732-679-6102. Specializing in ABC plates and mugs

Abingdon Pottery Collectors Club
Elaine Westover, Membership and Treasurer
210 Knox Hwy. 5, Abingdon, IL 61410; 309-462-3267. Dues $8 for single, $10 per couple. Specializing in collecting and preservation of Abingdon pottery

Akro Agate Collectors Club and *Clarksburg Crow* quarterly newsletter
Roger Hardy
10 Bailey St., Clarksburg, WV 26301-2524; 304-624-4523 (evenings) or West End Antiques, 97 Milford St., Clarksburg, WV 26301; 304-624-7600 (week days). Club website: www.akro-agate.com Annual membership fee: $25

The Akro Arsenal, quarterly catalog
Larry D. Wells
6301 Walnut Valley Dr., Ft. Wayne, IN 46818; 219-489-5842

Alex G. Malloy, Inc.
PO Box 38, South Salem, NY 10590; 203-438-0396. Specialized catalogs on antiquities, and ancient and medieval coins

The Aluminist
Dannie Woodard, Publisher
PO Box 1346, Weatherford, TX 76086. Subscription: $20 (includes membership)

America West Archives
Anderson, Warren
PO Box 100, Cedar City, UT 84721; 435-586-9497; e-mail: warren@americawestarchives.com. 26-page illustrated catalogs issued 6 times a year; Has both fixed-price and auction sections offering early western documents, letters, stock certificates, autographs, and other important ephemera; Subscription: $15 per year
American Antique Deck Collectors

52 Plus Joker Club
Clear the Decks, quarterly publication
Rhonda Hawes, Membership
204 Gorham Ave., Hamden, CT 06514 ($25 in US and Canada, $35 foreign). Specializing in antique playing cards

American Bell Association, Int., Inc.
c/o The Bell Tower
PO Box 19443, Indianapolis, IN 46219. Dorothy Malone Anthony, Past President

American Hatpin Society
Virginia Woodbury, President
20 Montecillo, Rolling Hills Estates, CA 90274; 310-326-2196. Newsletter published quarterly; Meetings also quarterly

Antique and Art Glass Salt Shaker Collectors' Society (AAGSSCS)
17460 Caloosa Trace Circle, Ft. Myers, FL 33912

Antique & Collectors Reproduction News
Antiques Coast to Coast
Mark Chervenka, Editor
PO Box 12130, Des Moines, IA 50312-9403; 515-274-5886 or (subscriptions only) 800-227-5531. 12 monthly issues: $32 per year in US; $41 in Canada; $59 all other foreign

Antique Advertising Association of America (AAAA)
PO Box 1121, Morton Grove, IL 60053; 708-466-0904. Publishes *Past Times* Newsletter; Subscription: $35

Antique Bottle & Glass Collector Magazine
Jim Hagenbuch, Publisher
102 Jefferson St., PO Box 180, East Greenville, PA 18041. Subscription: (12 issues) $21 in US ($24 in Canada)

Antique Comb Collectors Club International
Antique Comb Collector Newsletter
Belva Green, Editor
90 S. Highland Ave., #1204, Tarpon Springs, FL 34689-5351; 727-942-7354; e-mail: comber@gte.net

Antique Journal
Michael F. Shores, Publisher
Jeffrey Hill, Editor/General Manager
2329 Santa Clara Ave., #207, Alameda, CA 94501; 800-791-8592

Antique Journal Northwest
Michael F. Shores, Publisher
Jeffrey Hill, Editor/General Manager
3439 North East Sandy Blvd., Suite #275, Portland, OR 97232; 888-845-3201

Antique Purses Catalog: $4
Bayhouse
PO Box 40443, Cleveland, OH 44140; 216-871-8584. Includes colored photos of beaded and enameled mesh purses

Antique Radio Classified (ARC)
PO Box 2, Carlisle, MA 01741; 978-371-0512

Antique Souvenir Collectors News
Gary Leveille, Editor
PO Box 562, Great Barrington, MA 01230

Antique Stove Association
Macy Stern, Editor of *Antique Stove Association Quarterly*, 2617 Riverside Dr., Houston, TX 77004; 713-528-2990

Antique Telephone Collectors Association
Box 94, Abilene, KS 67410; 785-263-1757. An international organization associated with the Museum of Independent Telephony

Antique Trader Weekly
Nancy Crowley, Editor
PO Box 1050, Dubuque, IA 52004-1050. Featuring news about antiques and collectibles, auctions and events; Listing over 165,000 buyers and sellers in every edition; Subscription: $37 (52 issues) per year; Toll free for subscriptions only: 800-334-7165

Antique Wireless Association
Ormiston Rd., Breesport, NY 14816

Appraisers National Association
120 S. Bradford Ave., Placentia, CA 92870; 714-579-1082. Founded in 1982 by Dr. David Long, Ph.D., President of the College for Appraisers, to provide for a standardization of educational requirements for certification of its appraiser members and assure the public that A.N.A. appraisers not only have a broad range of knowledge in personal property valuation, but are held to the highest ethical and professional standards in the industry

Association of Coffee Mill Enthusiasts (ACME)
c/o Lucy Fullinwider, Treasurer
PO Box 5761, Midland, TX 79704. Quarterly newsletter, annual convention; Dues are $30 ($40 outside the continental US and Canada), covers cost of quarterly newsletter and copy of membership roster

Auction Times for the West
Michael F. Shores, Publisher
Jeffrey Hill, Editor/General Manager
2329 Santa Clara Ave., Suite 207, Alamedo, CA 94501. 800-791-8592

Autograph Times
2303 N. 44th St., #225, Phoenix, AZ 85008; 602-947-3112 or fax 602-947-8363. Subscription: $15 (US) per year

Autographs of America
Tim Anderson
PO Box 461, Provo, UT 84603; 801-226-1787 (please call in the afternoon); www.AutographsOfAmerica.com

Autumn Leaf
Bill Swanson, Editor
807 Roaring Springs Dr., Allen, TX 75002-2112; 972-727-5527
Gwynne Harrison, President
PO Box 1, Mira Loma, CA 91752-0001; 951-685-5434

Avon Times (National Avon collectors' newsletter)
c/o Dwight or Vera Young
PO Box 9868, Dept. P., Kansas City, MO 64134. Inquiries should be accompanied by LSASE.

Beatlefan
PO Box 33515, Decatur, GA 30033. Subscription: $7 (US) for 6 issues or $21 (Canada and Mexico)

Black Memorabilia Illustrated Sales List ($2 and LSASE)
Judy Posner
June - September: R.D. 1, Box 273 SC, Effort, PA 18330, fax: 717-629-0521; October - May: PO Box 2194 SC, Englewood, FL 34295, fax: 941-475-2645; e-mail: judyandjef@aol.com or www.judyposner.com. Buy-Sell-Collect

Bojo
PO Box 1403, Cranberry Township, PA 16066-0403. Send $3 for 38 pages of Beatles, toys, dolls, jewelry, autographs, Yellow Submarine items, etc.

Bookend Collector Club
c/o Louis Kuritzky, M.D.
4510 NW 17th Place, Gainesville, FL 32650; 352-377-3193; e-mail: lkuritzky@aol.com. Quarterly full-color glossy newsletter, $25 per yr

Bossons Briefs, quarterly magazine
Available through membership of International Bossons Collectors Society, 1787 Morgan Valley Rd., Rockmart, GA 30153

Boyd's Art Glass Collectors Guild
PO Box 52, Hatboro, PA 19040-0052

Boyd's Crystal Art Glass
Jody & Darrell's Glass Collectibles Newsletter
PO Box 180833, Arlington, TX 76096-0833. Publishes 6 times a year. Subscription includes an exclusive glass collectible produced by Boyd's Crystal Art Glass. LSASE for current subscription rates. Sample copy of newsletter: $3

British Royal Commemorative Sou venirs Mail Order Catalog
Audrey Zeder
1320 SW 10th St. #S, North Bend, WA 98045

Buckeye Marble Collectors Club
209 Crocus Court, Newark, OH 43055

The Buttonhook Society
Box 287, White Marsh, MD 21162. Publishes bimonthly newsletter *The Boutonneur*, which promotes collecting of buttonhooks and shares research and information contributed by members

Candy Container Collectors of America
The Candy Gram Newsletter
Joyce L. Doyle
PO Box 426, North Reading, MA 01864-0426. Send SASE for application

Candy Containers of America
Contact: Jeff Bradfield
90 Main St., Dayton, VA 22821

The Cane Collector's Chronicle
Linda Beeman
15 2nd St. N.E., Washington, D.C. 20002. $30 for 4 issues

Cane Collectors Club
PO Box 1004, Englewood Cliff, NJ 07632; 201-886-8826; e-mail: liela@walkingstickworld.com

The Carnival Pump
International Carnival Glass Assoc., Inc.
Lee Markley
Box 306, Mentone, IN 46539. Dues: $20 per family per year in US and Canada or $25 overseas, payable each July 1st

The Carousel News & Trader
87 Parke Ave. W., Suite 206, Mansfield, OH 44902. A monthly magazine for the carousel enthusiast; Subscription: $22 per year; Sample: $3

The Carousel Shopper Resource Catalog
Box 47, Dept. PC, Millwood, NY 10546. Only $2 (+50¢ postage); A full-color catalog featuring dealers of antique carousel art offering single figures or complete carousels, museums, restoration services, organizations, full-size reproductions, books, cards, posters, auction services, and other hard-to-find items for carousel enthusiasts

Cast Iron Marketplace
PO Box 16466, Saint Paul, MN 55116. Available to hobbyists/dealers on a monthly basis to buy/sell/trade products made by the great foundries from our industrial past. Subscription: $30 per year (includes free ads up to 200 words per issue)

A Catalog Collection
Kenneth E. Schneringer
271 Sabrina Ct., Woodstock, GA 30188-4228; 770-926-9383; e-mail: trademan68@aol.com. Specializing in catalogs, promochures, ciew books, labels, trade cards, special paper needs

Central Florida Insulator Collectors
3557 Nicklaus Dr., Titusville, FL 32780-5356; 407-267-9170; e-mail: bluebellwt@aol.com. Dues: $10 per year for single or family membership (checks payable to Jacqueline C. Linscott); Dues covers the cost of *Newsnotes*, the club's monthly newsletter, which informs members of meetings and shows, articles of interest on insulators and other collectibles. Members are invited to use free advertising of items for sale or trade. The club meets quarterly in members' homes and hosts a show each January which is open to the public. For club information send SASE to above address.

Ceramic Arts Studio Catalog Reprints
Wellman, BA
PO Box 673, Westminster, MA 01473-0673; e-mail: BAWELLMAN@NET1PLUS.COM. Also offers many other catalog reprints from dinnerware to art pottery; Specializing in all areas of American ceramics, art pottery, dinnerware and figurines

Ceramic Arts Studio Collector's Association
PO Box 46, Madison, WI 53701; 608-241-9138. Publishes newsletter, *CAS Collector*, a quarterly newsletter; Annual membership: $15; Sample copy: $3; Inventory record and price guide also available

Chicagoland Antique Amusements Slot Machine & Jukebox Gazette
Ken Durham, Editor
909 26 St., N.W., Suite 502, Washington, D.C. 20037; website: www.GameRoomAntiques.com; 20-page newspaper published twice a year; Subscription: 4 issues for $20; Sample: $10; Send SASE for free list of books

China Specialties, Inc.
Fiesta Collector's Quarterly Newsletter
PO Box 471, Valley City, OH 44280

Chintz Connection Newsletter
PO Box 222, Riverdale, MD 20738. Dedicated to helping collectors share information and find matchings; Subscription: 4 issues per year for $25

Coin-Op Newsletter
Ken Durham, Publisher
909 26th St. N.W., Suite 502, Washington, D.C. 20037. Subscription: $15 per year; Sample: $5; Send SASE for free list of books; website: www.GameRoomAntiques.com

The Cola Clan
Alice Fisher, Treasurer
2084 Continental Dr., N.E., Atlanta, GA 30345

Collector's Life
The World's Foremost Publication for Steiff Enthusiasts
Beth Savino
PO Box 798; Holland, OH 43528; 1-800-862-TOYS; fax: 419-473-3947; www.toystorenet.com

Collector Glass News
Box 308, Slippery Rock, PA 16057
724-946-2838; fax: 724-946-9012;
e-mail: cgn@glassnews.com or website: www.glassnews.com. An international publication providing current news to collectors of cartoon, fast-food, and promotional glassware

Collectors of Findlay Glass
PO Box 256, Findlay, OH 45840. An organization dedicated to the study and recognition of Findlay glass; Newsletter *The Melting Pot*, published quarterly; Annual convention; Membership: $10 per year

Compact Collectors
Roselyn Gerson
PO Box 40, Lynbrook, NY 11563; 516-593-8746 or fax 516-593-0610; e-mail: compactlady@aol.com. Publishes *Powder Puff* Newsletter, which contains articles covering all aspects of compact collecting, restoration, vintage ads, patents, history, and articles by members and prominent guest writers; Seeker and sellers column offered free to members

Cookie Crumbs
Cookie Cutter Collectors Club
Ruth Capper, Secretary/Treasurer
1167 Teal Road S.W., Dellroy, OH 44620. Subscription $12 per year (4 issues); Payable to CCCC

Cookie Jarrin' With Joyce: The Cookie Jar Newsletter
1501 Maple Ridge Rd., Walterboro, SC 29488

Cookies
Rosemary Henry
9610 Greenview Lane, Manassas, VA 20109-3320. Subscription: $12 per year (6 issues); Payable to Cookies

The Copley Courier
1639 N. Catalina St., Burbank, CA 91505

Cowan Pottery Museum Associates
For information write: CPMA, PO Box 16765, Rocky River, OH 44116 or contact Victoria Naumann Peltz, Curatorial Associate, Cowan Pottery Museum at Rocky River Public Library, 1600 Hampton Rd., Rocky River, OH 44116; 440-333-7610, ext. 214. Annual dues: $35, includes subscription to biannual *Cowan Pottery Journal* Newsletter

Cracker Jack® Collector's Assoc.
The Prize Insider Newsletter
Roberta Bowen
305 E. Minton Dr., Tempe, AZ 85282; 602-831-1402. Subscription/membership: $18 per year (single) or $24 (family)

Creamers, quarterly newsletter
PO Box 11, Lake Villa, IL 60046-0011. Subscription: $5 per year

Currier & Ives Catalog
Rudisill's Alt Print Haus
PO Box 199, Worton, MD 21678. Please include LSASE

(Currier & Ives) C&I Dinnerware Collector Club
E.R. Aupperle, Treasurer
29470 Saxon Road, Toulton, IL 61483; 309-896-3331; fax: 309-856-6005

Czechoslovakian Collectors Guild International
PO Box 901395, Kansas City, MO 64190

The DAZE, Inc. (formerly *The Depres sion Glass DAZE*)
Teri Steele (Cox), Publisher
The Nation's Marketplace and Meetingplace for American glass, china, and pottery collectors, Box 57, Otisville, MI 48463; e-mail at dgdaze@aol.com or call 800-336-9927 for trial subscription offer

The Dedham Pottery Collectors Society Newsletter
Jim Kaufman, Publisher
248 Highland St., Dedham, MA 02026; 800-283-8070

Disneyana Illustrated Sales List ($2 and LSASE)
Judy Posner
June - September: R.D. 1, Box 273 SC, Effort, PA 18330, fax: 717-629-0521; October - May: PO Box 2194 SC, Englewood, FL 34295, fax: 941-475-2645.e-mail: judyandjef@aol.com or www.judyposner.com. Buy-Sell-Collect

Docks, L.R. 'Les'
Shellac Shack
Box 691035, San Antonio, TX 78269-1035. Send $2 for a 72-page catalog of 78s that Docks wants to buy, the prices he will pay, and shipping instructions

Doorstop Collectors of America
Doorstopper Newsletter
Jeanie Bertoia
2413 Madison Ave., Vineland, NJ 08630; 609-692-4092. Membership: $20 per year, includes 2 newsletters and convention; Send 2-stamp SASE for sample

Dorothy Kamm's Porcelain Collector's Companion
PO Box 7460, Port St. Lucie, FL 34985-7460; 561-465-4008 or fax 561-460-9050; e-mail: dorothy.kamm@usa.net. Published bimonthly, Subscription: $28 per year

Dragonware Club
c/o Suzi Hibbard
e-mail:SRHACS@Pacbell.net

Drawing Room of Newport
Gacher, John
152 Spring St., Newport, RI 02840; 401-841-5060; website: www.drawrm.com. Book on Zsolnay available

Ed Taylor Radio Museum
245 N. Oakland Ave., Indianapolis, IN 46201-3360; 317-638-1641

Eggcup Collector's Corner
67 Stevens Ave., Old Bridge, NJ 08857. Issued quarterly; Subscription: $18 per year (payable to Joan George). Sample copy: $5

The Elegance of Old Ivory Newsletter
Box 1004, Wilsonville, OR 97070

Fenton Art Glass Collectors of America, Inc.
Butterfly Net newsletter
PO Box 384, 702 W. 5th St., Williamstown, WV 26187. Dues $20 per year for full membership, $5 for each associate membership. Children under 12 free

Fiesta Collector's Quarterly Newsletter
PO Box 471, Valley City, OH 44280. Subscription: $12 per year

Figural Bottle Opener Collectors
Linda Fitzsimmons, 9697 Gwynn Park Dr., Ellicott City, MD 21042; 410-465-9296. Please include SASE when requesting information.

Florence Collector's Club Newsletter
Rita Bee, Editor;
Beth Dunigan, Publisher;
c/o Florence Collector's Club Membership Chairman
PO Box 122, Richland, WA 99353. Subscription: (6 issues per year) $20

Fostoria Glass Society of America, Inc.
PO Box 826, Moundsville, WV 26041

Frankoma Family Collectors Association
c/o Nancy Littrell
PO Box 32571, Oklahoma City, OK 73123-0771. Membership dues: $25 (includes quarterly newsletter); Annual convention

Friends of Degenhart
c/o Degenhart Museum
PO Box 186, Cambridge, OH 43725; 740-432-2626. Membership: $5 ($10 for family) includes *Heartbeat* Newsletter (printed quarterly) and free admission to museum

H.C. Fry Society
PO Box 41, Beaver, PA 15009. Founded in 1983 for the sole purpose of learning about Fry glass; Publishes *Shards*, quarterly newsletter

The Glass Menagerie, bimonthly newsletter
Susan Candelaria, Editor
5440 El Arbol, Carlsbad, CA 92008

Goofus Glass Gazette
Steve Gillespie, Publisher
400 Martin Blvd., Village of the Oaks, MO 64118; 888-452-5554 or fax 816-452-5554; e-mail: goofus@midwest.net

The Gonder Collector
917 Hurl Dr.
Pittsburgh, PA 15236

Grandpa's Depot
John 'Grandpa' White
6720 E. Mississippi Ave., Unit B, Denver, CO 80224; 303-300-3984 or 303-758-8540. Publishes catalogs on railroad-related collectibles

Griswold & Cast Iron Cookware Association
Grant Windsor
PO Box 72606, Richmond, VA 23235-2606; 804-320-0386. Membership: $15 (for single) or $20 (for 2 members per address) payable to club

Haeger Pottery Collectors of America
Lanette Clarke
5021 Toyon Way, Antioch, CA 94509; 925-776-7784. Newsletter published 6 times per year; Dues: $20

The Hagen-Renaker Collector's Club Newsletter
c/o Jenny Palmer
3651 Polish Line Rd., Cheboygan, MI 49721-9045

Hall China Collector's Club Newsletter
PO Box 360488, Cleveland, OH 44136

Head Hunters Newsletter
c/o Maddy Gordon
PO Box 83H, Scarsdale, NY 10583. Subscription: $24 yearly (quarterly issues)

Homer Laughlin China Collector Association (HLCCA)
The Dish magazine (a 16-pg quarterly included with membership)
PO Box 26021 Crystal City, VA 22215-6021. Single: $25 couple/family: $40

Homer Laughlin Eagle
c/o Richard Racheter
1270 63rd Terrace South, St. Petersburg, FL 33705

How To Open and Operate a Home-Based Antiques Business; How To Rec ognize and Refinish Antiques for Plea sure and Profit and *How to Start a Home-Based Antique Business*
Jacquelyn Peake, author
Globe Pequot Press
PO Box 833, Old Saybrook, CT 06475 or any book store

Ice Screamer
c/o Duvall Sollers
PO Box 132, Monkton, MD 21111. Published quarterly; Dues: $15 per year; Annual convention held in late June in Lancaster, PA

Ideal Collectors Club
c/o Judith Izen
PO Box 623, Lexington, MA 02173; e-mail: jizenres@aol.com. Membership: $20 per year, includes a quarterly newsletter; Subscribers get free want-ed/for sale ads in each issue

The Illustrator Collector's News (TICN)
Denis C. Jackson, Editor
PO Box 1958, Sequim, WA 98382; e-mail: ticn@olypen.com. Subscription: $18 per year; $3 for sample copy of bimonthly publication; Publishes price and identification guides on various illustrators and old magazines, write for further information

Indiana Historical Radio Society
245 N. Oakland Ave., Indianapolis, IN 46201-3360; 317-638-1641

International Association of Calculator Collectors,
International Calculator Collector Newsletter
Guy Ball, Co-Editor
PO Box 345, Tustin, CA 92781-0345; e-mail: mrcalc@usa.net. Subscription: $16 per year ($20 foreign); Sample copy: $3

International Association of R.S. Prussia, Inc.
Theresa Newcomer, Secretary
PO Box 446, Mount Joy, PA 17522. Membership: $20 per household; Yearly convention

International Club for Collectors of Hatpins and Hatpin Holders (ICC of H&HH)
Audrae Heath, Managing Editor
PO Box 1009, Bonners Ferry, ID 83805-1009. Bimonthly *Points* newsletter and *Pictorial Journal*

International Golliwog Collector Club
Beth Savino
PO Box 798; Holland, OH 43528; 1-800-862-TOYS; fax:419-473-3947; www.toystorenet.com

International Ivory Society
Robert Weisblut, Co-Founder
11109 Nicholas Dr., Wheaton, MD 20902; 301-649-4002. $10 annual membership fee includes 4 newsletters

International Nippon Collectors Club (INCC)
c/o David Przech
1531 Independence Ave. S.E., Washington, D.C. 20003. Publishes newsletter 6 times a year; Holds annual convention

International Perfume and Scent Bottle Collectors Association
Randall B. Monsen, President
PO Box 529, Vienna, VA 22183 or fax: 703-242-1357. Membership: $35 (USA) or $48 (Foreign); Newsletter published quarterly

International Rose O'Neill Club
Contact Karen Stewart
PO Box 668, Branson, MO 65616. Publishes quarterly newsletter *Kewpiesta Kourier*. Dues: (includes newsletter) $7 (single) or $10 (family)

International Society of Antique Scale Collectors
Jan Macho, Executive Secretary
3616 Noakes St., Los Angeles, CA 90023; 323-263-6878. Publishes *Equilibrium* Magazine; Quarterly Newsletter; Annual membership directory and out-of-print scale catalogs; Annual convention. Please include SASE when requesting information.

International Vintage Poster Dealers Association (IVPDA)
Nancy Steinbock, Charter Member
800-438-1577. Specializing in posters

Iron Talk
Jimmy Walker, Editor
PO Box 68, Waelder, TX 78959. Journal of antique pressing irons; News of prices, patents, markets, collectibles, collectors, history, reference, advice and much more; One-year bimonthly subscription: $30 in US; $35 airmail delivery in Canada or Mexico; $40 other. *Year 2000 Pressing Iron Price Guide* $20 +$2

John F. Rinaldi
Nautical Antiques and Related Items (Appointment only)
Box 765, Dock Square, Kennebunkport, ME 04046; 207-967-3218; or fax 207-967-2918. Illustrated catalog: $5

Josef Originals Newsletter
Jim and Kaye Whitaker
PO Box 475, Dept. S, Lynnwood, WA 98046. Subscription (4 issues): $10 per year

Lang's Sporting Collectables, Inc.
14 Fishermans Lane, Raymond, ME 04071; phone/fax: 207-655-4265. Specializing in fishing tackle and related accessories

The Laughlin Eagle
Joan Jasper, Publisher
Richard Racheter, Editor
1270 63rd Terrace S., St. Petersburg, FL 33705. Subscription: $14 (4 issues) per year; Sample: $4

Les Amis de Vieux Quimper (Friends of Old Quimper)
c/o Mark and Adela Meadows
PO Box 819, Carnelian Bay, CA 96140; e-mail: meadows@cwo.com. SASE required for written reply

License Plate Collectors Hobby Magazine
Drew Steitz, Editor
PO Box 222, East Texas, PA 18046; phone/fax: 610-791-7979. Bimonthly publication with many photographs, classifieds, etc.; $18 per year (1st class, US); Sample: $2

Liddle Kiddle Convention
Paris Langford
415 Dodge Ave. Jefferson, LA 70121; e-mail: BBEAN415@AOL.COM. Send SASE for information about convention to be held in Atlanta in the fall of 2000

Line Jewels, NIA #1380
3557 Nicklaus Dr., Titusville, FL 32780

Mabel Lucie Attwell Catalogs
J. David Ehrhard
7212 Valmont St., Tujunga, CA 91042

Majolica International Society
Suite #103, 1275 First Ave., New York, NY 10021. Dues: $35 per year, entitles member to attend annual meeting and to receive the quarterly newsletter *Majolica Matters*

Marble Collectors' Society of America
Claire Block, Secretary
PO Box 222, Trumbull, CT 06611. Publishes *Marble Mania;* Gathers and disseminates information to further the hobby of marbles and marble collecting; $12 adds your name to the contributor mailing list ($21 covers 2 years)

Marble Collectors Unlimited
PO Box 206, Northboro, MA 01532

Martha's Kidlit Newsletter
Martha Rasmussen, Editor and Publisher
Box 1488, Ames IA 50014; 515-292-9309; e-mail: mart515@aol.com. For children's booklovers and collectors; Subscription: $30 in US, all others: $31

Midwest Open Salt Society
c/o Ed Bowman
2411 W. 500 North, Hartford City, IN 47348; Dues: $10 ($6 for spouse)

Midwest Sad Iron Collector Club
c/o Lynette Conrad, Secretary
24 Nob Hill Dr., St. Louis, MO 63138-1458; 314-741-4171

Miniature Bottle Club of the Great Lakes
19745 Woodmont, Harper Woods, MI 48225. Dues $5 per year; 4 meetings per year

Mt. Washington Art Glass Society
PO Box 107, Hyde Park, NY 12538-1122. Publishes *MWAGS Review,* to educate, inform and provide helpful information to anyone interested in art glass; Holds annual convention; Subscription/membership: $30 (single) or $40 for (2 persons in 1 household)

Murray Hudson Antiquarian Books and Maps
109 S. Church St., Box 163, Halls, TN 38040; 800-748-9946 or 901-836-9057; fax: 901-836-9017. Buyer and seller of antiquarian maps (especially pocket, wall, US Civil War, and railroad maps) and books with maps (atlases, travel guides, geographies, gazetteers, explorations, land surveys, etc.), especially of Southeastern and Southwestern US prior to 1900; Also world globes, map jigsaw puzzles and gameboards prior to 1950; Contact for catalog

Mystic Lights of the Aladdin Knights, bimonthly newsletter
c/o J.W. Courter
3935 Kelley Rd., Kevil, KY 40253; 270-488-2116. Information requires LSASE

National Association of Avon Collectors
c/o Connie Clark
6100 Walnut, Dept. P, Kansas City, MO 64113. Information requires LSASE

National Association Breweriana Advertising
2343 Met-To-Wee Lane, Wauwatosa, WI 53226; 414-257-0158. Membership: $20 (US), $30 (Canada) or $40 (Overseas); Publishes *The Breweriana Collector* and Membership Directory; Holds annual convention

National Association of Watch & Clock Collectors, Inc. (NAWCC)
514 Poplar St., Columbia, PA 17512-2130; 717-684-8261 (Headquarters, Museum, Library, School); www.nawc.org. Benefits include annual subscriptions to two publications, free research, participation in national and regional meetings, and the camaraderie of 35,000 fellow collectors worldwide. Call/write for information/application

National Autumn Leaf Collectors' Club
Bill Swanson, Newsletter Editor
807 Roaring Springs Dr., Allen, TX 75002-2112; 972-727-5527 or fax 972-727-2107; e-mail: bescom@home.com or Gwynne Harrison, President
PO Box 1, Mira Loma, CA 91752-0001; 909-685-5434 or fax 909-681-1692; e-mail: morgan99@pe.net

National Blue Ridge Newsletter
Norma Lilly
144 Highland Dr., Blountville, TN 37617. Subscription: $15 per year (6 issues)

National Bobbin Heads Club
Larkins, Barry
PO Box 9297, Daytona Beach, FL 32120; 904-253-7040

National Cambridge Collectors, Inc.
PO Box 416, Cambridge, OH 43725; 740-432-4245 or fax 740-439-9223; e-mail: NCC-Crystal-Ball@compuserve.com or website: www.Cambridgeglass.org

National Cuff Link Society
c/o Eugene R. Klompus
PO Box 5700, Vernon Hills, IL 60061; Phone/fax: 847-816-0035. $30 annual dues includes subscription to *The Link,* a quarterly magazine

National Depression Glass Association
Anita Woods
PO Box 69843, Odessa, TX 79769; 915-337-1297. Publishes *News and Views*

National Graniteware Society
PO Box 9248, Cedar Rapids, IA 52409-9248

National Greentown Glass Association
1807 W. Madison, Kokomo, IN 46901

National Imperial Glass Collectors' Society, Inc.
PO Box 534, Bellaire, OH 43906. Dues: $15 per year (+$3 for each additional member of household); Quarterly newsletter; Convention every June

National Insulator Association
1315 Old Mill Path, Broadview Heights, OH 44147

National Milk Glass Collectors' Society and *Opaque News,* quarterly newsletter
c/o Helen D. Storey
46 Almond Dr., Cocoa Townes, Hershey, PA 17033. Please include SASE

National Reamer Association
c/o Debbie Gillham
47 Midline Ct., Gaithersburg, MD 20878

National Shaving Mug Collectors Association
Penelope G. Nader, President
320 S. Greenwood St., Allerton, PA 18104; 610-437-2534. To stimulate the study, collection and preservation of shaving mugs and all related barbering items; Provides quarterly newsletter, bibliography, and directory; Holds 2 meetings per year; Dues: $15 per year

National Shelley China Club
Rochelle Hart, Secretary/Treasurer
591 West 67th Ave., Anchorage, AK 99518-1555. Membership: $25 per year, 4 quarterly newsletters plus many other benefits and publications, 9 years old, 550 members and growing, 1999 conference in Atlanta, GA; 10th-year anniversary in 2000 — Portland, OR

National Society of Lefton Collectors
c/o Loretta DeLozier
PO Box 50201, Knoxville, TN 37950-0201. Quarterly newsletter, annual convention; Dues: $25 per year

National Toothpick Holder Collectors Society
Toby Shugart, Membership
PO Box 417, Safety Harbor, FL 34695-0417. Dues: $15 (single) or $20 (couple); Includes 10 *Toothpick Bulletin* newsletters per year; Annual convention held in August; Exclusive toothpick holder annually

National Valentine Collectors Association
Evalene Pulati
PO Box 1404, Santa Ana, CA 92702; 714-547-1355. Specializing in Valentines and love tokens

NM (Nelson McCoy) Xpress
Carol Seman
8934 Brecksville Rd., Suite 406, Brecksville, OH 44141-2318

New England Society of Open Salt Collectors
Chuck Keys
21 Overbrook Lane, East Greenwich, RI 02818. Dues: $7 per year

Newspaper Collector's Society of America
Rick Brown
Lansing, MI, 517-887-1255; website: www.historybuff.com or e-mail: help@historybuff.com. An extensive, searchable, 300,000-word reference library of American history with an emphasis on newspapers publishing speeches; interactive crossword puzzles; regular auctions of ephemera, historic documents, and newspapers; a mall with over one hundred different online catalogs of paper collectibles; and much, much more!

Night Light Club
Culver, Bob
38619 Wakefield Ct., Northville, MI 48167; 248-473-8575. Specializing in miniature oil lamps

North American Torquay Society
Jerry and Gerry Kline, 2 of the founding members and archivists; Also members of Torquay Pottery Collectors' Society
604 Orchard View Dr., Maumee, OH 43537. Quarterly newsletter sent to members; Information and membership form requires #10 SASE

North American Trap Collectors' Association
c/o Tom Parr
PO Box 94, Galloway, OH 43119-0094. Dues: $15 per year; Publishes bimonthly newsletter

North Dakota Pottery Collectors Society and Newsletter
c/o Sandy Short
Box 14, Beach, ND 58621. Membership $15 per year including spouse; Annual convention in June; Quarterly newsletters

Novelty Salt & Pepper Shakers Club
Lula Fuller
PO Box 679388, Orlando, FL 32867-7388; 407-678-1219. Publishes quarterly newsletter; Holds annual convention; Dues: $20 per year in US, Canada and Mexico ($5 extra for couple)

Nutcracker Collectors' Club and Newsletter
Susan Otto, Editor
12204 Fox Run Dr., Chesterland, OH 44026. $15 for membership and quarterly newsletters ($17 foreign), free classifieds for members

The Occupied Japan Club
c/o Florence Archambault
29 Freeborn St., Newport, RI 02840-1821; e-mail: florence@aiconnect.com. Publishes *The Upside Down World of an O.J. Collector*, a bimonthly newsletter. Information requires SASE.

Old Sleepy Eye Collectors Club of America, Inc.
PO Box 12, Monmouth, IL 61462. Membership: $10 per year with additional $1 for spouse (if joining)

Old Stuff
Donna and Ron Miller, Publishers
2115 McDonald Lane, PO Box 1084, McMinnville, OR 97540. Published 6 times annually; Copies by mail: $3.50 each; Annual subscription: $18 ($32 in Canada)

On the LIGHTER Side Newsletter (bimonthly publication)
International Lighter Collectors
Judith Sanders, Editor
136 Circle Dr., Quitman, TX 75783; 903-763-2795 or fax 903-763-4953. Annual convention held in different cities in the US; Subscription fees: Overseas rate, US and Canada rate, and a Junior and Senior Citizen rate. Please include SASE when requesting information.

Open Salt Collectors of the Atlantic Regions (O.S.C.A.R.)
Wilbur Rudisill, Treasurer
1844 York Rd., Gettysburg, PA 17325. Dues: $5 per year

Open Salt Seekers of the West, Northern California Chapter
Sara Conley
84 Margaret Dr., Walnut Creek, CA 94596. Dues: $7 per year

Open Salt Seekers of the West, Southern California Chapter
Janet Hudson
2525 E. Vassar Court, Visalia, CA 93277. Dues: $5 per year

Pacific Northwest Fenton Association
PO Box 881, Tillamook, OR 97141; 503-842-4815; website: www.glasscastle.com/pnwfa.htm or e-mail: jshirley@pacifier.com. Newsletter subscription: $20 per year (published quarterly, includes annual piece of glass made only for subscribers)

Paper Collectors' Marketplace
PO Box 128, Scandinavia, WI 54977-0128; 715-467-2379 or fax 715-467-2243; e-mail: pcmpaper@gglbbs.com or website: www.pcmpaper.com. Subscription: $19.95 in US (12 issues)

Paper Pile Quarterly Magazine
Ada Fitzsimmons, Editor
PO Box 337, San Anselmo, CA 94960; 415-454-5552 or fax 415-454-2947; e-mail: apaperpile@aol.com or website: www.paperpilecollectibles.com. Sales and features magazine for paper buyers & sellers since 1980. Quarterly cataloged sales of paper items, large for-sale and wanted sections, auction results, book reviews, quarterly price guide & show schedule; Subscription: $20 per year (shipped 1st class); Sample copy: $5 (returnable as credit toward subscription or advertising)

Paperweight Collectors' Association, Inc.
PO Box 1263, Beltsville, MD 20704; 410-828-5722. Membership: for 1 or 2 people at 1 US address is $25 per year; $35 for non-US addresses. Sustaining membership for 1 or 2 people at 1 US address is $55 per year and includes a copy of the Annual Bulletin. Sustaining membership for 1 or 2 people at 1 non-US address is $65 per year if the Annual Bulletin is sent surface ($75 for airmail); Publishes 4 newsletters a year; The Annual Bulletin is now hard-cover, The next convention will be in 2001 with unconfirmed location

Peanut Pals
Robert Walthall, President
PO Box 4465, Huntsville, AL 35815; 205-881-9198. Associated collectors of Planters Peanuts memorabilia, bimonthly newsletter *Peanut Papers;* Annual directory sent to members; Annual convention and regional conventions; Dues: $20 per year (+$3 for each additional household member); Membership information: PO Box 652, St. Clairsville, OH, 43950. Sample newsletter: $2

Pen Collectors of America
PO Box 821449, Houston, TX 77282-1449; Phone/fax: 713-496-2290. Quarterly newsletter, *Pennant;* Annual membership fee: $25 (Includes newsletter and access to extensive reference library)

Pen Fancier's Club
1169 Overcash Dr., Dunedin, FL 34698; 727-734-4742 or fax: 727-738-0476; e-mail: penfanc@aol.com. Publishes quarterly catalog of vintage pens and mechanical pencils, books, parts, and information; Subscription: $20 per year; Sample: $4

Pepsi-Cola Collectors Club Express
Bob Stoddard, Editor
PO Box 817; Claremont, CA 91711

Perrault-Rago Gallery
17 S. Main St., Lambertville, NJ 08530. Specializing in 20th-century decorative arts, particularly art pottery and decorative tiles

Petroleum Collectibles Monthly
Scott Benjamin and Wayne Henderson, Publishers
PO Box 556, LaGrange, OH 44050-0556; 440-355-6608; www.pcmpublishing.com (visit website or call). Suscription: $29.95 per year US, Canada $38.50, International $65.95, Samples $5. Scott advises Gasoline Globes and is devoted to gas and oil collectibles

Phoenix and Consolidated Glass Collectors' Club
Tom Jiamachello, Secretary
41 River View Drive, Essex Junction, VT 05452; 802-878-2682; e-mail: TOPofVT@aol.com. Membership: $25 (single), $35 (family) per year. Please make checks payable to club

Phoenix Bird Collectors of America (PBCA)
685 S. Washington, Constantine, MI 49042; 616-435-8353. Membership: (payable to Joan Oates) $15 per year, includes *Phoenix Bird Discoveries*, published 3 times a year; Also available: 1996 Updated Value Guide to be used in conjunction with Books 1-IV: $6 ppd

Pickard Collectors Club, Ltd.
Membership office: 300 E. Grove St., Bloomington, IL 61701; 309-828-5533 or fax 309-829-2266. Membership (includes newsletter): $20 a year (single) or $25 (family)

Political Collectors of Indiana Club
Michael McQuillen
PO Box 50022, Indianapolis, IN 46250-0022; 317-845-1721; e-mail: buttons@oaktree.net or website: www.politicalparade.com. Official APIC (American Political Items Collectors) Chapter comprised of over 100 collectors of presidential and local political items

Porcelain Collector's Companion
c/o Dorothy Kamm
PO Box 7460, Port St. Lucie, FL 34985-4760; 561-464-4008 or fax 561-460-9050

Powder Puff Compact Collectors' Chronicle
Roselyn Gerson
PO Box 40, Lynbrook, NY 11563; 516-593-8746 or fax 516-593-0610; e-mail: compactlady@aol.com

The Prize Insider Newsletter for Cracker Jack Collectors
Larry White
108 Central St., Rowley, MA 01969; 508-948-8187

Psalm Card Collectors
contact: Chuck Thompson, Editor of newsletter
10802 Greencreek Dr., #703, Houston, TX 77070-5367. For all interested in holy cards, religion, literature, poetry, hobbies and clubs. Starter pack available: includes selection of 3 different size Psalm cards and more information, send name and address (2 postage stamps)

Purinton Pastimes
PO Box 9394, Arlington, VA 22219. Newsletter for Purinton pottery enthusiasts; Subscription: $10 per year

R. Lalique
John Danis
11028 Raleigh Ct., Rockford, IL 61115; 815-877-2410 or fax 815-877-6042; e-mail: danis6033@aol.com

R.A. Fox Collector's Club
c/o Pat Gibson
38280 Guava Dr., Newark, CA, 94560; 510-792-0586

Ribbon Tin News Newsletter (quarterly publication)
Hobart D. Van Deusen, Editor
28 The Green, Watertown, CT 06795; 860-945-3456; e-mail: rtn.hoby@worldnet.att.net. $30 per year for 24+ color plates. For collectors of typewriters, typewriter ribbon tins and go-withs. Indexed subscribers' list and participation in occasional mail/phone auctions

Rose Bowl Collectors
Johanna S. Billings, Co-Founder
P.O. Box 244; Danielsville, PA 18038-0244; 610-261-4775; fax: 610-261-4782; e-mail: bankie@concentric.net. Issues quartlery newsletter

Rosevilles of the Past Newsletter
Nancy Bomm, Editor
PO Box 656, Clarcona, FL 32710-0656. $19.95 per year for 6 newsletters

Salt & Pepper Illustrated Sales List ($2 and LSASE)
Judy Posner
June - September: R.D. 1, Box 273 SC, Effort, PA 18330, fax: 717-629-0521; October - May: PO Box 2194 SC, Englewood, FL 34295, fax: 941-475-2645; e-mail: judyandjef@aol.com or www.judyposner.com. Buy-Sell-Collect

Schoenhut Collectors Club
c/o Pat Girbach
1003 w. Huron St., Ann Arbor, MI 48103-4217 for membership information

Shawnee Pottery Collectors' Club
PO Box 713, New Smyrna Beach, FL 32170-0713. Monthly nation-wide newsletter. SASE (c/o Pamela Curran) required when requesting information; $3 for sample of current newsletter

Shot Glass Exchange @
PO Box 219, Western Springs, IL 60558; 708-246-1559. Primarily prepro-hibition glasses. Subscription: (includes 2 semi-annual issues, available in US only) $13 per year, single copy $8

Society of Inkwell Collectors
5136 Thomas Ave. South, Minneapolis, MN 55410; e-mail: soic@concentric.net or website: www.soic.com. Membership: $25.00 per year, includes subscription to *The Stained Finger*, a quarterly publication

Southern California Marble Club
18361-1 Strothern St., Reseda, CA 91335

Southern Folk Pottery Collectors Society Newsletter
1828 N. Howard Mill Rd., Robbins, NC 27325; 910-454-3961 or fax: 910-464-2530. Specializing in historical research and documentation, education, and promotion of the traditional southern folk potter (past and present) to a modern collecting audience. Membership dues includes biannual absentee auction catalogs (at discounted prices), access to member pieces, opportunities to meet potters, participate in events, newsletter information, various printings, and more.

Southern Oregon Antiques & Collectibles Club
PO Box 508, Talent, OR 97540; 541-535-1231 or fax: 541-535-5109. Meets 1st Wednesday of the month; Promotes 2 shows a year in Medford, OR

Stangl/Fulper Collectors Club
PO Box 538, Flemington, NJ 08822. Yearly membership: $25 (includes quarterly newsletter); Annual auction in June; American pottery and dinnerware show and sale in October

Stevengraph Collectors Assn.
David L. Brown
2103-2829 Arbutus Rd., Victoria, British Columbia, Canada, V8N 5X5; 250-477-9896

Still Bank Collectors Club of America
c/o Larry Egelhoff
4175 Millersville Rd., Indianapolis, IN 46205. Membership: $35 per year

Stretch Glass Society
PO Box 573, Hampshire, IL 60140. Membership: $22; Quarterly newsletter with color photos; Annual Spring convention

Style: 1900 The Quarterly Journal of the Arts & Crafts Movement
David Rago
333 N. Main St., Lambertville, 08530; 609-397-4104

Surveyors Historical Society Identification Committee
D.R. Beeks
PO Box 117, Mt. Vernon, IA 52314; 391-895-0506; e-mail dbeeksci@aol.com

Susie Cooper Catalogs
J. David Ehrhard
7212 Valmont St., Tujunga, CA 91042

Swan Seekers Network
9470 Campo Rd., Suite 134, Spring Valley, CA 91977; 619-462-5517; e-mail: jimer@swanseekers.com or Web page: www.swanseekers.com. Business hours: 10:00 a.m. – 4:00 p.m. Pacific Time, Monday – Thursday; Publishes *Swan Seekers News* and *Swan Seekers Crystal Gallery* periodicals ($30 per year US, $45 foreign); Specializing in retired Swarovski crystal

Table Toppers
1340 West Irving Park Rd., PO Box 161, Chicago, IL 60613; 312-769-3184. Membership: $18 (single) per year, which includes *Table Topics*, a bimonthly newsletter for those interested in table-top collectibles

The Tanner Restraints Collection
6442 Canyon Creek Way, Elk Grove, CA 95758-5431; 916-684-4006. 40-page catalog of magician/escape artist equipment from trick and regulation padlocks, handcuffs, leg shackles, and straight jackets to picks and pick sets; Books on all of the above and much more; Catalog: $3

Tarrant, Jenny
Holly Daze Antiques
4 Gardenview, St. Peters, MO 63376; e-mail: JennyJOL@aol.com or website: business.fortunecity.com/JV/712/index. Specializing in Halloween, Christmas, Easter, etc.; Buying & selling halloween and holiday items

Tea Leaf Club International
Maxine Johnson, Membership Chairman
PO Box 377, Belton, MO 64012. Publishes *Tea Leaf Readings* Newsletter; Membership: $20 (single) or $25 (couple) per year

Tea Talk
Tina M. Carter, Teapot Columnist
Diana Rosen/Lucy Roman, Editors
PO Box 860, Sausalito, CA 94966; 415-331-1557

The TeaTime Gazette
Linda Ashley Leamer
PO Box 40276, St. Paul, MN 55104

THCKK
The Hardware Companies Kollector's Klub
For information contact Jerry Heuring, 28450 US Highway 61, Scott City, MO 63780; 573-264-3947. Membership: $15 per year

Thermometer Collectors' Club of America
Richard Porter, Vice President
PO Box 944, Onset, MA 02558

Thimble Collectors International
6411 Montego Rd., Louisville, KY 40228

Three Rivers Depression Era Glass Society
Meetings held 1st Monday of each month at 6:00 p.m. at Old Country Bouffet, Heidleburg, PA
For more information call: Edith A. Putanko at John's Antiques & Edie's Glassware, Rte. 88 & Broughton Rd., Bethel Park, PA 15102; 412-831-2702

Tiffin Glass Collectors
PO Box 554, Tiffin, OH 44883. Meetings at Seneca County Museum on 2nd Tuesday of each month; Tiffin Glass Museum, 25 S. Washington, Tiffin, OH, Wednesday – Sunday from 1:00 p.m. – 5:00 p.m.

Tins 'n Signs
Box 440101, Aurora, CO 80044. Subscription: $25 per year

Tops & Bottoms Club (Rene Lalique perfumes only)
c/o Madeleine France
PO Box 15555, Ft. Lauderdale, FL 33318

Toy Shop
Mark Williams, Publisher
700 E. State St., Iola, WI 54990-0001; 715-445-2214 or fax: 715-445-4087; website: www.toyshopmag.com. Subscription $33 (26 issues) in US

Trick or Treat Trader
PO Box 499, Winchester, NH 03470; 603-239-8875. Subscription: $15 per year for 4 quarterly issues

TW List (Typewriters)
Chuck Dilts/Rich Cincotta
PO Box 286, Southboro, MA 01772; 508-229-2064; typewriters@writeme.com or visit www.erols.com/chuck101/home.htm (has List info on Links page)

Twin Winton Collectors Club
www.twinwinton.com

Uhl Collectors' Society
Beverly Leslie, Secretary/Treasurer
801 Poplar St., Boonville, IN, 47601; 812-897-3681.
Dave and Donna Swick, Newsletter
506 Martin St., Newton, IL 62488; 618-783-3455

Vaseline Glass Collectors, Inc.
Madolyn Courter
PO Box 125
Russellville, MO 65074; e-mail: mcourter@socketis.net. An organization whose sole purpose is to unify vaseline glass collectors; newsletter *Glowing Report* published bimonthly; Convention held annually. Membership $20 per year

Vaseline Glass Newsletter
Jerry Chambers
2163 Pomona Place, Fairfield, CA 94533; 707-425-6166 after 4:30 p.m. P.S.T.

Vernon Views, newsletter for Vernon Kilns collectors
PO Box 945, Scottsdale, AZ 85252. Published quarterly beginning with the Spring issue, $10 per year

Vetri: Italian Glass News
Howard Lockwood, Publisher
PO Box 191, Fort Lee, NJ 07024; 201-969-0373. Quarterly newsletter about 20th-century Italian glass

Vintage Fashion & Costume Jewelry Newsletter/Club
PO Box 265, Glen Oaks, NY 11004; 718-939-3095; fax: 718-939-7988; e-mail: VFCJ@aol.com. Year's subscription (4 issues): $15 in US, $20 in Canada, $25 International. Back issues available at $5 each

Vintage TVs
Harry Poster
Box 1883, S. Hackensack, 07606; Days: 201-794-9606; 24-hour fax: 201-794-9553; Catalog available on line: www.harryposter.com. Specializes in vintage TVs, transister radios, 3-D stereo cameras

The Wade Watch
Wade Watch Ltd.
8199 Pierson Ct., Arvada, CO 80005; 303-421-9655 or 303-424-4401; fax 303-421-0317. Year's subscription (4 issues): $8 in US; $14 International; Articles and photos welcome, but if to be returned, enclose SASE

Walking Stick Notes
Marilyn Vlahos, Editor
2611 Catalpa Ave., Pascagoula, MS 39567-1806. Please write to Marilyn Vlahos at the above address for information about her publication plans

The Wallace Nutting Collector's Club
PO Box 22475, Beachwood, OH 44122. Established in 1973, holds annual conventions, usually in the northeastern portion of the country; Generally recognized national center of Wallace Nutting-like activity are Michael Ivankovich's Wallace Nutting & Wallace Nutting-Like Specialty Auctions, held 4 times each year. These auctions provide the opportunity for collectors and dealers to compete for the largest variety of Wallace Nutting and Wallace Nutting-Like pictures available anywhere. These auctions also give sellers the opportunity to place their items in front of the country's leading enthusiasts. When writing for information please enclude a close-up photograph which includes the picture's frame, and a SASE.

Warwick China Collectors Club
Pat & Don Hoffmann, Sr.
1291 N. Elmwood Dr., Aurora, IL 60506-1309; 630-859-3435; Web page: www.skognet.com/~warwick or e-mail: warwick@skognet.com

Watt's News Newsletter, for Watt pottery enthusiasts
c/o Watt Collectors Association
PO Box 1995, Iowa City, IA 52244. Subscription: $12 per year; quarterly newsletter, annual convention

The Wedgwood Society of New York
7 Palatine Ct., Syosset, NY 11791-1105. Membership: $27.50 (single) or $32.50 (family). Publishes newsletter (6 times per year) and a scholarly magazine, *Ars Ceramica*, of original articles published by the Society; 6 meetings per year

Westmoreland Glass Collector's Newsletter
PO Box 143, North Liberty, IA 52317. Subscription: $16 per year. This publication is dedicated to the purpose of preserving Westmoreland Glass and its history.

Westmoreland Glass Society
Jim Fisher, President
513 5th Ave., Coralville, IA 52241; 319-354-5011. Membership: $15 (single) or $25 (household)

The Whimsey Club
c/o Lon Knickerbocker
PO Box 312, Dansville, NY, 14437. *Whimsical Notions*, quarterly newsletter with colored photos; Dues: $8 per year; Annual get together

The White Ironstone China Association, Inc.
Diane Dorman, Membership Chairman
PO Box 855, Fairport, NY 14450-0855. Newsletter available for: $25 (single) or $30 (2 individuals at same address)

Willow Review
PO Box 41312, Nashville, TN 37204. Send SASE for information

World's Fair Collectors' Society, Inc.
Fair News Newsletter (bimonthly publication for members)
Michael R. Pender, Editor
PO Box 20806, Sarasota, FL 34276-3806; 941-923-2590. Dues: $17 per year in US, $20 in Canada, and $30 overseas

The Zsolnay Store
152 Spring St., Newport, RI 02840; 401-841-5060; website: www.drawrm.com. Zsolnay book available

Index